LAROUSSE

POCKET

DICCIONARIO

ESPAÑOL-INGLÉS
INGLÉS-ESPAÑOL

LAROUSSE

P9-DXJ-059

Realizado por / Produced by
LAROUSSE
Idiomas • Language Reference

© **Larousse, 1994**

ISBN 2-03-401115-5
Larousse, Paris

ISBN 2-03-420800-5
Distribución /Sales Larousse Kingfisher Chambers Inc., New York

Library of Congress Catalog Card Number
93-086206

ISBN 2-03-430800-X
Distribución /Sales Larousse plc, London

ISBN 84-8016-113-2
Distribución /Sales Larousse Planeta, Barcelona

Printed in France

LAROUSSE
POCKET

SPANISH-ENGLISH

ENGLISH-SPANISH

DICTIONARY

LAROUSSE

A NUESTROS LECTORES

El Diccionario POCKET Larousse es ideal para todas las situaciones lingüísticas, desde el aprendizaje de idiomas en la escuela y en casa hasta los viajes al extranjero.

Este diccionario resulta muy manejable y está pensado para responder de manera práctica y rápida a los diferentes problemas que plantea la lectura del inglés actual. Con sus más de 55.000 palabras y expresiones y por encima de las 80.000 traducciones, este diccionario permitirá al lector comprender con claridad un amplio espectro de textos y realizar traducciones del inglés de uso corriente con rapidez y corrección.

De entre las características de esta obra, nueva en su totalidad, cabe destacar el tratamiento totalmente al día de las siglas y abreviaturas, nombres propios y términos comerciales e informáticos más comunes.

A través de un tratamiento claro y detallado del vocabulario básico, así como de los indicadores de sentido que guían hacia la traducción más adecuada, se permite al usuario escribir en inglés con precisión y seguridad.

Se ha puesto especial cuidado en la presentación de las entradas, tanto desde el punto de vista de su estructura como de la tipografía empleada. Para aquellos lectores que todavía están en un nivel básico o intermedio en su aprendizaje del inglés, el POCKET es el diccionario ideal.

Le invitamos a que se ponga en contacto con nosotros si tiene cualquier observación o crítica que hacer; entre todos podemos hacer del POCKET un diccionario aún mejor.

EL EDITOR

TO OUR READERS

The Larousse POCKET dictionary is ideal for all your language needs, from language learning at school and at home to travelling abroad.

This handy dictionary is designed to provide fast and practical solutions to the various problems encountered when reading present-day Spanish. With over 55,000 references and 80,000 translations, it enables the user to read and enjoy a wide range of texts and to translate everyday Spanish quickly and accurately. This new dictionary also features up-to-date coverage of common abbreviations and acronyms, proper names, business terms and computing vocabulary.

Writing basic Spanish accurately and confidently is no longer a problem thanks to the POCKET's detailed coverage of essential vocabulary, and helpful sense-markers which guide the user to the most appropriate translation.

Careful thought has gone into the presentation of the entries, both in terms of layout and typography. The POCKET is the ideal reference work for all learners from beginners up to intermediate level.

Send us your comments or queries – you will be helping to make this dictionary an even better book.

THE PUBLISHER

ABBREVIATIONS _____ ABREVIATURAS

abbreviation	*abbr/abrev*	abreviatura
adjective	*adj*	adjetivo
adjective only used in feminine form	*adj f*	adjetivo femenino
administration, administrative	ADMIN	administración
adverb	*adv*	adverbio
aeronautics, aviation	AERON	aeronáutica, aviación
agriculture, farming	AGR	agricultura
American English	*Am*	inglés americano
Latin American Spanish	*Amer*	español latinoamericano
anatomy	ANAT	anatomía
before noun	*antes de sust*	antes de sustantivo
– indicates that the translation is always used directly before the noun which it modifies		– indica que la traducción siempre se utiliza en inglés antepuesta al sustantivo al que modifica
archeology	ARCHEOL	arqueología
architecture	ARCHIT/ARQUIT	arquitectura
article	*art*	artículo
astrology	ASTROL	astrología
astronomy	ASTRON	astronomía
automobile, cars	AUT(OM)	automovilismo, coches
biology	BIOL	biología
botany	BOT	botánica
British English	*Br*	inglés británico
Canadian English	*Can*	inglés canadiense
chemistry	CHEM	química
cinema, film-making	CIN(EMA)	cine
commerce, business	COM(M)	comercio, negocios
compound	*comp*	sustantivo antepuesto a otro
comparative	*compar*	comparativo
computers, computer science	COMPUT	informática
conjunction	*conj*	conjunción
construction, building	CONSTR	construcción
continuous	*cont*	continuo
culinary, cooking	CULIN	cocina
definite	*def*	determinado
demonstrative	*demos*	demostrativo
sport	DEP	deporte
juridical, legal	DER	derecho, jurídico
pejorative	*despec*	despectivo, peyorativo
dated	*desus*	desusado
ecology	ECOLOG	ecología
economics	ECON	economía
school, education	EDUC	educación
electricity	ELEC(TR)	electricidad
electronics	ELECTRON/ELECTRÓN	electrónica

especially	*esp*	especialmente
exclamation	*excl*	interjección
feminine noun	*f*	sustantivo femenino
informal	*fam*	familiar
pharmacology, pharmaceutics	FARM	farmacología, farmacia
railways	FERROC	ferrocarril
figurative	*fig*	figurado
finance, financial	FIN	finanzas
physics	FÍS	física
formal	*fml*	formal, culto
photography	FOT	fotografía
soccer	FTBL	fútbol
inseparable	*fus*	inseparable

– shows that a phrasal verb is "fused", i.e. inseparable, e.g. **look after** where the object can not come between the verb and the particle, e.g. *I looked after him* but not * *I looked him after*

– indica que una locución verbal o "phrasal verb" (verbo + preposición o adverbio) es inseparable y el objeto no puede aparecer entre el verbo en sí y la partícula, p. ej. en **look after** se dice *I looked after him* no * *I looked him after*

generally, in most cases	*gen*	generalmente, en general
geography, geographical	GEOGR	geografía
geology, geological	GEOL	geología
geometry	GEOM	geometría
grammar	GRAM(M)	gramática
history	HIST	historia
humorous	*hum*	humorístico
industry	IND	industria
indefinite	*indef*	indeterminado
informal	*inf*	familiar
infinitive	*infin*	infinitivo
computers, computer science	INFORM	informática
exclamation	*interj*	interjección
invariable	*inv*	invariable
ironic	*iro/irón*	irónico
juridical, legal	JUR	derecho, jurídico
linguistics	LING	lingüística
literal	*lit*	literal
literature	LITER	literatura
phrase(s)	*loc*	locución, locuciones
adjectival phrase	*loc adj*	locución adjetiva
adverbial phrase	*loc adv*	locución adverbial
conjunctive phrase	*loc conj*	locución conjuntiva
prepositional phrase	*loc prep*	locución preposicional

– adjectives, adverbs etc consisting of more than one word, e.g. **a pesar de, a horcajadas**

– construcciones fijas de más de una palabra con función adjetiva, adverbial, etc; p.ej. **a pesar de, a horcajadas**

masculine noun	*m*	sustantivo masculino
mathematics	MAT(H)	matemáticas

mechanical engineering	MEC	mecánica
medicine	MED	medicina
metallurgy	METAL	metalurgia
weather, meteorology	METEOR	meteorología
very informal	*mfam*	muy familiar
military	MIL	militar
mining	MIN	minería
mythology	MITOL	mitología
music	MUS/MÚS	música
mythology	MYTH	mitología
noun	*n*	sustantivo
nautical, maritime	NAUT/NÁUT	náutica, marítimo
numeral	*num/núm*	número
oneself	*o.s.*	
pejorative	*pej*	peyorativo, despectivo
personal	*pers*	personal
pharmacology,	PHARM	farmacología,
pharmaceutics		farmacia
photography	PHOT	fotografía
phrase(s)	*phr*	locución, locuciones
physics	PHYS	física
plural	*pl*	plural
politics	POL(ÍT)	política
possessive	*poss/poses*	posesivo
past participle	*pp*	participio pasado
press, journalism	PRENS	periodismo, prensa
preposition	*prep*	preposición
pronoun	*pron*	pronombre
psychology, psychiatry	PSYCH/PSICOL	psicología
past tense	*pt*	pasado, pretérito
chemistry	QUÍM	química
registered trademark	®	marca registrada
railways	RAIL	ferrocarril
relative	*relat*	relativo
religion	RELIG	religión
someone, somebody	*sb*	
school, education	SCH	educación
Scottish English	*Scot*	inglés escocés
separable	*sep*	separable
– shows that a phrasal verb is separable, e.g. **let in,** where the object can come between the verb and the particle, e.g. *I let her in*		–indica que una locución verbal o "phrasal verb" (verbo + preposición o adverbio) es separable y el objeto puede aparecer entre el verbo en sí y la partícula, p. ej. en **let in,** se dice *I let her in*
singular	*sg*	singular
slang	*sl*	argot
sociology	SOCIOL	sociología
stock exchange	ST EX	bolsa
something	*sthg*	
subject	*subj/suj*	sujeto
superlative	*superl*	superlativo

bullfighting	TAUROM	tauromaquia
theatre	TEATR	teatro
technology, technical	TECH/TECN	tecnología, técnico
telecommunications	TELEC(OM)	telecomunicaciones
television	TV	televisión
printing, typography	TYPO	imprenta
uncountable noun	*U*	sustantivo "incontable"

   – i.e. an English noun which is never used in the plural or with "a"; used when the Spanish word is or can be a plural, e.g. **infighting** *n* (*U*) disputas *fpl* internas, **balido** *m* bleat, bleating (*U*)

   – esto es, sustantivo inglés que jamás se usa en plural o con el artículo "a"; utilizado cuando la palabra española es o puede ser plural, p. ej. **infighting** *n* (*U*) disputas *fpl* internas, **balido** *m* bleat, bleating (*U*)

university	UNIV	universidad
usually	*usu*	normalmente
auxiliary verb	*vaux*	verbo auxiliar
verb	*vb/v*	verbo
veterinary science	VETER	veterinaria
intransitive verb	*vi*	verbo intransitivo
impersonal verb	*v impers*	verbo impersonal
very informal	*v inf*	muy familiar
pronominal verb	*vpr*	verbo pronominal
transitive verb	*vt*	verbo transitivo
vulgar	*vulg*	vulgar
zoology	ZOOL	zoología
cultural equivalent	≃	equivalente cultural

SPANISH ALPHABETICAL ORDER

As this dictionary follows international alphabetical order, the Spanish letter combinations **ch** and **ll** are *not* treated as separate letters. Thus entries with **ch** appear after **cg** and not at the end of **c**. Similarly, entries with **ll** appear after **lk** and not at the end of **l**. Note, however, that **ñ** *is* treated as a separate letter and follows **n** in alphabetical order.

ENGLISH COMPOUNDS

A compound is a word or expression which has a single meaning but is made up of more than one word, e.g. **point of view, kiss of life, virtual reality, West Indies** and **Confederation of British Industry.** It is a feature of this dictionary that English compounds appear in the A-Z list in strict alphabetical order. The compound **blood poisoning** will therefore come after **bloodhound** which itself follows **blood group.**

LA ORDENACIÓN ALFABÉTICA EN ESPAÑOL

En este diccionario se ha seguido la ordenación alfabética internacional; por lo tanto, las consonantes **ch** y **ll** *no* se consideran letras aparte. Esto significa que las entradas con **ch** aparecerán después de **cg** y no al final de **c**; del mismo modo las entradas con **ll** vendrán después de **lk** y no al final de **l**. Adviértase, sin embargo, que la letra **ñ** *sí* se considera letra aparte y sigue a la **n** en orden alfabético.

LOS COMPUESTOS EN INGLÉS

En inglés se llama compuesto a una locución sustantiva de significado único pero formada por más de una palabra; p.ej. **point of view, kiss of life, virtual reality, West Indies** o **Confederation of British Industry.** Uno de los rasgos distintivos de este diccionario es la inclusión de estos compuestos con entrada propia y en riguroso orden alfabético. De esta forma **blood poisoning** vendrá después de **bloodhound**, el cual sigue a **blood group.**

PHONETIC TRANSCRIPTION____TRANSCRIPCIÓN FONÉTICA

English Vowels

[ɪ] pit, big, rid
[e] pet, tend
[æ] pat, bag, mad
[ʌ] putt, cut
[ɒ] pot, log
[ʊ] put, full
[ə] mother, suppose
[iː] bean, weed
[ɑː] barn, car, laugh
[ɔː] born, lawn
[uː] loop, loose
[ɜː] burn, learn, bird

Vocales españolas

[i] piso, imagen
[e] tela, eso
[a] pata, amigo
[o] bola, otro
[u] luz, una

English Diphthongs

[eɪ] bay, late, great
[aɪ] buy, light, aisle
[ɔɪ] boy, foil
[əʊ] no, road, blow
[aʊ] now, shout, town
[ɪə] peer, fierce, idea
[eə] pair, bear, share
[ʊə] poor, sure, tour

Diptongos españoles

[ei] ley, peine
[ai] aire, caiga
[oi] soy, boina
[au] causa, aura
[eu] Europa, feudo

Semi-vowels

you, spaniel [j]
wet, why, twin [w]

Semivocales

hierba, miedo
agua, hueso

Consonants

pop, people	[p]	papá, campo
bottle, bib	[b]	vaca, bomba
	[ß]	curvo, caballo
train, tip	[t]	toro, pato
dog, did	[d]	donde, caldo
come, kitchen	[k]	que, cosa
gag, great	[g]	grande, guerra
	[ɣ]	aguijón, bulldog
chain, wretched	[tʃ]	ocho, chusma
jig, fridge	[dʒ]	
fib, physical	[f]	fui, afable
vine, livid	[v]	
think, fifth	[θ]	cera, paz
this, with	[ð]	cada, pardo
seal, peace	[s]	solo, paso
zip, his	[z]	
sheep, machine	[ʃ]	
usual, measure	[ʒ]	
	[x]	gema, jamón
how, perhaps	[h]	
metal, comb	[m]	madre, cama

Consonantes

night, din**n**er	[n]	**n**o, pe**n**a	
su**ng**, parki**ng**	[ŋ]		
	[ɲ]	ca**ñ**a	
litt**l**e, he**l**p	[l]	a**l**a, **l**uz	
right, car**r**y	[r]	ata**r**, pa**r**o	
	[rr]	pe**rr**o, **r**osa	
	[ʎ]	**ll**ave, co**ll**ar	

The symbol [ˈ] indicates that the following syllable carries primary stress and the symbol [ˌ] that the following syllable carries secondary stress.

Los símbolos [ˈ] y [ˌ] indican que la sílaba siguiente lleva un acento primario o secundario respectivamente.

The symbol [ʳ] in English phonetics indicates that the final "r" is pronounced only when followed by a word beginning with a vowel. Note that it is nearly always pronounced in American English.

El símbolo [ʳ] en fonética inglesa indica que la "r" al final de palabra se pronuncia sólo cuando precede a una palabra que comienza por vocal. Adviértase que casi siempre se pronuncia en inglés americano.

Since Spanish pronunciation follows regular rules, phonetics are only provided in this dictionary for loan words from other languages, when these are difficult to pronounce. All one-word English headwords have phonetics. For English compound headwords, whether hyphenated or of two or more words, phonetics are given for any element which does not appear elsewhere in the dictionary as a headword in its own right.

Las palabras españolas no llevan transcripción fonética en este diccionario; sólo algunos préstamos lingüísticos procedentes de otras lenguas y de difícil pronunciación aparecen transcritos. Todas las entradas inglesas que constan de una palabra llevan transcripción fonética. En el caso de los compuestos ingleses (ya sea cuando lleven guiones o cuando no) se proporciona la transcripción fonética de todo aquel elemento que no aparezca en alguna otra parte del diccionario como entrada en sí misma.

Cuadro de Conjugación

Abreviaturas: *pres ind* = present indicative, *imperf ind* = imperfect,
pret perf sim = preterite, *fut* = future, *cond* = conditional,
pres subj = present subjunctive, *imperf indic* = imperfect,
imperf subj = imperfect subjunctive, *imperat* = imperative,
ger = gerund, *partic* = past participle

N.B. Todas las formas del *imperf subj* pueden conjugarse
con las terminaciones: -se, -ses, -se, -semos, -seis, -sen

acertar: *pres ind* acierto, acertamos, etc., *pres subj* acierte, acertemos, etc.,
imperat acierta, acertemos, acertad, etc.

adquirir: *pres ind* adquiero, adquirimos, etc., *pres subj* adquiera, adquiramos,
etc., *imperat* adquiere, adquiramos, adquirid, etc.

AMAR: *pres ind* amo, amas, ama, amamos, amáis, aman, *imperf ind* amaba,
amabas, amaba, amábamos, amabais, amaban, *pret perf sim* amé, amaste,
amó, amamos, amasteis, amaron, *fut* amaré, amarás, amará, amaremos,
amaréis, amarán, *cond* amaría, amarías, amaría, amaríamos, amaríais,
amarían, *pres subj* ame, ames, ame, amemos, améis, amen, *imperf subj* amara,
amaras, amara, amáramos, amarais, amaran, *imperat* ama, ame, amemos,
amad, amen, *ger* amando, *partic* amado, -da

andar: *pret perf sim* anduve, anduvimos, etc., *imperf subj* anduviera,
anduviéramos, etc.

asir: *pres ind* asgo, ase, asimos, etc., *pres subj* asga, asgamos, etc., *imperat* ase,
asga, asgamos, asgad, etc.

avergonzar: *pres ind* avergüenzo, avergonzamos, etc., *pret perf
sim* avergoncé, avergonzó, avergonzamos, etc., *pres subj* avergüence,
avergoncemos, etc., *imperat* avergüenza, avergüence, avergoncemos,
avergonzad, etc.

caber: *pres ind* quepo, cabe, cabemos, etc., *pret perf sim* cupe, cupimos, etc.,
fut cabré, cabremos, etc., *cond* cabría, cabríamos, etc., *pres subj* quepa,
quepamos, cabed, etc., *imperf subj* cupiera, cupiéramos, etc., *imperat* cabe,
quepa, quepamos, etc.

caer: *pres ind* caigo, cae, caemos, etc., *pret perf sim* cayó, caímos, cayeron,
etc., *pres subj* caiga, caigamos, etc., *imperf subj* cayera, cayéramos, etc.,
imperat cae, caiga, caigamos, caed, etc., *ger* cayendo

conducir: *pres ind* conduzco, conduce, conducimos, etc.,
pret perf sim conduje, condujimos, etc., *pres subj* conduzca, conduzcamos,
etc., *imperf subj* condujera, condujéramos, etc., *imperat* conduce, conduzca,
conduzcamos, conducid, etc.

conocer: *pres ind* conozco, conoce, conocemos, etc., *pres subj* conozca,
conozcamos, etc., *imperat* conoce, conozca, conozcamos, etc.

dar: *pres ind* doy, da, damos, etc., *pret perf sim* di, dio, dimos, etc.,
pres subj dé, demos, etc., *imperf subj* diera, diéramos, etc., *imperat* da, dé,
demos, dad, etc.

decir: *pres ind* digo, dice, decimos, etc., *pret perf sim* dije, dijimos, etc.,
fut diré, diremos, etc., *cond* diría, diríamos, etc., *pres subj* diga, digamos, etc.,
imperf subj dijera, dijéramos, etc., *imperat* di, diga, digamos, decid, etc.,
ger diciendo, *partic* dicho, -cha

discernir: *pres ind* discierno, discernimos, etc., *pres subj* discierna,
discernamos, etc., *imperat* discierne, discierna, discernamos, discernid, etc.

dormir: *pres ind* duermo, dormimos, etc., *pret perf sim* durmió, dormimos, durmieron, etc., *pres subj* duerma, durmamos, etc., *imperf subj* durmiera, durmiéramos, etc., *imperat* duerme, duerma, durmamos, dormid, etc., *ger* durmiendo

errar: *pres ind* yerro, erramos, etc., *pres subj* yerre, erremos, etc., *imperat* yerra, yerre, erremos, errad, etc.

estar: *pres ind* estoy, está, estamos, etc., *pret perf sim* estuve, estuvimos, etc., *pres subj* esté, estemos, etc., *imperf subj* estuviera, estuviéramos, etc., *imperat* está, esté, estemos, estad, etc.,

HABER: *pres ind* he, has, ha, hemos, habéis, han, *imperf ind* había, habías, había, habíamos, habíais, habían, *pret perf sim* hube, hubiste, hubo, hubimos, hubisteis, hubieron, *fut* habré, habrás, habrá, habremos, habréis, habrán, *cond* habría, habrías, habría, habríamos, habríais, habrían, *pres subj* haya, hayas, haya, hayamos, hayáis, hayan, *imperf subj* hubiera, hubieras, hubiera, hubiéramos, hubierais, hubieran, *imperat* he, haya, hayamos, habed, hayan, *ger* habiendo, *partic* habido, -da

hacer: *pres ind* hago, hace, hacemos, etc., *pret perf sim* hice, hizo, hicimos, etc., *fut* haré, haremos, etc., *cond* haría, haríamos, etc., *pres subj* haga, hagamos, etc., *imperf subj* hiciera, hiciéramos, etc., *imperat* haz, haga, hagamos, haced, etc., *partic* hecho, -cha

huir: *pres ind* huyo, huimos, etc., *pret perf sim* huyó, huimos, huyeron, etc., *pres subj* huya, huyamos, etc., *imperf subj* huyera, huyéramos, etc., *imperat* huye, huya, huyamos, huid, etc., *ger* huyendo

ir: *pres ind* voy, va, vamos, etc., *pret perf sim* fui, fue, fuimos, etc., *pres subj* vaya, vayamos, etc., *imperf subj* fuera, fuéramos, etc., *imperat* ve, vaya, vayamos, id, etc., *ger* yendo

leer: *pret perf sim* leyó, leímos, leyeron, etc., *imperf subj* leyera, leyéramos, etc., *ger* leyendo

lucir: *pres ind* luzco, luce, lucimos, etc., *pres subj* luzca, luzcamos, etc., *imperat* luce, luzca, luzcamos, lucid, etc.

mover: *pres ind* muevo, movemos, etc., *pres subj* mueva, movamos, etc., *imperat* mueve, mueva, movamos, moved, etc.

nacer: *pres ind* nazco, nace, nacemos, etc., *pres subj* nazca, nazcamos, etc., *imperat* nace, nazca, nazcamos, naced, etc.

oír: *pres ind* oigo, oye, oímos, etc., *pret perf sim* oyó, oímos, oyeron, etc., *pres subj* oiga, oigamos, etc., *imperf subj* oyera, oyéramos, etc., *imperat* oye, oiga, oigamos, oíd, etc., *ger* oyendo

oler: *pres ind* huelo, olemos, etc., *pres subj* huela, olamos, etc., *imperat* huele, huela, olamos, oled, etc.

parecer: *pres ind* parezco, parece, parecemos, etc., *pres subj* parezca, parezcamos, etc., *imperat* parece, parezca, parezcamos, pareced, etc.,

PARTIR: *pres ind* parto, partes, parte, partimos, partís, parten, *imperf ind* partía, partías, partía, partíamos, partíais, partían, *pret perf sim* partí, partiste, partió, partimos, partisteis, partieron, *fut* partiré, partirás, partirá, partiremos, partiréis, partirán, *cond* partiría, partirías, partiría, partiríamos, partiríais, partirían, *pres subj* parta, partas, parta, partamos, partáis, partan, *imperf subj* partiera, partieras, partiera, partiéramos, partierais, partieran, *imperat* parte, parta, partamos, partid, partan, *ger* partiendo, *partic* partido, -da

pedir: *pres ind* pido, pedimos, etc., *pret perf sim* pidió, pedimos, pidieron, etc., *pres subj* pida, pidamos, etc., *imperf subj* pidiera, pidiéramos, etc., *imperat* pide, pida, pidamos, pedid, etc., *ger* pidiendo

poder: *pres ind* puedo, podemos, etc., *pret perf sim* pude, pudimos, etc., *fut* podré, podremos, etc., *cond* podría, podríamos, etc., *pres subj* pueda, podamos, etc., *imperf subj* pudiera, pudiéramos, etc., *imperat* puede, pueda, podamos, poded, etc., *ger* pudiendo

poner: *pres ind* pongo, pone, ponemos, etc., *pret perf sim* puse, pusimos, etc., *fut* pondré, pondremos, etc., *cond* pondría, pondríamos, etc., *pres subj* ponga, pongamos, etc., *imperf subj* pusiera, pusiéramos, etc., *imperat* pon, ponga, pongamos, poned, etc., *partic* puesto, -ta

predecir: se conjuga como **decir** excepto en la segunda persona del singular del *imperat* predice

querer: *pres ind* quiero, queremos, etc., *pret perf sim* quise, quisimos, etc., *fut* querré, querremos, etc., *cond* querría, querríamos, etc., *pres subj* quiera, queramos, etc., *imperf subj* quisiera, quisiéramos, etc., *imperat* quiere, quiera, queramos, quered, etc.

reír: *pres ind* río, reímos, etc., *pret perf sim* rió, reímos, rieron, etc., *pres subj* ría, riamos, etc., *imperf subj* riera, riéramos, etc., *imperat* ríe, ría, riamos, reíd, etc., *ger* riendo

saber: *pres ind* sé, sabe, sabemos, etc., *pret perf sim* supe, supimos, etc., *fut* sabré, sabremos, etc., *cond* sabría, sabríamos, etc., *pres subj* sepa, sepamos, etc., *imperf subj* supiera, supiéramos, etc., *imperat* sabe, sepa, sepamos, sabed, etc.

salir: *pres ind* salgo, sale, salimos, etc., *fut* saldré, saldremos, etc., *cond* saldría, saldríamos, etc., *pres subj* salga, salgamos, etc., *imperat* sal, salga, salgamos, salid, etc.

sentir: *pres ind* siento, sentimos, etc., *pret perf sim* sintió, sentimos, sintieron, etc., *pres subj* sienta, sintamos, etc., *imperf subj* sintiera, sintiéramos, etc., *imperat* siente, sienta, sintamos, sentid, etc., *ger* sintiendo

SER: *pres ind* soy, eres, es, somos, sois, son, *imperf ind* era, eras, era, éramos, erais, eran, *pret perf sim* fui, fuiste, fue, fuimos, fuisteis, fueron, *fut* seré, serás, será, seremos, seréis, serán, *cond* sería, serías, sería, seríamos, seríais, serían, *pres subj* sea, seas, sea, seamos, seáis, sean, *imperf subj* fuera, fueras, fuera, fuéramos, fuerais, fueran, *imperat* sé, sea, seamos, sed, sean, *ger* siendo, *partic* sido, -da

sonar: *pres ind* sueno, sonamos, etc., *pres subj* suene, sonemos, etc., *imperat* suena, suene, sonemos, sonad, etc.

TEMER: *pres ind* temo, temes, teme, tememos, teméis, temen, *imperf ind* temía, temías, temía, temíamos, temíais, temían, *pret perf sim* temí, temiste, temió, temimos, temisteis, temieron, *fut* temeré, temerás, temerá, temeremos, temeréis, temerán, *cond* temería, temerías, temería, temeríamos, temeríais, temerían, *pres subj* tema, temas, tema, temamos, temáis, teman, *imperf subj* temiera, temieras, temiera, temiéramos, temierais, temieran, *imperat* teme, tema, temamos, temed, teman, *ger* temiendo, *partic* temido, -da

tender: *pres ind* tiendo, tendemos, etc., *pres subj* tienda, tendamos, etc., *imperat* tiende, tendamos, etc.

tener: *pres ind* tengo, tiene, tenemos, etc., *pret perf sim* tuve, tuvimos, etc., *fut* tendré, tendremos, etc., *cond* tendría, tendríamos, etc., *pres subj* tenga, tengamos, etc., *imperf subj* tuviera, tuviéramos, etc., *imperat* ten, tenga, tengamos, tened, etc.

traer: *pres ind* traigo, trae, traemos, etc., *pret perf sim* traje, trajimos, etc., *pres subj* traiga, traigamos, etc., *imperf subj* trajera, trajéramos, etc., *imperat* trae, traiga, traigamos, traed, etc., *ger* trayendo

valer: *pres ind* valgo, vale, valemos, etc., *fut* valdré, valdremos, etc., *cond* valdría, valdríamos, etc., *pres subj* valga, valgamos, etc., *imperat* vale, valga, valgamos, valed, etc.

venir: *pres ind* vengo, viene, venimos, etc., *pret perf sim* vine, vinimos, etc., *fut* vendré, vendremos, etc., *cond* vendría, vendríamos, etc., *pres subj* venga, vengamos, etc., *imperf subj* viniera, viniéramos, etc., *imperat* ven, venga, vengamos, venid, etc., *ger* viniendo

ver: *pres ind* veo, ve, vemos, etc., *pret perf sim* vi, vio, vimos, etc., *imperf subj* viera, viéramos, etc., *imperat* ve, vea, veamos, ved, etc., *ger* viendo, etc., *partic* visto, -ta

ENGLISH IRREGULAR VERBS

Infinitive	Past Tense	Past Participle
arise	arose	arisen
awake	awoke	awoken
be	was, were	been
bear	bore	born(e)
beat	beat	beaten
befall	befell	befallen
begin	began	begun
behold	beheld	beheld
bend	bent	bent
beseech	besought	besought
beset	beset	beset
bet	bet (also betted)	bet (also betted)
bid	bid (also bade)	bid (also bidden)
bind	bound	bound
bite	bit	bitten
bleed	bled	bled
blow	blew	blown
break	broke	broken
breed	bred	bred
bring	brought	brought
build	built	built
burn	burnt (also burned)	burnt (also burned)
burst	burst	burst
buy	bought	bought
can	could	–
cast	cast	cast
catch	caught	caught
choose	chose	chosen
cling	clung	clung
come	came	come
cost	cost	cost
creep	crept	crept
cut	cut	cut
deal	dealt	dealt
dig	dug	dug
do	did	done
draw	drew	drawn
dream	dreamed (also dreamt)	dreamed (also dreamt)
drink	drank	drunk
drive	drove	driven
dwell	dwelt	dwelt
eat	ate	eaten
fall	fell	fallen
feed	fed	fed
feel	felt	felt
fight	fought	fought
find	found	found
flee	fled	fled
fling	flung	flung
fly	flew	flown
forget	forgot	forgotten
forsake	forsook	forsaken

Infinitive	Past Tense	Past Participle
freeze	froze	frozen
get	got	got (Am gotten)
give	gave	given
go	went	gone
grind	ground	ground
grow	grew	grown
hang	hung (also hanged)	hung (also hanged)
have	had	had
hear	heard	heard
hide	hid	hidden
hit	hit	hit
hold	held	held
hurt	hurt	hurt
keep	kept	kept
kneel	knelt (also kneeled)	knelt (also kneeled)
know	knew	known
lay	laid	laid
lead	led	led
lean	leant (also leaned)	leant (also leaned)
leap	leapt (also leaped)	leapt (also leaped)
learn	learnt (also learned)	learnt (also learned)
leave	left	left
lend	lent	lent
let	let	let
lie	lay	lain
light	lit (also lighted)	lit (also lighted)
lose	lost	lost
make	made	made
may	might	–
mean	meant	meant
meet	met	met
mow	mowed	mown (also mowed)
pay	paid	paid
put	put	put
quit	quit (also quitted)	quit (also quitted)
read	read	read
rend	rent	rent
rid	rid	rid
ride	rode	ridden
ring	rang	rung
rise	rose	risen
run	ran	run
saw	sawed	sawn
say	said	said
see	saw	seen
seek	sought	sought
sell	sold	sold
send	sent	sent
set	set	set
shake	shook	shaken
shall	should	–
shear	sheared	shorn (also sheared)
shed	shed	shed
shine	shone	shone

Infinitive	Past Tense	Past Participle
shoot	shot	shot
show	showed	shown
shrink	shrank	shrunk
shut	shut	shut
sing	sang	sung
sink	sank	sunk
sit	sat	sat
slay	slew	slain
sleep	slept	slept
slide	slid	slid
sling	slung	slung
slit	slit	slit
smell	smelt (also smelled)	smelt (also smelled)
sow	sowed	sown (also sowed)
speak	spoke	spoken
speed	sped (also speeded)	sped (also speeded)
spell	spelt (also spelled)	spelt (also spelled)
spend	spent	spent
spill	spilt (also spilled)	spilt (also spilled)
spin	spun	spun
spit	spat	spat
split	split	split
spoil	spoiled (also spoilt)	spoiled (also spoilt)
spread	spread	spread
spring	sprang	sprung
stand	stood	stood
steal	stole	stolen
stick	stuck	stuck
sting	stung	stung
stink	stank	stunk
stride	strode	stridden
strike	struck	struck (also stricken)
strive	strove	striven
swear	swore	sworn
sweep	swept	swept
swell	swelled	swollen (also swelled)
swim	swam	swum
swing	swung	swung
take	took	taken
teach	taught	taught
tear	tore	torn
tell	told	told
think	thought	thought
throw	threw	thrown
thrust	thrust	thrust
tread	trod	trodden
wake	woke (also waked)	woken (also waked)
wear	wore	worn
weave	wove (also weaved)	woven (also weaved)
wed	wedded	wedded
weep	wept	wept
win	won	won
wind	wound	wound
wring	wrung	wrung
write	wrote	written

a¹ (*pl* aes), **A** (*pl* Aes) *f* [letra] a, A.

a² *prep* (*a* + *el* = **al**) **-1.** [periodo de tiempo]: **a las pocas semanas** a few weeks later; **al día siguiente** the following day. **-2.** [momento preciso] at; **a las siete** at seven o'clock; **a los 11 años** at the age of 11; **al caer la noche** at nightfall; **al oír la noticia se desmayó** on hearing the news, she fainted. **-3.** [frecuencia] per, every; **40 horas a la semana** 40 hours per ○ a week; **tres veces al día** three times a day. **-4.** [dirección] to; **voy a Sevilla** I'm going to Seville; **me voy al extranjero** I'm going abroad; **llegó a Barcelona/la fiesta** he arrived in Barcelona/at the party. **-5.** [posición]: **a la puerta** at the door; **está a la derecha/izquierda** it's on the right/left. **-6.** [distancia]: **está a más de cien kilómetros** it's more than a hundred kilometres away. **-7.** [con complemento indirecto] to; **dáselo a Juan** give it to Juan; **dile a Juan que venga** tell Juan to come. **-8.** [con complemento directo]: **quiere a sus hijos/su gato** she loves her children/her cat. **-9.** [cantidad, medida, precio]: **a cientos/miles/docenas** by the hundred/thousand/dozen; **a ... kilómetros por hora** at ... kilometres per hour; **¿a cuánto están las peras?** how much are the pears?; **ganaron tres a cero** they won three nil. **-10.** [modo]: **lo hace a la antigua** he does it the old way; **a lo Mozart** in Mozart's style; **a escondidas** secretly. **-11.** [instrumento]: **escribir a máquina** to use a typewriter; **a lápiz** in pencil; **a mano** by hand. **-12.** (*después de verbo y antes de infin*) [finalidad] to; **entró a pagar** he came in to pay; **aprender a nadar** to learn to swim. **-13.** (*después de sust y antes de infin*) [complemento de nombre]: **temas a tratar** matters to be discussed. **-14.** [en oraciones imperativas]: **¡a la cama!** go to bed!; **¡a bailar!** let's dance!

abad, -desa *m y f* abbot (*f* abbess).

abadía *f* abbey.

abajo ◇ *adv* **-1.** [posición - gen] below; [- en edificio] downstairs; **vive (en el piso de) ~** she lives downstairs; **está aquí/allí ~** it's down here/there; **más ~** further down. **-2.** [dirección] down; **ve ~** [en edificio] go downstairs; **hacia/para ~** down, downwards; **calle/escaleras ~** down the street/stairs; **río ~** downstream. **-3.** [en un texto] below. ◇ *interj*: **¡~ la dictadura!** down with the dictatorship! ◆ **de abajo** *loc adj* bottom.

abalanzarse *vpr*: **~ sobre** to fall upon; **~ hacia** to rush towards.

abalear *vt Amer* to shoot.

abalorio *m* (*gen pl*) [bisutería] trinket.

abanderado *m lit* & *fig* standard-bearer.

abandonado, -da *adj* **-1.** [desierto] deserted. **-2.** [desamparado] abandoned. **-3.** [descuidado - jardín, casa] neglected.

abandonar *vt* **-1.** [gen] to abandon; [lugar, profesión, cónyuge] to leave. **-2.** [desatender - obligaciones, estudios] to neglect. ◆ **abandonarse** *vpr* [a una emoción]: **~se a** [desesperación, dolor] to succumb to; [vicio] to give o.s. over to.

abandono *m* **-1.** [acción - gen] abandonment; [- de lugar, profesión, cónyuge] leaving; [- de obligaciones, estudios] neglect. **-2.** [estado] state of abandon. **-3.** DEP: **ganar por ~** to win by default.

abanicar *vt* to fan.

abanico m [para dar aire] fan.
abaratar vt to reduce the price of.
◆ **abaratarse** vpr to become cheaper.
abarcar vt [incluir] to embrace, to cover.
abarrotado, -da adj: ~ (de) [teatro, autobús] packed (with); [desván, baúl] crammed (with).
abarrotar vt: ~ algo (de ○ con) [teatro, autobús] to pack sthg (with); [desván, baúl] to cram sthg full (of).
abarrotería f Amer grocer's (store).
abarrotes mpl Amer groceries.
abastecer vt: ~ algo/a alguien (de) to supply sthg/sb (with).
abastecimiento m supply, supplying.
abasto m: no dar ~ (a algo/para hacer algo) to be unable to cope (with sthg/with doing sthg).
abatible adj folding.
abatido, -da adj dejected.
abatir vt **-1.** [derribar - muro] to knock down; [- avión] to shoot down. **-2.** [desanimar] to depress. ◆ **abatirse** vpr: ~se (sobre) to swoop (down on).
abdicación f abdication.
abdicar vi to abdicate.
abdomen m abdomen.
abdominal adj abdominal.
abecé m lit & fig ABC.
abecedario m [alfabeto] alphabet.
abedul m birch (tree).
abeja f bee.
abejorro m bumblebee.
aberración f perverse ○ evil thing.
abertura f opening.
abertzale [aßer'tʃale] adj, m y f Basque nationalist.
abeto m fir.
abierto, -ta ◇ pp → **abrir.** ◇ adj [gen] open; **dejar el grifo** ~ to leave the tap on; **bien** ○ **muy** ~ wide open.
abigarrado, -da adj multi-coloured;· fig motley.
abismal adj vast, colossal.
abismo m [profundidad] abyss.
abjurar [culto] vi: ~ de algo to abjure sthg.
ablandar vt [material] to soften. ◆ **ablandarse** vpr [material] to soften.
abnegación f abnegation, self-denial.
abochornar vt to embarrass. ◆ **abochornarse** vpr to get embarrassed.
abofetear vt to slap.
abogacía f legal profession.
abogado, -da m y f DER lawyer; ~ de-

fensor counsel for the defence; ~ **del estado** public prosecutor.
abogar vi fig [defender]: ~ **por algo** to advocate sthg; ~ **por alguien** to stand up for sb.
abolengo m lineage.
abolición f abolition.
abolir vt to abolish.
abolladura f dent.
abollar vt to dent.
abominable adj abominable.
abonado, -da m y f [a telefónica, revista] subscriber; [al fútbol, teatro] season-ticket holder.
abonar vt **-1.** [pagar - factura etc] to pay; ~ **algo en la cuenta de alguien** to credit sb's account with sthg. **-2.** [tierra] to fertilize. ◆ **abonarse** vpr: ~se (a) [revista] to subscribe (to); [fútbol, teatro] to buy a season ticket (for).
abono m **-1.** [pase] season ticket. **-2.** [fertilizante] fertilizer. **-3.** [pago] payment. **-4.** Amer [plazo] instalment.
abordar vt **-1.** [embarcación] to board. **-2.** fig [tema, tarea] to tackle.
aborigen adj [indígena] indigenous; [de Australia] aboriginal.
aborrecer vt to abhor, to loathe.
abortar vi [MED - espontáneamente] to have a miscarriage; [- intencionadamente] to have an abortion.
aborto m [MED - espontáneo] miscarriage; [- intencionado] abortion.
abotonar vt to button up. ◆ **abotonarse** vpr to do one's buttons up; [abrigo, camisa] to button up.
abovedado, -da adj arched, vaulted.
abrasar vt **-1.** [quemar - casa, bosque] to burn down; [- persona, mano, garganta] to burn. **-2.** [desecar - suj: sol, calor, lejía] to scorch; [- suj: sed] to parch.
abrazadera f TECN brace, bracket; [en carpintería] clamp.
abrazar vt [con los brazos] to hug, to embrace. ◆ **abrazarse** vpr to hug ○ embrace (each other).
abrazo m embrace, hug; **un (fuerte)** ~ [en cartas] best wishes.
abrebotellas m inv bottle opener.
abrecartas m inv paper knife.
abrelatas m inv tin opener Br, can opener Am.
abreviar vt [gen] to shorten; [texto] to abridge; [palabra] to abbreviate; [viaje, estancia] to cut short.
abreviatura f abbreviation.
abridor m **-1.** [abrebotellas] (bottle)

opener. **-2.** [abrelatas] (tin) opener *Br*, (can) opener *Am*.

abrigar *vt* **-1.** [arropar - suj: persona] to wrap up; [- suj: ropa] to keep warm. **-2.** *fig* [albergar - esperanza] to cherish; [- sospechas, malas intenciones] to harbour. ◆ **abrigarse** *vpr* [arroparse] to wrap up.

abrigo *m* **-1.** [prenda] coat, overcoat. **-2.** [refugio] shelter.

abril *m* April; *ver también* **septiembre**.

abrillantar *vt* to polish.

abrir ◇ *vt* **-1.** [gen] to open; [alas] to spread; [melón] to cut open. **-2.** [cerradura] to unlock, to open; [pestillo] to pull back; [grifo] to turn on; [cremallera] to undo. **-3.** [túnel] to dig; [canal, camino] to build; [agujero, surco] to make. ◇ *vi* [establecimiento] to open. ◆ **abrirse** *vpr* **-1.** [sincerarse]: ~**se a alguien** to open up to sb. **-2.** [cielo] to clear.

abrochar *vt* to do up; [cinturón] to fasten. ◆ **abrocharse** *vpr* to do up; [cinturón] to fasten.

abrumar *vt* [agobiar] to overwhelm.

abrupto, -ta *adj* [escarpado] sheer; [accidentado] rugged.

absceso *m* abscess.

absentismo *m* [de terrateniente] absentee landownership.

ábside *m* apse.

absolución *f* **-1.** DER acquittal. **-2.** RELIG absolution.

absoluto, -ta *adj* [gen] absolute; [silencio, obediencia] total. ◆ **en absoluto** *loc adv* [en negativas] at all; [tras pregunta] not at all; ¿**te gusta?** — **en** ~ do you like it? — not at all; **nada en** ~ nothing at all.

absolver *vt*: ~ **a alguien (de algo)** DER to acquit sb (of sthg); RELIG to absolve sb (of sthg).

absorbente *adj* **-1.** [que empapa] absorbent. **-2.** [actividad] absorbing.

absorber *vt* **-1.** [gen] to absorb. **-2.** [consumir, gastar] to soak up.

absorción *f* absorption.

absorto, -ta *adj*: ~ **(en)** absorbed ○ engrossed (in).

abstemio, -mia *adj* teetotal.

abstención *f* abstention.

abstenerse *vpr*: ~ **(de algo/de hacer algo)** to abstain (from sthg/from doing sthg).

abstinencia *f* abstinence.

abstracción *f* [gen] abstraction.

abstracto, -ta *adj* abstract.

abstraer *vt* to consider separately.

abstraído, -da *adj* lost in thought.

absuelto, -ta *pp* → **absolver**.

absurdo, -da *adj* absurd. ◆ **absurdo** *m*: **decir/hacer un** ~ to say/do something ridiculous.

abuchear *vt* to boo.

abuelo, -la *m y f* [familiar] grandfather (*f* grandmother). ◆ **abuelos** *mpl* grandparents.

abulia *f* apathy, lethargy.

abúlico, -ca *adj* apathetic, lethargic.

abultado, -da *adj* [paquete] bulky; [labios] thick.

abultar ◇ *vt* **-1.** [hinchar] to swell. **-2.** [exagerar] to blow up. ◇ *vi* [ser difícil de manejar] to be bulky.

abundancia *f* **-1.** [gran cantidad] abundance; **en** ~ in abundance. **-2.** [riqueza] plenty, prosperity.

abundante *adj* abundant.

abundar *vi* [ser abundante] to abound.

aburguesarse *vpr* to adopt middle-class ways.

aburrido, -da ◇ *adj* **-1.** [harto, fastidiado] bored; **estar** ~ **de hacer algo** to be fed up with doing sthg. **-2.** [que aburre] boring. ◇ *m y f* bore.

aburrimiento *m* boredom.

aburrir *vt* to bore. ◆ **aburrirse** *vpr* to get bored; [estar aburrido] to be bored.

abusado, -da *adj Amer* astute, shrewd.

abusar *vi* **-1.** [excederse] to go too far; ~ **de algo** to abuse sthg; ~ **de alguien** to take advantage of sb. **-2.** [forzar sexualmente]: ~ **de alguien** to sexually abuse sb.

abusivo, -va *adj* [trato] very bad, appalling; [precio] extortionate.

abuso *m* [uso excesivo]: ~ **(de)** abuse (of); ~ **de confianza** breach of confidence; ~**s deshonestos** sexual abuse (*U*).

abyecto, -ta *adj culto* vile, wretched.

a/c *abrev de* **a cuenta**.

a. C. (*abrev de* **antes de Cristo**) BC.

acá *adv* **-1.** [lugar] here; **de** ~ **para allá** back and forth. **-2.** [tiempo]: **de una semana** ~ during the last week.

acabado, -da *adj* **-1.** [completo] perfect, consummate. **-2.** [fracasado] finished. ◆ **acabado** *m* [de producto] finish; [de piso] décor.

acabar ◇ *vt* **-1.** [concluir] to finish. **-2.** [consumir - provisiones, dinero] to use up; [- comida] to finish. ◇ *vi* **-1.** [gen] to finish, to end; ~ **de hacer algo** to finish doing sthg. **-2.** [haber hecho recientemente]: ~ **de hacer algo** to have just done sthg; **acabo de llegar** I've just arrived. **-3.** [terminar por - persona]: ~ **por hacer algo**, ~ **haciendo algo** to end up doing sthg. **-4.** [destruir]: ~ **con** [gen] to destroy; [salud] to ruin; [paciencia] to exhaust; [violencia, crimen] to put an end to. ◆ **acabarse** *vpr* **-1.** [agotarse] to be used up; **se nos ha acabado el petróleo** we're out of petrol; **se ha acabado la comida** there's no more food left, all the food has gone. **-2.** [concluir] to finish. **-3.** *loc*: **¡se acabó!** [¡basta ya!] that's enough!; [se terminó] that's it, then!

acabóse *m fam*: **¡es el ~!** it really is the limit!

academia *f* **-1.** [colegio] school, academy. **-2.** [sociedad] academy. ◆ **Real Academia Española** *f institution that sets lexical and syntactical standards for Spanish.*

académico, -ca *adj* academic.

acaecer *v impers culto* to occur.

acallar *vt* to silence.

acalorado, -da *adj* **-1.** [por calor] hot. **-2.** [apasionado - debate] heated.

acalorar *vt* [excitar]: ~ **a alguien** to make sb hot under the collar. ◆ **acalorarse** *vpr* [excitarse] to get aroused O excited.

acampanado, -da *adj* flared.

acampar *vi* to camp.

acanalado, -da *adj* [columna] fluted; [tejido] ribbed; [hierro, uralita] corrugated.

acantilado *m* cliff.

acaparar *vt* **-1.** [monopolizar] to monopolize; [mercado] to corner. **-2.** [guardarse] to hoard.

acápite *m Amer* paragraph.

acaramelado, -da *adj fig* [afectado] sickly sweet.

acariciar *vt* **-1.** [persona] to caress; [animal] to stroke. **-2.** *fig* [idea, proyecto] to cherish.

acarrear *vt* **-1.** [transportar] to carry; [carbón] to haul. **-2.** *fig* [ocasionar] to bring, to give rise to.

acaso *adv* perhaps; **¿~ no lo sabías?** are you trying to tell me you didn't know?; **por si ~** (just) in case. ◆ **si acaso** ◇ *loc adv* [en todo caso] if anything. ◇ *loc conj* [en caso de que] if.

acatar *vt* to respect, to comply with.

acatarrarse *vpr* to catch a cold.

acaudalado, -da *adj* well-to-do.

acaudillar *vt* to lead.

acceder *vi* **-1.** [consentir]: ~ **(a algo/ hacer algo)** to agree (to sthg/to do

sthg). **-2.** [tener acceso]: ~ **a** to enter. **-3.** [alcanzar]: ~ **a** [trono] to accede to; [poder] to come to; [grado] to obtain.

accesible *adj* [gen] accessible.

accésit *m inv* consolation prize.

acceso *m* **-1.** [entrada]: ~ **(a)** entrance (to). **-2.** [paso]: ~ **(a)** access (to). **-3.** [carretera] access road. **-4.** *fig* [ataque] fit; [de fiebre, gripe] bout.

accesorio, -ria *adj* incidental. ◆ **accesorio** *m* (*gen pl*) accessory.

accidentado, -da ◇ *adj* **-1.** [vida] turbulent. **-2.** [viaje - en coche, tren, avión] bumpy. **-3.** [terreno, camino] rough, rugged. ◇ *m y f* injured person, victim.

accidental *adj* [imprevisto] accidental; [encuentro] chance.

accidentarse *vpr* to be involved in O have an accident.

accidente *m* **-1.** [desgracia] accident; ~ **de avión/coche** plane/car crash; ~ **de tráfico** road accident. **-2.** (*gen pl*) [del terreno] unevenness (*U*).

acción *f* **-1.** [gen] action. **-2.** [hecho] deed, act. **-3.** FIN share; ~ **ordinaria/ preferente** ordinary/preference share.

accionar *vt* to activate.

accionista *m y f* shareholder.

acechar *vt* **-1.** [vigilar] to keep under surveillance; [suj: cazador] to stalk. **-2.** [amenazar] to be lying in wait for.

acecho *m*: **estar al ~ de** to lie in wait for; *fig* to be on the lookout for.

aceite *m* oil; ~ **de colza/girasol/oliva** rapeseed/sunflower/olive oil.

aceitera *f* oil can. ◆ **aceiteras** *fpl* cruet (*sg*).

aceitoso, -sa *adj* oily.

aceituna *f* olive.

aceleración *f* acceleration.

acelerador, -ra *adj* accelerating. ◆ **acelerador** *m* accelerator.

acelerar ◇ *vt* [avivar] to speed up; TECN to accelerate. ◇ *vi* to accelerate. ◆ **acelerarse** *vpr* to hurry up.

acelga *f* chard.

acento *m* **-1.** [gen] accent. **-2.** [intensidad] stress, accent.

acentuación *f* accentuation.

acentuar *vt* **-1.** [palabra, letra - al escribir] to put an accent on; [- al hablar] to stress. **-2.** *fig* [realzar] to accentuate. ◆ **acentuarse** *vpr* [intensificarse] to deepen, to increase.

acepción *f* meaning, sense.

aceptable *adj* acceptable.

aceptación *f* **-1.** [aprobación] acceptance. **-2.** [éxito] success, popularity.

aceptar *vt* to accept.

acequia *f* irrigation channel.

acera *f* [para peatones] pavement *Br*, sidewalk *Am*.

acerbo, -ba *adj culto* [mordaz] caustic.

acerca ◇ **acerca de** *loc adv* about.

acercar *vt* to bring nearer ○ closer; ¡acércame el pan! could you pass me the bread? ◆ **acercarse** *vpr* [arrimarse - viniendo] to come closer; [- yendo] to go over.

acero *m* steel; ~ **inoxidable** stainless steel.

acérrimo, -ma *adj* [defensor] diehard (*antes de sust*); [enemigo] bitter.

acertado, -da *adj* **-1.** [con acierto - respuesta] correct; [- comentario] appropriate. **-2.** [oportuno] good, clever.

acertar ◇ *vt* **-1.** [adivinar] to guess (correctly). **-2.** [el blanco] to hit. **-3.** [elegir bien] to choose well. ◇ *vi* **-1.** [atinar]: ~ **(al hacer algo)** to be right (to do sthg). **-2.** [conseguir]: ~ **a hacer algo** to manage to do sthg. **-3.** [hallar]: ~ **con** to find.

acertijo *m* riddle.

acervo *m* [patrimonio] heritage.

achacar *vt*: ~ **algo a alguien/algo** to attribute sthg to sb/sthg.

achantar *vt fam* to put the wind up. ◆ **achantarse** *vpr fam* to get the wind up.

achaparrado, -da *adj* squat.

achaque *m* ailment.

achatado, -da *adj* flattened.

achicar *vt* **-1.** [tamaño] to make smaller. **-2.** [agua - de barco] to bale out. **-3.** *fig* [acobardar] to intimidate.

achicharrar *vt* [chamuscar] to burn. ◆ **achicharrarse** *vpr* **-1.** *fig* [de calor] to fry. **-2.** [chamuscarse] to burn.

achicoria *f* chicory.

achuchado, -da *adj fam* hard, tough.

achuchar *vt fam* [abrazar] to hug.

achurar *vt Amer* **-1.** [acuchillar] to stab to death. **-2.** [animal] to disembowel.

aciago, -ga *adj culto* black, fateful.

acicalar *vt* [arreglar] to do up. ◆ **acicalarse** *vpr* to do o.s. up.

acicate *m fig* [estímulo] incentive.

acidez *f* **-1.** [cualidad] acidity. **-2.** MED: ~ **de estómago** heartburn.

ácido, -da *adj* **-1.** QUÍM acidic. **-2.** [bebida, sabor, carácter] acid, sour. ◆ **ácido** *m* QUÍM acid.

acierto *m* **-1.** [a pregunta] correct answer. **-2.** [habilidad, tino] good ○ sound judgment. **-3.** [éxito] success.

aclamación *f* [ovación] acclamation, acclaim; **por** ~ unanimously.

aclamar *vt* to acclaim.

aclaración *f* explanation.

aclarar *vt* **-1.** [ropa] to rinse. **-2.** [explicar] to clarify, to explain. **-3.** ~ **la voz** [carraspeando] to clear one's throat. ◆ **aclararse** *vpr* **-1.** [entender] to understand. **-2.** [explicarse] to explain o.s.

aclaratorio, -ria *adj* explanatory.

aclimatación *f* acclimatization.

aclimatar *vt* **-1.** [al clima]: ~ **algo/a alguien (a)** to acclimatize sthg/sb (to). **-2.** [a ambiente]: ~ **algo/a alguien a algo** to get sthg/sb used to sthg. ◆ **aclimatarse** *vpr* **-1.** [al clima]: ~**se (a algo)** to acclimatize (to sthg). **-2.** [a ambiente] to settle in; ~**se a algo** to get used to sthg.

acné *m* acne.

acobardar *vt* to frighten, to scare. ◆ **acobardarse** *vpr* to get frightened ○ scared; ~**se ante** to shrink back from.

acodarse *vpr*: ~**se (en)** to lean (on).

acogedor, -ra *adj* [país, persona] welcoming; [casa, ambiente] cosy.

acoger *vt* **-1.** [recibir] to welcome. **-2.** [dar refugio] to take in. ◆ **acogerse a** *vpr* [inmunidad parlamentaria etc] to take refuge in; [ley] to have recourse to.

acogida *f* **-1.** [de persona] welcome. **-2.** [de idea, película etc] reception.

acolchar *vt* to pad.

acometer ◇ *vt* **-1.** [atacar] to attack. **-2.** [emprender] to undertake. ◇ *vi* [embestir]: ~ **contra** to hurtle into.

acometida *f* **-1.** [ataque] attack, charge. **-2.** [de luz, gas etc] (mains) connection.

acomodado, -da *adj* [rico] well-off.

acomodador, -ra *m y f* usher (*f* usherette).

acomodar *vt* **-1.** [instalar - persona] to seat, to instal; [- cosa] to place. **-2.** [adaptar] to fit. ◆ **acomodarse** *vpr* [instalarse] to make o.s. comfortable; ~**se en** to settle down in.

acomodaticio, -cia *adj* [complaciente] accommodating, easy-going.

acompañamiento *m* CULIN & MÚS accompaniment.

acompañante *m y f* companion.

acompañar *vt* **-1.** [ir con]: ~ **a alguien** [gen] to go with ○ accompany sb; [a la puerta] to show sb out; [a casa] to walk sb home. **-2.** [estar con]: ~ **a alguien** to keep sb company. **-3.** [adjuntar] to enclose. **-4.** MÚS to accompany.

acompasar *vt:* ~ **algo (a)** to synchronize sthg (with).

acomplejar *vt* to give a complex.
◆ **acomplejarse** *vpr* to develop a complex.

acondicionado, -da *adj* equipped.

acondicionador *m* (air) conditioner.

acondicionar *vt* **-1.** [reformar] to convert, to upgrade. **-2.** [preparar] to prepare, to get ready.

acongojar *vt* to distress.

aconsejar *vt* [dar consejos]: ~ **a alguien (que haga algo)** to advise sb (to do sthg).

acontecer *v impers* to take place, to happen.

acontecimiento *m* event; **adelantarse** ○ **anticiparse a los** ~**s** to jump the gun; [prevenir] to take preemptive measures.

acopio *m* stock, store.

acoplar *vt* **-1.** [encajar] to attach, to fit together. **-2.** FERROC to couple. **-3.** *fig* [adaptar] to adapt, to fit.

acorazado, -da *adj* armour-plated.
◆ **acorazado** *m* battleship.

acordar *vt:* ~ **algo/hacer algo** to agree on sthg/to do sthg. ◆ **acordarse** *vpr:* ~**se (de algo/de hacer algo)** to remember (sthg/to do sthg).

acorde ○ *adj* [en consonancia]: ~ **con** in keeping with. ○ *m* MÚS chord.

acordeón *m* accordion.

acordonar *vt* [cercar] to cordon off.

acorralar *vt lit & fig* to corner.

acortar *vt* **-1.** [falda, pantalón etc] to take up; [cable] to shorten. **-2.** [tiempo] to cut short. **-3.** [extensión] to shorten.
◆ **acortarse** *vpr* [días] to get shorter; [reunión] to end early.

acosar *vt* **-1.** [hostigar] to harass. **-2.** [perseguir] to pursue relentlessly.

acoso *m* [hostigamiento] harassment; ~ **sexual** sexual harassment.

acostar *vt* [en la cama] to put to bed.
◆ **acostarse** *vpr* **-1.** [irse a la cama] to go to bed. **-2.** [tumbarse] to lie down. *fam* [tener relaciones sexuales]: ~**se con alguien** to sleep with sb.

acostumbrado, -da *adj* **-1.** [habitual] usual. **-2.** [habituado]: **estar** ~ **a** to be used to.

acostumbrar ○ *vt* [habituar]: ~ **a alguien a algo/a hacer algo** to get sb used to sthg/to doing sthg. ○ *vi* [soler]: ~ **a hacer algo** to be in the habit of doing sthg, usually to do sthg.
◆ **acostumbrarse** *vpr* [habituarse]: ~**se a**

algo/a hacer algo to get used to sthg/ to doing sthg.

acotación *f* [nota] note in the margin.

acotar *vt* **-1.** [terreno, campo] to enclose; *fig* [tema etc] to delimit. **-2.** [texto] to write notes in the margin of.

acrecentar *vt* to increase.

acreditado, -da *adj* **-1.** [médico, abogado etc] distinguished; [marca] reputable. **-2.** [embajador, representante] accredited.

acreditar *vt* **-1.** [certificar] to certify; [autorizar] to authorize. **-2.** [confirmar] to confirm. **-3.** [embajador] to accredit. **-4.** FIN to credit.

acreedor, -ra ○ *adj:* **hacerse** ~ **de algo** to earn sthg, to show o.s. to be worthy of sthg. ○ *m y f* creditor.

acribillar *vt* [herir]: ~ **(a)** to pepper ○ riddle (with).

acrílico, -ca *adj* acrylic.

acrimonia = **acritud**.

acritud, acrimonia *f* **-1.** [de olor] acridity, pungency; [de sabor] bitterness. **-2.** *fig* [mordacidad] venom. **-3.** [desavenencia] acrimony.

acrobacia *f* [en circo] acrobatics (*pl*).

acróbata *m y f* acrobat.

acta *f* (*el*) **-1.** [de junta, reunión] minutes (*pl*); **levantar** ~ to take the minutes. **-2.** [de defunción etc] certificate; ~ **notarial** affidavit. ◆ **actas** *fpl* minutes.

actitud *f* [disposición de ánimo] attitude.

activar *vt* **-1.** [gen] to activate. **-2.** [explosivo] to detonate.

actividad *f* activity.

activo, -va *adj* **-1.** [gen & GRAM] active. **-2.** [trabajador] hard-working. ◆ **activo** *m* FIN assets (*pl*).

acto *m* **-1.** [acción] act; **hacer** ~ **de presencia** to show one's face; ~ **de solidaridad** show of solidarity. **-2.** [ceremonia] ceremony. **-3.** TEATR act. ◆ **en el acto** *loc adv* on the spot.

actor, -triz *m y f* actor (*f* actress).

actuación *f* **-1.** [conducta, proceder] conduct, behaviour. **-2.** [interpretación] performance.

actual *adj* **-1.** [existente] present, current. **-2.** [de moda] modern, present-day. **-3.** [de actualidad] topical.

actualidad *f* **-1.** [momento presente] current situation; **de** ~ [moderno] in fashion; [de interés actual] topical; **en la** ~ at the present time, these days. **-2.** [noticia] news (*U*); **ser** ~ to be making the news.

actualizar *vt* to update; [tecnología, industria] to modernize.

actualmente adv [hoy día] these days, nowadays; [en este momento] at the (present) moment.

actuar vi [gen] to act; ~ **de** to act as.

acuarela f watercolour.

acuario m aquarium. ◆ **Acuario** ◇ m [zodiaco] Aquarius. ◇ m y f [persona] Aquarius.

acuartelar vt -1. [alojar] to quarter. -2. [retener] to confine to barracks.

acuático, -ca adj aquatic.

acuchillar vt -1. [apuñalar] to stab. -2. [mueble, parquet] to grind down.

acuciar vt culto [suj: persona] to goad; [suj: necesidad, deseo] to press.

acuclillarse vpr to squat (down).

acudir vi -1. [ir] to go; [venir] to come. -2. [recurrir]: ~ **a** to go ○ turn to. -3. [presentarse]: ~ **(a)** [escuela, iglesia] to attend; [cita, examen] to turn up (for); fig [memoria, mente] to come (to).

acueducto m aqueduct.

acuerdo m agreement; **de** ~ all right, O.K.; **de** ~ **con** [conforme a] in accordance with; **estar de** ~ **(con alguien/en hacer algo)** to agree (with sb/to do sthg); **llegar a un** ~, **ponerse de** ~ to reach agreement.

acumular vt to accumulate.

acunar vt to rock.

acuñar vt -1. [moneda] to mint. -2. [palabra] to coin.

acuoso, -sa adj [gen] watery.

acupuntura f acupuncture.

acurrucarse vpr to crouch down; [por frío] to huddle up; [por miedo] to cower; [en sitio agradable] to curl up.

acusación f [inculpación] charge.

acusado, -da ◇ adj [marcado] marked. ◇ m y f [procesado] accused, defendant.

acusar vt -1. [culpar] to accuse; JUR to charge; ~ **a alguien de algo** [gen] to accuse sb of sthg; JUR to charge sb with sthg. -2. [mostrar] to show.

acusativo m accusative.

acuse ◆ **acuse de recibo** m acknowledgement of receipt.

acústico, -ca adj acoustic. ◆ **acústica** f [de local] acoustics (pl).

a.D. (abrev de anno Domini) AD.

adagio m [sentencia breve] adage.

adaptación f -1. [aclimatación]: ~ **(a)** adjustment (to). -2. [modificación] adaptation.

adaptar vt -1. [acomodar, ajustar] to adjust. -2. [modificar] to adapt. ◆ **adaptarse** vpr: ~**se (a)** to adjust (to).

adecentar vt to tidy up.

adecuado, -da adj appropriate, suitable.

adecuar vt to adapt. ◆ **adecuarse a** vpr -1. [ser adecuado] to be appropriate for. -2. [adaptarse] to adjust to.

adefesio m fam [persona fea] fright.

a. de JC., a.JC. (abrev de antes de Jesucristo) BC.

adelantado, -da adj advanced; **llevo el reloj** ~ my watch is fast; **por** ~ in advance.

adelantamiento m AUTOM overtaking.

adelantar ◇ vt -1. [dejar atrás] to overtake. -2. [mover hacia adelante] to move forward; [pie, reloj] to put forward. -3. [en el tiempo - trabajo, viaje] to bring forward; [- dinero] to pay in advance. ◇ vi -1. [progresar] to make progress. -2. [reloj] to be fast. ◆ **adelantarse** vpr -1. [en el tiempo] to be early; [frío, verano] to arrive early; [reloj] to gain; ~**se a alguien** to beat sb to it. -2. [en el espacio] to go on ahead.

adelante ◇ adv forward, ahead; **(de ahora) en** ~ from now on, in future; **más** ~ [en el tiempo] later (on); [en el espacio] further on. ◇ interj: ¡~! [¡siga!] go ahead!; [¡pase!] come in!

adelanto m advance; ~ **de dinero** advance.

adelgazar ◇ vi to lose weight, to slim. ◇ vt to lose.

ademán m [gesto - con manos etc] gesture; [- con cara] face, expression; **en** ~ **de** as if to.

además adv moreover, besides; [también] also; ~ **de** as well as, in addition to.

adentrarse vpr: ~ **en** [jungla etc] to enter the heart of; [tema etc] to study in depth.

adentro adv inside; **tierra** ~ inland; **mar** ~ out to sea.

adepto, -ta m y f: ~ **(a)** follower (of).

aderezar vt [sazonar - ensalada] to dress; [- comida] to season.

aderezo m [aliño - de ensalada] dressing; [- de comida] seasoning.

adeudar vt -1. [deber] to owe. -2. COM to debit. ◆ **adeudarse** vpr to get into debt.

adherir vt to stick. ◆ **adherirse** vpr -1. [pegarse] to stick. -2. [mostrarse de acuerdo]: ~**se a** to adhere to.

adhesión f [apoyo] support.

adhesivo, -va adj adhesive. ◆ **adhesivo** m [pegatina] sticker.

adicción f: ~ **(a)** addiction (to).

adición f addition.

adicional adj additional.

adicto, -ta ◇ adj: ~ **(a)** addicted (to).
◇ m y f: ~ **(a)** addict (of).

adiestrar vt to train; ~ **a alguien en algo/para hacer algo** to train sb in sthg/to do sthg.

adinerado, -da adj wealthy.

adiós ◇ m goodbye. ◇ interj: ¡~! goodbye!; [al cruzarse con alguien] hello!

adiposo, -sa adj fatty, adipose.

aditivo m additive.

adivinanza f riddle.

adivinar vt **-1.** [predecir] to foretell; [el futuro] to tell. **-2.** [acertar] to guess (correctly).

adivino, -na m y f fortune-teller.

adjetivo m adjective.

adjudicación f awarding.

adjudicar vt [asignar] to award. ◆ **adjudicarse** vpr [apropiarse] to take for o.s.

adjuntar vt to enclose.

adjunto, -ta ◇ adj [incluido] enclosed; ~ **le remito ...** please find enclosed .... ◇ m y f [auxiliar] assistant.

administración f **-1.** [suministro] supply; [de medicamento, justicia] administering. **-2.** [gestión] administration. **-3.** [gerentes] management; [oficina] manager's office. ◆ **Administración** f [gobierno] administration; **Administración local** local government; **Administración pública** civil service.

administrador, -ra m y f **-1.** [de empresa] manager. **-2.** [de bienes ajenos] administrator.

administrar vt **-1.** [gestionar - empresa, finca etc] to manage, to run; [- casa] to run. **-2.** [país] to run the affairs of. **-3.** [suministrar] to administer.

administrativo, -va adj administrative.

admirable adj admirable.

admiración f **-1.** [sentimiento] admiration. **-2.** [signo ortográfico] exclamation mark.

admirar vt **-1.** [gen] to admire. **-2.** [sorprender] to amaze. ◆ **admirarse** vpr: ~**se (de)** to be amazed (by).

admisible adj acceptable.

admisión f **-1.** [de persona] admission. **-2.** [de solicitudes etc] acceptance.

admitir vt **-1.** [acoger, reconocer] to admit; ~ **a alguien en** to admit sb to. **-2.** [aceptar] to accept.

ADN (abrev de **ácido desoxirribonucleico**) m DNA.

adobar vt to marinate.

adobe m adobe.

adobo m [salsa] marinade.

adoctrinar vt to instruct.

adolecer ◆ **adolecer de** vi **-1.** [enfermedad] to suffer from. **-2.** [defecto] to be guilty of.

adolescencia f adolescence.

adolescente adj, m y f adolescent.

adonde adv where; **la ciudad** ~ **vamos** the city we are going to, the city where we are going.

adónde adv where.

adopción f [de hijo, propuesta] adoption; [de ley] passing.

adoptar vt [hijo, propuesta] to adopt; [ley] to pass.

adoptivo, -va adj [hijo, país] adopted; [padre] adoptive.

adoquín (pl **adoquines**) m cobblestone.

adorable adj [persona] adorable; [ambiente, película] wonderful.

adoración f adoration; **sentir** ~ **por alguien** to worship sb.

adorar vt **-1.** [reverenciar] to worship. **-2.** [pirrarse por] to adore.

adormecer vt [producir sueño] to lull to sleep. ◆ **adormecerse** vpr to nod off.

adormilarse vpr to doze.

adornar vt to decorate.

adorno m decoration.

adosado, -da adj [casa] semi-detached.

adquirir vt **-1.** [comprar] to acquire, to purchase. **-2.** [conseguir - conocimientos, hábito, cultura] to acquire; [- éxito, popularidad] to achieve; [- enfermedad] to catch, to get.

adquisición f **-1.** [compra, cosa comprada] purchase. **-2.** [obtención] acquisition.

adquisitivo, -va adj purchasing (antes de sust).

adrede adv on purpose, deliberately.

adrenalina f adrenalin.

adscribir vt **-1.** [asignar] to assign. **-2.** [destinar] to appoint ○ assign to. ◆ **adscribirse** vpr: ~**se (a)** [grupo, partido] to become a member (of); [ideología] to subscribe to.

adscrito, -ta ◇ pp → **adscribir.** ◇ adj assigned.

aduana f [administración] customs (pl).

aducir vt to adduce.

adueñarse ◆ **adueñarse de** vpr **-1.** [apoderarse] to take over. **-2.** [dominar] to take hold of.

adulación f flattery.

adulador, -ra adj flattering.

adular *vt* to flatter.

adulterar *vt* [alimento] to adulterate.

adulterio *m* adultery.

adúltero, -ra ◇ *adj* adulterous. ◇ *m y f* adulterer (*f* adulteress).

adulto, -ta *adj, m y f* adult.

adusto, -ta *adj* dour.

advenedizo, -za *adj, m y f* parvenu (*f* parvenue).

advenimiento *m* advent; [al trono] accession.

adverbio *m* adverb.

adversario, -ria *m y f* adversary.

adversidad *f* adversity.

adverso, -sa *adj* adverse; [destino] unkind; [suerte] bad; [viento] unfavourable.

advertencia *f* warning; **servir de ~** to serve as a warning.

advertir *vt* **-1.** [notar] to notice. **-2.** [prevenir, avisar] to warn; **te advierto que no deberías hacerlo** I'd advise against you doing it; **te advierto que no me sorprende** mind you, it doesn't surprise me.

adviento *m* Advent.

adyacente *adj* adjacent.

aéreo, -a *adj* **-1.** [del aire] aerial. **-2.** AERON air (*antes de sust*).

aerobic [ae'roßik] *m* aerobics (*U*).

aeroclub (*pl* **aeroclubs**) *m* flying club.

aerodeslizador *m* hovercraft.

aerodinámico, -ca *adj* **-1.** FÍS aerodynamic. **-2.** [forma, línea] streamlined.

aeródromo *m* airfield, aerodrome.

aeroespacial *adj* aerospace (*antes de sust*).

aerógrafo *m* airbrush.

aerolínea *f* airline.

aeromoza *f Amer* air hostess.

aeronauta *m y f* aeronaut.

aeronaval *adj* air and sea (*antes de sust*).

aeronave *f* [gen] aircraft; [dirigible] airship.

aeroplano *m* aeroplane.

aeropuerto *m* airport.

aerosol *m* aerosol.

aeroespacial = **aeroespacial**.

aerostático, -ca *adj* aerostatic.

aeróstato *m* hot-air balloon.

aerotaxi *m* light aircraft (*for hire*).

afabilidad *f* affability.

afable *adj* affable.

afamado, -da *adj* famous.

afán *m* **-1.** [esfuerzo] hard work (*U*). **-2.** [anhelo] urge.

afanador, -ra *m y f Amer* cleaner.

afanar *vt fam* [robar] to pinch.
◆ **afanarse** *vpr* [esforzarse]: **~se (por hacer algo)** to do everything one can (to do sthg).

afanoso, -sa *adj* **-1.** [trabajoso, penoso] demanding. **-2.** [que se afana] eager.

afear *vt* to make ugly, to scar.

afección *f* MED complaint, disease.

afectación *f* affectation.

afectado, -da *adj* **-1.** [gen] affected. **-2.** [afligido] upset, badly affected.

afectar *vt* **-1.** [gen] to affect. **-2.** [afligir] to upset, to affect badly.

afectísimo, -ma *adj* [en cartas]: **suyo ~** yours faithfully.

afectivo, -va *adj* **-1.** [emocional] emotional. **-2.** [cariñoso] affectionate.

afecto *m* affection, fondness; **sentir ~ por alguien, tenerle ~ a alguien** to be fond of sb.

afectuoso, -sa *adj* affectionate, loving.

afeitar *vt* [pelo] to shave. ◆ **afeitarse** *vpr* to shave.

afeminado, -da *adj* effeminate.

aferrarse *vpr*: **~ a** *lit & fig* to cling to.

Afganistán Afghanistan.

afianzamiento *m* [en cargo, liderazgo] consolidation.

afianzar *vt* [objeto] to secure.
◆ **afianzarse** *vpr* to steady o.s.; **~se en algo** [opinión etc] to become sure O convinced of sthg; [cargo, liderazgo] to consolidate sthg.

afiche *m Amer* poster.

afición *f* **-1.** [inclinación] fondness, liking; **por ~** as a hobby; **tener ~ a algo** to be keen on sthg. **-2.** [aficionados] fans (*pl*).

aficionado, -da ◇ *adj* **-1.** [interesado] keen; **ser ~ a algo** to be keen on sthg. **-2.** [amateur] amateur. ◇ *m y f* **-1.** [interesado] fan; **~ al cine** film fan. **-2.** [amateur] amateur.

aficionar *vt*: **~ a alguien a algo** to make sb keen on sthg. ◆ **aficionarse** *vpr*: **~se a algo** to become keen on sthg.

afilado, -da *adj* [fino] sharp; [dedos] pointed.

afilar *vt* to sharpen.

afiliado, -da *m y f*: **~ (a)** member (of).

afiliarse *vpr*: **~ a** to join, to become a member of.

afín *adj* [semejante] similar, like.

afinar *vt* **-1.** MÚS [instrumento] to tune; **~ la voz** to sing in tune. **-2.** [perfeccionar, mejorar] to fine-tune. **-3.** [pulir] to refine.

afinidad f [gen & QUÍM] affinity.

afirmación f statement, assertion.

afirmar vt **-1.** [confirmar] to confirm. **-2.** [decir] to say, to declare. **-3.** [consolidar] to reaffirm. **-4.** CONSTR to reinforce.

afirmativo, -va adj affirmative.

aflicción f suffering, sorrow.

afligir vt to afflict; [causar pena] to distress.

aflojar ◇ vt [destensar] to loosen; [cuerda] to slacken. ◇ vi **-1.** [disminuir] to abate, to die down. **-2.** fig [ceder] to ease off. ◆ **aflojarse** vpr [gen] to come loose; [cuerda] to slacken.

aflorar vi fig [surgir] to (come to the) surface, to show.

afluencia f stream, volume.

afluente m tributary.

afluir ◆ **afluir a** vi **-1.** [gente] to flock to. **-2.** [sangre, fluido] to flow to.

afonía f loss of voice.

afónico, -ca adj: **quedarse ~** to lose one's voice.

aforo m [cabida] seating capacity.

afortunadamente adv fortunately.

afortunado, -da adj **-1.** [agraciado] lucky, fortunate. **-2.** [feliz, oportuno] happy, felicitous.

afrenta f [ofensa, agravio] affront.

África Africa.

africano, -na adj, m y f African.

afrontar vt [hacer frente a] to face.

afuera adv outside; **por (la parte de) ~** on the outside. ◆ **afueras** fpl: **las ~s** the outskirts.

afuerita adv Amer fam right outside.

afusilar vt Amer fam to shoot.

agachar vt to lower; [la cabeza] to bow. ◆ **agacharse** vpr [acuclillarse] to crouch down; [inclinar la cabeza] to stoop.

agalla f ZOOL gill. ◆ **agallas** fpl fig guts.

agarradero m **-1.** [asa] hold. **-2.** fam fig [pretexto] pretext, excuse.

agarrado, -da adj **-1.** [asido]: **~ (de)** gripped (by); **~s del brazo** arm in arm; **~s de la mano** hand in hand. **-2.** fam [tacaño] tight, stingy.

agarrar vt **-1.** [asir] to grab. **-2.** [pillar - ladrón, enfermedad] to catch. ◆ **agarrarse** vpr [sujetarse] to hold on.

agarrón m [tirón] pull, tug.

agarrotar vt [parte del cuerpo] to cut off the circulation in; [mente] to numb. ◆ **agarrotarse** vpr **-1.** [parte del cuerpo] to go numb. **-2.** [mecanismo] to seize up.

agasajar vt to lavish attention on.

ágata f (el) agate.

agazaparse vpr **-1.** [para esconderse] to crouch. **-2.** [agacharse] to bend down.

agencia f **-1.** [empresa] agency; **~ matrimonial** marriage bureau; **~ de viajes** travel agency. **-2.** [sucursal] branch.

agenda f **-1.** [de notas, fechas] diary; [de teléfonos, direcciones] book. **-2.** [de trabajo] agenda.

agente ◇ m y f [persona] agent; **~ de policía** ○ **de la autoridad** policeman (f policewoman); **~ de aduanas** customs officer; **~ de cambio (y bolsa)** stockbroker; **~ secreto** secret agent. ◇ m [causa activa] agent.

ágil adj [movimiento, persona] agile.

agilidad f agility.

agilizar vt to speed up.

agitación f **-1.** [intranquilidad] restlessness. **-2.** [jaleo] racket, commotion. **-3.** [conflicto] unrest.

agitar vt **-1.** [mover - botella etc] to shake; [- líquido] to stir; [- brazos] to wave. **-2.** [inquietar] to perturb, to worry. **-3.** [alterar, perturbar] to stir up. ◆ **agitarse** vpr [inquietarse] to get worried.

aglomeración f build-up; [de gente] crowd.

aglomerar vt to bring together. ◆ **aglomerarse** vpr to amass.

agnóstico, -ca adj, m y f agnostic.

agobiado, -da adj: **~ (de)** [trabajo] snowed under (with); [problemas] weighed down (with).

agobiar vt to overwhelm. ◆ **agobiarse** vpr to feel overwhelmed, to let things get one down.

agobio m **-1.** [físico] choking, suffocation. **-2.** [psíquico] pressure.

agolparse vpr [gente] to crowd round; [sangre] to rush.

agonía f **-1.** [pena] agony. **-2.** [del moribundo] death throes (pl).

agonizante adj dying.

agonizar vi [expirar] to be dying.

agosto m **-1.** [mes] August; ver también **septiembre. -2.** loc: **hacer su ~** to line one's pockets.

agotado, -da adj **-1.** [cansado]: **~ (de)** exhausted (from). **-2.** [producto] out of stock, sold out. **-3.** [pila, batería] flat.

agotador, -ra adj exhausting.

agotamiento m [cansancio] exhaustion.

agotar vt [gen] to exhaust; [producto] to sell out of; [agua] to drain. ◆ **agotarse** vpr **-1.** [cansarse] to tire o.s. out. **-2.** [acabarse] to run out; [libro, disco, entradas] to be sold out; [pila, batería] to go flat.

agraciado, -da *adj* **-1.** [atractivo] attractive, fetching. **-2.** [afortunado]: ~ **con algo** lucky enough to win sthg.

agraciar *vt* [embellecer] to make more attractive O fetching.

agradable *adj* pleasant.

agradar *vt* to please.

agradecer *vt* [suj: persona]: ~ **algo a alguien** [dar las gracias] to thank sb for sthg; [estar agradecido] to be grateful to sb for sthg.

agradecido, -da *adj* grateful.

agradecimiento *m* gratitude.

agrado *m* [gusto] pleasure; **ésto no es de mi** ~ this is not to my liking.

agrandar *vt* to make bigger.

agrario, -ria *adj* [reforma] agrarian; [producto, política] agricultural.

agravante ◇ *adj* aggravating. ◇ *m o f* **-1.** [problema] additional problem. **-2.** DER aggravating circumstance.

agravar *vt* to aggravate; [impuestos etc] to increase (the burden of). ◆ **agravarse** *vpr* to get worse.

agraviar *vt* to offend.

agravio *m* **-1.** [ofensa] offence, insult. **-2.** [perjuicio] wrong.

agredir *vt* to attack.

agregado, -da *m y f* **-1.** EDUC assistant teacher. **-2.** [de embajada] attaché; ~ **cultural** cultural attaché. ◆ **agregado** *m* [añadido] addition.

agregar *vt*: ~ **(algo a algo)** to add (sthg to sthg).

agresión *f* [ataque] act of aggression, attack.

agresividad *f* aggression.

agresivo, -va *adj lit & fig* aggressive.

agresor, -ra *m y f* attacker, assailant.

agreste *adj* [abrupto, rocoso] rugged.

agriar *vt* [vino, leche] to (turn) sour. ◆ **agriarse** *vpr lit & fig* to turn sour.

agrícola *adj* agricultural; [pueblo] farming (*antes de sust*).

agricultor, -ra *m y f* farmer.

agricultura *f* agriculture.

agridulce *adj* bittersweet; CULIN sweet and sour.

agrietar *vt* **-1.** [muro, tierra] to crack. **-2.** [labios, manos] to chap. ◆ **agrietarse** *vpr* [la piel] to chap.

agrio, agria *adj* **-1.** [ácido] sour. **-2.** *fig* [áspero] acerbic, bitter.

agronomía *f* agronomy.

agropecuario, -ria *adj* farming and livestock (*antes de sust*).

agrupación *f* [asociación] group.

agrupamiento *m* [concentración] grouping.

agrupar *vt* to group (together). ◆ **agruparse** *vpr* **-1.** [congregarse] to gather (round). **-2.** [unirse] to form a group.

agua *f* (*el*) water; ~ **mineral sin gas/con gas** still/sparkling mineral water; **venir como** ~ **de mayo** to be a godsend. ◆ **aguas** *fpl* **-1.** [manantial] waters, spring (*sg*). **-2.** [de río, mar] waters; ~**s territoriales** O **jurisdiccionales** territorial waters. **-3.** [de diamantes, telas] water (*U*). ◆ **agua de colonia** *f* eau de cologne. ◆ **agua oxigenada** *f* hydrogen peroxide. ◆ **aguas residuales** *fpl* sewage (*U*).

aguacate *m* [fruto] avocado (pear).

aguacero *m* shower.

aguachirle *f* dishwater (*U*), revolting drink.

aguado, -da *adj* [con demasiada agua] watery; [diluido a propósito] watered-down.

aguafiestas *m y f inv* spoilsport.

aguafuerte *m* etching.

aguamarina *f* aquamarine.

aguanieve *f* sleet.

aguantar *vt* **-1.** [sostener] to hold. **-2.** [resistir - peso] to bear. **-3.** [tolerar, soportar] to bear, to stand; **no sé cómo la aguantas** I don't know how you put up with her. **-4.** [contener - risa] to contain; [- respiración] to hold. ◆ **aguantarse** *vpr* **-1.** [contenerse] to restrain o.s. **-2.** [resignarse]: **no quiere** ~**se** he refuses to put up with it.

aguante *m* **-1.** [paciencia] self-restraint. **-2.** [resistencia] strength; [de persona] stamina.

aguar *vt* **-1.** [mezclar con agua] to water down. **-2.** *fig* [estropear] to spoil.

aguardar *vt* to wait for, to await.

aguardiente *m* spirit, liquor.

aguarrás *m* turpentine.

agudeza *f* [gen] sharpness.

agudizar *vt* [fig] [acentuar] to exacerbate. ◆ **agudizarse** *vpr* [crisis] to get worse.

agudo, -da *adj* **-1.** [gen] sharp; [crisis, problema, enfermedad] serious, acute. **-2.** *fig* [perspicaz] keen, sharp. **-3.** *fig* [ingenioso] witty. **-4.** MÚS [nota, voz] high, high-pitched.

agüero *m*: **de buen/mal** ~ that bodes well/ill.

aguijón m -1. [de insecto] sting. -2. fig [estímulo] spur, stimulus.

aguijonear vt -1. [espolear]: ~ a alguien para que haga algo to goad sb into doing sthg. -2. fig [estimular] to drive on.

águila f (el) -1. [ave] eagle. -2. fig [vivo, listo] sharp ○ perceptive person.

aguileño, -ña adj aquiline.

aguilucho m eaglet.

aguinaldo m Christmas box.

aguja f -1. [de coser, jeringuilla] needle; [de hacer punto] knitting needle. -2. [de reloj] hand; [de brújula] pointer; [de iglesia] spire. -3. FERROC point. -4. [de tocadiscos] stylus, needle. ◆ **agujas** fpl [de res] ribs.

agujerear vt to make a hole ○ holes in.

agujero m hole.

agujetas fpl: tener ~ to feel stiff.

aguzar vt -1. [afilar] to sharpen. -2. fig [apetito] to whet; [ingenio] to sharpen.

ah interj ¡~! [admiración] oooh!; [sorpresa] oh!; [pena] ah!

ahí adv there; **vino por** ~ he came that way; **la solución está** ~ that's where the solution lies; ¡~ **tienes!** there you are!, there you go!; **de** ~ **que** [por eso] and consequently, so; **está por** ~ [en lugar indefinido] he/she is around (somewhere); [en la calle] he/she is out; **por** ~, **por** ~ fig something like that; **por** ~ **va la cosa** you're not too far wrong.

ahijado, -da m y f [de padrinos] godson (f goddaughter).

ahijuna, aijuna interj Amer fam: ¡~! wow!

ahínco m enthusiasm, devotion.

ahíto, -ta adj culto [saciado]: **estar** ~ to be full.

ahogar vt -1. [asfixiar - en el agua] to drown; [- cubriendo la boca y nariz] to smother, to suffocate. -2. [estrangular] to strangle. -3. [extinguir] to extinguish, to put out. -4. fig [dominar - levantamiento] to quell; [- pena] to hold back. ◆ **ahogarse** vpr -1. [en el agua] to drown. -2. [asfixiarse] to suffocate.

ahogo m -1. [asfixia] breathlessness. -2. fig [económico] financial difficulty.

ahondar vi [profundizar] to go into detail; ~ **en** [penetrar] to penetrate deep into; [profundizar] to study in depth.

ahora ◇ adv -1. [en el presente] now; ~ **mismo** right now; **por** ~ for the time being. -2. [pronto] in a second ○ moment. ◇ conj [pero] but, however; ~ **que** but, though; ~ **bien** but, however.

ahorcar vt to hang. ◆ **ahorcarse** vpr to hang o.s.

ahorita, ahoritita adv Amer fam right now.

ahorrador, -ra ◇ adj thrifty, careful with money. ◇ m y f thrifty person.

ahorrar vt to save. ◆ **ahorrarse** vpr: ~**se algo** to save ○ spare o.s. sthg.

ahorro m -1. [gen] saving. -2. (gen pl) [cantidad ahorrada] savings (pl).

ahuecar vt [poner hueco - manos] to cup.

ahuevado, -da adj Amer fam [tonto] daft.

ahumado, -da adj smoked.

ahumar vt -1. [jamón, pescado] to smoke. -2. [habitación etc] to fill with smoke.

ahuyentar vt -1. [espantar, asustar] to scare away. -2. fig [apartar] to drive away.

aijuna = **ahijuna**.

airado, -da adj angry.

airar vt to anger, to make angry. ◆ **airarse** vpr to get angry.

aire m -1. [fluido] air; **al** ~ exposed; **al** ~ **libre** in the open air; **estar en el** ~ to be in the air; **tomar el** ~ to go for a breath of fresh air. -2. [viento] wind; [corriente] draught; **hoy hace (mucho)** ~ it's (very) windy today. -3. fig [aspecto] air, appearance. ◆ **aires** mpl [vanidad] airs (and graces). ◆ **aire (acondicionado)** m air-conditioning.

airear vt fig [contar] to air (publicly). ◆ **airearse** vpr to get a breath of fresh air.

airoso, -sa adj -1. [garboso] graceful. -2. [triunfante]: **salir** ~ **de algo** to come out of sthg with flying colours.

aislado, -da adj -1. [gen] isolated. -2. TECN insulated.

aislar vt -1. [gen] to isolate. -2. TECN to insulate.

ajá interj ¡~! [sorpresa] aha!; fam [aprobación] great!

ajar vt [flores] to wither, to cause to fade; [piel] to wrinkle; [colores] to make faded; [ropa] to wear out. ◆ **ajarse** vpr [flores] to fade, to wither; [piel] to wrinkle, to become wrinkled.

ajardinado, -da adj landscaped.

a.JC. = **a. de JC**.

ajedrez m inv chess.

ajeno, -na adj -1. [de otro] of others; **jugar en campo** ~ to play away from home. -2. [extraño]: ~ **a** having nothing to do with; ~ **a nuestra voluntad** beyond our control.

ajetreo m **-1.** [tarea] running around, hard work. **-2.** [animación] (hustle and) bustle.

ají m Amer chilli (pepper).

ajiaco m Amer [estofado] stew.

ajillo ◆ **al ajillo** loc adj CULIN in a sauce made with oil, garlic and chilli.

ajo m garlic; **andar** O **estar en el** ~ fig to be in on it.

ajustado, -da adj [ceñido - ropa] tight-fitting; [- tuerca, pieza] tight; [- resultado, final] close.

ajustadores mpl Amer bra (sg).

ajustar vt **-1.** [arreglar] to adjust. **-2.** [apretar] to tighten. **-3.** [encajar - piezas de motor] to fit; [- puerta, ventana] to push to. **-4.** [pactar - matrimonio] to arrange; [- pleito] to settle; [- paz] to negotiate; [- precio] to fix, to agree.

ajuste m [de pieza] fitting; [de mecanismo] adjustment; [de salario] agreement; ~ **de cuentas** fig settling of scores.

al → **a**.

ala f (el) **-1.** POLÍT & ZOOL wing. **-2.** [parte lateral - de tejado] eaves (pl); [- de sombrero] brim. **-3.** DEP winger, wing. ◆ **ala delta** f [aparato] hang glider.

alabanza f praise.

alabar vt to praise.

alabastro m alabaster.

alacena f recess for storing food.

alacrán m [animal] scorpion.

alado, -da adj [con alas] winged.

alambique m still.

alambre m wire; ~ **de espino** O **púas** barbed wire.

alameda f **-1.** [sitio con álamos] poplar grove. **-2.** [paseo] tree-lined avenue.

álamo m poplar.

alano m [perro] mastiff.

alarde m: ~ **(de)** show O display (of); **hacer** ~ **de algo** to show sthg off.

alardear vi: ~ **de** to show off about.

alargador m extension lead.

alargar vt **-1.** [ropa etc] to lengthen. **-2.** [viaje, visita, plazo] to extend; [conversación] to spin out. ◆ **alargarse** vpr [hacerse más largo - días] to get longer; [- reunión] to be prolonged.

alarido m shriek, howl.

alarma f [gen] alarm; **dar la** ~ to raise the alarm.

alarmante adj alarming.

alarmar vt **-1.** [avisar] to alert. **-2.** fig [asustar] to alarm. ◆ **alarmarse** vpr [inquietarse] to be alarmed.

alarmista m y f alarmist.

alazán, -ana adj chestnut.

alba f (el) [amanecer] dawn.

albacea m y f executor (f executrix).

albahaca f basil.

albanés, -esa adj, m y f Albanian. ◆ **albanés** m [lengua] Albanian.

Albania Albania.

albañil m bricklayer.

albañilería f [obra] brickwork.

albarán m delivery note.

albaricoque m apricot.

albedrío m [antojo, elección] fancy, whim; **a su** ~ as takes his/her fancy; **libre** ~ free will; **a su libre** ~ of his/her own free will.

alberca f **-1.** [depósito] water tank. **-2.** Amer [piscina] swimming pool.

albergar vt **-1.** [personas] to accommodate, to put up. **-2.** [odio] to harbour; [esperanzas] to cherish. ◆ **albergarse** vpr to stay.

albergue m accommodation (U), lodgings (pl); [de montaña] shelter, refuge; ~ **de cuentas** O **juvenil** youth hostel.

albino, -na adj, m y f albino.

albis ◆ **in albis** loc adv: **estar in** ~ to be in the dark; **quedarse in** ~ not to have a clue O the faintest idea.

albóndiga f meatball.

alborada f [amanecer] dawn.

alborear v impers: **empezaba a** ~ dawn was breaking.

albornoz m bathrobe.

alborotar ◇ vi to be noisy O rowdy. ◇ vt [amotinar] to stir up, to rouse. ◆ **alborotarse** vpr [perturbarse] to get worked up.

alboroto m **-1.** [ruido] din. **-2.** [jaleo] fuss, to-do.

alborozar vt to delight.

alborozo m delight, joy.

albufera f lagoon.

álbum (pl **álbumes**) m album.

alcachofa f BOT artichoke.

alcahuete, -ta m y f [mediador] go-between.

alcalde, -desa m y f mayor (f mayoress).

alcaldía f [cargo] mayoralty.

alcance m **-1.** [de arma, misil, emisora] range; **de corto/largo** ~ short-/long-range. **-2.** [de persona]: **a mi/a tu** etc ~ within my/your etc reach; **al** ~ **de la vista** within sight; **fuera del** ~ **de** beyond the reach of. **-3.** [de reformas etc] scope, extent.

alcanfor *m* camphor.

alcantarilla *f* sewer; [boca] drain.

alcantarillado *m* sewers (*pl*).

alcanzar ◇ *vt* **-1.** [llegar a] to reach. **-2.** [igualarse con] to catch up with. **-3.** [entregar] to pass. **-4.** [suj: bala etc] to hit. **-5.** [autobús, tren] to manage to catch. ◇ *vi* **-1.** [ser suficiente]: ~ **para algo/ hacer algo** to be enough for sthg/to do sthg. **-2.** [poder]: ~ **a hacer algo** to be able to do sthg.

alcaparra *f* caper.

alcayata *f* hook.

alcázar *m* fortress.

alce *m* elk, moose.

alcoba *f* bedroom.

alcohol *m* alcohol.

alcohólico, -ca *adj, m y f* alcoholic.

alcoholímetro *m* [para la sangre] Breathalyzer® *Br*, drunkometer *Am*.

alcoholismo *m* alcoholism.

alcohotest (*pl* **alcohotests**) *m* Breathalyzer® *Br*, drunkometer *Am*.

alcornoque *m* **-1.** [árbol] cork oak. **-2.** *fig* [persona] idiot, fool.

aldaba *f* [llamador] doorknocker.

aldea *f* small village.

aldeano, -na *m y f* villager.

aleación *f* [producto] alloy.

aleatorio, -ria *adj* [número] random; [suceso] chance (*antes de sust*).

aleccionar *vt* to instruct, to teach.

alegación *f* allegation.

alegar *vt* [motivos, pruebas] to put forward; ~ **que** to claim (that).

alegato *m* **-1.** DER & *fig* plea. **-2.** [ataque] diatribe.

alegoría *f* allegory.

alegórico, -ca *adj* allegorical.

alegrar *vt* [persona] to cheer up, to make happy; [fiesta] to liven up. ◆ **alegrarse** *vpr* [sentir alegría]: ~**se (de algo/por alguien)** to be pleased (about sthg/for sb).

alegre *adj* **-1.** [contento] happy. **-2.** [que da alegría] cheerful, bright. **-3.** *fam* [borracho] tipsy.

alegría *f* **-1.** [gozo] happiness, joy. **-2.** [motivo de gozo] joy.

alegrón *m* *fam* pleasant surprise.

alejamiento *m* **-1.** [lejanía] remoteness. **-2.** [distancia] distance. **-3.** [separación - de objetos etc] separation; [- entre personas] estrangement.

alejar *vt* **-1.** [poner más lejos] to move away. **-2.** *fig* [ahuyentar] to drive out. ◆ **alejarse** *vpr*: ~**se (de)** [ponerse más le-jos] to go ○ move away (from); [retirarse] to leave.

aleluya *interj*: ¡~! Hallelujah!

alemán, -ana *adj, m y f* German. ◆ **alemán** *m* [lengua] German.

Alemania Germany.

alentador, -ra *adj* encouraging.

alentar *vt* to encourage.

alergia *f* *lit* & *fig* allergy; **tener** ~ **a algo** to be allergic to sthg.

alérgico, -ca *adj* *lit* & *fig*: ~ **(a)** allergic (to).

alero *m* **-1.** [del tejado] eaves (*pl*). **-2.** DEP winger, wing.

alerta ◇ *adj inv & adv* alert. ◇ *f* alert.

alertar *vt* to alert.

aleta *f* **-1.** [de pez] fin. **-2.** [de buzo, foca] flipper. **-3.** [de coche] wing.

aletargar *vt* to make drowsy. ◆ **aletargarse** *vpr* to become drowsy ○ sleepy.

aletear *vi* to flap ○ flutter its wings.

alevín *m* **-1.** [cría de pez] fry, young fish. **-2.** *fig* [persona] novice, beginner.

alevosía *f* [traición] treachery.

alfabetizar *vt* **-1.** [personas] to teach to read and write. **-2.** [palabras, letras] to put into alphabetical order.

alfabeto *m* alphabet.

alfalfa *f* alfalfa, lucerne.

alfarería *f* [técnica] pottery.

alféizar *m* window-sill.

alférez *m* ≃ second lieutenant.

alfil *m* bishop.

alfiler *m* **-1.** [aguja] pin; ~ **de gancho** *Amer* safety pin. **-2.** [joya] brooch, pin.

alfombra *f* carpet; [alfombrilla] rug.

alfombrar *vt* to carpet.

alfombrilla *f* **-1.** [alfombra pequeña] rug. **-2.** [felpudo] doormat. **-3.** [del baño] bathmat.

alforja *f* (*gen pl*) [de caballo] saddlebag.

alga *f* (*el*) [de mar] seaweed (*U*); [de río] algae (*pl*).

algarroba *f* [fruto] carob ○ locust bean.

álgebra *f* (*el*) algebra.

álgido, -da *adj* [culminante] critical.

algo ◇ *pron* **-1.** [alguna cosa] something; [en interrogativas] anything; **¿te pasa** ~**?** is anything the matter?; ~ **es** ~ something is better than nothing; **por** ~ **lo habrá dicho** he must have said it for a reason. **-2.** [cantidad pequeña] a bit, a little; ~ **de** some, a little. **-3.** *fig* [cosa importante] something; **se cree que es** ~ he thinks he's something (special). ◇ *adv* [un poco] **rather, somewhat.**

algodón *m* cotton; ~ **(hidrófilo)** FARM cotton wool *Br*, absorbent cotton *Am*.

algoritmo *m* INFORM **algorithm.**

alguacil *m* [del juzgado] **bailiff.**

alguien *pron* **-1.** [alguna persona] **someone, somebody;** [en interrogativas] **anyone, anybody;** *¿hay* ~ *ahí?* is anyone there? **-2.** *fig* [persona de importancia] **somebody; se cree** ~ she thinks she's somebody (special).

alguno, -na ◇ *adj* (*antes de sust masculino* **algún**) **-1.** [indeterminado] **some;** [en interrogativas] **any;** *¿tienes algún libro?* do you have any books?; **algún día** some ○ one day; **ha surgido algún (que otro) problema** the odd problem has come up. **-2.** (*después de sust*) [ninguno] **any; no tengo interés** ~ I have no interest, I haven't any interest. ◇ *pron* **-1.** [persona] **someone, somebody;** (*pl*) **some people;** [en interrogativas] **anyone, anybody;** *¿conocisteis a* ~*s?* did you get to know any?; ~**s de, ~s (de) entre** some ○ a few of. **-2.** [cosa] **the odd one,** (*pl*) **some,** (*pl*) **a few;** [en interrogativas] **any; me salió mal** ~ I got the odd one wrong; ~ **de** some ○ a few of.

alhaja *f* [joya] **jewel.**

alhelí (*pl* **alhelíes**) *m* **wallflower.**

aliado, -da *adj* **allied.**

alianza *f* **-1.** [pacto, parentesco] **alliance. -2.** [anillo] **wedding ring.**

aliar *vt* [naciones] **to ally.** ◆ **aliarse** *vpr* to form an alliance.

alias ◇ *adv* **alias.** ◇ *m inv* **alias;** [entre amigos] **nickname.**

alicaído, -da *adj* [triste] **depressed.**

alicates *mpl* **pliers.**

aliciente *m* **-1.** [incentivo] **incentive. -2.** [atractivo] **attraction.**

alienación *f* **-1.** [gen] **alienation. -2.** [trastorno psíquico] **derangement.**

aliento *m* [respiración] **breath; cobrar** ~ to catch one's breath; **sin** ~ **breathless.**

aligerar *vt* **-1.** [peso] **to lighten. -2.** [ritmo] **to speed up;** [el paso] **to quicken. -3.** *fig* [aliviar] **to relieve, to ease.**

alijo *m* contraband (*U*).

alimaña *f* **pest** (*fox, weasel etc*).

alimentación *f* **-1.** [acción] **feeding. -2.** [comida] **food. -3.** [régimen alimenticio] **diet.**

alimentar *vt* [gen] **to feed;** [motor, co-

che] **to fuel.** ◆ **alimentarse** *vpr* [comer]: ~**se de** to live on.

alimenticio, -cia *adj* **nourishing; productos** ~**s** **foodstuffs.**

alimento *m* [gen] **food;** [valor nutritivo] **nourishment.**

alineación *f* **-1.** [en el espacio] **alignment. -2.** DEP **line-up.**

alinear *vt* **-1.** [en el espacio] **to line up. -2.** DEP **to select.** ◆ **alinearse** *vpr* POLÍT to align.

aliñar *vt* [ensalada] **to dress;** [carne] **to season.**

aliño *m* [para ensalada] **dressing;** [para carne] **seasoning.**

alioli *m* **garlic mayonnaise.**

alisar *vt* **to smooth (down).**

alistarse *vpr* **to enlist.**

aliviar *vt* **-1.** [atenuar] **to soothe. -2.** [aligerar - persona] **to relieve;** [- carga] **to lighten.**

alivio *m* **relief.**

aljibe *m* [de agua] **cistern.**

allá *adv* **-1.** [espacio] **over there;** ~ **abajo/arriba** down/up there; **más** ~ further on; **más** ~ **de** beyond. **-2.** [tiempo]: ~ **por los años cincuenta** back in the 50s; ~ **para el mes de agosto** around August some time. **-3.** *loc:* ~ **él/ella** *etc* that's his/her *etc* problem.

allanamiento *m* **forceful entry;** ~ **de morada** breaking and entering.

allanar *vt* **-1.** [terreno] **to flatten, to level. -2.** [irrumpir en] **to break into.**

allegado, -da *m y f* **-1.** [familiar] **relative. -2.** [amigo] **close friend.**

allí *adv* **there;** ~ **abajo/arriba** down/up there; ~ **mismo** right there; **está por** ~ it's around there somewhere.

alma *f* (*el*) **-1.** [gen] **soul. -2.** [de bastón, ovillo] **core.**

almacén *m* **warehouse.** ◆ **(grandes) almacenes** *mpl* **department store** (*sg*).

almacenar *vt* **-1.** [gen & INFORM] **to store. -2.** [reunir] **to collect.**

almendra *f* **almond.**

almendro *m* **almond (tree).**

almíbar *m* **syrup.**

almidón *m* **starch.**

almidonar *vt* **to starch.**

almirantazgo *m* [dignidad] **admiralty.**

almirante *m* **admiral.**

almirez *m* **mortar.**

almizcle *m* **musk.**

almohada *f* **pillow.**

almohadilla *f* [gen, TECN & ZOOL] **pad;** [cojín] **small cushion.**

almorrana f (gen pl) piles (pl).
almorzar ◇ vt [al mediodía] to have for lunch. ◇ vi [al mediodía] to have lunch.
almuerzo m [al mediodía] lunch.
aló interj Amer [al teléfono] hello.
alocado, -da m y f crazy person.
alojamiento m accommodation.
alojar vt to put up. ◆**alojarse** vpr **-1.** [hospedarse] to stay. **-2.** [introducirse] to lodge.
alondra f lark.
alpargata f (gen pl) espadrille.
Alpes mpl: los ~ the Alps.
alpinismo m mountaineering.
alpinista m y f mountaineer.
alpiste m [semilla] birdseed.
alquilar vt [casa, TV, oficina] to rent; [coche] to hire. ◆**alquilarse** vpr [casa, TV, oficina] to be for rent; [coche] to be for hire; "se alquila" "to let".
alquiler m **-1.** [acción - de casa, TV, oficina] renting; [- de coche] hiring; **de ~** [casa] rented; [coche] hire (antes de sust); **tenemos pisos de ~** we have flats to let Br, we have apartments to rent Am. **-2.** [precio - de casa, oficina] rent; [- de televisión] rental; [- de coche] hire charge.
alquimia f alchemy.
alquitrán m tar.
alrededor adv **-1.** [en torno] around; **mira a tu ~** look around you; **de ~** surrounding. **-2.** [aproximadamente]: **~ de** around, about. ◆**alrededores** mpl surrounding area (sg). ◆**alrededor de** loc prep around.
alta → alto.
altanero, -ra adj haughty.
altar m altar.
altavoz m [para anuncios] loudspeaker; [de tocadiscos] speaker.
alteración f **-1.** [cambio] alteration. **-2.** [excitación] agitation. **-3.** [alboroto] disturbance; **~ del orden público** breach of the peace.
alterar vt **-1.** [cambiar] to alter. **-2.** [perturbar - persona] to agitate, to fluster; [- orden público] to disrupt. ◆**alterarse** vpr [perturbarse] to get agitated ○ flustered.
altercado m argument, row.
alternar ◇ vt to alternate. ◇ vi **-1.** [relacionarse]: **~ (con)** to mix (with), to socialize (with). **-2.** [sucederse]: **~ con** to alternate with. ◆**alternarse** vpr **-1.** [en el tiempo] to take turns. **-2.** [en el espacio] to alternate.
alternativa → alternativo.

alternativamente adv [moverse] alternately.
alternativo, -va adj **-1.** [movimiento] alternating. **-2.** [posibilidad] alternative. ◆**alternativa** f [opción] alternative.
alterno, -na adj alternate; ELECTR alternating.
alteza f fig [de sentimientos] loftiness. ◆**Alteza** f [tratamiento] Highness; **Su Alteza Real** His Royal Highness (f Her Royal Highness).
altibajos mpl fig [de vida etc] ups and downs.
altiplano m high plateau.
altisonante adj high-sounding.
altitud f altitude.
altivez f haughtiness.
altivo, -va adj haughty.
alto, -ta adj **-1.** [gen] high; [persona, árbol, edificio] tall; [piso] top, upper. **-2.** [ruidoso] loud. **-3.** [avanzado] late; **a altas horas de la noche** late at night, in the small hours. ◆**alto** ◇ m **-1.** [altura] height; **mide dos metros de ~** [cosa] it's two metres high; [persona] he's two metres tall. **-2.** [interrupción] stop. **-3.** [lugar elevado] height; **en lo ~ de** at the top of. **-4.** MÚS alto. **-5.** loc: **pasar por ~ algo** to pass over sthg. ◇ adv **-1.** [arriba] high (up). **-2.** [hablar etc] loud. ◇ interj: **¡~!** halt!, stop! ◆**alta** f (el) [del hospital] discharge; **dar de alta** ○ **el alta a alguien** to discharge sb (from hospital).
altoparlante m Amer loudspeaker.
altramuz m lupin.
altruismo m altruism.
altura f **-1.** [gen] height; [en el mar] depth; **tiene dos metros de ~** [gen] it's two metres high; [persona] he's two metres tall. **-2.** [nivel] level; **está a la ~ del ayuntamiento** it's next to the town hall. **-3.** [latitud] latitude. ◆**alturas** fpl [el cielo] Heaven (sg); **a estas ~s** fig this far on, this late.
alubia f bean.
alucinación f hallucination.
alucinado, -da adj **-1.** MED hallucinating. **-2.** fam [sorprendido] gobsmacked.
alucinante adj **-1.** MED hallucinatory. **-2.** fam [extraordinario] amazing.
alucinar ◇ vi MED to hallucinate. ◇ vt fam fig [seducir] to captivate.
alud m lit & fig avalanche.
aludido, -da m y f: **el ~** the aforesaid; **darse por ~** [ofenderse] to take it personally; [reaccionar] to take the hint.

aludir *vi*: ~ **a** [sin mencionar] to allude to; [mencionando] to refer to.

alumbrado *m* lighting.

alumbramiento *m* [parto] delivery.

alumbrar *vt* **-1.** [iluminar] to light up. **-2.** [instruir] to enlighten. **-3.** [dar a luz] to give birth to.

aluminio *m* aluminium.

alumnado *m* [de escuela] pupils (*pl*); [de universidad] students (*pl*).

alumno, -na *m y f* [de escuela, profesor particular] pupil; [de universidad] student.

alunizar *vi* to land on the moon.

alusión *f* [sin mencionar] allusion; [mencionando] reference.

alusivo, -va *adj* allusive.

aluvión *m* **-1.** [gen] flood. **-2.** GEOL alluvium.

alza *f* (*el*) rise; **en ~** FIN rising; *fig* gaining in popularity.

alzamiento *m* uprising, revolt.

alzar *vt* **-1.** [levantar] to lift, to raise; [voz] to raise; [vela] to hoist; [cuello de abrigo] to turn up; [mangas] to pull up. **-2.** [aumentar] to raise. ◆ **alzarse** *vpr* **-1.** [levantarse] to rise. **-2.** [sublevarse] to rise up, to revolt.

a.m. (*abrev de* **ante meridiem**) a.m.

ama → **amo.**

amabilidad *f* kindness; ¿tendría la ~ de ...? would you be so kind as to ...?

amable *adj* kind; ¿sería tan ~ de ...? would you be so kind as to ...?

amaestrado, -da *adj* [gen] trained; [en circo] performing.

amaestrar *vt* to train.

amagar ◇ *vt* **-1.** [dar indicios de] to show signs of. **-2.** [mostrar intención] to threaten; **le amagó un golpe** he threatened to hit him. ◇ *vi* [tormenta] to be imminent, to threaten.

amago *m* **-1.** [indicio] sign, hint. **-2.** [amenaza] threat.

amainar *vi lit & fig* to abate.

amalgama *f* QUÍM & *fig* amalgam.

amalgamar *vt* QUÍM & *fig* to amalgamate.

amamantar *vt* [animal] to suckle; [bebé] to breastfeed.

amanecer ◇ *m* dawn. ◇ *v impers*: **amaneció a las siete** dawn broke at seven.

amanerado, -da *adj* [afectado] mannered, affected.

amansar *vt* **-1.** [animal] to tame. **-2.** *fig* [persona] to calm down.

amante *m y f* **-1.** [querido] lover. **-2.** *fig* [aficionado]: **ser ~ de algo/hacer algo** to be keen on sthg/doing sthg; **los ~s del arte** art lovers.

amañar *vt* [falsear] to fix; [elecciones, resultado] to rig; [documento] to doctor.

amaño *m* (*gen pl*) [treta] ruse, trick.

amapola *f* poppy.

amar *vt* to love.

amarar *vi* [hidroavión] to land at sea; [vehículo espacial] to splash down.

amargado, -da *adj* [resentido] bitter.

amargar *vt* to make bitter; *fig* to spoil.

amargo, -ga *adj lit & fig* bitter.

amargoso, -sa *adj Amer* bitter.

amargura *f* [sentimiento] sorrow.

amarillento, -ta *adj* yellowish.

amarillo, -lla *adj* [color] yellow. ◆ **amarillo** *m* [color] yellow.

amarilloso, -sa *adj Amer* yellowish.

amarra *f* mooring rope ○ line.

amarrar *vt* **-1.** NÁUT to moor. **-2.** [atar] to tie (up); ~ **algo/a alguien a algo** to tie sthg/sb to sthg.

amarre *m* mooring.

amarrete *Amer adj* mean, tight.

amasar *vt* **-1.** [masa] to knead; [yeso] to mix. **-2.** *fam fig* [riquezas] to amass.

amasia *f Amer* mistress.

amasijo *m fam fig* [mezcla] hotchpotch.

amateur [ama'ter] (*pl* **amateurs**) *adj, m y f* amateur.

amatista *f* amethyst.

amazona *f fig* [jinete] horsewoman.

Amazonas *m*: **el ~** the Amazon.

ambages *mpl*: **sin ~** without beating about the bush, in plain English.

ámbar *m* amber.

ambición *f* ambition.

ambicionar *vt* to have as one's ambition.

ambicioso, -sa *adj* ambitious.

ambidextro, -tra ◇ *adj* ambidextrous. ◇ *m y f* ambidextrous person.

ambientación *f* **-1.** CIN, LITER & TEATR setting. **-2.** RADIO sound effects (*pl*).

ambientador *m* air freshener.

ambiental *adj* **-1.** [físico, atmosférico] ambient. **-2.** ECOLOG environmental.

ambiente *m* **-1.** [aire] air, atmosphere. **-2.** [circunstancias] environment. **-3.** [ámbito] world, circles (*pl*). **-4.** [animación] life, atmosphere. **-5.** *Amer* [habitación] room.

ambigüedad *f* ambiguity.

ambiguo, -gua *adj* [gen] ambiguous.

ámbito *m* **-1.** [espacio, límites] confines (*pl*); **una ley de ~ provincial** an act which is provincial in its scope. **-2.** [ambiente] world, circles (*pl*).

ambivalente *adj* ambivalent.

ambos, -bas ◇ *adj pl* both. ◇ *pron pl* both (of them).

ambulancia *f* ambulance.

ambulante *adj* travelling; [biblioteca] mobile.

ambulatorio *m* state-run surgery ○ clinic.

ameba *f* amoeba.

amedrentar *vt* to scare, to frighten.

amén *adv* [en plegaria] amen. ◆ **amén de** *loc prep* **-1.** [además de] in addition to. **-2.** [excepto] except for, apart from.

amenaza *f* threat; ~ **de bomba** bomb scare; ~ **de muerte** death threat.

amenazar *vt* to threaten; ~ **a alguien con hacerle algo** to threaten to do sthg to sb; ~ **a alguien con hacer algo** to threaten sb with doing sthg; **amenaza lluvia** it's threatening to rain.

amenidad *f* [entretenimiento] entertaining qualities (*pl*).

ameno, -na *adj* [entretenido] entertaining.

América America; ~ **del Sur** South America.

americana → **americano**.

americano, -na *adj, m y f* American. ◆ **americana** *f* [chaqueta] jacket.

ameritar *vt Amer* to deserve.

amerizar *vi* [hidroavión] to land at sea; [vehículo espacial] to splash down.

ametralladora *f* machine gun.

ametrallar *vt* [con ametralladora] to machinegun.

amianto *m* asbestos.

amígdala *f* tonsil.

amigdalitis *f inv* tonsillitis.

amigo, -ga ◇ *adj* **-1.** [gen] friendly. **-2.** [aficionado]: ~ **de algo/hacer algo** keen on sthg/doing sthg. ◇ *m y f* **-1.** [persona] friend; **hacerse** ~ **de** to make friends with; **hacerse** ~**s** to become friends. **-2.** *fam* [compañero, novio] partner; [amante] lover.

amigote, amiguete *m fam* pal.

amiguismo *m*: **hay mucho** ~ there are always jobs for the boys.

aminoácido *m* amino acid.

aminorar *vt* to reduce.

amistad *f* friendship; **hacer** ○ **trabar** ~ **(con)** to make friends (with). ◆ **amistades** *fpl* friends.

amistoso, -sa *adj* friendly.

amnesia *f* amnesia.

amnistía *f* amnesty.

amo, ama *m y f* **-1.** [gen] owner. **-2.** [de criado, situación etc] master (*f* mistress). ◆ **ama de casa** *f* housewife. ◆ **ama de llaves** *f* housekeeper.

amodorrarse *vpr* to get drowsy.

amoldar *vt* [adaptar]: ~ **(a)** to adapt (to). ◆ **amoldarse** *vpr* [adaptarse]: ~**se (a)** to adapt (to).

amonestación *f* **-1.** [reprimenda] reprimand. **-2.** DEP warning.

amonestar *vt* **-1.** [reprender] to reprimand. **-2.** DEP to warn.

amoníaco, amoniaco *m* [gas] ammonia.

amontonar *vt* **-1.** [apilar] to pile up. **-2.** [reunir] to accumulate. ◆ **amontonarse** *vpr* **-1.** [personas] to form a crowd. **-2.** [problemas, trabajo] to pile up; [ideas, solicitudes] to come thick and fast.

amor *m* love; **hacer el** ~ to make love; **por** ~ **al arte** for the love of it. ◆ **amor propio** *m* pride.

amoral *adj* amoral.

amoratado, -da *adj* [de frío] blue; [por golpes] black and blue.

amordazar *vt* [persona] to gag; [perro] to muzzle.

amorfo, -fa *adj* [sin forma] amorphous.

amorío *m fam* [romance] fling.

amoroso, -sa *adj* [gen] loving; [carta, relación] love (*antes de sust*).

amortajar *vt* [difunto] to shroud.

amortiguador, -ra *adj* [de ruido] muffling; [de golpe] softening, cushioning. ◆ **amortiguador** *m* AUTOM shock absorber.

amortiguar *vt* [ruido] to muffle; [golpe] to soften, to cushion.

amortización *f* ECON [de deuda, préstamo] paying-off; [de inversión, capital] recouping; [de bonos, acciones] redemption; [de bienes de equipo] depreciation.

amortizar *vt* **-1.** [sacar provecho] to get one's money's worth out of. **-2.** [ECON - deuda, préstamo] to pay off; [- inversión, capital] to recoup; [- bonos, acciones] to redeem.

amotinar *vt* to incite to riot; [a marineros] to incite to mutiny. ◆ **amotinarse** *vpr* to riot; [marineros] to mutiny.

amparar *vt* **-1.** [proteger] to protect. **-2.** [dar cobijo a] to give shelter to. ◆ **ampararse** *vpr* **-1.** *fig* [apoyarse]: ~**se en** [ley] to have recourse to; [excusas] to draw on. **-2.** [cobijarse]: ~**se de** ○ **contra** to (take) shelter from.

amparo *m* [protección] protection; **al** ~

de [persona, caridad] with the help of; [ley] under the protection of.

amperio *m* amp, ampere.

ampliación *f* **-1.** [aumento] expansion; [de edificio, plazo] extension. **-2.** FOT enlargement.

ampliar *vt* **-1.** [gen] to expand; [local] to add an extension to; [plazo] to extend. **-2.** FOT to enlarge, to blow up.

amplificación *f* amplification.

amplificador *m* ELECTRÓN amplifier.

amplificar *vt* to amplify.

amplio, -plia *adj* **-1.** [sala etc] roomy, spacious; [avenida, gama] wide. **-2.** [ropa] loose. **-3.** [explicación etc] comprehensive; **en el sentido más ~ de la palabra** in the broadest sense of the word.

amplitud *f* **-1.** [espaciosidad] roominess, spaciousness; [de avenida] wideness. **-2.** [de ropa] looseness. **-3.** *fig* [extensión] extent, comprehensiveness.

ampolla *f* **-1.** [en piel] blister. **-2.** [para inyecciones] ampoule. **-3.** [frasco] phial.

ampuloso, -sa *adj* pompous.

amputar *vt* to amputate.

Amsterdam Amsterdam.

amueblar *vt* to furnish.

amurallar *vt* to build a wall around.

anacronismo *m* anachronism.

anagrama *m* anagram.

anal *adj* ANAT anal.

anales *mpl* lit & *fig* annals.

analfabetismo *m* illiteracy.

analfabeto, -ta *adj, m y f* illiterate.

analgésico, -ca *adj* analgesic. ◆ **analgésico** *m* analgesic.

análisis *m inv* analysis; **~ de sangre** blood test.

analizar *vt* to analyse.

analogía *f* similarity; **por ~** by analogy.

analógico, -ca *adj* INFORM & TECN analogue, analog.

análogo, -ga *adj*: **~ (a)** analogous o similar (to).

ananá, ananás *m Amer* pineapple.

anaquel *m* shelf.

anarquía *f* **-1.** [falta de gobierno] anarchy. **-2.** [doctrina política] anarchism.

anárquico, -ca *adj* anarchic.

anarquista *adj, m y f* anarchist.

anatema *m* [maldición] curse.

anatomía *f* anatomy.

anca *f* (*el*) haunch; **~s de rana** frogs' legs.

ancestral *adj* ancestral; [costumbre] age-old.

ancho, -cha *adj* [gen] wide; [prenda] loose-fitting; **te va o está ~** it's too big for you; **a mis/tus** *etc* **anchas** *fig* at ease; **quedarse tan ~** not to care less. ◆ **ancho** *m* width; **a lo ~** crosswise; **cinco metros de ~** five metres wide; **a lo ~ de** across (the width of); **~ de vía** gauge.

anchoa *f* anchovy (*salted*).

anchura *f* **-1.** [medida] width. **-2.** [de ropa] bagginess.

anciano, -na ◇ *adj* old. ◇ *m y f* old person, old man (*f* old woman). ◆ **anciano** *m* [de tribu] elder.

ancla *f* (*el*) anchor.

anclar *vi* to anchor.

andadas *fpl*: **volver a las ~** *fam fig* to return to one's evil ways.

andadura *f* walking.

ándale, ándele *interj Amer fam*: **¡~!** come on!

Andalucía Andalusia.

andaluz, -za *adj, m y f* Andalusian.

andamio *m* scaffold.

andanada *f* MIL & *fig* broadside.

andando *interj*: **¡~!** come on!, let's get a move on!

andante *adj* [que anda] walking.

andanza *f* (*gen pl*) [aventura] adventure.

andar ◇ *vi* **-1.** [caminar] to walk; [moverse] to move. **-2.** [funcionar] to work, to go; **las cosas andan mal** things are going badly. **-3.** [estar] to be; **~ preocupado** to be worried; **~ tras algo/alguien** *fig* to be after sthg/sb. **-4.** (*antes de gerundio*): **~ haciendo algo** to be doing sthg; **anda echando broncas a todos** he's going round telling everybody off. **-5.** [ocuparse]: **~ en** [asuntos, líos] to be involved in; [papeleos, negocios] to be busy with. **-6.** [hurgar]: **~ en** to rummage around in. **-7.** [alcanzar, rondar]: **anda por los 60** he's about sixty. ◇ *vt* **-1.** [recorrer] to go, to travel. **-2.** *Amer* [llevar puesto] to wear. ◇ *m* gait, walk. ◆ **andarse** *vpr* [obrar]: **~se con cuidado/misterios** to be careful/ secretive. ◆ **andares** *mpl* [de persona] gait (*sg*). ◆ **anda** *interj*: **¡anda!** [sorpresa, desilusión] oh!; [¡vamos!] come on!; [¡por favor!] go on!; **¡anda ya!** [incredulidad] come off it!

ándele = ándale.

andén *m* FERROC platform.

Andes *mpl*: **los ~** the Andes.

andinismo *m Amer* mountaineering.

andinista m y f Amer mountaineer.
Andorra Andorra.
andorrano, -na adj, m y f Andorran.
andrajo m [harapo] rag.
andrajoso, -sa adj ragged.
andrógino, -na adj androgynous.
androide m [autómata] android.
anduviera etc → **andar**.
anécdota f anecdote.
anecdótico, -ca adj **-1.** [con historietas] anecdotal. **-2.** [no esencial] incidental.
anegar vt [inundar] to flood. ◆ **anegarse** vpr **-1.** [inundarse] to flood; **sus ojos se anegaron de lágrimas** tears welled up in his eyes. **-2.** [ahogarse] to drown.
anejo, -ja adj: ~ **(a)** [edificio] connected (to); [documento] attached (to). ◆ **anejo** m annexe.
anemia f anaemia.
anémona f anemone.
anestesia f anaesthesia.
anestésico, -ca adj anaesthetic. ◆ **anestésico** m anaesthetic.
anexar vt [documento] to attach.
anexión f annexation.
anexionar vt to annex.
anexo, -xa adj [edificio] connected; [documento] attached. ◆ **anexo** m annexe.
anfetamina f amphetamine.
anfibio, -bia adj lit & fig amphibious.
anfiteatro m **-1.** CIN & TEATR circle. **-2.** [edificio] amphitheatre.
anfitrión, -ona m y f host (f hostess).
ángel m lit & fig angel; ~ **custodio** O **de la guarda** guardian angel; **tener** ~ to have something special.
angelical adj angelic.
angina f (gen pl) [amigdalitis] sore throat; **tener** ~**s** to have a sore throat. ◆ **angina de pecho** f angina (pectoris).
anglicano, -na adj, m y f Anglican.
anglosajón, -ona adj, m y f Anglo-Saxon.
Angola Angola.
angora f [de conejo] angora; [de cabra] mohair.
angosto, -ta adj culto narrow.
angostura f [extracto] angostura.
anguila f eel.
angula f elver.
angular adj angular. ◆ **gran angular** m FOT wide-angle lens.
ángulo m **-1.** [gen] angle. **-2.** [rincón] corner.
anguloso, -sa adj angular.
angustia f [aflicción] anxiety.

angustiar vt to distress. ◆ **angustiarse** vpr [agobiarse]: ~**se (por)** to get worried (about).
angustioso, -sa adj [espera, momentos] anxious; [situación, noticia] distressing.
anhelante adj: ~ **(por algo/hacer algo)** longing (for sthg/to do sthg), desperate (for sthg/to do sthg).
anhelar vt to long O wish for; ~ **hacer algo** to long to do sthg.
anhelo m longing.
anhídrido m anhydride; ~ **carbónico** carbon dioxide.
anidar vi [pájaro] to nest.
anilla f ring.
anillo m [gen & ASTRON] ring; ~ **de boda** wedding ring.
ánima f (el) soul.
animación f **-1.** [alegría] liveliness. **-2.** [bullicio] hustle and bustle, activity. **-3.** CIN animation.
animado, -da adj **-1.** [con buen ánimo] cheerful. **-2.** [divertido] lively. **-3.** CIN animated.
animador, -ra m y f **-1.** [en espectáculo] compere. **-2.** [en fiesta de niños] children's entertainer. **-3.** [en béisbol etc] cheerleader.
animadversión f animosity.
animal ◇ adj **-1.** [reino, funciones] animal (antes de sust). **-2.** fam [persona - basto] rough; [- ignorante] ignorant. ◇ m y f fam fig [persona] animal, brute. ◇ m animal; ~ **doméstico** [de granja etc] domestic animal; [de compañía] pet.
animar vt **-1.** [estimular] to encourage. **-2.** [alegrar - persona] to cheer up. **-3.** [avivar - fuego, diálogo, fiesta] to liven up; [comercio] to stimulate. ◆ **animarse** vpr **-1.** [alegrarse - persona] to cheer up; [- fiesta etc] to liven up. **-2.** [decidir]: ~**se (a hacer algo)** to finally decide (to do sthg).
ánimo ◇ m **-1.** [valor] courage. **-2.** [aliento] encouragement; **dar** ~**s a alguien** to encourage sb. **-3.** [humor] disposition. ◇ interj [para alentar]: ¡~! come on!
animoso, -sa adj [valiente] courageous; [decidido] undaunted.
aniñado, -da adj [comportamiento] childish; [voz, rostro] childlike.
aniquilar vt to annihilate, to wipe out.
anís (pl anises) m **-1.** [grano] aniseed. **-2.** [licor] anisette.
aniversario m [gen] anniversary; [cumpleaños] birthday.
ano m anus.

anoche *adv* last night, yesterday evening; **antes de** ~ the night before last.

anochecer ◇ *m* dusk, nightfall; **al** ~ at dusk. ◇ *v impers* to get dark.

anodino, -na *adj* [sin gracia] dull, insipid.

anomalía *f* anomaly.

anómalo, -la *adj* anomalous.

anonadado, -da *adj* [sorprendido] astonished, bewildered.

anonimato *m* anonymity; **permanecer en el** ~ to remain nameless.

anónimo, -ma *adj* anonymous ◆ **anónimo** *m* anonymous letter.

anorak (*pl* anoraks) *m* anorak.

anorexia *f* anorexia.

anormal *adj* [anómalo] abnormal.

anotación *f* [gen] note; [en registro] entry.

anotar *vt* **-1.** [apuntar] to note down. **-2.** [tantear] to notch up.

anquilosamiento *m* **-1.** [estancamiento] stagnation. **-2.** MED paralysis.

anquilosarse *vpr* **-1.** [estancarse] to stagnate. **-2.** MED to become paralysed.

ansia *f* (*el*) **-1.** [afán]: ~ **de** longing O yearning for. **-2.** [ansiedad] anxiousness; [angustia] anguish.

ansiar *vt*: ~ **hacer algo** to long O be desperate to do sth.

ansiedad *f* **-1.** [inquietud] anxiety; **con** ~ anxiously. **-2.** PSICOL nervous tension.

ansioso, -sa *adj* [impaciente] impatient; **estar** ~ **por** O **de hacer algo** to be impatient to do sthg.

antagónico, -ca *adj* antagonistic.

antagonista *m y f* opponent.

antaño *adv* in days gone by.

antártico, -ca *adj* Antarctic. ◆ **Antártico** *m*: **el Antártico** the Antarctic; **el océano Glacial Antártico** the Antarctic Ocean.

Antártida *f*: **la** ~ the Antarctic.

ante¹ *m* **-1.** [piel] suede. **-2.** [animal] elk.

ante² *prep* **-1.** [delante de, en presencia de] before. **-2.** [frente a - hecho, circunstancia] in the face of. ◆ **ante todo** *loc adv* **-1.** [sobre todo] above all. **-2.** [en primer lugar] first of all.

anteanoche *adv* the night before last.

anteayer *adv* the day before yesterday.

antebrazo *m* forearm.

antecedente ◇ *adj* preceding, previous. ◇ *m* [precedente] precedent. ◆ **antecedentes** *mpl* [de persona] record (*sg*); [de asunto] background (*sg*); po-

ner a alguien en ~s de [informar] to fill sb in on.

anteceder *vt* to precede.

antecesor, -ra *m y f* [predecesor] predecessor.

antedicho, -cha *adj* aforementioned.

antelación *f*: **con** ~ in advance, beforehand; **con dos horas de** ~ two hours in advance.

antemano ◆ **de antemano** *loc adv* beforehand, in advance.

antena *f* **-1.** RADIO & TV aerial, antenna; ~ **parabólica** satellite dish. **-2.** ZOOL antenna.

anteojos *mpl* desus o *Amer* [gafas] spectacles.

antepasado, -da *m y f* ancestor.

antepenúltimo, -ma *adj, m y f* last but two.

anteponer *vt*: ~ **algo a algo** to put sthg before sthg.

anterior *adj* **-1.** [previo]: ~ **(a)** previous (to). **-2.** [delantero] front (*antes de sust*).

anterioridad *f*: **con** ~ beforehand; **con** ~ **a** before, prior to.

anteriormente *adv* previously.

antes *adv* **-1.** [gen] before; **no importa si venís** ~ it doesn't matter if you come earlier; **ya no nado como** ~ I can't swim as I used to; **lo** ~ **posible** as soon as possible. **-2.** [primero] first; **esta señora está** ~ this lady is first. **-3.** [expresa preferencia]: ~ **... que** rather ... than; **prefiero la sierra** ~ **que el mar** I like the mountains before than the sea; **iría a la cárcel** ~ **que mentir** I'd rather go to prison than lie. ◆ **antes de** *loc prep* before; ~ **de hacer algo** before doing sthg. ◆ **antes (de) que** *loc conj* before; ~ **(de) que llegarais** before you arrived.

antesala *f* anteroom; **estar en la** ~ **de** *fig* to be on the verge of.

antiadherente *adj* nonstick.

antiaéreo, -a *adj* anti-aircraft.

antibala, antibalas *adj inv* bullet-proof.

antibiótico, -ca *adj* antibiotic. ◆ **antibiótico** *m* antibiotic.

anticiclón *m* anticyclone.

anticipación *f* earliness; **con** ~ in advance; **con un mes de** ~ a month in advance; **con** ~ **a** prior to.

anticipado, -da *adj* [elecciones] early; [pago] advance; **por** ~ in advance.

anticipar *vt* **-1.** [prever] to anticipate. **-2.** [adelantar] to bring forward. **-3.** [pago] to pay in advance. ◆ **anticiparse** *vpr* **-1.** [suceder antes] to arrive early; **se anticipó a su tiempo** he was ahead of his time. **-2.** [adelantarse]: **~se a alguien** to beat sb to it.

anticipo *m* [de dinero] advance.

anticonceptivo, -va *adj* contraceptive. ◆ **anticonceptivo** *m* contraceptive.

anticongelante *adj & m* antifreeze.

anticonstitucional *adj* unconstitutional.

anticorrosivo, -va *adj* anticorrosive.

anticuado, -da *adj* old-fashioned.

anticuario, -ria *m y f* [comerciante] antique dealer; [experto] antiquarian.

anticuerpo *m* antibody.

antidepresivo, -va *adj* antidepressant. ◆ **antidepresivo** *m* antidepressant (drug).

antidisturbios *mpl* [policía] riot police.

antidopaje *m* doping tests (*pl*).

antidoping [anti'ðopin] *adj* doping (*antes de sust*).

antídoto *m* antidote.

antier *adv Amer fam* the day before yesterday.

antiestético, -ca *adj* unsightly.

antifaz *m* mask.

antigás *adj inv* gas (*antes de sust*).

antigualla *f despec* [cosa] museum piece; [persona] old fogey, old fossil.

antiguamente *adv* [hace mucho] long ago; [previamente] formerly.

antigubernamental *adj* anti-government.

antigüedad *f* **-1.** [gen] antiquity. **-2.** [veteranía] seniority. ◆ **antigüedades** *fpl* [objetos] antiques.

antiguo, -gua *adj* **-1.** [viejo] old; [inmemorial] ancient. **-2.** [anterior, previo] former.

antihéroe *m* antihero.

antihigiénico, -ca *adj* unhygienic.

antihistamínico *m* antihistamine.

antiinflamatorio *m* anti-inflammatory drug.

antílope *m* antelope.

antinatural *adj* unnatural.

antiniebla *adj inv* → **faro**.

antioxidante *m* rustproofing agent.

antipatía *f* dislike; **tener ~ a alguien** to dislike sb.

antipático, -ca *adj* unpleasant.

antípodas *fpl*: **las ~** the Antipodes.

antiquísimo, -ma *adj* ancient.

antirreglamentario, -ria *adj* DEP illegal, against the rules.

antirrobo *m* [en coche] antitheft device; [en edificio] burglar alarm.

antisemita *adj* anti-Semitic.

antiséptico, -ca *adj* antiseptic. ◆ **antiséptico** *m* antiseptic.

antiterrorista *adj* anti-terrorist.

antítesis *f inv* antithesis.

antitetánico, -ca *adj* anti-tetanus (*antes de sust*).

antivirus *m inv* INFORM antivirus system.

antojarse *vpr* **-1.** [capricho]: **se le antojaron esos zapatos** he fancied those shoes; **se le ha antojado ir al cine** he felt like going to the cinema; **cuando se me antoje** when I feel like it. **-2.** [posibilidad]: **se me antoja que ...** I have a feeling that ....

antojitos *mpl Amer* snacks, tapas.

antojo *m* **-1.** [capricho] whim; [de embarazada] craving; **a mi/tu** *etc* **~** my/your *etc* (own) way. **-2.** [lunar] birthmark.

antología *f* anthology.

antónimo *m* antonym.

antonomasia *f*: **por ~** par excellence.

antorcha *f* torch.

antracita *f* anthracite.

antro *m despec* dive, dump.

antropófago, -ga *m y f* cannibal.

antropología *f* anthropology.

anual *adj* annual.

anualidad *f* annuity, yearly payment.

anuario *m* yearbook.

anudar *vt* to knot, to tie in a knot.

anulación *f* [cancelación] cancellation; [de ley] repeal; [de matrimonio, contrato] annulment.

anular[1] *m* → **dedo**.

anular[2] *vt* **-1.** [cancelar - gen] to cancel; [- ley] to repeal; [- matrimonio, contrato] to annul. **-2.** [DEP - gol] to disallow; [- resultado] to declare void.

anunciación *f* announcement. ◆ **Anunciación** *f* RELIG Annunciation.

anunciante *m y f* advertiser.

anunciar *vt* **-1.** [notificar] to announce. **-2.** [hacer publicidad de] to advertise. **-3.** [presagiar] to herald. ◆ **anunciarse** *vpr*: **~se en** to advertise in, to put an advert in.

anuncio *m* **-1.** [notificación] announcement; [cartel, aviso] notice; [póster] poster. **-2.** **~ (publicitario)** advertisement, advert; **~s por palabras** classified adverts. **-3.** [presagio] sign, herald.

anverso *m* [de moneda] head, obverse; [de hoja] front.

anzuelo *m* [para pescar] (fish) hook.

añadido, -da *adj*: **~ (a)** added (to).

añadidura *f* addition; **por ~** in addition, what is more.

añadir *vt* to add.

añejo, -ja *adj* **-1.** [vino, licor] mature; [tocino] cured. **-2.** [costumbre] age-old.

añicos *mpl*: **hacer** ○ **hacerse ~** to shatter.

añil *adj & m* [color] indigo.

año *m* year; **en el ~ 1939** in 1939; **los ~s 30** the thirties; **~ académico/escolar/fiscal** academic/school/tax year; **~ bisiesto/solar** leap/solar year; **~ nuevo** New Year; **¡Feliz Año Nuevo!** Happy New Year! ◆ **años** *mpl* [edad] age (*sg*); **¿cuántos ~s tienes?** — **tengo 17 ~s** how old are you? — I'm 17 (years old); **cumplir ~s** to have one's birthday; **cumplo ~s el 25** it's my birthday on the 25th.

añoranza *f*: **~ (de)** [gen] nostalgia (for); [hogar, patria] homesickness (for).

añorar *vt* to miss.

apabullar *vt* to overwhelm.

apacentar *vt* to graze.

apacible *adj* [gen] mild, gentle; [lugar, ambiente] pleasant.

apaciguar *vt* **-1.** [tranquilizar] to calm down. **-2.** [aplacar - dolor etc] to soothe. ◆ **apaciguarse** *vpr* **-1.** [tranquilizarse] to calm down. **-2.** [aplacarse - dolor etc] to abate.

apadrinar *vt* **-1.** [niño] to act as a godparent to. **-2.** [artista] to sponsor.

apagado, -da *adj* **-1.** [luz, fuego] out; [aparato] off. **-2.** [color, persona] subdued. **-3.** [sonido] muffled; [voz] quiet.

apagar *vt* **-1.** [extinguir - fuego] to put out; [- luz] to put off; [- vela] to extinguish. **-2.** [desconectar] to turn ○ switch off. **-3.** [aplacar - sed] to quench. **-4.** [rebajar - sonido] to muffle. ◆ **apagarse** *vpr* [extinguirse - fuego, vela, luz] to go out; [- dolor, ilusión, rencor] to die down; [- sonido] to die away.

apagón *m* power cut.

apaisado, -da *adj* oblong.

apalabrar *vt* [concertar] to make a verbal agreement regarding; [contratar] to engage on the basis of a verbal agreement.

apalancar *vt* [para abrir] to lever open; [para mover] to lever.

apalear *vt* to beat up.

apañado, -da *adj fam* [hábil, mañoso] clever, resourceful.

apañar *vt fam* **-1.** [reparar] to mend. **-2.** [amañar] to fix, to arrange. ◆ **apañarse** *vpr fam* to cope, to manage; **apañárselas (para hacer algo)** to manage (to do sthg).

apaño *m fam* **-1.** [reparación] patch. **-2.** [chanchullo] fix, shady deal. **-3.** [acuerdo] compromise.

aparador *m* [mueble] sideboard.

aparato *m* **-1.** [máquina] machine; [de laboratorio] apparatus (*U*); [electrodoméstico] appliance. **-2.** [dispositivo] device. **-3.** [teléfono]: **¿quién está al ~?** who's speaking? **-4.** [MED - prótesis] aid; [- para dientes] brace. **-5.** ANAT system. **-6.** POLÍT machinery. **-7.** [ostentación] pomp, ostentation.

aparatoso, -sa *adj* **-1.** [ostentoso] ostentatious. **-2.** [espectacular] spectacular.

aparcamiento *m* **-1.** [acción] parking. **-2.** [parking] car park *Br*, parking lot *Am*; [hueco] parking place.

aparcar ◇ *vt* [estacionar] to park. ◇ *vi* [estacionar] to park.

aparcero, -ra *m y f* sharecropper.

aparear *vt* [animales] to mate. ◆ **aparearse** *vpr* [animales] to mate.

aparecer *vi* **-1.** [gen] to appear. **-2.** [acudir]: **~ por (un lugar)** to turn up at (a place). **-3.** [ser encontrado] to turn up.

aparejado, -da *adj*: **llevar ~** [acarrear] to entail.

aparejador, -ra *m y f* quantity surveyor.

aparejo *m* **-1.** [de caballerías] harness. **-2.** MEC block and tackle. **-3.** NÁUT rigging. ◆ **aparejos** *mpl* equipment (*U*); [de pesca] tackle (*U*).

aparentar ◇ *vt* **-1.** [fingir] to feign. **-2.** [edad] to look. ◇ *vi* [presumir] to show off.

aparente *adj* [falso, supuesto] apparent.

aparición *f* **-1.** [gen] appearance. **-2.** [de ser sobrenatural] apparition.

apariencia *f* [aspecto] appearance; **guardar las ~s** to keep up appearances; **las ~s engañan** appearances can be deceptive.

apartado, -da *adj* **-1.** [separado]: **~ de** away from. **-2.** [alejado] remote. ◆ **apartado** *m* [párrafo] paragraph; [sección] section. ◆ **apartado de correos** *m* PO Box.

apartamento *m* apartment.

apartar *vt* **-1.** [alejar] to move away; [quitar] to remove. **-2.** [separar] to separate. **-3.** [escoger] to take, to select. ◆ **apartarse** *vpr* **-1.** [hacerse a un lado] to move to one side. **-2.** [separarse] to separate; **~se de** [gen] to move away from; [tema] to get away from; [mundo, sociedad] to cut o.s. off from.

aparte ◇ adv **-1.** [en otro lugar, a un lado] aside, to one side; **bromas** ~ joking apart. **-2.** [además] besides; ~ **de fea** ... besides being ugly .... **-3.** [por separado] separately. ◇ m **-1.** [párrafo] new paragraph. **-2.** TEATR aside.
◆ **aparte de** loc prep [excepto] apart from, except from.

apasionado, -da ◇ adj passionate. ◇ m y f lover, enthusiast.

apasionante adj fascinating.

apasionar vt to fascinate; **le apasiona la música** he's mad about music.
◆ **apasionarse** vpr to get excited.

apatía f apathy.

apático, -ca adj apathetic.

apátrida adj stateless.

apdo. abrev de **apartado**.

apeadero m [de tren] halt.

apear vt [bajar] to take down.
◆ **apearse** vpr [bajarse]: ~**se (de)** [tren] to alight (from), to get off; [coche] to get out (of); [caballo] to dismount (from).

apechugar vi: ~ **con** to put up with, to live with.

apedrear vt [persona] to stone; [cosa] to throw stones at.

apegarse vpr: ~ **a** to become fond of O attached to.

apego m fondness, attachment; **tener/tomar** ~ **a** to be/become fond of.

apelación f appeal.

apelar vi **-1.** DER to (lodge an) appeal; ~ **ante/contra** to appeal to/against. **-2.** [recurrir]: ~ **a** [persona] to go to; [sentido común, bondad] to appeal to; [violencia] to resort to.

apelativo m name.

apellidarse vpr: **se apellida Suárez** her surname is Suárez.

apellido m surname.

apelmazar vt **-1.** [jersey] to shrink. **-2.** [arroz, bizcocho] to make stodgy.
◆ **apelmazarse** vpr **-1.** [jersey] to shrink. **-2.** [arroz, bizcocho] to go stodgy.

apelotonar vt to bundle up.
◆ **apelotonarse** vpr [gente] to crowd together.

apenado, -da adj Amer ashamed.

apenar vt to sadden.

apenas adv **-1.** [casi no] scarcely, hardly; ~ **me puedo mover** I can hardly move. **-2.** [tan sólo] only; ~ **hace dos minutos** only two minutes ago. **-3.**

[tan pronto como] as soon as; ~ **llegó, sonó el teléfono** no sooner had he arrived than the phone rang.

apéndice m appendix.

apendicitis f inv appendicitis.

apercibir vt [amonestar] to reprimand.
◆ **apercibirse de** vpr to notice.

aperitivo m [bebida] aperitif; [comida] appetizer.

apero m (gen pl) tool; ~**s de labranza** farming implements.

apertura f **-1.** [gen] opening; [de año académico, temporada] start. **-2.** POLÍT [liberalización] liberalization (especially that introduced in Spain by the Franco regime after 1970).

aperturista adj, m y f progressive.

apesadumbrar vt to weigh down.
◆ **apesadumbrarse** vpr to be weighed down.

apestar vi: ~ **(a)** to stink (of).

apetecer vi: ¿**te apetece un café?** do you fancy a coffee?; **me apetece salir** I feel like going out.

apetecible adj [comida] appetizing, tempting; [vacaciones etc] desirable.

apetito m appetite; **abrir el** ~ to whet one's appetite; **perder el** ~ to lose one's appetite; **tener** ~ to be hungry.

apetitoso, -sa adj [comida] appetizing.

apiadar vt to earn the pity of.
◆ **apiadarse** vpr to show compassion; ~**se de** to take pity on.

ápice m **-1.** [pizca] iota; **no ceder un** ~ not to budge an inch. **-2.** [punto culminante] peak, height.

apicultura f beekeeping.

apilar vt to pile up. ◆ **apilarse** vpr to pile up.

apiñar vt to pack O cram together.
◆ **apiñarse** vpr to crowd together; [para protegerse, por miedo] to huddle together.

apio m celery.

apisonadora f steamroller.

aplacar vt to placate; [hambre] to satisfy; [sed] to quench. ◆ **aplacarse** vpr to calm down; [dolor] to abate.

aplanar vt to level.

aplastante adj fig [apabullante] overwhelming, devastating.

aplastar vt **-1.** [por el peso] to flatten. **-2.** [derrotar] to crush.

aplatanar vt fam to make listless.

aplaudir vt & vi to applaud.

aplauso m **-1.** [ovación] round of applause; ~**s** applause (U). **-2.** fig [alabanza] applause.

aplazamiento *m* postponement.
aplazar *vt* to postpone.
aplicación *f* [gen & INFORM] application.
aplicado, -da *adj* [estudioso] diligent.
aplicar *vt* [gen] to apply; [nombre, calificativo] to give. ◆ **aplicarse** *vpr* [esmerarse]: ~se (en algo) to apply o.s. (to sthg).
aplique *m* wall lamp.
aplomo *m* composure; perder el ~ to lose one's composure.
apocado, -da *adj* timid.
apocalipsis *m o f inv* calamity. ◆ **Apocalipsis** *m o f* Apocalypse.
apocarse *vpr* [intimidarse] to be frightened ○ scared; [humillarse] to humble o.s.
apodar *vt* to nickname.
apoderado, -da *m y f* **-1.** [representante] (official) representative. **-2.** TAUROM agent, manager.
apoderar *vt* [gen] to authorize; DER to grant power of attorney to. ◆ **apoderarse de** *vpr* **-1.** [adueñarse de] to seize. **-2.** *fig* [dominar] to take hold of, to grip.
apodo *m* nickname.
apogeo *m fig* height, apogee; estar en (pleno) ~ to be at its height.
apolillar *vt* to eat holes in. ◆ **apolillarse** *vpr* to get moth-eaten.
apolítico, -ca *adj* apolitical.
apología *f* apology, eulogy.
apoltronarse *vpr* **-1.** [apalancarse]: ~ (en) to become lazy ○ idle (in). **-2.** [acomodarse]: ~ en to lounge in.
apoplejía *f* apoplexy.
apoquinar *vt & vi fam* to fork out.
aporrear *vt* to bang.
aportación *f* [contribución] contribution.
aportar *vt* [contribuir con] to contribute.
aposentar *vt* to put up, to lodge. ◆ **aposentarse** *vpr* to take up lodgings.
aposento *m* **-1.** [habitación] room. **-2.** [alojamiento] lodgings (*pl*).
apósito *m* dressing.
aposta, apostas *adv* on purpose.
apostar ◇ *vt* **-1.** [jugarse] to bet. **-2.** [emplazar] to post. ◇ *vi*: ~ (por) to bet (on). ◆ **apostarse** *vpr* [jugarse] to bet; ~se algo con alguien to bet sb sthg.
apostas = **aposta**.
apostilla *f* note.
apóstol *m lit & fig* apostle.
apóstrofo *m* GRAM apostrophe.
apoteósico, -ca *adj* tremendous.

apoyar *vt* **-1.** [inclinar] to lean, to rest. **-2.** *fig* [basar, respaldar] to support. ◆ **apoyarse** *vpr* **-1.** [sostenerse]: ~se en to lean on. **-2.** *fig* [basarse]: ~se en [suj: tesis, conclusiones] to be based on, to rest on; [suj: persona] to base one's arguments on. **-3.** [respaldarse] to support one another.
apoyo *m lit & fig* support.
apreciable *adj* **-1.** [perceptible] appreciable. **-2.** *fig* [estimable] worthy.
apreciación *f* [consideración] appreciation; [estimación] evaluation.
apreciar *vt* **-1.** [valorar] to appreciate; [sopesar] to appraise, to evaluate. **-2.** [sentir afecto por] to think highly of. **-3.** [percibir] to tell, to make out.
aprecio *m* esteem.
aprehender *vt* [coger - persona] to apprehend; [- alijo, mercancía] to seize.
aprehensión *f* [de persona] arrest, capture; [de alijo, mercancía] seizure.
apremiante *adj* pressing, urgent.
apremiar ◇ *vt* [meter prisa]: ~ a alguien para que haga algo to urge sb to do sthg. ◇ *vi* [ser urgente] to be pressing.
apremio *m* [urgencia] urgency.
aprender ◇ *vt* **-1.** [estudiar] to learn. **-2.** [memorizar] to memorize. ◇ *vi*: ~ (a hacer algo) to learn (to do sthg).
aprendiz, -za *m y f* **-1.** [ayudante] apprentice, trainee. **-2.** [novato] beginner.
aprendizaje *m* **-1.** [acción] learning. **-2.** [tiempo, situación] apprenticeship.
aprensión *f*: ~ (por) [miedo] apprehension (about); [escrúpulo] squeamishness (about).
aprensivo, -va *adj* **-1.** [miedoso] apprehensive. **-2.** [hipocondríaco] hypochondriac.
apresar *vt* [suj: animal] to catch; [suj: persona] to capture.
aprestar *vt* **-1.** [preparar] to prepare, to get ready. **-2.** [tela] to size. ◆ **aprestarse a** *vpr*: ~se a hacer algo to get ready to do sthg.
apresto *m* size.
apresurado, -da *adj* hasty, hurried.
apresurar *vt* to hurry along, to speed up; ~ a alguien para que haga algo to try to make sb do sthg more quickly. ◆ **apresurarse** *vpr* to hurry.
apretado, -da *adj* **-1.** [gen] tight; [triunfo] narrow; [esprint] close; [caligrafía] cramped. **-2.** [apiñado] packed.
apretar ◇ *vt* **-1.** [oprimir - botón, tecla] to press; [- gatillo] to pull; [- nudo, tuerca, cinturón] to tighten; el zapato me

aprieta my shoe is pinching. **-2.** [estrechar] to squeeze; [abrazar] to hug. **-3.** [comprimir - ropa, objetos] to pack tight. **-4.** [juntar - dientes] to grit; [- labios] to press together. ◇ *vi* [calor, lluvia] to intensify. ◆ **apretarse** *vpr* [agolparse] to crowd together; [acercarse] to squeeze up.

apretón *m* [estrechamiento] squeeze; ~ **de manos** handshake.

apretujar *vt* **-1.** [gen] to squash. **-2.** [hacer una bola con] to screw up. ◆ **apretujarse** *vpr* [en banco, autobús] to squeeze together; [por frío] to huddle up.

apretujón *m* *fam* [abrazo] bearhug.

aprieto *m* *fig* fix, difficult situation; **poner en un** ~ **a alguien** to put sb in a difficult position; **verse** ○ **estar en un** ~ to be in a fix.

aprisa *adv* quickly.

aprisionar *vt* **-1.** [encarcelar] to imprison. **-2.** [inmovilizar - atando, con camisa de fuerza] to strap down; [- suj: viga etc] to trap.

aprobación *f* approval.

aprobado, -da *adj* [aceptado] approved. ◆ **aprobado** *m* EDUC pass.

aprobar *vt* **-1.** [proyecto, moción, medida] to approve; [ley] to pass. **-2.** [comportamiento etc] to approve of. **-3.** [examen, asignatura] to pass.

apropiación *f* [robo] theft.

apropiado, -da *adj* suitable, appropriate.

apropiar *vt*: ~ **(a)** to adapt (to). ◆ **apropiarse de** *vpr* *lit* & *fig* to steal.

aprovechable *adj* usable.

aprovechado, -da *adj* **-1.** [caradura]: **es muy** ~ he's always sponging off other people. **-2.** [bien empleado - tiempo] well-spent; [- espacio] well-planned.

aprovechamiento *m* [utilización] use.

aprovechar ◇ *vt* **-1.** [gen] to make the most of; [oferta, ocasión] to take advantage of; [conocimientos, experiencia] to use, to make use of. **-2.** [lo inservible] to put to good use. ◇ *vi* [ser provechoso] to be beneficial; **¡que aproveche!** enjoy your meal! ◆ **aprovecharse** *vpr*: ~**se (de)** to take advantage (of).

aprovisionamiento *m* supplying.

aproximación *f* **-1.** [acercamiento] approach. **-2.** [en cálculo] approximation.

aproximadamente *adv* approximately.

aproximado, -da *adj* approximate.

aproximar *vt* to move closer. ◆ **aproximarse** *vpr* to come closer.

aptitud *f* ability, aptitude; **tener** ~ **para algo** to have an aptitude for sthg.

apto, -ta *adj* **-1.** [adecuado, conveniente]: ~ **(para)** suitable (for). **-2.** [capacitado - intelectualmente] capable, able; [- físicamente] fit. **-3.** CIN: ~/**no** ~ **para menores** suitable/unsuitable for children.

apuesta *f* bet.

apuesto, -ta *adj* dashing.

apuntador, -ra *m y f* prompter.

apuntalar *vt* *lit* & *fig* to underpin.

apuntar *vt* **-1.** [anotar] to note down; ~ **a alguien** [en lista] to put sb down. **-2.** [dirigir - dedo] to point; [- arma] to aim; ~ **a alguien** [con el dedo] to point at sb; [con un arma] to aim at sb. **-3.** TEATR to prompt. **-4.** *fig* [indicar] to point out. ◆ **apuntarse** *vpr* **-1.** [en lista] to put one's name down; [en curso] to enrol. **-2.** [participar]: ~**se (a hacer algo)** to join in (doing sthg).

apunte *m* [nota] note. ◆ **apuntes** *mpl* EDUC notes.

apuñalar *vt* to stab.

apurado, -da *adj* **-1.** [necesitado] in need; ~ **de** short of. **-2.** [avergonzado] embarrassed. **-3.** [difícil] awkward.

apurar *vt* **-1.** [agotar] to finish off; [existencias, la paciencia] to exhaust. **-2.** [meter prisa] to hurry. **-3.** [preocupar] to trouble. **-4.** [avergonzar] to embarrass. ◆ **apurarse** *vpr* **-1.** [preocuparse]: ~**se (por)** to worry (about). **-2.** [darse prisa] to hurry.

apuro *m* **-1.** [dificultad] fix; **estar en** ~**s** to be in a tight spot. **-2.** [penuria] hardship (*U*). **-3.** [vergüenza] embarrassment; **me da** ~ **(decírselo)** I'm embarrassed (to tell her).

aquejado, -da *adj*: ~ **de** suffering from.

aquejar *vt* to afflict.

aquel, aquella (*mpl* **aquellos,** *fpl* **aquellas**) *adj demos* that, (*pl*) those.

aquél, aquélla (*mpl* **aquéllos,** *fpl* **aquéllas**) *pron demos* **-1.** [ése] that (one), (*pl*) those (ones); **este cuadro me gusta pero** ~ **del fondo no** I like this picture, but I don't like that one at the back; ~ **fue mi último día en Londres** that was my last day in London. **-2.** [nombrado antes] the former. **-3.** [con oraciones relativas] whoever, anyone who; ~ **que quiera hablar que levante la mano** whoever wishes ○ anyone wishing to speak should raise their hand; **aquéllos que ...** those who ....

aquella → **aquel**.

aquélla → aquél.
aquello *pron demos* (*neutro*) that; ~ de su mujer es una mentira all that about his wife is a lie.
aquellos, aquellas → aquel.
aquéllos, aquéllas → aquél.
aquí *adv* **-1.** [gen] here; ~ abajo/arriba down/up here; ~ dentro/fuera in/out here; ~ mismo right here; por ~ over here. **-2.** [ahora] now; de ~ a mañana between now and tomorrow; de ~ a poco shortly, soon; de ~ a un mes a month from now, in a month.
ara *f* (*el*) *culto* [altar] altar. ◆ **en aras de** *loc prep culto* for the sake of.
árabe ◇ *adj* Arab, Arabian. ◇ *m y f* [persona] Arab. ◇ *m* [lengua] Arabic.
Arabia Saudí, Arabia Saudita Saudi Arabia.
arábigo, -ga *adj* **-1.** [de Arabia] Arab, Arabian. **-2.** [numeración] Arabic.
arado *m* plough.
arancel *m* tariff.
arándano *m* bilberry.
arandela *f* TECN washer.
araña *f* **-1.** [animal] spider. **-2.** [lámpara] chandelier.
arañar *vt* [gen] to scratch.
arañazo *m* scratch.
arar *vt* to plough.
arbitraje *m* **-1.** [DEP - en fútbol etc] refereeing; [- en tenis, críquet] umpiring. **-2.** DER arbitration.
arbitrar ◇ *vt* **-1.** [DEP - en fútbol etc] to referee; [- en tenis, críquet] to umpire. **-2.** DER to arbitrate. ◇ *vi* **-1.** [DEP - en fútbol etc] to referee; [- en tenis, críquet] to umpire. **-2.** DER to arbitrate.
arbitrariedad *f* [cualidad] arbitrariness.
arbitrario, -ria *adj* arbitrary.
arbitrio *m* [decisión] judgment.
árbitro *m* **-1.** [DEP - en fútbol etc] referee; [- en tenis, críquet] umpire. **-2.** DER arbitrator.
árbol *m* **-1.** BOT tree. **-2.** TECN shaft; ~ de levas camshaft. **-3.** NÁUT mast. ◆ **árbol genealógico** *m* family tree.
arboleda *f* wood.
arbusto *m* bush, shrub.
arca *f* (*el*) [arcón] chest. ◆ **arcas** *fpl* coffers; ~s públicas Treasury (*sg*).
arcada *f* **-1.** (*gen pl*) [de estómago] retching (*U*); me dieron ~s I retched. **-2.** [ARQUIT - arcos] arcade; [- de puente] arch.
arcaico, -ca *adj* archaic.
arce *m* maple.

arcén *m* [de autopista] hard shoulder; [de carretera] verge.
archiconocido, -da *adj fam* very well-known.
archiduque, -quesa *m y f* archduke (*f* archduchess).
archipiélago *m* archipelago.
archivador, -ra *m y f* archivist. ◆ **archivador** *m* filing cabinet.
archivar *vt* [guardar - documento, fichero etc] to file.
archivo *m* **-1.** [lugar] archive; [documentos] archives (*pl*); imágenes de ~ TV library pictures. **-2.** [informe, ficha] file. **-3.** INFORM file.
arcilla *f* clay.
arco *m* **-1.** GEOM arc. **-2.** ARQUIT arch; ~ de herradura horseshoe arch; ~ triunfal O de triunfo triumphal arch. **-3.** DEP, MIL & MÚS bow. ◆ **arco iris** *m* rainbow.
arcón *m* large chest.
arder *vi* to burn; [sin llama] to smoulder; ~ de *fig* to burn with; está que arde [persona] he's fuming; [reunión] it's getting pretty heated.
ardid *m* ruse, trick.
ardiente *adj* [gen] burning; [líquido] scalding; [admirador, defensor] ardent.
ardilla *f* squirrel.
ardor *m* **-1.** [quemazón] burning (sensation); ~ de estómago heartburn. **-2.** *fig* [entusiasmo] fervour.
arduo, -dua *adj* arduous.
área *f* (*el*) **-1.** [gen] area; ~ metropolitana/de servicio metropolitan/service area. **-2.** DEP: ~ (de castigo O penalti) (penalty) area.
arena *f* **-1.** [de playa etc] sand; ~s movedizas quicksand (*U*). **-2.** [para luchar] arena. **-3.** TAUROM bullring.
arenal *m* sandy ground (*U*).
arenga *f* harangue.
arenilla *f* [polvo] dust.
arenoso, -sa *adj* sandy.
arenque *m* herring.
argamasa *f* mortar.
Argel Algiers.
Argelia Algeria.
Argentina: (la) ~ Argentina.
argentino, -na *adj, m y f* Argentinian.
argolla *f* **-1.** [aro] (large) ring. **-2.** *Amer* [alianza] wedding ring.
argot *m* **-1.** [popular] slang. **-2.** [técnico] jargon.
argucia *f* sophism.
argüir ◇ *vt culto* **-1.** [argumentar] to ar-

gue. **-2.** [demostrar] to prove. ◇ *vi* [argumentar] to argue.

argumentación *f* line of argument.

argumentar *vt* **-1.** [teoría, opinión] to argue. **-2.** [razones, excusas] to allege.

argumento *m* **-1.** [razonamiento] argument. **-2.** [trama] plot.

aria *f* MÚS aria.

aridez *f* [gen] dryness; [de zona, clima] aridity.

árido, -da *adj* [gen] dry; [zona, clima] arid. ♦ **áridos** *mpl* dry goods.

Aries ◇ *m* [zodiaco] Aries. ◇ *m y f* [persona] Aries.

ariete *f* HIST & MIL battering ram.

ario, -ria *adj, m y f* Aryan.

arisco, -ca *adj* surly.

arista *f* edge.

aristocracia *f* aristocracy.

aristócrata *m y f* aristocrat.

aritmético, -ca *adj* arithmetic. ♦ **aritmética** *f* arithmetic.

arma *f* (*el*) **-1.** [instrumento] arm, weapon; ~ **blanca** blade, weapon with a sharp blade; ~ **de fuego** firearm; ~ **homicida** murder weapon. **-2.** *fig* [medio] weapon.

armada → **armado.**

armadillo *m* armadillo.

armado, -da *adj* **-1.** [con armas] armed. **-2.** [con armazón] reinforced. ♦ **armada** *f* [marina] navy; [escuadra] fleet.

armador, -ra *m y f* shipowner.

armadura *f* **-1.** [de barco, tejado] framework; [de gafas] frame. **-2.** [de guerrero] armour.

armamentista, armamentístico, -ca *adj* arms (*antes de sust*).

armamento *m* [armas] arms (*pl*).

armar *vt* **-1.** [montar - mueble etc] to assemble; [- tienda] to pitch. **-2.** [ejército, personas] to arm. **-3.** *fam fig* [provocar] to cause; ~**la** *fam* to cause trouble. ♦ **armarse** *vpr* **-1.** [con armas] to arm o.s. **-2.** [prepararse]: ~**se de** [valor, paciencia] to summon up. **-3.** *loc*: **se armó la gorda** O **la de San Quintín** O **la de Dios es Cristo** *fam* all hell broke loose.

armario *m* [para objetos] cupboard; [para ropa] wardrobe; ~ **empotrado** fitted cupboard/wardrobe.

armatoste *m* [mueble, objeto] unwieldy object; [máquina] contraption.

armazón *f* [gen] framework, frame; [de avión, coche] chassis; [de edificio] skeleton.

armería *f* **-1.** [museo] military O war

museum. **-2.** [depósito] armoury. **-3.** [tienda] gunsmith's (shop).

armiño *m* [piel] ermine; [animal] stoat.

armisticio *m* armistice.

armonía *f* harmony.

armónico, -ca *adj* harmonic. ♦ **armónica** *f* harmonica.

armonioso, -sa *adj* harmonious.

armonizar ◇ *vt* **-1.** [concordar] to match. **-2.** MÚS to harmonize. ◇ *vi* [concordar]: ~ **con** to match.

arnés *m* armour. ♦ **arneses** *mpl* [de animales] harness (*U*).

aro *m* **-1.** [círculo] hoop; TECN ring; **los** ~**s olímpicos** the Olympic rings. **-2.** *Amer* [pendiente] earring.

aroma *m* aroma; [de vino] bouquet; CULIN flavouring.

aromático, -ca *adj* aromatic.

arpa *f* (*el*) harp.

arpía *f* *fig* [mujer] old hag.

arpillera *f* sackcloth, hessian.

arpón *m* harpoon.

arquear *vt* [gen] to bend; [cejas, espalda, lomo] to arch. ♦ **arquearse** *vpr* to bend.

arqueología *f* archeology.

arqueólogo, -ga *m y f* archeologist.

arquero *m* DEP & MIL archer.

arquetipo *m* archetype.

arquitecto, -ta *m y f* architect.

arquitectura *f* *lit* & *fig* architecture.

arrabal *m* [barrio pobre] slum (*on city outskirts*); [barrio periférico] outlying district.

arrabalero, -ra *adj* **-1.** [periférico] outlying. **-2.** [barriobajero] rough, coarse.

arracimarse *vpr* to cluster together.

arraigado, -da *adj* [costumbre, idea] deeply rooted; [persona] established.

arraigar *vi* *lit* & *fig* to take root. ♦ **arraigarse** *vpr* [establecerse] to settle down.

arraigo *m* roots (*pl*); **tener mucho** ~ to be deeply rooted.

arrancar ◇ *vt* **-1.** [desarraigar - árbol] to uproot; [- malas hierbas, flor] to pull up. **-2.** [quitar, separar] to tear O to rip off; [cable, página, pelo] to tear out; [cartel, cortinas] to tear down; [muela] to pull out; [ojos] to gouge out. **-3.** [arrebatar]: ~ **algo a alguien** to grab O snatch sthg from sb. **-4.** AUTOM & TECN to start; INFORM to start up. **-5.** *fig* [obtener]: ~ **algo a alguien** [confesión, promesa, secreto] to extract sthg from sb; [sonrisa, dinero, ovación] to get sthg out of sb; [suspiro, carcajada] to bring sthg from sb. ◇ *vi* **-1.** [partir] to set off. **-2.** [suj: máquina, coche] to start. **-3.** [provenir]: ~ **de** to stem from.

arranque *m* **-1.** [comienzo] start. **-2.** AUTOM starter motor. **-3.** *fig* [arrebato] fit.

arrasar *vt* to destroy, to devastate.

arrastrar ◇ *vt* **-1.** [gen] to drag ○ pull along; [pies] to drag; [carro, vagón] to pull; [suj: corriente, aire] to carry away. **-2.** *fig* [convencer] to win over; ~ **a alguien a algo/a hacer algo** to lead sb into sthg/to do sthg; **dejarse** ~ **por algo/alguien** to allow o.s. to be swayed by sthg/sb. **-3.** *fig* [producir] to bring. ◇ *vi* [rozar el suelo] to drag (along) the ground. ◆ **arrastrarse** *vpr* to crawl; *fig* to grovel.

arrastre *m* **-1.** [acarreo] dragging. **-2.** [pesca] trawling. **-3.** *loc:* **estar para el** ~ to have had it, to be done for.

arre *interj:* ¡~! gee up!

arrear *vt* **-1.** [azuzar] to gee up. **-2.** *fam* [propinar] to give.

arrebatado, -da *adj* **-1.** [impetuoso] impulsive, impetuous. **-2.** [ruborizado] flushed. **-3.** [iracundo] enraged.

arrebatar *vt* **-1.** [arrancar]: ~ **algo a alguien** to snatch sthg from sb. **-2.** *fig* [cautivar] to captivate. ◆ **arrebatarse** *vpr* [enfurecerse] to get furious.

arrebato *m* **-1.** [arranque] fit, outburst; **un** ~ **de amor** a crush. **-2.** [furia] rage.

arrebujar *vt* [amontonar] to bundle (up). ◆ **arrebujarse** *vpr* [arroparse] to wrap o.s. up.

arreciar *vi* **-1.** [temporal etc] to get worse. **-2.** *fig* [críticas etc] to intensify.

arrecife *m* reef.

arreglado, -da *adj* **-1.** [reparado] fixed; [ropa] mended. **-2.** [ordenado] tidy. **-3.** [bien vestido] smart. **-4.** [solucionado] sorted out. **-5.** *fig* [precio] reasonable.

arreglar *vt* **-1.** [reparar] to fix, to repair; [ropa] to mend. **-2.** [ordenar] to tidy (up). **-3.** [solucionar] to sort out. **-4.** MÚS to arrange. **-5.** [acicalar] to smarten up; [cabello] to do. ◆ **arreglarse** *vpr* **-1.** [apañarse]: ~**se (con algo)** to make do (with sthg); **arreglárselas (para hacer algo)** to manage (to do sthg). **-2.** [acicalarse] to smarten up.

arreglo *m* **-1.** [reparación] mending, repair; [de ropa] mending. **-2.** [solución] settlement. **-3.** MÚS **(musical)** arrangement. **-4.** [acuerdo] agreement; **llegar a un** ~ to reach agreement.

arrellanarse *vpr* to settle back.

arremangar, remangar *vt* to roll up. ◆ **arremangarse** *vpr* to roll up one's sleeves.

arremeter ◆ **arremeter contra** *vi* to attack.

arremetida *f* attack.

arremolinarse *vpr* **-1.** *fig* [personas]: ~ **alrededor de** to crowd around. **-2.** [agua, hojas] to swirl (about).

arrendamiento, arriendo *m* **-1.** [acción] renting, leasing. **-2.** [precio] rent, lease.

arrendar *vt* **-1.** [dar en arriendo] to let, to lease. **-2.** [tomar en arriendo] to rent, to lease.

arrendatario, -ria *m y f* leaseholder, tenant.

arreos *mpl* harness (U).

arrepentido, -da ◇ *adj* repentant. ◇ *m y f* POLÍT *person who renounces terrorist activities.*

arrepentimiento *m* regret, repentance.

arrepentirse *vpr* to repent; ~ **de algo/ de haber hecho algo** to regret sthg/ having done sthg.

arrestar *vt* to arrest.

arresto *m* [detención] arrest.

arriar *vt* to lower.

arriba ◇ *adv* **-1.** [posición - gen] above; [- en edificio] upstairs; **vive (en el piso de)** ~ she lives upstairs; **está aquí/allí** ~ it's up here/there; ~ **del todo** right at the top; **más** ~ further up. **-2.** [dirección] up; **ve** ~ [en edificio] go upstairs; **hacia/para** ~ up, upwards; **calle/ escaleras** ~ up the street/stairs; **río** ~ upstream. **-3.** [en un texto] above; **el** ~ **mencionado ...** the above-mentioned .... **-4.** *loc:* **de** ~ **abajo** [cosa] from top to bottom; [persona] from head to toe ○ foot; **mirar a alguien de** ~ **abajo** [con desdén] to look sb up and down. ◇ *prep:* ~ **(de)** *Amer* [encima de] on top of. ◇ *interj:* ¡~ ...! up (with) ...!; ¡~ **los mineros!** up (with) the miners!; ¡~ **las manos!** hands up! ◆ **arriba de** *loc prep* more than. ◆ **de arriba** *loc adj* top; **el estante de** ~ the top shelf.

arribar *vi* to arrive; NÁUT to reach port.

arribeño, -ña *m y f Amer fam* highlander.

arribista *adj, m y f* arriviste.

arriendo → **arrendamiento**.

arriesgado, -da *adj* [peligroso] risky.

arriesgar *vt* to risk; [hipótesis] to venture, to suggest. ◆ **arriesgarse** *vpr* to take risks/a risk.

arrimar *vt* [acercar] to move ○ bring closer; ~ **algo a** [pared, mesa] to move sthg up against. ◆ **arrimarse** *vpr* [acercarse] to come closer ○ nearer; ~**se a algo** [acercándose] to move closer to sthg; [apoyándose] to lean on sthg.

arrinconar *vt* **-1.** [apartar] to put in a corner. **-2.** [abandonar] to discard, to put away. **-3.** *fig* [persona - dar de lado] to cold-shoulder; [- acorralar] to corner.

arrodillarse *vpr* to kneel down; *fig* to go down on one's knees, to grovel.

arrogancia *f* arrogance.

arrogante *adj* arrogant.

arrojar *vt* **-1.** [lanzar] to throw; [con violencia] to hurl, to fling. **-2.** [despedir - humo] to send out; [- olor] to give off; [- lava] to spew out. **-3.** [echar]: ~ **a alguien de** to throw sb out of. **-4.** [resultado] to produce, to yield. **-5.** [vomitar] to throw up. ◆ **arrojarse** *vpr* to hurl o.s.

arrojo *m* courage, fearlessness.

arrollador, -ra *adj* overwhelming; [belleza, personalidad] dazzling.

arrollar *vt* **-1.** [atropellar] to run over. **-2.** [tirar - suj: agua, viento] to sweep away. **-3.** [vencer] to crush.

arropar *vt* [con ropa] to wrap up; [en cama] to tuck up. ◆ **arroparse** *vpr* to wrap o.s. up.

arroyo *m* **-1.** [riachuelo] stream. **-2.** [de la calle] gutter.

arroz *m* rice; ~ **blanco** boiled rice; ~ **con leche** rice pudding.

arruga *f* **-1.** [en ropa, papel] crease. **-2.** [en piel] wrinkle, line.

arrugar *vt* **-1.** [ropa, papel] to crease, to crumple. **-2.** [piel] to wrinkle. ◆ **arrugarse** *vpr* **-1.** [ropa] to get creased. **-2.** [piel] to get wrinkled.

arruinar *vt lit* & *fig* to ruin. ◆ **arruinarse** *vpr* to go bankrupt, to be ruined.

arrullar *vt* to lull to sleep. ◆ **arrullarse** *vpr* [animales] to coo.

arrumar *vt Amer* to pile up.

arsenal *m* **-1.** [de barcos] shipyard. **-2.** [de armas] arsenal. **-3.** [de cosas] array.

arsénico *m* arsenic.

art. (*abrev de* **artículo**) art.

arte *m o f* (*en sg gen m; en pl f*) **-1.** [gen] art; ~ **dramático** drama. **-2.** [habilidad] artistry. **-3.** [astucia] artfulness, cunning; **malas** ~**s** trickery (*U*). ◆ **artes** *fpl* arts; **bellas** ~**s** fine arts.

artefacto *m* [aparato] device; [máquina] machine.

arteria *f lit* & *fig* artery.

artesa *f* trough.

artesanal *adj* [hecho a mano] handmade.

artesanía *f* craftsmanship; **de** ~ [producto] handmade.

artesano, -na *m y f* craftsman (*f* craftswoman).

ártico, -ca *adj* arctic. ◆ **Ártico** *m*: **el Ártico** the Arctic; **el océano Glacial Ártico** the Arctic Ocean.

articulación *f* **-1.** ANAT & TECN joint. **-2.** LING articulation.

articulado, -da *adj* articulated.

articular *vt* [palabras, piezas] to articulate.

artículo *m* [gen] article; ~ **de fondo** editorial, leader; ~ **de primera necesidad** basic commodity.

artífice *m y f fig* architect.

artificial *adj* artificial.

artificio *m fig* [falsedad] artifice; [artimaña] trick.

artificioso, -sa *adj fig* [engañoso] deceptive.

artillería *f* artillery.

artillero *m* artilleryman.

artilugio *m* gadget, contrivance.

artimaña *f* (*gen pl*) trick, ruse.

artista *m y f* **-1.** [gen] artist. **-2.** [de espectáculos] artiste.

artístico, -ca *adj* artistic.

artritis *f inv* arthritis.

arzobispo *m* archbishop.

as *m* **-1.** [carta, dado] ace. **-2.** [campeón]: **un** ~ **del volante** an ace driver.

asa *f* (*el*) handle.

asado *m* roast.

asador *m* **-1.** [aparato] roaster. **-2.** [varilla] spit.

asaduras *fpl* offal (*U*); [de pollo, pavo] giblets.

asalariado, -da *m y f* wage earner.

asalmonado, -da *adj* salmon (pink).

asaltante *m y f* [agresor] attacker; [atracador] robber.

asaltar *vt* **-1.** [atacar] to attack; [castillo, ciudad etc] to storm. **-2.** [robar] to rob. **-3.** *fig* [suj: dudas etc] to assail.

asalto *m* **-1.** [ataque] attack; [de castillo, ciudad] storming. **-2.** [robo] robbery. **-3.** DEP round.

asamblea *f* assembly; POLÍT mass meeting.

asar *vt* [alimentos - al horno] to roast; [- a la parrilla] to grill.

ascendencia *f* **-1.** [linaje] descent. **-2.** [extracción social] extraction. **-3.** *fig* [influencia] ascendancy.

ascender ◇ *vi* **-1.** [subir] to go up, to climb. **-2.** [aumentar, elevarse] to rise, to go up. **-3.** [en empleo, deportes]: ~ **(a)** to be promoted (to). **-4.** [totalizar - precio etc]: ~ **a** to come O amount to. ◇ *vt*: ~ **a alguien (a)** to promote sb (to).

ascendiente *m y f* [antepasado] ancestor.

ascensión *f* ascent. ◆ **Ascensión** *f* RELIG Ascension.

ascenso *m* **-1.** [en empleo, deportes] promotion. **-2.** [ascensión] ascent.

ascensor *m* lift *Br*, elevator *Am*.

ascético, -ca *adj* ascetic.

asco *m* [sensación] revulsion; **siento** ~ I feel sick; ¡**qué** ~ **de tiempo!** what foul weather!; **me da** ~ I find it disgusting; ¡**qué** ~! how disgusting O revolting!; **hacer** ~**s a** to turn one's nose up at; **estar hecho un** ~ *fam* [cosa] to be filthy; [persona] to be a real sight.

ascua *f* (*el*) ember.

aseado, -da *adj* [limpio] clean; [arreglado] smart.

asear *vt* to clean. ◆ **asearse** *vpr* to get washed and dressed.

asediar *vt* to lay siege to; *fig* to pester.

asedio *m* siege; *fig* pestering.

asegurado, -da *m y f* policy-holder.

asegurar *vt* **-1.** [fijar] to secure. **-2.** [garantizar] to assure; **te lo aseguro** I assure you; ~ **a alguien que ...** to assure sb that .... **-3.** COM: ~ **(contra)** to insure (against); ~ **algo en** [cantidad] to insure sthg for. ◆ **asegurarse** *vpr* [cerciorarse]: ~**se de que ...** to make sure that ....

asemejar ◆ **asemejarse** *vpr* to be similar O alike; ~**se a** to be similar to, to be like.

asentamiento *m* [campamento] settlement.

asentar *vt* **-1.** [instalar - empresa, campamento] to set up; [- comunidad, pueblo] to settle. **-2.** [asegurar] to secure; [cimientos] to lay. ◆ **asentarse** *vpr* **-1.** [instalarse] to settle down. **-2.** [sedimentarse] to settle.

asentir *vi* **-1.** [estar conforme]: ~ **(a)** to agree (to). **-2.** [afirmar con la cabeza] to nod.

aseo *m* [limpieza - acción] cleaning; [- cualidad] cleanliness. ◆ **aseos** *mpl* toilets *Br*, restroom (*sg*) *Am*.

aséptico, -ca *adj* MED aseptic.

asequible *adj* **-1.** [accesible, comprensible] accessible. **-2.** [razonable - precio, producto] affordable.

aserradero *m* sawmill.

aserrar *vt* to saw.

asesinar *vt* to murder; [rey, jefe de estado] to assassinate.

asesinato *m* murder; [de rey, jefe de estado] assassination.

asesino, -na *m y f* murderer (*f* murderess); [de rey, jefe de estado] assassin.

asesor, -ra *m y f* adviser; FIN consultant; ~ **fiscal** tax consultant.

asesorar *vt* to advise; FIN to provide with consultancy services. ◆ **asesorarse** *vpr* to seek advice; ~**se de** to consult.

asesoría *f* [oficina] consultant's office.

asestar *vt* [golpe] to deal; [tiro] to fire.

aseveración *f* assertion.

asfaltado *m* [acción] asphalting, surfacing; [asfalto] asphalt, (road) surface.

asfalto *m* asphalt.

asfixia *f* asphyxiation, suffocation.

asfixiar *vt* [ahogar] to asphyxiate, to suffocate. ◆ **asfixiarse** *vpr* [ahogarse] to asphyxiate, to suffocate.

así ◇ *adv* [de este modo] in this way, like this; [de ese modo] in that way, like that; **era** ~ **de largo** it was this/that long; ~ **es/era/fue como ...** that is how ...; ~ ~ [no muy bien] so so; **algo** ~ [algo parecido] something like that; ~ **es** [para asentir] that is correct, yes; **y** ~ **todos los días** and the same thing happens day after day; ~ **como** [también] as well as, and also; [tal como] just as, exactly as. ◇ *conj* **-1.** [de modo que]: ~ **(es) que** so. **-2.** [aunque] although. **-3.** [tan pronto como]: ~ **que** as soon as. **-4.** *Amer* [aun si] even if. ◇ *adj inv* [como como] like this; [como ése] like that. ◆ **así y todo, aun así** *loc adv* even so.

Asia Asia.

asiático, -ca *adj, m y f* Asian, Asiatic.

asidero *m* [agarradero] handle.

asiduidad *f* frequency.

asiduo, -dua *adj, m y f* regular.

asiento *m* [mueble, localidad] seat; **tomar** ~ to sit down.

asignación *f* **-1.** [atribución] allocation. **-2.** [sueldo] salary.

asignar *vt* **-1.** [atribuir]: ~ **algo a alguien** to assign O allocate sthg to sb. **-2.** [destinar]: ~ **a alguien a** to send sb to.

asignatura *f* EDUC subject.

asilado, -da *m y f* person living in an old people's home, convalescent home etc.

asilo *m* **-1.** [hospicio] home; ~ **de ancianos** old people's home. **-2.** *fig* [amparo] asylum; ~ **político** political asylum. **-3.** [hospedaje] accommodation.

asimilación *f* [gen & LING] assimilation.

asimilar *vt* [gen] to assimilate.

asimismo *adv* [también] also, as well; (*a principio de frase*) likewise.

asir *vt* to grasp, to take hold of.

asistencia *f* **-1.** [presencia - acción] attendance; [- hecho] presence. **-2.** [ayuda] assistance; ~ **médica** medical attention; ~ **sanitaria** health care; ~ **técnica** technical assistance. **-3.** [afluencia] audience. **-4.** DEP assist.

asistenta *f* cleaning lady.

asistente *m y f* **-1.** [ayudante] assistant, helper; ~ **social** social worker. **-2.** [presente] person present; **los** ~**s** the audience (*sg*).

asistido, -da *adj* AUTOM power (*antes de sust*); INFORM computer-assisted.

asistir ◇ *vt* [ayudar] to attend to. ◇ *vi*: ~ **a** to attend, to go to.

asma *f* (*el*) asthma.

asno *m lit & fig* ass.

asociación *f* association; ~ **de vecinos** residents' association.

asociado, -da ◇ *adj* [miembro] associate. ◇ *m y f* [miembro] associate, partner.

asociar *vt* [relacionar] to associate. ◆ **asociarse** *vpr* to form a partnership.

asolar *vt* to devastate.

asomar ◇ *vi* [gen] to peep up; [del interior de algo] to peep out. ◇ *vt* to stick; ~ **la cabeza por la ventana** to stick one's head out of the window. ◆ **asomarse** a *vpr* [ventana] to stick one's head out of; [balcón] to come/go out onto.

asombrar *vt* [causar admiración] to amaze; [causar sorpresa] to surprise. ◆ **asombrarse** *vpr*: ~**se (de)** [sentir admiración] to be amazed (at); [sentir sorpresa] to be surprised (at). •

asombro *m* [admiración] amazement; [sorpresa] surprise.

asombroso, -sa *adj* [sensacional] amazing; [sorprendente] surprising.

asomo *m* [indicio] trace, hint; [de esperanza] glimmer.

aspa *f* (*el*) X-shaped cross; [de molino] arms (*pl*).

aspaviento *m* (*gen pl*) furious gesticulations (*pl*).

aspecto *m* **-1.** [apariencia] appearance; **tener buen/mal** ~ [persona] to look well/awful; [cosa] to look nice/horrible.

-2. [faceta] aspect; **en todos los** ~**s** in every respect.

aspereza *f* roughness; *fig* sourness.

áspero, -ra *adj* **-1.** [rugoso] rough. **-2.** *fig* [desagradable] sharp, sour.

aspersión *f* [de jardín] sprinkling; [de cultivos] spraying.

aspersor *m* [para jardín] sprinkler; [para cultivos] sprayer.

aspiración *f* **-1.** [gen & LING] aspiration. **-2.** [de aire - por una persona] breathing in; [- por una máquina] suction.

aspirador *m*, **aspiradora** *f* vacuum cleaner.

aspirante *m y f*: ~ **(a)** candidate (for); [en deportes, concursos] contender (for).

aspirar ◇ *vt* [aire - suj: persona] to breathe in, to inhale. ◇ *vi*: ~ **a algo** [ansiar] to aspire to sthg.

aspirina® *f* aspirin.

asquear *vt* to disgust, to make sick.

asqueroso, -sa *adj* disgusting, revolting.

asta *f* (*el*) **-1.** [de bandera] flagpole, mast. **-2.** [de lanza] shaft; [de brocha] handle. **-3.** [de toro] horn.

asterisco *m* asterisk.

astigmatismo *m* astigmatism.

astilla *f* splinter.

astillero *m* shipyard.

astringente *adj* astringent.

astro *m* ASTRON heavenly body; *fig* star.

astrofísica *f* astrophysics (*U*).

astrología *f* astrology.

astrólogo, -ga *m y f* astrologer.

astronauta *m y f* astronaut.

astronomía *f* astronomy.

astrónomo, -ma *m y f* astronomer.

astroso, -sa *adj* [andrajoso] shabby.

astucia *f* **-1.** [picardía] cunning, astuteness. **-2.** (*gen pl*) [treta] cunning trick.

astuto, -ta *adj* [ladino, tramposo] cunning; [sagaz, listo] astute.

asueto *m* break, rest; **unos días de** ~ a few days off.

asumir *vt* **-1.** [gen] to assume. **-2.** [aceptar] to accept.

asunción *f* assumption. ◆ **Asunción** *f*: **la Asunción** RELIG the Assumption.

Asunción GEOGR Asunción.

asunto *m* **-1.** [tema - general] subject; [- específico] matter; [- de obra, libro] theme; ~**s a tratar** agenda (*sg*). **-2.** [cuestión, problema] issue. **-3.** [negocio] affair, business (*U*); **no es** ~ **tuyo** it's none of your business. ◆ **asuntos** *mpl*

POLÍT affairs; ~**s exteriores** foreign affairs.

asustado, -da *adj* frightened, scared.

asustar *vt* to frighten, to scare. ◆ **asustarse** *vpr*: ~**se (de)** to be frightened ○ scared (of).

atacar *vt* [gen] to attack.

atadura *f lit & fig* tie.

atajar ◇ *vi* [acortar]: ~ **(por)** to take a short cut (through). ◇ *vt* [contener] to put a stop to; [hemorragia, inundación] to stem.

atajo *m* **-1.** [camino corto, medio rápido] short cut; **coger** ○ **tomar un** ~ to take a short cut. **-2.** *despec* [panda] bunch.

atalaya *f* **-1.** [torre] watchtower. **-2.** [altura] vantage point.

atañer *vi* **-1.** [concernir]: ~ **a** to concern. **-2.** [corresponder]: ~ **a** to be the responsibility of.

ataque *m* **-1.** [gen & DEP] attack. **-2.** *fig* [acceso] fit, bout; ~ **cardíaco** ○ **al corazón** heart attack.

atar *vt* **-1.** [unir] to tie (up). **-2.** *fig* [constreñir] to tie down.

atardecer ◇ *m* dusk. ◇ *v impers* to get dark.

atareado, -da *adj* busy.

atascar *vt* to block (up). ◆ **atascarse** *vpr* **-1.** [obstruirse] to get blocked up. **-2.** *fig* [detenerse] to get stuck; [al hablar] to dry up.

atasco *m* **-1.** [obstrucción] blockage. **-2.** AUTOM traffic jam.

ataúd *m* coffin.

ataviar *vt* [cosa] to deck out; [persona] to dress up. ◆ **ataviarse** *vpr* to dress up.

atavío *m* [indumentaria] attire (U).

atemorizar *vt* to frighten. ◆ **atemorizarse** *vpr* to get frightened.

Atenas Athens.

atenazar *vt* **-1.** [sujetar] to clench. **-2.** *fig* [suj: dudas] to torment, to rack; [suj: miedo, nervios] to grip.

atención ◇ *f* **-1.** [interés] attention; **llamar la** ~ [atraer] to attract attention; **poner** ○ **prestar** ~ to pay attention. **-2.** [cortesía] attentiveness (U). ◇ *interj*: ¡~! [en aeropuerto, conferencia] your attention please! ◆ **atenciones** *fpl* attentions.

atender ◇ *vt* **-1.** [satisfacer - petición, ruego] to attend to; [- consejo, instrucciones] to heed; [- propuesta] to agree to. **-2.** [cuidar de - necesitados, invitados] to look after; [- enfermo] to care for; [- cliente] to serve; ¿**le atienden?** are

you being served? ◇ *vi* [estar atento]: ~ **(a)** to pay attention (to).

atenerse ◆ **atenerse a** *vpr* **-1.** [promesa, orden] to stick to; [ley, normas] to abide by. **-2.** [consecuencias] to bear in mind.

atentado *m*: ~ **contra alguien** attempt on sb's life; ~ **contra algo** crime against sthg.

atentamente *adv* [en cartas] Yours sincerely ○ faithfully.

atentar *vi*: ~ **contra (la vida de) alguien** to make an attempt on sb's life; ~ **contra algo** [principio etc] to be a crime against sthg.

atento, -ta *adj* **-1.** [pendiente] attentive; **estar** ~ **a** [explicación, programa, lección] to pay attention to; [ruido, sonido] to listen out for; [acontecimientos, cambios, avances] to keep up with. **-2.** [cortés] considerate, thoughtful.

atenuante *m* DER extenuating circumstance.

atenuar *vt* [gen] to diminish; [dolor] to ease; [luz] to filter.

ateo, -a ◇ *adj* atheistic. ◇ *m y f* atheist.

aterciopelado, -da *adj* velvety.

aterrador, -ra *adj* terrifying.

aterrar *vt* to terrify.

aterrizaje *m* landing.

aterrizar *vi* [avión] to land.

aterrorizar *vt* to terrify; [suj: agresor] to terrorize.

atesorar *vt* [riquezas] to amass.

atestado *m* official report.

atestar *vt* **-1.** [llenar] to pack, to cram. **-2.** DER to testify to.

atestiguar *vt* to testify to.

atiborrar *vt* to stuff full. ◆ **atiborrarse** *vpr fam fig*: ~**se (de)** to stuff one's face (with).

ático *m* penthouse.

atinar *vi* [adivinar] to guess correctly; [dar en el blanco] to hit the target; ~ **a hacer algo** to succeed in doing sthg; ~ **con** to hit upon.

atingencia *f Amer* [relación] connection.

atípico, -ca *adj* atypical.

atisbar *vt* **-1.** [divisar, prever] to make out. **-2.** [acechar] to observe, to spy on.

atisbo *m* (*gen pl*) trace, hint; [de esperanza] glimmer.

atizar *vt* **-1.** [fuego] to poke, to stir. **-2.** *fam* [puñetazo, patada] to land, to deal.

atlántico, -ca *adj* Atlantic. ◆ **Atlántico** *m*: **el (océano) Atlántico** the Atlantic (Ocean).

atlas *m inv* atlas.

atleta *m y f* athlete.

atlético, -ca *adj* athletic.

atletismo *m* athletics (*U*).

atmósfera *f lit* & *fig* atmosphere.

atolladero *m* [apuro] fix, jam; **meter en/sacar de un ~ a alguien** to put sb in/get sb out of a tight spot.

atolondrado, -da *adj* -**1.** [precipitado] hasty, disorganized. -**2.** [aturdido] bewildered.

atómico, -ca *adj* atomic; [central, armas] nuclear.

atomizador *m* atomizer, spray.

átomo *m lit* & *fig* atom.

atónito, -ta *adj* astonished, astounded.

atontado, -da *adj* -**1.** [aturdido] dazed. -**2.** [tonto] stupid.

atontar *vt* [aturdir] to daze.

atormentar *vt* to torture; *fig* to torment.

atornillar *vt* to screw.

atorón *m Amer* traffic jam.

atorrante *Amer adj* lazy.

atosigar *vt fig* to harass.

atracador, -ra *m y f* [de banco] armed robber; [en la calle] mugger.

atracar ◇ *vi* NÁUT: ~ **(en)** to dock (at). ◇ *vt* [banco] to rob; [persona] to mug. ◆ **atracarse** *vpr*: ~**se de** to eat one's fill of.

atracción *f* -**1.** [gen] attraction. -**2.** [espectáculo] act. -**3.** *fig* [centro de atención] centre of attention. -**4.** (*gen pl*) [diversión infantil] fairground attraction.

atraco *m* robbery.

atracón *m fam* feast; **darse un ~** to stuff one's face.

atractivo, -va *adj* attractive. ◆ **atractivo** *m* [de persona] attractiveness, charm; [de cosa] attraction.

atraer *vt* [gen] to attract.

atragantarse *vpr*: ~ **(con)** to choke (on).

atrancar *vt* -**1.** [cerrar] to bar. -**2.** [obturar] to block. ◆ **atrancarse** *vpr* -**1.** [atascarse] to get blocked. -**2.** *fig* [al hablar, escribir] to dry up.

atrapar *vt* [agarrar, alcanzar] to catch.

atrás *adv* -**1.** [detrás - posición] behind, at the back; [- movimiento] backwards; **quedarse ~** *fig* to fall behind. -**2.** [antes] earlier, before.

atrasado, -da *adj* -**1.** [en el tiempo] delayed; [reloj] slow; [pago] overdue, late; [número, copia] back (*antes de sust*). -**2.** [en evolución, capacidad] backward.

atrasar ◇ *vt* to put back. ◇ *vi* to be slow. ◆ **atrasarse** *vpr* -**1.** [demorarse] to

be late. -**2.** [quedarse atrás] to fall behind.

atraso *m* [de evolución] backwardness. ◆ **atrasos** *mpl fam* arrears.

atravesar *vt* -**1.** [interponer] to put across. -**2.** [cruzar] to cross. -**3.** [traspasar] to penetrate. -**4.** *fig* [vivir] to go through. ◆ **atravesarse** *vpr* [interponerse] to be in the way.

atrayente *adj* attractive.

atreverse *vpr*: ~ **(a hacer algo)** to dare (to do sthg).

atrevido, -da *adj* [osado] daring; [caradura] cheeky.

atrevimiento *m* -**1.** [osadía] daring. -**2.** [insolencia] cheek.

atribución *f* -**1.** [imputación] attribution. -**2.** [competencia] responsibility.

atribuir *vt* [imputar]: ~ **algo a** to attribute sthg to. ◆ **atribuirse** *vpr* [méritos] to claim for o.s.; [poderes] to assume.

atributo *m* attribute.

atril *m* [para libros] lectern; MÚS music stand.

atrocidad *f* [crueldad] atrocity.

atropellado, -da *adj* hasty.

atropellar *vt* -**1.** [suj: vehículo] to run over. -**2.** *fig* [suj: persona] to trample on. ◆ **atropellarse** *vpr* [al hablar] to trip over one's words.

atropello *m* -**1.** [por vehículo] running over. -**2.** *fig* [moral] abuse.

atroz *adj* atrocious; [dolor] awful.

ATS (*abrev de* **ayudante técnico sanitario**) *m y f* qualified nurse.

atte. *abrev de* **atentamente**.

atuendo *m* attire.

atún *m* tuna.

aturdido, -da *adj* dazed.

aturdir *vt* [gen] to stun; [suj: alcohol] to fuddle; [suj: ruido, luz] to bewilder.

audacia *f* [intrepidez] daring.

audaz *adj* [intrépido] daring.

audición *f* -**1.** [gen] hearing. -**2.** MÚS & TEATR audition.

audiencia *f* -**1.** [público, recepción] audience. -**2.** [DER - juicio] hearing; [- tribunal, edificio] court.

audífono *m* hearing aid.

audiovisual *adj* audiovisual.

auditivo, -va *adj* ear (*antes de sust*).

auditor, -ra *m y f* FIN auditor.

auditorio *m* -**1.** [público] audience. -**2.** [lugar] auditorium.

auge *m* [gen & ECON] boom.

augurar *vt* [suj: persona] to predict; [suj: suceso] to augur.

augurio *m* omen, sign.

aula *f* (*el*) [de escuela] classroom; [de universidad] lecture room.

aullar *vi* to howl.

aullido *m* howl.

aumentar ◇ *vt* -1. [gen] to increase; [peso] to put on. -2. [en óptica] to magnify. -3. [sonido] to amplify. ◇ *vi* to increase; [precios] to rise.

aumento *m* -1. [incremento] increase; [de sueldo, precios] rise; **ir en** ~ to be on the increase. -2. [en óptica] magnification.

aun ◇ *adv* even. ◇ *conj*: ~ **estando cansado, lo hizo** even though he was tired, he did it; **ni** ~ **puesta de puntillas logra ver** she can't see, even on tiptoe; ~ **cuando** even though.

aún *adv* [todavía] still; (*en negativas*) yet, still; **no ha llegado** ~ he hasn't arrived yet, he still hasn't arrived.

aunar *vt* to join, to pool. ◆ **aunarse** *vpr* [aliarse] to unite.

aunque *conj* -1. [a pesar de que] even though, although; [incluso si] even if. -2. [pero] although.

aúpa *interj*: ¡~! [¡levántate!] get up!; ¡~ **el Atleti!** up the Athletic!

aupar *vt* to help up; *fig* [animar] to cheer on. ◆ **auparse** *vpr* to climb up.

aureola *f* -1. ASTRON & RELIG halo. -2. *fig* [fama] aura.

auricular *m* [de teléfono] receiver. ◆ **auriculares** *mpl* [cascos] headphones.

aurora *f* first light of dawn.

auscultar *vt* to sound with a stethoscope.

ausencia *f* absence; **brillar por su** ~ to be conspicuous by one's/its absence.

ausentarse *vpr* to go away.

ausente ◇ *adj* -1. [no presente] absent; **estará** ~ **todo el día** he'll be away all day. -2. [distraído] absent-minded. ◇ *m y f* -1. [no presente]: **criticó a los** ~**s** he criticized the people who weren't there. -2. DER missing person.

auspicio *m* [protección] protection; **bajo los** ~**s de** under the auspices of.

austeridad *f* austerity.

austero, -ra *adj* [gen] austere.

austral ◇ *adj* southern. ◇ *m* [moneda] austral.

Australia Australia.

australiano, -na *adj, m y f* Australian.

Austria Austria.

austríaco, -ca *adj, m y f* Austrian.

autarquía *f* -1. POLÍT autarchy. -2. ECON autarky.

auténtico, -ca *adj* [gen] genuine; [piel, joyas] genuine, real; **un** ~ **imbécil** a real idiot.

auto *m* -1. *fam* [coche] car. -2. DER judicial decree.

autoadhesivo, -va *adj* self-adhesive.

autobiografía *f* autobiography.

autobús *m* bus.

autocar *m* coach.

autocontrol *m* self-control.

autóctono, -na *adj* indigenous.

autodefensa *f* self-defence.

autodeterminación *f* self-determination.

autodidacta *adj* self-taught.

autoescuela *f* driving school.

autoestop, autostop *m* hitch-hiking; **hacer** ~ to hitch-hike.

autoestopista, autostopista *m y f* hitch-hiker.

autógrafo *m* autograph.

autómata *m* *lit & fig* automaton.

automático, -ca *adj* automatic. ◆ **automático** *m* [botón] press-stud.

automatización *f* automation.

automóvil *m* car *Br*, automobile *Am*.

automovilismo *m* motoring; DEP motor racing.

automovilista *m y f* motorist, driver.

automovilístico, -ca *adj* motor (*antes de sust*); DEP motor-racing (*antes de sust*).

autonomía *f* [POLÍT - facultad] autonomy; [- territorio] autonomous region.

autonómico, -ca *adj* autonomous.

autónomo, -ma ◇ *adj* -1. POLÍT autonomous. -2. [trabajador] self-employed; [traductor, periodista] freelance. ◇ *m y f* self-employed person; [traductor, periodista] freelance.

autopista *f* motorway *Br*, freeway *Am*.

autopsia *f* autopsy, post-mortem.

autor, -ra *m y f* -1. LITER author. -2. [de crimen] perpetrator.

autoridad *f* -1. [gen] authority. -2. [ley]: **la** ~ the authorities (*pl*).

autoritario, -ria *adj, m y f* authoritarian.

autorización *f* authorization.

autorizado, -da *adj* -1. [permitido] authorized. -2. [digno de crédito] authoritative.

autorizar *vt* -1. [dar permiso] to allow; [en situaciones oficiales] to authorize. -2. [capacitar] to allow, to entitle.

autorretrato *m* self-portrait.

autoservicio *m* **-1.** [tienda] self-service shop. **-2.** [restaurante] self-service restaurant.

autostop = **autoestop.**

autostopista = **autoestopista.**

autosuficiencia *f* self-sufficiency.

autovía *f* dual carriageway *Br*, state highway *Am*.

auxiliar ◇ *adj* [gen & GRAM] auxiliary. ◇ *m y f* assistant; ~ **administrativo** office clerk. ◇ *vt* to assist, to help.

auxilio *m* assistance, help; **primeros ~s** first aid (*U*).

av., avda. (*abrev de* **avenida**) Ave.

aval *m* **-1.** [persona] guarantor. **-2.** [documento] guarantee, reference.

avalancha *f lit & fig* avalanche.

avalar *vt* to endorse, to guarantee.

avance *m* **-1.** [gen] advance. **-2.** FIN [anticipo] advance payment. **-3.** [RADIO & TV - meteorológico etc] summary; [- de futura programación] preview; ~ **informativo** news (*U*) in brief.

avanzar ◇ *vi* to advance. ◇ *vt* **-1.** [adelantar] to move forward. **-2.** [anticipar] to tell in advance.

avaricia *f* greed, avarice.

avaricioso, -sa *adj* avaricious.

avaro, -ra *adj* miserly, mean.

avasallar *vt* [arrollar] to overwhelm.

avatar *m* (*gen pl*) vagary.

avda. = **av.**

ave *f* (*el*) [gen] bird; ~ **rapaz** O **de rapiña** bird of prey.

AVE (*abrev de* **de alta velocidad española**) *m Spanish high-speed train*.

avecinarse *vpr* to be on the way.

avellana *f* hazelnut.

avemaría *f* (*el*) [oración] Hail Mary.

avena *f* [grano] oats (*pl*).

avenencia *f* [acuerdo] compromise.

avenida *f* avenue.

avenido, -da *adj*: **bien/mal ~s** on good/bad terms.

avenirse *vpr* [ponerse de acuerdo] to come to an agreement; ~ **a algo/a hacer algo** to agree on sthg/to do sthg.

aventajado, -da *adj* [adelantado] outstanding.

aventajar *vt* [rebasar] to overtake; [estar por delante de] to be ahead of; ~ **a alguien en algo** to surpass sb in sthg.

aventura *f* **-1.** [gen] adventure. **-2.** [relación amorosa] affair.

aventurado, -da *adj* risky.

aventurero, -ra ◇ *adj* adventurous. ◇ *m y f* adventurer (*f* adventuress).

avergonzar *vt* **-1.** [deshonrar] to shame. **-2.** [abochornar] to embarrass. ◆ **avergonzarse** *vpr*: ~**se (de)** [por remordimiento] to be ashamed (of); [por timidez] to be embarrassed (about).

avería *f* [de máquina] fault; AUTOM breakdown.

averiado, -da *adj* [máquina] out of order; [coche] broken down.

averiar *vt* to damage. ◆ **averiarse** *vpr* [máquina] to be out of order; AUTOM to break down.

averiguación *f* investigation.

averiguar *vt* to find out.

aversión *f* aversion.

avestruz *m* ostrich.

aviación *f* **-1.** [navegación] aviation. **-2.** [ejército] airforce.

aviador, -ra *m y f* aviator.

aviar *vt* [comida] to prepare.

avicultura *f* poultry farming.

avidez *f* eagerness.

ávido, -da *adj*: ~ **de** eager for.

avinagrado, -da *adj lit & fig* sour.

avío *m* **-1.** [preparativo] preparation. **-2.** [víveres] provisions (*pl*). ◆ **avíos** *mpl fam* [equipo] things, kit (*U*).

avión *m* plane; **en** ~ by plane; **por** ~ [en un sobre] airmail; ~ **a reacción** jet.

avioneta *f* light aircraft.

avisar *vt* **-1.** [informar]: ~ **a alguien** to let sb know, to tell sb. **-2.** [advertir]: ~ **(de)** to warn (of). **-3.** [llamar] to call, to send for.

aviso *m* **-1.** [advertencia, amenaza] warning. **-2.** [notificación] notice; [en teatros, aeropuertos] call; **hasta nuevo** ~ until further notice; **sin previo** ~ without notice.

avispa *f* wasp.

avispado, -da *adj fam* sharp, quick-witted.

avispero *m* [nido] wasp's nest.

avituallar *vt* to provide with food.

avivar *vt* **-1.** [sentimiento] to rekindle. **-2.** [color] to brighten. **-3.** [fuego] to stoke up.

axila *f* armpit.

axioma *m* axiom.

ay (*pl* **ayes**) *interj*: ¡~! [dolor físico] ouch!; [sorpresa, pena] oh!; ¡~ **de tí si te cojo!** Heaven help you if I catch you!

aya → **ayo.**

ayer ◇ *adv* yesterday; *fig* in the past; ~ **(por la) noche** last night; ~ **por la mañana** yesterday morning. ◇ *m fig* yesteryear.

ayo, aya *m y f* [tutor] tutor (*f* governess).

ayuda *f* help, assistance; ECON & POLÍT aid; ~ **en carretera** breakdown service.

ayudante *adj, m y f* assistant.

ayudar *vt* to help; ~ **a alguien a hacer algo** to help sb (to) do sthg; **¿en qué puedo** ~**le?** how can I help you?
◆ **ayudarse** *vpr:* ~**se de** to make use of.

ayunar *vi* to fast.

ayunas *fpl:* **en** ~ [sin comer] without having eaten; *fig* [sin enterarse] in the dark.

ayuno *m* fast; **hacer** ~ to fast.

ayuntamiento *m* **-1.** [corporación] ≃ town council. **-2.** [edificio] town hall.

azabache *m* jet; **negro como el** ~ jet-black.

azada *f* hoe.

azafata *f:* ~ **(de vuelo)** air hostess *Br*, air stewardess.

azafate *m Amer* [bandeja] tray.

azafrán *m* saffron.

azahar *m* [del naranjo] orange blossom; [del limonero] lemon blossom.

azalea *f* azalea.

azar *m* chance, fate; **al** ~ at random; **por (puro)** ~ by (pure) chance.

azorar *vt* to embarrass. ◆ **azorarse** *vpr* to be embarrassed.

azotar *vt* [suj: persona] to beat; [en el trasero] to smack; [con látigo] to whip.

azote *m* **-1.** [golpe] blow; [en el trasero] smack; [latigazo] lash. **-2.** *fig* [calamidad] scourge.

azotea *f* [de edificio] terraced roof.

azteca *adj, m y f* Aztec.

azúcar *m o f* sugar; ~ **blanquilla/ moreno** refined/brown sugar.

azucarado, -da *adj* sweet, sugary.

azucarero, -ra *adj* sugar (*antes de sust*). ◆ **azucarero** *m* sugar bowl.

azucena *f* white lily.

azufre *m* sulphur.

azul *adj & m* blue.

azulejo *m* (glazed) tile.

azuzar *vt* [animal] to set on.

B

b, B *f* [letra] b, B.

baba *f* [saliva - de niño] dribble; [- de adulto] saliva; [- de animal] foam.

babear *vi* [niño] to dribble; [adulto, animal] to slobber; *fig* to drool.

babero *m* bib.

babi *m* child's overall.

bable *m* Asturian dialect.

babor *m* port; **a** ~ to port.

baboso, -sa *adj Amer fam* [tonto] daft, stupid. ◆ **babosa** *f* ZOOL slug.

babucha *f* slipper.

baca *f* roof o luggage rack.

bacalao *m* [fresco] cod; [salado] dried salted cod; **partir** o **cortar el** ~ *fam fig* to be the boss.

bacanal *f* orgy.

bache *m* **-1.** [en carretera] pothole. **-2.** *fig* [dificultades] bad patch. **-3.** [en un vuelo] air pocket.

bachiller *m y f* person who has passed the "*bachillerato*".

bachillerato *m* (former) Spanish course of secondary studies for academically orientated 14-16-year-olds.

bacinica *f Amer* chamber pot.

bacon ['beikon] *m inv* bacon.

bacteria *f* germ; ~**s** bacteria.

badén *m* [de carretera] ditch.

bádminton *m inv* badminton.

bafle (*pl* **bafles**), **baffle** (*pl* **baffles**) *m* loudspeaker.

bagaje *m fig* background; ~ **cultural** cultural baggage.

bagatela *f* trifle.

Bahamas *fpl:* **las** ~ the Bahamas.

bahía *f* bay.

bailaor, -ra *m y f* flamenco dancer.

bailar ◇ *vt* to dance. ◇ *vi* [danzar] to dance.

bailarín, -ina *m y f* dancer; [de ballet] ballet dancer.

baile *m* **-1.** [gen] dance; ~ **clásico** ballet. **-2.** [fiesta] ball.

baja → **bajo**.

bajada *f* **-1.** [descenso] descent; ~ **de bandera** [de taxi] minimum fare. **-2.**

[pendiente] **(downward) slope.** -3. [disminución] **decrease, drop.**

bajamar f low tide.

bajar ◇ vt -1. [poner abajo - libro, cuadro etc] to take/bring down; [- telón, ventanilla, mano] to lower. -2. [descender - montaña, escaleras] to go/come down. -3. [precios, inflación, hinchazón] to reduce; [música, volumen, radio] to turn down; [fiebre] to bring down. -4. [ojos, cabeza, voz] to lower. ◇ vi -1. [descender] to go/come down; ~ **por algo** to go/come down sthg; ~ **corriendo** to run down. -2. [disminuir] to fall, to drop; [fiebre, hinchazón] to go/come down; [Bolsa] to suffer a fall. ◆ **bajarse** vpr: ~**se (de)** [coche] to get out of (of); [moto, tren, avión] to get off; [árbol, escalera, silla] to get/come down (from).

bajeza f -1. [cualidad] baseness. -2. [acción] nasty deed.

bajial m Amer lowland.

bajo, -ja adj -1. [gen] low; [persona, estatura] short; [piso] ground floor (antes de sust); [planta] ground (antes de sust); [sonido] soft, faint. -2. [territorio, época] lower; **el** ~ **Amazonas** the lower Amazon. -3. [pobre] lower-class. -4. [vil] base. ◆ **bajo** ◇ m -1. (gen pl) [dobladillo] hem. -2. [piso] ground floor flat. -3. [MÚS - instrumento, cantante] bass; [- instrumentista] bassist. ◇ adv -1. [gen] low. -2. [hablar] quietly. ◇ prep -1. [gen] under. -2. [con temperaturas] below. ◆ **baja** f -1. [descenso] drop, fall. -2. [cese] **dar de baja a alguien** [en una empresa] to lay sb off; [en un club, sindicato] to expel sb; **darse de baja (de)** [dimitir] to resign (from); [salirse] to drop out (of). -3. [por enfermedad - permiso] sick leave (U); [- documento] sick note; **estar/darse de baja** to be on/to take sick leave. -4. MIL loss, casualty.

bajón m slump; **dar un** ~ to slump. .

bajura → pesca.

bala f -1. [proyectil] bullet. -2. [fardo] bale.

balacear vt Amer [tirotear] to shoot.

balada f ballad.

balance m -1. [COM - operación] balance; [- documento] balance sheet. -2. [resultado] outcome; **hacer** ~ **(de)** to take stock (of).

balancear vt [cuna] to rock; [columpio] to swing. ◆ **balancearse** vpr [en cuna, mecedora] to rock; [en columpio] to swing; [barco] to roll.

balanceo m -1. [gen] swinging; [de cuna, mecedora] rocking; [de barco] roll. -2. Amer AUTOM wheel balance.

balancín m -1. [mecedora] rocking chair; [en el jardín] swing hammock. -2. [columpio] seesaw.

balanza f -1. [báscula] scales (pl). -2. COM: ~ **comercial/de pagos** balance of trade/payments.

balar vi to bleat.

balaustrada f balustrade; [de escalera] banister.

balazo m [disparo] shot; [herida] bullet wound.

balbucear, balbucir vi & vt to babble.

balbuceo m babbling.

balbucir = balbucear.

Balcanes mpl: **los** ~ the Balkans.

balcón m [terraza] balcony.

balde m pail, bucket. ◆ **en balde** loc adv in vain.

baldosa f [en casa, edificio] floor tile; [en la acera] paving stone.

baldosín m tile.

balear ◇ vt Amer to shoot. ◇ adj Balearic.

Baleares fpl: **las (islas)** ~ the Balearic Islands.

baleo m Amer [disparo] shot.

balido m bleat, bleating (U).

balín m pellet.

balístico, -ca adj ballistic.

baliza f NÁUT marker buoy; AERON beacon.

ballena f [animal] whale.

ballesta f -1. HIST crossbow. -2. AUTOM (suspension) spring.

ballet [ba'le] (pl **ballets**) m ballet.

balneario m spa.

balompié m football.

balón m [pelota] ball.

baloncesto m basketball.

balonmano m handball.

balonvolea m volleyball.

balsa f -1. [embarcación] raft. -2. [estanque] pond, pool.

bálsamo m -1. FARM balsam. -2. [alivio] balm.

Báltico m: **el (mar)** ~ the Baltic (Sea).

baluarte m -1. [fortificación] bulwark. -2. fig [bastión] bastion, stronghold.

bambolear vt to shake. ◆ **bambolearse** vpr [gen] to sway; [mesa, silla] to wobble.

bambú (pl **bambúes** O **bambús**) m bamboo.

banal adj banal.

banana *f* banana.

banca *f* **-1.** [actividad] banking. **-2.** [institución]: **la** ~ **the banks** (*pl*). **-3.** [en juegos] bank.

bancario, -ria *adj* banking (*antes de sust*).

bancarrota *f* bankruptcy; **en** ~ bankrupt.

banco *m* **-1.** [asiento] bench; [de iglesia] pew. **-2.** FIN bank. **-3.** [de peces] shoal. **-4.** [de ojos, semen etc] bank. **-5.** [de carpintero, artesano etc] workbench. ◆ **banco de arena** *m* sandbank. ◆ **Banco Mundial** *m*: **el Banco Mundial the World Bank.**

banda *f* **-1.** [cuadrilla] gang; ~ **armada** terrorist organization. **-2.** MÚS band. **-3.** [faja] sash. **-4.** [cinta] ribbon. **-5.** [franja] stripe. **-6.** RADIO waveband. **-7.** [margen] side; [en billar] cushion; [en fútbol] touchline. ◆ **banda magnética** *f* magnetic strip. ◆ **banda sonora** *f* soundtrack.

bandada *f* [de aves] flock; [de peces] shoal.

bandazo *m* [del barco] lurch; **dar** ~**s** [barco, borracho] to lurch; *fig* [ir sin rumbo] to chop and change.

bandear *vt* to buffet.

bandeja *f* tray; **servir** O **dar algo a alguien en** ~ *fig* to hand sthg to sb on a plate.

bandera *f* flag; **jurar** ~ to swear allegiance (to the flag).

banderilla *f* TAUROM banderilla, *barbed dart thrust into bull's back.*

banderín *m* [bandera] pennant.

bandido, -da *m y f* **-1.** [delincuente] bandit. **-2.** [granuja] rascal.

bando *m* **-1.** [facción] side; **pasarse al otro** ~ to change sides. **-2.** [edicto - de alcalde] edict.

bandolero, -ra *m y f* bandit. ◆ **bandolera** *f* [correa] bandoleer; **en bandolera** slung across one's chest.

bandurria *f* small 12-stringed guitar.

banjo ['banjo] *m* banjo.

banquero, -ra *m y f* banker.

banqueta *f* **-1.** [asiento] stool. **-2.** *Amer* [acera] pavement *Br*, sidewalk *Am*.

banquete *m* [comida] banquet.

banquillo *m* **-1.** [asiento] low stool. **-2.** DEP bench.

bañada *f Amer* [acción de bañarse] bath.

bañadera *f Amer* [bañera] bath.

bañador *m* [for women] swimsuit; [for men] swimming trunks (*pl*).

bañar *vt* **-1.** [asear] to bath; MED to bathe. **-2.** [sumergir] to soak, to submerge. **-3.** [revestir] to coat. ◆ **bañarse** *vpr* **-1.** [en el baño] to have O take a bath. **-2.** [en playa, piscina] to go for a swim.

bañera *f* bathtub, bath.

bañista *m y f* bather.

baño *m* **-1.** [acción - en bañera] bath; [en playa, piscina] swim; **darse un** ~ [en bañera] to have O take a bath; [en playa, piscina] to go for a swim. **-2.** [bañera] bathtub, bath. **-3.** [cuarto de aseo] bathroom. **-4.** [capa] coat.

baqueta *f* MÚS drumstick.

bar *m* bar.

barahúnda *f* racket, din.

baraja *f* pack (of cards).

barajar *vt* **-1.** [cartas] to shuffle. **-2.** [considerar - nombres, posibilidades] to consider; [- datos, cifras] to marshal, to draw on.

baranda, barandilla *f* handrail.

baratija *f* trinket, knick-knack.

baratillo *m* [tienda] junkshop; [mercadillo] flea market.

barato, -ta *adj* cheap. ◆ **barato** *adv* cheap, cheaply.

barba *f* beard; ~ **incipiente** stubble; **por** ~ [cada uno] per head.

barbacoa *f* barbecue.

barbaridad *f* **-1.** [cualidad] cruelty; **¡qué** ~**!** how terrible! **-2.** [disparate] nonsense (*U*). **-3.** [montón]: **una** ~ **(de)** tons (of); **se gastó una** ~ she spent a fortune.

barbarie *f* [crueldad - cualidad] cruelty, savagery; [- acción] atrocity.

barbarismo *m* **-1.** [extranjerismo] foreign word. **-2.** [incorrección] substandard usage.

bárbaro, -ra ◇ *adj* **-1.** HIST barbarian. **-2.** [cruel] barbaric, cruel. **-3.** [bruto] uncouth, coarse. **-4.** *fam* [extraordinario] brilliant, great. ◇ *m y f* HIST barbarian. ◆ **bárbaro** *adv fam* [magníficamente]: **pasarlo** ~ to have a wild time.

barbecho *m* fallow (land); [retirada de tierras] land set aside.

barbería *f* barber's (shop).

barbero, -ra *m y f* barber.

barbilampiño, -ña *adj* beardless.

barbilla *f* chin.

barbo *m* barbel; ~ **de mar** red mullet.

barbotar *vi & vt* to mutter.

barbudo, -da *adj* bearded.

barca *f* dinghy, small boat.

barcaza *f* lighter.

barco m [gen] boat; [de gran tamaño] ship; **en ~** by boat; **~ cisterna** tanker; **~ de guerra** warship; **~ mercante** cargo ship; **~ de vapor** steamer, steamboat; **~ de vela** sailing ship.

baremo m [escala] scale.

bario m barium.

barítono m baritone.

barman (pl **barmans**) m barman.

barniz m [para madera] varnish; [para loza, cerámica] glaze.

barnizar vt [madera] to varnish; [loza, cerámica] to glaze.

barómetro m barometer.

barón, -onesa m y f baron (f baroness).

barquero, -ra m y f boatman (f boatwoman).

barquillo m CULIN cornet, cone.

barra f **-1.** [gen] bar; [de hielo] block; [para cortinas] rod; [en bicicleta] crossbar; **la ~** [de tribunal] the bar; **~ de labios** lipstick; **~ de pan** baguette, French stick. **-2.** [de bar, café] bar (counter); **~ libre** unlimited drink for a fixed price. **-3.** [signo gráfico] slash, oblique stroke.

barrabasada f fam mischief (U).

barraca f **-1.** [chabola] shack. **-2.** [caseta de feria] stall. **-3.** [en Valencia y Murcia] thatched farmhouse.

barranco m **-1.** [precipicio] precipice. **-2.** [cauce] ravine.

barraquismo m shanty towns (pl).

barrena f drill.

barrenar vt [taladrar] to drill.

barrendero, -ra m y f street sweeper.

barreno m **-1.** [instrumento] large drill. **-2.** [agujero - para explosiones] blast hole.

barreño m washing-up bowl.

barrer vt **-1.** [con escoba, reflectores] to sweep. **-2.** [suj: viento, olas] to sweep away.

barrera f **-1.** [gen] barrier; FERROC crossing gate; [de campo, casa] fence; **~s arancelarias** tariff barriers. **-2.** DEP wall.

barriada f neighbourhood, area.

barricada f barricade.

barrido m **-1.** [con escoba] sweep, sweeping (U). **-2.** TECN scan, scanning (U). **-3.** CIN pan, panning (U).

barriga f belly.

barrigón, -ona adj paunchy.

barril m barrel; **de ~** [bebida] draught.

barrio m [vecindario] area, neighborhood Am.

barriobajero, -ra despec adj low-life (antes de sust).

barrizal m mire.

barro m **-1.** [fango] mud. **-2.** [arcilla] clay. **-3.** [grano] blackhead.

barroco, -ca adj ARTE baroque. ◆ **barroco** m ARTE baroque.

barrote m bar.

bartola ◆ **a la bartola** loc adv fam: **tumbarse a la ~** to lounge around.

bártulos mpl things, bits and pieces.

barullo m fam **-1.** [ruido] din, racket; **armar ~** to raise hell. **-2.** [desorden] mess.

basar vt [fundamentar] to base. ◆ **basarse en** vpr [suj: teoría, obra etc] to be based on; [suj: persona] to base one's argument on.

basca f [náusea] nausea.

báscula f scales (pl).

bascular vi to tilt.

base f **-1.** [gen, MAT & MIL] base; [de edificio] foundations (pl), [de edificio, origen] basis; **sentar las ~s para** to lay the foundations of. **-3.** [de partido, sindicato]: **las ~s** the grass roots (pl), the rank and file. **-4.** loc: **a ~ de** by (means of); **me alimento a ~ de verduras** I live on vegetables; **a ~ de bien** extremely well. ◆ **base de datos** f INFORM database.

básico, -ca adj basic; **lo ~ de** the basics of.

basílica f basilica.

basta interj ¡~! that's enough!; ¡~ **de chistes/tonterías!** that's enough jokes/ of this nonsense!

bastante ◇ adv **-1.** [suficientemente] enough; **es lo ~ lista para ...** she's smart enough to .... **-2.** [considerablemente - antes de adj o adv] quite, pretty; [- después de verbo] quite a lot; **me gustó ~** I quite enjoyed it, I enjoyed it quite a lot. ◇ adj **-1.** [suficiente] enough; **no tengo dinero ~** I haven't enough money. **-2.** [mucho]: **éramos ~s** there were quite a few of us; **tengo ~ frío** I'm quite ○ pretty cold.

bastar vi to be enough; **basta con que se lo digas** it's enough for you to tell her; **con ocho basta** eight will be enough. ◆ **bastarse** vpr to be self-sufficient.

bastardilla → **letra**.

bastardo, -da adj **-1.** [hijo etc] bastard (antes de sust). **-2.** despec [innoble] mean, base.

bastidor m [armazón] frame. ◆ **bastidores** mpl TEATR wings; **entre ~es** fig behind the scenes.

basto, -ta *adj* coarse. ◆**bastos** *mpl* [naipes] ≃ clubs.

bastón *m* **-1.** [para andar] **walking stick**. **-2.** [de mando] **baton**. **-3.** [para esquiar] **ski stick**.

basura *f lit* & *fig* **rubbish** *Br*, **garbage** *Am*; **tirar algo a la ~** to throw sthg away.

basurero *m* **-1.** [persona] **dustman** *Br*, **garbage man** *Am*. **-2.** [vertedero] **rubbish dump**.

bata *f* **-1.** [de casa] **housecoat**; [para baño, al levantarse] **dressing gown**. **-2.** [de trabajo] **overall**; [de médico] **white coat**; [de laboratorio] **lab coat**.

batacazo *m* **bump, bang**.

batalla *f* **battle**; **de ~** [de uso diario] **everyday**.

batallar *vi* [con armas] **to fight**.

batallón *m* MIL **battalion**.

batata *f* **sweet potato**.

bate *m* DEP **bat**.

batear ◇ *vt* to hit. ◇ *vi* to bat.

batería *f* **-1.** ELECTR & MIL **battery**. **-2.** MÚS **drums** (*pl*). **-3.** [conjunto] **set**; [de preguntas] **barrage**; **~ de cocina pots** (*pl*) **and pans**.

batido, -da *adj* **-1.** [nata] **whipped**; [claras] **whisked**. **-2.** [senda, camino] **well-trodden**. ◆**batido** *m* [bebida] **milk-shake**. ◆**batida** *f* **-1.** [de caza] **beat**. **-2.** [de policía] **combing, search**.

batidora *f* [eléctrica] **mixer**.

batín *m* **short dressing gown**.

batir *vt* **-1.** [gen] **to beat**; [nata] **to whip**; [récord] **to break**. **-2.** [suj: olas, lluvia, viento] **to beat against**. **-3.** [derribar] **to knock down**. **-4.** [explorar - suj: policía etc] **to comb, to search**. ◆**batirse** *vpr* [luchar] **to fight**.

batuta *f* **baton**; **llevar la ~** *fig* **to call the tune**.

baúl *m* **-1.** [cofre] **trunk**. **-2.** *Amer* [maletero] **boot** *Br*, **trunk** *Am*.

bautismo *m* **baptism**.

bautista *m y f* RELIG **Baptist**.

bautizar *vt* **-1.** RELIG **to baptize, to christen**. **-2.** *fam fig* [aguar] **to dilute**.

bautizo *m* RELIG **baptism, christening**.

baya *f* **berry**.

bayeta *f* **-1.** [tejido] **flannel**. **-2.** [para fregar] **cloth**.

bayo, -ya *adj* **bay**.

bayoneta *f* **bayonet**.

baza *f* **-1.** [en naipes] **trick**. **-2.** *loc*: **meter ~ en algo** to butt in on sthg; **no pude meter ~ (en la conversación)** I couldn't get a word in edgeways.

bazar *m* **bazaar**.

bazo *m* ANAT **spleen**.

bazofia *f* **-1.** [comida] **pigswill** (*U*). **-2.** *fig* [libro, película etc] **rubbish** (*U*).

bazuca, bazooka *m* **bazooka**.

beatificar *vt* **to beatify**.

beato, -ta *adj* **-1.** [beatificado] **blessed**. **-2.** [piadoso] **devout**. **-3.** *fig* [santurrón] **sanctimonious**.

bebe *m Amer fam* **baby**.

bebé *m* **baby**; **~ probeta test-tube baby**.

bebedero *m* [de jaula] **water dish**.

bebedor, -ra *m y f* [borrachín] **heavy drinker**.

beber ◇ *vt* [líquido] **to drink**. ◇ *vi* [tomar líquido] **to drink**.

bebida *f* **drink**.

bebido, -da *adj* **drunk**.

beca *f* [del gobierno] **grant**; [de organización privada] **scholarship**.

becar *vt* [suj: gobierno] **to award a grant to**; [suj: organización privada] **to award a scholarship to**.

becario, -ria *m y f* [del gobierno] **grant holder**; [de organización privada] **scholarship holder**.

becerro, -rra *m y f* **calf**.

bechamel [betʃa'mel], **besamel** *f* **béchamel sauce**.

bedel *m* **janitor**.

befa *f* **jeer**; **hacer ~ de** to jeer at.

begonia *f* **begonia**.

beige [beis] *adj inv & m inv* **beige**.

béisbol *m* **baseball**.

belén *m* [de Navidad] **crib, Nativity scene**.

belfo, -fa *adj* **thick-lipped**.

belga *adj, m y f* **Belgian**.

Bélgica **Belgium**.

Belgrado **Belgrade**.

Belice **Belize**.

bélico, -ca *adj* [gen] **war** (*antes de sust*); [actitud] **bellicose, warlike**.

belicoso, -sa *adj* **bellicose**; *fig* **aggressive**.

beligerante *adj, m y f* **belligerent**.

bellaco, -ca *m y f* **villain, scoundrel**.

belleza *f* **beauty**.

bello, -lla *adj* **beautiful**.

bellota *f* **acorn**.

bemol ◇ *adj* **flat**. ◇ *m* MÚS **flat**; **tener (muchos) ~es** [ser difícil] **to be tricky**; [tener valor] **to have guts**; [ser un abuso] **to be a bit rich** ○ **much**.

bendecir *vt* **to bless**.

bendición *f* **blessing**.

bendito, -ta *adj* **-1.** [santo] holy; [alma] blessed; ¡~ **sea Dios!** *fam fig* thank goodness! **-2.** [dichoso] lucky. **-3.** [para enfatizar] damned.

benefactor, -ra *m y f* benefactor (*f* benefactress).

beneficencia *f* charity.

beneficiar *vt* to benefit. ◆ **beneficiarse** *vpr* to benefit; ~**se de algo** to do well out of sthg.

beneficiario, -ria *m y f* beneficiary; [de cheque] payee.

beneficio *m* **-1.** [bien] benefit; **a** ~ **de** [gala, concierto] in aid of; **en** ~ **de** for the good of; **en** ~ **de todos** in everyone's interest; **en** ~ **propio** for one's own good. **-2.** [ganancia] profit.

beneficioso, -sa *adj*: ~ **(para)** beneficial (to).

benéfico, -ca *adj* **-1.** [favorable] beneficial. **-2.** [rifa, función] charity (*antes de sust*); [organización] charitable.

Benelux (*abrev de* **België-Nederland-Luxembourg**) *m*: **el** ~ Benelux.

beneplácito *m* consent.

benevolencia *f* benevolence.

benevolente, benévolo, -la *adj* benevolent.

bengala *f* **-1.** [para pedir ayuda, iluminar etc] flare. **-2.** [para fiestas etc] sparkler.

benigno, -na *adj* **-1.** [gen] benign. **-2.** [clima, temperatura] mild.

benjamín, -ina *m y f* youngest child.

berberecho *m* cockle.

berenjena *f* aubergine *Br*, eggplant *Am*.

Berlín Berlin.

bermejo, -ja *adj* reddish.

bermellón *adj inv & m* vermilion.

bermudas *fpl* Bermuda shorts.

Berna Berne.

berrear *vi* **-1.** [animal] to bellow. **-2.** [persona] to howl.

berrido *m* **-1.** [del becerro] bellow, bellowing (*U*). **-2.** [de persona] howl, howling (*U*).

berrinche *m fam* tantrum; **coger** ○ **agarrarse un** ~ to throw a tantrum.

berro *m* watercress.

berza *f* cabbage.

besamel = bechamel.

besar *vt* to kiss. ◆ **besarse** *vpr* to kiss.

beso *m* kiss.

bestia ◇ *adj* **-1.** [ignorante] thick, stupid. **-2.** [torpe] clumsy. **-3.** [maleducado] rude. ◇ *m y f* [ignorante, torpe] brute. ◇ *f* [animal] beast; ~ **de carga** beast of burden.

bestial *adj* **-1.** [brutal] animal, brutal; [apetito] tremendous. **-2.** *fam* [formidable] terrific.

bestialidad *f* **-1.** [brutalidad] brutality. **-2.** *fam* [tontería] rubbish (*U*), nonsense (*U*). **-3.** *fam* [montón]: **una** ~ **de** tons (*pl*) ○ stacks (*pl*) of.

best-seller [bes'seler] (*pl* **best-sellers**) *m* best-seller.

besucón, -ona *fam adj* kissy.

besugo *m* **-1.** [animal] sea bream. **-2.** *fam* [persona] idiot.

besuquear *fam vt* to smother with kisses. ◆ **besuquearse** *vpr fam* to smooch.

bético, -ca *adj* [andaluz] Andalusian.

betún *m* **-1.** [para calzado] shoe polish. **-2.** QUÍM bitumen.

bianual *adj* **-1.** [dos veces al año] twice-yearly. **-2.** [cada dos años] biennial.

biberón *m* (baby's) bottle; **dar el** ~ **a** to bottle-feed.

Biblia *f* Bible.

bibliografía *f* bibliography.

biblioteca *f* **-1.** [gen] library. **-2.** [mueble] bookcase.

bibliotecario, -ria *m y f* librarian.

bicarbonato *m* FARM bicarbonate of soda.

bicentenario *m* bicentenary.

bíceps *m inv* biceps.

bicho *m* **-1.** [animal] beast, animal; [insecto] bug. **-2.** [pillo] little terror.

bici *f fam* bike.

bicicleta *f* bicycle.

bicolor *adj* two-coloured.

bidé *m* bidet.

bidimensional *adj* two-dimensional.

bidón *m* drum (*for oil etc*); [lata] can, canister; [de plástico] (large) bottle.

biela *f* connecting rod.

bien ◇ *adv* **-1.** [como es debido, adecuado] well; **has hecho** ~ you did the right thing; **habla inglés** ~ she speaks English well; **cierra** ~ **la puerta** shut the door properly; **hiciste** ~ **en decírmelo** you were right to tell me. **-2.** [expresa opinión favorable]: **estar** ~ [de aspecto] to be nice; [de salud] to be ○ feel well; [de calidad] to be good; [de comodidad] to be comfortable; **está** ~ **que te vayas, pero antes despídete** it's all right for you to go, but say goodbye first; **oler** ~ to smell nice; **pasarlo** ~ to have a good time; **sentar** ~ **a alguien** [ropa] to suit sb; [comida] to agree with sb; [comentario] to please sb. **-3.** [muy, bastante] very; **hoy me he**

levantado ~ **temprano** I got up nice and early today; **quiero un vaso de agua** ~ **fría** I'd like a nice cold glass of water. **-4.** [vale, de acuerdo] all right, OK; **¿nos vamos?** — ~ shall we go? — all right ○ OK. **-5.** [de buena gana, fácilmente] quite happily; **ella** ~ **que lo haría, pero no la dejan** she'd be happy to do it, but they won't let her. **-6.** loc: **¡está ~!** [bueno, vale] all right then!; [es suficiente] that's enough; **¡ya está ~!** that's enough!; **¡muy ~!** very good!, excellent! ◇ adj inv [adinerado] well-to-do. ◇ conj: ~ ... ~ either ... or; **dáselo** ~ **a mi hermano,** ~ **a mi padre** either give it to my brother or my father. ◇ m good; **el** ~ **y el mal** good and evil; **por el** ~ **de** for the sake of; **lo hice por tu** ~ I did it for your own good. ◆ **bienes** mpl **-1.** [patrimonio] property (U); ~**es inmuebles** ○ **raíces** real estate (U); ~**es gananciales** shared possessions; ~**es muebles** personal property (U). **-2.** [productos] goods; ~**es de consumo** consumer goods. ◆ **más bien** loc adv rather; **no estoy contento, más** ~ **estupefacto** I'm not so much happy as stunned. ◆ **no bien** loc adv no sooner, as soon as; **no** ~ **me había marchado cuando empezaron a** ... no sooner had I gone than they started .... ◆ **si bien** loc conj although, even though.

bienal f biennial exhibition.

bienaventurado, -da m y f RELIG blessed person.

bienestar m wellbeing.

bienhechor, -ra m y f benefactor (f benefactress).

bienio m [periodo] two years (pl).

bienvenido, -da ◇ adj welcome. ◇ interj: ¡~! welcome! ◆ **bienvenida** f welcome; **dar la bienvenida a alguien** to welcome sb.

bies m inv bias binding; **al** ~ [costura] on the bias; [sombrero etc] at an angle.

bife m Amer steak.

bífido, -da adj forked.

biftec = **bistec**.

bifurcación f fork; TECN bifurcation.

bifurcarse vpr to fork.

bigamia f bigamy.

bígamo, -ma ◇ adj bigamous. ◇ m y f bigamist.

bigote m moustache.

bigotudo, -da adj with a big moustache.

bikini = **biquini**.

bilateral adj bilateral.

biliar adj bile (antes de sust).

bilingüe adj bilingual.

bilis f inv lit & fig bile.

billar m **-1.** [juego] billiards (U). **-2.** [sala] billiard hall.

billete m **-1.** [dinero] note Br, bill Am. **-2.** [de rifa, transporte etc] ticket; ~ **de ida y vuelta** return (ticket) Br, round-trip (ticket) Am; ~ **sencillo** single (ticket) Br, one-way (ticket) Am. **-3.** [de lotería] lottery ticket.

billetera f, **billetero** m wallet.

billón núm billion Br, trillion Am; ver también **seis**.

bingo m **-1.** [juego] bingo. **-2.** [sala] bingo hall. **-3.** [premio] (full) house.

binóculo m pince-nez.

biodegradable adj biodegradable.

biografía f biography.

biográfico, -ca adj biographical.

biógrafo, -fa m y f [persona] biographer.

biología f biology.

biológico, -ca adj biological.

biólogo, -ga m y f biologist.

biombo m (folding) screen.

biopsia f biopsy.

bioquímico, -ca ◇ adj biochemical. ◇ m y f [persona] biochemist. ◆ **bioquímica** f [ciencia] biochemistry.

biorritmo m biorhythm.

bipartidismo m two-party system.

bipartito, -ta adj bipartite.

biplaza m two-seater.

biquini, bikini m [bañador] bikini.

birlar vt fam to pinch, to nick.

Birmania Burma.

birra f mfam beer.

birrete m **-1.** [de clérigo] biretta. **-2.** [de catedrático] mortarboard.

birria f fam [fealdad - persona] sight, fright; [- cosa] monstrosity.

bis (pl **bises**) ◇ adj inv: **viven en el 150** ~ they live at 150a. ◇ m encore.

bisabuelo, -la m y f great-grandfather (f great-grandmother); ~**s** great-grandparents.

bisagra f hinge.

bisección f bisection.

bisectriz f bisector.

biselar vt to bevel.

bisexual adj, m y f bisexual.

bisiesto → **año**.

bisnieto, -ta m y f great-grandchild, great-grandson (f granddaughter).

bisonte *m* bison.

bisoño, -ña *m y f* novice.

bistec, biftec *m* steak.

bisturí (*pl* **bisturíes**) *m* scalpel.

bisutería *f* imitation jewellery.

bit [bit] (*pl* **bits**) *m* INFORM bit.

bíter, bitter *m* bitters (*U*).

bizco, -ca *adj* cross-eyed.

bizcocho *m* [de repostería] sponge.

bizquear *vi* to squint.

blanco, -ca ◇ *adj* white. ◇ *m y f* [persona] white (person). ◆ **blanco** *m* **-1.** [color] white. **-2.** [diana] target; **dar en el ~** DEP & MIL to hit the target; *fig* to hit the nail on the head. **-3.** *fig* [objetivo] target; [de miradas] object. **-4.** [espacio vacío] blank (space). ◆ **blanca** *f* MÚS minim; **estar** ○ **quedarse sin blanca** *fig* to be flat broke. ◆ **blanco del ojo** *m* white of the eye. ◆ **en blanco** *loc adv* **-1.** [gen] blank; **se quedó con la mente en ~** his mind went blank. **-2.** [sin dormir]: **una noche en ~** a sleepless night.

blancura *f* whiteness.

blandengue *adj lit & fig* weak.

blandir *vt* to brandish.

blando, -da *adj* **-1.** [gen] soft; [carne] tender. **-2.** *fig* [persona - débil] weak; [- indulgente] lenient, soft.

blandura *f* **-1.** [gen] softness; [de carne] tenderness. **-2.** *fig* [debilidad] weakness; [indulgencia] leniency.

blanquear *vt* **-1.** [ropa] to whiten; [con lejía] to bleach. **-2.** [con cal] to whitewash. **-3.** *fig* [dinero] to launder.

blanquecino, -na *adj* off-white.

blanqueo *m* **-1.** [de ropa] whitening; [con lejía] bleaching. **-2.** [encalado] whitewashing. **-3.** *fig* [de dinero] laundering.

blanquillo *m Amer* egg.

blasfemar *vi* RELIG: **~ (contra)** to blaspheme (against).

blasfemia *f* RELIG blasphemy.

blasfemo, -ma *adj* blasphemous.

bledo *m*: **me importa un ~ (lo que diga)** *fam* I don't give a damn (about what he says).

blindado, -da *adj* armour-plated; [coche] armoured.

bloc [blok] (*pl* **blocs**) *m* pad; **~ de dibujo** sketchpad.

bloque *m* **-1.** [gen & INFORM] block. **-2.** POLÍT bloc. **-3.** MEC cylinder block.

bloquear *vt* **-1.** [gen & DEP] to block. **-2.** [aislar - suj: ejército, barcos] to blockade; [- suj: nieve, inundación] to cut off. **-3.** FIN to freeze.

bloqueo *m* **-1.** [gen & DEP] blocking; **~ mental** mental block. **-2.** ECON & MIL blockade. **-3.** FIN freeze, freezing (*U*).

blues [blus] *m inv* MÚS blues.

blusa *f* blouse.

blusón *m* smock.

bluyín *m*, **bluyínes** *mpl Amer* jeans (*pl*).

boa *f* ZOOL boa.

bobada *f fam*: **decir ~s** to talk nonsense.

bobina *f* **-1.** [gen] reel; [en máquina de coser] bobbin. **-2.** ELECTR coil.

bobo, -ba ◇ *adj* **-1.** [tonto] stupid, daft. **-2.** [ingenuo] naïve. ◇ *m y f* **-1.** [tonto] idiot. **-2.** [ingenuo] simpleton.

boca *f* **-1.** [gen] mouth; **~ arriba/abajo** face up/down; **abrir ○ hacer ~** to whet one's appetite; **se me hace la ~ agua** it makes my mouth water. **-2.** [entrada] opening; [- de cañón] muzzle; **~ de metro** ○ **underground entrance** *Br*, **subway entrance** *Am*. ◆ **boca a boca** *m* mouth-to-mouth resuscitation.

bocacalle *f* [entrada] entrance (*to a street*); [calle] side street; **gire en la tercera ~** take the third turning.

bocadillo *m* CULIN sandwich.

bocado *m* **-1.** [comida] mouthful. **-2.** [mordisco] bite.

bocajarro ◆ **a bocajarro** *loc adv* point-blank; **se lo dije a ~** I told him to his face.

bocanada *f* [de líquido] mouthful; [de humo] puff; [de viento] gust.

bocata *m fam* sarnie.

bocazas *m y f inv fam despec* big mouth, blabbermouth.

boceto *m* sketch, rough outline.

bocha *f* [bolo] bowl. ◆ **bochas** *fpl* [juego] bowls (*U*).

bochorno *m* **-1.** [calor] stifling ○ muggy heat. **-2.** [vergüenza] embarrassment.

bochornoso, -sa *adj* **-1.** [tiempo] muggy. **-2.** [vergonzoso] embarrassing.

bocina *f* **-1.** AUTOM & MÚS horn. **-2.** [megáfono] megaphone, loudhailer.

boda *f* wedding.

bodega *f* **-1.** [cava] wine cellar. **-2.** [tienda] wine shop; [bar] bar. **-3.** [en buque, avión] hold.

bodegón *m* ARTE still life.

bodrio *m fam despec* [gen] rubbish (*U*); [comida] pigswill (*U*); **¡qué ~!** what a load of rubbish!

body ['boði] (*pl* **bodies**) *m* body (*garment*).

BOE (*abrev de* **Boletín Oficial del Estado**) *m official Spanish gazette.*

bofetada *f* slap (in the face).

bofetón *m* hard slap (in the face).

bofia *f fam:* **la** ~ the cops (*pl*).

boga *f:* **estar en** ~ to be in vogue.

bogavante *m* lobster.

Bogotá Bogotá.

bohemio, -mia *adj* **-1.** [vida etc] bohemian. **-2.** [de Bohemia] Bohemian.

boicot (*pl* **boicots**), **boycot** (*pl* **boycots**) *m* boycott.

boicotear, boycotear *vt* to boycott.

boina *f* beret.

boîte [bwat] (*pl* **boîtes**) *f* nightclub.

boj (*pl* **bojes**) *m* [árbol] box.

bol (*pl* **boles**) *m* bowl.

bola *f* **-1.** [gen] ball; [canica] marble; ~**s de naftalina** mothballs. **-2.** *fam* [mentira] fib.

bolada *f Amer fam* opportunity.

bolea *f* DEP volley.

bolear *vt Amer* to shine, to polish.

bolera *f* bowling alley.

boletería *f Amer* box office.

boletero, -ra *m y f Amer* box office attendant.

boletín *m* journal, periodical; ~ **de noticias** O **informativo** news bulletin; ~ **meteorológico** weather forecast; ~ **de prensa** press release.

boleto *m* **-1.** [de lotería, rifa] ticket; [de quinielas] coupon. **-2.** *Amer* [billete] ticket.

boli *m fam* Biro®.

boliche *m* **-1.** [en la petanca] jack. **-2.** [bolos] ten-pin bowling. **-3.** [bolera] bowling alley. **-4.** *Amer* [tienda] small grocery store.

bólido *m* racing car.

bolígrafo *m* ballpoint pen, Biro®.

bolívar *m* bolivar.

Bolivia Bolivia.

boliviano, -na *adj, m y f* Bolivian.

bollo *m* **-1.** [para comer - de pan] (bread) roll; [- dulce] bun. **-2.** [abolladura] dent; [abultamiento] bump.

bolo *m* **-1.** DEP [pieza] skittle. **-2.** [actuación] show. **-3.** *Amer* [borracho] drunk. ◆ **bolos** *mpl* [deporte] skittles.

bolsa *f* **-1.** [gen] bag; ~ **de aire** air pocket; ~ **de basura** bin liner; ~ **de deportes** holdall, sports bag; ~ **de plástico** [en tiendas] carrier O plastic bag; ~ **de viaje** travel bag. **-2.** FIN: ~ **(de valores)** stock exchange, stock market; **la** ~ **ha subido/bajado** share prices have gone up/down; **jugar a la** ~ to speculate on the stock market. **-3.** MIN pocket. **-4.** ANAT sac. **-5.** *Amer* [saco de dormir] sleeping bag.

bolsillo *m* pocket; **de** ~ pocket (*antes de sust*); **lo pagué de mi** ~ I paid for it out of my own pocket.

bolso *m* bag; [de mujer] handbag.

boludo, -da *m y f Amer mfam* prat *Br*, jerk *Am*.

bomba ◇ *f* **-1.** [explosivo] bomb; ~ **atómica** atom O nuclear bomb; ~ **de mano** (hand) grenade. **-2.** [máquina] pump. **-3.** *fig* [acontecimiento] bombshell. **-4.** *Amer* [gasolinera] petrol station *Br*, gas station *Am*. **-5.** *loc:* **pasarlo** ~ *fam* to have a great time. ◇ *adj inv fam* astounding.

bombachas *fpl Amer* knickers.

bombachos *mpl Amer* baggy trousers.

bombardear *vt lit & fig* to bombard.

bombardeo *m* bombardment.

bombardero *m* [avión] bomber.

bombazo *m fig* [noticia] bombshell.

bombear *vt* [gen & DEP] to pump.

bombero, -ra *m y f* **-1.** [de incendios] fireman (*f* firewoman). **-2.** *Amer* [de gasolinera] petrol-pump *Br* O gas-pump *Am* attendant.

bombilla *f* light bulb.

bombillo *m Amer* light bulb.

bombín *m* bowler (hat).

bombo *m* **-1.** MÚS bass drum. **-2.** *fam fig* [elogio] hype; **a** ~ **y platillo** with a lot of hype. **-3.** MEC drum.

bombón *m* [golosina] chocolate.

bombona *f* cylinder; ~ **de butano** (butane) gas cylinder.

bonachón, -ona *fam adj* kindly.

bonanza *f* **-1.** [de tiempo] fair weather; [de mar] calm at sea. **-2.** *fig* [prosperidad] prosperity.

bondad *f* [cualidad] goodness; [inclinación] kindness; **tener la** ~ **de hacer algo** to be kind enough to do sthg.

bondadoso, -sa *adj* kind, good-natured.

boniato *m* sweet potato.

bonificar *vt* **-1.** [descontar] to give a discount of. **-2.** [mejorar] to improve.

bonito, -ta *adj* pretty; [bueno] nice. ◆ **bonito** *m* bonito (tuna).

bono *m* **-1.** [vale] voucher. **-2.** COM bond.

bonobús *m* multiple-journey ticket.

bonoloto *m Spanish state-run lottery.*

boñiga *f* cowpat.

boquerón *m* (fresh) anchovy.

boquete m hole.

boquiabierto, -ta adj open-mouthed; fig astounded, speechless.

boquilla f -1. [para fumar] cigarette holder. -2. [de pipa, instrumento musical] mouthpiece. -3. [de tubo, aparato] nozzle.

borbotear, borbotar vi to bubble.

borbotón m: **salir a borbotones** to gush out.

borda f NÁUT gunwale. ◆ **fuera borda** m [barco] outboard motorboat; [motor] outboard motor.

bordado, -da adj embroidered. ◆ **bordado** m embroidery.

bordar vt [coser] to embroider.

borde ◇ adj mfam [antipático] stroppy, miserable. ◇ m [gen] edge; [de carretera] side; [del mar] shore, seaside; [de río] bank; [de vaso, botella] rim; **al ~ de** fig on the verge ○ brink of.

bordear vt [estar alrededor de] to border; [moverse alrededor de] to skirt (round).

bordillo m kerb.

bordo m NÁUT board, side. ◆ **a bordo** loc adv on board.

borla f tassel; [pompón] pompom.

borrachera f -1. [embriaguez] drunkenness (U). -2. fig [emoción] intoxication.

borracho, -cha ◇ adj [ebrio] drunk. ◇ m y f [persona] drunk. ◆ **borracho** m [bizcocho] ≈ rum baba.

borrador m -1. [escrito] rough draft. -2. [goma de borrar] rubber Br, eraser Am.

borrar vt -1. [hacer desaparecer - con goma] to rub out Br, to erase Am; [- en ordenador] to delete; [- en casete] to erase. -2. [tachar] to cross out; fig [de lista etc] to take off. -3. fig [olvidar] to erase.

borrasca f thunderstorm.

borrego, -ga m y f [animal] lamb.

borrón m blot; fig blemish; **hacer ~ y cuenta nueva** to wipe the slate clean.

borroso, -sa adj [foto, visión] blurred; [escritura, texto] smudgy.

Bosnia Bosnia.

Bosnia Herzegovina Bosnia Herzegovina.

bosnio, -nia adj, m y f Bosnian.

bosque m [pequeño] wood; [grande] forest.

bosquejar vt [esbozar] to sketch (out).

bosquejo m [esbozo] sketch.

bostezar vi to yawn.

bostezo m yawn.

bota f -1. [calzado] boot; ~s de agua ○

de lluvia wellingtons. -2. [de vino] small leather container in which wine is kept.

botana f Amer snack, tapa.

botánico, -ca ◇ adj botanical. ◇ m y f [persona] botanist. ◆ **botánica** f [ciencia] botany.

botar ◇ vt -1. NÁUT to launch. -2. fam [despedir] to throw ○ kick out. -3. [pelota] to bounce. -4. Amer [tirar] to throw away. ◇ vi -1. [saltar] to jump. -2. [pelota] to bounce.

bote m -1. [tarro] jar. -2. [lata] can. -3. [botella de plástico] bottle. -4. [barca] boat; ~ **salvavidas** lifeboat. -5. [salto] jump; **dar ~s** [gen] to jump up and down; [en tren, coche] to bump up and down. -6. [de pelota] bounce; **dar ~s** to bounce.

botella f bottle.

botellín m small bottle.

boticario, -ria m y f desus pharmacist.

botijo m earthenware jug.

botín m -1. [de guerra, atraco] plunder, loot. -2. [calzado] ankle boot.

botiquín m [caja] first-aid kit; [mueble] first-aid cupboard.

botón m button. ◆ **botones** m inv [de hotel] bellboy, bellhop Am; [de oficinas etc] errand boy.

boutique [bu'tik] f boutique.

bóveda f ARQUIT vault.

box (pl **boxes**) m [de coches] pit; **entrar en ~es** to make a pit stop.

boxeador, -ra m y f boxer.

boxear vi to box.

boxeo m boxing.

bóxer (pl **bóxers**) m boxer.

boya f -1. [en el mar] buoy. -2. [de una red] float.

boyante adj -1. [feliz] happy. -2. [próspero - empresa, negocio] prosperous; [- economía, comercio] buoyant.

boycot etc = **boicot**.

bozal m [gen] muzzle.

bracear vi [nadar] to swim.

braga f (gen pl) knickers (pl).

bragueta f flies (pl) Br, zipper Am.

braille ['braile] m Braille.

bramar vi -1. [animal] to bellow. -2. [persona - de dolor] to groan; [- de ira] to roar.

bramido m -1. [de animal] bellow. -2. [de persona - de dolor] groan; [- de ira] roar.

brandy, brandi m brandy.

branquia f (gen pl) gill.

brasa f ember; **a la ~** CULIN barbecued.

brasero *m* brazier.

brasier, **brassier** *m Amer* bra.

Brasil: (**el**) ~ Brazil.

brasileño, **-ña** *adj*, *m y f* Brazilian.

brasilero, **-ra** *adj*, *m y f Amer* Brazilian.

brassier = brasier.

bravata *f* (*gen pl*) **-1.** [amenaza] threat. **-2.** [fanfarronería] bravado (*U*).

braveza *f* bravery.

bravío, **-a** *adj* [salvaje] wild; [feroz] fierce.

bravo, **-va** *adj* **-1.** [valiente] brave. **-2.** [animal] wild. **-3.** [mar] rough. ◆ **bravo** ◇ *m* [aplauso] cheer. ◇ *interj*: ¡~! bravo!

bravuconear *vi despec* to brag.

bravura *f* **-1.** [de persona] bravery. **-2.** [de animal] ferocity.

braza *f* **-1.** DEP breaststroke; **nadar a** ~ to swim breaststroke. **-2.** [medida] fathom.

brazada *f* stroke.

brazalete *m* **-1.** [en la muñeca] bracelet. **-2.** [en el brazo] armband.

brazo *m* **-1.** [gen & ANAT] arm; [de animal] foreleg; **cogidos del** ~ arm in arm; **en** ~**s** in one's arms; **luchar a** ~ **partido** [con empeño] to fight tooth and nail; **quedarse** O **estarse con los** ~**s cruzados** *fig* to sit around doing nothing; **ser el** ~ **derecho de alguien** to be sb's right-hand man (*f* woman). **-2.** [de árbol, río, candelabro] branch; [de grúa] boom, jib. ◆ **brazo de gitano** *m* ≃ swiss roll.

brea *f* **-1.** [sustancia] tar. **-2.** [para barco] pitch.

brebaje *m* concoction, foul drink.

brecha *f* **-1.** [abertura] hole, opening. **-2.** MIL breach. **-3.** *fig* [impresión] impression.

bregar *vi* **-1.** [luchar] to struggle. **-2.** [trabajar] to work hard. **-3.** [reñir] to quarrel.

breña *f* scrub.

breve ◇ *adj* brief; **en** ~ [pronto] shortly; [en pocas palabras] in short. ◇ *f* MÚS breve.

brevedad *f* shortness; **a** O **con la mayor** ~ as soon as possible.

brezo *m* heather.

bribón, **-ona** *m y f* scoundrel, rogue.

bricolaje, **bricolage** *m* D.I.Y., do-it-yourself.

brida *f* [de caballo] bridle.

bridge *m* bridge.

brigada ◇ *m* MIL ≃ warrant officer. ◇ *f* **-1.** MIL brigade. **-2.** [equipo] squad,

team; ~ **antidisturbios/antidroga** riot/drug squad.

brillante ◇ *adj* **-1.** [reluciente - luz, astro] shining; [- metal, zapatos, pelo] shiny; [- ojos, sonrisa, diamante] sparkling. **-2.** [magnífico] brilliant. ◇ *m* diamond.

brillantina *f* brilliantine, Brylcreem®.

brillar *vi* lit & *fig* to shine.

brillo *m* **-1.** [resplandor - de luz] brilliance; [- de estrellas] shining; [- de zapatos] shine. **-2.** [lucimiento] splendour.

brilloso, **-sa** *adj Amer* shining.

brincar *vi* [saltar] to skip (about); ~ **de alegría** to jump for joy.

brinco *m* jump.

brindar ◇ *vi* to drink a toast; ~ **por algo/alguien** to drink to sthg/sb. ◇ *vt* to offer. ◆ **brindarse** *vpr*: ~**se a hacer algo** to offer to do sthg.

brindis *m inv* toast.

brío *m* [energía, decisión] spirit, verve.

brisa *f* breeze.

británico, **-ca** ◇ *adj* British. ◇ *m y f* British person, Briton; **los** ~**s** the British.

brizna *f* **-1.** [filamento - de hierba] blade; [- de tabaco] strand. **-2.** *fig* [un poco] trace, bit.

broca *f* (drill) bit.

brocha *f* brush; ~ **de afeitar** shaving brush.

brochazo *m* brushstroke.

broche *m* **-1.** [cierre] clasp, fastener. **-2.** [joya] brooch.

broma *f* [ocurrencia, chiste] joke; [jugarreta] prank, practical joke; **en** ~ as a joke; **gastar una** ~ **a alguien** to play a joke O prank on sb; **ni en** ~ *fig* no way, not on your life.

bromear *vi* to joke.

bromista *m y f* joker.

bronca → bronco.

bronce *m* [aleación] bronze.

bronceado, **-da** *adj* tanned. ◆ **bronceado** *m* tan.

bronceador, **-ra** *adj* tanning (*antes de sust*), suntan (*antes de sust*). ◆ **bronceador** *m* [loción] suntan lotion; [leche] suntan cream.

broncear *vt* to tan. ◆ **broncearse** *vpr* to get a tan.

bronco, **-ca** *adj* **-1.** [grave - voz] harsh; [- tos] throaty. **-2.** [brusco] gruff. ◆ **bronca** *f* **-1.** [jaleo] row. **-2.** [regañina] scolding; **echar una bronca a alguien** to give sb a row, to tell sb off.

bronquio *m* bronchial tube.

bronquitis *f inv* bronchitis.

brotar *vi* **-1.** [planta] to sprout, to bud. **-2.** [agua, sangre etc]: ~ **de** to well up out of. **-3.** *fig* [esperanza, sospechas, pasiones] to stir. **-4.** [en la piel]: **le brotó un sarpullido** he broke out in a rash.

brote *m* **-1.** [de planta] bud, shoot. **-2.** *fig* [inicios] sign, hint.

broza *f* [maleza] brush, scrub.

bruces ◆ **de bruces** *loc adv* face down; **se cayó de** ~ he fell headlong, he fell flat on his face.

bruja → **brujo.**

brujería *f* witchcraft, sorcery.

brujo, -ja *adj* [hechicero] enchanting. ◆ **brujo** *m* wizard, sorcerer. ◆ **bruja** ◇ *f* **-1.** [hechicera] witch, sorceress. **-2.** [mujer fea] hag. **-3.** [mujer mala] (old) witch. ◇ *adj inv Amer fam* [sin dinero] broke, skint.

brújula *f* compass.

bruma *f* [niebla] mist; [en el mar] sea mist.

bruñido *m* polishing.

brusco, -ca *adj* **-1.** [repentino, imprevisto] sudden. **-2.** [tosco, grosero] brusque.

Bruselas Brussels.

brusquedad *f* **-1.** [imprevisión] suddenness. **-2.** [grosería] brusqueness.

brutal *adj* [violento] brutal.

brutalidad *f* [cualidad] brutality.

bruto, -ta ◇ *adj* **-1.** [torpe] clumsy; [ignorante] thick, stupid; [maleducado] rude. **-2.** [sin tratar]: **en** ~ [diamante] uncut; [petróleo] crude. **-3.** [sueldo, peso etc] gross. ◇ *m y f* brute.

Bta. *abrev de* **beata.**

Bto. *abrev de* **beato.**

bubónica → **peste.**

bucal *adj* oral.

Bucarest Bucharest.

bucear *vi* [en agua] to dive.

buceo *m* (underwater) diving.

bucle *m* [rizo] curl, ringlet.

Budapest Budapest.

budismo *m* Buddhism.

buen → **bueno.**

buenas → **bueno.**

buenaventura *f* [adivinación] fortune; **leer la** ~ **a alguien** to tell sb's fortune.

bueno, -na (*compar* **mejor,** *superl* **el mejor,** *superl* **f la mejor**) *adj* (*antes de sust masculino:* **buen**) **-1.** [gen] good. **-2.** [bondadoso] kind, good; **ser** ~ **con alguien** to be good to sb. **-3.** [curado, sano] well, all right. **-4.** [apacible - tiempo, clima] nice, fine. **-5.** [aprovechable] all right; [comida] fresh. **-6.** [uso enfático]: **ese buen hombre** that good man;

un buen día one fine day. **-7.** *loc:* **de buen ver** good-looking; **de buenas a primeras** [de repente] all of a sudden; [a simple vista] at first sight; **estar** ~ *fam* [persona] to be a bit of all right, to be tasty; **estar de buenas** to be in a good mood; **lo** ~ **es que ...** the best thing about it is that .... ◆ **bueno** ◇ *m* CIN: **el** ~ the goody. ◇ *adv* **-1.** [vale, de acuerdo] all right, O.K. **-2.** [pues] well. ◇ *interj Amer* [al teléfono]: **¡~!** hello.

◆ **buenas** *interj:* **¡buenas!** hello!

Buenos Aires Buenos Aires.

buey (*pl* **bueyes**) *m* ox.

búfalo *m* buffalo.

bufanda *f* scarf.

bufar *vi* [toro, caballo] to snort.

bufé (*pl* **bufés**), **buffet** (*pl* **buffets**) *m* [en restaurante] buffet.

bufete *m* lawyer's practice.

buffet = **bufé.**

bufido *m* [de toro, caballo] snort.

bufón *m* buffoon, jester.

buhardilla *f* [habitación] attic.

búho *m* owl.

buitre *m lit* & *fig* vulture.

bujía *f* AUTOM spark plug.

bulbo *m* ANAT & BOT bulb.

buldozer (*pl* **buldozers**), **bulldozer** (*pl* **bulldozers**) [bul'doθer] *m* bulldozer.

bulevar (*pl* **bulevares**) *m* boulevard.

Bulgaria Bulgaria.

búlgaro, -ra *adj, m y f* Bulgarian. ◆ **búlgaro** *m* [lengua] Bulgarian.

bulla *f* racket, uproar; **armar** ~ to kick up a racket.

bulldozer = **buldozer.**

bullicio *m* [de ciudad, mercado] hustle and bustle; [de multitud] hubbub.

bullicioso, -sa *adj* **-1.** [agitado - reunión, multitud] noisy; [- calle, mercado] busy, bustling. **-2.** [inquieto] rowdy.

bullir *vi* **-1.** [hervir] to boil; [burbujear] to bubble. **-2.** *fig* [multitud] to bustle; [ratas, hormigas etc] to swarm; [mar] to boil; ~ **de** to seethe with.

bulto *m* **-1.** [volumen] bulk, size; **escurrir el** ~ [trabajo] to shirk; [cuestión] to evade the issue. **-2.** [abombamiento - en rodilla, superficie etc] bump; [- en maleta, bolsillo etc] bulge. **-3.** [forma imprecisa] blurred shape. **-4.** [paquete] package; [maleta] item of luggage; [fardo] bundle; ~ **de mano** piece ○ item of hand luggage.

bumerán (*pl* **bumeráns**), **bumerang** (*pl* **bumerangs**) *m* boomerang.

bungalow [buŋga'lo] (*pl* **bungalows**) *m* bungalow.

búnquer (*pl* **búnquers**), **bunker** (*pl* **bunkers**) *m* [refugio] bunker.

buñuelo *m* [CULIN - dulce] ≃ doughnut; [- de bacalao etc] ≃ dumpling.

BUP *m* *academically orientated secondary-school course taught in Spain for pupils aged 14-17.*

buque *m* ship; ~ **nodriza** supply ship.

burbuja *f* bubble; **hacer ~s** to bubble.

burbujear *vi* to bubble.

burdel *m* brothel.

burdo, -da *adj* [gen] crude; [tela] coarse.

burgués, -esa *adj* middle-class, bourgeois.

burguesía *f* middle class; HIST & POLÍT bourgeoisie.

burla *f* -1. [mofa] taunt; **hacer ~ de** to mock. -2. [broma] joke. -3. [engaño] trick.

burlar *vt* [esquivar] to evade; [ley] to flout. ◆ **burlarse de** *vpr* to make fun of.

burlesco, -ca *adj* [tono] jocular; LITER burlesque.

burlón, -ona *adj* [sarcástico] mocking.

burocracia *f* bureaucracy.

burócrata *m y f* bureaucrat.

burrada *f* [acción, dicho]: **hacer ~s** to act stupidly; **decir ~s** to talk nonsense.

burro, -rra *m y f* -1. [animal] donkey; **no ver tres en un ~** *fam* to be as blind as a bat. -2. *fam* [necio] dimwit.

bursátil *adj* stock-market (*antes de sust*).

bus (*pl* **buses**) *m* AUTOM & INFORM bus.

busca ◇ *f* search; **en ~ de** in search of; **la ~ de** the search for. ◇ *m* → **buscapersonas.**

buscapersonas, busca *m inv* bleeper.

buscar ◇ *vt* -1. [gen] to look for; [provecho, beneficio propio] to seek; **voy a ~ el periódico** I'm going for the paper ○ to get the paper; **ir a ~ a alguien** to pick sb up. -2. [en diccionario, índice, horario] to look up. -3. INFORM to search for. ◇ *vi* to look. ◆ **buscarse** *vpr* [personal, aprendiz etc]: **"se busca camarero"** "waiter wanted".

buscón, -ona *m y f* [estafador] swindler.

búsqueda *f* search.

busto *m* -1. [pecho] chest; [de mujer] bust. -2. [escultura] bust.

butaca *f* -1. [mueble] armchair. -2. [localidad] seat.

butano *m* butane (gas).

butifarra *f* *type of Catalan pork sausage.*

buzo *m* -1. [persona] diver. -2. *Amer* [chandal] tracksuit.

buzón *m* letter box; **echar algo al ~** to post sthg.

byte [bait] (*pl* **bytes**) *m* INFORM byte.

C

c, C *f* [letra] c, C.

c., c/ (*abrev de* **calle**) St.

c/ -1. (*abrev de* **cuenta**) a/c. -2. = **c**.

cabal *adj* -1. [honrado] honest. -2. [exacto] exact; [completo] complete. ◆ **cabales** *mpl*: **no estar en sus ~es** not to be in one's right mind.

cábala *f* (*gen pl*) [conjeturas] guess.

cabalgar *vi* to ride.

cabalgata *f* cavalcade, procession.

caballa *f* mackerel.

caballería *f* -1. [animal] mount, horse. -2. [cuerpo militar] cavalry.

caballeriza *f* stable.

caballero ◇ *adj* [cortés] gentlemanly. ◇ *m* -1. [gen] gentleman; [al dirigir la palabra] sir; **ser todo un ~** to be a real gentleman; **"caballeros"** [en aseos] "gents"; [en grandes almacenes] "menswear". -2. [miembro de una orden] knight.

caballete *m* -1. [de lienzo] easel. -2. [de mesa] trestle. -3. [de nariz] bridge.

caballito *m* small horse, pony. ◆ **caballitos** *mpl* [de feria] merry-go-round (*sg*).

caballo *m* -1. [animal] horse; **montar a ~** to ride. -2. [pieza de ajedrez] knight. -3. [naipe] ≃ queen. -4. MEC: ~ **(de fuerza** ○ **de vapor)** horsepower.

cabaña *f* -1. [choza] hut, cabin. -2. [ganado] livestock (*U*).

cabaret (*pl* **cabarets**) *m* cabaret.

cabecear *vi* -1. [persona - negando] to shake one's head; [- afirmando] to nod one's head. -2. [caballo] to toss its head. -3. [dormir] to nod (off).

cabecera *f* -1. [gen] head; [de cama] headboard. -2. [de texto] heading; [de periódico] headline. -3. [de río] headwaters (*pl*).

cabecilla *m y f* ringleader.

cabellera *f* long hair (*U*).

cabello *m* hair (*U*).

caber *vi* **-1.** [gen] to fit; **no cabe nadie más** there's no room for anyone else; **no me cabe en el dedo** it won't fit my finger. **-2.** MAT: **nueve entre tres caben a tres** three into nine goes three (times). **-3.** [ser posible] to be possible; **cabe destacar que ...** it's worth pointing out that ....

cabestrillo ◆ **en cabestrillo** *loc adj* in a sling.

cabestro *m* [animal] leading ox.

cabeza *f* **-1.** [gen] head; **por ~** per head; **obrar con ~** to use one's head; **tirarse de ~ (a)** to dive (into); **venir a la ~** to come to mind; **~ (lectora)** [gen] head; [de tocadiscos] pickup. **-2.** [pelo] hair. **-3.** [posición] front, head; **a la ~ en ~** [en competición etc] in front; [en lista] at the top ○ head. **-4.** *loc:* **andar** ○ **estar mal de la ~** to be funny in the head; **se le ha metido en la ~ que ...** he has got it into his head that ...; **sentar la ~** to settle down. ◆ **cabeza de ajo** *f* head of garlic. ◆ **cabeza de turco** *f* scapegoat.

cabezada *f* **-1.** [de sueño] nod, nodding (*U*); **dar ~s** to nod off. **-2.** [golpe] butt.

cabezal *m* [de aparato] head.

cabezón, -ona *adj* [terco] pigheaded, stubborn.

cabida *f* capacity.

cabina *f* **-1.** [locutorio] booth, cabin; **~ telefónica** phone box *Br*, phone booth. **-2.** [de avión] cockpit; [de camión] cab. **-3.** [vestuario - en playa] bathing hut; [- en piscina] changing cubicle.

cabinera *f Amer* air hostess.

cabizbajo, -ja *adj* crestfallen.

cable *m* cable.

cablegrafiar *vt* to cable.

cabo *m* **-1.** GEOGR cape. **-2.** NÁUT cable, rope. **-3.** MIL corporal. **-4.** [trozo] bit, piece; [trozo final] stub, stump; [de cuerda] end. **-5.** *loc:* **llevar algo a ~** to carry sthg out. ◆ **cabo suelto** *m* loose end. ◆ **al cabo de** *loc prep* after.

cabra *f* [animal] goat; **estar como una ~** *fam* to be off one's head.

cabré → **caber**.

cabrear *vt mfam:* **~ a alguien** to get sb's goat, to annoy sb.

cabría → **caber**.

cabriola *f* prance; **hacer ~s** to prance about.

cabrita *f Amer* popcorn.

cabrito *m* [animal] kid (goat).

cabro, -bra *m y f Amer fam* kid.

cabrón, -ona *vulg* ◇ *adj:* **¡qué ~ eres!** you bastard! ◇ *m y f* bastard (*f* bitch).

cabuya *f Amer* rope.

caca *f fam* **-1.** [excremento] pooh. **-2.** [cosa sucia] nasty ○ dirty thing.

cacahuate *m Amer* peanut.

cacahuete *m* [fruto] peanut.

cacao *m* **-1.** [bebida] cocoa. **-2.** [árbol] cacao.

cacarear *vi* [gallo] to cluck, to cackle.

cacatúa *f* [ave] cockatoo.

cacería *f* hunt.

cacerola *f* pot, pan.

cachalote *m* sperm whale.

cacharro *m* **-1.** [recipiente] pot; **fregar los ~s** to do the dishes. **-2.** *fam* [trasto] junk (*U*), rubbish (*U*). **-3.** [máquina] crock; [coche] banger.

cachear *vt* to frisk.

cachemir *m*, **cachemira** *f* cashmere.

cacheo *m* frisk, frisking (*U*).

cachet [ka'tʃe] *m* **-1.** [distinción] cachet. **-2.** [cotización de artista] fee.

cachetada *f Amer fam* smack.

cachete *m* **-1.** [moflete] chubby cheek. **-2.** [bofetada] slap.

cachirulo *m* [chisme] thingamajig.

cachivache *m fam* knick-knack.

cacho *m* **-1.** *fam* [pedazo] piece, bit. **-2.** *Amer* [asta] horn.

cachondearse *vpr fam:* **~ (de)** to take the mickey (out of).

cachondeo *m fam* **-1.** [diversión] lark. **-2.** *despec* [cosa poco seria] joke.

cachondo, -da *fam adj* **-1.** [divertido] funny. **-2.** [salido] randy.

cachorro, -rra *m y f* [de perro] puppy; [de gato] kitten; [de león, lobo, oso] cub.

cacique *m* **-1.** [persona influyente] cacique, local political boss. **-2.** [jefe indio] chief.

caco *m fam* thief.

cacto, cactus (*pl* **cactus**) *m* cactus.

cada *adj inv* **-1.** [gen] each; [con números, tiempo] every; **~ dos meses** every two months; **~ cosa a su tiempo** one thing at a time; **~ cual** each one, everyone; **~ uno de** each of. **-2.** [valor progresivo]: **~ vez más** more and more; **~ vez más largo** longer and longer; **~ día más** more and more each day. **-3.** [valor enfático] such; **¡se pone ~ sombrero!** she wears such hats!

cadalso *m* scaffold.

cadáver *m* corpse, (dead) body.

cadena *f* **-1.** [gen] chain; **en ~** [accidente] multiple. **-2.** TV channel. **-3.** [RADIO -

emisora] station; [- red de emisoras] **network**. **-4.** [de proceso industrial] line; ~ **de montaje** assembly line. **-5.** [aparato de música] **sound system. -6.** GEOGR range. ◆ **cadena perpetua** f life imprisonment.

cadencia f [ritmo] rhythm, cadence.

cadera f hip.

cadete m cadet.

caducar vi **-1.** [carnet, ley, pasaporte etc] to expire. **-2.** [medicamento] to pass its use-by date; [alimento] to pass its sell-by date.

caducidad f expiry.

caduco, -ca adj **-1.** [viejo] decrepit; [idea] outmoded. **-2.** [desfasado] no longer valid.

caer vi **-1.** [gen] to fall; [diente, pelo] to fall out; **dejar ~ algo** to drop sthg; **~ bajo** to sink (very) low; **estar al ~** to be about to arrive. **-2.** [al perder equilibrio] to fall over O down; **~ de un tejado/caballo** to fall from a roof/horse. **-3.** fig [sentar]: **~ bien/mal (a alguien)** [comentario, noticia etc] to go down well/badly (with sb). **-4.** fig [mostrarse]: **me cae bien/mal** I like/don't like him. **-5.** fig [estar situado]: **cae cerca de aquí** it's not far from here. **-6.** fig [recordar]: **~ (en algo)** to be able to remember (sthg). ◆ **caer en** vi **-1.** [entender] to get, to understand; [solución] to hit upon. **-2.** [coincidir - fecha] to fall on; **cae en domingo** it falls on a Sunday. **-3.** [incurrir] to fall into. ◆ **caerse** vpr **-1.** [persona] to fall over O down. **-2.** [objetos] to drop, to fall. **-3.** [desprenderse - diente, pelo etc] to fall out; [- botón] to fall off; [- cuadro] to fall down.

café (pl **cafés**) m **-1.** [gen] coffee; **~ solo/con leche** black/white coffee; **~ instantáneo** O **soluble** instant coffee. **-2.** [establecimiento] cafe.

cafeína f caffeine.

cafetera → **cafetero**.

cafetería f cafe.

cafetero, -ra m y f **-1.** [cultivador] coffee grower. **-2.** [comerciante] coffee merchant. ◆ **cafetera** f **-1.** [gen] coffee pot. **-2.** [en bares] expresso machine; [eléctrica] percolator, coffee machine.

cafiche m Amer fam pimp.

cagar vulg vi [defecar] to shit. ◆ **cagarse** vpr vulg lit & fig to shit o.s.

caído, -da adj [árbol, hoja] fallen. ◆ **caída** f **-1.** [gen] fall, falling (U); [de diente, pelo] loss. **-2.** [de paro, precios, terreno]: **caída (de)** drop (in). **-3.** [de falda, vestido etc] drape. ◆ **caídos** mpl: **los ~s** the fallen.

caiga etc → **caer**.

caimán m **-1.** [animal] alligator, cayman. **-2.** fig [persona] sly fox.

caja f **-1.** [gen] box; [para transporte, embalaje] crate; **una ~ de cervezas** a crate of beer; **~ torácica** thorax. **-2.** [de reloj] case; [de engranajes etc] housing; **~ de cambios** gearbox. **-3.** [ataúd] coffin. **-4.** [de dinero] cash box; **~ fuerte** O **de caudales** safe, strongbox. **-5.** [en tienda, supermercado] till; [en banco] cashier's desk. **-6.** [banco]: **~ (de ahorros)** savings bank. **-7.** [hueco - de chimenea, ascensor] shaft. **-8.** IMPRENTA case. **-9.** [de instrumento musical] body. ◆ **caja negra** f black box. ◆ **caja registradora** f cash register.

cajero, -ra m y f [en tienda] cashier; [en banco] teller. ◆ **cajero** m: **~ (automático)** cash machine, cash dispenser.

cajetilla f **-1.** [de cigarrillos] packet. **-2.** [de cerillas] box.

cajón m **-1.** [de mueble] drawer. **-2.** [recipiente] crate, case. ◆ **cajón de sastre** m muddle, jumble.

cajuela f Amer boot Br, trunk Am.

cal f lime.

cala f **-1.** [bahía pequeña] cove. **-2.** [del barco] hold.

calabacín m courgette Br, zucchini Am.

calabaza f pumpkin, gourd.

calabozo m cell.

calada → **calado**.

calado, -da adj soaked. ◆ **calado** m NÁUT draught. ◆ **calada** f [de cigarrillo] drag.

calamar m squid.

calambre m **-1.** [descarga eléctrica] (electric) shock. **-2.** [contracción muscular] cramp (U).

calamidad f calamity; **ser una ~** fig to be a dead loss.

calaña f despec: **de esa ~** of that ilk.

calar ◇ vt **-1.** [empapar] to soak. **-2.** fig [persona] to see through. **-3.** [gorro, sombrero] to jam on. **-4.** [fruta] to cut a sample of. **-5.** [perforar] to pierce. ◇ vi **-1.** NÁUT to draw. **-2.** fig [penetrar]: **~ en** to have an impact on. ◆ **calarse** vpr **-1.** [empaparse] to get soaked. **-2.** [motor] to stall.

calavera f [cráneo] skull. ◆ **calaveras** fpl Amer AUTOM rear lights.

calcar vt **-1.** [dibujo] to trace. **-2.** [imitar] to copy.

calce m -1. [cuña] wedge. -2. Amer DER footnote.

calceta f stocking; **hacer** ~ to knit.

calcetín m sock.

calcificarse vpr to calcify.

calcinar vt [quemar] to char.

calcio m calcium.

calco m -1. [reproducción] tracing. -2. fig [imitación] carbon copy.

calcomanía f transfer.

calculador, -ra adj lit & fig calculating. ◆ **calculadora** f calculator.

calcular vt -1. [cantidades] to calculate. -2. [suponer] to reckon.

cálculo m -1. [operación] calculation. -2. [ciencia] calculus. -3. [evaluación] estimate. -4. MED stone, calculus.

caldear vt -1. [calentar] to heat (up). -2. fig [excitar] to warm up, to liven up.

caldera f -1. [recipiente] cauldron. -2. [máquina] boiler.

calderilla f small change.

caldero m cauldron.

caldo m -1. [sopa] broth. -2. [caldillo] stock. -3. [vino] wine.

calefacción f heating; ~ **central** central heating.

calefactor m heater.

calendario m calendar; ~ **escolar/laboral** school/working year.

calentador m -1. [aparato] heater. -2. [prenda] legwarmer.

calentar ◇ vt [subir la temperatura de] to heat (up), to warm (up). ◇ vi [entrenarse] to warm up. ◆ **calentarse** vpr [por calor - suj: persona] to warm o.s., to get warm; [- suj: cosa] to heat up.

calentura f -1. [fiebre] fever, temperature. -2. [herida] cold sore.

calesitas fpl Amer merry-go-round (sg).

calibrar vt -1. [medir] to calibrate, to gauge. -2. [dar calibre a - arma] to bore. -3. fig [juzgar] to gauge.

calibre m -1. [diámetro - de pistola] calibre; [- de alambre] gauge; [- de tubo] bore. -2. [instrumento] gauge. -3. fig [tamaño] size.

calidad f -1. [gen] quality; **de** ~ quality (antes de sust); ~ **de vida** quality of life. -2. [clase] class. -3. [condición]: **en** ~ **de** in one's capacity as.

cálido, -da adj warm.

caliente adj -1. [gen] hot; [templado] warm; **en** ~ fig in the heat of the moment. -2. fig [acalorado] heated.

calificación f -1. [atributo] quality. -2. EDUC mark.

calificar vt -1. [denominar]: ~ **a alguien de algo** to call sb sthg, to describe sb as sthg. -2. EDUC to mark. -3. GRAM to qualify.

calificativo, -va adj qualifying. ◆ **calificativo** m epithet.

caligrafía f -1. [arte] calligraphy. -2. [rasgos] handwriting.

cáliz m RELIG chalice.

calizo, -za adj chalky. ◆ **caliza** f limestone.

callado, -da adj quiet, silent.

callar ◇ vi -1. [no hablar] to keep quiet, to be silent. -2. [dejar de hablar] to be quiet, to stop talking. ◇ vt -1. [ocultar] to keep quiet about; [secreto] to keep. -2. [acallar] to silence. ◆ **callarse** vpr -1. [no hablar] to keep quiet, to be silent. -2. [dejar de hablar] to be quiet, to stop talking; **¡cállate!** shut up! -3. [ocultar] to keep quiet about; [secreto] to keep.

calle f -1. [vía de circulación] street, road; ~ **arriba/abajo** up/down the street; ~ **de dirección única** one-way street; ~ **peatonal** pedestrian precinct. -2. DEP lane. -3. loc: **dejar a alguien en la** ~ to put sb out of a job; **echar a alguien a la** ~ [de un trabajo] to sack sb; [de un lugar público] to kick o throw sb out.

callejear vi to wander the streets.

callejero, -ra adj [gen] street (antes de sust); [perro] stray. ◆ **callejero** m [guía] street map.

callejón m alley; ~ **sin salida** cul-de-sac; fig blind alley, impasse.

callejuela f backstreet, side street.

callista m y f chiropodist.

callo m [dureza] callus; [en el pie] corn. ◆ **callos** mpl CULIN tripe (U).

calma f -1. [sin ruido o movimiento] calm; **en** ~ calm. -2. [sosiego] tranquility; **tómatelo con** ~ take it easy. -3. [apatía] sluggishness, indifference.

calmante ◇ adj soothing. ◇ m sedative.

calmar vt -1. [mitigar] to relieve. -2. [tranquilizar] to calm, to soothe. ◆ **calmarse** vpr to calm down; [dolor, tempestad] to abate.

caló m gypsy dialect.

calor m [gen] heat; [tibieza] warmth; **entrar en** ~ [gen] to get warm; [público, deportista] to warm up; **hacer** ~ to be warm o hot; **tener** ~ to be warm o hot.

caloría f calorie.

calumnia *f* [oral] slander; [escrita] libel.

calumniar *vt* [oralmente] to slander; [por escrito] to libel.

calumnioso, -sa *adj* [de palabra] slanderous; [por escrito] libellous.

caluroso, -sa *adj* **-1.** [gen] hot; [templado] warm. **-2.** *fig* [afectuoso] warm.

calva → **calvo.**

calvario *m fig* [sufrimiento] ordeal.

calvicie *f* baldness.

calvo, -va *adj* bald. ◆ **calva** *f* [en la cabeza] bald patch.

calza *f* [cuña] wedge, block.

calzado, -da *adj* [con zapatos] shod. ◆ **calzado** *m* footwear. ◆ **calzada** *f* road (surface).

calzar *vt* **-1.** [poner calzado] to put on. **-2.** [llevar un calzado] to wear; **¿qué número calza?** what size do you take? **-3.** [poner cuña a] to wedge. ◆ **calzarse** *vpr* to put on.

calzo *m* [cuña] wedge.

calzón *m* (*gen pl*) *desus* [pantalón] trousers (*pl*). ◆ **calzones** *mpl Amer* [bragas] knickers (*pl*).

calzoncillo *m* (*gen pl*) underpants (*pl*).

cama *f* bed; **estar en** ○ **guardar** ~ to be confined to bed; **hacer la** ~ to make the bed; ~ **individual/de matrimonio** single/double bed.

camada *f* litter.

camafeo *m* cameo.

camaleón *m lit* & *fig* chameleon.

cámara ◇ *f* **-1.** [gen & TECN] chamber; ~ **alta/baja** upper/lower house; ~ **de aire/gas** air/gas chamber. **-2.** CIN, FOT & TV camera; **a** ~ **lenta** *lit* & *fig* in slow motion. **-3.** [de balón, neumático] inner tube. **-4.** [habitáculo] cabin. ◇ *m y f* [persona] cameraman (*f* camerawoman).

camarada *m y f* POLÍT comrade.

camarero, -ra *m y f* [de restaurante] waiter (*f* waitress); [de hotel] steward (*f* chambermaid).

camarilla *f* clique; POLÍT lobby.

camarón *m* shrimp.

camarote *m* cabin.

cambiante *adj* changeable.

cambiar ◇ *vt* **-1.** [gen] to change; ~ **libras por pesetas** to change pounds into pesetas. **-2.** [canjear]: ~ **algo (por)** to exchange sthg (for). ◇ *vi* **-1.** [gen] to change; ~ **de** [gen] to change; [casa] to move; ~ **de trabajo** to move jobs. **-2.** AUTOM [de marchas] to change gear. ◆ **cambiarse** *vpr*: ~**se (de)** [ropa] to

change; [casa] to move; ~**se de vestido** to change one's dress.

cambio *m* **-1.** [gen] change. **-2.** [trueque] exchange; **a** ~ **(de)** in exchange ○ return (for). **-3.** [FIN - de acciones] price; [- de divisas] exchange rate; "**cambio**" "**bureau de change**". **-4.** AUTOM: ~ **de marchas** ○ **velocidades** gear change; ~ **de sentido** U-turn. ◆ **cambio de rasante** *m* brow of a hill. ◆ **libre cambio** *m* **-1.** ECON [librecambismo] free trade. **-2.** FIN [de divisas] floating exchange rates (*pl*). ◆ **en cambio** *loc adv* **-1.** [por otra parte] on the other hand, however. **-2.** [en su lugar] instead.

camelar *vt fam* [seducir, engañar] to butter up, to win over.

camelia *f* camellia.

camello, -lla *m y f* [animal] camel. ◆ **camello** *m fam* [traficante] drug pusher ○ dealer.

camellón *m Amer* central reservation.

camerino *m* dressing room.

camilla ◇ *f* [de psiquiatría, dentista] stretcher; couch. ◇ *adj* → **mesa**.

caminante *m y f* walker.

caminar ◇ *vi* **-1.** [a pie] to walk. **-2.** *fig* [ir]: ~ **(hacia)** to head (for). ◇ *vt* [una distancia] to travel, to cover.

caminata *f* long walk.

camino *m* **-1.** [sendero] path, track; [carretera] road; **abrir** ~ **a** to clear the way for; **abrirse** ~ to get on ○ ahead. **-2.** [ruta] way; **a medio** ~ halfway; **estar a medio** ~ to be halfway there; **quedarse a medio** ~ to stop halfway through; ~ **de** on the way to; **en el** ○ **de** ~ on the way. **-3.** [viaje] journey; **ponerse en** ~ to set off. **-4.** *fig* [medio] way.

camión *m* **-1.** [de mercancías] lorry *Br*, truck *Am*; ~ **cisterna** tanker; ~ **de la mudanza** removal van. **-2.** *Amer* [autobús] bus.

camionero, -ra *m y f* lorry driver *Br*, trucker *Am*.

camioneta *f* van.

camisa *f* **-1.** [prenda] shirt. **-2.** *loc*: **meterse en** ~ **de once varas** to complicate matters unnecessarily; **mudar** ○ **cambiar de** ~ to change sides. ◆ **camisa de fuerza** *f* straitjacket.

camisería *f* [tienda] outfitter's.

camiseta *f* **-1.** [ropa interior] vest. **-2.** [de verano] T-shirt. **-3.** [DEP - de tirantes] vest; [- de mangas] shirt.

camisola *f* **-1.** [prenda interior] camisole. **-2.** *Amer* DEP sports shirt.

camisón *m* nightdress.

camorra f trouble; **buscar** ~ to look for trouble.

campamento m camp.

campana f bell; ~ **extractora de humos** extractor hood.

campanada f **-1.** [de campana] peal. **-2.** [de reloj] stroke. **-3.** fig [suceso] sensation.

campanario m belfry, bell tower.

campanilla f **-1.** [de la puerta] (small) bell; [con mango] handbell. **-2.** [flor] campanula, bellflower.

campanilleo m tinkling (U).

campante adj fam: **estar** O **quedarse tan** ~ to remain quite unruffled.

campaña f [gen] campaign; **de** ~ MIL field (antes de sust).

campechano, -na adj fam genial, good-natured.

campeón, -ona m y f champion.

campeonato m championship; **de** ~ fig terrific, great.

campero, -ra adj country (antes de sust); [al aire libre] open-air. ◆ **campera** f **-1.** [bota] ≃ cowboy boot. **-2.** Amer [chaqueta] short leather jacket.

campesino, -na m y f farmer; [muy pobre] peasant.

campestre adj country (antes de sust).

camping ['kampin] (pl **campings**) m **-1.** [actividad] camping; **ir de** ~ to go camping. **-2.** [terreno] campsite.

campito m Amer property, estate.

campo m **-1.** [gen & INFORM] field; ~ **de aviación** airfield; ~ **de batalla** battlefield; ~ **de tiro** firing range; **dejar el** ~ **libre** fig to leave the field open. **-2.** [campiña] country, countryside; **a** ~ **traviesa** cross country. **-3.** [DEP - de fútbol] pitch; [- de tenis] court; [- de golf] course. ◆ **campo de concentración** m concentration camp.

camuflaje m camouflage.

cana → **cano**.

Canadá: (el) ~ Canada.

canadiense adj, m y f Canadian.

canal m **-1.** [cauce artificial] canal. **-2.** GEOGR [estrecho] channel, strait. **-3.** RADIO & TV channel. **-4.** ANAT canal, duct. **-5.** [de agua, gas] conduit, pipe. **-6.** fig [medio, vía] channel.

canalizar vt **-1.** [territorio] to canalize; [agua] to channel. **-2.** fig [orientar] to channel.

canalla m y f swine, dog.

canalón m [de tejado] gutter; [en la pared] drainpipe.

canapé m **-1.** CULIN canapé. **-2.** [sofá] sofa, couch.

Canarias: las (islas) ~ the Canary Islands, the Canaries.

canario, -ria ◇ adj of the Canary Islands. ◇ m y f [persona] Canary Islander. ◆ **canario** m [pájaro] canary.

canasta f [gen & DEP] basket.

canastilla f **-1.** [cesto pequeño] basket. **-2.** [de bebé] layette.

canasto m large basket.

cancela f wrought-iron gate.

cancelación f cancellation.

cancelar vt **-1.** [anular] to cancel. **-2.** [deuda] to pay, to settle.

cáncer m MED & fig cancer. ◆ **Cáncer** ◇ m [zodiaco] Cancer. ◇ m y f [persona] Cancer.

cancerígeno, -na adj carcinogenic.

canceroso, -sa adj [úlcera, tejido] cancerous; [enfermo] suffering from cancer.

canciller m **-1.** [de gobierno, embajada] chancellor. **-2.** [de asuntos exteriores] foreign minister.

canción f song; ~ **de cuna** lullaby.

cancionero m songbook.

candado m padlock.

candela f **-1.** [vela] candle. **-2.** Amer [fuego] fire.

candelabro m candelabra.

candelero m candlestick; **estar en el** ~ fig to be in the limelight.

candente adj **-1.** [incandescente] redhot. **-2.** fig [actual] burning (antes de sust).

candidato, -ta m y f candidate.

candidatura f [para un cargo] candidacy.

candidez f ingenuousness.

cándido, -da adj ingenuous, simple.

candil m **-1.** [lámpara] oil lamp. **-2.** Amer [araña] chandelier.

candilejas fpl footlights.

canelo, -la adj fam fig [inocentón] gullible. ◆ **canela** f cinnamon.

canelón m CULIN cannelloni (pl).

cangrejo m crab.

canguro ◇ m [animal] kangaroo. ◇ m y f fam [persona] babysitter; **hacer de** ~ to babysit.

caníbal m y f cannibal.

canica f [pieza] marble. ◆ **canicas** fpl [juego] marbles.

caniche m poodle.

canijo, -ja adj sickly.

canilla f **-1.** [espinilla] shinbone. **-2.** Amer [grifo] tap. **-3.** Amer [pierna] leg.

canillita m Amer newspaper seller.

canino, -na *adj* canine. ◆**canino** *m* [diente] canine (tooth).

canjear *vt* to exchange.

cano, -na *adj* grey. ◆**cana** *f* grey hair.

canoa *f* canoe.

canódromo *m* greyhound track.

canon *m* -1. [norma] canon. -2. [modelo] ideal. -3. [impuesto] tax. -4. MÚS canon.

canónigo *m* canon.

canonizar *vt* to canonize.

canoso, -sa *adj* grey; [persona] grey-haired.

cansado, -da *adj* -1. [gen] tired; ~ de algo/de hacer algo tired of sthg/of doing sthg. -2. [pesado, cargante] tiring.

cansador, -ra *adj Amer* boring.

cansancio *m* tiredness.

cansar ◇ *vt* to tire (out). ◇ *vi* to be tiring. ◆**cansarse** *vpr*: ~se (de) *lit & fig* to get tired (of).

Cantábrica → cordillera.

Cantábrico *m*: el (mar) ~ the Cantabrian Sea.

cantaleta *f Amer* nagging.

cantante ◇ *adj* singing. ◇ *m y f* singer.

cantaor, -ra *m y f* flamenco singer.

cantar ◇ *vt* -1. [canción] to sing. -2. [bingo, línea, el gordo] to call (out). ◇ *vi* -1. [persona, ave] to sing; [gallo] to crow; [insecto] to chirp. -2. *fam fig* [confesar] to talk.

cántaro *m* large pitcher; llover a ~s to rain cats and dogs.

cante *m*: ~ (jondo o hondo) flamenco singing.

cantera *f* [de piedra] quarry.

cantero *m Amer* flowerbed.

cantidad *f* -1. [medida] quantity. -2. [abundancia] abundance, large number; en ~ in abundance; ~ de lots of. -3. [número] number. -4. [suma de dinero] sum (of money).

cantilena, cantinela *f*: la misma ~ *fig* the same old story.

cantimplora *f* water bottle.

cantina *f* [de soldados] mess; [en fábrica] canteen; [en estación de tren] buffet.

cantinela = cantilena.

canto *m* -1. [acción, arte] singing. -2. [canción] song. -3. [lado, borde] edge; de ~ edgeways. -4. [de cuchillo] blunt edge. -5. [guijarro] pebble; ~ rodado [pequeño] pebble; [grande] boulder.

cantor, -ra *m y f* singer.

canturrear *vt & vi fam* to sing softly.

canuto *m* -1. [tubo] tube. -2. *fam* [porro] joint.

caña *f* -1. BOT cane; ~ de azúcar sugarcane. -2. [de cerveza] small glass of beer. ◆**caña de pescar** *f* fishing rod.

cañabrava *f Amer* kind of cane.

cáñamo *m* hemp.

cañería *f* pipe.

caño *m* [de fuente] jet.

cañón *m* -1. [arma] gun; HIST cannon. -2. [de fusil] barrel; [de chimenea] flue; [de órgano] pipe. -3. GEOGR canyon.

caoba *f* mahogany.

caos *m inv* chaos.

caótico, -ca *adj* chaotic.

cap. *(abrev de capítulo)* ch.

capa *f* -1. [manto] cloak, cape; andar de ~ caída to be in a bad way; de ~ y espada cloak and dagger. -2. [baño - de barniz, pintura] coat; [- de chocolate etc] coating. -3. [estrato] layer; GEOL stratum; ~ de ozono ozone layer. -4. [grupo social] stratum, class. -5. TAUROM cape.

capacidad *f* -1. [gen] capacity; con ~ para 500 personas with a capacity of 500. -2. [aptitud] ability; no tener ~ para algo/para hacer algo to be no good at sthg/at doing sthg.

capacitación *f* training.

capacitar *vt*: ~ a alguien para algo [habilitar] to qualify sb for sthg; [formar] to train sb for sthg.

capar *vt* to castrate.

caparazón *m lit & fig* shell.

capataz *m y f* foreman (*f* forewoman).

capaz *adj* -1. [gen] capable; ~ de algo/de hacer algo capable of sthg/of doing sthg. -2. [espacioso]: muy/poco ~ with a large/small capacity; ~ para with room for.

capazo *m* large wicker basket.

capellán *m* chaplain.

caperuza *f* [gorro] hood.

capicúa *adj inv* reversible.

capilla *f* chapel; ~ ardiente funeral chapel.

cápita ◆ per cápita *loc adj* per capita.

capital ◇ *adj* -1. [importante] supreme. -2. [principal] main. ◇ *m* ECON capital. ◇ *f* [ciudad] capital.

capitalismo *m* capitalism.

capitalista *adj, m y f* capitalist.

capitalizar *vt* -1. ECON to capitalize. -2. *fig* [sacar provecho] to capitalize on.

capitán, -ana *m y f* captain.

capitanear *vt* DEP & MIL to captain.

capitel *m* capital.

capitoste *m y f despec* big boss.

capitulación *f* capitulation, surrender.

capitular *vi* to capitulate, to surrender.

capítulo *m* **-1.** [sección, división] chapter. **-2.** *fig* [tema] subject.

capó, capot [ka'po] *m* bonnet *Br*, hood *Am*.

caporal *m* MIL ≃ corporal.

capot = **capó.**

capota *f* hood *Br*, top *Am*.

capote *m* **-1.** [capa] cape with sleeves; [militar] greatcoat. **-2.** TAUROM cape.

capricho *m* whim, caprice; **darse un ~** to treat o.s.

caprichoso, -sa *adj* capricious.

Capricornio ◇ *m* [zodiaco] Capricorn. ◇ *m y f* [persona] Capricorn.

cápsula *f* **-1.** [gen & ANAT] capsule. **-2.** [tapón] cap.

captar *vt* **-1.** [atraer - simpatía] to win; [- interés] to gain, to capture. **-2.** [entender] to grasp. **-3.** [sintonizar] to pick up, to receive.

captura *f* capture.

capturar *vt* to capture.

capucha *f* hood.

capuchón *m* cap, top.

capullo, -lla *vulg m y f* [persona] prat. ◆ **capullo** *m* **-1.** [de flor] bud. **-2.** [de gusano] cocoon.

caqui, kaki *adj inv* [color] khaki.

cara *f* **-1.** [rostro, aspecto] face; **~ a** face to face; **de ~** [sol, viento] in one's face. **-2.** [lado] side; GEOM face. **-3.** [de moneda] heads (*U*); **~ o cruz** heads or tails; **echar algo a ~ o cruz** to toss (a coin) for sthg. **-4.** *fam* [osadía] cheek; **tener (mucha) ~, tener la ~ muy dura** to have a cheek. **-5.** *loc*: **de ~ a** with a view to; **echar en ~ algo a alguien** to reproach sb for sthg; **romper** O **partir la ~ a alguien** to smash sb's face in; **verse las ~s** [pelearse] to have it out; [enfrentarse] to fight it out.

carabina *f* **-1.** [arma] carbine, rifle. **-2.** *fam fig* [mujer] chaperone.

Caracas Caracas.

caracol *m* **-1.** [animal] snail. **-2.** [concha] shell. **-3.** [rizo] curl.

caracola *f* conch.

carácter (*pl* **caracteres**) *m* character; **tener buen/mal ~** to be good-natured/bad-tempered; **una reunión de ~ privado/oficial** a private/official meeting; **caracteres de imprenta** typeface (*sg*).

característico, -ca *adj* characteristic. ◆ **característica** *f* characteristic.

caracterización *f* **-1.** [gen] characterization. **-2.** [maquillaje] make-up.

caracterizar *vt* **-1.** [definir] to characterize. **-2.** [representar] to portray. **-3.** [maquillar] to make up. ◆ **caracterizarse por** *vpr* to be characterized by.

caradura *fam adj* cheeky.

carajillo *m* coffee with a dash of liqueur.

carajo *mfam interj*: **¡~!** damn it!

caramba *interj*: **¡~!** [sorpresa] good heavens!; [enfado] for heaven's sake!

carambola *f* cannon (*in billiards*). ◆ **carambolas** *interj Amer*: **¡~s!** good heavens!

caramelo *m* **-1.** [golosina] sweet. **-2.** [azúcar fundido] caramel.

cárate = **kárate.**

carátula *f* **-1.** [de libro] front cover; [de disco] sleeve. **-2.** [máscara] mask.

caravana *f* **-1.** [gen] caravan. **-2.** [de coches] tailback. ◆ **caravanas** *fpl Amer* [pendientes] earrings.

caray *interj*: **¡~!** [sorpresa] good heavens!; [enfado] damn it!

carbón *m* [para quemar] coal.

carboncillo *m* charcoal.

carbonilla *f* [ceniza] cinder.

carbonizar *vt* to char, to carbonize.

carbono *m* carbon.

carburador *m* carburettor.

carburante *m* fuel.

carca *fam despec adj* old-fashioned.

carcajada *f* guffaw; **reír a ~s** to roar with laughter.

carcamal *m y f fam despec* old crock.

cárcel *f* prison.

carcelero, -ra *m y f* warder, jailer.

carcoma *f* **-1.** [insecto] woodworm. **-2.** [polvo] wood dust.

carcomer *vt lit & fig* to eat away at.

carcomido, -da *adj* [madera] worm-eaten.

cardar *vt* **-1.** [lana] to card. **-2.** [pelo] to backcomb.

cardenal *m* **-1.** RELIG cardinal. **-2.** [hematoma] bruise.

cardiaco, -ca, cardíaco, -ca *adj* cardiac, heart (*antes de sust*).

cárdigan, cardigán *m* cardigan.

cardinal *adj* cardinal.

cardiólogo, -ga *m y f* cardiologist.

cardo *m* [planta] thistle.

carecer *vi*: **~ de algo** to lack sthg.

carencia *f* [ausencia] lack; [defecto] deficiency.

carente *adj*: ~ **de** lacking (in).

carestía *f* [escasez] scarcity, shortage.

careta *f* -1. [máscara] mask; ~ **antigás** gas mask. -2. *fig* [engaño] front.

carey *m* [material] tortoiseshell.

carga *f* -1. [acción] loading. -2. [cargamento - de avión, barco] cargo; [- de tren] freight. -3. [peso] load. -4. *fig* [sufrimiento] burden. -5. [ataque, explosivo] charge; **volver a la** ~ *fig* to persist. -6. [de batería, condensador] charge. -7. [para mechero, bolígrafo] refill. -8. [impuesto] tax.

cargado, -da *adj* -1. [abarrotado]: ~ **(de)** loaded (with). -2. [arma] loaded. -3. [bebida] strong. -4. [bochornoso - habitación] stuffy; [- tiempo] sultry, close; [- cielo] overcast.

cargador *m* [de arma] chamber.

cargamento *m* cargo.

cargante *adj fam fig* annoying.

cargar ◇ *vt* -1. [gen] to load; [pluma, mechero] to refill. -2. [peso encima] to throw over one's shoulder. -3. ELECTR to charge. -4. *fig* [responsabilidad, tarea] to give, to lay upon. -5. [producir pesadez - suj: humo] to make stuffy; [- suj: comida] to bloat. -6. [gravar]: ~ **un impuesto a algo/alguien** to tax sthg/sb. -7. [importe, factura, deuda]: ~ **algo (a)** to charge sthg (to). ◇ *vi* [atacar]: ~ **(contra)** to charge. ◆ **cargar con** *vi* -1. [paquete etc] to carry away. -2. *fig* [coste, responsabilidad] to bear; [consecuencias] to accept; [culpa] to bear. ◆ **cargarse** *vpr* -1. *fam* [romper] to break. -2. *fam* [matar - persona] to bump off; [- animal] to kill. -3. [por el humo] to get stuffy.

cargo *m* -1. [gen, ECON & DER] charge; **correr a** ~ **de** to be borne by; **hacerse** ~ **de** [asumir el control de] to take charge of; [ocuparse de] to take care of; [comprender] to understand. -2. [empleo] post.

cargosear *vt Amer* to annoy, to pester.

carguero *m* cargo boat.

Caribe *m*: **el (mar)** ~ the Caribbean (Sea).

caribeño, -ña *adj* Caribbean.

caricatura *f* caricature.

caricia *f* caress; [a perro, gato etc] stroke.

caridad *f* charity.

caries *f inv* tooth decay.

cariño *m* -1. [afecto] affection; **tomar** ~ **a** to grow fond of. -2. [cuidado] loving care. -3. [apelativo] love.

cariñoso, -sa *adj* affectionate.

carisma *m* charisma.

carismático, -ca *adj* charismatic.

Cáritas *f charitable organization run by the Catholic Church.*

caritativo, -va *adj* charitable.

cariz *m* look, appearance; **tomar mal/buen** ~ to take a turn for the worse/better.

carmesí (*pl* **carmesíes**) *adj & m* crimson.

carmín ◇ *adj* [color] carmine. ◇ *m* -1. [color] carmine. -2. [lápiz de labios] lipstick.

carnada *f lit & fig* bait.

carnal *adj* -1. [de la carne] carnal. -2. [parientes] first (*antes de sust*).

carnaval *m* carnival.

carnaza *f lit & fig* bait.

carne *f* -1. [de persona, fruta] flesh; **en** ~ **viva** raw; **ser de** ~ **y hueso** *fig* to be human. -2. [alimento] meat; ~ **de cerdo** pork; ~ **de cordero** lamb; ~ **picada** mince; ~ **de ternera** veal; ~ **de vaca** beef. ◆ **carne de gallina** *f* gooseflesh.

carné (*pl* **carnés**), **carnet** (*pl* **carnets**) *m* [documento] card; ~ **de conducir** driving licence; ~ **de identidad** identity card.

carnicería *f* -1. [tienda] butcher's. -2. *fig* [masacre] carnage (*U*).

carnicero, -ra *m y f lit & fig* [persona] butcher.

carnívoro, -ra *adj* carnivorous. ◆ **carnívoro** *m* carnivore.

carnoso, -sa *adj* fleshy; [labios] full.

caro, -ra *adj* [precio] expensive. ◆ **caro** *adv*: **costar** ~ to be expensive; **vender** ~ **algo** to sell sthg at a high price; *fig* not to give sthg up easily; **pagar** ~ **algo** *fig* to pay dearly for sthg.

carozo *m Amer* stone (*of fruit*).

carpa *f* -1. [pez] carp. -2. [de circo] big top; [para fiestas etc] marquee.

carpeta *f* file, folder.

carpintería *f* -1. [arte] carpentry; [de puertas y ventanas] joinery. -2. [taller] carpenter's/joiner's shop.

carpintero, -ra *m y f* [carpenter; [de puertas y ventanas] joiner.

carraca *f* [instrumento] rattle.

carraspear *vi* [toser] to clear one's throat.

carraspera *f* hoarseness.

carrera f -1. [acción de correr] run, running (U). -2. DEP & fig race; ~ **armamentística** O **de armamentos** arms race; ~ **de coches** motor race; ~ **de obstáculos** steeplechase. -3. [trayecto] route. -4. [de taxi] ride. -5. [estudios] university course; **hacer la** ~ **de derecho** to study law (at university). -6. [profesión] career. -7. [en medias] ladder.

carreta f cart.

carrete m -1. [de hilo] bobbin, reel; [de alambre] coil. -2. FOT roll (of film). -3. [para pescar] reel. -4. [de máquina de escribir] spool.

carretera f road; ~ **de circunvalación** ring road; ~ **comarcal** ≃ B road Br; ~ **de cuota** Amer toll road; ~ **nacional** ≃ A road Br, state highway Am.

carretilla f wheelbarrow.

carril m -1. [de carretera] lane; ~ **bus** bus lane. -2. [de vía de tren] rail.

carrillo m cheek; **comer a dos ~s** fig to cram one's face with food.

carrito m trolley.

carro m -1. [vehículo] cart; ~ **de combate** MIL tank. -2. [de máquina de escribir] carriage. -3. Amer [coche] car; ~ **comedor** dining car.

carrocería f bodywork Br, body.

carromato m [carro] wagon.

carroña f carrion.

carroza f [coche] carriage.

carruaje m carriage.

carrusel m [tiovivo] carousel.

carta f -1. [escrito] letter; **echar una** ~ to post a letter; ~ **de recomendación** reference (letter). -2. [naipe] (playing) card; **echar las ~s a alguien** to tell sb's fortune (with cards). -3. [menú] menu. -4. [mapa] map; [documento] chart. -5. [documento] charter; ~ **verde** green card. -6. loc: **jugarse todo a una** ~ to put all one's eggs in one basket. ◆ **carta blanca** f carte blanche. ◆ **carta de ajuste** f test card.

cartabón m set square.

cartapacio m [carpeta] folder.

cartearse vpr to correspond.

cartel m [anuncio] poster; "**prohibido fijar ~es**" "billposters will be prosecuted".

cártel m cartel.

cartelera f -1. [tablón] hoarding, billboard. -2. PRENS entertainments page; **estar en** ~ to be showing; **lleva un año en** ~ it's been running for a year.

cárter m AUTOM housing.

cartera f -1. [para dinero] wallet. -2. [para documentos] briefcase; [sin asa] portfolio; [de colegial] satchel. -3. COM, FIN & POLÍT portfolio; [pedidos atrasados] backlog. -4. Amer [bolso] bag.

carterista m y f pickpocket.

cartero, -ra m y f postman (f postwoman).

cartílago m cartilage.

cartilla f -1. [documento] book; ~ **(de ahorros)** savings book. -2. [para aprender a leer] primer.

cartón m -1. [material] cardboard; ~ **piedra** papier mâché. -2. [de cigarrillos] carton.

cartucho m [de arma] cartridge.

cartujo, -ja adj Carthusian.

cartulina f card.

casa f -1. [edificio] house; ~ **adosada** semi-detached house; ~ **de campo** country house; ~ **unifamiliar** house (usually detached) on an estate; **echar** O **tirar la** ~ **por la ventana** to spare no expense; **ser de andar por** ~ [sencillo] to be simple O basic. -2. [hogar] home; **en** ~ at home; **ir a** ~ to go home; **pásate por mi** ~ come round to my place. -3. [empresa] company; ~ **de huéspedes** guesthouse. -4. [organismo] ~ **Consistorial** town hall; ~ **de socorro** first-aid post.

casaca f frock coat.

casado, -da adj: ~ **(con)** married (to).

casamiento m wedding, marriage.

casar ◇ vt -1. [en matrimonio] to marry. -2. [unir] to fit together. ◇ vi to match. ◆ **casarse** vpr: ~**se (con)** to get married (to).

cascabel m (small) bell.

cascada f [de agua] waterfall.

cascado, -da adj -1. fam [estropeado] bust; [persona, ropa] worn-out. -2. [ronco] rasping.

cascanueces m inv nutcracker.

cascar vt -1. [romper] to crack. -2. fam [pegar] to thump. ◆ **cascarse** vpr [romperse] to crack.

cáscara f -1. [de almendra, huevo etc] shell. -2. [de limón, naranja] skin, peel.

cascarilla f husk.

cascarón m eggshell.

cascarrabias m y f inv grouch.

casco m -1. [para la cabeza] helmet; [de motorista] crash helmet. -2. [de barco] hull. -3. [de ciudad]: ~ **antiguo** old (part of) town; ~ **urbano** city centre. -4. [de caballo] hoof. -5. [envase] empty bottle.

caserío *m* [casa de campo] country house.

casero, -ra ◇ *adj* **-1.** [de casa - comida] home-made; [- trabajos] **domestic**; [- reunión, velada] **at home**; [de la familia] family (*antes de sust*). **-2.** [hogareño] home-loving. ◇ *m y f* [propietario] landlord (*f* landlady).

caserón *m* large, rambling house.

caseta *f* **-1.** [casa pequeña] hut. **-2.** [en la playa] bathing hut. **-3.** [de feria] stall, booth. **-4.** [para perro] kennel.

casete, cassette [ka'sete] ◇ *f* [cinta] cassette. ◇ *m* [magnetófono] cassette recorder.

casi *adv* almost; ~ **me muero** I almost ○ nearly died; ~ **no dormí** I hardly slept at all; ~, ~ almost, just about; ~ **nunca** hardly ever.

casilla *f* **-1.** [de caja, armario] compartment; [para cartas] pigeonhole. **-2.** [en un impreso] box. **-3.** [de ajedrez etc] square.

casillero *m* **-1.** [mueble] set of pigeonholes. **-2.** [casilla] pigeonhole.

casino *m* [para jugar] casino.

caso *m* **-1.** [gen, DER & GRAM] case; **el ~ es que** the fact is (that); **en el mejor/peor de los ~s** at best/worst. **-2.** [ocasión] occasion; **en ~ de** in the event of; **en ~ de que** if; **(en) ~ de que venga** should she come; **en cualquier** ○ **todo ~** in any event ○ case. **-3.** *loc:* **hacer ~ a** to pay attention to; **no hacer** ○ **venir al ~** to be irrelevant.

caspa *f* dandruff.

casquete *m* [gorro] skullcap.

casquillo *m* **-1.** [de bala] case. **-2.** [de lámpara] socket, lampholder.

cassette = casete.

casta *f* **-1.** [linaje] lineage. **-2.** [especie, calidad] breed. **-3.** [en la India] caste.

castaña → castaño.

castañetear *vi* [dientes] to chatter.

castaño, -ña *adj* [color] chestnut. ◆ **castaño** *m* **-1.** [color] chestnut. **-2.** [árbol] chestnut (tree). ◆ **castaña** *f* [fruto] chestnut.

castañuela *f* castanet.

castellano, -na *adj, m y f* Castilian. ◆ **castellano** *m* [lengua] (Castilian) Spanish.

castidad *f* chastity.

castigador, -ra *fam adj* seductive.

castigar *vt* **-1.** [imponer castigo] to punish. **-2.** DEP to penalize. **-3.** [maltratar] to damage.

castigo *m* **-1.** [sanción] punishment. **-2.** [sufrimiento] suffering (*U*); [daño] damage (*U*). **-3.** DEP penalty.

Castilla-La Mancha Castile and La Mancha.

Castilla-León Castile and León.

castillo *m* [edificio] castle.

castizo, -za *adj* pure; [autor] purist.

casto, -ta *adj* chaste.

castor *m* beaver.

castrar *vt* [animal, persona] to castrate; [gato] to doctor.

castrense *adj* military.

casual *adj* chance, accidental.

casualidad *f* coincidence; **dio la ~ de que ...** it so happened that ...; **por ~** by chance; **¡qué ~!** what a coincidence!

casualmente *adv* by chance.

casulla *f* chasuble.

cataclismo *m* cataclysm.

catacumbas *fpl* catacombs.

catador, -ra *m y f* taster.

catalán, -ana *adj, m y f* Catalan, Catalonian. ◆ **catalán** *m* [lengua] Catalan.

catalejo *m* telescope.

catalizador, -ra *adj fig* [impulsor] catalysing (*antes de sust*). ◆ **catalizador** *m* **-1.** QUÍM & *fig* catalyst. **-2.** AUTOM catalytic converter.

catalogar *vt* **-1.** [en catálogo] to catalogue. **-2.** [clasificar]: ~ **a alguien (de)** to class sb (as).

catálogo *m* catalogue.

Cataluña Catalonia.

catamarán *m* catamaran.

cataplasma *f* MED poultice.

catapulta *f* catapult.

catar *vt* to taste.

catarata *f* **-1.** [de agua] waterfall. **-2.** (*gen pl*) MED cataract.

catarro *m* cold.

catastro *m* land registry.

catástrofe *f* catastrophe; [accidente de avión, tren etc] disaster.

catastrófico, -ca *adj* catastrophic.

catch [katʃ] *m* DEP all-in wrestling.

catchup ['ketʃup], **ketchup** *m inv* ketchup.

catear *vt fam* to fail.

catecismo *m* catechism.

cátedra *f* **-1.** [cargo - en universidad] chair; [- en instituto] post of head of department. **-2.** [departamento] department.

catedral *f* cathedral.

catedrático, -ca *m y f* [de universidad] professor; [de instituto] head of department.

categoría *f* -1. [gen] category. -2. [posición social] standing; **de ~** important. -3. [calidad] quality; **de (primera) ~** first-class.

categórico, -ca *adj* categorical.

catequesis *f inv* catechesis.

cateto, -ta *despec m y f* country bumpkin.

catolicismo *m* Catholicism.

católico, -ca ◇ *adj* Catholic. ◇ *m y f* Catholic.

catorce *núm* fourteen; *ver también* **seis**.

catorceavo, -va, catorzavo, -va *núm* fourteenth.

catre *m* [cama] camp bed.

catrín, -trina *m y f Amer fam* toff.

cauce *m* -1. AGR & *fig* channel. -2. [de río] river-bed.

caucho *m* [sustancia] rubber.

caudaloso, -sa *adj* -1. [río] with a large flow. -2. [persona] wealthy, rich.

caudillo *m* [en la guerra] leader, head.

causa *f* -1. [origen, ideal] cause. -2. [razón] reason; **a ~ de** because of. -3. DER case.

causalidad *f* causality.

causante *adj*: **la razón ~** the cause.

causar *vt* [gen] to cause; [impresión] to make; [placer] to give.

cáustico, -ca *adj lit* & *fig* caustic.

cautela *f* caution, cautiousness; **con ~** cautiously.

cauteloso, -sa *adj* cautious, careful.

cautivador, -ra ◇ *adj* captivating, enchanting. ◇ *m y f* charmer.

cautivar *vt* -1. [apresar] to capture. -2. [seducir] to captivate, to enchant.

cautiverio *m*, **cautividad** *f* captivity.

cautivo, -va *adj, m y f* captive.

cauto, -ta *adj* cautious, careful.

cava ◇ *m* [bebida] *Spanish champagne-type wine*. ◇ *f* [bodega] wine cellar.

cavar *vt & vi* [gen] to dig; [con azada] to hoe.

caverna *f* cave; [más grande] cavern.

cavernícola *m y f* caveman (*f* cavewoman).

caviar (*pl* **caviares**) *m* caviar.

cavidad *f* cavity; [formada con las manos] cup.

cavilar *vi* to think deeply, to ponder.

cayado *m* [de pastor] crook.

cayera *etc* → **caer**.

caza ◇ *f* -1. [acción de cazar] hunting; **salir** O **ir de ~** to go hunting. -2. [animales, carne] game. ◇ *m* fighter (plane).

cazabombardero *m* fighter-bomber.

cazador, -ra *m y f* [persona] hunter. ◆ **cazadora** *f* [prenda] bomber jacket.

cazalla *f* [bebida] aniseed-flavoured spirit.

cazar *vt* -1. [animales etc] to hunt. -2. *fig* [pillar, atrapar] to catch; [en matrimonio] to trap.

cazo *m* saucepan.

cazoleta *f* -1. [recipiente] pot. -2. [de pipa] bowl.

cazuela *f* -1. [recipiente] pot; [de barro] earthenware pot; [para el horno] casserole (dish). -2. [guiso] casserole, stew; **a la ~** casseroled.

cazurro, -rra *adj* [bruto] stupid.

c/c (*abrev de* **cuenta corriente**) a/c.

CC OO (*abrev de* **Comisiones Obreras**) *fpl Spanish communist-inspired trade union.*

CD *m* -1. (*abrev de* **club deportivo**) sports club; [en fútbol] FC. -2. (*abrev de* **compact disc**) CD.

CDS (*abrev de* **Centro Democrático y Social**) *m Spanish political party at the centre of the political spectrum.*

CE *f* (*abrev de* **Comunidad Europea**) EC.

cebada *f* barley.

cebar *vt* -1. [sobrealimentar] to fatten (up). -2. [máquina, arma] to prime. -3. [anzuelo] to bait. ◆ **cebarse en** *vpr* to take it out on.

cebo *m* -1. [para cazar] bait. -2. *fig* [para atraer] incentive.

cebolla *f* onion.

cebolleta *f* -1. BOT spring onion. -2. [en vinagre] pickled onion; [muy pequeña] silverskin onion.

cebollino *m* -1. BOT chive; [cebolleta] spring onion. -2. *fam* [necio] idiot.

cebra *f* zebra.

cecear *vi* to lisp.

ceceo *m* lisp.

cecina *f* dried, salted meat.

cedazo *m* sieve.

ceder ◇ *vt* -1. [traspasar, transferir] to hand over. -2. [conceder] to give up. ◇ *vi* -1. [venirse abajo] to give way. -2. [destensarse] to give, to become loose. -3. [disminuir] to abate. -4. [rendirse] to give up; **~ a** to give in to; **~ en** to give up on.

cedro *m* cedar.

cédula *f* document; **~ (de identidad)** *Amer* identity card.

CEE (*abrev de* **Comunidad Económica Europea**) *f* EEC.

cegar *vt* **-1.** [gen] to blind. **-2.** [tapar - ventana] to block off; [- tubo] to block up. ◆ **cegarse** *vpr lit* & *fig* to be blinded.

cegato, -ta *fam adj* short-sighted.

ceguera *m lit* & *fig* blindness.

CEI (*abrev de* **Confederación de Estados Independientes**) *f* CIS.

ceja *f* ANAT eyebrow; **se le metió entre ~ y ~** *fam* he got it into his head.

cejar *vi*: **~ en** to give up on.

celda *f* cell.

celebración *f* **-1.** [festejo] celebration. **-2.** [realización] holding.

celebrar *vt* **-1.** [festejar] to celebrate. **-2.** [llevar a cabo] to hold; [oficio religioso] to celebrate. **-3.** [alegrarse de] to be delighted with. **-4.** [alabar] to praise. ◆ **celebrarse** *vpr* **-1.** [festejarse] to be celebrated; **esa fiesta se celebra el 24 de Julio** that festivity falls on 24th July. **-2.** [llevarse a cabo] to take place.

célebre *adj* famous, celebrated.

celebridad *f* **-1.** [fama] fame. **-2.** [persona famosa] celebrity.

celeridad *f* speed.

celeste *adj* [del cielo] celestial, heavenly.

celestial *adj* celestial, heavenly.

celestina *f* lovers' go-between.

celibato *m* celibacy.

célibe *adj, m y f* celibate.

celo *m* **-1.** [esmero] zeal, keenness. **-2.** [devoción] devotion. **-3.** [de animal] heat; **en ~** on heat, in season. **-4.** [cinta adhesiva] Sellotape®. ◆ **celos** *mpl* jealousy (*U*); **dar ~s a alguien** to make sb jealous; **tener ~s de alguien** to be jealous of sb.

celofán *m* cellophane.

celosía *f* lattice window, jalousie.

celoso, -sa *adj* **-1.** [con celos] jealous. **-2.** [cumplidor] keen, eager.

celta ◇ *adj* Celtic. ◇ *m y f* [persona] Celt. ◇ *m* [lengua] Celtic.

céltico, -ca *adj* Celtic.

célula *f* cell. ◆ **célula fotoeléctrica** *f* photoelectric cell, electric eye.

celulitis *f inv* cellulitis.

celulosa *f* cellulose.

cementerio *m* **-1.** [de muertos] cemetery, graveyard. **-2.** [de cosas inutilizables] dump; **~ de automóviles** O **coches** scrapyard.

cemento *m* [gen] cement; [hormigón]

concrete; **~ armado** reinforced concrete.

cena *f* dinner, evening meal; **dar una ~** to give a dinner party.

cenagal *m* bog, marsh.

cenagoso, -sa *adj* muddy, boggy.

cenar ◇ *vt* to have for dinner. ◇ *vi* to have dinner.

cencerro *m* cowbell; **estar como un ~** *fam fig* to be as mad as a hatter.

cenefa *f* border.

cenicero *m* ashtray.

cenit = **zenit**.

cenizo, -za *adj* ashen, ash-grey. ◆ **cenizo** *m* **-1.** [mala suerte] bad luck. **-2.** [gafe] jinx. ◆ **ceniza** *f* ash. ◆ **cenizas** *fpl* [de cadáver] ashes.

censar *vt* to take a census of.

censo *m* **-1.** [padrón] census; **~ electoral** electoral roll. **-2.** [tributo] tax.

censor, -ra *m y f* [funcionario] censor.

censura *f* **-1.** [prohibición] censorship. **-2.** [organismo] censors (*pl*). **-3.** [reprobación] censure, severe criticism.

censurar *vt* **-1.** [prohibir] to censor. **-2.** [reprobar] to censure.

centavo, -va *núm* hundredth; **la centava parte** a hundredth.

centella *f* **-1.** [rayo] flash. **-2.** [chispa] spark.

centellear *vi* to sparkle; [estrella] to twinkle.

centelleo *m* sparkle, sparkling (*U*); [de estrella] twinkle, twinkling (*U*).

centena *f* hundred; **una ~ de** a hundred.

centenar *m* hundred; **un ~ de** a hundred.

centenario, -ria *adj* [persona] in one's hundreds; [cifra] three-figure (*antes de sust*). ◆ **centenario** *m* centenary; **quinto ~** five hundredth anniversary.

centeno *m* rye.

centésimo, -ma *núm* hundredth.

centígrado, -da *adj* Centigrade.

centigramo *m* centigram.

centilitro *m* centilitre.

centímetro *m* **-1.** [medida] centimetre. **-2.** [cinta] measuring tape.

céntimo *m* [moneda] cent.

centinela *m* sentry.

centollo *m* spider crab.

centrado, -da *adj* **-1.** [basado]: **~ en** based on. **-2.** [equilibrado] stable, steady. **-3.** [rueda, cuadro etc] centred.

central ◇ *adj* central. ◇ *f* **-1.** [oficina] headquarters, head office; [de correos, comunicaciones] main office; ~ **telefónica** telephone exchange. **-2.** [de energía] power station; ~ **nuclear** nuclear power station.

centralista *adj, m y f* centralist.

centralita *f* switchboard.

centralización *f* centralization.

centralizar *vt* to centralize.

centrar *vt* **-1.** [gen & DEP] to centre. **-2.** [arma] to aim. **-3.** [persona] to steady. **-4.** [atención, interés] to be the centre of. ◆ **centrarse** *vpr* **-1.** [concentrarse]: ~**se en** to concentrate O focus on. **-2.** [equilibrarse] to find one's feet.

céntrico, -ca *adj* central.

centrifugadora *f* [para secar ropa] spin-dryer.

centrifugar *vt* [ropa] to spin-dry.

centrista *adj* centre (*antes de sust*).

centro *m* **-1.** [gen] centre; **ser de ~** PO-LÍT to be at the centre of the political spectrum; ~ **de cálculo** computer centre; ~ **de planificación familiar** family planning clinic; ~ **social** community centre. **-2.** [de ciudad] town centre; **me voy al ~** I'm going to town. ◆ **centro comercial** *m* shopping centre. ◆ **centro de mesa** *m* centrepiece.

centrocampista *m y f* DEP midfielder.

ceñir *vt* **-1.** [apretar] to be tight on. **-2.** [abrazar] to embrace. ◆ **ceñirse** *vpr* **-1.** [apretarse] to tighten. **-2.** [limitarse]: ~**se a** to keep O stick to.

ceño *m* frown, scowl; **fruncir el ~** to frown, to knit one's brow.

CEOE (*abrev de* **Confederación Española de Organizaciones Empresariales**) *f* Spanish employers' organization, ≈ CBI Br.

cepa *f lit & fig* stock.

cepillar *vt* **-1.** [gen] to brush. **-2.** [madera] to plane.

cepillo *m* **-1.** [para limpiar] brush; ~ **de dientes** toothbrush. **-2.** [de carpintero] plane.

cepo *m* **-1.** [para cazar] trap. **-2.** [para vehículos] wheel clamp. **-3.** [para sujetar] clamp.

cera *f* [gen] wax; [de abeja] beeswax; ~ **depilatoria** hair-removing wax.

cerámica *f* **-1.** [arte] ceramics (*U*), pottery. **-2.** [objeto] piece of pottery.

ceramista *m y f* potter.

cerca ◇ *f* [valla] fence. ◇ *adv* near, close; **por aquí ~** nearby; **de ~** [examinar etc] closely; [afectar, vivir] deeply. ◆ **cerca de** *loc prep* **-1.** [en el espacio] near, close to. **-2.** [aproximadamente] nearly, about.

cercado *m* **-1.** [valla] fence. **-2.** [lugar] enclosure.

cercanía *f* [cualidad] nearness. ◆ **cercanías** *fpl* [lugar] outskirts, suburbs.

cercano, -na *adj* **-1.** [pueblo, lugar] nearby. **-2.** [tiempo] near. **-3.** [pariente, fuente de información]: ~ **a** close (to).

cercar *vt* **-1.** [vallar] to fence (off). **-2.** [rodear, acorralar] to surround.

cerciorar *vt* to assure; ~**se (de)** to make sure (of).

cerco *m* **-1.** [gen] circle, ring. **-2.** [de puerta, ventana] frame. **-3.** [asedio] siege.

cerdo, -da *m y f* **-1.** [animal] pig (*f* sow). **-2.** *fam fig* [persona] pig, swine. ◆ **cerda** *f* [pelo - de cerdo, jabalí] bristle; [- de caballo] horsehair.

cereal *m* cereal; ~**es** (breakfast) cereal (*U*).

cerebro *m* **-1.** [gen] brain. **-2.** *fig* [cabecilla] brains (*sg*). **-3.** *fig* [inteligencia] brains (*pl*).

ceremonia *f* ceremony.

ceremonial *adj & m* ceremonial.

ceremonioso, -sa *adj* ceremonious.

cereza *f* cherry.

cerezo *m* [árbol] cherry tree.

cerilla *f* match.

cerillo *m* Amer match.

cerner, cernir *vt* [cribar] to sieve. ◆ **cernerse** *vpr* **-1.** [ave, avión] to hover. **-2.** *fig* [amenaza, peligro] to loom.

cernícalo *m* **-1.** [ave] kestrel. **-2.** *fam* [bruto] brute.

cernir = **cerner**.

cero ◇ *adj inv* zero. ◇ *m* **-1.** [signo] nought, zero; [en fútbol] nil; [en tenis] love. **-2.** [cantidad] nothing. **-3.** FÍS & METEOR zero; **sobre/bajo ~** above/below zero. **-4.** *loc*: **ser un ~ a la izquierda** *fam* [un inútil] to be useless; [un don nadie] to be a nobody; **partir de ~** to start from scratch; *ver también* **seis**.

cerrado, -da *adj* **-1.** [al exterior] closed, shut; [con llave, pestillo etc] locked. **-2.** [tiempo, cielo] overcast; [noche] dark. **-3.** [rodeado] surrounded; [por montañas] walled in. **-4.** [circuito] closed. **-5.** [curva] sharp, tight. **-6.** [vocal] close. **-7.** [acento, deje] broad, thick.

cerradura *f* lock.

cerrajero, -ra *m y f* locksmith.

cerrar ◇ *vt* **-1.** [gen] to close; [puerta, cajón, boca] to shut, to close; [puños] to clench; [con llave, pestillo etc] to lock.

-2. [tienda, negocio - definitivamente] to close down. **-3.** [apagar] to turn off. **-4.** [bloquear - suj: accidente, inundación etc] to block; [- suj: policía etc] to close off. **-5.** [tapar - agujero, hueco] to fill, to block (up); [- bote] to put the lid ○ top on. **-6.** [cercar] to fence (off). **-7.** [cicatrizar] to heal. **-8.** [ir último en] to bring up the rear of. ◇ *vi* to close, to shut; [con llave, pestillo etc] to lock up. ◆ **cerrarse** *vpr* **-1.** [al exterior] to close, to shut. **-2.** [incomunicarse] to clam up; ~**se a** to close one's mind to. **-3.** [herida] to heal, to close up. **-4.** [acto, debate, discusión etc] to (come to a) close.

cerrazón *f* *fig* [obstinación] stubbornness, obstinacy.

cerro *m* hill.

cerrojo *m* bolt; **echar el ~** to bolt the door.

certamen *m* competition, contest.

certero, -ra *adj* **-1.** [tiro] accurate. **-2.** [opinión, respuesta etc] correct.

certeza *f* certainty.

certidumbre *f* certainty.

certificación *f* **-1.** [hecho] certification. **-2.** [documento] certificate.

certificado, -da *adj* [gen] certified; [carta, paquete] registered. ◆ **certificado** *m* certificate; ~ **médico** medical certificate.

certificar *vt* **-1.** [constatar] to certify. **-2.** [en correos] to register.

cerumen *m* earwax.

cervato *m* fawn.

cervecería *f* **-1.** [fábrica] brewery. **-2.** [bar] bar.

cervecero, -ra *m y f* [que hace cerveza] brewer.

cerveza *f* beer; ~ **de barril** draught beer; ~ **negra** stout; ~ **rubia** lager.

cesante *adj* **-1.** [destituido] sacked; [ministro] removed from office. **-2.** *Amer* [parado] unemployed.

cesantear *vt Amer* to make redundant.

cesar ◇ *vt* [destituir] to sack; [ministro] to remove from office. ◇ *vi* [parar]: ~ **(de hacer algo)** to stop ○ cease (doing sthg); **sin** ~ non-stop, incessantly.

cesárea *f* caesarean (section).

cese *m* **-1.** [detención, paro] stopping, ceasing. **-2.** [destitución] sacking; [de ministro] removal from office.

cesión *f* cession, transfer.

césped *m* [hierba] lawn, grass (U).

cesta *f* basket. ◆ **cesta de la compra** *f* *fig* cost of living.

cesto *m* [cesta] (large) basket.

cetro *m* **-1.** [vara] sceptre. **-2.** *fig* [reinado] reign.

cf., cfr. (*abrev de* **confróntese**) cf.

cg (*abrev de* **centigramo**) cg.

ch, Ch *f* ch, Ch.

ch/ *abrev de* **cheque.**

chabacano, -na *adj* vulgar. ◆ **chabacano** *m Amer* apricot.

chabola *f* shack; **barrios de ~s** shanty town (*sg*).

chacal *m* jackal.

chacarero, -ra *m y f Amer* farmer.

chacha *f* maid.

chachachá *m* cha-cha.

cháchara *f* *fam* chatter, nattering; **estar de ~** to have a natter.

chachi *adj inv fam* cool, neat *Am*.

chacra *f Amer* farm.

chafar *vt* **-1.** [aplastar] to flatten. **-2.** *fig* [estropear] to spoil, to ruin. ◆ **chafarse** *vpr* [estropearse] to be ruined.

chaflán *m* [de edificio] corner.

chagra *Amer* ◇ *m y f* peasant, person from the country. ◇ *f* farm.

chal *m* shawl.

chalado, -da *fam adj* crazy, mad.

chalar *vt* to drive round the bend.

chalé (*pl* **chalés**), **chalet** (*pl* **chalets**) *m* [gen] detached house (with garden); [en el campo] cottage; [de alta montaña] chalet.

chaleco *m* waistcoat, vest *Am*; [de punto] tank-top; ~ **salvavidas** life jacket.

chalet = **chalé.**

chamaco, -ca *m y f Amer fam* nipper, lad (*f* lass).

chamarra *f* sheepskin jacket.

chamiza *f* [hierba] thatch.

chamizo *m* **-1.** [leña] half-burnt wood (*U*). **-2.** [casa] thatched hut.

champán, champaña *m* champagne.

champiñón *m* mushroom.

champú (*pl* **champús** ○ **champúes**) *m* shampoo.

chamuscar *vt* to scorch; [cabello, barba, tela] to singe. ◆ **chamuscarse** *vpr* [cabello, barba, tela] to get singed.

chamusquina *f* scorch, scorching (*U*); **me huele a ~** *fam* *fig* it smells a bit fishy to me.

chance *f Amer* opportunity.

chanchada *f Amer* dirty trick.

chancho *m Amer* pig.

chanchullo *m fam* fiddle, racket.

chancla *f* [chancleta] low sandal; [para la playa] flip-flop.

chancleta *f* low sandal; [para la playa] flip-flop.

chándal (*pl* **chandals**), **chandal** (*pl* **chandals**) *m* tracksuit.

changarro *m Amer* small shop.

chanquete *m* tiny transparent fish eaten in Málaga.

chantaje *m* blackmail; **hacer ~ a** to blackmail.

chantajear *vt* to blackmail.

chanza *f* joke.

chao *interj fam*: ¡~! bye!, see you!

chapa *f* **-1.** [lámina - de metal] sheet; [- de madera] board; **de tres ~s** three-ply. **-2.** [tapón] top, cap. **-3.** [insignia] badge. **-4.** [ficha de guardarropa] metal token ○ disc. **-5.** *Amer* [cerradura] lock. ◆ **chapas** *fpl* [juego] *children's game played with bottle tops.*

chapado, -da *adj* [con metal] plated; [con madera] veneered; **~ a la antigua** *fig* stuck in the past, old-fashioned.

chaparro, -rra ◇ *adj* short and squat. ◇ *m y f* [persona] short, squat person.

chaparrón *m* downpour; *fam fig* [gran cantidad] torrent.

chapopote *m Amer* bitumen, pitch.

chapotear *vi* to splash about.

chapucear *vt* to botch (up).

chapucero, -ra ◇ *adj* [trabajo] shoddy; [persona] bungling. ◇ *m y f* bungler.

chapulín *m Amer* grasshopper.

chapurrear, **chapurrar** *vt* to speak badly.

chapuza *f* **-1.** [trabajo mal hecho] botch (job). **-2.** [trabajo ocasional] odd job.

chapuzón *m* dip; **darse un ~** to go for a dip.

chaqué (*pl* **chaqués**) *m* morning coat.

chaqueta *f* jacket; [de punto] cardigan.

chaquetón *m* long jacket.

charanga *f* [banda] brass band.

charca *f* pool, pond.

charco *m* puddle.

charcutería *f* **-1.** [tienda] *shop selling cold cooked meats and cheeses,* ≃ delicatessen. **-2.** [productos] cold cuts (*pl*) and cheese.

charla *f* **-1.** [conversación] chat. **-2.** [conferencia] talk.

charlar *vi* to chat.

charlatán, -ana ◇ *adj* talkative. ◇ *m y f* **-1.** [hablador] chatterbox. **-2.** [mentiroso] trickster, charlatan.

charlotada *f* [payasada] clowning around (*U*).

charlotear *vi* to chat.

charnego, -ga *m y f pejorative term referring to immigrant to Catalonia from another part of Spain.*

charol *m* **-1.** [piel] patent leather. **-2.** *Amer* [bandeja] tray.

charola *f Amer* tray.

chárter *adj inv* charter (*antes de sust*).

chasca *f Amer* mop of hair.

chascar ◇ *vt* **-1.** [lengua] to click. **-2.** [dedos] to snap. ◇ *vi* **-1.** [madera] to crack. **-2.** [lengua] to click.

chasco *m* [decepción] disappointment; **llevarse un ~** to be disappointed.

chasis *m inv* AUTOM chassis.

chasquear ◇ *vt* **-1.** [látigo] to crack. **-2.** [la lengua] to click. ◇ *vi* [madera] to crack.

chasquido *m* [de látigo, madera, hueso] crack; [de lengua, arma] click; [de dedos] snap.

chatarra *f* **-1.** [metal] scrap (metal). **-2.** [objetos, piezas] junk.

chateo *m* pub crawl; **ir de ~** to go out drinking.

chato, -ta ◇ *adj* **-1.** [nariz] snub; [persona] snub-nosed. **-2.** [aplanado] flat. ◇ *m y f fam* [apelativo] love, dear. ◆ **chato** *m* [de vino] small glass of wine.

chau, chaucito *interj Amer fam*: ¡~! see you later!

chauvinista = **chovinista**.

chaval, -la *m y f fam* kid, lad (*f* lass).

chavo *m fam* **-1.** [dinero] **no tener un ~** to be penniless. **-2.** *Amer* [hombre] guy, bloke.

checo, -ca *adj, m y f* Czech. ◆ **checo** *m* [lengua] Czech.

che, ché *interj*: ¡~! hey!

checoslovaco, -ca *adj, m y f* Czechoslovak, Czechoslovakian.

Checoslovaquia Czechoslovakia.

chef [ʃef] (*pl* **chefs**) *m* chef.

chelo, -la *adj Amer* blond (*f* blonde).

chelín, schilling ['ʃilin] *m* shilling.

cheque *m* cheque *Br*, check *Am*; **extender un ~** to make out a cheque; **~ cruzado** ○ **barrado** crossed cheque; **~ (de) gasolina** petrol voucher; **~ nominativo** cheque in favour of a specific person; **~ al portador** cheque payable to the bearer; **~ de viaje** traveller's cheque.

chequear *vt* **-1.** MED: **~ a alguien** to examine sb, to give sb a checkup. **-2.** [comprobar] to check.

chequeo *m* **-1.** MED checkup. **-2.** [comprobación] check, checking (*U*).

chequera f chequebook Br, checkbook Am.

chévere adj Amer fam great, fantastic.

chic adj inv chic.

chica f **-1.** [joven] girl. **-2.** [tratamiento] darling. **-3.** [criada] maid.

chicano, -na adj, m y f Chicano, Mexican-American. ◆**chicano** m [lengua] Chicano.

chicarrón, -ona m y f strapping lad (f strapping lass).

chícharo m Amer pea.

chicharra f ZOOL cicada.

chicharro m [pez] horse mackerel.

chicharrón m [frito] pork crackling. ◆**chicharrones** mpl [embutido] cold processed meat made from pork.

chichón m bump.

chicle m chewing gum.

chiclé, chicler m AUTOM jet.

chico, -ca adj [pequeño] small. ◆**chico** m **-1.** [joven] boy. **-2.** [tratamiento] sonny, mate. **-3.** [recadero] messenger, office-boy.

chicote m Amer whip.

chifla f [silbido] whistle.

chiflado, -da fam adj crazy, mad.

chiflar ◇ vt fam [encantar]: **me chiflan las patatas fritas** I'm mad about chips. ◇ vi [silbar] to whistle.

chiflido m Amer whistling.

chile m chilli.

Chile Chile.

chileno, -na adj, m y f Chilean.

chillar ◇ vi **-1.** [gritar - personas] to scream, to yell; [- aves, monos] to screech; [- cerdo] to squeal; [- ratón] to squeak. **-2.** [chirriar] to screech; [puerta, madera] to creak; [bisagras] to squeak. ◇ vt fam [reñir] to yell at.

chillido m [de persona] scream, yell; [de ave, mono] screech; [de cerdo] squeal; [de ratón] squeak.

chillón, -ona adj **-1.** [voz] piercing. **-2.** [persona] noisy. **-3.** [color] gaudy.

chilpayate, -ta m y f Amer kid.

chimenea f **-1.** [hogar] fireplace. **-2.** [tubo] chimney.

chimpancé m chimpanzee.

china → chino.

China: (la) ~ China.

chinchar vt fam to pester, to bug. ◆**chincharse** vpr fam: **ahora te chinchas** now you can lump it.

chinche ◇ adj fam fig annoying. ◇ f [insecto] bedbug.

chincheta f drawing pin Br, thumbtack Am.

chinchín m [brindis] toast; ¡~! cheers!

chinchón m strong aniseed liquor.

chingar ◇ vt **-1.** fam [molestar] to cheese off. **-2.** mfam [estropear] to bugger up. **-3.** Amer vulg [fornicar con] to fuck. ◇ vi vulg [fornicar] to screw. ◆**chingarse** vpr mfam [beberse] to knock back.

chino, -na adj, m y f Chinese. ◆**chino** m [lengua] Chinese. ◆**china** f [piedra] pebble.

chip (pl **chips**) m INFORM chip.

chipirón m baby squid.

Chipre Cyprus.

chipriota adj, m y f Cypriot.

chiquillo, -lla m y f kid.

chiquito, -ta adj tiny. ◆**chiquito** m [de vino] small glass of wine.

chiribita f [chispa] spark.

chirimbolo m fam thingamajig.

chirimoya f custard apple.

chiringuito m fam [bar] refreshment stall.

chiripa f fam fig fluke; **de** ○ **por** ~ by luck.

chirivía f BOT parsnip.

chirla f small clam.

chirona f fam clink, slammer; **en** ~ in the clink.

chirriar vi [gen] to screech; [puerta, madera] to creak; [bisagra, muelles] to squeak.

chirrido m [gen] screech; [de puerta, madera] creak; [de bisagra, muelles] squeak.

chis = chist.

chisme m **-1.** [cotilleo] rumour, piece of gossip. **-2.** fam [cosa] thingamajig.

chismorrear vi to spread rumours, to gossip.

chismoso, -sa ◇ adj gossipy. ◇ m y f gossip, scandalmonger.

chispa f **-1.** [de fuego, electricidad] spark; **echar** ~s fam to be hopping mad. **-2.** [de lluvia] spot (of rain). **-3.** fig [pizca] bit. **-4.** fig [agudeza] sparkle.

chispear ◇ vi **-1.** [chisporrotear] to spark. **-2.** [relucir] to sparkle. ◇ v impers [llover] to spit (with rain).

chisporrotear vi [fuego, leña] to crackle; [aceite] to splutter; [comida] to sizzle.

chist, chis interj ¡~! ssh!

chistar vi: **me fui sin** ~ I left without a word.

chiste m joke; **contar** ~s to tell jokes; ~ **verde** dirty joke.

chistera f [sombrero] top hat.

chistorra f type of cured pork sausage typical of Aragon and Navarre.

chistoso, -sa adj funny.

chita ◆ **a la chita callando** loc adv fam quietly, on the quiet.

chitón interj ¡~! quiet!

chivar vt fam to tell secretly. ◆ **chivarse** vpr fam: ~se (de/a) [niños] to split (on/to); [delincuentes] to grass (on/to).

chivatazo m fam tip-off; **dar el** ~ to grass.

chivato, -ta m y f fam [delator] grass, informer; [acusica] telltale.

chivo, -va m y f kid, young goat; **ser el** ~ **expiatorio** fig to be the scapegoat.

choc (pl **chocs**), **choque**, **shock** [tʃok] m shock.

chocante adj startling.

chocar ◇ vi **-1.** [colisionar]: ~ (**contra**) to crash (into), to collide (with). **-2.** fig [enfrentarse] to clash. ◇ vt fig [sorprender] to startle.

chochear vi [viejo] to be senile.

chocho, -cha adj **-1.** [viejo] senile. **-2.** fam fig [encariñado] soft, doting.

choclo m Amer corn Br, maize Am.

chocolate m [para comer, beber] chocolate; ~ (**a la taza**) thick drinking chocolate; ~ **blanco** white chocolate; ~ **con leche** milk chocolate.

chocolatina f chocolate bar.

chófer (pl **chóferes**) m y f chauffeur.

chollo m fam [producto, compra] bargain; [trabajo, situación] cushy number.

chomba, chompa f Amer jumper.

chongo m Amer [moño] bun.

chopo m poplar.

choque m **-1.** [impacto] impact; [de coche, avión etc] crash. **-2.** fig [enfrentamiento] clash. **-3.** = **choc**.

chorizar vt fam to nick, to pinch.

chorizo m **-1.** [embutido] highly seasoned pork sausage. **-2.** fam [ladrón] thief.

choro m Amer mussel.

chorrada f mfam rubbish (U); **decir** ~**s** to talk rubbish.

chorrear vi **-1.** [gotear - gota a gota] to drip; [- en un hilo] to trickle. **-2.** [brotar] to spurt (out), to gush (out).

chorro m **-1.** [de líquido - borbotón] jet, spurt; [- hilo] trickle; **salir a** ~**s** to spurt ○ gush out. **-2.** fig [de luz, gente etc] stream; **tiene un** ~ **de dinero** she has loads of money.

choteo m fam joking, kidding; **tomar algo a** ~ to take sth as a joke.

choto, -ta m y f **-1.** [cabrito] kid, young goat. **-2.** [ternero] calf.

chovinista, chauvinista [tʃoßi'nista] ◇ adj chauvinistic. ◇ m y f chauvinist.

choza f hut.

christmas = **crismas**.

chubasco m shower.

chubasquero m raincoat, mac.

chúcaro, -ra adj Amer fam wild.

chuchería f **-1.** [golosina] sweet. **-2.** [objeto] trinket.

chucho m fam mutt, dog.

chufa f [tubérculo] tiger nut.

chulear fam vi [fanfarronear]: ~ (**de**) to be cocky (about).

chulería f [valentonería] cockiness.

chuleta f **-1.** [de carne] chop. **-2.** [en exámenes] crib note.

chulo, -la ◇ adj **-1.** [descarado] cocky; **ponerse** ~ to get cocky. **-2.** fam [bonito] lovely. ◇ m y f [descarado] cocky person. ◆ **chulo** m [proxeneta] pimp.

chumbera f prickly pear.

chumbo → **higo**.

chungo, -ga fam adj [persona] horrible, nasty; [cosa] lousy. ◆ **chunga** f: **tomarse algo a** ~ to take sth as a joke.

chupa f fam coat.

chupachup® (pl **chupachups**) m lollipop.

chupado, -da adj **-1.** [delgado] skinny. **-2.** fam [fácil]: **estar** ~ to be dead easy ○ a piece of cake. ◆ **chupada** f [gen] suck; [fumando] puff, drag.

chupar vt **-1.** [succionar] to suck; [fumando] to puff at. **-2.** [absorber] to soak up. **-3.** [quitar]: ~**le algo a alguien** to milk sb for sth.

chupe m Amer stew.

chupete m dummy Br, pacifier Am.

chupi adj fam great, brill.

chupón, -ona m y f fam [gorrón] sponger, cadger. ◆ **chupón** m Amer [chupete] dummy Br, pacifier Am.

churrería f shop selling "churros".

churro m [para comer] dough formed into sticks or rings and fried in oil.

churrusco m piece of burnt toast.

churumbel m fam kid.

chusco, -ca adj funny. ◆ **chusco** m fam crust of stale bread.

chusma f rabble, mob.

chut (pl **chuts**) m kick.

chutar vi [lanzar] to shoot. ◆ **chutarse** vpr mfam to shoot up.

chute m mfam fix.

CIA (*abrev de* **Central Intelligence Agency**) *f* CIA.

cía., **Cía.** (*abrev de* **compañía**) Co.

cianuro *m* cyanide.

ciático, -ca *adj* sciatic. ◆ **ciática** *f* sciatica.

cicatero, -ra *adj* stingy, mean.

cicatriz *f* lit & *fig* scar.

cicatrizar ◇ *vi* to heal (up). ◇ *vt fig* to heal.

cicerone *m y f* guide.

cíclico, -ca *adj* cyclical.

ciclismo *m* cycling.

ciclista *m y f* cyclist.

ciclo *m* **-1.** [gen] cycle. **-2.** [de conferencias, actos] series.

ciclocrós *m* cyclo-cross.

ciclomotor *m* moped.

ciclón *m* cyclone.

cicuta *f* hemlock.

ciego, -ga ◇ *adj* **-1.** [gen] blind; **a ciegas** *lit* & *fig* blindly. **-2.** *fig* [enloquecido]: ~ **(de)** blinded (by). **-3.** [pozo, tubería] blocked (up). ◇ *m y f* [invidente] blind person; **los** ~**s** the blind.

cielo *m* **-1.** [gen] sky. **-2.** RELIG heaven. **-3.** [nombre cariñoso] my love, my dear. **-4.** *loc*: **como llovido del** ~ [inesperadamente] out of the blue; [oportunamente] at just the right moment; **ser un** ~ to be an angel. ◆ **cielos** *interj*: ¡~**s!** good heavens!

ciempiés *m inv* centipede.

cien = **ciento**.

ciénaga *f* marsh, bog.

ciencia *f* [gen] science. ◆ **ciencias** *fpl* EDUC science (*U*). ◆ **ciencia ficción** *f* science fiction. ◆ **a ciencia cierta** *loc adv* for certain.

cieno *m* mud, sludge.

científico, -ca ◇ *adj* scientific. ◇ *m y f* scientist.

ciento, cien *núm* a ○ one hundred; ~ **cincuenta** a ○ one hundred and fifty; **cien mil** a ○ one hundred thousand; ~**s de** hundreds of; **por** ~ per cent; ~ **por** ~, **cien por cien** a hundred per cent.

cierne ◆ **en ciernes** *loc adv*: **estar en** ~**s** to be in its infancy; **una campeona en** ~**s** a budding champion.

cierre *m* **-1.** [gen] closing, shutting; [de fábrica] shutdown; RADIO & TV closedown; ~ **patronal** lockout. **-2.** [mecanismo] fastener; ~ **metálico** [de tienda etc] metal shutter; ~ **relámpago** *Amer* zip.

cierto, -ta *adj* **-1.** [verdadero] true; **estar en lo** ~ to be right; **lo** ~ **es que** ... the fact is that .... **-2.** [seguro] certain, definite. **-3.** [algún] certain; ~ **hombre** a certain man; **en cierta ocasión** once, on one occasion. ◆ **cierto** *adv* right, certainly. ◆ **por cierto** *loc adv* by the way.

ciervo, -va *m y f* deer, stag (*f* hind).

CIF (*abrev de* **código de identificación fiscal**) *m* tax code.

cifra *f* [gen] figure.

cifrar *vt* **-1.** [codificar] to code. **-2.** *fig* [centrar] to concentrate, to centre. ◆ **cifrarse en** *vpr* to amount to.

cigala *f* Dublin Bay prawn.

cigarra *f* cicada.

cigarrillo *m* cigarette.

cigarro *m* **-1.** [habano] cigar. **-2.** [cigarrillo] cigarette.

cigüeña *f* stork.

cigüeñal *m* crankshaft.

cilindrada *f* cylinder capacity.

cilíndrico, -ca *adj* cylindrical.

cilindro *m* [gen] cylinder; [de imprenta] roller.

cima *f* **-1.** [punta - de montaña] peak, summit; [- de árbol] top. **-2.** *fig* [apogeo] peak, high point.

cimbrear *vt* **-1.** [vara] to waggle. **-2.** [caderas] to sway.

cimentar *vt* **-1.** [edificio] to lay the foundations of; [ciudad] to found, to build. **-2.** *fig* [idea, paz, fama] to cement.

cimiento *m* (*gen pl*) CONSTR foundation; **echar los** ~**s** *lit* & *fig* to lay the foundations.

cinc, zinc *m* zinc.

cincel *m* chisel.

cincelar *vt* to chisel.

cincha *f* girth.

cinco *núm* five; ¡**choca esos** ~! *fig* put it there!; *ver también* **seis**.

cincuenta *núm* fifty; **los (años)** ~ the fifties; *ver también* **seis**.

cincuentón, -ona *m y f* fifty-year-old.

cine *m* cinema; **hacer** ~ to make films.

cineasta *m y f* film maker ○ director.

cineclub *m* **-1.** [asociación] film society. **-2.** [sala] club cinema.

cinéfilo, -la *m y f* film buff.

cinematografía *f* cinematography.

cinematográfico, -ca *adj* film (*antes de sust*).

cinematógrafo *m* [local] cinema.

cínico, -ca ◇ *adj* cynical. ◇ *m y f* cynic.

cinismo *m* cynicism.
cinta *f* -1. [tira - de plástico, papel] strip, band; [- de tela] ribbon; ~ **adhesiva** O **autoadhesiva** adhesive O sticky tape; ~ **métrica** tape measure. -2. [de imagen, sonido, ordenadores] tape; ~ **magnetofónica** recording tape; ~ **de vídeo** videotape. -3. [mecanismo] belt; ~ **transportadora** conveyor belt. -4. [película] film.
cintura *f* waist.
cinturilla *f* waistband.
cinturón *m* -1. [cinto] belt. -2. AUTOM ring road. -3. [cordón] cordon. ◆ **cinturón de seguridad** *m* seat O safety belt.
ciprés *m* cypress.
circo *m* [gen] circus.
circuito *m* -1. DEP & ELECTRÓN circuit. -2. [viaje] tour.
circulación *f* -1. [gen] circulation. -2. [tráfico] traffic.
circular ◇ *adj & f* circular. ◇ *vi* -1. [pasar]: ~ **(por)** [líquido] to flow O circulate (through); [persona] to move O walk (around); [vehículos] to drive (along). -2. [de mano en mano] to circulate; [moneda] to be in circulation. -3. [difundirse] to go round.
círculo *m* lit & fig circle. ◆ **círculos** *mpl* [medios] circles. ◆ **círculo polar** *m* polar circle; **el** ~ **polar ártico/antártico** the Arctic/Antarctic Circle. ◆ **círculo vicioso** *m* vicious circle.
circuncisión *f* circumcision.
circundante *adj* surrounding.
circundar *vt* to surround.
circunferencia *f* circumference.
circunloquio *m* circumlocution.
circunscribir *vt* -1. [limitar] to restrict, to confine. -2. GEOM to circumscribe. ◆ **circunscribirse a** *vpr* to confine o.s. to.
circunscripción *f* [distrito] district; MIL division; POLÍT constituency.
circunscrito, -ta ◇ *pp* → **circunscribir**. ◇ *adj* restricted, limited.
circunstancia *f* circumstance; **en estas** ~**s** under the circumstances; ~ **atenuante/agravante/eximente** DER extenuating/aggravating/exonerating circumstance.
circunstancial *adj* [accidental] chance (*antes de sust*).
circunvalar *vt* to go round.
cirio *m* (wax) candle; **montar un** ~ to make a row.
cirrosis *f inv* cirrhosis.
ciruela *f* plum; ~ **pasa** prune.

cirugía *f* surgery; ~ **estética** O **plástica** cosmetic O plastic surgery.
cirujano, -na *m y f* surgeon.
cisco *m* -1. [carbón] slack; **hecho** ~ *fig* shattered. -2. *fam* [alboroto] row, rumpus.
cisma *m* -1. [separación] schism. -2. [discordia] split.
cisne *m* swan.
cisterna *f* [de retrete] cistern.
cistitis *f inv* cystitis.
cita *f* -1. [entrevista] appointment; [de novios] date; **darse** ~ to meet; **tener una** ~ to have an appointment. -2. [referencia] quotation.
citación *f* DER summons (*sg*).
citar *vt* -1. [convocar] to make an appointment with. -2. [aludir] to mention; [textualmente] to quote. -3. DER to summons. ◆ **citarse** *vpr*: ~**se (con alguien)** to arrange to meet (sb).
citología *f* -1. [análisis ginecológico] smear test. -2. BIOL cytology.
cítrico, -ca *adj* citric. ◆ **cítricos** *mpl* citrus fruits.
CiU (*abrev de* **Convergència i Unió**) *f* Catalan coalition party to the centre-right of the political spectrum.
ciudad *f* [localidad] city; [pequeña] town.
ciudadanía *f* -1. [nacionalidad] citizenship. -2. [población] citizens (*pl*).
ciudadano, -na *m y f* citizen.
Ciudad de México Mexico City.
cívico, -ca *adj* civic; [conducta] public-spirited.
civil ◇ *adj* lit & fig civil. ◇ *m* [no militar] civilian.
civilización *f* civilization.
civilizado, -da *adj* civilized.
civilizar *vt* to civilize.
civismo *m* -1. [urbanidad] community spirit. -2. [cortesía] civility, politeness.
cizaña *f* BOT darnel; **meter** O **sembrar** ~ to sow discord.
cl (*abrev de* **centilitro**) cl.
clamar *vt* -1. [expresar] to exclaim. -2. [exigir] to cry out for. ◇ *vi* -1. [implorar] to appeal. -2. [protestar] to cry out.
clamor *m* clamour.
clamoroso, -sa *adj* -1. [rotundo] resounding. -2. [vociferante] loud, clamorous.
clan *m* -1. [tribu, familia] clan. -2. [banda] faction.
clandestino, -na *adj* clandestine; POLÍT underground.
claqué *m* tap dancing.

claqueta f clapperboard.

clara → **claro**.

claraboya f skylight.

clarear v impers **-1.** [amanecer]: **empezaba a ~** dawn was breaking. **-2.** [despejarse] to clear up. ◆ **clarearse** vpr [transparentarse] to be see-through.

claridad f **-1.** [transparencia] clearness, clarity. **-2.** [luz] light. **-3.** [franqueza] candidness. **-4.** [lucidez] clarity.

clarificar vt **-1.** [gen] to clarify; [misterio] to clear up. **-2.** [purificar] to refine.

clarín m [instrumento] bugle.

clarinete m [instrumento] clarinet.

clarividencia f farsightedness.

claro, -ra adj **-1.** [gen] clear; **~ está que ...** of course ...; **dejar algo ~** to make sthg clear; **a las claras** clearly; **pasar una noche en ~** to spend a sleepless night; **poner algo en ~** to get sthg clear, to clear sthg up; **sacar algo en ~ (de)** to make sthg out (from). **-2.** [luminoso] bright. **-3.** [color] light. **-4.** [diluido - té, café] weak. ◆ **claro** ◇ m **-1.** [en bosque] clearing; [en multitud] space, gap. **-2.** METEOR bright spell. ◇ adv clearly. ◇ interj **¡~!** of course! ◆ **clara** f [de huevo] white.

clase f **-1.** [gen] class; **~ alta/media** upper/middle class; **~ obrera** O **trabajadora** working class; **~ preferente/turista** club/tourist class; **primera ~** first class. **-2.** [tipo] sort, kind; **toda ~ de** all sorts O kinds of. **-3.** [EDUC - asignatura, alumnos] class; [- aula] classroom; **dar ~s** [en un colegio] to teach; [en una universidad] to lecture; **~s particulares** private classes O lessons.

clásico, -ca ◇ adj **-1.** [de la Antigüedad] classical. **-2.** [ejemplar, prototípico] classic. **-3.** [peinado, estilo, música etc] classical. **-4.** [habitual] customary. **-5.** [peculiar]: **~ de** typical of. ◇ m y f [persona] classic.

clasificación f classification; DEP (league) table.

clasificar vt to classify. ◆ **clasificarse** vpr [ganar acceso]: **~se (para)** to qualify (for); DEP to get through (to).

clasista adj class-conscious; despec snobbish.

claudicar vi [ceder] to give in.

claustro m **-1.** ARQUIT & RELIG cloister. **-2.** [de universidad] senate.

claustrofobia f claustrophobia.

cláusula f clause.

clausura f **-1.** [acto solemne] closing ceremony. **-2.** [cierre] closing down.

clausurar vt **-1.** [acto] to close, to conclude. **-2.** [local] to close down.

clavadista m y f Amer diver.

clavado, -da adj **-1.** [en punto - hora] on the dot. **-2.** [parecido] almost identical; **ser ~ a alguien** to be the spitting image of sb.

clavar vt **-1.** [clavo, estaca etc] to drive; [cuchillo] to thrust; [chincheta, alfiler] to stick. **-2.** [cartel, placa etc] to nail, to fix. **-3.** fig [mirada, atención] to fix, to rivet.

clave ◇ adj inv key. ◇ m MÚS harpsichord. ◇ f **-1.** [código] code; **en ~** in code. **-2.** [solución] key. **-3.** MÚS clef. **-4.** INFORM key.

clavel m carnation.

clavicémbalo m harpsichord.

clavicordio m clavichord.

clavícula f collar bone.

clavija f **-1.** ELECTR & TECN pin; [de auriculares, teléfono] jack. **-2.** MÚS peg.

clavo m **-1.** [pieza metálica] nail; **agarrarse a un ~ ardiendo** to clutch at straws; **dar en el ~** to hit the nail on the head. **-2.** BOT & CULIN clove. **-3.** MED [para huesos] pin.

claxon (pl **cláxones**) m horn; **tocar el ~** to sound the horn.

clemencia f mercy, clemency.

clemente adj [persona] merciful.

cleptómano, -na m y f kleptomaniac.

clerical adj clerical.

clérigo m [católico] priest; [anglicano] clergyman.

clero m clergy.

cliché, clisé m **-1.** FOT negative. **-2.** IMPRENTA plate. **-3.** fig [tópico] cliché.

cliente, -ta m y f [de tienda, garaje, bar] customer; [de banco, abogado etc] client; [de hotel] guest.

clientela f [de tienda, garaje] customers (pl); [de banco, abogado etc] clients (pl); [de hotel] guests (pl); [de bar, restaurante] clientele.

clima m lit & fig climate.

climatizado, -da adj air-conditioned.

climatizar vt to air-condition.

climatología f **-1.** [tiempo] weather. **-2.** [ciencia] climatology.

clímax m inv climax.

clínico, -ca adj clinical. ◆ **clínica** f clinic.

clip m [para papel] paper clip.

clisé = cliché.

clítoris m inv clitoris.

cloaca f sewer.

cloquear vi to cluck.

cloro *m* chlorine.

cloroformo *m* chloroform.

cloruro *m* chloride.

clown *m* clown.

club (*pl* **clubs** ○ **clubes**) *m* club; ~ **de fans** fan club; ~ **náutico** yacht club.

cm (*abrev de* **centímetro**) cm.

CNT (*abrev de* **Confederación Nacional del Trabajo**) *f Spanish anarchist trade union federation created in 1911.*

Co. (*abrev de* **compañía**) Co.

coacción *f* coercion.

coaccionar *vt* to coerce.

coagular *vt* [gen] to coagulate; [sangre] to clot; [leche] to curdle. ◆ **coagularse** *vpr* [gen] to coagulate; [sangre] to clot; [leche] to curdle.

coágulo *m* clot.

coalición *f* coalition.

coartada *f* alibi.

coartar *vt* to limit, to restrict.

coba *f fam* [halago] flattery; **dar** ~ **a alguien** [hacer la pelota] to suck up ○ crawl to sb; [aplacar] to soft-soap sb.

cobalto *m* cobalt.

cobarde ◇ *adj* cowardly. ◇ *m y f* coward.

cobardía *f* cowardice.

cobertizo *m* -1. [tejado adosado] lean-to. -2. [barracón] shed.

cobertura *f* -1. [gen] cover. -2. [de un edificio] covering. -3. PRENS: ~ **informativa** news coverage.

cobija *f Amer* blanket.

cobijar *vt* -1. [albergar] to house. -2. [proteger] to shelter. ◆ **cobijarse** *vpr* to take shelter.

cobijo *m* shelter; **dar** ~ **a alguien** to give shelter to sb, to take sb in.

cobra *f* cobra.

cobrador, -ra *m y f* [del autobús] conductor (*f* conductress); [de deudas, recibos] collector.

cobrar ◇ *vt* -1. [COM - dinero] to charge; [- cheque] to cash; [- deuda] to collect; **cantidades por** ~ amounts due; **¿me cobra, por favor?** how much do I owe you? -2. [en el trabajo] to earn. -3. [adquirir - importancia] to get, to acquire; ~ **fama** to become famous. -4. [sentir - cariño, afecto] to start to feel. ◇ *vi* [en el trabajo] to get paid.

cobre *m* copper; **no tener un** ~ *Amer* to be flat broke.

cobrizo, -za *adj* [color, piel] copper (*antes de sust*).

cobro *m* [de talón] cashing; [de pago] collection; ~ **revertido** reverse charge.

coca *f* -1. [planta] coca. -2. *fam* [cocaína] coke.

Coca-Cola® *f* Coca-Cola®, Coke®.

cocaína *f* cocaine.

cocción *f* [gen] cooking; [en agua] boiling; [en horno] baking.

cóccix, coxis *m inv* coccyx.

cocear *vi* to kick.

cocer *vt* -1. [gen] to cook; [hervir] to boil; [en horno] to bake. -2. [cerámica, ladrillos] to fire. ◆ **cocerse** *vpr flg* [plan] to be afoot.

coche *m* -1. [automóvil] car, automobile *Am*; ~ **de bomberos** fire engine; ~ **de carreras** racing car; ~ **celular** police van; ~ **familiar** estate car. -2. [de tren] coach, carriage; ~ **cama** sleeping car, sleeper; ~ **restaurante** restaurant ○ dining car. -3. [de caballos] carriage. ◆ **coche bomba** *m* car bomb.

cochera *f* [para coches] garage; [de autobuses, tranvías] depot.

cochinilla *f* -1. [crustáceo] woodlouse. -2. [insecto] cochineal.

cochinillo *m* sucking pig.

cochino, -na ◇ *adj* -1. [persona] filthy. -2. [tiempo, dinero] lousy. ◇ *m y f* [animal - macho] pig; [- hembra] sow.

cocido *m* stew.

cociente *m* quotient.

cocina *f* -1. [habitación] kitchen. -2. [electrodoméstico] cooker, stove; ~ **eléctrica/de gas** electric/gas cooker. -3. [arte] cooking; ~ **española** Spanish cuisine ○ cooking; **libro/clase de** ~ cookery book/class.

cocinar *vt & vi* to cook.

cocinero, -ra *m y f* cook.

cocker *m* cocker spaniel.

coco *m* [árbol] coconut palm; [fruto] coconut.

cocodrilo *m* crocodile.

cocotero *m* coconut palm.

cóctel, coctel *m* -1. [bebida, comida] cocktail. -2. [reunión] cocktail party. ◆ **cóctel molotov** *m* Molotov cocktail.

coctelera *f* cocktail shaker.

codazo *m* nudge, jab (*with one's elbow*); **abrirse paso a** ~**s** to elbow one's way through.

codearse *vpr*: ~**se (con)** to rub shoulders (with).

codera *f* elbow patch.

codicia *f* [de riqueza] greed.

codiciar *vt* to covet.

codicioso, -sa *adj* greedy.

codificar *vt* -1. [ley] to codify. -2. [un mensaje] to encode. -3. INFORM to code.

código *m* [gen & INFORM] code; ~ **postal/territorial** post/area code; ~ **de barras/de señales** bar/signal code; ~ **de circulación** highway code; ~ **civil/penal** civil/penal code; ~ **máquina** machine code.

codillo *m* [de jamón] shoulder.

codo *m* [en brazo, tubería] elbow; **estaba de ~s sobre la mesa** she was leaning (with her elbows) on the table.

codorniz *f* quail.

COE (*abrev de* **Comité Olímpico Español**) *m* SOC.

coeficiente *m* -1. [gen] coefficient. -2. [índice] rate.

coercer *vt* to restrict, to constrain.

coetáneo, -a *adj, m y f* contemporary.

coexistir *vi* to coexist.

cofia *f* [de enfermera, camarera] cap; [de monja] coif.

cofradía *f* -1. [religiosa] brotherhood (*f* sisterhood). -2. [no religiosa] guild.

cofre *m* -1. [arca] chest, trunk. -2. [para joyas] jewel box.

coger ◇ *vt* -1. [asir, agarrar] to take. -2. [atrapar - ladrón, pez, pájaro] to catch. -3. [alcanzar - persona, vehículo] to catch up with. -4. [recoger - frutos, flores] to pick. -5. [quedarse con - propina, empleo, piso] to take. -6. [quitar]: ~ **algo (a alguien)** to take sthg (from sb). -7. [tren, autobús] to take, to catch. -8. [contraer - gripe, resfriado] to catch, to get. -9. [sentir - manía, odio, afecto] to start to feel; ~ **cariño/miedo a** to become fond/scared of. -10. [oír] to catch; [entender] to get. -11. [sorprender, encontrar]: ~ **a alguien haciendo algo** to catch sb doing sthg. -12. [sintonizar - canal, emisora] to get, to receive. -13. *Amer vulg* [fornicar] to screw. ◇ *vi* [dirigirse]: ~ **a la derecha/la izquierda** to turn right/left. ◆ **cogerse** *vpr* -1. [agarrarse]: ~**se a** ○ **a algo** to cling to ○ clutch sthg. -2. [pillarse]: ~**se los dedos/la falda en la puerta** to catch one's fingers/skirt in the door.

cogida *f* [de torero] goring.

cognac = **coñá**.

cogollo *m* -1. [de lechuga] heart. -2. [brote - de árbol, planta] shoot.

cogorza *f fam*: **agarrarse una ~** to get smashed, to get blind drunk.

cogote *m* nape, back of the neck.

cohabitar *vi* to cohabit, to live together.

cohecho *m* bribery.

coherencia *f* [de razonamiento] coherence.

coherente *adj* coherent.

cohesión *f* cohesion.

cohete *m* rocket.

cohibido, -da *adj* inhibited.

cohibir *vt* to inhibit. ◆ **cohibirse** *vpr* to become inhibited.

COI (*abrev de* **Comité Olímpico Internacional**) *m* IOC.

coima *f Amer fam* bribe.

coincidencia *f* coincidence.

coincidir *vi* -1. [superficies, versiones, gustos] to coincide. -2. [personas - encontrarse] to meet; [- estar de acuerdo] to agree.

coito *m* (sexual) intercourse.

coja → **coger**.

cojear *vi* -1. [persona] to limp. -2. [mueble] to wobble.

cojera *f* [acción] limp; [estado] lameness.

cojín *m* cushion.

cojinete *m* [en eje] bearing; [en un riel de ferrocarril] chair.

cojo, -ja ◇ *v* → **coger**. ◇ *adj* -1. [persona] lame. -2. [mueble] wobbly. ◇ *m y f* cripple.

cojón *m* (*gen pl*) *vulg* ball. ◆ **cojones** *interj vulg*: **¡cojones!** [enfado] for fuck's sake!

cojonudo, -da *adj vulg* bloody brilliant.

cojudo, -da *adj Amer mfam* bloody stupid.

col *f* cabbage; ~ **de Bruselas** Brussels sprout.

cola *f* -1. [de animal, avión] tail. -2. [fila] queue *Br*, line *Am*; **hacer ~** to queue (up) *Br*, to stand in line *Am*. -3. [pegamento] glue. -4. [de clase, lista] bottom; [de desfile] end. -5. [peinado]: ~ **(de caballo)** pony tail.

colaboración *f* -1. [gen] collaboration. -2. [de prensa] contribution, article.

colaborador, -ra *m y f* -1. [gen] collaborator. -2. [de prensa] contributor.

colaborar *vi* -1. [ayudar] to collaborate. -2. [en prensa]: ~ **en** ○ **con** to write for. -3. [contribuir] to contribute.

colación *f loc*: **sacar** ○ **traer algo a ~** [tema] to bring sthg up.

colado, -da *adj* -1. [líquido] strained. -2. [enamorado]: **estar ~ por alguien** *fam* to have a crush on sb. ◆ **colada** *f* [ropa] laundry; **hacer la ~** to do the washing.

colador *m* [para líquidos] strainer, sieve; [para verdura] colander.

colapsar ◇ *vt* to bring to a halt, to stop. ◇ *vi* to come ○ grind to a halt.

colapso *m* **-1.** MED collapse, breakdown. **-2.** [de actividad] stoppage; [de tráfico] traffic jam, hold-up.

colar ◇ *vt* [verdura, té] to strain; [café] to filter. ◇ *vi* [pasar por bueno]: **esto no colará** this won't wash. ◆ **colarse** *vpr* **-1.** [líquido]: ~ **por** to seep through. **-2.** [persona] to slip, to sneak; [en una cola] to jump the queue *Br* ○ line *Am*; **~se en una fiesta** to gatecrash a party.

colateral *adj* [lateral] on either side.

colcha *f* bedspread.

colchón *m* [de cama] mattress; ~ **inflable** air bed.

colchoneta *f* [para playa] beach mat; [en gimnasio] mat.

cole *m fam* school.

colear *vi* [animal] to wag its tail.

colección *f lit* & *fig* collection.

coleccionable ◇ *adj* collectable. ◇ *m* special supplement in serialized form.

coleccionar *vt* to collect.

coleccionista *m y f* collector.

colecta *f* collection.

colectividad *f* community.

colectivo, -va *adj* collective. ◆ **colectivo** *m* group.

colector, -ra *m y f* [persona] collector. ◆ **colector** *m* **-1.** [sumidero] sewer; ~ **de basuras** chute. **-2.** MEC [de motor] manifold.

colega *m y f* **-1.** [compañero profesional] colleague. **-2.** [homólogo] counterpart, opposite number. **-3.** *fam* [amigo] mate.

colegiado, -da *adj who belongs to a professional association.* ◆ **colegiado** *m* DEP referee.

colegial, -la *m y f* schoolboy (*f* schoolgirl).

colegio *m* **-1.** [escuela] school. **-2.** [de profesionales]: ~ **(profesional)** professional association. ◆ **colegio electoral** *m* [lugar] polling station; [votantes] ward. ◆ **colegio mayor** *m* hall of residence.

cólera ◇ *m* MED cholera. ◇ *f* [ira] anger, rage; **montar en** ~ to get angry.

colérico, -ca *adj* [carácter] bad-tempered.

colesterol *m* cholesterol.

coleta *f* pigtail.

coletilla *f* postscript.

colgado, -da *adj* **-1.** [cuadro, jamón etc]: ~ **(de)** hanging (from). **-2.** [teléfono] on the hook.

colgador *m* hanger, coathanger.

colgante ◇ *adj* hanging. ◇ *m* pendant.

colgar ◇ *vt* **-1.** [suspender, ahorcar] to hang; ~ **el teléfono** to hang up. **-2.** [imputar]: ~ **algo a alguien** to blame sthg on sb. ◇ *vi* **-1.** [pender]: ~ **(de)** to hang (from). **-2.** [hablando por teléfono] to hang up.

colibrí *m* hummingbird.

cólico *m* stomachache.

coliflor *f* cauliflower.

colilla *f* (cigarette) butt ○ stub.

colimba *f Amer fam* military service.

colina *f* hill.

colindante *adj* neighbouring, adjacent.

colisión *f* [de automóviles] collision, crash; [de ideas, intereses] clash.

colisionar *vi* [coche]: ~ **(contra)** to collide (with), to crash (into).

collar *m* **-1.** [de personas] necklace. **-2.** [para animales] collar.

collarín *m* surgical collar.

colmado, -da *adj*: ~ **(de)** full to the brim (with). ◆ **colmado** *m* grocer's (shop).

colmar *vt* **-1.** [recipiente] to fill (to the brim). **-2.** *fig* [aspiración, deseo] to fulfil.

colmena *f* beehive.

colmillo *m* **-1.** [de persona] eye-tooth. **-2.** [de perro] fang; [de elefante] tusk.

colmo *m* height; **para** ~ **de desgracias** to crown it all; **es el** ~ **de la locura** it's sheer madness; **¡eso es el ~!** *fam* that's the last straw!

colocación *f* **-1.** [acción] placing, positioning; [situación] place, position. **-2.** [empleo] position, job.

colocado, -da *adj* **-1.** [gen] placed; **estar muy bien** ~ to have a very good job. **-2.** *fam* [borracho] legless; [drogado] high, stoned.

colocar *vt* **-1.** [en su sitio] to place, to put. **-2.** [en un empleo] to find a job for. **-3.** [invertir] to place, to invest. ◆ **colocarse** *vpr* **-1.** [en un trabajo] to get a job. **-2.** *fam* [emborracharse] to get legless; [drogarse] to get high ○ stoned.

colofón *m* [remate, fin] climax.

Colombia Colombia.

colombiano, -na *adj, m y f* Colombian.

colon *m* colon.

colonia *f* **-1.** [gen] colony. **-2.** [perfume] eau de cologne. **-3.** *Amer* [barrio] district; ~ **proletaria** shanty town.

colonial *adj* colonial.

colonización *f* colonization.

colonizador, -ra *m y f* colonist.

colonizar *vt* to colonize.

colono *m* settler, colonist.

coloquial *adj* colloquial.

coloquio *m* **-1.** [conversación] conversation. **-2.** [debate] discussion, debate.

color *m* [gen] colour; ~ **rojo** red; ~ **azul** blue; ¿**de qué** ~? what colour?; **de** ~ [persona] coloured; **en** ~ [foto, televisor] colour.

colorado, -da *adj* [color] red; **ponerse** ~ to blush, to go red.

colorante *m* colouring.

colorear *vt* to colour (in).

colorete *m* rouge, blusher.

colorido *m* colours (*pl*).

colosal *adj* **-1.** [estatura, tamaño] colossal. **-2.** [extraordinario] great, enormous.

coloso *m* **-1.** [estatua] colossus. **-2.** *fig* [cosa, persona] giant.

columna *f* **-1.** [gen] column. **-2.** *fig* [pilar] pillar. ◆ **columna vertebral** *f* spinal column.

columnista *m y f* columnist.

columpiar *vt* to swing. ◆ **columpiarse** *vpr* to swing.

columpio *m* swing.

colza *f* BOT rape.

coma ◇ *m* MED coma; **en** ~ in a coma. ◇ *f* **-1.** GRAM comma. **-2.** MAT ≃ decimal point.

comadreja *f* weasel.

comadrona *f* midwife.

comandancia *f* **-1.** [rango] command. **-2.** [edificio] command headquarters.

comandante *m* [MIL - rango] major; [- de un puesto] commander, commandant.

comandar *vt* MIL to command.

comando *m* MIL commando.

comarca *f* region, area.

comba *f* **-1.** [juego] skipping; **jugar a la** ~ to skip. **-2.** [cuerda] skipping rope.

combar *vt* to bend. ◆ **combarse** *vpr* [gen] to bend; [madera] to warp; [pared] to bulge.

combate *m* [gen] fight; [batalla] battle.

combatiente *m y f* combatant, fighter.

combatir ◇ *vi:* ~ **(contra)** to fight (against). ◇ *vt* to combat, to fight.

combativo, -va *adj* combative.

combi *m* [frigorífico] fridge-freezer.

combinación *f* **-1.** [gen] combination. **-2.** [de bebidas] cocktail. **-3.** [prenda] slip. **-4.** [de medios de transporte] connections (*pl*).

combinado *m* **-1.** [bebida] cocktail. **-2.** DEP combined team. **-3.** *Amer* [radiograma] radiogram.

combinar *vt* **-1.** [gen] to combine. **-2.** [bebidas] to mix. **-3.** [colores] to match.

combustible ◇ *adj* combustible. ◇ *m* fuel.

combustión *f* combustion.

comecocos *m inv fam* [para convencer]: **este panfleto es un** ~ this pamphlet is designed to brainwash you.

comedia *f* comedy; *fig* [engaño] farce.

comediante, -ta *m y f* actor (*f* actress); *fig* [farsante] fraud.

comedido, -da *adj* moderate.

comedirse *vpr* to be restrained.

comedor *m* [habitación - de casa] dining room; [- de fábrica] canteen.

comensal *m y f* fellow diner.

comentar *vt* [opinar sobre] to comment on; [hablar de] to discuss.

comentario *m* **-1.** [observación] comment, remark. **-2.** [crítica] commentary. ◆ **comentarios** *mpl* [murmuraciones] gossip (*U*).

comentarista *m y f* commentator.

comenzar ◇ *vt* to start, to begin; ~ **a hacer algo** to start doing ○ to do sthg; ~ **diciendo que ...** to start ○ to begin by saying that .... ◇ *vi* to start, to begin.

comer ◇ *vi* [ingerir alimentos - gen] to eat; [- al mediodía] to have lunch. ◇ *vt* **-1.** [alimentos] to eat. **-2.** [en juegos de tablero] to take, to capture. **-3.** *fig* [consumir] to eat up. ◆ **comerse** *vpr* **-1.** [alimentos] to eat. **-2.** [desgastar - recursos] to eat up; [- metal] to corrode. **-3.** [en los juegos de tablero] to take, to capture. **-4.** *Amer vulg* [fornicar]: ~**se a** to fuck.

comercial *adj* commercial.

comercializar *vt* to market.

comerciante *m y f* tradesman (*f* tradeswoman); [tendero] shopkeeper.

comerciar *vi* to trade, to do business.

comercio *m* **-1.** [de productos] trade; ~ **exterior/interior** foreign/domestic trade; **libre** ~ free trade. **-2.** [actividad] business, commerce. **-3.** [tienda] shop.

comestible *adj* edible, eatable. ◆ **comestibles** *mpl* [gen] food (*U*); [en una tienda] groceries.

cometa ◇ *m* ASTRON comet. ◇ *f* kite.

cometer *vt* [crimen] to commit; [error] to make.

cometido *m* **-1.** [objetivo] mission, task. **-2.** [deber] duty.

comezón *f* [picor] itch, itching (*U*).

cómic (*pl* **cómics**), **comic** (*pl* **comics**) *m* (adult) comic.

comicios *mpl* elections.

cómico, -ca ◇ *adj* **-1.** [de la comedia] comedy (*antes de sust*), comic. **-2.** [gracioso] comic, comical. ◇ *m y f* [actor de teatro] actor (*f* actress); [humorista] comedian (*f* comedienne), comic.

comida *f* **-1.** [alimento] food (*U*). **-2.** [almuerzo, cena etc] meal. **-3.** [al mediodía] lunch.

comidilla *f fam*: **ser/convertirse en la ~ del pueblo** to be/to become the talk of the town.

comienzo *m* start, beginning; **a ~s de los años 50** in the early 1950s; **dar ~** to start, to begin.

comillas *fpl* inverted commas, quotation marks; **entre ~** in inverted commas.

comilona *f fam* [festín] blow-out.

comino *m* [planta] cumin, cummin; **me importa un ~** I don't give a damn.

comisaría *f* police station, precinct *Am*.

comisario, -ria *m y f* **-1. ~ (de policía)** police superintendent. **-2.** [delegado] commissioner.

comisión *f* **-1.** [de un delito] perpetration. **-2.** COM commission; **(trabajar) a ~** (to work) on a commission basis. **-3.** [delegación] commission, committee; **~ investigadora** committee of inquiry; **~ permanente** standing commission.

comisura *f* corner (*of mouth, eyes*).

comité *m* committee.

comitiva *f* retinue.

como ◇ *adv* **-1.** (*comparativo*): **tan ... ~ ... as ... as ...;** **es (tan) negro ~ el carbón** it's as black as coal; **ser ~ algo** to be like sthg; **vive ~ un rey** he lives like a king; **lo que dijo fue ~ para ruborizarse** his words were enough to make you blush. **-2.** [de la manera que] as; **lo he hecho ~ es debido** I did it as ○ the way it should be done; **me encanta ~ bailas** I love the way you dance. **-3.** [según] as; **~ te decía ayer ...** as I was telling you yesterday .... **-4.** [en calidad de] as; **trabaja ~ bombero** he works as a fireman; **dieron el dinero ~ anticipo** they gave the money as an advance. **-5.** [aproximadamente] about; **me quedan ~ mil pesetas** I've got about a thousand pesetas left; **tiene un sabor ~ a naranja** it tastes a bit like an orange. ◇ *conj* **-1.** [ya que] as, since; **~ no llegabas, nos fuimos** as ○ since you didn't arrive, we left. **-2.** [si] if; **~ no me hagas caso, lo pasarás mal** if you don't listen to me, there will be trouble. ◆ **como que** *loc conj* **-1.** [que] that; **le pareció ~ que lloraban** it

seemed to him (that) they were crying. **-2.** [expresa causa]: **pareces cansado — ~ que he trabajado toda la noche** you seem tired — well, I've been up all night working. ◆ **como quiera** *loc adv* [de cualquier modo] anyway, anyhow. ◆ **como quiera que** *loc conj* **-1.** [de cualquier modo que] whichever way, however; **~ quiera que sea** whatever the case may be. **-2.** [dado que] since, given that. ◆ **como si** *loc conj* as if.

cómo *adv* **-1.** [de qué modo, por qué motivo] how; **¿~ lo has hecho?** how did you do it?; **¿~ son?** what are they like?; **no sé ~ has podido decir eso** I don't know how you could say that; **¿~ que no la has visto nunca?** what do you mean you've never seen her?; **¿a ~ están los tomates?** how much are the tomatoes?; **¿~?** *fam* [¿qué dices?] sorry?, what? **-2.** [exclamativo] how; **¡~ pasan los años!** how time flies!; **¡~ no!** of course!; **está lloviendo, ¡y ~!** it isn't half raining!

cómoda *f* chest of drawers.

comodidad *f* comfort, convenience (*U*); **para su ~** for your convenience.

comodín *m* [naipe] joker.

cómodo, -da *adj* **-1.** [gen] comfortable. **-2.** [útil] convenient. **-3.** [oportuno, fácil] easy.

comoquiera *adv*: **~ que** [de cualquier manera que] whichever way, however; [dado que] since, seeing as.

compa *m y f Amer fam* mate, buddy.

compact *m* compact disc player.

compactar *vt* to compress.

compact disk, compact disc *m* compact disc.

compacto, -ta *adj* compact.

compadecer *vt* to pity, to feel sorry for. ◆ **compadecerse de** *vpr* to pity, to feel sorry for.

compadre *m fam* [amigo] friend, mate.

compadrear *vi Amer* to brag, to boast.

compaginar *vt* [combinar] to reconcile. ◆ **compaginarse** *vpr*: **~se con** to square with, to go together with.

compañerismo *m* comradeship.

compañero, -ra *m y f* **-1.** [pareja, acompañante] companion. **-2.** [colega] colleague; **~ de clase** classmate; **~ de piso** flatmate.

compañía *f* company; **en ~ de** accompanied by, in the company of; **hacer ~ a alguien** to keep sb company.

comparación *f* comparison; **en ~ con** in comparison with, compared to.

comparar *vt*: ~ **algo** (**con**) to compare sthg (to).

comparativo, -va *adj* comparative.

comparecer *vi* to appear.

comparsa ◇ *f* TEATR extras (*pl*). ◇ *m y f* **-1.** TEATR extra. **-2.** *fig* [en carreras, competiciones] also-ran; [en organizaciones, empresas] nobody.

compartimento, compartimiento *m* compartment.

compartir *vt* **-1.** [ganancias] to share (out). **-2.** [piso, ideas] to share.

compás *m* **-1.** [instrumento] pair of compasses. **-2.** [MÚS - periodo] bar; [- ritmo] rhythm, beat; **al** ~ (**de la música**) in time (with the music); **llevar el** ~ to keep time; **perder el** ~ to lose the beat.

compasión *f* compassion, pity.

compasivo, -va *adj* compassionate.

compatibilizar *vt* to make compatible.

compatible *adj* [gen & INFORM] compatible.

compatriota *m y f* compatriot, fellow countryman (*f* fellow countrywoman).

compendiar *vt* [cualidades, características] to summarize; [libro, historia] to abridge.

compendio *m* **-1.** [libro] compendium. **-2.** *fig* [síntesis] epitome, essence.

compenetración *f* mutual understanding.

compenetrarse *vpr* to understand each other.

compensación *f* [gen] compensation; **en** ~ (**por**) in return (for).

compensar *vt* **-1.** [valer la pena] to make up for; **no me compensa** (**perder tanto tiempo**) it's not worth my while (wasting all that time). **-2.** [indemnizar]: ~ **a alguien** (**de** ○ **por**) to compensate sb (for).

competencia *f* **-1.** [entre personas, empresas] competition. **-2.** [incumbencia] field, province. **-3.** [aptitud, atribuciones] competence.

competente *adj* competent; ~ **en materia de** responsible for.

competer ◆ **competer a** *vi* [gen] to be up to, to be the responsibility of; [una autoridad] to come under the jurisdiction of.

competición *f* competition.

competidor, -ra *m y f* competitor.

competir *vi*: ~ (**con/por**) to compete (with/for).

competitividad *f* competitiveness.

competitivo, -va *adj* competitive.

compilar *vt* [gen & INFORM] to compile.

compinche *m y f fam* crony.

complacencia *f* pleasure, satisfaction.

complacer *vt* to please.

complaciente *adj* **-1.** [amable] obliging, helpful. **-2.** [indulgente] indulgent.

complejo, -ja *adj* complex. ◆ **complejo** *m* complex; ~ **industrial** industrial park.

complementar *vt* to complement. ◆ **complementarse** *vpr* to complement each other.

complementario, -ria *adj* complementary.

complemento *m* **-1.** [añadido] complement. **-2.** GRAM object, complement.

completamente *adv* completely, totally.

completar *vt* to complete.

completo, -ta *adj* **-1.** [entero, perfecto] complete; **por** ~ completely; **un deportista muy** ~ an all-round sportsman. **-2.** [lleno] full.

complexión *f* build.

complicación *f* **-1.** [gen] complication. **-2.** [complejidad] complexity.

complicado, -da *adj* **-1.** [difícil] complicated. **-2.** [implicado]: ~ (**en**) involved (in).

complicar *vt* [dificultar] to complicate.

cómplice *m y f* accomplice.

complicidad *f* complicity.

complot, compló *m* plot, conspiracy.

componente *m* **-1.** [gen & ELECTR] component. **-2.** [persona] member.

componer *vt* **-1.** [formar un todo, ser parte de] to make up. **-2.** [música, versos] to compose. **-3.** [arreglar - algo roto] to repair. ◆ **componerse** *vpr* [estar formado]: ~**se de** to be made up of.

comportamiento *m* behaviour.

comportar *vt* to involve, to entail. ◆ **comportarse** *vpr* to behave.

composición *f* composition.

compositor, -ra *m y f* composer.

compostura *f* **-1.** [reparación] repair. **-2.** [de persona, rostro] composure. **-3.** [en comportamiento] restraint.

compota *f* CULIN stewed fruit (*U*).

compra *f* purchase; **ir de** ~**s** to go shopping; **ir a** ○ **hacer la** ~ to do the shopping; ~ **a plazos** hire purchase.

comprador, -ra *m y f* [gen] buyer; [en una tienda] shopper, customer.

comprar *vt* **-1.** [adquirir] to buy, to purchase. **-2.** [sobornar] to buy (off).

compraventa *f* buying and selling, trading.

comprender vt -1. [incluir] to include, to comprise. -2. [entender] to understand. ◆**comprenderse** vpr [personas] to understand each other.

comprensión f understanding.

comprensivo, -va adj understanding.

compresa f [para menstruación] sanitary towel Br, sanitary napkin Am.

comprimido, -da adj compressed. ◆**comprimido** m pill, tablet.

comprimir vt to compress.

comprobante m [documento] supporting document, proof; [recibo] receipt.

comprobar vt [averiguar] to check; [demostrar] to prove.

comprometer vt -1. [poner en peligro - éxito etc] to jeopardize; [- persona] to compromise. -2. [avergonzar] to embarrass. ◆**comprometerse** vpr -1. [hacerse responsable]: ~se (a hacer algo) to commit o.s. (to doing sthg). -2. [ideológicamente, moralmente]: ~se (en algo) to become involved (in sthg).

comprometido, -da adj -1. [con una idea] committed. -2. [difícil] compromising, awkward.

compromiso m -1. [obligación] commitment; [acuerdo] agreement. -2. [cita] engagement; ~ matrimonial engagement. -3. [dificultad] compromising o difficult situation.

compuerta f sluice, floodgate.

compuesto, -ta pp ◇ componer. ◇ adj [formado]: ~ de composed of. ◆**compuesto** m GRAM & QUÍM compound.

compungido, -da adj contrite.

computador m, **computadora** f computer.

computar vt [calcular] to calculate.

cómputo m calculation.

comulgar vi RELIG to take communion.

común adj -1. [gen] common; **por lo** ~ generally; **poco** ~ unusual. -2. [compartido - amigo, interés] mutual; [- bienes, pastos] communal. -3. [ordinario - vino etc] ordinary, average.

comuna f commune.

comunicación f -1. [gen] communication; **ponerse en** ~ **con alguien** to get in touch with sb. -2. [escrito oficial] communiqué; [informe] report. ◆**comunicaciones** fpl communications.

comunicado, -da adj: **bien** ~ [lugar] well-served, with good connections. ◆**comunicado** m announcement, statement; ~ **a la prensa** press release.

comunicar ◇ vt -1. [transmitir - sentimientos, ideas] to convey; [- movimiento, virus] to transmit. -2. [información]: ~ **algo a alguien** to inform sb of sthg, to tell sb sthg. ◇ vi -1. [hablar - gen] to communicate; [- al teléfono] to get through; [escribir] to get in touch. -2. [dos lugares]: ~ **con algo** to connect with sthg, to join sthg. -3. [el teléfono] to be engaged Br, to be busy Am; **está comunicando** the line's engaged. ◆**comunicarse** vpr -1. [hablarse] to communicate (with each other). -2. [dos lugares] to be connected.

comunicativo, -va adj communicative.

comunidad f [gen] community; ~ **autónoma** autonomous region; **Comunidad Económica Europea** European Economic Community.

comunión f lit & fig communion.

comunismo m communism.

comunista adj, m y f communist.

comunitario, -ria adj -1. [de la comunidad] community (antes de sust). -2. [de la CEE] Community (antes de sust), of the European Community.

con prep -1. [gen] with; ¿~ **quién vas?** who are you going with?; **lo ha conseguido** ~ **su esfuerzo** he has achieved it through his own efforts; **una cartera** ~ **varios documentos** a briefcase containing several documents. -2. [a pesar de] in spite of; ~ **todo** despite everything; ~ **lo estudioso que es, le suspendieron** for all his hard work, they still failed him. -3. [hacia]: **para** ~ towards; **es amable para** ~ **todos** she is friendly towards o with everyone. -4. (+ infin) [para introducir una condición] by (+ gerund); ~ **hacerlo así** by doing it this way; ~ **salir a las diez es suficiente** if we leave at ten, we'll have plenty of time. -5. [a condición de que]: ~ **(tal) que** (+ subjuntivo) as long as; ~ **que llegue a tiempo me conformo** I don't mind as long as he arrives on time.

conato m attempt; ~ **de robo** attempted robbery; **un** ~ **de incendio** the beginnings of a fire.

concatenar, concadenar vt to link together.

concavidad f [lugar] hollow.

cóncavo, -va adj concave.

concebir ◇ vt [plan, hijo] to conceive; [imaginar] to imagine. ◇ vi to conceive.

conceder vt -1. [dar] to grant; [premio] to award. -2. [asentir] to admit, to concede.

concejal, -la m y f (town) councillor.
concentración f -1. [gen] concentration. -2. [de gente] gathering.
concentrado m concentrate.
concentrar vt -1. [gen] to concentrate. -2. [reunir - gente] to bring together; [- tropas] to assemble. ◆ **concentrarse** vpr to concentrate.
concéntrico, -ca adj concentric.
concepción f conception.
concepto m -1. [idea] concept. -2. [opinión] opinion. -3. [motivo]: **bajo ningún** ~ under no circumstances; **en** ~ **de** by way of, as.
concernir v impers to concern; **en lo que concierne a** as regards; **por lo que a mí me concierne** as far as I'm concerned.
concertar ◇ vt [precio] to agree on; [cita] to arrange; [pacto] to reach. ◇ vi [concordar]: ~ **(con)** to tally (with), to fit in (with).
concertina f concertina.
concesión f -1. [de préstamo etc] granting; [de premio] awarding. -2. COM & fig concession.
concesionario, -ria m y f [persona con derecho exclusivo de venta] licensed dealer; [titular de una concesión] concessionaire, licensee.
concha f -1. [de los animales] shell. -2. [material] tortoiseshell.
conchabarse vpr fam: ~ **(contra)** to gang up (on).
conciencia, consciencia f -1. [conocimiento] consciousness, awareness; **tener/tomar** ~ **de** to be/become aware of. -2. [moral, integridad] conscience; **a** ~ conscientiously; **me remuerde la** ~ I have a guilty conscience.
concienciar vt to make aware. ◆ **concienciarse** vpr to become aware.
concienzudo, -da adj conscientious.
concierto m -1. [actuación] concert. -2. [composición] concerto.
conciliar vt to reconcile; ~ **el sueño** to get to sleep.
concilio m council.
concisión f conciseness.
conciso, -sa adj concise.
conciudadano, -na m y f fellow citizen.
cónclave, conclave m conclave.
concluir ◇ vt to conclude; ~ **haciendo** o **hacer algo** to end up doing sthg. ◇ vi to (come to an) end.
conclusión f conclusion; **llegar a una** ~ to come to o to reach a conclusion; **en** ~ in conclusion.
concluyente adj conclusive.
concordancia f [gen & GRAM] agreement.
concordar ◇ vt to reconcile. ◇ vi -1. [estar de acuerdo]: ~ **(con)** to agree o tally (with). -2. GRAM: ~ **(con)** to agree (with).
concordia f harmony.
concretar vt [precisar] to specify, to state exactly. ◆ **concretarse** vpr [materializarse] to take shape.
concreto, -ta adj specific, particular; **en** ~ [en resumen] in short; [específicamente] specifically; **nada en** ~ nothing definite. ◆ **concreto armado** m Amer concrete.
concurrencia f -1. [asistencia] attendance; [espectadores] crowd, audience. -2. [de sucesos] concurrence.
concurrido, -da adj [bar, calle] crowded; [espectáculo] well-attended.
concurrir vi -1. [reunirse]: ~ **a algo** to go to sthg, to attend sthg. -2. [participar]: ~ **a** [concurso] to take part in, to compete in; [examen] to sit Br, to take.
concursante m y f [en concurso] competitor, contestant; [en oposiciones] candidate.
concursar vi [competir] to compete; [en oposiciones] to be a candidate.
concurso m -1. [prueba - literaria, deportiva] competition; [- de televisión] game show. -2. [para una obra] tender; **salir a** ~ to be put out to tender. -3. [ayuda] cooperation.
condado m [territorio] county.
condal adj: **la Ciudad** ~ Barcelona.
conde, -desa m y f count (f countess).
condecoración f [insignia] medal.
condecorar vt to decorate.
condena f sentence.
condenado, -da adj -1. [a una pena] convicted, sentenced; [a un sufrimiento] condemned. -2. fam [maldito] damned.
condenar vt -1. [declarar culpable] to convict. -2. [castigar]: ~ **a alguien a algo** to sentence sb to sthg. -3. [recriminar] to condemn.
condensar vt lit & fig to condense.
condescendencia f [benevolencia] graciousness; [altivez] condescension.
condescender vi: ~ **a** [con amabilidad] to consent to, to accede to; [con desprecio] to deign to, to condescend to.
condescendiente adj obliging.

condición f **-1.** [gen] condition; **condiciones de un contrato** terms of a contract; **con una sola** ~ on one condition. **-2.** [naturaleza] nature. **-3.** [clase social] social class. ◆ **condiciones** fpl **-1.** [aptitud] talent (U), ability (U). **-2.** [circunstancias] conditions; **condiciones atmosféricas/de vida** weather/living conditions. **-3.** [estado] condition (U); **estar en condiciones de** O **para hacer algo** [físicamente] to be in a fit state to do sthg; [por la situación] to be in a position to do sthg; **no estar en condiciones** [carne, pescado] to be off.

condicional adj & m conditional.

condicionar vt: ~ **algo a algo** to make sthg dependent on sthg.

condimento m seasoning (U).

condolencia f condolence.

condolerse vpr: ~ **(de)** to feel pity (for).

condón m condom.

cóndor m condor.

conducción f [de vehículo] driving.

conducir ◇ vt **-1.** [vehículo] to drive. **-2.** [dirigir - empresa] to manage, to run; [- ejército] to lead; [- asunto] to handle. **-3.** [a una persona a un lugar] to lead. ◇ vi **-1.** [en vehículo] to drive. **-2.** [a sitio, situación]: ~ **a** to lead to.

conducta f behaviour, conduct.

conducto m **-1.** [de fluido] pipe. **-2.** fig [vía] channel. **-3.** ANAT duct.

conductor, -ra m y f **-1.** [de vehículo] driver. **-2.** FÍS conductor.

conectar vt: ~ **algo (a** O **con)** to connect sthg (to O up to).

conejillo ◆ **conejillo de Indias** m guinea pig.

conejo, -ja m y f rabbit (f doe).

conexión f **-1.** [gen] connection. **-2.** RADIO & TV link-up; ~ **vía satélite** satellite link.

conexo, -xa adj related, connected.

confabular ◆ **confabularse** vpr: ~**se (para)** to plot O conspire (to).

confección f **-1.** [de ropa] tailoring, dressmaking. **-2.** [de comida] preparation, making; [de lista] drawing up.

confeccionar vt **-1.** [ropa] to make (up); [lista] to draw up. **-2.** [plato] to prepare; [bebida] to mix.

confederación f confederation.

conferencia f **-1.** [charla] lecture; **dar una** ~ to give a talk O lecture. **-2.** [reunión] conference. **-3.** [por teléfono] (long-distance) call.

conferir vt **-1.** ~ **algo a alguien** [honor, dignidad] to confer O bestow sthg upon sb; [responsabilidades] to give sthg to sb. **-2.** [cualidad] to give.

confesar vt [gen] to confess; [debilidad] to admit. ◆ **confesarse** vpr RELIG: ~ **(de algo)** to confess (sthg).

confesión f **-1.** [gen] confession. **-2.** [credo] religion, (religious) persuasion.

confesionario m confessional.

confeti mpl confetti (U).

confiado, -da adj [seguro] confident; [crédulo] trusting.

confianza f **-1.** [seguridad]: ~ **(en)** confidence (in); ~ **en uno mismo** self-confidence. **-2.** [fe] trust; **de** ~ trustworthy. **-3.** [familiaridad] familiarity; **en** ~ in confidence.

confiar vt **-1.** [secreto] to confide. **-2.** [responsabilidad, persona, asunto]: ~ **algo a alguien** to entrust sthg to sb. ◆ **confiar en** vi **-1.** [tener fe] to trust in. **-2.** [suponer]: ~ **en que** to be confident that. ◆ **confiarse** vpr [despreocuparse] to be too sure (of o.s.).

confidencia f confidence, secret.

confidencial adj confidential.

confidente m y f **-1.** [amigo] confidant (f confidante). **-2.** [soplón] informer.

configurar vt [formar] to shape, to form.

confín m (gen pl) **-1.** [límite] border, boundary. **-2.** [extremo - del reino, universo] outer reaches (pl); **en los confines de** on the very edge of.

confinar vt **-1.** [detener]: ~ **(en)** to confine (to). **-2.** [desterrar]: ~ **(en)** to banish (to).

confirmación f [gen & RELIG] confirmation.

confirmar vt to confirm.

confiscar vt to confiscate.

confitado, -da adj candied; **frutas confitadas** crystallised fruit.

confite m sweet Br, candy Am.

confitería f **-1.** [tienda] sweetshop, confectioner's. **-2.** Amer [café] cafe.

confitura f preserve, jam.

conflagración f conflict, war.

conflictivo, -va adj [asunto] controversial; [situación] troubled; [trabajador] difficult.

conflicto m [gen] conflict; [de intereses, opiniones] clash; ~ **laboral** industrial dispute.

confluir vi **-1.** [corriente, cauce]: ~ **(en)** to converge O meet (at). **-2.** [personas]:

~ (en) to come together ○ to gather (in).

conformar vt [configurar] to shape. ◆ **conformarse con** vpr [suerte, destino] to resign o.s. to; [apañárselas con] to make do with; [contentarse con] to settle for.

conforme ◇ adj **-1.** [acorde]: **~ a** in accordance with. **-2.** [de acuerdo]: **~ (con)** in agreement (with). **-3.** [contento]: **~ (con)** happy (with). ◇ adv [gen] as; **~ envejecía** as he got older.

conformidad f [aprobación]: **~ (con)** approval (of).

conformista adj, m y f conformist.

confort (pl **conforts**) m comfort; "todo ~" "all mod cons".

confortable adj comfortable.

confortar vt to console, to comfort.

confrontar vt **-1.** [enfrentar] to confront. **-2.** [comparar] to compare.

confundir vt **-1.** [trastocar]: **~ una cosa con otra** to mistake one thing for another; **~ dos cosas** to get two things mixed up. **-2.** [liar] to confuse. **-3.** [mezclar] to mix up. ◆ **confundirse** vpr **-1.** [equivocarse] to make a mistake; **~se de piso** to get the wrong flat. **-2.** [liarse] to get confused. **-3.** [mezclarse - colores, siluetas]: **~se (en)** to merge (into); [- personas]: **~se entre la gente** to lose o.s. in the crowd.

confusión f **-1.** [gen] confusion. **-2.** [error] mix-up.

confuso, -sa adj **-1.** [incomprensible - estilo, explicación] obscure. **-2.** [poco claro - rumor] muffled; [- clamor, griterío] confused; [- contorno, forma] blurred. **-3.** [turbado] confused, bewildered.

congelación f **-1.** [de alimentos] freezing. **-2.** ECON [de precios, salarios] freeze.

congelador m freezer.

congelados mpl frozen foods.

congelar vt [gen & ECON] to freeze. ◆ **congelarse** vpr to freeze.

congeniar vi: **~ (con)** to get on (with).

congénito, -ta adj [enfermedad] congenital; [talento] innate.

congestión f congestion.

congestionar vt to block. ◆ **congestionarse** vpr **-1.** AUTOM & MED to become congested. **-2.** [cara - de rabia etc] to flush, to turn purple.

congoja f anguish.

congraciarse vpr: **~ con alguien** to win sb over.

congratular vt: **~ a alguien (por)** to congratulate sb (on).

congregación f congregation.

congregar vt to assemble.

congresista m y f **-1.** [en un congreso] delegate. **-2.** [político] congressman (f congresswoman).

congreso m **-1.** [de una especialidad] congress. **-2.** [asamblea nacional]: **~ de diputados** [en España] lower house of Spanish Parliament; ≃ House of Commons Br; ≃ House of Representatives Am; **el Congreso** [en Estados Unidos] Congress.

congrio m conger eel.

congruente adj consistent, congruous.

conjetura f conjecture; **hacer ~s, hacerse una ~** to conjecture.

conjugación f GRAM conjugation.

conjugar vt **-1.** GRAM to conjugate. **-2.** [opiniones] to bring together, to combine; [esfuerzos, ideas] to pool.

conjunción f ASTRON & GRAM conjunction.

conjunto, -ta adj [gen] joint; [hechos, acontecimientos] combined. ◆ **conjunto** m **-1.** [gen] set, collection; **un ~ de circunstancias** a number of reasons. **-2.** [de ropa] outfit. **-3.** [MÚS - de rock] group, band; [- de música clásica] ensemble. **-4.** [totalidad] whole; **en ~** overall, as a whole. **-5.** MAT set.

conjurar ◇ vi [conspirar] to conspire, to plot. ◇ vt **-1.** [exorcizar] to exorcize. **-2.** [evitar - un peligro] to ward off, to avert.

conjuro m spell, incantation.

conllevar vt [implicar] to entail.

conmemoración f commemoration.

conmemorar vt to commemorate.

conmigo pron pers with me; **~ mismo/misma** with myself.

conmoción f **-1.** [física o psíquica] shock; **~ cerebral** concussion. **-2.** fig [trastorno, disturbio] upheaval.

conmocionar vt **-1.** [psíquicamente] to shock. **-2.** [físicamente] to concuss.

conmovedor, -ra adj moving, touching.

conmover vt **-1.** [emocionar] to move, to touch. **-2.** [sacudir] to shake.

conmutador m **-1.** ELECTR switch. **-2.** Amer [centralita] switchboard.

connotación f connotation; **una ~ irónica** a hint of irony.

cono m cone.

conocedor, -ra m y f: **~ (de)** [gen] expert (on); [de vinos] connoisseur (of).

conocer vt -1. [gen] to know; **darse a ~** to make o.s. known; **~ bien un tema** to know a lot about a subject; **~ alguien de vista** to know sb by sight; **~ a alguien de oídas** to have heard of sb. -2. [descubrir - lugar, país] to get to know. -3. [a una persona - por primera vez] to meet. -4. [reconocer]: **~ a alguien (por algo)** to recognize sb (by sthg). ◆ **conocerse** vpr -1. [a uno mismo] to know o.s. -2. [dos o más personas - por primera vez] to meet, to get to know each other; [- desde hace tiempo] to know each other.

conocido, -da ◇ adj well-known. ◇ m y f acquaintance.

conocimiento m -1. [gen] knowledge. -2. MED [sentido] consciousness. ◆ **conocimientos** mpl knowledge (U); **tener muchos ~s** to be very knowledgeable.

conozca etc → conocer.

conque conj so; ¿**~ te has cansado?** so you're tired, are you?

conquista f [de tierras, persona] conquest.

conquistador, -ra m y f -1. [de tierras] conqueror. -2. HIST conquistador.

conquistar vt [tierras] to conquer.

consabido, -da adj [conocido] well-known; [habitual] usual.

consagrar vt -1. RELIG to consecrate. -2. [dedicar]: **~ algo a algo/alguien** [tiempo, espacio] to devote sthg to sthg/sb; [monumento, lápida] to dedicate sthg to sthg/sb. -3. [acreditar, confirmar] to confirm, to establish.

consciencia = conciencia.

consciente adj conscious; **ser ~ de** to be aware of; **estar ~** [físicamente] to be conscious.

consecución f [de un deseo] realization; [de un objetivo] attainment; [de un premio] winning.

consecuencia f [resultado] consequence; **a** ○ **como ~ de** as a consequence ○ result of.

consecuente adj [coherente] consistent.

consecutivo, -va adj consecutive.

conseguir vt [gen] to obtain, to get; [un objetivo] to achieve; **~ hacer algo** to manage to do sthg.

consejero, -ra m y f -1. [en asuntos personales] counsellor; [en asuntos técnicos] adviser, consultant. -2. [de un consejo de administración] member; POLÍT councillor.

consejo m -1. [advertencia] advice (U); **dar un ~** to give some advice. -2. [or-

ganismo] council; **~ de administración** board of directors. ◆ **consejo de guerra** m court martial. ◆ **consejo de ministros** m cabinet.

consenso m [acuerdo] consensus; [consentimiento] consent.

consentimiento m consent.

consentir ◇ vt -1. [tolerar] to allow, to permit. -2. [mimar] to spoil. ◇ vi: **~ en algo/en hacer algo** to agree to sthg/to do sthg.

conserje m y f [portero] porter; [encargado] caretaker.

conserjería f -1. [de un hotel] reception desk. -2. [de un edificio público o privado] porter's lodge.

conserva f: **~ de carne** tinned meat; **en ~** tinned, canned.

conservación f [gen] conservation; [de alimentos] preservation.

conservador, -ra ◇ adj [gen] conservative; [del partido conservador] Conservative. ◇ m y f -1. [por ideología] conservative; [miembro del partido conservador] Conservative. -2. [de museo] curator.

conservante m y f preservative.

conservar vt -1. [gen & CULIN] to preserve; [amistad] to keep up; [salud] to look after; [calor] to retain. -2. [guardar - libros, cartas, secreto] to keep. ◆ **conservarse** vpr to keep; **se conserva bien** he's keeping well.

conservatorio m conservatoire.

considerable adj [gen] considerable; [importante, eminente] notable.

consideración f -1. [valoración] consideration. -2. [respeto] respect; **tratar a alguien con ~** to be nice to sb; **en ~ a algo** in recognition of sthg. -3. [importancia]: **de ~** serious.

considerado, -da adj [atento] considerate, thoughtful; [respetado] respected.

considerar vt -1. [valorar] to consider. -2. [juzgar, estimar] to think.

consigna f -1. [órdenes] instructions (pl). -2. [para el equipaje] left-luggage office.

consignar vt -1. [poner por escrito] to record, to write down. -2. [enviar - mercancía] to dispatch. -3. [equipaje] to deposit in the left-luggage office.

consigo pron pers with him/her, (pl) with them; [con usted] with you; [con uno mismo] with o.s.; **~ mismo/misma** with himself/herself; **hablar ~ mismo** to talk to o.s.

consiguiente *adj* consequent; **por ~** consequently, therefore.

consistencia *f* lit & fig consistency.

consistente *adj* **-1.** [sólido - material] solid. **-2.** [coherente - argumento] sound. **-3.** [compuesto]: **~ en** consisting of.

consistir ◆ consistir en *vi* **-1.** [gen] to consist of. **-2.** [deberse a] to lie in, to be based on.

consola *f* **-1.** [mesa] console table. **-2.** INFORM & TECN console; **~ de videojuegos** video console.

consolación *f* consolation.

consolar *vt* to console.

consolidar *vt* to consolidate.

consomé *m* consommé.

consonancia *f* harmony; **en ~ con** in keeping with.

consonante *f* consonant.

consorcio *m* consortium.

conspiración *f* plot, conspiracy.

conspirador, -ra *m y f* conspirator.

conspirar *vi* to conspire, to plot.

constancia *f* **-1.** [perseverancia - en una empresa] **perseverance**; [- en las ideas, opiniones] **steadfastness. -2.** [testimonio] record; **dejar ~ de algo** [registrar] to put sthg on record; [probar] to demonstrate sthg.

constante ◇ *adj* **-1.** [persona - en una empresa] persistent. **-2.** [acción] constant. ◇ *f* constant.

constar *vi* **-1.** [una información]: **~ (en)** to appear (in), to figure (in); **~le a alguien** to be clear to sb; **me consta que** I am quite sure that; **que conste que ...** let it be clearly understood that ..., let there be no doubt that ...; **hacer ~** to put on record. **-2.** [estar constituido por]: **~ de** to consist of.

constatar *vt* [observar] to confirm; [comprobar] to check.

constelación *f* constellation.

consternación *f* consternation.

consternar *vt* to dismay.

constipado, -da ◇ *adj*: **estar ~** to have a cold. ◇ *m* cold.

constiparse *vpr* to catch a cold.

constitución *f* constitution.

constitucional *adj* constitutional.

constituir *vt* **-1.** [componer] to make up. **-2.** [ser] to be. **-3.** [crear] to set up.

constituyente *adj & m* constituent.

constreñir *vt* [oprimir, limitar] to restrict.

construcción *f* **-1.** [gen] construction; **en ~** under construction. **-2.** [edificio] building.

constructivo, -va *adj* constructive.

constructor, -ra *adj* building (*antes de sust*), construction (*antes de sust*). ◆ **constructor** *m* [de edificios] builder.

construir *vt* [edificio, barco] to build; [aviones, coches] to manufacture; [frase, teoría] to construct.

consuelo *m* consolation, solace.

cónsul, consulesa *m y f* consul.

consulado *m* [oficina] consulate; [cargo] consulship.

consulta *f* **-1.** [sobre un problema] consultation; **hacer una ~ a alguien** to seek sb's advice. **-2.** [despacho de médico] consulting room; **horas de ~** surgery hours.

consultar ◇ *vt* [dato, fecha] to look up; [libro, persona] to consult. ◇ *vi*: **~ con** to consult, to seek advice from.

consultor, -ra *m y f* consultant.

consultorio *m* **-1.** [de un médico] consulting room. **-2.** [en periódico] **problem page**; [en radio] *programme answering listeners' questions*. **-3.** [asesoría] **advice bureau**.

consumar *vt* [gen] to complete; [un crimen] to perpetrate; [el matrimonio] to consummate.

consumición *f* **-1.** [acción] consumption. **-2.** [bebida] drink; [comida] food.

consumidor, -ra *m y f* [gen] consumer; [en un bar, restaurante] patron.

consumir ◇ *vt* **-1.** [gen] to consume. **-2.** [destruir - suj: fuego] to destroy. ◇ *vi* to consume. ◆ **consumirse** *vpr* **-1.** [persona] to waste away. **-2.** [fuego] to burn out.

consumismo *m* consumerism.

consumo *m* consumption; **bienes/sociedad de ~** consumer goods/society.

contabilidad *f* **-1.** [oficio] accountancy. **-2.** [de persona, empresa] bookkeeping, accounting; **llevar la ~** to do the accounts.

contable *m y f* accountant.

contacto *m* **-1.** [gen] contact; **perder el ~** to lose touch. **-2.** AUTOM ignition.

contado, -da *adj* [raro] rare, infrequent; **contadas veces** very rarely. ◆ **al contado** *loc adv*: **pagar al ~** to pay (in) cash.

contador, -ra *m y f* Amer [persona] accountant. ◆ **contador** *m* [aparato] meter.

contagiar *vt* [persona] to infect; [enfermedad] to transmit. ◆ **contagiarse** *vpr* [enfermedad, risa] to be contagious; [persona] to become infected.

contagio *m* infection, contagion.

contagioso, -sa *adj* [enfermedad] contagious, infectious; [risa etc] infectious.

container = contenedor.

contaminación *f* [gen] contamination; [del medio ambiente] pollution.

contaminar *vt* [gen] to contaminate; [el medio ambiente] to pollute.

contar ◇ *vt* -1. [enumerar, incluir] to count. -2. [narrar] to tell. ◇ *vi* to count. ◆ **contar con** *vi* -1. [confiar en] to count on. -2. [tener, poseer] to have. -3. [tener en cuenta] to take into account; **con esto no contaba** I hadn't reckoned with that.

contemplación *f* contemplation.

contemplar *vt* [mirar, considerar] to contemplate.

contemporáneo, -a *adj, m y f* contemporary.

contenedor, -ra *adj* containing. ◆ **contenedor, container** *m* [gen] container; [para escombros] skip; ~ **de basura** *large rubbish bin for collecting rubbish from blocks of flats etc.*

contener *vt* -1. [encerrar] to contain. -2. [detener, reprimir] to restrain. ◆ **contenerse** *vpr* to restrain o.s.

contenido *m* [gen] contents (*pl*); [de discurso, redacción] content.

contentar *vt* to please, to keep happy. ◆ **contentarse** *vpr*: ~**se con** to make do with.

contento, -ta *adj* [alegre] happy; [satisfecho] pleased.

contestación *f* answer.

contestador ◆ **contestador (automático)** *m* answering machine.

contestar *vt* to answer.

contestatario, -ria *adj* antiestablishment.

contexto *m* context.

contienda *f* [competición, combate] contest; [guerra] conflict, war.

contigo *pron pers* with you; ~ **mismo/misma** with yourself.

contiguo, -gua *adj* adjacent.

continencia *f* self-restraint.

continental *adj* continental.

continente *m* GEOGR continent.

contingente ◇ *adj* unforeseeable. ◇ *m* -1. [grupo] contingent. -2. COM quota.

continuación *f* continuation; **a** ~ next, then.

continuar ◇ *vt* to continue, to carry on with. ◇ *vi* to continue, to go on; ~ **haciendo algo** to continue doing o to

do sthg; **continúa lloviendo** it's still raining.

continuidad *f* [en una sucesión] continuity; [permanencia] continuation.

continuo, -nua *adj* -1. [ininterrumpido] continuous. -2. [constante, perseverante] continual.

contonearse *vpr* [hombre] to swagger; [mujer] to swing one's hips.

contorno *m* -1. GEOGR contour; [línea] outline. -2. (*gen pl*) [vecindad] neighbourhood; [de una ciudad] outskirts (*pl*).

contorsionarse *vpr* [gen] to do contortions; [de dolor] to writhe.

contra ◇ *prep* against; **un jarabe** ~ **la tos** a cough syrup; **en** ~ against; **estar en** ~ **de algo** to be opposed to sthg; **en** ~ **de** [a diferencia de] contrary to. ◇ *m*: **los pros y los** ~**s** the pros and cons.

contraataque *m* counterattack.

contrabajo *m* -1. [instrumento] double-bass. -2. [voz, cantante] low bass.

contrabandista *m y f* smuggler.

contrabando *m* [acto] smuggling; [mercancías] contraband; **pasar algo de** ~ to smuggle sthg in; ~ **de armas** gunrunning.

contracción *f* contraction.

contrachapado, -da *adj* made of plywood. ◆ **contrachapado** *m* plywood.

contradecir *vt* to contradict.

contradicción *f* contradiction; **estar en** ~ **con** to be in (direct) contradiction to.

contradicho, -cha *pp* → contradecir.

contradictorio, -ria *adj* contradictory.

contraer *vt* -1. [gen] to contract. -2. [costumbre, acento etc] to acquire. -3. [enfermedad] to catch. ◆ **contraerse** *vpr* to contract.

contrafuerte *m* ARQUIT buttress.

contraindicación *f*: "**contraindicaciones: ...**" "not to be taken with ...".

contralor *m* Amer inspector of public spending.

contralto *m* [voz] contralto.

contraluz *m* back lighting; **a** ~ against the light.

contramaestre *m* -1. NÁUT boatswain; MIL warrant officer. -2. [capataz] foreman.

contrapartida *f* compensation; **como** ~ to make up for it.

contrapelo ◆ **a contrapelo** *loc adv* -1. [acariciar] the wrong way. -2. [vivir, actuar] against the grain.

contrapesar vt [físicamente] to counterbalance.

contrapeso m **-1.** [en ascensores, poleas] counterweight. **-2.** fig [fuerza que iguala] counterbalance.

contraponer vt [oponer]: ~ **(a)** to set up (against). ◆ **contraponerse** vpr to oppose.

contraportada f [of newspaper, magazine] back page; [of book, record] back cover.

contraproducente adj counterproductive.

contrariar vt **-1.** [contradecir] to go against. **-2.** [disgustar] to upset.

contrariedad f **-1.** [dificultad] setback. **-2.** [disgusto] annoyance.

contrario, -ria adj **-1.** [opuesto - dirección, sentido] opposite; [- parte] opposing; [- opinión] contrary; **ser** ~ **a algo** to be opposed to sthg. **-2.** [perjudicial]: ~ **a** contrary to. ◆ **contrario** m **-1.** [rival] opponent. **-2.** [opuesto] opposite; **al** ~, **por el** ~ on the contrary; **de lo** ~ otherwise; **todo lo** ~ quite the contrary.

contrarreloj adj inv: **etapa** ~ time trial.

contrarrestar vt [neutralizar] to counteract.

contrasentido m nonsense (U); **es un** ~ **hacer eso** it doesn't make sense to do that.

contraseña f password.

contrastar ◇ vi to contrast. ◇ vt **-1.** [probar - hechos] to check, to verify. **-2.** [resistir] to resist.

contraste m contrast.

contratar vt **-1.** [obreros, personal, detective] to hire; [deportista] to sign. **-2.** [servicio, obra, mercancía]: ~ **algo a alguien** to contract for sthg with sb.

contratiempo m [accidente] mishap; [dificultad] setback.

contratista m y f contractor.

contrato m contract.

contraventana f shutter.

contribución f **-1.** [gen] contribution. **-2.** [impuesto] tax.

contribuir vi **-1.** [gen]: ~ **(a)** to contribute (to); ~ **con algo para** to contribute sthg towards. **-2.** [pagar impuestos] to pay taxes.

contribuyente m y f taxpayer.

contrincante m y f rival, opponent.

control m **-1.** [gen] control; **bajo** ~ under control; **perder el** ~ to lose one's temper. **-2.** [verificación] examination, inspection; **(bajo)** ~ **médico** (under) medical supervision; ~ **antidoping** dope test. **-3.** [puesto policial] checkpoint.

controlador, -ra m y f [gen & INFORM] controller; ~ **aéreo** air traffic controller.

controlar vt **-1.** [gen] to control; [cuentas] to audit. **-2.** [comprobar] to check.

controversia f controversy.

contundente adj **-1.** [arma, objeto] blunt; [golpe] thudding. **-2.** fig [razonamiento, argumento] forceful.

contusión f bruise.

convalecencia f convalescence.

convaleciente adj convalescent.

convalidar vt [estudios] to recognize; [asignaturas] to validate.

convencer vt to convince; ~ **a alguien de algo** to convince sb of sthg. ◆ **convencerse** vpr: ~**se de** to become convinced of.

convencimiento m [certeza] conviction; [acción] convincing.

convención f convention.

convencional adj conventional.

conveniencia f **-1.** [utilidad] usefulness; [oportunidad] suitability. **-2.** [interés] convenience; **sólo mira su** ~ he only looks after his own interests.

conveniente adj [útil] useful; [oportuno] suitable, appropriate; [lugar, hora] convenient; [aconsejable] advisable; **sería** ~ **asistir** it would be a good idea to go.

convenio m agreement.

convenir vi **-1.** [venir bien] to be suitable; **conviene analizar la situación** it would be a good idea to analyse the situation; **no te conviene hacerlo** you shouldn't do it. **-2.** [acordar]: ~ **en** to agree on.

convento m [de monjas] convent; [de monjes] monastery.

converger vi to converge.

conversación f conversation. ◆ **conversaciones** fpl [negociaciones] talks.

conversada f Amer chat.

conversar vi to talk, to converse.

conversión f conversion.

converso, -sa adj converted.

convertir vt **-1.** RELIG to convert. **-2.** [transformar]: ~ **algo/a alguien en** to convert sthg/sb into, to turn sthg/sb into. ◆ **convertirse** vpr **-1.** RELIG: ~**se (a)** to convert (to). **-2.** [transformarse]: ~**se en** to become, to turn into.

convexo, -xa adj convex.

convicción f conviction; **tener la** ~ **de que** to be convinced that.

convicto, -ta *adj* convicted.

convidar *vt* [invitar] to invite.

convincente *adj* convincing.

convite *m* **-1.** [invitación] invitation. **-2.** [fiesta] banquet.

convivencia *f* living together.

convivir *vi* to live together; ~ **con** to live with.

convocar *vt* [reunión] to convene; [huelga, elecciones] to call.

convocatoria *f* **-1.** [anuncio, escrito] notice. **-2.** [de examen] diet.

convulsión *f* **-1.** [de músculos] convulsion. **-2.** [política, social] upheaval (*U*).

conyugal *adj* conjugal; **vida** ~ married life.

cónyuge *m y f* spouse; **los** ~**s** husband and wife.

coñá, coñac (*pl* **coñacs**), **cognac** (*pl* **cognacs**) *m* brandy, cognac.

coñazo *m fam* pain, drag.

coño *vulg* ◇ *m* [genital] cunt. ◇ *interj* **-1.** [enfado]: ¡~! for fuck's sake! **-2.** [asombro]: ¡~! fucking hell!

cooperación *f* cooperation.

cooperar *vi*: ~ **(con alguien en algo)** to cooperate (with sb in sthg).

cooperativo, -va *adj* cooperative.
◆ **cooperativa** *f* cooperative.

coordinador, -ra ◇ *adj* coordinating. ◇ *m y f* coordinator.

coordinar *vt* **-1.** [movimientos, gestos] to coordinate. **-2.** [esfuerzos, medios] to combine, to pool.

copa *f* **-1.** [vaso] glass; **ir de** ~**s** to go out drinking; **¿quieres (tomar) una** ~? would you like (to have) a drink? **-2.** [de árbol] top. **-3.** [en deporte] cup.
◆ **copas** *fpl* [naipes] *suit with pictures of goblets in Spanish playing cards.*

COPE (*abrev de* **Cadena de Ondas Populares Españolas**) *f private Spanish radio station.*

Copenhague Copenhagen.

copete *m* [de ave] crest.

copia *f* [reproducción] copy; ~ **de seguridad** INFORM backup.

copiar ◇ *vt* [gen] to copy; [al dictado] to take down. ◇ *vi* [en examen] to cheat, to copy.

copiloto *m y f* copilot.

copión, -ona *m y f* [imitador] copycat; [en examen] cheat.

copioso, -sa *adj* copious.

copla *f* **-1.** [canción] folksong, popular song. **-2.** [estrofa] verse, stanza.

copo *m* [de nieve, cereales] flake; ~**s de avena** rolled oats.

copropietario, -ria *m y f* co-owner.

copular *vi* to copulate.

copulativo, -va *adj* copulative.

coquetear *vi* to flirt.

coqueto, -ta *adj* [persona - que flirtea] flirtatious, coquettish; [- que se arregla mucho] concerned with one's appearance.

coraje *m* **-1.** [valor] courage. **-2.** [rabia] anger; **me da mucho** ~ it makes me furious.

coral ◇ *adj* choral. ◇ *m* coral. ◇ *f* **-1.** [coro] choir. **-2.** [composición] chorale.

Corán *m*: **el** ~ the Koran.

coraza *f* **-1.** [de soldado] cuirasse, armour. **-2.** [de tortuga] shell.

corazón *m* **-1.** [gen] heart; **de buen** ~ kindhearted. **-2.** [de frutas] core. **-3.** → **dedo**.

corazonada *f* **-1.** [presentimiento] hunch. **-2.** [impulso] sudden impulse.

corbata *f* tie.

Córcega Corsica.

corchea *f* quaver.

corchete *m* **-1.** [broche] hook and eye. **-2.** [signo ortográfico] square bracket.

corcho *m* cork.

corcholata *f Amer* metal bottle top.

cordel *m* cord.

cordero, -ra *m y f* lit & *fig* lamb.

cordial *adj* cordial.

cordialidad *f* cordiality.

cordillera *f* mountain range; **la** ~ **Cantábrica** the Cantabrian Mountains.

cordón *m* **-1.** [gen & ANAT] cord; [de zapato] lace; ~ **umbilical** umbilical cord. **-2.** [cable eléctrico] flex. **-3.** *fig* [para protección, vigilancia] cordon; ~ **sanitario** cordon sanitaire. **-4.** *Amer* [de la acera] kerb.

cordura *f* [juicio] sanity; [sensatez] sense.

Corea: ~ **del Norte/Sur** North/South Korea.

corear *vt* to chorus.

coreógrafo, -fa *m y f* choreographer.

corista *m y f* [en coro] chorus singer.

cornada *f* goring.

cornamenta *f* [de toro] horns (*pl*); [de ciervo] antlers (*pl*).

córner *m* corner (kick).

corneta *f* [instrumento] bugle.

cornisa *f* ARQUIT cornice.

coro *m* **-1.** [gen] choir; **contestar a** ~ to answer all at once. **-2.** [de obra musical] chorus.

corona f **-1.** [gen] crown. **-2.** [de flores] garland; ~ **fúnebre/de laurel** funeral/laurel wreath. **-3.** [de santos] halo.

coronación f [de monarca] coronation.

coronar vt **-1.** [persona] to crown. **-2.** fig [terminar] to complete; [culminar] to crown, to cap.

coronel m colonel.

coronilla f crown (of the head); **estar hasta la ~ (de)** to be sick and tired (of).

corpiño m bodice.

corporación f corporation.

corporal adj corporal.

corporativo, -va adj corporate.

corpulento, -ta adj corpulent.

corral m [gen] yard; [para cerdos, ovejas] pen.

correa f **-1.** [de bolso, reloj] strap; [de pantalón] belt; [de perro] lead, leash. **-2.** TECN belt; ~ **del ventilador** fan belt.

corrección f **-1.** [de errores] correction; ~ **de pruebas** proofreading. **-2.** [de exámenes] marking. **-3.** [de texto] revision. **-4.** [de comportamiento] correctness.

correctivo, -va adj corrective. ◆ **correctivo** m punishment.

correcto, -ta adj **-1.** [resultado, texto, respuesta] correct. **-2.** [persona] polite; [conducta] proper.

corredor, -ra ◇ adj running. ◇ m y f **-1.** [deportista] runner. **-2.** [intermediario]: ~ **de bolsa** stockbroker; ~ **de comercio** COM registered broker; ~ **de fincas** land agent. ◆ **corredor** m [pasillo] corridor.

corregir vt [gen] to correct; [exámenes] to mark. ◆ **corregirse** vpr to change for the better.

correlación f correlation.

correo m post, mail; **echar al ~** to post; **a vuelta de ~** by return (of post); ~ **aéreo** air mail; ~ **certificado** registered post O mail; ~ **electrónico** electronic mail; ~ **urgente** special delivery. ◆ **Correos** m [organismo] the post office.

correr ◇ vi **-1.** [andar de prisa] to run; **a todo ~** at full speed O pelt; **(ella) corre que se las pela** she runs like the wind. **-2.** [conducir de prisa] to drive fast. **-3.** [pasar por - río] to flow; [- camino, agua del grifo] to run. **-4.** [el tiempo, las horas] to pass, to go by. **-5.** [propagarse - noticia etc] to spread. ◇ vt **-1.** [recorrer - una distancia] to cover; **corrió los 100 metros** he ran the 100 metres. **-2.** [deslizar - mesa, silla] to move O pull up. **-3.** [cor-

tinas] to draw; ~ **el pestillo** to bolt the door. **-4.** [experimentar - aventuras, vicisitudes] to have; [- riesgo] to run. ◆ **correrse** vpr **-1.** [desplazarse - persona] to move over; [- cosa] to slide. **-2.** [pintura, colores] to run.

correspondencia f **-1.** [gen] correspondence. **-2.** [de metro, tren] connection.

corresponder vi **-1.** [compensar]: ~ **(con algo) a alguien/algo** to repay sb/sthg (with sthg). **-2.** [pertenecer] to belong. **-3.** [coincidir]: ~ **(a/con)** to correspond (to/with). **-4.** [tocar]: ~**le a alguien hacer algo** to be sb's responsibility to do sthg. **-5.** [a un sentimiento] to reciprocate. ◆ **corresponderse** vpr **-1.** [escribirse] to correspond. **-2.** [amarse] to love each other.

correspondiente adj **-1.** [gen]: ~ **(a)** corresponding (to). **-2.** [respectivo] respective.

corresponsal m y f PRENS correspondent.

corretear vi [correr] to run about.

corrido, -da adj [avergonzado] embarrassed. ◆ **corrida** f **-1.** TAUROM bullfight. **-2.** [acción de correr] run. ◆ **de corrido** loc prep by heart; **recitar algo de ~** to recite sthg parrot-fashion.

corriente ◇ adj **-1.** [normal] ordinary, normal. **-2.** [agua] running. **-3.** [mes, año, cuenta] current. ◇ f **-1.** [de río, electricidad] current; ~ **alterna/continua** alternating/direct current. **-2.** [de aire] draught. **-3.** fig [tendencia] trend, current; [de opinión] tide. **-4.** loc: **ir contra ~** to go against the tide; **estar al ~ de** to be up to date with.

corro m [círculo] circle, ring; **en ~** in a circle; **hacer ~** to form a circle.

corroborar vt to corroborate.

corroer vt [gen] to corrode; GEOL to erode.

corromper vt **-1.** [pudrir - madera] to rot; [- alimentos] to turn bad, to spoil. **-2.** [pervertir] to corrupt.

corrosivo, -va adj lit & fig corrosive.

corrupción f **-1.** [gen] corruption. **-2.** [de una substancia] decay.

corrusco m hard crust.

corsario, -ria adj pirate (antes de sust). ◆ **corsario** m corsair, pirate.

corsé m corset.

cortacésped (pl **cortacéspedes**) m lawnmower.

cortado, -da adj **-1.** [labios, manos] chapped. **-2.** [leche] sour, off; [salsa]

curdled. **-3.** *fam fig* [tímido] **inhibited;
quedarse ~** to be left speechless.
◆ **cortado** *m* [café] *small coffee with just a
little milk.*

cortafuego *m* firebreak.

cortante *adj* **-1.** [afilado] **sharp. -2.** *fig*
[tajante - frase, estilo] **cutting;** [- viento]
biting; [- frío] **bitter.**

cortapisa *f* limitation, restriction.

cortar ◇ *vt* **-1.** [seccionar - pelo, uñas] to
cut; [- papel] to cut up; [- ramas] to cut
off; [- árbol] to cut down. **-2.** [amputar]
to amputate, to cut off. **-3.** [tela, figura
de papel] to cut out. **-4.** [interrumpir - retirada, luz, teléfono] to cut off; [- carrete-
ra] to block (off); [- hemorragia] to stop,
to staunch; [- discurso, conversación] to
interrupt. **-5.** [labios, piel] to chap. ◇ *vi*
-1. [producir un corte] to cut. **-2.** [cesar
una relación] to break ○ split up.
◆ **cortarse** *vpr* **-1.** [herirse] to cut o.s.;
~se el pelo to have a haircut. **-2.** [ali-
mento] to curdle. **-3.** [turbarse] to become tongue-tied.

cortaúñas *m inv* nail clippers (*pl*).

corte ◇ *m* **-1.** [raja] cut; [en pantalones,
camisa etc] tear; **~ y confección** [para
mujeres] dressmaking; [para hombres]
tailoring. **-2.** [interrupción]: **~ de luz**
power cut. **-3.** [sección] section. **-4.**
[concepción, estilo] style. **-5.** *fam* [ver-
güenza] embarrassment; **dar ~ a alguien** to embarrass sb. ◇ *f* [palacio]
court. ◆ **Cortes** *fpl* POLÍT *the Spanish
parliament.*

cortejar *vt* to court.

cortejo *m* retinue; **~ fúnebre** funeral
cortège ○ procession.

cortés *adj* polite, courteous.

cortesía *f* courtesy; **de ~** courtesy.

corteza *f* **-1.** [del árbol] bark. **-2.** [de
pan] crust; [de queso, tocino, limón] rind;
[de naranja etc] peel. **-3.** [terrestre] crust.

cortina *f* [de tela] curtain; *fig:* **~ de
agua** sheet of water; **~ de humo**
smoke screen.

cortisona *f* cortisone.

corto, -ta *adj* **-1.** [gen] short. **-2.** [escaso
- raciones] meagre; [- disparo] short of
the target; **~ de vista** short-sighted.
-3. *fig* [bobo] dim, simple. **-4.** *loc:* **quedarse ~** [al calcular] to underestimate;
decir que es bueno es quedarse ~ it's
an understatement to call it good.

cortocircuito *m* short circuit.

cortometraje *m* short (film).

cosa *f* **-1.** [gen] thing; **¿queréis alguna
~?** is there anything you want?; **no es**

gran ~ it's not important, it's no big
deal; **poca ~** nothing much. **-2.** [asun-
to] matter. **-3.** [ocurrencia]: **¡qué ~ tienes!** you do say some funny things!
-4. *loc:* **hacer algo como quien no quiere la ~** [disimuladamente] to do sthg as
if one wasn't intending to; [sin querer]
to do sthg almost without realizing it;
como si tal ~ as if nothing had happened; **eso es ~ mía** that's my affair ○
business. ◆ **cosa de** *loc adv* about.

coscorrón *m* bump on the head.

cosecha *f* **-1.** [gen] harvest; **ser de la
(propia) ~ de alguien** to be made up ○
invented by sb. **-2.** [del vino] vintage.

cosechar ◇ *vt* **-1.** [cultivar] to grow. **-2.**
[recolectar] to harvest. ◇ *vi* to (bring in
the) harvest.

coser ◇ *vt* [con hilo] to sew; **~ un botón** to sew on a button. ◇ *vi* to sew;
ser cosa de ~ y cantar to be child's
play ○ a piece of cake.

cosido *m* stitching.

cosmético, -ca *adj* cosmetic (*antes de
sust*). ◆ **cosmético** *m* cosmetic. ◆ **cos-
mética** *f* cosmetics (*U*).

cosmopolita *adj, m y f* cosmopolitan.

cosmos *m* cosmos.

cosquillas *fpl:* **hacer ~** to tickle; **tener
~** to be ticklish.

costa *f* GEOGR coast. ◆ **a costa de** *loc
prep* at the expense of; **lo hizo a ~ de
grandes esfuerzos** he did it by dint of
much effort. ◆ **a toda costa** *loc prep* at
all costs.

costado *m* side.

costal *m* sack.

costanera *f Amer* seaside promenade.

costar ◇ *vt* **-1.** [dinero] to cost; **¿cuánto
cuesta?** how much is it? **-2.** [tiempo] to
take. ◇ *vi* [ser difícil]: **~le a alguien hacer algo** to be difficult for sb to do
sthg.

Costa Rica Costa Rica.

costarricense, costarriqueño, -ña *adj,
m y f* Costa Rican.

coste *m* [de producción] cost; [de un ob-
jeto] price; **~ de la vida** cost of living.

costear *vt* [pagar] to pay for.

costilla *f* **-1.** [de persona, barco] rib. **-2.**
[de animal] cutlet.

costo *m* [de una mercancía] price; [de un
producto, de la vida] cost.

costoso, -sa *adj* [operación, maquinaria]
expensive.

costra *f* [de herida] scab.

costumbre *f* habit, custom; **coger/
perder la ~ de hacer algo** to get into/

out of the habit of doing sthg; **como de** ~ as usual.

costura *f* **-1.** [labor] sewing, needlework. **-2.** [puntadas] seam. **-3.** [oficio] dressmaking; **alta** ~ haute couture.

costurero *m* [caja] sewing box.

cota *f* **-1.** [altura] altitude, height above sea level. **-2.** *fig* [nivel] level, height.

cotarro *m* riotous gathering; **dirigir el** ~ to rule the roost.

cotejar *vt* to compare.

cotejo *m* comparison.

cotidiano, -na *adj* daily.

cotilla *m y f fam* gossip, busybody.

cotillear *vi fam* to gossip.

cotilleo *m fam* gossip, tittle-tattle.

cotillón *m* New Year's Eve party.

cotización *f* **-1.** [valor] price. **-2.** [en Bolsa] quotation, price.

cotizar *vt* **-1.** [valorar] to quote, to price. **-2.** [pagar] to pay. ◆ **cotizarse** *vpr* **-1.** [estimarse - persona] to be valued O prized. **-2.** ~**se a** [producto] to sell for, to fetch; [bonos, valores] to be quoted at.

coto *m* preserve; ~ **de caza** game preserve; **poner** ~ **a** to put a stop to.

cotorra *f* [ave] parrot.

COU (*abrev de* **curso de orientación universitaria**) *m one-year course which prepares pupils aged 17-18 for Spanish university entrance examinations.*

coxis = **cóccix**.

coyote *m* coyote.

coyuntura *f* **-1.** [situación] moment; **la** ~ **económica** the economic situation. **-2.** ANAT joint.

coz *f* kick.

crac (*pl* **cracs**), **crack** (*pl* **cracks**) *m* FIN crash.

crack (*pl* **cracks**) *m* **-1.** FIN → **crac**. **-2.** [droga] crack.

cráneo *m* cranium, skull.

crápula *m y f* libertine.

cráter *m* crater.

creación *f* creation.

creador, -ra ◇ *adj* creative. ◇ *m y f:* creator.

crear *vt* **-1.** [gen] to create. **-2.** [fundar - una academia] to found.

creatividad *f* creativity.

creativo, -va *adj* creative.

crecer *vi* **-1.** [persona, planta] to grow. **-2.** [días, noches] to grow longer. **-3.** [río, marea] to rise. **-4.** [aumentar - animosidad etc] to grow, to increase; [- ru-

mores] to spread. ◆ **crecerse** *vpr* to become more self-confident.

creces ◆ **con creces** *adv* with interest.

crecido, -da *adj* [cantidad] large; [hijo] grown-up. ◆ **crecida** *f* spate, flood.

creciente *adj* [gen] growing; [luna] crescent.

crecimiento *m* [gen] growth; [de precios] rise.

credibilidad *f* credibility.

crédito *m* **-1.** [préstamo] loan; **a** ~ on credit; ~ **al consumo** ECON consumer credit. **-2.** [plazo de préstamo] credit. **-3.** [confianza] trust, belief; **digno de** ~ trustworthy; **dar** ~ **a algo** to believe sthg. **-4.** [en universidad] credit.

credo *m* [religioso] creed.

crédulo, -la *adj* credulous.

creencia *f* belief.

creer *vt* **-1.** [gen] to believe. **-2.** [suponer] to think. ◆ **creer en** *vi* to believe in. ◆ **creerse** *vpr* [considerarse] to believe o.s. to be.

creíble *adj* credible, believable.

creído, -da *m y f* [presumido] conceited.

crema *f* **-1.** [gen] cream. **-2.** [betún] shoe polish. **-3.** [licor] crème. **-4.** [dulce, postre] custard.

cremallera *f* [para cerrar] zip (fastener).

crematorio, -ria *adj*: **horno** ~ crematour. ◆ **crematorio** *m* crematorium.

cremoso, -sa *adj* creamy.

crepe [krep] *f* crepe.

crepitar *vi* to crackle.

crepúsculo *m* [al amanecer] first light; [al anochecer] twilight, dusk.

crespo, -pa *adj* tightly curled, frizzy.

cresta *f* **-1.** [gen] crest. **-2.** [del gallo] comb.

Creta Crete.

cretino, -na *m y f* cretin.

creyente *m y f* believer.

cría → **crío**.

criadero *m* [de animales] farm (*breeding place*); [de árboles, plantas] nursery.

criadillas *fpl* bull's testicles.

criado, -da *m y f* servant (*f* maid).

criador, -ra *m y f* [de animales] breeder; [de vinos] grower.

crianza *f* **-1.** [de animales] breeding. **-2.** [del vino] vintage. **-3.** [educación] breeding.

criar *vt* **-1.** [amamantar - suj: mujer] to breastfeed; [- suj: animal] to suckle. **-2.** [animales] to breed, to rear; [flores, árboles] to grow. **-3.** [vino] to mature, to

make. **-4.** [educar] to bring up.
◆ **criarse** *vpr* **-1.** [crecer] to grow up.

criatura *f* **-1.** [niño] child; [bebé] baby.
-2. [ser vivo] creature.

criba *f* **-1.** [tamiz] sieve. **-2.** [selección]
screening.

cricket = **criquet.**

crimen *m* crime.

criminal *adj, m y f* criminal.

crin *f* mane.

crío, cría *m y f* [niño] kid. ◆ **cría** *f* **-1.**
[hijo del animal] young. **-2.** [crianza - de
animales] breeding; [- de plantas] growing.

criollo, -lla *adj* **-1.** [persona] native to
Latin America. **-2.** [comida, lengua]
creole.

cripta *f* crypt.

criquet, cricket ['kriket] *m* cricket.

crisantemo *m* chrysanthemum.

crisis *f inv* [gen] crisis; ~ **económica** recession; ~ **nerviosa** nervous break-
down.

crisma *f fam* bonce, nut.

crismas, christmas *m inv* Christmas
card.

crispar *vt* [los nervios] to set on edge;
[los músculos] to tense; [las manos] to
clench.

cristal *m* **-1.** [material] glass (*U*); [vidrio
fino] crystal. **-2.** [en la ventana] (window) pane. **-3.** MIN crystal.

cristalera *f* [puerta] French window;
[techo] glass roof; [armario] glass-
fronted cabinet.

cristalino, -na *adj* crystalline.
◆ **cristalino** *m* crystalline lens.

cristalizar *vt* **-1.** [una sustancia] to crystallize. **-2.** *fig* [un asunto] to bring to a
head. ◆ **cristalizarse** *vpr* to crystallize.
◆ **cristalizarse en** *vpr fig* to develop
into.

cristiandad *f* Christianity.

cristianismo *m* Christianity.

cristiano, -na *adj, m y f* Christian.

cristo *m* crucifix. ◆ **Cristo** *m* Christ.

criterio *m* **-1.** [norma] criterion. **-2.** [jui-
cio] taste. **-3.** [opinión] opinion.

crítica → **crítico.**

criticar *vt* **-1.** [enjuiciar - literatura, arte]
to review. **-2.** [censurar] to criticize.

crítico, -ca ◇ *adj* critical. ◇ *m y f* [per-
sona] critic. ◆ **crítica** *f* **-1.** [juicio - sobre
arte, literatura] review. **-2.** [conjunto de
críticos]: **la** ~ the critics (*pl*). **-3.** [ata-
que] criticism.

criticón, -ona ◇ *adj* nit-picking. ◇ *m y
f* nitpicker.

Croacia Croatia.

croar *vi* to croak.

croata ◇ *adj* Croatian. ◇ *m y f* Croat.

croissant [krwa'san] (*pl* **croissants**) *m*
croissant.

crol *m* DEP crawl.

cromo *m* **-1.** [metal] chrome. **-2.** [estam-
pa] transfer.

cromosoma *m* chromosome.

crónico, -ca *adj* chronic. ◆ **crónica** *f*
-1. [de la historia] chronicle. **-2.** [de un
periódico] column; [de la televisión] feature, programme.

cronista *m y f* [historiador] chronicler;
[periodista] columnist.

cronología *f* chronology.

cronometrar *vt* to time.

cronómetro *m* DEP stopwatch; TECN
chronometer.

croqueta *f* croquette.

croquis *m inv* sketch.

cross *m inv* [DEP - carrera] cross-country
race; [- deporte] cross-country (running).

cruce *m* **-1.** [de líneas] crossing, intersection; [de carreteras] crossroads. **-2.**
[de animales] cross.

crucero *m* **-1.** [viaje] cruise. **-2.** [barco]
cruiser. **-3.** [de iglesias] transept.

crucial *adj* crucial.

crucificar *vt* [en una cruz] to crucify.

crucifijo *m* crucifix.

crucifixión *f* crucifixion.

crucigrama *m* crossword (puzzle).

crudeza *f* **-1.** [gen] harshness. **-2.** [de
descripción, imágenes] brutality.

crudo, -da *adj* **-1.** [natural] raw; [petró-
leo] crude. **-2.** [sin cocer completamente]
undercooked. **-3.** [realidad, clima, tiem-
po] harsh; [novela] harshly realistic,
hard-hitting. **-4.** [cruel] cruel. ◆ **crudo**
m crude (oil).

cruel *adj* [gen] cruel.

crueldad *f* **-1.** [gen] cruelty; [del clima]
harshness. **-2.** [acción cruel] act of
cruelty.

cruento, -ta *adj* bloody.

crujido *m* [de madera] creak, creaking
(*U*); [de hojas secas] crackle, crackling
(*U*).

crujiente *adj* [madera] creaky; [hojas se-
cas] rustling; [patatas fritas] crunchy.

crujir *vi* [madera] to creak; [patatas fritas,
nieve] to crunch; [hojas secas] to crackle;
[dientes] to grind.

cruz *f* **-1.** [gen] cross; ~ **gamada**
swastika. **-2.** [de una moneda] tails (*U*).

-3. *fig* [aflicción] burden. ◆ **Cruz Roja** *f* Red Cross.

cruza *f Amer* cross, crossbreed.

cruzado, -da *adj* **-1.** [cheque, piernas, brazos] crossed. **-2.** [un animal] crossbred. **-3.** [abrigo, chaqueta] double-breasted. ◆ **cruzada** *f lit & fig* crusade.

cruzar *vt* **-1.** [gen] to cross. **-2.** [unas palabras] to exchange. ◆ **cruzarse** *vpr* **-1.** [gen] to cross; ~**se de brazos** to fold one's arms. **-2.** [personas]: ~**se con alguien** to pass sb.

cta. (*abrev de* **cuenta**) a/c.

cte. (*abrev de* **corriente**) inst.

CTNE (*abrev de* **Compañía Telefónica Nacional de España**) *f Spanish state telephone company.*

cuaderno *m* [gen] notebook; [en el colegio] exercise book. ◆ **cuaderno de bitácora** *m* logbook.

cuadra *f* **-1.** [de caballos] stable. **-2.** *Amer* [manzana] block.

cuadrado, -da *adj* [gen & MAT] square. ◆ **cuadrado** *m* square.

cuadragésimo, -ma *núm* fortieth.

cuadrar ◇ *vi* **-1.** [información, hechos]: ~ **(con)** to square ○ agree (with). **-2.** [números, cuentas] to tally, to add up. ◇ *vt* [gen] to square. ◆ **cuadrarse** *vpr* MIL to stand to attention.

cuadrícula *f* grid.

cuadrilátero *m* **-1.** GEOM quadrilateral. **-2.** DEP ring.

cuadrilla *f* [de amigos, trabajadores] group; [de maleantes] gang.

cuadro *m* **-1.** [pintura] painting, picture. **-2.** [escena] scene, spectacle. **-3.** [descripción] portrait. **-4.** [cuadrado] square; [de flores] bed; **a ~s** check (*antes de sust*). **-5.** [equipo] team. **-6.** [gráfico] chart, diagram. **-7.** [de la bicicleta] frame. **-8.** TEATR scene.

cuádruple *m* quadruple.

cuajar ◇ *vt* **-1.** [solidificar - leche] to curdle; [- huevo] to set; [- sangre] to clot, to coagulate. **-2.** ~ **de** [llenar] to fill with; [cubrir] to cover with. ◇ *vi* **-1.** [lograrse - acuerdo] to be settled; [- negocio] to take off, to get going. **-2.** [ser aceptado - persona] to fit in; [- moda] to catch on. **-3.** [nieve] to settle. ◆ **cuajarse** *vpr* **-1.** [leche] to curdle; [sangre] to clot, to coagulate. **-2.** [llenarse]: ~**se de** to fill (up) with.

cuajo *m* rennet. ◆ **de cuajo** *loc adv*: **arrancar de** ~ [árbol] to uproot; [brazo etc] to tear right off.

cual *pron relat*: **el/la** ~ *etc* [de persona] (*sujeto*) who; (*complemento*) whom; [de cosa] which; **lo** ~ which; **conoció a una española, la** ~ **vivía en Buenos Aires** he met a Spanish girl who lived in Buenos Aires; **está muy enfadada, lo** ~ **es comprensible** she's very angry, which is understandable; **todo lo** ~ all of which; **sea** ~ **sea** ○ **fuere su decisión** whatever his decision (may be).

cuál *pron* (*interrogativo*) what; [en concreto, especificando] which one; **¿** ~ **es tu nombre?** what is your name?; **¿** ~ **es la diferencia?** what's the difference?; **no sé** ~**es son mejores** I don't know which are best; **¿** ~ **prefieres?** which one do you prefer?

cualesquiera *pl* → **cualquiera**.

cualidad *f* quality.

cualificado, -da *adj* skilled.

cualitativo, -va *adj* qualitative.

cualquiera (*pl* **cualesquiera**) ◇ *adj* (*antes de sust*: **cualquier**) any; **cualquier día vendré a visitarte** I'll drop by one of these days; **en cualquier momento** at any time; **en cualquier lugar** anywhere. ◇ *pron* anyone; ~ **te lo dirá** anyone will tell you; ~ **que** [persona] anyone who; [cosa] whatever; ~ **que sea la razón** whatever the reason (may be). ◇ *m y f* [don nadie] nobody.

cuan *adv* [todo lo que]: **se desplomó** ~ **largo era** he fell flat on the ground.

cuán *adv* how.

cuando ◇ *adv* when; **de** ~ **en** ~, **de vez en** ~ from time to time, now and again. ◇ *conj* **-1.** [de tiempo] when; ~ **llegue el verano iremos de viaje** when summer comes we'll go travelling. **-2.** [si] if; ~ **tú lo dices será verdad** it must be true if you say so. **-3.** (*después de "aun"*) [aunque]: **no mentiría aun** ~ **le fuera en ello la vida** she wouldn't lie even if her life depended on it. ◆ **cuando más** *loc adv* at the most. ◆ **cuando menos** *loc adv* at least. ◆ **cuando quiera que** *loc conj* whenever.

cuándo *adv* when; **¿** ~ **vas a venir?** when are you coming?; **quisiera saber** ~ **sale el tren** I'd like to know when ○ at what time the train leaves.

cuantía *f* [suma] quantity; [alcance] extent.

cuantificar *vt* to quantify.

cuantioso, -sa *adj* large, substantial.

cuantitativo, -va *adj* quantitative.

cuanto, -ta ◇ *adj* **-1.** [todo]: **despilfarra ~ dinero gana** he squanders all the money he earns; **soporté todas cuantas críticas me hizo** I put up with every single criticism he made of me. **-2.** (*antes de adv*) [compara cantidades]: **cuantas más mentiras digas, menos te creerán** the more you lie, the less people will believe you. ◇ *pron relat* (*gen pl*) [de personas] everyone who; [de cosas] everything (that); **~s fueron alabaron el espectáculo** everyone who went said the show was excellent; **dio las gracias a todos ~s le ayudaron** he thanked everyone who helped him. ◆ **cuanto** ◇ *pron relat* (*neutro*) **-1.** [todo lo que] everything, as much as; **come ~ quieras** eat as much as you like; **comprendo ~ dice** I understand everything he says; **todo ~** everything. **-2.** [compara cantidades]: **~ más se tiene, más se quiere** the more you have, the more you want. ◇ *adv* [compara cantidades]: **más come, ~ más gordo está** the more he eats, the fatter he gets. ◆ **cuanto antes** *loc adv* as soon as possible. ◆ **en cuanto** ◇ *loc conj* [tan pronto como] as soon as; **en ~ acabe** as soon as I've finished. ◇ *loc prep* [en calidad de] as; **en ~ cabeza de familia** as head of the family. ◆ **en cuanto a** *loc prep* as regards.

cuánto, -ta ◇ *adj* **-1.** (*interrogativo*) how much, (*pl*) how many; **¿cuántas manzanas tienes?** how many apples do you have?; **¿~ pan quieres?** how much bread do you want?; **no sé ~s hombres había** I don't know how many men were there. **-2.** (*exclamativo*) what a lot of; **¡cuánta gente (había)!** what a lot of people (were there)! ◇ *pron* (*gen pl*) **-1.** (*interrogativo*) how much, (*pl*) how many; **¿~s han venido?** how many came?; **dime cuántas quieres** tell me how many you want. **-2.** (*exclamativo*): **¡~s quisieran conocerte!** there are so many people who would like to meet you! ◆ **cuánto** *pron* (*neutro*) **-1.** (*interrogativo*) how much; **¿~ quieres?** how much do you want? **me gustaría saber ~ te costarán** I'd like to know how much they'll cost you. **-2.** (*exclamativo*): **¡~ han cambiado las cosas!** how things have changed!

cuarenta *núm* forty; **los (años) ~** the forties.

cuarentena *f* [por epidemia] quarantine.

cuaresma *f* Lent.

cuartear *vt* to cut ○ chop up.

cuartel *m* MIL barracks (*pl*); **~ general** headquarters (*pl*).

cuartelazo *m* Amer military uprising.

cuarteto *m* quartet.

cuarto, -ta *núm* fourth; **la cuarta parte** a quarter. ◆ **cuarto** *m* **-1.** [parte] quarter; **un ~ de hora** a quarter of an hour; **son las dos y/menos ~** it's a quarter past/to two. **-2.** [habitación] room; **~ de baño** bathroom; **~ de estar** living room. ◆ **cuarta** *f* [palmo] span.

cuarzo *m* quartz.

cuate *m y f inv* Amer [amigo] friend.

cuatro ◇ *núm* four; *ver también* **seis**. ◇ *adj fig* [poco] a few; **hace ~ días** a few days ago.

cuatrocientos, -tas *núm* four hundred; *ver también* **seis**.

cuba *f* barrel, cask; **estar como una ~** to be legless ○ blind drunk.

Cuba Cuba.

cubalibre *m* rum and coke.

cubano, -na *adj, m y f* Cuban.

cubertería *f* set of cutlery, cutlery (*U*).

cúbico, -ca *adj* cubic.

cubierto, -ta ◇ *pp* → **cubrir**. ◇ *adj* **-1.** [gen]: **~ (de)** covered (with); **estar a ~** [protegido] to be under cover; [con saldo acreedor] to be in the black; **ponerse a ~** to take cover. **-2.** [cielo] overcast. ◆ **cubierto** *m* **-1.** [pieza de cubertería] piece of cutlery. **-2.** [para cada persona] place setting. ◆ **cubierta** *f* **-1.** [gen] cover. **-2.** [de neumático] tyre. **-3.** [de barco] deck.

cubilete *m* [en juegos] cup; [molde] mould.

cubito *m* [de hielo] ice cube.

cubo *m* **-1.** [recipiente] bucket; **~ de la basura** rubbish bin. **-2.** GEOM & MAT cube; **elevar al ~** to cube.

cubrecama *m* bedspread.

cubrir *vt* **-1.** [gen] to cover. **-2.** [proteger] to protect. **-3.** [disimular] to cover up, to hide. **-4.** [puesto, vacante] to fill. ◆ **cubrir de** *vt*: **~ de algo a alguien** to heap sthg on sb. ◆ **cubrirse** *vpr* **-1.** [taparse]: **~se (de)** to become covered (with). **-2.** [protegerse]: **~se (de)** to shelter (from). **-3.** [con sombrero] to put one's hat on. **-4.** [con ropa]: **~se (con)** to cover o.s. (with). **-5.** [cielo] to cloud over.

cucaracha *f* cockroach.

cuchara *f* [para comer] spoon.

cucharada *f* spoonful.

cucharilla *f* teaspoon.
cucharón *m* ladle.
cuchichear *vi* to whisper.
cuchilla *f* blade; ~ **de afeitar** razor blade.
cuchillo *m* knife.
cuchitril *m* hovel.
cuclillas ◆ **en cuclillas** *loc adv* squatting; **ponerse en** ~ to squat (down).
cuclillo *m* cuckoo.
cuco, -ca *adj fam* **-1.** [bonito] pretty. **-2.** [astuto] shrewd, canny. ◆ **cuco** *m* cuckoo.
cucurucho *m* **-1.** [de papel] paper cone. **-2.** [para helado] cornet, cone.
cuello *m* **-1.** [gen] neck; ~ **de botella** bottleneck. **-2.** [de prendas] collar.
cuenca *f* **-1.** [de río] basin. **-2.** [del ojo] (eye) socket. **-3.** [región minera] coalfield.
cuenco *m* earthenware bowl.
cuenta *f* **-1.** [acción de contar] count; **echar ~s** to reckon up; **llevar/perder la** ~ **de** to keep/lose count of; ~ **atrás** countdown. **-2.** [cálculo] sum. **-3.** BANCA & COM account; **abonar algo en** ~ **a alguien** to credit sthg to sb's account; ~ **de gastos** expenditure account; **pagar mil pesetas a** ~ to pay a thousand pesetas down; ~ **de ahorros** savings account; ~ **corriente** current account; ~ **de crédito** current account with an overdraft facility; ~ **deudora** overdrawn account; ~ **a plazo fijo** deposit account. **-4.** [factura] bill; **pasar la** ~ to send the bill; ~ **por cobrar/pagar** account receivable/payable. **-5.** [bolita de collar, rosario] bead. **-6.** *loc:* **a fin de** ~**s** in the end; **ajustarle a alguien las** ~**s** to settle an account ○ a score with sb; **caer en la** ~ **de algo** to realize sthg; **darse** ~ **de algo** to realize sthg; **más de la** ~ too much; **por mi/tu** *etc* ~ on my/your *etc* own; **tener en** ~ **algo** to bear sthg in mind.
cuentagotas *m inv* dropper; **a** ○ **con** ~ in dribs and drabs.
cuentakilómetros *m inv* [de distancia recorrida] ≃ milometer; [de velocidad] speedometer.
cuentarrevoluciones *m inv* tachometer, rev counter.
cuento *m* **-1.** [fábula] tale; ~ **de hadas** fairy tale. **-2.** [narración] short story. **-3.** [mentira, exageración] story, lie; ~ **chino** tall story. **-4.** *loc:* **tener** ~ to put it on.
cuerda *f* **-1.** [para atar - fina] string; [- más gruesa] rope; ~ **floja** tightrope.

-2. [de instrumento] **string. -3.** [de reloj] spring; **dar** ~ **a** [reloj] to wind up. **-4.** GEOM chord. ◆ **cuerdas vocales** *fpl* vocal cords.
cuerdo, -da *adj* **-1.** [sano de juicio] sane. **-2.** [sensato] sensible.
cuerno *m* [gen] horn; [de ciervo] antler.
cuero *m* **-1.** [piel de animal] skin; [piel curtida] hide; ~ **cabelludo** scalp; **en ~s, en ~s vivos** stark naked. **-2.** [material] leather.
cuerpo *m* **-1.** [gen] body; **a** ~ without a coat on; **luchar a** ~ to fight hand-to-hand; **tomar** ~ to take shape; **en** ~ **y alma** body and soul. **-2.** [tronco] trunk. **-3.** [corporación consular, militar etc] corps; ~ **de bomberos** fire brigade; ~ **diplomático** diplomatic corps.
cuervo *m* crow.
cuesta *f* slope; ~ **arriba** uphill; ~ **abajo** downhill; **a** ~**s** on one's back, over one's shoulders.
cuestión *f* **-1.** [pregunta] question. **-2.** [problema] problem. **-3.** [asunto] matter, issue.
cuestionar *vt* to question.
cuestionario *m* questionnaire.
cueva *f* cave.
cuicos *mpl Amer fam* cops.
cuidado ◇ *m* care; **tener** ~ **con** to be careful with; ~**s intensivos** intensive care (*U*); **eso me tiene** ○ **trae sin** ~ I couldn't care less about that. ◇ *interj:* ¡~! careful!, look out!
cuidadoso, -sa *adj* careful.
cuidar *vt* [gen] to look after; [estilo etc] to take care over; [detalles] to pay attention to. ◆ **cuidar de** *vi* to look after; **cuida de que no lo haga** make sure she doesn't do it. ◆ **cuidarse** *vpr* to take care of ○ to look after o.s.; ~**se de** to worry about.
culata *f* **-1.** [de arma] butt. **-2.** [de motor] cylinder head.
culebra *f* snake.
culebrón *m* TV soap opera.
culinario, -ria *adj* culinary.
culminación *f* culmination.
culminar ◇ *vt:* ~ **(con)** to crown (with). ◇ *vi* to finish, to culminate.
culo *m fam* **-1.** [de personas] backside, bum *Br*. **-2.** [de objetos] bottom.
culpa *f* [responsabilidad] fault; **tener la** ~ **de algo** to be to blame for sthg; **echar la** ~ **a alguien (de)** to blame sb (for); **por** ~ **de** because of.
culpabilidad *f* guilt.

culpable ◇ *adj*: ~ **(de)** guilty (of); **declararse** ~ to plead guilty. ◇ *m y f* DER guilty party; **tú eres el** ~ you're to blame.

culpar *vt*: ~ **a alguien (de)** [atribuir la culpa] to blame sb (for); [acusar] to accuse sb (of).

cultivar *vt* [tierra] to farm, to cultivate; [plantas] to grow. ✦ **cultivarse** *vpr* [persona] to improve o.s.

cultivo *m* **-1.** [de tierra] **farming**; [de plantas] **growing. -2.** [plantación] **crop.**

culto, -ta *adj* [persona] cultured, educated; [estilo] refined; [palabra] literary. ✦ **culto** *m* **-1.** [devoción] **worship. -2.** [religión] **cult.**

cultura *f* **-1.** [de sociedad] **culture. -2.** [sabiduría] **learning, knowledge.**

cultural *adj* cultural.

culturismo *m* body-building.

cumbre *f* **-1.** [de montaña] **summit. -2.** *fig* [punto culminante] **peak. -3.** POLÍT summit (conference).

cumpleaños *m inv* birthday.

cumplido, -da *adj* **-1.** [completo, lleno] full, complete. **-2.** [cortés] courteous. ✦ **cumplido** *m* compliment.

cumplidor, -ra *adj* reliable.

cumplimentar *vt* **-1.** [felicitar] to congratulate. **-2.** [cumplir - orden] to carry out; [- contrato] to fulfil.

cumplimiento *m* [de un deber] performance; [de contrato, promesa] fulfilment; [de la ley] observance; [de órdenes] carrying out; [de condena] completion; [de plazo] expiry.

cumplir ◇ *vt* **-1.** [orden] to carry out; [promesa] to keep; [ley] to observe; [contrato] to fulfil. **-2.** [años] to reach; **mañana cumplo los 20** I'm 20 ○ it's my 20th birthday tomorrow. **-3.** [condena] to serve; [servicio militar] to do. ◇ *vi* **-1.** [plazo, garantía] to expire. **-2.** [realizar el deber] to do one's duty; ~ **con el deber** to do one's duty; ~ **con la palabra** to keep one's word.

cúmulo *m* **-1.** [de objetos] **pile. -2.** *fig* [de asuntos, acontecimientos] **series.**

cuna *f* [para dormir] cot, cradle.

cundir *vi* **-1.** [propagarse] to spread. **-2.** [dar de sí - comida, reservas, tiempo] to go a long way.

cuneta *f* [de una carretera] ditch; [de una calle] gutter.

cuña *f* **-1.** [pieza] wedge. **-2.** [de publicidad] commercial break.

cuñado, -da *m y f* brother-in-law (*f* sister-in-law).

cuño *m* **-1.** [troquel] **die. -2.** [sello, impresión] **stamp.**

cuota *f* **-1.** [contribución - a entidad, club] membership fee, subscription. **-2.** [cupo] quota.

cupiera *etc* → **caber.**

cuplé *m* popular song.

cupo ◇ *v* → **caber.** ◇ *m* **-1.** [cantidad máxima] **quota. -2.** [cantidad proporcional] **share**; [de una cosa racionada] **ration.**

cupón *m* [gen] coupon; [de lotería, rifa] ticket.

cúpula *f* **-1.** ARQUIT dome, cupola. **-2.** *fig* [mandos] **leaders** (*pl*).

cura ◇ *m* priest. ◇ *f* **-1.** [curación] recovery. **-2.** [tratamiento] **treatment, cure.**

curación *f* **-1.** [de un enfermo - recuperación] recovery; [- tratamiento] **treatment;** [de una herida] **healing. -2.** [de jamón] curing.

curado, -da *adj* [alimento] cured; [pieles] tanned; ~ **de espanto** unshockable.

curandero, -ra *m y f* quack.

curar ◇ *vt* **-1.** [gen] to cure. **-2.** [herida] to dress. **-3.** [pieles] to tan. ◇ *vi* [enfermo] to recover; [herida] to heal up. ✦ **curarse** *vpr* **-1.** [sanar]: ~**se (de)** to recover (from). **-2.** [alimento] to cure.

curiosear ◇ *vi* [fisgonear] to nose around; [por una tienda] to browse round. ◇ *vt* [libros, revistas] to browse through.

curiosidad *f* [gen] curiosity.

curioso, -sa ◇ *adj* **-1.** [por saber, averiguar] curious, inquisitive. **-2.** [raro] odd, strange. ◇ *m y f* onlooker.

curita *f Amer* sticking plaster.

currante *fam adj* hard-working.

currar, currelar *vi fam* to work.

curre = **curro.**

currelar = **currar.**

currículum (vitae) [ku'rrikulum ('bite)] (*pl* **currícula (vitae)** ○ **currículums**), **currículo** (*pl* **currículos**) *m* curriculum vitae.

curro, curre *m fam* work.

cursar *vt* **-1.** [estudiar] to study. **-2.** [enviar] to send. **-3.** [dar - órdenes etc] to give, to issue. **-4.** [tramitar] to submit.

cursi *adj fam* [vestido, canción etc] naff, tacky; [modales, persona] affected.

cursilería *f* [cualidad] tackiness.

cursillo *m* [curso] short course.

cursiva → **letra.**

curso *m* **-1.** [año académico] **year. -2.** [asignatura] course; ~ **intensivo** crash course. **-3.** [dirección - de río, acontecímientos] course; [- de la economía] trend; **seguir su ~** to go on, to continue; **en ~** [mes, año] current; [trabajo] in progress.

cursor *m* INFORM cursor.

curtido, -da *adj* **-1.** [piel, cuero] tanned. **-2.** *fig* [experimentado] seasoned.

curtir *vt* **-1.** [piel] to tan. **-2.** *fig* [persona] to harden.

curva → curvo.

curvatura *f* curvature.

curvo, -va *adj* [gen] curved; [doblado] bent. ◆ **curva** *f* [gen] curve; [en carretera] bend; **~ de nivel** contour line.

cúspide *f.* **-1.** [de montaña] summit, top. **-2.** *fig* [apogeo] peak. **-3.** GEOM apex.

custodia *f* **-1.** [de cosas] safekeeping. **-2.** [de personas] custody.

custodiar *vt* **-1.** [vigilar] to guard. **-2.** [proteger] to look after.

custodio *m* guard.

cutáneo, -a *adj* skin (*antes de sust*).

cutícula *f* cuticle.

cutis *m inv* skin, complexion.

cutre *adj fam* **-1.** [de bajo precio, calidad] cheap and nasty. **-2.** [sórdido] shabby. **-3.** [tacaño] tight, stingy.

cutter (*pl* **cutters**) *m* (artist's) scalpel (*with retractable blade*).

cuyo, -ya *adj* [posesión - por parte de personas] whose; [- por parte de cosas] of which, whose; **ésos son los amigos en cuya casa nos hospedamos** those are the friends in whose house we spent the night; **ese señor, ~ hijo conociste ayer** that man, whose son you met yesterday; **un equipo cuya principal estrella ...** a team, the star player of which ○ whose star player ...; **en ~ caso** in which case.

CV (*abrev de* **curriculum vitae**) *m* CV.

D

d, D *f* [letra] d, D.

D. *abrev de* **don.**

dactilar → huella.

dádiva *f* [regalo] gift; [donativo] donation.

dado, -da *adj* given; **en un momento ~** at a certain point; **ser ~ a** to be fond of. ◆ **dado** *m* dice, die. ◆ **dado que** *loc conj* since, seeing as.

daga *f* dagger.

dale *interj*: **¡~!** — **¡otra vez con lo mismo!** there you go again!

dalia *f* dahlia.

dálmata *adj, m y f* [perro] Dalmatian.

daltónico, -ca *adj* colour-blind.

daltonismo *m* colour blindness.

dama *f* **-1.** [mujer] lady. **-2.** [en damas] king; [en ajedrez, naipes] queen. ◆ **damas** *fpl* [juego] draughts (*U*).

damisela *f desus* damsel.

damnificar *vt* [cosa] to damage; [persona] to harm, to injure.

danés, -esa ◇ *adj* Danish. ◇ *m y f* [persona] Dane. ◆ **danés** *m* [lengua] Danish.

danza *f* [gen] dancing; [baile] dance.

danzar *vi* **-1.** [bailar] to dance. **-2.** *fig* [ir de un sitio a otro] to run about.

dañar *vt* [vista, cosecha] to harm, to damage; [persona] to hurt; [pieza, objeto] to damage. ◆ **dañarse** *vpr* [persona] to hurt oneself; [cosa] to become damaged.

dañino, -na *adj* harmful.

daño *m* **-1.** [dolor] pain, hurt; **hacer ~ a alguien** to hurt sb; **hacerse ~** to hurt oneself. **-2.** [perjuicio - a algo] damage; [- a persona] harm; **~s y perjuicios** damages.

dar ◇ *vt* **-1.** [gen] to give; [baile, fiesta] to hold, to give; [naipes] to deal; **~ algo a alguien** to give sthg to sb, to give sb sthg. **-2.** [producir - gen] to give, to produce; [- frutos, flores] to bear; [- beneficios, intereses] to yield. **-3.** [suj: reloj] to strike; **el reloj ha dado las doce** the clock struck twelve. **-4.** [suministrar luz etc - por primera vez] to connect; [- tras un corte] to turn back on; [encender] to turn ○ switch on. **-5.** [CIN, TEATR & TV] to show; [concierto, interpretación] to give. **-6.** [mostrar - señales etc] to show. **-7.** [untar con] to apply; **~ barniz a una silla** to varnish a chair. **-8.** [provocar - gusto, escalofríos etc] to give; **me da vergüenza/pena** it makes me ashamed/sad; **me da risa** it makes me laugh; **me da miedo** it frightens me. **-9.** [expresa acción]: **~ un grito** to give a cry; **~le un golpe/una puñalada a alguien** to hit/stab sb; **voy a ~ un paseo** I'm going (to go) for a walk. **-10.** [considerar]: **~ algo por** to consider sthg as; **eso lo doy por hecho** I take that for granted; **~ a alguien por muerto** to give sb up for dead. ◇ *vi* **-1.** [repartir -

en naipes] to deal. **-2.** [horas] to strike; **han dado las tres en el reloj** three o'clock struck. **-3.** [golpear]: **le dieron en la cabeza** they hit him on the head; **la piedra dio contra el cristal** the stone hit the window. **-4.** [accionar]: ~ **a** [llave de paso] to turn; [botón, timbre] to press. **-5.** [estar orientado]: ~ **a** [suj: ventana, balcón] to look out onto, to overlook; [suj: pasillo, puerta] to lead to; [suj: casa, fachada] to face. **-6.** [encontrar]: ~ **con algo/alguien** to find sthg/sb; **he dado con la solución** I've hit upon the solution. **-7.** [proporcionar]: ~ **de beber a alguien** to give sb sthg to drink; **le da de mamar a su hijo** she breast-feeds her son. **-8.** *loc*: ~ **de sí** [ropa, calzado] to give, to stretch. ◆ **darse** *vpr* **-1.** [suceder] to occur, to happen; **se da pocas veces** it rarely happens. **-2.** [entregarse]: ~**se a** [droga etc] to take to. **-3.** [golpearse]: ~**se contra** to bump into. **-4.** [tener aptitud]: **se me da bien/mal el latín** I'm good/bad at Latin. **-5.** [considerarse]: ~**se por** to consider o.s. (to be); ~**se por vencido** to give in. **-6.** *loc*: **dársela a alguien** [engañar] to take sb in; **se las da de listo** he makes out (that) he is clever.

dardo *m* dart.

dársena *f* dock.

datar *vt* to date. ◆ **datar de** *vi* to date from.

dátil *m* BOT & CULIN date.

dato *m* [gen] piece of information, fact; ~**s** [gen] information; INFORM data; ~**s personales** personal details.

dcha. (*abrev de* **derecha**) rt.

d. de JC., d.JC. (*abrev de* **después de Jesucristo**) AD.

de *prep* (*de* + *el* = **del**) **-1.** [posesión, pertenencia] of; **el coche** ~ **mi padre/mis padres** my father's/parents' car; **es** ~ **ella** it's hers; **la pata** ~ **la mesa** the table leg. **-2.** [materia] (made) of; **un vaso** ~ **plástico** a plastic cup; **un reloj** ~ **oro** a gold watch. **-3.** [en descripciones]: **un vaso** ~ **agua** a glass of water; ~ **fácil manejo** user-friendly; **la señora** ~ **verde** the lady in green; **el chico** ~ **la coleta** the boy with the ponytail; **he comprado las peras** ~ **100 ptas el kilo** I bought the pears that were ○ at 100 pesetas a kilo; **un sello** ~ **50 ptas** a 50 peseta stamp. **-4.** [asunto] about; **hablábamos** ~ **ti** we were talking about you; **libros** ~ **historia** history books. **-5.** [uso]: **una bici** ~ **carreras** a racer;

ropa ~ **deporte** sportswear. **-6.** [en calidad de] as; **trabaja** ~ **bombero** he works as a fireman. **-7.** [tiempo - desde] from; [- durante] in; **trabaja** ~ **nueve a cinco** she works from nine to five; ~ **madrugada** early in the morning; **a las cuatro** ~ **la tarde** at four in the afternoon; **trabaja** ~ **noche y duerme** ~ **día** he works at night and sleeps during the day. **-8.** [procedencia, distancia] from; **salir** ~ **casa** to leave home; **soy** ~ **Bilbao** I'm from Bilbao. **-9.** [causa, modo] with; **morirse** ~ **hambre** to die of hunger; **llorar** ~ **alegría** to cry with joy; ~ **una patada** with a kick; ~ **una sola vez** in one go. **-10.** [con superlativos]: **el mejor** ~ **todos** the best of all; **el más importante del mundo** the most important in the world. **-11.** [en comparaciones]: **más/menos** ~ **...** more/less than .... **-12.** (*antes de infin*) [condición] if; ~ **querer ayudarme, lo haría** if she wanted to help me, she'd do it; ~ **no ser por ti, me hubiese hundido** if it hadn't been for you, I wouldn't have made it. **-13.** (*después de adj y antes de sust*) [enfatiza cualidad]: **el idiota** ~ **tu hermano** your stupid brother. **-14.** (*después de adj y antes de infin*): **es difícil** ~ **creer** it's hard to believe.

dé → **dar**.

deambular *vi* to wander (about).

debajo *adv* underneath; ~ **de** underneath, under; **por** ~ **de lo normal** below normal.

debate *m* debate.

debatir *vt* to debate. ◆ **debatirse** *vpr* [luchar] to struggle.

debe *m* debit (side).

deber ◇ *vt* [adeudar] to owe; ~ **algo a alguien** to owe sb sthg, to owe sthg to sb. ◇ *vi* **-1.** (*antes de infin*) [expresa obligación]: **debo hacerlo** I have to do it, I must do it; **deberían abolir esa ley** they ought to ○ should abolish that law; **debes dominar tus impulsos** you must ○ should control your impulses. **-2.** [expresa posibilidad]: ~ **de: el tren debe de llegar alrededor de las diez** the train should arrive at about ten; **deben de ser las diez** it must be ten o'clock; **no debe de ser muy mayor** she can't be very old. ◇ *m* duty. ◆ **deberse a** *vpr* **-1.** [ser consecuencia de] to be due to. **-2.** [dedicarse a] to have a responsibility towards. ◆ **deberes** *mpl* [trabajo escolar] homework (*U*).

debidamente *adv* properly.

debido, -da adj [justo, conveniente] due, proper; **como es ~** properly. ♦ **debido a** loc conj (a principio de frase) owing to; (en mitad de frase) due to.

débil adj **-1.** [persona - sin fuerzas] weak. **-2.** [voz, sonido] faint; [luz] dim.

debilidad f [gen] weakness; **tener ~ por** to have a soft spot for.

debilitar vt to weaken. ♦ **debilitarse** vpr to become ○ grow weak.

debutar vi to make one's debut.

década f decade.

decadencia f [gen] decadence.

decadente adj decadent.

decaer vi [gen] to decline; [enfermo] to get weaker; [salud] to fail; [entusiasmo] to flag; [restaurante etc] to go downhill.

decaído, -da adj [desalentado] gloomy, downhearted; [débil] frail.

decaimiento m [desaliento] gloominess; [decadencia] decline; [falta de fuerzas] weakness.

decano, -na m y f [de corporación, facultad] dean.

decapitar vt to decapitate, to behead.

decena f ten; **una ~ de veces** about ten times.

decencia f **-1.** [gen] decency; [en el vestir] modesty. **-2.** [dignidad] dignity.

decenio m decade.

decente adj **-1.** [gen] decent. **-2.** [en el comportamiento] proper; [en el vestir] modest. **-3.** [limpio] clean.

decepción f disappointment.

decepcionar vt to disappoint.

decibelio m decibel.

decidido, -da adj determined.

decidir ◇ vt **-1.** [gen] to decide; **~ hacer algo** to decide to do sthg. **-2.** [determinar] to determine. ◇ vi to decide. ♦ **decidirse** vpr to decide, to make up one's mind; **~se a hacer algo** to decide to do sthg; **~se por** to decide on, to choose.

décima → **décimo**.

decimal adj [sistema] decimal.

décimo, -ma núm tenth; **la décima parte** a tenth. ♦ **décimo** m **-1.** [fracción] tenth. **-2.** [en lotería] tenth part of a lottery ticket. ♦ **décima** f [en medidas] tenth; **una décima de segundo** a tenth of a second.

decir vt **-1.** [gen] to say; **~ que sí/no** to say yes/no; **¿cómo se dice "estación" en inglés?** how do you say "estación" in English?; **¿diga?, ¿dígame?** [al teléfono] hello? **-2.** [contar, ordenar] to tell; **~ a alguien que haga algo** to tell sb to

do sthg; **se dice que** they ○ people say (that); **~ la verdad** to tell the truth. **-3.** fig [revelar] to tell, to show; **eso lo dice todo** that says it all. **-4.** loc: **~ para sí** to say to o.s.; **es ~** that is, that's to say; **(o) mejor dicho** or rather; **querer ~** to mean; **¿qué quieres ~ con eso?** what do you mean by that?

decisión f **-1.** [dictamen, resolución] decision; **tomar una ~** to make ○ take a decision. **-2.** [empeño, tesón] determination; [seguridad, resolución] decisiveness.

decisivo, -va adj decisive.

declamar vt & vi to declaim, to recite.

declaración f [gen] statement; [de amor, impuestos, guerra] declaration; **prestar ~** to give evidence; **~ del impuesto sobre la renta** income tax return.

declarar ◇ vt [gen] to declare; [afirmar] to state, to say; **~ culpable/inocente a alguien** to find sb guilty/not guilty. ◇ vi DER to testify, to give evidence. ♦ **declararse** vpr **-1.** [incendio, epidemia] to break out. **-2.** [confesar el amor] to declare one's feelings ○ love. **-3.** [dar una opinión]: **~se a favor de algo** to say that one supports sthg; **~se en contra de algo** to say one is opposed to sthg; **~se culpable/inocente** to plead guilty/ not guilty.

declinar ◇ vt [gen & GRAM] to decline; [responsabilidad] to disclaim. ◇ vi [día, tarde] to draw to a close; [fiebre] to subside; [economía] to decline.

declive m **-1.** [decadencia] decline, fall; **en ~** in decline. **-2.** [pendiente] slope.

decodificador = **descodificador**.

decoración f **-1.** [acción] decoration; [efecto] décor. **-2.** [adorno] decorations (pl).

decorado m CIN & TEATR set.

decorar vt to decorate.

decorativo, -va adj decorative.

decoro m [pudor] decency.

decoroso, -sa adj [decente] decent; [correcto] seemly, proper.

decrecer vi [gen] to decrease, to decline; [caudal del río] to go down.

decrépito, -ta adj despec [viejo] decrepit; [civilización] decadent, declining.

decretar vt to decree.

decreto m decree; **~ ley** decree, ≃ order in council Br.

dedal m thimble.

dedicación f dedication.

dedicar vt **-1.** [tiempo, dinero, energía] to devote. **-2.** [libro, monumento] to dedicate. ♦ **dedicarse a** vpr **-1.** [a una profesión]: **¿a qué se dedica usted?** what do you do for a living?; **se dedica a la enseñanza** she works as a teacher. **-2.** [a una actividad, persona] to spend time on; **los domingos me dedico al estudio** I spend Sundays studying.

dedicatoria f dedication.

dedo m **-1.** [de la mano] finger; **dos ~s de whisky** two fingers of whisky; **~ anular/corazón** ring/middle finger; **~ gordo ○ pulgar** thumb; **~ índice/meñique** index/little finger. **-2.** [del pie] toe. **-3.** loc: **hacer ~** fam to hitchhike; **nombrar a alguien a ~** to handpick sb; **pillarse ○ cogerse los ~s** fig to get one's fingers burnt; **poner el ~ en la llaga** to put one's finger on it.

deducción f deduction.

deducir vt **-1.** [inferir] to guess, to deduce. **-2.** [descontar] to deduct.

defecar vi to defecate.

defecto m [físico] defect; [moral] fault; **~ de pronunciación** speech defect. ◆ **por defecto** loc adv by default.

defectuoso, -sa adj [mercancía] defective, faulty; [trabajo] inaccurate.

defender vt [gen] to defend; [amigo etc] to stand up for. ◆ **defenderse** vpr [protegerse]: **~se (de)** to defend o.s. (against).

defensa ◇ f defence. ◇ m y f DEP defender; **~ central** centre-back.

defensivo, -va adj defensive. ◆ **defensiva** f: **ponerse/estar a la defensiva** to go/be on the defensive.

defensor, -ra ◇ adj **▷ abogado.** ◇ m y f [gen] defender; [abogado] counsel for the defence; [adalid] champion; **~ del pueblo** ≃ ombudsman.

deferencia f deference.

deficiencia f [defecto] deficiency, shortcoming; [insuficiencia] lack.

deficiente adj [defectuoso - gen] deficient; **~ en** lacking ○ deficient in; [audición, vista] defective. ◆ **deficiente (mental)** m y f mentally handicapped person.

déficit (pl **déficits**) m ECON deficit.

deficitario, -ria adj [empresa, operación] loss-making; [balance] negative.

definición f **-1.** [gen] definition. **-2.** [en televisión] resolution.

definir vt [gen] to define. ◆ **definirse** vpr to take a clear stance.

definitivamente adv **-1.** [sin duda] definitely. **-2.** [para siempre] for good.

definitivo, -va adj [texto etc] definitive;

[respuesta] definite; **en definitiva** in short, anyway.

deforestación f deforestation.

deformación f [de huesos, objetos etc] deformation; [de la verdad etc] distortion; **~ física** (physical) deformity; **tener ~ profesional** to be always acting as if one were still at work.

deformar vt **-1.** [huesos, objetos etc] to deform. **-2.** [la verdad etc] to distort. ◆ **deformarse** vpr to go out of shape.

deforme adj [cuerpo] deformed; [imagen] distorted; [objeto] misshapen.

defraudar vt **-1.** [decepcionar] to disappoint. **-2.** [estafar] to defraud; **~ a Hacienda** to practise tax evasion.

defunción f decease, death.

degeneración f degeneration.

degenerado, -da adj, m y f degenerate.

degenerar vi: **~ (en)** to degenerate (into).

deglutir vt & vi to swallow.

degollar vt [cortar la garganta] to cut ○ slit the throat of; [decapitar] to behead.

degradar vt **-1.** [moralmente] to degrade. **-2.** [de un cargo] to demote. ◆ **degradarse** vpr to degrade ○ lower o.s.

degustación f tasting (of wines etc).

dehesa f meadow.

dejadez f neglect; [en aspecto] slovenliness.

dejado, -da adj careless; [aspecto] slovenly.

dejar ◇ vt **-1.** [gen] to leave; **deja esa pera en el plato** put that pear on the plate; **deja el abrigo en la percha** leave your coat on the hanger; **~ a alguien en algún sitio** [con el coche] to drop sb off somewhere; **deja algo de café para mí** leave some coffee for me; **~ algo/a alguien a alguien** [encomendar] to leave sthg/sb with sb. **-2.** [prestar]: **~ algo a alguien** to lend sb sthg, to lend sthg to sb. **-3.** [abandonar - casa, trabajo, país] to leave; [- tabaco, estudios] to give up; [- familia] to abandon; **~ algo por imposible** to give sthg up as a lost cause; **~ a alguien atrás** to leave sb behind. **-4.** [permitir]: **~ a alguien hacer algo** to let sb do sthg, to allow sb to do sthg; **sus gritos no me dejaron dormir** his cries prevented me from sleeping; **deja que tu hijo venga con nosotros** let your son come with us; **~ correr algo** fig to let sthg be. **-5.** [omitir] to leave out; **~ algo por ○ sin hacer** to fail to do sthg; **dejó lo más importante por**

resolver he left the most important question unsolved. **-6.** [esperar]: ~ **que** to wait until; **dejó que acabara de llover para salir** he waited until it had stopped raining before going out. ◇ *vi* **-1.** [parar]: ~ **de hacer algo** to stop doing sthg; **no deja de venir ni un solo día** he never fails to come. **-2.** [expresando promesa]: **no** ~ **de** to be sure to; **¡no dejes de escribirme!** be sure to write to me! ◆ **dejarse** *vpr* **-1.** [olvidar]: ~**se algo en algún sitio** to leave sthg somewhere. **-2.** [permitir]: ~**se engañar** to allow o.s. to be taken in.

deje *m* [acento] accent.

dejo *m* [acento] accent.

del → **de**.

delantal *m* apron.

delante *adv* **-1.** [en primer lugar, en la parte delantera] in front; **el de** ~ the one in front; **el asiento de** ~ the seat in front. **-2.** [enfrente] opposite. **-3.** [presente] present. ◆ **delante de** *loc prep* in front of.

delantero, -ra ◇ *adj* front. ◇ *m y f* DEP forward; ~ **centro** centre forward. ◆ **delantera** *f* **-1.** DEP forwards (*pl*), attack. **-2.** *loc*: **coger** o **tomar la delantera** to take the lead; **coger** o **tomar la delantera a alguien** to beat sb to it; **llevar la delantera** to be in the lead.

delatar *vt* to denounce; *fig* [suj: sonrisa, ojos etc] to betray. ◆ **delatarse** *vpr* to give o.s. away.

delator, -ra *m y f* informer.

delegación *f* **-1.** [autorización, embajada] delegation; ~ **de poderes** devolution (of power). **-2.** [sucursal] branch. **-3.** [oficina pública] local office.

delegado, -da *m y f* **-1.** [gen] delegate; ~ **de curso** form monitor. **-2.** COM representative.

delegar *vt*: ~ **algo (en** o **a)** to delegate sthg (to).

deleite *m* delight.

deletrear *vt* to spell (out).

deleznable *adj fig* [malo - clima, libro, actuación] **appalling**; [- excusa, razón] contemptible.

delfín *m* [animal] dolphin.

delgado, -da *adj* [gen] thin; [esbelto] slim.

deliberación *f* deliberation.

deliberar *vi* to deliberate.

delicadeza *f* **-1.** [miramiento - con cosas] care; [- con personas] kindness, attentiveness. **-2.** [finura - de perfume, rostro]

delicacy; [- de persona] sensitivity. **-3.** [de un asunto, situación] delicacy.

delicado, -da *adj* **-1.** [gen] delicate; [perfume, gusto] subtle; [paladar] refined. **-2.** [persona - sensible] sensitive; [- muy exigente] fussy; [- educado] polite; **estar** ~ **de salud** to be very weak.

delicia *f* delight.

delicioso, -sa *adj* [comida] delicious; [persona] lovely, delightful.

delimitar *vt* [finca etc] to set out the boundaries of; [funciones etc] to define.

delincuencia *f* crime; ~ **juvenil** juvenile delinquency.

delincuente *m y f* criminal.

delineante *m y f* draughtsman (*f* draughtswoman).

delinquir *vi* to commit a crime.

delirante *adj* [gen] delirious.

delirar *vi* [un enfermo] to be delirious; [desbarrar] to talk nonsense.

delirio *m* [por la fiebre] delirium; [de un enfermo mental] ravings (*pl*); ~**s de grandeza** delusions of grandeur.

delito *m* crime, offence.

delta ◇ *m* delta. ◇ *f* delta.

demacrado, -da *adj* gaunt.

demagogo, -ga *m y f* demagogue.

demanda *f* **-1.** [petición] request; [reivindicación] demand; ~ **salarial** wage claim; **en** ~ **de** asking for. **-2.** ECON demand. **-3.** DER lawsuit; [por daños y perjuicios] claim; **presentar una** ~ **contra** to take legal action against.

demandante *m y f* plaintiff.

demandar *vt* **-1.** DER: ~ **a alguien (por)** to sue sb (for). **-2.** [pedir] to ask for.

demarcación *f* **-1.** [señalización] demarcation. **-2.** [territorio demarcado] area; [jurisdicción] district.

demás ◇ *adj* other; **los** ~ **invitados** the other o remaining guests. ◇ *pron*: **lo** ~ the rest; **todo lo** ~ everything else; **los/las** ~ the others, the rest; **por lo** ~ apart from that, otherwise; **y** ~ and so on.

demasiado, -da ◇ *adj* too much, (*pl*) too many; **demasiada comida** too much food; ~**s niños** too many children. ◇ *adv* [gen] too much; (*antes de adj o adv*) too; **habla** ~ she talks too much; **iba** ~ **rápido** she was going too fast.

demencia *f* madness, insanity.

demencial *adj* [disparatado] chaotic.

demente *adj* mad.

democracia *f* democracy.

demócrata ◇ *adj* democratic. ◇ *m y f* democrat.

democrático, -ca *adj* democratic.

demografía *f* demography.

demoler *vt* [edificio] to demolish, to pull down; *fig* to destroy.

demolición *f* demolition.

demonio *m* **-1.** *lit* & *fig* devil. **-2.** [para enfatizar]: ¿qué/dónde ~s ...? what/where the hell ...? ◆ **demonios** *interj*: ¡~s! damn (it)!

demora *f* delay.

demorar *vt* to delay. ◆ **demorarse** *vpr* **-1.** [retrasarse] to be delayed. **-2.** [detenerse] to stop (somewhere).

demostración *f* **-1.** [gen] demonstration. **-2.** [de un teorema] proof. **-3.** [exhibición] display; [señal] sign; [prueba] proof.

demostrar *vt* **-1.** [hipótesis, teoría, verdad] to prove. **-2.** [alegría, impaciencia, dolor] to show. **-3.** [funcionamiento, procedimiento] to demonstrate, to show.

denegar *vt* to turn down, to reject.

denigrante *adj* [humillante] degrading; [insultante] insulting.

denigrar *vt* [humillar] to denigrate, to vilify; [insultar] to insult.

denominación *f* naming; "~ de origen" "appellation d'origine".

denominador *m* denominator.

denotar *vt* to indicate, to show.

densidad *f* [gen & INFORM] density; ~ de población population density; alta/doble ~ INFORM high/double density.

denso, -sa *adj* [gen] dense; [líquido] thick.

dentadura *f* teeth (*pl*); ~ postiza false teeth (*pl*), dentures (*pl*).

dentera *f*: dar ~ a alguien to set sb's teeth on edge.

dentífrico, -ca *adj* tooth (*antes de sust*). ◆ **dentífrico** *m* toothpaste.

dentista *m y f* dentist.

dentro *adv* inside; está ahí ~ it's in there; hacia/para ~ inwards; por ~ (on the) inside; *fig* inside, deep down. ◆ **dentro de** *loc prep* in; ~ del coche ○ inside the car; ~ de poco/un año in a while/a year; ~ de lo posible as far as possible.

denuedo *m* [valor] courage; [esfuerzo] resolve.

denuncia *f* [acusación] accusation; [condena] denunciation; [a la policía] complaint; presentar una ~ contra to file a complaint against.

denunciar *vt* to denounce; [delito] to report.

departamento *m* **-1.** [gen] department. **-2.** [división territorial] administrative district; [en Francia] department. **-3.** [de maleta, cajón, tren] compartment.

dependencia *f* **-1.** [de una persona] dependence; [de país, drogas, alcohol] dependency. **-2.** [departamento] section; [sucursal] branch. ◆ **dependencias** *fpl* [habitaciones] rooms; [edificios] outbuildings.

depender *vi* to depend; depende ... it depends .... ◆ **depender de** *vi*: ~ de algo to depend on sthg; ~ de alguien to be dependent on sb; depende de ti it's up to you.

dependienta *f* shop assistant, saleswoman.

dependiente ◇ *adj* dependent. ◇ *m* shop assistant, salesman.

depilar *vt* [gen] to remove the hair from; [cejas] to pluck; [con cera] to wax.

depilatorio, -ria *adj* hair-removing. ◆ **depilatorio** *m* hair-remover.

deplorable *adj* [suceso, comportamiento] deplorable; [aspecto] sorry, pitiful.

deponer *vt* **-1.** [abandonar - actitud] to drop, to set aside; [las armas] to lay down. **-2.** [destituir - ministro, secretario] to remove from office; [- líder, rey] to depose.

deportar *vt* to deport.

deporte *m* sport; hacer ~ to do ○ practise sports; practicar un ~ to do a sport.

deportista *m y f* sportsman (*f* sportswoman).

deportivo, -va *adj* **-1.** [revista, evento] sports (*antes de sust*). **-2.** [conducta, espíritu] sportsmanlike. ◆ **deportivo** *m* sports car.

depositar *vt* **-1.** [gen] to place; ~ algo en alguien [confianza, ilusiones] to place sthg in sb. **-2.** [en el banco etc] to deposit. ◆ **depositarse** *vpr* [asentarse] to settle.

depositario, -ria *m y f* **-1.** [de dinero] trustee. **-2.** [de confianza etc] repository. **-3.** [de mercancías etc] depositary.

depósito *m* **-1.** [almacén - de mercancías] store, warehouse; [- de armas] dump; ~ de cadáveres morgue, mortuary. **-2.** [recipiente] tank. **-3.** [de dinero] deposit.

depravado, -da *adj* depraved.

depreciar *vt* to (cause to) depreciate. ◆ **depreciarse** *vpr* to depreciate.

depredador, -ra ◇ *adj* predatory. ◇ *m y f* predator.

depresión *f* [gen] depression; ~ **nerviosa** nervous breakdown.

depresivo, -va ◇ *adj* PSICOL depressive; [deprimente] depressing. ◇ *m y f* depressive.

deprimido, -da *adj* depressed.

deprimir *vt* to depress. ◆ **deprimirse** *vpr* to get depressed.

deprisa, de prisa *adv* fast, quickly; ¡~! quick!

depuración *f* **-1.** [de agua, metal, gas] purification. **-2.** *fig* [de organismo, sociedad] purge.

depurar *vt* **-1.** [agua, metal, gas] to purify. **-2.** *fig* [organismo, sociedad] to purge.

derecha → **derecho**.

derecho, -cha ◇ *adj* **-1.** [diestro] right. **-2.** [vertical] upright. **-3.** [recto] straight. ◇ *adv* **-1.** [en posición vertical] upright. **-2.** [directamente] straight. ◆ **derecho** *m* **-1.** [leyes, estudio] law; ~ **civil/penal** civil/criminal law. **-2.** [prerrogativa] right; **el** ~ **al voto** the right to vote; ¡**no hay** ~! it's not fair!; **reservado el** ~ **de admisión** the management reserves the right of admission; ~**s civiles/ humanos** civil/human rights. **-3.** [de una tela, prenda] right side; **del** ~ right side out. ◆ **derecha** *f* **-1.** [contrario de izquierda] right, right-hand side; **a la** ~ to the right; **girar a la** ~ to turn right. **-2.** POLÍT right (wing); **ser de** ~**s** to be right-wing. ◆ **derechos** *mpl* [tasas] duties; [profesionales] fees; ~**s de aduana** customs duty (U); ~**s de inscripción** membership fee (*sg*); ~**s de autor** [potestad] copyright (U); [dinero] royalties.

deriva *f* drift; **a la** ~ adrift; **ir a la** ~ to drift.

derivado, -da *adj* GRAM derived. ◆ **derivado** *m* **-1.** [producto] by-product. **-2.** QUÍM derivative.

derivar ◇ *vt* **-1.** [desviar] to divert. **-2.** MAT to derive. ◇ *vi* [desviarse] to change direction, to drift. ◆ **derivar de** *vi* **-1.** [proceder] to derive from. **-2.** GRAM to be derived from.

derogación *f* repeal.

derramamiento *m* spilling; ~ **de sangre** bloodshed.

derramar *vt* [por accidente] to spill; [verter] to pour; ~ **lágrimas/sangre** to shed tears/blood.

derrame *m* **-1.** MED discharge. **-2.** [de líquido] spilling; [de sangre] shedding.

derrapar *vi* to skid.

derretir *vt* [gen] to melt; [nieve] to thaw. ◆ **derretirse** *vpr* [metal, mantequilla] to melt; [hielo, nieve] to thaw.

derribar *vt* **-1.** [construcción] to knock down, to demolish. **-2.** [hacer caer - árbol] to fell; [- avión] to bring down. **-3.** [gobierno, gobernante] to overthrow.

derribo *m* [material] rubble.

derrocar *vt* [gobierno] to bring down, to overthrow; [ministro] to oust.

derrochar *vt* [malgastar] to squander.

derroche *m* [malgaste] waste, squandering.

derrota *f* [fracaso] defeat.

derrotar *vt* to defeat.

derrotero *m* [camino] direction; **tomar diferentes** ~**s** to follow a different course.

derrotista *adj, m y f* defeatist.

derruir *vt* to demolish.

derrumbamiento *m* **-1.** [de puente, edificio - por accidente] collapse; [- intencionado] demolition. **-2.** *fig* [de imperio] fall; [de empresa etc] collapse.

derrumbar *vt* [puente, edificio] to demolish. ◆ **derrumbarse** *vpr* [puente, edificio] to collapse; [techo] to fall O cave in.

desabotonar *vt* to unbutton. ◆ **desabotonarse** *vpr* [suj: persona] to undo one's buttons; [suj: ropa] to come undone.

desabrochar *vt* to undo. ◆ **desabrocharse** *vpr* [suj: persona] to undo one's buttons; [suj: ropa] to come undone.

desacato *m* **-1.** [gen]: ~ **(a)** lack of respect (for), disrespect (for). **-2.** DER contempt of court.

desacierto *m* [error] error.

desaconsejar *vt*: ~ **algo (a alguien)** to advise (sb) against sthg; ~ **a alguien que haga algo** to advise sb not to do sthg.

desacorde *adj* [opiniones] conflicting.

desacreditar *vt* to discredit.

desactivar *vt* to defuse.

desacuerdo *m* disagreement.

desafiante *adj* defiant.

desafiar *vt* **-1.** [persona] to challenge; ~ **a alguien a algo/a que haga algo** to challenge sb to sthg/to do sthg. **-2.** [peligro] to defy.

desafinar *vi* MÚS to be out of tune.

desafío *m* challenge.

desaforado, -da *adj* **-1.** [excesivo - apetito] uncontrolled. **-2.** [furioso - grito] furious, wild.

desafortunadamente *adv* unfortunately.

desafortunado, -da *adj* **-1.** [gen] unfortunate. **-2.** [sin suerte] unlucky.

desagradable *adj* unpleasant.

desagradar *vi* to displease; **me desagrada su actitud** I don't like her attitude.

desagradecido, -da *m y f* ungrateful person.

desagrado *m* displeasure; **con ~** reluctantly.

desagraviar *vt*: **~ a alguien por algo** [por una ofensa] to make amends to sb for sthg; [por un perjuicio] to compensate sb for sthg.

desagüe *m* [vaciado] drain; [cañería] drainpipe.

desaguisado *m* [destrozo] damage (*U*).

desahogado, -da *adj* **-1.** [de espacio] spacious. **-2.** [de dinero] well-off.

desahogar *vt* [ira] to vent; [pena] to relieve, to ease. ◆ **desahogarse** *vpr* **-1.** [contar penas]: **~se con alguien** to pour out one's woes o to tell one's troubles to sb. **-2.** [desfogarse] to let off steam.

desahogo *m* **-1.** [moral] relief. **-2.** [de espacio] space, room. **-3.** [económico] ease.

desahuciar *vt* **-1.** [inquilino] to evict. **-2.** [enfermo]: **~ a alguien** to give up all hope of saving sb.

desahucio *m* eviction.

desaire *m* snub, slight; **hacer un ~ a alguien** to snub sb.

desajuste *m* **-1.** [de piezas] misalignment; [de máquina] breakdown. **-2.** [de declaraciones] inconsistency; [económico etc] imbalance.

desalentar *vt* to discourage.

desaliento *m* dismay, dejection.

desaliñado, -da *adj* [aspecto] scruffy; [pelo] dishevelled.

desaliño *m* [del aspecto] scruffiness; [del pelo] dishevelment.

desalmado, -da *adj* heartless.

desalojar *vt* **-1.** [por una emergencia - edificio, personas] to evacuate. **-2.** [por la fuerza - suj: policía, ejército] to clear; [- inquilinos etc] to evict. **-3.** [por propia voluntad] to abandon, to move out of.

desamor *m* [falta de afecto] indifference, coldness; [odio] dislike.

desamparado, -da *adj* [niño] helpless; [lugar] desolate, forsaken.

desamparar *vt* to abandon.

desamparo *m* [abandono] abandonment; [aflicción] helplessness.

desangrar *vt* **-1.** [animal, persona] to bleed. **-2.** *fig* [económicamente] to bleed dry. ◆ **desangrarse** *vpr* to lose a lot of blood.

desanimado, -da *adj* [persona] downhearted.

desanimar *vt* to discourage. ◆ **desanimarse** *vpr* to get downhearted o discouraged.

desánimo *m* [gen] dejection; [depresión] depression.

desapacible *adj* unpleasant.

desaparecer *vi* **-1.** [gen] to disappear. **-2.** [en guerra, accidente] to go missing.

desaparecido, -da *m y f* missing person.

desaparición *f* disappearance.

desapego *m* indifference.

desapercibido, -da *adj*: **pasar ~** to go unnoticed.

desaprensivo, -va *m y f* unscrupulous person.

desaprobar *vt* [gen] to disapprove of; [un plan etc] to reject.

desaprovechar *vt* to waste.

desarmador *m Amer* screwdriver.

desarmar *vt* **-1.** [gen] to disarm. **-2.** [desmontar] to take apart, to dismantle.

desarme *m* MIL & POLÍT disarmament.

desarraigar *vt* **-1.** [vicio, costumbre] to root out. **-2.** [persona, pueblo] to banish, to drive (out).

desarraigo *m* [de árbol] uprooting; [de vicio, costumbre] rooting out; [de persona, pueblo] banishment.

desarreglar *vt* [armario, pelo] to mess up; [planes, horario] to upset.

desarreglo *m* [de cuarto, persona] untidiness; [de vida] disorder.

desarrollado, -da *adj* developed.

desarrollar *vt* **-1.** [mejorar - crecimiento, país] to develop. **-2.** [exponer - teoría, tema, fórmula] to expound. **-3.** [realizar - actividad, trabajo] to carry out. ◆ **desarrollarse** *vpr* **-1.** [crecer, mejorar] to develop. **-2.** [suceder - reunión] to take place; [- película] to be set.

desarrollo *m* **-1.** [mejora] development. **-2.** [crecimiento] growth.

desarticular *vt* **-1.** [huesos] to dislocate. **-2.** *fig* [organización, banda] to break up; [plan] to foil.

desasosegar *vt* to make uneasy.

desasosiego *m* **-1.** [mal presentimiento] unease. **-2.** [nerviosismo] restlessness.

desastrado, -da *adj* [desaseado] scruffy; [sucio] dirty.

desastre *m* disaster; **su madre es un ~** her mother is hopeless.

desastroso, -sa *adj* disastrous.

desatar *vt* **-1.** [nudo, lazo] to untie; [paquete] to undo; [animal] to unleash. **-2.** *fig* [tormenta, iras, pasión] to unleash; [entusiasmo] to arouse; [lengua] to loosen. ◆ **desatarse** *vpr* **-1.** [nudo, lazo] to come undone. **-2.** *fig* [desencadenarse - tormenta] to break; [- ira, cólera] to erupt.

desatascar *vt* to unblock.

desatender *vt* **-1.** [obligación, persona] to neglect. **-2.** [ruegos, consejos] to ignore.

desatino *m* **-1.** [locura] foolishness. **-2.** [desacierto] foolish act.

desautorizar *vt* **-1.** [desmentir - noticia] to deny. **-2.** [prohibir - manifestación, huelga] to ban. **-3.** [desacreditar] to discredit.

desavenencia *f* [desacuerdo] friction, tension; [riña] quarrel.

desavenirse *vpr* to fall out.

desayunar ◇ *vi* to have breakfast. ◇ *vt* to have for breakfast.

desayuno *m* breakfast.

desazón *f* unease, anxiety.

desazonar *vt* to worry.

desbancar *vt fig* [ocupar el puesto de] to oust, to replace.

desbandada *f* breaking up, scattering; **a la ~** in great disorder.

desbarajuste *m* disorder, confusion.

desbaratar *vt* to ruin, to wreck.

desbloquear *vt* [cuenta] to unfreeze; [país] to lift the blockade on; [negociación] to end the deadlock in.

desbocado, -da *adj* [caballo] runaway.

desbocarse *vpr* [caballo] to bolt.

desbordar *vt* **-1.** [cauce, ribera] to overflow, to burst. **-2.** [límites, previsiones] to exceed; [paciencia] to push beyond the limit. ◆ **desbordarse** *vpr* **-1.** [líquido]: ~**se (de)** to overflow (from). **-2.** [río] to overflow. **-3.** *fig* [sentimiento] to erupt.

descabalgar *vi* to dismount.

descabellado, -da *adj* crazy.

descafeinado, -da *adj* [sin cafeína] decaffeinated. ◆ **descafeinado** *m* decaffeinated coffee.

descalabro *m* setback, damage (*U*).

descalificar *vt* **-1.** [en una competición] to disqualify. **-2.** [desprestigiar] to discredit.

descalzar *vt*: ~ **a alguien** to take sb's shoes off. ◆ **descalzarse** *vpr* to take off one's shoes.

descalzo, -za *adj* barefoot.

descaminado, -da *adj fig* [equivocado]: **andar** ○ **ir** ~ to be on the wrong track.

descampado *m* open country.

descansar *vi* **-1.** [reposar] to rest. **-2.** [dormir] to sleep; **¡que descanses!** sleep well!

descansillo *m* landing.

descanso *m* **-1.** [reposo] rest; **tomarse un ~** to take a rest; **día de ~** day off. **-2.** [pausa] break; CIN & TEATR interval; DEP half-time. **-3.** *fig* [alivio] relief.

descapotable *adj & m* convertible.

descarado, -da *adj* **-1.** [desvergonzado - persona] cheeky, impertinent. **-2.** [flagrante - intento etc] barefaced.

descarga *f* **-1.** [de mercancías] unloading. **-2.** [de electricidad] shock. **-3.** [disparo] firing, shots (*pl*).

descargar *vt* **-1.** [vaciar - mercancías, pistola] to unload. **-2.** [disparar - munición, arma, ráfaga]: ~ **(sobre)** to fire (at). **-3.** ELECTR to run down. ◆ **descargarse** *vpr* **-1.** [desahogarse]: ~**se con alguien** to take it out on sb. **-2.** ELECTR to go flat.

descargo *m* **-1.** [excusa]: ~ **a** argument against. **-2.** DER defence. **-3.** [COM - de deuda] discharge; [- recibo] receipt.

descarnado, -da *adj* **-1.** [descripción] brutal. **-2.** [persona, animal] scrawny.

descaro *m* cheek, impertinence.

descarriarse *vpr* **-1.** [ovejas, ganado] to stray. **-2.** *fig* [pervertirse] to go astray.

descarrilamiento *m* derailment.

descarrilar *vi* to be derailed.

descartar *vt* [ayuda] to refuse, to reject; [posibilidad] to rule out.

descendencia *f* **-1.** [hijos] offspring. **-2.** [linaje] lineage, descent.

descender *vi* **-1.** [en estimación] to go down; ~ **a segunda** to be relegated to the second division. **-2.** [cantidad, valor, temperatura, nivel] to fall, to drop. ◆ **descender de** *vi* **-1.** [avión] to get off. **-2.** [linaje] to be descended from.

descenso *m* **-1.** [en el espacio] descent. **-2.** [de cantidad, valor, temperatura, nivel] drop.

descentralizar *vt* to decentralize.

descentrar *vt* **-1.** [sacar del centro] to knock off-centre. **-2.** *fig* [desconcentrar] to distract.

descifrar *vt* **-1.** [clave, mensaje] to decipher. **-2.** [motivos, intenciones] to work

out; [misterio] to **solve**; [problemas] to puzzle out.
descodificador, **decodificador** *m* decoder.
descolgar *vt* **-1.** [una cosa colgada] to take down. **-2.** [teléfono] to pick up. ◆ **descolgarse** *vpr* [bajar]: **~se (por algo)** to let oneself down o to slide down (sthg).
descolocar *vt* [objeto] to put out of place, to disturb.
descolorido, -da *adj* faded.
descompasado, -da *adj* excessive, uncontrollable.
descomponer *vt* **-1.** [pudrir - fruta] to rot; [- cadáver] to decompose. **-2.** [dividir] to break down; **~ algo en** to break sthg down into. **-3.** [desordenar] to mess up. **-4.** [estropear] to damage. ◆ **descomponerse** *vpr* **-1.** [pudrirse - fruta] to rot; [- cadáver] to decompose. **-2.** *Amer* [averiarse] to break down.
descomposición *f* **-1.** [de elementos] decomposition. **-2.** [putrefacción - de fruta] rotting; [- de cadáver] decomposition. **-3.** [alteración] distortion. **-4.** [diarrea] diarrhoea.
descompostura *f* **-1.** [falta de mesura] lack of respect, rudeness. **-2.** *Amer* [avería] breakdown.
descompuesto, -ta ◇ *pp* → **descomponer**. ◇ *adj* **-1.** [putrefacto - fruta] rotten; [- cadáver] decomposed. **-2.** [alterado - rostro] distorted, twisted.
descomunal *adj* enormous.
desconcentrar *vt* to distract.
desconcertante *adj* disconcerting.
desconcertar *vt* to disconcert, to throw. ◆ **desconcertarse** *vpr* to be thrown o bewildered.
desconchado *m* [de pintura] peeling paint; [de enyesado] peeling plaster.
desconcierto *m* [desorden] disorder; [desorientación, confusión] confusion.
desconectar *vt* [aparato] to switch off; [línea] to disconnect; [desenchufar] to unplug.
desconfianza *f* distrust.
desconfiar ◆ **desconfiar de** *vi* **-1.** [sospechar de] to distrust. **-2.** [no confiar en] to have no faith in.
descongelar *vt* **-1.** [producto] to thaw; [nevera] to defrost. **-2.** *fig* [precios] to free; [créditos, salarios] to unfreeze.
descongestionar *vt* **-1.** MED to clear. **-2.** *fig* [calle, centro de ciudad] to make less congested; **~ el tráfico** to reduce congestion.

desconocer *vt* [ignorar] not to know.
desconocido, -da ◇ *adj* [no conocido] unknown. ◇ *m y f* stranger.
desconocimiento *m* ignorance.
desconsiderado, -da *adj* thoughtless, inconsiderate.
desconsolar *vt* to distress.
desconsuelo *m* distress, grief.
descontado, -da *adj* discounted. ◆ **por descontado** *loc adv* obviously; **dar algo por ~** to take sthg for granted.
descontar *vt* **-1.** [una cantidad] to deduct. **-2.** COM to discount.
descontentar *vt* to upset.
descontento, -ta *adj* unhappy, dissatisfied. ◆ **descontento** *m* dissatisfaction.
desconvocar *vt* to cancel, to call off.
descorazonador, -ra *adj* discouraging.
descorazonar *vt* to discourage.
descorchar *vt* to uncork.
descorrer *vt* **-1.** [cortinas] to draw back. **-2.** [cerrojo, pestillo] to draw back.
descortés *adj* rude.
descoser *vt* to unstitch. ◆ **descoserse** *vpr* to come unstitched.
descosido, -da *adj* unstitched.
descoyuntar *vt* to dislocate.
descrédito *m* discredit; **ir en ~ de algo/alguien** to count against sthg/sb.
descreído, -da *m y f* non-believer.
descremado, -da *adj* skimmed.
describir *vt* to describe.
descripción *f* description.
descrito, -ta *pp* → **describir**.
descuartizar *vt* [persona] to quarter; [res] to carve up.
descubierto, -ta ◇ *pp* → **descubrir**. ◇ *adj* **-1.** [gen] uncovered; [coche] open. **-2.** [cielo] clear. **-3.** [sin sombrero] bareheaded. ◆ **descubierto** *m* [FIN - de empresa] deficit; [- de cuenta bancaria] overdraft. ◆ **al descubierto** *loc adv* **-1.** [al raso] in the open. **-2.** BANCA overdrawn.
descubrimiento *m* **-1.** [de continentes, invenciones] discovery. **-2.** [de placa, busto] unveiling. **-3.** [de complots] uncovering; [de asesinos] detection.
descubrir *vt* **-1.** [gen] to discover; [petróleo] to strike; [complot] to uncover. **-2.** [destapar - estatua, placa] to unveil. **-3.** [vislumbrar] to spot, to spy. **-4.** [delatar] to give away. ◆ **descubrirse** *vpr* [quitarse el sombrero] to take one's hat off; **~se ante algo** *fig* to take one's hat off to sthg.
descuento *m* discount; **hacer ~** to give

a discount; **con** ~ at a discount; **un** ~ **del 10%** 10% off.

descuidado, -da *adj* **-1.** [desaseado - persona, aspecto] **untidy**; [- jardín] **neglected. -2.** [negligente] **careless. -3.** [distraído] **off one's guard.**

descuidar ◇ *vt* [desatender] to **neglect.** ◇ *vi* [no preocuparse] not to **worry; descuida, que yo me encargo** don't worry, I'll take care of it. ◆ **descuidarse** *vpr* **-1.** [abandonarse] to **neglect** one's appearance. **-2.** [despistarse] not to be careful.

descuido *m* **-1.** [falta de aseo] **carelessness. -2.** [olvido] **oversight**; [error] **slip.**

desde *prep* **-1.** [tiempo] **since; no lo veo** ~ **el mes pasado/**~ **ayer** I haven't seen him since last month/yesterday; ~ **ahora** from now on; ~ **hace mucho/un mes** for ages/a month; ~ **... hasta ...** from ... until ...; ~ **el lunes hasta el viernes** from Monday till Friday; ~ **entonces** since then; ~ **que** since; ~ **que murió mi madre** since my mother died. **-2.** [espacio] **from;** ~ **... hasta ...** from ... to ...; ~ **aquí hasta el centro** from here to the centre. ◆ **desde luego** *loc adv* **-1.** [por supuesto] **of course. -2.** [en tono de reproche] **for goodness' sake!**

desdecir ◆ **desdecirse** *vpr* to go back on one's word; ~**se de** to go back on.

desdén *m* **disdain, scorn.**

desdeñar *vt* to **scorn.**

desdeñoso, -sa *adj* **disdainful.**

desdibujarse *vpr* to become **blurred.**

desdicha *f* [desgracia - situación] **misery**; [- suceso] **misfortune.**

desdichado, -da *adj* [decisión, situación] **unfortunate**; [persona - sin suerte] **unlucky**; [- sin felicidad] **unhappy.**

desdicho, -cha *pp* → **desdecir.**

desdoblar *vt* [servilleta, carta] to **unfold**; [alambre] to **straighten out.**

desear *vt* **-1.** [querer] to **want**; [anhelar] to **wish; ¿qué desea?** [en tienda] what can I do for you?; **desearía estar allí** I wish I was there. **-2.** [sexualmente] to **desire.**

desecar *vt* to dry out. ◆ **desecarse** *vpr* to dry out.

desechable *adj* **disposable.**

desechar *vt* **-1.** [tirar - ropa, piezas] to **throw out, to discard. -2.** [rechazar - ayuda, oferta] to **refuse, to turn down. -3.** [desestimar - idea] to **reject**; [- plan, proyecto] to **drop.**

desecho *m* [objeto usado] **unwanted object**; [ropa] **castoff; material de** ~ [gen] **waste products** (*pl*); [metal] **scrap.** ◆ **desechos** *mpl* [basura] **rubbish** (*U*); [residuos] **waste products.**

desembalar *vt* to **unpack.**

desembarazar *vt* to **clear.** ◆ **desembarazarse** *vpr*: ~**se de** to get rid of.

desembarcar ◇ *vt* [pasajeros] to **disembark**; [mercancías] to **unload.** ◇ *vi* **-1.** [de barco, avión] to **disembark. -2.** *Amer* [de autobús, tren] to **get off.** ◆ **desembarcarse** *vpr Amer* to **get off.**

desembarco *m* **-1.** [de pasajeros] **disembarkation. -2.** MIL **landing.**

desembarque *m* [de mercancías] **unloading.**

desembocadura *f* [de río] **mouth**; [de calle] **opening.**

desembocar ◆ **desembocar en** *vi* **-1.** [río] to **flow into. -2.** [asunto] to **result in.**

desembolso *m* **payment;** ~ **inicial down payment.**

desempaquetar *vt* [paquete] to **unwrap**; [caja] to **unpack.**

desempatar *vi* to decide the contest; **jugar para** ~ to have a **play-off.**

desempate *m* **final result; partido de** ~ **decider.**

desempeñar *vt* **-1.** [función, misión] to **carry out**; [cargo, puesto] to **hold. -2.** [papel] to **play. -3.** [joyas] to **redeem.**

desempeño *m* **-1.** [de función] **carrying out. -2.** [de papel] **performance. -3.** [de objeto] **redemption.**

desempleado, -da *adj* **unemployed.**

desempleo *m* **unemployment.**

desempolvar *vt* **-1.** [mueble, jarrón] to **dust. -2.** *fig* [recuerdos] to **revive.**

desencadenar *vt* **-1.** [preso, perro] to **unchain. -2.** *fig* [suceso, polémica] to give rise to; [pasión, furia] to **unleash.** ◆ **desencadenarse** *vpr* **-1.** [pasiones, odios, conflicto] to **erupt**; [guerra] to **break out. -2.** [viento] to **blow up**; [tormenta] to **burst**; [terremoto] to **strike.**

desencajar *vt* **-1.** [mecanismo, piezas - sin querer] to **knock out of place**; [- intencionadamente] to **take apart. -2.** [hueso] to **dislocate.** ◆ **desencajarse** *vpr* **-1.** [piezas] to **come apart. -2.** [rostro] to **distort, to become distorted.**

desencanto *m* **disappointment.**

desenchufar *vt* [quitar el enchufe] to **unplug**; [apagar] to **switch off.**

desenfadado, -da *adj* [persona, conducta] **relaxed, easy-going**; [comedia, programa de TV] light-hearted; [estilo] light; [en el vestir] casual.

desenfado m [seguridad en sí mismo] self-assurance; [desenvoltura] ease; [desparpajo] uninhibited nature.

desenfocado, -da adj [imagen] out of focus; [visión] blurred.

desenfrenado, -da adj [ritmo, baile] frantic, frenzied; [comportamiento] uncontrolled; [apetito] insatiable.

desenfreno m -1. [gen] lack of restraint. -2. [vicio] debauchery.

desenfundar vt [pistola] to draw.

desenganchar vt -1. [vagón] to uncouple. -2. [caballo] to unhitch. -3. [pelo, jersey] to free.

desengañar vt -1. [a una persona equivocada]: ~ a alguien to reveal the truth to sb. -2. [a una persona esperanzada] to disillusion.

desengaño m disappointment; **llevarse un ~ con alguien** to be disappointed in sb.

desenlace m denouement, ending.

desenmarañar vt -1. [ovillo, pelo] to untangle. -2. fig [asunto] to sort out; [problema] to resolve.

desenmascarar vt [descubrir] to unmask.

desenredar vt -1. [hilos, pelo] to untangle. -2. fig [asunto] to sort out; [problema] to resolve. ◆ **desenredarse** vpr: ~se (de algo) to extricate oneself (from sthg).

desenrollar vt [hilo, cinta] to unwind; [persiana] to roll down; [pergamino, papel] to unroll.

desenroscar vt to unscrew.

desentenderse vpr to pretend not to hear/know etc.

desenterrar vt [cadáver] to disinter; [tesoro, escultura] to dig up.

desentonar vi -1. [MÚS - cantante] to sing out of tune; [- instrumento] to be out of tune. -2. [color, cortinas, edificio]: ~ (con) to clash (with).

desentumecer vt to stretch. ◆ **desentumecerse** vpr to loosen up.

desenvoltura f [al moverse, comportarse] ease; [al hablar] fluency.

desenvolver vt to unwrap. ◆ **desenvolverse** vpr -1. [asunto, proceso] to progress; [trama] to unfold; [entrevista] to pass off. -2. [persona] to cope, to manage.

desenvuelto, -ta ◇ pp → desenvolver. ◇ adj [al moverse, comportarse] natural; [al hablar] fluent.

deseo m -1. [pasión] desire. -2. [anhelo] wish; **buenos ~s** good intentions.

deseoso, -sa adj: estar ~ de algo/hacer algo to long for sthg/to do sthg.

desequilibrado, -da adj -1. [persona] unbalanced. -2. [balanza, eje] off-centre.

desequilibrio m [mecánico] lack of balance; [mental] mental instability.

desertar vi to desert.

desértico, -ca adj [del desierto] desert (antes de sust); [despoblado] deserted.

desertización f [del terreno] desertification; [de la población] depopulation.

desertor, -ra m y f deserter.

desesperación f [falta de esperanza] despair, desperation; **con ~** in despair.

desesperado, -da adj [persona, intento] desperate; [estado, situación] hopeless; [esfuerzo] furious.

desesperante adj infuriating.

desesperar vt -1. [quitar la esperanza] to drive to despair. -2. [irritar, enojar] to exasperate, to drive mad. ◆ **desesperarse** vpr -1. [perder la esperanza] to be driven to despair. -2. [irritarse, enojarse] to get mad ○ exasperated.

desestabilizar vt to destabilize.

desestimar vt -1. [rechazar] to turn down. -2. [despreciar] to turn one's nose up at.

desfachatez f fam cheek.

desfalco m embezzlement.

desfallecer vi -1. [debilitarse] to be exhausted; ~ de to feel faint from. -2. [desmayarse] to faint.

desfasado, -da adj [persona] out of touch; [libro, moda] out of date.

desfase m [diferencia] gap.

desfavorable adj unfavourable.

desfigurar vt -1. [rostro, cuerpo] to disfigure. -2. fig [la verdad] to distort.

desfiladero m narrow mountain pass.

desfilar vi MIL to parade.

desfile m MIL parade; [de carrozas] procession.

desfogar vt to vent. ◆ **desfogarse** vpr to let off steam.

desgajar vt [página] to tear out; [rama] to break off; [libro, periódico] to rip up; [naranja] to split into segments. ◆ **desgajarse** vpr [rama] to break off; [hoja] to fall.

desgana f -1. [falta de hambre] lack of appetite. -2. [falta de ánimo] lack of enthusiasm; **con ~** unwillingly, reluctantly.

desganado, -da adj [sin apetito]: estar ~ to be off one's food.

desgarbado, -da *adj* clumsy, ungainly.

desgarrador, -ra *adj* harrowing.

desgarrar *vt* to rip; ~ **el corazón** to break one's heart.

desgarro *m* tear.

desgastar *vt* to wear out. ◆ **desgastarse** *vpr* to wear o.s. out.

desgaste *m* **-1.** [de tela, muebles etc] wear and tear; [de roca] erosion; [de pilas] running down; [de cuerdas] fraying; [de metal] corrosion. **-2.** [de persona] wear and tear; [de dirigentes] losing of one's touch.

desglosar *vt* to break down.

desglose *m* breakdown.

desgracia *f* **-1.** [mala suerte] misfortune; **por** ~ unfortunately. **-2.** [catástrofe] disaster; ~**s personales** casualties; **es una** ~ **que** ... it's a terrible shame that .... **-3.** *loc:* **caer en** ~ to fall into disgrace.

desgraciado, -da *adj* **-1.** [gen] unfortunate. **-2.** [sin suerte] unlucky. **-3.** [infeliz] unhappy.

desgravar *vt* to deduct from one's tax bill.

desgreñado, -da *adj* dishevelled.

desguace *m* [de coches] scrapping; [de buques] breaking.

deshabitado, -da *adj* uninhabited.

deshabituar *vt:* ~ **a alguien (de)** to get sb out of the habit (of).

deshacer *vt* **-1.** [costura, nudo, paquete] to undo; [maleta] to unpack; [tarta, castillo de arena] to destroy. **-2.** [disolver - helado, mantequilla] to melt; [- pastilla, terrón de azúcar] to dissolve. **-3.** [poner fin a - contrato, negocio] to cancel; [- pacto, tratado] to break; [- plan, intriga] to foil; [- organización] to dissolve. **-4.** [destruir - enemigo] to rout; [- matrimonio] to ruin. ◆ **deshacerse** *vpr* **-1.** [desvanecerse] to disappear. **-2.** *fig* [librarse]: ~**se de o de** to get rid of. **-3.** *fig:* ~**se en algo (con o hacia alguien)** [cumplidos] to lavish sthg (on sb); [insultos] to heap sthg (on sb).

desharrapado, -da *adj* ragged.

deshecho, -cha ◇ *pp* → **deshacer.** ◇ *adj* **-1.** [costura, nudo, paquete] **undone**; [cama] **unmade**; [maleta] **unpacked. -2.** [enemigo] **destroyed**; [tarta, matrimonio] **ruined. -3.** [derretido - pastilla, terrón de azúcar] **dissolved**; [- helado, mantequilla] **melted. -4.** [afligido] **devastated. -5.** [cansado] **tired out.**

desheredar *vt* to disinherit.

deshidratar *vt* to dehydrate.

deshielo *m* thaw.

deshilachar *vt* to unravel. ◆ **deshilacharse** *vpr* to fray.

deshinchar *vt* **-1.** [globo, rueda] to let down, to deflate. **-2.** [hinchazón] to reduce the swelling in. ◆ **deshincharse** *vpr* [globo, hinchazón] to go down; [neumático] to go flat.

deshojar *vt* [árbol] to strip the leaves off; [flor] to pull the petals off; [libro] to pull the pages out of. ◆ **deshojarse** *vpr* [árbol] to shed its leaves; [flor] to drop its petals.

deshonesto, -ta *adj* [sin honradez] dishonest; [sin pudor] indecent.

deshonor *m*, **deshonra** *f* dishonour.

deshonrar *vt* to dishonour.

deshora ◆ **a deshora, a deshoras** *loc adv* [en momento inoportuno] at a bad time; [en horas poco habituales] at an unearthly hour.

deshuesar *vt* [carne] to bone; [fruto] to stone.

desidia *f* [en el trabajo] neglect; [en el aspecto] slovenliness.

desierto, -ta *adj* **-1.** [gen] deserted. **-2.** [vacante - premio] deferred. ◆ **desierto** *m* desert.

designar *vt* **-1.** [nombrar] to appoint. **-2.** [fijar, determinar] to name, to fix.

designio *m* intention, plan.

desigual *adj* **-1.** [diferente] different; [terreno] uneven. **-2.** [tiempo, persona, humor] changeable; [alumno, actuación] inconsistent; [lucha] unevenly matched, unequal; [tratamiento] unfair, unequal.

desilusión *f* disappointment, disillusionment (*U*); **llevarse una** ~ to be disappointed.

desilusionar *vt* [desengañar] to reveal the truth to; [decepcionar] to disappoint, to disillusion. ◆ **desilusionarse** *vpr* [decepcionarse] to be disappointed o disillusioned; [desengañarse] to realize the truth.

desinfección *f* disinfection.

desinfectar *vt* to disinfect.

desinflar *vt* [quitar aire] to deflate. ◆ **desinflarse** *vpr* [perder aire - gen] to go down; [- neumático] to go flat.

desintegración *f* **-1.** [de objetos] disintegration. **-2.** [de grupos, organizaciones] breaking up.

desintegrar *vt* **-1.** [objetos] to disintegrate; [átomo] to split. **-2.** [grupos, organizaciones] to break up.

desinterés *m* **-1.** [indiferencia] disinterest. **-2.** [generosidad] unselfishness.

desinteresado, -da *adj* unselfish.

desinteresarse *vpr*: ~ **de** ○ **por algo** to lose interest in sthg.

desistir *vi*: ~ **(de hacer algo)** to give up ○ to stop (doing sthg).

desleal *adj*: ~ **(con)** disloyal (to); [competencia] unfair.

deslealtad *f* disloyalty.

desleír *vt* [sólido] to dissolve; [líquido] to dilute.

desligar *vt* **-1.** [desatar] to untie. **-2.** *fig* [separar]: ~ **algo (de)** to separate sthg (from). ◆ **desligarse** *vpr* **-1.** [desatarse] to untie oneself. **-2.** *fig* [separarse]: ~**se de** to become separated from; ~**se de un grupo** to distance o.s. from a group.

deslindar *vt* **-1.** [limitar] to mark out (the boundaries of). **-2.** *fig* [separar] to define.

desliz *m* slip, error; **tener** ○ **cometer un** ~ to slip up.

deslizar *vt* [mano, objeto]: ~ **algo en** to slip sthg into; ~ **algo por algo** to slide sthg along sthg. ◆ **deslizarse** *vpr* [resbalar]: ~**se por** to slide along.

deslomar *vt* [a golpes] to thrash.

deslucido, -da *adj* **-1.** [sin brillo] faded; [plata] tarnished. **-2.** [sin gracia - acto, ceremonia] dull; [- actuación] lacklustre.

deslumbrar *vt* *lit* & *fig* to dazzle.

desmadrarse *vpr* *fam* to go wild.

desmadre *m* *fam* chaos.

desmán *m* **-1.** [con la bebida, comida etc] excess. **-2.** [abuso de poder] abuse (of power).

desmandarse *vpr* **-1.** [desobedecer] to be disobedient. **-2.** [insubordinarse] to get out of hand.

desmantelar *vt* [casa, fábrica] to clear out, to strip; [organización] to disband; [arsenal, andamio] to dismantle; [barco] to unrig.

desmaquillador *m* make-up remover.

desmayar *vi* to lose heart. ◆ **desmayarse** *vpr* to faint.

desmayo *m* [físico] fainting fit; **sufrir** ~ to have fainting fits.

desmedido, -da *adj* excessive, disproportionate.

desmelenado, -da *adj* **-1.** [persona] reckless, wild. **-2.** [cabello] tousled.

desmembrar *vt* **-1.** [trocear - cuerpo] to dismember; [- miembro, extremidad] to cut off. **-2.** [disgregar] to break up.

desmemoriado, -da *adj* forgetful.

desmentir *vt* **-1.** [negar] to deny. **-2.** [no corresponder] to belie.

desmenuzar *vt* **-1.** [trocear - pan, pastel, roca] to crumble; [- carne] to chop up; [- papel] to tear up into little pieces. **-2.** *fig* [examinar, analizar] to scrutinize.

desmerecer ◇ *vt* to be unworthy of. ◇ *vi* to lose value; ~ **(en algo) de alguien** to be inferior to sb (in sthg).

desmesurado, -da *adj* [excesivo] excessive, disproportionate; [enorme] enormous.

desmitificar *vt* to demythologize.

desmontar *vt* **-1.** [desarmar - máquina] to take apart ○ to pieces; [- motor] to strip down; [- piezas] to dismantle; [- rueda] to remove, to take off; [- tienda de campaña] to take down; [- arma] to uncock. **-2.** [jinete - suj: caballo] to unseat; [- suj: persona] to help down.

desmoralizar *vt* to demoralize.

desmoronar *vt* [edificios, rocas] to cause to crumble. ◆ **desmoronarse** *vpr* [edificio, roca, ideales] to crumble.

desnatado, -da *adj* skimmed.

desnaturalizado, -da *adj* [sustancia] adulterated; [alcohol] denatured.

desnivel *m* [del terreno] irregularity, unevenness (*U*).

desnivelar *vt* to make uneven; [balanza] to tip.

desnucar *vt* to break the neck of.

desnudar *vt* **-1.** [persona] to undress. **-2.** *fig* [cosa] to strip. ◆ **desnudarse** *vpr* to get undressed.

desnudez *f* [de persona] nakedness, nudity; [de cosa] bareness.

desnudo, -da *adj* **-1.** [persona, cuerpo] naked. **-2.** *fig* [salón, hombro, árbol] bare; [verdad] plain; [paisaje] barren. ◆ **desnudo** *m* nude.

desnutrición *f* malnutrition.

desobedecer *vt* to disobey.

desobediencia *f* disobedience.

desobediente *adj* disobedient.

desocupado, -da *adj* **-1.** [persona - ocioso] free, unoccupied; [- sin empleo] unemployed. **-2.** [lugar] vacant.

desocupar *vt* [edificio] to vacate; [habitación, mesa] to leave.

desodorante *m* deodorant.

desolación *f* **-1.** [destrucción] desolation. **-2.** [desconsuelo] distress, grief.

desolar *vt* **-1.** [destruir] to devastate, to lay waste. **-2.** [afligir] to cause anguish to.

desorbitado, -da *adj* **-1.** [gen] disproportionate; [precio] exorbitant. **-2.** *loc*: **con los ojos** ~**s** pop-eyed.

desorden m -1. [confusión] disorder, chaos; [falta de orden] mess. -2. [disturbio] disturbance.

desordenado, -da adj [habitación, persona] untidy, messy; [documentos, fichas] jumbled (up).

desorganización f disorganization.

desorganizar vt to disrupt, to disorganize.

desorientar vt -1. [en el espacio] to disorientate, to mislead. -2. fig [en la mente] to confuse. ◆ **desorientarse** vpr to lose one's way ○ bearings.

despabilado, -da adj -1. [despierto] wide-awake. -2. [listo] smart, quick.

despabilar vt -1. [despertar] to wake up. -2. [hacer más avispado] to make streetwise. ◆ **despabilarse** vpr -1. [despertarse] to wake up. -2. [darse prisa] to hurry up.

despachar ◇ vt -1. [mercancía] to dispatch. -2. [en tienda - cliente] to serve; [- entradas, bebidas etc] to sell. -3. fam fig [terminar - trabajo, discurso] to finish off. -4. [asunto, negocio] to settle. -5. Amer [facturar] to check in. ◇ vi [en una tienda] to serve.

despacho m -1. [oficina] office; [en casa] study. -2. [comunicación oficial] dispatch. -3. [venta] sale; [lugar de venta]: ~ de billetes/localidades ticket/box office.

despacio adv slowly.

desparpajo m fam forwardness, self-assurance.

desparramar vt [líquido] to spill; [objetos] to spread, to scatter.

despecho m [rencor, venganza] spite; [desengaño] bitterness; (hacer algo) por ~ (to do sthg) out of spite.

despectivo, -va adj -1. [despreciativo] contemptuous. -2. GRAM pejorative.

despedazar vt -1. [físicamente] to tear apart. -2. fig [moralmente] to shatter.

despedida f [adiós] farewell.

despedir vt -1. [decir adiós] to say goodbye to; **fuimos a ~le a la estación** we went to see him off at the station. -2. [echar - de un empleo] to dismiss, to sack; [- de un club] to throw out. -3. [lanzar, arrojar] to fling; **salir despedido de/por/hacia algo** to fly out of/through/towards sthg. -4. fig [difundir, desprender] to give off. ◆ **despedirse** vpr: ~**se (de)** to say goodbye (to).

despegar ◇ vt to unstick. ◇ vi [avión] to take off. ◆ **despegarse** vpr [etiqueta, pegatina, sello] to come unstuck.

despegue m takeoff.

despeinar vt [pelo] to ruffle; ~ **a alguien** to mess up sb's hair. ◆ **despeinarse** vpr to mess up one's hair.

despejado, -da adj -1. [tiempo, día] clear. -2. fig [persona, mente] alert. -3. [espacio - ancho] spacious; [- sin estorbos] clear, uncluttered.

despejar vt [gen] to clear. ◆ **despejarse** vpr -1. [persona - espabilarse] to clear one's head; [- despertarse] to wake o.s. up. -2. [tiempo] to clear up; [cielo] to clear.

despeje m DEP clearance.

despellejar vt [animal] to skin.

despensa f larder, pantry.

despeñadero m precipice.

despeñar vt to throw over a cliff. ◆ **despeñarse** vpr to fall over a cliff.

desperdiciar vt [tiempo, comida] to waste; [dinero] to squander; [ocasión] to throw away.

desperdicio m -1. [acción] waste. -2. [residuo]: ~**s** scraps.

desperdigar vt to scatter, to disperse.

desperezarse vpr to stretch.

desperfecto m [deterioro] damage (U); [defecto] flaw, imperfection.

despertador m alarm clock.

despertar ◇ vt -1. [persona, animal] to wake (up). -2. fig [reacción] to arouse. -3. fig [recuerdo] to revive, to awaken. ◇ vi to wake up. ◇ m awakening. ◆ **despertarse** vpr to wake up.

despiadado, -da adj pitiless, merciless.

despido m dismissal, sacking.

despierto, -ta adj -1. [sin dormir] awake. -2. fig [espabilado, listo] sharp.

despilfarrar vt [dinero] to squander; [electricidad, agua etc] to waste.

despilfarro m [de dinero] squandering; [de energía, agua etc] waste.

despiole m Amer fam rumpus, shindy.

despistado, -da adj absent-minded.

despistar vt -1. [dar esquinazo] to throw off the scent. -2. fig [confundir] to mislead. ◆ **despistarse** vpr -1. [perderse] to lose one's way, to get lost. -2. fig [distraerse] to get confused.

despiste m [distracción] absent-mindedness; [error] mistake, slip.

desplante m rude remark.

desplazamiento m -1. [viaje] journey; [traslado] move. -2. NÁUT displacement.

desplazar vt -1. [trasladar] to move. -2. fig [desbancar] to take the place of; ~ **a alguien/algo de** to remove sb/sthg from. ◆**desplazarse** *vpr* [viajar] to travel.

desplegar *vt* **-1.** [tela, periódico, mapa] to unfold; [alas] to spread, to open; [bandera] to unfurl. **-2.** [cualidad] to display. **-3.** MIL to deploy.

despliegue *m* **-1.** [de cualidad] display. **-2.** MIL deployment.

desplomarse *vpr* [gen] to collapse; [techo] to fall in.

desplumar *vt* **-1.** [ave] to pluck. **-2.** *fig* [estafar] to fleece.

despoblado, -da *adj* unpopulated, deserted.

despojar *vt*: ~ **a alguien de algo** to strip sb of sthg. ◆**despojarse** *vpr*: ~**se de algo** [bienes, alimentos] to give sthg up; [abrigo, chandal] to take sthg off.

despojo *m* [acción] plundering. ◆**despojos** *mpl* **-1.** [sobras, residuos] leftovers. **-2.** [de animales] offal (*U*).

desposar *vt* to marry. ◆**desposarse** *vpr* to get married.

desposeer *vt*: ~ **a alguien de** to dispossess sb of.

déspota *m y f* despot.

despotricar *vi*: ~ **(contra)** to rant on (at).

despreciar *vt* **-1.** [desdeñar] to scorn. **-2.** [rechazar] to spurn.

desprecio *m* scorn, contempt.

desprender *vt* **-1.** [lo que estaba fijo] to remove, to detach. **-2.** [olor, luz] to give off. ◆**desprenderse** *vpr* **-1.** [caerse, soltarse] to come ◇ fall off. **-2.** *fig* [deducirse]: **de sus palabras se desprende que ...** from his words it is clear ◇ it can be seen that .... **-3.** [librarse]: ~**se de** to get rid of.

desprendimiento *m* [separación] detachment; ~ **de tierras** landslide.

despreocupado, -da *adj* [libre de preocupaciones] **unworried, unconcerned;** [en el vestir] casual.

despreocuparse ◆**despreocuparse de** *vpr* [asunto] to stop worrying about.

desprestigiar *vt* to discredit.

desprevenido, -da *adj* unprepared; **coger** ◇ **pillar a** ~ **a alguien** to catch sb unawares, to take sb by surprise.

desproporcionado, -da *adj* disproportionate.

despropósito *m* stupid remark.

desprovisto, -ta *adj*: ~ **de** lacking in, devoid of.

después *adv* **-1.** [en el tiempo - más tarde] afterwards, later; [- entonces] then; [- justo lo siguiente] next; **poco** ~ soon after; **años** ~ years later; **ellos llegaron** ~ they arrived later; **llamé primero y** ~ **entré** I knocked first and then I went in; **yo voy** ~ it's my turn next. **-2.** [en el espacio] next, after; **¿qué viene** ~? what comes next ◇ after?; **hay una farmacia y** ~ **está mi casa** there's a chemist's and then there's my house. **-3.** [en una lista] further down. ◆**después de** *loc prep* after; **llegó** ~ **de ti** she arrived after you; ~ **de él, nadie lo ha conseguido** since he did it, no one else has; ~ **de hacer algo** after doing sthg. ◆**después de todo** *loc adv* after all.

despuntar ◇ *vt* [romper] to break the point off; [desgastar] to blunt. ◇ *vi* **-1.** *fig* [persona] to excel. **-2.** [alba] to break; [día] to dawn.

desquiciar *vt* *fig* [desequilibrar] to derange; [sacar de quicio] to drive mad.

desquite *m* revenge.

destacamento *m* detachment.

destacar ◇ *vt* **-1.** [poner de relieve] to emphasize, to highlight; **cabe** ~ **que ...** it is important to point out that .... **-2.** MIL to detach, to post. ◇ *vi* [sobresalir] to stand out. ◆**destacarse** *vpr*: ~**se (de/por)** to stand out (from/because of).

destajo *m* piecework; **trabajar a** ~ [por trabajo hecho] to do piecework; *fig* [afanosamente] to work flat out.

destapar *vt* **-1.** [abrir - caja, botella] to open; [olla] to take the lid off; [descorchar] to uncork. **-2.** [descubrir] to uncover. ◆**destaparse** *vpr* [desabrigarse] to lose the covers.

destartalado, -da *adj* [viejo, deteriorado] dilapidated; [desordenado] untidy.

destello *m* **-1.** [de luz, brillo] sparkle; [de estrella] twinkle. **-2.** *fig* [manifestación momentánea] glimmer.

destemplado, -da *adj* **-1.** [persona] out of sorts. **-2.** [tiempo, clima] unpleasant. **-3.** [carácter, actitud] irritable.

desteñir ◇ *vt* to fade, to bleach. ◇ *vi* to run, not to be colour fast.

desternillarse *vpr*: ~ **de risa** to split one's sides laughing ◇ with laughter.

desterrar *vt* [persona] to banish, to exile.

destetar *vt* to wean.

destiempo ◆**a destiempo** *loc adv* at the wrong time.

destierro *m* exile; **en el** ~ in exile.

destilar *vt* [agua, petróleo] to distil.

destilería *f* distillery.

destinar vt -1. ~ algo a O para [cantidad, edificio] to set sthg aside for; [empleo, cargo] to assign sthg to; [carta] to address sthg to; [medidas, programa, publicación] to aim sthg at. -2. ~ a alguien a [cargo, empleo] to appoint sb to; [plaza, lugar] to post sb to.

destinatario, -ria m y f addressee.

destino m -1. [sino] destiny, fate. -2. [rumbo] destination; (ir) con ~ a (to be) bound for O going to; un vuelo con ~ a ... a flight to .... -3. [empleo, plaza] position, post. -4. [finalidad] function.

destitución f dismissal.

destituir vt to dismiss.

destornillador m screwdriver.

destornillar vt to unscrew.

destreza f skill, dexterity.

destrozar vt -1. [físicamente - romper] to smash; [- estropear] to ruin. -2. [moralmente - persona] to shatter, to devastate; [- vida] to ruin.

destrozo m damage (U); ocasionar grandes ~s to cause a lot of damage.

destrucción f destruction.

destruir vt -1. [gen] to destroy; [casa, argumento] to demolish. -2. [proyecto] to ruin, to wreck; [ilusión] to dash.

desuso m disuse; caer en ~ to become obsolete, to fall into disuse.

desvaído, -da adj [color] pale, washed-out; [forma, contorno] blurred; [mirada] vague.

desvalido, -da adj needy, destitute.

desvalijar vt [casa] to burgle; [persona] to rob.

desván m attic, loft.

desvanecer vt -1. [humo, nubes] to dissipate. -2. [sospechas, temores] to dispel. ◆ **desvanecerse** vpr -1. [desmayarse] to faint. -2. [disiparse - humo, nubes] to clear, to disappear; [- sonido, sospechas, temores] to fade away.

desvanecimiento m [desmayo] fainting fit.

desvariar vi [delirar] to be delirious; [decir locuras] to talk nonsense, to rave.

desvarío m -1. [dicho] raving; [hecho] act of madness. -2. [delirio] delirium.

desvelar vt -1. [quitar el sueño] to keep awake. -2. [noticia, secreto etc] to reveal. ◆ **desvelarse por** vpr: ~se por hacer algo to make every effort to do sthg.

desvelo m [esfuerzo] effort.

desvencijado, -da adj [silla, mesa] rickety; [camión, coche] battered.

desventaja f disadvantage; en ~ at a disadvantage.

desventura f misfortune.

desvergonzado, -da adj shameless.

desvergüenza f [atrevimiento, frescura] shamelessness.

desvestir vt to undress. ◆ **desvestirse** vpr to undress (oneself).

desviación f -1. [de dirección, cauce, norma] deviation. -2. [en la carretera] diversion, detour.

desviar vt [río, carretera, tráfico] to divert; [dirección] to change; [golpe] to parry; [pelota, disparo] to deflect; [pregunta] to evade; [conversación] to change the direction of; [mirada, ojos] to avert. ◆ **desviarse** vpr [cambiar de dirección - conductor] to take a detour; [- avión, barco] to go off course; ~se de to turn off.

desvío m diversion, detour.

desvirtuar vt [gen] to detract from; [estropear] to spoil; [verdadero sentido] to distort.

desvivirse vpr [desvelarse]: ~ (por alguien/algo) to do everything one can (for sb/sthg); ~ por hacer algo to bend over backwards to do sthg.

detallado, -da adj detailed, thorough.

detallar vt [historia, hechos] to detail, to give a rundown of; [cuenta, gastos] to itemize.

detalle m -1. [gen] detail; con ~ in detail; entrar en ~s to go into detail. -2. [atención] kind gesture O thought; tener un ~ con alguien to be thoughtful O considerate to sb. ◆ **al detalle** loc adv COM retail.

detallista m y f COM retailer.

detectar vt to detect.

detective m y f detective.

detener vt -1. [arrestar] to arrest. -2. [parar] to stop; [retrasar] to hold up. ◆ **detenerse** vpr -1. [pararse] to stop. -2. [demorarse] to linger.

detenidamente adv carefully, thoroughly.

detenido, -da ◇ adj -1. [detallado] thorough. -2. [arrestado] (estar) ~ (to be) under arrest. ◇ m y f prisoner.

detenimiento ◆ **con detenimiento** loc adv carefully, thoroughly.

detergente m detergent.

deteriorar vt to damage, to spoil. ◆ **deteriorarse** vpr fig [empeorar] to deteriorate, to get worse.

deterioro m [daño] damage; [empeoramiento] deterioration.

determinación f **-1.** [fijación - de precio etc] settling, fixing. **-2.** [resolución] determination, resolution. **-3.** [decisión]: **tomar una ~** to take a decision.

determinado, -da adj **-1.** [concreto] specific; [en particular] particular. **-2.** [resuelto] determined. **-3.** GRAM definite.

determinar vt **-1.** [fijar - fecha, precio] to settle, to fix. **-2.** [averiguar] to determine. **-3.** [motivar] to cause, to bring about. **-4.** [decidir] to decide; **~ hacer algo** to decide to do sthg. ◆ **determinarse** vpr: **~se a hacer algo** to make up one's mind to do sthg.

detestar vt to detest.

detonante m [explosivo] explosive.

detractor, -ra m y f detractor.

detrás adv **-1.** [en el espacio] behind; **tus amigos vienen ~** your friends are coming on behind; **el interruptor está ~** the switch is at the back. **-2.** [en el orden] then, afterwards; **Portugal y ~ Puerto Rico** Portugal and then Puerto Rico. ◆ **detrás de** loc prep [gen] behind. ◆ **por detrás** loc adv at the back; **hablar de alguien por ~** to talk about sb behind his/her back.

detrimento m damage; **en ~ de** to the detriment of.

detrito m BIOL detritus. ◆ **detritos** mpl [residuos] waste (U).

deuda f debt; **~ pública** ECON national debt Br, public debt Am.

deudor, -ra ◇ adj [saldo] debit (antes de sust); [entidad] indebted. ◇ m y f debtor.

devaluación f devaluation.

devaluar vt to devalue.

devanar vt to wind.

devaneos mpl [amoríos] affairs; [coqueteos] flirting (U).

devastar vt to devastate.

devenir ◇ m transformation. ◇ vi [convertirse]: **~ en** to become, to turn into.

devoción f: **~ (por)** devotion (to).

devocionario m prayer book.

devolución f [gen] return; [de dinero] refund.

devolver ◇ vt **-1.** [restituir]: **~ algo (a)** [coche, dinero etc] to give sthg back (to); [producto defectuoso, carta] to return sthg (to). **-2.** [restablecer, colocar en su sitio]: **~ algo a** to return sthg to. **-3.** [favor, agravio] to pay back for; [visita] to return. **-4.** [vomitar] to bring ◇ throw up. ◇ vi to throw up. ◆ **devolverse** vpr Amer to come back.

devorar vt lit & fig to devour.

devoto, -ta ◇ adj [piadoso] devout; **ser ~ de** to have a devotion for. ◇ m y f [admirador] devotee.

devuelto, -ta pp → devolver.

dg (abrev de decigramo) dg.

di etc **-1.** → dar. **-2.** → decir.

día m **-1.** [gen] day; **me voy el ~ ocho** I'm going on the eighth; **¿a qué ~ estamos?** what day is it today?; **¿qué tal ~ hace?** what's the weather like today?; **todos los ~s** every day; **~ de los inocentes** 28th December, ≈ April Fools' Day; **~ de pago** payday; **~ festivo** (public) holiday; **~ hábil** ◇ **laborable** ◇ **de trabajo** working day; **de ~ en ~** from day to day, day by day; **del ~** fresh; **hoy (en) ~** nowadays; **todo el (santo) ~** all day long; **el ~ de mañana** in the future; **al ~ siguiente** on the following day; **un ~ sí y otro no** every other day; **menú del ~** today's menu. **-2.** [luz] daytime, day; **es de ~** it's daytime; **hacer algo de ~** to do sthg in the daytime ◇ during the day; **~ y noche** day and night; **en pleno ~, a plena luz del ~** in broad daylight. **-3.** loc: **estar/ponerse al ~ (de)** to be/get up to date (with); **poner algo/a alguien al ~** to update sthg/sb; **vivir al ~** to live from hand to mouth. ◆ **buen día** interj Amer: **¡buen ~!** good morning! ◆ **buenos días** interj: **¡buenos ~s!** [gen] hello!; [por la mañana] good morning!

diabético, -ca adj, m y f diabetic.

diablo m lit & fig devil; **pobre ~** poor devil.

diablura f prank.

diabólico, -ca adj **-1.** [del diablo] diabolic. **-2.** fig [muy malo, difícil] diabolical.

diadema f [para el pelo] hairband.

diáfano, -na adj **-1.** [transparente] transparent, diaphanous. **-2.** fig [claro] clear.

diafragma m diaphragm.

diagnosticar vt to diagnose.

diagnóstico m diagnosis.

diagonal adj & f diagonal.

diagrama m diagram.

dial m dial.

dialecto m dialect.

dialogar vi: **~ (con)** [hablar] to have a conversation (with), to talk (to); [negociar] to hold a dialogue ◇ talks (with).

diálogo m [conversación] conversation; LITER & POLÍT dialogue.

diamante m [piedra preciosa] diamond.

diámetro m diameter.

diana f -1. [en blanco de tiro] bull's-eye, bull. -2. [en cuartel] reveille.

diapasón m tuning fork.

diapositiva f slide, transparency.

diario, -ria adj daily; **a** ~ every day; **ropa de** ~ everyday clothes. ◆ **diario** m -1. [periódico] newspaper, daily. -2. [relación día a día] diary; ~ **de sesiones** parliamentary report.

diarrea f diarrhoea.

dibujante m y f [gen] sketcher; [de dibujos animados] cartoonist; [de dibujo técnico] draughtsman (f draughtswoman).

dibujar vt & vi to draw, to sketch.

dibujo m -1. [gen] drawing; ~**s animados** cartoons; ~ **artístico** art; ~ **lineal** technical drawing. -2. [de tela, prenda etc] pattern.

diccionario m dictionary.

dice → **decir.**

dicha f [alegría] joy.

dicho, -cha ◇ pp → **decir.** ◇ adj said, aforementioned; ~**s hombres** the said men, these men; **lo** ~ what I/we etc said; **o mejor** ~ or rather; ~ **y hecho** no sooner said than done. ◆ **dicho** m saying.

dichoso, -sa adj [feliz] happy; [afortunado] fortunate.

diciembre m December; ver también **septiembre.**

dicotomía f dichotomy.

dictado m dictation; **escribir al** ~ to take dictation.

dictador, -ra m y f dictator.

dictadura f dictatorship.

dictáfono m Dictaphone®.

dictamen m [opinión] opinion, judgment; [informe] report.

dictar vt -1. [texto] to dictate. -2. [emitir - sentencia, fallo] to pronounce, to pass; [- ley] to enact; [- decreto] to issue.

didáctico, -ca adj didactic.

diecinueve núm nineteen; ver también **seis.**

dieciocho núm eighteen; ver también **seis.**

dieciséis núm sixteen; ver también **seis.**

diecisiete núm seventeen; ver también **seis.**

diente m tooth; ~ **de leche** milk tooth; **armado hasta los** ~**s** armed to the teeth; **hablar entre** ~**s** to mumble, to mutter. ◆ **diente de ajo** m clove of garlic.

diera → **dar.**

diéresis f inv diaeresis.

dieron etc → **dar.**

diesel, diésel adj diesel.

diestro, -tra adj [hábil]: ~ **(en)** skilful (at); **a** ~ **y siniestro** fig left, right and centre, all over the place.

dieta f MED diet. ◆ **dietas** fpl COM expenses.

dietético, -ca adj dietetic, dietary. ◆ **dietética** f dietetics (U).

diez ◇ núm ten; ver también **seis.** ◇ m [en la escuela] A, top marks (pl).

difamar vt [verbalmente] to slander; [por escrito] to libel.

diferencia f difference.

diferenciar ◇ vt: ~ **(de)** to distinguish (from). ◇ vi: ~ **(entre)** to distinguish O differentiate (between). ◆ **diferenciarse** vpr [diferir]: ~**se (de/en)** to differ (from/in), to be different (from/in).

diferente ◇ adj: ~ **(de** O **a)** different (from O to). ◇ adv differently.

diferido ◆ **en diferido** loc adv TV recorded.

diferir vi [diferenciarse] to differ.

difícil adj difficult; ~ **de hacer** difficult to do; **es** ~ **que ganen** they are unlikely to win.

dificultad f -1. [calidad de difícil] difficulty. -2. [obstáculo] problem.

dificultar vt [estorbar] to hinder; [obstruir] to obstruct.

difuminar vt to blur.

difundir vt -1. [noticia, doctrina, epidemia] to spread. -2. [luz, calor] to diffuse; [emisión radiofónica] to broadcast. ◆ **difundirse** vpr -1. [noticia, doctrina, epidemia] to spread. -2. [luz, calor] to be diffused.

difunto, -ta m y f: **el** ~ the deceased.

difusión f -1. [de cultura, noticia, doctrina] dissemination. -2. [de programa] broadcasting.

diga → **decir.**

digerir vt to digest; fig [hechos] to assimilate, to take in.

digestión f digestion.

digestivo, -va adj digestive.

digital adj INFORM & TECN digital.

dígito m digit.

dignarse vpr: ~ **a** to deign to.

dignidad f [cualidad] dignity.

digno, -na adj -1. [noble - actitud, respuesta] dignified; [- persona] honourable, noble. -2. [merecedor]: ~ **de** worthy of; ~ **de elogio** praiseworthy; ~ **de mención/de ver** worth mentioning/seeing. -3. [adecuado]: ~ **de** appropriate for, fitting for. -4. [decente - sueldo, actuación etc] decent.

digo → decir.

digresión f digression.

dijera etc → decir.

dilapidar vt to squander, to waste.

dilatar vt -1. [extender] to expand; [partes del cuerpo] to dilate. -2. [prolongar] to prolong. -3. [demorar] to delay.

dilema m dilemma.

diligencia f -1. [esmero, cuidado] diligence. -2. [trámite, gestión] business (U). -3. [vehículo] stagecoach. ◆ **diligencias** fpl DER proceedings; **instruir ~s** to start proceedings.

diligente adj diligent.

diluir vt to dilute. ◆ **diluirse** vpr to dissolve.

diluvio m lit & fig flood.

dimensión f dimension; **las dimensiones de la tragedia** the extent of the tragedy.

diminutivo m diminutive.

diminuto, -ta adj tiny, minute.

dimisión f resignation; **presentar la ~** to hand in one's resignation.

dimitir vi: ~ **(de)** to resign (from).

dimos → dar.

Dinamarca Denmark.

dinámico, -ca adj dynamic.

dinamismo m dynamism.

dinamita f dynamite.

dinamo, dínamo f dynamo.

dinastía f dynasty.

dineral m fam fortune.

dinero m money; **andar bien/mal de ~** to be well off for/short of money; ~ **en metálico** cash; ~ **negro** O **sucio** illegally obtained money.

dinosaurio m dinosaur.

dintel m ARQUIT lintel.

dio → dar.

diócesis f diocese.

dios, -sa m y f god (f goddess). ◆ **Dios** m God; **a la buena de Dios** any old how; **¡Dios mío!** good God!, (oh) my God!; **¡por Dios!** for God's sake!; **¡vaya por Dios!** for Heaven's sake!, honestly!

diploma m diploma.

diplomacia f [gen] diplomacy.

diplomado, -da adj qualified.

diplomático, -ca ◇ adj lit & fig diplomatic. ◇ m y f diplomat.

diptongo m diphthong.

diputación f [corporación] committee; ~ **provincial** governing body of each province of an autonomous region in Spain; ≈ county council Br.

diputado, -da m y f ≈ Member of Parliament, MP Br, representative Am.

dique m -1. [en río] dike. -2. [en puerto] dock.

dirá → decir.

dirección f -1. [sentido, rumbo] direction; **calle de ~ única** one-way street; **en ~ a** towards, in the direction of. -2. [domicilio] address. -3. [mando - de empresa, hospital] **management**; [- de partido] **leadership**; [- de colegio] **headship**; [- de periódico] **editorship**; [- de una película] **direction**; [- de una obra de teatro] **production**; [- de una orquesta] **conducting**. -4. [junta directiva] management. -5. [de un vehículo] **steering**; ~ **asistida** power steering. ◆ **Dirección** f: **Dirección General de Tráfico** traffic department (part of the Ministry of the Interior).

directivo, -va ◇ adj managerial. ◇ m y f [jefe] **manager**. ◆ **directiva** f [junta] **board** (of directors).

directo, -ta adj -1. [gen] direct. -2. [derecho] straight. ◆ **directo** adv straight; ~ **a** straight to. ◆ **directa** f AUTOM top gear. ◆ **en directo** loc adv live.

director, -ra m y f -1. [de empresa] **director**; [de hotel, hospital] **manager** (f **manageress**); [de periódico] **editor**; [de cárcel] **governor**. -2. [de obra artística]: ~ **de cine** film director; ~ **de orquesta** **conductor**. -3. [de colegio] **headmaster** (f **headmistress**). -4. [de tesis, trabajo de investigación] **supervisor**; ~ **técnico** DEP **trainer**.

directorio m [gen & INFORM] directory.

directriz f GEOM directrix. ◆ **directrices** fpl [normas] guidelines.

diría → decir.

dirigente m y f [de partido político] **leader**; [de empresa] **manager**.

dirigir vt -1. [conducir - coche, barco] to steer; [- avión] to pilot; fig [- mirada] to direct. -2. [llevar - empresa, hotel, hospital] to manage; [- colegio, cárcel, periódico] to run; [- partido, revuelta] to lead; [- expedición] to head. -3. [película, obra de teatro] to direct; [orquesta] to conduct. -4. [carta, paquete] to address. -5. [guiar - persona] to guide. -6. [dedicar]: ~ **algo a** to aim sthg at. ◆ **dirigirse** vpr -1. [encaminarse]: ~**se a** O **hacia** to head for. -2. [hablar]: ~**se a** to address, to speak to. -3. [escribir]: ~**se a** to write to.

discar vt Amer to dial.

discernir vt to discern, to distinguish.

disminuir

disciplina *f* discipline.
discípulo, -la *m y f* disciple.
disco *m* **-1.** ANAT, ASTRON & GEOM disc.
-2. [de música] record; ~ **compacto**
compact disc; ~ **de larga duración** LP,
long-playing record. **-3.** [semáforo]
(traffic) light. **-4.** DEP discus. **-5.** INFORM
disk; ~ **duro/flexible** hard/floppy disk.
discografía *f* records previously released (*by an artist or group*).
disconforme *adj* in disagreement; **estar ~ con** to disagree with.
disconformidad *f* disagreement.
discontinuo, -nua *adj* [esfuerzo] intermittent; [línea] broken, dotted.
discordante *adj* [sonidos] discordant;
[opiniones] clashing.
discordia *f* discord.
discoteca *f* [local] disco.
discreción *f* discretion. ◆ **a discreción**
loc adv as much as one wants, freely.
discrecional *adj* [gen] optional; [parada]
request (*antes de sust*).
discrepancia *f* [diferencia] difference,
discrepancy; [desacuerdo] disagreement.
discrepar *vi*: ~ **(de)** [diferenciarse] to
differ (from); [disentir] to disagree
(with).
discreto, -ta *adj* **-1.** [prudente] discreet.
-2. [cantidad] moderate, modest. **-3.**
[normal - actuación] fair, reasonable.
discriminación *f* discrimination.
discriminar *vt* **-1.** [cosa]: ~ **algo de** to
discriminate ⊙ distinguish sthg from.
-2. [persona, colectividad] to discriminate against.
disculpa *f* [pretexto] excuse; [excusa, per-
dón] apology; **dar ~s** to make excuses;
pedir ~s a alguien (por) to apologize
to sb (for).
disculpar *vt* to excuse; ~ **a alguien (de**
⊙ **por algo)** to forgive sb (for sthg).
◆ **disculparse** *vpr*: ~**se (de** ⊙ **por algo)**
to apologize (for sthg).
discurrir *vi* **-1.** [pasar - personas] to
wander, to walk; [- tiempo, vida, sesión]
to go by, to pass; [- río, tráfico] to flow.
-2. [pensar] to think, to reflect.
discurso *m* speech.
discusión *f* [conversación] discussion;
[pelea] argument.
discutible *adj* debatable.
discutir ◇ *vi* **-1.** [hablar] to discuss. **-2.**
[pelear]: ~ **(de)** to argue (about). ◇ *vt*
[hablar] to discuss; [contradecir] to dispute.
disecar *vt* [cadáver] to dissect; [animal]
to stuff; [planta] to dry.

diseminar *vt* [semillas] to scatter; [ideas]
to disseminate.
disentir *vi*: ~ **(de/en)** to disagree
(with/on).
diseñar *vt* to design.
diseño *m* design; **ropa de ~** designer
clothes; ~ **asistido por ordenador** IN-
FORM computer-aided design; ~ **gráfico**
graphic design.
disertación *f* [oral] lecture, discourse;
[escrita] dissertation.
disfraz *m* [gen] disguise; [para baile, fiesta etc] fancy dress (*U*).
disfrazar *vt* to disguise. ◆ **disfrazarse**
vpr to disguise o.s.; ~**se de** to dress up
as.
disfrutar ◇ *vi* **-1.** [sentir placer] to enjoy
o.s. **-2.** [disponer de]: ~ **de algo** to enjoy sthg. ◇ *vt* to enjoy.
disgregar *vt* **-1.** [multitud, manifestación]
to disperse. **-2.** [roca, imperio, estado] to
break up; [átomo] to split. ◆ **disgregarse** *vpr* **-1.** [multitud, manifestación]
to disperse. **-2.** [roca, imperio, estado] to
break up.
disgustar *vt* [suj: comentario, críticas, no-
ticia] to upset. ◆ **disgustarse** *vpr*: ~**se
(con alguien/por algo)** [sentir enfado] to
get upset (with sb/about sthg); [ene-
mistarse] to fall out (with sb/over sthg).
disgusto *m* **-1.** [enfado] annoyance; [pe-
sadumbre] sorrow; **dar un ~ a alguien**
to upset sb; **llevarse un ~** to be upset.
-2. [pelea]: **tener un ~ con alguien** to
have a quarrel with sb.
disidente *m y f* [político] dissident; [reli-
gioso] dissenter.
disimular ◇ *vt* to hide, to conceal. ◇
vi to pretend.
disimulo *m* pretence, concealment.
disipar *vt* **-1.** [dudas, sospechas] to dispel; [ilusiones] to shatter. **-2.** [fortuna,
herencia] to squander, to throw away.
◆ **disiparse** *vpr* **-1.** [dudas, sospechas] to
be dispelled; [ilusiones] to be shattered.
-2. [niebla, humo, vapor] to vanish.
diskette = **disquete**.
dislexia *m* dyslexia.
dislocar *vt* to dislocate. ◆ **dislocarse**
vpr to dislocate.
disminución *f* decrease, drop.
disminuido, -da *adj* handicapped.
disminuir ◇ *vt* to reduce, to decrease.
◇ *vi* [gen] to decrease; [precios, tempera-
tura] to drop, to fall; [vista, memoria] to
fail; [días] to get shorter; [beneficios] to
fall off.

disolución *f* **-1.** [en un líquido] dissolving. **-2.** [de matrimonio, sociedad, partido] dissolution. **-3.** [mezcla] solution.

disolvente *adj & m* solvent.

disolver *vt* **-1.** [gen] to dissolve. **-2.** [reunión, manifestación, familia] to break up. ◆ **disolverse** *vpr* **-1.** [gen] to dissolve. **-2.** [reunión, manifestación, familia] to break up.

disparar ◇ *vt* to shoot; [pedrada] to throw. ◇ *vi* to shoot, to fire.

disparatado, -da *adj* absurd, crazy.

disparate *m* [comentario, acción] silly thing; [idea] crazy idea.

disparidad *f* difference, disparity.

disparo *m* shot.

dispensar *vt* **-1.** [disculpar] to excuse, to forgive. **-2.** [rendir]: ~ **algo (a alguien)** [honores] to confer sthg (upon sb); [bienvenida, ayuda] to give sthg (to sb). **-3.** [eximir]: ~ **a alguien de** to excuse O exempt sb from.

dispensario *m* dispensary.

dispersar *vt* **-1.** [esparcir - objetos] to scatter. **-2.** [disolver - gentío] to disperse; [- manifestación] to break up. ◆ **dispersarse** *vpr* to scatter.

dispersión *f* [de objetos] scattering.

disperso, -sa *adj* scattered.

disponer ◇ *vt* **-1.** [gen] to arrange. **-2.** [cena, comida] to lay on. **-3.** [decidir - suj: persona] to decide; [suj: ley] to stipulate. ◇ *vi* **-1.** [poseer]: ~ **de** to have. **-2.** [usar]: ~ **de** to make use of. ◆ **disponerse** *a vpr*: ~**se a hacer algo** to prepare O get ready to do sthg.

disponibilidad *f* [gen] availability.

disponible *adj* [gen] available; [tiempo] free, spare.

disposición *f* **-1.** [colocación] arrangement, layout. **-2.** [orden] order; [de ley] provision. **-3.** [uso]: **a** ~ **de** at the disposal of.

dispositivo *m* device; ~ **intrauterino** intrauterine device, IUD.

dispuesto, -ta ◇ *pp* → **disponer**. ◇ *adj* [preparado] ready; **estar** ~ **a hacer algo** to be prepared to do sthg.

disputa *f* dispute.

disputar *vt* **-1.** [cuestión, tema] to argue about. **-2.** [trofeo, puesto] to compete for; [carrera, partido] to compete in.

disquete, diskette [dis'kete] *m* INFORM diskette, floppy disk.

disquetera *f* INFORM disk drive.

distancia *f* **-1.** [gen] distance; **a** ~ from a distance; **mantener a** ~ to keep at a distance. **-2.** [en el tiempo] gap, space.

distanciar *vt* [gen] to drive apart; [rival] to forge ahead of. ◆ **distanciarse** *vpr* [alejarse - afectivamente] to grow apart; [- físicamente] to distance o.s.

distante *adj* **-1.** [en el espacio]: ~ **(de)** far away (from). **-2.** [en el trato] distant.

distar *vi* [hallarse a]: **ese sitio dista varios kilómetros de aquí** that place is several kilometres away from here.

diste *etc* → **dar**.

distendido, -da *adj* [informal] relaxed, informal.

distensión *f* **-1.** [entre países] détente; [entre personas] easing of tension. **-2.** MED strain.

distinción *f* **-1.** [diferencia] distinction; **a** ~ **de** in contrast to, unlike; **sin** ~ alike. **-2.** [privilegio] privilege. **-3.** [modales] refinement.

distinguido, -da *adj* **-1.** [notable] distinguished. **-2.** [elegante] refined.

distinguir *vt* **-1.** [diferenciar] to distinguish; ~ **algo de algo** to tell sthg from sthg. **-2.** [separar] to pick out. **-3.** [caracterizar] to characterize. ◆ **distinguirse** *vpr* [destacarse] to stand out.

distintivo, -va *adj* distinctive; [señal] distinguishing. ◆ **distintivo** *m* badge.

distinto, -ta *adj* [diferente] different. ◆ **distintos, -tas** *adj pl* [varios] various.

distorsión *f* [de tobillo, rodilla] sprain; [de imágenes, sonidos, palabras] distortion.

distracción *f* **-1.** [entretenimiento] entertainment; [pasatiempo] hobby, pastime. **-2.** [despiste] slip; [falta de atención] absent-mindedness.

distraer *vt* **-1.** [divertir] to amuse, to entertain. **-2.** [despistar] to distract. ◆ **distraerse** *vpr* **-1.** [divertirse] to enjoy o.s.; [pasar el tiempo] to pass the time. **-2.** [despistarse] to let one's mind wander.

distraído, -da *adj* **-1.** [entretenido] amusing, entertaining. **-2.** [despistado] absent-minded.

distribución *f* **-1.** [gen] distribution; ~ **de premios** prizegiving. **-2.** [de correo, mercancías] delivery. **-3.** [de casa, habitaciones] layout.

distribuidor, -ra ◇ *adj* [entidad] wholesale; [red] supply (*antes de sust*). ◇ *m y f* [persona] deliveryman (*f* deliverywoman). ◆ **distribuidor** *m* [aparato] vending machine.

distribuir *vt* **-1.** [gen] to distribute; [carga, trabajo] to spread; [pastel, ganancias] to divide up. **-2.** [correo, mercancías] to deliver. **-3.** [casa, habitaciones] to arrange.

distrito *m* district.

disturbio *m* disturbance; [violento] riot.

disuadir *vt*: ~ **(de)** to dissuade (from).

disuasión *f* deterrence.

disuasivo, -va *adj* deterrent.

disuelto, -ta *pp* → **disolver**.

DIU (*abrev de* **dispositivo intrauterino**) *m* IUD.

diurno, -na *adj* [gen] daytime (*antes de sust*); [planta, animal] diurnal.

diva → **divo**.

divagar *vi* to digress.

diván *m* divan; [de psiquiatra] couch.

divergencia *f* **-1.** [de líneas] divergence. **-2.** [de opinión] difference of opinion.

divergir *vi* **-1.** [calles, líneas] to diverge. **-2.** *fig* [opiniones]: ~ **(en)** to differ (on).

diversidad *f* diversity.

diversificar *vt* to diversify.

diversión *f* entertainment, amusement.

diverso, -sa *adj* [diferente] different. ◆ **diversos, -sas** *adj pl* [varios] several, various.

divertido, -da *adj* [entretenido - película, libro] entertaining; [- fiesta] enjoyable; [que hace reír] funny.

divertir *vt* to entertain, to amuse. ◆ **divertirse** *vpr* to enjoy o.s.

dividendo *m* FIN & MAT dividend.

dividir *vt*: ~ **(en)** to divide (into); ~ **entre** [gen] to divide between; MAT to divide by.

divinidad *f* divinity, god.

divino, -na *adj lit* & *fig* divine.

divisa *f* **-1.** (*gen pl*) [moneda] foreign currency. **-2.** [distintivo] emblem.

divisar *vt* to spy, to make out.

división *f* [gen] division; [partición] splitting up.

divo, -va *m y f* [MÚS - mujer] diva, prima donna; [- hombre] opera singer.

divorciado, -da ◇ *adj* divorced. ◇ *m y f* divorcé (*f* divorcée).

divorciar *vt lit* & *fig* to divorce. ◆ **divorciarse** *vpr* to get divorced.

divorcio *m* DER divorce.

divulgar *vt* [noticia, secreto] to reveal; [rumor] to spread; [cultura, ciencia, doctrina] to popularize.

dizque *adv Amer* apparently.

DNI (*abrev de* **documento nacional de identidad**) *m* ID card.

Dña *abrev de* **doña.**

do *m* MÚS C; [en solfeo] doh.

dobladillo *m* [de traje, vestido] hem; [de pantalón] turn-up *Br*, cuff *Am*.

doblado, -da *adj* **-1.** [papel, camisa] folded. **-2.** [voz, película] dubbed.

doblar ◇ *vt* **-1.** [duplicar] to double. **-2.** [plegar] to fold. **-3.** [torcer] to bend. **-4.** [esquina] to turn, to go round. **-5.** [voz, actor] to dub. ◇ *vi* **-1.** [girar] to turn. **-2.** [campanas] to toll. ◆ **doblarse** *vpr* [someterse]: ~**se a** to give in to.

doble ◇ *adj* double; **tiene ~ número de habitantes** it has double ○ twice the number of inhabitants; **es ~ de ancho** it's twice as wide; **una frase de ~ sentido** a phrase with a double meaning. ◇ *m y f* [gen & CIN] double. ◇ *m* [duplo]: **el ~** twice as much; **gana el ~ que yo** she earns twice as much as I do, she earns double what I do. ◇ *adv* double; **trabajar ~** to work twice as hard. ◆ **dobles** *mpl* DEP doubles.

doblegar *vt* [someter] to bend, to cause to give in. ◆ **doblegarse** *vpr*: ~**se (ante)** to give in ○ yield (to).

doblez *m* [pliegue] fold, crease.

doce *núm* twelve; *ver también* **seis.**

doceavo, -va *núm* twelfth.

docena *f* dozen; **a ~s** by the dozen.

docente *adj* teaching.

dócil *adj* obedient.

docto, -ta *adj* learned.

doctor, -ra *m y f*: ~ **(en)** doctor (of).

doctrina *f* doctrine.

documentación *f* [identificación personal] papers (*pl*).

documentado, -da *adj* [informado - película, informe] researched; [- persona] informed.

documental *adj & m* documentary.

documentar *vt* **-1.** [evidenciar] to document. **-2.** [informar] to brief. ◆ **documentarse** *vpr* to do research.

documento *m* **-1.** [escrito] document; ~ **nacional de identidad** identity card. **-2.** [testimonio] record.

dogma *m* dogma.

dogmático, -ca *adj* dogmatic.

dólar *m* dollar.

dolencia *f* pain.

doler *vi* to hurt; **me duele la pierna** my leg hurts; **¿te duele?** does it hurt?; **me duele la garganta/la cabeza** I have a sore throat/a headache. ◆ **dolerse** *vpr*:

~se de ○ por algo [quejarse] to complain about sthg; [arrepentirse] to be sorry about sthg.

dolido, -da adj hurt.

dolor m -1. [físico] pain; **siento un ~ en el brazo** I have a pain in my arm; **(tener) ~ de cabeza** (to have a) headache; **~ de estómago** stomachache; **~ de muelas** toothache. -2. [moral] grief, sorrow.

dolorido, -da adj [físicamente] sore; [moralmente] grieving, sorrowing.

doloroso, -sa adj [físicamente] painful; [moralmente] distressing.

domador, -ra m y f [de caballos] breaker; [de leones] tamer.

domar vt [gen] to tame; [caballo] to break in; fig [personas] to control.

domesticar vt lit & fig to tame.

doméstico, -ca adj domestic.

domiciliación f: **~ (bancaria)** standing order, direct debit (U).

domiciliar vt [pago] to pay by direct debit ○ standing order.

domicilio m -1. [vivienda] residence, home; **a ~** house (antes de sust). -2. [dirección] address; **sin ~ fijo** of no fixed abode; **~ social** head office.

dominante adj -1. [nación, religión, tendencia] dominant; [vientos] prevailing. -2. [persona] domineering.

dominar ○ vt -1. [controlar - país, territorio] to dominate, to rule (over); [- pasión, nervios, caballo] to control; [- situación] to be in control of; [- incendio] to bring under control; [- rebelión] to put down. -2. [divisar] to overlook. -3. [conocer - técnica, tema] to master; [- lengua] to be fluent in. ○ vi [predominar] to predominate. ◆ **dominarse** vpr to control o.s.

domingo m Sunday; ver también **sábado**.

dominguero, -ra fam despec m y f Sunday tripper/driver etc.

Dominica Dominica.

dominical adj Sunday (antes de sust).

dominicano, -na adj, m y f Dominican.

dominico, -ca adj, m y f Dominican.

dominio m -1. [dominación, posesión]: **~ (sobre)** control (over). -2. [autoridad] authority, power. -3. fig [territorio] domain; [ámbito] realm. -4. [conocimiento - de arte, técnica] mastery; [- de idiomas] command.

dominó m -1. [juego] dominoes (U). -2. [fichas] set of dominoes.

don m -1. [tratamiento]: **~ Luis García** [gen] Mr Luis García; [en cartas] Luis García Esquire; **~ Luis** not translated in modern English or translated as "Mr" + surname, if known. -2. [habilidad] gift; **el ~ de la palabra** the gift of the gab.

donaire m [al expresarse] wit; [al andar etc] grace.

donante m y f donor; **~ de sangre** blood donor.

donar vt to donate.

donativo m donation.

doncella f maid.

donde ◇ adv where; **el bolso está ~ lo dejaste** the bag is where you left it; **puedes marcharte ~ quieras** you can go wherever you want; **hasta ~** as far as, up to where; **por ~** wherever. ◇ pron where; **la casa ~ nací** the house where I was born; **la ciudad de ~ viene** the town (where) she comes from, the town from which she comes. ◆ **de donde** loc adv [de lo cual] from which.

dónde adv (interrogativo) where; **¿~ está el niño?** where's the child?; **no sé ~ se habrá metido** I don't know where she can be; **¿a ~ vas?** where are you going?; **¿de ~ eres?** where are you from?; **¿hacia ~ vas?** where are you heading?; **¿por ~?** whereabouts?; **¿por ~ se va al teatro?** how do you get to the theatre from here?

dondequiera ◆ **dondequiera que** adv wherever.

doña f: **~ Luisa García** Mrs Luisa García; **~ Luisa** not translated in modern English or translated as "Mrs" + surname, if known.

dopado, -da adj having taken performance-enhancing drugs.

dopar vt to dope.

doping ['dopin] m doping.

doquier ◆ **por doquier** loc adv everywhere.

dorado, -da adj lit & fig golden. ◆ **dorada** f [pez] gilthead.

dorar vt -1. [cubrir con oro] to gild. -2. [alimento] to brown.

dormilón, -ona fam m y f [persona] sleepyhead.

dormir ◇ vt [niño, animal] to put to bed; **~ la siesta** to have an afternoon nap. ◇ vi to sleep. ◆ **dormirse** vpr -1. [persona] to fall asleep. -2. [brazo, mano] to go to sleep.

dormitar vi to doze.

dormitorio *m* [de casa] bedroom; [de colegio] dormitory.

dorsal ◇ *adj* dorsal. ◇ *m* number (*on player's back*).

dorso *m* back; **al ~**, **en el ~** on the back; **"véase al ~"** "see overleaf".

dos *núm* two; **cada ~ por tres** every five minutes; *ver también* **seis**.

doscientos, **-tas** *núm* two hundred; *ver también* **seis**.

dosificar *vt* fig [fuerzas, palabras] to use sparingly.

dosis *f inv* & fig dose.

dossier [do'sjer] *m inv* dossier, file.

dotación *f* **-1.** [de dinero, armas, medios] amount granted. **-2.** [personal] personnel; [tripulantes] crew; [patrulla] squad.

dotado, **-da** *adj* gifted; **~ de** [persona] blessed with; [edificio, instalación, aparato] equipped with.

dotar *vt* **-1.** [proveer]: **~ algo de** to provide sthg with. **-2.** fig [suj: la naturaleza]: **~ a algo/alguien de** to endow sthg/sb with.

dote *f* [en boda] dowry. ◆ **dotes** *fpl* [dones] qualities.

doy → **dar**.

Dr. (*abrev de* **doctor**) Dr.

Dra. (*abrev de* **doctora**) Dr.

dragar *vt* to dredge.

dragón *m* dragon.

drama *m* [gen] drama; [obra] play.

dramático, **-ca** *adj* dramatic.

dramatizar *vt* to dramatize.

dramaturgo, **-ga** *m y f* playwright, dramatist.

drástico, **-ca** *adj* drastic.

drenar *vt* to drain.

driblar *vt* DEP to dribble.

droga *f* drug; **la ~** drugs (*pl*).

drogadicto, **-ta** *m y f* drug addict.

drogar *vt* to drug. ◆ **drogarse** *vpr* to take drugs.

droguería *f shop selling paint, cleaning materials etc*.

dromedario *m* dromedary.

dto. *abrev de* **descuento**.

dual *adj* dual.

Dublín Dublin.

ducha *f* shower; **tomar** ○ **darse una ~** to have ○ take a shower.

duchar *vt* to shower. ◆ **ducharse** *vpr* to have a shower.

duda *f* doubt; **poner algo en ~** to call sthg into question; **salir de ~s** to set one's mind at rest; **sin ~** doubtless; **no cabe ~** there is no doubt about it.

dudar ◇ *vi* **-1.** [desconfiar]: **~ de algo/alguien** to have one's doubts about sthg/sb. **-2.** [no estar seguro]: **~ sobre algo** to be unsure about sthg. **-3.** [vacilar] to hesitate; **~ entre hacer una cosa u otra** to be unsure whether to do one thing or another. ◇ *vt* to doubt; **dudo que venga** I doubt whether he'll come.

dudoso, **-sa** *adj* **-1.** [improbable]: **ser ~ (que)** to be doubtful (whether), to be unlikely (that). **-2.** [vacilante] hesitant, indecisive. **-3.** [sospechoso] suspect.

duelo *m* **-1.** [combate] duel. **-2.** [sentimiento] grief, sorrow.

duende *m* [personaje] imp, goblin.

dueño, **-ña** *m y f* [gen] owner; [de piso etc] landlord (*f* landlady).

duerma *etc* → **dormir**.

dulce ◇ *adj* **-1.** [gen] sweet. **-2.** [agua] fresh. **-3.** [mirada] tender. ◇ *m* [caramelo, postre] sweet; [pastel] cake, pastry.

dulcificar *vt* [endulzar] to sweeten.

dulzura *f* [gen] sweetness.

duna *f* dune.

dúo *m* **-1.** MÚS duet. **-2.** [pareja] duo; **a ~ together.

duodécimo, **-ma** *núm* twelfth.

dúplex, **duplex** *m inv* [piso] duplex.

duplicado, **-da** *adj* in duplicate. ◆ **duplicado** *m*: **(por) ~** (in) duplicate.

duplicar *vt* **-1.** [cantidad] to double. **-2.** [documento] to duplicate. ◆ **duplicarse** *vpr* to double.

duque, **-sa** *m y f* duke (*f* duchess).

duración *f* length.

duradero, **-ra** *adj* [gen] lasting; [ropa, zapatos] hard-wearing.

durante *prep* during; **le escribí ~ las vacaciones** I wrote to him during the holidays; **estuve escribiendo ~ una hora** I was writing for an hour; **~ toda la semana** all week.

durar *vi* [gen] to last; [permanecer, subsistir] to remain, to stay; [ropa] to wear well; **aún dura la fiesta** the party's still going on.

dureza *f* **-1.** [de objeto, metal etc] hardness. **-2.** [de clima, persona] harshness.

durmiera *etc* → **dormir**.

duro, **-ra** *adj* **-1.** [gen] hard; [carne] tough. **-2.** [resistente] tough. **-3.** [palabras, clima] harsh. ◇ *m* [moneda] five-peseta piece. ◇ *adv* hard.

d/v (*abrev de* **días vista**): **15 ~** within 15 days.

E

e¹, E *f* [letra] e, E.

e² *conj* (*en lugar de "y" ante palabras que empiecen por "i" o "hi"*) and.

EA (*abrev de* **Eusko Alkartasuna**) *f Basque nationalist political party*.

ebanista *m y f* cabinet-maker.

ébano *m* ebony.

ebrio, ebria *adj* [borracho] drunk.

Ebro *m*: **el ~** the Ebro.

ebullición *f* boiling.

eccema *m* eczema.

echar ◇ *vt* -1. [tirar] to throw; [red] to cast. -2. [añadir]: ~ **algo** (**a** ○ **en algo**) [vino etc] to pour sthg (into sthg); [sal, azúcar etc] to add sthg (to sthg). -3. [carta, postal] to post. -4. [humo, vapor, chispas] to give off, to emit. -5. [hojas, flores] to shoot. -6. [expulsar]: ~ **a alguien** (**de**) to throw sb out (of). -7. [despedir]: ~ **a alguien** (**de**) to sack sb (from). -8. [accionar]: ~ **la llave/el cerrojo** to lock/bolt the door; ~ **el freno** to brake, to put the brakes on. -9. [acostar] to lie (down). -10. *fam* [en televisión, cine] to show; **¿qué echan esta noche en la tele?** what's on telly tonight? -11. *loc*: ~ **abajo** [edificio] to pull down, to demolish; [gobierno] to bring down; [proyecto] to ruin; ~ **a perder** [vestido, alimentos, plan] to ruin; [ocasión] to waste; ~ **de menos** to miss. ◇ *vi* [empezar]: ~ **a hacer algo** to begin to do sthg, to start doing sthg; ~ **a correr** to break into a run; ~ **a llorar** to burst into tears; ~ **a reír** to burst out laughing. ◆ **echarse** *vpr* -1. [acostarse] to lie down. -2. [apartarse]: ~**se** (**a un lado**) to move (aside); ~**se atrás** *fig* to back out. -3. *loc*: ~**se a perder** [comida] to go off, to spoil; [plan] to fall through.

echarpe *m* shawl.

eclesiástico, -ca *adj* ecclesiastical.

eclipsar *vt lit & fig* to eclipse.

eclipse *m* eclipse.

eco *m* [gen] echo; **hacerse ~ de** to report; **tener ~** to arouse interest.

ecología *f* ecology.

ecológico, -ca *adj* [gen] ecological; [alimentos] organic.

ecologista ◇ *adj* environmental, ecological. ◇ *m y f* environmentalist.

economato *m* company cooperative shop.

economía *f* -1. [gen] economy; ~ **sumergida** black economy ○ market. -2. [estudio] economics (U); ~ **familiar** home economics. -3. [ahorro] saving.

económico, -ca *adj* -1. [problema, doctrina etc] economic. -2. [barato] cheap, low-cost. -3. [que gasta poco - motor etc] economical; [- persona] thrifty.

economista *m y f* economist.

economizar *vt lit & fig* to save.

ecosistema *m* ecosystem.

ecu (*abrev de* **unidad de cuenta europea**) *m* ecu.

ecuación *f* equation.

ecuador *m* equator.

Ecuador Ecuador.

ecuánime *adj* -1. [en el ánimo] levelheaded. -2. [en el juicio] impartial.

ecuatoriano, -na *adj, m y f* Ecuadorian, Ecuadoran.

ecuestre *adj* equestrian.

edad *f* age; **¿qué ~ tienes?** how old are you?; **tiene 25 años de ~** she's 25 (years old); **una persona de ~** an elderly person; ~ **escolar** school age; **Edad Media** Middle Ages (*pl*); ~ **del pavo** awkward age; **la tercera ~** [ancianos] senior citizens (*pl*).

edén *m* RELIG Eden; *fig* paradise.

edición *f* -1. [acción - IMPRENTA] publication; [- INFORM, RADIO & TV] editing. -2. [ejemplares] edition.

edicto *m* edict.

edificante *adj* [conducta] exemplary; [libro, discurso] edifying.

edificar *vt* [construir] to build.

edificio *m* building.

edil *m* (town) councillor.

Edimburgo Edinburgh.

editar *vt* -1. [libro, periódico] to publish; [disco] to release. -2. INFORM, RADIO & TV to edit.

editor, -ra ◇ *adj* publishing (*antes de sust*). ◇ *m y f* -1. [de libro, periódico] publisher. -2. RADIO & TV editor.

editorial ◇ *adj* publishing (*antes de sust*). ◇ *m* editorial, leader. ◇ *f* publisher, publishing house.

edredón *m* duvet, eiderdown.

educación *f* -1. [enseñanza] education. -2. [modales] good manners (*pl*); **¡qué**

poca ~! how rude!; **mala** ~ bad manners (*pl*).

educado, -da *adj* polite, well-mannered; **mal** ~ rude, ill-mannered.

educador, -ra *m y f* teacher.

educar *vt* **-1.** [enseñar] to educate. **-2.** [criar] to bring up. **-3.** [cuerpo, voz, oído] to train.

edulcorante *m* sweetener.

edulcorar *vt* to sweeten.

EE (*abrev de* **Euskadiko Ezquerra**) *m* Basque political party to the left of the political spectrum.

EE UU (*abrev de* **Estados Unidos**) *mpl* USA.

efectivamente *adv* [en respuestas] precisely, exactly.

efectividad *f* effectiveness.

efectivo, -va *adj* **-1.** [útil] effective. **-2.** [real] actual, true; **hacer** ~ [gen] to carry out; [promesa] to keep; [dinero, crédito] to pay; [cheque] to cash. ◆ **efectivo** *m* [dinero] cash; **en** ~ in cash. ◆ **efectivos** *mpl* [personal] forces.

efecto *m* **-1.** [gen] effect; ~ **invernadero** greenhouse effect; ~ **óptico** optical illusion; ~**s sonoros/visuales** sound/visual effects; ~**s especiales** special effects; ~**s secundarios** side effects. **-2.** [finalidad] aim, purpose; **a tal** ~ to that end; **a** ~**s para los** ~**s de algo** as far as sthg is concerned. **-3.** [impresión] impression; **producir buen/mal** ~ to make a good/bad impression. **-4.** [de balón, bola] spin; **dar** ~ **a** to put spin on. **-5.** COM [documento] bill. ◆ **efectos personales** *mpl* personal possessions O effects. ◆ **en efecto** *loc adv* indeed.

efectuar *vt* [gen] to carry out; [compra, pago, viaje] to make. ◆ **efectuarse** *vpr* to take place.

efeméride *f* [suceso] major event; [conmemoración] anniversary.

efervescencia *f* [de líquido] effervescence; [de bebida] fizziness.

efervescente *adj* [bebida] fizzy.

eficacia *f* [eficiencia] efficiency; [efectividad] effectiveness.

eficaz *adj* **-1.** [eficiente] efficient. **-2.** [efectivo] effective.

eficiencia *f* efficiency.

eficiente *adj* efficient.

efímero, -ra *adj* ephemeral.

efusión *f* [cordialidad] effusiveness.

efusivo, -va *adj* effusive.

EGB (*abrev de* **educación general básica**) *f* Spanish primary education system for pupils aged 6-14.

egipcio, -cia *adj, m y f* Egyptian.

Egipto Egypt.

egocéntrico, -ca *adj* egocentric.

egoísmo *m* selfishness, egoism.

egoísta ◇ *adj* egoistic, selfish. ◇ *m y f* egoist, selfish person.

ególatra ◇ *adj* egotistical. ◇ *m y f* egotist.

egresado, -da *m y f* Amer **-1.** [de escuela] student who has completed a course. **-2.** [de universidad] graduate.

egresar *vi* Amer **-1.** [de escuela] to leave school after graduation. **-2.** [de universidad] to graduate.

egreso *m* Amer **-1.** [de escuela] completion of course. **-2.** [de universidad] graduation.

eh *interj*: ¡~! hey!

ej. *abrev de* **ejemplar**.

eje *m* **-1.** [de rueda] axle; [de máquina] shaft. **-2.** GEOM axis. **-3.** *fig* [idea central] central idea, basis.

ejecución *f* **-1.** [realización] carrying out. **-2.** [de condenado] execution. **-3.** [de concierto] performance, rendition.

ejecutar *vt* **-1.** [realizar] to carry out. **-2.** [condenado] to execute. **-3.** [concierto] to perform. **-4.** INFORM [programa] to run.

ejecutivo, -va ◇ *adj* executive. ◇ *m y f* [persona] executive. ◆ **ejecutivo** *m* POLÍT: **el** ~ the government.

ejem *interj*: ¡~! [expresa duda] um!; [expresa ironía] ahem!

ejemplar ◇ *adj* exemplary. ◇ *m* [de libro] copy; [de revista] issue; [de moneda] example; [de especie, raza] specimen.

ejemplificar *vt* to exemplify.

ejemplo *m* example; **por** ~ for example; **predicar con el** ~ to practise what one preaches.

ejercer ◇ *vt* **-1.** [profesión] to practise; [cargo] to hold. **-2.** [poder, derecho] to exercise; [influencia, dominio] to exert; ~ **presión sobre** to put pressure on. ◇ *vi* to practise (one's profession); ~ **de** to practise O work as.

ejercicio *m* **-1.** [gen] exercise; **hacer** ~ to (do) exercise. **-2.** [de profesión] practising; [de cargo, funciones] carrying out. **-3.** [de poder, derecho] exercising. **-4.** MIL drill. **-5.** ECON: ~ **económico/fiscal** financial/tax year.

ejercitar *vt* [derecho] to exercise. ◆ **ejercitarse** *vpr*: ~**se (en)** to train (in).

ejército *m* MIL & *fig* army.

ejote *m* Amer green bean.

el, la (*mpl* **los**, *fpl* **las**) *art* (**el** antes de sustantivo femenino que empiece por "a" o

"ha" tónica; a + el = al; de + el = del)
-1. [gen] the; [en sentido genérico] *no se traduce*; ~ **coche** the car; **la casa** the house; **los niños** the children; ~ **agua/hacha/águila** the water/axe/eagle; **fui a recoger a los niños** I went to pick up the children; **los niños imitan a los adultos** children copy adults. **-2.** [con sustantivo abstracto] *no se traduce*; ~ **amor** love; **la vida** life. **-3.** [indica posesión, pertenencia]: **se partió la pierna** he broke his leg; **se quitó los zapatos** she took her shoes off; **tiene** ~ **pelo oscuro** he has dark hair. **-4.** [con días de la semana]: **vuelven** ~ **sábado** they're coming back on Saturday. **-5.** [con nombres propios geográficos] the; ~ **Sena** the (River) Seine; ~ **Everest** (Mount) Everest; **la España de la postguerra** post-war Spain. **-6.** [con complemento de nombre, especificativo]: ~ **de** the one; **he perdido** ~ **tren, cogeré** ~ **de las nueve** I've missed the train, I'll get the nine o'clock one; ~ **de azul** the one in blue. **-7.** [con complemento de nombre, posesivo]: **mi hermano y** ~ **de Juan** my brother and Juan's. **-8.** [antes de frase]: ~ **que** [cosa] the one, whichever; [persona] whoever; **coge** ~ **que quieras** take whichever you like; ~ **que más corra** whoever runs fastest. **-9.** [antes de adjetivo]: **prefiero** ~ **rojo al azul** I prefer the red one to the blue one.

él, ella *pron pers* **-1.** [sujeto, predicado - persona] he (*f* she); [- animal, cosa] it; **mi hermana es ella** she's the one who is my sister. **-2.** (*después de prep*) [complemento] him (*f* her); **voy a ir de vacaciones con ella** I'm going on holiday with her; **díselo a ella** tell her it. **-3.** [posesivo]: **de** ~ his; **de ella** hers.

elaborar *vt* [producto] to make, to manufacture; [idea] to work out; [plan, informe] to draw up.

elasticidad *f* [gen] elasticity.

elástico, -ca *adj* [gen] elastic. ◆ **elástico** *m* [cinta] elastic.

elección *f* **-1.** [nombramiento] election. **-2.** [opción] choice. ◆ **elecciones** *fpl* POLÍT election (*sg*).

electo, -ta *adj* elect; **el presidente** ~ the president elect.

elector, -ra *m y f* voter, elector.

electorado *m* electorate.

electoral *adj* electoral.

electricidad *f* electricity.

electricista *m y f* electrician.

eléctrico, -ca *adj* electric.

electrificar *vt* to electrify.

electrizar *vt fig* [exaltar] to electrify.

electrocutar *vt* to electrocute.

electrodoméstico *m* (*gen pl*) electrical household appliance.

electromagnético, -ca *adj* electromagnetic.

electrón *m* electron.

electrónico, -ca *adj* [de la electrónica] electronic. ◆ **electrónica** *f* electronics (*U*).

elefante, -ta *m y f* elephant.

elegancia *f* elegance.

elegante *adj* **-1.** [persona, traje, estilo] elegant. **-2.** [conducta, actitud, respuesta] dignified.

elegantoso, -sa *adj Amer* elegant.

elegía *f* elegy.

elegir *vt* [escoger] to choose, to select; [por votación] to elect.

elemental *adj* **-1.** [básico] basic. **-2.** [obvio] obvious.

elemento *m* **-1.** [gen] element. **-2.** [factor] factor. **-3.** [persona - en equipo, colectivo] individual.

elenco *m* [reparto] cast.

elepé *m* LP (record).

elevación *f* **-1.** [de pesos, objetos etc] lifting; [de nivel, altura, precios] rise. **-2.** [de terreno] elevation, rise.

elevado, -da *adj* [alto] high; *fig* [sublime] lofty.

elevador *m* **-1.** [montacargas] hoist. **-2.** *Amer* [ascensor] lift *Br*, elevator *Am*.

elevalunas *m inv* window winder.

elevar *vt* **-1.** [gen & MAT] to raise; [peso, objeto] to lift. **-2.** [ascender]: ~ **a alguien (a)** to elevate sb (to). ◆ **elevarse** *vpr* [gen] to rise; [edificio, montaña] to rise up; ~**se a** [altura] to reach; [gastos, daños] to amount O come to.

elidir *vt* to elide.

eliminar *vt* [gen] to eliminate; [contaminación, enfermedad] to get rid of.

eliminatorio, -ria *adj* qualifying (*antes de sust*). ◆ **eliminatoria** *f* [gen] qualifying round; [en atletismo] heat.

elipse *f* ellipse.

elipsis *f inv* ellipsis.

élite, elite *f* elite.

elitista *adj, m y f* elitista.

elixir, elíxir *m* **-1.** FARM: ~ **bucal** mouthwash. **-2.** *fig* [remedio milagroso] elixir.

ella → **él**.

ellas → **ellos**.

ello *pron pers* (*neutro*) it; **no nos llevamos bien, pero** ~ **no nos impide for-**

mar un buen equipo we don't get on very well, but it ○ that doesn't stop us making a good team; **no quiero hablar de ~** I don't want to talk about it; **por ~** for that reason.

ellos, ellas *pron pers* **-1.** [sujeto, predicado] they; **los invitados son ~** they are the guests, it is they who are the guests. **-2.** (*después de prep*) [complemento] them; **me voy al bar con ellas** I'm going with them to the bar; **díselo a ~** tell them it. **-3.** [posesivo]: **de ~/ellas** theirs.

elocuencia *f* eloquence.

elocuente *adj* eloquent; **se hizo un silencio ~** the silence said it all.

elogiar *vt* to praise.

elogio *m* praise.

El Salvador El Salvador.

elucidar *vt* to elucidate.

elucubración *f* **-1.** [reflexión] reflection, meditation. **-2.** *despec* [divagación] mental meandering.

elucubrar *vt* **-1.** [reflexionar] to reflect ○ meditate upon. **-2.** *despec* [divagar] to theorize about.

eludir *vt* [gen] to avoid; [perseguidores] to escape.

emanar ◆ **emanar de** *vi* to emanate from.

emancipación *f* [de mujeres, esclavos] emancipation; [de menores de edad] coming of age; [de países] obtaining of independence.

emancipar *vt* [gen] to emancipate; [países] to grant independence (to). ◆ **emanciparse** *vpr* to free o.s., to become independent.

embadurnar *vt*: **~ algo (de)** to smear sthg (with).

embajada *f* [edificio] embassy.

embajador, -ra *m y f* ambassador.

embalaje *m* [acción] packing.

embalar *vt* to wrap up, to pack. ◆ **embalarse** *vpr* [acelerar - corredor] to race away; [- vehículo] to pick up speed.

embalsamar *vt* to embalm.

embalse *m* reservoir.

embarazada ◇ *adj f* pregnant; **dejar ~ a alguien** to get sb pregnant; **quedarse ~** to get pregnant. ◇ *f* pregnant woman.

embarazar *vt* **-1.** [impedir] to restrict. **-2.** [cohibir] to inhibit.

embarazo *m* **-1.** [preñez] pregnancy. **-2.** [timidez] embarrassment. **-3.** [impedimento] obstacle.

embarazoso, -sa *adj* awkward, embarrassing.

embarcación *f* [barco] craft, boat.

embarcadero *m* jetty.

embarcar ◇ *vt* [personas] to board; [mercancías] to ship. ◇ *vi* to board. ◆ **embarcarse** *vpr* [para viajar] to board.

embargar *vt* **-1.** DER to seize. **-2.** [suj: emoción etc] to overcome.

embargo *m* **-1.** DER seizure. **-2.** ECON embargo. ◆ **sin embargo** *loc adv* however, nevertheless.

embarque *m* [de personas] boarding; [de mercancías] embarkation.

embarrancar *vi* to run aground.

embarullar *vt* *fam* to mess up. ◆ **embarullarse** *vpr* *fam* to get into a muddle.

embaucar *vt* to swindle, to deceive.

embeber *vt* to soak up. ◆ **embeberse** *vpr*: **~se (en algo)** [ensimismarse] to become absorbed (in sthg); *fig* [empaparse] to immerse o.s. (in sthg).

embellecer *vt* to adorn, to embellish.

embestida *f* [gen] attack; [de toro] charge.

embestir *vt* [gen] to attack; [toro] to charge.

emblema *m* **-1.** [divisa, distintivo] emblem, badge. **-2.** [símbolo] symbol.

embobar *vt* to captivate.

embocadura *f* [de instrumento] mouthpiece.

embolia *f* clot, embolism.

émbolo *m* AUTOM piston.

embolsarse *vpr* [ganar] to earn.

embonar *vt* *Amer fam* to suit.

emborrachar *vt* to make drunk. ◆ **emborracharse** *vpr* to get drunk.

emborronar *vt* [garabatear] to scribble on; [manchar] to smudge.

emboscada *f* *lit* & *fig* ambush.

embotellado, -da *adj* bottled.

embotellamiento *m* [de tráfico] traffic jam.

embotellar *vt* [líquido] to bottle.

embozar *vt* **-1.** [conducto] to block. **-2.** [rostro] to cover (up). ◆ **embozarse** *vpr* **-1.** [conducto] to get blocked (up). **-2.** [persona] to cover one's face.

embragar *vi* to engage the clutch.

embrague *m* clutch.

embriagar *vt* **-1.** [extasiar] to intoxicate. **-2.** [emborrachar] to make drunk. ◆ **embriagarse** *vpr* [emborracharse]: **~se (con)** to get drunk (on).

embriaguez f -1. [borrachera] drunkenness. -2. [éxtasis] intoxication.

embrión m embryo.

embrionario, -ria adj fig [inicial] embryonic.

embrollo m -1. [de hilos] tangle. -2. fig [lío] mess; [mentira] lie.

embromado, -da adj Amer fam tricky.

embrujar vt lit & fig to bewitch.

embrujo m [maleficio] curse, spell; fig [de ciudad, ojos] charm, magic.

embrutecer vt to brutalize. ◆ **embrutecerse** vpr to become brutalized.

embuchado, -da adj: carne embuchada cured cold meat.

embudo m funnel.

embuste m lie.

embustero, -ra ◇ adj lying. ◇ m y f liar.

embute m Amer fam bribe.

embutido m [comida] cold cured meat.

embutir vt lit & fig to stuff.

emergencia f -1. [urgencia] emergency; en caso de ~ in case of emergency. -2. [brote] emergence.

emerger vi [salir del agua] to emerge; [aparecer] to come into view, to appear.

emigración f [de personas] emigration; [de aves] migration.

emigrante adj, m y f emigrant.

emigrar vi [persona] to emigrate; [ave] to migrate.

eminencia f [persona] leading light. ◆ **Eminencia** f: Su Eminencia His Eminence.

eminente adj [distinguido] eminent.

emirato m emirate.

Emiratos Árabes Unidos mpl: los ~ United Arab Emirates.

emisión f -1. [de energía, rayos etc] emission. -2. [de bonos, sellos, monedas] issue. -3. [RADIO & TV - transmisión] broadcasting; [- programa] programme, broadcast.

emisor, -ra adj transmitting (antes de sust). ◆ **emisora** f radio station.

emitir ◇ vt -1. [rayos, calor, sonidos] to emit. -2. [moneda, sellos, bonos] to issue. -3. [expresar - juicio, opinión] to express; [- fallo] to pronounce. -4. RADIO & TV to broadcast. ◇ vi to broadcast.

emoción f -1. [conmoción, sentimiento] emotion. -2. [expectación] excitement; ¡qué ~! how exciting!

emocionante adj -1. [conmovedor] moving, touching. -2. [apasionante] exciting, thrilling.

emocionar vt -1. [conmover] to move. -2. [excitar, apasionar] to thrill, to excite. ◆ **emocionarse** vpr -1. [conmoverse] to be moved. -2. [excitarse, apasionarse] to get excited.

emotivo, -va adj [persona] emotional; [escena, palabras] moving.

empachar vt to give indigestion to. ◆ **empacharse** vpr [hartarse] to stuff o.s.; [sufrir indigestión] to get indigestion.

empacho m [indigestión] upset stomach, indigestion.

empadronar vt ≃ to register on the electoral roll. ◆ **empadronarse** vpr ≃ to register on the electoral roll.

empalagoso, -sa adj sickly, cloying.

empalizada f [cerca] fence; MIL stockade.

empalmar ◇ vt [tubos, cables] to connect, to join. ◇ vi -1. [autocares, trenes] to connect. -2. [carreteras] to link o join (up).

empalme m -1. [entre cables, tubos] joint, connection. -2. [de líneas férreas, carreteras] junction.

empanada f pasty.

empanadilla f small pasty.

empanar vt CULIN to coat in breadcrumbs.

empantanar vt to flood. ◆ **empantanarse** vpr -1. [inundarse] to be flooded o waterlogged. -2. fig [atascarse] to get bogged down.

empañar vt -1. [cristal] to mist o steam up. -2. fig [reputación] to tarnish. ◆ **empañarse** vpr to mist o steam up.

empapar vt -1. [humedecer] to soak. -2. [absorber] to soak up. ◆ **empaparse** vpr [persona, traje] to get soaked.

empapelar vt [pared] to paper.

empaquetar vt to pack, to package.

emparedado, -da adj confined. ◆ **emparedado** m sandwich.

emparedar vt to lock away.

emparejar vt [aparejar - personas] to pair off; [- zapatos etc] to match (up).

emparentar vi: ~ con to marry into.

empastar vt to fill.

empaste m filling.

empatar vi DEP to draw; [en elecciones etc] to tie; ~ a cero to draw nil-nil.

empate m [resultado] draw; un ~ a cero/dos a goalless/two-two draw.

empedernido, -da adj [bebedor, fumador] heavy; [criminal, jugador] hardened.

empedrado m paving.

empedrar vt to pave.

empeine m [de pie, zapato] instep.

empeñado, -da adj **-1.** [en préstamo] in pawn. **-2.** [obstinado] determined; **estar ~ en hacer algo** to be determined to do sthg.

empeñar vt [joyas etc] to pawn. ◆ **empeñarse** vpr **-1.** [obstinarse] to insist; **~se en hacer algo** [obstinarse] to insist on doing sthg; [persistir] to persist in doing sthg. **-2.** [endeudarse] to get into debt.

empeño m **-1.** [de joyas etc] pawning; **casa de ~s** pawnshop. **-2.** [obstinación] determination; **tener ~ en hacer algo** to be determined to do sthg.

empeorar vi to get worse, to deteriorate.

empequeñecer vt [quitar importancia] to diminish; [en una comparación] to overshadow, to dwarf.

emperador, emperatriz m y f emperor (f empress). ◆ **emperador** m [pez] swordfish.

emperifollar vt fam to doll O tart up.

emperrarse vpr: **~ (en hacer algo)** to insist (on doing sthg).

empezar ◇ vt to begin, to start. ◇ vi: **~ (a hacer algo)** to begin O start (to do sthg); **~ (por hacer algo)** to begin O start (by doing sthg); **para ~** to begin O start with.

empinado, -da adj steep.

empinar vt [levantar] to raise. ◆ **empinarse** vpr **-1.** [animal] to stand up on its hind legs. **-2.** [persona] to stand on tiptoe.

empírico, -ca adj empirical.

emplasto m FARM poultice.

emplazamiento m [ubicación] location.

emplazar vt **-1.** [situar] to locate; MIL to position. **-2.** [citar] to summon; DER to summons.

empleado, -da m y f [gen] employee; [de banco, administración, oficina] clerk.

emplear vt **-1.** [usar - objetos, materiales etc] to use; [- tiempo] to spend; **~ algo en hacer algo** to use sthg to do sthg. **-2.** [contratar] to employ. ◆ **emplearse** vpr **-1.** [colocarse] to find a job. **-2.** [usarse] to be used.

empleo m **-1.** [uso] use. **-2.** [trabajo] employment; [puesto] job; **estar sin ~** to be out of work.

emplomadura f Amer [diente] filling.

empobrecer vt to impoverish. ◆ **empobrecerse** vpr to get poorer.

empollar ◇ vt **-1.** [huevo] to incubate.

-2. fam [estudiar] to swot up on. ◇ vi fam to swot.

empollón, -ona fam m y f swot.

empolvarse vpr to powder one's face.

empotrado, -da adj fitted, built-in.

empotrar vt to fit, to build in.

emprendedor, -ra adj enterprising.

emprender vt [trabajo] to start; [viaje, marcha] to set off on; **~ vuelo** to fly off.

empresa f **-1.** [sociedad] company; **pequeña y mediana ~** small and medium-sized business. **-2.** [acción] enterprise, undertaking.

empresarial adj management (antes de sust). ◆ **empresariales** fpl business studies.

empresario, -ria m y f [patrono] employer; [hombre, mujer de negocios] businessman (f businesswoman); [de teatro] impresario.

empréstito m debenture loan.

empujar vt to push; **~ a alguien a que haga algo** to push sb into doing sthg.

empuje m **-1.** [presión] pressure. **-2.** [energía] energy, drive.

empujón m [empellón] shove, push; **abrirse paso a empujones** to shove O push one's way through.

empuñadura f handle; [de espada] hilt.

empuñar vt to take hold of, to grasp.

emulsión f emulsion.

en prep **-1.** [lugar - en el interior de] in; [- sobre la superficie de] on; [- en un punto concreto de] at; **viven ~ la capital** they live in the capital; **tiene el dinero ~ el banco** he keeps his money in the bank; **~ la mesa/el plato** on the table/plate; **~ casa/el trabajo** at home/work. **-2.** [dirección] into; **el avión cayó ~ el mar** the plane fell into the sea; **entraron ~ la habitación** they came into the room. **-3.** [tiempo - mes, año etc] in; [- día] on; **nació ~ 1940/mayo** he was born in 1940/May; **~ aquel día** on that day; **~ Nochebuena** at Christmas Eve; **~ Navidades** at Christmas; **~ aquella época** at that time, in those days; **~ un par de días** in a couple of days. **-4.** [medio de transporte] by; **ir ~ tren/coche/avión/barco** to go by train/car/plane/boat. **-5.** [modo] in; **~ voz baja** in a low voice; **lo dijo ~ inglés** she said it in English; **pagar ~ libras** to pay in pounds; **la inflación aumentó ~ un 10%** inflation increased by 10%; **todo se lo gasta ~ ropa** he spends everything on clothes. **-6.** [precio] in;

las **ganancias se calculan** ~ **millones** profits are calculated in millions; **te lo dejo en 5.000** I'll let you have it for 5,000. **-7.** [tema]: **es un experto** ~ **la materia** he's an expert on the subject; **es doctor** ~ **medicina** he's a doctor of medicine. **-8.** [causa] from; **lo detecté** ~ **su forma de hablar** I could tell from the way he was speaking. **-9.** [materia] in, made of; ~ **seda** in silk. **-10.** [cualidad] in terms of; **le supera** ~ **inteligencia** she is more intelligent than he is.

enagua *f* (*gen pl*) petticoat.

enajenación *f*, **enajenamiento** *m* [locura] insanity; [éxtasis] rapture.

enajenar *vt* **-1.** [volver loco] to drive mad; [extasiar] to enrapture. **-2.** [propiedad] to alienate.

enaltecer *vt* to praise.

enamoradizo, -za *adj* who falls in love easily.

enamorado, -da ◇ *adj*: ~ **(de)** in love (with). ◇ *m y f* lover.

enamorar *vt* to win the heart of. ◆ **enamorarse** *vpr*: ~**se (de)** to fall in love (with).

enano, -na *adj, m y f* dwarf.

enarbolar *vt* [bandera] to raise, to hoist; [pancarta] to hold up; [arma] to brandish.

enardecer *vt* [gen] to inflame; [persona, multitud] to fill with enthusiasm.

encabezamiento *m* [de carta, escrito] heading; [de artículo periodístico] headline; [preámbulo] foreword.

encabezar *vt* **-1.** [artículo de periódico] to headline; [libro] to write the foreword for. **-2.** [lista, carta] to head. **-3.** [marcha, expedición] to lead.

encabritarse *vpr* **-1.** [caballo, moto] to rear up. **-2.** *fam* [persona] to get shirty.

encadenar *vt* **-1.** [atar] to chain (up). **-2.** [enlazar] to link (together).

encajar ◇ *vt* **-1.** [meter ajustando]: ~ **(en)** to fit (into). **-2.** [meter con fuerza]: ~ **(en)** to push (into). **-3.** [hueso dislocado] to set. **-4.** [recibir - golpe, noticia, críticas] to take. ◇ *vi* **-1.** [piezas, objetos] to fit. **-2.** [hechos, declaraciones, datos]: ~ **(con)** to square (with), to match.

encaje *m* [tejido] lace.

encalar *vt* to whitewash.

encallar *vi* [barco] to run aground.

encaminar *vt* **-1.** [persona, pasos] to direct. **-2.** [medidas, leyes, actividades] to aim; **encaminado a** aimed at. ◆ **encaminarse** *vpr*: ~**se a/hacia** to set off for/towards.

encandilar *vt* to dazzle.

encantado, -da *adj* **-1.** [contento] delighted; ~ **de conocerle** pleased to meet you. **-2.** [hechizado - casa, lugar] haunted; [- persona] bewitched.

encantador, -ra *adj* delightful, charming.

encantar *vt* **-1.** [gustar]: ~**le a alguien algo/hacer algo** to love sthg/doing sthg. **-2.** [embrujar] to cast a spell on.

encanto *m* **-1.** [atractivo] charm; **ser un** ~ to be a treasure ◇ a delight. **-2.** [hechizo] spell.

encapotado, -da *adj* overcast.

encapotarse *vpr* to cloud over.

encapricharse *vpr* [obstinarse]: ~ **con algo/hacer algo** to set one's mind on sthg/doing sthg.

encapuchado, -da *adj* hooded.

encaramar *vt* to lift up. ◆ **encaramarse** *vpr*: ~**se (a ◇ en)** to climb up (onto).

encarar *vt* [hacer frente a] to confront, to face up to. ◆ **encararse** *vpr* [enfrentarse]: ~**se a ◇ con** to stand up to.

encarcelar *vt* to imprison.

encarecer *vt* [productos, precios] to make more expensive. ◆ **encarecerse** *vpr* to become more expensive.

encarecidamente *adv* earnestly.

encarecimiento *m* [de producto, coste] increase in price.

encargado, -da ◇ *adj*: ~ **(de)** responsible (for), in charge (of). ◇ *m y f* [gen] person in charge; COM manager (*f* manageress).

encargar *vt* **-1.** [poner al cargo]: ~ **a alguien de algo** to put sb in charge of sthg; ~ **a alguien que haga algo** to tell sb to do sthg. **-2.** [pedir] to order. ◆ **encargarse** *vpr* [ocuparse]: ~**se de** to be in charge of; **yo me encargaré de eso** I'll take care of ◇ see to that.

encargo *m* **-1.** [pedido] order; **por** ~ to order. **-2.** [recado] errand. **-3.** [tarea] task, assignment.

encariñarse *vpr*: ~ **con** to become fond of.

encarnación *f* [personificación - cosa] embodiment; [- persona] personificación.

encarnado, -da *adj* **-1.** [personificado] incarnate. **-2.** [color] red.

encarnizado, -da *adj* bloody, bitter.

encarnizarse *vpr*: ~ **con** [presa] to fall upon; [prisionero, enemigo] to treat savagely.

encarrilar *vt* *fig* [negocio, situación] to put on the right track.

encasillar *vt* [clasificar] to pigeonhole; TEATR to typecast.

encasquetar *vt* **-1.** [imponer]: ~ **algo a alguien** [idea, teoría] to drum sthg into sb; [discurso, lección] to force sb to sit through sthg. **-2.** [sombrero] to pull on.

encasquillarse *vpr* to get jammed.

encauzar *vt* **-1.** [corriente] to channel. **-2.** [orientar] to direct.

encendedor *m* lighter.

encender *vt* **-1.** [vela, cigarro, chimenea] to light. **-2.** [aparato] to switch on. **-3.** *fig* [avivar - entusiasmo, ira] to arouse; [- pasión, discusión] to inflame. ◆ **encenderse** *vpr* **-1.** [fuego, gas] to ignite; [luz, estufa] to come on. **-2.** *fig* [ojos] to light up; [persona, rostro] to go red, to blush; [de ira] to flare up.

encendido, -da *adj* [luz, colilla] burning; **la luz está encendida** the light is on. ◆ **encendido** *m* AUTOM ignition.

encerado, -da *adj* waxed, polished. ◆ **encerado** *m* [pizarra] blackboard.

encerar *vt* to wax, to polish.

encerrar *vt* **-1.** [recluir - gen] to shut (up ○ in); [- con llave] to lock (up ○ in); [- en la cárcel] to lock away ○ up. **-2.** [contener] to contain. ◆ **encerrarse** *vpr* [gen] to shut o.s. away; [con llave] to lock o.s. away.

encestar *vt* & *vi* to score (*in basketball*).

enceste *m* basket.

encharcar *vt* to waterlog. ◆ **encharcarse** *vpr* **-1.** [terreno] to become waterlogged. **-2.** [pulmones] to become flooded.

enchilarse *vpr* *Amer* *fam* to get angry.

enchufado, -da *adj* *fam*: **estar** ~ to get where one is through connections.

enchufar *vt* **-1.** [aparato] to plug in. **-2.** *fam* [a una persona] to pull strings for.

enchufe *m* **-1.** [ELECTR - macho] plug; [- hembra] socket. **-2.** *fam* [recomendación] connections (*pl*); **obtener algo por** ~ to get sthg by pulling strings ○ through one's connections.

encía *f* gum.

encíclica *f* encyclical.

enciclopedia *f* encyclopedia.

encierro *m* [protesta] sit-in.

encima *adv* **-1.** [arriba] on top; **yo vivo** ~ I live upstairs; **por** ~ [superficialmente] superficially. **-2.** [además] on top of that. **-3.** [sobre sí]: **lleva un abrigo** ~ she has a coat on; **¿llevas dinero** ~?

have you got any money on you? ◆ **encima de** *loc prep* **-1.** [en lugar superior que] above; **vivo** ~ **de tu casa** I live upstairs from you. **-2.** [sobre, en] on (top of); **el pan está** ~ **de la mesa** the bread is on (top of) the table. **-3.** [además] on top of. ◆ **por encima de** *loc prep* **-1.** [gen] over; **vive por** ~ **de sus posibilidades** he lives beyond his means. **-2.** *fig* [más que] more than; **por** ~ **de todo** more than anything else.

encina *f* holm oak.

encinta *adj* *f* pregnant.

enclave *m* enclave.

enclenque *adj* sickly, frail.

encoger ◇ *vt* **-1.** [ropa] to shrink. **-2.** [miembro, músculo] to contract. ◇ *vi* to shrink. ◆ **encogerse** *vpr* **-1.** [ropa] to shrink; [músculos etc] to contract; ~**se de hombros** to shrug one's shoulders. **-2.** *fig* [apocarse] to cringe.

encolar *vt* [silla etc] to glue; [pared] to size, to paste.

encolerizar *vt* to infuriate, to enrage. ◆ **encolerizarse** *vpr* to get angry.

encomendar *vt* to entrust. ◆ **encomendarse** *vpr*: ~**se a** [persona] to entrust o.s. to; [Dios, santos] to put one's trust in.

encomienda *f* **-1.** [encargo] assignment, mission. **-2.** *Amer* [paquete] parcel.

encontrado, -da *adj* conflicting.

encontrar *vt* **-1.** [gen] to find. **-2.** [dificultades] to encounter. **-3.** [persona] to meet, to come across. ◆ **encontrarse** *vpr* **-1.** [hallarse] to be; **se encuentra en París** she's in Paris. **-2.** [coincidir]: ~**se (con alguien)** to meet (sb); **me encontré con Juan** I ran into ○ met Juan. **-3.** *fig* [de ánimo] to feel. **-4.** [chocar] to collide.

encorvar *vt* to bend. ◆ **encorvarse** *vpr* to bend down ○ over.

encrespar *vt* **-1.** [pelo] to curl; [mar] to make choppy ○ rough. **-2.** [irritar] to irritate. ◆ **encresparse** *vpr* **-1.** [mar] to get rough. **-2.** [persona] to get irritated.

encrucijada *f* *lit* & *fig* crossroads (*sg*).

encuadernación *f* binding.

encuadernador, -ra *m* *y* *f* bookbinder.

encuadernar *vt* to bind.

encuadrar *vt* **-1.** [enmarcar - cuadro, tema] to frame. **-2.** [encerrar] to contain. **-3.** [encajar] to fit.

encubierto, -ta ◇ *pp* → **encubrir**. ◇ *adj* [intento] covert; [insulto, significado] hidden.

encubridor, -ra *m y f*: ~ **(de)** accessory (to).

encubrir *vt* [delito] to conceal; [persona] to harbour.

encuentro *m* **-1.** [acción] meeting, encounter. **-2.** DEP game, match. **-3.** [hallazgo] find.

encuesta *f* **-1.** [de opinión] survey, opinion poll. **-2.** [investigación] investigation, inquiry.

encuestador, -ra *m y f* pollster.

encuestar *vt* to poll.

endeble *adj* [persona, argumento] weak, feeble; [objeto] fragile.

endémico, -ca *adj* MED & *fig* endemic.

endemoniado, -da *adj* **-1.** *fam fig* [molesto - niño] **wicked**; [- trabajo] very tricky. **-2.** [desagradable] terrible, foul. **-3.** [poseído] possessed (of the devil).

endenantes *adv Amer fam* before.

enderezar *vt* **-1.** [poner derecho] to straighten. **-2.** [poner vertical] to put upright. **-3.** *fig* [corregir] to set right. ◆ **enderezarse** *vpr* [sentado] to sit up straight; [de pie] to stand up straight.

endeudamiento *m* debt.

endeudarse *vpr* to get into debt.

endiablado, -da *adj* [persona] wicked; [tiempo, genio] foul; [problema, crucigrama] fiendishly difficult.

endibia = **endivia**.

endiñar *vt fam*: ~ **algo a alguien** [golpe] to land ○ deal sb sthg; [trabajo, tarea] to lumber sb with sthg.

endivia, endibia *f* endive.

endomingado, -da *adj fam* dolled-up.

endosar *vt* **-1.** *fig* [tarea, trabajo]: ~ **algo a alguien** to lumber sb with sthg. **-2.** COM to endorse.

endulzar *vt* [con azúcar] to sweeten; *fig* [con dulzura] to ease.

endurecer *vt* **-1.** [gen] to harden. **-2.** [fortalecer] to strengthen.

enemigo, -ga ◇ *adj* enemy (*antes de sust*); **ser** ~ **de algo** to hate sthg. ◇ *m y f* enemy.

enemistad *f* enmity.

enemistar *vt* to make enemies of. ◆ **enemistarse** *vpr*: ~**se (con)** to fall out (with).

energético, -ca *adj* energy (*antes de sust*).

energía *f* **-1.** [gen] energy; ~ **atómica** ○ **nuclear** nuclear power; ~ **eólica/hidráulica** wind/water power; ~ **solar** solar energy ○ power. **-2.** [fuerza] strength.

enérgico, -ca *adj* [gen] energetic; [carácter] forceful; [gesto, medida] vigorous; [decisión, postura] emphatic.

energúmeno, -na *m y f fig* madman (*f* madwoman).

enero *m* January; *ver también* **septiembre**.

enervar *vt* **-1.** [debilitar] to sap, to weaken. **-2.** [poner nervioso] to exasperate.

enésimo, -ma *adj* **-1.** MAT nth. **-2.** *fig* umpteenth; **por enésima vez** for the umpteenth time.

enfadado, -da *adj* angry.

enfadar *vt* to anger. ◆ **enfadarse** *vpr*: ~**se (con)** to get angry (with).

enfado *m* anger.

énfasis *m inv* emphasis; **poner** ~ **en algo** to emphasize sthg.

enfático, -ca *adj* emphatic.

enfatizar *vt* to emphasize, to stress.

enfermar ◇ *vt* [causar enfermedad] to make ill. ◇ *vi* to fall ill; ~ **del pecho** to develop a chest complaint.

enfermedad *f* [física] illness; ~ **infecciosa/venérea** infectious/venereal disease.

enfermera → **enfermero**.

enfermería *f* sick bay.

enfermero, -ra *m y f* male nurse (*f* nurse).

enfermizo, -za *adj lit & fig* unhealthy.

enfermo, -ma ◇ *adj* ill, sick. ◇ *m y f* [gen] invalid, sick person; [en el hospital] patient.

enfilar *vt* **-1.** [ir por - camino] to go ○ head straight along. **-2.** [apuntar - arma] to aim.

enflaquecer *vi* to grow thin.

enfocar *vt* **-1.** [imagen, objetivo] to focus. **-2.** [suj: luz, foco] to shine on. **-3.** *fig* [tema, asunto] to approach, to look at.

enfoque *m* **-1.** [de una imagen] focus. **-2.** *fig* [de un asunto] approach, angle.

enfrascar *vt* to bottle. ◆ **enfrascarse en** *vpr* [riña] to get embroiled in; [lectura, conversación] to become engrossed in.

enfrentar *vt* **-1.** [hacer frente] to confront, to face. **-2.** [poner frente a frente] to bring face to face. ◆ **enfrentarse** *vpr* **-1.** [luchar, encontrarse] to meet, to clash. **-2.** [oponerse]: ~**se con alguien** to confront sb.

enfrente *adv* **-1.** [delante] opposite; **la tienda de** ~ the shop across the road;

~ de opposite. **-2.** [en contra]: **tiene a todos ~** everyone's against her.

enfriamiento *m* **-1.** [catarro] cold. **-2.** [acción] cooling.

enfriar *vt lit* & *fig* to cool. ◆ **enfriarse** *vpr* **-1.** [líquido, pasión, amistad] to cool down. **-2.** [quedarse demasiado frío] to go cold. **-3.** MED to catch a cold.

enfundar *vt* [espada] to sheathe; [pistola] to put away.

enfurecer *vt* to infuriate, to madden. ◆ **enfurecerse** *vpr* [gen] to get furious.

enfurruñarse *vpr fam* to sulk.

engalanar *vt* to decorate. ◆ **engalanarse** *vpr* to dress up.

enganchar *vt* **-1.** [agarrar - vagones] to couple; [- remolque, caballos] to hitch up; [- pez] to hook. **-2.** [colgar de un gancho] to hang up. ◆ **engancharse** *vpr* **-1.** [prenderse]: **~se algo con algo** to catch sthg on sthg. **-2.** [alistarse] to enlist, to join up. **-3.** [hacerse adicto]: **~se (a)** to get hooked (on).

enganche *m* **-1.** [de trenes] coupling. **-2.** [gancho] hook. **-3.** [reclutamiento] enlistment. **-4.** *Amer* [depósito] deposit.

engañar *vt* **-1.** [gen] to deceive; **engaña a su marido** she cheats on her husband. **-2.** [estafar] to cheat, to swindle. ◆ **engañarse** *vpr* **-1.** [hacerse ilusiones] to delude o.s. **-2.** [equivocarse] to be wrong.

engaño *m* [gen] deceit; [estafa] swindle.

engañoso, -sa *adj* [persona, palabras] deceitful; [aspecto, apariencia] deceptive.

engarzar *vt* **-1.** [encadenar - abalorios] to thread; [- perlas] to string. **-2.** [enlazar - palabras] to string together.

engatusar *vt fam* to get round; **~ a alguien para que haga algo** to coax ○ cajole sb into doing sthg.

engendrar *vt* **-1.** [procrear] to give birth to. **-2.** *fig* [originar] to give rise to.

engendro *m* **-1.** [obra de mala calidad] monstrosity. **-2.** [ser deforme] freak; [niño] malformed child.

englobar *vt* to bring together.

engomar *vt* [pegar] to stick, to glue.

engordar ◇ *vt* **-1.** to fatten up. **-2.** *fig* [aumentar] to swell. ◇ *vi* to put on weight.

engorroso, -sa *adj* bothersome.

engranaje *m* **-1.** [piezas - de reloj, piñón] cogs (*pl*); AUTOM gears (*pl*). **-2.** [aparato - político, burocrático] machinery.

engrandecer *vt* **-1.** *fig* [enaltecer] to exalt. **-2.** [aumentar] to increase, to enlarge.

engrasar *vt* [gen] to lubricate; [bisagra, mecanismo] to oil; [eje, bandeja] to grease.

engreído, -da *adj* conceited, full of one's own importance.

engrosar *vt fig* [aumentar] to swell.

engullir *vt* to gobble up.

enhebrar *vt* [gen] to thread; [perlas] to string.

enhorabuena ◇ *f* congratulations (*pl*). ◇ *adv*: **¡~ (por ...)!** congratulations (on ...)!

enigma *m* enigma.

enigmático, -ca *adj* enigmatic.

enjabonar *vt* [con jabón] to soap.

enjambre *m lit* & *fig* swarm.

enjaular *vt* [en jaula] to cage; *fam fig* [en prisión] to jail, to lock up.

enjuagar *vt* to rinse.

enjuague *m* rinse.

enjugar *vt* **-1.** [secar] to dry, to wipe away. **-2.** *fig* [pagar - deuda] to pay off; [- déficit] to cancel out.

enjuiciar *vt* **-1.** DER to try. **-2.** [opinar] to judge.

enjuto, -ta *adj* [delgado] lean.

enlace *m* **-1.** [acción] link. **-2.** [persona] go-between; **~ sindical** shop steward. **-3.** [casamiento]: **~ (matrimonial)** marriage. **-4.** [de trenes] connection; **estación de ~** junction; **vía de ~** crossover.

enlatar *vt* to can, to tin.

enlazar ◇ *vt*: **~ algo a** [atar] to tie sthg up to; [trabar, relacionar] to link ○ connect sthg with. ◇ *vi*: **~ en** [trenes] to connect at.

enloquecer ◇ *vt* **-1.** [volver loco] to drive mad. **-2.** *fig* [gustar mucho] to drive wild ○ crazy. ◇ *vi* to go mad.

enlutado, -da *adj* in mourning.

enmarañar *vt* **-1.** [enredar] to tangle (up). **-2.** [complicar] to complicate. ◆ **enmarañarse** *vpr* **-1.** [enredarse] to become tangled. **-2.** [complicarse] to become confused ○ complicated.

enmarcar *vt* to frame.

enmascarado, -da *adj* masked.

enmascarar *vt* [rostro] to mask; *fig* [encubrir] to disguise.

enmendar *vt* [error] to correct; [ley, dictamen] to amend; [comportamiento] to mend; [daño, perjuicio] to redress. ◆ **enmendarse** *vpr* to mend one's ways.

enmienda *f* **-1.** [en un texto] corrections (*pl*). **-2.** POLÍT amendment.

enmohecer *vt* [gen] to turn mouldy; [metal] to rust. ◆ **enmohecerse** *vpr*

[gen] to grow mouldy; [metal, conocimientos] to go rusty.

enmoquetar vt to carpet.

enmudecer ◇ vt to silence. ◇ vi [callarse] to fall silent, to go quiet; [perder el habla] to be struck dumb.

ennegrecer vt [gen] to blacken; [suj: nubes] to darken. ◆ **ennegrecerse** vpr [gen] to become blackened; [nublarse] to darken, to grow dark.

ennoblecer vt -1. fig [dignificar] to lend distinction to. -2. [dar un título] to ennoble.

enojar vt [enfadar] to anger; [molestar] to annoy. ◆ **enojarse** vpr: ~se (con) [enfadarse] to get angry (with); [molestarse] to get annoyed (with).

enojo m [enfado] anger; [molestia] annoyance.

enojoso, -sa adj [molesto] annoying; [delicado, espinoso] awkward.

enorgullecer vt to fill with pride. ◆ **enorgullecerse de** vpr to be proud of.

enorme adj [en tamaño] enormous, huge; [en gravedad] monstrous.

enormidad f [de tamaño] enormity, hugeness.

enrarecer vt -1. [contaminar] to pollute. -2. [rarificar] to rarefy. ◆ **enrarecerse** vpr -1. [contaminarse] to become polluted. -2. [rarificarse] to become rarefied. -3. fig [situación, ambiente] to become tense.

enredadera f creeper.

enredar vt -1. [madeja, pelo] to tangle up; [situación, asunto] to complicate, to confuse. -2. fig [implicar]: ~ a alguien (en) to embroil sb (in), to involve sb (in). ◆ **enredarse** vpr [plantas] to climb; [madeja, asunto] to get tangled up; [situación, asunto] to become confused.

enredo m -1. [maraña] tangle, knot. -2. [lío] mess, complicated affair; [asunto ilícito] shady affair. -3. [amoroso] (love) affair.

enrejado m -1. [barrotes - de balcón, verja] railings (pl); [- de jaula, celda, ventana] bars (pl). -2. [de cañas] trellis.

enrevesado, -da adj complex, complicated.

enriquecer vt -1. [hacer rico] to make rich. -2. fig [engrandecer] to enrich. ◆ **enriquecerse** vpr to get rich.

enrojecer ◇ vt [gen] to redden; [rostro, mejillas] to cause to blush. ◇ vi [por calor] to flush; [por turbación] to blush.

◆ **enrojecerse** vpr [por calor] to flush; [por turbación] to blush.

◆ **enrolar** vt to enlist. ◆ **enrolarse en** vpr [la marina] to enlist in; [un buque] to sign up for.

enrollar vt -1. [arrollar] to roll up. -2. fam [gustar]: me enrolla mucho I love it, I think it's great.

enroscar vt -1. [atornillar] to screw in. -2. [enrollar] to roll up; [cuerpo, cola] to curl up.

ensaimada f cake made of sweet coiled pastry.

ensalada f [de lechuga etc] salad.

ensaladilla f: ~ (rusa) Russian salad.

ensalzar vt to praise.

ensambladura f, **ensamblaje** m [acción] assembly; [pieza] joint.

ensanchar vt [orificio, calle] to widen; [ropa] to let out; [ciudad] to expand.

ensanche m -1. [de calle etc] widening. -2. [en la ciudad] new suburb.

ensangrentar vt to cover with blood.

ensañarse vpr: ~ con to torment, to treat cruelly.

ensartar vt -1. [perlas] to string; [aguja] to thread. -2. [atravesar - torero] to gore; [puñal] to plunge, to bury.

ensayar vt -1. [gen] to test. -2. TEATR to rehearse.

ensayista m y f essayist.

ensayo m -1. TEATR rehearsal; ~ general dress rehearsal. -2. [prueba] test. -3. LITER essay. -4. [en rugby] try.

enseguida adv [inmediatamente] immediately, at once; [pronto] very soon; llegará ~ he'll be here any minute now.

ensenada f cove, inlet.

enseñanza f [gen] education; [instrucción] teaching; ~ primaria/media primary/secondary education.

enseñar vt -1. [instruir, aleccionar] to teach; ~ a alguien a hacer algo to teach sb (how) to do sthg. -2. [mostrar] to show.

enseres mpl -1. [efectos personales] belongings. -2. [utensilios] equipment (U).

ensillar vt to saddle up.

ensimismarse vpr [enfrascarse] to become absorbed; [abstraerse] to be lost in thought.

ensombrecer vt lit & fig to cast a shadow over. ◆ **ensombrecerse** vpr to darken.

ensoñación f daydream.

ensopar vt Amer to soak.

ensordecer ◇ *vt* [suj: sonido] to deafen. ◇ *vi* to go deaf.

ensortijar *vt* to curl.

ensuciar *vt* to (make) dirty; *fig* [desprestigiar] to sully, to tarnish. ◆ **ensuciarse** *vpr* to get dirty.

ensueño *m lit* & *fig* dream; **de ~** dream (*antes de sust*), ideal.

entablado *m* [armazón] wooden platform; [suelo] floorboards (*pl*).

entablar *vt* [iniciar - conversación, amistad] to strike up.

entallar *vt* -1. [prenda] to cut, to tailor. -2. [madera] to carve, to sculpt.

entarimado *m* [plataforma] wooden platform; [suelo] floorboards (*pl*).

ente *m* -1. [ser] being. -2. [corporación] body, organization; **~ público** [gen] state-owned body ○ institution; [televisión] Spanish state broadcasting company.

entender ◇ *vt* -1. [gen] to understand. -2. [darse cuenta] to realize. -3. [oír] to hear. -4. [juzgar] to think; **yo no lo entiendo así** I don't see it that way. ◇ *vi* -1. [comprender] to understand. -2. [saber]: **~ de** ○ **en algo** to be an expert on sthg; **~ poco/algo de** to know very little/a little about. ◇ *m*: **a mi ~ ...** the way I see it .... ◆ **entenderse** *vpr* -1. [comprenderse - uno mismo] to know what one means; [- dos personas] to understand each other. -2. [llevarse bien] to get on. -3. [ponerse de acuerdo] to reach an agreement. -4. [comunicarse] to communicate (with each other).

entendido, -da *m y f*: **~ (en)** expert (on). ◆ **entendido** *interj*: ¡~! all right!, okay!

entendimiento *m* [comprensión] understanding; [juicio] judgment; [inteligencia] mind, intellect.

enterado, -da *adj*: **~ (en)** well-informed (about); **estar ~ de algo** to be aware of sthg; **no darse por ~** to turn a deaf ear.

enterar *vt*: **~ a alguien de algo** to inform sb about sthg. ◆ **enterarse** *vpr* -1. [descubrir]: **~se (de)** to find out (about). -2. *fam* [comprender] to get it, to understand. -3. [darse cuenta]: **~se (de algo)** to realize (sthg).

entereza *f* [serenidad] composure; [honradez] integrity; [firmeza] firmness.

enternecer *vt* to move, to touch. ◆ **enternecerse** *vpr* to be moved.

entero, -ra *adj* -1. [completo] whole.

-2. [sereno] composed. -3. [honrado] upright, honest.

enterrador, -ra *m y f* gravedigger.

enterrar *vt* [gen] to bury.

entibiar *vt* -1. [enfriar] to cool. -2. [templar] to warm. ◆ **entibiarse** *vpr* [sentimiento] to cool.

entidad *f* -1. [corporación] body; [empresa] firm, company. -2. FILOSOFÍA entity. -3. [importancia] importance.

entierro *m* [acción] burial; [ceremonia] funeral.

entlo. *abrev de* **entresuelo.**

entoldado *m* [toldo] awning; [para fiestas, bailes] marquee.

entomólogo, -ga *m y f* entomologist.

entonación *f* intonation.

entonar ◇ *vt* -1. [cantar] to sing. -2. [tonificar] to pick up. ◇ *vi* -1. [al cantar] to sing in tune. -2. [armonizar]: **~ (con algo)** to match (sthg).

entonces ◇ *adv* then; **desde ~** since then; **en** ○ **por aquel ~** at that time. ◇ *interj*: ¡~! well, then!

entornar *vt* to half-close.

entorno *m* environment, surroundings (*pl*).

entorpecer *vt* -1. [debilitar - movimientos] to hinder; [- mente] to cloud. -2. [dificultar] to obstruct, to hinder.

entrada *f* -1. [acción] entry; [llegada] arrival; **"prohibida la ~"** "no entry". -2. [lugar] entrance; [puerta] doorway. TECN inlet, intake. -4. [en espectáculos - billete] ticket; [- recaudación] receipts (*pl*), takings (*pl*); **~ libre** admission free; **sacar una ~** to buy a ticket. -5. [público] audience; DEP attendance. -6. [pago inicial] down payment. -7. [en contabilidad] income. -8. [plato] starter. -9. [en la frente]: **tener ~s** to have a receding hairline. -10. [en un diccionario] entry. -11. [principio]: **de ~** right from the beginning ○ the word go.

entrante ◇ *adj* [año, mes] coming; [presidente, gobierno] incoming. ◇ *m* -1. [plato] starter. -2. [hueco] recess.

entraña *f* (*gen pl*) -1. [víscera] entrails (*pl*), insides (*pl*). -2. *fig* [centro, esencia] heart.

entrañable *adj* intimate.

entrañar *vt* to involve.

entrar ◇ *vi* -1. [introducirse - viniendo] to enter, to come in; [- yendo] to enter, to go in; **~ en algo** to enter sthg, to come/go into sthg; **entré por la ventana** I got in through the window. -2. [penetrar - clavo etc] to go in; **~ en algo**

to go into sthg. **-3.** [caber]: ~ **(en)** to fit (in); **este anillo no te entra** this ring won't fit you. **-4.** [incorporarse]: ~ **(en algo)** [colegio, empresa] to start (at sthg); [club, partido político] to join (sthg); ~ **de** [botones etc] to start off as. **-5.** [estado físico o de ánimo]: **le entraron ganas de hablar** he suddenly felt like talking; **me está entrando frío** I'm getting cold; **me entró mucha pena** I was filled with pity. **-6.** [periodo de tiempo] to start; ~ **en** [edad, vejez] to reach; [año nuevo] to enter. **-7.** [cantidad]: **¿cuántos entran en un kilo?** how many do you get to the kilo? **-8.** [concepto, asignatura etc]: **no le entra la geometría** he can't get the hang of geometry. **-9.** AUTOM to engage. ◇ *vt* [introducir] to bring in.

entre *prep* **-1.** [gen] between; ~ **nosotros** [en confianza] between you and me, between ourselves; ~ **una cosa y otra** with one thing and another. **-2.** [en medio de muchos] among, amongst; **estaba ~ los asistentes** she was among those present; ~ **sí** amongst themselves; **discutían ~ sí** they were arguing with each other.

entreabierto, -ta *pp* → **entreabrir.**

entreabrir *vt* to half-open.

entreacto *m* interval.

entrecejo *m* space between the brows; **fruncir el ~** to frown.

entrecortado, -da *adj* [voz, habla] faltering; [respiración] laboured; [señal, sonido] intermittent.

entrecot, entrecote *m* entrecôte.

entredicho *m*: **estar en ~** to be in doubt; **poner en ~** to question, to call into question.

entrega *f* **-1.** [gen] handing over; [de pedido, paquete] delivery; [de premios] presentation; ~ **a domicilio** home delivery. **-2.** [dedicación]: ~ **(a)** devotion (to). **-3.** [fascículo] instalment.

entregar *vt* [gen] to hand over; [pedido, paquete] to deliver; [examen, informe] to hand in; [persona] to turn over. ◆ **entregarse** *vpr* [rendirse - soldado, ejército] to surrender; [- criminal] to turn o.s. in. ◆ **entregarse a** *vpr* **-1.** [persona, trabajo] to devote o.s. to. **-2.** [vicio, pasión] to give o.s. over to.

entreguerras ◆ **de entreguerras** *loc adj* between the wars.

entrelazar *vt* to interlace, to interlink.

entremés *m* CULIN (*gen pl*) hors d'œuvres.

entremeter *vt* to insert, to put in. ◆ **entremeterse** *vpr* [inmiscuirse]: ~**se (en)** to meddle (in).

entremezclar *vt* to mix up. ◆ **entremezclarse** *vpr* to mix.

entrenador, -ra *m y f* coach; [seleccionador] manager.

entrenamiento *m* training.

entrenar *vt & vi* to train. ◆ **entrenarse** *vpr* to train.

entrepierna *f* crotch.

entresacar *vt* to pick out.

entresijos *mpl* ins and outs.

entresuelo *m* mezzanine.

entretanto *adv* meanwhile.

entretención *f Amer* entertainment.

entretener *vt* **-1.** [despistar] to distract. **-2.** [retrasar] to hold up, to keep. **-3.** [divertir] to entertain. ◆ **entretenerse** *vpr* **-1.** [despistarse] to get distracted. **-2.** [divertirse] to amuse o.s. **-3.** [retrasarse] to be held up.

entretenido, -da *adj* entertaining, enjoyable.

entretenimiento *m* **-1.** [acción] entertainment. **-2.** [pasatiempo] pastime.

entrever *vt* [vislumbrar] to barely make out; [por un instante] to glimpse.

entrevero *m Amer* tangle, mess.

entrevista *f* interview.

entrevistar *vt* to interview. ◆ **entrevistarse** *vpr*: ~**se (con)** to have a meeting (with).

entrevisto, -ta *pp* → **entrever.**

entristecer *vt* to make sad. ◆ **entristecerse** *vpr* to become sad.

entrometerse *vpr*: ~ **(en)** to interfere (in).

entrometido, -da *m y f* meddler.

entroncar *vi* **-1.** [trenes etc] to connect. **-2.** *fig* [relacionarse]: ~ **(con)** to be related (to).

entuerto *m* wrong, injustice.

entumecer *vt* to numb. ◆ **entumecerse** *vpr* to become numb.

entumecido, -da *adj* numb.

enturbiar *vt lit & fig* to cloud. ◆ **enturbiarse** *vpr lit & fig* to become cloudy.

entusiasmar *vt* **-1.** [animar] to fill with enthusiasm. **-2.** [gustar]: **le entusiasma la música** he loves music. ◆ **entusiasmarse** *vpr*: ~**se (con)** to get excited (about).

entusiasmo *m* enthusiasm.

entusiasta ◇ *adj* enthusiastic. ◇ *m y f* enthusiast.

enumeración *f* enumeration, listing.

enumerar vt to enumerate, to list.

enunciar vt to formulate, to enunciate.

envainar vt to sheathe.

envalentonar vt to urge on, to fill with courage. ◆ **envalentonarse** vpr to become daring.

envanecer vt to make vain. ◆ **envanecerse** vpr to become vain.

envasado m [en botellas] bottling; [en latas] canning; [en paquetes] packing.

envasar vt [gen] to pack; [en latas] to can; [en botellas] to bottle.

envase m **-1.** [envasado - en botellas] bottling; [- en latas] canning; [- en paquetes] packing. **-2.** [recipiente] container; [botella] bottle; ~ **desechable** disposable container; ~ **sin retorno** non-returnable bottle.

envejecer ◇ vi [hacerse viejo] to grow old; [parecer viejo] to age. ◇ vt to age.

envejecimiento m ageing.

envenenamiento m poisoning.

envenenar vt to poison.

envergadura f **-1.** [importancia] size, extent; [complejidad] complexity; **una reforma de gran** ~ a wide-ranging reform. **-2.** [anchura] span.

envés m reverse (side), back; [de tela] wrong side.

enviado, -da m y f POLÍT envoy; PRENS correspondent.

enviar vt to send.

enviciar vt to addict, to get hooked. ◆ **enviciarse** vpr to become addicted.

envidia f envy; **tener** ~ **de** to envy.

envidiar vt to envy.

envidioso, -sa adj envious.

envilecer vt to debase.

envío m **-1.** COM dispatch; [de correo] delivery; [de víveres, mercancías] consignment. **-2.** [paquete] package.

envite m [en el juego] raise.

enviudar vi to be widowed.

envoltorio m, **envoltura** f wrapper, wrapping.

envolver vt **-1.** [embalar] to wrap (up). **-2.** [enrollar] to wind. **-3.** [implicar]: ~ **a alguien en** to involve sb in.

envuelto, -ta pp → **envolver**.

enyesar vt **-1.** MED to put in plaster. **-2.** CONSTR to plaster.

enzarzar vt to entangle, to embroil. ◆ **enzarzarse** vpr: ~**se en** to get entangled o embroiled in.

enzima f enzyme.

e.p.d. (abrev de **en paz descanse**) RIP.

épica → **épico**.

épico, -ca adj epic. ◆ **épica** f epic.

epidemia f epidemic.

epígrafe m heading.

epilepsia f epilepsy.

epílogo m epilogue.

episodio m [gen] episode.

epístola f culto [carta] epistle; RELIG Epistle.

epitafio m epitaph.

epíteto m epithet.

época f period; [estación] season; **de** ~ period (antes de sust); **en aquella** ~ at that time.

epopeya f **-1.** [gen] epic. **-2.** fig [hazaña] feat.

equidad f fairness.

equidistante adj equidistant.

equilibrado, -da adj **-1.** [gen] balanced. **-2.** [sensato] sensible.

equilibrar vt to balance.

equilibrio m balance; **mantenerse/perder el** ~ to keep/lose one's balance; **hacer** ~**s** fig to perform a balancing act.

equilibrista m y f [trapecista] trapeze artist; [funambulista] tightrope walker.

equino, -na adj equine.

equinoccio m equinox.

equipaje m luggage Br, baggage Am; **hacer el** ~ to pack; ~ **de mano** hand luggage.

equipar vt: ~ **(de)** [gen] to equip (with); [ropa] to fit out (with).

equiparar vt to compare. ◆ **equipararse** vpr to be compared.

equipo m **-1.** [equipamiento] equipment. **-2.** [personas, jugadores] team; ~ **de rescate** rescue team. **-3.** [de música] system.

equis adj X; **un número** ~ **de personas** x number of people.

equitación f [arte] equestrianism; [actividad] horse riding.

equitativo, -va adj fair, even-handed.

equivalente adj & m equivalent.

equivaler ◆ **equivaler a** vi to be equivalent to; fig [significar] to amount to.

equivocación f mistake; **por** ~ by mistake.

equivocado, -da adj mistaken.

equivocar vt to choose wrongly; ~ **algo con algo** to mistake sthg for sthg. ◆ **equivocarse** vpr to be wrong; ~**se en** to make a mistake in; **se equivocó de nombre** he got the wrong name.

equívoco, -ca *adj* **-1.** [ambiguo] ambiguous, equivocal. **-2.** [sospechoso] suspicious. ◆ **equívoco** *m* misunderstanding.

era ◇ *v* → **ser.** ◇ *f* [periodo] era.

erario *m* funds (*pl*).

erección *f* erection.

erecto, -ta *adj* erect.

eres → **ser.**

erguir *vt* to raise. ◆ **erguirse** *vpr* to rise up.

erigir *vt* [construir] to erect, to build.

erizado, -da *adj* [de punta] on end; [con púas o espinas] spiky.

erizar *vt* to cause to stand on end. ◆ **erizarse** *vpr* [pelo] to stand on end; [persona] to stiffen.

erizo *m* **-1.** [mamífero] hedgehog. **-2.** [pez] globefish; ~ **de mar** sea urchin.

ermita *f* hermitage.

erosionar *vt* to erode. ◆ **erosionarse** *vpr* to erode.

erótico, -ca *adj* erotic.

erotismo *m* eroticism.

erradicación *f* eradication.

erradicar *vt* to eradicate.

errante *adj* wandering.

errar ◇ *vt* [vocación, camino] to choose wrongly; [disparo, golpe] to miss. ◇ *vi* **-1.** [vagar] to wander. **-2.** [equivocarse] to make a mistake. **-3.** [al disparar] to miss.

errata *f* misprint.

erróneo, -a *adj* mistaken.

error *m* mistake, error; **estar en un** ~ to be mistaken; **salvo** ~ **u omisión** errors and omissions excepted; ~ **de imprenta** misprint.

ertzaintza [er'tʃaintʃa] *f Basque regional police force.*

eructar *vi* to belch.

eructo *m* belch.

erudito, -ta *adj* erudite.

erupción *f* **-1.** GEOL eruption; **en** ~ erupting. **-2.** MED rash.

es → **ser.**

esa → **ese².**

ésa → **ése.**

esbelto, -ta *adj* slender, slim.

esbozar *vt* to sketch, to outline; [sonrisa] to give a hint of.

esbozo *m* sketch, outline.

escabechado, -da *adj* CULIN marinated.

escabeche *m* CULIN marinade.

escabroso, -sa *adj* **-1.** [abrupto] rough. **-2.** [obsceno] risqué. **-3.** [espinoso] awkward, thorny.

escabullirse *vpr* [desaparecer]: ~ **(de)** to slip away (from).

escacharrar *vt fam* to knacker.

escafandra *f* diving suit.

escala *f* **-1.** [gen] scale; [de colores] range; **a** ~ [gráfica] to scale; **a** ~ **mundial** *fig* on a worldwide scale; **a gran** ~ on a large scale. **-2.** [en un viaje] stopover; **hacer** ~ to stop over.

escalada *f* **-1.** [de montaña] climb. **-2.** [de violencia, precios] escalation, rise.

escalador, -ra *m y f* [alpinista] climber.

escalafón *m* scale, ladder.

escalar *vt* to climb.

escaldar *vt* to scald.

escalera *f* **-1.** [gen] stairs (*pl*), staircase; [escala] ladder; ~ **mecánica** O **automática** escalator; ~ **de caracol** spiral staircase. **-2.** [en naipes] run.

escalfar *vt* to poach.

escalinata *f* staircase.

escalofriante *adj* spine-chilling.

escalofrío *m* (*gen pl*) shiver; **dar** ~**s a alguien** to give sb the shivers.

escalón *m* step; *fig* grade.

escalonar *vt* **-1.** [gen] to spread out. **-2.** [terreno] to terrace.

escalope *m* escalope.

escama *f* **-1.** [de peces, reptiles] scale. **-2.** [de jabón, en la piel] flake.

escamar *vt fam fig* [mosquear] to make suspicious.

escamotear *vt*: ~ **algo a alguien** [estafar] to do O swindle sb out of sthg; [hurtar] to rob sb of sthg.

escampar *v impers* to stop raining.

escandalizar *vt* to scandalize, to shock. ◆ **escandalizarse** *vpr* to be shocked.

escándalo *m* **-1.** [inmoralidad] scandal; [indignación] outrage. **-2.** [alboroto] uproar; **armar un** ~ to kick up a fuss.

escandaloso, -sa *adj* **-1.** [inmoral] outrageous. **-2.** [ruidoso] very noisy.

Escandinavia Scandinavia.

escandinavo, -va *adj, m y f* Scandinavian.

escáner (*pl* **escáners**) *m* INFORM & MED scanner.

escaño *m* **-1.** [cargo] seat (*in parliament*). **-2.** [asiento] bench (*in parliament*).

escapada *f* **-1.** [huida] escape, flight; DEP breakaway. **-2.** [viaje] quick trip.

escapar *vi* [huir]: ~ **(de)** to get away O escape (from). ◆ **escaparse** *vpr* **-1.** [huir]: ~**se (de)** to get away O escape (from); **~se de casa** to run away from home. **-2.** [salir - gas, agua etc] to leak.

escaparate *m* (shop) window.

escapatoria *f* [fuga] escape; **no tener ~** to have no way out.

escape *m* [de gas etc] leak; [de coche] exhaust; **a ~** in a rush, at high speed.

escaquearse *vpr fam* to duck out; **~ de algo/de hacer algo** to worm one's way out of sthg/doing sthg.

escarabajo *m* beetle.

escaramuza *f* MIL & *fig* skirmish.

escarbar *vt* to scratch, to scrape.

escarcha *f* frost.

escarlata *adj & m* scarlet.

escarlatina *f* scarlet fever.

escarmentar *vi* to learn (one's lesson).

escarmiento *m* lesson; **servir de ~** to serve as a lesson.

escarnio *m* mockery, ridicule.

escarola *f* endive.

escarpado, -da *adj* [inclinado] steep; [abrupto] craggy.

escasear *vi* to be scarce.

escasez *f* [insuficiencia] shortage; [pobreza] poverty.

escaso, -sa *adj* **-1.** [insuficiente - conocimientos, recursos] limited, scant; [- tiempo] short; [- cantidad, número] low; [- víveres, trabajo] scarce; [- visibilidad, luz] poor; **andar ~ de** to be short of. **-2.** [casi completo]: **un metro ~** barely a metre.

escatimar *vt* [gastos, comida] to be sparing with, to skimp on; [esfuerzo, energías] to use as little as possible; **no ~ gastos** to spare no expense.

escay, skai *m* Leatherette®.

escayola *f* CONSTR plaster of Paris; MED plaster.

escena *f* **-1.** [gen] scene; **hacer una ~** to make a scene. **-2.** [escenario] stage; **poner en ~** to stage.

escenario *m* **-1.** [tablas, escena] stage; CIN & TEATR [lugar de la acción] setting. **-2.** *fig* [de suceso] scene.

escenificar *vt* [novela] to dramatize; [obra de teatro] to stage.

escenografía *f* set design.

escepticismo *m* scepticism.

escéptico, -ca ◇ *adj* [incrédulo] sceptical. ◇ *m y f* sceptic.

escindir *vt* to split. ◆ **escindirse** *vpr*: **~se (en)** to split (into).

escisión *f* [del átomo] splitting; [de partido político] split.

esclarecer *vt* to clear up, to shed light on.

esclava → **esclavo**.

esclavitud *f lit* & *fig* slavery.

esclavizar *vt lit* & *fig* to enslave.

esclavo, -va *m y f lit* & *fig* [persona] slave.

esclerosis *f inv* MED sclerosis.

esclusa *f* [de canal] lock; [compuerta] floodgate.

escoba *f* broom.

escocedura *f* [sensación] stinging.

escocer *vi lit* & *fig* to sting.

escocés, -esa ◇ *adj* [gen] Scottish; [whisky] Scotch; [tejido] tartan, plaid. ◇ *m y f* [persona] Scot, Scotsman (*f* Scotswoman); **los escoceses** the Scottish, the Scots. ◆ **escocés** *m* [lengua] Scots (U).

Escocia Scotland.

escoger *vt* to choose.

escogido, -da *adj* [elegido] selected, chosen; [selecto] choice, select.

escolar ◇ *adj* school (*antes de sust*). ◇ *m y f* pupil, schoolboy (*f* schoolgirl).

escolarizar *vt* to provide with schools.

escollo *m* **-1.** [en el mar] reef. **-2.** *fig* stumbling block.

escolta *f* escort.

escoltar *vt* to escort.

escombros *mpl* rubble (U), debris (U).

esconder *vt* to hide, to conceal. ◆ **esconderse** *vpr*: **~se (de)** to hide (from).

escondido, -da *adj* [lugar] secluded. ◆ **a escondidas** *loc adv* in secret.

escondite *m* **-1.** [lugar] hiding place. **-2.** [juego] hide-and-seek.

escondrijo *m* hiding place.

escopeta *f* shotgun; **~ de aire comprimido** air gun; **~ de cañones recortados** sawn-off shotgun.

escoria *f fig* dregs (*pl*), scum.

Escorpio, Escorpión ◇ *m* [zodiaco] Scorpio. ◇ *m y f* [persona] Scorpio.

escorpión *m* scorpion. ◆ **Escorpión** = **Escorpio**.

escotado, -da *adj* low-cut.

escote *m* [de prendas] neckline; [de persona] neck; **pagar a ~** to go Dutch.

escotilla *f* hatch, hatchway.

escozor *m* stinging.

escribiente *m y f* clerk.

escribir *vt & vi* to write. ◆ **escribirse** *vpr* **-1.** [personas] to write to one another. **-2.** [palabras]: **se escribe con "h"** it is spelt with an "h".

escrito, -ta ◇ *pp* → **escribir**. ◇ *adj* written; **por ~** in writing. ◆ **escrito** *m*

[gen] text; [documento] **document**; [obra literaria] **writing, work.**

escritor, **-ra** *m y f* writer.

escritorio *m* [mueble] **desk, bureau.**

escritura *f* **-1.** [arte] **writing. -2.** [sistema de signos] **script. -3.** DER **deed.**

escrúpulo *m* **-1.** [duda, recelo] **scruple. -2.** [minuciosidad] **scrupulousness, great care. -3.** [aprensión] **qualm; le da ~** he has qualms about it.

escrupuloso, **-sa** *adj* **-1.** [gen] **scrupulous. -2.** [aprensivo] **particular, fussy.**

escrutar *vt* [con la mirada] **to scrutinize, to examine;** [votos] **to count.**

escrutinio *m* **count** (*of votes*).

escuadra *f* **-1.** GEOM **square. -2.** [de buques] **squadron. -3.** [de soldados] **squad.**

escuadrilla *f* **squadron.**

escuadrón *m* **squadron; ~ de la muerte death squad.**

escuálido, **-da** *adj culto* **emaciated.**

escucha *f* **listening-in, monitoring; estar** O **permanecer a la ~ to listen in; ~s telefónicas telephone tapping** (*U*).

escuchar ◇ *vt* **to listen to.** ◇ *vi* **to listen.**

escudería *f* **team** (*in motor racing*).

escudo *m* **-1.** [arma] **shield. -2.** [moneda] **escudo. -3.** [emblema] **coat of arms.**

escudriñar *vt* [examinar] **to scrutinize, to examine;** [otear] **to search.**

escuela *f* **school; ~ normal teacher training college; ~ privada private school, public school** *Br*; **~ pública state school; ~ universitaria university** *which awards degrees after three years of study.*

escueto, **-ta** *adj* [sucinto] **concise;** [sobrio] **plain, unadorned.**

escuincle, **-cla** *m y f Amer* **nipper, kid.**

esculpir *vt* **to sculpt, to carve.**

escultor, **-ra** *m y f* **sculptor** (*f* **sculptress**).

escultura *f* **sculpture.**

escupidera *f* **spittoon.**

escupir ◇ *vi* **to spit.** ◇ *vt* [suj: persona, animal] **to spit out;** [suj: volcán, chimenea etc] **to belch out.**

escupitajo *m* **gob, spit.**

escurreplatos *m inv* **dish rack.**

escurridizo, **-za** *adj lit & fig* **slippery.**

escurridor *m* **colander.**

escurrir ◇ *vt* [gen] **to drain;** [ropa] **to wring out;** [en lavadora] **to spin-dry.** ◇ *vi* [gotear] **to drip.** ◆ **escurrirse** *vpr* [resbalarse] **to slip.**

ese¹ *f* [figura] **zigzag; hacer ~s** [en carretera] **to zigzag;** [al andar] **to stagger about.**

ese² (*pl* **esos**), **esa** *adj demos* **-1.** [gen] **that,** (*pl*) **those. -2.** (*después de sust*) *fam* [despectivo] **that,** (*pl*) **those; el hombre ~ no me inspira confianza** I don't trust that guy.

ése (*pl* **ésos**), **ésa** *pron demos* **-1.** [gen] **that one,** (*pl*) **those ones. -2.** [mencionado antes] **the former. -3.** *fam* [despectivo]: **~ fue el que me pegó** that's the guy who hit me. **-4.** *loc*: **¡a ~!** stop that man!; **ni por ésas** not even then; **no me lo vendió ni por ésas** even then he wouldn't sell me it.

esencia *f* **essence.**

esencial *adj* **essential; lo ~ the fundamental thing.**

esfera *f* **-1.** [gen] **sphere. -2.** [de reloj] **face. -3.** [círculo social] **circle.**

esférico, **-ca** *adj* **spherical.**

esfinge *f* **sphinx.**

esforzar *vt* [voz] **to strain.** ◆ **esforzarse** *vpr* **to make an effort; ~se en** O **por hacer algo to try very hard to do sthg, to do one's best to do sthg.**

esfuerzo *m* **effort; sin ~ effortlessly.**

esfumarse *vpr* [esperanzas, posibilidades] **to fade away;** [persona] **to vanish.**

esgrima *f* **fencing.**

esgrimir *vt* **-1.** [arma] **to brandish, to wield. -2.** [argumento, hecho, idea] **to use, to employ.**

esguince *m* **sprain.**

eslabón *m* **link.**

eslip (*pl* **eslips**) *m* **briefs** (*pl*).

eslogan (*pl* **eslóganes**) *m* **slogan.**

eslora *f* NÁUT **length.**

eslovaco, **-ca** *adj*, *m y f* **Slovak, Slovakian.** ◆ **eslovaco** *m* [lengua] **Slovak.**

Eslovaquia **Slovakia.**

esmaltar *vt* **to enamel.**

esmalte *m* [sustancia - en dientes, cerámica etc] **enamel;** [- de uñas] **(nail) varnish** O **polish.**

esmerado, **-da** *adj* [persona] **painstaking, careful;** [trabajo] **polished.**

esmeralda *f* **emerald.**

esmerarse *vpr*: **~se (en algo/hacer algo)** [esforzarse] **to take great pains (over sthg/doing sthg).**

esmerilar *vt* [pulir] **to polish with emery.**

esmero *m* **great care.**

esmoquin (*pl* **esmóquines**) *m* **dinner jacket** *Br*, **tuxedo** *Am*.

esnifar *vt fam* **to sniff** (*drugs*).

esnob (*pl* **esnobs**) *m y f* person who wants to be trendy.

eso *pron demos* (*neutro*) that; ~ **es la Torre Eiffel** that's the Eiffel Tower; ~ **es lo que yo pienso** that's just what I think; ~ **que propones es irrealizable** what you're proposing is impossible; ~ **de vivir solo no me gusta** I don't like the idea of living on my own; ¡~, ~! that's right!, yes!; ¡~ **es!** that's it; **¿cómo es ~?, ¿y ~?** [¿por qué?] how come?; **para ~ es mejor no ir** if that's all it is, you might as well not go; **por** ~ **vine** that's why I came. ◆**a eso de** *loc prep* (at) about ○ around. ◆**en eso** *loc adv* at that very moment. ◆**y eso que** *loc conj* even though.

esófago *m* oesophagus.

esos, esas → **ese²**.

ésos, ésas → **ése**.

esotérico, -ca *adj* esoteric.

espabilar *vt* **-1.** [despertar] to wake up. **-2.** [avispar]: ~ **a alguien** to sharpen sb's wits. ◆**espabilarse** *vpr* **-1.** [despertarse] to wake up, to brighten up. **-2.** [darse prisa] to get a move on. **-3.** [avisparse] to sharpen one's wits.

espacial *adj* space (*antes de sust*).

espaciar *vt* to space out.

espacio *m* **-1.** [gen] space; **no tengo mucho** ~ I don't have much room; **a doble** ~ double-spaced; **por** ~ **de** over a period of; ◆ **aéreo** air space. **-2.** RADIO & TV programme.

espacioso, -sa *adj* spacious.

espada *f* [arma] sword; **estar entre la** ~ **y la pared** to be between the devil and the deep blue sea. ◆**espadas** *fpl* [naipes] ≃ spades.

espagueti *m* spaghetti (U).

espalda *f* **-1.** [gen] back; **de** ~**s a alguien** with one's back turned on sb; **tumbarse de** ~**s** to lie on one's back; **cubrirse las** ~**s** to cover o.s.; **hablar de uno a sus** ~**s** to talk about sb behind their back; **volver la** ~ **a alguien** to turn one's back on sb. **-2.** [en natación] backstroke.

espantadizo, -za *adj* nervous, easily frightened.

espantajo *m* [persona fea] fright, sight.

espantapájaros *m inv* scarecrow.

espantar *vt* **-1.** [ahuyentar] to frighten ○ scare away. **-2.** [asustar] to frighten, to scare. ◆**espantarse** *vpr* to get frightened ○ scared.

espanto *m* fright; **¡qué** ~**!** how terrible!

espantoso, -sa *adj* **-1.** [terrorífico] horrific. **-2.** [enorme] terrible. **-3.** [feísimo] frightful, horrible.

España Spain.

español, -la ◇ *adj* Spanish. ◇ *m y f* [persona] Spaniard. ◆**español** *m* [lengua] Spanish.

esparadrapo *m* (sticking) plaster, Band-Aid® *Am*.

esparcido, -da *adj* scattered.

esparcir *vt* [gen] to spread; [semillas, papeles, objetos] to scatter. ◆**esparcirse** *vpr* to spread (out).

espárrago *m* asparagus (U).

esparto *m* esparto (grass).

espasmo *m* spasm.

espasmódico, -ca *adj* spasmodic.

espatarrarse *vpr fam* to sprawl (with one's legs wide open).

espátula *f* CULIN & MED spatula; ARTE palette knife; CONSTR bricklayer's trowel; [de empapelar] stripping knife.

especia *f* spice.

especial *adj* **-1.** [gen] special; ~ **para** specially for; **en** ~ especially, particularly; **¿alguno en** ~? any one in particular? **-2.** [peculiar - carácter, gusto, persona] peculiar, strange.

especialidad *f* speciality, specialty *Am*.

especialista *m y f* **-1.** [experto]: ~ **(en)** specialist (in). **-2.** CIN stuntman (*f* stuntwoman).

especializado, -da *adj*: ~ **en** specialized (in).

especializar *vt* to specialize.

especie *f* **-1.** BIOL species (sg). **-2.** [clase] kind, sort; **pagar en** ~ ○ ~ **s** to pay in kind.

especificar *vt* to specify.

específico, -ca *adj* specific.

espécimen (*pl* **especímenes**) *m* specimen.

espectacular *adj* spectacular.

espectáculo *m* **-1.** [diversión] entertainment. **-2.** [función] show, performance. **-3.** [suceso, escena] sight.

espectador *m y f* TV viewer; CIN & TEATR member of the audience; DEP spectator; [de suceso, discusión] onlooker.

espectro *m* **-1.** [fantasma] spectre, ghost. **-2.** FÍS & MED spectrum.

especulación *f* speculation.

especular *vi*: ~ **(sobre)** to speculate (about); ~ **en** COM to speculate on.

espejismo *m* mirage; *fig* illusion.

espejo *m lit & fig* mirror.

espeleología *f* potholing.

espeluznante *adj* hair-raising, lurid.

espera *f* [acción] wait; **en ~ de, a la ~ de** waiting for, awaiting.

esperanza *f* [deseo, ganas] hope; [confianza, expectativas] expectation; **perder la ~** to lose hope; **tener ~ de hacer algo** to hope to be able to do sthg; **~ de vida** life expectancy.

esperanzar *vt* to give hope to, to encourage.

esperar ◇ *vt* **-1.** [aguardar] to wait for. **-2.** [tener esperanza de]: **~ que** to hope that; **espero que sí** I hope so; **~ hacer algo** to hope to do sthg. **-3.** [tener confianza en] to expect; **~ que** to expect (that); **~ algo de alguien** to expect sthg from sb, to hope for sthg from sb. ◇ *vi* **-1.** [aguardar] to wait. **-2.** [ser inevitable] to await; **como era de ~** as was to be expected. ◆ **esperarse** *vpr* **-1.** [imaginarse, figurarse] to expect. **-2.** [aguardar] to wait.

esperma ◇ *m o f* BIOL sperm. ◇ *f Amer* [vela] candle.

esperpento *m* [persona] grotesque sight; [cosa] piece of nonsense.

espeso, -sa *adj* [gen] thick; [bosque, niebla] dense; [nieve] deep.

espesor *m* **-1.** [grosor] thickness; **tiene 2 metros de ~** it's 2 metres thick. **-2.** [densidad - de niebla, bosque] density; [- de nieve] depth.

espesura *f* **-1.** [vegetación] thicket. **-2.** [grosor] thickness; [densidad] density.

espía *m y f* spy.

espiar *vt* to spy on.

espiga *f* **-1.** [de trigo etc] ear. **-2.** [en telas] herringbone. **-3.** [pieza - de madera] peg; [- de hierro] pin.

espigado, -da *adj* [persona] tall and slim.

espigón *m* breakwater.

espina *f* [de pez] bone; [de planta] thorn; **me da mala ~** it makes me uneasy, there's something fishy about it; **tener una ~ clavada** to bear a great burden. ◆ **espina dorsal** *f* spine.

espinaca *f* (*gen pl*) spinach (*U*).

espinazo *m* spine, backbone.

espinilla *f* **-1.** [hueso] shin, shinbone. **-2.** [grano] blackhead.

espinoso, -sa *adj lit & fig* thorny.

espionaje *m* espionage.

espiral *f lit & fig* spiral; **en ~** [escalera, forma] spiral.

espirar *vi & vt* to exhale, to breathe out.

espiritista *adj* spiritualist.

espíritu *m* [gen] spirit; RELIG soul. ◆ **Espíritu Santo** *m* Holy Ghost.

espiritual *adj & m* spiritual.

espléndido, -da *adj* **-1.** [magnífico] splendid, magnificent. **-2.** [generoso] generous, lavish.

esplendor *m* **-1.** [magnificencia] splendour. **-2.** [apogeo] greatness.

espliego *m* lavender.

espoleta *f* [de proyectil] fuse.

espolvorear *vt* to dust, to sprinkle.

esponja *f* sponge.

esponjoso, -sa *adj* spongy.

espontaneidad *f* spontaneity.

espontáneo, -a *adj* spontaneous.

esporádico, -ca *adj* sporadic.

esport *adj inv*: **(de) ~** sports (*antes de sust*).

esposa → **esposo**.

esposar *vt* to handcuff.

esposo, -sa *m y f* [persona] husband (*f* wife). ◆ **esposas** *fpl* [objeto] handcuffs.

espot (*pl* **espots**) *m* advertising spot, commercial.

espray (*pl* **esprays**) *m* spray.

esprint (*pl* **esprints**) *m* sprint.

espuela *f* [gen] spur.

espuma *f* **-1.** [gen] foam; [de cerveza] head; [de jabón] lather; [de olas] surf; [de un caldo] scum. **-2.** [para pelo] (styling) mousse.

espumadera *f* skimmer.

espumoso, -sa *adj* [gen] foamy, frothy; [vino] sparkling; [jabón] lathery.

esputo *m* [gen] spittle; MED sputum.

esqueje *m* cutting.

esquela *f* obituary.

esqueleto *m* [de persona] skeleton.

esquema *m* [gráfico] diagram; [resumen] outline.

esquemático, -ca *adj* schematic.

esquí (*pl* **esquíes** ○ **esquís**) *m* **-1.** [instrumento] ski. **-2.** [deporte] skiing; **~ náutico** ○ **acuático** water-skiing.

esquiador, -ra *m y f* skier.

esquiar *vi* to ski.

esquilar *vt* to shear.

esquimal *adj, m y f* Eskimo.

esquina *f* corner; **a la vuelta de la ~** just round the corner; **doblar la ~** to turn the corner.

esquinazo *m* corner; **dar (el) ~ a alguien** to give sb the slip.

esquirol *m fam* blackleg, scab.

esquivar *vt* [gen] to avoid; [golpe] to dodge.

esquivo, -va *adj* shy.

esquizofrenia *f* schizophrenia.

esta → **este²**.

ésta → **éste**.

estabilidad *f* stability.

estabilizar *vt* to stabilize. ◆ **estabilizarse** *vpr* to stabilize.

estable *adj* **-1.** [firme] stable. **-2.** [permanente - huésped] **permanent**; [- cliente] regular.

establecer *vt* **-1.** [gen] to establish; [récord] to set. **-2.** [negocio, campamento] to set up. **-3.** [inmigrantes etc] to settle. ◆ **establecerse** *vpr* **-1.** [instalarse] to settle. **-2.** [poner un negocio] to set up a business.

establecimiento *m* **-1.** [gen] establishment; [de récord] setting. **-2.** [de negocio, colonia] setting up.

establo *m* cowshed.

estaca *f* **-1.** [para clavar, delimitar] stake; [de tienda de campaña] peg. **-2.** [garrote] cudgel.

estación *f* **-1.** [gen & INFORM] station; ~ **de autocares/de tren** coach/railway station; ~ **de esquí** ski resort; ~ **de gasolina** petrol station; ~ **de servicio** service station; ~ **de trabajo** workstation; ~ **meteorológica** weather station. **-2.** [del año, temporada] season.

estacionamiento *m* AUTOM parking; ~ **indebido** parking offence.

estacionar *vt* AUTOM to park.

estacionario, -ria *adj* [gen] stationary; ECON stagnant.

estadio *m* **-1.** DEP stadium. **-2.** [fase] stage.

estadista *m y f* statesman (*f* stateswoman).

estadístico, -ca *adj* statistical. ◆ **estadística** *f* **-1.** [ciencia] statistics (*U*). **-2.** [datos] statistics (*pl*).

estado *m* state; **su** ~ **es grave** his condition is serious; **estar en buen/mal** ~ [coche, terreno etc] to be in good/bad condition; [alimento, bebida] to be fresh/off; ~ **de ánimo** state of mind; ~ **civil** marital status; ~ **de bienestar** welfare state; ~ **de excepción** ○ **emergencia** state of emergency; ~ **de salud** (state of) health; **estar en** ~ **(de esperanza** ○ **buena esperanza)** to be expecting. ◆ **Estado** *m* [gobierno] State; **Estado Mayor** MIL general staff. ◆ **Estados Unidos (de América)** United States (of America).

estadounidense ◇ *adj* United States (*antes de sust*). ◇ *m y f* United States citizen.

estafa *f* [gen] swindle; COM fraud.

estafador, -ra *m y f* swindler.

estafar *vt* [gen] to swindle; COM to defraud.

estafeta *f* sub-post office.

estallar *vi* **-1.** [reventar - bomba] to explode; [- neumático] to burst. **-2.** *fig* [guerra, epidemia etc] to break out.

estallido *m* **-1.** [de bomba] explosion; [de trueno] crash; [de látigo] crack. **-2.** *fig* [de guerra etc] outbreak.

Estambul Istanbul.

estamento *m* stratum, class.

estampa *f* **-1.** [imagen, tarjeta] print. **-2.** [aspecto] appearance.

estampado, -da *adj* printed. ◆ **estampado** *m* [dibujo] (cotton) print.

estampar *vt* **-1.** [imprimir - gen] to print; [- metal] to stamp. **-2.** [escribir]: ~ **la firma** to sign one's name.

estampida *f* stampede.

estampido *m* report, bang.

estampilla *f* **-1.** [para marcar] rubber stamp. **-2.** *Amer* [de correos] stamp.

estancado, -da *adj* [agua] stagnant; [situación, proyecto] at a standstill.

estancarse *vpr* [líquido] to stagnate; [situación] to come to a standstill.

estancia *f* **-1.** [tiempo] stay. **-2.** [habitación] room. **-3.** *Amer* [hacienda] cattle ranch.

estanciero *m Amer* ranch owner.

estanco, -ca *adj* watertight. ◆ **estanco** *m* tobacconist's.

estándar (*pl* **estándares**) *adj & m* standard.

estandarizar *vt* to standardize.

estandarte *m* standard, banner.

estanque *m* **-1.** [alberca] pond; [para riego] reservoir. **-2.** *Amer* [depósito] tank (*of petrol*).

estanquero *m y f* tobacconist.

estante *m* shelf.

estantería *f* [gen] shelves (*pl*), shelving (*U*); [para libros] bookcase.

estaño *m* tin.

estar ◇ *vi* **-1.** [hallarse] to be; **¿dónde está la llave?** where is the key?; **¿está María?** is Maria in?; **no está** she's not in. **-2.** [con fechas]: **¿a qué estamos hoy?** what's the date today?; **hoy estamos a martes/a 15 de julio** today is Tuesday/the 15th of July; **estábamos en octubre** it was October. **-3.** [quedarse] to stay, to be; **estaré un par de horas y me iré** I'll stay a couple of hours and then I'll go. **-4.** (*antes de "a"*) [expresa valores, grados]: **estamos a veinte**

grados it's twenty degrees here; **el dólar está a 95 pesetas** the dollar is at 95 pesetas; **están a 100 ptas el kilo** they're 100 pesetas a kilo. **-5.** [hallarse listo] to be ready; **¿aún no está ese trabajo?** is that piece of work still not ready? **-6.** [servir]: ~ **para** to be (there) for; **para eso están los amigos** that's what friends are for. **-7.** (*antes de gerundio*) [expresa duración] to be; **están golpeando la puerta** they're banging on the door. **-8.** (*antes de "sin" + infin*) [expresa negación]: **estoy sin dormir desde ayer** I haven't slept since yesterday; **está sin acabar** it's not finished. **-9.** [faltar]: **eso está aún por escribir** that has yet to be written. **-10.** [hallarse a punto de]: ~ **por hacer algo** to be on the verge of doing sthg. **-11.** [expresa disposición]: ~ **para algo** to be in the mood for sthg. ◇ *v copulativo* **-1.** (*antes de adj*) [expresa cualidad, estado] to be; **los pasteles están ricos** the cakes are delicious; **esta calle está sucia** this street is dirty. **-2.** (*antes de "con" o "sin" + sust*) [expresa estado] to be; **estamos sin agua** we have no water, we're without water. **-3.** [expresa situación, acción]: ~ **de**: ~ **de camarero** to work as a waiter, to be a waiter; ~ **de vacaciones** to be on holiday; ~ **de viaje** to be on a trip; ~ **de mudanza** to be (in the process of) moving. **-4.** [expresa permanencia]: ~ **en uso** to be in use; ~ **en guardia** to be on guard. **-5.** [expresa apoyo, predilección]: ~ **por** to be in favour of. **-6.** [expresa ocupación]: ~ **como** to be; **está como cajera** she's a checkout girl. **-7.** [consistir]: ~ **en** to be, to lie in; **el problema está en la fecha** the problem is the date. **-8.** [sentar - ropa]: **este traje te está bien** this suit looks good on you. **-9.** (*antes de "que" + verbo*) [expresa actitud]: **está que muerde porque ha suspendido** he's furious because he failed. ◆ **estarse** *vpr* [permanecer] to stay; **te puedes** ~ **con nosotros unos días** you can stay ○ spend a few days with us.

estárter (*pl* **estárters**) *m* starter.

estatal *adj* state (*antes de sust*).

estático, -ca *adj* [inmóvil] stock-still.

estatua *f* statue.

estatura *f* height.

estatus *m inv* status.

estatutario, -ria *adj* statutory.

estatuto *m* [gen] statute; [de empresa] article (of association); [de ciudad] by-law.

este[1] ◇ *adj* [posición, parte] east, eastern; [dirección, viento] easterly. ◇ *m* east; **los países del** ~ the Eastern bloc countries.

este[2] (*pl* **estos**), **esta** *adj demos* **-1.** [gen] this, (*pl*) these; **esta camisa** this shirt; ~ **año** this year. **-2.** *fam* [despectivo] that, (*pl*) those; **no soporto a la niña esta** I can't stand that girl.

éste (*pl* **éstos**), **ésta** *pron demos* **-1.** [gen] this one, (*pl*) these (ones); **dame otro boli**; ~ **no funciona** give me another pen; this one doesn't work; **aquellos cuadros no están mal, aunque éstos me gustan más** those paintings aren't bad, but I like these (ones) better; **ésta ha sido la semana más feliz de mi vida** this has been the happiest week of my life. **-2.** [recién mencionado] the latter; **entraron Juan y Pedro,** ~ **con un abrigo verde** Juan and Pedro came in, the latter wearing a green coat. **-3.** *fam* [despectivo]: ~ **es el que me pegó** this is the guy who hit me. ◆ **en éstas** *loc adv fam* just then, at that very moment.

estela *f* **-1.** [de barco] wake; [de avión, estrella fugaz] trail. **-2.** *fig* [rastro] trail.

estelar *adj* **-1.** ASTRON stellar. **-2.** CIN & TEATR star (*antes de sust*).

estepa *f* steppe.

estera *f* [tejido] matting; [alfombrilla] mat.

estéreo *adj inv & m* stereo.

estereofónico, -ca *adj* stereo.

estereotipo *m* stereotype.

estéril *adj* **-1.** [persona, terreno, imaginación] sterile. **-2.** *fig* [inútil] futile.

esterilizar *vt* to sterilize.

esterlina → **libra**.

esternón *m* breastbone, sternum.

esteroides *mpl* steroids.

esteta *m y f* aesthete.

estética → **estético**.

esteticista, **esthéticienne** [esteti'θjen] *f* beautician.

estético, -ca *adj* aesthetic. ◆ **estética** *f* FILOSOFÍA aesthetics (*U*).

esthéticienne = **esteticista**.

estiércol *m* [excrementos] dung; [abono] manure.

estigma *m fig* [deshonor] stigma.

estilarse *vpr fam* to be in (fashion).

estilo *m* **-1.** [gen] style; ~ **de vida** lifestyle. **-2.** [en natación] stroke. **-3.** GRAM speech; ~ **directo/indirecto** direct/

indirect speech. **-4.** *loc*: **algo por el ~** something of the sort.

estilográfica *f* fountain pen.

estima *f* esteem, respect.

estimación *f* **-1.** [aprecio] esteem, respect. **-2.** [valoración] valuation. **-3.** [en impuestos] assessment.

estimado, -da *adj* [querido] esteemed, respected; **Estimado señor** Dear Sir.

estimar *vt* **-1.** [valorar - gen] to value; [- valor] to estimate. **-2.** [apreciar] to think highly of. **-3.** [creer] to consider.

estimulante ◇ *adj* [que excita] stimulating. ◇ *m* stimulant.

estimular *vt* **-1.** [animar] to encourage. **-2.** [excitar] to stimulate.

estímulo *m* **-1.** [aliciente] incentive; [ánimo] encouragement. **-2.** [de un órgano] stimulus.

estío *m culto* summer.

estipendio *m* stipend, remuneration.

estipulación *f* **-1.** [acuerdo] agreement. **-2.** DER stipulation.

estipular *vt* to stipulate.

estirado, -da *adj* [persona - altanero] haughty; [- adusto] uptight.

estirar ◇ *vt* **-1.** [alargar - gen] to stretch; [- el cuello] to crane. **-2.** [desarrugar] to straighten. **-3.** *fig* [el dinero etc] to make last; [discurso, tema] to spin out. ◇ *vi*: **~ (de)** to pull. ◆ **estirarse** *vpr* **-1.** [desperezarse] to stretch. **-2.** [tumbarse] to stretch out.

estirón *m* [acción] tug, pull.

estirpe *f* stock, lineage.

estival *adj* summer (*antes de sust*).

esto *pron demos* (*neutro*) this thing; **~ es tu regalo de cumpleaños** this is your birthday present; **~ que acabas de decir no tiene sentido** what you just said doesn't make sense; **~ de trabajar de noche no me gusta** I don't like this business of working at night; **~ es** that is (to say). ◆ **en esto** *loc adv* just then, at that very moment.

estoc (*pl* **estocs**) *m* stock.

Estocolmo Stockholm.

estofa *f*: **de baja ~** [gente] low-class; [cosas] poor-quality.

estofado *m* stew.

estofar *vt* CULIN to stew.

estoicismo *m* stoicism.

estoico, -ca *adj* stoic, stoical.

estomacal *adj* [dolencia] stomach (*antes de sust*); [bebida] digestive.

estómago *m* stomach.

Estonia Estonia.

estop = **stop**.

estorbar ◇ *vt* [obstaculizar] to hinder; [molestar] to bother. ◇ *vi* [estar en medio] to be in the way.

estorbo *m* [obstáculo] hindrance; [molestia] nuisance.

estornudar *vi* to sneeze.

estos, -tas → este².

éstos, -tas → éste.

estoy → estar.

estrabismo *m* squint.

estrado *m* platform.

estrafalario *adj* outlandish, eccentric.

estragón *m* tarragon.

estragos *mpl*: **causar O hacer ~ en** [físicos] to wreak havoc with; [morales] to destroy, to ruin.

estrambótico, -ca *adj* outlandish.

estrangulador, -ra *m y f* strangler.

estrangular *vt* [ahogar] to strangle; MED to strangulate.

estraperlo *m* black market; **de ~** black market (*antes de sust*).

estratagema *f* MIL stratagem; *fig* [astucia] artifice, trick.

estrategia *f* strategy.

estratégico, -ca *adj* strategic.

estrato *m* GEOL & *fig* stratum.

estrechar *vt* **-1.** [hacer estrecho - gen] to narrow; [- ropa] to take in. **-2.** *fig* [relaciones] to make closer. **-3.** [apretar] to squeeze, to hug; **~ la mano a alguien** to shake sb's hand. ◆ **estrecharse** *vpr* [hacerse estrecho] to narrow.

estrechez *f* **-1.** [falta de anchura] narrowness; [falta de espacio] lack of space; [de ropa] tightness; **~ de miras** narrow-mindedness. **-2.** *fig* [falta de dinero] hardship; **pasar estrecheces** to be hard up. **-3.** [intimidad] closeness.

estrecho, -cha *adj* **-1.** [no ancho - gen] narrow; [- ropa] tight; [- habitación] cramped; **~ de miras** narrow-minded. **-2.** *fig* [íntimo] close. ◆ **estrecho** *m* GEOGR strait.

estrella *f* [gen] star; *fig* [destino] fate; **~ fugaz** shooting star. ◆ **estrella de mar** *f* starfish.

estrellado, -da *adj* **-1.** [con estrellas] starry. **-2.** [por la forma] star-shaped.

estrellar *vt* [arrojar] to smash. ◆ **estrellarse** *vpr* [chocar]: **~se (contra)** [gen] to smash (against); [avión, coche] to crash (into).

estrellón *m Amer* crash.

estremecer *vt* to shake. ◆ **estremecerse** *vpr*: **~se (de)** [horror, miedo] to tremble O shudder (with); [frío] to shiver (with).

estremecimiento *m* [de miedo] shudder; [de frío] shiver.

estrenar *vt* **-1.** [gen] to use for the first time; [ropa] to wear for the first time; [piso] to move into. **-2.** CIN to release; TEATR to premiere. ◆ **estrenarse** *vpr* [persona] to make one's debut, to start.

estreno *m* [de espectáculo] premiere, first night; [de cosa] first use; [en un empleo] debut.

estreñido, -da *adj* constipated.

estreñimiento *m* constipation.

estrépito *m* [ruido] racket, din; *fig* [ostentación] fanfare.

estrepitoso, -sa *adj* **-1.** [gen] noisy; [aplausos] deafening. **-2.** [derrota] resounding; [fracaso] spectacular.

estrés *m inv* stress.

estría *f* [gen] groove; [en la piel] stretch mark.

estribación *f* (*gen pl*) foothills (*pl*).

estribar ◆ **estribar en** *vi* to be based on, to lie in.

estribillo *m* MÚS chorus; LITER refrain.

estribo *m* **-1.** [de montura] stirrup. **-2.** [de coche, tren] step. **-3.** *loc*: **perder los ~s** to fly off the handle.

estribor *m* starboard.

estricto, -ta *adj* strict.

estridente *adj* **-1.** [ruido] strident, shrill. **-2.** [color] garish, loud.

estrofa *f* stanza, verse.

estropajo *m* scourer.

estropear *vt* **-1.** [averiar] to break. **-2.** [dañar] to damage. **-3.** [echar a perder] to ruin, to spoil. ◆ **estropearse** *vpr* **-1.** [máquina] to break down. **-2.** [comida] to go off, to spoil; [piel] to get damaged. **-3.** [plan] to fall through.

estropicio *m*: **hacer** ○ **causar un ~** to wreak havoc.

estructura *f* structure.

estruendo *m* **-1.** [estrépito] din, roar; [de trueno] crash. **-2.** [alboroto] uproar, tumult.

estrujar *vt* **-1.** [limón] to squeeze; [trapo, ropa] to wring (out); [papel] to screw up; [caja] to crush. **-2.** [abrazar - persona, mano] to squeeze. **-3.** *fig* [sacar partido] to bleed dry.

estuario *m* estuary.

estuche *m* **-1.** [caja] case; [de joyas] jewellery box. **-2.** [utensilios] set.

estuco *m* stucco.

estudiante *m y f* student.

estudiantil *adj* student (*antes de sust*).

estudiar ◇ *vt* [gen] to study. ◇ *vi* to study; **~ para médico** to be studying to be a doctor.

estudio *m* **-1.** [gen] study; **estar en ~** to be under consideration; **~ de mercado** [técnica] market research; [investigación] market survey. **-2.** [oficina] study; [de fotógrafo, pintor] studio. **-3.** [apartamento] studio apartment. **-4.** (*gen pl*) CIN, RADIO & TV studio. ◆ **estudios** *mpl* [serie de cursos] studies; [educación] education (*U*); **~s primarios/secundarios** primary/secondary education.

estudioso, -sa *adj* studious.

estufa *f* heater, fire.

estupefaciente *m* narcotic, drug.

estupefacto, -ta *adj* astonished.

estupendamente *adv* wonderfully; **estoy ~** I feel wonderful.

estupendo, -da *adj* great, fantastic. ◆ **estupendo** *interj*: ¡~! great!

estupidez *f* stupidity; **decir/hacer una ~** to say/do sthg stupid.

estúpido, -da *adj* stupid.

estupor *m* astonishment.

esturión *m* sturgeon.

estuviera *etc* → **estar**.

esvástica *f* swastika.

ETA *f* ETA, *terrorist Basque separatist organization.*

etapa *f* stage; **por ~s** in stages.

etarra *m y f* member of ETA.

ETB (*abrev de* **Euskal Telebista**) *f Basque television network.*

etc. (*abrev de* **etcétera**) etc.

etcétera *adv* etcetera.

etéreo, -a *adj fig* ethereal.

eternidad *f* eternity; **hace una ~ que no la veo** *fam* it's ages since I last saw her.

eterno, -na *adj* eternal; *fam* [larguísimo] never-ending, interminable.

ético, -ca *adj* ethical. ◆ **ética** *f* [moralidad] ethics (*pl*).

etílico, -ca *adj* QUÍM ethyl (*antes de sust*); **intoxicación etílica** alcohol poisoning.

etimología *f* etymology.

Etiopía Ethiopia.

etiqueta *f* **-1.** [gen & INFORM] label. **-2.** [ceremonial] etiquette; **de ~** formal.

etiquetar *vt lit & fig* to label; **~ a alguien de algo** to label sb sthg.

etnia *f* ethnic group.

étnico, -ca *adj* ethnic.

EUA (*abrev de* **Estados Unidos de América**) *mpl* USA.

eucalipto *m* eucalyptus.
eucaristía *f*: **la ~** the Eucharist.
eufemismo *m* euphemism.
euforia *f* euphoria, elation.
eufórico, -ca *adj* euphoric, elated.
eunuco *m* eunuch.
eurocheque *m* eurocheque *Br*, euro-check *Am*.
eurócrata *adj, m y f* Eurocrat.
eurodiputado, -da *m y f* Euro-M.P., M.E.P.
Europa Europe.
europarlamentario, -ria *m y f* Euro-M.P., M.E.P.
europeo, -a *adj, m y f* European.
Euskadi the Basque Country.
euskara, euskera *m* Basque.
eutanasia *f* euthanasia.
evacuación *f* evacuation.
evacuar *vt* [gen] to evacuate; [vientre] to empty, to void.
evadir *vt* to evade; [respuesta, peligro] to avoid. ◆ **evadirse** *vpr*: **~se (de)** to escape (from).
evaluación *f* -1. [gen] evaluation. -2. [EDUC - examen] assessment.
evaluar *vt* to evaluate, to assess.
evangélico, -ca *adj, m y f* evangelical.
evangelio *m* RELIG gospel.
evaporar *vt* to evaporate. ◆ **evaporarse** *vpr* [líquido etc] to evaporate.
evasión *f* -1. [huida] escape. -2. [de dinero]: **~ de capitales** ○ **divisas** capital flight; **~ fiscal** tax evasion. -3. *fig* [entretenimiento] amusement, recreation; [escapismo] escapism; **de ~** escapist.
evasivo, -va *adj* evasive. ◆ **evasiva** *f* evasive answer.
evento *m* event.
eventual *adj* -1. [no fijo - trabajador] temporary, casual; [- gastos] incidental. -2. [posible] possible.
eventualidad *f* -1. [temporalidad] temporariness. -2. [hecho incierto] eventuality; [posibilidad] possibility.
Everest *m*: **el ~** (Mount) Everest.
evidencia *f* -1. [prueba] evidence, proof. -2. [claridad] obviousness; **poner algo en ~** to demonstrate sthg; **poner a alguien en ~** to show sb up.
evidenciar *vt* to show, to demonstrate. ◆ **evidenciarse** *vpr* to be obvious ○ evident.
evidente *adj* evident, obvious.
evitar *vt* [gen] to avoid; [desastre, accidente] to avert; **~ que alguien haga algo** to prevent sb from doing sthg.

evocación *f* recollection, evocation.
evocar *vt* [recordar] to evoke.
evolución *f* -1. [gen] evolution; [de enfermedad] development, progress. -2. MIL manoeuvre.
evolucionar *vi* -1. [gen] to evolve; [enfermedad] to develop, to progress; [cambiar] to change. -2. MIL to carry out manoeuvres.
ex *prep* ex; **el ~ presidente** the ex-president, the former president.
exacerbar *vt* -1. [agudizar] to exacerbate, to aggravate. -2. [irritar] to irritate, to infuriate.
exactitud *f* accuracy, precision; [puntualidad] punctuality.
exacto, -ta *adj* -1. [justo - cálculo, medida] exact; **tres metros ~s** exactly three metres. -2. [preciso] accurate, precise; [correcto] correct, right. -3. [idéntico]: **~ (a)** identical (to), exactly the same (as). ◆ **exacto** *interj*: ¡~! exactly!, precisely!
exageración *f* exaggeration; **este precio es una ~** this price is over the top.
exagerado, -da *adj* [gen] exaggerated; [persona] overly dramatic; [precio] exorbitant; [gesto] flamboyant.
exagerar *vt & vi* to exaggerate.
exaltado, -da *adj* [jubiloso] elated; [acalorado - persona] worked up; [- discusión] heated; [excitable] hotheaded.
exaltar *vt* -1. [elevar] to promote, to raise. -2. [glorificar] to exalt. ◆ **exaltarse** *vpr* to get excited ○ worked up.
examen *m* -1. [ejercicio] exam, examination; **presentarse a un ~** to sit an exam; **~ de conducir** driving test; **~ final/oral** final/oral (exam); **~ parcial** ≃ end-of-term exam. -2. [indagación] consideration, examination.
examinar *vt* to examine. ◆ **examinarse** *vpr* to sit ○ take an exam.
exánime *adj* -1. [muerto] dead. -2. [desmayado] lifeless.
exasperar *vt* to exasperate. ◆ **exasperarse** *vpr* to get exasperated.
excavación *f* [lugar] dig, excavation.
excavar *vt* [gen] to dig; [en arqueología] to excavate.
excedencia *f* leave (of absence); EDUC sabbatical.
excedente ◇ *adj* [producción etc] surplus. ◇ *m* COM surplus.
exceder *vt* to exceed, to surpass. ◆ **excederse** *vpr* -1. [pasarse de la raya]: **~se (en)** to go too far ○ overstep the

mark (in). **-2.** [rebasar el límite]: **se exce-de en el peso** it's too heavy.

excelencia f [cualidad] excellence; **por ~ par** excellence. ◆ **Su Excelencia** m y f His Excellency (f Her Excellency).

excelente adj excellent.

excelentísimo, -ma adj most excellent.

excentricidad f eccentricity.

excéntrico, -ca adj, m y f eccentric.

excepción f exception; **a** ○ **con ~ de** with the exception of, except for. ◆ **de excepción** loc adj exceptional.

excepcional adj exceptional.

excepto adv except (for).

exceptuar vt: **~ (de)** [excluir] to exclude (from); [eximir] to exempt (from); **ex-ceptuando a ...** excluding ....

excesivo, -va adj excessive.

exceso m [demasía] excess; **~ de equi-paje** excess baggage; **~ de peso** [obesi-dad] excess weight.

excitación f [nerviosismo] agitation; [por enfado, sexo] arousal.

excitado, -da adj [nervioso] agitated; [por enfado, sexo] aroused.

excitante m stimulant.

excitar vt **-1.** [inquietar] to upset, to agitate. **-2.** [estimular - sentidos] to stimulate; [- apetito] to whet; [- pasión, curiosidad, persona] to arouse. ◆ **excitarse** vpr [alterarse] to get worked up ○ excited.

exclamación f [interjección] exclama-tion; [grito] cry.

exclamar vt & vi to exclaim, to shout out.

excluir vt to exclude; [hipótesis, opción] to rule out; [hacer imposible] to pre-clude; **~ a alguien de algo** to exclude sb from sthg.

exclusión f exclusion.

exclusivo, -va adj exclusive. ◆ **ex-clusiva** f **-1.** PRENS exclusive. **-2.** COM ex-clusive ○ sole right.

Excma. abrev de **Excelentísima.**

Excmo. abrev de **Excelentísimo.**

excombatiente m y f ex-serviceman (f ex-servicewoman) Br, war veteran Am.

excomulgar vt to excommunicate.

excomunión f excommunication.

excremento m (gen pl) excrement (U).

exculpar vt to exonerate; DER to acquit.

excursión f [viaje] excursion, trip; **ir de ~** to go on an outing ○ a trip.

excursionista m y f [en la ciudad] sight-seer, tripper; [en el campo] rambler; [en la montaña] hiker.

excusa f **-1.** [gen] excuse. **-2.** [petición de perdón] apology; **presentar uno sus ~s** to apologize, to make one's ex-cuses.

excusar vt [disculpar a] to excuse; [dis-culparse por] to apologize for. ◆ **excusarse** vpr to apologize.

exento, -ta adj exempt; **~ de** [sin] free from, without; [eximido de] exempt from.

exequias fpl funeral (sg), funeral rites.

exhalación f [emanación] exhalation, vapour; [suspiro] breath.

exhalar vt **-1.** [aire] to exhale, to breathe out; [suspiros] to heave. **-2.** [olor] to give off. **-3.** [quejas] to utter.

exhaustivo, -va adj exhaustive.

exhausto, -ta adj exhausted.

exhibición f **-1.** [demostración] show, display. **-2.** [deportiva, artística etc] exhi-bition. **-3.** [de películas] showing.

exhibir vt **-1.** [exponer - cuadros, fotogra-fías] to exhibit; [- modelos] to show; [- productos] to display. **-2.** [lucir - joyas, cualidades etc] to show off. **-3.** [película] to show, to screen.

exhortación f exhortation.

exhortar vt: **~ a** to exhort to.

exigencia f **-1.** [obligación] demand, re-quirement. **-2.** [capricho] fussiness (U).

exigente adj demanding.

exigir vt **-1.** [gen] to demand; **~ algo de** ○ **a alguien** to demand sthg from sb. **-2.** [requerir, necesitar] to require.

exiguo, -gua adj [escaso] meagre, pal-try; [pequeño] minute.

exiliado, -da ◇ adj exiled, in exile. ◇ m y f exile.

exiliar vt to exile. ◆ **exiliarse** vpr to go into exile.

exilio m exile.

eximir vt: **~ (de)** to exempt (from).

existencia f existence. ◆ **existencias** fpl COM stock (U).

existir vi to exist; **existe mucha pobre-za** there is a lot of poverty.

éxito m **-1.** [gen] success; **con ~** suc-cessfully; **tener ~** to be successful. **-2.** [libro] bestseller; [canción] hit.

exitoso, -sa adj successful.

éxodo m exodus.

exorbitante adj exorbitant.

exorcizar vt to exorcize.

exótico, -ca adj exotic.

expandir vt to spread; FÍS to expand. ◆ **expandirse** vpr to spread; FÍS to ex-pand.

expansión f **-1.** FÍS expansion. **-2.** ECON growth; **en ~** expanding. **-3.** [recreo] relaxation, amusement.

expansionarse vpr **-1.** [desahogarse]: **~ (con)** to open one's heart (to). **-2.** [divertirse] to relax, to let off steam. **-3.** [desarrollarse] to expand.

expansivo, -va adj **-1.** [gen] expansive. **-2.** fig [persona] open, frank.

expatriar vt to expatriate; [exiliar] to exile. ◆ **expatriarse** vpr to emigrate; [exiliarse] to go into exile.

expectación f expectancy, anticipation.

expectativa f [espera] expectation; [esperanza] hope; [perspectiva] prospect; **estar a la ~** to wait and see; **estar a la ~ de** [atento] to be on the lookout for; [a la espera] to be hoping for; **~ de vida** life expectancy.

expedición f [viaje, grupo] expedition.

expediente m **-1.** [documentación] documents (pl); [ficha] file. **-2.** [historial] record; **~ académico** academic record. **-3.** [investigación] inquiry; **abrir ~ a alguien** [castigar] to take disciplinary action against sb; [investigar] to start proceedings against sb.

expedir vt [carta, pedido] to send, to dispatch; [pasaporte, decreto] to issue; [contrato, documento] to draw up.

expedito, -ta adj clear, free.

expeler vt [humo - suj: persona] to blow out; [- suj: chimenea, tubo de escape] to emit; [- suj: extractor, volcán] to expel.

expendedor, -ra m y f dealer; [de lotería] seller, vendor.

expendeduría f [de tabaco] tobacconist's Br, cigar store Am.

expensas fpl [gastos] expenses, costs. ◆ **a expensas de** loc prep at the expense of.

experiencia f [gen] experience; **por (propia) ~** from (one's own) experience.

experimentado, -da adj [persona] experienced; [método] tried and tested.

experimentar vt **-1.** [gen] to experience; [derrota, pérdidas] to suffer. **-2.** [probar] to test; [hacer experimentos con] to experiment with o on.

experimento m experiment.

experto, -ta adj, m y f expert.

expiar vt to atone for, to expiate.

expirar vi to expire.

explanada f [llanura] flat o level ground (U).

explayar vt to extend. ◆ **explayarse** vpr **-1.** [divertirse] to amuse o.s., to enjoy o.s. **-2.** [hablar mucho] to talk at length. **-3.** [desahogarse]: **~se (con)** to pour out one's heart (to).

explicación f explanation.

explicar vt [gen] to explain; [teoría] to expound. ◆ **explicarse** vpr **-1.** [comprender] to understand; **no me lo explico** I can't understand it. **-2.** [dar explicaciones] to explain o.s. **-3.** [expresarse] to make o.s. understood.

explícito, -ta adj explicit.

exploración f [gen & MED] exploration.

explorador, -ra m y f explorer; [scout] boy scout (f girl guide).

explorar vt **-1.** [gen] to explore; MIL to scout. **-2.** MED to examine; [internamente] to explore, to probe.

explosión f lit & fig explosion; **hacer ~** to explode.

explosivo, -va adj [gen] explosive. ◆ **explosivo** m explosive.

explotación f **-1.** [acción] exploitation; [de fábrica etc] running; [de yacimiento minero] mining; [agrícola] farming; [de petróleo] drilling. **-2.** [instalaciones]: **~ agrícola** farm.

explotar ◇ vt **-1.** [gen] to exploit. **-2.** [fábrica] to run, to operate; [terreno] to farm; [mina] to work. ◇ vi to explode.

expoliar vt to pillage, to plunder.

exponer vt **-1.** [gen] to expose. **-2.** [teoría] to expound; [ideas, propuesta] to set out, to explain. **-3.** [cuadro, obra] to exhibit; [objetos en vitrinas] to display. **-4.** [vida, prestigio] to risk. ◆ **exponerse** vpr [arriesgarse]: **~se (a)** to run the risk (of); [a la muerte] to expose o.s. (to).

exportación f **-1.** [acción] export. **-2.** [mercancías] exports (pl).

exportar vt COM & INFORM to export.

exposición f **-1.** [gen & FOT] exposure. **-2.** [de arte etc] exhibition; [de objetos en vitrina] display; **~ universal** world fair. **-3.** [de teoría] exposition; [de ideas, propuesta] setting out, explanation.

expositor, -ra m y f [de arte] exhibitor; [de teoría] exponent.

exprés ◇ adj **-1.** [tren] express. **-2.** [café] espresso. ◇ m = **expreso**.

expresado, -da adj [mencionado] abovementioned.

expresamente adv [a propósito] expressly; [explícitamente] explicitly.

expresar vt to express; [suj: rostro] to show.

expresión f expression.

expresivo, -va adj expressive; [cariñoso] affectionate.

expreso, -sa adj [explícito] specific; [deliberado] express; [claro] clear. ◆ **expreso** ◇ m -1. [tren] express train. -2. [café] expresso. ◇ adv on purpose, expressly.

exprimidor m squeezer.

exprimir vt [fruta] to squeeze; [zumo] to squeeze out.

expropiar vt to expropriate.

expuesto, -ta ◇ pp → exponer. ◇ adj -1. [dicho] stated, expressed. -2. [desprotegido]: ~ **(a)** exposed (to). -3. [arriesgado] dangerous, risky. -4. [exhibido] on display.

expulsar vt -1. [persona - de clase, local, asociación] to throw out; [- de colegio] to expel. -2. DEP to send off. -3. [humo] to emit, to give off.

expulsión f [gen] expulsion; [de clase, local, asociación] throwing-out; DEP sending-off.

exquisitez f [cualidad] exquisiteness.

exquisito, -ta adj exquisite; [comida] delicious, sublime.

extasiarse vpr: ~ **(ante** O **con)** to go into ecstasies (over).

éxtasis m inv ecstasy.

extender vt -1. [desplegar - tela, plano, alas] to spread (out); [- brazos, piernas] to stretch out. -2. [esparcir - mantequilla] to spread; [- pintura] to smear; [- objetos etc] to spread out. -3. [ampliar - castigo, influencia etc] to extend. -4. [documento] to draw up; [cheque] to make out; [pasaporte, certificado] to issue. ◆ **extenderse** vpr -1. [ocupar]: ~se **(por)** to stretch O extend across. -2. [hablar mucho]: ~se **(en)** to enlarge O expand (on). -3. [durar] to extend, to last. -4. [difundirse]: ~se **(por)** to spread (across). -5. [tenderse] to stretch out.

extensión f -1. [superficie - de terreno etc] area, expanse. -2. [amplitud - de país etc] size; [- de conocimientos] extent. -3. [duración] duration, length. -4. [sentido - de concepto, palabra] range of meaning; **en toda la** ~ **de la palabra** in every sense of the word. -5. INFORM & TELECOM extension.

extensivo, -va adj extensive.

extenso, -sa adj extensive; [país] vast; [libro, película] long.

extenuar vt to exhaust completely.

exterior ◇ adj -1. [de fuera] outside; [capa] outer, exterior. -2. [visible] outward. -3. [extranjero] foreign. ◇ m -1.

[superficie] outside; **en el** ~ outside. -2. [extranjero] foreign countries (pl); **en el** ~ abroad. -3. [aspecto] appearance. ◆ **exteriores** mpl CIN outside shots; **rodar en** ~es to film on location.

exteriorizar vt to show, to reveal.

exterminar vt [aniquilar] to exterminate.

exterminio m extermination.

externo, -na adj -1. [gen] external; [parte, capa] outer; [influencia] outside; [signo, aspecto] outward. -2. [alumno] day (antes de sust).

extinción f [gen] extinction; [de esperanzas] loss.

extinguir vt [incendio] to put out, to extinguish; [raza] to wipe out; [afecto, entusiasmo] to put an end to. ◆ **extinguirse** vpr [fuego, luz] to go out; [animal, raza] to become extinct; [ruido] to die out; [afecto] to die.

extinto, -ta adj extinguished; [animal, volcán] extinct.

extintor m fire extinguisher.

extirpar vt [tumor] to remove; [muela] to extract; fig to eradicate.

extorsión f -1. [molestia] trouble, bother. -2. DER extortion.

extorsionista m y f extortionist.

extra ◇ adj -1. [adicional] extra. -2. [de gran calidad] top quality, superior. ◇ m y f CIN extra. ◇ m [gasto etc] extra. ◇ f → paga.

extracción f -1. [gen] extraction. -2. [en sorteos] draw. -3. [de carbón] mining.

extracto m -1. [resumen] summary, résumé; ~ **de cuentas** statement (of account). -2. [concentrado] extract.

extraditar vt to extradite.

extraer vt: ~ **(de)** [gen] to extract (from); [sangre] to draw (from); [carbón] to mine (from); [conclusiones] to come to O draw (from).

extralimitarse vpr fig to go too far.

extranjero, -ra ◇ adj foreign. ◇ m y f [persona] foreigner. ◆ **extranjero** m [territorio] foreign countries (pl); **estar en el/ir al** ~ to be/go abroad.

extrañar vt -1. [sorprender] to surprise; **me extraña (que digas esto)** I'm surprised (that you should say that). -2. [echar de menos] to miss. ◆ **extrañarse de** vpr [sorprenderse de] to be surprised at.

extrañeza f [sorpresa] surprise.

extraño, -ña ◇ adj -1. [gen] strange. -2. [ajeno] detached, uninvolved. -3. MED foreign. ◇ m y f stranger.

extraoficial *adj* unofficial.
extraordinario, -ria *adj* **-1.** [gen] extraordinary. **-2.** [gastos] additional; [edición, suplemento] special. ◆ **extraordinario** *m* **-1.** PRENS special edition. **-2.** → **paga**.
extrapolar *vt* to generalize about.
extrarradio *m* outskirts (*pl*), suburbs (*pl*).
extraterrestre *adj, m y f* extraterrestrial.
extravagancia *f* eccentricity.
extravagante *adj* eccentric, outlandish.
extravertido, -da = extrovertido.
extraviado, -da *adj* [perdido] lost; [animal] stray.
extraviar *vt* **-1.** [objeto] to lose, to mislay. **-2.** [excursionista] to mislead. ◆ **extraviarse** *vpr* **-1.** [persona] to get lost. **-2.** [objeto] to go missing.
extravío *m* [pérdida] loss, mislaying.
extremado, -da *adj* extreme.
extremar *vt* to go to extremes with. ◆ **extremarse** *vpr* to take great pains O care.
extremaunción *f* extreme unction.
extremidad *f* [extremo] end. ◆ **extremidades** *fpl* ANAT extremities.
extremista *adj, m y f* extremist.
extremo, -ma *adj* [gen] extreme; [en el espacio] far, furthest. ◆ **extremo** *m* **-1.** [punta] end. **-2.** [límite] extreme; **en último** ~ as a last resort. **-3.** DEP: ~ **derecho/izquierdo** outside right/left.
extrovertido, -da, extravertido, -da *adj, m y f* extrovert.
exuberancia *f* exuberance.
exuberante *adj* exuberant.
exudar *vt* to exude, to ooze.
exultante *adj* exultant.
eyaculación *f* ejaculation.
eyacular *vi* to ejaculate.

F

f, F *f* [letra] f, F. ◆ **23 F** *m* 23rd February, day of the failed coup d'état in Spain in 1981.
f. -1. (*abrev de* **factura**) inv. **-2.** (*abrev de* **folio**) f.
fa *m* MÚS F; [en solfeo] fa.

fabada *f* Asturian stew made of beans, pork sausage and bacon.
fábrica *f* [establecimiento] factory; ~ **de papel** paper mill.
fabricación *f* manufacture; **de** ~ **casera** home-made; ~ **en serie** mass production.
fabricante *m y f* manufacturer.
fabricar *vt* **-1.** [producir] to manufacture, to make. **-2.** [construir] to build, to construct. **-3.** *fig* [inventar] to fabricate, to make up.
fábula *f* LITER fable; [leyenda] legend.
fabuloso, -sa *adj* **-1.** [ficticio] mythical. **-2.** [muy bueno] fabulous, fantastic.
facción *f* POLÍT faction. ◆ **facciones** *fpl* [rasgos] features.
faceta *f* facet.
facha *f* **-1.** [aspecto] appearance, look. **-2.** [mamarracho] mess; **vas hecho una** ~ you look a mess.
fachada *f* ARQUIT façade.
facial *adj* facial.
fácil *adj* **-1.** [gen] easy; ~ **de hacer** easy to do. **-2.** [probable] likely.
facilidad *f* **-1.** [simplicidad] ease, easiness. **-2.** [aptitud] aptitude; **tener** ~ **para algo** to have a gift for sthg. ◆ **facilidades** *fpl* [comodidades] facilities; ~**es de pago** easy (payment) terms.
facilitar *vt* **-1.** [simplificar] to facilitate, to make easy; [posibilitar] to make possible. **-2.** [proporcionar] to provide.
facsímil, facsímile *m* facsimile.
factible *adj* feasible.
fáctico, -ca → **poder**.
factor *m* [gen] factor.
factoría *f* [fábrica] factory.
factótum (*pl* **factotums**) *m y f* factotum.
factura *f* **-1.** [por mercancías, trabajo realizado] invoice. **-2.** [de gas, teléfono] bill; [en tienda, hotel] bill.
facturación *f* **-1.** [ventas] turnover *Br*, net revenue *Am*. **-2.** [de equipaje - en aeropuerto] checking-in; [- en estación] registration; **mostrador de** ~ check-in desk.
facturar *vt* **-1.** [cobrar]: ~**le a alguien algo** to invoice O bill sb for sthg. **-2.** [vender] to turn over. **-3.** [equipaje - en aeropuerto] to check in; [- en estación] to register.
facultad *f* **-1.** [gen] faculty. **-2.** [poder] power, right.
facultativo, -va ◇ *adj* **-1.** [voluntario]

optional. **-2.** [médico] medical. ◇ *m y f* doctor.

faena *f* [tarea] task, work (*U*).

faenar *vi* to fish.

fagot *m* [instrumento] bassoon.

faisán *m* pheasant.

faja *f* **-1.** [prenda de mujer, terapéutica] corset; [banda] sash, cummerbund. **-2.** [de terreno - pequeña] strip; [- grande] belt.

fajo *m* [de billetes, papel] wad; [de leña, cañas] bundle.

falacia *f* deceit, trick.

falaz *adj* false.

falda *f* **-1.** [prenda] skirt; ~ **escocesa** kilt; ~ **pantalón** culottes (*pl*). **-2.** [de montaña] slope, mountainside.

faldón *m* [de ropa] tail; [de cortina, mesa camilla] folds (*pl*).

falla *f* [gen & GEOL] fault. ◆ **fallas** *fpl* [fiesta] *celebrations in Valencia during which cardboard figures are burnt.*

fallar ◇ *vt* **-1.** [sentenciar] to pass sentence on; [premio] to award. **-2.** [equivocar - respuesta] to get wrong; [- tiro] to miss. ◇ *vi* **-1.** [equivocarse] to get it wrong; [no acertar] to miss. **-2.** [fracasar, flaquear] to fail; [- plan] to go wrong. **-3.** [decepcionar]: ~**le a alguien** to let sb down. **-4.** [sentenciar]: ~ **a favor/en contra de** to find in favour of/against.

fallecer *vi* to pass away, to die.

fallecimiento *m* decease, death.

fallo *m* **-1.** [error] mistake; DEP miss. **-2.** [sentencia - de juez, jurado] verdict.

fallutería *f Amer fam* hypocrisy.

falo *m* phallus.

falsear *vt* [hechos, historia] to falsify, to distort; [moneda, firma] to forge.

falsedad *f* **-1.** [falta de verdad, autenticidad] falseness. **-2.** [mentira] falsehood.

falsete *m* falsetto.

falsificar *vt* to forge.

falso, -sa *adj* **-1.** [rumor, excusa etc] false, untrue. **-2.** [dinero, firma, cuadro] forged; [joyas] fake; **jurar en** ~ to commit perjury. **-3.** [hipócrita] deceitful.

falta *f* **-1.** [carencia] lack; **hacer** ~ to be necessary; **me hace** ~ **suerte** I need some luck; **por** ~ **de** for want ◇ lack of. **-2.** [escasez] shortage. **-3.** [ausencia] absence; **echar en** ~ **algo/a alguien** [notar la ausencia de] to notice that sthg/sb is missing; [echar de menos] to miss sthg/sb. **-4.** [imperfección] fault; [error] mistake; ~ **de educación** bad manners (*pl*); ~ **de ortografía** spelling mistake. **-5.** DEP foul; [en tenis] fault. **-6.** DER of-

fence. ◆ **a falta de** *loc prep* in the absence of. ◆ **sin falta** *loc adv* without fail.

faltar *vi* **-1.** [no haber] to be lacking, to be needed; **falta aire** there's not enough air; **falta sal** it needs a bit of salt. **-2.** [estar ausente] to be absent ◇ missing; **falta Elena** Elena is missing. **-3.** [carecer]: **le faltan las fuerzas** he lacks ◇ doesn't have the strength. **-4.** [hacer falta]: **me falta tiempo** I need time. **-5.** [quedar]: **falta un mes para las vacaciones** there's a month to go till the holidays; **sólo te falta firmar** all you have to do is sign; **¿cuánto falta para Leeds?** how much further is it to Leeds?; **falta mucho por hacer** there is still a lot to be done; **falta poco para que llegue** it won't be long till he arrives. **-6.** *loc*: **¡no faltaba** ◇ **faltaría más!** [asentimiento] of course!; [rechazo] that tops it all!, that's a bit much! ◆ **faltar a** *vi* **-1.** [palabra, promesa] to break, not to keep; [deber, obligación] to neglect. **-2.** [cita, trabajo] not to turn up at; **¡no faltes (a la cita)!** don't miss it!, be there! **-3.** [no respetar] to be disrespectful towards; ~ **a alguien en algo** to offend sb in sthg.

falto, -ta *adj*: ~ **de** lacking in, short of.

fama *f* **-1.** [renombre] fame. **-2.** [reputación] reputation.

famélico, -ca *adj* starving, famished.

familia *f* family; **en** ~ in private.

familiar ◇ *adj* **-1.** [de familia] family (*antes de sust*). **-2.** [en el trato - agradable] friendly; [- en demasía] overly familiar. **-3.** [lenguaje, estilo] informal. **-4.** [conocido] familiar. ◇ *m y f* relative, relation.

familiaridad *f* familiarity.

familiarizar *vt*: ~ **(con)** to familiarize (with). ◆ **familiarizarse** *vpr*: ~**se con** [estudiar] to familiarize o.s. with; [acostumbrarse a] to get used to.

famoso, -sa *adj* famous.

fanático, -ca ◇ *adj* fanatical. ◇ *m y f* [gen] fanatic; DEP fan.

fanatismo *m* fanaticism.

fanfarria *f* **-1.** *fam* [jactancia] bragging. **-2.** [de música] fanfare; [banda] brass band.

fanfarrón, -ona *adj* boastful.

fango *m* mud.

fantasear *vi* to fantasize.

fantasía *f* [imaginación] imagination; [cosa imaginada] fantasy; **de** ~ [ropa] fancy; [bisutería] imitation.

fantasma ◇ *m* [espectro] ghost, phantom. ◇ *m y f fam* [fanfarrón] show-off.
fantástico, -ca *adj* fantastic.
fantoche *m* **-1.** [títere] puppet. **-2.** [mamarracho] (ridiculous) sight.
fardo *m* bundle.
farfullar *vt & vi* to gabble, to splutter.
faringitis *f inv* sore throat.
farmacéutico, -ca ◇ *adj* pharmaceutical. ◇ *m y f* chemist, pharmacist.
farmacia *f* [establecimiento] chemist's (shop) *Br*, pharmacy, drugstore *Am*; ~ de turno ○ de guardia duty chemist's.
fármaco *m* medicine, drug.
faro *m* **-1.** [para barcos] lighthouse. **-2.** [de coche] headlight, headlamp; ~ antiniebla foglamp.
farol *m* [farola] street lamp ○ light; [linterna] lantern, lamp.
farola *f* [farol] street lamp ○ light; [poste] lamppost.
farsa *f lit & fig* farce.
farsante *adj* deceitful.
fascículo *m* part, instalment (*of serialization*).
fascinante *adj* fascinating.
fascinar *vt* to fascinate.
fascismo *m* fascism.
fascista *adj, m y f* fascist.
fase *f* phase.
fastidiado, -da *adj* [de salud] ill; **ando ~ del estómago** I've got a bad stomach.
fastidiar *vt* **-1.** [estropear - fiesta etc] to spoil, to ruin; [- máquina, objeto etc] to break. **-2.** [molestar] to annoy, to bother. ◆ **fastidiarse** *vpr* **-1.** [estropearse - fiesta etc] to be ruined; [- máquina] to break down. **-2.** [aguantarse] to put up with it.
fastidio *m* **-1.** [molestia] nuisance, bother. **-2.** [enfado] annoyance.
fastidioso, -sa *adj* [molesto] annoying.
fastuoso, -sa *adj* lavish, sumptuous.
fatal ◇ *adj* **-1.** [mortal] fatal. **-2.** [muy malo] terrible, awful. **-3.** [inevitable] inevitable. ◇ *adv* terribly; **sentirse ~** to feel terrible.
fatalidad *f* **-1.** [destino] fate, destiny. **-2.** [desgracia] misfortune.
fatalismo *m* fatalism.
fatídico, -ca *adj* fateful, ominous.
fatiga *f* [cansancio] tiredness, fatigue. ◆ **fatigas** *fpl* [penas] hardships.
fatigar *vt* to tire, to weary. ◆ **fatigarse** *vpr* to get tired.
fatigoso, -sa *adj* tiring, fatiguing.

fatuo, -tua *adj* **-1.** [necio] fatuous, foolish. **-2.** [engreído] conceited.
fauna *f* fauna.
favor *m* favour; **a ~ de** in favour of; **hacerle un ~ a alguien** [ayudar a] to do sb a favour; *fam fig* [acostarse con] to go to bed with sb; **pedir un ~ a alguien** to ask sb a favour; **tener a ○ en su ~ a alguien** to enjoy sb's support. ◆ **por favor** *loc adv* please.
favorable *adj* favourable; **ser ~ a algo** to be in favour of sthg.
favorecer *vt* **-1.** [gen] to favour; [ayudar] to help, to assist. **-2.** [sentar bien] to suit.
favoritismo *m* favouritism.
favorito, -ta *adj, m y f* favourite.
fax *m inv* **-1.** [aparato] fax (machine); **mandar algo por ~** to fax sthg. **-2.** [documento] fax.
fayuquero *m Amer* dealer in contraband.
faz *f culto* **-1.** [cara] countenance, face. **-2.** [del mundo, de la tierra] face.
fe *f* **-1.** [gen] faith; **hacer algo de buena ~** to do sthg in good faith. **-2.** [documento] certificate; ~ de erratas errata (*pl*). **-3.** *loc*: **dar ~ de que** to testify that.
fealdad *f* [de rostro etc] ugliness.
febrero *m* February; *ver también* **septiembre**.
febril *adj* feverish; *fig* [actividad] hectic.
fecha *f* [gen] date; [momento actual] current date; **hasta la ~** to date, so far; ~ de caducidad [de alimentos] sell-by date; [de carné, pasaporte] expiry date; [de medicamento] "use before" date; ~ tope ○ límite deadline.
fechar *vt* to date.
fechoría *f* bad deed, misdemeanour.
fécula *f* starch (*in food*).
fecundación *f* fertilization; ~ artificial artificial insemination; ~ in vitro in vitro fertilization.
fecundar *vt* **-1.** [fertilizar] to fertilize. **-2.** [hacer productivo] to make fertile.
fecundo, -da *adj* [gen] fertile; [artista] prolific.
federación *f* federation.
federal *adj, m y f* federal.
federar *vt* to federate. ◆ **federarse** *vpr* **-1.** [formar federación] to become ○ form a federation. **-2.** [ingresar en federación] to join a federation.
feedback ['fidbak] (*pl* **feedbacks**) *m* feedback.
fehaciente *adj* irrefutable.

felicidad f happiness. ◆ **felicidades** interj: ¡~es! [gen] congratulations!; [en cumpleaños] happy birthday!

felicitación f -1. [acción]: **felicitaciones** congratulations. -2. [postal] greetings card.

felicitar vt to congratulate.

feligrés, -esa m y f parishioner.

felino, -na adj feline.

feliz adj -1. [gen] happy. -2. [afortunado] lucky. -3. [oportuno] timely.

felpa f [de seda] plush; [de algodón] towelling.

felpudo m doormat.

femenino, -na adj [gen] feminine; BOT & ZOOL female. ◆ **femenino** m GRAM feminine.

fémina f woman, female.

feminismo m feminism.

feminista adj, m y f feminist.

fémur (pl **fémures**) m femur, thighbone.

fénix m inv [ave] phoenix.

fenomenal adj [magnífico] wonderful.

fenómeno ◇ m [gen] phenomenon. ◇ adv fam brilliantly, fantastically; **pasarlo ~** to have a great time. ◇ interj: ¡~! great!, terrific!

feo, -a adj -1. [persona] ugly. -2. [aspecto, herida, conducta] nasty; **es ~ escupir** it's rude to spit.

féretro m coffin.

feria f -1. [gen] fair; **~ (de muestras)** trade fair. -2. [fiesta popular] festival.

fermentación f fermentation.

fermentar vt & vi to ferment.

ferocidad f ferocity, fierceness.

feroz adj -1. [animal, bestia] fierce, ferocious. -2. fig [criminal, asesino] cruel, savage. -3. fig [dolor, angustia] terrible.

férreo, -a adj lit & fig iron (antes de sust).

ferretería f ironmonger's (shop) Br, hardware store.

ferrocarril m [sistema, medio] railway, railroad Am; [tren] train; **por ~** by train.

ferroviario, -ria adj railway (antes de sust) Br, rail (antes de sust), railroad (antes de sust) Am.

ferry m ferry.

fértil adj lit & fig fertile.

fertilidad f lit & fig fertility.

fertilizante m fertilizer.

fertilizar vt to fertilize.

ferviente adj fervent.

fervor m fervour.

festejar vt [celebrar] to celebrate.

festejo m [fiesta] party. ◆ **festejos** mpl [fiestas] public festivities.

festín m banquet, feast.

festival m festival.

festividad f festivity.

festivo, -va adj -1. [de fiesta] festive; **día ~** (public) holiday. -2. [alegre] cheerful, jolly; [chistoso] funny, witty.

fetiche m fetish.

fétido, -da adj fetid, foul-smelling.

feto m foetus.

feudal adj feudal.

FF AA (abrev de **Fuerzas Armadas**) fpl Spanish armed forces.

fiable adj [máquina] reliable; [persona] trustworthy.

fiador, -ra m y f guarantor, surety; **salir ~ por** to vouch for.

fiambre m [comida] cold meat Br, cold cut Am.

fiambrera f lunch o sandwich box.

fianza f -1. [depósito] deposit. -2. DER bail; **bajo ~** on bail. -3. [garantía] security, bond.

fiar ◇ vt COM to sell on credit. ◇ vi COM to sell on credit; **ser de ~** fig to be trustworthy. ◆ **fiarse** vpr: ¡no te fíes! don't be too sure (about it)!; **~se de algo/alguien** to trust sthg/sb.

fiasco m fiasco.

FIBA (abrev de **Federación Internacional de Baloncesto Amateur**) f IABF.

fibra f [gen] fibre; [de madera] grain; **~ de vidrio** fibreglass.

ficción f [gen] fiction.

ficha f -1. [tarjeta] (index) card; [con detalles personales] file, record card. -2. [de guardarropa, aparcamiento] ticket. -3. [de teléfono] token. -4. [de juego - gen] counter; [en ajedrez] piece; [en un casino] chip. -5. INFORM card.

fichaje m DEP [contratación] signing (up); [importe] transfer fee.

fichar ◇ vt -1. [archivar] to note down on an index card, to file. -2. [suj: policía] to put on police files o records. -3. DEP to sign up. ◇ vi -1. [suj: trabajador - al entrar] to clock in; [- al salir] to clock out. -2. DEP: **~ (por)** to sign up (for).

fichero m INFORM file.

ficticio, -cia adj [imaginario] fictitious.

ficus m inv rubber plant.

fidedigno, -na adj reliable.

fidelidad f -1. [lealtad] loyalty; [de cónyuge, perro] faithfulness. -2. [precisión] accuracy; **alta ~** high fidelity.

fideo m noodle.

fiebre f fever; **tener** ~ to have a temperature; ~ **del heno** hay fever.

fiel adj **-1.** [leal - amigo, seguidor] loyal; [- cónyuge, perro] faithful. **-2.** [preciso] accurate. ◆ **fieles** mpl RELIG: **los** ~**es** the faithful.

fieltro m felt.

fiero, -ra adj savage, ferocious. ◆ **fiera** f [animal] wild animal.

fierro m Amer **-1.** [hierro] iron. **-2.** [navaja] penknife.

fiesta f **-1.** [reunión] party; [de pueblo etc] (local) festivities (pl); ~ **mayor** local celebrations for the festival of a town's patron saint. **-2.** [día] public holiday; **ser** ~ to be a public holiday; **hacer** ~ to be on holiday. ◆ **fiestas** fpl [vacaciones] holidays.

figura f **-1.** [gen] figure; [forma] shape. **-2.** [en naipes] picture card.

figuraciones fpl imaginings.

figurado, -da adj figurative.

figurar ◇ vi **-1.** [aparecer] ~ **(en)** to appear (in), to figure (in). **-2.** [ser importante] to be prominent ◇ important. ◇ vt **-1.** [representar] to represent. **-2.** [simular] to feign, to simulate. ◆ **figurarse** vpr [imaginarse] to imagine; **ya me lo figuraba yo** I thought as much.

fijación f **-1.** [gen & FOT] fixing. **-2.** [obsesión] fixation.

fijador m [líquido] fixative; ~ **de pelo** [crema] hair gel; [espray] hair spray.

fijar vt **-1.** [gen] to fix; [asegurar] to fasten; [cartel] to stick up; [sello] to stick on. **-2.** [significado] to establish; ~ **el domicilio** to take up residence; ~ **la mirada/la atención** to fix one's gaze/attention on. ◆ **fijarse** vpr to pay attention; ~**se en algo** [darse cuenta] to notice sthg; [prestar atención] to pay attention to sthg.

fijo, -ja adj **-1.** [gen] fixed; [sujeto] secure. **-2.** [cliente] regular. **-3.** [fecha] definite. **-4.** [empleado, trabajo] permanent.

fila f [hilera - gen] line; [- de asientos] row; **en** ~, **en** ~ **india** in line, in single file; **ponerse en** ~ to line up. ◆ **filas** fpl MIL ranks; **cerrar** ~**s** fig to close ranks.

filántropo, -pa m y f philanthropist.

filarmónico, -ca adj philharmonic.

filatelia f philately.

filete m [CULIN - grueso] (fillet) steak; [- delgado] fillet; [solomillo] sirloin.

filiación f POLÍT affiliation.

filial ◇ adj **-1.** [de hijo] filial. **-2.** [de empresa] subsidiary. ◇ f subsidiary.

filigrana f [en orfebrería] filigree.

Filipinas fpl: **(las)** ~ the Philippines (sg).

filipino, -na adj, m y f Filipino. ◆ **filipino** m [lengua] Filipino.

film = **filme**.

filmar vt to film, to shoot.

filme (pl **filmes**), **film** (pl **films**) m film Br, movie Am.

filmoteca f [archivo] film library; [sala de cine] film institute.

filo m (cutting) edge; **de doble** ~, **de dos** ~**s** lit & fig double-edged. ◆ **al filo de** loc prep just before.

filología f **-1.** [ciencia] philology. **-2.** [carrera] language and literature.

filón m **-1.** [de carbón etc] seam. **-2.** fig [mina] gold mine.

filoso, -sa, filudo, -da adj Amer sharp.

filosofía f [ciencia] philosophy.

filósofo, -fa m y f philosopher.

filtración f **-1.** [de agua] filtration. **-2.** fig [de noticia etc] leak.

filtrar vt **-1.** [tamizar] to filter. **-2.** fig [datos, noticia] to leak. ◆ **filtrarse** vpr **-1.** [penetrar]: ~**se (por)** to filter ◇ seep (through). **-2.** fig [datos, noticia] to be leaked.

filtro m **-1.** [gen] filter; [de cigarrillo] filter, filter tip. **-2.** [pócima] philtre.

filudo, -da = **filoso**.

fin m **-1.** [final] end; **dar** ◇ **poner** ~ **a algo** to put an end to sthg; **tocar a su** ~ to come to a close; ~ **de semana** weekend; **a** ~**es de** at the end of; **al** ◇ **por** ~ at last, finally; **a** ~ **de cuentas** after all; **al** ~ **y al cabo** after all. **-2.** [objetivo] aim, goal. ◆ **a fin de** loc conj in order to. ◆ **en fin** loc adv anyway.

final ◇ adj final, end (antes de sust). ◇ m end; ~ **feliz** happy ending; **a** ~**es de** at the end of; **al** ~ [en conclusión] in the end. ◇ f final.

finalidad f aim, purpose.

finalista m y f finalist.

finalizar ◇ vt to finish, to complete. ◇ vi: ~ **(con)** to end ◇ finish (in).

financiación f financing.

financiar vt to finance.

financiero, -ra ◇ adj financial. ◇ m y f [persona] financier. ◆ **financiera** f [firma] finance company.

financista m y f Amer financier.

finanzas fpl finance (U).

finca f [gen] property; [casa de campo] country residence.

fingir ◇ *vt* to feign. ◇ *vi* to pretend.
finiquito *m* settlement.
finito, -ta *adj* finite.
finlandés, -esa ◇ *adj* Finnish. ◇ *m y f* [persona] Finn. ◆**finlandés** *m* [lengua] Finnish.
Finlandia Finland.
fino, -na *adj* **-1.** [gen] fine; [delgado] thin; [cintura] slim. **-2.** [cortés] refined. **-3.** [agudo - oído, olfato] sharp, keen; [- gusto, humor, ironía] refined. ◆**fino** *m* dry sherry.
finura *f* [gen] fineness; [delgadez] thinness; [cortesía] refinement; [de oído, olfato] sharpness, keenness; [de gusto, humor, ironía] refinement.
firma *f* **-1.** [rúbrica] **signature**; [acción] signing. **-2.** [empresa] firm.
firmamento *m* firmament.
firmar *vt* to sign.
firme *adj* **-1.** [gen] firm; [mueble, andamio, edificio] stable. **-2.** [argumento, base] solid. **-3.** [carácter, actitud, paso] resolute.
firmeza *f* **-1.** [gen] firmness; [de mueble, edificio] stability. **-2.** [de argumento] solidity. **-3.** [de carácter, actitud] resolution.
fiscal ◇ *adj* tax (*antes de sust*), fiscal. ◇ *m y f* public prosecutor *Br*, district attorney *Am*.
fisco *m* treasury, exchequer.
fisgar, fisgonear *vi* [gen] to pry; [escuchando] to eavesdrop.
fisgón, -ona *m y f* nosy parker.
fisgonear = fisgar.
físico, -ca ◇ *adj* physical. ◇ *m y f* [persona] physicist. ◆**físico** *m* [complexión] physique. ◆**física** *f* [ciencia] physics (*U*).
fisiológico, -ca *adj* physiological.
fisionomía, fisonomía *f* features (*pl*), appearance.
fisioterapeuta *m y f* physiotherapist.
fisonomía = fisonomía.
fisura *f* [grieta] fissure.
flacidez, flaccidez *f* flabbiness.
flácido, -da, fláccido, -da *adj* flaccid, flabby.
flaco, -ca *adj* thin, skinny.
flagelar *vt* to flagellate.
flagrante *adj* flagrant.
flamante *adj* [vistoso] resplendent; [nuevo] brand-new.
flambear *vt* to flambé.
flamenco, -ca ◇ *adj* **-1.** MÚS flamenco (*antes de sust*). **-2.** [de Flandes] Flemish. ◇ *m y f* [de Flandes] Fleming. ◆**fla-**
menco *m* **-1.** [ave] flamingo. **-2.** [lengua] Flemish. **-3.** MÚS flamenco.
flan *m* crème caramel; **estar hecho** O **como un** ~ to shake like a jelly, to be a bundle of nerves.
flanco *m* flank.
flanquear *vt* to flank.
flaquear *vi* to weaken; *fig* to flag.
flaqueza *f* weakness.
flash [flaʃ] (*pl* **flashes**) *m* **-1.** FOT flash. **-2.** [informativo] newsflash.
flato *m*: **tener** ~ to have a stitch.
flatulento, -ta *adj* flatulent.
flauta ◇ *f* flute; ~ **dulce** recorder; **de la gran** ~ *Amer fig* tremendous. ◇ *interj*: **¡(la gran)** ~! *Amer* good grief!, good heavens!
flecha *f* [gen] arrow; ARQUIT spire.
flechazo *m fam fig* [amoroso]: **fue un** ~ it was love at first sight.
fleco *m* [adorno] fringe.
flema *f* phlegm.
flemático, -ca *adj* [tranquilo] phlegmatic.
flemón *m* gumboil.
flequillo *m* fringe.
flete *m* **-1.** [precio] freightage. **-2.** [carga] cargo, freight.
flexible *adj* flexible.
flexo *m* adjustable table lamp O light.
flipar *fam vi* **-1.** [disfrutar] to have a wild time. **-2.** [asombrarse] to be gobsmacked. **-3.** [con una droga] to be stoned O high.
flirtear *vi* to flirt.
flojear *vi* [decaer - piernas, fuerzas etc] to weaken; [- memoria] to be failing; [- película, libro] to flag; [- calor, trabajo] to ease off; [- ventas] to fall off.
flojera *f* lethargy, feeling of weakness.
flojo, -ja *adj* **-1.** [suelto] loose. **-2.** [débil - persona, bebida] weak; [- sonido] faint; [- tela] thin; [- salud] poor; [- viento] light. **-3.** [inactivo - mercado, negocio] slack.
flor *f* **-1.** BOT flower; **echar** ~**es** **a alguien** to pay sb compliments. **-2.** [lo mejor]: **la** ~ **(y nata)** the crème de la crème, the cream. ◆**a flor de** *loc adv*: **a** ~ **de agua/tierra** at water/ground level.
flora *f* flora.
florecer *vi* to flower; *fig* to flourish.
floreciente *adj fig* flourishing.
florero *m* vase.
florido, -da *adj* [con flores] flowery; [estilo, lenguaje] florid.

florista *m y f* florist.

floristería *f* florist's (shop).

flota *f* fleet.

flotación *f* [gen & ECON] flotation.

flotador *m* **-1.** [para nadar] rubber ring. **-2.** [de caña de pescar] float.

flotar *vi* [gen & ECON] to float; [banderas] to flutter.

flote ♦ a flote *loc adv* afloat; **salir a ~** *fig* to get back on one's feet.

flotilla *f* flotilla.

fluctuar *vi* [variar] to fluctuate.

fluidez *f* **-1.** [gen] fluidity; [del tráfico] free flow; [de relaciones] smoothness. **-2.** *fig* [en el lenguaje] fluency.

fluido, -da *adj* **-1.** [gen] fluid; [tráfico] free-flowing. **-2.** [relaciones] smooth. **-3.** *fig* [lenguaje] fluent. **♦ fluido** *m* fluid; **~ eléctrico** electric current O power.

fluir *vi* to flow.

flujo *m* flow; **~ de caja** cash flow.

flúor *m* fluorine.

fluorescente *m* strip light.

fluvial *adj* river (*antes de sust*).

FM (*abrev de* **frecuencia modulada**) *f* FM.

FMI (*abrev de* **Fondo Monetario Internacional**) *m* IMF.

fobia *f* phobia.

foca *f* seal.

foco *m* **-1.** *fig* [centro] centre, focal point. **-2.** [lámpara - para un punto] spotlight; [- para una zona] floodlight. **-3.** FÍS & GEOM focus. **-4.** *Amer* [bombilla] light bulb.

fofo, -fa *adj* flabby.

fogata *f* bonfire, fire.

fogón *m* [para cocinar] stove.

fogoso, -sa *adj* passionate.

fogueo *m*: **de ~** blank.

foie-gras [fwaˈɣras] *m* (pâté de) foie-gras.

folclore, folclor, folklor *m* folklore.

folio *m* [hoja] leaf, sheet; [tamaño] folio.

folklor = **folclore**.

follaje *m* foliage.

folletín *m* [dramón] melodrama.

folleto *m* [turístico, publicitario] brochure; [explicativo, de instrucciones] leaflet.

follón *m fam* **-1.** [discusión] row; **se armó ~** there was an almighty row. **-2.** [lío] mess; **¡vaya ~!** what a mess!

fomentar *vt* to encourage, to foster.

fomento *m* encouragement, fostering.

fonda *f* boarding house.

fondear ◇ *vi* to anchor. ◇ *vt* [sondear] to sound; [registrar - barco] to search.

fondo *m* **-1.** [de recipiente, mar, piscina] bottom; **tocar ~** [embarcación] to scrape along the sea/river bed; *fig* to hit rock bottom; **doble ~** false bottom. **-2.** [de habitación etc] back; **al ~ de** [calle, pasillo] at the end of; [sala] at the back of. **-3.** [dimensión] depth. **-4.** [de tela, cuadro, foto] background; **al ~** in the background. **-5.** [de asunto, tema] heart, bottom. **-6.** ECON fund; **a ~ perdido** non-returnable; **~ común** kitty; **~ de amortización/de inversión/de pensiones** ECON sinking/investment/pension fund. **-7.** [de biblioteca, archivo] catalogue, collection. **-8.** DEP stamina. **-9.** *Amer* [combinación] petticoat. **♦ fondos** *mpl* ECON [capital] funds; **recaudar ~s** to raise funds. **♦ a fondo** ◇ *loc adv* thoroughly. ◇ *loc adj* thorough. **♦ en el fondo** *loc adv* **-1.** [en lo más íntimo] deep down. **-2.** [en lo esencial] basically.

fonético, -ca *adj* phonetic. **♦ fonética** *f* [ciencia] phonetics (*U*).

fontanería *f* plumbing.

fontanero, -ra *m y f* plumber.

football = **fútbol**.

footing [ˈfutin] *m* jogging; **hacer ~** to go jogging.

forajido, -da *m y f* outlaw.

foráneo, -a *adj* foreign.

forastero, -ra *m y f* stranger.

forcejear *vi* to struggle.

fórceps *m inv* forceps.

forense ◇ *adj* forensic. ◇ *m y f* pathologist.

forestal *adj* forest (*antes de sust*).

forja *f* [fragua] forge; [forjadura] forging.

forjar *vt* **-1.** [metal] to forge. **-2.** *fig* [inventarse] to invent; [crear] to build up. **♦ forjarse** *vpr fig* [labrarse] to carve out for o.s.

forma *f* **-1.** [gen] shape, form; **en ~ de** in the shape of; **guardar las ~s** to keep up appearances. **-2.** [manera] way, manner; **de cualquier ~, de todas ~s** anyway, in any case; **de esta ~** in this way; **de ~ que** in such a way that, so that. **-3.** ARTE & LITER form. **-4.** [condición física] fitness; **estar en ~** to be fit. **♦ formas** *fpl* **-1.** [silueta] figure (*sg*). **-2.** [modales] social conventions.

formación *f* **-1.** [gen & MIL] formation. **-2.** [educación] training; **~ profesional** vocational training. **-3.** [conjunto] grouping.

formal *adj* **-1.** [gen] formal. **-2.** [que se porta bien] well-behaved, good. **-3.** [de confianza] reliable. **-4.** [serio] serious.

formalidad *f* **-1.** [gen] formality. **-2.** [educación] **(good) manners** (*pl*). **-3.** [fiabilidad] reliability. **-4.** [seriedad] seriousness.

formalizar *vt* to formalize.

formar ◇ *vt* **-1.** [gen] to form. **-2.** [educar] to train, to educate. ◇ *vi* MIL to fall in. ◆ **formarse** *vpr* **-1.** [gen] to form. **-2.** [educarse] to be trained ○ educated.

formatear *vt* INFORM to format.

formato® *m* [gen & INFORM] format.

formica® *f* Formica®.

formidable *adj* [enorme] tremendous; [extraordinario] amazing, fantastic.

fórmula *f* formula; **~ uno** formula one.

formular *vt* to formulate.

formulario *m* form.

fornido, -da *adj* well-built.

foro *m* **-1.** [tribunal] court (of law). **-2.** TEATR back of the stage. **-3.** [debate] forum.

forofo, -fa *m y f fam* fan, supporter.

forraje *m* fodder.

forrar *vt*: **~ (de)** [libro] to cover (with); [ropa] to line (with); [asiento] to upholster (with).

forro *m* [de libro] cover; [de ropa] lining; [de asiento] upholstery.

fortalecer *vt* to strengthen.

fortaleza *f* **-1.** [gen] strength. **-2.** [recinto] fortress.

fortificación *f* fortification.

fortuito, -ta *adj* chance (*antes de sust*).

fortuna *f* **-1.** [suerte] **(good) luck; por ~** fortunately, luckily. **-2.** [destino] fortune, fate. **-3.** [riqueza] fortune.

forúnculo, furúnculo *m* boil.

forzado, -da *adj* forced.

forzar *vt* **-1.** [gen] to force; **~ la vista** to strain one's eyes. **-2.** [violar] to rape.

forzoso, -sa *adj* [obligatorio] obligatory, compulsory; [inevitable] inevitable; [necesario] necessary.

forzudo, -da *adj* strong.

fosa *f* **-1.** [sepultura] grave. **-2.** ANAT cavity; **~s nasales** nostrils. **-3.** [hoyo] pit; **~ marina** ocean trough.

fosfato *m* phosphate.

fosforescente *adj* phosphorescent.

fósforo *m* **-1.** QUÍM phosphorus. **-2.** [cerilla] match.

fósil *m* CIENCIA fossil.

foso *m* [hoyo] ditch; [de fortaleza] moat; [de garaje] pit; DEP & TEATR pit.

foto *f* photo.

fotocomponer *vt* IMPRENTA to typeset.

fotocopia *f* [objeto] photocopy.

fotocopiadora *f* photocopier.

fotocopiar *vt* to photocopy.

fotoeléctrico, -ca *adj* photoelectric.

fotogénico, -ca *adj* photogenic.

fotografía *f* **-1.** [arte] photography. **-2.** [objeto] photograph.

fotografiar *vt* to photograph.

fotógrafo, -fa *m y f* photographer.

fotomatón *m* passport photo machine.

fotonovela *f* photo story.

fotorrobot (*pl* **fotorrobots**) *f* Identikit® picture.

fotosíntesis *f inv* photosynthesis.

FP (*abrev de* **formación profesional**) *f vocationally orientated secondary education in Spain for pupils aged 14-18.*

fra. (*abrev de* **factura**) inv.

frac (*pl* **fracs**) *m* tails (*pl*), dress coat.

fracasar *vi*: **~ (en/como)** to fail (at/as).

fracaso *m* failure; **todo fue un ~** the whole thing was a disaster.

fracción *f* **-1.** [gen] fraction. **-2.** POLÍT faction.

fraccionario, -ria *adj* fractional; **moneda fraccionaria** small change.

fractura *f* fracture.

fragancia *f* fragrance.

fraganti ◆ **in fraganti** *loc adv*: **coger a alguien in ~** to catch sb red-handed ○ in the act.

fragata *f* frigate.

frágil *adj* [objeto] fragile; [persona] frail.

fragilidad *f* [de objeto] fragility; [de persona] frailty.

fragmentar *vt* [romper] to fragment; [dividir] to divide.

fragmento *m* fragment, piece; [de obra] excerpt.

fragor *m* [de batalla] clamour; [de trueno] crash.

fragua *f* forge.

fraguar ◇ *vt* **-1.** [forjar] to forge. **-2.** *fig* [idear] to think up. ◇ *vi* to set, to harden. ◆ **fraguarse** *vpr* to be in the offing.

fraile *m* friar.

frambuesa *f* raspberry.

francés, -esa ◇ *adj* French. ◇ *m y f* Frenchman (*f* Frenchwoman); **los franceses** the French. ◆ **francés** *m* [lengua] French.

Francia France.

francmasonería *f* Freemasonry.

franco, -ca *adj* **-1.** [sincero] frank, open; [directo] frank. **-2.** [sin obstáculos, gastos] free. ◆ **franco** *m* [moneda] franc.

francotirador, -ra *m* y *f* MIL sniper.

franela *f* flannel.

franja *f* strip; [en bandera, uniforme] stripe.

franquear *vt* **-1.** [paso, camino] to clear. **-2.** [río, montaña etc] to negotiate, to cross. **-3.** [correo] to frank.

franqueo *m* postage.

franqueza *f* [sinceridad] frankness.

franquicia *f* exemption.

franquismo *m*: el ~ [régimen] the Franco regime; [doctrina] Franco's doctrine.

frasco *m* small bottle.

frase *f* **-1.** [oración] sentence. **-2.** [locución] expression; ~ **hecha** [modismo] set phrase; [tópico] cliché.

fraternidad, fraternización *f* brotherhood, fraternity.

fraterno, -na *adj* brotherly, fraternal.

fraude *m* fraud; ~ **fiscal** tax evasion.

fraudulento, -ta *adj* fraudulent.

fray *m* brother.

frazada *f* *Amer* blanket; ~ **eléctrica** electric blanket.

frecuencia *f* frequency; **con** ~ often; ~ **modulada, modulación de** ~ frequency modulation.

frecuentar *vt* [lugar] to frequent; [persona] to see, to visit.

frecuente *adj* [reiterado] frequent; [habitual] common.

fregadero *m* (kitchen) sink.

fregado, -da *adj* *Amer fam* troublesome, annoying.

fregar *vt* **-1.** [limpiar] to wash; ~ **los platos** to do the washing-up. **-2.** [frotar] scrub. **-3.** *Amer fam* [molestar] to bother, to pester.

fregona *f* **-1.** *despec* [criada] skivvy. **-2.** [utensilio] mop.

freidora *f* [gen] deep fat fryer; [para patatas fritas] chip pan.

freír *vt* CULIN to fry.

frenar ◇ *vt* **-1.** AUTOM to brake. **-2.** [contener] to check. ◇ *vi* to stop; AUTOM to brake.

frenazo *m* **-1.** AUTOM: **dar un** ~ to brake hard. **-2.** *fig* [parón] sudden stop.

frenesí (*pl* **frenesíes**) *m* frenzy.

frenético, -ca *adj* **-1.** [colérico] furious, mad. **-2.** [enloquecido] frenzied, frantic.

freno *m* **-1.** AUTOM brake. **-2.** [de caballerías] bit. **-3.** *fig* [contención] check; **poner** ~ **a** to put a stop to.

frenopático, -ca *adj* psychiatric.

frente ◇ *f* forehead; ~ **a** ~ face to face. ◇ *m* front; **estar al** ~ **(de)** to be at the head (of); **hacer** ~ **a** to face up to; ~ **frío** cold front. ◆ **de frente** *loc adv* **-1.** [hacia delante] forwards. **-2.** [uno contra otro] head on. ◆ **frente a** *loc prep* **-1.** [enfrente de] opposite. **-2.** [con relación a] towards.

fresa *f* [planta, fruto] strawberry.

fresco, -ca ◇ *adj* **-1.** [gen] fresh; [temperatura] cool; [pintura, tinta] wet. **-2.** [caradura] cheeky. ◇ *m* y *f* [caradura] cheeky person. ◆ **fresco** *m* **-1.** ARTE fresco; **al** ~ in fresco. **-2.** [frescor] coolness; **hace** ~ it's chilly; **tomar el** ~ to get a breath of fresh air.

frescor *m* coolness, freshness.

frescura *f* **-1.** [gen] freshness. **-2.** [descaro] cheek, nerve.

fresno *m* ash (tree).

fresón *m* large strawberry.

frialdad *f* lit & fig coldness.

fricción *f* [gen] friction; [friega] rub, massage.

friega *f* massage.

frigidez *f* frigidity.

frigorífico, -ca *adj* [camión] refrigerator (*antes de sust*); [cámara] cold. ◆ **frigorífico** *m* refrigerator, fridge *Br*, icebox *Am*.

frijol, fríjol *m* *Amer* bean.

frío, -a *adj* [gen] cold; [inmutable] cool; **dejar a alguien** ~ to leave sb cold. ◆ **frío** *m* cold; **hacer un** ~ **que pela** to be freezing cold; **tener** ~ to be cold; **coger a alguien en** ~ *fig* to catch sb on the hop.

friolento, -ta *adj* *Amer* sensitive to the cold.

friolero, -ra *adj* sensitive to the cold.

frisar *vt* to be getting on for (*a certain age*).

frito, -ta ◇ *pp* → **freír**. ◇ *adj* **-1.** [alimento] fried. **-2.** *fam fig* [persona - harta] fed up (to the back teeth); [- dormida] flaked out, asleep. ◆ **frito** *m* (*gen pl*) fried food (*U*).

frívolo, -la *adj* frivolous.

frondoso, -sa *adj* leafy.

frontal *adj* frontal.

frontera *f* border; *fig* [límite] bounds (*pl*).

fronterizo, -za *adj* border (*antes de sust*).

frontispicio *m* **-1.** [de edificio - remate] pediment. **-2.** [de libro] frontispiece.

frontón *m* [deporte] **pelota**; [cancha] pelota court.

frotar *vt* to rub. ◆ **frotarse** *vpr*: ~**se las manos** to rub one's hands.

fructífero, -ra *adj* fruitful.

frugal *adj* frugal.

fruncir *vt* **-1.** [labios] to purse; ~ **el ceño** to frown. **-2.** [tela] to gather.

fruslería *f* triviality, trifle.

frustración *f* frustration.

frustrar *vt* [persona] to frustrate. ◆ **frustrarse** *vpr* **-1.** [persona] to get frustrated. **-2.** [ilusiones] to be thwarted; [proyecto] to fail.

fruta *f* fruit.

frutal *m* fruit tree.

frutería *f* fruit shop.

frutero, -ra *m y f* [persona] fruiterer. ◆ **frutero** *m* [recipiente] fruit bowl.

frutilla *f Amer* strawberry.

fruto *m* **-1.** [naranja, plátano etc] fruit; [nuez, avellana etc] nut; ~**s secos** dried fruit and nuts. **-2.** [resultado] fruit; **dar** ~ to bear fruit; **sacar** ~ **a** ○ **de algo** to profit from sthg.

fucsia *f* [planta] fuchsia.

fue -1. → **ir. -2.** → **ser.**

fuego *m* **-1.** [gen & MIL] fire; [de cocina, fogón] ring, burner; **a** ~ **lento/vivo** CULIN over a low/high heat; **pegar** ~ **a algo** to set sthg on fire, to set fire to sthg; **pedir/dar** ~ to ask for/give a light; **¿tiene** ~? have you got a light?; ~**s artificiales** fireworks. **-2.** [apasionamiento] passion, ardour.

fuelle *m* [gen] bellows (*pl*).

fuente *f* **-1.** [manantial] spring. **-2.** [construcción] fountain. **-3.** [bandeja] (serving) dish. **-4.** *fig* [origen] source; ~**s oficiales** official sources.

fuera ◇ *v* **-1.** → **ir. -2.** → **ser.** ◇ *adv* **-1.** [en el exterior] outside; **le echó** ~ she threw him out; **hacia** ~ outwards; **por** ~ (on the) outside. **-2.** [en otro lugar] away; [en el extranjero] abroad; **de** ~ [extranjero] from abroad. **-3.** *fig* [alejado]: ~ **de** [alcance, peligro] out of; [cálculos, competencia] outside; **estar** ~ **de sí** to be beside o.s. (with rage). **-4.** DEP: ~ **de juego** offside. ◇ *interj* **¡~!** [gen] (get) out!; [en el teatro] (get) off! ◆ **fuera de** *loc prep* [excepto] except for, apart from. ◆ **fuera de serie** *adj* exceptional.

fueraborda *m inv* outboard motor ○ engine.

fuero *m* **-1.** [ley local] (*gen pl*) ancient regional law still existing in some parts of Spain. **-2.** [jurisdicción] code of laws.

fuerte ◇ *adj* **-1.** [gen] strong. **-2.** [carácter] unpleasant. **-3.** [frío, dolor, color] intense; [lluvia] heavy; [ruido] loud; [golpe, pelea] hard. **-4.** [comida, salsa] rich. **-5.** [nudo] tight. ◇ *adv* **-1.** [intensamente - gen] hard; [- abrazar, agarrar] tight. **-2.** [abundantemente] **a lot. -3.** [en voz alta] loudly. ◇ *m* **-1.** [fortificación] fort. **-2.** [punto fuerte] strong point, forte.

fuerza *f* **-1.** [gen] strength; [violencia] force; [de sonido] loudness; [de dolor] intensity; **por** ~ of necessity; **tener** ~**s para** to have the strength to; **mayor** DER force majeure; [en seguros] act of God; **no llegué por un caso de** ~ **mayor** I didn't make it due to circumstances beyond my control; ~ **de voluntad** willpower; **a** ~ **de** by dint of; **a la** ~ [contra la voluntad] by force; [por necesidad] of necessity; **por la** ~ by force. **-2.** FÍS & MIL force; ~**s armadas** armed forces; ~**s del orden público** police (*pl*). **-3.** ELECTR power. ◆ **fuerzas** *fpl* [grupo] forces.

fuese -1. → **ir. -2.** → **ser.**

fuga *f* **-1.** [huida] escape. **-2.** [escape] leak. **-3.** MÚS fugue.

fugarse *vpr* to escape; ~ **de casa** to run away from home; ~ **con alguien** to run off with sb.

fugaz *adj* fleeting.

fugitivo, -va *m y f* fugitive.

fui → **ir.**

fulano, -na *m y f* what's his/her name, so-and-so. ◆ **fulana** *f* [prostituta] tart, whore.

fulgor *m* shining; [de disparo] flash.

fulminante *adj fig* [despido, muerte] sudden; [enfermedad] devastating; [mirada] withering.

fulminar *vt* [suj: enfermedad] to strike down; ~ **a alguien con la mirada** to look daggers at sb.

fumador, -ra *m y f* smoker; ~ **pasivo** passive smoker; **no** ~ nonsmoker.

fumar *vt & vi* to smoke.

fumigar *vt* to fumigate.

función *f* **-1.** [gen] function; [trabajo] duty; **director en funciones** acting director; **entrar en funciones** to take up one's duties. **-2.** CIN & TEATR show. ◆ **en función de** *loc prep* depending on.

funcional *adj* functional.

funcionamiento *m* operation, functioning.

funcionar *vi* to work; ~ **con gasolina** to run on petrol; **"no funciona"** "out of order".

funcionario, -ria *m y f* civil servant.

funda *f* [de sofá, máquina de escribir] cover; [de almohada] **case**; [de disco] sleeve; [de pistola] **sheath**.

fundación *f* foundation.

fundador, -ra *m y f* founder.

fundamental *adj* fundamental.

fundamentar *vt* **-1.** *fig* [basar] to base. **-2.** CONSTR to lay the foundations of. ◆ **fundamentarse en** *vpr fig* [basarse] to be based ○ founded on.

fundamento *m* **-1.** [base] foundation, basis. **-2.** [razón] reason, grounds (*pl*); **sin ~** unfounded, groundless.

fundar *vt* **-1.** [crear] to found. **-2.** [basar]: ~ **(en)** to base (on). ◆ **fundarse** *vpr* [basarse]: ~**se (en)** to be based (on).

fundición *f* **-1.** [fusión - de vidrio] melting; [- de metal] **smelting**. **-2.** [taller] foundry.

fundir *vt* **-1.** [METAL - plomo] to melt; [- hierro] to smelt. **-2.** ELECTR to fuse; [bombilla, fusible] to blow. **-3.** COM & *fig* to merge. ◆ **fundirse** *vpr* **-1.** ELECTR to blow. **-2.** [derretirse] to melt. **-3.** COM & *fig* to merge.

fúnebre *adj* funeral (*antes de sust*).

funeral *m* (*gen pl*) funeral.

funerario, -ria *adj* funeral (*antes de sust*). ◆ **funeraria** *f* undertaker's *Br*, mortician's *Am*.

funesto, -ta *adj* fateful, disastrous.

fungir *vi Amer* to act, to serve.

funicular *m* **-1.** [por tierra] funicular. **-2.** [por aire] cable car.

furgón *m* AUTOM van; FERROC wagon.

furgoneta *f* van.

furia *f* fury.

furioso, -sa *adj* furious.

furor *m* **-1.** [enfado] fury, rage. **-2.** *loc*: **hacer ~** to be all the rage.

furtivo, -va *adj* [mirada, sonrisa] furtive.

furúnculo = **forúnculo**.

fusible *m* fuse.

fusil *m* rifle.

fusilar *vt* [ejecutar] to execute by firing squad, to shoot.

fusión *f* **-1.** [agrupación] merging. **-2.** [de empresas, bancos] **merger**. **-3.** [derretimiento] melting. **-4.** FÍS fusion.

fusionar *vt* [gen & ECON] to merge. **-2.** FÍS to fuse. ◆ **fusionarse** *vpr* ECON to merge.

fusta *f* riding crop.

fustán *m Amer* petticoat.

fuste *m* shaft.

fútbol, football ['fudbol] *m* football; ~ **sala** indoor five-a-side.

futbolín *m* table football.

futbolista *m y f* footballer.

fútil *adj* trivial.

futilidad *f* triviality.

futón *m* futon.

futuro, -ra *adj* future. ◆ **futuro** *m* [gen & GRAM] future. ◆ **futuros** *mpl* ECON futures.

futurología *f* futurology.

G

g¹, G *f* [letra] g, G.

g² (*abrev de* **gramo**) g.

gabacho, -cha *fam despec m y f* Frog, *pejorative term referring to a French person.*

gabán *m* overcoat.

gabardina *f* [prenda] raincoat, mac.

gabinete *m* **-1.** [gobierno] cabinet. **-2.** [despacho] office. **-3.** [sala] study.

gacela *f* gazelle.

gaceta *f* gazette.

gachas *fpl* CULIN (corn) porridge (*U*).

gacho, -cha *adj* drooping.

gafas *fpl* glasses; ~ **graduales** prescription glasses; ~ **de sol** sunglasses.

gafe ◇ *adj* jinxed. ◇ *m y f* jinxed person.

gaita *f* [instrumento] bagpipes (*pl*).

gajes *mpl*: ~ **del oficio** occupational hazards.

gajo *m* [trozo de fruta] segment.

gala *f* **-1.** [fiesta] gala; **ropa/uniforme de gala** [ropa] full dress/uniform; **cena de gala** black tie dinner, formal dinner. **-2.** [ropa]: **galas** finery (*U*), best clothes. **-3.** [actuación] show. **-4.** *loc*: **hacer gala de algo** [preciarse] to be proud of sthg; [exhibir] to demonstrate sthg.

galán *m* TEATR leading man, lead.

galante *adj* gallant.

galantear *vt* to court, to woo.

galantería *f* **-1.** [cualidad] politeness. **-2.** [acción] gallantry, compliment.

galápago *m* turtle.

galardón *m* award, prize.

galaxia f galaxy.

galera f galley.

galería f **-1.** [gen] gallery; [corredor descubierto] verandah. **-2.** fig [vulgo] masses (pl). ◆ **galerías (comerciales)** fpl shopping arcade (sg).

Gales: [el país de] ~ Wales.

galés, -esa ◇ adj Welsh. ◇ m y f Welshman m (f Welshwoman); **los galeses** the Welsh. ◆ **galés** m [lengua] Welsh.

galgo m greyhound.

galimatías m inv [lenguaje] gibberish (U); [lío] jumble.

gallardía f **-1.** [valentía] bravery. **-2.** [elegancia] elegance.

gallego, -ga adj, m y f Galician. ◆ **gallego** m [lengua] Galician.

galleta f CULIN biscuit.

gallina ◇ f [ave] hen; **la ~ ciega** blind man's buff. ◇ m y f fam [persona] chicken, coward.

gallinero m **-1.** [corral] henhouse. **-2.** fam TEATR gods (sg).

gallo m **-1.** [ave] cock, cockerel; **en menos que canta un ~** fam in no time at all. **-2.** [al cantar] false note; [al hablar] squeak. **-3.** [pez] John Dory.

galo, -la ◇ adj HIST Gallic; [francés] French. ◇ m y f [persona] Gaul.

galón m **-1.** [adorno] braid; MIL stripe. **-2.** [medida] gallon.

galopar vi to gallop.

galope m gallop; **al ~** at a gallop; **a ~ tendido** at full gallop.

galpón m Amer shed.

gama f [gen] range; MÚS scale.

gamba f prawn.

gamberro, -rra ◇ adj loutish. ◇ m y f vandal; [en fútbol etc] hooligan.

gamo m fallow deer.

gamonal m Amer village chief.

gamuza f **-1.** [tejido] chamois (leather); [trapo] duster. **-2.** [animal] chamois.

gana f **-1.** [afán]: ~ **(de)** desire ○ wish (to); **de buena ~** willingly; **de mala ~** unwillingly; **me da/no me da la ~ hacerlo** I damn well feel like/don't damn well feel like doing it. **-2.** [apetito] appetite. ◆ **ganas** fpl [deseo]: **tener ~s de algo/hacer algo, sentir ~s de algo/hacer algo** to feel like sthg/doing sthg; **quedarse con ~s de hacer algo** not to manage to do sthg; **no tengo ~s de que me pongan una multa** I don't fancy getting a fine; **tenerle ~s a alguien** to have it in for sb.

ganadería f **-1.** [actividad] livestock farming. **-2.** [ganado] livestock.

ganado m livestock, stock; **~ porcino** pigs (pl); **~ vacuno** cattle (pl).

ganador, -ra ◇ adj winning. ◇ m y f winner.

ganancia f [rendimiento] profit; [ingreso] earnings (pl); **~s y pérdidas** profit and loss; **~ líquida** net profit.

ganancial → **bien**.

ganar ◇ vt **-1.** [gen] to win; [sueldo, dinero] to earn; [peso, tiempo, terreno] to gain. **-2.** [derrotar] to beat. **-3.** [aventajar]: ~ **a alguien en algo** to be better than sb as regards sthg. **-4.** [cima etc] to reach. **-5.** [ciudad etc] to take, to capture. ◇ vi **-1.** [vencer] to win. **-2.** [lograr dinero] to earn money. **-3.** [mejorar]: ~ **en algo** to gain in sthg. ◆ **ganarse** vpr **-1.** [conquistar - simpatía, respeto] to earn; [- persona] to win over. **-2.** [merecer] to deserve.

ganchillo m [aguja] crochet hook; [labor] crochet; **hacer ~** to crochet.

gancho m **-1.** [gen] hook; [de percha] peg. **-2.** [cómplice - de timador] decoy; [- de vendedor] person who attracts buyers. **-3.** fam [atractivo] sex appeal.

gandul, -la fam ◇ adj lazy. ◇ m y f lazybones, layabout.

ganga f fam snip, bargain.

gangrena f gangrene.

gángster (pl **gángsters**) m gangster.

ganso, -sa m y f **-1.** [ave - hembra] goose; [- macho] gander. **-2.** fam [persona] idiot, fool.

garabatear vi & vt to scribble.

garabato m scribble.

garaje m garage.

garante m y f guarantor; **salir ~** to act as guarantor.

garantía f **-1.** [gen] guarantee; **de ~** reliable, dependable; **ser ~ de algo** to guarantee sthg; **~s constitucionales** constitutional rights. **-2.** [fianza] surety.

garantizar vt **-1.** [gen] to guarantee; ~ **algo a alguien** to assure sb of sthg. **-2.** [avalar] to vouch for.

garbanzo m chickpea.

garbeo m fam stroll; **dar un ~** to go for ○ take a stroll.

garbo m [de persona] grace; [de escritura] stylishness, style.

garete m: **ir** ○ **irse al ~** fam to come adrift.

garfio m hook.

gargajo m phlegm.

garganta f **-1.** ANAT throat. **-2.** [desfiladero] gorge.

gargantilla f choker, necklace.

gárgara f (gen pl) gargle, gargling (U); **hacer ~s** to gargle; **mandar a alguien a hacer ~s** fam to send sb packing; **¡vete a hacer ~s!** fam get lost!

gárgola f gargoyle.

garita f [gen] cabin; [de conserje] porter's lodge; MIL sentry box.

garito m despec [casa de juego] gambling den; [establecimiento] dive.

garra f [de animal] claw; [de ave de rapiña] talon; despec [de persona] paw, hand; **caer en las ~s de alguien** to fall into sb's clutches; **tener ~** [persona] to have charisma; [novela, canción etc] to be gripping.

garrafa f carafe.

garrafal adj monumental, enormous.

garrapata f tick.

garrapiñar vt [fruta] to candy; [almendras etc] to coat with sugar.

garrote m **-1.** [palo] club, stick. **-2.** [instrumento] garotte.

garúa f Amer drizzle.

garza f heron; **~ real** grey heron.

gas m gas; **~ ciudad/natural** town/ natural gas; **~ butano** butane (gas); **~ lacrimógeno** tear gas. ◆ **gases** mpl [en el estómago] wind (U). ◆ **a todo gas** loc adv flat out.

gasa f gauze.

gaseoducto m gas pipeline.

gaseoso, -sa adj gaseous; [bebida] fizzy. ◆ **gaseosa** f lemonade.

gasóleo m diesel oil.

gasolina f petrol Br, gas Am; **poner ~** to fill up (with petrol).

gasolinera f petrol station Br, gas station Am.

gastado, -da adj [ropa, pieza etc] worn out; [frase, tema] hackneyed; [persona] broken, burnt out.

gastar ◇ vt **-1.** [consumir - dinero, tiempo] to spend; [- gasolina, electricidad] to use (up); [- ropa, zapatos] to wear out. **-2.** fig [usar - gen] to use; [- ropa] to wear; [- número de zapatos] to take; **~ una broma (a alguien)** to play a joke (on sb). **-3.** [malgastar] to waste. ◇ vi [despilfarrar] to spend (money). ◆ **gastarse** vpr **-1.** [deteriorarse] to wear out. **-2.** [terminarse] to run out.

gasto m [acción de gastar] outlay, expenditure; [cosa que pagar] expense; [de energía, gasolina] consumption; [despilfarro] waste; **cubrir ~s** to cover costs, to break even; **~ público** public expenditure; **~s fijos** COM fixed charges O costs; [en una casa] overheads; **~s generales** overheads; **~s de mantenimiento** maintenance costs; **~s de representación** entertainment allowance (sg).

gastritis f inv gastritis.

gastronomía f gastronomy.

gastrónomo, -ma m y f gourmet.

gatas ◆ **a gatas** loc adv on all fours.

gatear vi to crawl.

gatillo m trigger.

gato, -ta m y f cat; **dar ~ por liebre a alguien** to swindle O cheat sb; **buscar tres pies al ~** to overcomplicate matters; **aquí hay ~ encerrado** there's something fishy going on here. ◆ **gato** m AUTOM jack.

gauchada f Amer favour.

gaucho, -cha adj, m y f gaucho.

gavilán m sparrowhawk.

gavilla f sheaf.

gaviota f seagull.

gay adj inv, m y f gay (homosexual).

gazmoño, -ña adj sanctimonious.

gazpacho m gazpacho, Andalusian soup made from tomatoes, peppers, cucumbers and bread, served chilled.

géiser, géyser (pl géyseres) m geyser.

gel m gel.

gelatina f [de carne] gelatine; [de fruta] jelly.

gema f gem.

gemelo, -la ◇ adj twin (antes de sust). ◇ m y f [persona] twin. ◆ **gemelo** m [músculo] calf. ◆ **gemelos** mpl **-1.** [de camisa] cufflinks. **-2.** [prismáticos] binoculars; [para teatro] opera glasses.

gemido m [de persona] moan, groan; [de animal] whine.

Géminis ◇ m [zodiaco] Gemini. ◇ m y f [persona] Gemini.

gemir vi **-1.** [persona] to moan, to groan; [animal] to whine. **-2.** [viento] to howl.

gene, gen m gene.

genealogía f genealogy.

generación f generation.

generador, -ra adj generating. ◆ **generador** m generator.

general ◇ adj **-1.** [gen] general; **por lo ~, en ~** in general, generally. **-2.** [usual] usual. ◇ m MIL general; **~ de brigada** brigadier Br, brigadier general Am; **~ de división** major general.

generalidad f **-1.** [mayoría] majority. **-2.** [vaguedad] generalization.

generalísimo *m* supreme commander, generalissimo.

Generalitat [ʒenerali'tat] *f* Generalitat, *autonomous government of Catalonia or Valencia.*

generalizar ◇ *vt* to spread, to make widespread. ◇ *vi* to generalize. ◆ **generalizarse** *vpr* to become widespread.

generalmente *adv* generally.

generar *vt* [gen] to generate; [engendrar] to create.

genérico, -ca *adj* [común] generic.

género *m* -1. [clase] kind, type. -2. GRAM gender. -3. LITER genre. -4. BIOL genus; **el ~ humano** the human race. -5. [productos] merchandise, goods (*pl*). -6. [tejido] cloth, material.

generosidad *f* generosity.

generoso, -sa *adj* generous.

genético, -ca *adj* genetic. ◆ **genética** *f* genetics (*U*).

genial *adj* -1. [autor, compositor etc] of genius. -2. *fig* [estupendo] brilliant, great.

genio *m* -1. [talento] genius. -2. [carácter] nature, disposition. -3. [mal carácter] bad temper; **estar de/tener mal ~** to be in a mood/bad-tempered. -4. [ser sobrenatural] genie.

genital *adj* genital. ◆ **genitales** *mpl* genitals.

genocidio *m* genocide.

gente *f* -1. [gen] people (*pl*); **~ bien** well-to-do people; **~ menuda** kids (*pl*). -2. *fam* [familia] folks (*pl*).

gentileza *f* courtesy, kindness.

gentío *m* crowd.

gentuza *f* riffraff.

genuflexión *f* genuflection.

genuino, -na *adj* genuine.

GEO (*abrev de* **Grupo Especial de Operaciones**) *m specially trained police force,* ≃ SAS *Br,* ≃ SWAT *Am.*

geografía *f* geography; *fig:* **varios puntos de la ~ nacional** several parts of the country.

geógrafo, -fa *m y f* geographer.

geología *f* geology.

geólogo, -ga *m y f* geologist.

geometría *f* geometry.

geranio *m* geranium.

gerencia *f* [gen] management.

gerente *m y f* manager, director.

geriatría *f* geriatrics (*U*).

germen *m lit & fig* germ.

germinar *vi lit & fig* to germinate.

gerundio *m* gerund.

gestar *vi* to gestate. ◆ **gestarse** *vpr:* **se estaba gestando un cambio sin precedentes** the seeds of an unprecedented change had been sown.

gesticulación *f* gesticulation; [de cara] face-pulling.

gesticular *vi* to gesticulate; [con la cara] to pull faces.

gestión *f* -1. [diligencia] step, thing that has to be done; **tengo que hacer unas gestiones** I have a few things to do. -2. [administración] management.

gestionar *vt* -1. [tramitar] to negotiate. -2. [administrar] to manage.

gesto *m* -1. [gen] gesture. -2. [mueca] face, grimace; **hacer un ~** to pull a face.

gestor, -ra ◇ *adj* managing (*antes de sust*). ◇ *m y f person who carries out dealings with public bodies on behalf of private customers or companies, combining the role of solicitor and accountant.*

géyser = **géiser**.

ghetto = **gueto**.

giba *f* [de camello] hump.

Gibraltar Gibraltar.

gibraltareño, -ña *adj, m y f* Gibraltarian.

gigabyte [xiɣa'ßait] *m* INFORM gigabyte.

gigante, -ta *m y f* giant. ◆ **gigante** *adj* gigantic.

gigantesco, -ca *adj* gigantic.

gil, -la *m y f Amer fam* twit, idiot.

gilipollada, jilipollada *f fam:* **hacer/decir una ~** to do/say sthg bloody stupid.

gilipollas, jilipollas *fam* ◇ *adj inv* daft, dumb *Am.* ◇ *m y f inv* prat.

gimnasia *f* [deporte] gymnastics (*U*); [ejercicio] gymnastics (*pl*).

gimnasio *m* gymnasium.

gimnasta *m y f* gymnast.

gimotear *vi* to whine, to whimper.

gin [jin] ◆ **gin tonic** *m* gin and tonic.

ginebra *f* gin.

Ginebra Geneva.

ginecología *f* gynaecology.

ginecólogo, -ga *m y f* gynaecologist.

gira *f* tour.

girar ◇ *vi* -1. [dar vueltas, torcer] to turn; [rápidamente] to spin. -2. *fig* [centrarse]: **~ en torno a** ○ **alrededor de** to be centred around, to centre on. ◇ *vt* -1. [hacer dar vueltas] to turn; [rápidamente] to spin. -2. COM to draw. -3. [dinero - por correo, telégrafo] to transfer, to remit.

girasol m sunflower.

giratorio, -ria adj revolving; [silla] swivel (antes de sust).

giro m -1. [gen] turn. -2. [postal, telegráfico] money order; ~ **postal** postal order. -3. [de letras, órdenes de pago] draft. -4. [expresión] turn of phrase.

gis m Amer chalk.

gitano, -na m y f gypsy.

glacial adj glacial; [viento, acogida] icy.

glaciar ◇ adj glacial. ◇ m glacier.

gladiolo, gladíolo m gladiolus.

glándula f gland.

glicerina f glycerine.

global adj global, overall.

globo m -1. [Tierra] globe, earth. -2. [aeróstato, juguete] balloon. -3. [esfera] sphere.

glóbulo m MED corpuscle; ~ **blanco/rojo** white/red corpuscle.

gloria f -1. [gen] glory. -2. [placer] delight.

glorieta f -1. [de casa, jardín] arbour. -2. [plaza - redonda] circus, roundabout Br, traffic circle Am.

glorificar vt to glorify.

glorioso, -sa adj [importante] glorious.

glosa f marginal note.

glosar vt -1. [anotar] to annotate. -2. [comentar] to comment on.

glosario m glossary.

glotón, -ona ◇ adj gluttonous, greedy. ◇ m y f glutton.

glúcido m carbohydrate.

glucosa f glucose.

gluten m gluten.

gnomo, nomo m gnome.

gobernador, -ra m y f governor.

gobernanta f cleaning and laundry staff manageress.

gobernante ◇ adj ruling (antes de sust). ◇ m y f ruler, leader.

gobernar vt -1. [gen] to govern, to rule; [casa, negocio] to run, to manage. -2. [barco] to steer; [avión] to fly.

gobierno m -1. [gen] government. -2. [administración, gestión] running, management. -3. [control] control.

goce m pleasure.

godo, -da ◇ adj Gothic. ◇ m y f HIST Goth.

gol (pl **goles**) m goal.

goleador, -ra m y f goalscorer.

golear vt to score a lot of goals against, to thrash.

golf m golf.

golfear vi fam [vaguear] to loaf around.

golfista m y f golfer.

golfo, -fa m y f [gamberro] lout; [vago] layabout. ◆ **golfo** m GEOGR gulf, bay. ◆ **Golfo Pérsico** m: **el Golfo Pérsico** the Persian Gulf.

golondrina f [ave] swallow.

golosina f [dulce] sweet; [exquisitez] titbit, delicacy.

goloso, -sa adj sweet-toothed.

golpe m -1. [gen] blow; [bofetada] smack; [con puño] punch; [en puerta etc] knock; [en tenis, golf] shot; [entre coches] bump, collision; **a ~s** by force; fig in fits and starts; **un ~ bajo** DEP & fig a blow below the belt; ~ **de castigo** [en rugby] penalty (kick); ~ **franco** free kick. -2. [disgusto] blow. -3. [atraco] raid, job, heist Am. -4. POLÍT: ~ (**de Estado**) coup (d'état). -5. loc: **no dar o pegar** ~ not to lift a finger, not to do a stroke of work. ◆ **de golpe** loc adv suddenly. ◆ **de un golpe** loc adv at one fell swoop, all at once. ◆ **golpe de gracia** m coup de grâce. ◆ **golpe de suerte** m stroke of luck. ◆ **golpe de vista** m glance; **al primer ~ de vista** at a glance.

golpear vt & vi [gen] to hit; [puerta] to bang; [con puño] to punch.

golpista m y f person involved in military coup.

golpiza f Amer beating.

goma f -1. [sustancia viscosa, pegajosa] gum; ~ **arábiga** gum arabic; ~ **de mascar** chewing gum; ~ **de pegar** glue, gum. -2. [tira elástica] rubber band, elastic band Br; ~ **elástica** elastic. -3. [caucho] rubber; ~ **espuma** foam rubber; ~ **de borrar** rubber Br, eraser Am. ◆ **Goma 2** f plastic explosive.

gomina f hair gel.

gong m inv gong.

gordinflón, -ona m y f fatty.

gordo, -da ◇ adj -1. [persona] fat; **me cae ~** I can't stand him. -2. [grueso] thick. -3. [grande] big. -4. [grave] big, serious. ◇ m y f -1. [persona obesa] fat man (f fat woman); **armar la gorda** fig to kick up a row o stink. -2. Amer [querido] sweetheart, darling. ◆ **gordo** m [en lotería] first prize, jackpot; **el ~** first prize in the Spanish national lottery.

gordura f fatness.

gorgorito m warble.

gorila m -1. ZOOL gorilla. -2. fig [guardaespaldas] bodyguard. -3. fig [en discoteca etc] bouncer.

gorjear vi to chirp, to twitter.

gorra f (peaked) cap; **de ~** for free; **vivir de ~** to scrounge.

gorrear = **gorronear**.

gorrinada f [guarrada - acción] disgusting behaviour (*U*); [- lugar] **pigsty**.

gorrión m **sparrow**.

gorro m [gen] **cap**; [de niño] **bonnet**.

gorrón, -ona fam m y f **sponger**.

gorronear, gorrear vt & vi fam to sponge, to scrounge.

gota f **-1.** [gen] **drop**; [de sudor] **bead**; **caer cuatro ~s** to spit (with rain); **ni ~** anything; **no se veía ni ~** you couldn't see a thing; **sudar la ~ gorda** to sweat blood, to work very hard. **-2.** fig [de aire] **breath**; [de sensatez etc] **ounce**. **-3.** MED **gout**. ◆ **gota a gota** m MED intravenous drip. ◆ **gota fría** f METEOR cold front that remains in one place for some time, causing continuous heavy rain.

gotear ◇ vi [líquido] to **drip**; [techo, depósito etc] to **leak**; fig to **trickle through**. ◇ v impers [chispear] to **spit**, to **drizzle**.

gotera f [filtración] **leak**.

gótico, -ca adj **Gothic**.

gourmet → **gurmet**.

gozada f fam absolute delight.

gozar vi to enjoy o.s.; **~ de algo** to enjoy sthg; **~ con** to take delight in.

gozne m **hinge**.

gozo m **joy, pleasure**.

gr abrev de **grado**.

grabación f **recording**.

grabado m **-1.** [gen] **engraving**; [en madera] **carving**. **-2.** [en papel - acción] **printing**; [- lámina] **print**.

grabar vt **-1.** [gen] to **engrave**; [en madera] to **carve**; [en papel] to **print**. **-2.** [sonido, cinta] to **record**. ◆ **grabarse en** vpr fig: **grabársele a alguien en la memoria** to become engraved on sb's mind.

gracia f **-1.** [humor, comicidad] **humour**; **hacer ~ a alguien** to amuse sb; **no me hizo ~** I didn't find it funny; **tener ~** [ser divertido] to be funny; **tiene ~** [es curioso] it's funny; **caer en ~** to be liked. **-2.** [arte, habilidad] **skill, natural ability**. **-3.** [encanto] **grace, elegance**. **-4.** [chiste] **joke**. ◆ **gracias** fpl **thank you, thanks**; **dar las ~s a alguien (por)** to thank sb (for); **muchas ~s** thank you, thanks very much.

gracioso, -sa ◇ adj **-1.** [divertido] **funny, amusing**. **-2.** [curioso] **funny**; **es ~ que ...** it's funny how .... ◇ m y f TEATR **fool, clown**.

grada f **-1.** [peldaño] **step**. **-2.** TEATR **row**. ◆ **gradas** fpl DEP **terraces**.

gradación f [escalonamiento] **scale**.

gradería f, **graderío** m TEATR **rows** (*pl*); DEP **terraces** (*pl*).

grado m **-1.** [gen] **degree**. **-2.** [fase] **stage, level**; [índice, nivel] **extent, level**; **en ~ sumo** **greatly**. **-3.** [rango - gen] **grade**; MIL **rank**. **-4.** EDUC **year, class, grade** Am. **-5.** [voluntad]: **hacer algo de buen/mal ~** to do sthg willingly/ unwillingly.

graduación f **-1.** [acción] **grading**; [de la vista] **eye-test**. **-2.** EDUC **graduation**. **-3.** [de bebidas] **strength**, ≃ **proof**. **-4.** MIL **rank**.

graduado, -da m y f [persona] **graduate**. ◆ **graduado** m [título - gen] **certificate**; **~ escolar** basic school-leaving certificate.

gradual adj **gradual**.

graduar vt **-1.** [medir] to **gauge**, to **measure**; [regular] to **regulate**; [vista] to **test**. **-2.** [escalonar] to **stagger**; [publicación] to **serialize**. **-3.** EDUC to **confer a degree on**. **-4.** MIL to **commission**. ◆ **graduarse** vpr: **~se (en)** to **graduate (in)**.

grafía f **written symbol**.

gráfico, -ca adj **graphic**. ◆ **gráfico** m [gráfica] **graph, chart**; [dibujo] **diagram**. ◆ **gráfica** f **graph, chart**.

gragea f MED **pill, tablet**.

grajo m **rook**.

gral. (abrev de **general**) **gen**.

gramática → **gramático**.

gramatical adj **grammatical**.

gramático, -ca adj **grammatical**. ◆ **gramática** f [disciplina, libro] **grammar**.

gramo m **gram**.

gramófono m **gramophone**.

gramola f **gramophone**.

gran = **grande**.

granada f **-1.** [fruta] **pomegranate**. **-2.** [proyectil] **grenade**.

granate ◇ m **garnet**. ◇ adj inv **garnet- coloured**.

Gran Bretaña f **Great Britain**.

grande ◇ adj (antes de sust: **gran**) **-1.** [de tamaño] **big, large**; [de altura] **tall**; [de intensidad, importancia] **great**; **este traje me está ~** this suit is too big for me. **-2.** fig & irón [enojoso] just great, a bit rich. **-3.** loc: **pasarlo en ~** fam to have a great time. ◇ m [noble] **grandee**. ◆ **grandes** mpl [adultos] **grown-ups**. ◆ **a lo grande** loc adv **in style**.

grandeza f -1. [de tamaño] (great) size. -2. [de sentimientos] **generosity**.

grandioso, -sa adj grand, splendid.

grandullón, -ona m y f big boy (f big girl).

granel ◆ a granel loc adv [sin envase - gen] loose; [- en gran cantidad] in bulk.

granero m granary.

granito m granite.

granizada f METEOR hailstorm.

granizado m iced drink.

granizar v impers to hail.

granizo m hail.

granja f farm.

granjearse vpr to gain, to earn.

granjero, -ra m y f farmer.

grano m -1. [semilla - de cereales] grain; ~ **de café** coffee bean; ~ **de pimienta** peppercorn. -2. [partícula] grain. -3. [en la piel] spot, pimple. -4. loc: **ir al** ~ to get to the point.

granuja m y f [pillo] rogue, scoundrel; [canalla] trickster, swindler.

granulado, -da adj granulated.

grapa f [para papeles etc] staple; [para heridas] stitch, (wire) suture.

grapadora f stapler.

grapar vt to staple.

GRAPO (abrev de **Grupos de Resistencia Antifascista Primero de Octubre**) mpl former left-wing Spanish terrorist group.

grasa → graso.

grasiento, -ta adj greasy.

graso, -sa adj [gen] greasy; [con alto contenido en grasas] fatty. ◆ **grasa** f -1. [en comestibles] fat; [de cerdo] lard. -2. [lubricante] grease, oil. -3. [suciedad] grease.

gratén m gratin; **al** ~ au gratin.

gratificación f -1. [moral] reward. -2. [monetaria] bonus.

gratificante adj rewarding.

gratificar vt [complacer] to reward; [retribuir] to give a bonus to; [dar propina] to tip.

gratinado, -da adj au gratin.

gratis adv [sin dinero] free, for nothing; [sin esfuerzo] for nothing.

gratitud f gratitude.

grato, -ta adj pleasant; **nos es** ~ **comunicarle que ...** we are pleased to inform you that ....

gratuito, -ta adj -1. [sin dinero] free. -2. [arbitrario] gratuitous; [infundado] unfair, uncalled for.

grava f gravel.

gravamen m -1. [impuesto] tax. -2. [obligación moral] burden.

gravar vt [con impuestos] to tax.

grave adj -1. [gen] serious; [estilo] formal; **estar** ~ to be seriously ill. -2. [sonido, voz] low, deep.

gravedad f -1. [cualidad de grave] seriousness. -2. FÍS gravity.

gravilla f gravel.

gravitar vi to gravitate; fig [pender]: ~ **sobre** to hang ○ loom over.

graznar vi [cuervo] to caw; [ganso] to honk; [pato] to quack; fig [persona] to squawk.

graznido m [de cuervo] caw, cawing (U); [de ganso] honk, honking (U); [de pato] quack, quacking (U); fig [de personas] squawk, squawking (U).

Grecia Greece.

gremio m [sindicato] (trade) union; [profesión] profession, trade; HIST guild.

greña f (gen pl) tangle of hair.

gres m stoneware.

gresca f row.

griego, -ga adj, m y f Greek. ◆ **griego** m [lengua] Greek.

grieta f crack; [entre montañas] crevice; [que deja pasar luz] chink.

grifería f taps (pl), plumbing.

grifo m [llave] tap Br, faucet Am.

grillado, -da adj fam crazy, loopy.

grillete m shackle.

grillo m cricket.

grima f [dentera]: **dar** ~ to set one's teeth on edge.

gringo, -ga adj, m y f gringo.

gripa f Amer flu.

gripe f flu.

gris ◇ adj grey; fig [triste] gloomy, miserable. ◇ m grey.

gritar ◇ vi [hablar alto] to shout; [chillar] to scream, to yell. ◇ vt: ~ **(algo) a alguien** to shout (sth) at sb.

griterío m screaming, shouting.

grito m [gen] shout; [de dolor, miedo] cry, scream; [de sorpresa, de animal] cry; **dar** ○ **pegar un** ~ to shout ○ scream (out); **a** ~ **limpio** ○ **pelado** at the top of one's voice; **pedir algo a** ~s fig to be crying out for sthg; **poner el** ~ **en el cielo** to hit the roof; **ser el último** ~ to be the latest fashion ○ craze, to be the in thing.

Groenlandia Greenland.

grogui adj lit & fig groggy.

grosella f redcurrant; ~ **negra** blackcurrant; ~ **silvestre** gooseberry.

grosería f [cualidad] rudeness; [acción] rude thing; [palabrota] swear word.

grosero, -ra adj **-1.** [maleducado] rude, crude. **-2.** [tosco] coarse, rough.

grosor m thickness.

grosso ◆ **a grosso modo** loc adv roughly.

grotesco, -ca adj grotesque.

grúa f **-1.** CONSTR crane. **-2.** AUTOM breakdown truck.

grueso, -sa adj **-1.** [espeso] thick. **-2.** [corpulento] thickset; [obeso] fat. **-3.** [grande] large, big. **-4.** [mar] stormy. ◆ **grueso** m [grosor] thickness.

grulla f crane.

grumete m cabin boy.

grumo m [gen] lump; [de sangre] clot.

gruñido m **-1.** [gen] growl; [del cerdo] grunt. **-2.** fig [de personas] grumble.

gruñir vi **-1.** [gen] to growl; [cerdo] to grunt. **-2.** fig [personas] to grumble.

gruñón, -ona fam adj grumpy.

grupa f hindquarters.

grupo m [gen] group; [de árboles] cluster; TECN unit, set; **en ~** in a group; **~ electrógeno** generator. ◆ **grupo sanguíneo** m blood group.

gruta f grotto.

guacal m Amer **-1.** [calabaza] pumpkin. **-2.** [jaula] cage.

guachada f Amer fam mean trick.

guachimán m Amer night watchman.

guacho, -cha m y f Amer fam illegitimate child.

Guadalquivir m: **el ~** the Guadalquivir.

guadaña f scythe.

guagua f Amer **-1.** [autobús] bus. **-2.** [niño] baby.

guajolote m Amer turkey.

guampa f Amer horn.

guanajo m Amer turkey.

guantazo m fam slap.

guante m glove; **echarle el ~ a algo** to get hold of sthg, to get one's hands on sthg.

guantera f glove compartment.

guapo, -pa adj [gen] good-looking; [hombre] handsome; [mujer] pretty.

guarango, -ga adj Amer coarse, vulgar.

guarda ◇ m y f [vigilante] guard, keeper; **~ jurado** security guard. ◇ f **-1.** [tutela] guardianship. **-2.** [de libros] flyleaf.

guardabarros m inv mudguard Br, fender Am.

guardabosque m y f forest ranger.

guardacoches m y f inv parking attendant.

guardacostas m inv [barco] coastguard boat.

guardaespaldas m y f inv bodyguard.

guardameta m y f goalkeeper.

guardapolvo m overalls (pl).

guardar vt **-1.** [gen] to keep; [en su sitio] to put away. **-2.** [vigilar] to keep watch over; [proteger] to guard. **-3.** [reservar, ahorrar]: **~ algo (a O para alguien)** to save sthg (for sb). **-4.** [cumplir - ley] to observe; [- secreto, promesa] to keep. ◆ **guardarse de** vpr: **~se de hacer algo** [evitar] to avoid doing sthg; [abstenerse de] to be careful not to do sthg.

guardarropa m [gen] wardrobe; [de cine, discoteca etc] cloakroom.

guardarropía f TEATR wardrobe.

guardería f nursery; [en el lugar de trabajo] crèche.

guardia ◇ f **-1.** [gen] guard; [vigilancia] watch, guard; **montar (la) ~** to mount guard; **~ municipal** urban police. **-2.** [turno] duty; **estar de ~** to be on duty. ◇ m y f [policía] policeman (f policewoman); **~ de tráfico** traffic warden. ◆ **Guardia Civil** f: **la Guardia Civil** the Civil Guard, military-style Spanish security force who police rural areas, highways and borders.

guardián, -ana m y f [de persona] guardian; [de cosa] watchman, keeper.

guarecer vt: **~ (de)** to protect O shelter (from). ◆ **guarecerse** vpr: **~se (de)** to shelter (from).

guarida f lair; fig hideout.

guarnición f **-1.** CULIN garnish. **-2.** MIL garrison.

guarrería f **-1.** [suciedad] filth, muck. **-2.** [acción] filthy thing.

guarro, -rra ◇ adj filthy. ◇ m y f **-1.** [animal] pig. **-2.** fam [persona] filthy O dirty pig.

guarura m Amer fam bodyguard.

guasa f fam [gracia] humour; [ironía] irony; **estar de ~** to be joking.

guasearse vpr fam: **~ (de)** to take the mickey (out of).

guasón, -ona m y f joker, tease.

Guatemala -1. [país] Guatemala. **-2.** [ciudad] Guatemala City.

guatemalteco, -ca, guatemaltés, -esa adj, m y f Guatemalan.

guau m woof.

guay adj fam cool, neat.

guayín m Amer fam van.

gubernativo, **-va** *adj* government (*antes de sust*).

guepardo *m* cheetah.

güero, **-ra** *adj Amer fam* blond (*f* blonde).

guerra *f* war; [referido al tipo de conflicto] warfare; [pugna] struggle, conflict; [de intereses, ideas] conflict; **declarar la** ~ to declare war; **en** ~ at war; ~ **civil/mundial** civil/world war; ~ **fría** cold war; ~ **de guerrillas** guerrilla warfare; **dar** ~ to be a pain, to be annoying.

guerrear *vi* to (wage) war.

guerrero, **-ra** ◇ *adj* warlike. ◇ *m y f* [luchador] warrior.

guerrilla *f* [grupo] guerrilla group.

guerrillero, **-ra** *m y f* guerrilla.

gueto, **ghetto** ['geto] *m* ghetto.

güevón *m Amer vulg* bloody idiot.

guía ◇ *m y f* [persona] guide; ~ **turístico** tourist guide. ◇ *f* **-1.** [indicación] guidance. **-2.** [libro] guide (book); ~ **de ferrocarriles** train timetable; ~ **telefónica** telephone book ○ directory.

guiar *vt* **-1.** [indicar dirección] to guide, to lead; [aconsejar] to guide, to direct. **-2.** AUTOM to drive; NÁUT to steer. ◆ **guiarse** *vpr*: **~se por algo** to be guided by ○ to follow sthg.

guijarro *m* pebble.

guillotina *f* guillotine.

guinda *f* morello cherry.

guindilla *f* chilli (pepper).

guiñapo *m* [persona] (physical) wreck.

guiño *m* wink.

guiñol *m* puppet theatre.

guión *m* **-1.** CIN & TV script. **-2.** GRAM [signo] hyphen.

guionista *m y f* scriptwriter.

guiri *fam despec m y f* foreigner.

guirigay *m fam* [jaleo] racket.

guirlache *m brittle sweet made of roasted almonds or hazelnuts and toffee*.

guirnalda *f* garland.

guisa *f* way; **a** ~ **de** by way of.

guisado *m* stew.

guisante *m* pea.

guisar *vt & vi* to cook. ◆ **guisarse** *vpr fig* to be cooking, to be going on.

guiso *m* dish.

güisqui, **whisky** *m* whisky.

guitarra *f* guitar.

guitarrista *m y f* guitarist.

gula *f* gluttony.

gurí, **-isa** *m y f Amer fam* kid, child.

gurmet, **gourmet** [gur'met] *m y f* gourmet.

guru, **gurú** *m* guru.

gusanillo *m fam*: **el** ~ **de la conciencia** conscience; **entrarle a uno el** ~ **de los videojuegos** to be bitten by the videogame bug; **matar el** ~ [bebiendo] to have a drink on an empty stomach; [comiendo] to have a snack between meals; **sentir un** ~ **en el estómago** to have butterflies (in one's stomach).

gusano *m lit & fig* worm.

gustar ◇ *vi* [agradar] to be pleasing; **me gusta esa chica/ir al cine** I like that girl/going to the cinema; **me gustan las novelas** I like novels; **como guste** as you wish. ◇ *vt* to taste, to try.

gustazo *m fam* great pleasure.

gusto *m* **-1.** [gen] taste; [sabor] taste, flavour; **de buen/mal** ~ in good/bad taste; **tener buen/mal** ~ to have good/bad taste. **-2.** [placer] pleasure; **con mucho** ~ gladly, with pleasure; **da** ~ **estar aquí** it's a real pleasure to be here; **mucho** ○ **tanto** ~ pleased to meet you; **tomar** ~ **a algo** to take a liking to sthg. ◆ **a gusto** *loc adv*: **hacer algo a** ~ [de buena gana] to do sthg willingly ○ gladly; [cómodamente] to do sthg comfortably; **estar a** ~ to be comfortable ○ at ease.

gustoso, **-sa** *adj* **-1.** [sabroso] tasty. **-2.** [con placer]: **hacer algo** ~ to do sthg gladly ○ willingly.

gutural *adj* guttural.

Guyana *f* Guyana.

Guyana francesa *f*: **la** ~ French Guyana.

h¹, **H** *f* [letra] h, H; **por h o por b** *fig* for one reason or another.

h², **h.** (*abrev de* **hora**) hr, h.

ha ◇ *v* → **haber**. ◇ (*abrev de* **hectárea**) ha.

haba *f* broad bean.

habano, **-na** *adj* Havanan. ◆ **habano** *m* Havana cigar.

haber ◇ *vaux* **-1.** [en tiempos compuestos] to have; **lo he/había hecho** I have/had done it; **los niños ya han comido** the children have already eaten; **en el estreno ha habido mucha gente** there were a lot of people at the premiere. **-2.** [expresa reproche]: ~ **venido antes** you could have come a bit earlier; ¡~**lo dicho!** why didn't you say so? **-3.** [expresa obligación]: ~ **de hacer algo** to have to do sthg; **has de estudiar más** you have to study more. ◇ *v impers* **-1.** [existir, estar]: **hay** there is/are; **hay mucha gente en la calle** there are a lot of people in the street; **había/hubo muchos problemas** there were many problems; **habrá dos mil** [expresa futuro] there will be two thousand; [expresa hipótesis] there must be two thousand. **-2.** [expresa obligación]: ~ **que hacer algo** to have to do sthg; **hay que hacer más ejercicio** one ◇ you should do more exercise; **habrá que soportar su mal humor** we'll have to put up with his bad mood. **-3.** *loc:* **algo habrá** there must be something in it; **allá se las haya** that's his/her/your *etc* problem; **habérselas con alguien** to face ◇ confront sb; ¡**hay que ver!** well I never!; **no hay de qué** don't mention it; ¿**qué hay?** *fam* [saludo] how are you doing? ◇ *m* **-1.** [bienes] assets (*pl*). **-2.** [en cuentas, contabilidad] credit (side). ◆**haberes** *mpl* [sueldo] remuneration (*U*).

habichuela *f* bean.

hábil *adj* **-1.** [diestro] skilful; [inteligente] clever. **-2.** [utilizable - lugar] suitable, fit. **-3.** DER: **días** ~**es** working days.

habilidad *f* [destreza] skill; [inteligencia] cleverness; **tener** ~ **para algo** to be good at sthg.

habilitar *vt* **-1.** [acondicionar] to fit out, to equip. **-2.** [autorizar] to authorize.

habiloso, -sa *adj Amer* shrewd, astute.

habitación *f* [gen] room; [dormitorio] bedroom; ~ **doble** [con cama de matrimonio] double room; [con dos camas] twin room; ~ **individual** ◇ **simple** single room.

habitante *m* [de ciudad, país] inhabitant; [de barrio] resident.

habitar ◇ *vi* to live. ◇ *vt* to live in, to inhabit.

hábitat (*pl* **hábitats**) *m* [gen] habitat.

hábito *m* habit; **tener el** ~ **de hacer algo** to be in the habit of doing sthg.

habitual *adj* habitual; [cliente, lector] regular.

habituar *vt*: ~ **a alguien a** to accustom sb to. ◆**habituarse** *vpr*: ~**se a** [gen] to get used ◇ accustomed to; [drogas etc] to become addicted to.

habla *f* (*el*) **-1.** [idioma] language; [dialecto] dialect; **de** ~ **española** Spanish-speaking. **-2.** [facultad] speech; **quedarse sin** ~ to be left speechless. **-3.** LING discourse. **-4.** [al teléfono]: **estar al** ~ **con alguien** to be on the line to sb.

hablador, -ra *adj* talkative.

habladurías *fpl* [rumores] rumours; [chismes] gossip (*U*).

hablante ◇ *adj* speaking. ◇ *m y f* speaker.

hablar ◇ *vi*: ~ (**con**) to talk (to), to speak (to); ~ **de** to talk about; ~ **bien/mal de** to speak well/badly of; ~ **en voz alta/baja** to speak loudly/softly; ¡**ni** ~! no way! ◇ *vt* **-1.** [idioma] to speak. **-2.** [asunto]: ~ **algo (con)** to discuss sthg (with). ◆**hablarse** *vpr* to speak (to each other); **no** ~**se** not to be speaking, not to be on speaking terms; **"se habla inglés"** "English spoken".

habrá *etc* → **haber.**

hacendado, -da *m y f* landowner.

hacer ◇ *vt* **-1.** [elaborar, crear, cocinar] to make; ~ **un vestido/planes** to make a dress/plans; ~ **un poema/una sinfonía** to write a poem/symphony; **para** ~ **la carne ...** to cook the meat .... **-2.** [construir] to build; **han hecho un edificio nuevo** they've put up a new building. **-3.** [generar] to produce; **el árbol hace sombra** the tree gives shade; **la carretera hace una curva** there's a bend in the road. **-4.** [movimientos, sonidos, gestos] to make; **le hice señas** I signalled to her; **el reloj hace tic-tac** the clock goes tick-tock; ~ **ruido** to make a noise. **-5.** [obtener - fotocopia] to make; [- retrato] to paint; [- fotografía] to take. **-6.** [realizar - trabajo, estudios] to do; [- viaje] to make; [- comunión] to take; **hoy hace guardia** she's on duty today; **estoy haciendo segundo** I'm in my second year. **-7.** [practicar - gen] to do; [- tenis, fútbol] to play; **debes** ~ **deporte** you should start doing some sport. **-8.** [arreglar - casa, colada] to do; [- maleta] to make. **-9.** [transformar en]: ~ **a alguien feliz** to make sb happy; **la guerra no le hizo un hombre** the war didn't make him (into) a man; **hizo pedazos el pa-**

pel he tore the paper to pieces; ~ de algo/alguien algo to make sthg/sb into sthg; hizo de ella una buena cantante he made a good singer of her. **-10.** [comportarse como]: ~ **el tonto** to act the fool; ~ **el vándalo** to act like a hooligan. **-11.** [causar]: ~ **daño a alguien** to hurt sb; **me hizo gracia** I thought it was funny. **-12.** CIN & TEATR to play; **hace el papel de la hija del rey** she plays (the part of) the king's daughter. **-13.** [ser causa de]: ~ **que alguien haga algo** to make sb do sthg; **me hizo reír** it made me laugh; **has hecho que se enfadara** you've made him angry. **-14.** [mandar]: ~ **que se haga algo** to have sthg done; **voy a ~ teñir este traje** I'm going to have the dress dyed. ◇ vi **-1.** [actuar]: ~ **de** CIN & TEATR to play; [trabajar] to act as. **-2.** [aparentar]: ~ **como si** to act as if; **haz como que no te importa** act as if you don't care. **-3.** [procurar, intentar]: ~ **por hacer algo** to try to do sthg; **haré por verle esta noche** I'll try to see him tonight. **-4.** loc: ¿hace? all right? ◇ v impers **-1.** [tiempo meteorológico]: **hace frío/sol/viento** it's cold/sunny/windy; **hace un día precioso** it's a beautiful day. **-2.** [tiempo transcurrido]: **hace diez años ten** years ago; **hace mucho/poco** a long time/not long ago; **hace un mes que llegué** it's a month since I arrived; **no la veo desde hace un año** I haven't seen her for a year. ◆ **hacerse** vpr **-1.** [formarse] to form. **-2.** [desarrollarse, crecer] to grow. **-3.** [guisarse, cocerse] to cook. **-4.** [convertirse] to become; ~**se musulmán** to become a Moslem. **-5.** [crearse en la mente]: ~**se ilusiones** to get one's hopes up; ~**se una idea de algo** to imagine what sthg is like. **-6.** [mostrarse]: **se hace el gracioso/el simpático** he tries to act the comedian/the nice guy; ~**se el distraído** to pretend to be miles away.

hacha f (el) axe.

hachís, hash [xaʃ] m hashish.

hacia prep **-1.** [dirección, tendencia, sentimiento] towards; ~ **aquí/allí** this/that way; ~ **abajo** downwards; ~ **arriba** upwards; ~ **atrás** backwards; ~ **adelante** forwards. **-2.** [tiempo] around, about; ~ **las diez** around ○ about ten o'clock.

hacienda f **-1.** [finca] country estate ○ property. **-2.** [bienes] property; ~ pú-

blica public purse. ◆**Hacienda** f: **Ministerio de Hacienda** m the Treasury.

hada f (el) fairy.

haga etc → **hacer.**

Haití Haiti.

hala interj ¡~! [para dar ánimo, prisa] come on!; [para expresar incredulidad] no!, you're joking!; [para expresar admiración, sorpresa] wow!

halagador, -ra adj flattering.

halagar vt to flatter.

halago m flattery.

halagüeño, -ña adj [prometedor] promising, encouraging.

halcón m **-1.** ZOOL falcon, hawk. **-2.** Amer fam [matón] government-paid killer.

hálito m [aliento] breath.

halitosis f inv bad breath.

hall [xol] (pl halls) m foyer.

hallar vt [gen] to find; [averiguar] to find out. ◆**hallarse** vpr **-1.** [en un lugar - persona] to be, to find o.s.; [- casa etc] to be (situated). **-2.** [en una situación] to be; ~**se enfermo** to be ill.

hallazgo m **-1.** [descubrimiento] discovery. **-2.** [objeto] find.

halo m [de astros, santos] halo; [de objetos, personas] aura.

halógeno, -na adj QUÍM halogenous; [faro] halogen (antes de sust).

halterofilia f weightlifting.

hamaca f **-1.** [para colgar] hammock. **-2.** [tumbona - silla] deckchair; [- canapé] sunlounger.

hambre f **-1.** [apetito] hunger; [inanición] starvation; **tener ~** to be hungry; **matar el ~** to satisfy one's hunger. **-2.** [epidemia] famine. **-3.** fig [deseo]: ~ **de** hunger ○ thirst for.

hambriento, -ta adj starving.

hamburguesa f hamburger.

hampa f (el) underworld.

hámster ['xamster] (pl hámsters) m hamster.

hándicap ['xandikap] (pl hándicaps) m handicap.

hará etc → **hacer.**

haraganear vi to laze about.

harapiento, -ta adj ragged, tattered.

harapo m rag, tatter.

hardware ['xarwar] m INFORM hardware.

harén m harem.

harina f flour.

harinoso, -sa adj floury; [manzana] mealy.

hartar vt **-1.** [atiborrar] to stuff (full). **-2.** [fastidiar]: ~ **a alguien** to annoy sb, to get on sb's nerves. ◆**hartarse** *vpr* **-1.** [atiborrarse] to stuff O gorge o.s. **-2.** [cansarse]: ~**se (de)** to get fed up (with). **-3.** [no parar]: ~**se de algo** to do sthg non-stop.

hartazgo, hartón *m* fill; **darse un ~ (de)** to have one's fill (of).

harto, -ta *adj* **-1.** [de comida] full. **-2.** [cansado]: ~ **(de)** tired (of), fed up (with). ◆**harto** *adv* somewhat, rather.

hartón = hartazgo.

hash = hachís.

hasta ◇ *prep* **-1.** [en el espacio] as far as, up to; **desde aquí ~ allí** from here to there; *¿*~ **dónde va este tren?** where does this train go? **-2.** [en el tiempo] until, till; ~ **ahora** (up) until now, so far; ~ **el final** right up until the end; ~ **luego** O **pronto** O **la vista** see you (later). **-3.** [con cantidades] up to. ◇ *adv* [incluso] even. ◆**hasta que** *loc conj* until, till.

hastiar *vt* [aburrir] to bore; [asquear] to sicken, to disgust. ◆**hastiarse de** *vpr* to tire of.

hastío *m* [tedio] boredom (*U*); [repugnancia] disgust.

hatillo *m* bundle of clothes.

haya ◇ *v* → **haber**. ◇ *f* [árbol] beech (tree); [madera] beech (wood).

haz ◇ *v* → **hacer**. ◇ *m* **-1.** [de leña] bundle; [de cereales] sheaf. **-2.** [de luz] beam.

hazaña *f* feat, exploit.

hazmerreír *m* laughing stock.

HB (*abrev de* **Herri Batasuna**) *f political wing of ETA*.

he → **haber**.

hebilla *f* buckle.

hebra *f* [de hilo] thread; [de judías, puerros] string; [de tabaco] strand (of tobacco).

hebreo, -a *adj, m y f* Hebrew. ◆**hebreo** *m* [lengua] Hebrew.

hechicero, -ra *m y f* wizard (*f* witch), sorcerer (*f* sorceress).

hechizar *vt* to cast a spell on; *fig* to bewitch, to captivate.

hechizo *m* **-1.** [maleficio] spell. **-2.** *fig* [encanto] magic, charm.

hecho, -cha ◇ *pp* → **hacer**. ◇ *adj* **-1.** [acabado - persona] mature; **estás ~ un artista** you've become quite an artist; **una mujer hecha y derecha** a fully-grown woman. **-2.** [carne] done; **quiero el filete muy/poco ~** I'd like the steak well done/rare. ◆**hecho** *m* **-1.** [obra] action, deed. **-2.** [suceso] event. **-3.**

[realidad, dato] fact. ◆**de hecho** *loc adv* in fact, actually.

hechura *f* **-1.** [de traje] cut. **-2.** [forma] shape.

hectárea *f* hectare.

heder *vi* [apestar] to stink, to reek.

hediondo, -da *adj* [pestilente] stinking.

hedor *m* stink, stench.

hegemonía *f* [gen] dominance; POLÍT hegemony.

helada → **helado**.

heladería *f* [tienda] ice-cream parlour; [puesto] ice-cream stall.

helado, -da *adj* **-1.** [hecho hielo - agua] frozen; [- lago] frozen over. **-2.** [muy frío - manos, agua] freezing. ◆**helado** *m* ice-cream. ◆**helada** *f* frost.

helar ◇ *vt* [líquido] to freeze. ◇ *v impers*: **ayer heló** there was a frost last night. ◆**helarse** *vpr* to freeze; [plantas] to be frostbitten.

helecho *m* fern, bracken.

hélice *f* **-1.** TECN propeller. **-2.** [espiral] spiral.

helicóptero *m* helicopter.

helio *m* helium.

Helsinki Helsinki.

hematoma *m* bruise, haematoma MED.

hembra *f* **-1.** BIOL female; [mujer] woman; [niña] girl. **-2.** [del enchufe] socket.

hemiciclo *m* [en el parlamento] floor.

hemisferio *m* hemisphere.

hemofilia *f* haemophilia.

hemorragia *f* haemorrhage; ~ **nasal** nosebleed.

hemorroides *fpl* haemorrhoids, piles.

henchir *vt* to fill (up).

hender, hendir *vt* [carne, piel] to carve open, to cleave; [piedra, madera] to crack open; [aire, agua] to cut O slice through.

hendidura *f* [en carne, piel] cut, split; [en piedra, madera] crack.

hendir = hender.

heno *m* hay.

hepatitis *f inv* hepatitis.

herbicida *m* weedkiller.

herbolario, -ria *m y f* [persona] herbalist.

hercio, hertz ['erθjo] *m* hertz.

heredar *vt*: ~ **(de)** to inherit (from).

heredero, -ra *m y f* heir (*f* heiress).

hereditario, -ria *adj* hereditary.

hereje *m y f* heretic.

herejía *f* heresy.

herencia f [de bienes] inheritance; [de características] legacy; BIOL heredity.

herido, -da ◇ adj [gen] injured; [en lucha, atentado] wounded; [sentimentalmente] hurt, wounded. ◇ m y f [gen] injured person; [en lucha, atentado] wounded person; **no hubo ~s** there were no casualties; **los ~s** the wounded. ◆ **herida** f [lesión] injury; [en lucha, atentado] wound.

herir vt -1. [físicamente] to injure; [en lucha, atentado] to wound; [vista] to hurt; [oído] to pierce. -2. [sentimentalmente] to hurt.

hermanado, -da adj [gen] united, joined; [ciudades] twinned.

hermanar vt [ciudades] to twin.

hermanastro, -tra m y f stepbrother (f stepsister).

hermandad f [asociación] association; [RELIG - de hombres] brotherhood; [- de mujeres] sisterhood.

hermano, -na m y f brother (f sister).

hermético, -ca adj -1. [al aire] airtight, hermetic; [al agua] watertight, hermetic. -2. fig [persona] inscrutable.

hermoso, -sa adj [gen] beautiful, lovely; [hombre] handsome; [excelente] wonderful.

hermosura f [gen] beauty; [de hombre] handsomeness.

hernia f hernia, rupture.

herniarse vpr MED to rupture o.s.

héroe m hero.

heroico, -ca adj heroic.

heroína f -1. [mujer] heroine. -2. [droga] heroin.

heroinómano, -na m y f heroin addict.

heroísmo m heroism.

herpes m inv herpes (U).

herradura f horseshoe.

herramienta f tool.

herrería f [taller] smithy, forge.

herrero m blacksmith, smith.

herrumbre f [óxido] rust.

hertz = hercio.

hervidero m -1. [de pasiones, intrigas] hotbed. -2. [de gente - muchedumbre] swarm, throng; [- sitio] place throbbing ○ swarming with people.

hervir ◇ vt to boil. ◇ vi -1. [líquido] to boil. -2. fig [lugar]: **~ de** to swarm with.

hervor m boiling; **dar un ~ a algo** to blanch sthg.

heterodoxo, -xa adj unorthodox.

heterogéneo, -a adj heterogeneous.

heterosexual adj, m y f heterosexual.

hexágono m hexagon.

hez f lit & fig dregs (pl). ◆ **heces** fpl [excrementos] faeces.

hibernar vi to hibernate.

híbrido, -da adj lit & fig hybrid. ◆ **híbrido** m [animal, planta] hybrid.

hice etc → hacer.

hidalgo, -ga m y f nobleman (f noblewoman).

hidratante m moisturizing cream.

hidratar vt [piel] to moisturize; QUÍM to hydrate.

hidrato m: **~ de carbono** carbohydrate.

hidráulico, -ca adj hydraulic.

hidroavión m seaplane.

hidroeléctrico, -ca adj hydroelectric.

hidrógeno m hydrogen.

hidroplano m [barco] hydrofoil.

hiedra f ivy.

hiel f -1. [bilis] bile. -2. fig [mala intención] spleen, bitterness.

hielo m ice; **romper el ~** fig to break the ice.

hiena f hyena.

hierático, -ca adj solemn.

hierba, yerba f -1. [planta] herb; **mala ~** weed. -2. [césped] grass. -3. fam [droga] grass.

hierbabuena f mint.

hierro m [metal] iron; **de ~** [severo] iron (antes de sust); **~ forjado** wrought iron; **~ fundido** cast iron.

hígado m liver.

higiene f hygiene.

higiénico, -ca adj hygienic.

higienizar vt to sterilize.

higo m fig; **~ chumbo** prickly pear; **~s a brevas** once in a blue moon.

higuera f fig tree.

hijastro, -tra m y f stepson (f stepdaughter).

hijo, -ja m y f [descendiente] son (f daughter); **~ de papá** fam daddy's boy; **~ único** only child. ◆ **hijo** m [hijo o hija] child. ◆ **hijos** mpl children.

hilacha f loose thread.

hilada f row.

hilar vt [hilo, tela] to spin; [ideas, planes] to think up.

hilaridad f hilarity.

hilatura f spinning.

hilera f row.

hilo m -1. [fibra, hebra] thread; **colgar ○ pender de un ~** to be hanging by a thread; **mover los ~s** to pull some strings. -2. [tejido] linen. -3. [de metal, teléfono] wire. **-4.** [de agua, sangre] trickle. **-5.** MÚS: ~ **musical®** piped music. **-6.** *fig* [de pensamiento] train; [de discurso, conversación] thread; **perder el** ~ to lose the thread; **seguir el** ~ to follow (the thread).

hilvanar *vt* **-1.** [ropa] to tack *Br*, to baste *Am*. **-2.** *fig* [coordinar - ideas] to piece together.

Himalaya *m*: **el** ~ the Himalayas (*pl*).

himno *m* hymn; ~ **nacional** national anthem.

hincapié *m*: **hacer** ~ **en** [insistir] to insist on; [subrayar] to emphasize.

hincar *vt* ~ **algo en** to stick sthg into. ◆ **hincarse** *vpr*: ~**se de rodillas** to fall to one's knees.

hincha *m y f* [seguidor] fan.

hinchado, -da *adj* **-1.** [rueda, globo] inflated; [cara, tobillo] swollen. **-2.** *fig* [persona] bigheaded, conceited; [lenguaje, estilo] bombastic.

hinchar *vt lit* & *fig* to blow up. ◆ **hincharse** *vpr* **-1.** [pierna, mano] to swell (up). **-2.** *fig* [de comida]: ~**se (a)** to stuff o.s. (with). ◆ **hincharse a** *vpr* [no parar de]: ~**se a hacer algo** to do sthg a lot.

hinchazón *f* swelling.

hindú (*pl* **hindúes**) *adj, m y f* **-1.** [de la India] Indian. **-2.** RELIG Hindu.

hinduismo *m* Hinduism.

hinojo *m* fennel.

hipar *vi* to hiccup, to have hiccups.

hiper *m fam* hypermarket.

hiperactivo, -va *adj* hyperactive.

hipérbola *f* hyperbola.

hipermercado *m* hypermarket.

hipertensión *f* high blood pressure.

hípico, -ca *adj* [de las carreras] horseracing (*antes de sust*); [de la equitación] showjumping (*antes de sust*). ◆ **hípica** *f* [carreras de caballos] horseracing; [equitación] showjumping.

hipnosis *f inv* hypnosis.

hipnótico, -ca *adj* hypnotic.

hipnotismo *m* hypnotism.

hipnotizador, -ra *adj* hypnotic; *fig* spellbinding, mesmerizing.

hipnotizar *vt* to hypnotize; *fig* to mesmerize.

hipo *m* hiccups (*pl*); **tener** ~ to have (the) hiccups; **quitar el** ~ **a uno** *fig* to take one's breath away.

hipocondriaco, -ca *adj, m y f* hypochondriac.

hipocresía *f* hypocrisy.

hipócrita ◇ *adj* hypocritical. ◇ *m y f* hypocrite.

hipodérmico, -ca *adj* hypodermic.

hipódromo *m* racecourse, racetrack.

hipopótamo *m* hippopotamus.

hipoteca *f* mortgage.

hipotecar *vt* [bienes] to mortgage.

hipotecario, -ria *adj* mortgage (*antes de sust*).

hipotenusa *f* hypotenuse.

hipótesis *f inv* hypothesis.

hipotético, -ca *adj* hypothetical.

hippy, hippie ['xipi] (*pl* **hippies**) *adj, m y f* hippy.

hiriente *adj* [palabras] hurtful, cutting.

hirsuto, -ta *adj* [cabello] wiry; [brazo, pecho] hairy.

hispánico, -ca *adj, m y f* Hispanic, Spanish-speaking.

hispanidad *f* [cultura] Spanishness; [pueblos] Spanish-speaking world.

hispano, -na ◇ *adj* [español] Spanish; [hispanoamericano] Spanish-American; [en Estados Unidos] Hispanic. ◇ *m y f* [español] Spaniard; [estadounidense] Hispanic.

hispanoamericano, -na ◇ *adj* Spanish-American. ◇ *m y f* Spanish American.

hispanohablante ◇ *adj* Spanish-speaking. ◇ *m y f* Spanish speaker.

histeria *f* MED & *fig* hysteria.

histérico, -ca *adj* MED & *fig* hysterical; **ponerse** ~ to get hysterical.

histerismo *m* MED & *fig* hysteria.

historia *f* **-1.** [gen] history; ~ **del arte** art history; **pasar a la** ~ to go down in history. **-2.** [narración, chisme] story; **dejarse de** ~**s** to stop beating about the bush.

historiador, -ra *m y f* historian.

historial *m* [gen] record; [profesional] curriculum vitae, résumé *Am*; ~ **médico** ○ **clínico** medical ○ case history.

histórico, -ca *adj* **-1.** [de la historia] historical. **-2.** [verídico] factual. **-3.** [importante] historic.

historieta *f* **-1.** [chiste] funny story, anecdote. **-2.** [tira cómica] comic strip.

hito *m lit* & *fig* milestone.

hizo → **hacer**.

hmnos. (*abrev de* **hermanos**) bros.

hobby ['xoβi] (*pl* **hobbies**) *m* hobby.

hocico *m* [de perro] muzzle; [de gato] nose; [de cerdo] snout.

hockey ['xokei] *m* hockey; ~ **sobre**

hielo/patines ice/roller hockey; ~ **sobre hierba** (field) hockey.

hogar *m* **-1.** [de chimenea] fireplace; [de horno, cocina] **grate. -2.** [domicilio] home. **-3.** [familia] family.

hogareño, -ña *adj* [gen] family (*antes de sust*); [amante del hogar] home-loving.

hogaza *f* large loaf.

hoguera *f* bonfire; **morir en la** ~ to be burned at the stake.

hoja *f* **-1.** [de plantas] leaf; [de flor] petal; [de hierba] **blade. -2.** [de papel] sheet (of paper); [de libro] page. **-3.** [de cuchillo] blade; ~ **de afeitar** razor blade. **-4.** [de puertas, ventanas] leaf. ◆ **hoja de cálculo** *f* INFORM spreadsheet.

hojalata *f* tinplate.

hojaldre *m* puff pastry.

hojarasca *f* **-1.** [hojas secas] (dead) leaves (*pl*); [frondosidad] tangle of leaves. **-2.** *fig* [paja] rubbish.

hojear *vt* to leaf through.

hola *interj*: ¡~! hello!

Holanda Holland.

holandés, -esa ◇ *adj* Dutch. ◇ *m y f* [persona] Dutchman (*f* Dutchwoman). ◆ **holandés** *m* [lengua] Dutch. ◆ **holandesa** *f* [papel] *piece of paper measuring 22 x 28cm.*

holding ['xoldin] (*pl* **holdings**) *m* holding company.

holgado, -da *adj* **-1.** [ropa] baggy, loose-fitting; [habitación, espacio] roomy. **-2.** [victoria, situación económica] comfortable.

holgar *vi* [sobrar] to be unnecessary; **huelga decir que ...** needless to say ....

holgazán, -ana ◇ *adj* idle, good-for-nothing. ◇ *m y f* good-for-nothing.

holgazanear *vi* to laze about.

holgura *f* **-1.** [anchura - de espacio] room; [- de ropa] bagginess, looseness; [- entre piezas] play, give. **-2.** [bienestar] comfort, affluence.

hollar *vt* to tread (on).

hollín *m* soot.

holocausto *m* holocaust.

hombre ◇ *m* man; **el** ~ [la humanidad] man, mankind; **el** ~ **de la calle** ○ **de a pie** the man in the street; ~ **de las cavernas** caveman; ~ **de negocios** businessman; ~ **de palabra** man of his word; **un pobre** ~ a nobody; ¡**pobre** ~! poor chap *Br* ○ guy!; **de** ~ **a** ~ man to man. ◇ *interj*: ¡~! ¡**qué alegría verte!** (hey,) how nice to see you! ◆ **hombre orquesta** (*pl* **hombres orquesta**) *m*

one-man band. ◆ **hombre rana** (*pl* **hombres rana**) *m* frogman.

hombrera *f* [de traje, vestido] shoulder pad; [de uniforme] epaulette.

hombría *f* manliness.

hombro *m* shoulder; **a** ~**s** over one's shoulders; **encogerse de** ~**s** to shrug one's shoulders; **arrimar el** ~ *fig* to lend a hand.

hombruno, -na *adj* mannish.

homenaje *m* [gen] tribute; [al soberano] homage; **partido (de)** ~ testimonial (match); **en** ~ **de** ○ **a** in honour of, as a tribute to; **rendir** ~ **a** to pay tribute to.

homenajeado, -da *m y f* guest of honour.

homenajear *vt* to pay tribute to.

homeopatía *f* homeopathy.

homicida ◇ *adj* [mirada etc] murderous; **arma** ~ murder weapon. ◇ *m y f* murderer.

homicidio *m* homicide, murder.

homilía *f* homily, sermon.

homogeneizar *vt* to homogenize.

homogéneo, -a *adj* homogenous.

homologar *vt* **-1.** [equiparar]: ~ (**con**) to bring into line (with), to make comparable (with). **-2.** [dar por válido - producto] to authorize officially; [- récord] to confirm officially.

homólogo, -ga ◇ *adj* [semejante] equivalent. ◇ *m y f* counterpart.

homosexual *adj, m y f* homosexual.

hondo, -da *adj* **-1.** *lit & fig* [gen] deep; **lo** ~ the depths (*pl*); **calar** ~ **en** to strike a chord with; **en lo más** ~ **de** in the depths of. **-2.** → **cante.** ◆ **honda** *f* sling.

hondonada *f* hollow.

hondura *f* depth.

Honduras Honduras.

hondureño, -ña *adj, m y f* Honduran.

honestidad *f* [honradez] honesty; [decencia] modesty, decency; [justicia] fairness.

honesto, -ta *adj* [honrado] honest; [decente] modest, decent; [justo] fair.

hongo *m* **-1.** [planta - comestible] mushroom; [- no comestible] toadstool. **-2.** [enfermedad] fungus.

honor *m* honour; **hacer** ~ **a** to live up to; **en** ~ **a la verdad** to be (quite) honest. ◆ **honores** *mpl* [ceremonial] honours.

honorable *adj* honourable.

honorar *vt* to honour.

honorario, **-ria** *adj* honorary.
◆ **honorarios** *mpl* fees.

honorífico, **-ca** *adj* honorific.

honra *f* honour; ¡y a mucha ~! and proud of it! ◆ **honras fúnebres** *fpl* funeral (*sg*).

honradez *f* honesty.

honrado, **-da** *adj* honest.

honrar *vt* to honour. ◆ **honrarse** *vpr*: ~**se** (**con algo/de hacer algo**) to be honoured (by sthg/to do sthg).

honroso, **-sa** *adj* **-1.** [que da honra] honorary. **-2.** [respetable] honourable, respectable.

hora *f* **-1.** [del día] hour; **a primera ~** first thing in the morning; **a última ~** [al final del día] at the end of the day; [en el último momento] at the last moment; **dar la ~** to strike the hour; **de última ~** [noticia] latest, up-to-the-minute; [preparativos] last-minute; "**última ~**" "stop press"; (**pagar**) **por ~s** (to pay) by the hour; ~**s de oficina/trabajo** office/working hours; ~ **oficial** official time; ~ **punta** rush hour; ~**s extraordinarias** overtime (*U*); ~**s de visita** visiting times; **media ~** half an hour. **-2.** [momento determinado] time; **¿a qué ~ sale?** what time ○ when does it leave?; **es ~ de irse** it's time to go; **a la ~** on time; **en su ~** when the time comes, at the appropriate time; **¿qué ~ es?** what time is it? **-3.** [cita] appointment; **pedir/dar ~** to ask for/give an appointment; **tener ~ en/con** to have an appointment at/with. **-4.** *loc*: **a altas ~s de la noche** in the small hours; **en mala ~** unluckily; **la ~ de la verdad** the moment of truth; ¡**ya era ~**! and about time too!

horadar *vt* to pierce; [con máquina] to bore through.

horario, **-ria** *adj* time (*antes de sust*). ◆ **horario** *m* timetable; ~ **comercial/laboral** opening/working hours (*pl*); ~ **intensivo** *working day without a long break for lunch*; ~ **de visitas** visiting hours (*pl*).

horca *f* **-1.** [patíbulo] gallows (*pl*). **-2.** AGR pitchfork.

horcajadas ◆ **a horcajadas** *loc adv* astride.

horchata *f* *cold drink made from ground tiger nuts or almonds, milk and sugar.*

horizontal *adj* horizontal.

horizonte *m* horizon.

horma *f* [gen] mould, pattern; [para

arreglar zapatos] **last**; [para conservar zapatos] **shoe tree**; [de sombrero] **hat block**.

hormiga *f* ant.

hormigón *m* concrete; ~ **armado** reinforced concrete.

hormigueo *m* pins and needles (*pl*).

hormiguero ◇ *adj* → **oso**. ◇ *m* ants' nest.

hormona *f* hormone.

hornada *f* *lit* & *fig* batch.

hornear *vt* to bake.

hornillo *m* [para cocinar] **camping** ○ portable **stove**; [de laboratorio] small furnace.

horno *m* CULIN oven; TECN furnace; [de cerámica, ladrillos] kiln; **alto ~** blast furnace; **altos ~s** [factoría] iron and steelworks; ~ **eléctrico** electric oven; ~ **microondas** microwave (oven).

horóscopo *m* **-1.** [signo zodiacal] star sign. **-2.** [predicción] horoscope.

horquilla *f* [para el pelo] hairpin.

horrendo, **-da** *adj* [gen] horrendous; [muy malo] terrible, awful.

horrible *adj* [gen] horrible; [muy malo] terrible, awful.

horripilante *adj* [terrorífico] horrifying, spine-chilling.

horripilar *vt* to terrify.

horror *m* **-1.** [miedo] terror, horror; ¡**qué ~**! how awful! **-2.** (*gen pl*) [atrocidad] atrocity.

horrorizado, **-da** *adj* terrified, horrified.

horrorizar *vt* to terrify, to horrify. ◆ **horrorizarse** *vpr* to be terrified ○ horrified.

horroroso, **-sa** *adj* **-1.** [gen] awful. **-2.** [muy feo] horrible, hideous.

hortaliza *f* (garden) vegetable.

hortelano, **-na** *m y f* market gardener.

hortensia *f* hydrangea.

hortera *fam adj* tasteless, tacky.

horticultura *f* horticulture.

hosco, **-ca** *adj* [persona] sullen, gruff; [lugar] grim, gloomy.

hospedar *vt* to put up. ◆ **hospedarse** *vpr* to stay.

hospicio *m* [para niños] children's home; [para pobres] poorhouse.

hospital *m* hospital.

hospitalario, **-ria** *adj* [acogedor] hospitable.

hospitalidad *f* hospitality.

hospitalizar *vt* to hospitalize, to take ○ send to hospital.

hosquedad *f* sullenness, gruffness.

hostal *m* guesthouse.

hostelería *f* catering.

hostia *f* **-1.** RELIG host. **-2.** *vulg* [bofetada] bash, punch. **-3.** *vulg* [accidente] smash-up. ◆ **hostias** *interj vulg*: ¡~s! bloody hell!, damn it!

hostiar *vt vulg* to bash.

hostigar *vt* **-1.** [acosar] to pester, to bother. **-2.** MIL to harass.

hostil *adj* hostile.

hostilidad *f* [sentimiento] hostility. ◆ **hostilidades** *fpl* MIL hostilities.

hotel *m* hotel.

hotelero, -ra *adj* hotel (*antes de sust*).

hoy *adv* **-1.** [en este día] today; **de ~ en adelante** from now on. **-2.** [en la actualidad] nowadays, today; **~ día, ~ en día, ~ por ~** these days, nowadays.

hoyo *m* [gen] hole, pit; [de golf] hole.

hoyuelo *m* dimple.

hoz *f* sickle; **la ~ y el martillo** the hammer and sickle.

huacal *m Amer* **-1.** [jaula] cage. **-2.** [cajón] drawer.

hubiera *etc* → **haber**.

hucha *f* moneybox.

hueco, -ca *adj* **-1.** [vacío] hollow. **-2.** [sonido] resonant, hollow. **-3.** [sin ideas] empty. ◆ **hueco** *m* **-1.** [cavidad - gen] hole; [- en pared] recess. **-2.** [tiempo libre] spare moment. **-3.** [espacio libre] space, gap; [de escalera] well; [de ascensor] shaft.

huela *etc* → **oler**.

huelga *f* strike; **estar/declararse en ~** to be/to go on strike; **~ de brazos caídos** o **cruzados** sit-down (strike); **~ de celo** work-to-rule; **~ de hambre** hunger strike; **~ general** general strike; **~ salvaje** wildcat strike.

huelguista *m y f* striker.

huella *f* **-1.** [de persona] footprint; [de animal, rueda] track; **~ digital** o **dactilar** fingerprint. **-2.** *fig* [vestigio] trace. **-3.** *fig* [impresión profunda] mark; **dejar ~** to leave one's mark.

huérfano, -na *adj, m y f* orphan.

huerta *f* [huerto] market garden *Br*, truck farm *Am*.

huerto *m* [de hortalizas] vegetable garden; [de frutales] orchard.

hueso *m* **-1.** [del cuerpo] bone; **ser un ~ duro de roer** to be a hard nut to crack. **-2.** [de fruto] stone *Br*, pit *Am*. **-3.** *Amer fam* [enchufe] contacts (*pl*), influence.

huésped, -da *m y f* guest.

huesudo, -da *adj* bony.

hueva *f* roe.

huevada *f Amer vulg* bollocks (*U*), crap.

huevo *m* **-1.** [de animales] egg; **~ a la copa** o **tibio** *Amer* boiled egg; **~ escalfado/frito** poached/fried egg; **~ pasado por agua/duro** soft-boiled/hard-boiled egg; **~s revueltos** scrambled eggs. **-2.** (*gen pl*) *vulg* [testículos] balls (*pl*); **costar un ~** [ser caro] to cost a packet o bomb; [ser difícil] to be bloody hard.

huevón *m Amer vulg* stupid bastard.

huida *f* escape, flight.

huidizo, -za *adj* shy, elusive.

huir *vi* **-1.** [escapar]: **~ (de)** [gen] to flee (from); [de cárcel etc] to escape (from); **~ del país** to flee the country. **-2.** [evitar]: **~ de algo** to avoid sthg, to keep away from sthg.

hule *m* oilskin.

humanidad *f* humanity. ◆ **humanidades** *fpl* [letras] humanities.

humanitario, -ria *adj* humanitarian.

humanizar *vt* to humanize.

humano, -na *adj* **-1.** [del hombre] human. **-2.** [compasivo] humane. ◆ **humano** *m* human being; **los ~s** mankind (*U*).

humareda *f* cloud of smoke.

humear *vi* [salir humo] to (give off) smoke; [salir vapor] to steam.

humedad *f* **-1.** [gen] dampness; [en pared, techo] damp; [de algo chorreando] wetness; [de piel, ojos etc] moistness. **-2.** [de atmósfera etc] humidity.

humedecer *vt* to moisten. ◆ **humedecerse** *vpr* to become moist; **~se los labios** to moisten one's lips.

húmedo, -da *adj* **-1.** [gen] damp; [chorreando] wet; [piel, ojos etc] moist. **-2.** [aire, clima, atmósfera] humid.

humidificar *vt* to humidify.

humildad *f* humility.

humilde *adj* humble.

humillación *f* humiliation.

humillado, -da *adj* humiliated.

humillante *adj* humiliating.

humillar *vt* to humiliate. ◆ **humillarse** *vpr* to humble o.s.

humo *m* [gen] smoke; [vapor] steam; [de coches etc] fumes (*pl*). ◆ **humos** *mpl fig* [aires] airs; **bajarle a alguien los ~s** *fig* to take sb down a peg or two.

humor *m* **-1.** [estado de ánimo] mood; [carácter] temperament; **estar de buen/mal ~** to be in a good/bad mood. **-2.** [gracia] humour; **un programa de ~** a comedy programme; **~ negro** black

humour. -3. [ganas] mood; **no estoy de ~** I'm not in the mood.
humorismo *m* humour; TEATR & TV comedy.
humorista *m y f* humorist; TEATR & TV comedian (*f* comedienne).
humorístico, -ca *adj* humorous.
hundimiento *m* **-1.** [naufragio] sinking. **-2.** [ruina] collapse.
hundir *vt* **-1.** [gen] to sink; **~ algo en el agua** to put sthg underwater. **-2.** *fig* [afligir] to devastate, to destroy. **-3.** *fig* [hacer fracasar] to ruin. ◆ **hundirse** *vpr* **-1.** [sumergirse] to sink; [intencionadamente] to dive. **-2.** [derrumbarse] to collapse; [techo] to cave in. **-3.** *fig* [fracasar] to be ruined.
húngaro, -ra *adj, m y f* Hungarian. ◆ **húngaro** *m* [lengua] Hungarian.
Hungría Hungary.
huracán *m* hurricane.
huraño, -ña *adj* unsociable.
hurgar *vi*: **~ (en)** [gen] to rummage around (in); [con el dedo, un palo] to poke around (in). ◆ **hurgarse** *vpr*: **~se la nariz** to pick one's nose; **~se los bolsillos** to rummage around in one's pockets.
hurgonear *vt* to poke.
hurón *m* ZOOL ferret.
hurra *interj* ¡~! hurray!
hurtadillas ◆ **a hurtadillas** *loc adv* on the sly, stealthily.
hurtar *vt* to steal.
hurto *m* theft.
husmear ◇ *vt* [olfatear] to sniff out, to scent. ◇ *vi* [curiosear] to nose around.
huso *m* spindle; [en máquina] bobbin.
huy *interj* ¡~! [dolor] ouch!; [sorpresa] gosh!

I

i, I *f* [letra] i, I.
IAE (*abrev de* **Impuesto sobre Actividades Económicas**) *m Spanish tax paid by professionals and shop owners.*
iba → **ir**.
ibérico, -ca *adj* Iberian.
íbero, -ra *adj, m y f* Iberian. ◆ **íbero, ibero** *m* [lengua] Iberian.

iberoamericano, -na *adj, m y f* Latin American.
iceberg (*pl* **icebergs**) *m* iceberg.
Icona (*abrev de* **Instituto Nacional para la Conservación de la Naturaleza**) *m Spanish national institute for conservation,* ≃ NCC *Br.*
icono *m* icon.
iconoclasta *m y f* iconoclast.
id → **ir**.
ida *f* outward journey; **(billete de) ~ y vuelta** return (ticket).
idea *f* **-1.** [gen] idea; [propósito] intention; **con la ~ de** with the idea ○ intention of; **~ fija** obsession; **no tener ni ~ (de)** not to have a clue (about). **-2.** [opinión] impression; **cambiar de ~** to change one's mind.
ideal *adj & m* ideal.
idealista ◇ *adj* idealistic. ◇ *m y f* idealist.
idealizar *vt* to idealize.
idear *vt* **-1.** [planear] to think up, to devise. **-2.** [inventar] to invent.
ideario *m* ideology.
ídem *pron* ditto.
idéntico, -ca *adj*: **~ (a)** identical (to).
identidad *f* [gen] identity.
identificación *f* identification.
identificar *vt* to identify. ◆ **identificarse** *vpr*: **~se (con)** to identify (with).
ideología *f* ideology.
idílico, -ca *adj* idyllic.
idilio *m* love affair.
idioma *m* language.
idiosincrasia *f* individual character.
idiota ◇ *adj despec* [tonto] stupid. ◇ *m y f* idiot.
idiotez *f* [tontería] stupid thing, stupidity (*U*).
ido, ida *adj* mad, touched.
idolatrar *vt* to worship; *fig* to idolize.
ídolo *m* idol.
idóneo, -a *adj*: **~ (para)** suitable (for).
iglesia *f* church.
iglú (*pl* **iglúes**) *m* igloo.
ignorancia *f* ignorance.
ignorante ◇ *adj* ignorant. ◇ *m y f* ignoramus.
ignorar *vt* **-1.** [desconocer] not to know, to be ignorant of. **-2.** [no tener en cuenta] to ignore.
igual ◇ *adj* **-1.** [idéntico]: **~ (que)** the same (as); **llevan jerseys ~es** they're wearing the same jumper; **son ~es** they're the same. **-2.** [parecido]: **~**

(que) similar (to). **-3.** [equivalente]: ~ **(a)** equal (to). **-4.** [liso] even. **-5.** [constante - velocidad] constant; [- clima, temperatura] even. **-6.** MAT: **A más B es ~ a C** A plus B equals C. ◇ *m y f* equal; **sin ~** without equal, unrivalled. ◇ *adv* **-1.** [de la misma manera] the same; **yo pienso ~** I think the same, I think so too; **al ~ que** just like; **por ~** equally. **-2.** [posiblemente] perhaps; ~ **llueve** it could well rain. **-3.** DEP: **van ~es** the scores are level. **-4.** *loc*: **dar** ○ **ser ~ a alguien** to be all the same to sb; **es** ○ **da ~** it doesn't matter, it doesn't make any difference.

igualado, -da *adj* level.

igualar *vt* **-1.** [gen] to make equal; DEP to equalize; ~ **algo a** ○ **con** to equate sthg with. **-2.** [persona] to be equal to; **nadie le iguala en generosidad** nobody is as generous as he is. **-3.** [terreno] to level; [superficie] to smooth. ◆ **igualarse** *vpr* **-1.** [gen] to be equal. **-2.** [a otra persona]: ~**se a** ○ **con alguien** to treat sb as an equal.

igualdad *f* **-1.** [equivalencia] equality; **en ~ de condiciones** on equal terms; ~ **de oportunidades** equal opportunities (*pl*). **-2.** [identidad] sameness.

igualitario, -ria *adj* egalitarian.

igualmente *adv* **-1.** [también] also, likewise. **-2.** [fórmula de cortesía] the same to you, likewise.

ikurriña *f* Basque national flag.

ilegal *adj* illegal.

ilegible *adj* illegible.

ilegítimo, -ma *adj* illegitimate.

ileso, -sa *adj* unhurt, unharmed; **salir** ○ **resultar ~** to escape unharmed.

ilícito, -ta *adj* illicit.

ilimitado, -da *adj* unlimited, limitless.

iluminación *f* **-1.** [gen] lighting; [acción] illumination. **-2.** RELIG enlightenment.

iluminar *vt* [gen] to illuminate, to light up. ◆ **iluminarse** *vpr* to light up.

ilusión *f* **-1.** [esperanza - gen] hope; [- infundada] delusion, illusion; **hacerse** ○ **forjarse ilusiones** to build up one's hopes. **-2.** [emoción] thrill, excitement (*U*); **¡qué ~!** how exciting!; **me hace mucha ~** I'm really looking forward to it. **-3.** [espejismo] illusion.

ilusionar *vt* **-1.** [esperanzar]: ~ **a alguien (con algo)** to build up sb's hopes (about sthg). **-2.** [emocionar] to excite, to thrill. ◆ **ilusionarse** *vpr* [emocionarse]: ~**se (con)** to get excited (about).

ilusionista *m y f* conjurer.

iluso, -sa *adj* gullible.

ilusorio, -ria *adj* illusory; [promesa] empty.

ilustración *f* **-1.** [estampa] illustration. **-2.** [cultura] learning. ◆ **Ilustración** *f* HIST: **la Ilustración** the Enlightenment.

ilustrado, -da *adj* **-1.** [publicación] illustrated. **-2.** [persona] learned. **-3.** HIST enlightened.

ilustrar *vt* **-1.** [explicar] to illustrate, to explain. **-2.** [publicación] to illustrate.

ilustre *adj* [gen] illustrious, distinguished.

imagen *f* [gen] image; TV picture; **ser la viva ~ de alguien** to be the spitting image of sb.

imaginación *f* **-1.** [facultad] imagination; **pasar por la ~ de alguien** to occur to sb, to cross sb's mind. **-2.** (*gen pl*) [idea falsa] delusion.

imaginar *vt* **-1.** [gen] to imagine. **-2.** [idear] to think up, to invent. ◆ **imaginarse** *vpr* to imagine; **¡imagínate!** just think ○ imagine!; **me imagino que sí** I suppose so.

imaginario, -ria *adj* imaginary.

imaginativo, -va *adj* imaginative.

imán *m* [para atraer] magnet.

imbécil ◇ *adj* stupid. ◇ *m y f* idiot.

imbecilidad *f* stupidity; **decir/hacer una ~** to say/do sthg stupid.

imborrable *adj fig* indelible; [recuerdo] unforgettable.

imbuir *vt*: ~ **(de)** to imbue (with).

imitación *f* imitation; [de humorista] impersonation; **a ~ de** in imitation of; **piel de ~** imitation leather.

imitador, -ra *m y f* imitator; [humorista] impersonator.

imitar *vt* [gen] to imitate, to copy; [a personajes famosos] to impersonate; [producto, material] to simulate.

impaciencia *f* impatience.

impacientar *vt* to make impatient. ◆ **impacientarse** *vpr* to grow impatient.

impaciente *adj* impatient; ~ **por hacer algo** impatient ○ anxious to do sthg.

impactar ◇ *vt* [suj: noticia] to have an impact on. ◇ *vi* [bala] to hit.

impacto *m* **-1.** [gen] impact; [de bala] hit. **-2.** [señal] (impact) mark; ~**s de bala** bullethole.

impagado, -da *adj* unpaid.

impar *adj* MAT odd.

imparable *adj* unstoppable.

imparcial *adj* impartial.

impartir *vt* to give.

impase, impasse [im'pas] *m* impasse.

impasible *adj* impassive.

impávido, -da *adj* [valeroso] fearless, courageous; [impasible] impassive.

impecable *adj* impeccable.

impedido, -da *adj* disabled; **estar ~ de un brazo** to have the use of only one arm.

impedimento *m* [gen] obstacle; [contra un matrimonio] impediment.

impedir *vt* -1. [imposibilitar] to prevent; **~ a alguien hacer algo** to prevent sb from doing sth. -2. [dificultar] to hinder, to obstruct.

impenetrable *adj* lit & fig impenetrable.

impensable *adj* unthinkable.

imperante *adj* prevailing.

imperar *vi* to prevail.

imperativo, -va *adj* -1. [gen & GRAM] imperative. -2. [autoritario] imperious. ◆**imperativo** *m* [gen & GRAM] imperative.

imperceptible *adj* imperceptible.

imperdible *m* safety pin.

imperdonable *adj* unforgivable.

imperfección *f* -1. [cualidad] imperfection. -2. [defecto] flaw, defect.

imperfecto, -ta *adj* [gen] imperfect; [defectuoso] faulty, defective. ◆**imperfecto** *m* GRAM imperfect.

imperial *adj* imperial.

imperialismo *m* imperialism.

impericia *f* lack of skill; [inexperiencia] inexperience.

imperio *m* -1. [territorio] empire. -2. [dominio] rule.

imperioso, -sa *adj* -1. [autoritario] imperious. -2. [apremiante] urgent.

impermeable ◇ *adj* waterproof. ◇ *m* raincoat, mac *Br*.

impersonal *adj* impersonal.

impertinencia *f* -1. [gen] impertinence. -2. [comentario] impertinent remark.

impertinente *adj* impertinent.

imperturbable *adj* imperturbable.

ímpetu *m* -1. [brusquedad] force. -2. [energía] energy. -3. FÍS impetus.

impetuoso, -sa *adj* -1. [olas, viento, ataque] violent. -2. fig [persona] impulsive, impetuous.

impío, -a *adj* godless, impious.

implacable *adj* implacable, relentless.

implantar *vt* -1. [establecer] to introduce. -2. MED to insert. ◆**implantarse** *vpr* [establecerse] to be introduced.

implicación *f* -1. [participación] involvement. -2. (*gen pl*) [consecuencia] implication.

implicar *vt* -1. [involucrar]: **~ (en)** to involve (in); DER to implicate (in). -2. [significar] to mean. ◆**implicarse** *vpr* DER to incriminate o.s.; **~se en** to become involved in.

implícito, -ta *adj* implicit.

implorar *vt* to implore.

imponente *adj* -1. [impresionante] imposing, impressive. -2. [estupendo] sensational, terrific.

imponer ◇ *vt* -1. **~ algo (a alguien)** [gen] to impose sth (on sb); [respeto] to command sth (from sb). -2. [moda] to set; [costumbre] to introduce. ◇ *vi* to be imposing. ◆**imponerse** *vpr* -1. [hacerse respetar] to command respect, to show authority. -2. [prevalecer] to prevail. -3. [ser necesario] to be necessary. -4. DEP to win, to prevail.

impopular *adj* unpopular.

importación *f* [acción] importing; [artículo] import.

importador, -ra *m y f* importer.

importancia *f* importance; **dar ~ a algo** to attach importance to sthg; **quitar ~ a algo** to play sthg down; **darse ~** to give o.s. airs, to show off.

importante *adj* -1. [gen] important; [lesión] serious. -2. [cantidad] considerable.

importar ◇ *vt* -1. [gen & INFORM] to import. -2. [suj: factura, coste] to amount to, to come to. ◇ *vi* -1. [preocupar] to matter; **no me importa** I don't care, it doesn't matter to me; **¿y a ti qué te importa?** what's it got to do with you? -2. [en preguntas] to mind; **¿le importa que me siente?** do you mind if I sit down?; **¿te importaría acompañarme?** would you mind coming with me? ◇ *v impers* to matter; **no importa** it doesn't matter.

importe *m* [gen] price, cost; [de factura] total.

importunar *vt* to bother, to pester.

importuno, -na = **inoportuno**.

imposibilidad *f* impossibility; **su ~ para contestar la pregunta** his inability to answer the question.

imposibilitado, -da *adj* disabled; **estar ~ para hacer algo** to be unable to do sthg.

imposibilitar *vt*: **~ a alguien para hacer algo** to make it impossible for sb to do sthg, to prevent sb from doing sthg.

imposible *adj* **-1.** [irrealizable] impossible. **-2.** [insoportable] **unbearable**, impossible.

imposición *f* **-1.** [obligación] imposition. **-2.** [impuesto] tax. **-3.** BANCA deposit.

impostor, -ra *m y f* [suplantador] impostor.

impotencia *f* impotence.

impotente *adj* impotent.

impracticable *adj* **-1.** [irrealizable] impracticable. **-2.** [intransitable] impassable.

imprecisión *f* imprecision, vagueness (U).

impreciso, -sa *adj* imprecise, vague.

impredecible *adj* unforeseeable; [variable] unpredictable.

impregnar *vt*: ~ **(de)** to impregnate (with). ◆ **impregnarse** *vpr*: ~se **(de)** to become impregnated (with).

imprenta *f* **-1.** [arte] printing. **-2.** [máquina] (printing) **press**. **-3.** [establecimiento] printing house.

imprescindible *adj* indispensable, essential.

impresentable *adj* unpresentable.

impresión *f* **-1.** [gen] impression; [sensación física] **feeling**; **causar (una) buena/mala** ~ to make a good/bad impression; **dar la** ~ **de** to give the impression of; **tener la** ~ **de que** to have the impression that. **-2.** [huella] imprint; ~ **digital** O **dactilar** fingerprint. **-3.** [IMPRENTA - acción] **printing**; [- edición] **edition**.

impresionable *adj* impressionable.

impresionante *adj* impressive; [error] enormous.

impresionar ◇ *vt* **-1.** [maravillar] to impress. **-2.** [conmocionar] to move. **-3.** [horrorizar] to shock. **-4.** FOT to expose. ◇ *vi* [maravillar] to make an impression. ◆ **impresionarse** *vpr* **-1.** [maravillarse] to be impressed. **-2.** [conmocionarse] to be moved. **-3.** [horrorizarse] to be shocked.

impreso, -sa ◇ *pp* → **imprimir**. ◇ *adj* printed. ◆ **impreso** *m* **-1.** [texto] printed matter (U). **-2.** [formulario] form.

impresor, -ra *m y f* [persona] printer. ◆ **impresora** *f* INFORM printer; **impresora láser/térmica** laser/thermal printer; **impresora de matriz** O **de agujas** dot-

matrix printer; **impresora de chorro de tinta** ink-jet printer.

imprevisible *adj* unforeseeable; [variable] unpredictable.

imprevisto, -ta *adj* unexpected. ◆ **imprevisto** *m* [hecho]: **salvo** ~s barring accidents.

imprimir *vt* **-1.** [gen] to print; [huella, paso] to leave. **-2.** *fig* [transmitir]: ~ **algo a** to impart O bring sthg to.

improbable *adj* improbable, unlikely.

improcedente *adj* **-1.** [inoportuno] inappropriate. **-2.** DER inadmissible.

improperio *m* insult.

impropio, -pia *adj*: ~ **(de)** improper (for), unbecoming (to).

improvisado, -da *adj* [gen] improvised; [discurso, truco] **impromptu**; [comentario] ad-lib; [cama etc] makeshift.

improvisar ◇ *vt* [gen] to improvise; [comida] to rustle up; ~ **una cama** to make (up) a makeshift bed. ◇ *vi* [gen] to improvise; MÚS to extemporize.

improviso ◆ **de improviso** *loc adv* unexpectedly, suddenly; **coger a alguien de** ~ to catch sb unawares.

imprudencia *f* [en los actos] carelessness (U); [en los comentarios] indiscretion.

imprudente *adj* [en los actos] careless, rash; [en los comentarios] indiscreet.

impúdico, -ca *adj* immodest, indecent.

impuesto, -ta *pp* → **imponer**. ◆ **impuesto** *m* tax; ~ **sobre el valor añadido** value-added tax; ~ **sobre la renta** ≃ income tax.

impugnar *vt* to contest, to challenge.

impulsar *vt* **-1.** [empujar] to propel, to drive. **-2.** [incitar]: ~ **a alguien (a algo/a hacer algo)** to drive sb (to sthg/to do sthg). **-3.** [promocionar] to stimulate.

impulsivo, -va *adj* impulsive.

impulso *m* **-1.** [progreso] stimulus, boost. **-2.** [fuerza] momentum. **-3.** [motivación] impulse, urge.

impulsor, -ra *m y f* dynamic force.

impune *adj* unpunished.

impunidad *f* impunity.

impureza *f (gen pl)* impurity.

impuro, -ra *adj lit & fig* impure.

imputación *f* accusation.

imputar *vt* [atribuir]: ~ **algo a alguien** [delito] to accuse sb of sthg; [fracaso, error] to attribute sthg to sb.

in → **fraganti, vitro**.

inabarcable *adj* unmanageable.

inacabable *adj* interminable, endless.

inaccesible *adj* inaccessible.

inaceptable *adj* unacceptable.

inactividad *f* inactivity.

inactivo, -va *adj* inactive.

inadaptado, -da *adj* maladjusted.

inadecuado, -da *adj* [inapropiado] unsuitable, inappropriate.

inadmisible *adj* inadmissible.

inadvertido, -da *adj* unnoticed; **pasar ~ to** go unnoticed.

inagotable *adj* inexhaustible.

inaguantable *adj* unbearable.

inalámbrico, -ca *adj* cordless.

inalcanzable *adj* unattainable.

inalterable *adj* **-1.** [gen] unalterable; [salud] stable; [amistad] undying. **-2.** [color] fast. **-3.** [rostro, carácter] impassive. **-4.** [resultado, marcador] unchanged.

inamovible *adj* immovable, fixed.

inanición *f* starvation.

inanimado, -da *adj* inanimate.

inánime *adj* lifeless.

inapreciable *adj* **-1.** [incalculable] invaluable. **-2.** [insignificante] imperceptible.

inapropiado, -da *adj* inappropriate.

inaudito, -ta *adj* unheard-of.

inauguración *f* inauguration, opening.

inaugurar *vt* to inaugurate, to open.

inca *adj, m y f* Inca.

incalculable *adj* incalculable.

incalificable *adj* unspeakable.

incandescente *adj* incandescent.

incansable *adj* untiring, tireless.

incapacidad *f* **-1.** [imposibilidad] inability. **-2.** [inaptitud] incompetence. **-3.** DER incapacity.

incapacitado, -da *adj* [DER - gen] disqualified; [- para testar] incapacitated; [- para trabajar] unfit.

incapacitar *vt*: ~ **(para)** [gen] to disqualify (from); [para trabajar etc] to render unfit (for).

incapaz *adj* **-1.** [gen]: ~ **de** incapable of. **-2.** [sin talento]: ~ **para** incompetent at, no good at. **-3.** DER incompetent.

incautación *f* seizure, confiscation.

incautarse ◆ **incautarse de** *vpr* DER to seize, to confiscate.

incauto, -ta *adj* gullible.

incendiar *vt* to set fire to. ◆ **incendiarse** *vpr* to catch fire.

incendiario, -ria ◇ *adj* **-1.** [bomba etc] incendiary. **-2.** *fig* [artículo, libro etc] inflammatory. ◇ *m y f* arsonist.

incendio *m* fire; ~ **provocado** arson.

incentivo *m* incentive.

incertidumbre *f* uncertainty.

incesto *m* incest.

incidencia *f* **-1.** [repercusión] impact, effect. **-2.** [suceso] event.

incidente *m* incident.

incidir ◆ **incidir en** *vi* **-1.** [incurrir en] to fall into, to lapse into. **-2.** [insistir en] to focus on. **-3.** [influir en] to have an impact on, to affect.

incienso *m* incense.

incierto, -ta *adj* **-1.** [dudoso] uncertain. **-2.** [falso] untrue.

incineración *f* [de cadáver] cremation; [de basura] incineration.

incinerar *vt* [cadáver] to cremate; [basura] to incinerate.

incipiente *adj* incipient; [estado, etapa] early.

incisión *f* incision.

incisivo, -va *adj* **-1.** [instrumento] sharp, cutting. **-2.** *fig* [mordaz] incisive.

inciso, -sa *adj* cut. ◆ **inciso** *m* passing remark.

incitante *adj* [instigador] inciting; [provocativo] provocative.

incitar *vt*: ~ **a alguien a algo** [violencia, rebelión etc] to incite sb to sthg; ~ **a alguien a la fuga/venganza** to urge sb to flee/avenge himself; ~ **a alguien a hacer algo** [rebelarse etc] to incite sb to do sthg; [fugarse, vengarse] to urge sb to do sthg.

inclemencia *f* harshness, inclemency.

inclinación *f* **-1.** [desviación] slant, inclination; [de terreno] slope. **-2.** *fig* [afición]: ~ **(a ○ por)** penchant ○ propensity (for). **-3.** [cariño]: ~ **hacia alguien** fondness towards sb. **-4.** [saludo] bow.

inclinar *vt* **-1.** [doblar] to bend; [ladear] to tilt. **-2.** [cabeza] to bow. ◆ **inclinarse** *vpr* **-1.** [doblarse] to lean. **-2.** [para saludar]: ~**se (ante)** to bow (before). ◆ **inclinarse a** *vi* [tender a] to be ○ feel inclined to. ◆ **inclinarse por** *vi* [preferir] to favour, to lean towards.

incluir *vt* [gen] to include; [adjuntar - en cartas] to enclose.

inclusive *adv* inclusive.

incluso, -sa *adj* enclosed. ◆ **incluso** *adv & prep* even.

incógnito, -ta *adj* unknown. ◆ **incógnita** *f* **-1.** MAT unknown quantity. **-2.** [misterio] mystery. ◆ **de incógnito** *loc adv* incognito.

incoherencia *f* **-1.** [cualidad] incoherence. **-2.** [comentario] nonsensical remark.

incoherente *adj* **-1.** [inconexo] incoherent. **-2.** [inconsecuente] inconsistent.

incoloro, -ra adj lit & fig colourless.
incomodar vt -1. [causar molestia] to bother, to inconvenience. -2. [enfadar] to annoy. ◆ **incomodarse** vpr [enfadarse]: ~se (por) to get annoyed (about).
incomodidad f -1. [de silla etc] uncomfortableness. -2. [de situación, persona] awkwardness.
incómodo, -da adj -1. [silla etc] uncomfortable. -2. [situación, persona] awkward, uncomfortable.
incomparable adj incomparable.
incompatible adj: ~ (con) incompatible (with).
incompetencia f incompetence.
incompetente adj incompetent.
incompleto, -ta adj -1. [gen] incomplete. -2. [inacabado] unfinished.
incomprendido, -da adj misunderstood.
incomprensible adj incomprehensible.
incomprensión f lack of understanding.
incomprensivo, -va adj unsympathetic.
incomunicado, -da adj -1. [gen] isolated. -2. [por la nieve etc] cut off. -3. [preso] in solitary confinement.
inconcebible adj inconceivable.
inconcluso, -sa adj unfinished.
incondicional ◇ adj unconditional; [ayuda] wholehearted; [seguidor] staunch. ◇ m y f staunch supporter.
inconexo, -xa adj [gen] unconnected; [pensamiento, texto] disjointed.
inconformista adj, m y f nonconformist.
inconfundible adj unmistakable; [prueba] irrefutable.
incongruente adj incongruous.
inconsciencia f -1. [gen] unconsciousness. -2. fig [falta de juicio] thoughtlessness.
inconsciente adj -1. [gen] unconscious. -2. fig [irreflexivo] thoughtless.
inconsecuente adj inconsistent.
inconsistente adj [tela, pared etc] flimsy; [salsa] runny; [argumento, discurso etc] lacking in substance.
inconstancia f -1. [en el trabajo, la conducta] unreliability. -2. [de opinión, ideas] changeability.
inconstante adj -1. [en el trabajo, la conducta] unreliable. -2. [de opinión, ideas] changeable.
inconstitucional adj unconstitutional.
incontable adj [innumerable] countless.
incontestable adj indisputable.

incontinencia f MED incontinence.
incontrolable adj uncontrollable.
inconveniencia f -1. [inoportunidad] inappropriateness. -2. [comentario] tactless remark; [acto] mistake.
inconveniente ◇ adj -1. [inoportuno] inappropriate. -2. [descortés] rude. ◇ m -1. [dificultad] obstacle, problem. -2. [desventaja] drawback.
incordiar vt fam to bother, to pester.
incorporación f: ~ (a) [gen] incorporation (into); [a un puesto] induction (into).
incorporar vt -1. [añadir]: ~ (a) [gen] to incorporate (into); CULIN to mix (into). -2. [levantar] to sit up. ◆ **incorporarse** vpr -1. [empezar]: ~se (a) [equipo] to join; [trabajo] to start. -2. [levantarse] to sit up.
incorrección f -1. [inexactitud] incorrectness; [error gramatical] mistake. -2. [descortesía] lack of courtesy, rudeness (U).
incorrecto, -ta adj -1. [equivocado] incorrect, wrong. -2. [descortés] rude, impolite.
incorregible adj incorrigible.
incredulidad f incredulity.
incrédulo, -la adj sceptical, incredulous; RELIG unbelieving.
increíble adj -1. [difícil de creer] unconvincing. -2. fig [extraordinario] incredible. -3. fig [inconcebible] unbelievable.
incrementar vt to increase. ◆ **incrementarse** vpr to increase.
incremento m increase; [de temperatura] rise.
increpar vt -1. [reprender] to reprimand. -2. [insultar] to abuse, insult.
incriminar vt to accuse.
incruento, -ta adj bloodless.
incrustar vt -1. TECN to inlay; [en joyería] to set. -2. fam fig [empotrar]: ~ algo en algo to sink sthg into sthg. ◆ **incrustarse** vpr [cal etc] to become encrusted.
incubar vt -1. [huevo] to incubate. -2. [enfermedad] to be sickening for.
inculcar vt: ~ algo a alguien to instil sthg into sb.
inculpar vt: ~ a alguien (de) [gen] to accuse sb (of); DER to charge sb (with).
inculto, -ta ◇ adj [persona] uneducated. ◇ m y f ignoramus.
incumbencia f: es/no es de nuestra ~ it is/isn't a matter for us, it falls/doesn't fall within our area of responsibility.

incumbir ◆ **incumbir a** *vi*: ~ **a alguien** to be a matter for sb; **esto no te incumbe** this is none of your business.

incumplimiento *m* [de deber] failure to fulfil; [de orden, ley] non-compliance; [de promesa] failure to keep; ~ **de contrato** breach of contract.

incumplir *vt* [deber] to fail to fulfil, to neglect; [orden, ley] to fail to comply with; [promesa] to break; [contrato] to breach.

incurable *adj* incurable.

incurrir ◆ **incurrir en** *vi* **-1.** [delito, falta] to commit; [error] to make. **-2.** [desprecio etc] to incur.

incursión *f* incursion.

indagación *f* investigation, inquiry.

indagar ◇ *vt* to investigate, to inquire into. ◇ *vi* to investigate, to inquire.

indecencia *f* **-1.** [cualidad] indecency. **-2.** [acción] outrage, crime.

indecente *adj* **-1.** [impúdico] indecent. **-2.** [indigno] miserable, wretched.

indecible *adj* [alegría] indescribable; [dolor] unspeakable.

indecisión *f* indecisiveness.

indeciso, -sa *adj* **-1.** [persona - inseguro] indecisive; [- que está dudoso] undecided. **-2.** [pregunta, respuesta] hesitant; [resultado] undecided.

indefenso, -sa *adj* defenceless.

indefinido, -da *adj* **-1.** [ilimitado] indefinite; [contrato] open-ended. **-2.** [impreciso] vague. **-3.** GRAM indefinite.

indeleble *adj* culto indelible.

indemne *adj* unhurt, unharmed.

indemnización *f* [gen] compensation; [por despido] severance pay.

indemnizar *vt*: ~ **a alguien (por)** to compensate sb (for).

independencia *f* independence; **con** ~ **de** independently of.

independiente *adj* **-1.** [gen] independent. **-2.** [aparte] separate.

independizar *vt* to grant independence to. ◆ **independizarse** *vpr*: ~**se (de)** to become independent (of).

indeseable *adj* undesirable.

indeterminación *f* indecisiveness.

indeterminado, -da *adj* **-1.** [sin determinar] indeterminate; **por tiempo** ~ indefinitely. **-2.** [impreciso] vague.

indexar *vt* INFORM to index.

India: (la) ~ India.

indiano, -na *m y f* **-1.** [indígena] (Latin American) Indian. **-2.** [emigrante] *Spanish emigrant to Latin America who returned to Spain having made his fortune.*

indicación *f* **-1.** [señal, gesto] sign, signal. **-2.** (*gen pl*) [instrucción] instruction; [para llegar a un sitio] directions (*pl*). **-3.** [nota, corrección] note.

indicado, -da *adj* suitable, appropriate.

indicador, -ra *adj* indicating (*antes de sust*). ◆ **indicador** *m* [gen] indicator; TECN gauge, meter.

indicar *vt* [señalar] to indicate; [suj: aguja etc] to read.

indicativo, -va *adj* indicative. ◆ **indicativo** *m* GRAM indicative.

índice *m* **-1.** [gen] index; [proporción] level, rate; ~ **de natalidad** birth rate; ~ **de precios al consumo** retail price index. **-2.** [señal] sign, indicator. **-3.** [catálogo] catalogue. **-4.** [dedo] index finger.

indicio *m* sign; [pista] clue; [cantidad pequeña] trace.

Índico *m*: **el (océano)** ~ the Indian Ocean.

indiferencia *f* indifference.

indiferente *adj* indifferent; **me es** ~ [me da igual] I don't mind, it's all the same to me; [no me interesa] I'm not interested in it.

indígena ◇ *adj* indigenous, native. ◇ *m y f* native.

indigencia *f* culto destitution.

indigente *adj* destitute.

indigestarse *vpr* to get indigestion.

indigestión *f* indigestion.

indigesto, -ta *adj* indigestible; *fam fig* [pesado] stodgy, heavy.

indignación *f* indignation.

indignar *vt* to anger. ◆ **indignarse** *vpr*: ~**se (por)** to get angry o indignant (about).

indigno, -na *adj* **-1.** [gen]: ~ **(de)** unworthy (of). **-2.** [impropio] not fitting, wrong. **-3.** [vergonzoso] contemptible.

indio, -dia ◇ *adj* Indian. ◇ *m y f* Indian; **hacer el** ~ to play the fool.

indirecto, -ta *adj* indirect. ◆ **indirecta** *f* hint; **lanzar una indirecta a alguien** to drop a hint to sb.

indisciplina *f* indiscipline.

indiscreción *f* **-1.** [cualidad] indiscretion. **-2.** [comentario] indiscreet remark.

indiscreto, -ta *adj* indiscreet.

indiscriminado, -da *adj* indiscriminate.

indiscutible *adj* [gen] indisputable; [poder] undisputed.

indispensable *adj* indispensable.

indisponer *vt* **-1.** [enfermar] to make ill, to upset. **-2.** [enemistar] to set at odds.

indisposición *f* [malestar] indisposition.

indispuesto, -ta ◇ *pp* → **indisponer**. ◇ *adj* indisposed, unwell.

indistinto, -ta *adj* **-1.** [indiferente]: **es ~** it doesn't matter, it makes no difference. **-2.** [cuenta, cartilla] joint. **-3.** [perfil, figura] indistinct, blurred.

individual *adj* **-1.** [gen] individual; [habitación, cama] single; [despacho] personal. **-2.** [prueba, competición] singles (*antes de sust*). ◆ **individuales** *mpl* DEP singles.

individualizar *vi* to single people out.

individuo, -dua *m y f* person; *despec* individual.

indocumentado, -da *adj* **-1.** [sin documentación] without identity papers. **-2.** [ignorante] ignorant.

índole *f* [naturaleza] nature; [tipo] type, kind.

indolencia *f* indolence, laziness.

indoloro, -ra *adj* painless.

indómito, -ta *adj* **-1.** [animal] untameable. **-2.** [carácter] rebellious; [pueblo] unruly.

Indonesia Indonesia.

inducir *vt* [incitar]: **~ a alguien a algo/a hacer algo** to lead sb into sthg/into doing sthg; **~ a error** to mislead.

inductor, -ra *adj* instigating.

indudable *adj* undoubted; **es ~ que ...** there is no doubt that ....

indulgencia *f* indulgence.

indultar *vt* to pardon.

indulto *m* pardon.

indumentaria *f* attire.

industria *f* [gen] industry.

industrial ◇ *adj* industrial. ◇ *m y f* industrialist.

industrializar *vt* to industrialize.

inédito, -ta *adj* **-1.** [no publicado] unpublished. **-2.** [sorprendente] unprecedented.

INEF (*abrev de* **Instituto Nacional de Educación Física**) *m Spanish university for training physical education teachers.*

inefable *adj* ineffable, inexpressible.

ineficaz *adj* **-1.** [de bajo rendimiento] inefficient. **-2.** [de baja efectividad] ineffective.

ineficiente *adj* **-1.** [de bajo rendimiento] inefficient. **-2.** [de baja efectividad] ineffective.

ineludible *adj* unavoidable.

INEM (*abrev de* **Instituto Nacional de Empleo**) *m Spanish department of employment.*

inenarrable *adj* spectacular.

ineptitud *f* ineptitude.

inepto, -ta *adj* inept.

inequívoco, -ca *adj* [apoyo, resultado] unequivocal; [señal, voz] unmistakeable.

inercia *f* *lit & fig* inertia.

inerme *adj* [sin armas] unarmed; [sin defensa] defenceless.

inerte *adj* **-1.** [materia] inert. **-2.** [cuerpo, cadáver] lifeless.

inesperado, -da *adj* unexpected.

inestable *adj* *lit & fig* unstable.

inevitable *adj* inevitable.

inexacto, -ta *adj* **-1.** [impreciso] inaccurate. **-2.** [erróneo] incorrect, wrong.

inexistente *adj* nonexistent.

inexperiencia *f* inexperience.

inexperto, -ta *adj* **-1.** [falto de experiencia] inexperienced. **-2.** [falto de habilidad] unskilful.

inexpresivo, -va *adj* expressionless.

infalible *adj* infallible.

infame *adj* vile, base.

infamia *f* [deshonra] infamy, disgrace.

infancia *f* [periodo] childhood.

infante, -ta *m y f* **-1.** [niño] infant. **-2.** [hijo del rey] infante (*f* infanta), prince (*f* princess).

infantería *f* infantry.

infantil *adj* **-1.** [para niños] children's; [de niños] child (*antes de sust*). **-2.** *fig* [inmaduro] infantile, childish.

infarto *m*: **~ (de miocardio)** heart attack.

infatigable *adj* indefatigable, tireless.

infección *f* infection.

infeccioso, -sa *adj* infectious.

infectar *vt* to infect. ◆ **infectarse** *vpr* to become infected.

infecundo, -da *adj* [tierra] infertile.

infeliz *adj* **-1.** [desgraciado] unhappy. **-2.** *fig* [ingenuo] gullible.

inferior ◇ *adj*: **~ (a)** [en espacio, cantidad] lower (than); [en calidad] inferior (to); **una cifra ~ a 100** a figure under o below 100. ◇ *m y f* inferior.

inferioridad *f* inferiority.

inferir *vt* **-1.** [deducir]: **~ (de)** to deduce (from), to infer (from). **-2.** [ocasionar - herida] to inflict; [- mal] to cause.

infernal *adj* *lit & fig* infernal.

infestar *vt* to infest; [suj: carteles, propaganda etc] to be plastered across.

infidelidad *f* [conyugal] infidelity; [a la patria, un amigo] disloyalty.

infiel ◇ *adj* **-1.** [desleal - cónyuge] unfaithful; [- amigo] disloyal. **-2.** [inexacto] inaccurate, unfaithful. ◇ *m y f* RELIG infidel.

infiernillo *m* portable stove.

infierno *m lit & fig* hell; ¡vete al ~! go to hell!

infiltrado, -da *m y f* infiltrator.

infiltrar *vt* [inyectar] to inject. ◆ **infiltrarse en** *vpr* to infiltrate.

ínfimo, -ma *adj* [calidad, categoría] extremely low; [precio] **giveaway**; [importancia] minimal.

infinidad *f*: **una ~ de** an infinite number of; *fig* masses of; **en ~ de ocasiones** on countless occasions.

infinitivo *m* infinitive.

infinito, -ta *adj lit & fig* infinite. ◆ **infinito** *m* infinity.

inflación *f* ECON inflation.

inflamable *adj* inflammable.

inflamación *f* MED inflammation.

inflamar *vt* MED & *fig* to inflame. ◆ **inflamarse** *vpr* [hincharse] to become inflamed.

inflamatorio, -ria *adj* inflammatory.

inflar *vt* **-1.** [soplando] to blow up, to inflate; [con bomba] to pump up. **-2.** *fig* [exagerar] to blow up, to exaggerate. ◆ **inflarse** *vpr*: ~**se (de)** [hartarse] to stuff o.s. (with).

inflexible *adj lit & fig* inflexible.

inflexión *f* inflection.

infligir *vt* to inflict; [castigo] to impose.

influencia *f* influence.

influenciar *vt* to influence.

influir ◇ *vt* to influence. ◇ *vi* to have influence; ~ **en** to influence.

influjo *m* influence.

influyente *adj* influential.

información *f* **-1.** [conocimiento] information. **-2.** [PRENS - noticias] news (*U*); [- noticia] report, piece of news; [- sección] section, news (*U*); ~ **meteorológica** weather report O forecast. **-3.** [oficina] information office; [mostrador] information desk. **-4.** TELECOM directory enquiries (*pl*) *Br*, directory assistance *Am*.

informal *adj* **-1.** [desenfadado] informal. **-2.** [irresponsable] unreliable.

informante *m y f* informant.

informar ◇ *vt*: ~ **a alguien (de)** to inform O tell sb (about). ◇ *vi* to inform; PRENS to report. ◆ **informarse** *vpr* to find out (details); ~**se de** to find out about.

informático, -ca ◇ *adj* computer (*antes de sust*). ◇ *m y f* [persona] computer expert. ◆ **informática** *f* [ciencia] information technology, computing.

informativo, -va *adj* **-1.** [instructivo, esclarecedor] informative. **-2.** [que da noticias] **news** (*antes de sust*); [que da información] information (*antes de sust*). ◆ **informativo** *m* news (bulletin).

informatizar *vt* to computerize.

informe ◇ *adj* shapeless. ◇ *m* **-1.** [gen] report. **-2.** DER plea. ◆ **informes** *mpl* [gen] information (*U*); [sobre comportamiento] report (*sg*); [para un empleo] references.

infortunio *m* misfortune, bad luck (*U*).

infracción *f* infringement; [de circulación] offence.

infraestructura *f* [de organización] infrastructure.

infrahumano, -na *adj* subhuman.

infranqueable *adj* impassable; *fig* insurmountable.

infrarrojo, -ja *adj* infrared.

infravalorar *vt* to undervalue, to underestimate.

infringir *vt* [quebrantar] to infringe, to break.

infundado, -da *adj* unfounded.

infundir *vt*: ~ **algo a alguien** to fill sb with sthg, to inspire sthg in sb; ~ **miedo** to inspire fear.

infusión *f* infusion; ~ **de manzanilla** camomile tea.

ingeniar *vt* to invent, to devise. ◆ **ingeniarse** *vpr*: **ingeniárselas** to manage, to engineer it; **ingeniárselas para hacer algo** to manage O contrive to do sthg.

ingeniería *f* engineering.

ingeniero, -ra *m y f* engineer; ~ **de caminos, canales y puertos** civil engineer.

ingenio *m* **-1.** [inteligencia] ingenuity. **-2.** [agudeza] wit. **-3.** [máquina] device.

ingenioso, -sa *adj* [inteligente] ingenious, clever; [agudo] witty.

ingenuidad *f* ingenuousness, naivety.

ingenuo, -nua *adj* ingenuous, naive.

ingerencia = injerencia.

ingerir *vt* to consume, to ingest.

Inglaterra England.

ingle *f* groin.

inglés, -esa ◇ *adj* English. ◇ *m y f* [persona] Englishman (*f* Englishwoman); **los ingleses** the English. ◆ **inglés** *m* [lengua] English.

ingratitud *f* ingratitude.

ingrato, -ta *adj* ungrateful; [trabajo] thankless.

ingrávido, -da *adj* weightless.

ingrediente *m* ingredient.

ingresar ◇ *vt* BANCA to deposit, to pay in. ◇ *vi*: ~ **(en)** [asociación, ejército] to join; [hospital] to be admitted (to); [convento, universidad] to enter; ~ **cadáver** to be dead on arrival.

ingreso *m* **-1.** [gen] entry; [en asociación, ejército] joining; [en hospital, universidad] admission. **-2.** BANCA deposit. ◆ **ingresos** *mpl* **-1.** [sueldo etc] income (*U*). **-2.** [recaudación] revenue (*U*).

inhabilitar *vt* to disqualify.

inhabitable *adj* uninhabitable.

inhabitado, -da *adj* uninhabited.

inhalador *m* inhaler.

inhalar *vt* to inhale.

inherente *adj*: ~ **(a)** inherent (in).

inhibir *vt* to inhibit. ◆ **inhibirse de** *vpr* [gen] to keep out of, to stay away from; [responsabilidades] to shirk.

inhóspito, -ta *adj* inhospitable.

inhumano, -na *adj* [despiadado] inhuman; [desconsiderado] inhumane.

INI (*abrev de* **Instituto Nacional de Industria**) *m Spanish governmental organization that promotes industry.*

iniciación *f* **-1.** [gen] initiation. **-2.** [de suceso, curso] start, beginning.

inicial *adj & f* initial.

inicializar *vt* INFORM to initialize.

iniciar *vt* [gen] to start, to initiate; [debate, discusión] to start off.

iniciativa *f* initiative.

inicio *m* start, beginning.

inigualable *adj* unrivalled.

ininteligible *adj* unintelligible.

ininterrumpido, -da *adj* uninterrupted.

injerencia, ingerencia *f* interference, meddling.

injerir *vt* to introduce, to insert. ◆ **injerirse** *vpr* [entrometerse]: ~**se (en)** to interfere (in), to meddle (in).

injertar *vt* to graft.

injerto *m* graft.

injuria *f* [insulto] insult, abuse (*U*); [agravio] offence; DER slander.

injuriar *vt* [insultar] to insult, to abuse; [agraviar] to offend; DER to slander.

injurioso, -sa *adj* insulting, abusive; DER slanderous.

injusticia *f* injustice.

injustificado, -da *adj* unjustified.

injusto, -ta *adj* unfair, unjust.

inmadurez *f* immaturity.

inmaduro, -ra *adj* [persona] immature.

inmediaciones *fpl* [de localidad] surrounding area (*sg*); [de lugar, casa] vicinity (*sg*).

inmediatamente *adv* immediately.

inmediato, -ta *adj* **-1.** [gen] immediate; **de** ~ immediately. **-2.** [contiguo] next, adjoining.

inmejorable *adj* unbeatable.

inmensidad *f* [grandeza] immensity.

inmenso, -sa *adj* [gen] immense.

inmersión *f* immersion; [de submarinista] dive.

inmerso, -sa *adj*: ~ **(en)** immersed (in).

inmigración *f* immigration.

inmigrante *m y f* immigrant.

inmigrar *vi* to immigrate.

inminente *adj* imminent, impending.

inmiscuirse *vpr*: ~ **(en)** to interfere O meddle (in).

inmobiliario, -ria *adj* property (*antes de sust*), real estate *Am* (*antes de sust*). ◆ **inmobiliaria** *f* [agencia] estate agency *Br*, real estate agent *Am*.

inmoral *adj* immoral.

inmortal *adj* immortal.

inmortalizar *vt* to immortalize.

inmóvil *adj* motionless, still; [coche, tren] stationary.

inmovilizar *vt* to immobilize.

inmueble ◇ *adj*: **bienes** ~**s** real estate (*U*). ◇ *m* [edificio] building.

inmundicia *f* [suciedad] filth, filthiness; [basura] rubbish.

inmundo, -da *adj* filthy, dirty.

inmune *adj* MED immune.

inmunidad *f* immunity.

inmunizar *vt* to immunize.

inmutar *vt* to upset, to perturb. ◆ **inmutarse** *vpr* to get upset, to be perturbed; **ni se inmutó** he didn't bat an eyelid.

innato, -ta *adj* innate.

innecesario, -ria *adj* unnecessary.

innoble *adj* ignoble.

innovación *f* innovation.

innovador, -ra ◇ *adj* innovative. ◇ *m y f* innovator.

innovar *vt* [método, técnica] to improve on.

innumerable *adj* countless, innumerable.

inocencia *f* innocence.

inocentada *f* practical joke, trick.

inocente *adj* **-1.** [gen] innocent. **-2.** [ingenuo - persona] naive, innocent. **-3.** [sin maldad - persona] harmless.

inodoro, -ra adj odourless. ◆**inodoro** m toilet Br, washroom Am.

inofensivo, -va adj inoffensive, harmless.

inolvidable adj unforgettable.

inoperante adj ineffective.

inoportuno, -na, importuno, -na adj **-1.** [en mal momento] inopportune, untimely. **-2.** [molesto] inconvenient. **-3.** [inadecuado] inappropriate.

inoxidable adj rustproof; [acero] stainless.

inquebrantable adj unshakeable; [lealtad] unswerving.

inquietar vt to worry, to trouble. ◆**inquietarse** vpr to worry.

inquieto, -ta adj **-1.** [preocupado]: ~ **(por)** worried o anxious (about). **-2.** [agitado, emprendedor] restless.

inquietud f [preocupación] worry, anxiety.

inquilino, -na m y f tenant.

inquirir vt culto to inquire into, to investigate.

inquisición f [indagación] inquiry, investigation. ◆**Inquisición** f [tribunal] Inquisition.

inquisidor, -ra adj inquisitive. ◆**inquisidor** m inquisitor.

insaciable adj insatiable.

insalubre adj culto insalubrious, unhealthy.

Insalud (abrev de **Instituto Nacional de la Salud**) m ≃ NHS Br, ≃ Medicaid Am.

insatisfecho, -cha adj **-1.** [descontento] dissatisfied. **-2.** [no saciado] not full, unsatisfied.

inscribir vt **-1.** [grabar]: ~ **algo (en)** to engrave o inscribe sthg (on). **-2.** [apuntar]: ~ **algo/a alguien (en)** to register sthg/sb (on). ◆**inscribirse** vpr: ~**se (en)** [gen] to enrol (on); [asociación] to enrol (with); [concurso] to enter.

inscripción f **-1.** EDUC registration, enrolment; [en censo, registro] **registration**; [en partido etc] enrolment; [en concursos etc] entry. **-2.** [escrito] inscription.

inscrito, -ta pp → **inscribir**.

insecticida m insecticide.

insecto m insect.

inseguridad f **-1.** [falta de confianza] insecurity. **-2.** [duda] uncertainty. **-3.** [peligro] lack of safety.

inseguro, -ra adj **-1.** [sin confianza] insecure. **-2.** [dudoso] uncertain. **-3.** [peligroso] unsafe.

inseminación f insemination; ~ **artificial** artificial insemination.

insensatez f foolishness; **hacer/decir una** ~ to do/say sthg foolish.

insensato, -ta ◇ adj foolish, senseless. ◇ m y f fool.

insensibilidad f [emocional] insensitivity; [física] numbness.

insensible adj **-1.** [indiferente]: ~ **(a)** insensitive (to). **-2.** [entumecido] numb. **-3.** [imperceptible] imperceptible.

insertar vt [gen & COMPUT]: ~ **(en)** to insert (into).

inservible adj useless, unserviceable.

insidioso, -sa adj malicious.

insigne adj distinguished, illustrious.

insignia f **-1.** [distintivo] badge; MIL insignia. **-2.** [bandera] flag, banner.

insignificante adj insignificant.

insinuar vt: ~ **algo (a)** to hint at o insinuate sthg (to). ◆**insinuarse** vpr **-1.** [amorosamente]: ~**se (a)** to make advances (to). **-2.** [asomar]: ~**se detrás de algo** to peep out from behind sthg.

insípido, -da adj lit & fig insipid.

insistencia f insistence.

insistir vi: ~ **(en)** to insist (on).

insociable adj unsociable.

insolación f MED sunstroke (U).

insolencia f insolence; **hacer/decir una** ~ to do/say sthg insolent.

insolente adj [descarado] insolent; [orgulloso] haughty.

insolidario, -ria adj lacking in solidarity.

insólito, -ta adj very unusual.

insoluble adj insoluble.

insolvencia f insolvency.

insolvente adj insolvent.

insomnio m insomnia.

insondable adj lit & fig unfathomable.

insonorizar vt to soundproof.

insoportable adj unbearable, intolerable.

insostenible adj untenable.

inspección f inspection; [policial] search.

inspeccionar vt to inspect; [suj: policía] to search.

inspector, -ra m y f inspector; ~ **de aduanas** customs official; ~ **de Hacienda** tax inspector.

inspiración f **-1.** [gen] inspiration. **-2.** [respiración] inhalation, breath.

inspirar vt **-1.** [gen] to inspire. **-2.** [respirar] to inhale, to breathe in. ◆**ins-**

pirarse *vpr.* ~**se (en)** to be inspired (by).

instalación *f* **-1.** [gen] installation; ~ **eléctrica** wiring. **-2.** [de gente] settling. ◆ **instalaciones** *fpl* [deportivas etc] facilities.

instalar *vt* **-1.** [montar - antena etc] to instal, to fit; [- local, puesto etc] to set up. **-2.** [situar - objeto] to place; [- gente] to settle. ◆ **instalarse** *vpr* [establecerse]: ~**se en** to settle (down) in; [nueva casa] to move into.

instancia *f* **-1.** [solicitud] application (form). **-2.** [ruego] request; **a** ~**s de** at the request ◇ bidding of; **en última** ~ as a last resort.

instantáneo, -a *adj* **-1.** [momentáneo] momentary. **-2.** [rápido] instantaneous. ◆ **instantánea** *f* snapshot, snap.

instante *m* moment; **a cada** ~ all the time, constantly; **al** ~ instantly, immediately; **en un** ~ in a second.

instar *vt*: ~ **a alguien a que haga algo** to urge ◇ press sb to do sthg.

instaurar *vt* to establish, to set up.

instigar *vt*: ~ **a alguien (a que haga algo)** to instigate sb (to do sthg); ~ **a algo** to incite to sthg.

instintivo, -va *adj* instinctive.

instinto *m* instinct; **por** ~ instinctively.

institución *f* **-1.** [gen] institution; **ser una** ~ *fig* to be an institution. **-2.** [de ley, sistema] introduction; [de organismo] establishment; [de premio] foundation.

instituir *vt* [fundar - gobierno] to establish; [- premio, sociedad] to found; [- sistema, reglas] to introduce.

instituto *m* **-1.** [corporación] institute. **-2.** EDUC: ~ **(de Bachillerato** ◇ **Enseñanza Media)** state secondary school; ~ **de Formación Profesional** ≈ technical college. ◆ **instituto de belleza** *m* beauty salon.

institutriz *f* governess.

instrucción *f* **-1.** [conocimientos] education; [docencia] instruction. **-2.** [DER - investigación] preliminary investigation; [- curso del proceso] proceedings (*pl*). ◆ **instrucciones** *fpl* [de uso] instructions.

instructivo, -va *adj* [gen] instructive; [juguete, película] educational.

instructor, -ra ◇ *adj* training. ◇ *m y f* [gen] instructor, teacher; DEP coach.

instruido, -da *adj* educated.

instruir *vt* [enseñar] to instruct.

instrumental *m* instruments (*pl*).

instrumentista *m y f* **-1.** MÚS instrumentalist. **-2.** MED surgeon's assistant.

instrumento *m* **-1.** MUS & *fig* instrument. **-2.** [herramienta] tool, instrument.

insubordinado, -da *adj* insubordinate.

insubordinar *vt* to incite to rebellion. ◆ **insubordinarse** *vpr* to rebel.

insubstancial = **insustancial**.

insuficiencia *f* **-1.** [escasez] lack, shortage. **-2.** MED failure.

insuficiente ◇ *adj* insufficient. ◇ *m* [nota] fail.

insufrible *adj* intolerable, insufferable.

insular *adj* insular, island (*antes de sust*).

insulina *f* insulin.

insulso, -sa *adj* *lit* & *fig* bland, insipid.

insultar *vt* to insult.

insulto *m* insult.

insumiso, -sa ◇ *adj* rebellious. ◇ *m y f* [gen] rebel; MIL *person who refuses to do military or community service.*

insuperable *adj* **-1.** [inmejorable] unsurpassable. **-2.** [sin solución] insurmountable, insuperable.

insurgente *adj* insurgent.

insurrección *f* insurrection, revolt.

insustancial, insubstancial *adj* insubstantial.

intachable *adj* irreproachable.

intacto, -ta *adj* untouched; *fig* intact.

integral *adj* **-1.** [total] total, complete. **-2.** [sin refinar - pan, harina, pasta] wholemeal; [- arroz] brown.

integrante ◇ *adj* integral, constituent; **estado** ~ **de la CE** member state of the EC. ◇ *m y f* member.

integrar *vt* **-1.** [gen & MAT] to integrate. **-2.** [componer] to make up. ◆ **integrarse** *vpr* to integrate.

integridad *f* [gen] integrity; [totalidad] wholeness.

íntegro, -gra *adj* **-1.** [completo] whole, entire; [versión etc] unabridged. **-2.** [honrado] honourable.

intelecto *m* intellect.

intelectual *adj, m y f* intellectual.

inteligencia *f* intelligence; ~ **artificial** INFORM artificial intelligence.

inteligente *adj* [gen & COMPUT] intelligent.

inteligible *adj* intelligible.

intemperie *f*: **a la** ~ in the open air.

intempestivo, -va *adj* [clima, comentario] harsh; [hora] ungodly, unearthly; [proposición, visita] inopportune.

intención f intention; **tener la ~ de** to intend to; **buena/mala ~** good/bad intentions (pl).

intencionado, -da adj intentional, deliberate; **bien ~** [acción] well-meant; [persona] well-meaning; **mal ~** [acción] ill-meant; [persona] malevolent.

intensidad f [gen] intensity; [de lluvia] heaviness; [de luz, color] brightness; [de amor] passion, strength.

intensificar vt to intensify. ◆ **intensificarse** vpr to intensify.

intensivo, -va adj intensive.

intenso, -sa adj [gen] intense; [lluvia] heavy; [luz, color] bright; [amor] passionate, strong.

intentar vt: **~ (hacer algo)** to try (to do sthg).

intento m [tentativa] attempt; [intención] intention; **~ de golpe/robo** attempted coup/robbery.

interactivo, -va adj INFORM interactive.

intercalar vt to insert, to put in.

intercambiable adj interchangeable.

intercambio m exchange; **~ comercial** trade.

interceder vi: **~ (por alguien)** to intercede (on sb's behalf).

interceptar vt **-1.** [detener] to intercept. **-2.** [obstruir] to block.

intercesión f intercession.

interés m **-1.** [gen & FIN] interest; **de ~** interesting; **tener ~ en o por** to be interested in; **tengo ~ en que venga pronto** it's in my interest that he should come soon; **intereses creados** vested interests. **-2.** [egoísmo] self-interest; **por ~** out of selfishness.

interesado, -da ◇ adj **-1.** [gen]: **~ (en o por)** interested (in). **-2.** [egoísta] selfish, self-interested. ◇ m y f [deseoso] interested person; **los ~s** those interested.

interesante adj interesting.

interesar vi to interest; **le interesa el arte** she's interested in art. ◆ **interesarse** vpr: **~se (en o por)** to take an interest (in), to be interested (in); **se interesó por tu salud** she asked after your health.

interfaz f INFORM interface.

interferencia f interference.

interferir ◇ vt **-1.** [gen & RADIO, TELECOM & TV] to jam. **-2.** [interponerse] to interfere with. ◇ vi: **~ (en)** to interfere (in).

interfono m intercom.

interino, -na ◇ adj [gen] temporary; [presidente, director etc] acting; [gobierno]

interim. ◇ m y f [gen] stand-in; [médico, juez] locum; [profesor] supply teacher. ◆ **interina** f [asistenta] cleaning lady.

interior ◇ adj **-1.** [gen] inside, inner; [patio, jardín etc] interior, inside; [habitación, vida] inner. **-2.** POLÍT domestic. **-3.** GEOGR inland. ◇ m **-1.** [parte de dentro] inside, interior. **-2.** GEOGR interior. **-3.** [de una persona] inner self; **en mi ~** deep down.

interiorismo m interior design.

interiorizar vt to internalize; [sentimientos] to bottle up.

interjección f interjection.

interlocutor, -ra m y f interlocutor, speaker; **su ~** the person she was speaking to.

intermediario, -ria m y f [gen] intermediary; COM middleman; [en disputas] mediator.

intermedio, -dia adj **-1.** [etapa] intermediate, halfway; [calidad] average; [tamaño] medium. **-2.** [tiempo] intervening; [espacio] in between. ◆ **intermedio** m [gen & TEATR] interval; CIN intermission.

interminable adj endless, interminable.

intermitente ◇ adj intermittent. ◇ m indicator.

internacional adj international.

internado, -da adj [en manicomio] confined; [en colegio] boarding; POLÍT interned. ◆ **internado** m [colegio] boarding school.

internar vt: **~ (en)** [internado] to send to boarding school (at); [manicomio] to commit (to); [campo de concentración] to intern (in). ◆ **internarse** vpr: **~se (en)** [un lugar] to go o penetrate deep (into); [un tema] to become deeply involved (in).

interno, -na ◇ adj **-1.** [gen] internal; POLÍT domestic. **-2.** [alumno] boarding. ◇ m y f **-1.** [alumno] boarder. **-2.** → médico. **-3.** [preso] prisoner, inmate.

interpelación f formal question.

interpolar vt to interpolate, to put in.

interponer vt **-1.** [gen] to interpose, to put in. **-2.** DER to lodge, to make. ◆ **interponerse** vpr to intervene.

interpretación f **-1.** [explicación] interpretation. **-2.** [artística] performance. **-3.** [traducción] interpreting.

interpretar vt **-1.** [gen] to interpret. **-2.** [artísticamente] to perform.

intérprete m y f **-1.** [traductor & INFORM] interpreter. **-2.** [artista] performer.

interpuesto, -ta *pp* → interponer.
interrogación *f* **-1.** [acción] questioning. **-2.** [signo] question mark.
interrogante *m o f* [incógnita] question mark.
interrogar *vt* [gen] to question; [con amenazas etc] to interrogate.
interrogatorio *m* [gen] questioning; [con amenazas] interrogation.
interrumpir *vt* **-1.** [gen] to interrupt. **-2.** [discurso, trabajo] to break off; [viaje, vacaciones] to cut short.
interrupción *f* **-1.** [gen] interruption. **-2.** [de discurso, trabajo] breaking-off; [de viaje, vacaciones] cutting-short.
interruptor *m* switch.
intersección *f* intersection.
interurbano, -na *adj* inter-city; TELECOM long-distance.
intervalo *m* **-1.** [gen & MÚS] interval; [de espacio] space, gap; **a ~s** at intervals. **-2.** [duración]: **en el ~ de un mes** in the space of a month.
intervención *f* **-1.** [gen] intervention. **-2.** [discurso] speech; [interpelación] contribution. **-3.** COM auditing. **-4.** MED operation. **-5.** TELECOM tapping.
intervenir ◇ *vi* **-1.** [participar]: ~ **(en)** [gen] to take part (in); [pelea] to get involved (in); [discusión etc] to make a contribution (to). **-2.** [dar un discurso] to make a speech. **-3.** [interferir]: ~ **(en)** to intervene (in). **-4.** MED to operate. ◇ *vt* **-1.** MED to operate on. **-2.** TELECOM to tap. **-3.** [incautar] to seize. **-4.** COM to audit.
interventor, -ra *m y f* COM auditor.
interviú (*pl* interviús) *f* interview.
intestino, -na *adj* internecine. ◆ **intestino** *m* intestine.
intimar *vi*: ~ **(con)** to become intimate ○ very friendly (with).
intimidad *f* **-1.** [vida privada] private life; [privacidad] privacy; **en la ~** in private. **-2.** [amistad] intimacy.
íntimo, -ma ◇ *adj* **-1.** [vida, fiesta] private; [ambiente, restaurante] intimate. **-2.** [relación, amistad] close. **-3.** [sentimiento etc] innermost. ◇ *m y f* close friend.
intolerable *adj* intolerable, unacceptable; [dolor, ruido] unbearable.
intolerancia *f* [actitud] intolerance.
intoxicación *f* poisoning (U); ~ **alimenticia** food poisoning.
intoxicar *vt* to poison.
intranquilizar *vt* to worry. ◆ **intranquilizarse** *vpr* to get worried.

intranquilo, -la *adj* [preocupado] worried, uneasy; [nervioso] restless.
intranscendente = intrascendente.
intransferible *adj* non-transferable.
intransigente *adj* intransigent.
intransitable *adj* impassable.
intrascendente, intranscendente *adj* insignificant, unimportant.
intrépido, -da *adj* intrepid.
intriga *f* **-1.** [curiosidad] curiosity; **de ~** suspense (*antes de sust*). **-2.** [maquinación] intrigue. **-3.** [trama] plot.
intrigar *vt & vi* to intrigue.
intrincado, -da *adj* [problema etc] intricate.
intríngulis *m inv fam* [dificultad] snag, catch; [quid] crux.
intrínseco, -ca *adj* intrinsic.
introducción *f*: ~ **(a)** introduction (to).
introducir *vt* **-1.** [meter - llave, carta etc] to put in, to insert. **-2.** [mercancías etc] to bring in, to introduce. **-3.** [dar a conocer]: ~ **a alguien en** to introduce sb to; ~ **algo en** to introduce ○ bring sthg to. ◆ **introducirse** *vpr*: ~**se en** to get into.
introductorio, -ria *adj* introductory.
intromisión *f* meddling, interfering.
introspectivo, -va *adj* introspective.
introvertido, -da *adj, m y f* introvert.
intruso, -sa *m y f* intruder.
intuición *f* intuition.
intuir *vt* to know by intuition, to sense.
intuitivo, -va *adj* intuitive.
inundación *f* flood, flooding (U).
inundar *vt* to flood; *fig* to inundate. ◆ **inundarse** *vpr* to be flooded; ~**se de** *fig* to be inundated ○ swamped with.
inusitado, -da *adj* uncommon, rare.
inútil *adj* **-1.** [gen] useless; [intento, esfuerzo] unsuccessful, vain. **-2.** [inválido] disabled.
inutilidad *f* [gen] uselessness; [falta de sentido] pointlessness.
inutilizar *vt* [gen] to make unusable; [máquinas, dispositivos] to disable.
invadir *vt* to invade; **le invade la tristeza** she's overcome by sadness.
invalidez *f* **-1.** MED disability; ~ **permanente/temporal** permanent/temporal disability. **-2.** DER invalidity.
inválido, -da ◇ *adj* **-1.** MED disabled. **-2.** DER invalid. ◇ *m y f* invalid, disabled person; **los ~s** the disabled.
invariable *adj* invariable.
invasión *f* invasion.

invasor, -ra ◇ *adj* invading. ◇ *m y f* invader.

invención *f* invention.

inventar *vt* [gen] to invent; [narración, falsedades] to make up. ◆**inventarse** *vpr* to make up.

inventario *m* inventory; **hacer el ~** COM to do the stocktaking.

inventiva *f* inventiveness.

invento *m* invention.

inventor, -ra *m y f* inventor.

invernadero, invernáculo *m* greenhouse.

invernar *vi* [pasar el invierno] to (spend the) winter; [hibernar] to hibernate.

inverosímil *adj* unlikely, improbable.

inversión *f* **-1.** [del orden] inversion. **-2.** [de dinero, tiempo] investment.

inverso, -sa *adj* opposite, inverse; **a la inversa** the other way round; **en orden ~** in reverse order.

inversor, -ra *m y f* COM & FIN investor.

invertebrado, -da *adj* **-1.** ZOOL invertebrate. **-2.** *fig* [incoherente] disjointed. ◆**invertebrado** *m* invertebrate.

invertido, -da *adj* **-1.** [al revés] reversed, inverted; [sentido, dirección] opposite. **-2.** [homosexual] homosexual.

invertir *vt* **-1.** [gen] to reverse; [poner boca abajo] to turn upside down. **-2.** [dinero, tiempo, esfuerzo] to invest. **-3.** [tardar - tiempo] to spend.

investidura *f* investiture.

investigación *f* **-1.** [estudio] research; **~ y desarrollo** research and development. **-2.** [indagación] investigation, inquiry.

investigador, -ra *m y f* **-1.** [estudioso] researcher. **-2.** [detective] investigator.

investigar ◇ *vt* **-1.** [estudiar] to research. **-2.** [indagar] to investigate. ◇ *vi* **-1.** [estudiar] to do research. **-2.** [indagar] to investigate.

investir *vt*: **~ a alguien con algo** to invest sb with sthg.

inveterado, -da *adj* deep-rooted.

inviable *adj* impractical, unviable.

invidente *m y f* blind ○ sightless person; **los ~s** the blind.

invierno *m* winter.

invisible *adj* invisible.

invitación *f* invitation.

invitado, -da *m y f* guest.

invitar ◇ *vt* **-1.** [convidar]: **~ a alguien (a algo/a hacer algo)** to invite sb (to sthg/to do sthg). **-2.** [pagar]: **os invito** it's my treat, this one's on me; **te invito a cenar fuera** I'll take you out for

dinner. ◇ *vi* to pay; **invita la casa** it's on the house. ◆**invitar a** *vi fig* [incitar]: **~ a algo** to encourage sthg; **la lluvia invita a quedarse en casa** the rain makes you want to stay at home.

in vitro *loc adv* **-1.** [de probeta] in vitro. **-2.** → **fecundación**.

invocar *vt* to invoke.

involucrar *vt*: **~ a alguien (en)** to involve sb (in). ◆**involucrarse** *vpr*: **~se (en)** to get involved (in).

involuntario, -ria *adj* [espontáneo] involuntary; [sin querer] unintentional.

inyección *f* injection.

inyectar *vt* to inject. ◆**inyectarse** *vpr* [drogas] to take drugs intravenously; **~se algo** to inject o.s. with sthg.

iodo = **yodo**.

ion *m* ion.

IPC (*abrev de* **índice de precios al consumo**) *m Spanish cost of living index*, ≃ RPI *Br*.

ir *vi* **-1.** [gen] to go; **~ hacia el sur/al cine** to go south/to the cinema; **~ en autobús/coche** to go by bus/car; **~ andando** to go on foot, to walk; **¡vamos!** let's go! **-2.** [expresa duración gradual]: **~ haciendo algo** to be (gradually) doing sthg; **va anocheciendo** it's getting dark; **voy mejorando mi estilo** I'm working on improving my style. **-3.** [expresa intención, opinión]: **~ a hacer algo** to be going to do sthg; **voy a decírselo a tu padre** I'm going to tell your father. **-4.** [cambiar]: **~ a mejor/peor** *etc* to get better/worse *etc*. **-5.** [funcionar] to work; **la manivela va floja** the crank is loose; **la televisión no va** the television isn't working. **-6.** [desenvolverse] to go; **le va bien en su nuevo trabajo** things are going well for him in his new job; **su negocio va mal** his business is going badly; **¿cómo te va?** how are you doing? **-7.** [vestir]: **~ en/con** to wear; **iba en camisa y con corbata** he was wearing a shirt and tie; **~ de azul/de uniforme** to be dressed in blue/in uniform. **-8.** [tener aspecto físico] to look like; **iba hecho un pordiosero** he looked like a beggar. **-9.** [vacaciones, tratamiento]: **~le bien a alguien** to do sb good. **-10.** [ropa]: **~le (bien) a alguien** to suit sb; **~ con algo** to go with sthg. **-11.** [comentario, indirecta]: **~ con ○ por alguien** to be meant for sb, to be aimed at sb. **-12.** *loc:* **fue y dijo que ...** he went and said that ...; **ni me va ni me viene** *fam* I don't care;

¡qué va! you must be joking!; ser el no va más to be the ultimate. ◆ ir de *vi* -1. [película, novela] to be about. -2. *fig* [persona] to think o.s.; va de listo he thinks he's clever. ◆ ir por *vi* -1. [buscar]: ~ por algo/alguien to go and get sthg/sb, to go and fetch sthg/sb. -2. [alcanzar]: va por el cuarto vaso de vino he's already on his fourth glass of wine; vamos por la mitad de la asignatura we covered about half the subject. ◆ irse *vpr* -1. [marcharse] to go, to leave; ~se a to go to; ¡vete! go away! -2. [gastarse, desaparecer] to go. -3. *loc*: ~se abajo [edificio] to fall down; [negocio] to collapse; [planes] to fall through.

ira *f* anger, rage.

IRA (*abrev de* **Irish Republican Army**) *m* IRA.

iracundo, -da *adj* angry, irate; [irascible] irascible.

Irán: (el) ~ Iran.

iraní (*pl* iraníes) *adj, m y f* Iranian.

Iraq: (el) ~ Iraq.

iraquí (*pl* iraquíes) *adj, m y f* Iraqi.

irascible *adj* irascible.

iris *m inv* iris.

Irlanda Ireland.

irlandés, -esa ◇ *adj* Irish. ◇ *m y f* [persona] Irishman (*f* Irishwoman); los irlandeses the Irish. ◆ **irlandés** *m* [lengua] Irish.

ironía *f* irony.

irónico, -ca *adj* ironic, ironical.

ironizar ◇ *vt* to ridicule. ◇ *vi*: ~ (sobre) to be ironical (about).

IRPF (*abrev de* **Impuesto sobre la Renta de las Personas Físicas**) *m* Spanish personal income tax.

irracional *adj* irrational.

irradiar *vt lit & fig* to radiate.

irreal *adj* unreal.

irreconciliable *adj* irreconcilable.

irreconocible *adj* unrecognizable.

irrecuperable *adj* irretrievable.

irreflexión *f* rashness.

irreflexivo, -va *adj* rash.

irrefutable *adj* irrefutable.

irregular *adj* [gen] irregular; [terreno, superficie] uneven.

irrelevante *adj* irrelevant.

irremediable *adj* irremediable.

irreparable *adj* irreparable.

irresistible *adj* irresistible.

irresoluto, -ta *adj culto* irresolute.

irrespetuoso, -sa *adj* disrespectful.

irrespirable *adj* unbreathable.

irresponsable *adj* irresponsible.

irreverente *adj* irreverent.

irreversible *adj* irreversible.

irrevocable *adj* irrevocable.

irrigar *vt* to irrigate.

irrisorio, -ria *adj* -1. [excusa etc] laughable, derisory. -2. [precio etc] ridiculously low.

irritable *adj* irritable.

irritar *vt* to irritate. ◆ **irritarse** *vpr* -1. [enfadarse] to get angry o annoyed. -2. [suj: piel etc] to become irritated.

irrompible *adj* unbreakable.

irrupción *f* bursting in.

isla *f* island.

islam *m* Islam.

islamismo *m* Islam.

islandés, -esa ◇ *adj* Icelandic. ◇ *m y f* [persona] Icelander. ◆ **islandés** *m* [lengua] Icelandic.

Islandia Iceland.

isleño, -ña ◇ *adj* island (*antes de sust*). ◇ *m y f* islander.

islote *m* small, rocky island.

Israel Israel.

israelí (*pl* israelíes) *adj, m y f* Israeli.

istmo *m* isthmus.

Italia Italy.

italiano, -na *adj, m y f* Italian. ◆ **italiano** *m* [lengua] Italian.

itálico, -ca *adj* → **letra**.

itinerante *adj* itinerant; [embajador] roving.

itinerario *m* route, itinerary.

ITV (*abrev de* **inspección técnica de vehículos**) *f* annual technical inspection for motor vehicles of ten years or more, ≃ MOT *Br*.

IVA (*abrev de* **impuesto sobre el valor añadido**) *m* VAT.

izar *vt* to raise, to hoist.

izda (*abrev de* **izquierda**) L, l.

izquierda → **izquierdo**.

izquierdo, -da *adj* left. ◆ **izquierda** *f* -1. [lado] left; a la izquierda (de) on o to the left (of); girar a la izquierda to turn left. -2. [mano] left hand. -3. POLÍT left (wing); de izquierdas left-wing.

J

j, J *f* [letra] j, J.
ja *interj*: ¡~! ha!
jabalí (*pl* jabalíes) *m y f* wild boar.
jabalina *f* DEP javelin.
jabón *m* soap; ~ **de afeitar/tocador** shaving/toilet soap.
jabonar *vt* to soap.
jabonera *f* soap dish.
jaca *f* [caballo pequeño] pony; [yegua] mare.
jacal *m Amer* hut.
jacinto *m* hyacinth.
jactarse *vpr*: ~ **(de)** to boast (about o of).
jacuzzi® [ja'kusi] (*pl* jacuzzis) *m* Jacuzzi®.
jadear *vi* to pant.
jadeo *m* panting.
jaguar (*pl* jaguars) *m* jaguar.
jaiba *f Amer* [cangrejo de río] crayfish.
jalea *f* jelly; ~ **real** royal jelly.
jalear *vt* to cheer on.
jaleo *m* **-1.** *fam* [alboroto] row, rumpus. **-2.** *fam* [lío] mess, confusion.
jalonar *vt* to stake o mark out; *fig* to mark.
Jamaica Jamaica.
jamás *adv* never; **no le he visto** ~ I've never seen him; **la mejor película que** ~ **se haya hecho** the best film ever made; ~ **de los jamases** never ever.
jamón *m* ham; ~ **(de) York** o **(en) dulce** boiled ham; ~ **serrano** cured ham, ≃ Parma ham.
Japón: **(el)** ~ Japan.
japonés, -esa *adj, m y f* Japanese. ◆**japonés** *m* [lengua] Japanese.
jaque *m*: ~ **mate** checkmate.
jaqueca *f* migraine.
jarabe *m* syrup; ~ **para la tos** cough mixture o syrup.
jarana *f* [juerga]: **estar/irse de** ~ to be/go out on the town.
jaranero, -ra *adj* fond of partying.
jardín *m* garden; ~ **botánico** botanical garden. ◆**jardín de infancia** *m* kindergarten, nursery school.

jardinera → jardinero.
jardinería *f* gardening.
jardinero, -ra *m y f* gardener. ◆**jardinera** *f* flowerpot stand.
jarra *f* **-1.** [para servir] jug. **-2.** [para beber] tankard. ◆**en jarras** *loc adv* [postura] hands on hips.
jarro *m* jug.
jarrón *m* vase.
jaspeado, -da *adj* mottled, speckled.
jauja *f fam* paradise.
jaula *f* cage.
jauría *f* pack of dogs.
jazmín *m* jasmine.
jazz [jas] *m* jazz.
JC (*abrev de* Jesucristo) JC.
je *interj*: ¡~! ha!
jeep [jip] (*pl* jeeps) *m* jeep.
jefa → jefe.
jefatura *f* **-1.** [cargo] leadership. **-2.** [organismo] headquarters, head office.
jefe, -fa *m y f* [gen] boss; COM manager (*f* manageress); [líder] leader; [de tribu, ejército] chief; [de departamento etc] head; **en** ~ MIL in-chief; ~ **de cocina** chef; ~ **de estación** stationmaster; ~ **de Estado** head of state; ~ **de estudios** deputy head; ~ **de producción/ventas** production/sales manager; ~ **de redacción** editor-in-chief.
jengibre *m* ginger.
jeque *m* sheikh.
jerarquía *f* **-1.** [organización] hierarchy. **-2.** [persona] high-ranking person, leader.
jerárquico, -ca *adj* hierarchical.
jerez *m* sherry.
jerga *f* jargon; [argot] slang.
jeringuilla *f* syringe.
jeroglífico, -ca *adj* hieroglyphic. ◆**jeroglífico** *m* **-1.** [inscripción] hieroglyphic. **-2.** [pasatiempo] rebus.
jerséi (*pl* jerséis), **jersey** *m* (*pl* jerseys) jumper, pullover.
Jerusalén Jerusalem.
jesuita *adj & m* Jesuit.
jesús *interj*: ¡~! [sorpresa] good heavens!; [tras estornudo] bless you!
jet [jet] (*pl* jets) ◇ *m* jet. ◇ *f* → jet-set.
jeta *mfam f* [cara] mug, face; **tener (mucha)** ~ to be a cheeky bugger.
jet-set ['jetset] *f* jet set.
Jibuti Djibouti.
jilguero *m* goldfinch.
jilipollada = gilipollada.
jilipollas = gilipollas.
jinete *m y f* rider; [yóquey] jockey.

jirafa f ZOOL giraffe.

jirón m [andrajo] shred, rag; **hecho jirones** in tatters.

jitomate m Amer variety of tomato.

JJ OO (abrev de **juegos olímpicos**) mpl Olympic Games.

jockey ['jokei] = **yóquey**.

jocoso, -sa adj jocular.

joder vulg vi **-1.** [copular] to fuck. **-2.** [fastidiar] to be a pain in the arse; **¡no jodas!** [incredulidad] bollocks!, pull the other one!

jofaina f wash basin.

jolgorio m merrymaking.

jolín, jolines interj fam: **¡~!, ¡jolines!** hell!, Christ!

jondo → **cante**.

jornada f **-1.** [de trabajo] working day; **~ intensiva** working day from 8 to 3 with only a short lunch break; **media ~** half day; **~ partida** typical Spanish working day from 9 to 1 and 4 to 7. **-2.** [de viaje] day's journey. **-3.** DEP round of matches, programme. ◆ **jornadas** fpl [conferencia] conference (sg).

jornal m day's wage.

jornalero, -ra m y f day labourer.

joroba f hump.

jorobado, -da ◇ adj [con joroba] hunchbacked. ◇ m y f hunchback.

jorongo m Amer **-1.** [manta] blanket. **-2.** [poncho] poncho.

jota f **-1.** [baile] Aragonese folk song and dance. **-2.** [loc]: **no entender** O **saber ni ~** fam fig not to understand O know a thing.

joto m y f Amer fam despec queer Br, faggot Am.

joven ◇ adj young. ◇ m y f young man (f young woman); **los jóvenes** young people.

jovial adj jovial, cheerful.

joya f jewel; fig gem.

joyería f **-1.** [tienda] jeweller's (shop). **-2.** [arte, comercio] jewellery.

joyero, -ra m y f [persona] jeweller. ◆ **joyero** m [estuche] jewellery box.

Jr. (abrev de **junior**) Jr.

juanete m bunion.

jubilación f [retiro] retirement; **~ anticipada** early retirement.

jubilado, -da ◇ adj retired. ◇ m y f pensioner Br, senior citizen.

jubilar vt: **~ a alguien (de)** to pension sb off O retire sb (from). ◆ **jubilarse** vpr to retire.

jubileo m RELIG jubilee.

júbilo m jubilation, joy.

judía f bean; **~ blanca/verde** haricot/green bean.

judicial adj judicial.

judío, -a ◇ adj Jewish. ◇ m y f Jew (f Jewess).

judo = **yudo**.

juega → **jugar**.

juego m **-1.** [gen & DEP] game; [acción] play, playing; [con dinero] gambling; **estar/poner en ~** to be/put at stake; **~ de azar** game of chance; **~ de manos** conjuring trick; **~ de palabras** play on words, pun; **Juegos Olímpicos** Olympic Games; **~ sucio/limpio** foul/clean play; **descubrirle el ~ a alguien** to see through sb; **estar (en) fuera de ~** DEP to be offside; fig not to know what's going on. **-2.** [conjunto de objetos] set; **~ de herramientas** tool kit; **~ de té/café** tea/coffee service; **hacer ~ (con)** to match.

juerga f fam rave-up; **irse/estar de ~** to go/be out on the town.

juerguista fam m y f reveller.

jueves m inv Thursday; **Jueves Santo** Maundy Thursday; ver también **sábado**.

juez m y f **-1.** DER judge; **~ de paz** Justice of the Peace. [DEP - gen] judge; [- en atletismo] official; **~ de línea** [fútbol] linesman; [rugby] touch judge; **~ de salida** starter; **~ de silla** umpire.

jugada f **-1.** DEP period of play; [en tenis, ping-pong] rally; [en fútbol, rugby etc] move; [en ajedrez etc] move; [en billar] shot. **-2.** [treta] dirty trick; **hacer una mala ~ a alguien** to play a dirty trick on sb.

jugador, -ra m y f [gen] player; [de juego de azar] gambler.

jugar ◇ vi **-1.** [gen] to play; **~ al ajedrez** to play chess; **~ en un equipo** to play for a team; **te toca ~** it's your turn O go. **-2.** [con dinero]: **~ (a)** to gamble (on); **~ (a la Bolsa)** to speculate (on the Stock Exchange). ◇ vt **-1.** [gen] to play; [ficha, pieza] to move. **-2.** [dinero]: **~ algo (a algo)** to gamble sthg (on sthg). ◆ **jugarse** vpr **-1.** [apostarse] to bet. **-2.** [arriesgar] to risk. **-3.** loc: **jugársela a alguien** to play a dirty trick on sb.

jugarreta f fam dirty trick.

juglar m minstrel.

jugo m **-1.** [gen & ANAT] juice; BOT sap. **-2.** [interés] meat, substance; **sacar ~ a algo/alguien** to get the most out of sthg/sb.

jugoso, -sa adj -1. [con jugo] juicy. -2. fig [picante] juicy; [sustancioso] meaty, substantial.

juguete m lit & fig toy; **de** ~ toy (antes de sust).

juguetear vi to play (around); ~ **con algo** to toy with sthg.

juguetería f toy shop.

juguetón, -ona adj playful.

juicio m -1. DER trial. -2. [sensatez] (sound) judgement; [cordura] sanity, reason; **estar/no estar en su (sano)** ~ to be/not to be in one's right mind; **perder el** ~ to lose one's reason. -3. [opinión] opinion; **a mi** ~ in my opinion. ◆**Juicio Final** m: **el Juicio Final** the Last Judgement.

juicioso, -sa adj sensible, wise.

julio m -1. [mes] July; ver también **septiembre**. -2. FÍS joule.

junco m -1. [planta] rush, reed. -2. [embarcación] junk.

jungla f jungle.

junio m June; ver también **septiembre**.

júnior (pl **juniors**) adj -1. DEP under-21. -2. [hijo] junior.

junta f -1. [gen] committee; [de empresa, examinadores] board; ~ **directiva** board of directors; ~ **militar** military junta. -2. [reunión] meeting. -3. [juntura] joint; ~ **de culata** gasket.

juntar vt [gen] to put together; [fondos] to raise; [personas] to bring together. ◆**juntarse** vpr -1. [reunirse - personas] to get together; [- ríos, caminos] to meet. -2. [arrimarse] to draw O move closer. -3. [convivir] to live together.

junto, -ta ◇ adj -1. [gen] together. -2. [próximo] close together. ◇ adv: **todo** ~ [ocurrir etc] all at the same time; [escribirse] as one word. ◆**junto a** loc prep -1. [al lado de] next to. -2. [cerca de] right by, near. ◆**junto con** loc prep together with.

juntura f joint.

Júpiter m Jupiter.

jurado, -da adj -1. [declaración etc] sworn. -2. → **guarda**. ◆**jurado** m -1. [tribunal] jury. -2. [miembro] member of the jury.

juramento m -1. [promesa] oath. -2. [blasfemia] oath, curse.

jurar ◇ vt to swear; [constitución etc] to pledge allegiance to; **te lo juro I** promise; ~ **por ... que** to swear by ... that. ◇ vi [blasfemar] to swear.

jurel m scad, horse mackerel.

jurídico, -ca adj legal.

jurisdicción f jurisdiction.

jurisdiccional adj jurisdictional; [aguas] territorial.

jurisprudencia f [ciencia] jurisprudence; [casos previos] case law.

jurista m y f jurist.

justa f HIST joust.

justamente adv -1. [con justicia] justly. -2. [exactamente] exactly.

justicia f -1. [gen] justice; [equidad] fairness, justice; **hacer** ~ to do justice; **ser de** ~ to be only fair. -2. [organización]: **la** ~ the law.

justiciero, -ra adj righteous.

justificación f [gen & IMPRENTA] justification.

justificante m documentary evidence (U).

justificar vt -1. [gen & IMPRENTA] to justify. -2. [excusar]: ~ **a alguien** to make excuses for sb. ◆**justificarse** vpr [suj: persona] to justify O excuse o.s.

justo, -ta adj -1. [equitativo] fair. -2. [merecido - recompensa, victoria] deserved; [- castigo] just. -3. [exacto - medida, hora] exact. -4. [idóneo] right. -5. [apretado] tight; **estar** O **venir** ~ to be a tight fit. ◆**justo** adv just; ~ **ahora iba a llamarte I** was just about to ring you; ~ **en medio** right in the middle.

juvenil adj youthful; DEP youth (antes de sust).

juventud f -1. [edad] youth. -2. [conjunto] young people (pl).

juzgado m [tribunal] court; ~ **de guardia** court open during the night or at other times when ordinary courts are shut.

juzgar vt -1. [enjuiciar] to judge; DER to try; ~ **mal a alguien** to misjudge sb; **a** ~ **por (como)** judging by (how). -2. [estimar] to consider, to judge.

K

k, K f [letra] k, K.

kaki = **caqui**.

kárate, cárate m karate.

kart (pl **karts**) m go-kart.

Kenia Kenya.

ketchup ['ketʃup] m ketchup.

kg (abrev de **kilogramo**) kg.

kibutz [ki'ßuθ] (*pl* **kibutzim**) *m* kibutz.

kilo, quilo *m* [peso] kilo.

kilogramo, quilogramo *m* kilogram.

kilometraje, quilometraje *m* ≃ mileage, distance in kilometres.

kilométrico, -ca, quilométrico, -ca *adj* [distancia] kilometric.

kilómetro, quilómetro *m* kilometre; ~ **cuadrado** square kilometre.

kilovatio, quilovatio *m* kilowatt.

kiosco = **quiosco**.

kiwi (*pl* **kiwis**) *m* [fruto] kiwi (fruit).

km (*abrev de* **kilómetro**) km.

km/h (*abrev de* **kilómetro por hora**) km/h.

KO (*abrev de* **knockout**) *m* KO.

kurdo, -da ◇ *adj* Kurdish. ◇ *m y f* Kurd.

Kuwait [ku'ßait] Kuwait.

L

l¹, L *f* [letra] l, L.

l² (*abrev de* **litro**) l.

la¹ *m* MÚS A; [en solfeo] lah.

la² ◇ *art* → **el**. ◇ *pron* → **lo**.

laberinto *m lit* & *fig* labyrinth.

labia *f fam* smooth talk; **tener mucha ~** to have the gift of the gab.

labio *m* -1. ANAT lip. -2. [borde] edge.

labor *f* -1. [trabajo] work; [tarea] task; **~es domésticas** household chores; **ser de profesión sus ~es** to be a housewife. -2. [de costura] needlework.

laborable → **día**.

laboral *adj* labour; [semana, condiciones] working (*antes de sust*).

laboratorio *m* laboratory; **~ de idiomas** O **lenguas** language laboratory.

laborioso, -sa *adj* [difícil] laborious.

laborista ◇ *adj* Labour. ◇ *m y f* Labour Party supporter O member; **los ~s** Labour.

labrador, -ra *m y f* [agricultor] farmer; [trabajador] farm worker.

labranza *f* farming.

labrar *vt* -1. [campo - cultivar] to cultivate; [- arar] to plough. -2. [piedra, metal etc] to work. -3. *fig* [desgracia etc] to bring about; [porvenir, fortuna] to carve

out. ◆ **labrarse** *vpr* [porvenir etc] to carve out for o.s.

labriego, -ga *m y f* farmworker.

laca *f* -1. [gen] lacquer; [para cuadros] lake. -2. [para el pelo] hairspray.

lacar *vt* to lacquer.

lacayo *m* footman; *fig* lackey.

lacerar *vt* to lacerate; *fig* to wound.

lacio, -cia *adj* -1. [cabello - liso] straight; [- sin fuerza] lank. -2. [planta] wilted. -3. *fig* [sin fuerza] limp.

lacón *m* shoulder of pork.

lacónico, -ca *adj* laconic.

lacra *f* scourge.

lacrar *vt* to seal with sealing wax.

lacre *m* sealing wax.

lacrimógeno, -na *adj* -1. [novela etc] weepy, tear-jerking. -2. → **gas**.

lacrimoso, -sa *adj* -1. [ojos etc] tearful. -2. [historia etc] weepy, tear-jerking.

lactancia *f* lactation; **~ materna** breastfeeding.

lactante *m y f* breast-fed baby.

lácteo, -a *adj* [gen] milk (*antes de sust*); [industria, productos] dairy.

ladear *vt* to tilt.

ladera *f* slope, mountainside.

ladino, -na *adj* crafty. ◆ **ladino** *m* [dialecto] Ladino.

lado *m* -1. [gen] side; **en el ~ de arriba/abajo** on the top/bottom; **a ambos ~s** on both sides; **estoy de su ~** I'm on her side; **de ~** [torcido] crooked; **dormir de ~** to sleep on one's side; **por un ~** on the one hand; **por otro ~** on the other hand. -2. [lugar] place; **debe estar en otro ~** it must be somewhere else. -3. *loc*: **dar de ~ a alguien** to cold-shoulder sb; **dejar algo de ~** O **a un ~** [prescindir] to leave sthg to one side. ◆ **al lado** *loc adv* [cerca] nearby. ◆ **al lado de** *loc prep* [junto a] beside. ◆ **de al lado** *loc adj* next door; **la casa de al ~** the house next door.

ladrar *vi lit* & *fig* to bark.

ladrido *m lit* & *fig* bark, barking (*U*).

ladrillo *m* CONSTR brick.

ladrón, -ona *m y f* [persona] thief, robber. ◆ **ladrón** *m* [para varios enchufes] adapter.

lagartija *f* (small) lizard.

lagarto, -ta *m y f* ZOOL lizard.

lago *m* lake.

lágrima *f* tear; **llorar a ~ viva** to cry buckets.

lagrimal *m* corner of the eye.

laguna *f* -1. [lago] lagoon. -2. *fig* [en co-

lección, memoria] **gap**; [en leyes, reglamento] **loophole**.
La Habana Havana.
La Haya The Hague.
laico, -ca *adj* lay, secular.
lama *m* lama.
lamber *vt Amer fam* to lick.
La Meca Mecca.
lamentable *adj* **-1.** [triste] terribly sad. **-2.** [malo] lamentable, deplorable.
lamentar *vt* to regret, to be sorry about; **lo lamento** I'm very sorry.
lamento *m* moan.
lamer *vt* to lick. ◆ **lamerse** *vpr* to lick o.s.
lamido, -da *adj* skinny. ◆ **lamido** *m* lick.
lámina *f* **-1.** [plancha] sheet; [placa] plate. **-2.** [rodaja] slice. **-3.** [plancha grabada] engraving. **-4.** [dibujo] plate.
laminar *vt* **-1.** [hacer láminas] to roll. **-2.** [cubrir con láminas] to laminate.
lámpara *f* **-1.** [aparato] lamp; ~ **de pie** standard lamp. **-2.** [bombilla] bulb. **-3.** TECN valve.
lamparón *m* grease stain.
lampiño, -ña *adj* [sin barba] beardless, hairless.
lamprea *f* lamprey.
lana ◇ *f* wool; **de** ~ woollen. ◇ *m Amer fam* dosh, dough.
lance *m* **-1.** [en juegos, deportes] incident; [acontecimiento] event. **-2.** [riña] dispute.
lanceta *f Amer* sting.
lancha *f* [embarcación - grande] launch; [- pequeña] boat; ~ **salvavidas** lifeboat.
lanero, -ra *adj* wool (*antes de sust*).
langosta *f* **-1.** [crustáceo] lobster. **-2.** [insecto] locust.
langostino *m* king prawn.
languidecer *vi* to languish; [conversación, entusiasmo] to flag.
languidez *f* [debilidad] listlessness; [falta de ánimo] disinterest.
lánguido, -da *adj* [débil] listless; [falto de ánimo] disinterested.
lanilla *f* **-1.** [pelillo] nap. **-2.** [tejido] flannel.
lanolina *f* lanolin.
lanza *f* [arma - arrojadiza] **spear**; [- en justas, torneos] **lance**.
lanzado, -da *adj* [atrevido] forward; [valeroso] fearless.
lanzagranadas *m inv* grenade launcher.
lanzamiento *m* **-1.** [de objeto] throwing; [de cohete] launching. **-2.** [DEP - con

la mano] **throw**; [- con el pie] **kick**; [- en béisbol] **pitch**; ~ **de peso** shot put. **-3.** [de producto, artista] **launch**; [de disco] **release**.
lanzamisiles *m inv* rocket launcher.
lanzar *vt* **-1.** [gen] to throw; [con fuerza] to hurl, to fling; [de una patada] to kick; [bomba] to drop; [flecha, misil] to fire; [cohete] to launch. **-2.** [proferir] to let out; [acusación, insulto] to hurl; [suspiro] to heave. **-3.** [COM - producto, artista, periódico] to launch; [- disco] to release. ◆ **lanzarse** *vpr* **-1.** [tirarse] to throw o.s. **-2.** [abalanzarse]: ~**se (sobre)** to throw o.s. (upon).
lapa *f* ZOOL limpet.
La Paz La Paz.
lapicera *f Amer* [bolígrafo] biro, pen.
lapicero *m* pencil.
lápida *f* memorial stone; ~ **mortuoria** tombstone.
lapidar *vt* to stone.
lapidario, -ria *adj* solemn.
lápiz (*pl* **lápices**) *m* pencil; ~ **de labios** lipstick; ~ **de ojos** eyeliner; ~ **óptico** INFORM light pen.
lapón, -ona *adj, m y f* Lapp. ◆ **lapón** *m* [lengua] Lapp.
lapso *m* space, interval.
lapsus *m inv* lapse, slip.
larga → **largo**.
largar *vt* **-1.** [aflojar] to pay out. **-2.** *fam* [dar, decir] to give; **le largué un bofetón** I gave him a smack. ◆ **largarse** *vpr fam* to clear off.
largavistas *m inv Amer* binoculars (*pl*).
largo, -ga *adj* **-1.** [en espacio, tiempo] long. **-2.** [alto] tall. **-3.** [sobrado]: **media hora larga** a good half hour. ◆ **largo** ◇ *m* length; **a lo** ~ lengthways; **tiene dos metros de** ~ it's two metres long; **pasar de** ~ to pass by; **a lo** ~ **de** [en el espacio] along; [en el tiempo] throughout; **¡**~ **de aquí!** go away! ◇ *adv* at length; ~ **y tendido** at great length. ◆ **larga** *f*: **a la larga** in the long run; **dar largas a algo** to put sthg off.
largometraje *m* feature film.
larguero *m* **-1.** CONSTR main beam. **-2.** DEP crossbar.
largura *f* length.
laringe *f* larynx.
laringitis *f inv* laryngitis.
larva *f* larva.
las ◇ *art* → **el**. ◇ *pron* → **lo**.
lasaña *f* lasagne, lasagna.
lascivo, -va *adj* lascivious, lewd.
láser ◇ *adj inv* → **rayo**. ◇ *m inv* laser.

lástex *m inv* Lastex®.

lástima *f* **-1.** [compasión] pity. **-2.** [pena] shame, pity; **da ~ ver gente así** it's sad to see people in that state; **¡qué ~!** what a shame O pity!; **quedarse hecho una ~** to be a sorry O pitiful sight.

lastimar *vt* to hurt. ◆ **lastimarse** *vpr* to hurt o.s.

lastimoso, -sa *adj* pitiful, woeful.

lastre *m* **-1.** [peso] ballast. **-2.** *fig* [estorbo] burden.

lata *f* **-1.** [envase] can, tin; [de bebidas] can; **en ~** tinned, canned. **-2.** *fam* [fastidio] pain; **¡qué ~!** what a pain!; **dar la ~ a alguien** to pester sb.

latente *adj* latent.

lateral ◇ *adj* [del lado - *gen*] lateral; [- puerta, pared] side. ◇ *m* **-1.** [lado] side. **-2.** DEP: **~ derecho/izquierdo** right/left back.

latido *m* [del corazón] beat; [en dedo etc] throb, throbbing (*U*).

latifundio *m* large rural estate.

latigazo *m* **-1.** [golpe] lash. **-2.** [chasquido] crack (of the whip).

látigo *m* whip.

latín *m* Latin; **saber (mucho) ~** *fig* to be sharp, to be on the ball.

latinajo *m fam despec* Latin word used in an attempt to sound academic.

latino, -na *adj, m y f* Latin.

latinoamericano, -na *adj, m y f* Latin American.

latir *vi* [suj: corazón] to beat.

latitud *f* GEOGR latitude. ◆ **latitudes** *fpl* [parajes] region (*sg*), area (*sg*).

latón *m* brass.

latoso, -sa *fam adj* tiresome.

laúd *m* lute.

laureado, -da *adj* prize-winning.

laurel *m* BOT laurel; CULIN bay leaf. ◆ **laureles** *mpl* [honores] laurels; **dormirse en los ~es** *fig* to rest on one's laurels.

lava *f* lava.

lavabo *m* **-1.** [objeto] washbasin. **-2.** [habitación] lavatory *Br*, washroom *Am*.

lavadero *m* [en casa] laundry room; [público] washing place.

lavado *m* wash, washing (*U*); **~ de cerebro** brainwashing.

lavadora *f* washing machine.

lavamanos *m inv* washbasin.

lavanda *f* lavender.

lavandería *f* laundry; [automática] launderette.

lavaplatos *m inv* [aparato] dishwasher.

lavar *vt* [limpiar] to wash; **~ y marcar** shampoo and set. ◆ **lavarse** *vpr* [gen] to wash o.s.; [cara, manos, pelo] to wash; [dientes] to clean.

lavativa *f* enema.

lavavajillas *m inv* dishwasher.

laxante *m* MED laxative.

laxar *vt* [vientre] to loosen.

lazada *f* bow.

lazarillo *m* **-1.** [persona] blind person's guide. **-2.** → **perro**.

lazo *m* **-1.** [atadura] bow. **-2.** [trampa] snare; [de vaquero] lasso. **-3.** (*gen pl*) *fig* [vínculo] tie, bond.

Lda. *abrev de* **licenciada**.

Ldo. *abrev de* **licenciado**.

le *pron pers* **-1.** (*complemento indirecto*) [hombre] (to) him; [mujer] (to) her; [cosa] to it; [usted] to you; **~ expliqué el motivo** I explained the reason to him/her; **~ tengo miedo** I'm afraid of him/her; **ya ~ dije lo que pasaría** [a usted] I told you what would happen. **-2.** (*complemento directo*) him; [usted] you. **-3.** → **se**.

leal *adj*: **~ (a)** loyal (to).

lealtad *f*: **~ (a)** loyalty (to).

leasing ['lisin] (*pl* **leasings**) *m* system of leasing whereby the lessee has the option of purchasing the property after a certain time.

lección *f* lesson; **dar a alguien una ~** [como advertencia] to teach sb a lesson; [como ejemplo] to give sb a lesson.

lechal *m* sucking lamb.

leche *f* **-1.** [gen] milk; **~ condensada/en polvo** condensed/powdered milk; **~ descremada** O **desnatada** skimmed milk; **~ merengada** *drink made from milk, egg whites, sugar and cinnamon*. **-2.** *mfam* [bofetada]: **pegar una ~ a alguien** to belt O clobber sb. **-3.** *mfam* [malhumor] bloody awful mood; **estar de mala ~** to be in a bloody awful mood; **tener mala ~** to be a miserable git.

lechera → **lechero**.

lechería *f* dairy.

lechero, -ra ◇ *adj* milk (*antes de sust*), dairy. ◇ *m y f* [persona] milkman (*f* milkwoman). ◆ **lechera** *f* [para transportar] milk churn; [para beber] milk jug.

lecho *m* [gen] bed.

lechón *m* sucking pig.

lechuga *f* [planta] lettuce.

lechuza *f* (barn) owl.

lectivo, -va *adj* school (*antes de sust*).

lector, -ra *m y f* **-1.** [gen] reader. **-2.** EDUC language assistant. ◆ **lector** *m* [de microfilms etc] **reader, scanner;** ~ **óptico** optical scanner.

lectura f -1. [gen] reading. -2. [de tesis] viva voce. -3. [escrito] reading (matter) (U). -4. [de datos] scanning; ~ **óptica** optical scanning.

leer ◇ vt [gen & INFORM] to read. ◇ vi to read; ~ **de corrido** to read fluently.

legado m -1. [herencia] legacy. -2. [representante - persona] legate.

legajo m file.

legal adj -1. [gen] legal; [hora] standard. -2. fam [persona] honest, decent.

legalidad f legality.

legalizar vt [gen] to legalize.

legañas fpl sleep (U) (in the eyes).

legañoso, -sa adj full of sleep.

legar vt -1. [gen] to bequeath. -2. [delegar] to delegate.

legendario, -ria adj legendary.

legible adj legible.

legión f lit & fig legion.

legionario, -ria adj legionary. ◆ **legionario** m HIST legionary; MIL legionnaire.

legislación f [leyes] legislation.

legislar vi to legislate.

legislatura f [periodo] period of office.

legitimar vt -1. [legalizar] to legitimize. -2. [certificar] to authenticate.

legítimo, -ma adj [gen] legitimate; [auténtico] real, genuine; [oro] pure.

lego, -ga ◇ adj -1. [gen] lay. -2. [ignorante] ignorant. ◇ m y f [gen] layman (f laywoman).

legua f league; ~ **marina** marine league.

leguleyo, -ya m y f despec bad lawyer.

legumbre f (gen pl) pulse, pod vegetable.

lehendakari, lendakari [lenda'kari] m president of the autonomous Basque government.

leído, -da adj [persona] well-read. ◆ **leída** f reading.

leitmotiv [leitmo'tif] (pl **leitmotivs**) m leitmotiv.

lejanía f distance.

lejano, -na adj distant; **no está** ~ it's not far (away).

lejía f bleach.

lejos adv -1. [en el espacio] far (away); ¿está ~? is it far?; **a lo** ~ in the distance; **de** ○ **desde** ~ from a distance. -2. [en el pasado] long ago; [en el futuro] far in the future; **eso queda ya** ~ that happened a long time ago. ◆ **lejos de** ◇ loc conj far from; ~ **de mejorar ... far**

from getting better .... ◇ loc prep far (away) from.

lelo, -la ◇ adj stupid. ◇ m y f idiot.

lema m -1. [norma] motto; [político, publicitario] slogan. -2. LING & MAT lemma.

lencería f -1. [ropa] linen. -2. [tienda] draper's.

lendakari = **lehendakari**.

lengua f -1. [gen] tongue; ~ **de víbora** ○ **viperina** malicious tongue; **irse de la** ~ to let the cat out of the bag; **morderse la** ~ to bite one's tongue; **tirar a alguien de la** ~ to draw sb out. -2. [idioma, lenguaje] language; ~ **materna** mother tongue.

lenguado m sole.

lenguaje m [gen & INFORM] language; ~ **cifrado** code; ~ **corporal** body language; ~ **gestual** gestures (pl); ~ **máquina** machine language; ~ **de programación** programming language; ~ **de los sordomudos** sign language.

lengüeta f [gen & MÚS] tongue.

lengüetazo m, **lengüetada** f lick.

lente f lens; ~s **de contacto** contact lenses. ◆ **lentes** mpl [gafas] glasses.

lenteja f lentil.

lentejuela f sequin.

lentilla f (gen pl) contact lens.

lentitud f slowness; **con** ~ slowly.

lento, -ta adj slow; [veneno] slow-working; [agonía, enfermedad] lingering.

leña f [madera] firewood; **echar** ~ **al fuego** to add fuel to the flames ○ fire.

leñador, -ra m y f woodcutter.

leño m [de madera] log; **dormir como un** ~ to sleep like a log.

Leo ◇ m [zodiaco] Leo. ◇ m y f [persona] Leo.

león, -ona m y f lion (f lioness); fig fierce person; **no es tan fiero el** ~ **como lo pintan** proverb he/it etc is not as bad as he/it etc is made out to be. ◆ **león marino** m sea lion.

leonera f fam fig [cuarto sucio] pigsty.

leonino, -na adj [contrato, condiciones] one-sided.

leopardo m leopard.

leotardo m -1. (gen pl) [medias] stockings (pl), thick tights (pl). -2. [de gimnasta etc] leotard.

lépero, -ra adj Amer fam coarse, vulgar.

lepra f leprosy.

leproso, -sa m y f leper.

lerdo, -da adj [idiota] dim, slow-witted; [torpe] useless.

les *pron pers pl* **-1.** (*complemento indirecto*) (to) them; [ustedes] (to) you; ~ **expliqué el motivo** I explained the reason to them; ~ **tengo miedo** I'm afraid of them; **ya** ~ **dije lo que pasaría** [a ustedes] I told you what would happen. **-2.** (*complemento directo*) them; [ustedes] you. **-3.** → **se**.

lesbiano, -na *adj* lesbian. ◆ **lesbiana** *f* lesbian.

lesión *f* **-1.** [herida] injury. **-2.** DER: ~ **grave** grievous bodily harm.

lesionado, -da ◇ *adj* injured. ◇ *m y f* injured person.

lesionar *vt* to injure; *fig* to damage, to harm. ◆ **lesionarse** *vpr* to injure o.s.

letal *adj* lethal.

letanía *f* (*gen pl*) *lit* & *fig* litany.

letargo *m* ZOOL hibernation.

Letonia Latvia.

letra *f* **-1.** [signo] letter. **-2.** [caligrafía] handwriting. **-3.** [estilo] script; IMPRENTA typeface; ~ **bastardilla** O **cursiva** O **itálica** italic type, italics (*pl*); ~ **de imprenta** O **molde** IMPRENTA print; [en formularios etc] block capitals (*pl*); ~ **mayúscula/minúscula** capital/small letter; ~ **negrita** O **negrilla** bold (face); **leer la** ~ **pequeña** *fig* to read the small print; **mandar cuatro** ~**s a alguien** to drop sb a line. **-4.** [de una canción] lyrics (*pl*). **-5.** COM: ~ **(de cambio)** bill of exchange. ◆ **letras** *fpl* EDUC arts.

letrado, -da ◇ *adj* learned. ◇ *m y f* lawyer.

letrero *m* sign.

letrina *f* latrine.

leucemia *f* leukaemia.

leva *f* MIL levy.

levadura *f* yeast; ~ **de cerveza** brewer's yeast.

levantamiento *m* **-1.** [sublevación] uprising. **-2.** [elevación] raising; ~ **de pesas** DEP weightlifting. **-3.** [supresión] lifting, removal.

levantar *vt* **-1.** [gen] to raise; [peso, capó, trampilla] to lift; ~ **el ánimo** to cheer up; ~ **la vista** O **mirada** to look up. **-2.** [separar - pintura, venda, tapa] to remove. **-3.** [recoger - campamento] to strike; [- tienda de campaña, puesto] to take down; [- mesa] to clear. **-4.** [encender - protestas, polémica] to stir up; ~ **a alguien contra** to stir sb up against. **-5.** [suspender - embargo, prohibición] to lift; [- pena, castigo] to suspend; [- sesión] to adjourn. **-6.** [redactar - acta, atestado] to draw up. ◆ **levantarse** *vpr* **-1.** [ponerse

de pie] to stand up. **-2.** [de la cama] to get up. **-3.** [elevarse - avión etc] to take off; [- niebla] to lift. **-4.** [sublevarse] to rise up. **-5.** [empezar - viento, oleaje] to get up; [- tormenta] to gather.

levante *m* **-1.** [este] east; [región] east coast. **-2.** [viento] east wind.

levar *vt* to weigh.

leve *adj* **-1.** [gen] light; [olor, sabor, temblor] slight. **-2.** [pecado, falta, herida] minor. **-3.** [enfermedad] mild, slight.

levedad *f* lightness; [de temblor etc] slightness; [de pecado, falto, herida] minor nature; [de enfermedad] mildness.

levita *f* frock coat.

levitar *vi* to levitate.

léxico, -ca *adj* lexical. ◆ **léxico** *m* [vocabulario] vocabulary.

lexicografía *f* lexicography.

lexicón *m* lexicon.

ley *f* **-1.** [gen] law; [parlamentaria] act; ~ **de incompatibilidades** *act regulating which other positions may be held by people holding public office*; **con todas las de la** ~ in due form, properly. **-2.** [regla] rule; ~ **del embudo** one law for o.s. and another for everyone else; ~ **de la oferta y de la demanda** law of supply and demand. **-3.** [de un metal: **de** ~ [oro] pure; [plata] sterling. ◆ **leyes** *fpl* [derecho] law (*sg*).

leyenda *f* [narración] legend.

liar *vt* **-1.** [atar] to tie up. **-2.** [envolver - cigarrillo] to roll; ~ **algo en** [papel] to wrap sthg up in; [toalla etc] to roll sthg up in. **-3.** [involucrar]: ~ **a alguien (en)** to get sb mixed up (in). **-4.** [complicar - asunto etc] to confuse; **¡ya me has liado!** now you've really got me confused! ◆ **liarse** *vpr* **-1.** [enredarse] to get muddled up. **-2.** [empezar] to begin, to start.

Líbano *m*: **el** ~ the Lebanon.

libélula *f* dragonfly.

liberación *f* [gen] liberation; [de preso] release.

liberado, -da *adj* [gen] liberated; [preso] freed.

liberal *adj, m y f* liberal.

liberar *vt* [gen] to liberate; [preso] to free; ~ **de algo a alguien** to free sb from sthg. ◆ **liberarse** *vpr* to liberate o.s.; ~**se de algo** to free O liberate o.s. from sthg.

Liberia Liberia.

libertad *f* freedom, liberty; **dejar** O **poner a alguien en** ~ to set sb free, to release sb; **tener** ~ **para hacer algo** to be free to do sthg; **tomarse la ~ de hacer algo** to take the liberty of doing sthg; **~ condicional** probation; **~ de expresión** freedom of speech; **~ de imprenta** O **prensa** freedom of the press.

libertar *vt* [gen] to liberate; [preso] to set free.

libertino, -na ◇ *adj* licentious. ◇ *m y f* libertine.

Libia Libya.

libido *f* libido.

libra *f* [peso, moneda] pound; **~ esterlina** pound sterling. ◆ **Libra** ◇ *m* [zodiaco] Libra. ◇ *m y f* [persona] Libran.

librador, -ra *m y f* drawer.

libramiento *m*, **libranza** *f* order of payment.

librar ◇ *vt* **-1.** [eximir]: **~ a alguien (de algo/de hacer algo)** [gen] to free sb (from sthg/from doing sthg); [pagos, impuestos] to exempt sb (from sthg/ from doing sthg). **-2.** [entablar - pelea, lucha] to engage in; [- batalla, combate] to join, to wage. **-3.** COM to draw. ◇ *vi* [no trabajar] to be off work. ◆ **librarse** *vpr* **-1.** [salvarse]: **~se (de hacer algo)** to escape (from doing sthg); **de buena te libraste** you had a narrow escape. **-2.** [deshacerse]: **~se de algo/alguien** to get rid of sthg/sb.

libre *adj* **-1.** [gen] free; [rato, tiempo] spare; [camino, vía] clear; [espacio, piso, lavabo] empty, vacant; **200 metros ~s** 200 metres freestyle; **~ de** [gen] free from; [exento] exempt from; **~ de franqueo** post-free; **~ de impuestos** tax-free; **ir por ~** to go it alone. **-2.** [alumno] external; **estudiar por ~** to be an external student.

librecambio *m* free trade.

librería *f* **-1.** [tienda] bookshop. **-2.** [mueble] bookcase.

librero, -ra ◇ *m y f* [persona] bookseller. ◇ *m Amer* [mueble] bookshelf.

libreta *f* **-1.** [para escribir] notebook. **-2.** [del banco]: **~ (de ahorros)** savings book.

libreto *m* **-1.** MÚS libretto. **-2.** *Amer* CIN script.

libro *m* [gen & COM] book; **llevar los ~s** to keep the books; **~ de bolsillo** paperback; **~ de consulta/cuentos** reference/story book; **~ de escolaridad** school report; **~ de familia** *document containing personal details of the members of a family*; **~ de reclamaciones** complaints book; **~ de registro (de entradas)** register; **~ de texto** textbook.

Lic. *abrev de* **licenciado**.

licencia *f* **-1.** [documento] licence, permit; [autorización] permission; **~ de armas/caza** gun/hunting licence; **~ de obras** planning permission; **~ poética** poetic licence. **-2.** MIL discharge. **-3.** [confianza] licence, freedom.

licenciado, -da *m y f* **-1.** EDUC graduate; **~ en económicas** economics graduate. **-2.** MIL discharged soldier.

licenciar *vt* MIL to discharge. ◆ **licenciarse** *vpr* **-1.** EDUC: **~se (en)** to graduate (in). **-2.** MIL to be discharged.

licenciatura *f* degree.

licencioso, -sa *adj* licentious.

liceo *m* EDUC lycée.

licitador, -ra *m y f* bidder.

lícito, -ta *adj* **-1.** [legal] lawful. **-2.** [correcto] right. **-3.** [justo] fair.

licor *m* liquor.

licuadora *f* liquidizer, blender.

licuar *vt* CULIN to liquidize.

líder ◇ *adj* leading. ◇ *m y f* leader.

liderato, liderazgo *m* **-1.** [primer puesto] lead; [en liga] first place. **-2.** [dirección] leadership.

lidia *f* **-1.** [arte] bullfighting. **-2.** [corrida] bullfight.

lidiar ◇ *vi* [luchar]: **~ (con)** to struggle (with). ◇ *vt* TAUROM to fight.

liebre *f* ZOOL hare.

Liechtenstein ['litʃenstein] Liechtenstein.

lienzo *m* **-1.** [para pintar] canvas. **-2.** [cuadro] painting.

lifting ['liftin] (*pl* **liftings**) *m* facelift.

liga *f* **-1.** [gen] league. **-2.** [de medias] suspender.

ligadura *f* **-1.** MED & MÚS ligature. **-2.** [atadura] bond, tie.

ligamento *m* ANAT ligament.

ligar ◇ *vt* [gen & CULIN] to bind; [atar] to tie (up). ◇ *vi* **-1.** [coincidir]: **~ (con)** to tally (with). **-2.** *fam* [conquistar]: **~ (con)** to get off (with).

ligazón *f* link, connection.

ligereza *f* **-1.** [levedad - gen] lightness. **-2.** [agilidad] agility. **-3.** [irreflexión - cualidad] rashness; [- acto] rash act.

ligero, -ra *adj* **-1.** [gen] light; [dolor, rumor, descenso] slight; [traje, tela] thin. **-2.** [ágil] agile, nimble. **-3.** [rápido] quick, swift. **-4.** [irreflexivo] flippant; **a la ligera** lightly; **juzgar a alguien a la ligera** to be quick to judge sb.

light [lait] *adj inv* [comida] low-calorie; [refresco] diet (*antes de sust*); [cigarrillos] light.

ligón, -ona *fam adj*: **es muy ~** he's always getting off with sb or other.

liguero, -ra *adj* DEP league (*antes de sust*). ◆ **liguero** *m* suspender belt *Br*, garter belt *Am*.

lija *f* [papel] sandpaper.

lila ◇ *f* [flor] lilac. ◇ *adj inv & m* [color] lilac.

lima *f* **-1.** [utensilio] file; **~ de uñas** nail file. **-2.** BOT lime.

Lima Lima.

limar *vt* **-1.** [pulir] to file down. **-2.** [perfeccionar] to polish.

limitación *f* **-1.** [restricción] limitation, limit. **-2.** [distrito] boundaries (*pl*).

limitado, -da *adj* **-1.** [gen] limited. **-2.** *fig* [poco inteligente] dim-witted.

limitar ◇ *vt* **-1.** [gen] to limit. **-2.** [terreno] to mark out. **-3.** [atribuciones, derechos etc] to set out, to define. ◇ *vi:* **~ (con)** to border (on). ◆ **limitarse a** *vpr* to limit o.s. to.

límite ◇ *adj inv* **-1.** [precio, velocidad, edad] maximum. **-2.** [situación] extreme; [caso] borderline. ◇ *m* **-1.** [tope] limit; **dentro de un ~** within limits; **su pasión no tiene ~** her passion knows no bounds; **~ de velocidad** speed limit. **-2.** [confín] boundary.

limítrofe *adj* [país, territorio] bordering; [terreno, finca] neighbouring.

limón *m* lemon.

limonada *f* lemonade.

limonero, -ra *adj* lemon (*antes de sust*). ◆ **limonero** *m* lemon tree.

limosna *f* alms (*pl*); **pedir ~** to beg.

limpia *f Amer* cleaning.

limpiabotas *m y f inv* shoeshine, bootblack *Br*.

limpiacristales *m inv* window-cleaning fluid.

limpiamente *adv* **-1.** [con destreza] cleanly. **-2.** [honradamente] honestly.

limpiaparabrisas *m inv* windscreen wiper *Br*, windshield wiper *Am*.

limpiar *vt* **-1.** [gen] to clean; [con trapo] to wipe; [mancha] to wipe away; [zapatos] to polish. **-2.** *fig* [desembarazar]: **~ algo de algo** to clear sthg of sthg.

limpieza *f* **-1.** [cualidad] cleanliness. **-2.** [acción] cleaning; **~ en seco** dry cleaning. **-3.** *fig* [destreza] skill, cleanness. **-4.** *fig* [honradez] honesty.

limpio, -pia *adj* **-1.** [gen] clean; [pulcro] neat; [cielo, imagen] clear. **-2.** [neto - sueldo etc] net. **-3.** [honrado] honest; [intenciones] honourable; [juego] clean. **-4.** [sin culpa]: **estar ~** to be in the clear.

◆ **limpio** *adv* cleanly, fair; **pasar a O poner en ~** to make a fair copy of; **sacar algo en ~ de** to make sthg out from.

linaje *m* lineage.

linaza *f* linseed.

lince *m* lynx; **ser un ~ para algo** to be very sharp at sthg.

linchar *vt* to lynch.

lindar ◆ **lindar con** *vi* **-1.** [terreno] to adjoin, to be next to. **-2.** [conceptos, ideas] to border on.

linde *m o f* boundary.

lindero, -ra *adj* [terreno] adjoining. ◆ **lindero** *m* boundary.

lindo, -da *adj* pretty, lovely; **de lo ~** a great deal.

línea *f* **-1.** [gen, DEP & TELECOM] line; **cortar la ~ (telefónica)** to cut off the phone; **~ aérea** airline; **~ de conducta** course of action; **~ continua** AUTOM solid white line; **~ de puntos** dotted line. **-2.** [de un coche etc] lines (*pl*), shape. **-3.** [silueta] figure; **guardar la ~** to watch one's figure. **-4.** [estilo] style; **de ~ clásica** classical. **-5.** [categoría] class, category; **de primera ~** first-rate. **-6.** INFORM: **en ~** on-line; **fuera de ~** off-line. **-7.** *loc:* **en ~s generales** in broad terms; **leer entre ~s** to read between the lines.

lingote *m* ingot.

lingüista *m y f* linguist.

lingüístico, -ca *adj* linguistic. ◆ **lingüística** *f* linguistics.

linier [li'njer] (*pl* **liniers**) *m* linesman.

linimento *m* liniment.

lino *m* **-1.** [planta] flax. **-2.** [tejido] linen.

linterna *f* **-1.** [farol] lantern, lamp. **-2.** [de pilas] torch *Br*, flashlight *Am*.

lío *m* **-1.** [paquete] bundle. **-2.** *fam* [enredo] mess; **hacerse un ~** to get muddled up; **meterse en ~s** to get into trouble. **-3.** *fam* [jaleo] racket, row. **-4.** *fam* [amorío] affair.

liposucción *f* liposuction.

liquen *m* lichen.

liquidación *f* **-1.** [pago] settlement, payment. **-2.** [rebaja] clearance sale. **-3.** [fin] liquidation.

liquidar *vt* **-1.** [pagar - deuda] to pay; [- cuenta] to settle. **-2.** [rebajar] to sell off. **-3.** [malgastar] to throw away. **-4.** [acabar - asunto] to settle; [- negocio, sociedad] to wind up.

líquido, -da *adj* **-1.** [gen] liquid. **-2.** ECON [neto] net. ◆ **líquido** *m* **-1.** [gen] liquid. **-2.** ECON liquid assets (*pl*). **-3.** MED fluid.

lira *f* **-1.** MÚS lyre. **-2.** [moneda] lira.

lírico, -ca *adj* LITER lyrical. ◆ **lírica** *f* lyric poetry.

lirio *m* iris.

lirón *m* ZOOL dormouse; **dormir como un ~** *fig* to sleep like a log.

lis *f* iris.

Lisboa Lisbon.

lisiado, -da ◇ *adj* crippled. ◇ *m y f* cripple.

lisiar *vt* to maim, to cripple.

liso, -sa ◇ *adj* **-1.** [llano] flat; [sin asperezas] smooth; [pelo] straight; **los 400 metros ~s** the 400 metres; **lisa y llanamente** quite simply; **hablando lisa y llanamente** to put it plainly. **-2.** [no estampado] plain. ◇ *m y f Amer* coarse O rude person.

lisonja *f* flattering remark.

lisonjear *vt* to flatter.

lista *f* **-1.** [enumeración] list; **pasar ~** to call the register; **~ de boda/de espera/ de precios** wedding/waiting/price list. **-2.** [de tela, madera] strip; [de papel] slip; [de color] stripe. ◆ **lista de correos** *f* poste restante.

listado, -da *adj* striped.

listín ◆ **listín (de teléfonos)** *m* (telephone) directory.

listo, -ta *adj* **-1.** [inteligente, hábil] clever, smart; **dárselas de ~** to make o.s. out to be clever; **pasarse de ~** to be too clever by half; **ser más ~ que el hambre** to be nobody's fool. **-2.** [preparado] ready; **¿estáis ~s?** are you ready?; **estás** O **vas ~ (si crees que ...)** you've got another think coming (if you think that ...).

listón *m* lath; DEP bar.

litera *f* **-1.** [cama] bunk (bed); [de barco] berth; [de tren] couchette. **-2.** [vehículo] litter.

literal *adj* literal.

literario, -ria *adj* literary.

literato, -ta *m y f* writer.

literatura *f* literature.

litigar *vi* to go to law.

litigio *m* DER litigation (U); *fig* dispute; **en ~** in dispute.

litografía *f* **-1.** [arte] lithography. **-2.** [grabado] lithograph.

litoral ◇ *adj* coastal. ◇ *m* coast.

litro *m* litre.

Lituania Lithuania.

liturgia *f* liturgy.

liviano, -na *adj* **-1.** [ligero - blusa] thin; [- carga] light. **-2.** [sin importancia] slight.

lívido, -da *adj* **-1.** [pálido] very pale. **-2.** [amoratado] livid.

ll, Ll *f* [letra] ll, Ll.

llaga *f* lit & fig wound.

llagar *vt* to wound.

llama *f* **-1.** [de fuego, pasión] flame; **en ~s** ablaze. **-2.** ZOOL llama.

llamada *f* **-1.** [gen] call; [a la puerta] knock; [con timbre] ring. **-2.** TELECOM telephone call; **hacer una ~** to make a phone call; **~ urbana/interrurbana/a cobro revertido** local/long-distance/ reverse-charge call.

llamado, -da *adj* so-called. ◆ **llamado** *m Amer* [de teléfono] call.

llamamiento *m* [apelación] appeal, call.

llamar ◇ *vt* **-1.** [gen] to call; [con gestos] to beckon. **-2.** [por teléfono] to phone, to call. **-3.** [convocar] to summon, to call; **~ (a filas)** MIL to call up. **-4.** [atraer] to attract, to call. ◇ *vi* **-1.** [a la puerta etc - con golpes] to knock; [- con timbre] to ring; **están llamando** there's somebody at the door. **-2.** [por teléfono] to phone. ◆ **llamarse** *vpr* [tener por nombre] to be called; **¿cómo te llamas?** what's your name?; **me llamo Pepe** my name's Pepe.

llamarada *f* [de fuego, ira etc] blaze.

llamativo, -va *adj* [color] bright, gaudy; [ropa] showy.

llamear *vi* to burn, to blaze.

llano, -na *adj* **-1.** [campo, superficie] flat. **-2.** [trato, persona] natural, straightforward. **-3.** [pueblo, clase] ordinary. **-4.** [lenguaje, expresión] simple, plain. ◆ **llano** *m* [llanura] plain.

llanta *f* rim.

llanto *m* tears (*pl*), crying.

llanura *f* plain.

llave *f* **-1.** [gen] key; **bajo ~** under lock and key; **echar la ~** to lock up; **~ en mano** [vivienda] ready for immediate occupation; **~ de contacto** ignition key; **~ maestra** master key. **-2.** [del agua, gas] tap *Br*, faucet *Am*; [de la electricidad] switch; **cerrar la ~ de paso** to turn the water/gas off at the mains. **-3.** [herramienta] spanner; **~ inglesa** monkey wrench. **-4.** [de judo etc] hold, lock. **-5.** [signo ortográfico] curly bracket.

llavero *m* keyring.

llavín *m* latchkey.

llegada *f* **-1.** [gen] arrival. **-2.** DEP finish.

llegar *vi* **-1.** [a un sitio]: ~ **(de)** to arrive (from); ~ **a un hotel/una ciudad** to arrive at a hotel/in a city; **llegaré pronto** I'll be there early. **-2.** [un tiempo, la noche etc] to come. **-3.** [durar]: ~ **a** O **hasta** to last until. **-4.** [alcanzar]: ~ **a** to reach; **no llego al techo** I can't reach the ceiling; ~ **hasta** to reach up to. **-5.** [ser suficiente]: ~ **(para)** to be enough (for). **-6.** [lograr]: ~ **a (ser)** algo to get to be sthg, to become sthg; **si llego a saberlo** if I get to know of it. ◆ **llegarse a** *vpr* to go round to.

llenar *vt* **-1.** [ocupar]: ~ **algo (de)** [vaso, hoyo, habitación] to fill sthg (with); [pared, suelo] to cover sthg (with). **-2.** [satisfacer] to satisfy. **-3.** [rellenar - impreso] to fill in O out. **-4.** [colmar]: ~ **a alguien de** to fill sb with. ◆ **llenarse** *vpr* **-1.** [ocuparse] to fill up. **-2.** [saciarse] to be full. **-3.** [cubrirse]: ~**se de** to become covered in.

lleno, -na *adj* **-1.** [gen] full; [cubierto] covered; ~ **de** [gen] full of; [manchas, pósters] covered in. **-2.** *fam* [regordete] chubby. ◆ **de lleno** *loc adv* full in the face; **acertó de ~** he was bang on target.

llevadero, -ra *adj* bearable.

llevar ◇ *vt* **-1.** [gen] to carry. **-2.** [acompañar, coger y depositar] to take; ~ **algo/a alguien a** to take sthg/sb to; **me llevó en coche** he drove me there. **-3.** [prenda, objeto personal] to wear; **llevo gafas** I wear glasses; **no llevo dinero** I haven't got any money on me. **-4.** [caballo, coche etc] to handle. **-5.** [conducir]: ~ **a alguien a algo** to lead sb to sthg; ~ **a alguien a hacer algo** to lead O cause sb to do sthg. **-6.** [ocuparse de, dirigir] to be in charge of; [casa, negocio] to run; **lleva la contabilidad** she keeps the books. **-7.** [hacer - de alguna manera]: **lleva muy bien sus estudios** he's doing very well in his studies. **-8.** [tener - de alguna manera] to have; ~ **el pelo largo** to have long hair; **llevas las manos sucias** your hands are dirty. **-9.** [soportar] to deal O cope with. **-10.** [mantener] to keep; ~ **el paso** to keep in step. **-11.** [pasarse - tiempo]: **lleva tres semanas sin venir** she hasn't come for three weeks now, it's three weeks since she came last. **-12.** [ocupar - tiempo] to take; **me llevó un día hacer este guiso** it took me a day to make this dish. **-13.** [sobrepasar en]: **te llevo seis puntos** I'm six points ahead

of you; **me lleva dos centímetros** he's two centimetres taller than me. **-14.** *loc*: ~ **consigo** [implicar] to lead to, to bring about; ~ **las de perder** to be heading for defeat. ◇ *vi* **-1.** [conducir]: ~ **a** to lead to; **esta carretera lleva al norte** this road leads north. **-2.** (*antes de participio*) [haber]: **llevo leída media novela** I'm halfway through the novel; **llevo dicho esto mismo docenas de veces** I've said the same thing time and again. **-3.** (*antes de gerundio*) [estar]: ~ **mucho tiempo haciendo algo** to have been doing sthg for a long time. ◆ **llevarse** *vpr* **-1.** [coger] to take, to steal. **-2.** [conseguir] to get; **se ha llevado el premio** she has carried off the prize; **yo me llevo siempre las culpas** I always get the blame. **-3.** [recibir - susto, sorpresa etc] to get, to receive; **me llevé un disgusto** I was upset. **-4.** [entenderse]: ~**se bien/mal (con alguien)** to get on well/badly (with sb). **-5.** [estar de moda] to be in (fashion); **este año se lleva el verde** green is in this year. **-6.** MAT: **me llevo una** carry (the) one.

llorar *vi* [con lágrimas] to cry.

lloriquear *vi* to whine, to snivel.

lloro *m* crying (*U*), tears (*pl*).

llorón, -ona *m y f* crybaby.

lloroso, -sa *adj* tearful.

llover *v impers* to rain; **está lloviendo** it's raining.

llovizna *f* drizzle.

lloviznar *v impers* to drizzle.

lluvia *f* METEOR rain; **bajo la ~** in the rain; ~ **ácida** acid rain; ~ **radiactiva** (nuclear) fallout.

lluvioso, -sa *adj* rainy.

lo, la (*mpl* **los**, *fpl* **las**) *pron pers* (*complemento directo*) [cosa] it; (*pl*) them; [persona] him (*f* her); (*pl*) them; [usted] you. ◆ **lo** ◇ *pron pers* (*neutro*) (*predicado*) it; **su hermana es muy guapa pero él no ~ es** his sister is very good-looking, but he isn't; **es muy bueno aunque no ~ parezca** it's very good, even if it doesn't look it. ◇ *art det* (*neutro*): **antiguo me gusta más que ~ moderno** I like old things better than modern things; ~ **mejor/peor** the best/worst part; **no te imaginas ~ grande que era** you can't imagine how big it was. ◆ **lo de** *loc prep*: **¿y ~ de la fiesta?** what about the party, then?; **siento ~ de ayer** I'm sorry about yesterday. ◆ **lo que** *loc conj* what;

acepté ~ que me ofrecieron I accepted what they offered me.

loa f **-1.** [gen] praise. **-2.** LITER eulogy.

loable adj praiseworthy.

loar vt to praise.

lobato = lobezno.

lobby ['loßi] (pl lobbies) m lobby, pressure group.

lobezno, lobato m wolf cub.

lobo, -ba m y f wolf. ◆ **lobo de mar** m [marinero] sea dog.

lóbrego, -ga adj gloomy, murky.

lóbulo m lobe.

local ◇ adj local. ◇ m **-1.** [edificio] premises (pl). **-2.** [sede] headquarters (pl).

localidad f **-1.** [población] place, town. **-2.** [asiento] seat. **-3.** [entrada] ticket; **"no hay ~es"** "sold out".

localizar vt **-1.** [encontrar] to locate. **-2.** [circunscribir] to localize.

loción f lotion.

loco, -ca ◇ adj **-1.** [gen] mad; **estar ~ de/por** to be mad with/about; **volverse ~ por** to be mad about; **~ de atar** O **remate** stark raving mad; **a lo ~** [sin pensar] hastily; [temerariamente] wildly. **-2.** [extraordinario - interés, ilusión] tremendous; [- amor, alegría] wild. ◇ m y f lit & fig madman (f madwoman), lunatic.

locomoción f transport; [de tren] locomotion.

locomotor, -ra O **-triz** adj locomotive. ◆ **locomotora** f engine, locomotive.

locuaz adj loquacious, talkative.

locución f phrase.

locura f **-1.** [demencia] madness. **-2.** [imprudencia] folly.

locutor, -ra m y f [de radio] announcer; [de televisión] presenter.

locutorio m **-1.** TELECOM phone box O booth. **-2.** RADIO studio.

lodo m lit & fig mud.

logaritmo m logarithm.

lógico, -ca adj logical; **es ~ que se enfade** it stands to reason that he should get angry. ◆ **lógica** f [ciencia] logic.

logístico, -ca adj logistic. ◆ **logística** f logistics (pl).

logopeda m y f speech therapist.

logotipo m logo.

logrado, -da adj [bien hecho] accomplished.

lograr vt [gen] to achieve; [puesto, beca, divorcio] to get, to obtain; [resultado] to obtain, to achieve; [perfección] to attain; [victoria, premio] to win; [deseo, aspiración] to fulfil; **~ hacer algo** to manage to do sthg; **~ que alguien haga algo** to manage to get sb to do sthg.

logro m achievement.

LOGSE (abrev de **Ley Orgánica de Ordenación General del Sistema Educativo**) f Spanish Education Act.

loma f hillock.

lombriz f earthworm, worm.

lomo m **-1.** [espalda] back. **-2.** [carne] loin. **-3.** [de libro] spine.

lona f canvas.

loncha f slice; [de beicon] rasher.

londinense ◇ adj London (antes de sust). ◇ m y f Londoner.

Londres London.

longaniza f type of spicy, cold pork sausage.

longitud f **-1.** [dimensión] length; **tiene medio metro de ~** it's half a metre long; **~ de onda** wavelength. **-2.** ASTRON & GEOGR longitude.

lonja f **-1.** [loncha] slice. **-2.** [edificio] exchange; **~ de pescado** fish market.

loro m [animal] parrot.

los ◇ art → el. ◇ pron → lo.

losa f paving stone, flagstone; [de tumba] tombstone.

loseta f floor tile.

lote m **-1.** [parte] share. **-2.** [conjunto] batch, lot.

lotería f **-1.** [gen] lottery; **jugar a la ~** to play the lottery; **le tocó la ~** she won the lottery; **~ primitiva** twice-weekly state-run lottery. **-2.** [juego de mesa] lotto.

loza f **-1.** [material] earthenware; [porcelana] china. **-2.** [objetos] crockery.

lozanía f [de persona] youthful vigour.

lozano, -na adj **-1.** [planta] lush. **-2.** [persona] youthfully vigorous.

Ltd., ltda. (abrev de **limitada**) Ltd.

lubina f sea bass.

lubricante, lubrificante ◇ adj lubricating. ◇ m lubricant.

lubricar, lubrificar vt to lubricate.

lucero m bright star.

lucha f fight; fig struggle; **~ libre** all-in wrestling.

luchar vi to fight; fig to struggle; **~ contra/por** to fight against/for.

lucidez f lucidity, clarity.

lúcido, -da adj lucid.

luciérnaga f glow-worm.

lucimiento m [de ceremonia etc] sparkle; [de actriz etc] brilliant performance.

lucir ◇ *vi* **-1.** [gen] to shine. **-2.** [llevar puesto] to wear. **-3.** *Amer* [parecer] to seem. ◇ *vt* [gen] to show off; [ropa] to sport. ◆ **lucirse** *vpr* **-1.** [destacar]: ~**se (en)** to shine (at). **-2.** *fam fig* & *irón* [quedar mal] to mess things up.

lucrativo, -va *adj* lucrative; **no** ~ non profit-making.

lucro *m* profit, gain.

lucubrar *vt* to rack one's brains over.

lúdico, -ca *adj* [del juego] **game** (*antes de sust*); [ocioso] of enjoyment, of pleasure.

ludopatía *f* pathological addiction to gambling.

luego ◇ *adv* **-1.** [justo después] then, next; **primero aquí y** ~ **allí** first here and then there. **-2.** [más tarde] later; **hazlo** ~ do it later. **-3.** *Amer* [pronto] soon. ◇ *conj* [así que] so, therefore. ◆ **luego luego** *loc adv Amer* right away.

lugar *m* **-1.** [gen] place; [localidad] place, town; [del crimen, accidente etc] scene; [para acampar, merendar etc] spot; **en primer** ~ in the first place, firstly; **fuera de** ~ out of place; **no hay** ~ **a duda** there's no room for doubt; **tener** ~ to take place; **yo en tu** ~ if I were you. **-2.** [motivo] cause, reason; **dar** ~ **a** to bring about, to cause. **-3.** [puesto] position. ◆ **en lugar de** *loc prep* instead of. ◆ **lugar común** *m* platitude.

lugareño, -ña *m y f* villager.

lúgubre *adj* gloomy, mournful.

lujo *m* luxury; *fig* profusion; **permitirse el** ~ **de algo/de hacer algo** to be able to afford sthg/to do sthg.

lujoso, -sa *adj* luxurious.

lujuria *f* lust.

lumbago *m* lumbago.

lumbre *f* [fuego] fire; **dar** ~ **a alguien** to give sb a light.

lumbrera *f fam* leading light.

luminoso, -sa *adj* [gen] bright; [fuente, energía] light (*antes de sust*).

luna *f* **-1.** [astro] moon; ~ **llena/nueva** full/new moon. **-2.** [cristal] window (pane). **-3.** *loc*: **estar en la** ~ to be miles away. ◆ **luna de miel** *f* honeymoon.

lunar ◇ *adj* lunar. ◇ *m* **-1.** [en la piel] mole, beauty spot. **-2.** [en telas] spot; **a** ~**es** spotted.

lunático, -ca *m y f* lunatic.

lunes *m inv* Monday; *ver también* **sábado.**

luneta *f* [de coche] windscreen; ~ **térmica** demister.

lupa *f* magnifying glass.

lustrabotas *m inv*, **lustrador** *m Amer* bootblack.

lustrar *vt* to polish.

lustre *m* [brillo] shine.

lustro *m* five-year period.

lustroso, -sa *adj* shiny.

luto *m* mourning; **de** ~ in mourning.

luxación *f* dislocation.

Luxemburgo Luxembourg.

luxemburgués, -esa ◇ *adj* Luxembourg (*antes de sust*). ◇ *m y f* Luxembourger.

luz *f* [gen] light; [electricidad] electricity; [destello] flash (of light); **apagar la** ~ to switch off the light; **cortar la** ~ to cut off the electricity supply; **dar** O **encender la** ~ to switch on the light; **pagar (el recibo de) la** ~ to pay the electricity (bill); **se ha ido la** ~ the lights have gone out; ~ **solar** sunlight; **a la** ~ **de** in the light of; **arrojar** ~ **sobre** to shed light on; **dar a** ~ **(un niño)** to give birth (to a child); **sacar a la** ~ to bring to light. ◆ **luces** *fpl* AUTOM lights; **poner las luces de carretera** O **largas** to put (one's headlights) on full beam; **luces de cruce** O **cortas** dipped headlights; **luces de posición** O **situación** sidelights.

lycra® *f* Lycra®.

m¹, M *f* [letra] m, M.

m² (*abrev de* **metro**) m.

macabro, -bra *adj* macabre.

macana *f Amer fam* [disparate] stupid thing.

macarra *m fam* [de prostitutas] pimp; [rufián] thug.

macarrón *m* [tubo] sheath (*of cable*). ◆ **macarrones** *mpl* [pasta] macaroni (U).

macedonia *f* salad; ~ **de frutas** fruit salad.

macerar *vt* CULIN to soak, to macerate.

maceta *f* [tiesto] flowerpot.

macetero *m* flowerpot holder.

machaca *m y f fam* [currante] dogsbody.

machacar ◇ *vt* **-1.** [triturar] to crush.
-2. *fig* [insistir] to keep going on about.
◇ *vi fig*: ~ **(sobre)** to go on (about).

machete *m* machete.

machista *adj, m y f* male chauvinist.

macho ◇ *adj* **-1.** BIOL male. **-2.** *fig*
[hombre] macho. ◇ *m* **-1.** BIOL male. **-2.**
fig [hombre] he-man. **-3.** TECN male
part; [de enchufe] pin. ◇ *interj fam*: ¡oye,
~! oy, mate!

macizo, -za *adj* solid; **estar** ~ [hombre]
to be hunky; [mujer] to be gorgeous.
◆ **macizo** *m* **-1.** GEOGR massif. **-2.** BOT:
~ **de flores** flowerbed.

macro *f* INFORM macro.

macrobiótico, -ca *adj* macrobiotic.

mácula *f* spot; *fig* blemish.

macuto *m* backpack.

madeja *f* hank, skein.

madera *f* **-1.** [gen] wood; CONSTR timber; [tabla] piece of wood; **de** ~ wood-
en; ~ **contrachapada** plywood. **-2.** *fig*
[disposición]: **tener** ~ **de algo** to have
the makings of sthg.

madero *m* [tabla] log.

madrastra *f* stepmother.

madrazo *m Amer* hard blow.

madre *f* **-1.** [gen] mother; ~ **adoptiva/
de alquiler** foster/surrogate mother; ~
política mother-in-law; ~ **soltera** single mother; ~ **superiora** mother superior; **me vale** ~ *Amer fig* I couldn't
care less. **-2.** [poso] dregs (*pl*). ◆ **madre mía** *interj*: ¡~ **mía!** Jesus!, Christ!

Madrid Madrid.

madriguera *f* [gen & *fig*] den; [de cone-
jo] burrow.

madrileño, -ña *m y f* native/inhabitant
of Madrid.

madrina *f* [gen] patroness; [de boda]
bridesmaid; [de bautizo] godmother.

madroño *m* **-1.** [árbol] strawberry tree.
-2. [fruto] strawberry-tree berry.

madrugada *f* **-1.** [amanecer] dawn. **-2.**
[noche] early morning; **las tres de la** ~
three in the morning.

madrugador, -ra *adj* early-rising.

madrugar *vi* to get up early; *fig* to be
quick off the mark.

madurar ◇ *vt* **-1.** [gen] to mature; [fru-
ta, mies] to ripen. **-2.** [idea, proyecto etc]
to think through. ◇ *vi* [gen] to mature;
[fruta] to ripen.

madurez *f* **-1.** [cualidad - gen] maturity;
[- de fruta, mies] ripeness. **-2.** [edad adul-
ta] adulthood.

maduro, -ra *adj* [gen] mature; [fruta,

mies] ripe; **de edad madura** middle-
aged.

maestra → **maestro**.

maestría *f* [habilidad] mastery, skill.

maestro, -tra ◇ *adj* **-1.** [perfecto] masterly. **-2.** [principal] main; [llave] **master**
(*antes de sust*). ◇ *m y f* **-1.** [profesor]
teacher. **-2.** [sabio] master. **-3.** MÚS
maestro. **-4.** [director]: ~ **de ceremonias**
master of ceremonies; ~ **de cocina**
chef; ~ **de obras** foreman; ~ **de orquesta** conductor.

mafia *f* mafia.

mafioso, -sa *m y f* mafioso.

magdalena *f* fairy cake.

magia *f* magic.

mágico, -ca *adj* **-1.** [con magia] magic.
-2. [atractivo] magical.

magisterio *m* **-1.** [enseñanza] teaching.
-2. [profesión] teaching profession.

magistrado, -da *m y f* [juez] judge.

magistral *adj* **-1.** [de maestro] magiste-
rial. **-2.** [genial] masterly.

magistratura *f* **-1.** [jueces] magistra-
ture. **-2.** [tribunal] tribunal; ~ **de trabajo** industrial tribunal.

magnánimo, -ma *adj* magnanimous.

magnate *m* magnate; ~ **del petróleo/
de la prensa** oil/press baron.

magnesia *f* magnesia.

magnesio *m* magnesium.

magnético, -ca *adj lit* & *fig* magnetic.

magnetizar *vt* to magnetize; *fig* to
mesmerize.

magnetofónico, -ca *adj* [cinta] magnetic.

magnetófono *m* tape recorder.

magnicidio *m* assassination (*of somebody important*).

magnificencia *f* magnificence.

magnífico, -ca *adj* wonderful, magnificent.

magnitud *f* magnitude.

magnolia *f* magnolia.

mago, -ga *m y f* **-1.** [prestidigitador] magician. **-2.** [en cuentos etc] wizard.

magro, -gra *adj* **-1.** [sin grasa] lean. **-2.**
[pobre] poor. ◆ **magro** *m* lean meat.

magulladura *f* bruise.

magullar *vt* to bruise.

mahometano, -na *adj, m y f* Muslim.

mahonesa = **mayonesa**.

maicena *f* cornflour *Br*, cornstarch *Am*.

maíz *m* maize *Br*, corn *Am*; ~ **dulce**
sweetcorn.

maja → **majo**.

majadero, -ra *m y f* idiot.

majareta *fam* ◇ *adj* nutty. ◇ *m y f* nutcase.

majestad *f* majesty. ◆ **Su Majestad** *f* His/Her Majesty.

majestuoso, -sa *adj* majestic.

majo, -ja *adj* **-1.** [simpático] nice. **-2.** [bonito] pretty.

mal ◇ *adj* → **malo.** ◇ *m* **-1.** [perversión]: **el** ~ evil. **-2.** [daño] harm, damage. **-3.** [enfermedad] illness; ~ **de montaña** altitude ○ mountain sickness; ~ **de ojo** evil eye. **-4.** [inconveniente] bad thing; **un** ~ **necesario** a necessary evil. ◇ *adv* **-1.** [incorrectamente] wrong; **esto está** ~ **hecho** this has been done wrong; **has escrito** ~ **esta palabra** you've spelt that word wrong. **-2.** [inadecuadamente] badly; **la fiesta salió** ~ the party went off badly; **oigo/veo** ~ I can't hear/see very well; **encontrarse** ~ [enfermo] to feel ill; [incómodo] to feel uncomfortable; **oler** ~ [tener mal olor] to smell bad; *fam* [tener mal cariz] to smell fishy; **saber** ~ [tener mal sabor] to taste bad; **sentar** ~ **a alguien** [ropa] not to suit sb; [comida] to disagree with sb; [comentario, actitud] to upset sb; **tomar algo a** ~ to take sthg the wrong way. **-3.** [difícilmente] hardly; ~ **puede saberlo si no se lo cuentas** he's hardly going to know it if you don't tell him. **-4.** *loc*: **estar a** ~ **con alguien** to have fallen out with sb; **ir de** ~ **en peor** to go from bad to worse; **no estaría** ~ **que ...** it would be nice if .... ◆ **mal que** *loc conj* although, even though. ◆ **mal que bien** *loc adv* somehow or other.

malabarismo *m* lit & *fig* juggling (U).

malabarista *m y f* juggler.

malacostumbrado, -da *adj* spoiled.

malaria *f* malaria.

Malasia Malaysia.

malcriado, -da *adj* spoiled.

maldad *f* **-1.** [cualidad] evil. **-2.** [acción] evil thing.

maldecir ◇ *vt* to curse. ◇ *vi* to curse.

maldición *f* curse.

maldito, -ta *adj* **-1.** [embrujado] cursed. **-2.** *fam* [para enfatizar] damned; **¡maldita sea!** damn it!

maleable *adj* lit & *fig* malleable.

maleante *m y f* crook.

malecón *m* [atracadero] jetty.

maleducado, -da *adj* rude.

maleficio *m* curse.

malentendido *m* misunderstanding.

malestar *m* **-1.** [dolor] upset, discomfort; **siento un** ~ **en el estómago** I've got an upset stomach; **sentir** ~ **general** to feel unwell. **-2.** *fig* [inquietud] uneasiness, unrest.

maleta *f* suitcase; **hacer** ○ **preparar la** ~ to pack (one's bags).

maletero *m* boot *Br*, trunk *Am*.

maletín *m* briefcase.

malévolo, -la *adj* malevolent, wicked.

maleza *f* [arbustos] undergrowth; [malas hierbas] weeds (*pl*).

malformación *f* malformation.

malgastar *vt* [dinero, tiempo] to waste; [salud] to ruin.

malhablado, -da *adj* foul-mouthed.

malhechor, -ra *adj, m y f* criminal.

malhumorado, -da *adj* bad-tempered; [enfadado] in a bad mood.

malicia *f* [maldad] wickedness, evil; [mala intención] malice.

malicioso, -sa *adj* [malo] wicked, evil; [malintencionado] malicious.

maligno, -na *adj* malignant.

malla *f* **-1.** [tejido] mesh; ~ **de alambre** wire mesh. **-2.** [red] net. **-3.** *Amer* [traje de baño] swimsuit. ◆ **mallas** *fpl* **-1.** [de gimnasia] leotard (*sg*); [de ballet] tights. **-2.** [de portería] net (*sg*).

Mallorca Majorca.

malo, -la, mal (*compar* **peor,** *superl* **el peor**) *adj* (*antes de sust masculino*: "*mal*") **-1.** [gen] bad; [calidad] poor, bad; **lo** ~ **fue que ...** the problem was (that) .... **-2.** [malicioso] wicked. **-3.** [enfermo] ill, sick; **estar/ponerse** ~ to be/fall ill. **-4.** [travieso] naughty. ◆ **malo, -la** *m y f* [de película etc] villain, baddie. ◆ **malas** *fpl*: **estar de malas** to be in a bad mood; **por las malas** by force.

malograr *vt* to waste. ◆ **malograrse** *vpr* **-1.** [fracasar] to fail. **-2.** [morir] to die before one's time.

malparado, -da *adj*: **salir** ~ **de algo** to come out of sthg badly.

malpensado, -da *adj* malicious, evil-minded.

malsano, -na *adj* unhealthy.

malsonante *adj* rude.

malta *m* malt.

Malta Malta.

maltés, -esa *adj, m y f* Maltese.

maltratar *vt* **-1.** [pegar, insultar] to ill-treat. **-2.** [estropear] to damage.

maltrecho, -cha *adj* battered.

malva ◇ *f* BOT mallow. ◇ *adj inv* mauve. ◇ *m* [color] mauve.

malvado, -da *adj* evil, wicked.

malversación f: ~ (**de fondos**) embez-zlement (of funds).

malversar vt to embezzle.

Malvinas fpl: **las (islas)** ~ the Falkland Islands, the Falklands.

malvivir vi to scrape together an exist-ence.

mama f **-1.** [órgano - de mujer] breast; [- ZOOL] udder. **-2.** fam [madre] mum.

mamá (pl **mamás**) f fam mum, mum-my; ~ **grande** Amer fam grandma.

mamadera f Amer (baby's) bottle.

mamar ◇ vt **-1.** [suj: bebé] to suckle. **-2.** fig [aprender]: **lo mamó desde pe-queño** he was immersed in it as a child. ◇ vi to suckle.

mamarracho m [fantoche] mess.

mambo m mambo.

mamífero, -ra adj mammal. ◆ **ma-mífero** m mammal.

mamografía f MED **-1.** [técnica] breast scanning, mammography. **-2.** [resulta-do] breast scan.

mamotreto m **-1.** despec [libro] hefty tome. **-2.** [objeto grande] monstrosity.

mampara f screen.

manada f [ZOOL - gen] herd; [- de lobos] pack; [- de ovejas] flock; [- de leones] pride.

manager (pl **managers**) m manager.

Managua Managua.

manantial m spring; fig source.

manar vi lit & fig: ~ (**de**) to flow (from).

manazas adj inv clumsy.

mancha f **-1.** [gen] stain, spot; [de tinta] blot; [de colour] spot, mark. **-2.** ASTRON spot. **-3.** fig [deshonra] blemish.

manchar vt **-1.** [ensuciar]: ~ **algo (de** O **con)** [gen] to make sthg dirty (with); [con manchas] to stain sthg (with); [em-borronar] to smudge sthg (with). **-2.** fig [deshonrar] to tarnish.

manchego, -ga adj of/relating to La Mancha. ◆ **manchego** m → **queso**.

mancillar vt to tarnish.

manco, -ca adj [sin una mano] one-handed; [sin manos] handless; [sin un brazo] one-armed; [sin brazos] armless.

mancomunidad f association.

mancorna, mancuerna f Amer cufflink.

mandado, -da m y f [subordinado] underling. ◆ **mandado** m [recado] er-rand.

mandamás (pl **mandamases**) m y f bigwig.

mandamiento m **-1.** [orden - militar] or-der, command; [- judicial] writ. **-2.** RELIG commandment.

mandar ◇ vt **-1.** [dar órdenes] to order; ~ **a alguien hacer algo** to order sb to do sthg; ~ **hacer algo** to have sthg done. **-2.** [enviar] to send. **-3.** [dirigir, gobernar] to lead, to be in charge of; [país] to rule. ◇ vi **-1.** [gen] to be in charge; [jefe de estado] to rule. **-2.** des-pec [dar órdenes] to order people around. **-3.** loc: **¿mande?** fam eh?, you what?

mandarina f mandarin.

mandatario, -ria m y f representative, agent.

mandato m **-1.** [gen] order, command. **-2.** [poderes de representación, disposi-ción] mandate; ~ **judicial** warrant. **-3.** POLÍT term of office; [reinado] period of rule.

mandíbula f jaw.

mandil m [delantal] apron.

mando m **-1.** [poder] command, authority; **al** ~ **de** in charge of. **-2.** [periodo en poder] term of office. **-3.** (gen pl) [autoridades] leadership (U); MIL command (U); ~**s intermedios** middle management (sg). **-4.** [dispositivo] con-trol; ~ **automático/a distancia** auto-matic/remote control.

mandolina f mandolin.

mandón, -ona ◇ adj bossy. ◇ m y f bossy-boots.

manecilla f [del reloj] hand.

manejable adj [gen] manageable; [herra-mienta] easy to use.

manejar vt **-1.** [conocimientos, datos] to use, to marshal. **-2.** [máquina, mandos] to operate; [caballo, bicicleta] to handle; [arma] to wield. **-3.** [negocio etc] to manage, to run; [gente] to handle. **-4.** Amer [conducir] to drive. ◆ **manejarse** vpr **-1.** [moverse] to move O get about. **-2.** [desenvolverse] to manage.

manejo m **-1.** [de máquina, mandos] operation; [de armas, herramientas] use; **de fácil** ~ user-friendly. **-2.** [de conoci-mientos, datos] marshalling; [de idiomas] command. **-3.** [de caballo, bicicleta] handling. **-4.** [de negocio etc] manage-ment, running. **-5.** (gen pl) fig [intriga] intrigue.

manera f way, manner; **a mi** ~ **de ver** the way I see it; **de cualquier** ~ [sin cuidado] any old how; [de todos modos] anyway, in any case; **de esta** ~ in this way; **de ninguna** ~, **en** ~ **alguna** [re-fuerza negación] by no means, under no circumstances; [respuesta exclamativa] no way!, certainly not!; **de todas ~s** anyway; **en cierta ~** in a way; **~ de ser** way of being, nature; **de ~ que** [para] so (that); **no hay ~** there is no way, it's impossible. ◆**maneras** *fpl* [modales] manners.

manga *f* **-1.** [de prenda] sleeve; **en ~s de camisa** in shirt sleeves. **-2.** [manguera] hosepipe. **-3.** [de pastelería] forcing ○ piping bag. **-4.** DEP stage, round.

mangante *fam m y f* thief.

mango *m* **-1.** [asa] handle. **-2.** [árbol] mango tree; [fruta] mango.

mangonear *vi fam* **-1.** [entrometerse] to meddle. **-2.** [mandar] to be bossy. **-3.** [manipular] to fiddle about.

manguera *f* hosepipe; [de bombero] fire hose.

manía *f* **-1.** [idea fija] obsession. **-2.** [peculiaridad] idiosyncracy. **-3.** [mala costumbre] bad habit. **-4.** [afición exagerada] mania, craze. **-5.** *fam* [ojeriza] dislike. **-6.** PSICOL mania.

maniaco, -ca, maníaco, -ca ◇ *adj* manic. ◇ *m y f* maniac.

maniatar *vt* to tie the hands of.

maniático, -ca ◇ *adj* fussy. ◇ *m y f* fussy person; **es un ~ del fútbol** he's football-crazy.

manicomio *m* mental ○ psychiatric hospital *Br*, insane asylum *Am*.

manicuro, -ra *m y f* [persona] manicurist. ◆**manicura** *f* [técnica] manicure.

manido, -da *adj* [tema etc] hackneyed.

manifestación *f* **-1.** [de alegría, dolor etc] show, display; [de opinión] declaration, expression; [indicio] sign. **-2.** [por la calle] demonstration.

manifestar *vt* **-1.** [alegría, dolor etc] to show. **-2.** [opinión etc] to express. ◆**manifestarse** *vpr* **-1.** [por la calle] to demonstrate. **-2.** [hacerse evidente] to become clear ○ apparent.

manifiesto, -ta *adj* clear, evident; **poner de ~ algo** [revelar] to reveal sthg; [hacer patente] to make sthg clear. ◆**manifiesto** *m* manifesto.

manillar *m* handlebars (*pl*).

maniobra *f* **-1.** [gen] manoeuvre; **hacer ~s** to manoeuvre. **-2.** *fig* [treta] trick.

maniobrar *vi* to manoeuvre.

manipulación *f* **-1.** [gen] handling. **-2.** [engaño] manipulation.

manipular *vt* **-1.** [manejar] to handle. **-2.** [mangonear - información, resultados] to manipulate; [- negocios, asuntos] to interfere in.

maniquí (*pl* **maniquíes**) ◇ *m* dummy. ◇ *m y f* [modelo] model.

manirroto, -ta ◇ *adj* extravagant. ◇ *m y f* spendthrift.

manitas *m y f inv* handy person.

manito, mano *m Amer fam* mate, chum.

manivela *f* crank.

manjar *m* delicious food (*U*).

mano *f* **-1.** [gen] hand; **a ~** [cerca] to hand, handy; [sin máquina] by hand; **a ~ armada** armed; **dar** ○ **estrechar la ~ a alguien** to shake hands with sb; **darse** ○ **estrecharse la ~** to shake hands; **echar/tender una ~** to give/offer a hand; **¡~s arriba!, ¡arriba las ~s!** hands up!; **~ de obra** [capacidad de trabajo] labour; [trabajadores] workforce. **-2.** [ZOOL - gen] forefoot; [- de perro, gato] (front) paw; [- de cerdo] (front) trotter. **-3.** [lado]: **a ~ derecha/izquierda** on the right/left. **-4.** [de pintura etc] coat. **-5.** [influencia] influence. **-6.** [partida de naipes] game. **-7.** *fig* [serie, tanda] series. **-8.** *loc*: **bajo ~** secretly; **caer en ~s de alguien** to fall into sb's hands; **con las ~s cruzadas, ~ sobre ~** sitting around doing nothing; **coger a alguien con las ~s en la masa** to catch sb red-handed ○ in the act; **de primera ~** [coche etc] brand new; [noticias etc] first-hand; **de segunda ~** second-hand; **~ a ~** tête-à-tête; **¡~s a la obra!** let's get down to it!; **tener buena ~ para algo** to have a knack for sthg.

manojo *m* bunch.

manoletina *f* [zapato] *type of open, low-heeled shoe, often with a bow.*

manómetro *m* pressure gauge.

manopla *f* mitten.

manosear *vt* **-1.** [gen] to handle roughly; [papel, tela] to rumple. **-2.** [persona] to fondle.

manotazo *m* slap.

mansalva ◆**a mansalva** *loc adv* [en abundancia] in abundance.

mansedumbre *f* [gen] calmness, gentleness; [de animal] tameness.

mansión *f* mansion.

manso, -sa *adj* **-1.** [apacible] calm, gentle. **-2.** [domesticado] tame.

manta *f* [abrigo] blanket; **liarse la ~ a la cabeza** *fig* to take the plunge.

manteca *f* fat; [mantequilla] butter; **~ de cacao** cocoa butter; **~ de cerdo** lard.

mantecado *m* **-1.** [pastel] shortcake. **-2.**

[helado] *ice-cream made of milk, eggs and sugar.*

mantel *m* tablecloth.

mantener *vt* **-1.** [sustentar, aguantar] to support. **-2.** [conservar] to keep; [en buen estado] to maintain, to service. **-3.** [tener - relaciones, conversación] to have. **-4.** [defender - opinión] to stick to, to maintain; [- candidatura] to refuse to withdraw. ◆ **mantenerse** *vpr* **-1.** [sustentarse] to subsist, to support o.s. **-2.** [permanecer, continuar] to remain; [edificio] to remain standing; ~**se aparte** [en discusión] to stay out of it.

mantenimiento *m* **-1.** [sustento] sustenance. **-2.** [conservación] upkeep, maintenance.

mantequilla *f* butter.

mantilla *f* **-1.** [de mujer] mantilla. **-2.** [de bebé] shawl.

manto *m* [gen] cloak.

mantón *m* shawl.

manual ◇ *adj* [con las manos] manual. ◇ *m* manual.

manubrio *m* crank.

manufacturar *vt* to manufacture.

manuscrito, -ta *adj* handwritten. ◆ **manuscrito** *m* manuscript.

manutención *f* **-1.** [sustento] support, maintenance. **-2.** [alimento] food.

manzana *f* **-1.** [fruta] apple. **-2.** [grupo de casas] block (of houses).

manzanilla *f* **-1.** [planta] camomile. **-2.** [infusión] camomile tea.

manzano *m* apple tree.

maña *f* **-1.** [destreza] skill. **-2.** [astucia] wits (*pl*), guile (U).

mañana ◇ *f* morning; **a las dos de la** ~ at two in the morning. ◇ *m:* **el** ~ tomorrow, the future. ◇ *adv* tomorrow; **¡hasta** ~! see you tomorrow!; **por la** ~ tomorrow morning; **pasado** ~ the day after tomorrow.

mañoso, -sa *adj* skilful.

mapa *m* map.

mapamundi *m* world map.

maqueta *f* **-1.** [reproducción a escala] (scale) model. **-2.** [de libro] dummy.

maquillaje *m* **-1.** [producto] make-up. **-2.** [acción] making-up.

maquillar *vt* [pintar] to make up. ◆ **maquillarse** *vpr* to make o.s. up.

máquina *f* **-1.** [gen] machine; **a toda** ~ at full pelt; **escribir a** ~ to type; **hecho a** ~ machine-made; ~ **de coser** sewing machine; ~ **de escribir** typewriter; ~ **fotográfica** camera; ~ **tragaperras, ~ traganíqueles** *Amer* slot machine, fruit

machine. **-2.** [locomotora] engine; ~ **de vapor** steam engine. **-3.** [mecanismo] mechanism. **-4.** *Amer* [coche] car. **-5.** *fig* [de estado, partido etc] machinery (U).

maquinación *f* machination.

maquinal *adj* mechanical.

maquinar *vt* to machinate, to plot.

maquinaria *f* **-1.** [gen] machinery. **-2.** [de reloj etc] mechanism.

maquinilla *f:* ~ **de afeitar** razor; ~ **eléctrica** electric razor.

maquinista *m y f* [de tren] engine driver *Br*, engineer *Am*; [de barco] engineer.

mar *m o f lit & fig* sea; **alta** ~ high seas (*pl*); **el** ~ **del Norte** the North Sea; **llover a** ~**es** to rain buckets; **la** ~ **de** really, very.

marabunta *f fig* [muchedumbre] crowd.

maraca *f* maraca.

maraña *f* **-1.** [maleza] thicket. **-2.** *fig* [enredo] tangle.

maratón *m lit & fig* marathon.

maravilla *f* **-1.** [gen] marvel, wonder; **es una** ~ it's wonderful; **hacer** ~**s** to do ○ work wonders; **a las mil** ~**s, de** ~ wonderfully; **venir de** ~ to be just the thing ○ ticket. **-2.** BOT marigold.

maravillar *vt* to amaze. ◆ **maravillarse** *vpr:* ~**se (con)** to be amazed (by).

maravilloso, -sa *adj* marvellous, wonderful.

marca *f* **-1.** [señal] mark; [de rueda, animal] track; [en ganado] brand; [en papel] watermark. **-2.** [COM - de tabaco, café etc] brand; [- de coche, ordenador etc] make; **de** ~ designer (*antes de sust*); ~ **de fábrica** trademark; ~ **registrada** registered trademark. **-3.** [etiqueta] label. **-4.** [DEP - gen] performance; [- en carreras] time; [- plusmarca] record.

marcado, -da *adj* [gen] marked. ◆ **marcado** *m* **-1.** [señalado] marking. **-2.** [peinado] set.

marcador, -ra *adj* marking. ◆ **marcador** *m* **-1.** [tablero] scoreboard. **-2.** [DEP - defensor] marker; [- goleador] scorer.

marcapasos *m inv* pacemaker.

marcar ◇ *vt* **-1.** [gen] to mark. **-2.** [poner precio a] to price. **-3.** [indicar] to indicate. **-4.** [resaltar] to emphasise. **-5.** [número de teléfono] to dial. **-6.** [suj: termómetro, contador etc] to read; [suj: reloj] to say. **-7.** [DEP - tanto] to score; [- a un jugador] to mark. **-8.** [cabello] to set. ◇ *vi* **-1.** [dejar secuelas] to leave a mark. **-2.** DEP [anotar un tanto] to score.

marcha f **-1.** [partida] departure. **-2.** [ritmo] speed; **en ~** [motor] running; [plan] underway; **poner en ~** [gen] to start; [dispositivo, alarma] to activate; **hacer algo sobre la ~** to do sthg as one goes along. **-3.** AUTOM gear; **~ atrás** reverse; **dar ~ atrás** AUTOM to reverse; *fig* to back out. **-4.** MIL & POLÍT march. **-5.** MÚS march. **-6.** [transcurso] course; [progreso] progress. **-7.** DEP walk. **-8.** *fam* [animación] liveliness, life; **hay mucha ~** there's a great atmosphere.

marchar vi **-1.** [andar] to walk. **-2.** [partir] to leave, to go. **-3.** [funcionar] to work. **-4.** [desarrollarse] to progress; **el negocio marcha** business is going well. ◆ **marcharse** vpr to leave, to go.

marchitar vt *lit* & *fig* to wither. ◆ **marchitarse** vpr **-1.** [planta] to fade, to wither. **-2.** *fig* [persona] to languish.

marchito, -ta adj [planta] faded.

marcial adj martial.

marco m **-1.** [cerco] frame. **-2.** *fig* [ambiente, paisaje] setting. **-3.** [ámbito] framework. **-4.** [moneda] mark. **-5.** [portería] goalmouth.

marea f [del mar] tide; **~ alta/baja** high/low tide; **~ negra** oil slick.

marear vt **-1.** [provocar náuseas] to make sick; [en coche, avión etc] to make travelsick. **-2.** [aturdir] to make dizzy. **-3.** *fam fig* [fastidiar] to annoy. ◆ **marearse** vpr **-1.** [tener náuseas] to feel sick; [en coche, avión etc] to feel travelsick. **-2.** [estar aturdido] to get dizzy. **-3.** [emborracharse] to get drunk.

marejada f [mar rizada] heavy sea.

maremoto m tidal wave.

mareo m **-1.** [náuseas] sickness; [en coches, aviones etc] travelsickness. **-2.** [aturdimiento] dizziness. **-3.** *fam fig* [fastidio] drag, pain.

marfil m ivory.

margarina f margarine.

margarita f **-1.** BOT daisy. **-2.** IMPRENTA daisy wheel.

margen m o f **-1.** (gen f) [de río] bank; [de camino] side. **-2.** (gen m) [de página] margin. **-3.** (gen m) COM margin. **-4.** (gen m) [límites] leeway; **dejar al ~** to exclude; **estar al ~ de** to have nothing to do with; **mantenerse al ~ de** to keep out of; **~ de error** margin of error. **-5.** (gen m) [ocasión]: **dar ~ a alguien para hacer algo** to give sb the chance to do sthg.

marginación f exclusion.

marginado, -da ◇ adj excluded. ◇ m y f outcast.

maría f *Amer fam* migrant from country to urban areas.

marica m *mfam despec* queer, poof.

Maricastaña → **tiempo**.

maricón m *mfam despec* queer, poof.

marido m husband.

marihuana f marijuana.

marimacho m *fam* mannish woman; *despec* butch woman.

marina → **marino**.

marinero, -ra adj [gen] sea (antes de sust); [buque] seaworthy; [pueblo] seafaring. ◆ **marinero** m sailor.

marino, -na adj sea (antes de sust), marine. ◆ **marino** m sailor. ◆ **marina** f MIL: **~ (de guerra)** navy.

marioneta f [muñeco] marionette, puppet. ◆ **marionetas** fpl [teatro] puppet show (sg).

mariposa f **-1.** [insecto] butterfly. **-2.** [en natación] butterfly.

mariquita f [insecto] ladybird Br, ladybug Am.

marisco m seafood (U), shellfish (U).

marisma f salt marsh.

marisquería f seafood restaurant.

marítimo, -ma adj [del mar] maritime; [cercano al mar] seaside (antes de sust).

marketing ['marketin] m marketing.

mármol m marble.

marmota f marmot.

mar Muerto npr m: **el ~** the Dead Sea.

mar Negro m: **el ~** the Black Sea.

marqués, -esa m marquis (f marchioness).

marquesina f glass canopy; [parada de autobús] bus-shelter.

marrano, -na m y f **-1.** [animal] pig. **-2.** *fam fig* [sucio] (filthy) pig.

mar Rojo m: **el ~** the Red Sea.

marrón adj & m brown.

marroquí (pl marroquíes) adj, m y f Moroccan.

Marruecos Morocco.

Marte m Mars.

martes m inv Tuesday; **~ de Carnaval** Shrove Tuesday; **~ y trece** ≈ Friday 13th; ver también **sábado**.

martillear, martillar vt to hammer.

martillo m hammer.

mártir m y f lit & fig martyr.

martirio m **-1.** RELIG martyrdom. **-2.** *fig* [sufrimiento] trial, torment.

martirizar vt **-1.** [torturar] to martyr. **-2.** *fig* [hacer sufrir] to torment.

marxismo m Marxism.

marxista adj, m y f Marxist.

marzo m March; ver también **septiembre**.

mas conj but.

más ◇ adv **-1.** (comparativo) more; **Pepe es ~ alto/ambicioso** Pepe is taller/more ambitious; **tener ~ hambre** to be hungrier ᴏ more hungry; **~ de/ que** more than; **~ ... que ...** more ... than ...; **Juan es ~ alto que tú** Juan is taller than you; **de ~** [de sobra] left over; **hay 100 ptas de ~** there are 100 pesetas left over; **eso está de ~** that's not necessary. **-2.** (superlativo) **el/la/lo ~ the** most; **el ~ listo/ambicioso** the cleverest/most ambitious. **-3.** (en frases negativas) any more; **no necesito ~ (trabajo)** I don't need any more (work). **-4.** (con pron interrogativos e indefinidos) else; **¿qué/quién ~?** what/ who else?; **nadie ~ vino** nobody else came. **-5.** [indica suma] plus; **dos ~ dos igual a cuatro** two plus two is four. **-6.** [indica intensidad]: **no le aguanto, ¡es ~ tonto!** I can't stand him, he's so stupid!; **¡qué día ~ bonito!** what a lovely day! **-7.** [indica preferencia]: **~ vale que nos vayamos a casa** it would be better for us to go home. **-8.** loc: **el que ~ y el que menos** everyone; **es ~** indeed, what is more; **~ bien** rather; **~ o menos** more or less; **¿qué ~ da?** what difference does it make?; **sin ~ (ni ~)** just like that. ◇ m inv MAT plus (sign); **tiene sus ~ y sus menos** it has its good points and its bad points. ◆ **por más que** loc conj however much; **por ~ que lo intente no lo conseguirá** however much ᴏ hard she tries, she'll never manage it.

masa f **-1.** [gen] mass. **-2.** CULIN dough. **-3.** Amer [pastelillo] small cake. ◆ **masas** fpl: **las ~s** the masses.

masacre f massacre.

masaje m massage.

masajista m masseur (f masseuse).

mascar vt & vi to chew.

máscara f [gen] mask; **~ antigás** gas mask.

mascarilla f **-1.** MED mask. **-2.** [cosmética] face pack.

mascota f mascot.

masculino, -na adj **-1.** BIOL male. **-2.** [varonil] manly. **-3.** GRAM masculine.

mascullar vt to mutter.

masificación f overcrowding.

masilla f putty.

masivo, -va adj mass (antes de sust).

masón, -ona ◇ adj masonic. ◇ m y f mason, freemason.

masoquista ◇ adj masochistic. ◇ m y f masochist.

máster (pl masters) m Master's (degree).

masticar vt [mascar] to chew.

mástil m **-1.** NÁUT mast. **-2.** [palo] pole. **-3.** MÚS neck.

mastín m mastiff.

masturbación f masturbation.

masturbar vt to masturbate. ◆ **masturbarse** vpr to masturbate.

mata f [arbusto] bush, shrub; [matojo] tuft; **~s** scrub. ◆ **mata de pelo** f mop of hair.

matadero m abattoir, slaughterhouse.

matador, -ra fam adj [cansado] killing, exhausting. ◆ **matador** m matador.

matambre m Amer cold cooked meat.

matamoscas m inv [pala] flyswat; [espray] flyspray.

matanza f [masacre] slaughter.

matar vt **-1.** [gen] to kill; **~las callando** to be up to sthg on the quiet. **-2.** [apagar - sed] to quench; [- hambre] to stay. ◆ **matarse** vpr **-1.** [morir] to die. **-2.** [suicidarse, esforzarse] to kill o.s.

matasellos m y f inv postmark.

mate ◇ adj matt. ◇ m **-1.** [en ajedrez] mate, checkmate. **-2.** [en baloncesto] dunk; [en tenis] smash. **-3.** BOT [bebida] maté.

matemático, -ca ◇ adj mathematical. ◇ m y f [científico] mathematician. ◆ **matemáticas** fpl [ciencia] mathematics (U).

materia f **-1.** [sustancia, asunto] matter. **-2.** [material] material; **~ prima, primera ~** raw material. **-3.** [asignatura] subject; **en ~ de** on the subject of, concerning.

material ◇ adj **-1.** [gen] physical; [daños, consecuencias] material. **-2.** [real] real, actual. ◇ m **-1.** [gen] material. **-2.** [instrumentos] equipment.

materialismo m materialism.

materialista ◇ adj materialistic. ◇ m y f materialist.

materializar vt **-1.** [idea, proyecto] to realize. **-2.** [hacer tangible] to produce. ◆ **materializarse** vpr to materialize.

maternal adj motherly, maternal.

maternidad f **-1.** [cualidad] motherhood. **-2.** [hospital] maternity hospital.

materno, -na adj maternal; [lengua] mother (antes de sust).

matinal *adj* morning (*antes de sust*).

matiz *m* **-1.** [variedad - de color, opinión] shade; [- de sentido] nuance, shade of meaning. **-2.** [atisbo] trace, hint.

matizar *vt* **-1.** [teñir]: ~ **(de)** to tinge (with). **-2.** *fig* [distinguir - rasgos, aspectos] to distinguish; [- tema] to explain in detail. **-3.** *fig* [dar tono especial] to tinge. **-4.** ARTE to blend.

matojo *m* [mata] tuft; [arbusto] bush, shrub.

matón, -ona *m y f fam* bully.

matorral *m* thicket.

matraca *f* [instrumento] rattle.

matriarcado *m* matriarchy.

matrícula *f* **-1.** [inscripción] registration. **-2.** [documento] registration document. **-3.** AUTOM number plate. ◆ **matrícula de honor** *f* top marks (*pl*).

matricular *vt* to register. ◆ **matricularse** *vpr* to register.

matrimonial *adj* marital; [vida] married.

matrimonio *m* **-1.** [gen] marriage. **-2.** [pareja] married couple.

matriz ◇ *f* **-1.** ANAT womb. **-2.** [de talonario] (cheque) stub. **-3.** [molde] mould. **-4.** MAT matrix. ◇ *adj* [empresa] parent (*antes de sust*); [casa] head (*antes de sust*); [iglesia] mother (*antes de sust*).

matrona *f* **-1.** [madre] matron. **-2.** [comadrona] midwife.

matutino, -na *adj* morning (*antes de sust*).

maullar *vi* to miaow.

maxilar *m* jaw.

máxima → **máximo**.

máxime *adv* especially.

máximo, -ma ◇ *superl* → **grande**. ◇ *adj* maximum; [galardón, puntuación] highest. ◆ **máximo** *m* maximum; **al** ~ to the utmost; **llegar al** ~ to reach the limit; **como** ~ [a más tardar] at the latest; [como mucho] at the most. ◆ **máxima** *f* **-1.** [sentencia, principio] maxim. **-2.** [temperatura] high, highest temperature.

mayo *m* May; *ver también* **septiembre**.

mayonesa, mahonesa *f* mayonnaise.

mayor ◇ *adj* **-1.** (*comparativo*): ~ **(que)** [de tamaño] bigger (than); [de importancia etc] greater (than); [de edad] older (than); [de número] higher (than). **-2.** (*superlativo*): **el/la** ~ ... [de tamaño] the biggest ...; [de importancia etc] the greatest ...; [de edad] the oldest ...; [de número] the highest .... **-3.** [adulto] grown-up. **-4.** [anciano] elderly. **-5.** MÚS: **en do** ~ in C major. **-6.** *loc*: **al por** ~ COM wholesale. ◇ *m y f*: **el/la** ~ [hijo, hermano] the eldest. ◇ *m* MIL major. ◆ **mayores** *mpl* **-1.** [adultos] grown-ups. **-2.** [antepasados] ancestors.

mayoral *m* [capataz] foreman.

mayordomo *m* butler.

mayoreo *m* Amer wholesale.

mayoría *f* majority; **la** ~ **de** most of; **la** ~ **de los españoles** most Spaniards; **en su** ~ in the main. ◆ **mayoría de edad** *f*: **llegar a la** ~ **de edad** to come of age.

mayorista *m y f* wholesaler.

mayoritario, -ria *adj* majority (*antes de sust*).

mayúscula → **letra**.

mayúsculo, -la *adj* tremendous, enormous.

maza *f* mace; [del bombo] drumstick.

mazapán *m* marzipan.

mazmorra *f* dungeon.

mazo *m* **-1.** [martillo] mallet. **-2.** [de mortero] pestle. **-3.** [conjunto - de naipes] balance (of the deck).

me *pron pers* **-1.** (*complemento directo*) me; **le gustaría verme** she'd like to see me. **-2.** (*complemento indirecto*) (to) me; ~ **lo dio** he gave it to me; ~ **tiene miedo** he's afraid of me. **-3.** (*reflexivo*) myself.

mear *vi vulg* to piss.

MEC (*abrev de* **Ministerio de Educación y Ciencia**) *m Spanish ministry of education and science.*

mecachis *interj fam eufemismo*: ¡~! sugar! *Br*, shoot! *Am*.

mecánico, -ca ◇ *adj* mechanical. ◇ *m y f* [persona] mechanic. ◆ **mecánica** *f* **-1.** [ciencia] mechanics (*U*). **-2.** [funcionamiento] mechanics (*pl*).

mecanismo *m* [estructura] mechanism.

mecanografía *f* typing.

mecanógrafo, -fa *m y f* typist.

mecapal *m Amer* porter's leather harness.

mecedora *f* rocking chair.

mecenas *m y f inv* patron.

mecer *vt* to rock. ◆ **mecerse** *vpr* to rock back and forth; [en columpio] to swing.

mecha *f* **-1.** [de vela] wick. **-2.** [de explosivos] fuse. **-3.** [de pelo] streak.

mechero *m* (cigarette) lighter.

mechón *m* [de pelo] lock; [de lana] tuft.

medalla *f* medal.

medallón *m* **-1.** [joya] medallion. **-2.** [rodaja] médaillon; ~ **de pescado** [empanado] fishcake.

media → medio.
mediación f mediation; **por** ~ **de** through.
mediado, -da adj [medio lleno] half-full; **mediada la película** halfway through the film. ◆ **a mediados de** loc prep in the middle of, halfway through.
mediana → mediano.
mediano, -na adj **-1.** [intermedio - de tamaño] medium; [- de calidad] average. **-2.** [mediocre] average, ordinary. ◆ **mediana** f **-1.** GEOM median. **-2.** [de carretera] central reservation.
medianoche (pl **mediasnoches**) f [hora] midnight; **a** ~ **at midnight**.
mediante prep by means of.
mediar vi **-1.** [llegar a la mitad] to be halfway through; **mediaba julio** it was mid-July. **-2.** [estar en medio - tiempo, distancia, espacio]: ~ **entre** to be between; **media un jardín/un kilómetro entre las dos casas** there is a garden/ one kilometre between the two houses; **medió una semana** a week passed by. **-3.** [intervenir]: ~ **(en/entre)** to mediate (in/between). **-4.** [interceder]: ~ **(en favor de** ○ **por)** to intercede (on behalf of ○ for).
mediatizar vt to determine.
medicación f medication.
medicamento m medicine.
medicar vt to give medicine to. ◆ **medicarse** vpr to take medicine.
medicina f medicine.
medicinal adj medicinal.
medición f measurement.
médico, -ca ◇ adj medical. ◇ m y f doctor; ~ **de cabecera** ○ **familia** family doctor, general practitioner; ~ **de guardia** duty doctor; ~ **interno** houseman Br, intern Am.
medida f **-1.** [gen] measure; [medición] measurement; **a (la)** ~ [gen] custombuilt; [ropa] made-to-measure. **-2.** [disposición] measure, step; **tomar** ~**s** to take measures ○ steps. **-3.** [moderación] moderation. **-4.** [grado] extent, degree; **en cierta/gran** ~ to some/a large extent; **en la** ~ **de lo posible** as far as possible; **a** ~ **que entraban** as they were coming in. ◆ **medidas** fpl [del cuerpo] measurements.
medieval adj medieval.
medievo, medioevo m Middle Ages (pl).
medio, -dia adj **-1.** [gen] half; **a** ~ **camino** [en viaje] halfway there; [en trabajo etc] halfway through; **media do-**

cena/hora half a dozen/an hour; ~ **pueblo estaba allí** half the town was there; **a media luz** in the half-light; **hacer algo a medias** to half-do sthg; **pagar a medias** to go halves, to share the cost; **un kilo y** ~ one and a half kilos; **son (las dos) y media** it's half past (two). **-2.** [intermedio - estatura, tamaño] medium; [- posición, punto] middle. **-3.** [de promedio - temperatura, velocidad] average. ◆ **medio** ◇ adv half; ~ **borracho** half drunk; **a** ~ **hacer** half done. ◇ m **-1.** [mitad] half. **-2.** [centro] middle, centre; **en** ~ **(de)** in the middle (of); **estar por (en)** ~ to be in the way; **quitar de en** ~ **a alguien** to get rid of sb, to get sb out of the way. **-3.** [sistema, manera] means, method; **por** ~ **de** by means of, through. **-4.** [elemento físico] environment; ~ **ambiente** environment. **-5.** [ambiente social] circle; **en** ~**s bien informados** in well-informed circles. **-6.** DEP midfielder. ◆ **medios** mpl [recursos] means, resources; **los** ~**s de comunicación** ○ **información** the media. ◆ **media** f **-1.** [promedio] average. **-2.** [hora]: **al dar la** ~ on the halfhour. **-3.** (gen pl) [prenda] tights (pl), stockings (pl). **-4.** DEP midfielders (pl).
medioambiental adj environmental.
mediocre adj mediocre, average.
mediodía (pl **mediodías**) m [hora] midday, noon; **al** ~ at noon ○ midday.
medioevo = medievo.
mediofondo m middle-distance running.
medir vt **-1.** [gen] to measure; **¿cuánto mides?** how tall are you?; **mido 1,80** ≈ I'm 6 foot (tall); **mide diez metros** it's ten metres long. **-2.** [pros, contras etc] to weigh up. **-3.** [palabras] to weigh carefully.
meditar ◇ vi: ~ **(sobre)** to meditate (on). ◇ vt **-1.** [gen] to meditate, to ponder. **-2.** [planear] to plan, to think through.
mediterráneo, -a adj Mediterranean. ◆ **Mediterráneo** m: **el (mar) Mediterráneo** the Mediterranean (Sea).
médium m y f inv medium.
médula f **-1.** ANAT (bone) marrow; ~ **espinal** spinal cord. **-2.** [esencia] core.
medusa f jellyfish.
megafonía f public-address system.
megáfono m megaphone.
mejicano, -na = mexicano.
Méjico = México.
mejilla f cheek.

mejillón *m* mussel.

mejor ◇ *adj* **-1.** (*comparativo*): ~ **(que)** better (than). **-2.** (*superlativo*): **el/la** ~ ... the best .... ◇ *m y f*: **el/la** ~ **(de)** the best (in); **el** ~ **de todos** the best of all; **lo** ~ **fue que** ... the best thing was that .... ◇ *adv* **-1.** (*comparativo*): ~ **(que)** better (than); **ahora veo** ~ I can see better now; **es** ~ **que no vengas** it would be better if you didn't come; **estar** ~ [no tan malo] to feel better; [recuperado] to be better. **-2.** (*superlativo*) best; **el que la conoce** ~ the one who knows her best. ◆ **a lo mejor** *loc adv* maybe, perhaps. ◆ **mejor dicho** *loc adv* (or) rather.

mejora *f* [progreso] improvement.

mejorar ◇ *vt* [gen] to improve; [enfermo] to make better. ◇ *vi* to improve, to get better. ◆ **mejorarse** *vpr* to improve, to get better; **¡qué te mejores!** get well soon!

mejoría *f* improvement.

mejunje *m* lit & fig concoction.

melancolía *f* melancholy.

melancólico, -ca *adj* melancholic.

melaza *f* molasses (*pl*).

melena *f* **-1.** [de persona] long hair (*U*). **-2.** [de león] mane.

melenudo, -da *despec adj* with a mop of hair.

mellado, -da *adj* **-1.** [con hendiduras] nicked. **-2.** [sin dientes] gap-toothed.

mellizo, -za *adj, m y f* twin.

melocotón *m* peach.

melodía *f* melody, tune.

melódico, -ca *adj* melodic.

melodioso, -sa *adj* melodious.

melodrama *m* melodrama.

melómano, -na *m y f* music lover.

melón *m* [fruta] melon.

meloso, -sa *adj* **-1.** [como la miel] honey; *fig* sweet. **-2.** [empalagoso] sickly.

membrana *f* membrane.

membrete *m* letterhead.

membrillo *m* **-1.** [fruto] quince. **-2.** [dulce] quince jelly.

memorable *adj* memorable.

memorándum (*pl* **memorándums** o **memorandos**) *m* **-1.** [cuaderno] notebook. **-2.** [nota diplomática] memorandum.

memoria *f* **-1.** [gen & INFORM] memory; **de** ~ by heart; **hacer** ~ to try to remember; **traer a la** ~ to call to mind. **-2.** [recuerdo] remembrance. **-3.** [disertación] (academic) paper. **-4.** [informe] ~ (anual) (annual) report. ◆ **memorias** *fpl* [biografía] memoirs.

memorizar *vt* to memorize.

menaje *m* household goods and furnishings (*pl*); ~ **de cocina** kitchenware.

mención *f* mention.

mencionar *vt* to mention.

menda ◇ *pron fam* [el que habla] yours truly. ◇ *m y f* [uno cualquiera]: **vino un** ~ **y** ... this bloke came along and ....

mendigar ◇ *vt* to beg for. ◇ *vi* to beg.

mendigo, -ga *m y f* beggar.

mendrugo *m* crust (of bread).

menear *vt* [mover - gen] to move; [- la cabeza] to shake; [- la cola] to wag; [- las caderas] to wiggle. ◆ **menearse** *vpr* **-1.** [moverse] to move (about); [agitarse] to shake; [oscilar] to sway. **-2.** [darse prisa, espabilarse] to get a move on.

menester *m* necessity. ◆ **menesteres** *mpl* [asuntos] business (*U*), matters (*pl*).

menestra *f* vegetable stew.

mengano, -na *m y f* so-and-so.

menguante *adj* [luna] waning.

menguar ◇ *vi* [disminuir] to decrease, to diminish; [luna] to wane. ◇ *vt* [disminuir] to lessen, to diminish.

menopausia *f* menopause.

menor ◇ *adj* **-1.** (*comparativo*): ~ **(que)** [de tamaño] smaller (than); [de edad] younger (than); [de importancia etc] less o lesser (than); [de número] lower (than). **-2.** (*superlativo*): **el/la** ~ ... [de tamaño] the smallest ...; [de edad] the youngest ...; [de importancia] the slightest ...; [de número] the lowest .... **-3.** [de poca importancia] minor; **un problema** ~ a minor problem. **-4.** [joven]: **ser** ~ **de edad** [para votar, conducir etc] to be under age; DER to be a minor. **-5.** MÚS: **en do** ~ in C minor. **-6.** *loc*: **al por** ~ COM retail. ◇ *m y f* **-1.** (*superlativo*): **el/la** ~ [hijo, hermano] the youngest. **-2.** DER [niño] minor.

Menorca Minorca.

menos ◇ *adj inv* **-1.** (*comparativo*) [cantidad] less; [número] fewer; ~ **aire** less air; ~ **manzanas** fewer apples; ~ ... **que** ... less/fewer ... than ...; **tiene** ~ **experiencia que tú** she has less experience than you; **hace** ~ **calor que ayer** it's not as hot as it was yesterday. **-2.** (*superlativo*) [cantidad] the least; [número] the fewest; **el que compró** ~ **acciones** the one who bought the fewest shares; **lo que** ~ **tiempo llevó** the thing that took the least time. **-3.** *fam* [peor]: **éste es ~ coche que el mío** that car isn't as good as mine. ◇ *adv* **-1.** (*comparativo*) less; **~ de/que** less than; **estás ~ gordo** you're not as fat. **-2.** (*superlativo*): **el/la/lo ~** the least; **él es el ~ indicado para criticar** he's the last person who should be criticizing; **ella es la ~ adecuada para el cargo** she's the least suitable person for the job; **es lo ~ que puedo hacer** it's the least I can do. **-3.** [expresa resta] minus; **tres ~ dos igual a uno** three minus two is one. **-4.** [con las horas] to; **son (las dos) ~ diez** it's ten to (two). **-5.** *loc*: **es lo de ~** that's the least of it; **hacer de ~ a alguien** to snub sb; **¡~ mal!** just as well!, thank God!; **no es para ~** not without (good) reason; **venir a ~** to go down in the world. ◇ *m inv* MAT minus (sign). ◇ *prep* [excepto] except (for); **todo ~ eso** anything but that. ◆ **al menos, por lo menos** *loc adv* at least. ◆ **a menos que** *loc conj* unless; **no iré a ~ que me acompañes** I won't go unless you come with me. ◆ **de menos** *loc adj* [que falta] missing; **hay 100 ptas de ~** there's 100 pesetas missing.

menoscabar *vt* [fama, honra etc] to damage; [derechos, intereses, salud] to harm; [belleza, perfección] to diminish.

menospreciar *vt* [despreciar] to scorn, to despise; [infravalorar] to undervalue.

mensaje *m* [gen & INFORM] message.

mensajero, -ra *m y f* [gen] messenger; [de mensajería] courier.

menstruación *f* menstruation.

menstruar *vi* to menstruate, to have a period.

mensual *adj* monthly; **5.000 ptas ~es** 5,000 pesetas a month.

mensualidad *f* **-1.** [sueldo] monthly salary. **-2.** [pago] monthly payment O instalment.

menta *f* mint.

mental *adj* mental.

mentalidad *f* mentality.

mentalizar *vt* to put into a frame of mind. ◆ **mentalizarse** *vpr* to get into a frame of mind.

mentar *vt* to mention.

mente *f* [gen] mind; **traer a la ~** to bring to mind.

mentecato, -ta *m y f* idiot.

mentir *vi* to lie.

mentira *f* lie; [acción] lying; **aunque parezca ~** strange as it may seem; **de ~**

pretend, false; **parece ~ (que ...)** it hardly seems possible (that ...).

mentirijillas ◆ **de mentirijillas** *fam* ◇ *loc adv* [en broma] as a joke, in fun. ◇ *loc adj* [falso] pretend, make-believe.

mentiroso, -sa ◇ *adj* lying; [engañoso] deceptive. ◇ *m y f* liar.

mentón *m* chin.

menú (*pl* **menús**) *m* **-1.** [lista] menu; [comida] food; **~ del día** set meal. **-2.** INFORM menu.

menudencia *f* trifle, insignificant thing.

menudeo *m Amer* retailing.

menudillos *mpl* giblets.

menudo, -da *adj* **-1.** [pequeño] small. **-2.** [insignificante] trifling, insignificant. **-3.** (*antes de sust*) [para enfatizar] what!; **¡~ lío/gol!** what a mess/goal! ◆ **a menudo** *loc adv* often.

meñique → **dedo**.

meollo *m* core, heart.

mercader *m y f* trader.

mercadería *f* merchandise, goods (*pl*).

mercadillo *m* flea market.

mercado *m* market; **~ común** Common Market.

mercancía *f* merchandise (*U*), goods (*pl*). ◆ **mercancías** *m inv* FERROC goods train, freight train *Am*.

mercante *adj* merchant.

mercantil *adj* mercantile, commercial.

mercenario, -ria *adj, m y f* mercenary.

mercería *f* [tienda] haberdasher's (shop) *Br*, notions store *Am*.

mercurio *m* mercury.

Mercurio *m* Mercury.

merecedor, -ra *adj*: **~ de** worthy of.

merecer ◇ *vt* to deserve, to be worthy of; **la isla merece una visita** the island is worth a visit; **no merece la pena** it's not worth it. ◇ *vi* to be worthy.

merecido *m*: **recibir su ~** to get one's just deserts.

merendar ◇ *vi* to have tea (*as a light afternoon meal*). ◇ *vt* to have for tea.

merendero *m* open-air café or bar (*in the country or on the beach*).

merengue *m* **-1.** CULIN meringue. **-2.** [baile] merengue.

meridiano, -na *adj* **-1.** [hora etc] midday. **-2.** *fig* [claro] crystal-clear. ◆ **meridiano** *m* meridian.

merienda *f* tea (*as a light afternoon meal*); [en el campo] picnic.

mérito *m* **-1.** [cualidad] merit. **-2.** [valor] value, worth; **tiene mucho ~** it's no mean achievement; **de ~** worthy.

merluza f [pez, pescado] hake.

merma f decrease, reduction.

mermar ◇ vi to diminish, to lessen. ◇ vt to reduce, to diminish.

mermelada f jam; ~ **de naranja** marmalade.

mero, -ra adj (antes de sust) mere. ◆ **mero** m grouper.

merodear vi: ~ **(por)** to snoop O prowl (about).

mes m **-1.** [del año] month. **-2.** [salario] monthly salary.

mesa f **-1.** [gen] table; [de oficina, despacho] desk; **bendecir la** ~ to say grace; **poner/quitar la** ~ to set/clear the table; ~ **camilla** small round table under which a heater is placed; ~ **de mezclas** mixing desk; ~ **plegable** folding table. **-2.** [comité] board, committee; [en un debate etc] panel; ~ **directiva** executive board O committee. ◆ **mesa redonda** f [coloquio] round table.

mesero, -ra m y f Amer waiter m (f waitress).

meseta f plateau, tableland.

mesías m fig Messiah.

mesilla f small table; ~ **de noche** bedside table.

mesón m **-1.** HIST inn. **-2.** [bar-restaurante] old, country-style restaurant and bar.

mestizo, -za ◇ adj [persona] half-caste; [animal, planta] cross-bred. ◇ m y f half-caste.

mesura f **-1.** [moderación] moderation, restraint; **con** ~ [moderadamente] in moderation. **-2.** [cortesía] courtesy.

meta f **-1.** [DEP - llegada] finishing line; [- portería] goal. **-2.** fig [objetivo] aim, goal.

metabolismo m metabolism.

metáfora f metaphor.

metal m **-1.** [material] metal. **-2.** MÚS brass.

metálico, -ca ◇ adj [sonido, color] metallic; [objeto] metal. ◇ m: **pagar en** ~ to pay (in) cash.

metalizado, -da adj [pintura] metallic.

metalurgia f metallurgy.

metamorfosis f inv lit & fig metamorphosis.

metedura ◆ **metedura de pata** f clanger.

meteorito m meteorite.

meteoro m meteor.

meteorología f meteorology.

meteorológico, -ca adj meteorological.

meteorólogo, -ga m y f meteorologist; RADIO & TV weatherman (f weatherwoman).

meter vt **-1.** [gen] to put in; ~ **algo/a alguien en algo** to put sthg/sb in sthg; ~ **la llave en la cerradura** to get the key into the lock; **le metieron en la cárcel** they put him in prison; ~ **dinero en el banco** to put money in the bank. **-2.** [hacer participar]: ~ **a alguien en algo** to get sb into sthg. **-3.** [obligar a]: ~ **a alguien a hacer algo** to make sb start doing sthg. **-4.** [causar]: ~ **prisa/miedo a alguien** to rush/scare sb; ~ **ruido** to make a noise. **-5.** fam [asestar] to give; **le metió un puñetazo** he gave him a punch. **-6.** [estrechar - prenda] to take in; ~ **el bajo de una falda** to take up a skirt. ◆ **meterse** vpr **-1.** [entrar] to get in; ~**se en** to get into. **-2.** (en frase interrogativa) [estar] to get to; **¿dónde se ha metido ese chico?** where has that boy got to? **-3.** [dedicarse]: ~**se a** to become; ~**se a torero** to become a bullfighter. **-4.** [involucrarse]: ~**se (en)** to get involved (in). **-5.** [entrometerse] to meddle; **se mete en todo** he never minds his own business; ~**se por medio** to interfere. **-6.** [empezar]: ~**se a hacer algo** to get started on doing sthg. ◆ **meterse con** vpr **-1.** [incordiar] to hassle. **-2.** [atacar] to go for.

meterete, metete adj Amer fam meddling, meddlesome.

meticuloso, -sa adj meticulous.

metido, -da adj **-1.** [envuelto]: **andar** O **estar** ~ **en** to be involved in. **-2.** [abundante]: ~ **en años** elderly; ~ **en carnes** plump.

metódico, -ca adj methodical.

método m **-1.** [sistema] method. **-2.** EDUC course.

metodología f methodology.

metomentodo fam m y f busybody.

metralla f shrapnel.

metralleta f submachine gun.

métrico, -ca adj [del metro] metric.

metro m **-1.** [gen] metre. **-2.** [transporte] underground Br, tube Br, subway Am. **-3.** [cinta métrica] tape measure.

metrópoli f, **metrópolis** f inv [ciudad] metropolis.

metropolitano, -na adj metropolitan.

mexicanismo, mejicanismo m Mexicanism.

mexicano, -na, mejicano, -na adj, m y f Mexican.

México, Méjico Mexico.

mezcla f **-1.** [gen] mixture; [tejido] blend; [de una grabación] mix. **-2.** [acción] mixing.

mezclar vt **-1.** [gen] to mix; [combinar, armonizar] to blend. **-2.** [confundir, desordenar] to mix up. **-3.** fig [implicar]: ~ a alguien en to get sb mixed up in. ◆ **mezclarse** vpr **-1.** [gen]: ~se (con) to mix (with). **-2.** [esfumarse]: ~se entre to disappear o blend into. **-3.** fig [implicarse]: ~se en to get mixed up in.

mezquino, -na adj mean.

mezquita f mosque.

mg (abrev de **miligramo**) mg.

mi¹ m MÚS E; [en solfeo] mi.

mi² (pl **mis**) adj poses my; ~ casa my house; ~s libros my books.

mí pron pers (después de prep) **-1.** [gen] me; este trabajo no es para ~ this job isn't for me; no se fía de ~ he doesn't trust me. **-2.** (reflexivo) myself. **-3.** loc: ¡a ~ qué! so what?, why should I care?; para ~ [yo creo] as far as I'm concerned, in my opinion; por ~ as far as I'm concerned; por ~, no hay inconveniente it's fine by me.

mía → **mío**.

miaja f crumb; fig tiny bit.

miau m miaow.

michelines mpl fam spare tyre (sg).

mico m fam [persona] ugly devil.

micro ◇ m fam (abrev de **micrófono**) mike. ◇ m o f Amer [microbús] minibus.

microbio m germ, microbe.

microbús m minibus.

microfilm (pl **microfilms**), **microfilme** m microfilm.

micrófono m microphone.

microondas m inv microwave (oven).

microordenador m INFORM microcomputer.

microprocesador m INFORM microprocessor.

microscópico, -ca adj microscopic.

microscopio m microscope; ~ electrónico electron microscope.

miedo m fear; dar ~ to be frightening; me de ~ conducir I'm afraid o frightened of driving; temblar de ~ to tremble with fear; tener ~ a o de (hacer algo) to be afraid of (doing sthg); de ~ fam fig [estupendo] smashing.

miedoso, -sa adj fearful.

miel f honey.

miembro m **-1.** [gen] member. **-2.** [extremidad] limb, member; ~ (viril) penis.

mientras ◇ conj **-1.** [al tiempo que] while; leía ~ comía she was reading

while eating; ~ más ando más sudo the more I walk, the more I sweat. **-2.** [hasta que]: ~ no se pruebe lo contrario until proved otherwise. **-3.** [por el contrario]: ~ (que) whereas, whilst. ◇ adv: ~ (tanto) meanwhile, in the meantime.

miércoles m Wednesday; ~ de ceniza Ash Wednesday; ver también **sábado**.

mierda vulg f **-1.** [excremento] shit. **-2.** [suciedad] filth, shit. **-3.** [cosa sin valor]: es una ~ it's (a load of) crap. **-4.** loc: ¡vete a la ~! go to hell!, piss off!

mies f [cereal] ripe corn. ◆ **mieses** fpl [campo] cornfields.

miga f [de pan] crumb; [ser complicado] to have more to it than meets the eye. ◆ **migas** fpl CULIN fried breadcrumbs; hacer buenas/malas ~s fam to get on well/badly.

migración f migration.

migraña f migraine.

migrar vi to migrate.

migratorio, -ria adj migratory.

mijo m millet.

mil núm thousand; dos ~ two thousand; ~ pesetas a thousand pesetas; ver también **seis**.

milagro m miracle; de ~ miraculously.

milagroso, -sa adj miraculous; fig amazing.

milenario, -ria adj ancient. ◆ **milenario** m millennium.

milenio m millennium.

milésimo, -ma núm thousandth.

mili f fam military service; hacer la ~ to do one's military service.

milicia f **-1.** [profesión] military (profession). **-2.** [grupo armado] militia.

miliciano, -na m y f militiaman (f female soldier).

miligramo m milligram.

milímetro m millimetre.

militante adj, m y f militant.

militar ◇ adj military. ◇ m y f soldier; los ~es the military. ◇ vi: ~ (en) to be active (in).

milla f mile; ~ (marina) nautical mile.

millar m thousand; un ~ de personas a thousand people.

millón núm million; dos millones two million; un ~ de personas a million people; un ~ de cosas que hacer a million things to do; un ~ de gracias thanks a million. ◆ **millones** mpl [dineral] a fortune (sg).

millonario, -ria m y f millionaire (f millionairess).

millonésimo, -ma *núm* millionth.

mimado, -da *adj* spoilt.

mimar *vt* to spoil, to pamper.

mimbre *m* wicker; **de ~** wickerwork.

mímico, -ca *adj* mime (*antes de sust*).

◆ **mímica** *f* -1. [mimo] mime. -2. [lenguaje] sign language.

mimo *m* -1. [zalamería] mollycoddling. -2. [cariño] show of affection. -3. TEATR mime.

mimosa *f* BOT mimosa.

min (*abrev de* **minuto**) min.

mina *f* -1. GEOL & MIL mine; **~ de carbón** coalmine. -2. *fig* [chollo] goldmine.

minar *vt* -1. MIL to mine. -2. *fig* [aminorar] to undermine.

mineral ◇ *adj* mineral. ◇ *m* -1. GEOL mineral. -2. MIN ore.

minería *f* -1. [técnica] mining. -2. [sector] mining industry.

minero, -ra ◇ *adj* mining (*antes de sust*); [producción, riqueza] mineral. ◇ *m y f* miner.

miniatura *f* miniature.

minicadena *f* midi system.

minifalda *f* mini skirt.

minigolf (*pl* **minigolfs**) *m* [juego] crazy golf.

mínimo, -ma ◇ *superl* → **pequeño**. ◇ *adj* -1. [lo más bajo posible o necesario] minimum. -2. [lo más bajo temporalmente] lowest. -3. [muy pequeño - efecto, importancia etc] minimal, very small; [- protesta, ruido etc] slightest; **no tengo la más mínima idea** I haven't the slightest idea; **como ~** at the very least; **en lo más ~** in the slightest. ◆ **mínimo** *m* [límite] minimum. ◆ **mínima** *f* METEOR low, lowest temperature.

ministerio *m* -1. POLÍT ministry *Br*, department *Am*. -2. RELIG ministry. ◆ **Ministerio de Asuntos Exteriores** *m* ≃ Foreign Office *Br*, ≃ State Department *Am*. ◆ **Ministerio de Economía y Hacienda** *m* ≃ Treasury *Br*, ≃ Treasury Department *Am*. ◆ **Ministerio del Interior** *m* ≃ Home Office *Br*, ≃ Department of the Interior *Am*.

ministro, -tra *m y f* POLÍT minister *Br*, secretary *Am*; **primer ~** prime minister.

minoría *f* minority; **~s étnicas** ethnic minorities.

minorista ◇ *adj* retail. ◇ *m y f* retailer.

minoritario, -ria *adj* minority (*antes de sust*).

minucia *f* trifle, insignificant thing.

minucioso, -sa *adj* -1. [meticuloso] meticulous. -2. [detallado] highly detailed.

minúsculo, -la *adj* -1. [tamaño] tiny, minute. -2. [letra] small; IMPRENTA lower-case. ◆ **minúscula** *f* small letter; IMPRENTA lower-case letter.

minusvalía *f* [física] handicap, disability.

minusválido, -da ◇ *adj* disabled, handicapped. ◇ *m y f* disabled o handicapped person.

minuta *f* -1. [factura] fee. -2. [menú] menu.

minutero *m* minute hand.

minuto *m* minute.

mío, mía ◇ *adj poses* mine; **este libro es ~** this book is mine; **un amigo ~** a friend of mine; **no es asunto ~** it's none of my business. ◇ *pron poses*: **el ~** mine; **el ~ es rojo** mine is red; **esta es la mía** *fam* this is the chance I've been waiting for; **lo ~ es el teatro** [lo que me va] theatre is what I should be doing; **los ~s** *fam* [mi familia] my folks; [mi bando] my lot, my side.

miope *adj* shortsighted, myopic.

miopía *f* shortsightedness, myopia.

mira ◇ *f* sight; *fig* intention; **con ~s a** with a view to. ◇ *interj*: **¡~! look!**

mirado, -da *adj* [prudente] careful; **bien ~** [bien pensado] if you look at it closely. ◆ **mirada** *f* [gen] look; [rápida] glance; [de cariño, placer, admiración] gaze; **mirada fija** stare; **apartar la mirada** to look away; **dirigir** o **lanzar la mirada** a to glance at; **echar una mirada (a algo)** to glance o to have a quick look (at sthg); **fulminar con la mirada a alguien** to look daggers at sb; **levantar la mirada** to look up.

mirador *m* -1. [balcón] enclosed balcony. -2. [para ver un paisaje] viewpoint.

miramiento *m* circumspection; **andarse con ~s** to stand on ceremony; **sin ~s** just like that.

mirar ◇ *vt* -1. [gen] to look at; [observar] to watch; [fijamente] to stare at; **~ algo de cerca/lejos** to look at sthg closely/from a distance; **~ algo por encima** to glance over sthg, to have a quick look at sthg; **~ a alguien bien/mal** to think highly/poorly of sb. -2. [fijarse en] to keep an eye on. -3. [examinar, averiguar] to check, to look through; **le miraron todas las maletas** they searched all her luggage; **mira si ha llegado la carta** go and see if the letter has arrived. -4. [considerar] to consider, to take a look at. ◇ *vi* **-1.** [gen] to look; [observar] to watch; [fijamente] to stare; **mira, yo creo que ...** look, I think that .... **-2.** [buscar] to check, to look; **he mirado en todas partes** I've looked everywhere. **-3.** [orientarse]: ~ **a** to face. **-4.** [cuidar]: ~ **por alguien/algo** to look after sb/sthg. ◆ **mirarse** *vpr* [uno mismo] to look at o.s.; **si bien se mira** *fig* if you really think about it.

mirilla *f* spyhole.

mirlo *m* blackbird.

mirón, -ona *fam m y f* **-1.** [espectador] onlooker. **-2.** [curioso] nosy parker. **-3.** [voyeur] peeping Tom.

misa *f* mass; **ir a** ~ to go to mass O church; *fam fig* to be gospel.

misal *m* missal.

misántropo, -pa *m ý f* misanthropist.

miscelánea *f* miscellany.

miserable ◇ *adj* **-1.** [pobre] poor; [vivienda] wretched, squalid. **-2.** [penoso, insuficiente] miserable. **-3.** [vil] contemptible, base. **-4.** [tacaño] mean. ◇ *m y f* [ruin] wretch, vile person.

miseria *f* **-1.** [pobreza] poverty. **-2.** [desgracia] misfortune. **-3.** [tacañería] meanness. **-4.** [vileza] baseness. **-5.** [poco dinero] pittance.

misericordia *f* compassion; **pedir** ~ to beg for mercy.

mísero, -ra *adj* [pobre] wretched; **ni un** ~ ... not even a measly O miserable ....

misil (*pl* **misiles**) *m* missile; ~ **de crucero** cruise missile.

misión *f* **-1.** [gen] mission; [cometido] task. **-2.** [expedición científica] expedition.

misionero, -ra *adj, m y f* missionary.

misiva *f culto* missive.

mismo, -ma ◇ *adj* **-1.** [igual] same; **el** ~ **piso** the same flat; **del** ~ **color que** the same colour as. **-2.** [para enfatizar]: **yo** ~ I myself; **en este** ~ **cuarto** in this very room; **en su misma calle** right in the street where he lives; **por mí/ti** ~ by myself/yourself; **¡tú** ~! it's up to you. ◇ *pron*: **el** ~ the same; **el** ~ **que vi ayer** the same one I saw yesterday; **lo** ~ the same (thing); **lo** ~ **que** the same as; **da** O **es lo** ~ it doesn't matter, it doesn't make any difference; **me da lo** ~ I don't care. ◆ **mismo** *adv* (*después de sust*) **-1.** [para enfatizar]: **lo vi desde mi casa** ~ I saw it from my own house; **ahora/aquí** ~ right now/here; **ayer** ~ only yesterday; **por eso**

~ precisely for that reason. **-2.** [por ejemplo]: **escoge uno cualquiera** — **este** ~ choose any — this one, for instance.

misógino, -na *adj* misogynistic.

miss (*pl* **misses**) *f* beauty queen.

misterio *m* mystery.

misterioso, -sa *adj* mysterious.

mística → **místico**.

místico, -ca *adj* mystical. ◆ **mística** *f* [práctica] mysticism.

mitad *f* **-1.** [gen] half; **a** ~ **de precio** at half price; **a** ~ **de camino** halfway there; **a** ~ **de película** halfway through the film; **a** ~ **de half** (of); **la** ~ **del tiempo no está** half the time she's not in; ~ **y** ~ half and half. **-2.** [centro] middle; **en** ~ **de** in the middle of; **(cortar algo) por la** ~ (to cut sthg) in half.

mítico, -ca *adj* mythical.

mitigar *vt* **-1.** [gen] to alleviate, to reduce; [ánimos] to calm; [sed] to slake; [hambre] to take the edge off; [choque, golpe] to soften; [dudas, sospechas] to allay. **-2.** [justificar] to mitigate.

mitin (*pl* **mítines**) *m* rally, meeting.

mito *m* [gen] myth.

mitología *f* mythology.

mitote *m Amer fam* [alboroto] racket.

mixto, -ta *adj* mixed; [comisión] joint.

ml (*abrev de* **mililitro**) ml.

mm (*abrev de* **milímetro**) mm.

mobiliario *m* furniture.

mocasín *m* moccasin.

mochila *f* backpack.

mochuelo *m* little owl.

moción *f* motion.

moco *m fam* snot (*U*); MED mucus (*U*); **limpiarse los** ~s to wipe one's nose.

mocoso, -sa *m y f fam despec* brat.

moda *f* [gen] fashion; [furor pasajero] craze; **estar de** ~ to be fashionable O in fashion; **estar pasado de** ~ to be unfashionable O out of fashion.

modal *adj* modal. ◆ **modales** *mpl* manners.

modalidad *f* form, type; DEP discipline.

modelar *vt* to model; *fig* to shape.

modelo ◇ *adj* model. ◇ *m y f* model. ◇ *m* **-1.** [gen] model. **-2.** [prenda de vestir] number.

modem ['moðem] (*pl* **modems**) *m* INFORM modem.

moderación *f* moderation.

moderado, -da *adj, m y f* moderate.

moderador, -ra m y f chair, chairperson.

moderar vt -1. [gen] to moderate; [velocidad] to reduce. -2. [debate] to chair.
◆ **moderarse** vpr to restrain o.s.

modernizar vt to modernize.

moderno, -na adj modern.

modestia f modesty.

modesto, -ta adj modest.

módico, -ca adj modest.

modificar vt -1. [variar] to alter. -2. GRAM to modify.

modista m y f -1. [diseñador] fashion designer. -2. [que cose] tailor (f dressmaker).

modisto m -1. [diseñador] fashion designer. -2. [sastre] tailor.

modo m [manera, forma] way; **a ∼ de** as, by way of; **de ese ∼** in that way; **de ningún ∼** in no way; **de todos ∼s** in any case, anyway; **de un ∼ u otro** one way or another; **en cierto ∼** in some ways; **∼ de empleo** instructions (pl) for use; **de ∼ que** [de manera que] in such a way that; [así que] so.
◆ **modos** mpl [modales] manners; **buenos/malos ∼s** good/bad manners.

modorra f fam drowsiness.

modoso, -sa adj [recatado] modest; [formal] well-behaved.

modular vt to modulate.

módulo m -1. [gen] module. -2. [de muebles] unit.

mofa f mockery.

mofarse vpr to scoff; **∼ de** to mock.

moflete m chubby cheek.

mogollón m mfam -1. [muchos]: **∼ de** tons (pl) of, loads (pl) of. -2. [lío] row, commotion.

mohair [mo'er] m mohair.

moho m -1. [hongo] mould. -2. [herrumbre] rust.

mohoso, -sa adj -1. [con hongo] mouldy. -2. [oxidado] rusty.

moisés m inv Moses basket.

mojado, -da adj wet; [húmedo] damp.

mojar vt to wet; [humedecer] to dampen; [comida] to dunk. ◆ **mojarse** vpr [con agua] to get wet.

mojigato, -ta adj -1. [beato] prudish. -2. [con falsa humildad] sanctimonious.

mojón m [piedra] milestone; [poste] milepost.

molar mfam vi to be bloody gorgeous.

molcajete m Amer mortar.

molde m mould.

moldeado m -1. [del pelo] soft perm. -2. [de figura, cerámica] moulding.

moldear vt -1. [gen] to mould. -2. [modelar] to cast. -3. [cabello] to give a soft perm to.

mole f hulk.

molécula f molecule.

moler vt -1. [gen] to grind; [aceitunas] to press; [trigo] to mill. -2. fam fig [cansar] to wear out.

molestar vt -1. [perturbar] to annoy; **¿le molesta que fume?** do you mind if I smoke?; **perdone que le moleste ...** I'm sorry to bother you .... -2. [doler] to hurt. -3. [ofender] to offend. ◆ **molestarse** vpr -1. [incomodarse] to bother; **∼se en hacer algo** to bother to do sthg; **∼se por alguien/algo** to put o.s. out for sb/sthg. -2. [ofenderse]: **∼se (por algo)** to take offence (at sthg).

molestia f -1. [incomodidad] nuisance; **si no es demasiada ∼** if it's not too much trouble. -2. [malestar] discomfort.

molesto, -ta adj -1. [incordiante] annoying; [visita] inconvenient. -2. [irritado]: **∼ (con)** annoyed (with). -3. [con malestar] in discomfort.

molido, -da adj fam fig [cansado] worn out; **estar ∼ de** to be worn out from.

molinero, -ra m y f miller.

molinillo m grinder.

molino m mill; **∼ de viento** windmill.

molla f [parte blanda] flesh.

molleja f gizzard.

mollera f fam [juicio] brains (pl).

molusco m mollusc.

momentáneo, -a adj [de un momento] momentary; [pasajero] temporary.

momento m [gen] moment; [periodo] time; **llegó un ∼ en que ...** there came a time when ...; **a cada ∼** all the time; **al ∼** straightaway; **de ∼, por el ∼** for the time being ○ moment; **del ∼** [actual] of the day; **de un ∼ a otro** any minute now; **desde el ∼ (en) que ...** [tiempo] from the moment that ...; [causa] seeing as ....

momia f mummy.

Mónaco Monaco.

monada f -1. [persona] little beauty. -2. [cosa] lovely thing. -3. [gracia] antic.

monaguillo m altar boy.

monarca m monarch.

monarquía f monarchy.

monárquico, -ca adj monarchic.

monasterio m [de monjes] monastery; [de monjas] convent.

Moncloa f: **la ∼** residence of the Spanish premier which by extension refers to the Spanish government.

monda f [acción] peeling; [piel] peel; **ser la ~** mfam [extraordinario] to be amazing; [gracioso] to be a scream.

mondadientes m inv toothpick.

mondadura f [piel] peel.

mondar vt to peel. ◆ **mondarse** vpr: **~se (de risa)** fam to laugh one's head off.

moneda f **-1.** [pieza] coin; **ser ~ corriente** to be commonplace. **-2.** [divisa] currency.

monedero m purse.

monegasco, -ca adj, m y f Monegasque.

monetario, -ria adj monetary.

mongólico, -ca MED m y f Down's syndrome person.

mongolismo m Down's syndrome.

monigote m **-1.** [muñeco] rag ○ paper doll. **-2.** [dibujo] doodle. **-3.** fig [persona] puppet.

monitor, -ra m y f [persona] instructor. ◆ **monitor** m INFORM & TECN monitor.

monja f nun.

monje m monk.

mono, -na ◇ adj lovely. ◇ m y f [animal] monkey; **ser el último ~** to be bottom of the heap. ◆ **mono** m **-1.** [prenda - con peto] dungarees (pl); [- con mangas] overalls (pl). **-2.** fam [abstinencia] cold turkey.

monóculo m monocle.

monogamia f monogamy.

monografía f monograph.

monolingüe adj monolingual.

monólogo m monologue; TEATR soliloquy.

monopatín m skateboard.

monopolio m monopoly.

monopolizar vt lit & fig to monopolize.

monosílabo, -ba adj monosyllabic. ◆ **monosílabo** m monosyllable.

monotonía f [uniformidad] monotony.

monótono, -na adj monotonous.

monseñor m Monsignor.

monserga f fam drivel (U).

monstruo ◇ adj inv [grande] enormous, monster (antes de sust). ◇ m **-1.** [gen] monster. **-2.** fam [prodigio] giant, marvel.

monstruosidad f **-1.** [crueldad] monstrosity, atrocity. **-2.** [fealdad] hideousness. **-3.** [anomalía] freak.

monstruoso, -sa adj **-1.** [cruel] monstrous. **-2.** [feo] hideous. **-3.** [enorme] huge, enormous. **-4.** [deforme] terribly deformed.

monta f **-1.** [importancia] importance; **de poca/mucha ~** of little/great importance. **-2.** [en un caballo] ride, riding (U).

montacargas m inv goods lift Br, freight elevator Am.

montaje m **-1.** [de una máquina] assembly. **-2.** TEATR staging. **-3.** FOT montage. **-4.** CIN editing. **-5.** [farsa] put-up job.

montante m **-1.** [ventanuco] fanlight. **-2.** [importe] total; **~s compensatorios** COM compensating duties.

montaña f lit & fig mountain; **ir de excursión a la ~** to go camping in the mountains; **~ rusa** roller coaster; **hacer una ~ de un grano de arena** to make a mountain out of a molehill.

montañero, -ra m y f mountaineer.

montañismo m mountaineering.

montañoso, -sa adj mountainous.

montar ◇ vt **-1.** [ensamblar - máquina, estantería] to assemble; [- tienda de campaña, tenderete] to put up. **-2.** [encajar]: **~ algo en algo** to fit sthg into sthg. **-3.** [organizar - negocio, piso] to set up. **-4.** [cabalgar] to ride. **-5.** [poner encima]: **~ a alguien en** to lift sb onto. **-6.** [CULIN - nata] to whip; [- claras, yemas] to beat. **-7.** TEATR to stage. **-8.** CIN to cut, to edit. ◇ vi **-1.** [subir] to get on; [en un coche] to get in; **~ en** [gen] to get onto; [coche] to get into; [animal] to mount. **-2.** [ir montado] to ride; **~ en bicicleta/a caballo** to ride a bicycle/a horse. ◆ **montarse** vpr [gen] to get on; [en un coche] to get in; [en un animal] to mount; **~se en** [gen] to get onto; [coche] to get into; [animal] to mount.

montaraz adj mountain (antes de sust).

monte m [elevación] mountain; [terreno] woodland; **~ bajo** scrub. ◆ **monte de piedad** m state pawnbroker's.

montepío m mutual aid society.

montés adj wild.

Montevideo Montevideo.

montículo m hillock.

monto m total.

montón m **-1.** [pila] heap, pile; **a ○ en ~** everything together ○ at once; **del ~** fig run-of-the-mill. **-2.** fig [muchos] loads; **un ~ de** loads of.

montura f **-1.** [cabalgadura] mount. **-2.** [arreos] harness; [silla] saddle. **-3.** [soporte - de gafas] frame.

monumental adj **-1.** [ciudad, lugar] famous for its monuments. **-2.** fig [fracaso etc] monumental.

monumento m monument.

monzón m monsoon.

moña f fam [borrachera]: **coger una ~** to get smashed.

moño m bun (of hair); **estar hasta el ~ (de)** to be sick to death (of).

MOPU (abrev de **Ministerio de Obras Públicas y Urbanismo**) m Spanish ministry of public works and town planning.

moquear vi to have a runny nose.

moqueta f fitted carpet.

mora f **-1.** [de la zarzamora] blackberry. **-2.** [del moral] mulberry.

morada f culto dwelling.

morado, -da adj purple. ◆ **morado** m [color] purple.

moral ◇ adj moral. ◇ f **-1.** [ética] morality. **-2.** [ánimo] morale.

moraleja f moral.

moralizar vi to moralize.

morbo m fam [placer malsano] morbid pleasure.

morboso, -sa adj morbid.

morcilla f CULIN ≃ black pudding Br, ≃ blood sausage Am.

mordaz adj caustic, biting.

mordaza f gag.

mordedura f bite.

morder ◇ vt **-1.** [con los dientes] to bite. **-2.** [gastar] to eat into. ◇ vi to bite; **estar que muerde** to be hopping mad. ◆ **morderse** vpr: ~**se la lengua/las uñas** to bite one's tongue/nails.

mordida f Amer fam [soborno] bribe.

mordisco m bite.

mordisquear vt to nibble (at).

moreno, -na ◇ adj **-1.** [pelo, piel] dark; [por el sol] tanned; **ponerse ~** to get a tan. **-2.** [pan, azúcar] brown. ◇ m y f [por el pelo] dark-haired person; [por la piel] dark-skinned person.

morera f white mulberry.

moretón m bruise.

morfina f morphine.

moribundo, -da adj dying.

morir vi **-1.** [gen] to die. **-2.** [río, calle] to come out. **-3.** [fuego] to die down; [luz] to go out; [día] to come to a close. ◆ **morirse** vpr **-1.** [fallecer]: ~**se (de)** to die (of). **-2.** fig [sentir con fuerza]: ~**se de envidia/ira** to be burning with envy/rage; **me muero de ganas de ir a bailar** I'm dying to go dancing; **me muero de hambre/frío** I'm starving/freezing; ~**se por algo** to be dying for sthg; ~**se por alguien** to be crazy about sb.

mormón, -ona adj, m y f Mormon.

moro, -ra ◇ adj HIST Moorish. ◇ m y f **-1.** HIST Moor; ~**s y cristianos** traditional Spanish festival involving mock battle between Moors and Christians. **-2.** [árabe] Arab (N.B.: the term 'moro' is considered to be racist).

moroso, -sa COM ◇ adj defaulting. ◇ m y f defaulter, bad debtor.

morral m MIL haversack; [de cazador] gamebag.

morrear mfam vt & vi to snog.

morriña f [por el país de uno] homesickness; [por el pasado] nostalgia.

morro m **-1.** [hocico] snout. **-2.** fam [de coche, avión] nose.

morsa f walrus.

morse m (en aposición inv) Morse (code).

mortadela f Mortadella.

mortaja f shroud.

mortal ◇ adj mortal; [caída, enfermedad] fatal; [aburrimiento, susto, enemigo] deadly. ◇ m y f mortal.

mortalidad f mortality.

mortandad f mortality.

mortero m mortar.

mortífero, -ra adj deadly.

mortificar vt to mortify.

mortuorio, -ria adj death (antes de sust).

mosaico, -ca adj Mosaic. ◆ **mosaico** m mosaic.

mosca f fly; **por si las** ~**s** just in case; **¿qué ~ te ha picado?** what's up with you? ◆ **mosca muerta** m y f slyboots.

moscardón m ZOOL blowfly.

moscón m ZOOL bluebottle.

moscovita adj, m y f Muscovite.

Moscú Moscow.

mosquearse vpr fam [enfadarse] to get cross; [sospechar] to smell a rat.

mosquete m musket.

mosquetero m musketeer.

mosquitero m mosquito net.

mosquito m mosquito.

mosso d'Esquadra m member of the Catalan police force.

mostacho m moustache.

mostaza f mustard.

mosto m [residuo] must; [zumo de uva] grape juice.

mostrador m [en tienda] counter; [en bar] bar.

mostrar vt to show. ◆ **mostrarse** vpr to appear, to show o.s.; **se mostró muy interesado** he expressed great interest.

mota f [de polvo] **speck**; [en una tela] **dot**.

mote m **nickname**.

moteado, -da adj **speckled**; [vestido] **dotted**.

motel m **motel**.

motín m [del pueblo] **uprising, riot**; [de las tropas] **mutiny**.

motivación f **motive, motivation** (U).

motivar vt **-1.** [causar] **to cause**; [impulsar] **to motivate**. **-2.** [razonar] **to explain, to justify**.

motivo m **-1.** [causa] **reason, cause**; [de crimen] **motive**; **con ~ de** [por causa de] **because of**; [para celebrar] **on the occasion of**; [con el fin de] **in order to**; **sin ~** **for no reason**. **-2.** ARTE, LITER & MÚS **motif**.

moto f **motorbike** Br, **motorcycle**.

motocicleta f **motorbike, motorcycle**.

motociclismo m **motorcycling**.

motociclista m y f **motorcyclist**.

motocross m **motocross**.

motoneta f Amer **scooter, moped**.

motor (f **motora** O **motriz**) adj **motor**. ◆ **motor** m **-1.** [aparato] **motor, engine**. **-2.** [fuerza] **dynamic force**. ◆ **motora** f **motorboat**.

motorismo m **motorcycling**.

motorista m y f **motorcyclist**.

motriz → **motor**.

mountain bike ['maunten 'bike] m DEP **mountain biking**.

mousse [mus] m inv CULIN **mousse**.

movedizo, -za adj [movible] **movable, easily moved**.

mover vt **-1.** [gen & INFORM] **to move**; [mecánicamente] **to drive**. **-2.** [cabeza - afirmativamente] **to nod**; [- negativamente] **to shake**. **-3.** [suscitar] **to provoke**. **-4.** fig [empujar]: **~ a alguien a algo/a hacer algo to drive sb to sthg/to do sthg**. ◆ **mover a** vi **-1.** [incitar] **to incite to**. **-2.** [causar] **to provoke, to cause**. ◆ **moverse** vpr **-1.** [gen] **to move**; [en la cama] **to toss and turn**. **-2.** [darse prisa] **to get a move on**.

movido, -da adj **-1.** [debate, torneo] **lively**; [persona] **active, restless**; [jornada, viaje] **hectic**. **-2.** FOT **blurred, fuzzy**. ◆ **movida** f fam [ambiente] **scene**; **la movida madrileña** the Madrid scene of the late 1970s.

móvil ◇ adj **mobile, movable**. ◇ m **-1.** [motivo] **motive**. **-2.** [juguete] **mobile**.

movilidad f **mobility**.

movilizar vt **to mobilize**.

movimiento m **-1.** [gen & POLÍT] **movement**. **-2.** FÍS & TECN **motion**; **~ sísmico earth tremor**. **-3.** [circulación - gen] **activity**; [- de personal, mercancías] **turnover**; [- de vehículos] **traffic**; **~ de capital cash flow**. **-4.** [MÚS - parte de la obra] **movement**.

moviola f **editing projector**.

moza → **mozo**.

mozárabe ◇ adj **Mozarabic**, Christian in the time of Moorish Spain. ◇ m [lengua] **Mozarabic**.

mozo, -za ◇ adj [joven] **young**; [soltero] **single**. ◇ m y f **young boy** (f **young girl**), **young lad** (f **young lass**). ◆ **mozo** m **-1.** [trabajador] **assistant (worker)**; **~ de estación (station) porter**. **-2.** [recluta] **conscript**. **-3.** Amer [camarero] **waiter**.

mu m [mugido] **moo**; **no decir ni ~ not to say a word**.

mucamo, -ma m y f Amer **servant**.

muchacho, -cha m y f **boy** (f **girl**). ◆ **muchacha** f [sirvienta] **maid**.

muchedumbre f [de gente] **crowd, throng**; [de cosas] **great number, masses** (pl).

mucho, -cha ◇ adj **-1.** [gran cantidad] (en sg) **a lot of**; (en pl) **many, a lot of**; (en interrogativas y negativas) **much, a lot of**; **tengo ~ sueño I'm very sleepy**; **~s días several days**; **no tengo ~ tiempo I haven't got much time**. **-2.** (en sg) [demasiado]: **hay ~ niño aquí there are too many kids here**. ◇ pron (en sg) **a lot**; (en pl) **many, a lot**; **tengo ~ que contarte I have a lot to tell you**; **¿queda dinero? - no ~ is there any money left? - not much** O **not a lot**; **~s piensan igual a lot of** O **many people think the same**. ◆ **mucho** adv **-1.** [gen] **a lot**; **habla ~ he talks a lot**; **me canso ~ I get really** O **very tired**; **me gusta ~ I like it a lot** O **very much**; **no me gusta ~ I don't like it much**; **(no) ~ más tarde (not) much later**. **-2.** [largo tiempo]: **hace ~ que no vienes I haven't seen you for a long time**; **¿vienes ~ por aquí? do you come here often?**; **¿dura ~ la obra? is the play long?**; **~ antes/después long before/after**. **-3.** loc: **como ~ at the most**; **con ~ by far, easily**; **ni ~ menos by no means**; **no está ni ~ menos decidido it is by no means decided**. ◆ **por mucho que** loc conj **no matter how much, however much**; **por ~ que insistas no matter how much** O **however much you insist**.

mucosidad f **mucus**.

muda *f* [ropa interior] change of underwear.

mudanza *f* **-1.** [cambio] change; [de carácter] fickleness; [de plumas, piel] moulting. **-2.** [de casa] move; **estar de ~** to be moving.

mudar ◇ *vt* **-1.** [gen] to change; [casa] to move; **cuando mude la voz** when his voice breaks. **-2.** [piel, plumas] to moult. ◇ *vi* [cambiar]: **~ de** [opinión, color] to change; [domicilio] to move. ◆ **mudarse** *vpr*: **~se (de casa)** to move (house); **~se (de ropa)** to change.

mudéjar *adj, m y f* Mudejar.

mudo, -da *adj* **-1.** [sin habla] dumb. **-2.** [callado] silent, mute; **se quedó ~** he was left speechless. **-3.** [sin sonido] silent.

mueble ◇ *m* piece of furniture; **los ~s** the furniture (*U*); **~ bar** cocktail cabinet. ◇ *adj* → **bien**.

mueca *f* [gen] face, expression; [de dolor] grimace.

muela *f* [diente - gen] tooth; [- molar] molar.

muelle *m* **-1.** [de colchón, reloj] spring. **-2.** [en el puerto] dock, quay; [en el río] wharf.

muera → **morir**.

muérdago *m* mistletoe.

muermo *m fam* bore, drag; **tener ~** to be bored.

muerte *f* **-1.** [gen] death; **de mala ~** third-rate, lousy. **-2.** [homicidio] murder.

muerto, -ta ◇ *pp* → **morir**. ◇ *adj* [gen] dead; **estar ~ de miedo/frío** to be scared/freezing to death; **estar ~ de hambre** to be starving. ◇ *m y f* dead person; [cadáver] corpse; **hubo dos ~s** two people died; **hacer el ~** to float on one's back.

muesca *f* **-1.** [concavidad] notch, groove. **-2.** [corte] nick.

muestra *f* **-1.** [pequeña cantidad] sample. **-2.** [señal] sign, show; [prueba] proof; [de cariño, aprecio] token; **dar ~s de** to show signs of. **-3.** [modelo] model, pattern. **-4.** [exposición] show, exhibition.

muestrario *m* collection of samples.

muestreo *m* sample; [acción] sampling.

mugido *m* [de vaca] moo, mooing (*U*); [de toro] bellow, bellowing (*U*).

mugir *vi* [vaca] to moo; [toro] to bellow.

mugre *f* filth, muck.

mugriento, -ta *adj* filthy.

mujer *f* woman; [cónyuge] wife; **~ de la limpieza** cleaning lady; **~ de negocios** businesswoman.

mujeriego, -ga *adj* fond of the ladies. ◆ **mujeriego** *m* womanizer.

mujerzuela *f despec* loose woman.

mulato, -ta *adj, m y f* mulatto.

muleta *f* **-1.** [para andar] crutch; *fig* prop, support. **-2.** TAUROM muleta, *red cape hanging from a stick used to tease the bull.*

Mulhacén *m*: **el ~** Mulhacén.

mullido, -da *adj* soft, springy.

mulo, -la *m y f* ZOOL mule.

multa *f* fine; **poner una ~ a alguien** to fine sb.

multar *vt* to fine.

multicopista *f* duplicator.

multimedia *adj inv* INFORM multimedia.

multimillonario, -ria *m y f* multimillionaire.

multinacional *adj & f* multinational.

múltiple *adj* [variado] multiple. ◆ **múltiples** *adj pl* [numerosos] many, numerous.

multiplicación *f* multiplication.

multiplicar *vt & vi* to multiply. ◆ **multiplicarse** *vpr* **-1.** [esforzarse] to do lots of things at the same time. **-2.** BIOL to multiply.

múltiplo, -pla *adj* multiple. ◆ **múltiplo** *m* multiple.

multitud *f* [de personas] crowd; **una ~ de cosas** loads of O countless things.

multitudinario, -ria *adj* extremely crowded; [manifestación] mass (*antes de sust*).

multiuso *adj inv* multipurpose.

mundanal *adj* worldly.

mundano, -na *adj* **-1.** [del mundo] worldly, of the world. **-2.** [de la vida social] (high) society.

mundial ◇ *adj* [política, economía, guerra] world (*antes de sust*); [tratado, organización, fama] worldwide. ◇ *m* World Championships (*pl*); [en fútbol] World Cup.

mundo *m* **-1.** [gen] world; **el tercer ~** the Third World; **se la cayó el ~ encima** his world fell apart; **todo el ~** everyone, everybody; **venir al ~** to come into the world, to be born. **-2.** [experiencia]: **hombre/mujer de ~** man/woman of the world.

munición *f* ammunition.

municipal ◇ *adj* town (*antes de sust*), municipal; [elecciones] local; [instalaciones] public. ◇ *m y f* → **guardia**.

municipio *m* **-1.** [corporación] town council. **-2.** [territorio] town, municipality.

muñeco, -ca *m y f* [juguete] doll; [marioneta] puppet. ◆ **muñeco** *m fig* puppet. ◆ **muñeca** *f* **-1.** ANAT wrist. **-2.** *Amer fam* [enchufe]: **tener ~** to have friends in high places. ◆ **muñeco de nieve** *m* snowman.

muñequera *f* wristband.

muñón *m* stump.

mural ◇ *adj* [pintura] mural; [mapa] wall. ◇ *m* mural.

muralla *f* wall.

murciélago *m* bat.

murmullo *m* [gen] murmur, murmuring (*U*); [de hojas] rustle, rustling (*U*); [de insectos] buzz, buzzing (*U*).

murmuración *f* gossip (*U*).

murmurar ◇ *vt* to murmur. ◇ *vi* **-1.** [susurrar - persona] to murmur, to whisper; [- agua, viento] to murmur, to gurgle. **-2.** [criticar]: **~ (de)** to gossip o backbite (about). **-3.** [rezongar, quejarse] to grumble.

muro *m lit & fig* wall.

mus *m inv* card game played in pairs with bidding and in which players communicate by signs.

musa *f* [inspiración] muse.

musaraña *f* ZOOL shrew; **mirar a las ~s** to stare into space o thin air.

muscular *adj* muscular.

musculatura *f* muscles (*pl*).

músculo *m* muscle.

musculoso, -sa *adj* muscular.

museo *m* museum; **~ de arte** art gallery.

musgo *m* moss.

música → **músico**.

músico, -ca ◇ *adj* musical. ◇ *m y f* [persona] musician. ◆ **música** *f* music; **música ambiental** background music.

musitar *vt* to mutter, to mumble.

muslo *m* thigh; [de pollo] drumstick.

mustio, -tia *adj* **-1.** [flor, planta] withered, wilted. **-2.** [persona] gloomy.

musulmán, -ana *adj, m y f* Muslim.

mutación *f* [cambio] sudden change; BIOL mutation.

mutante *adj, m y f* mutant.

mutar *vt* to mutate.

mutilado, -da *adj* mutilated.

mutilar *vt* [gen] to mutilate; [estatua] to deface.

mutismo *m* [silencio] silence.

mutua → **mutuo**.

mutualidad *f* [asociación] mutual benefit society.

mutuo, -tua *adj* mutual. ◆ **mutua** *f* mutual benefit society.

muy *adv* very; **~ bueno/cerca** very good/near; **~ de mañana** very early in the morning; **¡~ bien!** [vale] OK!, all right!; [qué bien] very good!, well done!; **eso es ~ de ella** that's just like her; **eso es ~ de los americanos** that's typically American; **¡el ~ idiota!** what an idiot!

N

n, N *f* [letra] n, N. ◆ **N** *m*: **el 20 N** *20th November, the date of Franco's death.*

n/ *abrev de* **nuestro**.

nabo *m* turnip.

nácar *m* mother-of-pearl.

nacer *vi* **-1.** [venir al mundo - niño, animal] to be born; [- planta] to sprout; [- pájaro] to hatch (out); **~ para algo** to be born to be sthg; **ha nacido cantante** she's a born singer. **-2.** [surgir - pelo] to grow; [- río] to rise; [- costumbre, actitud, duda] to have its roots.

nacido, -da ◇ *adj* born. ◇ *m y f*: **los ~s hoy** those born today; **recién ~** new-born baby; **ser un mal ~** to be a wicked o vile person.

naciente *adj* **-1.** [día] dawning; [sol] rising. **-2.** [gobierno, estado] new, fledgling; [interés] growing.

nacimiento *m* **-1.** [gen] birth; [de planta] sprouting; **de ~** from birth. **-2.** [de río] source. **-3.** [origen] origin, beginning. **-4.** [belén] Nativity scene.

nación *f* [gen] nation; [territorio] country. ◆ **Naciones Unidas** *fpl* United Nations.

nacional *adj* national; [mercado, vuelo] domestic; [asuntos] home (*antes de sust*).

nacionalidad *f* nationality.

nacionalismo *m* nationalism.

nacionalista *adj, m y f* nationalist.

nacionalizar *vt* **-1.** [banca, bienes] to nationalize. **-2.** [persona] to naturalize.

◆ **nacionalizarse** *vpr* to become naturalized.

nada ◇ *pron* nothing; (*en negativas*) anything; **no he leído** ~ **de este autor** I haven't read anything by this author; ~ **más** nothing else, nothing more; **no quiero** ~ **más** I don't want anything else; **no dijo** ~ **de** ~ he didn't say anything at all; **de** ~ [respuesta a "gracias"] you're welcome; **como si** ~ as if nothing had happened. ◇ *adv* **-1.** [en absoluto] at all; **la película no me ha gustado** ~ I didn't like the film at all. **-2.** [poco] a little, a bit; **no hace** ~ **que salió** he left just a minute ago; ~ **menos que** [cosa] no less than; [persona] none other than. ◇ *f*: **la** ~ nothingness, the void. ◆ **nada más** *loc conj* no sooner, as soon as; ~ **más salir de casa se puso a llover** no sooner had I left the house than it started to rain, as soon as I left the house, it started to rain.

nadador, -ra *m y f* swimmer.

nadar *vi* [gen] to swim; [flotar] to float.

nadería *f* trifle, little thing.

nadie *pron* nobody, no one; ~ **lo sabe** nobody knows; **no se lo dije a** ~ I didn't tell anybody; **no ha llamado** ~ nobody phoned.

nado ◆ **a nado** *loc adv* swimming.

naïf [na'if] *adj* naïve, primitivistic.

nailon, nilón, nylon® *m* nylon.

naipe *m* (playing) card. ◆ **naipes** *mpl* cards.

nalga *f* buttock.

nana *f* [canción] lullaby.

naranja ◇ *adj inv* orange. ◇ *m* [color] orange. ◇ *f* [fruto] orange. ◆ **media naranja** *f fam fig* other ○ better half.

naranjo *m* [árbol] orange tree.

narciso *m* BOT narcissus.

narcótico, -ca *adj* narcotic. ◆ **narcótico** *m* narcotic; [droga] drug.

narcotizar *vt* to drug.

narcotraficante *m y f* drug trafficker.

narcotráfico *m* drug trafficking.

nardo *m* nard, spikenard.

narigudo, -da *adj* big-nosed.

nariz *f* **-1.** [órgano] nose. **-2.** [orificio] nostril. **-3.** *fig* [olfato] sense of smell. **-4.** *loc:* **estar hasta las narices (de algo)** to be fed up to the back teeth (with sthg); **meter las narices en algo** to poke ○ stick one's nose into sthg.

narración *f* **-1.** [cuento, relato] narrative, story. **-2.** [acción] narration.

narrador, -ra *m y f* narrator.

narrar *vt* [contar] to recount, to tell.

narrativo, -va *adj* narrative. ◆ **narrativa** *f* narrative.

nasal *adj* nasal.

nata *f* **-1.** [gen & fig] cream; ~ **batida** ○ **montada** whipped cream. **-2.** [de leche hervida] skin.

natación *f* swimming.

natal *adj* [país] native; [ciudad, pueblo] home (*antes de sust*).

natalicio *m* [cumpleaños] birthday.

natalidad *f* birth rate.

natillas *fpl* custard (*U*).

nativo, -va *adj, m y f* native.

nato, -ta *adj* [gen] born; [cargo, título] ex officio.

natural ◇ *adj* **-1.** [gen] natural; [flores, fruta, leche] fresh; **al** ~ [persona] in one's natural state; [fruta] in its own juice; **ser** ~ **en alguien** to be natural ○ normal for sb. **-2.** [nativo] native; **ser** ~ **de** to come from. ◇ *m y f* [nativo] native. ◇ *m* [talante] nature, disposition.

naturaleza *f* **-1.** [gen] nature; **por** ~ by nature. **-2.** [complexión] constitution.

naturalidad *f* naturalness; **con** ~ naturally.

naturalizar *vt* to naturalize. ◆ **naturalizarse** *vpr* to become naturalized.

naturista *m y f person favouring return to nature.*

naufragar *vi* [barco] to sink, to be wrecked; [persona] to be shipwrecked.

naufragio *m* [de barco] shipwreck.

náufrago, -ga *m y f* castaway.

náusea *f* (*gen pl*) nausea (*U*), sickness (*U*); **me da** ~**s** it makes me sick.

nauseabundo, -da *adj* nauseating.

náutico, -ca *adj* [gen] nautical; DEP water (*antes de sust*). ◆ **náutica** *f* navigation, seamanship.

navaja *f* **-1.** [cuchillo - pequeño] penknife; [- más grande] jackknife. **-2.** [molusco] razor-shell.

navajero, -ra *m y f thug who carries a knife.*

naval *adj* naval.

Navarra Navarre.

navarro, -rra *adj, m y f* Navarrese.

nave *f* **-1.** [barco] ship; **quemar las** ~**s** to burn one's boats ○ bridges. **-2.** [vehículo] craft; ~ **espacial** spaceship. **-3.** [de fábrica] shop, plant; [almacén] warehouse. **-4.** [de iglesia] nave.

navegación *f* navigation.

navegante *m y f* navigator.

navegar *vi & vt* [barco] to sail; [avión] to fly.

Navidad f **-1.** [día] Christmas (Day). **-2.** (gen pl) [periodo] Christmas (time); **felices Navidades** Merry Christmas.

navideño, -ña adj Christmas (antes de sust).

naviero, -ra adj shipping. ◆ **naviero** m [armador] shipowner. ◆ **naviera** f [compañía] shipping company.

navío m large ship.

nazi adj, m y f Nazi.

nazismo m Nazism.

neblina f mist.

nebuloso, -sa adj **-1.** [con nubes] cloudy; [de niebla] foggy. **-2.** fig [idea, mirada] vague. ◆ **nebulosa** f ASTRON nebula.

necedad f **-1.** [estupidez] stupidity, foolishness. **-2.** [dicho, hecho] stupid ○ foolish thing; **decir ~es** to talk nonsense.

necesario, -ria adj necessary; **es ~ hacerlo** it needs to be done; **no es ~ que lo hagas** you don't need to do it; **si fuera ~** if need be.

neceser m toilet bag ○ case.

necesidad f **-1.** [gen] need. **-2.** [obligación] necessity; **por ~** out of necessity. **-3.** [hambre] hunger. ◆ **necesidades** fpl: **hacer (uno) sus ~** eufemismo to answer the call of nature.

necesitado, -da ◇ adj needy. ◇ m y f needy ○ poor person; **los ~s** the poor.

necesitar vt to need; **necesito que me lo digas** I need you to tell me; **"se necesita piso"** "flat wanted". ◆ **necesitar de** vi to have need of.

necio, -cia adj stupid, foolish.

necrología f obituary; [lista de esquelas] obituary column.

néctar m nectar.

nectarina f nectarine.

nefasto, -ta adj [funesto] ill-fated; [dañino] bad, harmful; [pésimo] terrible, awful.

negación f **-1.** [desmentido] denial. **-2.** [negativa] refusal. **-3.** [lo contrario] antithesis, negation. **-4.** GRAM negative.

negado, -da adj useless.

negar vt **-1.** [rechazar] to deny. **-2.** [denegar] to refuse, to deny; **~le algo a alguien** to refuse ○ deny sb sthg. ◆ **negarse** vpr: **~se (a)** to refuse (to).

negativo, -va adj [gen] negative. ◆ **negativo** m FOT negative. ◆ **negativa** f **-1.** [rechazo] refusal. **-2.** [mentís] denial.

negligencia f negligence.

negligente adj negligent.

negociable adj negotiable.

negociación f negotiation.

negociante m y f [comerciante] businessman (f businesswoman).

negociar ◇ vi **-1.** [comerciar] to do business; **~ con** to deal ○ trade with. **-2.** [discutir] to negotiate. ◇ vt to negotiate.

negocio m **-1.** [gen] business; **el mundo de los ~s** the business world. **-2.** [transacción] deal, (business) transaction; **~ sucio** shady deal. **-3.** [operación ventajosa] good deal, bargain; **hacer ~** to do well. **-4.** [comercio] trade.

negra → negro.

negrero, -ra m y f **-1.** HIST slave trader. **-2.** fig [explotador] slave driver.

negrita, negrilla → letra.

negro, -gra ◇ adj **-1.** [gen] black. **-2.** [furioso] furious; **ponerse ~** to get mad ○ angry. **-3.** CIN: **cine ~** film noir. ◇ m y f black man (f black woman). ◆ **negro** m [color] black. ◆ **negra** f **-1.** MÚS crotchet. **-2.** loc: **tener la negra** to have bad luck.

negrura f blackness.

nene, -na m y f fam [niño] baby.

nenúfar m water lily.

neocelandés, -esa, neozelandés, -esa m y f New Zealander.

neologismo m neologism.

neón m QUÍM neon.

neoyorquino, -na ◇ adj New York (antes de sust), of/relating to New York. ◇ m y f New Yorker.

neozelandés, -esa = neocelandés.

Nepal: el ~ Nepal.

Neptuno Neptune.

nervio m **-1.** ANAT nerve. **-2.** [de carne] sinew. **-3.** [vigor] energy, vigour. ◆ **nervios** mpl [estado mental] nerves; **tener ~s** to be nervous; **poner los ~s de punta a alguien** to get on sb's nerves; **tener los ~s de punta** to be on edge.

nerviosismo m nervousness, nerves (pl).

nervioso, -sa adj **-1.** [ANAT - sistema, enfermedad] nervous; [- tejido, célula, centro] nerve (antes de sust). **-2.** [inquieto] nervous; **ponerse ~** to get nervous. **-3.** [irritado] worked-up; **ponerse ~** to get uptight ○ worked up.

nervudo, -da adj sinewy.

neto, -ta adj **-1.** [claro] clear, clean; [verdad] simple, plain. **-2.** [peso, sueldo] net.

neumático, -ca adj pneumatic. ◆ **neu-**

mático *m* tyre; ~ **de repuesto** spare tyre.

neumonía *f* pneumonia.

neurálgico, -ca *adj* **-1.** MED neuralgic. **-2.** *fig* [importante] critical.

neurastenia *f* nervous exhaustion.

neurología *f* neurology.

neurólogo, -ga *m y f* neurologist.

neurona *f* neuron, nerve cell.

neurosis *f inv* neurosis.

neurótico, -ca *adj, m y f* neurotic.

neutral *adj, m y f* neutral.

neutralidad *f* neutrality.

neutralizar *vt* to neutralize.

neutro, -tra *adj* **-1.** [gen] neutral. **-2.** BIOL & GRAM neuter.

neutrón *m* neutron.

nevado, -da *adj* snowy. ◆ **nevada** *f* snowfall.

nevar *v impers* to snow.

nevera *f* fridge *Br*, icebox *Am*.

nevisca *f* snow flurry.

nexo *m* link, connection; [relación] relation, connection.

ni ◇ *conj*: ~ ... ~ ... neither ... nor ...; ~ **mañana** ~ **pasado** neither tomorrow nor the day after; **no** ... ~ ... neither ... nor ..., not ... or ... (either); **no es alto** ~ **bajo** he's neither tall nor short, he's not tall or short (either); **no es rojo** ~ **verde** ~ **azul** it's neither red nor green nor blue; ~ **un/una** ... not a single ...; **no me quedaré** ~ **un minuto más** I'm not staying a minute longer; ~ **uno/una** not a single one; **no he aprobado** ~ **una** I haven't passed a single one; ~ **que** as if; ¡~ **que yo fuera tonto!** as if I were that stupid! ◇ *adv* not even; **anda tan atareado que** ~ **tiene tiempo para comer** he's so busy he doesn't even have time to eat.

Nicaragua Nicaragua.

nicaragüense *adj, m y f* Nicaraguan.

nicho *m* niche.

nicotina *f* nicotine.

nido *m* [gen] nest.

niebla *f* [densa] fog; [neblina] mist; **hay** ~ it's foggy.

nieto, -ta *m y f* grandson (*f* granddaughter).

nieve *f* METEOR snow. ◆ **nieves** *fpl* [nevada] snows, snowfall (*sg*).

NIF (*abrev de* **número de identificación fiscal**) *m* ≃ National Insurance number *Br*, *identification number for tax purposes*.

Nilo *m*: **el** ~ the (river) Nile.

nilón = **nailon**.

nimiedad *f* **-1.** [cualidad] insignificance, triviality. **-2.** [dicho, hecho] trifle.

nimio, -mia *adj* insignificant, trivial.

ninfa *f* nymph.

ninfómana *f* nymphomaniac.

ninguno, -na ◇ *adj* (*antes de sust masculino:* **ningún**) no; **ninguna respuesta se dio** no answer was given; **no tengo ningún interés en hacerlo** I've no interest in doing it, I'm not at all interested in doing it; **no tengo ningún hijo/ninguna buena idea** I don't have any children/good ideas; **no tiene ninguna gracia** it's not funny. ◇ *pron* [cosa] none, not any; [persona] nobody, no one; ~ **funciona** none of them works; **no hay** ~ there aren't any, there are none; ~ **lo sabrá** no one o nobody will know; ~ **de** none of; ~ **de ellos** none of them; ~ **de los dos** neither of them.

niña → **niño**.

niñería *f* **-1.** [cualidad] childishness (*U*). **-2.** *fig* [tontería] silly o childish thing.

niñero, -ra *adj* fond of children. ◆ **niñera** *f* nanny.

niñez *f* [infancia] childhood.

niño, -ña ◇ *adj* young. ◇ *m y f* [crío] child, boy (*f* girl); [bebé] baby; **los** ~**s** the children; ~ **bien** *despec* spoilt brat; ~ **prodigio** child prodigy; **ser el** ~ **bonito de alguien** to be sb's pet o blue-eyed boy. ◆ **niña** *f* [del ojo] pupil; **la niña de los ojos** *fig* the apple of one's eye.

nipón, -ona *adj, m y f* Japanese.

níquel *m* nickel.

niquelar *vt* to nickel-plate.

niqui *m* T-shirt.

níspero *m* medlar.

nitidez *f* clarity; [de imágenes, colores] sharpness.

nítido, -da *adj* clear; [imágenes, colores] sharp.

nitrato *m* nitrate.

nitrógeno *m* nitrogen.

nivel *m* **-1.** [gen] level; [altura] height; **al** ~ **de** level with; **al** ~ **del mar** at sea level. **-2.** [grado] level, standard; **al mismo** ~ **(que)** on a level o par (with); **a** ~ **europeo** at a European level; ~ **de vida** standard of living.

nivelador, -ra *adj* levelling. ◆ **niveladora** *f* bulldozer.

nivelar *vt* **-1.** [allanar] to level. **-2.** [equilibrar] to even out; FIN to balance.

no ◇ *adv* **-1.** [expresa negación - gen] not; [- en respuestas] no; [- con sustantivos] non-; ~ **sé** I don't know; ~ **veo nada** I can't see anything; ~ **es fácil** it's not easy, it isn't easy; ~ **tiene dinero** he has no money, he hasn't got any money; **todavía** ~ not yet; **¿~ vienes? - ~,** ~ **creo** aren't you coming? - no, I don't think so; ~ **fumadores** non-smokers; ~ **bien** as soon as; ~ **ya ... sino que ...** not only ... but (also) ...; **¡a que** ~ **lo haces!** I bet you don't do it!; **¿cómo** ~**?** of course; **pues** ~**, eso sí que** ~ certainly not; **¡que** ~**!** I said no! **-2.** [expresa duda, extrañeza]: **¿~ irás a venir?** you're not coming, are you?; **estamos de acuerdo, ¿~?** we're agreed then, are we?; **es español, ¿~?** he's Spanish, isn't he? ◇ *m* no.

n.º *(abrev de* **número)** no.

nobiliario, -ria *adj* noble.

noble *adj, m y f* noble; **los ~s** the nobility.

nobleza *f* nobility.

noche *f* night; [atardecer] evening; **ayer por la ~** last night; **esta ~** tonight; **hacer** ~ **en** to stay the night in; **hacerse de** ~ to get dark; **por la ~, de** ~ at night; **buenas ~s** [despedida] good night; [saludo] good evening; **de la ~ a la mañana** overnight.

Nochebuena *f* Christmas Eve.

nochero *m Amer* **-1.** [vigilante] night watchman. **-2.** [mesita] bedside table.

Nochevieja *f* New Year's Eve.

noción *f* [concepto] notion; **tener ~ (de)** to have an idea (of). ◆ **nociones** *fpl* [conocimiento básico]: **tener nociones de** to have a smattering of.

nocivo, -va *adj* [gen] harmful; [gas] noxious.

noctámbulo, -la *m y f* night owl.

nocturno, -na *adj* **-1.** [club, tren, vuelo] night *(antes de sust)*; [clase] evening *(antes de sust)*. **-2.** [animales, plantas] nocturnal.

nodriza *f* wet nurse.

Noel → **papá**.

nogal *m* walnut.

nómada ◇ *adj* nomadic. ◇ *m y f* nomad.

nombramiento *m* appointment.

nombrar *vt* **-1.** [citar] to mention. **-2.** [designar] to appoint.

nombre *m* **-1.** [gen] name; ~ **y apellidos** full name; ~ **compuesto** compound name; ~ **de pila** first o Christian name; ~ **de soltera** maiden name; **en** ~ **de** on behalf of. **-2.** [fama] reputation; **tener mucho** ~ to be renowned

o famous. **-3.** GRAM noun; ~ **común/propio** common/proper noun.

nomenclatura *f* nomenclature.

nómina *f* **-1.** [lista de empleados] payroll. **-2.** [hoja de salario] payslip.

nominal *adj* nominal.

nominar *vt* to nominate.

nomo, gnomo *m* gnome.

non *m* odd number. ◆ **nones** *adv* [no] no way.

nonagésimo, -ma *núm* ninetieth.

nordeste = **noreste**.

nórdico, -ca *adj* **-1.** [del norte] northern, northerly. **-2.** [escandinavo] Nordic.

noreste, nordeste ◇ *adj* [posición, parte] northeast, northeastern; [dirección, viento] northeasterly. ◇ *m* north-east.

noria *f* **-1.** [para agua] water wheel. **-2.** [de feria] big wheel *Br*, Ferris wheel.

norma *f* standard; [regla] rule; **es la ~ hacerlo así** it's usual to do it this way.

normal *adj* normal.

normalidad *f* normality.

normalizar *vt* **-1.** [volver normal] to return to normal. **-2.** [estandarizar] to standardize. ◆ **normalizarse** *vpr* to return to normal.

normativo, -va *adj* normative. ◆ **normativa** *f* regulations *(pl)*.

noroeste ◇ *adj* [posición, parte] northwest, northwestern; [dirección, viento] northwesterly. ◇ *m* northwest.

norte ◇ *adj* [posición, parte] north, northern; [dirección, viento] northerly. ◇ *m* GEOGR north.

norteamericano, -na *adj, m y f* North American, American.

Noruega Norway.

noruego, -ga *adj, m y f* Norwegian. ◆ **noruego** *m* [lengua] Norwegian.

nos *pron pers* **-1.** *(complemento directo)* us; **le gustaría vernos** she'd like to see us. **-2.** *(complemento indirecto)* (to) us; ~ **lo dio** he gave it to us; ~ **tiene miedo** he's afraid of us. **-3.** *(reflexivo)* ourselves. **-4.** *(recíproco)* each other; ~ **enamoramos** we fell in love (with each other).

nosocomio *m Amer* hospital.

nosotros, -tras *pron pers* **-1.** *(sujeto)* we. **-2.** *(predicado)*: **somos ~** it's us. **-3.** *(después de prep)* *(complemento)* us; **vente a comer con** ~ come and eat with us. **-4.** *loc*: **entre** ~ between you and me.

nostalgia *f* [del pasado] nostalgia; [de país, amigos] homesickness.

nota f **-1.** [gen & MÚS] note; **tomar ~ de algo** [apuntar] to note sthg down; [fijarse] to take note of sthg; **~ dominante** prevailing mood. **-2.** EDUC mark; **sacar** O **tener buenas ~s** to get good marks. **-3.** [cuenta] bill. **-4.** loc: **dar la ~** to make o.s. conspicuous.

notable ◇ adj remarkable, outstanding. ◇ m EDUC merit, second class.

notar vt **-1.** [advertir] to notice; **te noto cansado** you look tired to me; **hacer ~ algo** to point sthg out. **-2.** [sentir] to feel. ◆ **notarse** vpr to be apparent; **se nota que le gusta** you can tell she likes it.

notaría f [oficina] notary's office.

notario, -ria m y f notary (public).

noticia f news (U); **una ~** a piece of news; **¿tienes ~s suyas?** have you heard from him? ◆ **noticias** fpl: **las ~s** RADIO & TV the news.

notificación f notification.

notificar vt to notify, to inform.

notoriedad f [fama] fame.

notorio, -ria adj **-1.** [evidente] obvious. **-2.** [conocido] widely-known.

novato, -ta ◇ adj inexperienced. ◇ m y f novice, beginner.

novecientos, -tas núm nine hundred; ver también **seis**.

novedad f **-1.** [cualidad - de nuevo] newness; [- de novedoso] novelty. **-2.** [cambio] change. **-3.** [noticia] news (U); **sin ~** without incident; MIL all quiet. ◆ **novedades** fpl [libros, discos] new releases; [moda] latest fashion (sg).

novedoso, -sa adj novel, new.

novel adj new, first-time.

novela f novel; **~ policíaca** detective story.

novelesco, -ca adj **-1.** [de la novela] fictional. **-2.** [fantástico] fantastic.

novelista m y f novelist.

noveno, -na núm ninth.

noventa núm ninety; **los (años) ~** the nineties; ver también **seis**.

noviazgo m engagement.

noviembre m November; ver también **septiembre**.

novillada f TAUROM bullfight with young bulls.

novillo, -lla m y f young bull or cow; **hacer ~** fam to play truant Br, to play hooky Am.

novio, -via m y f **-1.** [compañero] boyfriend (f girlfriend). **-2.** [prometido] fiancé (f fiancée). **-3.** [recién casado] bridegroom (f bride); **los ~s** the newly-weds.

nubarrón m storm cloud.

nube f **-1.** [gen & fig] cloud; **poner algo/a alguien por las ~s** fig to praise sthg/sb to the skies; **por las ~s** [caro] sky-high, terribly expensive. **-2.** [de personas, moscas] swarm.

nublado, -da adj **-1.** [encapotado] cloudy, overcast. **-2.** fig [turbado] clouded.

nublar vt lit & fig to cloud. ◆ **nublarse** vpr **-1.** [suj: cielo] to cloud over. **-2.** fig [turbarse, oscurecerse] to become clouded.

nubosidad f cloudiness, clouds (pl).

nuca f nape, back of the neck.

nuclear adj nuclear.

núcleo m **-1.** [centro] nucleus; fig centre. **-2.** [grupo] core.

nudillo m knuckle.

nudismo m nudism.

nudo m **-1.** [gen] knot; **se le hizo un ~ en la garganta** she got a lump in her throat. **-2.** [cruce] junction. **-3.** fig [vínculo] tie, bond. **-4.** fig [punto principal] crux.

nudoso, -sa adj knotty, gnarled.

nuera f daughter-in-law.

nuestro, -tra ◇ adj poses our; **~ coche** our car; **este libro es ~** this book is ours, this is our book; **un amigo ~** a friend of ours; **no es asunto ~** it's none of our business. ◇ pron poses: **el ~** ours; **el ~ es rojo** ours is red; **esta es la nuestra** fam this is the chance we have been waiting for; **lo ~ es el teatro** [lo que nos va] theatre is what we should be doing; **los ~s** fam [nuestra familia] our folks; [nuestro bando] our lot, our side.

nueva → **nuevo**.

Nueva York New York.

Nueva Zelanda New Zealand.

nueve núm nine; ver también **seis**.

nuevo, -va ◇ adj [gen] new; [patatas, legumbres] new, fresh; [vino] young; **ser ~ en** to be new to. ◇ m y f newcomer. ◆ **buena nueva** f good news (U). ◆ **de nuevo** loc adv again.

nuez f **-1.** BOT [gen] nut; [de nogal] walnut. **-2.** ANAT Adam's apple. ◆ **nuez moscada** f nutmeg.

nulidad f **-1.** [no validez] nullity. **-2.** [ineptitud] incompetence.

nulo, -la adj **-1.** [sin validez] null and void. **-2.** fam [incapacitado]: **~ (para)** useless (at).

núm. (*abrev de* **número**) No.
numeración *f* **-1.** [acción] numbering. **-2.** [sistema] numerals (*pl*), numbers (*pl*).
numeral *adj* numeral.
numerar *vt* to number.
numérico, -ca *adj* numerical.
número *m* **-1.** [gen] number; ~ **de matrícula** AUTOM registration number; ~ **redondo** round number; **en ~s rojos** in the red; **hacer ~s** to reckon up. **-2.** [tamaño, talla] size. **-3.** [de publicación] issue; ~ **atrasado** back number. **-4.** [de lotería] ticket. **-5.** [de un espectáculo] turn, number; **montar el ~** *fam* to make O cause a scene.
numeroso, -sa *adj* numerous; **un grupo ~** a large group.
nunca *adv* (*en frases afirmativas*) never; (*en frases negativas*) ever; **casi ~ viene** he almost never comes, he hardly ever comes; **¿~ le has visto?** have you never seen her?, haven't you ever seen her?; **más que ~** more than ever; ~ **jamás** O **más** never more O again.
nuncio *m* nuncio.
nupcial *adj* wedding (*antes de sust*).
nupcias *fpl* wedding (*sg*), nuptials.
nutria *f* otter.
nutrición *f* nutrition.
nutrido, -da *adj* **-1.** [alimentado] nourished; **mal ~** undernourished. **-2.** [numeroso] large.
nutrir *vt* **-1.** [alimentar] ~ **(con** O **de)** to nourish O feed (with). **-2.** *fig* [fomentar] to feed, to nurture. **-3.** *fig* [suministrar]: ~ **(de)** to supply (with). ◆ **nutrirse** *vpr* **-1.** [gen]: ~**se de** O **con** to feed on. **-2.** *fig* [proveerse]: ~**se de** O **con** to supply O provide o.s. with.
nutritivo, -va *adj* nutritious.
nylon® ['nailon] = **nailon**.

ñ, Ñ *f* [letra] ñ, Ñ, *15th letter of the Spanish alphabet*.
ñoñería, ñoñez *f* inanity, insipidness (U).
ñoño, -ña *adj* **-1.** [remilgado] squeam-ish; [quejica] whining. **-2.** [soso] dull, insipid.
ñudo *Amer* ◆ **al ñudo** *loc adv* in vain.

o¹, O *f* [letra] o, O.
o² *conj* ("u" *en vez de* "o" *antes de palabras que empiezan por* "o" *u* "ho") or; ~ ... ~ either ... or; ~ **sea (que)** in other words.
o/ *abrev de* **orden**.
oasis *m inv* lit & fig oasis.
obcecar *vt* to blind. ◆ **obcecarse** *vpr* to become stubborn; ~**se en hacer algo** to insist on doing sthg.
obedecer ◇ *vt*: ~ **(a alguien)** to obey (sb). ◇ *vi* **-1.** [acatar] to obey. **-2.** [someterse]: ~ **a** to respond to. **-3.** [estar motivado]: ~ **a** to be due to.
obediencia *f* obedience.
obediente *adj* obedient.
obertura *f* overture.
obesidad *f* obesity.
obeso, -sa *adj* obese.
óbice *m*: **no ser ~ para** not to be an obstacle to.
obispo *m* bishop.
objeción *f* objection; **poner objeciones a** to raise objections to; **tener objeciones** to have objections; ~ **de conciencia** conscientious objection.
objetar *vt* to object to; **no tengo nada que ~** I have no objection.
objetivo, -va *adj* objective. ◆ **objetivo** *m* **-1.** [finalidad] objective, aim. **-2.** MIL target. **-3.** FOT lens.
objeto *m* **-1.** [gen] object; **ser ~ de** to be the object of; ~**s de valor** valuables; ~**s perdidos** lost property (U). **-2.** [propósito] purpose, object; **sin ~** [inútilmente] to no purpose, pointlessly; **al** O **con ~ de** [para] in order to.
objetor, -ra *m y f* objector; ~ **de conciencia** conscientious objector.
oblicuo, -cua *adj* [inclinado] oblique; [mirada] sidelong.
obligación *f* **-1.** [gen] obligation, duty; **por ~** out of a sense of duty. **-2.** FIN (*gen pl*) bond, security.

obligar vt: ~ **a alguien (a hacer algo)** to oblige O force sb (to do sthg).
◆**obligarse** vpr: ~se **a hacer algo** to undertake to do sthg.
obligatorio, -ria adj obligatory, compulsory.
oboe m [instrumento] oboe.
obra f -1. [gen] work (U); **es ~ suya** it's his doing; **poner en ~** to put into effect; ~ **de caridad** [institución] charity; ~**s sociales** community work (U); **por ~ (y gracia) de** thanks to. -2. ARTE work (of art); TEATR play; LITER book; MÚS opus; ~ **maestra** masterpiece; ~**s completas** complete works. -3. CONSTR [lugar] building site; [reforma] alteration; "~**s**" [en carretera] "roadworks"; ~**s públicas** public works.
obrar ◇ vi -1. [actuar] to act. -2. [causar efecto] to work, to take effect. -3. [estar en poder]: ~ **en manos de** to be in the possession of. ◇ vt to work.
obrero, -ra ◇ adj [clase] working; [movimiento] labour (antes de sust). ◇ m y f [en fábrica] worker; [en obra] workman; ~ **cualificado** skilled worker.
obscenidad f obscenity.
obsceno, -na adj obscene.
obscurecer = oscurecer.
obscuridad = oscuridad.
obscuro, -ra = oscuro.
obsequiar vt: ~ **a alguien con algo** to present sb with sthg.
obsequio m gift, present.
observación f -1. [gen] observation. -2. [nota] note. -3. [cumplimiento] observance.
observador, -ra ◇ adj observant. ◇ m y f observer.
observar vt -1. [contemplar] to observe, to watch. -2. [advertir] to notice, to observe. -3. [acatar - ley, normas] to observe; [- conducta, costumbre] to follow. ◆**observarse** vpr to be noticed.
observatorio m observatory.
obsesión f obsession.
obsesionar vt to obsess. ◆**obsesionarse** vpr to be obsessed.
obsesivo, -va adj obsessive.
obseso, -sa ◇ adj obsessed. ◇ m y f obsessed O obsessive person.
obstaculizar vt to hinder, to hamper.
obstáculo m obstacle; **un ~ para an** obstacle to; **poner ~s a algo/alguien** to hinder sthg/sb.
obstante ◆**no obstante** loc adv nevertheless, however.
obstetricia f obstetrics (U).

obstinado, -da adj [persistente] persistent; [terco] obstinate, stubborn.
obstinarse vpr to refuse to give way; ~ **en** to persist in.
obstrucción f lit & fig obstruction.
obstruir vt -1. [bloquear] to block, to obstruct. -2. [obstaculizar] to obstruct, to impede. ◆**obstruirse** vpr to get blocked (up).
obtener vt [beca, cargo, puntos] to get; [premio, victoria] to win; [ganancias] to make; [satisfacción] to gain.
obturar vt to block.
obtuso, -sa adj -1. [sin punta] blunt. -2. fig [tonto] obtuse, stupid.
obús (pl obuses) m [proyectil] shell.
obviar vt to avoid, to get round.
obvio, -via adj obvious.
oca f [animal] goose.
ocasión f -1. [oportunidad] opportunity, chance. -2. [momento] moment, time; [vez] occasion; **en dos ocasiones** on two occasions; **en alguna ~** sometimes; **en cierta ~** once; **en otra ~** some other time. -3. [motivo]: **con ~ de** on the occasion of. -4. [ganga] bargain; **de ~** [precio, artículos etc] bargain (antes de sust).
ocasional adj -1. [accidental] accidental. -2. [irregular] occasional.
ocasionar vt to cause.
ocaso m -1. [puesta del sol] sunset. -2. fig [decadencia] decline.
occidental adj western.
occidente m west. ◆**Occidente** m [bloque de países] the West.
OCDE (abrev de **Organización para la Cooperación y el Desarrollo Económico**) f OECD.
Oceanía Oceania.
océano m ocean; fig [inmensidad] sea, host.
ochenta núm eighty; **los (años) ~** the eighties; ver también **seis**.
ocho núm eight; **de aquí en ~ días** [en una semana] a week today; ver también **seis**.
ochocientos, -tas núm eight hundred; ver también **seis**.
ocio m [tiempo libre] leisure; [inactividad] idleness.
ocioso, -sa adj -1. [inactivo] idle. -2. [innecesario] unnecessary; [inútil] pointless.
ocre ◇ m ochre. ◇ adj inv ochre.
octágono, -na adj octagonal. ◆**octágono** m octagon.
octano m octane.

octava *f* → octavo.

octavilla *f* **-1.** [de propaganda política] pamphlet, leaflet. **-2.** [tamaño] octavo.

octavo, -va *núm* eighth. ◆ **octavo** *m* [parte] eighth. ◆ **octava** *f* MÚS octave.

octeto *m* INFORM byte.

octogenario, -ria *adj, m y f* octogenarian.

octogésimo, -ma *núm* eightieth.

octubre *m* October; *ver también* **septiembre.**

ocular *adj* eye (*antes de sust*).

oculista *m y f* ophthalmologist.

ocultar *vt* **-1.** [gen] to hide. **-2.** *fig* [delito] to cover up. ◆ **ocultarse** *vpr* to hide.

oculto, -ta *adj* hidden.

ocupación *f* **-1.** [gen] occupation; ~ **ilegal de viviendas** squatting. **-2.** [empleo] job.

ocupado, -da *adj* **-1.** [persona] busy. **-2.** [teléfono, lavabo etc] engaged. **-3.** [lugar - gen, por ejército] occupied; [plaza] taken.

ocupante *m y f* occupant; ~ **ilegal de viviendas** squatter.

ocupar *vt* **-1.** [gen] to occupy. **-2.** [superficie, espacio] to take up; [habitación, piso] to live in; [mesa] to sit at; [sillón] to sit in. **-3.** [suj: actividad] to take up. **-4.** [cargo] to hold. **-5.** [dar trabajo a] to find O provide work for. ◆ **ocuparse** *vpr* [encargarse]: ~**se de** [gen] to deal with; [niños, enfermos, finanzas] to look after.

ocurrencia *f* **-1.** [idea] bright idea. **-2.** [dicho gracioso] witty remark.

ocurrir *vi* **-1.** [acontecer] to happen. **-2.** [pasar, preocupar]: **¿qué le ocurre a Juan?** what's up with Juan? ◆ **ocurrirse** *vpr* [venir a la cabeza]: **no se me ocurre ninguna solución** I can't think of a solution; **¡ni se te ocurra!** don't even think about it!; **se me ocurre que ... it** occurs to me that ....

odiar *vt & vi* to hate.

odio *m* hatred; **tener ~ a algo/alguien** to hate sthg/sb.

odioso, -sa *adj* hateful, horrible.

odontólogo, -ga *m y f* dentist, dental surgeon.

OEA (*abrev de* **Organización de Estados Americanos**) *f* OAS.

oeste ◇ *adj* [posición, parte] west, western; [dirección, viento] westerly. ◇ *m* west.

ofender *vt* [injuriar] to insult; [suj: palabras] to offend, to hurt. ◆ **ofenderse** *vpr*: ~**se (por)** to take offence (at).

ofensa *f* **-1.** [acción]: ~ **(a)** offence (against). **-2.** [injuria] slight, insult.

ofensivo, -va *adj* offensive. ◆ **ofensiva** *f* offensive.

oferta *f* **-1.** [gen] offer; "~**s de trabajo**" "situations vacant". **-2.** ECON [suministro] supply; **la ~ y la demanda** supply and demand; ~ **monetaria** money supply. **-3.** [rebaja] bargain, special offer; **de ~** bargain (*antes de sust*), on offer. **-4.** FIN [proposición] bid, tender; ~ **pública de adquisición** COM takeover bid.

ofertar *vt* to offer.

office ['ofis] *m inv* scullery.

oficial, -la *m y f* [obrero] journeyman; [aprendiz] trainee. ◆ **oficial** ◇ *adj* official. ◇ *m* **-1.** MIL officer. **-2.** [funcionario] clerk.

oficialismo *m Amer* [gobierno]: **el ~** the Government.

oficiar *vt* to officiate at.

oficina *f* office; ~ **de empleo** job centre; ~ **de turismo** tourist office.

oficinista *m y f* office worker.

oficio *m* **-1.** [profesión manual] trade; **de ~** by trade. **-2.** [trabajo] job. **-3.** [experiencia]: **tener mucho ~** to be very experienced. **-4.** RELIG service.

oficioso, -sa *adj* unofficial.

ofimática *f* office automation.

ofrecer *vt* **-1.** [gen] to offer; [una fiesta] to give, to throw; ~**le algo a alguien** to offer sb sthg. **-2.** [un aspecto] to present. ◆ **ofrecerse** *vpr* [presentarse] to offer, to volunteer; ~**se a** O **para hacer algo** to offer to do sthg.

ofrecimiento *m* offer.

ofrenda *f* RELIG offering; *fig* [por gratitud, amor] gift.

ofrendar *vt* to offer up.

oftalmología *f* ophthalmology.

ofuscar *vt* **-1.** [deslumbrar] to dazzle. **-2.** [turbar] to blind. ◆ **ofuscarse** *vpr*: ~**se (con)** to be blinded (by).

ogro *m* ogre.

oh *interj*: **¡~!** oh!

oídas ◆ de oídas *loc adv* by hearsay.

oído *m* **-1.** [órgano] ear; **de ~** by ear; **hacer ~s sordos** to turn a deaf ear. **-2.** [sentido] (sense of) hearing; **ser duro de ~** to be hard of hearing; **tener ~, tener buen ~** to have a good ear.

oír ◇ *vt* **-1.** [gen] to hear. **-2.** [atender] to listen to. ◇ *vi* to hear; **¡oiga, por favor!** excuse me!; **¡oye!** *fam* hey!

OIT (*abrev de* **Organización Internacional del Trabajo**) *f* ILO.

ojal *m* buttonhole.

ojalá *interj*: ¡~! if only (that were so)!; ¡~ **lo haga!** I hope she does it!; ¡~ **fuera ya domingo!** I wish it were Sunday!

ojeada *f* glance, look; **echar una ~ a algo/alguien** to take a quick glance at sthg/sb, to take a quick look at sthg/sb.

ojear *vt* to have a look at.

ojera *f* (*gen pl*) bags (*pl*) under the eyes.

ojeriza *f fam* dislike; **tener ~ a alguien** to have it in for sb.

ojeroso, -sa *adj* haggard.

ojo ◇ *m* -1. ANAT eye; ~s **saltones** popping eyes. -2. [agujero - de aguja] eye; [- de puente] span; ~ **de la cerradura** keyhole. -3. *loc*: **a ~ (de buen cubero)** roughly, approximately; **andar con (mucho) ~** to be (very) careful; **comerse con los ~s a alguien** *fam* to drool over sb; **echar el ~ a algo** to have one's eye on sthg; **en un abrir y cerrar de ~s** in the twinkling of an eye; **mirar algo con buenos/malos ~s** to look favourably/unfavourably on sthg; **no pegar ~** not to get a wink of sleep; **tener (buen) ~** to have a good eye. ◇ *interj*: ¡~! watch out!

OK, okey [o'kei] (*abrev de* **all correct**) *interj* OK.

okupa *m y f mfam* squatter.

ola *f* wave; ~ **de calor** heatwave; ~ **de frío** cold spell.

ole, olé *interj*: ¡~! bravo!

oleada *f* -1. [del mar] swell. -2. *fig* [abundancia] wave.

oleaje *m* swell.

óleo *m* oil (painting).

oleoducto *m* oil pipeline.

oler ◇ *vt* to smell. ◇ *vi* -1. [despedir olor]: ~ **(a)** to smell (of). -2. *fig* [parecer]: ~ **a** to smack of. ◆ **olerse** *vpr*: ~**se algo** *fig* to sense sthg.

olfatear *vt* -1. [olisquear] to sniff. -2. *fig* [barruntar] to smell, to sense. ◆ **olfatear en** *vi* [indagar] to pry into.

olfato *m* -1. [sentido] sense of smell. -2. *fig* [sagacidad] nose, instinct; **tener ~ para algo** to be a good judge of sthg.

oligarquía *f* oligarchy.

olimpiada, olimpíada *f* Olympic Games (*pl*); **las ~s** the Olympics.

olisquear *vt* to sniff (at).

oliva *f* olive.

olivar *m* olive grove.

olivera *f* olive tree.

olivo *m* olive tree.

olla *f* pot; ~ **exprés** O **a presión** pressure cooker; ~ **podrida** CULIN stew.

olmo *m* elm (tree).

olor *m* smell; ~ **a** smell of.

oloroso, -sa *adj* fragrant. ◆ **oloroso** *m* oloroso (sherry).

OLP (*abrev de* **Organización para la Liberación de Palestina**) *f* PLO.

olvidadizo, -za *adj* forgetful.

olvidar *vt* -1. [gen] to forget. -2. [dejarse] to leave; **olvidé las llaves en la oficina** I left my keys at the office. ◆ **olvidarse** *vpr* -1. [gen] to forget; ~**se de algo/hacer algo** to forget sthg/to do sthg. -2. [dejarse] to leave.

olvido *m* -1. [de un nombre, hecho etc] forgetting; **caer en el ~** to fall into oblivion. -2. [descuido] oversight.

ombligo *m* ANAT navel.

omisión *f* omission.

omitir *vt* to omit.

ómnibus *m inv* omnibus; FERROC local train.

omnipotente *adj* omnipotent.

omnívoro, -ra *adj* omnivorous.

omoplato, omóplato *m* shoulderblade.

OMS (*abrev de* **Organización Mundial de la Salud**) *f* WHO.

once *núm* eleven; *ver también* **seis**.

ONCE (*abrev de* **Organización Nacional de Ciegos Españoles**) *f Spanish association for the blind, famous for its national lottery*.

onceavo, -va *núm* eleventh.

onda *f* wave; ~ **corta/larga/media** short/long/medium wave; ~ **expansiva** shock wave; **estar en la ~** *fam* to be on the ball.

ondear *vi* to ripple.

ondulación *f* [acción] rippling.

ondulado, -da *adj* wavy.

ondular ◇ *vi* [agua] to ripple; [terreno] to undulate. ◇ *vt* to wave.

ónice, ónix *m o f* onyx.

onomástico, -ca *adj culto* onomastic. ◆ **onomástica** *f culto* name day.

ONU (*abrev de* **Organización de las Naciones Unidas**) *f* UN.

onza *f* [unidad de peso] ounce.

OPA *f* (*abrev de* **oferta pública de adquisición**) takeover bid.

opaco, -ca *adj* opaque.

ópalo *m* opal.

opción *f* -1. [elección] option; **no hay ~** there is no alternative. -2. [derecho] right; **dar ~ a** to give the right to; **te-**

ner ~ **a** [empleo, cargo] to be eligible for.

opcional *adj* optional.

OPEP (*abrev de* **Organización de Países Exportadores de Petróleo**) *f* OPEC.

ópera *f* opera; ~ **bufa** comic opera, opera buffa.

operación *f* **-1.** [gen] operation; ~ **quirúrgica** (surgical) operation; ~ **retorno** *police operation to assist return of holidaymakers to their city homes, minimizing traffic congestion and maximizing road safety.* **-2.** COM transaction.

operador, -ra *m y f* **-1.** INFORM & TELECOM operator. **-2.** [de la cámara] cameraman; [del proyector] projectionist. ◆ **operador** *m* MAT operator. ◆ **operador turístico** *m* tour operator.

operar ◇ *vt* **-1.** [enfermo: ~ **a alguien (de algo)** [enfermedad] to operate on sb (for sthg); **le operaron del hígado** they've operated on his liver. **-2.** [cambio etc] to bring about, to produce. ◇ *vi* **-1.** [gen] to operate. **-2.** [actuar] to act. **-3.** COM & FIN to deal. ◆ **operarse** *vpr* **-1.** [enfermo] to be operated on, to have an operation; **me voy a** ~ **del hígado** I'm going to have an operation on my liver. **-2.** [cambio etc] to occur.

operario, -ria *m y f* worker.

operativo, -va *adj* operative.

opereta *f* operetta.

opinar ◇ *vt* to believe, to think. ◇ *vi* to give one's opinion; ~ **de algo/alguien,** ~ **sobre algo/alguien** to think about sthg/sb.

opinión *f* [parecer] opinion; **expresar** O **dar una** ~ to give an opinion; **la** ~ **pública** public opinion.

opio *m* opium.

opíparo, -ra *adj* sumptuous.

oponente *m y f* opponent.

oponer *vt* **-1.** [resistencia] to put up. **-2.** [argumento, razón] to put forward, to give. ◆ **oponerse** *vpr* **-1.** [no estar de acuerdo] to be opposed; ~**se a algo** [desaprobar] to oppose sthg; [contradecir] to contradict sthg; **me opongo a creerlo** I refuse to believe it. **-2.** [obstaculizar]: ~**se a** to impede.

oporto *m* port (wine).

oportunidad *f* [ocasión] opportunity, chance.

oportunismo *m* opportunism.

oportunista *m y f* opportunist.

oportuno, -na *adj* **-1.** [pertinente] appropriate. **-2.** [propicio] timely; **el momento** ~ the right time.

oposición *f* **-1.** [gen] opposition. **-2.** [resistencia] resistance. **-3.** (*gen pl*) [examen] public entrance examination; ~ **a profesor** public examination to be a teacher; **preparar oposiciones** to be studying for a public entrance examination.

opositar *vi*: ~ **(a)** to sit a public entrance examination (for).

opositor, -ra *m y f* **-1.** [a un cargo] *candidate in a public entrance examination.* **-2.** [oponente] opponent.

opresión *f fig* [represión] oppression.

opresivo, -va *adj* oppressive.

opresor, -ra *m y f* oppressor.

oprimir *vt* **-1.** [apretar - botón etc] to press; [- garganta, brazo etc] to squeeze. **-2.** [suj: zapatos, cinturón] to pinch. **-3.** *fig* [reprimir] to oppress. **-4.** *fig* [angustiar] to weigh down on, to burden.

optar *vi* [escoger]: ~ **(por algo)** to choose (sthg); ~ **por hacer algo** to choose to do sthg; ~ **entre** to choose between.

optativo, -va *adj* optional.

óptico, -ca ◇ *adj* optic. ◇ *m y f* [persona] optician. ◆ **óptica** *f* **-1.** FÍS optics (U). **-2.** [tienda] optician's (shop). **-3.** *fig* [punto de vista] point of view.

optimismo *m* optimism.

optimista ◇ *adj* optimistic. ◇ *m y f* optimist.

óptimo, -ma ◇ *superl* → **bueno.** ◇ *adj* optimum.

opuesto, -ta ◇ *pp* → **oponer.** ◇ *adj* **-1.** [contrario] conflicting; ~ **a** opposed O contrary to. **-2.** [de enfrente] opposite.

opulencia *f* [riqueza] opulence; [abundancia] abundance.

opulento, -ta *adj* [rico] opulent.

opus *m* MÚS opus. ◆ **Opus Dei** *m*: **el Opus Dei** the Opus Dei, *traditionalist religious organization, the members of which are usually professional people or public figures.*

oración *f* **-1.** [rezo] prayer. **-2.** GRAM sentence; ~ **principal/subordinada** main/subordinate clause.

orador, -ra *m y f* speaker.

oral ◇ *adj* oral. ◇ *m* → **examen.**

órale *interj Amer fam*: ¡~! come on!

orangután *m* orangutang.

orar *vi* to pray.

órbita *f* **-1.** ASTRON orbit. **-2.** [de ojo] eye socket.

orca *f* killer whale.

orden ◇ *m* **-1.** [gen] order; **en** ~ [bien colocado] tidy, in its place; [como debe ser] in order; **por** ~ in order; **las fuerzas del** ~ the forces of law and order; ~ **público** law and order. **-2.** [tipo] type, order; **problemas de** ~ **económico** economic problems. ◇ *f* order; **por** ~ **de** by order of; **estar a la** ~ **del día** to be the order of the day. ◆ **del orden de** *loc prep* around, approximately. ◆ **orden del día** *m* agenda.

ordenado, -da *adj* [lugar, persona] tidy.

ordenador *m* INFORM computer; ~ **personal** personal computer; ~ **portátil** laptop computer.

ordenanza ◇ *m* [de oficina] messenger. ◇ *f* (*gen pl*) ordinance, law; ~**s municipales** by-laws.

ordenar *vt* **-1.** [poner en orden - gen] to arrange; [- habitación, armario etc] to tidy (up). **-2.** [mandar] to order. **-3.** RELIG to ordain. ◆ **ordenarse** *vpr* RELIG to be ordained.

ordeñar *vt* to milk.

ordinariez *f* commonness, coarseness; **decir/hacer una** ~ to say/do sthg rude.

ordinario, -ria *adj* **-1.** [común] ordinary, usual. **-2.** [vulgar] common, coarse. **-3.** [no selecto] unexceptional. **-4.** [no especial - presupuesto, correo] daily; [- tribunal] of first instance.

orégano *m* oregano.

oreja *f* ANAT ear.

orfanato, orfelinato *m* orphanage.

orfandad *f* orphanhood; *fig* abandonment.

orfebre *m y f* [de plata] silversmith; [de oro] goldsmith.

orfebrería *f* [obra - de plata] silver work; [- de oro] gold work.

orfelinato = **orfanato**.

orgánico, -ca *adj* organic.

organigrama *m* [gen & INFORM] flowchart.

organillo *m* barrel organ.

organismo *m* **-1.** BIOL organism. **-2.** ANAT body. **-3.** *fig* [entidad] organization, body.

organización *f* organization.

organizar *vt* to organize.

órgano *m* organ.

orgasmo *m* orgasm.

orgía *f* orgy.

orgullo *m* pride.

orgulloso, -sa *adj* proud.

orientación *f* **-1.** [dirección - acción] guiding; [- rumbo] direction. **-2.** [posicionamiento - acción] positioning; [- lugar] position. **-3.** *fig* [información] guid-

ance; ~ **profesional** careers advice ○ guidance.

oriental ◇ *adj* [gen] eastern; [del Lejano Oriente] oriental. ◇ *m y f* oriental.

orientar *vt* **-1.** [dirigir] to direct; [casa] to build facing. **-2.** *fig* [medidas etc]: ~ **hacia** to direct towards ○ at. **-3.** *fig* [aconsejar] to give advice ○ guidance to. ◆ **orientarse** *vpr* **-1.** [dirigirse - foco etc]: ~**se a** to point towards ○ at. **-2.** [encontrar el camino] to get one's bearings. **-3.** *fig* [encaminarse]: ~**se hacia** to be aiming at.

oriente *m* east. ◆ **Oriente** *m*: **el Oriente** the East, the Orient; **Oriente Medio/Próximo** Middle/Near East; **Lejano** ○ **Extremo Oriente** Far East.

orificio *m* hole; TECN opening.

origen *m* **-1.** [gen] origin; [ascendencia] origins (*pl*), birth; **de** ~ **español** of Spanish origin. **-2.** [causa] cause; **dar** ~ **a** to give rise to.

original ◇ *adj* **-1.** [gen] original. **-2.** [raro] eccentric, different. ◇ *m* original.

originalidad *f* **-1.** [gen] originality. **-2.** [extravagancia] eccentricity.

originar *vt* to cause. ◆ **originarse** *vpr* to be caused.

originario, -ria *adj* **-1.** [inicial, primitivo] original. **-2.** [procedente]: **ser** ~ **de** [costumbres etc] to come from (originally); [persona] to be a native of.

orilla *f* **-1.** [ribera - de río] bank; [- de mar] shore; **a** ~**s del mar** by the sea. **-2.** [borde] edge. **-3.** [acera] pavement.

orillar *vt* [dificultad, obstáculo] to skirt around.

orín *m* [herrumbre] rust. ◆ **orines** *mpl* [orina] urine (*U*).

orina *f* urine.

orinal *m* chamberpot.

orinar *vi & vt* to urinate. ◆ **orinarse** *vpr* to wet o.s.

oriundo, -da *adj*: ~ **de** native of.

ornamentación *f* ornamentation.

ornamento *m* [objeto] ornament.

ornar *vt* to decorate, to adorn.

ornitología *f* ornithology.

oro *m* gold; *fig* riches (*pl*); **hacerse de** ~ to make one's fortune; **pedir el** ~ **y el moro** to ask the earth. ◆ **oros** *mpl* [naipes] *suit of Spanish cards bearing gold coins*. ◆ **oro negro** *m* oil.

orografía *f* [relieve] terrain.

orquesta *f* **-1.** [músicos] orchestra. **-2.** [lugar] orchestra pit.

orquestar *vt* to orchestrate.

orquestina *f* dance band.

orquídea f orchid.

ortiga f (stinging) nettle.

ortodoxia f orthodoxy.

ortodoxo, -xa adj orthodox.

ortografía f spelling.

ortográfico, -ca adj spelling (antes de sust).

ortopedia f orthopaedics (U).

ortopédico, -ca adj orthopaedic.

ortopedista m y f orthopaedist.

oruga f caterpillar.

orujo m strong spirit made from grape pressings.

orzuelo m stye.

os pron pers **-1.** (complemento directo) you; **me gustaría veros** I'd like to see you. **-2.** (complemento indirecto) (to) you; ~ **lo dio** he gave it to you; ~ **tengo miedo** I'm afraid of you. **-3.** (reflexivo) yourselves. **-4.** (recíproco) each other; ~ **enamorasteis** you fell in love (with each other).

osadía f **-1.** [valor] boldness, daring. **-2.** [descaro] audacity, cheek.

osado, -da adj **-1.** [valeroso] daring, bold. **-2.** [descarado] impudent, cheeky.

osamenta f skeleton.

osar vi to dare.

oscilación f **-1.** [movimiento] swinging; FÍS oscillation. **-2.** fig [variación] fluctuation.

oscilar vi **-1.** [moverse] to swing; FÍS to oscillate. **-2.** fig [variar] to fluctuate.

oscurecer ◇ vt **-1.** [privar de luz] to darken. **-2.** fig [mente] to confuse, to cloud. ◇ v impers [anochecer] to get dark. ◆ **oscurecerse** vpr to grow dark.

oscuridad f **-1.** [falta de luz] darkness. **-2.** [zona oscura]: **en la** ~ in the dark. **-3.** fig [falta de claridad] obscurity.

oscuro, -ra adj **-1.** [gen] dark; **a oscuras** in the dark. **-2.** [nublado] overcast. **-3.** fig [inusual] obscure. **-4.** fig [intenciones, asunto] shady.

óseo, -a adj bone (antes de sust).

Oslo Oslo.

oso, osa m y f bear (f she-bear); ~ **de felpa** O **peluche** teddy bear; ~ **hormiguero** ant-eater; ~ **panda** panda; ~ **polar** polar bear.

ostensible adj evident, clear.

ostentación f ostentation, show.

ostentar vt [poseer] to hold, to have.

ostentoso, -sa adj ostentatious.

osteópata m y f osteopath.

ostra f oyster; **aburrirse como una** ~ fam to be bored to death. ◆ **ostras** interj fam: ¡~s! blimey!

OTAN (abrev de **Organización del Tratado del Atlántico Norte**) f NATO.

OTI (abrev de **Organización de Televisiones Iberoamericanas**) f association of all Spanish-speaking television networks.

otitis f inv inflammation of the ear.

otoñal adj autumn Br (antes de sust), autumnal Br, fall Am (antes de sust).

otoño m lit & fig autumn Br, fall Am.

otorgar vt to grant; [premio] to award, to present; DER to execute.

otorrino, -na m y f fam ear, nose and throat specialist.

otorrinolaringología f ear, nose and throat medicine.

otro, -tra ◇ adj **-1.** [distinto] (sg) another, (pl) other; ~ **chico** another boy; **el** ~ **chico** the other boy; **(los)** ~s **chicos** (the) other boys; **no hacer otra cosa que llorar** to do nothing but cry; **el** ~ **día** [pasado] the other day. **-2.** [nuevo] another; **estamos ante** ~ **Dalí** this is another Dali; ~s **tres goles** another three goals. ◇ pron (sg) another (one), (pl) others; **dame** ~ give me another (one); **el** ~ the other one; **(los)** ~s (the) others; **yo no lo hice, fue** ~ it wasn't me, it was somebody else; ~ **habría abandonado, pero no él** anyone else would have given up, but not him; ¡**otra!** [en conciertos] encore!

output ['autput] (pl **outputs**) m INFORM output (U).

ovación f ovation.

ovacionar vt to give an ovation to.

oval adj oval.

ovalado, -da adj oval.

ovario m ovary.

oveja f sheep, ewe. ◆ **oveja negra** f black sheep.

ovillo m ball (of wool etc); **hacerse un** ~ to curl up into a ball.

ovino, -na adj ovine, sheep (antes de sust).

ovni ['ofni] m (abrev de **objeto volador no identificado**) UFO.

ovulación f ovulation.

ovular ◇ adj ovular. ◇ vi to ovulate.

oxidación f rusting.

oxidar vt to rust; QUÍM to oxidize. ◆ **oxidarse** vpr to get rusty.

óxido m **-1.** QUÍM oxide. **-2.** [herrumbre] rust.

oxigenado, -da adj **-1.** QUÍM oxygenated. **-2.** [cabello] peroxide (antes de sust), bleached.

oxigenar vt QUÍM to oxygenate. ◆ **oxi-**

genarse *vpr* [airearse] to get a breath of fresh air.

oxígeno *m* oxygen.

oye → **oír**.

oyente *m y f* **-1.** RADIO listener. **-2.** [alumno] unregistered student.

ozono *m* ozone.

P

p, P *f* [letra] p, P.

p. -1. = pág. **-2.** *abrev de* paseo.

pabellón *m* **-1.** [edificio] pavilion. **-2.** [parte de un edificio] block, section. **-3.** [en parques, jardines] summerhouse. **-4.** [tienda de campaña] bell tent. **-5.** [bandera] flag.

pábilo *m* wick.

PAC (*abrev de* **política agrícola común**) *f* CAP.

pacer *vi* to graze.

pachá (*pl* **pachaes**) *m* pasha; **vivir como un ~** *fam* to live like a lord.

pachanga *f fam* rowdy celebration.

pacharán *m liqueur made from brandy and sloes.*

pachorra *f fam* calmness.

pachucho, -cha *adj fam* off-colour.

paciencia *f* patience; **perder la ~** to lose one's patience.

paciente *adj, m y f* patient.

pacificación *f* pacification.

pacificar *vt* **-1.** [país] to pacify. **-2.** [ánimos] to calm.

pacífico, -ca *adj* [gen] peaceful; [persona] peaceable.

Pacífico *m*: **el (océano) ~** the Pacific (Ocean).

pacifismo *m* pacifism.

pacifista *adj, m y f* pacifist.

paco, -ca *m y f Amer fam* cop.

pacotilla *f*: **de ~** trashy, third-rate.

pactar ◇ *vt* to agree to. ◇ *vi*: **~ (con)** to strike a deal (with).

pacto *m* [gen] agreement, pact; [entre países] treaty.

padecer ◇ *vt* to suffer, to endure; [enfermedad] to suffer from. ◇ *vi* to suffer; [enfermedad] **~ de** to suffer from.

padecimiento *m* suffering.

padrastro *m* **-1.** [pariente] stepfather. **-2.** [pellejo] hangnail.

padre ◇ *m* [gen & RELIG] father. ◇ *adj inv fam* incredible. ◆ **padres** *mpl* [padre y madre] parents.

padrenuestro (*pl* **padrenuestros**) *m* Lord's Prayer.

padrino *m* **-1.** [de bautismo] godfather; [de boda] best man. **-2.** [en duelos, torneos etc] second. **-3.** *fig* [protector] patron. ◆ **padrinos** *mpl* [padrino y madrina] godparents.

padrísimo *adj Amer fam* fantastic, great.

padrón *m* [censo] census; [para votar] electoral roll ο register.

padrote *m Amer fam* pimp.

paella *f* paella.

paellera *f large frying-pan or earthenware dish for cooking paella.*

pág., p. (*abrev de* **página**) p.

paga *f* payment; [salario] salary, wages (*pl*); [de niño] pocket money; **~ extra** ο **extraordinaria** *bonus paid twice a year to Spanish workers.*

pagadero, -ra *adj* payable; **~ a 90 días/a la entrega** payable within 90 days/on delivery.

pagano, -na *adj, m y f* pagan, heathen.

pagar ◇ *vt* [gen] to pay; [deuda] to pay off, to settle; [ronda, gastos, delito] to pay for; [ayuda, favor] to repay; **me las pagarás** *fam* you'll pay for this. ◇ *vi* to pay.

pagaré (*pl* **pagarés**) *m* COM promissory note, IOU; **~ del Tesoro** Treasury note.

página *f* page; **las ~s amarillas** the Yellow Pages.

pago *m* payment; *fig* reward, payment; **en ~ de** [en recompensa por] as a reward for; [a cambio de] in return for; **~ anticipado/inicial** advance/down payment. ◆ **pagos** *mpl* [lugar]: **por estos ~s** around here.

paila *f Amer* **-1.** [sartén] frying pan. **-2.** [huevos fritos] fried eggs (*pl*).

país *m* country; **los ~es bálticos** the Baltic States.

paisaje *m* [gen] landscape; [vista panorámica] scenery (*U*), view.

paisano, -na *m y f* [del mismo país] compatriot. ◆ **paisano** *m* [civil] civilian; **de ~** MIL in civilian clothes; **de ~** [policía] in plain clothes.

Países Bajos *mpl*: **los ~** the Netherlands.

País Vasco *m*: el ~ the Basque Country.

paja *f* **-1.** [gen] straw. **-2.** *fig* [relleno] waffle. **-3.** *vulg* [masturbación] wank.

pajar *m* straw loft.

pájara *f fig* crafty ○ sly woman.

pajarería *f* pet shop.

pajarita *f* [corbata] bow tie.

pájaro *m* ZOOL bird; ~ **bobo** penguin; ~ **carpintero** woodpecker; ~ **de mal agüero** bird of ill omen; **más vale** ~ **en mano que ciento volando** *proverb* a bird in the hand is worth two in the bush; **matar dos** ~**s de un tiro** to kill two birds with one stone; **tener** ~**s en la cabeza** to be scatterbrained ○ empty-headed.

paje *m* page.

pajilla, pajita *f* (drinking) straw.

Pakistán, Paquistán Pakistan.

pala *f* **-1.** [herramienta] spade; [para recoger] shovel; CULIN slice; ~ **mecánica** ○ **excavadora** excavator, digger. **-2.** [de frontón, ping-pong] bat. **-3.** [de remo, hélice] blade.

palabra *f* **-1.** [gen] word; **de** ~ by word of mouth; **no tener** ~ to go back on one's word; **tomar** ○ **coger la** ~ a alguien to hold sb to their word; ~ **de honor** word of honour. **-2.** [habla] speech. **-3.** [derecho de hablar] right to speak; **dar la** ~ a alguien to give the floor to sb. **-4.** *loc*: **en una** ~ in a word. ◆ **palabras** *fpl* [discurso] words.

palabrería *f fam* hot air.

palabrota *f* swearword; **decir** ~**s** to swear.

palacete *m* mansion, small palace.

palacio *m* palace; ~ **de congresos** conference centre.

palada *f* **-1.** [al cavar] spadeful, shovelful. **-2.** [de remo] stroke.

paladar *m* palate.

paladear *vt* to savour.

palanca *f* [barra, mando] lever; ~ **de cambio** gear lever ○ stick, gearshift *Am*; ~ **de mando** joystick.

palangana *f* [para fregar] washing-up bowl; [para lavarse] wash bowl.

palco *m* box (*at theatre*).

Palestina Palestine.

palestino, -na *adj*, *m y f* Palestinian.

paleta *f* [gen] small shovel, small spade; [llana] trowel; CULIN slice; ARTE palette.

paletilla *f* shoulder blade.

paleto, -ta ◇ *adj* coarse, uncouth. ◇ *m y f* yokel, hick *Am*.

paliar *vt* **-1.** [atenuar] to ease, to relieve. **-2.** [disculpar] to excuse, to justify.

palidecer *vi* [ponerse pálido] to go ○ turn pale.

palidez *f* paleness.

pálido, -da *adj* pale; *fig* dull.

palillero *m* toothpick holder.

palillo *m* **-1.** [mondadientes] toothpick. **-2.** [baqueta] drumstick. **-3.** [para comida china] chopstick.

palique *m fam* chat, natter; **estar de** ~ to have a chat ○ a natter.

paliza *f* **-1.** [golpes, derrota] beating. **-2.** [esfuerzo] hard grind.

palma *f* **-1.** [de mano] palm. **-2.** [palmera] palm (tree); [hoja de palmera] palm leaf. ◆ **palmas** *fpl* [aplausos] applause (*U*); **batir** ~**s** to clap (one's hands).

palmada *f* **-1.** [golpe] pat; [más fuerte] slap. **-2.** [aplauso] clap; ~**s** clapping (*U*).

palmar¹ *m* palm grove.

palmar² *fam vi* to kick the bucket.

palmarés *m* **-1.** [historial] record. **-2.** [lista] list, roll.

palmear *vi* to clap, to applaud.

palmera *f* [árbol] palm (tree); [datilera] date palm.

palmito *m* **-1.** [árbol] palmetto, fan palm. **-2.** CULIN palm heart.

palmo *m* handspan; *fig* small amount; ~ **a** ~ bit by bit; **dejar a alguien con un** ~ **de narices** to let sb down.

palmotear *vi* to clap.

palo *m* **-1.** [gen] stick; [de golf] club; [de portería] post; [de la escoba] handle. **-2.** [mástil] mast. **-3.** [golpe] blow (*with a stick*). **-4.** [de baraja] suit. **-5.** *fig* [pesadez] bind, drag. **-6.** *loc*: **a** ~ **seco** [gen] without anything else; [bebida] neat.

paloma → **palomo**.

palomar *m* dovecote; [grande] pigeon shed.

palomilla *f* **-1.** [insecto] grain moth. **-2.** [tornillo] wing nut. **-3.** [soporte] bracket.

palomita *f*: ~**s** popcorn (*U*).

palomo, -ma *m y f* dove, pigeon; **paloma mensajera** carrier ○ homing pigeon.

palpable *adj* touchable, palpable; *fig* obvious, clear.

palpar ◇ *vt* **-1.** [tocar] to feel, to touch; MED to palpate. **-2.** *fig* [percibir] to feel. ◇ *vi* to feel around.

palpitación *f* beat, beating (*U*); [con fuerza] throb, throbbing (*U*). ◆ **palpitaciones** *fpl* MED palpitations.

palpitante *adj* **-1.** [que palpita] beating; [con fuerza] throbbing. **-2.** *fig* [interesante - interés, deseo, cuestión] burning.

palpitar *vi* [latir] to beat; [con fuerza] to throb.

palta *f Amer* avocado.

paludismo *m* malaria.

palurdo, -da *m y f* yokel, hick *Am.*

pamela *f* sun hat.

pampa *f*: la ~ the pampas (*pl*).

pamplina *f* (*gen pl*) *fam* trifle, unimportant thing.

pan *m* **-1.** [alimento] bread; ~ **de molde** O **inglés** sliced bread; ~ **integral** wholemeal bread; ~ **moreno** O **negro** [integral] brown bread; ~ **rallado** breadcrumbs (*pl*). **-2.** [hogaza] loaf. **-3.** *loc*: **contigo** ~ **y cebolla** I'll go through thick and thin with you; **llamar al** ~ ~ **y al vino vino** to call a spade a spade; **ser** ~ **comido** to be a piece of cake; **ser el** ~ **nuestro de cada día** to be commonplace; **ser más bueno que el** ~ to be kindness itself.

pana *f* corduroy.

panacea *f lit & fig* panacea.

panadería *f* bakery, baker's.

panadero, -ra *m y f* baker.

panal *m* honeycomb.

Panamá Panama.

panameño, -ña *adj, m y f* Panamanian.

pancarta *f* placard, banner.

panceta *f* bacon.

pancho, -cha *adj fam* calm, unruffled; **estar/quedarse tan** ~ to be/remain perfectly calm.

páncreas *m inv* pancreas.

panda ◇ *m* → **oso.** ◇ *f* gang.

pandemónium (*pl* **pandemóniums**) *m* pandemonium.

pandereta *f* tambourine.

pandero *m* MÚS tambourine.

pandilla *f* gang.

panecillo *m* bread roll.

panegírico, -ca *adj* panegyrical. ◆ **panegírico** *m* panegyric.

panel *m* **-1.** [gen] panel. **-2.** [pared, biombo] screen. **-3.** [tablero] board.

panera *f* bread basket.

pánfilo, -la *adj* simple, foolish.

panfleto *m* pamphlet.

pánico *m* panic.

panificadora *f* (large) bakery.

panocha *f* ear, cob.

panorama *m* **-1.** [vista] panorama. **-2.** *fig* [situación] overall state; [perspectiva] outlook.

panorámico, -ca *adj* panoramic. ◆ **panorámica** *f* panorama.

pantaletas *fpl Amer* knickers.

pantalla *f* **-1.** [gen & INFORM] screen; ~ **de cristal líquido** liquid crystal display; **la pequeña** ~ the small screen, television. **-2.** [de lámpara] lampshade.

pantalón *m* (*gen pl*) trousers (*pl*), pants (*pl*) *Am*; ~ **tejano** O **vaquero** jeans (*pl*); ~ **pitillo** drainpipe trousers (*pl*).

pantano *m* **-1.** [ciénaga] marsh; [laguna] swamp. **-2.** [embalse] reservoir.

pantanoso, -sa *adj* **-1.** [cenagoso] marshy, boggy. **-2.** *fig* [difícil] tricky.

panteón *m* pantheon; [familiar] mausoleum, vault.

pantera *f* panther.

pantimedias *fpl Amer* tights.

pantorrilla *f* calf.

pantufla *f* (*gen pl*) slipper.

panty (*pl* **pantys**) *m* tights (*pl*).

panza *f* belly.

panzada *f fam* [hartura] bellyful.

pañal *m* nappy *Br*, diaper *Am*; **estar en** ~**es** [en sus inicios] to be in its infancy; [sin conocimientos] not to have a clue.

pañería *f* [producto] drapery; [tienda] draper's (shop), dry-goods store *Am.*

paño *m* **-1.** [tela] cloth, material. **-2.** [trapo] cloth; [para polvo] duster; [de cocina] tea towel. **-3.** [lienzo] panel. ◆ **paños** *mpl* [vestiduras] drapes; ~**s menores** underwear (*U*).

pañoleta *f* shawl, wrap.

pañuelo *m* [de nariz] handkerchief; [para el cuello] scarf; [para la cabeza] headscarf; ~ **de papel** paper handkerchief, tissue.

papa *f* potato; **no saber ni** ~ *fam* not to have a clue. ◆ **Papa** *m* Pope.

papá *m fam* dad, daddy, pop *Am.* ◆ **Papá Noel** *m* Father Christmas.

papachador, -ra *adj Amer* comforting.

papachar *vt Amer* to spoil.

papada *f* [de persona] double chin; [de animal] dewlap.

papagayo *m* parrot.

papalote *m Amer* [cometa] kite.

papamoscas *m inv* flycatcher.

papanatas *m y f inv fam* sucker.

papaya *f* [fruta] papaya, pawpaw.

papel *m* **-1.** [gen] paper; [hoja] sheet of paper; ~ **celofán** Cellophane, cellophane; ~ **continuo** INFORM continuous paper; ~ **de embalar** O **de embalaje** wrapping paper; ~ **de estaño** O **de aluminio** O **de plata** tin O aluminium foil; ~ **de fumar**

cigarette paper; ~ **de lija** sandpaper; ~ **higiénico** toilet paper; ~ **madera** *Amer* cardboard; ~ **milimetrado** graph paper; ~ **pintado** wallpaper. **-2.** CIN, TEATR & *fig* role, part; ~ **principal/ secundario** main/minor part; **hacer buen/mal** ~ to do well/badly. **-3.** FIN stocks and shares (*pl*); ~ **moneda** paper money. ◆ **papeles** *mpl* [documentos] papers.

papeleo *m* paperwork, red tape.

papelera → papelero.

papelería *f* stationer's (shop).

papelero, -ra *adj* paper (*antes de sust*). ◆ **papelera** *f* [cesto - en oficina etc] wastepaper basket ○ bin; [- en la calle] litter bin.

papeleta *f* **-1.** [boleto] ticket, slip (of paper); [de votación] ballot paper. **-2.** EDUC *slip of paper with university exam results*.

paperas *fpl* mumps.

papi *m fam* daddy, dad.

papilla *f* [para niños] baby food; **hecho** ~ [cansado] shattered; [roto] smashed to bits.

papiro *m* papyrus.

paquete *m* **-1.** [de libros, regalos etc] parcel; ~ **bomba** parcel bomb; ~ **postal** parcel. **-2.** [de cigarrillos, klínex, folios etc] pack, packet; [de azúcar, arroz] bag. **-3.** [de medidas] package; ~ **turístico** package tour. **-4.** INFORM package.

Paquistán = Pakistán.

par ◇ *adj* **-1.** MAT even. **-2.** [igual] equal. ◇ *m* **-1.** [pareja - de zapatos etc] pair. **-2.** [dos - veces etc] couple. **-3.** [número indeterminado] few, couple; **un** ~ **de copas** a couple of ○ a few drinks. **-4.** [en golf] par. **-5.** [noble] peer. ◆ **a la par** *loc adv* **-1.** [simultáneamente] at the same time. **-2.** [a igual nivel] at the same level. ◆ **de par en par** *loc adj:* **abierto de** ~ **en** ~ wide open. ◆ **sin par** *loc adj* matchless.

para *prep* **-1.** [finalidad] for; **es** ~ **ti** it's for you; **una mesa** ~ **el salón** a table for the living room; **esta agua no es buena** ~ **beber** this water isn't fit for drinking ○ to drink; **te lo repetiré** ~ **que te enteres** I'll repeat it so you understand; **¿**~ **qué?** what for? **-2.** [motivación] (in order) to; ~ **conseguir sus propósitos** in order to achieve his aims; **lo he hecho** ~ **agradarte** I did it to please you. **-3.** [dirección] towards; **ir** ~ **casa** to head (for) home; **salir** ~ **el aeropuerto** to leave for the airport. **-4.**

[tiempo] for; **tiene que estar acabado** ~ **mañana** it has to be finished by ○ for tomorrow. **-5.** [comparación]: **está muy delgado** ~ **lo que come** he's very thin considering how much he eats; ~ **ser verano hace mucho frío** considering it's summer, it's very cold. **-6.** (*después de adj y antes de infin*) [inminencia, propósito] to; **la comida está lista** ~ **servir** the meal is ready to be served; **el atleta está preparado** ~ **ganar** the athlete is ready to win. ◆ **para con** *loc prep* towards; **es buena** ~ **con los demás** she is kind towards other people.

parabién (*pl* parabienes) *m* congratulations (*pl*).

parábola *f* **-1.** [alegoría] parable. **-2.** GEOM parabola.

parabólico, -ca *adj* parabolic.

parabrisas *m inv* windscreen, windshield *Am*.

paracaídas *m inv* parachute.

paracaidista *m y f* parachutist; MIL paratrooper.

parachoques *m inv* AUTOM bumper, fender *Am*; FERROC buffer.

parada → parado.

paradero *m* **-1.** [de persona] whereabouts (*pl*). **-2.** *Amer* [parada de autobús] bus stop.

paradisiaco, -ca, paradisíaco, -ca *adj* heavenly.

parado, -da ◇ *adj* **-1.** [inmóvil - coche] stationary, standing; [- persona] still, motionless; [- fábrica, proyecto] at a standstill. **-2.** *fam* [sin empleo] unemployed. **-3.** *loc:* **salir bien/mal** ~ **de algo** to come off well/badly out of sthg. ◇ *m y f fam* [desempleado] unemployed person; **los** ~**s** the unemployed. ◆ **parada** *f* **-1.** [detención] stop, stopping (*U*). **-2.** DEP save. **-3.** [de autobús] (bus) stop; [de taxis] taxi rank; [de metro] (underground) station; **parada discrecional** request stop. **-4.** MIL parade.

paradoja *f* paradox.

paradójico, -ca *adj* paradoxical, ironical.

parador *m* **-1.** [mesón] roadside inn. **-2.** [hotel]: ~ **(nacional)** *state-owned luxury hotel, usually a building of historic or artistic importance.*

parafernalia *f* paraphernalia.

parafrasear *vt* to paraphrase.

paráfrasis *f inv* paraphrase.

paraguas *m inv* umbrella.

Paraguay: (el) ~ Paraguay.

paraguayo, -ya *adj, m y f* Paraguayan.

paragüero *m* umbrella stand.

paraíso *m* RELIG Paradise; *fig* paradise.

paraje *m* spot, place.

paralelismo *m* **-1.** GEOM parallelism. **-2.** [semejanza] similarity, parallels (*pl*).

paralelo, -la *adj*: ~ **(a)** parallel (to). ◆ **paralelo** *m* GEOGR parallel. ◆ **paralela** *f* GEOM parallel (line).

parálisis *f inv* paralysis; ~ **cerebral** cerebral palsy.

paralítico, -ca *adj, m y f* paralytic.

paralizar *vt* to paralyse. ◆ **paralizarse** *vpr* to become paralysed; [producción etc] to come to a standstill.

parámetro *m* parameter.

páramo *m* moor, moorland (*U*); *fig* wilderness.

parangón *m* paragon; **sin** ~ unparalleled.

paranoia *f* paranoia.

paranormal *adj* paranormal.

parapente *m* parapente, paraskiing.

parapetarse *vpr lit & fig*: ~ **(tras)** to take refuge (behind).

parapeto *m* [antepecho] parapet; [barandilla] bannister; [barricada] barricade.

parapléjico, -ca *adj, m y f* paraplegic.

parapsicología *f* parapsychology.

parar ◇ *vi* **-1.** [gen] to stop; ~ **de hacer algo** to stop doing sthg; **sin** ~ nonstop. **-2.** [alojarse] to stay. **-3.** [recaer]: ~ **en manos de alguien** to come into the possession of sb. **-4.** [acabar] to end up; **¿en qué parará este lío?** where will it all end? ◇ *vt* **-1.** [gen] to stop; [golpe] to parry. **-2.** [preparar] to prepare. **-3.** *Amer* [levantar] to raise. ◆ **pararse** *vpr* **-1.** [detenerse] to stop. **-2.** *Amer* [ponerse de pie] to stand up.

pararrayos *m inv* lightning conductor.

parásito, -ta *adj* BIOL parasitic. ◆ **parásito** *m* BIOL & *fig* parasite. ◆ **parásitos** *mpl* [interferencias] statics (*pl*).

parasol *m* parasol.

parcela *f* plot (of land).

parche *m* **-1.** [gen] patch. **-2.** [chapuza - para salir del paso] makeshift solution.

parchís *m inv* ludo.

parcial ◇ *adj* **-1.** [no total] partial. **-2.** [no ecuánime] biased. ◇ *m* [examen] end-of-term exam at university.

parcialidad *f* **-1.** [tendenciosidad] bias, partiality. **-2.** [bando] faction.

parco, -ca *adj* [escaso] meagre; [cena] frugal; [explicación] brief, concise.

pardillo, -lla ◇ *adj* **-1.** [ingenuo] naive. **-2.** [palurdo] countrified. ◇ *m y f* **-1.** [in-genuo] naive person. **-2.** [palurdo] bumpkin.

pardo, -da *adj* greyish-brown, dull brown.

parecer ◇ *m* **-1.** [opinión] opinion. **-2.** [apariencia]: **de buen** ~ good-looking. ◇ *vi* (*antes de sust*) to look like; **parece un palacio** it looks like a palace. ◇ *v copulativo* to look, to seem; **pareces cansado** you look ○ seem tired. ◇ *v impers* **-1.** [opinar]: **me parece que ...** I think ○ it seems to me that ...; **me parece que sí/no** I think/don't think so; **¿qué te parece?** what do you think (of it)? **-2.** [tener aspecto de]: **parece que va a llover** it looks like it's going to rain; **parece que le gusta** it looks as if ○ it seems that she likes it; **eso parece** so it seems; **al** ~ apparently. ◆ **parecerse** *vpr*: ~**se (en)** to be alike (in); ~**se a alguien** [físicamente] to look like sb; [en carácter] to be like sb.

parecido, -da *adj* similar; **bien** ~ [atractivo] good-looking. ◆ **parecido** *m*: ~ **(con/entre)** resemblance (to/between).

pared *f* **-1.** [gen] wall; **las** ~**es oyen** walls have ears; **subirse por las** ~**es** to hit the roof. **-2.** [de montaña] side.

paredón *m* [thick] wall; [de fusilamiento] (execution) wall.

parejo, -ja *adj*: ~ **(a)** similar (to). ◆ **pareja** *f* **-1.** [gen] pair; [de novios] couple; **por parejas** in pairs. **-2.** [miembro del par - persona] partner; **la pareja de este calcetín** the other sock of this pair.

parentela *f* relations (*pl*), family.

parentesco *m* relationship.

paréntesis *m inv* **-1.** [signo] bracket; **entre** ~ in brackets, in parentheses. **-2.** [intercalación] digression. **-3.** [interrupción] break.

paria *m y f* pariah.

parida *f fam* tripe (*U*), nonsense (*U*).

pariente, -ta *m y f* [familiar] relation, relative.

parir ◇ *vi* to give birth. ◇ *vt* to give birth to.

París Paris.

parking ['parkin] (*pl* **parkings**) *m* car park, parking lot *Am*.

parlamentar *vi* to negotiate.

parlamentario, -ria ◇ *adj* parliamentary. ◇ *m y f* member of parliament.

parlamento *m* POLÍT parliament.

parlanchín, -ina ◇ *adj* talkative. ◇ *m y f* chatterbox.

parlante *adj* talking.

parlotear *vi fam* to chatter.

paro *m* **-1.** [desempleo] unemployment. **-2.** [cesación - acción] shutdown; [- estado] stoppage; ~ **cardiaco** cardiac arrest.

parodia *f* parody.

parodiar *vt* to parody.

parpadear *vi* **-1.** [pestañear] to blink. **-2.** [centellear] to flicker.

párpado *m* eyelid.

parque *m* **-1.** [gen] park; ~ **acuático** waterpark; ~ **de atracciones** amusement park; ~ **nacional** national park; ~ **tecnológico** science park; (~) **zoológico** zoo. **-2.** [vehículos] fleet; ~ **de bomberos** fire station. **-3.** [para niños] playpen.

parqué (*pl* **parqués**), **parquet** [par'ke] (*pl* **parquets**) *m* parquet (floor).

parqueadero *m Amer* car park.

parquear *vt Amer* to park.

parquet = **parqué**.

parquímetro *m* parking meter.

parra *f* grapevine.

parrafada *f* earful, dull monologue.

párrafo *m* paragraph.

parranda *f fam* [juerga]: **irse de** ~ to go out on the town.

parrilla *f* [utensilio] grill; **a la** ~ grilled.

parrillada *f* mixed grill.

párroco *m* parish priest.

parroquia *f* **-1.** [iglesia] parish church. **-2.** [jurisdicción] parish. **-3.** [clientela] clientele.

parroquiano, -na *m y f* **-1.** [feligrés] parishioner. **-2.** [cliente] customer.

parsimonia *f* deliberation; **con** ~ unhurriedly.

parte ◇ *m* report; **dar** ~ **(a alguien de algo)** to report (sthg to sb); ~ **facultativo** O **médico** medical report; ~ **meteorológico** weather forecast. ◇ *f* [gen] part; [bando] side; DER party; **la mayor** ~ **de la gente** most people; **la tercera** ~ **de a** third of; **en alguna** ~ somewhere; **no lo veo por ninguna** ~ I can't find it anywhere; **en** ~ to a certain extent, partly; **estar/ponerse de** ~ **de alguien** to be on/to take sb's side; **por mi** ~ for my part; **por** ~ **de padre/madre** on one's father's/ mother's side; **por** ~**s** bit by bit; **por una** ~ ... **por la otra** ... on the one hand ... on the other (hand) ...; **tomar** ~ **en algo** to take part in sthg. ◆ **de parte de** *loc prep* on behalf of, for; **¿de** ~ **de (quién)?** TELECOM who is calling,

please? ◆ **por otra parte** *loc adv* [además] what is more, besides.

partera *f* midwife.

parterre *m* flowerbed.

partición *f* [reparto] sharing out; [de territorio] partitioning.

participación *f* **-1.** [colaboración] participation. **-2.** [de lotería] share of a lottery ticket. **-3.** [comunicación] notice.

participante *m y f* participant.

participar ◇ *vi* [colaborar]: ~ **(en)** to take part O participate (in); FIN to have a share (in). ◇ *vt*: ~ **algo a alguien** to notify sb of sthg.

partícipe ◇ *adj*: ~ **(de)** involved (in); **hacer** ~ **de algo a alguien** [notificar] to notify sb of sthg; [compartir] to share sthg with sb. ◇ *m y f* participant.

partícula *f* particle.

particular ◇ *adj* **-1.** [gen] particular; **tiene su sabor** ~ it has its own particular taste; **en** ~ in particular. **-2.** [no público - domicilio, clases etc] private. **-3.** [no corriente - habilidad etc] uncommon. ◇ *m y f* [persona] member of the public. ◇ *m* [asunto] matter.

particularizar ◇ *vt* [caracterizar] to characterize. ◇ *vi* **-1.** [detallar] to go into details. **-2.** [personalizar]: ~ **en alguien** to single sb out.

partida *f* **-1.** [marcha] departure. **-2.** [en juego] game. [documento] certificate; ~ **de defunción/matrimonio/nacimiento** death/marriage/birth certificate. **-3.** [COM - mercancía] consignment; [- entrada] item, entry.

partidario, -ria ◇ *adj*: ~ **de** in favour of. ◇ *m y f* supporter.

partidista *adj* partisan, biased.

partido *m* **-1.** POLÍT party. **-2.** DEP match; ~ **amistoso** friendly (match). **-3.** *loc*: **sacar** ~ **de** to make the most of; **tomar** ~ **por** to side with.

partir ◇ *vt* **-1.** [dividir] to divide, to split. **-2.** [repartir] to share out. **-3.** [romper] to break open; [cascar] to crack; [tronco, loncha etc] to cut. ◇ *vi* **-1.** [marchar] to leave, to set off. **-2.** [basarse]: ~ **de** to start from. ◆ **partirse** *vpr* **-1.** [romperse] to split. **-2.** [rajarse] to crack. ◆ **a partir de** *loc prep* starting from; **a** ~ **de aquí** from here on.

partitura *f* score.

parto *m* birth; **estar de** ~ to be in labour.

parvulario *m* nursery school, kindergarten.

pasa f [fruta] raisin; ~ **de Corinto** currant; ~ **de Esmirna** sultana.

pasable adj passable.

pasada → pasado.

pasadizo m passage.

pasado, -da adj **-1.** [gen] past; ~ **un año** a year later; **lo** ~, ~ **está** let bygones be bygones. **-2.** [último] last; **el año** ~ last year. **-3.** [podrido] off, bad. **-4.** [hecho - filete, carne] well done. ♦ **pasado** m [gen] past; GRAM past (tense). ♦ **pasada** f [con el trapo] wipe; [con la brocha] coat. ♦ **de pasada** loc adv in passing. ♦ **mala pasada** f dirty trick.

pasador m **-1.** [cerrojo] bolt. **-2.** [para el pelo] slide.

pasaje m **-1.** [billete] ticket, fare. **-2.** [pasajeros] passengers (pl). **-3.** [calle] passage. **-4.** [fragmento] passage.

pasajero, -ra ◇ adj passing. ◇ m y f passenger.

pasamanos m inv [de escalera interior] bannister; [de escalera exterior] handrail.

pasamontañas m inv balaclava (helmet).

pasaporte m passport.

pasapuré m, **pasapurés** m inv food mill.

pasar ◇ vt **-1.** [gen] to pass; [noticia, aviso] to pass on; **¿me pasas la sal?** would you pass me the salt?; ~ **algo por** [filtrar] to pass sthg through. **-2.** [cruzar] to cross; ~ **la calle** to cross the road; **pasé el río a nado** I swam across the river. **-3.** [traspasar] to pass through. **-4.** [trasladar]: ~ **algo a** to move sthg to. **-5.** [llevar adentro] to show in; **el criado nos pasó al salón** the butler showed us into the living room. **-6.** [contagiar]: ~ **algo a alguien** to give sthg to sb, to infect sb with sthg; **me has pasado la tos** you've given me your cough. **-7.** [admitir - instancia etc] to accept. **-8.** [consentir]: ~ **algo a alguien** to let sb get away with sthg. **-9.** [rebasar - en el espacio] to go through; [- en el tiempo] to have been through; ~ **un semáforo en rojo** to go through a red light. **-10.** [emplear - tiempo] to spend; **pasó dos años en Roma** he spent two years in Rome. **-11.** [padecer] to go through, to suffer; **pasarlo mal** to have a hard time of it. **-12.** [sobrepasar]: **ya ha pasado los veinticinco** he's over twenty-five now; **mi hijo me pasa ya dos centímetros** my son is already two centimetres

taller than me. **-13.** [adelantar - coche, contrincante etc] to overtake. **-14.** CIN to show. ◇ vi **-1.** [gen] to pass, to go; **pasó por mi lado** he passed by my side; **el autobús pasa por mi casa** the bus goes past O passes in front of my house; **el Manzanares pasa por Madrid** the Manzanares goes O passes through Madrid; **he pasado por tu calle** I went down your street; ~ **de ... a ...** to go O pass from ... to ...; ~ **de largo** to go by. **-2.** [entrar] to go/come in; **¡pase!** come in! **-3.** [poder entrar]: ~ **(por)** to go (through); **por ahí no pasa** it won't go through there. **-4.** [ir un momento] to pop in; **pasaré por mi oficina/por tu casa** I'll pop into my office/round to your place. **-5.** [suceder] to happen; **¿qué pasa aquí?** what's going on here?; **¿qué pasa?** what's the matter?; **pase lo que pase** whatever happens, come what may. **-6.** [terminarse] to be over; **pasó la Navidad** Christmas is over. **-7.** [transcurrir] to go by. **-8.** [cambiar - acción]: ~ **a** to move on to; **pasemos a otra cosa** let's move on to something else. **-9.** [conformarse]: ~ **(con/sin algo)** to make do (with/without sthg); **tendrá que** ~ **sin coche** she'll have to make do without a car. **-10.** [servir] to be all right, to be usable; **puede** ~ it'll do. **-11.** fam [prescindir]: ~ **de algo/alguien** to want nothing to do with sthg/sb; **paso de política** I'm not into politics. **-12.** [tolerar]: ~ **por algo** to put up with sthg. ♦ **pasarse** vpr **-1.** [acabarse] to pass; **siéntate hasta que se te pase** sit down until you feel better. **-2.** [emplear - tiempo] to spend, to pass; **se pasaron el día hablando** they spent all day talking. **-3.** [desaprovecharse] to slip by; **se me pasó la oportunidad** I missed my chance. **-4.** [estropearse - comida] to go off; [- flores] to fade. **-5.** [cambiar de bando]: ~**se a** to go over to. **-6.** [omitir] to miss out; **te has pasado una página** you've missed a page out. **-7.** [olvidarse]: **pasársele a alguien** to slip sb's mind; **se me pasó decírtelo** I forgot to mention it to you. **-8.** [no fijarse]: **pasársele a alguien** to escape sb's attention; **no se le pasa nada** he never misses a thing. **-9.** [excederse]: ~**se de generoso/bueno** to be far too generous/kind. **-10.** fam [propasarse] to go over the top; **te has pasado diciéndole eso** what you said went too far O was over the top. **-11.** [divertirse]: **¿qué**

tal te lo estás pasando? how are you enjoying yourself?; **pasárselo bien/mal** to have a good/bad time.

pasarela f **-1.** [puente] footbridge; [para desembarcar] gangway. **-2.** [en un desfile] catwalk.

pasatiempo m [hobby] pastime, hobby.

Pascua f **-1.** [de los judíos] Passover. **-2.** [de los cristianos] Easter. ◆ **Pascuas** fpl [Navidad] Christmas (sg); **¡felices Pascuas!** Merry Christmas!; **de Pascuas a Ramos** once in a blue moon.

pase m **-1.** [gen, DEP & TAUROM] pass. **-2.** [proyección] showing, screening. **-3.** [desfile] parade; ~ **de modelos** fashion parade.

pasear ◇ vi to go for a walk. ◇ vt to take for a walk; [perro] to walk; fig to show off, to parade.

paseo m **-1.** [acción - a pie] walk; [- en coche] drive; [- a caballo] ride; [- en barca] row; **dar un** ~ [a pie] to go for a walk. **-2.** [lugar] avenue; ~ **marítimo** promenade. **-3.** loc: **mandar** O **enviar a alguien a** ~ to send sb packing.

pasillo m corridor.

pasión f passion. ◆ **Pasión** f RELIG Passion.

pasivo, -va adj **-1.** [gen & GRAM] passive. **-2.** [población etc] inactive. ◆ **pasivo** m COM liabilities (pl).

pasmado, -da adj **-1.** [asombrado] astonished, astounded. **-2.** [atontado] stunned.

pasmar vt to astound. ◆ **pasmarse** vpr to be astounded.

pasmo m astonishment.

pasmoso, -sa adj astonishing.

paso m **-1.** [gen] step; [huella] footprint. **-2.** [acción] passing; [cruce] crossing; [camino de acceso] way through, thoroughfare; **abrir** ~ **a alguien** lit & fig to make way for sb; **ceder el** ~ (**a alguien**) to let sb past; AUTOM to give way (to sb); **"ceda el** ~" "give way"; **"prohibido el** ~" "no entry"; ~ **elevado** flyover; ~ **a nivel** level crossing; ~ **peatonal** O **de peatones** pedestrian crossing; ~ **de cebra** zebra crossing. **-3.** [forma de andar] walk; [ritmo] pace. **-4.** [GEOGR - en montaña] pass; [- en el mar] strait. **-5.** (gen pl) [gestión] step; [progreso] advance; **dar los** ~**s necesarios para** to take the necessary steps. **-6.** loc: **a cada** ~ every other minute; **está a dos** O **cuatro** ~**s** it's just down the road; **¡a este** ~ ...! fig at that rate ...!; **estar de** ~ to be passing through; ~ **a**

~ **step by step; salir del** ~ to get out of trouble. ◆ **de paso** loc adv in passing.

pasodoble m paso doble.

pasota fam ◇ adj apathetic. ◇ m y f dropout.

pasta f **-1.** [masa] paste; [de papel] pulp; ~ **dentífrica** toothpaste. **-2.** [CULIN - espaguetti etc] pasta; [- de pasteles] pastry; [- de pan] dough. **-3.** [pastelillo] pastry. **-4.** fam [dinero] dough. **-5.** [encuadernación]: **en** ~ hardback.

pastar vi to graze.

pastel m **-1.** [CULIN - dulce] cake; [- salado] pie. **-2.** ARTE pastel.

pastelería f **-1.** [establecimiento] cake shop, patisserie. **-2.** [repostería] pastries (pl).

pasteurizado [pasteuri'θaðo], **-da** adj pasteurized.

pastiche m pastiche.

pastilla f **-1.** MED pill, tablet. **-2.** [de jabón, chocolate] bar.

pasto m **-1.** [acción] grazing; [sitio] pasture. **-2.** [hierba] fodder. **-3.** loc: **ser** ~ **de las llamas** to go up in flames.

pastón m fam: **vale un** ~ it costs a bomb.

pastor, -ra m y f [de ganado] shepherd (f shepherdess). ◆ **pastor** m **-1.** [sacerdote] minister. **-2.** → **perro**.

pastoso, -sa adj **-1.** [blando] pasty; [arroz] sticky. **-2.** [seco] dry.

pata f **-1.** [pierna] leg. **-2.** [pie - gen] foot; [- de perro, gato] paw; [- de vaca, caballo] hoof. **-3.** fam [de persona] leg; **a cuatro** ~**s** on all fours; **ir a la** ~ **coja** to hop. **-4.** [de mueble] leg; [de gafas] arm. **-5.** loc: **meter la** ~ to put one's foot in it; **poner/estar** ~**s arriba** to turn/be upside down; **tener mala** ~ to be unlucky. ◆ **patas** fpl Amer fam [poca vergüenza] cheek (U). ◆ **pata de gallo** f [en la cara] crow's feet (pl).

patada f kick; [en el suelo] stamp; **dar una** ~ **a** to kick; **tratar a alguien a** ~**s** to treat sb like dirt.

patalear vi to kick about; [en el suelo] to stamp one's feet.

pataleo m kicking (U); [en el suelo] stamping (U).

pataleta f tantrum.

patán m bumpkin.

patata f potato; ~**s fritas** [de sartén] chips; [de bolsa] crisps.

paté m paté.

patear ◇ vt [dar un puntapié] to kick;

[pisotear] to stamp on. ◇ *vi* [patalear] to stamp one's feet.

patentado, -da *adj* patent, patented.

patente ◇ *adj* obvious; [demostración, prueba] clear. ◇ *f* [de invento] patent.

paternal *adj* fatherly, paternal; *fig* paternal.

paternidad *f* fatherhood; DER paternity.

paterno, -na *adj* paternal.

patético, -ca *adj* pathetic, moving.

patetismo *m* pathos (*U*).

patidifuso, -sa *adj fam* stunned.

patilla *f* **-1.** [de pelo] sideboard, sideburn. **-2.** [de gafas] arm.

patín *m* **-1.** [calzado - de cuchilla] ice skate; [- de ruedas] roller skate. **-2.** [patinete] scooter. **-3.** [embarcación] pedal boat.

pátina *f* patina.

patinaje *m* skating.

patinar *vi* **-1.** [sobre hielo] to skate; [sobre ruedas] to roller-skate. **-2.** [resbalar - coche] to skid; [- persona] to slip. **-3.** *fam fig* [meter la pata] to put one's foot in it.

patinazo *m* **-1.** [de coche] skid; [de persona] slip. **-2.** *fam fig* [planchazo] blunder.

patinete *m* scooter.

patio *m* [gen] patio, courtyard; [de escuela] playground; [de cuartel] parade ground.

patitieso, -sa *adj* **-1.** [de frío] frozen stiff. **-2.** [de sorpresa] aghast, amazed.

pato, -ta *m y f* duck; **pagar el ~** to carry the can.

patológico, -ca *adj* pathological.

patoso, -sa *adj fam* clumsy.

patria → patrio.

patriarca *m* patriarch.

patrimonio *m* **-1.** [bienes - heredados] inheritance; [- propios] wealth; [económico] national wealth. **-2.** *fig* [de una colectividad] exclusive birthright.

patrio, -tria *adj* native. ◆ **patria** *f* native country.

patriota *m y f* patriot.

patriotismo *m* patriotism.

patrocinador, -ra *m y f* sponsor.

patrocinar *vt* to sponsor.

patrocinio *m* sponsorship.

patrón, -ona *m y f* **-1.** [de obreros] boss; [de criados] master (*f* mistress). **-2.** [de pensión etc] landlord (*f* landlady). **-3.** [santo] patron saint. ◆ **patrón** *m* **-1.** [de barco] skipper. **-2.** [en costura] pattern.

patronal ◇ *adj* [empresarial] management (*antes de sust*). ◇ *f* **-1.** [de empresa] management. **-2.** [de país] employers' organisation.

patronato *m* [gen] board; [con fines benéficos] trust.

patrono, -na *m y f* **-1.** [de empresa - encargado] boss; [- empresario] employer. **-2.** [santo] patron saint.

patrulla *f* patrol; **~ urbana** vigilante group.

patrullar *vt & vi* to patrol.

patuco *m* (*gen pl*) bootee.

paulatino, -na *adj* gradual.

pausa *f* pause, break; MÚS rest; **con ~** unhurriedly.

pausado, -da *adj* deliberate, slow.

pauta *f* **-1.** [gen] standard, model. **-2.** [en un papel] guideline.

pava → pavo.

pavimentación *f* [de una carretera] road surfacing; [de la acera] paving; [de un suelo] flooring.

pavimento *m* [de carretera] road surface; [de acera] paving; [de suelo] flooring.

pavo, -va *m y f* [ave] turkey; **~ real** peacock (*f* peahen).

pavonearse *vpr despec*: **~ (de)** to boast o brag (about).

pavor *m* terror.

paya *f Amer improvised poem accompanied by guitar.*

payasada *f* clowning (*U*); **hacer ~s** to clown around.

payaso, -sa *m y f* clown.

payo, -ya *m y f* non-gipsy.

paz *f* peace; [tranquilidad] peacefulness; **dejar a alguien en ~** to leave sb alone o in peace; **estar** o **quedar en ~** to be quits; **hacer las paces** to make (it) up; **que en ~ descanse, que descanse en ~** may he/she rest in peace.

PC *m* (*abrev de* **personal computer**) PC.

PD, PS (*abrev de* **posdata**) PS.

pdo. *abrev de* **pasado.**

peaje *m* toll.

peana *f* pedestal.

peatón *m* pedestrian.

peca *f* freckle.

pecado *m* sin.

pecador, -ra *m y f* sinner.

pecaminoso, -sa *adj* sinful.

pecar *vi* **-1.** RELIG to sin. **-2.** [pasarse]: **~ de confiado/generoso** to be overconfident/too generous.

pecera *f* fish tank; [redonda] fish bowl.

pecho *m* **-1.** [gen] chest; [de mujer] bosom. **-2.** [mama] breast; **dar el ~ a** to breastfeed. **-3.** *loc*: **a lo hecho, ~** it's no use crying over spilt milk; **tomarse algo a ~** to take sthg to heart.

pechuga *f* [de ave] breast (*meat*).

pecoso, -sa *adj* freckly.

pectoral *adj* ANAT pectoral, chest (*antes de sust*).

peculiar *adj* **-1.** [característico] typical, characteristic. **-2.** [curioso] peculiar.

peculiaridad *f* **-1.** [cualidad] uniqueness. **-2.** [detalle] particular feature O characteristic.

pedagogía *f* education, pedagogy.

pedagogo, -ga *m y f* educator; [profesor] teacher.

pedal *m* pedal.

pedalear *vi* to pedal.

pedante *adj* pompous.

pedantería *f* pomposity (*U*).

pedazo *m* piece, bit; **hacer ~s** to break to bits; *fig* to destroy.

pedernal *m* flint.

pedestal *m* pedestal, stand.

pedestre *adj* on foot.

pediatra *m y f* pediatrician.

pedicuro, -ra *m y f* chiropodist *Br*, podiatrist *Am*.

pedido *m* COM order; **hacer un ~** to place an order.

pedigrí, pedigree [peði'ɣɾi] *m* pedigree.

pedir ◇ *vt* **-1.** [gen] to ask for; [en comercios, restaurantes] to order; **~ a alguien que haga algo** to ask sb to do sthg; **~ a alguien (en matrimonio)** to ask for sb's hand (in marriage); **~ prestado algo a alguien** to borrow sthg from sb. **-2.** [exigir] to demand. **-3.** [requerir] to call for, to need. **-4.** [poner precio]: **~ (por)** to ask (for); **pide un millón por la moto** he's asking a million for the motorbike. ◇ *vi* [mendigar] to beg.

pedo *m vulg* [ventosidad] fart; **tirarse un ~** to fart.

pedrada *f* [golpe]: **a ~s** by stoning.

pedregullo *m Amer* gravel.

pedrería *f* precious stones (*pl*).

pedrusco *m* rough stone.

peeling ['pilin] (*pl* **peelings**) *m* face mask O pack.

pega *f* [obstáculo] difficulty, hitch; **poner ~s (a)** to find problems (with).

pegadizo, -za *adj* **-1.** [música] catchy. **-2.** *fig* [contagioso] catching.

pegajoso, -sa *adj* sticky; *despec* clinging.

pegamento *m* glue.

pegar ◇ *vt* **-1.** [adherir] to stick; [con pegamento] to glue; [póster, cartel] to fix, to put up; [botón] to sew on. **-2.** [arrimar]: **~ algo a** to put O place sthg against. **-3.** [golpear] to hit. **-4.** [propinar - bofetada, paliza etc] to give; [- golpe] to deal. **-5.** [contagiar]: **~ algo a alguien** to give sb sthg, to pass sthg on to sb. ◇ *vi* **-1.** [adherir] to stick. **-2.** [golpear] to hit. **-3.** [armonizar] to go together, to match; **~ con** to go with. **-4.** [sol] to beat down. ◆ **pegarse** *vpr* **-1.** [adherirse] to stick. **-2.** [agredirse] to fight. **-3.** [golpearse]: **~se (un golpe) con algo** to hit o.s. against sthg. **-4.** *fig* [contagiarse - enfermedad] to be transmitted; **se me pegó su acento** I picked up his accent.

pegatina *f* sticker.

pegote *m fam* **-1.** [masa pegajosa] sticky mess. **-2.** [chapucería] botch.

peinado *m* hairdo; [estilo, tipo] hairstyle.

peinar *vt lit & fig* to comb. ◆ **peinarse** *vpr* to comb one's hair.

peine *m* comb.

peineta *f comb worn in the back of the hair.*

p.ej. (*abrev de* **por ejemplo**) e.g.

Pekín Peking, Beijing.

pela *f fam* peseta; **no tengo ~s** I'm skint.

peladilla *f* sugared almond.

pelado, -da *adj* **-1.** [cabeza] shorn. **-2.** [piel, cara etc] peeling; [fruta] peeled. **-3.** [habitación, monte, árbol] bare. **-4.** [número] exact, round; **saqué un aprobado ~** I passed, but only just. **-5.** *fam* [sin dinero] broke, skint.

pelaje *m* [de gato, oso, conejo] fur; [de perro, caballo] coat.

pelar *vt* **-1.** [persona] to cut the hair of. **-2.** [fruta, patatas] to peel; [guisantes, marisco] to shell. **-3.** [aves] to pluck; [conejos etc] to skin. ◆ **pelarse** *vpr* **-1.** [cortarse el pelo] to have one's hair cut. **-2.** [piel, espalda etc] to peel.

peldaño *m* step; [de escalera de mano] rung.

pelea *f* **-1.** [a golpes] fight. **-2.** [riña] row, quarrel.

pelear *vi* **-1.** [a golpes] to fight. **-2.** [a gritos] to have a row O quarrel. **-3.** [esforzarse] to struggle. ◆ **pelearse** *vpr* **-1.** [a golpes] to fight. **-2.** [a gritos] to have a row O quarrel.

pelele *m fam despec* [persona] puppet.

peletería *f* [tienda] fur shop, furrier's.

peliagudo, -da *adj* tricky.

pelícano, pelícano *m* pelican.

película *f* [gen] film; ~ **muda/de terror** silent/horror film; ~ **del Oeste** western; **de** ~ amazing.

peligro *m* danger; **correr** ~ **(de)** to be in danger (of); **estar/poner en** ~ to be/put at risk; **fuera de** ~ out of danger; ¡~ **de muerte!** danger!

peligroso, -sa *adj* dangerous.

pelín *m fam* mite, tiny bit.

pelirrojo, -ja ◇ *adj* ginger, red-headed. ◇ *m y f* redhead.

pellejo *m* [piel, vida] skin.

pellizcar *vt* [gen] to pinch.

pellizco *m* pinch.

pelma, pelmazo, -za *fam despec* ◇ *adj* annoying, tiresome. ◇ *m y f* bore, pain.

pelo *m* **-1.** [gen] hair. **-2.** [de oso, conejo, gato] fur; [de perro, caballo] coat. **-3.** [de una tela] nap. **-4.** *loc:* **con** ~**s y señales** with all the details; **no tener** ~**s en la lengua** *fam* not to mince one's words; **poner a alguien los** ~**s de punta** *fam* to make sb's hair stand on end; **por los** ~**s, por un** ~ by the skin of one's teeth; **tomar el** ~ **a alguien** *fam* to pull sb's leg. ◆ **a contra pelo** *loc adv lit &* *fig* against the grain.

pelota ◇ *f* **-1.** [gen & DEP] ball; **jugar a la** ~ to play ball; ~ **vasca pelota; hacer la** ~ **(a alguien)** *fam* to suck up (to sb). **-2.** *fam* [cabeza] nut. ◇ *m y f* [persona] crawler, creep.

pelotera *f fam* scrap, fight.

pelotón *m* [de soldados] squad; [de gente] crowd; DEP pack.

pelotudo, -da *adj Amer fam* stupid.

peluca *f* wig.

peluche *m* plush.

peludo, -da *adj* hairy.

peluquería *f* **-1.** [establecimiento] hairdresser's (shop). **-2.** [oficio] hairdressing.

peluquero, -ra *m y f* hairdresser.

peluquín *m* toupee.

pelusa *f* **-1.** [de tela] fluff. **-2.** [vello] down.

pelvis *f inv* pelvis.

pena *f* **-1.** [lástima] shame, pity; ¡**qué** ~! what a shame ○ pity!; **dar** ~ to inspire pity; **el pobre me da** ~ I feel sorry for the poor chap. **-2.** [tristeza] sadness, sorrow. **-3.** (*gen pl*) [desgracia] problem, trouble. **-4.** (*gen pl*) [dificultad] struggle (*U*); **a duras** ~**s** with great difficulty. **-5.** [castigo] punish-

ment; ~ **capital** ○ **de muerte** death penalty. **-6.** *Amer* [vergüenza] shame, embarrassment; **me da** ~ I'm ashamed of it. **-7.** *loc.* **(no) valer** ○ **merecer la** ~ (not) to be worthwhile ○ worth it.

penacho *m* **-1.** [de pájaro] crest. **-2.** [adorno] plume.

penal ◇ *adj* criminal. ◇ *m* prison.

penalidad *f* (*gen pl*) suffering (*U*), hardship.

penalización *f* **-1.** [acción] penalization. **-2.** [sanción] penalty.

penalti, penalty *m* DEP penalty.

penar ◇ *vt* [castigar] to punish. ◇ *vi* [sufrir] to suffer.

pender *vi* **-1.** [colgar]: ~ **(de)** to hang (from). **-2.** *fig* [amenaza etc]: ~ **sobre** to hang over.

pendiente ◇ *adj* **-1.** [por resolver] pending; [deuda] outstanding; **estar** ~ **de** [atento a] to keep an eye on; [a la espera de] to be waiting for. **-2.** [asignatura] failed. ◇ *m* earring. ◇ *f* slope.

pendón, -ona *m y f fam* libertine.

péndulo *m* pendulum.

pene *m* penis.

penene *m y f untenured teacher or lecturer.*

penetración *f* **-1.** [gen] penetration. **-2.** [sagacidad] astuteness.

penetrante *adj* **-1.** [intenso - dolor] acute; [- olor] sharp; [- frío] biting; [- mirada] penetrating; [- voz, sonido etc] piercing. **-2.** [sagaz] sharp, penetrating.

penetrar ◇ *vi:* ~ **en** [internarse en] to enter; [filtrarse por] to get into, to penetrate; [perforar] to pierce; [llegar a conocer] to get to the bottom of. ◇ *vt* **-1.** [introducirse en - suj: arma, sonido etc] to pierce, to penetrate; [- suj: humedad, líquido] to permeate; [- suj: emoción, sentimiento] to pierce. **-2.** [llegar a conocer - secreto etc] to get to the bottom of. **-3.** [sexualmente] to penetrate.

penicilina *f* penicillin.

península *f* peninsula.

peninsular *adj* peninsular.

penitencia *f* penance.

penitenciaría *f* penitentiary.

penoso, -sa *adj* **-1.** [trabajoso] laborious. **-2.** [lamentable] distressing; [aspecto, espectáculo] sorry.

pensador, -ra *m y f* thinker.

pensamiento *m* **-1.** [gen] thought; [mente] mind; [idea] idea. **-2.** BOT pansy.

pensar ◇ *vi* to think; ~ **en algo/en alguien/en hacer algo** to think about sthg/about sb/ about doing sthg; ~ **sobre algo** to think about sthg; **piensa en**

un **número/buen regalo** think of a number/good present; **dar que ~ a alguien** to give sb food for thought. ◇ *vt* **-1.** [reflexionar] to think about ○ over. **-2.** [opinar, creer] to think; **~ algo de alguien/algo** to think sthg of sb/sthg; **pienso que no vendrá** I don't think she'll come. **-3.** [idear] to think up. **-4.** [tener la intención de]: **~ hacer algo** to intend to do sthg. ◆ **pensarse** *vpr*: **~se algo** to think sthg over.

pensativo, -va *adj* pensive, thoughtful.

pensión *f* **-1.** [dinero] pension. **-2.** [de huéspedes] ≈ guest house; **media ~** [en hotel] half board; **estar a media ~** [en colegio] to have school dinners; **~ completa** full board.

pensionista *m y f* [jubilado] pensioner.

pentágono *m* pentagon.

pentagrama *m* MÚS stave.

penúltimo, -ma *adj, m y f* penultimate, last but one.

penumbra *f* half-light.

penuria *f* **-1.** [pobreza] penury, poverty. **-2.** [escasez] paucity, dearth.

peña *f* **-1.** [roca] crag, rock; [monte] cliff. **-2.** [grupo de amigos] circle, group; [club] club; [quinielística] pool.

peñasco *m* large crag ○ rock.

peñón *m* rock. ◆ **Peñón** *m*: **el Peñón (de Gibraltar)** the Rock (of Gibraltar).

peón *m* **-1.** [obrero] unskilled labourer. **-2.** [en ajedrez] pawn.

peonza *f* (spinning) top.

peor ◇ *adj* **-1.** (*comparativo*): **~ (que)** worse (than). **-2.** (*superlativo*): **el/la ~ ... the worst ....** ◇ *pron*: **el/la ~ (de)** the worst (in), of; **lo ~ de todos** the worst of all; **lo ~ fue que ...** the worst thing was that .... ◇ *adv* **-1.** (*comparativo*): **~ (que)** worse (than); **ahora veo ~** I see worse now; **estar ~** [enfermo] to get worse; **estoy ~** [de salud] I feel worse. **-2.** (*superlativo*) worst; **el que lo hizo ~** the one who did it (the) worst.

pepinillo *m* gherkin.

pepino *m* BOT cucumber; **me importa un ~** I couldn't care less.

pepita *f* **-1.** [de fruta] pip. **-2.** [de oro] nugget.

peppermint = **pipermín**.

pequeñez *f* **-1.** [gen] smallness. **-2.** *fig* [insignificancia] trifle.

pequeño, -ña *adj* small, little; [hermano] little; [posibilidad] slight; [ingresos, cifras etc] low.

pequinés, -esa *m* [perro] Pekinese.

pera *f* **-1.** [fruta] pear. **-2.** [para ducha etc] (rubber) bulb. **-3.** *loc*: **pedir ~s al olmo** to ask (for) the impossible; **ser la ~** *fam* to be the limit.

peral *m* pear-tree.

percance *m* mishap.

percatarse *vpr*: **~ (de algo)** to notice (sthg).

percebe *m* [pez] barnacle.

percepción *f* **-1.** [de los sentidos] perception. **-2.** [cobro] receipt, collection.

perceptible *adj* [por los sentidos] noticeable, perceptible.

percha *f* **-1.** [de armario] (coat) hanger. **-2.** [de pared] coat rack. **-3.** [de pie] coat stand. **-4.** [para pájaros] perch.

perchero *m* [de pared] coat rack; [de pie] coat stand.

percibir *vt* **-1.** [con los sentidos] to perceive, to notice; [por los oídos] to hear; [ver] to see. **-2.** [cobrar] to receive, to get.

percusión *f* percussion.

perdedor, -ra *m y f* loser.

perder ◇ *vt* **-1.** [gen] to lose. **-2.** [desperdiciar] to waste. **-3.** [tren, oportunidad] to miss. ◇ *vi* **-1.** [salir derrotado] to lose. **-2.** *loc*: **echar algo a ~** to spoil sthg; **echarse a ~** [alimento] to go off. ◆ **perderse** *vpr* **-1.** [gen] to get lost. **-2.** [desaparecer] to disappear. **-3.** [desperdiciarse] to be wasted. **-4.** [desaprovechar]: **¡no te lo pierdas!** don't miss it! **-5.** *fig* [por los vicios] to be beyond salvation.

perdición *f* ruin, undoing.

pérdida *f* **-1.** [gen] loss; **no tiene ~** you can't miss it. **-2.** [de tiempo, dinero] waste. **-3.** [escape] leak. ◆ **pérdidas** *fpl* **-1.** FIN & MIL losses. **-2.** [daños] damage (*U*).

perdidamente *adv* hopelessly.

perdido, -da *adj* **-1.** [extraviado] lost; [animal, bala] stray. **-2.** [sucio] filthy. **-3.** *fam* [de remate] complete, utter. **-4.** *loc*: **estar ~** to be done for ○ lost.

perdigón *m* pellet.

perdiz *f* partridge.

perdón *m* pardon, forgiveness; **no tener ~** to be unforgivable; **¡~!** sorry!

perdonar *vt* **-1.** [gen] to forgive; **~le algo a alguien** to forgive sb for sthg; **perdone que le moleste** sorry to bother you. **-2.** [eximir de - deuda, condena]: **~ algo a alguien** to let sb off sthg; **~le la vida a alguien** to spare sb their life.

perdonavidas *m y f inv fam* bully.

perdurable *adj* **-1.** [que dura siempre] eternal. **-2.** [que dura mucho] long-lasting.

perdurar *vi* **-1.** [durar mucho] to endure, to last. **-2.** [persistir] to persist.

perecedero, -ra *adj* **-1.** [productos] perishable. **-2.** [naturaleza] transitory.

perecer *vi* to perish, to die.

peregrinación *f* RELIG pilgrimage; *fig* [a un lugar] trek.

peregrinaje *m* RELIG pilgrimage; *fig* [a un lugar] trek.

peregrino, -na ◇ *adj* **-1.** [ave] migratory. **-2.** *fig* [extraño] strange. ◇ *m y f* [persona] pilgrim.

perejil *m* parsley.

perenne *adj* **-1.** BOT perennial. **-2.** [recuerdo] enduring. **-3.** [continuo] constant.

pereza *f* idleness.

perezoso, -sa *adj* **-1.** [vago] lazy. **-2.** [lento] slow, sluggish.

perfección *f* perfection; **es de una gran ~** it's exceptionally good.

perfeccionar *vt* **-1.** [redondear] to perfect. **-2.** [mejorar] to improve.

perfeccionista *adj, m y f* perfectionist.

perfecto, -ta *adj* perfect.

perfidia *f* perfidy, treachery.

perfil *m* **-1.** [contorno] outline, shape. **-2.** [de cara, cuerpo] profile; **de ~** in profile. **-3.** *fig* [característica] characteristic. **-4.** *fig* [retrato moral] profile. **-5.** GEOM cross section.

perfilar *vt* to outline. ◆ **perfilarse** *vpr* **-1.** [destacarse] to be outlined. **-2.** [concretarse] to shape up.

perforación *f* **-1.** [gen & MED] perforation. **-2.** [taladro] bore-hole.

perforar *vt* [horadar] to perforate; [agujero] to drill; INFORM to punch.

perfume *m* perfume.

perfumería *f* **-1.** [tienda, arte] perfumery. **-2.** [productos] perfumes (*pl*).

pergamino *m* parchment.

pericia *f* skill.

periferia *f* periphery; [alrededores] outskirts (*pl*).

periférico, -ca *adj* peripheral; [barrio] outlying.

perifollos *mpl fam* frills (and fripperies).

perífrasis *f inv*: **~ (verbal)** wordy explanation.

perilla *f* goatee; **venir de ~(s)** to be just the right thing.

perímetro *m* perimeter.

periódico, -ca *adj* [gen] periodic. ◆ **periódico** *m* newspaper.

periodismo *m* journalism.

periodista *m y f* journalist.

periodo, período *m* period; DEP half.

peripecia *f* incident, sudden change.

peripuesto, -ta *adj fam* dolled-up.

periquete *m*: **en un ~** *fam* in a jiffy.

periquito *m* parakeet.

periscopio *m* periscope.

peritar *vt* [casa] to value; [coche] to assess the damage to.

perito *m* **-1.** [experto] expert; **~ agrónomo** agronomist. **-2.** [ingeniero técnico] technician.

perjudicar *vt* to damage, to harm.

perjudicial *adj*: **~ (para)** harmful (to).

perjuicio *m* harm (*U*), damage (*U*).

perjurar *vi* [jurar en falso] to commit perjury.

perla *f* pearl; *fig* [maravilla] gem, treasure; **de ~s** great, fine; **me viene de ~s** it's just the right thing.

perlé *m* beading.

permanecer *vi* **-1.** [en un lugar] to stay. **-2.** [en un estado] to remain, to stay.

permanencia *f* **-1.** [en un lugar] staying, continued stay. **-2.** [en un estado] continuation.

permanente ◇ *adj* permanent; [comisión] standing. ◇ *f* perm; **hacerse la ~** to have a perm.

permeable *adj* permeable.

permisible *adj* permissible, acceptable.

permisivo, -va *adj* permissive.

permiso *m* **-1.** [autorización] permission; **con ~** if I may. **-2.** [documento] licence, permit; **~ de armas** gun licence; **~ de conducir** driving licence *Br*, driver's license *Am*. **-3.** [vacaciones] leave.

permitir *vt* to allow; **~ a alguien hacer algo** to allow sb to do sthg; **¿me permite?** may I? ◆ **permitirse** *vpr* to allow o.s. (the luxury of); **no puedo permitírmelo** I can't afford it.

permuta, permutación *f* exchange.

pernicioso, -sa *adj* damaging, harmful.

pero ◇ *conj* but; **la casa es vieja ~ céntrica** the house may be old, but it's central; **~ ¿qué es tanto ruido?** what on earth is all this noise about? ◇ *m* snag, fault; **poner ~s a todo** to find fault with everything.

perol *m* casserole (dish).

perorata *f* long-winded speech.

perpendicular *adj* perpendicular; **ser ~ a algo** to be at right angles to sthg.

perpetrar *vt* to perpetrate, to commit.
perpetuar *vt* to perpetuate. ◆ **perpetuarse** *vpr* to last, to endure.
perpetuo, -tua *adj* -1. [gen] perpetual. -2. [para toda la vida] lifelong; DER life (*antes de sust*).
perplejo, -ja *adj* perplexed, bewildered.
perra *f* -1. [rabieta] tantrum; **coger una** ~ to throw a tantrum. -2. [dinero] penny; **estoy sin una** ~ I'm flat broke. -3. → **perro**.
perrera → **perrero**.
perrería *f fam*: **hacer** ~**s a alguien** to play dirty tricks on sb.
perrero, -ra *m y f* [persona] dogcatcher. ◆ **perrera** *f* -1. [lugar] kennels (*pl*). -2. [vehículo] dogcatcher's van.
perro, -rra *m y f* [animal] dog (*f* bitch); ~ **callejero** stray dog; ~ **de caza** hunting dog; ~ **lazarillo** guide dog; ~ **lobo** alsatian; ~ **pastor** sheepdog; ~ **policía** police dog; **ser** ~ **viejo** to be an old hand. ◆ **perro caliente** *m* hot dog.
persecución *f* -1. [seguimiento] pursuit. -2. [acoso] persecution.
perseguir *vt* -1. [seguir, tratar de obtener] to pursue. -2. [acosar] to persecute. -3. [suj: mala suerte, problema etc] to dog.
perseverante *adj* persistent.
perseverar *vi*: ~ **(en)** to persevere (with), to persist (in).
persiana *f* blind.
persistente *adj* persistent.
persistir *vi*: ~ **(en)** to persist (in).
persona *f* -1. [individuo] person; **cien** ~**s** a hundred people; **en** ~ in person; **por** ~ per head; **ser buena** ~ to be nice; ~ **mayor** adult, grown-up. -2. DER party. -3. GRAM person.
personaje *m* -1. [persona importante] important person, celebrity. -2. [de obra] character.
personal ◇ *adj* [gen] personal; [teléfono, dirección] private, home (*antes de sust*). ◇ *m* [trabajadores] staff, personnel.
personalidad *f* -1. [características] personality. -2. [identidad] identity. -3. [persona importante] important person, celebrity.
personalizar *vi* -1. [nombrar] to name names. -2. [aludir] to get personal.
personarse *vpr* to turn up.
personificar *vt* to personify.
perspectiva *f* -1. [gen] perspective. -2. [paisaje] view. -3. [futuro] prospect; **en** ~ in prospect.
perspicacia *f* insight, perceptiveness.

perspicaz *adj* sharp, perceptive.
persuadir *vt* to persuade; ~ **a alguien para que haga algo** to persuade sb to do sthg. ◆ **persuadirse** *vpr* to convince o.s.; ~**se de algo** to become convinced of sthg.
persuasión *f* persuasion.
persuasivo, -va *adj* persuasive. ◆ **persuasiva** *f* persuasive power.
pertenecer *vi* -1. [gen]: ~ **a** to belong to. -2. [corresponder] to be a matter for.
perteneciente *adj*: **ser** ~ **a** to belong to.
pertenencia *f* -1. [propiedad] ownership. -2. [afiliación] membership. ◆ **pertenencias** *fpl* [enseres] belongings.
pértiga *f* -1. [vara] pole. -2. DEP polevault.
pertinaz *adj* -1. [terco] stubborn. -2. [persistente] persistent.
pertinente *adj* -1. [adecuado] appropriate. -2. [relativo] relevant, pertinent.
pertrechos *mpl* -1. MIL supplies and ammunition. -2. *fig* [utensilios] gear (*U*).
perturbación *f* -1. [desconcierto] disquiet, unease. -2. [disturbio] disturbance; ~ **del orden público** breach of the peace. -3. MED mental imbalance.
perturbado, -da *adj* -1. MED disturbed. -2. [desconcertado] perturbed.
perturbador, -ra ◇ *adj* unsettling. ◇ *m y f* troublemaker.
perturbar *vt* -1. [trastornar] to disrupt. -2. [inquietar] to disturb, to unsettle. -3. [enloquecer] to perturb.
Perú: **(el)** ~ Peru.
peruano, -na *adj, m y f* Peruvian.
perversión *f* perversion.
perverso, -sa *adj* depraved.
pervertido, -da *m y f* pervert.
pervertir *vt* to corrupt. ◆ **pervertirse** *vpr* to be corrupted.
pesa *f* -1. [gen] weight. -2. (*gen pl*) DEP weights (*pl*).
pesadez *f* -1. [peso] weight. -2. [sensación] heaviness. -3. [molestia, fastidio] drag, pain. -4. [aburrimiento] ponderousness.
pesadilla *f* nightmare.
pesado, -da ◇ *adj* -1. [gen] heavy. -2. [caluroso] sultry. -3. [lento] ponderous, sluggish. -4. [duro] difficult, tough. -5. [aburrido] boring. -6. [molesto] annoying, tiresome; **¡qué** ~ **eres!** you're so annoying! ◇ *m y f* bore, pain.
pesadumbre *f* grief, sorrow.

pésame *m* sympathy, condolences (*pl*); **dar el ~** to offer one's condolences.

pesar ◇ *m* **-1.** [tristeza] grief. **-2.** [arrepentimiento] remorse. ◇ *vt* **-1.** [determinar el peso de] to weigh. **-2.** [examinar] to weigh up. ◇ *vi* **-1.** [tener peso] to weigh. **-2.** [ser pesado] to be heavy. **-3.** [importar] to play an important part. **-4.** [entristecer]: **me pesa tener que decirte esto** I'm sorry to have to tell you this. ◆ **a pesar de** *loc prep* despite; **a ~ mío** against my will. ◆ **a pesar de que** *loc conj* in spite of the fact that.

pesca *f* **-1.** [acción] fishing; **ir de ~** to go fishing; **~ de bajura/altura** coastal/deep-sea fishing. **-2.** [lo pescado] catch.

pescadería *f* fishmonger's (shop).

pescadilla *f* whiting.

pescado *m* fish; **~ azul/blanco** blue/white fish.

pescador, -ra *m y f* fisherman (*f* fisherwoman).

pescar ◇ *vt* **-1.** [peces] to catch. **-2.** *fig* [enfermedad] to catch. **-3.** *fam fig* [conseguir] to get o.s., to land. **-4.** *fam fig* [atrapar] to catch. ◇ *vi* to fish, to go fishing.

pescuezo *m* neck.

pese ◆ **pese a** *loc prep* despite.

pesebre *m* **-1.** [para los animales] manger. **-2.** [belén] crib, Nativity scene.

pesero *m Amer* fixed-rate taxi service.

peseta *f* [unidad] peseta. ◆ **pesetas** *fpl fig* [dinero] money (*U*).

pesetero, -ra *adj* money-grubbing.

pesimismo *m* pessimism.

pesimista ◇ *adj* pessimistic. ◇ *m y f* pessimist.

pésimo, -ma ◇ *superl* → **malo**. ◇ *adj* terrible, awful.

peso *m* **-1.** [gen] weight; **tiene un kilo de ~** it weighs a kilo; **de ~** [razones] weighty; [persona] influential; **~ bruto/neto** gross/net weight; **~ muerto** dead weight. **-2.** [moneda] peso. **-3.** [de atletismo] shot. **-4.** [balanza] scales (*pl*).

pespunte *m* backstitch.

pesquero, -ra *adj* fishing. ◆ **pesquero** *m* fishing boat.

pesquisa *f* investigation, inquiry.

pestaña *f* [de párpado] eyelash; **quemarse las ~s** *fig* to burn the midnight oil.

pestañear *vi* to blink; **sin ~** [con serenidad] without batting an eyelid; [con atención] without losing concentration once.

peste *f* **-1.** [enfermedad, plaga] plague; **~ bubónica** bubonic plague. **-2.** *fam* [mal olor] stink, stench. **-3.** *loc*: **decir ~s de alguien** to heap abuse on sb.

pesticida *m* pesticide.

pestilencia *f* stench.

pestillo *m* [cerrojo] bolt; [mecanismo, en verjas] latch; **correr** o **echar el ~** to shoot the bolt.

petaca *f* **-1.** [para cigarrillos] cigarette case; [para tabaco] tobacco pouch. **-2.** [para bebidas] flask. **-3.** *Amer* [maleta] suitcase.

pétalo *m* petal.

petanca *f* game similar to bowls played in parks, on beach etc.

petardo *m* [cohete] firecracker.

petate *m* kit bag.

petición *f* **-1.** [acción] request; **a ~ de** at the request of. **-2.** DER [escrito] petition.

petiso, -sa *adj Amer fam* short.

peto *m* [de prenda] bib.

petrificar *vt lit & fig* to petrify.

petrodólar *m* petrodollar.

petróleo *m* oil, petroleum.

petrolero, -ra *adj* oil (*antes de sust*). ◆ **petrolero** *m* oil tanker.

petrolífero, -ra *adj* oil (*antes de sust*).

petulante *adj* opinionated.

peúco *m* (*gen pl*) bootee.

peyorativo, -va *adj* pejorative.

pez *m* fish; **~ de río** freshwater fish; **~ espada** swordfish; **estar ~ (en algo)** to have no idea (about sthg). ◆ **pez gordo** *m fam fig* big shot.

pezón *m* [de pecho] nipple.

pezuña *f* hoof.

piadoso, -sa *adj* **-1.** [compasivo] kindhearted. **-2.** [religioso] pious.

pianista *m y f* pianist.

piano *m* piano.

pianola *f* pianola.

piar *vi* to cheep, to tweet.

PIB (*abrev de* **producto interior bruto**) *m* GDP.

pibe, -ba *m y f Amer fam* kid, boy (*f* girl).

pica *f* **-1.** [naipe] spade. **-2.** [lanza] pike; **poner una ~ en Flandes** to do the impossible. ◆ **picas** *fpl* [palo de baraja] spades.

picadero *m* [de caballos] riding school.

picadillo *m* [de carne] mince; [de verdura] chopped vegetables (*pl*).

picado, -da *adj* **-1.** [marcado - piel] pockmarked; [- fruta] bruised. **-2.** [agujereado] perforated; ~ **de polilla** moth-eaten. **-3.** [triturado - alimento] chopped; [- carne] minced; [- tabaco] cut. **-4.** [vino] sour. **-5.** [diente] decayed. **-6.** [mar] choppy. **-7.** *fig* [enfadado] annoyed.

picador, -ra *m y f* TAUROM picador.

picadora *f* mincer.

picadura *f* **-1.** [de mosquito, serpiente] bite; [de avispa, ortiga, escorpión] sting. **-2.** [tabaco] (cut) tobacco (U).

picante ◇ *adj* **-1.** [comida etc] spicy, hot. **-2.** *fig* [obsceno] saucy. ◇ *m* [comida] spicy food; [sabor] spiciness.

picantería *f Amer* cheap restaurant.

picapica → **polvo**.

picaporte *m* [aldaba] doorknocker; [barrita] latch.

picar ◇ *vt* **-1.** [suj: mosquito, serpiente] to bite; [suj: avispa, escorpión, ortiga] to sting. **-2.** [escocer] to itch; **me pican los ojos** my eyes are stinging. **-3.** [triturar - verdura] to chop; [- carne] to mince. **-4.** [suj: ave] to peck. **-5.** [aperitivo] to pick at. **-6.** [tierra, piedra, hielo] to hack at. **-7.** *fig* [enojar] to irritate. **-8.** *fig* [estimular - persona, caballo] to spur on; [- curiosidad] to prick. **-9.** [perforar - billete, ficha] to punch. ◇ *vi* **-1.** [alimento] to be spicy ○ hot. **-2.** [pez] to bite. **-3.** [escocer] to itch. **-4.** [ave] to peck. **-5.** [tomar un aperitivo] to nibble. **-6.** [sol] to burn. **-7.** [dejarse engañar] to take the bait. ◆ **picarse** *vpr* **-1.** [vino] to turn sour. **-2.** [mar] to get choppy. **-3.** [diente] to get a cavity. **-4.** [oxidarse] to go rusty. **-5.** *fig* [enfadarse] to get annoyed ○ cross.

picardía *f* **-1.** [astucia] craftiness. **-2.** [travesura] naughty trick, mischief (U). **-3.** [atrevimiento] brazenness.

picaresco, -ca *adj* mischievous, roguish. ◆ **picaresca** *f* **-1.** LITER picaresque literature. **-2.** [modo de vida] roguery.

pícaro, -ra *m y f* **-1.** [astuto] sly person, rogue. **-2.** [travieso] rascal. **-3.** [atrevido] brazen person.

picatoste *m* crouton.

pichi *m* pinafore (dress).

pichichi *m* DEP top scorer.

pichincha *f Amer fam* snip, bargain.

pichón *m* ZOOL young pigeon.

picnic (*pl* **picnics**) *m* picnic.

pico *m* **-1.** [de ave] beak. **-2.** [punta, saliente] corner. **-3.** [herramienta] pick, pickaxe. **-4.** [cumbre] peak. **-5.** [cantidad indeterminada]: **cincuenta y** ~ fifty-odd; **llegó a las cinco y** ~ he got there just

after five. **-6.** *fam* [boca] gob, mouth; **cerrar el** ~ [callar] to shut up.

picor *m* [del calor] burning; [que irrita] itch.

picoso, -sa *adj Amer* spicy, hot.

picotear *vt* [suj: ave] to peck.

pida, pidiera *etc* → **pedir**.

pie *m* **-1.** [gen & ANAT] foot; **a** ~ on foot; **estar de** ○ **en** ~ to be on one's feet ○ standing; **ponerse de** ○ **en** ~ to stand up; **de** ~**s a cabeza** *fig* from head to toe; **seguir en** ~ [vigente] to be still valid; **en** ~ **de igualdad** on an equal footing; **en** ~ **de guerra** at war; ~ **de foto** caption. **-2.** [de micrófono, lámpara etc] stand; [de copa] stem. **-3.** *loc*: **al** ~ **de la letra** to the letter, word for word; **andar con** ~**s de plomo** to tread carefully; **buscarle (los) tres** ~**s al gato** to split hairs; **dar** ~ **a alguien para que haga algo** to give sb cause to do sthg; **no tener ni** ~ **s ni cabeza** to make no sense at all; **pararle los** ~**s a alguien** to put sb in their place; **tener un** ~ **en la tumba** to have one foot in the grave.

piedad *f* **-1.** [compasión] pity; **tener** ~ **de** to take pity on. **-2.** [religiosidad] piety.

piedra *f* **-1.** [gen] stone; ~ **angular** *lit* & *fig* cornerstone; ~ **pómez** pumice stone; ~ **preciosa** precious stone. **-2.** [de mechero] flint.

piel *f* **-1.** ANAT skin; ~ **roja** redskin (*N.B.: the term "piel roja" is considered to be racist*); **dejar** ○ **jugarse la** ~ to risk one's neck. **-2.** [cuero] leather. **-3.** [pelo] fur. **-4.** [cáscara] skin, peel.

piensa *etc* → **pensar**.

pierda *etc* → **perder**.

pierna *f* leg; **estirar las** ~**s** to stretch one's legs.

pieza *f* **-1.** [gen] piece; [de mecanismo] part; ~ **de recambio** ○ **repuesto** spare part, extra *Am*; **dejar/quedarse de una** ~ to leave/be thunderstruck. **-2.** [obra dramática] play. **-3.** [habitación] room.

pifiar *vt*: ~**la** *fam* to put one's foot in it.

pigmento *m* pigment.

pijama *m* pyjamas (*pl*).

pila *f* **-1.** [generador] battery. **-2.** [montón] pile; **tiene una** ~ **de deudas** he's up to his neck in debt. **-3.** [fregadero] sink.

pilar *m* *lit* & *fig* pillar.

píldora *f* pill; [anticonceptivo]: **la** ~ the pill; **dorar la** ~ to sugar the pill.

pileta *f Amer* swimming pool.

pillaje *m* pillage.

pillar ◇ *vt* **-1.** [gen] to catch. **-2.** [chiste, explicación] to get. **-3.** [atropellar] to knock down. ◇ *vi* [hallarse]: **me pilla lejos** it's out of the way for me; **me pilla de camino** it's on my way. ◆ **pillarse** *vpr* [dedos etc] to catch.

pillo, -lla *fam* ◇ *adj* **-1.** [travieso] mischievous. **-2.** [astuto] crafty. ◇ *m y f* [pícaro] rascal.

pilotar *vt* [avión] to fly, to pilot; [coche] to drive; [barco] to steer.

piloto ◇ *m y f* [gen] pilot; [de coche] driver; ~ **automático** automatic pilot. ◇ *m* [luz - de coche] tail light; [- de aparato] pilot lamp. ◇ *adj inv* pilot (*antes de sust*).

piltrafa *f* (*gen pl*) scrap; *fam* [persona débil] wreck.

pimentón *m* paprika.

pimienta *f* pepper.

pimiento *m* [fruto] pepper, capsicum; [planta] pimiento, pepper plant; ~ **morrón** sweet pepper.

pimpollo *m* **-1.** [de rama, planta] shoot; [de flor] bud. **-2.** *fam fig* [persona atractiva] gorgeous person.

pinacoteca *f* art gallery.

pinar *m* pine wood O grove.

pinaza *f* pine needles (*pl*).

pincel *m* [para pintar] paintbrush; [para maquillar etc] brush.

pinchadiscos *m y f inv* disc jockey.

pinchar ◇ *vt* **-1.** [punzar - gen] to prick; [- rueda] to puncture; [- globo, balón] to burst. **-2.** [penetrar] to pierce. **-3.** [fijar]: ~ **algo en la pared** to pin sthg to the wall. **-4.** *fam* [teléfono] to tap. **-5.** *fig* [irritar] to torment. **-6.** *fig* [incitar]: ~ **a alguien para que haga algo** to urge sb to do sthg. ◇ *vi* **-1.** [rueda] to get a puncture. **-2.** [punzarse - persona] to prick o.s.; [- rueda] to get a puncture. ◆ **pincharse** *vpr* **-1.** [punzarse - persona] to prick o.s.; [- rueda] to get a puncture. **-2.** [inyectarse]: ~**se (algo)** [medicamento] to inject o.s. (with sthg); *fam* [droga] to shoot up (with sthg).

pinchazo *m* **-1.** [punzada] prick. **-2.** [marca] needle mark. **-3.** [de neumático, balón etc] puncture, flat *Am*.

pinche ◇ *m y f* kitchen boy (*f* kitchen maid). ◇ *adj Amer fam* damned.

pinchito *m* CULIN **-1.** [tapa] aperitif on a stick. **-2.** [pincho moruno] shish kebab.

pincho *m* **-1.** [punta] (sharp) point. **-2.** [espina - de planta] prickle, thorn. **-3.** CULIN aperitif on a stick; ~ **moruno** shish kebab.

pinga *f Amer vulg* prick, cock.

pingajo *m fam despec* rag.

pingo *m fam despec* [pingajo] rag.

ping-pong [pin'pon] *m* table-tennis.

pingüino *m* penguin.

pinitos *mpl*: hacer ~ *lit* & *fig* to take one's first steps.

pino *m* pine; **en el quinto** ~ in the middle of nowhere.

pinta → **pinto**.

pintado, -da *adj* **-1.** [coloreado] coloured; "**recién** ~" "wet paint". **-2.** [maquillado] made-up. **-3.** [moteado] speckled. ◆ **pintada** *f* [escrito] graffiti (U).

pintalabios *m inv* lipstick.

pintar ◇ *vt* to paint; ~ **algo de negro** to paint sthg black. ◇ *vi* **-1.** [con pintura] to paint. **-2.** [significar, importar] to count; **aquí no pinto nada** there's no place for me here; **¿qué pinto yo en este asunto?** where do I come in? ◆ **pintarse** *vpr* **-1.** [maquillarse] to make o.s. up.

pinto, -ta *adj* speckled, spotted. ◆ **pinta** *f* **-1.** [lunar] spot. **-2.** *fig* [aspecto] appearance; **tener pinta de algo** to look O seem sthg; **tiene buena pinta** it looks good. **-3.** [unidad de medida] pint. **-4.** *Amer* [pintada] graffiti (U).

pintor, -ra *m y f* painter; *despec* dauber.

pintoresco, -ca *adj* picturesque; *fig* [extravagante] colourful.

pintura *f* **-1.** ARTE painting; ~ **a la acuarela** watercolour; ~ **al óleo** oil painting; **no poder ver a alguien ni en** ~ *fig* not to be able to stand the sight of sb. **-2.** [materia] paint.

pinza *f* (*gen pl*) **-1.** [gen] tweezers (*pl*); [de tender ropa] peg, clothespin *Am*. **-2.** [de animal] pincer, claw. **-3.** [pliegue] fold.

piña *f* **-1.** [del pino] pine cone. **-2.** [ananás] pineapple. **-3.** *fig* [conjunto de gente] close-knit group.

piñata *f pot full of sweets*.

piñón *m* **-1.** [fruto] pine nut. **-2.** [rueda dentada] pinion.

pío, -a *adj* pious. ◆ **pío** *m* cheep, cheeping (U); [de gallina] cluck, clucking (U); **no decir ni** ~ *fig* not to make a peep.

piojo *m* louse.

piola *adj Amer fam* **-1.** [astuto] shrewd. **-2.** [estupendo] fabulous.

pionero, -ra *m y f* pioneer.

pipa f -1. [para fumar] pipe. -2. [pepita] seed, pip; ~s (de girasol) sunflower seeds coated in salt. -3. loc: pasarlo O pasárselo ~ to have a whale of a time.

pipermín, peppermint [piper'min] m peppermint liqueur.

pipí m fam wee-wee; hacer ~ to have a wee-wee.

pique m -1. [enfado] grudge. -2. [rivalidad] rivalry. -3. loc: irse a ~ [barco] to sink; [negocio] to go under; [plan] to fail.

piquete m [grupo]: ~ de ejecución firing squad; ~ (de huelga) picket.

pirado, -da adj fam crazy.

piragua f canoe.

piragüismo m canoeing.

pirámide f pyramid.

piraña f piranha.

pirarse vpr fam to clear off.

pirata ◇ adj pirate (antes de sust); [disco] bootleg. ◇ m y f lit & fig pirate; ~ informático hacker.

piratear ◇ vi -1. [gen] to be involved in piracy. -2. INFORM to hack. ◇ vt INFORM to hack into.

pirenaico, -ca adj Pyrenean.

pírex, pyrex® m Pyrex®.

Pirineos mpl: los ~ the Pyrenees.

piripi adj fam tipsy.

pirómano, -na m y f pyromaniac.

piropo m fam flirtatious remark, ≈ wolf whistle.

pirotecnia f pyrotechnics (U).

pirrarse vpr fam: ~ por algo/alguien to be dead keen on sthg/sb.

pirueta f pirouette; hacer ~s fig [esfuerzo] to perform miracles.

piruleta f lollipop.

pirulí (pl pirulís) m lollipop.

pis (pl pises) m fam pee.

pisada f -1. [acción] footstep; seguir las ~s de alguien to follow in sb's footsteps. -2. [huella] footprint.

pisapapeles m inv paperweight.

pisar vt -1. [con el pie] to tread on; ~ fuerte fig to be firing on all cylinders. -2. [uvas] to tread. -3. fig [llegar a] to set foot in. -4. fig [despreciar] to trample on. -5. fig [anticiparse]: ~ un contrato a alguien to beat sb to a contract; ~ una idea a alguien to think of something before sb.

piscina f swimming pool.

Piscis ◇ m [zodiaco] Pisces. ◇ m y f [persona] Pisces.

piscolabis m inv fam snack.

piso m -1. [vivienda] flat. -2. [planta] floor. -3. [suelo - de carretera] surface; [- de edificio] floor. -4. [capa] layer.

pisotear vt -1. [con el pie] to trample on. -2. [humillar] to scorn.

pista f -1. [gen] track; ~ de aterrizaje runway; ~ de baile dance floor; ~ de esquí ski slope; ~ de hielo ice rink; ~ de tenis tennis court. -2. fig [indicio] clue.

pistacho m pistachio.

pisto m ≈ ratatouille.

pistola f -1. [arma - con cilindro] gun; [- sin cilindro] pistol. -2. [pulverizador] spraygun; pintar a ~ to spray-paint.

pistolero, -ra m y f [persona] gunman. ◆ **pistolera** f [funda] holster.

pistón m -1. MEC piston. -2. [MÚS - corneta] cornet; [- llave] key.

pitada f Amer fam drag, puff.

pitar ◇ vt -1. [arbitrar - partido] to referee; [- falta] to blow for. -2. [abuchear]: ~ a alguien to whistle at sb in disapproval. -3. Amer fam [dar una calada a] to puff (on). ◇ vi -1. [tocar el pito] to blow a whistle; [del coche] to toot one's horn. -2. loc: salir/irse pitando to rush out/off.

pitido m whistle.

pitillera f cigarette case.

pitillo m [cigarrillo] cigarette.

pito m -1. [silbato] whistle. -2. [claxon] horn.

pitón m [cuerno] horn.

pitonisa f fortune-teller.

pitorrearse vpr fam: ~ (de) to take the mickey (out of).

pitorro m spout.

pivote (pl pivotes), **pívot** (pl pivots) m y f DEP pivot.

pizarra f -1. [roca, material] slate. -2. [encerado] blackboard.

pizca f fam -1. [gen] tiny bit; [de sal] pinch. -2. Amer [cosecha] harvest, crop.

pizza ['pitsa] f pizza.

pizzería [pitse'ria] f pizzeria.

placa f -1. [lámina] plate; [de madera] sheet; ~ solar solar panel. -2. [inscripción] plaque; [de policía] badge. -3. [matrícula] number plate. -4. [de cocina] ring. -5. ELECTRÓN board. -6. ~ dental dental plaque.

placaje m tackle.

placenta f placenta.

placentero, -ra adj pleasant.

placer m pleasure; ha sido un ~ (conocerle) it has been a pleasure meeting you.

plácido, -da *adj* [persona] placid; [día, vida, conversación] peaceful.

plafón *m* ARQUIT soffit.

plaga *f* **-1.** [gen] plague; AGR blight; [animal] pest. **-2.** [epidemia] epidemic.

plagado, -da *adj*: ~ **(de)** infested (with).

plagar *vt*: ~ **de** [propaganda etc] to swamp with; [moscas etc] to infest with.

plagiar *vt* [copiar] to plagiarize.

plagio *m* [copia] plagiarism.

plan *m* **-1.** [proyecto, programa] plan. **-2.** *fam* [ligue] date. **-3.** *fam* [modo, forma]: **lo dijo en ~ serio** he was serious about it; **¡vaya ~ de vida!** what a life!; **si te pones en ese ~** ... if you're going to be like that about it ....

plana → **plano**.

plancha *f* **-1.** [para planchar] iron. **-2.** [para cocinar] grill; **a la ~** grilled. **-3.** [placa] plate; [de madera] sheet. **-4.** IMPRENTA plate.

planchado *m* ironing.

planchar *vt* to iron.

planeador *m* glider.

planear ◇ *vt* to plan. ◇ *vi* **-1.** [hacer planes] to plan. **-2.** [en el aire] to glide.

planeta *m* planet.

planicie *f* plain.

planificación *f* planning; ~ **familiar** family planning.

planificar *vt* to plan.

planilla *f* *Amer* [formulario] form.

plano, -na *adj* flat. ◆ **plano** *m* **-1.** [diseño, mapa] plan. **-2.** [nivel, aspecto] level. **-3.** CIN shot; **primer ~** close-up. **-4.** GEOM plane. **-5.** *loc*: **de ~** [golpear] right, directly; [negar] flatly. ◆ **plana** *f* [página] page; **en primera plana** on the front page.

planta *f* **-1.** BOT & IND plant; ~ **depuradora** purification plant. **-2.** [piso] floor; ~ **baja** ground floor. **-3.** [del pie] sole.

plantación *f* **-1.** [terreno] plantation. **-2.** [acción] planting.

plantado, -da *adj* standing, planted; **dejar ~ a alguien** *fam* [cortar la relación] to walk out on sb; [no acudir] to stand sb up; **ser bien ~** to be good-looking.

plantar *vt* **-1.** [sembrar]: ~ **algo (de)** to plant sthg (with). **-2.** [fijar - tienda de campaña] to pitch; [- poste] to put in. **-3.** *fam* [asestar] to deal, to land. ◆ **plantarse** *vpr* **-1.** [gen] to plant o.s. **-2.** [en un sitio con rapidez]: ~**se en** to get to, to reach.

planteamiento *m* **-1.** [exposición] raising, posing. **-2.** [enfoque] approach.

plantear *vt* **-1.** [exponer - problema] to pose; [- posibilidad, dificultad, duda] to raise. **-2.** [enfocar] to approach. ◆ **plantearse** *vpr*: ~**se algo** to consider sthg, to think about sthg.

plantel *m* *fig* [conjunto] group.

plantilla *f* **-1.** [de empresa] staff. **-2.** [suela interior] insole. **-3.** [patrón] pattern, template.

plantón *m*: **dar un ~ a alguien** *fam* to stand sb up.

plañidero, -ra *adj* plaintive.

plañir *vi* to moan, to wail.

plasmar *vt* **-1.** *fig* [reflejar] to give shape to. **-2.** [modelar] to shape, to mould. ◆ **plasmarse** *vpr* to take shape.

plasta ◇ *adj mfam*: **ser ~** to be a pain. ◇ *m y f mfam* [pesado] pain, drag.

plástico, -ca *adj* [gen] plastic. ◆ **plástico** *m* [gen] plastic.

plastificar *vt* to plasticize.

plastilina® *f* ≃ Plasticine®.

plata *f* **-1.** [metal] silver; ~ **de ley** sterling silver; **hablar en ~** *fam* to speak bluntly. **-2.** [objetos de plata] silverware. **-3.** *Amer* [dinero] money.

plataforma *f* **-1.** [gen] platform. **-2.** ~ **petrolífera** oil rig. **-3.** *fig* [punto de partida] launching pad. **-4.** GEOL shelf.

platal *m* *Amer fam*: **un ~** a fortune.

plátano *m* **-1.** [fruta] banana. **-2.** [árbol] banana tree.

platea *f* stalls (*pl*).

plateado, -da *adj* **-1.** [con plata] silver-plated. **-2.** *fig* [color] silvery.

plática *f* [charla] talk, chat.

platicar *vi* to talk, to chat.

platillo *m* **-1.** [plato pequeño] small plate; [de taza] saucer. **-2.** [de una balanza] pan. **-3.** (*gen pl*) MÚS cymbal. ◆ **platillo volante** *m* flying saucer.

platina *f* [de microscopio] slide.

platino *m* [metal] platinum. ◆ **platinos** *mpl* AUTOM & MEC contact points.

plato *m* **-1.** [recipiente] plate, dish; **lavar los ~s** to do the washing-up; **pagar los ~s rotos** to carry the can. **-2.** [parte de una comida] course; **primer ~** first course, starter; **de primer ~** for starters; **segundo ~** second course, main course. **-3.** [comida] dish; ~ **combinado** *single-course meal which usually consists of meat or fish accompanied by chips and vegetables*; ~ **principal** main course. **-4.** [de tocadiscos, microondas] turntable.

plató *m* set.

platónico, -ca *adj* Platonic.

platudo, -da *adj Amer fam* loaded, rolling in it.

plausible *adj* **-1.** [admisible] acceptable. **-2.** [posible] plausible.

playa *f* **-1.** [en el mar] beach; **ir a la ~ de vacaciones** to go on holiday to the seaside. **-2.** *Amer* [aparcamiento]: **~ de estacionamiento** car park.

play-back ['pleißak] (*pl* **play-backs**) *m*: **hacer ~** to mime (the lyrics).

playero, -ra *adj* beach (*antes de sust*). ◆ **playeras** *fpl* **-1.** [de deporte] tennis shoes. **-2.** [para la playa] canvas shoes.

plaza *f* **-1.** [en una población] square. **-2.** [sitio] place. **-3.** [asiento] seat; **de dos ~s** two-seater (*antes de sust*). **-4.** [puesto de trabajo] position, job; **~ vacante** vacancy. **-5.** [mercado] market, marketplace. **-6.** TAUROM: **~ (de toros)** bullring.

plazo *m* **-1.** [de tiempo] period (of time); **en un ~ de un mes** within a month; **mañana termina el ~ de inscripción** the deadline for registration is tomorrow; **a corto/largo ~** [gen] in the short/long term; ECON short/long term. **-2.** [de dinero] instalment; **a ~s** in instalments, on hire purchase.

plazoleta *f* small square.

plebe *f*: **la ~** *lit & fig* the plebs.

plebeyo, -ya *adj* **-1.** HIST plebeian. **-2.** [vulgar] common.

plebiscito *m* plebiscite.

plegable *adj* collapsible, foldaway; [chair] folding.

plegar *vt* to fold; [mesita, hamaca] to fold away.

plegaria *f* prayer.

pleito *m* DER [litigio] legal action (*U*), lawsuit; [disputa] dispute.

plenario, -ria *adj* plenary.

plenilunio *m* full moon.

plenitud *f* **-1.** [totalidad] completeness, fullness. **-2.** [abundancia] abundance.

pleno, -na *adj* full, complete; [derecho] perfect; **en ~ día** in broad daylight; **en plena guerra** in the middle of the war; **le dio en plena cara** she hit him right in the face; **en ~ uso de sus facultades** in full command of his faculties; **en plena forma** on top form. ◆ **pleno** *m* [reunión] plenary meeting.

pletina *f* cassette deck.

pletórico, -ca *adj*: **~ de** full of.

pliego *m* **-1.** [hoja] sheet (of paper). **-2.** [carta, documento] sealed document ○ letter; **~ de condiciones** specifications (*pl*). **-3.** IMPRENTA signature.

pliegue *m* **-1.** [gen & GEOL] fold. **-2.** [en un plisado] pleat.

plisado *m* pleating.

plomería *f Amer* plumber's.

plomero *m Amer* plumber.

plomizo, -za *adj* [color] leaden.

plomo *m* **-1.** [metal] lead; **caer a ~** to fall ○ drop like a stone. **-2.** [pieza de metal] lead weight. **-3.** [fusible] fuse.

pluma ◇ *f* **-1.** [de ave] feather. **-2.** [para escribir] (fountain) pen; HIST quill; **~ estilográfica** fountain pen. ◇ *adj inv* DEP featherweight.

plum-cake [pluŋ'keik] (*pl* **plum-cakes**) *m* fruit cake.

plumero *m* feather duster; **vérsele a alguien el ~** *fam* to see through sb.

plumier (*pl* **plumiers**) *m* pencil box.

plumilla *f* nib.

plumón *m* [de ave] down.

plural *adj & m* plural.

pluralidad *f* diversity.

pluralismo *m* pluralism.

pluralizar *vi* to generalize.

pluriempleo *m*: **hacer ~** to have more than one job.

plus (*pl* **pluses**) *m* bonus.

pluscuamperfecto *adj & m* pluperfect.

plusmarca *f* record.

plusvalía *f* ECON appreciation, added value.

Plutón Pluto.

pluvial *adj* rain (*antes de sust*).

p.m. (*abrev de* **post meridiem**) p.m.

PM (*abrev de* **policía militar**) *f* MP.

PNB (*abrev de* **producto nacional bruto**) *m* GNP.

PNV (*abrev de* **Partido Nacionalista Vasco**) *m* Basque nationalist party.

población *f* **-1.** [ciudad] town, city; [pueblo] village. **-2.** [habitantes] population.

poblado, -da *adj* **-1.** [habitado] inhabited; **una zona muy poblada** a densely populated area. **-2.** *fig* [lleno] full; [barba, cejas] bushy. ◆ **poblado** *m* settlement.

poblador, -ra *m y f* settler.

poblar *vt* **-1.** [establecerse en] to settle, to colonize. **-2.** *fig* [llenar]: **~ (de)** [plantas, árboles] to plant (with); [peces etc] to stock (with). **-3.** [habitar] to inhabit. ◆ **poblarse** *vpr*: **~se (de)** to fill up (with).

pobre ◇ adj poor; ¡~ **hombre!** poor man!; ¡~ **de mí!** poor me! ◇ m y f **-1.** [gen] poor person; **los ~s** the poor; ¡el ~! poor thing! **-2.** [mendigo] beggar.

pobreza f [escasez] poverty; ~ **de** lack ◇ scarcity of.

pochismo m Amer fam language mistake caused by English influence.

pocho, -cha adj **-1.** [persona] off-colour. **-2.** [fruta] over-ripe. **-3.** Amer fam [americanizado] Americanized.

pocilga f lit & fig pigsty.

pocillo m Amer small cup.

pócima f [poción] potion.

poción f potion.

poco, -ca ◇ adj little, not much, (pl) few, not many; **poca agua** not much water; **de poca importancia** of little importance; **hay ~s árboles** there aren't many trees; **pocas personas lo saben** few ◇ not many people know it; **tenemos ~ tiempo** we don't have much time; **hace ~ tiempo** not long ago; **dame unos ~s días** give me a few days. ◇ pron little, not much, (pl) few, not many; **queda ~** there's not much left; **tengo muy ~s** I don't have very many, I have very few; **~s hay que sepan tanto** not many people know so much; **un ~** a bit; ¿**me dejas un ~?** can I have a bit?; **un ~ de** a bit of; **un ~ de sentido común** a bit of common sense; **unos ~s** a few. ◆ **poco** adv **-1.** [escasamente] not much; **este niño come ~** this boy doesn't eat much; **es ~ común** it's not very common; **es un ~ triste** it's rather sad; **por ~** almost, nearly. **-2.** [brevemente]: **tardaré muy ~** I won't be long; **al ~ de ...** shortly after ...; **dentro de ~** soon, in a short time; **hace ~** not long ago; **~ a ~** [progresivamente] little by little; ¡~ **a ~!** [despacio] steady on!

podar vt to prune.

podenco m hound.

poder ◇ m **-1.** [gen] power; **estar en/hacerse con el ~** to be in/to seize power; **~ adquisitivo** purchasing power; **tener ~ de convocatoria** to be a crowd-puller; **~es fácticos** the church, military and press. **-2.** [posesión]: **estar en ~ de alguien** to be in sb's hands. **-3.** (gen pl) [autorización] power, authorization; **dar ~es a alguien para que haga algo** to authorize sb to do sthg; **por ~es** by proxy. ◇ vi **-1.** [tener facultad] can, to be able to; **no puedo decírtelo** I can't tell you, I'm unable to tell you.

-2. [tener permiso] can, may; **no puedo salir por la noche** I'm not allowed to ◇ I can't go out at night; ¿**se puede fumar aquí?** may I smoke here? **-3.** [ser capaz moralmente] can; **no podemos portarnos así con él** we can't treat him like that. **-4.** [tener posibilidad, ser posible] may, can; **podías haber cogido el tren** you could have caught the train; **puede estallar la guerra** war could ◇ may break out; ¡**hubiera podido invitarnos!** [expresa enfado] she could ◇ might have invited us! **-5.** loc: **a ◇ hasta más no ~** as much as can be; **es avaro a más no ~** he's as miserly as can be; **no ~ más** [estar cansado] to be too tired to carry on; [estar harto de comer] to be full (up); [estar enfadado] to have had enough; ¿**se puede?** may I come in? ◇ v impers [ser posible] may; **puede que llueva** it may ◇ might rain; ¿**vendrás mañana? - puede** will you come tomorrow? - I may do; **puede ser** perhaps, maybe. ◇ vt [ser más fuerte que] to be stronger than. ◆ **poder con** vi + prep **-1.** [enfermedad, rival] to be able to overcome. **-2.** [tarea, problema] to be able to cope with. **-3.** [soportar]: **no ~ con algo/alguien** not to be able to stand sthg/sb; **no puedo con la hipocresía** I can't stand hypocrisy.

poderío m [poder] power.

poderoso, -sa adj powerful.

podio, podium m podium.

podólogo, -ga m y f chiropodist.

podrá → **poder.**

podrido, -da ◇ pp → **pudrir.** ◇ adj rotten.

poema m poem.

poesía f **-1.** [género literario] poetry. **-2.** [poema] poem.

poeta m y f poet.

poético, -ca adj poetic.

poetisa f female poet.

póker = **póquer.**

polaco, -ca adj, m y f Polish. ◆ **polaco** m [lengua] Polish.

polar adj polar.

polarizar vt fig [miradas, atención, esfuerzo] to concentrate. ◆ **polarizarse** vpr [vida política, opinión pública] to become polarized.

polaroid® f inv Polaroid®.

polca f polka.

polea f pulley.

polémico, -ca adj controversial. ◆ **polémica** f controversy.

polemizar vi to argue, to debate.

polen *m* pollen.

poleo *m* pennyroyal.

poli *fam* ◇ *m y f* cop. ◇ *f* cops (*pl*).

polichinela *m* **-1.** [personaje] Punchinello. **-2.** [títere] puppet, marionette.

policía ◇ *m y f* policeman (*f* policewoman). ◇ *f*: **la ~** the police.

policiaco, -ca, policíaco, -ca *adj* police (*antes de sust*); [novela, película] detective (*antes de sust*).

policial *adj* police (*antes de sust*).

polideportivo, -va *adj* multi-sport; [gimnasio] multi-use. ◆ **polideportivo** *m* sports centre.

poliéster *m inv* polyester.

polietileno *m* polythene *Br*, polyethylene *Am*.

polifacético, -ca *adj* multifaceted, versatile.

poligamia *f* polygamy.

polígamo, -ma *adj* polygamous.

polígloto, -ta, polígloto, -ta *adj, m y f* polyglot.

polígono *m* **-1.** GEOM polygon. **-2.** [terreno]: **~ industrial/residencial** industrial/housing estate; **~ de tiro** firing range.

polilla *f* moth.

poliomelitis, polio *f inv* polio.

polipiel *f* artificial skin.

Polisario (*abrev de* **Frente Popular para la Liberación de Sakiet el Hamra y Río de Oro**) *m*: **el (Frente) ~** the Polisario Front.

politécnico, -ca *adj* polytechnic. ◆ **politécnica** *f* polytechnic.

político, -ca *adj* **-1.** [de gobierno] political. **-2.** [pariente]: **hermano ~** brother-in-law; **familia política** in-laws (*pl*). ◆ **político** *m* politician. ◆ **política** *f* **-1.** [arte de gobernar] politics (*U*). **-2.** [modo de gobernar, táctica] policy.

politizar *vt* to politicize. ◆ **politizarse** *vpr* to become politicized.

polivalente *adj* [vacuna, suero] polyvalent.

póliza *f* **-1.** [de seguro] (insurance) policy. **-2.** [sello] *stamp on a document showing that a certain tax has been paid.*

polizón *m* stowaway.

polla → **pollo**.

pollera *f Amer* skirt.

pollería *f* poultry shop.

pollito *m* chick.

pollo, -lla *m y f* ZOOL chick. ◆ **pollo** *m* CULIN chicken. ◆ **polla** *f vulg* cock, prick.

polo *m* **-1.** [gen] pole; **~ norte/sur** North/South Pole; **ser ~s opuestos** *fig* to be poles apart. **-2.** ELECTR terminal. **-3.** [helado] ice lolly. **-4.** [jersey] polo shirt. **-5.** DEP polo.

pololo, -la *m y f Amer fam* boyfriend (*f* girlfriend).

Polonia Poland.

poltrón, -ona *adj* lazy. ◆ **poltrona** *f* easy chair.

polución *f* [contaminación] pollution.

polvareda *f* dust cloud.

polvera *f* powder compact.

polvo *m* **-1.** [en el aire] dust; **limpiar** O **quitar el ~** to do the dusting. **-2.** [de un producto] powder; **en ~** powdered; **~s de talco** talcum powder; **~s picapica** itching powder; **estar hecho ~** *fam* to be knackered; **hacer ~ algo** to smash sthg. ◆ **polvos** *mpl* [maquillaje] powder (*U*); **ponerse ~s** to powder one's face.

pólvora *f* [sustancia explosiva] gunpowder; **correr como la ~** to spread like wildfire.

polvoriento, -ta *adj* [superficie] dusty; [sustancia] powdery.

polvorín *m* munitions dump.

polvorón *m crumbly sweet made from flour, butter and sugar.*

pomada *f* ointment.

pomelo *m* [fruto] grapefruit.

pómez → **piedra**.

pomo *m* knob.

pompa *f* **-1.** [suntuosidad] pomp. **-2.** [ostentación] show, ostentation. **-3.** ~ (**de jabón**) (soap) bubble. ◆ **pompas fúnebres** *fpl* [servicio] undertaker's (*sg*).

pompis *m inv fam* bottom, backside.

pompón *m* pompom.

pomposo, -sa *adj* **-1.** [suntuoso] sumptuous; [ostentoso] showy. **-2.** [lenguaje] pompous.

pómulo *m* [hueso] cheekbone.

ponchar *vt Amer* to puncture.

ponche *m* punch.

poncho *m* poncho.

ponderar *vt* **-1.** [alabar] to praise. **-2.** [considerar] to weigh up.

ponedero *m* nesting box.

ponedor, -ra *adj* egg-laying.

ponencia *f* [conferencia] lecture, paper; [informe] report.

poner ◇ *vt* **-1.** [gen] to put; [colocar] to place, to put. **-2.** [vestir]: **~ algo a alguien** to put sthg on sb. **-3.** [contribuir, invertir] to put in; **~ dinero en el negocio** to put money into the business; **~**

algo de mi/tu *etc* **parte** to do my/your *etc* bit. **-4.** [hacer estar de cierta manera]: ~ **a alguien en un aprieto/de mal humor** to put sb in a difficult position/in a bad mood; **le has puesto colorado** you've made him blush. **-5.** [calificar]: ~ **a alguien de algo** to call sb sthg. **-6.** [oponer]: ~ **obstáculos a algo** to hinder sthg; ~ **pegas a algo** to raise objections to sthg. **-7.** [asignar - precio, medida] to fix, to settle; [- multa, tarea] to give; **le pusieron Mario** they called him Mario. **-8.** [TELECOM - telegrama, fax] to send; [- conferencia] to make; **¿me pones con él?** can you put me through to him? **-9.** [conectar - televisión etc] to switch O put on; [- despertador] to set; [- instalación, gas] to put in. **-10.** CIN, TEATR & TV to show; **¿qué ponen en la tele?** what's on the telly? **-11.** [montar - negocio] to set up; **ha puesto una tienda** she has opened a shop. **-12.** [decorar] to do up; **han puesto su casa con mucho lujo** they've done up their house in real style. **-13.** [suponer] to suppose; **pongamos que sucedió así** (let's) suppose that's what happened; **pon que necesitemos cinco días** suppose we need five days; **poniendo que todo salga bien** assuming everything goes according to plan. **-14.** [decir] to say; **¿qué pone ahí?** what does it say? **-15.** [huevo] to lay. ◇ *vi* [ave] to lay (eggs). ◆ **ponerse** ◇ *vpr* **-1.** [colocarse] to put o.s.; ~**se de pie** to stand up; **ponte en la ventana** stand by the window. **-2.** [ropa, gafas, maquillaje] to put on. **-3.** [estar de cierta manera] to go, to become; **se puso rojo de ira** he went red with anger; **se puso colorado** he blushed; **se puso muy guapa** she made herself attractive. **-4.** [iniciar]: ~**se a hacer algo** to start doing sthg. **-5.** [de salud]: ~**se malo** O **enfermo** to fall ill; ~**se bien** to get better. **-6.** [llenarse]: ~**se de algo** to get covered in sthg; **se puso de barro hasta las rodillas** he got covered in mud up to the knees. **-7.** [suj: astro] to set. **-8.** [llegar]: ~**se en** to get to. ◇ *v impers Amer fam* [parecer]: **se me pone que ...** it seems to me that ....

poney = poni.

pongo → poner.

poni, poney ['poni] *m* pony.

poniente *m* [occidente] West; [viento] west wind.

pontífice *m* Pope, Pontiff.

pontón *m* pontoon.

pop *adj* pop.

popa *f* stern.

pope *m fam fig* [pez gordo] big shot.

popote *m Amer* drinking straw.

populacho *m despec* mob, masses (*pl*).

popular *adj* **-1.** [del pueblo] of the people; [arte, música] folk. **-2.** [famoso] popular.

popularidad *f* popularity.

popularizar *vt* to popularize. ◆ **popularizarse** *vpr* to become popular.

popurrí *m* potpourri.

póquer, póker *m* [juego] poker.

por *prep* **-1.** [causa] because of; **se enfadó ~ tu comportamiento** she got angry because of your behaviour. **-2.** [finalidad] (*antes de infin*) (in order) to; (*antes de sust, pron*) for; **lo hizo ~ complacerte** he did it to please you; **lo hice ~ ella** I did it for her. **-3.** [medio, modo, agente] by; ~ **mensajero/fax** by courier/fax; ~ **escrito** in writing; **lo cogieron ~ el brazo** they took him by the arm; **el récord fue batido ~ el atleta** the record was broken by the athlete. **-4.** [tiempo aproximado]: **creo que la boda será ~ abril** I think the wedding will be some time in April. **-5.** [tiempo concreto]: ~ **la mañana/tarde** in the morning/afternoon; ~ **la noche** at night; **ayer salimos ~ la noche** we went out last night; ~ **unos días** for a few days. **-6.** [lugar - aproximadamente en]: **¿~ dónde vive?** whereabouts does he live?; **vive ~ las afueras** he lives somewhere on the outskirts; **había papeles ~ el suelo** there were papers all over the floor. **-7.** [lugar - a través de] through; **iba paseando ~ el bosque/la calle** she was walking through the forest/along the street; **pasar ~ la aduana** to go through customs. **-8.** [a cambio de, en lugar de] for; **lo ha comprado ~ poco dinero** she bought it for very little; **cambió el coche ~ la moto** he exchanged his car for a motorbike; **él lo hará ~ mí** he'll do it for me. **-9.** [distribución] per; **cien pesetas ~ unidad** a hundred pesetas each; **20 kms ~ hora** 20 km an O per hour. **-10.** MAT: **dos ~ dos igual a cuatro** two times two is four. **-11.** [en busca de] for; **baja ~ tabaco** go down to the shops for some cigarettes; **a ~ for**; **vino a ~ las entradas** she came for the tickets. **-12.** [concesión]: ~ **más** O **mucho que lo intentes no lo conseguirás** however hard you try O try as you might, you'll never manage it; **no me cae bien, ~ (muy) simpático que te parezca** you may think he's nice, but I don't like him. ◆ **por qué** *pron* why; *¿~* **qué lo dijo?** why did she say it?; *¿~* **qué no vienes?** why don't you come?

porcelana *f* [material] porcelain, china.

porcentaje *m* percentage.

porche *m* [soportal] arcade; [entrada] porch.

porción *f* portion, piece.

pordiosero, -ra *m y f* beggar.

porfía *f* [insistencia] persistence; [tozudez] stubbornness.

porfiar *vi* **-1.** [disputar] to argue obstinately. **-2.** [empeñarse]: ~ **en** to be insistent on.

pormenor *m* (*gen pl*) detail.

porno *adj fam* porno.

pornografía *f* pornography.

pornográfico, -ca *adj* pornographic.

poro *m* pore.

poroso, -sa *adj* porous.

porque *conj* **-1.** [debido a que] because. **-2.** [para que] so that, in order that.

porqué *m* reason; **el ~ de** the reason for.

porquería *f* **-1.** [suciedad] filth. **-2.** [cosa de mala calidad] rubbish (U).

porra *f* **-1.** [palo] club; [de policía] truncheon. **-2.** *loc*: **mandar a alguien a la ~** *fam* to tell sb to go to hell.

porrazo *m* [golpe] bang, blow; [caída] bump.

porro *m fam* [de droga] joint.

porrón *m glass wine jar used for drinking wine from its long spout*.

portaaviones = **portaviones**.

portada *f* **-1.** [de libro] title page; [de revista] (front) cover; [de periódico] front page. **-2.** [de disco] sleeve.

portador, -ra *m y f* carrier, bearer; **al ~** COM to the bearer.

portaequipajes *m inv* boot *Br*, trunk *Am*.

portafolios *m inv*, **portafolio** *m* [carpeta] file; [maletín] attaché case.

portal *m* [entrada] entrance hall; [puerta] main door.

portalámparas *m inv* socket.

portamonedas *m inv* purse.

portar *vt* to carry. ◆ **portarse** *vpr* to behave; **se ha portado bien conmigo** she has treated me well; *~***se mal** to misbehave.

portátil *adj* portable.

portaviones, portaaviones *m inv* aircraft carrier.

portavoz *m y f* [persona] spokesman (*f* spokeswoman).

portazo *m*: **dar un ~** to slam the door.

porte *m* **-1.** (*gen pl*) [gasto de transporte] carriage; ~ **debido/pagado** COM carriage due/paid. **-2.** [transporte] **carriage**, transport. **-3.** [aspecto] **bearing**, demeanour.

portento *m* wonder, marvel.

portentoso, -sa *adj* wonderful, amazing.

portería *f* **-1.** [de casa, colegio] caretaker's office ○ lodge; [de hotel, ministerio] porter's office ○ lodge. **-2.** DEP goal, goalmouth.

portero, -ra *m y f* **-1.** [de casa, colegio] caretaker; [de hotel, ministerio] porter; ~ **automático** ○ **electrónico** ○ **eléctrico** entry-phone. **-2.** DEP goalkeeper.

pórtico *m* **-1.** [fachada] portico. **-2.** [arcada] arcade.

portillo *m* [puerta pequeña] wicket gate.

portuario, -ria *adj* port (*antes de sust*); [de los muelles] dock (*antes de sust*); **trabajador ~** docker.

Portugal Portugal.

portugués, -esa *adj, m y f* Portuguese. ◆ **portugués** *m* [lengua] Portuguese.

porvenir *m* future.

pos ◆ **en pos de** *loc prep* **-1.** [detrás de] behind. **-2.** [en busca de] after.

posada *f* **-1.** [fonda] inn, guest house. **-2.** [hospedaje] lodging, accommodation.

posaderas *fpl fam* backside (*sg*), bottom (*sg*).

posar ◇ *vt* to put ○ lay down; [mano, mirada] to rest. ◇ *vi* to pose. ◆ **posarse** *vpr* **-1.** [gen] to settle. **-2.** [pájaro] to perch; [nave, helicóptero] to come down.

posavasos *m inv* coaster; [en pub] beer mat.

posdata, postdata *f* postscript.

pose *f* pose.

poseedor, -ra *m y f* owner; [de cargo, acciones, récord] holder.

poseer *vt* [ser dueño de] to own; [estar en poder de] to have, to possess.

poseído, -da *adj*: ~ **por** possessed by.

posesión *f* possession.

posesivo, -va *adj* possessive.

poseso, -sa *m y f* possessed person.

posgraduado, -da, postgraduado, -da *adj, m y f* postgraduate.

posguerra, postguerra f post-war period.

posibilidad f possibility, chance; **cabe la ~ de que ...** there is a chance that ....

posibilitar vt to make possible.

posible adj possible; **es ~ que llueva** it could rain; **dentro de lo ~, en lo ~** as far as possible; **de ser ~** if possible; **hacer (todo) lo ~** to do everything possible; **lo antes ~** as soon as possible.

posición f **-1.** [gen] position. **-2.** [categoría - social] status (U); [- económica] situation.

posicionarse vpr to take a position o stance.

positivo, -va adj [gen & ELECTR] positive.

poso m sediment; fig trace.

posponer vt **-1.** [relegar] to put behind, to relegate. **-2.** [aplazar] to postpone.

pospuesto, -ta pp → **posponer**.

posta ✦ **a posta** loc adv on purpose.

postal ◇ adj postal. ◇ f postcard.

postdata = **posdata**.

poste m post, pole; DEP post.

póster (pl **posters**) m poster.

postergar vt **-1.** [retrasar] to postpone.✦ **-2.** [relegar] to put behind, to relegate.

posteridad f **-1.** [generación futura] posterity. **-2.** [futuro] future.

posterior adj **-1.** [en el espacio] rear, back. **-2.** [en el tiempo] subsequent, later; **~ a** subsequent to, after.

posteriori ✦ **a posteriori** loc adv later, afterwards.

posterioridad f: **con ~** later, subsequently.

postgraduado, -da = **posgraduado**.

postguerra = **posguerra**.

postigo m [contraventana] shutter.

postín m showiness; **darse ~** to show off; **de ~** posh.

postizo, -za adj [falso] false. ✦ **postizo** m hairpiece.

postor, -ra m y f bidder.

postrado, -da adj prostrate.

postre m dessert, pudding; **a la ~** fig in the end.

postrero, -ra adj (antes de sust masculino sg: **postrer**) culto last.

postrimerías fpl final stages.

postulado m postulate.

postular ◇ vt [exigir] to call for. ◇ vi [para colectas] to collect.

póstumo, -ma adj posthumous.

postura f **-1.** [posición] position, posture. **-2.** [actitud] attitude, stance.

potable adj [bebible] drinkable; **agua ~** drinking water.

potaje m [CULIN - guiso] vegetable stew; [- caldo] vegetable stock.

potasio m potassium.

pote m pot.

potencia f [gen, MAT & POLÍT] power; **tiene mucha ~** it's very powerful.

potencial ◇ adj [gen & FÍS] potential. ◇ m **-1.** [fuerza] power. **-2.** [posibilidades] potential. **-3.** GRAM conditional.

potenciar vt **-1.** [fomentar] to encourage, to promote. **-2.** [reforzar] to boost.

potente adj powerful.

potra → **potro**.

potrero m Amer field, pasture.

potro, -tra m y f ZOOL colt (f filly). ✦ **potro** m DEP vaulting horse.

pozo m well; [de mina] shaft.

p.p. -1. (abrev de **por poder**) pp. **-2.** (abrev de **porte pagado**) c/p.

PP (abrev de **Partido Popular**) m Spanish political party to the right of the political spectrum.

práctica → **práctico**.

practicante ◇ adj practising. ◇ m y f **-1.** [de deporte] practitioner; [de religión] practising member of a Church. **-2.** MED medical assistant.

practicar ◇ vt **-1.** [gen] to practise; [deporte] to play. **-2.** [realizar] to carry out, to perform. ◇ vi to practise.

práctico, -ca adj practical. ✦ **práctica** f **-1.** [gen] practice; [de un deporte] playing; **en la práctica** in practice. **-2.** [clase no teórica] practical.

pradera f large meadow, prairie.

prado m meadow. ✦ **Prado** m: **el (Museo del) Prado** the Prado (Museum).

Praga Prague.

pragmático, -ca ◇ adj pragmatic. ◇ m y f [persona] pragmatist.

pral. abrev de **principal**.

praliné m praline.

preacuerdo m draft agreement.

preámbulo m [introducción - de libro] foreword, preface; [- de congreso, conferencia] introduction.

precalentar vt **-1.** CULIN to pre-heat. **-2.** DEP to warm up.

precario, -ria adj precarious.

precaución f **-1.** [prudencia] caution, care. **-2.** [medida] precaution; **tomar precauciones** to take precautions.

precaver vt to guard against. ✦ **precaverse** vpr to take precautions.

precavido, -da *adj* [prevenido] prudent; **es muy ~** he always comes prepared.
precedente ◇ *adj* previous, preceding. ◇ *m* precedent.
preceder *vt* to go before, to precede.
preceptivo, -va *adj* obligatory, compulsory. ◆ **preceptiva** *f* rules (*pl*).
precepto *m* precept.
preciado, -da *adj* valuable, prized.
preciar *vt* to appreciate. ◆ **preciarse** *vpr* to have self-respect; **~se de** to be proud of.
precintar *vt* to seal.
precinto *m* seal.
precio *m lit* & *fig* price; **a cualquier ~** at any price; **al ~ de** *fig* at the cost of; **~ de fábrica/de coste** factory/cost price; **~ de salida** starting price; **~ de venta (al público)** retail price.
preciosidad *f* [cosa bonita]: **¡es una ~!** it's lovely ○ beautiful!
precioso, -sa *adj* **-1.** [valioso] precious. **-2.** [bonito] lovely, beautiful.
precipicio *m* precipice.
precipitación *f* **-1.** [apresuramiento] haste. **-2.** [lluvia] rainfall (*U*).
precipitado, -da *adj* hasty.
precipitar *vt* **-1.** [arrojar] to throw ○ hurl down. **-2.** [acelerar] to speed up. ◆ **precipitarse** *vpr* **-1.** [caer] to plunge (down). **-2.** [acelerarse - acontecimientos etc] to speed up. **-3.** [apresurarse]: **~se (hacia)** to rush (towards). **-4.** [obrar irreflexivamente] to act rashly.
precisamente *adv* [justamente]: **¡~!** exactly!, precisely!; **~ por eso** for that very reason; **~ tú lo sugeriste** in fact it was you who suggested it.
precisar *vt* **-1.** [determinar] to fix, to set; [aclarar] to specify exactly. **-2.** [necesitar] to need, to require.
precisión *f* accuracy, precision.
preciso, -sa *adj* **-1.** [determinado, conciso] precise. **-2.** [necesario]: **ser ~ para (algo/hacer algo)** to be necessary (for sthg/to do sthg); **es ~ que vengas** you must come.
precocinado, -da *adj* pre-cooked.
preconcebido, -da *adj* [idea] preconceived; [plan] drawn up in advance.
preconcebir *vt* draw up in advance.
preconizar *vt* to recommend.
precoz *adj* [persona] precocious.
precursor, -ra *m y f* precursor.
predecesor, -ra *m y f* predecessor.
predecir *vt* to predict.
predestinado, -da *adj*: **~ (a)** predestined (to).

predestinar *vt* to predestine.
predeterminar *vt* to predetermine.
prédica *f* sermon.
predicado *m* GRAM predicate.
predicador, -ra *m y f* preacher.
predicar *vt* & *vi* to preach.
predicción *f* prediction; [del tiempo] forecast.
predicho, -cha *pp* → **predecir**.
predilección *f*: **~ (por)** preference (for).
predilecto, -ta *adj* favourite.
predisponer *vt*: **~ (a)** to predispose (to).
predisposición *f* **-1.** [aptitud]: **~ para** aptitude for. **-2.** [tendencia]: **~ a** predisposition to.
predispuesto, -ta ◇ *pp* → **predisponer**. ◇ *adj*: **~ (a)** predisposed (to).
predominante *adj* predominant; [viento, actitudes] prevailing.
predominar *vi*: **~ (sobre)** to predominate ○ prevail (over).
predominio *m* preponderance, predominance (*U*).
preelectoral *adj* pre-election (*antes de sust*).
preeminente *adj* preeminent.
preescolar *adj* nursery (*antes de sust*), preschool.
prefabricado, -da *adj* prefabricated.
prefabricar *vt* to prefabricate.
prefacio *m* preface.
preferencia *f* preference; **con ○ de ~** preferably; **tener ~** AUTOM to have right of way; **tener ~ por** to have a preference for.
preferente *adj* preferential.
preferentemente *adv* preferably.
preferible *adj*: **~ (a)** preferable (to).
preferido, -da *adj* favourite.
preferir *vt*: **~ algo (a algo)** to prefer sthg (to sthg).
prefijo *m* **-1.** GRAM prefix. **-2.** TELECOM (telephone) dialling code.
pregón *m* [discurso] speech; [bando] proclamation.
pregonar *vt* **-1.** [bando etc] to proclaim. **-2.** *fig* [secreto] to spread about.
pregunta *f* question; **hacer una ~** to ask a question.
preguntar ◇ *vt* to ask; **~ algo a alguien** to ask sb sthg. ◇ *vi*: **~ por** to ask about ○ after. ◆ **preguntarse** *vpr*: **~se (si)** to wonder (whether).
prehistoria *f* prehistory.
prehistórico, -ca *adj* prehistoric.

prejuicio m prejudice.

preliminar ◇ adj preliminary. ◇ m (gen pl) preliminary.

preludio m [gen & MÚS] prelude.

prematrimonial adj premarital.

prematuro, -ra adj premature.

premeditación f premeditation.

premeditar vt to think out in advance.

premiar vt **-1.** [recompensar] to reward. **-2.** [dar un premio a] to give a prize to.

premier (pl premiers) m British prime minister.

premio m [en competición] prize; [recompensa] reward; ~ **gordo** first prize.

premisa f premise.

premonición f premonition.

premura f [urgencia] urgency.

prenatal adj prenatal, antenatal.

prenda f **-1.** [vestido] garment, article of clothing. **-2.** [garantía] pledge; **dejar algo en** ~ to leave sthg as a pledge. **-3.** [de un juego] forfeit. **-4.** loc: **no soltar** ~ not to say a word.

prendar vt to enchant.

prender ◇ vt **-1.** [arrestar] to arrest, to apprehend. **-2.** [sujetar] to fasten. **-3.** [encender] to light. **-4.** [agarrar] to grip. ◇ vi [arder] to catch (fire). ◆ **prenderse** vpr [arder] to catch fire.

prendido, -da adj caught.

prensa f **-1.** [gen] press; ~ **del corazón** romantic magazines (pl). **-2.** [imprenta] printing press.

prensar vt to press.

preñado, -da adj **-1.** [mujer] pregnant. **-2.** fig [lleno]: ~ **de** full of.

preocupación f concern, worry.

preocupado, -da adj: ~ **(por)** worried ○ concerned (about).

preocupar vt **-1.** [inquietar] to worry. **-2.** [importar] to bother. ◆ **preocuparse** vpr **-1.** [inquietarse]: ~**se (por)** to worry (about), to be worried (about). **-2.** [encargarse]: ~**se de algo** to take care of sthg; ~**se de hacer algo** to see to it that sthg is done; ~**se de que ...** to make sure that ....

preparación f **-1.** [gen] preparation. **-2.** [conocimientos] training.

preparado, -da adj **-1.** [dispuesto] ready; [de antemano] prepared. **-2.** CULIN ready-cooked. ◆ **preparado** m FARM preparation.

preparar vt **-1.** [gen] to prepare; [trampa] to set, to lay; [maletas] to pack. **-2.** [examen] to prepare for. **-3.** DEP to train. ◆ **prepararse** vpr: ~**se (para algo)** to prepare o.s. ○ get ready (for sthg); ~**se**

para hacer algo to prepare ○ get ready to do sthg.

preparativo, -va adj preparatory, preliminary. ◆ **preparativos** mpl preparations.

preposición f preposition.

prepotente adj [arrogante] domineering.

prerrogativa f prerogative.

presa f **-1.** [captura - de cazador] catch; [- de animal] prey; **hacer** ~ **en alguien** to seize ○ grip sb; **ser** ~ **de** to be prey to; **ser** ~ **del pánico** to be panic-stricken. **-2.** [dique] dam.

presagiar vt [felicidad, futuro] to foretell; [tormenta, problemas] to warn of.

presagio m **-1.** [premonición] premonition. **-2.** [señal] omen.

presbítero m priest.

prescindir ◆ **prescindir de** vi **-1.** [renunciar a] to do without. **-2.** [omitir] to dispense with.

prescribir ◇ vt to prescribe. ◇ vi **-1.** [ordenar] to prescribe. **-2.** DER to expire.

prescripción f prescription.

prescrito, -ta pp → **prescribir**.

presencia f [asistencia, aspecto] presence; **en** ~ **de** in the presence of. ◆ **presencia de ánimo** f presence of mind.

presencial → **testigo**.

presenciar vt [asistir] to be present at; [ser testigo de] to witness.

presentación f **-1.** [gen] presentation. **-2.** [entre personas] introduction.

presentador, -ra m y f presenter.

presentar vt **-1.** [gen] to present; [dimisión] to tender; [tesis, pruebas, propuesta] to submit; [solicitud, recurso, denuncia] to lodge; [moción] to propose. **-2.** [ofrecer - disculpas, excusas] to make; [- respetos] to pay. **-3.** [persona, amigos etc] to introduce. **-4.** [tener - aspecto etc] to have, to show; **presenta difícil solución** it's going to be difficult to solve. **-5.** [proponer]: ~ **a alguien para** to propose sb for. ◆ **presentarse** vpr **-1.** [aparecer] to turn up. **-2.** [en juzgado, comisaría]: ~**se (en)** to report (to); ~**se a un examen** to sit an exam. **-3.** [darse a conocer] to introduce o.s. **-4.** [para un cargo]: ~**se (a)** to stand ○ run (for). **-5.** [futuro] to appear, to look. **-6.** [problema etc] to arise.

presente ◇ adj **-1.** [gen] present; **aquí** ~ here present; **tener** ~ [recordar] to remember; [tener en cuenta] to bear in mind. **-2.** [en curso] current; **del** ~ **mes** of this month. ◇ m y f [escrito]: **por la**

~ **le informo** ... I hereby inform you .... ◇ *m* **-1.** [gen & GRAM] present. **-2.** [regalo] gift, present. **-3.** [corriente]: **el ~** [mes] the current month; [año] the current year.

presentimiento *m* presentiment, feeling.

presentir *vt* to foresee; ~ **que algo va a pasar** to have a feeling that sthg is going to happen; ~ **lo peor** to fear the worst.

preservar *vt* to protect.

preservativo, -va *adj* protective. ◆ **preservativo** *m* condom.

presidencia *f* [de nación] presidency; [de asamblea, empresa] chairmanship.

presidente, -ta *m y f* [de nación] president; [de asamblea, empresa] chairman (*f* chairwoman); ~ **(del gobierno)** ≃ prime minister.

presidiario, -ria *m y f* convict.

presidio *m* prison.

presidir *vt* **-1.** [ser presidente de] to preside over; [reunión] to chair. **-2.** [predominar] to dominate.

presión *f* pressure.

presionar *vt* **-1.** [apretar] to press. **-2.** *fig* [coaccionar] to pressurize.

preso, -sa *m y f* prisoner.

prestación *f* [de servicio - acción] provision; [- resultado] service. ◆ **prestaciones** *fpl* [de coche etc] performance features.

prestado, -da *adj* on loan; **dar ~ algo** to lend sthg; **pedir/tomar ~ algo** to borrow sthg.

prestamista *m y f* moneylender.

préstamo *m* **-1.** [acción - de prestar] lending; [- de pedir prestado] borrowing. **-2.** [cantidad] loan.

prestar *vt* **-1.** [dejar - dinero etc] to lend, to loan. **-2.** [dar - ayuda etc] to give, to offer; [- servicio] to provide; [- atención] to pay; [- declaración, juramento] to make. ◆ **prestarse a** *vpr* **-1.** [ofrecerse a] to offer to. **-2.** [acceder a] to consent to. **-3.** [dar motivo a] to be open to.

presteza *f* promptness.

prestidigitador, -ra *m y f* conjuror.

prestigio *m* prestige.

prestigioso, -sa *adj* prestigious.

presto, -ta *adj* [dispuesto]: ~ **(a)** ready (to).

presumible *adj* probable, likely.

presumido, -da *adj* conceited, vain.

presumir ◇ *vt* [suponer] to presume. ◇ *vi* **-1.** [jactarse] to show off. **-2.** [ser vanidoso] to be conceited ○ vain.

presunción *f* **-1.** [suposición] presumption. **-2.** [vanidad] conceit, vanity.

presunto, -ta *adj* presumed, supposed; [criminal, robo etc] alleged.

presuntuoso, -sa *adj* [vanidoso] conceited; [pretencioso] pretentious.

presuponer *vt* to presuppose.

presupuesto, -ta *pp* → **presuponer.** ◆ **presupuesto** *m* **-1.** [cálculo] budget; [de costo] estimate. **-2.** [suposición] assumption.

prêt-à-porter [pretapor'te] (*pl* **prêts-à-porter**) *m* off-the-peg clothing.

pretencioso, -sa *adj* [persona] pretentious; [cosa] showy.

pretender *vt* **-1.** [intentar]: ~ **hacer algo** to try to do sthg. **-2.** [aspirar a]: ~ **hacer algo** to aspire ○ want to do sthg; ~ **que alguien haga algo** to want sb to do sthg; **¿qué pretendes decir?** what do you mean? **-3.** [afirmar] to claim. **-4.** [cortejar] to court.

pretendido, -da *adj* supposed.

pretendiente ◇ *m y f* **-1.** [aspirante]: ~ **(a)** candidate (for). **-2.** [a un trono]: ~ **(a)** pretender (to). ◇ *m* [a una mujer] suitor.

pretensión *f* **-1.** [intención] aim, intention. **-2.** [aspiración] aspiration. **-3.** [supuesto derecho]: ~ **(a ○ sobre)** claim (to). **-4.** [afirmación] claim. **-5.** (*gen pl*) [exigencia] demand.

pretérito, -ta *adj* past. ◆ **pretérito** *m* GRAM preterite, past.

pretexto *m* pretext, excuse.

prevalecer *vi*: ~ **(sobre)** to prevail (over).

prevaler *vi*: ~ **(sobre)** to prevail (over).

prevención *f* [acción] prevention; [medida] precaution.

prevenido, -da *adj* **-1.** [previsor]: **ser ~** to be cautious. **-2.** [avisado, dispuesto]: **estar ~** to be prepared.

prevenir *vt* **-1.** [evitar] to prevent; **más vale ~ que curar** *proverb* prevention is better than cure *proverb*. **-2.** [avisar] to warn. **-3.** [prever] to foresee. **-4.** [predisponer]: ~ **a alguien contra algo/alguien** to prejudice sb against sthg/sb.

preventivo, -va *adj* [medicina, prisión] preventive; [medida] precautionary.

prever *vt* **-1.** [conjeturar] to foresee. **-2.** [planear] to plan. **-3.** [predecir] to forecast.

previniera *etc* → **prevenir.**

previo, -via *adj* prior; ~ **pago de multa** on payment of a fine.

previó → **prever.**

previsible *adj* foreseeable.
previsión *f* **-1.** [predicción] forecast. **-2.** [visión de futuro] foresight.
previsor, -ra *adj* prudent, farsighted.
previsto, -ta ◇ *pp* → **prever.** ◇ *adj* [conjeturado] predicted; [planeado] planned.
prieto, -ta *adj* **-1.** [ceñido] tight. **-2.** *Amer fam* [moreno] dark-haired.
prima → **primo.**
primacía *f* primacy.
primar *vi:* ~ **(sobre)** to have priority (over).
primario, -ria *adj* primary; *fig* primitive.
primavera *f* [estación] spring.
primaveral *adj* spring (*antes de sust*).
primer, primera → **primero.**
primerizo, -za *m y f* [principiante] beginner.
primero, -ra ◇ *núm adj* (*antes de sust masculino sg:* **primer**) **-1.** [para ordenar] first. **-2.** [en importancia] main, basic; **lo** ~ the most important ○ main thing. ◇ *núm m y f* **-1.** [en orden]: **el** ~ the first one; **llegó el** ~ he came first; **es el** ~ **de la clase** he's top of the class; **a** ~**s de mes** at the beginning of the month. **-2.** [mencionado antes]: **vinieron Pedro y Juan, el** ~ **con ...** Pedro and Juan arrived, the former with .... ◆ **primero** ◇ *adv* **-1.** [en primer lugar] first. **-2.** [antes, todo menos]: ~ **morir que traicionarle** I'd rather die than betray him. ◇ *m* **-1.** [piso] first floor. **-2.** [curso] first year. ◆ **primera** *f* **-1.** AUTOM first (gear). **-2.** AERON & FERROC first class. **-3.** DEP first division. **-4.** *loc:* **de primera** first-class.
primicia *f* scoop, exclusive.
primitivo, -va *adj* **-1.** [gen] primitive. **-2.** [original] original.
primo, -ma *m y f* **-1.** [pariente] cousin. **-2.** *fam* [tonto] sucker; **hacer el** ~ to be taken for a ride. ◆ **prima** *f* **-1.** [paga extra] bonus. **-2.** [de un seguro] premium. ◆ **prima dona** *f* prima donna.
primogénito, -ta *adj, m y f* first-born.
primor *m* fine thing.
primordial *adj* fundamental.
primoroso, -sa *adj* **-1.** [delicado] exquisite, fine. **-2.** [hábil] skilful.
princesa *f* princess.
principado *m* principality.
principal *adj* main, principal; [puerta] front.
príncipe *m* prince.

principiante, -ta ◇ *adj* inexperienced. ◇ *m y f* novice.
principio *m* **-1.** [comienzo] beginning, start; **a** ~**s** de at the beginning of; **en un** ~ at first. **-2.** [fundamento, ley] principle; **en** ~ in principle; **por** ~ on principle. **-3.** [origen] origin, source. **-4.** [elemento] element. ◆ **principios** *mpl* **-1.** [reglas de conducta] principles. **-2.** [nociones] rudiments.
pringar *vt* **-1.** [ensuciar] to make greasy. **-2.** [mojar] to dip.
pringoso, -sa *adj* [grasiento] greasy; [pegajoso] sticky.
pringue ◇ *m* [suciedad] muck, dirt; [grasa] grease.
priori ◆ **a priori** *loc adv* in advance, a priori.
prioridad *f* priority; AUTOM right of way.
prioritario, -ria *adj* priority (*antes de sust*).
prisa *f* haste, hurry; **a** ○ **de** ~ quickly; **correr** ~ to be urgent; **darse** ~ to hurry (up); **meter** ~ **a alguien** to hurry ○ rush sb; **tener** ~ to be in a hurry.
prisión *f* **-1.** [cárcel] prison. **-2.** [encarcelamiento] imprisonment.
prisionero, -ra *m y f* prisoner.
prisma *m* **-1.** FÍS & GEOM prism. **-2.** *fig* [perspectiva] perspective.
prismático, -ca *adj* prismatic. ◆ **prismáticos** *mpl* binoculars.
privación *f* [gen] deprivation; [de libertad] loss.
privado, -da *adj* private; **en** ~ in private.
privar *vt* **-1.** [quitar]: ~ **a alguien/algo de** to deprive sb/sthg of. **-2.** [prohibir]: ~ **a alguien de hacer algo** to forbid sb to do sthg. ◆ **privarse de** *vpr* to go without.
privativo, -va *adj* exclusive.
privilegiado, -da *adj* **-1.** [favorecido] privileged. **-2.** [excepcional] exceptional.
privilegiar *vt* [persona] to favour; [intereses] to put first.
privilegio *m* privilege.
pro ◇ *prep* for, supporting; **una asociación** ~ **derechos humanos** a human rights organization. ◇ *m* advantage; **los** ~**s y los contras** the pros and cons. ◆ **en pro de** *loc prep* for, in support of.
proa *f* NÁUT prow, bows (*pl*); AERON nose.
probabilidad *f* probability; [oportunidad] chance.

probable *adj* probable, likely; **es ~ que lleva** it'll probably rain.

probador *m* fitting room.

probar ◇ *vt* **-1.** [demostrar, indicar] to prove. **-2.** [comprobar] to test, to check. **-3.** [experimentar] to try. **-4.** [degustar] to taste, to try. ◇ *vi*: **~ a hacer algo** to try to do sthg. ◆ **probarse** *vpr* [ropa] to try on.

probeta *f* test tube.

problema *m* problem.

problemático, -ca *adj* problematic. ◆ **problemática** *f* problems (*pl*).

procedencia *f* **-1.** [origen] origin. **-2.** [punto de partida] point of departure; **con ~ de** (arriving) from.

procedente *adj* **-1.** [originario]: **~ de** [gen] originating in; AERON & FERROC (arriving) from. **-2.** [oportuno] appropriate; DER right and proper.

proceder ◇ *m* conduct, behaviour. ◇ *vi* **-1.** [originarse]: **~ de** to come from. **-2.** [actuar]: **~ (con)** to act (with). **-3.** [empezar]: **~ (a algo/a hacer algo)** to proceed (with sthg/to do sthg). **-4.** [ser oportuno] to be appropriate.

procedimiento *m* **-1.** [método] procedure, method. **-2.** DER proceedings (*pl*).

procesado, -da *m y f* accused, defendant.

procesador *m* INFORM processor; **~ de textos** word processor.

procesar *vt* **-1.** DER to prosecute. **-2.** INFORM to process.

procesión *f* RELIG & *fig* procession.

proceso *m* **-1.** [gen] process. **-2.** [desarrollo, intervalo] course. **-3.** [DER - juicio] trial; [- causa] lawsuit.

proclama *f* proclamation.

proclamar *vt* **-1.** [nombrar] to proclaim. **-2.** [anunciar] to declare. ◆ **proclamarse** *vpr* **-1.** [nombrarse] to proclaim o.s. **-2.** [conseguir un título]: **~se campeón** to become champion.

proclive *adj*: **~ a** prone to.

procreación *f* procreation.

procrear *vi* to procreate.

procurador, -ra *m y f* DER attorney.

procurar *vt* **-1.** [intentar]: **~ hacer algo** to try to do sthg; **~ que ...** to make sure that .... **-2.** [proporcionar] to get, to secure. ◆ **procurarse** *vpr* to get, to obtain (for o.s.).

prodigar *vt*: **~ algo a alguien** to lavish sthg on sb.

prodigio *m* [suceso] miracle; [persona] prodigy.

prodigioso, -sa *adj* **-1.** [sobrenatural] miraculous. **-2.** [extraordinario] wonderful.

pródigo, -ga *adj* [generoso] generous, lavish.

producción *f* **-1.** [gen & CIN] production; **~ en serie** ECON mass production. **-2.** [productos] products (*pl*).

producir *vt* **-1.** [gen & CIN] to produce. **-2.** [causar] to cause, to give rise to. **-3.** [interés, fruto] to yield, to bear. ◆ **producirse** *vpr* [ocurrir] to take place.

productividad *f* productivity.

productivo, -va *adj* productive; [que da beneficio] profitable.

producto *m* **-1.** [gen & MAT] product; AGR produce (*U*); **~ interior/nacional bruto** gross domestic/national product; **~ químico** chemical. **-2.** [ganancia] profit. **-3.** *fig* [resultado] result.

productor, -ra ◇ *adj* producing. ◇ *m y f* CIN [persona] producer. ◆ **productora** *f* CIN [firma] production company.

proeza *f* exploit, deed.

profanar *vt* to desecrate.

profano, -na ◇ *adj* **-1.** [no sagrado] profane, secular. **-2.** [ignorante] ignorant, uninitiated. ◇ *m y f* layman (*f* laywoman).

profecía *f* [predicción] prophecy.

proferir *vt* to utter; [insultos] to hurl.

profesar *vt* **-1.** [una religión] to follow; [una profesión] to practise. **-2.** [admiración etc] to profess.

profesión *f* profession.

profesional *adj, m y f* professional.

profesionista *m y f* *Amer* professional.

profesor, -ra *m y f* [gen] teacher; [de universidad] lecturer; [de autoescuela, esquí etc] instructor.

profesorado *m* [plantilla] teaching staff, faculty *Am*; [profesión] teachers (*pl*), teaching profession.

profeta *m* prophet.

profetisa *f* prophetess.

profetizar *vt* to prophesy.

profiera *etc* → **proferir**.

prófugo, -ga *adj, m y f* fugitive.

profundidad *f* *lit* & *fig* depth; **tiene dos metros de ~** it's two metres deep.

profundizar ◇ *vt* *fig* to study in depth. ◇ *vi* to go into detail; **~ en** to study in depth.

profundo, -da *adj* **-1.** [gen] deep. **-2.** *fig* [respeto, libro, pensamiento] profound, deep; [dolor] intense.

profusión *f* profusion.

progenitor, -ra *m y f* father (*f* mother).
◆ **progenitores** *mpl* parents.

programa *m* -1. [gen] programme. -2. [de actividades] schedule, programme; [de estudios] syllabus. -3. INFORM program.

programación *f* -1. INFORM programming. -2. TV scheduling; **la ~ del lunes** Monday's programmes.

programador, -ra *m y f* [persona] programmer.

programar *vt* -1. [vacaciones, reforma etc] to plan. -2. CIN & TV to put on, to show. -3. TECN to programme; INFORM to program.

progre *fam m y f* progressive.

progresar *vi* to progress.

progresión *f* [gen & MAT] progression; [mejora] progress, advance.

progresista *adj, m y f* progressive.

progresivo, -va *adj* progressive.

progreso *m* progress; **hacer ~s** to make progress.

prohibición *f* ban, banning (U).

prohibido, -da *adj* prohibited, banned; "**~ aparcar/fumar**" "no parking/smoking", "parking/smoking prohibited"; "**prohibida la entrada**" "no entry"; "**dirección prohibida**" AUTOM "no entry".

prohibir *vt* -1. [gen] to forbid; **~ a alguien hacer algo** to forbid sb to do sthg; "**se prohíbe el paso**" "no entry". -2. [por ley - de antemano] to prohibit; [- a posteriori] to ban.

prohibitivo, -va *adj* prohibitive.

prójimo *m* fellow human being.

prole *f* offspring.

proletariado *m* proletariat.

proletario, -ria *adj, m y f* proletarian.

proliferación *f* proliferation.

proliferar *vi* to proliferate.

prolífico, -ca *adj* prolific.

prolijo, -ja *adj* [extenso] long-winded.

prólogo *m* [de libro] preface, foreword; [de obra de teatro] prologue; *fig* prelude.

prolongación *f* extension.

prolongado, -da *adj* long; *fig* [dilatado] lengthy.

prolongar *vt* [gen] to extend; [espera, visita, conversación] to prolong; [cuerda, tubo] to lengthen.

promedio *m* average.

promesa *f* [compromiso] promise.

prometer ◇ *vt* to promise. ◇ *vi* [tener futuro] to show promise. ◆ **prometerse** *vpr* to get engaged.

prometido, -da ◇ *m y f* fiancé (*f* fiancée). ◇ *adj* [para casarse] engaged.

prominente *adj* -1. [abultado] protruding. -2. [elevado, ilustre] prominent.

promiscuo, -cua *adj* promiscuous.

promoción *f* -1. [gen & DEP] promotion. -2. [curso] class, year.

promocionar *vt* to promote.

promotor, -ra *m y f* promoter; [de una rebelión] instigator.

promover *vt* -1. [iniciar - fundación etc] to set up; [- rebelión] to stir up. -2. [ocasionar] to cause. -3. [ascender]: **~ a alguien** to promote sb to.

promulgar *vt* [ley] to pass.

pronombre *m* pronoun.

pronosticar *vt* to predict, to forecast.

pronóstico *m* -1. [predicción] forecast. -2. MED prognosis; **de ~ grave** serious, in a serious condition.

pronto, -ta *adj* quick, fast; [respuesta] prompt, early; [curación, tramitación] speedy. ◆ **pronto** ◇ *adv* -1. [rápidamente] quickly; **tan ~ como** as soon as. -2. [temprano] early; **salimos ~** we left early. -3. [dentro de poco] soon; **¡hasta ~!** see you soon! ◇ *m fam* sudden impulse. ◆ **al pronto** *loc adv* at first. ◆ **de pronto** *loc adv* suddenly. ◆ **por lo pronto** *loc adv* -1. [de momento] for the time being. -2. [para empezar] to start with.

pronunciación *f* pronunciation.

pronunciado, -da *adj* [facciones] pronounced; [curva] sharp; [pendiente, cuesta] steep; [nariz] prominent.

pronunciamiento *m* -1. [sublevación] uprising. -2. DER pronouncement.

pronunciar *vt* -1. [decir - palabra] to pronounce; [- discurso] to deliver, to make. -2. DER to pass. ◆ **pronunciarse** *vpr* -1. [definirse]: **~se (sobre)** to state an opinion (on). -2. [sublevarse] to revolt.

propagación *f* -1. [gen] spreading (U). -2. BIOL & FÍS propagation.

propaganda *f* -1. [publicidad] advertising (U). -2. [política, religiosa] propaganda.

propagar *vt* [gen] to spread; [razas, especies] to propagate. ◆ **propagarse** *vpr* -1. [gen] to spread. -2. BIOL & FÍS to propagate.

propasarse *vpr*: **~ (con algo)** to go too far (with sthg); **~ con alguien** [sexualmente] to take liberties with sb.

propensión *f* propensity, tendency.

propenso, -sa *adj*: **~ a algo/a hacer algo** prone to sthg/doing sthg.

propicio, -cia *adj* **-1.** [favorable] propitious, favourable. **-2.** [adecuado] suitable, appropriate.

propiedad *f* **-1.** [derecho] ownership; [bienes] property; ~ **privada** private property; ~ **pública** public ownership. **-2.** [facultad] property. **-3.** [exactitud] accuracy; **usar una palabra con** ~ to use a word properly.

propietario, -ria *m y f* [de bienes] owner; [de cargo] holder.

propina *f* tip.

propinar *vt* [paliza] to give; [golpe] to deal.

propio, -pia *adj* **-1.** [gen] own; **tiene coche** ~ she has a car of her own, she has her own car; **por tu** ~ **bien** for your own good. **-2.** [peculiar]: ~ **de** typical O characteristic of; **no es** ~ **de él** it's not like him. **-3.** [apropiado]: ~ **(para)** suitable O right (for). **-4.** [correcto] proper, true. **-5.** [en persona] himself (*f* herself); **el** ~ **compositor** the composer himself.

proponer *vt* to propose; [candidato] to put forward. ◆ **proponerse** *vpr*: ~**se hacer algo** to plan O intend to do sthg.

proporción *f* **-1.** [gen & MAT] proportion. **-2.** (*gen pl*) [importancia] extent, size. ◆ **proporciones** *fpl* [tamaño] size (*sg*).

proporcionado, -da *adj*: ~ **(a)** [estatura, sueldo] commensurate (with); [medidas] proportionate (to); **bien** ~ well-proportioned.

proporcionar *vt* **-1.** [ajustar]: ~ **algo a algo** to adapt sthg to sthg. **-2.** [facilitar]: ~ **algo a alguien** to provide sb with sthg. **-3.** *fig* [conferir] to lend, to add.

proposición *f* [propuesta] proposal.

propósito *m* **-1.** [intención] intention. **-2.** [objetivo] purpose. ◆ **a propósito** ◇ *loc adj* [adecuado] suitable. ◇ *loc adv* **-1.** [adrede] on purpose. **-2.** [por cierto] by the way. ◆ **a propósito de** *loc prep* with regard to.

propuesta *f* proposal; [de empleo] offer.

propuesto, -ta *pp* → **proponer**.

propugnar *vt* to advocate, to support.

propulsar *vt* **-1.** [impeler] to propel. **-2.** *fig* [promover] to promote.

propulsión *f* propulsion; ~ **a chorro** jet propulsion.

propulsor, -ra *m y f* [persona] promoter. ◆ **propulsor** *m* **-1.** [dispositivo] engine. **-2.** [combustible] propellent.

propusiera *etc* → **proponer**.

prórroga *f* **-1.** [gen] extension; [de estudios, servicio militar] deferment. **-2.** DEP extra time.

prorrogar *vt* [alargar] to extend; [aplazar] to defer, to postpone.

prorrumpir *vi*: ~ **en** to burst into.

prosa *f* LITER prose.

proscrito, -ta ◇ *adj* [prohibido] banned. ◇ *m y f* **-1.** [desterrado] exile. **-2.** [fuera de la ley] outlaw.

proseguir ◇ *vt* to continue. ◇ *vi* to go on, to continue.

prosiga *etc* → **proseguir**.

prosiguiera *etc* → **proseguir**.

prospección *f* [gen] exploration; [petrolífera, minera] prospecting.

prospecto *m* leaflet; COM & EDUC prospectus.

prosperar *vi* [mejorar] to prosper.

prosperidad *f* **-1.** [mejora] prosperity. **-2.** [éxito] success.

próspero, -ra *adj* prosperous.

prostíbulo *m* brothel.

prostitución *f* [gen] prostitution.

prostituir *vt* *lit* & *fig* to prostitute. ◆ **prostituirse** *vpr* to become a prostitute.

prostituta *f* prostitute.

protagonista *m y f* [gen] main character, hero (*f* heroine); TEATR lead, leading role.

protagonizar *vt* **-1.** [obra, película] to play the lead in, to star in. **-2.** *fig* [crimen, hazaña] to be responsible for.

protección *f* protection.

proteccionismo *m* protectionism.

protector, -ra ◇ *adj* protective. ◇ *m y f* [persona] protector.

proteger *vt* [gen] to protect; ~ **algo de algo** to protect sthg from sthg. ◆ **protegerse** *vpr* to take cover O refuge.

protege-slips *m inv* panty pad O liner.

protegido, -da *m y f* protégé (*f* protégée).

proteína *f* protein.

prótesis *f inv* MED prosthesis; [miembro] artificial limb.

protesta *f* protest; DER objection.

protestante *adj, m y f* Protestant.

protestar *vi* **-1.** [quejarse]: ~ **(por/contra)** to protest (about/against); **¡protesto!** DER objection! **-2.** [refunfuñar] to grumble.

protocolo *m* **-1.** [gen & INFORM] protocol. **-2.** [ceremonial] etiquette.

prototipo *m* **-1.** [modelo] archetype. **-2.** [primer ejemplar] prototype.

protuberancia *f* protuberance, bulge.

provecho *m* **-1.** [gen] benefit; **buen ~** enjoy your meal!; **de ~** [persona] worthy; **sacar ~ de** to make the most of, to take advantage of. **-2.** [rendimiento] good effect.

provechoso, -sa *adj* **-1.** [ventajoso] beneficial, advantageous. **-2.** [lucrativo] profitable.

proveedor, -ra *m y f* supplier.

proveer *vt* **-1.** [abastecer] to supply, to provide. **-2.** [puesto, cargo] to fill. ◆ **proveerse de** *vpr* **-1.** [ropa, víveres] to stock up on. **-2.** [medios, recursos] to arm o.s. with.

provenir *vi*: **~ de** to come from.

proverbial *adj* proverbial.

proverbio *m* proverb.

providencia *f* [medida] measure.

providencial *adj lit & fig* providential.

proviene *etc* → **provenir**.

provincia *f* [división administrativa] province. ◆ **provincias** *fpl* [no la capital] the provinces.

provinciano, -na *adj, m y f despec* provincial.

proviniera *etc* → **provenir**.

provisión *f* **-1.** (*gen pl*) [suministro] supply, provision; [de una plaza] filling (U). **-2.** [disposición] measure.

provisional *adj* provisional.

provisto, -ta *pp* → **proveer**.

provocación *f* [hostigamiento] provocation.

provocar *vt* **-1.** [incitar] to incite. **-2.** [irritar] to provoke. **-3.** [ocasionar - gen] to cause. **-4.** [excitar sexualmente] to arouse. **-5.** *Amer fig* [apetecer]: **¿te provoca hacerlo?** do you feel like doing it?

provocativo, -va *adj* provocative.

próximamente *adv* soon, shortly; CIN coming soon.

proximidad *f* [cercanía] closeness, proximity. ◆ **proximidades** *fpl* **-1.** [de ciudad] surrounding area (*sg*). **-2.** [de lugar] vicinity (*sg*).

próximo, -ma *adj* **-1.** [cercano] near, close; [casa, ciudad] nearby; **en fecha próxima** shortly. **-2.** [siguiente] next; **el ~ año** next year.

proyección *f* **-1.** [gen & GEOM] projection. **-2.** CIN screening. **-3.** *fig* [trascendencia] importance.

proyectar *vt* **-1.** [dirigir - focos etc] to shine, to direct. **-2.** [mostrar - película]

to screen; [- sombra] to cast; [- diapositivas] to show. **-3.** [planear - viaje, operación, edificio] to plan; [- puente, obra] to design. **-4.** [arrojar] to throw forwards.

proyectil *m* projectile, missile.

proyecto *m* **-1.** [intención] project. **-2.** [plan] plan. **-3.** [diseño - ARQUIT] design; [- IND & TECN] plan. **-4.** [borrador] draft; **~ de ley** bill. **-5.** EDUC: **~ fin de carrera** *design project forming part of doctoral thesis for architecture students etc*; **~ de investigación** [de un grupo] research project; [de una persona] dissertation.

proyector, -ra *adj* projecting. ◆ **proyector** *m* [de cine, diapositivas] projector.

prudencia *f* [cuidado] caution, care; [previsión, sensatez] prudence; [moderación] moderation; **con ~** in moderation.

prudente *adj* **-1.** [cuidadoso] careful, cautious; [previsor, sensato] sensible. **-2.** [razonable] reasonable.

prueba ◇ *v* → **probar**. ◇ *f* **-1.** [demostración] proof; DER evidence, proof; **no tengo ~s** I have no proof. **-2.** [manifestación] sign, token. **-3.** EDUC & MED test; **~ de acceso** entrance examination. **-4.** [comprobación] test; **a O de ~** [trabajador] on trial; [producto comprado] on approval; **es a ~ de agua/balas** it's waterproof/bulletproof; **poner a ~** to (put to the) test. **-5.** DEP event. **-6.** IMPRENTA proof.

PS = **PD**.

pseudónimo *m* pseudonym.

psicoanálisis *m inv* psychoanalysis.

psicoanalista *m y f* psychoanalyst.

psicodélico, -ca *adj* psychedelic.

psicología *f lit & fig* psychology.

psicológico, -ca *adj* psychological.

psicólogo, -ga *m y f* psychologist.

psicópata *m y f* psychopath.

psicosis *f inv* psychosis.

psicosomático, -ca *adj* psychosomatic.

psiquiatra *m y f* psychiatrist.

psiquiátrico, -ca *adj* psychiatric.

psíquico, -ca *adj* psychic.

PSOE [pe'soe, soe] (*abrev de* **Partido Socialista Obrero Español**) *m major Spanish political party to the centre-left of the political spectrum.*

pta. (*abrev de* **peseta**) pta.

púa *f* **-1.** [de planta] thorn; [de erizo] quill; [de peine] tooth; [de tenedor] prong. **-2.** MÚS plectrum.

pub [pap] (*pl* **pubs**) *m upmarket pub*, ≃ wine bar.

pubertad *f* puberty.

pubis *m inv* pubes (*pl*).
publicación *f* publication.
publicar *vt* **-1.** [editar] to publish. **-2.** [difundir] to publicize; [ley] to pass; [aviso] to issue.
publicidad *f* **-1.** [difusión] publicity; **dar ~ a algo** to publicize sthg. **-2.** COM advertising; TV adverts (*pl*), commercials (*pl*).
publicitario, -ria *adj* advertising (*antes de sust*).
público, -ca *adj* public; **ser ~** [conocido] to be common knowledge; **en ~** in public. ◆ **público** *m* **-1.** CIN, TEATR & TV audience; DEP crowd. **-2.** [comunidad] public; **el gran ~** the (general) public.
publirreportaje *m* [anuncio de televisión] promotional film; [en revista] advertising spread.
puchero *m* **-1.** [perola] cooking pot. **-2.** [comida] stew. ◆ **pucheros** *mpl* [gesto] pout (*sg*); **hacer ~s** to pout.
pucho *m Amer* [colilla] cigarette butt.
pudding = pudin.
púdico, -ca *adj* modest.
pudiente *adj* wealthy.
pudiera *etc* → poder.
pudin (*pl* púdines), **pudding** ['puðin] (*pl* puddings) *m* (plum) pudding.
pudor *m* **-1.** [recato] (sense of) shame. **-2.** [timidez] bashfulness.
pudoroso, -sa *adj* **-1.** [recatado] modest. **-2.** [tímido] bashful.
pudrir *vt* to rot. ◆ **pudrirse** *vpr* to rot.
puebla *etc* → poblar.
pueblerino, -na *adj* village (*antes de sust*); *despec* provincial.
pueblo *m* **-1.** [población - pequeña] village; [- grande] town. **-2.** [nación] people.
pueda *etc* → poder.
puente *m* **-1.** [gen] bridge. **-2.** [días festivos]: **hacer ~** *to take an extra day off between two public holidays*. ◆ **puente aéreo** *m* [civil] air shuttle; [militar] airlift.
puenting *m* bungee-jumping.
puerco, -ca ◇ *adj* filthy. ◇ *m y f* [animal] pig (*f* sow).
puercoespín *m* porcupine.
puericultor, -ra *m y f* pediatrician.
pueril *adj fig* childish.
puerro *m* leek.
puerta *f* **-1.** [de casa] door; [de jardín, ciudad etc] gate; **de ~ en ~** from door to door; **~ principal/trasera** front/back door. **-2.** *fig* [posibilidad] gateway, opening. **-3.** DEP goalmouth. **-4.** *loc*: **a**

las ~s de on the verge of; **a ~ cerrada** [gen] behind closed doors; [juicio] in camera.
puerto *m* **-1.** [de mar] port; **~ deportivo** marina. **-2.** [de montaña] pass. **-3.** INFORM port. **-4.** *fig* [refugio] haven.
Puerto Rico Puerto Rico.
pues *conj* **-1.** [dado que] since, as. **-2.** [por lo tanto] therefore, so; **creo, ~, que** ... so, I think that .... **-3.** [así que] so; **querías verlo, ~ ahí está** you wanted to see it, so here it is. **-4.** [enfático]: **¡~ ya está!** well, that's it!; **¡~ claro!** but of course!
puesto, -ta ◇ *pp* → poner. ◇ *adj*: **ir muy ~** to be all dressed up. ◆ **puesto** *m* **-1.** [empleo] post, position. **-2.** [en fila, clasificación etc] place. **-3.** [tenderete] stall, stand. **-4.** MIL post; **~ de policía** police station; **~ de socorro** first-aid post. ◆ **puesta** *f* [acción]: **puesta a punto** [de una técnica] perfecting; [de un motor] tuning; **puesta al día** updating; **puesta en escena** staging, production; **puesta en marcha** [de máquina] starting, start-up; [de acuerdo, proyecto] implementation. ◆ **puesta de sol** *f* sunset. ◆ **puesto que** *loc conj* since, as.
puf (*pl* pufs) *m* pouf, pouffe.
púgil *m* boxer.
pugna *f* fight, battle.
pugnar *vi fig* [esforzarse]: **~ por** to struggle ○ fight (for).
puja *f* [en subasta - acción] bidding; [- cantidad] bid.
pujar ◇ *vi* [en subasta] to bid higher. ◇ *vt* to bid.
pulcro, -cra *adj* neat, tidy.
pulga *f* flea.
pulgada *f* inch.
pulgar → dedo.
pulgón *m* aphid.
pulimentar *vt* to polish.
pulir *vt* to polish. ◆ **pulirse** *vpr* [gastarse] to blow.
pulmón *m* lung.
pulmonía *f* pneumonia.
pulpa *f* pulp; [de fruta] flesh.
púlpito *m* pulpit.
pulpo *m* [animal] octopus.
pulque *m Amer fermented maguey juice.*
pulsación *f* **-1.** [del corazón] beat, beating (*U*). **-2.** [en máquina de escribir] keystroke.
pulsador *m* button, push button.
pulsar *vt* [botón, timbre etc] to press; [teclas de ordenador] to hit, to strike; [teclas

de piano] to play; [cuerdas de guitarra] to pluck.

pulsera f bracelet.

pulso m **-1.** [latido] pulse; **tomar el ~ a algo/alguien** fig to sound sthg/sb out. **-2.** [firmeza]: **tener buen ~** to have a steady hand; **a ~** unaided.

pulular vi to swarm.

pulverizador, -ra adj spray (antes de sust). ◆ **pulverizador** m spray.

pulverizar vt **-1.** [líquido] to spray. **-2.** [sólido] to reduce to dust; TECN to pulverize. **-3.** fig [aniquilar] to pulverize.

puma m puma.

punción f puncture.

punición f punishment.

punk [paŋk] (pl **punks**), **punki** adj, m y f punk.

punta f **-1.** [extremo - gen] point; [- de pan, pelo] end; [- de dedo, cuerno] tip; **sacar ~ a (un lápiz)** to sharpen (a pencil); **a ~ (de) pala** by the dozen O bucket. **-2.** [pizca] touch, bit; [de sal] pinch.

puntada f [pespunte] stitch.

puntal m [madero] prop; fig [apoyo] mainstay.

puntapié m kick.

puntear vt to pluck.

punteo m guitar solo.

puntera → **puntero**.

puntería f **-1.** [destreza] marksmanship. **-2.** [orientación] aim.

puntero, -ra ◇ adj leading. ◇ m y f [líder] leader. ◆ **puntera** f [de zapato] toecap.

puntiagudo, -da adj pointed.

puntilla f point lace. ◆ **de puntillas** loc adv on tiptoe.

puntilloso, -sa adj **-1.** [susceptible] touchy. **-2.** [meticuloso] punctilious.

punto m **-1.** [gen] point; **~ débil/fuerte** weak/strong point; **~ de ebullición/fusión** boiling/melting point; **~ culminante** high point; **~s a tratar** matters to be discussed; **poner ~ final a algo** to bring sthg to a close. **-2.** [signo ortográfico] dot; **~ y coma** semi-colon; **~s suspensivos** suspension points; **dos ~s** colon. **-3.** [marca] spot, dot. **-4.** [lugar] spot, place; **~ de venta** COM point of sale. **-5.** [momento] point, moment; **estar a ~** to be ready; **estar a ~ de hacer algo** to be on the point of doing sthg. **-6.** [estado] state, condition; **llegar a un ~ en que ...** to reach the stage where ...; **poner a ~** [gen] to fine-tune; [motor] to tune. **-7.** [cláusula] clause. **-8.** [punta-

da - en costura, cirugía] stitch; **~ de cruz** cross-stitch; **hacer ~** to knit; **un jersey de ~** a knitted jumper. **-9.** [estilo de tejer] knitting; **~ de ganchillo** crochet. **-10.** [objetivo] target. ◆ **en punto** loc adv on the dot. ◆ **hasta cierto punto** loc adv up to a point. ◆ **punto de partida** m starting point. ◆ **punto de vista** m point of view. ◆ **punto muerto** m **-1.** AUTOM neutral. **-2.** [en un proceso] deadlock; **estar en un ~ muerto** to be deadlocked.

puntuación f **-1.** [calificación] mark; [en concursos, competiciones] score. **-2.** [ortográfica] punctuation.

puntual adj **-1.** [en el tiempo] punctual. **-2.** [exacto, detallado] detailed. **-3.** [aislado] isolated, one-off.

puntualidad f **-1.** [en el tiempo] punctuality. **-2.** [exactitud] exactness.

puntualizar vt to specify, to clarify.

puntuar ◇ vt **-1.** [calificar] to mark; DEP to award marks to. **-2.** [escrito] to punctuate. ◇ vi **-1.** [calificar] to mark. **-2.** [entrar en el cómputo]: **~ (para)** to count (towards).

punzada f **-1.** [pinchazo] prick. **-2.** [dolor intenso] stabbing pain (U); fig pang.

punzante adj **-1.** [que pincha] sharp. **-2.** [intenso] sharp. **-3.** [mordaz] caustic.

punzar vt **-1.** [pinchar] to prick. **-2.** [suj: dolor] to stab; fig [suj: actitud] to wound.

punzón m punch.

puñado m handful.

puñal m dagger.

puñalada f stab; [herida] stab wound.

puñeta ◇ f fam [tontería]: **mandar a alguien a hacer ~s** to tell sb to get lost. ◇ interj fam: **¡~!, ¡~s!** damn it!

puñetazo m punch.

puñetero, -ra fam ◇ adj **-1.** [persona] damn. **-2.** [cosa] tricky. ◇ m y f pain.

puño m **-1.** [mano cerrada] fist; **de su ~ y letra** in his/her own handwriting. **-2.** [de manga] cuff. **-3.** [empuñadura - de espada] hilt; [- de paraguas] handle.

pupila f pupil.

pupilo, -la m y f [discípulo] pupil.

pupitre m desk.

puré m CULIN purée; [sopa] thick soup; **~ de patatas** mashed potatoes (pl).

pureza f purity.

purga f fig [depuración] purge.

purgante adj & m purgative.

purgar vt lit & fig to purge.

purgatorio m purgatory.

purificar *vt* to purify; [mineral, metal] to refine.

puritano, -na *adj, m y f* puritan.

puro, -ra *adj* **-1.** [gen] pure; [oro] solid. **-2.** [cielo, atmósfera] clear. **-3.** [conducta, persona] decent, honourable. **-4.** [mero] sheer; [verdad] plain; **por pura casualidad** by pure chance. ◆ **puro** *m* cigar.

púrpura ◇ *adj inv* purple. ◇ *m* purple.

purpúreo, -a *adj culto* purple.

pus *m* pus.

pusilánime *adj* cowardly.

puso → **poner**.

puta ◇ *adj* → **puto**. ◇ *f vulg* whore.

putear *vulg vt* [fastidiar] to piss off.

puto, -ta *adj vulg* [maldito] bloody. ◆ **puto** *m vulg* male prostitute.

putrefacción *f* rotting, putrefaction.

puzzle ['puθle], **puzle** *m* jigsaw puzzle.

PVP (*abrev de* precio de venta al público) *m* ≈ RRP.

PYME (*abrev de* Pequeña y Mediana Empresa) *f* SME.

pyrex® = **pírex**.

pza. (*abrev de* plaza) Sq.

Q

q, Q *f* [letra] q, Q.

q.e.p.d. (*abrev de* que en paz descanse) RIP.

que ◇ *pron relat* **-1.** (*sujeto*) [persona] who, that; [cosa] that, which; **la mujer ~ me saluda** the woman (who o that is) waving to me; **el ~ me lo compró** the one who bought it from me; **la moto ~ me gusta** the motorbike (that) I like. **-2.** (*complemento directo*) [persona] whom, that; [cosa] that, which; **el hombre ~ conociste ayer** the man (whom o that) you met yesterday; **ese coche es el ~ me quiero comprar** that car is the one (that o which) I want to buy. **-3.** (*complemento indirecto*): **al/a la ~** (to) whom; **ese es el chico al ~ presté dinero** that's the boy to whom I lent some money. **-4.** (*complemento circunstancial*): **la playa a la ~ fui** the beach where o to which I went; **la mujer con la ~ hablas** the woman to whom you are talking; **la mesa sobre la ~ escribes** the table on which you are writing. **-5.** (*complemento de tiempo*): **(en) ~** when; **el día (en) ~ me fui** the day (when) I left. ◇ *conj* **-1.** (*con oraciones de sujeto*) that; **es importante ~ me escuches** it's important that you listen to me. **-2.** (*con oraciones de complemento directo*) that; **me ha confesado ~ me quiere** he has told me that he loves me. **-3.** (*comparativo*) than; **es más rápido ~ tú** he's quicker than you; **antes morir ~ vivir la guerra** I'd rather die than live through a war. **-4.** [expresa causa]: **hemos de esperar, ~ todavía no es la hora** we'll have to wait, as it isn't time yet. **-5.** [expresa consecuencia] that; **tanto me lo pidió ~ se lo di** he asked me for it so insistently that I gave it to him. **-6.** [expresa finalidad] so (that); **ven aquí ~ te vea** come over here so (that) I can see you. **-7.** (+ *subjuntivo*) [expresa deseo] that; **quiero ~ lo hagas** I want you to do it; **espero ~ te diviertas** I hope (that) you have fun. **-8.** (*en oraciones exclamativas*): **¡~ te diviertas!** have fun!; **¡~ te doy un bofetón!** do that again and I'll slap you! **-9.** (*en oraciones interrogativas*): **¿~ quiere venir? pues que venga** so she wants to come? then let her. **-10.** [expresa disyunción] or; **quieras ~ no, harás lo que yo mando** you'll do what I tell you, whether you like it or not. **-11.** [expresa hipótesis] if; **~ no quieres hacerlo, pues no pasa nada** it doesn't matter if you don't want to do it. **-12.** [expresa reiteración] and; **estaban charla ~ charla** they were talking and talking.

qué ◇ *adj* [gen] what; [al elegir, al concretar] which; **¿~ hora es?** what's the time?; **¿~ coche prefieres?** which car do you prefer?; **¿a ~ distancia?** how far away? ◇ *pron* (*interrogativo*) what; **¿~ te dijo?** what did he tell you?; **no sé ~ hacer** I don't know what to do; **¿~? [¿cómo?]** sorry?, pardon? ◇ *adv* **-1.** [exclamativo] how; **¡~ horror!** how awful!; **¡~ tonto eres!** how stupid you are!, you're so stupid!; **¡~ casa más bonita!** what a lovely house!; **¡y ~!** so what? **-2.** [expresa gran cantidad]: **¡~ de ...!** what a lot of ...!; **¡~ de gente hay aquí!** what a lot of people there are here!

quebradero ◆ **quebradero de cabeza** *m* headache, problem.

quebradizo, -za *adj* **-1.** [frágil] fragile, brittle. **-2.** [débil] frail. **-3.** [voz] weak.

quebrado, -da *adj* [terreno] rough, uneven; [perfil] rugged.

quebradura *f* [grieta] crack, fissure.

quebrantar *vt* **-1.** [incumplir - promesa, ley] to break; [- obligación] to fail in. **-2.** [debilitar] to weaken; [moral, resistencia] to break. ◆ **quebrantarse** *vpr* [debilitarse] to deteriorate.

quebranto *m* **-1.** [pérdida] loss. **-2.** [debilitamiento] weakening, debilitation.

quebrar ◇ *vt* [romper] to break. ◇ *vi* FIN to go bankrupt. ◆ **quebrarse** *vpr* **-1.** [romperse] to break. **-2.** [voz] to break, to falter. **-3.** [deslomarse] to rupture o.s.

quechua *m* [idioma] Quechua.

quedar *vi* **-1.** [permanecer] to remain, to stay. **-2.** [haber aún, faltar] to be left, to remain; **¿queda azúcar?** is there any sugar left?; **nos quedan 100 pesetas** we have 100 pesetas left; **¿cuánto queda para León?** how much further is it to León?; **~ por hacer** to remain to be done; **queda por fregar el suelo** the floor has still to be cleaned. **-3.** [mostrarse]: **~ como** to come across as; **~ bien/mal (con alguien)** to make a good/bad impression (on sb). **-4.** [llegar a ser, resultar]: **el trabajo ha quedado perfecto** the job turned out perfectly; **el cuadro queda muy bien ahí** the picture looks great there. **-5.** [acabar]: **~ en** to end in; **~ en nada** to come to nothing. **-6.** [sentar] to look; **te queda un poco corto el traje** your suit is a bit too short; **~ bien/mal a alguien** to look good/bad on sb; **~ bien/mal con algo** to go well/badly with sthg. **-7.** [citarse]: **~ (con alguien)** to arrange to meet (sb); **hemos quedado el lunes** we've arranged to meet on Monday. **-8.** [acordar]: **~ en algo/en hacer algo** to agree on sthg/to do sthg; **~ en que ...** to agree that ...; **¿en qué quedamos?** what's it to be, then? **-9.** *fam* [estar situado] to be; **¿por dónde queda?** whereabouts is it? ◆ **quedarse** *vpr* **-1.** [permanecer - en un lugar] to remain. **-2.** [terminar - en un estado]: **~se ciego/sordo** to go blind/deaf; **~se triste** to be o feel sad; **~se sin dinero** to be left penniless; **la pared se ha quedado limpia** the wall is clean now. **-3.** [comprar] to take; **me quedo éste** I'll take this one. ◆ **quedarse con** *vpr* **-1.**

[retener, guardarse] to keep. **-2.** [preferir] to go for, to prefer.

quedo, -da *adj* quiet, soft. ◆ **quedo** *adv* quietly, softly.

quehacer *m* (*gen pl*) task; **~es domésticos** housework (*U*).

queja *f* **-1.** [lamento] moan, groan. **-2.** [protesta] complaint.

quejarse *vpr* **-1.** [lamentar] to groan, to cry out. **-2.** [protestar] to complain; **~ de** to complain about.

quejica *despec adj* whining, whingeing.

quejido *m* cry, moan.

quejoso, -sa *adj*: **~ (de)** annoyed o upset (with).

quemado, -da *adj* **-1.** [gen] burnt; [por agua hirviendo] scalded; [por electricidad] burnt-out; [fusible] blown. **-2.** [por sol] sunburnt. **-3.** *loc*: **estar ~** [agotado] to be burnt-out; [harto] to be fed up.

quemador *m* burner.

quemadura *f* [por fuego] burn; [por agua hirviendo] scald.

quemar ◇ *vt* **-1.** [gen] to burn; [suj: agua hirviendo] to scald; [suj: electricidad] to blow. **-2.** *fig* [malgastar] to fritter away. **-3.** *fig* [desgastar] to burn out. **-4.** *fig* [hartar] to make fed up. ◇ *vi* [estar caliente] to be (scalding) hot. ◆ **quemarse** *vpr* **-1.** [por fuego] to burn down; [por agua hirviendo] to get scalded; [por calor] to burn; [por electricidad] to blow. **-2.** [por el sol] to get burned. **-3.** *fig* [desgastarse] to burn out. **-4.** *fig* [hartarse] to get fed up.

quemarropa ◆ **a quemarropa** *loc adv* point-blank.

quemazón *f* burning; [picor] itch.

quepa → **caber**.

querella *f* **-1.** DER [acusación] charge. **-2.** [discordia] dispute.

querer ◇ *vt* **-1.** [gen] to want; **quiero una bicicleta** I want a bicycle; **¿quieren ustedes algo más?** would you like anything else?; **~ que alguien haga algo** to want sb to do sthg; **quiero que lo hagas tú** I want you to do it; **~ que pase algo** to want sthg to happen; **queremos que las cosas te vayan bien** we want things to go well for you; **quisiera hacerlo, pero ...** I'd like to do it, but .... **-2.** [amar] to love. **-3.** [en preguntas - con amabilidad]: **¿quiere decirle a su amigo que pase?** could you tell your friend to come in, please? **-4.** [pedir - precio]: **~ algo (por)** to want sthg (for); **¿cuánto quieres por el coche?** how much do you want for the car?

-5. *fig* & *irón* [dar motivos para]: **tú lo que quieres es que te pegue** you're asking for a smack. **-6.** *loc*: **como quien no quiere la cosa** as if it were nothing; **quien bien te quiere te hará llorar** *proverb* you have to be cruel to be kind *proverb*. ◇ *vi* to want; **ven cuando quieras** come whenever you like ○ want; **no me voy porque no quiero** I'm not going because I don't want to; **queriendo** on purpose; **sin ~** accidentally; **~ decir** to mean; **¿qué quieres decir con eso?** what do you mean by that?; **~ es poder** where there's a will there's a way. ◇ *v impers* [haber atisbos]: **parece que quiere llover** it looks like rain. ◇ *m* love.
◆ **quererse** *vpr* to love each other.

querido, -da ◇ *adj* dear. ◇ *m y f* lover; [apelativo afectuoso] darling.

queso *m* cheese; **~ de bola** Dutch cheese; **~ manchego** *hard mild yellow cheese made in La Mancha*; **~ rallado** grated cheese.

quibutz [ki'ßuθ] (*pl* **quibutzs**), **kibutz** (*pl* **kibutzim**) *m* kibbutz.

quicio *m* jamb; **estar fuera de ~** *fig* to be out of kilter; **sacar de ~ a alguien** *fig* to drive sb mad.

quiebra *f* **-1.** [ruina] bankruptcy; [en bolsa] crash. **-2.** *fig* [pérdida] collapse.

quiebro *m* [ademán] swerve.

quien *pron* **-1.** (*relativo*) [sujeto] who; [complemento] whom; **fue mi hermano ~ me lo explicó** it was my brother who explained it to me; **era Pepe a ~ vi/de ~ no me fiaba** it was Pepe (whom) I saw/didn't trust. **-2.** (*indefinido*): **~es quieran verlo que se acerquen** whoever wants to see it will have to come closer; **hay ~ lo niega** there are those who deny it. **-3.** *loc*: **más ~ menos** everyone.

quién *pron* (*interrogativo*) [sujeto] who; [complemento] who, whom; **¿~ es ese hombre?** who's that man?; **no sé ~ viene** I don't know who is coming; **¿a ~es has invitado?** who ○ whom have you invited?; **¿de ~ es?** whose is it?; **¿~ es?** [en la puerta] who is it?; [al teléfono] who's calling?

quienquiera (*pl* **quienesquiera**) *pron* whoever; **~ que venga** whoever comes.

quiera *etc* → **querer**.

quieto, -ta *adj* [parado] still; **¡estáte ~!** keep still!; **¡~ ahí!** don't move!

quietud *f* **-1.** [inmovilidad] stillness. **-2.** [tranquilidad] quietness.

quijada *f* jaw.

quijotesco, -ca *adj* quixotic.

quilate *m* carat.

quilla *f* NÁUT keel.

quilo *etc* = **kilo**.

quimbambas *fpl*: **irse a las ~** to go to the ends of the earth.

quimera *f* fantasy.

quimérico, -ca *adj* fanciful.

químico, -ca ◇ *adj* chemical. ◇ *m y f* [científico] chemist. ◆ **química** *f* [ciencia] chemistry.

quina *f* [bebida] quinine.

quincalla *f* trinket.

quince *núm* fifteen; **~ días** a fortnight; *ver también* **seis**.

quinceañero, -ra *m y f* teenager.

quinceavo, -va *núm* fifteenth.

quincena *f* fortnight.

quincenal *adj* fortnightly.

quincuagésimo, -ma *núm* fiftieth.

quiniela *f* [boleto] pools coupon. ◆ **quinielas** *fpl* [apuestas] (football) pools. ◆ **quiniela hípica** *f* sweepstake.

quinientos, -tas *núm* five hundred; *ver también* **seis**.

quinina *f* quinine.

quinqué *m* oil lamp.

quinquenio *m* [periodo] five-year period.

quinqui *m y f fam* delinquent.

quinta → **quinto**.

quinteto *m* quintet.

quinto, -ta *núm* fifth. ◆ **quinto** *m* **-1.** [parte] fifth. **-2.** MIL recruit. ◆ **quinta** *f* **-1.** [finca] country house. **-2.** MIL call-up year.

quintuplicar *vt* to increase fivefold. ◆ **quintuplicarse** *vpr* to increase fivefold.

quiosco, kiosco *m* kiosk; [de periódicos] newspaper stand; **~ de música** bandstand.

quiosquero, -ra *m y f* owner of a newspaper stand.

quirófano *m* operating theatre.

quiromancia *f* palmistry, chiromancy.

quiromasaje *m* (manual) massage.

quirúrgico, -ca *adj* surgical.

quisiera *etc* → **querer**.

quisque *m*: **cada ○ todo ~** every man Jack.

quisquilloso, -sa *adj* **-1.** [detallista] pernickety. **-2.** [susceptible] touchy.

quiste *m* cyst.

quitaesmalte *m* nail-polish remover.

quitaipón ◆ **de quitaipón** *loc adj* removable; [capucha] detachable.

quitamanchas *m inv* stain remover.

quitanieves *m inv* snow plough.

quitar *vt* **-1.** [gen] to remove; [ropa, zapatos etc] to take off; **~le algo a alguien** to take sthg away from sb; **de quita y pon** removable; [capucha] detachable. **-2.** [dolor, ansiedad] to take away, to relieve; [sed] to quench. **-3.** [tiempo] to take up. **-4.** [robar] to take, to steal. **-5.** [impedir]: **esto no quita que sea un vago** that doesn't change the fact that he's a layabout. **-6.** [exceptuar]: **quitando el queso, me gusta todo** apart from cheese, I'll eat anything. **-7.** [desconectar] to switch off. ◆ **quitarse** *vpr* **-1.** [apartarse] to get out of the way. **-2.** [ropa] to take off. **-3.** [suj: mancha] to come out. **-4.** *loc*: **~se a alguien de encima** ○ **de en medio** to get rid of sb.

quitasol *m* sunshade *Br*, parasol.

quite *m* DEP parry; **estar al ~** to be on hand to help.

Quito Quito.

quizá, quizás *adv* perhaps; **~ lluevá mañana** it might rain tomorrow; **~ no lo creas** you may not believe it; **~ sí** maybe; **~ no** maybe not.

R

r, R *f* [letra] r, R.

rábano *m* radish; **me importa un ~** I couldn't care less.

rabí *m* rabbi.

rabia *f* **-1.** [ira] rage; **me da ~** it makes me mad; **tenerle ~ a alguien** *fig* not to be able to stand sb. **-2.** [enfermedad] rabies.

rabiar *vi* **-1.** [sufrir] to writhe in pain. **-2.** [enfadarse] to be furious. **-3.** [desear]: **~ por algo/hacer algo** to be dying for sthg/to do sthg.

rabieta *f fam* tantrum.

rabillo *m* corner; **mirar algo con el ~ del ojo** to look at sthg out of the corner of one's eye.

rabioso, -sa *adj* **-1.** [furioso] furious. **-2.**

[excesivo] terrible. **-3.** [enfermo de rabia] rabid. **-4.** [chillón] loud, gaudy.

rabo *m* **-1.** [de animal] tail; **~ de buey** oxtail. **-2.** [de hoja, fruto] stem.

rácano, -na *fam adj* **-1.** [tacaño] mean, stingy. **-2.** [gandul] idle, lazy.

RACE (*abrev de* **Real Automóvil Club de España**) *m* Spanish automobile association, ≈ AA *Br*, ≈ AAA *Am*.

racha *f* **-1.** [ráfaga] gust (of wind). **-2.** [época] spell; [serie] string; **buena/mala ~** good/bad patch; **a ~s** in fits and starts.

racial *adj* racial.

racimo *m* **-1.** [de frutos] bunch. **-2.** [de flores] raceme.

raciocinio *m* [razón] (power of) reason.

ración *f* **-1.** [porción] portion. **-2.** [en bar, restaurante] *large portion of a dish served as a snack.*

racional *adj* rational.

racionalizar *vt* to rationalize.

racionar *vt* to ration.

racismo *m* racism.

racista *adj, m y f* racist.

radar (*pl* **radares**) *m* radar.

radiación *f* radiation.

radiactivo, -va, radioactivo, -va *adj* radioactive.

radiador *m* radiator.

radiante *adj* radiant.

radiar *vt* **-1.** [irradiar] to radiate. **-2.** [por radio] to broadcast.

radical *adj, m y f* radical.

radicar *vi*: **~ en** [suj: problema etc] to lie in; [suj: población] to be (situated) in. ◆ **radicarse** *vpr* [establecerse]: **~se (en)** to settle (in).

radio ◇ *m* **-1.** ANAT & GEOM radius. **-2.** [de rueda] spoke. **-3.** QUÍM radium. ◇ *f* radio; **oír algo por la ~** to hear sthg on the radio.

radioactivo, -va = **radiactivo**.

radioaficionado, -da *m y f* radio ham.

radiocasete *m* radio cassette (player).

radiocontrol *m* remote control.

radiodespertador *m* clock radio.

radiodifusión *f* broadcasting.

radioescucha *m y f inv* listener.

radiofónico, -ca *adj* radio (*antes de sust*).

radiografía *f* [fotografía] X-ray; [ciencia] radiography.

radionovela *f* radio soap opera.

radiorreloj *m* clock radio.

radiotaxi *m* taxi (with radio link).

radioteléfono *m* radiotelephone.

radioterapia *f* radiotherapy.
radioyente *m y f* listener.
RAE *abrev de* Real Academia Española.
raer *vt* to scrape (off).
ráfaga *f* [de aire, viento] gust; [de disparos] burst; [de luces] flash.
raído, -da *adj* threadbare; [por los bordes] frayed.
raigambre *f* [tradición] tradition.
rail, raíl *m* rail.
raíz (*pl* **raíces**) *f* [gen & MAT] root; ~ **cuadrada/cúbica** square/cube root; **a ~ de** as a result of, following; **echar raíces** to put down roots.
raja *f* -1. [porción] slice. -2. [grieta] crack.
rajar *vt* -1. [partir] to crack; [melón] to slice. -2. *mfam* [apuñalar] to slash. ◆ **rajarse** *vpr* -1. [partirse] to crack. -2. *fam* [echarse atrás] to chicken out.
rajatabla ◆ **a rajatabla** *loc adv* to the letter, strictly.
ralentí *m* neutral.
rallado, -da *adj* grated. ◆ **rallado** *m* grating.
rallador *m* grater.
ralladura *f* (*gen pl*) grating.
rallar *vt* to grate.
rally ['rali] (*pl* **rallys**) *m* rally.
RAM (*abrev de* **random access memory**) *f* RAM.
rama *f* branch; **andarse por las ~s** *fam* to beat about the bush.
ramaje *m* branches (*pl*).
ramal *m* [de carretera, ferrocarril] branch.
ramalazo *m* -1. *fam* [hecho que delata] giveaway sign. -2. [ataque] fit.
rambla *f* [avenida] avenue, boulevard.
ramera *f* whore, hooker *Am*.
ramificación *f* -1. [gen] ramification. -2. [de carretera, ferrocarril, ciencia] branch.
ramificarse *vpr* -1. [bifurcarse] to branch out. -2. [subdividirse]: ~ **(en)** to subdivide (into).
ramillete *m* bunch, bouquet.
ramo *m* -1. [de flores] bunch, bouquet. -2. [rama] branch; **el ~ de la construcción** the building industry.
rampa *f* -1. [para subir y bajar] ramp. -2. [cuesta] steep incline.
rana *f* frog.
ranchero, -ra *m y f* rancher. ◆ **ranchera** *f* -1. MÚS *popular Mexican song*. -2. AUTOM estate car.
rancho *m* -1. [comida] mess. -2. [granja] ranch.

rancio, -cia *adj* -1. [pasado] rancid. -2. [antiguo] ancient. -3. [añejo - vino] mellow.
rango *m* -1. [social] standing. -2. [jerárquico] rank.
ranking ['raŋkin] (*pl* **rankings**) *m* ranking.
ranura *f* groove; [de máquina tragaperras, cabina telefónica] slot.
rapaces *fpl* → **rapaz**.
rapapolvo *m fam* ticking-off.
rapar *vt* [barba, bigote] to shave off; [cabeza] to shave; [persona] to shave the hair of.
rapaz, -za *m y f fam* lad (*f* lass). ◆ **rapaz** *adj* -1. [que roba] rapacious, greedy. -2. ZOOL → **ave**. ◆ **rapaces** *fpl* ZOOL birds of prey.
rape *m* angler fish; **cortar el pelo al ~ a alguien** to crop sb's hair.
rapé *m* (*en aposición inv*) snuff.
rápidamente *adv* quickly.
rapidez *f* speed.
rápido, -da *adj* quick, fast; [coche] fast; [beneficio, decisión] quick. ◆ **rápido** ◇ *adv* quickly; **más** ~ quicker; **¡ven, ~!** come, quick! ◇ *m* [tren] express train. ◆ **rápidos** *mpl* [de río] rapids.
rapiña *f* -1. [robo] robbery with violence. -2. → **ave**.
rappel ['rapel] (*pl* **rappels**) *m* DEP abseiling; **hacer** ~ to abseil.
rapsodia *f* rhapsody.
raptar *vt* to abduct, to kidnap.
rapto *m* -1. [secuestro] abduction, kidnapping. -2. [ataque] fit.
raqueta *f* [para jugar - al tenis] racquet; [- al ping pong] bat.
raquítico, -ca *adj* -1. MED rachitic. -2. [insuficiente] miserable.
rareza *f* -1. [poco común, extraño] rarity. -2. [extravagancia] eccentricity.
raro, -ra *adj* -1. [extraño] strange; **¡qué ~!** how odd ○ strange! -2. [excepcional] unusual, rare; [visita] infrequent. -3. [extravagante] odd, eccentric. -4. [escaso] rare; **rara vez** rarely.
ras *m*: **a ~ de** level with; **a ~ de tierra** at ground level; **volar a ~ de tierra** to fly low.
rasante *f* [de carretera] gradient.
rascacielos *m inv* skyscraper.
rascador *m* [herramienta] scraper.
rascar ◇ *vt* -1. [con uñas, clavo] to scratch. -2. [con espátula] to scrape (off); [con cepillo] to scrub. ◇ *vi* to be rough. ◆ **rascarse** *vpr* to scratch o.s.
rasera *f* fish slice.

rasgar vt to tear; [sobre] to tear open.

rasgo m -1. [característica] **trait, characteristic**. -2. [trazo] **flourish, stroke.** ◆ **rasgos** mpl -1. [del rostro] **features.** -2. [letra] **handwriting** (U). ◆ **a grandes rasgos** loc adv in general terms.

rasguear vt to strum.

rasguñar vt to scratch.

rasguño m scratch.

raso, -sa adj -1. [terreno] **flat**. -2. [cucharada etc] **level. -3.** [a poca altura] **low. -4.** MIL: **soldado** ~ **private.** ◆ **raso** m [tela] **satin.**

raspa f backbone (of fish).

raspadura f (gen pl) **scraping**; [señal] scratch.

raspar vt -1. [rascar] to scrape (off). -2. [rasar] to graze, to shave.

rasposo, -sa adj rough.

rastras ◆ **a rastras** loc adv: **llevar algo/a alguien a** ~ lit & fig to drag sthg/sb along.

rastreador, -ra m y f tracker.

rastrear vt [seguir las huellas de] to track.

rastrero, -ra adj despicable.

rastrillo m -1. [en jardinería] **rake.** -2. [mercado] **flea market**; [benéfico] **jumble sale.**

rastro m -1. [pista] **trail**; **perder el** ~ **de alguien** to lose track of sb; **sin dejar** ~ without trace. -2. [vestigio] **trace.** -3. [mercado] **flea market.**

rastrojo m stubble.

rasurar vt to shave. ◆ **rasurarse** vpr to shave.

rata f rat.

ratero, -ra m y f petty thief.

ratificar vt to ratify. ◆ **ratificarse en** vpr to stand by.

rato m while; **estuvimos hablando mucho** ~ we were talking for quite a while; **al poco** ~ **(de)** shortly after; **pasar el** ~ to kill time; **pasar un mal** ~ to have a hard time of it; ~**s libres** spare time (U); **a** ~**s** at times.

ratón m [gen & INFORM] mouse.

ratonera f -1. [para ratas] **mousetrap.** -2. fig [trampa] **trap.**

raudal m -1. [de agua] **torrent.** -2. fig [montón] **abundance**; [de lágrimas] **flood**; [de desgracias] **string**; **a** ~**es** in abundance, by the bucket.

ravioli m (gen pl) ravioli (U).

raya f -1. [línea] **line**; [en tejido] **stripe**; **a** ~**s** striped. -2. [del pelo] **parting**; **hacerse la** ~ to part one's hair. -3. [de pantalón] **crease.** -4. fig [límite] **limit**; **pasarse**

de la ~ to overstep the mark. -5. [señal - en disco, pintura etc] **scratch.** -6. [pez] **ray.** -7. [guión] **dash.**

rayado, -da adj -1. [a rayas - tela] **striped**; [- papel] **ruled.** -2. [estropeado] **scratched.** ◆ **rayado** m [rayas] **stripes** (pl).

rayar ◇ vt -1. [marcar] to scratch. -2. [trazar rayas] to rule lines on. ◇ vi -1. [aproximarse]: ~ **en algo** to border on sthg; **raya en los cuarenta** he's pushing forty. -2. [alba] to break. ◆ **rayarse** vpr to get scratched.

rayo m -1. [de luz] **ray**; ~ **solar** sunbeam. -2. FÍS **beam, ray**; ~ **láser** laser beam; ~**s infrarrojos/ultravioleta/uva** infrared/ultraviolet/UVA rays; ~**s X** X-rays; **caer como un** ~ fig to be a bombshell. -3. METEOR **bolt of lightning**; ~**s lightning** (U).

rayón m rayon.

rayuela f Amer [juego en que se salta a la pata coja] **hopscotch.**

raza f -1. [humana] **race**; ~ **humana** human race. -2. [animal] **breed**; **de** ~ [caballo] **thoroughbred**; [perro] **pedigree.** -3. Amer fam [cara] **cheek, nerve.**

razón f -1. [gen] **reason**; **dar la** ~ **a alguien** to say that sb is right; **en** ~ **de** O **a** in view of; ~ **de ser** raison d'être; **tener** ~ **(en hacer algo)** to be right (to do sthg); **no tener** ~ to be wrong; **y con** ~ and quite rightly so. -2. [información]: **se vende piso:** ~ **aquí** flat for sale: enquire within; **dar** ~ **de** to give an account of. -3. MAT **ratio.** ◆ **a razón de** loc adv at a rate of.

razonable adj reasonable.

razonamiento m reasoning (U).

razonar ◇ vt [argumentar] to reason out. ◇ vi [pensar] to reason.

re m MÚS **D**; [en solfeo] **re.**

reacción f reaction; ~ **en cadena** chain reaction.

reaccionar vi to react.

reaccionario, -ria adj, m y f reactionary.

reacio, -cia adj stubborn; **ser** ~ **a** O **en hacer algo** to be reluctant to do sthg.

reactivación f revival.

reactor m -1. [propulsor] **reactor.** -2. [avión] **jet (plane).**

readmitir vt to accept O take back.

reafirmar vt to confirm. ◆ **reafirmarse** vpr to assert o.s.; ~**se en algo** to become confirmed in sthg.

reajuste m -1. [cambio] **readjustment**; ~ **ministerial** cabinet reshuffle. -2.

[ECON - de precios, impuestos] increase; [- de sector] **streamlining**; [- de salarios] reduction; ~ **de plantilla** redundancies (pl).

real adj -1. [verdadero] real. -2. [de monarquía] **royal**.

realce m -1. [esplendor] glamour; **dar ~ a algo/alguien** to enhance sthg/sb. -2. [en pintura] highlight.

realeza f [monarcas] royalty.

realidad f -1. [mundo real] reality; ~ **virtual** INFORM virtual reality. -2. [verdad] truth; **en ~** actually, in fact.

realista ◇ adj realistic. ◇ m y f ARTE realist.

realización f -1. [ejecución] carrying-out; [de proyecto, medidas] implementation; [de sueños, deseos] fulfilment. -2. [obra] achievement. -3. CIN production.

realizador, -ra m y f CIN & TV director.

realizar vt -1. [ejecutar - esfuerzo, viaje, inversión] to make; [- operación, experimento, trabajo] to perform; [- encargo] to carry out; [- plan, reformas] to implement; [- desfile] to go on. -2. [hacer real] to fulfil, to realize. -3. CIN to produce. ◆ **realizarse** vpr -1. [en un trabajo] to find fulfilment. -2. [hacerse real - sueño, predicción, deseo] to come true; [- esperanza, ambición] to be fulfilled. -3. [ejecutarse] to be carried out.

realmente adv -1. [en verdad] in fact, actually. -2. [muy] really, very.

realquilado, -da m y f sub-tenant.

realquilar vt to sublet.

realzar vt -1. [resaltar] to enhance. -2. [en pintura] to highlight.

reanimar vt -1. [físicamente] to revive. -2. [moralmente] to cheer up. -3. MED to resuscitate.

reanudar vt [conversación, trabajo] to resume; [amistad] to renew.

reaparición f reappearance.

rearme m rearmament.

reavivar vt to revive.

rebaja f -1. [acción] reduction. -2. [descuento] discount. ◆ **rebajas** fpl COM sales; "**grandes ~s**" "massive reductions"; **estar de ~s** to have a sale on.

rebajado, -da adj -1. [precio] reduced. -2. [humillado] humiliated.

rebajar vt -1. [precio] to reduce; **te rebajo 100 pesetas** I'll knock 100 pesetas off for you. -2. [persona] to humiliate. -3. [intensidad] to tone down. -4. [altura] to lower. ◆ **rebajarse** vpr [persona] to humble o.s.; **~se a hacer algo** to lower o.s. o stoop to do sthg.

rebanada f slice.

rebañar vt to scrape clean.

rebaño m flock; [de vacas] herd.

rebasar vt to exceed, to surpass; [agua] to overflow; AUTOM to overtake.

rebatir vt to refute.

rebeca f cardigan.

rebelarse vpr to rebel.

rebelde ◇ adj -1. [sublevado] rebel (antes de sust). -2. [desobediente] rebellious. ◇ m y f [sublevado, desobediente] rebel.

rebeldía f -1. [cualidad] rebelliousness. -2. [acción] (act of) rebellion.

rebelión f rebellion.

rebenque m Amer [látigo] whip.

reblandecer vt to soften.

rebobinar vt to rewind.

rebosante adj: ~ **(de)** brimming o overflowing (with).

rebosar ◇ vt to overflow with. ◇ vi to overflow; ~ **de** to be overflowing with; fig [persona] to brim with.

rebotar vi: ~ **(en)** to bounce (off), to rebound (off).

rebote m -1. [bote] bounce, bouncing (U). -2. DEP rebound; **de ~** on the rebound.

rebozado, -da adj CULIN coated in batter o breadcrumbs.

rebozar vt CULIN to coat in batter o breadcrumbs.

rebuscado, -da adj recherché, pretentious.

rebuznar vi to bray.

recabar vt [pedir] to ask for; [conseguir] to manage to get.

recadero, -ra m y f messenger.

recado m -1. [mensaje] message. -2. [encargo] errand; **hacer ~s** to run errands.

recaer vi -1. [enfermo] to have a relapse. -2. [ir a parar]: ~ **sobre** to fall on. -3. [reincidir]: ~ **en** to relapse into.

recaída f relapse.

recalcar vt to stress, to emphasize.

recalcitrante adj recalcitrant.

recalentar vt -1. [volver a calentar] to warm up. -2. [calentar demasiado] to overheat.

recámara f -1. [de arma de fuego] chamber. -2. Amer [dormitorio] bedroom.

recamarera f Amer maid.

recambio m spare (part); [para pluma] refill; **de ~** spare.

recapacitar vi to reflect, to think.

recapitulación f recap, recapitulation.

recargado, -da *adj* [estilo etc] over-elaborate.

recargar *vt* **-1.** [volver a cargar - encendedor, recipiente] to refill; [- batería, pila] to recharge; [- fusil, camión] to reload. **-2.** [cargar demasiado] to overload. **-3.** [adornar en exceso] to overelaborate. **-4.** [cantidad]: ~ **1.000 pesetas a alguien** to charge sb 1,000 pesetas extra. **-5.** [poner en exceso]: ~ **algo de algo** to put too much of sthg in sthg.

recargo *m* extra charge, surcharge.

recatado, -da *adj* [pudoroso] modest, demure.

recato *m* [pudor] modesty, demureness.

recauchutar *vt* to retread.

recaudación *f* **-1.** [acción] collection. **-2.** [cantidad] takings (*pl*); DEP gate.

recaudador, -ra *m y f*: ~ **(de impuestos)** tax collector.

recaudar *vt* to collect.

recelar ◇ *vt* **-1.** [sospechar] to suspect. **-2.** [temer] to fear. ◇ *vi*: ~ **de** to mistrust.

recelo *m* mistrust, suspicion.

receloso, -sa *adj* mistrustful, suspicious.

recepción *f* [gen] reception.

recepcionista *m y f* receptionist.

receptáculo *m* receptacle.

receptivo, -va *adj* receptive.

receptor, -ra *m y f* [persona] recipient. ◆ **receptor** *m* [aparato] receiver.

recesión *f* recession.

receta *f* **-1.** CULIN & *fig* recipe. **-2.** MED prescription.

rechazar *vt* **-1.** [gen & MED] to reject; [oferta] to turn down. **-2.** [repeler - a una persona] to push away; MIL to repel.

rechazo *m* **-1.** [gen & MED] rejection; [hacia una ley, un político] disapproval; ~ **a hacer algo** refusal to do sthg. **-2.** [negación] denial.

rechinar *vi* **-1.** [puerta] to creak; [dientes] to grind; [frenos, ruedas] to screech; [metal] to clank. **-2.** [dando dentera] to grate.

rechistar *vi* to answer back.

rechoncho, -cha *adj fam* chubby.

rechupete ◆ de rechupete *loc adv fam* [gen] brilliant, great; [comida] scrumptious.

recibidor *m* entrance hall.

recibimiento *m* reception, welcome.

recibir ◇ *vt* **-1.** [gen] to receive; [clase, instrucción] to have. **-2.** [dar la bienvenida a] to welcome. **-3.** [ir a buscar] to meet. ◇ *vi* [atender visitas] to receive visitors.

recibo *m* receipt; **acusar** ~ **de** to acknowledge receipt of.

reciclaje *m* **-1.** [de residuos] recycling. **-2.** [de personas] retraining.

reciclar *vt* [residuos] to recycle.

recién *adv* recently, newly; **el** ~ **casado** the newly-wed; **los** ~ **llegados** the newcomers; **el** ~ **nacido** the newborn baby.

reciente *adj* **-1.** [acontecimiento etc] recent. **-2.** [pintura, pan etc] fresh.

recientemente *adv* recently.

recinto *m* [zona cercada] enclosure; [área] place, area; [alrededor de edificios] grounds (*pl*); ~ **ferial** fairground (*of trade fair*).

recio, -cia *adj* **-1.** [persona] robust. **-2.** [voz] gravelly. **-3.** [objeto] solid. **-4.** [material, tela] tough, strong.

recipiente *m* container, receptacle.

reciprocidad *f* reciprocity.

recíproco, -ca *adj* mutual, reciprocal.

recital *m* **-1.** [de música clásica] recital; [de rock] concert. **-2.** [de lectura] reading.

recitar *vt* to recite.

reclamación *f* **-1.** [petición] claim, demand. **-2.** [queja] complaint.

reclamar ◇ *vt* [pedir, exigir] to demand, to ask for. ◇ *vi* [protestar]: ~ **(contra)** to protest (against), to complain (about).

reclamo *m* **-1.** [para atraer] inducement. **-2.** [para cazar] decoy, lure.

reclinar *vt*: ~ **algo (sobre)** to lean sthg (on). ◆ **reclinarse** *vpr* to lean back.

recluir *vt* to shut ○ lock away. ◆ **recluirse** *vpr* to shut o.s. away.

reclusión *f* **-1.** [encarcelamiento] imprisonment. **-2.** *fig* [encierro] seclusion.

recluso, -sa *m y f* [preso] prisoner.

recluta *m* [obligatorio] conscript; [voluntario] recruit.

reclutamiento *m* [de soldados - obligatorio] conscription; [- voluntario] recruitment.

recobrar *vt* [gen] to recover; [conocimiento] to regain; [tiempo perdido] to make up for. ◆ **recobrarse** *vpr*: ~**se (de)** to recover (from).

recodo *m* bend.

recogedor *m* dustpan.

recoger *vt* **-1.** [coger] to pick up. **-2.** [reunir] to collect, to gather. **-3.** [ordenar, limpiar - mesa] to clear; [- habitación, cosas] to tidy ○ clear up. **-4.** [ir a buscar] to pick up, to fetch. **-5.** [albergar] to take in. **-6.** [cosechar] to gather, to harvest; [fruta] to pick. ◆ **recogerse** *vpr* **-1.** [a dormir, meditar] to retire. **-2.** [cabello] to put up.

recogido, -da *adj* **-1.** [lugar] withdrawn, secluded. **-2.** [cabello] tied back. ◆ **recogida** *f* **-1.** [gen] collection. **-2.** [cosecha] harvest, gathering; [de fruta] picking.

recolección *f* **-1.** [cosecha] harvest, gathering. **-2.** [recogida] collection.

recolector, -ra *m y f* **-1.** [gen] collector. **-2.** [de cosecha] harvester; [de fruta] picker.

recomendación *f* (*gen pl*) **-1.** [gen] recommendation. **-2.** [referencia] reference.

recomendado, -da *m y f* protégé (*f* protégée).

recomendar *vt* to recommend; ~ **a alguien que haga algo** to recommend that sb do sthg.

recompensa *f* reward; **en ~ por** in return for.

recompensar *vt* [premiar] to reward.

recomponer *vt* to repair, to mend.

recompuesto, -ta *pp* → **recomponer.**

reconciliación *f* reconciliation.

reconciliar *vt* to reconcile. ◆ **reconciliarse** *vpr* to be reconciled.

recóndito, -ta *adj* hidden, secret.

reconfortar *vt* **-1.** [anímicamente] to comfort. **-2.** [físicamente] to revitalize.

reconocer *vt* **-1.** [gen] to recognize. **-2.** MED to examine. **-3.** [terreno] to survey. ◆ **reconocerse** *vpr* **-1.** [identificarse] to recognize each other. **-2.** [confesarse]: ~**se culpable** to admit one's guilt.

reconocido, -da *adj* **-1.** [admitido] recognized, acknowledged. **-2.** [agradecido] grateful.

reconocimiento *m* **-1.** [gen] recognition. **-2.** [agradecimiento] gratitude. **-3.** MED examination. **-4.** MIL reconnaissance.

reconquista *f* reconquest, recapture. ◆ **Reconquista** *f*: **la Reconquista** HIST *the Reconquest of Spain, when the Christian Kings retook the country from the Muslims.*

reconstruir *vt* **-1.** [edificio, país etc] to rebuild. **-2.** [suceso] to reconstruct.

reconversión *f* restructuring; ~ **industrial** rationalization of industry.

recopilación *f* [texto - de poemas, artículos] compilation, collection; [- de leyes] code.

recopilar *vt* **-1.** [recoger] to collect, to gather. **-2.** [escritos, leyes] to compile.

récord (*pl* **récords**) ◇ *m* record; **batir un ~** to break a record. ◇ *adj inv* record.

recordar ◇ *vt* **-1.** [acordarse de] to remember. **-2.** [traer a la memoria] to remind; **me recuerda a un amigo mío** he reminds me of a friend of mine. ◇ *vi* to remember; **si mal no recuerdo** as far as I can remember.

recordatorio *m* [aviso] reminder.

recordman [re'korðman] (*pl* **recordmen** o **recordmans**) *m* record holder.

recorrer *vt* **-1.** [atravesar - lugar, país] to travel through o across, to cross; [- ciudad] to go round. **-2.** [distancia] to cover. **-3.** *fig* [con la mirada] to look over.

recorrida *f Amer* trip.

recorrido *m* **-1.** [trayecto] route, path. **-2.** [viaje] journey.

recortado, -da *adj* **-1.** [cortado] cut. **-2.** [borde] jagged.

recortar *vt* **-1.** [cortar - lo que sobra] to cut off o away; [- figuras de un papel] to cut out. **-2.** [pelo, flequillo] to trim. **-3.** *fig* [reducir] to cut. ◆ **recortarse** *vpr* [figura etc] to stand out.

recorte *m* **-1.** [pieza cortada] cut, trimming; [de periódico, revista] cutting. **-2.** [reducción] cut, cutback.

recostar *vt* to lean (back). ◆ **recostarse** *vpr* to lie down.

recoveco *m* **-1.** [rincón] nook. **-2.** [curva] bend. **-3.** *fig* [lo más oculto]: **los ~s del alma** the innermost recesses of the mind.

recreación *f* re-creation.

recrear *vt* **-1.** [volver a crear] to recreate. **-2.** [entretener] to amuse, to entertain. ◆ **recrearse** *vpr* **-1.** [entretenerse] to amuse o.s., to entertain o.s. **-2.** [regodearse] to take delight o pleasure.

recreativo, -va *adj* recreational.

recreo *m* **-1.** [entretenimiento] recreation, amusement. **-2.** [EDUC - en primaria] playtime; [- en secundaria] break.

recriminar *vt* to reproach.

recrudecer *vi* to get worse. ◆ **recrudecerse** *vpr* to get worse.

recta → **recto.**

rectángulo *m* rectangle.

rectificar *vt* **-1.** [error] to rectify, to correct. **-2.** [conducta, actitud etc] to improve. **-3.** [ajustar] to put right.

rectitud *f* straightness; *fig* rectitude.

recto, -ta *adj* **-1.** [sin curvas, vertical] straight. **-2.** *fig* [íntegro] honourable. ◆ **recto** ◇ *m* ANAT rectum. ◇ *adv* straight on ◯ ahead. ◆ **recta** *f* straight line; **la recta final** *lit* & *fig* the home straight.

rector, -ra ◇ *adj* governing. ◇ *m y f* [de universidad] vice-chancellor *Br*, president *Am*. ◆ **rector** *m* RELIG rector.

recuadro *m* box.

recubrir *vt* [gen] to cover; [con pintura, barniz] to coat.

recuento *m* recount.

recuerdo *m* **-1.** [rememoración] memory. **-2.** [objeto - de viaje] souvenir; [- de persona] keepsake. ◆ **recuerdos** *mpl* [saludos] regards; **dale ~s de mi parte** give her my regards.

recular *vi* [retroceder] to go ◯ move back.

recuperable *adj* [gen] recoverable; [fiestas, horas de trabajo] that can be made up later.

recuperación *f* **-1.** [de lo perdido, la salud, la economía] recovery. **-2.** [fisioterapia] physiotherapy.

recuperar *vt* [lo perdido] to recover; [horas de trabajo] to catch up; [conocimiento] to regain. ◆ **recuperarse** *vpr* **-1.** [enfermo] to recuperate, to recover. **-2.** [de una crisis] to recover; [negocio] to pick up; **~se de algo** to get over sthg.

recurrir *vi* **-1.** [buscar ayuda]: **~ a alguien** to turn to sb; **~ a algo** to resort to sthg. **-2.** DER to appeal.

recurso *m* **-1.** [medio] resort; **como último ~** as a last resort. **-2.** DER appeal. ◆ **recursos** *mpl* [fondos] resources; [financieros] means; **~s propios** ECON equities.

red *f* **-1.** [malla] net; [para cabello] hairnet. **-2.** [sistema] network, system; [de electricidad, agua] mains (*sg*); **~ viaria** road network ◯ system. **-3.** [organización - de espionaje] ring; [- de tiendas] chain. **-4.** INFORM network.

redacción *f* **-1.** [acción - gen] writing; [- de periódico etc] editing. **-2.** [estilo] wording. **-3.** [equipo de redactores] editorial team ◯ staff. **-4.** [oficina] editorial office. **-5.** EDUC essay.

redactar *vt* to write (up); [carta] to draft.

redactor, -ra *m y f* [PRENS - escritor] writer; [- editor] editor; **~ jefe** editor-in-chief.

redada *f* *fig* [de policía - en un solo lugar] raid; [- en varios lugares] round-up.

redención *f* redemption.

redil *m* fold, pen.

redimir *vt* **-1.** [gen] to redeem. **-2.** [librar] to free, to exempt. ◆ **redimirse** *vpr* to redeem o.s.

rédito *m* interest (*U*), yield (*U*).

redoblar ◇ *vt* to redouble. ◇ *vi* to roll.

redomado, -da *adj* out-and-out.

redondear *vt* **-1.** [hacer redondo] to make round. **-2.** [negocio, acuerdo] to round off. **-3.** [cifra, precio] to round up/down.

redondel *m* **-1.** [gen] circle, ring. **-2.** TAUROM bullring.

redondo, -da *adj* **-1.** [circular, esférico] round; **a la redonda** around; **caerse ~** *fig* to collapse in a heap. **-2.** [perfecto] excellent.

reducción *f* **-1.** [gen] reduction. **-2.** [sometimiento] suppression.

reducido, -da *adj* **-1.** [pequeño] small. **-2.** [limitado] limited. **-3.** [estrecho] narrow.

reducir *vt* **-1.** [gen] to reduce. **-2.** [someter - país, ciudad] to suppress; [- sublevados, atracadores] to bring under control. **-3.** MAT [convertir] to convert. ◆ **reducirse a** *vpr* **-1.** [limitarse a] to be reduced to. **-2.** [equivaler a] to boil ◯ come down to.

reducto *m* **-1.** [fortificación] redoubt. **-2.** *fig* [refugio] stronghold, bastion.

redundancia *f* redundancy, superfluousness.

redundante *adj* redundant, superfluous.

redundar *vi*: **~ en algo** to have an effect on sthg; **redunda en beneficio nuestro** it is to our advantage.

reeditar *vt* to bring out a new edition of; [reimprimir] to reprint.

reelección *f* re-election.

reembolsar, reembolsar *vt* [gastos] to reimburse; [fianza, dinero] to refund; [deuda] to repay.

reembolso, reembolso *m* [de gastos] reimbursement; [de fianza, dinero] refund; [de deuda] repayment; **contra ~** cash on delivery.

reemplazar, remplazar *vt* [gen & INFORM] to replace.

reemplazo, remplazo *m* **-1.** [gen & INFORM] replacement. **-2.** MIL call-up, draft.

reemprender *vt* to start again.

reencarnación *f* reincarnation.

reencuentro *m* reunion.

reestructurar *vt* to restructure.

refacción f Amer **-1.** [reparaciones] repairs (pl). **-2.** [recambios] **spare parts** (pl).

refaccionar vt Amer to repair, to fix.

refaccionaria f Amer repair workshop.

referencia f reference; **con ~** a with reference to. ◆ **referencias** fpl [información] information (U).

referéndum (pl **referéndums**) m referendum.

referente adj: **~ a** concerning, relating to.

referir vt **-1.** [narrar] to tell, to recount. **-2.** [remitir]: **~ a alguien a** to refer sb to. **-3.** [relacionar]: **~ algo a** to relate sthg to. ◆ **referirse a** vpr to refer to; **¿a qué te refieres?** what do you mean?; **por lo que se refiere a ...** as far as ... is concerned.

refilón ◆ **de refilón** loc adv **-1.** [de lado] sideways; **mirar algo de ~** to look at sthg out of the corner of one's eye. **-2.** fig [de pasada] briefly.

refinado, -da adj refined.

refinamiento m refinement.

refinar vt to refine.

refinería f refinery.

reflector m ELECTR spotlight; MIL searchlight.

reflejar vt lit & fig to reflect. ◆ **reflejarse** vpr lit & fig: **~se (en)** to be reflected (in).

reflejo, -ja adj [movimiento, dolor] reflex (antes de sust). ◆ **reflejo** m **-1.** [gen] reflection. **-2.** [destello] glint, gleam. **-3.** ANAT reflex. ◆ **reflejos** mpl [de peluquería] highlights.

reflexión f reflection; **con ~** on reflection; **sin previa ~** without thinking.

reflexionar vi to reflect, to think.

reflexivo, -va adj **-1.** [que piensa] thoughtful. **-2.** GRAM reflexive.

reflujo m ebb (tide).

reforma f **-1.** [modificación] reform; **~ agraria** agrarian reform. **-2.** [en local, casa etc] alterations (pl). ◆ **Reforma** f: **la Reforma** RELIG the Reformation.

reformar vt **-1.** [gen & RELIG] to reform. **-2.** [local, casa etc] to renovate. ◆ **reformarse** vpr to mend one's ways.

reformatorio m ≃ youth custody centre Br, ≃ borstal Br, reformatory Am; [de menores de 15 años] ≃ remand home.

reforzar vt to reinforce.

refractario, -ria adj **-1.** [material] refractory. **-2.** [opuesto]: **~ a** averse to.

refrán m proverb, saying.

refregar vt **-1.** [frotar] to scrub. **-2.** fig [reprochar]: **~ algo a alguien** to reproach sb for sthg.

refrenar vt to curb, to restrain.

refrendar vt [aprobar] to approve.

refrescante adj refreshing.

refrescar ◇ vt **-1.** [gen] to refresh; [bebidas] to chill. **-2.** fig [conocimientos] to brush up. ◇ vi **-1.** [tiempo] to cool down. **-2.** [bebida] to be refreshing. ◆ **refrescarse** vpr **-1.** [tomar aire fresco] to get a breath of fresh air. **-2.** [beber algo] to have a drink. **-3.** [mojarse con agua fría] to splash o.s. down.

refresco m **-1.** [bebida] soft drink; **~s** refreshments. **-2.** MIL: **de ~** new, fresh.

refriega f scuffle; MIL skirmish.

refrigeración f **-1.** [aire acondicionado] air-conditioning. **-2.** [de alimentos] refrigeration. **-3.** [de máquinas] cooling.

refrigerador, -ra adj cooling. ◆ **refrigerador** m [de alimentos] refrigerator, fridge Br, icebox Am.

refrigerar vt **-1.** [alimentos] to refrigerate. **-2.** [local] to air-condition. **-3.** [máquina] to cool.

refrigerio m snack.

refrito, -ta adj [demasiado frito] overfried; [frito de nuevo] re-fried. ◆ **refrito** m fig [cosa rehecha] rehash.

refuerzo m reinforcement.

refugiado, -da m y f refugee.

refugiar vt to give refuge to. ◆ **refugiarse** vpr to take refuge; **~se de algo** to shelter from sthg.

refugio m **-1.** [lugar] shelter, refuge; **~ atómico** nuclear bunker. **-2.** fig [amparo, consuelo] refuge, comfort.

refulgir vi to shine brightly.

refunfuñar vi to grumble.

refutar vt to refute.

regadera f **-1.** [para regar] watering can. **-2.** Amer [chubasco] shower.

regadío m irrigated land.

regalado, -da adj **-1.** [muy barato] dirt cheap. **-2.** [agradable] comfortable.

regalar vt **-1.** [dar - de regalo] to give (as a present); [- gratis] to give away. **-2.** [agasajar]: **~ a alguien con algo** to shower sb with sthg.

regaliz m liquorice.

regalo m **-1.** [obsequio] present, gift. **-2.** [placer] joy, delight.

regalón, -ona adj Amer fam spoilt.

regañadientes ◆ **a regañadientes** loc adv fam unwillingly, reluctantly.

regañar ◇ vt [reprender] to tell off. ◇ vi [pelearse] to fall out, to argue.

regañina *f* [reprimenda] ticking off.

regañón, -ona *adj* grumpy.

regar *vt* **-1.** [con agua - planta] to water; [- calle] to hose down. **-2.** [suj: río] to flow through.

regata *f* NÁUT regatta, boat race.

regatear ◇ *vt* **-1.** [escatimar] to be sparing with; **no ha regateado esfuerzos** he has spared no effort. **-2.** DEP to beat, to dribble past. **-3.** [precio] to haggle over. ◇ *vi* **-1.** [negociar el precio] to barter. **-2.** NÁUT to race.

regateo *m* bartering, haggling.

regazo *m* lap.

regeneración *f* regeneration; [moral] reform.

regenerar *vt* to regenerate; [moralmente] to reform.

regentar *vt* [país] to run, to govern; [negocio] to run, to manage; [puesto] to hold.

regente ◇ *adj* regent. ◇ *m y f* **-1.** [de un país] regent. **-2.** [administrador - de tienda] manager; [- de colegio] governor. **-3.** *Amer* [alcalde] mayor (*f* mayoress).

regidor, -ra *m y f* TEATR stage manager; CIN & TV assistant director.

régimen (*pl* **regímenes**) *m* **-1.** [sistema político] regime; **Antiguo ~** ancien régime. **-2.** [normativa] rules (*pl*). **-3.** [dieta] diet. **-4.** [de vida, lluvias etc] pattern.

regimiento *m* MIL & *fig* regiment.

regio, -gia *adj* lit & *fig* royal.

región *f* region; MIL district.

regir ◇ *vt* **-1.** [reinar en] to rule, to govern. **-2.** [administrar] to run, to manage. **-3.** *fig* [determinar] to govern, to determine. ◇ *vi* [ley] to be in force, to apply. ◆ **regirse por** *vpr* to trust in.

registrador, -ra *m y f* registrar.

registrar *vt* **-1.** [inspeccionar - zona, piso] to search; [- persona] to frisk. **-2.** [nacimiento, temperatura etc] to register, to record. **-3.** [grabar] to record. ◆ **registrarse** *vpr* **-1.** [suceder] to occur. **-2.** [observarse] to be recorded.

registro *m* **-1.** [oficina] registry (office); **~ civil** registry (office). **-2.** [libro] register. **-3.** [inspección] search, searching (*U*). **-4.** INFORM record. **-5.** LING & MÚS register.

regla *f* **-1.** [para medir] ruler, rule. **-2.** [norma] rule; **en ~** in order; **por ~ general** as a rule. **-3.** MAT operation. **-4.** *fam* [menstruación] period.

reglamentación *f* [acción] regulation; [reglas] rules (*pl*), regulations (*pl*).

reglamentar *vt* to regulate.

reglamentario, -ria *adj* lawful; [arma, balón] regulation (*antes de sust*); DER statutory.

reglamento *m* regulations (*pl*), rules (*pl*).

reglar *vt* to regulate.

regocijar ◆ **regocijarse** *vpr*: **~se (de o con)** to rejoice (in).

regocijo *m* joy, delight.

regodeo *m* delight, pleasure; [malicioso] (cruel) delight o pleasure.

regordete *adj* chubby.

regresar ◇ *vi* [yendo] to go back, to return; [viniendo] to come back, to return. ◇ *vt* *Amer* [devolver] to give back.

regresión *f* **-1.** [de epidemia] regression. **-2.** [de exportaciones] drop, decline.

regresivo, -va *adj* regressive.

regreso *m* return; **estar de ~** to be back.

reguero *m* [de sangre, agua] trickle; [de harina etc] trail; **correr como un ~ de pólvora** to spread like wildfire.

regulación *f* [gen] regulation; [de nacimientos, tráfico] control; [de mecanismo] adjustment.

regulador, -ra *adj* regulatory.

regular ◇ *adj* **-1.** [gen] regular; [de tamaño] medium; **de un modo ~** regularly. **-2.** [mediocre] average, fair. **-3.** [normal] normal, usual. ◇ *adv* all right; [de salud] so-so. ◇ *vt* [gen] to control, to regulate; [mecanismo] to adjust. ◆ **por lo regular** *loc adv* as a rule, generally.

regularidad *f* regularity; **con ~** regularly.

regularizar *vt* [legalizar] to regularize.

regusto *m* aftertaste; [semejanza, aire] flavour, hint.

rehabilitación *f* **-1.** [de personas] rehabilitation; [en un puesto] reinstatement. **-2.** [de local] restoration.

rehabilitar *vt* **-1.** [personas] to rehabilitate; [en un puesto] to reinstate. **-2.** [local] to restore.

rehacer *vt* **-1.** [volver a hacer] to redo, to do again. **-2.** [reconstruir] to rebuild. ◆ **rehacerse** *vpr* [recuperarse] to recuperate, to recover.

rehecho, -cha *pp* → **rehacer**.

rehén (*pl* **rehenes**) *m* hostage.

rehogar *vt* to fry over a low heat.

rehuir *vt* to avoid.

rehusar *vt & vi* to refuse.

Reikiavik Reykjavik.

reimpresión *f* [tirada] reprint; [acción] reprinting.

reina f [monarca] queen.

reinado m lit & fig reign.

reinante adj **-1.** [monarquía, persona] reigning, ruling. **-2.** [viento] prevailing; [frío, calor] current.

reinar vi lit & fig to reign.

reincidir vi: ~ **en** [falta, error] to relapse into, to fall back into; [delito] to repeat.

reincorporar vt to reincorporate. ◆ **reincorporarse** vpr: ~se (a) to rejoin.

reino m CIENCIA & POLÍT kingdom; fig realm.

Reino Unido: el ~ the United Kingdom.

reintegrar vt **-1.** [a un puesto] to reinstate. **-2.** [dinero] to reimburse. ◆ **reintegrarse** vpr: ~se (a) to return (to).

reintegro m **-1.** [de dinero] reimbursement; BANCA withdrawal. **-2.** [en lotería] return of one's stake (in lottery).

reír ◇ vi to laugh. ◇ vt to laugh at. ◆ **reírse** vpr: ~se (de) to laugh (at).

reiterar vt to reiterate.

reiterativo, -va adj repetitious.

reivindicación f claim, demand.

reivindicar vt **-1.** [derechos, salario etc] to claim, to demand. **-2.** [atentado] to claim responsibility for.

reivindicativo, -va adj: **plataforma reivindicativa** (set of) demands; **jornada reivindicativa** day of protest.

reja f [gen] bars (pl); [en el suelo] grating; [celosía] grille.

rejego, -ga adj Amer fam [terco] stubborn.

rejilla f **-1.** [enrejado] grid, grating; [de ventana] grille; [de cocina] grill (on stove); [de horno] gridiron. **-2.** [para sillas, muebles] wickerwork. **-3.** [para equipaje] luggage rack.

rejón m TAUROM type of "banderilla" used by mounted bullfighter.

rejoneador, -ra m y f TAUROM bullfighter on horseback who uses the "rejón".

rejuntarse vpr fam to live together.

rejuvenecer vt & vi to rejuvenate.

relación f **-1.** [nexo] relation, connection; **con** ~ **a, en** ~ **con** in relation to; ~ **precio-calidad** value for money. **-2.** [comunicación, trato] relations (pl), relationship; **relaciones diplomáticas/públicas** diplomatic/public relations. **-3.** [lista] list. **-4.** [descripción] account. **-5.** [informe] report. **-6.** (gen pl) [noviazgo] relationship. **-7.** MAT ratio.

◆ **relaciones** fpl [contactos] connections.

relacionar vt [vincular] to relate, to connect. ◆ **relacionarse** vpr: ~se (con) [alternar] to mix (with).

relajación f relaxation.

relajar vt to relax. ◆ **relajarse** vpr to relax.

relajo m Amer fam [alboroto] racket, din.

relamer vt to lick repeatedly. ◆ **relamerse** vpr **-1.** [persona] to lick one's lips. **-2.** [animal] to lick its chops.

relamido, -da adj prim and proper.

relámpago m [descarga] flash of lightning, lightning (U); [destello] flash.

relampaguear vi fig to flash.

relatar vt [suceso] to relate, to recount; [historia] to tell.

relatividad f relativity.

relativo, -va adj **-1.** [gen] relative. **-2.** [escaso] limited.

relato m [exposición] account, report; [cuento] tale.

relax m inv **-1.** [relajación] relaxation. **-2.** [sección de periódico] personal column.

relegar vt: ~ (a) to relegate (to); ~ **algo al olvido** to banish sthg from one's mind.

relevante adj outstanding, important.

relevar vt **-1.** [sustituir] to relieve, to take over from. **-2.** [destituir]: ~ (de) to dismiss (from), to relieve (of). **-3.** [eximir]: ~ (de) to free (from). **-4.** [DEP - en partidos] to substitute; [- en relevos] to take over from.

relevo m **-1.** MIL relief, changing. **-2.** DEP [acción] relay. **-3.** loc: **tomar el** ~ to take over. ◆ **relevos** mpl DEP [carrera] relay (race) (sg).

relieve m **-1.** [gen, ARTE & GEOGR] relief; **bajo** ~ bas-relief. **-2.** [importancia] importance; **poner de** ~ to underline (the importance of).

religión f religion.

religioso, -sa ◇ adj religious. ◇ m y f [monje] monk (f nun).

relinchar vi to neigh, to whinny.

reliquia f relic; [familiar] heirloom.

rellano m [de escalera] landing.

rellenar vt **-1.** [volver a llenar] to refill. **-2.** [documento, formulario] to fill in ○ out. **-3.** [pollo, cojín etc] to stuff; [tarta, pastel] to fill.

relleno, -na adj [gen] stuffed; [tarta, pastel] filled. ◆ **relleno** m [de pollo] stuffing; [de pastel] filling.

reloj m [de pared] clock; [de pulsera] watch; ~ **de arena** hourglass; ~ **de pulsera** watch, wristwatch; **hacer algo contra** ~ to do sthg against the clock.

relojero, -ra m y f watchmaker.

reluciente adj shining, gleaming.

relucir vi lit & fig to shine; **sacar algo a** ~ to bring sthg up, to mention sthg.

remachar vt -1. [machacar] to rivet. -2. fig [recalcar] to drive home, to stress.

remache m [clavo] rivet.

remanente m -1. [de géneros] surplus stock; [de productos agrícolas] surplus. -2. [en cuenta bancaria] balance.

remangar = arremangar.

remanso m still pool.

remar vi to row.

rematado, -da adj utter, complete.

rematar ◇ vt -1. [acabar] to finish. -2. [matar - persona] to finish off; [- animal] to put out of its misery. -3. DEP to shoot. -4. [liquidar, vender] to sell off cheaply. ◇ vi [en fútbol] to shoot; [de cabeza] to head at goal.

remate m -1. [fin, colofón] end. -2. [en fútbol] shot; [de cabeza] header at goal. ◆ **de remate** loc adv totally, completely.

rembolsar = reembolsar.

rembolso = reembolso.

remedar vt to imitate; [por burla] to ape.

remediar vt [daño] to remedy, to put right; [problema] to solve; [peligro] to avoid.

remedio m -1. [solución] solution, remedy; **como último** ~ as a last resort; **no hay** ○ **queda más** ~ **que ...** there's nothing for it but ...; **no tener más** ~ to have no alternative ○ choice; **sin** ~ [sin cura, solución] hopeless; [ineludiblemente] inevitably. -2. [consuelo] consolation. -3. [medicamento] remedy, cure.

rememorar vt to remember, to recall.

remendar vt to mend, to darn.

remero, -ra m y f [persona] rower. ◆ **remera** f Amer [prenda] T-shirt.

remesa f [de productos] consignment; [de dinero] remittance.

remeter vt to tuck in.

remezón m Amer earth tremor.

remiendo m [parche] mend, darn.

remilgado, -da adj -1. [afectado] affected. -2. [escrupuloso] squeamish; [con comida] fussy.

remilgo m -1. [afectación] affectation.

remitente m y f sender.

remisión f Amer dismissal, sacking.

reminiscencia f reminiscence; **tener** ~**s de** to be reminiscent of.

remiso, -sa adj: **ser** ~ **a hacer algo** to be reluctant to do sthg.

remite m sender's name and address.

remitente m y f sender.

remitir ◇ vt -1. [enviar] to send. -2. [perdonar] to forgive, to remit. -3. [traspasar]: ~ **algo a** to refer sthg to. ◇ vi -1. [en texto]: ~ **a** to refer to. -2. [disminuir] to subside. ◆ **remitirse a** vpr -1. [atenerse a] to abide by. -2. [referirse a] to refer to.

remo m -1. [pala] oar. -2. [deporte] rowing.

remoción f Amer dismissal, sacking.

remodelar vt [gen] to redesign; [gobierno] to reshuffle.

remojar vt [humedecer] to soak.

remojo m: **poner en** ~ to leave to soak; **estar en** ~ to be soaking.

remolacha f beetroot Br, beet Am; [azucarera] (sugar) beet.

remolcador, -ra adj [coche] tow (antes de sust); [barco] tug (antes de sust). ◆ **remolcador** m [camión] breakdown lorry; [barco] tug, tugboat.

remolcar vt [coche] to tow; [barco] to tug.

remolino m -1. [de agua] eddy, whirlpool; [de viento] whirlwind; [de humo] cloud, swirl. -2. [de gente] throng, mass. -3. [de pelo] cowlick.

remolón, -ona adj lazy.

remolque m -1. [acción] towing. -2. [vehículo] trailer.

remontar vt [pendiente, río] to go up; [obstáculo] to overcome; [puestos] to catch up. ◆ **remontarse** vpr -1. [ave, avión] to soar, to climb high. -2. [gastos]: ~**se a** to amount ○ come to. -3. fig [datar]: ~**se a** to go ○ date back to.

remorder vt fig: ~**le a alguien** to fill sb with remorse.

remordimiento m remorse.

remoto, -ta adj remote; **no tengo ni la más remota idea** I haven't got the faintest idea.

remover vt -1. [agitar - sopa, café] to stir; [- ensalada] to toss; [- bote, frasco] to shake; [- tierra] to dig up. -2. [desplazar] to move, to shift. -3. [reavivar - recuerdos, pasado] to rake up. -4. Amer [despedir] to dismiss, to sack. ◆ **removerse** vpr to move about; [mar] to get rough.

remplazar = reemplazar.

remplazo = reemplazo.

remuneración f remuneration.

remunerar vt **-1.** [pagar] to remunerate. **-2.** [recompensar] to reward.

renacer vi **-1.** [gen] to be reborn; [flores, hojas] to grow again. **-2.** [alegría, esperanza] to return, to revive.

renacimiento m [gen] rebirth; [de flores, hojas] budding. ◆ **Renacimiento** m: el Renacimiento the Renaissance.

renacuajo m tadpole; fam fig tiddler.

renal adj renal, kidney (antes de sust).

rencilla f quarrel.

rencor m resentment, bitterness.

rencoroso, -sa adj resentful, bitter.

rendición f surrender.

rendido, -da adj **-1.** [agotado] exhausted. **-2.** [sumiso] submissive; [admirador] devoted.

rendija f crack, gap.

rendimiento m **-1.** [de inversión, negocio] yield, return; [de trabajador, fábrica] productivity; [de tierra, cosecha] yield. **-2.** [de motor] performance.

rendir ◇ vt **-1.** [cansar] to tire out. **-2.** [rentar] to yield. **-3.** [vencer] to defeat, to subdue. **-4.** [ofrecer] to give, to present; [pleitesía] to pay. ◇ vi [máquina] to perform well; [negocio] to be profitable; [fábrica, trabajador] to be productive. ◆ **rendirse** vpr **-1.** [entregarse] to surrender. **-2.** [ceder]: ~se a to give in to. **-3.** [desanimarse] to give in ○ up.

renegado, -da adj, m y f renegade.

renegar vi **-1.** [repudiar]: ~ de RELIG to renounce; [familia] to disown. **-2.** fam [gruñir] to grumble.

Renfe (abrev de Red Nacional de los Ferrocarriles Españoles) f Spanish state railway network.

renglón m line; COM item.

reno m reindeer.

renombrar vt INFORM to rename.

renombre m renown, fame.

renovación f [de carné, contrato] renewal; [de mobiliario, local] renovation.

renovar vt **-1.** [cambiar - mobiliario, local] to renovate; [- vestuario] to clear out; [- personal, plantilla] to shake out. **-2.** [rehacer - carné, contrato, ataques] to renew. **-3.** [restaurar] to restore. **-4.** [innovar] to rethink, to revolutionize; POLÍT to reform.

renquear vi to limp, to hobble; fig to struggle along.

renta f **-1.** [ingresos] income; ~ **fija** fixed income; ~ **per cápita** ○ **por habitante** per capita income. **-2.** [alquiler] rent. **-3.** [beneficios] return. **-4.** [intereses] interest.

rentable adj profitable.

rentar ◇ vt **-1.** [rendir] to produce, to yield. **-2.** Amer [alquilar] to rent. ◇ vi to be profitable.

rentista m y f person of independent means.

renuncia f [abandono] giving up; [dimisión] resignation.

renunciar vi **-1.** [abandonar] to give up. **-2.** [dimitir] to resign. ◆ **renunciar a** vi **-1.** [prescindir de] to give up; [plan, proyecto] to drop; ~ **al tabaco** to give up ○ stop smoking. **-2.** [rechazar]: ~ **(a hacer algo)** to refuse (to do sthg).

reñido, -da adj **-1.** [enfadado]: ~ **(con)** on bad terms ○ at odds (with); **están** ~**s** they've fallen out. **-2.** [disputado] hard-fought. **-3.** [incompatible]: **estar** ~ **con** to be incompatible with.

reñir ◇ vt **-1.** [regañar] to tell off. **-2.** [disputar] to fight. ◇ vi [enfadarse] to argue, to fall out.

reo, -a m y f [culpado] offender, culprit; [acusado] accused, defendant.

reojo m: **mirar algo de** ~ to look at sthg out of the corner of one's eye.

repantigarse vpr to sprawl out.

reparación f **-1.** [arreglo] repair, repairing (U); **en** ~ under repair. **-2.** [compensación] reparation, redress.

reparador, -ra adj [descanso, sueño] refreshing.

reparar ◇ vt [coche etc] to repair, to fix; [error, daño etc] to make amends for; [fuerzas] to restore. ◇ vi [advertir]: ~ **en algo** to notice sthg; **no** ~ **en gastos** to spare no expense.

reparo m **-1.** [objeción] objection. **-2.** [apuro]: **no tener** ~**s en** not to be afraid to.

repartición f [reparto] sharing out.

repartidor, -ra m y f [gen] distributor; [de butano, carbón] deliveryman (f deliverywoman); [de leche] milkman (f milklady); [de periódicos] paperboy (f papergirl).

repartir vt **-1.** [dividir - gen] to share out, to divide; [- territorio, nación] to partition. **-2.** [distribuir - leche, periódicos, correo] to deliver; [- naipes] to deal (out). **-3.** [asignar - trabajo, órdenes] to give out, to allocate; [- papeles] to assign.

reparto m **-1.** [división] division, distribution; ~ **de beneficios** ECON profit sharing; ~ **de premios** prizegiving. **-2.** [distribución - de leche, periódicos, correo] **delivery. -3.** [asignación] **allocation. -4.** CIN & TEATR **cast.**

repasador *m Amer* tea towel.

repasar *vt* **-1.** [revisar] to go over; [lección] to revise. **-2.** [zurcir] to darn, to mend.

repaso *m* [revisión] revision; [de ropa] darning, mending; **curso de ~** refresher course.

repatriar *vt* to repatriate.

repecho *m* steep slope.

repelente *adj* **-1.** [desagradable, repugnante] repulsive. **-2.** [ahuyentador] repellent.

repeler *vt* **-1.** [rechazar] to repel. **-2.** [repugnar] to repulse, to disgust.

repelús *m*: **me da ~** it gives me the shivers.

repente *m* [arrebato] fit. ◆ **de repente** *loc adv* suddenly.

repentino, -na *adj* sudden.

repercusión *f* **-1.** *fig* [consecuencia] repercussion. **-2.** [resonancia] echoes (*pl*).

repercutir *vi fig* [afectar]: ~ **en** to have repercussions on.

repertorio *m* **-1.** [obras] repertoire. **-2.** *fig* [serie] selection.

repesca *f* **-1.** EDUC resit. **-2.** DEP repêchage.

repetición *f* repetition; [de una jugada] action replay.

repetidor, -ra *m y f* EDUC student repeating a year. ◆ **repetidor** *m* ELECTR repeater.

repetir ◇ *vt* to repeat; [ataque] to renew; [en comida] to have seconds of. ◇ *vi* **-1.** [alumno] to repeat a year. **-2.** [sabor, alimento]: ~ **(a alguien)** to repeat (on sb). **-3.** [comensal] to have seconds. ◆ **repetirse** *vpr* **-1.** [fenómeno] to recur. **-2.** [persona] to repeat o.s.

repicar *vi* [campanas] to ring; [tambor] to sound.

repique *m* peal, ringing (*U*).

repiqueteo *m* [de campanas] **pealing;** [de tambor] **beating;** [de timbre] **ringing;** [de lluvia, dedos] **drumming.**

repisa *f* [estante] shelf; [sobre chimenea] mantelpiece.

replantear *vt* **-1.** [reenfocar] to reconsider, to restate. **-2.** [volver a mencionar] to bring up again.

replegar *vt* [ocultar] to retract. ◆ **replegarse** *vpr* [retirarse] to withdraw, to retreat.

repleto, -ta *adj*: ~ **(de)** packed (with).

réplica *f* **-1.** [respuesta] reply. **-2.** [copia] replica.

replicar ◇ *vt* [responder] to answer; [objetar] to answer back, to retort. ◇ *vi* [objetar] to answer back.

repliegue *m* **-1.** [retirada] withdrawal, retreat. **-2.** [pliegue] fold.

repoblación *f* [con gente] repopulation; [con peces] restocking; ~ **forestal** reafforestation.

repoblar *vt* [con gente] to repopulate; [con peces] to restock; [con árboles] to replant.

repollo *m* cabbage.

reponer *vt* **-1.** [gen] to replace. **-2.** CIN & TEATR to re-run; TV to repeat. **-3.** [replicar]: ~ **que** to reply that.

reportaje *m* RADIO & TV report; PRENS article.

reportar *vt* **-1.** [traer] to bring. **-2.** *Amer* [informar] to report.

reporte *m Amer* report.

reportero, -ra, repórter *m y f* reporter.

reposado, -da *adj* relaxed, calm.

reposar *vi* **-1.** [descansar] to (have a) rest. **-2.** [sedimentarse] to stand.

reposera *f Amer* easy chair.

reposición *f* **-1.** CIN rerun; TEATR revival; TV repeat. **-2.** [de existencias, pieza etc] replacement.

reposo *m* [descanso] rest.

repostar ◇ *vi* [coche] to fill up; [avión] to refuel. ◇ *vt* **-1.** [gasolina] to fill up with. **-2.** [provisiones] to stock up on.

repostería *f* [oficio, productos] confectionery.

reprender *vt* [a niños] to tell off; [a empleados] to reprimand.

represión *f* [a niños] telling-off; [a empleados] reprimand.

represalia *f* (*gen pl*) reprisal; **tomar ~s** to retaliate, to take reprisals.

representación *f* **-1.** [gen & COM] representation; **en ~ de** on behalf of. **-2.** TEATR performance.

representante ◇ *adj* representative. ◇ *m y f* **-1.** [gen & COM] representative. **-2.** [de artista] agent.

representar *vt* **-1.** [gen & COM] to represent. **-2.** [aparentar] to look; **representa unos 40 años** she looks about 40. **-3.** [significar] to mean; **representa el 50% del consumo interno** it accounts for 50% of domestic consumption. **-4.** [TEATR - función] to perform; [- papel] to play.

representativo, -va *adj* **-1.** [simbolizador]: **ser ~ de** to represent. **-2.** [característico, relevante]: ~ **(de)** representative (of).

represión f repression.

reprimenda f reprimand.

reprimir vt [gen] to suppress; [minorías, disidentes] to repress. ◆ **reprimirse** vpr: ~**se (de hacer algo)** to restrain o.s. (from doing sthg).

reprobar vt to censure, to condemn.

reprochar vt: ~ **algo a alguien** to reproach sb for sthg. ◆ **reprocharse** vpr: ~**se algo (uno mismo)** to reproach o.s. for sthg.

reproche m reproach.

reproducción f reproduction.

reproducir vt [gen & ARTE] to reproduce; [gestos] to copy, to imitate. ◆ **reproducirse** vpr **-1.** [volver a suceder] to recur. **-2.** [procrear] to reproduce.

reproductor, -ra adj reproductive.

reptil m reptile.

república f republic.

República Checa f Czech Republic.

República Dominicana f Dominican Republic.

republicano, -na adj, m y f republican.

repudiar vt **-1.** [condenar] to repudiate. **-2.** [rechazar] to disown.

repuesto, -ta ◇ pp → **reponer**. ◇ adj: ~ **(de)** recovered (from). ◆ **repuesto** m [gen] reserve; AUTOM spare part; **la rueda de** ~ the spare wheel.

repugnancia f disgust.

repugnante adj disgusting.

repugnar vt: **me repugna ese olor/su actitud** I find that smell/her attitude disgusting; **me repugna hacerlo** I'm loathe to do it.

repujar vt to emboss.

repulsa f [censura] condemnation.

repulsión f repulsion.

repulsivo, -va adj repulsive.

reputación f reputation; **tener mucha** ~ to be very famous.

reputar vt to consider.

requemado, -da adj burnt.

requerimiento m **-1.** [demanda] entreaty. **-2.** [DER - intimación] writ, injunction; [- aviso] summons (sg).

requerir vt **-1.** [necesitar] to require. **-2.** [ordenar] to demand. **-3.** [pedir]: ~ **a alguien (para) que haga algo** to ask sb to do sthg. **-4.** DER to order. ◆ **requerirse** vpr [ser necesario] to be required O necessary.

requesón m cottage cheese.

requisa f [requisición - MIL] requisition; [- en aduana] seizure.

requisito m requirement; ~ **previo** prerequisite.

res f beast, animal.

resabio m **-1.** [sabor] nasty aftertaste. **-2.** [vicio] persistent bad habit.

resaca f **-1.** fam [de borrachera] hangover. **-2.** [de las olas] undertow.

resalado, -da adj fam charming.

resaltar ◇ vi **-1.** [destacar] to stand out. **-2.** [en edificios - decoración] to stand out. ◇ vt [destacar] to highlight.

resarcir vt: ~ **a alguien (de)** to compensate sb (for). ◆ **resarcirse** vpr to be compensated; ~**se de** [daño, pérdida] to be compensated for; [desengaño, derrota] to make up for.

resbalada f Amer fam slip.

resbaladizo, -za adj lit & fig slippery.

resbalar vi **-1.** [caer]: ~ **(con** O **sobre)** to slip (on). **-2.** [deslizarse] to slide. **-3.** [estar resbaladizo] to be slippery. ◆ **resbalarse** vpr to slip (over).

resbalón m slip.

rescatar vt **-1.** [liberar, salvar] to rescue; [pagando rescate] to ransom. **-2.** [recuperar - herencia etc] to recover.

rescate m **-1.** [liberación, salvación] rescue. **-2.** [dinero] ransom. **-3.** [recuperación] recovery.

rescindir vt to rescind.

rescisión f cancellation.

rescoldo m ember; fig lingering feeling.

resecar vt [piel] to dry out. ◆ **resecarse** vpr **-1.** [piel] to dry out. **-2.** [tierra] to become parched.

reseco, -ca adj **-1.** [piel, garganta, pan] very dry. **-2.** [tierra] parched. **-3.** [flaco] emaciated.

resentido, -da adj bitter, resentful; **estar** ~ **con alguien** to be really upset with sb.

resentimiento m resentment, bitterness.

resentirse vpr **-1.** [debilitarse] to be weakened; [salud] to deteriorate. **-2.** [sentir molestias]: ~ **de** to be suffering from. **-3.** [ofenderse] to be offended.

reseña f [de libro, concierto] review; [de partido, conferencia] report.

reseñar vt **-1.** [criticar - libro, concierto] to review; [- partido, conferencia] to report on. **-2.** [describir] to describe.

reserva f [de hotel, avión etc] reservation. **-2.** [provisión] reserves (pl); **tener algo de** ~ to keep sthg in reserve. **-3.** [objeción] reservation. **-4.** [de indígenas] reservation. **-5.** [de animales] reserve; ~ **natural** nature reserve. **-6.** MIL reserve. ◆ **reservas** *fpl* **-1.** [energía acumulada] energy reserves. **-2.** [recursos] resources.

reservado, -da *adj* **-1.** [gen] reserved. **-2.** [tema, asunto] confidential. ◆ **reservado** *m* [en restaurante] private room; FERROC reserved compartment.

reservar *vt* **-1.** [habitación, asiento etc] to reserve, to book. **-2.** [guardar - dinero, pasteles etc] to set aside; [- sorpresa] to keep. **-3.** [callar - opinión, comentarios] to reserve. ◆ **reservarse** *vpr* **-1.** [esperar]: ~**se para** to save o.s. for. **-2.** [guardar para sí - secreto] to keep to o.s.; [- dinero, derecho] to retain (for o.s.).

resfriado, -da *adj*: estar ~ to have a cold. ◆ **resfriado** *m* cold.

resfriar *vt* to make cold. ◆ **resfriarse** *vpr* [constiparse] to catch a cold.

resfrío *m Amer* cold.

resguardar *vt & vi*: ~ **de** to protect against. ◆ **resguardarse** *vpr*: ~**se de** [en un portal] to shelter from; [con abrigo, paraguas] to protect o.s. against.

resguardo *m* **-1.** [documento] receipt. **-2.** [protección] protection.

residencia *f* **-1.** [estancia] stay. **-2.** [localidad, domicilio] residence. **-3.** [establecimiento - de estudiantes] hall of residence; [- de ancianos] old people's home; [- de oficiales] residence. **-4.** [hospital] hospital. **-5.** [permiso para extranjeros] residence permit.

residencial *adj* residential.

residente *adj, m y f* resident.

residir *vi* **-1.** [vivir] to reside. **-2.** [radicar]: ~ **en** to lie in.

residuo *m* **-1.** (*gen pl*) [material inservible] waste; QUÍM residue; ~**s nucleares** nuclear waste (*U*). **-2.** [restos] leftovers (*pl*).

resignación *f* resignation.

resignarse *vpr*: ~ (**a hacer algo**) to resign o.s. (to doing sthg).

resina *f* resin.

resistencia *f* **-1.** [gen, ELECTR & POLÍT] resistance; **ofrecer** ~ to put up resistance. **-2.** [de puente, cimientos] strength. **-3.** [física - para correr etc] stamina.

resistente *adj* [gen] tough, strong; ~ **al calor** heat-resistant.

resistir ◇ *vt* **-1.** [dolor, peso, críticas] to withstand. **-2.** [tentación, impulso, deseo] to resist. **-3.** [tolerar] to tolerate, to stand. ◇ *vi* **-1.** [ejército, ciudad etc]: ~ (**a algo/a alguien**) to resist (sthg/sb). **-2.**

[corredor etc] to keep going; ~ **a algo** to stand up to sthg, to withstand sthg. **-3.** [mesa, dique etc] to take the strain; ~ **a algo** to withstand sthg. **-4.** [mostrarse firme - ante tentaciones etc] to resist (it); ~ **a algo** to resist sthg. ◆ **resistirse** *vpr*: ~**se** (**a algo**) to resist (sthg); **me resisto a creerlo** I refuse to believe it; **se le resisten las matemáticas** she just can't get the hang of maths.

resma *f* ream.

resollar *vi* to gasp (for breath); [jadear] to pant.

resolución *f* **-1.** [solución - de una crisis] resolution; [- de un crimen] solution. **-2.** [firmeza] determination. **-3.** [decisión] decision; DER ruling. **-4.** [de Naciones Unidas etc] resolution.

resolver *vt* **-1.** [solucionar - duda, crisis] to resolve; [- problema, caso] to solve. **-2.** [decidir]: ~ **hacer algo** to decide to do sthg. **-3.** [partido, disputa, conflicto] to settle. ◆ **resolverse** *vpr* **-1.** [solucionarse - duda, crisis] to be resolved; [- problema, caso] to be solved. **-2.** [decidirse]: ~**se a hacer algo** to decide to do sthg.

resonancia *f* **-1.** [gen & FÍS] resonance (*U*). **-2.** *fig* [importancia] repercussions (*pl*).

resonante *adj* resounding; FÍS resonant; *fig* important.

resonar *vi* to resound, to echo.

resoplar *vi* [de cansancio] to pant; [de enfado] to snort.

resoplido *m* [por cansancio] pant; [por enfado] snort.

resorte *m* spring; *fig* means (*pl*); **tocar todos los** ~**s** to pull out all the stops.

respaldar *vt* to back, to support. ◆ **respaldarse** *vpr fig* [apoyarse]: ~**se en** to fall back on.

respaldo *m* **-1.** [de asiento] back. **-2.** *fig* [apoyo] backing, support.

respectar *v impers*: **por lo que respecta a alguien/a algo, en lo que respecta a alguien/a algo** as far as sb/sthg is concerned.

respectivo, -va *adj* respective; **en lo** ~ **a** with regard to.

respecto *m*: **al** ~, **a este** ~ in this respect; **no sé nada al** ~ I don't know anything about it; (**con**) ~ **a,** ~ **de** regarding.

respetable *adj* [venerable] respectable.

respetar *vt* [gen] to respect; [la palabra] to honour.

respeto m: ~ (a O por) respect (for); **es una falta de** ~ it shows a lack of respect; **por** ~ a out of consideration for.

respetuoso, -sa adj: ~ (**con**) respectful (of).

respingo m [movimiento] start, jump.

respingón, -ona adj snub.

respiración f breathing; MED respiration.

respirar ◇ vt [aire] to breathe. ◇ vi to breathe; fig [sentir alivio] to breathe again; **sin** ~ [sin descanso] without a break; [atentamente] with great attention.

respiratorio, -ria adj respiratory.

respiro m -1. [descanso] rest. -2. [alivio] relief, respite.

resplandecer vi -1. [brillar] to shine. -2. fig [destacar] to shine, to stand out.

resplandeciente adj shining; [sonrisa] beaming; [época] glittering; [vestimenta, color] resplendent.

resplandor m -1. [luz] brightness; [de fuego] glow. -2. [brillo] gleam.

responder ◇ vt to answer. ◇ vi -1. [contestar]: ~ (**a algo**) to answer (sthg). -2. [reaccionar]: ~ (**a**) to respond (to). -3. [responsabilizarse]: ~ **de algo/por alguien** to answer for sthg/for sb. -4. [replicar] to answer back.

respondón, -ona adj insolent.

responsabilidad f responsibility; DER liability; **tener la** ~ **de algo** to be responsible for sthg; ~ **limitada** limited liability.

responsabilizar vt: ~ **a alguien (de algo)** to hold sb responsible (for sthg). ◆ **responsabilizarse** vpr: ~**se (de)** to accept responsibility (for).

responsable ◇ adj responsible; ~ **de** responsible for. ◇ m y f -1. [culpable] person responsible. -2. [encargado] person in charge.

respuesta f -1. [gen] answer, reply; [en exámenes] answer; **en** ~ **a** in reply to. -2. fig [reacción] response.

resquebrajar vt to crack. ◆ **resquebrajarse** vpr to crack.

resquicio m -1. [abertura] chink; [grieta] crack. -2. fig [pizca] glimmer.

resta f MAT subtraction.

restablecer vt to reestablish, to restore. ◆ **restablecerse** vpr [curarse]: ~**se (de)** to recover (from).

restallar vt & vi [látigo] to crack; [lengua] to click.

restante adj remaining; **lo** ~ the rest.

restar ◇ vt -1. MAT to subtract. -2. [disminuir]: ~ **importancia a algo/méritos a alguien** to play down the importance of sthg/sb's qualities. ◇ vi [faltar] to be left.

restauración f restoration.

restaurante m restaurant.

restaurar vt to restore.

restitución f return.

restituir vt [devolver - objeto] to return; [- salud] to restore.

resto m: **el** ~ [gen] the rest; MAT the remainder. ◆ **restos** mpl -1. [sobras] leftovers. -2. [cadáver] remains. -3. [ruinas] ruins.

restregar vt to rub hard; [para limpiar] to scrub. ◆ **restregarse** vpr [frotarse] to rub.

restricción f restriction.

restrictivo, -va adj restrictive.

restringir vt to limit, to restrict.

resucitar ◇ vt [person] to bring back to life; [costumbre] to revive. ◇ vi [persona] to rise from the dead.

resuello m gasp, gasping (U); [jadeo] pant, panting (U).

resuelto, -ta ◇ pp → **resolver**. ◇ adj [decidido] determined.

resulta f: **de** ~s **de** as a result of.

resultado m result.

resultante adj & f resultant.

resultar ◇ vi -1. [acabar siendo]: ~ (**ser**) to turn out (to be); **resultó ileso** he was uninjured; **nuestro equipo resultó vencedor** our team came out on top. -2. [salir bien] to work (out), to be a success. -3. [originarse]: ~ **de** to result from. -4. [ser] to be; **resulta sorprendente** it's surprising; **me resultó imposible terminar antes** I was unable to finish earlier. -5. [venir a costar]: ~ **a** to come to, to cost. ◇ v impers [suceder]: ~ **que** to turn out that; **ahora resulta que no quiere alquilarlo** now it seems that she doesn't want to rent it.

resumen m summary; **en** ~ in short.

resumir vt to summarize; [discurso] to sum up. ◆ **resumirse en** vpr -1. [sintetizarse en] to be able to be summed up in. -2. [reducirse a] to boil down to.

resurgir vi to undergo a resurgence.

resurrección f resurrection.

retablo m altarpiece.

retaguardia f [tropa] rearguard; [territorio] rear.

retahíla f string, series.

retal m remnant.

retardar *vt* [retrasar] to delay; [frenar] to hold up, to slow down.

retazo *m* remnant; *fig* fragment.

rete *adv Amer fam* very.

retén *m* reserve.

retención *f* **-1.** [en el sueldo] deduction. **-2.** (*gen pl*) [de tráfico] hold-up.

retener *vt* **-1.** [detener] to hold back; [en comisaría] to detain. **-2.** [contener - impulso, ira] to hold back, to restrain. **-3.** [conservar] to retain. **-4.** [quedarse con] to hold on to, to keep. **-5.** [memorizar] to remember. **-6.** [deducir del sueldo] to deduct.

reticente *adj* [reacio] unwilling, reluctant.

retina *f* retina.

retintín *m* [ironía] sarcastic tone.

retirado, -da *adj* **-1.** [jubilado] retired. **-2.** [solitario, alejado] isolated, secluded. ◆ **retirada** *f* **-1.** MIL retreat; **batirse en retirada** to beat a retreat. **-2.** [de fondos, moneda, carné] withdrawal. **-3.** [de competición, actividad] withdrawal.

retirar *vt* **-1.** [quitar - gen] to remove; [- dinero, moneda, carné] to withdraw; [- nieve] to clear. **-2.** [jubilar - a deportista] to force to retire; [- a empleado] to retire. **-3.** [retractarse de] to take back. ◆ **retirarse** *vpr* **-1.** [gen] to retire. **-2.** [de competición, elecciones] to withdraw; [de reunión] to leave. **-3.** [de campo de batalla] to retreat. **-4.** [apartarse] to move away.

retiro *m* **-1.** [jubilación] retirement; [pensión] pension. **-2.** [refugio, ejercicio] retreat.

reto *m* challenge.

retocar *vt* to touch up; [prenda de vestir] to alter.

retoño *m* BOT sprout, shoot; *fig* offspring (*U*).

retoque *m* touching-up (*U*); [de prenda de vestir] alteration; **dar los últimos ~s a** to put the finishing touches to.

retorcer *vt* [torcer - brazo, alambre] to twist; [- ropa, cuello] to wring. ◆ **retorcerse** *vpr* [contraerse]: ~**se (de)** [risa] to double up (with); [dolor] to writhe about (in).

retorcido, -da *adj* **-1.** [torcido - brazo, alambre] twisted. **-2.** *fig* [rebuscado] complicated.

retornable *adj* returnable; **no ~** non-returnable.

retornar *vt & vi* to return.

retorno *m* [gen & INFORM] return; ~ **de carro** carriage return.

retortijón *m* (*gen pl*) stomach cramp.

retozar *vi* to frolic; [amantes] to romp about.

retractarse *vpr* [de una promesa] to go back on one's word; [de una opinión] to take back what one has said; ~ **de** [lo dicho] to retract, to take back.

retraer *vt* [encoger] to retract. ◆ **retraerse** *vpr* **-1.** [encogerse] to retract. **-2.** [retroceder] to withdraw, to retreat.

retraído, -da *adj* withdrawn, retiring.

retransmisión *f* broadcast; ~ **en directo/diferido** live/recorded broadcast.

retransmitir *vt* to broadcast.

retrasado, -da ◇ *adj* **-1.** [país, industria] backward; [reloj] slow; [tren] late, delayed. **-2.** [en el pago, los estudios] behind. **-3.** MED retarded, backward. ◇ *m y f*: ~ **(mental)** mentally retarded person.

retrasar *vt* **-1.** [aplazar] to postpone. **-2.** [demorar] to delay, to hold up. **-3.** [hacer más lento] to slow down, to hold up. **-4.** [en el pago, los estudios] to set back. **-5.** [reloj] to put back. ◆ **retrasarse** *vpr* **-1.** [llegar tarde] to be late. **-2.** [quedarse atrás] to fall behind. **-3.** [aplazarse] to be put off. **-4.** [reloj] to lose time.

retraso *m* **-1.** [por llegar tarde] delay; **llegar con (15 minutos de)** ~ to be (15 minutes) late. **-2.** [por sobrepasar una fecha]: **llevo en mi trabajo un ~ de 20 páginas** I'm 20 pages behind with my work. **-3.** [subdesarrollo] backwardness. **-4.** MED mental deficiency.

retratar *vt* **-1.** [fotografiar] to photograph. **-2.** [dibujar] to do a portrait of. **-3.** *fig* [describir] to portray.

retrato *m* **-1.** [dibujo] portrait; [fotografía] photograph; ~ **robot** photofit picture; **ser el vivo ~ de alguien** to be the spitting image of sb. **-2.** *fig* [reflejo] portrayal.

retrete *m* toilet.

retribución *f* [pago] payment; [recompensa] reward.

retribuir *vt* [pagar] to pay; [recompensar] to reward.

retro *adj* reactionary.

retroactivo, -va *adj* [ley] retroactive; [pago] backdated.

retroceder *vi* to go back; *fig* to back down.

retroceso *m* [regresión - gen] backward movement; [- en negociaciones] setback; [- en la economía] recession.

retrógrado, -da *adj, m y f* reactionary.
retroproyector *m* overhead projector.
retrospectivo, -va *adj* retrospective.
retrovisor *m* rear-view mirror.
retumbar *vi* [resonar] to resound.
reuma, reúma *m o f* rheumatism.
reumatismo *m* rheumatism.
reunión *f* meeting.
reunir *vt* **-1.** [público, accionistas etc] to bring together. **-2.** [objetos, textos etc] to collect, to bring together; [fondos] to raise. **-3.** [requisitos] to meet; [cualidades] to possess, to combine. ◆ **reunirse** *vpr* [congregarse] to meet.
revalidar *vt* to confirm.
revalorar = revalorizar.
revalorizar, revalorar *vt* **-1.** [aumentar el valor] to increase the value of; [moneda] to revalue. **-2.** [restituir el valor] to reassess in a favourable light. ◆ **revalorizarse** *vpr* [aumentar de valor] to appreciate; [moneda] to be revalued.
revancha *f* **-1.** [venganza] revenge. **-2.** DEP return match.
revelación *f* revelation.
revelado *m* FOT developing.
revelador, -ra *adj* [aclarador] revealing.
revelar *vt* **-1.** [declarar] to reveal. **-2.** [evidenciar] to show. **-3.** FOT to develop. ◆ **revelarse** *vpr*: ~se como to show o.s. to be.
revendedor, -ra *m y f* ticket tout.
reventa *f* resale; [de entradas] touting.
reventar ◇ *vt* **-1.** [explotar] to burst. **-2.** [echar abajo] to break down; [con explosivos] to blow up. ◇ *vi* [explotar] to burst. ◆ **reventarse** *vpr* [explotar] to explode; [rueda] to burst.
reventón *m* **-1.** [pinchazo] blowout, flat *Am*, puncture *Br*. **-2.** [estallido] burst.
reverberación *f* [de sonido] reverberation; [de luz, calor] reflection.
reverberar *vi* [sonido] to reverberate; [luz, calor] to reflect.
reverdecer *vi fig* [amor] to revive.
reverencia *f* **-1.** [respeto] reverence. **-2.** [saludo - inclinación] bow; [- flexión de piernas] curtsy.
reverenciar *vt* to revere.
reverendo, -da *adj* reverend. ◆ **reverendo** *m* reverend.
reverente *adj* reverent.
reversible *adj* reversible.
reverso *m* back, other side.
revertir *vi* **-1.** [volver, devolver] to revert. **-2.** [resultar]: ~ en to result in; ~ en beneficio/perjuicio de to be to the advantage/detriment of.

revés *m* **-1.** [parte opuesta - de papel, mano] back; [- de tela] other o wrong side; **al** ~ [en sentido contrario] the wrong way round; [en forma opuesta] the other way round; **del** ~ [lo de detrás, delante] the wrong way round, back to front; [lo de dentro, fuera] inside out; [lo de arriba, abajo] upside down. **-2.** [bofetada] slap. **-3.** DEP backhand. **-4.** [contratiempo] setback.
revestimiento *m* covering.
revestir *vt* **-1.** [recubrir]: ~ (de) [gen] to cover (with); [pintura] to coat (with); [forro] to line (with). **-2.** [poseer - solemnidad, gravedad etc] to take on, to have.
revisar *vt* **-1.** [repasar] to go over again. **-2.** [inspeccionar] to inspect; [cuentas] to audit. **-3.** [modificar] to revise.
revisión *f* **-1.** [repaso] revision. **-2.** [inspección] inspection; ~ de cuentas audit; ~ médica check-up. **-3.** [modificación] amendment. **-4.** [AUTOM - puesta a punto] service; [- anual] ≃ MOT (test).
revisor, -ra *m y f* [en tren] ticket inspector; [en autobús] (bus) conductor.
revista *f* **-1.** [publicación] magazine; ~ del corazón gossip magazine. **-2.** [sección de periódico] section, review. **-3.** [espectáculo teatral] revue. **-4.** [inspección] inspection; **pasar** ~ **a** MIL to inspect; [examinar] to examine.
revistero *m* [mueble] magazine rack.
revivir ◇ *vi* to revive. ◇ *vt* [recordar] to revive memories of.
revocar *vt* [gen] to revoke.
revolcar *vt* to upend. ◆ **revolcarse** *vpr* to roll about.
revolotear *vi* to flutter (about).
revoltijo, revoltillo *m* jumble.
revoltoso, -sa ◇ *adj* rebellious. ◇ *m y f* troublemaker.
revolución *f* revolution.
revolucionar *vt* [transformar] to revolutionize.
revolucionario, -ria *adj, m y f* revolutionary.
revolver *vt* **-1.** [dar vueltas] to turn around; [líquido] to stir. **-2.** [mezclar] to mix; [ensalada] to toss. **-3.** [desorganizar] to mess up; [cajones] to turn out. **-4.** [irritar] to upset; **me revuelve el estómago** o **las tripas** it makes my stomach turn. ◆ **revolver en** *vi* [cajones etc] to rummage around in. ◆ **revolverse** *vpr* **-1.** [volverse] to turn around. **-2.** [el mar] to become rough; [el tiempo] to turn stormy.
revólver *m* revolver.

revuelo m [agitación] commotion; **armar un gran ~** to cause a great stir.

revuelto, -ta ◇ pp → **revolver**. ◇ adj **-1.** [desordenado] in a mess. **-2.** [alborotado - época etc] turbulent. **-3.** [clima] unsettled. **-4.** [aguas] choppy. ◆ **revuelto** m CULIN scrambled eggs (pl). ◆ **revuelta** f [disturbio] riot, revolt.

revulsivo, -va adj fig stimulating, revitalizing. ◆ **revulsivo** m fig kick-start.

rey m king. ◆ **Reyes** mpl: **los Reyes** the King and Queen; **(Día de) Reyes** Twelfth Night.

reyerta f fight, brawl.

rezagado, -da adj: **ir ~** to lag behind.

rezar vi **-1.** [orar]: **~ (a)** to pray (to). **-2.** [decir] to read, to say. **-3.** [corresponderse]: **~ con** to have to do with.

rezo m [oración] prayer.

rezumar ◇ vt **-1.** [transpirar] to ooze. **-2.** fig [manifestar] to be overflowing with. ◇ vi to ooze ◇ seep out.

ría f estuary.

riachuelo m brook, stream.

riada f lit & fig flood.

ribera f [del río] bank; [del mar] shore.

ribete m edging (U), trimming (U); fig touch, nuance.

ricino m [planta] castor oil plant.

rico, -ca ◇ adj **-1.** [gen] rich. **-2.** [abundante]: **~ (en)** rich (in). **-3.** [sabroso] delicious. **-4.** [simpático] cute. ◇ m y f rich person; **los ~s** the rich.

rictus m inv **-1.** [de ironía] smirk. **-2.** [de desprecio] sneer. **-3.** [de dolor] wince.

ridiculez f **-1.** [payasada] silly thing, nonsense (U). **-2.** [nimiedad] trifle; **cuesta una ~** it costs next to nothing.

ridiculizar vt to ridicule.

ridículo, -la adj ridiculous; [precio, suma] laughable, derisory. ◆ **ridículo** m ridicule; **hacer el ~** to make a fool of o.s.; **poner** ◇ **dejar en ~ a alguien** to make sb look stupid; **quedar en ~** to look like a fool.

riego m [de campo] irrigation; [de jardín] watering.

riel m **-1.** [de vía] rail. **-2.** [de cortina] (curtain) rail.

rienda f [de caballería] rein; **dar ~ suelta a** fig to give free rein to. ◆ **riendas** fpl fig [dirección] reins.

riesgo m risk; **a todo ~** [seguro, póliza] comprehensive.

rifa f raffle.

rifar vt to raffle. ◆ **rifarse** vpr fig to fight over.

rifle m rifle.

rigidez f **-1.** [de un cuerpo, objeto etc] rigidity. **-2.** [del rostro] stoniness. **-3.** fig [severidad] strictness, harshness.

rígido, -da adj **-1.** [cuerpo, objeto etc] rigid. **-2.** [rostro] stony. **-3.** [severo - normas etc] harsh; [- carácter] inflexible.

rigor m **-1.** [severidad] strictness. **-2.** [exactitud] accuracy, rigour. **-3.** [inclemencia] harshness. ◆ **de rigor** loc adj essential.

riguroso, -sa adj **-1.** [severo] strict. **-2.** [exacto] rigorous. **-3.** [inclemente] harsh.

rimar vt & vi to rhyme.

rimbombante adj [estilo, frases] pompous.

rímel, rimmel m mascara.

rincón m corner (inside).

rinconera f corner piece.

ring (pl **rings**) m (boxing) ring.

rinoceronte m rhinoceros.

riña f [disputa] quarrel; [pelea] fight.

riñón m kidney.

riñonera f [pequeño bolso] bum bag Br, fanny pack Am.

río m lit & fig river; **ir ~ arriba/abajo** to go upstream/downstream; **cuando el ~ suena, agua lleva** proverb there's no smoke without fire proverb.

rioja m Rioja (wine).

riojano, -na adj, m y f Riojan.

riqueza f **-1.** [fortuna] wealth. **-2.** [abundancia] richness.

risa f laugh, laughter (U); **me da ~** I find it funny; **¡qué ~!** how funny!; **de ~ funny.**

risotada f guffaw.

ristra f lit & fig string.

ristre ◆ **en ristre** loc adv at the ready.

risueño, -ña adj [alegre] smiling.

ritmo m **-1.** [gen] rhythm; [cardíaco] beat. **-2.** [velocidad] pace.

rito m **-1.** RELIG rite. **-2.** [costumbre] ritual.

ritual adj & m ritual.

rival adj, m y f rival.

rivalidad f rivalry.

rivalizar vi: **~ (con)** to compete (with).

rizado, -da adj **-1.** [pelo] curly. **-2.** [mar] choppy. ◆ **rizado** m [en peluquería]: **hacerse un ~** to have one's hair curled.

rizar vt [pelo] to curl. ◆ **rizarse** vpr [pelo] to curl.

rizo, -za adj [pelo] curly. ◆ **rizo** m **-1.** [de pelo] curl. **-2.** [del agua] ripple. **-3.** [de avión] loop. **-4.** loc: **rizar el ~** to split hairs.

RNE (*abrev de* **Radio Nacional de España**) *f Spanish national radio station.*

roast-beef [ros'ßif] (*pl* **roast-beefs**), **rosbif** (*pl* **rosbifs**) *m* roast beef.

robar *vt* **-1.** [gen] to steal; [casa] to burgle; ~ **a alguien** to rob sb. **-2.** [en naipes] to draw. **-3.** [cobrar caro] to rob.

roble *m* **-1.** BOT oak. **-2.** *fig* [persona] strong person.

robo *m* [delito] robbery, theft; [en casa] burglary.

robot (*pl* **robots**) *m* [gen & INFORM] robot.

robótica *f* robotics (U).

robustecer *vt* to strengthen. ◆ **robustecerse** *vpr* to get strong.

robusto, -ta *adj* robust.

roca *f* rock.

rocalla *f* rubble.

roce *m* **-1.** [rozamiento - gen] rub, rubbing (U); [- suave] brush, brushing (U); FÍS friction. **-2.** [desgaste] wear. **-3.** [rasguño - en piel] graze; [- en zapato, puerta] scuffmark; [- en metal] scratch. **-4.** [trato] close contact. **-5.** [desavenencia] brush.

rociar *vt* [arrojar gotas] to sprinkle; [con espray] to spray.

rocío *m* dew.

rock, rock and roll *m inv* [estilo] rock; [de los 50] rock and roll.

rockero, -ra, roquero, -ra *m y f* **-1.** [músico] rock musician. **-2.** [fan] rock fan.

rocoso, -sa *adj* rocky.

rodaballo *m* turbot.

rodado, -da *adj* **-1.** [piedra] rounded. **-2.** [tráfico] road (*antes de sust*). **-3.** *loc*: **estar muy** ~ [persona] to be very experienced; **venir** ~ **para** to be the perfect opportunity to.

rodaja *f* slice.

rodaje *m* **-1.** [filmación] shooting. **-2.** [de motor] running-in. **-3.** [experiencia] experience.

Ródano *m*: **el** ~ the (River) Rhône.

rodapié *m* skirting board.

rodar ◇ *vi* **-1.** [deslizar] to roll. **-2.** [circular] to travel, to go. **-3.** [caer]: ~ **(por)** to tumble (down). **-4.** [ir de un lado a otro] to go around. **-5.** CIN to shoot. ◇ *vt* **-1.** CIN to shoot. **-2.** [automóvil] to run in.

rodear *vt* **-1.** [gen] to surround; **le rodeó el cuello con los brazos** she put her arms around his neck. **-2.** [dar la vuelta a] to go around. **-3.** [eludir] to

skirt around. ◆ **rodearse** *vpr*: ~**se de** to surround o.s. with.

rodeo *m* **-1.** [camino largo] detour; **dar un** ~ to make a detour. **-2.** (*gen pl*) [evasiva] evasiveness (U); **andar** o **ir con** ~**s** to beat about the bush. **-3.** [espectáculo] rodeo.

rodilla *f* knee; **de** ~**s** on one's knees.

rodillera *f* [protección] knee pad.

rodillo *m* [gen] roller; [para repostería] rolling pin.

rodríguez *m inv* grass widower.

roedor, -ra *adj* ZOOL rodent (*antes de sust*). ◆ **roedor** *m* rodent.

roer *vt* **-1.** [con dientes] to gnaw (at). **-2.** *fig* [gastar] to eat away (at).

rogar *vt* [implorar] to beg; [pedir] to ask; ~ **a alguien que haga algo** to ask o beg sb to do sthg; **le ruego me perdone** I beg your pardon; **"se ruega silencio"** "silence, please".

rogativa *f* (*gen pl*) rogation.

rojizo, -za *adj* reddish.

rojo, -ja ◇ *adj* red; **ponerse** ~ [gen] to turn red; [ruborizarse] to blush. ◇ *m y f* POLÍT red. ◆ **rojo** *m* [color] red; **al** ~ **vivo** [en incandescencia] red hot; *fig* heated.

rol (*pl* **roles**) *m* [papel] role.

rollizo, -za *adj* chubby, plump.

rollo *m* **-1.** [cilindro] roll; ~ **de primavera** CULIN spring roll. **-2.** CIN roll. **-3.** *fam* [discurso]: **el** ~ **de costumbre** the same old story; **tener mucho** ~ to witter on. **-4.** *fam* [embuste] tall story. **-5.** *fam* [pelmazo, pesadez] bore, drag.

ROM (*abrev de* **read-only memory**) *f* ROM.

Roma Rome.

romance *m* **-1.** LING Romance language. **-2.** [idilio] romance.

románico, -ca *adj* **-1.** ARQUIT & ARTE Romanesque. **-2.** LING Romance.

romano, -na *m y f* Roman.

romanticismo *m* **-1.** ARTE & LITER Romanticism. **-2.** [sentimentalismo] romanticism.

romántico, -ca *adj, m y f* **-1.** ARTE & LITER Romantic. **-2.** [sentimental] romantic.

rombo *m* **-1.** GEOM rhombus. **-2.** IMPRENTA lozenge.

romería *f* [peregrinación] pilgrimage.

romero, -ra *m y f* [peregrino] pilgrim. ◆ **romero** *m* BOT rosemary.

romo, -ma *adj* [sin filo] blunt.

rompecabezas *m inv* **-1.** [juego] jigsaw. **-2.** *fam* [problema] puzzle.

rompeolas *m inv* breakwater.

romper ◇ *vt* **-1.** [gen] to break; [hacer añicos] to smash; [rasgar] to tear. **-2.** [desgastar] to wear out. **-3.** [interrumpir - monotonía, silencio, hábito] to break; [- hilo del discurso] to break off; [- tradición] to put an end to. **-4.** [terminar - relaciones etc] to break off. ◇ *vi* **-1.** [terminar una relación]: ~ **(con alguien)** to break ○ split up **(with sb)**. **-2.** [olas, el día] to break; [hostilidades] to break out; **al** ○ **el alba** ○ **día at** daybreak. **-3.** [empezar]: ~ **a hacer algo** to suddenly start doing sthg; ~ **a llorar** to burst into tears; ~ **a reír** to burst out laughing. ◆ **romperse** *vpr* [partirse] to break; [rasgarse] to tear; **se ha roto una pierna** he has broken a leg.

rompimiento *m* breaking; [de relaciones] breaking-off.

ron *m* rum.

roncar *vi* to snore.

roncha *f* red blotch.

ronco, -ca *adj* **-1.** [afónico] hoarse. **-2.** [bronco] harsh.

ronda *f* **-1.** [de vigilancia, visitas] rounds (*pl*); **hacer la** ~ to do one's rounds. **-2.** *fam* [de bebidas, en el juego etc] round.

rondar ◇ *vt* **-1.** [vigilar] to patrol. **-2.** [rayar - edad] to be around. ◇ *vi* [merodear]: ~ **(por)** to wander ○ hang around.

ronquera *f* hoarseness.

ronquido *m* snore, snoring (*U*).

ronronear *vi* to purr.

ronroneo *m* purr, purring (*U*).

roña ◇ *adj fam* [tacaño] stingy. ◇ *f* **-1.** [suciedad] filth, dirt. **-2.** VETER mange.

roñoso, -sa ◇ *adj* **-1.** [sucio] dirty. **-2.** [tacaño] mean. ◇ *m y f* miser.

ropa *f* clothes (*pl*); ~ **blanca** linen; ~ **de abrigo** warm clothes (*pl*); ~ **de cama** bed linen; ~ **hecha** ready-to-wear clothes; ~ **interior** underwear.

ropaje *m* robes (*pl*).

ropero *m* **-1.** [armario] wardrobe. **-2.** [habitación] walk-in wardrobe, TEATR cloakroom.

roquero = **rockero**.

rosa ◇ *f* [flor] rose; **estar (fresco) como una** ~ to be as fresh as a daisy. ◇ *m* [color] pink. ◇ *adj inv* [color] pink. ◆ **rosa de los vientos** *f* NÁUT compass.

rosado, -da *adj* pink. ◆ **rosado** *m* → **vino**.

rosal *m* [arbusto] rose bush.

rosario *m* **-1.** RELIG rosary; **rezar el** ~ to say one's rosary. **-2.** [sarta] string.

rosca *f* **-1.** [de tornillo] thread. **-2.** [forma - de anillo] ring; [- espiral] coil. **-3.** CULIN ring doughnut. **-4.** *loc:* **pasarse de** ~ [persona] to go over the top.

rosco *m* ring-shaped bread roll.

roscón *m* ring-shaped bread roll; ~ **de reyes** *roll eaten on 6th January.*

rosetón *m* [ventana] rose window.

rosquilla *f* ring doughnut.

rostro *m* face.

rotación *f* **-1.** [giro] rotation; ~ **de cultivos** crop rotation. **-2.** [alternancia] rota; **por** ~ in turn.

rotativo, -va *adj* rotary, revolving. ◆ **rotativo** *m* newspaper. ◆ **rotativa** *f* rotary press.

roto, -ta ◇ *pp* → **romper.** ◇ *adj* **-1.** [gen] broken; [tela, papel] torn. **-2.** *fig* [deshecho - vida etc] destroyed; [- corazón] broken. **-3.** *fig* [exhausto] shattered. ◇ *m y f Amer* [trabajador] worker. ◆ **roto** *m* [en tela] tear, rip.

rotonda *f* [plaza] circus.

rotoso, -sa *adj Amer* ragged.

rótula *f* kneecap.

rotulador *m* felt-tip pen; [fluorescente] marker pen.

rótulo *m* **-1.** [letrero] sign. **-2.** [encabezamiento] headline, title.

rotundo, -da *adj* **-1.** [categórico - negativa, persona] categorical; [- lenguaje, estilo] emphatic. **-2.** [completo] total.

rotura *f* [gen] break, breaking (*U*); [de hueso] fracture; [en tela] rip, hole.

roturar *vt* to plough.

roulotte [ru'lot], **rulot** *f* caravan *Br*, trailer *Am*.

rozadura *f* **-1.** [señal] scratch, scrape. **-2.** [herida] graze.

rozamiento *m* [fricción] rub, rubbing (*U*); FÍS friction (*U*).

rozar *vt* **-1.** [gen] to rub; [suavemente] to brush; [suj: zapato] to graze. **-2.** [pasar cerca de] to skim. ◆ **rozar con** *vi* **-1.** [tocar] to brush against. **-2.** *fig* [relacionarse con] to touch on. ◆ **rozarse** *vpr* **-1.** [tocarse] to touch. **-2.** [pasar cerca] to brush past each other. **-3.** [herirse - rodilla etc] to graze. **-4.** *fig* [tener trato]: ~**se con** to rub shoulders with.

Rte. *abrev de* **remitente.**

RTVE (*abrev de* **Radiotelevisión Española**) *f Spanish state broadcasting company.*

rubeola, rubéola *f* German measles (*U*).

rubí (*pl* **rubís** ○ **rubíes**) *m* ruby.

rubio, -bia ◇ adj -1. [pelo, persona] blond (f blonde), fair. -2. [tabaco] Virginia (antes de sust). -3. [cerveza] lager (antes de sust). ◇ m y f [persona] blond (f blonde).

rubor m -1. [vergüenza] embarrassment. -2. [sonrojo] blush.

ruborizar vt [avergonzar] to embarrass. ◆ **ruborizarse** vpr to blush.

rúbrica f -1. [de firma] flourish. -2. [conclusión] final flourish; **poner ~ a algo** to complete sthg.

rubricar vt -1. fig [confirmar] to confirm. -2. fig [concluir] to complete.

rucio, -cia adj [gris] grey. ◆ **rucio** m ass, donkey.

rudeza f -1. [tosquedad] roughness. -2. [grosería] coarseness.

rudimentario, -ria adj rudimentary.

rudimentos mpl rudiments.

rudo, -da adj -1. [tosco] rough. -2. [brusco] sharp, brusque. -3. [grosero] rude, coarse.

rueda f -1. [pieza] wheel; **~ delantera/trasera** front/rear wheel; **~ de repuesto** spare wheel; **ir sobre ~s** fig to go smoothly. -2. [corro] circle. ◆ **rueda de prensa** f press conference.

ruedo m TAUROM bullring.

ruega etc → **rogar**.

ruego m request; **~s y preguntas** any other business.

rufián m villain.

rugby m rugby.

rugido m [gen] roar; [de persona] bellow.

rugir vi [gen] to roar; [persona] to bellow.

rugoso, -sa adj -1. [áspero - material, terreno] rough. -2. [con arrugas - rostro etc] wrinkled; [- tejido] crinkled.

ruido m -1. [gen] noise; [sonido] sound; **mucho ~ y pocas nueces** much ado about nothing. -2. fig [escándalo] row.

ruidoso, -sa adj -1. [que hace ruido] noisy. -2. fig [escandaloso] sensational.

ruin adj -1. [vil] low, contemptible. -2. [avaro] mean.

ruina f -1. [gen] ruin; **amenazar ~** [edificio] to be about to collapse; **estar en la ~** to be ruined. -2. [destrucción] destruction. -3. [fracaso - persona] wreck; **estar hecho una ~** to be a wreck. ◆ **ruinas** fpl [históricas] ruins.

ruindad f -1. [cualidad] baseness. -2. [acto] vile deed.

ruinoso, -sa adj -1. [poco rentable] ruinous. -2. [edificio] ramshackle.

ruiseñor m nightingale.

ruleta f roulette.

ruletero m Amer taxi driver.

rulo m [para el pelo] roller.

rulot = **roulotte**.

ruma f Amer heap, pile.

Rumanía Romania.

rumano, -na adj, m y f Romanian. ◆ **rumano** m [lengua] Romanian.

rumba f rumba.

rumbo m -1. [dirección] direction, course; **ir con ~ a** to be heading for; **perder el ~** [barco] to go off course; fig [persona] to lose one's way. -2. fig [camino] path, direction.

rumiante adj & m ruminant.

rumiar ◇ vt [suj: rumiante] to chew; fig to chew over. ◇ vi [masticar] to ruminate, to chew the cud.

rumor m -1. [ruido sordo] murmur. -2. [chisme] rumour.

rumorearse v impers: **~ que ...** to be rumoured that ....

runrún m -1. [ruido confuso] hum, humming (U). -2. [chisme] rumour.

rupestre adj cave (antes de sust).

ruptura f [gen] break; [de relaciones, conversaciones] breaking-off; [de contrato] breach.

rural adj rural.

Rusia Russia.

ruso, -sa adj, m y f Russian. ◆ **ruso** m [lengua] Russian.

rústico, -ca adj -1. [del campo] country (antes de sust). -2. [tosco] rough, coarse. ◆ **en rústica** loc adj paperback.

ruta f route; fig way, course.

rutina f [gen & INFORM] routine; **por ~** as a matter of course.

rutinario, -ria adj routine.

S

s¹, S f [letra] s, S. ◆ **S** (abrev de **san**) St.

s² (abrev de **segundo**) s.

s., sig. (abrev de **siguiente**) foll.

SA (abrev de **sociedad anónima**) f ≃ Ltd., ≃ PLC.

sábado m Saturday; **¿qué día es hoy? - (es) ~** what day is it (today)? - (it's) Saturday; **cada ~, todos los ~s** every

Saturday; **cada dos ~s, un ~ sí y otro no** every other Saturday; **caer en ~** to be on a Saturday; **te llamo el ~** I'll call you on Saturday; **el próximo ~, el ~ que viene** next Saturday; **el ~ pasado** last Saturday; **el ~ por la mañana/ tarde/noche** Saturday morning/ afternoon/night; **en ~** on Saturdays; **nací en ~** I was born on a Saturday; **este ~** [pasado] last Saturday; [próximo] this (coming) Saturday; **¿trabajas los ~s?** do you work (on) Saturdays?; **trabajar un ~** to work on a Saturday; **un ~ cualquiera** on any Saturday.

sábana f sheet.

sabandija f fig [persona] worm.

sabañón m chilblain.

sabático, -ca adj [del sábado] Saturday (antes de sust).

saber ◇ m knowledge. ◇ vt **-1.** [conocer] to know; **ya lo sé** I know; **hacer ~ algo a alguien** to inform sb of sthg, to tell sb sthg. **-2.** [ser capaz de]: **~ hacer algo** to know how to do sthg, to be able to do sthg; **sabe hablar inglés/ montar en bici** she can speak English/ ride a bike. **-3.** [enterarse] to learn, to find out; **lo supe ayer** I only found out yesterday. **-4.** [entender de] to know about; **sabe mucha física** he knows a lot about physics. ◇ vi **-1.** [tener sabor]: **~ (a)** to taste (of); **~ bien/mal** to taste good/bad; **~ mal a alguien** fig to upset ○ annoy sb. **-2.** [entender]: **~ de algo** to know about sthg. **-3.** [tener noticia]: **~ de alguien** to hear from sb; **~ de algo** to learn of sthg. **-4.** [parecer]: **eso me sabe a disculpa** that sounds like an excuse to me. **-5.** Amer fam [soler]: **~ hacer algo** to be wont to do sthg. **-6.** loc: **que yo sepa** as far as I know. ◆ **saberse** vpr: **~se algo** to know sthg. ◆ **a saber** loc adv [es decir] namely.

sabido, -da adj: **como es (bien) ~** as everyone knows.

sabiduría f **-1.** [conocimientos] knowledge, learning. **-2.** [prudencia] wisdom.

sabiendas ◆ **a sabiendas** loc adv knowingly.

sabihondo, -da, sabiondo, -da adj, m y f know-all.

sabio, -bia adj **-1.** [sensato, inteligente] wise. **-2.** [docto] learned. **-3.** [amaestrado] trained.

sabiondo, -da = sabihondo.

sablazo m fam fig [de dinero] scrounging (U); **dar un ~ a alguien** to scrounge money off sb.

sable m sabre.

sablear vi fam to scrounge money.

sabor m **-1.** [gusto] taste, flavour; **tener ~ a algo** to taste of sthg; **dejar mal/ buen ~ (de boca)** fig to leave a nasty taste in one's mouth/a warm feeling. **-2.** fig [estilo] flavour.

saborear vt lit & fig to savour.

sabotaje m sabotage.

sabotear vt to sabotage.

sabrá etc → saber.

sabroso, -sa adj **-1.** [gustoso] tasty. **-2.** fig [substancioso] tidy, considerable.

sabueso m **-1.** [perro] bloodhound. **-2.** fig [policía] sleuth.

saca f sack.

sacacorchos m inv corkscrew.

sacapuntas m inv pencil sharpener.

sacar ◇ vt **-1.** [poner fuera, hacer salir] to take out; [lengua] to stick out; **~ algo de** to take sthg out of; **nos sacaron algo de comer** they gave us something to eat. **-2.** [quitar]: **~ algo (de)** to remove sthg (from). **-3.** [librar, salvar]: **~ a alguien de** to get sb out of. **-4.** [obtener - carné, buenas notas] to get, to obtain; [- premio] to win; [- foto] to take; [- fotocopia] to make; [- dinero del banco] to withdraw. **-5.** [sonsacar]: **~ algo a alguien** to get sthg out of sb. **-6.** [extraer - producto]: **~ algo de** to extract sthg from. **-7.** [fabricar] to produce. **-8.** [crear - modelo, disco etc] to bring out. **-9.** [exteriorizar] to show. **-10.** [resolver - crucigrama etc] to do, to finish. **-11.** [deducir] to gather, to understand; [conclusión] to come to. **-12.** [mostrar] to show; **le sacaron en televisión** he was on television. **-13.** [comprar - entradas etc] to get, to buy. **-14.** [prenda - de ancho] to let out; [- de largo] to let down. **-15.** [aventajar]: **sacó tres minutos a su rival** he was three minutes ahead of his rival. **-16.** [DEP - con la mano] to throw in; [- con la raqueta] to serve. ◇ vi DEP to put the ball into play; [con la raqueta] to serve. ◆ **sacarse** vpr [carné etc] to get. ◆ **sacar adelante** vt **-1.** [hijos] to bring up. **-2.** [negocio] to make a go of.

sacarina f saccharine.

sacerdote, -tisa m y f [pagano] priest (f priestess). ◆ **sacerdote** m [cristiano] priest.

saciar vt [satisfacer - sed] to quench; [- hambre] to satisfy.

saco m **-1.** [bolsa] sack, bag; **~ de dormir** sleeping bag. **-2.** Amer jacket. **-3.**

loc: **entrar a ~ en** to sack, to pillage; **no echar algo en ~ roto** to take good note of sthg.

sacramento *m* sacrament.

sacrificar *vt* **-1.** [gen] to sacrifice. **-2.** [animal - para consumo] to slaughter.

sacrificio *m lit & fig* sacrifice.

sacrilegio *m lit & fig* sacrilege.

sacristán, -ana *m y f* sacristan, sexton.

sacristía *f* sacristy.

sacro, -cra *adj* [sagrado] holy, sacred.

sacudida *f* **-1.** [gen] shake; [de la cabeza] toss; [de tren, coche] jolt; **~ eléctrica** electric shock. **-2.** [terremoto] tremor.

sacudir *vt* **-1.** [agitar] to shake. **-2.** [golpear - alfombra etc] to beat. **-3.** *fig* [conmover] to shake, to shock. **-4.** *fam fig* [pegar] to smack.

sádico, -ca ◇ *adj* sadistic. ◇ *m y f* sadist.

sadismo *m* sadism.

saeta *f* **-1.** [flecha] arrow. **-2.** MÚS *flamenco-style song sung on religious occasions.*

safari *m* [expedición] safari.

saga *f* saga.

sagacidad *f* astuteness.

sagaz *adj* astute, shrewd.

Sagitario ◇ *m* [zodiaco] Sagittarius. ◇ *m y f* [persona] Sagittarian.

sagrado, -da *adj* holy, sacred; *fig* sacred.

Sahara *m:* **el (desierto del) ~** the Sahara (Desert).

sal *f* CULIN & QUÍM salt. ◆ **sales** *fpl* **-1.** [para reanimar] smelling salts. **-2.** [para baño] bath salts.

sala *f* **-1.** [habitación - gen] room; [- de una casa] lounge, living room; [- de hospital] ward; **~ de espera** waiting room; **~ de estar** lounge, living room; **~ de partos** delivery room. **-2.** [local - de conferencias, conciertos] hall; [- de cine, teatro] auditorium; **~ de fiestas** discothèque. **-3.** [DER - lugar] court (room); [- magistrados] bench.

salado, -da *adj* **-1.** [con sal] salted; [agua] salt (*antes de sust*); [con demasiada sal] salty. **-2.** *fig* [gracioso] witty. **-3.** *Amer* unfortunate.

salamandra *f* [animal] salamander.

salami, salame *m* salami.

salar *vt* **-1.** [para conservar] to salt. **-2.** [para cocinar] to add salt to.

salarial *adj* wage (*antes de sust*).

salario *m* salary, wages (*pl*); [semanal] wage.

salchicha *f* sausage.

salchichón *m* ≃ salami.

saldar *vt* **-1.** [pagar - cuenta] to close; [- deuda] to settle. **-2.** *fig* [poner fin a] to settle. **-3.** COM to sell off. ◆ **saldarse** *vpr* [acabar]: **~se con** to produce; **la pelea se saldó con 11 heridos** 11 people were injured in the brawl.

saldo *m* **-1.** [de cuenta] balance; **~ acreedor/deudor** credit/debit balance. **-2.** [de deudas] settlement. **-3.** (*gen pl*) [restos de mercancías] remnant; [rebajas] sale; **de ~** bargain. **-4.** *fig* [resultado] balance.

saldrá *etc* → **salir.**

saledizo, -za *adj* projecting.

salero *m* **-1.** [recipiente] salt cellar. **-2.** *fig* [gracia] wit; [donaire] charm.

salga *etc* → **salir.**

salida *f* **-1.** [acción de partir - gen] leaving; [- de tren, avión] departure. **-2.** DEP start. **-3.** [lugar] exit, way out. **-4.** [momento]: **quedamos a la ~ del trabajo** we agreed to meet after work. **-5.** [viaje] trip. **-6.** [aparición - de sol, luna] rise; [- de revista, nuevo modelo] appearance. **-7.** [COM - posibilidades] market; [- producción] output. **-8.** *fig* [solución] way out; **si no hay otra ~** if there's no alternative. **-9.** *fig* [futuro - de carreras etc] opening, opportunity.

salido, -da *adj* **-1.** [saliente] projecting, sticking out; [ojos] bulging. **-2.** [animal] on heat. **-3.** *mfam* [persona] horny.

saliente ◇ *adj* POLÍT outgoing. ◇ *m* projection.

salino, -na *adj* saline.

salir *vi* **-1.** [ir fuera] to go out; [venir fuera] to come out; **~ de** to go/come out of; **¿salimos al jardín?** shall we go out into the garden?; **¡sal aquí fuera!** come out here! **-2.** [ser novios]: **~ (con alguien)** to go out (with sb). **-3.** [marcharse]: **~ (de/para)** to leave (from/for). **-4.** [desembocar - calle]: **~ a** to open out onto. **-5.** [resultar] to turn out; **ha salido muy estudioso** he has turned out to be very studious; **¿qué salió en la votación?** what was the result of the vote?; **~ elegida actriz del año** to be voted actress of the year; **~ bien/mal** to turn out well/badly; **~ ganando/perdiendo** to come off well/badly. **-6.** [proceder]: **~ de** to come from; **el vino sale de la uva** wine comes from grapes. **-7.** [surgir - luna, estrellas, planta] to come out; [- sol] to rise; [- dientes] to come through; **le ha salido un sarpullido en la espalda** her back has come out in a rash. **-8.** [aparecer - publicación, producto, traumas] to come out; [- moda, ley] to come in; [- en imagen, prensa, televisión] to appear; **¡qué bien sales en la foto!** you look great in the photo!; **ha salido en los periódicos** it's in the papers; ~ **de** CIN & TEATR to appear as. **-9.** [costar]: ~ **(a** ○ **por)** to work out (at); ~ **caro** [de dinero] to be expensive; [por las consecuencias] to be costly. **-10.** [parecerse]: ~ **a alguien** to take after sb. **-11.** [en juegos] to lead; **te toca** ~ **a ti** it's your lead. **-12.** [quitarse - manchas] to come out. **-13.** [librarse]: ~ **de** [gen] to get out of; [problema] to get round. **-14.** INFORM: ~ **(de)** to quit, to exit. ◆ **salirse** *vpr* **-1.** [marcharse - de lugar, asociación etc]: ~**se (de)** to leave. **-2.** [filtrarse]: ~**se (por)** [líquido, gas] to leak ○ **escape (through)**; [humo, aroma] to come out (through). **-3.** [rebosar] to overflow; [leche] to boil over; **el río se salió del cauce** the river broke its banks. **-4.** [desviarse]: ~**se (de)** to come off; **el coche se salió de la carretera** the car came off ○ left the road. **-5.** *fig* [escaparse]: ~**se de** [gen] to deviate from; [límites] to go beyond; ~**se del tema** to digress. **-6.** *loc*: ~**se con la suya** to get one's own way. ◆ **salir adelante** *vi* **-1.** [persona, empresa] to get by. **-2.** [proyecto, propuesta, ley] to be successful.

salitre *m* saltpetre.

saliva *f* saliva.

salivar *vi* to salivate.

salmo *m* psalm.

salmón ◇ *m* [pez] salmon. ◇ *adj & m inv* [color] salmon (pink).

salmonete *m* red mullet.

salmuera *f* brine.

salobre *adj* salty.

salón *m* **-1.** [habitación - en casa] lounge, sitting room; [- en residencia, edificio público] reception hall. **-2.** [local - de sesiones etc] hall; ~ **de actos** assembly hall. **-3.** [feria] show, exhibition. **-4.** [establecimiento] shop; ~ **de belleza/masaje** beauty/massage parlour; ~ **de té** tearoom.

salpicadera *f Amer* mudguard *Br*, fender *Am*.

salpicadero *m* dashboard.

salpicar *vt* [rociar] to splash.

salpimentar *vt* to season.

salpullido = sarpullido.

salsa *f* **-1.** [CULIN - gen] sauce; [- de carne] gravy; ~ **bechamel** ○ **besamel** bechamel ○ white sauce; ~ **rosa** thou-

sand island dressing; **en su propia** ~ *fig* in one's element. **-2.** *fig* [interés] spice. **-3.** MÚS salsa.

salsera *f* gravy boat.

saltamontes *m inv* grasshopper.

saltar ◇ *vt* **-1.** [obstáculo] to jump (over). **-2.** [omitir] to skip, to miss out. **-3.** [hacer estallar] to blow up. ◇ *vi* **-1.** [gen] to jump; [a la comba] to skip; [al agua] to dive; ~ **sobre alguien** [abalanzarse] to set upon sb; ~ **de un tema a otro** to jump (around) from one subject to another. **-2.** [levantarse] to jump up; ~ **de la silla** to jump out of one's seat. **-3.** [salir para arriba - objeto] to jump (up); [- champán, aceite] to spurt (out); [- corcho, válvula] to pop out. **-4.** [explotar] to explode, to blow up. **-5.** [romperse] to break. **-6.** [reaccionar violentamente] to explode. ◆ **saltarse** *vpr* **-1.** [omitir] to skip, to miss out. **-2.** [salir despedido] to pop off. **-3.** [no respetar - cola, semáforo] to jump; [- ley, normas] to break.

salteado, -da *adj* **-1.** CULIN sautéed. **-2.** [espaciado] unevenly spaced.

salteador, -ra *m y f*: ~ **de caminos** highwayman.

saltear *vt* CULIN to sauté.

saltimbanqui *m y f* acrobat.

salto *m* **-1.** [gen & DEP] jump; [grande] leap; [al agua] dive; ~ **de altura/longitud** high/long jump. **-2.** *fig* [diferencia, omisión] gap. **-3.** *fig* [progreso] leap forward. ◆ **salto de agua** *m* waterfall. ◆ **salto de cama** *m* negligée.

saltón, -ona *adj* [ojos] bulging; [dientes] sticking out.

salubre *adj* healthy.

salud ◇ *f lit & fig* health; **estar bien/ mal de** ~ to be well/unwell; **beber** ○ **brindar a la** ~ **de alguien** to drink to sb's health. ◇ *interj*: **¡~!** [para brindar] cheers!; [después de estornudar] bless you!

saludable *adj* **-1.** [sano] healthy. **-2.** *fig* [provechoso] beneficial.

saludar *vt* to greet; MIL to salute; **saluda a Ana de mi parte** give my regards to Ana; **le saluda atentamente** yours faithfully. ◆ **saludarse** *vpr* to greet one another.

saludo *m* greeting; MIL salute; **Ana te manda** ~**s** [en cartas] Ana sends you her regards; [al teléfono] Ana says hello; **un** ~ **afectuoso** [en cartas] yours sincerely.

salva *f* MIL salvo; **una ~ de aplausos** *fig* a round of applause.

salvación *f* **-1.** [remedio]: **no tener ~** to be beyond hope. **-2.** [rescate] **rescue. -3.** RELIG salvation.

salvado *m* bran.

salvador, -ra *m y f* [persona] saviour. ◆ **Salvador** *m* GEOGR: **El Salvador** El Salvador.

salvadoreño, -ña *adj, m y f* Salvadoran.

salvaguardar *vt* to safeguard.

salvaje ◇ *adj* **-1.** [gen] wild. **-2.** [pueblo, tribu] savage. ◇ *m y f* **-1.** [primitivo] savage. **-2.** [bruto] maniac.

salvamanteles *m inv* [llano] table mat; [con pies] trivet.

salvamento *m* rescue, saving; **equipo de ~** rescue team.

salvar *vt* **-1.** [gen & INFORM] to save. **-2.** [rescatar] to rescue. **-3.** [superar - moralmente] to overcome; [- físicamente] to go over O around. **-4.** [recorrer] to cover. **-5.** [exceptuar]: **salvando algunos detalles** except for a few details. ◆ **salvarse** *vpr* **-1.** [librarse] to escape. **-2.** RELIG to be saved.

salvavidas ◇ *adj inv* life (*antes de sust*). ◇ *m* [chaleco] lifejacket; [flotador] lifebelt.

salvedad *f* exception.

salvia *f* sage.

salvo, -va *adj* safe; **estar a ~** to be safe; **poner algo a ~** to put sthg in a safe place. ◆ **salvo** *adv* except; **~ que** unless.

salvoconducto *m* safe-conduct, pass.

san *adj* Saint; **~ José** Saint Joseph.

sanar ◇ *vt* [persona] to cure; [herida] to heal. ◇ *vi* [persona] to get better; [herida] to heal.

sanatorio *m* sanatorium, nursing home.

sanción *f* [castigo] **punishment**; ECON sanction.

sancionar *vt* [castigar] to punish.

sandalia *f* sandal.

sandez *f* silly thing, nonsense (*U*).

sandía *f* watermelon.

sándwich ['sanwitʃ] (*pl* **sándwiches**) *m* toasted sandwich.

saneamiento *m* **-1.** [higienización - de edificio] **disinfection. -2.** *fig* [FIN - de moneda etc] **stabilization**; [- de economía] putting back on a sound footing.

sanear *vt* **-1.** [higienizar - tierras] to drain; [- un edificio] to disinfect. **-2.**

[FIN - moneda] to stabilize; [- economía] to put back on a sound footing.

sanfermines *mpl* festival held in Pamplona when bulls are run through the streets of the town.

sangrar ◇ *vi* to bleed. ◇ *vt* **-1.** [sacar sangre] to bleed. **-2.** IMPRENTA to indent.

sangre *f* blood; **no llegó la ~ al río** it didn't get too nasty. ◆ **sangre fría** *f* sangfroid; **a ~ fría** in cold blood.

sangría *f* **-1.** [bebida] sangria. **-2.** MED bloodletting. **-3.** *fig* [ruina] drain.

sangriento, -ta *adj* [ensangrentado, cruento] bloody.

sanguijuela *f lit & fig* leech.

sanguinario, -ria *adj* bloodthirsty.

sanguíneo, -a *adj* blood (*antes de sust*).

sanidad *f* **-1.** [salubridad] health, healthiness. **-2.** [servicio] public health; [ministerio] health department.

sanitario, -ria *adj* health (*antes de sust*). ◆ **sanitarios** *mpl* [instalación] bathroom fittings (*pl*).

San José San José.

sano, -na *adj* **-1.** [saludable] healthy; **~ y salvo** safe and sound. **-2.** [positivo - principios, persona etc] sound; [- ambiente, educación] wholesome. **-3.** [entero] intact.

San Salvador San Salvador.

santero, -ra *adj* pious.

Santiago (de Chile) Santiago.

santiamén ◆ **en un santiamén** *loc adv fam* in a flash.

santidad *f* saintliness, holiness.

santiguar *vt* to make the sign of the cross over. ◆ **santiguarse** *vpr* [persignarse] to cross o.s.

santo, -ta ◇ *adj* **-1.** [sagrado] holy. **-2.** [virtuoso] saintly. **-3.** *fam fig* [dichoso] damn; **todo el ~ día** all day long. ◇ *m y f* RELIG saint. ◆ **santo** *m* **-1.** [onomástica] saint's day. **-2.** *loc*: **¿a ~ de qué?** why on earth? ◆ **santo y seña** *m* MIL password.

Santo Domingo Santo Domingo.

santuario *m* shrine; *fig* sanctuary.

saña *f* viciousness, malice.

sapo *m* toad.

saque *m* **-1.** [en fútbol]: **~ de banda** throw-in; **~ inicial** O **de centro** kick-off; **~ de esquina/meta** corner/goal kick. **-2.** [en tenis etc] serve.

saquear *vt* **-1.** [rapiñar - ciudad] to sack; [- tienda etc] to loot. **-2.** *fam* [vaciar] to ransack.

saqueo *m* [de ciudad] sacking; [de tienda etc] looting.

sarampión *m* measles (*U*).

sarao *m* [fiesta] party.

sarcasmo *m* sarcasm.

sarcástico, -ca *adj* sarcastic.

sarcófago *m* sarcophagus.

sardana *f* *traditional Catalan dance and music*.

sardina *f* sardine; **como ~s en canasta** O **en lata** like sardines.

sardónico, -ca *adj* sardonic.

sargento *m y f* MIL ≃ sergeant.

sarpullido, salpullido *m* rash.

sarro *m* [de dientes] tartar.

sarta *f* *lit* & *fig* string.

sartén *f* frying pan; **tener la ~ por el mango** to be in control.

sastre, -tra *m y f* tailor.

sastrería *f* [oficio] tailoring; [taller] tailor's (shop).

Satanás *m* Satan.

satélite ◇ *m* satellite. ◇ *adj* *fig* satellite (*antes de sust*).

satén *m* satin; [de algodón] sateen.

satinado, -da *adj* glossy.

sátira *f* satire.

satírico, -ca ◇ *adj* satirical. ◇ *m y f* satirist.

satirizar *vt* to satirize.

satisfacción *f* satisfaction.

satisfacer *vt* **-1.** [gen] to satisfy; [sed] to quench. **-2.** [deuda, pago] to pay, to settle. **-3.** [ofensa, daño] to redress. **-4.** [duda, pregunta] to answer. **-5.** [cumplir - requisitos, exigencias] to meet.

satisfactorio, -ria *adj* satisfactory.

satisfecho, -cha ◇ *pp* → **satisfacer**. ◇ *adj* satisfied; **~ de sí mismo** self-satisfied; **darse por ~** to be satisfied.

saturar *vt* to saturate. ◆ **saturarse** *vpr*: **~se (de)** to become saturated (with).

saturnismo *m* lead poisoning.

Saturno Saturn.

sauce *m* willow; **~ llorón** weeping willow.

sauna *f* sauna.

savia *f* sap; *fig* vitality; **~ nueva** *fig* new blood.

saxo *m* [instrumento] sax.

saxofón, saxófono *m* [instrumento] saxophone.

saxófono = **saxofón**.

sazón *f* **-1.** [madurez] ripeness; **en ~** ripe. **-2.** [sabor] seasoning. ◆ **a la sazón** *loc adv* then, at that time.

sazonado, -da *adj* seasoned.

sazonar *vt* to season.

scanner [es'kaner] = **escáner**.

schilling = **chelín**.

scout [es'kaut] (*pl* **scouts**) *m* scout.

se *pron pers* **-1.** (*reflexivo*) [de personas] himself (*f* herself), (*pl*) themselves; [usted mismo] yourself, (*pl*) yourselves; [de cosas, animales] itself, (*pl*) themselves; **~ está lavando, está lavándo~** she is washing (herself); **~ lavó los dientes** she cleaned her teeth; **espero que ~ diviertan** I hope you enjoy yourselves; **el perro ~ lame** the dog is licking itself; **~ lame la herida** it's licking its wound; **~ levantaron y ~ fueron** they got up and left. **-2.** (*reflexivo impersonal*) oneself; **hay que afeitar~ todos los días** one has to shave every day, you have to shave every day. **-3.** (*recíproco*) each other, one another; **~ aman** they love each other; **~ escriben cartas** they write to each other. **-4.** [en construcción pasiva]: **~ ha suspendido la reunión** the meeting has been cancelled; **"~ prohíbe fumar"** "no smoking"; **"~ habla inglés"** "English spoken". **-5.** (*impersonal*): **en esta sociedad ya no ~ respeta a los ancianos** in our society old people are no longer respected; **~ dice que ...** it is said that ..., people say that .... **-6.** (*en vez de "le" o "les" antes de "lo", "la", "los" o "las"*) (*complemento indirecto*) [gen] to him (*f* to her), (*pl*) to them; [de cosa, animal] to it, (*pl*) to them; [usted, ustedes] to you; **~ lo dio** he gave it to him/her *etc*; **~ lo dije, pero no me hizo caso** I told her, but she didn't listen; **si usted quiere, yo ~ lo arreglo en un minuto** if you like, I'll sort it out for you in a minute.

sé **-1.** → **saber**. **-2.** → **ser**.

sebo *m* fat; [para jabón, velas] tallow.

secador *m* dryer; **~ de pelo** hair-dryer.

secadora *f* clothes O tumble dryer.

secar *vt* **-1.** [desecar] to dry. **-2.** [enjugar] to wipe away; [con fregona] to mop up. ◆ **secarse** *vpr* [gen] to dry up; [ropa, vajilla, suelo] to dry.

sección *f* **-1.** [gen & GEOM] section. **-2.** [departamento] department.

seccionar *vt* **-1.** [cortar] to cut; TECN to section. **-2.** [dividir] to divide (up).

secesión *f* secession.

seco, -ca *adj* **-1.** [gen] dry; [plantas, flores] withered; [higos, pasas] dried; **lavar en ~** to dry-clean. **-2.** [tajante] brusque. **-3.** *loc*: **parar en ~** to stop dead. ◆ **a secas** *loc adv* simply, just; **llámame Juan a secas** just call me Juan.

secretaría f **-1.** [oficina, lugar] secretary's office. **-2.** [organismo] secretariat.

secretariado m EDUC secretarial skills (pl).

secretario, -ria m y f secretary.

secreto, -ta adj [gen] secret; [tono] confidential; **en ~** in secret. ◆ **secreto** m **-1.** [gen] secret. **-2.** [sigilo] secrecy.

secta f sect.

sector m **-1.** [gen] sector; [grupo] group. **-2.** [zona] area.

secuaz m y f despec minion.

secuela f consequence.

secuencia f sequence.

secuestrador, -ra m y f kidnapper.

secuestrar vt **-1.** [raptar] to kidnap. **-2.** [avión] to hijack. **-3.** [embargar] to seize.

secuestro m **-1.** [rapto] kidnapping. **-2.** [de avión, barco] hijack. **-3.** [de bienes etc] seizure, confiscation.

secular adj **-1.** [seglar] secular, lay. **-2.** [centenario] age-old.

secundar vt to support, to back (up); [propuesta] to second.

secundario, -ria adj secondary.

sed ◇ v → **ser**. ◇ f thirst; **tener ~** to be thirsty; **~ de** fig thirst for.

seda f silk.

sedal m fishing line.

sedante ◇ adj MED sedative; [música] soothing. ◇ m sedative.

sede f **-1.** [emplazamiento] headquarters (pl); [de gobierno] seat; **~ social** head office. **-2.** RELIG see. ◆ **Santa Sede** f: **la Santa Sede** the Holy See.

sedentario, -ria adj sedentary.

sedición f sedition.

sediento, -ta adj **-1.** [de agua] thirsty. **-2.** fig [deseoso]: **~ de** hungry for.

sedimentar vt to deposit. ◆ **sedimentarse** vpr [líquido] to settle.

sedimento m **-1.** [poso] sediment. **-2.** GEOL deposit. **-3.** fig [huella] residue.

sedoso, -sa adj silky.

seducción f **-1.** [cualidad] seductiveness. **-2.** [acción - gen] attraction, charm; [- sexual] seduction.

seducir vt **-1.** [atraer] to attract, to charm; [sexualmente] to seduce. **-2.** [persuadir]: **~ a alguien para que haga algo** to tempt sb to do sthg.

seductor, -ra ◇ adj [gen] charming; [sexualmente] seductive; [persuasivo] tempting. ◇ m y f seducer.

segador, -ra m y f [agricultor] reaper.

segar vt **-1.** AGR to reap. **-2.** [cortar] to cut off. **-3.** fig [truncar] to put an end to.

seglar m lay person.

segmento m **-1.** GEOM & ZOOL segment. **-2.** [trozo] piece.

segregación f **-1.** [separación, discriminación] segregation; **~ racial** racial segregation. **-2.** [secreción] secretion.

segregar vt **-1.** [separar, discriminar] to segregate. **-2.** [secretar] to secrete.

seguidilla f **-1.** (gen pl) [baile] traditional Spanish dance. **-2.** [cante] mournful flamenco song.

seguido, -da adj **-1.** [consecutivo] consecutive; **diez años ~s** ten years in a row. **-2.** [sin interrupción - gen] one after the other; [- línea, pitido etc] continuous. ◆ **seguido** adv **-1.** [inmediatamente después] straight after. **-2.** [en línea recta] straight on. ◆ **en seguida** loc adv straight away, at once; **en seguida nos vamos** we're going in a minute.

seguidor, -ra m y f follower.

seguimiento m [de noticia] following; [de clientes] follow-up.

seguir ◇ vt **-1.** [gen] to follow. **-2.** [perseguir] to chase. **-3.** [reanudar] to continue, to resume. ◇ vi **-1.** [sucederse]: **~ a algo** to follow sthg; **a la tormenta siguió la lluvia** the storm was followed by rain. **-2.** [continuar] to continue, to go on; ¡**sigue**! ¡**no te pares**! go ○ carry on, don't stop!; **sigo trabajando en la fábrica** I'm still working at the factory; **debes ~ haciéndolo** you should keep on ○ carry on doing it; **sigo pensando que está mal** I still think it's wrong; **sigue enferma/en el hospital** she's still ill/at the hospital. ◆ **seguirse** vpr to follow; **~se de algo** to follow ○ be deduced from sthg; **de esto se sigue que estás equivocado** it therefore follows that you are wrong.

según ◇ prep **-1.** [de acuerdo con] according to; **~ su opinión, ha sido un éxito** in his opinion ○ according to him, it was a success; **~ yo/tú** etc in my/your etc opinion. **-2.** [dependiendo de] depending on; **~ la hora que sea** depending on the time. ◇ adv **-1.** [como] (just) as; **todo permanecía ~ lo recordaba** everything was just as she remembered it; **actuó ~ se le recomendó** he did as he had been advised. **-2.** [a medida que] as; **entrarás en forma ~ vayas entrenando** you'll get fit as you train. **-3.** [dependiendo]: **¿te gusta la música?** - **~** do you like music? - it depends; **lo intentaré ~ esté de tiempo** I'll try to do it, depending on how much time I have. ◆ **según que** *loc adv* depending on whether. ◆ **según qué** *loc adj* certain; ~ **qué días la clase es muy aburrida** some days the class is really boring.

segunda → segundo.

segundero *m* second hand.

segundo, -da ◇ *núm adj* second. ◇ *núm m y f* **-1.** [en orden]: **el** ~ the second one; **llegó el** ~ he came second. **-2.** [mencionado antes]: **vinieron Pedro y Juan, el** ~ **con ...** Pedro and Juan arrived, the latter with .... **-3.** [ayudante] number two; ~ **de abordo** NÁUT first mate. ◆ **segundo** *m* **-1.** [gen] second. **-2.** [piso] second floor. ◆ **segunda** *f* **-1.** AUTOM second (gear). **-2.** AERON & FERROC second class. **-3.** DEP second division. ◆ **con segundas** *loc adv* with an ulterior motive.

seguramente *adv* probably; ~ **iré, pero aún no lo sé** the chances are I'll go, but I'm not sure yet.

seguridad *f* **-1.** [fiabilidad, ausencia de peligro] **safety**; [protección, estabilidad] **security**; **de** ~ [cinturón, cierre] **safety** (*antes de sust*); [puerta, guardia] **security** (*antes de sust*); ~ **vial** road safety. **-2.** [certidumbre] **certainty**; **con** ~ for sure, definitely. **-3.** [confianza] **confidence**; **en sí mismo** self-confidence. ◆ **Seguridad Social** *f* Social Security.

seguro, -ra *adj* **-1.** [fiable, sin peligro] **safe**; [protegido, estable] **secure**. **-2.** [infalible - prueba, negocio etc] **reliable**. **-3.** [confiado] **sure**; **estar** ~ **de algo** to be sure about sthg. **-4.** [indudable - nombramiento, fecha etc] **definite, certain; tener por** ~ **que** to be sure that. ◆ **seguro** ◇ *m* **-1.** [contrato] **insurance** (*U*); ~ **a todo riesgo/a terceros** comprehensive/third party insurance; ~ **de incendios/de vida** fire/life insurance; ~ **de paro** O **de desempleo** unemployment benefit; ~ **del coche** car insurance; ~ **mutuo** joint insurance. **-2.** [dispositivo] **safety device**; [de armas] **safety catch**. **-3.** *Amer* [imperdible] **safety pin**. ◇ *adv* for sure, definitely; ~ **vendrá** she's bound to come.

seis ◇ *núm adj inv* **-1.** [para contar] **six**; **tiene** ~ **años** she's six (years old). **-2.** [para ordenar] (number) **six**; **la página** ~ page six. ◇ *núm m* **-1.** [número] **six**; **el** ~ number six; **doscientos** ~ two hundred and six; **treinta y** ~ thirty-six. **-2.** [en fechas] **sixth**; **el** ~ **de agosto** the sixth of August. **-3.** [en direcciones]: **ca-**

lle Mayor (número) ~ number six calle Mayor. **-4.** [en naipes] **six**; **el** ~ **de diamantes** the six of diamonds; **echar** O **tirar un** ~ to play a six. ◇ *núm mpl* **-1.** [referido a grupos]: **invité a diez y sólo vinieron** ~ I invited ten and only six came along; **somos** ~ there are six of us; **de** ~ **en** ~ in sixes; **los** ~ the six of them. **-2.** [en temperaturas]: **estamos a** ~ **bajo cero** the temperature is six below zero. **-3.** [en puntuaciones]: **empatar a** ~ to draw six all; ~ **a cero** six-nil. ◇ *núm fpl* [hora]: **las** ~ six o'clock; **son las** ~ it's six o'clock.

seiscientos, -tas *núm* six hundred; *ver también* seis.

seísmo *m* earthquake.

selección *f* **-1.** [gen] **selection**; [de personal] **recruitment**. **-2.** [equipo] **team**; ~ **nacional** national team.

seleccionador, -ra *m y f* **-1.** DEP **selector**, ≃ **manager**. **-2.** [de personal] **recruiter**.

seleccionar *vt* to pick, to select.

selectividad *f* [examen] university entrance examination.

selectivo, -va *adj* selective.

selecto, -ta *adj* **-1.** [excelente] **fine, excellent. -2.** [escogido] **exclusive, select.**

self-service *m inv* self-service restaurant.

sellar *vt* **-1.** [timbrar] to stamp. **-2.** [lacrar] to seal.

sello *m* **-1.** [gen] **stamp**. **-2.** [tampón] **rubber stamp**. **-3.** [lacre] **seal**. **-4.** *fig* [carácter] **hallmark**.

selva *f* [gen] **jungle**; [bosque] **forest**.

semáforo *m* traffic lights (*pl*).

semana *f* week; **entre** ~ during the week; ~ **laboral** working week. ◆ **Semana Santa** *f* Easter; RELIG Holy Week.

semanal *adj* weekly.

semanario, -ria *adj* weekly. ◆ **semanario** *m* [publicación semanal] weekly.

semántico, -ca *adj* semantic. ◆ **semántica** *f* semantics (*U*).

semblante *m* countenance, face.

semblanza *f* portrait, profile.

sembrado, -da *adj fig* [lleno]: ~ **de** scattered O plagued with.

sembrar *vt* **-1.** [plantar] to sow. **-2.** *fig* [llenar] to scatter. **-3.** *fig* [confusión, pánico etc] to sow.

semejante ◇ *adj* **-1.** [parecido]: ~ **(a)** similar (to). **-2.** [tal] such; **jamás aceptaría** ~ **invitación** I would never accept such an invitation. ◇ *m* (*gen pl*) fellow (human) being.

semejanza *f* similarity.

semejar *vt* to resemble. ◆ **semejarse** *vpr* to be alike.

semen *m* semen.

semental *m* stud; [caballo] stallion.

semestral *adj* half-yearly, six-monthly.

semestre *m* period of six months, semester *Am*; **cada** ~ every six months.

semidirecto ◇ *adj* express. ◇ *m* → **tren**.

semifinal *f* semifinal.

semilla *f* seed.

seminario *m* -1. [escuela para sacerdotes] seminary. -2. [EDUC - curso, conferencia] seminar; [- departamento] department.

sémola *f* semolina.

Sena *m*: **el** ~ the (river) Seine.

senado *m* senate.

senador, -ra *m* y *f* senator.

sencillez *f* -1. [facilidad] simplicity. -2. [modestia] unaffectedness. -3. [discreción] plainness.

sencillo, -lla *adj* -1. [fácil, sin lujo, llano] simple. -2. [campechano] unaffected. -3. [billete, unidad etc] single. ◆ **sencillo** *m* -1. [disco] single. -2. *Amer fam* [cambio] loose change.

senda *f*, **sendero** *m* path.

sendos, -das *adj pl* each, respective; **llegaron los dos con** ~ **paquetes** they arrived each carrying a parcel.

Senegal: (**el**) ~ Senegal.

senil *adj* senile.

senior (*pl* **seniors**) *adj & m* senior.

seno *m* -1. [pecho] breast. -2. [pechera] bosom; **en el** ~ **de** *fig* within. -3. [útero]: ~ (**materno**) womb. -4. *fig* [amparo, cobijo] refuge, shelter. -5. ANAT [de la nariz] sinus.

sensación *f* -1. [percepción] feeling, sensation. -2. [efecto] sensation. -3. [premonición] feeling.

sensacional *adj* sensational.

sensacionalista *adj* sensationalist.

sensatez *f* wisdom, common sense.

sensato, -ta *adj* sensible.

sensibilidad *f* -1. [perceptibilidad] feeling. -2. [sentimentalismo] sensitivity. -3. [don especial] feel. -4. [de emulsión fotográfica, balanza etc] sensitivity.

sensibilizar *vt* -1. [concienciar] to raise the awareness of. -2. FOT to sensitize.

sensible *adj* -1. [gen] sensitive. -2. [evidente] perceptible; [pérdida] significant.

sensiblero, -ra *adj despec* mushy, sloppy.

sensitivo, -va *adj* -1. [de los sentidos] sensory. -2. [receptible] sensitive.

sensor *m* sensor.

sensorial *adj* sensory.

sensual *adj* sensual.

sentado, -da *adj* -1. [en asiento] seated; **estar** ~ to be sitting down. -2. [establecido]: **dar algo por** ~ to take sthg for granted; **dejar** ~ **que ...** to make it clear that ....

sentar ◇ *vt* -1. [en asiento] to seat, to sit. -2. [establecer] to establish. ◇ *vi* -1. [ropa, color] to suit. -2. [comida]: ~ **bien/mal a alguien** to agree/disagree with sb. -3. [vacaciones, medicamento]: ~ **bien a alguien** to do sb good. -4. [comentario, consejo]: **le sentó mal** it upset her; **le sentó bien** she appreciated it. ◆ **sentarse** *vpr* to sit down.

sentencia *f* -1. DER sentence. -2. [proverbio, máxima] maxim.

sentenciar *vt* DER: ~ (**a alguien a algo**) to sentence (sb to sthg).

sentido, -da *adj* [profundo] heartfelt. ◆ **sentido** *m* -1. [gen] sense; **tener** ~ to make sense; ~ **común** common sense; ~ **del humor** sense of humour; **sexto** ~ sixth sense. -2. [conocimiento] consciousness; **perder/recobrar el** ~ to lose/regain consciousness. -3. [significado] meaning, sense; **sin** ~ [ilógico] meaningless; [inútil, irrelevante] pointless; **doble** ~ double meaning. -4. [dirección] direction; **de** ~ **único** one-way.

sentimental *adj* sentimental.

sentimentaloide *adj* mushy, sloppy.

sentimiento *m* -1. [gen] feeling. -2. [pena, aflicción]: **le acompaño en el** ~ my deepest sympathy.

sentir ◇ *vt* -1. [gen] to feel. -2. [lamentar] to regret, to be sorry about; **siento que no puedas venir** I'm sorry you can't come; **lo siento (mucho)** I'm (really) sorry. -3. [oír] to hear. ◇ *vi* to feel; **sin** ~ *fig* without noticing. ◇ *m* feelings (*pl*), sentiments (*pl*). ◆ **sentirse** *vpr* to feel; **me siento mareada** I feel sick.

seña *f* [gesto, indicio, contraseña] sign, signal. ◆ **señas** *fpl* -1. [dirección] address (*sg*); ~**s personales** (personal) description (*sg*). -2. [gesto, indicio] signs; **dar** ~**s de algo** to show signs of sthg; (**hablar**) **por** ~**s** (to talk) in sign language; **hacer** ~**s (a alguien)** to signal (to sb). **-3.** [detalle] details; **para** O **por más** ~s to be precise.

señal f **-1.** [gen & TELECOM] signal; [de teléfono] tone; ~ **de alarma/salida** alarm/starting signal. **-2.** [indicio, símbolo] sign; **dar** ~**es de vida** to show signs of life; ~ **de la Cruz** sign of the Cross; ~ **de tráfico** road sign; **en** ~ **de** as a mark O sign of. **-3.** [marca, huella] mark; **no dejó ni** ~ she didn't leave a trace. **-4.** [cicatriz] scar, mark. **-5.** [fianza] deposit.

señalado, -da adj [importante - fecha] special; [- personaje] distinguished.

señalar vt **-1.** [marcar, denotar] to mark; [hora, temperatura etc] to indicate, to say. **-2.** [indicar - con el dedo, con un comentario] to point out. **-3.** [fijar] to set, to fix.

señalización f **-1.** [conjunto de señales] signs (pl). **-2.** [colocación de señales] signposting.

señalizar vt to signpost.

señor, -ra adj [refinado] noble, refined. ◆ **señor** m **-1.** [tratamiento - antes de nombre, cargo] Mr; [- al dirigir la palabra] Sir; **el** ~ **López** Mr López; **¡**~ **presidente!** Mr President!; **¿qué desea el** ~? what would you like, Sir?; **Muy** ~ **mío** [en cartas] Dear Sir. **-2.** [hombre] man. **-3.** [caballero] gentleman. **-4.** [dueño] owner. **-5.** [amo - de criado] master. ◆ **señora** f **-1.** [tratamiento - antes de nombre, cargo] Mrs; [- al dirigir la palabra] Madam; **la señora López** Mrs López; **¡señora presidenta!** Madam President!; **¿qué desea la señora?** what would you like, Madam?; **¡señoras y** ~**es!** ... Ladies and Gentlemen! ...; **Estimada señora** [en cartas] Dear Madam. **-2.** [mujer] lady. **-3.** [dama] lady. **-4.** [dueña] owner. **-5.** [ama - de criado] mistress. **-6.** [esposa] wife. ◆ **señores** mpl [matrimonio]: **los** ~**es Ruiz** Mr & Mrs Ruiz.

señoría f lordship (f ladyship).

señorial adj [majestuoso] stately.

señorío m **-1.** [dominio] dominion, rule. **-2.** [distinción] nobility.

señorito, -ta adj fam despec [refinado] lordly. ◆ **señorito** m **-1.** desus [hijo del amo] master. **-2.** fam despec [niñato] rich kid. ◆ **señorita** f **-1.** [soltera, tratamiento] Miss. **-2.** [joven] young lady. **-3.** [maestra]: **la** ~ miss, the teacher. **-4.** desus [hija del amo] mistress.

señuelo m **-1.** [reclamo] decoy. **-2.** fig [trampa] bait, lure.

sepa → **saber**.

separación f **-1.** [gen] separation. **-2.** [espacio] space, distance.

separado, -da adj **-1.** [gen] separate; **está muy** ~ **de la pared** it's too far away from the wall; **por** ~ separately. **-2.** [del cónyuge] separated.

separar vt **-1.** [gen] to separate; ~ **algo de** to separate sthg from. **-2.** [desunir] to take off, to remove. **-3.** [apartar - silla etc] to move away. **-4.** [reservar] to put aside. **-5.** [destituir]: ~ **de** to remove O dismiss from. ◆ **separarse** vpr **-1.** [apartarse] to move apart. **-2.** [ir por distinto lugar] to part company. **-3.** [matrimonio]: ~**se (de alguien)** to separate (from sb). **-4.** [desprenderse] to come away O off.

separatismo m separatism.

separo m Amer cell.

sepia f [molusco] cuttlefish.

septentrional adj northern.

septiembre, setiembre m September; **el 1 de** ~ the 1st of September; **uno de los** ~**s más lluviosos de la última década** one of the rainiest Septembers in the last decade; **a principios/mediados/finales de** ~ at the beginning/in the middle/at the end of September; **el pasado/próximo (mes de)** ~ last/next September; **en** ~ in September; **en pleno** ~ in mid-September; **este (mes de)** ~ [pasado] (this) last September; [próximo] next September, this coming September; **para** ~ by September.

séptimo, -ma, sétimo, -ma núm seventh.

septuagésimo, -ma núm seventieth.

sepulcral adj fig [profundo - voz, silencio] lugubrious, gloomy.

sepulcro m tomb.

sepultar vt to bury.

sepultura f **-1.** [enterramiento] burial. **-2.** [fosa] grave.

sepulturero, -ra m y f gravedigger.

sequedad f **-1.** [falta de humedad] dryness. **-2.** fig [antipatía] brusqueness.

sequía f drought.

séquito m [comitiva] retinue, entourage.

ser ◇ vaux (antes de participio forma la voz pasiva) to be; **fue visto por un testigo** he was seen by a witness. ◇ v copulativo **-1.** [gen] to be; **es alto/gracioso** he is tall/funny; **es azul/difícil** it's blue/difficult; **es un amigo/el dueño** he is a friend/the owner. **-2.** [empleo, dedicación] to be; **soy abogado/actriz** I'm a lawyer/an actress; **son estudiantes**

they're students. ◇ *vi* **-1.** [gen] to be; **fue aquí** it was here; **lo importante es decidirse** the important thing is to reach a decision; ~ **de** [estar hecho de] to be made of; [provenir de] to be from; [ser propiedad de] to belong to; [formar parte de] to be a member of; **¿de dónde eres?** where are you from?; **los juguetes son de mi hijo** the toys are my son's. **-2.** [con precios, horas, números] to be; **¿cuánto es?** how much is it?; **son 300 pesetas** that'll be 300 pesetas; **¿qué (día) es hoy?** what day is it today?; **mañana será 15 de julio** tomorrow (it) will be the 15th of July; **¿qué hora es?** what time is it?, what's the time?; **son las tres (de la tarde)** it's three o'clock (in the afternoon), it's three (pm). **-3.** [servir, ser adecuado]: ~ **para** to be for; **este trapo es para (limpiar) las ventanas** this cloth is for (cleaning) the windows; **este libro es para niños** this book is (meant) for children. **-4.** (*uso partitivo*): ~ **de los que ...** to be one of those (people) who ...; **ése es de los que están en huelga** he is one of those on strike. ◇ *v impers* **-1.** [expresa tiempo] to be; **es muy tarde** it's rather late; **era de noche/de día** it was night/day. **-2.** [expresa necesidad, posibilidad]: **es de desear que ...** it is to be hoped that ...; **es de suponer que aparecerá** presumably, he'll turn up. **-3.** [expresa motivo]: **es que no vine porque estaba enfermo** the reason I didn't come is that I was ill. **-4.** *loc*: **a no** ~ **que** unless; **como sea** somehow or other; **de no** ~ **por** had it not been for; **érase una vez, érase que se era** once upon a time; **no es para menos** not without reason; **o sea** that is (to say), I mean; **por si fuera poco** as if that wasn't enough. ◇ *m* [ente] being; ~ **humano/vivo** human/living being.

SER (*abrev de* **Sociedad Española de Radiodifusión**) *f Spanish independent radio company.*

Serbia Serbia.

serenar *vt* [calmar] to calm. ◆ **serenarse** *vpr* **-1.** [calmarse] to calm down. **-2.** [estabilizarse - tiempo] to clear up; [- aguas] to grow calm.

serenata *f* MÚS serenade.

serenidad *f* **-1.** [tranquilidad] calm. **-2.** [quietud] tranquility.

sereno, -na *adj* calm. ◆ **sereno** *m* [vigilante] night watchman.

serial *m* serial.

serie *f* **-1.** [gen & TV] series (*sg*); [de hechos, sucesos] chain; [de mentiras] string. **-2.** [de sellos, monedas] set. **-3.** *loc*: **ser un fuera de** ~ to be unique. ◆ **de serie** *loc adj* [equipamiento] (fitted) as standard. ◆ **en serie** *loc adv* [fabricación]: **fabricar en** ~ to mass-produce.

seriedad *f* **-1.** [gravedad] seriousness. **-2.** [responsabilidad] sense of responsibility. **-3.** [formalidad - de persona] reliability.

serio, -ria *adj* **-1.** [gen] serious; **estar** ~ to look serious. **-2.** [responsable, formal] responsible. **-3.** [sobrio] sober. ◆ **en serio** *loc adv* seriously; **lo digo en** ~ I'm serious; **tomar(se) algo/a alguien en** ~ to take sthg/sb seriously.

sermón *m lit & fig* sermon.

seropositivo, -va MED ◇ *adj* HIV-positive. ◇ *m y f* HIV-positive person.

serpentear *vi* **-1.** [río, camino] to wind. **-2.** [culebra] to wriggle.

serpentina *f* streamer.

serpiente *f* [culebra] snake; LITER serpent.

serranía *f* mountainous region.

serrano, -na *adj* **-1.** [de la sierra] mountain (*antes de sust*). **-2.** [jamón] cured.

serrar *vt* to saw (up).

serrín *m* sawdust.

serrucho *m* handsaw.

servicial *adj* attentive, helpful.

servicio *m* **-1.** [gen] service; ~ **de prensa/de urgencias** press/casualty department; ~ **de mesa** dinner service; ~ **militar** military service; ~ **de té** tea set. **-2.** [servidumbre] servants (*pl*). **-3.** [turno] duty. **-4.** (*gen pl*) [WC] toilet, lavatory. **-5.** DEP serve, service.

servidor, -ra *m y f* **-1.** [en cartas]: **su seguro** ~ yours faithfully. **-2.** [yo] yours truly, me. ◆ **servidor** *m* INFORM server.

servidumbre *f* **-1.** [criados] servants (*pl*). **-2.** [dependencia] servitude.

servil *adj* servile.

servilleta *f* serviette, napkin.

servilletero *m* serviette O napkin ring.

servir ◇ *vt* to serve; **sírvanos dos cervezas** bring us two beers; **¿te sirvo más patatas?** would you like some more potatoes?; **¿en qué puedo ~le?** what can I do for you? ◇ *vi* **-1.** [gen] to serve; ~ **en el gobierno** to be a government minister. **-2.** [valer, ser útil] to serve, to be useful; **no sirve para estudiar** he's no good at studying; **de nada sirve que se lo digas** it's no use telling

him; ~ **de algo** to serve as sthg.
◆ **servirse** *vpr* **-1.** [aprovecharse]: ~**se de**
to make use of; **sírvase llamar cuando
quiera** please call whenever you want.
-2. [comida, bebida] to help o.s.
sésamo *m* sesame.
sesenta *núm* sixty; **los (años)** ~ the
sixties; *ver también* **seis.**
sesgo *m* **-1.** [oblicuidad] slant. **-2.** *fig*
[rumbo] course, path.
sesión *f* **-1.** [reunión] meeting, session;
DER sitting, session. **-2.** [proyección, re-
presentación] show, performance; ~
continua continuous showing; ~ **matinal** matinée; ~ **de tarde** afternoon
matinée; ~ **de noche** evening showing. **-3.** [periodo] session.
seso *m* (*gen pl*) **-1.** [cerebro] brain. **-2.**
[sensatez] brains (*pl*), sense; **sorber el**
~ O **los** ~**s a alguien** to brainwash sb.
sesudo, -da *adj* [inteligente] brainy.
set (*pl* **sets**) *m* DEP set.
seta *f* mushroom; ~ **venenosa** toadstool.
setecientos, -tas *núm* seven hundred;
ver también **seis.**
setenta *núm* seventy; **los (años)** ~ the
seventies; *ver también* **seis.**
setiembre = **septiembre.**
sétimo, -ma = **séptimo.**
seto *m* fence; ~ **vivo** hedge.
seudónimo = **pseudónimo.**
severidad *f* **-1.** [rigor] severity. **-2.** [in-
transigencia] strictness.
severo, -ra *adj* **-1.** [castigo] severe,
harsh. **-2.** [persona] strict.
Sevilla Seville.
sevillano, -na *adj, m y f* Sevillian.
◆ **sevillanas** *fpl* Andalusian dance and
song.
sexagésimo, -ma *núm* sixtieth.
sexi, sexy (*pl* **sexys**) *adj* sexy.
sexista *adj, m y f* sexist.
sexo *m* [gen] sex.
sexteto *m* MÚS sextet.
sexto, -ta *núm* sixth.
sexual *adj* [gen] sexual; [educación, vida]
sex (*antes de sust*).
sexualidad *f* sexuality.
sexy = **sexi.**
sha [sa, ʃa] *m* shah.
shock = **choc.**
shorts [ʃorts] *mpl* shorts.
show [ʃou] (*pl* **shows**) *m* show.
si¹ (*pl* **sis**) *m* MÚS B; [en solfeo] ti.
si² *conj* **-1.** (*condicional*) if; ~ **viene él
yo me voy** if he comes, then I'm

going; ~ **hubieses venido te habrías
divertido** if you had come, you would
have enjoyed yourself. **-2.** (*en oraciones
interrogativas indirectas*) if, whether; **ig-
noro** ~ **lo sabe** I don't know if O
whether she knows. **-3.** [expresa protes-
ta] but; **¡**~ **te dije que no lo hicieras!**
but I told you not to do it!
sí (*pl* **síes**) ◇ *adv* **-1.** [afirmación] yes;
¿vendrás? - ~, **iré** will you come? -
yes, I will; **claro que** ~ of course; **creo
que** ~ I think so; **¿están de acuerdo? -
algunos** ~ do they agree? - some do.
-2. [uso enfático]: ~ **que** really, certainly; ~ **que me gusta** I really O certainly like it. **-3.** *loc*: **no creo que puedas hacerlo - ¡a que** ~! I don't think
you can do it - I bet I can!; **porque** ~
[sin razón] because (I/you *etc* felt like
it); **¿**~? [incredulidad] really? ◇ *pron pers*
-1. (*reflexivo*) [de personas] himself (*f*
herself), (*pl*) themselves; [usted] yourself, (*pl*) yourselves; [de cosas, animales]
itself, (*pl*) themselves; **lo quiere todo
para** ~ (**misma**) she wants everything
for herself; **se acercó la silla hacia** ~ he
drew the chair nearer (himself); **de
(por)** ~ [cosa] in itself. **-2.** (*reflexivo impersonal*) oneself; **cuando uno piensa
en** ~ **mismo** when one thinks about
oneself, when you think about yourself. ◇ *m* consent; **dar el** ~ to give
one's consent.
siamés, -esa *adj* Siamese. ◆ **siamés** *m*
[gato] Siamese.
Siberia Siberia.
Sicilia Sicily.
sicoanálisis *etc* = **psicoanálisis.**
sicodélico, -ca = **psicodélico.**
sicología *etc* = **psicología.**
sicópata = **psicópata.**
sicosis = **psicosis.**
sicosomático, -ca = **psicosomático.**
sida (*abrev de* **síndrome de inmuno-
deficiencia adquirida**) *m* AIDS.
siderurgia *f* iron and steel industry.
siderúrgico, -ca *adj* IND iron and steel
(*antes de sust*).
sidra *f* cider.
siega *f* **-1.** [acción] reaping, harvesting.
-2. [época] harvest (time).
siembra *f* **-1.** [acción] sowing. **-2.** [épo-
ca] sowing time.
siempre *adv* **-1.** [gen] always; **como** ~
as usual; **de** ~ usual; **lo de** ~ the
usual; **somos amigos de** ~ we've always been friends; **es así desde** ~ it
has always been that way; **para** ~,

para ~ jamás for ever and ever. **-2.** *Amer* [sin duda] really. ◆ **siempre que** *loc conj* **-1.** [cada vez que] whenever. **-2.** [con tal de que] provided that, as long as. ◆ **siempre y cuando** *loc conj* provided that, as long as.

sien *f* temple.

sienta *etc* **-1.** → sentar. **-2.** → sentir.

sierra *f* **-1.** [herramienta] saw. **-2.** [cordillera] mountain range. **-3.** [región montañosa] mountains (*pl*).

siervo, -va *m y f* **-1.** [esclavo] serf. **-2.** RELIG servant.

siesta *f* siesta, nap; **dormir** ○ **echarse la ~** to have an afternoon nap.

siete ◇ *núm* seven; *ver también* seis. ◇ *f Amer fig:* **de la gran ~** amazing; **¡la gran ~!** good heavens!

sífilis *f inv* syphilis.

sifón *m* **-1.** [agua carbónica] soda (water). **-2.** [tubo] siphon.

sig. = s.

sigilo *m* [gen] secrecy; [al robar, escapar] stealth.

sigiloso, -sa *adj* [discreto] secretive; [al robar, escapar] stealthy.

siglas *fpl* acronym.

siglo *m* **-1.** [cien años] century; **el ~ XX** the 20th century. **-2.** *fig* [mucho tiempo]: **hace ~s que no la veo** I haven't seen her for ages.

signatura *f* **-1.** [en biblioteca] catalogue number. **-2.** [firma] signature.

significación *f* **-1.** [importancia] significance. **-2.** [significado] meaning.

significado, -da *adj* important. ◆ **significado** *m* [sentido] meaning.

significar ◇ *vt* **-1.** [gen] to mean. **-2.** [expresar] to express. ◇ *vi* [tener importancia]: **no significa nada para mí** it means nothing to me.

significativo, -va *adj* significant.

signo *m* **-1.** [gen] sign; **~ de multiplicar/dividir** multiplication/division sign; **~ del zodiaco** sign of the zodiac. **-2.** [en la escritura] mark; **~ de admiración/interrogación** exclamation/question mark. **-3.** [símbolo] symbol.

sigo *etc* → seguir.

siguiente ◇ *adj* **-1.** [en el tiempo, espacio] next. **-2.** [a continuación] following. ◇ *m y f* **-1.** [el que sigue]: **el ~** the next one; **¡el ~!** next, please! **-2.** [lo que sigue]: **lo ~** the following.

sílaba *f* syllable.

silabear *vt* to spell out syllable by syllable.

silbar ◇ *vt* **-1.** [gen] to whistle. **-2.** [abuchear] to hiss. ◇ *vi* **-1.** [gen] to whistle. **-2.** [abuchear] to hiss. **-3.** *fig* [oídos] to ring.

silbato *m* whistle.

silbido, silbo *m* **-1.** [gen] whistle. **-2.** [para abuchear, del serpiente] hiss, hissing (*U*).

silenciador *m* silencer.

silenciar *vt* to hush up, to keep quiet.

silencio *m* **-1.** [gen] silence; **guardar ~ (sobre algo)** to keep silent (about sthg); **romper el ~** to break the silence. **-2.** MÚS rest.

silencioso, -sa *adj* silent, quiet.

silicona *f* silicone.

silla *f* **-1.** [gen] chair; **~ de ruedas** wheelchair; **~ eléctrica** electric chair. **-2.** [de caballo]: **~ (de montar)** saddle.

sillín *m* saddle, seat.

sillón *m* armchair.

silueta *f* **-1.** [cuerpo] figure. **-2.** [contorno] outline. **-3.** [dibujo] silhouette.

silvestre *adj* wild.

simbólico, -ca *adj* symbolic.

simbolizar *vt* to symbolize.

símbolo *m* symbol.

simetría *f* symmetry.

simiente *f culto* seed.

símil *m* **-1.** [paralelismo] similarity, resemblance. **-2.** LITER simile.

similar *adj*: **~ (a)** similar (to).

similitud *f* similarity.

simio, -mia *m y f* simian, ape.

simpatía *f* **-1.** [cordialidad] friendliness. **-2.** [cariño] affection; **coger ~ a alguien** to take a liking to sb; **tener ~ a, sentir ~ por** to like. **-3.** MED sympathy.

simpático, -ca *adj* **-1.** [gen] nice, likeable; [abierto, cordial] friendly. **-2.** [anécdota, comedia etc] amusing, entertaining. **-3.** [reunión, velada etc] pleasant, agreeable.

simpatizante *m y f* sympathizer.

simpatizar *vi*: **~ (con)** [persona] to hit it off (with); [cosa] to sympathize (with).

simple ◇ *adj* **-1.** [gen] simple. **-2.** [fácil] easy, simple. **-3.** [único, sin componentes] single; **dame una ~ razón** give me one single reason. **-4.** [mero] mere; **por ~ estupidez** through sheer stupidity. ◇ *m y f* [persona] simpleton.

simplemente *adv* simply.

simpleza *f* **-1.** [de persona] simplemindedness. **-2.** [tontería] trifle.

simplicidad *f* simplicity.

simplificar *vt* to simplify.

simplista *adj* simplistic.

simposio, simposium *m* symposium.

simulacro *m* simulation; ~ **de combate** mock battle.

simular *vt* **-1.** [sentimiento, desmayo etc] to feign; **simuló que no me había visto** he pretended not to have seen me. **-2.** [combate, salvamento] to simulate.

simultáneo, -nea *adj* simultaneous.

sin *prep* without; ~ **alcohol** alcohol-free; **estoy** ~ **una peseta** I'm penniless; **ha escrito cinco libros** ~ **(contar) las novelas** he has written five books, not counting his novels; **está** ~ **hacer** it hasn't been done yet; **estamos** ~ **vino** we're out of wine; ~ **que** (+ *subjuntivo*) without (+ *gerund*); ~ **que nadie se enterara** without anyone noticing. ◆ **sin embargo** *conj* however.

sinagoga *f* synagogue.

sincerarse *vpr*: ~ **(con alguien)** to open one's heart (to sb).

sinceridad *f* sincerity; [llaneza, franqueza] frankness; **con toda** ~ in all honesty.

sincero, -ra *adj* sincere; [abierto, directo] frank; **para ser** ~ to be honest.

síncope *m* blackout.

sincronizar *vt* **-1.** [regular] to synchronize. **-2.** FÍS to tune.

sindical *adj* (trade) union (*antes de sust*).

sindicalista *m y f* trade unionist.

sindicato *m* trade union, labor union *Am*.

síndrome *m* syndrome; ~ **de abstinencia** withdrawal symptoms (*pl*); ~ **de Down** Down's syndrome; ~ **tóxico** *toxic syndrome caused by ingestion of adulterated rapeseed oil.*

sinfín *m* vast number; **un** ~ **de problemas** no end of problems.

sinfonía *f* symphony.

sinfónico, -ca *adj* symphonic.

Singapur Singapore.

single ['singel] *m* single.

singular ◇ *adj* **-1.** [raro] peculiar, odd. **-2.** [único] unique. **-3.** GRAM singular. ◇ *m* GRAM singular; **en** ~ in the singular.

singularidad *f* **-1.** [rareza, peculiaridad] peculiarity. **-2.** [exclusividad] uniqueness.

singularizar *vt* to distinguish, to single out. ◆ **singularizarse** *vpr* to stand out.

siniestro, -tra *adj* **-1.** [perverso] sinister. **-2.** [desgraciado] disastrous. ◆ **siniestro** *m* disaster; [accidente de coche] accident, crash; [incendio] fire.

sinnúmero *m*: **un** ~ **de** countless.

sino *conj* **-1.** [para contraponer] but; **no lo hizo él,** ~ **ella** he didn't do it, she did; **no sólo es listo,** ~ **también trabajador** he's not only clever but also hardworking. **-2.** [para exceptuar] except, but; **¿quién** ~ **tú lo haría?** who else but you would do it?; **no quiero** ~ **que se haga justicia** I only want justice to be done.

sinónimo, -ma *adj* synonymous. ◆ **sinónimo** *m* synonym.

sinopsis *f inv* synopsis.

síntesis *f inv* synthesis; **en** ~ in short.

sintético, -ca *adj* [artificial] synthetic.

sintetizador, -ra *adj* synthesizing. ◆ **sintetizador** *m* synthesizer.

sintetizar *vt* **-1.** [resumir] to summarize. **-2.** [fabricar artificialmente] to synthesize.

sintiera *etc* → **sentir**.

síntoma *m* symptom.

sintonía *f* **-1.** [música] signature tune. **-2.** [conexión] tuning. **-3.** *fig* [compenetración] harmony.

sintonizar ◇ *vt* [conectar] to tune in to. ◇ *vi* **-1.** [conectar]: ~ **(con)** to tune in (to). **-2.** *fig* [compenetrarse]: ~ **en algo (con alguien)** to be on the same wavelength (as sb) about sthg.

sinuoso, -sa *adj* **-1.** [camino] winding. **-2.** [movimiento] sinuous.

sinvergüenza *m y f* **-1.** [canalla] rogue. **-2.** [fresco, descarado] cheeky person.

sionismo *m* Zionism.

siquiatra = psiquiatra.

siquiátrico, -ca = psiquiátrico.

síquico, -ca = psíquico.

siquiera ◇ *conj* [aunque] even if; **ven** ~ **por pocos días** do come, even if it's only for a few days. ◇ *adv* [por lo menos] at least; **dime** ~ **tu nombre** (you could) at least tell me your name. ◆ **ni (tan) siquiera** *loc conj* not even; **ni (tan)** ~ **me hablaron** they didn't even speak to me.

sirena *f* **-1.** MITOL mermaid, siren. **-2.** [señal] siren.

Siria Syria.

sirimiri *m* drizzle.

sirviente, -ta *m y f* servant.

sisa *f* [en costura] dart; [de manga] armhole.

sisear *vt & vi* to hiss.

sísmico, -ca *adj* seismic.

sistema *m* **-1.** [gen & INFORM] system; ~ **monetario/nervioso/solar** monetary/nervous/solar system; ~ **exper-**

to/operativo INFORM expert/operating system; ~ **dual** TV *system enabling dubbed TV programmes to be heard in the original language*; ~ **métrico (decimal)** metric (decimal) system; ~ **monetario europeo** European Monetary System; ~ **montañoso** mountain chain o range; ~ **periódico de los elementos** periodic table of elements. **-2.** [método, orden] method. ◆**por sistema** *loc adv* systematically.

Sistema Ibérico *m*: **el** ~ **the** Iberian mountain chain.

sistemático, -ca *adj* systematic.

sistematizar *vt* to systematize.

sitiar *vt* [cercar] to besiege.

sitio *m* **-1.** [lugar] place; **cambiar de** ~ **(con alguien)** to change places (with sb); **en otro** ~ elsewhere. **-2.** [espacio] room, space; **hacer** ~ **a alguien** to make room for sb. **-3.** [cerco] siege.

situación *f* **-1.** [circunstancias] situation; [legal, social] status. **-2.** [condición, estado] state, condition. **-3.** [ubicación] location.

situado, -da *adj* **-1.** [acomodado] comfortably off. **-2.** [ubicado] located.

situar *vt* **-1.** [colocar] to place, to put; [edificio, ciudad] to site, to locate. **-2.** [en clasificación] to place, to rank. **-3.** [localizar] to locate, to find. ◆**situarse** *vpr* **-1.** [colocarse] to take up position. **-2.** [ubicarse] to be located. **-3.** [acomodarse, establecerse] to get o.s. established. **-4.** [en clasificación] to be placed; **se sitúa entre los mejores** he's (ranked) amongst the best.

skai [es'kai] = **escay.**

ski [es'ki] = **esquí.**

SL (*abrev de* **sociedad limitada**) *f* ≈ Ltd.

slip [es'lip] = **eslip.**

slogan [es'loɣan] = **eslogan.**

SME (*abrev de* **sistema monetario europeo**) *m* EMS.

smoking [es'mokin] = **esmoquin.**

s/n *abrev de* **sin número.**

snob = **esnob.**

so ◇ *prep* under; ~ **pretexto de** under the pretext of. ◇ *adv*: **¡**~ **tonto!** you idiot! ◇ *interj*: **¡**~**!** whoa!

sobaco *m* armpit.

sobado, -da *adj* **-1.** [cuello, puños etc] worn, shabby; [libro] dog-eared. **-2.** *fig* [argumento, excusa] hackneyed. ◆**sobado** *m* CULIN shortcrust pastry.

sobar *vt* **-1.** [tocar] to finger, to paw. **-2.** *despec* [acariciar, besar] to touch up.

soberanía *f* sovereignty.

soberano, -na ◇ *adj* **-1.** [independiente] sovereign. **-2.** *fig* [grande] massive; [paliza] thorough; [belleza, calidad] unrivalled. ◇ *m y f* sovereign.

soberbio, -bia *adj* **-1.** [arrogante] proud, arrogant. **-2.** [magnífico] superb. ◆**soberbia** *f* **-1.** [arrogancia] pride, arrogance. **-2.** [magnificencia] grandeur.

sobornar *vt* to bribe.

soborno *m* **-1.** [acción] bribery. **-2.** [dinero, regalo] bribe.

sobra *f* excess, surplus; **de** ~ [en exceso] more than enough; [de más] superfluous; **lo sabemos de** ~ we know it only too well. ◆**sobras** *fpl* [de comida] leftovers.

sobrado, -da *adj* **-1.** [de sobra] more than enough, plenty of. **-2.** [de dinero] well off.

sobrante *adj* remaining.

sobrar *vi* **-1.** [quedar, restar] to be left over; **nos sobró comida** we had some food left over. **-2.** [haber de más] to be more than enough; **parece que van a** ~ **bocadillos** it looks like there are going to be too many sandwiches. **-3.** [estar de más] to be superfluous; **lo que dices sobra** that goes without saying.

sobrasada *f* Mallorcan spiced sausage.

sobre¹ *m* **-1.** [para cartas] envelope. **-2.** [para alimentos] sachet, packet.

sobre² *prep* **-1.** [encima de] on (top of); **el libro está** ~ **la mesa** the book is on (top of) the table. **-2.** [por encima de] over, above; **el pato vuela** ~ **el lago** the duck is flying over the lake. **-3.** [acerca de] about, on; **un libro** ~ **el amor** a book about o on love; **una conferencia** ~ **el desarme** a conference on disarmament. **-4.** [alrededor de] about; **llegarán** ~ **las diez** they'll arrive at about ten o'clock. **-5.** [acumulación] upon; **nos contó mentira** ~ **mentira** he told us lie upon lie o one lie after another. **-6.** [cerca de] upon; **la desgracia estaba ya** ~ **nosotros** the disaster was already upon us.

sobrecarga *f* **-1.** [exceso de carga] excess weight. **-2.** [saturación] overload.

sobrecargo *m* COM surcharge.

sobrecoger *vt* to startle. ◆**sobrecogerse** *vpr* to be startled.

sobredosis *f inv* overdose.

sobreentender = **sobrentender.**

sobregiro *m* COM overdraft.

sobremesa *f* after-dinner period.

sobrenatural *adj* [extraordinario] supernatural.

sobrenombre *m* nickname.

sobrentender, sobreentender *vt* to understand, to deduce. ◆ **sobrentenderse** *vpr* to be inferred ○ implied.

sobrepasar *vt* **-1.** [exceder] to exceed. **-2.** [aventajar]: ~ **a alguien** to overtake sb.

sobrepeso *m* excess weight.

sobreponer, superponer *vt* *fig* [anteponer]: ~ **algo a algo** to put sthg before sthg. ◆ **sobreponerse** *vpr*: ~**se a algo** to overcome sthg.

sobreproducción, superproducción *f* ECON overproduction (*U*).

sobrepuesto, -ta, superpuesto, -ta *adj* superimposed. ◆ **sobrepuesto, -ta** *pp* → **sobreponer**.

sobresaliente ◇ *adj* [destacado] outstanding. ◇ *m* [en escuela] excellent, ≃ A; [en universidad] ≃ first class.

sobresalir *vi* **-1.** [en tamaño] to jut out. **-2.** [en importancia] to stand out.

sobresaltar *vt* to startle. ◆ **sobresaltarse** *vpr* to be startled, to start.

sobresalto *m* start, fright.

sobrestimar *vt* to overestimate.

sobretodo *m* overcoat.

sobrevenir *vi* to happen, to ensue; **sobrevino la guerra** the war intervened.

sobreviviente = **superviviente**.

sobrevivir *vi* to survive.

sobrevolar *vt* to fly over.

sobriedad *f* **-1.** [moderación] restraint, moderation. **-2.** [no embriaguez] soberness.

sobrino, -na *m y f* nephew (*f* niece).

sobrio, -bria *adj* **-1.** [moderado] restrained. **-2.** [no excesivo] simple. **-3.** [austero, no borracho] sober.

socarrón, -ona *adj* sarcastic.

socavar *vt* [excavar por debajo] to dig under; *fig* [debilitar] to undermine.

socavón *m* **-1.** [hoyo] hollow; [en la carretera] pothole. **-2.** MIN gallery.

sociable *adj* sociable.

social *adj* **-1.** [gen] social. **-2.** COM company (*antes de sust*).

socialdemócrata *m y f* social democrat.

socialismo *m* socialism.

socialista *adj, m y f* socialist.

sociedad *f* **-1.** [gen] society; ~ **de consumo** consumer society; ~ **deportiva** sports club; ~ **literaria** literary society. **-2.** COM [empresa] company; ~ **anónima** public (limited) company *Br*, incorporated company *Am*; ~ **(de responsa-**

bilidad) limitada private limited company.

socio, -cia *m y f* **-1.** COM partner. **-2.** [miembro] member.

sociología *f* sociology.

sociólogo, -ga *m y f* sociologist.

socorrer *vt* to help.

socorrismo *m* first aid; [en la playa] life-saving.

socorrista *m y f* first aid worker; [en la playa] lifeguard.

socorro ◇ *m* help, aid. ◇ *interj*: ¡~! help!

soda *f* [bebida] soda water.

sodio *m* sodium.

soez *adj* vulgar, dirty.

sofá (*pl* **sofás**) *m* sofa; ~ **cama** ○ **nido** sofa bed.

Sofía Sofia.

sofisticación *f* sophistication.

sofisticado, -da *adj* sophisticated.

sofocar *vt* **-1.** [ahogar] to suffocate. **-2.** [incendio] to put out. **-3.** *fig* [rebelión] to quell. **-4.** *fig* [avergonzar] to mortify. ◆ **sofocarse** *vpr* **-1.** [ahogarse] to suffocate. **-2.** *fig* [irritarse]: ~**se (por)** to get hot under the collar (about).

sofoco *m* **-1.** [ahogo] breathlessness (*U*); [sonrojo, bochorno] hot flush. **-2.** *fig* [vergüenza] mortification. **-3.** *fig* [disgusto]: **llevarse un** ~ to have a fit.

sofreír *vt* to fry lightly over a low heat.

sofrito, -ta *pp* → **sofreír**. ◆ **sofrito** *m* fried tomato and onion sauce.

software ['sofwer] *m* INFORM software.

soga *f* rope; [para ahorcar] noose.

sois → **ser**.

soja *f* soya.

sol *m* **-1.** [astro] sun; **hace** ~ it's sunny; **no dejar a alguien ni a** ~ **ni a sombra** not to give sb a moment's peace. **-2.** [rayos, luz] sunshine, sun; **tomar el** ~ to sunbathe. **-3.** MÚS G; [en solfeo] so. **-4.** [moneda] sol.

solamente *adv* only, just; **vino** ~ **él** only he came.

solapa *f* **-1.** [de prenda] lapel. **-2.** [de libro, sobre] flap.

solapado, -da *adj* underhand, devious.

solar ◇ *adj* solar. ◇ *m* undeveloped plot (of land).

solario, solárium (*pl* **solariums**) *m* solarium.

solazar *vt* to amuse, to entertain.

soldada *f* pay.

soldado *m* soldier; ~ **raso** private.

soldador, **-ra** *m y f* [persona] welder.
♦ **soldador** *m* [aparato] soldering iron.
soldar *vt* to solder, to weld.
soleado, **-da** *adj* sunny.
soledad *f* loneliness; *culto* solitude.
solemne *adj* **-1.** [con pompa] formal. **-2.**
[grave] solemn. **-3.** *fig* [enorme] utter.
solemnidad *f* **-1.** [suntuosidad] pomp,
solemnity. **-2.** [acto] ceremony.
soler *vi*: ~ **hacer algo** to do sthg usually; **aquí suele llover mucho** it usually
rains a lot here; **solíamos ir a la playa
cada día** we used to go to the beach
every day.
solera *f* **-1.** [tradición] tradition. **-2.** [del
vino] sediment; **de** ~ vintage.
solfeo *m* MÚS solfeggio, singing of
scales.
solicitar *vt* **-1.** [pedir] to request; [un
empleo] to apply for; ~ **algo a** O **de alguien** to request sthg of sb. **-2.** [perso-
na] to pursue; **estar muy solicitado** to
be much sought after.
solícito, **-ta** *adj* solicitous, obliging.
solicitud *f* **-1.** [petición] request. **-2.**
[documento] application. **-3.** [atención]
care.
solidaridad *f* solidarity.
solidario, **-ria** *adj* **-1.** [adherido]: ~
(con) sympathetic (to). **-2.** [obligación,
compromiso] mutually binding.
solidez *f* [física] solidity.
solidificar *vt* to solidify. ♦ **solidi-
ficarse** *vpr* to solidify.
sólido, **-da** *adj* **-1.** [gen] solid; [cimien-
tos, fundamento] firm. **-2.** [argumento, conocimiento, idea] sound. ♦ **sólido** *m*
solid.
soliloquio *m* soliloquy.
solista ◇ *adj* solo. ◇ *m y f* soloist.
solitario, **-ria** ◇ *adj* **-1.** [sin compañía]
solitary. **-2.** [lugar] lonely, deserted. ◇
m y f [persona] loner. ♦ **solitario** *m* [jue-
go] patience.
sollozar *vi* to sob.
sollozo *m* sob.
solo, **-la** *adj* **-1.** [sin nadie] alone; **se
quedó** ~ **a temprana edad** he was on
his own from an early age; **a solas**
alone, by oneself. **-2.** [sin nada] on its
own; [café] black; [whisky] neat. **-3.**
[único] single, sole; **ni una sola gota**
not a (single) drop; **dame una sola
cosa** give me just one thing. **-4.** [solita-
rio] lonely. ♦ **solo** *m* MÚS solo.
sólo *adv* only, just; **no** ~ ... **sino (también)** ... not only ... but (also) ...; ~
que ... only ....

solomillo *m* sirloin.
soltar *vt* **-1.** [desasir] to let go of. **-2.**
[desatar - gen] to unfasten; [- nudo] to
untie; [- hebilla, cordones] to undo. **-3.**
[dejar libre] to release. **-4.** [desenrollar -
cable etc] to let O pay out. **-5.** [patada,
grito, suspiro etc] to give; **no suelta ni
un duro** you can't get a penny out of
her. **-6.** [decir bruscamente] to come out
with. ♦ **soltarse** *vpr* **-1.** [desasirse] to
break free. **-2.** [desatarse] to come undone. **-3.** [desprenderse] to come off. **-4.**
[perder timidez] to let go.
soltero, **-ra** ◇ *adj* single, unmarried. ◇
m y f bachelor (*f* single woman).
solterón, **-ona** ◇ *adj* unmarried. ◇ *m y
f* old bachelor (*f* spinster, old maid).
soltura *f* **-1.** [gen] fluency. **-2.** [seguridad
de sí mismo] assurance.
soluble *adj* **-1.** [que se disuelve] soluble.
-2. [que se soluciona] solvable.
solución *f* solution.
solucionar *vt* to solve; [disputa] to resolve.
solventar *vt* **-1.** [pagar] to settle. **-2.** [re-
solver] to resolve.
solvente *adj* **-1.** [económicamente] solvent. **-2.** *fig* [fuentes etc] reliable.
Somalia Somalia.
sombra *f* **-1.** [proyección - fenómeno]
shadow; [- zona] shade; **dar** ~ **a** to cast
a shadow over. **-2.** [en pintura] shade.
-3. *fig* [anonimato] background; **permanecer en la** ~ to stay out of the limelight. **-4.** [suerte]: **buena/mala** ~ good/
bad luck. ♦ **sombras** *fpl* [oscuridad, in-
quietud] darkness (*U*).
sombrero *m* [prenda] hat.
sombrilla *f* sunshade, parasol; **me vale**
~ *Amer fig* I couldn't care less.
sombrío, **-bría** *adj* **-1.** [oscuro] gloomy,
dark. **-2.** *fig* [triste] sombre, gloomy.
somero, **-ra** *adj* superficial.
someter *vt* **-1.** [a rebeldes] to subdue.
-2. [presentar]: ~ **algo a la aprobación
de alguien** to submit sthg for sb's approval; ~ **algo a votación** to put sthg
to the vote. **-3.** [subordinar] to subordinate. **-4.** [a operación, interrogatorio etc]:
~ **a alguien a algo** to subject sb to
sthg. ♦ **someterse** *vpr* **-1.** [rendirse] to
surrender. **-2.** [conformarse]: ~**se a algo**
to yield O bow to sthg. **-3.** [a operación,
interrogatorio etc]: ~**se a algo** to undergo sthg.
somier (*pl* **somieres**) *m* [de muelles]
bed springs (*pl*); [de tablas] slats (*of
bed*).

somnífero, -ra *adj* somniferous.
◆ **somnífero** *m* sleeping pill.

somos → **ser**.

son ◇ *v* → **ser**. ◇ *m* **-1.** [sonido] sound. **-2.** [estilo] way; **en ~ de** in the manner of; **en ~ de paz** in peace.

sonajero *m* rattle.

sonambulismo *m* sleepwalking.

sonámbulo, -la *m y f* sleepwalker.

sonar¹ *m* sonar.

sonar² *vi* **-1.** [gen] to sound; **(así o tal) como suena** literally, in so many words. **-2.** [timbre] to ring. **-3.** [hora]: **sonaron las doce** the clock struck twelve. **-4.** [ser conocido, familiar] to be familiar; **me suena** it rings a bell; **no me suena su nombre** I don't remember hearing her name before. **-5.** [pronunciarse - letra] to be pronounced. **-6.** [rumorearse] to be rumoured. ◆ **sonarse** *vpr* to blow one's nose.

sonda *f* **-1.** MED & TECN probe. **-2.** NÁUT sounding line. **-3.** MIN drill, bore.

sondear *vt* **-1.** [indagar] to sound out. **-2.** [MIN - terreno] to test; [- roca] to drill.

sondeo *m* **-1.** [encuesta] (opinion) poll. **-2.** MIN drilling (*U*). **-3.** NÁUT sounding.

sonido *m* sound.

sonoro, -ra *adj* **-1.** [gen] sound (*antes de sust*); [película] talking. **-2.** [ruidoso, resonante, vibrante] resonant.

sonreír *vi* [reír levemente] to smile. ◆ **sonreírse** *vpr* to smile.

sonriente *adj* smiling.

sonrisa *f* smile.

sonrojar *vt* to cause to blush. ◆ **sonrojarse** *vpr* to blush.

sonrojo *m* blush, blushing (*U*).

sonrosado, -da *adj* rosy.

sonsacar *vt*: **~ algo a alguien** [conseguir] to wheedle sthg out of sb; [hacer decir] to extract sthg from sb; **~ a alguien** to pump sb for information.

sonso, -sa *adj Amer fam* silly.

soñador, -ra *m y f* dreamer.

soñar ◇ *vt lit & fig* to dream; **¡ni ~lo!** not on your life! ◇ *vi lit & fig*: **~ (con)** to dream (of o about).

soñoliento, -ta *adj* sleepy, drowsy.

sopa *f* **-1.** [guiso] soup. **-2.** [de pan] sop, piece of soaked bread.

sopapo *m* slap.

sopero, -ra *adj* soup (*antes de sust*). ◆ **sopero** *m* [plato] soup plate. ◆ **sopera** *f* [recipiente] soup tureen.

sopesar *vt* to try the weight of; *fig* to weigh up.

sopetón ◆ **de sopetón** *loc adv* suddenly, abruptly.

soplar ◇ *vt* **-1.** [vela, fuego] to blow out. **-2.** [ceniza, polvo] to blow off. **-3.** [globo etc] to blow up. **-4.** [vidrio] to blow. **-5.** *fig* [pregunta, examen] to prompt. ◇ *vi* [gen] to blow.

soplete *m* blowlamp.

soplido *m* blow, puff.

soplo *m* **-1.** [soplido] blow, puff. **-2.** MED murmur. **-3.** *fam* [chivatazo] tip-off.

soplón, -ona *m y f fam* grass.

soponcio *m fam* fainting fit.

sopor *m* drowsiness.

soporífero, -ra *adj lit & fig* soporific.

soportar *vt* **-1.** [sostener] to support. **-2.** [resistir, tolerar] to stand; **¡no le soporto!** I can't stand him! **-3.** [sobrellevar] to endure, to bear.

soporte *m* **-1.** [apoyo] support. **-2.** INFORM medium; **~ físico** hardware; **~ lógico** software.

soprano *m y f* soprano.

sor *f* sister RELIG.

sorber *vt* **-1.** [beber] to sip; [haciendo ruido] to slurp. **-2.** [absorber] to soak up. **-3.** [atraer] to draw o suck in.

sorbete *m* sorbet.

sorbo *m* [acción] gulp, swallow; [pequeño] sip; **beber a ~s** to sip.

sordera *f* deafness.

sórdido, -da *adj* **-1.** [miserable] squalid. **-2.** [obsceno, perverso] sordid.

sordo, -da ◇ *adj* **-1.** [que no oye] deaf. **-2.** [ruido, dolor] dull. ◇ *m y f* [persona] deaf person; **los ~s** the deaf.

sordomudo, -da ◇ *adj* deaf and dumb. ◇ *m y f* deaf-mute.

sorna *f* sarcasm.

sorprendente *adj* surprising.

sorprender *vt* **-1.** [asombrar] to surprise. **-2.** [atrapar]: **~ a alguien (haciendo algo)** to catch sb (doing sthg). **-3.** [coger desprevenido] to catch unawares. ◆ **sorprenderse** *vpr* to be surprised.

sorprendido, -da *adj* surprised.

sorpresa *f* surprise; **de o por ~** by surprise.

sorpresivo, -va *adj Amer* unexpected.

sortear *vt* **-1.** [rifar] to raffle. **-2.** [echar a suertes] to draw lots for. **-3.** *fig* [esquivar] to dodge.

sorteo *m* **-1.** [lotería] draw. **-2.** [rifa] raffle.

sortija *f* ring.

sortilegio *m* [hechizo] spell.

SOS (*abrev de save our souls*) *m* SOS.

sosa *f* soda.

sosegado, -da *adj* calm.

sosegar *vt* to calm. ◆ **sosegarse** *vpr* to calm down.

soseras *m y f inv fam* dull person, bore.

sosias *m inv* double, lookalike.

sosiego *m* calm.

soslayo ◆ **de soslayo** *loc adv* [oblicuamente] sideways, obliquely; **mirar a alguien de** ~ to look at sb out of the corner of one's eye.

soso, -sa *adj* **-1.** [sin sal] bland, tasteless. **-2.** [sin gracia] dull, insipid.

sospecha *f* suspicion; **despertar** ~**s** to arouse suspicion.

sospechar ◇ *vt* [creer, suponer] to suspect; **sospecho que no lo terminará** I doubt whether she'll finish it. ◇ *vi:* ~ **de** to suspect.

sospechoso, -sa ◇ *adj* suspicious. ◇ *m y f* suspect.

sostén *m* **-1.** [apoyo] support. **-2.** [sustento] main support; [alimento] sustenance. **-3.** [sujetador] bra.

sostener *vt* **-1.** [sujetar] to support, to hold up. **-2.** [defender - idea, opinión, tesis] to defend; [- promesa, palabra] to stand by, to keep; ~ **que ...** to maintain that .... **-3.** [tener - conversación] to hold, to have; [- correspondencia] to keep up. ◆ **sostenerse** *vpr* to hold o.s. up; [en pie] to stand up; [en el aire] to hang.

sostenido, -da *adj* **-1.** [persistente] sustained. **-2.** MÚS sharp.

sota *f* ≈ jack.

sotabarba *f* double chin.

sotana *f* cassock.

sótano *m* basement.

soterrar *vt* [enterrar] to bury; *fig* to hide.

soufflé [su'fle] (*pl* **soufflés**) *m* soufflé.

soul *m* MÚS soul (music).

soviético, -ca ◇ *adj* **-1.** [del soviet] soviet. **-2.** [de la URSS] Soviet. ◇ *m y f* Soviet.

soy → **ser**.

spaghetti [espa'xeti] = **espagueti**.

sport [es'port] = **esport**.

spot [es'pot] = **espot**.

spray [es'prai] = **espray**.

sprint [es'prin] = **esprint**.

squash [es'kwaʃ] *m inv* squash.

Sr. (*abrev de* **señor**) Mr.

Sra. (*abrev de* **señora**) Mrs.

Sres. (*abrev de* **señores**) Messrs.

Srta. (*abrev de* **señorita**) Miss.

s.s.s. (*abrev de* **su seguro servidor**) *formula used in letters*.

Sta. (*abrev de* **santa**) St.

standard [es'tandar] = **estándar**.

standarizar [estandari'θar] = **estandarizar**.

starter [es'tarter] = **estárter**.

status [es'tatus] = **estatus**.

stereo [es'tereo] = **estéreo**.

sterling [es'terlin] = **esterlina**.

Sto. (*abrev de* **santo**) St.

stock [es'tok] = **estoc**.

stop, estop [es'top] *m* **-1.** AUTOM stop sign. **-2.** [en telegrama] stop.

stress [es'tres] = **estrés**.

strip-tease [es'triptis] *m inv* striptease.

su (*pl* **sus**) *adj poses* [de él] his; [de ella] her; [de cosa, animal] its; [de uno] one's; [de ellos, ellas] their; [de usted, ustedes] your.

suave *adj* **-1.** [gen] soft. **-2.** [liso] smooth. **-3.** [sabor, olor, color] delicate. **-4.** [apacible - persona, carácter] gentle; [- clima] mild. **-5.** [fácil - cuesta, tarea, ritmo] gentle; [- dirección de un coche] smooth.

suavidad *f* **-1.** [gen] softness. **-2.** [lisura] smoothness. **-3.** [de sabor, olor, color] delicacy. **-4.** [de carácter] gentleness. **-5.** [de clima] mildness. **-6.** [de cuesta, tarea, ritmo] gentleness; [de la dirección de un coche] smoothness.

suavizante *m* conditioner; ~ **para la ropa** fabric conditioner.

suavizar *vt* **-1.** [gen] to soften; [ropa, cabello] to condition. **-2.** [ascensión, conducción, tarea] to ease; [clima] to make milder. **-3.** [sabor, olor, color] to tone down. **-4.** [alisar] to smooth.

subacuático, -ca *adj* subaquatic.

subalquilar *vt* to sublet.

subalterno, -na *m y f* [empleado] subordinate.

subasta *f* **-1.** [venta pública] auction; **sacar algo a** ~ to put sthg up for auction. **-2.** [contrata pública] tender; **sacar algo a** ~ to put sthg out to tender.

subastar *vt* to auction.

subcampeón, -ona *m y f* runner-up.

subconsciente *adj & m* subconscious.

subdesarrollado, -da *adj* underdeveloped.

subdesarrollo *m* underdevelopment.

subdirector, -ra *m y f* assistant manager.

subdirectorio *m* INFORM subdirectory.

súbdito, -ta *m y f* **-1.** [subordinado] subject. **-2.** [ciudadano] citizen, national.

subdivisión *f* subdivision.

subestimar *vt* to underestimate; [infravalorar] to underrate. ◆ **subestimarse** *vpr* to underrate o.s.

subido, -da *adj* **-1.** [intenso] strong, intense. **-2.** *fam* [atrevido] risqué. ◆ **subida** *f* **-1.** [cuesta] hill. **-2.** [ascensión] ascent, climb. **-3.** [aumento] increase, rise.

subir ◇ *vi* **-1.** [a piso, azotea] to go/come up; [a montaña, cima] to climb. **-2.** [aumentar - precio, temperatura] to go up, to rise; [- cauce, marea] to rise. **-3.** [montar - en avión, barco] to get on; [- en coche] to get in; **sube al coche** get into the car. **-4.** [cuenta, importe]: ~ **a** to come ○ amount to. **-5.** [de categoría] to be promoted. ◇ *vt* **-1.** [ascender - calle, escaleras] to go/come up; [- pendiente, montaña] to climb. **-2.** [poner arriba] to lift up; [llevar arriba] to take/bring up. **-3.** [aumentar - precio, peso] to put up, to increase; [- volumen de radio etc] to turn up. **-4.** [montar]: ~ **algo/a alguien a** to lift sthg/sb onto. **-5.** [alzar - mano, bandera, voz] to raise; [- persiana] to roll up; [- ventanilla] to wind up. ◆ **subirse** *vpr* **-1.** [ascender]: ~se a [árbol] to climb up; [mesa] to climb onto; [piso] to go/come up to. **-2.** [montarse] ~se a [tren, avión] to get on, to board; [caballo, bicicleta] to mount; [coche] to get into; **el taxi paró y me subí** the taxi stopped and I got in. **-3.** [alzarse - pernera, mangas] to roll up; [- cremallera] to do up; [- pantalones, calcetines] to pull up.

súbito, -ta *adj* sudden.

subjetivo, -va *adj* subjective.

sub júdice [suß'djuðiθe] *adj* DER sub judice.

subjuntivo, -va *adj* subjunctive. ◆ **subjuntivo** *m* subjunctive.

sublevación *f*, **sublevamiento** *m* uprising.

sublevar *vt* **-1.** [amotinar] to stir up. **-2.** [indignar] to infuriate. ◆ **sublevarse** *vpr* [amotinarse] to rebel.

sublime *adj* sublime.

submarinismo *m* skin-diving.

submarinista *m y f* skin-diver.

submarino, -na *adj* underwater. ◆ **submarino** *m* submarine.

subnormal ◇ *adj* **-1.** *ofensivo* [minusválido] subnormal. **-2.** *fig & despec* [imbécil] moronic. ◇ *m y f* *fig & despec* [imbécil] moron.

suboficial *m* MIL non-commissioned officer.

subordinado, -da *adj, m y f* subordinate.

subordinar *vt* [gen & GRAM] to subordinate.

subproducto *m* by-product.

subrayar *vt* *lit* & *fig* to underline.

subsanar *vt* **-1.** [solucionar] to resolve. **-2.** [corregir] to correct.

subscribir = suscribir.

subscripción = suscripción.

subscriptor = suscriptor.

subsecretario, -ria *m y f* **-1.** [de secretario] assistant secretary. **-2.** [de ministro] undersecretary.

subsidiario, -ria *adj* DER ancillary.

subsidio *m* benefit, allowance; ~ **de invalidez** disability allowance; ~ **de paro** unemployment benefit.

subsiguiente *adj* subsequent.

subsistencia *f* **-1.** [vida] subsistence. **-2.** [conservación] continued existence. ◆ **subsistencias** *fpl* [provisiones] provisions.

subsistir *vi* **-1.** [vivir] to live, to exist. **-2.** [sobrevivir] to survive.

substancia = sustancia.

substancial = sustancial.

substancioso = sustancioso.

substantivo = sustantivo.

substitución = sustitución.

substituir = sustituir.

substituto = sustituto.

substracción = sustracción.

substraer = sustraer.

subsuelo *m* subsoil.

subterráneo, -a *adj* subterranean, underground. ◆ **subterráneo** *m* underground tunnel.

subtítulo *m* [gen & CIN] subtitle.

suburbio *m* poor suburb.

subvención *f* subsidy.

subvencionar *vt* to subsidize.

subversión *f* subversion.

subversivo, -va *adj* subversive.

subyacer *vi* [ocultarse]: ~ **bajo algo** to underlie sthg.

subyugar *vt* **-1.** [someter] to subjugate. **-2.** *fig* [dominar] to quell, to master. **-3.** *fig* [atraer] to captivate.

succionar *vt* [suj: raíces] to suck up; [suj: bebé] to suck.

sucedáneo, -a *adj* ersatz, substitute. ◆ **sucedáneo** *m* substitute.

suceder ◇ *v impers* [ocurrir] to happen; **suceda lo que suceda** whatever happens. ◇ *vi* [venir después]: ~ **a** to come after, to follow; **a la guerra sucedieron años muy tristes** the war was followed by years of misery.

sucesión *f* [gen] succession.

sucesivamente *adv* successively; **y así** ~ and so on.

sucesivo, -va *adj* **-1.** [consecutivo] successive, consecutive. **-2.** [siguiente]: **en días** ~**s les informaremos** we'll let you know over the next few days; **en lo** ~ in future.

suceso *m* **-1.** [acontecimiento] event. **-2.** (*gen pl*) [hecho delictivo] **crime**; [incidente] incident.

sucesor, -ra *m y f* successor.

suciedad *f* **-1.** [cualidad] dirtiness (*U*). **-2.** [porquería] dirt, filth (*U*).

sucinto, -ta *adj* [conciso] succinct.

sucio, -cia *adj* **-1.** [gen] dirty; [al comer, trabajar] messy; **en** ~ in rough. **-2.** [juego] dirty.

suculento, -ta *adj* tasty.

sucumbir *vi* **-1.** [rendirse, ceder]: ~ **(a)** to succumb (to). **-2.** [fallecer] to die.

sucursal *f* branch.

sudadera *f* [prenda] sweatshirt.

Sudáfrica South Africa.

sudafricano, -na *adj, m y f* South African.

Sudán Sudan.

sudar *vi* [gen] to sweat.

sudeste, sureste ◇ *adj* [posición, parte] southeast, southeastern; [dirección, viento] southeasterly. ◇ *m* southeast.

sudoeste, suroeste ◇ *adj* [posición, parte] southwest, southwestern; [dirección, viento] southwesterly. ◇ *m* southwest.

sudor *m* [gen] sweat (*U*).

sudoroso, -sa *adj* sweaty.

Suecia Sweden.

sueco, -ca ◇ *adj* Swedish. ◇ *m y f* [persona] Swede. ◆ **sueco** *m* [lengua] Swedish.

suegro, -gra *m y f* father-in-law (*f* mother-in-law).

suela *f* sole.

sueldo *m* salary, wages (*pl*); [semanal] wage; **a** ~ [asesino] hired; [empleado] salaried.

suelo ◇ *v* → **soler**. ◇ *m* **-1.** [pavimento - en interiores] floor; [- en el exterior] ground. **-2.** [terreno, territorio] soil; [para edificar] land. **-3.** [base] bottom. **-4.** *loc*: **echar por el** ~ **un plan** to ruin a project; **estar por los** ~**s** [persona, precio] to be at rock bottom; [productos] to

be dirt cheap; **poner** O **tirar por los** ~**s** to run down, to criticize.

suelto, -ta *adj* **-1.** [gen] loose; [cordones] undone; **¿tienes cinco duros** ~**s?** have you got 25 pesetas in loose change?; **andar** ~ [en libertad] to be free; [en fuga] to be at large; [con diarrea] to have diarrhoea. **-2.** [separado] separate; [desparejado] odd; **no los vendemos** ~**s** we don't sell them separately. **-3.** [arroz] fluffy. **-4.** [lenguaje, estilo] fluent. **-5.** [desenvuelto] comfortable. ◆ **suelto** *m* [calderilla] loose change.

suena *etc* → **sonar²**.

sueño *m* **-1.** [ganas de dormir] sleepiness; [por medicamento etc] drowsiness; **¡qué** ~**!** I'm really sleepy!; **tener** ~ to be sleepy. **-2.** [estado] sleep; **coger el** ~ to get to sleep. **-3.** [imagen mental, objetivo, quimera] dream; **en** ~**s** in a dream.

suero *m* **-1.** MED serum; ~ **artificial** saline solution. **-2.** [de la leche] whey.

suerte *f* **-1.** [azar] chance; **la** ~ **está echada** the die is cast. **-2.** [fortuna] luck; **por** ~ luckily; **¡qué** ~**!** that was lucky!; **tener** ~ to be lucky. **-3.** [destino] fate. **-4.** [situación] situation, lot. **-5.** *culto* [clase]: **toda** ~ **de** all manner of. **-6.** *culto* [manera] manner, fashion; **de** ~ **que** in such a way that.

suéter (*pl* **suéteres**) *m* sweater.

suficiencia *f* **-1.** [capacidad] proficiency. **-2.** [presunción] smugness.

suficiente ◇ *adj* **-1.** [bastante] enough; [medidas, esfuerzos] adequate; **no llevo (dinero)** ~ I don't have enough (money) on me; **no tienes la estatura** ~ you're not tall enough. **-2.** [presuntuoso] smug. ◇ *m* [nota] pass.

sufragar *vt* to defray.

sufragio *m* suffrage.

sufragista *m y f* suffragette.

sufrido, -da *adj* **-1.** [resignado] patient, uncomplaining; [durante mucho tiempo] long-suffering. **-2.** [resistente - tela] hardwearing; [- color] that does not show the dirt.

sufrimiento *m* suffering.

sufrir ◇ *vt* **-1.** [gen] to suffer; [accidente] to have. **-2.** [soportar] to bear, to stand; **tengo que** ~ **sus manías** I have to put up with his idiosyncrasies. **-3.** [experimentar - cambios etc] to undergo. ◇ *vi* [padecer] to suffer; ~ **del estómago** *etc* to have a stomach *etc* complaint.

sugerencia *f* suggestion.

sugerente *adj* evocative.

sugerir *vt* **-1.** [proponer] to suggest. **-2.** [evocar] to evoke.

sugestión *f* suggestion.

sugestionar *vt* to influence.

sugestivo, -va *adj* attractive.

suich *m Amer* switch.

suicida ◇ *adj* suicidal. ◇ *m y f* [por naturaleza] suicidal person; [suicidado] person who has committed suicide.

suicidarse *vpr* to commit suicide.

suicidio *m* suicide.

Suiza Switzerland.

suizo, -za *adj, m y f* Swiss.

sujeción *f* **-1.** [atadura] fastening. **-2.** [sometimiento] subjection.

sujetador *m* bra.

sujetar *vt* **-1.** [agarrar] to hold down. **-2.** [aguantar] to fasten; [papeles] to fasten together. **-3.** [someter] to subdue; [a niños] to control. ◆ **sujetarse** *vpr* **-1.** [agarrarse]: ~se a to hold on to, to cling to. **-2.** [aguantarse] to keep in place. **-3.** [someterse]: ~se a to keep o stick to.

sujeto, -ta *adj* **-1.** [agarrado - objeto] fastened. **-2.** [expuesto]: ~ a subject to. ◆ **sujeto** *m* **-1.** [gen & GRAM] subject. **-2.** [individuo] individual.

sulfato *m* sulphate.

sulfurar *vt* [encolerizar] to infuriate. ◆ **sulfurarse** *vpr* [encolerizarse] to get mad.

sultán *m* sultan.

sultana *f* sultana.

suma *f* **-1.** [MAT - acción] addition; [- resultado] total. **-2.** [conjunto - de conocimientos, datos] total, sum; [- de dinero] sum. **-3.** [resumen]: **en** ~ in short.

sumamente *adv* extremely.

sumar *vt* **-1.** MAT to add together; **tres y cinco suman ocho** three and five are o make eight. **-2.** [costar] to come to. ◆ **sumarse** *vpr*: ~se (a) to join (in).

sumario, -ria *adj* **-1.** [conciso] brief. **-2.** DER summary. ◆ **sumario** *m* **-1.** DER indictment. **-2.** [resumen] summary.

sumergible *adj* waterproof.

sumergir *vt* [hundir] to submerge; [- con fuerza] to plunge; [bañar] to dip. ◆ **sumergirse** *vpr* [hundirse] to submerge; [- con fuerza] to plunge.

sumidero *m* drain.

suministrador, -ra *m y f* supplier.

suministrar *vt* to supply; ~ **algo a alguien** to supply sb with sthg.

suministro *m* [gen] supply; [acto] supplying.

sumir *vt*: ~ **a alguien en** to plunge sb into. ◆ **sumirse en** *vpr* **-1.** [depresión, sueño etc] to sink into. **-2.** [estudio, tema] to immerse o.s. in.

sumisión *f* **-1.** [obediencia - acción] submission; [- cualidad] submissiveness. **-2.** [rendición] surrender.

sumiso, -sa *adj* submissive.

sumo, -ma *adj* **-1.** [supremo] highest, supreme. **-2.** [gran] extreme, great.

sunnita ◇ *adj* Sunni. ◇ *m y f* Sunnite.

suntuoso, -sa *adj* sumptuous.

supeditar *vt*: ~ **(a)** to subordinate (to); **estar supeditado a** to be dependent on. ◆ **supeditarse** *vpr*: ~se a to submit to.

súper ◇ *m fam* supermarket. ◇ *f*: **(gasolina)** ~ ≃ four-star (petrol).

superable *adj* surmountable.

superar *vt* **-1.** [gen] to beat; [récord] to break; ~ **algo/a alguien en algo** to beat sthg/sb in sthg. **-2.** [adelantar - corredor] to overtake, to pass. **-3.** [época, técnica]: **estar superado** to have been superseded. **-4.** [resolver - dificultad etc] to overcome. ◆ **superarse** *vpr* **-1.** [mejorar] to better o.s. **-2.** [lucirse] to excel o.s.

superávit *m inv* surplus.

superdotado, -da *m y f* extremely gifted person.

superficial *adj lit & fig* superficial.

superficie *f* **-1.** [gen] surface. **-2.** [área] area.

superfluo, -flua *adj* superfluous; [gasto] unnecessary.

superior, -ra RELIG *m y f* superior (*f* mother superior). ◆ **superior** ◇ *adj* **-1.** [de arriba] top. **-2.** [mayor]: ~ **(a)** higher (than). **-3.** [mejor]: ~ **(a)** superior (to). **-4.** [excelente] excellent. **-5.** ANAT & GEOGR upper. **-6.** EDUC higher. ◇ *m* (*gen pl*) [jefe] superior.

superioridad *f lit & fig* superiority.

superlativo, -va *adj* **-1.** [belleza etc] exceptional. **-2.** GRAM superlative.

supermercado *m* supermarket.

superpoblación *f* overpopulation.

superponer = sobreponer.

superpotencia *f* superpower.

superpuesto, -ta ◇ *adj* = sobrepuesto. ◇ *pp* → superponer.

supersónico, -ca *adj* supersonic.

superstición *f* superstition.

supersticioso, -sa *adj* superstitious.

supervisar *vt* to supervise.

supervisor, -ra *m y f* supervisor.

supervivencia *f* survival.

superviviente, sobreviviente ◇ *adj* surviving. ◇ *m y f* survivor.

supiera *etc* → **saber**.

suplementario, -ria *adj* supplementary, extra.

suplemento *m* **-1.** [gen & PRENS] supplement. **-2.** [complemento] attachment.

suplente *m y f* **-1.** [gen] stand-in. **-2.** TEATR understudy. **-3.** DEP substitute.

supletorio, -ria *adj* additional, extra. ◆ **supletorio** *m* TELECOM extension.

súplica *f* **-1.** [ruego] plea, entreaty. **-2.** DER petition.

suplicar *vt* [rogar]: ~ **algo (a alguien)** to plead for sthg (with sb); ~ **a alguien que haga algo** to beg sb to do sthg.

suplicio *m lit* & *fig* torture.

suplir *vt* **-1.** [sustituir]: ~ **algo/a alguien (con)** to replace sthg/sb (with). **-2.** [compensar]: ~ **algo (con)** to compensate for sthg (with).

supo → **saber**.

suponer ◇ *vt* **-1.** [creer, presuponer] to suppose. **-2.** [implicar] to involve, to entail. **-3.** [significar] to mean. **-4.** [conjeturar] to imagine; **lo suponía** I guessed as much; **te suponía mayor** I thought you were older. ◇ *m*: **ser un** ~ to be conjecture. ◆ **suponerse** *vpr* to suppose.

suposición *f* assumption.

supositorio *m* suppository.

supremacía *f* supremacy.

supremo, -ma *adj lit* & *fig* supreme.

supresión *f* **-1.** [de ley, impuesto, derecho] abolition; [de sanciones, restricciones] lifting. **-2.** [de palabras, texto] deletion. **-3.** [de puestos de trabajo, proyectos] axing.

suprimir *vt* **-1.** [ley, impuesto, derecho] to abolish; [sanciones, restricciones] to lift. **-2.** [palabras, texto] to delete. **-3.** [puestos de trabajo, proyectos] to axe.

supuesto, -ta ◇ *pp* → **suponer**. ◇ *adj* supposed; [culpable, asesino] alleged; [nombre] false; **por** ~ of course. ◆ **supuesto** *m* assumption; **en el** ~ **de que ...** assuming ....

supurar *vi* to fester.

sur ◇ *adj* [posición, parte] south, southern; [dirección, viento] southerly. ◇ *m* south.

surcar *vt* [tierra] to plough; [aire, agua] to cut ⊙ slice through.

surco *m* **-1.** [zanja] furrow. **-2.** [señal - de disco] groove; [- de rueda] rut. **-3.** [arruga] line, wrinkle.

sureño, -ña ◇ *adj* southern; [viento] southerly. ◇ *m y f* southerner.

sureste = **sudeste**.

surf, surfing *m* surfing.

surgir *vi* **-1.** [brotar] to spring forth. **-2.** [aparecer] to appear. **-3.** *fig* [producirse] to arise.

suroeste = **sudoeste**.

surrealista *adj, m y f* surrealist.

surtido, -da *adj* [variado] assorted. ◆ **surtido** *m* **-1.** [gama] range. **-2.** [caja surtida] assortment.

surtidor *m* [de gasolina] pump; [de un chorro] spout.

surtir ◇ *vt* [proveer]: ~ **a alguien (de)** to supply sb (with). ◇ *vi* [brotar]: ~ **(de)** to spout ⊙ spurt (from). ◆ **surtirse de** *vpr* [proveerse de] to stock up on.

susceptible *adj* **-1.** [sensible] oversensitive. **-2.** [posible]: ~ **de** liable to.

suscitar *vt* to provoke; [interés, dudas, sospechas] to arouse.

suscribir *vt* **-1.** [firmar] to sign. **-2.** [ratificar] to endorse. **-3.** COM [acciones] to subscribe for. ◆ **suscribirse** *vpr* **-1.** PRENS: ~**se (a)** to subscribe (to). **-2.** COM: ~**se a** to take out an option on.

suscripción *f* subscription.

suscriptor, -ra *m y f* subscriber.

susodicho, -cha *adj* above-mentioned.

suspender *vt* **-1.** [colgar] to hang (up). **-2.** EDUC to fail. **-3.** [interrumpir] to suspend; [sesión] to adjourn. **-4.** [aplazar] to postpone. **-5.** [de un cargo] to suspend.

suspense *m* suspense.

suspensión *f* **-1.** [gen & AUTOM] suspension. **-2.** [aplazamiento] postponement; [de reunión, sesión] adjournment.

suspenso, -sa *adj* **-1.** [colgado]: ~ **de** hanging from. **-2.** [no aprobado]: **estar** ~ to have failed. **-3.** *fig* [interrumpido]: **en** ~ pending. ◆ **suspenso** *m* failure.

suspensores *mpl Amer* braces.

suspicacia *f* suspicion.

suspicaz *adj* suspicious.

suspirar *vi* [dar suspiros] to sigh.

suspiro *m* [aspiración] sigh.

sustancia *f* **-1.** [gen] substance; **sin** ~ lacking in substance. **-2.** [esencia] essence. **-3.** [de alimento] nutritional value.

sustancial *adj* substantial, significant.

sustancioso, -sa *adj* substantial.

sustantivo, -va *adj* GRAM noun (*antes de sust*). ◆ **sustantivo** *m* GRAM noun.

sustentar *vt* **-1.** [gen] to support. **-2.** *fig* [mantener - argumento, teoría] to defend.

sustento *m* **-1.** [alimento] sustenance; [mantenimiento] livelihood. **-2.** [apoyo] support.

sustitución *f* [cambio] replacement.

sustituir *vt*: ~ **(por)** to replace (with).

sustituto, -ta *m y f* substitute, replacement.

susto *m* fright.

sustracción *f* **-1.** [robo] theft. **-2.** MAT subtraction.

sustraer *vt* **-1.** [robar] to steal. **-2.** MAT to subtract. ◆ **sustraerse** *vpr*: ~**se a** ○ **de** [obligación, problema] to avoid.

susurrar *vt & vi* to whisper.

susurro *m* whisper; *fig* murmur.

sutil *adj* [gen] subtle; [velo, tejido] delicate, thin; [brisa] gentle; [hilo, línea] fine.

sutileza *f* subtlety; [de velo, tejido] delicacy, thinness; [de brisa] gentleness; [de hilo, línea] fineness.

sutura *f* suture.

suyo, -ya ◇ *adj poses* [de él] his; [de ella] hers; [de uno] one's (own); [de ellos, ellas] theirs; [de usted, ustedes] yours; **este libro es** ~ this book is his/hers *etc*; **un amigo** ~ a friend of his/hers *etc*; **no es asunto** ~ it's none of his/her *etc* business; **es muy** ~ *fam fig* he/she is really selfish. ◇ *pron poses* **-1. el** ~ [de él] his; [de ella] hers; [de cosa, animal] its (own); [de uno] one's own; [de ellos, ellas] theirs; [de usted, ustedes] yours. **-2.** *loc*: **de** ~ in itself; **hacer de las suyas** to be up to his/her *etc* usual tricks; **hacer** ~ to make one's own; **lo** ~ **es el teatro** he/she *etc* should be on the stage; **lo** ~ **sería volver** the proper thing to do would be to go back; **los** ~**s** *fam* [su familia] his/her *etc* folks; [su bando] his/her *etc* lot.

svástica = esvástica.

t¹, T *f* [letra] t, T.

t² **-1.** (*abrev de* **tonelada**) t. **-2.** *abrev de* **tomo**.

tabacalero, -ra *adj* tobacco (*antes de sust*). ◆ **Tabacalera** *f* state tobacco monopoly in Spain.

tabaco *m* **-1.** [planta] tobacco plant. **-2.** [picadura] tobacco. **-3.** [cigarrillos] cigarettes (*pl*).

tábano *m* horsefly.

tabarra *f fam*: **dar la** ~ to be a pest.

taberna *f country-style bar, usually cheap.*

tabernero, -ra *m y f* [propietario] landlord (*f* landlady); [encargado] barman (*f* barmaid).

tabique *m* [pared] partition (wall).

tabla *f* **-1.** [plancha] plank; ~ **de planchar** ironing board. **-2.** [pliegue] pleat. **-3.** [lista, gráfico] table. **-4.** NÁUT [de surf, vela etc] board. **-5.** ARTE panel. ◆ **tablas** *fpl* **-1.** [en ajedrez]: **quedar en** ○ **hacer** ~**s** to end in stalemate. **-2.** TEATR stage (*sg*), boards.

tablado *m* [de teatro] stage; [de baile] dancefloor; [plataforma] platform.

tablao *m* flamenco show.

tablero *m* **-1.** [gen] board. **-2.** [en baloncesto] backboard. **-3.** ~ **(de mandos)** [de avión] instrument panel; [de coche] dashboard.

tableta *f* **-1.** MED tablet. **-2.** [de chocolate] bar.

tablón *m* plank; [en el techo] beam; ~ **de anuncios** notice board.

tabú (*pl* **tabúes** ○ **tabús**) *adj & m* taboo.

tabular *vt & vi* to tabulate.

taburete *m* stool.

tacaño, -ña *adj* mean, miserly.

tacha *f* **-1.** [defecto] flaw, fault; **sin** ~ faultless. **-2.** [clavo] tack.

tachar *vt* **-1.** [lo escrito] to cross out. **-2.** *fig* [acusar]: ~ **a alguien de mentiroso** *etc* to accuse sb of being a liar *etc*.

tacho *m Amer* bucket.

tachón *m* **-1.** [tachadura] correction, crossing out. **-2.** [clavo] stud.

tachuela *f* tack.

tácito, -ta *adj* tacit; [norma, regla] unwritten.

taciturno, -na *adj* taciturn.

taco *m* **-1.** [tarugo] plug. **-2.** [cuña] wedge. **-3.** *fam fig* [palabrota] swearword. **-4.** [de billar] cue. **-5.** [de hojas, billetes de banco] wad; [de billetes de autobús, metro] book. **-6.** [de jamón, queso] hunk. **-7.** *Amer* CULIN taco. **-8.** *Amer* [tacón] heel.

tacón *m* heel.

táctico, -ca *adj* tactical. ◆ **táctica** *f lit* & *fig* tactics (*pl*).

tacto *m* **-1.** [sentido] sense of touch. **-2.** [textura] feel. **-3.** *fig* [delicadeza] tact.

tafetán *m* taffeta.

Tailandia Thailand.

taimado, -da *adj* crafty.

Taiwán [tai'wan] Taiwan.

tajada *f* **-1.** [rodaja] slice. **-2.** *fig* [parte] share; **sacar** ~ **de algo** to get sthg out of sthg.

tajante *adj* [categórico] categorical.

tajar *vt* to cut ○ slice up; [en dos] to slice in two.

tajo *m* **-1.** [corte] deep cut. **-2.** [acantilado] precipice.

Tajo *m*: **el (río)** ~ the (River) Tagus.

tal ◇ *adj* **-1.** [semejante, tan grande] such; **¡jamás se vio cosa** ~! you've never seen such a thing!; **lo dijo con** ~ **seguridad que ...** he said it with such conviction that ...; **dijo cosas** ~**es como ...** he said such things as .... **-2.** [sin especificar] such and such; **a** ~ **hora** at such and such a time. **-3.** [desconocido]: **un** ~ **Pérez** a (certain) Mr Pérez. ◇ *pron* **-1.** [alguna cosa] such a thing. **-2.** *loc*: **que si** ~ **que si cual** this, that and the other; **ser** ~ **para cual** to be two of a kind; ~ **y cual,** ~ **y** ~ this and that; **y** ~ [etcétera] and so on. ◇ *adv*: **¿qué** ~? how's it going?, how are you doing?; **déjalo** ~ **cual** leave it just as it is. ◆ **con tal de** *loc prep* as long as, provided; **con** ~ **de volver pronto ...** as long as we're back early .... ◆ **con tal (de) que** *loc conj* as long as, provided. ◆ **tal (y) como** *loc conj* just as ○ like. ◆ **tal que** *loc prep fam* [como por ejemplo] like.

taladrador, -ra *adj* drilling. ◆ **taladradora** *f* drill.

taladrar *vt* to drill; *fig* [suj: sonido] to pierce.

taladro *m* **-1.** [taladradora] drill. **-2.** [agujero] drill hole.

talante *m* **-1.** [humor] mood; **estar de buen** ~ to be in good humour. **-2.** [carácter] character, disposition.

talar *vt* to fell.

talco *m* talc, talcum powder.

talego *m* **-1.** [talega] sack. **-2.** *mfam* [mil pesetas] 1000 peseta note.

talento *m* **-1.** [don natural] talent. **-2.** [inteligencia] intelligence.

talgo (*abrev de* **tren articulado ligero de Goicoechea Oriol**) *m* *Spanish intercity high-speed train.*

talismán *m* talisman.

talla *f* **-1.** [medida] size; **¿qué** ~ **usas?** what size are you? **-2.** [estatura] height. **-3.** *fig* [capacidad] stature; **dar la** ~ to be up to it. **-4.** [ARTE - en madera] carving; [- en piedra] sculpture .

tallado, -da *adj* [madera] carved; [piedras preciosas] cut.

tallar *vt* **-1.** [esculpir - madera, piedra] to carve; [- piedra preciosa] to cut. **-2.** [medir] to measure (the height of).

tallarín *m* (*gen pl*) noodle.

talle *m* **-1.** [cintura] waist. **-2.** [figura, cuerpo] figure.

taller *m* **-1.** [gen] workshop. **-2.** AUTOM garage. **-3.** ARTE studio.

tallo *m* stem; [brote] sprout, shoot.

talón *m* **-1.** [gen & ANAT] heel; ~ **de Aquiles** *fig* Achilles' heel; **pisarle a alguien los talones** to be hot on sb's heels. **-2.** [cheque] cheque; [matriz] stub; ~ **cruzado/devuelto/en blanco** crossed/bounced/blank cheque; ~ **bancario** cashier's cheque *Br*, cashier's check *Am*.

talonario *m* [de cheques] cheque book; [de recibos] receipt book.

tamaño, -ña *adj* such; **¡cómo pudo decir tamaña estupidez!** how could he say such a stupid thing! ◆ **tamaño** *m* size; **de gran** ~ large; **de** ~ **natural** life-size.

tambalearse *vpr* **-1.** [bambolearse - persona] to stagger; [- mueble] to wobble; [- tren] to sway. **-2.** *fig* [gobierno, sistema] to totter.

también *adv* also, too; **yo** ~ me too; ~ **a mí me gusta** I like it too, I also like it.

tambor *m* **-1.** MÚS & TECN drum; [de pistola] cylinder. **-2.** ANAT eardrum. **-3.** AUTOM brake drum.

Támesis *m*: **el (río)** ~ the (River) Thames.

tamiz *m* [cedazo] sieve.

tamizar *vt* **-1.** [cribar] to sieve. **-2.** *fig* [seleccionar] to screen.

tampoco *adv* neither, not ... either; **ella no va y tú** ~ she's not going and neither are you, she's not going and you aren't either; **¿no lo sabías? - yo** ~ **didn't you know? - me neither** ○ **neither did I.**

tampón *m* **-1.** [sello] stamp; [almohadilla] inkpad. **-2.** [para la menstruación] tampon.

tan *adv* **-1.** [mucho] so; ~ **grande/ deprisa** so big/quickly; **¡qué película** ~ **larga!** what a long film!; ~ ... **que** ... so ... that ...; ~ **es así que** ... so much so that .... **-2.** [en comparaciones]: ~ ... **como** ... as ... as .... ◆ **tan sólo** *loc adv* only.

tanda *f* **-1.** [grupo, lote] group, batch. **-2.** [serie] series; [de inyecciones] course. **-3.** [turno de trabajo] shift.

tándem (*pl* **tándemes**) *m* **-1.** [bicicleta] tandem. **-2.** [pareja] duo, pair.

tangente *f* tangent.

tangible *adj* tangible.

tango *m* tango.

tanque *m* **-1.** MIL tank. **-2.** [vehículo cisterna] tanker. **-3.** [depósito] tank.

tantear ◇ *vt* **-1.** [sopesar - peso, precio, cantidad] to try to guess; [- problema, posibilidades, ventajas] to weigh up. **-2.** [probar, sondear] to test (out). **-3.** [toro, contrincante etc] to size up. ◇ *vi* **-1.** [andar a tientas] to feel one's way. **-2.** [apuntar los tantos] to (keep) score.

tanteo *m* **-1.** [prueba, sondeo] testing out. **-2.** [de posibilidades, ventajas] weighing up. **-3.** [de contrincante, puntos débiles] sizing up. **-4.** [puntuación] score. ◆ **a tanteo** *loc adv* roughly.

tanto, -ta ◇ *adj* **-1.** [gran cantidad] so much, (*pl*) so many; ~ **dinero** so much money, such a lot of money; **tanta gente** so many people; **tiene** ~ **entusiasmo/~s amigos que** ... she has so much enthusiasm/so many friends that .... **-2.** [cantidad indeterminada] so much, (*pl*) so many; **nos daban tantas pesetas al día** they used to give us so many pesetas per day; **cuarenta y ~s** forty-something, forty-odd; **nos conocimos en el sesenta y ~s** we met sometime in the Sixties. **-3.** [en comparaciones]: ~ ... **como** as much ... as, (*pl*) as many ... as. ◇ *pron* **-1.** [gran cantidad] so much, (*pl*) so many; **¿cómo puedes tener ~s?** how can you have so many? **-2.** [cantidad indetermi-

nada] so much, (*pl*) so many; **a ~s de agosto** on such and such a date in August. **-3.** [igual cantidad] as much, (*pl*) as many; **había mucha gente aquí, allí no había tanta** there were a lot of people here, but not as many there; **otro** ~ as much again, the same again; **otro** ~ **le ocurrió a los demás** the same thing happened to the rest of them. **-4.** *loc*: **ser uno de** ~**s** to be nothing special. ◆ **tanto** ◇ *m* **-1.** [punto] point; [gol] goal; **marcar un** ~ to score. **-2.** *fig* [ventaja] point; **apuntarse un** ~ **a favor** to earn o.s. a point in one's favour. **-3.** [cantidad indeterminada]: **un** ~ so much, a certain amount; ~ **por ciento** percentage. **-4.** *loc*: **estar al** ~ **(de)** to be on the ball (about). ◇ *adv* **-1.** [mucho]: ~ **(que ...)** [cantidad] so much (that ...); [tiempo] so long (that ...); **no bebas** ~ don't drink so much; ~ **mejor/peor** so much the better/worse; ~ **más cuanto que** ... all the more so because .... **-2.** [en comparaciones]: **como** as much as; ~ **hombres como mujeres** both men and women; ~ **si estoy como si no** whether I'm there or not. **-3.** *loc*: **¡y** ~**!** most certainly!, you bet! ◆ **tantas** *fpl fam*: **eran las tantas** it was very late. ◆ **en tanto (que)** *loc conj* while. ◆ **entre tanto** *loc adv* meanwhile. ◆ **por (lo) tanto** *loc conj* therefore, so. ◆ **tanto (es así) que** *loc conj* so much so that. ◆ **un tanto** *loc adv* [un poco] a bit, rather.

tañido *m* [de campana] ringing.

tapa *f* **-1.** [para cerrar] lid. **-2.** CULIN snack, tapa. **-3.** [portada - de libro] cover. **-4.** [de zapato] heel plate. **-5.** *Amer* [de botella] top; [de frasco] stopper.

tapadera *f* **-1.** [para encubrir] front. **-2.** [tapa] lid.

tapar *vt* **-1.** [cerrar - ataúd, cofre] to close (the lid of); [- olla, caja] to put the lid on; [- botella] to put the top on. **-2.** [ocultar, cubrir] to cover; [no dejar ver] to block out. **-3.** [abrigar - en la cama] to tuck in; [- con ropa] to wrap up. **-4.** [encubrir] to cover up. ◆ **taparse** *vpr* **-1.** [cubrirse] to cover (up). **-2.** [abrigarse - con ropa] to wrap up; [- en la cama] to tuck o.s. in.

taparrabos *m inv* **-1.** [de hombre primitivo] loincloth. **-2.** [tanga] tanga briefs (*pl*).

tapete *m* [paño] runner; [en mesa de billar, para cartas] baize.

tapia *f* (stone) wall.

tapiar vt -1. [obstruir] to brick up. -2. [cercar] to wall in.

tapicería f -1. [tela] upholstery. -2. [tienda - para muebles] upholsterer's. -3. [tapices] tapestries (pl).

tapiz m [para la pared] tapestry; [para el suelo] carpet.

tapizado m -1. [de mueble] upholstery. -2. [de pared] tapestries (pl).

tapizar vt [mueble] to upholster.

tapón m -1. [para tapar - botellas, frascos] stopper; [- de corcho] cork; [- de metal, plástico] cap, top; [- de bañera, lavabo] plug. -2. [atasco] traffic jam. -3. [en el oído - de cerumen] wax (U) in the ear; [- de algodón] earplug. -4. [en baloncesto] block.

taponar vt [cerrar - botella] to put the top on; [- lavadero] to put the plug in; [- salida] to block; [- tubería] to stop up.

tapujo m subterfuge; **hacer algo con/sin ~s** to do sthg deceitfully/openly.

taquigrafía f shorthand.

taquilla f -1. [ventanilla - gen] ticket office; [- CIN & TEATR] box office. -2. [armario] locker. -3. [recaudación] takings (pl).

taquillero, -ra ◇ adj: **es un espectáculo ~** the show is a box-office hit. ◇ m y f ticket clerk.

taquimecanógrafo, -fa m y f shorthand typist.

tara f -1. [defecto] defect. -2. [peso] tare.

tarántula f tarantula.

tararear vt to hum.

tardanza f lateness.

tardar vi -1. [llevar tiempo] to take; **tardó un año en hacerlo** she took a year to do it; **¿cuánto tardarás (en hacerlo)?** how long will it take you (to do it)? -2. [retrasarse] to be late; [ser lento] to be slow; **~ en hacer algo** to take a long time to do sthg; **no tardaron en hacerlo** they were quick to do it; **a más ~** at the latest.

tarde ◇ f [hasta las cinco] afternoon; [después de las cinco] evening; **por la ~** [hasta las cinco] in the afternoon; [después de las cinco] in the evening; **buenas ~s** [hasta las cinco] good afternoon; [después de las cinco] good evening; **de ~ en ~** from time to time. ◇ adv [gen] late; [en demasía] too late; **ya es ~ para eso** it's too late for that now; **~ o temprano** sooner or later.

tardío, -a adj [gen] late; [consejo, decisión] belated.

tarea f [gen] task; EDUC homework.

tarifa f -1. [precio] charge; COM tariff; [en transportes] fare. -2. (gen pl) [lista] price list.

tarima f platform.

tarjeta f [gen & INFORM] card; **~ de crédito** credit card; **~ de embarque** boarding pass; **~ postal** postcard; **~ de visita** visiting O calling card.

tarot m tarot.

tarrina f terrine.

tarro m [recipiente] jar.

tarta f [gen] cake; [plana, con base de pasta dura] tart; [plana, con base de bizcocho] flan.

tartaleta f tartlet.

tartamudear vi to stammer, to stutter.

tartamudo, -da ◇ adj stammering. ◇ m y f stammerer.

tartana f fam [coche viejo] banger.

tártaro, -ra ◇ adj [pueblo] Tartar. ◇ m y f Tartar.

tartera f [fiambrera] lunch box.

tarugo m -1. fam [necio] blockhead. -2. [de madera] block of wood.

tasa f -1. [índice] rate; **~ de mortalidad/natalidad** death/birth rate. -2. [impuesto] tax. -3. EDUC fee. -4. [tasación] valuation.

tasación f valuation.

tasar vt -1. [valorar] to value. -2. [fijar precio] to fix a price for.

tasca f ≃ pub.

tatarabuelo, -la m y f great-great-grandfather (f -grandmother).

tatuaje m -1. [dibujo] tattoo. -2. [acción] tattooing.

tatuar vt to tattoo.

taurino, -na adj bullfighting (antes de sust).

tauro ◇ m [zodiaco] Taurus. ◇ m y f [persona] Taurean.

tauromaquia f bullfighting.

TAV (abrev de **tren de alta velocidad**) m Spanish high-speed train.

taxativo, -va adj precise, exact.

taxi m taxi.

taxidermista m y f taxidermist.

taxímetro m taximeter.

taxista m y f taxi driver.

taza f -1. [para beber] cup. -2. [de retrete] bowl.

tazón m bowl.

te pron pers -1. (complemento directo) you; **le gustaría verte** she'd like to see you. -2. (complemento indirecto) (to) you; **~ lo dio** he gave it to you; **~ tiene**

miedo he's afraid of you. **-3.** (*reflexivo*) yourself. **-4.** *fam* [valor impersonal]: **si ~ dejas pisar, estás perdido** if you let people walk all over you, you've had it.

té (*pl* **tés**) *m* tea.

tea *f* [antorcha] torch.

teatral *adj* **-1.** [de teatro - gen] theatre (*antes de sust*); [- grupo] drama (*antes de sust*). **-2.** [exagerado] theatrical.

teatro *m* **-1.** [gen] theatre. **-2.** *fig* [fingimiento] playacting.

tebeo® *m* (children's) comic.

techo *m* **-1.** [gen] roof; [dentro de casa] ceiling; **~ deslizante** O **corredizo** AUTOM sun roof; **bajo ~** under cover. **-2.** *fig* [límite] ceiling.

techumbre *f* roof.

tecla *f* [gen, INFORM & MÚS] key.

teclado *m* [gen & MÚS] keyboard.

teclear *vt & vi* [en ordenador etc] to type; [en piano] to play.

técnico, -ca ◇ *adj* technical. ◇ *m y f* **-1.** [mecánico] technician. **-2.** [experto] expert. **técnica** *f* **-1.** [gen] technique. **-2.** [tecnología] technology.

tecnicolor *m* Technicolor®.

tecnócrata *m y f* technocrat.

tecnología *f* technology; **~ punta** state-of-the-art technology.

tecnológico, -ca *adj* technological.

tecolote *m Amer* owl.

tedio *m* boredom, tedium.

tedioso, -sa *adj* tedious.

Tegucigalpa Tegucigalpa.

Teide *m*: **el ~** (Mount) Teide.

teja *f* [de tejado] tile.

tejado *m* roof.

tejano, -na ◇ *adj* **-1.** [de Texas] Texan. **-2.** [tela] denim. ◇ *m y f* [persona] Texan. **tejanos** *mpl* [pantalones] jeans.

tejemaneje *m fam* **-1.** [maquinación] intrigue. **-2.** [ajetreo] to-do, fuss.

tejer ◇ *vt* **-1.** [gen] to weave. **-2.** [labor de punto] to knit. **-3.** [telaraña] to spin. ◇ *vi* [hacer ganchillo] to crochet; [hacer punto] to knit.

tejido *m* **-1.** [tela] fabric, material; IND textile. **-2.** ANAT tissue.

tejo *m* **-1.** [juego] hopscotch. **-2.** BOT yew.

tejón *m* badger.

tel., teléf. (*abrev de* **teléfono**) tel.

tela *f* **-1.** [tejido] fabric, material; [retal] piece of material; **~ de araña** cobweb; **~ metálica** wire netting. **-2.** ARTE [lienzo] canvas. **-3.** *fam* [dinero] dough. **-4.** *fam* [cosa complicada]: **tener (mucha) ~** [ser difícil] to be (very) tricky. **-5.** *loc*: **poner en ~ de juicio** to call into question.

telar *m* **-1.** [máquina] loom. **-2.** (*gen pl*) [fábrica] textiles mill.

telaraña *f* spider's web, cobweb.

tele *f fam* telly.

telearrastre *m* ski-tow.

telecomedia *f* television comedy programme.

telecomunicación *f* [medio] telecommunication. **telecomunicaciones** *fpl* [red] telecommunications.

telediario *m* television news (*U*).

teledirigido, -da *adj* remote-controlled.

teléf. = **tel.**

telefax *m inv* telefax, fax.

teleférico *m* cable-car.

telefilme, telefilm (*pl* **telefilms**) *m* TV film.

telefonear *vi* to phone.

telefónico, -ca *adj* telephone (*antes de sust*). **Telefónica** *f Spanish national telephone monopoly.*

telefonista *m y f* telephonist.

teléfono *m* **-1.** [gen] telephone, phone; **hablar por ~** to be on the phone; **~ inalámbrico** O **móvil** cordless O mobile phone; **~ público** public phone. **-2.** **(número de) ~** telephone number.

telegrafía *f* telegraphy.

telegráfico, -ca *adj lit* & *fig* telegraphic.

telégrafo *m* [medio, aparato] telegraph.

telegrama *m* telegram.

telejuego *m* television game show.

telele *m*: **le dio un ~** [desmayo] he had a fainting fit; [enfado] he had a fit.

telemando *m* remote control.

telemática *f* telematics (*U*).

telenovela *f* television soap opera.

telepatía *f* telepathy.

telescópico, -ca *adj* telescopic.

telescopio *m* telescope.

telesilla *m* chair lift.

telespectador, -ra *m y f* viewer.

telesquí *m* ski lift.

teletexto *m* Teletext®.

teletipo *m* **-1.** [aparato] teleprinter. **-2.** [texto] Teletype®.

televenta *f* **-1.** [por teléfono] telesales (*pl*). **-2.** [por televisión] *TV advertising in which a phone number is given for clients to contact.*

televidente *m y f* viewer.

televisar *vt* to televise.

televisión *f* television.

televisor *m* television (set).

télex *m inv* telex.

telón *m* [de escenario - delante] curtain; [- detrás] backcloth; ~ **de acero** *fig* Iron Curtain; ~ **de fondo** *fig* backdrop.

telonero, -ra *m y f* [cantante] support artist; [grupo] support band.

tema *m* **-1.** [gen] subject. **-2.** MÚS theme.

temario *m* [de una asignatura] curriculum; [de oposiciones] list of topics; [de reunión, congreso] agenda.

temático, -ca *adj* thematic. ◆ **temática** *f* subject matter.

temblar *vi* **-1.** [tiritar]: ~ **(de)** [gen] to tremble (with); [de frío] to shiver (with). **-2.** [vibrar - suelo etc] to shudder, to shake.

temblor *m* shaking (*U*), trembling (*U*).

tembloroso, -sa *adj* trembling, shaky.

temer ◇ *vt* **-1.** [tener miedo de] to fear, to be afraid of. **-2.** [sospechar] to fear. ◇ *vi* to be afraid; **no temas** don't worry; ~ **por** to fear for. ◆ **temerse** *vpr*: ~**se que** to be afraid that; **me temo que no vendrá** I'm afraid she won't come.

temerario, -ria *adj* rash; [conducción] reckless.

temeridad *f* **-1.** [cualidad] recklessness. **-2.** [acción] folly (*U*), reckless act.

temeroso, -sa *adj* [receloso] fearful.

temible *adj* fearsome.

temor *m*: ~ **(a** ○ **de)** fear (of).

temperamental *adj* **-1.** [cambiante] temperamental. **-2.** [impulsivo] impulsive.

temperamento *m* temperament.

temperatura *f* temperature.

tempestad *f* storm.

tempestuoso, -sa *adj lit* & *fig* stormy.

templado, -da *adj* **-1.** [tibio - agua, bebida, comida] lukewarm. **-2.** GEOGR [clima, zona] temperate. **-3.** [nervios] steady. **-4.** [persona, carácter] calm, composed. **-5.** MÚS in tune.

templanza *f* **-1.** [serenidad] composure. **-2.** [moderación] moderation. **-3.** [benignidad - del clima] mildness.

templar *vt* **-1.** [entibiar - lo frío] to warm (up); [- lo caliente] to cool down. **-2.** [calmar - nervios, ánimos] to calm; [- ira, pasiones] to restrain; [- voz] to soften. **-3.** TECN [metal etc] to temper. **-4.** MÚS to tune. **-5.** [tensar] to tighten (up). ◆ **templarse** *vpr* to warm up.

temple *m* **-1.** [serenidad] composure. **-2.** TECN tempering. **-3.** ARTE tempera.

templete *m* pavilion.

templo *m* [edificio - gen] temple; [- católico, protestante] church; [- judío] synagogue.

temporada *f* **-1.** [periodo concreto] season; [de exámenes] period; **de** ~ [fruta, trabajo] seasonal; [en turismo] peak (*antes de sust*); ~ **alta/baja** high/low season; ~ **media** mid-season. **-2.** [periodo indefinido] (period of) time; **pasé una** ~ **en el extranjero** I spent some time abroad.

temporal ◇ *adj* **-1.** [provisional] temporary. **-2.** ANAT & RELIG temporal. ◇ *m* [tormenta] storm.

temporero, -ra *m y f* casual labourer.

temporizador *m* timing device.

temprano, -na *adj* early. ◆ **temprano** *adv* early.

ten *v* → **tener.** ◆ **ten con ten** *m fam* tact.

tenacidad *f* tenacity.

tenacillas *fpl* tongs; [para vello] tweezers; [para rizar el pelo] curling tongs.

tenaz *adj* [perseverante] tenacious.

tenaza *f* (*gen pl*) **-1.** [herramienta] pliers (*pl*). **-2.** [pinzas] tongs (*pl*). **-3.** ZOOL pincer.

tendedero *m* **-1.** [armazón] clothes horse; [cuerda] clothes line. **-2.** [lugar] drying place.

tendencia *f* tendency, trend; ~ **a hacer algo** tendency to do sthg.

tendenciosidad *f* tendentiousness.

tendencioso, -sa *adj* tendentious.

tender *vt* **-1.** [colgar - ropa] to hang out. **-2.** [tumbar] to lay (out). **-3.** [extender] to stretch (out); [mantel] to spread. **-4.** [dar - cosa] to hand; [- mano] to hold out, to offer. **-5.** [entre dos puntos - cable, vía] to lay; [- puente] to build. **-6.** *fig* [preparar - trampa etc] to lay. ◆ **tender a** *vi*: ~ **a hacer algo** to tend to do something; ~ **a la depresión** to have a tendency to get depressed. ◆ **tenderse** *vpr* to stretch out, to lie down.

tenderete *m* [presto] stall.

tendero, -ra *m y f* shopkeeper.

tendido, -da *adj* **-1.** [extendido, tumbado] stretched out. **-2.** [colgado - ropa] hung out, on the line. ◆ **tendido** *m* **-1.** [instalación - de cable] laying; ~ **eléctrico** electrical installation. **-2.** TAUROM front rows (*pl*).

tendón *m* tendon.

tendrá *etc* → **tener.**

tenebroso, -sa adj dark, gloomy; fig shady, sinister.

tenedor¹ m [utensilio] fork.

tenedor², -ra m y f [poseedor] holder; ~ **de libros** COM bookkeeper.

teneduría f COM bookkeeping.

tenencia f possession; ~ **ilícita de armas** illegal possession of arms.

tener ◇ vaux **-1.** (antes de participio) [haber]: **teníamos pensado ir al teatro** we had thought of going to the theatre. **-2.** (antes de adj) [hacer estar]: **me tuvo despierto** it kept me awake; **eso la tiene despistada** that has confused her. **-3.** [expresa obligación]: ~ **que hacer algo** to have to do sthg; **tiene que ser así** it has to be this way. **-4.** [expresa propósito]: **tenemos que ir a cenar un día** we ought to ○ should go for dinner some time. ◇ vt **-1.** [gen] to have; **tengo un hermano** I have ○ I've got a brother; ~ **fiebre** to have a temperature; **tuvieron una pelea** they had a fight; ~ **un niño** to have a baby; **¡que tengan buen viaje!** have a good journey!; **hoy tengo clase** I have to go to school today. **-2.** [medida, años, sensación, cualidad] to be; **tiene 3 metros de ancho** it's 3 metres wide; **¿cuántos años tienes?** how old are you?; **tiene diez años** she's ten (years old); ~ **hambre/miedo** to be hungry/afraid; ~ **mal humor** to be bad-tempered; **le tiene lástima** he feels sorry for her. **-3.** [sujetar] to hold; **tenlo por el asa** hold it by the handle. **-4.** [tomar]: **ten el libro que me pediste** here's the book you asked me for; **¡aquí tienes!** here you are! **-5.** [recibir] to get; **tuve un verdadero desengaño** I was really disappointed; **tendrá una sorpresa** he'll get a surprise. **-6.** [valorar]: **me tienen por tonto** they think I'm stupid; ~ **a alguien en mucho** to think the world of sb. **-7.** [guardar, contener] to keep. **-8.** loc: **no las tiene todas consigo** he is not too sure about it; ~ **a bien hacer algo** to be kind enough to do sthg; ~ **que ver con algo/alguien** [existir relación] to have something to do with sthg/sb; [existir semejanza] to be in the same league as sthg/sb. ◆ **tenerse** vpr **-1.** [sostenerse]: ~**se de pie** to stand upright. **-2.** [considerarse]: **se tiene por listo** he thinks he's clever.

tengo → tener.

tenia f tapeworm.

teniente m lieutenant.

tenis m inv tennis; ~ **de mesa** table tennis.

tenista m y f tennis player.

tenor m **-1.** MÚS tenor. **-2.** [estilo] tone. ◆ **a tenor de** loc prep in view of.

tensar vt to tauten; [arco] to draw.

tensión f **-1.** [gen] tension; ~ **nerviosa** nervous tension. **-2.** TECN [estiramiento] stress. **-3.** MED: ~ **(arterial)** blood pressure; **tener la ~ alta/baja** to have high/low blood pressure. **-4.** ELECTR voltage; **alta ~** high voltage.

tenso, -sa adj taut; fig tense.

tentación f [deseo] temptation; **caer en la ~** to give in to temptation; **tener la ~ de** to be tempted to.

tentáculo m tentacle.

tentador, -ra adj tempting.

tentar vt **-1.** [palpar] to feel. **-2.** [atraer, incitar] to tempt.

tentativa f attempt; ~ **de asesinato** attempted murder.

tentempié (pl tentempiés) m snack.

tenue adj **-1.** [tela, hilo, lluvia] fine. **-2.** [luz, sonido, dolor] faint. **-3.** [relación] tenuous.

teñir vt **-1.** [ropa, pelo]: ~ **algo (de rojo** etc) to dye sthg (red etc). **-2.** fig [matizar]: ~ **algo (de)** to tinge sthg (with). ◆ **teñirse** vpr: ~**se (el pelo)** to dye one's hair.

teología f theology; ~ **de la liberación** liberation theology.

teólogo, -ga m y f theologian.

teorema m theorem.

teoría f theory; **en ~** in theory.

teórico, -ca ◇ adj theoretical. ◇ m y f [persona] theorist. ◆ **teórica** f [teoría] theory (U).

teorizar vi to theorize.

tequila m o f tequila.

TER (abrev de **tren español rápido**) m Spanish high-speed train.

terapéutico, -ca adj therapeutic.

terapia f therapy; ~ **ocupacional/de grupo** occupational/group therapy.

tercer → tercero.

tercera → tercero.

tercermundista adj third-world (antes de sust).

tercero, -ra núm (antes de sust masculino sg: **tercer**) third. ◆ **tercero** m **-1.** [piso] third floor. **-2.** [curso] third year. **-3.** [mediador, parte interesada] third party. ◆ **tercera** f AUTOM third (gear).

terceto m MÚS trio.

terciar ◇ vt [poner en diagonal - gen] to place diagonally; [- sombrero] to tilt. ◇

vi -**1.** [mediar]: ~ **(en)** to mediate (in).
-**2.** [participar] to intervene, to take part. ◆ **terciarse** *vpr* to arise; **si se tercia** if the opportunity arises.
tercio *m* -**1.** [tercera parte] third. -**2.** TAUROM stage (*of bullfight*).
terciopelo *m* velvet.
terco, -ca *adj* stubborn.
tergal® *m* Tergal®.
tergiversar *vt* to distort, to twist.
termal *adj* thermal.
termas *fpl* [baños] hot baths, spa (*sg*).
térmico, -ca *adj* thermal.
terminación *f* -**1.** [finalización] completion. -**2.** [parte final] end. -**3.** GRAM ending.
terminal ◇ *adj* [gen] final; [enfermo] terminal. ◇ *m* ELECTR & INFORM terminal. ◇ *f* [de aeropuerto] terminal; [de autobuses] terminus.
terminante *adj* categorical; [prueba] conclusive.
terminar ◇ *vt* to finish. ◇ *vi* -**1.** [acabar] to end; [tren] to stop, to terminate; ~ **en** [objeto] to end in. -**2.** [ir a parar]: ~ **(de/en)** to end up (as/in); ~ **por hacer algo** to end up doing sthg. ◆ **terminarse** *vpr* -**1.** [finalizarse] to finish. -**2.** [agotarse] to run out.
término *m* -**1.** [fin, extremo] end; **poner ~ a algo** to put a stop to sthg. -**2.** [territorio]: ~ **(municipal)** district. -**3.** [plazo] period; **en el ~ de un mes** within (the space of) a month. -**4.** [lugar, posición] place; **en primer ~** ARTE & FOT in the foreground; **en último ~** ARTE & FOT in the background; *fig* [si es necesario] as a last resort; [en resumidas cuentas] in the final analysis. -**5.** [elemento] point; ~ **medio** [media] average; [compromiso] compromise; **por ~ medio** on average. -**6.** LING & MAT term; **en ~s generales** generally speaking. ◆ **términos** *mpl* [palabras] terms; **los ~s del contrato** the terms of the contract.
terminología *f* terminology.
termo *m* Thermos® (flask).
termómetro *m* thermometer.
termostato *m* thermostat.
terna *f* POLÍT shortlist of three candidates.
ternasco *m* suckling lamb.
ternero, -ra *m y f* [animal] calf. ◆ **ternera** *f* [carne] veal.
ternilla *f* -**1.** CULIN gristle. -**2.** ANAT cartilage.
ternura *f* tenderness.
terquedad *f* stubbornness.
terracota *f* terracotta.

terrado *m* terrace roof.
terral, tierral *m Amer* dust cloud.
terraplén *m* embankment.
terráqueo, -a *adj* Earth (*antes de sust*), terrestrial.
terrateniente *m y f* landowner.
terraza *f* -**1.** [balcón] balcony. -**2.** [de café] terrace, patio. -**3.** [azotea] terrace roof. -**4.** [bancal] terrace.
terregal *m* earthquake.
terrenal *adj* earthly.
terreno, -na *adj* earthly. ◆ **terreno** *m* -**1.** [suelo - gen] land; [- GEOL] terrain; [- AGR] soil. -**2.** [solar] plot (of land). -**3.** DEP: ~ **(de juego)** field, pitch. -**4.** *fig* [ámbito] field.
terrestre *adj* -**1.** [del planeta] terrestrial. -**2.** [de la tierra] land (*antes de sust*).
terrible *adj* -**1.** [gen] terrible. -**2.** [aterrador] terrifying.
terrícola *m y f* earthling.
territorial *adj* territorial.
territorio *m* territory; **por todo el ~ nacional** across the country, nationwide.
terrón *m* -**1.** [de tierra] clod of earth. -**2.** [de harina etc] lump.
terror *m* terror; CIN horror; **dar ~ to** terrify.
terrorífico, -ca *adj* terrifying.
terrorismo *m* terrorism.
terrorista *adj, m y f* terrorist.
terroso, -sa *adj* -**1.** [parecido a la tierra] earthy. -**2.** [con tierra] muddy.
terso, -sa *adj* -**1.** [piel, superficie] smooth. -**2.** [aguas, mar] clear. -**3.** [estilo, lenguaje] polished.
tersura *f* -**1.** [de piel, superficie] smoothness. -**2.** [de aguas, mar] clarity.
tertulia *f* regular meeting of people for informal discussion of a particular issue of common interest; ~ **literaria** literary circle.
tesina *f* (undergraduate) dissertation.
tesis *f inv* thesis.
tesitura *f* [circunstancia] circumstances (*pl*).
tesón *m* -**1.** [tenacidad] tenacity, perseverance. -**2.** [firmeza] firmness.
tesorero, -ra *m y f* treasurer.
tesoro *m* -**1.** [botín] treasure. -**2.** [hacienda pública] treasury, exchequer. ◆ **Tesoro** *m* ECON: **el Tesoro** the Treasury.
test (*pl* tests) *m* test.
testamentario, -ria ◇ *adj* testamentary. ◇ *m y f* executor.

testamento *m* will; **hacer** ~ to write one's will. ◆**Antiguo Testamento** *m* Old Testament. ◆**Nuevo Testamento** *m* New Testament.

testar *vi* to make a will.

testarudo, -da *adj* stubborn.

testículo *m* testicle.

testificar ◇ *vt* to testify; *fig* to testify to. ◇ *vi* to testify, to give evidence.

testigo ◇ *m y f* [persona] witness; ~ **de cargo/descargo** witness for the prosecution/defence; ~ **ocular** O **presencial** eyewitness. ◇ *m* DEP baton. ◆**testigo de Jehová** *m y f* Jehovah's Witness.

testimonial *adj* [documento, prueba etc] testimonial.

testimoniar *vt* to testify; *fig* to testify to.

testimonio *m* **-1.** DER testimony. **-2.** [prueba] proof; **como** ~ **de** as proof of; **dar** ~ **de** to prove.

teta *f* **-1.** *fam* [de mujer] tit. **-2.** [de animal] teat.

tétanos *m inv* tetanus.

tetera *f* teapot.

tetilla *f* **-1.** [de hombre, animal] nipple. **-2.** [de biberón] teat.

tetina *f* teat.

tetrapléjico, -ca *adj, m y f* quadriplegic.

tétrico, -ca *adj* gloomy.

textil *adj & m* textile.

texto *m* **-1.** [gen] text. **-2.** [pasaje] passage.

textual *adj* **-1.** [del texto] textual. **-2.** [exacto] exact.

textura *f* [de tela etc] texture.

tez *f* complexion.

ti *pron pers* (*después de prep*) **-1.** [gen] you; **siempre pienso en** ~ I'm always thinking about you; **me acordaré de** ~ I'll remember you. **-2.** [reflexivo] yourself; **sólo piensas en** ~ **(mismo)** you only think about yourself.

tía → **tío.**

tianguis *m inv Amer* open-air market.

Tibet *m*: **el** ~ Tibet.

tibia *f* shinbone, tibia.

tibieza *f* [calidez] warmth; [falta de calor] lukewarmness.

tibio, -bia *adj* **-1.** [cálido] warm; [falto de calor] tepid, lukewarm. **-2.** *fig* [frío] lukewarm.

tiburón *m* [gen] shark.

tic *m* tic.

ticket = **tíquet.**

tictac *m* tick tock.

tiempo *m* **-1.** [gen] time; **al poco** ~ soon afterwards; **a** ~ **(de hacer algo)** in time (to do sthg); **a un** ~ at the same time; **con el** ~ in time; **del** ~ [fruta] of the season; [bebida] at room temperature; **estar a** O **tener** ~ **de** to have time to; **fuera de** ~ at the wrong moment; **ganar** ~ to save time; **perder el** ~ to waste time; ~ **libre** O **de ocio** spare time; **a** ~ **parcial** O **partido** parttime; **en** ~**s de Mariacastaña** donkey's years ago; **engañar** O **matar el** ~ to kill time. **-2.** [periodo largo] long time; **con** ~ in good time; **hace** ~ **que** it is a long time since; **hace** ~ **que no vive aquí** he hasn't lived here for some time; **tomarse uno su** ~ to take one's time. **-3.** [edad] age; **¿qué** ~ **tiene?** how old is he? **-4.** [movimiento] movement; **motor de cuatro** ~**s** four-stroke engine. **-5.** METEOR weather; **hizo buen/mal** ~ the weather was good/bad; **si el** ~ **lo permite** O **no lo impide** weather permitting; **hace un** ~ **de perros** it's a foul day. **-6.** DEP half. **-7.** GRAM tense. **-8.** [MÚS - compás] time; [- ritmo] tempo.

tienda *f* **-1.** [establecimiento] shop. **-2.** [para acampar]: ~ **(de campaña)** tent.

tiene → **tener.**

tienta ◆**a tientas** *loc adv* blindly; **andar a** ~**s** to grope along.

tierno, -na *adj* **-1.** [blando, cariñoso] tender. **-2.** [del día] fresh.

tierra *f* **-1.** [gen] land; ~ **adentro** inland; ~ **firme** terra firma. **-2.** [materia inorgánica] earth, soil; **un camino de** ~ a dirt track. **-3.** [suelo] ground; **caer a** ~ to fall to the ground; **tomar** ~ to touch down. **-4.** [patria] homeland, native land. **-5.** ELECTR earth *Br*, ground *Am*. ◆**Tierra** *f*: **la Tierra** the Earth.

tierral = **terral.**

tieso, -sa *adj* **-1.** [rígido] stiff. **-2.** [erguido] erect. **-3.** *fig* [engreído] haughty.

tiesto *m* flowerpot.

tifoideo, -a *adj* typhoid (*antes de sust*).

tifón *m* typhoon.

tifus *m inv* typhus.

tigre *m* tiger.

tigresa *f* tigress.

tijera *f* (*gen pl*) scissors (*pl*); [de jardinero, esquilador] shears (*pl*); **unas** ~**s** a pair of scissors/shears.

tijereta *f* [insecto] earwig.

tila *f* [infusión] lime blossom tea.

tildar *vt*: ~ **a alguien de algo** to brand O call sb sthg.

tilde *f* -1. [signo ortográfico] tilde. -2. [acento gráfico] accent.

tiliches *mpl Amer* bits and pieces.

tilín *m* tinkle, tinkling (*U*); **me hace ~** *fam* I fancy him.

tilo *m* [árbol] linden ○ lime tree.

timar *vt* [estafar]: **~ a alguien** to swindle sb; **~ algo a alguien** to swindle sb out of sthg.

timbal *m* [MÚS - de orquesta] kettledrum.

timbrar *vt* to stamp.

timbre *m* -1. [aparato] bell; **tocar el ~** to ring the bell. -2. [de voz, sonido] tone; TECN timbre. -3. [sello - de documentos] stamp; [- de impuestos] seal.

timidez *f* shyness.

tímido, -da *adj* shy.

timo *m* [estafa] swindle.

timón *m* -1. AERON & NÁUT rudder. -2. *fig* [gobierno] helm; **llevar el ~ de** to be at the helm of. -3. *Amer* [volante] steering wheel.

timonel, timonero *m* NÁUT helmsman.

timorato, -ta *adj* [mojigato] prudish.

tímpano *m* ANAT eardrum.

tina *f* -1. [tinaja] pitcher. -2. [gran cuba] vat. -3. [bañera] bathtub.

tinaja *f* (large) pitcher.

tinglado *m* -1. [cobertizo] shed. -2. [armazón] platform. -3. *fig* [lío] fuss. -4. *fig* [maquinación] plot.

tinieblas *fpl* darkness (*U*); *fig* confusion (*U*), uncertainty (*U*).

tino *m* -1. [puntería] good aim. -2. *fig* [habilidad] skill. -3. *fig* [juicio] sense, good judgment.

tinta *f* ink; **~ china** Indian ink; **cargar** ○ **recargar las ~s** to exaggerate; **saberlo de buena ~** to have it on good authority; **sudar ~** to sweat blood. ◆ **medias tintas** *fpl*: **andarse con medias ~s** to be wishy-washy.

tinte *m* -1. [sustancia] dye. -2. [operación] dyeing. -3. [tintorería] dry cleaner's. -4. *fig* [tono] shade, tinge.

tintero *m* [frasco] ink pot; [en la mesa] inkwell.

tintinear *vi* to jingle, to tinkle.

tinto, -ta *adj* -1. [teñido] dyed. -2. [manchado] stained. -3. [vino] red. ◆ **tinto** *m* [vino] red wine.

tintorera *f* blue shark.

tintorería *f* dry cleaner's.

tiña *f* MED ringworm.

tío, -a *m y f* -1. [familiar] uncle (*f* aunt). -2. *fam* [individuo] guy (*f* bird). -3. *mfam* [apelativo] mate (*f* darling).

tiovivo *m* merry-go-round.

típico, -ca *adj* typical; [traje, restaurante etc] traditional; **~ de** typical of.

tipificar *vt* -1. [gen & DER] to classify. -2. [simbolizar] to typify.

tiple *m y f* [cantante] soprano.

tipo, -pa *m y f mfam* guy (*f* bird). ◆ **tipo** *m* -1. [clase] type, sort; **todo ~ de** all sorts of. -2. [cuerpo - de mujer] figure; [- de hombre] build. -3. ECON rate; **~ de interés/cambio** interest/exchange rate. -4. IMPRENTA & ZOOL type.

tipografía *f* -1. [procedimiento] printing. -2. [taller] printing works (*sg*).

tipográfico, -ca *adj* typographical.

tipógrafo, -fa *m y f* printer.

tíquet (*pl* **tíquets**), **ticket** ['tiket] (*pl* **tickets**) *m* ticket.

tiquismiquis ◇ *adj inv fam* [maniático] pernickety. ◇ *m y f inv fam* [maniático] fusspot. ◇ *mpl* -1. [riñas] squabbles. -2. [bagatelas] trifles.

TIR (*abrev de* **transport international routier**) *m* International Road Transport, ≃ HGV *Br*.

tira *f* -1. [banda cortada] strip. -2. [de viñetas] comic strip. -3. *loc*: **la ~ de** *fam* loads (*pl*) of.

tirabuzón *m* [rizo] curl.

tirachinas *m inv* catapult.

tiradero *m Amer* rubbish dump.

tirado, -da *adj* -1. *fam* [barato] dirt cheap. -2. *fam* [fácil] simple, dead easy; **estar ~** to be a cinch. -3. *loc*: **dejar ~ a alguien** to leave sb in the lurch. ◆ **tirada** *f* -1. [lanzamiento] throw. -2. [IMPRENTA - número de ejemplares] print run; [- reimpresión] reprint; [- número de lectores] circulation. -3. [sucesión] series. -4. [distancia]: **de** ○ **en una tirada** in one go.

tirador, -ra *m y f* [persona] marksman. ◆ **tirador** *m* [mango] handle. ◆ **tiradores** *mpl Amer* [tirantes] braces.

Tirana Tirana.

tiranía *f* tyranny.

tirano, -na ◇ *adj* tyrannical. ◇ *m y f* tyrant.

tirante ◇ *adj* -1. [estirado] taut. -2. *fig* [violento, tenso] tense. ◇ *m* -1. [de tela] strap. -2. ARQUIT brace. ◆ **tirantes** *mpl* [para pantalones] braces *Br*, suspenders *Am*.

tirantez *f fig* tension.

tirar ◇ *vt* -1. [lanzar] to throw; **~ algo a alguien/algo** [para hacer daño] to throw sthg at sb/sthg; **tírame una manzana** throw me an apple. -2. [dejar caer] to **drop**; [derramar] to **spill**; [volcar] to **knock over**. **-3.** [desechar, malgastar] to **throw away**. **-4.** [disparar] to **fire**; [- bomba] to **drop**; [- petardo, cohete] to **let off**. **-5.** [derribar] to **knock down**. **-6.** [jugar - carta] to **play**; [- dado] to **throw**. **-7.** [DEP - falta, penalti etc] to **take**; [- balón] to **pass**. **-8.** [imprimir] to **print**. ◇ vi **-1.** [estirar, arrastrar]: ~ **(de algo)** to **pull (sthg)**; **tira y afloja** give and take. **-2.** [disparar] to **shoot**. **-3.** fam [atraer] to **have a pull**; **me tira la vida del campo** I feel drawn towards life in the country. **-4.** [cigarrillo, chimenea etc] to **draw**. **-5.** [dirigirse] to **go, to head**. **-6.** fam [apañárselas] to **get by**; **ir tirando** to **get by**; **voy tirando** I'm O.K. **-7.** [parecerse]: **tira a gris** it's greyish; **tira a su abuela** she takes after her grandmother; **tirando a** approaching. **-8.** [tender]: ~ **para algo** [persona] to **have the makings of sthg**; **este programa tira a (ser) hortera** this programme is a bit on the tacky side; **el tiempo tira a mejorar** the weather looks as if it's getting better. **-9.** [DEP - con el pie] to **kick**; [- con la mano] to **throw**; [- a meta, canasta etc] to **shoot**. ◆ **tirarse** vpr **-1.** [lanzarse]: ~**se (a)** [agua] to **dive (into)**; [aire] to **jump (into)**; ~**se sobre alguien** to **jump on top of sb**. **-2.** [tumbarse] to **stretch out**. **-3.** [tiempo] to **spend**.

tirita® f (sticking) **plaster** Br, **Bandaid**® Am.

tiritar vi: ~ **(de)** to **shiver (with)**.

tiro m **-1.** [gen] **shot**; **pegar un** ~ **a alguien** to **shoot sb**; **pegarse un** ~ to **shoot o.s.**; **ni a** ~**s** never in a million years. **-2.** [acción] **shooting**; ~ **al blanco** [deporte] **target shooting**; [lugar] shooting range; ~ **con arco** archery. **-3.** [huella, marca] **bullet mark**; [herida] gunshot wound. **-4.** [alcance] **range**; **a** ~ **de** within the range of; **a** ~ **de piedra** a stone's throw away. **-5.** [de chimenea, horno] **draw**. **-6.** [de caballos] **team**.

tiroides m inv **thyroid (gland)**.

tirón m **-1.** [estirón] **pull**. **-2.** [robo] **bagsnatching**. ◆ **de un tirón** loc adv in one go.

tirotear ◇ vt to **fire at**. ◇ vi to **shoot**.

tiroteo m [tiros] **shooting**; [intercambio de disparos] **shootout**.

tisana f **herbal tea**.

tisis f inv MED **(pulmonary) tuberculosis**.

titánico, -ca adj **titanic**.

títere m lit & fig **puppet**; **no dejar** ~ **con cabeza** [destrozar] to **destroy everything in sight**; [criticar] to **spare nobody**. ◆ **títeres** mpl [guiñol] **puppet show** (sg).

titilar, titilear vi [estrella, luz] to **flicker**.

titiritar vi: ~ **(de)** to **shiver (with)**.

titiritero, -ra m y f **-1.** [de títeres] **puppeteer**. **-2.** [acróbata] **acrobat**.

titubeante adj **-1.** [actitud] **hesitant**. **-2.** [voz] **stuttering**. **-3.** [al andar] **tottering**.

titubear vi **-1.** [dudar] to **hesitate**. **-2.** [al hablar] to **stutter**.

titubeo m (gen pl) **-1.** [duda] **hesitation**. **-2.** [al hablar] **stutter, stuttering** (U). **-3.** [al andar] **tottering**.

titulado, -da m y f [diplomado] **holder of a qualification**; [licenciado] **graduate**.

titular ◇ adj [profesor, médico] **official**. ◇ m y f [poseedor] **holder**. ◇ m (gen pl) PRENS **headline**. ◇ vt [llamar] to **title, to call**. ◆ **titularse** vpr **-1.** [llamarse] to be **titled** ○ **called**. **-2.** [licenciarse]: ~**se (en)** to **graduate (in)**. **-3.** [diplomarse]: ~**se (en)** to **obtain a qualification (in)**.

título m **-1.** [gen] **title**; ~ **de propiedad** title deed. **-2.** [licenciatura] **degree**; [diploma] **diploma**; **tiene muchos** ~**s** she has a lot of qualifications. **-3.** fig [derecho] **right**; **a** ~ **de** as.

tiza f **chalk**; **una** ~ a **piece of chalk**.

tiznar vt to **blacken**.

tizne m o f **soot**.

tizón m **burning stick** ○ **log**.

tlapalería f Amer **ironmonger's (shop)**.

toalla f [para secarse] **towel**; ~ **de ducha/manos** bath/hand towel; **arrojar** ○ **tirar la** ~ to **throw in the towel**.

toallero m **towel rail**.

tobillo m **ankle**.

tobogán m [rampa] **slide**; [en parque de atracciones] **helter-skelter**; [en piscina] **flume**.

toca f **wimple**.

tocadiscos m inv **record player**.

tocado, -da adj **-1.** [chiflado] **soft in the head**. ◆ **tocado** m [prenda] **headgear** (U).

tocador m **-1.** [mueble] **dressing table**. **-2.** [habitación - en lugar público] **powder room**; [- en casa] **boudoir**.

tocar ◇ vt **-1.** [gen] to **touch**; [palpar] to **feel**; [suj: país, jardín] to **border on**. **-2.** [instrumento, canción] to **play**; [bombo] to **bang**; [sirena, alarma] to **sound**; [campana, timbre] to **ring**; **el reloj tocó las doce** the clock struck twelve. **-3.** [abordar - tema etc] to **touch on**. **-4.** fig [conmover] to touch; [herir] to wound. **-5.** *fig* [concernir]: **por lo que a mí me toca/a eso le toca** as far as I'm/that's concerned. ◇ *vi* **-1.** [entrar en contacto] to touch. **-2.** [estar próximo]: ~ **(con)** [gen] to be touching; [país, jardín] to border (on). **-3.** [llamar - a la puerta, ventana] to knock. **-4.** [corresponder - en un reparto]: ~ **a alguien** to be due to sb; **tocamos a mil cada uno** we're due a thousand each; **le tocó la mitad** he got half of it; **te toca a ti hacerlo** [turno] it's your turn to do it; [responsabilidad] it's up to you to do it. **-5.** [caer en suerte]: **me ha tocado la lotería** I've won the lottery; **le ha tocado sufrir mucho** he has had to suffer a lot. **-6.** [llegar el momento]: **nos toca pagar ahora** it's time (for us) to pay now. ◆ **tocarse** *vpr* to touch.

tocayo, -ya *m y f* namesake.

tocinería *f* pork butcher's (shop).

tocino *m* [para cocinar] lard; [para comer] fat (*of bacon*). ◆ **tocino de cielo** *m* CULIN *dessert made of syrup and eggs.*

todavía *adv* **-1.** [aún] still; [con negativo] yet, still; ~ **no lo he recibido** I still haven't got it yet, I haven't got it yet; ~ **ayer** as late as yesterday; ~ **no** not yet. **-2.** [sin embargo] still. **-3.** [incluso] even.

todo, -da ◇ *adj* **-1.** [gen] all; ~ **el mundo** everybody; ~ **el libro** the whole book, all (of) the book; ~ **el día** all day. **-2.** [cada, cualquier]: ~**s los días/lunes** every day/Monday; ~ **español** every Spaniard, all Spaniards. **-3.** [para enfatizar]: **es** ~ **un hombre** he's every bit a man; **ya es toda una mujer** she's a big girl now; **fue** ~ **un éxito** it was a great success. ◇ *pron* **-1.** [todas las cosas] everything, (*pl*) all of them; **lo vendió** ~ he sold everything, he sold it all; ~**s están rotos** they're all broken, all of them are broken; **ante** ~ [sobre todo] above all; [en primer lugar] first of all; **con** ~ despite everything; **sobre** ~ above all; **está en** ~ he/she always makes sure everything is just so. **-2.** [todas las personas]: ~**s** everybody; **todas vinieron** everybody ○ they all came. ◆ **todo** ◇ *m* whole. ◇ *adv* completely, all. ◆ **del todo** *loc adv*: **no estoy del** ~ **contento** I'm not entirely happy; **no lo hace mal del** ~ she doesn't do it at all badly. ◆ **todo terreno** *m* Jeep®.

todopoderoso, -sa *adj* almighty.

toffee ['tofi] (*pl* **toffees**) *m* coffee-flavoured toffee.

toga *f* **-1.** [manto] toga. **-2.** [traje] gown.

Togo Togo.

toldo *m* [de tienda] awning; [de playa] sunshade.

tolerancia *f* tolerance.

tolerante *adj* tolerant.

tolerar *vt* **-1.** [consentir aceptar] to tolerate; ~ **que alguien haga algo** to tolerate sb doing sthg. **-2.** [aguantar] to stand.

toma *f* **-1.** [de biberón, papilla] feed. **-2.** [de medicamento] dose; [de sangre] sample. **-3.** [de ciudad etc] capture. **-4.** [de agua, aire] inlet; ~ **de corriente** ELECTR socket. **-5.** CIN [de escena] take. **-6.** *loc*: **ser un** ~ **y daca** to be give and take. ◆ **toma de posesión** *f* **-1.** [de gobierno, presidente] investiture. **-2.** [de cargo] undertaking.

tomar ◇ *vt* **-1.** [gen] to take; [actitud, costumbre] to adopt. **-2.** [datos, información] to take down. **-3.** [comida, bebida] to have; **¿qué quieres** ~? what would you like (to drink/eat)? **-4.** [autobús, tren etc] to catch; [taxi] to take. **-5.** [considerar, confundir]: ~ **a alguien por algo/alguien** to take sb for sthg/sb. **-6.** *loc*: ~**la** ○ ~**las con alguien** *fam* to have it in for sb; **¡toma!** [al dar algo] here you are!; [expresando sorpresa] well I never! ◇ *vi* [encaminarse] to go, to head. ◆ **tomarse** *vpr* **-1.** [comida, bebida] to have; [medicina, drogas] to take. **-2.** [interpretar] to take; ~**se algo a mal/bien** to take sthg badly/well.

tomate *m* [fruto] tomato.

tómbola *f* tombola.

tomillo *m* thyme.

tomo *m* [volumen] volume.

ton ◆ **sin ton ni son** *loc adv* for no apparent reason.

tonada *f* tune.

tonadilla *f* ditty.

tonalidad *f* [de color] tone.

tonel *m* [recipiente] barrel.

tonelada *f* tonne.

tonelaje *m* tonnage.

tónico, -ca *adj* **-1.** [reconstituyente] revitalizing. **-2.** GRAM & MÚS tonic. ◆ **tónico** *m* [reconstituyente] tonic. ◆ **tónica** *f* **-1.** [tendencia] trend. **-2.** MÚS tonic. **-3.** [bebida] tonic water.

tonificar *vt* to invigorate.

tono *m* **-1.** [gen] tone; **fuera de** ~ out of place. **-2.** [MÚS - tonalidad] key; [- altura] pitch. **-3.** [de color] shade; ~ **de piel** complexion.

tonsura f tonsure.

tontear vi [hacer el tonto] to fool about.

tontería f **-1.** [estupidez] stupid thing; **decir una** ~ to talk nonsense; **hacer una** ~ to do sthg foolish. **-2.** [cosa sin importancia o valor] trifle.

tonto, -ta ◇ adj stupid. ◇ m y f idiot; **hacer el** ~ to play the fool; **hacerse el** ~ to act innocent. ◆ **a tontas y a locas** loc adv haphazardly.

top (pl **tops**) m [prenda] short top.

topacio m topaz.

topadora f Amer bulldozer.

topar vi [encontrarse]: ~ **con alguien** to bump into sb; ~ **con algo** to come across sthg.

tope ◇ adj inv [máximo] top, maximum; [fecha] last. ◇ m **-1.** [pieza] block; [para puerta] doorstop. **-2.** FERROC buffer. **-3.** [límite máximo] limit; [de plazo] deadline. **-4.** [freno]: **poner** ~ **a** to rein in, to curtail. **-5.** loc: **estar hasta los** ~**s** to be bursting at the seams. ◆ **a tope** loc adv **-1.** [de velocidad, intensidad] flat out. **-2.** fam [lleno - lugar] packed.

topetazo m bump.

tópico, -ca adj **-1.** MED topical. **-2.** [manido] clichéd. ◆ **tópico** m cliché.

topo m ZOOL & fig mole.

topógrafo, -fa m y f topographer.

topónimo m place name.

toque m **-1.** [gen] touch; **dar los (últimos)** ~**s a algo** to put the finishing touches to sthg. **-2.** [aviso] warning; **dar un** ~ **a alguien** [llamar] to call sb; [amonestar] to prod sb, to warn sb. **-3.** [sonido - de campana] chime, chiming (U); [- de tambor] beat, beating (U); [- de sirena etc] blast; ~ **de diana** reveille; ~ **de difuntos** death knell; ~ **de queda** curfew.

toquetear vt [manosear - cosa] to fiddle with; [- persona] to fondle.

toquilla f shawl.

tórax m inv thorax.

torbellino m **-1.** [remolino - de aire] whirlwind; [- de agua] whirlpool; [- de polvo] dustcloud. **-2.** fig [mezcla confusa] spate.

torcedura f **-1.** [torsión] twist, twisting (U). **-2.** [esguince] sprain.

torcer ◇ vt **-1.** [gen] to twist; [doblar] to bend. **-2.** [girar] to turn. ◇ vi [girar] to turn. ◆ **torcerse** vpr **-1.** [retorcerse] to twist; [doblarse] to bend; **me tuerzo al andar/escribir** I can't walk/write in

a straight line. **-2.** [dislocarse] to sprain. **-3.** [ir mal - esperanzas, negocios, día] to go wrong; [- persona] to go astray.

torcido, -da adj [enroscado] twisted; [doblado] bent; [cuadro, corbata] crooked.

tordo, -da adj dappled. ◆ **tordo** m [pájaro] thrush.

torear ◇ vt **-1.** [lidiar] to fight (bulls). **-2.** fig [eludir] to dodge. **-3.** fig [burlarse de]: ~ **a alguien** to mess sb about. ◇ vi [lidiar] to fight bulls.

toreo m bullfighting.

torero, -ra m y f [persona] bullfighter; **saltarse algo a la torera** fig to flout sthg. ◆ **torera** f [prenda] bolero (jacket).

tormenta f lit & fig storm.

tormento m torment.

tormentoso, -sa adj stormy; [sueño] troubled.

tornado m tornado.

tornar culto ◇ vt [convertir]: ~ **algo en (algo)** to turn sthg into (sthg). ◇ vi **-1.** [regresar] to return. **-2.** [volver a hacer]: ~ **a hacer algo** to do sthg again. ◆ **tornarse** vpr [convertirse]: ~**se (en)** to turn (into), to become.

torneado, -da adj [cerámica] turned.

torneo m tournament.

tornillo m screw; [con tuerca] bolt; **le falta un** ~ fam he has a screw loose.

torniquete m MED tourniquet.

torno m **-1.** [de alfarero] (potter's) wheel. **-2.** [para pesos] winch. ◆ **en torno a** loc prep **-1.** [alrededor de] around. **-2.** [acerca de] about; **girar en** ~ **a** to be about.

toro m bull. ◆ **toros** mpl [lidia] bullfight (sg), bullfighting (U).

toronja f grapefruit.

torpe adj **-1.** [gen] clumsy. **-2.** [necio] slow, dim-witted.

torpedear vt to torpedo.

torpedero m torpedo boat.

torpedo m [proyectil] torpedo.

torpeza f **-1.** [gen] clumsiness; **fue una** ~ **hacerlo/decirlo** it was a clumsy thing to do/say. **-2.** [falta de inteligencia] slowness.

torre f **-1.** [construcción] tower; ELECTR pylon; ~ **(de apartamentos)** tower block; ~ **de control** control tower; ~ **de perforación** oil derrick. **-2.** [en ajedrez] rook, castle. **-3.** MIL turret.

torrefacto, -ta adj high-roast (antes de sust).

torrencial adj torrential.

torrente *m* torrent; **un ~ de** *fig* [gente, palabras etc] a stream O flood of; [dinero, energía] masses of.

torreta *f* -1. MIL turret. -2. ELECTR pylon.

torrezno *m* chunk of fried bacon.

tórrido, -da *adj* torrid.

torrija *f* French toast (*U*).

torsión *f* -1. [del cuerpo, brazo] twist, twisting (*U*). -2. MEC torsion.

torso *m* culto torso.

torta *f* -1. CULIN cake. -2. *fam* [bofetada] thump; **dar** O **pegar una ~ a alguien** to thump sb. ◆ **ni torta** *loc adv fam* not a thing.

tortazo *m* -1. [bofetada] thump. -2. [accidente] crash.

tortícolis *f inv* crick in the neck.

tortilla *f* omelette; **~ (a la) española** Spanish O potato omelette; **~ (a la) francesa** French O plain omelette.

tórtola *f* turtledove.

tortolito, -ta *m y f* (*gen pl*) *fam* [enamorado] lovebird.

tortuga *f* [terrestre] tortoise; [marina] turtle; [fluvial] terrapin.

tortuoso, -sa *adj* -1. [sinuoso] tortuous, winding. -2. *fig* [perverso] devious.

tortura *f* torture.

torturar *vt* to torture.

tos *f* cough; **~ ferina** = **tosferina**.

tosco, -ca *adj* -1. [basto] crude. -2. *fig* [ignorante] coarse.

toser *vi* to cough.

tosferina, tos ferina *f* whooping cough.

tostado, -da *adj* -1. [pan, almendras] toasted. -2. [color] brownish. -3. [piel] tanned. ◆ **tostada** *f* piece of toast.

tostador *m*, **tostadora** *f* toaster.

tostar *vt* -1. [dorar, calentar - pan, almendras] to toast; [- carne] to brown. -2. [broncear] to tan. ◆ **tostarse** *vpr* to get brown.

tostón *m fam fig* [rollo, aburrimiento] bore, drag.

total ◇ *adj* total. ◇ *m* -1. [suma] total. -2. [totalidad, conjunto] whole; **el ~ del grupo** the whole group; **en ~** in all. ◇ *adv* anyway; **~ que me marché** so anyway, I left.

totalidad *f* whole; **en su ~** as a whole.

totalitario, -ria *adj* totalitarian.

totalizar *vt* to amount to.

tóxico, -ca *adj* toxic, poisonous. ◆ **tóxico** *m* poison.

toxicómano, -na *m y f* drug addict.

toxina *f* toxin.

tozudo, -da *adj* stubborn.

traba *f fig* [obstáculo] obstacle; **poner ~s (a alguien)** to put obstacles in the way (of sb).

trabajador, -ra ◇ *adj* hard-working. ◇ *m y f* worker.

trabajar ◇ *vi* -1. [gen] to work; **~ de/ en** to work as/in; **~ en una empresa** to work for a firm. -2. CIN & TEATR to act. ◇ *vt* -1. [hierro, barro, tierra] to work; [masa] to knead. -2. [mejorar] to work on O at.

trabajo *m* -1. [gen] work; **hacer un buen ~** to do a good job; **~ intelectual/físico** mental/physical effort; **~ manual** manual labour; **~s manuales** [en el colegio] arts and crafts. -2. [empleo] job; **no tener ~** to be out of work. -3. [estudio escrito] essay. -4. POLÍT labour. -5. *fig* [esfuerzo] effort.

trabajoso, -sa *adj* -1. [difícil] hard, difficult. -2. [molesto] tiresome.

trabalenguas *m inv* tongue-twister.

trabar *vt* -1. [sujetar] to fasten; [a preso] to shackle. -2. [unir] to join. -3. [iniciar - conversación, amistad] to strike up. -4. [obstaculizar] to hinder. -5. CULIN to thicken. ◆ **trabarse** *vpr* -1. [enredarse] to get tangled. -2. *loc*: **se le trabó la lengua** he got tongue-tied.

trabazón *f fig* [conexión, enlace] link, connection.

trabucar *vt* to mix up.

tracción *f* traction; **~ delantera/trasera** front-wheel/rear-wheel drive.

tractor, -ra *adj* tractive. ◆ **tractor** *m* tractor.

tradición *f* tradition.

tradicional *adj* traditional.

tradicionalismo *m* traditionalism; POLÍT conservatism.

traducción *f* translation.

traducir ◇ *vt* [a otro idioma] to translate. ◇ *vi*: **~ (de/a)** to translate (from/ into). ◆ **traducirse** *vpr* [a otro idioma]: **~se (por)** to be translated (by O as).

traductor, -ra *m y f* translator.

traer *vt* -1. [trasladar, provocar] to bring; [consecuencias] to carry, to have; **~ consigo** [implicar] to mean, to lead to. -2. [llevar] to carry; **¿qué traes ahí?** what have you got there? -3. [llevar adjunto, dentro] to have; **trae un artículo interesante** it has an interesting article in it. -4. [llevar puesto] to wear. ◆ **traerse** *vpr*: **traérselas** *fam fig* to be a real handful.

traficante *m y f* [de drogas, armas etc] trafficker.

traficar *vi*: ~ **(en/con algo)** to traffic (in sthg).

tráfico *m* [gen] traffic.

tragaluz *m* skylight.

traganíqueles *f inv Amer fam* → **máquina**.

tragaperras *f inv* slot machine.

tragar ◇ *vt* **-1.** [ingerir, creer] to swallow. **-2.** [absorber] to swallow up. **-3.** *fig* [soportar] to put up with. ◇ *vi* to swallow. ◆ **tragarse** *vpr fig* [soportarse]: **no se tragan** they can't stand each other.

tragedia *f* tragedy.

trágico, -ca *adj* tragic.

trago *m* **-1.** [de líquido] mouthful; **de un** ~ in one gulp. **-2.** *fam* [copa] drink. **-3.** *fam fig* [disgusto]: **ser un** ~ **para alguien** to be tough on sb.

tragón, -ona *fam* ◇ *adj* greedy. ◇ *m y f* pig, glutton.

traición *f* **-1.** [infidelidad] betrayal. **-2.** DER treason.

traicionar *vt lit & fig* [ser infiel] to betray.

traicionero, -ra *adj* [desleal] treacherous; DER treasonous.

traidor, -ra ◇ *adj* treacherous; DER treasonous. ◇ *m y f* traitor.

traiga *etc* → **traer**.

trailer ['trailer] (*pl* **trailers**) *m* **-1.** CIN trailer. **-2.** AUTOM articulated lorry.

traje *m* **-1.** [con chaqueta] suit; [de una pieza] dress; ~ **de baño** swimsuit; ~ **de chaqueta** woman's two-piece suit. **-2.** [regional, de época etc] costume; ~ **de luces** matador's outfit. **-3.** [ropa] clothes (*pl*); ~ **de paisano** [de militar] civilian clothes; [de policía] plain clothes.

trajeado, -da *adj fam* [arreglado] spruced up.

trajín *m fam fig* [ajetreo] bustle.

trajinar *vi fam fig* to bustle about.

trajo → **traer**.

trama *f* **-1.** [de hilos] weft. **-2.** *fig* [confabulación] intrigue. **-3.** LITER plot.

tramar *vt* **-1.** [hilo] to weave. **-2.** *fam fig* [planear] to plot; [complot] to hatch; **estar tramando algo** to be up to something.

tramitar *vt* **-1.** [suj: autoridades - pasaporte, permiso] to take the necessary steps to obtain; [- solicitud, dimisión] to process. **-2.** [suj: solicitante]: ~ **un permiso** to be in the process of applying for a licence.

trámite *m* [gestión] formal step; **de** ~ routine, formal. ◆ **trámites** *mpl* **-1.** [proceso] procedure (*sg*). **-2.** [papeleo] paperwork (*U*).

tramo *m* **-1.** [espacio] section, stretch. **-2.** [de escalera] flight (of stairs).

tramoya *f* TEATR stage machinery (*U*).

trampa *f* **-1.** [para cazar] trap. **-2.** *fig* [engaño] trick; **tender una** ~ **(a alguien)** to set ○ lay a trap (for sb); **hacer ~s** to cheat. **-3.** *fig* [deuda] debt.

trampear *vi fam* [estafar] to swindle money.

trampilla *f* [en el suelo] trapdoor.

trampolín *m* [de piscina] diving board; [de esquí] ski jump; [en gimnasia] springboard.

tramposo, -sa ◇ *adj* [fullero] cheating. ◇ *m y f* [fullero] cheat.

tranca *f* **-1.** [de puerta o ventana] bar. **-2.** [arma] cudgel. **-3.** *loc*: **a ~s y barrancas** with great difficulty.

trance *m* **-1.** [apuro] difficult situation; **estar en** ~ **de hacer algo** to be about to do sthg; **pasar por un mal** ~ to go through a bad patch. **-2.** [estado hipnótico] trance.

tranquilidad *f* peacefulness, calmness; **para mayor** ~ to be on the safe side.

tranquilizante *m* FARM tranquilizer.

tranquilizar *vt* **-1.** [calmar] to calm (down). **-2.** [dar confianza] to reassure. ◆ **tranquilizarse** *vpr* **-1.** [calmarse] to calm down. **-2.** [ganar confianza] to feel reassured.

tranquillo *m fam*: **coger el** ~ **a algo** to get the knack of sthg.

tranquilo, -la *adj* **-1.** [sosegado - lugar, música] peaceful; [- persona, tono de voz, mar] calm; [- viento] gentle; **¡(tú) ~!** *fam* don't you worry! **-2.** [velada, charla, negocio] quiet. **-3.** [mente] untroubled; [conciencia] clear. **-4.** [despreocupado] casual, laid-back.

transacción *f* COM transaction.

transar *vi Amer* to compromise.

transatlántico, -ca *adj* transatlantic. ◆ **transatlántico** *m* NÁUT (ocean) liner.

transbordador *m* **-1.** NÁUT ferry. **-2.** AERON: ~ **(espacial)** space shuttle.

transbordar ◇ *vt* to transfer. ◇ *vi* to change (*trains etc*).

transbordo *m*: **hacer** ~ to change (*trains etc*).

transcendencia *f* importance; **tener una gran** ~ to be deeply significant.

transcendental *adj* **-1.** [importante] momentous. **-2.** [meditación] transcendental.

transcendente *adj* momentous.

transcender *vi* **-1.** [extenderse]: ~ **(a algo)** to spread (across sthg). **-2.** [filtrarse] to be leaked. **-3.** [sobrepasar]: ~ **de** to transcend, to go beyond.

transcribir *vt* [escribir] to transcribe.

transcurrir *vi* **-1.** [tiempo] to pass, to go by. **-2.** [ocurrir] to take place.

transcurso *m* **-1.** [paso de tiempo] passing. **-2.** [periodo de tiempo]: **en el** ~ **de** in the course of.

transeúnte *m y f* [paseante] passer-by.

transexual *adj, m y f* transsexual.

transferencia *f* transfer.

transferir *vt* to transfer.

transfigurar *vt* to transfigure.

transformación *f* transformation.

transformador, -ra *adj* transforming. ◆ **transformador** *m* ELECTRÓN transformer.

transformar *vt* **-1.** [cambiar radicalmente]: ~ **algo/a alguien (en)** to transform sthg/sb (into). **-2.** [convertir]: ~ **algo (en)** to convert sthg (into). **-3.** [en rugby] to convert. ◆ **transformarse** *vpr* **-1.** [cambiar radicalmente] to be transformed. **-2.** [convertirse]: ~**se en algo** to be converted into sthg.

tránsfuga *m y f* POLÍT defector.

transfusión *f* transfusion.

transgredir *vt* to transgress.

transgresor, -ra *m y f* transgressor.

transición *f* transition; **periodo de** ~ transition period; ~ **democrática** transition to democracy.

transido, -da *adj*: ~ **(de)** stricken (with); ~ **de pena** grief-stricken.

transigir *vi* **-1.** [ceder] to compromise. **-2.** [ser tolerante] to be tolerant.

transistor *m* transistor.

transitar *vi* to go (along).

tránsito *m* **-1.** [circulación - gen] movement; [- de coches] traffic. **-2.** [transporte] transit.

transitorio, -ria *adj* [gen] transitory; [residencia] temporary; [régimen, medida] transitional, interim.

translúcido, -da *adj* translucent.

transmisión *f* **-1.** [gen & AUTOM] transmission; [de saludos, noticias] passing on. **-2.** RADIO & TV broadcast, broadcasting (*U*). **-3.** [de herencia, poderes etc] transference.

transmisor, -ra *adj* transmission (*antes de sust*). ◆ **transmisor** *m* transmitter.

transmitir *vt* **-1.** [gen] to transmit; [saludos, noticias] to pass on. **-2.** RADIO & TV to broadcast. **-3.** [ceder] to transfer.

transparencia *f* transparency.

transparentarse *vpr* [tela] to be see-through; [vidrio, líquido] to be transparent.

transparente *adj* [gen] transparent; [tela] see-through.

transpiración *f* perspiration; BOT transpiration.

transpirar *vi* to perspire; BOT to transpire.

transplantar *vt* to transplant.

transplante *m* transplant, transplanting (*U*).

transponer *vt* [cambiar] to switch. ◆ **transponerse** *vpr* [adormecerse] to doze off.

transportador *m* [para medir ángulos] protractor.

transportar *vt* **-1.** [trasladar] to transport. **-2.** [embelesar] to captivate. ◆ **transportarse** *vpr* [embelesarse] to go into raptures.

transporte *m* transport; ~ **público** O **colectivo** public transport.

transportista *m y f* carrier.

transvase *m* **-1.** [de líquido] decanting. **-2.** [de río] transfer.

transversal *adj* transverse.

tranvía *m* tram, streetcar *Am*.

trapecio *m* [de gimnasia] trapeze.

trapecista *m y f* trapeze artist.

trapero, -ra *m y f* rag-and-bone man.

trapío *m culto* TAUROM good bearing.

trapisonda *f fam* [enredo] scheme.

trapo *m* **-1.** [trozo de tela] rag. **-2.** [gamuza, bayeta] cloth; **poner a alguien como un** ~ to tear sb to pieces. ◆ **trapos** *mpl fam* [ropa] clothes.

tráquea *f* windpipe, trachea MED.

traquetear ◇ *vt* to shake. ◇ *vi* [hacer ruido] to rattle.

traqueteo *m* [ruido] rattling.

tras *prep* **-1.** [detrás de] behind. **-2.** [después de, en pos de] after; **uno** ~ **otro** one after the other; **andar** ~ **algo** to be after sthg.

trasatlántico, -ca = transatlántico.

trasbordador = transbordador.

trasbordar = transbordar.

trasbordo = transbordo.

trascendencia = transcendencia.

trascendental = transcendental.

trascendente = transcendente.

trascender = transcender.

trascribir = transcribir.

trascurrir = transcurrir.

trascurso = transcurso.

trasegar vt [desordenar] to rummage about amongst.

trasero, -ra adj back (antes de sust), rear (antes de sust). ◆ **trasero** m fam backside.

trasferencia = transferencia.

trasferir = transferir.

trasfigurar = transfigurar.

trasfondo m background; [de palabras, intenciones] undertone.

trasformación = transformación.

trasformador, -ra = transformador.

trasformar = transformar.

trásfuga = tránsfuga.

trasfusión = transfusión.

trasgredir = transgredir.

trasgresor, -ra = transgresor.

trashumante adj seasonally migratory.

trasiego m [movimiento] comings and goings (pl).

traslación f ASTRON passage.

trasladar vt -1. [desplazar] to move. -2. [a empleado, funcionario] to transfer. -3. [reunión, fecha] to postpone. ◆ **trasladarse** vpr -1. [desplazarse] to go. -2. [mudarse] to move; **me traslado de piso** I'm moving flat.

traslado m -1. [de casa, empresa, muebles] move, moving (U). -2. [de trabajo] transfer. -3. [de personas] movement.

traslúcido, -da = translúcido.

trasluz m reflected light; **al ~** against the light.

trasmisión = transmisión.

trasmisor, -ra = transmisor.

trasmitir = transmitir.

trasnochar vi to stay up late.

traspapelar vt [papeles, documentos] to mislay.

trasparencia = transparencia.

trasparentarse = transparentarse.

trasparente = transparente.

traspasar vt -1. [atravesar] to go through, to pierce. -2. [cruzar] to cross (over); [puerta] to pass through. -3. [suj: líquido] to soak through. -4. [jugador] to transfer. -5. [negocio] to sell (as a going concern). -6. fig [exceder] to go beyond.

traspaso m [venta - de jugador] transfer; [- de negocio] sale (as a going concern).

traspié (pl **traspiés**) m -1. [resbalón] trip, stumble; **dar un ~** to trip up. -2. fig [error] slip.

traspiración = transpiración.

traspirar = transpirar.

trasplantar = transplantar.

trasplante = transplante.

trasponer = transponer.

trasportar etc = transportar.

trasquilar vt [esquilar] to shear.

trastabillar vi Amer to stagger.

trastada f dirty trick; **hacer una ~ a alguien** to play a dirty trick on sb.

traste m -1. MÚS fret. -2. loc: **dar al ~ con algo** to ruin sthg; **irse al ~** to fall through.

trastero m junk room.

trastienda f backroom.

trasto m -1. [utensilio inútil] piece of junk, junk (U). -2. fam fig [persona traviesa] menace, nuisance. ◆ **trastos** mpl fam [pertenencias, equipo] things, stuff (U); **tirarse los ~s a la cabeza** to have a flaming row.

trastocar vt [cambiar] to turn upside down. ◆ **trastocarse** vpr [enloquecer] to go mad.

trastornado, -da adj disturbed, unbalanced.

trastornar vt -1. [volver loco] to drive mad. -2. [inquietar] to worry, to trouble. -3. [alterar] to turn upside down; [planes] to disrupt. ◆ **trastornarse** vpr [volverse loco] to go mad.

trastorno m -1. [mental] disorder; [digestivo] upset. -2. [alteración - por huelga, nevada] disruption (U); [- por guerra etc] upheaval.

trastrocar vt [cambiar de orden] to switch o change round.

trasvase = transvase.

tratable adj easy-going, friendly.

tratado m -1. [convenio] treaty. -2. [escrito] treatise.

tratamiento m -1. [gen & MED] treatment. -2. [título] title, form of address. -3. INFORM processing; **~ de datos/textos** data/word processing; **~ por lotes** batch processing.

tratar ◇ vt -1. [gen & MED] to treat. -2. [discutir] to discuss. -3. INFORM to process. -4. [dirigirse a]: **~ a alguien de** [usted, tú etc] to address sb as. ◇ vi -1. [versar]: **~ de/sobre** to be about. -2. [tener relación]: **~ con alguien** to mix with sb, to have dealings with sb. -3. [intentar]: **~ de hacer algo** to try to do sthg. -4. [utilizar]: **~ con** to deal with, to use. -5. [comerciar]: **~ en** to deal in. ◆ **tratarse** vpr -1. [relacionarse]: **~se con** to mix with, to have dealings with.

-2. [versar]: ~**se de** to be about; **¿de qué se trata?** what's it about?

tratativas *fpl Amer* procedure (*sg*).

trato *m* **-1.** [comportamiento, conducto] treatment; **de ~ agradable** pleasant; **malos ~s** battering (*U*) (*of child, wife*). **-2.** [relación] dealings (*pl*). **-3.** [acuerdo] deal; **cerrar** O **hacer un ~** to do O make a deal; **¡~ hecho!** it's a deal! **-4.** [tratamiento] title, term of address.

trauma *m* trauma.

traumatólogo, -ga *m y f* traumatologist.

través ◆ a través de *loc prep* **-1.** [de un lado a otro del espacio] across, over. **-2.** [por, por medio de] through. **◆ de través** *loc adv* [transversalmente] crossways; [de lado] sideways.

travesaño *m* **-1.** ARQUIT crosspiece. **-2.** DEP crossbar.

travesía *f* **-1.** [viaje - por mar] voyage, crossing. **-2.** [calle] cross-street.

travestido, -da, travestí (*pl* **travestís**) *m y f* transvestite.

travesura *f* prank, mischief (*U*).

traviesa *f* **-1.** FERROC sleeper (*on track*). **-2.** CONSTR crossbeam.

travieso, -sa *adj* mischievous.

trayecto *m* **-1.** [distancia] distance; **final de ~** end of the line. **-2.** [viaje] journey, trip. **-3.** [ruta] route.

trayectoria *f* **-1.** [recorrido] trajectory. **-2.** *fig* [evolución] path.

traza *f* [aspecto] appearance (*U*), looks (*pl*).

trazado *m* **-1.** [trazo] outline, sketching. **-2.** [diseño] plan, design. **-3.** [recorrido] route.

trazar *vt* **-1.** [dibujar] to draw, to trace; [ruta] to plot. **-2.** [indicar, describir] to outline. **-3.** [idear] to draw up.

trazo *m* **-1.** [de dibujo, rostro] line. **-2.** [de letra] stroke.

trébol *m* [planta] clover. **◆ tréboles** *mpl* [naipes] clubs.

trece *núm* thirteen; *ver también* **seis**.

treceavo, -va *núm* thirteenth.

trecho *m* [espacio] distance; [tiempo] time.

tregua *f* truce; *fig* respite.

treinta *núm* thirty; **los (años) ~** the Thirties; *ver también* **seis**.

treintena *f* thirty.

tremendo, -da *adj* [enorme] tremendous, enormous. **◆ tremenda** *f*: **tomar** O **tomarse algo a la tremenda** to take sthg hard.

trémulo, -la *adj* [voz] trembling; [luz] flickering.

tren *m* **-1.** [ferrocarril] train; **~ de alta velocidad/largo recorrido** high-speed/long-distance train; **~ semidirecto** *through train, a section of which becomes a stopping train*; **estar como (para parar) un ~** to be really gorgeous; **perder el ~** *fig* to miss the boat. **-2.** TECN line; **~ de aterrizaje** undercarriage; **~ de lavado** car wash.

trenza *f* **-1.** [de pelo] plait. **-2.** [de fibras] braid.

trenzar *vt* **-1.** [pelo] to plait. **-2.** [fibras] to braid.

trepa *m y f fam* social climber.

trepador, -ra ◇ *adj*: **planta trepadora** creeper. ◇ *m y f fam* social climber.

trepar ◇ *vt* to climb. ◇ *vi* **-1.** [subir] to climb. **-2.** *fam fig* [medrar] to be a social climber.

trepidar *vi* to shake, to vibrate.

tres *núm* three; **ni a la de ~** for anything in the world, no way; *ver también* **seis**. **◆ tres cuartos** *m inv* [abrigo] three-quarter-length coat. **◆ tres en raya** *m* noughts and crosses (*U*) *Br*, tick-tack-toe *Am*.

trescientos, -tas *núm* three hundred; *ver también* **seis**.

tresillo *m* [sofá] three-piece suite.

treta *f* [engaño] trick.

triangular *adj* triangular.

triángulo *m* GEOM & MÚS triangle.

triates *mpl Amer* triplets.

tribu *f* tribe.

tribulación *f* tribulation.

tribuna *f* **-1.** [estrado] rostrum, platform; [del jurado] jury box. **-2.** [DEP - localidad] stand; [- graderío] stand. **-3.** PRENS: **~ de prensa** press box; **~ libre** open forum.

tribunal *m* **-1.** [gen] court; **llevar a alguien/acudir a los ~es** to take sb/go to court. **-2.** [de examen] board of examiners; [de concurso] panel.

tributable *adj* taxable.

tributar *vt* [homenaje] to pay; [respeto, admiración] to have.

tributo *m* **-1.** [impuesto] tax. **-2.** *fig* [precio] price. **-3.** [homenaje] tribute.

triciclo *m* tricycle.

tricornio *m* three-cornered hat.

tricot *m inv* knitting (*U*).

tricotar *vt & vi* to knit.

tricotosa *f* knitting machine.

tridimensional *adj* three-dimensional.

trifulca *f fam* row, squabble.

tropel

trigésimo, -ma *núm* thirtieth.

trigo *m* wheat.

trigonometría *f* trigonometry.

trillado, -da *adj fig* trite.

trillar *vt* to thresh.

trillizo, -za *m y f* triplet.

trilogía *f* trilogy.

trimestral *adj* three-monthly, quarterly; [exámenes, notas] end-of-term (*antes de sust*).

trimestre *m* three months (*pl*), quarter; [en escuela, universidad] term.

trinar *vi* to chirp; **está que trina** *fig* she's fuming.

trincar *fam* ◇ *vt* [detener] to nick, to arrest. ◇ *vi* [beber] to guzzle.

trincha *f* strap.

trinchante *m* [tenedor] meat fork.

trinchar *vt* to carve.

trinchera *f* MIL trench.

trineo *m* [pequeño] sledge; [grande] sleigh.

Trinidad *f*: **la (Santísima) ~** the (Holy) Trinity.

Trinidad y Tobago Trinidad and Tobago.

trino *m* [de pájaros] chirp, chirping (*U*); MÚS trill.

trío *m* [gen] trio.

tripa *f* **-1.** [intestino] gut, intestine. **-2.** *fam* [barriga] gut, belly. ◆ **tripas** *fpl fig* [interior] insides.

triple ◇ *adj* triple. ◇ *m*: **el ~** three times as much; **el ~ de gente** three times as many people.

triplicado *m* second copy, triplicate.

triplicar *vt* to triple, to treble. ◆ **triplicarse** *vpr* to triple, to treble.

trípode *m* tripod.

tripulación *f* crew.

tripulante *m y f* crew member.

tripular *vt* to man.

tris *m*: **estar en un ~ de** *fig* to be within a whisker of.

triste *adj* **-1.** [gen] sad; [día, tiempo, paisaje] gloomy, dreary; **es ~ que** it's a shame ○ pity that. **-2.** *fig* [color, vestido, luz] pale. **-3.** (*antes de sust*) [humilde] poor; [sueldo] sorry, miserable.

tristeza *f* [gen] sadness; [de paisaje, día] gloominess, dreariness.

triturador *m* [de basura] waste-disposal unit; [de papeles] shredder.

triturar *vt* **-1.** [moler, desmenuzar] to crush, to grind; [papel] to shred. **-2.** [mascar] to chew.

triunfador, -ra *m y f* winner.

triunfal *adj* triumphant.

triunfar *vi* **-1.** [vencer] to win, to triumph. **-2.** [tener éxito] to succeed, to be successful.

triunfo *m* [gen] triumph; [en encuentro, elecciones] victory, win.

trivial *adj* trivial.

trivializar *vt* to trivialize.

trizas *fpl* piece (*sg*), bit (*sg*); **hacer ~ algo** [hacer añicos] to smash sthg to pieces; [desgarrar] to tear sthg to shreds; **estar hecho ~** [persona] to be shattered.

trocar *vt* **-1.** [transformar]: **~ algo (en algo)** to change sthg (into sthg). **-2.** [intercambiar] to swap.

trocear *vt* to cut up (into pieces).

trocha *f Amer* path.

troche ◆ **a troche y moche** *loc adv* haphazardly.

trofeo *m* trophy.

troglodita *m y f* **-1.** [cavernícola] cave dweller, troglodyte. **-2.** *fam* [bárbaro, tosco] roughneck.

trola *f fam* fib, lie.

trolebús *m* trolleybus.

trombón *m* [MÚS - instrumento] trombone; [- músico] trombonist.

trombosis *f inv* thrombosis.

trompa *f* **-1.** MÚS horn. **-2.** [de elefante] trunk; [de oso hormiguero] snout. **-3.** *fam* [borrachera]: **coger ○ pillar una ~** to get plastered.

trompazo *m* bang.

trompear *vt Amer fam* to punch. ◆ **trompearse** *vpr Amer fam* to have a fight.

trompeta *f* trumpet.

trompetista *m y f* trumpeter.

trompicón *m* [tropezón] stumble; **a trompicones** in fits and starts.

trompo *m* spinning top.

tronado, -da *adj fam* [radio etc] old, broken-down. ◆ **tronada** *f* thunderstorm.

tronar *v impers & vi* to thunder. ◆ **tronarse** *vpr Amer fam* to shoot o.s.

tronchar *vt* [partir] to snap. ◆ **troncharse** *vpr fam*: **~se (de risa)** to split one's sides laughing.

tronco *m* ANAT & BOT trunk; [talado y sin ramas] log; **dormir como un ~**, **estar hecho un ~** to sleep like a log.

tronera *f* **-1.** ARQUIT & HIST embrasure. **-2.** [en billar] pocket.

trono *m* throne.

tropa *f* (*gen pl*) MIL troops (*pl*).

tropel *m* [de personas] mob, crowd.

tropero *m Amer* cowboy.

tropezar *vi* [con pie]: ~ **(con)** to trip o stumble (on). ◆ **tropezarse** *vpr fam* [encontrarse] to bump into each other; ~**se con alguien** to bump into sb. ◆ **tropezar con** *vi* [problema, persona] to run into, to come across.

tropezón *m* **-1.** [tropiezo] trip, stumble; **dar un** ~ to trip up, to stumble. **-2.** *fig* [desacierto] **slip-up.** ◆ **tropezones** *mpl* CULIN small chunks of meat.

tropical *adj* tropical.

trópico *m* tropic.

tropiezo *m* **-1.** [tropezón] trip, stumble; **dar un** ~ to trip up, to stumble. **-2.** *fig* [equivocación] **slip-up. -3.** [revés] setback.

troquel *m* [molde] mould, die.

trotamundos *m y f inv* globe-trotter.

trotar *vi* to trot; *fam fig* [andar mucho] to dash o run around.

trote *m* [de caballo] trot; **al** ~ at a trot.

troupe [trup, 'trupe] (*pl* **troupes**) *f* troupe.

trovador *m* troubadour.

trozo *m* [gen] piece; [de obra, película] extract; **cortar algo a** ~**s** to cut sthg into pieces.

trucar *vt* to doctor; [motor] to soup up.

trucha *f* [pez] trout.

truco *m* **-1.** [trampa, engaño] trick. **-2.** [habilidad, técnica] knack; **coger el** ~ to get the knack; ~ **publicitario** advertising gimmick.

truculento, -ta *adj* horrifying, terrifying.

trueno *m* METEOR clap of thunder, thunder (U).

trueque *m* **-1.** COM & HIST barter. **-2.** [intercambio] exchange, swap.

trufa *f* [hongo, bombón] truffle.

truhán, -ana *m y f* rogue, crook.

truncar *vt* [frustrar - vida, carrera] to cut short; [- planes, ilusiones] to spoil, to ruin.

trusa *f Amer* **-1.** [calzoncillos] underpants (*pl*). **-2.** [bragas] knickers (*pl*).

tu (*pl* **tus**) *adj poses* (*antes de sust*) your.

tú *pron pers* you; **es más alta que** ~ she's taller than you; **de** ~ **a** ~ [lucha] evenly matched; **hablar** o **tratar de** ~ **a alguien** to address sb as "tú".

tubérculo *m* tuber, root vegetable.

tuberculosis *f inv* tuberculosis.

tubería *f* **-1.** [cañerías] pipes (*pl*), pipework. **-2.** [tubo] pipe.

tubo *m* **-1.** [tubería] pipe; ~ **de escape** AUTOM exhaust (pipe); ~ **del desagüe** drainpipe. **-2.** [recipiente] tube; ~ **de ensayo** test tube. **-3.** ANAT tract; ~ **digestivo** digestive tract.

tuerca *f* nut.

tuerto, -ta *adj* [sin un ojo] one-eyed; [ciego de un ojo] blind in one eye.

tuétano *m* ANAT (bone) marrow.

tufillo *m* whiff.

tufo *m* [mal olor] stench.

tugurio *m* hovel.

tul *m* tulle.

tulipa *f* [tulipán] tulip.

tulipán *m* tulip.

tullido, -da ◇ *adj* crippled. ◇ *m y f* cripple, disabled person.

tumba *f* grave, tomb; **ser (como) una** ~ to be as silent as the grave.

tumbar *vt* [derribar] to knock over o down. ◆ **tumbarse** *vpr* [acostarse] to lie down.

tumbo *m* jolt, jerk.

tumbona *f* [en la playa] deck chair; [en el jardín] (sun) lounger.

tumor *m* tumour.

tumulto *m* **-1.** [disturbio] riot, disturbance. **-2.** [alboroto] uproar, tumult.

tumultuoso, -sa *adj* **-1.** [conflictivo] tumultuous. **-2.** [turbulento] rough, stormy.

tuna *f* → **tuno.**

tunante, -ta *m y f* crook, scoundrel.

tunda *f fam* [paliza] thrashing.

túnel *m* tunnel. ◆ **túnel de lavado** *m* AUTOM car wash.

Túnez -1. [capital] Tunis. **-2.** [país] Tunisia.

túnica *f* tunic.

Tunicia Tunisia.

tuno, -na *m y f* rogue, scoundrel. ◆ **tuna** *f* group of student minstrels.

tuntún ◆ **al tuntún** *loc adv* without thinking.

tupé *m* [cabello] quiff.

tupido, -da *adj* thick, dense.

turba *f* **-1.** [combustible] peat, turf. **-2.** [muchedumbre] mob.

turbación *f* **-1.** [desconcierto] upset, disturbance. **-2.** [azoramiento] embarrassment.

turbante *m* turban.

turbar *vt* **-1.** [alterar] to disturb. **-2.** [emocionar] to upset. **-3.** [desconcertar] to trouble, to disconcert. ◆ **turbarse** *vpr* [emocionarse] to get upset.

turbina *f* turbine.

turbio, -bia *adj* **-1.** [agua etc] cloudy. **-2.** [vista] blurred. **-3.** *fig* [negocio etc] shady. **-4.** *fig* [época etc] turbulent.

turbulencia *f* **-1.** [de fluido] turbulence. **-2.** [alboroto] uproar, clamour.

turbulento, -ta *adj* **-1.** [gen] turbulent. **-2.** [revoltoso] unruly, rebellious.

turco, -ca ◇ *adj* Turkish. ◇ *m y f* [persona] Turk. ◆ **turco** *m* [lengua] Turkish.

turismo *m* **-1.** [gen] tourism; **hacer ~ (por)** to go touring (round). **-2.** AUTOM private car.

turista *m y f* tourist.

turístico, -ca *adj* tourist (*antes de sust*).

turnarse *vpr*: **~ (con alguien)** to take turns (with sb).

turno *m* **-1.** [tanda] turn, go. **-2.** [de trabajo] shift; **~ de día/noche** day/night shift.

turquesa ◇ *f* [mineral] turquoise. ◇ *adj inv* [color] turquoise. ◇ *m* [color] turquoise.

Turquía Turkey.

turrón *m Christmas sweet similar to marzipan or nougat, made with almonds and honey.*

tururú *interj fam*: **¡~!** you must be joking!

tute *m* [juego] *card game similar to whist.*

tutear *vt* to address as "tú". ◆ **tutearse** *vpr* to address each other as "tú".

tutela *f* **-1.** DER guardianship. **-2.** [cargo]: **~ (de)** responsibility (for); **bajo la ~ de** under the protection of.

tutelar ◇ *adj* DER tutelary. ◇ *vt* to act as guardian to.

tutor, -ra *m y f* **-1.** DER guardian. **-2.** [profesor - privado] tutor; [- de un curso] form teacher.

tutoría *f* DER guardianship.

tutú (*pl* **tutús**) *m* tutu.

tuviera *etc* → **tener**.

tuyo, -ya ◇ *adj poses* yours; **este libro es ~** this book is yours; **un amigo ~** a friend of yours; **no es asunto ~** it's none of your business. ◇ *pron poses*: **el ~** yours; **el ~ es rojo** yours is red; **ésta es la tuya** *fam* this is the chance you've been waiting for; **lo ~ es el teatro** [lo que haces bien] you should be on the stage; **los ~s** *fam* [tu familia] your folks; [tu bando] your lot.

TV (*abrev de* **televisión**) *f* TV.

TV3 (*abrev de* **Televisión de Cataluña, SA**) *f Catalan television channel.*

TVE (*abrev de* **Televisión Española**) *f Spanish state television network.*

TVG (*abrev de* **Televisión de Galicia**) *f Galician television channel.*

TVV (*abrev de* **Televisión Valenciana, SA**) *f Valencian television channel.*

u¹, U *f* [letra] u, U.

u² *conj* or; *ver también* **o².**

ubicación *f* position, location.

ubicar *vt* to place, to position; [edificio etc] to locate. ◆ **ubicarse** *vpr* [edificio etc] to be situated.

ubre *f* udder.

Ucrania the Ukraine.

Ud., Vd. *abrev de* **usted.**

Uds., Vds. *abrev de* **ustedes.**

UEFA (*abrev de* **Unión de Asociaciones Europeas de Fútbol**) *f* UEFA.

ufanarse *vpr*: **~ de** to boast about.

ufano, -na *adj* **-1.** [satisfecho] proud, pleased. **-2.** [engreído] boastful, conceited.

Uganda Uganda.

UGT (*abrev de* **Unión General de los Trabajadores**) *f major socialist Spanish trade union.*

UHF (*abrev de* **ultra high frequency**) *f* UHF.

ujier (*pl* **ujieres**) *m* usher.

újule *interj Amer*: **¡~!** wow!

úlcera *f* MED ulcer.

ulcerar *vt* to ulcerate. ◆ **ulcerarse** *vpr* MED to ulcerate.

ulterior *adj culto* [en el tiempo] subsequent, ulterior.

ulteriormente *adv culto* subsequently.

ultimador, -ra *m y f Amer* killer.

últimamente *adv* recently.

ultimar *vt* **-1.** [gen] to conclude, to complete. **-2.** *Amer* [matar] to kill.

ultimátum (*pl* **ultimátums** ○ **ultimatos**) *m* ultimatum.

último, -ma ◇ *adj* **-1.** [gen] last; **por ~** lastly, finally. **-2.** [más reciente] latest, most recent. **-3.** [más remoto] furthest, most remote. **-4.** [más bajo] bottom. **-5.** [más alto] top. **-6.** [de más atrás] back. ◇ *m y f* **-1.** [en fila, carrera etc]: **el ~** the last (one); **llegar el ~** to come last. **-2.**

(*en comparaciones, enumeraciones*): **éste** ~
... the latter ....

ultra *m y f* POLÍT right-wing extremist.

ultraderecha *f* extreme right (wing).

ultraizquierda *f* extreme left (wing).

ultrajar *vt* to insult, to offend.

ultraje *m* insult.

ultramar *m* overseas (*pl*); **de** ~ overseas (*antes de sust*).

ultramarino, -na *adj* overseas (*antes de sust*). ◆ **ultramarinos** *mpl* **-1.** [comestibles] groceries. **-2.** [tienda] grocer's (shop) (*sg*).

ultranza ◆ **a ultranza** *loc adv* **-1.** [con decisión] to the death. **-2.** [acérrimamente] out-and-out.

ultrasonido *m* ultrasound.

ultratumba *f*: **de** ~ from beyond the grave.

ultravioleta *adj inv* ultraviolet.

ulular *vi* **-1.** [viento, lobo] to howl. **-2.** [búho] to hoot.

umbilical *adj* → **cordón**.

umbral *m* **-1.** [gen] threshold. **-2.** *fig* [límite] bounds (*pl*), realms (*pl*).

un, una ◇ *art* (*antes de sust femenino que empiece por "a" o "ha" tónica:* **un**) a, an (*ante sonido vocálico*); ~ **hombre/coche** a man/car; **una mujer/mesa** a woman/table; ~ **águila/hacha** an eagle/axe; **una hora** an hour. ◇ *adj* → **uno**.

unánime *adj* unanimous.

unanimidad *f* unanimity; **por** ~ unanimously.

unción *f* unction.

undécimo, -ma *núm* eleventh.

UNED (*abrev de* **Universidad Nacional de Educación a Distancia**) *f Spanish open university.*

ungüento *m* ointment.

únicamente *adv* only, solely.

único, -ca *adj* **-1.** [sólo] only; **es lo** ~ **que quiero** it's all I want. **-2.** [excepcional] unique. **-3.** [precio, función, razón] single.

unicornio *m* unicorn.

unidad *f* **-1.** [gen, MAT & MIL] unit; **25 pesetas la** ~ 25 pesetas each; ~ **central de proceso** INFORM central processing unit; ~ **de disco** INFORM disk drive. **-2.** [cohesión, acuerdo] unity.

unido, -da *adj* united; [familia, amigo] close.

unifamiliar *adj* detached.

unificar *vt* **-1.** [unir] to unite, to join; [países] to unify. **-2.** [uniformar] to standardize.

uniformar *vt* **-1.** [igualar] to standardize. **-2.** [poner uniforme] to put into uniform.

uniforme ◇ *adj* uniform; [superficie] even. ◇ *m* uniform.

uniformidad *f* uniformity; [de superficie] evenness.

unión *f* **-1.** [gen] union; **en** ~ **de** together with. **-2.** [suma, adherimiento] joining together. **-3.** TECN join, joint.

unir *vt* **-1.** [pedazos, habitaciones etc] to join. **-2.** [empresas, estados, facciones] to unite. **-3.** [comunicar - ciudades etc] to link. **-4.** [suj: amistad, circunstancias etc] to bind. **-5.** [casar] to join, to marry. **-6.** [combinar] to combine. **-7.** [mezclar] to mix ○ blend in. ◆ **unirse** *vpr* **-1.** [gen] to join together; ~**se a algo** to join sthg. **-2.** [casarse]: ~**se en matrimonio** to be joined in wedlock.

unisexo, unisex *adj inv* unisex.

unísono ◆ **al unísono** *loc adv* in unison.

unitario, -ria *adj* **-1.** [de una unidad - estado, nación] single; [- precio] unit (*antes de sust*). **-2.** POLÍT unitarian.

universal *adj* **-1.** [gen] universal. **-2.** [mundial] world (*antes de sust*).

universidad *f* university.

universitario, -ria ◇ *adj* university (*antes de sust*). ◇ *m y f* [estudiante] university student.

universo *m* **-1.** ASTRON universe. **-2.** *fig* [mundo] world.

unívoco, -ca *adj* univocal, unambiguous.

uno, una ◇ *adj* (*antes de sust masculino sg:* **un**) **-1.** [indefinido] one; **un día volveré** one ○ some day I'll return; **había** ~**s coches mal aparcados** there were some badly parked cars; **había** ~**s 12 muchachos** there were about ○ some 12 boys there. **-2.** [numeral] one; **un hombre, un voto** one man, one vote; **la fila** ~ row one. ◇ *pron* **-1.** [indefinido] one; **coge** ~ take one; ~ **de vosotros** one of you; ~**s ... otros ...** some ... others ...; ~ **a otro**, ~**s a otros** each other, one another; ~ **y otro** both; ~**s y otros** all of them. **-2.** *fam* [cierta persona] someone, somebody; **hablé con** ~ **que te conoce** I spoke to someone who knows you; **me lo han contado** ~**s** certain people told me so. **-3.** [yo] one; ~ **ya no está para estos trotes** one isn't really up to this sort of thing any more. **-4.** *loc*: **a una** [en armonía, a la vez] together; **de** ~ **en** ~, ~ **a** ~, ~

por ~ one by one; **juntar varias cosas en una** to combine several things into one; **lo ~ por lo otro** it all evens out in the end; **más de ~** many people; **una de dos** it's either one thing or the other; ~**s cuantos** a few; **una y no más** once bitten, twice shy. ◆ **uno** m [número] (number) one; **el ~** number one; *ver también* **seis**. ◆ **una** f [hora]: **la una** one o'clock.

untar vt -1. [pan, tostada]: ~ **(con)** to spread (with); [piel, cara etc] to smear (with). -2. [máquina, bisagra etc] to grease.

untuoso, -sa adj greasy, oily.

uña f -1. [de mano] fingernail, nail; **ser ~ y carne** to be as thick as thieves. -2. [de pie] toenail. -3. [garra] claw.

UPG (abrev de **Unión del Pueblo Gallego**) f Galician nationalist party.

UPN (abrev de **Unión del Pueblo Navarro**) f Navarrese nationalist party.

uralita® f CONSTR material made of asbestos and cement, usually corrugated and used mainly for roofing.

uranio m uranium.

Urano Uranus.

urbanidad f politeness, courtesy.

urbanismo m town planning.

urbanización f -1. [acción] urbanization. -2. [zona residencial] (housing) estate.

urbanizar vt to develop, to urbanize.

urbano, -na adj urban, city (antes de sust).

urbe f large city.

urdir vt -1. [planear] to plot, to forge. -2. [hilos] to warp.

urgencia f -1. [cualidad] urgency. -2. [necesidad] urgent need; **en caso de ~** in case of emergency. ◆ **urgencias** fpl MED casualty (department) (sg).

urgente adj -1. [apremiante] urgent. -2. [correo] express.

urgir vi to be urgently necessary; **me urge hacerlo** I urgently need to do it.

urinario, -ria adj urinary. ◆ **urinario** m urinal, comfort station Am.

urna f -1. [vasija] urn. -2. [caja de cristal] glass case. -3. [para votar] ballot box.

urraca f magpie.

URSS (abrev de **Unión de Repúblicas Socialistas Soviéticas**) f USSR.

urticaria f nettle rash.

Uruguay: **(el) ~** Uruguay.

uruguayo, -ya adj, m y f Uruguayan.

usado, -da adj -1. [utilizado] used; **muy ~** widely-used. -2. [gastado] worn-out, worn.

usanza f: **a la vieja ~** in the old way o style.

usar vt -1. [gen] to use. -2. [prenda] to wear. ◆ **usarse** vpr -1. [emplearse] to be used. -2. [estar de moda] to be worn.

uso m -1. [gen] use; **al ~** fashionable; **al ~ andaluz** in the Andalusian style. -2. (gen pl) [costumbre] custom. -3. LING usage. -4. [desgaste] wear and tear.

usted pron pers -1. [tratamiento de respeto - sg] you; [- pl]: ~**es** you (pl); **contesten ~es a las preguntas** please answer the questions; **me gustaría hablar con ~** I'd like to talk to you. -2. [tratamiento de respeto - posesivo]: **de ~/~es** yours.

usual adj usual.

usuario, -ria m y f user.

usufructo m DER usufruct, use.

usura f usury.

usurero, -ra m y f usurer.

usurpar vt to usurp.

utensilio m [gen] tool, implement; CULIN utensil; ~**s de pesca** fishing tackle.

útero m womb, uterus MED.

útil ◇ adj [beneficioso, aprovechable] useful. ◇ m (gen pl) [herramienta] tool; AGR implement.

utilidad f -1. [cualidad] usefulness. -2. [beneficio] profit.

utilitario, -ria adj AUTOM utility. ◆ **utilitario** m AUTOM utility car.

utilización f use.

utilizar vt [gen] to use.

utopía f utopia.

utópico, -ca adj utopian.

uva f grape; **estar de mala ~** to be in a bad mood; **tener mala ~** to be a nasty piece of work; ~**s de la suerte** grapes eaten for good luck as midnight chimes on New Year's Eve.

UVI (abrev de **unidad de vigilancia intensiva**) f ICU.

uy interj: ¡~! ahh!, oh!

v, V ['uße] *f* [letra] v, V. ◆ **v doble** *f* W.

v. = **vid.**

va → **ir.**

vaca *f* **-1.** [animal] cow. **-2.** [carne] beef.

vacaciones *fpl* holiday (*sg*), holidays *Br*, vacation (*sg*) *Am*; **estar/irse de** ~ to be/go on holiday.

vacante ◇ *adj* vacant. ◇ *f* vacancy.

vaciar *vt* **-1.** [gen]: ~ **algo (de)** to empty sthg (of). **-2.** [dejar hueco] to hollow (out). **-3.** ARTE to cast, to mould.

vacilación *f* **-1.** [duda] hesitation; [al elegir] indecision. **-2.** [oscilación] swaying; [de la luz] flickering.

vacilante *adj* **-1.** [gen] hesitant; [al elegir] indecisive. **-2.** [luz] flickering; [pulso] irregular; [paso] swaying, unsteady.

vacilar *vi* **-1.** [dudar] to hesitate; [al elegir] to be indecisive. **-2.** [voz, principios, régimen] to falter. **-3.** [fluctuar - luz] to flicker; [- pulso] to be irregular. **-4.** [tambalearse] to wobble, to sway. **-5.** *fam* [chulear] to swank. **-6.** *fam* [bromear] to take the mickey.

vacilón, -ona *fam m y f* **-1.** [chulo] show-off. **-2.** [bromista] tease. ◆ **vacilón** *m Amer fam* [fiesta] party.

vacío, -a *adj* empty. ◆ **vacío** *m* **-1.** FÍS vacuum; **envasar al** ~ to vacuum-pack. **-2.** [abismo, carencia] void. **-3.** [hueco] space, gap.

vacuna *f* vaccine.

vacunar *vt* to vaccinate.

vacuno, -na *adj* bovine.

vadear *vt* to ford; *fig* to overcome.

vado *m* **-1.** [en acera] lowered kerb; "~ **permanente**" "keep clear". **-2.** [de río] ford.

vagabundear *vi* [vagar]: ~ **(por)** to wander, to roam.

vagabundo, -da ◇ *adj* [persona] vagrant; [perro] stray. ◇ *m y f* tramp, bum *Am*.

vagancia *f* **-1.** [holgazanería] laziness, idleness. **-2.** [vagabundeo] vagrancy.

vagar *vi*: ~ **(por)** to wander, to roam.

vagina *f* vagina.

vago, -ga *adj* **-1.** [perezoso] lazy, idle. **-2.** [impreciso] vague.

vagón *m* [de pasajeros] carriage; [de mercancías] wagon.

vagoneta *f* wagon.

vaguedad *f* **-1.** [cualidad] vagueness. **-2.** [dicho] vague remark.

vahído *m* blackout, fainting fit.

vaho *m* **-1.** [vapor] steam. **-2.** [aliento] breath.

vaina *f* **-1.** [gen] sheath. **-2.** [BOT - envoltura] pod. **-3.** *Amer fam* [engreído] pain in the neck.

vainilla *f* vanilla.

vaivén *m* **-1.** [balanceo - de barco] swaying, rocking; [- de péndulo, columpio] swinging. **-2.** [altibajo] ups-and-downs (*pl*).

vajilla *f* crockery; **una** ~ a dinner service.

vale ◇ *m* **-1.** [bono] coupon, voucher. **-2.** [entrada gratuita] free ticket. **-3.** [comprobante] receipt. **-4.** [pagaré] I.O.U. ◇ *interj* → **valer.**

valedero, -ra *adj* valid.

valenciano, -na *adj, m y f* [de Valencia] Valencian.

valentía *f* [valor] bravery.

valer ◇ *vt* **-1.** [costar - precio] to cost; [tener un valor de] to be worth; **¿cuánto vale?** [de precio] how much does it cost?, how much is it? **-2.** [suponer] to earn. **-3.** [merecer] to deserve, to be worth. **-4.** [equivaler] to be equivalent ○ equal to. ◇ *vi* **-1.** [merecer aprecio] to be worthy; **hacerse** ~ to show one's worth. **-2.** [servir]: ~ **para algo** to be for sthg; **eso aún vale** you can still use that; **¿para qué vale?** what's it for? **-3.** [ser válido] to be valid; [en juegos] to be allowed. **-4.** [ayudar] to help, to be of use. **-5.** [tener calidad] to be of worth; **no** ~ **nada** to be worthless ○ useless. **-6.** [equivaler]: ~ **por** to be worth. **-7.** *loc*: **más vale tarde que nunca** better late than never; **más vale que te calles/vayas** it would be better if you shut up/left; **¿vale?** okay?, all right?; **¡vale!** okay!, all right! ◆ **valerse** *vpr* **-1.** [servirse]: ~**se de algo/alguien** to use sthg/sb. **-2.** [desenvolverse]: ~**se (por sí mismo)** to manage on one's own.

valeroso, -sa *adj* brave, courageous.

valía *f* value, worth.

validar *vt* to validate.

validez *f* validity; **dar** ~ **a** to validate.

válido, -da *adj* valid.

valiente *adj* [valeroso] brave.

valija *f* **-1.** [maleta] case, suitcase; **~ diplomática** diplomatic bag. **-2.** [de correos] mailbag.

valioso, -sa *adj* **-1.** [gen] valuable. **-2.** [intento, esfuerzo] worthy.

valla *f* **-1.** [cerca] fence. **-2.** DEP hurdle. ◆ **valla publicitaria** *f* billboard, hoarding.

vallar *vt* to put a fence round.

valle *m* valley.

valor *m* **-1.** [gen, MAT & MÚS] value; **joyas por ~ de ...** jewels worth ...; **sin ~** worthless. **-2.** [importancia] importance; **dar ~ a** to give ○ attach importance to; **quitar ~ a algo** to take away from sthg. **-3.** [valentía] bravery. ◆ **valores** *mpl* **-1.** [principios] values. **-2.** FIN securities, bonds; **~es en cartera** investments.

valoración *f* **-1.** [de precio, pérdidas] valuation. **-2.** [de mérito, cualidad, ventajas] evaluation, assessment.

valorar *vt* **-1.** [tasar, apreciar] to value. **-2.** [evaluar] to evaluate, to assess.

vals (*pl* **valses**) *m* waltz.

valuar *vt* to value.

válvula *f* valve. ◆ **válvula de escape** *f* *fig* means of letting off steam.

vampiresa *f* *fam* vamp, femme fatale.

vampiro *m* [personaje] vampire.

vanagloriarse *vpr:* **~ (de)** to boast (about), to show off (about).

vandalismo *m* vandalism.

vanguardia *f* **-1.** MIL vanguard; **ir a la ~ de** *fig* to be at the forefront of. **-2.** [cultural] avant-garde, vanguard.

vanidad *f* **-1.** [orgullo] vanity. **-2.** [inutilidad] futility.

vanidoso, -sa *adj* vain, conceited.

vano, -na *adj* **-1.** [gen] vain; **en ~** in vain. **-2.** [vacío, superficial] shallow, superficial.

vapor *m* **-1.** [emanación] vapour; [de agua] steam; **al ~** CULIN steamed; **de ~** [máquina etc] steam (*antes de sust*); **~ de agua** FÍS & QUÍM water vapour. **-2.** [barco] steamship.

vaporizador *m* **-1.** [pulverizador] spray. **-2.** [para evaporar] vaporizer.

vaporoso, -sa *adj* **-1.** [con vapor - ducha, baño] steamy; [- cielo] hazy, misty. **-2.** [fino - tela etc] diaphanous.

vapulear *vt* to beat, to thrash; *fig* to slate.

vaquero, -ra ◇ *adj* cowboy (*antes de sust*). ◇ *m y f* [persona] cowboy (*f* cowgirl), cowherd. ◆ **vaqueros** *mpl* [pantalón] jeans.

vara *f* **-1.** [rama, palo] stick. **-2.** [de metal etc] rod. **-3.** [insignia] staff.

variable *adj* changeable, variable.

variación *f* variation; [del tiempo] change.

variado, -da *adj* varied; [galletas, bombones] assorted.

variante ◇ *adj* variant. ◇ *f* **-1.** [variación] variation; [versión] version. **-2.** AUTOM by-pass.

variar ◇ *vt* **-1.** [modificar] to alter, to change. **-2.** [dar variedad] to vary. ◇ *vi* [cambiar]: **para ~ irón** (just) for a change.

varicela *f* chickenpox.

varicoso, -sa *adj* varicose.

variedad *f* variety. ◆ **variedades, variétés** *fpl* TEATR variety (*U*), music hall (*U*).

varilla *f* **-1.** [barra larga] rod, stick. **-2.** [tira larga - de abanico, paraguas] spoke, rib; [- de gafas] arm; [- de corsé] bone, stay.

vario, -ria *adj* [variado] varied, different; (*pl*) various, several. ◆ **varios, -rias** *pron pl* several.

variopinto, -ta *adj* diverse.

varita *f* wand; **~ mágica** magic wand.

variz *f* (*gen pl*) varicose vein.

varón *m* [hombre] male, man; [chico] boy.

varonil *adj* masculine, male.

Varsovia Warsaw.

vasallo, -lla *m y f* [siervo] vassal.

vasco, -ca *adj, m y f* Basque. ◆ **vasco** *m* [lengua] Basque.

vascuence *m* [lengua] Basque.

vasectomía *f* vasectomy.

vaselina® *f* Vaseline®.

vasija *f* [de barro] earthenware vessel.

vaso *m* **-1.** [recipiente, contenido] glass; **un ~ de plástico** a plastic cup. **-2.** ANAT vessel; **~s sanguíneos** blood vessels.

vástago *m* **-1.** [descendiente] offspring (*U*). **-2.** [brote] shoot. **-3.** [varilla] rod.

vasto, -ta *adj* vast.

váter = **wáter**.

vaticinar *vt* to prophesy, to predict.

vatio, watio ['batio] *m* watt.

vaya ◇ *v* → **ir**. ◇ *interj* **-1.** [sorpresa]: **¡~!** well! **-2.** [énfasis]: **¡~ moto!** what a motorbike!

VB *abrev de* **visto bueno**.

Vd. = **Ud**.

Vda. *abrev de* **viuda**.

Vds. = **Uds**.

ve → **ir**.

véase → ver.

vecinal adj [camino, impuestos] local.

vecindad f -1. [vecindario] neighbourhood. -2. [alrededores] vicinity.

vecindario m [de barrio] neighbourhood; [de población] community, inhabitants (pl).

vecino, -na ◇ adj [cercano] neighbouring. ◇ m y f -1. [de la misma casa, calle] neighbour; [de un barrio] resident. -2. [de una localidad] inhabitant.

vector m vector.

veda f -1. [prohibición] ban (on hunting and fishing); **levantar la** ~ to open the season. -2. [periodo] close season.

vedado, -da adj prohibited. ◆**vedado** m reserve.

vedar vt to prohibit.

vedette [be'ðet] (pl **vedettes**) f star.

vegetación f vegetation.

vegetal ◇ adj -1. BIOL vegetable, plant (antes de sust). -2. [sandwich] salad (antes de sust). ◇ m vegetable.

vegetar vi to vegetate.

vegetariano, -na adj, m y f vegetarian.

vehemencia f [pasión, entusiasmo] vehemence.

vehemente adj [apasionado, entusiasta] vehement.

vehículo m [gen] vehicle; [de infección] carrier.

veinte núm twenty; **los (años)** ~ the twenties; ver también seis.

veinteavo, -va núm twentieth.

veintena f -1. [veinte] twenty. -2. [aproximadamente]: **una** ~ **(de)** about twenty.

vejación f, **vejamen** m humiliation.

vejestorio m despec old fogey.

vejez f old age.

vejiga f bladder; ~ **de la bilis** gall bladder.

vela f -1. [para dar luz] candle; **estar a dos** ~**s** not to have two halfpennies to rub together. -2. [de barco] sail. -3. DEP sailing. -4. [vigilia] vigil; **pasar la noche en** ~ [adrede] to stay awake all night; [desvelado] to have a sleepless night.

velada f evening.

velado, -da adj -1. [oculto] veiled, hidden. -2. FOT blurred.

velar ◇ vi -1. [cuidar]: ~ **por** to look after, to watch over. -2. [no dormir] to stay awake. ◇ vt -1. [de noche - muerto] to keep a vigil over. -2. [ocultar] to mask, to veil. -3. FOT to blur. ◆**velarse** vpr FOT to blur.

veleidad f -1. [inconstancia] fickleness. -2. [antojo, capricho] whim, caprice.

velero m sailing boat/ship.

veleta f weather vane.

vello m -1. [pelusilla] down. -2. [pelo] hair.

velloso, -sa adj hairy.

velo m lit & fig veil.

velocidad f -1. [gen] speed; TECN velocity; **a toda** ~ at full speed; **de alta** ~ high-speed; ~ **punta** top speed. -2. AUTOM [marcha] gear; **cambiar de** ~ to change gear.

velocímetro m speedometer.

velódromo m cycle track, velodrome.

veloz adj fast, quick.

ven → venir.

vena f -1. [gen, ANAT & MIN] vein. -2. [inspiración] inspiration. -3. [don] vein, streak; **tener** ~ **de algo** to have a gift for doing sthg.

venado m ZOOL deer; CULIN venison.

vencedor, -ra ◇ adj winning, victorious. ◇ m y f winner.

vencer ◇ vt -1. [ganar] to beat, to defeat. -2. [derrotar - suj: sueño, cansancio, emoción] to overcome. -3. [aventajar]: ~ **a alguien** a ○ **en algo** to outdo sb at sthg. -4. [superar - miedo, obstáculos] to overcome; [- tentación] to resist. ◇ vi -1. [ganar] to win, to be victorious. -2. [caducar - garantía, contrato, plazo] to expire; [- deuda, pago] to fall due; [- bono] to mature. -3. [prevalecer] to prevail. ◆**vencerse** vpr [estante etc] to give way, to collapse.

vencido, -da adj -1. [derrotado] defeated; **darse por** ~ to give up. -2. [caducado - garantía, contrato, plazo] expired; [- pago, deuda] due, payable.

vencimiento m [término - de garantía, contrato, plazo] expiry; [- de pago, deuda] falling due.

venda f bandage.

vendaje m bandaging.

vendar vt to bandage; ~ **los ojos a alguien** to blindfold sb.

vendaval m gale.

vendedor, -ra m y f [gen] seller; [en tienda] shop ○ sales assistant; [de coches, seguros] salesman (f saleswoman).

vender vt lit & fig to sell; ~ **algo a** ○ **por** to sell sthg for. ◆**venderse** vpr -1. [ser vendido] to be sold ○ on sale; **"se vende"** "for sale". -2. [dejarse sobornar] to sell o.s., to be bribed.

vendimia f grape harvest.

vendrá etc → venir.

veneno *m* [gen] poison; [de serpiente, insecto] venom.

venenoso, -sa *adj* **-1.** [gen] poisonous. **-2.** *fig* [malintencionado] venomous.

venerable *adj* venerable.

venerar *vt* to venerate, to worship.

venéreo, -a *adj* venereal.

venezolano, -na *adj*, *m y f* Venezuelan.

Venezuela Venezuela.

venga *interj* ¡~! come on!

venganza *f* vengeance, revenge.

vengar *vt* to avenge. ◆ **vengarse** *vpr*: ~se (de) to take revenge (on).

vengativo, -va *adj* vengeful, vindictive.

vengo → venir.

venia *f* **-1.** [permiso] permission. **-2.** DER [perdón] pardon.

venial *adj* petty, venial.

venida *f* **-1.** [llegada] arrival. **-2.** [regreso] return.

venidero, -ra *adj* coming, future.

venir ◇ *vi* **-1.** [gen] to come; ~ a/de hacer algo to come ○ to do sthg/from doing sthg; ~ de algo [proceder, derivarse] to come from sthg; no me vengas con exigencias don't come to me making demands; el año que viene next year. **-2.** [llegar] to arrive; vino a las doce he arrived at twelve o'clock. **-3.** [hallarse] to be; su foto viene en primera página his photo is ○ appears on the front page; el texto viene en inglés the text is in English. **-4.** [acometer, sobrevenir] me viene sueño I'm getting sleepy; le vinieron ganas de reír he was seized by a desire to laugh; le vino una tremenda desgracia he suffered a great misfortune. **-5.** [ropa, calzado]: ~ a alguien to fit sb; ¿qué tal te viene? does it fit all right?; el abrigo le viene pequeño the coat is too small for her. **-6.** [convenir]: ~ bien/mal a alguien to suit/not to suit sb. **-7.** [aproximarse]: viene a costar un millón it costs almost a million. **-8.** *loc*: ¿a qué viene esto? what do you mean by that?; ~ a menos [negocio] to go downhill; [persona] to go down in the world; ~ a parar en to end in; ~ a ser to amount to. ◇ *vaux* **-1.** (*antes de gerundio*) [haber estado]: ~ haciendo algo to have been doing sthg. **-2.** (*antes de participio*) [estar]: los cambios vienen motivados por la presión de la oposición the changes have resulted from pressure on the part of the opposition. ◆ **venirse** *vpr* **-1.** [volver]: ~se (de) to come back ○ return (from). **-2.** *loc*: ~se abajo [techo,

estante etc] to collapse; [ilusiones] to be dashed.

venta *f* **-1.** [acción] sale, selling; estar en ~ to be for sale; ~ al contado cash sale; ~ a plazos sale by instalments. **-2.** (*gen pl*) [cantidad] sales (*pl*).

ventaja *f* **-1.** [hecho favorable] advantage. **-2.** [en competición] lead; llevar ~ a alguien to have a lead over sb.

ventajoso, -sa *adj* advantageous.

ventana *f* [gen & INFORM] window.

ventanilla *f* **-1.** [de vehículo, sobre] window. **-2.** [taquilla] counter.

ventilación *f* ventilation.

ventilador *m* [airear] to air. **-2.** [resolver] to clear up. **-3.** [discutir] to air. ◆ **ventilarse** *vpr* [airearse] to air.

ventilar *vt* **-1.** [airear] to air. **-2.** [resolver] to clear up. **-3.** [discutir] to air. ◆ **ventilarse** *vpr* [airearse] to air.

ventiscar, ventisquear *v impers* to blow a blizzard.

ventisquero *m* [nieve amontonada] snowdrift.

ventolera *f* [viento] gust of wind.

ventosa *f* [gen & ZOOL] sucker.

ventosidad *f* wind, flatulence.

ventoso, -sa *adj* windy.

ventrílocuo, -cua *m y f* ventriloquist.

ventura *f* **-1.** [suerte] luck; a la (buena) ~ [al azar] at random, haphazardly; [sin nada previsto] without planning ○ a fixed plan. **-2.** [casualidad] fate, fortune.

Venus Venus.

ver ◇ *vi* **-1.** [gen] to see. **-2.** *loc*: a ~ [veamos] let's see; ¿a ~? [mirando con interés] let me see; ¡a ~! [¡pues claro!] what do you expect?; [al empezar algo] right!; dejarse ~ (por un sitio) to show one's face (somewhere); eso está por ~ that remains to be seen; ya veremos we'll see. ◇ *vt* **-1.** [gen] to see; [mirar] to look at; [televisión, partido de fútbol] to watch; ¿ves algo? can you see anything?; he estado viendo tu trabajo I've been looking at your work; ya veo que estás de mal humor I can see you're in a bad mood; ¿ves lo que quiero decir? do you see what I mean?; ir a ~ lo que pasa to go and see what's going on; es una manera de ~ las cosas that's one way of looking at it; yo no lo veo tan mal I don't think it's that bad. **-2.** *loc*: eso habrá que ~lo that remains to be seen; ¡hay que ~ qué lista es! you wouldn't believe how clever she is!; no puedo verle (ni en pintura) *fam* I can't stand him; si no lo veo, no lo creo you'll never believe it; ~ venir a alguien to see what sb is up to. ◇ *m*: **estar de buen ~** to be good-looking. ◆ **verse** *vpr* **-1.** [mirarse, imaginarse] to see o.s.; **~se en el espejo** to see o.s. in the mirror. **-2.** [percibirse]: **desde aquí se ve el mar** you can see the sea from here. **-3.** [encontrarse] to meet, to see each other; **hace mucho que no nos vemos** we haven't seen each other for a long time. **-4.** [darse, suceder] to be seen. **-5.** *loc*: **vérselas y deseárselas para hacer algo** to have a real struggle doing sthg. ◆ **véase** *vpr* [en textos] see. ◆ **por lo visto, por lo que se ve** *loc adv* apparently.

vera *f* **-1.** [orilla - de río, lago] bank; [- de camino] edge, side. **-2.** *fig* [lado] side; **a la ~ de** next to.

veracidad *f* truthfulness.

veraneante *m y f* holidaymaker, (summer) vacationer *Am*.

veranear *vi*: **~ en** to spend one's summer holidays in.

veraneo *m* summer holidays (*pl*); **de ~** holiday (*antes de sust*).

veraniego, -ga *adj* summer (*antes de sust*).

verano *m* summer.

veras *fpl* truth (*U*); **de ~** [verdaderamente] really; [en serio] seriously.

veraz *adj* truthful.

verbal *adj* verbal.

verbena *f* [fiesta] street party (*on the eve of certain saints' days*).

verbo *m* GRAM verb.

verdad *f* **-1.** [gen] truth; **a decir ~** to tell the truth. **-2.** [principio aceptado] fact. **-3.** *loc*: **no te gusta, ¿~?** you don't like it, do you?; **está bueno, ¿~?** it's good, isn't it? ◆ **verdades** *fpl* [opinión sincera] true thoughts; **cantarle** o **decirle a alguien cuatro ~es** *fig* to tell sb a few home truths. ◆ **de verdad** ◇ *loc adv* **-1.** [en serio] seriously. **-2.** [realmente] really. ◇ *loc adj* [auténtico] real.

verdadero, -ra *adj* **-1.** [cierto, real] true, real; **fue un ~ lío** it was a real mess. **-2.** [sin falsificar] real. **-3.** [enfático] real.

verde ◇ *adj* **-1.** [gen] green; **poner ~ a alguien** to criticize sb. **-2.** [fruta] unripe, green. **-3.** *fig* [obsceno] blue, dirty. **-4.** *fig* [inmaduro - proyecto etc] in its early stages. ◇ *m* [color] green. ◆ **Verdes** *mpl* [partido]: **los Verdes** the Greens.

verdor *m* **-1.** [color] greenness. **-2.** [madurez] lushness.

verdugo *m* **-1.** [de preso] executioner; [que ahorca] hangman. **-2.** [pasamontañas] balaclava helmet.

verdulería *f* greengrocer's (shop).

verdulero, -ra *m y f* [tendero] greengrocer.

verdura *f* vegetables (*pl*), greens (*pl*).

vereda *f* **-1.** [senda] path. **-2.** *Amer* [acera] pavement *Br*, sidewalk *Am*.

veredicto *m* verdict.

vergonzoso, -sa *adj* **-1.** [deshonroso] shameful. **-2.** [tímido] bashful.

vergüenza *f* **-1.** [turbación] embarrassment; **dar ~** to embarrass; **¡qué ~!** how embarrassing!; **sentir ~** to feel embarrassed. **-2.** [timidez] bashfulness. **-3.** [remordimiento] shame; **sentir ~** to feel ashamed. **-4.** [dignidad] pride, dignity. **-5.** [deshonra, escándalo] disgrace; **¡es una ~!** it's disgraceful!

verídico, -ca *adj* [cierto] true, truthful.

verificar *vt* **-1.** [comprobar - verdad, autenticidad] to check, to verify. **-2.** [examinar - funcionamiento, buen estado] to check, to test. **-3.** [confirmar - fecha, cita] to confirm. **-4.** [llevar a cabo] to carry out. ◆ **verificarse** *vpr* [tener lugar] to take place.

verja *f* **-1.** [puerta] iron gate. **-2.** [valla] railings (*pl*). **-3.** [enrejado] grille.

vermú (*pl* vermús), **vermut** (*pl* vermuts) *m* **-1.** [bebida] vermouth. **-2.** *Amer* CIN & TEATR matinee.

vernáculo, -la *adj* vernacular.

verosímil *adj* **-1.** [creíble] believable, credible. **-2.** [probable] likely, probable.

verruga *f* wart.

versado, -da *adj*: **~ (en)** versed (in).

versar *vi*: **~ sobre** to be about, to deal with.

versátil *adj* **-1.** [voluble] fickle. **-2.** (*considerado incorrecto*) [polifacético] versatile.

versículo *m* verse.

versión *f* [gen] version; [en música pop] cover version; **~ original** CIN original (version).

verso *m* **-1.** [género] verse. **-2.** [unidad rítmica] line (*of poetry*). **-3.** [poema] poem.

vértebra *f* vertebra.

vertebrado, -da *adj* vertebrate. ◆ **vertebrados** *mpl* ZOOL vertebrates.

vertedero *m* [de basuras] rubbish tip o dump; [de agua] overflow.

verter *vt* **-1.** [derramar] to spill. **-2.** [vaciar - líquido] to pour (out); [- recipiente] to empty. **-3.** [tirar - basura, residuos] to

dump. **-4.** *fig* [decir] to tell. ◆ **verterse**
vpr [derramarse] to spill.

vertical ◇ *adj* GEOM vertical; [derecho]
upright. ◇ *f* GEOM vertical.

vértice *m* [gen] vertex; [de cono] apex.

vertido *m* **-1.** (*gen pl*) [residuo] waste
(*U*). **-2.** [acción] dumping.

vertiente *f* **-1.** [pendiente] slope. **-2.** *fig*
[aspecto] side, aspect.

vertiginoso, -sa *adj* **-1.** [mareante] dizzy. **-2.** *fig* [raudo] giddy.

vértigo *m* [enfermedad] vertigo; [mareo]
dizziness; **trepar me da ~** climbing
makes me dizzy.

vesícula *f*: **~ biliar** gall bladder.

vespertino, -na *adj* evening (*antes de
sust*).

vestíbulo *m* [de casa] (entrance) hall;
[de hotel, oficina] lobby, foyer.

vestido, -da *adj* dressed. ◆ **vestido** *m*
-1. [indumentaria] clothes (*pl*). **-2.**
[prenda femenina] dress.

vestidura *f* (*gen pl*) clothes (*pl*); RELIG
vestments (*pl*); **rasgarse las ~s** to
make a fuss.

vestigio *m* vestige; *fig* sign, trace.

vestimenta *f* clothes (*pl*), wardrobe.

vestir ◇ *vt* **-1.** [gen] to dress. **-2.** [llevar
puesto] to wear. **-3.** [cubrir] to cover.
-4. *fig* [encubrir]: **~ algo de** to invest
sthg with. ◇ *vi* **-1.** [llevar ropa] to
dress. **-2.** *fig* [estar bien visto] to be the
done thing. ◆ **vestirse** *vpr* **-1.** [ponerse
ropa] to get dressed, to dress. **-2.**
[adquirir ropa]: **~se en** to buy one's
clothes at.

vestuario *m* **-1.** [vestimenta] clothes
(*pl*), wardrobe; TEATR costumes (*pl*).
-2. [guardarropa] cloakroom. **-3.** [para
cambiarse] changing room; [de actores]
dressing room.

veta *f* **-1.** [filón] vein, seam. **-2.** [faja, lis-
ta] grain.

vetar *vt* to veto.

veterano, -na *adj*, *m y f* veteran.

veterinario, -ria ◇ *adj* veterinary. ◇ *m
y f* [persona] vet, veterinary surgeon.
◆ **veterinaria** *f* [ciencia] veterinary science O medicine.

veto *m* veto; **poner ~ a algo** to veto
sthg.

vetusto, -ta *adj culto* ancient, very old.

vez *f* **-1.** [gen] time; **una ~** once; **dos
veces** twice; **tres veces** three times;
¿has estado allí alguna ~? have you
ever been there?; **a la ~ (que)** at the
same time (as); **cada ~ (que)** every
time; **cada ~ más** more and more;

cada ~ menos less and less; **cada ~ la
veo más feliz** she seems happier and
happier; **de una ~** in one go; **de una ~
para siempre** O **por todas** once and for
all; **muchas veces** often, a lot; **otra ~**
again; **pocas veces, rara ~** rarely, seldom; **por última ~** for the last time;
una ~ más once again; **una y otra ~**
time and again; **érase una ~** once
upon a time. **-2.** [turno] turn. ◆ **a veces, algunas veces** *loc adv* sometimes,
at times. ◆ **de vez en cuando** *loc adv*
from time to time, now and again.
◆ **en vez de** *loc prep* instead of. ◆ **tal
vez** *loc adv* perhaps, maybe. ◆ **una vez
que** *loc conj* once, after.

VHF (*abrev de* **very high frequency**) *f*
VHF.

VHS (*abrev de* **video home system**) *m*
VHS.

vía ◇ *f* **-1.** [medio de transporte] route;
por ~ aérea [gen] by air; [correo] (by)
airmail; **por ~ marítima** by sea; **por ~
terrestre** overland, by land; **~ fluvial**
waterway. **-2.** [calzada, calle] road; **~
pública** public thoroughfare. **-3.** [FE-
RROC - raíl] rails (*pl*), track; [- andén]
platform; **~ férrea** [ruta] railway line.
-4. [proceso]: **estar en ~s de** to be in
the process of; **país en ~s de desarrollo** developing country; **una especie en
~s de extinción** an endangered species. **-5.** ANAT tract. **-6.** [opción] channel, path; **por ~ oficial/judicial** through
official channels/the courts. **-7.** [cami-
no] way; **dar ~ libre** [dejar paso] to give
way; [dar libertad de acción] to give a
free rein. **-8.** DER procedure. ◇ *prep*
via. ◆ **Vía Láctea** *f* Milky Way.

viabilidad *f* viability.

viable *adj fig* [posible] viable.

viaducto *m* viaduct.

viajante *m y f* travelling salesperson.

viajar *vi* **-1.** [trasladarse, irse]: **~ (en)** to
travel (by). **-2.** [circular] to run.

viaje *m* **-1.** [gen] journey, trip; [en barco]
voyage; **¡buen ~!** have a good journey
O trip!; **estar/ir de ~** to be/go away
(on a trip); **hay 11 días de ~** it's an
11-day journey; **~ de ida/de vuelta**
outward/return journey; **~ de ida y
vuelta** return journey O trip; **~ de no-
vios** honeymoon. **-2.** *fig* [recorrido] trip.
◆ **viajes** *mpl* [singladuras] travels.

viajero, -ra ◇ *adj* [persona] travelling;
[ave] migratory. ◇ *m y f* [gen] traveller;
[en transporte público] passenger.

vial *adj* road (*antes de sust*).

viandante *m y f* **-1.** [peatón] pedestrian. **-2.** [transeúnte] passer-by.

viario, -ria *adj* road (*antes de sust*).

víbora *f* viper.

vibración *f* vibration.

vibrante *adj* **-1.** [oscilante] vibrating. **-2.** *fig* [emocionante] vibrant.

vibrar *vi* **-1.** [oscilar] to vibrate. **-2.** *fig* [voz, rodillas etc] to shake. **-3.** *fig* [público] to get excited.

vicaría *f* [residencia] vicarage.

vicario *m* vicar.

vicepresidente, -ta *m y f* [de país, asociación] vice-president; [de comité, empresa] vice-chairman.

viceversa *adv* vice versa.

viciado, -da *adj* [maloliente] foul; [contaminado] polluted.

viciar *vt* **-1.** [pervertir] to corrupt. **-2.** [contaminar] to pollute. **-3.** [adulterar] to adulterate. ◆ **viciarse** *vpr* **-1.** [pervertirse] to become ○ get corrupted; [enviciarse] to take to vice. **-2.** [contaminarse] to become polluted.

vicio *m* **-1.** [mala costumbre] bad habit, vice. **-2.** [libertinaje] vice. **-3.** [defecto físico, de dicción etc] defect.

vicioso, -sa ◇ *adj* **-1.** [depravado] depraved. **-2.** [defectuoso] defective. ◇ *m y f* [depravado] depraved person.

vicisitud *f* [inestabilidad] instability, changeability. ◆ **vicisitudes** *fpl* [avatares] vicissitudes, ups and downs.

víctima *f* victim; [en accidente, guerra] casualty; **ser ~ de** to be the victim of.

victoria *f* victory; **cantar ~** to claim victory.

victorioso, -sa *adj* victorious.

vid *f* vine.

vid., v. (*abrev de* **véase**) v., vid.

vida *f* life; **de por ~** for life; **en ~ de** during the life ○ lifetime of; **en mi/tu** *etc* **~** never (in my/your *etc* life); **estar con ~** to be alive; **ganarse la ~** to earn a living; **pasar a mejor ~** to pass away; **perder la ~** to lose one's life; **quitar la ~ a alguien** to kill sb; **¡así es la ~!** that's life!; **darse ○ pegarse la gran ~**, **darse ○ pegarse la ~ padre** to live the life of Riley.

vidente *m y f* clairvoyant.

vídeo, video *m* **-1.** [gen] video; **grabar en ~** to videotape. **-2.** [aparato filmador] camcorder.

videocámara *f* camcorder.

videocasete *m* video, videocassette.

videoclip *m* (pop) video.

videoclub (*pl* **videoclubes**) *m* video club.

videojuego *m* video game.

videotexto *m*, **videotex** *m inv* [por señal de televisión] teletext; [por línea telefónica] videotext, viewdata.

vidriero, -ra *m y f* **-1.** [que fabrica cristales] glass merchant ○ manufacturer. **-2.** [que coloca cristales] glazier. ◆ **vidriera** *f* [puerta] glass door; [ventana] glass window; [en catedrales] stained glass window.

vidrio *m* [material] glass.

vidrioso, -sa *adj* **-1.** *fig* [tema, asunto] thorny, delicate. **-2.** *fig* [ojos] glazed.

vieira *f* scallop.

viejo, -ja ◇ *adj* old; **hacerse ~** to get ○ grow old. ◇ *m y f* **-1.** [anciano] old man (*f* old lady); **los ~s** the elderly; **~ verde** dirty old man (*f* dirty old woman). **-2.** *fam* [padres] old man (*f* old girl); **mis ~s** my folks. **-3.** *Amer fam* [amigo] pal, mate. ◆ **Viejo de Pascua** *m Amer* Father Christmas.

Viena Vienna.

viene → **venir**.

vienés, -esa *adj*, *m y f* Viennese.

viento *m* **-1.** [aire] wind; **~ de costado** ○ **de lado** crosswind. **-2.** [cuerda] guy (rope). **-3.** *loc*: **contra ~ y marea** in spite of everything; **mis esperanzas se las llevó el ~** my hopes flew out of the window; **~ en popa** splendidly.

vientre *m* ANAT stomach.

viera → **ver**.

viernes *m inv* Friday; *ver también* **sábado**. ◆ **Viernes Santo** *m* RELIG Good Friday.

Vietnam Vietnam.

vietnamita *adj*, *m y f* Vietnamese.

viga *f* [de madera] beam, rafter; [de metal] girder.

vigencia *f* [de ley etc] validity; [de costumbre] use.

vigente *adj* [ley etc] in force; [costumbre] in use.

vigésimo, -ma *núm* twentieth.

vigía *m y f* lookout.

vigilancia *f* **-1.** [cuidado] vigilance, care. **-2.** [vigilantes] guards (*pl*).

vigilante ◇ *adj* vigilant. ◇ *m y f* guard; **~ nocturno** night watchman.

vigilar ◇ *vt* [enfermo] to watch over; [presos, banco] to guard; [niños, bolso] to keep an eye on; [proceso] to oversee. ◇ *vi* to keep watch.

vigilia *f* [vela] wakefulness; **estar de ~** to be awake.

vigor *m* **-1.** [gen] vigour. **-2.** [vigencia]: **entrar en** ~ to come into force.

vigorizar *vt* [fortalecer] to fortify.

vigoroso, -sa *adj* [gen] vigorous; [colorido] strong.

vikingo, -ga *adj, m y f* Viking.

vil *adj* vile, despicable; [metal] base.

vileza *f* **-1.** [acción] vile O despicable act. **-2.** [cualidad] vileness.

villa *f* **-1.** [población] small town. **-2.** [casa] villa, country house.

villancico *m* [navideño] Christmas carol.

villano, -na *m y f* villain.

vilo ◇ **en vilo** *loc adv* **-1.** [suspendido] in the air, suspended. **-2.** [inquieto] on tenterhooks; **tener a alguien en** ~ to keep sb in suspense.

vinagre *m* vinegar.

vinagrera *f* [vasija] vinegar bottle. ◆ **vinagreras** *fpl* CULIN [convoy] cruet (*sg*).

vinagreta *f* vinaigrette, French dressing.

vinculación *f* link, linking (*U*).

vincular *vt* **-1.** [enlazar] to link; [por obligación] to tie, to bind. **-2.** DER to entail.

vínculo *m* [lazo - entre hechos, países] link; [- personal, familiar] tie, bond.

vinícola *adj* [país, región] wine-producing (*antes de sust*); [industria] wine (*antes de sust*).

vinicultura *f* wine producing.

vino ◇ *v* → **venir**. ◇ *m* wine; ~ **blanco/tinto** white/red wine; ~ **dulce/seco** sweet/dry wine; ~ **rosado** rosé.

viña *f* vineyard.

viñedo *m* (large) vineyard.

viñeta *f* **-1.** [de tebeo] (individual) cartoon. **-2.** [de libro] vignette.

vio → **ver**.

viola *f* viola.

violación *f* **-1.** [de ley, derechos] violation, infringement. **-2.** [de persona] rape.

violador, -ra *adj, m y f* rapist.

violar *vt* **-1.** [ley, derechos, domicilio] to violate, to infringe. **-2.** [persona] to rape.

violencia *f* **-1.** [agresividad] violence. **-2.** [fuerza - de viento, pasiones] force. **-3.** [incomodidad] embarrassment, awkwardness.

violentar *vt* **-1.** [incomodar] to embarrass. **-2.** [forzar - domicilio] to break into. ◆ **violentarse** *vpr* [incomodarse] to feel awkward.

violento, -ta *adj* **-1.** [gen] violent; [goce] intense. **-2.** [incómodo] awkward.

violeta ◇ *f* [flor] violet. ◇ *adj inv & m* [color] violet.

violín *m* violin.

violón *m* double bass.

violonchelo, violoncelo *m* cello.

VIP (*abrev de* **very important person**) *m y f* VIP.

viperino, -na *adj fig* venomous.

viraje *m* **-1.** [giro - AUTOM] turn; NÁUT tack. **-2.** [curva] bend, curve. **-3.** *fig* [cambio] change of direction.

virar ◇ *vt* [girar] to turn (round); NÁUT to tack. ◇ *vi* [girar] to turn (round).

virgen ◇ *adj* [gen] virgin; [cinta] blank; [película] unused. ◇ *m y f* [persona] virgin. ◇ *f* ARTE Madonna. ◆ **Virgen** *f*: **la Virgen** RELIG the (Blessed) Virgin.

virgo *m* [virginidad] virginity. ◆ **Virgo** ◇ *m* [zodiaco] Virgo. ◇ *m y f* [persona] Virgo.

virguería *f fam* gem.

viril *adj* virile, manly.

virilidad *f* virility.

virtual *adj* **-1.** [posible] possible, potential. **-2.** [casi real] virtual.

virtud *f* **-1.** [cualidad] virtue. **-2.** [poder] power; **tener la** ~ **de** to have the power O ability to. ◆ **en virtud de** *loc prep* by virtue of.

virtuoso, -sa ◇ *adj* [honrado] virtuous. ◇ *m y f* [genio] virtuoso.

viruela *f* **-1.** [enfermedad] smallpox. **-2.** [pústula] pockmark; **picado de** ~**s** pockmarked.

virulé ◆ **a la virulé** *loc adj* **-1.** [torcido] crooked. **-2.** [hinchado]: **un ojo a la** ~ a black eye.

virulencia *f* MED & *fig* virulence.

virus *m inv* [gen & INFORM] virus.

viruta *f* shaving.

visado *m* visa.

víscera *f* internal organ; ~**s** entrails.

visceral *adj* ANAT & *fig* visceral; **un sentimiento/una reacción** ~ a gut feeling/reaction.

viscoso, -sa *adj* [gen] viscous; [baboso] slimy. ◆ **viscosa** *f* [tejido] viscose.

visera *f* **-1.** [de gorra] peak. **-2.** [de casco, suelta] visor. **-3.** [de automóvil] sun visor.

visibilidad *f* visibility.

visible *adj* visible.

visigodo, -da *m y f* Visigoth.

visillo *m* (*gen pl*) net/lace curtain.

visión f -1. [sentido, lo que se ve] sight. -2. [alucinación, lucidez] **vision; ver visiones** to be seeing things. -3. [punto de vista] (point of) view.

visionar vt to view privately.

visionario, -ria adj, m y f visionary.

visita f -1. [gen] visit; [breve] call; **hacer una ~ a alguien** to visit sb, to pay sb a visit; **pasar ~** MED to see one's patients. -2. [visitante] visitor; **tener ~** O **~s** to have visitors.

visitante m y f visitor.

visitar vt [gen] to visit; [suj: médico] to call on.

vislumbrar vt -1. [entrever] to make out, to discern. -2. [adivinar] to have an inkling of. ◆ **vislumbrarse** vpr -1. [entreverse] to be barely visible. -2. [adivinarse] to become a little clearer.

vislumbre m o f lit & fig glimmer.

viso m -1. [aspecto]: **tener ~s de** to seem; **tiene ~s de hacerse realidad** it could become a reality. -2. [reflejo - de tejido] sheen; [- de metal] glint.

visón m mink.

víspera f [día antes] day before, eve; **en ~s de** on the eve of.

vista → **visto**.

vistazo m glance, quick look; **echar** O **dar un ~ a** to have a quick look at.

visto, -ta pp → **ver**. ◇ adj: **estar bien/mal ~** to be considered good/ frowned upon. ◆ **vista** ◇ v → **vestir**. ◇ f -1. [sentido] sight, eyesight; [ojos] eyes (pl). -2. [observación] watching. -3. [mirada] gaze; **fijar la vista en** to fix one's eyes on; **a primera** O **simple vista** [aparentemente] at first sight, on the face of it; **estar a la vista** [visible] to be visible; [muy cerca] to be staring one in the face. -4. [panorama] view. -5. DER hearing. -6. loc: **conocer a alguien de vista** to know sb by sight; **hacer la vista gorda** to turn a blind eye; **¡hasta la vista!** see you!; **no perder de vista a alguien/algo** [vigilar] not to let sb/sthg out of one's sight; [tener en cuenta] not to lose sight of sb/sthg; **perder de vista** [dejar de ver] to lose sight of; [perder contacto] to lose touch with; **saltar a la vista** to be blindingly obvious. ◆ **vistas** fpl [panorama] view (sg); **con vistas al mar** with a sea view. ◆ **visto bueno** m: **el ~ bueno** the go-ahead; **"~ bueno"** "approved". ◆ **a la vista** loc adv BANCA at sight. ◆ **con vistas a** loc prep with a view to. ◆ **en vista de** loc prep in view of. ◆ **en vista de que** loc conj

since, seeing as. ◆ **por lo visto** loc adv apparently. ◆ **visto que** loc conj seeing O given that.

vistoso, -sa adj eye-catching.

visual ◇ adj visual. ◇ f line of sight.

visualizar vt -1. [gen] to visualize. -2. INFORM to display.

vital adj [gen] vital; [ciclo] life (antes de sust); [persona] full of life, vivacious.

vitalicio, -cia adj for life, life (antes de sust).

vitalidad f vitality.

vitamina f vitamin.

vitaminado, -da adj vitamin-enriched.

vitamínico, -ca adj vitamin (antes de sust).

viticultor, -ra m y f wine grower.

viticultura f wine growing, viticulture.

vitorear vt to cheer.

vítreo, -a adj vitreous.

vitrina f [en casa] display cabinet; [en tienda] showcase, glass case.

vitro ◆ **in vitro** loc adv in vitro.

vituperar vt to criticize harshly.

viudedad f -1. [viudez - de mujer] widowhood; [- de hombre] widowerhood. -2. **(pensión de) ~** widow's/ widower's pension.

viudo, -da m y f widower (f widow).

viva ◇ m cheer. ◇ interj: **¡~!** hurrah!; **¡~ el rey!** long live the King!

vivac = vivaque.

vivacidad f liveliness.

vivales m y f inv crafty person.

vivamente adv -1. [relatar, describir] vividly. -2. [afectar, emocionar] deeply.

vivaque, vivac m bivouac.

vivaz adj [despierto] alert, sharp.

vivencia f (gen pl) experience.

víveres mpl provisions, supplies.

vivero m -1. [de plantas] nursery. -2. [de peces] fish farm; [de moluscos] bed.

viveza f -1. [de colorido, descripción] vividness. -2. [de persona, discusión, ojos] liveliness; [de ingenio, inteligencia] sharpness.

vívido, -da adj vivid.

vividor, -ra m y f despec scrounger.

vivienda f -1. [alojamiento] housing. -2. [morada] dwelling.

viviente adj living.

vivir ◇ vt [experimentar] to experience, to live through. ◇ vi [gen] to live; [estar vivo] to be alive; [en armonía] to be happy; **~ para ver** who'd have thought it?

vivito *adj*: ~ y coleando *fam* alive and kicking.

vivo, -va *adj* **-1.** [existente - ser, lengua etc] living; **estar** ~ [persona, costumbre, recuerdo] to be alive. **-2.** [dolor, deseo, olor] intense; [luz, color, tono] bright. **-3.** [gestos, ojos, descripción] lively, vivid. **-4.** [activo - ingenio, niño] quick, sharp; [- ciudad] lively. **-5.** [genio] quick, hot. ◆ **vivos** *mpl*: **los ~s** the living. ◆ **en vivo** *loc adv* [en directo] live.

Vizcaya Vizcaya; **Golfo de** ~ Bay of Biscay.

vizconde, -desa *m y f* viscount (*f* viscountess).

vocablo *m* word, term.

vocabulario *m* **-1.** [riqueza léxica] vocabulary. **-2.** [diccionario] dictionary.

vocación *f* vocation.

vocacional *adj* vocational.

vocal ◇ *adj* vocal. ◇ *f* vowel.

vocalizar *vi* to vocalize.

vocear ◇ *vt* **-1.** [gritar] to shout ○ call out. **-2.** [llamar] to shout ○ call to. **-3.** [pregonar - mercancía] to hawk. ◇ *vi* [gritar] to shout.

vociferar *vi* to shout.

vodka ['boθka] *m o f* vodka.

vol. (*abrev de* **volumen**) vol.

volador, -ra *adj* flying.

volandas ◆ **en volandas** *loc adv* in the air.

volante ◇ *adj* flying. ◇ *m* **-1.** [para conducir] (steering) wheel. **-2.** [de tela] frill, flounce. **-3.** [del médico] (referral) note. **-4.** [en bádminton] shuttlecock.

volar ◇ *vt* [en guerras, atentados] to blow up; [caja fuerte, puerta] to blow open; [edificio en ruinas] to demolish (*with explosives*); MIN to blast. ◇ *vi* **-1.** [gen] to fly; [papeles etc] to blow away; ~ **a** [una altura] to fly at; [un lugar] to fly to; **echar(se) a** ~ to fly away ○ off. **-2.** *fam* [desaparecer] to disappear, to vanish.

volátil *adj* QUÍM & *fig* volatile.

vol-au-vent = **volován**.

volcán *m* volcano.

volcánico, -ca *adj* volcanic.

volcar ◇ *vt* **-1.** [tirar] to knock over; [carretilla] to tip up. **-2.** [vaciar] to empty out. ◇ *vi* [coche, camión] to overturn; [barco] to capsize. ◆ **volcarse** *vpr* [esforzarse]: ~**se (con/en)** to bend over backwards (for/in).

volea *f* volley.

voleibol *m* volleyball.

voleo *m* volley; **a** ○ **al** ~ [arbitrariamente] randomly, any old how.

volován (*pl* **volovanes**), **vol-au-vent** [bolo'ßan] (*pl* **vol-au-vents**) *m* vol-au-vent.

volquete *m* dumper truck, dump truck *Am*.

voltaje *m* voltage.

voltear *vt* **-1.** [heno, crepe, torero] to toss; [tortilla - con plato] to turn over; [mesa, silla] to turn upside-down. **-2.** *Amer* [derribar] to knock over. ◆ **voltearse** *vpr Amer* **-1.** [volverse] to turn around. **-2.** [volcarse] to overturn.

voltereta *f* [en el suelo] handspring; [en el aire] somersault; ~ **lateral** cartwheel.

voltio *m* volt.

voluble *adj* changeable, fickle.

volumen *m* **-1.** [gen & COM] volume; ~ **de negocio** ○ **ventas** turnover. **-2.** [espacio ocupado] size, bulk.

voluminoso, -sa *adj* bulky.

voluntad *f* **-1.** [determinación] will, willpower; ~ **de hierro** iron will. **-2.** [intención] intention; **buena** ~ goodwill; **mala** ~ ill will. **-3.** [deseo] wishes (*pl*), will; **contra la** ~ **de alguien** against sb's will. **-4.** [albedrío] free will; **a** ~ [cuanto se quiere] as much as one likes; **por** ~ **propia** of one's own free will.

voluntariado *m* voluntary enlistment.

voluntario, -ria ◇ *adj* voluntary. ◇ *m y f* volunteer.

voluntarioso, -sa *adj* [esforzado] willing.

voluptuoso, -sa *adj* voluptuous.

volver ◇ *vt* **-1.** [dar la vuelta a] to turn round; [lo de arriba abajo] to turn over. **-2.** [poner del revés - boca abajo] to turn upside down; [- lo de dentro fuera] to turn inside out; [- lo de detrás delante] to turn back to front. **-3.** [cabeza, ojos etc] to turn. **-4.** [convertir en]: **eso le volvió un delincuente** that turned him into a criminal. ◇ *vi* [ir de vuelta] to go back, to return; [venir de vuelta] to come back, to return; **yo allí no vuelvo** I'm not going back there; **vuelve, no te vayas** come back, don't go; ~ **en sí** to come to. ◆ **volver a** *vi* [reanudar] to return to; ~ **a hacer algo** [hacer otra vez] to do sthg again. ◆ **volverse** *vpr* **-1.** [darse la vuelta, girar la cabeza] to turn round. **-2.** [ir de vuelta] to go back, to return; [venir de vuelta] to come back, to return. **-3.** [convertirse en] to become; ~**se loco/pálido** to go mad/pale. **-4.** *loc*: ~**se atrás** [de una afirmación, promesa] to go back on one's word; [de una decisión] to back out; ~**se (en) contra (de) alguien** to turn against sb.

vomitar ◇ *vt* [devolver] to vomit, to bring up. ◇ *vi* to vomit, to be sick.

vómito *m* [substancia] vomit (*U*).

voraz *adj* -1. [persona, apetito] voracious. -2. *fig* [fuego, enfermedad] raging.

vos *pron pers* [tú] you.

vosotros, -tras *pron pers* you (*pl*).

votación *f* vote, voting (*U*); **decidir algo por** ~ to put sthg to the vote; ~ **a mano alzada** show of hands.

votante *m y f* voter.

votar ◇ *vt* -1. [partido, candidato] to vote for; [ley] to vote on. -2. [aprobar] to pass, to approve (*by vote*). ◇ *vi* to vote; ~ **por** [emitir un voto por] to vote for; *fig* [estar a favor de] to be in favour of; ~ **por que ...** to vote (that) ...; ~ **en blanco** to return a blank ballot paper.

voto *m* -1. [gen] vote; ~ **de confianza/censura** vote of confidence/no confidence. -2. RELIG vow.

voy → **ir**.

vóytelas *interj Amer fam* good grief!

voz *f* -1. [gen & GRAM] voice; **a media** ~ in a low voice, under one's breath; **a** ~ **en cuello** ○ **grito** at the top of one's voice; **alzar** ○ **levantar la** ~ **a alguien** to raise one's voice to sb; **en** ~ **alta** aloud; **en** ~ **baja** softly, in a low voice; ~ **en off** CIN voice-over; TEATR voice offstage. -2. [grito] shout; **a voces** shouting; **dar voces** to shout. -3. [vocablo] word. -4. [derecho a expresarse] say, voice; **no tener ni** ~ **ni voto** to have no say in the matter. -5. [rumor] rumour.

vudú *m* (*en aposición inv*) voodoo.

vuelco *m* upset; **dar un** ~ [coche] to overturn; [relaciones] to change completely; [empresa] to go to ruin; **me dio un** ~ **el corazón** my heart missed ○ skipped a beat.

vuelo *m* -1. [gen & AERON] flight; **alzar** ○ **emprender** ○ **levantar el** ~ [despegar] to take flight, to fly off; *fig* [irse de casa] to fly the nest; **coger algo al** ~ [en el aire] to catch sthg in flight; *fig* [rápido] to catch on to sthg very quickly; **remontar el** ~ to soar; ~ **chárter/regular** charter/scheduled flight; ~ **libre** hang gliding; ~ **sin motor** gliding. -2. [de vestido]: **una falda de** ~ a full skirt.

vuelta *f* -1. [gen] turn; [acción] turning; **darse la** ~ to turn round; **dar ~s (a algo)** [girándolo] to turn (sthg) round;

media ~ MIL about-turn; AUTOM U-turn. -2. DEP lap; ~ **(ciclista)** tour. -3. [regreso, devolución] return; **a la** ~ [volviendo] on the way back; [al llegar] on one's return; **estar de** ~ to be back. -4. [paseo]: **dar una** ~ to go for a walk. -5. [dinero sobrante] change. -6. [ronda, turno] round. -7. [parte opuesta] back, other side; **a la** ~ **de la página** over the page. -8. [cambio, avatar] change. -9. *loc*: **a** ~ **de correo** by return of post; **dar la** ~ **a la tortilla** *fam* to turn the tables; **dar una** ~/**dos** *etc* ~**s de campana** [coche] to turn over once/twice *etc*; **darle** ~**s a algo** to turn sthg over in one's mind; **estar de** ~ **de algo** to be blasé about sthg; **no tiene** ~ **de hoja** there are no two ways about it.

vuelto, -ta ◇ *pp* → **volver**. ◇ *adj* turned. ◆ **vuelto** *m Amer* change.

vuestro, -tra ◇ *adj poses* your; ~ **libro/amigo** your book/friend; **este libro es** ~ this book is yours; **un amigo** ~ a friend of yours; **no es asunto** ~ it's none of your business. ◇ *pron poses*: **el** ~ yours; **los** ~**s están en la mesa** yours are on the table; **lo** ~ **es el teatro** [lo que hacéis bien] you should be on the stage; **los** ~**s** *fam* [vuestra familia] your folks; [vuestro bando] your lot.

vulgar *adj* -1. [no refinado] vulgar. -2. [corriente, ordinario] ordinary, common.

vulgaridad *f* -1. [grosería] vulgarity; **hacer/decir una** ~ to do/say sthg vulgar. -2. [banalidad] banality.

vulgarizar *vt* to popularize.

vulgo *m despec*: **el** ~ [plebe] the masses (*pl*); [no expertos] the lay public (*U*).

vulnerable *adj* vulnerable.

vulnerar *vt* -1. [prestigio etc] to harm, to damage. -2. [ley, pacto etc] to violate, to break.

vulva *f* vulva.

VV *abrev de* **ustedes**.

w, W *f* [letra] w, W.
walkie-talkie ['walki'talki] (*pl* **walkie-talkies**) *m* walkie-talkie.
walkman® ['walman] (*pl* **walkmans**) *m* Walkman®.
Washington ['wafinton] Washington.
wáter ['bater] (*pl* **wáteres**), **váter** (*pl* **váteres**) *m* toilet.
waterpolo [water'polo] *m* water polo.
watio = vatio.
WC (*abrev de* **water closet**) *m* WC.
whisky ['wiski] = güisqui.
windsurf ['winsurf], **windsurfing** ['winsurfin] *m* windsurfing.

x, X *f* [letra] x, X. ◆**X** *m y f*: **la señora X** Mrs X.
xenofobia *f* xenophobia.
xilofón, xilófono *m* xylophone.

y¹, Y *f* [letra] y, Y.
y² *conj* **-1.** [gen] and; **un ordenador** ~ **una impresora** a computer and a printer; **horas** ~ **horas de espera** hours and hours of waiting. **-2.** [pero] and yet; **sabía que no lo conseguiría** ~ **seguía intentándolo** she knew she wouldn't manage it and yet she kept on trying. **-3.** [en preguntas] what about; ¿~ **tu mujer?** what about your wife?

ya ◇ *adv* **-1.** [en el pasado] already; ~ **me lo habías contado** you had already told me; ~ **en 1926** as long ago as 1926. **-2.** [ahora] now; [inmediatamente] at once; **hay que hacer algo** ~ something has to be done now/at once; **bueno, yo** ~ **me voy** right, I'm off now; ~ **no es así** it's no longer like that. **-3.** [en el futuro]: ~ **te llamaré** I'll give you a ring some time; ~ **hablaremos** we'll talk later; ~ **nos habremos ido** we'll already have gone; ~ **verás** you'll (soon) see. **-4.** [refuerza al verbo]: ~ **entiendo/lo sé** I understand/know. ◇ *conj* [distributiva]: ~ **(sea) por ...** ~ **(sea) por ...** whether for ... or .... ◇ *interj*: ¡~! [expresa asentimiento] right!; [expresa comprensión] yes!; ¡~, ~! *irón* sure!, yes, of course! ◆**ya no** *loc adv*: ~ **no ... sino not only ...**, and. ◆**ya que** *loc conj* since; ~ **que has venido, ayúdame con esto** since you're here, give me a hand with this.
yacer *vi* to lie.
yacimiento *m* **-1.** [minero] bed, deposit; ~ **de petróleo** oilfield. **-2.** [arqueológico] site.
yanqui *m y f* **-1.** HIST Yankee. **-2.** *fam* [estadounidense] *pejorative term referring to a person from the US*, yank.
yate *m* yacht.
yegua *f* mare.
yema *f* **-1.** [de huevo] yolk. **-2.** [de planta] bud, shoot. **-3.** [de dedo] fingertip.
Yemen: (**el**) ~ Yemen.
yen (*pl* **yenes**) *m* yen.
yerba = hierba.
yerbatero *m Amer* healer.
yermo, -ma *adj* [estéril] barren.
yerno *m* son-in-law.
yeso *m* **-1.** GEOL gypsum. **-2.** CONSTR plaster. **-3.** ARTE gesso.
yeyé *adj* sixties.
yo *pron pers* **-1.** (*sujeto*) I; ~ **me llamo Luis** I'm called Luis. **-2.** (*predicado*): **soy** ~ it's me. **-3.** *loc*: ~ **que tú/él** *etc* if I were you/him *etc*.
yodo, iodo *m* iodine.
yoga *m* yoga.
yogur (*pl* **yogures**), **yogurt** (*pl* **yogurts**) *m* yoghurt.
yonqui *m y f fam* junkie.
yóquey (*pl* **yóqueys**), **jockey** (*pl* **jockeys**) *m* jockey.
yoyó *m* yoyo.
yuca *f* **-1.** BOT yucca. **-2.** CULIN cassava.
yudo, judo ['juðo] *m* judo.

yugo *m lit* & *fig* yoke.
Yugoslavia Yugoslavia.
yugoslavo, -va ◇ *adj* Yugoslavian. ◇ *m y f* Yugoslav.
yugular *adj* & *f* jugular.
yunque *m* anvil.
yuppie (*pl* **yuppies**), **yuppi** *m y f* yuppie.
yuxtaponer *vt* to juxtapose.
yuxtaposición *f* juxtaposition.
yuxtapuesto, -ta *pp* → yuxtaponer.

Z

z, Z *f* [letra] z, Z.
zafio, -fia *adj* rough, uncouth.
zafiro *m* sapphire.
zaga *f* DEP defence; **a la ~** behind, at the back; **no irle a la ~ a alguien** to be every bit ○ just as good as sb.
zaguán *m* (entrance) hall.
Zaire Zaire.
zalamería *f* (*gen pl*) flattery (*U*).
zalamero, -ra *m y f* flatterer; *despec* smooth talker.
zamarra *f* sheepskin jacket.
zambo, -ba *m y f* knock-kneed person.
zambullir *vt* to dip, to submerge. ◆ **zambullirse** *vpr*: ~**se (en)** [agua] to dive (into); [actividad] to immerse o.s. (in).
zampar *fam vi* to gobble. ◆ **zamparse** *vpr* to wolf down.
zanahoria *f* carrot.
zanca *f* [de ave] leg, shank.
zancada *f* stride.
zancadilla *f* trip; **poner una** ○ **la ~ a alguien** [hacer tropezar] to trip sb up; [engañar] to trick sb.
zancadillear *vt* [hacer tropezar] to trip up.
zanco *m* stilt.
zancudo, -da *adj* long-legged. ◆ **zancudo** *m Amer* mosquito.
zángano, -na *m y f fam* [persona] lazy oaf. ◆ **zángano** *m* [abeja] drone.
zanja *f* ditch.
zanjar *vt* [poner fin a] to put an end to; [resolver] to settle, to resolve.
zapallo *m Amer* courgette.

zapata *f* [de freno] shoe.
zapateado *m type of flamenco music and dance.*
zapatear *vi* to stamp one's feet.
zapatería *f* **-1.** [oficio] shoemaking. **-2.** [taller] shoemaker's. **-3.** [tienda] shoe shop.
zapatero, -ra *m y f* **-1.** [fabricante] shoemaker. **-2.** [reparador]: ~ **(de viejo** ○ **remendón)** cobbler. **-3.** [vendedor] shoe seller.
zapatilla *f* **-1.** [de baile] shoe, pump; [de estar en casa] **slipper**; [de deporte] **sports shoe, trainer. -2.** [de grifo] washer.
zapato *m* shoe.
zapping ['θapin] *m inv* channel-hopping; **hacer ~** to channel-hop.
zar, zarina *m y f* tsar (*f* tsarina), czar (*f* czarina).
zarandear *vt* **-1.** [cosa] to shake. **-2.** [persona] to jostle, to knock about.
zarcillo *m* (*gen pl*) earring.
zarpa *f* [de animal - uña] **claw**; [- mano] **paw.**
zarpar *vi* to weigh anchor, to set sail.
zarpazo *m* clawing (*U*).
zarza *f* bramble, blackberry bush.
zarzal *m* bramble patch.
zarzamora *f* blackberry.
zarzaparrilla *f* sarsaparilla.
zarzuela *f* MÚS zarzuela, *Spanish light opera.*
zas *interj*: ¡~! wham!, bang!
zenit, cenit *m lit* & *fig* zenith.
zepelín (*pl* **zepelines**) *m* zeppelin.
zigzag (*pl* **zigzags** ○ **zigzagues**) *m* zigzag.
zigzaguear *vi* to zigzag.
zinc = cinc.
zíper *m Amer* zip.
zócalo *m* **-1.** [de pared] skirting board. **-2.** [de edificio, pedestal] plinth.
zoco *m* souk, Arabian market.
zodíaco, zodiaco *m* zodiac.
zombi, zombie *m y f lit* & *fig* zombie.
zona *f* zone, area; ~ **azul** AUTOM restricted parking zone; ~ **verde** [grande] park; [pequeño] lawn.
zoo *m* zoo.
zoología *f* zoology.
zoológico, -ca *adj* zoological. ◆ **zoológico** *m* zoo.
zoólogo, -ga *m y f* zoologist.
zopenco, -ca *fam m y f* nitwit.
zoquete ◇ *m Amer* [calcetín] ankle sock. ◇ *m y f* [tonto] blockhead.

zorro, -rra *m y f lit & fig* fox. ◆ **zorro** *m* [piel] fox (fur).

zozobra *f* anxiety, worry.

zozobrar *vi* **-1.** [naufragar] to be shipwrecked. **-2.** *fig* [fracasar] to fall through.

zueco *m* clog.

zulo *m* hideout.

zulú (*pl* **zulúes**) *adj, m y f* Zulu.

zumbar *vi* [gen] to buzz; [máquinas] to whirr, to hum; **me zumban los oídos** my ears are buzzing.

zumbido *m* [gen] buzz, buzzing (*U*); [de máquinas] whirr, whirring (*U*).

zumo *m* juice.

zurcido *m* **-1.** [acción] darning. **-2.** [remiendo] darn.

zurcir *vt* to darn.

zurdo, -da *adj* [mano etc] left; [persona] left-handed. ◆ **zurda** *f* [mano] left hand.

zurrar *vt* [pegar] to beat, to thrash.

zutano, -na *m y f* so-and-so, what's-his-name (*f* what's-her-name).

a¹ (*pl* as OR a's), **A** (*pl* As OR A's) [eɪ] *n* [letter] a *f*, A *f.* ◆**A** *n* **-1.** MUS la *m.* **-2.** SCH [mark] ≃ sobresaliente *m.*

a² [*stressed* eɪ, *unstressed* ə] (*before vowel or silent "h":* **an** [*stressed* æn, *unstressed* ən]) *indef art* **-1.** [gen] un (una); **a boy** un chico; **a table** una mesa; **an orange** una naranja; **an eagle** un águila; **a hundred/thousand pounds** cien/mil libras. **-2.** [referring to occupation]: **to be a dentist/teacher** ser dentista/maestra. **-3.** [to express prices, ratios etc] por; **£10 a person** 10 libras por persona; **50 km an hour** 50 kms. por hora; **20p a kilo** 20 peniques el kilo; **twice a week/month** dos veces a la semana/al mes.

AA *n* **-1.** (*abbr of* **Automobile Association**) *asociación británica del automóvil,* ≃ RACE *m.* **-2.** (*abbr of* **Alcoholics Anonymous**) AA *mpl.*

AAA *n* (*abbr of* **American Automobile Association**) *asociación estadounidense del automóvil,* ≃ RACE *m.*

AB (*abbr of* **Bachelor of Arts**) *n Am (titular de una) licenciatura de letras.*

aback [ə'bæk] *adv*: **to be taken** ~ quedarse atónito(ta) OR estupefacto(ta).

abandon [ə'bændən] ◇ *vt* abandonar. ◇ *n*: **with** ~ con desenfreno.

abashed [ə'bæʃt] *adj* avergonzado(da).

abate [ə'beɪt] *vi* [storm] amainar; [noise] debilitarse; [fear] apaciguarse.

abattoir [ˈæbətwɑːr] *n* matadero *m.*

abbey [ˈæbɪ] *n* abadía *f.*

abbot [ˈæbət] *n* abad *m.*

abbreviate [ə'briːvɪeɪt] *vt* abreviar.

abbreviation [ə,briːvɪ'eɪʃn] *n* abreviatura *f.*

ABC *n lit* & *fig* abecé *m.*

abdicate [ˈæbdɪkeɪt] ◇ *vi* abdicar. ◇ *vt* [responsibility] abdicar de.

abdomen [ˈæbdəmen] *n* abdomen *m.*

abduct [əb'dʌkt] *vt* raptar.

aberration [,æbə'reɪʃn] *n* aberración *f.*

abet [ə'bet] *vt* → **aid.**

abeyance [ə'beɪəns] *n*: **in** ~ [custom] en desuso; [law] en suspenso.

abhor [əb'hɔːr] *vt* aborrecer.

abide [ə'baɪd] *vt* soportar, aguantar. ◆**abide by** *vt fus* [law, ruling] acatar; [principles, own decision] atenerse a.

ability [ə'bɪlətɪ] *n* **-1.** [capability] capacidad *f.* **-2.** [skill] dotes *fpl.*

abject [ˈæbdʒekt] *adj* **-1.** [poverty] vil, indigente. **-2.** [person] sumiso(sa); [apology] humillante.

ablaze [ə'bleɪz] *adj* [on fire] en llamas.

able [ˈeɪbl] *adj* **-1.** [capable]: **to be** ~ **to do sthg** poder hacer algo. **-2.** [skilful] capaz, competente.

ably [ˈeɪblɪ] *adv* eficientemente.

abnormal [æb'nɔːml] *adj* anormal.

aboard [ə'bɔːd] ◇ *adv* a bordo. ◇ *prep* [ship, plane] a bordo de; [bus, train] en.

abode [ə'bəʊd] *n fml*: **of no fixed** ~ sin domicilio fijo.

abolish [ə'bɒlɪʃ] *vt* abolir.

abolition [,æbə'lɪʃn] *n* abolición *f.*

abominable [ə'bɒmɪnəbl] *adj* abominable, deplorable.

aborigine [,æbə'rɪdʒənɪ] *n* aborigen *m y f* de Australia.

abort [ə'bɔːt] *vt* **-1.** [pregnancy, plan, project] abortar; [pregnant woman] provocar el aborto a. **-2.** COMPUT abortar.

abortion [ə'bɔːʃn] *n* aborto *m*; **to have an** ~ abortar.

abortive [ə'bɔːtɪv] *adj* frustrado(da).

abound [ə'baʊnd] *vi* **-1.** [be plentiful] abundar. **-2.** [be full]: **to ~ with** OR **in** abundar en.

about [ə'baʊt] ◇ *adv* **-1.** [approximately] más o menos, como; **there were ~ fifty/a hundred** había (como) unos cincuenta/cien o así; **at ~ five o'clock** a eso de las cinco. **-2.** [referring to place] por ahí; **to leave things lying ~** dejar las cosas por ahí; **to walk ~** ir andando por ahí; **to jump ~** dar saltos. **-3.** [on the point of]: **to be ~ to do sthg** estar a punto de hacer algo. ◇ *prep* **-1.** [relating to, concerning] sobre, acerca de; **a film ~ Paris** una película sobre París; **what is it ~?** ¿de qué trata?; **there's something odd ~ that man** hay algo raro en ese hombre; **how ~ ...?** → **how**; **what ~ ...?** → **what**. **-2.** [referring to place] por; **to wander ~ the streets** vagar por las calles.

about-turn, about-face *n* MIL media vuelta *f*; *fig* cambio *m* radical.

above [ə'bʌv] ◇ *adv* **-1.** [on top, higher up] arriba; **the flat ~** el piso de arriba; **see ~** [in text] véase más arriba. **-2.** [more, over]: **children aged five and ~** niños de cinco años en adelante. ◇ *prep* **-1.** [on top of] encima de. **-2.** [higher up than, over] por encima de. **-3.** [more than, superior to] por encima de; **children ~ the age of 15** niños mayores de 15 años. ◆ **above all** *adv* sobre todo.

aboveboard [ə,bʌv'bɔːd] *adj* honrado(da), sin tapujos.

abrasive [ə'breɪsɪv] *adj* **-1.** [substance] abrasivo(va). **-2.** [person] mordaz.

abreast [ə'brest] ◇ *adv* hombro con hombro. ◇ *prep*: **to keep ~ of** mantenerse OR estar al día de.

abridged [ə'brɪdʒd] *adj* abreviado(da).

abroad [ə'brɔːd] *adv* en el extranjero; **to go ~** ir al extranjero.

abrupt [ə'brʌpt] *adj* **-1.** [sudden] repentino(na). **-2.** [brusque] brusco(ca).

abscess ['æbsɪs] *n* absceso *m*.

abscond [əb'skɒnd] *vi*: **to ~ (with/from)** escaparse OR fugarse (con/de).

abseil ['æbseɪl] *vi*: **to ~ (down sthg)** descolgarse OR descender haciendo rappel (por algo).

absence ['æbsəns] *n* **-1.** [of person] ausencia *f*. **-2.** [of thing] falta *f*.

absent ['æbsənt] *adj* [not present] ausente; **to be ~ from** faltar a, ausentarse de.

absentee [,æbsən'tiː] *n* ausente *m* y *f*.

absent-minded [-'maɪndɪd] *adj* [person] despistado(da); [behaviour] distraído(da).

absolute ['æbsəluːt] *adj* absoluto(ta).

absolutely ['æbsəluːtlɪ] ◇ *adv* [completely] completamente, absolutamente. ◇ *excl* ¡desde luego!

absolve [əb'zɒlv] *vt*: **to ~ sb (from)** absolver a alguien (de).

absorb [əb'sɔːb] *vt* [gen] absorber; **to be ~ed in sthg** *fig* estar absorto OR embebido en algo.

absorbent [əb'sɔːbənt] *adj* absorbente.

absorption [əb'sɔːpʃn] *n* [of liquid] absorción *f*.

abstain [əb'steɪn] *vi*: **to ~ (from)** abstenerse (de).

abstemious [æb'stiːmjəs] *adj fml* sobrio(bria), moderado(da).

abstention [əb'stenʃn] *n* abstención *f*.

abstract ['æbstrækt] ◇ *adj* abstracto(ta). ◇ *n* [summary] resumen *m*, sinopsis *f*.

absurd [əb'sɜːd] *adj* absurdo(da).

ABTA ['æbtə] (*abbr of* **Association of British Travel Agents**) *n* asociación británica de agencias de viajes.

abundant [ə'bʌndənt] *adj* abundante.

abundantly [ə'bʌndəntlɪ] *adv* [extremely]: **it's ~ clear** está clarísimo.

abuse [*n* ə'bjuːs, *vb* ə'bjuːz] ◇ *n* (*U*) **-1.** [offensive remarks] insultos *mpl*. **-2.** [misuse, maltreatment] abuso *m*. ◇ *vt* **-1.** [insult] insultar. **-2.** [maltreat, misuse] abusar de.

abusive [ə'bjuːsɪv] *adj* [person] grosero(ra); [behaviour, language] insultante.

abysmal [ə'bɪzml] *adj* pésimo(ma), nefasto(ta).

abyss [ə'bɪs] *n* abismo *m*, sima *f*.

a/c (*abbr of* **account (current)**) c/c.

AC *n* (*abbr of* **alternating current**) CA *f*.

academic [,ækə'demɪk] ◇ *adj* **-1.** [of college, university] académico(ca). **-2.** [studious] estudioso(sa). **-3.** [hypothetical] teórico(ca). ◇ *n* [university lecturer] profesor *m* universitario, profesora *f* universitaria.

academy [ə'kædəmɪ] *n* academia *f*.

ACAS ['eɪkæs] (*abbr of* **Advisory, Conciliation and Arbitration Service**) *n* organización británica para el arbitraje en conflictos laborales, ≃ IMAC *m*.

accede [æk'siːd] *vi* **-1.** [agree]: **to ~ to** acceder a. **-2.** [monarch]: **to ~ to the throne** subir al trono.

accelerate [ək'seləreɪt] *vi* **-1.** [car, driver] acelerar. **-2.** [inflation, growth] dispararse.

acceleration [ək,selə'reɪʃn] *n* aceleración *f*.

accelerator [ək'seləreɪtər] *n* acelerador *m*.

accent ['æksent] *n lit & fig* acento *m*.

accept [ək'sept] *vt* -1. [gen] aceptar. -2. [difficult situation, problem] asimilar. -3. [defeat, blame, responsibility] asumir. -4. [agree]: **to ~ that** admitir que. -5. [subj: machine - coins, tokens] admitir.

acceptable [ək'septəbl] *adj* aceptable.

acceptance [ək'septəns] *n* -1. [gen] aceptación *f*. -2. [of piece of work, article] aprobación *f*. -3. [of defeat, blame, responsibility] reconocimiento *m*. -4. [of person - as part of group etc] admisión *f*.

access ['ækses] *n* -1. [entry] acceso *m*. -2. [opportunity to use or see] libre acceso *m*; **to have ~ to** tener acceso a.

accessible [ək'sesəbl] *adj* -1. [place] accesible. -2. [service, book, film] asequible.

accessory [ək'sesərɪ] *n* -1. [of car, vacuum cleaner] accesorio *m*. -2. JUR cómplice *m y f*. ◆ **accessories** *npl* complementos *mpl*.

accident ['æksɪdənt] *n* accidente *m*; **it was an ~** fue sin querer; **by ~** [by chance] por casualidad.

accidental [,æksɪ'dentl] *adj* accidental.

accidentally [,æksɪ'dentəlɪ] *adv* -1. [by chance] por casualidad. -2. [unintentionally] sin querer.

accident-prone *adj* propenso(sa) a los accidentes.

acclaim [ə'kleɪm] ◇ *n* (U) elogio *m*, alabanza *f*. ◇ *vt* elogiar, alabar.

acclimatize, -ise [ə'klaɪmətaɪz], **acclimate** *Am* ['æklɪmeɪt] *vi*: **to ~ (to)** aclimatarse (a).

accolade ['ækəleɪd] *n* [praise] elogio *m*, halago *m*; [award] galardón *m*.

accommodate [ə'kɒmədeɪt] *vt* -1. [provide room for people - subj: person] alojar; [- subj: building, place] albergar. -2. [oblige] complacer.

accommodating [ə'kɒmədeɪtɪŋ] *adj* complaciente, servicial.

accommodation [ə,kɒmə'deɪʃn] *n Br*, **accommodations** [ə,kɒmə'deɪʃnz] *npl Am* [lodging] alojamiento *m*.

accompany [ə'kʌmpənɪ] *vt* acompañar.

accomplice [ə'kʌmplɪs] *n* cómplice *m y f*.

accomplish [ə'kʌmplɪʃ] *vt* [achieve] conseguir, alcanzar.

accomplished [ə'kʌmplɪʃt] *adj* competente, experto(ta).

accomplishment [ə'kʌmplɪʃmənt] *n* -1. [action] realización *f*. -2. [achievement] logro *m*.

accord [ə'kɔːd] ◇ *n*: **to do sthg of one's own ~** hacer algo por propia voluntad. ◇ *vt*: **to ~ sb sthg, to ~ sthg to sb** conceder algo a alguien.

accordance [ə'kɔːdəns] *n*: **in ~ with** acorde con, conforme a.

according [ə'kɔːdɪŋ] ◆ **according to** *prep* -1. [as stated or shown by] según; **to go ~ to plan** ir según lo planeado. -2. [with regard to] de acuerdo con, conforme a.

accordingly [ə'kɔːdɪŋlɪ] *adv* -1. [appropriately] como corresponde. -2. [consequently] por lo tanto.

accordion [ə'kɔːdjən] *n* acordeón *m*.

accost [ə'kɒst] *vt* abordar.

account [ə'kaʊnt] *n* -1. [with bank, shop etc] cuenta *f*. -2. [report - spoken] relato *m*; [- written] informe *m*. -3. *phr*: **to take ~ of sthg, to take sthg into ~** tener en cuenta algo; **of no ~** indiferente, de poca importancia; **on no ~** bajo ningún pretexto OR concepto. ◆ **accounts** *npl* [of business] cuentas *fpl*. ◆ **by all accounts** *adv* a decir de todos, según todo el mundo. ◆ **on account of** *prep* debido a. ◆ **account for** *vt fus* -1. [explain] justificar. -2. [represent] representar.

accountable [ə'kaʊntəbl] *adj* [responsible]: ~ **(for)** responsable (de).

accountancy [ə'kaʊntənsɪ] *n* contabilidad *f*.

accountant [ə'kaʊntənt] *n* contable *m y f*, contador *m*, -ra *f Amer*.

accrue [ə'kruː] *vi* acumularse.

accumulate [ə'kjuːmjuleɪt] ◇ *vt* acumular. ◇ *vi* [money, things] acumularse; [problems] amontonarse.

accuracy ['ækjʊrəsɪ] *n* -1. [of description, report] veracidad *f*. -2. [of weapon, marksman] precisión *f*; [of typing, figures] exactitud *f*.

accurate ['ækjʊrət] *adj* -1. [description, report] veraz. -2. [weapon, marksman, typist] preciso(sa); [figures, estimate] exacto(ta).

accurately ['ækjʊrətlɪ] *adv* -1. [truthfully] verazmente. -2. [precisely] con precisión.

accusation [,ækjuː'zeɪʃn] *n* -1. [charge] acusación *f*. -2. JUR denuncia *f*.

accuse [ə'kjuːz] *vt*: **to ~ sb of sthg/of doing sthg** acusar a alguien de algo/de hacer algo.

accused [ə'kjuːzd] (*pl inv*) *n* JUR: **the ~** el acusado, la acusada.

accustomed [ə'kʌstəmd] *adj*: **~ to** acostumbrado(da) a.

ace [eɪs] *n* [playing card] as *m*.

ache [eɪk] ◇ *n* [pain] dolor *m*. ◇ *vi* [hurt] doler; **my back ~s** me duele la espalda.

achieve [ə'tʃiːv] *vt* [success, goal, fame] alcanzar, lograr; [ambition] realizar.

achievement [ə'tʃiːvmənt] *n* **-1.** [accomplishment] logro *m*, éxito *m*. **-2.** [act of achieving] consecución *f*, realización *f*.

achiever [ə'tʃiːvəʳ] *n*: **low ~** [at school] estudiante *m* y *f* de bajo rendimiento escolar.

Achilles' tendon [ə'kɪliːz-] *n* tendón *m* de Aquiles.

acid ['æsɪd] ◇ *adj* **-1.** CHEM ácido(da). **-2.** [sharp-tasting] agrio (agria). **-3.** *fig* [person, remark] mordaz. ◇ *n* ácido *m*.

acid rain *n* lluvia *f* ácida.

acknowledge [ək'nɒlɪdʒ] *vt* **-1.** [accept] reconocer. **-2.** [greet] saludar. **-3.** [letter etc]: **to ~ receipt of** acusar recibo de. **-4.** [recognize]: **to ~ sb as** reconocer OR considerar a alguien como.

acknowledg(e)ment [ək'nɒlɪdʒmənt] *n* **-1.** [acceptance] reconocimiento *m*. **-2.** [confirmation of receipt] acuse *m* de recibo. ◆ **acknowledg(e)ments** *npl* agradecimientos *mpl*.

acne ['æknɪ] *n* acné *m*.

acorn ['eɪkɔːn] *n* bellota *f*.

acoustic [ə'kuːstɪk] *adj* acústico(ca). ◆ **acoustics** *npl* acústica *f*.

acquaint [ə'kweɪnt] *vt* **-1.** [make familiar]: **to ~ sb with sthg** [information] poner a alguien al corriente de algo; [method, technique] familiarizar a alguien con algo. **-2.** [make known]: **to be ~ed with sb** conocer a alguien.

acquaintance [ə'kweɪntəns] *n* conocido *m*, -da *f*.

acquire [ə'kwaɪəʳ] *vt* **-1.** [buy, adopt] adquirir. **-2.** [obtain - information, document] procurarse.

acquisitive [ə'kwɪzɪtɪv] *adj* consumista.

acquit [ə'kwɪt] *vt* **-1.** JUR: **to ~ sb of sthg** absolver a alguien de algo. **-2.** [perform]: **to ~ o.s. well/badly** hacer un buen/mal papel.

acquittal [ə'kwɪtl] *n* JUR absolución *f*.

acre ['eɪkəʳ] *n* acre *m*.

acrid ['ækrɪd] *adj lit* & *fig* acre.

acrimonious [,ækrɪ'məʊnjəs] *adj* [words] áspero(ra); [dispute] enconado(da).

acrobat ['ækrəbæt] *n* acróbata *m* y *f*.

acronym ['ækrənɪm] *n* siglas *fpl*.

across [ə'krɒs] ◇ *adv* **-1.** [from one side to the other] de un lado a otro; **to walk/run ~** cruzar andando/corriendo. **-2.** [in measurements]: **the river is 2 km ~** el río tiene 2 kms de ancho. ◇ *prep* **-1.** [from one side to the other of] a través de, de un lado a otro de; **to walk/run ~ the road** cruzar la carretera andando/corriendo. **-2.** [on the other side of] al otro lado de. ◆ **across from** *prep* enfrente de.

acrylic [ə'krɪlɪk] ◇ *adj* acrílico(ca). ◇ *n* acrílico *m*.

act [ækt] ◇ *n* **-1.** [action, deed] acto *m*, acción *f*; **to be in the ~ of doing sthg** estar haciendo algo. **-2.** [pretence] farsa *f*. **-3.** [in parliament] ley *f*. **-4.** [THEATRE - part of play] acto *m*; [- routine, turn] número *m*. ◇ *vi* **-1.** [gen] actuar; **to ~ as** [person] hacer de; [thing] actuar como. **-2.** [behave]: **to ~ (as if/like)** comportarse (como si/como). **-3.** *fig* [pretend] fingir. ◇ *vt* [part - in play, film] interpretar.

acting ['æktɪŋ] ◇ *adj* [interim] en funciones. ◇ *n* actuación *f*; **I like ~** me gusta actuar.

action ['ækʃn] *n* **-1.** [gen & MIL] acción *f*; **to take ~** tomar medidas; **in ~** [person] en acción; [machine] en funcionamiento; **out of ~** [person] fuera de combate; [machine] averiado(da). **-2.** [deed] acto *m*, acción *f*. **-3.** JUR demanda *f*.

action replay *n* repetición *f* (de la jugada).

activate ['æktɪveɪt] *vt* [device] activar; [machine] poner en funcionamiento.

active ['æktɪv] *adj* **-1.** [person, campaigner] activo(va). **-2.** [encouragement etc] enérgico(ca). **-3.** [volcano] en actividad; [bomb] activado(da).

actively ['æktɪvlɪ] *adv* [encourage, discourage] enérgicamente.

activity [æk'tɪvətɪ] *n* **-1.** [movement, action] actividad *f*. **-2.** [pastime, hobby] afición *f*.

actor ['æktəʳ] *n* actor *m*.

actress ['æktrɪs] *n* actriz *f*.

actual ['æktʃʊəl] *adj* [emphatic]: **the ~ cost is £10** el coste real es de 10 libras; **the ~ spot where it happened** el sitio mismo en que ocurrió.

actually ['æktʃʊəlɪ] *adv* **-1.** [really, in truth]: **do you ~ like him?** ¿de verdad que te gusta?; **no-one ~ saw her** en realidad, nadie la vio. **-2.** [by the way]:

~, **I was there yesterday** pues yo estuve ayer por allí.

acumen ['ækjumen] *n*: **business ~** vista *f* para los negocios.

acupuncture ['ækjupʌŋktʃəʳ] *n* acupuntura *f*.

acute [ə'kjuːt] *adj* **-1.** [illness] agudo(da); [pain, danger] extremo(ma). **-2.** [perceptive - person] perspicaz. **-3.** [hearing, smell] muy fino(na).

ad [æd] (*abbr of* **advertisement**) *n* anuncio *m*.

AD (*abbr of* **Anno Domini**) d. C.

adamant ['ædəmənt] *adj*: **to be ~ (that)** mostrarse inflexible (en que).

Adam's apple ['ædəmz-] *n* bocado *m* OR nuez *f* de Adán.

adapt [ə'dæpt] ♦ *vt* adaptar. ♦ *vi*: **to ~ (to)** adaptarse OR amoldarse (a).

adaptable [ə'dæptəbl] *adj* [person] capaz de adaptarse.

adapter, adaptor [ə'dæptəʳ] *n* [ELEC - for several devices] ladrón *m*; [- for different socket] adaptador *m*.

add [æd] *vt* **-1.** [gen]: **to ~ sthg (to sthg)** añadir algo (a algo). **-2.** [numbers] sumar. ◆ **add on** *vt sep* [to bill, total]: **to ~ sthg on (to sthg)** añadir OR incluir algo (en algo). ◆ **add to** *vt fus* aumentar, acrecentar. ◆ **add up** ♦ *vt sep* [numbers] sumar. ♦ *vi inf* [make sense]: **it doesn't ~ up** no tiene sentido.

adder ['ædəʳ] *n* víbora *f*.

addict ['ædɪkt] *n* **-1.** [taking drugs] adicto *m*, -ta *f*; **drug ~** drogadicto *m*, -ta *f*, toxicómano *m*, -na *f*. **-2.** *fig* [fan] fanático *m*, -ca *f*.

addicted [ə'dɪktɪd] *adj* **-1.** [to drug]: **~ (to)** adicto(ta) (a). **-2.** *fig* [to food, TV]: **to be ~ (to)** ser un fanático (de).

addiction [ə'dɪkʃn] *n* **-1.** [to drug]: **~ (to)** adicción *f* (a). **-2.** *fig* [to food, TV]: **~ (to)** vicio *m* (por).

addictive [ə'dɪktɪv] *adj lit & fig* adictivo(va).

addition [ə'dɪʃn] *n* **-1.** MATH suma *f*. **-2.** [extra thing] adición *f*. **-3.** [act of adding] incorporación *f*; **in ~** además; **in ~ to** además de.

additional [ə'dɪʃənl] *adj* adicional.

additive ['ædɪtɪv] *n* aditivo *m*.

address [ə'dres] ♦ *n* **-1.** [of person, organization] dirección *f*, domicilio *m*. **-2.** [speech] discurso *m*. ♦ *vt* **-1.** [letter, parcel, remark]: **to ~ sthg to** dirigir algo a. **-2.** [meeting, conference] dirigirse a. **-3.** [issue]: **to ~ o.s. to sthg** enfrentarse a OR abordar algo.

address book *n* agenda *f* de direcciones.

adenoids ['ædɪnɔɪdz] *npl* vegetaciones *fpl* (adenoideas).

adept ['ædept] *adj*: **to be ~ (at sthg/at doing sthg)** ser experto(ta) (en algo/en hacer algo).

adequate ['ædɪkwət] *adj* **-1.** [sufficient] suficiente. **-2.** [good enough] aceptable.

adhere [əd'hɪəʳ] *vi* **-1.** [to surface, principle]: **to ~ (to)** adherirse (a). **-2.** [to rule, decision]: **to ~ to** respetar, observar.

adhesive [əd'hiːsɪv] ♦ *adj* adhesivo(va), adherente. ♦ *n* adhesivo *m*.

adhesive tape *n* cinta *f* adhesiva.

adjacent [ə'dʒeɪsənt] *adj*: **~ (to)** adyacente OR contiguo(gua) (a).

adjective ['ædʒɪktɪv] *n* adjetivo *m*.

adjoining [ə'dʒɔɪnɪŋ] ♦ *adj* [table] adyacente; [room] contiguo(gua). ♦ *prep* junto a.

adjourn [ə'dʒɜːn] ♦ *vt* [decision] aplazar; [session] levantar; [meeting] interrumpir. ♦ *vi* aplazarse, suspenderse.

adjudge [ə'dʒʌdʒ] *vt* declarar, juzgar.

adjudicate [ə'dʒuːdɪkeɪt] *vi* actuar como juez; **to ~ on** OR **upon sthg** emitir un fallo OR un veredicto sobre algo.

adjust [ə'dʒʌst] ♦ *vt* [machine, setting] ajustar; [clothing] arreglarse. ♦ *vi*: **to ~ (to)** adaptarse OR amoldarse (a).

adjustable [ə'dʒʌstəbl] *adj* [machine, chair] regulable, graduable.

adjustment [ə'dʒʌstmənt] *n* **-1.** [modification] modificación *f*, reajuste *m*. **-2.** (*U*) [change in attitude]: **~ (to)** adaptación *f* OR amoldamiento *m* (a).

ad lib [ˌæd'lɪb] ♦ *adj* [improvised] improvisado(da). ♦ *adv* [without preparation] improvisando; [without limit] a voluntad. ◆ **ad-lib** *vi* improvisar.

administer [əd'mɪnɪstəʳ] *vt* [gen] administrar; [punishment] aplicar.

administration [əd,mɪnɪ'streɪʃn] *n* [gen] administración *f*; [of punishment] aplicación *f*.

administrative [əd'mɪnɪstrətɪv] *adj* administrativo(va).

admirable ['ædmərəbl] *adj* admirable.

admiral ['ædmərəl] *n* almirante *m*.

admiration [ˌædmə'reɪʃn] *n* admiración *f*.

admire [əd'maɪəʳ] *vt*: **to ~ sb (for)** admirar a alguien (por).

admirer [əd'maɪərəʳ] *n* admirador *m*, -ra *f*.

admission [əd'mɪʃn] *n* **-1.** [permission to enter] admisión *f*, ingreso *m*. **-2.** [cost of entrance] **entrada** f. **-3.** [of guilt, mistake] reconocimiento m.

admit [əd'mɪt] ◇ vt **-1.** [acknowledge, confess]: **to ~ (that)** admitir OR reconocer (que); **to ~ doing sthg** reconocer haber hecho algo; **to ~ defeat** fig darse por vencido. **-2.** [allow to enter or join] admitir; **to be admitted to hospital** Br OR **to the hospital** Am ser ingresado en el hospital. ◇ vi: **to ~ to sthg** confesar algo.

admittance [əd'mɪtəns] n: **to gain ~ to** conseguir entrar en; **"no ~"** "prohibido el paso".

admittedly [əd'mɪtɪdlɪ] adv sin duda.

admonish [əd'mɒnɪʃ] vt amonestar.

ad nauseam [,æd'nɔːzɪæm] adv hasta la saciedad.

ado [ə'duː] n: **without further** OR **more ~** sin más preámbulos, sin mayor dilación.

adolescence [,ædə'lesns] n adolescencia f.

adolescent [,ædə'lesnt] ◇ adj **-1.** [teenage] adolescente. **-2.** pej [immature] pueril. ◇ n [teenager] adolescente m y f.

adopt [ə'dɒpt] vt & vi adoptar.

adoption [ə'dɒpʃn] n adopción f.

adore [ə'dɔːr] vt **-1.** [love deeply] adorar. **-2.** [like very much]: **I ~ chocolate** me encanta el chocolate.

adorn [ə'dɔːn] vt adornar.

adrenalin [ə'drenəlɪn] n adrenalina f.

Adriatic [,eɪdrɪ'ætɪk] n: **the ~ (Sea)** el (mar) Adriático.

adrift [ə'drɪft] ◇ adj [boat] a la deriva. ◇ adv: **to go ~** fig irse a la deriva.

adult ['ædʌlt] ◇ adj **-1.** [fully grown] adulto(ta). **-2.** [mature] maduro(ra). **-3.** [suitable for adults only] para adultos OR mayores. ◇ n adulto m, -ta f.

adultery [ə'dʌltərɪ] n adulterio m.

advance [əd'vɑːns] ◇ n **-1.** [gen] avance m. **-2.** [money] anticipo m. ◇ comp: **~ notice** OR **warning** previo aviso m; **~ booking** reserva f anticipada. ◇ vt **-1.** [improve] promover. **-2.** [bring forward in time] adelantar. **-3.** [give in advance]: **to ~ sb sthg** adelantarle a alguien algo. ◇ vi avanzar. ◆ **advances** npl: **to make ~s to sb** [sexual] hacerle proposiciones a alguien, insinuarse a alguien; [business] hacerle una propuesta a alguien. ◆ **in advance** adv [pay] por adelantado; [book] con antelación; [know] de antemano.

advanced [əd'vɑːnst] adj **-1.** [developed]

avanzado(da). **-2.** [student, pupil] adelantado(da); [studies] superior.

advantage [əd'vɑːntɪdʒ] n: **~ (over)** ventaja f (sobre); **to be to one's ~** en beneficio de uno; **to take ~ of sthg** aprovechar algo; **to take ~ of sb** aprovecharse de alguien.

advent ['ædvənt] n [arrival] advenimiento m. ◆ **Advent** n RELIG Adviento m.

adventure [əd'ventʃər] n aventura f.

adventure playground n Br parque m infantil.

adventurous [əd'ventʃərəs] adj **-1.** [daring] aventurero(ra). **-2.** [dangerous] arriesgado(da).

adverb ['ædvɜːb] n adverbio m.

adverse ['ædvɜːs] adj adverso(sa).

advert ['ædvɜːt] Br = **advertisement**.

advertise ['ædvətaɪz] ◇ vt anunciar. ◇ vi anunciarse, poner un anuncio; **to ~ for** buscar (mediante anuncio).

advertisement [əd'vɜːtɪsmənt] n anuncio m.

advertiser ['ædvətaɪzər] n anunciante m y f.

advertising ['ædvətaɪzɪŋ] n publicidad f.

advice [əd'vaɪs] n (U) consejos mpl; **to take sb's ~** seguir el consejo de alguien; **a piece of ~** un consejo; **to give sb ~** aconsejar a alguien.

advisable [əd'vaɪzəbl] adj aconsejable.

advise [əd'vaɪz] ◇ vt **-1.** [give advice to]: **to ~ sb to do sthg** aconsejar a alguien que haga algo; **to ~ sb against sthg/against doing sthg** desaconsejar a alguien algo/que haga algo. **-2.** [professionally]: **to ~ sb on sthg** asesorar a alguien en algo. **-3.** fml [inform]: **to ~ sb (of sthg)** informar a alguien (de algo). ◇ vi **-1.** [give advice]: **to ~ against sthg** desaconsejar algo; **to ~ against doing sthg** aconsejar no hacer algo. **-2.** [professionally]: **to ~ on** asesorar en (materia de).

advisedly [əd'vaɪzɪdlɪ] adv [deliberately] deliberadamente; [after careful consideration] con conocimiento de causa.

adviser Br, **advisor** Am [əd'vaɪzər] n consejero m, -ra f, asesor m, -ra f.

advisory [əd'vaɪzərɪ] adj [body] consultivo(va), asesor(ra).

advocate [n 'ædvəkət, vb 'ædvəkeɪt] ◇ n **-1.** JUR abogado m, -da f. **-2.** [supporter] defensor m, -ra f. ◇ vt abogar por.

Aegean [iː'dʒiːən] n: **the ~ (Sea)** el mar Egeo.

aerial ['eərɪəl] ◇ adj aéreo(a). ◇ n Br [antenna] antena f.

aerobics [eə'rəʊbɪks] *n* (*U*) aerobic *m*.
aerodynamic [,eərəʊdaɪ'næmɪk] *adj* aerodinámico(ca).
aeroplane ['eərəpleɪn] *n Br* avión *m*.
aerosol ['eərəsɒl] *n* aerosol *m*.
aesthetic, esthetic *Am* [iːs'θetɪk] *adj* estético(ca).
afar [ə'fɑːʳ] *adv*: **from ~** desde lejos.
affable ['æfəbl] *adj* afable.
affair [ə'feəʳ] *n* **-1.** [event, do] acontecimiento *m*. **-2.** [concern, matter] asunto *m*. **-3.** [extra-marital relationship] aventura *f* (amorosa).
affect [ə'fekt] *vt* **-1.** [influence, move emotionally] afectar. **-2.** [put on] fingir.
affected [ə'fektɪd] *adj* [insincere] afectado(da).
affection [ə'fekʃn] *n* cariño *m*, afecto *m*.
affectionate [ə'fekʃnət] *adj* cariñoso(sa).
affirm [ə'fɜːm] *vt* afirmar.
affix [ə'fɪks] *vt* fijar, pegar.
afflict [ə'flɪkt] *vt* aquejar, afligir.
affluence ['æfluəns] *n* opulencia *f*.
affluent ['æfluənt] *adj* pudiente.
afford [ə'fɔːd] *vt* **-1.** [gen]: **to be able to ~** poder permitirse (el lujo de); **we can't ~ to let this happen** no podemos permitirnos el lujo de dejar que esto ocurra. **-2.** *fml* [provide, give] brindar.
affront [ə'frʌnt] *n* afrenta *f*.
Afghanistan [æf'gænɪstæn] *n* Afganistán.
afield [ə'fiːld] *adv*: **far ~** lejos.
afloat [ə'fləʊt] *adj lit* & *fig* a flote.
afoot [ə'fʊt] *adj* [plan] en marcha; **there is a rumour ~ that** corre el rumor de que.
afraid [ə'freɪd] *adj* **-1.** [gen] asustado(da); **to be ~ of sb** tenerle miedo a alguien; **to be ~ of sthg** tener miedo de algo; **to be ~ of doing** OR **to do sthg** tener miedo de hacer algo. **-2.** [in apologies]: **to be ~ that** temerse que; **I'm ~ so/not** me temo que sí/no.
afresh [ə'freʃ] *adv* de nuevo.
Africa ['æfrɪkə] *n* África.
African ['æfrɪkən] ◇ *adj* africano(na). ◇ *n* africano *m*, -na *f*.
African American *n* negro *m* americano, negra *f* americana.
aft [ɑːft] *adv* en popa.
after ['ɑːftəʳ] ◇ *prep* **-1.** [gen] después de; **~ all my efforts** después de todos mis esfuerzos; **~ you!** ¡usted primero!; **day ~ day** día tras día; **the day ~ tomorrow** pasado mañana; **the week ~ next** no la semana que viene sino la otra. **-2.** *inf* [in search of]: **to be ~ sthg**

buscar algo; **to be ~ sb** andar detrás de alguien. **-3.** [with the name of]: **to be named ~ sb/sthg** llamarse así por alguien/algo. **-4.** [towards retreating person]: **to run ~ sb** correr tras alguien. **-5.** *Am* [telling the time]: **it's twenty ~ three** son las tres y veinte. ◇ *adv* más tarde, después. ◇ *conj* después (de) que; **~ you had done it** después de que lo hubieras hecho. ◆ **afters** *npl Br inf* postre *m*. ◆ **after all** *adv* **-1.** [in spite of everything] después de todo. **-2.** [it should be remembered] al fin y al cabo.
aftereffects ['ɑːftəɪ,fekts] *npl* secuelas *fpl*, efectos *mpl* secundarios.
afterlife ['ɑːftəlaɪf] (*pl* **-lives** [-laɪvz]) *n* más allá *m*, vida *f* de ultratumba.
aftermath ['ɑːftəmæθ] *n* [time] periodo *m* posterior; [situation] situación *f* posterior.
afternoon [,ɑːftə'nuːn] *n* tarde *f*; **in the ~** por la tarde; **good ~** buenas tardes.
aftershave ['ɑːftəʃeɪv] *n* loción *f* para después del afeitado.
aftertaste ['ɑːftəteɪst] *n* **-1.** [of food, drink] resabio *m*. **-2.** *fig* [of unpleasant experience] mal sabor *m* de boca.
afterthought ['ɑːftəθɔːt] *n* idea *f* a posteriori.
afterward(s) ['ɑːftəwəd(z)] *adv* después, más tarde.
again [ə'gen] *adv* **-1.** [gen] otra vez, de nuevo; **never ~** nunca jamás; **he's well ~ now** ya está bien; **to do sthg ~** volver a hacer algo; **to say sthg ~** repetir algo; **~ and ~** una y otra vez; **all over ~** otra vez desde el principio; **time and ~** una y otra vez. **-2.** *phr*: **half as much ~** la mitad otra vez; **twice as much ~** dos veces lo mismo otra vez; **then** OR **there ~** por otro lado, por otra parte.
against [ə'genst] ◇ *prep* contra; **I'm ~ it** estoy (en) contra (de) ello; **to lean ~ sthg** apoyarse en algo; **(as) ~** a diferencia de. ◇ *adv* en contra.
age [eɪdʒ] (*cont* **ageing** OR **aging**) ◇ *n* **-1.** [gen] edad *f*; **to come of ~** hacerse mayor de edad; **to be under ~** ser menor (de edad); **what ~ are you?** ¿qué edad tienes? **-2.** [state of being old] vejez *f*. ◇ *vt* & *vi* envejecer. ◆ **ages** *npl* [long time]: **~s ago** hace siglos; **I haven't seen her for ~s** hace siglos que no la veo.
aged [*adj* eɪdʒd, *npl* 'eɪdʒɪd] ◇ *adj* [of the stated age]: **children ~ between 8 and**

15 niños de entre 8 y 15 años de edad. ◇ *npl*: **the ~** los ancianos.

age group *n* (grupo *m* de) edad *f*.

agency ['eɪdʒənsɪ] *n* **-1.** [business] agencia *f*. **-2.** [organization, body] organismo *m*, instituto *m*.

agenda [ə'dʒendə] *n* orden *m* del día.

agent ['eɪdʒənt] *n* **-1.** COMM [of company] representante *m* y *f*; [of actor] agente *m* y *f*. **-2.** [substance] agente *m*. **-3.** [secret agent] agente *m* (secreto).

aggravate ['ægrəveɪt] *vt* **-1.** [make worse] agravar, empeorar. **-2.** [annoy] irritar.

aggregate ['ægrɪgət] ◇ *adj* global, total. ◇ *n* [total] conjunto *m*, total *m*.

aggressive [ə'gresɪv] *adj* **-1.** [belligerent - person] agresivo(va). **-2.** [forceful - person, campaign] audaz, emprendedor(ra).

aggrieved [ə'griːvd] *adj* ofendido(da).

aghast [ə'gɑːst] *adj*: **~ (at)** horrorizado(da) (ante).

agile [*Br* 'ædʒaɪl, *Am* 'ædʒəl] *adj* ágil.

agitate ['ædʒɪteɪt] ◇ *vt* **-1.** [disturb, worry] inquietar. **-2.** [shake about] agitar. ◇ *vi* [campaign]: **to ~ for/against** hacer campaña a favor de/en contra de.

AGM *n abbr of* **annual general meeting.**

agnostic [æg'nɒstɪk] ◇ *adj* agnóstico(ca). ◇ *n* agnóstico *m*, -ca *f*.

ago [ə'gəʊ] *adv*: **a long time/three days/three years ~** hace mucho tiempo/tres días/tres años.

agog [ə'gɒg] *adj* ansioso(sa), expectante.

agonizing ['ægənaɪzɪŋ] *adj* angustioso(sa).

agony ['ægənɪ] *n* **-1.** [physical pain] dolor *m* muy intenso; **to be in ~** tener tremendos dolores. **-2.** [mental pain] angustia *f*; **to be in ~** estar angustiado.

agony aunt *n Br inf* consejera *f* sentimental.

agree [ə'griː] ◇ *vi* **-1.** [be of same opinion]: **to ~ (with sb about sthg)** estar de acuerdo (con alguien acerca de algo); **to ~ on sthg** ponerse de acuerdo en algo. **-2.** [consent]: **to ~ (to sthg)** acceder (a algo). **-3.** [approve]: **to ~ with sthg** estar de acuerdo con algo. **-4.** [be consistent] concordar. **-5.** [food]: **to ~ with sb** sentarle bien a alguien. **-6.** GRAMM: **to ~ (with)** concordar (con). ◇ *vt* **-1.** [fix] acordar, convenir. **-2.** [be of same opinion]: **to ~ that** estar de acuerdo en que. **-3.** [agree, consent]: **to ~ to do sthg** acordar hacer algo. **-4.** [concede]: **to ~ (that)** reconocer que.

agreeable [ə'griːəbl] *adj* **-1.** [pleasant] agradable. **-2.** [willing]: **to be ~ to sthg/doing sthg** estar conforme con algo/hacer algo.

agreed [ə'griːd] ◇ *adj*: **to be ~ on sthg** estar de acuerdo sobre algo. ◇ *adv* [admittedly] de acuerdo que.

agreement [ə'griːmənt] *n* **-1.** [accord, settlement, contract] acuerdo *m*; **to be in ~ with** estar de acuerdo con. **-2.** [consent] aceptación *f*. **-3.** [consistency] correspondencia *f*. **-4.** GRAMM concordancia *f*.

agricultural [,ægrɪ'kʌltʃərəl] *adj* agrícola.

agriculture ['ægrɪkʌltʃə^r] *n* agricultura *f*.

aground [ə'graʊnd] *adv*: **to run ~** encallar.

ahead [ə'hed] *adv* **-1.** [in front] delante. **-2.** [forwards] adelante, hacia delante; **go ~!** ¡por supuesto!; **right** OR **straight ~** todo recto OR de frente. **-3.** [winning]: **to be ~** [in race] ir en cabeza; [in football, rugby etc] ir ganando. **-4.** [in better position] por delante; **to get ~** [be successful] abrirse camino. **-5.** [in time]: **to look** OR **think ~** mirar hacia el futuro. ◆ **ahead of** *prep* **-1.** [in front of] frente a. **-2.** [beating]: **to be two points ~ of** llevar dos puntos de ventaja a. **-3.** [in better position than] por delante de. **-4.** [in time] con anterioridad a; **~ of schedule** por delante de lo previsto.

aid [eɪd] ◇ *n* ayuda *f*; **medical ~** asistencia *f* médica; **in ~ of** a beneficio de. ◇ *vt* **-1.** [help] ayudar. **-2.** JUR: **to ~ and abet** ser cómplice de.

aide [eɪd] *n* POL ayudante *m* y *f*.

AIDS, Aids [eɪdz] (*abbr of* **acquired immune deficiency syndrome**) ◇ *n* SIDA *m*. ◇ *comp*: **~ patient** sidoso *m*, -sa *f*.

ailing ['eɪlɪŋ] *adj* **-1.** [ill] achacoso(sa). **-2.** *fig* [economy] debilitado(da), renqueante.

ailment ['eɪlmənt] *n* achaque *m*, molestia *f*.

aim [eɪm] ◇ *n* **-1.** [objective] objetivo *m*, intención *f*. **-2.** [in firing gun] puntería *f*; **to take ~ at** apuntar a. ◇ *vt* **-1.** [weapon]: **to ~ sthg at** apuntar algo a. **-2.** [plan, action]: **to be ~ed at doing sthg** ir dirigido OR encaminado a hacer algo. **-3.** [campaign, publicity, criticism]: **to ~ sthg at sb** dirigir algo a alguien. ◇ *vi* **-1.** [point weapon]: **to ~ (at sthg)** apuntar (a algo). **-2.** [intend]: **to ~ at** OR **for sthg** apuntar a OR pretender algo; **to ~ to do sthg** aspirar a OR pretender hacer algo.

aimless ['eɪmlɪs] *adj* sin un objetivo claro.

ain't [eɪnt] *inf* = **am not, are not, is not, have not, has not.**

air [eə'] ◇ *n* **-1.** [gen] aire *m*; **into the ~** al aire; **by ~** en avión; **(up) in the ~** *fig* en el aire. **-2.** RADIO & TV: **on the ~** en el aire. ◇ *comp* aéreo(a). ◇ *vt* **-1.** [clothes, sheets] **airear;** [cupboard, room] ventilar. **-2.** [views, opinions] **expresar.** **-3.** *Am* [broadcast] **emitir.** ◇ *vi* [clothes, sheets] **airearse;** [cupboard, room] ventilarse.

airbag ['eəbæg] *n* AUT *colchón que se infla automáticamente en caso de accidente para proteger a los pasajeros.*

airbase ['eəbeɪs] *n* base *f* aérea.

airbed ['eəbed] *n* Br colchón *m* inflable.

airborne ['eəbɔːn] *adj* **-1.** [troops] aerotransportado(da); [attack] aéreo(a). **-2.** [plane] en el aire, en vuelo.

air-conditioned [-kən'dɪʃnd] *adj* climatizado(da), con aire acondicionado.

air-conditioning [-kən'dɪʃnɪŋ] *n* aire *m* acondicionado.

aircraft ['eəkrɑːft] (*pl inv*) *n* [plane] avión *m*; [any flying machine] aeronave *m*.

aircraft carrier *n* portaaviones *m inv.*

airfield ['eəfiːld] *n* campo *m* de aviación.

airforce ['eəfɔːs] *n*: **the ~** las fuerzas aéreas.

air freshener [-'freʃnə'] *n* ambientador *m*.

airgun ['eəgʌn] *n* pistola *f* de aire comprimido.

airhostess ['eə,həʊstɪs] *n* azafata *f*, aeromoza *f Amer.*

airlift ['eəlɪft] ◇ *n* puente *m* aéreo. ◇ *vt* transportar por avión.

airline ['eəlaɪn] *n* línea *f* aérea.

airliner ['eəlaɪnə'] *n* avión *m* (grande) de pasajeros.

airlock ['eəlɒk] *n* **-1.** [in tube, pipe] bolsa *f* de aire. **-2.** [airtight chamber] cámara *f* OR esclusa *f* de aire.

airmail ['eəmeɪl] *n*: **by ~** por correo aéreo.

airplane ['eəpleɪn] *n Am* avión *m*.

airport ['eəpɔːt] *n* aeropuerto *m*.

air raid *n* ataque *m* aéreo.

airsick ['eəsɪk] *adj*: **to be ~** marearse (*en el avión*).

airspace ['eəspeɪs] *n* espacio *m* aéreo.

air steward *n* auxiliar *m* de vuelo.

airstrip ['eəstrɪp] *n* pista *f* de aterrizaje.

air terminal *n* terminal *f* aérea.

airtight ['eətaɪt] *adj* hermético(ca).

air-traffic controller *n* controlador aéreo *m*, controladora aérea *f*.

airy ['eərɪ] *adj* **-1.** [room] espacioso(sa) y bien ventilado(da). **-2.** [fanciful] ilusorio(ria). **-3.** [nonchalant] despreocupado(da).

aisle [aɪl] *n* **-1.** [in church] nave *f* lateral. **-2.** [in plane, theatre, supermarket] pasillo *m*.

ajar [ə'dʒɑː'] *adj* entreabierto(ta).

aka (*abbr of* **also known as**) alias.

akin [ə'kɪn] *adj*: **~ to sthg/to doing sthg** semejante a algo/a hacer algo.

alacrity [ə'lækrətɪ] *n* presteza *f*.

alarm [ə'lɑːm] ◇ *n* alarma *f*; **to raise** OR **sound the ~** dar la (voz de) alarma. ◇ *vt* alarmar, asustar.

alarm clock *n* despertador *m*.

alarming [ə'lɑːmɪŋ] *adj* alarmante.

alas [ə'læs] *excl literary* ¡ay!

Albania [æl'beɪnjə] *n* Albania.

Albanian [æl'beɪnjən] ◇ *adj* albanés(esa). ◇ *n* **-1.** [person] albanés *m*, -esa *f*. **-2.** [language] albanés *m*.

albeit [ɔːl'biːɪt] *conj fml* aunque, si bien.

album ['ælbəm] *n* **-1.** [of stamps, photos] álbum *m*. **-2.** [record] elepé *m*.

alcohol ['ælkəhɒl] *n* alcohol *m*.

alcoholic [,ælkə'hɒlɪk] ◇ *adj* alcohólico(ca). ◇ *n* alcohólico *m*, -ca *f*.

alcove ['ælkəʊv] *n* hueco *m*.

alderman ['ɔːldəmən] (*pl* -men [-mən]) *n* ≃ concejal *m*, -la *f*.

ale [eɪl] *n* tipo de cerveza.

alert [ə'lɜːt] ◇ *adj* **-1.** [vigilant] atento(ta). **-2.** [perceptive] despierto(ta). **-3.** [aware]: **to be ~ to** ser consciente de. ◇ *n* [gen] MIL: **on the ~** alerta. ◇ *vt* alertar; **to ~ sb to sthg** alertar a alguien de algo.

A level (*abbr of* **Advanced level**) *n Br* SCH *nivel escolar necesario para acceder a la universidad.*

alfresco [æl'freskəʊ] *adj & adv* al aire libre.

algae ['ældʒiː] *npl* algas *fpl*.

algebra ['ældʒɪbrə] *n* álgebra *f*.

Algeria [æl'dʒɪərɪə] *n* Argelia.

alias ['eɪlɪəs] (*pl* -es) ◇ *adv* alias. ◇ *n* alias *m*.

alibi ['ælɪbaɪ] *n* coartada *f*.

alien ['eɪljən] ◇ *adj* **-1.** [from outer space] extraterrestre. **-2.** [unfamiliar] extraño(ña), ajeno(na). ◇ *n* **-1.** [from outer space] extraterrestre *m y f*. **-2.** JUR [foreigner] extranjero *m*, -ra *f*.

alienate ['eɪljəneɪt] *vt* [make unsympathetic] ganarse la antipatía de.

alight [ə'laɪt] (*pt* & *pp* **-ed**) ◇ *adj* [on fire] ardiendo. ◇ *vi fml* **-1.** [land] posarse. **-2.** [get off]: **to ~ from** apearse de.

align [ə'laɪn] *vt* [line up] alinear.

alike [ə'laɪk] ◇ *adj* parecido(da). ◇ *adv* de la misma forma; **to look ~** parecerse.

alimony ['ælɪmənɪ] *n* pensión *f* alimenticia.

alive [ə'laɪv] *adj* **-1.** [living] vivo(va). **-2.** [active, lively] lleno(na) de vida; **to come ~** [story, description] cobrar vida; [person, place] animarse.

alkali ['ælkəlaɪ] (*pl* **-s** OR **-ies**) *n* álcali *m*.

all [ɔːl] ◇ *adj* **-1.** (*with sg noun*) todo(da); **~ the drink** toda la bebida; **~ day** todo el día; **~ night** toda la noche; **~ the time** todo el tiempo OR el rato. **-2.** (*with pl noun*) todos(das); **~ the boxes** todas las cajas; **~ men** todos los hombres; **~ three died** los tres murieron. ◇ *pron* **-1.** (*sg*) [the whole amount] todo *m*, -da *f*; **she drank it ~, she drank ~ of it** se lo bebió todo. **-2.** (*pl*) [everybody, everything] todos *mpl*, -das *fpl*; **~ of them came, they ~ came** vinieron todos. **-3.** (*with superl*) **he's the cleverest of ~** es el más listo de todos; **the most amazing thing of ~** lo más impresionante de todo; **best/worst of ~ ...** lo mejor/peor de todo es que ...; **above ~ → above**; **after ~ → after**; **at ~ → at.** ◇ *adv* **-1.** [entirely] completamente; **I'd forgotten ~ about that** me había olvidado completamente de eso; **~ alone** completamente solo(la). **-2.** [in sport, competitions]: **the score is two ~** el resultado es de empate a dos. **-3.** (*with compar*): **to run ~ the faster** correr aun más rápido. ◆ **all but** *adv* casi. ◆ **all in all** *adv* en conjunto. ◆ **all that** *adv*: **she's not ~ that pretty** no es tan guapa. ◆ **in all** *adv* en total.

Allah ['ælə] *n* Alá *m*.

all-around *Am* = **all-round.**

allay [ə'leɪ] *vt fml* apaciguar, mitigar.

all clear *n* **-1.** [signal] señal *f* de cese de peligro. **-2.** *fig* [go-ahead] luz *f* verde.

allegation [,ælɪ'geɪʃn] *n* acusación *f*.

allege [ə'ledʒ] *vt* alegar; **to be ~d to have done/said** ser acusado de haber hecho/dicho.

allegedly [ə'ledʒɪdlɪ] *adv* presuntamente.

allegiance [ə'liːdʒəns] *n* fidelidad *f*.

allergic [ə'lɜːdʒɪk] *adj lit* & *fig*: **~ (to sthg)** alérgico(ca) (a algo).

allergy ['ælədʒɪ] *n* alergia *f*.

alleviate [ə'liːvɪeɪt] *vt* aliviar.

alley(way) ['ælɪ(weɪ)] *n* callejuela *f*.

alliance [ə'laɪəns] *n* alianza *f*.

allied ['ælaɪd] *adj* **-1.** [powers, troops] aliado(da). **-2.** [subjects] afín.

alligator ['ælɪgeɪtər] (*pl inv* OR **-s**) *n* caimán *m*.

all-important *adj* crucial.

all-in *adj Br* [inclusive] todo incluido. ◆ **all in** ◇ *adj inf* [tired] hecho(cha) polvo. ◇ *adv* [inclusive] todo incluido.

all-night *adj* [party etc] que dura toda la noche; [chemist, bar] abierto(ta) toda la noche.

allocate ['æləkeɪt] *vt*: **to ~ sthg to sb** [money, resources] destinar algo a alguien; [task, tickets, seats] asignar algo a alguien.

allot [ə'lɒt] *vt* [job, time] asignar; [money, resources] destinar.

allotment [ə'lɒtmənt] *n* **-1.** *Br* [garden] parcela municipal arrendada para su cultivo. **-2.** [share - of money, resources] asignación *f*; [- of time] espacio *m* (de tiempo) concedido.

all-out *adj* [effort] supremo(ma); [war] sin cuartel.

allow [ə'laʊ] *vt* **-1.** [permit] permitir, dejar; **to ~ sb to do sthg** permitir OR dejar a alguien hacer algo. **-2.** [set aside - money] destinar; [- time] dejar. **-3.** [officially accept - subj: person] conceder; [- subj: law] admitir. **-4.** [concede]: **to ~ that** admitir OR reconocer que. ◆ **allow for** *vt fus* contar con.

allowance [ə'laʊəns] *n* **-1.** [money received - from government] subsidio *m*; [- from employer] dietas *fpl*. **-2.** *Am* [pocket money] paga *f*. **-3.** FIN desgravación *f*. **-4.** **to make ~s for sthg/sb** [forgive] disculpar algo/a alguien; [take into account] tener en cuenta algo/a alguien.

alloy ['ælɔɪ] *n* aleación *f*.

all right ◇ *adv* **-1.** [gen] bien. **-2.** *inf* [only just acceptably] (más o menos) bien. **-3.** *inf* [in answer - yes] vale, bueno. ◇ *adj* **-1.** [gen] bien. **-2.** *inf* [not bad]: **it's ~, but ...** no está mal, pero .... **-3.** *inf* [OK]: **sorry - that's ~** lo siento - no importa.

all-round *Br*, **all-around** *Am adj* [multi-skilled] polifacético(ca).

all-time *adj* de todos los tiempos.

allude [ə'luːd] *vi*: to ~ to aludir a.

alluring [ə'ljuərɪŋ] *adj* [person] atrayente; [thing] tentador(ra).

allusion [ə'luːʒn] *n* alusión *f*.

ally ['ælaɪ] *n* aliado *m*, -da *f*.

almighty [ɔːl'maɪtɪ] *adj inf* [very big] descomunal.

almond ['ɑːmənd] *n* [nut] almendra *f*.

almost ['ɔːlməʊst] *adv* casi.

alms [ɑːmz] *npl dated* limosna *f*.

aloft [ə'lɒft] *adv* [in the air] en lo alto.

alone [ə'ləʊn] ◇ *adj* solo(la); **to be ~ with** estar a solas con. ◇ *adv* **-1.** [without others] solo(la). **-2.** [only] sólo. **-3.** *phr*: **to leave sthg/sb ~** dejar algo/a alguien en paz. ◆ **let alone** *conj* y mucho menos.

along [ə'lɒŋ] ◇ *adv* **-1.** [forward] hacia delante; **to go** OR **walk ~** avanzar; **she was walking ~** iba andando. **-2.** [to this or that place]: **to come ~** venir; **to go ~** ir. ◇ *prep* [towards one end of, beside] por, a lo largo de. ◆ **all along** *adv* todo el rato, siempre. ◆ **along with** *prep* junto con.

alongside [ə,lɒŋ'saɪd] ◇ *prep* **-1.** [next to] junto a. **-2.** [together with] junto con. ◇ *adv*: **to come ~** ponerse a la misma altura.

aloof [ə'luːf] ◇ *adj* frío(a), distante. ◇ *adv* distante; **to remain ~ (from)** mantenerse a distancia (de).

aloud [ə'laʊd] *adv* en alto, en voz alta.

alphabet ['ælfəbet] *n* alfabeto *m*.

alphabetical [,ælfə'betɪkl] *adj* alfabético(ca); **in ~ order** en OR por orden alfabético.

Alps [ælps] *npl*: **the ~** los Alpes.

already [ɔːl'redɪ] *adv* ya.

alright [,ɔːl'raɪt] = **all right**.

Alsatian [æl'seɪʃn] *n* [dog] pastor *m* alemán.

also ['ɔːlsəʊ] *adv* también.

altar ['ɔːltər] *n* altar *m*.

alter ['ɔːltər] ◇ *vt* [modify] alterar, modificar. ◇ *vi* cambiar.

alteration [,ɔːltə'reɪʃn] *n* alteración *f*.

alternate [*adj Br* ɔːl'tɜːnət, *Am* 'ɔːltərnət, *vb* 'ɔːltərneɪt] ◇ *adj* **-1.** [by turns] alternativo(va), alterno(na). **-2.** [every other]: **on ~ days/weeks** cada dos días/semanas. ◇ *vi*: **to ~ (with/between)** alternar (con/entre).

alternating current ['ɔːltəneɪtɪŋ-] *n* ELEC corriente *f* alterna.

alternative [ɔːl'tɜːnətɪv] ◇ *adj* alternativo(va). ◇ *n* alternativa *f*, opción *f*; **to**

have no ~ (but to do sthg) no tener más remedio (que hacer algo).

alternatively [ɔːl'tɜːnətɪvlɪ] *adv* o bien, por otra parte.

alternator ['ɔːltəneɪtər] *n* ELEC alternador *m*.

although [ɔːl'ðəʊ] *conj* aunque.

altitude ['æltɪtjuːd] *n* altitud *f*.

alto ['æltəʊ] (*pl* **-s**) *n* [male voice] contralto *m*; [female voice] contralto *f*.

altogether [,ɔːltə'geðər] *adv* **-1.** [completely] completamente; **not ~** no del todo. **-2.** [considering all things] en conjunto. **-3.** [in total] en total.

aluminium *Br* [,æljʊ'mɪnɪəm], **aluminum** *Am* [ə'luːmɪnəm] *n* aluminio *m*.

always ['ɔːlweɪz] *adv* siempre.

am [æm] → **be**.

a.m. (*abbr of* **ante meridiem**): **at 3 ~** a las tres de la mañana.

AM (*abbr of* **amplitude modulation**) *n* AM *f*.

amalgamate [ə'mælgəmeɪt] ◇ *vt* [unite] amalgamar. ◇ *vi* [unite] amalgamarse.

amass [ə'mæs] *vt* amasar.

amateur ['æmətər] ◇ *adj* aficionado(da); *pej* chapucero(ra). ◇ *n* aficionado *m*, -da *f*; *pej* chapucero *m*, -ra *f*.

amateurish [,æmə'tɜːrɪʃ] *adj* chapucero(ra).

amaze [ə'meɪz] *vt* asombrar.

amazed [ə'meɪzd] *adj* asombrado(da).

amazement [ə'meɪzmənt] *n* asombro *m*.

amazing [ə'meɪzɪŋ] *adj* asombroso(sa).

Amazon ['æməzn] *n* **-1.** [river]: **the ~** el Amazonas. **-2.** [region]: **the ~ (Basin)** la cuenca amazónica; **the ~ rain forest** la selva amazónica.

ambassador [æm'bæsədər] *n* embajador *m*, -ra *f*.

amber ['æmbər] ◇ *adj* **-1.** [amber-coloured] de color ámbar. **-2.** *Br* [traffic light] ámbar. ◇ *n* ámbar *m*.

ambiguous [æm'bɪgjʊəs] *adj* ambiguo(gua).

ambition [æm'bɪʃn] *n* ambición *f*.

ambitious [æm'bɪʃəs] *adj* ambicioso(sa).

amble ['æmbl] *vi* [walk] deambular, pasear.

ambulance ['æmbjʊləns] *n* ambulancia *f*.

ambush ['æmbʊʃ] ◇ *n* emboscada *f*. ◇ *vt* emboscar.

amenable [ə'miːnəbl] *adj* razonable; **~ to** favorable a.

amend [ə'mend] *vt* [law] enmendar; [text] corregir. ◆ **amends** *npl*: **to make ~s for sthg** reparar algo.

amendment [ə'mendmənt] *n* [change - to law] enmienda *f*; [- to text] corrección *f*.

amenities [ə'mi:nətız] *npl* [of town] facilidades *fpl*; [of building] comodidades *fpl*.

America [ə'merıkə] *n* América.

American [ə'merıkn] ◇ *adj* americano(na). ◇ *n* [person] americano *m*, -na *f*.

American Indian *n* amerindio *m*, -dia *f*.

amiable ['eımjəbl] *adj* amable, agradable.

amicable ['æmıkəbl] *adj* amigable, amistoso(sa).

amid(st) [ə'mıd(st)] *prep fml* entre, en medio de.

amiss [ə'mıs] ◇ *adj* mal. ◇ *adv*: **to take sthg** ~ tomarse algo a mal.

ammonia [ə'məunjə] *n* amoniaco *m*.

ammunition [ˌæmjʊ'nıʃn] *n* (U) MIL municiones *fpl*.

amnesia [æm'ni:zjə] *n* amnesia *f*.

amnesty ['æmnəstı] *n* amnistía *f*.

amok [ə'mɒk] *adv*: **to run** ~ enloquecer atacando a gente de forma indiscriminada.

among(st) [ə'mʌŋ(st)] *prep* entre.

amoral [ˌeı'mɒrəl] *adj* amoral.

amorous ['æmərəs] *adj* amoroso(sa).

amount [ə'maunt] *n* cantidad *f*.
◆ **amount to** *vt fus* **-1.** [total] ascender a. **-2.** [be equivalent to] venir a ser.

amp [æmp] *n abbr of* **ampere.**

ampere ['æmpeəʳ] *n* amperio *m*.

amphibian [æm'fıbıən] *n* anfibio *m*.

ample ['æmpl] *adj* **-1.** [enough] suficiente; [more than enough] sobrado(da). **-2.** [garment, room] amplio(plia); [stomach, bosom] abundante.

amplifier ['æmplıfaıəʳ] *n* amplificador *m*.

amputate ['æmpjʊteıt] *vt & vi* amputar.

Amsterdam [ˌæmstə'dæm] *n* Amsterdam.

Amtrak ['æmtræk] *n organismo que regula y coordina las líneas férreas en Estados Unidos.*

amuck [ə'mʌk] = **amok.**

amuse [ə'mju:z] *vt* **-1.** [make laugh, smile] divertir. **-2.** [entertain] distraer.

amused [ə'mju:zd] *adj* **-1.** [person, look] divertido(da); **I was not** ~ **at** OR **by that** no me hizo gracia eso. **-2.** [entertained]: **to keep o.s.** ~ entretenerse, distraerse.

amusement [ə'mju:zmənt] *n* **-1.** [enjoyment] regocijo *m*, diversión *f*. **-2.** [diversion, game] atracción *f*.

amusement arcade *n* salón *m* de juegos.

amusement park *n* parque *m* de atracciones.

amusing [ə'mju:zıŋ] *adj* divertido(da).

an [stressed æn, unstressed ən] → **a²**.

anabolic steroid [ˌænə'bɒlık-] *n* esteroide *m* anabolizante.

anaemic *Br*, **anemic** *Am* [ə'ni:mık] *adj* [ill] anémico(ca).

anaesthetic *Br*, **anesthetic** *Am* [ˌænıs'θetık] *n* anestesia *f*; **local/general** ~ anestesia local/general.

analogue, analog *Am* ['ænəlɒg] ◇ *adj* [watch, clock] analógico(ca). ◇ *n fml* equivalente *m*.

analogy [ə'nælədʒı] *n* analogía *f*.

analyse *Br*, **analyze** *Am* ['ænəlaız] *vt* analizar.

analysis [ə'næləsıs] (*pl* **analyses** [ə'næləsi:z]) *n* análisis *m inv*.

analyst ['ænəlıst] *n* **-1.** [gen] analista *m y f*. **-2.** [psychoanalyst] psicoanalista *m y f*.

analytic(al) [ˌænə'lıtık(l)] *adj* analítico(ca).

analyze *Am* = **analyse.**

anarchist ['ænəkıst] *n* anarquista *m y f*.

anarchy ['ænəkı] *n* anarquía *f*.

anathema [ə'næθəmə] *n*: **the idea is** ~ **to me** la idea me parece aberrante.

anatomy [ə'nætəmı] *n* anatomía *f*.

ANC (*abbr of* **African National Congress**) *n* ANC *m*.

ancestor ['ænsestəʳ] *n lit & fig* antepasado *m*.

anchor ['æŋkəʳ] ◇ *n* NAUT ancla *f*; **to drop** ~ echar el ancla; **to weigh** ~ levar anclas. ◇ *vt* **-1.** [secure] sujetar. **-2.** TV presentar. ◇ *vi* NAUT anclar.

anchovy ['æntʃəvı] (*pl inv* OR **-ies**) *n* [salted] anchoa *f*; [fresh] boquerón *m*.

ancient ['eınʃənt] *adj* **-1.** [gen] antiguo(gua). **-2.** *hum* [very old] vetusto(ta).

ancillary [æn'sılərı] *adj* auxiliar.

and [strong form ænd, weak form ənd, ən] *conj* **-1.** [gen] y; [before "i" or "hi"] e; **faster** ~ **faster** cada vez más rápido; **it's nice** ~ **easy** es sencillito. **-2.** [in numbers]: **one hundred** ~ **eighty** ciento ochenta; **one** ~ **a half** uno y medio; **2** ~ **2 is 4** 2 y 2 son 4. **-3.** [to]: **try** ~ **come** intenta venir; **come** ~ **see the kids** ven a ver a los niños; **wait** ~ **see** espera a ver. ◆ **and so on, and so forth** *adv* etcétera, y cosas así.

Andalusia [ˌændə'lu:zıə] *n* Andalucía.

Andes ['ændi:z] *npl*: **the** ~ los Andes.

Andorra [æn'dɔːrə] *n* Andorra.

anecdote ['ænɪkdəʊt] *n* anécdota *f*.

anemic *Am* = **anaemic**.

anesthetic *etc Am* = **anaesthetic** *etc*.

anew [ə'njuː] *adv* de nuevo, nuevamente.

angel ['eɪndʒəl] *n* RELIG ángel *m*.

anger ['æŋgəʳ] ◇ *n* ira *f*, furia *f*. ◇ *vt* enfurecer.

angina [æn'dʒaɪnə] *n* angina *f* de pecho.

angle ['æŋgl] *n* -1. [gen] ángulo *m*; **at an ~** [aslant] torcido. -2. [point of view] enfoque *m*.

angler ['æŋgləʳ] *n* pescador *m*, -ra *f* (*con caña*).

Anglican ['æŋglɪkən] ◇ *adj* anglicano(na). ◇ *n* anglicano *m*, -na *f*.

angling ['æŋglɪŋ] *n* pesca *f* con caña.

Anglo-Saxon [ˌæŋgləʊ'sæksn] ◇ *adj* anglosajón(ona). ◇ *n* -1. [person] anglosajón *m*, -ona *f*. -2. [language] anglosajón *m*.

angry ['æŋgrɪ] *adj* [person] enfadado(da); [letter, look, face] furioso(sa), airado(da); **to be ~ at** OR **with sb** estar enfadado con alguien; **to get ~ with sb** enfadarse con alguien.

anguish ['æŋgwɪʃ] *n* angustia *f*.

angular ['æŋgjʊləʳ] *adj* [face, body] anguloso(sa).

animal ['ænɪml] ◇ *adj* animal. ◇ *n* animal *m*; *pej* animal *m y f*.

animate ['ænɪmət] *adj* animado(da).

animated ['ænɪmeɪtɪd] *adj* animado(da).

aniseed ['ænɪsiːd] *n* anís *m*.

ankle ['æŋkl] ◇ *n* tobillo *m*. ◇ *comp*: **~ boots** botines *mpl*; **~ socks** calcetines *mpl* por el tobillo.

annex ['æneks] ◇ *n* edificio *m* anejo. ◇ *vt* anexionar.

annexe ['æneks] = **annex**.

annihilate [ə'naɪəleɪt] *vt* [destroy] aniquilar.

anniversary [ˌænɪ'vɜːsərɪ] *n* aniversario *m*.

announce [ə'naʊns] *vt* anunciar.

announcement [ə'naʊnsmənt] *n* anuncio *m*.

announcer [ə'naʊnsəʳ] *n*: **radio/ television ~** presentador *m*, -ra *f* OR locutor *m*, -ra *f* de radio/televisión.

annoy [ə'nɔɪ] *vt* fastidiar, molestar.

annoyance [ə'nɔɪəns] *n* molestia *f*.

annoyed [ə'nɔɪd] *adj*: **~ at sthg/with sb** molesto(ta) por algo/con alguien.

annoying [ə'nɔɪɪŋ] *adj* fastidioso(sa).

annual ['ænjʊəl] ◇ *adj* anual. ◇ *n* -1. [plant] planta *f* anual. -2. [book] anuario *m*.

annual general meeting *n* junta *f* general anual.

annul [ə'nʌl] *vt* anular.

annum ['ænəm] *n*: **per ~** al año.

anomaly [ə'nɒməlɪ] *n* anomalía *f*.

anonymous [ə'nɒnɪməs] *adj* anónimo(ma).

anorak ['ænəræk] *n* chubasquero *m*, anorak *m*.

anorexia (nervosa) [ˌænə'reksɪə(nɜː-'vəʊsə)] *n* anorexia *f*.

anorexic [ˌænə'reksɪk] ◇ *adj* anoréxico(ca). ◇ *n* anoréxico *m*, -ca *f*.

another [ə'nʌðəʳ] ◇ *adj* otro(tra); **in ~ few minutes** en unos minutos más. ◇ *pron* otro *m*, -tra *f*; **one after ~** uno tras otro, una tras otra; **one ~** el uno al otro, la una a la otra; **we love one ~** nos queremos.

answer ['ɑːnsəʳ] ◇ *n* respuesta *f*; **in ~ to** en respuesta a. ◇ *vt* -1. [reply to] responder a, contestar a. -2. [respond to]: **to ~ the door** abrir la puerta; **to ~ the phone** coger OR contestar el teléfono. ◇ *vi* responder, contestar.
◆ **answer back** *vt sep & vi* replicar.
◆ **answer for** *vt fus* -1. [accept responsibility for] responder por. -2. [suffer consequences of] responder de.

answerable ['ɑːnsərəbl] *adj*: **~ (to sb/for sthg)** responsable (ante alguien/de algo).

answering machine ['ɑːnsərɪŋ-] *n* contestador *m* automático.

ant [ænt] *n* hormiga *f*.

antagonism [æn'tægənɪzm] *n* antagonismo *m*.

antagonize, -ise [æn'tægənaɪz] *vt* provocar la hostilidad de.

Antarctic [æn'tɑːktɪk] ◇ *adj* antártico(ca). ◇ *n*: **the ~** el Antártico.

Antarctica [æn'tɑːktɪkə] *n* (la) Antártida.

antelope ['æntɪləʊp] (*pl inv* OR **-s**) *n* antílope *m*.

antenatal [ˌæntɪ'neɪtl] *adj* prenatal.

antenatal clinic *n* maternidad *f*.

antenna [æn'tenə] (*pl sense 1* **-nae** [-niː], *pl sense 2* **-s**) *n* -1. [of insect] antena *f*. -2. *Am* [aerial] antena *f*.

anthem ['ænθəm] *n* himno *m*.

anthology [æn'θɒlədʒɪ] *n* antología *f*.

antibiotic [ˌæntɪbaɪ'ɒtɪk] *n* antibiótico *m*.

antibody ['æntɪˌbɒdɪ] *n* anticuerpo *m*.

anticipate [æn'tısıpeıt] *vt* **-1.** [expect] prever. **-2.** [look forward to] esperar ansiosamente. **-3.** [competitor] adelantarse a.

anticipation [æn,tısı'peıʃn] *n* expectación *f*; **in ~ of** en previsión de.

anticlimax [æntı'klaımæks] *n* anticlímax *m*.

anticlockwise [,æntı'klɒkwaız] *Br adv* en sentido contrario al de las agujas del reloj.

antics ['æntıks] *npl* payasadas *fpl*.

anticyclone [,æntı'saıkləʊn] *n* anticiclón *m*.

antidepressant [,æntıdı'presnt] *n* antidepresivo *m*.

antidote ['æntıdəʊt] *n lit* & *fig:* **~ (to)** antídoto *m* (contra).

antifreeze ['æntıfriːz] *n* anticongelante *m*.

antihistamine [,æntı'hıstəmın] *n* antihistamínico *m*.

antiperspirant [,æntı'pɜːspərənt] *n* antitranspirante *m*.

antiquated ['æntıkweıtıd] *adj* anticuado(da).

antique [æn'tiːk] ◇ *adj* [furniture, object] antiguo(gua). ◇ *n* antigüedad *f*.

antique shop *n* tienda *f* de antigüedades.

anti-Semitism [,æntı'semıtızm] *n* antisemitismo *m*.

antiseptic [,æntı'septık] ◇ *adj* antiséptico(ca). ◇ *n* antiséptico *m*.

antisocial [,æntı'səʊʃl] *adj* **-1.** [against society] antisocial. **-2.** [unsociable] poco sociable.

antlers ['æntləz] *npl* cornamenta *f*.

anus ['eınəs] *n* ano *m*.

anvil ['ænvıl] *n* yunque *m*.

anxiety [æŋ'zaıətı] *n* **-1.** [worry] ansiedad *f*, inquietud *f*. **-2.** [cause of worry] preocupación *f*. **-3.** [keenness] afán *m*, ansia *f*.

anxious ['æŋkʃəs] *adj* **-1.** [worried] preocupado(da); **to be ~ about** estar preocupado por. **-2.** [keen]: **to be ~ that/to do sthg** estar ansioso(sa) por que/por hacer algo.

any ['enı] ◇ *adj* **-1.** (*with negative*) ninguno(na); **I haven't read ~ books** no he leído ningún libro; **I haven't got ~ money** no tengo nada de dinero. **-2.** [some] algún(una); **are there ~ cakes left?** ¿queda algún pastel?; **is there ~ milk left?** ¿queda algo de leche?; **have you got ~ money?** ¿tienes dinero? **-3.** [no matter which] cualquier; **~ box will**

do cualquier caja vale; *see also* **case, day, moment, rate.** ◇ *pron* **-1.** (*with negative*) ninguno *m*, -na *f*; **I didn't get ~ a mí** no me tocó ninguno. **-2.** [some] alguno *m*, -na *f*; **can ~ of you do it?** ¿sabe alguno de vosotros hacerlo?; **I need some matches, do you have ~?** necesito cerillas, ¿tienes? **-3.** [no matter which] cualquiera; **take ~ you like** coge cualquiera que te guste. ◇ *adv* **-1.** (*with negative*): **I can't see it ~ more** ya no lo veo; **he's not feeling ~ better** no se siente nada mejor; **I can't stand it ~ longer** no lo aguanto más. **-2.** [some, a little]: **do you want ~ more potatoes?** ¿quieres más patatas?; **is that ~ better/different?** ¿es así mejor/diferente?

anybody ['enı,bɒdı] = **anyone**.

anyhow ['enıhaʊ] *adv* **-1.** [in spite of that] de todos modos. **-2.** [carelessly] de cualquier manera. **-3.** [in any case] en cualquier caso.

anyone ['enıwʌn] *pron* **-1.** (*in negative sentences*) nadie; **I don't know ~** no conozco a nadie. **-2.** (*in questions*) alguien. **-3.** [any person] cualquiera.

anyplace *Am* = **anywhere**.

anything ['enıθıŋ] *pron* **-1.** (*in negative sentences*) nada; **I don't want ~** no quiero nada. **-2.** (*in questions*) algo; **would you like ~ else?** ¿quiere algo más? **-3.** [any object, event] cualquier cosa.

anyway ['enıweı] *adv* **-1.** [in any case] de todas formas OR maneras. **-2.** [in conversation] en cualquier caso.

anywhere ['enıweəʳ], **anyplace** *Am* ['enıpleıs] *adv* **-1.** (*in negative sentences*) en ningún sitio; **I didn't go ~** no fui a ninguna parte. **-2.** (*in questions*) en algún sitio; **did you go ~?** ¿fuiste a algún sitio? **-3.** [any place] cualquier sitio; **~ you like** donde quieras.

apart [ə'pɑːt] *adv* **-1.** [separated] aparte; **we're living ~** vivimos separados. **-2.** [aside] aparte; **joking ~** bromas aparte. ◆ **apart from** *prep* **-1.** [except for] salvo. **-2.** [as well as] aparte de.

apartheid [ə'pɑːtheıt] *n* apartheid *m*.

apartment [ə'pɑːtmənt] *n* piso *m*, apartamento *m*.

apartment building *n Am* bloque *m* de pisos.

apathy ['æpəθı] *n* apatía *f*.

ape [eıp] ◇ *n* simio *m*. ◇ *vt pej* imitar.

aperitif [əperə'tiːf] *n* aperitivo *m*.

aperture ['æpə,tjʊəʳ] *n* abertura *f*.

apex ['eɪpeks] (*pl* **-es** OR **apices**) *n* [top] vértice *m*.

APEX ['eɪpeks] (*abbr of* **advance purchase excursion**) *n Br* (tarifa *f*) APEX *f*.

apices ['eɪpɪsiːz] *pl* → **apex**.

apiece [ə'piːs] *adv* cada uno(na).

apocalypse [ə'pɒkəlɪps] *n* apocalipsis *m inv*.

apologetic [ə,pɒlə'dʒetɪk] *adj* [tone, look] lleno(na) de disculpas; **to be ~ (about)** no hacer más que disculparse (por).

apologize, -ise [ə'pɒlədʒaɪz] *vi*: **to ~ (to sb for sthg)** disculparse (con alguien por algo).

apology [ə'pɒlədʒɪ] *n* disculpa *f*.

apostle [ə'pɒsl] *n* RELIG apóstol *m*.

apostrophe [ə'pɒstrəfɪ] *n* apóstrofo *m*.

appal, appall *Am* [ə'pɔːl] *vt* horrorizar.

appalling [ə'pɔːlɪŋ] *adj* **-1.** [shocking] horroroso(sa). **-2.** *inf* [very bad] fatal.

apparatus [,æpə'reɪtəs] (*pl inv* OR **-es**) *n* [gen & POL] aparato *m*.

apparel [ə'pærəl] *n Am* ropa *f*.

apparent [ə'pærənt] *adj* **-1.** [evident] evidente, patente. **-2.** [seeming] aparente.

apparently [ə'pærəntlɪ] *adv* **-1.** [it seems] por lo visto. **-2.** [seemingly] aparentemente.

appeal [ə'piːl] ◇ *vi* **-1.** [request]: **to ~ (to sb for sthg)** solicitar (de alguien algo). **-2.** [to sb's honour, common sense]: **to ~ to** apelar a. **-3.** JUR: **to ~ (against)** apelar (contra). **-4.** [attract, interest]: **to ~ (to)** atraer (a). ◇ *n* **-1.** [request] llamamiento *m*, súplica *f*; [fund-raising campaign] campaña *f* para recaudar fondos. **-2.** JUR apelación *f*. **-3.** [charm, interest] atractivo *m*.

appealing [ə'piːlɪŋ] *adj* [attractive] atractivo(va).

appear [ə'pɪəʳ] *vi* **-1.** [gen] aparecer. **-2.** [seem]: **to ~ (to be/to do sthg)** parecer (ser/hacer algo); **it would ~ that ...** parece que .... **-3.** [in play, film, on TV]: **to ~ on TV/in a film** salir en televisión/en una película. **-4.** JUR: **to ~ (before)** comparecer (ante).

appearance [ə'pɪərəns] *n* **-1.** [gen] aparición *f*; **to make an ~** aparecer. **-2.** [look - of person, place, object] aspecto *m*.

appease [ə'piːz] *vt* aplacar, apaciguar.

append [ə'pend] *vt fml*: **to ~ sthg (to sthg)** agregar algo (a algo).

appendices [ə'pendɪsiːz] *pl* → **appendix**.

appendicitis [ə,pendɪ'saɪtɪs] *n* (*U*) apendicitis *f inv*.

appendix [ə'pendɪks] (*pl* **-dixes** OR **-dices**) *n* [gen & MED] apéndice *m*.

appetite ['æpɪtaɪt] *n* **-1.** [for food] apetito *m*; **~ for ganas** *fpl* de. **-2.** *fig* [enthusiasm]: **~ for entusiasmo** *m* OR **ilusión** *f* por.

appetizer, -iser ['æpɪtaɪzəʳ] *n* aperitivo *m*.

appetizing, -ising ['æpɪtaɪzɪŋ] *adj* [food] apetitoso(sa).

applaud [ə'plɔːd] *vt & vi lit & fig* aplaudir.

applause [ə'plɔːz] *n* (*U*) aplausos *mpl*.

apple ['æpl] *n* manzana *f*.

apple tree *n* manzano *m*.

appliance [ə'plaɪəns] *n* aparato *m*.

applicable [ə'plɪkəbl] *adj*: **to be ~ (to)** aplicarse (a).

applicant ['æplɪkənt] *n*: **~ (for)** solicitante *m y f* (de).

application [,æplɪ'keɪʃn] *n* **-1.** [gen] aplicación *f*. **-2.** [for job, college, club]: **~ (for)** solicitud *f* (para). **-3.** COMPUT: **~ (program)** aplicación *f*.

application form *n* impreso *m* de solicitud.

applied [ə'plaɪd] *adj* [science] aplicado(da).

apply [ə'plaɪ] ◇ *vt* [gen] aplicar; [brakes] echar. ◇ *vi* **-1.** [for work, grant] presentar una solicitud; **to ~ to sb for sthg** solicitar a alguien algo. **-2.** [be relevant] aplicarse; **to ~ to** concernir a.

appoint [ə'pɔɪnt] *vt* **-1.** [to job, position]: **to ~ sb (to sthg)** nombrar a alguien (para algo); **to ~ sb as sthg** nombrar a alguien algo. **-2.** *fml* [time, place] señalar, fijar.

appointment [ə'pɔɪntmənt] *n* **-1.** [to job, position] nombramiento *m*. **-2.** [job, position] puesto *m*, cargo *m*. **-3.** [with businessman, lawyer] cita *f*; [with doctor, hairdresser] hora *f*; **to have an ~** [with businessman] tener una cita; [with doctor] tener hora; **to make an ~** concertar una cita.

apportion [ə'pɔːʃn] *vt* [money] repartir; [blame] adjudicar.

appraisal [ə'preɪzl] *n* evaluación *f*.

appreciable [ə'priːʃəbl] *adj* apreciable.

appreciate [ə'priːʃɪeɪt] ◇ *vt* **-1.** [value, like] apreciar. **-2.** [recognize, understand] darse cuenta de. **-3.** [be grateful for] agradecer. ◇ *vi* FIN encarecerse.

appreciation [ə,priːʃɪ'eɪʃn] *n* **-1.** [liking] aprecio *m*. **-2.** [recognition, understanding] entendimiento *m*. **-3.** [gratitude] agradecimiento *m*. **-4.** FIN encarecimiento *m*.

appreciative [əˈpriːʃətɪv] *adj* [person, remark] agradecido(da); [audience] entendido(da).

apprehensive [ˌæprɪˈhensɪv] *adj* aprensivo(va).

apprentice [əˈprentɪs] *n* aprendiz *m*, -za *f*.

apprenticeship [əˈprentɪʃɪp] *n* aprendizaje *m*.

approach [əˈprəʊtʃ] ◇ *n* **-1.** [arrival] llegada *f*. **-2.** [way in] acceso *m*. **-3.** [method] enfoque *m*. **-4.** [to person]: **to makes ~es to sb** hacerle propuestas a alguien. ◇ *vt* **-1.** [come near to] acercarse a. **-2.** [ask]: **to ~ sb about sthg** hacer una propuesta OR dirigirse a alguien acerca de algo. **-3.** [problem, situation] abordar. **-4.** [level, speed] aproximarse a. ◇ *vi* acercarse.

approachable [əˈprəʊtʃəbl] *adj* accesible.

appropriate [*adj* əˈprəʊprɪət, *vb* əˈprəʊprieɪt] ◇ *adj* apropiado(da). ◇ *vt* JUR [take] apropiarse de.

approval [əˈpruːvl] *n* **-1.** [admiration] aprobación *f*. **-2.** [official sanctioning] visto *m* bueno. **-3.** COMM: **on ~ a prueba.**

approve [əˈpruːv] ◇ *vi* estar de acuerdo; **to ~ of sthg/sb** ver con buenos ojos algo/a alguien. ◇ *vt* aprobar.

approx. [əˈprɒks] (*abbr of* **approximately**) aprox.

approximate [əˈprɒksɪmət] *adj* aproximado(da).

approximately [əˈprɒksɪmətlɪ] *adv* aproximadamente.

apricot [ˈeɪprɪkɒt] *n* [fruit] albaricoque *m*, chabacano *m Amer*.

April [ˈeɪprəl] *n* abril *m*; *see also* **September**.

April Fools' Day *n* primero *m* de abril, ≈ Día *m* de los Santos Inocentes.

apron [ˈeɪprən] *n* [clothing] delantal *m*, mandil *m*.

apt [æpt] *adj* **-1.** [pertinent] acertado(da). **-2.** [likely]: **~ to do sthg** propenso(sa) a hacer algo.

aptitude [ˈæptɪtjuːd] *n* aptitud *f*.

aptly [ˈæptlɪ] *adv* apropiadamente.

aqualung [ˈækwəlʌŋ] *n* escafandra *f* autónoma.

aquarium [əˈkweərɪəm] (*pl* **-riums** OR **-ria** [-rɪə]) *n* acuario *m*.

Aquarius [əˈkweərɪəs] *n* Acuario *m*.

aquatic [əˈkwætɪk] *adj* acuático(ca).

aqueduct [ˈækwɪdʌkt] *n* acueducto *m*.

Arab [ˈærəb] ◇ *adj* árabe. ◇ *n* [person] árabe *m y f*.

Arabic [ˈærəbɪk] ◇ *adj* árabe. ◇ *n* [language] árabe *m*.

Arabic numeral *n* número *m* arábigo.

arable [ˈærəbl] *adj* cultivable.

arbitrary [ˈɑːbɪtrərɪ] *adj* [random] arbitrario(ria).

arbitration [ˌɑːbɪˈtreɪʃn] *n* arbitraje *m*.

arcade [ɑːˈkeɪd] *n* **-1.** [shopping arcade] galería *f* OR centro *m* comercial. **-2.** [covered passage] arcada *f*, galería *f*.

arch [ɑːtʃ] ◇ *n* **-1.** ARCHIT arco *m*. **-2.** [of foot] puente *m*. ◇ *vt* arquear.

archaeologist [ˌɑːkɪˈɒlədʒɪst] *n* arqueólogo *m*, -ga *f*.

archaeology [ˌɑːkɪˈɒlədʒɪ] *n* arqueología *f*.

archaic [ɑːˈkeɪɪk] *adj* arcaico(ca).

archbishop [ˌɑːtʃˈbɪʃəp] *n* arzobispo *m*.

archenemy [ˌɑːtʃˈenɪmɪ] *n* peor enemigo *m*, enemigo acérrimo.

archeology *etc* [ˌɑːkɪˈɒlədʒɪ] = **archaeology** *etc*.

archer [ˈɑːtʃər] *n* arquero *m*.

archery [ˈɑːtʃərɪ] *n* tiro *m* con arco.

archetypal [ˌɑːkɪˈtaɪpl] *adj* arquetípico(ca).

architect [ˈɑːkɪtekt] *n* **-1.** [of buildings] arquitecto *m*, -ta *f*. **-2.** *fig* [of plan, event] artífice *m y f*.

architecture [ˈɑːkɪtektʃər] *n* [gen & COMPUT] arquitectura *f*.

archives [ˈɑːkaɪvz] *npl* [of documents] archivos *mpl*.

archway [ˈɑːtʃweɪ] *n* [passage] arcada *f*; [entrance] entrada *f* en forma de arco.

Arctic [ˈɑːktɪk] ◇ *adj* GEOGR ártico(ca). ◇ *n*: **the ~** el Ártico.

ardent [ˈɑːdənt] *adj* ardoroso(sa), ferviente.

arduous [ˈɑːdjʊəs] *adj* arduo(dua).

are [*weak form* ər, *strong form* ɑːr] → **be**.

area [ˈeərɪə] *n* **-1.** [region, designated space] zona *f*, área *f*; **in the ~** en la zona. **-2.** *fig* [approximate size, number]: **in the ~ of** del orden de, alrededor de. **-3.** [surface size] superficie *f*, área *f*. **-4.** [of knowledge, interest] campo *m*.

area code *n* prefijo *m* (telefónico).

arena [əˈriːnə] *n* **-1.** SPORT pabellón *m*. **-2.** *fig* [area of activity]: **she entered the political ~** saltó al ruedo político.

aren't [ɑːnt] = **are not**.

Argentina [ˌɑːdʒənˈtiːnə] *n* (la) Argentina.

Argentine [ˈɑːdʒəntaɪn] *adj* argentino(na).

Argentinian [ˌɑːdʒənˈtɪnɪən] ◊ *adj* argentino(na). ◊ *n* argentino *m*, -na *f*.

arguably [ˈɑːgjʊəblɪ] *adv* probablemente.

argue [ˈɑːgjuː] ◊ *vi* **-1.** [quarrel]: **to ~ (with sb about sthg)** discutir (con alguien de algo). **-2.** [reason]: **to ~ (for/against)** argumentar (a favor de/contra). ◊ *vt*: **to ~ that** argumentar que.

argument [ˈɑːgjʊmənt] *n* **-1.** [gen] discusión *f*; **to have an ~ (with)** tener una discusión (con). **-2.** [reason] argumento *m*.

argumentative [ˌɑːgjʊˈmentətɪv] *adj* muy propenso(sa) a discutir.

arid [ˈærɪd] *adj lit & fig* árido(da).

Aries [ˈeəriːz] *n* Aries *m*.

arise [əˈraɪz] (*pt* **arose**, *pp* **arisen** [əˈrɪzn]) *vi* [appear]: **to ~ (from)** surgir OR provenir (de).

aristocrat [*Br* ˈærɪstəkræt, *Am* əˈrɪstəkræt] *n* aristócrata *m y f*.

arithmetic [əˈrɪθmətɪk] *n* aritmética *f*.

ark [ɑːk] *n* arca *f*.

arm [ɑːm] ◊ *n* **-1.** [of person, chair] brazo *m*; **~ in ~** del brazo; **to twist sb's ~** *fig* persuadir a alguien. **-2.** [of garment] manga *f*. ◊ *vt* armar. ◆ **arms** *npl* [weapons] armas *fpl*.

armaments [ˈɑːməmənts] *npl* armamento *m*.

armchair [ˈɑːmtʃeəʳ] *n* sillón *m*.

armed [ɑːmd] *adj* **-1.** [police, thieves] armado(da). **-2.** *fig* [with information]: **~ with** provisto(ta) de.

armed forces *npl* fuerzas *fpl* armadas.

armhole [ˈɑːmhəʊl] *n* sobaquera *f*, sisa *f*.

armour *Br*, **armor** *Am* [ˈɑːməʳ] *n* **-1.** [for person] armadura *f*. **-2.** [for military vehicle] blindaje *m*.

armoured car [ɑːməd-] *n* MIL carro *m* blindado.

armoury *Br*, **armory** *Am* [ˈɑːmərɪ] *n* arsenal *m*.

armpit [ˈɑːmpɪt] *n* sobaco *m*, axila *f*.

armrest [ˈɑːmrest] *n* brazo *m*.

arms control [ˈɑːmz-] *n* control *m* armamentístico.

army [ˈɑːmɪ] *n lit & fig* ejército *m*.

A road *n Br* ≃ carretera *f* nacional.

aroma [əˈrəʊmə] *n* aroma *m*.

arose [əˈrəʊz] *pt* → **arise**.

around [əˈraʊnd] ◊ *adv* **-1.** [about, round] por ahí; **to walk/look ~** andar/

mirar por ahí. **-2.** [on all sides] alrededor. **-3.** [present, available]: **is John ~?** [there] ¿está John por ahí?; [here] ¿está John por aquí? **-4.** [turn, look]: **to turn ~** volverse; **to look ~** volver la cabeza. ◊ *prep* **-1.** [on all sides of] alrededor de. **-2.** [about, round - place] por. **-3.** [in the area of] cerca de. **-4.** [approximately] alrededor de.

arouse [əˈraʊz] *vt* [excite - feeling] levantar, despertar; [- person] excitar.

arrange [əˈreɪndʒ] *vt* **-1.** [flowers, books, furniture] colocar. **-2.** [event, meeting, party] organizar; **to ~ to do sthg** acordar hacer algo; **to ~ sthg for sb** organizarle algo a alguien. **-3.** MUS arreglar.

arrangement [əˈreɪndʒmənt] *n* **-1.** [agreement] acuerdo *m*; **to come to an ~** llegar a un acuerdo. **-2.** [of flowers, furniture] disposición *f*. **-3.** MUS arreglo *m*. ◆ **arrangements** *npl* preparativos *mpl*.

array [əˈreɪ] *n* [of objects] surtido *m*.

arrears [əˈrɪəz] *npl* [money owed] atrasos *mpl*; **in ~** [retrospectively] con retraso; [late] atrasado en el pago.

arrest [əˈrest] ◊ *n* arresto *m*, detención *f*; **under ~** bajo arresto. ◊ *vt* **-1.** [subj: police] detener. **-2.** [sb's attention] captar. **-3.** *fml* [stop] poner freno a.

arrival [əˈraɪvl] *n* llegada *f*; **late ~** [of train, bus, mail] retraso *m*; **new ~** [person] recién llegado *m*, recién llegada *f*; [baby] recién nacido *m*, recién nacida *f*.

arrive [əˈraɪv] *vi* **-1.** [gen] llegar; **to ~ at** [conclusion, decision] llegar a. **-2.** [baby] nacer.

arrogant [ˈærəgənt] *adj* arrogante.

arrow [ˈærəʊ] *n* flecha *f*.

arse [ɑːs], **ass** *Am* [æs] *n v inf* [bottom] culo *m*.

arsenic [ˈɑːsnɪk] *n* arsénico *m*.

arson [ˈɑːsn] *n* incendio *m* premeditado.

art [ɑːt] *n* arte *m*. ◆ **arts** *npl* **-1.** SCH & UNIV [humanities] letras *fpl*. **-2.** [fine arts]: **the ~s** las bellas artes.

artefact [ˈɑːtɪfækt] = **artifact**.

artery [ˈɑːtərɪ] *n* arteria *f*.

art gallery *n* [public] museo *m* (de arte); [commercial] galería *f* (de arte).

arthritis [ɑːˈθraɪtɪs] *n* artritis *f inv*.

artichoke [ˈɑːtɪtʃəʊk] *n* alcachofa *f*.

article [ˈɑːtɪkl] *n* artículo *m*; **~ of clothing** prenda *f* de vestir.

articulate [*adj* ɑːˈtɪkjʊlət, *vb* ɑːˈtɪkjʊleɪt] ◊ *adj* [person] elocuente; [speech] claro(ra), bien articulado(da). ◊ *vt* [express clearly] expresar.

articulated lorry [ɑːˈtɪkjʊleɪtɪd-] *n Br* camión *m* articulado.

artifact [ˈɑːtɪfækt] *n* artefacto *m*.

artificial [ˌɑːtɪˈfɪʃl] *adj* artificial.

artillery [ɑːˈtɪlərɪ] *n* [guns] artillería *f*.

artist [ˈɑːtɪst] *n* artista *m y f*.

artiste [ɑːˈtiːst] *n* artista *m y f*.

artistic [ɑːˈtɪstɪk] *adj* **-1.** [gen] artístico(ca). **-2.** [good at art] con sensibilidad artística.

artistry [ˈɑːtɪstrɪ] *n* maestría *f*.

artless [ˈɑːtlɪs] *adj* ingenuo(nua).

as [unstressed əz, stressed æz] ◇ *conj* **-1.** [referring to time - while] mientras; [- when] cuando; **she told it to me ~ we walked along** me lo contó mientras paseábamos; **~ time goes by** a medida que pasa el tiempo; **she rang (just) ~ I was leaving** llamó justo cuando iba a salir. **-2.** [referring to manner, way] como; **do ~ I say** haz lo que te digo. **-3.** [introducing a statement] como; **~ you know, ...** como (ya) sabes, ... **-4.** [because] como, ya que. **-5.** *phr*: **~ it is** (ya) de por sí. ◇ *prep* como; **I'm speaking ~ a friend** te hablo como amigo; **she works ~ a nurse** trabaja de OR como enfermera; **~ a boy, I lived in Spain** de niño vivía en España; **it came ~ a shock** fue una gran sorpresa. ◇ *adv* (*in comparisons*): **~ ... ~** tan ... como; **~ tall ~ I am** tan alto como yo; **I've lived ~ long ~ she has** he vivido durante tanto tiempo como ella; **twice ~ big** el doble de grande; **it's just ~ fast** es igual de rápido; **~ much ~** tanto como; **~ many ~** tantos(tas) como; **~ much wine ~** tanto vino como quieras. **◆ as for, as to** *prep* en cuanto a. **◆ as from, as of** *prep* a partir de. **◆ as if, as though** *conj* como si. **◆ as to** *prep Br* con respecto a.

a.s.a.p. (*abbr of* **as soon as possible**) a la mayor brevedad posible.

asbestos [æsˈbestəs] *n* asbesto *m*, amianto *m*.

ascend [əˈsend] ◇ *vt* subir. ◇ *vi* ascender.

ascendant [əˈsendənt] *n*: **in the ~** en auge.

ascent [əˈsent] *n* **-1.** [climb] ascensión *f*. **-2.** [upward slope] subida *f*, cuesta *f*. **-3.** *fig* [progress] ascenso *m*.

ascertain [ˌæsəˈteɪn] *vt* determinar.

ASCII [ˈæskɪ] (*abbr of* **American Standard Code for Information**) *n* ASCII *m*.

ascribe [əˈskraɪb] *vt*: **to ~ sthg to** atribuir algo a.

ash [æʃ] *n* **-1.** [from cigarette, fire] ceniza *f*. **-2.** [tree] fresno *m*.

ashamed [əˈʃeɪmd] *adj* avergonzado(da), apenado(da) *Amer*; **I'm ~ to do it** me avergüenza hacerlo; **to be ~ of** avergonzarse de, achuncharse de *Amer*.

ashen-faced [ˈæʃn,feɪst] *adj*: **to be ~** tener la cara pálida.

ashore [əˈʃɔːr] *adv* [swim] hasta la orilla; **to go ~** desembarcar.

ashtray [ˈæʃtreɪ] *n* cenicero *m*.

Ash Wednesday *n* miércoles *m inv* de ceniza.

Asia [*Br* ˈeɪʃə, *Am* ˈeɪʒə] *n* Asia.

Asian [*Br* ˈeɪʃn, *Am* ˈeɪʒn] ◇ *adj* asiático(ca). ◇ *n* asiático *m*, -ca *f*.

aside [əˈsaɪd] ◇ *adv* **-1.** [to one side] a un lado; **to move ~** apartarse; **to take sb ~** llevar a alguien aparte. **-2.** [apart] aparte; **~ from** aparte de. ◇ *n* **-1.** [in play] aparte *m*. **-2.** [remark] inciso *m*.

ask [ɑːsk] ◇ *vt* **-1.** [question - person]: **to ~ (sb sthg)** preguntar (a alguien algo). **-2.** [put - question]: **to ~ a question** hacer una pregunta. **-3.** [request, demand] pedir; **to ~ sb (to do sthg)** pedir a alguien (que haga algo); **to ~ sb for sthg** pedirle algo a alguien. **-4.** [invite] invitar. ◇ *vi* **-1.** [question] preguntar. **-2.** [request] pedir. **◆ ask after** *vt fus* preguntar por. **◆ ask for** *vt fus* **-1.** [person] preguntar por. **-2.** [thing] pedir.

askance [əˈskæns] *adv*: **to look ~ at sb** mirar a alguien con recelo.

askew [əˈskjuː] *adj* torcido(da).

asking price [ˈɑːskɪŋ-] *n* precio *m* inicial.

asleep [əˈsliːp] *adj* dormido(da); **to fall ~** quedarse dormido.

asparagus [əˈspærəgəs] *n* (*U*) [plant] espárrago *m*; [shoots] espárragos *mpl*.

aspect [ˈæspekt] *n* **-1.** [of subject, plan] aspecto *m*. **-2.** [appearance] cariz *m*, aspecto *m*. **-3.** [of building] orientación *f*.

aspersions [əˈspɜːʃnz] *npl*: **to cast ~ on sthg** poner en duda algo.

asphalt [ˈæsfælt] *n* asfalto *m*.

asphyxiate [əsˈfɪksɪeɪt] *vt* asfixiar.

aspiration [ˌæspəˈreɪʃn] *n* aspiración *f*.

aspire [əˈspaɪər] *vi*: **to ~ to** aspirar a.

aspirin [ˈæsprɪn] *n* aspirina *f*.

ass [æs] *n* **-1.** [donkey] asno *m*, -na *f*. **-2.** *Br inf* [idiot] burro *m*, -rra *f*. **-3.** *Am v inf* = **arse**.

assailant [əˈseɪlənt] *n* agresor *m*, -ra *f*.

assassin [əˈsæsɪn] *n* asesino *m*, -na *f*.

assassinate [əˈsæsɪneɪt] *vt* asesinar.

assassination [ə,sæsɪ'neɪʃn] *n* asesinato *m*.

assault [ə'sɔːlt] ◇ *n* **-1.** MIL: ~ **(on)** ataque *m* (contra). **-2.** [physical attack]: ~ **(on sb)** agresión *f* (contra alguien). ◇ *vt* [physically] asaltar, agredir; [sexually] abusar de.

assemble [ə'sembl] ◇ *vt* **-1.** [gather] juntar, reunir. **-2.** [fit together] montar. ◇ *vi* reunirse.

assembly [ə'semblɪ] *n* **-1.** [meeting, lawmaking body] asamblea *f*. **-2.** [gathering together] reunión *f*. **-3.** [fitting together] montaje *m*.

assembly line *n* cadena *f* de montaje.

assent [ə'sent] ◇ *n* consentimiento *m*. ◇ *vi*: **to ~ (to)** asentir (a).

assert [ə'sɜːt] *vt* **-1.** [fact, belief] afirmar. **-2.** [authority] imponer.

assertive [ə'sɜːtɪv] *adj* enérgico(ca).

assess [ə'ses] *vt* evaluar.

assessment [ə'sesmənt] *n* **-1.** [evaluation] evaluación *f*. **-2.** [calculation] cálculo *m*.

assessor [ə'sesər] *n* tasador *m*, -ra *f*.

asset ['æset] *n* **-1.** [valuable quality - of person] cualidad *f*; [- of thing] ventaja *f*. **-2.** [valuable person] elemento *m* importante. ◆ **assets** *npl* COMM activo *m*, bienes *mpl*.

assign [ə'saɪn] *vt* **-1.** [gen]: **to ~ sthg (to sb)** asignar OR encomendar algo (a alguien); **to ~ sb to sthg** asignar OR encomendar a alguien algo; **to ~ sb to do sthg** asignar OR encomendar a alguien que haga algo. **-2.** [designate for specific use, purpose]: **to ~ sthg (to)** destinar algo (a).

assignment [ə'saɪnmənt] *n* **-1.** [task] misión *f*; SCH trabajo *m*. **-2.** [act of assigning] asignación *f*.

assimilate [ə'sɪmɪleɪt] *vt* **-1.** [learn] asimilar. **-2.** [absorb]: **to ~ sb (into)** integrar a alguien (en).

assist [ə'sɪst] *vt*: **to ~ sb (with sthg/in doing sthg)** ayudar a alguien (con algo/a hacer algo).

assistance [ə'sɪstəns] *n* ayuda *f*, asistencia *f*; **to be of ~ (to)** ayudar (a).

assistant [ə'sɪstənt] ◇ *n* ayudante *m* y *f*; **(shop)** ~ dependiente *m*, -ta *f*. ◇ *comp* adjunto(ta); ~ **manager** director adjunto *m*, directora adjunta *f*.

associate [*adj* & *n* ə'səʊʃɪət, *vb* ə'səʊʃɪeɪt] ◇ *adj* asociado(da). ◇ *n* socio *m*, -cia *f*. ◇ *vt* asociar; **to ~ sthg/sb with** asociar algo/a alguien con; **to be ~d with** [organization, plan, opinion] estar relacionado con; [people] estar aso-

ciado con. ◇ *vi*: **to ~ with sb** relacionarse con alguien.

association [ə,səʊsɪ'eɪʃn] *n* **-1.** [organization, act of associating] asociación *f*; **in ~ with** en colaboración con. **-2.** [in mind] connotación *f*.

assorted [ə'sɔːtɪd] *adj* [of various types] variado(da).

assortment [ə'sɔːtmənt] *n* surtido *m*.

assume [ə'sjuːm] *vt* **-1.** [suppose] suponer. **-2.** [power, responsibility] asumir. **-3.** [appearance, attitude] adoptar.

assumed name [ə'sjuːmd-] *n* nombre *m* falso.

assuming [ə'sjuːmɪŋ] *conj* suponiendo que.

assumption [ə'sʌmpʃn] *n* **-1.** [supposition] suposición *f*. **-2.** [of power] asunción *f*.

assurance [ə'ʃʊərəns] *n* **-1.** [promise] garantía *f*. **-2.** [confidence] seguridad *f* de sí mismo. **-3.** [insurance] seguro *m*.

assure [ə'ʃʊər] *vt* asegurar, garantizar; **to ~ sb of sthg** garantizar a alguien algo; **to be ~d of sthg** tener algo garantizado.

assured [ə'ʃʊəd] *adj* [confident] seguro(ra).

asterisk ['æstərɪsk] *n* asterisco *m*.

astern [ə'stɜːn] *adv* NAUT a popa.

asthma ['æsmə] *n* asma *f*.

astonish [ə'stɒnɪʃ] *vt* asombrar.

astonishment [ə'stɒnɪʃmənt] *n* asombro *m*.

astound [ə'staʊnd] *vt* asombrar.

astray [ə'streɪ] *adv*: **to go ~** [become lost] extraviarse; **to lead sb ~** [into bad ways] llevar a alguien por el mal camino.

astride [ə'straɪd] ◇ *adv* a horcajadas. ◇ *prep* a horcajadas en.

astrology [ə'strɒlədʒɪ] *n* astrología *f*.

astronaut ['æstrənɔːt] *n* astronauta *m* y *f*.

astronomical [,æstrə'nɒmɪkl] *adj* astronómico(ca).

astronomy [ə'strɒnəmɪ] *n* astronomía *f*.

astute [ə'stjuːt] *adj* astuto(ta).

asylum [ə'saɪləm] *n* **-1.** [mental hospital] manicomio *m*. **-2.** [protection] asilo *m*.

at [*unstressed* ət, *stressed* æt] *prep* **-1.** [indicating place] en; ~ **my father's** en casa de mi padre; **standing ~ the window** de pie junto a la ventana; ~ **the bottom of the hill** al pie de la colina; ~ **school/work/home** en la escuela/el trabajo/casa. **-2.** [indicating direction] a; **to look ~ sthg/sb** mirar algo/a alguien.

-3. [indicating a particular time] en; ~ **a more suitable time** en un momento más oportuno; ~ **midnight/noon/ eleven o'clock** a medianoche/ mediodía/las once; ~ **night** por la noche; ~ **Christmas/Easter** en Navidades/Semana Santa. **-4.** [indicating speed, rate, price] a; ~ **100mph/high speed** a 100 millas por hora/gran velocidad; ~ **£50 (a pair)** a 50 libras (el par). **-5.** [indicating particular state, condition]: ~ **peace/war** en paz/guerra; **she's** ~ **lunch** está comiendo. **-6.** [indicating a particular age] a; ~ **52/your age** a los 52/tu edad. **-7.** (*after adjectives*): **delighted** ~ encantado con; **clever/ experienced** ~ listo/experimentado en; **puzzled/horrified** ~ perplejo/horrorizado ante; **he's good/bad** ~ **sport** se le dan bien/mal los deportes. ◆ **at all** *adv* **-1.** (*with negative*): **not** ~ **all** [when thanked] de nada; [when answering a question] en absoluto; **she's not** ~ **all happy** no está nada contenta. **-2.** [in the slightest]: **anything** ~ **all will do** cualquier cosa valdrá; **do you know her** ~ **all?** ¿la conoces (de algo)?

ate [*Br* et, *Am* eɪt] *pt* → **eat.**

atheist ['eɪθɪɪst] *n* ateo *m*, -a *f*.

Athens ['æθɪnz] *n* Atenas.

athlete ['æθliːt] *n* atleta *m y f*.

athletic [æθ'letɪk] *adj* atlético(ca). ◆ **athletics** *npl* atletismo *m*.

Atlantic [ət'læntɪk] ◇ *adj* atlántico(ca). ◇ *n*: **the** ~ **(Ocean)** el (océano) Atlántico.

atlas ['ætləs] *n* atlas *m inv*.

ATM (*abbr of* **automatic teller machine**) *n* cajero automático.

atmosphere ['ætmə,sfɪər] *n* **-1.** [of planet] atmósfera *f*. **-2.** [air in room, mood of place] ambiente *m*, atmósfera *f*.

atmospheric [,ætməs'ferɪk] *adj* **-1.** [pressure, pollution] atmosférico(ca). **-2.** [attractive, mysterious] cautivador(ra).

atom ['ætəm] *n* TECH átomo *m*.

atom bomb *n* bomba *f* atómica.

atomic [ə'tɒmɪk] *adj* atómico(ca).

atomic bomb = **atom bomb.**

atomizer, -iser ['ætəmaɪzər] *n* atomizador *m*.

atone [ə'təʊn] *vi*: **to** ~ **for** reparar.

A to Z *n* guía *f* alfabética; [map] callejero *m*.

atrocious [ə'trəʊʃəs] *adj* [very bad] atroz.

atrocity [ə'trɒsətɪ] *n* [terrible act] atrocidad *f*.

attach [ə'tætʃ] *vt* **-1.** [with pin, clip]: **to** ~ **sthg (to)** sujetar algo (a); [with string] atar algo (a). **-2.** [importance, blame]: **to** ~ **sthg (to sthg)** atribuir algo (a algo).

attaché case [ə'tæʃeɪ-] *n* maletín *m*.

attached [ə'tætʃt] *adj* **-1.** [fastened on]: ~ **to** adjunto(ta) (a). **-2.** [fond]: ~ **to** encariñado(da) con.

attachment [ə'tætʃmənt] *n* **-1.** [device] accesorio *m*. **-2.** [fondness]: ~ **(to)** cariño *m* (por).

attack [ə'tæk] ◇ *n*: ~ **(on)** ataque *m* (contra). ◇ *vt* **-1.** [gen] atacar. **-2.** [job, problem] acometer. ◇ *vi* atacar.

attacker [ə'tækər] *n* atacante *m y f*.

attain [ə'teɪn] *vt* lograr, alcanzar.

attainment [ə'teɪnmənt] *n* logro *m*.

attempt [ə'tempt] ◇ *n*: ~ **(at sthg)** intento *m* (de algo); ~ **on sb's life** atentado *m*. ◇ *vt*: **to** ~ **sthg/to do sthg** intentar algo/hacer algo.

attend [ə'tend] ◇ *vt* asistir a. ◇ *vi* **-1.** [be present] asistir. **-2.** [pay attention]: **to** ~ **(to)** atender (a). ◆ **attend to** *vt fus* **-1.** [matter] ocuparse de. **-2.** [customer] atender a; [patient] asistir a.

attendance [ə'tendəns] *n* asistencia *f*.

attendant [ə'tendənt] ◇ *adj* concomitante. ◇ *n* [at museum] vigilante *m y f*; [at petrol station] encargado *m*, -da *f*.

attention [ə'tenʃn] ◇ *n* (*U*) **-1.** [gen] atención *f*; **to bring sthg to sb's** ~, **to draw sb's** ~ **to sthg** llamar la atención de alguien sobre algo; **to attract** OR **catch sb's** ~ atraer OR captar la atención de alguien; **to pay/pay no** ~ **(to)** prestar/no prestar atención (a); **for the** ~ **of** COMM a la atención de. **-2.** [care] asistencia *f*. ◇ *excl* MIL ¡firmes!

attentive [ə'tentɪv] *adj* atento(ta).

attic ['ætɪk] *n* desván *m*, entretecho *m Amer*.

attitude ['ætɪtjuːd] *n* **-1.** [way of thinking, acting]: ~ **(to OR towards)** actitud *f* (hacia). **-2.** [posture] postura *f*.

attn. (*abbr of* **for the attention of**) a/a.

attorney [ə'tɜːnɪ] *n Am* abogado *m*, -da *f*.

attorney general (*pl* **attorneys general**) *n* fiscal *m* general del estado.

attract [ə'trækt] *vt* **-1.** [gen] atraer. **-2.** [support, criticism] atraerse, ganarse.

attraction [ə'trækʃn] *n* **-1.** [gen]: ~ **(to sb)** atracción *f* (hacia OR por alguien). **-2.** [attractiveness - of thing] atractivo *m*.

attractive [ə'træktɪv] *adj* atractivo(va).

attribute [*vb* ə'trɪbjuːt, *n* 'ætrɪbjuːt] ◇ *vt*:

to ~ sthg to atribuir algo a. ◇ n atributo m.

attrition [ə'trɪʃn] n desgaste m; **war of ~** guerra de desgaste.

aubergine ['əʊbəʒiːn] n Br berenjena f.

auburn ['ɔːbən] adj castaño rojizo.

auction ['ɔːkʃn] ◇ n subasta f. ◇ vt subastar.

auctioneer [,ɔːkʃə'nɪəʳ] n subastador m, -ra f.

audacious [ɔː'deɪʃəs] adj [daring] audaz; [cheeky] atrevido(da).

audible ['ɔːdəbl] adj audible.

audience ['ɔːdjəns] n -1. [of play, film] público m. -2. [formal meeting, TV viewers] audiencia f.

audiotypist ['ɔːdɪəʊ,taɪpɪst] n mecanógrafo m, -fa f por dictáfono.

audio-visual ['ɔːdɪəʊ-] adj audiovisual.

audit ['ɔːdɪt] ◇ n auditoría f. ◇ vt auditar.

audition [ɔː'dɪʃn] n prueba f (a un artista).

auditor ['ɔːdɪtəʳ] n auditor m, -ra f.

auditorium [,ɔːdɪ'tɔːrɪəm] (pl -riums OR -ria [-rɪə]) n auditorio m.

augment [ɔːg'ment] vt acrecentar.

augur ['ɔːgəʳ] vi: to ~ well/badly traer buenos/malos augurios.

August ['ɔːgəst] n agosto m; see also September.

Auld Lang Syne [,ɔːldlæŋ'saɪn] n canción escocesa en alabanza de los viejos tiempos.

aunt [ɑːnt] n tía f.

auntie, aunty ['ɑːntɪ] n inf tita f.

au pair [,əʊ'peəʳ] n au pair f.

aura ['ɔːrə] n aura f, halo m.

aural ['ɔːrəl] adj auditivo(va).

auspices ['ɔːspɪsɪz] npl: under the ~ of bajo los auspicios de.

auspicious [ɔː'spɪʃəs] adj prometedor(ra).

Aussie ['ɒzɪ] n inf australiano m, -na f.

austere [ɒ'stɪəʳ] adj austero(ra).

austerity [ɒ'sterətɪ] n austeridad f.

Australia [ɒ'streɪljə] n Australia f.

Australian [ɒ'streɪljən] ◇ adj australiano(na). ◇ n australiano m, -na f.

Austria ['ɒstrɪə] n Austria f.

Austrian ['ɒstrɪən] ◇ adj austriaco(ca). ◇ n austriaco m, -ca f.

authentic [ɔː'θentɪk] adj auténtico(ca).

author ['ɔːθəʳ] n autor m, -ra f.

authoritarian [ɔː,θɒrɪ'teərɪən] adj autoritario(ria).

authoritative [ɔː'θɒrɪtətɪv] adj -1. [per-son, voice] autoritario(ria). -2. [study] autorizado(da).

authority [ɔː'θɒrətɪ] n -1. [gen] autoridad f; to be an ~ on ser una autoridad en. -2. [permission] autorización f. ◆ **authorities** npl: the authorities las autoridades fpl.

authorize, -ise ['ɔːθəraɪz] vt: to ~ (sb to do sthg) autorizar (a alguien a hacer algo).

autistic [ɔː'tɪstɪk] adj autista.

auto ['ɔːtəʊ] (pl -s) n Am coche m, auto m.

autobiography [,ɔːtəbaɪ'ɒgrəfɪ] n autobiografía f.

autocratic [,ɔːtə'krætɪk] adj autocrático(ca).

autograph ['ɔːtəgrɑːf] ◇ n autógrafo m. ◇ vt autografiar.

automate ['ɔːtəmeɪt] vt automatizar.

automatic [,ɔːtə'mætɪk] ◇ adj automático(ca). ◇ n -1. Br [car] coche m automático. -2. [gun] arma f automática. -3. [washing machine] lavadora f automática.

automatically [,ɔːtə'mætɪklɪ] adv automáticamente.

automation [,ɔːtə'meɪʃn] n automatización f.

automobile ['ɔːtəməbiːl] n Am coche m, automóvil m.

autonomous [ɔː'tɒnəməs] adj autónomo(ma).

autonomy [ɔː'tɒnəmɪ] n autonomía f.

autopsy ['ɔːtɒpsɪ] n autopsia f.

autumn ['ɔːtəm] n otoño m.

auxiliary [ɔːg'zɪljərɪ] ◇ adj auxiliar. ◇ n [medical worker] auxiliar sanitario m, auxiliar sanitaria f.

Av. (abbr of avenue) Av.

avail [ə'veɪl] ◇ n: to no ~ en vano. ◇ vt: to ~ o.s. of sthg aprovechar algo.

available [ə'veɪləbl] adj -1. [product, service] disponible. -2. [person] libre, disponible.

avalanche ['ævəlɑːnʃ] n lit & fig avalancha f, alud m.

avant-garde [,ævɒŋ'gɑːd] adj de vanguardia, vanguardista.

avarice ['ævərɪs] n avaricia f.

Ave. (abbr of avenue) Avda.

avenge [ə'vendʒ] vt vengar.

avenue ['ævənjuː] n -1. [wide road] avenida f. -2. fig [method, means] vía f.

average ['ævərɪdʒ] ◇ adj -1. [mean, typical] medio(dia). -2. [mediocre] regular. ◇ n media f, promedio m; on ~ de media, por término medio. ◇ vt alcanzar un promedio de. ◆ **average out** vi: **to ~ out at** salir a una media de.

aversion [əˈvɜːʃn] n [dislike]: **~ (to)** aversión f (a).

avert [əˈvɜːt] vt **-1.** [problem, accident] evitar, prevenir. **-2.** [eyes, glance] apartar, desviar.

aviary [ˈeɪvjərɪ] n pajarera f.

avid [ˈævɪd] adj: **~ (for)** ávido(da) (de).

avocado [ˌævəˈkɑːdəʊ] (pl **-s** OR **-es**) n: **~ (pear)** aguacate m, palta f Amer.

avoid [əˈvɔɪd] vt: **to ~ (sthg/doing sthg)** evitar (algo/hacer algo).

avoidance [əˈvɔɪdəns] n → **tax avoidance**.

await [əˈweɪt] vt esperar, aguardar.

awake [əˈweɪk] (pt awoke OR awaked, pp awoken) ◇ adj [not sleeping] despierto(ta). ◇ vt lit & fig despertar. ◇ vi lit & fig despertarse.

awakening [əˈweɪknɪŋ] n lit & fig despertar m.

award [əˈwɔːd] ◇ n **-1.** [prize] premio m, galardón m. **-2.** [compensation] indemnización f. ◇ vt: **to ~ sb sthg, to ~ sthg to sb** [prize] conceder OR otorgar algo a alguien; [compensation] adjudicar algo a alguien.

aware [əˈweəʳ] adj **-1.** [conscious]: **~ of** consciente de. **-2.** [informed, sensitive] informado(da), al día; **~ of sthg** al día de algo; **to be ~ that** estar informado de que.

awareness [əˈweənɪs] n conciencia f.

awash [əˈwɒʃ] adj lit & fig: **~ (with)** inundado(da) (de).

away [əˈweɪ] ◇ adv **-1.** [move, walk, drive]: **to walk ~ (from)** marcharse (de); **to drive ~ (from)** alejarse (de) (en coche); **to turn** OR **look ~** apartar la vista. **-2.** [at a distance - in space, time]: **~ from** a distancia de; **4 miles ~** a 4 millas de distancia; **the exam is two days ~** faltan dos días para el examen. **-3.** [not at home or office] fuera. **-4.** [in safe place]: **to put sthg ~** poner algo en su sitio. **-5.** [indicating removal or disappearance]: **to fade ~** desvanecerse; **to give sthg ~** regalar algo; **to take sthg ~** llevarse algo. **-6.** [continuously]: **he was working ~ when ...** estaba muy concentrado trabajando cuando .... ◇ adj SPORT visitante; **~ game** partido m fuera de casa.

awe [ɔː] n sobrecogimiento m; **to be in ~ of sb** estar sometido a alguien.

awesome [ˈɔːsəm] adj impresionante.

awful [ˈɔːful] adj **-1.** [terrible] terrible, espantoso(sa); **I feel ~** me siento fatal. **-2.** inf [very great] tremendo(da).

awfully [ˈɔːflɪ] adv inf [very] tremendamente.

awhile [əˈwaɪl] adv literary un rato.

awkward [ˈɔːkwəd] adj **-1.** [clumsy - movement] torpe; [- person] desgarbado(da). **-2.** [embarrassed, embarrassing] incómodo(da). **-3.** [unreasonable] difícil. **-4.** [inconvenient] poco manejable.

awning [ˈɔːnɪŋ] n toldo m.

awoke [əˈwəʊk] pt → **awake**.

awoken [əˈwəʊkn] pp → **awake**.

awry [əˈraɪ] ◇ adj torcido(da), ladeado(da). ◇ adv: **to go ~** salir mal.

axe Br, **ax** Am [æks] ◇ n hacha f. ◇ vt [project, jobs] suprimir.

axes [ˈæksiːz] pl → **axis**.

axis [ˈæksɪs] (pl axes) n eje m.

axle [ˈæksl] n eje m.

aye [aɪ] ◇ adv sí. ◇ n sí m.

azalea [əˈzeɪljə] n azalea f.

Aztec [ˈæztek] ◇ adj azteca. ◇ n [person] azteca m y f.

B

b (pl b's OR bs), **B** (pl B's OR Bs) [biː] n [letter] b f, B f. ◆ **B** n **-1.** MUS si m. **-2.** SCH [mark] ≃ bien m.

BA n (abbr of **Bachelor of Arts**) (titular de una) licenciatura de letras.

babble [ˈbæbl] vi [person] farfullar.

baboon [bəˈbuːn] n babuino m.

baby [ˈbeɪbɪ] n **-1.** [newborn child] bebé m; [infant] niño m. **-2.** inf [term of affection] cariño m.

baby buggy n **-1.** Br [foldable pushchair] sillita f de niño (con ruedas). **-2.** Am = **baby carriage**.

baby carriage n Am cochecito m de niños.

baby-sit vi cuidar a niños.

baby-sitter [-ˈsɪtəʳ] n canguro m y f.

bachelor [ˈbætʃələʳ] n soltero m.

Bachelor of Arts n ≃ licenciado m, -da f en Letras.

Bachelor of Science n ≃ licenciado m, -da f en Ciencias.

back [bæk] ◇ *adv* **-1.** [in position] **atrás;** **stand ~!** ¡échense para atrás!; **to push ~** empujar hacia atrás. **-2.** [to former position or state] **de vuelta; to come ~** volver; **to go ~** volver; **to look ~** volver la mirada; **to walk ~** volver andando; **to give sthg ~** devolver algo; **to be ~ (in fashion)** estar de vuelta; **he has been there and ~** ha estado allí y ha vuelto; **I spent all day going ~ and forth** pasé todo el día yendo y viniendo. **-3.** [in time]: **two weeks ~** hace dos semanas; **it dates ~ to 1960** data de 1960; **~ in March** allá en marzo. **-4.** [phone, write] **de vuelta.** ◇ *n* **-1.** [of person] **espalda** *f;* [of animal] **lomo** *m;* **behind sb's ~** a las espaldas de alguien. **-2.** [of hand, cheque] **dorso** *m;* [of coin, page] **reverso** *m;* [of car, book, head] **parte** *f* **trasera;** [of chair] **respaldo** *m;* [of room, cupboard] **fondo** *m.* **-3.** SPORT [player] **defensa** *m.* ◇ *adj* (*in compounds*) **-1.** [at the back - door, legs, seat] **trasero(ra);** [- page] **último(ma). -2.** [overdue - pay, rent] **atrasado(da).** ◇ *vt* **-1.** [reverse] **dar marcha atrás a. -2.** [support] **respaldar. -3.** [bet on] **apostar por. -4.** [line with material] **forrar.** ◇ *vi* [drive backwards] **ir marcha atrás;** [walk backwards] **ir hacia atrás.** ◆ **back to back** *adv* [with backs facing] **espalda con espalda.** ◆ **back to front** *adv* **al revés.** ◆ **back down** *vi* **echarse** OR **volverse atrás.** ◆ **back out** *vi* **echarse** OR **volverse atrás.** ◆ **back up** ◇ *vt sep* **-1.** [support] **apoyar. -2.** COMPUT **hacer un archivo de seguridad de.** ◇ *vi* [reverse] **ir marcha atrás.**

backache ['bækeɪk] *n* **dolor** *m* **de espalda.**

backbencher [,bæk'bentʃər] *n* Br **diputado sin cargo en el gabinete del gobierno o la oposición.**

backbone ['bækbəʊn] *n lit & fig* **columna** *f* **vertebral.**

backcloth ['bækklɒθ] *n* Br **= backdrop.**

backdate [,bæk'deɪt] *vt:* **a pay rise ~d to March** un aumento de sueldo con efecto retroactivo desde marzo.

back door *n* **puerta** *f* **trasera.**

backdrop ['bækdrɒp] *n lit & fig* **telón** *m* **de fondo.**

backfire [,bæk'faɪər] *vi* **-1.** [motor vehicle] **petardear. -2.** [go wrong]: **it ~d on him** le salió el tiro por la culata.

backgammon ['bæk,gæmən] *n* **backgammon** *m.*

background ['bækgraʊnd] *n* **-1.** [in picture, view] **fondo** *m;* **in the ~** [of painting etc] **al fondo;** [out of the limelight] **en la sombra. -2.** [of event, situation] **trasfondo** *m.* **-3.** [upbringing] **origen** *m;* **family ~ antecedentes** *mpl* **familiares.**

backhand ['bækhænd] *n* **revés** *m.*

backhanded ['bækhændɪd] *adj fig* **equívoco(ca).**

backhander ['bækhændər] *n* Br *inf:* **to give sb a ~** untarle la mano a alguien.

backing ['bækɪŋ] *n* **-1.** [support] **apoyo** *m,* **respaldo** *m.* **-2.** [lining] **refuerzo** *m.* **-3.** MUS **acompañamiento** *m.*

backlash ['bæklæʃ] *n* **reacción** *f* **violenta.**

backlog ['bæklɒg] *n* **acumulación** *f.*

back number *n* **número** *m* **atrasado.**

backpack ['bækpæk] *n* **mochila** *f.*

back pay *n* (*U*) **atrasos** *mpl.*

back seat *n* **asiento** *m* **trasero** OR **de atrás.**

backside [,bæk'saɪd] *n inf* **trasero** *m.*

backstage [,bæk'steɪdʒ] *adv* **entre bastidores.**

back street *n* Br **callejuela** *f* **de barrio.**

backstroke ['bækstrəʊk] *n* **espalda** *f* (*en natación*).

backup ['bækʌp] ◇ *adj* **-1.** [plan] **de emergencia;** [team] **de apoyo. -2.** COMPUT **de seguridad.** ◇ *n* **-1.** [support] **apoyo** *m.* **-2.** COMPUT **copia** *f* **de seguridad.**

backward ['bækwəd] ◇ *adj* **-1.** [movement, look] **hacia atrás. -2.** [country, person] **atrasado(da).** ◇ *adv* Am **= backwards.**

backwards ['bækwədz], **backward** Am *adv* **-1.** [move, go] **hacia atrás; ~ and forwards** [movement] **de un lado a otro. -2.** [back to front] **al** OR **del revés.**

backwater ['bæk,wɔːtər] *n fig* **páramo** *m,* **lugar** *m* **atrasado.**

backyard [,bæk'jɑːd] *n* **-1.** Br [yard] **patio** *m.* **-2.** Am [garden] **jardín** *m* (**trasero**).

bacon ['beɪkən] *n* **bacon** *m,* **tocino** *m.*

bacteria [bæk'tɪərɪə] *npl* **bacterias** *fpl.*

bad [bæd] (*compar* **worse,** *superl* **worst**) ◇ *adj* **-1.** [gen] **malo(la); he's ~ at French** se le da mal el francés; **to go ~** [food] **echarse a perder; too ~!** ¡qué pena!; **it's not ~ (at all)** no está nada mal; **how are you? — not ~** ¿qué tal? **— bien. -2.** [illness] **fuerte, grave. -3.** [guilty]: **to feel ~ about sthg** sentirse mal por algo. ◇ *adv* Am **= badly.**

badge [bædʒ] *n* **-1.** [for decoration - metal, plastic] **chapa** *f;* [sewn-on] **insignia** *f.* **-2.** [for identification] **distintivo** *m.*

badger ['bædʒəʳ] ◇ n tejón m. ◇ vt: **to ~ sb (to do sthg)** ponerse pesado(da) con alguien (para que haga algo).

badly ['bædlɪ] (*compar* **worse**, *superl* **worst**) *adv* **-1.** [not well] mal. **-2.** [seriously] gravemente; **I'm ~ in need of help** necesito ayuda urgentemente.

badly-off *adj* **-1.** [poor] apurado(da) de dinero. **-2.** [lacking]: **to be ~ for sthg** estar OR andar mal de algo.

bad-mannered [-'mænəd] *adj* maleducado(da).

badminton ['bædmɪntən] n bádminton m.

bad-tempered [-'tempəd] *adj* **-1.** [by nature] de mal genio. **-2.** [in a bad mood] malhumorado(da).

baffle ['bæfl] vt desconcertar.

bag [bæg] ◇ n **-1.** [container, bagful] bolsa f; **to pack one's ~s** fig hacer las maletas. **-2.** [handbag] bolso m, cartera f *Amer*. ◇ vt *Br inf* [reserve] pedirse, reservarse. ◆ **bags** *npl* **-1.** [under eyes] ojeras fpl. **-2.** [lots]: **~s of** *inf* un montón de.

bagel ['beɪgəl] n bollo de pan en forma de rosca.

baggage ['bægɪdʒ] n (U) equipaje m.

baggage reclaim n recogida f de equipajes.

baggy ['bægɪ] *adj* holgado(da).

bagpipes ['bægpaɪps] *npl* gaita f.

baguette [bə'get] n barra f de pan.

Bahamas [bə'hɑːməz] *npl*: **the ~** (las) Bahamas.

bail [beɪl] n (U) fianza f; **on ~** bajo fianza. ◆ **bail out** ◇ vt sep **-1.** [pay bail for] obtener la libertad bajo fianza de. **-2.** [rescue] sacar de apuros. ◇ vi [from plane] tirarse en paracaídas.

bailiff ['beɪlɪf] n alguacil m.

bait [beɪt] ◇ n lit & fig cebo m. ◇ vt **-1.** [put bait on] cebar. **-2.** [tease, torment] hacer sufrir, cebarse con.

bake [beɪk] ◇ vt [food] cocer al horno. ◇ vi [food] cocerse al horno.

baked beans [beɪkt-] *npl* alubias fpl cocidas en salsa de tomate.

baked potato [beɪkt-] n patata f asada OR al horno.

baker ['beɪkəʳ] n panadero m; **~'s (shop)** panadería f.

bakery ['beɪkərɪ] n panadería f.

baking ['beɪkɪŋ] n cocción f.

balaclava (helmet) [bælə'klɑːvə-] n pasamontañas m inv.

balance ['bæləns] ◇ n **-1.** [equilibrium] equilibrio m; **to keep/lose one's ~** mantener/perder el equilibrio; **it caught me off ~** me pilló desprevenido(da). **-2.** fig [counterweight] contrapunto m. **-3.** [of evidence etc] peso m. **-4.** [scales] balanza f. **-5.** [of account] saldo m. ◇ vt **-1.** [keep in balance] poner en equilibrio. **-2.** [compare] sopesar. **-3.** [in accounting]: **to ~ the books/a budget** hacer que cuadren las cuentas/cuadre un presupuesto. ◇ vi **-1.** [maintain equilibrium] sostenerse en equilibrio. **-2.** [in accounting] cuadrar. ◆ **on balance** *adv* tras pensarlo detenidamente.

balanced diet ['bælənst-] n dieta f equilibrada.

balance of payments n balanza f de pagos.

balance of trade n balanza f comercial.

balance sheet n balance m.

balcony ['bælkənɪ] n **-1.** [on building - big] terraza f; [- small] balcón m. **-2.** [in theatre] anfiteatro m, galería f.

bald [bɔːld] *adj* **-1.** [without hair] calvo(va). **-2.** [without tread] desgastado(da). **-3.** fig [blunt] escueto(ta).

bale [beɪl] n bala f, fardo m. ◆ **bale out** vi *Br* **-1.** [remove water] achicar agua. **-2.** [from plane] tirarse en paracaídas.

Balearic Islands [bælɪ'ærɪk-], **Balearics** [bælɪ'ærɪks] *npl*: **the ~** las Baleares.

baleful ['beɪlful] *adj* maligno(na).

balk [bɔːk] vi: **to ~ (at doing sthg)** resistirse (a hacer algo).

Balkans ['bɔːlkənz], **Balkan States** *npl*: **the ~** los países balcánicos.

ball [bɔːl] n **-1.** [for tennis, cricket] pelota f; [for golf, billiards] bola f; [for football] balón m; **to be on the ~** fig estar al tanto de todo. **-2.** [round shape] bola f. **-3.** [of foot] pulpejo m. **-4.** [dance] baile m. ◆ **balls** v inf ◇ npl [testicles] pelotas fpl. ◇ n (U) [nonsense] gilipolleces fpl.

ballad ['bæləd] n balada f.

ballast ['bæləst] n lastre m.

ball bearing n cojinete m de bolas.

ball boy n recogepelotas m inv.

ballerina [bælə'riːnə] n bailarina f.

ballet ['bæleɪ] n ballet m.

ballet dancer n bailarín m, -ina f.

ball game n *Am* [baseball match] partido m de béisbol.

balloon [bə'luːn] n **-1.** [toy] globo m. **-2.** [hot-air balloon] globo m (aerostático). **-3.** [in cartoon] bocadillo m.

ballot ['bælət] ◇ n [voting process] votación f. ◇ vt: **to ~ the members on an**

issue someter un asunto a votación entre los miembros.

ballot box n [container] urna f.

ballot paper n voto m, papeleta f.

ball park n Am estadio m de béisbol.

ballpoint (pen) ['bɔːlpɔɪnt-] n bolígrafo m.

ballroom ['bɔːlrʊm] n salón m de baile.

ballroom dancing n (U) baile m de salón.

balm [bɑːm] n bálsamo m.

balmy ['bɑːmɪ] adj apacible.

balsa ['bɒlsə], **balsawood** ['bɒlsəwʊd] n balsa f.

Baltic ['bɔːltɪk] ◇ adj báltico(ca). ◇ n: the ~ (Sea) el (mar) Báltico.

Baltic Republic n: the ~s las repúblicas bálticas.

bamboo [bæm'buː] n bambú m.

bamboozle [bæm'buːzl] vt inf camelar, engatusar.

ban [bæn] ◇ n: ~ (on) prohibición f (de). ◇ vt: to ~ sb (from doing sthg) prohibir a alguien (hacer algo).

banal [bə'nɑːl] adj pej banal.

banana [bə'nɑːnə] n plátano m, banana f Amer.

band [bænd] n **-1.** [musical group - pop] grupo m; [- jazz, military] banda f. **-2.** [of thieves etc] banda f. **-3.** [strip] cinta f. **-4.** [stripe, range] franja f. ◆ **band together** vi juntarse.

bandage ['bændɪdʒ] ◇ n venda f. ◇ vt vendar.

Band-Aid® n ≈ tirita® f.

b and b, B and B n abbr of bed and breakfast.

bandit ['bændɪt] n bandido m, -da f.

bandstand ['bændstænd] n quiosco m de música.

bandwagon ['bændwægən] n: to jump on the ~ subirse OR apuntarse al carro.

bandy ['bændɪ] adj de piernas arqueadas. ◆ **bandy about, bandy around** vt sep sacar a relucir.

bandy-legged [-,legd] adj de piernas arqueadas.

bang [bæŋ] ◇ n **-1.** [blow] golpe m. **-2.** [loud noise] estampido m, estruendo m. ◇ vt **-1.** [hit - drum, desk] golpear; [- knee, head] golpearse. **-2.** [slam] cerrar de golpe. ◇ vi golpear. ◇ adv [exactly]: ~ in the middle of justo en mitad de; ~ on muy acertado(da). ◆ **bangs** npl Am flequillo m.

banger ['bæŋə'] n Br **-1.** inf [sausage] salchicha f. **-2.** inf [old car] carraca f, cacharro m. **-3.** [firework] petardo m.

Bangladesh [,bæŋglə'deʃ] n Bangladesh.

bangle ['bæŋgl] n brazalete m.

banish ['bænɪʃ] vt lit & fig desterrar.

banister ['bænɪstə'] n, **banisters** ['bænɪstəz] npl barandilla f, pasamanos m inv.

bank [bæŋk] ◇ n **-1.** [gen & FIN] banco m. **-2.** [by river, lake] ribera f, orilla f. **-3.** [slope] loma f. **-4.** [of clouds etc] masa f. ◇ vi **-1.** FIN: to ~ with tener una cuenta en. **-2.** [plane] ladearse. ◆ **bank on** vt fus contar con.

bank account n cuenta f bancaria.

bank balance n saldo m.

bank card = banker's card.

bank charges npl comisiones fpl bancarias.

bank draft n giro m bancario.

banker ['bæŋkə'] n banquero m, -ra f.

banker's card n Br tarjeta f de identificación bancaria.

bank holiday n Br día m festivo.

banking ['bæŋkɪŋ] n banca f.

bank manager n director m, -ra f de banco.

bank note n billete m de banco.

bank rate n tipo m de interés bancario.

bankrupt ['bæŋkrʌpt] ◇ adj [financially] quebrado(da), en quiebra; to go ~ quebrar. ◇ vt llevar a la quiebra.

bankruptcy ['bæŋkrəptsɪ] n quiebra f, bancarrota f; fig [of ideas] agotamiento m, falta f total.

bank statement n extracto m de cuenta.

banner ['bænə'] n pancarta f.

bannister ['bænɪstə'], **bannisters** ['bænɪstəz] = banister(s).

banquet ['bæŋkwɪt] n banquete m.

banter ['bæntə'] n (U) bromas fpl.

bap [bæp] n Br bollo m de pan.

baptism ['bæptɪzm] n bautismo m.

baptize, -ise [Br bæp'taɪz, Am 'bæptaɪz] vt bautizar.

bar [bɑːr] ◇ n **-1.** [of soap] pastilla f; [of chocolate] tableta f; [of gold] lingote m; [of wood] tabla f; [of metal] barra f; to be behind ~s estar entre rejas. **-2.** fig [obstacle] barrera f; [ban] prohibición f. **-3.** [drinking place] bar m. **-4.** [counter] barra f. **-5.** MUS compás m. ◇ vt **-1.** [close with a bar] atrancar. **-2.** [block]: to ~ sb's way impedir el paso a alguien. **-3.** [ban]: to ~ sb (from doing sthg) prohibir a alguien (hacer algo); to ~ sb from somewhere prohibir a alguien la entrada en un sitio. ◇ prep [except] me-

nos, salvo; ~ **none** sin excepción.
◆ **Bar** *n* JUR: **the Bar** *Br* conjunto de los abogados que ejercen en tribunales superiores; *Am* la abogacía.

barbaric [bɑːˈbærɪk] *adj* bárbaro(ra).

barbecue [ˈbɑːbɪkjuː] *n* barbacoa *f*.

barbed wire [bɑːbd-] *n* alambre *m* de espino.

barber [ˈbɑːbəʳ] *n* barbero *m*; ~'**s** barbería *f*.

barbiturate [bɑːˈbɪtjʊrət] *n* barbitúrico *m*.

bar code *n* código *m* de barras.

bare [beəʳ] ◇ *adj* -**1.** [without covering - legs, trees, hills] desnudo(da); [- feet] descalzo(za). -**2.** [absolute, minimum] esencial. -**3.** [empty] vacío(a). ◇ *vt* descubrir; **to** ~ **one's teeth** enseñar los dientes.

bareback [ˈbeəbæk] *adj & adv* a pelo.

barefaced [ˈbeəfeɪst] *adj* descarado(da).

barefoot(ed) [ˌbeəˈfʊt(ɪd)] *adj & adv* descalzo(za).

barely [ˈbeəlɪ] *adv* [scarcely] apenas.

bargain [ˈbɑːgɪn] ◇ *n* -**1.** [agreement] trato *m*, acuerdo *m*; **into the** ~ por añadidura, además. -**2.** [good buy] ganga *f*. ◇ *vi*: **to** ~ **(with sb for sthg)** negociar (con alguien para obtener algo).
◆ **bargain for, bargain on** *vt fus* contar con.

barge [bɑːdʒ] ◇ *n* barcaza *f*. ◇ *vi inf*: **to** ~ **into** [person] chocarse con; [room] irrumpir en. ◆ **barge in** *vi inf*: **to** ~ **in (on)** [conversation etc] entrometerse (en).

baritone [ˈbærɪtəʊn] *n* barítono *m*.

bark [bɑːk] ◇ *n* -**1.** [of dog] ladrido *m*. -**2.** [on tree] corteza *f*. ◇ *vi*: **to** ~ **(at)** ladrar (a).

barley [ˈbɑːlɪ] *n* cebada *f*.

barley sugar *n Br* azúcar *m o f* cande.

barley water *n Br* hordiate *m*.

barmaid [ˈbɑːmeɪd] *n* camarera *f*.

barman [ˈbɑːmən] (*pl* -**men** [-mən]) *n* camarero *m*, barman *m*.

barn [bɑːn] *n* granero *m*.

barometer [bəˈrɒmɪtəʳ] *n* barómetro *m*; *fig* [of public opinion etc] piedra *f* de toque.

baron [ˈbærən] *n* barón *m*.

baroness [ˈbærənɪs] *n* baronesa *f*.

barrack [ˈbærək] *vt Br* abroncar.
◆ **barracks** *npl* cuartel *m*.

barrage [ˈbærɑːʒ] *n* -**1.** [of firing] bombardeo *m*, fuego *m* intenso de artillería. -**2.** [of questions] aluvión *m*, alud *m*. -**3.** *Br* [dam] presa *f*, dique *m*.

barrel [ˈbærəl] *n* -**1.** [for beer, wine, oil] barril *m*. -**2.** [of gun] cañón *m*.

barren [ˈbærən] *adj* estéril.

barricade [ˌbærɪˈkeɪd] ◇ *n* barricada *f*. ◇ *vt* levantar barricadas en.

barrier [ˈbærɪəʳ] *n lit & fig* barrera *f*.

barring [ˈbɑːrɪŋ] *prep* salvo.

barrister [ˈbærɪstəʳ] *n Br* abogado *m*, -da *f* (*de tribunales superiores*).

barrow [ˈbærəʊ] *n* carrito *m*.

bartender [ˈbɑːtendəʳ] *n* camarero *m*, -ra *f*.

barter [ˈbɑːtəʳ] ◇ *n* trueque *m*. ◇ *vt*: **to** ~ **(sthg for sthg)** trocar (algo por algo).

base [beɪs] ◇ *n* base *f*. ◇ *vt* -**1.** [place, establish] emplazar; **he's** ~**d in Paris** trabaja en París. -**2.** [use as starting point]: **to** ~ **sthg on** OR **upon** basar algo en. ◇ *adj pej* bajo(ja), vil.

baseball [ˈbeɪsbɔːl] *n* béisbol *m*.

baseball cap *n* gorra *f* de béisbol.

basement [ˈbeɪsmənt] *n* sótano *m*.

base rate *n* tipo *m* de interés base.

bases [ˈbeɪsiːz] *pl* → **basis**.

bash [bæʃ] *inf* ◇ *n* -**1.** [attempt]: **to have a** ~ **at sthg** intentar algo. -**2.** [party] juerga *f*. ◇ *vt* [hit - person, thing] darle un porrazo a; [- one's head, knee] darse un porrazo en.

bashful [ˈbæʃfʊl] *adj* [person] vergonzoso(sa); [smile] tímido(da).

basic [ˈbeɪsɪk] *adj* básico(ca). ◆ **basics** *npl* -**1.** [rudiments] principios *mpl* básicos. -**2.** [essentials] lo imprescindible.

BASIC [ˈbeɪsɪk] (*abbr of* **Beginner's All-purpose Symbolic Instruction Code**) *n* BASIC *m*.

basically [ˈbeɪsɪklɪ] *adv* -**1.** [essentially] esencialmente. -**2.** [really] en resumen.

basil [ˈbæzl] *n* albahaca *f*.

basin [ˈbeɪsn] *n* -**1.** *Br* [bowl] balde *m*, barreño *m*. -**2.** [wash basin] lavabo *m*. -**3.** GEOGR cuenca *f*.

basis [ˈbeɪsɪs] (*pl* **bases**) *n* base *f*; **on the** ~ **of** de acuerdo con, a partir de; **on a weekly/monthly** ~ de forma semanal/mensual.

bask [bɑːsk] *vi* [sunbathe]: **to** ~ **in the sun** tostarse al sol.

basket [ˈbɑːskɪt] *n* cesto *m*, cesta *f*.

basketball [ˈbɑːskɪtbɔːl] *n* baloncesto *m*.

Basque [bɑːsk] ◇ *adj* vasco(ca). ◇ *n* -**1.** [person] vasco *m*, -ca *f*. -**2.** [language] vascuence *m*, euskera *m*.

Basque Country [bɑːsk-] *n*: **the** ~ el País Vasco, Euskadi.

bass [beɪs] ◇ *adj* bajo(ja). ◇ *n* -**1.**

[singer, bass guitar] bajo m. **-2.** [double bass] contrabajo m.

bass drum [beɪs-] n bombo m.

bass guitar [beɪs-] n bajo m.

bassoon [bəˈsuːn] n fagot m.

bastard [ˈbɑːstəd] n **-1.** [illegitimate child] bastardo m, -da f. **-2.** v inf pej cabrón m, -ona f.

bastion [ˈbæstɪən] n bastión m.

bat [bæt] n **-1.** [animal] murciélago m. **-2.** [for cricket, baseball] bate m. **-3.** [for table-tennis] pala f, paleta f.

batch [bætʃ] n **-1.** [of letters etc] remesa f. **-2.** [of work] montón m, serie f. **-3.** [of products] lote m.

bated [ˈbeɪtɪd] adj: with ~ breath con el aliento contenido.

bath [bɑːθ] ◇ n **-1.** [bathtub] bañera f, bañadera f Amer. **-2.** [act of washing] baño m, bañada f Amer; **to have** OR **take a ~** darse un baño, bañarse. ◇ vt bañar. ◆ **baths** npl Br [public swimming pool] piscina f municipal.

bathe [beɪð] ◇ vt [wound] lavar. ◇ vi bañarse.

bathing [ˈbeɪðɪŋ] n (U) baños mpl.

bathing cap n gorro m de baño.

bathing costume, bathing suit n traje m de baño, bañador m, malla f Amer.

bathrobe [ˈbɑːθrəʊb] n **-1.** [made of towelling] albornoz m. **-2.** [dressing gown] batín m, bata f.

bathroom [ˈbɑːθrʊm] n **-1.** Br [room with bath] (cuarto m de) baño m. **-2.** Am [toilet] servicio m.

bath towel n toalla f de baño.

bathtub [ˈbɑːθtʌb] n bañera f.

baton [ˈbætən] n **-1.** [of conductor] batuta f. **-2.** [in relay race] testigo m. **-3.** Br [of policeman] porra f.

batsman [ˈbætsmən] (pl -men [-mən]) n bateador m.

battalion [bəˈtæljən] n batallón m.

batten [ˈbætn] n listón m (de madera).

batter [ˈbætər] ◇ n pasta f para rebozar. ◇ vt **-1.** [child, woman] pegar. **-2.** [door, ship] sacudir, golpear. ◆ **batter down** vt sep echar abajo.

battered [ˈbætəd] adj **-1.** [child, woman] maltratado(da). **-2.** [car, hat] abollado(da).

battery [ˈbætərɪ] n [of radio] pila f; [of car, guns] batería f.

battle [ˈbætl] ◇ n **-1.** [in war] batalla f. **-2.** [struggle]: ~ **(for/against/with)** lucha f (por/contra/con). ◇ vi: **to ~ (for/against/with)** luchar (por/contra/con).

battlefield [ˈbætlfiːld], **battleground** [ˈbætlgraʊnd] n lit & fig campo m de batalla.

battlements [ˈbætlmənts] npl almenas fpl.

battleship [ˈbætlʃɪp] n acorazado m.

bauble [ˈbɔːbl] n baratija f.

baulk [bɔːk] = balk.

bawdy [ˈbɔːdɪ] adj verde, picante.

bawl [bɔːl] vi **-1.** [shout] vociferar. **-2.** [cry] berrear.

bay [beɪ] ◇ n **-1.** [of coast] bahía f. **-2.** [for loading] zona f de carga y descarga. **-3.** [for parking] plaza f. **-4.** phr: **to keep sthg/sb at ~** mantener algo/a alguien a raya. ◇ vi aullar.

bay leaf n (hoja f de) laurel m.

bay window n balcón OR acristalado.

bazaar [bəˈzɑːr] n **-1.** [market] bazar m. **-2.** Br [charity sale] mercadillo m benéfico.

B & B abbr of bed and breakfast.

BBC (abbr of British Broadcasting Corporation) n BBC f, compañía estatal británica de radiotelevisión.

BC (abbr of before Christ) a.C.

be [biː] (pt **was** OR **were**, pp **been**) ◇ aux vb **-1.** (in combination with present participle: to form cont tense) estar; **what is he doing?** ¿qué hace OR está haciendo?; **it's snowing** está nevando; **I'm leaving tomorrow** me voy mañana; **they've been promising it for years** han estado prometiéndolo durante años. **-2.** (in combination with pp: to form passive) ser; **to ~ loved** ser amado; **there was no one to ~ seen** no se veía a nadie; **ten people were killed** murieron diez personas. **-3.** (in question tags): **you're not going now, are you?** no irás a marcharte ya ¿no?; **the meal was delicious, wasn't it?** la comida fue deliciosa ¿verdad? **-4.** (followed by "to" + infin): **I'm to be promoted** me van a ascender; **you're not to tell anyone** no debes decírselo a nadie. ◇ copulative vb **-1.** (with adj, n) [indicating innate quality, permanent condition] ser; [indicating state, temporary condition] estar; **snow is white** la nieve es blanca; **she's intelligent/tall** es inteligente/alta; **to ~ a doctor/plumber** ser médico/fontanero; **I'm Scottish** soy escocés; **1 and 1 are 2** 1 y 1 son 2; **your hands are cold** tus manos están frías; **I'm tired/angry** estoy cansado/enfadado; **he's in a difficult position** está en una situación difícil. **-2.** [referring to health] estar; **she's ill/better** está enferma/mejor; **how are you?** ¿cómo estás? **-3.** [referring to age]: **how old are you?** ¿qué edad OR cuántos años tienes?; **I'm 20 (years old)** tengo 20 años. **-4.** [cost] ser, costar; **how much is it?** ¿cuánto es?; **that will ~ £10, please** son 10 libras; **apples are only 20p a kilo today** hoy las manzanas están a tan sólo 20 peniques el kilo. ◇ vi **-1.** [exist] ser, existir; **the worst prime minister that ever was** el peor primer ministro que jamás existió; **~ that as it may** aunque así sea; **there is/are** hay; **is there life on Mars?** ¿hay vida en Marte? **-2.** [referring to place] estar; **Valencia is in Spain** Valencia está en España; **he will ~ here tomorrow** estará aquí mañana. **-3.** [referring to movement] estar; **where have you been?** ¿dónde has estado? ◇ impersonal vb **-1.** [referring to time, dates] ser; **it's two o'clock** son las dos; **it's the 17th of February** estamos a 17 de febrero. **-2.** [referring to distance]: **it's 3 km to the next town** hay 3 kms hasta el próximo pueblo. **-3.** [referring to the weather]: **it's hot/cold/windy** hace calor/frío/viento. **-4.** [for emphasis] ser; **it's me** soy yo.

beach [biːtʃ] ◇ n playa f. ◇ vt varar.

beacon ['biːkən] n **-1.** [warning fire] almenara f. **-2.** [lighthouse] faro m, fanal m. **-3.** [radio beacon] radiofaro m.

bead [biːd] n **-1.** [of wood, glass] cuenta f, abalorio m. **-2.** [of sweat] gota f.

beagle ['biːgl] n sabueso m.

beak [biːk] n pico m.

beaker ['biːkər] n taza f (sin asa).

beam [biːm] ◇ n **-1.** [of wood, concrete] viga f. **-2.** [of light] rayo m. ◇ vt transmitir. ◇ vi **-1.** [smile] sonreír resplandeciente. **-2.** [shine] resplandecer.

bean [biːn] n CULIN [haricot] judía f, habichuela f; [of coffee] grano m.

beanbag ['biːnbæg] n cojín grande relleno de polietileno.

beanshoot ['biːnʃuːt], **beansprout** ['biːnspraʊt] n brote m de soja.

bear [beər] ◇ n [animal] oso m, -sa f. ◇ vt **-1.** [carry] llevar. **-2.** [support] soportar. **-3.** [responsibility] cargar con. **-4.** [marks, signs] llevar. **-5.** [endure] aguantar. **-6.** [fruit, crop] dar. **-7.** [feeling] guardar, albergar. ◇ vi: **to ~ left** torcer OR doblar a la izquierda; **to bring pressure/influence to ~ on** ejercer presión/influencia sobre. ◆ **bear down** vi: **to ~ down on** echar-

se encima de. ◆ **bear out** vt sep corroborar. ◆ **bear up** vi resistir. ◆ **bear with** vt fus tener paciencia con.

beard [bɪəd] n barba f.

bearer ['beərər] n **-1.** [of stretcher, news, cheque] portador m, -ra f. **-2.** [of passport] titular m y f.

bearing ['beərɪŋ] n **-1.** [connection]: **~ (on)** relación f (con). **-2.** [deportment] porte m. **-3.** [for shaft] cojinete m. **-4.** [on compass] rumbo m; **to get one's ~s** orientarse; **to lose one's ~s** desorientarse.

beast [biːst] n lit & fig bestia f.

beastly ['biːstlɪ] adj dated atroz.

beat [biːt] (pt **beat**, pp **beaten**) ◇ n **-1.** [of drum] golpe m. **-2.** [of heart, pulse] latido m. **-3.** MUS [rhythm] ritmo m; [individual unit of time] golpe m (de compás). **-4.** [of policeman] ronda f. ◇ vt **-1.** [hit - person] pegar; [- thing] golpear. **-2.** [wings, eggs, butter] batir. **-3.** [defeat] ganar; **it ~s me** inf no me lo explico. **-4.** [be better than] ser mucho mejor que. **-5.** phr: **~ it!** inf ¡largo! ◇ vi **-1.** [rain] golpear. **-2.** [heart, pulse] latir. ◆ **beat off** vt sep repeler. ◆ **beat up** vt sep inf dar una paliza a.

beating ['biːtɪŋ] n **-1.** [hitting] paliza f. **-2.** [defeat] derrota f.

beautiful ['bjuːtɪfʊl] adj **-1.** [person] guapo(pa). **-2.** [thing, animal] precioso(sa). **-3.** inf [very good - shot, weather] espléndido(da).

beautifully ['bjuːtəflɪ] adv **-1.** [attractively] bellamente. **-2.** inf [very well] espléndidamente.

beauty ['bjuːtɪ] n belleza f.

beauty parlour n salón f de belleza.

beauty salon = **beauty parlour**.

beauty spot n **-1.** [picturesque place] bello paraje m. **-2.** [on skin] lunar m.

beaver ['biːvər] n castor m.

became [bɪ'keɪm] pt → **become**.

because [bɪ'kɒz] conj porque. ◆ **because of** prep por, a causa de.

beck [bek] n: **to be at sb's ~ and call** estar siempre a disposición de alguien.

beckon ['bekən] ◇ vt [signal to] llamar (con un gesto). ◇ vi [signal]: **to ~ to sb** llamar (con un gesto) a alguien.

become [bɪ'kʌm] (pt **became**, pp **become**) vi hacerse; **to ~ happy** ponerse contento; **to ~ angry** enfadarse; **he became Prime Minister in 1991** en 1991 se convirtió en primer ministro.

becoming [bɪ'kʌmɪŋ] adj **-1.** [attractive]

favorecedor(ra). -2. [appropriate] **apropiado(da).**

bed [bed] *n* **-1.** [to sleep on] **cama** *f*; **to go to ~ irse a la cama; to make the ~ hacer la cama; to go to ~ with** *euphemism* **acostarse con. -2.** [flowerbed] **macizo** *m*. **-3.** [of sea] **fondo** *m*; [of river] **lecho** *m*.

bed and breakfast *n* [service] **cama** *f* **y desayuno;** [hotel] **pensión** *f*.

bedclothes ['bedkləʊðz] *npl* **ropa** *f* **de cama.**

bedlam ['bedləm] *n* **jaleo** *m*, **alboroto** *m*.

bed linen *n* **ropa** *f* **de cama.**

bedraggled [bɪ'drægld] *adj* **mojado y sucio** (mojada y sucia).

bedridden ['bed,rɪdn] *adj* **postrado(da) en cama.**

bedroom ['bedrum] *n* **dormitorio** *m*, **recámara** *f Amer*.

bedside ['bedsaɪd] *n* [side of bed] **lado** *m* **de la cama;** [of ill person] **lecho** *m*; **~ table mesita** *f* **de noche.**

bed-sit(ter) *n Br* **habitación** *alquilada con cama.*

bedsore ['bedsɔːʳ] *n* **úlcera** *f* **por decúbito.**

bedspread ['bedspred] *n* **colcha** *f*.

bedtime ['bedtaɪm] *n* **hora** *f* **de dormir.**

bee [biː] *n* **abeja** *f*.

beech [biːtʃ] *n* **haya** *f*.

beef [biːf] *n* **carne** *f* **de vaca.** ◆ **beef up** *vt sep inf* **reforzar.**

beefburger ['biːf,bɜːgəʳ] *n* **hamburguesa** *f*.

Beefeater ['biːf,iːtəʳ] *n guardián de la Torre de Londres.*

beefsteak ['biːf,steɪk] *n* **bistec** *m*.

beehive ['biːhaɪv] *n* [for bees] **colmena** *f*.

beeline ['biːlaɪn] *n*: **to make a ~ for** *inf* **irse derechito(ta) hacia.**

been [biːn] *pp* → **be.**

beer [bɪəʳ] *n* **cerveza** *f*.

beet [biːt] *n* **remolacha** *f*.

beetle ['biːtl] *n* **escarabajo** *m*.

beetroot ['biːtruːt] *n* **remolacha** *f*.

before [bɪ'fɔːʳ] ◇ *adv* **antes; we went the year ~ fuimos el año anterior.** ◇ *prep* **-1.** [in time] **antes de; they arrived ~ us llegaron antes que nosotros. -2.** [in space - facing] **ante, frente a.** ◇ *conj* **antes de; ~ it's too late antes de que sea demasiado tarde.**

beforehand [bɪ'fɔːhænd] *adv* **con antelación, de antemano.**

befriend [bɪ'frend] *vt* **hacer** OR **entablar amistad con.**

beg [beg] ◇ *vt* **-1.** [money, food] **mendigar, pedir. -2.** [favour, forgiveness] **suplicar; to ~ sb to do sthg rogar a alguien que haga algo; to ~ sb for sthg rogar algo a alguien.** ◇ *vi* **-1.** [for money, food]: **to ~ (for sthg) pedir** OR **mendigar (algo). -2.** [for favour, forgiveness]: **to ~ (for sthg) suplicar** OR **rogar (algo).**

began [bɪ'gæn] *pt* → **begin.**

beggar ['begəʳ] *n* **mendigo** *m*, **-ga** *f*.

begin [bɪ'gɪn] (*pt* **began,** *pp* **begun,** *cont* **-ning**) ◇ *vt*: **to ~ (doing** OR **to do sthg) empezar** OR **comenzar (a hacer algo).** ◇ *vi* **empezar, comenzar; to ~ with para empezar, de entrada.**

beginner [bɪ'gɪnəʳ] *n* **principiante** *m* **y** *f*.

beginning [bɪ'gɪnɪŋ] *n* **comienzo** *m*, **principio** *m*; **at the ~ of the month a principios de mes.**

begrudge [bɪ'grʌdʒ] *vt* **-1.** [envy]: **to ~ sb sthg envidiar a alguien algo. -2.** [give, do unwillingly]: **to ~ doing sthg hacer algo de mala gana** OR **a regañadientes.**

begun [bɪ'gʌn] *pp* → **begin.**

behalf [bɪ'hɑːf] *n*: **on ~ of** *Br*, **in ~ of** *Am* **en nombre** OR **en representación de.**

behave [bɪ'heɪv] ◇ *vt*: **to ~ o.s. portarse bien.** ◇ *vi* **-1.** [in a particular way] **comportarse, portarse. -2.** [in an acceptable way] **comportarse** OR **portarse bien.**

behaviour *Br*, **behavior** *Am* [bɪ'heɪvjəʳ] *n* **comportamiento** *m*, **conducta** *f*.

behead [bɪ'hed] *vt* **decapitar.**

beheld [bɪ'held] *pt & pp* → **behold.**

behind [bɪ'haɪnd] ◇ *prep* **-1.** [in space] **detrás de. -2.** [causing, responsible for] **detrás de. -3.** [in support of]: **we're ~ you nosotros te apoyamos. -4.** [in time]: **to be ~ schedule ir retrasado(da). -5.** [less successful than] **por detrás de.** ◇ *adv* **-1.** [in space] **detrás. -2.** [in time]: **to be ~ (with) ir atrasado(da) (con). -3.** [less successful] **por detrás.** ◇ *n inf* **trasero** *m*.

behold [bɪ'həʊld] (*pt & pp* **beheld**) *vt literary* **contemplar.**

beige [beɪʒ] *adj* **beige.**

being ['biːɪŋ] *n* **-1.** [creature] **ser** *m*. **-2.** [state of existing]: **in ~ en vigor; to come into ~ ver la luz, nacer.**

belated [bɪ'leɪtɪd] *adj* **tardío(a).**

belch [beltʃ] ◇ *vt* **arrojar.** ◇ *vi* **-1.** [person] **eructar. -2.** [smoke, fire] **brotar.**

beleaguered [bɪ'liːgəd] *adj* **-1.** MIL **ase-**

diado(da). **-2.** *fig* [harassed] atosigado(da).

Belgian ['beldʒən] ◇ *adj* belga. ◇ *n* belga *m y f*.

Belgium ['beldʒəm] *n* Bélgica.

Belgrade [,bel'greɪd] *n* Belgrado.

belie [bɪ'laɪ] (*cont* **belying**) *vt* **-1.** [disprove] desmentir. **-2.** [give false idea of] encubrir.

belief [bɪ'li:f] *n* **-1.** [faith, principle]: ~ **(in)** creencia *f* (en). **-2.** [opinion] opinión *f*.

believe [bɪ'li:v] ◇ *vt* creer; ~ **it or not** lo creas o no. ◇ *vi* [know to exist, be good]: **to** ~ **in** creer en.

believer [bɪ'li:vər] *n* **-1.** [religious person] creyente *m y f*. **-2.** [in idea, action]: ~ **in** sthg partidario *m*, -ria *f* de algo.

belittle [bɪ'lɪtl] *vt* menospreciar.

bell [bel] *n* [of church] campana *f*; [handbell, on door, bike] timbre *m*.

belligerent [bɪ'lɪdʒərənt] *adj* **-1.** [at war] beligerante. **-2.** [aggressive] belicoso(sa).

bellow ['beləʊ] *vi* **-1.** [person] rugir. **-2.** [bull] mugir, bramar.

bellows ['beləʊz] *npl* fuelle *m*.

belly ['belɪ] *n* **-1.** [of person] barriga *f*. **-2.** [of animal] vientre *m*.

bellyache ['belɪeɪk] *inf* ◇ *n* dolor *m* de barriga. ◇ *vi* gruñir.

belly button *n inf* ombligo *m*.

belong [bɪ'lɒŋ] *vi* **-1.** [be property]: **to** ~ **to** pertenecer a. **-2.** [be member]: **to** ~ **to** ser miembro de. **-3.** [be situated in right place]: **where does this book** ~? ¿dónde va este libro?; **he felt he didn't** ~ **there** sintió que no encajaba allí.

belongings [bɪ'lɒŋɪŋz] *npl* pertenencias *fpl*.

beloved [bɪ'lʌvd] ◇ *adj* querido(da). ◇ *n* amado *m*, -da *f*.

below [bɪ'ləʊ] ◇ *adv* **-1.** [gen] abajo; **the flat** ~ el piso de abajo. **-2.** [in text] más abajo; **see** ~ véase más abajo. ◇ *prep* **-1.** [lower than in position] (por) debajo de, bajo. **-2.** [lower than in rank, number] por debajo de.

belt [belt] ◇ *n* **-1.** [for clothing] cinturón *m*. **-2.** TECH [wide] cinta *f*; [narrow] correa *f*. **-3.** [of land, sea] franja *f*. ◇ *vt* inf arrear. ◇ *vi Br inf* ir a toda mecha.

beltway ['belt,weɪ] *n Am* carretera *f* de circunvalación.

bemused [bɪ'mju:zd] *adj* atónito(ta).

bench [bentʃ] *n* **-1.** [seat] banco *m*. **-2.** [in lab, workshop] mesa *f* de trabajo. **-3.** *Br* POL escaño *m*.

bend [bend] (*pt & pp* **bent**) ◇ *n* curva *f*; **round the** ~ *inf* majareta. ◇ *vt* doblar. ◇ *vi* [person] agacharse; [tree] doblarse; **to** ~ **over backwards for** hacer todo lo humanamente posible por.

beneath [bɪ'ni:θ] ◇ *adv* debajo. ◇ *prep* **-1.** [under] bajo. **-2.** [unworthy of] indigno(na) de.

benefactor ['benɪfæktər] *n* benefactor *m*.

beneficial [,benɪ'fɪʃl] *adj*: ~ **(to)** beneficioso(sa) (para).

beneficiary [,benɪ'fɪʃərɪ] *n* **-1.** JUR [of will] beneficiario *m*, -ria *f*. **-2.** [of change in law, new rule] beneficiado *m*, -da *f*.

benefit ['benɪfɪt] ◇ *n* **-1.** [advantage] ventaja *f*; **for the** ~ **of** en atención a; **to be to sb's** ~, **to be of** ~ **to sb** ir en beneficio de alguien. **-2.** ADMIN [allowance of money] subsidio *m*. ◇ *vt* beneficiar. ◇ *vi*: **to** ~ **from** beneficiarse de.

Benelux ['benɪlʌks] *n* (el) Benelux; **the** ~ **countries** los países del Benelux.

benevolent [bɪ'nevələnt] *adj* benevolente.

benign [bɪ'naɪn] *adj* **-1.** [person] bondadoso(sa). **-2.** MED benigno(na).

bent [bent] ◇ *pt & pp* → **bend**. ◇ *adj* **-1.** [wire, bar] torcido(da). **-2.** [person, body] encorvado(da). **-3.** *Br inf* [dishonest] corrupto(ta). **-4.** [determined]: **to be** ~ **on sthg/on doing sthg** estar empeñado(da) en algo/en hacer algo. ◇ *n* [natural tendency] inclinación *f*; ~ **for** don *m* OR talento *m* para.

bequeath [bɪ'kwi:ð] *vt lit & fig*: **to** ~ **sb sthg**, **to** ~ **sthg to sb** legar algo a alguien.

bequest [bɪ'kwest] *n* legado *m*.

berate [bɪ'reɪt] *vt* regañar.

bereaved [bɪ'ri:vd] (*pl inv*) *n*: **the** ~ la persona más allegada al difunto.

beret ['bereɪ] *n* boina *f*.

berk [bɜ:k] *n Br inf* gilipollas *m y f inv*.

Berlin [bɜ:'lɪn] *n* Berlín.

berm [bɜ:m] *n Am* arcén *m*.

Bermuda [bə'mju:də] *n* las Bermudas.

Bern [bɜ:n] *n* Berna.

berry ['berɪ] *n* baya *f*.

berserk [bə'zɜ:k] *adj*: **to go** ~ ponerse hecho(cha) una fiera.

berth [bɜ:θ] ◇ *n* **-1.** [in harbour] amarradero *m*, atracadero *m*. **-2.** [in ship, train] litera *f*. ◇ *vt & vi* atracar.

beseech [bɪ'si:tʃ] (*pt & pp* **besought** OR **beseeched**) *vt literary*: **to** ~ **(sb to do sthg)** suplicar (a alguien que haga algo).

beset [bɪ'set] (*pt* & *pp* **beset**) ◇ *adj*: ~ **with** OR **by** [subj: person] acosado(da) por; [subj: plan] plagado(da) de. ◇ *vt* acosar.

beside [bɪ'saɪd] *prep* **-1.** [next to] al lado de, junto a. **-2.** [compared with] comparado(da) con. **-3.** *phr*: **that's ~ the point** eso no viene al caso; **to be ~ o.s. with rage** estar fuera de sí; **to be ~ o.s. with joy** estar loco(ca) de alegría.

besides [bɪ'saɪdz] ◇ *adv* además. ◇ *prep* aparte de.

besiege [bɪ'siːdʒ] *vt lit* & *fig* asediar.

besotted [bɪ'sɒtɪd] *adj*: ~ **with** borracho(cha) de.

besought [bɪ'sɔːt] *pt* & *pp* → **beseech**.

best [best] ◇ *adj* mejor. ◇ *adv* mejor; **which did you like ~?** ¿cuál te gustó más? ◇ *n*: **to do one's ~** hacerlo lo mejor que uno puede; **to make the ~ of sthg** sacarle el mayor partido posible a algo; **for the ~** para bien; **all the ~** [ending letter] un abrazo; [saying goodbye] que te vaya bien. ◆ **at best** *adv* en el mejor de los casos.

best man *n* ≃ padrino *m* de boda.

bestow [bɪ'stəʊ] *vt fml*: **to ~ sthg on sb** [gift] otorgar OR conceder algo a alguien; [praise] dirigir algo a alguien; [title] conferir algo a alguien.

best-seller *n* [book] best seller *m*, éxito *m* editorial.

bet [bet] (*pt* & *pp* **bet** OR **-ted**) ◇ *n* **-1.** [gen]: ~ **(on)** apuesta *f* (a). **-2.** *fig* [prediction] predicción *f*. ◇ *vt* apostar. ◇ *vi* **-1.** [gamble]: **to ~ (on)** apostar (a). **-2.** [predict]: **to ~ on sthg** contar con (que pase) algo.

betray [bɪ'treɪ] *vt* **-1.** [person, trust, principles] traicionar. **-2.** [secret] revelar. **-3.** [feeling] delatar.

betrayal [bɪ'treɪəl] *n* **-1.** [of person, trust, principles] traición *f*. **-2.** [of secret] revelación *f*.

better ['betə*r*] ◇ *adj* (*compar of good*) mejor. ◇ *adv* (*compar of well*) **-1.** [in quality] mejor. **-2.** [more]: **I like it ~** me gusta más. **-3.** [preferably]: **we had ~ be going** más vale que nos vayamos ya. ◇ *n* [best one] mejor *m y f*; **to get the ~ of sb** poder con alguien. ◇ *vt* mejorar; **to ~ o.s.** mejorarse.

better off *adj* **-1.** [financially] mejor de dinero. **-2.** [in better situation]: **you'd be ~ going by bus** sería mejor si vas en autobús.

betting ['betɪŋ] *n* (U) apuestas *fpl*.

betting shop *n Br* casa *f* de apuestas.

between [bɪ'twiːn] ◇ *prep* entre; **closed ~ 1 and 2** cerrado de 1 a 2. ◇ *adv*: **(in) ~** en medio, entremedio.

beverage ['bevərɪdʒ] *n fml* bebida *f*.

beware [bɪ'weə*r*] *vi*: **to ~ (of)** tener cuidado (con).

bewildered [bɪ'wɪldəd] *adj* desconcertado(da).

bewitching [bɪ'wɪtʃɪŋ] *adj* hechizante.

beyond [bɪ'jɒnd] ◇ *prep* más allá de; ~ **midnight** pasada la medianoche; ~ **my reach/responsibility** fuera de mi alcance/competencia. ◇ *adv* más allá.

bias ['baɪəs] *n* **-1.** [prejudice] prejuicio *m*. **-2.** [tendency] tendencia *f*, inclinación *f*.

biased ['baɪəst] *adj* parcial; **to be ~ towards/against** tener prejuicios en favor/en contra de.

bib [bɪb] *n* [for baby] babero *m*.

Bible ['baɪbl] *n*: **the ~** la Biblia.

bicarbonate of soda [baɪ'kɑːbənət-] *n* bicarbonato *m*.

biceps ['baɪseps] (*pl inv*) *n* bíceps *m inv*.

bicker ['bɪkə*r*] *vi* reñir.

bicycle ['baɪsɪkl] *n* bicicleta *f*.

bicycle path *n* camino *m* para bicicletas.

bicycle pump *n* bomba *f*.

bid [bɪd] (*pt* & *pp* **bid**) ◇ *n* **-1.** [attempt]: ~ **(for)** intento *m* (de hacerse con). **-2.** [at auction] puja *f*. **-3.** [financial offer]: ~ **(for sthg)** oferta *f* (para adquirir algo). ◇ *vt* [money] pujar. ◇ *vi* [at auction]: **to ~ (for)** pujar (por).

bidder ['bɪdə*r*] *n* postor *m*, -ra *f*.

bidding ['bɪdɪŋ] *n* (U) [at auction] puja *f*.

bide [baɪd] *vt*: **to ~ one's time** esperar el momento oportuno.

bifocals [,baɪ'fəʊklz] *npl* gafas *fpl* bifocales.

big [bɪg] *adj* **-1.** [large, important] grande; **a ~ problem** un gran problema; ~ **problems** grandes problemas. **-2.** [older] mayor. **-3.** [successful] popular.

bigamy ['bɪgəmɪ] *n* bigamia *f*.

big deal *inf* ◇ *n*: **it's no ~** no tiene (la menor) importancia. ◇ *excl* ¡y a mí qué!

Big Dipper [-'dɪpə*r*] *n Br* [rollercoaster] montaña *f* rusa.

bigheaded [,bɪg'hedɪd] *adj inf pej* creído(da).

bigot ['bɪgət] *n* fanático *m*, -ca *f*.

bigoted ['bɪgətɪd] *adj* fanático(ca).

bigotry ['bɪgətrɪ] *n* fanatismo *m*.

big time n inf: **the ~** el éxito, la fama.

big toe n dedo m gordo (del pie).

big top n carpa f.

big wheel n Br [at fairground] noria f.

bike [baɪk] n inf [bicycle] bici f; [motorcycle] moto f.

bikeway ['baɪkweɪ] n Am [lane] carril-bici m.

bikini [bɪ'kiːnɪ] n biquini m, bikini m.

bile [baɪl] n [fluid] bilis f.

bilingual [baɪ'lɪŋgwəl] adj bilingüe.

bill [bɪl] ◇ n **-1.** [statement of cost]: **~ (for)** [meal] cuenta f (de); [electricity, phone] factura f (de). **-2.** [in parliament] proyecto m de ley. **-3.** [of show, concert] programa m. **-4.** Am [banknote] billete m. **-5.** [poster]: **"post** OR **stick no ~s"** "prohibido fijar carteles". **-6.** [beak] pico m. ◇ vt [send a bill]: **to ~ sb for** mandar la factura a alguien por.

billboard ['bɪlbɔːd] n cartelera f.

billet ['bɪlɪt] n acantonamiento m.

billfold ['bɪlfəʊld] n Am billetera f.

billiards ['bɪljədz] n billar m.

billion ['bɪljən] num **-1.** Am [thousand million] millar m de millones. **-2.** Br [million million] billón m.

Bill of Rights n: **the ~** las diez primeras enmiendas de la Constitución estadounidense.

bimbo ['bɪmbəʊ] (pl **-s** OR **-es**) n inf pej niña f mona, mujer joven, guapa y poco inteligente.

bin [bɪn] n **-1.** Br [for rubbish] cubo m de la basura; [for paper] papelera f. **-2.** [for grain, coal] depósito m.

bind [baɪnd] (pt & pp **bound**) vt **-1.** [tie up] atar. **-2.** [unite - people] unir. **-3.** [bandage] vendar. **-4.** [book] encuadernar. **-5.** [constrain] obligar.

binder ['baɪndəʳ] n [cover] carpeta f.

binding ['baɪndɪŋ] ◇ adj obligatorio(ria). ◇ n [on book] encuadernación f.

binge [bɪndʒ] inf n: **to go on a ~** irse de juerga.

bingo ['bɪŋgəʊ] n bingo m.

binoculars [bɪ'nɒkjʊləz] npl gemelos mpl, prismáticos mpl.

biochemistry [,baɪəʊ'kemɪstrɪ] n bioquímica f.

biodegradable [,baɪəʊdɪ'greɪdəbl] adj biodegradable.

biography [baɪ'ɒgrəfɪ] n biografía f.

biological [,baɪə'lɒdʒɪkl] adj biológico(ca).

biology [baɪ'ɒlədʒɪ] n biología f.

birch [bɜːtʃ] n [tree] abedul m.

bird [bɜːd] n **-1.** [animal - large] ave f; [- small] pájaro m. **-2.** inf [woman] tía f.

birdie ['bɜːdɪ] n [in golf] birdie m.

bird's-eye view n vista f panorámica.

bird-watcher [-,wɒtʃəʳ] n observador m, -ra f de pájaros.

Biro® ['baɪərəʊ] n bolígrafo m, lapicera f Amer.

birth [bɜːθ] n [gen] nacimiento m; [delivery] parto m; **to give ~ (to)** dar a luz (a).

birth certificate n partida f de nacimiento.

birth control n control m de natalidad.

birthday ['bɜːθdeɪ] n cumpleaños m inv.

birthmark ['bɜːθmɑːk] n antojo m.

birthrate ['bɜːθreɪt] n índice m de natalidad.

Biscay ['bɪskɪ] n: **the Bay of ~** el golfo de Vizcaya.

biscuit ['bɪskɪt] n [in UK] galleta f; [in US] tipo de bollo.

bisect [baɪ'sekt] vt dividir en dos.

bishop ['bɪʃəp] n **-1.** [in church] obispo m. **-2.** [in chess] alfil m.

bison ['baɪsn] (pl inv OR **-s**) n bisonte m.

bit [bɪt] ◇ pt → **bite.** ◇ n **-1.** [piece] trozo m; **a ~ of** un poco de; **a ~ of news** una noticia; **~s and pieces** Br [objects] cosillas fpl; [possessions] bártulos mpl; **to take sthg to ~s** desmontar algo. **-2.** [amount]: **a ~ of** un poco de; **a ~ of shopping** algunas compras; **quite a ~ of** bastante. **-3.** [short time]: **(for) a ~** un rato. **-4.** [of drill] broca f. **-5.** [of bridle] bocado m, freno m. **-6.** COMPUT bit m. ◆ **a bit** adv un poco. ◆ **bit by bit** adv poco a poco.

bitch [bɪtʃ] n **-1.** [female dog] perra f. **-2.** v inf pej [unpleasant woman] bruja f. ◇ vi inf [talk unpleasantly]: **to ~ about** poner a parir a.

bitchy ['bɪtʃɪ] adj inf: **to be ~** tener mala uva.

bite [baɪt] (pt **bit**, pp **bitten**) ◇ n **-1.** [by dog, person] mordisco m; [by insect, snake] picotazo m. **-2.** inf [food]: **a ~ (to eat)** un bocado. **-3.** [wound - from dog] mordedura f; [- from insect, snake] picadura f. ◇ vt **-1.** [subj: person, animal] morder. **-2.** [subj: insect, snake] picar. ◇ vi **-1.** [animal, person]: **to ~ (into sthg)** morder (algo); **to ~ off** sthg arrancar algo de un mordisco. **-2.** [insect, snake] picar. **-3.** [grip] agarrar.

biting ['baɪtɪŋ] adj **-1.** [very cold] gélido(da), cortante. **-2.** [caustic] mordaz.

bitten ['bɪtn] *pp* → bite.
bitter ['bɪtəʳ] ◇ *adj* **-1.** [coffee, chocolate] amargo(ga); [lemon] agrio(gria). **-2.** [icy] gélido(da). **-3.** [causing pain] amargo(ga). **-4.** [acrimonious] enconado(da). **-5.** [resentful] amargado(da). ◇ *n Br* [beer] *tipo de cerveza amarga.*
bitter lemon *n* bíter *m* de limón.
bitterness ['bɪtənɪs] *n* **-1.** [of taste] amargor *m*. **-2.** [of wind, weather] gelidez *f*. **-3.** [resentment] resentimiento *m*.
bizarre [bɪ'zɑːʳ] *adj* [behaviour, appearance] extravagante; [machine, remark] singular, extraordinario(ria).
blab [blæb] *vi inf* irse de la lengua.
black [blæk] ◇ *adj* **-1.** [gen] negro(gra); ~ **and blue** amoratado(da); ~ **and white** [films, photos] en blanco y negro; [clear-cut] extremadamente nítido(da). **-2.** [without milk] solo. **-3.** [angry] furioso(sa). ◇ *n* **-1.** [colour] negro *m*. **-2.** [person] negro *m*, -gra *f*. **-3.** *phr*: **in** ~ **and white** [in writing] por escrito; **to be in the** ~ tener saldo positivo. ◇ *vt Br* [boycott] boicotear. ◆ **black out** *vi* desmayarse.
blackberry ['blækbərɪ] *n* mora *f*, zarzamora *f*.
blackbird ['blækbɜːd] *n* mirlo *m*.
blackboard ['blækbɔːd] *n* pizarra *f*.
blackcurrant [,blæk'kʌrənt] *n* grosella *f* negra, casis *m*.
blacken ['blækn] *vt* **-1.** [make dark] ennegrecer. **-2.** [tarnish] manchar.
black eye *n* ojo *m* morado.
blackhead ['blækhed] *n* barrillo *m*.
black ice *n* hielo *transparente en el suelo.*
blackleg ['blækleg] *n pej* esquirol *m*.
blacklist ['blæklɪst] *n* lista *f* negra.
blackmail ['blækmeɪl] ◇ *n lit & fig* chantaje *m*. ◇ *vt lit & fig* chantajear.
black market *n* mercado *m* negro.
blackout ['blækaʊt] *n* **-1.** [in wartime, power cut] apagón *m*. **-2.** [of news] censura *f*. **-3.** [fainting fit] desmayo *m*.
black pudding *n Br* morcilla *f*.
Black Sea *n*: **the** ~ el mar Negro.
black sheep *n* oveja *f* negra.
blacksmith ['blæksmɪθ] *n* herrero *m*.
black spot *n* punto *m* negro.
bladder ['blædəʳ] *n* ANAT vejiga *f*.
blade [bleɪd] *n* **-1.** [of knife, saw] hoja *f*. **-2.** [of propeller] aleta *f*, paleta *f*. **-3.** [of grass] brizna *f*, hoja *f*.
blame [bleɪm] ◇ *n* culpa *f*; **to take the** ~ **for** hacerse responsable de; **to be to** ~ **for** ser el culpable de. ◇ *vt* echar la culpa a, culpar; **to** ~ **sthg on sthg/sb,**

to ~ **sthg/sb for sthg** culpar algo/a alguien de algo.
bland [blænd] *adj* soso(sa).
blank [blæŋk] ◇ *adj* **-1.** [wall] liso(sa); [sheet of paper] en blanco. **-2.** *fig* [look] vacío(a). ◇ *n* **-1.** [empty space] espacio *m* en blanco. **-2.** MIL [cartridge] cartucho *m* de fogueo.
blank cheque *n* cheque *m* en blanco; *fig* carta *f* blanca.
blanket ['blæŋkɪt] *n* **-1.** [bed cover] manta *f*, frazada *f Amer.* **-2.** [layer] manto *m*.
blare [bleəʳ] *vi* resonar, sonar.
blasé [*Br* 'blɑːzeɪ, *Am* ,blɑː'zeɪ] *adj*: **to be** ~ **about** estar de vuelta de.
blasphemy ['blæsfəmɪ] *n* blasfemia *f*.
blast [blɑːst] ◇ *n* **-1.** [of bomb] explosión *f*. **-2.** [of wind] ráfaga *f*. ◇ *vt* [hole, tunnel] perforar (*con explosivos*). ◇ *excl Br inf* ¡maldita sea! ◆ **(at) full blast** *adv* a todo trapo.
blasted ['blɑːstɪd] *adj inf* maldito(ta).
blast-off *n* despegue *m*.
blatant ['bleɪtənt] *adj* descarado(da).
blaze [bleɪz] ◇ *n* **-1.** [fire] incendio *m*. **-2.** *fig* [of colour] explosión *f*; [of light] resplandor *m*; **a** ~ **of publicity** una ola de publicidad. ◇ *vi lit & fig* arder.
blazer ['bleɪzəʳ] *n* chaqueta *f* de sport generalmente con la insignia de un equipo, colegio etc.
bleach [bliːtʃ] ◇ *n* lejía *f*. ◇ *vt* [hair] blanquear; [clothes] desteñir.
bleached [bliːtʃt] *adj* [hair] teñido(da) de rubio; [jeans] desteñido(da).
bleachers ['bliːtʃəz] *npl Am* SPORT graderío *m* descubierto.
bleak [bliːk] *adj* **-1.** [future] negro(gra). **-2.** [place, person, face] sombrío(a). **-3.** [weather] desapacible.
bleary-eyed [,blɪərɪ'aɪd] *adj* con los ojos nublados.
bleat [bliːt] *vi* **-1.** [sheep] balar. **-2.** *fig* [person] gimotear.
bleed [bliːd] (*pt & pp* bled) ◇ *vt* [radiator etc] vaciar. ◇ *vi* sangrar.
bleeper ['bliːpəʳ] *n* busca *m*.
blemish ['blemɪʃ] *n* [mark] señal *f*, marca *f*; *fig* mancha *f*.
blend [blend] ◇ *n lit & fig* mezcla *f*. ◇ *vt*: **to** ~ **(sthg with sthg)** mezclar (algo con algo). ◇ *vi*: **to** ~ **(with)** combinarse (con).
blender ['blendəʳ] *n* licuadora *f*.
bless [bles] (*pt & pp* **-ed** OR blest) *vt* **-1.** RELIG bendecir. **-2.** *phr*: ~ **you!** [after sneezing] ¡jesús!; [thank you] ¡gracias!

blessing ['blesiŋ] n -1. RELIG bendición f. -2. fig [good wishes] aprobación f.

blest [blest] pt & pp → **bless**.

blew [bluː] pt → **blow**.

blight [blaɪt] vt malograr, arruinar.

blimey ['blaɪmɪ] excl Br inf ¡ostias!

blind [blaɪnd] ◇ adj -1. [unsighted, irrational] ciego(ga). -2. fig [unaware]: **to be ~ to** sthg no ver algo. ◇ n [for window] persiana f. ◇ npl: **the ~** los ciegos. ◇ vt [permanently] dejar ciego(ga); [temporarily] cegar; **to ~ sb to sthg** fig no dejar a alguien ver algo.

blind alley n lit & fig callejón m sin salida.

blind corner n curva f sin visibilidad.

blind date n cita f a ciegas.

blinders ['blaɪndəz] npl Am anteojeras fpl.

blindfold ['blaɪndfəʊld] ◇ adv con los ojos vendados. ◇ n venda f. ◇ vt vendar los ojos a.

blindly ['blaɪndlɪ] adv -1. [unable to see] a ciegas. -2. fig [guess] a boleo; [accept] ciegamente.

blindness ['blaɪndnɪs] n lit & fig: **~ (to)** ceguera f (ante).

blind spot n -1. [when driving] ángulo m muerto. -2. fig [inability to understand] punto m débil.

blink [blɪŋk] ◇ vt -1. [eyes]: **to ~ one's eyes** parpadear. -2. Am AUT: **to ~ one's lights** dar las luces (intermitentemente). ◇ vi parpadear.

blinkers ['blɪŋkəz] npl Br anteojeras fpl.

bliss [blɪs] n gloria f, dicha f.

blissful ['blɪsful] adj dichoso(sa), feliz.

blister ['blɪstər] ◇ n ampolla f. ◇ vi ampollarse.

blithely ['blaɪðlɪ] adv alegremente.

blitz [blɪts] n MIL bombardeo m aéreo.

blizzard ['blɪzəd] n ventisca f (de nieve).

bloated ['bləʊtɪd] adj hinchado(da).

blob [blɒb] n -1. [drop] gota f. -2. [indistinct shape] bulto m borroso.

bloc [blɒk] n bloque m.

block [blɒk] ◇ n -1. [gen] bloque m. -2. Am [of buildings] manzana f, cuadra f Amer. -3. [obstruction - physical or mental] bloqueo m. ◇ vt -1. [road] cortar; [pipe] obstruir. -2. [view] tapar. -3. [prevent] bloquear, obstaculizar.

blockade [blɒ'keɪd] ◇ n bloqueo m. ◇ vt bloquear.

blockage ['blɒkɪdʒ] n obstrucción f.

blockbuster ['blɒkbʌstər] n inf [book]

(gran) éxito m editorial; [film] (gran) éxito de taquilla.

block capitals npl mayúsculas fpl (de imprenta).

block letters npl mayúsculas fpl (de imprenta).

bloke [bləʊk] n Br inf tío m, tipo m.

blond [blɒnd] adj rubio(bia).

blonde [blɒnd] ◇ adj rubia. ◇ n [woman] rubia f.

blood [blʌd] n sangre f; **in cold ~** a sangre fría.

bloodbath ['blʌdbɑːθ, pl -bɑːðz] n matanza f, carnicería f.

blood cell n glóbulo m.

blood donor n donante m y f de sangre.

blood group n grupo m sanguíneo.

bloodhound ['blʌdhaʊnd] n sabueso m.

blood poisoning n septicemia f.

blood pressure n tensión f arterial; **to have high/low ~** tener la tensión alta/baja.

bloodshed ['blʌdʃed] n derramamiento m de sangre.

bloodshot ['blʌdʃɒt] adj inyectado(da) (de sangre).

bloodstream ['blʌdstriːm] n flujo m sanguíneo, sangre f.

blood test n análisis m inv de sangre.

bloodthirsty ['blʌd,θɜːstɪ] adj sediento(ta) de sangre.

blood transfusion n transfusión f de sangre.

bloody ['blʌdɪ] ◇ adj -1. [war, conflict] sangriento(ta). -2. [face, hands] ensangrentado(da). -3. Br v inf maldito(ta), pinche Amer. ◇ adv Br v inf: **he's ~ useless** es un puto inútil; **it's ~ brilliant** es de puta madre.

bloody-minded [-'maɪndɪd] adj Br inf puñetero(ra), que lleva la contraria.

bloom [bluːm] ◇ n flor f. ◇ vi florecer.

blooming ['bluːmɪŋ] ◇ adj Br inf [to show annoyance] condenado(da). ◇ adv Br inf condenadamente.

blossom ['blɒsəm] ◇ n flor f; **in ~** en flor. ◇ vi lit & fig florecer.

blot [blɒt] ◇ n [of ink] borrón m; fig mancha f. ◇ vt -1. [paper] emborronar. -2. [ink] secar. ◆ **blot out** vt sep [gen] cubrir, ocultar; [memories] borrar.

blotchy ['blɒtʃɪ] adj lleno(na) de marcas.

blotting paper ['blɒtɪŋ-] n (U) papel m secante.

blouse [blaʊz] n blusa f.

blow [bləʊ] (*pt* **blew**, *pp* **blown**) ◇ *vi* **-1.** [gen] soplar. **-2.** [in wind] salir volando, volar. **-3.** [fuse] fundirse. ◇ *vt* **-1.** [subj: wind] hacer volar. **-2.** [whistle, horn] tocar, hacer sonar. **-3.** [bubbles] hacer. **-4.** [kiss] mandar. **-5.** [fuse] fundir. **-6.** [clear]: **to ~ one's nose** sonarse la nariz. **-7.** *inf* [money] ventilarse. ◇ *n* [hit, shock] golpe *m*. ◆ **blow out** ◇ *vt sep* apagar. ◇ *vi* **-1.** [candle] apagarse. **-2.** [tyre] reventar. ◆ **blow over** *vi* **-1.** [storm] amainar. **-2.** [argument] disiparse. ◆ **blow up** ◇ *vt sep* **-1.** [inflate] inflar. **-2.** [destroy] volar. **-3.** [photograph] ampliar. ◇ *vi* saltar por los aires, estallar.

blow-dry *n* secado *m* (*con secador*).

blowlamp *Br* ['bləʊlæmp], **blowtorch** ['bləʊtɔːtʃ] *n* soplete *m*.

blown [bləʊn] *pp* → **blow**.

blowout ['bləʊaʊt] *n* [of tyre] pinchazo *m*, reventón *m*.

blowtorch = **blowlamp**.

blubber ['blʌbər] *vi pej* lloriquear.

bludgeon ['blʌdʒən] *vt* apalear.

blue [bluː] ◇ *adj* **-1.** [colour] azul. **-2.** *inf* [sad] triste. **-3.** [pornographic - film] equis (*inv*), porno; [- joke] verde. ◇ *n* azul *m*; **out of the ~** en el momento menos pensado. ◆ **blues** *npl* **-1.** MUS blues *m inv*. **-2.** *inf* [sad feeling] depre *f*.

bluebell ['bluːbel] *n* campanilla *f*.

blueberry ['bluːbəri] *n* arándano *m*.

bluebottle ['bluːˌbɒtl] *n* moscardón *m*, moscón *m*.

blue cheese *n* queso *m* azul.

blue-collar *adj*: **~ worker** obrero *m*, -ra *f*.

blue jeans *npl Am* vaqueros *mpl*, tejanos *mpl*.

blueprint ['bluːprint] *n* **-1.** CONSTR cianotipo *m*. **-2.** *fig* [description] proyecto *m*.

bluff [blʌf] ◇ *adj* brusco(ca). ◇ *n* [deception] fanfarronada *f*; **to call sb's ~** desafiar a alguien a que haga lo que dice. ◇ *vi* fanfarronear.

blunder ['blʌndər] ◇ *n* metedura *f* de pata. ◇ *vi* **-1.** [make mistake] meter la pata. **-2.** [move clumsily] ir tropezando.

blunt [blʌnt] *adj* **-1.** [knife] desafilado(da). **-2.** [object] romo(ma). **-3.** [forthright] directo(ta), franco(ca).

blur [blɜːr] ◇ *n* imagen *f* borrosa. ◇ *vt* **-1.** [vision] nublar. **-2.** [distinction] desdibujar.

blurb [blɜːb] *n inf texto publicitario en la cubierta o solapa de un libro.*

blurt [blɜːt] ◆ **blurt out** *vt sep* espetar, decir de repente.

blush [blʌʃ] ◇ *n* rubor *m*. ◇ *vi* ruborizarse.

blusher ['blʌʃər] *n* colorete *m*.

blustery ['blʌstəri] *adj* borrascoso(sa).

BMX (*abbr of* **bicycle motorcross**) *n mountain-bike.*

BO *n* (*abbr of* **body odour**) OC *m*.

boar [bɔːr] *n* **-1.** [male pig] verraco *m*. **-2.** [wild pig] jabalí *m*.

board [bɔːd] ◇ *n* **-1.** [plank] tabla *f*. **-2.** [for notices] tablón *m*. **-3.** [for games] tablero *m*. **-4.** [blackboard] pizarra *f*. **-5.** COMPUT placa *f*. **-6.** [of company]: **~ (of directors)** (junta *f*) directiva *f*. **-7.** [committee] comité *m*, junta *f*. **-8.** *Br* [at hotel, guesthouse] pensión *f*; **~ and lodging** comida y habitación; **full ~** pensión completa; **half ~** media pensión. **-9. on ~** [ship, plane] a bordo; [bus, train] dentro. **-10.** *phr*: **above ~** en regla. ◇ *vt* [ship, plane] embarcar en; [train, bus] subirse a.

boarder ['bɔːdər] *n* **-1.** [lodger] huésped *m y f*. **-2.** [at school] interno *m*, -na *f*.

boarding card ['bɔːdɪŋ-] *n* tarjeta *f* de embarque.

boardinghouse ['bɔːdɪŋhaʊs, *pl* -haʊzɪz] *n* casa *f* de huéspedes.

boarding school ['bɔːdɪŋ-] *n* internado *m*.

Board of Trade *n Br*: **the ~** ≃ el Ministerio de Comercio.

boardroom ['bɔːdrʊm] *n* sala *f* de juntas.

boast [bəʊst] ◇ *vt* disfrutar de. ◇ *vi*: **to ~ (about)** alardear OR jactarse (de).

boastful ['bəʊstfʊl] *adj* fanfarrón(ona).

boat [bəʊt] *n* [large] barco *m*; [small] barca *f*; **by ~** en barco/barca.

boater ['bəʊtər] *n* [hat] canotié *m*.

boatswain ['bəʊsn] *n* NAUT contramaestre *m*.

bob [bɒb] ◇ *n* **-1.** [hairstyle] corte *m* de chico. **-2.** *Br inf dated* [shilling] chelín *m*. **-3.** = **bobsleigh**. ◇ *vi* [boat] balancearse.

bobbin ['bɒbin] *n* bobina *f*.

bobby ['bɒbi] *n Br inf* poli *m*.

bobsleigh ['bɒbslei] *n* bobsleigh *m*.

bode [bəʊd] *vi literary*: **to ~ ill/well for** traer malos/buenos presagios para.

bodily ['bɒdɪli] ◇ *adj* corporal. ◇ *adv*: **to lift/move sb ~** levantar/mover a alguien por la fuerza.

body ['bɒdi] *n* **-1.** [gen] cuerpo *m*. **-2.** [corpse] cadáver *m*. **-3.** [organization] entidad f; **a ~ of thought/opinion** una corriente de pensamiento/opinión. **-4.** [of car] carrocería f; [of plane] fuselaje m.

body building n culturismo m.

bodyguard ['bɒdɪgɑːd] n guardaespaldas m inv, guarura m Amer.

body odour n olor m corporal.

bodywork ['bɒdɪwɜːk] n carrocería f.

bog [bɒg] n **-1.** [marsh] cenagal m. **-2.** Br v inf [toilet] meódromo m.

bogged down [ˌbɒgd-] adj **-1.** [in details, work]: **~ (in)** empantanado(da) (en). **-2.** [in mud, snow]: **~ in** atascado(da) en.

boggle ['bɒgl] vi: **the mind ~s!** ¡me da vueltas la cabeza!, ¡es increíble!

bogus ['bəʊgəs] adj falso(sa).

boil [bɔɪl] ◇ n **-1.** MED pústula f, grano m. **-2.** [boiling point]: **to bring sthg to the ~** poner algo a hervir; **to come to the ~** romper a hervir. ◇ vt **-1.** [water] hervir. **-2.** [pan, kettle] poner a hervir. **-3.** [food] cocer. ◇ vi hervir. ◆ **boil down to** vt fus reducirse a. ◆ **boil over** vi **-1.** [liquid] rebosar. **-2.** fig [feelings] desbordarse.

boiled [bɔɪld] adj cocido(da); **~ egg** huevo m pasado por agua; **~ sweets** Br caramelos mpl (duros).

boiler ['bɔɪlər] n caldera f.

boiler suit n Br mono m.

boiling ['bɔɪlɪŋ] adj inf [hot]: **I'm ~** estoy asado(da) de calor; **it's ~** hace un calor de muerte.

boiling point n punto m de ebullición.

boisterous ['bɔɪstərəs] adj ruidoso(sa), alborotador(ra).

bold [bəʊld] adj **-1.** [brave, daring] audaz. **-2.** [lines, design] marcado(da). **-3.** [colour] vivo(va). **-4.** TYPO: **type** OR **print** negrita f.

Bolivia [bəˈlɪvɪə] n Bolivia.

Bolivian [bəˈlɪvɪən] ◇ adj boliviano(na). ◇ n boliviano m, -na f.

bollard ['bɒlɑːd] n [on road] poste m.

bollocks ['bɒləks] Br v inf npl cojones mpl.

bolster ['bəʊlstər] vt reforzar. ◆ **bolster up** vt fus reforzar.

bolt [bəʊlt] ◇ n **-1.** [on door, window] cerrojo m. **-2.** [type of screw] tornillo m, perno m. ◇ adv: **~ upright** muy derecho(cha). ◇ vt **-1.** [fasten together] atornillar. **-2.** [door, window] echar el cerrojo a. **-3.** [food] tragarse. ◇ vi salir disparado(da).

bomb [bɒm] ◇ n bomba f. ◇ vt bombardear.

bombard [bɒmˈbɑːd] vt MIL & fig: **to ~ (with)** bombardear (a).

bombastic [bɒmˈbæstɪk] adj grandilocuente, rimbombante.

bomb disposal squad n equipo m de artificieros.

bomber ['bɒmər] n **-1.** [plane] bombardero m. **-2.** [person] persona f que pone bombas.

bombing ['bɒmɪŋ] n bombardeo m.

bombshell ['bɒmʃel] n fig bombazo m.

bona fide ['bəʊnəˈfaɪdɪ] adj de buena fe.

bond [bɒnd] ◇ n **-1.** [between people] lazo m, vínculo m. **-2.** [binding promise] compromiso m. **-3.** FIN bono m. ◇ vt [glue] adherir; fig [people] unir.

bondage ['bɒndɪdʒ] n literary [servitude] esclavitud f, vasallaje m.

bone [bəʊn] ◇ n [gen] hueso m; [of fish] raspa f, espina f. ◇ vt [fish] limpiar; [meat] deshuesar.

bone-dry adj bien seco(ca).

bone-idle adj haragán(ana), gandul(la).

bonfire ['bɒnfaɪər] n hoguera f.

bonfire night n Br noche del 5 de noviembre en que se encienden hogueras y fuegos artificiales.

Bonn [bɒn] n Bonn.

bonnet ['bɒnɪt] n **-1.** Br [of car] capó m. **-2.** [hat] toca f.

bonny ['bɒnɪ] adj Scot majo(ja).

bonus ['bəʊnəs] (pl **-es**) n [extra money] paga f extra, prima f; fig beneficio m adicional.

bony ['bəʊnɪ] adj **-1.** [person, hand] huesudo(da). **-2.** [meat] lleno(na) de huesos; [fish] espinoso(sa).

boo [buː] (pl **-s**) ◇ excl ¡bu! ◇ n abucheo m. ◇ vt & vi abuchear.

boob [buːb] n inf [mistake] metedura f de pata. ◆ **boobs** npl Br v inf [woman's breasts] tetas fpl.

booby trap ['buːbɪ-] n [bomb] bomba f camuflada.

book [bʊk] ◇ n **-1.** [for reading] libro m. **-2.** [of stamps] librillo m; [of tickets, cheques] talonario m; [of matches] cajetilla f. ◇ vt **-1.** [reserve] reservar; **to be fully ~ed** estar completo. **-2.** inf [subj: police] multar. **-3.** Br FTBL amonestar. ◇ vi hacer reserva. ◆ **books** npl COMM libros mpl. ◆ **book up** vt sep: **to be ~ed up** estar completo.

bookcase ['bʊkkeɪs] n estantería f.

bookie ['bʊkɪ] n inf corredor m, -ra f de apuestas.

booking ['bʊkɪŋ] n **-1.** [reservation] reserva f. **-2.** Br FTBL amonestación f.

booking office n taquilla f.

bookkeeping ['bʊk,kiːpɪŋ] n contabilidad f.

booklet ['bʊklɪt] n folleto m.

bookmaker ['bʊk,meɪkər] n corredor m, -ra f de apuestas.

bookmark ['bʊkmɑːk] n separador m.

bookseller ['bʊk,selər] n librero m, -ra f.

bookshelf ['bʊkʃelf] (pl **-shelves** [-ʃelvz]) n [shelf] estante m; [bookcase] estantería f, librero m Amer.

bookshop Br ['bʊkʃɒp], **bookstore** Am ['bʊkstɔːr] n librería f.

book token n vale m para comprar libros.

boom [buːm] ⋄ n -1. [loud noise] estampido m. -2. [increase] auge m, boom m. -3. [for TV camera, microphone] jirafa f. ⋄ vi -1. [make noise] tronar. -2. ECON estar en auge.

boon [buːn] n ayuda f.

boost [buːst] ⋄ n -1. [in profits, production] incremento m. -2. [to popularity, spirits] empujón m. ⋄ vt -1. [increase] incrementar. -2. [improve] levantar.

booster ['buːstər] n MED inyección f de revacunación.

boot [buːt] ⋄ n -1. [item of footwear] bota f; [ankle boot] botín m. -2. Br [of car] maletero m, cajuela f Amer. ⋄ vt inf dar una patada a. ◆ **to boot** adv además. ◆ **boot out** vt sep inf echar, poner (de patitas) en la calle.

booth [buːð] n -1. [at fair] puesto m. -2. [for phoning, voting] cabina f.

booty ['buːtɪ] n literary botín m.

booze [buːz] inf ⋄ n (U) bebida f, alcohol m. ⋄ vi pimplar, empinar el codo.

bop [bɒp] inf ⋄ n [disco, dance] baile m. ⋄ vi bailar.

border ['bɔːdər] ⋄ n -1. [between countries] frontera f. -2. [edge] borde m. -3. [in garden] arriate m. ⋄ vt -1. [country] limitar con. -2. [edge] bordear. ◆ **border on** vt fus rayar en.

borderline ['bɔːdəlaɪn] ⋄ adj: **a ~ case** un caso dudoso. ⋄ n fig límite m.

bore [bɔːr] ⋄ pt → **bear**. ⋄ n -1. pej [person] pelmazo m, -za f; [situation, event] rollo m, lata f. -2. [of gun] calibre m. ⋄ vt -1. [not interest] aburrir; **to ~ sb stiff** OR **to tears** OR **to death** aburrir a alguien un montón. -2. [drill] horadar.

bored [bɔːd] adj aburrido(da); **to be ~ with sthg** estar harto de algo.

boredom ['bɔːdəm] n aburrimiento m.

boring ['bɔːrɪŋ] adj aburrido(da).

born [bɔːn] adj -1. [given life] nacido(da); **to be ~** nacer. -2. [natural] nato(ta).

borne [bɔːn] pp → **bear**.

borough ['bʌrə] n [area of town] distrito m; [town] municipio m.

borrow ['bɒrəʊ] vt: **to ~ sthg from sb** coger OR tomar algo prestado a alguien; **can I ~ your bike?** ¿me prestas tu bici?

Bosnia ['bɒznɪə] n Bosnia.

Bosnia-Herzegovina [-,hɜːtsəgə'viːnə] n Bosnia-Hercegovina.

Bosnian ['bɒznɪən] ⋄ adj bosnio(nia). ⋄ n bosnio m, -nia f.

bosom ['bʊzəm] n [of woman] busto m, pecho m.

boss [bɒs] ⋄ n jefe m, -fa f. ⋄ vt pej mangonear, dar órdenes a. ◆ **boss about**, **boss around** vt sep pej mangonear, dar órdenes a.

bossy ['bɒsɪ] adj mandón(ona).

bosun ['bəʊsn] = **boatswain**.

botany ['bɒtənɪ] n botánica f.

botch [bɒtʃ] ◆ **botch up** vt sep inf estropear, hacer chapuceramente.

both [bəʊθ] ⋄ adj los dos, las dos, ambos(bas). ⋄ pron: - **(of them)** los dos (las dos), ambos mpl, -bas fpl; - **of us are coming** vamos los dos. ⋄ adv: **she is ~ pretty and intelligent** es guapa e inteligente.

bother ['bɒðər] ⋄ vt -1. [worry] preocupar; [irritate] fastidiar; **I/she can't be ~ed to do it** no tengo/tiene ganas de hacerlo. -2. [pester] molestar. ⋄ vi: **to ~ (doing** OR **to do sthg)** molestarse (en hacer algo); **to ~ about** preocuparse por. ⋄ n (U) -1. [inconvenience] problema m. -2. [pest, nuisance] molestia f.

bothered ['bɒðəd] adj preocupado(da).

bottle ['bɒtl] ⋄ n -1. [gen] botella f. -2. [of shampoo, medicine - plastic] bote m; [- glass] frasco m. -3. [for baby] biberón m. -4. (U) Br inf [courage] agallas fpl. ⋄ vt [wine] embotellar. ◆ **bottle up** vt sep reprimir, tragarse.

bottle bank n contenedor m de vidrio (para reciclaje).

bottleneck ['bɒtlnek] n -1. [in traffic] embotellamiento m. -2. [in production] freno m.

bottle-opener n abrebotellas m inv.

bottom ['bɒtəm] ⋄ adj -1. [lowest] más bajo(ja), de abajo del todo. -2. [least successful] peor. ⋄ n -1. [lowest part - of glass, bottle] culo m; [- of bag, mine, sea] fondo m; [- of ladder, hill] pie m; [- of page, list] final *m*. **-2.** [farthest point] final *m*, fondo *m*. **-3.** [of class etc] parte *f* más baja. **-4.** [buttocks] trasero *m*. **-5.** [root]: **to get to the ~ of** llegar al fondo de. ◆ **bottom out** *vi* tocar fondo.

bottom line *n fig*: **the ~ is ...** a fin de cuentas ....

bough [baʊ] *n* rama *f*.

bought [bɔːt] *pt & pp* → **buy**.

boulder ['bəʊldəʳ] *n* canto *m* rodado.

bounce [baʊns] ◇ *vi* **-1.** [gen] rebotar. **-2.** [person]: **to ~ (on sthg)** dar botes (en algo). **-3.** *inf* [cheque] ser rechazado(da) por el banco. ◇ *vt* botar. ◇ *n* bote *m*.

bouncer ['baʊnsəʳ] *n inf* matón *m*, gorila *m* (*de una local*).

bound [baʊnd] ◇ *pt & pp* → **bind**. ◇ *adj* **-1.** [certain]: **it's ~ to happen** seguro que va a pasar. **-2.** [obliged]: **~ (by sthg/to do sthg)** obligado(da) (por algo/a hacer algo); **I'm ~ to say** OR **admit** tengo que decir OR admitir. **-3.** [for place]: **to be ~ for** ir rumbo a. ◇ *n* salto *m*. ◇ *vi* ir dando saltos. ◆ **bounds** *npl* [limits] límites *mpl*; **out of ~s** (en) zona prohibida.

boundary ['baʊndərı] *n* [gen] límite *m*; [between countries] frontera *f*.

bouquet [bəʊ'keɪ] *n* [of flowers] ramo *m*.

bourbon ['bɜːbən] *n* bourbon *m*.

bourgeois ['bɔːʒwɑː] *adj pej* burgués(esa).

bout [baʊt] *n* **-1.** [attack] ataque *m*, acceso *m*. **-2.** [session] racha *f*. **-3.** [boxing match] pelea *f*, combate *m*.

bow¹ [baʊ] ◇ *n* **-1.** [act of bowing] reverencia *f*. **-2.** [of ship] proa *f*. ◇ *vt* inclinar. ◇ *vi* **-1.** [make a bow] inclinarse. **-2.** [defer]: **to ~ to sthg** ceder OR doblegarse ante algo.

bow² [bəʊ] *n* **-1.** [weapon, musical instrument] arco *m*. **-2.** [knot] lazo *m*.

bowels ['baʊəlz] *npl lit & fig* entrañas *fpl*.

bowl [bəʊl] ◇ *n* [gen] cuenco *m*, bol *m*; [for soup] tazón *m*; [for washing clothes] barreño *m*, balde *m*. ◇ *vi* lanzar la bola. ◆ **bowls** *n* (*U*) bochas *fpl*. ◆ **bowl over** *vt sep* **-1.** [knock over] atropellar. **-2.** *fig* [surprise, impress] dejar atónito(ta).

bow-legged [,bəʊ'legɪd] *adj* de piernas arqueadas, estevado(da).

bowler ['bəʊləʳ] *n* **-1.** CRICKET lanzador *m*. **-2.** **~ (hat)** bombín *m*, sombrero *m* hongo.

bowling ['bəʊlɪŋ] *n* (*U*) bolos *mpl*.

bowling alley *n* **-1.** [building] bolera *f*. **-2.** [alley] calle *f*.

bowling green *n* campo de césped para jugar a las bochas.

bow tie [bəʊ-] *n* pajarita *f*.

box [bɒks] ◇ *n* **-1.** [container, boxful] caja *f*; [for jewels] estuche *m*. **-2.** THEATRE palco *m*. **-3.** *Br inf* [television]: **the ~** la caja tonta. ◇ *vt* [put in boxes] encajonar. ◇ *vi* boxear.

boxer ['bɒksəʳ] *n* **-1.** [fighter] boxeador *m*, púgil *m*. **-2.** [dog] bóxer *m*.

boxer shorts *npl* calzón *m* (de boxeo).

boxing ['bɒksɪŋ] *n* boxeo *m*.

Boxing Day *n* fiesta nacional en Inglaterra y Gales el 26 de diciembre (salvo domingos) en que tradicionalmente se da el aguinaldo.

boxing glove *n* guante *m* de boxeo.

box office *n* taquilla *f*, boletería *f Amer*.

boxroom ['bɒksrʊm] *n Br* trastero *m*.

boy [bɔɪ] ◇ *n* **-1.** [male child] chico *m*, niño *m*, pibe *m Amer*. **-2.** *inf* [young man] chaval *m*. ◇ *excl*: **(oh) ~!** ¡jolín!, ¡vaya, vaya!

boycott ['bɔɪkɒt] ◇ *n* boicot *m*. ◇ *vt* boicotear.

boyfriend ['bɔɪfrend] *n* novio *m*.

boyish ['bɔɪɪʃ] *adj* [man] juvenil.

BR (*abbr of* **British Rail**) *n* ferrocarriles *británicos*, ≈ Renfe *f*.

bra [brɑː] *n* sujetador *m*.

brace [breɪs] ◇ *n* **-1.** [on teeth] aparato *m* corrector. **-2.** [pair] par *m*. ◇ *vt* [steady] tensar; **to ~ o.s. (for)** *lit & fig* prepararse (para). ◆ **braces** *npl Br* tirantes *mpl*, tiradores *mpl Amer*.

bracelet ['breɪslɪt] *n* brazalete *m*, pulsera *f*.

bracing ['breɪsɪŋ] *adj* tonificante.

bracken ['brækn] *n* helecho *m*.

bracket ['brækɪt] ◇ *n* **-1.** [support] soporte *m*, palomilla *f*. **-2.** [parenthesis - round] paréntesis *m inv*; [- square] corchete *m*; **in ~s** entre paréntesis. **-3.** [group] sector *m*, banda *f*. ◇ *vt* [enclose in brackets] poner entre paréntesis.

brag [bræg] *vi* fanfarronear, jactarse.

braid [breɪd] ◇ *n* **-1.** [on uniform] galón *m*. **-2.** [hairstyle] trenza *f*. ◇ *vt* trenzar.

brain [breɪn] *n lit & fig* cerebro *m*. ◆ **brains** *npl* cerebro *m*, seso *m*.

brainchild ['breɪntʃaɪld] *n inf* invención *f*, idea *f*.

brainwash ['breɪnwɒʃ] *vt* lavar el cerebro a.

brainwave ['breɪnweɪv] *n* idea *f* genial.

brainy ['breɪnı] *adj inf* listo(ta).

brake [breɪk] ◇ n lit & fig freno m. ◇ vi frenar.

brake light n luz f de freno.

bramble ['bræmbl] n [bush] zarza f, zarzamora f; [fruit] mora f.

bran [bræn] n salvado m.

branch [brɑːntʃ] ◇ n -1. [of tree, of subject] rama f. -2. [of river] afluente m; [of railway] ramal m. -3. [of company, bank] sucursal f. ◇ vi bifurcarse. ◆ **branch out** vi [person] ampliar horizontes; [firm] expandirse, diversificarse.

brand [brænd] ◇ n -1. [of product] marca f. -2. fig [type] tipo m, estilo m. -3. [mark] hierro m. ◇ vt -1. [cattle] marcar (con hierro). -2. fig [classify]: **to** ~ **sb (as sthg)** tildar a alguien (de algo).

brandish ['brændɪʃ] vt [weapon] blandir; [letter etc] agitar.

brand name n marca f.

brand-new adj flamante.

brandy ['brændɪ] n coñac m.

brash [bræʃ] adj pej insolente.

brass [brɑːs] n -1. [metal] latón m. -2. MUS: **the** ~ el metal.

brass band n banda f de metal.

brassiere [Br 'bræsɪər, Am brəˈzɪr] n sostén m, sujetador m.

brat [bræt] n inf pej mocoso m, -sa f.

bravado [brəˈvɑːdəʊ] n bravuconería f.

brave [breɪv] ◇ adj valiente. ◇ vt [weather, storm] desafiar; [sb's anger] hacer frente a.

bravery ['breɪvərɪ] n valentía f.

brawl [brɔːl] n gresca f, reyerta f.

brawn [brɔːn] n (U) -1. [muscle] musculatura f, fuerza f física. -2. Br [meat] carne de cerdo en gelatina.

bray [breɪ] vi [donkey] rebuznar.

brazen ['breɪzn] adj [person] descarado(da); [lie] burdo(da). ◆ **brazen out** vt sep: **to** ~ **it out** echarle cara.

brazier ['breɪzjər] n brasero m.

Brazil [brəˈzɪl] n (el) Brasil.

Brazilian [brəˈzɪljən] ◇ adj brasileño(ña), brasilero(ra) Amer. ◇ n brasileño m, -ña f, brasilero m, -ra f Amer.

brazil nut n nuez f de Pará.

breach [briːtʃ] ◇ n -1. [act of disobedience] incumplimiento m; ~ **of confidence** abuso m de confianza; **to be in** ~ **of sthg** incumplir algo; **breach of contract** incumplimiento de contrato. -2. [opening, gap] brecha f. -3. fig [in friendship, marriage] ruptura f. ◇ vt -1. [disobey] incumplir. -2. [make hole in] abrir (una) brecha en.

breach of the peace n alteración f del orden público.

bread [bred] n -1. [food] pan m; ~ **and butter** [buttered bread] pan con mantequilla; fig [main income] sustento m diario. -2. inf [money] pasta f.

bread bin Br, **bread box** Am n panera f.

breadcrumbs ['bredkrʌmz] npl migas fpl (de pan); CULIN pan m rallado.

breadline ['bredlaɪn] n: **to be on the** ~ vivir en la miseria.

breadth [bretθ] n -1. [in measurements] anchura f. -2. fig [scope] amplitud f.

breadwinner ['bred,wɪnər] n cabeza m y f de familia.

break [breɪk] (pt **broke**, pp **broken**) ◇ n -1. [gap - in clouds] claro m; [- in transmission] corte m. -2. [fracture] fractura f. -3. [pause]: ~ **(from)** descanso m (de); **to have** OR **take a** ~ tomarse un descanso. -4. [playtime] recreo m. -5. inf [chance] oportunidad f; **a lucky** ~ un golpe de suerte. ◇ vt -1. [gen] romper; [arm, leg etc] romperse; **to** ~ **sb's hold** escaparse OR liberarse de alguien. -2. [machine] estropear. -3. [journey, contact] interrumpir. -4. [habit, health] acabar con; [strike] reventar. -5. [law, rule] violar; [appointment, word] faltar a. -6. [record] batir. -7. [tell]: **to** ~ **the news (of sthg to sb)** dar la noticia (de algo a alguien). ◇ vi -1. [come to pieces] romperse. -2. [stop working] estropearse. -3. [pause] parar; [weather] cambiar. -4. [start - day] romper; [- storm] estallar. -5. [escape]: **to** ~ **loose** OR **free** escaparse. -6. [voice] cambiar. -7. [news] divulgarse. -8. phr: **to** ~ **even** salir sin pérdidas ni beneficios. ◆ **break away** vi [escape] escaparse; **to** ~ **away (from)** [end connection] separarse (de); POL escindirse (de). ◆ **break down** ◇ vt sep -1. [destroy - gen] derribar; [- resistance] vencer. -2. [analyse] descomponer. ◇ vi -1. [collapse, disintegrate, fail] venirse abajo. -2. [stop working] estropearse. -3. [lose emotional control] perder el control. -4. [decompose] descomponerse. ◆ **break in** ◇ vi -1. [enter by force] entrar por la fuerza. -2. [interrupt]: **to** ~ **in (on sthg/sb)** interrumpir (algo/a alguien). ◇ vt sep -1. [horse, shoes] domar. -2. [person] amoldar, poner al tanto. ◆ **break into** vt fus -1. [house, shop] entrar (por la fuerza) en; [box, safe] forzar. -2. [begin suddenly]: **to** ~ **into song/a run** echarse a cantar/correr. ◆ **break off** ◇ vt sep

-1. [detach] **partir. -2.** [end] **romper;** [holiday] **interrumpir.** ◇ *vi* **-1.** [become detached] **partirse. -2.** [stop talking] **interrumpirse.** ◆ **break out** *vi* **-1.** [fire, fighting, panic] **desencadenarse;** [war] **estallar. -2.** [escape]: **to ~ out (of)** escapar (de). ◆ **break up** ◇ *vt sep* **-1.** [ice] **hacer pedazos;** [car] **desguazar. -2.** [relationship] **romper;** [talks] **poner fin a;** [fight, crowd] **disolver.** ◇ *vi* **-1.** [into smaller pieces] **hacerse pedazos. -2.** [relationship] **deshacerse;** [conference] **concluir;** [school, pupils] **terminar el curso; to ~ up with sb** romper con alguien. **-3.** [crowd] **disolverse.**

breakage ['breɪkɪdʒ] *n* **rotura** *f*.

breakdown ['breɪkdaʊn] *n* **-1.** [of car, train] **avería** *f*; [of talks, in communications] **ruptura** *f*; [of law and order] **colapso** *m*. **-2.** [analysis] **desglose** *m*.

breakfast ['brekfəst] *n* **desayuno** *m*.

breakfast television *n Br* **programación** *f* **matinal de televisión.**

break-in *n* **robo** *m* (*con allanamiento de morada*).

breaking ['breɪkɪŋ] *n*: **~ and entering** JUR **allanamiento** *m* **de morada.**

breakneck ['breɪknek] *adj*: **at ~ speed** a (una) **velocidad de vértigo.**

breakthrough ['breɪkθruː] *n* **avance** *m*.

breakup ['breɪkʌp] *n* **ruptura** *f*.

breast [brest] *n* **-1.** [of woman] **pecho** *m*, **seno** *m*; [of man] **pecho.** **-2.** [meat of bird] **pechuga** *f*.

breast-feed *vt* & *vi* **amamantar.**

breaststroke ['breststrəʊk] *n* **braza** *f*.

breath [breθ] *n* **respiración** *f*, **aliento** *m*; **to take a deep ~** respirar hondo; **to get one's ~ back** recuperar el aliento; **to say sthg under one's ~** decir algo en voz baja; **out of ~** sin aliento.

breathalyse *Br*, **-yze** *Am* ['breθəlaɪz] *vt* **hacer la prueba del alcohol a.**

breathe [briːð] ◇ *vi* **respirar.** ◇ *vt* **-1.** [inhale] **respirar. -2.** [exhale] **despedir.** ◆ **breathe in** *vt sep* & *vi* **aspirar.** ◆ **breathe out** *vi* **espirar.**

breather ['briːðər] *n inf* **respiro** *m*.

breathing ['briːðɪŋ] *n* **respiración** *f*.

breathless ['breθlɪs] *adj* **-1.** [out of breath] **jadeante. -2.** [with excitement] **sin aliento (por la emoción).**

breathtaking ['breθ,teɪkɪŋ] *adj* **sobrecogedor(ra), impresionante.**

breed [briːd] (*pt* & *pp* **bred** [bred]) ◇ *n* **-1.** [of animal] **raza** *f*. **-2.** *fig* [sort] **generación** *f*, **especie** *f*. ◇ *vt* [animals] **criar;** [plants] **cultivar.** ◇ *vi* **procrear.**

breeding ['briːdɪŋ] *n* **-1.** [of animals] **cría** *f*; [of plants] **cultivo** *m*. **-2.** [manners] **educación** *f*.

breeze [briːz] ◇ *n* **brisa** *f*. ◇ *vi*: **to ~ in/out** entrar/salir como si tal cosa.

breezy ['briːzɪ] *adj* **-1.** [windy]: **it's ~** hace aire. **-2.** [cheerful] **jovial, despreocupado(da).**

brevity ['brevɪtɪ] *n* **brevedad** *f*.

brew [bruː] ◇ *vt* [beer] **elaborar;** [tea, coffee] **preparar.** ◇ *vi* **-1.** [tea] **reposar. -2.** [trouble] **fraguarse.**

brewer ['bruːər] *n* **cervecero** *m*, **-ra** *f*.

brewery ['bruːərɪ] *n* **fábrica** *f* **de cerveza.**

bribe [braɪb] ◇ *n* **soborno** *m*. ◇ *vt*: **to ~ (sb to do sthg)** **sobornar (a alguien para que haga algo).**

bribery ['braɪbərɪ] *n* **soborno** *m*.

bric-a-brac ['brɪkəbræk] *n* **baratijas** *fpl*.

brick [brɪk] *n* **ladrillo** *m*.

bricklayer ['brɪk,leɪər] *n* **albañil** *m*.

bridal ['braɪdl] *adj* **nupcial; ~ dress** **traje** *m* **de novia.**

bride [braɪd] *n* **novia** *f*.

bridegroom ['braɪdgrʊm] *n* **novio** *m*.

bridesmaid ['braɪdzmeɪd] *n* **dama** *f* **de honor.**

bridge [brɪdʒ] ◇ *n* **-1.** [gen] **puente** *m*. **-2.** [on ship] **puente** *m* **de mando. -3.** [of nose] **caballete** *m*. **-4.** [card game] **bridge** *m*. ◇ *vt fig* [gap] **llenar.**

bridle ['braɪdl] *n* **brida** *f*.

bridle path *n* **camino** *m* **de herradura.**

brief [briːf] ◇ *adj* **-1.** [short, to the point] **breve; in ~** en resumen. **-2.** [clothes] **corto(ta).** ◇ *n* **-1.** JUR [statement] **sumario** *m*, **resumen** *m*. **-2.** *Br* [instructions] **instrucciones** *fpl*. ◇ *vt*: **to ~ sb (on)** **informar a alguien (acerca de).** ◆ **briefs** *npl* [underpants] **calzoncillos** *mpl*; [knickers] **bragas** *fpl*.

briefcase ['briːfkeɪs] *n* **maletín** *m*, **portafolios** *m inv*.

briefing ['briːfɪŋ] *n* [meeting] **reunión** *f* **informativa;** [instructions] **instrucciones** *fpl*.

briefly ['briːflɪ] *adv* **-1.** [for a short time] **brevemente. -2.** [concisely] **en pocas palabras.**

brigade [brɪˈgeɪd] *n* **brigada** *f*.

brigadier [,brɪgəˈdɪər] *n* **brigadier** *m*, **general** *m* **de brigada.**

bright [braɪt] *adj* **-1.** [light] **brillante;** [day, room] **luminoso(sa);** [weather] **despejado(da). -2.** [colour] **vivo(va), fuerte. -3.** [lively - eyes] **brillante;** [- smile] **radiante. -4.** [intelligent - person] **listo(ta);**

[- idea] **genial. -5.** [hopeful] prometedor(ra).

brighten ['braɪtn] vi **-1.** [become lighter] despejarse. **-2.** [become more cheerful] alegrarse. ◆ **brighten up** ◇ vt sep animar, alegrar. ◇ vi **-1.** [become more cheerful] animarse. **-2.** [weather] despejarse.

brilliance ['brɪljəns] n **-1.** [cleverness] brillantez f. **-2.** [of colour, light] brillo m.

brilliant ['brɪljənt] adj **-1.** [clever] genial, fantástico(ca). **-2.** [colour] vivo(va). **-3.** [light, career, future] brillante. **-4.** inf [wonderful] fenomenal, genial.

Brillo pad® ['brɪləʊ-] n estropajo m (jabonoso) de aluminio.

brim [brɪm] ◇ n **-1.** [edge] borde m. **-2.** [of hat] ala f. ◇ vi lit & fig: **to ~ with** rebosar de.

brine [braɪn] n salmuera f.

bring [brɪŋ] (pt & pp **brought**) vt [gen] traer; **to ~ sthg to an end** poner fin a algo. ◆ **bring about** vt sep producir. ◆ **bring around** vt sep [make conscious] reanimar. ◆ **bring back** vt sep **-1.** [books etc] devolver; [person] traer de vuelta. **-2.** [memories] traer (a la memoria). **-3.** [practice, hanging] volver a introducir; [fashion] recuperar. ◆ **bring down** vt sep **-1.** [plane, bird] derribar; [government, tyrant] derrocar. **-2.** [prices] reducir. ◆ **bring forward** vt sep **-1.** [meeting, elections etc] adelantar. **-2.** [in bookkeeping] sumar a la siguiente columna. ◆ **bring in** vt sep **-1.** [introduce - law] implantar; [- bill] presentar. **-2.** [earn] ganar. ◆ **bring off** vt sep [plan] sacar adelante; [deal] cerrar. ◆ **bring out** vt sep **-1.** [new product, book] sacar. **-2.** [the worst etc in sb] revelar, despertar. ◆ **bring round, bring to** = **bring around.** ◆ **bring up** vt sep **-1.** [raise - children] criar. **-2.** [mention] sacar a relucir. **-3.** [vomit] devolver.

brink [brɪŋk] n: **on the ~ of** al borde de.

brisk [brɪsk] adj **-1.** [quick] rápido(da). **-2.** [busy] boyante, activo(va). **-3.** [efficient, confident - manner] enérgico(ca); [- person] eficaz.

bristle ['brɪsl] ◇ n [gen] cerda f; [of person] pelillo m. ◇ vi **-1.** [stand up] erizarse, ponerse de punta. **-2.** [react angrily]: **to ~ (at)** enfadarse (por).

Brit [brɪt] n inf británico m, -ca f.

Britain ['brɪtn] n Gran Bretaña.

British ['brɪtɪʃ] adj británico(ca).

British Council n: **the ~** el British Council.

British Isles npl: **the ~** las islas Británicas.

British Rail n compañía ferroviaria británica, ≃ Renfe f.

British Telecom [-'telɪkɒm] n principal empresa británica de telecomunicaciones, ≃ Telefónica f.

Briton ['brɪtn] n británico m, -ca f.

brittle ['brɪtl] adj quebradizo(za), frágil.

broach [brəʊtʃ] vt abordar.

B road n Br ≃ carretera f comarcal.

broad [brɔːd] adj **-1.** [shoulders, river, street] ancho(cha); [grin] amplio(plia). **-2.** [range, interests] amplio(plia). **-3.** [description, outline] general. **-4.** [hint] claro(ra). **-5.** [accent] cerrado(da). **-6.** phr: **in ~ daylight** a plena luz del día.

broad bean n haba f.

broadcast ['brɔːdkɑːst] (pt & pp **broadcast**) ◇ n emisión f. ◇ vt emitir.

broaden ['brɔːdn] ◇ vt **-1.** [road, pavement] ensanchar. **-2.** [scope, appeal] ampliar. ◇ vi [river, road] ensancharse; [smile] hacerse más amplia.

broadly ['brɔːdlɪ] adv **-1.** [generally] en general. **-2.** [smile] abiertamente.

broadminded [,brɔːd'maɪndɪd] adj abierto(ta), liberal.

broadsheet ['brɔːdʃiːt] n periódico con hojas de gran tamaño.

broccoli ['brɒkəlɪ] n brécol m.

brochure ['brəʊʃə] n folleto m.

broil [brɔɪl] vt Am asar a la parrilla.

broke [brəʊk] ◇ pt → **break.** ◇ adj inf sin blanca, sin un duro.

broken ['brəʊkn] ◇ pp → **break.** ◇ adj **-1.** [gen] roto(ta). **-2.** [not working] estropeado(da). **-3.** [interrupted - sleep] entrecortado(da); [- journey] discontinuo(nua). **-4.** [hesitant, inaccurate] macarrónico(ca).

broker ['brəʊkə] n [of stock] corredor m; [of insurance] agente m y f.

brolly ['brɒlɪ] n Br inf paraguas m inv.

bronchitis [brɒŋ'kaɪtɪs] n (U) bronquitis f.

bronze [brɒnz] n [metal, sculpture] bronce m.

brooch [brəʊtʃ] n broche m, alfiler m.

brood [bruːd] ◇ n **-1.** [of animals] cría f, nidada f. **-2.** inf [of children] prole f. ◇ vi: **to ~ (over** OR **about)** dar vueltas (a).

brook [brʊk] n arroyo m.

broom [bruːm] n [brush] escoba f.

broomstick ['bruːmstɪk] n palo m de escoba.

Bros., bros. (*abbr of* **brothers**) Hnos.
broth [brɒθ] *n* caldo *m*.
brothel ['brɒθl] *n* burdel *m*.
brother ['brʌðər] *n* [relative, monk] hermano *m*.
brother-in-law (*pl* **brothers-in-law**) *n* cuñado *m*.
brought [brɔːt] *pt & pp* → **bring**.
brow [brau] *n* -1. [forehead] frente *f*. -2. [eyebrow] ceja *f*. -3. [of hill] cima *f*.
brown [braun] ◇ *adj* -1. [gen] marrón; [hair, eyes] castaño(ña). -2. [tanned] moreno(na). ◇ *n* marrón *m*. ◇ *vt* [food] dorar.
Brownie (Guide) ['brauni-] *n* guía *f* (7-10 años).
brown paper *n* (*U*) papel *m* de embalar.
brown rice *n* arroz *m* integral.
brown sugar *n* azúcar *m* moreno.
browse [brauz] *vi* [person] echar un ojo, mirar; **to ~ through** hojear.
bruise [bruːz] ◇ *n* cardenal *m*. ◇ *vt* -1. [person, arm] magullar; [fruit] estropear. -2. *fig* [feelings] herir.
brunch [brʌntʃ] *n* brunch *m, combinación de desayuno y almuerzo que se toma por la mañana tarde.*
brunette [bruːˈnet] *n* morena *f*.
brunt [brʌnt] *n*: **to bear** OR **take the ~ of** aguantar lo peor de.
brush [brʌʃ] ◇ *n* -1. [for hair, teeth] cepillo *m*; [for shaving, painting] brocha *f*; [of artist] pincel *m*; [broom] escoba *f*. -2. [encounter] roce *m*. ◇ *vt* -1. [clean with brush] cepillar. -2. [move with hand] quitar, apartar. -3. [touch lightly] rozar. ◆ **brush aside** *vt sep* rechazar. ◆ **brush off** *vt sep* [dismiss] hacer caso omiso de. ◆ **brush up** ◇ *vt sep fig* [revise] repasar. ◇ *vi*: **to ~ up on** repasar.
brushwood ['brʌʃwʊd] *n* leña *f*.
brusque [bruːsk] *adj* brusco(ca).
Brussels ['brʌslz] *n* Bruselas.
brussels sprout *n* col *f* de Bruselas.
brutal ['bruːtl] *adj* brutal.
brute [bruːt] ◇ *adj* bruto(ta). ◇ *n* -1. [large animal] bestia *f*, bruto *m*. -2. [bully] bestia *m y f*.
BSc (*abbr of* **Bachelor of Science**) *n* (*titular de una*) licenciatura de ciencias.
BT *n abbr of* **British Telecom**.
bubble ['bʌbl] ◇ *n* [gen] burbuja *f*; [of soap] pompa *f*. ◇ *vi* -1. [produce bubbles] burbujear. -2. [make a bubbling sound] borbotar.
bubble bath *n* espuma *f* de baño.
bubble gum *n* chicle *m* (de globo).

bubblejet printer ['bʌbldʒet-] *n* COMPUT impresora *f* de inyección.
Bucharest [ˌbuːkəˈrest] *n* Bucarest.
buck [bʌk] (*pl inv* OR **-s**) ◇ *n* -1. [male animal] macho *m*. -2. *inf* [dollar] dólar *m*. -3. *inf* [responsibility]: **to pass the ~ to sb** echarle el muerto a alguien. ◇ *vt* [subj: horse] tirar. ◇ *vi* corcovear. ◆ **buck up** *inf* ◇ *vt sep* [improve] mejorar; **~ your ideas up** más vale que espabiles. ◇ *vi* -1. [hurry up] darse prisa. -2. [cheer up] animarse.
bucket ['bʌkɪt] *n* [container, bucketful] cubo *m*.
Buckingham Palace ['bʌkɪŋəm-] *n* el palacio de Buckingham.
buckle ['bʌkl] ◇ *n* hebilla *f*. ◇ *vt* -1. [fasten] abrochar con hebilla. -2. [bend] combar, torcer. ◇ *vi* [wheel] combarse, torcerse; [knees] doblarse.
bud [bʌd] ◇ *n* [shoot] brote *m*; [flower] capullo *m*. ◇ *vi* brotar, echar brotes.
Budapest [ˌbjuːdəˈpest] *n* Budapest.
Buddha ['budə] *n* Buda *m*.
Buddhism ['budɪzm] *n* budismo *m*.
budding ['bʌdɪŋ] *adj* en ciernes.
buddy ['bʌdɪ] *n inf* [friend] amiguete *m*, -ta *f*, colega *m y f*.
budge [bʌdʒ] ◇ *vt* mover. ◇ *vi* [move] moverse; [give in] ceder.
budgerigar ['bʌdʒərɪgɑːr] *n* periquito *m*.
budget ['bʌdʒɪt] ◇ *adj* económico(ca). ◇ *n* presupuesto *m*. ◆ **budget for** *vt fus* contar con.
budgie ['bʌdʒɪ] *n inf* periquito *m*.
buff [bʌf] ◇ *adj* color de ante. ◇ *n inf* [expert] aficionado *m*, -da *f*.
buffalo ['bʌfələu] (*pl inv* OR **-s** OR **-es**) *n* búfalo *m*.
buffer ['bʌfər] *n* -1. *Br* [for trains] tope *m*. -2. [protection] defensa *f*, salvaguarda *f*. -3. COMPUT memoria *f* intermedia.
buffet[1] [*Br* 'bufeɪ, *Am* bəˈfeɪ] *n* -1. [meal] bufé *m*. -2. [cafeteria] cafetería *f*.
buffet[2] ['bʌfɪt] *vt* [physically] golpear.
buffet car ['bufeɪ-] *n* coche *m* restaurante (*sólo mostrador*).
bug [bʌg] ◇ *n* -1. [small insect] bicho *m*. -2. *inf* [germ] microbio *m*. -3. *inf* [listening device] micrófono *m* oculto. -4. COMPUT error *m*. -5. [enthusiasm] manía *f*. ◇ *vt* -1. *inf* [spy on - room] poner un micrófono oculto en; [- phone] pinchar. -2. *inf* [annoy] fastidiar, jorobar.
bugger ['bʌgər] *Br v inf n* [unpleasant person] cabrón *m*, -ona *f*. ◆ **bugger off** *vi v inf*: **~ off!** ¡vete a tomar por culo!

buggy ['bʌgɪ] n -1. [carriage] calesa f. -2. [pushchair] sillita f de ruedas; Am [pram] cochecito m de niño.

bugle ['bjuːgl] n corneta f, clarín m.

build [bɪld] (pt & pp **built**) ◇ vt -1. [construct] construir. -2. fig [form, create] crear. ◇ n complexión f, constitución f. ◆ **build (up)on** ◇ vt fus [further] desarrollar. ◇ vt sep [base on] fundar en. ◆ **build up** ◇ vt sep -1. [business - establish] poner en pie; [- promote] fomentar. -2. [person] fortalecer. ◇ vi acumularse.

builder ['bɪldəʳ] n constructor m, -ra f.

building ['bɪldɪŋ] n -1. [structure] edificio m. -2. [profession] construcción f.

building and loan association n Am ≃ caja f de ahorros.

building site n solar m (de construcción), obra f.

building society n Br ≃ caja f de ahorros.

buildup ['bɪldʌp] n [increase] acumulación f.

built [bɪlt] pt & pp → **build**.

built-in adj -1. [physically integral] empotrado(da). -2. [inherent] incorporado(da).

built-up adj urbanizado(da).

bulb [bʌlb] n -1. [for lamp] bombilla f. -2. [of plant] bulbo m.

Bulgaria [bʌl'geərɪə] n Bulgaria.

Bulgarian [bʌl'geərɪən] ◇ adj búlgaro(ra). ◇ n -1. [person] búlgaro m, -ra f. -2. [language] búlgaro m.

bulge [bʌldʒ] ◇ n [lump] protuberancia f, bulto m. ◇ vi: **to ~ (with)** rebosar (de), estar atestado(da) (de).

bulk [bʌlk] ◇ n -1. [mass] bulto m, volumen m. -2. [large quantity]: **in ~** a granel. -3. [majority, most of]: **the ~ of** la mayor parte de. ◇ adj a granel.

bulky ['bʌlkɪ] adj abultado(da), voluminoso(sa).

bull [bʊl] n -1. [male cow] toro m. -2. [male animal] macho m.

bulldog ['bʊldɒg] n buldog m.

bulldozer ['bʊldəʊzəʳ] n bulldozer m.

bullet ['bʊlɪt] n bala f.

bulletin ['bʊlətɪn] n -1. [news] boletín m; [medical report] parte m. -2. [regular publication] boletín m, gaceta f.

bullet-proof adj a prueba de balas.

bullfight ['bʊlfaɪt] n corrida f (de toros).

bullfighter ['bʊl,faɪtəʳ] n torero m, -ra f.

bullfighting ['bʊl,faɪtɪŋ] n toreo m.

bullion ['bʊljən] n (U) lingotes mpl.

bullock ['bʊlək] n buey m, toro m castrado.

bullring ['bʊlrɪŋ] n plaza f (de toros).

bull's-eye n diana f.

bully ['bʊlɪ] ◇ n abusón m, matón m. ◇ vt abusar de, intimidar.

bum [bʌm] n -1. v inf [bottom] culo m. -2. Am inf pej [tramp] vagabundo m, -da f.

bumblebee ['bʌmblbiː] n abejorro m.

bump [bʌmp] ◇ n -1. [lump - on head] chichón m; [- on road] bache m. -2. [knock, blow, noise] golpe m. ◇ vt [car] chocar con OR contra; [head, knee] golpearse en; **I ~ed my head on the door** me di con la cabeza en la puerta. ◆ **bump into** vt fus [meet by chance] toparse con.

bumper ['bʌmpəʳ] ◇ adj abundante; **~ edition** edición especial. ◇ n -1. AUT parachoques m inv. -2. Am RAIL tope m.

bumptious ['bʌmpʃəs] adj pej engreído(da).

bumpy ['bʌmpɪ] adj -1. [road] lleno(na) de baches. -2. [ride, journey] con muchas sacudidas.

bun [bʌn] n -1. [cake, bread roll] bollo m. -2. [hairstyle] moño m.

bunch [bʌntʃ] ◇ n [of people] grupo m; [of flowers] ramo m; [of fruit] racimo m; [of keys] manojo m. ◇ vi agruparse. ◆ **bunches** npl [hairstyle] coletas fpl.

bundle ['bʌndl] ◇ n [of clothes] lío m, bulto m; [of notes, papers] fajo m; [of wood] haz m. ◇ vt [clothes] empaquetar de cualquier manera; [person] empujar. ◆ **bundle up** vt sep [put into bundles] liar, envolver.

bung [bʌŋ] ◇ n tapón m. ◇ vt Br inf -1. [throw] tirar. -2. [pass] alcanzar.

bungalow ['bʌŋgələʊ] n bungalow m.

bungle ['bʌŋgl] vt chapucear.

bunion ['bʌnjən] n juanete m.

bunk [bʌŋk] n [bed] litera f.

bunk bed n litera f.

bunker ['bʌŋkəʳ] n -1. [shelter, in golf] búnker m. -2. [for coal] carbonera f.

bunny ['bʌnɪ] n: **~ (rabbit)** conejito m, -ta f.

bunting ['bʌntɪŋ] n (U) [flags] banderitas fpl.

buoy [Br bɔɪ, Am 'buːɪ] n boya f. ◆ **buoy up** vt sep [encourage] alentar.

buoyant ['bɔɪənt] adj -1. [able to float] boyante. -2. [optimistic - gen] optimista; [- market] con tendencia alcista.

burden ['bɜːdn] ◇ n -1. [heavy load] carga f. -2. fig [heavy responsibility]: **~**

on carga f para. ◇ vt: **to ~ sb with** cargar a alguien con.

bureau ['bjuərəu] (pl **-x**) n **-1.** [government department] departamento m. **-2.** [office] oficina f. **-3.** Br [desk] secreter m; Am [chest of drawers] cómoda f.

bureaucracy [bjuə'rɒkrəsɪ] n burocracia f.

bureaux ['bjuərəuz] pl → **bureau**.

burger ['bɜːgə[r]] n hamburguesa f.

burglar ['bɜːglə[r]] n ladrón m, -ona f.

burglar alarm n alarma f antirrobo.

burglarize Am = **burgle**.

burglary ['bɜːglərɪ] n robo m (de una casa).

burgle ['bɜːgl], **burglarize** ['bɜːglərɪz] Am vt robar, desvalijar (una casa).

burial ['berɪəl] n entierro m.

burly ['bɜːlɪ] adj fornido(da).

Burma ['bɜːmə] n Birmania.

burn [bɜːn] (pt & pp **burnt** OR **-ed**) ◇ vt **-1.** [gen] quemar. **-2.** [injure - by heat, fire] quemarse. ◇ vi **-1.** [gen] arder. **-2.** [be alight] estar encendido(da). **-3.** [food] quemar. **-4.** [cause burning sensation] escocer. **-5.** [become sunburnt] quemarse. ◇ n quemadura f. ◆ **burn down** ◇ vt sep incendiar. ◇ vi [be destroyed by fire] incendiarse.

burner ['bɜːnə[r]] n quemador m.

Burns' Night n fiesta celebrada en Escocia el 25 de enero en honor del poeta escocés Robert Burns.

burnt [bɜːnt] pt & pp → **burn**.

burp [bɜːp] inf vi eructar.

burrow ['bʌrəu] ◇ n madriguera f. ◇ vi **-1.** [dig] escarbar (un agujero). **-2.** fig [in order to search] hurgar.

bursar ['bɜːsə[r]] n tesorero m, -ra f.

bursary ['bɜːsərɪ] n Br beca f.

burst [bɜːst] (pt & pp **burst**) ◇ vi **-1.** [gen] reventarse; [bag] romperse; [tyre] pincharse. **-2.** [explode] estallar. ◇ vt [gen] reventar; [tyre] pinchar. ◇ n [of gunfire, enthusiasm] estallido m; [of song] clamor m. ◆ **burst into** vt fus **-1.** [tears, song]: **to ~ into tears/song** romper a llorar/cantar. **-2.** [flames] estallar en. ◆ **burst out** vi [begin suddenly]: **to ~ out laughing/crying** echarse a reír/llorar.

bursting ['bɜːstɪŋ] adj **-1.** [full] lleno(na) a estallar. **-2.** [with emotion]: **~ with** rebosando de. **-3.** [eager]: **to be ~ to do sthg** estar deseando hacer algo.

bury ['berɪ] vt **-1.** [in ground] enterrar. **-2.** [hide - face, memory] ocultar.

bus [bʌs] n autobús m; **by ~** en autobús.

bush [buʃ] n **-1.** [plant] arbusto m. **-2.** [open country]: **the ~** el campo abierto, el monte. **-3.** phr: **to beat about the ~** andarse por las ramas.

bushy ['buʃɪ] adj poblado(da), espeso(sa).

business ['bɪznɪs] n **-1.** (U) [commerce, amount of trade] negocios mpl; **to be away on ~** estar en viaje de negocios; **to mean ~** inf ir en serio; **to go out of ~** quebrar. **-2.** [company] negocio m, empresa f. **-3.** [concern, duty] oficio m, ocupación f; **mind your own ~!** inf ¡no te metas donde no te llaman! **-4.** (U) [affair, matter] asunto m.

business class n clase f preferente.

businesslike ['bɪznɪslaɪk] adj formal, práctico(ca).

businessman ['bɪznɪsmæn] (pl **-men** [-men]) n empresario m, hombre m de negocios.

business trip n viaje m de negocios.

businesswoman ['bɪznɪs,wumən] (pl **-women** [-,wimin]) n empresaria f, mujer f de negocios.

busker ['bʌskə[r]] n Br músico m ambulante OR callejero.

bus-shelter n marquesina f (de parada de autobús).

bus station n estación f de autobuses.

bus stop n parada f de autobús, paradero m Amer.

bust [bʌst] (pt & pp **-ed** OR **bust**) ◇ adj inf **-1.** [broken] fastidiado(da), roto(ta). **-2.** [bankrupt]: **to go ~** quebrar. ◇ n [bosom, statue] busto m. ◇ vt inf [break] fastidiar, estropear.

bustle ['bʌsl] ◇ n bullicio m. ◇ vi apresurarse.

busy ['bɪzɪ] ◇ adj **-1.** [active] activo(va). **-2.** [hectic - life, week] ajetreado(da); [- town, office] concurrido(da). **-3.** [occupied] ocupado(da); **to be ~ doing sthg** estar ocupado haciendo algo. ◇ vt: **to ~ o.s. (doing sthg)** ocuparse (haciendo algo).

busybody ['bɪzɪ,bɒdɪ] n pej entrometido m, -da f.

busy signal n Am TELEC señal f de comunicando.

but [bʌt] ◇ conj pero; **we were poor ~ happy** éramos pobres pero felices; **she owns not one ~ two houses** tiene no una sino dos casas. ◇ prep menos, excepto; **everyone ~ Jane was there** todos estaban allí, menos Jane; **we've**

had nothing ~ bad weather no hemos tenido más que mal tiempo; **he has no one ~ himself to blame** la culpa no es de otro más que él OR sino de él. ◇ *adv fml*: **had I ~ known** de haberlo sabido; **we can ~ try** por intentarlo que no quede. ◆ **but for** *conj* de no ser por.
butcher ['bʊtʃər] ◇ *n* **-1.** [occupation] carnicero *m*, -ra *f*; ~'s **(shop)** carnicería *f*. **-2.** [indiscriminate killer] carnicero *m*, -ra *f*, asesino *m*, -na *f*. ◇ *vt* [animal - for meat] **matar**; *fig* [kill indiscriminately] hacer una carnicería con.
butler ['bʌtlər] *n* mayordomo *m*.
butt [bʌt] ◇ *n* **-1.** [of cigarette, cigar] colilla *f*. **-2.** [of rifle] culata *f*. **-3.** [for water] tina *f*. **-4.** [target] blanco *m*. ◇ *vt* topetar. ◆ **butt in** *vi* [interrupt]: **to ~ in on sb** cortar a alguien; **to ~ in on sthg** entrometerse en algo.
butter ['bʌtər] ◇ *n* mantequilla *f*. ◇ *vt* untar con mantequilla.
buttercup ['bʌtəkʌp] *n* ranúnculo *m*.
butter dish *n* mantequera *f*.
butterfly ['bʌtəflaɪ] *n* **-1.** [insect] mariposa *f*. **-2.** [swimming style] **(estilo** *m***)** mariposa *f*.
buttocks ['bʌtəks] *npl* nalgas *fpl*.
button ['bʌtn] ◇ *n* **-1.** [gen & COMPUT] botón *m*. **-2.** *Am* [badge] chapa *f*. ◇ *vt* = **button up.** ◆ **button up** *vt sep* abotonar, abrochar.
button mushroom *n* champiñón *m* pequeño.
buttress ['bʌtrɪs] *n* contrafuerte *m*.
buxom ['bʌksəm] *adj* [woman] maciza, pechugona.
buy [baɪ] (*pt* & *pp* **bought**) ◇ *vt lit* & *fig* comprar; **to ~ sthg from sb** comprar algo a alguien. ◇ *n* compra *f*. ◆ **buy up** *vt sep* acaparar.
buyer ['baɪər] *n* [purchaser] comprador *m*, -ra *f*.
buyout ['baɪaʊt] *n adquisición de la mayoría de las acciones de una empresa.*
buzz [bʌz] ◇ *n* [of insect, machinery] zumbido *m*; [of conversation] rumor *m*; **to give sb a ~** *inf* [on phone] dar un toque OR llamar a alguien. ◇ *vi* **-1.** [make noise] zumbar. **-2.** *fig* [be active]: **to ~ (with)** bullir (de).
buzzer ['bʌzər] *n* timbre *m*.
buzzword ['bʌzwɜːd] *n inf* palabra *f* de moda.
by [baɪ] *prep* **-1.** [indicating cause, agent] por; **caused/written ~** causado/escrito por; **a book ~ Joyce** un libro de Joyce. **-2.** [indicating means, method, manner]: **to**

travel ~ bus/train/plane/ship viajar en autobús/tren/avión/barco; **to pay ~ cheque** pagar con cheque; **he got rich ~ buying land** se hizo rico comprando terrenos; **~ profession/trade** de profesión/oficio. **-3.** [beside, close to] **junto a**; **~ the sea** junto al mar. **-4.** [past] por delante de; **to walk ~ sb/sthg** pasear por delante de alguien/algo; **we drove ~ the castle** pasamos por el castillo (conduciendo). **-5.** [via, through] por; **we entered ~ the back door** entramos por la puerta trasera. **-6.** [with time - at or before, during] para; **I'll be there ~ eight** estaré allí para las ocho; **~ now** ya; **~ day/night** de día/noche. **-7.** [according to] según; **~ law/my standards** según la ley/mis criterios. **-8.** [in division] entre; [in multiplication, measurements] por; **divide 20 ~ 2** dividir 20 entre 2; **multiply 20 ~ 2** multiplicar 20 por 2; **twelve feet ~ ten** doce pies por diez. **-9.** [in quantities, amounts] por; ~ **the thousand** OR **thousands** por miles; **~ the day/hour** por día/horas; **prices were cut ~ 50%** los precios fueron rebajados (en) el 50%. **-10.** [indicating gradual change]: **day ~ day** día a OR tras día; **one ~ one** uno a uno. **-11.** [to explain a word or expression]: **what do you mean ~ "all right"?** ¿qué quieres decir con "bien"?; **what do you understand ~ the word "subsidiary"?** ¿qué entiendes por "subsidiariedad"? **-12.** *phr*: **(all) ~ oneself** solo(la); **did you do it all ~ yourself?** ¿lo hiciste tú solo?
bye(-bye) [baɪ(baɪ)] *excl inf* ¡hasta luego!
bye-election = **by-election.**
byelaw ['baɪlɔː] = **bylaw.**
by-election *n* elección *f* parcial.
bygone ['baɪgɒn] *adj* pasado(da). ◆ **bygones** *npl*: **let ~s be ~s** lo pasado, pasado está.
bylaw ['baɪlɔː] *n* reglamento *m* OR estatuto *m* local.
bypass ['baɪpɑːs] ◇ *n* **-1.** [road] carretera *f* de circunvalación. **-2.** MED: **~ (operation)** (operación *f* de) by-pass *m*. ◇ *vt* evitar.
by-product *n* **-1.** [product] subproducto *m*. **-2.** [consequence] consecuencia *f*.
bystander ['baɪ,stændər] *n* espectador *m*, -ra *f*.
byte [baɪt] *n* COMPUT byte *m*, octeto *m*.
byword ['baɪwɜːd] *n*: ~ **(for)** símbolo *m* (de), equivalente *m* (a).

C

c¹ (*pl* **c's** OR **cs**), **C** (*pl* **C's** OR **Cs**) [siː] *n* [letter] c *f*, C *f*. ◆ **C** *n* -1. MUS do *m*. -2. (*abbr of* **celsius, centigrade**) C.

c² (*abbr of* **cent(s)**) cént.

c. (*abbr of* **circa**) h.

c/a (*abbr of* **current account**) c/c.

cab [kæb] *n* -1. [taxi] taxi *m*. -2. [of lorry] cabina *f*.

cabaret ['kæbəreɪ] *n* cabaret *m*.

cabbage ['kæbɪdʒ] *n* col *f*, repollo *m*.

cabin ['kæbɪn] *n* -1. [on ship] camarote *m*. -2. [in aircraft] cabina *f*. -3. [house] cabaña *f*.

cabin class *n* clase *f* económica OR de cámara.

cabinet ['kæbɪnɪt] *n* -1. [cupboard] armario *m*. -2. POL consejo *m* de ministros, gabinete *m*.

cable ['keɪbl] ◇ *n* -1. [rope, wire] cable *m*. -2. [telegram] cablegrama *m*. ◇ *vt* cablegrafiar.

cable car *n* teleférico *m*.

cable television, cable TV *n* televisión *f* por cable.

cache [kæʃ] *n* -1. [store] alijo *m*. -2. COMPUT memoria *f* de acceso rápido.

cackle ['kækl] *vi* -1. [hen] cacarear. -2. [person] reírse.

cactus ['kæktəs] (*pl* **-tuses** OR **-ti** [-taɪ]) *n* cactus *m inv*.

cadet [kə'det] *n* cadete *m*.

cadge [kædʒ] *Br inf vt*: **to ~ sthg** (**off** OR **from sb**) gorronear algo (a alguien).

caesarean (section) *Br*, **cesarean (section)** *Am* [sɪ'zeərɪən-] *n* cesárea *f*.

cafe, café ['kæfeɪ] *n* café *m*, cafetería *f*.

cafeteria [,kæfɪ'tɪərɪə] *n* (restaurante *m*) autoservicio *m*, cantina *f*.

caffeine ['kæfiːn] *n* cafeína *f*.

cage [keɪdʒ] *n* jaula *f*.

cagey ['keɪdʒɪ] (*compar* **-ier**, *superl* **-iest**) *adj inf* reservado(da).

cagoule [kə'guːl] *n Br* chubasquero *m*.

cajole [kə'dʒəʊl] *vt*: **to ~ sb** (**into doing sthg**) engatusar a alguien (para que haga algo).

cake [keɪk] *n* -1. [sweet food] pastel *m*, tarta *f*; **to be a piece of ~** *inf* ser pan

comido. -2. [of fish, potato] medallón *m* empanado. -3. [of soap] pastilla *f*.

caked [keɪkt] *adj*: **~ with mud** cubierto(ta) de barro seco.

calcium ['kælsɪəm] *n* calcio *m*.

calculate ['kælkjʊleɪt] *vt* -1. [work out] calcular. -2. [plan]: **to be ~d to do sthg** estar pensado(da) para hacer algo.

calculating ['kælkjʊleɪtɪŋ] *adj pej* calculador(ra).

calculation [,kælkjʊ'leɪʃn] *n* cálculo *m*.

calculator ['kælkjʊleɪtə'] *n* calculadora *f*.

calendar ['kælɪndə'] *n* calendario *m*.

calendar month *n* mes *m* civil.

calendar year *n* año *m* civil.

calf [kɑːf] (*pl* **calves**) *n* -1. [young animal - of cow] ternero *m*, -ra *f*, becerro *m*, -rra *f*; [- of other animals] cría *f*. -2. [leather] piel *f* de becerro. -3. [of leg] pantorrilla *f*.

calibre, caliber *Am* ['kælɪbə'] *n* -1. [quality] nivel *m*. -2. [size] calibre *m*.

California [,kælɪ'fɔːnjə] *n* California.

calipers *Am* = **callipers**.

call [kɔːl] ◇ *n* -1. [cry, attraction, vocation] llamada *f*; [cry of bird] reclamo *m*. -2. [visit] visita *f*; **to pay a ~ on sb** hacerle una visita a alguien. -3. [demand]: **~ for** petición *f* de. -4. [summons]: **on ~** de guardia. -5. TELEC llamada *f*. ◇ *vt* -1. [gen & TELEC] llamar; **I'm ~ed Joan** me llamo Joan; **what is it ~ed?** ¿cómo se llama?; **he ~ed my name** me llamó por el nombre; **we'll ~ it £10** dejémoslo en 10 libras. -2. [announce - flight] anunciar; [- strike, meeting, election] convocar. ◇ *vi* -1. [gen & TELEC] llamar; **who's ~ing?** ¿quién es? -2. [visit] pasar. ◆ **call back** ◇ *vt sep* -1. [on phone] volver a llamar. -2. [ask to return] hacer volver. ◇ *vi* -1. [on phone] volver a llamar. -2. [visit again] volver a pasarse. ◆ **call for** *vt fus* -1. [collect] ir a buscar. -2. [demand] pedir. ◆ **call in** *vt sep* -1. [send for] llamar. -2. [recall - product, banknotes] retirar; [- loan] exigir pago de. ◆ **call off** *vt sep* -1. [meeting, party] suspender; [- strike] desconvocar. -2. [dog etc] llamar (*para que no ataque*). ◆ **call on** *vt fus* -1. [visit] visitar. -2. [ask]: **to ~ on sb to do sthg** pedir a alguien que haga algo. ◆ **call out** ◇ *vt sep* -1. [order to help - troops] movilizar; [- police, firemen] hacer intervenir. -2. [cry out] gritar. ◇ *vi* gritar. ◆ **call round** *vi* pasarse. ◆ **call up** *vt sep* -1. MIL llamar a filas a. -2. [on telephone] llamar (por teléfono). **-3.** COMPUT hacer aparecer en pantalla.

call box *n Br* cabina *f* telefónica.

caller ['kɔːləʳ] *n* **-1.** [visitor] visita *f*. **-2.** [on telephone] persona *f* que llama.

call-in *n Am* RADIO & TV programa *m* a micrófono abierto.

calling ['kɔːlɪŋ] *n* **-1.** [profession] profesión *f*. **-2.** [vocation] vocación *f*.

calling card *n Am* tarjeta *f* de visita.

callipers *Br*, **calipers** *Am* ['kælɪpəz] *npl* **-1.** MED aparato *m* ortopédico. **-2.** MATH compás *m* de grueso.

callous ['kæləs] *adj* despiadado(da).

calm [kɑːm] ◇ *adj* **-1.** [not worried or excited] tranquilo(la). **-2.** [evening, weather] apacible. **-3.** [water] en calma. ◇ *n* calma *f*. ◇ *vt* calmar. ◆ **calm down** ◇ *vt sep* calmar. ◇ *vi* calmarse.

Calor gas® ['kæləʳ-] *n Br* (gas *m*) butano *m*.

calorie ['kælərɪ] *n* caloría *f*.

calves [kɑːvz] *pl* → **calf**.

camber ['kæmbəʳ] *n* bombeo *m*.

Cambodia [kæm'bəʊdjə] *n* Camboya.

camcorder ['kæm,kɔːdəʳ] *n* camcorder *m*, cámara *f* de vídeo con micrófono.

came [keɪm] *pt* → **come**.

camel ['kæml] *n* camello *m*.

cameo ['kæmɪəʊ] (*pl* **-s**) *n* **-1.** [jewellery] camafeo *m*. **-2.** [in acting] *actuación breve y memorable*; [in writing] *excelente descripción*.

camera ['kæmərə] *n* cámara *f*. ◆ **in camera** *adv fml* a puerta cerrada.

cameraman ['kæmərəmæn] (*pl* **-men** [-mən]) *n* cámara *m*.

camouflage ['kæməflɑːʒ] ◇ *n* camuflaje *m*. ◇ *vt* camuflar.

camp [kæmp] ◇ *n* **-1.** [gen & MIL] campamento *m*. **-2.** [temporary mass accommodation] campo *m*. **-3.** [faction] bando *m*. ◇ *vi* acampar. ◆ **camp out** *vi* acampar (al aire libre).

campaign [kæm'peɪn] ◇ *n* campaña *f*. ◇ *vi*: **to ~ (for/against)** hacer campaña (a favor de/en contra de).

camp bed *n* cama *f* de campaña.

camper ['kæmpəʳ] *n* **-1.** [person] campista *m y f*. **-2. ~ (van)** caravana *f*.

campground ['kæmpɡraʊnd] *n Am* camping *m*.

camping ['kæmpɪŋ] *n* camping *m*.

camping site, **campsite** ['kæmpsaɪt] *n* camping *m*.

campus ['kæmpəs] (*pl* **-es**) *n* campus *m inv*, ciudad *f* universitaria.

can¹ [kæn] (*pt & pp* **-ned**, *cont* **-ning**) ◇ *n* [for drink, food] lata *f*, bote *m*; [for oil, paint] lata. ◇ *vt* enlatar.

can² [*weak form* kən, *strong form* kæn] (*pt & conditional* **could**, *negative* **cannot** OR **can't**) *modal vb* **-1.** [be able to] poder; **~ you come to lunch?** ¿puedes venir a comer?; **~ you see/hear something?** ¿ves/oyes algo? **-2.** [know how to] saber; **I ~ speak French/play the piano** sé hablar francés/tocar el piano. **-3.** [indicating permission, in polite requests] poder; **you ~ use my car if you like** puedes utilizar mi coche si quieres; **~ I speak to John, please?** ¿puedo hablar con John, por favor? **-4.** [indicating disbelief, puzzlement]: **you ~'t be serious** estás de broma ¿no?; **what ~ she have done with it?** ¿qué puede haber hecho con ello? **-5.** [indicating possibility] poder; **you could have done it** podrías haberlo hecho; **I could see you tomorrow** podríamos vernos mañana.

Canada ['kænədə] *n* (el) Canadá.

Canadian [kə'neɪdjən] ◇ *adj* canadiense. ◇ *n* [person] canadiense *m y f*.

canal [kə'næl] *n* canal *m*.

canary [kə'neərɪ] *n* canario *m*.

Canary Islands, **Canaries** [kə'neərɪz] *npl*: **the ~** las (islas) Canarias.

cancel ['kænsl] *vt* **-1.** [call off] cancelar, suspender. **-2.** [invalidate - cheque, debt] cancelar. ◆ **cancel out** *vt sep* anular.

cancellation [,kænsə'leɪʃn] *n* suspensión *f*.

cancer ['kænsəʳ] *n* [disease] cáncer *m*. ◆ **Cancer** *n* Cáncer *m*.

candelabra [,kændɪ'lɑːbrə] *n* candelabro *m*.

candid ['kændɪd] *adj* franco(ca).

candidate ['kændɪdət] *n*: **~ (for)** candidato *m*, -ta *f* (a).

candle ['kændl] *n* vela *f*.

candlelight ['kændllaɪt] *n* luz *f* de una vela.

candlelit ['kændllɪt] *adj* a la luz de las velas.

candlestick ['kændlstɪk] *n* candelero *m*.

candour *Br*, **candor** *Am* ['kændəʳ] *n* franqueza *f*, sinceridad *f*.

candy ['kændɪ] *n* **-1.** (U) [confectionery] golosinas *fpl*; **~ bar** chocolatina *f*. **-2.** [sweet] caramelo *m*.

candyfloss *Br* ['kændɪflɒs], **cotton candy** *Am* *n* azúcar *m* hilado, algodón *m*.

cane [keɪn] *n* **-1.** (U) [for making furniture, supporting plant] caña *f*, mimbre *m*.

-2. [walking stick] bastón *m*. **-3.** [for punishment]: **the ~** la vara.

canine ['keɪnaɪn] ◇ *adj* canino(na). ◇ *n*: **~ (tooth)** (diente *m*) canino *m*, colmillo *m*.

canister ['kænɪstə'] *n* [for tea] bote *m*; [for film] lata *f*; [for gas] bombona *f*; **smoke ~** bote de humo.

cannabis ['kænəbɪs] *n* canabis *m*.

canned [kænd] *adj* [food, drink] enlatado(da), en lata.

cannibal ['kænɪbl] *n* caníbal *m y f*.

cannon ['kænən] (*pl inv* OR **-s**) *n* cañón *m*.

cannonball ['kænənbɔːl] *n* bala *f* de cañón.

cannot ['kænɒt] *fml* → **can²**.

canny ['kænɪ] *adj* [shrewd] astuto(ta).

canoe [kə'nuː] *n* [gen] canoa *f*, SPORT piragua *f*.

canoeing [kə'nuːɪŋ] *n* piragüismo *m*.

canon ['kænən] *n* **-1.** [clergyman] canónigo *m*. **-2.** [general principle] canon *m*.

can opener *n* abrelatas *m inv*.

canopy ['kænəpɪ] *n* [over bed, seat] dosel *m*.

can't [kɑːnt] = **cannot**.

cantankerous [kæn'tæŋkərəs] *adj* [person] refunfuñón(ona); [behaviour] arisco(ca).

canteen [kæn'tiːn] *n* **-1.** [restaurant] cantina *f*. **-2.** [set of cutlery] (juego *m* de) cubertería *f*.

canter ['kæntə'] ◇ *n* medio galope *m*. ◇ *vi* ir a medio galope.

cantilever ['kæntɪliːvə'] *n* voladizo *m*.

Cantonese [,kæntə'niːz] ◇ *adj* cantonés(esa). ◇ *n* **-1.** [person] cantonés *m*, -esa *f*. **-2.** [language] cantonés *m*.

canvas ['kænvəs] *n* **-1.** [cloth] lona *f*. **-2.** [for painting on, finished painting] lienzo *m*.

canvass ['kænvəs] ◇ *vt* **-1.** POL [person] solicitar el voto a. **-2.** [opinion] pulsar. ◇ *vi solicitar votos yendo de puerta en puerta*.

canyon ['kænjən] *n* cañón *m*.

cap [kæp] ◇ *n* **-1.** [hat - peaked] gorra *f*; [- with no peak] gorro *m*. **-2.** [on bottle] tapón *m*; [on jar] tapa *f*; [on pen] capuchón *m*. **-3.** *Br* [contraceptive device] diafragma *m*. ◇ *vt* **-1.** [top]: **to be capped with** estar coronado(da) de. **-2.** [outdo]: **to ~ it all** para colmo.

capability [,keɪpə'bɪlətɪ] *n* capacidad *f*.

capable ['keɪpəbl] *adj* **-1.** [able]: **to be ~ of sthg/of doing sthg** ser capaz de

algo/de hacer algo. **-2.** [competent] hábil.

capacity [kə'pæsɪtɪ] *n* **-1.** [gen]: **~ (for)** capacidad *f* (de); **seating ~** aforo *m*; **~ for doing** OR **to do sthg** capacidad de hacer algo. **-2.** [position] calidad *f*.

cape [keɪp] *n* **-1.** GEOGR cabo *m*. **-2.** [cloak] capa *f*.

caper ['keɪpə'] *n* **-1.** [food] alcaparra *f*. **-2.** *inf* [escapade] treta *f*.

capita → **per capita**.

capital ['kæpɪtl] ◇ *adj* **-1.** [letter] mayúscula. **-2.** [punishable by death] capital. ◇ *n* **-1.** [of country, main centre] capital *f*. **-2.** **~ (letter)** mayúscula *f*. **-3.** [money] capital *m*; **to make ~ (out) of** *fig* sacar partido de.

capital expenditure *n* (*U*) inversión *f* de capital.

capital gains tax *n* impuesto *m* sobre plusvalías.

capital goods *npl* bienes *mpl* de capital.

capitalism ['kæpɪtəlɪzm] *n* capitalismo *m*.

capitalist ['kæpɪtəlɪst] ◇ *adj* capitalista. ◇ *n* capitalista *m y f*.

capitalize, -ise ['kæpɪtəlaɪz] *vi*: **to ~ on sthg** capitalizar algo.

capital punishment *n* (*U*) pena *f* capital.

Capitol Hill ['kæpɪtl-] *n* el Capitolio, *ubicación del Congreso estadounidense, en Washington*.

capitulate [kə'pɪtjuleɪt] *vi*: **to ~ (to)** capitular (ante).

Capricorn ['kæprɪkɔːn] *n* Capricornio *m*.

capsize [kæp'saɪz] ◇ *vt* hacer volcar OR zozobrar. ◇ *vi* volcar, zozobrar.

capsule ['kæpsjuːl] *n* cápsula *f*.

captain ['kæptɪn] *n* capitán *m*, -ana *f*.

caption ['kæpʃn] *n* [under picture etc] leyenda *f*; [heading] encabezamiento *m*.

captivate ['kæptɪveɪt] *vt* cautivar.

captive ['kæptɪv] ◇ *adj* **-1.** [imprisoned] en cautividad. **-2.** *fig* [market] asegurado(da). ◇ *n* cautivo *m*, -va *f*.

captivity [kæp'tɪvətɪ] *n*: **in ~** en cautividad, en cautiverio.

captor ['kæptə'] *n* apresador *m*, -ra *f*.

capture ['kæptʃə'] ◇ *vt* **-1.** [gen & COMPUT] capturar. **-2.** [audience, share of market] hacerse con; [city] tomar. **-3.** [scene, mood, attention] captar. ◇ *n* captura *f*.

car [kɑː'] ◇ *n* **-1.** [motorcar] coche *m*, automóvil *m*, carro *m* *Amer*. **-2.** [on train] vagón *m*. ◇ *comp* [door, tyre etc] del coche; [industry] del automóvil; [accident] de automóvil.

carafe [kəˈræf] n garrafa f.

caramel [ˈkærəmel] n **-1.** [burnt sugar] caramelo m (líquido), azúcar m quemado. **-2.** [sweet] tofe m.

carat [ˈkærət] n Br quilate m.

caravan [ˈkærəvæn] n caravana f, roulotte f.

caravan site n Br camping m para caravanas OR roulottes.

carbohydrate [ˌkɑːbəʊˈhaɪdreɪt] n CHEM hidrato m de carbono. ◆ **carbohydrates** npl [in food] féculas fpl.

carbon [ˈkɑːbən] n [element] carbono m.

carbonated [ˈkɑːbəneɪtɪd] adj con gas.

carbon copy n [document] copia f en papel carbón; fig [exact copy] calco m.

carbon dioxide [-daɪˈɒksaɪd] n bióxido m OR dióxido m de carbono.

carbon monoxide [-mɒˈnɒksaɪd] n monóxido m de carbono.

carbon paper n (U) papel m carbón.

car-boot sale n venta de objetos usados colocados en el portaequipajes del coche.

carburettor Br, **carburetor** Am [ˌkɑːbəˈretər] n carburador m.

carcass [ˈkɑːkəs] n [gen] cadáver m (de animal); [of bird] carcasa f; [at butcher's] canal m.

card [kɑːd] n **-1.** [playing card] carta f, naipe m. **-2.** [for information, greetings, computers] tarjeta f. **-3.** [postcard] postal f. **-4.** [cardboard] cartulina f. ◆ **cards** npl las cartas, los naipes. ◆ **on the cards** Br, **in the cards** Am adv inf más que probable.

cardboard [ˈkɑːdbɔːd] ◇ n (U) cartón m. ◇ comp de cartón.

cardboard box n caja f de cartón.

cardiac [ˈkɑːdɪæk] adj cardíaco(ca).

cardigan [ˈkɑːdɪgən] n rebeca f.

cardinal [ˈkɑːdɪnl] ◇ adj capital. ◇ n RELIG cardenal m.

card index n Br fichero m.

card table n mesita f plegable (para jugar a cartas).

care [keər] ◇ n **-1.** [gen] cuidado m; in sb's ~ al cargo OR cuidado de alguien; to be in/be taken into ~ estar/ser internado en un centro de protección de menores; to take ~ of [look after] cuidar de; [deal with] encargarse de; take ~! ¡nos vemos!, ¡cuídate!; to take ~ (to do sthg) tener cuidado (de hacer algo). **-2.** [cause of worry] preocupación f. ◇ vi **-1.** [be concerned]: to ~ (about) preocuparse (de OR por). **-2.** [mind] importar; I don't ~ no me importa.
◆ **care of** prep al cuidado de, en casa de. ◆ **care for** vt fus dated [like]: I don't ~ for cheese no me gusta el queso.

career [kəˈrɪər] ◇ n carrera f. ◇ vi ir a toda velocidad.

careers adviser n persona que aconseja sobre salidas profesionales.

carefree [ˈkeəfriː] adj despreocupado(da).

careful [ˈkeəfʊl] adj [gen] cuidadoso(sa); [driver] prudente; [work] esmerado(da); to be ~ with ser mirado OR cuidadoso con; to be ~ to do sthg tener cuidado de hacer algo.

carefully [ˈkeəflɪ] adv **-1.** [cautiously] con cuidado, cuidadosamente. **-2.** [thoroughly] detenidamente.

careless [ˈkeəlɪs] adj **-1.** [inattentive] descuidado(da). **-2.** [unconcerned] despreocupado(da).

caress [kəˈres] ◇ n caricia f. ◇ vt acariciar.

caretaker [ˈkeəˌteɪkər] n Br conserje m y f.

car ferry n transbordador m de coches.

cargo [ˈkɑːgəʊ] (pl -es OR -s) n carga f, cargamento m.

car hire n Br alquiler m de coches.

Caribbean [Br kærɪˈbɪən, Am kəˈrɪbɪən] n: the ~ (Sea) el (mar) Caribe.

caring [ˈkeərɪŋ] adj solícito(ta), dedicado(da).

carnage [ˈkɑːnɪdʒ] n carnicería f.

carnal [ˈkɑːnl] adj literary carnal.

carnation [kɑːˈneɪʃn] n clavel m.

carnival [ˈkɑːnɪvl] n carnaval m.

carnivorous [kɑːˈnɪvərəs] adj carnívoro(ra).

carol [ˈkærəl] n villancico m.

carousel [ˌkærəˈsel] n **-1.** [at fair] tiovivo m. **-2.** [at airport] cinta f transportadora.

carp [kɑːp] (pl inv OR -s) ◇ n carpa f. ◇ vi: to ~ (about) refunfuñar OR renegar (de).

car park n Br aparcamiento m, parqueadero m Amer.

carpenter [ˈkɑːpəntər] n carpintero m, -ra f.

carpentry [ˈkɑːpəntrɪ] n carpintería f.

carpet [ˈkɑːpɪt] ◇ n lit & fig alfombra f; fitted ~ moqueta f. ◇ vt [fit with carpet] enmoquetar.

carpet slipper n zapatilla f.

carpet sweeper [-ˈswiːpər] n cepillo m mecánico (de alfombras).

car phone n teléfono m de coche.

car rental n Am alquiler m de coches.

carriage ['kærɪdʒ] *n* **-1.** [horsedrawn vehicle] carruaje *m*. **-2.** *Br* [railway coach] vagón *m*. **-3.** [transport of goods] transporte *m*; ~ **paid** OR **free** *Br* porte pagado. **-4.** [on typewriter] carro *m*.

carriage return *n* retorno *m* de carro.

carriageway ['kærɪdʒweɪ] *n Br* carril *m*.

carrier ['kærɪə'] *n* **-1.** COMM transportista *m* y *f*. **-2.** [of disease] portador *m*, -ra *f*. **-3.** = carrier bag.

carrier bag *n* bolsa *f* (*de papel o plástico*).

carrot ['kærət] *n* **-1.** [vegetable] zanahoria *f*. **-2.** *inf* [incentive] aliciente *m*.

carry ['kærɪ] ◇ *vt* **-1.** [transport] llevar. **-2.** [disease] transmitir. **-3.** [involve] acarrear, conllevar. **-4.** [motion, proposal] aprobar. **-5.** [be pregnant with] estar embarazada de. **-6.** MATH llevarse. ◇ *vi* [sound] oírse. ◆ **carry away** *vt fus*: **to get carried away** exaltarse. ◆ **carry forward** *vt sep* llevar a la página siguiente; **carried forward** suma y sigue. ◆ **carry off** *vt sep* **-1.** [make a success of] llevar a cabo. **-2.** [win] llevarse. ◆ **carry on** ◇ *vt fus* **-1.** [continue] continuar, seguir; **to ~ on doing sthg** continuar OR seguir haciendo algo. **-2.** [conversation] sostener. ◇ *vi* **-1.** [continue]: **to ~ on (with)** continuar OR seguir (con). **-2.** *inf* [make a fuss] exagerar la nota. ◆ **carry out** *vt fus* **-1.** [perform] llevar a cabo. **-2.** [fulfil] cumplir. ◆ **carry through** *vt sep* [accomplish] llevar a cabo.

carryall ['kærɪɔːl] *n Am* bolsa *f* de viaje.

carrycot ['kærɪkɒt] *n* moisés *m*.

carry-out *n* comida *f* para llevar.

carsick ['kɑːˌsɪk] *adj* mareado(da) (*al ir en coche*).

cart [kɑːt] ◇ *n* carro *m*, carreta *f*. ◇ *vt inf* acarrear.

carton ['kɑːtn] *n* **-1.** [strong cardboard box] caja *f* de cartón. **-2.** [for liquids] cartón *m*, envase *m*.

cartoon [kɑː'tuːn] *n* **-1.** [satirical drawing] chiste *m* (en viñeta). **-2.** [comic strip] tira *f* cómica. **-3.** [film] dibujos *mpl* animados.

cartridge ['kɑːtrɪdʒ] *n* **-1.** [for gun, camera] cartucho *m*. **-2.** [for pen] recambio *m*.

cartwheel ['kɑːtwiːl] *n* voltereta *f* lateral.

carve [kɑːv] ◇ *vt* **-1.** [wood] tallar; [stone] esculpir. **-2.** [meat] trinchar. **-3.** [cut] grabar. ◇ *vi* trinchar. ◆ **carve out** *vt sep* [niche, place] conquistar. ◆ **carve up** *vt sep* repartir.

carving ['kɑːvɪŋ] *n* **-1.** [art, work - wooden] tallado *m*; [- stone] labrado *m*. **-2.** [object - wooden] talla *f*; [- stone] escultura *f*.

carving knife *n* cuchillo *m* de trinchar.

car wash *n* lavado *m* de coches.

case [keɪs] *n* **-1.** [gen] caso *m*; **to be the ~** ser el caso; **in that/which ~** en ese/ cuyo caso; **as** OR **whatever the ~ may be** según sea el caso; **in ~ of** en caso de. **-2.** [argument] argumento *m*; **the ~ for/against (sthg)** los argumentos a favor/en contra (de algo). **-3.** JUR [trial, inquiry] pleito *m*, causa *f*. **-4.** [container - of leather] funda *f*; [- of hard material] estuche *m*. **-5.** *Br* [suitcase] maleta *f*. ◆ **in any case** *adv* en cualquier caso. ◆ **in case** *conj & adv* por si acaso.

cash [kæʃ] ◇ *n* **-1.** [notes and coins] (dinero *m*) efectivo *m*; **to pay (in) ~** pagar al contado OR en efectivo. **-2.** *inf* [money] dinero *m*. **-3.** [payment]: ~ **in advance** pago *m* al contado por adelantado; ~ **on delivery** entrega *f* contra reembolso. ◇ *vt* cobrar, hacer efectivo. ◆ **cash in** *vi*: **to ~ in on** *inf* sacar partido de.

cash and carry *n* almacén *m* de venta al por mayor.

cashbook ['kæʃbʊk] *n* libro *m* de caja.

cash box *n* caja *f* con cerradura (para el dinero).

cash card *n* tarjeta *f* de cajero automático.

cash desk *n Br* caja *f*.

cash dispenser [-dɪ'spensə'] *n* cajero *m* automático.

cashew (nut) ['kæʃuː-] *n* (nuez *m* de) anacardo *m*.

cashier [kæ'ʃɪə'] *n* cajero *m*, -ra *f*.

cash machine = cash dispenser.

cashmere [kæʃ'mɪə'] *n* cachemira *f*.

cash register *n* caja *f* (registradora).

casing ['keɪsɪŋ] *n* revestimiento *m*.

casino [kə'siːnəʊ] (*pl* **-s**) *n* casino *m*.

cask [kɑːsk] *n* tonel *m*, barril *m*.

casket ['kɑːskɪt] *n* **-1.** [for jewels] estuche *m*. **-2.** *Am* [coffin] ataúd *m*.

casserole ['kæsərəʊl] *n* **-1.** [stew] guiso *m*. **-2.** [pan] cazuela *f*, cacerola *f*.

cassette [kæ'set] *n* cinta *f*, casete *f*.

cassette player *n* casete *m*, magnetófono *m*.

cassette recorder *n* casete *m*, magnetófono *m*.

cast [kɑːst] (*pt* & *pp* **cast**) ◇ *n* [of play, film] reparto *m*. ◇ *vt* **-1.** [look] echar, lanzar; **to ~** doubt on sthg poner algo en duda. **-2.** [light] irradiar; [shadow] proyectar. **-3.** [throw] arrojar, lanzar. **-4.** [choose for play]: **to ~** sb as asignar a alguien el papel de. **-5.** [vote] emitir. **-6.** [metal, statue] fundir. ◆ **cast aside** *vt sep* [person] abandonar; [idea] rechazar. ◆ **cast off** *vi* NAUT soltar amarras.

castanets [,kæstə'nets] *npl* castañuelas *fpl*.

castaway ['kɑːstəweɪ] *n* náufrago *m*, -ga *f*.

caste [kɑːst] *n* casta *f*.

caster ['kɑːstə'] *n* [wheel] ruedecilla *f*.

caster sugar *n Br* azúcar *m* extrafino.

Castile [kæs'tiːl], **Castilla** [kæs'tiʎə] *n* Castilla.

casting vote ['kɑːstɪŋ-] *n* voto *m* de calidad.

cast iron *n* hierro *m* fundido.

castle ['kɑːsl] *n* **-1.** [building] castillo *m*. **-2.** [in chess] torre *f*.

castor ['kɑːstə'] = **caster**.

castor oil *n* aceite *m* de ricino.

castor sugar = **caster sugar**.

castrate [kæ'streɪt] *vt* castrar.

casual ['kæʒʊəl] *adj* **-1.** [relaxed, indifferent] despreocupado(da). **-2.** *pej* [offhand] descuidado(da), informal. **-3.** [chance - visitor] ocasional; [- remark] casual. **-4.** [informal] de sport, informal. **-5.** [irregular - labourer etc] eventual.

casually ['kæʒʊəlɪ] *adv* **-1.** [in a relaxed manner, indifferently] con aire despreocupado. **-2.** [informally] informalmente.

casualty ['kæʒjʊəltɪ] *n* **-1.** [gen] víctima *m y f*. **-2.** (U) [ward] urgencias *fpl*.

casualty department *n* unidad *f* de urgencias.

cat [kæt] *n* **-1.** [domestic] gato *m*, -ta *f*. **-2.** [wild] felino *m*.

Catalan ['kætə,læn] ◇ *adj* catalán(ana). ◇ *n* **-1.** [person] catalán *m*, -ana *f*. **-2.** [language] catalán *m*.

catalogue *Br*, **catalog** *Am* ['kætəlɒg] ◇ *n* **-1.** [of items] catálogo *m*. **-2.** *fig* [list] serie *f*, cadena *f*. ◇ *vt* **-1.** [make official list of] catalogar. **-2.** *fig* [list] enumerar.

Catalonia [,kætə'ləʊnɪə] *n* Cataluña.

Catalonian [,kætə'ləʊnɪən] ◇ *adj* catalán(ana). ◇ *n* [person] catalán *m*, -ana *f*.

catalyst ['kætəlɪst] *n lit* & *fig* catalizador *m*.

catalytic convertor [,kætə'lɪtɪk kən'vɜːtə'] *n* catalizador *m*.

catapult ['kætəpʌlt] *Br n* **-1.** HIST [handheld] **tirachinas** *m inv*. **-2.** HIST [machine] catapulta *f*.

cataract ['kætərækt] *n* [in eye, waterfall] catarata *f*.

catarrh [kə'tɑː'] *n* (U) catarro *m*.

catastrophe [kə'tæstrəfɪ] *n* catástrofe *f*.

catch [kætʃ] (*pt* & *pp* **caught**) ◇ *vt* **-1.** [gen] coger, agarrar *Amer*. **-2.** [fish] pescar; [stop - person] parar. **-3.** [be in time for]: **to ~ the (last)** post *Br* llegar a la (última) recogida del correo. **-4.** [hear clearly] entender, llegar a oír. **-5.** [interest, imagination] despertar. **-6.** [see]: **to ~ sight OR a glimpse of** alcanzar a ver. **-7.** [hook - shirt etc] engancharse; [shut in door - finger] pillarse. **-8.** [strike] golpear. ◇ *vi* **-1.** [become hooked, get stuck] engancharse. **-2.** [start to burn] prenderse. ◇ *n* **-1.** [of ball etc] parada *f*. **-2.** [of fish] pesca *f*, captura *f*. **-3.** [fastener] pestillo *m*. **-4.** [snag] trampa *f*. ◆ **catch on** *vi* **-1.** [become popular] hacerse popular. **-2.** *inf* [understand]: **to ~ on (to)** caer en la cuenta (de). ◆ **catch out** *vt sep* [trick] pillar en un error. ◆ **catch up** ◇ *vt sep* alcanzar. ◇ *vi*: **we'll soon ~ up** pronto nos pondremos a la misma altura; **to ~ up on** [sleep] recuperar; [work, reading] ponerse al día con. ◆ **catch up with** *vt fus* **-1.** [group etc] alcanzar. **-2.** [criminal] pillar, descubrir.

catching ['kætʃɪŋ] *adj* contagioso(sa).

catchment area ['kætʃmənt-] *n Br* zona *f* de captación.

catchphrase ['kætʃfreɪz] *n* muletilla *f*.

catchy ['kætʃɪ] *adj* pegadizo(za).

categorically [,kætɪ'gɒrɪklɪ] *adv* [state] categóricamente; [deny] rotundamente.

category ['kætəgərɪ] *n* categoría *f*.

cater ['keɪtə'] *vi* proveer comida. ◆ **cater for** *vt fus Br* [tastes, needs] atender a; [social group] estar destinado(da) a; **I hadn't ~ed for that** no había contado con eso. ◆ **cater to** *vt fus* complacer.

caterer ['keɪtərə'] *n* proveedor *m*, -ra *f*.

catering ['keɪtərɪŋ] *n* [at wedding etc] servicio *m* de banquetes; [trade] hostelería *f*.

caterpillar ['kætəpɪlə'] *n* oruga *f*.

caterpillar tracks *npl* (rodado *m* de) oruga *f*.

cathedral [kə'θiːdrəl] *n* catedral *f*.

Catholic ['kæθlɪk] ◇ *adj* católico(ca). ◇ *n* católico *m*, -ca *f*. ◆ **catholic** *adj* diverso(sa).

Catseyes® ['kætsaɪz] *npl Br* catafaros *mpl*.

cattle ['kætl] *npl* ganado *m* (vacuno).

catty ['kætɪ] *adj inf pej* [spiteful] rencoroso(sa).

catwalk ['kætwɔːk] *n* pasarela *f*.

caucus ['kɔːkəs] *n* [political group] comité *m*. ◆ **Caucus** *n Am* congreso de los principales partidos estadounidenses.

caught [kɔːt] *pt & pp* → **catch**.

cauliflower ['kɒlɪ,flaʊəʳ] *n* coliflor *f*.

cause [kɔːz] ◇ *n* **-1.** [gen] causa *f*. **-2.** [grounds]: ~ **(for)** motivo *m* (para); ~ **for complaint** motivo de queja; ~ **to do sthg** motivo para hacer algo. ◇ *vt* causar; **to** ~ **sb to do sthg** hacer que alguien haga algo.

caustic ['kɔːstɪk] *adj* **-1.** CHEM cáustico(ca). **-2.** [comment] mordaz, hiriente.

caution ['kɔːʃn] ◇ *n* **-1.** (U) [care] precaución *f*, cautela *f*. **-2.** [warning] advertencia *f*. ◇ *vt* **-1.** [warn - against danger] prevenir; [- against behaving rudely etc] advertir. **-2.** *Br* [subj: policeman]: **to** ~ **sb (for)** amonestar a alguien (por).

cautious ['kɔːʃəs] *adj* prudente, precavido(da).

cavalier [,kævə'lɪəʳ] *adj* arrogante, desdeñoso(sa).

cavalry ['kævlrɪ] *n* caballería *f*.

cave [keɪv] *n* cueva *f*. ◆ **cave in** *vi* [roof, ceiling] hundirse.

caveman ['keɪvmæn] (*pl* **-men** [-men]) *n* cavernícola *m y f*.

caviar(e) ['kævɪɑːʳ] *n* caviar *m*.

cavity ['kævətɪ] *n* **-1.** [in object, structure] cavidad *f*. **-2.** [in tooth] caries *f inv*.

cavort [kə'vɔːt] *vi* retozar, brincar.

CB *n abbr of* **citizens' band**.

CBI *abbr of* **Confederation of British Industry**.

cc ◇ *n* (*abbr of* **cubic centimetre**) cc. ◇ (*abbr of* **carbon copy**) cc.

CD *n* (*abbr of* **compact disc**) CD *m*.

CD player *n* reproductor *m* de CD.

CD-ROM [,siːdiː'rɒm] (*abbr of* **compact disc read only memory**) *n* CD-ROM *m*.

cease [siːs] *fml* ◇ *vt* cesar; **to** ~ **doing** OR **to do sthg** dejar de hacer algo. ◇ *vi* cesar.

cease-fire *n* alto *m* el fuego.

ceaseless ['siːslɪs] *adj fml* incesante.

cedar (tree) ['siːdəʳ-] *n* cedro *m*.

ceiling ['siːlɪŋ] *n* **-1.** [of room] techo *m*. **-2.** [limit] tope *m*, límite *m*.

celebrate ['selɪbreɪt] ◇ *vt* celebrar. ◇ *vi* divertirse.

celebrated ['selɪbreɪtɪd] *adj* célebre.

celebration [,selɪ'breɪʃn] *n* **-1.** (U) [activity, feeling] celebración *f*. **-2.** [event] fiesta *f*, festejo *m*.

celebrity [sɪ'lebrətɪ] *n* celebridad *f*.

celery ['selərɪ] *n* apio *m*.

celibate ['selɪbət] *adj* célibe.

cell [sel] *n* **-1.** BIOL, COMPUT & POL célula *f*. **-2.** [prisoner's, nun's or monk's room] celda *f*.

cellar ['seləʳ] *n* **-1.** [basement] sótano *m*. **-2.** [stock of wine] bodega *f*.

cello ['tʃeləʊ] (*pl* **-s**) *n* violoncelo *m*.

Cellophane® ['seləfeɪn] *n* celofán® *m*.

Celsius ['selsɪəs] *adj* centígrado(da); **20 degrees** ~ 20 grados centígrados.

Celt [kelt] *n* celta *m y f*.

Celtic ['keltɪk] ◇ *adj* celta. ◇ *n* celta *m*.

cement [sɪ'ment] ◇ *n* **-1.** [for concrete] cemento *m*. **-2.** [glue] cola *f*. ◇ *vt* **-1.** [glue] encolar. **-2.** [agreement, relationship] cimentar, fortalecer.

cement mixer *n* hormigonera *f*.

cemetery ['semɪtrɪ] *n* cementerio *m*.

censor ['sensəʳ] ◇ *n* censor *m*, -ra *f*. ◇ *vt* censurar.

censorship ['sensəʃɪp] *n* censura *f*.

censure ['senʃəʳ] *vt* censurar.

census ['sensəs] (*pl* **-uses**) *n* censo *m*.

cent [sent] *n* centavo *m*.

centenary *Br* [sen'tiːnərɪ], **centennial** *Am* [sen'tenjəl] *n* centenario *m*.

center *Am* = **centre**.

centigrade ['sentɪgreɪd] *adj* centígrado(da); **20 degrees** ~ 20 grados centígrados.

centilitre *Br*, **centiliter** *Am* ['sentɪ,liːtəʳ] *n* centilitro *m*.

centimetre *Br*, **centimeter** *Am* ['sentɪ,miːtəʳ] *n* centímetro *m*.

centipede ['sentɪpiːd] *n* ciempiés *m inv*.

central ['sentrəl] *adj* **-1.** [gen] central; **in** ~ **Spain** en el centro de España. **-2.** [easily reached] céntrico(ca).

Central America *n* Centroamérica *f*.

central heating *n* calefacción *f* central.

centralize, -ise ['sentrəlaɪz] *vt* centralizar.

central locking [-'lɒkɪŋ] *n* cierre *m* centralizado.

central reservation *n Br* mediana *f*.

centre *Br*, **center** *Am* ['sentəʳ] ◇ *n* centro *m*; **the** ~ POL el centro. ◇ *adj* **-1.** [middle] central. **-2.** POL centrista. ◇ *vt* centrar.

centre back *n* defensa *m y f* central.

centre forward *n* delantero *m*, -ra *f* centro *inv*.

centre half = centre back.

century ['sentʃʊrɪ] *n* siglo *m*.

ceramic [sɪ'ræmɪk] *adj* de cerámica, cerámico(ca). ◆ **ceramics** *n* cerámica *f*.

cereal ['sɪərɪəl] *n* -1. [crop] cereal *m*. -2. [breakfast food] cereales *mpl*.

ceremonial [ˌserɪ'məʊnjəl] *adj* ceremonial.

ceremony ['serɪmənɪ] *n* ceremonia *f*; **to stand on** ~ andarse con cumplidos OR ceremonias.

certain ['sɜːtn] *adj* -1. [gen] seguro(ra); **he's** ~ **to be late** (es) seguro que llega tarde; **to be** ~ **(of)** estar seguro (de); **to make** ~ **(of)** asegurarse (de); **for** ~ seguro, con toda seguridad. -2. [particular, some] cierto(ta); **to a** ~ **extent** hasta cierto punto. -3. [named person]: **a** ~ ... un (una) tal ....

certainly ['sɜːtnlɪ] *adv* desde luego; ~ **not!** ¡claro que no!

certainty ['sɜːtntɪ] *n* seguridad *f*.

certificate [sə'tɪfɪkət] *n* [gen] certificado *m*; SCH & UNIV diploma *m*, título *m*; [of birth, death] partida *f*.

certified ['sɜːtɪfaɪd] *adj* [document] certificado(da); [person] diplomado(da).

certified mail *n* Am correo *m* certificado.

certified public accountant *n* Am contable diplomado *m*, contable diplomada *f*.

certify ['sɜːtɪfaɪ] *vt* -1. [declare true] certificar. -2. [declare insane] declarar demente.

cervical [sə'vaɪkl] *adj* cervical.

cervical smear *n* citología *f*, frotis *f* cervical.

cervix ['sɜːvɪks] (*pl* -ices [-ɪsiːz]) *n* [of womb] cuello *m* del útero.

cesarean (section) = caesarean (section).

cesspit ['sespɪt], **cesspool** ['sespuːl] *n* pozo *m* negro.

cf. (*abbr of* confer) cf., cfr.

CFC (*abbr of* chlorofluorocarbon) *n* CFC *m*.

Chad [tʃæd] *n* el Chad.

chafe [tʃeɪf] *vt* [rub] rozar.

chaffinch ['tʃæfɪntʃ] *n* pinzón *m*.

chain [tʃeɪn] ◇ *n* cadena *f*; ~ **of events** serie *f* OR cadena *f* de acontecimientos. ◇ *vt* [person, object] encadenar.

chain reaction *n* reacción *f* en cadena.

chain saw *n* sierra *f* (mecánica) continua OR de cinta.

chain-smoke *vi* fumar un cigarrillo tras otro.

chain store *n* grandes almacenes *mpl*.

chair [tʃeər] ◇ *n* -1. [gen] silla *f*; [armchair] sillón *m*. -2. [university post] cátedra *f*. -3. [of meeting] presidencia *f*. ◇ *vt* presidir.

chair lift *n* telesilla *m*.

chairman ['tʃeəmən] (*pl* -men [-mən]) *n* presidente *m*.

chairperson ['tʃeəˌpɜːsn] (*pl* -s) *n* presidente *m*, -ta *f*.

chalet ['ʃæleɪ] *n* chalé *m*, chalet *m*.

chalk [tʃɔːk] *n* -1. [type of rock] creta *f*. -2. [for drawing] tiza *f*, gis *m* Amer.

chalkboard ['tʃɔːkbɔːd] *n* Am pizarra *f*.

challenge ['tʃælɪndʒ] ◇ *n* desafío *m*, reto *m*. ◇ *vt* -1. [to fight, competition]: **to** ~ **sb (to sthg/to do sthg)** desafiar a alguien (a algo/a que haga algo). -2. [question] poner en tela de juicio.

challenging ['tʃælɪndʒɪŋ] *adj* -1. [task, job] estimulante, que supone un reto. -2. [look, tone of voice] desafiante.

chamber ['tʃeɪmbər] *n* [room] cámara *f*.

chambermaid ['tʃeɪmbəmeɪd] *n* [at hotel] camarera *f*.

chamber music *n* música *f* de cámara.

chamber of commerce *n* cámara *f* de comercio.

chameleon [kə'miːljən] *n* camaleón *m*.

champagne [ˌʃæm'peɪn] *n* champán *m*.

champion ['tʃæmpjən] *n* -1. [of competition] campeón *m*, -ona *f*. -2. [of cause] defensor *m*, -ra *f*.

championship ['tʃæmpjənʃɪp] *n* campeonato *m*.

chance [tʃɑːns] ◇ *n* -1. [luck] azar *m*, suerte *f*; **by** ~ por casualidad. -2. [likelihood] posibilidad *f*; **not to stand a** ~ **(of)** no tener ninguna posibilidad (de); **by any** ~ por casualidad, acaso. -3. [opportunity] oportunidad *f*. -4. [risk] riesgo *m*; **to take a** ~ **(on)** correr un riesgo OR arriesgarse (con). ◇ *adj* fortuito(ta), casual. ◇ *vt* arriesgar; **to** ~ **it** arriesgarse.

chancellor ['tʃɑːnsələr] *n* -1. [chief minister] canciller *m*. -2. UNIV ≃ rector *m*, -ra *f*.

Chancellor of the Exchequer *n* Br Ministro *m*, -tra *f* de Economía y Hacienda.

chandelier [ˌʃændə'lɪər] *n* (lámpara *f* de) araña *f*.

change [tʃeɪndʒ] ◇ *n* -1. [gen] cambio *m*; ~ **of clothes** muda *f*; **for a** ~ para variar. -2. [from payment] vuelta *f*, cambio *m*, vuelto *m* Amer. -3. [coins] suelto *m*, calderilla *f*. -4. [money in exchange]:

have you got ~ for £5? ¿tienes cambio de 5 libras? ◇ *vt* **-1.** [gen] cambiar; **to ~ sthg into** transformar algo en; **to ~ pounds into francs** cambiar libras en francos; **to ~ direction** cambiar de rumbo; **to ~ one's mind** cambiar de idea OR opinión. **-2.** [goods in shop] descambiar. **-3.** [switch - job, gear, train] cambiar de; **to ~ one's clothes** cambiarse de ropa. ◇ *vi* **-1.** [alter] cambiar; **to ~ into sthg** transformarse en algo. **-2.** [change clothes] cambiarse. **-3.** [change trains, buses] hacer transbordo. ◆ **change over** *vi* [convert]: **to ~ over** to cambiar a.

changeable ['tʃeɪndʒəbl] *adj* variable.

change machine *n* máquina *f* de cambio.

changeover ['tʃeɪndʒ,əʊvəʳ] *n*: ~ **(to)** cambio *m* (a).

changing ['tʃeɪndʒɪŋ] *adj* cambiante.

changing room *n* vestuario *m*.

channel ['tʃænl] ◇ *n* canal *m*. ◇ *vt lit & fig* canalizar. ◆ **Channel** *n*: **the (English) Channel** el Canal de la Mancha. ◆ **channels** *npl* [procedure] conductos *mpl*, medios *mpl*.

Channel Islands *npl*: **the ~** las islas del canal de la Mancha.

Channel tunnel *n*: **the ~** el túnel del Canal de la Mancha.

chant [tʃɑːnt] ◇ *n* **-1.** RELIG canto *m*. **-2.** [repeated words] soniquete *m*. ◇ *vt* **-1.** RELIG cantar. **-2.** [words] corear.

chaos ['keɪɒs] *n* caos *m*.

chaotic [keɪ'ɒtɪk] *adj* caótico(ca).

chap [tʃæp] *n Br inf* chico *m*, tío *m*.

chapel ['tʃæpl] *n* capilla *f*.

chaperon(e) ['ʃæpərəʊn] ◇ *n* carabina *f*, acompañanta *f*. ◇ *vt* acompañar.

chaplain ['tʃæplɪn] *n* capellán *m*.

chapped [tʃæpt] *adj* agrietado(da).

chapter ['tʃæptəʳ] *n lit & fig* capítulo *m*.

char [tʃɑːʳ] ◇ *n Br* [cleaner] mujer *f* de la limpieza. ◇ *vt* [burn] carbonizar, calcinar.

character ['kærəktəʳ] *n* **-1.** [nature, quality, letter] carácter *m*. **-2.** [in film, book, play] personaje *m*. **-3.** *inf* [person of stated kind] tipo *m*. **-4.** *inf* [person with strong personality]: **to be a ~** ser todo un carácter.

characteristic [,kærəktə'rɪstɪk] ◇ *adj* característico(ca). ◇ *n* característica *f*.

characterize, -ise ['kærəktəraɪz] *vt* **-1.** [typify] caracterizar. **-2.** [portray]: **to ~ sthg as** definir algo como.

charade [ʃə'rɑːd] *n* farsa *f*. ◆ **charades** *n* (U) charadas *fpl*.

charcoal ['tʃɑːkəʊl] *n* [for barbecue etc] carbón *m* (vegetal); [for drawing] carboncillo *m*.

charge [tʃɑːdʒ] ◇ *n* **-1.** [cost] precio *m*, coste *m*; **free of ~** gratis. **-2.** JUR cargo *m*, acusación *f*. **-3.** [responsibility]: **to have ~ of sthg** tener algo al cargo de uno; **to take ~ (of)** hacerse cargo (de); **to be in ~** ser el encargado (la encargada); **in ~ of** encargado(da) de. **-4.** ELEC carga *f*. **-5.** MIL [of cavalry] carga *f*. ◇ *vt* **-1.** [customer, sum] cobrar; **to ~ sthg to sb** cargar algo en la cuenta de alguien. **-2.** [suspect, criminal]: **to ~ sb (with)** acusar a alguien (de). **-3.** [attack] cargar contra. **-4.** [battery] cargar. ◇ *vi* [rush] cargar; **to ~ in/out** entrar/salir en tromba.

charge card *n* tarjeta *f* de crédito de un establecimiento comercial.

charger ['tʃɑːdʒəʳ] *n* [for batteries] cargador *m*.

chariot ['tʃærɪət] *n* carro *m*, cuadriga *f*.

charisma [kə'rɪzmə] *n* carisma *m*.

charitable ['tʃærətəbl] *adj* **-1.** [person, remark] caritativo(va). **-2.** [organization] benéfico(ca).

charity ['tʃærətɪ] *n* **-1.** [kindness, money] caridad *f*. **-2.** [organization] institución *f* benéfica.

charm [tʃɑːm] ◇ *n* **-1.** [appeal, attractiveness] encanto *m*. **-2.** [spell] hechizo *m*. **-3.** [on bracelet] dije *m*, amuleto *m*. ◇ *vt* dejar encantado(da).

charming ['tʃɑːmɪŋ] *adj* encantador(ra).

chart [tʃɑːt] ◇ *n* **-1.** [diagram] gráfico *m*. **-2.** [map] carta *f*. ◇ *vt* **-1.** [plot, map] representar en un mapa. **-2.** *fig* [record] trazar. ◆ **charts** *npl*: **the ~s** la lista de éxitos.

charter ['tʃɑːtəʳ] ◇ *n* [document] carta *f*. ◇ *comp* chárter (*inv*). ◇ *vt* [plane, boat] fletar.

chartered accountant ['tʃɑːtəd-] *n Br* contable colegiado *m*, contable colegiada *f*.

charter flight *n* vuelo *m* chárter.

chase [tʃeɪs] ◇ *n* [pursuit] persecución *f*. ◇ *vt* **-1.** [pursue] perseguir. **-2.** [drive away] ahuyentar. **-3.** [money, jobs] ir detrás de.

chasm ['kæzm] *n* [deep crack] sima *f*; *fig* [divide] abismo *m*.

chassis ['ʃæsɪ] (*pl inv*) *n* [of vehicle] chasis *m inv*.

chaste [tʃeɪst] *adj* casto(ta).

chat [tʃæt] ◇ *n* charla *f*. ◇ *vi* charlar.
◆ **chat up** *vt sep Br inf* ligar con.

chat show *n Br* programa *m* de entrevistas.

chatter ['tʃætər] ◇ *n* **-1.** [of person] cháchara *f*. **-2.** [of bird] gorjeo *m*; [of monkey] chillidos *mpl*. ◇ *vi* **-1.** [person] parlotear. **-2.** [teeth] castañetear.

chatterbox ['tʃætəbɒks] *n inf* parlanchín *m*, -ina *f*.

chatty ['tʃæti] *adj* **-1.** [person] dicharachero(ra). **-2.** [letter] informal.

chauffeur ['ʃəʊfər] *n* chófer *m y f*.

chauvinist ['ʃəʊvɪnɪst] *n* **-1.** [sexist] sexista *m y f*; **male** ~ machista *m*. **-2.** [nationalist] chovinista *m y f*.

cheap [tʃiːp] ◇ *adj* **-1.** [inexpensive] barato(ta). **-2.** [low-quality] de mala calidad. **-3.** [vulgar - joke etc] de mal gusto. ◇ *adv* barato.

cheapen ['tʃiːpn] *vt* [degrade] rebajar.

cheaply ['tʃiːplɪ] *adv* barato.

cheat [tʃiːt] ◇ *n* tramposo *m*, -sa *f*. ◇ *vt* timar, estafar; **to** ~ **sb out of sthg** estafar algo a alguien. ◇ *vi* [in exam] copiar; [at cards] hacer trampas.

check [tʃek] ◇ *n* **-1.** [inspection, test]: ~ **(on)** inspección *f* OR comprobación *f* (de); **to keep a** ~ **on** llevar un control de. **-2.** [restraint]: ~ **(on)** restricción *f* (en). **-3.** *Am* [cheque] cheque *m*. **-4.** *Am* [bill] cuenta *f*. **-5.** [pattern] cuadros *mpl*. ◇ *vt* **-1.** [test, verify] comprobar; [inspect] inspeccionar. **-2.** [restrain, stop] refrenar. ◇ *vi* comprobar; **to** ~ **(for/on sthg)** comprobar (algo). ◆ **check in** ◇ *vt sep* [luggage, coat] facturar. ◇ *vi* **-1.** [at hotel] inscribirse, registrarse. **-2.** [at airport] facturar. ◆ **check out** ◇ *vt sep* **-1.** [luggage, coat] recoger. **-2.** [investigate] comprobar. ◇ *vi* [from hotel] dejar el hotel. ◆ **check up** *vi*: **to** ~ **up (on)** informarse (acerca de).

checkbook *Am* = **chequebook**.

checked [tʃekt] *adj* a cuadros.

checkered *Am* = **chequered**.

checkers ['tʃekəz] *n Am* (U) damas *fpl*.

check-in *n* facturación *f* de equipajes.

checking account ['tʃekɪŋ-] *n Am* cuenta *f* corriente.

checkmate ['tʃekmeɪt] *n* jaque *m* mate.

checkout ['tʃekaʊt] *n* caja *f*.

checkpoint ['tʃekpɔɪnt] *n* control *m*.

checkup ['tʃekʌp] *n* chequeo *m*.

Cheddar (cheese) ['tʃedər-] *n* (queso *m*) cheddar *m*.

cheek [tʃiːk] *n* **-1.** [of face] mejilla *f*. **-2.** *inf* [impudence] cara *f*, descaro *m*.

cheekbone ['tʃiːkbəʊn] *n* pómulo *m*.

cheeky ['tʃiːkɪ] *adj* descarado(da).

cheer [tʃɪər] ◇ *n* [shout] aclamación *f*; ~**s** vítores *mpl*. ◇ *vt* **-1.** [shout approval, encouragement at] aclamar. **-2.** [gladden] animar. ◇ *vi* gritar con entusiasmo. ◆ **cheers** *excl* [when drinking] ¡salud!; *inf* [thank you] ¡gracias!; *inf* [goodbye] ¡hasta luego! ◆ **cheer up** ◇ *vt sep* animar. ◇ *vi* animarse.

cheerful ['tʃɪəful] *adj* [gen] alegre.

cheerio [,tʃɪərɪ'əʊ] *excl inf* ¡hasta luego!

cheese [tʃiːz] *n* queso *m*.

cheeseboard ['tʃiːzbɔːd] *n* tabla *f* de quesos.

cheeseburger ['tʃiːz,bɜːgər] *n* hamburguesa *f* de queso.

cheesecake ['tʃiːzkeɪk] *n* pastel *m* OR tarta *f* de queso.

cheetah ['tʃiːtə] *n* guepardo *m*, onza *f*.

chef [ʃef] *n* chef *m*, jefe *m* de cocina.

chemical ['kemɪkl] ◇ *adj* químico(ca). ◇ *n* sustancia *f* química.

chemist ['kemɪst] *n* **-1.** *Br* [pharmacist] farmacéutico *m*, -ca *f*; ~**'s (shop)** farmacia *f*. **-2.** [scientist] químico *m*, -ca *f*.

chemistry ['kemɪstrɪ] *n* [science] química *f*.

cheque *Br*, **check** *Am* [tʃek] *n* cheque *m*, talón *m*.

chequebook *Br*, **checkbook** *Am* ['tʃekbʊk] *n* talonario *m* de cheques, chequera *f Amer*.

cheque card *n Br* tarjeta *f* de identificación bancaria.

chequered *Br* ['tʃekəd], **checkered** *Am* ['tʃekerd] *adj* **-1.** [patterned] a cuadros. **-2.** [varied] lleno(na) de altibajos.

cherish ['tʃerɪʃ] *vt* **-1.** [hope, memory] abrigar. **-2.** [privilege, right] apreciar. **-3.** [person, thing] tener mucho cariño a.

cherry ['tʃerɪ] *n* [fruit] cereza *f*; ~ **(tree)** cerezo *m*.

chess [tʃes] *n* ajedrez *m*.

chessboard ['tʃesbɔːd] *n* tablero *m* de ajedrez.

chessman ['tʃesmæn] (*pl* **-men** [-men]) *n* pieza *f*.

chest [tʃest] *n* **-1.** ANAT pecho *m*. **-2.** [box, trunk - gen] arca *f*, cofre *m*; [- for tools] caja *f*.

chestnut ['tʃesnʌt] ◇ *adj* [colour] castaño(ña). ◇ *n* [nut] castaña *f*; ~ **(tree)** castaño *m*.

chest of drawers (*pl* **chests of drawers**) *n* cómoda *f*.

chew [tʃuː] *vt* **-1.** [food] masticar. **-2.** [nails] morderse; [carpet] morder.

◆ **chew up** vt sep [food] masticar; [slippers] mordisquear.

chewing gum ['tʃuːɪŋ-] n chicle m.

chic [ʃiːk] adj chic (inv), elegante.

chick [tʃɪk] n [baby bird] polluelo m.

chicken ['tʃɪkɪn] n **-1.** [bird] gallina f. **-2.** [food] pollo m. **-3.** inf [coward] gallina m y f. ◆ **chicken out** vi inf: to ~ out (of sthg/of doing sthg) rajarse (a la hora de algo/de hacer algo).

chickenpox ['tʃɪkɪnpɒks] n varicela f.

chickpea ['tʃɪkpiː] n garbanzo m.

chicory ['tʃɪkərɪ] n achicoria f.

chief [tʃiːf] ◇ adj principal. ◇ n jefe m, -fa f.

chief executive n [head of company] director m, -ra f general.

chiefly ['tʃiːflɪ] adv **-1.** [mainly] principalmente. **-2.** [especially, above all] por encima de todo.

chiffon ['ʃɪfɒn] n gasa f.

chilblain ['tʃɪlbleɪn] n sabañón m.

child [tʃaɪld] (pl **children**) n **-1.** [boy, girl] niño m, -ña f. **-2.** [son, daughter] hijo m, -ja f.

child benefit n (U) Br subsidio pagado a todas las familias por cada hijo.

childbirth ['tʃaɪldbɜːθ] n (U) parto m.

childhood ['tʃaɪldhʊd] n infancia f.

childish ['tʃaɪldɪʃ] adj pej infantil.

childlike ['tʃaɪldlaɪk] adj [person] como un niño; [smile, trust] de niño.

childminder ['tʃaɪld,maɪndər] n Br niñera f (durante el día).

childproof ['tʃaɪldpruːf] adj a prueba de niños.

children ['tʃɪldrən] pl → child.

children's home n hogar m infantil.

Chile ['tʃɪlɪ] n Chile.

Chilean ['tʃɪlɪən] ◇ adj chileno(na). ◇ n chileno m, -na f.

chili ['tʃɪlɪ] = **chilli**.

chill [tʃɪl] ◇ n **-1.** [illness] resfriado m. **-2.** [in temperature]: there's a ~ in the air hace un poco de fresco. ◇ vt **-1.** [drink, food] (dejar) enfriar. **-2.** [person - with cold] enfriar; [- with fear] hacer sentir escalofríos.

chilli ['tʃɪlɪ] (pl **-ies**) n guindilla f, chile m, ají m Amer.

chilling ['tʃɪlɪŋ] adj **-1.** [very cold] helado(da). **-2.** [frightening] escalofriante.

chilly ['tʃɪlɪ] adj frío(a).

chime [tʃaɪm] ◇ n campanada f. ◇ vi [bell] repicar; [clock] sonar.

chimney ['tʃɪmnɪ] n chimenea f.

chimneypot ['tʃɪmnɪpɒt] n cañón m de chimenea.

chimneysweep ['tʃɪmnɪswiːp] n deshollinador m, -ra f.

chimp [tʃɪmp], **chimpanzee** [,tʃɪmpən'ziː] n chimpancé m y f.

chin [tʃɪn] n barbilla f.

china ['tʃaɪnə] n porcelana f, loza f.

China ['tʃaɪnə] n la China.

Chinese [,tʃaɪ'niːz] ◇ adj chino(na). ◇ n **-1.** [person] chino m, -na f. **-2.** [language] chino m. ◇ npl: the ~ los chinos.

Chinese leaves npl Br (hojas fpl de) col f china.

chink [tʃɪŋk] ◇ n **-1.** [narrow opening] grieta f; [of light] resquicio m. **-2.** [sound] tintineo m. ◇ vi tintinear.

chip [tʃɪp] ◇ n **-1.** Br [fried potato chip] patata f frita; Am [potato crisp] patata f frita (de bolsa o de churrería). **-2.** [fragment - gen] pedacito m; [- of wood] viruta f; [- of stone] lasca f. **-3.** [flaw - in cup, glass] desportilladura f. **-4.** COMPUT chip m. **-5.** [token] ficha f. ◇ vt [damage] desportillar. ◆ **chip in** inf vi **-1.** [pay money] poner dinero. **-2.** [interrupt] interrumpir. ◆ **chip off** vt sep desconchar.

chipboard ['tʃɪpbɔːd] n aglomerado m.

chip shop n Br tienda en la que se vende pescado y patatas fritas.

chiropodist [kɪ'rɒpədɪst] n podólogo m, -ga f, pedicuro m, -ra f.

chirp [tʃɜːp] vi [bird] piar; [insect] chirriar.

chirpy ['tʃɜːpɪ] adj inf alegre.

chisel ['tʃɪzl] n [for wood] formón m, escoplo m; [for stone] cincel m.

chit [tʃɪt] n [note] nota f firmada.

chitchat ['tʃɪttʃæt] n (U) inf cotilleos mpl.

chivalry ['ʃɪvlrɪ] n **-1.** literary [of knights] caballería f. **-2.** [good manners] caballerosidad f.

chives [tʃaɪvz] npl cebollana f.

chlorine ['klɔːriːn] n cloro m.

choc-ice ['tʃɒkaɪs] n Br helado m cubierto de chocolate.

chock [tʃɒk] n cuña f, calzo m.

chock-a-block, chock-full adj inf: ~ (with) hasta los topes (de).

chocolate ['tʃɒkələt] ◇ n **-1.** [food, drink] chocolate m. **-2.** [sweet] bombón m. ◇ comp de chocolate.

choice [tʃɔɪs] ◇ n **-1.** [gen] elección f; to have no ~ but to do sthg no tener más remedio que hacer algo. **-2.** [person chosen] **preferido** m, **-da** f; [thing chosen] **alternativa** f **preferida**. **-3.** [variety, selection] **surtido** m. ◇ adj de primera calidad.

choir ['kwaɪəʳ] n coro m.

choirboy ['kwaɪəbɔɪ] n niño m de coro.

choke [tʃəuk] ◇ n AUT **estárter** m. ◇ vt **-1.** [subj: person, fumes] **asfixiar**; [subj: fishbone etc] **hacer atragantarse**. **-2.** [block - pipes, gutter] **atascar**. ◇ vi [on fishbone etc] **atragantarse**; [to death] **asfixiarse**.

cholera ['kɒlərə] n cólera m.

choose [tʃuːz] (pt **chose**, pp **chosen**) ◇ vt **-1.** [select] **elegir**, **escoger**. **-2.** [decide]: **to ~ to do sthg decidir hacer algo**; **do whatever you ~ haz lo que quieras**. ◇ vi **elegir**, **escoger**.

choos(e)y ['tʃuːzɪ] (compar **-ier**, superl **-iest**) adj [gen] **quisquilloso(sa)**; [about food] **exigente**, **remilgado(da)**.

chop [tʃɒp] ◇ n **-1.** CULIN **chuleta** f. **-2.** [blow - with axe] **hachazo** m. ◇ vt **-1.** [cut up] **cortar**. **-2.** phr: **to ~ and change cambiar cada dos por tres**. ◆ **chops** npl inf **morros** mpl, **jeta** f. ◆ **chop down** vt sep **talar**. ◆ **chop up** vt sep [vegetables, meat] **picar**; [wood] **cortar**.

chopper ['tʃɒpəʳ] n **-1.** [for wood] **hacha** f; [for meat] **cuchillo** m de carnicero. **-2.** inf [helicopter] **helicóptero** m.

choppy ['tʃɒpɪ] adj **picado(da)**.

chopsticks ['tʃɒpstɪks] npl **palillos** mpl.

chord [kɔːd] n MUS **acorde** m.

chore [tʃɔːʳ] n **tarea** f, **faena** f.

chortle ['tʃɔːtl] vi **reírse con satisfacción**.

chorus ['kɔːrəs] n **-1.** [part of song, refrain] **estribillo** m. **-2.** [choir, group of singers or dancers] **coro** m.

chose [tʃəuz] pt → **choose**.

chosen ['tʃəuzn] pp → **choose**.

Christ [kraɪst] n **Cristo** m.

christen ['krɪsn] vt **bautizar**.

christening ['krɪsnɪŋ] n **bautizo** m.

Christian ['krɪstʃən] ◇ adj **cristiano(na)**. ◇ n **cristiano** m, **-na** f.

Christianity [ˌkrɪstɪ'ænətɪ] n **cristianismo** m.

Christian name n **nombre** m de pila.

Christmas ['krɪsməs] n **Navidad** f; **happy** OR **merry ~! ¡Felices Navidades!**

Christmas card n **crismas** m inv.

Christmas Day n **día** m de Navidad.

Christmas Eve n **Nochebuena** f.

Christmas pudding n Br **pudín** de frutas que se come caliente el día de Navidad.

Christmas tree n **árbol** m de Navidad.

chrome [krəum], **chromium** ['krəumɪəm] ◇ n **cromo** m. ◇ comp **cromado(da)**.

chronic ['krɒnɪk] adj **-1.** [illness, unemployment] **crónico(ca)**. **-2.** [liar, alcoholic] **empedernido(da)**.

chronicle ['krɒnɪkl] n **crónica** f.

chronological [ˌkrɒnə'lɒdʒɪkl] adj **cronológico(ca)**.

chrysanthemum [krɪ'sænθəməm] (pl **-s**) n **crisantemo** m.

chubby ['tʃʌbɪ] adj [person, hands] **rechoncho(cha)**; [cheeks] **mofletudo(da)**.

chuck [tʃʌk] vt inf **-1.** [throw] **tirar**, **arrojar**; **to ~ sb out echar a alguien**. **-2.** [job, girlfriend] **dejar**. ◆ **chuck away**, **chuck out** vt sep inf **tirar**.

chuckle ['tʃʌkl] vi **reírse entre dientes**.

chug [tʃʌg] vi [train] **traquetear**; [car] **resoplar**.

chum [tʃʌm] n inf [gen] **amiguete** m, **-ta** f, **manito** m Amer; [at school] **compañero** m, **-ra** f.

chunk [tʃʌŋk] n [piece] **trozo** m.

church [tʃɜːtʃ] n **iglesia** f; **to go to ~ ir a misa**.

Church of England n: **the ~ la Iglesia Anglicana**.

churchyard ['tʃɜːtʃjɑːd] n **cementerio** m, **camposanto** m.

churlish ['tʃɜːlɪʃ] adj **descortés**.

churn [tʃɜːn] ◇ n **-1.** [for making butter] **mantequera** f. **-2.** [for transporting milk] **lechera** f. ◇ vt [stir up] **agitar**. ◆ **churn out** vt sep inf **hacer como churros** OR **en cantidades industriales**.

chute [ʃuːt] n [for water] **vertedor** m; [slide] **tobogán** m; [for waste] **rampa** f.

chutney ['tʃʌtnɪ] n **salsa agridulce y picante de fruta y semillas**.

CIA (abbr of **Central Intelligence Agency**) n **CIA** f.

CID (abbr of **Criminal Investigation Department**) n Br ≃ **Brigada** f de Policía Judicial.

cider ['saɪdəʳ] n **sidra** f.

cigar [sɪ'gɑːʳ] n **puro** m.

cigarette [ˌsɪgə'ret] n **cigarillo** m.

cigarette paper n **papel** m de fumar.

cinch [sɪntʃ] n inf: **it's a ~ está tirado**, **es pan comido**.

cinder ['sɪndəʳ] n **ceniza** f.

Cinderella [ˌsɪndə'relə] n **Cenicienta** f.

cine-camera ['sɪnɪ-] n **cámara** f **cinematográfica**.

cine-film ['sɪnɪ-] n **película** f **cinematográfica**.

cinema ['sɪnəmə] *n* cine *m*, biógrafo *m* Amer.

cinnamon ['sɪnəmən] *n* canela *f*.

cipher ['saɪfəʳ] *n* [secret writing system] código *m*, cifra *f*.

circa ['sɜːkə] *prep* hacia.

circle ['sɜːkl] ◇ *n* -1. [gen] círculo *m*; **to go round in ~s** darle (mil) vueltas al mismo tema. -2. [in theatre] anfiteatro *m*; [in cinema] entresuelo *m*. ◇ *vt* -1. [draw a circle round] rodear con un círculo. -2. [move round] describir círculos alrededor de. ◇ *vi* dar vueltas.

circuit ['sɜːkɪt] *n* -1. [gen] circuito *m*. -2. [of track] vuelta *f*.

circuitous [sə'kjuːɪtəs] *adj* tortuoso(sa).

circular ['sɜːkjələʳ] ◇ *adj* [gen] circular. ◇ *n* circular *f*.

circulate ['sɜːkjuleɪt] ◇ *vi* -1. [gen] circular. -2. [socialize] alternar. ◇ *vt* [rumour, document] hacer circular.

circulation [,sɜːkju'leɪʃn] *n* -1. [of blood, money] circulación *f*. -2. [of magazine, newspaper] tirada *f*.

circumcise ['sɜːkəmsaɪz] *vt* circuncidar.

circumference [sə'kʌmfərəns] *n* circunferencia *f*.

circumspect ['sɜːkəmspekt] *adj* circunspecto(ta).

circumstances ['sɜːkəmstənsɪz] *npl* circunstancias *fpl*; **under** OR **in no ~s** bajo ningún concepto; **in** OR **under the ~** dadas las circunstancias.

circumvent [,sɜːkəm'vent] *vt fml* burlar.

circus ['sɜːkəs] *n* -1. [for entertainment] circo *m*. -2. [in place names] glorieta *f*.

CIS (*abbr of* **Commonwealth of Independent States**) *n* CEI *f*.

cistern ['sɪstən] *n* -1. *Br* [in roof] depósito *m* de agua. -2. [in toilet] cisterna *f*.

cite [saɪt] *vt* citar.

citizen ['sɪtɪzn] *n* ciudadano *m*, -na *f*.

Citizens' Advice Bureau *n* oficina británica de información y asistencia al ciudadano.

Citizens' Band *n* banda de radio reservada para radioaficionados y conductores.

citizenship ['sɪtɪznʃɪp] *n* ciudadanía *f*.

citrus fruit ['sɪtrəs-] *n* cítrico *m*.

city ['sɪtɪ] *n* ciudad *f*. ◆ **City** *n Br:* **the City** la City, *centro financiero de Londres*.

city centre *n* centro *m* de la ciudad.

city hall *n Am* ayuntamiento *m*.

city technology college *n Br* centro de formación profesional financiado por la industria.

civic ['sɪvɪk] *adj* -1. [leader, event] público(ca). -2. [duty, pride] cívico(ca).

civic centre *n Br* zona de la ciudad donde se encuentran los edificios públicos.

civil ['sɪvl] *adj* -1. [involving ordinary citizens] civil. -2. [polite] cortés.

civil engineering *n* ingeniería *f* civil.

civilian [sɪ'vɪljən] ◇ *n* civil *m* y *f*. ◇ *comp* [organization] civil; [clothes] de paisano.

civilization [,sɪvɪlaɪ'zeɪʃn] *n* civilización *f*.

civilized ['sɪvɪlaɪzd] *adj* civilizado(da).

civil law *n* derecho *m* civil.

civil liberties *npl* libertades *fpl* civiles.

civil rights *npl* derechos *mpl* civiles.

civil servant *n* funcionario *m*, -ria *f*.

civil service *n* administración *f* pública.

civil war *n* guerra *f* civil.

clad [klæd] *adj literary:* **~ in** vestido(da) de.

claim [kleɪm] ◇ *n* -1. [for pay, insurance, expenses] reclamación *f*. -2. [of right] reivindicación *f*; **to lay ~ to sthg** reclamar algo. -3. [assertion] afirmación *f*. ◇ *vt* -1. [allowance, expenses, lost property] reclamar. -2. [responsibility, credit] atribuirse. -3. [maintain]: **to ~ (that)** mantener que. ◇ *vi:* **to ~ on one's insurance** reclamar al seguro; **to ~ for sthg** reclamar algo.

claimant ['kleɪmənt] *n* [to throne] pretendiente *m* y *f*; [of unemployment benefit] solicitante *m* y *f*; JUR demandante *m* y *f*.

clairvoyant [kleə'vɔɪənt] *n* clarividente *m* y *f*.

clam [klæm] *n* almeja *f*.

clamber ['klæmbəʳ] *vi* trepar.

clammy ['klæmɪ] *adj* [hands] húmedo(da), pegajoso(sa); [weather] bochornoso(sa).

clamour *Br*, **clamor** *Am* ['klæməʳ] ◇ *n* (U) -1. [noise] clamor *m*. -2. [demand]: **~ (for)** exigencias *fpl* OR demandas *fpl* (de). ◇ *vi:* **to ~ for sthg** exigir a voces algo.

clamp [klæmp] ◇ *n* [gen] abrazadera *f*; [for car wheel] cepo *m*. ◇ *vt* -1. [with clamp] sujetar (con abrazadera). -2. [with wheel clamp] poner un cepo a. ◆ **clamp down** *vi:* **to ~ down on** poner freno a.

clan [klæn] *n* clan *m*.

clandestine [klæn'destɪn] *adj* clandestino(na).

clang [klæŋ] *vi* hacer un ruido metálico.

clap [klæp] ◇ *vt*: **to ~ one's hands** dar palmadas. ◇ *vi* aplaudir.

clapping ['klæpɪŋ] *n* (*U*) aplausos *mpl*.

claret ['klærət] *n* burdeos *m inv*.

clarify ['klærɪfaɪ] *vt* aclarar.

clarinet [,klærə'net] *n* clarinete *m*.

clarity ['klærətɪ] *n* claridad *f*.

clash [klæʃ] ◇ *n* **-1.** [difference - of interests] conflicto *m*; [- of personalities] choque *m*. **-2.** [fight, disagreement]: ~ **(with)** conflicto *m* (con). **-3.** [noise] estruendo *m*. ◇ *vi* **-1.** [fight, disagree]: **to ~ (with)** enfrentarse (con). **-2.** [opinions, policies] estar en desacuerdo. **-3.** [date, event]: **to ~ (with)** coincidir (con). **-4.** [colour]: **to ~ (with)** desentonar (con).

clasp [klɑːsp] ◇ *n* [on necklace, bracelet] broche *m*; [on belt] cierre *m*. ◇ *vt* [person] abrazar (agarrando); [thing] agarrar.

class [klɑːs] ◇ *n* **-1.** [gen] clase *f*. **-2.** [category] clase *f*, tipo *m*. ◇ *vt*: **to ~ sb (as)** clasificar a alguien (de).

classic ['klæsɪk] ◇ *adj* [typical] clásico(ca). ◇ *n* clásico *m*.

classical ['klæsɪkl] *adj* clásico(ca).

classified ['klæsɪfaɪd] *adj* [secret] reservado(da), secreto(ta).

classified ad *n* anuncio *m* por palabras.

classify ['klæsɪfaɪ] *vt* clasificar.

classmate ['klɑːsmeɪt] *n* compañero *m*, -ra *f* de clase.

classroom ['klɑːsrʊm] *n* aula *f*, clase *f*.

classy ['klɑːsɪ] *adj inf* con clase.

clatter ['klætər] *n* [gen] estrépito *m*; [of pots, pans, dishes] ruido *m* (de cacharros); [of hooves] chacoloteo *m*.

clause [klɔːz] *n* **-1.** [in legal document] cláusula *f*. **-2.** GRAMM oración *f*.

claw [klɔː] ◇ *n* **-1.** [of animal, bird] garra *f*; [of cat] uña *f*. **-2.** [of crab, lobster] pinza *f*. ◇ *vi*: **to ~ at sthg** [cat] arañar algo; [person] intentar agarrarse a algo.

clay [kleɪ] *n* arcilla *f*.

clean [kliːn] ◇ *adj* **-1.** [gen] limpio(pia). **-2.** [page] en blanco. **-3.** [record, reputation] impecable; [driving licence] sin multas. **-4.** [joke] inocente. **-5.** [outline] nítido(da); [movement] suelto(ta). ◇ *vt* & *vi* limpiar. ♦ **clean out** *vt sep* **-1.** [clear out] limpiar el interior de. **-2.** *inf* [take everything from]: **they ~ed us out** (los ladrones) nos limpiaron la casa. ♦ **clean up** *vt sep* [clear up] ordenar, limpiar; **to ~ o.s. up** asearse.

cleaner ['kliːnər] *n* **-1.** [person] limpia-

dor *m*, -ra *f*. **-2.** [substance] producto *m* de limpieza.

cleaning ['kliːnɪŋ] *n* limpieza *f*.

cleanliness ['klenlɪnɪs] *n* limpieza *f*.

cleanse [klenz] *vt* [gen] limpiar; [soul] purificar; **to ~ sthg/sb of sthg** limpiar algo/a alguien de algo.

cleanser ['klenzər] *n* crema *f* OR loción *f* limpiadora.

clean-shaven [-'ʃeɪvn] *adj* [never growing a beard] barbilampiño(ña); [recently shaved] bien afeitado(da).

clear [klɪər] ◇ *adj* **-1.** [gen] claro(ra); [day, road, view] despejado(da); **to make sthg ~ (to)** dejar algo claro (a); **it's ~ that ...** está claro que ...; **are you ~ about it?** ¿lo entiendes?; **to make o.s. ~** explicarse con claridad. **-2.** [transparent] transparente. **-3.** [free of blemishes - skin] terso(sa). **-4.** [free - time] libre. **-5.** [complete - day, week] entero(ra); [- profit, wages] neto(ta). ◇ *adv* [out of the way]: **stand ~!** ¡aléjate!; **to jump/step ~** saltar/dar un paso para hacerse a un lado. ◇ *vt* **-1.** [remove objects, obstacles from] despejar; [pipe] desatascar; **to ~ sthg of sthg** quitar algo de algo; **to ~ a space** hacer sitio; **to ~ the table** quitar la mesa. **-2.** [remove] quitar. **-3.** [jump] saltar. **-4.** [pay] liquidar. **-5.** [authorize] aprobar. **-6.** [prove not guilty] declarar inocente, **to be ~ed of sthg** salir absuelto de algo. ◇ *vi* despejarse. ♦ **clear away** *vt sep* poner en su sitio. ♦ **clear off** *vi Br inf* largarse. ♦ **clear out** *vt sep* limpiar a fondo. ♦ **clear up** ◇ *vt sep* **-1.** [room, mess] limpiar; [toys, books] ordenar. **-2.** [mystery, disagreement] aclarar, resolver. ◇ *vi* **-1.** [weather] despejarse; [infection] desaparecer. **-2.** [tidy up] ordenar, recoger.

clearance ['klɪərəns] *n* **-1.** [removal - of rubbish, litter] despeje *m*, limpieza *f*; [of slums, houses] eliminación *f*. **-2.** [permission] autorización *f*, permiso *m*. **-3.** [free space] distancia *f* de seguridad.

clear-cut *adj* [issue, plan] bien definido(da); [division] nítido(da).

clearing ['klɪərɪŋ] *n* claro *m*.

clearing bank *n Br* banco asociado a la cámara de compensación.

clearly ['klɪəlɪ] *adv* **-1.** [gen] claramente. **-2.** [plainly] obviamente.

clearway ['klɪəweɪ] *n Br* carretera donde no se puede parar.

cleavage ['kliːvɪdʒ] *n* [between breasts] escote *m*.

cleaver ['kli:vər] n cuchillo m OR cuchilla f de carnicero.

clef [klef] n clave f.

cleft [kleft] n grieta f.

clench [klentʃ] vt apretar.

clergy ['klɜ:dʒɪ] npl: **the ~** el clero.

clergyman ['klɜ:dʒɪmən] (pl **-men** [-mən]) n clérigo m.

clerical ['klerɪkl] adj **-1.** [in office] de oficina. **-2.** [in church] clerical.

clerk [Br klɑ:k, Am klɜ:rk] n **-1.** [in office] oficinista m y f. **-2.** [in court] secretario m. **-3.** Am [shop assistant] dependiente m, -ta f.

clever ['klevər] adj **-1.** [intelligent] listo(ta), inteligente. **-2.** [idea, invention] ingenioso(sa); [with hands] hábil.

cliché ['kli:ʃeɪ] n cliché m.

click [klɪk] ◇ vt chasquear. ◇ vi **-1.** [heels] sonar con un taconazo; [camera] hacer clic. **-2.** inf [fall into place]: **suddenly, it ~ed (with me)** de pronto, caí en la cuenta.

client ['klaɪənt] n cliente m, -ta f.

cliff [klɪf] n [on coast] acantilado m; [inland] precipicio m.

climate ['klaɪmɪt] n [weather] clima m; fig [atmosphere] ambiente m.

climax ['klaɪmæks] n [culmination] clímax m, culminación f.

climb [klaɪm] ◇ n escalada f. ◇ vt [stairs, ladder] subir; [tree] trepar a; [mountain] escalar. ◇ vi **-1.** [clamber]: to **~ over sthg** trepar por algo; to **~ into sthg** subirse a algo. **-2.** [plant] trepar; [road, plane] subir. **-3.** [increase] subir.

climb-down n rectificación f.

climber ['klaɪmər] n [mountaineer] escalador m, -ra f.

climbing ['klaɪmɪŋ] n montañismo m.

clinch [klɪntʃ] vt [deal] cerrar.

cling [klɪŋ] (pt & pp clung) vi **-1.** [hold tightly]: to **~ (to)** agarrarse (a). **-2.** [clothes, person]: to **~ (to sb)** pegarse (a alguien).

clingfilm ['klɪŋfɪlm] n Br film m de plástico adherente.

clinic ['klɪnɪk] n clínica f.

clinical ['klɪnɪkl] adj **-1.** MED clínico(ca). **-2.** [cold] frío(a).

clink [klɪŋk] vi tintinear.

clip [klɪp] ◇ n **-1.** [for paper] clip m; [for hair] horquilla f; [on earring] cierre m. **-2.** [of film] fragmento m, secuencias fpl. ◇ vt **-1.** [fasten] sujetar. **-2.** [cut - lawn, newspaper cutting] recortar; [punch - tickets] picar.

clipboard ['klɪpbɔ:d] n tabloncillo m con pinza sujetapapeles.

clippers ['klɪpəz] npl [for nails] cortaúñas m inv; [for hair] maquinilla f para cortar el pelo; [for hedges, grass] tijeras fpl de podar.

clipping ['klɪpɪŋ] n **-1.** [from newspaper] recorte m. **-2.** [of nails] corte m.

clique [kli:k] n pej camarilla f.

cloak [kləuk] n [garment] capa f, manto m.

cloakroom ['kləukrum] n **-1.** [for clothes] guardarropa m. **-2.** Br [toilets] servicios mpl.

clock [klɒk] n **-1.** [timepiece] reloj m; **round the ~** día y noche, las 24 horas. **-2.** [mileometer] cuentakilómetros m inv. ◆ **clock in, clock on** vi Br fichar (a la entrada). ◆ **clock off, clock out** vi Br fichar (a la salida).

clockwise ['klɒkwaɪz] adj & adv en el sentido de las agujas del reloj.

clockwork ['klɒkwɜ:k] comp de cuerda.

clog [klɒg] vt atascar, obstruir. ◆ **clogs** npl zuecos mpl. ◆ **clog up** ◇ vt sep [drain, pipe] atascar; [eyes, nose] congestionar. ◇ vi atascarse.

close¹ [kləus] ◇ adj **-1.** [near] cercano(na); **~ to** cerca de; **~ to tears/laughter** a punto de llorar/reír; **~ up, ~ to** de cerca; **~ by, ~ at hand** muy cerca; **it was a ~ shave** OR **thing** OR **call** nos libramos por los pelos. **-2.** [relationship, friend] íntimo(ma); **to be ~ to sb** estar muy unido(a) a alguien. **-3.** [relative, family] cercano(na); [resemblance] grande; [link, tie, cooperation] estrecho(cha). **-4.** [questioning] minucioso(sa); [examination] detallado(da); [look] de cerca; [watch] estrecho(cha). **-5.** [room, air] cargado(da); [weather] bochornoso(sa). **-6.** [contest, race] reñido(da); [result] apretado(da). ◇ adv cerca. ◆ **close on, close to** prep [almost] cerca de.

close² [kləuz] ◇ vt **-1.** [gen] cerrar. **-2.** [meeting] clausurar; [discussion, speech] terminar. ◇ vi cerrarse. ◇ n final m. ◆ **close down** ◇ vt sep cerrar (definitivamente). ◇ vi [factory etc] cerrarse (definitivamente).

closed [kləuzd] adj cerrado(da).

close-knit [,kləus-] adj muy unido(da).

closely ['kləuslɪ] adv **-1.** [of connection, relation etc] estrechamente; **to be ~ involved in sthg** estar muy metido en algo; [of resemblance] fielmente. **-2.** [carefully] atentamente.

closet ['klɒzɪt] ◇ *adj inf* en secreto. ◇ *n Am* armario *m*.

close-up ['kləʊs-] *n* primer plano *m*.

closing time *n* hora *f* de cierre.

closure ['kləʊʒə*r*] *n* cierre *m*.

clot [klɒt] ◇ *n* **-1.** [in blood] coágulo *m*; [in liquid] grumo *m*. **-2.** *Br inf* [fool] bobo *m*, -ba *f*. ◇ *vi* [blood] coagularse.

cloth [klɒθ] *n* **-1.** (U) [fabric] tela *f*. **-2.** [piece of cloth] trapo *m*.

clothe [kləʊð] *vt fml* vestir.

clothes [kləʊðz] *npl* ropa *f*; **to put one's ~ on** vestirse; **to take one's ~ off** quitarse la ropa.

clothes brush *n* cepillo *m* para la ropa.

clothesline ['kləʊðzlaɪn] *n* cuerda *f* para tender la ropa.

clothes peg *Br*, **clothespin** *Am* ['kləʊðzpɪn] *n* pinza *f* (para la ropa).

clothing ['kləʊðɪŋ] *n* ropa *f*.

cloud [klaʊd] *n* nube *f*. ◆ **cloud over** *vi lit* & *fig* nublarse.

cloudy ['klaʊdɪ] *adj* **-1.** [overcast] nublado(da). **-2.** [murky] turbio(bia).

clout [klaʊt] *inf n* **-1.** [blow] tortazo *m*. **-2.** (U) [influence] influencia *f*.

clove [kləʊv] *n*: **a ~ of garlic** un diente de ajo. ◆ **cloves** *npl* [spice] clavos *mpl*.

clover ['kləʊvə*r*] *n* trébol *m*.

clown [klaʊn] ◇ *n* [performer] payaso *m*. ◇ *vi* hacer payasadas.

cloying ['klɔɪɪŋ] *adj* empalagoso(sa).

club [klʌb] ◇ *n* **-1.** [organization, place] club *m*. **-2.** [weapon] porra *f*, garrote *m*. **-3.** (golf) ~ palo *m* de golf. ◇ *vt* apalear, aporrear. ◆ **clubs** *npl* [cards] tréboles *mpl*. ◆ **club together** *vi Br* recolectar dinero.

club car *n Am* RAIL vagón *m* restaurante.

clubhouse ['klʌbhaʊs, *pl* -haʊzɪz] *n* [for golfers] (edificio *m* del) club *m*.

cluck [klʌk] *vi* [hen] cloquear.

clue [kluː] *n* **-1.** [in crime] pista *f*; **not to have a ~ (about)** no tener ni idea (de). **-2.** [in crossword] pregunta *f*, clave *f*.

clued-up [kluːd-] *adj Br inf* al tanto.

clump [klʌmp] *n* [of bushes] mata *f*; [of trees, flowers] grupo *m*.

clumsy ['klʌmzɪ] *adj* **-1.** [ungraceful] torpe. **-2.** [unwieldy] difícil de manejar. **-3.** [tactless] torpe, sin tacto.

clung [klʌŋ] *pt* & *pt* → **cling**.

cluster ['klʌstə*r*] ◇ *n* [group] grupo *m*; [of grapes] racimo *m*. ◇ *vi* agruparse.

clutch [klʌtʃ] ◇ *n* AUT embrague *m*. ◇ *vt* [hand] estrechar; [arm, baby] agarrar.

◇ *vi*: **to ~ at sthg** tratar de agarrarse a algo.

clutter ['klʌtə*r*] ◇ *n* desorden *m*. ◇ *vt* cubrir desordenadamente.

cm (*abbr of* **centimetre**) cm.

CND (*abbr of* **Campaign for Nuclear Disarmament**) *n* organización británica *contra el armamento nuclear*.

c/o (*abbr of* **care of**) c/d.

Co. **-1.** (*abbr of* **Company**) Cía. **-2.** *abbr of* **County**.

coach [kəʊtʃ] ◇ *n* **-1.** [bus] autocar *m*. **-2.** RAIL coche *m*, vagón *m*. **-3.** [horse-drawn] carruaje *m*. **-4.** SPORT entrenador *m*, -ra *f*. **-5.** [tutor] profesor *m*, -ra *f* particular. ◇ *vt* **-1.** SPORT entrenar. **-2.** [tutor] dar clases particulares a.

coal [kəʊl] *n* carbón *m*.

coalfield ['kəʊlfiːld] *n* cuenca *f* minera.

coalition [ˌkəʊə'lɪʃn] *n* coalición *f*.

coalman ['kəʊlmæn] (*pl* **-men** [-men]) *n Br* carbonero *m*.

coalmine ['kəʊlmaɪn] *n* mina *f* de carbón.

coarse [kɔːs] *adj* **-1.** [skin, hair, sandpaper] áspero(ra); [fabric] basto(ta). **-2.** [person, joke] ordinario(ria).

coast [kəʊst] ◇ *n* costa *f*. ◇ *vi* **-1.** [in car] ir en punto muerto. **-2.** [progress easily] ir holgadamente OR sin esfuerzos.

coastal ['kəʊstl] *adj* costero(ra).

coaster ['kəʊstə*r*] *n* [small mat] posavasos *m inv*.

coastguard ['kəʊstgɑːd] *n* [person] guardacostas *m* y *f inv*.

coastline ['kəʊstlaɪn] *n* litoral *m*.

coat [kəʊt] ◇ *n* **-1.** [garment] abrigo *m*. **-2.** [of animal] pelo *m*, pelaje *m*. **-3.** [layer] capa *f*. ◇ *vt*: **to ~ sthg (with)** cubrir algo (de).

coat hanger *n* percha *f*.

coating ['kəʊtɪŋ] *n* [of dust etc] capa *f*; [of chocolate, silver] baño *m*.

coat of arms (*pl* **coats of arms**) *n* escudo *m* de armas.

coax [kəʊks] *vt*: **to ~ sb (to do** OR **into doing sthg)** engatusar a alguien (para que haga algo).

cob [kɒb] *n* → **corn**.

cobbled ['kɒbld] *adj* adoquinado(da).

cobbler ['kɒblə*r*] *n* zapatero (remendón) *m*, zapatera (remendona) *f*.

cobbles ['kɒblz], **cobblestones** ['kɒblstəʊnz] *npl* adoquines *mpl*.

cobweb ['kɒbweb] *n* telaraña *f*.

Coca-Cola® [ˌkəʊkə'kəʊlə] *n* Coca-Cola® *f*.

cocaine [kəʊ'keɪn] *n* cocaína *f*.
cock [kɒk] ◇ *n* -1. [male chicken] gallo *m*. -2. [male bird] macho *m*. ◇ *vt* -1. [gun] amartillar. -2. [head] ladear.
◆ **cock up** *vt sep Br v inf* jorobar.
cockerel ['kɒkrəl] *n* gallo *m* joven.
cockeyed ['kɒkaɪd] *adj inf* -1. [lopsided] torcido(da). -2. [foolish] disparatado(da).
cockle ['kɒkl] *n* berberecho *m*.
Cockney ['kɒknɪ] (*pl* **Cockneys**) *n* -1. [person] cockney *m y f*, persona procedente del este de Londres. -2. [dialect, accent] cockney *m*, dialecto del este de Londres.
cockpit ['kɒkpɪt] *n* [in plane] cabina *f*.
cockroach ['kɒkrəʊtʃ] *n* cucaracha *f*.
cocksure [ˌkɒk'ʃʊəʳ] *adj* presuntuoso(sa).
cocktail ['kɒkteɪl] *n* cóctel *m*.
cock-up *n v inf* chapuza *f*, pifia *f*.
cocky ['kɒkɪ] *adj inf* chulo(la), chuleta.
cocoa ['kəʊkəʊ] *n* -1. [powder] cacao *m*. -2. [drink] chocolate *m*.
coconut ['kəʊkənʌt] *n* coco *m*.
cod [kɒd] (*pl inv* OR **-s**) *n* bacalao *m*.
COD (*abbr of* **cash on delivery**) *contra reembolso*, ≃ CAE.
code [kəʊd] ◇ *n* -1. [gen] código *m*. -2. [for telephone] prefijo *m*. ◇ *vt* [encode] codificar, cifrar.
cod-liver oil *n* aceite *m* de hígado de bacalao.
coed [ˌkəʊ'ed] *adj* (*abbr of* **coeducational**) mixto(ta).
coerce [kəʊ'ɜːs] *vt*: **to ~ sb (into doing sthg)** coaccionar a alguien (para que haga algo).
coffee ['kɒfɪ] *n* café *m*.
coffee bar *n Br* cafetería *f*.
coffee break *n* pausa para descansar en el trabajo por la mañana y por la tarde.
coffee morning *n Br* reunión matinal, generalmente benéfica, en la que se sirve café.
coffeepot ['kɒfɪpɒt] *n* cafetera *f*.
coffee shop *n* -1. *Br* [shop] cafetería *f*. -2. *Am* [restaurant] café *m*.
coffee table *n* mesita *f* baja (de salón).
coffin ['kɒfɪn] *n* ataúd *m*.
cog [kɒg] *n* [tooth on wheel] diente *m*; [wheel] rueda *f* dentada.
cognac ['kɒnjæk] *n* coñac *m*.
coherent [kəʊ'hɪərənt] *adj* coherente.
cohesive [kəʊ'hiːsɪv] *adj* unido(da).
coil [kɔɪl] ◇ *n* -1. [of rope, wire] rollo *m*; [of hair] tirabuzón *m*; [of smoke] espiral *f*. -2. ELEC bobina *f*. -3. *Br* [contraceptive device] DIU *m*, espiral *m*. ◇ *vi* enrollar-

se, enroscarse. ◇ *vt* enrollar, enroscar.
◆ **coil up** *vt sep* enrollar.
coin [kɔɪn] ◇ *n* moneda *f*. ◇ *vt* [invent] acuñar, inventar.
coinage ['kɔɪnɪdʒ] *n* [currency] moneda *f*.
coin-box *n Br* teléfono *m* público.
coincide [ˌkəʊɪn'saɪd] *vi*: **to ~ (with)** coincidir (con).
coincidence [kəʊ'ɪnsɪdəns] *n* coincidencia *f*.
coincidental [kəʊˌɪnsɪ'dentl] *adj* fortuito(ta).
coke [kəʊk] *n* [fuel] coque *m*.
Coke® [kəʊk] *n* Coca-Cola® *f*.
cola ['kəʊlə] *n* (bebida *f* de) cola *f*.
colander ['kʌləndəʳ] *n* colador *m*, escurridor *m*.
cold [kəʊld] ◇ *adj* frío(a); **it's ~** hace frío; **my hands are ~** tengo las manos frías; **I'm ~** tengo frío; **to get ~** enfriarse. ◇ *n* -1. [illness] resfriado *m*, constipado *m*; **to catch (a) ~** resfriarse, coger un resfriado. -2. [low temperature] frío *m*.
cold-blooded [-'blʌdɪd] *adj* -1. [animal] de sangre fría. -2. [person] despiadado(da); [killing] a sangre fría.
cold sore *n* calentura *f*, pupa *f*.
cold war *n*: **the ~** la guerra fría.
coleslaw ['kəʊlslɔː] *n* ensalada de col, zanahoria, cebolla y mayonesa.
colic ['kɒlɪk] *n* cólico *m*.
collaborate [kə'læbəreɪt] *vi*: **to ~ (with)** colaborar (con).
collapse [kə'læps] ◇ *n* -1. [of building] derrumbamiento *m*; [of roof] hundimiento *m*. -2. [of marriage, system] fracaso *m*; [of government, currency] caída *f*; [of empire] derrumbamiento *m*. -3. MED colapso *m*. ◇ *vi* -1. [building, person] derrumbarse; [roof] hundirse; **to ~ with laughter** partirse de risa. -2. [plan, business] venirse abajo. -3. MED sufrir un colapso.
collapsible [kə'læpsəbl] *adj* plegable.
collar ['kɒləʳ] *n* -1. [on clothes] cuello *m*. -2. [for dog] collar *m*. -3. TECH collar *m*.
collarbone ['kɒləbəʊn] *n* clavícula *f*.
collate [kə'leɪt] *vt* -1. [compare] cotejar. -2. [put in order] poner en orden.
collateral [kɒ'lætərəl] *n* garantía *f* subsidiaria, seguridad *f* colateral.
colleague ['kɒliːg] *n* colega *m y f*.
collect [kə'lekt] ◇ *vt* -1. [gather together] reunir, juntar; **to ~ o.s.** recobrar el dominio de sí mismo. -2. [as a hobby] coleccionar. -3. [go to get - person, par-

cel] recoger. -4. [money, taxes] recaudar. ◇ vi -1. [gather] congregarse, reunirse. -2. [accumulate] acumularse. -3. [for charity, gift] hacer una colecta. ◇ adv Am TELEC: **to call (sb)** ~ llamar (a alguien) a cobro revertido.

collection [kə'lekʃn] n -1. [of stamps, art etc] colección f. -2. [of poems, stories etc] recopilación f. -3. [of rubbish, mail] recogida f; [of taxes] recaudación f. -4. [of money] colecta f.

collective [kə'lektɪv] ◇ adj colectivo(va). ◇ n colectivo m.

collector [kə'lektər] n -1. [as a hobby] coleccionista m y f. -2. [of taxes] recaudador m, -ra f. -3. [of debts, rent] cobrador m, -ra f.

college ['kɒlɪdʒ] n -1. [for further education] instituto m, escuela f. -2. [of university] colegio universitario que forma parte de ciertas universidades. -3. [organized body] colegio m.

college of education n escuela de formación de profesores de enseñanza primaria y secundaria.

collide [kə'laɪd] vi: **to** ~ **(with)** [gen] chocar (con); [vehicles] colisionar OR chocar (con).

collie ['kɒlɪ] n collie m.

colliery ['kɒljərɪ] n mina f de carbón.

collision [kə'lɪʒn] n lit & fig: ~ **(with/between)** choque m (con/entre), colisión f (con/entre).

colloquial [kə'ləukwɪəl] adj coloquial.

collude [kə'luːd] vi: **to** ~ **with** estar en connivencia con.

Colombia [kə'lɒmbɪə] n Colombia.

Colombian [kə'lɒmbɪən] ◇ adj colombiano(na). ◇ n colombiano m, -na f.

colon ['kəulən] n -1. ANAT colon m. -2. [punctuation mark] dos puntos mpl.

colonel ['kɜːnl] n coronel m y f.

colonial [kə'ləunjəl] adj colonial.

colonize, -ise ['kɒlənaɪz] vt colonizar.

colony ['kɒlənɪ] n colonia f.

color etc Am = **colour** etc.

colossal [kə'lɒsl] adj colosal.

colour Br, **color** Am ['kʌlər] ◇ n color m; **in** ~ en color. ◇ adj en color. ◇ vt -1. [give colour to] dar color a; [with pen, crayon] colorear. -2. [dye] teñir. -3. [affect] influenciar. ◇ vi [blush] ruborizarse.

colour bar n discriminación f racial.

colour-blind adj daltónico(ca).

coloured Br, **colored** Am ['kʌləd] adj -1. [pens, sheets etc] de colores. -2. [with stated colour]: **maroon-**~ de color

granate; **brightly-**~ de vivos colores. -3. [person - black] de color.

colourful Br, **colorful** Am ['kʌləful] adj -1. [brightly coloured] de vivos colores. -2. [story] animado(da). -3. [person] pintoresco(ca).

colouring Br, **coloring** Am ['kʌlərɪŋ] n -1. [dye] colorante m. -2. [complexion, hair] tez f. -3. [of animal's skin] color m.

colour scheme n combinación f de colores.

colt [kəult] n potro m.

column ['kɒləm] n -1. [gen] columna f. -2. [of people, vehicles] hilera f.

columnist ['kɒləmnɪst] n columnista m y f.

coma ['kəumə] n coma m.

comb [kəum] ◇ n peine m. ◇ vt lit & fig peinar.

combat ['kɒmbæt] ◇ n combate m. ◇ vt combatir.

combination [ˌkɒmbɪ'neɪʃn] n combinación f.

combine [vb kəm'baɪn, n 'kɒmbaɪn] ◇ vt: **to** ~ **sthg (with)** combinar algo (con). ◇ vi combinarse. ◇ n -1. [group] grupo m. -2. = **combine harvester**.

combine harvester [-'hɑːvɪstər] n cosechadora f.

come [kʌm] (pt **came**, pp **come**) vi -1. [move] venir; [arrive] llegar; **the news came as a shock** la noticia constituyó un duro golpe; **coming!** ¡ahora voy! -2. [reach]: **to** ~ **up/down to** llegar hasta. -3. [happen] pasar; ~ **what may** pase lo que pase. -4. [become]: **to** ~ **true** hacerse realidad; **to** ~ **unstuck** despegarse; **my shoelaces have** ~ **undone** se me han desatado los cordones. -5. [begin gradually]: **to** ~ **to do sthg** llegar a hacer algo. -6. [be placed in order]: **to** ~ **first/last in a race** llegar el primero/el último en una carrera; **she came second in the exam** quedó segunda en el examen; **P** ~**s before Q** la P viene antes de la Q. ◆ **to come** adv: **in (the) days/years to** ~ en días/años venideros. ◆ **come about** vi [happen] pasar, ocurrir. ◆ **come across** vt fus [find] cruzarse con. ◆ **come along** vi -1. [arrive by chance - opportunity] surgir; [- bus] aparecer, llegar. -2. [improve] ir; **the project is coming along nicely** el proyecto va muy bien. ◆ **come apart** vi deshacerse. ◆ **come back** vi -1. [in talk, writing]: **to** ~ **back to sthg** volver a algo. -2. [memory]: **to** ~ **back to sb** volverle a la memoria a alguien. ◆ **come**

by vt fus [get, obtain] conseguir. ◆ **come down** vi -1. [decrease] bajar. -2. [descend - plane, parachutist] aterrizar; [- rain] caer. ◆ **come down to** vt fus reducirse a. ◆ **come down with** vt fus coger, agarrar (enfermedad). ◆ **come forward** vi presentarse. ◆ **come from** vt fus [noise etc] venir de; [person] ser de. ◆ **come in** vi -1. [enter] entrar, pasar; ~ in! ¡pase! -2. [arrive - train, letters, donations] llegar. ◆ **come in for** vt fus [criticism etc] recibir, llevarse. ◆ **come into** vt fus -1. [inherit] heredar. -2. [begin to be]: **to ~ into being** nacer, ver la luz. ◆ **come off** vi -1. [button] descoserse; [label] despegarse; [lid] soltarse; [stain] quitarse. -2. [plan, joke] salir bien. -3. phr: ~ **off it!** inf ¡venga ya! ◆ **come on** vi -1. [start] empezar. -2. [start working - lights, heating] encenderse. -3. [progress, improve] ir; **it's coming on nicely** va muy bien. -4. phr: ~ **on!** [expressing encouragement, urging haste] ¡vamos!; [expressing disbelief] ¡venga ya! ◆ **come out** vi -1. [become known] salir a la luz. -2. [appear - product, book, sun] salir; [- film] estrenarse. -3. [go on strike] ponerse en huelga. ◆ **come over** vt fus [subj: feeling] sobrevenir; **I don't know what has ~ over her** no sé qué le pasa. ◆ **come round** vi -1. [change opinion]: **to ~ round (to sthg)** terminar por aceptar (algo). -2. [regain consciousness] volver en sí. ◆ **come through** vt fus [difficult situation, period] pasar por; [operation, war] sobrevivir a. ◆ **come to** ◇ vt fus -1. [reach]: **to ~ to an end** tocar a su fin; **to ~ to a decision** alcanzar una decisión. -2. [amount to] ascender a. ◇ vi [regain consciousness] volver en sí. ◆ **come under** vt fus -1. [be governed by] **estar bajo.** -2. [suffer]: **to ~ under attack** ser víctima de críticas. ◆ **come up** vi -1. [name, topic, opportunity] surgir. -2. [be imminent] estar al llegar. -3. [sun, moon] salir. ◆ **come up against** vt fus tropezarse OR toparse con. ◆ **come up with** vt fus [idea] salir con; [solution] encontrar.

comeback ['kʌmbæk] n [return] reaparición f; **to make a ~** [fashion] volver (a ponerse de moda); [actor] hacer una reaparición.

comedian [kə'miːdjən] n cómico m.

comedown ['kʌmdaʊn] n inf desilusión f, decepción f.

comedy ['kɒmədɪ] n comedia f.

comet ['kɒmɪt] n cometa m.

come-uppance [ˌkʌm'ʌpəns] n: **to get one's ~** inf llevarse uno su merecido.

comfort ['kʌmfət] ◇ n -1. [gen] comodidad f. -2. [solace] consuelo m. ◇ vt consolar, confortar.

comfortable ['kʌmftəbl] adj -1. [gen] cómodo(da). -2. [financially secure] acomodado(da). -3. [victory, job, belief] fácil; [lead, majority] amplio(plia).

comfortably ['kʌmftəblɪ] adv -1. [sit, sleep] cómodamente. -2. [without financial difficulty] sin aprietos. -3. [easily] fácilmente.

comfort station n Am euphemism aseos mpl públicos.

comic ['kɒmɪk] ◇ adj cómico(ca). ◇ n -1. [comedian] cómico m, -ca f. -2. [magazine - for children] tebeo m; [- for adults] cómic m.

comical ['kɒmɪkl] adj cómico(ca).

comic strip n tira f cómica.

coming ['kʌmɪŋ] ◇ adj [future] próximo(ma). ◇ n: **~s and goings** idas fpl y venidas.

comma ['kɒmə] n coma f.

command [kə'mɑːnd] ◇ n -1. [order] orden f. -2. (U) [control] mando m. -3. [of language, skill] dominio m. -4. COMPUT comando m. ◇ vt -1. [order]: **to ~ sb (to do sthg)** ordenar OR mandar a alguien (que haga algo). -2. MIL [control] comandar. -3. [deserve - respect, attention] hacerse acreedor(ra) de.

commandeer [ˌkɒmən'dɪəʳ] vt requisar.

commander [kə'mɑːndəʳ] n -1. [in army] comandante m y f. -2. [in navy] capitán m, -ana f de fragata.

commandment [kə'mɑːndmənt] n RELIG mandamiento m.

commando [kə'mɑːndəʊ] (pl -s OR -es) n comando m.

commemorate [kə'meməreɪt] vt conmemorar.

commemoration [kəˌmemə'reɪʃn] n conmemoración f.

commence [kə'mens] fml ◇ vt: **to ~ (doing sthg)** comenzar OR empezar (a hacer algo). ◇ vi comenzar, empezar.

commend [kə'mend] vt -1. [praise] alabar. -2. [recommend]: **to ~ sthg (to)** recomendar algo (a).

commensurate [kə'menʃərət] adj fml: ~ **with** acorde OR en proporción con.

comment ['kɒment] ◇ n comentario m; **no ~** sin comentarios. ◇ vi comentar; **to ~ on** hacer comentarios sobre.

commentary ['kɒməntrɪ] n comentario m.

commentator ['kɒmənteɪtə'] *n* comentarista *m y f*.

commerce ['kɒmɜːs] *n* (U) comercio *m*.

commercial [kə'mɜːʃl] ◇ *adj* comercial. ◇ *n* anuncio *m* (*televisivo o radiofónico*).

commercial break *n* pausa *f* para la publicidad.

commiserate [kə'mɪzəreɪt] *vi*: **to ~ (with)** compadecerse (de).

commission [kə'mɪʃn] ◇ *n* **-1.** [money, investigative body] comisión *f*. **-2.** [piece of work] encargo *m*. ◇ *vt* encargar; **to ~ sb (to do sthg)** encargar a alguien (que haga algo).

commissionaire [kə,mɪʃə'neə'] *n* Br portero *m* (uniformado).

commissioner [kə'mɪʃnə'] *n* comisario *m*, -ria *f*.

commit [kə'mɪt] *vt* **-1.** [crime, sin etc] cometer. **-2.** [pledge - money, resources] destinar; **to ~ o.s. (to)** comprometerse (a). **-3.** [consign - to mental hospital] ingresar; **to ~ sthg to memory** aprender algo de memoria.

commitment [kə'mɪtmənt] *n* compromiso *m*.

committee [kə'mɪtɪ] *n* comisión *f*, comité *m*.

commodity [kə'mɒdətɪ] *n* mercancía *f*, producto *m*.

common ['kɒmən] ◇ *adj* **-1.** [gen]: ~ **(to)** común (a). **-2.** [ordinary - man, woman] corriente, de la calle. **-3.** Br pej [vulgar] vulgar, ordinario(ria). ◇ *n* campo *m* común. ◆ **in common** *adv* en común.

common law *n* derecho *m* consuetudinario. ◆ **common-law** *adj* [wife, husband] de hecho.

commonly ['kɒmənlɪ] *adv* generalmente, comúnmente.

Common Market *n*: **the ~** el Mercado Común.

commonplace ['kɒmənpleɪs] *adj* corriente, común.

common room *n* sala *f* de estudiantes.

Commons ['kɒmənz] *npl* Br: **the ~** (la Cámara de) los Comunes.

common sense *n* sentido *m* común.

Commonwealth ['kɒmənwelθ] *n*: **the ~** la Commonwealth.

Commonwealth of Independent States *n*: **the ~** la Comunidad de Estados Independientes.

commotion [kə'məʊʃn] *n* alboroto *m*.

communal ['kɒmjʊnl] *adj* comunal.

commune [*n* 'kɒmjuːn, *vb* kə'mjuːn] ◇ *n* comuna *f*. ◇ *vi*: **to ~ with** estar en comunión OR comulgar con.

communicate [kə'mjuːnɪkeɪt] ◇ *vt* transmitir, comunicar. ◇ *vi*: **to ~ (with)** comunicarse (con).

communication [kə,mjuːnɪ'keɪʃn] *n* **-1.** [contact] comunicación *f*. **-2.** [letter, phone call] comunicado *m*.

communication cord *n* Br alarma *f* (*de un tren o metro*).

communion [kə'mjuːnjən] *n* [communication] comunión *f*. ◆ **Communion** *n* (U) RELIG comunión *f*.

communiqué [kə'mjuːnɪkeɪ] *n* comunicado *m* oficial.

Communism ['kɒmjʊnɪzm] *n* comunismo *m*.

Communist ['kɒmjʊnɪst] ◇ *adj* comunista. ◇ *n* comunista *m y f*.

community [kə'mjuːnətɪ] *n* comunidad *f*.

community centre *n* centro *m* social.

community charge *n* Br impuesto municipal pagado por todos los adultos, ≃ contribución *f* urbana.

commutation ticket [,kɒmjuː'teɪʃn-] *n* Am billete *m* de abono.

commute [kə'mjuːt] ◇ *vt* JUR conmutar. ◇ *vi* [to work] viajar diariamente al lugar de trabajo, esp en tren.

commuter [kə'mjuːtə'] *n* persona que viaja diariamente al lugar de trabajo, esp en tren.

compact [*adj* kəm'pækt, *n* 'kɒmpækt] ◇ *adj* [small and neat] compacto(ta). ◇ *n* **-1.** [for face powder] polvera *f*. **-2.** Am [car] utilitario *m*.

compact disc *n* compact disc *m*.

compact disc player *n* compact *m* (disc), reproductor *m* de discos compactos.

companion [kəm'pænjən] *n* compañero *m*, -ra *f*.

companionship [kəm'pænjənʃɪp] *n* compañerismo *m*.

company ['kʌmpənɪ] *n* [gen] compañía *f*; [business] empresa *f*, compañía *f*; **to keep sb ~** hacer compañía a alguien; **to part ~ (with)** separarse (de).

company secretary *n* ejecutivo de una empresa encargado de llevar las cuentas, asuntos legales etc.

comparable ['kɒmprəbl] *adj*: ~ **(to** OR **with)** comparable (a).

comparative [kəm'pærətɪv] *adj* **-1.** [relative] relativo(va). **-2.** [study] comparado(da). **-3.** GRAMM comparativo(va).

comparatively [kəm'pærətɪvlɪ] *adv* relativamente.

compare [kəm'peəʳ] ◇ *vt*: **to ~ sthg/sb (with), to ~ sthg/sb (to)** comparar algo/a alguien (con); **~d with** OR **to** [as opposed to] comparado con; [in comparison with] en comparación con. ◇ *vi*: **to ~ (with)** compararse (con).

comparison [kəm'pærɪsn] *n* comparación *f*; **in ~ (with** OR **to)** en comparación (con).

compartment [kəm'pɑːtmənt] *n* **-1.** [container] compartimento *m*. **-2.** RAIL departamento *m*, compartimento *m*.

compass ['kʌmpəs] *n* [magnetic] brújula *f*. ◆ **compasses** *npl* compás *m*.

compassion [kəm'pæʃn] *n* compasión *f*.

compassionate [kəm'pæʃənət] *adj* compasivo(va).

compatible [kəm'pætəbl] *adj*: **~ (with)** compatible (con).

compel [kəm'pel] *vt* [force] obligar; **to ~ sb to do sthg** forzar OR obligar a alguien a hacer algo.

compelling [kəm'pelɪŋ] *adj* [forceful] convincente.

compensate ['kɒmpenseɪt] ◇ *vt*: **to ~ sb for sthg** [financially] compensar OR indemnizar a alguien por algo. ◇ *vi*: **to ~ for sthg** compensar algo.

compensation [,kɒmpen'seɪʃn] *n* **-1.** [money]: **~ (for)** indemnización *f* (por). **-2.** [way of compensating]: **~ (for)** compensación *f* (por).

compete [kəm'piːt] *vi* **-1.** [gen]: **to ~ (for/in)** competir (por/en); **to ~ (with** OR **against)** competir (con). **-2.** [be in conflict] rivalizar.

competence ['kɒmpɪtəns] *n* [proficiency] competencia *f*, aptitud *f*.

competent ['kɒmpɪtənt] *adj* competente, capaz.

competition [,kɒmpɪ'tɪʃn] *n* **-1.** [rivalry] competencia *f*. **-2.** [race, sporting event] competición *f*. **-3.** [contest] concurso *m*.

competitive [kəm'petətɪv] *adj* **-1.** [person, spirit] competidor(ra). **-2.** [match, exam, prices] competitivo(va).

competitor [kəm'petɪtəʳ] *n* competidor *m*, -ra *f*.

compile [kəm'paɪl] *vt* recopilar.

complacency [kəm'pleɪsnsɪ] *n* autosatisfacción *f*, autocomplacencia *f*.

complacent [kəm'pleɪsnt] *adj* autocomplaciente.

complain [kəm'pleɪn] *vi* **-1.** [moan]: **to ~ (about)** quejarse (de). **-2.** MED: **to ~ of sthg** sufrir algo.

complaint [kəm'pleɪnt] *n* **-1.** [gen] queja *f*. **-2.** MED dolencia *f*.

complement [*n* 'kɒmplɪmənt, *vb* 'kɒmplɪ,ment] ◇ *n* **-1.** [gen & GRAMM] complemento *m*. **-2.** [number]: **a full ~ of** la totalidad de. ◇ *vt* complementar.

complementary [,kɒmplɪ'mentərɪ] *adj* complementario(ria).

complete [kəm'pliːt] ◇ *adj* **-1.** [total] total. **-2.** [lacking nothing] completo(ta); **bathroom ~ with shower** baño con ducha. **-3.** [finished] terminado(da). ◇ *vt* **-1.** [make whole - collection] completar; [- disappointment, amazement] colmar. **-2.** [finish] terminar. **-3.** [form] rellenar.

completely [kəm'pliːtlɪ] *adv* completamente.

completion [kəm'pliːʃn] *n* finalización *f*, terminación *f*.

complex ['kɒmpleks] ◇ *adj* complejo(ja). ◇ *n* complejo *m*.

complexion [kəm'plekʃn] *n* [of face] tez *f*, cutis *m*.

compliance [kəm'plaɪəns] *n* [obedience]: **~ (with)** acatamiento *m* (de).

complicate ['kɒmplɪkeɪt] *vt* complicar.

complicated ['kɒmplɪkeɪtɪd] *adj* complicado(da).

complication [,kɒmplɪ'keɪʃn] *n* complicación *f*.

compliment [*n* 'kɒmplɪmənt, *vb* 'kɒmplɪment] ◇ *n* cumplido *m*. ◇ *vt*: **to ~ sb (on)** felicitar a alguien (por). ◆ **compliments** *npl fml* saludos *mpl*.

complimentary [,kɒmplɪ'mentərɪ] *adj* **-1.** [remark] elogioso(sa); [person] halagador(ra). **-2.** [drink, seats] gratis (*inv*).

complimentary ticket *n* entrada *f* gratuita.

comply [kəm'plaɪ] *vi*: **to ~ with sthg** [standards] cumplir (con) algo; [request] acceder a algo; [law] acatar algo.

component [kəm'pəʊnənt] *n* [gen] elemento *m*; TECH pieza *f*.

compose [kəm'pəʊz] *vt* **-1.** [constitute] componer; **to be ~d of** estar compuesto OR componerse de. **-2.** [music, poem, letter] componer. **-3.** [calm]: **to ~ o.s.** calmarse.

composed [kəm'pəʊzd] *adj* tranquilo(la).

composer [kəm'pəʊzəʳ] *n* compositor *m*, -ra *f*.

composition [,kɒmpə'zɪʃn] *n* **-1.** [gen] composición *f*. **-2.** [essay] redacción *f*.

compost [*Br* 'kɒmpɒst, *Am* 'kɒmpəʊst] *n* abono *m*.

composure [kəm'pəʊʒəʳ] n calma f.

compound ['kɒmpaʊnd] n **-1.** [gen & CHEM] compuesto m. **-2.** [enclosed area] recinto m.

compound fracture n fractura f complicada.

comprehend [,kɒmprɪ'hend] vt comprender.

comprehension [,kɒmprɪ'henʃn] n comprensión f.

comprehensive [,kɒmprɪ'hensɪv] ◇ adj **-1.** [wide-ranging] amplio(plia). **-2.** [insurance] a todo riesgo. ◇ n Br = comprehensive school.

comprehensive school n instituto de enseñanza media no selectiva en Gran Bretaña.

compress [kəm'pres] vt **-1.** [squeeze, press] comprimir. **-2.** [shorten] reducir.

comprise [kəm'praɪz] vt **-1.** [consist of] comprender. **-2.** [form] constituir.

compromise ['kɒmprəmaɪz] ◇ n arreglo m, término m medio. ◇ vt comprometer. ◇ vi llegar a un arreglo, transigir.

compulsion [kəm'pʌlʃn] n **-1.** [strong desire] ganas fpl irrefrenables. **-2.** (U) [force] obligación f.

compulsive [kəm'pʌlsɪv] adj **-1.** [gambler] empedernido(da); [liar] compulsivo(va). **-2.** [fascinating, compelling] absorbente.

compulsory [kəm'pʌlsərɪ] adj [gen] obligatorio(ria); [retirement] forzoso(sa).

computer [kəm'pju:təʳ] n ordenador m.

computer game n videojuego m.

computerized [kəm'pju:təraɪzd] adj informatizado(da), computerizado(da).

computing [kəm'pju:tɪŋ], **computer science** n informática f.

comrade ['kɒmreɪd] n camarada m y f.

con [kɒn] inf ◇ n [trick] timo m. ◇ vt timar, estafar; to ~ sb out of sthg timarle algo a alguien; to ~ sb into doing sthg engañar a alguien para que haga algo.

concave [,kɒn'keɪv] adj concavo(va).

conceal [kən'si:l] vt [object, substance, information] ocultar; [feelings] disimular; to ~ sthg from sb ocultarle algo a alguien.

concede [kən'si:d] ◇ vt [defeat, a point] admitir, reconocer. ◇ vi [gen] ceder; [in sports, chess] rendirse.

conceit [kən'si:t] n vanidad f.

conceited [kən'si:tɪd] adj engreído(da).

conceive [kən'si:v] ◇ vt concebir. ◇ vi **-1.** MED concebir. **-2.** [imagine] to ~ of sthg imaginarse algo.

concentrate ['kɒnsəntreɪt] ◇ vt concentrar. ◇ vi: to ~ (on) concentrarse (en).

concentration [,kɒnsən'treɪʃn] n concentración f.

concentration camp n campo m de concentración.

concept ['kɒnsept] n concepto m.

concern [kən'sɜ:n] ◇ n **-1.** [worry, anxiety] preocupación f. **-2.** [company] negocio m, empresa f. ◇ vt **-1.** [worry] preocupar; to be ~ed about preocuparse por. **-2.** [involve] concernir; to be ~ed with [subj: person] estar involucrado en; to ~ o.s. with sthg preocuparse de OR por algo; as far as ... is ~ed por lo que a ... respecta.

concerning [kən'sɜ:nɪŋ] prep sobre, acerca de.

concert ['kɒnsət] n concierto m.

concerted [kən'sɜ:tɪd] adj conjunto(ta).

concert hall n sala f de conciertos.

concertina [,kɒnsə'ti:nə] n concertina f.

concerto [kən'tʃeətəʊ] (pl -s) n concierto m.

concession [kən'seʃn] n **-1.** [allowance, franchise] concesión f. **-2.** [special price] descuento m, rebaja f; [reduced ticket] entrada f de descuento.

conciliatory [kən'sɪlɪətrɪ] adj conciliador(ra).

concise [kən'saɪs] adj conciso(sa).

conclude [kən'klu:d] ◇ vt **-1.** [bring to an end] concluir, terminar. **-2.** [deduce] to ~ (that) concluir que. **-3.** [agreement] llegar a; [business deal] cerrar; [treaty] firmar. ◇ vi terminar, concluir.

conclusion [kən'klu:ʒn] n **-1.** [decision] conclusión f. **-2.** [ending] final m. **-3.** [of business deal] cierre m; [of treaty] firma f; [of agreement] alcance m.

conclusive [kən'klu:sɪv] adj concluyente, irrebatible.

concoct [kən'kɒkt] vt **-1.** [excuse, story] ingeniar. **-2.** [food] confeccionar; [drink] preparar.

concoction [kən'kɒkʃn] n [drink] brebaje m; [food] mezcla f.

concourse ['kɒŋkɔ:s] n [of station etc] vestíbulo m.

concrete ['kɒŋkri:t] ◇ adj [definite, real] concreto(ta). ◇ n hormigón m, concreto m Amer. ◇ comp [made of concrete] de hormigón.

concur [kən'kɜ:ʳ] vi [agree] to ~ (with) estar de acuerdo, coincidir (con).

concurrently [kən'kʌrəntlɪ] adv simultáneamente, al mismo tiempo.

concussion [kən'kʌʃn] *n* conmoción *f* cerebral.

condemn [kən'dem] *vt* **-1.** [gen]: **to ~ sb (for/to)** condenar a alguien (por/a). **-2.** [building] declarar en ruinas.

condensation [ˌkɒnden'seɪʃn] *n* [on glass] vaho *m*.

condense [kən'dens] ◇ *vt* condensar. ◇ *vi* condensarse.

condensed milk [kən'denst-] *n* leche *f* condensada.

condescending [ˌkɒndɪ'sendɪŋ] *adj* altanero(ra), altivo(va).

condition [kən'dɪʃn] ◇ *n* **-1.** [state] estado *m*; **in good/bad ~** en buen/mal estado; **to be out of ~** no estar en forma. **-2.** MED [disease, complaint] afección *f*. **-3.** [provision] condición *f*; **on ~ that** a condición de que; **on one ~** con una condición. ◇ *vt* [gen] condicionar.

conditional [kən'dɪʃənl] *adj* condicional; **to be ~ on** OR **upon** depender de.

conditioner [kən'dɪʃnər] *n* suavizante *m*.

condolences [kən'dəʊlənsɪz] *npl* pésame *m*; **to offer one's ~** dar uno su más sentido pésame.

condom ['kɒndəm] *n* condón *m*.

condominium [ˌkɒndə'mɪnɪəm] *n* Am **-1.** [apartment] piso *m*, apartamento *m*. **-2.** [apartment block] bloque *m* de pisos OR apartamentos.

condone [kən'dəʊn] *vt* perdonar.

conducive [kən'djuːsɪv] *adj*: **~ to** favorable para.

conduct [*n* 'kɒndʌkt, *vb* kən'dʌkt] ◇ *n* **-1.** [behaviour] conducta *f*. **-2.** [carrying out] dirección *f*. ◇ *vt* **-1.** [carry out] dirigir, llevar a cabo. **-2.** [behave]: **to ~ o.s. well/badly** comportarse bien/mal. **-3.** MUS dirigir. **-4.** PHYSICS conducir.

conducted tour [kən'dʌktɪd-] *n* excursión *f* con guía.

conductor [kən'dʌktər] *n* **-1.** [of orchestra, choir] director *m*, -ra *f*. **-2.** [on bus] cobrador *m*. **-3.** Am [on train] revisor *m*, -ra *f*.

conductress [kən'dʌktrɪs] *n* cobradora *f*.

cone [kəʊn] *n* **-1.** [shape] cono *m*. **-2.** [for ice cream] cucurucho *m*. **-3.** [from tree] piña *f*.

confectioner [kən'fekʃnər] *n* confitero *m*, -ra *f*; **~'s (shop)** confitería *f*.

confectionery [kən'fekʃnərɪ] *n* (*U*) dulces *mpl*, golosinas *fpl*.

confederation [kənˌfedə'reɪʃn] *n* confederación *f*.

Confederation of British Industry *n*: **the ~** *organización patronal británica*, ≃ la CEOE.

confer [kən'fɜːr] ◇ *vt fml*: **to ~ sthg (on)** otorgar OR conferir algo (a). ◇ *vi*: **to ~ (with)** consultar (con).

conference ['kɒnfərəns] *n* congreso *m*, conferencia *f*.

confess [kən'fes] ◇ *vt* confesar. ◇ *vi* **-1.** [to crime] confesarse; **to ~ to sthg** confesar algo. **-2.** [admit]: **to ~ to sthg** admitir algo.

confession [kən'feʃn] *n* confesión *f*.

confetti [kən'fetɪ] *n* confeti *m*.

confide [kən'faɪd] *vi*: **to ~ (in)** confiar (en).

confidence ['kɒnfɪdəns] *n* **-1.** [self-assurance] confianza *f* OR seguridad *f* (en sí mismo/misma). **-2.** [trust] confianza *f*. **-3.** [secrecy]: **in ~** en secreto. **-4.** [secret] intimidad *f*, secreto *m*.

confidence trick *n* timo *m*, estafa *f*.

confident ['kɒnfɪdənt] *adj* **-1.** [self-assured - person] seguro de sí mismo (segura de sí misma); [- smile, attitude] confiado(da). **-2.** [sure]: **~ (of)** seguro(ra) (de).

confidential [ˌkɒnfɪ'denʃl] *adj* [gen] confidencial; [person] de confianza.

confine [kən'faɪn] *vt* **-1.** [limit, restrict] limitar, restringir; **to be ~d to** limitarse a. **-2.** [shut up] recluir, encerrar.

confined [kən'faɪnd] *adj* reducido(da).

confinement [kən'faɪnmənt] *n* [imprisonment] reclusión *f*.

confines ['kɒnfaɪnz] *npl* confines *mpl*.

confirm [kən'fɜːm] *vt* confirmar.

confirmation [ˌkɒnfə'meɪʃn] *n* confirmación *f*.

confirmed [kən'fɜːmd] *adj* [non-smoker] inveterado(da); [bachelor] empedernido.

confiscate ['kɒnfɪskeɪt] *vt* confiscar.

conflict [*n* 'kɒnflɪkt, *vb* kən'flɪkt] ◇ *n* conflicto *m*. ◇ *vi*: **to ~ (with)** estar en desacuerdo (con).

conflicting [kən'flɪktɪŋ] *adj* contrapuesto(ta).

conform [kən'fɔːm] *vi* **-1.** [behave as expected] amoldarse a las normas sociales. **-2.** [be in accordance]: **to ~ (to** OR **with)** [expectations] corresponder (a); [rules] ajustarse (a).

confound [kən'faʊnd] *vt* [confuse, defeat] confundir, desconcertar.

confront [kən'frʌnt] *vt* **-1.** [problem, task] hacer frente a. **-2.** [subj: problem, task] presentarse a. **-3.** [enemy etc] enfrentar-

se con. -4. [challenge]: **to ~ sb (with)** poner a alguien cara a cara (con).

confrontation [,kɒnfrʌn'teɪʃn] *n* enfrentamiento *m*, confrontación *f*.

confuse [kən'fjuːz] *vt* **-1.** [bewilder] desconcertar. **-2.** [mix up]: **to ~ (with)** confundir (con). **-3.** [complicate, make less clear] complicar.

confused [kən'fjuːzd] *adj* **-1.** [not clear] confuso(sa). **-2.** [bewildered] desconcertado(da).

confusing [kən'fjuːzɪŋ] *adj* confuso(sa).

confusion [kən'fjuːʒn] *n* **-1.** [gen] confusión *f*. **-2.** [of person] desconcierto *m*.

congeal [kən'dʒiːl] *vi* coagularse.

congenial [kən'dʒiːnjəl] *adj* ameno(na), agradable.

congested [kən'dʒestɪd] *adj* **-1.** [area] superpoblado(da); [road] congestionado(da). **-2.** MED congestionado(da).

congestion [kən'dʒestʃn] *n* (*U*) **-1.** [of traffic] retención *f*, congestión *f*. **-2.** MED congestión *f*.

conglomerate [kən'glɒmərət] *n* COMM conglomerado *m*.

congratulate [kən'grætʃʊleɪt] *vt*: **to ~ sb (on)** felicitar a alguien (por).

congratulations [kən,grætʃʊ'leɪʃənz] ◇ *npl* felicitaciones *fpl*. ◇ *excl* ¡enhorabuena!

congregate ['kɒŋgrɪgeɪt] *vi* [people] congregarse; [animals] juntarse.

congregation [,kɒŋgrɪ'geɪʃn] *n* RELIG feligreses *mpl*.

congress ['kɒŋgres] *n* congreso *m*. ◆ **Congress** *n* [in US]: **(the) Congress** el Congreso.

congressman ['kɒŋgresmən] (*pl* **-men** [-mən]) *n* miembro *m* del Congreso.

conifer ['kɒnɪfəʳ] *n* conífera *f*.

conjugate ['kɒndʒʊgeɪt] *vt* conjugar.

conjugation [,kɒndʒʊ'geɪʃn] *n* conjugación *f*.

conjunction [kən'dʒʌŋkʃn] *n* **-1.** GRAMM conjunción *f*. **-2.** [combination]: **in ~ with** juntamente con.

conjunctivitis [kən,dʒʌŋktɪ'vaɪtɪs] *n* conjuntivitis *f inv*.

conjure ['kʌndʒəʳ] *vi* hacer juegos de manos. ◆ **conjure up** *vt sep* [evoke] evocar.

conjurer ['kʌndʒərəʳ] *n* prestidigitador *m*, -ra *f*.

conk [kɒŋk] *n inf* [nose] napia *f*. ◆ **conk out** *vi inf* escacharrarse.

conker ['kɒŋkəʳ] *n Br* castaña *f* (*del castaño de Indias*).

conman ['kɒnmæn] (*pl* **-men** [-men]) *n* estafador *m*, timador *m*.

connect [kə'nekt] ◇ *vt* **-1.** [join]: **to ~ sthg (to)** unir algo (con). **-2.** [on telephone]: **I'll ~ you now** ahora le paso OR pongo. **-3.** [associate]: **to ~ sthg/sb (with)** asociar algo/a alguien (con). **-4.** ELEC: **to ~ sthg to** conectar algo a. ◇ *vi* [train, plane, bus]: **to ~ (with)** enlazar (con).

connected [kə'nektɪd] *adj* [related]: **~ (with)** relacionado(da) (con).

connection [kə'nekʃn] *n* **-1.** [gen & ELEC]: **~ (between/with)** conexión *f* (entre/con); **in ~ with** con relación OR respecto a. **-2.** [plane, train, bus] enlace *m*. **-3.** [professional acquaintance] contacto *m*; **to have good ~s** tener mucho enchufe.

connive [kə'naɪv] *vi* **-1.** [plot]: **to ~ (with)** confabularse (con). **-2.** [allow to happen]: **to ~ at sthg** hacer la vista gorda con algo.

connoisseur [,kɒnə's3ːʳ] *n* entendido *m*, -da *f*, experto *m*, -ta *f*.

conquer ['kɒŋkəʳ] *vt* **-1.** [take by force] conquistar. **-2.** [gain control of, overcome] doblegar, vencer.

conqueror ['kɒŋkərəʳ] *n* conquistador *m*, -ra *f*.

conquest ['kɒŋkwest] *n* conquista *f*.

cons [kɒnz] *npl* **-1.** *Br inf*: **all mod ~** con todas las comodidades. **-2.** → **pro**.

conscience ['kɒnʃəns] *n* conciencia *f*.

conscientious [,kɒnʃɪ'enʃəs] *adj* concienzudo(da).

conscious ['kɒnʃəs] *adj* **-1.** [gen] consciente; **to be ~ of** ser consciente de. **-2.** [intentional] deliberado(da).

consciousness ['kɒnʃəsnɪs] *n* **-1.** [gen] conciencia *f*. **-2.** [state of being awake] conocimiento *m*; **to lose/regain ~** perder/recobrar el conocimiento.

conscript ['kɒnskrɪpt] *n* recluta *m* y *f*.

conscription [kən'skrɪpʃn] *n* servicio *m* militar obligatorio.

consecutive [kən'sekjʊtɪv] *adj* consecutivo(va); **on three ~ days** tres días seguidos.

consent [kən'sent] ◇ *n* (*U*) **-1.** [permission] consentimiento *m*. **-2.** [agreement] acuerdo *m*. ◇ *vi*: **to ~ (to)** consentir (en).

consequence ['kɒnsɪkwəns] *n* **-1.** [result] consecuencia *f*; **in ~** por consiguiente. **-2.** [importance] importancia *f*.

consequently ['kɒnsɪkwəntlɪ] *adv* por consiguiente.

conservation [ˌkɒnsə'veɪʃn] n conservación f.

conservative [kən'sɜːvətɪv] adj **-1.** [not modern] conservador(ra). **-2.** [estimate, guess] moderado(da). ◆ **Conservative** POL ◇ adj conservador(ra). ◇ n conservador m, -ra f.

Conservative Party n: **the** ~ el partido Conservador británico.

conservatory [kən'sɜːvətrɪ] n pequeña habitación acristalada aneja a la casa.

conserve [n 'kɒnsɜːv, vb kən'sɜːv] ◇ n compota f. ◇ vt [energy, supplies] ahorrar; [nature, wildlife] conservar.

consider [kən'sɪdər] vt **-1.** [gen] considerar; **to** ~ **doing sthg** pensarse si hacer algo. **-2.** [take into account] tener en cuenta; **all things** ~**ed** teniéndolo todo en cuenta.

considerable [kən'sɪdrəbl] adj considerable.

considerably [kən'sɪdrəblɪ] adv considerablemente, sustancialmente.

considerate [kən'sɪdərət] adj considerado(da).

consideration [kən,sɪdə'reɪʃn] n consideración f; **to take sthg into** ~ tomar OR tener algo en cuenta.

considering [kən'sɪdərɪŋ] ◇ prep habida cuenta de. ◇ conj después de todo.

consign [kən'saɪn] vt: **to** ~ **sthg/sb to** relegar algo/a alguien a.

consignment [ˌkən'saɪnmənt] n remesa f.

consist [kən'sɪst] ◆ **consist in** vt fus consistir en, basarse en. ◆ **consist of** vt fus consistir en, constar de.

consistency [kən'sɪstənsɪ] n **-1.** [coherence - of behaviour, policy] consecuencia f, coherencia f; [of work] regularidad f. **-2.** [texture] consistencia f.

consistent [kən'sɪstənt] adj **-1.** [regular] constante. **-2.** [coherent]: ~ **(with)** consecuente (con).

consolation [ˌkɒnsə'leɪʃn] n consuelo m.

console [n 'kɒnsəʊl, vt kən'səʊl] ◇ n consola f. ◇ vt consolar.

consonant ['kɒnsənənt] n consonante f.

consortium [kən'sɔːtjəm] (pl **-tiums** OR **-tia** [-tjə]) n consorcio m.

conspicuous [kən'spɪkjʊəs] adj [building] visible; [colour] llamativo(va).

conspiracy [kən'spɪrəsɪ] n conspiración f.

conspire [kən'spaɪər] ◇ vt: **to** ~ **to do sthg** conspirar para hacer algo. ◇ vi **-1.** [plan secretly]: **to** ~ **(against/with)** conspirar (contra/con). **-2.** [combine] confabularse.

constable ['kʌnstəbl] n policía m y f.

constabulary [kən'stæbjʊlərɪ] n policía f (de una zona determinada).

constant ['kɒnstənt] adj [gen] constante.

constantly ['kɒnstəntlɪ] adv [forever] constantemente.

consternation [ˌkɒnstə'neɪʃn] n consternación f.

constipated ['kɒnstɪpeɪtɪd] adj estreñido(da).

constipation [ˌkɒnstɪ'peɪʃn] n estreñimiento m.

constituency [kən'stɪtjʊənsɪ] n [area] distrito m electoral.

constituent [kən'stɪtjʊənt] n **-1.** [voter] votante m y f. **-2.** [element] componente m, constituyente m.

constitute ['kɒnstɪtjuːt] vt constituir.

constitution [ˌkɒnstɪ'tjuːʃn] n constitución f.

constraint [kən'streɪnt] n **-1.** [restriction]: ~ **(on)** limitación f (de). **-2.** [self-control] autocontrol m. **-3.** [coercion] coacción f.

construct [kən'strʌkt] vt lit & fig construir.

construction [kən'strʌkʃn] n construcción f.

constructive [kən'strʌktɪv] adj constructivo(va).

construe [kən'struː] vt fml: **to** ~ **sthg as** interpretar algo como.

consul ['kɒnsəl] n cónsul m y f.

consulate ['kɒnsjʊlət] n consulado m.

consult [kən'sʌlt] ◇ vt consultar. ◇ vi: **to** ~ **with sb** consultar a OR con alguien.

consultant [kən'sʌltənt] n **-1.** [expert] asesor m, -ra f. **-2.** Br [hospital doctor] (médico) especialista m, (médica) especialista f.

consultation [ˌkɒnsəl'teɪʃn] n **-1.** [gen] consulta f. **-2.** [discussion] discusión f.

consulting room [kən'sʌltɪŋ-] n consultorio m, consulta f.

consume [kən'sjuːm] vt lit & fig consumir.

consumer [kən'sjuːmər] n consumidor m, -ra f.

consumer goods npl bienes mpl de consumo.

consumer society n sociedad f de consumo.

consummate [adj kən'sʌmət, vb 'kɒnsəmeɪt] ◇ adj **-1.** [skill, ease] absoluto(ta). **-2.** [liar, politician, snob] consumado(da). ◇ vt [marriage] consumar.

consumption [kən'sʌmpʃn] *n* [use] consumo *m*.

contact ['kɒntækt] ◇ *n* contacto *m*; **in ~ (with)** en contacto (con); **to lose ~ with** perder (el) contacto con; **to make ~ with** ponerse en contacto con. ◇ *vt* ponerse en contacto con.

contact lens *n* lentilla *f*, lente *f* de contacto.

contagious [kən'teɪdʒəs] *adj* contagioso(sa).

contain [kən'teɪn] *vt* contener; **to ~ o.s.** contenerse.

container [kən'teɪnər] *n* **-1.** [box, bottle etc] recipiente *m*, envase *m*. **-2.** [for transporting goods] contenedor *m*.

contaminate [kən'tæmɪneɪt] *vt* contaminar.

cont'd *abbr of* **continued**.

contemplate ['kɒntempleɪt] ◇ *vt* **-1.** [consider] considerar, pensar en. **-2.** *fml* [look at] contemplar. ◇ *vi* reflexionar.

contemporary [kən'tempərəri] ◇ *adj* contemporáneo(a). ◇ *n* contemporáneo *m*, -a *f*.

contempt [kən'tempt] *n* **-1.** [scorn]: **~ (for)** desprecio *m* OR desdén *m* (por). **-2.** JUR desacato *m*.

contemptuous [kən'temptʃuəs] *adj* despreciativo(va); **to be ~ of sthg** despreciar algo.

contend [kən'tend] ◇ *vi* **-1.** [deal]: **to ~ with** enfrentarse a. **-2.** [compete]: **to ~ for/against** competir por/contra. ◇ *vt fml*: **to ~ that** sostener OR afirmar que.

contender [kən'tendər] *n* [gen] contendiente *m* y *f*; [for title] aspirante *m* y *f*.

content [*n* 'kɒntent, *adj & vb* kən'tent] ◇ *adj*: **~ (with)** contento(ta) OR satisfecho(cha) (con); **to be ~ to do sthg** contentarse con hacer algo. ◇ *n* contenido *m*. ◇ *vt*: **to ~ o.s. with sthg/with doing sthg** contentarse con algo/con hacer algo. ◆ **contents** *npl* contenido *m*.

contented [kən'tentɪd] *adj* satisfecho(cha), contento(ta).

contention [kən'tenʃn] *n fml* **-1.** [argument, assertion] argumento *m*. **-2.** (*U*) [disagreement] disputas *fpl*. **-3.** [competition]: **to be in ~** entrar en liza.

contest [*n* 'kɒntest, *vb* kən'test] ◇ *n* **-1.** [competition] competición *f*, concurso *m*. **-2.** [for power, control] lucha *f*. ◇ *vt* **-1.** [seat, election] presentarse como candidato(ta) a. **-2.** [dispute - statement] disputar; [- decision] impugnar.

contestant [kən'testənt] *n* [in quiz show] concursante *m* y *f*; [in race] participante *m* y *f*; [in boxing match] contrincante *m* y *f*.

context ['kɒntekst] *n* contexto *m*.

continent ['kɒntɪnənt] *n* continente *m*. ◆ **Continent** *n Br*: **the Continent** la Europa continental.

continental [ˌkɒntɪ'nentl] *adj* **-1.** GEOGR continental. **-2.** [European] de la Europa continental.

continental breakfast *n* desayuno *m* continental.

continental quilt *n Br* edredón *m*.

contingency [kən'tɪndʒənsɪ] *n* contingencia *f*.

contingency plan *n* plan *m* de emergencia.

continual [kən'tɪnjʊəl] *adj* continuo(nua), constante.

continually [kən'tɪnjʊəlɪ] *adv* continuamente, constantemente.

continuation [kənˌtɪnjʊ'eɪʃn] *n* continuación *f*.

continue [kən'tɪnjuː] ◇ *vt*: **to ~ (doing** OR **to do sthg)** continuar (haciendo algo); **to be ~d** continuará. ◇ *vi*: **to ~ (with sthg)** continuar (con algo).

continuous [kən'tɪnjuəs] *adj* continuo(nua).

continuously [kən'tɪnjʊəslɪ] *adv* continuamente, ininterrumpidamente.

contort [kən'tɔːt] *vt* retorcer.

contortion [kən'tɔːʃn] *n* contorsión *f*.

contour ['kɒnˌtʊər] *n* **-1.** [outline] contorno *m*. **-2.** [on map] curva *f* de nivel.

contraband ['kɒntrəbænd] ◇ *adj* de contrabando. ◇ *n* contrabando *m*.

contraception [ˌkɒntrə'sepʃn] *n* anticoncepción *f*.

contraceptive [ˌkɒntrə'septɪv] ◇ *adj* anticonceptivo(va). ◇ *n* anticonceptivo *m*.

contract [*n* 'kɒntrækt, *vb* kən'trækt] ◇ *n* contrato *m*. ◇ *vt* **-1.** [through legal agreement]: **to ~ sb (to do sthg)** contratar a alguien (para hacer algo); **to ~ to do sthg** comprometerse a hacer algo (por contrato). **-2.** *fml* [illness, disease] contraer. ◇ *vi* [decrease in size, length] contraerse.

contraction [kən'trækʃn] *n* contracción *f*.

contractor [kən'træktər] *n* contratista *m* y *f*.

contradict [ˌkɒntrə'dɪkt] *vt* contradecir.

contradiction [ˌkɒntrə'dɪkʃn] *n* contradicción *f*.

contraflow ['kɒntrəfləʊ] *n* estrechamiento (de la autopista) a una carretera de dos direcciones.

contraption [kən'træpʃn] *n* chisme *m*, artilugio *m*.

contrary ['kɒntrərɪ, *adj sense 2* kən'treərɪ] ◇ *adj* **-1.** [opposite] contrario(ria); ~ **to** en contra de. **-2.** [awkward] obstinado(da). ◇ *n:* **the ~** lo contrario; **on the ~** al contrario. ◆ **contrary to** *prep* en contra de.

contrast [*n* 'kɒntrɑːst, *vb* kən'trɑːst] ◇ *n:* ~ **(between** OR **with)** contraste *m* (entre); **by** OR **in ~** en cambio; **in ~ with** OR **to** a diferencia de. ◇ *vt:* **to ~ sthg with** contrastar algo con. ◇ *vi:* **to ~ (with)** contrastar (con).

contravene [,kɒntrə'viːn] *vt* contravenir.

contribute [kən'trɪbjuːt] ◇ *vt* [give] contribuir, aportar. ◇ *vi* **-1.** [gen] **to ~ (to)** contribuir (a). **-2.** [write material]: **to ~** to colaborar con.

contribution [,kɒntrɪ'bjuːʃn] *n* **-1.** [gen]: ~ **(to)** contribución *f* (a). **-2.** [article] colaboración *f*.

contributor [kən'trɪbjʊtər] *n* **-1.** [of money] contribuyente *m* y *f*. **-2.** [to magazine, newspaper] colaborador *m*, -ra *f*.

contrive [kən'traɪv] *fml vt* **-1.** [engineer] maquinar, idear. **-2.** [manage]: **to ~ to do sthg** lograr hacer algo.

contrived [kən'traɪvd] *adj* inverosímil.

control [kən'trəʊl] ◇ *n* **-1.** [gen & COMPUT] control *m*; [on spending] restricción *f*; **in ~ of** al mando de; **to be in ~ of the situation** dominar la situación; **out of/under ~** fuera de/bajo control. **-2.** [of emotions] dominio *m*. ◇ *vt* **-1.** [gen] controlar; **to ~ o.s.** dominarse. **-2.** [operate - machine, plane] manejar; [- central heating] regular. ◆ **controls** *npl* [of machine, vehicle] controles *mpl*.

controller [kən'trəʊlər] *n* FIN interventor *m*, -ra *f*; RADIO & TV director *m*, -ra *f*.

control panel *n* tablero *m* de instrumentos OR de mandos.

control tower *n* torre *f* de control.

controversial [,kɒntrə'vɜːʃl] *adj* polémico(ca).

controversy ['kɒntrəvɜːsɪ, *Br* kən'trɒvəsɪ] *n* controversia *f*, polémica *f*.

convalesce [,kɒnvə'les] *vi* convalecer.

convene [kən'viːn] ◇ *vt* convocar. ◇ *vi* reunirse.

convenience [kən'viːnjəns] *n* comodidad *f*; **do it at your ~** hágalo cuando le venga bien.

convenience store *n Am* tienda *f* que abre hasta tarde.

convenient [kən'viːnjənt] *adj* **-1.** [suitable] conveniente; **is Monday ~?** ¿te viene bien el lunes? **-2.** [handy - size] práctico(ca); [- position] adecuado(da); ~ **for** [well-situated] bien situado para.

convent ['kɒnvənt] *n* convento *m*.

convention [kən'venʃn] *n* convención *f*.

conventional [kən'venʃənl] *adj* convencional.

converge [kən'vɜːdʒ] *vi lit & fig:* **to ~ (on)** converger (en).

conversant [kən'vɜːsənt] *adj fml:* ~ **with** familiarizado(da) con.

conversation [,kɒnvə'seɪʃn] *n* conversación *f*.

conversational [,kɒnvə'seɪʃənl] *adj* coloquial.

converse [*n* 'kɒnvɜːs, *vb* kən'vɜːs] ◇ *n:* **the ~** lo contrario OR opuesto. ◇ *vi fml:* **to ~ (with)** conversar (con).

conversely [kən'vɜːslɪ] *adv fml* a la inversa.

conversion [kən'vɜːʃn] *n* [gen & RELIG] conversión *f*.

convert [*vb* kən'vɜːt, *n* 'kɒnvɜːt] ◇ *vt* **-1.** [gen]: **to ~ sthg (to** OR **into)** convertir algo (en). **-2.** [change belief of]: **to ~ sb (to)** convertir a alguien (a). ◇ *n* converso *m*, -sa *f*.

convertible [kən'vɜːtəbl] ◇ *adj* **-1.** [sofa]: ~ **sofa** sofá-cama *m*. **-2.** [currency] convertible. **-3.** [car] descapotable. ◇ *n* (coche *m*) descapotable *m*.

convex [kɒn'veks] *adj* convexo(xa).

convey [kən'veɪ] *vt* **-1.** [transport] transportar. **-2.** [express]: **to ~ sthg (to)** expresar OR transmitir algo (a).

conveyer belt [kən'veɪər-] *n* cinta *f* transportadora.

convict [*n* 'kɒnvɪkt, *vb* kən'vɪkt] ◇ *n* presidiario *m*, -ria *f*. ◇ *vt:* **to ~ sb of** condenar a alguien por.

conviction [kən'vɪkʃn] *n* **-1.** [belief, fervour] convicción *f*. **-2.** JUR condena *f*.

convince [kən'vɪns] *vt:* **to ~ sb (of sthg/to do sthg)** convencer a alguien (de algo/para que haga algo).

convincing [kən'vɪnsɪŋ] *adj* convincente.

convoluted ['kɒnvəluːtɪd] *adj* [tortuous] retorcido(da).

convoy ['kɒnvɔɪ] *n* convoy *m*.

convulse [kən'vʌls] *vt:* **to be ~d with** [pain] retorcerse de; [laughter] troncharse de.

convulsion [kən'vʌlʃn] *n* MED convulsión *f*.

coo [kuː] *vi* arrullar.

cook [kuk] ◇ *n* cocinero *m*, -ra *f*. ◇ *vt* -1. [gen] cocinar, guisar; [prepare] preparar. -2. [in oven] asar, hacer en el horno. ◇ *vi* -1. [prepare food] cocinar, guisar. -2. [in oven] cocerse. ◆ **cook up** *vt sep* [plan, deal] tramar, urdir; [excuse] inventarse.

cookbook ['kuk,buk] = **cookery book**.

cooker ['kukər] *n* cocina *f* (*aparato*).

cookery ['kukərɪ] *n* cocina *f* (*arte*).

cookery book *n* libro *m* de cocina.

cookie ['kukɪ] *n Am* galleta *f*.

cooking ['kukɪŋ] *n* [food] cocina *f*.

cool [kuːl] ◇ *adj* -1. [not warm] fresco(ca). -2. [calm] tranquilo(la). -3. [unfriendly] frío(a). -4. *inf* [hip] guay, chachi. ◇ *vt* refrescar. ◇ *vi* [become less warm] enfriarse. ◇ *n*: **to keep/lose one's ~** mantener/perder la calma. ◆ **cool down** *vi* -1. [become less warm] enfriarse. -2. [become less angry] calmarse.

cool box *n* nevera *f* portátil.

coop [kuːp] *n* gallinero *m*. ◆ **coop up** *vt sep inf* encerrar.

Co-op ['kəu,ɒp] (*abbr of* **co-operative society**) *n* Coop. *f*.

cooperate [kəu'ɒpəreɪt] *vi*: **to ~ (with)** cooperar (con).

cooperation [kəu,ɒpə'reɪʃn] *n* (U) cooperación *f*.

cooperative [kəu'ɒpərətɪv] ◇ *adj* -1. [helpful] servicial. -2. [collective] cooperativo(va). ◇ *n* cooperativa *f*.

coordinate [*n* kəu'ɔːdɪnət, *vt* kəu'ɔːdɪneɪt] ◇ *n* coordenada *f*. ◇ *vt* coordinar. ◆ **coordinates** *npl* [clothes] conjunto *m*.

coordination [kəu,ɔːdɪ'neɪʃn] *n* coordinación *f*.

cop [kɒp] *n inf* poli *m*, paco *m Amer*.

cope [kəup] *vi* arreglárselas; **to ~ with** [work] poder con; [problem, situation] hacer frente a.

Copenhagen [,kəupən'heɪgən] *n* Copenhague *f*.

copier ['kɒpɪər] *n* fotocopiadora *f*.

cop-out *n inf* escaqueo *m*.

copper ['kɒpər] *n* -1. [metal] cobre *m*. -2. *Br inf* [policeman] poli *m*.

coppice ['kɒpɪs], **copse** [kɒps] *n* bosquecillo *m*.

copy ['kɒpɪ] ◇ *n* -1. [imitation, duplicate] copia *f*. -2. [of book, magazine] ejemplar

m. ◇ *vt* -1. [imitate] copiar. -2. [photocopy] fotocopiar.

copyright ['kɒpɪraɪt] *n* (U) derechos *mpl* de autor.

coral ['kɒrəl] *n* coral *m*.

cord [kɔːd] *n* -1. [string] cuerda *f*; [for tying clothes] cordón *m*. -2. [wire] cable *m*, cordón *m*. -3. [fabric] pana *f*. ◆ **cords** *npl* pantalones *mpl* de pana.

cordial ['kɔːdjəl] ◇ *adj* cordial, afectuoso(sa). ◇ *n* bebida de frutas concentrada.

cordon ['kɔːdn] *n* cordón *m*. ◆ **cordon off** *vt sep* acordonar.

corduroy ['kɔːdərɔɪ] *n* pana *f*.

core [kɔːr] ◇ *n* -1. [of fruit] corazón *m*. -2. [of Earth, nuclear reactor, group] núcleo *m*. -3. [of issue, matter] meollo *m*. ◇ *vt* quitar el corazón de.

Corfu [kɔː'fuː] *n* Corfú.

corgi ['kɔːgɪ] (*pl* **-s**) *n* perro *m* galés.

coriander [,kɒrɪ'ændər] *n* cilantro *m*.

cork [kɔːk] *n* corcho *m*.

corkscrew ['kɔːkskruː] *n* sacacorchos *m inv*.

corn [kɔːn] *n* -1. *Br* [wheat, barley, oats] cereal *m*. -2. *Am* [maize] maíz *m*, choclo *m Amer*; **~ on the cob** mazorca *f*. -3. [callus] callo *m*.

cornea ['kɔːnɪə] (*pl* **-s**) *n* córnea *f*.

corned beef [kɔːnd-] *n* carne de vaca cocinada y enlatada.

corner ['kɔːnər] ◇ *n* -1. [angle - on outside] esquina *f*; [- on inside] rincón *m*. -2. [bend - in street, road] curva *f*; **just around the ~** a la vuelta de la esquina. -3. [faraway place] rincón *m*. -4. [in football] córner *m*. ◇ *vt* -1. [trap] arrinconar. -2. [monopolize] acaparar.

corner shop *n* tienda pequeña de barrio que vende comida, artículos de limpieza etc.

cornerstone ['kɔːnəstəun] *n fig* piedra *f* angular.

cornet ['kɔːnɪt] *n* -1. [instrument] corneta *f*. -2. *Br* [ice-cream cone] cucurucho *m*.

cornflakes ['kɔːnfleɪks] *npl* copos *mpl* de maíz, cornflakes *mpl*.

cornflour *Br* ['kɔːnflauər], **cornstarch** *Am* ['kɔːnstɑːtʃ] *n* harina *f* de maíz, maicena *f*.

Cornwall ['kɔːnwɔːl] *n* Cornualles *f*.

corny ['kɔːnɪ] *adj inf* trillado(da).

coronary ['kɒrənrɪ], **coronary thrombosis** [-θrɒm'bəusɪs] (*pl* **coronary thromboses** [-θrɒm'bəusiːz]) *n* trombosis *f inv* coronaria.

coronation [,kɒrə'neɪʃn] *n* coronación *f*.

coroner ['kɒrənəʳ] *n* ≃ juez *m y f* de instrucción.

Corp. (*abbr of* **corporation**) Corp.

corporal ['kɔ:pərəl] *n* cabo *m y f.*

corporal punishment *n* castigo *m* corporal.

corporate ['kɔ:pərət] *adj* **-1.** [business] corporativo(va). **-2.** [collective] colectivo(va).

corporation [,kɔ:pə'reɪʃn] *n* **-1.** [council] ayuntamiento *m*. **-2.** [large company] ≃ sociedad *f* mercantil.

corps [kɔ:ʳ] (*pl inv*) *n* cuerpo *m.*

corpse [kɔ:ps] *n* cadáver *m.*

correct [kə'rekt] ◇ *adj* **-1.** [accurate - time, amount, forecast] exacto(ta); [- answer] correcto(ta). **-2.** [socially acceptable] correcto(ta). **-3.** [appropriate, required] apropiado(da). ◇ *vt* corregir.

correction [kə'rekʃn] *n* corrección *f.*

correctly [kə'rektlɪ] *adv* **-1.** [gen] correctamente. **-2.** [appropriately, as required] apropiadamente.

correlation [,kɒrə'leɪʃn] *n*: ~ **(between)** correlación *f* (entre).

correspond [,kɒrɪ'spɒnd] *vi* **-1.** [correlate]: to ~ **(with** OR **to)** corresponder (con OR a). **-2.** [match]: to ~ **(with** OR **to)** coincidir (con). **-3.** [write letters]: to ~ **(with)** cartearse (con).

correspondence [,kɒrɪ'spɒndəns] *n*: ~ **(with/between)** correspondencia *f* (con/entre).

correspondence course *n* curso *m* por correspondencia.

correspondent [,kɒrɪ'spɒndənt] *n* [reporter] corresponsal *m y f.*

corridor ['kɒrɪdɔ:ʳ] *n* pasillo *m.*

corroborate [kə'rɒbəreɪt] *vt* corroborar.

corrode [kə'rəud] ◇ *vt* corroer. ◇ *vi* corroerse.

corrosion [kə'rəuʒn] *n* corrosión *f.*

corrugated ['kɒrəgeɪtɪd] *adj* ondulado(da).

corrugated iron *n* chapa *f* ondulada.

corrupt [kə'rʌpt] ◇ *adj* [gen & COMPUT] corrupto(ta). ◇ *vt* corromper; to ~ **a minor** pervertir a un menor.

corruption [kə'rʌpʃn] *n* corrupción *f.*

corset ['kɔ:sɪt] *n* corsé *m*, faja *f.*

Corsica ['kɔ:sɪkə] *n* Córcega *f.*

cortege, cortège [kɔ:'teɪʒ] *n* cortejo *m.*

cosh [kɒʃ] ◇ *n* porra *f.* ◇ *vt* aporrear.

cosmetic [kɒz'metɪk] ◇ *n* cosmético *m.* ◇ *adj fig* superficial.

cosmopolitan [kɒzmə'pɒlɪtn] *adj* cosmopolita.

cosset ['kɒsɪt] *vt* mimar.

cost [kɒst] (*pt* & *pp* **cost** OR **-ed**) ◇ *n* **-1.** [price] coste *m*, precio *m*. **-2.** *fig* [loss, damage] coste *m*, costo *m*; at the ~ of a costa de; at all ~s a toda costa. ◇ *vt* **-1.** [gen] costar; it ~ **us £20/a lot of effort** nos costó 20 libras/mucho esfuerzo; how much does it ~? ¿cuánto cuesta OR vale? **-2.** [estimate] presupuestar, preparar un presupuesto de.

◆ **costs** *npl* JUR litisexpensas *fpl.*

co-star ['kəu-] *n* coprotagonista *m y f.*

Costa Rica [,kɒstə'ri:kə] *n* Costa Rica.

Costa Rican [,kɒstə'ri:kən] ◇ *adj* costarricense. ◇ *n* costarricense *m y f.*

cost-effective *adj* rentable.

costing ['kɒstɪŋ] *n* cálculo *m* del coste.

costly ['kɒstlɪ] *adj* costoso(sa).

cost of living *n*: the ~ el coste de la vida.

cost price *n* precio *m* de coste.

costume ['kɒstju:m] *n* **-1.** [gen] traje *m*. **-2.** [swimming costume] traje *m* de baño.

costume jewellery *n* (*U*) bisutería *f.*

cosy *Br*, **cozy** *Am* ['kəuzɪ] ◇ *adj* **-1.** [warm and comfortable - room] acogedor(ra). **-2.** [intimate] agradable, amigable. ◇ *n* funda *f* para tetera.

cot [kɒt] *n* **-1.** *Br* [for child] cuna *f.* **-2.** *Am* [folding bed] cama *f* plegable.

cottage ['kɒtɪdʒ] *n* casa *f* de campo, chalé *m.*

cottage cheese *n* requesón *m.*

cottage pie *n* *Br* pastel de carne picada con una capa de puré de patatas.

cotton ['kɒtn] *n* **-1.** [fabric] algodón *m*. **-2.** [thread] hilo *m* (de algodón).

◆ **cotton on** *vi inf*: to ~ **on (to)** caer en la cuenta (de).

cotton candy *n* *Am* azúcar *m* hilado, algodón *m.*

cotton wool *n* algodón *m* (hidrófilo).

couch [kautʃ] *n* **-1.** [sofa] sofá *m*, diván *m*. **-2.** [in doctor's surgery] camilla *f.* ◇ *vt*: to ~ **sthg in** formular algo en.

couchette [ku:'ʃet] *n* *Br* litera *f.*

cough [kɒf] ◇ *n* tos *f.* ◇ *vi* toser.

cough mixture *n* *Br* jarabe *m* para la tos.

cough sweet *n* *Br* caramelo *m* para la tos.

cough syrup = **cough mixture.**

could [kud] *pt* → **can²**.

couldn't ['kudnt] = **could not.**

could've ['kudəv] = **could have.**

council ['kaunsl] *n* **-1.** [of a town] ayuntamiento *m*; [of a county] ≃ diputación *f.* **-2.** [group, organization] consejo *m.* **-3.** [meeting] junta *f*, consejo *m.*

council estate *n* urbanización *f* de viviendas de protección oficial.

council house *n Br* ≃ casa *f* de protección oficial.

councillor ['kaʊnsələ'] *n* concejal *m y f.*

council tax *n Br* impuesto municipal basado en el valor de la propiedad, ≃ contribución *f* urbana.

counsel ['kaʊnsəl] *n* **-1.** (U) *fml* [advice] consejo *m.* **-2.** [lawyer] abogado *m*, -da *f.*

counsellor *Br*, **counselor** *Am* ['kaʊnsələ'] *n* **-1.** [gen] consejero *m*, -ra *f.* **-2.** *Am* [lawyer] abogado *m*, -da *f.*

count [kaʊnt] ◇ *n* **-1.** [total] total *m*; [of votes] recuento *m*; **to keep/lose ~ of** llevar/perder la cuenta de. **-2.** [aristocrat] conde *m.* ◇ *vt* **-1.** [add up] contar; [total, cost] calcular. **-2.** [consider]: **to ~ sb as** considerar a alguien como. **-3.** [include] incluir, contar. ◇ *vi* contar; **to ~ (up) to** contar hasta; **to ~ for** valer.
◆ **count against** *vt fus* perjudicar.
◆ **count (up)on** *vt fus* contar con.
◆ **count up** *vt fus* contar.

countdown ['kaʊntdaʊn] *n* cuenta *f* atrás.

counter ['kaʊntə'] ◇ *n* **-1.** [in shop] mostrador *m*; [in bank] ventanilla *f.* **-2.** [in board game] ficha *f.* ◇ *vt*: **to ~ sthg with** responder a algo mediante; **to ~ sthg by doing sthg** contrarrestar algo haciendo algo. ◆ **counter to** *adv* contrario a.

counteract [,kaʊntə'rækt] *vt* contrarrestar.

counterattack [,kaʊntərə'tæk] ◇ *n* contraataque *m.* ◇ *vt & vi* contraatacar.

counterclockwise [,kaʊntə'klɒkwaɪz] *adv Am* en sentido opuesto a las agujas del reloj.

counterfeit ['kaʊntəfɪt] ◇ *adj* falsificado(da). ◇ *vt* falsificar.

counterfoil ['kaʊntəfɔɪl] *n* matriz *f.*

countermand [,kaʊntə'mɑːnd] *vt* revocar.

counterpart ['kaʊntəpɑːt] *n* homólogo *m*, -ga *f.*

counterproductive [,kaʊntəprə'dʌktɪv] *adj* contraproducente.

countess ['kaʊntɪs] *n* condesa *f.*

countless ['kaʊntlɪs] *adj* innumerable.

country ['kʌntrɪ] ◇ *n* **-1.** [nation] país *m.* **-2.** [population]: **the ~** el pueblo. **-3.** [countryside]: **the ~** el campo. **-4.** [terrain] terreno *m.* ◇ *comp* campestre.

country dancing *n* (U) baile *m* tradicional.

country house *n* casa *f* de campo.

countryman ['kʌntrɪmən] (*pl* **-men** [-mən]) *n* [from same country] compatriota *m.*

country park *n Br* parque natural abierto al público.

countryside ['kʌntrɪsaɪd] *n* [land] campo *m*; [landscape] paisaje *m.*

county ['kaʊntɪ] *n* condado *m.*

county council *n Br* organismo que gobierna un condado, ≃ diputación *f* provincial.

coup [kuː] *n* **-1.** [rebellion]: **~ (d'état)** golpe *m* (de estado). **-2.** [masterstroke] éxito *m.*

couple ['kʌpl] ◇ *n* **-1.** [two people in relationship] pareja *f.* **-2.** [two objects, people]: **a ~ (of)** un par (de). **-3.** [a few - objects, people]: **a ~ (of)** un par (de), unos(nas). ◇ *vt* [join]: **to ~ sthg (to)** enganchar algo (con).

coupon ['kuːpɒn] *n* [gen] cupón *m*; [for pools] boleto *m.*

courage ['kʌrɪdʒ] *n* valor *m.*

courageous [kə'reɪdʒəs] *adj* valiente.

courgette [kɔː'ʒet] *n Br* calabacín *m.*

courier ['kʊrɪə'] *n* **-1.** [on holiday] guía *m y f.* **-2.** [to deliver letters, packages] mensajero *m*, -ra *f.*

course [kɔːs] *n* **-1.** [gen] curso *m*; [of lectures] ciclo *m*; UNIV carrera *f*; **~ of treatment** MED tratamiento *m*; **off ~** fuera de su rumbo; **~ (of action)** medida *f*; **in the ~ of** a lo largo de. **-2.** [of meal] plato *m.* **-3.** SPORT [for golf] campo *m* (de golf); [for horse racing] hipódromo *m.*
◆ **of course** *adv* **-1.** [inevitably, not surprisingly] naturalmente. **-2.** [certainly] claro; **of ~ not** claro que no.

coursebook ['kɔːsbʊk] *n* libro *m* de texto.

coursework ['kɔːswɜːk] *n* (U) trabajo *m* realizado durante el curso.

court [kɔːt] ◇ *n* **-1.** [place of trial, judge, jury etc] tribunal *m*; **to take sb to ~** llevar a alguien a juicio. **-2.** SPORT cancha *f*, pista *f.* **-3.** [of king, queen etc] corte *f.* ◇ *vi dated* [go out together] cortejarse.

courteous ['kɜːtjəs] *adj* cortés.

courtesy ['kɜːtɪsɪ] ◇ *n* cortesía *f.* ◇ *comp* de cortesía. ◆ **(by) courtesy of** *prep* [the author] con permiso de; [a company] por cortesía OR gentileza de.

courthouse ['kɔːthaʊs, *pl* -haʊzɪz] *n Am* palacio *m* de justicia.

courtier ['kɔːtjə'] *n* cortesano *m.*

court-martial (*pl* **court-martials** OR **courts-martial**) *n* consejo *m* de guerra.

courtroom ['kɔːtrʊm] *n* sala *f* del tribunal.

courtyard ['kɔːtjɑːd] *n* patio *m*.

cousin ['kʌzn] *n* primo *m*, -ma *f*.

cove [kəʊv] *n* cala *f*, ensenada *f*.

covenant ['kʌvənənt] *n* **-1.** [of money] *compromiso escrito para el pago regular de una contribución esp con fines caritativos.* **-2.** [agreement] convenio *m*.

Covent Garden [ˌkɒvənt-] *n famosa galería comercial londinense donde se dan cita todo tipo de artistas callejeros.*

cover ['kʌvər] ◇ *n* **-1.** [covering] cubierta *f*; [lid] tapa *f*; [for seat, typewriter] funda *f*. **-2.** [of book] tapa *f*, cubierta *f*; [of magazine - at the front] portada *f*; [- at the back] contraportada *f*. **-3.** [protection, shelter] refugio *m*; **to take ~** [from weather, gunfire] refugiarse; **under ~** [from weather] a cubierto. **-4.** [concealment] tapadera *f*; **under ~ of** al amparo OR abrigo de. **-5.** [insurance] cobertura *f*. **-6.** [blanket] manta *f*. ◇ *vt* **-1.** [gen]: **to ~ sthg (with)** cubrir algo (de); [with lid] tapar algo (con). **-2.** [insure]: **to ~ sb (against)** cubrir OR asegurar a alguien (contra). **-3.** [include] abarcar. **-4.** [report on] informar sobre. **-5.** [discuss, deal with] abarcar. ◆ **cover up** *vt sep* **-1.** [place sthg over] tapar. **-2.** [conceal] encubrir.

coverage ['kʌvərɪdʒ] *n* [of news] reportaje *m*, cobertura *f* informativa.

cover charge *n* precio *m* del cubierto.

covering ['kʌvərɪŋ] *n* **-1.** [for floor etc] cubierta *f*. **-2.** [of snow, dust] capa *f*.

covering letter *Br*, **cover letter** *Am n* [with CV] carta *f* de presentación; [with parcel, letter] nota *f* aclaratoria.

cover note *n Br* póliza *f* provisional.

covert ['kʌvət] *adj* [operation] encubierto(ta), secreto(ta); [glance] furtivo(va).

cover-up *n* encubrimiento *m*.

covet ['kʌvɪt] *vt* codiciar.

cow [kaʊ] ◇ *n* **-1.** [female type of cattle] vaca *f*. **-2.** [female elephant, whale, seal] hembra *f*. **-3.** *Br inf pej* [woman] bruja *f*, foca *f*. ◇ *vt* acobardar, intimidar.

coward ['kaʊəd] *n* cobarde *m y f*.

cowardly ['kaʊədlɪ] *adj* cobarde.

cowboy ['kaʊbɔɪ] *n* [cattleman] vaquero *m*, tropero *m Amer*.

cower ['kaʊər] *vi* encogerse.

cox [kɒks], **coxswain** ['kɒksən] *n* timonel *m y f*.

coy [kɔɪ] *adj* gazmoño(ña) (*afectada*).

cozy *Am* = **cosy**.

crab [kræb] *n* cangrejo *m*.

crab apple *n* manzana *f* silvestre.

crack [kræk] ◇ *n* **-1.** [split - in wood, ground] grieta *f*; [- in glass, pottery] raja *f*. **-2.** [gap] rendija *f*. **-3.** [sharp noise - of whip] chasquido *m*; [- of twigs] crujido *m*. **-4.** *inf* [attempt]: **to have a ~ at sthg** intentar algo. **-5.** *drugs sl* [cocaine] crack *m*. ◇ *adj* de primera. ◇ *vt* **-1.** [cause to split] romper, partir. **-2.** [egg, nut] cascar. **-3.** [whip etc] chasquear. **-4.** [bang - head] golpearse. **-5.** [solve] dar con la clave de. **-6.** *inf* [make - joke] contar. ◇ *vi* **-1.** [split - skin, wood, ground] agrietarse; [- pottery, glass] partirse. **-2.** [break down] hundirse. **-3.** [make sharp noise - whip] chasquear; [- twigs] crujir. **-4.** *Br inf* [act quickly]: **to get ~ing** ponerse manos a la obra. ◆ **crack down** *vi*: **to ~ down (on)** tomar medidas severas (contra). ◆ **crack up** *vi* venirse abajo.

cracker ['krækər] *n* **-1.** [biscuit] galleta *f* (salada). **-2.** *Br* [for Christmas] *tubo con sorpresa típico de Navidades.*

crackers ['krækəz] *adj Br inf* majara.

crackle ['krækl] *vi* [fire] crujir, chasquear; [radio] sonar con interferencias.

cradle ['kreɪdl] ◇ *n* [baby's bed, birthplace] cuna *f*. ◇ *vt* acunar, mecer.

craft [krɑːft] (*pl sense 2 inv*) *n* **-1.** [trade] oficio *m*; [skill] arte *m*. **-2.** [boat] embarcación *f*.

craftsman ['krɑːftsmən] (*pl* **-men** [-mən]) *n* artesano *m*.

craftsmanship ['krɑːftsmənʃɪp] *n* (*U*) **-1.** [skill] destreza *f*, habilidad *f*. **-2.** [skilled work] artesanía *f*.

craftsmen *pl* → **craftsman**.

crafty ['krɑːftɪ] *adj* astuto(ta).

crag [kræg] *n* peñasco *m*.

cram [kræm] ◇ *vt* **-1.** [push - books, clothes] embutir; [people] apiñar. **-2.** [overfill]: **to ~ sthg with** atiborrar OR atestar algo de; **to be crammed (with)** estar repleto(ta) (de). ◇ *vi* empollar.

cramp [kræmp] *n* calambre *m*; **stomach ~s** retortijones *mpl* de vientre.

cranberry ['krænbərɪ] *n* arándano *m* (agrio).

crane [kreɪn] *n* **-1.** [machine] grúa *f*. **-2.** [bird] grulla *f*.

crank [kræŋk] ◇ *n* **-1.** TECH manivela *f*. **-2.** *inf* [eccentric] majareta *m y f*. ◇ *vt* [wind] girar.

crankshaft ['kræŋkʃɑːft] *n* cigüeñal *m*.

cranny ['krænɪ] *n* → **nook**.

crescent

crap [kræp] n (U) v inf mierda f.

crash [kræʃ] ◇ n -1. [accident] choque m. -2. [loud noise] estruendo m. FIN crac m. ◇ vt estrellar. ◇ vi -1. [collide - two vehicles] **chocar**; [one vehicle - into wall etc] **estrellarse**; **to ~ into sthg** chocar OR estrellarse contra algo. -2. FIN quebrar. -3. COMPUT bloquearse.

crash course n cursillo m intensivo de introducción, curso m acelerado.

crash helmet n casco m protector.

crash-land vi realizar un aterrizaje forzoso.

crass [kræs] adj burdo(da); **a ~ error** un craso error.

crate [kreɪt] n caja f (para embalaje o transporte).

crater ['kreɪtəʳ] n -1. [hole in ground] socavón m. -2. [of volcano, on the moon] cráter m.

cravat [krə'væt] n pañuelo m (de hombre).

crave [kreɪv] ◇ vt ansiar. ◇ vi: **to ~ for sthg** ansiar algo.

crawl [krɔːl] ◇ vi -1. [baby] andar a gatas. -2. [insect, person] arrastrarse. -3. [move slowly, with difficulty] avanzar lentamente. -4. inf [grovel]: **to ~ (to)** arrastrarse (ante). ◇ n [swimming stroke]: **the ~** el crol.

crayfish ['kreɪfɪʃ] (pl inv OR -es) n [freshwater] cangrejo m de río; [spiny lobster] langosta f.

crayon ['kreɪɒn] n lápiz m de cera.

craze [kreɪz] n moda f.

crazy ['kreɪzɪ] adj inf -1. [mad - person] loco(ca); [- idea] disparatado(da). -2. [enthusiastic]: **to be ~ about** estar loco(ca) por.

creak [kriːk] vi [floorboard, bed] crujir; [door, hinge] chirriar.

cream [kriːm] ◇ adj [in colour] (color) crema (inv). ◇ n -1. [food] nata f. -2. [cosmetic, mixture for food] crema f. -3. [colour] (color m) crema m. -4. [elite]: **the ~** la flor y nata, la crema.

cream cake n Br pastel m de nata.

cream cheese n queso m cremoso OR blanco.

cream cracker n Br galleta sin azúcar que generalmente se come con queso.

cream tea n Br merienda de té con bollos, nata y mermelada.

crease [kriːs] ◇ n [deliberate - in shirt] pliegue m; [- in trousers] raya f; [accidental] arruga f. ◇ vt arrugar. ◇ vi [gen] arrugarse; [forehead] fruncirse.

create [kriː'eɪt] vt [gen] crear; [interest] producir.

creation [kriː'eɪʃn] n creación f.

creative [kriː'eɪtɪv] adj [gen] creativo(va); [energy] creador(ra); **~ writing** redacciones fpl.

creature ['kriːtʃəʳ] n criatura f.

crèche [kreʃ] n Br guardería f (infantil).

credence ['kriːdns] n: **to give** OR **lend ~** to dar crédito a.

credentials [krɪ'denʃlz] npl credenciales fpl.

credibility [ˌkredə'bɪlətɪ] n credibilidad f.

credit ['kredɪt] ◇ n -1. [financial aid] crédito m; **in ~** con saldo acreedor OR positivo; **on ~** a crédito. -2. (U) [praise] reconocimiento m; **to give sb ~ for** reconocer a alguien el mérito de. -3. SCH & UNIV crédito m. -4. [money credited] saldo m acreedor OR positivo. ◇ vt -1. FIN [add] abonar; **we'll ~ your account** lo abonaremos en su cuenta. -2. inf [believe] creer. -3. [give the credit to]: **to ~ sb with** atribuir a alguien el mérito de. ◆ **credits** npl [on film] títulos mpl.

credit card n tarjeta f de crédito.

credit note n pagaré m.

creditor ['kredɪtəʳ] n acreedor m, -ra f.

creed [kriːd] n credo m.

creek [kriːk] n -1. [inlet] cala f. -2. Am [stream] riachuelo m.

creep [kriːp] (pt & pp **crept**) ◇ vi -1. [insect] arrastrarse; [traffic etc] avanzar lentamente. -2. [person] deslizarse, andar con sigilo. -3. inf [grovel]: **to ~ (to sb)** hacer la pelota (a alguien). ◇ n inf [person] pelotillero m, -ra f. ◆ **creeps** npl: **to give sb the ~s** inf ponerle a alguien la piel de gallina.

creeper ['kriːpəʳ] n enredadera f.

creepy ['kriːpɪ] adj inf horripilante.

creepy-crawly [-'krɔːlɪ] (pl -ies) n inf bicho m.

cremate [krɪ'meɪt] vt incinerar.

crematorium Br [ˌkremə'tɔːrɪəm] (pl -riums OR -ria [-rɪə]), **crematory** Am ['kremətrɪ] n (horno m) crematorio m.

crepe [kreɪp] n -1. [cloth] crespón m. -2. [rubber] crepé m. -3. [thin pancake] crepe f.

crepe bandage n Br venda f de gasa.

crepe paper n (U) papel m seda.

crept [krept] pt & pp → **creep**.

crescendo [krɪ'ʃendəʊ] (pl -s) n crescendo m.

crescent ['kresnt] n -1. [shape] media luna f. -2. [street] calle f en forma de arco.

cress [kres] *n* berro *m*.

crest [krest] *n* **-1.** [on bird's head, of wave] cresta *f*. **-2.** [of hill] cima *f*, cumbre *f*. **-3.** [on coat of arms] blasón *m*.

crestfallen ['krest,fɔːln] *adj* alicaído(da).

Crete [kriːt] *n* Creta.

cretin ['kretɪn] *n inf* [idiot] cretino *m*, -na *f*.

crevasse [krɪ'væs] *n* grieta *f*, fisura *f*.

crevice ['krevɪs] *n* grieta *f*, hendidura *f*.

crew [kruː] *n* **-1.** [of ship, plane] tripulación *f*. **-2.** [on film set etc] equipo *m*.

crew cut *n* rapado *m*, corte *m* al cero.

crew-neck(ed) [-nek(t)] *adj* con cuello redondo.

crib [krɪb] ◇ *n* [cot] cuna *f*. ◇ *vt inf*: to ~ **sthg off** OR **from sb** copiar algo de alguien.

crick [krɪk] *n* [in neck] tortícolis *f*.

cricket ['krɪkɪt] *n* **-1.** [game] críquet *m*. **-2.** [insect] grillo *m*.

crime [kraɪm] ◇ *n* **-1.** [criminal behaviour - serious] criminalidad *f*; [- less serious] delincuencia *f*. **-2.** [serious offence] crimen *m*; [less serious offence] delito *m*. **-3.** [immoral act] crimen *m*. ◇ *comp*: ~ **novel** novela *f* policíaca.

criminal ['krɪmɪnl] ◇ *adj* **-1.** JUR [act, behaviour] criminal, delictivo(va); [law] penal; [lawyer] criminalista. **-2.** *inf* [shameful] criminal. ◇ *n* [serious] criminal *m y f*; [less serious] delincuente *m y f*.

crimson ['krɪmzn] ◇ *adj* [in colour] carmesí. ◇ *n* carmesí *m*.

cringe [krɪndʒ] *vi* **-1.** [out of fear] encogerse. **-2.** *inf* [with embarrassment]: to ~ **(at)** encogerse de vergüenza (ante).

crinkle ['krɪŋkl] *vt* arrugar.

cripple ['krɪpl] ◇ *n dated* & *offensive* tullido *m*, -da *f*. ◇ *vt* **-1.** MED dejar inválido(da). **-2.** [country, industry] paralizar; [ship, plane] dejar inutilizado(da).

crisis ['kraɪsɪs] (*pl* crises ['kraɪsiːz]) *n* crisis *f inv*.

crisp [krɪsp] *adj* **-1.** [pastry, bacon, snow] crujiente; [banknote, vegetables, weather] fresco(ca). **-2.** [brisk] directo(ta). ◆ **crisps** *npl* patatas *fpl* fritas (*de bolsa*).

crisscross ['krɪskrɒs] *adj* entrecruzado(da).

criterion [kraɪ'tɪərɪən] (*pl* -ria [-rɪə] OR -rions) *n* criterio *m*.

critic ['krɪtɪk] *n* crítico *m*, -ca *f*.

critical ['krɪtɪkl] *adj* [gen] crítico(ca); [illness] grave; **to be** ~ **of** criticar a.

critically ['krɪtɪklɪ] *adv* [gen] críticamente; [ill] gravemente.

criticism ['krɪtɪsɪzm] *n* crítica *f*.

criticize, -ise ['krɪtɪsaɪz] *vt* & *vi* criticar.

croak [krəʊk] *vi* **-1.** [frog] croar; [raven] graznar. **-2.** [person] ronquear.

Croat ['krəʊæt], **Croatian** [krəʊ'eɪʃn] ◇ *adj* croata. ◇ *n* **-1.** [person] croata *m y f*. **-2.** [language] croata *m*.

Croatia [krəʊ'eɪʃə] *n* Croacia.

Croatian = **Croat**.

crochet ['krəʊʃeɪ] *n* ganchillo *m*.

crockery ['krɒkərɪ] *n* loza *f*, vajilla *f*.

crocodile ['krɒkədaɪl] (*pl inv* OR **-s**) *n* cocodrilo *m*.

crocus ['krəʊkəs] (*pl* **-es**) *n* azafrán *m*.

croft [krɒft] *n Br* granja o terreno pequeño que pertenece a una familia y les proporciona sustento.

crony ['krəʊnɪ] *n inf* amiguete *m*, -ta *f*, amigote *m*.

crook [krʊk] *n* **-1.** [criminal] ratero *m*, -ra *f*. **-2.** *inf* [dishonest person] ladrón *m*, -ona *f*, sinvergüenza *m y f*. **-3.** [shepherd's staff] cayado *m*.

crooked ['krʊkɪd] *adj* **-1.** [back] encorvado(da); [path] sinuoso(sa). **-2.** [teeth, tie] torcido(da). **-3.** *inf* [dishonest - person, policeman] corrupto(ta).

crop [krɒp] ◇ *n* **-1.** [kind of plant] cultivo *m*. **-2.** [harvested produce] cosecha *f*. **-3.** [whip] fusta *f*. ◇ *vt* [cut short] cortar (muy corto). ◆ **crop up** *vi* surgir, salir.

croquette [krɒ'ket] *n* croqueta *f*.

cross [krɒs] ◇ *adj* enfadado(da); **to get** ~ **(with)** enfadarse (con). ◇ *n* **-1.** [gen] cruz *f*. **-2.** [hybrid] cruce *m*; **a** ~ **between** [combination] una mezcla de. ◇ *vt* **-1.** [gen & FIN] cruzar. **-2.** [face - subj: expression] reflejarse en. **-3.** RELIG: **to** ~ **o.s.** santiguarse. ◇ *vi* [intersect] cruzarse. ◆ **cross off, cross out** *vt sep* tachar.

crossbar ['krɒsbɑːʳ] *n* **-1.** [on goal] travesaño *m*. **-2.** [on bicycle] barra *f*.

cross-Channel *adj* [ferry] que hace la travesía del Canal de la Mancha; [route] a través del Canal de la Mancha.

cross-country ◇ *adj* & *adv* a campo traviesa. ◇ *n* cross *m*.

cross-examine *vt* interrogar (*para comprobar veracidad*).

cross-eyed ['krɒsaɪd] *adj* bizco(ca).

crossfire ['krɒs,faɪəʳ] *n* fuego *m* cruzado.

crossing ['krɒsɪŋ] *n* **-1.** [on road] cruce *m*, paso *m* de peatones; [on railway line] paso a nivel. **-2.** [sea journey] travesía *f*.

cross-legged ['krɒslegd] *adv* con las piernas cruzadas.

cross-purposes *npl*: **to be at ~ with** sufrir un malentendido con.

cross-reference *n* remisión *f*, referencia *f*.

crossroads ['krɒsrəʊdz] (*pl inv*) *n* cruce *m*.

cross-section *n* **-1.** [drawing] sección *f* transversal. **-2.** [sample] muestra *f* representativa.

crosswalk ['krɒswɔːk] *n Am* paso *m* de peatones.

crosswind ['krɒswɪnd] *n* viento *m* de costado.

crosswise ['krɒswaɪz] *adv* en diagonal.

crossword (puzzle) ['krɒswɜːd-] *n* crucigrama *m*.

crotch [krɒtʃ] *n* entrepierna *f*.

crotchety ['krɒtʃɪtɪ] *adj Br inf* refunfuñón(ona).

crouch [kraʊtʃ] *vi* [gen] agacharse; [ready to spring] agazaparse.

crow [krəʊ] ◇ *n* cuervo *m*. ◇ *vi* **-1.** [cock] cantar. **-2.** *inf* [gloat] darse pisto.

crowbar ['krəʊbɑːʳ] *n* palanca *f*.

crowd [kraʊd] ◇ *n* **-1.** [mass of people] multitud *f*, muchedumbre *f*; [at football match etc] público *m*. **-2.** [particular group] gente *f*. ◇ *vi* agolparse, apiñarse. ◇ *vt* **-1.** [room, theatre etc] llenar. **-2.** [people] meter, apiñar.

crowded ['kraʊdɪd] *adj*: **~ (with)** repleto(ta) OR atestado(da) (de).

crown [kraʊn] ◇ *n* **-1.** [of royalty, on tooth] corona *f*. **-2.** [of hat] copa *f*; [of head] coronilla *f*; [of hill] cumbre *f*, cima *f*. ◇ *vt* [gen] coronar. ◆ **Crown** *n*: **the Crown** [monarchy] la corona.

crown jewels *npl* joyas *fpl* de la corona.

crown prince *n* príncipe *m* heredero.

crow's feet *npl* patas *fpl* de gallo.

crucial ['kruːʃl] *adj* crucial.

crucifix ['kruːsɪfɪks] *n* crucifijo *m*.

Crucifixion [,kruːsɪ'fɪkʃn] *n*: **the ~** la crucifixión.

crude [kruːd] *adj* **-1.** [rubber, oil, joke] crudo(da). **-2.** [person, behaviour] basto(ta). **-3.** [drawing, sketch] tosco(ca).

crude oil *n* crudo *m*.

cruel [krʊəl] *adj* [gen] cruel; [winter] crudo(da).

cruelty ['krʊəltɪ] *n* (*U*) crueldad *f*.

cruet ['kruːɪt] *n* vinagreras *fpl*.

cruise [kruːz] ◇ *n* crucero *m*. ◇ *vi* **-1.** [sail] hacer un crucero. **-2.** [drive, fly] ir a velocidad de crucero.

cruiser ['kruːzəʳ] *n* **-1.** [warship] crucero *m*. **-2.** [cabin cruiser] yate *m* (para cruceros).

crumb [krʌm] *n* **-1.** [of food] miga *f*, migaja *f*. **-2.** [of information] pizca *f*.

crumble ['krʌmbl] ◇ *n* compota de fruta con una pasta seca por encima. ◇ *vt* desmigajar. ◇ *vi* **-1.** [building, cliff] desmoronarse; [plaster] caerse. **-2.** *fig* [relationship, hopes] venirse abajo.

crumbly ['krʌmblɪ] *adj* que se desmigaja con facilidad.

crumpet ['krʌmpɪt] *n* [food] *bollo que se come tostado*.

crumple ['krʌmpl] *vt* [dress, suit] arrugar; [letter] estrujar.

crunch [krʌntʃ] ◇ *n* crujido *m*. ◇ *vt* **-1.** [with teeth] ronzar. **-2.** [underfoot] hacer crujir.

crunchy ['krʌntʃɪ] *adj* crujiente.

crusade [kruː'seɪd] *n lit & fig* cruzada *f*.

crush [krʌʃ] ◇ *n* **-1.** [crowd] gentío *m*. **-2.** *inf* [infatuation]: **to have a ~ on sb** estar colado(da) OR loco(ca) por alguien. ◇ *vt* **-1.** [squash] aplastar. **-2.** [grind - garlic, grain] triturar; [- ice] picar; [- grapes] exprimir. **-3.** [destroy] demoler.

crust [krʌst] *n* **-1.** [on bread] corteza *f*. **-2.** [on pie] pasta *f* (dura). **-3.** [of snow, earth] corteza *f*.

crutch [krʌtʃ] *n* **-1.** [stick] muleta *f*; *fig* [support] apoyo *m*. **-2.** [crotch] entrepierna *f*.

crux [krʌks] *n*: **the ~ of the matter** el quid de la cuestión.

cry [kraɪ] ◇ *n* **-1.** [weep] llorera *f*. **-2.** [shout] grito *m*. ◇ *vi* **-1.** [weep] llorar. **-2.** [shout] gritar. ◆ **cry off** *vi* volverse atrás.

crystal ['krɪstl] *n* cristal *m*.

crystal clear *adj* **-1.** [transparent] cristalino(na). **-2.** [clearly stated] claro(ra) como el agua.

CSE (*abbr of* **Certificate of Secondary Education**) *n antiguo título de enseñanza secundaria en Gran Bretaña para alumnos de bajo rendimiento escolar.*

CTC *n abbr of* **city technology college**.

cub [kʌb] *n* **-1.** [young animal] cachorro *m*. **-2.** [boy scout] boy scout *de entre 8 y 11 años*.

Cuba ['kjuːbə] *n* Cuba.

Cuban ['kjuːbən] ◇ *adj* cubano(na). ◇ *n* [person] cubano *m*, -na *f*.

cubbyhole ['kʌbɪhəʊl] *n* [room] cuchitril *m*; [cupboard] armario *m*.

cube [kju:b] ◇ n [gen] cubo m; [of sugar] terrón m. ◇ vt MATH elevar al cubo.

cubic ['kju:bɪk] adj cúbico(ca).

cubicle ['kju:bɪkl] n [at swimming pool] caseta f; [in shop] probador m.

Cub Scout n boy scout de entre 8 y 11 años.

cuckoo ['kuku:] n cuco m, cuclillo m.

cuckoo clock n reloj m de cuco.

cucumber ['kju:kʌmbəʳ] n pepino m.

cuddle ['kʌdl] ◇ n abrazo m. ◇ vt abrazar. ◇ vi abrazarse.

cuddly toy ['kʌdlɪ-] n muñeco m de peluche.

cue [kju:] n -1. RADIO, THEATRE & TV entrada f; on ~ justo en aquel instante. -2. fig [stimulus, signal] señal f. -3. [in snooker, pool] taco m.

cuff [kʌf] n -1. [of sleeve] puño m; off the ~ improvisado(da), sacado(da) de la manga. -2. Am [of trouser leg] vuelta f. -3. [blow] cachete m.

cuff link n gemelo m, collera f Amer.

cuisine [kwɪ'zi:n] n cocina f.

cul-de-sac ['kʌldəsæk] n callejón m sin salida.

cull [kʌl] vt -1. [animals] eliminar. -2. fml [information, facts] recoger.

culminate ['kʌlmɪneɪt] vi: to ~ in culminar en.

culmination [,kʌlmɪ'neɪʃn] n culminación f.

culottes [kju:'lɒts] npl falda f pantalón.

culpable ['kʌlpəbl] adj fml: ~ (of) culpable (de); ~ **homicide** homicidio m involuntario.

culprit ['kʌlprɪt] n culpable m y f.

cult [kʌlt] ◇ n RELIG culto m. ◇ comp de culto.

cultivate ['kʌltɪveɪt] vt -1. [gen] cultivar. -2. [get to know - person] hacer amistad con.

cultivated ['kʌltɪveɪtɪd] adj -1. [cultured] culto(ta). -2. [land] cultivado(da).

cultivation [,kʌltɪ'veɪʃn] n (U) cultivo m.

cultural ['kʌltʃərəl] adj cultural.

culture ['kʌltʃəʳ] n -1. [gen] cultura f. -2. [of bacteria] cultivo m.

cultured ['kʌltʃəd] adj culto(ta).

cumbersome ['kʌmbəsəm] adj -1. [parcel] abultado(da); [machinery] aparatoso(sa). -2. [system] torpe.

cunning ['kʌnɪŋ] ◇ adj [gen] astuto(ta); [device, idea] ingenioso(sa). ◇ n (U) astucia f.

cup [kʌp] ◇ n -1. [gen] taza f. -2. [prize, of bra] copa f. ◇ vt ahuecar.

cupboard ['kʌbəd] n armario m.

Cup Final n: the ~ ≃ la final de la Copa.

cup tie n Br partido m de copa.

curate ['kjuərət] n coadjutor m, -ra f.

curator [,kjuə'reɪtəʳ] n conservador m, -ra f, director m, -ra f.

curb [kɜ:b] ◇ n -1. [control]: ~ **(on)** control m OR restricción f (de); **to put a** ~ **on sthg** poner freno a algo. -2. Am [in road] bordillo m. ◇ vt controlar, contener.

curdle ['kɜ:dl] vi [milk] cuajarse; fig [blood] helarse.

cure [kjuəʳ] ◇ n -1. MED: ~ **(for)** cura f (para). -2. [solution]: ~ **(for)** remedio m (a). ◇ vt -1. MED curar. -2. [problem, inflation] remediar. -3. [food, tobacco] curar; [leather] curtir.

cure-all n panacea f.

curfew ['kɜ:fju:] n toque m de queda.

curio ['kjuərɪəʊ] (pl -s) n curiosidad f.

curiosity [,kjuərɪ'ɒsɪtɪ] n curiosidad f.

curious ['kjuərɪəs] adj curioso(sa); **to be** ~ **about** sentir curiosidad por.

curl [kɜ:l] ◇ n [of hair] rizo m. ◇ vt -1. [hair] rizar. -2. [twist] enroscar. ◇ vi -1. [hair] rizarse. -2. [paper] abarquillarse.
◆ **curl up** vi [person, animal] acurrucarse; [leaf, paper] abarquillarse.

curler ['kɜ:ləʳ] n rulo m.

curling tongs npl tenacillas fpl de rizar.

curly ['kɜ:lɪ] adj [hair] rizado(da); [pig's tail] enroscado(da).

currant ['kʌrənt] n [dried grape] pasa f.

currency ['kʌrənsɪ] n -1. FIN moneda f; **foreign** ~ divisa f. -2. fml [acceptability]: **to gain** ~ ganar aceptación.

current ['kʌrənt] ◇ adj [price, method, girlfriend] actual; [year] en curso; [issue] último(ma); [ideas, expressions, customs] corriente. ◇ n corriente f.

current account n Br cuenta f corriente.

current affairs npl temas mpl de actualidad.

currently ['kʌrəntlɪ] adv actualmente.

curriculum [kə'rɪkjələm] (pl -lums OR -la [-lə]) n [course of study] temario m, plan m de estudios.

curriculum vitae [-'vi:taɪ] (pl curricula vitae) n currículum m vitae.

curry ['kʌrɪ] n curry m.

curse [kɜ:s] ◇ n -1. [evil charm] maldición f. -2. [swearword] taco m, palabrota f. ◇ vt maldecir. ◇ vi [swear] soltar tacos.

cursor ['kɜːsəʳ] *n* COMPUT cursor *m*.

cursory ['kɜːsərɪ] *adj* superficial.

curt [kɜːt] *adj* brusco(ca), seco(ca).

curtail [kɜːˈteɪl] *vt* **-1.** [visit] acortar. **-2.** [expenditure] reducir; [rights] restringir.

curtain ['kɜːtn] *n* **-1.** [gen] cortina *f*. **-2.** [in theatre] telón *m*.

curts(e)y ['kɜːtsɪ] (*pt* & *pp* **curtsied**) ◇ *n* reverencia *f* (*de mujer*). ◇ *vi* hacer una reverencia (*una mujer*).

curve [kɜːv] ◇ *n* curva *f*. ◇ *vi* [river] hacer una curva; [surface] curvarse.

cushion ['kʊʃn] ◇ *n* **-1.** [for sitting on] cojín *m*. **-2.** [protective layer] colchón *m*. ◇ *vt lit* & *fig* amortiguar.

cushy ['kʊʃɪ] *adj inf* cómodo(da); **a ~ job** OR **number** un chollo (de trabajo).

custard ['kʌstəd] *n* (*U*) [sauce] natillas *fpl*.

custodian [kʌˈstəʊdjən] *n* [of building, museum] conservador *m*, -ra *f*.

custody ['kʌstədɪ] *n* custodia *f*; **to take sb into ~** detener a alguien; **in ~** bajo custodia.

custom ['kʌstəm] *n* **-1.** [tradition, habit] costumbre *f*. **-2.** (*U*) *fml* [trade] clientela *f*. ◆ **customs** *n* [place] aduana *f*.

customary ['kʌstəmrɪ] *adj* acostumbrado(da), habitual.

customer ['kʌstəməʳ] *n* **-1.** [client] cliente *m y f*. **-2.** *inf* [person] tipo *m*.

customize, -ise ['kʌstəmaɪz] *vt* personalizar.

Customs and Excise *n* (*U*) *Br* oficina del gobierno británico encargada de la recaudación de derechos arancelarios.

customs duty *n* (*U*) derechos *mpl* de aduana, aranceles *mpl*.

customs officer *n* empleado *m*, -da *f* de aduana.

cut [kʌt] (*pt* & *pp* **cut**) ◇ *n* **-1.** [gen] corte *m*. **-2.** [reduction]: **~ (in)** reducción *f* (de). **-3.** *inf* [share] parte *f*. ◇ *vt* **-1.** [gen] cortar; [one's finger etc] cortarse. **-2.** [spending, staff etc] reducir, recortar. **-3.** *inf* [lecture] fumarse. ◆ **cut back** *vt sep* **-1.** [plant] podar. **-2.** [expenditure, budget] recortar. ◆ **cut down** ◇ *vt sep* **-1.** [chop down] cortar, talar. **-2.** [reduce] reducir. ◇ *vi*: **to ~ down on smoking** OR **cigarettes** fumar menos. ◆ **cut in** *vi* **-1.** [interrupt]: **to ~ in (on sb)** cortar OR interrumpir (a alguien). **-2.** [in car] colarse. ◆ **cut off** *vt sep* **-1.** [gen] cortar. **-2.** [separate]: **to be ~ off (from)** [person] estar aislado(da) (de); [town, village] quedarse incomunicado(da) (de). ◆ **cut out** *vt sep* **-1.** [re-

move] recortar. **-2.** [dress, pattern etc] cortar. **-3.** [stop]: **to ~ out smoking** OR **cigarettes** dejar de fumar; **~ it out!** *inf* ¡basta ya! **-4.** [exclude - light etc] eliminar; **to ~ sb out of one's will** desheredar a alguien. ◆ **cut up** *vt sep* [chop up] cortar, desmenuzar.

cutback ['kʌtbæk] *n*: **~ (in)** recorte *m* OR reducción *f* (en).

cute [kjuːt] *adj* [appealing] mono(na), lindo(da).

cuticle ['kjuːtɪkl] *n* cutícula *f*.

cutlery ['kʌtlərɪ] *n* (*U*) cubertería *f*.

cutlet ['kʌtlɪt] *n* chuleta *f*.

cutout ['kʌtaʊt] *n* **-1.** [on machine] cortacircuitos *m inv*. **-2.** [shape] recorte *m*.

cut-price, cut-rate *Am adj* de oferta.

cutthroat ['kʌtθrəʊt] *adj* [ruthless] encarnizado(da).

cutting ['kʌtɪŋ] ◇ *adj* [sarcastic] cortante, mordaz. ◇ *n* **-1.** [of plant] esqueje *m*. **-2.** [from newspaper] recorte *m*. **-3.** *Br* [for road, railway] desmonte *m*.

CV (*abbr of* **curriculum vitae**) *n* CV *m*.

cwt. *abbr of* **hundredweight**.

cyanide ['saɪənaɪd] *n* cianuro *m*.

cycle ['saɪkl] ◇ *n* **-1.** [series of events, poems, songs] ciclo *m*. **-2.** [bicycle] bicicleta *f*. ◇ *comp*: **~ path** camino *m* para bicicletas. ◇ *vi* ir en bicicleta.

cycling ['saɪklɪŋ] *n* ciclismo *m*; **to go ~** ir en bicicleta.

cyclist ['saɪklɪst] *n* ciclista *m y f*.

cygnet ['sɪgnɪt] *n* pollo *m* de cisne.

cylinder ['sɪlɪndəʳ] *n* **-1.** [shape, engine component] cilindro *m*. **-2.** [container - for gas] bombona *f*.

cymbals ['sɪmblz] *npl* platillos *mpl*.

cynic ['sɪnɪk] *n* cínico *m*, -ca *f*.

cynical ['sɪnɪkl] *adj* cínico(ca).

cynicism ['sɪnɪsɪzm] *n* cinismo *m*.

cypress ['saɪprəs] *n* ciprés *m*.

Cypriot ['sɪprɪət] ◇ *adj* chipriota. ◇ *n* chipriota *m y f*.

Cyprus ['saɪprəs] *n* Chipre *m*.

cyst [sɪst] *n* quiste *m*.

cystitis [sɪsˈtaɪtɪs] *n* cistitis *f inv*.

czar [zɑːʳ] *n* zar *m*.

Czech [tʃek] ◇ *adj* checo(ca). ◇ *n* **-1.** [person] checo *m*, -ca *f*. **-2.** [language] checo *m*.

Czechoslovak [ˌtʃekəˈsləʊvæk] = **Czechoslovakian**.

Czechoslovakia [ˌtʃekəsləˈvækɪə] *n* Checoslovaquia.

Czechoslovakian [ˌtʃekəsləˈvækɪən] ◇

adj checoslovaco(ca). ◇ *n* [person] checoslovaco *m*, -ca *f*.

D

d (*pl* **d's** OR **ds**), **D** (*pl* **D's** OR **Ds**) [diː] *n* [letter] d *f*, D *f*. ◆**D** *n* MUS re *m*.

DA *n abbr of* **district attorney**.

dab [dæb] ◇ *n* [small amount] toque *m*, pizca *f*; [of powder] pizca *f*. ◇ *vt* **-1.** [skin, wound] dar ligeros toques en. **-2.** [cream, ointment]: **to ~ sthg on** OR **onto** aplicar algo sobre.

dabble ['dæbl] *vi*: **to ~ (in)** pasar el tiempo OR entretenerse (con).

dachshund ['dækshund] *n* perro *m* salchicha.

dad [dæd], **daddy** ['dædɪ] *n inf* papá *m*.

daddy longlegs [-'lɒŋlegz] (*pl inv*) *n* típula *f*.

daffodil ['dæfədɪl] *n* narciso *m*.

daft [dɑːft] *adj Br inf* tonto(ta).

dagger ['dægər] *n* daga *f*, puñal *m*.

daily ['deɪlɪ] ◇ *adj* diario(ria). ◇ *adv* diariamente; **twice ~** dos veces al día. ◇ *n* [newspaper] diario *m*.

dainty ['deɪntɪ] *adj* delicado(da), fino(na).

dairy ['deərɪ] *n* **-1.** [on farm] vaquería *f*. **-2.** [shop] lechería *f*.

dairy farm *n* granja *f* (de productos lácteos).

dairy products *npl* productos *mpl* lácteos.

dais ['deɪɪs] *n* tarima *f*, estrado *m*.

daisy ['deɪzɪ] *n* margarita *f*.

daisy wheel *n* margarita *f* (*de máquina de escribir*).

dale [deɪl] *n* valle *m*.

dam [dæm] ◇ *n* [across river] presa *f*. ◇ *vt* represar.

damage ['dæmɪdʒ] ◇ *n* **-1.** [physical harm]: **~ (to)** daño *m* (a). **-2.** [harmful effect]: **~ (to)** perjuicio *m* (a). ◇ *vt* dañar. ◆**damages** *npl* JUR daños *mpl* y perjuicios.

damn [dæm] ◇ *adj inf* maldito(ta). ◇ *adv* inf tela de, muy. ◇ *n inf*: **I don't give** OR **care a ~ (about it)** me importa un bledo. ◇ *vt* **-1.** RELIG [condemn] con-

denar. **-2.** *v inf* [curse]: **~ it!** ¡maldita sea!

damned [dæmd] *inf* ◇ *adj* maldito(ta); **I'm ~ if ...** que me maten si ...; **well I'll be** OR **I'm ~!** ¡ostras! ◇ *adv* tela de, muy.

damning ['dæmɪŋ] *adj* comprometedor(ra).

damp [dæmp] ◇ *adj* húmedo(da). ◇ *n* humedad *f*. ◇ *vt* [make wet] humedecer.

dampen ['dæmpən] *vt* **-1.** [make wet] humedecer. **-2.** *fig* [emotion] apagar.

damson ['dæmzn] *n* (ciruela *f*) damascena *f*.

dance [dɑːns] ◇ *n* baile *m*. ◇ *vi* **-1.** [to music] bailar. **-2.** [move quickly and lightly] agitarse, moverse.

dancer ['dɑːnsər] *n* bailarín *m*, -ina *f*.

dancing ['dɑːnsɪŋ] *n* (U) baile *m*.

dandelion ['dændɪlaɪən] *n* diente *m* de león.

dandruff ['dændrʌf] *n* caspa *f*.

Dane [deɪn] *n* danés *m*, -esa *f*.

danger ['deɪndʒər] *n*: **~ (to)** peligro *m* (para); **in/out of ~** en/fuera de peligro; **to be in ~ of doing sthg** correr el riesgo de hacer algo.

dangerous ['deɪndʒərəs] *adj* peligroso(sa).

dangle ['dæŋgl] ◇ *vt* colgar; *fig*: **to ~ sthg before sb** poner los dientes largos a alguien con algo. ◇ *vi* colgar, pender.

Danish ['deɪnɪʃ] ◇ *adj* danés(esa). ◇ *n* **-1.** [language] danés *m*. **-2.** *Am* = **Danish pastry**. ◇ *npl* [people]: **the ~** los daneses.

Danish pastry *n* pastel de hojaldre con crema o manzana o almendras etc.

dank [dæŋk] *adj* húmedo(da) e insalubre.

dapper ['dæpər] *adj* pulcro(cra).

dappled ['dæpld] *adj* **-1.** [light] moteado(da). **-2.** [horse] rodado(da).

dare [deər] ◇ *vt* **-1.** [be brave enough]: **to ~ to do sthg** atreverse a hacer algo, osar hacer algo. **-2.** [challenge]: **to ~ sb to do sthg** desafiar a alguien a hacer algo. **-3.** *phr*: **I ~ say (...)** supongo OR me imagino (que ...). ◇ *vi* atreverse, osar; **how ~ you!** ¿cómo te atreves? ◇ *n* desafío *m*, reto *m*.

daredevil ['deə,devl] *n* temerario *m*, -ria *f*.

daring ['deərɪŋ] ◇ *adj* atrevido(da), audaz. ◇ *n* audacia *f*.

dark [dɑːk] ◇ *adj* **-1.** [night, colour, hair] oscuro(ra). **-2.** [person, skin] moreno(na). **-3.** [thoughts, days, mood] sombrío(a), triste. **-4.** [look, comment, side of character etc] siniestro(tra). ◇ *n* **-1.** [darkness]: **the ~** la oscuridad; **to be in the ~ about sthg** estar a oscuras sobre algo. **-2.** [night]: **before/after ~** antes/después del anochecer.

darken ['dɑːkn] ◇ *vt* oscurecer. ◇ *vi* [become darker] oscurecerse.

dark glasses *npl* gafas *fpl* oscuras.

darkness ['dɑːknɪs] *n* oscuridad *f*.

darkroom ['dɑːkrum] *n* PHOT cuarto *m* oscuro.

darling ['dɑːlɪŋ] ◇ *adj* [dear] querido(da). ◇ *n* **-1.** [loved person] encanto *m*. **-2.** *inf* [addressing any woman] maja *f*.

darn [dɑːn] ◇ *adj inf* maldito(ta), condenado(da). ◇ *adv inf* tela de, muy. ◇ *vt* zurcir. ◇ *excl inf* ¡maldita sea!

dart [dɑːt] ◇ *n* [arrow] dardo *m*. ◇ *vi* precipitarse. ◆ **darts** *n* (U) [game] dardos *mpl*.

dartboard ['dɑːtbɔːd] *n* blanco *m*, diana *f*.

dash [dæʃ] ◇ *n* **-1.** [of liquid, colour] gotas *fpl*, chorrito *m*. **-2.** [in punctuation] guión *m*. **-3.** [rush]: **to make a ~ for sthg** salir disparado hacia algo. ◇ *vt* **-1.** *literary* [throw] arrojar. **-2.** [hopes] frustrar, malograr. ◇ *vi* ir de prisa.

dashboard ['dæʃbɔːd] *n* salpicadero *m*.

dashing ['dæʃɪŋ] *adj* gallardo(da).

data ['deɪtə] *n* (U) datos *mpl*.

database ['deɪtəbeɪs] *n* COMPUT base *f* de datos.

data processing *n* proceso *m* de datos.

date [deɪt] ◇ *n* **-1.** [in time] fecha *f*; **to ~** hasta la fecha. **-2.** [appointment] cita *f*. **-3.** *Am* [person] pareja *f* (*con la que se sale*). **-4.** [fruit] dátil *m*. ◇ *vt* **-1.** [establish the date of] datar. **-2.** [mark with the date] fechar. **-3.** *Am* [go out with] salir con.

dated ['deɪtɪd] *adj* anticuado(da).

date of birth *n* fecha *f* de nacimiento.

daub [dɔːb] *vt*: **to ~ sthg with** embadurnar algo con.

daughter ['dɔːtə'] *n* hija *f*.

daughter-in-law (*pl* **daughters-in-law**) *n* nuera *f*.

daunting ['dɔːntɪŋ] *adj* amedrantador(ra).

dawdle ['dɔːdl] *vi* remolonear.

dawn [dɔːn] ◇ *n* **-1.** [of day] amanecer *m*, alba *f*. **-2.** [of era, period] albores *mpl*. ◇ *vi* [day] amanecer. ◆ **dawn (up)on** *vt*

fus: **it ~ed on me that ...** caí en la cuenta de que ....

day [deɪ] *n* **-1.** [gen] día *m*; **the ~ before/after** el día anterior/siguiente; **the ~ before yesterday** anteayer; **the ~ after tomorrow** pasado mañana; **any ~ now** cualquier día de estos; **one** OR **some ~, one of these ~s** uno de estos días; **to make sb's ~** dar un alegrón a alguien. **-2.** [period in history]: **in my/your** *etc* **~** en mis/tus *etc* tiempos; **in those ~s** en aquellos tiempos. ◆ **days** *adv* de día.

daybreak ['deɪbreɪk] *n* amanecer *m*, alba *f*; **at ~** al amanecer.

daycentre ['deɪsentə'] *n Br* (*centro estatal diurno donde se da*) acogida y cuidado a niños, ancianos, minusválidos etc.

daydream ['deɪdriːm] ◇ *n* sueño *m*, ilusión *f*. ◇ *vi* soñar despierto(ta).

daylight ['deɪlaɪt] *n* **-1.** [light] luz *f* del día. **-2.** [dawn] amanecer *m*.

day off (*pl* **days off**) *n* día *m* libre.

day return *n Br* billete *m* de ida y vuelta para un día.

daytime ['deɪtaɪm] ◇ *n* (U) día *m*. ◇ *comp* de día, diurno(na).

day-to-day *adj* cotidiano(na).

day trip *n* excursión *f* (de un día).

daze [deɪz] ◇ *n*: **in a ~** aturdido(da). ◇ *vt lit & fig* aturdir.

dazzle ['dæzl] *vt lit & fig* deslumbrar.

DC *n* (*abbr of* **direct current**) CC *f*.

D-day ['diːdeɪ] *n* el día D.

DEA (*abbr of* **Drug Enforcement Administration**) *n* organismo estadounidense para la lucha contra la droga.

deacon ['diːkən] *n* diácono *m*.

deactivate [,diː'æktɪveɪt] *vt* desactivar.

dead [ded] ◇ *adj* **-1.** [person, animal, plant] muerto(ta); **to shoot sb ~** matar a alguien a tiros. **-2.** [numb - leg, arm] entumecido(da). **-3.** [telephone] cortado(da); [car battery] descargado(da). **-4.** [silence] absoluto(ta). **-5.** [lifeless - town, party] sin vida. ◇ *adv* **-1.** [directly, precisely] justo. **-2.** [completely] totalmente, completamente; **"~ slow"** "al paso". **-3.** *inf* [very] la mar de, muy. **-4.** [suddenly]: **to stop ~** parar en seco. ◇ *npl*: **the ~** los muertos.

deaden ['dedn] *vt* atenuar.

dead end *n lit & fig* callejón *m* sin salida.

dead heat *n* empate *m*.

deadline ['dedlaɪn] *n* plazo *m*, fecha *f* tope.

deadlock ['dedlɒk] *n* punto *m* muerto.

dead loss n inf **-1.** [person] inútil m y f. **-2.** [thing] inutilidad f.

deadly ['dedlɪ] ◇ adj **-1.** [gen] mortal. **-2.** [accuracy] absoluto(ta). ◇ adv [boring] mortalmente, terriblemente; [serious] totalmente.

deadpan ['dedpæn] adj inexpresivo(va), serio(ria).

deaf [def] ◇ adj [unable to hear] sordo(da). ◇ npl: **the ~** los sordos.

deaf-aid n Br audífono m.

deaf-and-dumb adj sordomudo(da).

deafen ['defn] vt ensordecer.

deaf-mute n sordomudo m, -da f.

deafness ['defnɪs] n sordera f.

deal [di:l] (pt & pp **dealt**) ◇ n **-1.** [quantity]: **a good** OR **great ~ (of)** mucho. **-2.** [business agreement] trato m, transacción f; **to do** OR **strike a ~ with sb** hacer un trato con alguien. **-3.** inf [treatment] trato m; **big ~!** ¡vaya cosa! ◇ vt **-1.** [strike]: **to ~ sb/sthg a blow, to ~ a blow to sb/sthg** lit & fig asestar un golpe a alguien/algo. **-2.** [cards] repartir, dar. ◇ vi **-1.** [in cards] repartir, dar. **-2.** [in drugs] traficar con droga. ◆ **deal in** vt fus COMM comerciar en. ◆ **deal out** vt sep repartir. ◆ **deal with** vt fus **-1.** [handle - situation, problem] hacer frente a, resolver; [- customer] tratar con. **-2.** [be about] tratar de. **-3.** [be faced with] enfrentarse a.

dealer ['di:lər] n **-1.** [trader] comerciante m y f. **-2.** [in cards] repartidor m, -ra f.

dealing ['di:lɪŋ] n comercio m. ◆ **dealings** npl [personal] trato m; [in business] tratos mpl.

dealt [delt] pt & pp → **deal**.

dean [di:n] n **-1.** [of university] ≃ decano m, -na f. **-2.** [of church] deán m.

dear [dɪər] ◇ adj **-1.** [loved] querido(da); **~ to sb** preciado(da) para alguien. **-2.** [expensive] caro(ra). **-3.** [in letter]: **Dear Sir** Estimado señor, Muy señor mío; **Dear Madam** Estimada señora. ◇ n querido m, -da f. ◇ excl: **oh ~!** ¡vaya por Dios!

dearly ['dɪəlɪ] adv [love, wish] profundamente.

death [deθ] n muerte f; **to frighten sb to ~** dar un susto de muerte a alguien; **to be sick to ~ of sthg/of doing sthg** estar hasta las narices de algo/de hacer algo.

death certificate n partida f OR certificado m de defunción.

death duty Br, **death tax** Am n impuesto m de sucesiones.

deathly ['deθlɪ] ◇ adj sepulcral. ◇ adv: **he was ~ pale** estaba pálido como un muerto.

death penalty n pena f de muerte.

death rate n índice m OR tasa f de mortalidad.

death tax Am = **death duty**.

death trap n inf trampa f mortal, sitio m peligroso.

debar [di:'ba:r] vt: **to ~ sb from somewhere/from doing sthg** privar a alguien del acceso a algún lugar/de hacer algo.

debase [dɪ'beɪs] vt: **to ~ o.s.** rebajarse.

debate [dɪ'beɪt] ◇ n debate m; **that's open to ~** eso está por ver. ◇ vt **-1.** [issue] discutir, debatir. **-2.** [what to do]: **to ~ (whether to do sthg)** pensarse (si hacer algo). ◇ vi discutir, debatir.

debating society [dɪ'beɪtɪŋ-] n asociación de debates especialmente universitaria.

debauchery [dɪ'bɔ:tʃərɪ] n depravación f, libertinaje m.

debit ['debɪt] ◇ n debe m, débito m. ◇ vt: **to ~ sb's account with an amount, to ~ an amount to sb** adeudar OR cargar una cantidad en la cuenta de alguien.

debit note n pagaré m.

debris ['deɪbri:] n (U) [of building] escombros mpl; [of aircraft] restos mpl.

debt [det] n deuda f; **to be in ~ (to sb)** tener una deuda (con alguien).

debt collector n cobrador m, -ra f de morosos.

debtor ['detər] n deudor m, -ra f.

debug [,di:'bʌg] vt COMPUT suprimir fallos de.

debunk [,di:'bʌŋk] vt desmentir.

debut ['deɪbju:] n debut m.

decade ['dekeɪd] n década f.

decadent ['dekədənt] adj decadente.

decaffeinated [dɪ'kæfɪneɪtɪd] adj descafeinado(da).

decamp [dɪ'kæmp] vi inf escabullirse.

decanter [dɪ'kæntər] n licorera f.

decathlon [dɪ'kæθlɒn] n decatlón m.

decay [dɪ'keɪ] ◇ n (U) [of tooth] caries f; [of body, plant] descomposición f. **-2.** fig [of building] deterioro m; [of society] degradación f. ◇ vi **-1.** [tooth] picarse; [body, plant] pudrirse. **-2.** fig [building] deteriorarse; [society] degradarse.

deceased [dɪ'si:st] (pl inv) fml n: **the ~** el difunto (la difunta).

deceit [dɪ'si:t] n engaño m.

deceitful [dɪ'siːtful] *adj* [person, smile] embustero(ra); [behaviour] falso(sa).

deceive [dɪ'siːv] *vt* engañar; **to ~ o.s.** engañarse (a uno mismo/una misma).

December [dɪ'sembər] *n* diciembre *m*; *see also* **September.**

decency ['diːsnsɪ] *n* **-1.** [respectability] decencia *f*. **-2.** [consideration]: **to have the ~ to do sthg** tener la delicadeza de hacer algo.

decent ['diːsnt] *adj* **-1.** [gen] decente. **-2.** [considerate]: **that's very ~ of you** es muy amable de tu parte.

deception [dɪ'sepʃn] *n* engaño *m*.

deceptive [dɪ'septɪv] *adj* engañoso(sa).

decide [dɪ'saɪd] ◇ *vt* **-1.** [gen]: **to ~ (to do sthg)** decidir (hacer algo); **to ~ (that)** decidir que. **-2.** [person] hacer decidirse. **-3.** [issue, case] resolver. ◇ *vi* decidir. ◆ **decide (up)on** *vt fus* decidirse por.

decided [dɪ'saɪdɪd] *adj* **-1.** [advantage, improvement] indudable. **-2.** [person] decidido(da); [opinion] categórico(ca).

decidedly [dɪ'saɪdɪdlɪ] *adv* **-1.** [clearly] decididamente. **-2.** [resolutely] con decisión.

deciduous [dɪ'sɪdjʊəs] *adj* de hoja caduca.

decimal ['desɪml] ◇ *adj* decimal. ◇ *n* (número *m*) decimal *m*.

decimal point *n* coma *f* decimal.

decimate ['desɪmeɪt] *vt* diezmar.

decipher [dɪ'saɪfər] *vt* descifrar.

decision [dɪ'sɪʒn] *n* decisión *f*; **to make a ~** tomar una decisión.

decisive [dɪ'saɪsɪv] *adj* **-1.** [person] decidido(da). **-2.** [factor, event] decisivo(va).

deck [dek] *n* **-1.** [of ship] cubierta *f*; [of bus] piso *m*. **-2.** [of cards] baraja *f*. **-3.** *Am* [of house] entarimado *m* (*junto a una casa*).

deckchair ['dektʃeər] *n* tumbona *f*.

declaration [,deklə'reɪʃn] *n* declaración *f*.

Declaration of Independence *n*: **the ~** la declaración de independencia estadounidense de 1776.

declare [dɪ'kleər] *vt* declarar.

decline [dɪ'klaɪn] ◇ *n* declive *m*; **in ~** en decadencia; **on the ~** en declive. ◇ *vt* [offer] declinar; [request] denegar; **to ~ to do sthg** rehusar hacer algo. ◇ *vi* **-1.** [deteriorate] disminuir. **-2.** [refuse] negarse.

decode [,diː'kəʊd] *vt* descodificar.

decompose [,diːkəm'pəʊz] *vi* descomponerse.

decongestant [,diːkən'dʒestənt] *n* decongestivo *m*.

décor ['deɪkɔːʳ] *n* decoración *f*.

decorate ['dekəreɪt] *vt* **-1.** [make pretty]: **to ~ sthg (with)** decorar algo (de). **-2.** [with paint] pintar; [with wallpaper] empapelar. **-3.** [with medal] condecorar.

decoration [,dekə'reɪʃn] *n* **-1.** [gen] decoración *f*. **-2.** [ornament] adorno *m*. **-3.** [medal] condecoración *f*.

decorator ['dekəreɪtəʳ] *n* [painter] pintor *m*, -ra *f*; [paperhanger] empapelador *m*, -ra *f*.

decorum [dɪ'kɔːrəm] *n* decoro *m*.

decoy [*n* 'diːkɔɪ, *vb* dɪ'kɔɪ] ◇ *n* señuelo *m*. ◇ *vt* desviar (*mediante señuelo*).

decrease [*n* 'diːkriːs, *vb* dɪ'kriːs] ◇ *n*: **~ (in)** disminución *f* (en). ◇ *vt & vi* disminuir.

decree [dɪ'kriː] ◇ *n* **-1.** [order, decision] decreto *m*. **-2.** *Am* [judgment] sentencia *f*, fallo *m*. ◇ *vt* decretar.

decree nisi [-'naɪsaɪ] (*pl* **decrees nisi**) *n Br* JUR sentencia *f* provisional de divorcio.

decrepit [dɪ'krepɪt] *adj* decrépito(ta).

dedicate ['dedɪkeɪt] *vt* dedicar; **to ~ o.s. to sthg** consagrarse OR dedicarse a algo.

dedication [,dedɪ'keɪʃn] *n* **-1.** [commitment] dedicación *f*. **-2.** [in book] dedicatoria *f*.

deduce [dɪ'djuːs] *vt*: **to ~ (sthg from sthg)** deducir (algo de algo).

deduct [dɪ'dʌkt] *vt*: **to ~ (from)** deducir (de), descontar (de).

deduction [dɪ'dʌkʃn] *n* deducción *f*.

deed [diːd] *n* **-1.** [action] acción *f*, obra *f*. **-2.** JUR escritura *f*.

deem [diːm] *vt fml* estimar.

deep [diːp] ◇ *adj* **-1.** [gen] profundo(da); **to be 10 feet ~** tener 10 pies de profundidad. **-2.** [sigh, breath] hondo(da). **-3.** [colour] intenso(sa). **-4.** [sound, voice] grave. ◇ *adv* [dig, cut] hondo; **~ down** OR **inside** por dentro.

deepen ['diːpn] ◇ *vt* [hole, channel] ahondar. ◇ *vi* **-1.** [river, sea] ahondarse. **-2.** [crisis, recession] agudizarse; [emotion, darkness] hacerse más intenso(sa).

deep freeze *n* congelador *m*.

deep fry *vt* freír (con mucho aceite).

deeply ['diːplɪ] *adv* [gen] profundamente; [dig, breathe, sigh] hondo.

deep-sea *adj*: **~ diving** buceo *m* de profundidad.

deer [dɪəʳ] (*pl inv*) *n* ciervo *m*.

deface [dɪ'feɪs] *vt* pintarrajear.

defamatory [dɪ'fæmətrɪ] *adj fml* difamatorio(ria).

default [dɪ'fɔːlt] ◇ *n* **-1.** [on payment, agreement] incumplimiento *m*; [failure to attend] incomparecencia *f*; **by ~** [win] por incomparecencia. **-2.** COMPUT: **~ (value)** valor *m* de ajuste (por defecto). ◇ *vi* incumplir un compromiso.

defeat [dɪ'fiːt] ◇ *n* derrota *f*; **to admit ~** darse por vencido(da). ◇ *vt* [team, opponent] derrotar; [motion] rechazar; [plans] frustrar.

defeatist [dɪ'fiːtɪst] *adj* derrotista.

defect [*n* 'diːfekt, *vb* dɪ'fekt] ◇ *n* [fault] defecto *m*. ◇ *vi* POL: **to ~ to the other side** pasarse al otro bando.

defective [dɪ'fektɪv] *adj* defectuoso(sa).

defence Br, **defense** Am [dɪ'fens] *n* defensa *f*.

defenceless Br, **defenseless** Am [dɪ'fenslɪs] *adj* indefenso(sa).

defend [dɪ'fend] *vt* defender.

defendant [dɪ'fendənt] *n* acusado *m*, -da *f*.

defender [dɪ'fendəʳ] *n* **-1.** [gen] defensor *m*, -ra *f*. **-2.** SPORT defensa *m y f*.

defense Am = **defence**.

defenseless Am = **defenceless**.

defensive [dɪ'fensɪv] ◇ *adj* **-1.** [weapons, tactics] defensivo(va). **-2.** [person] receloso(sa). ◇ *n*: **on the ~** a la defensiva.

defer [dɪ'fɜːʳ] ◇ *vt* deferir, aplazar. ◇ *vi*: **to ~ to sb** deferir con OR a alguien.

deferential [,defə'renʃl] *adj* deferente.

defiance [dɪ'faɪəns] *n* desafío *m*; **in ~ of** en desafío de, a despecho de.

defiant [dɪ'faɪənt] *adj* desafiante.

deficiency [dɪ'fɪʃnsɪ] *n* **-1.** [lack] escasez *f*. **-2.** [inadequacy] deficiencia *f*.

deficient [dɪ'fɪʃnt] *adj* **-1.** [lacking]: **to be ~ in** ser deficitario(ria) en, estar falto(ta) de. **-2.** [inadequate] deficiente.

deficit ['defɪsɪt] *n* déficit *m inv*.

defile [dɪ'faɪl] *vt* [desecrate] profanar; *fig* [mind, purity] corromper.

define [dɪ'faɪn] *vt* definir.

definite ['defɪnɪt] *adj* **-1.** [plan, date, answer] definitivo(va). **-2.** [improvement, difference] indudable. **-3.** [confident - person] tajante; **I am quite ~ (about it)** estoy totalmente seguro (de ello).

definitely ['defɪnɪtlɪ] *adv* **-1.** [without doubt] sin duda. **-2.** [for emphasis] desde luego, con (toda) seguridad.

definition [defɪ'nɪʃn] *n* **-1.** [gen] definición *f*; **by ~** por definición. **-2.** [clarity] nitidez *f*.

deflate [dɪ'fleɪt] ◇ *vt* [balloon] desinflar; *fig* [person] bajar los humos a. ◇ *vi* desinflarse.

deflation [dɪ'fleɪʃn] *n* ECON deflación *f*.

deflect [dɪ'flekt] *vt* [gen] desviar; [criticism] soslayar.

defogger [,diː'fɒgəʳ] *n* Am AUT dispositivo *m* antivaho, luneta *f* térmica.

deformed [dɪ'fɔːmd] *adj* deforme.

defraud [dɪ'frɔːd] *vt* defraudar, estafar.

defrost [,diː'frɒst] ◇ *vt* **-1.** [gen] descongelar. **-2.** Am AUT [demist] desempañar. ◇ *vi* descongelarse.

deft [deft] *adj* habilidoso(sa), diestro(tra).

defunct [dɪ'fʌŋkt] *adj* [plan] desechado(da); [body, organization] desaparecido(da).

defuse [,diː'fjuːz] *vt* Br **-1.** [bomb] desactivar. **-2.** [situation] neutralizar.

defy [dɪ'faɪ] *vt* **-1.** [disobey - person, authority] desafiar, desobedecer; [law, rule] violar. **-2.** [challenge]: **to ~ sb to do sthg** retar OR desafiar a alguien a hacer algo. **-3.** [description, analysis] hacer imposible; [attempts, efforts] hacer inútil.

degenerate [*adj* dɪ'dʒenərət, *vb* dɪ'dʒenəreɪt] ◇ *adj* degenerado(da). ◇ *vi*: **to ~ (into)** degenerar (en).

degrading [dɪ'greɪdɪŋ] *adj* denigrante.

degree [dɪ'griː] *n* **-1.** [unit of measurement, amount] grado *m*; **by ~s** poco a poco. **-2.** [qualification] título *m* universitario, ≃ licenciatura *f*; **to have/take a ~ (in sthg)** tener/hacer una licenciatura (en algo).

dehydrated [,diːhaɪ'dreɪtɪd] *adj* deshidratado(da).

de-ice [diː'aɪs] *vt* descongelar.

deign [deɪn] *vt*: **to ~ to do sthg** dignarse a hacer algo.

deity ['diːɪtɪ] *n* deidad *f*.

dejected [dɪ'dʒektɪd] *adj* abatido(da).

delay [dɪ'leɪ] ◇ *n* retraso *m*. ◇ *vt* retrasar; **to ~ starting sthg** retrasar el comienzo de algo. ◇ *vi*: **to ~ (in doing sthg)** retrasarse (en hacer algo).

delayed [dɪ'leɪd] *adj*: **to be ~** [person] retrasarse; [train] ir con retraso.

delectable [dɪ'lektəbl] *adj* **-1.** [food] deleitable. **-2.** [person] apetecible.

delegate [*n* 'delɪgət, *vb* 'delɪgeɪt] ◇ *n* delegado *m*, -da *f*. ◇ *vt*: **to ~ sthg (to sb)** delegar algo (en alguien); **to ~ sb to do sthg** delegar a alguien para hacer algo.

delegation [,delɪ'geɪʃn] *n* delegación *f*.

delete [dɪ'liːt] vt [gen & COMPUT] borrar.

deli ['delɪ] n inf abbr of **delicatessen**.

deliberate [adj dɪ'lɪbərət, vb dɪ'lɪbəreɪt] ◇ adj **-1.** [intentional] deliberado(da). **-2.** [slow] pausado(da). ◇ vi fml deliberar.

deliberately [dɪ'lɪbərətlɪ] adv **-1.** [on purpose] adrede. **-2.** [slowly] pausadamente.

delicacy ['delɪkəsɪ] n **-1.** [gracefulness, tact] delicadeza f. **-2.** [food] exquisitez f, manjar m.

delicate ['delɪkət] adj **-1.** [gen] delicado(da). **-2.** [subtle - colour, taste] suave, sutil. **-3.** [tactful] prudente; [instrument] sensible.

delicatessen [,delɪkə'tesn] n ≃ charcutería f, ≃ (tienda f de) ultramarinos m inv.

delicious [dɪ'lɪʃəs] adj delicioso(sa).

delight [dɪ'laɪt] n [great pleasure] gozo m, regocijo m; **to take ~ in doing sthg** disfrutar haciendo algo. ◇ vt encantar. ◇ vi: **to ~ in sthg/in doing sthg** disfrutar con algo/haciendo algo.

delighted [dɪ'laɪtɪd] adj encantado(da), muy contento(ta); **~ by** OR **with** encantado con; **to be ~ to do sthg/that** estar encantado de hacer algo/de que; **I'd be ~ (to come)** me encantaría (ir).

delightful [dɪ'laɪtful] adj [gen] encantador(ra); [meal] delicioso(sa); [view] muy agradable.

delinquent [dɪ'lɪŋkwənt] ◇ adj [behaviour] delictivo(va); [child] delincuente. ◇ n delincuente m y f.

delirious [dɪ'lɪrɪəs] adj [with fever] delirante; fig [ecstatic] enfervorizado(da).

deliver [dɪ'lɪvər] vt **-1.** [distribute] repartir; [hand over] entregar; **to ~ sthg to sb** entregar algo a alguien. **-2.** [give - speech, verdict, lecture] pronunciar; [- message] entregar; [- warning, ultimatum] lanzar; [- blow, kick] asestar. **-3.** [baby] traer al mundo. **-4.** fml [free] liberar, libertar. **-5.** Am POL [votes] captar.

delivery [dɪ'lɪvərɪ] n **-1.** [distribution] reparto m; [handing over] entrega f. **-2.** [goods delivered] partida f. **-3.** [way of speaking] (estilo m de) discurso m. **-4.** [birth] parto m.

delude [dɪ'luːd] vt engañar; **to ~ o.s.** engañarse (a uno mismo/una misma).

deluge ['deljuːdʒ] n [flood] diluvio m; fig [huge number] aluvión m.

delusion [dɪ'luːʒn] n espejismo m, engaño m.

de luxe [də'lʌks] adj de lujo.

delve [delv] vi: **to ~ (into)** [bag, cupboard] hurgar (en); fig [mystery] profundizar (en).

demand [dɪ'mɑːnd] ◇ n **-1.** [claim, firm request] exigencia f, reclamación f; **on ~ a petición. -2.** [need]: **~ for** demanda f de; **in ~** solicitado(da). ◇ vt [gen] exigir; [pay rise] reclamar, demandar; **to ~ to do sthg** exigir hacer algo.

demanding [dɪ'mɑːndɪŋ] adj **-1.** [exhausting] que exige mucho esfuerzo. **-2.** [not easily satisfied] exigente.

demean [dɪ'miːn] vt: **to ~ o.s.** humillarse, rebajarse.

demeaning [dɪ'miːnɪŋ] adj denigrante.

demeanour Br, **demeanor** Am [dɪ'miːnər] n (U) fml proceder m, comportamiento m.

demented [dɪ'mentɪd] adj demente.

demise [dɪ'maɪz] n fml **-1.** [death] defunción f. **-2.** [end] hundimiento m.

demister [,diː'mɪstər] n Br AUT dispositivo m antivaho, luneta f térmica.

demo ['deməʊ] n (abbr of **demonstration**) n inf mani f.

democracy [dɪ'mɒkrəsɪ] n democracia f.

democrat ['deməkræt] n demócrata m y f. ◆**Democrat** n Am demócrata m y f.

democratic [demə'krætɪk] adj democrático(ca). ◆**Democratic** adj Am demócrata.

Democratic Party n Am Partido m Demócrata (de Estados Unidos).

demolish [dɪ'mɒlɪʃ] vt [building] demoler; [argument, myth] destrozar.

demonstrate ['demənstreɪt] ◇ vt **-1.** [prove] demostrar. **-2.** [show] hacer una demostración de. ◇ vi manifestarse.

demonstration [demən'streɪʃn] n **-1.** [of machine, product] demostración f. **-2.** [public meeting] manifestación f.

demonstrator ['demənstreɪtər] n **-1.** [in march] manifestante m y f. **-2.** [of machine, product] persona que hace demostraciones.

demoralized [dɪ'mɒrəlaɪzd] adj desmoralizado(da).

demote [,diː'məʊt] vt descender de categoría.

demure [dɪ'mjʊər] adj recatado(da).

den [den] n [lair] guarida f.

denial [dɪ'naɪəl] n **-1.** [refutation] negación f, rechazo m. **-2.** [refusal] denegación f.

denier ['denɪər] n denier m.

denigrate ['denɪgreɪt] vt fml desacreditar.

denim ['denɪm] n tela f vaquera.
◆ **denims** npl (pantalones mpl) vaqueros mpl.
denim jacket n cazadora f vaquera.
Denmark ['denmɑːk] n Dinamarca.
denomination [dɪ,nɒmɪ'neɪʃn] n -1. [religious group] confesión f. -2. [of money] valor m.
denounce [dɪ'naʊns] vt denunciar.
dense [dens] adj -1. [gen] denso(sa); [trees] tupido(da). -2. inf [stupid] bruto(ta).
density ['densətɪ] n densidad f.
dent [dent] ◇ n [on car] abolladura f; [in wall] melladura f. ◇ vt [car] abollar; [wall] mellar.
dental ['dentl] adj dental.
dental floss n hilo m OR seda f dental.
dental surgeon n odontólogo m, -ga f.
dentist ['dentɪst] n dentista m y f; to go to the ~'s ir al dentista.
dentures ['dentʃəz] npl dentadura f postiza.
deny [dɪ'naɪ] vt -1. [refute] negar, rechazar; to ~ doing sthg negar haber hecho algo. -2. fml [refuse] to ~ sb sthg denegar algo a alguien.
deodorant [diː'əʊdərənt] n desodorante m.
depart [dɪ'pɑːt] vi fml -1. [leave] to ~ (from) salir (de); this train will ~ from Platform 2 este tren efectuará su salida de la vía 2. -2. [differ] to ~ from sthg apartarse de algo.
department [dɪ'pɑːtmənt] n -1. [gen] departamento m. -2. [in government] ministerio m.
department store n grandes almacenes mpl.
departure [dɪ'pɑːtʃər] n -1. [of train, plane] salida f; [of person] marcha f. -2. [change]: ~ (from) abandono m (de); a new ~ un nuevo enfoque.
departure lounge n [in airport] sala f de embarque; [in coach station] vestíbulo m de salidas.
depend [dɪ'pend] vi: to ~ on depender de; you can ~ on me puedes confiar en mí; it ~s depende; ~ing on según.
dependable [dɪ'pendəbl] adj fiable.
dependant [dɪ'pendənt] n persona dependiente del cabeza de familia.
dependent [dɪ'pendənt] adj -1. [gen]: to be ~ (on) depender (de). -2. [addicted] adicto(ta).
depict [dɪ'pɪkt] vt -1. [in picture] retratar. -2. [describe]: to ~ sthg/sb as sthg describir algo/a alguien como algo.

deplete [dɪ'pliːt] vt mermar, reducir.
deplorable [dɪ'plɔːrəbl] adj deplorable.
deplore [dɪ'plɔːr] vt deplorar.
deploy [dɪ'plɔɪ] vt desplegar.
depopulation [diː,pɒpjʊ'leɪʃn] n despoblación f.
deport [dɪ'pɔːt] vt deportar.
depose [dɪ'pəʊz] vt deponer.
deposit [dɪ'pɒzɪt] ◇ n -1. GEOL yacimiento m. -2. [sediment] poso m, sedimento m. -3. [payment into bank] ingreso m. -4. [down payment - on house, car] entrada f; [- on hotel room] señal f, adelanto m; [- on hired goods] fianza f; [- on bottle] dinero m del envase OR casco. ◇ vt -1. [put down] depositar. -2. [in bank] ingresar.
deposit account n Br cuenta f de ahorro a plazo fijo.
depot ['depəʊ] n -1. [storage facility] almacén m; [for buses] cochera f. -2. Am [bus or train terminus] terminal f.
depreciate [dɪ'priːʃɪeɪt] vi depreciarse.
depress [dɪ'pres] vt -1. [person] deprimir. -2. [economy] desactivar. -3. [price, share value] reducir.
depressed [dɪ'prest] adj deprimido(da).
depressing [dɪ'presɪŋ] adj deprimente.
depression [dɪ'preʃn] n -1. [gen & ECON] depresión f. -2. fml [in pillow] hueco m.
deprivation [,deprɪ'veɪʃn] n -1. [poverty] miseria f. -2. [lack] privación f.
deprive [dɪ'praɪv] vt: to ~ sb of sthg privar a alguien de algo.
depth [depθ] n profundidad f; in ~ a fondo; he was out of his ~ with that job ese trabajo le venía grande. ◆ **depths** npl: in the ~s of winter en pleno invierno; to be in the ~s of despair estar en un abismo de desesperación.
deputation [,depjʊ'teɪʃn] n delegación f.
deputize, -ise ['depjʊtaɪz] vi: to ~ (for) actuar en representación (de).
deputy ['depjʊtɪ] ◇ adj: ~ head subdirector m, -ra f; ~ chairman/president vicepresidente m. ◇ n -1. [second-in-command] asistente m y f, suplente m y f. -2. Am [deputy sheriff] ayudante m y f del sheriff.
derail [dɪ'reɪl] vt & vi [train] descarrilar.
deranged [dɪ'reɪndʒd] adj perturbado(da), trastornado(da).
derby [Br 'dɑːbɪ, Am 'dɜːbɪ] n -1. [sports event] derby m (local). -2. Am [hat] sombrero m hongo.
deregulate [,diː'regjʊleɪt] vt liberalizar.
derelict ['derəlɪkt] adj abandonado(da).

deride [dɪ'raɪd] *vt* mofarse de.

derisory [də'raɪzərɪ] *adj* **-1.** [puny, trivial] irrisorio(ria). **-2.** [derisive] burlón(ona).

derivative [dɪ'rɪvətɪv] *n* derivado *m*.

derive [dɪ'raɪv] ◇ *vt* **-1.** [draw, gain]: **to ~ sthg from sthg** encontrar algo en algo. **-2.** [come]: **to be ~d from** derivar de. ◇ *vi*: **to ~ from** derivar de.

derogatory [dɪ'rɒgətrɪ] *adj* despectivo(va).

derrick ['derɪk] *n* **-1.** [crane] grúa *f*. **-2.** [over oil well] torre *f* de perforación.

derv [dɜːv] *n Br* gasóleo *m*, gasoil *m*.

descend [dɪ'send] ◇ *vt fml* [go down] descender por. ◇ *vi* **-1.** *fml* [go down] descender. **-2.** [subj: silence, gloom]: **to ~ (on sthg/sb)** invadir (algo/a alguien). **-3.** [stoop]: **to ~ to sthg/to doing sthg** rebajarse a algo/a hacer algo.

descendant [dɪ'sendənt] *n* descendiente *m y f*.

descended [dɪ'sendɪd] *adj*: **to be ~ from** ser descendiente de, descender de.

descent [dɪ'sent] *n* **-1.** [downwards movement] descenso *m*, bajada *f*. **-2.** [origin] ascendencia *f*.

describe [dɪ'skraɪb] *vt* describir.

description [dɪ'skrɪpʃn] *n* **-1.** [account] descripción *f*. **-2.** [type]: **of all ~s** de todas clases.

desecrate ['desɪkreɪt] *vt* profanar.

desert [*n* 'dezət, *vb* dɪ'zɜːt] ◇ *n* GEOGR desierto *m*. ◇ *vt* abandonar. ◇ *vi* MIL desertar.

deserted [dɪ'zɜːtɪd] *adj* abandonado(da).

deserter [dɪ'zɜːtə^r] *n* desertor *m*, -ra *f*.

desert island ['dezət-] *n* isla *f* desierta.

deserve [dɪ'zɜːv] *vt* merecer.

deserving [dɪ'zɜːvɪŋ] *adj* encomiable.

design [dɪ'zaɪn] ◇ *n* **-1.** [gen] diseño *m*; [of garment] corte *m*. **-2.** [pattern] dibujo *m*. **-3.** *fml* [intention] designio *m*; **by ~** adrede; **to have ~s on** tener las miras puestas en. ◇ *vt* **-1.** [draw plans for] diseñar. **-2.** [plan, prepare] concebir.

designate [*adj* 'dezɪgnət, *vb* 'dezɪgneɪt] ◇ *adj* designado(da). ◇ *vt* designar.

designer [dɪ'zaɪnə^r] ◇ *adj* [clothes] de diseño; [glasses] de marca. ◇ *n* [gen] diseñador *m*, -ra *f*; THEATRE escenógrafo *m*, -fa *f*.

desirable [dɪ'zaɪərəbl] *adj* **-1.** *fml* [appropriate] deseable, conveniente. **-2.** [attractive] atractivo(va), apetecible.

desire [dɪ'zaɪə^r] ◇ *n*: **~ (for sthg/to do sthg)** deseo *m* (de algo/de hacer algo). ◇ *vt* desear.

desk [desk] *n* **-1.** [gen] mesa *f*, escritorio *m*; [in school] pupitre *m*. **-2.** [service area]: **information ~** (mostrador *m* de) información *f*.

desktop publishing *n* COMPUT autoedición *f* de textos.

desolate ['desələt] *adj* [place, person] desolado(da); [feeling] desolador(ra).

despair [dɪ'speə^r] ◇ *n* desesperación *f*. ◇ *vi* desesperarse; **to ~ of sb** desesperarse con alguien; **to ~ of sthg/doing sthg** desesperar de algo/hacer algo.

despairing [dɪ'speərɪŋ] *adj* desesperado(da).

despatch [dɪ'spætʃ] = **dispatch**.

desperate ['desprət] *adj* desesperado(da); **to be ~ for sthg** necesitar desesperadamente algo.

desperately ['desprətlɪ] *adv* **-1.** [want, fight, love] desesperadamente. **-2.** [ill] gravemente; [poor, unhappy, shy] tremendamente.

desperation [,despə'reɪʃn] *n* desesperación *f*; **in ~** con desesperación.

despicable [dɪ'spɪkəbl] *adj* despreciable.

despise [dɪ'spaɪz] *vt* despreciar.

despite [dɪ'spaɪt] *prep* a pesar de, pese a.

despondent [dɪ'spɒndənt] *adj* descorazonado(da).

dessert [dɪ'zɜːt] *n* postre *m*.

dessertspoon [dɪ'zɜːtspuːn] *n* [spoon] cuchara *f* de postre.

destination [,destɪ'neɪʃn] *n* destino *m*.

destined ['destɪnd] *adj* **-1.** [fated, intended]: **~ for sthg/to do sthg** destinado(da) a algo/a hacer algo. **-2.** [bound]: **~ for rumbo a**, con destino a.

destiny ['destɪnɪ] *n* destino *m*.

destitute ['destɪtjuːt] *adj* indigente.

destroy [dɪ'strɔɪ] *vt* **-1.** [ruin] destruir. **-2.** [put down] matar, sacrificar.

destruction [dɪ'strʌkʃn] *n* destrucción *f*.

detach [dɪ'tætʃ] *vt* **-1.** [pull off]: **to ~ sthg (from)** quitar OR separar algo (de). **-2.** [disassociate]: **to ~ o.s. from sthg** distanciarse de algo.

detachable [dɪ'tætʃəbl] *adj* [handle etc] de quita y pon; [collar] postizo(za).

detached [dɪ'tætʃt] *adj* [unemotional] objetivo(va).

detached house *n* casa *f* OR chalet *m* individual.

detachment [dɪ'tætʃmənt] *n* **-1.** [aloofness] distanciamiento *m*. **-2.** MIL destacamento *m*.

detail ['diːteɪl] ◇ *n* **-1.** [small point] detalle *m*, pormenor *m*. **-2.** (*U*) [facts,

points] **detalles** *mpl*; **to go into ~ entrar en detalles**; **in ~ con detalle. -3.** MIL **destacamento** *m.* ◇ *vt* [list] **detallar.**
◆ **details** *npl* [gen] **información** *f*; [personal] **datos** *mpl.*

detailed ['di:teɪld] *adj* **detallado(da).**

detain [dɪ'teɪn] *vt* [gen] **retener**; [in police station] **detener.**

detect [dɪ'tekt] *vt* [gen] **detectar**; [difference] **notar, percibir.**

detection [dɪ'tekʃn] *n* (U) **-1.** [gen] **detección** *f.* **-2.** [of crime] **investigación** *f*; [of drugs] **descubrimiento** *m.*

detective [dɪ'tektɪv] *n* [private] **detective** *m y f*; [policeman] **agente** *m y f.*

detective novel *n* **novela** *f* **policíaca.**

détente [deɪ'tɒnt] *n* POL **distensión** *f.*

detention [dɪ'tenʃn] *n* **-1.** [of suspect, criminal] **detención** *f*, **arresto** *m.* **-2.** [at school] **castigo de permanecer en la escuela después de clase.**

deter [dɪ'tɜːr] *vt*: **to ~ sb (from doing sthg) disuadir a alguien (de hacer algo).**

detergent [dɪ'tɜːdʒənt] *n* **detergente** *m.*

deteriorate [dɪ'tɪərɪəreɪt] *vi* [health, economy] **deteriorarse**; [weather] **empeorar.**

determination [dɪ,tɜːmɪ'neɪʃn] *n* **determinación** *f.*

determine [dɪ'tɜːmɪn] *vt* **determinar.**

determined [dɪ'tɜːmɪnd] *adj* **decidido(da)**; **~ to do sthg decidido** OR **resuelto a hacer algo.**

deterrent [dɪ'terənt] *n* **fuerza** *f* **disuasoria**; **nuclear ~ armas** *fpl* **nucleares disuasorias.**

detest [dɪ'test] *vt* **detestar.**

detonate ['detəneɪt] *vt & vi* **detonar.**

detour ['di:,tʊər] *n* **desviación** *f*, **desvío** *m*; **to make a ~ dar un rodeo.**

detract [dɪ'trækt] *vi*: **to ~ from sthg** [gen] **mermar algo, aminorar algo**; [achievement] **restar importancia a algo.**

detriment ['detrɪmənt] *n*: **to the ~ of en detrimento de.**

detrimental [,detrɪ'mentl] *adj* **perjudicial.**

deuce [djuːs] *n* (U) TENNIS **deuce** *m*, **iguales** *mpl* **(a cuarenta).**

devaluation [,diːvæljʊ'eɪʃn] *n* **devaluación** *f.*

devastated ['devəsteɪtɪd] *adj* [area, city] **asolado(da)**; *fig* [person] **desolado(da).**

devastating ['devəsteɪtɪŋ] *adj* **-1.** [destructive - hurricane etc] **devastador(ra). -2.** [effective - remark, argument] **abrumador(ra). -3.** [upsetting - news, experience]

desolador(ra). -4. [attractive] **imponente, irresistible.**

develop [dɪ'veləp] ◇ *vt* **-1.** [land] **urbanizar. -2.** [illness] **contraer, coger**; [habit] **adquirir**; **to ~ a fault fallar, estropearse. -3.** [product] **elaborar. -4.** [idea, argument, resources] **desarrollar. -5.** PHOT **revelar.** ◇ *vi* **-1.** [grow] **desarrollarse. -2.** [appear] **presentarse, darse.**

developing country [dɪ'veləpɪŋ-] *n* **país** *m* **en vías de desarrollo.**

development [dɪ'veləpmənt] *n* (U) **-1.** [growth] **desarrollo** *m.* **-2.** [of design, product] **elaboración** *f.* **-3.** [developed land] **urbanización** *f.* **-4.** [new event] **(nuevo) acontecimiento** *m.* **-5.** [advance - in science etc] **avance** *m.*

deviate ['diːvɪeɪt] *vi*: **to ~ from sthg apartarse** OR **desviarse de algo.**

device [dɪ'vaɪs] *n* **dispositivo** *m*, **mecanismo** *m.*

devil ['devl] *n* **diablo** *m*, **demonio** *m*; **poor ~ pobre diablo**; **you lucky ~! ¡vaya suerte que tienes!**; **who/where/why the ~ ...? ¿quién/dónde/por qué demonios ...?** ◆ **Devil** *n* [Satan]: **the Devil el Diablo.**

devious ['diːvjəs] *adj* **-1.** [person, scheme] **malévolo(la), retorcido(da)**; [means] **dudoso(sa). -2.** [route] **sinuoso(sa).**

devise [dɪ'vaɪz] *vt* [instrument, system] **diseñar**; [plan] **trazar.**

devoid [dɪ'vɔɪd] *adj fml*: **~ of desprovisto(ta) de.**

devolution [,diːvə'luːʃn] *n* POL ≃ **autonomía** *f*, ≃ **traspaso** *m* **de competencias.**

devote [dɪ'vəʊt] *vt*: **to ~ sthg to dedicar** OR **consagrar algo a.**

devoted [dɪ'vəʊtɪd] *adj* [person] **leal**; **to be ~ to sb tener veneración por alguien.**

devotee [,devə'tiː] *n* [fan] **devoto** *m*, **-ta** *f*, **admirador** *m*, **-ra** *f.*

devotion [dɪ'vəʊʃn] *n* (U) **-1.** [commitment]: **~ (to) dedicación** *f* **(a). -2.** RELIG **devoción** *f.*

devour [dɪ'vaʊər] *vt literary lit* & *fig* **devorar.**

devout [dɪ'vaʊt] *adj* RELIG **devoto(ta).**

dew [djuː] *n* **rocío** *m.*

dexterity [dek'sterətɪ] *n* **destreza** *f.*

diabetes [,daɪə'biːtiːz] *n* **diabetes** *f inv.*

diabetic [,daɪə'betɪk] ◇ *adj* [person] **diabético(ca).** ◇ *n* **diabético** *m*, **-ca** *f.*

diabolic(al) [,daɪə'bɒlɪk(l)] *adj inf* [very bad] **demencial, pésimo(ma).**

diagnose ['daɪəgnəʊz] *vt* MED diagnosticar.

diagnosis [ˌdaɪəg'nəʊsɪs] (*pl* **-oses** [-əʊsiːz]) *n* MED [verdict] diagnóstico *m*; [science, activity] **diagnosis** *f inv*.

diagonal [daɪ'ægənl] ◇ *adj* diagonal. ◇ *n* diagonal *f*.

diagram ['daɪəgræm] *n* diagrama *m*, dibujo *m* esquemático.

dial ['daɪəl] ◇ *n* **-1.** [of watch, clock, meter] esfera *f*. **-2.** [of telephone, radio] dial *m*. ◇ *vt* [number] marcar.

dialect ['daɪəlekt] *n* dialecto *m*.

dialling code ['daɪəlɪŋ-] *n Br* prefijo *m* (telefónico).

dialling tone *Br* ['daɪəlɪŋ-], **dial tone** *Am n* señal *f* de llamada.

dialogue *Br*, **dialog** *Am* ['daɪəlɒg] *n* diálogo *m*.

dial tone *Am* = **dialling tone**.

dialysis [daɪ'ælɪsɪs] *n* diálisis *f inv*.

diameter [daɪ'æmɪtər] *n* diámetro *m*.

diamond ['daɪəmənd] *n* **-1.** [gem, playing card] diamante *m*. **-2.** [shape] rombo *m*.
◆ **diamonds** *npl* diamantes *mpl*.

diaper ['daɪpər] *n Am* pañal *m*.

diaphragm ['daɪəfræm] *n* diafragma *m*.

diarr(h)oea [ˌdaɪə'rɪə] *n* diarrea *f*.

diary ['daɪərɪ] *n* **-1.** [appointment book] agenda *f*. **-2.** [journal] diario *m*.

dice [daɪs] (*pl inv*) ◇ *n* dado *m*. ◇ *vt* cortar en cuadraditos.

dictate [dɪk'teɪt] *vt*: **to ~ sthg (to sb)** dictar algo (a alguien).

dictation [dɪk'teɪʃn] *n* dictado *m*; **to take** OR **do ~** escribir al dictado.

dictator [dɪk'teɪtər] *n* dictador *m*, -ra *f*.

dictatorship [dɪk'teɪtəʃɪp] *n* dictadura *f*.

dictionary ['dɪkʃənrɪ] *n* diccionario *m*.

did [dɪd] *pt* → **do**.

diddle ['dɪdl] *vt inf* timar.

didn't ['dɪdnt] = **did not**.

die [daɪ] (*pl* **dice**, *pt* & *pp* **died**, *cont* **dying**) ◇ *vi* **-1.** [gen] morir, morirse; **to be dying** estar muriéndose OR agonizando; **to be dying for sthg/to do sthg** morirse por algo/por hacer algo. **-2.** *literary* [feeling] extinguirse. ◇ *n* [dice] dado *m*. ◆ **die away** *vi* desvanecerse.
◆ **die down** *vi* [wind] amainar; [sound] apaciguarse; [fire] remitir; [excitement, fuss] calmarse. ◆ **die out** *vi* extinguirse.

diehard ['daɪhɑːd] *n* reaccionario *m*, -ria *f*.

diesel ['diːzl] *n* **-1.** [vehicle] vehículo *m* diesel. **-2.** [fuel] gasóleo *m*, gasoil *m*.

diesel engine *n* AUT motor *m* diesel; RAIL locomotora *f* diesel.

diesel fuel, **diesel oil** *n* gasóleo *m*.

diet ['daɪət] ◇ *n* **-1.** [eating pattern] dieta *f*. **-2.** [to lose weight] régimen *m*; **to be on a ~** estar a régimen. ◇ *comp* [low-calorie] light (*inv*). ◇ *vi* estar a régimen.

differ ['dɪfər] *vi* **-1.** [be different] diferir, ser diferente; **to ~ from sthg** distinguirse OR diferir de algo. **-2.** [disagree]: **to ~ with sb (about sthg)** disentir OR discrepar de alguien (en algo).

difference ['dɪfrəns] *n* diferencia *f*; **it doesn't make any ~** da lo mismo.

different ['dɪfrənt] *adj*: **~ (from)** diferente OR distinto(ta) (de).

differentiate [ˌdɪfə'renʃɪeɪt] ◇ *vt*: **to ~ (sthg from sthg)** diferenciar OR distinguir (algo de algo). ◇ *vi*: **to ~ between** diferenciar OR distinguir entre.

difficult ['dɪfɪkəlt] *adj* difícil.

difficulty ['dɪfɪkəltɪ] *n* dificultad *f*; **to have ~ in doing sthg** tener dificultad en OR para hacer algo.

diffident ['dɪfɪdənt] *adj* retraído(da).

diffuse [dɪ'fjuːz] *vt* difundir.

dig [dɪg] (*pt* & *pp* **dug**) ◇ *vt* **-1.** [hole - with spade] cavar; [- with hands, paws] escarbar. **-2.** [garden] cavar en; [mine] excavar. **-3.** [press]: **to ~ sthg into** clavar OR hundir algo en. ◇ *vi* **-1.** [with spade] cavar; [with hands, paws] escarbar. **-2.** [press]: **to ~ into** clavarse OR hundirse en. ◇ *n* **-1.** *fig* [unkind remark] pulla *f*. **-2.** ARCHEOL excavación *f*. ◆ **dig out** *vt sep inf* [find - letter] desempolvar; [- information] extraer. ◆ **dig up** *vt sep* [gen] desenterrar; [tree] arrancar.

digest [*n* 'daɪdʒest, *vb* dɪ'dʒest] ◇ *n* compendio *m*. ◇ *vt lit* & *fig* digerir.

digestion [dɪ'dʒestʃn] *n* digestión *f*.

digestive biscuit [dɪ'dʒestɪv-] *n Br* galleta hecha con harina integral.

digit ['dɪdʒɪt] *n* **-1.** [figure] dígito *m*. **-2.** [finger, toe] dedo *m*.

digital ['dɪdʒɪtl] *adj* digital.

dignified ['dɪgnɪfaɪd] *adj* [gen] solemne; [behaviour] ceremonioso(sa).

dignity ['dɪgnətɪ] *n* dignidad *f*.

digress [daɪ'gres] *vi* apartarse del tema; **to ~ from** apartarse OR desviarse de.

digs [dɪgz] *npl Br inf* alojamiento *m*; **to live in ~** vivir de patrona.

dike [daɪk] *n* [wall, bank] dique *m*.

dilapidated [dɪ'læpɪdeɪtɪd] *adj* destartalado(da), derruido(da).

dilate [daɪ'leɪt] *vi* dilatarse.

dilemma [dɪ'lemə] *n* dilema *m*.

diligent ['dɪlɪdʒənt] *adj* diligente.

dilute [daɪ'luːt] *vt* diluir; [wine, beer] aguar.

dim [dɪm] ◇ *adj* **-1.** [light] tenue; [room] sombrío(a). **-2.** [outline, figure] difuso(sa). **-3.** [eyesight] nublado(da). **-4.** [memory] vago(ga). **-5.** *inf* [stupid] tonto(ta), torpe. ◇ *vt* atenuar. ◇ *vi* [light] atenuarse.

dime [daɪm] *n Am* moneda de diez centavos.

dimension [dɪ'menʃn] *n* dimensión *f*.

diminish [dɪ'mɪnɪʃ] *vt & vi* disminuir.

diminutive [dɪ'mɪnjʊtɪv] *fml* ◇ *adj* diminuto(ta). ◇ *n* GRAMM diminutivo *m*.

dimmer ['dɪməʳ], **dimmer switch** *n* potenciómetro *m*.

dimmers ['dɪməz] *npl Am* [dipped headlights] luces *fpl* cortas OR de cruce; [parking lights] luces de posición OR situación.

dimmer switch = **dimmer**.

dimple ['dɪmpl] *n* hoyuelo *m*.

din [dɪn] *n inf* estrépito *m*.

dine [daɪn] *vi fml* cenar. ◆ **dine out** *vi* cenar fuera.

diner ['daɪnəʳ] *n* **-1.** [person] comensal *m y f* (*en cena*). **-2.** *Am* [restaurant - cheap] restaurante *m* barato; [- on the road] ≈ restaurante *m* OR parador *m* de carretera.

dinghy ['dɪŋgɪ] *n* bote *m*.

dingy ['dɪndʒɪ] *adj* [room, street] lóbrego(ga); [clothes, carpet] deslustrado(da).

dining car ['daɪnɪŋ-] *n* vagón *m* restaurante.

dining room ['daɪnɪŋ-] *n* comedor *m*.

dinner ['dɪnəʳ] *n* **-1.** [evening meal] cena *f*; [midday meal] comida *f*, almuerzo *m*. **-2.** [formal event] cena *f* de gala, banquete *m*.

dinner jacket *n* esmoquin *m*.

dinner party *n* cena *f* (*de amigos en casa*).

dinnertime ['dɪnətaɪm] *n* [in the evening] la hora de la cena; [at midday] la hora del almuerzo OR de la comida.

dinosaur ['daɪnəsɔːʳ] *n* [reptile] dinosaurio *m*.

dint [dɪnt] *n fml*: **by ~ of** a base de.

dip [dɪp] ◇ *n* **-1.** [in road, ground] pendiente *f*, declive *m*. **-2.** [sauce] salsa *f*. **-3.** [swim] chapuzón *m*; **to go for/take a ~** ir a darse/darse un chapuzón. ◇ *vt* **-1.** [into liquid]: **to ~ sthg in** OR **into sthg** mojar algo en algo. **-2.** *Br* [headlights]: **to ~ one's lights** poner las luces de cruce. ◇ *vi* descender suavemente.

diploma [dɪ'pləʊmə] (*pl* **-s**) *n* diploma *m*.

diplomacy [dɪ'pləʊməsɪ] *n* diplomacia *f*.

diplomat ['dɪpləmæt] *n* **-1.** [official] diplomático *m*, -ca *f*. **-2.** [tactful person] persona *f* diplomática.

diplomatic [ˌdɪplə'mætɪk] *adj* diplomático(ca).

dipstick ['dɪpstɪk] *n* AUT varilla *f* (para medir el nivel) del aceite.

dire ['daɪəʳ] *adj* [consequences] grave; [warning] estremecedor(ra); [need, poverty] extremo(ma).

direct [dɪ'rekt] ◇ *adj* directo(ta). ◇ *vt* **-1.** [gen]: **to ~ sthg at sb** dirigir algo a alguien. **-2.** [person to place]: **to ~ sb (to)** indicar a alguien el camino (a). **-3.** [order]: **to ~ sb to do sthg** mandar a alguien hacer algo. ◇ *adv* directamente.

direct current *n* corriente *f* continua.

direct debit *n Br* domiciliación *f* (de pago).

direction [dɪ'rekʃn] *n* dirección *f*; **sense of ~** sentido *m* de la orientación. ◆ **directions** *npl* **-1.** [instructions to place] señas *fpl*, indicaciones *fpl*. **-2.** [instructions for use] modo *m* de empleo.

directly [dɪ'rektlɪ] *adv* **-1.** [gen] directamente. **-2.** [immediately] inmediatamente. **-3.** [very soon] pronto, en breve.

director [dɪ'rektəʳ] *n* director *m*, -ra *f*.

directory [dɪ'rektərɪ] *n* **-1.** [gen] guía *f* (alfabética). **-2.** COMPUT directorio *m*.

directory enquiries *n Br* (servicio *m* de) información *f* telefónica.

dire straits *npl*: **in ~** en serios aprietos.

dirt [dɜːt] *n* (*U*) **-1.** [mud, dust] suciedad *f*. **-2.** [earth] tierra *f*.

dirt cheap *inf* ◇ *adj* tirado(da) de precio. ◇ *adv* a precio de ganga.

dirty ['dɜːtɪ] ◇ *adj* **-1.** [gen] sucio(cia). **-2.** [joke] verde; [film] pornográfico(ca); [book, language] obsceno(na). ◇ *vt* ensuciar.

disability [ˌdɪsə'bɪlətɪ] *n* minusvalía *f*.

disabled [dɪs'eɪbld] ◇ *adj* [person] minusválido(da). ◇ *npl*: **the ~** los minusválidos.

disadvantage [ˌdɪsəd'vɑːntɪdʒ] *n* desventaja *f*; **to be at a ~** estar en desventaja.

disagree [ˌdɪsə'griː] *vi* **-1.** [have different opinions]: **to ~ (with)** no estar de acuerdo (con). **-2.** [differ] contradecirse, no concordar. **-3.** [subj: food, drink]: **to ~ with sb** sentar mal a alguien.

disagreeable [ˌdɪsə'griːəbl] *adj* desagradable.

disagreement [ˌdɪsə'griːmənt] *n* **-1.** [fact of disagreeing] desacuerdo *m*. **-2.** [argument] discusión *f*.

disallow [ˌdɪsə'laʊ] *vt* **-1.** [appeal, claim] rechazar. **-2.** [goal] anular.

disappear [ˌdɪsə'pɪər] *vi* desaparecer.

disappearance [ˌdɪsə'pɪərəns] *n* desaparición *f*.

disappoint [ˌdɪsə'pɔɪnt] *vt* [person] decepcionar; [expectations, hopes] defraudar.

disappointed [ˌdɪsə'pɔɪntɪd] *adj* **-1.** [person]: ~ **(in** OR **with sthg)** decepcionado(da) **(con algo). -2.** [expectations, hopes] defraudado(da).

disappointing [ˌdɪsə'pɔɪntɪŋ] *adj* decepcionante.

disappointment [ˌdɪsə'pɔɪntmənt] *n* decepción *f*, desilusión *f*.

disapproval [ˌdɪsə'pruːvl] *n* desaprobación *f*.

disapprove [ˌdɪsə'pruːv] *vi*: **to** ~ **(of sthg/sb)** censurar (algo/a alguien).

disarm [dɪs'ɑːm] ◇ *vt lit* & *fig* desarmar. ◇ *vi* desarmarse.

disarmament [dɪs'ɑːməmənt] *n* desarme *m*.

disarray [ˌdɪsə'reɪ] *n*: **in** ~ [clothes, hair] en desorden; [army, political party] sumido(da) en el desconcierto.

disaster [dɪ'zɑːstər] *n* desastre *m*.

disastrous [dɪ'zɑːstrəs] *adj* desastroso(sa).

disband [dɪs'bænd] ◇ *vt* disolver, disgregar. ◇ *vi* disolverse, disgregarse.

disbelief [ˌdɪsbɪ'liːf] *n*: **in** OR **with** ~ con incredulidad.

disc *Br*, **disk** *Am* [dɪsk] *n* disco *m*.

discard [dɪ'skɑːd] *vt* [old clothes etc] desechar; [possibility] descartar.

discern [dɪ'sɜːn] *vt* **-1.** [gen] discernir; [improvement] percibir. **-2.** [figure, outline] distinguir.

discerning [dɪ'sɜːnɪŋ] *adj* refinado(da); [audience] entendido(da).

discharge [*n* 'dɪstʃɑːdʒ, *vb* dɪs'tʃɑːdʒ] ◇ *n* **-1.** [of patient] alta *f*; [of prisoner, defendant] puesta *f* en libertad; [of soldier] licencia *f*. **-2.** [of gas, smoke] emisión *f*; [- of sewage] vertido *m*. **-3.** [MED - from wound] supuración *f*. **-4.** ELEC descarga *f*. ◇ *vt* **-1.** [patient] dar de alta; [prisoner, defendant] poner en libertad; [soldier] licenciar. **-2.** *fml* [duty etc] cumplir. **-3.** [gas, smoke] despedir; [sewage] verter; [cargo] descargar. **-4.** [debt] saldar.

disciple [dɪ'saɪpl] *n* **-1.** [follower] discípulo *m*, -la *f*. **-2.** RELIG discípulo *m*.

discipline ['dɪsɪplɪn] ◇ *n* disciplina *f*. ◇ *vt* **-1.** [control] disciplinar. **-2.** [punish] castigar.

disc jockey *n* pinchadiscos *m* y *f inv*.

disclaim [dɪs'kleɪm] *vt fml* negar.

disclose [dɪs'kləʊz] *vt* desvelar, revelar.

disclosure [dɪs'kləʊʒər] *n* revelación *f*.

disco ['dɪskəʊ] (*pl* **-s**) (*abbr of* **discotheque**) *n* [place] discoteca *f*; [event] baile *m*.

discomfort [dɪs'kʌmfət] *n* incomodidad *f*.

disconcert [ˌdɪskən'sɜːt] *vt* desconcertar.

disconnect [ˌdɪskə'nekt] *vt* **-1.** [detach] quitar, separar. **-2.** [from gas, electricity - appliance] desconectar; [- house, subscriber] cortar el suministro a. **-3.** [on phone - number] cortar la línea a.

disconsolate [dɪs'kɒnsələt] *adj* desconsolado(da).

discontent [ˌdɪskən'tent] *n*: ~ **(with)** descontento *m* (con).

discontented [ˌdɪskən'tentɪd] *adj* descontento(ta).

discontinue [ˌdɪskən'tɪnjuː] *vt* interrumpir.

discord ['dɪskɔːd] *n* **-1.** [disagreement] discordia *f*. **-2.** MUS disonancia *f*.

discotheque ['dɪskəʊtek] *n* discoteca *f*.

discount [*n* 'dɪskaʊnt, *vb Br* dɪs'kaʊnt, *Am* 'dɪskaʊnt] ◇ *n* descuento *m*. ◇ *vt* [report, claim] descartar.

discourage [dɪ'skʌrɪdʒ] *vt* **-1.** [dispirit] desanimar. **-2.** [deter] desaconsejar; **to** ~ **sb from doing sthg** disuadir a alguien de hacer algo.

discover [dɪ'skʌvər] *vt* descubrir.

discovery [dɪ'skʌvərɪ] *n* descubrimiento *m*.

discredit [dɪs'kredɪt] ◇ *n* descrédito *m*. ◇ *vt* **-1.** [person, organization] desacreditar. **-2.** [idea, report] refutar.

discreet [dɪ'skriːt] *adj* discreto(ta).

discrepancy [dɪ'skrepənsɪ] *n*: ~ **(in/ between)** desigualdad *f* (en/entre).

discretion [dɪ'skreʃn] *n* (*U*) **-1.** [tact] discreción *f*. **-2.** [judgment] capacidad *f* de decisión; **at the** ~ **of** a voluntad de.

discriminate [dɪ'skrɪmɪneɪt] *vi* **-1.** [distinguish]: **to** ~ **(between)** discriminar OR distinguir (entre). **-2.** [treat unfairly]: **to** ~ **against sb** discriminar a alguien.

discriminating [dɪ'skrɪmɪneɪtɪŋ] *adj* refinado(da); [audience] entendido(da).

discrimination [dɪˌskrɪmɪˈneɪʃn] *n* **-1.** [prejudice]: ~ **(against)** discriminación *f* (hacia). **-2.** [judgment] **(buen)** gusto *m*.

discus [ˈdɪskəs] (*pl* **-es**) *n* disco *m* (*en atletismo*).

discuss [dɪˈskʌs] *vt* **-1.** [gen]: **to ~ sthg (with sb)** discutir algo (con alguien). **-2.** [subj: book, lecture] tratar de.

discussion [dɪˈskʌʃn] *n* discusión *f*.

disdain [dɪsˈdeɪn] *fml* ◇ *n*: ~ **(for)** desdén *m* OR desprecio *m* (hacia). ◇ *vt* desdeñar, despreciar.

disease [dɪˈziːz] *n lit* & *fig* enfermedad *f*.

disembark [ˌdɪsɪmˈbɑːk] *vi* desembarcar.

disenchanted [ˌdɪsɪnˈtʃɑːntɪd] *adj*: ~ **(with)** desencantado(da) (con).

disengage [ˌdɪsɪnˈɡeɪdʒ] *vt* **-1.** [release]: **to ~ sthg (from)** soltar OR desenganchar algo (de). **-2.** TECH [gears] quitar; [clutch] soltar.

disfavour *Br*, **disfavor** *Am* [dɪsˈfeɪvəʳ] *n* **-1.** [disapproval] desaprobación *f*. **-2.** [state of being disapproved of] desgracia *f*.

disfigure [dɪsˈfɪɡəʳ] *vt* desfigurar.

disgrace [dɪsˈɡreɪs] ◇ *n* vergüenza *f*; **he's a ~ to his family** es una deshonra para su familia; **to be in ~** [minister, official] estar desprestigiado(da); [child, pet] estar castigado(da). ◇ *vt* deshonrar.

disgraceful [dɪsˈɡreɪsfʊl] *adj* vergonzoso(sa).

disgruntled [dɪsˈɡrʌntld] *adj* disgustado(da).

disguise [dɪsˈɡaɪz] ◇ *n* disfraz *m*; **in ~** [policeman, personality] de incógnito. ◇ *vt* disfrazar.

disgust [dɪsˈɡʌst] ◇ *n*: ~ **(at)** [physical] asco *m* (hacia); [moral] indignación *f* (ante). ◇ *vt* [physically] asquear; [morally] indignar.

disgusting [dɪsˈɡʌstɪŋ] *adj* [physically] asqueroso(sa); [morally] indignante.

dish [dɪʃ] *n* **-1.** [container] fuente *f*. **-2.** [course] plato *m*. **-3.** *Am* [plate] plato *m*. ◆ **dishes** *npl* platos *mpl*; **to do OR wash the ~es** fregar (los platos). ◆ **dish out** *vt sep inf* repartir. ◆ **dish up** *vt sep inf* servir.

dish aerial *Br*, **dish antenna** *Am n* (antena *f*) parabólica *f*.

dishcloth [ˈdɪʃklɒθ] *n* trapo *m* de fregar los platos.

disheartened [dɪsˈhɑːtnd] *adj* descorazonado(da).

dishevelled *Br*, **disheveled** *Am* [dɪˈʃevəld] *adj* desaliñado(da); [hair] despeinado(da).

dishonest [dɪsˈɒnɪst] *adj* deshonesto(ta), nada honrado(da).

dishonor *etc Am* = **dishonour** *etc*.

dishonour *Br*, **dishonor** *Am* [dɪsˈɒnəʳ] *fml* ◇ *n* deshonra *f*. ◇ *vt* deshonrar.

dishonourable *Br*, **dishonorable** *Am* [dɪsˈɒnərəbl] *adj* deshonroso(sa).

dish soap *n Am* detergente *m* para vajillas.

dish towel *n Am* paño *m* de cocina.

dishwasher [ˈdɪʃˌwɒʃəʳ] *n* [machine] lavavajillas *m inv*.

disillusioned [ˌdɪsɪˈluːʒnd] *adj* desilusionado(da).

disincentive [ˌdɪsɪnˈsentɪv] *n* freno *m*, traba *f*.

disinclined [ˌdɪsɪnˈklaɪnd] *adj*: **to be ~ to do sthg** ser reacio(cia) a hacer algo.

disinfect [ˌdɪsɪnˈfekt] *vt* desinfectar.

disinfectant [ˌdɪsɪnˈfektənt] *n* desinfectante *m*.

disintegrate [dɪsˈɪntɪɡreɪt] *vi lit* & *fig* desintegrarse.

disinterested [ˌdɪsˈɪntrəstɪd] *adj* **-1.** [objective] desinteresado(da). **-2.** *inf* [uninterested]: ~ **(in)** indiferente (a).

disjointed [dɪsˈdʒɔɪntɪd] *adj* deslabazado(da).

disk [dɪsk] *n* **-1.** COMPUT disquete *m*. **-2.** *Am* = **disc**.

disk drive *Br*, **diskette drive** *Am n* COMPUT disquetera *f*.

diskette [dɪskˈet] *n* disquete *m*.

diskette drive *n Am* = **disk drive**.

dislike [dɪsˈlaɪk] ◇ *n* **-1.** [feeling]: ~ **(for)** [things] aversión *f* (a); [people] antipatía *f* (por); **to take a ~ to** cogerle manía a. **-2.** [person, thing not liked] fobia *f*. ◇ *vt* [thing] tener aversión a; [person] tener antipatía a.

dislocate [ˈdɪsləkeɪt] *vt* MED dislocar.

dislodge [dɪsˈlɒdʒ] *vt*: **to ~ sthg/sb (from)** desalojar algo/a alguien (de).

disloyal [ˌdɪsˈlɔɪəl] *adj*: ~ **(to)** desleal (a).

dismal [ˈdɪzml] *adj* **-1.** [weather, future] sombrío(a); [place, atmosphere] deprimente. **-2.** [attempt, failure] lamentable.

dismantle [dɪsˈmæntl] *vt* [machine] desmontar; [organization] desmantelar.

dismay [dɪsˈmeɪ] ◇ *n* (*U*) consternación *f*. ◇ *vt* consternar.

dismiss [dɪsˈmɪs] *vt* **-1.** [refuse to take seriously] desechar. **-2.** [from job]: **to ~**

sb (from) despedir a alguien (de). **-3.** [allow to leave] dar permiso para irse a.

dismissal [dɪsˈmɪsl] n [from job] despido m.

dismount [ˌdɪsˈmaʊnt] vi: **to ~ (from sthg)** desmontar (de algo).

disobedience [ˌdɪsəˈbiːdjəns] n desobediencia f.

disobedient [ˌdɪsəˈbiːdjənt] adj: **~ (to)** desobediente (con).

disobey [ˌdɪsəˈbeɪ] vt & vi desobedecer.

disorder [dɪsˈɔːdəʳ] n **-1.** [disarray]: **in ~** en desorden. **-2.** (U) [rioting] disturbios mpl. **-3.** MED [physical] afección f, dolencia f; [mental] trastorno m.

disorderly [dɪsˈɔːdəlɪ] adj **-1.** [untidy] desordenado(da). **-2.** [unruly - behaviour] incontrolado(da).

disorganized, -ised [dɪsˈɔːgənaɪzd] adj desorganizado(da).

disorientated Br [dɪsˈɔːrɪənteɪtɪd], **disoriented** Am [dɪsˈɔːrɪəntɪd] adj desorientado(da).

disown [dɪsˈəʊn] vt renegar de.

disparaging [dɪˈspærɪdʒɪŋ] adj menospreciativo(va).

dispassionate [dɪˈspæʃnət] adj desapasionado(da).

dispatch [dɪˈspætʃ] ◇ n despacho m. ◇ vt [goods, parcel] expedir; [message, messenger, troops] enviar.

dispel [dɪˈspel] vt disipar.

dispensary [dɪˈspensərɪ] n dispensario m.

dispense [dɪˈspens] vt **-1.** [advice] ofrecer; [justice] administrar. **-2.** [drugs, medicine] despachar, dispensar. ◆ **dispense with** vt fus prescindir de.

dispensing chemist Br, **dispensing pharmacist** Am [dɪˈspensɪŋ-] n farmacéutico m, -ca f.

disperse [dɪˈspɜːs] ◇ vt dispersar. ◇ vi dispersarse.

dispirited [dɪˈspɪrɪtɪd] adj desanimado(da).

displace [dɪsˈpleɪs] vt [supplant] reemplazar, sustituir.

display [dɪˈspleɪ] ◇ n **-1.** [arrangement - in shop window] escaparate m; [- in museum] exposición f; [- on stall, pavement] muestrario m. **-2.** [demonstration, public event] demostración f. **-3.** COMPUT visualización f. ◇ vt **-1.** [arrange] exponer. **-2.** [show] demostrar.

displease [dɪsˈpliːz] vt [annoy] disgustar; [anger] enfadar.

displeasure [dɪsˈpleʒəʳ] n [annoyance] disgusto m; [anger] enfado m.

disposable [dɪˈspəʊzəbl] adj desechable; **~ income** ingresos mpl disponibles.

disposal [dɪˈspəʊzl] n **-1.** [removal] eliminación f. **-2.** [availability]: **at sb's ~** a la disposición de alguien.

dispose [dɪˈspəʊz] ◆ **dispose of** vt fus [rubbish] deshacerse de; [problem] quitarse de encima OR de en medio.

disposed [dɪˈspəʊzd] adj **-1.** [willing]: **to be ~ to do sthg** estar dispuesto(ta) a hacer algo. **-2.** [friendly]: **to be well ~ to OR towards sb** tener buena disposición hacia alguien.

disposition [ˌdɪspəˈzɪʃn] n [temperament] carácter m.

disproportionate [dɪsprəˈpɔːʃnət] adj: **~ (to)** desproporcionado(da) (a).

disprove [ˌdɪsˈpruːv] vt refutar.

dispute [dɪˈspjuːt] ◇ n **-1.** [quarrel] disputa f. **-2.** (U) [disagreement] conflicto m, desacuerdo m. **-3.** INDUSTRY conflicto m laboral. ◇ vt cuestionar.

disqualify [ˌdɪsˈkwɒlɪfaɪ] vt **-1.** [subj: authority, illness etc]: **to ~ sb (from doing sthg)** incapacitar a alguien (para hacer algo). **-2.** SPORT descalificar. **-3.** Br [from driving] retirar el permiso de conducir a.

disquiet [dɪsˈkwaɪət] n inquietud f.

disregard [ˌdɪsrɪˈgɑːd] ◇ n: **~ (for)** indiferencia f (a), despreocupación f (por). ◇ vt hacer caso omiso de.

disrepair [ˌdɪsrɪˈpeəʳ] n: **in a state of ~** en mal estado.

disreputable [dɪsˈrepjʊtəbl] adj [person, company] de mala fama; [behaviour] vergonzante.

disrepute [ˌdɪsrɪˈpjuːt] n: **to bring sthg into ~** desprestigiar OR desacreditar algo.

disrupt [dɪsˈrʌpt] vt [meeting] interrumpir; [transport system] trastornar, perturbar; [class] revolucionar, enredar en.

disruption [dɪsˈrʌpʃn] n [of meeting] interrupción f; [of transport system] trastorno m, desbarajuste m.

dissatisfaction [ˈdɪsˌsætɪsˈfækʃn] n descontento m.

dissatisfied [ˌdɪsˈsætɪsfaɪd] adj: **~ (with)** insatisfecho(cha) OR descontento(ta) (con).

dissect [dɪˈsekt] vt MED disecar; fig [study] analizar minuciosamente.

disseminate [dɪˈsemɪneɪt] vt difundir.

dissent [dɪˈsent] ◇ n [gen] disconformidad f, disentimiento m; SPORT: **he was booked for ~** le amonestaron por protestar. ◇ vi: **to ~ (from)** disentir (de).

dissertation [ˌdɪsə'teɪʃn] n tesina f.
disservice [ˌdɪs'sɜːvɪs] n: **to do sb a ~** hacer un flaco servicio a alguien.
dissident ['dɪsɪdənt] n disidente m y f.
dissimilar [ˌdɪ'sɪmɪləʳ] adj: **~ (to)** distinto(ta) (de).
dissipate ['dɪsɪpeɪt] vt -1. [heat] disipar. -2. [efforts, money] desperdiciar.
dissociate [dɪ'səʊʃɪeɪt] vt disociar.
dissolute ['dɪsəluːt] adj disoluto(ta).
dissolve [dɪ'zɒlv] ◇ vt disolver. ◇ vi -1. [substance] disolverse. -2. fig [disappear] desvanecerse, desaparecer.
dissuade [dɪ'sweɪd] vt: **to ~ sb (from doing sthg)** disuadir a alguien (de hacer algo).
distance ['dɪstəns] n distancia f; **at a ~** a distancia; **from a ~** desde lejos; **in the ~** a lo lejos.
distant ['dɪstənt] adj -1. [place, time, relative] lejano(na); **~ from** distante de. -2. [person, manner] frío(a), distante.
distaste [dɪs'teɪst] n: **~ (for)** desagrado m (por).
distasteful [dɪs'teɪstful] adj desagradable.
distended [dɪ'stendɪd] adj dilatado(da).
distil Br, **distill** Am [dɪ'stɪl] vt [liquid] destilar.
distillery [dɪ'stɪlərɪ] n destilería f.
distinct [dɪ'stɪŋkt] adj -1. [different]: **~ (from)** distinto(ta) (de); **as ~ from** a diferencia de. -2. [clear - improvement] notable, visible; [- possibility] claro(ra).
distinction [dɪ'stɪŋkʃn] n -1. [difference, excellence] distinción f; **to draw** OR **make a ~ between** hacer una distinción entre. -2. [in exam result] sobresaliente m.
distinctive [dɪ'stɪŋktɪv] adj característico(ca), particular.
distinguish [dɪ'stɪŋgwɪʃ] vt [gen]: **to ~ sthg (from)** distinguir algo (de).
distinguished [dɪ'stɪŋgwɪʃt] adj distinguido(da).
distinguishing [dɪ'stɪŋgwɪʃɪŋ] adj distintivo(va).
distort [dɪ'stɔːt] vt -1. [shape, face] deformar; [sound] distorsionar. -2. [truth, facts] tergiversar.
distract [dɪ'strækt] vt [person, attention]: **to ~ sb (from)** distraer a alguien (de).
distracted [dɪ'stræktɪd] adj distraído(da).
distraction [dɪ'strækʃn] n [interruption, diversion] distracción f.
distraught [dɪ'strɔːt] adj muy turbado(da).

distress [dɪ'stres] ◇ n -1. [anxiety] angustia f; [pain] dolor m. -2. [danger, difficulty] peligro m. ◇ vt afligir, apenar.
distressing [dɪ'stresɪŋ] adj angustioso(sa), doloroso(sa).
distribute [dɪ'strɪbjuːt] vt [gen] distribuir, repartir.
distribution [ˌdɪstrɪ'bjuːʃn] n [gen] distribución f.
distributor [dɪ'strɪbjʊtəʳ] n -1. COMM distribuidor m, -ra f. -2. AUT delco® m.
district ['dɪstrɪkt] n -1. [area - of country] zona f, región f; [- of town] barrio m. -2. [administrative area] distrito m.
district attorney n Am fiscal m y f (del distrito).
district council n Br ADMIN ≃ municipio m.
district nurse n Br enfermera encargada de atender a domicilio a los pacientes de una zona.
distrust [dɪs'trʌst] ◇ n desconfianza f. ◇ vt desconfiar de.
disturb [dɪ'stɜːb] vt -1. [interrupt - person] molestar; [- concentration] perturbar. -2. [upset, worry] inquietar. -3. [alter - surface, arrangement] alterar; [- papers] desordenar.
disturbance [dɪ'stɜːbəns] n -1. [fight] tumulto m. -2. [interruption] interrupción f. -3. [of mind, emotions] trastorno m.
disturbed [dɪ'stɜːbd] adj -1. [upset, ill] trastornado(da). -2. [worried] inquieto(ta).
disturbing [dɪ'stɜːbɪŋ] adj inquietante.
disuse [ˌdɪs'juːs] n: **to fall into ~** [regulation] caer en desuso; [building, mine] verse paulatinamente abandonado(da).
disused [ˌdɪs'juːzd] adj abandonado(da).
ditch [dɪtʃ] ◇ n [gen] zanja f; [by road] cuneta f. ◇ vt inf -1. [end relationship with] romper con. -2. [get rid of] deshacerse de.
dither ['dɪðəʳ] vi vacilar.
ditto ['dɪtəʊ] adv ídem, lo mismo.
dive [daɪv] (Br pt & pp -d, Am pt -d OR **dove**, pp -d) ◇ vi -1. [into water - person] zambullirse; [- submarine, bird, fish] sumergirse. -2. [with breathing apparatus] bucear. -3. [through air - person] lanzarse; [- plane] caer en picado. -4. [into bag, cupboard]: **to ~ into** meter la mano en. ◇ n -1. [of person - into water] zambullida f. -2. [of submarine] inmersión f. -3. [of person - through air] salto m; [- in football etc] estirada f. -4. [of plane] pi-

cado *m*. **-5.** *inf pej* [bar, restaurant] garito *m*, antro *m*.

diver ['daɪvər] *n* [underwater] buceador *m*, -ra *f*; [professional] buzo *m*; [from diving board] saltador *m*, -ra *f* (de trampolín).

diverge [daɪ'vɜːdʒ] *vi* **-1.** [gen]: **to ~ (from)** divergir (de). **-2.** [disagree] discrepar.

diversify [daɪ'vɜːsɪfaɪ] ◇ *vt* diversificar. ◇ *vi* diversificarse.

diversion [daɪ'vɜːʃn] *n* **-1.** [distraction] distracción *f*. **-2.** [of traffic, river, funds] desvío *m*.

diversity [daɪ'vɜːsəti] *n* diversidad *f*.

divert [daɪ'vɜːt] *vt* **-1.** [traffic, river, funds] desviar. **-2.** [person, attention] distraer.

divide [dɪ'vaɪd] ◇ *vt*: **to ~ sthg (between** OR **among)** dividir algo (entre); **to ~ sthg into** dividir algo en; **to ~ sthg by** dividir algo entre OR por; **~ 3 into 89** divide 89 entre 3. ◇ *vi* **-1.** [river, road, wall] bifurcarse. **-2.** [group] dividirse.

dividend ['dɪvɪdend] *n* FIN dividendo *m*; [profit] beneficio *m*.

divine [dɪ'vaɪn] *adj* divino(na).

diving ['daɪvɪŋ] *n* (U) **-1.** [into water] salto *m*. **-2.** [with breathing apparatus] buceo *m*.

divingboard ['daɪvɪŋbɔːd] *n* trampolín *m*.

divinity [dɪ'vɪnəti] *n* **-1.** [godliness, deity] divinidad *f*. **-2.** [study] teología *f*.

division [dɪ'vɪʒn] *n* **-1.** [gen] división *f*. **-2.** [of labour, responsibility] repartición *f*.

divorce [dɪ'vɔːs] ◇ *n* divorcio *m*. ◇ *vt* [husband, wife] divorciarse de.

divorced [dɪ'vɔːst] *adj* divorciado(da).

divorcee [dɪvɔː'siː] *n* divorciado *m*, -da *f*.

divulge [daɪ'vʌldʒ] *vt* divulgar, revelar.

DIY *n abbr of* **do-it-yourself**.

dizzy ['dɪzɪ] *adj* **-1.** [because of illness etc] mareado(da). **-2.** [because of heights]: **to feel ~** sentir vértigo.

DJ *n abbr of* **disc jockey**.

DNA (*abbr of* **deoxyribonucleic acid**) *n* ADN *m*.

do [duː] (*pt* **did**, *pp* **done**, *pl* **dos** OR **do's**) ◇ *aux vb* **-1.** (*in negatives*): **don't leave it there** no lo dejes ahí. **-2.** (*in questions*): **what did he want?** ¿qué quería?; **~ you think she'll come?** ¿crees que vendrá? **-3.** (*referring back to previous verb*): **~ you think so? - yes, I ~** ¿tú crees? - sí; **she reads more than**

I **~** lee más que yo; **so ~ I/they** yo/ellos también. **-4.** (*in question tags*): **you know her, don't you?** la conoces ¿no?; **so you think you can dance, ~ you?** así que te crees que sabes bailar ¿no? **-5.** (*for emphasis*): **I did tell you but you've forgotten** sí que te lo dije, pero te has olvidado; **~ come in** ¡pase, por favor! ◇ *vt* **-1.** [gen] hacer; **to ~ the cooking/cleaning** hacer la comida/limpieza; **to ~ one's hair** peinarse; **to ~ one's teeth** lavarse los dientes; **he did his duty** cumplió con su deber; **what can I ~ for you?** ¿en qué puedo servirle?; **what can we ~?** ¿qué vamos a hacer? **-2.** [referring to job]: **what ~ you ~?** ¿a qué te dedicas? **-3.** [study] hacer; **I did physics at school** hice física en la escuela. **-4.** [travel at a particular speed] ir a; **the car can ~ 110 mph** el coche puede ir a 110 millas por hora. **-5.** [be good enough for]: **will that ~ you?** ¿te vale eso? ◇ *vi* **-1.** [gen] hacer; **~ as she says** haz lo que te dice; **they're ~ing really well** les va muy bien; **he could ~ better** lo podría hacer mejor; **how did you ~ in the exam?** ¿qué tal te salió el examen? **-2.** [be good enough, sufficient] servir, valer; **this kind of behaviour won't ~** ese tipo de comportamiento no es aceptable; **that will ~ (nicely)** con eso vale; **that will ~!** [showing annoyance] ¡basta ya! *phr*: **how ~ you ~** [greeting] ¿cómo está usted?; [answer] mucho gusto. ◇ *n* [party] fiesta *f*. ◆ **dos** *npl*: **~s and don'ts** normas *fpl* de conducta. ◆ **do away with** *vt fus* [disease, poverty] acabar con; [law, reforms] suprimir. ◆ **do down** *vt sep inf*: **to ~ sb down** menospreciar a alguien. ◆ **do up** *vt sep* **-1.** [fasten - shoelaces, tie] atar; [- coat, buttons] abrochar; **~ your shoes up** átate los zapatos. **-2.** [decorate] renovar, redecorar. **-3.** [wrap up] envolver. ◆ **do with** *vt fus* **-1.** [need]: **I could ~ with a drink/new car** no me vendría mal una copa/un coche nuevo. **-2.** [have connection with]: **that has nothing to ~ with it** eso no tiene nada que ver (con ello). ◆ **do without** ◇ *vt fus* pasar sin; **I can ~ without your sarcasm** podrías ahorrarte tu sarcasmo. ◇ *vi* apañárselas.

Doberman ['dəubəmən] (*pl* **-s**) *n*: **~ (pinscher)** doberman *m*.

docile [*Br* 'dəusaɪl, *Am* 'dɒsəl] *adj* dócil.

dock [dɒk] ◇ *n* **-1.** [in harbour] dársena

f, **muelle** *m.* **-2.** [in court] **banquillo** *m* (de los acusados). ◇ *vi* **atracar.**

docker ['dɒkər] *n* **estibador** *m.*

docklands ['dɒkləndz] *npl Br* **muelles** *mpl.*

dockyard ['dɒkjɑːd] *n* **astillero** *m.*

doctor ['dɒktər] ◇ *n* **-1.** [of medicine] **médico** *m,* **-ca** *f;* **to go to the ~'s** ir al médico. **-2.** [holder of PhD] **doctor** *m,* **-ra** *f.* ◇ *vt* **-1.** [results, text] **amañar. -2.** [food, drink] **adulterar.**

doctorate ['dɒktərət], **doctor's degree** *n* **doctorado** *m.*

doctrine ['dɒktrɪn] *n* **doctrina** *f.*

document ['dɒkjʊmənt] *n* **documento** *m.*

documentary [ˌdɒkjʊ'mentərɪ] ◇ *adj* **documental.** ◇ *n* **documental** *m.*

dodge [dɒdʒ] ◇ *n inf* [fraud] **artimaña** *f.* ◇ *vt* **esquivar.** ◇ *vi* **echarse a un lado.**

dodgy ['dɒdʒɪ] *adj Br inf* [business, plan] **arriesgado(da), comprometido(da);** [chair, brakes] **poco fiable.**

doe [dəʊ] *n* **-1.** [female deer] **gama** *f.* **-2.** [female rabbit] **coneja** *f.*

does [weak form dəz, strong form dʌz] → **do.**

doesn't ['dʌznt] = **does not.**

dog [dɒg] ◇ *n* **-1.** [animal] **perro** *m. Am* [hot dog] **perrito** *m* **caliente.** ◇ *vt* **-1.** [subj: person] **seguir. -2.** [subj: problems, bad luck] **perseguir.**

dog collar *n* **-1.** [of dog] **collar** *m* de perro. **-2.** [of priest] **alzacuello** *m.*

dog-eared [-ɪəd] *adj* **manoseado(da).**

dogged ['dɒgɪd] *adj* **tenaz.**

dogsbody ['dɒgzˌbɒdɪ] *n Br inf* **último mono** *m,* **burro** *m* **de carga.**

doing ['duːɪŋ] *n:* **this is all your ~** tú eres responsable por esto. ◆ **doings** *npl* **actividades** *fpl.*

do-it-yourself *n* **bricolaje** *m.*

doldrums ['dɒldrəmz] *npl fig:* **to be in the ~** [trade] **estar estancado(da);** [person] **estar abatido(da).**

dole [dəʊl] *n* (subsidio *m* de) **paro** *m;* **to be on the ~** estar **parado(da).** ◆ **dole out** *vt sep* **distribuir, repartir.**

doleful ['dəʊlful] *adj* **lastimero(ra).**

doll [dɒl] *n* [toy] **muñeca** *f.*

dollar ['dɒlər] *n* **dólar** *m.*

dolphin ['dɒlfɪn] *n* **delfín** *m.*

domain [də'meɪn] *n* **-1.** [sphere of interest] **campo** *m,* **ámbito** *m.* **-2.** [land] **dominios** *mpl.*

dome [dəʊm] *n* [roof] **cúpula** *f;* [ceiling] **bóveda** *f.*

domestic [də'mestɪk] ◇ *adj* **-1.** [internal - policy, flight] **nacional. -2.** [chores, water supply, animal] **doméstico(ca). -3.** [home-loving] **hogareño(ña), casero(ra).** ◇ *n* **criado** *m,* **-da** *f.*

domestic appliance *n* **electrodoméstico** *m.*

dominant ['dɒmɪnənt] *adj* **dominante.**

dominate ['dɒmɪneɪt] *vt* **dominar.**

domineering [ˌdɒmɪ'nɪərɪŋ] *adj* **dominante, tiránico(ca).**

dominion [də'mɪnjən] *n* **-1.** (U) [power] **dominio** *m.* **-2.** [land] **dominios** *mpl.*

domino ['dɒmɪnəʊ] (*pl* **-es**) *n* **dominó** *m.* ◆ **dominoes** *npl* **dominó** *m.*

don [dɒn] *n Br UNIV* **profesor** *m,* **-ra** *f* de universidad.

donate [də'neɪt] *vt* **donar.**

done [dʌn] ◇ *pp* → **do.** ◇ *adj* **-1.** [finished] **listo(ta). -2.** [cooked] **hecho(cha); well-~** muy hecho. ◇ *adv* [to conclude deal]: **~!** ¡(trato) hecho!

donkey ['dɒŋkɪ] (*pl* **donkeys**) *n* **burro** *m,* **-rra** *f.*

donor ['dəʊnər] *n* **donante** *m y f.*

donor card *n* **carné** *m* de donante.

don't [dəʊnt] = **do not.**

doodle ['duːdl] *vi* **garabatear.**

doom [duːm] *n* **perdición** *f,* **fatalidad** *f.*

doomed [duːmd] *adj* [plan, mission] **condenado(da) al fracaso; to be ~ to sthg/to do sthg** estar condenado a algo/a hacer algo.

door [dɔːʳ] *n* **-1.** [gen] **puerta** *f.* **-2.** [doorway] **entrada** *f.*

doorbell ['dɔːbel] *n* **timbre** *m* (de la puerta).

doorknob ['dɔːnɒb] *n* **pomo** *m.*

doorman ['dɔːmən] (*pl* **-men** [-mən]) *n* **portero** *m.*

doormat ['dɔːmæt] *n* [mat] **felpudo** *m.*

doorstep ['dɔːstep] *n* **peldaño** *m* de la puerta.

doorway ['dɔːweɪ] *n* **entrada** *f,* **portal** *m.*

dope [dəʊp] ◇ *n inf* **-1.** drugs sl [cannabis] **maría** *f.* **-2.** [for athlete, horse] **estimulante** *m.* **-3.** [fool] **bobo** *m,* **-ba** *f.* ◇ *vt* **drogar, dopar.**

dopey ['dəʊpɪ] (*compar* **-ier,** superl **-iest**) *adj inf* **-1.** [groggy] **atontado(da), grogui. -2.** [stupid] **imbécil.**

dormant ['dɔːmənt] *adj* [volcano] **inactivo(va).**

dormitory ['dɔːmətrɪ] *n* **dormitorio** *m.*

Dormobile® ['dɔːməˌbiːl] *n* **combi** *m.*

DOS [dɒs] (abbr of **disk operating system**) *n* **DOS** *m.*

dose [dəʊs] *n lit & fig* dosis *f inv.*

dosser ['dɒsə'] *n Br inf* gandul *m*, -la *f.*

dosshaus ['dɒshaʊs, *pl* -haʊzɪz] *n Br inf* pensión *f* de mala muerte.

dot [dɒt] ◇ *n* punto *m*; **on the ~** en punto. ◇ *vt* salpicar.

dote [dəʊt] ◆ **dote (up)on** *vt fus* adorar.

dot-matrix printer *n* COMPUT impresora *f* matricial de agujas.

double ['dʌbl] ◇ *adj* **-1.** [gen] doble. **-2.** [repeated] repetido(da); **~ three eight two** treinta y tres, ochenta y dos. ◇ *adv* **-1.** [twice] doble; **~ the amount** el doble. **-2.** [in two - fold] en dos; **to bend ~** doblarse, agacharse. ◇ *n* **-1.** [twice as much] el doble. **-2.** [drink] doble. **-3.** [lookalike] doble *m y f.* ◇ *vt* doblar. ◇ *vi* [increase twofold] doblarse. ◆ **doubles** *npl* TENNIS (partido *m* de) dobles *mpl.*

double-barrelled *Br*, **double-barreled** *Am* [-'bærəld] *adj* **-1.** [shotgun] de dos cañones. **-2.** [name] *con dos apellidos unidos con guión.*

double bass [-beɪs] *n* contrabajo *m.*

double bed *n* cama *f* de matrimonio.

double-breasted [-'brestɪd] *adj* cruzado(da).

double-check *vt & vi* verificar dos veces.

double chin *n* papada *f.*

double cream *n* nata *f* enriquecida.

double-cross *vt* traicionar, timar.

double-decker [-'dekə'] *n* autobús *m* de dos pisos.

double-dutch *n Br hum*: **it's ~ to me** me suena a chino.

double-glazing [-'gleɪzɪŋ] *n* doble acristalamiento *m.*

double room *n* habitación *f* doble.

double vision *n* vista *f* doble.

doubly ['dʌblɪ] *adv* doblemente.

doubt [daʊt] ◇ *n* duda *f*; **there is no ~ that** no hay de qué cabe duda de que; **without (a) ~** sin duda (alguna); **to be in ~ about sthg** estar dudando acerca de algo; **to cast ~ on** poner en duda; **no ~** sin duda. ◇ *vt* **-1.** [not trust] dudar de. **-2.** [consider unlikely] dudar; **to ~ whether** OR **if** dudar que.

doubtful ['daʊtful] *adj* **-1.** [gen] dudoso(sa). **-2.** [unsure] incierto(ta); **to be ~ about** OR **of** tener dudas acerca de.

doubtless ['daʊtlɪs] *adv* sin duda.

dough [dəʊ] *n (U)* **-1.** [for baking] masa *f*, pasta *f.* **-2.** *v inf* [money] pasta *f.*

doughnut ['dəʊnʌt] *n* [without hole] buñuelo *m*; [with hole] dónut® *m.*

douse [daʊs] *vt* **-1.** [put out] apagar. **-2.** [drench] mojar, empapar.

dove[1] [dʌv] *n* paloma *f.*

dove[2] [dəʊv] *Am pt* → **dive.**

dovetail ['dʌvteɪl] *vt & vi* encajar.

dowdy ['daʊdɪ] *adj* poco elegante.

down [daʊn] ◇ *adv* **-1.** [downwards] (hacia) abajo; **to fall ~** caer; **to bend ~** agacharse; **~** here/there aquí/allí abajo. **-2.** [along]: **I'm going ~ the pub** voy a acercarme al pub. **-3.** [southwards] hacia el sur; **we're going ~ to Brighton** vamos a bajar a Brighton. **-4.** [lower in amount]: **prices are coming ~** van bajando los precios. **-5.** [including]: **~ to the last detail** hasta el último detalle. **-6.** [as deposit]: **to pay £5 ~** pagar 5 libras ahora (y el resto después). ◇ *prep* **-1.** [downwards]: **they ran ~ the hill** corrieron cuesta abajo; **he walked ~ the stairs** bajó la escalera; **rain poured ~ the window** la lluvia resbalaba por la ventana. **-2.** [along]: **she was walking ~ the street** iba andando por la calle. ◇ *adj* **-1.** *inf* [depressed] deprimido(da). **-2.** [not in operation]: **the computer is ~ again** el ordenador se ha estropeado otra vez. ◇ *n* [feathers] plumón *m*; [hair] pelusa *f*, vello *m.* ◇ *vt* **-1.** [knock over] derribar. **-2.** [swallow] beberse de un trago. ◆ **downs** *npl Br* montes del sur de Inglaterra. ◆ **down with** *excl*: **~ with the King!** ¡abajo el rey!

down-and-out *n* vagabundo *m*, -da *f.*

down-at-heel *adj* desastrado(da).

downbeat ['daʊnbiːt] *adj inf* pesimista.

downcast ['daʊnkɑːst] *adj fml* [sad] alicaído(da), triste.

downfall ['daʊnfɔːl] *n (U)* ruina *f*, caída *f.*

downhearted [ˌdaʊn'hɑːtɪd] *adj* desanimado(da).

downhill [ˌdaʊn'hɪl] ◇ *adj* cuesta abajo. ◇ *adv* **-1.** [downwards] cuesta abajo. **-2.** [worse] en declive. ◇ *n* SKIING descenso *m.*

Downing Street ['daʊnɪŋ-] *n calle londinense donde se encuentran las residencias del Primer Ministro y el ministro de Finanzas; por extensión el gobierno británico.*

down payment *n* entrada *f.*

downpour ['daʊnpɔː'] *n* chaparrón *m.*

downright ['daʊnraɪt] ◇ *adj* patente, manifiesto(ta). ◇ *adv* completamente.

downstairs [ˌdaʊnˈsteəz] ◇ *adj* de abajo. ◇ *adv* abajo; **to come/go ~** bajar (la escalera).

downstream [ˌdaʊnˈstriːm] *adv* río OR aguas abajo.

down-to-earth *adj* realista.

downtown [ˌdaʊnˈtaʊn] ◇ *adj* céntrico(ca), del centro (de la ciudad). ◇ *adv* [live] en el centro; [go] al centro.

downturn [ˈdaʊntɜːn] *n*: **~ (in)** descenso *m* (en).

down under *adv* en/a Australia o Nueva Zelanda.

downward [ˈdaʊnwəd] ◇ *adj* **-1.** [towards ground] hacia abajo. **-2.** [decreasing] descendente. ◇ *adv Am* = **downwards**.

downwards [ˈdaʊnwədz] *adv* [gen] hacia abajo; **face ~** boca abajo.

dowry [ˈdaʊərɪ] *n* dote *f*.

doze [dəʊz] ◇ *n* sueñecito *m*; **to have a ~** echar una cabezada. ◇ *vi* dormitar. ◆ **doze off** *vi* quedarse adormilado(da).

dozen [ˈdʌzn] ◇ *num adj*: **a ~ eggs** una docena de huevos. ◇ *n* docena *f*; **50p a ~** 50 peniques la docena. ◆ **dozens** *npl inf*: **~s of** montones *mpl* OR miles *mpl* de.

dozy [ˈdəʊzɪ] *adj* **-1.** [sleepy] soñoliento(ta), amodorrado(da). **-2.** *Br inf* [stupid] tonto(ta).

Dr. -1. (*abbr of* **Drive**) c/. **-2.** (*abbr of* **Doctor**) Dr.

drab [dræb] *adj* [colour] apagado(da); [building, clothes] sobrio(bria); [lives] monótono(na).

draft [drɑːft] ◇ *n* **-1.** [early version] borrador *m*. **-2.** [money order] letra *f* de cambio, giro *m*. **-3.** *Am* MIL: **the ~** la llamada a filas. **-4.** *Am* = **draught**. ◇ *vt* **-1.** [write] redactar, hacer un borrador de. **-2.** *Am* MIL llamar a filas. **-3.** [transfer - staff etc] transferir.

draftsman *Am* = **draughtsman**.

drafty *Am* = **draughty**.

drag [dræg] ◇ *vt* **-1.** [gen] arrastrar. **-2.** [lake, river] dragar. ◇ *vi* **-1.** [dress, coat] arrastrarse. **-2.** [time, play] ir muy despacio. ◇ *n inf* **-1.** [bore - thing] rollo *m*; [- person] pesado *m*, **-da** *f*. **-2.** [on cigarette] calada *f*. **-3.** [cross-dressing]: **in ~** vestido de mujer. ◆ **drag on** *vi* ser interminable.

dragon [ˈdrægən] *n* **-1.** [beast] dragón *m*. **-2.** *inf* [woman] bruja *f*.

dragonfly [ˈdrægnflaɪ] *n* libélula *f*.

drain [dreɪn] ◇ *n* [for water] desagüe *m*; [for sewage] alcantarilla *f*; [grating] sumidero *m*. ◇ *vt* **-1.** [marsh, field] drenar; [vegetables] escurrir. **-2.** [energy, resources] agotar. **-3.** [drink, glass] apurar. ◇ *vi* **-1.** [dishes] escurrirse. **-2.** [colour, blood, tension] desaparecer poco a poco.

drainage [ˈdreɪnɪdʒ] *n* **-1.** [pipes, ditches] alcantarillado *m*. **-2.** [of land] drenaje *m*.

draining board *Br* [ˈdreɪnɪŋ-], **drainboard** *Am* [ˈdreɪnbɔːrd] *n* escurridero *m*.

drainpipe [ˈdreɪnpaɪp] *n* tubo *m* de desagüe.

dram [dræm] *n* trago *m*.

drama [ˈdrɑːmə] *n* **-1.** [gen] drama *m*. **-2.** [subject] teatro *m*.

dramatic [drəˈmætɪk] *adj* **-1.** [concerned with theatre] dramático(ca). **-2.** [gesture, escape, improvement] espectacular.

dramatist [ˈdræmətɪst] *n* dramaturgo *m*, **-ga** *f*.

dramatize, -ise [ˈdræmətaɪz] *vt* **-1.** [rewrite as play] adaptar, escenificar. **-2.** *pej* [make dramatic] dramatizar, exagerar.

drank [dræŋk] *pt* → **drink**.

drape [dreɪp] *vt*: **to ~ sthg over sthg** cubrir algo con algo; **~d with** OR **in** cubierto con. ◆ **drapes** *npl Am* cortinas *fpl*.

draper [ˈdreɪpər] *n* pañero *m*, **-ra** *f*.

drastic [ˈdræstɪk] *adj* **-1.** [extreme, urgent] drástico(ca). **-2.** [noticeable] radical.

draught *Br*, **draft** *Am* [drɑːft] *n* **-1.** [air current] corriente *f* de aire. **-2.** **on ~** [beer] de barril. ◆ **draughts** *n Br* damas *fpl*.

draught beer *n Br* cerveza *f* de barril.

draughtboard [ˈdrɑːftbɔːd] *n Br* tablero *m* de damas.

draughtsman *Br* (*pl* **-men** [-mən]), **draftsman** *Am* (*pl* **-men** [-mən]) [ˈdrɑːftsmən] *n* delineante *m y f*.

draughty *Br*, **drafty** *Am* [ˈdrɑːftɪ] *adj* que tiene corrientes de aire.

draw [drɔː] (*pt* **drew**, *pp* **drawn**) ◇ *vt* **-1.** [sketch] dibujar; [line, circle] trazar. **-2.** [pull - cart etc] tirar de; **she drew the comb through her hair** se pasó el peine por el cabello. **-3.** [curtains - open] descorrer; [- close] correr. **-4.** [gun, sword] sacar. **-5.** [conclusion] llegar a. **-6.** [distinction, comparison] señalar. **-7.** [attract - criticism, praise, person] atraer; **to ~ sb's attention to sthg** llamar la atención de alguien hacia algo. ◇ *vi* **-1.** [sketch] dibujar. **-2.** [move] moverse; **to ~ away** alejarse; **to ~ closer** acercarse. **-3.** SPORT: **to ~ (with)** empatar (con). ◇ *n* **-1.** SPORT empate *m*. **-2.** [lottery] sorteo *m*. ◆ **draw out** *vt sep* **-1.** [encourage to talk] hacer hablar. **-2.** [prolong] prolongar. **-3.** [money] sacar. ◆ **draw up** ◇ *vt sep* [draft] preparar, redactar. ◇ *vi* [stop] pararse.

drawback ['drɔːbæk] *n* inconveniente *m*, desventaja *f*.

drawbridge ['drɔːbrɪdʒ] *n* puente *m* levadizo.

drawer [drɔːr] *n* [in desk, chest] cajón *m*.

drawing ['drɔːɪŋ] *n* dibujo *m*.

drawing board *n* tablero *m* de delineante.

drawing pin *n Br* chincheta *f*.

drawing room *n* salón *m*.

drawl [drɔːl] *n* manera lenta y poco clara de hablar, alargando las vocales.

drawn [drɔːn] *pp* → **draw**.

dread [dred] ◇ *n* pavor *m*. ◇ *vt*: **to ~ (doing sthg)** temer (hacer algo).

dreadful ['dredful] *adj* **-1.** [very unpleasant - pain, weather] terrible. **-2.** [poor - play, English] horrible, fatal. **-3.** [for emphasis - waste, bore] espantoso(sa).

dreadfully ['dredfulɪ] *adv* terriblemente.

dream [driːm] (*pt & pp* **-ed** OR **dreamt**) ◇ *n lit & fig* sueño *m*; **bad ~** pesadilla *f*. ◇ *adj* ideal. ◇ *vt*: **to ~ (that)** soñar que. ◇ *vi lit & fig*: **to ~ of** doing sthg soñar con hacer algo; **to ~ (of** OR **about)** soñar (con); **I wouldn't ~ of it** ¡ni hablar!, ¡de ninguna manera! ◆ **dream up** *vt sep* inventar, idear.

dreamt [dremt] *pp* → **dream**.

dreamy ['driːmɪ] *adj* **-1.** [distracted] soñador(ra). **-2.** [peaceful, dreamlike] de ensueño.

dreary ['drɪərɪ] *adj* **-1.** [weather, day] triste. **-2.** [job, life] monótono(na), aburrido(da); [persona] gris.

dredge [dredʒ] *vt* dragar. ◆ **dredge up** *vt sep* **-1.** [with dredger] extraer (del agua) con draga. **-2.** *fig* [from past] sacar a (la) luz.

dregs [dregz] *npl* **-1.** [of liquid] sedimento *m*. **-2.** *fig* [of society] hez *f*.

drench [drentʃ] *vt* empapar; **~ed to the skin** calado hasta los huesos.

dress [dres] ◇ *n* **-1.** [woman's garment] vestido *m*. **-2.** (*U*) [clothing] traje *m*. ◇ *vt* **-1.** [clothe] vestir; **to be ~ed in** ir vestido de; **to be ~ed** estar vestido; **to get ~ed** vestirse. **-2.** [bandage] vendar. **-3.** CULIN aliñar. ◇ *vi* **-1.** [put on clothing] vestirse. **-2.** [wear clothes] vestir; **to ~ well/badly** vestir bien/mal.

dress circle *n* piso *m* principal.

dresser ['dresər] *n* **-1.** [for dishes] aparador *m*. **-2.** *Am* [chest of drawers] cómoda *f*.

dressing ['dresɪŋ] *n* **-1.** [bandage] vendaje *m*. **-2.** [for salad] aliño *m*. **-3.** *Am* [for turkey etc] relleno *m*.

dressing gown *n* bata *f*.

dressing room *n* THEATRE camerino *m*; SPORT vestuario *m*.

dressing table *n* tocador *m*.

dressmaker ['dres,meɪkər] *n* costurero *m*, -ra *f*, modisto *m*, -ta *f*.

dressmaking ['dres,meɪkɪŋ] *n* costura *f*.

dress rehearsal *n* ensayo *m* general.

dressy ['dresɪ] *adj* elegante.

drew [druː] *pt* → **draw**.

dribble ['drɪbl] ◇ *n* **-1.** [saliva] baba *f*. **-2.** [trickle] hilo *m*. ◇ *vt* SPORT [ball] regatear. ◇ *vi* **-1.** [drool] babear. **-2.** [spill] gotear, caer gota a gota.

dried [draɪd] *adj* [gen] seco(ca); [milk, eggs] en polvo.

dried fruit *n* (*U*) fruta *f* pasa.

drier ['draɪər] = **dryer**.

drift [drɪft] ◇ *n* **-1.** [trend, movement] movimiento *m*, tendencia *f*; [of current] flujo *m*. **-2.** [meaning] significado *m*, sentido *m*. **-3.** [mass - of snow] ventisquero *m*; [- of sand, leaves] montículo *m*. ◇ *vi* **-1.** [boat] ir a la deriva. **-2.** [snow, sand, leaves] amontonarse.

driftwood ['drɪftwud] *n* madera *f* de deriva.

drill [drɪl] ◇ *n* **-1.** [tool - gen] taladro *m*; [- bit] broca *f*; [- dentist's] fresa *f*; [- in mine, oilfield] perforadora *f*. **-2.** [exercise - for fire, battle] simulacro *m*. ◇ *vt* **-1.** [tooth, wood, oil well] perforar. **-2.** [instruct - people, pupils] adiestrar, entrenar; [- soldiers] instruir. ◇ *vi*: **to ~ into/for** perforar en/en busca de.

drink [drɪŋk] (*pt* **drank**, *pp* **drunk**) ◇ *n* **-1.** [gen] bebida *f*; **a ~ of water** un trago de agua. **-2.** [alcoholic beverage] copa *f*; **would you like a ~?** ¿quieres tomar algo (de beber)?; **to have a ~** tomar algo, tomar una copa. ◇ *vt* beber. ◇ *vi* beber.

drink-driving *Br*, **drunk-driving** *Am n* conducción *f* en estado de embriaguez.

drinker ['drɪŋkər] *n* **-1.** [of alcohol] bebedor *m*, -ra *f*. **-2.** [of tea, coffee]: **tea/coffee ~** persona que bebe té/café.

drinking water ['drɪŋkɪŋ-] *n* agua *f* potable.

drip [drɪp] ◇ n -1. [drop] gota f; [drops] goteo m. -2. MED gota a gota m inv. ◇ vi [liquid, tap, nose] **gotear**.

drip-dry adj de lava y pon.

drive [draɪv] (pt **drove**, pp **driven**) ◇ n -1. [outing] paseo m (en coche); **to go for a ~** ir a dar una vuelta en coche. -2. [journey] viaje m (en coche); **it's a two-hour ~ (away)** está a dos horas en coche. -3. [urge] instinto m. -4. [campaign] campaña f. -5. [energy] vigor m, energía f. -6. [road to house] camino m (de entrada). -7. SPORT drive m. -8. COMPUT unidad f de disco. ◇ vt -1. [vehicle] **conducir, manejar** Amer. -2. [passenger] **llevar** (en coche). -3. [fuel, power] **impulsar**. -4. [force to move - gen] **arrastrar**; [- cattle] **arrear**. -5. [motivate] **motivar**. -6. [force]: **to ~ sb to do sthg conducir** OR **llevar a alguien a hacer algo; to ~ sb to despair** hacer desesperar a alguien; **to ~ sb mad** OR **crazy volver loco a alguien**. -7. [hammer] **clavar**. ◇ vi AUT **conducir**; **I don't ~** no sé conducir.

drivel ['drɪvl] n inf (U) tonterías fpl.

driven ['drɪvn] pp → drive.

driver ['draɪvə'] n [gen] conductor m, -ra f; RAIL maquinista m y f; [of racing car] piloto m y f.

driver's license Am = driving licence.

drive shaft n (eje m de) transmisión f.

driveway ['draɪvweɪ] n camino m de entrada.

driving ['draɪvɪŋ] ◇ adj [rain] torrencial; [wind] huracanado(da). ◇ n (U) conducción f, el conducir.

driving instructor n instructor m, -ra f de conducción.

driving lesson n clase f de conducir OR conducción.

driving licence Br, **driver's license** Am n carné m OR permiso m de conducir.

driving mirror n retrovisor m.

driving school n autoescuela f.

driving test n examen m de conducir.

drizzle ['drɪzl] ◇ n llovizna f. ◇ v impers **lloviznar**.

droll [drəʊl] adj **gracioso(sa)**.

drone [drəʊn] n -1. [hum] **zumbido** m. -2. [bee] **zángano** m.

drool [druːl] vi -1. [dribble] **babear**. -2. fig [admire]: **to ~ over caérsele la baba con**.

droop [druːp] vi [shoulders] **encorvarse**; [eyelids] **cerrarse**; [head] **inclinarse**; [flower] **marchitarse**.

drop [drɒp] ◇ n -1. [of liquid, milk, whisky] gota f. -2. [sweet] pastilla f. -3. [decrease]: **~ (in)** [price] caída f (de); [temperature] descenso m (de); [demand, income] disminución f (en). -4. [distance down] caída f. ◇ vt -1. [let fall - gen] **dejar caer**; [- bomb] **lanzar**. -2. [decrease] **reducir**. -3. [voice] **bajar**. -4. [abandon - subject, course] **dejar**; [- charges] **retirar**; [- person, lover] **abandonar**; [- player] **excluir, no seleccionar**. -5. [utter - hint, remark] **lanzar, soltar**. -6. [write - letter, postcard] **poner, escribir**. -7. [let out of car] **dejar**. ◇ vi -1. [fall down] **caer**; **to ~ to one's knees arrodillarse**; **we walked until we dropped** estuvimos andando hasta no poder más. -2. [fall away - ground] **ceder**. -3. [decrease - temperature, price, voice] **bajar**; [- attendance, demand, unemployment] **disminuir**; [- wind] **amainar**. ◆ **drops** npl MED **gotas** fpl.
◆ **drop in** vi inf: **to ~ in on pasarse por casa de**. ◆ **drop off** ◇ vt sep [person, letter] **dejar**. ◇ vi -1. [fall asleep] **quedarse dormido(da)**. -2. [grow less] **bajar**.
◆ **drop out** vi: **to ~ out (of** OR **from)** [school, college] **dejar de asistir (a)**; [competition] **retirarse (de)**.

dropout ['drɒpaʊt] n [from society] **marginado** m, -da f; [from university] **persona** f que ha dejado los estudios.

droppings ['drɒpɪŋz] npl **excremento** m (de animales).

drought [draʊt] n **sequía** f.

drove [drəʊv] pt → drive.

drown [draʊn] ◇ vt [kill] **ahogar**. ◇ vi **ahogarse**.

drowsy ['draʊzɪ] adj [person] **somnoliento(ta)**.

drudgery ['drʌdʒərɪ] n **trabajo pesado y monótono**.

drug [drʌg] ◇ n -1. [medicine] **medicamento** m. -2. [narcotic] **droga** f; **to be on** OR **take ~s drogarse**. ◇ vt -1. [person] **drogar**. -2. [food, drink] **echar droga a**.

drug abuse n **consumo** m **de drogas**.

drug addict n **drogadicto** m, **-ta** f.

druggist ['drʌgɪst] n Am **farmacéutico** m, **-ca** f.

drugstore ['drʌgstɔːʳ] n Am **farmacia** f (que también vende productos de perfumería etc).

drum [drʌm] ◇ n -1. [instrument] **tambor** m; **~s batería** f. -2. [container, cylinder] **bidón** m. ◇ vt [fingers] **tamborilear con**. ◇ vi [rain, hoofs] **golpetear**.
◆ **drum up** vt sep **intentar conseguir**.

drummer ['drʌmər] *n* [in orchestra] **tambor** *m y f*; [in pop group] **batería** *m y f*.

drumstick ['drʌmstɪk] *n* **-1.** [for drum] **palillo** *m*. **-2.** [food] **muslo** *m*.

drunk [drʌŋk] ◇ *pp* → **drink**. ◇ *adj* [on alcohol] **borracho(cha); to get ~ emborracharse; to be ~ estar borracho.** ◇ *n* **borracho** *m*, **-cha** *f*.

drunkard ['drʌŋkəd] *n* **borracho** *m*, **-cha** *f*.

drunk-driving *Am* = **drink-driving**.

drunken ['drʌŋkn] *adj* **-1.** [person] **borracho(cha). -2.** [talk, steps, stupor] de **borracho(cha).**

drunken driving = **drink-driving**.

dry [draɪ] ◇ *adj* **-1.** [gen] **seco(ca). -2.** [day] **sin lluvia. -3.** [earth, soil] **árido(da).** ◇ *vt* [gen] **secar;** [hands, hair] **secarse; to ~ o.s** **secarse; to ~ one's eyes** **secarse las lágrimas.** ◇ *vi* **secarse.** ◆ **dry up** ◇ *vt sep* **secar.** ◇ *vi* **-1.** [river, well] **secarse. -2.** [stop - supply] **agotarse. -3.** [stop speaking] **cortarse. -4.** [dry dishes] **secar.**

dry cleaner *n*: **~'s (shop) tintorería** *f*.

dryer ['draɪər] *n* [for clothes] **secadora** *f*.

dry land *n* **tierra** *f* **firme.**

dry rot *n* **putrefacción** *f* **de la madera.**

dry ski slope *n* **pista** *f* **de esquí artificial.**

DSS (*abbr of* **Department of Social Security**) *n* **ministerio británico de la seguridad social.**

DTI (*abbr of* **Department of Trade and Industry**) *n* **ministerio británico de comercio e industria.**

DTP (*abbr of* **desktop publishing**) *n* **autoed.** *f*.

dual ['djuːəl] *adj* **doble.**

dual carriageway *n* **Br carretera de dos sentidos y doble vía separados,** ≃ **autovía** *f*.

dubbed [dʌbd] *adj* **-1.** CINEMA **doblado(da). -2.** [nicknamed] **apodado(da).**

dubious ['djuːbjəs] *adj* **-1.** [questionable - person, deal, reasons] **sospechoso(sa);** [- honour, distinction] **paradójico(ca). -2.** [uncertain, undecided] **dudoso(sa); to feel** OR **be ~ (about) tener dudas (sobre).**

Dublin ['dʌblɪn] *n* **Dublín.**

duchess ['dʌtʃɪs] *n* **duquesa** *f*.

duck [dʌk] ◇ *n* **-1.** [bird] **pato** *m*, **-ta** *f*. **-2.** [food] **pato** *m*. ◇ *vt* **-1.** [lower] **agachar, bajar. -2.** [try to avoid - duty] **esquivar.** ◇ *vi* [lower head] **agacharse.**

duckling ['dʌklɪŋ] *n* **patito** *m*.

duct [dʌkt] *n* **conducto** *m*.

dud [dʌd] ◇ *adj* [gen] **falso(sa);** [mine] **que no estalla;** [cheque] **sin fondos.** ◇ *n* **persona o cosa inútil.**

dude [djuːd] *n* **Am inf** [man] **tío** *m*.

due [djuː] ◇ *adj* **-1.** [expected] **esperado(da); it's ~ out in May saldrá en mayo; she's ~ back soon tendría que volver dentro de poco; the train's ~ in half an hour el tren debe llegar dentro de media hora. -2.** [appropriate] **oportuno(na), debido(da); with all ~ respect sin ganas de ofender; in ~ course** [at appropriate time] **a su debido tiempo;** [eventually] **al final. -3.** [owed, owing] **pagadero(ra); I'm ~ a bit of luck ya sería hora que tuviera un poco de suerte; to be ~ to deberse a.** ◇ *n* [deserts]: **to give sb their ~ hacer justicia a alguien.** ◇ *adv*: **~ north/south derecho hacia el norte/sur.** ◆ **dues** *npl* **cuota** *f*. ◆ **due to** *prep* **debido a.**

duel ['djuːəl] *n* **duelo** *m*.

duet [djuː'et] *n* **dúo** *m*.

duffel bag ['dʌfl-] *n* **morral** *m*.

duffel coat ['dʌfl-] *n* **trenca** *f*.

duffle bag ['dʌfl-] = **duffel bag.**

duffle coat ['dʌfl-] = **duffel coat.**

dug [dʌg] *pt & pp* → **dig.**

duke [djuːk] *n* **duque** *m*.

dull [dʌl] ◇ *adj* **-1.** [boring] **aburrido(da). -2.** [listless] **torpe. -3.** [dim] **apagado(da). -4.** [cloudy] **gris, triste. -5.** [thud, boom, pain] **sordo(da).** ◇ *vt* [senses] **embotar, entorpecer;** [pain] **aliviar;** [pleasure, memory] **enturbiar.**

duly ['djuːlɪ] *adv* **-1.** [properly] **debidamente. -2.** [as expected] **como era de esperar.**

dumb [dʌm] *adj* **-1.** [unable to speak] **mudo(da); to be struck ~ quedarse de una pieza. -2.** **inf** [stupid] **estúpido(da).**

dumbfound [dʌm'faund] *vt* **dejar mudo(da) de asombro; to be ~ed quedar mudo de asombro.**

dummy ['dʌmɪ] ◇ *adj* **falso(sa).** ◇ *n* **-1.** [of ventriloquist] **muñeco** *m*; [in shop window] **maniquí** *m*. **-2.** [copy] **imitación** *f*. **-3.** **Br** [for baby] **chupete** *m*. **-4.** SPORT **amago** *m*.

dump [dʌmp] ◇ *n* **-1.** [for rubbish] **basurero** *m*, **vertedero** *m*. **-2.** [for ammunition] **depósito** *m*. **-3.** **inf** [ugly place - house] **casucha** *f*. ◇ *vt* **-1.** [put down - sand, load] **descargar;** [- bags, washing] **dejar. -2.** [dispose of] **deshacerse de.**

dumper (truck) **Br** ['dʌmpər-], **dump truck** **Am** *n* **volquete** *m*.

dumping ['dʌmpɪŋ] n vertido m; "no ~" "prohibido verter basura".

dumpling ['dʌmplɪŋ] n bola de masa que se guisa al vapor con carne y verduras.

dump truck Am = dumper (truck).

dumpy ['dʌmpɪ] adj inf bajito y regordete (bajita y regordeta).

dunce [dʌns] n zoquete m y f.

dune [dju:n] n duna f.

dung [dʌŋ] n [of animal] excremento m; [used as manure] estiércol m.

dungarees [ˌdʌŋgə'ri:z] npl Br [for work] mono m; [fashion garment] pantalones mpl de peto.

dungeon ['dʌndʒən] n calabozo m.

duo ['dju:əʊ] n dúo m.

dupe [dju:p] ◇ n primo m, -ma f, inocente m y f. ◇ vt: to ~ sb (into doing sthg) embaucar a uno (a que haga algo).

duplex ['dju:pleks] n Am -1. [apartment] dúplex m, piso m que las habitaciones están distribuidas entre dos plantas. -2. [house] casa f adosada.

duplicate [adj & n 'dju:plɪkət, vb 'dju:plɪkeɪt] ◇ adj duplicado(da). ◇ n copia f, duplicado m; in ~ por duplicado. ◇ vt [copy] duplicar.

durable ['djʊərəbl] adj duradero(ra).

duration [dju'reɪʃn] n duración f; for the ~ of durante.

duress [djʊ'res] n: under ~ por coacción f.

Durex® ['djʊəreks] n [condom] preservativo m, condón m.

during ['djʊərɪŋ] prep durante.

dusk [dʌsk] n crepúsculo m, anochecer m.

dust [dʌst] ◇ n polvo m. ◇ vt -1. [clean] quitar el polvo a, limpiar. -2. [cover with powder]: to ~ sthg (with) espolvorear algo (con).

dustbin ['dʌstbɪn] n Br cubo m de la basura.

dustcart ['dʌstkɑ:t] n Br camión m de la basura.

duster ['dʌstər] n [cloth] bayeta f, trapo m (de quitar el polvo).

dust jacket n sobrecubierta f.

dustman ['dʌstmən] (pl -men [-mən]) n Br basurero m.

dustpan ['dʌstpæn] n recogedor m.

dusty ['dʌstɪ] adj [covered in dust] polvoriento(ta).

Dutch [dʌtʃ] ◇ adj holandés(esa). ◇ n [language] holandés m. ◇ npl: the ~ los holandeses.

Dutch elm disease n hongo que ataca a los olmos.

dutiful ['dju:tɪfʊl] adj obediente, sumiso(sa).

duty ['dju:tɪ] n -1. (U) [moral, legal responsibility] deber m; to do one's ~ cumplir uno con su deber. -2. [work] servicio m; to be on/off ~ estar/no estar de servicio. -3. [tax] impuesto m. ◆ duties npl tareas fpl.

duty-free adj libre de impuestos.

duvet ['du:veɪ] n Br edredón m.

duvet cover n Br funda f del edredón.

dwarf [dwɔ:f] (pl -s OR dwarves [dwɔ:vz]) ◇ n enano m, -na f. ◇ vt achicar, empequeñecer.

dwell [dwel] (pt & pp -ed OR dwelt) vi literary morar, habitar. ◆ dwell on vt fus darle vueltas a.

dwelling ['dwelɪŋ] n literary morada f.

dwelt [dwelt] pt & pp ⟩ dwell.

dwindle ['dwɪndl] vi ir disminuyendo.

dye [daɪ] ◇ n tinte m. ◇ vt teñir.

dying ['daɪɪŋ] ◇ cont ⟩ die. ◇ adj -1. [person, animal] moribundo(da). -2. [activity, practice] en vías de desaparición.

dyke [daɪk] = dike.

dynamic [daɪ'næmɪk] adj dinámico(ca).

dynamite ['daɪnəmaɪt] n lit & fig dinamita f.

dynamo ['daɪnəməʊ] (pl -s) n dinamo f.

dynasty [Br 'dɪnəstɪ, Am 'daɪnəstɪ] n dinastía f.

dyslexia [dɪs'leksɪə] n dislexia f.

dyslexic [dɪs'leksɪk] adj disléxico(ca).

E

e (pl e's OR es), **E** (pl E's OR Es) [i:] n [letter] e f, E f. ◆ **E** n -1. MUS mi m. -2. (abbr of east) E m.

each [i:tʃ] ◇ adj cada. ◇ pron cada uno m, una f; one ~ uno cada uno; ~ of us/the boys cada uno de nosotros/los niños; two of ~ dos de cada (uno); ~ other el uno al otro; they kissed ~ other se besaron; we know ~ other nos conocemos.

eager ['i:gər] adj [pupil] entusiasta; [smile, expression] de entusiasmo; to be ~ for sthg/to do sthg ansiar algo/de hacer algo, desear vivamente algo/hacer algo.

eagle ['iːgl] *n* águila *f*.

ear [ɪəʳ] *n* **-1.** [of person, animal] oreja *f*. **-2.** [of corn] espiga *f*.

earache ['ɪəreɪk] *n* dolor *m* de oídos.

eardrum ['ɪədrʌm] *n* tímpano *m*.

earl [ɜːl] *n* conde *m*.

earlier ['ɜːlɪəʳ] ◇ *adj* anterior. ◇ *adv* antes; ~ **on** antes.

earliest ['ɜːlɪəst] ◇ *adj* primero(ra). ◇ *n*: **at the** ~ como muy pronto.

earlobe ['ɪələʊb] *n* lóbulo *m* (de la oreja).

early ['ɜːlɪ] ◇ *adj* **-1.** [before expected time, in day] temprano(na); **she was** ~ llegó temprano OR con adelanto; **I'll take an** ~ **lunch** almorzaré pronto OR temprano; **to get up** ~ madrugar. **-2.** [at beginning]: ~ **morning** la madrugada; **in the** ~ **1950s** a principios de los años 50. ◇ *adv* **-1.** [before expected time] temprano, pronto; **we got up** ~ nos levantamos temprano; **it arrived ten minutes** ~ llegó con diez minutos de adelanto. **-2.** [at beginning]: **as** ~ **as 1920** ya en 1920; ~ **this morning** esta mañana temprano; ~ **in the year** a principios de año; ~ **on** temprano.

early retirement *n* jubilación *f* anticipada.

earmark ['ɪəmɑːk] *vt*: **to be** ~ed **for** estar destinado(da) a.

earn [ɜːn] *vt* **-1.** [be paid] ganar. **-2.** [generate - wage]: business, product] generar. **-3.** *fig* [gain - respect, praise] ganarse.

earnest ['ɜːnɪst] *adj* [gen] serio(ria); [wish] sincero(ra). ◆ **in earnest** *adv* [seriously] en serio.

earnings ['ɜːnɪŋz] *npl* ingresos *mpl*.

earphones ['ɪəfəʊnz] *npl* auriculares *mpl*.

earplugs ['ɪəplʌgz] *npl* tapones *mpl* para los oídos.

earring ['ɪərɪŋ] *n* pendiente *m*, caravana *f Amer*.

earshot ['ɪəʃɒt] *n*: **within/out of** ~ al alcance/fuera del alcance del oído.

earth [ɜːθ] ◇ *n* **-1.** [gen] tierra *f*; **how/ what/where/why on** ~ ...? ¿cómo/ qué/dónde/por qué demonios ...? **-2.** [in electric plug, appliance] toma *f* de tierra. ◇ *vt Br*: **to be** ~ed estar conectado(da) a tierra.

earthenware ['ɜːθnweəʳ] *n* loza *f*.

earthquake ['ɜːθkweɪk] *n* terremoto *m*.

earthworm ['ɜːθwɜːm] *n* lombriz *f* (de tierra).

earthy ['ɜːθɪ] *adj* **-1.** [rather crude] natural, desinhibido(da). **-2.** [of, like earth] terroso(sa).

earwig ['ɪəwɪg] *n* tijereta *f*.

ease [iːz] ◇ *n* (*U*) **-1.** [lack of difficulty] facilidad *f*; **with** ~ con facilidad. **-2.** [comfort] comodidad *f*; **at** ~ cómodo(da); **ill at** ~ incómodo(da). ◇ *vt* **-1.** [pain, grief] calmar, aliviar; [problems, tension] atenuar. **-2.** [move carefully]: **to** ~ **sthg open** abrir algo con cuidado; **to** ~ **o.s. out of sthg** levantarse despacio de algo. ◇ *vi* [problem] atenuarse; [pain] calmarse; [rain] amainar; [grip] relajarse. ◆ **ease off** *vi* [problem] atenuarse; [pain] calmarse; [rain] amainar. ◆ **ease up** *vi* **-1.** *inf* [treat less severely]: **to** ~ **up on sb** no ser muy duro(ra) con alguien. **-2.** [rain] amainar. **-3.** [relax - person] tomarse las cosas con más calma.

easel ['iːzl] *n* caballete *m*.

easily ['iːzɪlɪ] *adv* **-1.** [without difficulty] fácilmente. **-2.** [without doubt] sin lugar a dudas. **-3.** [in a relaxed manner] tranquilamente, relajadamente.

east [iːst] ◇ *n* **-1.** [direction] este *m*. **-2.** [region]: **the** ~ el este. ◇ *adj* oriental; [wind] del este. ◇ *adv*: ~ (**of**) al este (de). ◆ **East** *n*: **the East** POL el Este; [Asia] el Oriente.

East End *n*: **the** ~ el este de Londres.

Easter ['iːstəʳ] *n* Semana *f* Santa.

Easter egg *n* huevo *m* de Pascua.

easterly ['iːstəlɪ] *adj* del este.

eastern ['iːstən] *adj* del este, oriental. ◆ **Eastern** *adj* [gen & POL] del Este; [from Asia] oriental.

East German ◇ *adj* de Alemania Oriental. ◇ *n* [person] alemán *m*, -ana *f* oriental.

East Germany *n*: (**the former**) ~ (la antigua) Alemania Oriental.

eastward ['iːstwəd] ◇ *adj* hacia el este. ◇ *adv* = **eastwards**.

eastwards ['iːstwədz] *adv* hacia el este.

easy ['iːzɪ] *adj* **-1.** [not difficult] fácil. **-2.** [life, time] cómodo(da). **-3.** [manner] relajado(da).

easy chair *n* [armchair] sillón *m*.

easygoing [ˌiːzɪ'gəʊɪŋ] *adj* [person] tolerante; [manner] relajado(da).

eat [iːt] (*pt* **ate**, *pp* **eaten**) *vt & vi* comer. ◆ **eat away, eat into** *vt sep* **-1.** [corrode] corroer. **-2.** [deplete] mermar.

eaten ['iːtn] *pp* → **eat**.

eau de cologne [ˌəʊdəkə'ləʊn] *n* (agua *f* de) colonia *f*.

eaves ['i:vz] *npl* alero *m*.

eavesdrop ['i:vzdrɒp] *vi*: **to ~ (on)** escuchar secretamente (a).

ebb [eb] ◇ *n* reflujo *m*. ◇ *vi* [tide, sea] bajar.

ebony ['ebənɪ] *n* ébano *m*.

EC (*abbr of* **European Community**) *n* CE *f*.

eccentric [ɪk'sentrɪk] ◇ *adj* excéntrico(ca). ◇ *n* excéntrico *m*, -ca *f*.

echo ['ekəʊ] (*pl* -es) ◇ *n lit & fig* eco *m*. ◇ *vt* [words] repetir; [opinion] hacerse eco de. ◇ *vi* resonar.

eclipse [ɪ'klɪps] ◇ *n lit & fig* eclipse *m*. ◇ *vt fig* eclipsar.

ecological [,i:kə'lɒdʒɪkl] *adj* **-1.** [pattern, balance, impact] ecológico(ca). **-2.** [group, movement, person] ecologista.

ecology [ɪ'kɒlədʒɪ] *n* ecología *f*.

economic [,i:kə'nɒmɪk] *adj* **-1.** [of money, industry] económico(ca). **-2.** [profitable] rentable.

economical [,i:kə'nɒmɪkl] *adj* económico(ca).

economics [,i:kə'nɒmɪks] ◇ *n* (U) economía *f*. ◇ *npl* [of plan, business] aspecto *m* económico.

economize, -ise [ɪ'kɒnəmaɪz] *vi*: **to ~ (on)** economizar (en).

economy [ɪ'kɒnəmɪ] *n* economía *f*.

economy class *n* clase *f* económica OR turista.

ecstasy ['ekstəsɪ] *n* [great happiness] éxtasis *m inv*.

ecstatic [ek'stætɪk] *adj* extático(ca).

ECU, Ecu ['ekju:] (*abbr of* **European Currency Unit**) *n* ECU *m*, ecu *m*.

Ecuador ['ekwədɔ:r] *n* (el) Ecuador.

Ecuadoran [,ekwə'dɔ:rən], **Ecuadorian** [,ekwə'dɔ:rɪən] ◇ *adj* ecuatoriano(na). ◇ *n* ecuatoriano *m*, -na *f*.

eczema ['eksɪmə] *n* eczema *m*.

Eden ['i:dn] *n*: **(the Garden of) ~** (el jardín del) Edén *m*.

edge [edʒ] ◇ *n* **-1.** [of cliff, table, garden] borde *m*; **to be on the ~ of** estar al borde de. **-2.** [of coin] canto *m*; [of knife] filo *m*. **-3.** [advantage]: **to have an ~ over** OR **the ~ on** llevar ventaja a. ◇ *vi*: **to ~ away/closer** ir alejándose/ acercándose poco a poco. ◆ **on edge** *adj* con los nervios de punta.

edgeways ['edʒweɪz], **edgewise** ['edʒwaɪz] *adv* de lado.

edgy ['edʒɪ] *adj* nervioso(sa).

edible ['edɪbl] *adj* comestible.

edict ['i:dɪkt] *n* edicto *m*.

Edinburgh ['edɪnbrə] *n* Edimburgo.

edit ['edɪt] *vt* **-1.** [correct - text] corregir, revisar. **-2.** [select material for - book] recopilar. **-3.** CINEMA, RADIO & TV montar. **-4.** [run - newspaper, magazine] dirigir.

edition [ɪ'dɪʃn] *n* edición *f*.

editor ['edɪtər] *n* **-1.** [of newspaper, magazine] director *m*, -ra *f*. **-2.** [of section of newspaper, programme, text] redactor *m*, -ra *f*. **-3.** [compiler - of book] autor *m*, -ra *f* de la edición. **-4.** CINEMA, RADIO & TV montador *m*, -ra *f*.

editorial [,edɪ'tɔ:rɪəl] ◇ *adj* editorial; **~ staff** redacción *f*. ◇ *n* editorial *m*.

educate ['edʒʊkeɪt] *vt* **-1.** [at school, college] educar. **-2.** [inform] informar.

education [,edʒʊ'keɪʃn] *n* (U) **-1.** [activity, sector] enseñanza *f*. **-2.** [process or result of teaching] educación *f*.

educational [,edʒʊ'keɪʃənl] *adj* educativo(va); [establishment] docente.

EEC (*abbr of* **European Economic Community**) *n* CEE *f*.

eel [i:l] *n* anguila *f*.

eerie ['ɪərɪ] *adj* espeluznante.

efface [ɪ'feɪs] *vt* borrar.

effect [ɪ'fekt] ◇ *n* efecto *m*; **to have an ~ on** tener OR surtir efecto en; **to take ~** [law, rule] entrar en vigor; [drug] hacer efecto; **to put sthg into ~** hacer entrar algo en vigor; **words to that ~** palabras por el estilo. ◇ *vt* efectuar, llevar a cabo. ◆ **effects** *npl*: **(special) ~s** efectos *mpl* especiales.

effective [ɪ'fektɪv] *adj* **-1.** [successful] eficaz. **-2.** [actual, real] efectivo(va). **-3.** [law, ceasefire] operativo(va).

effectively [ɪ'fektɪvlɪ] *adv* **-1.** [well, successfully] eficazmente. **-2.** [in fact] de hecho.

effectiveness [ɪ'fektɪvnɪs] *n* eficacia *f*.

effeminate [ɪ'femɪnət] *adj pej* afeminado(da).

effervescent [,efə'vesənt] *adj* efervescente.

efficiency [ɪ'fɪʃənsɪ] *n* [gen] eficiencia *f*; [of machine] rendimiento *m*.

efficient [ɪ'fɪʃənt] *adj* [gen] eficiente; [machine] de buen rendimiento.

effluent ['efluənt] *n* aguas *fpl* residuales.

effort ['efət] *n* **-1.** [gen] esfuerzo *m*; **to be worth the ~** merecer la pena; **to make the ~ to do sthg** hacer el esfuerzo de hacer algo; **to make an/no ~ to do sthg** hacer un esfuerzo/no hacer ningún esfuerzo por hacer algo. **-2.** *inf* [result of trying] tentativa *f*.

effortless ['efətlɪs] *adj* sin gran esfuerzo.

effusive [ɪ'fjuːsɪv] *adj* efusivo(va).

e.g. (*abbr of* **exempli gratia**) *adv* p. ej.

egg [eg] *n* [gen] huevo *m*. ◆ **egg on** *vt sep* incitar.

eggcup ['egkʌp] *n* huevera *f*.

eggplant ['egplɑːnt] *n Am* berenjena *f*.

eggshell ['egʃel] *n* cáscara *f* de huevo.

egg white *n* clara *f* (de huevo).

egg yolk [-jəʊk] *n* yema *f* (de huevo).

ego ['iːgəʊ] (*pl* **-s**) *n* [opinion of self] amor *m* propio, ego *m*.

egoism ['iːgəʊɪzm] *n* egoísmo *m*.

egoistic [ˌiːgəʊ'ɪstɪk] *adj* egoísta.

egotistic(al) [ˌiːgə'tɪstɪk(l)] *adj* egotista.

Egypt ['iːdʒɪpt] *n* Egipto.

Egyptian [ɪ'dʒɪpʃn] ◇ *adj* egipcio(cia). ◇ *n* [person] egipcio *m*, -cia *f*.

eiderdown ['aɪdədaʊn] *n* edredón *m*.

eight [eɪt] *num* ocho; *see also* **six**.

eighteen [ˌeɪ'tiːn] *num* dieciocho; *see also* **six**.

eighth [eɪtθ] *num* octavo(va); *see also* **sixth**.

eighty ['eɪtɪ] *num* ochenta; *see also* **sixty**.

Eire ['eərə] *n* Eire.

either ['aɪðə', 'iːðə'] ◇ *adj* **-1.** [one or the other] cualquiera de los dos; **she couldn't find** ~ **jumper** no podía encontrar ninguno de los dos jerseys; ~ **way** de cualquiera de las formas. **-2.** [each] cada; **on** ~ **side** a ambos lados. ◇ *pron*: ~ **(of them)** cualquiera (de ellos (ellas)); **I don't like** ~ **(of them)** no me gusta ninguno de ellos (ninguna de ellas). ◇ *adv* (*in negatives*) tampoco; **she can't and I can't** ~ ella no puede y yo tampoco. ◇ *conj*: ~ **... or o** ~ ... o; ~ **you or me** o tú o yo; **I don't like** ~ **him or his wife** no me gusta ni él ni su mujer (tampoco).

eject [ɪ'dʒekt] *vt* **-1.** [object] expulsar, despedir. **-2.** [person]: **to** ~ **sb (from)** expulsar a alguien (de).

eke [iːk] ◆ **eke out** *vt sep* alargar *fig*, estirar *fig*.

elaborate [*adj* ɪ'læbrət, *vb* ɪ'læbəreɪt] ◇ *adj* [ceremony] complicado(da); [carving] trabajado(da); [explanation, plan] detallado(da). ◇ *vi*: **to** ~ **on sthg** ampliar algo, explicar algo con más detalle.

elapse [ɪ'læps] *vi* transcurrir.

elastic [ɪ'læstɪk] ◇ *adj* **-1.** [gen] elástico(ca). **-2.** *fig* [flexible] flexible. ◇ *n* elástico *m*.

elasticated [ɪ'læstɪkeɪtɪd] *adj* elástico(ca).

elastic band *n Br* gomita *f*.

elated [ɪ'leɪtɪd] *adj* eufórico(ca).

elbow ['elbəʊ] *n* codo *m*.

elder ['eldə'] ◇ *adj* mayor. ◇ *n* **-1.** [older person] mayor *m y f*. **-2.** [of tribe, church] anciano *m*. **-3.** ~ **(tree)** saúco *m*.

elderly ['eldəlɪ] ◇ *adj* mayor, anciano(na). ◇ *npl*: **the** ~ los ancianos.

eldest ['eldɪst] *adj* mayor.

elect [ɪ'lekt] ◇ *adj* electo(ta); **the president** ~ el presidente electo. ◇ *vt* **-1.** [by voting] elegir; **to** ~ **sb (as) sthg** elegir a alguien (como) algo. **-2.** *fml* [choose]: **to** ~ **to do sthg** optar por OR decidir hacer algo.

election [ɪ'lekʃn] *n* elección *f*; **to have** OR **hold an** ~ celebrar (unas) elecciones.

electioneering [ɪˌlekʃə'nɪərɪŋ] *n usu pej* electoralismo *m*.

elector [ɪ'lektə'] *n* elector *m*, -ra *f*.

electorate [ɪ'lektərət] *n*: **the** ~ el electorado.

electric [ɪ'lektrɪk] *adj* [gen] eléctrico(ca). ◆ **electrics** *npl Br inf* sistema *m* eléctrico.

electrical [ɪ'lektrɪkl] *adj* eléctrico(ca).

electrical shock *Am* = **electric shock**.

electric blanket *n* manta *f* eléctrica.

electric cooker *n* cocina *f* eléctrica.

electric fire *n* estufa *f* eléctrica.

electrician [ˌɪlek'trɪʃn] *n* electricista *m y f*.

electricity [ˌɪlek'trɪsətɪ] *n* electricidad *f*.

electric shock *Br*, **electrical shock** *Am n* descarga *f* eléctrica.

electrify [ɪ'lektrɪfaɪ] *vt* **-1.** [rail line] electrificar. **-2.** *fig* [excite] electrizar.

electrocute [ɪ'lektrəkjuːt] *vt*: **to** ~ **o.s.**, **to be** ~**d** electrocutarse.

electrolysis [ˌɪlek'trɒləsɪs] *n* electrólisis *f inv*.

electron [ɪ'lektrɒn] *n* electrón *m*.

electronic [ˌɪlek'trɒnɪk] *adj* electrónico(ca). ◆ **electronics** ◇ *n* (*U*) [technology] electrónica *f*. ◇ *npl* [equipment] sistema *m* electrónico.

electronic data processing *n* proceso *m* electrónico de datos.

electronic mail *n* COMPUT correo *m* electrónico.

elegant ['elɪgənt] *adj* elegante.

element ['elɪmənt] *n* **-1.** [gen] elemento *m*. **-2.** [amount, proportion] toque *m*. **-3.** [in heater, kettle] resistencia *f*. ◆ **elements** *npl* **-1.** [basics] elementos *mpl*. **-2.** [weather]: **the** ~**s** los elementos.

elementary [ˌelɪ'mentərɪ] *adj* elemental; ~ **education** enseñanza *f* primaria.

elementary school *n Am* escuela *f* primaria.

elephant ['elɪfənt] (*pl inv* OR **-s**) *n* elefante *m*.

elevate ['elɪveɪt] *vt*: **to** ~ **sthg/sb** (**to** OR **into**) elevar algo/a alguien (a la categoría de).

elevator ['elɪveɪtəʳ] *n Am* ascensor *m*, elevador *m Amer*.

eleven [ɪ'levn] *num* once *m*; *see also* **six**.

elevenses [ɪ'levnzɪz] *n* (*U*) *Br* tentempié *m* que se toma sobre las once.

eleventh [ɪ'levnθ] *num* undécimo(ma); *see also* **sixth**.

elicit [ɪ'lɪsɪt] *vt fml* **-1.** [response, reaction]: **to** ~ **sthg** (**from sb**) provocar algo (en alguien). **-2.** [information]: **to** ~ **sthg** (**from sb**) sacar algo (a alguien).

eligible ['elɪdʒəbl] *adj* [suitable, qualified] elegible; **to be** ~ **for sthg/to do sthg** reunir los requisitos para algo/para hacer algo.

eliminate [ɪ'lɪmɪneɪt] *vt* eliminar; **to be** ~**d from sthg** ser eliminado(da) de algo.

elite [ɪ'liːt] ◇ *adj* selecto(ta). ◇ *n* élite *f*.

elitist [ɪ'liːtɪst] *pej adj* elitista.

elk [elk] (*pl inv* OR **-s**) *n* alce *m*.

elm [elm] *n*: ~ (**tree**) olmo *m*.

elocution [ˌelə'kjuːʃn] *n* dicción *f*.

elongated ['iːlɒŋgeɪtɪd] *adj* alargado(da).

elope [ɪ'ləʊp] *vi*: **to** ~ (**with**) fugarse (con).

eloquent ['eləkwənt] *adj* elocuente.

El Salvador [ˌel'sælvədɔːʳ] *n* El Salvador.

else [els] *adv*: **anything** ~? ¿algo más?; **I don't need anything** ~ no necesito nada más; **everyone** ~ todos los demás (todas las demás); **everywhere** ~ en/a todas las otras partes; **little** ~ poco más; **nothing/nobody** ~ nada/nadie más; **someone/something** ~ otra persona/cosa; **somewhere** ~ en/a otra parte; **who** ~? ¿quién si no?; **what** ~? ¿qué más?; **where** ~? ¿en/a qué otro sitio? ◆ **or else** *conj* [or if not] si no, de lo contrario.

elsewhere [els'weəʳ] *adv* a/en otra parte.

elude [ɪ'luːd] *vt* [gen] escaparse de, eludir a; [blow] esquivar.

elusive [ɪ'luːsɪv] *adj* [person, success] esquivo(va); [quality] difícil de encontrar.

emaciated [ɪ'meɪʃɪeɪtɪd] *adj* demacrado(da).

E-mail (*abbr of* **electronic mail**) *n* COMPUT correo *m* electrónico.

emanate ['eməneɪt] *fml vi*: **to** ~ **from** emanar de.

emancipate [ɪ'mænsɪpeɪt] *vt*: **to** ~ **sb** (**from**) emancipar a alguien (de).

embankment [ɪm'bæŋkmənt] *n* **-1.** RAIL terraplén *m*. **-2.** [of river] dique *m*.

embark [ɪm'bɑːk] *vi*: **to** ~ **on** *lit* & *fig* embarcarse en.

embarkation [ˌembɑː'keɪʃn] *n* [gen] embarque *m*; [of troops] embarco *m*.

embarrass [ɪm'bærəs] *vt* **-1.** [gen] avergonzar; **it** ~**es me** me da vergüenza. **-2.** [financially] poner en un aprieto.

embarrassed [ɪm'bærəst] *adj* avergonzado(da), violento(ta).

embarrassing [ɪm'bærəsɪŋ] *adj* embarazoso(sa), violento(ta); **how** ~! ¡qué vergüenza!

embarrassment [ɪm'bærəsmənt] *n* [feeling] vergüenza *f*, pena *f Amer*.

embassy ['embəsɪ] *n* embajada *f*.

embedded [ɪm'bedɪd] *adj* [buried]: ~ (**in**) incrustado(da) (en).

embellish [ɪm'belɪʃ] *vt*: **to** ~ **sthg** (**with**) adornar OR embellecer algo (con).

embers ['embəz] *npl* rescoldos *mpl*.

embezzle [ɪm'bezl] *vt* malversar.

embittered [ɪm'bɪtəd] *adj* amargado(da), resentido(da).

emblem ['embləm] *n* emblema *m*.

embody [ɪm'bɒdɪ] *vt* personificar, encarnar; **to be embodied in sthg** estar plasmado en algo.

embossed [ɪm'bɒst] *adj* **-1.** [heading, design]: ~ (**on**) [paper] estampado(da) (en); [leather, metal] repujado(da) (en). **-2.** [paper]: ~ (**with**) estampado(da) (con). **-3.** [leather, metal]: ~ (**with**) repujado(da) (con).

embrace [ɪm'breɪs] ◇ *n* abrazo *m*. ◇ *vt* **-1.** [hug] abrazar, dar un abrazo a. **-2.** *fml* [convert to] convertirse a. **-3.** *fml* [include] abarcar. ◇ *vi* abrazarse.

embroider [ɪm'brɔɪdəʳ] *vt* **-1.** SEWING bordar. **-2.** *pej* [embellish] adornar.

embroidery [ɪm'brɔɪdərɪ] *n* (*U*) bordado *m*.

embroil [ɪm'brɔɪl] *vt*: **to get/be** ~**ed** (**in**) enredarse/estar enredado (en).

embryo ['embrɪəʊ] (*pl* **-s**) *n* embrión *m*.

emerald ['emərəld] ◇ *adj* [colour] esmeralda *m inv*. ◇ *n* [stone] esmeralda *f*.

emerge [ɪ'mɜːdʒ] ◇ *vi* **-1.** [gen]: **to** ~ (**from**) salir (de). **-2.** [come into existence, become known] surgir, emerger. ◇ *vt*: **it** ~**d that** ... resultó que ....

emergence [ɪ'mɜːdʒəns] *n* surgimiento *m*, aparición *f*.

emergency [ɪ'mɜːdʒənsɪ] ◇ *adj* [case, exit, services] de emergencia; [ward] de urgencia; [supplies] de reserva; [meeting] extraordinario(ria). ◇ *n* emergencia *f*.

emergency exit *n* salida *f* de emergencia.

emergency landing *n* aterrizaje *m* forzoso.

emergency services *npl* servicios *mpl* de urgencia.

emery board ['emərɪ-] *n* lima *f* de uñas.

emigrant ['emɪgrənt] *n* emigrante *m* y *f*.

emigrate ['emɪgreɪt] *vi*: to ~ (to/from) emigrar (a/de).

eminent ['emɪnənt] *adj* eminente.

emission [ɪ'mɪʃn] *n* emisión *f*.

emit [ɪ'mɪt] *vt* [gen] emitir; [smell, smoke] despedir.

emotion [ɪ'məʊʃn] *n* emoción *f*.

emotional [ɪ'məʊʃənl] *adj* **-1.** [gen] emotivo(va). **-2.** [needs, problems] emocional.

emperor ['empərər] *n* emperador *m*.

emphasis ['emfəsɪs] (*pl* **-ases** [-əsiːz]) *n*: ~ (on) énfasis *m* *inv* (en); to lay OR place ~ on poner énfasis en, hacer hincapié en.

emphasize, -ise ['emfəsaɪz] *vt* [word, syllable] acentuar; [point, fact, feature] subrayar, hacer hincapié en; to ~ that ... poner de relieve OR subrayar que ....

emphatic [ɪm'fætɪk] *adj* [forceful] rotundo(da), categórico(ca).

emphatically [ɪm'fætɪklɪ] *adv* **-1.** [with emphasis] rotundamente, enfáticamente. **-2.** [certainly] ciertamente.

empire ['empaɪər] *n* imperio *m*.

employ [ɪm'plɔɪ] *vt* **-1.** [give work to] emplear; to be ~ed as estar empleado de. **-2.** *fml* [use] utilizar, emplear; to ~ sthg as sthg/to do sthg utilizar algo de algo/para hacer algo.

employee [ɪm'plɔɪiː] *n* empleado *m*, -da *f*.

employer [ɪm'plɔɪər] *n* patrono *m*, -na *f*, empresario *m*, -ria *f*.

employment [ɪm'plɔɪmənt] *n* empleo *m*; to be in ~ tener trabajo.

employment agency *n* agencia *f* de trabajo.

empower [ɪm'paʊər] *vt* *fml*: to be ~ed to do sthg estar autorizado(da) a OR para hacer algo.

empress ['emprɪs] *n* emperatriz *f*.

empty ['emptɪ] ◇ *adj* **-1.** [gen] vacío(a); [town] desierto(ta). **-2.** *pej* [words, threat, promise] vano(na). ◇ *vt* vaciar; to ~ sthg into sthg vaciar algo en algo. ◇ *vi* vaciarse. ◇ *n* *inf* casco *m*.

empty-handed [-'hændɪd] *adv* con las manos vacías.

EMS (*abbr of* **European Monetary System**) *n* SME *m*.

emulate ['emjʊleɪt] *vt* emular.

emulsion [ɪ'mʌlʃn] *n*: ~ (paint) pintura *f* mate.

enable [ɪ'neɪbl] *vt*: to ~ sb to do sthg permitir a alguien hacer algo.

enact [ɪ'nækt] *vt* **-1.** JUR promulgar. **-2.** [act] representar.

enamel [ɪ'næml] *n* **-1.** [gen] esmalte *m*. **-2.** [paint] pintura *f* de esmalte.

encampment [ɪn'kæmpmənt] *n* campamento *m*.

encapsulate [ɪn'kæpsjʊleɪt] *vt*: to ~ sthg (in) sintetizar algo (en).

encase [ɪn'keɪs] *vt*: ~d in encajonado(da) en.

enchanted [ɪn'tʃɑːntɪd] *adj*: ~ (by OR with) encantado(da) (con).

enchanting [ɪn'tʃɑːntɪŋ] *adj* encantador(ra).

encircle [ɪn'sɜːkl] *vt* rodear.

enclose [ɪn'kləʊz] *vt* **-1.** [surround, contain] rodear; ~d by OR with rodeado de; an ~d space un espacio cerrado. **-2.** [put in envelope] adjuntar; please find ~d ... envío adjunto ....

enclosure [ɪn'kləʊʒər] *n* **-1.** [place] recinto *m* (vallado). **-2.** [in letter] anexo *m*.

encompass [ɪn'kʌmpəs] *vt* *fml* [include] abarcar.

encore ['ɒŋkɔːr] ◇ *n* bis *m*. ◇ *excl* ¡otra!

encounter [ɪn'kaʊntər] ◇ *n* encuentro *m*. ◇ *vt* *fml* encontrarse con.

encourage [ɪn'kʌrɪdʒ] *vt* **-1.** [give confidence to]: to ~ sb (to do sthg) animar a alguien (a hacer algo). **-2.** [foster] fomentar.

encouragement [ɪn'kʌrɪdʒmənt] *n* aliento *m*; [of industry] fomento *m*.

encroach [ɪn'krəʊtʃ] *vi*: to ~ on OR upon [rights, territory] usurpar; [privacy, time] invadir.

encyclop(a)edia [ɪn,saɪklə'piːdjə] *n* enciclopedia *f*.

end [end] ◇ *n* **-1.** [last part, finish] fin *m*, final *m*; at the ~ of May/1992 a finales de mayo/1992; at an ~ terminando; to bring sthg to an ~ poner fin a algo; to come to an ~ llegar a su fin, terminarse; "the ~" [in films] "FIN"; to put an ~ to sthg poner fin a algo; in the ~ [finally] finalmente, por fin. **-2.** [of two-ended thing] **extremo** m, **punta** f; [of phone line] **lado** m; ~ **to** ~ extremo con extremo; **cigarette** ~ colilla f. **-3.** fml [purpose] **fin** m. ◇ vt: **to** ~ **sthg (with)** terminar algo (con). ◇ vi [finish] acabarse, terminarse; **to** ~ **in/with** acabar en/con, terminar en/con. ◆ **on end** adv **-1.** [upright - hair] de punta; [- object] de pie. **-2.** [continuously]: **for days on** ~ día tras día. ◆ **end up** vi acabar, terminar; **to** ~ **up doing sthg** acabar por hacer algo/haciendo algo; **to** ~ **up in** ir a parar a.

endanger [ɪn'deɪndʒəʳ] vt poner en peligro.

endearing [ɪn'dɪərɪŋ] adj simpático(ca).

endeavour Br, **endeavor** Am [ɪn'devəʳ] fml ◇ n esfuerzo m. ◇ vt: **to** ~ **to do sthg** procurar hacer algo.

ending ['endɪŋ] n final m, desenlace m.

endive ['endaɪv] n **-1.** [salad vegetable] endibia f. **-2.** [chicory] achicoria f.

endless ['endlɪs] adj [gen] interminable; [patience, resources] inagotable.

endorse [ɪn'dɔːs] vt **-1.** [approve] apoyar, respaldar. **-2.** [cheque] endosar.

endorsement [ɪn'dɔːsmənt] n **-1.** [approval] apoyo m, respaldo m. **-2.** Br [on driving licence] nota de sanción que consta en el carnet de conducir.

endow [ɪn'daʊ] vt **-1.** fml [equip]: **to be** ~**ed with** estar dotado(da) de. **-2.** [donate money to] donar fondos a.

endurance [ɪn'djʊərəns] n resistencia f.

endure [ɪn'djʊəʳ] ◇ vt soportar, aguantar. ◇ vi fml perdurar.

endways Br ['endweɪz], **endwise** Am ['endwaɪz] adv **-1.** [not sideways] de lado. **-2.** [with ends touching] extremo con extremo.

enemy ['enɪmɪ] n enemigo m, -ga f.

energetic [,enə'dʒetɪk] adj **-1.** [lively, physically taxing] enérgico(ca). **-2.** [enthusiastic] activo(va), vigoroso(sa).

energy ['enədʒɪ] n energía f.

enforce [ɪn'fɔːs] vt [law] hacer cumplir, aplicar; [standards] imponer.

enforced [ɪn'fɔːst] adj forzoso(sa).

engage [ɪn'geɪdʒ] ◇ vt **-1.** [attract] atraer. **-2.** [TECH - clutch] pisar; [- gear] meter. **-3.** fml [employ] contratar; **to be** ~**d in** OR **on** dedicarse a. ◇ vi [be involved]: **to** ~ **in** [gen] meterse en, dedicarse a; [conversation] entablar.

engaged [ɪn'geɪdʒd] adj **-1.** [to be married]: ~ **(to)** prometido(da) (con); **to get** ~ prometerse. **-2.** [busy, in use] ocupa-

do(da); ~ **in sthg** ocupado en algo. **-3.** TELEC comunicando.

engaged tone n Br señal f de comunicando.

engagement [ɪn'geɪdʒmənt] n **-1.** [to be married] compromiso m; [period] noviazgo m. **-2.** [appointment] cita f.

engagement ring n anillo m de compromiso.

engaging [ɪn'geɪdʒɪŋ] adj atractivo(va).

engender [ɪn'dʒendəʳ] vt fml engendrar.

engine ['endʒɪn] n **-1.** [of vehicle] motor m. **-2.** RAIL locomotora f, máquina f.

engine driver n Br maquinista m y f.

engineer [,endʒɪ'nɪəʳ] ◇ n **-1.** [gen] ingeniero m, -ra f. **-2.** Am [engine driver] maquinista m y f. ◇ vt **-1.** [construct] construir. **-2.** [contrive] tramar.

engineering [,endʒɪ'nɪərɪŋ] n ingeniería f.

England ['ɪŋglənd] n Inglaterra f.

English ['ɪŋglɪʃ] ◇ adj inglés(esa). ◇ n [language] inglés m. ◇ npl [people]: **the** ~ los ingleses.

English breakfast n desayuno m inglés.

English Channel n: **the** ~ el canal de la Mancha.

Englishman ['ɪŋglɪʃmən] (pl **-men** [-mən]) n inglés m.

Englishwoman ['ɪŋglɪʃ,wʊmən] (pl **-women** [-,wɪmɪn]) n inglesa f.

engrave [ɪn'greɪv] vt lit & fig: **to** ~ **sthg (on)** grabar algo (en).

engraving [ɪn'greɪvɪŋ] n grabado m.

engrossed [ɪn'grəʊst] adj: **to be** ~ **(in)** estar absorto(ta) (en).

engulf [ɪn'gʌlf] vt: **to be** ~**ed in** [flames etc] verse devorado(da) por; [fear, despair] verse sumido(da) en.

enhance [ɪn'hɑːns] vt [gen] aumentar; [status, position] elevar; [beauty] realzar.

enjoy [ɪn'dʒɔɪ] vt **-1.** [like] disfrutar de; **did you** ~ **the film/book?** ¿te gustó la película/el libro?; **she** ~**s reading** le gusta leer; ~ **your meal!** ¡que aproveche!; **to** ~ **o.s.** pasarlo bien, divertirse. **-2.** fml [possess] gozar OR disfrutar de.

enjoyable [ɪn'dʒɔɪəbl] adj agradable.

enjoyment [ɪn'dʒɔɪmənt] n [pleasure] placer m.

enlarge [ɪn'lɑːdʒ] vt [gen & PHOT] ampliar. ◆ **enlarge (up)on** vt fus ampliar.

enlargement [ɪn'lɑːdʒmənt] n [gen & PHOT] ampliación f.

enlighten [ɪn'laɪtn] vt fml iluminar.

enlightened [ɪn'laɪtnd] adj amplio(plia) de miras.

enlightenment [ɪnˈlaɪtnmənt] *n* (U) aclaración *f*. ◆ **Enlightenment** *n*: the Enlightenment la Ilustración.

enlist [ɪnˈlɪst] ◇ *vt* -1. [person] alistar, reclutar. -2. [support] obtener. ◇ *vi* MIL: to ~ (in) alistarse (en).

enmity [ˈenmətɪ] *n* enemistad *f*.

enormity [ɪˈnɔːmətɪ] *n* [extent] enormidad *f*.

enormous [ɪˈnɔːməs] *adj* enorme.

enough [ɪˈnʌf] ◇ *adj* bastante, suficiente. ◇ *pron* bastante; **more than** ~ más que suficiente; **that's** ~ [sufficient] ya está bien; **to have had** ~ (**of**) [expressing annoyance] estar harto (de). ◇ *adv* bastante, suficientemente; **I was stupid** ~ **to believe him** fui lo bastante tonto como para creerle; **he was good** ~ **to lend me his car** *fml* tuvo la bondad de dejarme su coche; **strangely** ~ curiosamente.

enquire [ɪnˈkwaɪəʳ] *vi* [ask for information] informarse; **to** ~ **about sthg** informarse de algo; **to** ~ **when/how/ whether/if** ... preguntar cuándo/cómo/ si .... ◆ **enquire into** *vt fus* investigar.

enquiry [ɪnˈkwaɪərɪ] *n* -1. [question] pregunta *f*; "Enquiries" "Información". -2. [investigation] investigación *f*.

enraged [ɪnˈreɪdʒd] *adj* enfurecido(da).

enrol *Br*, **enroll** *Am* [ɪnˈrəʊl] ◇ *vt* matricular. ◇ *vi*: to ~ (on) matricularse (en).

en route [ˌɒnˈruːt] *adv*: ~ (**from/to**) en el camino (de/a).

ensign [ˈensaɪn] *n* -1. [flag] bandera *f*. -2. *Am* [sailor] = alférez *m* de fragata.

ensue [ɪnˈsjuː] *vi fml* originarse; [war] sobrevenir.

ensure [ɪnˈʃʊəʳ] *vt*: to ~ (**that**) asegurar que.

ENT (*abbr of* **Ear, Nose & Throat**) *n* otorrinolaringología *f*.

entail [ɪnˈteɪl] *vt* [involve] conllevar, suponer.

enter [ˈentəʳ] ◇ *vt* -1. [gen] entrar en. -2. [join - profession, parliament] ingresar en; [- university] matricularse en; [- army, navy] alistarse en. -3. [become involved in - politics etc] meterse en; [- race, examination etc] presentarse a. -4. [register]: **to** ~ **sthg/sb for sthg** inscribir algo/a alguien en algo. -5. [write down] apuntar. -6. [appear in] presentarse OR aparecer en. -7. COMPUT dar entrada a. ◇ *vi* -1. [come or go in] entrar. -2. [participate]: **to** ~ (**for sthg**) presentarse (a algo). ◆ **enter into** *vt fus*

entrar en; [agreement] comprometerse a.

enter key *n* COMPUT tecla *f* de entrada.

enterprise [ˈentəpraɪz] *n* empresa *f*.

enterprise zone *n* zona del Reino Unido donde se fomenta la actividad industrial y empresarial.

enterprising [ˈentəpraɪzɪŋ] *adj* emprendedor(ra).

entertain [ˌentəˈteɪn] *vt* -1. [amuse] divertir, entretener. -2. [invite] recibir (en casa). -3. *fml* [idea, proposal] considerar.

entertainer [ˌentəˈteɪnəʳ] *n* artista *m* y *f*.

entertaining [ˌentəˈteɪnɪŋ] *adj* divertido(da), entretenido(da).

entertainment [ˌentəˈteɪnmənt] *n* -1. (U) [amusement] diversión *f*. -2. [show] espectáculo *m*.

enthral, enthrall *Am* [ɪnˈθrɔːl] *vt* embelesar.

enthusiasm [ɪnˈθjuːzɪæzm] *n* -1. [passion, eagerness]: ~ (**for**) entusiasmo *m* (por). -2. [interest] pasión *f*, interés *m*.

enthusiast [ɪnˈθjuːzɪæst] *n* entusiasta *m* y *f*.

enthusiastic [ɪnˌθjuːzɪˈæstɪk] *adj* [person] entusiasta; [cry, response] entusiástico(ca).

entice [ɪnˈtaɪs] *vt* seducir, atraer.

entire [ɪnˈtaɪəʳ] *adj* entero(ra); **the** ~ **evening** toda la noche.

entirely [ɪnˈtaɪəlɪ] *adv* enteramente; **I'm not** ~ **sure** no estoy del todo seguro.

entirety [ɪnˈtaɪrətɪ] *n fml*: **in its** ~ en su totalidad.

entitle [ɪnˈtaɪtl] *vt* [allow]: **to** ~ **sb to sthg** dar a alguien derecho a algo; **to** ~ **sb to do sthg** autorizar a alguien a hacer algo.

entitled [ɪnˈtaɪtld] *adj* -1. [allowed]: **to be** ~ **to sthg/to do sthg** tener derecho a algo/a hacer algo. -2. [having the title] titulado(da).

entourage [ˌɒntʊˈrɑːʒ] *n* séquito *m*.

entrails [ˈentreɪlz] *npl* entrañas *fpl*.

entrance [*n* ˈentrəns, *vb* ɪnˈtrɑːns] ◇ *n*: ~ (**to**) entrada *f* (a OR de); **to gain** ~ **to** *fml* [building] lograr acceso a; [society, university] lograr el ingreso en. ◇ *vt* encantar, hechizar.

entrance examination *n* examen *m* de ingreso.

entrance fee *n* (precio *m* de) entrada *f*.

entrant [ˈentrənt] *n* participante *m* y *f*.

entreat [ɪnˈtriːt] *vt*: **to** ~ **sb (to do sthg)** suplicar OR rogar a alguien (que haga algo).

entrenched [ɪn'trentʃt] *adj* [firm] arraigado(da).

entrepreneur [,ɒntrəprə'nɜːʳ] *n* empresario *m*, -ria *f*.

entrust [ɪn'trʌst] *vt*: **to ~ sthg to sb, to ~ sb with sthg** confiar algo a alguien.

entry ['entri] *n* **-1.** [gen]: **~ (into)** entrada *f* (en); **no ~** se prohibe la entrada, prohibido el paso. **-2.** *fig* [joining - of group, society] ingreso *m*. **-3.** [in competition] participante *m y f*. **-4.** [in diary] anotación *f*; [in ledger] partida *f*.

entry form *n* boleto *m* OR impreso *m* de inscripción.

entry phone *n* Br portero *m* automático.

envelop [ɪn'veləp] *vt*: **to ~ sthg/sb in** envolver algo/a alguien en.

envelope ['envələʊp] *n* sobre *m*.

envious ['envɪəs] *adj* [person] envidioso(sa); [look] de envidia.

environment [ɪn'vaɪərənmənt] *n* **-1.** [surroundings] entorno *m*. **-2.** [natural world]: **the ~** el medio ambiente.

environmental [ɪn,vaɪərən'mentl] *adj* medioambiental; **~ pollution** contaminación *f* del medio ambiente.

environmentally [ɪn,vaɪərən'mentəlɪ] *adv* ecológicamente; **~ friendly** ecológico(ca).

envisage [ɪn'vɪzɪdʒ], **envision** Am [ɪn'vɪʒn] *vt* prever.

envoy ['envɔɪ] *n* enviado *m*, -da *f*.

envy ['envɪ] ◇ *n* envidia *f*. ◇ *vt*: **to ~ (sb sthg)** envidiar (algo a alguien).

epic ['epɪk] ◇ *adj* épico(ca). ◇ *n* epopeya *f*.

epidemic [,epɪ'demɪk] *n* epidemia *f*.

epileptic [,epɪ'leptɪk] ◇ *adj* epiléptico(ca). ◇ *n* epiléptico *m*, -ca *f*.

episode ['epɪsəʊd] *n* **-1.** [event] episodio *m*. **-2.** [of story, TV series] capítulo *m*.

epistle [ɪ'pɪsl] *n* epístola *f*.

epitaph ['epɪtɑːf] *n* epitafio *m*.

epitome [ɪ'pɪtəmɪ] *n*: **the ~ of** [person] la personificación de; [thing] el vivo ejemplo de.

epitomize, -ise [ɪ'pɪtəmaɪz] *vt* [subj: person] personificar; [subj: thing] representar el paradigma de.

epoch ['iːpɒk] *n* época *f*.

equable ['ekwəbl] *adj* [calm, reasonable] ecuánime.

equal ['iːkwəl] ◇ *adj* igual; **~ to** [sum] igual a; **to be ~ to** [task etc] estar a la altura de. ◇ *n* igual *m y f*. ◇ *vt* **-1.** MATH ser igual a. **-2.** [person, quality] igualar.

equality [iː'kwɒlətɪ] *n* igualdad *f*.

equalize, -ise ['iːkwəlaɪz] *vi* SPORT empatar.

equalizer ['iːkwəlaɪzəʳ] *n* SPORT (gol *m* de la) igualada *f*.

equally ['iːkwəlɪ] *adv* **-1.** [gen] igualmente; **~ important** igual de importante. **-2.** [share, divide] a partes iguales, por igual.

equal opportunities *npl* igualdad *f* de oportunidades.

equanimity [,ekwə'nɪmətɪ] *n* ecuanimidad *f*.

equate [ɪ'kweɪt] *vt*: **to ~ sthg with** equiparar algo con.

equation [ɪ'kweɪʒn] *n* ecuación *f*.

equator [ɪ'kweɪtəʳ] *n*: **the ~** el ecuador.

equilibrium [,iːkwɪ'lɪbrɪəm] *n* equilibrio *m*.

equip [ɪ'kwɪp] *vt* **-1.** [provide with equipment]: **to ~ sthg (with)** equipar algo (con); **to ~ sb (with)** proveer a alguien (de). **-2.** [prepare]: **to be equipped for** estar bien dotado(da) para.

equipment [ɪ'kwɪpmənt] *n* (U) equipo *m*.

equitable ['ekwɪtəbl] *adj* equitativo(va).

equities ['ekwətɪz] *npl* ST EX acciones *fpl* ordinarias.

equivalent [ɪ'kwɪvələnt] ◇ *adj* equivalente; **to be ~ to** equivaler a. ◇ *n* equivalente *m*.

equivocal [ɪ'kwɪvəkl] *adj* equívoco(ca).

er [ɜːʳ] *excl* ¡ejem!

era ['ɪərə] (*pl* **-s**) *n* era *f*, época *f*.

eradicate [ɪ'rædɪkeɪt] *vt* erradicar.

erase [ɪ'reɪz] *vt* lit & fig borrar.

eraser [ɪ'reɪzəʳ] *n* goma *f* de borrar.

erect [ɪ'rekt] ◇ *adj* [person, posture] erguido(da). ◇ *vt* **-1.** [building, statue] erigir, levantar. **-2.** [tent] montar.

erection [ɪ'rekʃn] *n* **-1.** (U) [of building, statue] construcción *f*. **-2.** [erect penis] erección *f*.

ERM (*abbr of* **Exchange Rate Mechanism**) *n* mecanismo de tipos de cambio del SME.

ermine ['ɜːmɪn] *n* armiño *m*.

erode [ɪ'rəʊd] *vt* **-1.** [rock, soil] erosionar; [metal] desgastar. **-2.** [confidence, rights] mermar.

erosion [ɪ'rəʊʒn] *n* **-1.** [of rock, soil] erosión *f*; [of metal] desgaste *m*. **-2.** [of confidence, rights] merma *f*.

erotic [ɪ'rɒtɪk] *adj* erótico(ca).

err [ɜːʳ] *vi* equivocarse, errar.

errand ['erənd] *n* recado *m*, mandado *m*.

erratic [ɪ'rætɪk] *adj* irregular.

error ['erə'] *n* error *m*; **spelling** ~ falta *f* de ortografía; **in** ~ por equivocación.

erupt [ɪ'rʌpt] *vi* [volcano] entrar en erupción; *fig* [violence, war] estallar.

eruption [ɪ'rʌpʃn] *n* **-1.** [of volcano] erupción *f*. **-2.** [of violence, war] estallido *m*.

escalate ['eskəleɪt] *vi* **-1.** [conflict] intensificarse. **-2.** [costs] ascender.

escalator ['eskəleɪtə'] *n* escalera *f* mecánica.

escapade [,eskə'peɪd] *n* aventura *f*.

escape [ɪ'skeɪp] ◇ *n* **-1.** [gen] fuga *f*. **-2.** [leakage - of gas, water] escape *m*. ◇ *vt* **-1.** [avoid] escapar a, eludir. **-2.** [subj: fact, name]: **her name** ~**s me** ahora mismo no caigo en su nombre. ◇ *vi* **-1.** [gen]: **to** ~ **(from)** escaparse (de). **-2.** [survive] escapar.

escapism [ɪ'skeɪpɪzm] *n* (*U*) evasión *f*.

escort [*n* 'eskɔːt, *vb* ɪ'skɔːt] ◇ *n* **-1.** [guard] escolta *f*. **-2.** [companion] acompañante *m* y *f*. ◇ *vt* escoltar; **to** ~ **sb home** acompañar a alguien a casa.

Eskimo ['eskɪməʊ] (*pl* **-s**) *n* [person] esquimal *m* y *f*.

espadrille [,espə'drɪl] *n* alpargata *f*.

especially [ɪ'speʃəlɪ] *adv* **-1.** [in particular] sobre todo. **-2.** [more than usually, specifically] especialmente.

espionage ['espɪə,nɑːʒ] *n* espionaje *m*.

esplanade [,esplə'neɪd] *n* paseo *m* marítimo.

Esquire [ɪ'skwaɪə'] *n* Sr. Don; **B. Jones** ~ Sr. Don B. Jones.

essay ['eseɪ] *n* **-1.** SCH redacción *f*; UNIV trabajo *m*. **-2.** LITERATURE ensayo *m*.

essence ['esns] *n* esencia *f*.

essential [ɪ'senʃl] *adj* **-1.** [absolutely necessary]: ~ **(to** OR **for)** esencial OR indispensable (para). **-2.** [basic] fundamental, esencial. ◆ **essentials** *npl* **-1.** [basic commodities] lo indispensable. **-2.** [most important elements] elementos *mpl* esenciales.

essentially [ɪ'senʃəlɪ] *adv* [basically] esencialmente.

establish [ɪ'stæblɪʃ] *vt* **-1.** [gen] establecer. **-2.** [facts, cause] verificar.

establishment [ɪ'stæblɪʃmənt] *n* establecimiento *m*. ◆ **Establishment** *n*: **the Establishment** el sistema.

estate [ɪ'steɪt] *n* **-1.** [land, property] finca *f*. **-2. (housing)** ~ urbanización *f*. **-3. (industrial)** ~ polígono *m* industrial. **-4.** JUR [inheritance] herencia *f*.

estate agency *n Br* agencia *f* inmobiliaria.

estate agent *n Br* agente inmobiliario *m*, agente inmobiliaria *f*.

estate car *n Br* ranchera *f*.

esteem [ɪ'stiːm] ◇ *n* estima *f*, consideración *f*. ◇ *vt* estimar, apreciar.

esthetic *etc Am* = **aesthetic** *etc*.

estimate [*n* 'estɪmət, *vb* 'estɪmeɪt] ◇ *n* **-1.** [calculation, judgment] cálculo *m*, estimación *f*. **-2.** [written quote] presupuesto *m*. ◇ *vt* estimar.

estimation [,estɪ'meɪʃn] *n* **-1.** [opinion] juicio *m*. **-2.** [calculation] cálculo *m*.

Estonia [e'stəʊnɪə] *n* Estonia.

estranged [ɪ'streɪndʒd] *adj* [husband, wife] separado(da); **his** ~ **son** su hijo con el que no se habla.

estuary ['estjʊərɪ] *n* estuario *m*.

etc. (*abbr of* **et cetera**) etc.

etching ['etʃɪŋ] *n* aguafuerte *m* o *f*.

eternal [ɪ'tɜːnl] *adj* [gen] eterno(na); *fig* [complaints, whining] perpetuo(tua).

eternity [ɪ'tɜːnətɪ] *n* eternidad *f*.

ethic ['eθɪk] *n* ética *f*. ◆ **ethics** ◇ *n* (*U*) [study] ética *f*. ◇ *npl* [morals] moralidad *f*.

ethical ['eθɪkl] *adj* ético(ca).

Ethiopia [,iːθɪ'əʊpɪə] *n* Etiopía.

ethnic ['eθnɪk] *adj* **-1.** [traditions, groups, conflict] étnico(ca). **-2.** [food] *típico de una cultura distinta a la occidental*.

ethos ['iːθɒs] *n* código *m* de valores.

etiquette ['etɪket] *n* etiqueta *f*.

euphemism ['juːfəmɪzm] *n* eufemismo *m*.

euphoria [juː'fɔːrɪə] *n* euforia *f*.

Eurocheque ['jʊərə,tʃek] *n* eurocheque *m*.

Euro MP *n* eurodiputado *m*, -da *f*.

Europe ['jʊərəp] *n* Europa *f*.

European [,jʊərə'piːən] ◇ *adj* europeo(a). ◇ *n* europeo *m*, -a *f*.

European Community *n*: **the** ~ la Comunidad Europea.

European Monetary System *n*: **the** ~ el Sistema Monetario Europeo.

European Parliament *n*: **the** ~ el Parlamento Europeo.

euthanasia [,juːθə'neɪzjə] *n* eutanasia *f*.

evacuate [ɪ'vækjʊeɪt] *vt* evacuar.

evade [ɪ'veɪd] *vt* eludir.

evaluate [ɪ'væljʊeɪt] *vt* evaluar.

evaporate [ɪ'væpəreɪt] *vi* [liquid] evaporarse; *fig* [feeling] desvanecerse.

evaporated milk [ɪ'væpəreɪtɪd-] *n* leche *f* evaporada.

evasion [ɪ'veɪʒn] n **-1.** [of responsibility, payment etc] evasión f. **-2.** [lie] evasiva f.

evasive [ɪ'veɪsɪv] adj evasivo(va).

eve [iːv] n: **on the ~ of** en la víspera de.

even ['iːvn] ◇ adj **-1.** [regular] uniforme, constante. **-2.** [calm] sosegado(da). **-3.** [flat, level] llano(na), liso(sa). **-4.** [equal - contest, chance] igualado(da); [- chance] igual; **to get ~ with** ajustarle las cuentas a. **-5.** [number] par. ◇ adv **-1.** [gen] incluso, hasta; **~ now/then** incluso ahora/entonces; **not ~** ni siquiera. **-2.** [in comparisons] aun; **~ more** aun más. ◆ **even if** conj aunque, así Amer. ◆ **even so** conj aun así. ◆ **even though** conj aunque. ◆ **even out** vi igualarse.

evening ['iːvnɪŋ] n **-1.** [end of day - early part] tarde f; [- later part] noche f. **-2.** [event, entertainment] velada f. ◆ **evenings** adv [early] por la tarde; [late] por la noche.

evening class n clase f nocturna.

evening dress n **-1.** [worn by man] traje m de etiqueta. **-2.** [worn by woman] traje m de noche.

event [ɪ'vent] n **-1.** [happening] acontecimiento m, suceso m; **in the ~ of** en caso de; **in the ~ that it rains** (en) caso de que llueva. **-2.** SPORT prueba f. ◆ **in any event** adv en todo caso. ◆ **in the event** adv Br al final.

eventful [ɪ'ventfʊl] adj accidentado(da).

eventual [ɪ'ventʃʊəl] adj final.

eventuality [ɪ,ventʃʊ'ælətɪ] n eventualidad f.

eventually [ɪ'ventʃʊəlɪ] adv finalmente.

ever ['evər] adv **-1.** [at any time] alguna vez; **have you ~ done it?** ¿lo has hecho alguna vez?; **hardly ~** casi nunca. **-2.** [all the time] siempre; **as ~** como siempre; **for ~** para siempre. **-3.** [for emphasis]: **~ so muy; ~ such a mess** un lío tan grande; **why/how ~ did you do it?** ¿por qué/cómo diablos lo hiciste?; **what ~ can it be?** ¿qué diablos puede ser? ◆ **ever since** ◇ adv desde entonces. ◇ conj desde que. ◇ prep desde.

evergreen ['evəgriːn] ◇ adj de hoja perenne. ◇ n árbol m de hoja perenne.

everlasting [,evə'lɑːstɪŋ] adj eterno(na).

every ['evrɪ] adj cada; **~ day** cada día, todos los días. ◆ **every now and then, every so often** adv de vez en cuando. ◆ **every other** adj: **~ other day** un día sí y otro no, cada dos días.

everybody ['evrɪ,bɒdɪ] = **everyone**.

everyday ['evrɪdeɪ] adj diario(ria), cotidiano(na).

everyone ['evrɪwʌn] pron todo el mundo, todos(das).

everyplace Am = **everywhere**.

everything ['evrɪθɪŋ] pron todo; **money isn't ~** el dinero no lo es todo.

everywhere ['evrɪweər], **everyplace** Am ['evrɪ,pleɪs] adv en OR por todas partes; [with verbs of motion] a todas partes.

evict [ɪ'vɪkt] vt: **to ~ sb from** desahuciar a alguien de.

evidence ['evɪdəns] n (U) **-1.** [proof] prueba f. **-2.** JUR [of witness] declaración f; **to give ~** dar testimonio.

evident ['evɪdənt] adj evidente, manifiesto(ta).

evidently ['evɪdəntlɪ] adv **-1.** [seemingly] por lo visto, al parecer. **-2.** [obviously] evidentemente, obviamente.

evil ['iːvl] ◇ adj [person] malo(la), malvado(da); [torture, practice] perverso(sa), vil. ◇ n **-1.** [evil quality] maldad f. **-2.** [evil thing] mal m.

evocative [ɪ'vɒkətɪv] adj evocador(ra).

evoke [ɪ'vəʊk] vt **-1.** [memory, emotion] evocar. **-2.** [response] producir.

evolution [,iːvə'luːʃn] n **-1.** BIOL evolución f. **-2.** [development] desarrollo m.

evolve [ɪ'vɒlv] ◇ vt desarrollar. ◇ vi **-1.** BIOL: **to ~ (into/from)** evolucionar (en/de). **-2.** [develop] desarrollarse.

ewe [juː] n oveja f.

ex- [eks] prefix ex-.

exacerbate [ɪg'zæsəbeɪt] vt exacerbar.

exact [ɪg'zækt] ◇ adj exacto(ta); **to be ~** para ser exacto. ◇ vt: **to ~ sthg (from)** exigir algo (de).

exacting [ɪg'zæktɪŋ] adj **-1.** [job, work] arduo(dua). **-2.** [standards] severo(ra); [person] exigente.

exactly [ɪg'zæktlɪ] ◇ adv [precisely] exactamente; **it's ~ ten o'clock** son las diez en punto. ◇ excl ¡exacto!

exaggerate [ɪg'zædʒəreɪt] vt & vi exagerar.

exaggeration [ɪg,zædʒə'reɪʃn] n exageración f.

exalted [ɪg'zɔːltɪd] adj [person, position] elevado(da).

exam [ɪg'zæm] (abbr of **examination**) n examen m; **to take** OR **sit an ~** presentarse a un examen.

examination [ɪg,zæmɪ'neɪʃn] n **-1.** = **exam**. **-2.** [inspection] inspección f, examen m. **-3.** MED reconocimiento m. **-4.** [consideration] estudio m.

examine [ɪg'zæmɪn] *vt* **-1.** [gen] examinar. **-2.** MED reconocer. **-3.** [consider - idea, proposal] estudiar, considerar. **-4.** JUR interrogar.

examiner [ɪg'zæmɪnəʳ] *n* examinador *m*, -ra *f*.

example [ɪg'zɑːmpl] *n* ejemplo *m*; for ~ por ejemplo.

exasperate [ɪg'zæspəreɪt] *vt* exasperar.

exasperation [ɪg,zæspə'reɪʃn] *n* exasperación *f*, irritación *f*.

excavate ['ekskəveɪt] *vt* excavar.

exceed [ɪk'siːd] *vt* **-1.** [amount, number] exceder, pasar. **-2.** [limit, expectations] rebasar.

exceedingly [ɪk'siːdɪŋlɪ] *adv* extremadamente.

excel [ɪk'sel] *vi*: to ~ (in OR at) sobresalir (en); to ~ o.s. *Br* lucirse.

excellence ['eksələns] *n* excelencia *f*.

excellent ['eksələnt] *adj* excelente.

except [ɪk'sept] ◇ *prep & conj*: ~ (for) excepto, salvo. ◇ *vt*: to ~ sb (from) exceptuar OR excluir a alguien (de).

excepting [ɪk'septɪŋ] *prep & conj* = except.

exception [ɪk'sepʃn] *n* **-1.** [exclusion]: ~ (to) excepción *f* (a); with the ~ of a excepción de. **-2.** [offence]: to take ~ to ofenderse por.

exceptional [ɪk'sepʃənl] *adj* excepcional.

excerpt ['eksɜːpt] *n*: ~ (from) extracto *m* (de).

excess [ɪk'ses, *before nouns* 'ekses] ◇ *adj* excedente. ◇ *n* exceso *m*.

excess baggage *n* exceso *m* de equipaje.

excess fare *n Br* suplemento *m*.

excessive [ɪk'sesɪv] *adj* excesivo(va).

exchange [ɪks'tʃeɪndʒ] ◇ *n* **-1.** [gen] intercambio *m*; in ~ (for) a cambio (de). **-2.** FIN cambio *m*. **-3.** TELEC: (telephone) ~ central *f* telefónica. **-4.** *fml* [conversation]: a heated ~ una acalorada discusión. ◇ *vt* [swap] intercambiar, cambiar; to ~ sthg for sthg cambiar algo por algo; to ~ sthg with sb intercambiar algo con alguien.

exchange rate *n* FIN tipo *m* de cambio.

Exchequer [ɪks'tʃekəʳ] *n Br*: the ~ ≃ Hacienda.

excise ['eksaɪz] *n* (U) impuestos *mpl* sobre el consumo interior.

excite [ɪk'saɪt] *vt* **-1.** [person] emocionar. **-2.** [suspicion, interest] despertar.

excited [ɪk'saɪtɪd] *adj* emocionado(da).

excitement [ɪk'saɪtmənt] *n* emoción *f*.

exciting [ɪk'saɪtɪŋ] *adj* emocionante.

exclaim [ɪk'skleɪm] ◇ *vt* exclamar. ◇ *vi*: to ~ (at) exclamar (ante).

exclamation [,eksklə'meɪʃn] *n* exclamación *f*.

exclamation mark *Br*, **exclamation point** *Am n* signo *m* de admiración.

exclude [ɪk'skluːd] *vt*: to ~ sthg/sb (from) excluir algo/a alguien (de).

excluding [ɪk'skluːdɪŋ] *prep* excepto, con excepción de.

exclusive [ɪk'skluːsɪv] ◇ *adj* **-1.** [highclass] selecto(ta). **-2.** [sole] exclusivo(va). ◇ *n* [news story] exclusiva *f*.
◆ **exclusive of** *prep* excluyendo.

excrement ['ekskrɪmənt] *n* excremento *m*.

excruciating [ɪk'skruːʃɪeɪtɪŋ] *adj* insoportable.

excursion [ɪk'skɜːʃn] *n* excursión *f*.

excuse [*n* ɪk'skjuːs, *vb* ɪk'skjuːz] ◇ *n* excusa *f*; to make an ~ dar una excusa, excusarse. ◇ *vt* **-1.** [gen]: to ~ sb (for sthg/for doing sthg) perdonar a alguien (por algo/por haber hecho algo). **-2.** [let off]: to ~ sb (from) dispensar a alguien (de). **-3.** *phr*: ~ me [to attract attention] oiga (por favor); [when coming past] ¿me deja pasar?; [apologizing] perdone; *Am* [pardon me?] ¿perdón?, ¿cómo?

ex-directory *adj Br* que no figura en la guía telefónica.

execute ['eksɪkjuːt] *vt* [gen & COMPUT] ejecutar.

execution [,eksɪ'kjuːʃn] *n* ejecución *f*.

executioner [,eksɪ'kjuːʃnəʳ] *n* verdugo *m*.

executive [ɪg'zekjʊtɪv] ◇ *adj* [decisionmaking] ejecutivo(va). ◇ *n* **-1.** [person] ejecutivo *m*, -va *f*. **-2.** [committee] ejecutiva *f*, órgano *m* ejecutivo.

executive director *n* director ejecutivo *m*, directora ejecutiva *f*.

executor [ɪg'zekjʊtəʳ] *n* albacea *m*.

exemplify [ɪg'zemplɪfaɪ] *vt* ejemplificar.

exempt [ɪg'zempt] ◇ *adj*: ~ (from) exento(ta) (de). ◇ *vt*: to ~ sthg/sb (from) eximir algo/a alguien (de).

exercise ['eksəsaɪz] ◇ *n* **-1.** [gen] ejercicio *m*. **-2.** MIL maniobra *f*. ◇ *vt* **-1.** [dog] llevar de paseo; [horse] entrenar. **-2.** *fml* [power, right] ejercer; [caution, restraint] mostrar. ◇ *vi* hacer ejercicio.

exercise book *n* cuaderno *m* de ejercicios.

exert [ɪg'zɜːt] *vt* ejercer; to ~ o.s. esforzarse.

exertion [ɪgˈzɜːʃn] *n* esfuerzo *m*.

exhale [eksˈheɪl] ◇ *vt* exhalar, despedir. ◇ *vi* espirar.

exhaust [ɪgˈzɔːst] ◇ *n* (U) [fumes] gases *mpl* de combustión; ~ (**pipe**) tubo *m* de escape. ◇ *vt* agotar.

exhausted [ɪgˈzɔːstɪd] *adj* [person] agotado(da).

exhausting [ɪgˈzɔːstɪŋ] *adj* agotador(ra).

exhaustion [ɪgˈzɔːstʃn] *n* agotamiento *m*.

exhaustive [ɪgˈzɔːstɪv] *adj* exhaustivo(va).

exhibit [ɪgˈzɪbɪt] ◇ *n* **-1.** ART objeto *m* expuesto. **-2.** JUR prueba *f* (instrumental). ◇ *vt* **-1.** *fml* [feeling] mostrar, manifestar. **-2.** ART exponer.

exhibition [ˌeksɪˈbɪʃn] *n* **-1.** ART exposición *f*. **-2.** [of feeling] manifestación *f*.

exhilarating [ɪgˈzɪləreɪtɪŋ] *adj* estimulante.

exile [ˈeksaɪl] ◇ *n* **-1.** [condition] exilio *m*; **in** ~ en el exilio. **-2.** [person] exiliado *m*, -da *f*. ◇ *vt*: **to** ~ **sb** (**from/to**) exiliar a alguien (de/a).

exist [ɪgˈzɪst] *vi* existir.

existence [ɪgˈzɪstəns] *n* existencia *f*; **to be in** ~ existir; **to come into** ~ nacer.

existing [ɪgˈzɪstɪŋ] *adj* existente, actual.

exit [ˈeksɪt] ◇ *n* salida *f*. ◇ *vi fml* salir; THEATRE hacer mutis.

exodus [ˈeksədəs] *n* éxodo *m*.

exonerate [ɪgˈzɒnəreɪt] *vt*: **to** ~ **sb** (**from**) exonerar a alguien (de).

exorbitant [ɪgˈzɔːbɪtənt] *adj* [cost] excesivo(va); [demand, price] exorbitante.

exotic [ɪgˈzɒtɪk] *adj* exótico(ca).

expand [ɪkˈspænd] ◇ *vt* extender, ampliar. ◇ *vi* extenderse, ampliarse; [materials, fluids] expandirse, dilatarse.

◆ **expand (up)on** *vt fus* desarrollar.

expanse [ɪkˈspæns] *n* extensión *f*.

expansion [ɪkˈspænʃn] *n* expansión *f*.

expect [ɪkˈspekt] ◇ *vt* **-1.** [gen] esperar; **to** ~ **sb to do sthg** esperar que alguien haga algo; **to** ~ **sthg (from sb)** esperar algo (de alguien); **as** ~**ed** como era de esperar. **-2.** [suppose] imaginarse, suponer; **I** ~ **so** supongo que sí. ◇ *vi* **-1.** [anticipate]: **to** ~ **to do sthg** esperar hacer algo. **-2.** [be pregnant]: **to be** ~**ing** estar embarazada OR en estado.

expectancy → **life expectancy**.

expectant [ɪkˈspektənt] *adj* expectante.

expectant mother *n* futura madre *f*.

expectation [ˌekspekˈteɪʃn] *n* esperanza *f*; **against all** ~ OR ~**s, contrary to all** ~ OR ~**s** contrariamente a lo que se es-

peraba; **to live up to/fall short of sb's** ~**s** estar/no estar a la altura de lo esperado.

expedient [ɪkˈspiːdjənt] *fml* ◇ *adj* conveniente. ◇ *n* recurso *m*.

expedition [ˌekspɪˈdɪʃn] *n* **-1.** [journey] expedición *f*. **-2.** [outing] salida *f*.

expel [ɪkˈspel] *vt* **-1.** [person]: **to** ~ **sb** (**from**) expulsar a alguien (de). **-2.** [gas, liquid]: **to** ~ **sthg (from)** expeler algo (de).

expend [ɪkˈspend] *vt*: **to** ~ **sthg (on)** emplear algo (en).

expendable [ɪkˈspendəbl] *adj* reemplazable.

expenditure [ɪkˈspendɪtʃər] *n* (U) gasto *m*.

expense [ɪkˈspens] *n* (U) gasto *m*; **at the** ~ **of** [sacrificing] a costa de; **at sb's** ~ *lit* & *fig* a costa de alguien.

◆ **expenses** *npl* COMM gastos *mpl*.

expense account *n* cuenta *f* de gastos.

expensive [ɪkˈspensɪv] *adj* caro(ra).

experience [ɪkˈspɪərɪəns] ◇ *n* experiencia *f*. ◇ *vt* experimentar.

experienced [ɪkˈspɪərɪənst] *adj*: ~ (**at** OR **in**) experimentado(da) (en).

experiment [ɪkˈsperɪmənt] ◇ *n* experimento *m*. ◇ *vi*: **to** ~ (**with/on**) experimentar (con), hacer experimentos (con).

expert [ˈekspɜːt] ◇ *adj*: ~ (**at sthg/at doing sthg**) experto(ta) (en algo/en hacer algo). ◇ *n* experto *m*, -ta *f*.

expertise [ˌekspɜːˈtiːz] *n* (U) competencia *f*, aptitud *f*.

expire [ɪkˈspaɪər] *vi* [licence, membership] caducar; [lease] vencer.

expiry [ɪkˈspaɪərɪ] *n* [of licence] caducación *f*; [of lease] vencimiento *m*.

explain [ɪkˈspleɪn] ◇ *vt*: **to** ~ **sthg (to sb)** explicar algo (a alguien). ◇ *vi* explicar; **to** ~ **to sb about sthg** explicarle algo a alguien.

explanation [ˌekspləˈneɪʃn] *n*: ~ (**for**) explicación *f* (de).

explicit [ɪkˈsplɪsɪt] *adj* explícito(ta).

explode [ɪkˈspləʊd] ◇ *vt* [bomb] hacer explotar; [building etc] volar; *fig* [theory] reventar. ◇ *vi lit* & *fig* estallar.

exploit [*n* ˈeksplɔɪt, *vb* ɪkˈsplɔɪt] ◇ *n* proeza *f*, hazaña *f*. ◇ *vt* explotar.

exploitation [ˌeksplɔɪˈteɪʃn] *n* (U) explotación *f*.

exploration [ˌekspləˈreɪʃn] *n* exploración *f*.

explore [ɪkˈsplɔːr] *vt* & *vi lit* & *fig* explorar.

explorer [ɪk'splɔːrəʳ] *n* explorador *m*, -ra *f*.

explosion [ɪk'spləʊʒn] *n* explosión *f*.

explosive [ɪk'spləʊsɪv] ◇ *adj* explosivo(va). ◇ *n* explosivo *m*.

exponent [ɪk'spəʊnənt] *n* **-1.** [supporter] partidario *m*, -ria *f*. **-2.** [expert] experto *m*, -ta *f*.

export [*n & comp* 'ekspɔːt, *vb* ɪk'spɔːt] ◇ *n* **-1.** [act] exportación *f*. **-2.** [exported product] artículo *m* de exportación. ◇ *comp* de exportación. ◇ *vt* exportar.

exporter [ek'spɔːtəʳ] *n* exportador *m*, -ra *f*.

expose [ɪk'spəʊz] *vt lit & fig* descubrir; **to be ~d to sthg** estar OR verse expuesto a algo.

exposed [ɪk'spəʊzd] *adj* [land, house, position] expuesto(ta), al descubierto.

exposure [ɪk'spəʊʒəʳ] *n* **-1.** [to light, radiation] exposición *f*. **-2.** MED hipotermia *f*. **-3.** PHOT [time] (tiempo *m* de) exposición *f*; [photograph] fotografía *f*. **-4.** [publicity] publicidad *f*.

exposure meter *n* fotómetro *m*.

expound [ɪk'spaʊnd] *fml vt* exponer.

express [ɪk'spres] ◇ *adj* **-1.** *Br* [letter, delivery] urgente. **-2.** [train, coach] rápido(da). **-3.** *fml* [specific] expreso(sa). ◇ *adv* urgente. ◇ *n* [train] expreso *m*. ◇ *vt* expresar; **to ~ o.s.** expresarse.

expression [ɪk'spreʃn] *n* expresión *f*.

expressive [ɪk'spresɪv] *adj* [full of feeling] expresivo(va).

expressly [ɪk'spreslɪ] *adv* [specifically] expresamente.

expressway [ɪk'spresweɪ] *n Am* autopista *f*.

exquisite [ɪk'skwɪzɪt] *adj* exquisito(ta).

ext., extn. *(abbr of extension)* ext.

extend [ɪk'stend] ◇ *vt* **-1.** [gen] extender; [house] ampliar; [road, railway] prolongar; [visa] prorrogar. **-2.** [offer - welcome, help] brindar; [- credit] conceder. ◇ *vi* **-1.** [become longer] extenderse. **-2.** [from surface, object] sobresalir.

extension [ɪk'stenʃn] *n* **-1.** [gen & TELEC] extensión *f*. **-2.** [to building] ampliación *f*. **-3.** [of visit] prolongación *f*; [of deadline, visa] prórroga *f*. **-4.** ELEC: ~ **(lead)** alargador *m*.

extension cable *n* alargador *m*.

extensive [ɪk'stensɪv] *adj* [gen] extenso(sa); [changes] profundo(da); [negotiations] amplio(plia).

extensively [ɪk'stensɪvlɪ] *adv* extensamente.

extent [ɪk'stent] *n* **-1.** [size] extensión *f*. **-2.** [of problem, damage] alcance *m*. **-3.** [degree]: **to what ~ ...?** ¿hasta qué punto ...?; **to the ~ that** [in that, in so far as] en la medida en que; [to the point where] hasta tal punto que; **to some/a certain ~** hasta cierto punto; **to a large** OR **great ~** en gran medida.

extenuating circumstances [ɪk'stenjʊeɪtɪŋ-] *npl* circunstancias *fpl* atenuantes.

exterior [ɪk'stɪərɪəʳ] ◇ *adj* exterior. ◇ *n* exterior *m*.

exterminate [ɪk'stɜːmɪneɪt] *vt* exterminar.

external [ɪk'stɜːnl] *adj* externo(na).

extinct [ɪk'stɪŋkt] *adj* extinto(ta).

extinguish [ɪk'stɪŋgwɪʃ] *vt fml* [gen] extinguir; [cigarette] apagar.

extinguisher [ɪk'stɪŋgwɪʃəʳ] *n* extintor *m*.

extn. = **ext.**

extol, extoll *Am* [ɪk'stəʊl] *vt* [merits, values] ensalzar.

extort [ɪk'stɔːt] *vt*: **to ~ sthg from sb** [confession, promise] arrancar algo a alguien; [money] sacar algo a alguien.

extortionate [ɪk'stɔːʃnət] *adj* desorbitado(da), exorbitante.

extra ['ekstrə] ◇ *adj* [additional] extra (*inv*), adicional; [spare] de más; **take ~ care** pon sumo cuidado. ◇ *n* **-1.** [additional] extra *m*. **-2.** [additional charge] suplemento *m*. **-3.** CINEMA & THEATRE extra *m y f*. ◇ *adv* extra; **to pay/charge ~** pagar/cobrar un suplemento.

extra- ['ekstrə] *prefix* extra-.

extract [*n* 'ekstrækt, *vb* ɪk'strækt] ◇ *n* **-1.** [from book, piece of music] fragmento *m*. **-2.** CHEM extracto *m*. ◇ *vt*: **to ~ sthg (from)** [gen] extraer algo (de); [confession] arrancar algo (de).

extradite ['ekstrədaɪt] *vt*: **to ~ sb (from/to)** extraditar OR extradir a alguien (de/a).

extramarital [,ekstrə'mærɪtl] *adj* fuera del matrimonio.

extramural [,ekstrə'mjʊərəl] *adj* UNIV *fuera de la universidad pero organizado por ella.*

extraordinary [ɪk'strɔːdnrɪ] *adj* extraordinario(ria).

extraordinary general meeting *n* junta *f* (general) extraordinaria.

extravagance [ɪk'strævəgəns] *n* **-1.** (*U*) [excessive spending] derroche *m*, despilfarro *m*. **-2.** [luxury] extravagancia *f*.

extravagant [ɪk'strævəgənt] *adj* **-1.** [wasteful] derrochador(ra). **-2.** [expensive] caro(ra). **-3.** [exaggerated] extravagante.

extreme [ɪk'striːm] ◇ *adj* extremo(ma). ◇ *n* [furthest limit] extremo *m*.

extremely [ɪk'striːmlɪ] *adv* [very] sumamente, extremadamente.

extremist [ɪk'striːmɪst] ◇ *adj* extremista. ◇ *n* extremista *m y f*.

extricate ['ekstrɪkeɪt] *vt*: **to ~ sthg from** lograr sacar algo de; **to ~ o.s. from** lograr salirse de.

extrovert ['ekstrəvɜːt] ◇ *adj* extrovertido(da). ◇ *n* extrovertido *m*, -da *f*.

exultant [ɪg'zʌltənt] *adj* jubiloso(sa).

eye [aɪ] (*cont* **eyeing** OR **eying**) ◇ *n* ojo *m*; **to cast** OR **run one's ~ over sthg** echar un ojo OR un vistazo a algo; **to have one's ~ on sthg** echar el ojo a algo; **to keep one's ~s open for**, **to keep an ~ out for** estar atento a; **to keep an ~ on sthg** echar un ojo a algo, vigilar algo. ◇ *vt* mirar.

eyeball ['aɪbɔːl] *n* globo *m* ocular.

eyebath ['aɪbɑːθ] *n* lavaojos *m inv*.

eyebrow ['aɪbraʊ] *n* ceja *f*.

eyebrow pencil *n* lápiz *m* de cejas.

eyedrops ['aɪdrɒps] *npl* colirio *m*.

eyelash ['aɪlæʃ] *n* pestaña *f*.

eyelid ['aɪlɪd] *n* párpado *m*.

eyeliner ['aɪˌlaɪnəʳ] *n* lápiz *m* de ojos.

eye-opener *n inf* [revelation] revelación *f*; [surprise] sorpresa *f*.

eye shadow *n* sombra *f* de ojos.

eyesight ['aɪsaɪt] *n* vista *f*.

eyesore ['aɪsɔːʳ] *n* monstruosidad *f*.

eyestrain ['aɪstreɪn] *n* vista *f* cansada.

eyewitness [ˌaɪ'wɪtnɪs] *n* testigo *m y f* ocular.

F

f (*pl* **f's** OR **fs**), **F** (*pl* **F's** OR **Fs**) [ef] *n* [letter] f *f*, F *f*. ◆ **F** ◇ *n* MUS fa *m*. ◇ *adj* (*abbr of* **Fahrenheit**) F.

fable ['feɪbl] *n* [traditional story] fábula *f*.

fabric ['fæbrɪk] *n* **-1.** [cloth] tela *f*, tejido *m*. **-2.** [of building, society] estructura *f*.

fabrication [ˌfæbrɪ'keɪʃn] *n* **-1.** [lying, lie] invención *f*. **-2.** [manufacture] fabricación *f*.

fabulous ['fæbjʊləs] *adj inf* [excellent] fabuloso(sa).

facade [fə'sɑːd] *n* fachada *f*.

face [feɪs] ◇ *n* **-1.** [of person] cara *f*, rostro *m*; **~ to ~** cara a cara; **to lose ~** quedar mal; **to save ~** salvar las apariencias; **to say sthg to sb's ~** decir algo a alguien en su cara. **-2.** [expression] semblante *m*; **to make** OR **pull a ~** hacer muecas. **-3.** [of cliff, mountain, coin] cara *f*; [of building] fachada *f*. **-4.** [of clock, watch] esfera *f*. **-5.** [appearance, nature] aspecto *m*. **-6.** [surface] superficie *f*; **on the ~ of it** a primera vista. ◇ *vt* **-1.** [point towards] mirar a. **-2.** [confront, accept, deal with] hacer frente a. **-3.** *inf* [cope with] aguantar, soportar. ◇ *vi*: **~ forwards/south** mirar hacia delante/al sur. ◆ **face down** *adv* boca abajo. ◆ **face up** *adv* boca arriba. ◆ **in the face of** *prep* [in spite of] a pesar de. ◆ **face up to** *vt fus* hacer frente a.

facecloth ['feɪsklɒθ] *n Br* toallita *f* (*para lavarse*).

face cream *n* crema *f* facial.

face-lift *n* [on face] lifting *m*; *fig* [on building etc] lavado *m* de cara.

face powder *n* (*U*) polvos *mpl* para la cara.

face-saving [-'seɪvɪŋ] *adj* para salvar las apariencias.

facet ['fæsɪt] *n* faceta *f*.

facetious [fə'siːʃəs] *adj* guasón(ona).

face value *n* [of coin, stamp] valor *m* nominal; **to take sthg at ~** tomarse algo literalmente.

facility [fə'sɪlətɪ] *n* [feature] dispositivo *m*. ◆ **facilities** *npl* [amenities] instalaciones *fpl*; [services] servicios *mpl*.

facing ['feɪsɪŋ] *adj* opuesto(ta).

facsimile [fæk'sɪmɪlɪ] *n* facsímil *m*.

fact [fækt] *n* **-1.** [piece of information] hecho *m*; **to know sthg for a ~** saber algo a ciencia cierta. **-2.** (*U*) [truth] realidad *f*. ◆ **in fact** *conj & adv* de hecho, en realidad.

fact of life *n* hecho *m* ineludible. ◆ **facts of life** *npl euphemism*: **to tell sb (about) the facts of life** contar a alguien cómo nacen los niños.

factor ['fæktəʳ] *n* factor *m*.

factory ['fæktərɪ] *n* fábrica *f*.

fact sheet *n Br* hoja *f* informativa.

factual ['fæktʃʊəl] *adj* basado(da) en hechos reales.

faculty ['fækltɪ] *n* **-1.** [gen] facultad *f*. **-2.** *Am* [in college]: **the ~** el profesorado.

fad [fæd] n [of person] capricho m; [of society] moda f pasajera.

fade [feɪd] ◇ vt descolorar, desteñir. ◇ vi **-1.** [jeans, curtains, paint] descolorarse, desteñirse; [flower] marchitarse. **-2.** [light, sound, smile] irse apagando. **-3.** [memory, feeling, interest] desvanecerse.

faeces Br, **feces** Am ['fiːsiːz] npl heces fpl.

fag [fæg] n inf **-1.** Br [cigarette] pitillo m. **-2.** Am pej [homosexual] marica m.

Fahrenheit ['færənhaɪt] adj Fahrenheit (inv).

fail [feɪl] ◇ vt **-1.** [exam, test, candidate] suspender. **-2.** [not succeed]: **to ~ to do sthg** no lograr hacer algo. **-3.** [neglect]: **to ~ to do sthg** no hacer algo. **-4.** [let down] fallar. ◇ vi **-1.** [not succeed] fracasar. **-2.** [not pass exam] suspender. **-3.** [stop functioning] fallar. **-4.** [weaken] debilitarse.

failing ['feɪlɪŋ] ◇ n [weakness] fallo m. ◇ prep a falta de; **~ that** en su defecto.

failure ['feɪljər] n **-1.** [lack of success, unsuccessful thing] fracaso m. **-2.** [person] fracasado m, -da f. **-3.** [in exam] suspenso m. **-4.** [act of neglecting]: **her ~ to do it** el que no lo hiciera. **-5.** [breakdown, malfunction] avería f, fallo m.

faint [feɪnt] ◇ adj **-1.** [weak, vague] débil; [outline] impreciso(sa); [memory, longing] vago(ga); [trace, hint, smell] leve. **-2.** [chance] reducido(da). **-3.** [dizzy] mareado(da). ◇ vi desmayarse.

fair [feər] ◇ adj **-1.** [just] justo(ta); **it's not ~!** ¡no hay derecho! **-2.** [quite large] considerable. **-3.** [quite good] bastante bueno(na). **-4.** [hair] rubio(bia). **-5.** [skin, complexion] blanco(ca), claro(ra). **-6.** [weather] bueno(na). ◇ n **-1.** Br [funfair] parque m de atracciones. **-2.** [trade fair] feria f. ◇ adv [fairly] limpio. ◆ **fair enough** adv Br inf vale.

fair-haired [-'heəd] adj rubio(bia).

fairly ['feəlɪ] adv **-1.** [moderately] bastante. **-2.** [justly] justamente.

fairness ['feənɪs] n [justness] justicia f.

fair play n juego m limpio.

fairy ['feərɪ] n hada f.

fairy tale n cuento m de hadas.

faith [feɪθ] n fe f.

faithful ['feɪθful] ◇ adj fiel. ◇ npl RELIG: **the ~** los fieles.

faithfully ['feɪθfulɪ] adv fielmente; **Yours ~** Br [in letter] le saluda atentamente.

fake [feɪk] ◇ adj falso(sa). ◇ n **-1.** [object, painting] falsificación f. **-2.** [person] impostor m, -ra f. ◇ vt **-1.** [results, signature] falsificar. **-2.** [illness, emotions] fingir. ◇ vi [pretend] fingir.

falcon ['fɔːlkən] n halcón m.

Falkland Islands ['fɔːklənd-], **Falklands** ['fɔːkləndz] npl: **the ~** las (Islas) Malvinas.

fall [fɔːl] (pt **fell**, pp **fallen**) ◇ vi **-1.** [gen] caer; **he fell off the chair** se cayó de la silla; **to ~ to bits** OR **pieces** hacerse pedazos; **to ~ flat** fig no causar el efecto deseado. **-2.** [decrease] bajar. **-3.** [become]: **to ~ ill** ponerse enfermo(ma); **to ~ asleep** dormirse; **to ~ in love** enamorarse. ◇ n **-1.** [gen] caída f. **-2.** [of snow] nevada f. **-3.** [MIL - of city] derrota f. **-4.** [decrease]: **~ (in)** descenso m (de). **-5.** Am [autumn] otoño m. ◆ **falls** npl cataratas fpl. ◆ **fall apart** vi [book, chair] romperse; fig [country, person] desmoronarse. ◆ **fall back** vi [person, crowd] retroceder atrás, retroceder. ◆ **fall back on** vt fus [resort to] recurrir a. ◆ **fall behind** vi **-1.** [in race] quedarse atrás. **-2.** [with rent, work] retrasarse. ◆ **fall for** vt fus **-1.** inf [fall in love with] enamorarse de. **-2.** [trick, lie] tragarse. ◆ **fall in** vi **-1.** [roof, ceiling] desplomarse, hundirse. **-2.** MIL formar filas. ◆ **fall off** vi **-1.** [branch, handle] desprenderse. **-2.** [demand, numbers] disminuir. ◆ **fall out** vi **-1.** [hair, tooth]: **his hair is ~ing out** se le está cayendo el pelo. **-2.** [friends] pelearse, discutir. **-3.** MIL romper filas. ◆ **fall over** vi [person, chair etc] caerse. ◆ **fall through** vi [plan, deal] fracasar.

fallacy ['fæləsɪ] n concepto m erróneo, error m.

fallen ['fɔːln] pp → **fall**.

fallible ['fæləbl] adj falible.

fallout ['fɔːlaut] n [radiation] lluvia f radiactiva.

fallout shelter n refugio m atómico.

fallow ['fæləu] adj en barbecho.

false [fɔːls] adj [gen] falso(sa); [eyelashes, nose] postizo(za).

false alarm n falsa alarma f.

false teeth npl dentadura f postiza.

falsify ['fɔːlsɪfaɪ] vt [facts, accounts] falsificar.

falter ['fɔːltər] vi vacilar.

fame [feɪm] n fama f.

familiar [fə'mɪljər] adj **-1.** [known] familiar, conocido(da). **-2.** [conversant]: **~ with** familiarizado(da) con. **-3.** pej [too informal - tone, manner] demasiado amistoso(sa).

familiarity [fə‚mɪlɪ'ærətɪ] n (U) [knowledge]: ~ **with** conocimiento m de.

familiarize, -ise [fə'mɪljəraɪz] vt: to ~ **o.s./sb with** sthg familiarizarse/ familiarizar a alguien con algo.

family ['fæmlɪ] n familia f.

family credit n (U) Br ≃ prestación f OR ayuda f familiar.

family doctor n médico m de cabecera.

family planning n planificación f familiar.

famine ['fæmɪn] n hambruna f.

famished ['fæmɪʃt] adj inf [very hungry] muerto(ta) de hambre, famélico(ca).

famous ['feɪməs] adj: ~ **(for)** famoso(sa) (por).

famously ['feɪməslɪ] adv dated: to get on OR along ~ **(with sb)** llevarse de maravilla (con alguien).

fan [fæn] ◇ n **-1.** [of paper, silk] abanico m. **-2.** [electric or mechanical] ventilador m. **-3.** [enthusiast] fan m y f, admirador m, -ra f; FTBL hincha m y f. ◇ vt **-1.** [cool] abanicar. **-2.** [stimulate - fire, feelings] avivar. ◆ **fan out** vi desplegarse en abanico.

fanatic [fə'nætɪk] n fanático m, -ca f.

fan belt n correa f del ventilador.

fanciful ['fænsɪfʊl] adj [odd] rocambolesco(ca).

fancy ['fænsɪ] ◇ vt **-1.** inf [feel like]: I ~ a cup of tea/going to the cinema me apetece una taza de té/ir al cine. **-2.** inf [desire]: do you ~ her? ¿te gusta?, ¿te mola? **-3.** [imagine]: ~ **that!** ¡imagínate! **-4.** dated [think] creer. ◇ n [desire, liking] capricho m; to take a ~ to encapricharse con. ◇ adj **-1.** [elaborate] elaborado(da). **-2.** [expensive] de lujo, caro(ra); [prices] exorbitante.

fancy dress n (U) disfraz m.

fancy-dress party n fiesta f de disfraces.

fanfare ['fænfeəʳ] n fanfarria f.

fang [fæŋ] n colmillo m.

fan heater n convector m.

fanny ['fænɪ] n Am inf [buttocks] nalgas fpl.

fantasize, -ise ['fæntəsaɪz] vi fantasear; to ~ **about** sthg/about doing sthg soñar con algo/con hacer algo.

fantastic [fæn'tæstɪk] adj [gen] fantástico(ca).

fantasy ['fæntəsɪ] n fantasía f.

fao (abbr of **for the attention of**) a/a.

far [fɑːʳ] (compar **farther** OR **further**, superl **farthest** OR **furthest**) ◇ adv **-1.** [in distance, time] lejos; is it ~? ¿está lejos?; how ~ is it? ¿a qué distancia está?; how ~ is it to Prague? ¿cuánto hay de aquí a Praga?; ~ **away** OR **off** [a long way away, a long time away] lejos; so ~ por ahora, hasta ahora; ~ **and wide** por todas partes; as ~ as hasta. **-2.** [in degree or extent]: ~ **more/better/ stronger** mucho más/mejor/más fuerte; how ~ **have you got?** ¿hasta dónde has llegado?; as ~ **as I know** que yo sepa; as ~ **as I'm concerned** for OR en lo que a mí respecta; as ~ **as possible** en (la medida de) lo posible; ~ **and away, by** ~ con mucho; ~ **from it** en absoluto, todo lo contrario; so ~ hasta un cierto punto. ◇ adj [extreme] extremo(ma).

faraway ['fɑːrəweɪ] adj **-1.** [land etc] lejano(na). **-2.** [look, expression] ausente.

farce [fɑːs] n lit & fig farsa f.

farcical ['fɑːsɪkl] adj absurdo(da).

fare [feəʳ] n **-1.** [payment] (precio m del) billete m; [in taxi] tarifa f; [passenger] cliente m y f (de taxi). **-2.** (U) fml [food] comida f.

Far East n: the ~ el Extremo Oriente.

farewell [‚feə'wel] ◇ n adiós m, despedida f. ◇ excl literary ¡vaya con Dios!

farm [fɑːm] ◇ n granja f, chacra f Amer. ◇ vt [land] cultivar; [livestock] criar.

farmer ['fɑːməʳ] n agricultor m, -ra f, granjero m, -ra f, chacarero m, -ra f Amer.

farmhand ['fɑːmhænd] n peón m.

farmhouse ['fɑːmhaʊs, pl -haʊzɪz] n granja f, caserío m.

farming ['fɑːmɪŋ] n (U) **-1.** AGR [industry] agricultura f. **-2.** [act - of crops] cultivo m; [- of animals] cría f, crianza f.

farm labourer = **farmhand**.

farmland ['fɑːmlænd] n (U) tierras fpl de labranza.

farmstead ['fɑːmsted] n Am granja f.

farm worker = **farmhand**.

farmyard ['fɑːmjɑːd] n corral m.

far-reaching [-'riːtʃɪŋ] adj trascendental, de amplio alcance.

farsighted [‚fɑː'saɪtɪd] adj **-1.** [gen] con visión de futuro. **-2.** Am [long-sighted] présbita.

fart [fɑːt] v inf ◇ n [flatulence] pedo m. ◇ vi tirarse un pedo.

farther ['fɑːðəʳ] compar → **far**.

farthest ['fɑːðəst] superl → **far**.

fascinate ['fæsɪneɪt] *vt* fascinar.
fascinating ['fæsɪneɪtɪŋ] *adj* fascinante.
fascination [ˌfæsɪ'neɪʃn] *n* fascinación *f*.
fascism ['fæʃɪzm] *n* fascismo *m*.
fashion ['fæʃn] ◇ *n* **-1.** [clothing, style, vogue] moda *f*; **in/out of** ~ de/pasado de moda. **-2.** [manner] manera *f*. ◇ *vt fml* elaborar; *fig* forjar.
fashionable ['fæʃnəbl] *adj* de moda.
fashion show *n* pase *m* OR desfile *m* de modelos.
fast [fɑːst] ◇ *adj* **-1.** [rapid] rápido(da). **-2.** [clock, watch] que adelanta. **-3.** [dye, colour] que no destiñe. ◇ *adv* **-1.** [rapidly] de prisa, rápidamente. **-2.** [firmly]: **stuck** ~ bien pegado(da); ~ **asleep** profundamente dormido. ◇ *n* ayuno *m*. ◇ *vi* ayunar.
fasten ['fɑːsn] *vt* **-1.** [gen] sujetar; [clothes, belt] abrochar; **he ~ed his coat** se abrochó el abrigo. **-2.** [attach]: **to** ~ **sthg to sthg** fijar algo a algo.
fastener ['fɑːsnər] *n* cierre *m*, broche *m*; [zip] cremallera *f*.
fastening ['fɑːsnɪŋ] *n* [of door, window] cerrojo *m*, pestillo *m*.
fast food *n* (U) comida *f* rápida.
fastidious [fə'stɪdɪəs] *adj* [fussy] quisquilloso(sa).
fat [fæt] ◇ *adj* **-1.** [gen] gordo(da); **to get** ~ engordar. **-2.** [meat] con mucha grasa. **-3.** [book, package] grueso(sa). ◇ *n* **-1.** [gen] grasa *f*. **-2.** [for cooking] manteca *f*.
fatal ['feɪtl] *adj* **-1.** [serious] fatal, funesto(ta). **-2.** [mortal] mortal.
fatality [fə'tælətɪ] *n* [accident victim] víctima *f* mortal, muerto *m*.
fate [feɪt] *n* **-1.** [destiny] destino *m*; **to tempt** ~ tentar a la suerte. **-2.** [result, end] final *m*, suerte *f*.
fateful ['feɪtful] *adj* fatídico(ca).
father ['fɑːðər] *n lit* & *fig* padre *m*.
Father Christmas *n Br* Papá *m* Noel.
father-in-law (*pl* **father-in-laws** OR **fathers-in-law**) *n* suegro *m*.
fatherly ['fɑːðəlɪ] *adj* paternal.
fathom ['fæðəm] ◇ *n* braza *f*. ◇ *vt*: **to** ~ **sthg/sb (out)** llegar a comprender algo/a alguien.
fatigue [fə'tiːg] *n* fatiga *f*.
fatten ['fætn] *vt* engordar.
fattening ['fætnɪŋ] *adj* que engorda.
fatty ['fætɪ] ◇ *adj* graso(sa). ◇ *n inf pej* gordinflón *m*, -ona *f*.
fatuous ['fætjʊəs] *adj* necio(cia).
faucet ['fɔːsɪt] *n Am* grifo *m*.

fault [fɔːlt] ◇ *n* **-1.** [responsibility] culpa *f*; **to be at** ~ tener la culpa. **-2.** [mistake, imperfection] defecto *m*; **to find** ~ **with** encontrar defectos a. **-3.** GEOL falla *f*. **-4.** [in tennis] falta *f*. ◇ *vt*: **to** ~ **sb (on sthg)** criticar a alguien (en algo).
faultless ['fɔːltlɪs] *adj* impecable.
faulty ['fɔːltɪ] *adj* [machine, system] defectuoso(sa); [reasoning, logic] imperfecto(ta).
fauna ['fɔːnə] *n* fauna *f*.
faux pas [ˌfəʊ'pɑː] (*pl inv*) *n* plancha *f*.
favour *Br*, **favor** *Am* ['feɪvər] ◇ *n* [gen] favor *m*; **in sb's** ~ a favor de alguien; **to be in/out of** ~ **(with)** ser/dejar de ser popular (con); **to do sb a** ~ hacerle un favor a alguien. ◇ *vt* **-1.** [prefer] decantarse por, preferir. **-2.** [treat better, help] favorecer. ◆ **in favour** *adv* [in agreement] a favor. ◆ **in favour of** *prep* **-1.** [in preference to] en favor de. **-2.** [in agreement with]: **to be in** ~ **of sthg/of doing sthg** estar a favor de algo/de hacer algo.
favourable *Br*, **favorable** *Am* ['feɪvrəbl] *adj* [positive] favorable.
favourite *Br*, **favorite** *Am* ['feɪvrɪt] ◇ *adj* favorito(ta). ◇ *n* favorito *m*, -ta *f*.
favouritism *Br*, **favoritism** *Am* ['feɪvrɪtɪzm] *n* favoritismo *m*.
fawn [fɔːn] ◇ *adj* pajizo(za), beige (*inv*). ◇ *n* [animal] cervato *m*, cervatillo *m*. ◇ *vi*: **to** ~ **on sb** adular a alguien.
fax [fæks] ◇ *n* fax *m*. ◇ *vt* **-1.** [send fax to] mandar un fax a. **-2.** [send by fax] enviar por fax.
fax machine *n* fax *m*.
FBI (*abbr of* **Federal Bureau of Investigation**) *n* FBI *m*.
fear [fɪər] ◇ *n* **-1.** [gen] miedo *m*, temor *m*; **for** ~ **of** por miedo a. **-2.** [risk] peligro *m*. ◇ *vt* **-1.** [be afraid of] temer. **-2.** [anticipate] temerse; **to** ~ **(that)** ... temerse que ....
fearful ['fɪəful] *adj* **-1.** *fml* [frightened] temeroso(sa). **-2.** [frightening] terrible.
fearless ['fɪəlɪs] *adj* intrépido(da).
feasible ['fiːzəbl] *adj* factible, viable.
feast [fiːst] ◇ *n* [meal] banquete *m*, festín *m*. ◇ *vi*: **to** ~ **on** OR **off sthg** darse un banquete a base de algo.
feat [fiːt] *n* hazaña *f*.
feather ['feðər] *n* pluma *f*.
feature ['fiːtʃər] ◇ *n* **-1.** [characteristic] característica *f*. **-2.** [of face] rasgo *m*. **-3.** GEOGR accidente *m* geográfico. **-4.** [article] artículo *m* de fondo. **-5.** RADIO & TV [programme] programa *m* especial. **-6.**

CINEMA = **feature film**. ◇ *vt* [subj: film] tener como protagonista a; [subj: exhibition] tener como atracción principal a. ◇ *vi*: **to ~ (in)** aparecer OR figurar (en).

feature film *n* largometraje *m*.

February ['februərı] *n* febrero *m*; *see also* **September**.

feces *Am* = **faeces**.

fed [fed] *pt & pp* → **feed**.

federal ['fedrəl] *adj* federal.

federation [,fedə'reıʃn] *n* federación *f*.

fed up *adj*: **~ (with)** harto(ta) (de).

fee [fi:] *n* [to lawyer, doctor etc] honorarios *mpl*; **membership ~** cuota *f* de socio; **entrance ~** entrada *f*; **school ~s** (precio *m* de) matrícula *f*.

feeble ['fi:bəl] *adj* **-1.** [weak] débil. **-2.** [poor, silly] pobre, flojo(ja).

feed [fi:d] (*pt & pp* **fed**) ◇ *vt* **-1.** [gen] alimentar; [animal] dar de comer a. **-2.** [put, insert]: **to ~ sthg into sthg** introducir algo en algo. ◇ *vi* comer. ◇ *n* **-1.** [meal] comida *f*. **-2.** [animal food] pienso *m*.

feedback ['fi:dbæk] *n* (U) **-1.** [reaction] reacciones *fpl*. **-2.** COMPUT & ELEC realimentación *f*; [on guitar etc] feedback *m*.

feeding bottle ['fi:dıŋ-] *n Br* biberón *m*.

feel [fi:l] (*pt & pp* **felt**) ◇ *vt* **-1.** [touch] tocar. **-2.** [sense, notice, experience] sentir; **I felt myself blushing** noté que me ponía colorado. **-3.** [believe] creer; **to ~ (that)** creer OR pensar que. **-4.** *phr*: **not to ~ o.s.** no encontrarse bien. ◇ *vi* **-1.** [have sensation]: **to ~ hot/cold/sleepy** tener calor/frío/sueño. **-2.** [have emotion]: **to ~ safe/happy** sentirse seguro/feliz. **-3.** [seem] parecer (al tacto). **-4.** [by touch]: **to ~ for sthg** buscar algo a tientas. **-5.** [be in mood]: **do you ~ like a drink/eating out?** ¿te apetece beber algo/comer fuera? ◇ *n* **-1.** [sensation, touch] tacto *m*, sensación *f*. **-2.** [atmosphere] atmósfera *f*.

feeler ['fi:lə^r] *n* antena *f*.

feeling ['fi:lıŋ] *n* **-1.** [emotion] sentimiento *m*. **-2.** [sensation] sensación *f*. **-3.** [intuition] presentimiento *m*; **I have a OR get the ~ (that) ...** me da la sensación de que .... **-4.** [understanding] apreciación *f*, entendimiento *m*. ◆ **feelings** *npl* sentimientos *mpl*.

feet [fi:t] *pl* → **foot**.

feign [feın] *vt fml* fingir, aparentar.

fell [fel] ◇ *pt* → **fall**. ◇ *vt* [tree] talar. ◆ **fells** *npl* GEOGR monte *m*.

fellow ['feləʊ] ◇ *adj*: **~ students/ prisoners** compañeros de clase/celda. ◇ *n* **-1.** *dated* [man] tipo *m*. **-2.** [comrade, peer] camarada *m y f*. **-3.** [of society] miembro *m*. **-4.** [of college] miembro *m* del claustro de profesores.

fellowship ['feləʊʃıp] *n* **-1.** [comradeship] camaradería *f*. **-2.** [society] asociación *f*. **-3.** [of society or college] pertenencia *f*.

felony ['feлənı] *n* JUR delito *m* grave.

felt [felt] ◇ *pt & pp* → **feel**. ◇ *n* (U) fieltro *m*.

felt-tip pen *n* rotulador *m*.

female ['fi:meıl] ◇ *adj* [animal, plant, connector] hembra; [figure, sex] femenino(na). ◇ *n* **-1.** [female animal] hembra *f*. **-2.** [woman] mujer *f*.

feminine ['femının] ◇ *adj* femenino(na). ◇ *n* GRAMM femenino *m*.

feminist ['femınıst] *n* feminista *m y f*.

fence [fens] ◇ *n* valla *f*. ◇ *vt* cercar.

fencing ['fensıŋ] *n* SPORT esgrima *f*.

fend [fend] *vi*: **to ~ for o.s.** valerse por sí mismo. ◆ **fend off** *vt sep* [blows] defenderse de, desviar; [questions, reporters] eludir.

fender ['fendə^r] *n* **-1.** [round fireplace] guardafuego *m*. **-2.** [on boat] defensa *f*. **-3.** *Am* [on car] guardabarros *m inv*.

ferment [*n* 'fɜ:ment, *vb* fə'ment] ◇ *n* [unrest] agitación *f*. ◇ *vi* fermentar.

fern [fɜ:n] *n* helecho *m*.

ferocious [fə'rəʊʃəs] *adj* feroz.

ferret ['ferıt] *n* hurón *m*. ◆ **ferret about**, **ferret around** *vi inf* rebuscar.

ferris wheel ['ferıs-] *n* noria *f*.

ferry ['ferı] ◇ *n* [large, for cars] transbordador *m*, ferry *m*; [small] barca *f*. ◇ *vt* llevar, transportar.

ferryboat ['ferıbəʊt] *n* = **ferry**.

fertile ['fɜ:taıl] *adj* fértil.

fertilizer ['fɜ:tılaızə^r] *n* abono *m*.

fervent ['fɜ:vənt] *adj* ferviente.

fester ['festə^r] *vi* enconarse.

festival ['festəvl] *n* **-1.** [event, celebration] festival *m*. **-2.** [holiday] día *m* festivo.

festive ['festıv] *adj* festivo(va).

festive season *n*: **the ~** las Navidades.

festivities [fes'tıvətız] *npl* festividades *fpl*.

festoon [fe'stu:n] *vt* engalanar.

fetch [fetʃ] *vt* **-1.** [go and get] ir a buscar. **-2.** *inf* [raise - money] venderse por.

fetching ['fetʃıŋ] *adj* atractivo(va).

fete, fête [feıt] *n* fiesta *f* benéfica.

fetish ['fetıʃ] *n* **-1.** [object of sexual obsession] **fetiche** *m*. **-2.** [mania] **obsesión** *f*, **manía** *f*.

fetus ['fi:təs] = **foetus.**

feud [fju:d] ◇ *n* **enfrentamiento** *m* duradero. ◇ *vi* **pelearse.**

feudal ['fju:dl] *adj* **feudal.**

fever ['fi:vər] *n lit* & *fig* **fiebre** *f*; **to have a ~** **tener fiebre.**

feverish ['fi:vərɪʃ] *adj lit* & *fig* **febril.**

few [fju:] ◇ *adj* **pocos(cas); a ~** **algunos(nas); a ~ more potatoes algunas patatas más; quite a ~, a good ~** **bastantes; ~ and far between** **escasos,** **contados.** ◇ *pron* **pocos** *mpl*, **-cas** *fpl*; **a ~ (of them)** **algunos** *mpl*, **-nas** *fpl*.

fewer ['fju:ər] ◇ *adj* **menos.** ◇ *pron* **menos.**

fewest ['fju:əst] *adj* **menos.**

fiancé [fɪ'ɒnseɪ] *n* **prometido** *m*.

fiancée [fɪ'ɒnseɪ] *n* **prometida** *f*.

fiasco [fɪ'æskəʊ] (*Br pl* **-s,** *Am pl* **-es**) *n* **fiasco** *m*.

fib [fɪb] *inf n* **bola** *f*, **trola** *f*.

fibre *Br*, **fiber** *Am* ['faɪbər] *n* **fibra** *f*.

fibreglass *Br*, **fiberglass** *Am* ['faɪbəɡlɑːs] *n (U)* **fibra** *f* **de vidrio.**

fickle ['fɪkl] *adj* **voluble.**

fiction ['fɪkʃn] *n* **-1.** [stories] **(literatura** *f* **de) ficción** *f*. **-2.** [fabrication] **ficción** *f*.

fictional ['fɪkʃənl] *adj* **-1.** [literary] **novelesco(ca). -2.** [invented] **ficticio(cia).**

fictitious [fɪk'tɪʃəs] *adj* [false] **ficticio(cia).**

fiddle ['fɪdl] ◇ *n* **-1.** [violin] **violín** *m*. **-2.** *Br inf* [fraud] **timo** *m*. ◇ *vt Br inf* **falsear.** ◇ *vi* [play around]: **to ~ (with sthg)** **juguetear (con algo).**

fiddly ['fɪdlɪ] *adj Br* [job] **delicado(da);** [gadget] **intrincado(da).**

fidget ['fɪdʒɪt] *vi* **no estarse quieto(ta).**

field [fi:ld] *n* [gen & COMPUT] **campo** *m*; **in the ~** **sobre el terreno.**

field day *n*: **to have a ~** **disfrutar de lo lindo.**

field glasses *npl* **prismáticos** *mpl*.

field marshal *n* **mariscal** *m* **de campo.**

field trip *n* **excursión** *f* **para hacer trabajo de campo.**

fieldwork ['fi:ldwɜ:k] *n (U)* **trabajo** *m* **de campo.**

fiend [fi:nd] *n* [cruel person] **malvado** *m*, **-da** *f*.

fiendish ['fi:ndɪʃ] *adj* **-1.** [evil] **malévolo(la). -2.** *inf* [very difficult] **endiablado(da).**

fierce [fɪəs] *adj* [gen] **feroz;** [temper] **endiablado(da);** [loyalty] **ferviente;** [heat] **asfixiante.**

fiery ['faɪərɪ] *adj* **-1.** [burning] **ardiente. -2.** [volatile - temper] **endiablado(da);** [- speech] **encendido(da);** [- person] **apasionado(da).**

fifteen [fɪf'ti:n] *num* **quince;** *see also* **six.**

fifth [fɪfθ] *num* **quinto(ta);** *see also* **sixth.**

fifty ['fɪftɪ] *num* **cincuenta;** *see also* **sixty.**

fifty-fifty ◇ *adj* **al cincuenta por ciento; a ~ chance** **unas posibilidades del cincuenta por ciento.** ◇ *adv*: **to go ~** **ir a medias.**

fig [fɪg] *n* **higo** *m*.

fight [faɪt] (*pt* & *pp* **fought**) ◇ *n* **pelea** *f*; [fig] **lucha** *f*; **to have a ~ (with)** **pelearse (con); to put up a ~** **oponer resistencia.** ◇ *vt* [gen] **luchar contra;** [battle, campaign] **librar;** [war] **luchar en.** ◇ *vi* **-1.** [in punch-up] **pelearse;** [in war] **luchar. -2.** *fig* [battle, struggle]: **to ~ (for/ against)** **luchar (por/contra). -3.** [argue]: **to ~ (about** OR **over)** **pelearse** OR **discutir (por). ◆ fight back** ◇ *vt fus* **reprimir, contener.** ◇ *vi* **defenderse.**

fighter ['faɪtər] *n* **-1.** [plane] **caza** *m*. **-2.** [soldier] **combatiente** *m* **y** *f*. **-3.** [combative person] **luchador** *m*, **-ra** *f*.

fighting ['faɪtɪŋ] *n (U)* [punch-up] **pelea** *f*; [on streets, terraces] **peleas** *fpl*; [in war] **combate** *m*.

figment ['fɪgmənt] *n*: **a ~ of sb's imagination** **un producto de la imaginación de alguien.**

figurative ['fɪgərətɪv] *adj* **figurado(da).**

figure [*Br* 'fɪgər, *Am* 'fɪgjər] ◇ *n* **-1.** [statistic, number] **cifra** *f*; **to be in single/ double ~s** **no sobrepasar/sobrepasar la decena. -2.** [shape of person, personality] **figura** *f*. **-3.** [diagram] **gráfico** *m*, **diagrama** *m*. ◇ *vt* [suppose] **figurarse, suponer.** ◇ *vi* [feature] **figurar. ◆ figure out** *vt sep* [reason, motives] **figurarse;** [problem etc] **resolver.**

figurehead ['fɪgəhed] *n* [leader without real power] **testaferro** *m*.

figure of speech *n* **forma** *f* **de hablar.**

Fiji ['fi:dʒi:] *n* **Fiyi.**

file [faɪl] ◇ *n* **-1.** [folder] **carpeta** *f*. **-2.** [report] **expediente** *m*; **on ~, on the ~s** **archivado. -3.** COMPUT **fichero** *m*. **-4.** [tool] **lima** *f*. **-5.** [line]: **in single ~** **en fila india.** ◇ *vt* **-1.** [put in file] **archivar. -2.** JUR **presentar. -3.** [shape, smoothe] **limar.** ◇ *vi* [walk in single file] **ir en fila.**

filet *Am* = **fillet.**

filing cabinet ['faɪlɪŋ-] *n* **archivo** *m*, **fichero** *m*.

Filipino [ˌfɪlɪˈpiːnəʊ] (pl **-s**) ◇ adj filipino(na). ◇ n filipino m, -na f.

fill [fɪl] ◇ vt **-1.** [gen]: **to ~ sthg (with)** llenar algo (de). **-2.** [gap, hole, crack] rellenar; [tooth] empastar. **-3.** [need, vacancy etc] cubrir. ◇ n: **to eat one's ~** comer hasta hartarse. ◆ **fill in** ◇ vt sep **-1.** [complete] rellenar. **-2.** [inform]: **to ~ sb in (on)** poner a alguien al corriente (de). ◇ vi [substitute]: **to ~ in (for sb)** sustituir (a alguien). ◆ **fill out** vt sep [complete] rellenar. ◆ **fill up** ◇ vt sep llenar (hasta arriba). ◇ vi llenarse.

fillet Br, **filet** Am ['fɪlɪt] n filete m.

fillet steak n filete m (de carne).

filling ['fɪlɪŋ] ◇ adj [satisfying] que llena mucho. ◇ n **-1.** [in tooth] empaste m. **-2.** [in cake, sandwich] relleno m.

filling station n estación f de servicio.

film [fɪlm] ◇ n **-1.** [gen] película f. **-2.** (U) [footage] escenas fpl filmadas. ◇ vt & vi filmar, rodar.

film star n estrella f de cine.

Filofax® ['faɪləʊfæks] n agenda f (de hojas recambiables).

filter ['fɪltər] ◇ n filtro m. ◇ vt [purify] filtrar.

filter coffee n café m de filtro.

filter lane n Br carril m de giro.

filter-tipped [-'tɪpt] adj con filtro.

filth [fɪlθ] n (U) **-1.** [dirt] suciedad f. **-2.** [obscenity] obscenidades fpl.

filthy ['fɪlθɪ] adj **-1.** [very dirty] mugriento(ta), sucísimo(ma). **-2.** [obscene] obsceno(na).

fin [fɪn] n [on fish] aleta f.

final ['faɪnl] ◇ adj **-1.** [last] último(ma). **-2.** [at end] final. **-3.** [definitive] definitivo(va). ◇ n final f. ◆ **finals** npl UNIV exámenes mpl finales.

finale [fɪ'nɑːlɪ] n final m.

finalize, -ise ['faɪnəlaɪz] vt ultimar.

finally ['faɪnəlɪ] adv **-1.** [at last] por fin. **-2.** [lastly] finalmente, por último.

finance [n 'faɪnæns, vb faɪ'næns] ◇ n (U) **-1.** [money] fondos mpl. **-2.** [money management] finanzas fpl. ◇ vt financiar. ◆ **finances** npl finanzas fpl.

financial [fɪ'nænʃl] adj financiero(ra).

find [faɪnd] (pt & pp **found**) ◇ vt **-1.** [gen] encontrar. **-2.** [realize - fact] darse cuenta de, descubrir. **-3.** JUR: **to be found guilty/not guilty (of)** ser declarado(da) culpable/inocente (de). ◇ n hallazgo m, descubrimiento m. ◆ **find out** ◇ vi informarse. ◇ vt fus **-1.** [fact] averiguar. **-2.** [truth] descubrir. ◇ vt sep [person] descubrir.

findings ['faɪndɪŋz] npl conclusiones fpl.

fine [faɪn] ◇ adj **-1.** [excellent] excelente. **-2.** [perfectly satisfactory]: **it's/that's ~** está bien, perfecto; **how are you? – fine thanks** ¿qué tal? – muy bien. **-3.** [weather] bueno(na); **it will be ~ tomorrow** mañana hará buen día. **-4.** [thin, smooth] fino(na). **-5.** [minute - detail, distinction] sutil; [- adjustment, tuning] milimétrico(ca). ◇ adv [very well] muy bien. ◇ n multa f. ◇ vt multar.

fine arts npl bellas artes fpl.

finery ['faɪnərɪ] n (U) galas fpl.

finesse [fɪ'nes] n finura f, delicadeza f.

fine-tune vt poner a punto.

finger ['fɪŋgər] ◇ n dedo m. ◇ vt acariciar con los dedos.

fingernail ['fɪŋgəneɪl] n uña f (de las manos).

fingerprint ['fɪŋgəprɪnt] n huella f dactilar OR digital.

fingertip ['fɪŋgətɪp] n punta f OR yema f del dedo.

finicky ['fɪnɪkɪ] adj pej [person] melindroso(sa); [task] delicado(da).

finish ['fɪnɪʃ] ◇ n **-1.** [end] final m. **-2.** [surface texture] acabado m. ◇ vt: **to ~ sthg/doing sthg** acabar algo/de hacer algo, terminar algo/de hacer algo. ◇ vi acabar, terminar. ◆ **finish off** vt sep acabar OR terminar del todo. ◆ **finish up** vi acabar, terminar.

finishing line ['fɪnɪʃɪŋ-] n línea f de meta.

finishing school ['fɪnɪʃɪŋ-] n colegio privado donde se prepara a las alumnas de clase alta para entrar en sociedad.

finite ['faɪnaɪt] adj **-1.** [limited] finito(ta). **-2.** GRAMM conjugado(da).

Finland ['fɪnlənd] n Finlandia f.

Finn [fɪn] n [person] finlandés m, -esa f.

Finnish ['fɪnɪʃ] ◇ adj finlandés(esa). ◇ n [language] finlandés m.

fir [fɜːr] n abeto m.

fire ['faɪər] ◇ n **-1.** [gen] fuego m; **on ~** en llamas; **to catch ~** incendiarse; **to open ~ (on sb)** abrir fuego (contra alguien); **to set ~ to** prender fuego a. **-2.** [blaze] incendio m. **-3.** Br [heater]: **(electric/gas) ~** estufa f (eléctrica/de gas). ◇ vt **-1.** [shoot] disparar. **-2.** [dismiss] despedir. ◇ vi: **to ~ (on OR at)** disparar (contra).

fire alarm n alarma f antiincendios.

firearm ['faɪərɑːm] n arma f de fuego.

firebomb ['faɪəbɒm] n bomba f incendiaria.

fire brigade Br, **fire department** Am n cuerpo m de bomberos.

fire door n puerta f cortafuegos.

fire engine n coche m de bomberos.

fire escape n escalera f de incendios.

fire extinguisher n extintor m (de incendios).

fireguard ['faɪəgɑːd] n pantalla f (de chimenea).

firelighter ['faɪəlaɪtəʳ] n enciende-fuegos m inv, tea f.

fireman ['faɪəmən] (pl -men [-mən]) n bombero m.

fireplace ['faɪəpleɪs] n chimenea f.

fireproof ['faɪəpruːf] adj incombustible.

fireside ['faɪəsaɪd] n: **by the** ~ al calor de la chimenea.

fire station n parque m de bomberos.

firewood ['faɪəwʊd] n leña f.

firework ['faɪəwɜːk] n fuego m de artificio. ◆ **fireworks** npl fuegos mpl artificiales OR de artificio.

firing ['faɪərɪŋ] n (U) MIL disparos mpl.

firing squad n pelotón m de ejecución OR fusilamiento.

firm [fɜːm] ◇ adj **-1.** [gen] firme; **to stand** ~ mantenerse firme. **-2.** FIN [steady] estable. ◇ n firma f, empresa f.

first [fɜːst] ◇ adj primero(ra); **for the** ~ **time** por primera vez; ~ **thing (in the morning)** a primera hora (de la mañana). ◇ adv **-1.** [gen] primero; ~ **of all** en primer lugar. **-2.** [for the first time] por primera vez. ◇ n **-1.** [person] primero m, -ra f. **-2.** [unprecedented event] acontecimiento sin precedentes. **-3.** Br UNIV ≃ sobresaliente m. ◆ **at first** adv al principio. ◆ **at first hand** adv de primera mano.

first aid n (U) primeros auxilios mpl.

first-aid kit n botiquín m de primeros auxilios.

first-class adj **-1.** [excellent] de primera. **-2.** [letter, ticket] de primera clase.

first floor n **-1.** Br [above ground level] primer piso m. **-2.** Am [at ground level] planta f baja.

firsthand [,fɜːst'hænd] ◇ adj de primera mano. ◇ adv directamente.

first lady n primera dama f.

firstly ['fɜːstlɪ] adv en primer lugar.

first name n nombre m de pila.

first-rate adj de primera.

firtree ['fɜːtriː] = **fir**.

fish [fɪʃ] (pl inv) ◇ n **-1.** [animal] pez m. **-2.** (U) [food] pescado m. ◇ vt pescar en. ◇ vi [for fish]: **to** ~ **(for sthg)** pescar (algo).

fish and chips npl pescado m frito con patatas fritas.

fish and chip shop n Br tienda f de pescado frito con patatas fritas.

fishbowl ['fɪʃbəʊl] n pecera f.

fishcake ['fɪʃkeɪk] n pastelillo m de pescado.

fisherman ['fɪʃəmən] (pl -men [-mən]) n pescador m.

fish farm n piscifactoría f.

fish fingers Br, **fish sticks** Am npl palitos mpl de pescado.

fishing ['fɪʃɪŋ] n pesca f; **to go** ~ ir de pesca.

fishing boat n barco m pesquero.

fishing line n sedal m.

fishing rod n caña f de pescar.

fishmonger ['fɪʃ,mʌŋgəʳ] n pescadero m, -ra f; ~**'s (shop)** pescadería f.

fish sticks Am = **fish fingers**.

fishy ['fɪʃɪ] adj **-1.** [smell, taste] a pescado. **-2.** [suspicious] sospechoso(sa).

fist [fɪst] n puño m.

fit [fɪt] ◇ adj **-1.** [suitable] ~ **(for sthg/ to do sthg)** apto(ta) (para algo/para hacer algo); **do as you think** ~ haz lo que te parezca conveniente. **-2.** [healthy] en forma; **to keep** ~ mantenerse en forma. ◇ n **-1.** [of clothes, shoes etc]: **it's a good** ~ le/te etc sienta OR va bien. **-2.** [bout, seizure] ataque m; **he had a** ~ lit & fig le dio un ataque; **in** ~**s and starts** a trompicones. ◇ vt **-1.** [be correct size for] sentar bien a, ir bien a. **-2.** [place]: **to** ~ **sthg into** encajar algo en. **-3.** [provide]: **to** ~ **sthg with** equipar algo con; **to have an alarm fitted** poner una alarma. **-4.** [be suitable for] corresponder a. ◇ vi **-1.** [clothes, shoes] estar bien de talla. **-2.** [part - when assembling etc]: **this bit** ~**s in here** esta pieza encaja aquí. **-3.** [have enough room] caber. ◆ **fit in** ◇ vt sep [accommodate] hacer un hueco a. ◇ vi **-1.** [subj: person]: **to** ~ **in (with)** adaptarse (a). **-2.** [be compatible]: **it doesn't** ~ **in with our plans** no encaja con nuestros planes.

fitful ['fɪtfʊl] adj irregular, intermitente.

fitment ['fɪtmənt] n mueble m.

fitness ['fɪtnɪs] n (U) **-1.** [health] buen estado m físico. **-2.** [suitability]: ~ **(for)** idoneidad f (para).

fitted carpet ['fɪtəd-] n moqueta f.

fitted kitchen ['fɪtəd-] n Br cocina f de módulos.

fitter ['fɪtəʳ] n [mechanic] (mecánico m) ajustador m.

fitting ['fɪtɪŋ] ◇ *adj fml* conveniente, adecuado(da). ◇ *n* **-1.** [part] accesorio *m*. **-2.** [for clothing] prueba *f*. ◆ **fittings** *npl* accesorios *mpl*.

fitting room *n* probador *m*.

five [faɪv] *num* cinco; *see also* **six**.

fiver ['faɪvə'] *n Br inf (billete de)* cinco libras.

fix [fɪks] ◇ *vt* **-1.** [gen] fijar; **to ~ sthg (to)** fijar algo (a). **-2.** [repair] arreglar, refaccionar *Amer*. **-3.** *inf* [rig] amañar. **-4.** [prepare - food, drink] preparar. ◇ *n* **-1.** *inf* [difficult situation]: **to be in a ~** estar en un aprieto. **-2.** *drugs sl* dosis *f inv*. ◆ **fix up** *vt sep* **-1.** [provide]: **to ~ sb up with** proveer a alguien de. **-2.** [arrange] organizar, preparar.

fixation [fɪk'seɪʃn] *n*: **~ (on OR about)** fijación *f* (con).

fixed [fɪkst] *adj* fijo(ja).

fixture ['fɪkstʃə'] *n* **-1.** [furniture] instalación *f* fija. **-2.** [permanent feature] rasgo *m* característico. **-3.** [sports event] encuentro *m*.

fizz [fɪz] *vi* burbujear.

fizzle ['fɪzl] ◆ **fizzle out** *vi* [firework, fire] apagarse; *fig* disiparse.

fizzy ['fɪzɪ] *adj* gaseoso(sa).

flabbergasted ['flæbəgɑːstɪd] *adj* pasmado(da), boquiabierto(ta).

flabby ['flæbɪ] *adj* fofo(fa), gordo(da).

flag [flæg] ◇ *n* [banner] bandera *f*. ◇ *vi* decaer. ◆ **flag down** *vt sep*: **to ~ sb down** hacer señales a alguien para que se detenga.

flagpole ['flægpəʊl] *n* asta *f* (de bandera).

flagrant ['fleɪgrənt] *adj* flagrante.

flagstone ['flægstəʊn] *n* losa *f*.

flair [fleə'] *n* don *m*.

flak [flæk] *n* (*U*) **-1.** [gunfire] fuego *m* antiaéreo. **-2.** *inf* [criticism] críticas *fpl*.

flake [fleɪk] ◇ *n* [of skin] escama *f*; [of snow] copo *m*; [of paint] desconchón *m*. ◇ *vi* [skin] descamarse; [paint, plaster] descascarillarse, desconcharse.

flamboyant [flæm'bɔɪənt] *adj* **-1.** [person, behaviour] extravagante. **-2.** [clothes, design] vistoso(sa).

flame [fleɪm] *n* llama *f*; **in ~s** en llamas.

flamingo [flə'mɪŋgəʊ] (*pl* **-s** OR **-es**) *n* flamenco *m*.

flammable ['flæməbl] *adj* inflamable.

flan [flæn] *n* tarta *f* (*de fruta etc*).

flank [flæŋk] ◇ *n* **-1.** [of animal] costado *m*, ijada *f*. **-2.** [of army] flanco *m*. ◇ *vt*: **to be ~ed by** estar flanqueado(da) por.

flannel ['flænl] *n* **-1.** [fabric] franela *f*. **-2.** *Br* [facecloth] toallita *f* (de baño para lavarse).

flap [flæp] ◇ *n* [of skin] colgajo *m*; [of pocket, book, envelope] solapa *f*. ◇ *vt* agitar; [wings] batir. ◇ *vi* [flag, skirt] ondear; [wings] aletear.

flapjack ['flæpdʒæk] *n* **-1.** *Br* [biscuit] torta *f* de avena. **-2.** *Am* [pancake] torta *f*, crepe *f*.

flare [fleə'] ◇ *n* [signal] bengala *f*. ◇ *vi* **-1.** [burn brightly]: **to ~ (up)** llamear. **-2.** [intensify]: **to ~ (up)** estallar. ◆ **flares** *npl Br* pantalones *mpl* de campana.

flash [flæʃ] ◇ *n* **-1.** [of light] destello *m*; [of lightning] relámpago *m*, refucilo *m Amer*. **-2.** PHOT flash *m*. **-3.** [of genius, inspiration etc] momento *m*; [of anger] acceso *m*; **in a ~** en un instante. ◇ *vt* **-1.** [shine in specified direction] dirigir; [switch on briefly] encender intermitentemente. **-2.** [send out] lanzar. **-3.** [show - picture, image] mostrar; [- information, news] emitir. ◇ *vi* **-1.** [light] destellar. **-2.** [eyes] brillar. **-3.** [rush]: **to ~ by** OR **past** pasar como un rayo.

flashback ['flæʃbæk] *n* flashback *m*.

flashbulb ['flæʃbʌlb] *n* flash *m*.

flashgun ['flæʃgʌn] *n* disparador *m* de flash.

flashlight ['flæʃlaɪt] *n* [torch] linterna *f* eléctrica.

flashy ['flæʃɪ] *adj inf* chulo(la); *pej* ostentoso(sa).

flask [flɑːsk] *n* **-1.** [thermos flask] termo *m*. **-2.** [used in chemistry] matraz *m*. **-3.** [hip flask] petaca *f*.

flat [flæt] ◇ *adj* **-1.** [surface, ground] llano(na); [feet] plano. **-2.** [shoes] bajo(ja). **-3.** [tyre] desinflado(da). **-4.** [refusal, denial] rotundo(da). **-5.** [business, trade] flojo(ja); [voice, tone] monótono(na); [colour] soso(sa); [performance, writing] desangelado(da). **-6.** MUS [lower than correct note] desafinado(da); [lower than stated note] bemol (*inv*). **-7.** [fare, price] único(ca). **-8.** [beer, lemonade] muerto(ta). **-9.** [battery] descargado(da). ◇ *adv* **-1.** [level]: **to lie ~** estar totalmente extendido; **to fall ~** [person] caerse de bruces. **-2.** [of time]: **in five minutes ~** en cinco minutos justos. ◇ *n* **-1.** *Br* [apartment] piso *m*, apartamento *m*. **-2.** MUS bemol *m*. ◆ **flat out** *adv* a toda velocidad.

flatly ['flætlɪ] *adv* **-1.** [refuse, deny] de

plano, terminantemente. **-2.** [speak, perform] monótonamente.

flatmate ['flætmeɪt] n Br compañero m, -ra f de piso.

flat rate n tarifa f única.

flatten ['flætn] vt **-1.** [surface, paper, bumps] allanar, aplanar; [paper] alisar. **-2.** [building, city] arrasar. ◆ **flatten out** ◇ vi allanarse, nivelarse. ◇ vt sep allanar.

flatter ['flætəʳ] vt **-1.** [subj: person, report] adular, halagar. **-2.** [subj: clothes, colour, photograph] favorecer.

flattering ['flætərɪŋ] adj **-1.** [remark, interest] halagador(ra). **-2.** [clothes, colour, photograph] favorecedor(ra).

flattery ['flætərɪ] n (U) halagos mpl.

flaunt [flɔːnt] vt ostentar, hacer gala de.

flavour Br, **flavor** Am ['fleɪvəʳ] ◇ n **-1.** [taste] sabor m. **-2.** fig [atmosphere] aire m, toque m. ◇ vt condimentar.

flavouring Br, **flavoring** Am ['fleɪvərɪŋ] n (U) condimento m.

flaw [flɔː] n [fault] desperfecto m.

flawless ['flɔːlɪs] adj impecable.

flax [flæks] n lino m.

flea [fliː] n pulga f.

flea market n rastro m.

fleck [flek] n mota f.

fled [fled] pt & pp → **flee**.

flee [fliː] (pt & pp **fled**) ◇ vt huir de. ◇ vi: **to ~ (from/to)** huir (de/a).

fleece [fliːs] ◇ n vellón m. ◇ vt inf [cheat] desplumar.

fleet [fliːt] n **-1.** [of ships] flota f. **-2.** [of cars, buses] parque m (móvil).

fleeting ['fliːtɪŋ] adj fugaz.

Fleet Street n calle londinense que antiguamente fue el centro de la prensa inglesa y cuyo nombre todavía se utiliza para referirse a ésta.

Flemish ['flemɪʃ] ◇ adj flamenco(ca). ◇ n [language] flamenco m. ◇ npl: **the ~** los flamencos.

flesh [fleʃ] n **-1.** [of body] carne f; **in the ~** en persona. **-2.** [of fruit, vegetable] pulpa f.

flesh wound n herida f superficial.

flew [fluː] pt → **fly**.

flex [fleks] ◇ n ELEC cable m, cordón m. ◇ vt flexionar.

flexible ['fleksəbl] adj flexible.

flexitime ['fleksɪtaɪm] n (U) horario m flexible.

flick [flɪk] ◇ n **-1.** [of whip, towel] golpe m rápido. **-2.** [with finger] toba f. ◇ vt [switch] apretar, pulsar. ◆ **flick through** vt fus hojear rápidamente.

flicker ['flɪkəʳ] vi [eyes] parpadear; [flame] vacilar.

flick knife n Br navaja f automática.

flight [flaɪt] n **-1.** [gen] vuelo m. **-2.** [of steps, stairs] tramo m. **-3.** [of birds] bandada f. **-4.** [escape] huida f, fuga f.

flight attendant n auxiliar m de vuelo, azafata f.

flight crew n tripulación f de vuelo.

flight deck n **-1.** [of aircraft carrier] cubierta f de vuelo. **-2.** [of plane] cabina f del piloto.

flight recorder n registrador m de vuelo.

flimsy ['flɪmzɪ] adj **-1.** [dress, material] muy ligero(ra). **-2.** [structure] débil, poco sólido(da). **-3.** [excuse] flojo(ja).

flinch [flɪntʃ] vi **-1.** [shudder] estremecerse; **without ~ing** sin pestañear. **-2.** [be reluctant]: **to ~ (from sthg/from doing sthg)** retroceder (ante algo/ante hacer algo); **without ~ing** sin inmutarse.

fling [flɪŋ] (pt & pp **flung**) ◇ n [affair] aventura f amorosa. ◇ vt arrojar.

flint [flɪnt] n **-1.** [rock] sílex m. **-2.** [in lighter] piedra f.

flip [flɪp] ◇ vt **-1.** [turn] dar la vuelta a; **to ~ sthg open** abrir algo de golpe. **-2.** [switch] pulsar. ◇ n [of coin] papirotazo m.

flip-flop n [shoe] chancleta f.

flippant ['flɪpənt] adj frívolo(la).

flipper ['flɪpəʳ] n aleta f.

flirt [flɜːt] ◇ n coqueto m, -ta f. ◇ vi [with person]: **to ~ (with)** flirtear OR coquetear (con).

flirtatious [flɜːˈteɪʃəs] adj coqueto(ta).

flit [flɪt] vi [bird] revolotear.

float [fləʊt] ◇ n **-1.** [for fishing line] corcho m. **-2.** [buoyant object] flotador m. **-3.** [in procession] carroza f. **-4.** [supply of change] cambio m. ◇ vt [on water] hacer flotar. ◇ vi flotar.

flock [flɒk] n **-1.** [of sheep] rebaño m; [of birds] bandada f. **-2.** fig [of people] multitud f, tropel m.

flog [flɒg] vt **-1.** [whip] azotar. **-2.** Br inf [sell] vender.

flood [flʌd] ◇ n **-1.** [of water] inundación f. **-2.** [of letters, people] aluvión m, riada f. ◇ vt lit & fig: **to ~ sthg (with)** inundar algo de (de).

flooding ['flʌdɪŋ] n (U) inundación f.

floodlight ['flʌdlaɪt] n foco m.

floor [flɔːʳ] ◇ n **-1.** [of room, forest] suelo m; [of club, disco] pista f. **-2.** [of sea, valley] fondo m. **-3.** [of building] piso m,

planta *f.* **-4.** [at meeting, debate]: **to give/have the ~** dar/tener la palabra. ◇ *vt* **-1.** [knock down] derribar. **-2.** [baffle] desconcertar, dejar perplejo(ja).

floorboard ['flɔːbɔːd] *n* tabla *f* (del suelo).

floor show *n* espectáculo *m* de cabaret.

flop [flɒp] *inf n* [failure] fracaso *m*.

floppy ['flɒpɪ] *adj* caído(da), flojo(ja).

floppy (disk) *n* disco *m* flexible.

flora ['flɔːrə] *n* flora *f*.

florid ['flɒrɪd] *adj* **-1.** [red] rojizo(za). **-2.** [extravagant] florido(da).

florist ['flɒrɪst] *n* florista *m y f*; **~'s (shop)** floristería *f*.

flotsam ['flɒtsəm] *n* (*U*): **~ and jetsam** restos *mpl* del naufragio; *fig* desechos *mpl* de la humanidad.

flounce [flaʊns] ◇ *n* SEWING volante *m*. ◇ *vi*: **to ~ out** salir airadamente.

flounder ['flaʊndər] *vi* **-1.** [move with difficulty] debatirse. **-2.** [when speaking] titubear.

flour ['flaʊər] *n* harina *f*.

flourish ['flʌrɪʃ] ◇ *vi* florecer. ◇ *vt* agitar. ◇ *n*: **to do sthg with a ~** hacer algo con una floritura.

flout [flaʊt] *vt* incumplir, no obedecer.

flow [fləʊ] ◇ *n* [gen] flujo *m*; [of opinion] corriente *f*. ◇ *vi* **-1.** [gen] fluir, correr. **-2.** [hair, clothes] ondear.

flow chart, flow diagram *n* organigrama *m*, cuadro *m* sinóptico.

flower ['flaʊər] ◇ *n lit & fig* flor *f*. ◇ *vi lit & fig* florecer.

flowerbed ['flaʊəbed] *n* arriate *m*.

flowerpot ['flaʊəpɒt] *n* tiesto *m*.

flowery ['flaʊərɪ] *adj* **-1.** [patterned] de flores, floreado(da). **-2.** *pej* [elaborate] florido(da). **-3.** [sweet-smelling] con olor a flores.

flown [fləʊn] *pp* → **fly**.

flu [fluː] *n* gripe *f*.

fluctuate ['flʌktʃʊeɪt] *vi* fluctuar.

fluency ['fluːənsɪ] *n* soltura *f*, fluidez *f*.

fluent ['fluːənt] *adj* **-1.** [in foreign language]: **to be ~ in French, to speak ~ French** dominar el francés. **-2.** [style] elocuente, fluido(da).

fluff [flʌf] *n* pelusa *f*.

fluffy ['flʌfɪ] *adj* [jumper] de pelusa; [toy] de peluche.

fluid ['fluːɪd] ◇ *n* fluido *m*, líquido *m*. ◇ *adj* **-1.** [flowing] fluido(da). **-2.** [situation, opinion] incierto(ta).

fluid ounce *n* = 0,03 litre, onza *f* líquida.

fluke [fluːk] *n inf* chiripa *f*; **by a ~** por OR de chiripa.

flummox ['flʌməks] *vt Br inf* desconcertar, confundir.

flung [flʌŋ] *pt & pp* → **fling**.

flunk [flʌŋk] *vt & vi inf* catear.

fluorescent [flʊə'resnt] *adj* fluorescente.

fluoride ['flʊəraɪd] *n* fluoruro *m*.

flurry ['flʌrɪ] *n* **-1.** [shower] ráfaga *f*. **-2.** [burst] frenesí *m*.

flush [flʌʃ] ◇ *adj* [level]: **~ with** nivelado(da) con. ◇ *n* **-1.** [of lavatory] cadena *f*. **-2.** [blush] rubor *m*. **-3.** [sudden feeling] arrebato *m*. ◇ *vt* **-1.** [toilet] tirar de la cadena de. **-2.** [force out of hiding]: **to ~ sb out** hacer salir a alguien. ◇ *vi* [blush] ruborizarse.

flushed [flʌʃt] *adj* **-1.** [red-faced] encendido(da). **-2.** [excited]: **~ (with)** enardecido(da) (por).

flustered ['flʌstəd] *adj* aturullado(da).

flute [fluːt] *n* MUS flauta *f*.

flutter ['flʌtər] ◇ *n* **-1.** [of wings] aleteo *m*; [of eyelashes] pestañeo *m*. **-2.** *inf* [of excitement] arranque *m*. ◇ *vi* **-1.** [bird] aletear. **-2.** [flag, dress] ondear.

flux [flʌks] *n* [change]: **to be in a state of ~** cambiar constantemente.

fly [flaɪ] (*pt* **flew**, *pp* **flown**) ◇ *n* **-1.** [insect] mosca *f*. **-2.** [in trousers] bragueta *f*. ◇ *vt* **-1.** [plane] pilotar; [kite, model aircraft] hacer volar. **-2.** [passengers, supplies] transportar en avión. **-3.** [flag] ondear. ◇ *vi* **-1.** [bird, plane, person] volar. **-2.** [pilot a plane] pilotar. **-3.** [travel by plane] ir en avión. **-4.** [flag] ondear.

◆ **fly away** *vi* irse volando.

fly-fishing *n* pesca *f* con mosca.

flying ['flaɪɪŋ] ◇ *adj* [able to fly] volador(ra), volante. ◇ *n*: **I hate/love ~** odio/me encanta ir en avión; **her hobby is ~** es aficionada a la aviación.

flying colours *npl*: **to pass (sthg) with ~** salir airoso(sa) (de algo).

flying picket *n* piquete de apoyo proveniente de otra fábrica o sindicato.

flying saucer *n* platillo *m* volante.

flying squad *n* brigada *f* volante.

flying start *n*: **to get off to a ~** empezar con muy buen pie.

flying visit *n* visita *f* relámpago.

flyover ['flaɪˌəʊvər] *n Br* paso *m* elevado.

flysheet ['flaɪʃiːt] *n* doble techo *m*.

fly spray *n* matamoscas *m inv* (en aerosol).

FM (*abbr of* **frequency modulation**) FM *f*.

foal [fəʊl] *n* potro *m*.

foam [fəʊm] ◇ *n* **-1.** [bubbles] espuma *f*. **-2.** ~ **(rubber)** gomaespuma *f*. ◇ *vi* hacer espuma.

fob [fɒb] ◆ **fob off** *vt sep*: **to** ~ **sb off (with sthg)** dar largas a alguien (con algo); **to** ~ **sthg off on sb** endosar a alguien algo.

focal point ['fəʊkl-] *n* punto *m* focal OR central.

focus ['fəʊkəs] (*pl* **-cuses** OR **-ci** [-saɪ]) ◇ *n* [gen] foco *m*; **in** ~ enfocado; **out of** ~ desenfocado. ◇ *vt* **-1.** [eyes, lens, rays] enfocar. **-2.** [attention] fijar, centrar. ◇ *vi* **-1.** [eyes, lens]: **to** ~ **(on sthg)** enfocar (algo). **-2.** [attention]: **to** ~ **on sthg** centrarse en algo.

fodder ['fɒdər] *n* forraje *m*.

foe [fəʊ] *n literary* enemigo *m*, -ga *f*.

foetus ['fiːtəs] *n* feto *m*.

fog [fɒg] *n* niebla *f*.

foggy ['fɒgɪ] *adj* [misty] brumoso(sa); [day] de niebla.

foghorn ['fɒghɔːn] *n* sirena *f* (*de niebla*).

fog lamp *n* faro *m* antiniebla.

foible ['fɔɪbl] *n* manía *f*.

foil [fɔɪl] ◇ *n* (U) [metal sheet] papel *m* aluminio OR de plata. ◇ *vt* frustrar.

fold [fəʊld] ◇ *vt* [sheet, blanket] doblar; [chair, pram] plegar; **to** ~ **one's arms** cruzar los brazos. ◇ *vi* **-1.** [table, chair etc] plegarse. **-2.** *inf* [collapse] venirse abajo. ◇ *n* **-1.** [in material, paper] pliegue *m*. **-2.** [for animals] redil *m*. ◆ **fold up** ◇ *vt sep* **-1.** [bend] doblar. **-2.** [close up] plegar. ◇ *vi* **-1.** [bend] doblarse. **-2.** [close up] plegarse. **-3.** [collapse] venirse abajo.

folder ['fəʊldər] *n* [gen] carpeta *f*.

folding ['fəʊldɪŋ] *adj* plegable; [ladder] de tijera.

foliage ['fəʊlɪɪdʒ] *n* follaje *m*.

folk [fəʊk] ◇ *adj* popular. ◇ *npl* [people] gente *f*. ◇ *n* MUS música *f* folklórica OR popular. ◆ **folks** *npl inf* [relatives] familia *f*.

folklore ['fəʊklɔːr] *n* folklore *m*.

folk music *n* música *f* folklórica OR popular.

folk song *n* canción *f* popular.

follow ['fɒləʊ] ◇ *vt* **-1.** [gen] seguir. **-2.** [understand] comprender. ◇ *vi* **-1.** [gen] seguir. **-2.** [be logical] ser lógico(ca); **it** ~**s that** se deduce que. **-3.** [understand] comprender. ◆ **follow up** *vt sep* examinar en más detalle; **to** ~ **sthg up with** proseguir algo con.

follower ['fɒləʊər] *n* partidario *m*, -ria *f*.

following ['fɒləʊɪŋ] ◇ *adj* siguiente. ◇ *n* partidarios *mpl*; [of team] afición *f*. ◇ *prep* tras.

folly ['fɒlɪ] *n* (U) [foolishness] locura *f*.

fond [fɒnd] *adj* **-1.** [affectionate] afectuoso(sa), cariñoso(sa). **-2.** [having a liking]: **to be** ~ **of sb** tener cariño a alguien; **to be** ~ **of sthg/of doing sthg** ser aficionado(da) a algo/a hacer algo.

fondle ['fɒndl] *vt* acariciar.

font [fɒnt] *n* **-1.** [in church] pila *f* bautismal. **-2.** COMPUT: **hard/printer/screen** ~ grupo *m* de caracteres impreso/de impresora/de pantalla.

food [fuːd] *n* comida *f*.

food mixer *n* batidora *f* eléctrica.

food poisoning [-'pɔɪznɪŋ] *n* intoxicación *f* alimenticia.

food processor [-,prəʊsesər] *n* robot *m* de cocina.

foodstuffs ['fuːdstʌfs] *npl* comestibles *mpl*.

fool [fuːl] ◇ *n* **-1.** [idiot] tonto *m*, -ta *f*, imbécil *m* y *f*. **-2.** *Br* [dessert] mousse de fruta con nata. ◇ *vt* [deceive] engañar; [joke with] tomar el pelo a; **to** ~ **sb into doing sthg** embaucar a alguien para que haga algo. ◇ *vi* bromear. ◆ **fool about, fool around** *vi* **-1.** [behave foolishly]: **to** ~ **about (with sthg)** hacer el tonto (con algo). **-2.** [be unfaithful]: **to** ~ **about (with sb)** tontear (con alguien).

foolhardy ['fuːl,hɑːdɪ] *adj* temerario(ria).

foolish ['fuːlɪʃ] *adj* tonto(ta).

foolproof ['fuːlpruːf] *adj* infalible.

foot [fʊt] (*pl sense 1* **feet**, *pl sense 2 inv* OR **feet**) ◇ *n* **-1.** [gen] pie *m*; [of bird, animal] pata *f*; **to be on one's feet** estar de pie; **to get to one's feet** levantarse; **on** ~ a pie, andando; **to put one's** ~ **in it** meter la pata; **to put one's feet up** descansar (con los pies en alto). **-2.** [unit of measurement] = 30,48 cm, pie *m*. ◇ *vt inf*: **to** ~ **the bill (for sthg)** pagar la cuenta (de algo).

footage ['fʊtɪdʒ] *n* (U) secuencias *fpl*.

football ['fʊtbɔːl] *n* **-1.** [game - soccer] fútbol *m*; [- American football] fútbol americano. **-2.** [ball] balón *m*.

footballer ['fʊtbɔːlər] *n Br* futbolista *m* y *f*.

football ground *n Br* campo *m* de fútbol.

football player = **footballer**.

footbrake ['fʊtbreɪk] *n* freno *m* de pedal.

footbridge ['fʊtbrɪdʒ] *n* paso *m* elevado, pasarela *f*.

foothills ['fʊthɪlz] *npl* estribaciones *fpl*.

foothold ['fʊthəʊld] *n* punto *m* de apoyo para el pie.

footing ['fʊtɪŋ] *n* **-1.** [foothold] equilibrio *m*; **to lose one's ~** perder el equilibrio. **-2.** [basis] nivel *m*; **on an equal ~ (with)** en pie de igualdad (con).

footlights ['fʊtlaɪts] *npl* candilejas *fpl*.

footnote ['fʊtnəʊt] *n* nota *f* a pie de página.

footpath ['fʊtpɑːθ, *pl* -pɑːðz] *n* senda *f*.

footprint ['fʊtprɪnt] *n* huella *f*, pisada *f*.

footstep ['fʊtstep] *n* **-1.** [sound] paso *m*. **-2.** [footprint] pisada *f*.

footwear ['fʊtweəʳ] *n* calzado *m*.

for [fɔːʳ] ◇ *prep* **-1.** [indicating intention, destination, purpose] para; **this is ~ you** esto es para ti; **I'm going ~ the paper** voy (a) por el periódico; **the plane ~ Paris** [gen] el avión para OR de París; [in airport announcements] el avión con destino a París; **it's time ~ bed** es hora de irse a la cama; **we did it ~ a laugh** OR **~ fun** lo hicimos de broma OR por divertirnos; **to go ~ a walk** ir a dar un paseo; **what's it ~?** ¿para qué es OR sirve? **-2.** [representing, on behalf of] por; **the MP ~ Barnsley** el diputado por Barnsley; **let me do it ~ you** deja que lo haga por ti; **he plays ~ England** juega en la selección inglesa; **to work ~** trabajar para. **-3.** [because of] por; **a prize ~ bravery** un premio a la valentía; **to jump ~ joy** dar saltos de alegría; **~ fear of failing** por miedo a fracasar. **-4.** [with regard to] para; **it's not ~ me to say** no me toca a mí decidir; **he looks young ~ his age** aparenta ser más joven de lo que es. **-5.** [indicating amount of time, space] para; **there's no time/room ~ it** no hay tiempo/sitio para eso. **-6.** [indicating period of time - during] durante; [- by, in time for] para; **she cried ~ two hours** estuvo llorando durante dos horas; **I've lived here ~ three years** llevo tres años viviendo aquí, he vivido aquí (durante) tres años; **I've worked here ~ years** trabajo aquí desde hace años; **I'll do it ~ tomorrow** lo tendré hecho para mañana. **-7.** [indicating distance] en; **there were roadworks ~ 50 miles** había obras en 50 millas; **we walked ~ miles** andamos millas y millas. **-8.** [indicating particular occasion] para; **I got it ~ my birthday** me lo regalaron para OR por mi cumpleaños; **~ the first time** por vez primera. **-9.** [indicating amount of money, price] por; **I bought/sold it ~ £10** lo compré/vendí por 10 libras; **they're 50p ~ ten** son a 50 peniques cada diez. **-10.** [in favour of, in support of] a favor de, por; **to vote ~ sthg/sb** votar por algo/a alguien; **to be all ~ sthg** estar completamente a favor de algo. **-11.** [in ratios] por. **-12.** [indicating meaning]: **P ~ Peter** P de Pedro; **what's the Greek ~ "mother"?** ¿cómo se dice "madre" en griego? ◇ *conj fml* [as, since] ya que. ◆ **for all** ◇ *prep* **-1.** [in spite of] a pesar de; **~ all your moaning** a pesar de lo mucho que te quejas. **-2.** [considering how little] para; **~ all the good it has done me** para lo que me ha servido. ◇ *conj*: **~ all I care, she could be dead** por mí, como si se muere; **~ all I know** por lo que yo sé, que yo sepa.

forage ['fɒrɪdʒ] *vi* [search]: **to ~ (for sthg)** buscar (algo).

foray ['fɒreɪ] *n lit & fig*: **~ (into)** incursión *f* (en).

forbad [fə'bæd], **forbade** [fə'beɪd] *pt* → **forbid**.

forbid [fə'bɪd] (*pt* **-bade** OR **-bad**, *pp* **forbid** OR **-bidden**) *vt*: **to ~ sb (to do sthg)** prohibir a alguien (hacer algo).

forbidden [fə'bɪdn] *adj* prohibido(da).

forbidding [fə'bɪdɪŋ] *adj* [building, landscape] inhóspito(ta); [person, expression] severo(ra), austero(ra).

force [fɔːs] ◇ *n* fuerza *f*; **sales ~** personal *m* de ventas; **security ~s** fuerzas *fpl* de seguridad; **by ~** a la fuerza; **to be in/come into ~** estar/entrar en vigor; **in ~** [in large numbers] en masa, en gran número. ◇ *vt* forzar; **to ~ sb to do sthg** [gen] forzar a alguien a hacer algo; [subj: event, circumstances] obligar a alguien a hacer algo. ◆ **forces** *npl*: **the ~s** las fuerzas armadas; **to join ~s (with)** unirse (con).

force-feed *vt* alimentar a la fuerza.

forceful ['fɔːsfʊl] *adj* [person, impression] fuerte; [support, recommendation] enérgico(ca); [speech, idea, argument] contundente.

forceps ['fɔːseps] *npl* fórceps *m inv*.

forcibly ['fɔːsəblɪ] *adv* **-1.** [using physical force] por la fuerza. **-2.** [remind] vivamente; [express, argue, recommend] enérgicamente.

ford [fɔːd] *n* vado *m*.

fore [fɔːʳ] *n*: to come to the ~ empezar a destacar, emerger.

forearm ['fɔːrɑːm] *n* antebrazo *m*.

foreboding [fɔːˈbəʊdɪŋ] *n* **-1.** [presentiment] **presagio** *m*. **-2.** [apprehension] miedo *m*.

forecast ['fɔːkɑːst] (*pt* & *pp* **forecast** OR **-ed**) ◇ *n* [prediction] predicción *f*, previsión *f*; [of weather] pronóstico *m*. ◇ *vt* [predict] predecir; [weather] pronosticar.

foreclose [fɔːˈkləʊz] ◇ *vi*: to ~ on sb privar a alguien del derecho a redimir su hipoteca. ◇ *vt* ejecutar.

forecourt ['fɔːkɔːt] *n* patio *m*.

forefinger ['fɔːˌfɪŋgəʳ] *n* (dedo *m*) índice *m*.

forefront ['fɔːfrʌnt] *n*: in OR at the ~ of en OR a la vanguardia de.

forego [fɔːˈgəʊ] = **forgo**.

foregone conclusion ['fɔːgɒn-] *n*: it's a ~ es un resultado inevitable.

foreground ['fɔːgraʊnd] *n* primer plano *m*.

forehand ['fɔːhænd] *n* [stroke] golpe *m* natural, drive *m*.

forehead ['fɔːhed] *n* frente *f*.

foreign ['fɒrən] *adj* **-1.** [from abroad] extranjero(ra). **-2.** [external - policy] exterior; [- correspondent, holiday] en el extranjero. **-3.** [unwanted, harmful] extraño(ña). **-4.** [alien, untypical]: ~ (to sb/sthg) ajeno(na) (a alguien/algo).

foreign affairs *npl* asuntos *mpl* exteriores.

foreign currency *n* (U) divisa *f*.

foreigner ['fɒrənəʳ] *n* extranjero *m*, -ra *f*.

foreign minister *n* ministro *m*, -tra *f* de asuntos exteriores.

Foreign Office *n* Br: the ~ el Ministerio de Asuntos Exteriores británico.

Foreign Secretary *n* Br Ministro *m*, -tra *f* de Asuntos Exteriores.

foreleg ['fɔːleg] *n* pata *f* delantera.

foreman ['fɔːmən] (*pl* **-men** [-mən]) *n* **-1.** [of workers] capataz *m*. **-2.** [of jury] presidente *m*.

foremost ['fɔːməʊst] ◇ *adj* primero(ra). ◇ *adv*: **first and** ~ ante todo.

forensic [fəˈrensɪk] *adj* forense.

forensic science *n* ciencia *f* forense.

forerunner ['fɔːˌrʌnəʳ] *n* [precursor] precursor *m*, -ra *f*.

foresee [fɔːˈsiː] (*pt* **-saw** [-ˈsɔː], *pp* **-seen**) *vt* prever.

foreseeable [fɔːˈsiːəbl] *adj* previsible; **for/in the** ~ **future** en un futuro próximo.

foreseen [fɔːˈsiːn] *pp* → **foresee**.

foreshadow [fɔːˈʃædəʊ] *vt* presagiar.

foresight ['fɔːsaɪt] *n* (U) previsión *f*.

forest ['fɒrɪst] *n* bosque *m*.

forestall [fɔːˈstɔːl] *vt* anticiparse a.

forestry ['fɒrɪstrɪ] *n* silvicultura *f*.

foretaste ['fɔːteɪst] *n* anticipo *m*.

foretell [fɔːˈtel] (*pt* & *pp* **-told**) *vt* predecir.

forever [fəˈrevəʳ] *adv* **-1.** [eternally] para siempre. **-2.** *inf* [incessantly] siempre, continuamente.

forewarn [fɔːˈwɔːn] *vt* prevenir.

foreword ['fɔːwɜːd] *n* prefacio *m*.

forfeit ['fɔːfɪt] ◇ *n* precio *m*; [in game] prenda *f*. ◇ *vt* renunciar, perder.

forgave [fəˈgeɪv] *pt* → **forgive**.

forge [fɔːdʒ] ◇ *n* fragua *f*. ◇ *vt* **-1.** [gen] fraguar. **-2.** [falsify] falsificar. ◆ **forge ahead** *vi* hacer grandes progresos.

forger ['fɔːdʒəʳ] *n* falsificador *m*, -ra *f*.

forgery ['fɔːdʒərɪ] *n* falsificación *f*.

forget [fəˈget] (*pt* **-got**, *pp* **-gotten**) ◇ *vt*: to ~ (to do sthg) olvidar (hacer algo). ◇ *vi*: to ~ (about sthg) olvidarse (de algo).

forgetful [fəˈgetfʊl] *adj* olvidadizo(za).

forget-me-not *n* nomeolvides *m inv*.

forgive [fəˈgɪv] (*pt* **-gave**, *pp* **-given**) *vt*: to ~ sb (for sthg/for doing sthg) perdonar a alguien (algo/por haber hecho algo).

forgiveness [fəˈgɪvnɪs] *n* perdón *m*.

forgo [fɔːˈgəʊ] (*pt* **-went**, *pp* **-gone** [-ˈgɒn]) *vt* sacrificar, renunciar a.

forgot [fəˈgɒt] *pt* → **forget**.

forgotten [fəˈgɒtn] *pp* → **forget**.

fork [fɔːk] ◇ *n* **-1.** [for food] tenedor *m*. **-2.** [for gardening] horca *f*. **-3.** [in road etc] bifurcación *f*. ◇ *vi* bifurcarse. ◆ **fork out** *inf vi*: to ~ out for sthg soltar pelas para algo.

forklift truck ['fɔːklɪft-] *n* carretilla *f* elevadora.

forlorn [fəˈlɔːn] *adj* **-1.** [person, expression] consternado(da). **-2.** [place, landscape] desolado(da). **-3.** [hope, attempt] desesperado(da).

form [fɔːm] ◇ *n* **-1.** [shape, type] forma *f*; **in the** ~ **of** en forma de. **-2.** [fitness]: **on** ~ Br, **in** ~ Am en forma; **off** ~ en baja forma. **-3.** [document] impreso *m*, formulario *m*. **-4.** [figure - of person] figura *f*. **-5.** Br [class] clase *f*. ◇ *vt* formar; [plan] concebir; [impression, idea] formarse. ◇ *vi* formarse.

formal ['fɔːml] *adj* **-1.** [gen] formal;

[education] convencional. **-2.** [clothes, wedding, party] de etiqueta.

formality [fɔː'mælətɪ] *n* formalidad *f*.

format ['fɔːmæt] ◇ *n* [gen & COMPUT] formato *m*; [of meeting] plan *m*. ◇ *vt* COMPUT formatear.

formation [fɔː'meɪʃn] *n* formación *f*; [of ideas, plans] creación *f*.

formative ['fɔːmətɪv] *adj* formativo(va).

former ['fɔːmər] ◇ *adj* **-1.** [previous] antiguo(gua); **in ~ times** antiguamente. **-2.** [first of two] primero(ra). ◇ *n*: **the ~** el primero (la primera)/los primeros (las primeras).

formerly ['fɔːməlɪ] *adv* antiguamente.

formidable ['fɔːmɪdəbl] *adj* **-1.** [frightening] imponente, temible. **-2.** [impressive] formidable.

formula ['fɔːmjʊlə] (*pl* **-as** OR **-ae** [-iː]) *n* fórmula *f*.

formulate ['fɔːmjʊleɪt] *vt* formular.

forsake [fə'seɪk] (*pt* **forsook**, *pp* **forsaken**) *vt literary* abandonar.

forsaken [fə'seɪkn] *adj* abandonado(da).

forsook [fə'sʊk] *pt* → **forsake**.

fort [fɔːt] *n* fuerte *m*, fortaleza *f*.

forte ['fɔːtɪ] *n* fuerte *m*.

forth [fɔːθ] *adv literary* **-1.** [outwards, onwards] hacia adelante. **-2.** [into future]: **from that day ~** desde aquel día en adelante.

forthcoming [fɔːθ'kʌmɪŋ] *adj* **-1.** [election, book, events] próximo(ma). **-2.** [person] abierto(ta), amable.

forthright ['fɔːθraɪt] *adj* [person, manner, opinions] directo(ta), franco(ca); [opposition] rotundo(da).

forthwith [ˌfɔːθ'wɪθ] *adv fml* inmediatamente.

fortified wine ['fɔːtɪfaɪd-] *n* vino *m* licoroso.

fortify ['fɔːtɪfaɪ] *vt* **-1.** MIL fortificar. **-2.** [person, resolve] fortalecer.

fortnight ['fɔːtnaɪt] *n* quincena *f*.

fortnightly ['fɔːt,naɪtlɪ] ◇ *adj* quincenal. ◇ *adv* quincenalmente.

fortress ['fɔːtrɪs] *n* fortaleza *f*.

fortunate ['fɔːtʃnət] *adj* afortunado(da).

fortunately ['fɔːtʃnətlɪ] *adv* afortunadamente.

fortune ['fɔːtʃuːn] *n* **-1.** [money, luck] fortuna *f*. **-2.** [future]: **to tell sb's ~** decir a alguien la buenaventura.

fortune-teller [-,telər] *n* adivino *m*, -na *f*.

forty ['fɔːtɪ] *num* cuarenta; *see also* **sixty**.

forum ['fɔːrəm] (*pl* **-s**) *n lit* & *fig* foro *m*.

forward ['fɔːwəd] ◇ *adj* **-1.** [towards front - movement] hacia adelante; [near front - position etc] delantero(ra). **-2.** [towards future]: **~ planning** planificación *f* anticipada. **-3.** [advanced]: **we're (no) further ~** (no) hemos adelantado (nada). **-4.** [impudent] atrevido(da). ◇ *adv* **-1.** [ahead] hacia adelante; **to go** OR **move ~** avanzar. **-2.** [in time]: **to bring sthg ~** adelantar algo. ◇ *n* SPORT delantero *m*, -ra *f*. ◇ *vt* [send on] remitir; **"please ~"** "remítase al destinatario".

forwarding address ['fɔːwədɪŋ-] *n* nueva dirección *f* para reenvío de correo.

forwards ['fɔːwədz] *adv* = **forward**.

forwent [fɔː'went] *pt* → **forgo**.

fossil ['fɒsl] *n* fósil *m*.

foster ['fɒstər] *vt* **-1.** [child] acoger. **-2.** [idea, arts, relations] promover.

foster child *n* menor *m* y *f* en régimen de acogimiento familiar.

foster parents *npl* familia *f* de acogida.

fought [fɔːt] *pt* & *pp* → **fight**.

foul [faʊl] ◇ *adj* **-1.** [unclean - smell] fétido(da); [- taste] asqueroso(sa); [- water, language] sucio(cia). **-2.** [very unpleasant] horrible. ◇ *n* falta *f*. ◇ *vt* **-1.** [make dirty] ensuciar. **-2.** SPORT cometer una falta contra.

found [faʊnd] ◇ *pt* & *pp* → **find**. ◇ *vt*: **to ~ sthg (on)** fundar algo (en).

foundation [faʊn'deɪʃn] *n* **-1.** [organization, act of establishing] fundación *f*. **-2.** [basis] fundamento *m*, base *f*. **-3.** [make-up]: **~ (cream)** crema *f* base.
◆ **foundations** *npl* CONSTR cimientos *mpl*.

founder ['faʊndər] ◇ *n* fundador *m*, -ra *f*. ◇ *vi lit* & *fig* hundirse, irse a pique.

foundry ['faʊndrɪ] *n* fundición *f*.

fountain ['faʊntɪn] *n* **-1.** [structure] fuente *f*. **-2.** [jet] chorro *m*.

fountain pen *n* pluma (*f*) estilográfica *f*.

four [fɔːr] *num* cuatro; **on all ~s** a gatas; *see also* **six**.

four-letter word *n* palabrota *f*, taco *m*.

four-poster (bed) *n* cama *f* de columnas.

foursome ['fɔːsəm] *n* grupo *m* de cuatro personas.

fourteen [ˌfɔː'tiːn] *num* catorce; *see also* **six**.

fourth [fɔːθ] *num* cuarto(ta); *see also* **sixth**.

Fourth of July n: the ~ el cuatro de julio, día de la independencia estadounidense.

four-wheel drive n tracción f a cuatro ruedas.

fowl [faʊl] (pl inv OR **-s**) n ave f de corral.

fox [fɒks] ◇ n zorro m. ◇ vt [perplex] dejar perplejo(ja).

foxglove ['fɒksɡlʌv] n dedalera f.

foyer ['fɔɪeɪ] n vestíbulo m.

fracas ['fræka:, Am 'freɪkəs] (Br pl inv, Am pl **fracases**) n fml riña f, gresca f.

fraction ['frækʃn] n **-1.** MATH quebrado m, fracción f. **-2.** [small part] fracción f.

fractionally ['frækʃnəlɪ] adv ligeramente.

fracture ['fræktʃər] ◇ n fractura f. ◇ vt fracturar.

fragile ['frædʒaɪl] adj frágil.

fragment ['fræɡmənt] n [of glass, text] fragmento m; [of paper, plastic] trozo m.

fragrance ['freɪɡrəns] n fragancia f.

fragrant ['freɪɡrənt] adj fragante.

frail [freɪl] adj frágil.

frame [freɪm] ◇ n **-1.** [of picture, door] marco m; [of glasses] montura f; [of chair, bed] armadura f; [of bicycle] cuadro m; [of boat] armazón m o f. **-2.** [physique] cuerpo m. ◇ vt **-1.** [put in a frame] enmarcar. **-2.** [express] formular, expresar. **-3.** inf [set up] tender una trampa a, amañar la culpabilidad de.

frame of mind n estado m de ánimo.

framework ['freɪmwɜːk] n **-1.** [physical structure] armazón m o f, esqueleto m. **-2.** [basis] marco m.

France [frɑːns] n Francia.

franchise ['fræntʃaɪz] n **-1.** POL sufragio m, derecho m de voto. **-2.** COMM concesión f, licencia f exclusiva.

frank [fræŋk] ◇ adj franco(ca). ◇ vt franquear.

frankly ['fræŋklɪ] adv francamente.

frantic ['fræntɪk] adj frenético(ca).

fraternity [frə'tɜːnətɪ] n **-1.** fml [community] cofradía f. **-2.** [in American university] club m de estudiantes. **-3.** (U) fml [friendship] fraternidad f.

fraternize, -ise ['frætənaɪz] vi: to ~ (with) fraternizar (con).

fraud [frɔːd] n **-1.** (U) [deceit] fraude m. **-2.** pej [impostor] farsante m y f.

fraught [frɔːt] adj **-1.** [full]: ~ with lleno(na) OR cargado(da) de. **-2.** Br [frantic] tenso(sa).

fray [freɪ] ◇ vt fig [temper, nerves] crispar, poner de punta. ◇ vi **-1.** [sleeve, cuff] deshilacharse. **-2.** fig [temper,

nerves] crisparse. ◇ n literary: to enter the ~ saltar a la palestra.

frayed [freɪd] adj [sleeve, cuff] deshilachado(da).

freak [friːk] ◇ adj imprevisible. ◇ n **-1.** [strange creature - in appearance] monstruo m; [- in behaviour] estrafalario m, -ria f. **-2.** [unusual event] anormalidad f. **-3.** inf [fanatic: **film/fitness** ~ fanático m, -ca f del cine/ejercicio. ◆ **freak out** inf vi flipar, alucinar.

freckle ['frekl] n peca f.

free [friː] (compar **freer**, superl **freest**, pt & pp **freed**) ◇ adj **-1.** [gen]: ~ (from OR of) libre (de); **to be** ~ **to do sthg** ser libre de hacer algo; **feel** ~! ¡adelante!, ¡cómo no!; **to set** ~ liberar. **-2.** [not paid for] gratis (inv), gratuito(ta); ~ **of charge** gratis (inv). **-3.** [unattached] suelto(ta). **-4.** [generous]: **to be** ~ **with sthg** no regatear algo. ◇ adv **-1.** [without payment]: **(for)** ~ gratis. **-2.** [unrestricted] libremente. **-3.** [loose]: **to pull/cut sthg** ~ soltar algo tirando/cortando. ◇ vt **-1.** [release] liberar, libertar; **to** ~ **sb of sthg** librar a alguien de algo. **-2.** [make available] dejar libre. **-3.** [extricate - person] rescatar; [- one's arm, oneself] soltar.

freedom ['friːdəm] n libertad f; ~ **from** indemnidad f ante OR de.

freefone ['friːfəʊn] n (U) Br teléfono m OR número m gratuito.

free-for-all n refriega f.

free gift n obsequio m.

freehand ['friːhænd] adj & adv a pulso.

freehold ['friːhəʊld] n propiedad f absoluta.

free house n bar no controlado por una compañía cervecera.

free kick n tiro m libre.

freelance ['friːlɑːns] ◇ adj autónomo(ma). ◇ adv por libre. ◇ n (trabajador m, -ra f) autónomo m, -ma f.

freely ['friːlɪ] adv **-1.** [readily - admit, confess] sin reparos; [- available] fácilmente. **-2.** [openly] abiertamente, francamente. **-3.** [without restrictions] libremente. **-4.** [generously] liberalmente.

Freemason ['friː,meɪsn] n francmasón m, -ona f.

freephone ['friːfəʊn] = **freefone.**

freepost ['friːpəʊst] n franqueo m pagado.

free-range adj de granja.

freestyle ['friːstaɪl] n [in swimming] estilo m libre.

free trade n libre cambio m.

freeway ['fri:weɪ] *n Am* autopista *f*.

freewheel [,fri:'wi:l] *vi* [on bicycle] andar sin pedalear; [in car] ir en punto muerto.

free will *n* libre albedrío *m*; **to do sthg of one's own ~** hacer algo por voluntad propia.

freeze [fri:z] (*pt* **froze**, *pp* **frozen**) ◇ *vt* **-1.** [gen] helar. **-2.** [food, wages, prices] congelar. **-3.** [assets] bloquear. ◇ *vi* [gen] helarse. ◇ *v impers* METEOR helar. ◇ *n* **-1.** [cold weather] helada *f*. **-2.** [of wages, prices] congelación *f*.

freeze-dried [-'draɪd] *adj* liofilizado(da).

freezer ['fri:zər] *n* congelador *m*.

freezing ['fri:zɪŋ] ◇ *adj* helado(da); **it's ~ in here** hace un frío espantoso aquí. ◇ *n* = **freezing point**.

freezing point *n* punto *m* de congelación.

freight [freɪt] *n* (*U*) [goods] mercancías *fpl*, flete *m*.

freight train *n* (tren *m* de) mercancías *m inv*.

French [frentʃ] ◇ *adj* francés(esa). ◇ *n* [language] francés *m*. ◇ *npl*: **the ~** los franceses.

French bean *n* judía *f* verde.

French bread *n* (*U*) [in UK] pan *m* de barra.

French dressing *n* [in UK] [vinaigrette] vinagreta *f*; [in US] ≈ salsa *f* rosa.

French fries *npl* patatas *fpl* fritas.

Frenchman ['frentʃmən] (*pl* **-men** [-mən]) *n* francés *m*.

French stick *n Br* barra *f* de pan.

French windows *npl* puertaventanas *fpl*.

Frenchwoman ['frentʃ,wumən] (*pl* **-women** [-,wɪmɪn]) *n* francesa *f*.

frenetic [frə'netɪk] *adj* frenético(ca).

frenzy ['frenzɪ] *n* frenesí *m*.

frequency ['fri:kwənsɪ] *n* frecuencia *f*.

frequent [*adj* 'fri:kwənt, *vb* frɪ'kwent] ◇ *adj* frecuente. ◇ *vt* frecuentar.

frequently ['fri:kwəntlɪ] *adv* a menudo.

fresh [freʃ] *adj* **-1.** [gen] fresco(ca); [flavour, taste] refrescante. **-2.** [bread] del día. **-3.** [not canned] natural. **-4.** [water] dulce. **-5.** [pot of tea, fighting, approach] nuevo(va). **-6.** [bright and pleasant] alegre.

freshen ['freʃn] ◇ *vt* [air] refrescar. ◇ *vi* [wind] soplar más fuerte. ◆ **freshen up** *vi* [person] refrescarse, lavarse.

fresher ['freʃər] *n Br inf* estudiante *m y f* de primer año.

freshly ['freʃlɪ] *adv* recién.

freshman ['freʃmən] (*pl* **-men** [-mən]) *n* estudiante *m y f* de primer año.

freshness ['freʃnɪs] *n* (*U*) **-1.** [of food] buen estado *m*. **-2.** [originality] novedad *f*, originalidad *f*. **-3.** [brightness] pulcritud *f*. **-4.** [refreshing quality] frescor *m*. **-5.** [energy] vigor *m*.

freshwater ['freʃ,wɔːtər] *adj* de agua dulce.

fret [fret] *vi* preocuparse.

friar ['fraɪər] *n* fraile *m*.

friction ['frɪkʃn] *n* fricción *f*.

Friday ['fraɪdɪ] *n* viernes *m inv*; *see also* **Saturday**.

fridge [frɪdʒ] *n* nevera *f*.

fridge-freezer *n Br* nevera *f* congeladora.

fried [fraɪd] *adj* frito(ta).

friend [frend] *n* [close acquaintance] amigo *m*, **-ga** *f*; **to be ~s with sb** ser amigo de alguien; **to make ~s (with)** hacerse amigo (de), trabar amistad (con).

friendly ['frendlɪ] *adj* **-1.** [person] amable, simpático(ca); [attitude, manner, welcome] amistoso(sa); **to be ~ with sb** ser amigo de alguien. **-2.** [nation] amigo(ga). **-3.** [argument, game] amistoso(sa).

friendship ['frendʃɪp] *n* amistad *f*.

fries [fraɪz] = **French fries**.

frieze [fri:z] *n* friso *m*.

fright [fraɪt] *n* **-1.** [fear] miedo *m*; **to take ~** espantarse, asustarse. **-2.** [shock] susto *m*; **to give sb a ~** darle un susto a alguien.

frighten ['fraɪtn] *vt* asustar.

frightened ['fraɪtnd] *adj* asustado(da); **to be ~ of sthg/of doing sthg** tener miedo a algo/a hacer algo.

frightening ['fraɪtnɪŋ] *adj* aterrador(ra), espantoso(sa).

frightful ['fraɪtful] *adj* dated terrible.

frigid ['frɪdʒɪd] *adj* [sexually] frígido(da).

frill [frɪl] *n* **-1.** [decoration] volante *m*. **-2.** *inf* [extra] adorno *m*.

fringe [frɪndʒ] *n* **-1.** [decoration] flecos *mpl*. **-2.** *Br* [of hair] flequillo *m*. **-3.** [edge] periferia *f*. **-4.** [extreme] margen *m*. ◇ *vt* [edge] bordear.

fringe benefit *n* beneficio *m* complementario.

frisk [frɪsk] *vt* cachear, registrar.

frisky ['frɪskɪ] *adj inf* retozón(ona), juguetón(ona).

fritter ['frɪtər] *n* buñuelo *m*. ◆ **fritter away** *vt sep*: **to ~ money/time away on sthg** malgastar dinero/tiempo en algo.

frivolous ['frɪvələs] *adj* frívolo(la).

frizzy ['frɪzɪ] adj crespo(pa), ensortijado(da).

fro [frəʊ] adv → to.

frock [frɒk] n dated vestido m.

frog [frɒg] n [animal] rana f.

frogman ['frɒgmən] (pl -men) n hombre-rana m.

frogmen ['frɒgmən] pl → frogman.

frolic ['frɒlɪk] (pt & pp -ked, cont -king) vi retozar, triscar.

from [weak form frəm, strong form frɒm] prep -1. [indicating source, origin, removal] de; **where are you ~?** ¿de dónde eres?; **I got a letter ~ her today** hoy me ha llegado una carta suya; **a flight ~ Paris** un vuelo de París; **to translate ~ Spanish into English** traducir del español al inglés; **he's not back ~ work yet** no ha vuelto del trabajo aún; **to take sthg away ~ sb** quitarle algo a alguien. -2. [indicating a deduction]: **take 15 (away) ~ 19** quita 15 a 19; **to deduct sthg ~ sthg** deducir OR descontar algo de algo. -3. [indicating escape, separation] de; **he ran away ~ home** huyó de casa. -4. [indicating position] desde; **seen ~ above/below** visto desde arriba/abajo; **a light bulb hung ~ the ceiling** una bombilla colgaba del techo. -5. [indicating distance] de; **it's 60 km ~ here** está a 60 kms. de aquí. -6. [indicating material object is made out of] de; **it's made ~ wood/plastic** está hecho de madera/plástico. -7. [starting at a particular time] desde; **closed ~ 1 pm to 2 pm** cerrado de 13h a 14h; **~ the moment I saw him** desde el momento en que lo vi. -8. [indicating difference, change] de; **to be different ~** ser diferente de; **~ ... to ...** de ... a; **the price went up ~ £100 to £150** el precio subió de 100 a 150 libras. -9. [because of, as a result of] de; **to die ~ cold** morir de frío; **to suffer ~ cold/hunger** padecer frío/hambre. -10. [on the evidence of] por; **to speak ~ personal experience** hablar por propia experiencia. -11. [indicating lowest amount]: **prices range ~ £5 to £500** los precios oscilan entre 5 y 500 libras; **it could take anything ~ 15 to 20 weeks** podría llevar de 15 a 20 semanas.

front [frʌnt] ◇ n -1. [gen] parte f delantera; [- of house] fachada f. -2. METEOR, MIL & POL frente m. -3. [on coast]: **(sea) ~** paseo m marítimo. -4. [outward appearance] fachada f. ◇ adj [gen] delantero(ra); [page] primero(ra). ◆**in front**

adv -1. [further forward] delante. -2. [winning] en cabeza. ◆**in front of** prep delante de.

frontbench [,frʌnt'bentʃ] n Br en la Cámara de los Comunes, cada una de las dos filas de escaños ocupadas respectivamente por los ministros del Gobierno y los principales líderes de la oposición mayoritaria.

front door n puerta f principal.

frontier ['frʌn,tɪəʳ, Am frʌn'tɪər] n lit & fig frontera f.

front man n -1. [of group] portavoz m y f. -2. [of programme] presentador m.

front room n sala f de estar.

front-runner n favorito m, -ta f.

front-wheel drive n [vehicle] vehículo m de tracción delantera.

frost [frɒst] n -1. [layer of ice] escarcha f. -2. [weather] helada f.

frostbite ['frɒstbaɪt] n (U) congelación f MED.

frosted ['frɒstɪd] adj -1. [glass] esmerilado(da). -2. Am CULIN escarchado(da).

frosty ['frɒstɪ] adj -1. [very cold] de helada. -2. [covered with frost] escarchado(da). -3. fig [unfriendly] glacial.

froth [frɒθ] ◇ n espuma f. ◇ vi hacer espuma.

frown [fraʊn] vi fruncir el ceño. ◆**frown (up)on** vt fus desaprobar.

froze [frəʊz] pt → freeze.

frozen [frəʊzn] ◇ pp → freeze. ◇ adj -1. [gen] helado(da). -2. [preserved] congelado(da).

frugal ['fru:gl] adj frugal.

fruit [fru:t] (pl inv OR **fruits**) n -1. [food] fruta f. -2. [result] fruto m.

fruitcake ['fru:tkeɪk] n pastel m de frutas.

fruiterer ['fru:tərəʳ] n Br frutero m, -ra f; **~'s (shop)** frutería f.

fruitful ['fru:tfʊl] adj [successful] fructífero(ra).

fruition [fru:'ɪʃn] n: **to come to ~** [plan] realizarse; [hope] cumplirse.

fruit juice n zumo m de fruta.

fruitless ['fru:tlɪs] adj infructuoso(sa).

fruit machine n Br máquina f tragaperras.

fruit salad n macedonia f (de frutas).

frumpy ['frʌmpɪ] adj chapado(da) a la antigua.

frustrate [frʌ'streɪt] vt frustrar.

frustrated [frʌ'streɪtɪd] adj frustrado(da).

frustration [frʌ'streɪʃn] n frustración f.

fry [fraɪ] ◇ vt [food] freír. ◇ vi [food] freírse.

frying pan ['fraɪɪŋ-] n sartén f.

ft. abbr of **foot, feet**.

fuck [fʌk] vulg vt & vi joder, follar, chingar Amer. ◆ **fuck off** vi vulg: ~ **off!** ¡vete a tomar por culo!

fudge [fʌdʒ] n (U) [sweet] dulce de azúcar, leche y mantequilla.

fuel [fjʊəl] ◇ n combustible m. ◇ vt -1. [supply with fuel] alimentar. -2. [increase] agravar.

fuel tank n depósito m de gasolina.

fugitive ['fjuːdʒətɪv] n fugitivo m, -va f.

fulfil, fulfill Am [fʊl'fɪl] vt [promise, duty, threat] cumplir; [hope, ambition] realizar, satisfacer; [obligation] cumplir con; [role] desempeñar; [requirement] satisfacer.

fulfilment, fulfillment Am [fʊl'fɪlmənt] n -1. [satisfaction] satisfacción f, realización f (de uno mismo). -2. [of promise, duty, threat] cumplimiento m; [of hope, ambition] realización f; [of role] desempeño m; [of requirement] satisfacción f.

full [fʊl] ◇ adj -1. [filled]: ~ **(of)** lleno(na) (de); **I'm** ~! [after meal] ¡no puedo más! -2. [complete - recovery, employment, control] pleno(na); [- name, price, fare] completo(ta); [- explanation, information] detallado(da); [- member, professor] numerario(ria). -3. [maximum - volume, power etc] máximo(ma). -4. [plump] grueso(sa). -5. [wide] holgado(da), amplio(plia). ◇ adv [very]: **to know sthg** ~ **well** saber algo perfectamente. ◇ n: **in** ~ íntegramente.

full-blown [-'bləʊn] adj [gen] auténtico(ca); [AIDS] desarrollado(da).

full board n pensión f completa.

full-fledged Am = **fully-fledged**.

full moon n luna f llena.

full-scale adj -1. [life-size] de tamaño natural. -2. [complete] a gran escala.

full stop n punto m.

full time n Br SPORT final m del (tiempo reglamentario del) partido. ◆ **full-time** ◇ adj de jornada completa. ◇ adv a tiempo completo.

full up adj lleno(na).

fully ['fʊlɪ] adv -1. [completely] completamente. -2. [thoroughly] detalladamente.

fully-fledged Br, **full-fledged** Am [-'fledʒd] adj fig hecho(cha) y derecho(cha); [member] de pleno derecho.

fulsome ['fʊlsəm] adj exagerado(da).

fumble ['fʌmbl] vi hurgar; **to** ~ **for sthg** [for key, light switch] buscar algo a tientas; [for words] buscar algo titubeando.

fume [fjuːm] vi [with anger] rabiar. ◆ **fumes** npl humo m.

fumigate ['fjuːmɪgeɪt] vt fumigar.

fun [fʌn] n (U) -1. [pleasure, amusement] diversión f; **to have** ~ divertirse, pasarlo bien; **have** ~! ¡que te diviértas!; **for** ~, **for the** ~ **of it** por diversión. -2. [playfulness]: **he's full of** ~ le encanta todo lo que sea diversión. -3. [at sb else's expense]: **to make** ~ **of sb, to poke** ~ **at sb** reírse OR burlarse de alguien.

function ['fʌŋkʃn] ◇ n -1. [gen & MATH] función f. -2. [way of working] funcionamiento m. -3. [formal social event] acto m, ceremonia f. ◇ vi funcionar; **to** ~ **as** hacer de, actuar como.

functional ['fʌŋkʃnəl] adj -1. [practical] funcional. -2. [operational] en funcionamiento.

fund [fʌnd] ◇ n fondo m. ◇ vt financiar. ◆ **funds** npl fondos mpl.

fundamental [,fʌndə'mentl] adj: ~ **(to)** fundamental (para).

funding ['fʌndɪŋ] n financiación f.

funeral ['fjuːnərəl] n funeral m.

funeral parlour n funeraria f.

funfair ['fʌnfeəʳ] n parque m de atracciones.

fungus ['fʌŋgəs] (pl -**gi** [-gaɪ] OR -**guses**) n hongo m.

funnel ['fʌnl] n -1. [for pouring] embudo m. -2. [on ship] chimenea f.

funny ['fʌnɪ] adj -1. [amusing] divertido(da), gracioso(sa). -2. [odd] raro(ra). -3. [ill] pachucho(cha).

fur [fɜːʳ] n -1. [on animal] pelaje m, pelo m. -2. [garment] (prenda f de) piel f.

fur coat n abrigo m de OR pieles.

furious ['fjʊərɪəs] adj -1. [very angry] furioso(sa). -2. [frantic] frenético(ca).

furlong ['fɜːlɒŋ] n 201,17 metros.

furnace ['fɜːnɪs] n horno m.

furnish ['fɜːnɪʃ] vt -1. [fit out] amueblar. -2. fml [provide - goods, explanation] proveer; [- proof] aducir; **to** ~ **sb with sthg** proporcionar algo a alguien.

furnished ['fɜːnɪʃt] adj amueblado(da).

furnishings ['fɜːnɪʃɪŋz] npl mobiliario m.

furniture ['fɜːnɪtʃəʳ] n (U) muebles mpl, mobiliario m; **a piece of** ~ un mueble.

furrow ['fʌrəʊ] n lit & fig surco m.

furry ['fɜːrɪ] adj peludo(da).

further ['fɜːðəʳ] ◇ compar → **far**. ◇ adv -1. [in distance] más lejos; **how much** ~ **is it?** ¿cuánto queda (de camino)?; ~ **on** más adelante. -2. [in degree, extent, time] más; ~ **on/back** más adelante/atrás. **-3.** [in addition] además. ◇ *adj* otro(tra); **until** ~ **notice** hasta nuevo aviso. ◇ *vt* promover, fomentar.

further education *n* Br estudios postescolares no universitarios.

furthermore [,fɜːðə'mɔːr] *adv* lo que es más.

furthest ['fɜːðɪst] ◇ *superl* → **far**. ◇ *adj* **-1.** [in distance] más lejano(na). **-2.** [greatest - in degree, extent] extremo(ma). ◇ *adv* **-1.** [in distance] más lejos. **-2.** [to greatest degree, extent] más.

furtive ['fɜːtɪv] *adj* furtivo(va).

fury ['fjʊərɪ] *n* furia *f*.

fuse *esp* Br, **fuze** Am [fjuːz] ◇ *n* **-1.** ELEC fusible *m*, plomo *m*. **-2.** [of bomb, firework] mecha *f*. ◇ *vt* fundir. ◇ *vi* [gen & ELEC] fundirse.

fuse-box *n* caja *f* de fusibles.

fused [fjuːzd] *adj* [fitted with a fuse] con fusible.

fuselage ['fjuːzəlɑːʒ] *n* fuselaje *m*.

fuss [fʌs] ◇ *n* (*U*) **-1.** [excitement, anxiety] jaleo *m*; **to make a** ~ armar un escándalo. **-2.** [complaints] protestas *fpl*. ◇ *vi* apurarse, angustiarse.

fussy ['fʌsɪ] *adj* **-1.** [fastidious] quisquilloso(sa). **-2.** [over-decorated] recargado(da).

futile ['fjuːtaɪl] *adj* inútil, vano(na).

futon ['fuːtɒn] *n* futón *m*.

future ['fjuːtʃər] ◇ *n* futuro *m*; **in** ~ de ahora en adelante; **in the** ~ en el futuro; ~ **(tense)** futuro *m*. ◇ *adj* futuro(ra).

fuze Am = **fuse**.

fuzzy ['fʌzɪ] *adj* **-1.** [hair] rizado(da), ensortijado(da). **-2.** [photo, image] borroso(sa).

G

g¹ (*pl* **g's** OR **gs**), **G** (*pl* **G's** OR **Gs**) [dʒiː] *n* [letter] g *f*, G *f*. ◆**G** *n* **-1.** MUS sol *m*. **-2.** (*abbr of* **good**) B.

g² *n* (*abbr of* **gram**) g. *m*.

gab [gæb] *n* → **gift**.

gabble ['gæbl] ◇ *vt & vi* farfullar, balbucir. ◇ *n* farfulleo *m*.

gable ['geɪbl] *n* aguilón *m*.

gadget ['gædʒɪt] *n* artilugio *m*.

Gaelic ['geɪlɪk] *n* [language] gaélico *m*.

gaffe [gæf] *n* metedura *f* de pata.

gag [gæg] ◇ *n* **-1.** [for mouth] mordaza *f*. **-2.** *inf* [joke] chiste *m*. ◇ *vt* amordazar.

gage Am = **gauge**.

gaiety ['geɪətɪ] *n* alegría *f*, regocijo *m*.

gaily ['geɪlɪ] *adv* alegremente.

gain [geɪn] ◇ *n* **-1.** [profit] beneficio *m*, ganancia *f*. **-2.** [improvement] mejora *f*. ◇ *vt* [gen] ganar. ◇ *vi* **-1.** [advance]: **to** ~ **in sthg** ganar algo. **-2.** [benefit]: **to** ~ **(from** OR **by)** beneficiarse (de). **-3.** [watch, clock] adelantarse. ◆**gain on** *vt fus* ganar terreno a.

gait [geɪt] *n* forma *f* de andar.

gal. *abbr of* **gallon**.

gala ['gɑːlə] *n* [celebration] fiesta *f*.

galaxy ['gæləksɪ] *n* galaxia *f*.

gale [geɪl] *n* vendaval *m*.

gall [gɔːl] *n* [nerve]: **to have the** ~ **to do sthg** tener el descaro de hacer algo.

gallant [*sense 1* 'gælənt, *sense 2* gə'lænt, 'gælənt] *adj* **-1.** [courageous] valiente, valeroso(sa). **-2.** [polite to women] galante.

gall bladder *n* vesícula *f* biliar.

gallery ['gælərɪ] *n* **-1.** [for art] galería *f*. **-2.** [in courtroom, parliament] tribuna *f*. **-3.** [in theatre] paraíso *m*.

galley ['gælɪ] (*pl* **galleys**) *n* **-1.** [ship] galera *f*. **-2.** [kitchen] cocina *f*.

galling ['gɔːlɪŋ] *adj* indignante.

gallivant [,gælɪ'vænt] *vi inf* andar por ahí holgazaneando.

gallon ['gælən] *n* = 4,546 litros, galón *m*.

gallop ['gæləp] ◇ *n* galope *m*. ◇ *vi lit & fig* galopar.

gallows ['gæləʊz] (*pl inv*) *n* horca *f*.

gallstone ['gɔːlstəʊn] *n* cálculo *m* biliar.

galore [gə'lɔːr] *adj* en abundancia.

galvanize, -ise ['gælvənaɪz] *vt* **-1.** TECH galvanizar. **-2.** [impel]: **to** ~ **sb into action** impulsar a alguien a la acción.

gambit ['gæmbɪt] *n* táctica *f*.

gamble ['gæmbl] ◇ *n* [calculated risk] riesgo *m*, empresa *f* arriesgada. ◇ *vi* **-1.** [bet] jugar; **to** ~ **on** [race etc] apostar a; [stock exchange] jugar a. **-2.** [take risk]: **to** ~ **on** contar de antemano con que.

gambler ['gæmblər] *n* jugador *m*, -ra *f*.

gambling ['gæmblɪŋ] *n* (*U*) juego *m*.

game [geɪm] ◇ *n* **-1.** [gen] juego *m*. **-2.** [of football, rugby etc] partido *m*; [of snooker, chess, cards] partida *f*. **-3.** [hunted animals] caza *f*. ◇ *adj* **-1.** [brave] valiente. **-2.** [willing]: ~ **(for sthg/to do sthg)** dispuesto(ta) (a algo/a hacer algo). ◆ **games** ◇ *n* (U) [at school] deportes *mpl*. ◇ *npl* [sporting contest] juegos *mpl*.

gamekeeper ['geɪm,kiːpəʳ] *n* guarda *m* de caza.

game reserve *n* coto *m* de caza.

gammon ['gæmən] *n* jamón *m*.

gamut ['gæmət] *n* gama *f*.

gang [gæŋ] *n* **-1.** [of criminals] banda *f*. **-2.** [of young people] pandilla *f*. ◆ **gang up** *vi inf*: to ~ **up (on sb)** confabularse (contra alguien).

gangland ['gæŋlænd] *n* (U) bajos fondos *mpl*, mundo *m* del hampa.

gangrene ['gæŋgriːn] *n* gangrena *f*.

gangster ['gæŋstəʳ] *n* gángster *m*.

gangway ['gæŋweɪ] *n Br* [aisle] pasillo *m*.

gantry ['gæntrɪ] *n* pórtico *m* (*para grúas*).

gaol [dʒeɪl] *Br* = **jail**.

gap [gæp] *n* **-1.** [empty space] hueco *m*; [in traffic, trees, clouds] claro *m*; [in text] espacio *m* en blanco. **-2.** [interval] intervalo *m*. **-3.** *fig* [in knowledge, report] laguna *f*. **-4.** *fig* [great difference] desfase *m*.

gape [geɪp] *vi* **-1.** [person] mirar boquiabierto(ta). **-2.** [hole, wound] estar muy abierto(ta).

gaping ['geɪpɪŋ] *adj* **-1.** [open-mouthed] boquiabierto(ta). **-2.** [wide-open] abierto(ta).

garage [*Br* 'gærɑːʒ, 'gærɪdʒ, *Am* gə'rɑːʒ] *n* **-1.** [for keeping car] garaje *m*. **-2.** *Br* [for fuel] gasolinera *f*. **-3.** [for car repair] taller *m*. **-4.** *Br* [for selling cars] concesionario *m* de automóviles.

garbage ['gɑːbɪdʒ] *n* (U) **-1.** [refuse] basura *f*. **-2.** *inf* [nonsense] tonterías *fpl*.

garbage can *n Am* cubo *m* de la basura.

garbage truck *n Am* camión *m* de la basura.

garbled ['gɑːbld] *adj* confuso(sa).

garden ['gɑːdn] *n* jardín *m*.

garden centre *n* centro *m* de jardinería.

gardener ['gɑːdnəʳ] *n* jardinero *m*, -ra *f*.

gardening ['gɑːdnɪŋ] *n* jardinería *f*.

gargle ['gɑːgl] *vi* hacer gárgaras.

gargoyle ['gɑːgɔɪl] *n* gárgola *f*.

garish ['geərɪʃ] *adj* chillón(ona).

garland ['gɑːlənd] *n* guirnalda *f*.

garlic ['gɑːlɪk] *n* ajo *m*.

garlic bread *n* pan *m* de ajo.

garment ['gɑːmənt] *n* prenda *f* (de vestir).

garnish ['gɑːnɪʃ] *vt* guarnecer.

garrison ['gærɪsn] *n* guarnición *f*.

garrulous ['gærələs] *adj* parlanchín(ina).

garter ['gɑːtəʳ] *n* **-1.** [band round leg] liga *f*. **-2.** *Am* [suspender] portaligas *m inv*.

gas [gæs] (*pl* **-es** OR **-ses**) ◇ *n* **-1.** CHEM gas *m*. **-2.** *Am* [petrol] gasolina *f*. ◇ *vt* asfixiar con gas.

gas cooker *n Br* cocina *f* de gas.

gas cylinder *n* bombona *f* de gas.

gas fire *n Br* estufa *f* de gas.

gas gauge *n Am* indicador *m* del nivel de gasolina.

gash [gæʃ] ◇ *n* raja *f*. ◇ *vt* rajar.

gasket ['gæskɪt] *n* junta *f*.

gasman ['gæsmæn] (*pl* **-men** [-men]) *n* hombre *m* del gas.

gas mask *n* máscara *f* antigás.

gas meter *n* contador *m* del gas.

gasoline ['gæsəliːn] *n Am* gasolina *f*.

gasp [gɑːsp] ◇ *n* resuello *m*. ◇ *vi* **-1.** [breathe quickly] resollar, jadear. **-2.** [in shock, surprise] ahogar un grito.

gas pedal *n Am* acelerador *m*.

gas station *n Am* gasolinera *f*, grifo *m* Amer.

gas stove = **gas cooker**.

gas tank *n Am* depósito *m* de gasolina.

gas tap *n* llave *f* del gas.

gastroenteritis ['gæstrəʊ,entə'raɪtɪs] *n* (U) gastroenteritis *f inv*.

gastronomy [gæs'trɒnəmɪ] *n* gastronomía *f*.

gasworks ['gæswɜːks] (*pl inv*) *n* fábrica *f* de gas.

gate [geɪt] *n* **-1.** [gen] puerta *f*; [metal] verja *f*. **-2.** SPORT [takings] taquilla *f*; [attendance] entrada *f*.

gâteau ['gætəʊ] (*pl* **-x** [-z]) *n Br* tarta *f* (con nata).

gatecrash ['geɪtkræʃ] *inf vi* colarse de gorra.

gateway ['geɪtweɪ] *n* [entrance] puerta *f*, pórtico *m*.

gather ['gæðəʳ] ◇ *vt* **-1.** [collect] recoger; to ~ **together** reunir. **-2.** [increase - speed, strength] ganar, cobrar. **-3.** [understand]: to ~ **(that)** sacar en conclusión que. **-4.** [cloth] fruncir. ◇ *vi* [people, animals] reunirse; [clouds] acumularse.

gathering ['gæðərɪŋ] *n* [meeting] reunión *f*.

gauche [gəʊʃ] *adj* torpe.

gaudy ['gɔːdɪ] *adj* chillón(ona), llamativo(va).

gauge, gage Am [geɪdʒ] ◇ n **-1.** [for fuel, temperature] indicador m; [for width of tube, wire] calibrador m. **-2.** [calibre] calibre m. **-3.** RAIL ancho m de vía. ◇ vt lit & fig calibrar.

gaunt [gɔːnt] adj **-1.** [person, face] enjuto(ta). **-2.** [building, landscape] adusto(ta).

gauntlet ['gɔːntlɪt] n guante m; **to run the ~ of** sth exponerse a algo; **to throw down the ~ (to** sb) arrojar el guante (a alguien).

gauze [gɔːz] n gasa f.

gave [geɪv] pt → **give**.

gawky ['gɔːkɪ] adj desgarbado(da).

gawp [gɔːp] vi: **to ~ (at** sth/sb) mirar boquiabierto(a) (algo/a alguien).

gay [geɪ] ◇ adj **-1.** [homosexual] gay, homosexual. **-2.** [cheerful, lively, bright] alegre. ◇ n gay m y f.

gaze [geɪz] ◇ n mirada f fija. ◇ vi: **to ~ (at** sth/sb) mirar fijamente (algo/a alguien).

gazelle [gə'zel] (pl inv OR **-s**) gacela f.

gazetteer [ˌgæzɪ'tɪər] n índice m geográfico.

gazump [gə'zʌmp] vt Br inf: **to ~** sb acordar vender una casa a alguien y luego vendérsela a otro a un precio más alto.

GB (abbr of **Great Britain**) n GB f.

GCE (abbr of **General Certificate of Education**) n **-1.** [O level] antiguo examen final de enseñanza secundaria en Gran Bretaña para alumnos de buen rendimiento escolar. **-2.** = **A level**.

GCSE (abbr of **General Certificate of Secondary Education**) n examen final de enseñanza secundaria en Gran Bretaña.

GDP (abbr of **gross domestic product**) n PIB m.

gear [gɪər] ◇ n **-1.** [mechanism] engranaje m. **-2.** [speed - of car, bicycle] marcha f; **in ~** con una marcha metida; **out of ~** en punto muerto. **-3.** (U) [equipment, clothes] equipo m. ◇ vt: **to ~** sth to orientar OR encaminar algo hacia. ◆ **gear up** vi: **to ~ up for** sth/to do sth hacer preparativos para algo/para hacer algo.

gearbox ['gɪəbɒks] n caja f de cambios.

gear lever, gear stick Br, **gear shift** Am n palanca f de cambios.

gear wheel n rueda f dentada.

geese [giːs] pl → **goose**.

gel [dʒel] ◇ n [for shower] gel m; [for hair] gomina f. ◇ vi **-1.** [thicken] aglutinarse. **-2.** [plan] cuajar; [idea, thought] tomar forma.

gelatin ['dʒelətɪn], **gelatine** [ˌdʒelə'tiːn] n gelatina f.

gelignite ['dʒelɪgnaɪt] n gelignita f.

gem [dʒem] n lit & fig joya f.

Gemini ['dʒemɪnaɪ] n Géminis m inv.

gender ['dʒendər] n género m.

gene [dʒiːn] n gen m, gen m.

general ['dʒenərəl] ◇ adj general. ◇ n general m. ◆ **in general** adv **-1.** [as a whole] en general. **-2.** [usually] por lo general.

general anaesthetic n anestesia f general.

general delivery n Am lista f de correos.

general election n elecciones fpl generales.

generalization [ˌdʒenərəlaɪ'zeɪʃn] n generalización f.

general knowledge n cultura f general.

generally ['dʒenərəlɪ] adv en general.

general practitioner n médico m, -ca f de cabecera.

general public n: **the ~** el gran público.

generate ['dʒenəreɪt] vt generar.

generation [ˌdʒenə'reɪʃn] n generación f.

generator ['dʒenəreɪtər] n generador m.

generosity [ˌdʒenə'rɒsətɪ] n generosidad f.

generous ['dʒenərəs] adj generoso(sa); [cut of clothes] amplio(plia).

genetic [dʒɪ'netɪk] adj genético(ca). ◆ **genetics** n (U) genética f.

Geneva [dʒɪ'niːvə] n Ginebra f.

genial ['dʒiːnjəl] adj cordial, afable.

genitals ['dʒenɪtlz] npl genitales mpl.

genius ['dʒiːnjəs] (pl **-es**) n genio m.

gent [dʒent] n inf caballero m. ◆ **gents** n Br [toilets] servicio m de caballeros.

genteel [dʒen'tiːl] adj fino(na), refinado(da).

gentle ['dʒentl] adj **-1.** [kind] tierno(na), dulce. **-2.** [breeze, movement, slope] suave. **-3.** [scolding] ligero(ra); [hint] sutil.

gentleman ['dʒentlmən] (pl [-mən] -men) n **-1.** [well-behaved man] caballero m. **-2.** [man] señor m, caballero m.

gently ['dʒentlɪ] adv **-1.** [kindly] dulcemente. **-2.** [softly, smoothly] suavemente. **-3.** [carefully] con cuidado.

gentry ['dʒentrɪ] n alta burguesía f.

genuine ['dʒenjuɪn] adj **-1.** [real] auténtico(ca). **-2.** [sincere] sincero(ra).

geography [dʒɪ'ɒgrəfɪ] n geografía f.

geology [dʒɪ'ɒlədʒɪ] n geología f.

geometric(al) [ˌdʒɪə'metrɪk(l)] *adj* geométrico(ca).

geometry [dʒɪ'ɒmətrɪ] *n* geometría *f.*

geranium [dʒɪ'reɪnjəm] (*pl* **-s**) *n* geranio *m.*

gerbil ['dʒɜːbɪl] *n* jerbo *m*, gerbo *m.*

geriatric [ˌdʒerɪ'ætrɪk] *adj* **-1.** [of old people] geriátrico(ca). **-2.** *pej* [very old, inefficient] anticuado(da).

germ [dʒɜːm] *n* BIOL & *fig* germen *m*; MED microbio *m.*

German ['dʒɜːmən] ◇ *adj* alemán(ana). ◇ *n* **-1.** [person] alemán *m*, -ana *f.* **-2.** [language] alemán *m.*

German measles *n* rubéola *f.*

Germany ['dʒɜːmənɪ] *n* Alemania.

germinate ['dʒɜːmɪneɪt] *vt & vi lit & fig* germinar.

gerund ['dʒerənd] *n* gerundio *m.*

gesticulate [dʒes'tɪkjʊleɪt] *vi* gesticular.

gesture ['dʒestʃər] ◇ *n* gesto *m.* ◇ *vi:* **to ~ to** OR **towards sb** hacer gestos a alguien.

get [get] (*Br pt & pp* **got**, *Am pt* **got**, *pp* **gotten**) ◇ *vt* **-1.** [cause to do]: **to ~ sb to do sthg** hacer que alguien haga algo; **I'll ~ my sister to help** le pediré a mi hermana que ayude. **-2.** [cause to be done]: **to ~ sthg done** mandar hacer algo; **have you got the car fixed yet?** ¿te han arreglado ya el coche? **-3.** [cause to become]: **to ~ sthg ready** preparar algo; **to ~ sb pregnant** dejar a alguien preñada. **-4.** [cause to move]: **can you ~ it through the gap?** ¿puedes meterlo por el hueco?; **to ~ sthg/sb out of sthg** conseguir sacar algo/a alguien de algo. **-5.** [bring, fetch] traer; **can I ~ you something to eat/drink?** ¿te traigo algo de comer/beber?; **I'll ~ my coat** voy a por el abrigo; **could you ~ me the boss, please?** [when phoning] póngame con el jefe. **-6.** [obtain] conseguir; **she got top marks** sacó las mejores notas. **-7.** [receive] recibir; **what did you ~ for your birthday?** ¿qué te regalaron para tu cumpleaños?; **she ~s a good salary** gana un buen sueldo. **-8.** [experience - a sensation]: **do you ~ the feeling he doesn't like us?** ¿no te da la sensación de que no le gustamos? **-9.** [catch - bus, criminal, illness] coger, agarrar *Amer*; **I've got a cold** estoy resfriado; **he got cancer** contrajo cáncer. **-10.** [understand] entender; **I don't ~ it** *inf* no me aclaro, no lo entiendo; **he didn't seem to ~ the point** no pareció captar el sentido. **-11.** *inf* [annoy] po

ner negro(gra). **-12.** [find]: **you ~ a lot of artists here** hay mucho artista por aquí; *see also* **have.** ◇ *vi* **-1.** [become] ponerse; **to ~ angry/pale** ponerse furioso/pálido; **to ~ ready** prepararse; **to ~ dressed** vestirse; **I'm getting cold/bored** me estoy enfriando/aburriendo; **it's getting late** se está haciendo tarde. **-2.** [arrive] llegar; **how do I ~ there?** ¿cómo se llega (allí)?; **I only got back yesterday** regresé justo ayer. **-3.** [eventually succeed]: **to ~ to do sthg** llegar a hacer algo; **did you ~ to see him?** ¿conseguiste verlo? **-4.** [progress] llegar; **how far have you got?** ¿cuánto llevas?, ¿hasta dónde has llegado?; **now we're getting somewhere** ahora sí que vamos por buen camino; **we're getting nowhere** así no llegamos a ninguna parte. ◇ *aux vb:* **to ~ excited** emocionarse; **someone could ~ hurt** alguien podría resultar herido; **I got beaten up** me zurraron; **let's ~ going** OR **moving** vamos a ponernos en marcha. ◆ **get about, get around** *vi* **-1.** [move from place to place] salir a menudo. **-2.** [circulate - news etc] difundirse; *see also* **get around.** ◆ **get along** *vi* **-1.** [manage] arreglárselas. **-2.** [progress]: **how are you getting along?** ¿cómo te va? **-3.** [have a good relationship]: **to ~ along (with sb)** llevarse bien (con alguien). ◆ **get around, get round** ◇ *vt fus* [overcome - problem] solventar; [- obstacle] sortear. ◇ *vi* **-1.** [circulate - news etc] difundirse. **-2.** [eventually do]: **to ~ around to (doing) sthg** sacar tiempo para (hacer) algo; *see also* **get about.** ◆ **get at** *vt fus* **-1.** [reach] llegar a, alcanzar. **-2.** [imply] referirse a. **-3.** *inf* [criticize]: **stop getting at me!** ¡deja ya de meterte conmigo! ◆ **get away** *vi* **-1.** [leave] salir, irse. **-2.** [go on holiday]: **I really need to ~ away** necesito unas buenas vacaciones. **-3.** [escape] escaparse. ◆ **get away with** *vt fus* salir impune de; **she lets him ~ away with everything** ella se lo consiente todo. ◆ **get back** ◇ *vt sep* [recover, regain] recuperar. ◇ *vi* [move away] echarse atrás, apartarse. ◆ **get back to** *vt fus* **-1.** [return to previous state, activity] volver a; **to ~ back to sleep/normal** volver a dormirse/a la normalidad. **-2.** *inf* [phone back]: **I'll ~ back to you later** te llamo de vuelta más tarde. ◆ **get by** *vi* apañárselas, apañarse. ◆ **get down** *vt sep* **-1.** [depress] deprimir. **-2.** [fetch from higher level] bajar. ◆ **get down to** *vt fus:*

to ~ **down to doing sthg** ponerse a hacer algo. ◆ **get in** *vi* **-1.** [enter] entrar. **-2.** [arrive] llegar. ◆ **get into** *vt fus* **-1.** [car] subir a. **-2.** [become involved in] meterse en. **-3.** [enter into a particular situation, state]: **to ~ into a panic** OR **state** ponerse nerviosísimo; **to ~ into trouble** meterse en líos; **to ~ into the habit of doing sthg** adquirir el hábito OR coger la costumbre de hacer algo. **-4.** [be accepted as a student at]: **she managed to ~ into Oxford** consiguió entrar en Oxford. ◇ *vt fus* **-1.** [go away from] irse OR salirse de; **~ off my land!** ¡fuera de mis tierras! **-2.** [train, bus, etc] bajarse de. ◇ *vi* **-1.** [leave bus, train] bajarse, desembarcarse *Amer.* **-2.** [escape punishment] escaparse; **he got off lightly** salió bien librado. **-3.** [depart] irse, salir. ◆ **get off with** *vt fus Br inf* ligar con. ◆ **get on** ◇ *vt fus* [bus, train, horse] subirse a, montarse en. ◇ *vi* **-1.** [enter bus, train] subirse, montarse. **-2.** [have good relationship] llevarse bien. **-3.** [progress]: **how are you getting on?** ¿cómo te va? **-4.** [proceed]: **to ~ on with sthg** seguir OR continuar con algo. **-5.** [be successful professionally] triunfar. ◆ **get out** ◇ *vt sep* [remove - object, prisoner] sacar; [- stain etc] quitar; **she got a pen out of her bag** sacó un bolígrafo del bolso. ◇ *vi* **-1.** [leave car, bus, train] bajarse. **-2.** [become known - news] difundirse, filtrarse. ◆ **get out of** *vt fus* **-1.** [car etc] bajar de. **-2.** [escape from] escapar OR huir de. **-3.** [avoid]: **to ~ out of (doing) sthg** librarse de (hacer) algo. ◆ **get over** *vt fus* **-1.** [recover from] recuperarse de. **-2.** [overcome] superar. **-3.** [communicate] hacer comprender. ◆ **get round** = **get around.** ◆ **get through** ◇ *vt fus* **-1.** [job, task] terminar. **-2.** [exam] aprobar. **-3.** [food, drink] consumir. **-4.** [unpleasant situation] sobrevivir a. ◇ *vi* **-1.** [make oneself understood]: **to ~ through (to sb)** hacerse comprender (por alguien). **-2.** TELEC conseguir comunicar. ◆ **get to** *vt fus inf* [annoy] fastidiar, molestar. ◆ **get together** ◇ *vt sep* [organize - project, demonstration] organizar, montar; [- team] juntar; [- report] preparar. ◇ *vi* juntarse, reunirse. ◆ **get up** ◇ *vi* levantarse. ◇ *vt fus* [organize - petition etc] preparar, organizar. ◆ **get up to** *vt fus inf* hacer, montar.

getaway ['getəweɪ] *n* fuga *f*, huida *f*; **to make one's ~** darse a la fuga.

get-together *n inf* reunión *f*.

geyser ['giːzər] *n* **-1.** [hot spring] géiser *m*. **-2.** *Br* [water heater] calentador *m* de agua.

Ghana ['gɑːnə] *n* Ghana.

ghastly ['gɑːstlɪ] *adj* **-1.** *inf* [very bad, unpleasant] horrible, espantoso(sa). **-2.** [horrifying] horripilante. **-3.** [ill] fatal.

gherkin ['gɜːkɪn] *n* pepinillo *m*.

ghetto ['getəʊ] (*pl* **-s** OR **-es**) *n* gueto *m*.

ghetto blaster [-'blɑːstər] *n inf* radiocasete *m* portátil de gran tamaño y potencia.

ghost [gəʊst] *n* [spirit] fantasma *m*.

giant ['dʒaɪənt] ◇ *adj* gigantesco(ca). ◇ *n* gigante *m*.

gibberish ['dʒɪbərɪʃ] *n* galimatías *m inv*.

gibe [dʒaɪb] ◇ *n* pulla *f*, sarcasmo *m*. ◇ *vi*: **to ~ (at)** mofarse (de).

giblets ['dʒɪblɪts] *npl* menudillos *mpl*.

Gibraltar [dʒɪ'brɔːltər] *n* Gibraltar; **the Rock of ~** el Peñón.

giddy ['gɪdɪ] *adj* [dizzy] mareado(da).

gift [gɪft] *n* **-1.** [present] regalo *m*, obsequio *m*. **-2.** [talent] don *m*; **to have a ~ for sthg/for doing sthg** tener un don especial para algo/para hacer algo; **to have the ~ of the gab** tener un pico de oro.

gift certificate *Am* = **gift token.**

gifted ['gɪftɪd] *adj* **-1.** [talented] dotado(da). **-2.** [extremely intelligent] superdotado(da).

gift token, gift voucher *n Br* vale *m* OR cupón *m* para regalo.

gig [gɪg] *n inf* [concert] concierto *m*.

gigabyte ['gaɪgəbaɪt] *n* COMPUT gigaocteto *m*.

gigantic [dʒaɪ'gæntɪk] *adj* gigantesco(ca).

giggle ['gɪgl] ◇ *n* **-1.** [laugh] risita *f*, risa *f* tonta. **-2.** *Br inf* [fun]: **it's a real ~** es la mar de divertido; **to do sthg for a ~** hacer algo por puro cachondeo. ◇ *vi* [laugh] tener la risa tonta.

gilded ['gɪldɪd] = **gilt.**

gill [dʒɪl] *n* [unit of measurement] =0,142 *litros*.

gills [gɪlz] *npl* [of fish] agallas *fpl*.

gilt [gɪlt] ◇ *adj* dorado(da). ◇ *n* dorado *m*.

gilt-edged *adj* FIN de máxima garantía.

gimmick ['gɪmɪk] *n pej* artilugio *m* innecesario; **advertising ~** reclamo *m* publicitario.

gin [dʒɪn] *n* ginebra *f*; **~ and tonic** gintonic *m*.

ginger ['dʒɪndʒər] ◇ *adj Br* [hair] bermejo(ja); [cat] de color bermejo. ◇ *n* jengibre *m*.

ginger ale *n* [mixer] ginger-ale *m*.

ginger beer *n* [slightly alcoholic] refresco *m* de jengibre.

gingerbread ['dʒɪndʒəbred] *n* **-1.** [cake] pan *m* de jengibre. **-2.** [biscuit] galleta *f* de jengibre.

ginger-haired [-'heəd] *adj* pelirrojo(ja).

gingerly ['dʒɪndʒəlɪ] *adv* con mucho tiento.

gipsy ['dʒɪpsɪ] ◇ *adj* gitano(na). ◇ *n Br* gitano *m*, -na *f*.

giraffe [dʒɪ'rɑːf] (*pl inv* OR **-s**) *n* jirafa *f*.

girder ['gɜːdə^r] *n* viga *f*.

girdle ['gɜːdl] *n* [corset] faja *f*.

girl [gɜːl] *n* **-1.** [child] niña *f*. **-2.** [young woman] chica *f*, muchacha *f*. **-3.** [daughter] niña *f*, chica *f*. **-4.** *inf* [female friend]: **the ~s** las amigas, las chicas.

girlfriend ['gɜːlfrend] *n* **-1.** [female lover] novia *f*. **-2.** [female friend] amiga *f*.

girl guide *Br*, **girl scout** *Am n* [individual] exploradora *f*.

giro ['dʒaɪrəʊ] (*pl* **-s**) *n Br* **-1.** (*U*) [system] giro *m*. **-2.** **~ (cheque)** cheque *m* para giro bancario.

girth [gɜːθ] *n* **-1.** [circumference] circunferencia *f*. **-2.** [of horse] cincha *f*.

gist [dʒɪst] *n*: **the ~ of** lo esencial de; **to get the ~ (of sthg)** entender el sentido (de algo).

give [gɪv] (*pt* **gave**, *pp* **given**) ◇ *vt* **-1.** [gen] dar; [time, effort] dedicar; [attention] prestar; **to ~ sb/sthg sthg, to ~ sthg to sb/sthg** dar algo a alguien/algo. **-2.** [as present]: **to ~ sb sthg, to ~ sthg to sb** regalar algo a alguien. **-3.** [hand over]: **to ~ sb sthg, to ~ sthg to sb** entregar OR dar algo a alguien. ◇ *vi* [collapse, break] romperse, ceder. ♦ **give or take** *prep* o menos o más; **in half an hour ~ or take five minutes** en más o menos media hora. ♦ **give away** *vt sep* **-1.** [as present] regalar. **-2.** [reveal] revelar, descubrir. ♦ **give back** *vt sep* [return] devolver, regresar *Amer*. ♦ **give in** *vi* **-1.** [admit defeat] rendirse, darse por vencido(da). **-2.** [agree unwillingly]: **to ~ in to sthg** ceder ante algo. ♦ **give off** *vt fus* [produce, emit] despedir. ♦ **give out** ◇ *vt sep* [distribute] repartir, distribuir. ◇ *vi* [supply, strength] agotarse, acabarse; [legs, machine] fallar. ♦ **give up** ◇ *vt sep* **-1.** [stop] abandonar; **to ~ up chocolate** dejar de comer chocolate. **-2.** [job] dimitir de, renunciar a. **-3.** [surrender]: **to**

~ o.s. up (to sb) rendirse (a alguien). ◇ *vi* rendirse, darse por vencido(da).

given ['gɪvn] ◇ *adj* **-1.** [set, fixed] dado(da). **-2.** [prone]: **to be ~ to sthg/to doing sthg** ser dado(da) a algo/a hacer algo. ◇ *prep* [taking into account] dado(da); **~** that dado que.

given name *n* nombre *m* de pila.

glacier ['glæsjə^r] *n* glaciar *m*.

glad [glæd] *adj* **-1.** [happy, pleased] alegre, contento(ta); **to be ~ about/that** alegrarse de/de que. **-2.** [willing]: **to be ~ to do sthg** tener gusto en hacer algo. **-3.** [grateful]: **to be ~ of sthg** agradecer algo.

gladly ['glædlɪ] *adv* **-1.** [happily, eagerly] alegremente. **-2.** [willingly] con mucho gusto.

glamor *Am* = **glamour**.

glamorous ['glæmərəs] *adj* atractivo(va), lleno(na) de encanto.

glamour *Br*, **glamor** *Am* ['glæmə^r] *n* encanto *m*, atractivo *m*.

glance [glɑːns] ◇ *n* [quick look] mirada *f*, vistazo *m*; **at a ~** de un vistazo; **at first ~** a primera vista. ◇ *vi* [look quickly]: **to ~ at sb** lanzar una mirada a alguien; **to ~ at sthg** echar una ojeada OR un vistazo a algo. ♦ **glance off** *vt fus* rebotar en.

glancing ['glɑːnsɪŋ] *adj* oblicuo(cua).

gland [glænd] *n* glándula *f*.

glandular fever ['glændjʊlə^r-] *n* mononucleosis *f inv* infecciosa.

glare [gleə^r] ◇ *n* **-1.** [scowl] mirada *f* asesina. **-2.** [blaze, dazzle] destello *m*, deslumbramiento *m*. **-3.** (*U*) *fig* [of publicity] foco *m*. ◇ *vi* **-1.** [scowl]: **to ~ (at sthg/sb)** mirar con furia (algo/a alguien). **-2.** [blaze, dazzle] deslumbrar.

glaring ['gleərɪŋ] *adj* **-1.** [very obvious] evidente. **-2.** [blazing, dazzling] deslumbrante.

glasnost ['glæznɒst] *n* glasnost *f*.

glass [glɑːs] ◇ *n* **-1.** [material] vidrio *m*, cristal *m*. **-2.** [drinking vessel, glassful] vaso *m*; [with stem] copa *f*. ◇ *comp* de vidrio, de cristal. ♦ **glasses** *npl* [spectacles] gafas *fpl*.

glassware ['glɑːsweə^r] *n* (*U*) cristalería *f*.

glassy ['glɑːsɪ] *adj* **-1.** [smooth, shiny] cristalino(na). **-2.** [blank, lifeless] vidrioso(sa).

glaze [gleɪz] ◇ *n* [on pottery] vidriado *m*; [on food] glaseado *m*. ◇ *vt* [pottery] vidriar; [food] glasear.

glazier ['gleɪzjə^r] *n* vidriero *m*, -ra *f*.

gleam [gli:m] ◇ *n* destello *m*; [of hope] rayo *m*. ◇ *vi* relucir.

gleaming ['gli:mɪŋ] *adj* reluciente.

glean [gli:n] *vt* [gather] recoger.

glee [gli:] *n* (U) [joy, delight] alegría *f*, regocijo *m*.

glen [glen] *n* Scot cañada *f*.

glib [glɪb] *adj pej* de mucha labia.

glide [glaɪd] *vi* -1. [move smoothly] deslizarse. -2. [fly] planear.

glider ['glaɪdəʳ] *n* [plane] planeador *m*.

gliding ['glaɪdɪŋ] *n* [sport] vuelo *m* sin motor.

glimmer ['glɪməʳ] *n* -1. [faint light] luz *f* tenue. -2. *fig* [trace, sign] atisbo *m*; [of hope] rayo *m*.

glimpse [glɪmps] ◇ *n* -1. [look, sight] vislumbre *f*. -2. [idea, perception] asomo *m*, atisbo *m*. ◇ *vt* entrever, vislumbrar.

glint [glɪnt] ◇ *n* -1. [flash] destello *m*. -2. [in eyes] fulgor *m*. ◇ *vi* destellar.

glisten ['glɪsn] *vi* relucir, brillar.

glitter ['glɪtəʳ] *vi* relucir, brillar.

gloat [gləʊt] *vi*: to ~ (over sthg) regodearse (con algo).

global ['gləʊbl] *adj* [worldwide] mundial.

global warming [-'wɔːmɪŋ] *n* calentamiento *m* mundial.

globe [gləʊb] *n* -1. [gen] globo *m*. -2. [spherical map] globo *m* (terráqueo).

gloom [glu:m] *n* (U) -1. [darkness] penumbra *f*. -2. [unhappiness] pesimismo *m*, melancolía *f*.

gloomy ['glu:mɪ] *adj* -1. [dark, cloudy] oscuro(ra). -2. [unhappy] melancólico(ca). -3. [without hope - report, forecast] pesimista; [- situation, prospects] desalentador(ra).

glorious ['glɔːrɪəs] *adj* magnífico(ca).

glory ['glɔːrɪ] *n* -1. [gen] gloria *f*. -2. [beauty, splendour] esplendor *m*. ◆ **glory in** *vt fus* [relish] disfrutar de, regocijarse con.

gloss [glɒs] *n* -1. [shine] lustre *m*, brillo *m*. -2. ~ (paint) pintura *f* esmalte. ◆ **gloss over** *vt fus* tocar muy por encima.

glossary ['glɒsərɪ] *n* glosario *m*.

glossy ['glɒsɪ] *adj* -1. [smooth, shiny] lustroso(sa). -2. [on shiny paper] de papel satinado.

glove [glʌv] *n* guante *m*.

glove compartment *n* guantera *f*.

glow [gləʊ] ◇ *n* [light] fulgor *m*. ◇ *vi* [gen] brillar.

glower ['glaʊəʳ] *vi*: to ~ (at sthg/sb) mirar con furia (algo/a alguien).

glucose ['glu:kəʊs] *n* glucosa *f*.

glue [glu:] (*cont* **glueing** OR **gluing**) ◇ *n* [paste] pegamento *m*; [for glueing wood, metal etc] cola *f*. ◇ *vt* [paste] pegar (con pegamento); [wood, metal etc] encolar.

glum [glʌm] *adj* [unhappy] sombrío(a).

glut [glʌt] *n* superabundancia *f*.

glutton ['glʌtn] *n* [greedy person] glotón *m*, -ona *f*; to be a ~ for punishment ser un masoquista.

gnarled [nɑːld] *adj* nudoso(sa).

gnash [næʃ] *vt*: to ~ one's teeth hacer rechinar los dientes.

gnat [næt] *n* mosquito *m*.

gnaw [nɔː] *vt* [chew] roer; to ~ (away) at sb corroer a alguien.

gnome [nəʊm] *n* gnomo *m*.

GNP (*abbr of* gross national product) *n* PNB *m*.

go [gəʊ] (*pt* went, *pp* gone, *pl* goes) ◇ *vi* -1. [move, travel, attend] ir; where are you ~ing? ¿dónde vas?; he's gone to Portugal se ha ido a Portugal; we went by bus/train fuimos en autobús/tren; to ~ and do sthg ir a hacer algo; where does this path ~? ¿a dónde lleva este camino?; to ~ swimming/ shopping ir a nadar/de compras; to ~ for a walk/run ir a dar un paseo/a correr; to ~ to church/school ir a misa/la escuela. -2. [depart - person] irse, marcharse; [- bus] salir; I must ~, I have to ~ tengo que irme; it's time we went es hora de irse OR marcharse; let's ~! ¡vámonos! -3. [pass - time] pasar. -4. [progress] ir; to ~ well/badly ir bien/mal; how's it ~ing? *inf* [how are you?] ¿qué tal? -5. [belong, fit] ir; the plates ~ in the cupboard los platos van en el armario; it won't ~ into the suitcase no cabe en la maleta. -6. [become] ponerse; to ~ grey ponerse gris; to ~ mad volverse loco; to ~ blind quedarse ciego. -7. [indicating intention, certainty, expectation]: to be ~ing to do sthg ir a hacer algo; he said he was ~ing to be late dijo que llegaría tarde; it's ~ing to rain/snow va a llover/nevar. -8. [match, be compatible]: to ~ (with) ir bien (con); this blouse goes well with the skirt esta blusa va muy bien OR hace juego con la falda. -9. [function, work] funcionar. -10. [bell, alarm] sonar. -11. [stop working] estropearse; the fuse must have gone han debido de saltar los plomos. -12. [deteriorate]: her sight/hearing is ~ing está perdiendo la vista/el oído. -13. [be disposed of]: he'll have to ~ habrá que despedirle; every-

thing must ~! ¡gran liquidación! **-14.** *inf* [expressing irritation, surprise]: **now what's he gone and done?** ¿qué leches ha hecho ahora? **-15.** [in division]: **three into two won't ~** dos entre tres no cabe. ◇ *n* **-1.** [turn] turno *m*; **it's my ~ me toca a mí. -2.** *inf* [attempt]: **to have a ~ at sthg** intentar OR probar algo. **-3.** *phr*: **to have a ~ at sb** *inf* echar una bronca a alguien; **to be on the ~** *inf* no parar, estar muy liado. ◆ **to go** *adv* [remaining]: **there are only three days to ~** sólo quedan tres días. ◆ **go about** ◇ *vt fus* **-1.** [perform] hacer, realizar; **to ~ about one's business** ocuparse uno de sus asuntos. **-2.** [tackle]: **to ~ about doing sthg** apañárselas para hacer algo; **how do you intend ~ing about it?** ¿cómo piensas hacerlo? ◇ *vi* = **go around.** ◆ **go ahead** *vi* **-1.** [begin]: **to ~ ahead (with sthg)** seguir adelante (con algo); **~ ahead!** ¡adelante! **-2.** [take place] celebrarse. ◆ **go along** *vi* [proceed]: **as you ~ along** a medida que lo vayas haciendo. ◆ **go along with** *vt fus* estar de acuerdo con. ◆ **go around** *vi* **-1.** [associate]: **to ~ around with sb** juntarse con alguien. **-2.** [joke, illness, story] correr (por ahí). ◆ **go back on** *vt fus* [one's word, promise] faltar a. ◆ **go back to** *vt fus* **-1.** [return to activity] continuar OR seguir con; **to ~ back to sleep** volver a dormir. **-2.** [date from] remontarse a. ◆ **go by** ◇ *vi* [time] pasar. ◇ *vt fus* **-1.** [be guided by] guiarse por. **-2.** [judge from]: **~ing by her voice, I'd say she was French** a juzgar por su voz yo diría que es francesa. ◆ **go down** ◇ *vi* **-1.** [get lower - prices etc] bajar. **-2.** [be accepted]: **to ~ down well/badly** tener una buena/mala acogida. **-3.** [sun] ponerse. **-4.** [tyre, balloon] deshincharse. ◇ *vt fus* bajar. ◆ **go for** *vt fus* **-1.** [choose] decidirse por. **-2.** [be attracted to]: **I don't really ~ for men like him** no me gustan mucho los hombres como él. **-3.** [attack] lanzarse sobre, atacar. **-4.** [try to obtain - record, job] ir a por. ◆ **go in** *vi* entrar. ◆ **go in for** *vt fus* **-1.** [competition, exam] presentarse a. **-2.** *inf* [enjoy]: **I don't really ~ in for classical music** no me va la música clásica. ◆ **go into** *vt fus* **-1.** [investigate] investigar. **-2.** [take up as a profession] dedicarse a. ◆ **go off** ◇ *vi* **-1.** [explode - bomb] estallar; [- gun] dispararse. **-2.** [alarm] sonar. **-3.** [go bad - food] estropearse; [- milk] cortarse. **-4.** [lights, heat-

ing] apagarse. **-5.** [happen]: **to ~ off (well/badly)** salir (bien/mal). ◇ *vt fus inf* [lose interest in] perder el gusto a OR el interés en. ◆ **go on** ◇ *vi* **-1.** [take place] pasar, ocurrir. **-2.** [continue]: **to ~ on (doing sthg)** seguir (haciendo algo). **-3.** [proceed to further activity]: **to ~ on to sthg/to do sthg** pasar a algo/a hacer algo. **-4.** [heating etc] encenderse. **-5.** [talk for too long]: **to ~ on (about)** no parar de hablar (de). ◇ *vt fus* [be guided by] guiarse por. ◇ *excl* ¡venga!, ¡vamos! ◆ **go on at** *vt fus* [nag] dar la lata a. ◆ **go out** *vi* **-1.** [leave house] salir; **to ~ out for a meal** cenar fuera. **-2.** [as friends or lovers]: **to ~ out (with sb)** salir (con alguien). **-3.** [light, fire, cigarette] apagarse. ◆ **go over** *vt fus* **-1.** [examine] repasar. **-2.** [repeat] repetir. ◆ **go round** *vi* [revolve] girar, dar vueltas; *see also* **go around.** ◆ **go through** *vt fus* **-1.** [experience] pasar por, experimentar. **-2.** [study, search through] registrar; **she went through his pockets** le miró en los bolsillos. ◆ **go through with** *vt fus* llevar a cabo. ◆ **go towards** *vt fus* contribuir a. ◆ **go under** *vi lit & fig* hundirse. ◆ **go up** ◇ *vi* **-1.** [rise - prices, temperature, balloon] subir. **-2.** [be built] levantarse, construirse. ◇ *vt fus* subir. ◆ **go without** ◇ *vt fus* prescindir de. ◇ *vi* apañárselas.

goad [gəʊd] *vt* [provoke] aguijonear, incitar.

go-ahead ◇ *adj* [dynamic] dinámico(ca). ◇ *n* (U) [permission] luz *f* verde.

goal [gəʊl] *n* **-1.** SPORT [area between goalposts] portería *f*, arco *m* Amer; [point scored] gol *m*. **-2.** [aim] objetivo *m*, meta *f*.

goalkeeper ['gəʊl,kiːpər] *n* portero *m*, -ra *f*, arquero *m*, -ra *f* Amer.

goalmouth ['gəʊlmaʊθ] (*pl* -mauðz]) *n* portería *f*, meta *f*, arco *m* Amer.

goalpost ['gəʊlpəʊst] *n* poste *m* (de la portería).

goat [gəʊt] *n* [animal] cabra *f*.

gob [gɒb] *v inf n Br* [mouth] pico *m*.

gobble ['gɒbl] *vt* [food] engullir, tragar. ◆ **gobble down, gobble up** *vt sep* engullir, tragar.

go-between *n* intermediario *m*, -ria *f*.

gobsmacked ['gɒbsmækt] *adj Br inf* alucinado(da), flipado(da).

go-cart = **go-kart**.

god [gɒd] *n* dios *m*. ◆ **God** ◇ *n* Dios *m*; **God knows** sabe Dios; **for God's sake** ¡por el amor de Dios!; **thank God** ¡gracias a Dios! ◇ *excl*: **(my) God!** ¡Dios (mío)!

godchild ['gɒdtʃaɪld] (*pl* **-children** [-,tʃɪldrən]) *n* ahijado *m*, -da *f*.

goddaughter ['gɒd,dɔːtəʳ] *n* ahijada *f*.

goddess ['gɒdɪs] *n* diosa *f*.

godfather ['gɒd,fɑːðəʳ] *n* padrino *m*.

godforsaken ['gɒdfə,seɪkn] *adj* dejado(da) de la mano de Dios.

godmother ['gɒd,mʌðəʳ] *n* madrina *f*.

godsend ['gɒdsend] *n*: **to be a ~** venir como agua de mayo.

godson ['gɒdsʌn] *n* ahijado *m*.

goes [gəʊz] → **go**.

goggles ['gɒglz] *npl* [for swimming] gafas *fpl* submarinas; [for skiing] gafas de esquí; [for welding] gafas de protección.

going ['gəʊɪŋ] ◇ *adj* **-1.** *Br* [available] disponible. **-2.** [rate] actual. ◇ *n* (*U*) **-1.** [rate of advance] marcha *f*. **-2.** [conditions] condiciones *fpl*.

go-kart [-kɑːt] *n* kart *m*.

gold [gəʊld] ◇ *adj* [gold-coloured] dorado(da). ◇ *n* [gen] oro *m*. ◇ *comp* [made of gold] de oro.

golden ['gəʊldən] *adj* **-1.** [made of gold] de oro. **-2.** [gold-coloured] dorado(da).

goldfish ['gəʊldfɪʃ] (*pl inv*) *n* pez *m* de colores.

gold leaf *n* pan *m* de oro.

gold medal *n* medalla *f* de oro.

goldmine ['gəʊldmaɪn] *n* *lit* & *fig* mina *f* de oro.

gold-plated [-'pleɪtɪd] *adj* chapado(da) en oro.

goldsmith ['gəʊldsmɪθ] *n* orfebre *m* *y* *f*.

golf [gɒlf] *n* golf *m*.

golf ball *n* **-1.** [for golf] pelota *f* de golf. **-2.** [for typewriter] esfera *f* impresora.

golf club *n* **-1.** [society, place] club *m* de golf. **-2.** [stick] palo *m* de golf.

golf course *n* campo *m* de golf.

golfer ['gɒlfəʳ] *n* golfista *m* *y* *f*.

gone [gɒn] ◇ *pp* → **go**. ◇ *adj*: those days are ~ esos tiempos ya pasaron. ◇ *prep* [past]: it was ~ **six already** ya eran las seis pasadas.

gong [gɒŋ] *n* gong *m*.

good [gʊd] (*compar* **better**, *superl* **best**) ◇ *adj* **-1.** [gen] bueno(na); **it's ~ to see you** me alegro de verte; **she's ~ at it** se le da bien; **to be ~ with** saber manejárselas con; **she's ~ with her hands** es muy mañosa; **it's ~ for you** es bueno, es beneficioso; **to feel ~** sentirse fenomenal; **it's ~ that ...** está bien que ...; **to look ~** [attractive] estar muy guapo; [appetizing, promising] tener buena

pinta; **~ looks** atractivo *m*; **be ~!** ¡sé bueno!, ¡pórtate bien!; **~!** ¡muy bien!, ¡estupendo! **-2.** [kind] amable; **to be ~ to sb** ser amable con alguien; **to be ~ enough to do sthg** ser tan amable de hacer algo. ◇ *n* **-1.** (*U*) [benefit] bien *m*; **it will do him ~** le hará bien. **-2.** [use] beneficio *m*, provecho *m*; **what's the ~ of ...?** ¿de OR para qué sirve ...?; **it's no ~** no sirve para nada. **-3.** [morally correct behaviour] el bien; **to be up to no ~** estar tramando algo malo. ◆ **goods** *npl* **-1.** [COM - for sale] productos *mpl*; [- when transported] mercancías *fpl*. **-2.** ECON bienes *mpl*. ◆ **as good as** *adv* casi, prácticamente; **it's as ~ as new** está como nuevo. ◆ **for good** *adv* [forever] para siempre. ◆ **good afternoon** *excl* ¡buenas tardes! ◆ **good evening** *excl* [in the evening] ¡buenas tardes!; [at night] ¡buenas noches! ◆ **good morning** *excl* ¡buenos días!, ¡buen día! *Amer.* ◆ **good night** *excl* ¡buenas noches!

goodbye [,gʊd'baɪ] ◇ *excl* ¡adiós! ◇ *n* adiós *m*.

Good Friday *n* Viernes *m* Santo.

good-humoured [-'hjuːməd] *adj* jovial.

good-looking [-'lʊkɪŋ] *adj* [person] guapo(pa).

good-natured [-'neɪtʃəd] *adj* bondadoso(sa).

goodness ['gʊdnɪs] ◇ *n* (*U*) **-1.** [kindness] bondad *f*. **-2.** [nutritive quality] alimento *m*. ◇ *excl*: **(my) ~!** ¡Dios mío!; **for ~' sake!** ¡por Dios!; **thank ~** ¡gracias a Dios!

goods train [gʊdz-] *n* *Br* mercancías *m* *inv*.

goodwill [,gʊd'wɪl] *n* **-1.** [kind feelings] buena voluntad *f*. **-2.** COMM fondo *m* de comercio.

goody ['gʊdɪ] *inf* *n* bueno *m*, -na *f*.

goose [guːs] (*pl* **geese**) *n* [bird] ganso *m*, oca *f*.

gooseberry ['gʊzbərɪ] *n* [fruit] grosella *f* silvestre, uva *f* espina.

gooseflesh ['guːsfleʃ] *n*, **goose pimples** *Br*, **goosebumps** *Am* ['guːsbʌmps] *npl* carne *f* de gallina.

gore [gɔːʳ] ◇ *n* *literary* [blood] sangre *f* (derramada). ◇ *vt* cornear.

gorge [gɔːdʒ] ◇ *n* cañón *m*. ◇ *vt*: **to ~ o.s. on** OR **with** atracarse de.

gorgeous ['gɔːdʒəs] *adj* **-1.** [lovely] magnífico(ca), espléndido(da). **-2.** *inf* [good-looking]: **to be ~** estar como un tren.

gorilla [gə'rɪlə] n gorila m y f.

gormless ['gɔːmlɪs] adj Br inf memo(ma), lerdo(da).

gorse [gɔːs] n (U) tojo m.

gory ['gɔːrɪ] adj [death, scene] sangriento(ta); [details, film] escabroso(sa).

gosh [gɒʃ] excl inf ¡joroba!, ¡caray!

go-slow n Br huelga f de celo.

gospel ['gɒspl] n [doctrine] evangelio m.
◆ **Gospel** n [in Bible] Evangelio m.

gossip ['gɒsɪp] ◇ n -1. [conversation] cotilleo m. -2. [person] cotilla m y f, chismoso m, -sa f. ◇ vi cotillear.

gossip column n ecos mpl de sociedad.

got [gɒt] pt & pp → get.

gotten ['gɒtn] pp Am → get.

goulash ['guːlæʃ] n gulasch m.

gourmet ['guəmeɪ] ◇ n gastrónomo m, -ma f. ◇ comp para/de gastrónomos.

gout [gaut] n gota f.

govern ['gʌvən] ◇ vt -1. POL gobernar. -2. [control] dictar. ◇ vi POL gobernar.

governess ['gʌvənɪs] n institutriz f.

government ['gʌvnmənt] ◇ n gobierno m. ◇ comp gubernamental.

governor ['gʌvənər] n -1. POL gobernador m, -ra f. -2. [of school, bank, prison] director m, -ra f.

gown [gaun] n -1. [dress] vestido m, traje m. -2. [of judge etc] toga f.

GP (abbr of **general practitioner**) n médico de cabecera.

grab [græb] ◇ vt -1. [snatch away] arrebatar; [grip] agarrar, asir. -2. inf [appeal to] seducir. ◇ vi: **to ~ at sthg** intentar agarrar algo.

grace [greɪs] ◇ n -1. (U) [elegance] elegancia f, gracia f. -2. (U) [delay] prórroga f. -3. [prayer]: **to say ~** bendecir la mesa. ◇ vt fml -1. [honour] honrar. -2. [decorate] adornar, embellecer.

graceful ['greɪsful] adj -1. [beautiful] elegante. -2. [gracious] cortés.

gracious ['greɪʃəs] ◇ adj -1. [polite] cortés. -2. [elegant] elegante. ◇ excl: **(good) ~!** ¡Dios mío!

grade [greɪd] ◇ n -1. [level, quality] clase f, calidad f. -2. Am [class] curso m, clase f. -3. [mark] nota f. ◇ vt -1. [classify] clasificar. -2. [mark, assess] calificar.

grade crossing n Am paso m a nivel.

grade school n Am escuela f primaria.

gradient ['greɪdɪənt] n pendiente f.

gradual ['grædʒuəl] adj gradual.

gradually ['grædʒuəlɪ] adv gradualmente.

graduate [n 'grædʒuət, vb 'grædʒueɪt] ◇ n -1. [person with a degree] licenciado m,

-da f, egresado m, -da f Amer. -2. Am [of high school] ≃ bachiller m y f. ◇ vi -1. [with a degree]: **to ~ (from)** licenciarse (por), egresar (de) Amer. -2. Am [from high school]: **to ~ (from)** ≃ obtener el título de bachiller (en).

graduation [,grædʒu'eɪʃn] n graduación f, egreso m Amer.

graffiti [grə'fiːtɪ] n (U) pintadas fpl.

graft [grɑːft] ◇ n -1. BOT & MED injerto m. -2. Br inf [hard work] curro m muy duro. -3. Am inf [corruption] chanchullos mpl. ◇ vt BOT & MED: **to ~ sthg (onto sthg)** injertar algo (en algo).

grain [greɪn] n -1. [seed, granule] grano m. -2. (U) [crop] cereales mpl. -3. fig [small amount] pizca f. -4. [pattern] veta f.

gram [græm] n gramo m.

grammar ['græmər] n gramática f.

grammar school n [in UK] colegio subvencionado para mayores de once años con un programa de asignaturas tradicional; [in US] escuela f primaria.

grammatical [grə'mætɪkl] adj -1. [of grammar] gramatical. -2. [correct] (gramaticalmente) correcto(ta).

gramme [græm] Br = **gram**.

gramophone ['græməfəun] dated n gramófono m.

gran [græn] n Br inf abuelita f, yaya f.

grand [grænd] ◇ adj -1. [impressive] grandioso(sa), monumental. -2. [ambitious] ambicioso(sa). -3. [important] distinguido(da). -4. inf dated [excellent] fenomenal. ◇ n inf [thousand pounds or dollars]: **a ~** mil libras/dólares; **five ~** cinco mil libras/dólares.

grandchild ['græntʃaɪld] (pl **-children** [-,tʃɪldrən]) n nieto m, -ta f.

grand(d)ad ['grændæd] n inf abuelito m, yayo m.

granddaughter ['græn,dɔːtər] n nieta f.

grandeur ['grændʒər] n -1. [splendour] grandiosidad f. -2. [status] grandeza f.

grandfather ['grænd,fɑːðər] n abuelo m.

grandma ['grænmɑː] n inf abuelita f, yaya f, mamá f grande Amer.

grandmother ['græn,mʌðər] n abuela f.

grandpa ['grænpɑː] n inf abuelito m, yayo m, papá m grande Amer.

grandparents ['græn,peərənts] npl abuelos mpl.

grand piano n piano m de cola.

grand slam n SPORT [in tennis] gran slam m; [in rugby] gran chelem f.

grandson ['grænsʌn] n nieto m.

grandstand ['grændstænd] n tribuna f.

grand total *n* [total number] **cantidad** *f* total; [total sum, cost] **importe** *m* total.

granite ['grænɪt] *n* granito *m*.

granny ['grænɪ] *n inf* abuelita *f*, yaya *f*.

grant [grɑːnt] ◇ *n* subvención *f*; [for study] beca *f*. ◇ *vt fml* **-1.** [gen] conceder; **to take sthg/sb for ~ed** no apreciar algo/a alguien en lo que vale; **it is taken for ~ed that ...** se da por sentado que .... **-2.** [admit - truth, logic] admitir, aceptar.

granulated sugar ['grænjuleɪtɪd-] *n* azúcar *m* granulado.

granule ['grænjuːl] *n* gránulo *m*.

grape [greɪp] *n* uva *f*.

grapefruit ['greɪpfruːt] (*pl inv* OR **-s**) *n* pomelo *m*.

grapevine ['greɪpvaɪn] *n* **-1.** [plant] vid *f*; [against wall] parra *f*. **-2.** [information channel]: **I heard on the ~ that ...** me ha dicho un pajarito que ....

graph [grɑːf] *n* gráfica *f*.

graphic ['græfɪk] *adj lit* & *fig* gráfico(ca). ◆ **graphics** *npl* [pictures] ilustraciones *fpl*; **computer** ~**s** gráficos *mpl*.

graphite ['græfaɪt] *n* grafito *m*.

graph paper *n* (*U*) papel *m* cuadriculado.

grapple ['græpl] ◆ **grapple with** *vt fus* **-1.** [person] forcejear con. **-2.** [problem] esforzarse por resolver.

grasp [grɑːsp] ◇ *n* **-1.** [grip] agarre *m*, asimiento *m*. **-2.** [understanding] comprensión *f*; **to have a good ~ of sthg** dominar algo. ◇ *vt* **-1.** [grip, seize] agarrar, asir. **-2.** [understand] comprender. **-3.** [opportunity] aprovechar.

grasping ['grɑːspɪŋ] *adj pej* avaro(ra).

grass [grɑːs] ◇ *n* **-1.** [plant] hierba *f*; [lawn] césped *m*; [pasture] pasto *m*; **"keep off the ~" "prohibido pisar el césped".** **-2.** *drugs sl* [marijuana] hierba *f*, maría *f*. ◇ *vi Br crime sl*: **to ~ (on sb)** chivarse (de alguien).

grasshopper ['grɑːsˌhɒpə**r**] *n* saltamontes *m inv*.

grass roots ◇ *npl* bases *fpl*. ◇ *comp* de base.

grass snake *n* culebra *f*.

grate [greɪt] ◇ *n* parrilla *f*, rejilla *f*. ◇ *vt* rallar. ◇ *vi* rechinar, chirriar.

grateful ['greɪtful] *adj* [gen] agradecido(da); [smile, letter] de agradecimiento; **to be ~ to sb (for sthg)** estar agradecido a alguien (por algo); **I'm very ~ to you** te lo agradezco mucho.

grater ['greɪtə**r**] *n* rallador *m*.

gratify ['grætɪfaɪ] *vt* **-1.** [please - person]: **to be gratified** estar satisfecho. **-2.** [satisfy - wish] **satisfacer.**

grating ['greɪtɪŋ] ◇ *adj* chirriante. ◇ *n* [grille] reja *f*, enrejado *m*.

gratitude ['grætɪtjuːd] *n* (*U*): **~ (to sb for)** agradecimiento *m* OR gratitud *f* (a alguien por).

gratuitous [grə'tjuːɪtəs] *adj fml* gratuito(ta).

grave [greɪv] ◇ *adj* grave. ◇ *n* sepultura *f*, tumba *f*.

gravel ['grævl] *n* grava *f*, gravilla *f*.

gravestone ['greɪvstəʊn] *n* lápida *f* (sepulcral).

graveyard ['greɪvjɑːd] *n* cementerio *m*.

gravity ['grævətɪ] *n* gravedad *f*.

gravy ['greɪvɪ] *n* (*U*) [meat juice] salsa *f* OR jugo *m* de carne.

gray *Am* = **grey**.

graze [greɪz] ◇ *vt* **-1.** [feed on] pacer OR pastar en. **-2.** [skin, knee etc] rasguñar. **-3.** [touch lightly] rozar. ◇ *vi* pacer, pastar. ◇ *n* rasguño *m*.

grease [griːs] ◇ *n* grasa *f*. ◇ *vt* engrasar.

greaseproof paper [ˌgriːspruːf-] *n* (*U*) *Br* papel *m* de cera (para envolver).

greasy ['griːzɪ] *adj* grasiento(ta); [inherently] graso(sa).

great [greɪt] ◇ *adj* **-1.** [gen] grande; [heat] intenso(sa); **~ big** enorme. **-2.** *inf* [splendid] estupendo(da), fenomenal; **we had a ~ time** lo pasamos en grande; **~!** ¡estupendo! ◇ *n* grande *m* y *f*.

Great Britain *n* Gran Bretaña.

greatcoat ['greɪtkəʊt] *n* gabán *m*.

Great Dane *n* gran danés *m*.

great-grandchild *n* bisnieto *m*, -ta *f*.

great-grandfather *n* bisabuelo *m*.

great-grandmother *n* bisabuela *f*.

greatly ['greɪtlɪ] *adv* enormemente.

greatness ['greɪtnɪs] *n* grandeza *f*.

Greece [griːs] *n* Grecia.

greed [griːd] *n* (*U*): **~ (for)** [food] glotonería *f* (con); [money] codicia *f* (de); [power] ambición *f* (de).

greedy ['griːdɪ] *adj* **-1.** [for food] glotón(ona). **-2.** [for money, power]: **~ for** codicioso(sa) OR ávido(da) de.

Greek [griːk] ◇ *adj* griego(ga). ◇ *n* **-1.** [person] griego *m*, -ga *f*. **-2.** [language] griego *m*.

green [griːn] ◇ *adj* **-1.** [gen] verde. **-2.** *inf* [pale] pálido(da). **-3.** *inf* [inexperienced] novato(ta). ◇ *n* **-1.** [colour] verde *m*. **-2.** [in village] terreno *m* comunal. **-3.** [in golf] green *m*. ◆ **Green** *n* POL verde *m* y *f*, ecologista *m* y *f*; **the Greens** los verdes. ◆ **greens** *npl* [vegetables] verduras *fpl*.

greenback ['gri:nbæk] *n Am inf* billete *de banco americano.*

green belt *n Br* cinturón *m* verde.

green card *n* **-1.** *Br* [for vehicle] *seguro que cubre a conductores en el extranjero.* **-2.** *Am* [work permit] permiso *m* de trabajo (*en Estados Unidos*).

greenery ['gri:nərı] *n* vegetación *f*.

greenfly ['gri:nflaɪ] (*pl inv* OR **-ies**) *n* pulgón *m*.

greengage ['gri:ngeɪdʒ] *n* ciruela *f* claudia.

greengrocer ['gri:n,grəʊsəʳ] *n* verdulero *m*, -ra *f*; ~'s **(shop)** verdulería *f*.

greenhouse ['gri:nhaʊs, *pl* -haʊzɪz] *n* invernadero *m*.

greenhouse effect *n*: **the** ~ el efecto invernadero.

Greenland ['gri:nlənd] *n* Groenlandia.

green salad *n* ensalada *f* verde.

greet [gri:t] *vt* **-1.** [say hello to] saludar. **-2.** [receive] recibir.

greeting ['gri:tɪŋ] *n* saludo *m*; [welcome] recibimiento *m*. ◆ **greetings** *npl*: **Christmas/birthday** ~**s!** ¡feliz navidad/cumpleaños!; ~**s from ...** recuerdos de ....

greetings card *Br* ['gri:tɪŋz-], **greeting card** *Am n* tarjeta *f* de felicitación.

grenade [grə'neɪd] *n*: **(hand)** ~ granada *f* (de mano).

grew [gru:] *pt* → **grow**.

grey *Br*, **gray** *Am* [greɪ] ◇ *adj lit & fig* gris; **to go** ~ [grey-haired] echar canas, encanecer. ◇ *n* gris *m*.

grey-haired [-'heəd] *adj* canoso(sa).

greyhound ['greɪhaʊnd] *n* galgo *m*.

grid [grɪd] *n* **-1.** [grating] reja *f*, enrejado *m*. **-2.** [system of squares] cuadrícula *f*.

griddle ['grɪdl] *n* plancha *f*.

gridlock ['grɪdlɒk] *n Am* embotellamiento *m*, atasco *m*.

grief [gri:f] *n* (*U*) **-1.** [sorrow] dolor *m*, pesar *m*. **-2.** *inf* [trouble] problemas *mpl*. **-3.** *phr*: **to come to** ~ [person] sufrir un percance; [plans] irse al traste; **good** ~! ¡madre mía!

grievance ['gri:vns] *n* (motivo *m* de) queja *f*.

grieve [gri:v] *vi*: **to** ~ **(for)** llorar (por).

grievous ['gri:vəs] *adj fml* grave.

grievous bodily harm *n* (*U*) lesiones *fpl* graves.

grill [grɪl] ◇ *n* **-1.** [of cooker] parrilla *f*. **-2.** [food] parrillada *f*. ◇ *vt* **-1.** CULIN

asar a la parrilla. **-2.** *inf* [interrogate] someter a un duro interrogatorio.

grille [grɪl] *n* [on radiator, machine] rejilla *f*; [on window, door] reja *f*.

grim [grɪm] *adj* **-1.** [expression] adusto(ta); [determination] inexorable. **-2.** [place, facts, prospects] descorazonador(ra), lúgubre.

grimace [grɪ'meɪs] ◇ *n* mueca *f*. ◇ *vi* hacer una mueca.

grime [graɪm] *n* mugre *f*.

grimy ['graɪmɪ] *adj* mugriento(ta).

grin [grɪn] ◇ *n* sonrisa *f* (abierta). ◇ *vi*: **to** ~ **(at)** sonreír (a).

grind [graɪnd] (*pt & pp* **ground**) ◇ *vt* [crush] moler. ◇ *vi* [scrape] rechinar, chirriar. ◇ *n* [hard, boring work] rutina *f*. ◆ **grind down** *vt sep* [oppress] oprimir, acogotar. ◆ **grind up** *vt sep* pulverizar.

grinder ['graɪndəʳ] *n* molinillo *m*.

grip [grɪp] ◇ *n* **-1.** [grasp, hold]: **to have a** ~ **(on sthg/sb)** tener (algo/a alguien) bien agarrado. **-2.** [control, domination]: ~ **on** control *m* de, dominio *m* de; **to get to** ~**s with** llegar a controlar; **to get a** ~ **on o.s.** calmarse, controlarse. **-3.** [adhesion] sujeción *f*, adherencia *f*. **-4.** [handle] asidero *m*. **-5.** [bag] bolsa *f* de viaje. ◇ *vt* **-1.** [grasp] agarrar, asir; [hand] apretar; [weapon] empuñar. **-2.** [seize] apoderarse de.

gripe [graɪp] *inf* ◇ *n* [complaint] queja *f*. ◇ *vi*: **to** ~ **(about)** quejarse (de).

gripping ['grɪpɪŋ] *adj* apasionante.

grisly ['grɪzlɪ] *adj* [horrible, macabre] espeluznante.

gristle ['grɪsl] *n* cartílago *m*, ternilla *f*.

grit [grɪt] ◇ *n* **-1.** [stones] grava *f*; [sand, dust] arena *f*. **-2.** *inf* [courage] valor *m*. ◇ *vt* cubrir de arena (*las calles*).

gritty ['grɪtɪ] *adj inf* [brave] valiente.

groan [grəʊn] ◇ *n* gemido *m*. ◇ *vi* **-1.** [moan] gemir. **-2.** [creak] crujir.

grocer ['grəʊsəʳ] *n* tendero *m*, -ra *f*, abarrotero *m*, -ra *f Amer*; ~'s **(shop)** tienda *f* de comestibles OR ultramarinos, abarrotería *f Amer*.

groceries ['grəʊsərɪz] *npl* [foods] comestibles *mpl*, abarrotes *mpl Amer*.

grocery ['grəʊsərɪ] *n* [shop] tienda *f* de comestibles OR ultramarinos, abarrotería *f Amer*.

groggy ['grɒgɪ] *adj* atontado(da), mareado(da).

groin [grɔɪn] *n* ingle *f*.

groom [gru:m] ◇ *n* **-1.** [of horses] mozo *m* de cuadra. **-2.** [bridegroom] novio *m*. ◇ *vt* **-1.** [brush] cepillar, almohazar. **-2.**

[prepare]: **to ~ sb (for sthg)** preparar a alguien (para algo).

groove [gruːv] *n* [deep line] ranura *f*; [in record] surco *m*.

grope [grəup] ◇ *vt* **-1.** [fondle] meter mano a. **-2.** [try to find]: **to ~ one's way** andar a tientas. ◇ *vi*: **to ~ (about) for sthg** [object] buscar algo a tientas; [solution, remedy] buscar algo a ciegas.

gross [grəus] (*pl inv* OR **-es**) ◇ *adj* **-1.** [total] bruto(ta). **-2.** *fml* [serious, inexcusable] grave. **-3.** [coarse, vulgar] basto(ta), vulgar. **-4.** *inf* [obese] obeso(sa). ◇ *n* gruesa *f*. ◇ *vt* ganar en bruto.

grossly ['grəuslɪ] *adv* [seriously] enormemente.

grotesque [grəu'tesk] *adj* grotesco(ca).

grotto ['grɒtəu] (*pl* **-es** OR **-s**) *n* gruta *f*.

grotty ['grɒtɪ] *adj Br fml* [serious, inexcusable] asqueroso(sa).

ground [graund] ◇ *pt & pp* → **grind**. ◇ *n* **-1.** [surface of earth] suelo *m*, tierra *f*; **above/below ~** sobre/bajo tierra; **on the ~** en el suelo. **-2.** [area of land] terreno *m*; SPORT campo *m*, terreno *m* de juego. **-3.** [subject area] campo *m*. **-4.** [advantage]: **to gain/lose ~** ganar/perder terreno. ◇ *vt* **-1.** [base]: **to be ~ed on** OR **in sthg** basarse en algo. **-2.** [aircraft, pilot] hacer permanecer en tierra. **-3.** *Am inf* [child] castigar sin salir. **-4.** *Am* ELEC: **to be ~ed** estar conectado(da) a tierra. ◆ **grounds** *npl* **-1.** [reason]: **~s (for sthg/for doing sthg)** motivos *mpl* (para algo/para hacer algo); **on the ~s that** aduciendo que, debido a que. **-2.** [around building] jardines *mpl*. **-3.** [of coffee] poso *m*.

ground crew *n* personal *m* de tierra.

ground floor *n* planta *f* baja; **~ flat** (piso *m*) bajo *m*.

grounding ['graundɪŋ] *n*: **~ (in)** base *f* (de), conocimientos *mpl* básicos (de).

groundless ['graundlɪs] *adj* infundado(da).

groundsheet ['graundʃiːt] *n* lona *f* impermeable (*para camping etc*).

ground staff *n* **-1.** [at sports ground] personal *m* al cargo de las instalaciones. **-2.** *Br* = ground crew.

groundwork ['graundwɜːk] *n* (*U*) trabajo *m* preliminar.

group [gruːp] ◇ *n* grupo *m*. ◇ *vt* agrupar. ◇ *vi*: **to ~ (together)** agruparse.

groupie ['gruːpɪ] *n inf* groupie *f*.

grouse [graus] (*pl inv* OR **-s**) ◇ *n* [bird] urogallo *m*. ◇ *vi inf* quejarse.

grove [grəuv] *n* [of trees] arboleda *f*.

grovel ['grɒvl] *vi lit & fig*: **to ~ (to)** arrastrarse (ante).

grow [grəu] (*pt* grew, *pp* grown) ◇ *vi* **-1.** [gen] crecer. **-2.** [become] volverse, ponerse; **to ~ dark** oscurecer; **to ~ old** envejecer. ◇ *vt* **-1.** [plants] cultivar. **-2.** [hair, beard] dejarse crecer. ◆ **grow on** *vt fus inf* gustar cada vez más. ◆ **grow out of** *vt fus* **-1.** [become too big for]: **he has grown out of his clothes** se le ha quedado pequeña la ropa. **-2.** [lose habit etc] perder. ◆ **grow up** *vi* crecer; **~ up!** ¡no seas niño!

grower ['grəuər] *n* cultivador *m*, -ra *f*.

growl [graul] *vi* [dog, person] gruñir; [lion, engine] rugir.

grown [grəun] ◇ *pp* → **grow**. ◇ *adj* crecido(da), adulto(ta).

grown-up *n* persona *f* mayor.

growth [grəuθ] *n* **-1.** [gen]: **~ (of OR in)** crecimiento *m* (de). **-2.** MED tumor *m*.

grub [grʌb] *n* **-1.** [insect] larva *f*, gusano *m*. **-2.** *inf* [food] manduca *f*, papeo *m*.

grubby ['grʌbɪ] *adj* sucio(cia), mugriento(ta).

grudge [grʌdʒ] ◇ *n* rencor *m*; **to bear sb a ~, to bear a ~ against sb** guardar rencor a alguien. ◇ *vt*: **to ~ sb sthg** conceder algo a alguien a regañadientes; **to ~ doing sthg** hacer algo a regañadientes.

gruelling *Br*, **grueling** *Am* ['gruəlɪŋ] *adj* agotador(ra).

gruesome ['gruːsəm] *adj* horripilante.

gruff [grʌf] *adj* **-1.** [hoarse] bronco(ca). **-2.** [rough, unfriendly] hosco(ca).

grumble ['grʌmbl] *vi* **-1.** [complain] quejarse, refunfuñar; **to ~ about sthg** quejarse de algo, refunfuñar por algo. **-2.** [stomach] gruñir, hacer ruido.

grumpy ['grʌmpɪ] *adj inf* gruñón(ona).

grunt [grʌnt] *vi* gruñir.

G-string *n* taparrabos *m inv*, tanga *m*.

guarantee [,gærən'tiː] ◇ *n* garantía *f*. ◇ *vt* garantizar.

guard [gɑːd] ◇ *n* **-1.** [person] guardia *m* y *f*. **-2.** [group of guards, operation] guardia *f*; **to be on/stand ~** estar de/hacer guardia; **to catch sb off ~** coger a alguien desprevenido. **-3.** *Br* RAIL jefe *m* de tren. **-4.** [protective device - for body] protector *m*; [- for machine] cubierta *f* protectora. ◇ *vt* **-1.** [protect, hide] guardar. **-2.** [prevent from escaping] vigilar.

guard dog *n* perro *m* guardián.

guarded ['gɑːdɪd] *adj* cauteloso(sa).

guardian ['gɑːdjən] *n* **-1.** [of child] tutor

m, -ra *f*. **-2.** [protector] guardián *m*, -ana *f*, protector *m*, -ra *f*.

guardrail ['gɑːdreɪl] *n Am* [on road] pretil *m*.

guard's van *n Br* furgón *m* de cola.

Guatemala [ˌgwɑːtəˈmɑːlə] *n* Guatemala.

Guatemalan [ˌgwɑːtəˈmɑːlən] ◇ *adj* guatemalteco(ca). ◇ *n* guatemalteco *m*, -ca *f*.

guerilla [gəˈrɪlə] = **guerrilla**.

Guernsey ['gɜːnzɪ] *n* [place] Guernsey.

guerrilla [gəˈrɪlə] *n* guerrillero *m*, -ra *f*.

guerrilla warfare *n* (U) guerra *f* de guerrillas.

guess [ges] ◇ *n* suposición *f*, conjetura *f*; **to take a ~** intentar adivinar. ◇ *vt* adivinar; **~ what? ¿sabes qué?** ◇ *vi* **-1.** [conjecture] suponer, conjeturar; **to ~ at sthg** tratar de adivinar algo. **-2.** [suppose]: **I ~ (so)** supongo OR me imagino que sí.

guesswork ['gesw3ːk] *n* (U) conjeturas *fpl*, suposiciones *fpl*.

guest [gest] *n* **-1.** [at home] invitado *m*, -da *f*. **-2.** [at hotel] huésped *m y f*.

guesthouse ['gesthaus, *pl* -hauzɪz] *n* casa *f* de huéspedes.

guestroom ['gestrum] *n* cuarto *m* de los huéspedes.

guffaw [gʌˈfɔː] ◇ *n* carcajada *f*. ◇ *vi* reírse a carcajadas.

guidance ['gaɪdəns] *n* (U) **-1.** [help] orientación *f*. **-2.** [leadership] dirección *f*.

guide [gaɪd] ◇ *n* **-1.** [person] guía *m y f*. **-2.** [book] guía *f*. ◇ *vt* **-1.** [show by leading] guiar. **-2.** [control] conducir, dirigir. **-3.** [influence]: **to be ~d** by guiarse por. ◆ **Guide** *n* = Girl Guide.

guide book *n* guía *f*.

guide dog *n* perro *m* lazarillo.

guidelines ['gaɪdlaɪnz] *npl* directrices *fpl*.

guild [gɪld] *n* **-1.** HISTORY gremio *m*. **-2.** [association] corporación *f*.

guile [gaɪl] *n* (U) *literary* astucia *f*.

guillotine ['gɪləˌtiːn] *n* [gen] guillotina *f*.

guilt [gɪlt] *n* **-1.** [remorse] culpa *f*. **-2.** JUR culpabilidad *f*.

guilty ['gɪltɪ] *adj* [gen]: **~ (of)** culpable (de); **to be found ~/not ~** ser declarado culpable/inocente.

guinea pig ['gɪnɪ-] *n lit & fig* conejillo *m* de Indias.

guise [gaɪz] *n fml* apariencia *f*.

guitar [gɪˈtɑːr] *n* guitarra *f*.

guitarist [gɪˈtɑːrɪst] *n* guitarrista *m y f*.

gulf [gʌlf] *n* **-1.** [sea] golfo *m*. **-2.** [chasm] sima *f*, abismo *m*. **-3.** [big difference]: **~ (between)** abismo *m* (entre). ◆ **Gulf** *n*: **the Gulf** el Golfo.

gull [gʌl] *n* gaviota *f*.

gullet ['gʌlɪt] *n* esófago *m*.

gullible ['gʌləbl] *adj* crédulo(la).

gully ['gʌlɪ] *n* barranco *m*.

gulp [gʌlp] ◇ *n* trago *m*. ◇ *vt* [liquid] tragarse; [food] engullir. ◇ *vi* tragar saliva. ◆ **gulp down** *vt sep* [liquid] tragarse; [food] engullir.

gum [gʌm] ◇ *n* **-1.** [chewing gum] chicle *m*. **-2.** [adhesive] cola *f*, pegamento *m*. **-3.** ANAT encía *f*. ◇ *vt* pegar, engomar.

gumboots ['gʌmbuːts] *npl Br* botas *fpl* de agua OR de goma.

gun [gʌn] *n* **-1.** [pistol] pistola *f*; [rifle] escopeta *f*, fusil *m*. **-2.** [tool] pistola *f*. ◆ **gun down** *vt sep* abatir (a tiros).

gunboat ['gʌnbəʊt] *n* cañonero *m*.

gunfire ['gʌnfaɪər] *n* (U) disparos *mpl*, tiroteo *m*.

gunman ['gʌnmən] (*pl* -men [-mən]) *n* pistolero *m*.

gunpoint ['gʌnpɔɪnt] *n*: **at ~** a punta de pistola.

gunpowder ['gʌnˌpaʊdər] *n* pólvora *f*.

gunshot ['gʌnʃɒt] *n* tiro *m*, disparo *m*.

gunsmith ['gʌnsmɪθ] *n* armero *m*.

gurgle ['gɜːgl] *vi* **-1.** [water] gorgotear. **-2.** [baby] gorjear.

guru ['gʊruː] *n lit & fig* gurú *m*.

gush [gʌʃ] ◇ *n* chorro *m*. ◇ *vi* **-1.** [flow out] chorrear, manar. **-2.** *pej* [enthuse] ser muy efusivo(va).

gusset ['gʌsɪt] *n* escudete *m*.

gust [gʌst] *n* ráfaga *f*, racha *f*.

gusto ['gʌstəʊ] *n*: **with ~** con deleite.

gut [gʌt] ◇ *n* **-1.** MED intestino *m*. **-2.** [strong thread] sedal *m*. ◇ *vt* **-1.** [animal] destripar. **-2.** [building etc] destruir el interior de. ◆ **guts** *npl inf* **-1.** [intestines] tripas *fpl*; **to hate sb's ~s** odiar a alguien a muerte. **-2.** [courage] agallas *fpl*.

gutter ['gʌtər] *n* **-1.** [ditch] cuneta *f*. **-2.** [on roof] canalón *m*.

gutter press *n pej* prensa *f* amarilla OR sensacionalista.

guy [gaɪ] *n* **-1.** *inf* [man] tipo *m*, tío *m*, chavo *m Amer*. **-2.** *Br* [dummy] muñeco que se quema en Gran Bretaña la noche de Guy Fawkes.

Guy Fawkes' Night *n fiesta que se celebra el 5 de noviembre en Gran Bretaña en que se encienden hogueras y se lanzan fuegos artificiales.*

guy rope *n* viento *m*, cuerda *f* (*de tienda de campaña*).

guzzle ['gʌzl] ◇ *vt* zamparse. ◇ *vi* zampar.

gym [dʒɪm] *n* *inf* **-1.** [gymnasium] gimnasio *m*. **-2.** [exercises] gimnasia *f*.

gymnasium [dʒɪm'neɪzjəm] (*pl* **-siums** OR **-sia** [-zjə]) *n* gimnasio *m*.

gymnast ['dʒɪmnæst] *n* gimnasta *m y f*.

gymnastics [dʒɪm'næstɪks] *n* (*U*) gimnasia *f*.

gym shoes *npl* zapatillas *fpl* de gimnasia.

gymslip ['dʒɪm,slɪp] *n* *Br* bata *f* de colegio.

gynaecologist *Br*, **gynecologist** *Am* [,gaɪnə'kɒlədʒɪst] *n* ginecólogo *m*, -ga *f*.

gynaecology *Br*, **gynecology** *Am* [,gaɪnə'kɒlədʒɪ] *n* ginecología *f*.

gypsy ['dʒɪpsɪ] = **gipsy**.

gyrate [dʒaɪ'reɪt] *vi* girar.

h (*pl* **h's** OR **hs**), **H** (*pl* **H's** OR **Hs**) [eɪtʃ] *n* [letter] h *f*, H *f*.

haberdashery ['hæbədæʃərɪ] *n* mercería *f*.

habit ['hæbɪt] *n* **-1.** [custom] costumbre *f*, hábito *m*; **to make a ~ of doing sthg** tener por costumbre hacer algo. **-2.** [garment] hábito *m*.

habitat ['hæbɪtæt] *n* hábitat *m*.

habitual [hə'bɪtʃuəl] *adj* **-1.** [usual] habitual, acostumbrado(da). **-2.** [smoker, gambler] empedernido(da).

hack [hæk] ◇ *n* *pej* [writer] escritorzuelo *m*, -la *f*; [journalist] gacetillero *m*, -ra *f*. ◇ *vt* [cut] cortar en tajos, acuchillar.
◆ **hack into** *vt fus* piratear.

hacker ['hækər] *n*: **(computer) ~** pirata *m y f* informático.

hackneyed ['hæknɪd] *adj* *pej* trillado(da), gastado(da).

hacksaw ['hæksɔː] *n* sierra *f* para metales.

had [*weak form* həd, *strong form* hæd] *pt & pp* → **have**.

haddock ['hædək] (*pl inv*) *n* eglefino *m*.

hadn't ['hædnt] = **had not**.

haemophiliac [,hiːmə'fɪlɪæk] = **hemophiliac**.

haemorrhage ['hemərɪdʒ] = **hemorrhage**.

haemorrhoids ['hemərɔɪdz] = **hemorrhoids**.

haggard ['hægəd] *adj* ojeroso(sa).

haggis ['hægɪs] *n* plato típico escocés hecho con las asaduras del cordero.

haggle ['hægl] *vi*: **to ~ (with sb over** OR **about sthg)** regatear (algo con alguien).

Hague [heɪg] *n*: **The ~** La Haya.

hail [heɪl] ◇ *n* **-1.** METEOR granizo *m*, pedrisco *m*. **-2.** *fig* [large number] lluvia *f*. ◇ *vt* **-1.** [call] llamar. **-2.** [acclaim]: **to ~ sb as sthg** aclamar a alguien algo; **to ~ sthg as sthg** ensalzar algo catalogándolo de algo. ◇ *v impers* granizar.

hailstone ['heɪlstəun] *n* granizo *m*, piedra *f*.

hair [heər] *n* **-1.** (*U*) [gen] pelo *m*; **to do one's ~** arreglarse el pelo. **-2.** [on person's skin] vello *m*.

hairbrush ['heəbrʌʃ] *n* cepillo *m* para el pelo.

haircut ['heəkʌt] *n* corte *m* de pelo.

hairdo ['heəduː] (*pl* **-s**) *n* *inf* peinado *m*.

hairdresser ['heə,dresər] *n* peluquero *m*, -ra *f*; **~'s (salon)** peluquería *f*.

hairdryer ['heə,draɪər] *n* secador *m* (de pelo).

hair gel *n* gomina *f*.

hairgrip ['heəgrɪp] *n* *Br* horquilla *f*.

hairpin ['heəpɪn] *n* horquilla *f* de moño.

hairpin bend *n* curva *f* muy cerrada.

hair-raising [-,reɪzɪŋ] *adj* espeluznante.

hair remover [-rɪ,muːvər] *n* depilatorio *m*.

hair slide *n* *Br* pasador *m*.

hairspray ['heəspreɪ] *n* laca *f* (para el pelo).

hairstyle ['heəstaɪl] *n* peinado *m*.

hairy ['heərɪ] *adj* **-1.** [covered in hair] peludo(da). **-2.** *inf* [scary] espeluznante, espantoso(sa).

Haiti ['heɪtɪ] *n* Haití.

hake [heɪk] (*pl inv* OR **-s**) *n* merluza *f*.

half [*Br* hɑːf, *Am* hæf] (*pl senses 1 and 3* **halves**, *pl senses 2 and 4* **halves** OR **halfs**) ◇ *adj* medio(dia); **~ a dozen/ mile** media docena/milla; **~ an hour** media hora. ◇ *adv* **-1.** [gen]: **~ full/ open** lleno/abierto por la mitad; **~ and ~** mitad y mitad. **-2.** [by half]: **~ as big (as)** la mitad de grande (que). **-3.** [in telling the time]: ~ **past nine**, ~ **after nine** *Am* las nueve y media; **it's ~ past** son y media. ◊ *n* **-1.** [one of two parts] mitad *f*; ~ **(of) the group** la mitad del grupo; **a pound/mile and a ~** una libra/milla y media; **in ~** por la mitad, en dos; **to go halves (with sb)** ir a medias (con alguien). **-2.** [fraction, halfback, child's ticket] medio *m*. **-3.** [of sports match] tiempo *m*, mitad *f*. **-4.** [of beer] media pinta *f*. ◊ *pron* la mitad; ~ **of it/them** la mitad.

halfback ['hɑːfbæk] *n* medio *m*.

half board *n* media pensión *f*.

half-breed ◊ *adj* mestizo(za). ◊ *n* mestizo *m*, -za *f* (*atención: el término "half-breed" se considera racista*).

half-caste [-kɑːst] ◊ *adj* mestizo(za). ◊ *n* mestizo *m*, -za *f* (*atención: el término "half-caste" se considera racista*).

half-hearted [-'hɑːtɪd] *adj* poco entusiasta.

half hour *n* media hora *f*.

half-mast *n*: **at ~** [flag] a media asta.

half moon *n* media luna *f*.

half note *n Am* MUS blanca *f*.

halfpenny ['heɪpnɪ] (*pl* **-pennies** OR **-pence**) *n* medio penique *m*.

half-price *adj* a mitad de precio.

half term *n Br* breves vacaciones escolares a mitad de trimestre.

half time *n* (*U*) descanso *m*.

halfway [hɑːf'weɪ] ◊ *adj* intermedio(dia). ◊ *adv* **-1.** [in space]: **I was ~ down the street** llevaba la mitad de la calle andada. **-2.** [in time]: **the film was ~ through** la película iba por la mitad.

halibut ['hælɪbət] (*pl inv* OR **-s**) *n* halibut *m*.

hall [hɔːl] *n* **-1.** [in house] vestíbulo *m*. **-2.** [public building] sala *f*. **-3.** *Br* UNIV colegio *m* mayor. **-4.** [country house] mansión *f*, casa *f* solariega.

hallmark ['hɔːlmɑːk] *n* **-1.** [typical feature] sello *m* distintivo. **-2.** [on metal] contraste *m*.

hallo [hə'ləʊ] = **hello**.

hall of residence (*pl* **halls of residence**) *n Br* residencia *f* universitaria, colegio *m* mayor.

Hallowe'en [ˌhæləʊ'iːn] *n fiesta celebrada la noche del 31 de octubre.*

hallucinate [hə'luːsɪneɪt] *vi* alucinar.

hallway ['hɔːlweɪ] *n* vestíbulo *m*.

halo ['heɪləʊ] (*pl* **-es** OR **-s**) *n* halo *m*, aureola *f*.

halt [hɔːlt] ◊ *n* [stop]: **to come to a ~** [vehicle] pararse; [activity] interrumpirse;

to call a ~ to poner fin a. ◊ *vt* [person] parar, detener; [development, activity] interrumpir. ◊ *vi* [person, train] **pararse**, **detenerse**; [development, activity] interrumpirse.

halterneck ['hɔːltənek] *adj* escotado(da) por detrás.

halve [*Br* hɑːv, *Am* hæv] *vt* **-1.** [reduce by half] reducir a la mitad. **-2.** [divide] partir en dos.

halves [*Br* hɑːvz, *Am* hævz] *pl* → **half**.

ham [hæm] ◊ *n* [meat] jamón *m*. ◊ *comp* de jamón.

hamburger ['hæmbɜːgər] *n* **-1.** [burger] hamburguesa *f*. **-2.** (*U*) *Am* [mince] carne *f* picada.

hamlet ['hæmlɪt] *n* aldea *f*.

hammer ['hæmər] ◊ *n* [gen & SPORT] martillo *m*. ◊ *vt* **-1.** [with tool] martillear. **-2.** [with fist] aporrear. **-3.** *inf* [defeat] dar una paliza a. ◊ *vi* [with fist]: **to ~ (on sthg)** aporrear (algo). ◆ **hammer out** *vt fus* [solution, agreement] alcanzar con esfuerzo.

hammock ['hæmək] *n* hamaca *f*, chinchorro *m Amer*.

hamper ['hæmpər] ◊ *n* **-1.** [for food] cesta *f*. **-2.** *Am* [for laundry] cesto *m* de la ropa sucia. ◊ *vt* obstaculizar.

hamster ['hæmstər] *n* hámster *m*.

hamstring ['hæmstrɪŋ] *n* tendón *m* de la corva.

hand [hænd] ◊ *n* **-1.** [gen] mano *f*; **to hold ~s** ir cogidos de la mano; ~ **in** [people] (cogidos) de la mano; **by ~ a** mano; **in the ~s of** en manos de; **to have sthg on one's ~s** tener uno algo en sus manos; **to get** OR **lay one's ~s on sthg** hacerse con algo; **to get** OR **lay one's ~s on sb** pillar a alguien; **to get out of ~** [situation] hacerse incontrolable; [person] desmandarse; **to give** OR **lend sb a ~ (with)** echar una mano a alguien (con); **to have one's ~s full** estar muy ocupado; **to have time in ~** tener tiempo de sobra; **to take sb in ~** hacerse cargo OR ocuparse de alguien; **to try one's ~ at sthg** intentar hacer algo. **-2.** [influence] influencia *f*. **-3.** [worker - on farm] bracero *m*, peón *m*; [- on ship] tripulante *m*. **-4.** [of clock, watch] manecilla *f*, aguja *f*. **-5.** [handwriting] letra *f*. ◊ *vt*: **to ~ sthg to sb**, **to ~ sb sthg** dar OR entregar algo a alguien. ◆ **(close) at hand** *adv* cerca. ◆ **on hand** *adv* al alcance de la mano. ◆ **on the other hand** *conj* por otra parte. ◆ **out of hand** *adv* [completely] ter-

minantemente. ◆**to hand** *adv* a mano.
◆**hand down** *vt sep* [heirloom] pasar en
herencia; [knowledge] transmitir.
◆**hand in** *vt sep* entregar. ◆**hand out**
vt sep repartir, distribuir. ◆**hand over**
◇ *vt sep* **-1.** [baton, money] entregar. **-2.**
[responsibility, power] ceder. ◇ *vi:* **to ~**
over (to) dar paso (a).

handbag ['hændbæg] *n* bolso *m*.

handball ['hændbɔ:l] *n* balonmano *m*.

handbook ['hændbʊk] *n* manual *m*.

handbrake ['hændbreɪk] *n* freno *m* de
mano.

handcuffs ['hændkʌfs] *npl* esposas *fpl*.

handful ['hændfʊl] *n* [gen] puñado *m*.

handgun ['hændgʌn] *n* pistola *f*.

handicap ['hændɪkæp] ◇ *n* **-1.** [disabil-
ity] incapacidad *f*, minusvalía *f*. **-2.** [dis-
advantage] desventaja *f*, obstáculo *m*.
-3. SPORT hándicap *m*. ◇ *vt* estorbar.

handicapped ['hændɪkæpt] ◇ *adj* mi-
nusválido(da). ◇ *npl:* **the ~** los minusválidos.

handicraft ['hændɪkrɑːft] *n* [skill] trabajos *mpl* manuales, artesanía *f*.

handiwork ['hændɪwɜːk] *n* (U) [doing,
work] obra *f*.

handkerchief ['hæŋkətʃɪf] (*pl* -**chiefs** OR
-**chieves** [-tʃiːvz]) *n* pañuelo *m*.

handle ['hændl] ◇ *n* [of door, window]
pomo *m*; [of tool] mango *m*; [of suitcase,
cup, jug] asa *f*. ◇ *vt* [gen] manejar; [or-
der, complaint, application] encargarse
de; [negotiations, takeover] conducir;
[people] tratar.

handlebars ['hændlbɑːz] *npl* manillar *m*.

handler ['hændlər] *n* **-1.** [of animal] guardián *m*, -ana *f*. **-2.** [at airport]: (**baggage**)
~ mozo *m* de equipajes.

hand luggage *n* Br equipaje *m* de
mano.

handmade [,hænd'meɪd] *adj* hecho(cha)
a mano.

handout ['hændaʊt] *n* **-1.** [gift] donativo
m. **-2.** [leaflet] hojas *fpl* (informativas).

handrail ['hændreɪl] *n* pasamano *m*.

handset ['hændset] *n* auricular *m* (*de teléfono*); **to lift/replace the ~** descolgar/
colgar (el teléfono).

handshake ['hændʃeɪk] *n* apretón *m* de
manos.

handsome ['hænsəm] *adj* **-1.** [man] guapo, atractivo. **-2.** [literary] [woman] be-
lla. **-3.** [reward, profit] considerable.

handstand ['hændstænd] *n* pino *m*.

handwriting ['hænd,raɪtɪŋ] *n* letra *f*, caligrafía *f*.

handy ['hændɪ] *adj inf* **-1.** [useful] prácti-
co(ca); **to come in ~** venir bien. **-2.**
[skilful] mañoso(sa). **-3.** [near] a mano,
cerca.

handyman ['hændɪmæn] (*pl* -**men**
[-men]) *n*: **a good ~** un manitas.

hang [hæŋ] (*pt & pp sense 1* **hung**, *pt &
pp sense 2* **hung** OR **hanged**) ◇ *vt* **-1.**
[fasten] colgar. **-2.** [execute] ahorcar. ◇
vi **-1.** [be fastened] colgar, pender. **-2.**
[be executed] ser ahorcado(da). ◇ *n*: **to
get the ~ of sthg** *inf* coger el tranquillo
a algo. ◆**hang about, hang around** *vi*
pasar el rato; **they didn't ~ about se
pusieron en marcha sin perder un mi-
nuto. ◆**hang on** *vi* **-1.** [keep hold]: **to
~ on (to)** agarrarse (a). **-2.** *inf* [continue
waiting] esperar, aguardar. **-3.** [per-
severe] resistir. ◆**hang out** *vi inf* [spend
time] moverse, pasar el rato. ◆**hang
round** = **hang about.** ◆**hang up** ◇ *vt
sep* colgar. ◇ *vi* colgar. ◆**hang up on**
vt fus colgar.

hangar ['hæŋər] *n* hangar *m*.

hanger ['hæŋər] *n* percha *f*.

hanger-on (*pl* **hangers-on**) *n* lapa *f*,
moscón *m*, -ona *f*.

hang gliding *n* vuelo *m* con ala delta.

hangover ['hæŋ,əʊvər] *n* [from drinking]
resaca *f*.

hang-up *n inf* complejo *m*.

hanker ['hæŋkər] ◆**hanker after,
hanker for** *vt fus* anhelar.

hankie, hanky ['hæŋkɪ] (*abbr of* **handkerchief**) *n inf* pañuelo *m*.

haphazard [,hæp'hæzəd] *adj* caóti-
co(ca).

hapless ['hæplɪs] *adj literary* desventu-
rado(da), desgraciado(da).

happen ['hæpən] *vi* **-1.** [occur] pasar,
ocurrir; **to ~ to sb** pasarle OR sucederle
a alguien. **-2.** [chance]: **I ~ed to be
looking out of the window** ... dio la
casualidad de que estaba mirando por
la ventana ...; **do you ~ to have a pen
on you?** ¿no tendrás un boli acaso OR
por casualidad?; **as it ~s** ... da la casualidad de que ....

happening ['hæpənɪŋ] *n* suceso *m*,
acontecimiento *m*.

happily ['hæpɪlɪ] *adv* **-1.** [with pleasure]
alegremente, felizmente. **-2.** [fortu-
nately] afortunadamente.

happiness ['hæpɪnɪs] *n* [state] felicidad *f*;
[feeling] alegría *f*.

happy ['hæpɪ] *adj* **-1.** [gen] feliz, con-
tento(ta); **~ Christmas/birthday!** ¡Feliz
Navidad/cumpleaños!; **to be ~ with/**

about sthg estar contento con algo. **-2.** [causing contentment] **feliz, alegre. -3.** [fortunate] **feliz, oportuno(na). -4.** [willing]: **to be ~ to do sthg** estar más que dispuesto(ta) a hacer algo; **I'd be ~ to do it** yo lo haría con gusto.

happy-go-lucky *adj* despreocupado(da).

happy medium *n* término *m* medio.

harangue [həˈræŋ] ◇ *n* arenga *f*. ◇ *vt* arengar.

harass [ˈhærəs] *vt* acosar.

harbour *Br*, **harbor** *Am* [ˈhɑːbəʳ] ◇ *n* puerto *m*. ◇ *vt* **-1.** [feeling] abrigar. **-2.** [person] dar refugio a, encubrir.

hard [hɑːd] ◇ *adj* **-1.** [gen] duro(ra); [frost] fuerte; **to be ~ on sb/sthg** [subj: person] ser duro con alguien/algo; [subj: work, strain] perjudicar a alguien/algo; [subj: result] ser inmerecido para alguien/algo. **-2.** [difficult] difícil. **-3.** [forceful - push, kick etc] fuerte. **-4.** [fact, news] concreto(ta). **-5.** *Br* [extreme]: **~ left/right** extrema izquierda/derecha. ◇ *adv* **-1.** [try] mucho; [work, rain] intensamente; [listen] atentamente. **-2.** [push, kick] fuerte, con fuerza. **-3.** *phr*: **to be ~ pushed** OR **put** OR **pressed to do sthg** vérselas y deseárselas para hacer algo; **to feel ~ done by** sentirse tratado injustamente.

hardback [ˈhɑːdbæk] *n* edición *f* en pasta dura OR en tela.

hardboard [ˈhɑːdbɔːd] *n* madera *f* conglomerada.

hard-boiled *adj lit* & *fig* duro(ra).

hard cash *n* dinero *m* contante y sonante.

hard copy *n* COMPUT copia *f* impresa.

hard disk *n* COMPUT disco *m* duro.

harden [ˈhɑːdn] ◇ *vt* **-1.** [gen] endurecer. **-2.** [resolve, opinion] reforzar. ◇ *vi* **-1.** [gen] endurecerse. **-2.** [resolve, opinion] reforzarse.

hard-headed [-ˈhedɪd] *adj* realista.

hard-hearted [-ˈhɑːtɪd] *adj* insensible.

hard labour *n* (*U*) trabajos *mpl* forzados.

hard-liner *n* partidario *m*, -ria *f* de la línea dura.

hardly [ˈhɑːdlɪ] *adv* apenas; **~ ever/ anything** casi nunca/nada; **I'm ~ a communist, am I?** ¡pues sí que tengo yo mucho que ver con el comunismo!

hardness [ˈhɑːdnɪs] *n* **-1.** [firmness] dureza *f*. **-2.** [difficulty] dificultad *f*.

hardship [ˈhɑːdʃɪp] *n* **-1.** (*U*) [difficult

conditions] privaciones *fpl*. **-2.** [difficult circumstance] infortunio *m*.

hard shoulder *n Br* AUT arcén *m*.

hard up *adj inf* sin un duro; **to be ~ for sthg** andar escaso de algo.

hardware [ˈhɑːdweəʳ] *n* (*U*) **-1.** [tools, equipment] artículos *mpl* de ferretería. **-2.** COMPUT hardware *m*.

hardware shop *n* ferretería *f*.

hardwearing [ˌhɑːdˈweərɪŋ] *adj Br* resistente, duradero(ra).

hardworking [ˌhɑːdˈwɜːkɪŋ] *adj* trabajador(ra).

hardy [ˈhɑːdɪ] *adj* **-1.** [person, animal] fuerte, robusto(ta). **-2.** [plant] resistente.

hare [heəʳ] *n* liebre *f*.

harebrained [ˈheəˌbreɪnd] *adj inf* atolondrado(da).

harelip [ˌheəˈlɪp] *n* labio *m* leporino.

haricot (bean) [ˈhærɪkəʊ-] *n* judía *f*, alubia *f*.

Harley Street [ˈhɑːlɪ-] *n calle londinense famosa por sus médicos especialistas.*

harm [hɑːm] ◇ *n* daño *m*; **to do ~ to sthg/sb**, **to do sthg/sb ~** [physically] hacer daño a algo/alguien; *fig* perjudicar algo/a alguien; **to be out of ~'s way** estar a salvo. ◇ *vt* [gen] hacer daño a, dañar; [reputation, chances, interests] dañar.

harmful [ˈhɑːmfʊl] *adj*: **~ (to)** perjudicial OR dañino(na) (para).

harmless [ˈhɑːmlɪs] *adj* inofensivo(va).

harmonica [hɑːˈmɒnɪkə] *n* armónica *f*.

harmonize, -ise [ˈhɑːmənaɪz] ◇ *vi*: **to ~ (with)** armonizar (con). ◇ *vt* armonizar.

harmony [ˈhɑːmənɪ] *n* armonía *f*.

harness [ˈhɑːnɪs] ◇ *n* [for horse] arreos *mpl*, guarniciones *fpl*. ◇ *vt* **-1.** [horse] enjaezar. **-2.** [use] aprovechar.

harp [hɑːp] *n* arpa *f*. ◆ **harp on** *vi*: **to ~ on (about sthg)** dar la matraca (con algo).

harpoon [hɑːˈpuːn] *n* arpón *m*.

harpsichord [ˈhɑːpsɪkɔːd] *n* clavicordio *m*.

harrowing [ˈhærəʊɪŋ] *adj* pavoroso(sa).

harsh [hɑːʃ] *adj* **-1.** [life, conditions, winter] duro(ra). **-2.** [punishment, decision, person] severo(ra). **-3.** [texture, taste, voice] áspero(ra); [light, sound] violento(ta).

harvest [ˈhɑːvɪst] ◇ *n* [gen] cosecha *f*, pizca *f Amer*; [of grapes] vendimia *f*. ◇ *vt* cosechar.

has [*weak form* həz, *strong form* hæz] *3rd person sg* → **have**.

has-been *n inf pej* vieja gloria *f*.

hash [hæʃ] *n* **-1.** [meat] picadillo *m* (de carne). **-2.** *inf* [mess]: **to make a ~ of sthg** hacer algo fatal.

hashish [ˈhæʃiːʃ] *n* hachís *m*.

hasn't [ˈhæznt] = **has not**.

hassle [ˈhæsl] *inf* ◇ *n* (U) [annoyance] rollo *m*, lío *m*. ◇ *vt* dar la lata a.

haste [heɪst] *n* prisa *f*; **to do sthg in ~** hacer algo de prisa y corriendo.

hasten [ˈheɪsn] *fml* ◇ *vt* acelerar. ◇ *vi*: **to ~ (to do sthg)** apresurarse (a hacer algo).

hastily [ˈheɪstɪlɪ] *adv* **-1.** [quickly] de prisa, precipitadamente. **-2.** [rashly] a la ligera, sin reflexionar.

hasty [ˈheɪstɪ] *adj* **-1.** [quick] apresurado(da), precipitado(da). **-2.** [rash] irreflexivo(va).

hat [hæt] *n* sombrero *m*.

hatch [hætʃ] ◇ *vi* **-1.** [chick] romper el cascarón, salir del huevo. **-2.** [egg] romperse. ◇ *vt* **-1.** [chick, egg] incubar. **-2.** *fig* [scheme, plot] idear, tramar. ◇ *n* [for serving food] ventanilla *f*.

hatchback [ˈhætʃˌbæk] *n* coche *m* con puerta trasera.

hatchet [ˈhætʃɪt] *n* hacha *f*.

hatchway [ˈhætʃˌweɪ] *n* escotilla *f*.

hate [heɪt] ◇ *n* odio *m*. ◇ *vt* odiar; **to ~ doing sthg** odiar hacer algo.

hateful [ˈheɪtfʊl] *adj* odioso(sa).

hatred [ˈheɪtrɪd] *n* odio *m*.

hat trick *n* SPORT tres tantos marcados por un jugador en el mismo partido.

haughty [ˈhɔːtɪ] *adj* altanero(ra), altivo(va).

haul [hɔːl] ◇ *n* **-1.** [of stolen goods] botín *m*; [of drugs] alijo *m*. **-2.** [distance]: **long ~** largo camino *m*, largo trayecto *m*. ◇ *vt* [pull] tirar, arrastrar.

haulage [ˈhɔːlɪdʒ] *n* transporte *m*.

haulier *Br* [ˈhɔːlɪər], **hauler** *Am* [ˈhɔːlər] *n* transportista *m* y *f*.

haunch [hɔːntʃ] *n* **-1.** [of person] asentaderas *fpl*; **to squat on one's ~es** ponerse en cuclillas. **-2.** [of animal] pernil *m*.

haunt [hɔːnt] ◇ *n* sitio *m* favorito. ◇ *vt* **-1.** [subj: ghost] aparecer en. **-2.** [subj: memory, fear, problem] atormentar.

have [hæv] (*pt* & *pp* **had**) ◇ *aux vb* (*to form perfect tenses*) haber; **to ~ eaten** haber comido; **he hasn't gone yet, has he?** no se habrá ido ya ¿no?; **no, he hasn't (done it)** no, no lo ha hecho; **yes, he has (done it)** sí, lo ha hecho; **I was out of breath, having run all the way** estaba sin aliento después de haber corrido todo el camino. ◇ *vt* **-1.** [possess, receive]: **to ~ (got)** tener; **I no money, I haven't got any money** no tengo dinero; **he has big hands** tiene las manos grandes; **do you ~ a car?, ~ you got a car?** ¿tienes coche? **-2.** [experience, suffer] tener; **I had an accident** tuve un accidente; **to ~ a cold** tener un resfriado. **-3.** (*referring to an action, instead of another verb*): **to ~ a look** mirar, echar una mirada; **to ~ a swim** darse un baño, nadar; **to ~ breakfast** desayunar; **to ~ lunch** comer; **to ~ dinner** cenar; **to ~ a cigarette** fumarse un cigarro; **to ~ an operation** operarse. **-4.** [give birth to]: **to ~ a baby** tener un niño. **-5.** [cause to be done]: **to ~ sb do sthg** hacer que alguien haga algo; **to ~ sthg done** hacer que se haga algo; **to ~ one's hair cut** (ir a) cortarse el pelo. **-6.** [be treated in a certain way]: **I had my car stolen** me robaron el coche. **-7.** *inf* [cheat]: **you've been had** te han timado. **-8.** *phr*: **to ~ had it** [car, machine] estar para el arrastre. ◇ *modal vb* [be obliged]: **to ~ (got) to do sthg** tener que hacer algo; **do you ~ to go?, ~ you got to go?** ¿tienes que irte? ◆ **have on** *vt sep* **-1.** [be wearing] llevar (puesto). **-2.** [tease] tomar el pelo a. **-3.** [have to do]: **~ you got anything on on Friday?** ¿estás libre OR haces algo el viernes? ◆ **have out** *vt sep* **-1.** [have removed]: **to ~ one's tonsils out** operarse de las amígdalas. **-2.** [discuss frankly]: **to ~ it out with sb** poner las cuentas claras con alguien.

haven [ˈheɪvn] *n fig* refugio *m*, asilo *m*.

haven't [ˈhævnt] = **have not**.

haversack [ˈhævəsæk] *n* mochila *f*.

havoc [ˈhævək] *n* (U) caos *m*, estragos *mpl*; **to play ~ with sthg** causar estragos en algo.

Hawaii [həˈwaɪiː] *n* Hawai.

hawk [hɔːk] *n* halcón *m*.

hawker [ˈhɔːkər] *n* vendedor *m*, -ra *f* ambulante.

hay [heɪ] *n* heno *m*.

hay fever *n* (U) fiebre *f* del heno.

haystack [ˈheɪˌstæk] *n* almiar *m*.

haywire [ˈheɪˌwaɪər] *adj inf*: **to go ~** [person] volverse majara(ja); [plan] liarse, embrollarse; [computer, TV etc] changarse.

hazard [ˈhæzəd] ◇ *n* riesgo *m*, peligro *m*. ◇ *vt* [guess, suggestion] aventurar.

hazardous ['hæzədəs] *adj* arriesgado(da), peligroso(sa).

hazard warning lights *npl Br* señales *fpl* de emergencia.

haze [heɪz] *n* neblina *f.*

hazel ['heɪzl] *adj* color avellana (*inv*).

hazelnut ['heɪzl,nʌt] *n* avellana *f.*

hazy ['heɪzɪ] *adj* **-1.** [misty] neblinoso(sa). **-2.** [vague] vago(ga), confuso(sa).

he [hiː] ◇ *pers pron* él; ~'s tall/happy es alto/feliz; HE can't do it ÉL no puede hacerlo; there ~ is allí está. ◇ *comp*: ~-goat macho cabrío *m.*

head [hed] ◇ *n* **-1.** ANAT & COMPUT cabeza *f*; a OR per ~ por persona, por cabeza; to be soft in the ~ estar mal de la sesera; to be off one's ~ *Br*, to be out of one's ~ *Am* estar como una cabra; it went to her ~ se le subió a la cabeza; to keep/lose one's ~ no perder/ perder la cabeza; to laugh one's ~ off reír a mandíbula batiente. **-2.** [mind, brain] talento *m*, aptitud *f*; she has a ~ for figures se le dan bien las cuentas. **-3.** [top - gen] cabeza *f*; [- of bed] cabecera *f.* **-4.** [of flower] cabezuela *f*; [of cabbage] cogollo *m.* **-5.** [leader] jefe *m*, -fa *f.* **-6.** [head teacher] director *m*, -ra *f* (de colegio). ◇ *vt* **-1.** [procession, convoy, list] encabezar. **-2.** [organization, delegation] dirigir. **-3.** FTBL cabecear. ◇ *vi*: to ~ north/for home dirigirse hacia el norte/a casa. ◆ heads *npl* [on coin] cara *f*; ~s or tails? ¿cara o cruz? ◆ head for *vt fus* **-1.** [place] dirigirse a. **-2.** *fig* [trouble, disaster] ir camino a.

headache ['hedeɪk] *n* **-1.** MED dolor *m* de cabeza. **-2.** *fig* [problem] quebradero *m* de cabeza.

headband ['hedbænd] *n* cinta *f*, banda *f* (*para el pelo*).

head boy *n Br* [at school] *alumno delegado principal que suele representar a sus condiscípulos en actos escolares.*

headdress ['hed,dres] *n* tocado *m.*

header ['hedə*r*] *n* FTBL cabezazo *m.*

headfirst [,hed'fɜːst] *adv* de cabeza.

head girl *n Br* [in school] *alumna delegada principal que suele representar a sus condiscípulas en actos escolares.*

heading ['hedɪŋ] *n* encabezamiento *m.*

headlamp ['hedlæmp] *n Br* faro *m.*

headland ['hedlənd] *n* cabo *m*, promontorio *m.*

headlight ['hedlaɪt] *n* faro *m.*

headline ['hedlaɪn] *n* titular *m.*

headlong ['hedlɒŋ] *adv* **-1.** [headfirst] de cabeza. **-2.** [quickly, unthinkingly] precipitadamente.

headmaster [,hed'mɑːstə*r*] *n* director *m* (de colegio).

headmistress [,hed'mɪstrɪs] *n* directora *f* (de colegio).

head office *n* oficina *f* central.

head-on ◇ *adj* de frente, frontal. ◇ *adv* de frente.

headphones ['hedfəʊnz] *npl* auriculares *mpl.*

headquarters [,hed'kwɔːtəz] *npl* (oficina *f*) central *f*, sede *f*; MIL cuartel *m* general.

headrest ['hedrest] *n* reposacabezas *m inv.*

headroom ['hedrʊm] *n* (*U*) [in car] espacio *m* entre la cabeza y el techo; [below bridge] altura *f* libre, gálibo *m.*

headscarf ['hedskɑːf] (*pl* -scarves [-skɑːvz] OR -scarfs) *n* pañuelo *m* (para la cabeza).

headset ['hedset] *n* auriculares *mpl* con micrófono.

head start *n*: ~ (on OR over) ventaja *f* (con respecto a).

headstrong ['hedstrɒŋ] *adj* obstinado(da).

head waiter *n* jefe *m* de rango OR de camareros.

headway ['hedweɪ] *n*: to make ~ avanzar, hacer progresos.

headwind ['hedwɪnd] *n* viento *m* de proa.

heady ['hedɪ] *adj* **-1.** [exciting] emocionante. **-2.** [causing giddiness] embriagador(ra).

heal [hiːl] ◇ *vt* **-1.** [person] curar, sanar; [wound] cicatrizar. **-2.** *fig* [troubles, discord] remediar. ◇ *vi* cicatrizar.

healing ['hiːlɪŋ] *n* curación *f.*

health [helθ] *n* **-1.** [gen] salud *f*; to be in good/poor ~ estar bien/mal de salud. **-2.** *fig* [of country, organization] buen estado *m.*

health centre *n* ambulatorio *m*, centro *m* sanitario.

health food *n* dietética.

health food shop *n* tienda *f* de dietética.

health service *n* servicio *m* sanitario de la Seguridad Social, ≃ INSALUD *m.*

healthy ['helθɪ] *adj* **-1.** [gen] sano(na), saludable. **-2.** [profit] pingüe. **-3.** [attitude, respect] natural, sano(na).

heap [hiːp] ◇ *n* montón *m*, pila *f.* ◇ *vt* [pile up]: to ~ sthg (on OR onto sthg)

hear [hɪəʳ] (pt & pp **heard** [hɜːd]) ◇ vt **-1.** [gen] oír; **I ~ (that)** me dicen que. **-2.** JUR ver. ◇ vi **-1.** [gen] oír; **have you heard about that job yet?** ¿sabes algo del trabajo ése?; **to ~ from sb** tener noticias de alguien. **-2.** phr: **to have heard of** haber oído hablar de; **I won't ~ of it!** ¡de eso ni hablar!

hearing ['hɪərɪŋ] n **-1.** [sense] oído m; **hard of ~** duro de oído. **-2.** JUR vista f.

hearing aid n audífono m.

hearsay ['hɪəseɪ] n (U) habladurías fpl.

hearse [hɜːs] n coche m fúnebre.

heart [hɑːt] n **-1.** [gen] corazón m; **from the ~** con toda sinceridad; **to break sb's ~** partir el corazón a alguien. **-2.** [courage]: **I didn't have the ~ to tell her** no tuve valor para decírselo; **to lose ~** descorazonarse. **-3.** [centre of issue, problem] quid m; [- of city etc] centro m; [- of lettuce] cogollo m. ◆ **hearts** npl corazones mpl. ◆ **at heart** adv en el fondo. ◆ **by heart** adv de memoria.

heartache ['hɑːteɪk] n congoja f.

heart attack n infarto m.

heartbeat ['hɑːtbiːt] n latido m.

heartbroken ['hɑːt,brəʊkn] adj desolado(da), abatido(da).

heartburn ['hɑːtbɜːn] n ardor m de estómago.

heart failure n paro m cardíaco.

heartfelt ['hɑːtfelt] adj sincero(ra), de todo corazón.

hearth [hɑːθ] n hogar m.

heartless ['hɑːtlɪs] adj cruel.

heartwarming ['hɑːt,wɔːmɪŋ] adj gratificante, grato(ta).

hearty ['hɑːtɪ] adj **-1.** [laughter] bonachón(ona); [welcome, congratulations, thanks] cordial; [person] fuertote(ta). **-2.** [meal] abundante; [appetite] bueno(na). **-3.** [dislike, distrust] profundo(da).

heat [hiːt] ◇ n **-1.** [gen] calor m. **-2.** [specific temperature] temperatura f. **-3.** fig [pressure] tensión f; **in the ~ of the moment** en el calor del momento. **-4.** [eliminating round] serie f, prueba f eliminatoria. **-5.** ZOOL: **on** Br OR **in ~** en celo. ◇ vt calentar. ◆ **heat up** ◇ vt sep calentar. ◇ vi calentarse.

heated ['hiːtɪd] adj acalorado(da).

heater ['hiːtəʳ] n calentador m.

heath [hiːθ] n [place] brezal m.

heathen ['hiːðn] n pagano m, -na f.

heather ['heðəʳ] n brezo m.

heating ['hiːtɪŋ] n calefacción f.

heatstroke ['hiːtstrəʊk] n (U) insolación f.

heat wave n ola f de calor.

heave [hiːv] ◇ vt **-1.** [pull] tirar de, arrastrar; [push] empujar. **-2.** inf [throw] tirar. ◇ vi **-1.** [pull] tirar. **-2.** [rise and fall - waves] ondular; [- chest] palpitar.

heaven ['hevn] n [Paradise] cielo m. ◆ **heavens** npl: **the ~s** literary los cielos; **(good) ~s!** ¡cielos!

heavenly ['hevnlɪ] adj inf dated [delightful] divino(na).

heavily ['hevɪlɪ] adv **-1.** [smoke, drink] mucho; [rain] con fuerza; **in debt** con muchas deudas. **-2.** [solidly]: **~ built** corpulento(ta). **-3.** [breathe, sigh] profundamente. **-4.** [sit, move, fall] pesadamente. **-5.** [speak] pesarosamente.

heavy ['hevɪ] adj **-1.** [gen] pesado(da); [solid] sólido(da); **~ build** corpulencia f; **how ~ is it?** ¿cuánto pesa? **-2.** [traffic, rain, fighting] intenso(sa); **to be a ~ smoker/drinker** ser un fumador/bebedor empedernido. **-3.** [soil, mixture] denso(sa). **-4.** [blow] duro(ra). **-5.** [busy - schedule, day] apretado(da). **-6.** [work] duro(ra). **-7.** [weather, air, day] cargado(da).

heavy cream n Am nata f para montar.

heavy goods vehicle n Br vehículo m (de transporte) pesado.

heavyweight ['hevɪweɪt] SPORT ◇ adj de los pesos pesados. ◇ n peso m pesado.

Hebrew ['hiːbruː] ◇ adj hebreo(a). ◇ n **-1.** [person] hebreo m, -a f. **-2.** [language] hebreo m.

Hebrides ['hebrɪdiːz] npl: **the ~** las Hébridas.

heck [hek] excl: **what/where/why the ~ ...?** ¿qué/dónde/por qué demonios ...?; **a ~ of a lot of** la mar de.

heckle ['hekl] vt & vi interrumpir con exabruptos.

hectic ['hektɪk] adj ajetreado(da).

he'd [hiːd] = **he had, he would**.

hedge [hedʒ] ◇ n seto m. ◇ vi [prevaricate] contestar con evasivas.

hedgehog ['hedʒhɒg] n erizo m.

heed [hiːd] ◇ n: **to take ~ of sthg** tener algo en cuenta. ◇ vt fml tener en cuenta.

heedless ['hiːdlɪs] adj: **to be ~ of sthg** no hacer caso de algo.

heel [hiːl] n **-1.** [of foot] talón m. **-2.** [of shoe] tacón m, taco m Amer.

hefty ['heftɪ] adj inf **-1.** [person] fornido(da). **-2.** [salary, fee, fine] considerable, importante.

heifer ['hefəʳ] n vaquilla f.

height [haɪt] n **-1.** [gen] altura f; [of person] estatura f; **5 metres in ~** 5 metros de altura; **what ~ is it/are you?** ¿cuánto mide/mides? **-2.** [zenith]: **the ~ of** [gen] **el punto álgido de;** [ignorance, bad taste] el colmo de.

heighten ['haɪtn] ◇ vt intensificar, aumentar. ◇ vi intensificarse, aumentar.

heir [eəʳ] n heredero m.

heiress ['eərɪs] n heredera f.

heirloom ['eəluːm] n reliquia f de familia.

heist [haɪst] n inf golpe m, robo m.

held [held] pt & pp → **hold.**

helicopter ['helɪkɒptəʳ] n helicóptero m.

helium ['hiːlɪəm] n helio m.

hell [hel] ◇ n infierno m; **what/where/why the ~ ...?** inf ¿qué/dónde/por qué demonios ...?; **one** OR **a ~ of a nice guy** inf un tipo estupendo; **to do sthg for the ~ of it** inf hacer algo porque sí; **to give sb ~** inf hacérselas pasar canutas a alguien; **go to ~!** v inf ¡vete al infierno! ◇ excl inf ¡hostias!

he'll [hiːl] = **he will.**

hellish ['helɪʃ] adj inf diabólico(ca).

hello [hə'ləʊ] excl **-1.** [as greeting] ¡hola!; [on phone - when answering] ¡diga!, ¡bueno! Amer; [- when calling] ¡oiga! **-2.** [to attract attention] ¡oiga!

helm [helm] n lit & fig timón m.

helmet ['helmɪt] n casco m.

help [help] ◇ n **-1.** [gen] ayuda f; **with the ~ of** con la ayuda de; **to be a ~** ser una ayuda; **to be of ~** ayudar. **-2.** (U) [emergency aid] socorro m, ayuda f. ◇ vt **-1.** [assist]: **to ~ sb (to) do sthg/with sthg)** ayudar a alguien (a hacer algo/con algo); **can I ~ you?** [in shop, bank] ¿en qué puedo servirle? **-2.** [avoid]: **I can't ~ it/feeling sad** no puedo evitarlo/evitar que me dé pena. **-3.** [with food, drink]: **to ~ o.s. (to sthg)** servirse (algo). ◇ vi: **to ~ (with)** ayudar (con). ◇ excl ¡socorro!, ¡auxilio! ◆ **help out** ◇ vt sep echar una mano a. ◇ vi echar una mano.

helper ['helpəʳ] n **-1.** [gen] ayudante m y f. **-2.** Am [to do housework] mujer f OR señora f de la limpieza.

helpful ['helpfʊl] adj **-1.** [willing to help] servicial, atento(ta). **-2.** [providing assistance] útil.

helping ['helpɪŋ] n ración f; **would you like a second ~?** ¿quiere repetir?

helpless ['helplɪs] adj [child] indefenso(sa); [look, gesture] impotente.

helpline ['helplaɪn] n servicio m telefónico de ayuda.

Helsinki ['helsɪŋkɪ] n Helsinki.

hem [hem] n dobladillo m. ◆ **hem in** vt sep rodear, cercar.

hemisphere ['hemɪˌsfɪəʳ] n [of earth] hemisferio m.

hemline ['hemlaɪn] n bajo m (de falda).

hemophiliac [ˌhiːmə'fɪlɪæk] n hemofílico m, -ca f.

hemorrhage ['hemərɪdʒ] n hemorragia f.

hemorrhoids ['hemərɔɪdz] npl hemorroides fpl.

hen [hen] n **-1.** [female chicken] gallina f. **-2.** [female bird] hembra f.

hence [hens] adv fml **-1.** [therefore] por lo tanto, así pues. **-2.** [from now]: **five years ~** de aquí a cinco años.

henceforth [ˌhens'fɔːθ] adv fml de ahora en adelante.

henchman ['hentʃmən] (pl **-men** [-mən]) n pej esbirro m.

henpecked ['henpekt] adj pej calzonazos (inv).

hepatitis [ˌhepə'taɪtɪs] n hepatitis f inv.

her [hɜːʳ] ◇ pers pron **-1.** (direct - unstressed) la; (- stressed) ella; [- referring to ship, car etc] la; **I know ~** la conozco; **I like ~** me gusta; **it's ~** es ella; **if I were** OR **was ~** si (yo) fuera ella; **you can't expect HER to do it** no esperarás que ELLA lo haga; **fill ~ up!** AUT ¡llénemelo!, ¡lléneme el depósito! **-2.** (indirect - gen) le; (- with other third person pronouns) se; **he sent ~ a letter** le mandó una carta; **we spoke to ~** hablamos con ella; **I gave it to ~** se lo di. **-3.** (after prep, in comparisons etc) ella; **I'm shorter than ~** yo soy más bajo que ella. ◇ poss adj su, sus (pl); **~ coat** su abrigo; **~ children** sus niños; **~ name is Sarah** se llama Sarah; **it wasn't HER fault** no fue culpa suya OR su culpa; **she washed ~ hair** se lavó el pelo.

herald ['herəld] ◇ vt fml **-1.** [signify, usher in] anunciar. **-2.** [proclaim] proclamar. ◇ n **-1.** [messenger] heraldo m. **-2.** [sign] anuncio m.

herb [hɜːb] n hierba f (aromática o medicinal).

herd [hɜːd] ◇ n manada f, rebaño m. ◇ vt fig [push] conducir (en grupo) bruscamente.

here [hɪəʳ] *adv* aquí; ~ **he is/they are** aquí está/están; ~ **it is** aquí está; ~ **is the book** aquí tienes el libro; ~ **and there** aquí y allá; ~ **are the keys** aquí tienes las llaves.

hereabouts *Br* [ˈhɪərəˌbaʊts], **hereabout** *Am* [ˌhɪərəˈbaʊt] *adv* por aquí.

hereafter [ˌhɪərˈɑːftəʳ] ◇ *adv fml* [from now on] de ahora en adelante; [later on] más tarde. ◇ *n:* **the** ~ el más allá, la otra vida.

hereby [ˌhɪəˈbaɪ] *adv fml* **-1.** [in documents] por la presente. **-2.** [when speaking]: **I** ~ **declare you the winner** desde este momento te declaro vencedor.

hereditary [hɪˈredɪtrɪ] *adj* hereditario(ria).

heresy [ˈherəsɪ] *n* RELIG & *fig* herejía *f.*

herewith [ˌhɪəˈwɪð] *adv fml* [with letter]: **please find** ~ ... le mando adjunto ....

heritage [ˈherɪtɪdʒ] *n* patrimonio *m.*

hermetically [hɜːˈmetɪklɪ] *adv:* ~ **sealed** cerrado(da) herméticamente.

hermit [ˈhɜːmɪt] *n* ermitaño *m,* -ña *f.*

hernia [ˈhɜːnjə] *n* hernia *f* de hiato OR hiatal.

hero [ˈhɪərəʊ] (*pl* -es) *n* **-1.** [gen] héroe *m.* **-2.** [idol] ídolo *m.*

heroic [hɪˈrəʊɪk] *adj* heroico(ca).

heroin [ˈherəʊɪn] *n* heroína *f* (*droga*).

heroine [ˈherəʊɪn] *n* heroína *f.*

heron [ˈherən] (*pl inv* OR -s) *n* garza *f* real.

herring [ˈherɪŋ] (*pl inv* OR -s) *n* arenque *m.*

hers [hɜːz] *poss pron* suyo (suya); **that money is** ~ ese dinero es suyo; **those keys are** ~ esas llaves son suyas; **it wasn't his fault, it was** HERS no fue culpa de él sino de ella; **a friend of** ~ un amigo suyo, un amigo de ella; **mine is good, but** ~ **is bad** el mío es bueno pero el suyo es malo.

herself [hɜːˈself] *pron* **-1.** (*reflexive*) se; (*after prep*) sí misma; **with** ~ consigo misma. **-2.** (*for emphasis*) ella misma; **she did it** ~ lo hizo ella sola.

he's [hiːz] = **he is, he has.**

hesitant [ˈhezɪtənt] *adj* **-1.** [unsure of oneself] indeciso(sa), inseguro(ra). **-2.** [faltering, slow to appear] vacilante.

hesitate [ˈhezɪteɪt] *vi* vacilar, dudar; **to** ~ **to do sthg** dudar en hacer algo.

hesitation [ˌhezɪˈteɪʃn] *n* vacilación *f.*

heterogeneous [ˌhetərəˈdʒiːnjəs] *adj fml* heterogéneo(a).

heterosexual [ˌhetərəʊˈsekʃʊəl] ◇ *adj* heterosexual. ◇ *n* heterosexual *m y f.*

het up [het-] *adj inf* nervioso(sa), hecho(cha) un manojo de nervios.

hey [heɪ] *excl* ¡eh!, ¡oye!

heyday [ˈheɪdeɪ] *n* apogeo *m,* auge *m.*

HGV *n abbr of* **heavy goods vehicle.**

hi [haɪ] *excl inf* [hello] ¡hola!

hiatus [haɪˈeɪtəs] (*pl* -es) *n fml* [pause] pausa *f.*

hibernate [ˈhaɪbəneɪt] *vi* hibernar.

hiccough, hiccup [ˈhɪkʌp] ◇ *n* **-1.** [caused by wind] hipo *m;* **to have** ~**s** tener hipo. **-2.** *fig* [difficulty] contratiempo *m.* ◇ *vi* hipar.

hid [hɪd] *pt* → **hide.**

hidden [ˈhɪdn] ◇ *pp* → **hide.** ◇ *adj* oculto(ta).

hide [haɪd] (*pt* hid, *pp* hidden) ◇ *vt* **-1.** [conceal] esconder, ocultar; **to** ~ **sthg (from sb)** esconder OR ocultar algo (a alguien). **-2.** [cover] tapar, ocultar. ◇ *vi* esconderse. ◇ *n* **-1.** [animal skin] piel *f.* **-2.** [for watching birds, animals] puesto *m.*

hide-and-seek *n* escondite *m.*

hideaway [ˈhaɪdəweɪ] *n inf* escondite *m.*

hideous [ˈhɪdɪəs] *adj* horrible.

hiding [ˈhaɪdɪŋ] *n* **-1.** [concealment]: **in** ~ escondido(da). **-2.** *inf* [beating]: **to give sb/get a (good)** ~ darle a alguien/ recibir una (buena) paliza.

hiding place *n* escondite *m.*

hierarchy [ˈhaɪərɑːkɪ] *n* jerarquía *f.*

hi-fi [ˈhaɪfaɪ] *n* equipo *m* de alta fidelidad.

high [haɪ] ◇ *adj* **-1.** [gen] alto(ta); [wind] fuerte; [altitude] grande; **it's 6 metres** ~ tiene 6 metros de alto OR altura; **how** ~ **is it?** ¿cuánto mide?; **temperatures in the** ~ **20s** temperaturas cercanas a los 30 grados. **-2.** [ideals, principles, tone] elevado(da). **-3.** [high-pitched] agudo(da). **-4.** *drug sl* flipado(da). ◇ *adv* alto; **he threw the ball** ~ **in the air** lanzó la bola muy alto. ◇ *n* [highest point] punto *m* álgido.

highbrow [ˈhaɪbraʊ] *adj* culto(ta), intelectual.

high chair *n* trona *f.*

high-class *adj* [superior] de (alta) categoría.

High Court *n Br* tribunal *m* supremo.

higher [ˈhaɪəʳ] *adj* [exam, qualification] supe- rior. ◆ **Higher** *n:* Higher (Grade) *en Escocia, examen realizado al final de la enseñanza secundaria.*

higher education *n* enseñanza *f* superior.

high-handed [-'hændɪd] *adj* despótico(ca), arbitrario(ria).

high jump *n* salto *m* de altura.

Highland Games ['haɪlənd-] *npl fiesta de deportes escoceses.*

Highlands ['haɪləndz] *npl*: **the ~** [of Scotland] las Tierras Altas del Norte (de Escocia).

highlight ['haɪlaɪt] ◇ *n* [of event, occasion] punto *m* culminante. ◇ *vt* **-1.** [visually] subrayar, marcar. **-2.** [emphasize] destacar, resaltar. ◆ **highlights** *npl* [in hair] reflejos *mpl*.

highlighter (pen) ['haɪlaɪtər-] *n* rotulador *m*, marcador *m*.

highly ['haɪlɪ] *adv* **-1.** [very, extremely] muy, enormemente. **-2.** [in important position]: **~ placed** en un puesto importante. **-3.** [favourably]: **to think ~ of sb** tener a alguien en mucha estima.

highly-strung *adj* muy nervioso(sa).

Highness ['haɪnɪs] *n*: **His/Her/Your (Royal) ~** Su Alteza *f* (Real); **their (Royal) ~es** Sus Altezas (Reales).

high-pitched [-'pɪtʃt] *adj* agudo(da).

high point *n* [of occasion] momento *m* OR punto *m* culminante.

high-powered [-'pauəd] *adj* **-1.** [powerful] de gran potencia. **-2.** [prestigious - activity, place] prestigioso(sa); [- person] de altos vuelos.

high-ranking [-'ræŋkɪŋ] *adj* [in army etc] de alta graduación; [in government]: **~ official** alto cargo *m*.

high-rise *adj*: **~ building** edificio de muchos pisos.

high school *n* ≃ instituto *m* de bachillerato.

high season *n* temporada *f* alta.

high street *n* Br calle *f* mayor OR principal.

high tech [-'tek] *adj* de alta tecnología.

high tide *n* [of sea] marea *f* alta.

highway ['haɪweɪ] *n* **-1.** Am [main road between cities] autopista *f*. **-2.** Br [any main road] carretera *f*.

Highway Code *n* Br: **the ~** el código de la circulación.

hijack ['haɪdʒæk] *vt* [aircraft] secuestrar.

hijacker ['haɪdʒækər] *n* secuestrador *m*, -ra *f* (*de un avión*).

hike [haɪk] ◇ *n* [long walk] caminata *f*. ◇ *vi* [go for walk] ir de excursión.

hiker ['haɪkər] *n* excursionista *m* y *f*.

hiking ['haɪkɪŋ] *n* excursionismo *m*; **to go ~** ir de excursión.

hilarious [hɪ'leərɪəs] *adj* desternillante.

hill [hɪl] *n* **-1.** [mound] colina *f*. **-2.** [slope] cuesta *f*.

hillside ['hɪlsaɪd] *n* ladera *f*.

hilly ['hɪlɪ] *adj* montañoso(sa).

hilt [hɪlt] *n* puño *m*, empuñadura *f*; **to support/defend sb to the ~** apoyar/defender a alguien sin reservas.

him [hɪm] *pers pron* **-1.** (*direct - unstressed*) lo, le; (*- stressed*) él; **I know ~** lo OR le conozco; **I like ~** me gusta; **it's ~** es él; **if I were** OR **was ~** si (yo) fuera él; **you can't expect** HIM **to do it** no esperarás que ÉL lo haga. **-2.** (*indirect - gen*) le; (*- with other third person pronouns*) se; **she sent ~ a letter** le mandó una carta; **we spoke to ~** hablamos con él; **I gave it to ~** se lo di. **-3.** (*after prep, in comparisons etc*) él; **I'm shorter than ~** yo soy más bajo que él.

Himalayas [,hɪmə'leɪəz] *npl*: **the ~** el Himalaya.

himself [hɪm'self] *pron* **-1.** (*reflexive*) se; (*after prep*) sí mismo; **with ~** consigo mismo. **-2.** (*for emphasis*) él mismo; **he did it ~** lo hizo él solo.

hind [haɪnd] (*pl inv* OR **-s**) ◇ *adj* trasero(ra), posterior. ◇ *n* cierva *f*.

hinder ['hɪndər] *vt* [gen] estorbar; [progress, talks, attempts] entorpecer.

Hindi ['hɪndɪ] *n* [language] hindi *m*.

hindrance ['hɪndrəns] *n* **-1.** [obstacle] obstáculo *m*, impedimento *m*; [person] estorbo *m*. **-2.** (U) [delay] interrupciones *fpl*, retrasos *mpl*.

hindsight ['haɪndsaɪt] *n*: **with the benefit of ~** ahora que se sabe lo que pasó.

Hindu ['hɪnduː] (*pl* **-s**) ◇ *adj* hindú. ◇ *n* hindú *m* y *f*.

hinge [hɪndʒ] *n* [on door, window] bisagra *f*. ◆ **hinge (up)on** *vt fus* [depend on] depender de.

hint [hɪnt] ◇ *n* **-1.** [indication] indirecta *f*; **to drop a ~** lanzar una indirecta. **-2.** [piece of advice] consejo *m*. **-3.** [small amount, suggestion] asomo *m*; [of colour] pizca *f*. ◇ *vi*: **to ~ at sthg** insinuar algo. ◇ *vt*: **to ~ that** insinuar que.

hip [hɪp] *n* ANAT cadera *f*.

hippie ['hɪpɪ] *n* hippy *m* y *f*.

hippopotamus [,hɪpə'pɒtəməs] (*pl* **-muses** OR **-mi** [-maɪ]) *n* hipopótamo *m*.

hippy ['hɪpɪ] *n* = **hippie**.

hire ['haɪər] ◇ *n* (U) [of car, equipment] alquiler *m*; **for ~** [taxi] libre; **boats for ~** se alquilan barcos. ◇ *vt* **-1.** [rent] alquilar. **-2.** [employ] contratar. ◆ **hire**

out vt sep [car, equipment] alquilar; [one's services] ofrecer.

hire car n Br coche m de alquiler.

hire purchase n (U) Br compra f a plazos.

his [hɪz] ◇ poss adj su, sus (pl); ~ **house** su casa; ~ **children** sus niños; ~ **name is** Joe se llama Joe; **it wasn't HIS fault** no fue culpa suya OR su culpa; **he washed** ~ **hair** se lavó el pelo. ◇ poss pron suyo (suya); **that money is** ~ ese dinero es suyo; **those keys are** ~ esas llaves son suyas; **it wasn't her fault, it was HIS** no fue culpa de ella sino de él; **a friend of** ~ un amigo suyo, un amigo de él; **mine is good, but** ~ **is bad** el mío es bueno pero el suyo es malo.

Hispanic [hɪ'spænɪk] ◇ adj hispánico(ca). ◇ n hispano m, -na f.

hiss [hɪs] ◇ n -1. [of person] bisbiseo m, siseo m. -2. [of steam, gas, snake] silbido m. ◇ vi -1. [person] bisbisear, sisear; [to express disapproval] ≃ silbar, ≃ pitar. -2. [steam, gas, snake] silbar.

historic [hɪ'stɒrɪk] adj [significant] histórico(ca).

historical [hɪ'stɒrɪkəl] adj histórico(ca).

history ['hɪstərɪ] n -1. [gen] historia f. -2. [past record] historial m.

hit [hɪt] (pt & pp **hit**) ◇ n -1. [blow] golpe m. -2. [successful strike] impacto m. -3. [success] éxito m. ◇ comp de éxito. ◇ vt -1. [subj: person] pegar, golpear. -2. [crash into] chocar contra OR con. -3. [reach] alcanzar, llegar a; [bull's-eye] dar en. -4. [affect badly] afectar. -5. phr: **to** ~ **it off (with sb)** hacer buenas migas (con alguien).

hit-and-miss = hit-or-miss.

hit-and-run adj [driver] que se da a la fuga después de causar un accidente.

hitch [hɪtʃ] ◇ n [problem, snag] obstáculo m, pega f. ◇ vt -1. [catch]: **to** ~ **a lift** conseguir que le lleven en coche a uno. -2. [fasten]: **to** ~ **sthg on** OR **onto sthg** enganchar algo a algo. ◇ vi [hitchhike] hacer autoestop. ◆ **hitch up** vt sep [clothes] subirse.

hitchhike ['hɪtʃhaɪk] vi hacer autoestop.

hitchhiker ['hɪtʃhaɪkə(r)] n autoestopista m y f.

hi-tech [,haɪ'tek] = high tech.

hitherto [,hɪðə'tuː] adv fml hasta ahora.

hit-or-miss adj azaroso(sa).

HIV (abbr of **human immunodeficiency virus**) n VIH m, HIV m; **to be** ~-**positive** ser seropositivo.

hive [haɪv] n [for bees] colmena f; **a** ~ **of activity** un enjambre, un centro de actividad. ◆ **hive off** vt sep [separate] transferir.

HNC (abbr of **Higher National Certificate**) n diploma técnico en Gran Bretaña.

HND (abbr of **Higher National Diploma**) n diploma técnico superior en Gran Bretaña.

hoard [hɔːd] ◇ n [store] acopio m. ◇ vt [collect, save] acumular; [food] acaparar.

hoarding ['hɔːdɪŋ] n Br [for advertisements, posters] valla f publicitaria.

hoarfrost ['hɔːfrɒst] n escarcha f.

hoarse [hɔːs] adj -1. [voice] ronco(ca). -2. [person] afónico(ca).

hoax [həʊks] n engaño m; ~ **call** falsa alarma telefónica.

hob [hɒb] n Br [on cooker] encimera f.

hobble ['hɒbl] vi [limp] cojear.

hobby ['hɒbɪ] n [leisure activity] hobby m, distracción f favorita.

hobbyhorse ['hɒbɪhɔːs] n -1. [toy] caballo m de juguete. -2. [favourite topic] caballo m de batalla.

hobo ['həʊbəʊ] (pl -es OR -s) n Am [tramp] vagabundo m, -da f.

hockey ['hɒkɪ] n -1. [on grass] hockey m sobre hierba. -2. Am [ice hockey] hockey m sobre hielo.

hoe [həʊ] ◇ n azada f. ◇ vt azadonar.

hog [hɒg] ◇ n cerdo m; **to go the whole** ~ fig ir a por todas. ◇ vt inf [monopolize] acaparar.

Hogmanay ['hɒgməneɪ] n denominación escocesa de la Nochevieja.

hoist [hɔɪst] ◇ n [pulley, crane] grúa f; [lift] montacargas m inv. ◇ vt izar.

hold [həʊld] (pt & pp **held**) ◇ vt -1. [have hold of] tener cogido(da). -2. [embrace] abrazar. -3. [keep in position, sustain, support] sostener, aguantar. -4. [as prisoner] detener; **to** ~ **sb prisoner/hostage** tener a alguien como prisionero/rehén. -5. [have, possess] poseer. -6. [contain - gen] contener; [- fears, promise etc] guardar; [- number of people] tener cabida para. -7. [conduct, stage - event] celebrar; [- conversation] mantener. -8. fml [consider] considerar; **to** ~ **sb responsible for sthg** considerar a alguien responsable de algo. -9. [on telephone]: **please** ~ **the line** no cuelgue por favor. -10. [maintain - interest etc] mantener. -11. MIL ocupar, tener. -12. phr: ~ **it** OR **everything!** ¡para!, ¡espera!; **to** ~ **one's own** defenderse. ◇ vi -1. [luck, weather] continuar así; [promise, offer] **seguir en pie**; **to ~ still** OR **steady** estarse quieto. **-2.** [on phone] esterar. ◇ *n* **-1.** [grasp, grip]: **to have a firm ~ on sthg** tener algo bien agarrado; **to take** OR **lay ~ of sthg** agarrar algo; **to get ~ of sthg** [obtain] hacerse con algo; **to get ~ of sb** [find] localizar a alguien. **-2.** [of ship, aircraft] bodega *f*. **-3.** [control, influence] dominio *m*. ◆ **hold back** *vt sep* **-1.** [tears, anger] contener, reprimir. **-2.** [secret] ocultar. ◆ **hold down** *vt sep* [job] conservar. ◆ **hold off** *vt sep* [fend off] mantener a distancia. ◆ **hold on** *vi* **-1.** [wait] esperar; [on phone] no colgar. **-2.** [grip]: **to ~ on (to sthg)** agarrarse (a algo). ◆ **hold out** ◇ *vt sep* [hand, arms] extender, tender. ◇ *vi* **-1.** [last] durar. **-2.** [resist]: **to ~ out (against sthg/sb)** resistir (ante algo/a alguien). ◆ **hold up** *vt sep* **-1.** [raise] levantar, alzar. **-2.** [delay] retrasar.

holdall ['həʊldɔːl] *n* Br bolsa *f* de viaje.

holder ['həʊldər] *n* **-1.** [container] soporte *m*; [for candle] candelero *m*; [for cigarette] boquilla *f*. **-2.** [owner] titular *m* y *f*; [of ticket, record, title] poseedor *m*, -ra *f*.

holding ['həʊldɪŋ] *n* **-1.** [investment] participación *f*, acciones *fpl*. **-2.** [farm] propiedad *f*, terreno *m* de cultivo.

holdup ['həʊldʌp] *n* **-1.** [robbery] atraco *m* a mano armada. **-2.** [delay] retraso *m*.

hole [həʊl] *n* **-1.** [gen] agujero *m*; [in ground, road etc] hoyo *m*. **-2.** [in golf] hoyo *m*. **-3.** [horrible place] cuchitril *m*.

holiday ['hɒlɪdeɪ] *n* **-1.** [vacation] vacaciones *fpl*; **to be/go on ~** estar/ir de vacaciones. **-2.** [public holiday] fiesta *f*, día *m* festivo.

holiday camp *n* Br colonia *f* veraniega.

holidaymaker ['hɒlɪdeɪˌmeɪkər] *n* Br turista *m* y *f*.

holiday pay *n* Br sueldo *m* de vacaciones.

holiday resort *n* Br lugar *m* de veraneo.

holistic [həʊ'lɪstɪk] *adj* holístico(ca).

Holland ['hɒlənd] *n* Holanda.

holler ['hɒlər] *vt & vi inf* gritar.

hollow ['hɒləʊ] ◇ *adj* **-1.** [not solid] hueco(ca). **-2.** [cheeks, eyes] hundido(da). **-3.** [resonant] sonoro(ra), resonante. **-4.** [false, meaningless] vano(na); [laugh] falso(sa). ◇ *n* hueco *m*; [in ground] depresión *f*, hondonada *f*.

◆ **hollow out** *vt sep* **-1.** [make hollow] dejar hueco. **-2.** [make by hollowing] hacer ahuecando.

holly ['hɒlɪ] *n* acebo *m*.

holocaust ['hɒləkɔːst] *n* holocausto *m*. ◆ **Holocaust** *n*: **the Holocaust** el Holocausto.

holster ['həʊlstər] *n* pistolera *f*.

holy ['həʊlɪ] *adj* **-1.** [sacred] sagrado(da); [water] bendito(ta). **-2.** [pure and good] santo(ta).

Holy Ghost *n*: **the ~** el Espíritu Santo.

Holy Spirit *n*: **the ~** el Espíritu Santo.

homage ['hɒmɪdʒ] *n* (U) *fml* homenaje *m*; **to pay ~ to** rendir homenaje a.

home [həʊm] ◇ *n* **-1.** [house, flat] casa *f*; **to make one's ~ somewhere** establecerse en algún sitio. **-2.** [own country] tierra *f*; [own city] ciudad *f* natal. **-3.** [family] hogar *m*; **to leave ~** independizarse, irse de casa. **-4.** [place of origin] cuna *f*. **-5.** [institution] asilo *m*. ◇ *adj* **-1.** [not foreign] nacional. **-2.** [in one's own home - cooking] casero(ra); [- life] familiar; [- improvements] en la casa. **-3.** SPORT de casa. ◇ *adv* [to one's house] a casa; [at one's house] en casa. ◆ **at home** *adv* **-1.** [in one's house, flat] en casa. **-2.** [comfortable]: **at ~ (with)** a gusto (con); **to make o.s. at ~** acomodarse. **-3.** [in one's own country] en mi país.

home address *n* domicilio *m* particular.

home brew *n* (U) [beer] cerveza *f* casera.

home computer *n* ordenador *m* personal.

Home Counties *npl*: **the ~** *los condados de los alrededores de Londres.*

home economics *n* (U) economía *f* doméstica.

home help *n* Br *asistente empleado por el ayuntamiento para ayudar en las tareas domésticas a enfermos y ancianos.*

homeland ['həʊmlænd] *n* **-1.** [country of birth] tierra *f* natal, patria *f*. **-2.** [in South Africa] *territorio donde se confina a la población negra.*

homeless ['həʊmlɪs] *adj* sin hogar.

homely ['həʊmlɪ] *adj* **-1.** [simple] sencillo(lla). **-2.** [unattractive] feúcho(cha).

homemade [ˌhəʊm'meɪd] *adj* [clothes] de fabricación casera; [food] casero(ra).

Home Office *n* Br: **the ~** el Ministerio del Interior británico.

homeopathy [ˌhəʊmɪ'ɒpəθɪ] *n* homeopatía *f*.

Home Secretary n Br: **the ~** el Ministro del Interior británico.

homesick ['hǝumsɪk] adj nostálgico(ca); **to be ~** tener morriña.

hometown ['hǝumtaun] n pueblo m/ ciudad f natal.

homeward ['hǝumwǝd] ◇ adj de regreso OR **vuelta (a casa).** ◇ adv = **homewards.**

homewards ['hǝumwǝdz] adv hacia casa.

homework ['hǝumwɜːk] n (U) lit & fig deberes mpl.

homey, homy ['hǝumɪ] adj Am confortable, agradable.

homicide ['hɒmɪsaɪd] n fml homicidio m.

homoeopathy [ˌhǝumɪ'ɒpǝθɪ] etc = **homeopathy** etc.

homogeneous [ˌhɒmǝ'dʒiːnjǝs] adj homogéneo(a).

homosexual [ˌhɒmǝ'sekʃuǝl] ◇ adj homosexual. ◇ n homosexual m y f.

homy = **homey.**

Honduran [hɒn'djuǝrǝn] ◇ adj hondureño(ña). ◇ n hondureño m, -ña f.

Honduras [hɒn'djuǝrǝs] n Honduras.

hone [hǝun] vt **-1.** [sharpen] afilar. **-2.** [develop, refine] afinar.

honest ['ɒnɪst] ◇ adj **-1.** [trustworthy, legal] honrado(da). **-2.** [frank] franco(ca), sincero(ra); **to be ~ ...** si he de serte franco ... ◇ adv inf = **honestly 2.**

honestly ['ɒnɪstlɪ] ◇ adv **-1.** [truthfully] honradamente. **-2.** [expressing sincerity] de verdad, en serio. ◇ excl [expressing impatience, disapproval] ¡será posible!

honesty ['ɒnɪstɪ] n honradez f.

honey ['hʌnɪ] n **-1.** [food] miel f. **-2.** [form of address] cielo m, mi vida f.

honeycomb ['hʌnɪkǝum] n panal m.

honeymoon ['hʌnɪmuːn] n luna f de miel; fig periodo m idílico.

honeysuckle ['hʌnɪˌsʌkl] n madreselva f.

Hong Kong [ˌhɒŋ'kɒŋ] n Hong Kong.

honk [hɒŋk] ◇ vi **-1.** [motorist] tocar el claxon. **-2.** [goose] graznar. ◇ vt tocar.

honor Am etc = **honour** etc.

honorary [Br 'ɒnǝrǝrɪ, Am ɒnǝ'reǝrɪ] adj **-1.** [given as an honour] honorario(ria). **-2.** [unpaid] honorífico(ca).

honour Br, **honor** Am ['ɒnǝr] ◇ n **-1.** [gen] honor m, honra f; **in ~ of** en honor de. **-2.** [source of pride - person] honra f. ◇ vt **-1.** [promise, agreement] cumplir; [debt] **satisfacer**; [cheque] pagar, aceptar. **-2.** fml [bring honour to]

honrar. ◆ **honours** npl **-1.** [tokens of respect] honores mpl. **-2.** Br UNIV: **~s degree** licenciatura de cuatro años necesaria para acceder a un máster.

honourable Br, **honorable** Am ['ɒnrǝbl] adj **-1.** [proper] honroso(sa). **-2.** [morally upright] honorable.

hood [hud] n **-1.** [on cloak, jacket] capucha f. **-2.** [of cooker, pram, convertible car] capota f. **-3.** Am [car bonnet] capó m.

hoodlum ['huːdlǝm] n Am inf matón m.

hoof [huːf, huf] (pl -s OR **hooves**) n [of horse] casco m; [of cow etc] pezuña f.

hook [huk] ◇ n **-1.** [gen] gancho m; **off the ~** [phone] descolgado(da). **-2.** [for catching fish] anzuelo m. **-3.** [fastener] corchete m. ◇ vt **-1.** [attach with hook] enganchar. **-2.** [fish] pescar, coger. ◆ **hook up** vt sep: **to ~ sthg up to sthg** conectar algo a algo.

hooked [hukt] adj **-1.** [nose] aguileño(ña). **-2.** inf [addicted]: **to be ~ (on)** estar enganchado(da) (a algo).

hook(e)y ['hukɪ] n Am inf: **to play ~** hacer pellas OR novillos.

hooligan ['huːlɪgǝn] n gamberro m.

hoop [huːp] n aro m.

hooray [hu'reɪ] = **hurray.**

hoot [huːt] ◇ n **-1.** [of owl] grito m, ululato m. **-2.** [of horn] bocinazo m. ◇ vi **-1.** [owl] ulular. **-2.** [horn] sonar. ◇ vt tocar.

hooter ['huːtǝr] n [horn] claxon m, bocina f.

Hoover® ['huːvǝr] n Br aspiradora f. ◆ **hoover** vt pasar la aspiradora por.

hooves [huːvz] pl → **hoof.**

hop [hɒp] vi **-1.** [person] saltar a la pata coja. **-2.** [bird etc] dar saltitos. **-3.** inf [move nimbly] ponerse de un brinco. ◆ **hops** npl lúpulo m.

hope [hǝup] ◇ vi: **to ~ (for sthg)** esperar (algo); **I ~ so/not** espero que sí/no. ◇ vt: **to ~ (that)** esperar que; **to ~ to do sthg** esperar hacer algo. ◇ n esperanza f; **in the ~ of** con la esperanza de.

hopeful ['hǝupful] adj **-1.** [optimistic] optimista; **to be ~ of sthg/of doing sthg** tener esperanzas de algo/hacer algo. **-2.** [promising] prometedor(ra).

hopefully ['hǝupfǝlɪ] adv **-1.** [in a hopeful way] esperanzadamente. **-2.** [with luck] con suerte.

hopeless ['hǝuplɪs] adj **-1.** [despairing] desesperado(da). **-2.** [impossible] imposible. **-3.** inf [useless] inútil.

hopelessly ['həʊplɪslɪ] *adv* **-1.** [despairingly] desesperadamente. **-2.** [completely] totalmente.

horizon [hə'raɪzn] *n* [of sky] horizonte *m*; **on the ~** en el horizonte; *fig* a la vuelta de la esquina.

horizontal [,hɒrɪ'zɒntl] *adj* horizontal.

hormone ['hɔːməʊn] *n* hormona *f*.

horn [hɔːn] *n* **-1.** [of animal] cuerno *m*. **-2.** MUS [instrument] trompa *f*. **-3.** [on car] claxon *m*, bocina *f*; [on ship] sirena *f*.

hornet ['hɔːnɪt] *n* avispón *m*.

horny ['hɔːnɪ] *adj* **-1.** [scale, body, armour] córneo(a); [hand] calloso(sa). **-2.** *v inf* [sexually excited] cachondo(da), caliente.

horoscope ['hɒrəskəʊp] *n* horóscopo *m*.

horrendous [hɒ'rendəs] *adj* horrendo(da).

horrible ['hɒrəbl] *adj* horrible.

horrid ['hɒrɪd] *adj* [person] antipático(ca); [idea, place] horroroso(sa).

horrific [hɒ'rɪfɪk] *adj* horrendo(da).

horrify ['hɒrɪfaɪ] *vt* horrorizar.

horror ['hɒrəʳ] *n* horror *m*.

horror film *n* película *f* de terror OR de miedo.

hors d'oeuvre [ɔː'dɜːvr] (*pl* **hors d'oeuvres** [ɔː'dɜːvr]) *n* entremeses *mpl*.

horse [hɔːs] *n* [animal] caballo *m*.

horseback ['hɔːsbæk] ◇ *adj*: **~ riding** equitación *f*. ◇ *n*: **on ~** a caballo.

horse chestnut *n* [nut] castaña *f* de Indias; **~ (tree)** castaño *m* de Indias.

horseman ['hɔːsmən] (*pl* **-men** [-mən]) *n* jinete *m*.

horsepower ['hɔːs,paʊəʳ] *n* (*U*) caballos *mpl* de vapor.

horse racing *n* (*U*) carreras *fpl* de caballos.

horseradish ['hɔːs,rædɪʃ] *n* rábano *m* silvestre.

horse riding *n* equitación *f*; **to go ~** montar a caballo.

horseshoe ['hɔːsʃuː] *n* herradura *f*.

horsewoman ['hɔːs,wʊmən] (*pl* **-women** [-,wɪmɪn]) *n* amazona *f*.

horticulture ['hɔːtɪkʌltʃəʳ] *n* horticultura *f*.

hose [həʊz] *n* [hosepipe] manguera *f*.

hosepipe ['həʊzpaɪp] *n* = **hose**.

hosiery ['həʊzɪərɪ] *n* (*U*) medias *fpl* y calcetines.

hospice ['hɒspɪs] *n* hospicio *m*.

hospitable [hɒ'spɪtəbl] *adj* hospitalario(ria).

hospital ['hɒspɪtl] *n* hospital *m*.

hospitality [,hɒspɪ'tælətɪ] *n* hospitalidad *f*.

host [həʊst] ◇ *n* **-1.** [person, place, organization] anfitrión *m*, -ona *f*. **-2.** [compere] presentador *m*, -ra *f*. **-3.** *literary* [large number]: **a ~ of** una multitud de. **-4.** RELIG hostia *f*. ◇ *vt* [show] presentar; [event] ser el anfitrión de.

hostage ['hɒstɪdʒ] *n* rehén *m*.

hostel ['hɒstl] *n* albergue *m*.

hostess ['həʊstes] *n* **-1.** [at party] anfitriona *f*. **-2.** [in club etc] chica *f* de alterne.

hostile [*Br* 'hɒstaɪl, *Am* 'hɒstl] *adj* **-1.** [antagonistic, enemy]: **~ (to)** hostil (hacia). **-2.** [unfavourable] adverso(sa).

hostility [hɒ'stɪlətɪ] *n* [antagonism] hostilidad *f*. ◆ **hostilities** *npl* hostilidades *fpl*.

hot [hɒt] *adj* **-1.** [gen] caliente; **I'm ~** tengo calor. **-2.** [weather, climate] caluroso(sa); **it's (very) ~** hace (mucho) calor. **-3.** [spicy] picante, picoso(sa) *Amer*. **-4.** *inf* [expert]: **~ on** OR **at** experto(ta) en. **-5.** [recent] caliente, último(ma). **-6.** [temper] vivo(va).

hot-air balloon *n* aeróstato *m*, globo *m*.

hotbed ['hɒtbed] *n* semillero *m*.

hot-cross bun *n* bollo a base de especias y pasas con una cruz dibujada en una cara que se come en Semana Santa.

hot dog *n* perrito *m* caliente.

hotel [həʊ'tel] *n* hotel *m*.

hot flush *Br*, **hot flash** *Am n* sofoco *m*.

hotfoot ['hɒt,fʊt] *adv literary* presto.

hotheaded [,hɒt'hedɪd] *adj* irreflexivo(va).

hothouse ['hɒthaʊs, *pl* -haʊzɪz] *n* [greenhouse] invernadero *m*.

hot line *n* teléfono *m* rojo.

hotly ['hɒtlɪ] *adv* **-1.** [passionately] acaloradamente. **-2.** [closely]: **we were ~ pursued** nos pisaban los talones.

hotplate ['hɒtpleɪt] *n* calentador *m*, fuego *m*.

hot-tempered *adj* iracundo(da).

hot-water bottle *n* bolsa *f* de agua caliente.

hound [haʊnd] ◇ *n* [dog] perro *m* de caza, sabueso *m*. ◇ *vt* **-1.** [persecute] acosar. **-2.** [drive]: **to ~ sb out (of somewhere)** conseguir echar a alguien (de algún sitio) acosándolo.

hour ['aʊəʳ] *n* **-1.** [gen] hora *f*; **half an ~** media hora; **70 miles per** OR **an ~** 70 millas por hora; **on the ~** a la hora en punto cada hora. **-2.** *literary* [important time] momento *m*. ◆ **hours** *npl* **-1.** [of business] horas *fpl*. **-2.** [of person - routine] horario *m*.

hourly ['auəlɪ] ◇ *adj* **-1.** [happening every hour] de hora en hora, cada hora. **-2.** [per hour] por hora. ◇ *adv* **-1.** [every hour] cada hora. **-2.** [per hour] por hora.

house [*n* & *adj* haus, *pl* 'hauzɪz, *vb* hauz] ◇ *n* **-1.** [gen] casa *f*; **it's on the ~** la casa invita, es cortesía de la casa. **-2.** POL cámara *f*. **-3.** [in theatre] audiencia *f*; **to bring the ~ down** *inf* ser un exitazo, ser muy aplaudido. ◇ *vt* [person, family] alojar; [department, library, office] albergar. ◇ *adj* **-1.** [within business] de la empresa. **-2.** [wine] de la casa.

house arrest *n*: **under ~** bajo arresto domiciliario.

houseboat ['hausbəut] *n* casa *f* flotante.

housebreaking ['haus,breɪkɪŋ] *n* allanamiento *m* de morada.

housecoat ['hauskəut] *n* bata *f*.

household ['haushəuld] ◇ *adj* **-1.** [domestic] doméstico(ca), de la casa. **-2.** [word, name] conocido(da) por todos. ◇ *n* hogar *m*, casa *f*.

housekeeper ['haus,ki:pər] *n* ama *f* de llaves.

housekeeping ['haus,ki:pɪŋ] *n* (U) **-1.** [work] quehaceres *mpl* domésticos. **-2.** ~ **(money)** dinero *m* para los gastos de la casa.

house music *n* música *f* ácida OR house.

House of Commons *n Br*: **the ~** la Cámara de los Comunes.

House of Lords *n Br*: **the ~** la Cámara de los Lores.

House of Representatives *n Am*: **the ~** la Cámara de los Representantes.

houseplant ['hausplɑ:nt] *n* planta *f* interior.

Houses of Parliament *n*: **the ~** el Parlamento británico.

housewarming (party) ['haus,wɔ:mɪŋ-] *n* fiesta *f* de inauguración de una casa.

housewife ['hauswaɪf] (*pl* **-wives** [-waɪvz]) *n* ama *f* de casa.

housework ['hauswɜ:k] *n* (U) quehaceres *mpl* domésticos.

housing ['hauzɪŋ] *n* [houses] vivienda *f*; [act of accommodating] alojamiento *m*.

housing association *n Br* cooperativa *f* de viviendas.

housing benefit *n* (U) subsidio estatal *para ayudar con el pago del alquiler y otros gastos.*

housing estate *Br*, **housing project** *Am n* urbanización generalmente de protección oficial, ≈ fraccionamiento *m Amer*.

hovel ['hɒvl] *n* casucha *f*, tugurio *m*.

hover ['hɒvər] *vi* [fly] cernerse.

hovercraft ['hɒvəkrɑ:ft] (*pl inv* OR **-s**) *n* aerodeslizador *m*.

how [hau] *adv* **-1.** [gen] cómo; ~ **do you do it?** ¿cómo se hace?; **I found out ~ he did it** averigüé cómo lo hizo; ~ **are you?** ¿cómo estás?; ¿**cómo do you do?** mucho gusto. **-2.** [referring to degree, amount]: ~ **high is it?** ¿cuánto mide de alto OR de altura?; **he asked ~ high it was** preguntó cuánto medía de alto; ~ **expensive is it?** ¿cómo de caro es?, ¿es muy caro?; ~ **long have you been waiting?** ¿cuánto llevas esperando?; ~ **many people came?** ¿cuánta gente vino?; ~ **old are you?** ¿qué edad OR cuántos años tienes? **-3.** [in exclamations] qué; ~ **nice/awful!** ¡qué bonito/horrible!; ~ **I hate doing it!** ¡cómo OR cuánto odio tener que hacerlo! ◆ **how about** *adv*: ~ **about a drink?** ¿qué tal una copa?; ~ **about you?** ¿y qué te parece?, ¿y tú? ◆ **how much** ◇ *pron* cuánto(ta); ~ **much does it cost?** ¿cuánto cuesta? ◇ *adj* cuánto(ta); ~ **much bread?** ¿cuánto pan?

however [hau'evər] ◇ *adv* **-1.** [nevertheless] sin embargo, no obstante. **-2.** [no matter how]: ~ **difficult it may be** por (muy) difícil que sea; ~ **many times** OR **much I told her** por mucho que se lo dijera. **-3.** [how] cómo. ◇ *conj* comoquiera que; ~ **you want** como quieras.

howl [haul] ◇ *n* **-1.** [of animal] aullido *m*. **-2.** [of person - in pain, anger] alarido *m*, grito *m*; [- in laughter] carcajada *f*. ◇ *vi* **-1.** [animal] aullar. **-2.** [person - in pain, anger] gritar; [- in laughter] reírse a carcajadas. **-3.** [wind] bramar.

hp (*abbr of* **horsepower**) CV *m*, cv *m*.

HP *n* **-1.** *Br abbr of* **hire purchase**. **-2.** = **hp**.

HQ *n abbr of* **headquarters**.

hub [hʌb] *n* **-1.** [of wheel] cubo *m*. **-2.** [of activity] centro *m*, eje *m*.

hubbub ['hʌbʌb] *n* alboroto *m*.

hubcap ['hʌbkæp] *n* tapacubos *m inv*.

huddle ['hʌdl] *vi* **-1.** [crouch, curl up] acurrucarse. **-2.** [cluster] apretarse unos contra otros, apiñarse.

hue [hju:] *n* [colour] tono *m*, matiz *m*.

huff [hʌf] *n*: **in a ~** enojado(da).

hug [hʌg] ◇ *n* abrazo *m*; **to give sb a ~** abrazar a alguien. ◇ *vt* **-1.** [embrace, hold] **abrazar. -2.** [stay close to] **ceñirse** OR **ir pegado a.**

huge [hju:dʒ] *adj* **enorme.**

hulk [hʌlk] *n* **-1.** [of ship] **casco** *m* **abandonado. -2.** [person] **tiarrón** *m*, **-ona** *f.*

hull [hʌl] *n* **casco** *m.*

hullo [hə'ləʊ] = **hello.**

hum [hʌm] ◇ *vi* **-1.** [buzz] **zumbar. -2.** [sing] **canturrear, tararear. -3.** [be busy] **bullir, hervir.** ◇ *vt* **tararear, canturrear.**

human [hju:mən] ◇ *adj* **humano(na).** ◇ *n:* ~ **(being)** (ser *m*) **humano** *m.*

humane [hju:'meɪn] *adj* **humano(na), humanitario(ria).**

humanitarian [hju:,mænɪ'teərɪən] *adj* **humanitario(ria).**

humanity [hju:'mænətɪ] *n* **humanidad** *f.* ◆ **humanities** *npl:* **the humanities** **las humanidades.**

human race *n:* **the** ~ **la raza humana.**

human rights *npl* **derechos** *mpl* **humanos.**

humble ['hʌmbl] ◇ *adj* **humilde.** ◇ *vt* *fml* **humillar.**

humbug ['hʌmbʌg] *n* **-1.** (U) *dated* [hypocrisy] **farsa** *f*, **hipocresía** *f.* **-2.** *Br* [sweet] **caramelo** *m* **de menta.**

humdrum ['hʌmdrʌm] *adj* **rutinario(ria), aburrido(da).**

humid ['hju:mɪd] *adj* **húmedo(da).**

humidity [hju:'mɪdətɪ] *n* **humedad** *f.*

humiliate [hju:'mɪlɪeɪt] *vt* **humillar.**

humiliation [hju:,mɪlɪ'eɪʃn] *n* **humillación** *f.*

humility [hju:'mɪlətɪ] *n* **humildad** *f.*

humor *Am* = **humour.**

humorous ['hju:mərəs] *adj* **humorístico(ca).**

humour *Br*, **humor** *Am* ['hju:məʳ] ◇ *n* **-1.** [sense of fun, mood] **humor** *m*; **in good/bad** ~ **de buen/mal humor. -2.** [funny side] **gracia** *f.* ◇ *vt* **complacer.**

hump [hʌmp] *n* **-1.** [hill] **montículo** *m.* **-2.** [on back] **joroba** *f*, **giba** *f.*

humpbacked bridge ['hʌmpbækt-] *n* **puente** *m* **peraltado.**

hunch [hʌntʃ] ◇ *n* *inf* **presentimiento** *m.* ◇ *vt* **encorvar.**

hunchback ['hʌntʃbæk] *n* **jorobado** *m*, **-da** *f.*

hunched [hʌntʃt] *adj* **encorvado(da).**

hundred ['hʌndrəd] *num* **cien**; **a** OR **one** ~ **cien; a** OR **one** ~ **and eighty ciento ochenta;** *see also* **six.** ◆ **hundreds** *npl* **centenares** *mpl.*

hundredth ['hʌndrətθ] ◇ *num adj* **centésimo(ma).** ◇ *num n* [fraction] **centési-**

mo *m*; **a** ~ **of a second una centésima;** *see also* **sixth.**

hundredweight ['hʌndrədweɪt] *n* [in UK] = 50,8 kg; [in US] = 45,3 kg.

hung [hʌŋ] *pt & pp* → **hang.**

Hungarian [hʌŋ'geərɪən] ◇ *adj* **húngaro(ra).** ◇ *n* **-1.** [person] **húngaro** *m*, **-ra** *f.* **-2.** [language] **húngaro** *m.*

Hungary ['hʌŋgərɪ] *n* **Hungría.**

hunger ['hʌŋgəʳ] *n* **-1.** [for food] **hambre** *f.* **-2.** *literary* [for change, knowledge etc] **sed** *f.* ◆ **hunger after, hunger for** *vt fus literary* **anhelar, ansiar.**

hunger strike *n* **huelga** *f* **de hambre.**

hung over *adj inf:* **to be** ~ **tener resaca.**

hungry ['hʌŋgrɪ] *adj* [for food] **hambriento(ta); to be/go** ~ **tener/pasar hambre.**

hung up *adj inf:* **to be** ~ **(on** OR **about)** **estar neura (por culpa de).**

hunk [hʌŋk] *n* **-1.** [large piece] **pedazo** *m*, **trozo** *m.* **-2.** *inf* [attractive man] **tío** *m* **bueno, macizo** *m.*

hunt [hʌnt] ◇ *n* **-1.** [of animals, birds] **caza** *f*, **cacería** *f.* **-2.** [for person, clue etc] **busca** *f*, **búsqueda** *f.* ◇ *vi* **-1.** [for animals, birds] **cazar. -2.** [for person, clue etc]: **to** ~ **(for sthg) buscar (algo).** ◇ *vt* **-1.** [animals, birds] **cazar. -2.** [person] **perseguir.**

hunter ['hʌntəʳ] *n* [of animals, birds] **cazador** *m*, **-ra** *f.*

hunting ['hʌntɪŋ] *n* **-1.** [of animals] **caza** *f*; **to go** ~ **ir de caza** OR **cacería. -2.** *Br* [of foxes] **caza** *f* **del zorro.**

hurdle ['hɜ:dl] ◇ *n* **-1.** [in race] **valla** *f.* **-2.** [obstacle] **obstáculo** *m.* ◇ *vt* **saltar.**

hurl [hɜ:l] *vt* **-1.** [throw] **lanzar, arrojar. -2.** [shout] **proferir, soltar.**

hurray [hʊ'reɪ] *excl* **¡hurra!**

hurricane ['hʌrɪkən] *n* **huracán** *m.*

hurried ['hʌrɪd] *adj* [hasty] **apresurado(da), precipitado(da).**

hurriedly ['hʌrɪdlɪ] *adv* **apresuradamente, precipitadamente.**

hurry ['hʌrɪ] ◇ *vt* [person] **meter prisa a;** [work, speech] **apresurar.** ◇ *vi:* **to** ~ **(to do sthg) apresurarse (a hacer algo).** ◇ *n* **prisa** *f*; **to be in a** ~ **tener prisa; to do sthg in a** ~ **hacer algo de prisa** OR **apresuradamente.** ◆ **hurry up** *vi* **darse prisa.**

hurt [hɜ:t] (*pt & pp* **hurt**) ◇ *vt* **-1.** [physically - person] **hacer daño a;** [- one's leg, arm] **hacerse daño en. -2.** [emotionally] **herir. -3.** [harm] **perjudicar.** ◇ *vi* **-1.** [gen] **doler; my head** ~**s me duele**

la cabeza. **-2.** [cause physical pain, do harm] hacer daño. ◇ *adj* **-1.** [injured] herido(da). **-2.** [offended] dolido(da).

hurtful ['hɜːtfʊl] *adj* hiriente.

hurtle ['hɜːtl] *vi*: **to ~ past** pasar como un rayo.

husband ['hʌzbənd] *n* marido *m*.

hush [hʌʃ] ◇ *n* silencio *m*. ◇ *excl* ¡silencio!, ¡a callar!

husk [hʌsk] *n* [of seed, grain] cáscara *f*.

husky ['hʌskɪ] ◇ *adj* [hoarse] ronco(ca). ◇ *n* (perro *m*) samoyedo *m*, perro *m* esquimal.

hustle ['hʌsl] ◇ *vt* [hurry] meter prisa a. ◇ *n*: ~ **(and bustle)** bullicio *m*.

hut [hʌt] *n* **-1.** [rough house] cabaña *f*, choza *f*. **-2.** [shed] cobertizo *m*.

hutch [hʌtʃ] *n* conejera *f*.

hyacinth ['haɪəsɪnθ] *n* jacinto *m*.

hydrant ['haɪdrənt] *n* boca *f* de riego; [for fire] boca *f* de incendio.

hydraulic [haɪ'drɔːlɪk] *adj* hidráulico(ca).

hydroelectric [ˌhaɪdrəʊɪ'lektrɪk] *adj* hidroeléctrico(ca).

hydrofoil ['haɪdrəfɔɪl] *n* embarcación *f* con hidroala.

hydrogen ['haɪdrədʒən] *n* hidrógeno *m*.

hyena [haɪ'iːnə] *n* hiena *f*.

hygiene ['haɪdʒiːn] *n* higiene *f*.

hygienic [haɪ'dʒiːnɪk] *adj* higiénico(ca).

hymn [hɪm] *n* himno *m*.

hype [haɪp] *inf n* bombo *m*, publicidad *f* exagerada.

hyperactive [ˌhaɪpər'æktɪv] *adj* hiperactivo(va).

hypermarket ['haɪpəˌmɑːkɪt] *n* hipermercado *m*.

hyphen ['haɪfn] *n* guión *m*.

hypnosis [hɪp'nəʊsɪs] *n* hipnosis *f inv*.

hypnotic [hɪp'nɒtɪk] *adj* hipnótico(ca).

hypnotize, -ise ['hɪpnətaɪz] *vt* hipnotizar.

hypochondriac [ˌhaɪpə'kɒndrɪæk] *n* hipocondríaco *m*, -ca *f*.

hypocrisy [hɪ'pɒkrəsɪ] *n* hipocresía *f*.

hypocrite ['hɪpəkrɪt] *n* hipócrita *m* y *f*.

hypocritical [ˌhɪpə'krɪtɪkl] *adj* hipócrita.

hypothesis [haɪ'pɒθɪsɪs] (*pl* **-theses** [-θɪsiːz]) *n* hipótesis *f inv*.

hypothetical [ˌhaɪpə'θetɪkl] *adj* hipotético(ca).

hysteria [hɪs'tɪərɪə] *n* histeria *f*.

hysterical [hɪs'terɪkl] *adj* **-1.** [frantic] histérico(ca). **-2.** *inf* [very funny] tronchante.

hysterics [hɪs'terɪks] *npl* **-1.** [panic, excitement] histeria *f*, histerismo *m*. **-2.** *inf* [fits of laughter]: **to be in ~** troncharse OR partirse de risa.

i (*pl* **i's** OR **is**), **I** (*pl* **I's** OR **Is**) *n* [letter] i *f*, I *f*.

I [aɪ] *pers pron* yo; **I'm happy** soy feliz; **I'm leaving** me voy; **she and ~ were at college together** ella y yo fuimos juntos a la universidad; **it is ~** *fml* soy yo; **I can't do it** yo no puedo hacer esto.

ice [aɪs] ◇ *n* **-1.** [frozen water] hielo *m*. **-2.** *Br* [ice cream] helado *m*. **-3.** [on road] hielo transparente en el suelo. ◇ *vt* glasear, alcorzar. ◆ **ice over, ice up** *vi* helarse.

iceberg ['aɪsbɜːg] *n* iceberg *m*.

iceberg lettuce *n* lechuga *f* iceberg.

icebox ['aɪsbɒks] *n* **-1.** *Br* [in refrigerator] congelador *m*. **-2.** *Am* [refrigerator] refrigerador *m*.

ice cream *n* helado *m*.

ice cube *n* cubito *m* de hielo.

ice hockey *n* hockey *m* sobre hielo.

Iceland ['aɪslənd] *n* Islandia.

Icelandic [aɪs'lændɪk] ◇ *adj* islandés(esa). ◇ *n* [language] islandés *m*.

ice lolly *n Br* polo *m*.

ice pick *n* pico *m* para el hielo.

ice rink *n* pista *f* de (patinaje sobre) hielo.

ice skate *n* patín *m* de cuchilla. ◆ **ice-skate** *vi* patinar sobre hielo.

ice-skating *n* patinaje *m* sobre hielo.

icicle ['aɪsɪkl] *n* carámbano *m*.

icing ['aɪsɪŋ] *n* glaseado *m*.

icing sugar *n Br* azúcar *m* glas.

icon ['aɪkɒn] *n* COMPUT & RELIG icono *m*.

icy ['aɪsɪ] *adj* **-1.** [gen] helado(da). **-2.** *fig* [unfriendly] glacial.

I'd [aɪd] = **I would**, **I had**.

ID *n* (U) (*abbr of* **identification**) ≃ DNI *m*.

idea [aɪ'dɪə] *n* **-1.** [gen] idea *f*; **to have no ~** no tener ni idea; **to get the ~** *inf* captar la idea, hacerse una idea. **-2.** [intuition, feeling] sensación *f*, impresión *f*; **to have an ~ (that)** ... tener la sensación de que ....

ideal [aɪ'dɪəl] ◇ *adj*: **~ (for)** ideal (para). ◇ *n* ideal *m*.

ideally [aɪ'dɪəlɪ] *adv* **-1.** [perfectly] idealmente; [suited] perfectamente. **-2.** [preferably] a ser posible.

identical [aɪ'dentɪkl] *adj* idéntico(ca).

identification [aɪ,dentɪfɪ'keɪʃn] *n* **-1.** [gen]: **~ (with)** identificación *f* (con). **-2.** [documentation] documentación *f*.

identify [aɪ'dentɪfaɪ] ◇ *vt* identificar; **to ~ sb with sthg** relacionar a alguien con algo. ◇ *vi*: **to ~ with sb/sthg** identificarse con alguien/algo.

Identikit picture® [aɪ'dentɪkɪt-] *n* fotorrobot *f*.

identity [aɪ'dentətɪ] *n* identidad *f*.

identity card *n* carné *m* OR documento *m* de identidad, cédula *f Amer*.

identity parade *n* rueda *f* de identificación.

ideology [,aɪdɪ'ɒlədʒɪ] *n* ideología *f*.

idiom ['ɪdɪəm] *n* **-1.** [phrase] locución *f*, modismo *m*. **-2.** *fml* [style] lenguaje *m*.

idiomatic [,ɪdɪə'mætɪk] *adj* idiomático(ca).

idiosyncrasy [,ɪdɪə'sɪŋkrəsɪ] *n* rareza *f*, manía *f*.

idiot ['ɪdɪət] *n* [fool] idiota *m y f*.

idiotic [,ɪdɪ'ɒtɪk] *adj* idiota.

idle ['aɪdl] ◇ *adj* **-1.** [lazy] perezoso(sa), vago(ga). **-2.** [not working - machine, factory] parado(da); [- person] desocupado(da), sin trabajo. **-3.** [rumour] infundado(da); [threat, boast] vano(na); [curiosity] que no viene a cuento. ◇ *vi* estar en punto muerto. ◆ **idle away** *vt sep* desperdiciar.

idol ['aɪdl] *n* ídolo *m*.

idolize, -ise ['aɪdəlaɪz] *vt* idolatrar.

idyllic [ɪ'dɪlɪk] *adj* idílico(ca).

i.e. (*abbr of* **id est**) i.e.

if [ɪf] *conj* **-1.** [gen] si; **~ I were you** yo que tú, yo en tu lugar. **-2.** [though] aunque. ◆ **if not** *conj* por no decir. ◆ **if only** ◇ *conj* **-1.** [naming a reason] aunque sólo sea. **-2.** [expressing regret] si; **~ only I'd been quicker!** ¡ojalá hubiera sido más rápido! ◇ *excl* ¡ojalá!

igloo ['ɪgluː] (*pl* **-s**) *n* iglú *m*.

ignite [ɪg'naɪt] ◇ *vt* encender. ◇ *vi* encenderse.

ignition [ɪg'nɪʃn] *n* **-1.** [act of igniting] ignición *f*. **-2.** [in car] encendido *m*; **to switch on the ~** arrancar (el motor).

ignition key *n* llave *f* de contacto.

ignorance ['ɪgnərəns] *n* ignorancia *f*.

ignorant ['ɪgnərənt] *adj* **-1.** [uneducated, rude] ignorante. **-2.** *fml* [unaware]: **to be ~ of sthg** ignorar algo.

ignore [ɪg'nɔːr] *vt* [take no notice of] no hacer caso de, ignorar.

ilk [ɪlk] *n*: **of that ~** [of that sort] de ese tipo.

ill [ɪl] ◇ *adj* **-1.** [unwell] enfermo(ma); **to feel ~** encontrarse mal; **to be taken** OR **to fall ~** caer OR ponerse enfermo. **-2.** [bad] malo(la). ◇ *adv* **-1.** [badly] mal. **-2.** *fml* [unfavourably]: **to speak/think ~ of sb** hablar/pensar mal de alguien.

I'll [aɪl] = **I will, I shall**.

ill-advised [-əd'vaɪzd] *adj* [action] poco aconsejable; [person] imprudente.

ill at ease *adj* incómodo(da), violento(ta).

illegal [ɪ'liːgl] *adj* ilegal.

illegible [ɪ'ledʒəbl] *adj* ilegible.

illegitimate [,ɪlɪ'dʒɪtɪmət] *adj* ilegítimo(ma).

ill-equipped [-ɪ'kwɪpt] *adj*: **to be ~ to do sthg** estar mal preparado(da) para hacer algo.

ill-fated [-'feɪtɪd] *adj* desafortunado(da).

ill feeling *n* resentimiento *m*.

ill health *n* mala salud *f*.

illicit [ɪ'lɪsɪt] *adj* ilícito(ta).

illiteracy [ɪ'lɪtərəsɪ] *n* analfabetismo *m*.

illiterate [ɪ'lɪtərət] ◇ *adj* analfabeto(ta). ◇ *n* analfabeto *m*, -ta *f*.

illness ['ɪlnɪs] *n* enfermedad *f*.

illogical [ɪ'lɒdʒɪkl] *adj* ilógico(ca).

ill-suited *adj*: **~ (for)** poco adecuado(da) (para).

ill-timed [-'taɪmd] *adj* inoportuno(na).

ill-treat *vt* maltratar.

illuminate [ɪ'luːmɪneɪt] *vt* **-1.** [light up] iluminar. **-2.** [explain] ilustrar, aclarar.

illumination [ɪ,luːmɪ'neɪʃn] *n* [lighting] alumbrado *m*, iluminación *f*. ◆ **illuminations** *npl Br* iluminaciones *fpl*, alumbrado *m* decorativo.

illusion [ɪ'luːʒn] *n* **-1.** [gen] ilusión *f*; **to be under the ~ that** creer equivocadamente que. **-2.** [magic trick] truco *m* de ilusionismo.

illustrate ['ɪləstreɪt] *vt* ilustrar.

illustration [,ɪlə'streɪʃn] *n* ilustración *f*.

illustrious [ɪ'lʌstrɪəs] *adj fml* ilustre.

ill will *n* rencor *m*, animadversión *f*.

I'm [aɪm] = **I am**.

image ['ɪmɪdʒ] *n* imagen *f*.

imagery ['ɪmɪdʒrɪ] *n* (*U*) imágenes *fpl*.

imaginary [ɪˈmædʒɪnrɪ] *adj* imaginario(ria).

imagination [ɪˌmædʒɪˈneɪʃn] *n* imaginación *f*.

imaginative [ɪˈmædʒɪnətɪv] *adj* imaginativo(va).

imagine [ɪˈmædʒɪn] *vt* **-1.** [gen] imaginar; ~ **never having to work!** ¡imagina que nunca tuvieras que trabajar!; ~ **(that)!** ¡imagínate! **-2.** [suppose]: **to ~ (that)** imaginarse que.

imbalance [ˌɪmˈbæləns] *n* desequilibrio *m*.

imbecile [ˈɪmbɪsiːl] *n* imbécil *m y f*.

IMF (*abbr of* **International Monetary Fund**) *n* FMI *m*.

imitate [ˈɪmɪteɪt] *vt* imitar.

imitation [ˌɪmɪˈteɪʃn] ◇ *n* imitación *f*. ◇ *adj* de imitación.

immaculate [ɪˈmækjʊlət] *adj* **-1.** [clean and tidy] inmaculado(da); [taste] exquisito(ta). **-2.** [impeccable] impecable.

immaterial [ˌɪməˈtɪərɪəl] *adj* [irrelevant, unimportant] irrelevante.

immature [ˌɪməˈtjʊər] *adj* inmaduro(ra); [animal] joven.

immediate [ɪˈmiːdjət] *adj* **-1.** [gen] inmediato(ta); **in the ~ future** en el futuro más cercano. **-2.** [family] directo(ta).

immediately [ɪˈmiːdjətlɪ] ◇ *adv* **-1.** [at once] inmediatamente. **-2.** [directly] directamente. ◇ *conj* en cuanto.

immense [ɪˈmens] *adj* inmenso(sa).

immerse [ɪˈmɜːs] *vt* **-1.** [plunge]: **to ~ sthg in sthg** sumergir algo en algo. **-2.** [involve]: **to ~ o.s. in sthg** enfrascarse en algo.

immersion heater [ɪˈmɜːʃn-] *n* calentador *m* de inmersión.

immigrant [ˈɪmɪgrənt] *n* inmigrante *m y f*.

immigration [ˌɪmɪˈgreɪʃn] *n* inmigración *f*.

imminent [ˈɪmɪnənt] *adj* inminente.

immobilize, -ise [ɪˈməʊbɪlaɪz] *vt* inmovilizar.

immoral [ɪˈmɒrəl] *adj* inmoral.

immortal [ɪˈmɔːtl] *adj* inmortal.

immortalize, -ise [ɪˈmɔːtəlaɪz] *vt* inmortalizar.

immovable [ɪˈmuːvəbl] *adj* **-1.** [fixed] fijo(ja), inamovible. **-2.** [determined, decided] inconmovible, inflexible.

immune [ɪˈmjuːn] *adj* **-1.** [gen & MED]: **(to)** inmune (a). **-2.** [exempt]: ~ **(from)** exento(ta) (de).

immunity [ɪˈmjuːnɪtɪ] *n* **-1.** [gen & MED]: ~ **(to)** inmunidad *f* (a). **-2.** [exemption]: ~ **(from)** exención *f* (de).

immunize, -ise [ˈɪmjuːnaɪz] *vt*: **to ~ sb (against sthg)** inmunizar a alguien (contra algo).

imp [ɪmp] *n* **-1.** [creature] duendecillo *m*. **-2.** [naughty child] diablillo *m*.

impact [*n* ˈɪmpækt, *vb* ɪmˈpækt] ◇ *n* impacto *m*; **to make an ~ on** OR **upon** causar impacto en. ◇ *vt* [influence] influenciar.

impair [ɪmˈpeər] *vt* [sight, hearing] dañar, debilitar; [ability, efficiency] mermar; [movement] entorpecer.

impart [ɪmˈpɑːt] *vt fml* **-1.** [information]: **to ~ sthg (to sb)** comunicar algo (a alguien). **-2.** [feeling, quality]: **to ~ sthg (to sthg)** conferir algo (a algo).

impartial [ɪmˈpɑːʃl] *adj* imparcial.

impassable [ɪmˈpɑːsəbl] *adj* intransitable, impracticable.

impasse [æmˈpɑːs] *n* impasse *m*, callejón *m* sin salida.

impassive [ɪmˈpæsɪv] *adj* impasible.

impatience [ɪmˈpeɪʃns] *n* impaciencia *f*.

impatient [ɪmˈpeɪʃnt] *adj* impaciente; **to be ~ to do sthg** estar impaciente por hacer algo; **to be ~ for sthg** esperar algo con impaciencia.

impeccable [ɪmˈpekəbl] *adj* impecable.

impede [ɪmˈpiːd] *vt* dificultar.

impediment [ɪmˈpedɪmənt] *n* **-1.** [obstacle] impedimento *m*, obstáculo *m*. **-2.** [disability] defecto *m*.

impel [ɪmˈpel] *vt*: **to ~ sb to do sthg** impulsar OR impeler a alguien a hacer algo.

impending [ɪmˈpendɪŋ] *adj* inminente.

imperative [ɪmˈperətɪv] ◇ *adj* [essential] apremiante. ◇ *n* imperativo *m*.

imperfect [ɪmˈpɜːfɪkt] ◇ *adj* [not perfect] imperfecto(ta). ◇ *n* GRAMM: ~ **(tense)** (pretérito *m*) imperfecto *m*.

imperial [ɪmˈpɪərɪəl] *adj* **-1.** [of an empire or emperor] imperial. **-2.** [system of measurement]: ~ **system** sistema anglosajón de medidas.

imperialism [ɪmˈpɪərɪəlɪzm] *n* imperialismo *m*.

impersonal [ɪmˈpɜːsnl] *adj* impersonal.

impersonate [ɪmˈpɜːsəneɪt] *vt* [gen] hacerse pasar por; THEATRE imitar.

impersonation [ɪmˌpɜːsəˈneɪʃn] *n* **-1.** [pretending to be]: **charged with ~ of a policeman** acusado de hacerse pasar por policía. **-2.** [impression] imitación *f*; **to do ~s (of)** imitar (a), hacer imitaciones (de).

impertinent [ɪmˈpɜːtɪnənt] *adj* impertinente, insolente.

impervious [ɪmˈpɜːvjəs] *adj* [not influenced]: ~ **to** insensible a.

impetuous [ɪmˈpetʃʊəs] *adj* impetuoso(sa), irreflexivo(va).

impetus [ˈɪmpɪtəs] *n* (U) **-1.** [momentum] ímpetu *m*. **-2.** [stimulus] incentivo *m*, impulso *m*.

impinge [ɪmˈpɪndʒ] *vi*: **to ~ on sthg/sb** afectar algo/a alguien.

implant [*n* ˈɪmplɑːnt, *vb* ɪmˈplɑːnt] ◇ *n* injerto *m*. ◇ *vt* **-1.** [fix - idea etc]: **to ~ sthg in** OR **into** inculcar algo en. **-2.** MED: **to ~ sthg in** OR **into** implantar algo en.

implausible [ɪmˈplɔːzəbl] *adj* inverosímil.

implement [*n* ˈɪmplɪmənt, *vt* ˈɪmplɪment] ◇ *n* herramienta *f*. ◇ *vt* llevar a cabo, poner en práctica.

implication [ˌɪmplɪˈkeɪʃn] *n* **-1.** [involvement] implicación *f*. **-2.** [inference] consecuencia *f*; **by ~** de forma indirecta.

implicit [ɪmˈplɪsɪt] *adj* **-1.** [gen]: ~ **(in)** implícito(ta) (en). **-2.** [complete - belief] absoluto(ta); [- faith] incondicional.

implore [ɪmˈplɔːʳ] *vt*: **to ~ sb (to do sthg)** suplicar a alguien (que haga algo).

imply [ɪmˈplaɪ] *vt* **-1.** [suggest] insinuar, dar a entender. **-2.** [involve] implicar, suponer.

impolite [ˌɪmpəˈlaɪt] *adj* maleducado(da), descortés.

import [*n* ˈɪmpɔːt, *vt* ɪmˈpɔːt] ◇ *n* **-1.** [act of importing, product] importación *f*. **-2.** *fml* [meaning] sentido *m*, significado *m*. ◇ *vt lit* & *fig* importar.

importance [ɪmˈpɔːtns] *n* importancia *f*.

important [ɪmˈpɔːtnt] *adj*: ~ **(to)** importante (para); **it's not** ~ no importa.

importer [ɪmˈpɔːtəʳ] *n* importador *m*, -ra *f*.

impose [ɪmˈpəʊz] ◇ *vt*: **to ~ sthg (on)** imponer algo (a). ◇ *vi*: **to ~ (on)** abusar (de), molestar (a).

imposing [ɪmˈpəʊzɪŋ] *adj* imponente, impresionante.

imposition [ˌɪmpəˈzɪʃn] *n* **-1.** [enforcement] imposición *f*. **-2.** [cause of trouble] molestia *f*.

impossible [ɪmˈpɒsəbl] *adj* **-1.** [gen] imposible. **-2.** [person, behaviour] inaguantable, insufrible.

impostor, imposter *Am* [ɪmˈpɒstəʳ] *n* impostor *m*, -ra *f*.

impotent [ˈɪmpətənt] *adj* impotente.

impound [ɪmˈpaʊnd] *vt* incautarse.

impoverished [ɪmˈpɒvərɪʃt] *adj* [country, people, imagination] empobrecido(da).

impracticable [ɪmˈpræktɪkəbl] *adj* impracticable, irrealizable.

impractical [ɪmˈpræktɪkl] *adj* poco práctico(ca).

impregnable [ɪmˈpregnəbl] *adj lit* & *fig* inexpugnable, impenetrable.

impregnate [ˈɪmpregneɪt] *vt* **-1.** [introduce substance into]: **to ~ sthg (with)** impregnar OR empapar algo (de). **-2.** *fml* [fertilize] fecundar.

impress [ɪmˈpres] *vt* **-1.** [produce admiration in] impresionar. **-2.** [stress]: **to ~ sthg on sb** hacer comprender a alguien la importancia de algo.

impression [ɪmˈpreʃn] *n* **-1.** [gen] impresión *f*; **to make an ~** impresionar; **to make a good/bad ~** causar una buena/mala impresión; **to be under the ~ that** tener la impresión de que. **-2.** [imitation] imitación *f*.

impressive [ɪmˈpresɪv] *adj* impresionante.

imprint [ˈɪmprɪnt] *n* **-1.** [mark] huella *f*, impresión *f*. **-2.** [publisher's name] pie *m* de imprenta.

imprison [ɪmˈprɪzn] *vt* encarcelar.

improbable [ɪmˈprɒbəbl] *adj* [event] improbable; [story, excuse] inverosímil; [clothes, hat] estrafalario(ria); [contraption] extraño(ña).

impromptu [ɪmˈprɒmptjuː] *adj* improvisado(da).

improper [ɪmˈprɒpəʳ] *adj* **-1.** [unsuitable] impropio(pia). **-2.** [incorrect, illegal] indebido(da). **-3.** [rude] indecoroso(sa).

improve [ɪmˈpruːv] ◇ *vi* mejorar, mejorarse; **to ~ on** OR **upon sthg** mejorar algo. ◇ *vt* mejorar.

improvement [ɪmˈpruːvmənt] *n* **-1.** [gen]: ~ **(in/on)** mejora *f* (en/con respecto a). **-2.** [to home] reforma *f*.

improvise [ˈɪmprəvaɪz] *vt* & *vi* improvisar.

impudent [ˈɪmpjʊdənt] *adj* insolente.

impulse [ˈɪmpʌls] *n* impulso *m*; **on ~** sin pensar.

impulsive [ɪmˈpʌlsɪv] *adj* impulsivo(va), irreflexivo(va).

impunity [ɪmˈpjuːnətɪ] *n*: **with ~** impunemente.

impurity [ɪmˈpjʊərətɪ] *n* impureza *f*.

in [ɪn] ◇ *prep* **-1.** [indicating place, position] en; ~ **a box/the garden/the lake** en una caja/el jardín/el lago; ~ **Paris/Belgium/the country** en París/Bélgica/

el campo; ~ **here/there** aquí/allí dentro. **-2.** [wearing] con; **she was still ~ her nightclothes** todavía llevaba su vestido de noche. **-3.** [at a particular time]: **at four o'clock ~ the morning/afternoon** a las cuatro de la mañana/tarde; **~ the morning** por la mañana; **~ 1992/May/the spring** en 1992/mayo/primavera. **-4.** [within] en; **he learned to type ~ two weeks** aprendió a escribir a máquina en dos semanas; **I'll be ready ~ five minutes** estoy listo en cinco minutos. **-5.** [during] desde hace; **it's my first decent meal ~ weeks** es lo primero decente que como desde hace OR en semanas. **-6.** [indicating situation, circumstances]: **danger/difficulty** en peligro/dificultades; **~ the sun** al sol; **~ the rain** bajo la lluvia; **a rise ~ prices** un aumento de los precios. **-7.** [indicating manner, condition] en; **~ a loud/soft voice** en voz alta/baja; **~ pencil/ink** a lápiz/bolígrafo. **-8.** [indicating emotional state] con; **~ anger/joy** con enfado/alegría. **-9.** [specifying area of activity]: **advances ~ medicine** avances en la medicina; **he's ~ computers** está metido en informática. **-10.** [with numbers - showing quantity, age]: **large/small quantities** en grandes/pequeñas cantidades; **~ (their) thousands** a OR por millares; **she's ~ her sixties** andará por los sesenta. **-11.** [describing arrangement]: **~ a line/circle** en línea/círculo; **to stand ~ twos** estar en pares OR parejas. **-12.** [as regards] en; **~ these matters** en estos temas; **two metres ~ length/width** dos metros de largo/ancho; **a change ~ direction** un cambio de dirección. **-13.** [in ratios]: **one ~ ten** uno de cada diez; **five pence ~ the pound** cinco peniques por libra. **-14.** (*after superl*) de; **the best ~ the world** el mejor del mundo. **-15.** (+ *present participle*): **~ doing sthg** al hacer algo. ◇ *adv* **-1.** [inside] dentro; **to jump ~** saltar adentro; **do come ~** pasa por favor. **-2.** [at home, work]: **is Judith ~?** ¿está Judith?; **I'm staying ~ tonight** esta noche no salgo. **-3.** [of train, boat, plane]: **is the train ~ yet?** ¿ha llegado el tren? **-4.** [of tide]: **the tide's ~** la marea está alta. **-5.** *phr*: **you're ~ for a surprise** te vas a llevar una sorpresa; **to have it ~ for sb** tenerla tomada con alguien. ◇ *adj inf* de moda. ◆ **ins** *npl*: **the ~s and outs** los detalles, los pormenores.

in. *abbr of* **inch.**

inability [,ınə'bılətı] *n*: **~ (to do sthg)** incapacidad *f* (de hacer algo).

inaccessible [,ınək'sesəbl] *adj* inaccesible.

inaccurate [ın'ækjurət] *adj* incorrecto(ta), inexacto(ta).

inadequate [ın'ædıkwət] *adj* **-1.** [insufficient] insuficiente. **-2.** [person] incapaz.

inadvertently [,ınəd'vɜːtəntlı] *adv* sin querer, accidentalmente.

inadvisable [,ınəd'vaızəbl] *adj* poco aconsejable.

inane [ı'neın] *adj* necio(cia).

inanimate [ın'ænımət] *adj* inanimado(da).

inappropriate [,ınə'prəuprıət] *adj* [remark, clothing] impropio(pia); [time] inoportuno(na).

inarticulate [,ınɑː'tıkjulət] *adj* [person] incapaz de expresarse; [speech, explanation] mal pronunciado(da) OR expresado(da).

inasmuch [,ınəz'mʌtʃ] ◆ **inasmuch as** *conj* en la medida en que.

inaudible [ı'nɔːdıbl] *adj* inaudible.

inauguration [ı,nɔːgju'reıʃn] *n* **-1.** [of leader, president] investidura *f*. **-2.** [of building, system] inauguración *f*.

in-between *adj* intermedio(dia).

inborn [,ın'bɔːn] *adj* innato(ta).

inbound ['ınbaund] *adj Am* que se aproxima.

inbred [,ın'bred] *adj* **-1.** [closely related] endogámico(ca). **-2.** [inborn] innato(ta).

inbuilt [,ın'bılt] *adj* [in person] innato(ta); [in thing] inherente.

inc. (*abbr of* **inclusive**) inclus.

Inc. [ıŋk] (*abbr of* **incorporated**) ≃ S.A.

incapable [ın'keıpəbl] *adj* **-1.** [unable]: **to be ~ of sthg/of doing sthg** ser incapaz de algo/de hacer algo. **-2.** [useless] incompetente.

incapacitated [,ınkə'pæsıteıtıd] *adj* incapacitado(da).

incarcerate [ın'kɑːsəreıt] *vt fml* encarcelar.

incarnation [,ınkɑː'neıʃn] *n* **-1.** [personification] personificación *f*. **-2.** [existence] encarnación *f*.

incendiary device [ın'sendjərı-] *n* artefacto *m* incendiario.

incense [*n* 'ınsens, *vt* ın'sens] ◇ *n* incienso *m*. ◇ *vt* sulfurar, indignar.

incentive [ın'sentıv] *n* incentivo *m*.

incentive scheme *n* plan *m* de incentivos.

inception [ın'sepʃn] *n fml* inicio *m*.

incessant [ɪn'sesnt] *adj* incesante, constante.

incessantly [ɪn'sesntlɪ] *adv* incesantemente, constantemente.

incest ['ɪnsest] *n* incesto *m*.

inch [ɪntʃ] ◇ *n* = 2,5 cm, pulgada *f*. ◇ *vi* avanzar poco a poco.

incidence ['ɪnsɪdəns] *n* [of disease, theft] índice *m*.

incident ['ɪnsɪdənt] *n* incidente *m*, suceso *m*.

incidental [,ɪnsɪ'dentl] *adj* accesorio(ria).

incidentally [,ɪnsɪ'dentəlɪ] *adv* por cierto, a propósito.

incinerate [ɪn'sɪnəreɪt] *vt* incinerar.

incipient [ɪn'sɪpɪənt] *adj fml* incipiente.

incisive [ɪn'saɪsɪv] *adj* [comment, person] incisivo(va); [mind] penetrante.

incite [ɪn'saɪt] *vt* incitar, provocar; **to ~ sb to do sthg** incitar a alguien a que haga algo.

inclination [,ɪnklɪ'neɪʃn] *n* **-1.** (U) [liking, preference] inclinación *f*, propensión *f*. **-2.** [tendency]: **~ to do sthg** tendencia *f* a hacer algo.

incline [*n* 'ɪnklaɪn, *vb* ɪn'klaɪn] ◇ *n* pendiente *f*. ◇ *vt* [head] inclinar, ladear.

inclined [ɪn'klaɪnd] *adj* **-1.** [tending]: **to be ~ to sthg** ser propenso OR tener tendencia a algo; **to be ~ to do sthg** tener tendencia a hacer algo. **-2.** *fml* [wanting]: **to be ~ to do sthg** estar dispuesto a hacer algo. **-3.** [sloping] inclinado(da).

include [ɪn'kluːd] *vt* **-1.** [gen] incluir. **-2.** [with letter] adjuntar.

included [ɪn'kluːdɪd] *adj* incluido(da).

including [ɪn'kluːdɪŋ] *prep* inclusive; **six died, ~ a child** seis murieron, incluido un niño.

inclusive [ɪn'kluːsɪv] *adj* **-1.** [including everything] inclusivo(va); **one to nine ~** uno a nueve inclusive. **-2.** [including all costs]: **~ of VAT** con el IVA incluido; **£150 ~** 150 libras todo incluido.

incoherent [,ɪnkəʊ'hɪərənt] *adj* incoherente, ininteligible.

income ['ɪŋkʌm] *n* [gen] ingresos *mpl*; [from property] renta *f*; [from investment] réditos *mpl*.

income support *n* (U) *Br* subsidio para personas con muy bajos ingresos o desempleados sin derecho a subsidio de paro, ≃ salario *m* social.

income tax *n* impuesto *m* sobre la renta.

incompatible [,ɪnkəm'pætɪbl] *adj*: **~ (with)** incompatible (con).

incompetent [ɪn'kɒmpɪtənt] *adj* incompetente, incapaz.

incomplete [,ɪnkəm'pliːt] *adj* incompleto(ta).

incomprehensible [ɪn,kɒmprɪ'hensəbl] *adj* incomprensible.

inconceivable [,ɪnkən'siːvəbl] *adj* inconcebible.

inconclusive [,ɪnkən'kluːsɪv] *adj* [evidence, argument] poco convincente; [meeting, outcome] sin conclusión clara.

incongruous [ɪn'kɒŋgrʊəs] *adj* incongruente.

inconsequential [,ɪnkɒnsɪ'kwenʃl] *adj* intrascendente, de poca importancia.

inconsiderable [,ɪnkən'sɪdərəbl] *adj*: **not ~** nada insignificante OR despreciable.

inconsiderate [,ɪnkən'sɪdərət] *adj* desconsiderado(da).

inconsistency [,ɪnkən'sɪstənsɪ] *n* **-1.** [between theory and practice] inconsecuencia *f*; [between statements etc] falta *f* de correspondencia. **-2.** [contradictory point] contradicción *f*.

inconsistent [,ɪnkən'sɪstənt] *adj* **-1.** [translation, statement]: **~ (with)** falto(ta) de correspondencia (con). **-2.** [group, government, person] inconsecuente. **-3.** [erratic] irregular, desigual.

inconspicuous [,ɪnkən'spɪkjʊəs] *adj* discreto(ta).

inconvenience [,ɪnkən'viːnjəns] ◇ *n* **-1.** [difficulty, discomfort] molestia *f*, incomodidad *f*. **-2.** [inconvenient thing] inconveniente *m*. ◇ *vt* incomodar.

inconvenient [,ɪnkən'viːnjənt] *adj* [time] inoportuno(na); [position] incómodo(da); **that date is ~** esa fecha no me viene bien.

incorporate [ɪn'kɔːpəreɪt] *vt* **-1.** [integrate]: **to ~ sthg/sb (in)**, **to ~ sthg/sb (into)** incorporar algo/a alguien (en). **-2.** [include] incluir, comprender.

incorporated [ɪn'kɔːpəreɪtɪd] *adj* COMM: **~ company** sociedad *f* anónima.

incorrect [,ɪnkə'rekt] *adj* incorrecto(ta).

incorrigible [ɪn'kɒrɪdʒəbl] *adj* incorregible.

increase [*n* 'ɪnkriːs, *vb* ɪn'kriːs] ◇ *n*: **~ (in)** [gen] aumento *m* (de); [in price] subida *f* (de); **to be on the ~** ir en aumento. ◇ *vt* aumentar, incrementar. ◇ *vi* [gen] aumentar, aumentarse; [price] subir.

increasing [ɪn'kriːsɪŋ] *adj* creciente.

increasingly [ɪn'kriːsɪŋlɪ] *adv* cada vez más.

incredible [ɪn'kredəbl] *adj* increíble.

incredulous [ɪn'kredjʊləs] *adj* incrédulo(la).

increment ['ɪnkrɪmənt] *n* incremento *m*.

incriminating [ɪn'krɪmɪneɪtɪŋ] *adj* incriminatorio(ria).

incubator ['ɪnkjʊbeɪtə'] *n* [for baby] incubadora *f*.

incumbent [ɪn'kʌmbənt] *fml* ◇ *adj*: **to be ~ on** OR **upon sb to do sthg** incumbir a alguien hacer algo. ◇ *n* titular *m* y *f*.

incur [ɪn'kɜ:'] *vt* [wrath, criticism] incurrir en, atraerse; [loss] contraer; [expenses] incurrir en.

indebted [ɪn'detɪd] *adj* **-1.** [grateful]: **~ (to)** agradecido(da) (a). **-2.** [owing money]: **~ (to)** en deuda (con).

indecent [ɪn'di:snt] *adj* **-1.** [improper] indecente. **-2.** [unreasonable, excessive] desmedido(da).

indecent assault *n* atentado *m* contra el pudor.

indecent exposure *n* exhibicionismo *m*.

indecisive [ˌɪndɪ'saɪsɪv] *adj* **-1.** [person] indeciso(sa). **-2.** [result] no decisivo(va).

indeed [ɪn'di:d] *adv* **-1.** [certainly] ciertamente, realmente; **are you coming?** - **~ I am** ¿vienes tú? - por supuesto que sí. **-2.** [in fact] de hecho. **-3.** [for emphasis] realmente; **very big ~** grandísimo; **very few ~** poquísimos. **-4.** [to express surprise, disbelief]: **~?** ¿ah sí?

indefinite [ɪn'defɪnɪt] *adj* **-1.** [time, number] indefinido(da). **-2.** [answer, opinion] impreciso(sa).

indefinitely [ɪn'defɪnətlɪ] *adv* **-1.** [for unfixed period] indefinidamente. **-2.** [imprecisely] de forma imprecisa.

indemnity [ɪn'demnətɪ] *n* **-1.** [insurance] indemnidad *f*. **-2.** [compensation] indemnización *f*, compensación *f*.

indent [ɪn'dent] *vt* **-1.** [dent] mellar. **-2.** [text] sangrar.

independence [ˌɪndɪ'pendəns] *n* independencia *f*.

Independence Day *n* fiesta del 4 de julio en Estados Unidos en conmemoración de la Declaración de Independencia de este país en 1776.

independent [ˌɪndɪ'pendənt] *adj*: **~ (of)** independiente (de).

independent school *n* Br colegio *m* privado.

in-depth *adj* a fondo, exhaustivo(va).

indescribable [ˌɪndɪ'skraɪbəbl] *adj* indescriptible.

indestructible [ˌɪndɪ'strʌktəbl] *adj* indestructible.

index ['ɪndeks] (*pl* **-es** OR **indices**) *n* índice *m*.

index card *n* ficha *f*.

index finger *n* (dedo *m*) índice *m*.

index-linked [-lɪŋkt] *adj* ligado(da) al coste de la vida.

India ['ɪndjə] *n* (la) India.

Indian ['ɪndjən] ◇ *adj* **-1.** [from India] hindú, indio(dia). **-2.** [from the Americas] indio(dia). ◇ *n* **-1.** [from India] hindú *m* y *f*, indio *m*, -dia *f*. **-2.** [from the Americas] indio *m*, -dia *f*.

Indian Ocean *n*: **the ~** el océano Índico.

indicate ['ɪndɪkeɪt] ◇ *vt* indicar. ◇ *vi* [when driving]: **to ~ left/right** indicar a la izquierda/derecha.

indication [ˌɪndɪ'keɪʃn] *n* **-1.** [suggestion, idea] indicación *f*. **-2.** [sign] indicio *m*.

indicative [ɪn'dɪkətɪv] ◇ *adj*: **~ of sthg** indicativo(va) de algo. ◇ *n* GRAMM indicativo *m*.

indicator ['ɪndɪkeɪtə'] *n* **-1.** [sign] indicador *m*. **-2.** [on car] intermitente *m*.

indices ['ɪndɪsi:z] *pl* → **index**.

indict [ɪn'daɪt] *vt*: **to ~ sb (for)** acusar a alguien (de).

indictment [ɪn'daɪtmənt] *n* **-1.** JUR acusación *f*. **-2.** [criticism] crítica *f* severa.

indifference [ɪn'dɪfrəns] *n* indiferencia *f*.

indifferent [ɪn'dɪfrənt] *adj* **-1.** [uninterested]: **~ (to)** indiferente (a). **-2.** [mediocre] ordinario(ria), mediocre.

indigenous [ɪn'dɪdʒɪnəs] *adj* indígena.

indigestion [ˌɪndɪ'dʒestʃn] *n* (U) indigestión *f*.

indignant [ɪn'dɪgnənt] *adj*: **~ (at)** indignado(da) (por).

indignity [ɪn'dɪgnətɪ] *n* indignidad *f*.

indigo ['ɪndɪgəʊ] ◇ *adj* (color) añil. ◇ *n* añil *m*.

indirect [ˌɪndɪ'rekt] *adj* indirecto(ta).

indiscreet [ˌɪndɪ'skri:t] *adj* indiscreto(ta), imprudente.

indiscriminate [ˌɪndɪ'skrɪmɪnət] *adj* indiscriminado(da).

indispensable [ˌɪndɪ'spensəbl] *adj* indispensable, imprescindible.

indisputable [ˌɪndɪ'spju:təbl] *adj* incuestionable.

indistinct [ˌɪndɪ'stɪŋkt] *adj* [memory] confuso(sa); [picture, marking] borroso(sa).

indistinguishable [ˌɪndɪ'stɪŋgwɪʃəbl] *adj*: **~ (from)** indistinguible (de).

individual [,ɪndɪ'vɪdʒʊəl] ◇ *adj* **-1.** [gen] individual. **-2.** [tuition] particular. **-3.** [approach, style] personal. ◇ *n* individuo *m*.

individually [,ɪndɪ'vɪdʒʊəlɪ] *adv* [separately] individualmente, por separado.

indoctrination [ɪn,dɒktrɪ'neɪʃn] *n* adoctrinamiento *m*.

Indonesia [,ɪndə'niːzjə] *n* Indonesia.

indoor ['ɪndɔːr] *adj* [gen] interior; [shoes] de andar por casa; [plant] de interior; [sports] en pista cubierta; ~ **swimming pool** piscina *f* cubierta.

indoors [,ɪn'dɔːz] *adv* [gen] dentro; [at home] en casa.

induce [ɪn'djuːs] *vt* **-1.** [persuade]: **to ~ sb to do sthg** inducir OR persuadir a alguien a que haga algo. **-2.** [labour, sleep, anger] provocar.

inducement [ɪn'djuːsmənt] *n* [incentive] incentivo *m*, aliciente *m*.

induction [ɪn'dʌkʃn] *n* **-1.** [into official position]: ~ **into** introducción *f* OR inducción *f* a. **-2.** ELEC & MED inducción *f*. **-3.** [introduction to job] introducción *f*.

induction course *n* cursillo *m* introductorio.

indulge [ɪn'dʌldʒ] ◇ *vt* **-1.** [whim, passion] satisfacer. **-2.** [child, person] consentir. ◇ *vi*: **to ~ in sthg** permitirse algo.

indulgence [ɪn'dʌldʒəns] *n* **-1.** [act of indulging] indulgencia *f*. **-2.** [special treat] gratificación *f*, vicio *m*.

indulgent [ɪn'dʌldʒənt] *adj* indulgente.

industrial [ɪn'dʌstrɪəl] *adj* industrial.

industrial action *n* huelga *f*; **to take ~** declararse en huelga.

industrial estate *Br*, **industrial park** *Am n* polígono *m* industrial.

industrialist [ɪn'dʌstrɪəlɪst] *n* industrial *m y f*.

industrial park *Am* = **industrial estate**.

industrial relations *npl* relaciones *fpl* laborales.

industrial revolution *n* revolución *f* industrial.

industrious [ɪn'dʌstrɪəs] *adj* diligente, trabajador(ra).

industry ['ɪndəstrɪ] *n* **-1.** [gen] industria *f*. **-2.** [hard work] laboriosidad *f*.

inebriated [ɪ'niːbrɪeɪtɪd] *adj fml* ebrio (ebria).

inedible [ɪn'edɪbl] *adj* no comestible.

ineffective [,ɪnɪ'fektɪv] *adj* ineficaz, inútil.

ineffectual [,ɪnɪ'fektʃʊəl] *adj* ineficaz, inútil.

inefficiency [,ɪnɪ'fɪʃnsɪ] *n* ineficacia *f*.

inefficient [,ɪnɪ'fɪʃnt] *adj* ineficaz, ineficiente.

ineligible [ɪn'elɪdʒəbl] *adj*: ~ **(for)** inelegible (para).

inept [ɪ'nept] *adj* inepto(ta); ~ **at** incapaz para.

inequality [,ɪnɪ'kwɒlətɪ] *n* desigualdad *f*.

inert [ɪ'nɜːt] *adj* inerte.

inertia [ɪ'nɜːʃə] *n* inercia *f*.

inescapable [,ɪnɪ'skeɪpəbl] *adj* ineludible.

inevitable [ɪn'evɪtəbl] *adj* inevitable.

inevitably [ɪn'evɪtəblɪ] *adv* inevitablemente.

inexcusable [,ɪnɪk'skjuːzəbl] *adj* inexcusable, imperdonable.

inexhaustible [,ɪnɪg'zɔːstəbl] *adj* inagotable.

inexpensive [,ɪnɪk'spensɪv] *adj* barato(ta), económico(ca).

inexperienced [,ɪnɪk'spɪərɪənst] *adj* inexperto(ta).

inexplicable [,ɪnɪk'splɪkəbl] *adj* inexplicable.

infallible [ɪn'fæləbl] *adj* infalible.

infamous ['ɪnfəməs] *adj* infame.

infancy ['ɪnfənsɪ] *n* primera infancia *f*.

infant ['ɪnfənt] *n* **-1.** [baby] bebé *m*. **-2.** [young child] niño pequeño *m*, niña pequeña *f*.

infantry ['ɪnfəntrɪ] *n* infantería *f*.

infant school *n Br* colegio *m* preescolar.

infatuated [ɪn'fætjʊeɪtɪd] *adj*: ~ **(with)** encaprichado(da) (con).

infatuation [ɪn,fætjʊ'eɪʃn] *n*: ~ **(with)** encaprichamiento *m* (con).

infect [ɪn'fekt] *vt* [wound] infectar; [person]: **to ~ sb (with sthg)** contagiar a alguien (algo).

infection [ɪn'fekʃn] *n* **-1.** [disease] infección *f*. **-2.** [spreading of germs] contagio *m*.

infectious [ɪn'fekʃəs] *adj lit & fig* contagioso(sa).

infer [ɪn'fɜːr] *vt* **-1.** [deduce]: **to ~ (that)** deducir OR inferir que; **to ~ sthg (from sthg)** deducir OR inferir algo (de algo). **-2.** *inf* [imply] insinuar, sugerir.

inferior [ɪn'fɪərɪər] ◇ *adj*: ~ **(to)** inferior (a). ◇ *n* [in status] inferior *m y f*.

inferiority [ɪn,fɪərɪ'ɒrətɪ] *n* inferioridad *f*.

inferiority complex *n* complejo *m* de inferioridad.

inferno [ɪn'fɜːnəʊ] (*pl* **-s**) *n* infierno *m*.

infertile [ɪnˈfɜːtaɪl] *adj* estéril.

infested [ɪnˈfestɪd] *adj*: ~ **with** infestado(da) de.

infighting [ˈɪnˌfaɪtɪŋ] *n* (U) disputas *fpl* internas.

infiltrate [ˈɪnfɪltreɪt] *vt* infiltrar.

infinite [ˈɪnfɪnət] *adj* infinito(ta).

infinitive [ɪnˈfɪnɪtɪv] *n* infinitivo *m*.

infinity [ɪnˈfɪnətɪ] *n* **-1.** MATH infinito *m*. **-2.** [incalculable number]: **an ~ (of)** infinidad *f* (de).

infirm [ɪnˈfɜːm] ◇ *adj* achacoso(sa). ◇ *npl*: **the ~** los enfermos.

infirmary [ɪnˈfɜːmərɪ] *n* **-1.** [hospital] hospital *m*. **-2.** [room] enfermería *f*.

infirmity [ɪnˈfɜːmətɪ] *n* **-1.** [illness] dolencia *f*. **-2.** [state] enfermedad *f*.

inflamed [ɪnˈfleɪmd] *adj* MED inflamado(da).

inflammable [ɪnˈflæməbl] *adj* [burning easily] inflamable.

inflammation [ˌɪnfləˈmeɪʃn] *n* MED inflamación *f*.

inflatable [ɪnˈfleɪtəbl] *adj* inflable, hinchable.

inflate [ɪnˈfleɪt] *vt* **-1.** [gen] inflar, hinchar. **-2.** ECON inflar.

inflation [ɪnˈfleɪʃn] *n* ECON inflación *f*.

inflationary [ɪnˈfleɪʃnrɪ] *adj* ECON inflacionario(ria), inflacionista.

inflict [ɪnˈflɪkt] *vt*: **to ~ sthg on sb** infligir algo a alguien.

influence [ˈɪnfluəns] ◇ *n*: ~ **(on** OR **over sb)** influencia *f* (sobre alguien); ~ **(on sthg)** influencia (en algo); **under the ~ of** [person, group] bajo la influencia de; [alcohol, drugs] bajo los efectos de. ◇ *vt* influenciar.

influential [ˌɪnfluˈenʃl] *adj* influyente.

influenza [ˌɪnfluˈenzə] *n fml* gripe *f*.

influx [ˈɪnflʌks] *n* afluencia *f*.

inform [ɪnˈfɔːm] *vt*: **to ~ sb (of/about sthg)** informar a alguien (de/sobre algo). ◆ **inform on** *vt fus* delatar.

informal [ɪnˈfɔːml] *adj* informal; [language] familiar.

informant [ɪnˈfɔːmənt] *n* **-1.** [informer] delator *m*, -ra *f*. **-2.** [of researcher] fuente *f* de información (*persona*).

information [ˌɪnfəˈmeɪʃn] *n* (U): ~ **(on** OR **about)** información *f* OR datos *mpl* (sobre); **a piece of ~** un dato; **for your ~** para tu información.

information desk *n* (mostrador *m* de) información *f*.

information technology *n* informática *f*.

informative [ɪnˈfɔːmətɪv] *adj* informativo(va).

informer [ɪnˈfɔːməʳ] *n* delator *m*, -ra *f*.

infrared [ˌɪnfrəˈred] *adj* infrarrojo(ja).

infrastructure [ˈɪnfrəˌstrʌktʃəʳ] *n* infraestructura *f*.

infringe [ɪnˈfrɪndʒ] ◇ *vt* infringir, vulnerar. ◇ *vi*: **to ~ on sthg** infringir OR vulnerar algo.

infringement [ɪnˈfrɪndʒmənt] *n* violación *f*, transgresión *f*.

infuriating [ɪnˈfjuərɪeɪtɪŋ] *adj* exasperante.

ingenious [ɪnˈdʒiːnjəs] *adj* ingenioso(sa), inventivo(va).

ingenuity [ˌɪndʒɪˈnjuːətɪ] *n* ingenio *m*, inventiva *f*.

ingenuous [ɪnˈdʒenjuəs] *adj fml* ingenuo(nua).

ingot [ˈɪŋgət] *n* lingote *m*.

ingrained [ˌɪnˈgreɪnd] *adj* **-1.** [ground in] incrustado(da). **-2.** [deeply rooted] arraigado(da).

ingratiating [ɪnˈgreɪʃɪeɪtɪŋ] *adj* obsequioso(sa), lisonjero(ra).

ingredient [ɪnˈgriːdjənt] *n* ingrediente *m*.

inhabit [ɪnˈhæbɪt] *vt* habitar.

inhabitant [ɪnˈhæbɪtənt] *n* habitante *m* y *f*.

inhale [ɪnˈheɪl] ◇ *vt* inhalar. ◇ *vi* [gen] inspirar; [smoker] tragarse el humo.

inhaler [ɪnˈheɪləʳ] *n* MED inhalador *m*.

inherent [ɪnˈhɪərənt, ɪnˈherənt] *adj*: ~ **(in)** inherente (a).

inherently [ɪnˈhɪərəntlɪ, ɪnˈherəntlɪ] *adv* intrínsecamente.

inherit [ɪnˈherɪt] ◇ *vt*: **to ~ sthg (from sb)** heredar algo (de alguien). ◇ *vi* heredar.

inheritance [ɪnˈherɪtəns] *n* herencia *f*.

inhibit [ɪnˈhɪbɪt] *vt* [restrict] impedir.

inhibition [ˌɪnhɪˈbɪʃn] *n* inhibición *f*.

inhospitable [ˌɪnhɒˈspɪtəbl] *adj* **-1.** [unwelcoming] inhospitalario(ria). **-2.** [harsh] inhóspito(ta).

in-house ◇ *adj* [journal, report] de circulación interna; [staff] de plantilla. ◇ *adv* en la oficina.

inhuman [ɪnˈhjuːmən] *adj* **-1.** [cruel] inhumano(na). **-2.** [not human] infrahumano(na).

initial [ɪˈnɪʃl] ◇ *adj* inicial. ◇ *vt* poner las iniciales a. ◆ **initials** *npl* [of person] iniciales *fpl*.

initially [ɪˈnɪʃəlɪ] *adv* inicialmente.

initiate [ɪˈnɪʃɪeɪt] *vt* iniciar; **to ~ sb into sthg** iniciar a alguien en algo.

initiative [ɪ'nɪʃətɪv] *n* iniciativa *f*.

inject [ɪn'dʒekt] *vt* MED: **to ~ sb with sthg, to ~ sthg into sb** inyectarle algo a alguien.

injection [ɪn'dʒekʃn] *n* inyección *f*.

injunction [ɪn'dʒʌŋkʃn] *n* interdicto *m*.

injure ['ɪndʒəʳ] *vt* [gen] herir; [reputation] dañar; [chances] perjudicar.

injured ['ɪndʒəd] *adj* [gen] herido(da); [reputation] dañado(da).

injury ['ɪndʒərɪ] *n* **-1.** (U) [physical harm] lesiones *fpl*. **-2.** [wound] lesión *f*. **-3.** [to pride, reputation] agravio *m*.

injury time *n* (U) (tiempo *m* de) descuento *m*.

injustice [ɪn'dʒʌstɪs] *n* injusticia *f*; **to do sb an ~** no hacerle justicia a alguien.

ink [ɪŋk] *n* tinta *f*.

ink-jet printer *n* COMPUT impresora *f* de chorro de tinta.

inkling ['ɪŋklɪŋ] *n*: **to have an ~ of sthg** tener una vaga idea de algo.

inlaid [,ɪn'leɪd] *adj* incrustado(da); **~ with** [jewels] con incrustaciones de.

inland [*adj* 'ɪnlənd, *adv* ɪn'lænd] ◇ *adj* interior. ◇ *adv* hacia el interior.

Inland Revenue *n Br*: **the ~** ≃ Hacienda *f*.

in-laws *npl inf* suegros *mpl*.

inlet ['ɪnlet] *n* **-1.** [stretch of water] entrante *m*. **-2.** [way in] entrada *f*, admisión *f*.

inmate ['ɪnmeɪt] *n* [of prison] preso *m*, -sa *f*; [of mental hospital] interno *m*, -na *f*.

inn [ɪn] *n* fonda *f*; [pub] *pub decorado a la vieja usanza*.

innate [,ɪ'neɪt] *adj* innato(ta).

inner ['ɪnəʳ] *adj* **-1.** [gen] interior. **-2.** [feelings] íntimo(ma); [fears, doubts, meaning] interno(na).

inner city *n* núcleo *m* urbano deprimido.

inner tube *n* cámara *f* (de aire).

innings ['ɪnɪŋz] (*pl inv*) *n Br* [in cricket] entrada *f*, turno *m*.

innocence ['ɪnəsəns] *n* inocencia *f*.

innocent ['ɪnəsənt] ◇ *adj*: **~ (of)** inocente (de). ◇ *n* [naive person] inocente *m y f*.

innocuous [ɪ'nɒkjʊəs] *adj* inocuo(cua).

innovation [,ɪnə'veɪʃn] *n* innovación *f*.

innovative ['ɪnəvətɪv] *adj* innovador(ra).

innuendo [,ɪnju:'endəʊ] (*pl -es* OR *-s*) *n* **-1.** [individual remark] insinuación *f*, indirecta *f*. **-2.** (U) [style of speaking] insinuaciones *fpl*, indirectas *fpl*.

inoculate [ɪ'nɒkjʊleɪt] *vt*: **to ~ sb with sthg** inocular algo a alguien.

inordinately [ɪ'nɔ:dɪnətlɪ] *adv fml* desmesuradamente.

in-patient *n* paciente interno *m*, paciente interna *f*.

input ['ɪnpʊt] (*pt & pp* input OR *-ted*) ◇ *n* **-1.** [contribution] aportación *f*, contribución *f*. **-2.** COMPUT entrada *f*. ◇ *vt* COMPUT entrar.

inquest ['ɪnkwest] *n* investigación *f* judicial.

inquire [ɪn'kwaɪəʳ] ◇ *vi* [ask for information] informarse, pedir información; **to ~ about sthg** informarse de algo. ◇ *vt*: **to ~ when/if/how ...** preguntar cuándo/si/cómo .... ◆ **inquire after** *vt fus* preguntar por. ◆ **inquire into** *vt fus* investigar.

inquiry [ɪn'kwaɪərɪ] *n* **-1.** [question] pregunta *f*; **"Inquiries"** "Información". **-2.** [investigation] investigación *f*.

inquiry desk *n* (mostrador *m* de) información *f*.

inquisitive [ɪn'kwɪzətɪv] *adj* curioso(sa).

inroads ['ɪnrəʊdz] *npl*: **to make ~ into** [savings, supplies] mermar; [market, enemy territory] abrirse paso en.

insane [ɪn'seɪn] *adj* [mad] demente; *fig* [jealousy, person] loco(ca).

insanity [ɪn'sænətɪ] *n* [madness] demencia *f*; *fig* locura *f*.

insatiable [ɪn'seɪʃəbl] *adj* insaciable.

inscription [ɪn'skrɪpʃn] *n* **-1.** [engraved] inscripción *f*. **-2.** [written] dedicatoria *f*.

inscrutable [ɪn'skru:təbl] *adj* inescrutable.

insect ['ɪnsekt] *n* insecto *m*.

insecticide [ɪn'sektɪsaɪd] *n* insecticida *m*.

insect repellent *n* loción *f* antiinsectos.

insecure [,ɪnsɪ'kjʊəʳ] *adj* **-1.** [not confident] inseguro(ra). **-2.** [not safe] poco seguro(ra).

insensible [ɪn'sensəbl] *adj* **-1.** [unconscious] inconsciente. **-2.** [unaware]: **to be ~ of sthg** no ser consciente de algo. **-3.** [unable to feel]: **to be ~ to sthg** ser insensible a algo.

insensitive [ɪn'sensətɪv] *adj*: **~ (to)** insensible (a).

inseparable [ɪn'seprəbl] *adj*: **~ (from)** inseparable (de).

insert [*vb* ɪn'sɜ:t, *n* 'ɪnsɜ:t] ◇ *vt*: **to ~ sthg (in** OR **into)** [hole] introducir algo (en); [text] insertar algo (en). ◇ *n* PRESS encarte *m*.

insertion [ɪn'sɜːʃn] *n* inserción *f*.
in-service training *n Br* formación *f* en horas de trabajo.
inshore [*adj* 'ɪnʃɔːʳ, *adv* ɪn'ʃɔːʳ] ◇ *adj* costero(ra). ◇ *adv* hacia la orilla OR la costa.
inside [ɪn'saɪd] ◇ *prep* dentro de; ~ **three months** en menos de tres meses. ◇ *adv* [be, remain] dentro; [go, move etc] hacia dentro; *fig* [feel, hurt etc] interiormente; **come ~!** ¡metéos dentro! ◇ *adj* interior. ◇ *n* interior *m*; **from the ~** desde dentro; **to overtake on the ~** [of road] adelantar por dentro; **~ out** [wrong way] al revés; **to know sthg ~ out** conocer algo de arriba abajo OR al dedillo. ◆ **insides** *npl inf* tripas *fpl*. ◆ **inside of** *prep Am* [building, object] dentro de.
inside lane *n* AUT carril *m* de dentro.
insight ['ɪnsaɪt] *n* **-1.** (U) [power of understanding] perspicacia *f*. **-2.** [understanding] idea *f*.
insignificant [,ɪnsɪg'nɪfɪkənt] *adj* insignificante.
insincere [,ɪnsɪn'sɪəʳ] *adj* insincero(ra).
insinuate [ɪn'sɪnjueɪt] *pej vt*: **to ~ (that)** insinuar (que).
insipid [ɪn'sɪpɪd] *adj pej* soso(sa), insípido(da).
insist [ɪn'sɪst] ◇ *vt*: **to ~ that** insistir en que. ◇ *vi*: **to ~ on sthg** exigir algo; **to ~ (on doing sthg)** insistir (en hacer algo).
insistent [ɪn'sɪstənt] *adj* **-1.** [determined] insistente; **to be ~ on sthg** insistir en algo. **-2.** [continual] persistente.
insofar [,ɪnsəʊ'fɑːʳ] ◆ **insofar as** *conj* en la medida en que.
insole ['ɪnsəʊl] *n* plantilla *f*.
insolent ['ɪnsələnt] *adj* insolente.
insolvent [ɪn'sɒlvənt] *adj* insolvente.
insomnia [ɪn'sɒmnɪə] *n* insomnio *m*.
inspect [ɪn'spekt] *vt* inspeccionar; [troops] pasar revista a.
inspection [ɪn'spekʃn] *n* inspección *f*.
inspector [ɪn'spektəʳ] *n* inspector *m*, -ra *f*; [on bus, train] revisor *m*, -ra *f*.
inspiration [,ɪnspə'reɪʃn] *n* **-1.** [gen] inspiración *f*. **-2.** [source of inspiration]: **~ (for)** fuente *f* de inspiración (para).
inspire [ɪn'spaɪəʳ] *vt* **-1.** [stimulate, encourage]: **to ~ sb (to do sthg)** alentar OR animar a alguien (a hacer algo). **-2.** [fill]: **to ~ sb with sthg, to ~ sthg in sb** inspirar algo a alguien.
install *Br*, **instal** *Am* [ɪn'stɔːl] *vt* [gen & COMPUT] instalar.

installation [,ɪnstə'leɪʃn] *n* [gen & COMPUT] instalación *f*.
installment *Am* = instalment.
installment plan *n Am* compra *f* a plazos.
instalment *Br*, **installment** *Am* [ɪn'stɔːlmənt] *n* **-1.** [payment] plazo *m*; **in ~s** a plazos. **-2.** TV & RADIO episodio *m*; [of novel] entrega *f*.
instance ['ɪnstəns] *n* [example, case] ejemplo *m*; **for ~** por ejemplo; **in this ~** en este caso.
instant ['ɪnstənt] ◇ *adj* instantáneo(a). ◇ *n* [moment] instante *m*; **at that OR the same ~** en aquel mismo instante; **the ~ (that) ...** en cuanto ...; **this ~** ahora mismo.
instantly ['ɪnstəntlɪ] *adv* en el acto.
instead [ɪn'sted] *adv* en cambio. ◆ **instead of** *prep* en lugar de, en vez de.
instep ['ɪnstep] *n* [of foot] empeine *m*.
instigate ['ɪnstɪgeɪt] *vt* iniciar; **to ~ sb to do sthg** instigar a alguien a hacer algo.
instil *Br*, **instill** *Am* [ɪn'stɪl] *vt*: **to ~ sthg in OR into sb** inculcar OR infundir algo a alguien.
instinct ['ɪnstɪŋkt] *n* instinto *m*; **my first ~ was ...** mi primer impulso fue ....
instinctive [ɪn'stɪŋktɪv] *adj* instintivo(va).
institute ['ɪnstɪtjuːt] ◇ *n* instituto *m*. ◇ *vt* [proceedings] iniciar, entablar; [system] instituir.
institution [,ɪnstɪ'tjuːʃn] *n* **-1.** [gen] institución *f*. **-2.** [home - for children, old people] asilo *m*; [- for mentally-handicapped] hospital *m* psiquiátrico.
instruct [ɪn'strʌkt] *vt* **-1.** [tell, order]: **to ~ sb to do sthg** mandar OR ordenar a alguien que haga algo. **-2.** [teach]: **to ~ sb (in sthg)** instruir a alguien (en algo).
instruction [ɪn'strʌkʃn] *n* instrucción *f*. ◆ **instructions** *npl* [for use] instrucciones *fpl*.
instructor [ɪn'strʌktəʳ] *n* **-1.** [gen] instructor *m*. **-2.** [in skiing] monitor *m*. **-3.** [in driving] profesor *m*. **-4.** *Am* SCH profesor *m*, -ra *f*.
instrument ['ɪnstrʊmənt] *n* instrumento *m*.
instrumental [,ɪnstrʊ'mentl] *adj* [important, helpful]: **to be ~ in sthg** jugar un papel fundamental en algo.
instrument panel *n* tablero *m* de instrumentos.

insubordinate [ˌɪnsəˈbɔːdɪnət] *adj fml* insubordinado(da).

insubstantial [ˌɪnsəbˈstænʃl] *adj* [frame, structure] endeble; [meal] poco sustancioso(sa).

insufficient [ˌɪnsəˈfɪʃnt] *adj*: ~ (for) insuficiente (para).

insular [ˈɪnsjʊləʳ] *adj* estrecho(cha) de miras.

insulate [ˈɪnsjʊleɪt] *vt* aislar; **to ~ sb against** OR **from sthg** aislar a alguien de algo.

insulating tape [ˈɪnsjʊleɪtɪŋ-] *n Br* cinta *f* aislante.

insulation [ˌɪnsjʊˈleɪʃn] *n* [material, substance] aislamiento *m*.

insulin [ˈɪnsjʊlɪn] *n* insulina *f*.

insult [*vt* ɪnˈsʌlt, *n* ˈɪnsʌlt] ◇ *vt* [with words] insultar; [with actions] ofender. ◇ *n* [remark] insulto *m*; [action] ofensa *f*.

insuperable [ɪnˈsuːprəbl] *adj fml* insalvable, insuperable.

insurance [ɪnˈʃʊərəns] *n* **-1.** [against fire, accident, theft]: ~ (against) seguro *m* (contra). **-2.** *fig* [safeguard, protection]: ~ (against) prevención *f* (contra).

insurance policy *n* póliza *f* de seguros.

insure [ɪnˈʃʊəʳ] ◇ *vt* **-1.** [against fire, accident, theft]: **to ~ sthg/sb (against)** asegurar algo/a alguien (contra). **-2.** *Am* [make certain] asegurar. ◇ *vi* [prevent]: **to ~ (against)** prevenir OR prevenirse (contra).

insurer [ɪnˈʃʊərəʳ] *n* asegurador *m*, -ra *f*.

insurmountable [ˌɪnsəˈmaʊntəbl] *adj fml* infranqueable, insuperable.

intact [ɪnˈtækt] *adj* intacto(ta).

intake [ˈɪnteɪk] *n* **-1.** [of food, drink] ingestión *f*; [of air] inspiración *f*. **-2.** [in army] reclutamiento *m*; [in organization] número *m* de ingresos.

integral [ˈɪntɪɡrəl] *adj* integrante; **to be ~ to** ser parte integrante de.

integrate [ˈɪntɪɡreɪt] ◇ *vi*: **to ~ (with** OR **into)** integrarse (en). ◇ *vt*: **to ~ sthg/sb with sthg, to ~ sthg/sb into sthg** integrar algo/a alguien en algo.

integrity [ɪnˈteɡrətɪ] *n* integridad *f*.

intellect [ˈɪntəlekt] *n* [mind, cleverness] intelecto *m*, inteligencia *f*.

intellectual [ˌɪntəˈlektjʊəl] ◇ *adj* intelectual. ◇ *n* intelectual *m* y *f*.

intelligence [ɪnˈtelɪdʒəns] *n* (*U*) **-1.** [ability to think] inteligencia *f*. **-2.** [information service] servicio *m* secreto OR de espionaje. **-3.** [information] información *f* secreta.

intelligent [ɪnˈtelɪdʒənt] *adj* [clever] inteligente.

intelligent card *n* tarjeta *f* inteligente.

intend [ɪnˈtend] *vt* pretender, proponerse; **to be ~ed for/as sthg** [project, book] estar pensado para/como algo; **to ~ doing** OR **to do sthg** tener la intención de OR pretender hacer algo; **later than I had ~ed** más tarde de lo que había pensado.

intended [ɪnˈtendɪd] *adj* pretendido(da).

intense [ɪnˈtens] *adj* **-1.** [extreme, profound] intenso(sa). **-2.** [serious - person] muy serio(ria).

intensely [ɪnˈtenslɪ] *adv* **-1.** [very - boring, irritating] enormemente. **-2.** [very much - suffer] intensamente; [- dislike] profundamente.

intensify [ɪnˈtensɪfaɪ] ◇ *vt* intensificar. ◇ *vi* intensificarse.

intensity [ɪnˈtensətɪ] *n* intensidad *f*.

intensive [ɪnˈtensɪv] *adj* [concentrated] intensivo(va).

intensive care *n* (*U*): **(in) ~** (bajo) cuidados *mpl* intensivos.

intent [ɪnˈtent] ◇ *adj* **-1.** [absorbed] atento(ta). **-2.** [determined]: **to be ~ on** OR **upon doing sthg** estar empeñado(da) en hacer algo. ◇ *n fml* intención *f*; **to all ~s and purposes** para todos los efectos.

intention [ɪnˈtenʃn] *n* intención *f*.

intentional [ɪnˈtenʃənl] *adj* deliberado(da), intencionado(da).

intently [ɪnˈtentlɪ] *adv* atentamente.

interact [ˌɪntərˈækt] *vi* **-1.** [communicate, work together]: **to ~ (with sb)** comunicarse (con alguien). **-2.** [react]: **to ~ (with sthg)** interaccionar (con algo).

intercede [ˌɪntəˈsiːd] *vi fml*: **to ~ (with/for)** interceder (con/por).

intercept [ˌɪntəˈsept] *vt* interceptar.

interchange [*n* ˈɪntətʃeɪndʒ, *vb* ˌɪntəˈtʃeɪndʒ] ◇ *n* **-1.** [exchange] intercambio *m*. **-2.** [on motorway] cruce *m*. ◇ *vt* intercambiar.

interchangeable [ˌɪntəˈtʃeɪndʒəbl] *adj*: ~ (with) intercambiable (con).

intercity [ˌɪntəˈsɪtɪ] *n* red *de trenes rápidos que conecta las principales ciudades británicas.*

intercom [ˈɪntəkɒm] *n* [for block of flats] portero *m* automático; [within a building] interfono *m*.

intercourse [ˈɪntəkɔːs] *n* (*U*): **sexual ~** relaciones *fpl* sexuales, coito *m*.

interest [ˈɪntrəst] ◇ *n* **-1.** [gen & FIN]: ~ **(in)** interés *m* (en OR por); **that's of no**

~ eso no tiene interés. **-2.** [hobby] afición *f.* ◇ *vt* interesar.

interested ['ɪntrəstɪd] *adj* interesado(da); **to be ~ in sthg/in doing sthg** estar interesado en algo/en hacer algo.

interesting ['ɪntrəstɪŋ] *adj* interesante.

interest rate *n* tipo *m* de interés.

interface ['ɪntəfeɪs] *n* COMPUT interfaz *f.*

interfere [,ɪntə'fɪəʳ] *vi* **-1.** [meddle]: **to ~ (with OR in sthg)** entrometerse OR interferir (en algo). **-2.** [damage] interferir; **to ~ with sthg** [career, routine] interferir en algo; [work, performance] interrumpir algo.

interference [,ɪntə'fɪərəns] *n* (U) **-1.** [meddling]: **~ (with OR in)** intromisión *f* OR interferencia *f* (en). **-2.** [on radio, TV, telephone] interferencia *f.*

interim ['ɪntərɪm] ◇ *adj* [report] parcial; [measure] provisional; [government] interino(na). ◇ *n*: **in the ~** entre tanto.

interior [ɪn'tɪərɪəʳ] ◇ *adj* **-1.** [inner] interior. **-2.** POL [minister, department] del Interior. ◇ *n* interior *m.*

interior decorator, interior designer *n* diseñador *m*, -ra *f* de interiores.

interlock [,ɪntə'lɒk] *vi* [fingers] entrelazarse; [cogs] engranar.

interloper ['ɪntələʊpəʳ] *n* intruso *m*, -sa *f.*

interlude ['ɪntəluːd] *n* **-1.** [pause] intervalo *m.* **-2.** [interval] intermedio *m.*

intermediary [,ɪntə'miːdjərɪ] *n* intermediario *m*, -ria *f.*

intermediate [,ɪntə'miːdjət] *adj* intermedio(dia).

interminable [ɪn'tɜːmɪnəbl] *adj* interminable.

intermission [,ɪntə'mɪʃn] *n* [of film] descanso *m*; [of play, opera, ballet] entreacto *m.*

intermittent [,ɪntə'mɪtənt] *adj* intermitente.

intern [*vb* ɪn'tɜːn, *n* 'ɪntɜːn] ◇ *vt* recluir, internar. ◇ *n* médico *m* interno residente.

internal [ɪn'tɜːnl] *adj* **-1.** [gen] interno(na). **-2.** [within a country] interior, nacional; **~ flight** vuelo *m* nacional.

internally [ɪn'tɜːnəlɪ] *adv* **-1.** [gen] internamente. **-2.** [within a country] a nivel nacional.

Internal Revenue *n Am*: **the ~** ≃ Hacienda *f.*

international [,ɪntə'næʃənl] ◇ *adj* internacional. ◇ *n Br* SPORT **-1.** [match] encuentro *m* internacional. **-2.** [player] internacional *m y f.*

interpret [ɪn'tɜːprɪt] ◇ *vt* interpretar. ◇ *vi* hacer de intérprete.

interpreter [ɪn'tɜːprɪtəʳ] *n* [person] intérprete *m y f.*

interrelate [,ɪntərɪ'leɪt] *vi*: **to ~ (with)** interrelacionarse (con).

interrogate [ɪn'terəgeɪt] *vt* [gen & COMPUT] interrogar.

interrogation [ɪn,terə'geɪʃn] *n* interrogatorio *m.*

interrogation mark *n Am* signo *m* de interrogación.

interrogative [,ɪntə'rɒgətɪv] GRAMM *adj* interrogativo(va).

interrupt [,ɪntə'rʌpt] *vt & vi* interrumpir.

interruption [,ɪntə'rʌpʃn] *n* interrupción *f.*

intersect [,ɪntə'sekt] ◇ *vi* cruzarse, cortarse. ◇ *vt* cruzar, cortar.

intersection [,ɪntə'sekʃn] *n* [junction] intersección *f*, cruce *m.*

intersperse [,ɪntə'spɜːs] *vt*: **to be ~d with OR by** estar entremezclado con.

interstate (highway) ['ɪntərsteɪt-] *n* autopista *f* interestatal.

interval ['ɪntəvl] *n* **-1.** [gen & MUS]: **~ (between)** intervalo *m* (entre); **at ~s** [now and again] a ratos; [regularly] a intervalos; **at monthly/yearly ~s** a intervalos de un mes/un año. **-2.** *Br* [at play, concert] intermedio *m*, descanso *m.*

intervene [,ɪntə'viːn] *vi* **-1.** [gen]: **to ~ (in)** intervenir (en). **-2.** [prevent thing from happening] interponerse. **-3.** [pass] transcurrir.

intervention [,ɪntə'venʃn] *n* intervención *f.*

interview ['ɪntəvjuː] ◇ *n* entrevista *f.* ◇ *vt* entrevistar.

interviewer ['ɪntəvjuːəʳ] *n* entrevistador *m*, -ra *f.*

intestine [ɪn'testɪn] *n* intestino *m.*

intimacy ['ɪntɪməsɪ] *n*: **~ (between/ with)** intimidad *f* (entre/con).

intimate [*adj* 'ɪntɪmət, *vb* 'ɪntɪmeɪt] ◇ *adj* **-1.** [gen] íntimo(ma). **-2.** [knowledge] profundo(da). ◇ *vt fml*: **to ~ (that)** dar a entender (que).

intimidate [ɪn'tɪmɪdeɪt] *vt* intimidar.

into ['ɪntʊ] *prep* **-1.** [inside] en; **to put sthg ~ sthg** meter algo en algo; **to get ~ a car** subir a un coche. **-2.** [against] con; **to bump/crash ~** tropezar/chocar con. **-3.** [referring to change in condition etc]: **to turn** OR **develop ~** convertirse en; **to translate sthg ~ Spanish** traducir algo al español. **-4.** [concerning] en relación con; **research ~ electronics** investigación en torno a la electrónica. **-5.** MATH: **to divide 4 ~ 8** dividir 8 entre 4.

intolerable [ɪn'tɒlrəbl] *adj fml* [position, conditions] intolerable; [boredom, pain] inaguantable.

intolerance [ɪn'tɒlərəns] *n* intolerancia *f.*

intolerant [ɪn'tɒlərənt] *adj* intolerante.

intoxicated [ɪn'tɒksɪkeɪtɪd] *adj* **-1.** [drunk] embriagado(da). **-2.** *fig* [excited]: **~ (by** OR **with)** ebrio (ebria) (de).

intractable [ɪn'træktəbl] *adj fml* **-1.** [stubborn] intratable. **-2.** [insoluble] inextricable, insoluble.

intransitive [ɪn'trænzətɪv] *adj* intransitivo(va).

intravenous [,ɪntrə'viːnəs] *adj* intravenoso(sa).

in-tray *n* bandeja para cartas y documentos recién llegados a la oficina.

intricate ['ɪntrɪkət] *adj* intrincado(da).

intrigue [ɪn'triːg] ◇ *n* intriga *f.* ◇ *vt* intrigar.

intriguing [ɪn'triːgɪŋ] *adj* intrigante.

intrinsic [ɪn'trɪnsɪk] *adj* intrínseco(ca).

introduce [,ɪntrə'djuːs] *vt* **-1.** [present - person, programme] presentar; **to ~ sb (to sb)** presentar a alguien (a alguien); **to ~ o.s.** presentarse. **-2.** [bring in]: **to ~ sthg (to** OR **into)** introducir algo (en). **-3.** [show for first time]: **to ~ sb to sthg** iniciar a alguien en algo.

introduction [,ɪntrə'dʌkʃn] *n* **-1.** [gen]: **~ (to sthg)** introducción *f* (a algo). **-2.** [of people]: **~ (to sb)** presentación *f* (a alguien).

introductory [,ɪntrə'dʌktrɪ] *adj* [chapter] introductorio(ria); [remarks] preliminar.

introvert ['ɪntrəvɜːt] *n* introvertido *m,* -da *f.*

introverted ['ɪntrəvɜːtɪd] *adj* introvertido(da).

intrude [ɪn'truːd] *vi*: **to ~ (on** OR **upon sb)** inmiscuirse (en los asuntos de alguien); **to ~ (on** OR **upon sthg)** inmiscuirse (en algo).

intruder [ɪn'truːdər] *n* intruso *m,* -sa *f.*

intrusive [ɪn'truːsɪv] *adj* [person] entrometido(da); [presence] indeseado(da).

intuition [,ɪntjuː'ɪʃn] *n* intuición *f.*

inundate ['ɪnʌndeɪt] *vt* **-1.** *fml* [flood] inundar. **-2.** [overwhelm] desbordar; **to be ~d with** verse desbordado por.

invade [ɪn'veɪd] *vt* invadir.

invalid [*adj* ɪn'vælɪd, *n* 'ɪnvəlɪd] ◇ *adj* **-1.** [marriage, vote, ticket] nulo(la). **-2.** [argument, result] que no es válido(da). ◇ *n* inválido *m,* -da *f.*

invaluable [ɪn'væljuəbl] *adj*: **~ (to)** [information, advice] inestimable (para); [person] valiosísimo(ma) (para).

invariably [ɪn'veərɪəblɪ] *adv* siempre, invariablemente. ·

invasion [ɪn'veɪʒn] *n* invasión *f.*

invent [ɪn'vent] *vt* inventar.

invention [ɪn'venʃn] *n* **-1.** [gen] invención *f.* **-2.** [ability to invent] inventiva *f.*

inventive [ɪn'ventɪv] *adj* [person, mind] inventivo(va); [solution] ingenioso(sa).

inventor [ɪn'ventər] *n* inventor *m,* -ra *f.*

inventory ['ɪnvəntrɪ] *n* **-1.** [list] inventario *m.* **-2.** *Am* [goods] existencias *fpl.*

invert [ɪn'vɜːt] *vt fml* invertir.

inverted commas [ɪn'vɜːtɪd-] *npl Br* comillas *fpl;* **in ~** entre comillas.

invest [ɪn'vest] ◇ *vt* [money, time, energy]: **to ~ sthg (in)** invertir algo (en). ◇ *vi lit* & *fig*: **to ~ (in)** invertir (en).

investigate [ɪn'vestɪgeɪt] *vt* & *vi* investigar.

investigation [ɪn,vestɪ'geɪʃn] *n* [enquiry, examination]: **~ (into)** investigación *f* (en).

investment [ɪn'vestmənt] *n* inversión *f.*

investor [ɪn'vestər] *n* inversor *m,* -ra *f.*

inveterate [ɪn'vetərət] *adj* [liar] incorregible; [reader, smoker] empedernido(da).

invidious [ɪn'vɪdɪəs] *adj* [task, role] desagradable; [comparison] odioso(sa).

invigilate [ɪn'vɪdʒɪleɪt] *vt* & *vi Br* vigilar (*en un examen*).

invigorating [ɪn'vɪgəreɪtɪŋ] *adj* [bath, walk] vigorizante; [experience] estimulante.

invincible [ɪn'vɪnsɪbl] *adj* **-1.** [unbeatable] invencible. **-2.** [unchangeable] inalterable.

invisible [ɪn'vɪzɪbl] *adj* invisible.

invitation [,ɪnvɪ'teɪʃn] *n* invitación *f.*

invite [ɪn'vaɪt] *vt*: **to ~ sb (to sthg/to do sthg)** invitar a alguien (a algo/a hacer algo).

inviting [ɪn'vaɪtɪŋ] *adj* tentador(ra).

invoice ['ɪnvɔɪs] ◇ *n* factura *f.* ◇ *vt* **-1.** [send invoice to] mandar la factura a. **-2.** [prepare invoice for] facturar.

invoke [ɪn'vəʊk] *vt fml* [quote as justification] acogerse a.

involuntary [ɪn'vɒləntrɪ] *adj* involuntario(ria).

involve [ɪn'vɒlv] *vt* **-1.** [entail, require]: **to ~ sthg/doing sthg** conllevar algo/hacer algo; **it ~s working weekends** supone OR implica trabajar los fines de semana. **-2.** [concern, affect] afectar a. **-3.** [make part of sthg]: **to ~ sb (in)** involucrar a alguien (en).

involved [ɪn'vɒlvd] *adj* **-1.** [complex] enrevesado(da). **-2.** [participating]: **to be ~ in** estar metido(da) en. **-3.** [in a relationship]: **to be/get ~ with sb** estar liado(da)/liarse con alguien.

involvement [ɪn'vɒlvmənt] *n* **-1.** **~ (in)** [crime] implicación *f* (en); [running sthg] participación *f* (en). **-2.** [concern, enthusiasm]: **~ (in)** compromiso *m* (con).

inward ['ɪnwəd] ◇ *adj* **-1.** [inner] interno(na). **-2.** [towards the inside] hacia el interior. ◇ *adv Am* = **inwards**.

inwards ['ɪnwədz] *adv* hacia dentro.

iodine [*Br* 'aɪədiːn, *Am* 'aɪədaɪn] *n* yodo *m*.

iota [aɪ'əʊtə] *n* pizca *f*, ápice *m*.

IOU (*abbr of* **I owe you**) *n* pag. *m*.

IQ (*abbr of* **intelligence quotient**) *n* C.I. *m*.

IRA *n* (*abbr of* **Irish Republican Army**) IRA *m*.

Iran [ɪ'rɑːn] *n* (el) Irán.

Iranian [ɪ'reɪnjən] ◇ *adj* iraní. ◇ *n* [person] iraní *m y f*.

Iraq [ɪ'rɑːk] *n* (el) Irak.

Iraqi [ɪ'rɑːkɪ] ◇ *adj* iraquí. ◇ *n* [person] iraquí *m y f*.

irate [aɪ'reɪt] *adj* iracundo(da), airado(da).

Ireland ['aɪələnd] *n* Irlanda.

iris ['aɪərɪs] (*pl* **-es**) *n* **-1.** [flower] lirio *m*. **-2.** [of eye] iris *m inv*.

Irish ['aɪrɪʃ] ◇ *adj* irlandés(esa). ◇ *n* [language] irlandés *m*. ◇ *npl* [people]: **the ~** los irlandeses.

Irishman ['aɪrɪʃmən] (*pl* **-men** [-mən]) *n* irlandés *m*.

Irish Sea *n*: **the ~** el mar de Irlanda.

Irishwoman ['aɪrɪʃ,wʊmən] (*pl* **-women** [-,wɪmɪn]) *n* irlandesa *f*.

irksome ['ɜːksəm] *adj* fastidioso(sa).

iron ['aɪən] ◇ *adj lit & fig* de hierro. ◇ *n* **-1.** [metal] hierro *m*, fierro *m Amer*. **-2.** [for clothes] plancha *f*. **-3.** [golf club] hierro *m*. ◇ *vt* planchar. ◆ **iron out** *vt sep fig* [overcome] resolver.

Iron Curtain *n*: **the ~** el telón de acero.

ironic(al) [aɪ'rɒnɪk(l)] *adj* irónico(ca); **how ~!** ¡qué ironía!

ironing ['aɪənɪŋ] *n* **-1.** [work] planchado *m*. **-2.** [clothes to be ironed] ropa *f* para planchar.

ironing board *n* tabla *f* de planchar.

ironmonger ['aɪən,mʌŋgə^r] *n Br* ferretero *m*, -ra *f*; **~'s (shop)** ferretería *f*.

irony ['aɪrənɪ] *n* ironía *f*.

irrational [ɪ'ræʃənl] *adj* irracional.

irreconcilable [ɪ,rekən'saɪləbl] *adj* [completely different] irreconciliable.

irregular [ɪ'regjʊlə^r] *adj* [gen & GRAMM] irregular.

irrelevant [ɪ'reləvənt] *adj* irrelevante, que no viene al caso.

irreparable [ɪ'repərəbl] *adj* irreparable.

irreplaceable [,ɪrɪ'pleɪsəbl] *adj* irreemplazable, insustituible.

irrepressible [,ɪrɪ'presəbl] *adj* [enthusiasm] irreprimible; [person] imparable.

irresistible [,ɪrɪ'zɪstəbl] *adj* irresistible.

irrespective [,ɪrɪ'spektɪv] ◆ **irrespective of** *prep* con independencia de.

irresponsible [,ɪrɪ'spɒnsəbl] *adj* irresponsable.

irrigate ['ɪrɪgeɪt] *vt* regar, irrigar.

irrigation [,ɪrɪ'geɪʃn] *n* riego *m*.

irritable ['ɪrɪtəbl] *adj* irritable.

irritate ['ɪrɪteɪt] *vt* irritar.

irritating ['ɪrɪteɪtɪŋ] *adj* irritante.

irritation [ɪrɪ'teɪʃn] *n* **-1.** [anger, soreness] irritación *f*. **-2.** [cause of anger] motivo *m* de irritación.

IRS (*abbr of* **Internal Revenue Service**) *n Am*: **the ~** ≃ Hacienda *f*.

is [ɪz] → **be**.

Islam ['ɪzlɑːm] *n* [religion] islam *m*.

island ['aɪlənd] *n* **-1.** [in water] isla *f*. **-2.** [in traffic] isleta *f*, refugio *m*.

islander ['aɪləndə^r] *n* isleño *m*, -ña *f*.

isle [aɪl] *n* [as part of name] isla *f*; *literary* [island] ínsula *f*.

Isle of Man *n*: **the ~** la isla de Man.

Isle of Wight [-waɪt] *n*: **the ~** la isla de Wight.

isn't ['ɪznt] = **is not**.

isobar ['aɪsəbɑː^r] *n* isobara *f*.

isolate ['aɪsəleɪt] *vt*: **to ~ sb (from)** [physically] aislar a alguien (de); [socially] marginar a alguien (de).

isolated ['aɪsəleɪtɪd] *adj* aislado(da).

Israel ['ɪzreɪəl] *n* Israel.

Israeli [ɪz'reɪlɪ] ◇ *adj* israelí. ◇ *n* israelí *m y f*.

issue ['ɪʃuː] ◇ *n* **-1.** [important subject] cuestión *f*, tema *m*; **at ~** en cuestión; **to make an ~ of sthg** darle demasiada importancia a algo. **-2.** [of newspaper, magazine] número *m*, edición *f*. **-3.** [of stamps, shares, banknotes] emisión *f*. ◇ *vt* **-1.** [decree] promulgar; [statement, warning] hacer público(ca). **-2.** [stamps, shares, banknotes] emitir. **-3.** [passport, document]: **to ~ sthg to sb, to ~ sb with sthg** expedir algo a alguien.

isthmus ['ɪsməs] *n* istmo *m*.

it [ɪt] *pron* **-1.** [referring to specific thing or person - subj] él *m*, ella *f*; [- direct object] lo *m*, la *f*; [- indirect object] le; **~ is in my hand** está en mi mano; **did you find ~?** ¿lo encontraste?; **give ~ to me** dámelo; **he gave ~ a kick** le dio una patada. **-2.** (*with prepositions*) él *m*, ella *f*; [- meaning "this matter" etc] ello; **as if his life depended on ~** como si le fuera la vida en ello; **in ~** dentro; **have you been to ~ before?** ¿has estado antes?; **on ~** encima; **to talk about ~** hablar de él/ella/ello; **under/beneath ~** debajo; **beside ~** al lado; **from/of ~** de él/ella/ello; **over ~** por encima. **-3.** (*impersonal use*): **~ was raining** llovía; **~ is cold today** hace frío hoy; **~'s two o'clock** son las dos; **who is ~? - it's Mary/me** ¿quién es? - soy Mary/yo; **what day is ~?** ¿a qué (día) estamos hoy?

IT *n abbr of* **information technology.**

Italian [ɪ'tæljən] ◇ *adj* italiano(na). ◇ *n* **-1.** [person] italiano *m*, -na *f*. **-2.** [language] italiano *m*.

italic [ɪ'tælɪk] *adj* cursiva. ◆ **italics** *npl* cursiva *f*.

Italy ['ɪtəlɪ] *n* Italia.

itch [ɪtʃ] ◇ *n* picor *m*, picazón *f*. ◇ *vi* **-1.** [be itchy - person] tener picazón; [- arm, leg etc] picar. **-2.** *fig* [be impatient]: **to be ~ing to do sthg** estar deseando hacer algo.

itchy ['ɪtʃɪ] *adj* que pica.

it'd ['ɪtəd] = **it would, it had.**

item ['aɪtəm] *n* **-1.** [in collection] artículo *m*; [on list, agenda] asunto *m*, punto *m*. **-2.** [article in newspaper] artículo *m*; **news ~** noticia *f*.

itemize, -ise ['aɪtəmaɪz] *vt* detallar.

itinerary [aɪ'tɪnərərɪ] *n* itinerario *m*.

it'll [ɪtl] = **it will.**

its [ɪts] *poss adj* su, sus (*pl*); **the dog broke ~ leg** el perro se rompió la pata.

it's [ɪts] = **it is, it has.**

itself [ɪt'self] *pron* **-1.** (*reflexive*) se; (*after prep*) sí mismo(ma); **with ~** consigo mismo(ma). **-2.** (*for emphasis*): **the town ~** is lovely el pueblo en sí es bonito; **in ~** en sí.

ITV (*abbr of* **Independent Television**) *n* ITV *f*, canal privado de televisión en Gran Bretaña.

I've [aɪv] = **I have.**

ivory ['aɪvərɪ] *n* marfil *m*.

ivy ['aɪvɪ] *n* hiedra *f*.

Ivy League *n Am* grupo de ocho prestigiosas universidades del este de los EEUU.

J

j (*pl* **j's** OR **js**), **J** (*pl* **J's** OR **Js**) [dʒeɪ] *n* [letter] j *f*, J *f*.

jab [dʒæb] ◇ *n Br inf* [injection] pinchazo *m*. ◇ *vt*: **to ~ sthg into** clavar algo en; **to ~ sthg at** apuntarle algo a.

jabber ['dʒæbər] *vi* charlotear.

jack [dʒæk] *n* **-1.** [device] gato *m*. **-2.** [playing card] ≃ sota *f*. ◆ **jack up** *vt sep* **-1.** [lift with a jack] levantar con gato. **-2.** [force up] subir.

jackal ['dʒækəl] *n* chacal *m*.

jackdaw ['dʒækdɔː] *n* grajilla *f*.

jacket ['dʒækɪt] *n* **-1.** [garment] chaqueta *f*, americana *f*, saco *m* *Amer*. **-2.** [potato skin] piel *f*. **-3.** [book cover] sobrecubierta *f*. **-4.** *Am* [of record] cubierta *f*.

jacket potato *n* patata *f* asada con piel.

jackhammer ['dʒæk,hæmər] *n Am* martillo *m* neumático.

jack knife *n* navaja *f*. ◆ **jack-knife** *vi* derrapar la parte delantera.

jack plug *n* (enchufe *m* de) clavija *f*.

jackpot ['dʒækpɒt] *n* (premio *m*) gordo *m*.

jaded ['dʒeɪdɪd] *adj* [tired] agotado(da); [bored] hastiado(da).

jagged ['dʒægɪd] *adj* dentado(da).

jail [dʒeɪl] ◇ *n* cárcel *f*. ◇ *vt* encarcelar.

jailer ['dʒeɪlər] *n* carcelero *m*, -ra *f*.

jam [dʒæm] ◇ *n* **-1.** [preserve] mermelada *f*. **-2.** [of traffic] embotellamiento *m*, atasco *m*. **-3.** *inf* [difficult situation]: **to get into/be in a ~** meterse/estar en un apuro. ◇ *vt* **-1.** [place roughly] meter a la fuerza. **-2.** [fix] sujetar; **~ the door shut** atranca la puerta. **-3.** [pack tightly] apiñar. **-4.** [fill] abarrotar, atestar. **-5.** TELEC bloquear. **-6.** [cause to stick] atascar. **-7.** RADIO interferir. ◇ *vi* [stick] atascarse.

Jamaica [dʒə'meɪkə] *n* Jamaica.

jam-packed [-'pækt] *adj inf* a tope.

jangle ['dʒæŋgl] vi tintinear.

janitor ['dʒænɪtəʳ] n Am & Scot conserje m, portero m.

January ['dʒænjʊərɪ] n enero m; see also **September**.

Japan [dʒə'pæn] n (el) Japón.

Japanese [,dʒæpə'niːz] (pl inv) ◇ adj japonés(esa). ◇ n [language] japonés m. ◇ npl: **the ~** los japoneses.

jar [dʒɑːʳ] ◇ n tarro m. ◇ vt [shake] sacudir. ◇ vi **-1.** [upset]: **to ~ (on sb)** poner los nervios de punta (a alguien). **-2.** [clash - opinions] discordar; [- colours] desentonar.

jargon ['dʒɑːgən] n jerga f.

jaundice ['dʒɔːndɪs] n icteria f.

jaundiced ['dʒɔːndɪst] adj fig [attitude, view] desencantado(da).

jaunt [dʒɔːnt] n excursión f.

jaunty ['dʒɔːntɪ] adj [hat, wave] airoso(sa); [person] vivaz, desenvuelto(ta).

javelin ['dʒævlɪn] n jabalina f.

jaw [dʒɔː] n [of person] mandíbula f; [of animal] quijada f.

jawbone ['dʒɔːbəʊn] n [of person] mandíbula f, maxilar m; [of animal] quijada f.

jay [dʒeɪ] n arrendajo m.

jaywalker ['dʒeɪwɔːkəʳ] n peatón m imprudente.

jazz [dʒæz] n MUS jazz m. ◆ **jazz up** vt sep inf alegrar, avivar.

jazzy ['dʒæzɪ] adj [bright] llamativo(va).

jealous ['dʒeləs] adj **-1.** [envious]: **to be ~ (of)** tener celos OR estar celoso(sa) (de). **-2.** [possessive]: **to be ~ (of)** ser celoso(sa) (de).

jealousy ['dʒeləsɪ] n (U) celos mpl.

jeans [dʒiːnz] npl vaqueros mpl, tejanos mpl.

jeep [dʒiːp] n jeep m, campero m Amer.

jeer [dʒɪəʳ] ◇ vt [boo] abuchear; [mock] mofarse de. ◇ vi: **to ~ (at sb)** [boo] abuchear (a alguien); [mock] mofarse (de alguien).

Jehovah's Witness [dʒɪ'həʊvəz-] n testigo m y f de Jehová.

Jello® ['dʒeləʊ] n Am jalea f, gelatina f.

jelly ['dʒelɪ] n **-1.** [dessert] jalea f, gelatina f. **-2.** [jam] mermelada f.

jellyfish ['dʒelɪfɪʃ] (pl inv OR **-es**) n medusa f.

jeopardize, -ise ['dʒepədaɪz] vt poner en peligro, arriesgar.

jerk [dʒɜːk] ◇ n **-1.** [of head] movimiento m brusco; [of arm] tirón m; [of vehicle] sacudida f. **-2.** v inf [fool] idiota

m y f, majadero m, -ra f. ◇ vi [person] saltar; [vehicle] dar sacudidas.

jersey ['dʒɜːzɪ] (pl jerseys) n [sweater] jersey m.

Jersey ['dʒɜːzɪ] n Jersey.

jest [dʒest] n: **in ~** en broma.

Jesus (Christ) ['dʒiːzəs-] n Jesús m, Jesucristo m.

jet [dʒet] n **-1.** [aircraft] reactor m. **-2.** [stream] chorro m. **-3.** [nozzle, outlet] boquilla f.

jet-black adj negro(gra) azabache.

jet engine n reactor m.

jetfoil ['dʒetfɔɪl] n hidroplano m.

jet lag n aturdimiento tras un largo viaje en avión.

jetsam ['dʒetsəm] → flotsam.

jettison ['dʒetɪsən] vt [cargo] deshacerse de; fig [ideas] desechar.

jetty ['dʒetɪ] n embarcadero m.

Jew [dʒuː] n judío m, -a f.

jewel ['dʒuːəl] n **-1.** [gemstone] piedra f preciosa. **-2.** [jewellery] joya f.

jeweller Br, **jeweler** Am ['dʒuːələʳ] n joyero m, -ra f; **~'s (shop)** joyería f.

jewellery Br, **jewelry** Am ['dʒuːəlrɪ] n (U) joyas fpl, alhajas fpl.

Jewess ['dʒuːɪs] n judía f.

Jewish ['dʒuːɪʃ] adj judío(a).

jib [dʒɪb] n **-1.** [beam] aguilón m. **-2.** [sail] foque m.

jibe [dʒaɪb] n pulla f, burla f.

jiffy ['dʒɪfɪ] n inf: **in a ~** en un santiamén.

Jiffy bag® n sobre m acolchado.

jig [dʒɪg] n giga f.

jigsaw (puzzle) ['dʒɪgsɔː-] n rompecabezas m inv, puzzle m.

jilt [dʒɪlt] vt dejar plantado(da).

jingle ['dʒɪŋgl] ◇ n [song] sintonía de anuncio publicitario. ◇ vi tintinear.

jinx [dʒɪŋks] n gafe m.

jitters ['dʒɪtəz] npl inf: **to have the ~** estar como un flan.

job [dʒɒb] n **-1.** [paid employment] trabajo m, empleo m. **-2.** [task] trabajo m. **-3.** [difficult task]: **we had a ~ doing it** nos costó trabajo hacerlo. **-4.** [function] cometido m. **-5.** phr: **that's just the ~** Br inf eso me viene de perilla.

job centre n Br oficina f de empleo.

jobless ['dʒɒblɪs] adj desempleado(da).

jobsharing ['dʒɒbʃeərɪŋ] n (U) empleo m compartido.

jockey ['dʒɒkɪ] (pl **-s**) ◇ n jockey m, jinete m. ◇ vi: **to ~ for position** competir por colocarse en mejor posición.

jocular ['dʒɒkjʊləʳ] *adj* **-1.** [cheerful] bromista. **-2.** [funny] jocoso(sa).

jodhpurs ['dʒɒdpəz] *npl* pantalón *m* de montar.

jog [dʒɒg] ◇ *n* trote *m*; **to go for a ~** hacer footing. ◇ *vt* golpear ligeramente; **to ~ sb's memory** refrescar la memoria a alguien. ◇ *vi* hacer footing.

jogging ['dʒɒgɪŋ] *n* footing *m*.

john [dʒɒn] *n Am inf* [toilet] wáter *m*.

join [dʒɔɪn] ◇ *n* juntura *f*. ◇ *vt* **-1.** [unite] unir, juntar. **-2.** [get together with] reunirse con. **-3.** [become a member of - political party] afiliarse a; [- club] hacerse socio de; [- army] alistarse en. **-4.** [take part in] unirse a; **to ~ a queue** *Br*, **to ~ a line** *Am* meterse en la cola. ◇ *vi* **-1.** [rivers] confluir; [edges, pieces] unirse, juntarse. **-2.** [become a member of - political party] afiliarse; [- of club] hacerse socio; [- of army] alistarse. ◆ **join in** ◇ *vt fus* participar en. ◇ *vi* participar. ◆ **join up** *vi* MIL alistarse.

joiner ['dʒɔɪnəʳ] *n* carpintero *m*.

joinery ['dʒɔɪnərɪ] *n* carpintería *f*.

joint [dʒɔɪnt] ◇ *adj* [responsibility] compartido(da); [effort] conjunto(ta); **~ owner** copropietario *m*, -ria *f*. ◇ *n* **-1.** ANAT articulación *f*. **-2.** [place where things are joined] juntura *f*. **-3.** *Br* [of meat - uncooked] corte *m* para asar; [- cooked] asado *m*. **-4.** *inf pej* [place] antro *m*. **-5.** *drugs sl* porro *m*.

joint account *n* cuenta *f* conjunta.

jointly ['dʒɔɪntlɪ] *adv* conjuntamente.

joke [dʒəʊk] ◇ *n* [funny story] chiste *m*; [funny action] broma *f*; **to play a ~ on sb** gastarle una broma a alguien; **it's no ~** [not easy] no es (nada) fácil. ◇ *vi* bromear; **you're joking** estás de broma; **to ~ about sthg/with sb** bromear acerca de algo/con alguien.

joker ['dʒəʊkəʳ] *n* **-1.** [person] bromista *m* y *f*. **-2.** [playing card] comodín *m*.

jolly ['dʒɒlɪ] ◇ *adj* [person, laugh] alegre; [time] divertido(da). ◇ *adv Br inf* muy.

jolt [dʒəʊlt] ◇ *n lit* & *fig* sacudida *f*. ◇ *vt* [jerk] sacudir, zarandear.

Jordan ['dʒɔːdn] *n* Jordania.

jostle ['dʒɒsl] ◇ *vt* empujar, dar empujones a. ◇ *vi* empujar, dar empujones.

jot [dʒɒt] *n* pizca *f*. ◆ **jot down** *vt sep* apuntar, anotar.

jotter ['dʒɒtəʳ] *n* bloc *m*.

journal ['dʒɜːnl] *n* **-1.** [magazine] revista *f*, boletín *m*. **-2.** [diary] diario *m*.

journalism ['dʒɜːnəlɪzm] *n* periodismo *m*.

journalist ['dʒɜːnəlɪst] *n* periodista *m* y *f*.

journey ['dʒɜːnɪ] (*pl* -s) *n* viaje *m*.

jovial ['dʒəʊvjəl] *adj* jovial.

jowls [dʒaʊlz] *npl* carrillo *m*.

joy [dʒɔɪ] *n* **-1.** [happiness] alegría *f*, regocijo *m*. **-2.** [cause of joy] placer *m*.

joyful ['dʒɔɪfʊl] *adj* alegre.

joyous ['dʒɔɪəs] *adj* jubiloso(sa).

joyride ['dʒɔɪraɪd] (*pt* **-rode**, *pp* **-ridden**) *vi* darse una vuelta en un coche robado.

joystick ['dʒɔɪstɪk] *n* [of aircraft] palanca *f* de mando; [for video games, computers] joystick *m*.

JP *n abbr of* **Justice of the Peace**.

Jr. *Am* (*abbr of* **Junior**) jr.

jubilant ['dʒuːbɪlənt] *adj* [person] jubiloso(sa); [shout] alborozado(da).

jubilee ['dʒuːbɪliː] *n* aniversario *m*.

judge [dʒʌdʒ] ◇ *n* [gen & JUR] juez *m* y *f*. ◇ *vt* **-1.** [gen & JUR] juzgar. **-2.** [age, distance] calcular. ◇ *vi* juzgar; **to ~ from** OR **by, judging from** OR **by a** juzgar por.

judg(e)ment ['dʒʌdʒmənt] *n* **-1.** JUR fallo *m*, sentencia *f*. **-2.** [opinion] juicio *m*; **to pass ~ (on sb/sthg)** pronunciarse (sobre alguien/algo). **-3.** [ability to form opinion] juicio *m*.

judiciary [dʒuː'dɪʃərɪ] *n*: **the ~** el poder judicial.

judicious [dʒuː'dɪʃəs] *adj* juicioso(sa).

judo ['dʒuːdəʊ] *n* judo *m*.

jug [dʒʌg] *n* jarra *f*.

juggernaut ['dʒʌgənɔːt] *n* camión *m* grande.

juggle ['dʒʌgl] ◇ *vt* **-1.** [throw] hacer juegos malabares con. **-2.** [rearrange] jugar con. ◇ *vi* hacer juegos malabares.

juggler ['dʒʌgləʳ] *n* malabarista *m* y *f*.

jugular (vein) ['dʒʌgjʊləʳ-] *n* yugular *f*.

juice [dʒuːs] *n* **-1.** [from fruit, vegetables] zumo *m*, jugo *m*. **-2.** [from meat] jugo *m*.

juicy ['dʒuːsɪ] *adj* **-1.** [gen] jugoso(sa). **-2.** *inf* [scandalous] picante.

jukebox ['dʒuːkbɒks] *n* máquina *f* de discos.

July [dʒuː'laɪ] *n* julio *m*; *see also* **September**.

jumble ['dʒʌmbl] ◇ *n* [mixture] revoltijo *m*. ◇ *vt*: **to ~ (up)** revolver.

jumble sale *n Br* rastrillo *m* benéfico.

jumbo jet ['dʒʌmbəʊ-] *n* jumbo *m*.

jumbo-sized ['dʒʌmbəʊsaɪzd] *adj* gigante.

jump [dʒʌmp] ◇ n **-1.** [act of jumping] salto m. **-2.** [rapid increase] **incremento** m, salto m. ◇ vt **-1.** [cross by jumping] saltar. **-2.** inf [attack] **asaltar.** ◇ vi **-1.** [spring] saltar. **-2.** [make a sudden movement] **sobresaltarse. -3.** [increase rapidly] aumentar de golpe. ◆ **jump at** vt fus no dejar escapar.

jumper ['dʒʌmpəʳ] n **-1.** Br [pullover] jersey m. **-2.** Am [dress] pichi m.

jump leads npl cables mpl de empalme (de batería).

jump-start vt arrancar empujando.

jumpsuit ['dʒʌmpsuːt] n mono m.

jumpy ['dʒʌmpɪ] adj inquieto(ta).

junction ['dʒʌŋkʃn] n [of roads] cruce m; [of railway lines] empalme m.

June [dʒuːn] n junio m; see also **September.**

jungle ['dʒʌŋgl] n lit & fig selva f.

junior ['dʒuːnjəʳ] ◇ adj **-1.** [officer] subalterno(na); [partner, member] de menor antigüedad, júnior (inv). **-2.** Am [after name] júnior (inv), hijo(ja). ◇ n **-1.** [person of lower rank] subalterno m, -na f. **-2.** [younger person]: **he's my ~** soy mayor que él. **-3.** Am SCH & UNIV alumno de penúltimo año.

junior high school n Am ≃ instituto m de bachillerato (13-15 años).

junior school n Br ≃ escuela f primaria.

junk [dʒʌŋk] inf n (U) [unwanted things] trastos mpl.

junk food n (U) pej comida preparada poco nutritiva o saludable.

junkie ['dʒʌŋkɪ] n drugs sl yonqui m y f.

junk mail n (U) pej propaganda f (por correo).

junk shop n tienda f de objetos usados.

Jupiter ['dʒuːpɪtəʳ] n Júpiter m.

jurisdiction [,dʒʊərɪs'dɪkʃn] n jurisdicción f.

juror ['dʒʊərəʳ] n jurado m.

jury ['dʒʊərɪ] n jurado m.

just [dʒʌst] ◇ adv **-1.** [recently]: **he has ~ left/moved** acaba de salir/mudarse. **-2.** [at that moment]: **we were ~ leaving when ...** justo íbamos a salir cuando ...; **I'm ~ about to do it** voy a hacerlo ahora; **I couldn't do it ~ then** no lo podía hacer en aquel momento; **~ as I was leaving** justo en el momento en que salía. **-3.** [only, simply] sólo, solamente; **"~ add water"** "añada un poco de agua"; **~ a minute** OR **moment** OR **second** un momento. **-4.** [almost not]

apenas; **I (only) ~ did it** conseguí hacerlo por muy poco. **-5.** [for emphasis]: **I ~ know it!** ¡estoy seguro! **-6.** [exactly, precisely] **exactamente; ~ what I need** justo lo que necesito; **~ here/there** aquí/allí mismo. **-7.** [in requests]: **could you ~ open your mouth?** ¿podrías abrir la boca un momento, por favor? ◇ adj justo(ta). ◆ **just about** adv casi. ◆ **just as** adv: **~ as ... as tan ... como, igual de ... que.** ◆ **just now** adv **-1.** [a short time ago] hace un momento. **-2.** [at this moment] justo ahora, ahora mismo.

justice ['dʒʌstɪs] n justicia f; **to bring sb to ~** llevar a alguien ante los tribunales.

Justice of the Peace (pl **Justices of the Peace**) n juez m y f de paz.

justify ['dʒʌstɪfaɪ] vt: **to ~ (sthg/doing sthg)** justificar (algo/el haber hecho algo).

jut [dʒʌt] vi: **to ~ (out)** sobresalir.

juvenile ['dʒuːvənaɪl] ◇ adj **-1.** JUR juvenil. **-2.** [childish] infantil. ◇ n JUR menor m y f (de edad).

juxtapose [,dʒʌkstə'pəʊz] vt: **to ~ sthg (with)** yuxtaponer algo (a).

k (pl **k's** OR **ks**), **K** (pl **K's** OR **Ks**) [keɪ] n [letter] k f, K f. ◆ **K -1.** (abbr of kilobyte(s)) K. **-2.** abbr of **thousand.**

kaleidoscope [kə'laɪdəskəʊp] n lit & fig caleidoscopio m.

kangaroo [,kæŋgə'ruː] n canguro m.

karat ['kærət] n Am quilate m.

karate [kə'rɑːtɪ] n kárate m.

kayak ['kaɪæk] n kayac m.

KB n abbr of **kilobyte.**

kcal (abbr of kilocalorie) kcal.

kebab [kɪ'bæb] n pincho m moruno.

keel [kiːl] n quilla f; **on an even ~** en equilibrio estable.

keen [kiːn] adj **-1.** [enthusiastic] entusiasta; **to be ~ on sthg** ser aficionado(da) a algo; **she is ~ on you** tú le gustas; **to be ~ to do** OR **on doing sthg** tener ganas de hacer algo. **-2.** [intense - interest, desire] **profundo(da);** [- competition] reñido(da). **-3.** [sharp - sense of smell, hearing, vision] agudo(da); [- eye, ear] fino(na); [- mind] agudo.

keep [ki:p] (*pt & pp* **kept**) ◇ *vt* **-1.** [maintain in a particular place or state or position] mantener; **to ~ sb waiting/awake** tener a alguien esperando/despierto. **-2.** [retain] quedarse con; **~ the change** quédese con la vuelta. **-3.** [put aside, store] guardar. **-4.** [prevent]: **to ~ sb/sthg from doing sthg** impedir a alguien/algo hacer algo. **-5.** [detain] detener; **to ~ sb waiting** hacer esperar a alguien. **-6.** [fulfil, observe - appointment] acudir a; [- promise, vow] cumplir. **-7.** [not disclose]: **to ~ sthg from sb** ocultar algo a alguien; **to ~ sthg to o.s.** no contarle algo a nadie. **-8.** [in writing - record, account] llevar; [- diary] escribir; [- note] tomar. **-9.** [own - animals] criar; [- shop] tener. ◇ *vi* **-1.** [remain] mantenerse; **to ~ quiet** callarse. **-2.** [continue]: **to ~ doing sthg** [repeatedly] no dejar de hacer algo; [without stopping] continuar OR seguir haciendo algo; **to ~ going** seguir adelante. **-3.** [continue in a particular direction] continuar, seguir; **to ~ left/right** circular por la izquierda/derecha. **-4.** [food] conservarse. **-5.** *Br* [be in a particular state of health] andar. ◇ *n* [food, board etc] **to earn one's ~** ganarse el pan. ◆ **keeps** *n*: **for ~s** para siempre. ◆ **keep back** *vt sep* [information] ocultar; [money, salary] retener. ◆ **keep off** *vt fus*: "~ **off the grass**" "no pisar la hierba". ◆ **keep on** *vi* **-1.** [continue]: **to ~ on doing sthg** [continue to do] continuar OR seguir haciendo algo; [do repeatedly] no dejar de hacer algo. **-2.** [talk incessantly]: **to ~ on (about)** seguir dale que te pego (con). ◆ **keep out** *vt sep* no dejar pasar. ◇ *vi*: "~ **out**" "prohibida la entrada". ◆ **keep to** *vt fus* [follow] ceñirse a. ◆ **keep up** ◇ *vt sep* mantener. ◇ *vi* [maintain pace, level etc] mantener el ritmo; **to ~ up with sb/sthg** seguir el ritmo de alguien/algo.

keeper ['ki:pə˞] *n* guarda *m y f*.

keep-fit *Br n* (U) ejercicios *mpl* de mantenimiento.

keeping ['ki:pɪŋ] *n* **-1.** [care]: **in sb's ~** al cuidado de alguien; **in safe ~** en lugar seguro. **-2.** [conformity, harmony]: **in/out of ~ (with)** en armonía/desacuerdo (con).

keepsake ['ki:pseɪk] *n* recuerdo *m*.

keg [keg] *n* barrilete *m*.

kennel ['kenl] *n* **-1.** [for dog] caseta *f* del perro. **-2.** *Am* = **kennels**. ◆ **kennels** *npl Br* residencia *f* para perros.

Kenya ['kenjə] *n* Kenia.

Kenyan ['kenjən] ◇ *adj* keniano(na). ◇ *n* keniano *m*, -na *f*.

kept [kept] *pt & pp* → **keep**.

kerb [kɜ:b] *n Br* bordillo *m*.

kernel ['kɜ:nl] *n* [of nut, fruit] pepita *f*.

kerosene ['kerəsi:n] *n* queroseno *m*.

kestrel ['kestrəl] *n* cernícalo *m*.

ketchup ['ketʃəp] *n* catsup *m*.

kettle ['ketl] *n* tetera *f* para hervir.

key [ki:] ◇ *n* **-1.** [for lock] llave *f*. **-2.** [of typewriter, computer, piano] tecla *f*. **-3.** [explanatory list] clave *f*. **-4.** [solution, answer]: **the ~ (to)** la clave (de). **-5.** MUS [scale of notes] tono *m*. ◇ *adj* clave (*inv*).

keyboard ['ki:bɔ:d] *n* teclado *m*.

keyed up [ki:d-] *adj* nervioso(sa).

keyhole ['ki:həʊl] *n* ojo *m* de la cerradura.

keynote ['ki:nəʊt] *comp*: **~ speech** discurso *m* que marca la tónica.

keypad ['ki:pæd] *n* teclado *m* (*de teléfono, fax etc*).

key ring *n* llavero *m*.

kg (*abbr of* **kilogram**) kg *m*.

khaki ['kɑ:kɪ] ◇ *adj* caqui. ◇ *n* caqui *m*.

kick [kɪk] ◇ *n* **-1.** [from person] patada *f*, puntapié *m*; [from animal] coz *f*. **-2.** *inf* [excitement]: **to get a ~ from sthg** disfrutar con algo. ◇ *vt* **-1.** [hit with foot] dar una patada OR un puntapié a. **-2.** *inf* [give up] dejar. ◇ *vi* [person] dar patadas; [animal] dar coces, cocear. ◆ **kick about**, **kick around** *vi Br inf* andar rodando por ahí. ◆ **kick off** *vi* [football] hacer el saque inicial. ◆ **kick out** *vt sep inf* echar, poner de patitas en la calle.

kid [kɪd] ◇ *n* **-1.** *inf* [child] crío *m*, -a *f*. **-2.** *inf* [young person] chico *m*, -ca *f*, chaval *m*, -la *f*. **-3.** [young goat] cabrito *m*. **-4.** [leather] cabritilla *f*. ◇ *comp inf* [brother, sister] menor. ◇ *vt inf* **-1.** [tease] tomar el pelo a. **-2.** [delude]: **to ~ o.s.** hacerse ilusiones. ◇ *vi inf*: **to be kidding** estar de broma.

kidnap ['kɪdnæp] *vt* secuestrar, raptar, plagiar *Amer*.

kidnapper *Br*, **kidnaper** *Am* ['kɪdnæpə˞] *n* secuestrador *m*, -ra *f*, raptor *m*, -ra *f*, plagiario *m*, -ria *f Amer*.

kidnapping *Br*, **kidnaping** *Am*

['kɪdnæpɪŋ] n secuestro m, rapto m, plagio m Amer.

kidney ['kɪdnɪ] (pl **kidneys**) n ANAT & CULIN riñón m.

kidney bean n judía f pinta.

kill [kɪl] ◇ vt **-1.** [gen] matar. **-2.** fig [cause to end, fail] poner fin a. **-3.** [occupy]: **to ~ time** matar el tiempo. ◇ vi matar. ◇ n **-1.** [killing] matanza f. **-2.** [dead animal] pieza f.

killer ['kɪlə'] n [person, animal] asesino m, -na f.

killing ['kɪlɪŋ] n asesinato m.

killjoy ['kɪldʒɔɪ] n aguafiestas m y f inv.

kiln [kɪln] n horno m.

kilo ['kiːləʊ] (pl **-s**) (abbr of **kilogram**) n kilo m.

kilobyte ['kɪləbaɪt] n kilobyte m.

kilogram(me) ['kɪləgræm] n kilogramo m.

kilohertz ['kɪləhɜːtz] (pl inv) n kilohercio m.

kilometre Br ['kɪlə,miːtə'], **kilometer** Am [kɪ'lɒmɪtə'] n kilómetro m.

kilowatt ['kɪləwɒt] n kilovatio m.

kilt [kɪlt] n falda f escocesa.

kin [kɪn] → **kith**.

kind [kaɪnd] ◇ adj [person, gesture] amable; [thought] considerado(da). ◇ n tipo m, clase f; **a ~ of** una especie de; **~ of** Am inf un poco; **they're two of a ~** son tal para cual; **in ~** [payment] en especie.

kindergarten ['kɪndə,gɑːtn] n jardín m de infancia.

kind-hearted [-'hɑːtɪd] adj bondadoso(sa).

kindle ['kɪndl] vt **-1.** [fire] encender. **-2.** fig [idea, feeling] despertar.

kindly ['kaɪndlɪ] ◇ adj amable, bondadoso(sa). ◇ adv **-1.** [gently, favourably] amablemente. **-2.** [please]: **will you ~ ...?** ¿sería tan amable de ...?

kindness ['kaɪndnɪs] n **-1.** [gentleness] amabilidad f. **-2.** [helpful act] favor m.

kindred ['kɪndrɪd] adj [similar] afín; **~ spirit** alma f gemela.

king [kɪŋ] n rey m.

kingdom ['kɪŋdəm] n reino m.

kingfisher ['kɪŋ,fɪʃə'] n martín m pescador.

king-size(d) [-saɪz(d)] adj [cigarette] extra largo; [bed, pack] gigante.

kinky ['kɪŋkɪ] adj inf morboso(sa), pervertido(da).

kiosk ['kiːɒsk] n **-1.** [small shop] quiosco m. **-2.** Br [telephone box] cabina f telefónica.

kip [kɪp] Br inf ◇ n sueñecito m. ◇ vi dormir.

kipper ['kɪpə'] n arenque m ahumado.

kiss [kɪs] ◇ n beso m. ◇ vt besar. ◇ vi besarse.

kiss of life n [to resuscitate sb]: **the ~** la respiración boca a boca.

kit [kɪt] n **-1.** [set] utensilios mpl, equipo m. **-2.** Br [clothes] equipo m. **-3.** [to be assembled] modelo m para armar, kit m.

kit bag n macuto m, petate m.

kitchen ['kɪtʃɪn] n cocina f.

kitchen sink n fregadero m.

kitchen unit n módulo m OR armario m de cocina.

kite [kaɪt] n [toy] cometa f.

kith [kɪθ] n: **~ and kin** parientes mpl y amigos.

kitten ['kɪtn] n gatito m.

kitty ['kɪtɪ] n [for bills, drinks] fondo m común; [in card games] bote m, puesta f.

kiwi ['kiːwiː] n **-1.** [bird] kiwi m. **-2.** inf [New Zealander] persona f de Nueva Zelanda.

kiwi fruit n kiwi m.

km (abbr of **kilometre**) km.

km/h (abbr of **kilometres per hour**) km/h.

knack [næk] n: **it's easy once you've got the ~** es fácil cuando le coges el tranquillo; **he has the ~ of appearing at the right moment** tiene el don de aparecer en el momento adecuado.

knackered ['nækəd] adj Br inf hecho(cha) polvo.

knapsack ['næpsæk] n mochila f.

knead [niːd] vt amasar.

knee [niː] n rodilla f.

kneecap ['niːkæp] n rótula f.

kneel [niːl] (Br pt & pp **knelt**, Am pt & pp **-ed** OR **knelt**) vi arrodillarse.
◆ **kneel down** vi arrodillarse.

knelt [nelt] pt & pp → **kneel**.

knew [njuː] pt → **know**.

knickers ['nɪkəz] npl **-1.** Br [underwear] bragas fpl, calzonarios mpl Amer. **-2.** Am [knickerbockers] bombachos mpl.

knick-knack ['nɪknæk] n baratija f.

knife [naɪf] (pl **knives**) ◇ n cuchillo m. ◇ vt acuchillar.

knight [naɪt] ◇ n **-1.** HIST caballero m. **-2.** [knighted man] hombre con el título de "Sir". **-3.** [in chess] caballo m. ◇ vt conceder el título de "Sir" a.

knighthood ['naɪthʊd] n **-1.** [present-day title] título m de "Sir". **-2.** HIST título m de caballero.

knit [nɪt] (*pt* & *pp* **knit** OR **-ted**) ◇ *vt* [make with wool] tejer, tricotar. ◇ *vi* **-1.** [with wool] hacer punto, tricotar. **-2.** [join] soldarse.

knitting ['nɪtɪŋ] *n* (*U*) **-1.** [activity] labor *f* de punto. **-2.** [work produced] punto *m*, calceta *f*.

knitting needle *n* aguja *f* de hacer punto.

knitwear ['nɪtweəʳ] *n* (*U*) género *m* OR ropa *f* de punto.

knives [naɪvz] *pl* → **knife**.

knob [nɒb] *n* **-1.** [on door, drawer, bedstead] pomo *m*. **-2.** [on TV, radio etc] botón *m*.

knock [nɒk] ◇ *n* **-1.** [hit] golpe *m*. **-2.** *inf* [piece of bad luck] revés *m*. ◇ *vt* **-1.** [hit hard] golpear; **to ~ sb over** [gen] hacer caer a alguien; AUT atropellar a alguien; **to ~ sthg over** tirar OR volcar algo. **-2.** [make by hitting] hacer, abrir. **-3.** *inf* [criticize] poner por los suelos. ◇ *vi* **-1.** [on door]: **to ~ (at** OR **on)** llamar (a). **-2.** [car engine] traquetear. ◆ **knock down** *vt sep* **-1.** [subj: car, driver] atropellar. **-2.** [building] derribar. ◆ **knock off** *vi inf* [stop working] parar de currar. ◆ **knock out** *vt sep* **-1.** [subj: person, punch] dejar sin conocimiento; [subj: drug] dejar dormido a. **-2.** [eliminate from competition] eliminar.

knocker ['nɒkəʳ] *n* [on door] aldaba *f*.

knock-kneed [-'niːd] *adj* patizambo(ba).

knock-on effect *n Br* reacción *f* en cadena.

knockout ['nɒkaʊt] *n* K.O. *m*.

knot [nɒt] ◇ *n* **-1.** [gen] nudo *m*; **to tie/untie a ~** hacer/deshacer un nudo. **-2.** [of people] corrillo *m*. ◇ *vt* anudar.

knotty ['nɒtɪ] *adj* intrincado(da).

know [nəʊ] (*pt* **knew**, *pp* **known**) ◇ *vt* **-1.** [gen]: **to ~ (that)** saber (que); [language] saber hablar; **to ~ how to do sthg** saber hacer algo; **to get to ~ sthg** enterarse de algo; **to let sb ~ (about)** avisar a alguien (de). **-2.** [be familiar with - person, place] conocer; **to get to ~ sb** llegar a conocer a alguien. ◇ *vi* **-1.** [have knowledge] saber; **to ~ of** OR **about sthg** saber algo, estar enterado(da) de algo; **you ~** [to emphasize] ¿sabes?; [to remind] ¡ya sabes!, ¡sí hombre! **-2.** [be knowledgeable]: **to ~ about sthg** saber de algo. ◇ *n*: **to be in the ~** estar enterado(da).

know-all *n Br* sabelotodo *m y f*.

know-how *n* conocimientos *mpl*.

knowing ['nəʊɪŋ] *adj* cómplice.

knowingly ['nəʊɪŋlɪ] *adv* **-1.** [in knowing manner] con complicidad. **-2.** [intentionally] adrede.

know-it-all = **know-all**.

knowledge ['nɒlɪdʒ] *n* (*U*) conocimiento *m*; **to the best of my ~** por lo que yo sé.

knowledgeable ['nɒlɪdʒəbl] *adj* entendido(da).

known [nəʊn] *pp* → **know**.

knuckle ['nʌkl] *n* **-1.** ANAT nudillo *m*. **-2.** [of meat] jarrete *m*.

knuckle-duster *n* puño *m* americano.

koala (bear) [kəʊ'ɑːlə-] *n* koala *m*.

Koran [kɒ'rɑːn] *n*: **the ~** el Corán.

Korea [kə'rɪə] *n* Corea.

Korean [kə'rɪən] ◇ *adj* coreano(na). ◇ *n* **-1.** [person] coreano *m*, -na *f*. **-2.** [language] coreano *m*.

kosher ['kəʊʃəʳ] *adj* **-1.** [meat] *permitido por la religión judía.* **-2.** *inf* [reputable] limpio(pia), legal.

Koweit [kəʊ'weɪt] = **Kuwait**.

kung fu [ˌkʌŋ'fuː] *n* kung-fu *m*.

Kurd [kɜːd] *n* kurdo *m*, -da *f*.

Kuwait [kʊ'weɪt] *n* Kuwait.

l¹ (*pl* **l's** OR **ls**), **L** (*pl* **L's** OR **Ls**) [el] *n* [letter] l *f*, L *f*.

l² (*abbr of* **litre**) l.

lab [læb] *inf* = **laboratory**.

label ['leɪbl] ◇ *n* **-1.** [identification] etiqueta *f*. **-2.** [of record] sello *m* discográfico. ◇ *vt* **-1.** [fix label to] etiquetar. **-2.** *usu pej* [describe]: **to ~ sb (as)** calificar OR etiquetar a alguien (de).

labor *etc Am* = **labour** *etc*.

laboratory [*Br* lə'bɒrətrɪ, *Am* 'læbrə,tɔːrɪ] *n* laboratorio *m*.

laborious [lə'bɔːrɪəs] *adj* laborioso(sa).

labor union *n Am* sindicato *m*.

labour *Br*, **labor** *Am* ['leɪbəʳ] ◇ *n* **-1.** [hard work] trabajo *m*. **-2.** [piece of work] esfuerzo *m*. **-3.** [workers, work carried out] mano *f* de obra. **-4.** [giving birth] parto *m*. ◇ *vi* **-1.** [work hard] trabajar (duro). **-2.** [work with difficulty]: **to ~ at** OR **over** trabajar duro en. ◆ **Labour**

POL ◇ *adj* laborista. ◇ *n Br* (U) los laboristas.

laboured *Br*, **labored** *Am* ['leɪbəd] *adj* [style] trabajoso(sa); [gait, breathing] penoso(sa), fatigoso(sa).

labourer *Br*, **laborer** *Am* ['leɪbərəʳ] *n* obrero *m*, -ra *f*.

Labour Party *n Br*: **the** ~ el partido Laborista.

Labrador ['læbrədɔːʳ] *n* [dog] (perro *m* de) terranova *m*, labrador *m*.

labyrinth ['læbərɪnθ] *n* laberinto *m*.

lace [leɪs] ◇ *n* **-1.** [fabric] encaje *m*. **-2.** [shoelace] cordón *m*. ◇ *vt* **-1.** [shoe, boot] atar. **-2.** [drink, food]: **coffee ~d with brandy** café con unas gotas de coñac. ◆ **lace up** *vt sep* atar.

lack [læk] ◇ *n* falta *f*; **for** OR **through** ~ **of** por falta de; **no** ~ **of** abundancia de. ◇ *vt* carecer de. ◇ *vi*: **to be ~ing in** carecer de; **to be ~ing** faltar.

lackadaisical [ˌlækə'deɪzɪkl] *adj pej* apático(ca), desganado(da).

lacklustre *Br*, **lackluster** *Am* ['læk,lʌstəʳ] *adj pej* soso(sa), apagado(da).

laconic [lə'kɒnɪk] *adj* lacónico(ca).

lacquer ['lækəʳ] *n* laca *f*.

lad [læd] *n inf* [boy] chaval *m*.

ladder ['lædəʳ] ◇ *n* **-1.** [for climbing] escalera *f*. **-2.** *Br* [in tights] carrera *f*. ◇ *vt Br* [tights] hacerse una carrera en.

laden ['leɪdn] *adj*: ~ **(with)** cargado(da) (de).

ladies *Br* ['leɪdɪz], **ladies' room** *Am n* lavabo *m* de señoras.

ladle ['leɪdl] ◇ *n* cucharón *m*. ◇ *vt* servir con cucharón.

lady ['leɪdɪ] ◇ *n* **-1.** [woman] señora *f*. **-2.** [woman of high status] dama *f*. ◇ *comp* mujer; ~ **doctor** doctora *f*. ◆ **Lady** *n* [woman of noble rank] lady *f*.

ladybird *Br* ['leɪdɪbɜːd], **ladybug** *Am* ['leɪdɪbʌg] *n* mariquita *f*.

lady-in-waiting [-'weɪtɪŋ] (*pl* **ladies-in-waiting**) *n* dama *f* de honor.

ladylike ['leɪdɪlaɪk] *adj* distinguido(da), elegante.

Ladyship ['leɪdɪʃɪp] *n*: **her/your** ~ su señoría *f*.

lag [læg] ◇ *vi* **-1.** [move more slowly]: **to** ~ **(behind)** rezagarse. **-2.** [develop more slowly]: **to** ~ **(behind)** andar a la zaga. ◇ *vt* revestir. ◇ *n* [timelag] retraso *m*, demora *f*.

lager ['lɑːgəʳ] *n* cerveza *f* rubia.

lagoon [lə'guːn] *n* laguna *f*.

laid [leɪd] *pt & pp* → **lay**.

laid-back *adj inf* relajado(da).

lain [leɪn] *pp* → **lie**.

lair [leəʳ] *n* guarida *f*.

laity ['leɪətɪ] *n* RELIG: **the** ~ los seglares.

lake [leɪk] *n* lago *m*.

Lake District *n*: **the** ~ el Distrito de los Lagos al noroeste de Inglaterra.

lamb [læm] *n* cordero *m*.

lambswool ['læmzwʊl] ◇ *n* lana *f* de cordero. ◇ *comp* de lana de cordero.

lame [leɪm] *adj* **-1.** [person, horse] cojo(ja). **-2.** [excuse, argument] pobre.

lament [lə'ment] ◇ *n* lamento *m*. ◇ *vt* lamentar.

lamentable ['læməntəbl] *adj* lamentable.

laminated ['læmɪneɪtɪd] *adj* laminado(da).

lamp [læmp] *n* lámpara *f*.

lampoon [læm'puːn] ◇ *n* pasquín *m*, sátira *f*. ◇ *vt* satirizar.

lamppost ['læmppəʊst] *n* farol *m*.

lampshade ['læmpʃeɪd] *n* pantalla *f*.

lance [lɑːns] ◇ *n* lanza *f*. ◇ *vt* abrir con lanceta.

lance corporal *n* cabo *m* interino, soldado *m* de primero.

land [lænd] ◇ *n* **-1.** [gen] tierra *f*. **-2.** [property] tierras *fpl*, finca *f*. ◇ *vt* **-1.** [unload] desembarcar. **-2.** [catch - fish] pescar. **-3.** *inf* [obtain] conseguir, pillar. **-4.** [plane] hacer aterrizar. **-5.** *inf* [place]: **to** ~ **sb in sthg** meter a alguien en algo; **to** ~ **sb with sb/sthg** cargar a alguien con alguien/algo. ◇ *vi* **-1.** [by plane] aterrizar, tomar tierra. **-2.** [fall] caer. **-3.** [from ship] desembarcar. ◆ **land up** *vi inf*: **to** ~ **up (in)** acabar (en).

landing ['lændɪŋ] *n* **-1.** [of stairs] rellano *m*. **-2.** [of aeroplane] aterrizaje *m*. **-3.** [of person] desembarco *m*.

landing card *n* tarjeta *f* de desembarque.

landing gear *n* (U) tren *m* de aterrizaje.

landing stage *n* desembarcadero *m*.

landing strip *n* pista *f* de aterrizaje.

landlady ['lænd,leɪdɪ] *n* casera *f*, patrona *f*.

landlord ['lændlɔːd] *n* **-1.** [of rented room or building] dueño *m*, casero *m*. **-2.** [of pub] patrón *m*.

landmark ['lændmɑːk] *n* **-1.** [prominent feature] punto *m* de referencia. **-2.** *fig* [in history] hito *m*.

landowner ['lænd,əʊnəʳ] *n* terrateniente *m y f*.

landscape ['lændskeɪp] *n* paisaje *m*.

landslide ['lændslaɪd] *n* **-1.** [of earth, rocks] desprendimiento *m* de tierras. **-2.** POL victoria *f* arrolladora OR aplastante.

lane [leɪn] *n* **-1.** [road in country] camino *m*. **-2.** [road in town] callejuela *f*, callejón *m*. **-3.** [for traffic] carril *m*. **-4.** [in swimming pool, race track] calle *f*. **-5.** [for shipping, aircraft] ruta *f*.

language ['læŋgwɪdʒ] *n* **-1.** [gen] lengua *f*, idioma *m*. **-2.** [faculty or style of communication] lenguaje *m*.

language laboratory *n* laboratorio *m* de idiomas.

languid ['læŋgwɪd] *adj* lánguido(da).

languish ['læŋgwɪʃ] *vi* [in misery] languidecer; [in prison] pudrirse.

lank [læŋk] *adj* lacio(cia).

lanky ['læŋkɪ] *adj* larguirucho(cha).

lantern ['læntən] *n* farol *m*.

lap [læp] ◇ *n* **-1.** [of person] regazo *m*. **-2.** [of race] vuelta *f*. ◇ *vt* **-1.** [subj: animal] beber a lengüetadas. **-2.** [overtake in race] doblar. ◇ *vi* [water, waves] romper con suavidad.

lapel [lə'pel] *n* solapa *f*.

Lapland ['læplænd] *n* Laponia *f*.

lapse [læps] ◇ *n* **-1.** [failing] fallo *m*, lapsus *m inv*. **-2.** [in behaviour] desliz *m*. **-3.** [of time] lapso *m*, periodo *m*. ◇ *vi* **-1.** [membership] caducar; [treatment, agreement] cumplir, expirar. **-2.** [standards, quality] bajar momentáneamente; [tradition] extinguirse. **-3.** [subj: person]: **to ~ into** terminar cayendo en.

lap-top (computer) *n* COMPUT (pequeño) ordenador *m* portátil.

larceny ['lɑːsənɪ] *n* (U) latrocinio *m*.

lard [lɑːd] *n* manteca *f* de cerdo.

larder ['lɑːdər] *n* despensa *f*.

large [lɑːdʒ] *adj* [size] grande; [family] numeroso(sa); [sum] importante. ◆ **at large** *adv* **-1.** [as a whole] en general. **-2.** [escaped prisoner, animal] suelto(ta). ◆ **by and large** *adv* en general.

largely ['lɑːdʒlɪ] *adv* [mostly] en gran parte; [chiefly] principalmente.

lark [lɑːk] *n* **-1.** [bird] alondra *f*. **-2.** *inf* [joke] broma *f*. ◆ **lark about** *vi* hacer el gamberro.

laryngitis [,lærɪn'dʒaɪtɪs] *n* (U) laringitis *f inv*.

larynx ['lærɪŋks] *n* laringe *f*.

lasagna, lasagne [lə'zænjə] *n* (U) lasaña *f*.

laser ['leɪzər] *n* láser *m*.

laser printer *n* COMPUT impresora *f* láser.

lash [læʃ] ◇ *n* **-1.** [eyelash] pestaña *f*. **-2.** [blow with whip] latigazo *m*. ◇ *vt* **-1.** *lit* & *fig* [whip] azotar. **-2.** [tie]: **to ~ sthg (to)** amarrar algo (a). ◆ **lash out** *vi* **-1.** [physically]: **to ~ out (at** OR **against sb)** soltar un golpe (a alguien). **-2.** *Br inf* [spend money]: **to ~ out (on sthg)** derrochar el dinero (en algo).

lass [læs] *n* chavala *f*, muchacha *f*.

lasso [læ'suː] (*pl* **-s**) *n* lazo *m*.

last [lɑːst] ◇ *adj* último(ma); **~ month/Tuesday** el mes/martes pasado; **~ but one** penúltimo(ma); **~ but two** antepenúltimo(ma); **~ night** anoche. ◇ *adv* **-1.** [most recently] por última vez. **-2.** [finally, in final position] en último lugar; **he arrived ~** llegó el último. ◇ *pron*: **the year/Saturday before ~** no el año/sábado pasado, sino el anterior; **the ~ but one** el penúltimo (la penúltima); **the night before ~** anteanoche; **the time before ~** la vez anterior a la pasada; **to leave sthg till ~** dejar algo para lo último. ◇ *n*: **the ~ I saw/heard of him** la última vez que lo vi/que oí de él. ◇ *vi* durar; [food] conservarse. ◆ **at (long) last** *adv* por fin.

last-ditch *adj* último(ma), desesperado(da).

lasting ['lɑːstɪŋ] *adj* [peace, effect] duradero(ra); [mistrust] profundo(da).

lastly ['lɑːstlɪ] *adv* **-1.** [to conclude] por último. **-2.** [at the end] al final.

last-minute *adj* de última hora.

latch [lætʃ] *n* pestillo *m*. ◆ **latch onto** *vt fus inf* [person] pegarse OR engancharse a; [idea] pillar.

late [leɪt] ◇ *adj* **-1.** [not on time] con retraso; **to be ~ (for)** llegar tarde (a). **-2.** [near end of]: **in the ~ afternoon** al final de la tarde; **in ~ December** a finales de diciembre. **-3.** [later than normal] tardío(a); **we had a ~ breakfast** desayunamos tarde. **-4.** [former]: **the ~ president** el ex-presidente. **-5.** [dead] difunto(ta). ◇ *adv* **-1.** [gen] tarde. **-2.** [near end of period]: **~ in the day** al final del día; **~ in August** a finales de agosto. ◆ **of late** *adv* últimamente.

latecomer ['leɪt,kʌmər] *n* persona *f* que llega tarde.

lately ['leɪtlɪ] *adv* últimamente.

latent ['leɪtənt] *adj* latente.

later ['leɪtər] ◇ *adj* **-1.** [date, edition] posterior. **-2.** [near end of]: **in the ~**

15th century a finales del siglo XV. ◇ *adv* [at a later time]: ~ **(on)** más tarde.

lateral ['lætərəl] *adj* lateral.

latest ['leɪtɪst] ◇ *adj* [most recent] último(ma). ◇ *n*: **at the** ~ a más tardar, como muy tarde.

lathe [leɪð] *n* torno *m*.

lather ['lɑːðəʳ] ◇ *n* espuma *f* (de jabón). ◇ *vt* enjabonar.

Latin ['lætɪn] ◇ *adj* **-1.** [temperament, blood] latino(na). **-2.** [studies] de latín. ◇ *n* [language] latín *m*.

Latin America *n* América *f* Latina, Latinoamérica *f*.

Latin American ◇ *adj* latinoamericano(na). ◇ *n* [person] latinoamericano *m*, -na *f*.

latitude ['lætɪtjuːd] *n* GEOGR latitud *f*.

latter ['lætəʳ] ◇ *adj* **-1.** [near to end] último(ma). **-2.** [second] segundo(da). ◇ *n*: **the** ~ éste *m*, -ta *f*.

latterly ['lætəlɪ] *adv* últimamente.

lattice ['lætɪs] *n* enrejado *m*, celosía *f*.

Latvia ['lætvɪə] *n* Letonia *f*.

laudable ['lɔːdəbl] *adj* loable.

laugh [lɑːf] ◇ *n* **-1.** [sound] risa *f*. **-2.** *inf* [fun, joke]: **to have a** ~ reírse un rato; **to do sthg for** ~**s** OR **a** ~ hacer algo para divertirse OR en cachondeo. ◇ *vi* reírse. ◆ **laugh at** *vt fus* [mock] reírse de. ◆ **laugh off** *vt sep* [dismiss] restar importancia a, tomarse a risa.

laughable ['lɑːfəbl] *adj pej* [absurd] ridículo(la), risible.

laughingstock ['lɑːfɪŋstɒk] *n* hazmerreír *m*.

laughter ['lɑːftəʳ] *n* (*U*) risa *f*.

launch [lɔːntʃ] ◇ *n* **-1.** [of boat, ship] botadura *f*. **-2.** [of rocket, missile, product] lanzamiento *m*; [of book] publicación *f*. **-3.** [boat] lancha *f*. ◇ *vt* **-1.** [boat, ship] botar. **-2.** [missile, attack, product] lanzar; [book] publicar, sacar. **-3.** [strike] convocar; [company] fundar.

launch(ing) pad ['lɔːntʃ(ɪŋ)-] *n* plataforma *f* de lanzamiento.

launder ['lɔːndəʳ] *vt* **-1.** [wash] lavar. **-2.** *inf* [money] blanquear.

laund(e)rette [lɔːn'dret], **Laundromat®** *Am* ['lɔːndrəmæt] *n* lavandería *f* (automática).

laundry ['lɔːndrɪ] *n* **-1.** [clothes - about to be washed] colada *f*, ropa *f* sucia; [- newly washed] ropa *f* limpia. **-2.** [business, room] lavandería *f*.

laureate ['lɔːrɪət] → **poet laureate**.

lava ['lɑːvə] *n* lava *f*.

lavatory ['lævətrɪ] *n* **-1.** [receptacle] wáter *m*. **-2.** [room] servicio *m*.

lavender ['lævəndəʳ] *n* **-1.** [plant] lavanda *f*. **-2.** [colour] color *m* lavanda.

lavish ['lævɪʃ] ◇ *adj* **-1.** [person] pródigo(ga); [gifts, portions] muy generoso(sa); **to be** ~ **with** [praise, attention] ser pródigo en; [money] ser desprendido(da) con. **-2.** [sumptuous] espléndido(da), suntuoso(sa). ◇ *vt*: **to** ~ **sthg on** [praise, care] prodigar algo a; [time, money] gastar algo en.

law [lɔː] *n* **-1.** [gen] ley *f*; **against the** ~ contra la ley; **to break the** ~ infringir OR violar la ley; ~ **and order** el orden público. **-2.** [set of rules, study, profession] derecho *m*.

law-abiding [-ə,baɪdɪŋ] *adj* observante de la ley.

law court *n* tribunal *m* de justicia.

lawful ['lɔːful] *adj fml* legal, lícito(ta).

lawn [lɔːn] *n* [grass] césped *m*.

lawnmower ['lɔːn,məʊəʳ] *n* cortacésped *m* o *f*.

lawn tennis *n* tenis *m* sobre hierba.

law school *n* facultad *f* de derecho.

lawsuit ['lɔːsuːt] *n* pleito *m*.

lawyer ['lɔːjəʳ] *n* abogado *m*, -da *f*.

lax [læks] *adj* [discipline, morals] relajado(da); [person] negligente.

laxative ['læksətɪv] *n* laxante *m*.

lay [leɪ] (*pt* & *pp* **laid**) ◇ *pt* → **lie**. ◇ *vt* **-1.** [put, place] colocar, poner. **-2.** [prepare - plans] hacer; **to** ~ **the table** poner la mesa. **-3.** [put in position - bricks] poner; [- cable, trap] tender; [- foundations] echar. **-4.** [egg] poner. **-5.** [blame, curse] echar. ◇ *adj* **-1.** [not clerical] laico(ca). **-2.** [untrained, unqualified] lego(ga). ◆ **lay aside** *vt sep* **-1.** [store for future - food] guardar; [- money] ahorrar. **-2.** [put away] dejar a un lado. ◆ **lay down** *vt sep* **-1.** [set out] imponer, dictar. **-2.** [put down - arms] deponer, entregar; [- tools] dejar. ◆ **lay off** ◇ *vt sep* [make redundant] despedir. ◇ *vt fus inf* **-1.** [leave in peace] dejar en paz. **-2.** [stop, give up]: **to** ~ **off (doing sthg)** dejar (de hacer algo). ◆ **lay on** *vt sep Br* [provide, supply] proveer. ◆ **lay out** *vt sep* **-1.** [arrange, spread out] disponer. **-2.** [plan, design] diseñar el trazado de.

layabout ['leɪəbaʊt] *n Br inf* holgazán *m*, -ana *f*, gandul *m*, -la *f*.

lay-by (*pl* **lay-bys**) *n Br* área *f* de descanso.

layer ['leɪəʳ] *n* **-1.** [of substance, material] capa *f*. **-2.** *fig* [level] nivel *m*.

layman ['leɪmən] (*pl* **-men** [-mən]) *n* **-1.** [untrained, unqualified person] lego *m*, -ga *f*. **-2.** RELIG laico *m*, -ca *f*.

layout ['leɪaʊt] *n* [of building, garden] trazado *m*, diseño *m*; [of text] presentación *f*, composición *f*.

laze [leɪz] *vi*: **to ~ (about** OR **around)** gandulear, holgazanear.

lazy ['leɪzɪ] *adj* **-1.** [person] perezoso(sa), vago(ga). **-2.** [stroll, gesture] lento(ta); [afternoon] ocioso(sa).

lazybones ['leɪzɪbəʊnz] (*pl inv*) *n* gandul *m*, -la *f*.

lb (*abbr of* **pound**) lb.

LCD *n abbr of* **liquid crystal display**.

lead¹ [liːd] (*pt & pp* **led**) ◇ *n* **-1.** [winning position] delantera *f*; **to be in** OR **have the ~** llevar la delantera. **-2.** [amount ahead]: **to have a ~ of ...** llevar una ventaja de .... **-3.** [initiative, example] iniciativa *f*, ejemplo *m*; **to take the ~** [do sthg first] tomar la delantera. **-4.** THEATRE: **(to play) the ~** (hacer) el papel principal. **-5.** [clue] pista *f*. **-6.** [for dog] correa *f*. **-7.** [wire, cable] cable *m*. ◇ *adj* [singer, actor] principal; [story in newspaper] más destacado(da). ◇ *vt* **-1.** [be in front of] encabezar. **-2.** [take, guide, direct] conducir. **-3.** [be in charge of, take the lead in] estar al frente de, dirigir. **-4.** [life] llevar. **-5.** [cause]: **to ~ sb to do sthg** llevar a alguien a hacer algo. ◇ *vi* **-1.** [go]: **to ~ (to)** conducir OR llevar (a). **-2.** [give access to]: **to ~ (to** OR **into)** dar (a). **-3.** [be winning] ir en cabeza. **-4.** [result in]: **to ~ to** conducir a. ◆ **lead up to** *vt fus* **-1.** [build up to] conducir a, preceder. **-2.** [plan to introduce] apuntar a.

lead² [led] *n* **-1.** [metal] plomo *m*. **-2.** [in pencil] mina *f*.

leaded ['ledɪd] *adj* **-1.** [petrol] con plomo. **-2.** [window] emplomado(da).

leader ['liːdər] *n* **-1.** [of party etc, in competition] líder *m y f*. **-2.** *Br* [in newspaper] editorial *m*, artículo *m* de fondo.

leadership ['liːdəʃɪp] *n* (*U*) **-1.** [people in charge]: **the ~** los líderes. **-2.** [position of leader] liderazgo *m*. **-3.** [qualities of leader] dotes *fpl* de mando.

lead-free [led-] *adj* sin plomo.

leading ['liːdɪŋ] *adj* **-1.** [major - athlete, writer] destacado(da). **-2.** [at front] que va en cabeza.

leading lady *n* primera actriz *f*.

leading light *n* cerebro *m*, cabeza *f* pensante.

leading man *n* primer actor *m*.

leaf [liːf] (*pl* **leaves**) *n* **-1.** [of tree, book] hoja *f*. **-2.** [of table] hoja *f* abatible. ◆ **leaf through** *vt fus* hojear.

leaflet ['liːflɪt] *n* [small brochure] folleto *m*; [piece of paper] octavilla *f*.

league [liːg] *n* [gen & SPORT] liga *f*; **to be in ~ with** [work with] estar confabulado con.

leak [liːk] ◇ *n* **-1.** [hole - in tank, bucket] agujero *m*; [- in roof] gotera *f*. **-2.** [escape] escape *m*, fuga *f*. **-3.** [disclosure] filtración *f*. ◇ *vt* [make known] filtrar. ◇ *vi* **-1.** [bucket] tener un agujero; [roof] tener goteras; [water, gas] salirse, escaparse; **to ~ (out) from** salirse de. ◆ **leak out** *vi* **-1.** [liquid] escaparse. **-2.** *fig* [secret, information] trascender.

leakage ['liːkɪdʒ] *n* fuga *f*, escape *m*.

lean [liːn] (*pt & pp* **leant** OR **-ed**) ◇ *adj* **-1.** [person] delgado(da). **-2.** [meat] magro(gra), sin grasa. **-3.** [winter, year] de escasez. ◇ *vt* [support, prop]: **to ~ sthg against** apoyar algo contra. ◇ *vi* **-1.** [bend, slope] inclinarse. **-2.** [rest]: **to ~ on/against** apoyarse en/contra.

leaning ['liːnɪŋ] *n*: **~ (towards)** inclinación *f* (hacia OR por).

leant [lent] *pt & pp* → **lean**.

lean-to (*pl* **lean-tos**) *n* cobertizo *m*.

leap [liːp] (*pt & pp* **leapt** OR **-ed**) ◇ *n* salto *m*. ◇ *vi* [gen] saltar; [prices] dispararse.

leapfrog ['liːpfrɒg] ◇ *n* pídola *f*. ◇ *vt* saltar.

leapt [lept] *pt & pp* → **leap**.

leap year *n* año *m* bisiesto.

learn [lɜːn] (*pt & pp* **-ed** OR **learnt**) ◇ *vt* **-1.** [acquire knowledge of, memorize] aprender; **to ~ (how) to do sthg** aprender a hacer algo. **-2.** [hear]: **to ~ (that)** enterarse de (que). ◇ *vi* **-1.** [acquire knowledge] aprender. **-2.** [hear]: **to ~ (of** OR **about)** enterarse (de).

learned ['lɜːnɪd] *adj* erudito(ta).

learner ['lɜːnər] *n* principiante *m y f*.

learner (driver) *n* conductor *m* principiante OR en prácticas.

learning ['lɜːnɪŋ] *n* saber *m*, erudición *f*.

learnt [lɜːnt] *pt & pp* → **learn**.

lease [liːs] ◇ *n* JUR contrato *m* de arrendamiento, arriendo *m*. ◇ *vt* arrendar; **to ~ sthg from/to sb** arrendar algo de/ a alguien.

leasehold ['liːshəʊld] ◇ *adj* arrendado(da). ◇ *adv* en arriendo.

leash [liːʃ] *n* [for dog] correa *f*.

least [liːst] (*superl of* **little**) ◇ *adj* [smallest in amount, degree] menor; **he earns**

the ~ **money** es el que menos dinero gana. ◇ *pron* [smallest amount]: **the** ~ **lo** menos; **it's the** ~ **(that) he can do** es lo menos que puede hacer; **not in the** ~ en absoluto; **to say the** ~ por no decir otra cosa. ◇ *adv* [to the smallest amount, degree] menos. ◆ **at least** *adv* por lo menos. ◆ **least of all** *adv* y menos (todavía). ◆ **not least** *adv fml* en especial.

leather ['leðəʳ] ◇ *n* cuero *m*, piel *f*. ◇ *comp* [jacket, trousers] de cuero; [shoes, bag] de piel.

leave [liːv] (*pt & pp* **left**) ◇ *vt* **-1.** [gen] dejar; **he left it to her to decide** dejó que ella decidiera; **to** ~ **sb alone** dejar a alguien en paz. **-2.** [go away from - house, room] salir de; [- wife, home] abandonar. **-3.** [do not take, forget] dejarse. **-4.** [bequeath]: **to** ~ **sb sthg, to** ~ **sthg to sb** dejarle algo a alguien. ◇ *vi* [bus, train, plane] salir; [person] irse, marcharse. ◇ *n* [time off] permiso *m*; **to be on** ~ estar de permiso. ◆ **leave behind** *vt sep* **-1.** [abandon] dejar. **-2.** [forget] dejarse. ◆ **leave out** *vt sep* excluir.

leave of absence *n* excedencia *f*.

leaves [liːvz] *pl* → **leaf**.

Lebanon ['lebənən] *n*: **(the)** ~ (el) Líbano.

lecherous ['letʃərəs] *adj* lascivo(va).

lecture ['lektʃəʳ] ◇ *n* **-1.** [talk - at university] clase *f*; [- at conference] conferencia *f*. **-2.** [criticism, reprimand] sermón *m*. ◇ *vt* [scold] echar un sermón a. ◇ *vi* [give talk]: **to** ~ **(on/in)** [at university] dar una clase (de/en); [at conference] dar una conferencia (sobre/en).

lecturer ['lektʃərəʳ] *n* profesor *m*, -ra *f* de universidad.

led [led] *pt & pp* → **lead**[1].

ledge [ledʒ] *n* **-1.** [of window] alféizar *m*. **-2.** [of mountain] saliente *m*.

ledger ['ledʒəʳ] *n* libro *m* mayor.

leech [liːtʃ] *n lit & fig* sanguijuela *f*.

leek [liːk] *n* puerro *m*.

leer [lɪəʳ] *vi*: **to** ~ **at sb** mirar lascivamente a alguien.

leeway ['liːweɪ] *n* [room to manoeuvre] libertad *f* de acción OR movimientos.

left [left] ◇ *adj* **-1.** [remaining]: **there's no wine** ~ no queda vino. **-2.** [not right] izquierdo(da). ◇ *adv* a la izquierda. ◇ *n*: **on** ~ a la izquierda. ◆ **Left** *n* POL: **the Left** la izquierda.

left-hand *adj* izquierdo(da); **the** ~ **side** el lado izquierdo, la izquierda.

left-hand drive *adj* con el volante a la izquierda.

left-handed [-'hændɪd] *adj* **-1.** [person] zurdo(da). **-2.** [implement] para zurdos.

left luggage (office) *n Br* consigna *f*.

leftover ['leftəʊvəʳ] *adj* sobrante. ◆ **leftovers** *npl* sobras *fpl*.

left wing *n* POL izquierda *f*. ◆ **left-wing** *adj* izquierdista.

leg [leg] *n* **-1.** [of person] pierna *f*; **to pull sb's** ~ tomarle el pelo a alguien. **-2.** [of animal] pata *f*. **-3.** [of trousers] pernera *f*, pierna *f*. **-4.** CULIN [of lamb, pork] pierna *f*; [of chicken] muslo *m*. **-5.** [of furniture] pata *f*. **-6.** [of journey] etapa *f*; [of tournament] fase *f*, manga *f*.

legacy ['legəsɪ] *n lit & fig* legado *m*.

legal ['liːgl] *adj* **-1.** [concerning the law] jurídico(ca), legal. **-2.** [lawful] legal, lícito(ta).

legalize, -ise ['liːgəlaɪz] *vt* legalizar.

legal tender *n* moneda *f* de curso legal.

legend ['ledʒənd] *n lit & fig* leyenda *f*.

leggings ['legɪŋz] *npl* mallas *fpl*.

legible ['ledʒəbl] *adj* legible.

legislation [ˌledʒɪs'leɪʃn] *n* legislación *f*.

legislature ['ledʒɪsleɪtʃəʳ] *n* legislatura *f*.

legitimate [lɪ'dʒɪtɪmət] *adj* legítimo(ma).

legless ['leglɪs] *adj Br inf* [drunk] trompa, como una cuba.

legroom ['legrʊm] *n* (*U*) sitio *m* para las piernas.

leg-warmers [-ˌwɔːməz] *npl* calentadores *mpl*.

leisure [*Br* 'leʒəʳ, *Am* 'liːʒəʳ] *n* ocio *m*, tiempo *m* libre; **do it at your** ~ hazlo cuando tengas tiempo.

leisure centre *n* centro *m* deportivo y cultural.

leisurely [*Br* 'leʒəlɪ, *Am* 'liːʒərlɪ] ◇ *adj* lento(ta). ◇ *adv* con calma, sin prisa.

leisure time *n* tiempo *m* libre, ocio *m*.

lemon ['lemən] *n* [fruit] limón *m*.

lemonade [ˌlemə'neɪd] *n* **-1.** *Br* [fizzy drink] gaseosa *f*. **-2.** [made with fresh lemons] limonada *f*.

lemon juice *n* zumo *m* de limón.

lemon sole *n* platija *f*.

lemon squeezer [-'skwiːzəʳ] *n* exprimidor *m*, exprimelimones *m inv*.

lemon tea *n* té *m* con limón.

lend [lend] (*pt & pp* **lent**) *vt* **-1.** [loan] prestar, dejar; **to** ~ **sb sthg, to** ~ **sthg to sb** prestarle algo a alguien. **-2.** [offer]: **to** ~ **sthg (to sb)** prestar algo (a alguien); **to** ~ **itself to sthg** prestarse a algo. **-3.** [add]: **to** ~ **sthg to** prestar algo a.

lending rate ['lendıŋ-] n tipo m de interés (en un crédito).

length [leŋθ] n **-1.** [measurement] longitud f, largo m; **what ~ is it?** ¿cuánto mide de largo?; **in ~** de largo. **-2.** [whole distance, size] extensión f. **-3.** [of swimming pool] largo m. **-4.** [piece - of string, wood] trozo m alargado; [- of cloth] largo m. **-5.** [duration] duración f. **-6.** phr: **to go to great ~s to do sthg** hacer lo imposible para hacer algo. ◆ **at length** adv **-1.** [eventually] por fin. **-2.** [in detail - speak] largo y tendido; [- discuss] con detenimiento.

lengthen ['leŋθən] ◇ vt alargar. ◇ vi alargarse.

lengthways ['leŋθweiz] adv a lo largo.

lengthy ['leŋθı] adj [stay, visit] extenso(sa); [discussions, speech] prolongado(da).

lenient ['li:njənt] adj indulgente.

lens [lenz] n **-1.** [in glasses] lente f; [in camera] objetivo m. **-2.** [contact lens] lentilla f, lente f de contacto.

lent [lent] pt & pp → **lend**.

Lent [lent] n Cuaresma f.

lentil ['lentıl] n lenteja f.

Leo ['li:əʊ] n Leo m.

leopard ['lepəd] n leopardo m.

leotard ['li:ətɑːd] n malla f.

leper ['lepə^r] n leproso m, -sa f.

leprosy ['leprəsı] n lepra f.

lesbian ['lezbıən] n lesbiana f.

less [les] ◇ (compar of **little**) ◇ adj menos; **~ ... than** menos ... que; **~ and ~** cada vez menos. ◇ pron menos; **the ~ you work, the ~ you earn** cuanto menos trabajas, menos ganas; **it costs ~ than you think** cuesta menos de lo que piensas; **no ~ than** nada menos que. ◇ adv menos; **~ than five** menos de cinco; **~ and ~** cada vez menos. ◇ prep [minus] menos.

lessen ['lesn] ◇ vt aminorar, reducir. ◇ vi aminorarse, reducirse.

lesser ['lesə^r] adj menor; **to a ~ extent** OR **degree** en menor grado.

lesson ['lesn] n **-1.** [class] clase f. **-2.** [warning experience] lección f.

lest [lest] conj fml para que no; **~ we forget** no sea que nos olvidemos.

let [let] (pt & pp **let**) vt **-1.** [allow]: **to ~ sb do sthg** dejar a alguien hacer algo; **to ~ sthg happen** dejar que algo ocurra; **to ~ sb know sthg** avisar a alguien de algo; **to ~ go of sthg/sb** soltar algo/a alguien; **to ~ sthg/sb go** [release] liberar a algo/alguien, soltar a algo/

alguien. **-2.** [in verb forms]: **~'s go!** ¡vamos!; **~'s see** veamos; **~ him wait!** ¡déjale que espere! **-3.** [rent out - house, room] alquilar; [- land] arrendar; **"to ~"** "se alquila". ◆ **let alone** adv ni mucho menos. ◆ **let down** vt sep **-1.** [deflate] desinflar. **-2.** [disappoint] fallar, defraudar. ◆ **let in** vt sep **-1.** [admit] dejar entrar. **-2.** [leak] dejar pasar. ◆ **let off** vt sep **-1.** [excuse]: **to ~ sb off sthg** eximir a alguien de algo. **-2.** [not punish] perdonar. **-3.** [cause to explode - bomb] hacer estallar; [- gun] disparar. ◆ **let on** vi: **don't ~ on!** ¡no cuentes nada! ◆ **let out** vt sep **-1.** [allow to go out] dejar salir. **-2.** [emit - sound] soltar. ◆ **let up** vi **-1.** [heat, rain] cesar. **-2.** [person] parar.

letdown ['letdaʊn] n inf chasco m.

lethal ['li:θl] adj letal, mortífero(ra).

lethargic [lə'θɑːdʒık] adj [mood] letárgico(ca); [person] aletargado(da).

let's [lets] = **let us**.

letter ['letə^r] n **-1.** [written message] carta f. **-2.** [of alphabet] letra f.

letter bomb n carta f bomba.

letterbox ['letəbɒks] n Br buzón m.

letter of credit n carta f de crédito.

lettuce ['letıs] n lechuga f.

letup ['letʌp] n tregua f, respiro m.

leuk(a)emia [luː'kiːmıə] n leucemia f.

level ['levl] ◇ adj **-1.** [equal in speed, score] igualado(da); [equal in height] nivelado(da); **to be ~ (with sthg)** estar al mismo nivel (que algo). **-2.** [flat - floor, field] liso(sa), llano(na). ◇ n **-1.** [gen] nivel m. **-2.** phr: **to be on the ~** inf ir en serio. **-3.** Am [spirit level] nivel m de burbuja de aire. ◇ vt **-1.** [make flat] allanar. **-2.** [demolish - building] derribar; [- forest] arrasar. ◆ **level off, level out** vi **-1.** [stabilize, slow down] estabilizarse. **-2.** [ground] nivelarse; [plane] enderezarse. ◆ **level with** vt fus inf ser sincero(ra) con.

level crossing n Br paso m a nivel.

level-headed [-'hedıd] adj sensato(ta).

lever [Br 'liːvə^r, Am 'levər] n **-1.** [handle, bar] palanca f. **-2.** fig [tactic] resorte m.

leverage [Br 'liːvərıdʒ, Am 'levərıdʒ] n (U) **-1.** [force] fuerza f de apalanque. **-2.** fig [influence] influencia f.

levy ['levı] ◇ n: **~ (on)** [financial contribution] contribución f (a OR para); [tax] recaudación f OR impuesto m (sobre). ◇ vt recaudar.

lewd [ljuːd] adj [person, look] lascivo(va); [behaviour, song] obsceno(na); [joke] verde.

liability [ˌlaɪəˈbɪlətɪ] n **-1.** [hindrance] estorbo m. **-2.** [legal responsibility]: ~ **(for)** responsabilidad f (de OR por). ◆ **liabilities** npl FIN pasivo m.

liable ['laɪəbl] adj **-1.** [likely]: **that's ~ to happen** eso pueda que ocurra. **-2.** [prone]: **to be ~ to** ser propenso(sa) a. **-3.** [legally responsible]: **to be ~ (for)** ser responsable (de).

liaise [lɪˈeɪz] vi: **to ~ (with)** estar en contacto (con).

liaison [lɪˈeɪzɒn] n [contact, co-operation]: ~ **(with/between)** relación f (con/entre), enlace m (con/entre).

liar ['laɪər] n mentiroso m, -sa f.

libel ['laɪbl] ◇ n libelo m. ◇ vt publicar un libelo contra.

liberal ['lɪbərəl] ◇ adj **-1.** [tolerant] liberal. **-2.** [generous] generoso(sa). ◇ n liberal m y f. ◆ **Liberal** POL ◇ adj liberal. ◇ n (miembro m del partido) liberal m y f.

Liberal Democrat ◇ adj demócrata liberal. ◇ n (miembro m del partido) demócrata liberal m y f.

liberate ['lɪbəreɪt] vt liberar.

liberation [ˌlɪbəˈreɪʃn] n liberación f.

liberty ['lɪbətɪ] n libertad f; **at ~** en libertad; **to be at ~ to do sthg** ser libre de hacer algo; **to take liberties (with sb)** tomarse demasiadas libertades (con alguien).

Libra ['liːbrə] n Libra f.

librarian [laɪˈbreərɪən] n bibliotecario m, -ria f.

library ['laɪbrərɪ] (pl **-ies**) n [public institution] biblioteca f.

libretto [lɪˈbretəʊ] (pl **-s**) n libreto m.

Libya ['lɪbɪə] n Libia f.

lice [laɪs] pl → **louse**.

licence ['laɪsəns] ◇ n permiso m, licencia f. ◇ vt Am = **license**.

license ['laɪsəns] ◇ vt [person, organization] dar licencia a; [activity] autorizar. ◇ n Am = **licence**.

licensed ['laɪsənst] adj **-1.** [person]: **to be ~ to do sthg** estar autorizado(da) para hacer algo. **-2.** [object] registrado(da), con licencia. **-3.** Br [premises] autorizado(da) a vender alcohol.

license plate n Am (placa f de) matrícula f.

lick [lɪk] ◇ n inf [small amount]: **a ~ of paint** una mano de pintura. ◇ vt lit & fig lamer.

licorice ['lɪkərɪs] = **liquorice**.

lid [lɪd] n **-1.** [cover] tapa f, tapadera f. **-2.** [eyelid] párpado m.

lie [laɪ] (pt sense 1 **lied**, pt senses 2-5 **lay**, pp sense 1 **lied**, pp senses 2-5 **lain**, cont all senses **lying**) ◇ n mentira f; **to tell ~s** contar mentiras, mentir. ◇ vi **-1.** [tell lie] mentir; **to ~ to sb** mentirle a alguien. **-2.** [be horizontal, lie down] tumbarse, echarse; [be buried] yacer; **to be lying** estar tumbado(da). **-3.** [be situated] hallarse. **-4.** [be - solution, attraction] hallarse, encontrarse. **-5.** phr: **to ~ low** permanecer escondido(da). ◆ **lie about, lie around** vi estar OR andar tirado(da). ◆ **lie down** vi tumbarse, echarse. ◆ **lie in** vi Br quedarse en la cama hasta tarde.

Liechtenstein ['lɪktən,staɪn] n Liechtenstein.

lie-down n Br siesta f.

lie-in n Br: **to have a ~** quedarse en la cama hasta tarde.

lieu [ljuː, luː] ◆ **in lieu** adv: **in ~ of** en lugar de.

lieutenant [Br lefˈtenənt, Am luːˈtenənt] n teniente m.

life [laɪf] (pl **lives**) n [gen] vida f; **that's ~!** ¡así es la vida!; **for ~** de por vida, para toda la vida; **to come to ~** [thing] cobrar vida; [person] reanimarse de pronto; **to scare the ~ out of sb** pegarle a alguien un susto de muerte.

life assurance = **life insurance**.

life belt n flotador m, salvavidas m inv.

lifeboat ['laɪfbəʊt] n [on a ship] bote m salvavidas; [on shore] lancha f de salvamento.

life buoy n flotador m, salvavidas m inv.

life expectancy [-ɪkˈspektənsɪ] n expectativa f de vida.

lifeguard ['laɪfgɑːd] n socorrista m y f.

life imprisonment [-ɪmˈprɪznmənt] n cadena f perpetua.

life insurance n (U) seguro m de vida.

life jacket n chaleco m salvavidas.

lifeless ['laɪflɪs] adj **-1.** [dead] sin vida. **-2.** [listless] insulso(sa).

lifelike ['laɪflaɪk] adj realista, natural.

lifeline ['laɪflaɪn] n **-1.** [rope] cuerda f OR cable m (de salvamento). **-2.** [something vital for survival] cordón m umbilical.

lifelong ['laɪflɒŋ] adj de toda la vida.

life preserver [-prɪ,zɜːvər] n Am salvavidas m inv.

life raft n balsa f salvavidas.

lifesaver ['laɪf,seɪvər] n [person] socorrista m y f.

life sentence n (condena f a) cadena f perpetua.

life-size(d) [-saɪz(d)] *adj* (de) tamaño natural.

lifespan ['laɪfspæn] *n* [of person, animal, plant] vida *f*.

lifestyle ['laɪfstaɪl] *n* estilo *m* OR modo *m* de vida.

life-support system *n* aparato *m* de respiración artificial.

lifetime ['laɪftaɪm] *n* vida *f*.

lift [lɪft] ◇ *n* -1. [ride - in car etc]: **to give sb a ~ (somewhere)** acercar OR llevar a alguien (a algún sitio). -2. *Br* [elevator] ascensor *m*, elevador *m* *Amer*. ◇ *vt* -1. [gen] levantar; **to ~ sthg down** bajar algo. -2. [plagiarize] copiar. ◇ *vi* [disappear - mist] despejarse.

lift-off *n* despegue *m*.

light [laɪt] (*pt & pp* **lit** OR **-ed**) ◇ *adj* -1. [gen] ligero(ra); [rain] fino(na); [traffic] escaso(sa). -2. [not strenuous - duties, responsibilities] simple; [- work] suave; [- punishment] leve. -3. [bright] luminoso(sa), lleno(na) de luz; **it's growing ~** se hace de día. -4. [pale - colour] claro(ra). ◇ *n* -1. [brightness, source of light] luz *f*. -2. [for cigarette, pipe] fuego *m*, lumbre *f*; **have you got a ~?** ¿tienes fuego? -3. [perspective]: **in the ~ of** *Br*, **in ~ of** *Am* a la luz de. -4. *phr*: **to come to ~** salir a la luz (pública); **to set ~ to** prender fuego a. ◇ *vt* -1. [ignite] encender. -2. [illuminate] iluminar. ◇ *adv* con poco equipaje. ◆ **light up** ◇ *vt sep* [illuminate] iluminar. ◇ *vi* -1. [look happy] iluminarse, encenderse. -2. *inf* [start smoking] ponerse a fumar.

light bulb *n* bombilla *f*, foco *m* *Amer*.

lighten ['laɪtn] ◇ *vt* -1. [make brighter - room] iluminar. -2. [make less heavy] aligerar. ◇ *vi* [brighten] aclararse.

lighter ['laɪtə'] *n* [cigarette lighter] encendedor *m*, mechero *m*.

light-headed [-'hedɪd] *adj* mareado(da).

light-hearted [-'hɑːtɪd] *adj* -1. [cheerful] alegre. -2. [amusing] frívolo(la).

lighthouse ['laɪthaʊs, *pl* -haʊzɪz] *n* faro *m*.

lighting ['laɪtɪŋ] *n* iluminación *f*; **street ~** alumbrado *m* público.

lightly ['laɪtlɪ] *adv* -1. [gently] suavemente. -2. [slightly] ligeramente. -3. [frivolously] a la ligera.

light meter *n* fotómetro *m*.

lightning ['laɪtnɪŋ] *n* (*U*) relámpago *m*.

lightweight ['laɪtweɪt] ◇ *adj* [object] ligero(ra). ◇ *n* [boxer] peso *m* ligero.

likable ['laɪkəbl] *adj* simpático(ca).

like [laɪk] ◇ *prep* -1. [gen] como; (*in questions or indirect questions*) cómo; **what did it taste ~?** ¿a qué sabía?; **what did it look ~?** ¿cómo era?; **tell me what it's ~** dime cómo es; **something ~ £100** algo así como cien libras; **something ~ that** algo así, algo por el estilo. -2. [in the same way as] como, igual que; **~ this/that** así. -3. [typical of] propio(pia) OR típico(ca) de. ◇ *vt* -1. [find pleasant, approve of] gustar; **I ~ cheese** me gusta el queso; **I ~ it/them** me gusta/gustan; **he ~s doing** OR **to do sthg** (a él) le gusta hacer algo. -2. [want] querer; **I don't ~ to bother her** no quiero molestarla; **would you ~ some more?** ¿quieres un poco más?; **I'd ~ to come tomorrow** querría OR me gustaría venir mañana; **I'd ~ you to come to dinner** me gustaría que vinieras a cenar; [in shops, restaurants]: **I'd ~ a kilo of apples/the soup** póngame un kilo de manzanas/la sopa. ◇ *n*: **the ~ of sb/sthg** alguien/algo del estilo. ◆ **likes** *npl* [things one likes] gustos *mpl*, preferencias *fpl*.

likeable ['laɪkəbl] = **likable**.

likelihood ['laɪklɪhʊd] *n* (*U*) probabilidad *f*.

likely ['laɪklɪ] *adj* -1. [probable] probable; **rain is ~** es probable que llueva; **he's ~ to come** es probable que venga. -2. [suitable] indicado(da).

liken ['laɪkn] *vt*: **to ~ sthg/sb to** comparar algo/a alguien con.

likeness ['laɪknɪs] *n* -1. [resemblance]: **~ (to)** parecido *m* (con). -2. [portrait] retrato *m*.

likewise ['laɪkwaɪz] *adv* [similarly] de la misma forma; **to do ~** hacer lo mismo.

liking ['laɪkɪŋ] *n*: **to have a ~ for sthg** tener afición *f* por OR a algo; **to take a ~ to sb** tomar OR coger cariño *m* a alguien; **to be to sb's ~** ser del gusto de alguien; **for my/his** *etc* **~** para mi/su *etc* gusto.

lilac ['laɪlək] ◇ *adj* [colour] lila. ◇ *n* -1. [tree] lila *f*. -2. [colour] lila *m*.

Lilo® ['laɪləʊ] (*pl* -s) *n* *Br* colchoneta *f*, colchón *m* hinchable.

lily ['lɪlɪ] *n* lirio *m*, azucena *f*.

lily of the valley (*pl* **lilies of the valley**) *n* lirio *m* de los valles.

limb [lɪm] *n* -1. [of body] miembro *m*, extremidad *f*. -2. [of tree] rama *f*.

limber ['lɪmbə'] ◆ **limber up** *vi* desentumecerse.

limbo ['lɪmbəʊ] (*pl* **-s**) *n* (U) [uncertain state]: **to be in** ~ estar en un estado de incertidumbre.

lime [laɪm] *n* **-1.** [fruit] lima *f*. **-2.** [drink]: ~ **(juice)** lima *f*. **-3.** CHEM cal *f*.

limelight ['laɪmlaɪt] *n*: **in the** ~ en (el) candelero.

limerick ['lɪmərɪk] *n copla humorística de cinco versos.*

limestone ['laɪmstəʊn] *n* (U) (piedra *f*) caliza *f*.

limey ['laɪmɪ] (*pl* **limeys**) *n Am inf término peyorativo que designa a un inglés.*

limit ['lɪmɪt] ◇ *n* **-1.** [gen] límite *m*. **-2.** *phr*: **off** ~**s** en zona prohibida; **within** ~**s** dentro de un límite. ◇ *vt* limitar, restringir.

limitation [,lɪmɪ'teɪʃn] *n* limitación *f*.

limited ['lɪmɪtɪd] *adj* [restricted] limitado(da); **to be** ~ **to** estar limitado a.

limited (liability) company *n* sociedad *f* limitada.

limousine ['lɪməziːn] *n* limusina *f*.

limp [lɪmp] ◇ *adj* flojo(ja). ◇ *vi* cojear.

limpet ['lɪmpɪt] *n* lapa *f*.

line [laɪn] ◇ *n* **-1.** [gen] línea *f*. **-2.** [row] fila *f*. **-3.** [queue] cola *f*; **to stand** OR **wait in** ~ hacer cola. **-4.** [course - direction] línea *f*; [- of action] camino *m*; **what's his** ~ **of business?** ¿a qué negocios se dedica? **-5.** [length - of rope] cuerda *f*; [- for fishing] sedal *m*; [- of wire] hilo *m*. **-6.** TELEC: **(telephone)** ~ línea *f* (telefónica); **hold the** ~, **please** no cuelgue, por favor; **the** ~ **is busy** está comunicando; **it's a bad** ~ hay interferencias. **-7.** [on page] línea *f*, renglón *m*; [of poem - song] verso *m*; [letter]: **to drop sb a** ~ *inf* mandar unas letras a alguien. **-8.** [system of transport]: **(railway)** ~ [track] vía *f* (férrea); [route] línea *f* (férrea). **-9.** [wrinkle] arruga *f*. **-10.** [borderline] límite *m*. **-11.** COMM línea *f*. **-12.** *phr*: **to draw the** ~ **at sthg** no pasar por algo, negarse a algo. ◇ *vt* [coat, curtains] forrar; [drawer] cubrir el interior de. ◆ **out of line** *adv*: **to be out of** ~ estar fuera de lugar. ◆ **line up** ◇ *vt sep* **-1.** [make into a row or queue] alinear. **-2.** [arrange] programar, organizar. ◇ *vi* [form a queue] alinearse.

lined [laɪnd] *adj* **-1.** [of paper] de rayos. **-2.** [wrinkled] arrugado(da).

linen ['lɪnɪn] *n* **-1.** [cloth] lino *m*. **-2.** [tablecloths, sheets] ropa *f* blanca OR de hilo; **bed** ~ ropa *f* de cama.

liner ['laɪnə'] *n* [ship] transatlántico *m*.

linesman ['laɪnzmən] (*pl* **-men** [-mən]) *n* juez *m y f* de línea.

lineup ['laɪnʌp] *n* **-1.** [of players, competitors] alineación *f*. **-2.** *Am* [identification parade] rueda *f* de identificación.

linger ['lɪŋgə'] *vi* **-1.** [remain - over activity] entretenerse; [- in a place] rezagarse. **-2.** [persist] persistir.

lingerie ['lænʒərɪ] *n* ropa *f* interior femenina.

lingo ['lɪŋgəʊ] (*pl* **-es**) *n inf* [foreign language] idioma *m*; [jargon] jerga *f*.

linguist ['lɪŋgwɪst] *n* **-1.** [someone good at languages] persona *f* con facilidad para las lenguas. **-2.** [student or teacher of linguistics] lingüista *m y f*.

linguistics [lɪŋ'gwɪstɪks] *n* (U) lingüística *f*.

lining ['laɪnɪŋ] *n* **-1.** [gen & AUT] forro *m*. **-2.** [of stomach, nose] paredes *fpl* interiores.

link [lɪŋk] ◇ *n* **-1.** [of chain] eslabón *m*. **-2.** [connection] conexión *f*, enlace *m*; ~**s (between/with)** lazos *mpl* (entre/con), vínculos *mpl* (entre/con). ◇ *vt* **-1.** [connect - cities] comunicar; [- computers] conectar; [- facts] relacionar; **to** ~ **sthg with** OR **to** relacionar OR asociar algo con. **-2.** [join - arms] enlazar. ◆ **link up** *vt sep*: **to** ~ **sthg up (with)** conectar algo (con).

links [lɪŋks] (*pl inv*) *n* campo *m* de golf.

lino ['laɪnəʊ], **linoleum** [lɪ'nəʊljəm] *n* linóleo *m*.

lintel ['lɪntl] *n* dintel *m*.

lion ['laɪən] *n* león *m*.

lioness ['laɪənes] *n* leona *f*.

lip [lɪp] *n* **-1.** [of mouth] labio *m*. **-2.** [of cup] borde *m*; [of jug] pico *m*.

lip-read *vi* leer en los labios.

lip salve [-sælv] *n Br* vaselina® *f*, cacao *m*.

lip service *n*: **to pay** ~ **to sthg** hablar en favor de algo sin hacer nada al respeto.

lipstick ['lɪpstɪk] *n* **-1.** [container] lápiz *m* OR barra *f* de labios. **-2.** [substance] carmín *m*, lápiz *m* de labios.

liqueur [lɪ'kjʊə'] *n* licor *m*.

liquid ['lɪkwɪd] ◇ *adj* líquido(da). ◇ *n* líquido *m*.

liquidation [,lɪkwɪ'deɪʃn] *n* liquidación *f*.

liquid crystal display *n* pantalla *f* de cristal líquido.

liquidize, -ise ['lɪkwɪdaɪz] *vt Br* licuar.

liquidizer ['lɪkwɪdaɪzə'] *n Br* licuadora *f*.

liquor ['lɪkəʳ] n (U) alcohol m, bebida f alcohólica.

liquorice ['lɪkərɪʃ, 'lɪkərɪs] n (U) regaliz m.

liquor store n Am tienda donde se venden bebidas alcohólicas para llevar.

Lisbon ['lɪzbən] n Lisboa.

lisp [lɪsp] ◇ n ceceo m. ◇ vi cecear.

list [lɪst] ◇ n lista f. ◇ vt **-1.** [in writing] hacer una lista de. **-2.** [in speech] enumerar. ◇ vi NAUT escorar.

listed building [,lɪstɪd-] n Br edificio declarado de interés histórico y artístico.

listen ['lɪsn] vi **-1.** [give attention]: to ~ (to sthg/sb) escuchar (algo/a alguien); to ~ for estar atento a. **-2.** [heed advice]: to ~ (to sb/sthg) hacer caso (a alguien/de algo); to ~ to reason atender a razones.

listener ['lɪsnəʳ] n **-1.** [person listening] oyente m y f. **-2.** [to radio] radioyente m y f.

listless ['lɪstlɪs] adj apático(ca).

lit [lɪt] pt & pp → **light**.

litany ['lɪtənɪ] (pl **-ies**) n lit & fig letanía f.

liter Am = **litre**.

literacy ['lɪtərəsɪ] n alfabetización f.

literal ['lɪtərəl] adj literal.

literally ['lɪtərəlɪ] adv literalmente; to take sthg ~ tomarse algo al pie de la letra.

literary ['lɪtərərɪ] adj **-1.** [gen] literario(ria). **-2.** [person] literato(ta).

literate ['lɪtərət] adj **-1.** [able to read and write] alfabetizado(da). **-2.** [well-read] culto(ta), instruido(da).

literature ['lɪtrətʃəʳ] n **-1.** [novels, plays, poetry] literatura f. **-2.** [books on a particular subject] publicaciones fpl. **-3.** [printed information] documentación f.

lithe [laɪð] adj ágil.

Lithuania [,lɪθjʊ'eɪnɪə] n Lituania.

litigation [,lɪtɪ'geɪʃn] n fml litigio m.

litre Br, **liter** Am ['liːtəʳ] n litro m.

litter ['lɪtəʳ] ◇ n **-1.** [waste material] basura f. **-2.** [newborn animals] camada f. ◇ vt: **papers ~ed the floor** los papeles estaban esparcidos por el suelo.

litterbin ['lɪtə,bɪn] n Br papelera f.

little ['lɪtl] (compar sense 3 **less**, superl sense 3 **least**) ◇ adj **-1.** [small in size, younger] pequeño(ña). **-2.** [short in length] corto(ta); **a ~ while** un ratito. **-3.** [not much] poco(ca); **he speaks ~ English** habla poco inglés; **he speaks a ~ English** habla un poco de inglés. ◇ pron: **I understood very ~** entendí muy

poco; **a ~** un poco; **a ~ (bit)** un poco; **give me a ~ (bit)** dame un poco. ◇ adv poco; **~ by ~** poco a poco.

little finger n dedo m meñique.

live[1] [lɪv] ◇ vi [gen] vivir. ◇ vt llevar; **to ~ a quiet life** llevar una vida tranquila. ◆**live down** vt sep lograr hacer olvidar. ◆**live off** vt fus [savings, land] vivir de; [people] vivir a costa de. ◆**live on** ◇ vt fus **-1.** [survive on] vivir con OR de. **-2.** [eat] vivir de. ◇ vi [memory, feeling] permanecer, perdurar. ◆**live together** vi vivir juntos. ◆**live up to** vt fus estar a la altura de. ◆**live with** vt fus **-1.** [live in same house as] vivir con. **-2.** [accept - situation, problem] aceptar.

live[2] [laɪv] adj **-1.** [living] vivo(va). **-2.** [burning] encendido(da). **-3.** [unexploded] sin explotar. **-4.** ELEC cargado(da). **-5.** [performance] en directo.

livelihood ['laɪvlɪhʊd] n sustento m, medio m de vida.

lively ['laɪvlɪ] adj **-1.** [person, debate, time] animado(da). **-2.** [mind] agudo(da), perspicaz. **-3.** [colours] vivo(va), llamativo(va).

liven ['laɪvn] ◆**liven up** ◇ vt sep animar. ◇ vi animarse.

liver ['lɪvəʳ] n hígado m.

livery ['lɪvərɪ] n [of servant] librea f; [of company] uniforme m.

lives [laɪvz] pl → **life**.

livestock ['laɪvstɒk] n ganado m.

livid ['lɪvɪd] adj **-1.** [angry] furioso(sa). **-2.** [blue-grey] lívido(da).

living ['lɪvɪŋ] ◇ adj [relatives, language] vivo(va); [artist etc] contemporáneo(a). ◇ n **-1.** [means of earning money]: **what do you do for a ~?** ¿cómo te ganas la vida? **-2.** [lifestyle] vida f.

living conditions npl condiciones fpl de vida.

living room n cuarto m de estar, salón m.

living standards npl nivel m de vida.

living wage n salario m OR sueldo m mínimo.

lizard ['lɪzəd] n [small] lagartija f; [big] lagarto m.

llama ['lɑːmə] (pl inv OR **-s**) n llama f.

load [ləʊd] ◇ n **-1.** [something carried] carga f. **-2.** [amount of work]: **a heavy/light ~** mucho/poco trabajo. **-3.** [large amount]: **~s of** inf montones OR un montón de; **it was a ~ of rubbish** inf fue una porquería. ◇ vt **-1.** [gen & COMPUT]: **to ~ sthg/sb (with)** cargar algo/a alguien (de). **-2.** [camera, video recorder]: **he ~ed the camera with a film** cargó la cámara con una película. ◆**load up** *vt sep & vi* cargar.

loaded ['ləʊdɪd] *adj* **-1.** [question, statement] con doble sentido OR intención. **-2.** *inf* [rich] forrado(da).

loading bay ['ləʊdɪŋ-] *n* zona *f* de carga y descarga.

loaf [ləʊf] (*pl* **loaves**) *n* [of bread] (barra *f* de) pan *m*.

loafer ['ləʊfər] *n* [shoe] mocasín *m*.

loan [ləʊn] ◇ *n* [something lent] préstamo *m*; **on ~** prestado(da). ◇ *vt* prestar; **to ~ sthg to sb, to ~ sb sthg** prestar algo a alguien.

loath [ləʊθ] *adj*: **to be ~ to do sthg** ser reacio(cia) a hacer algo.

loathe [ləʊð] *vt*: **to ~ (doing sthg)** aborrecer OR detestar (hacer algo).

loathsome ['ləʊðsəm] *adj* [smell] repugnante; [person, behaviour] odioso(sa).

loaves [ləʊvz] *pl* → **loaf**.

lob [lɒb] *n* TENNIS lob *m*.

lobby ['lɒbɪ] ◇ *n* **-1.** [hall] vestíbulo *m*. **-2.** [pressure group] grupo *m* de presión, lobby *m*. ◇ *vt* ejercer presión (política) sobre.

lobe [ləʊb] *n* lóbulo *m*.

lobster ['lɒbstər] *n* langosta *f*.

local ['ləʊkl] ◇ *adj* local. ◇ *n inf* **-1.** [person]: **the ~s** [in village] los lugareños; [in town] los vecinos del lugar. **-2.** *Br* [pub] bar *m* del barrio. **-3.** *Am* [bus, train] omnibús *m*.

local authority *n Br* autoridad *f* local.

local call *n* llamada *f* local.

local government *n* gobierno *m* municipal.

locality [ləʊ'kælətɪ] *n* localidad *f*.

locally ['ləʊkəlɪ] *adv* **-1.** [on local basis] en el lugar. **-2.** [nearby] por la zona.

locate [*Br* ləʊ'keɪt, *Am* 'ləʊkeɪt] *vt* **-1.** [find] localizar. **-2.** [situate] ubicar.

location [ləʊ'keɪʃn] *n* **-1.** [place] localización *f*, situación *f*. **-2.** CINEMA: **on ~** en exteriores.

loch [lɒk , lɒx] *n Scot* lago *m*.

lock [lɒk] ◇ *n* **-1.** [of door] cerradura *f*; [of bicycle] candado *m*. **-2.** [on canal] esclusa *f*. **-3.** AUT [steering lock] ángulo *m* de giro. **-4.** *literary* [of hair] mechón *m*. ◇ *vt* **-1.** [with key] cerrar con llave; [with padlock] cerrar con candado. **-2.** [keep safely] poner bajo llave. **-3.** [immobilize] bloquear. ◇ *vi* **-1.** [with key] cerrarse con llave; [with padlock] cerrarse con candado. **-2.** [become immobi-

lized] bloquearse. ◆**lock in** *vt sep* encerrar. ◆**lock out** *vt sep* **-1.** [accidentally] dejar fuera al cerrar accidentalmente la puerta; **to ~ o.s. out** quedarse fuera (*por olvidarse la llave dentro*). **-2.** [deliberately] dejar fuera a. ◆**lock up** ◇ *vt sep* **-1.** [person - in prison] encerrar; [- in asylum] internar. **-2.** [house] cerrar (con llave).

locker ['lɒkər] *n* taquilla *f*, armario *m*.

locker room *n Am* vestuario *m* con taquillas.

locket ['lɒkɪt] *n* guardapelo *m*.

locksmith ['lɒksmɪθ] *n* cerrajero *m*, -ra *f*.

locomotive ['ləʊkə,məʊtɪv] *n* locomotora *f*.

locum ['ləʊkəm] (*pl* **-s**) *n* interino *m*, -na *f*.

locust ['ləʊkəst] *n* langosta *f*.

lodge [lɒdʒ] ◇ *n* **-1.** [caretaker's etc room] portería *f*. **-2.** [of manor house] casa *f* del guarda. **-3.** [of freemasons] logia *f*. **-4.** [for hunting] refugio *m* de caza. ◇ *vi* **-1.** [stay]: **to ~ (with sb)** alojarse (con alguien). **-2.** [become stuck] alojarse. ◇ *vt fml* [register] presentar.

lodger ['lɒdʒər] *n* huésped *m* y *f*.

lodging ['lɒdʒɪŋ] → **board**. ◆**lodgings** *npl* habitación *f* (alquilada).

loft [lɒft] *n* [in house] desván *m*, entrecho *m Amer*; [for hay] pajar *m*.

lofty ['lɒftɪ] *adj* **-1.** [noble, elevado(da). **-2.** *pej* [haughty] arrogante, altanero(ra). **-3.** *literary* [high] elevado(da).

log [lɒg] ◇ *n* **-1.** [of wood] tronco *m*. **-2.** [written record - of ship] diario *m* de a bordo; [- of plane] diario *m* de vuelo. ◇ *vt* anotar. ◆**log in** *vi* COMPUT entrar (en el sistema). ◆**log out** *vi* COMPUT salir (del sistema).

logbook ['lɒgbʊk] *n* **-1.** [of ship] diario *m* de a bordo; [of plane] diario *m* de vuelo. **-2.** [of car] documentación *f*.

loggerheads ['lɒgəhedz] *n*: **to be at ~** estar a matar.

logic ['lɒdʒɪk] *n* lógica *f*.

logical ['lɒdʒɪkl] *adj* lógico(ca).

logistics [lə'dʒɪstɪks] ◇ *n* (U) logística *f*. ◇ *npl* logística *f*.

logo ['ləʊgəʊ] (*pl* **-s**) *n* logotipo *m*.

loin [lɔɪn] *n* lomo *m*.

loiter ['lɔɪtər] *vi* [for bad purpose] merodear; [hang around] vagar.

loll [lɒl] *vi* **-1.** [sit, lie about] repantigarse. **-2.** [hang down] colgar.

lollipop ['lɒlɪpɒp] *n* pirulí *m*.

lollipop lady n Br mujer encargada de parar el tráfico en un paso de cebra para que crucen los niños.

lollipop man n Br hombre encargado de parar el tráfico en un paso de cebra para que crucen los niños.

lolly ['lɒlɪ] n inf **-1.** [lollipop] pirulí m. **-2.** Br [ice lolly] polo m.

London ['lʌndən] n Londres.

Londoner ['lʌndənəʳ] n londinense m y f.

lone [ləʊn] adj solitario(ria).

loneliness ['ləʊnlɪnɪs] n soledad f.

lonely ['ləʊnlɪ] adj **-1.** [person] solo(la). **-2.** [time, childhood] solitario(ria). **-3.** [place] solitario(ria), aislado(da).

lonesome ['ləʊnsəm] adj Am inf **-1.** [person] solo(la). **-2.** [place] solitario(ria).

long [lɒŋ] ◇ adj largo(ga); **two days ~** de dos días de duración; **the table is 5m ~** la mesa mide OR tiene 5m de largo; **the journey is 50km ~** el viaje es de 50 km; **the book is 500 pages ~** el libro tiene 500 páginas. ◇ adv mucho tiempo; **how ~ will it take?** ¿cuánto se tarda?; **how ~ will you be?** ¿cuánto tardarás?; **how ~ have you been waiting?** ¿cuánto tiempo llevas esperando?; **how ~ is the journey?** ¿cuánto hay de viaje?; **I'm no ~er young** ya no soy joven; **I can't wait any ~er** ya no puedo esperar más; **so ~** inf hasta luego OR pronto; **before ~** pronto; **for ~** mucho tiempo. ◇ vt: **to ~ to do sthg** desear ardientemente hacer algo. ◆ **as long as, so long as** conj mientras; **as ~ as you do it, so will I** siempre y cuando tú lo hagas, yo también lo haré. ◆ **long for** vt fus desear ardientemente.

long-distance adj [runner] de fondo; [lorry driver] para distancias grandes.

long-distance call n conferencia f (telefónica).

longhand ['lɒŋhænd] n escritura f a mano.

long-haul adj de larga distancia.

longing ['lɒŋɪŋ] ◇ adj anhelante. ◇ n **-1.** [desire] anhelo m, deseo m; [nostalgia] nostalgia f, añoranza f. **-2.** [strong wish]: **(a) ~ (for)** (un) ansia f (de).

longitude ['lɒndʒɪtjuːd] n longitud f.

long jump n salto m de longitud.

long-life adj de larga duración.

long-playing record [-'pleɪɪŋ-] n disco m de larga duración.

long-range adj **-1.** [missile, bomber] de

largo alcance. **-2.** [plan, forecast] a largo plazo.

long shot n posibilidad f remota.

longsighted [,lɒŋ'saɪtɪd] adj présbita.

long-standing adj antiguo(gua).

longsuffering [,lɒŋ'sʌfərɪŋ] adj sufrido(da).

long term n: **in the ~** a largo plazo.

long wave n (U) onda f larga.

long weekend n puente m.

longwinded [,lɒŋ'wɪndɪd] adj prolijo(ja).

loo [luː] (pl **-s**) n Br inf wáter m.

look [lʊk] ◇ n **-1.** [with eyes] mirada f; **to give sb a ~** dirigir la mirada hacia OR a alguien; **to take** OR **have a ~ (at sthg)** echar una mirada OR ojeada (a algo). **-2.** [search]: **to have a ~ (for sthg)** buscar (algo). **-3.** [appearance] aspecto m; **by the ~** OR **~s of it, it has been here for ages** parece que hace años que está aquí. ◇ vi **-1.** [with eyes]: **to ~ (at sthg/sb)** mirar (algo/a alguien). **-2.** [search]: **to ~ (for sthg/sb)** buscar (algo/a alguien). **-3.** [building, window]: **to ~ (out) onto** dar a. **-4.** [have stated appearance] verse; [seem] parecer; **it ~s like rain** OR **as if it will rain** parece que va a llover; **she ~s like her mother** se parece a su madre. ◇ vt **-1.** [look at] mirar. **-2.** [appear]: **to ~ one's age** representar la edad que se tiene. ◆ **looks** npl belleza f. ◆ **look after** vt fus **-1.** [take care of] cuidar. **-2.** [be responsible for] encargarse de. ◆ **look at** vt fus **-1.** [see, glance at] mirar; [examine] examinar. **-2.** [judge] estudiar. ◆ **look down on** vt fus [condescend to] despreciar. ◆ **look for** vt fus buscar. ◆ **look forward to** vt fus esperar (con ilusión). ◆ **look into** vt fus [problem, possibility] estudiar; [issue] investigar. ◆ **look on** vi mirar, observar. ◆ **look out** vi tener cuidado; **~ out!** ¡cuidado! ◆ **look out for** vt fus estar atento(ta) a. ◆ **look round** ◇ vt fus [shop] echar un vistazo; [castle, town] visitar. ◇ vi volver la cabeza. ◆ **look to** vt fus **-1.** [depend on] recurrir a. **-2.** [think about] pensar en. ◆ **look up** ◇ vt sep **-1.** [in book] buscar. **-2.** [visit - person] ir a ver OR visitar. ◇ vi [improve] mejorar. ◆ **look up to** vt fus respetar, admirar.

lookout ['lʊkaʊt] n **-1.** [place] puesto m de observación. **-2.** [person] centinela m y f. **-3.** [search]: **to be on the ~ for** estar al acecho de.

loom [luːm] ◇ n telar m. ◇ vi **-1.** [rise up] surgir OR aparecer amenazante. **-2.**

fig [be imminent] ser inminente. ◆ **loom up** *vi* divisarse sombríamente.

loony ['lu:nɪ] *inf* ◇ *adj* majara. ◇ *n* majara *m y f*.

loop [lu:p] *n* **-1.** [shape] lazo *m*. **-2.** COMPUT bucle *m*.

loophole ['lu:phəʊl] *n* laguna *f*.

loose [lu:s] *adj* **-1.** [not firmly fixed] flojo(ja). **-2.** [unattached - paper, sweets, hair] suelto(ta). **-3.** [clothes, fit] holgado(da). **-4.** *dated* [promiscuous] promiscuo(cua). **-5.** [inexact - translation] impreciso(sa).

loose change *n* (dinero *m*) suelto *m*.

loose end *n*: to be at a ~ *Br*, to be at ~s *Am* estar desocupado(da).

loosely ['lu:slɪ] *adv* **-1.** [not firmly] holgadamente, sin apretar. **-2.** [inexactly] vagamente.

loosen ['lu:sn] *vt* aflojar. ◆ **loosen up** *vi* **-1.** [before game, race] desentumecerse. **-2.** *inf* [relax] relajarse.

loot [lu:t] ◇ *n* botín *m*. ◇ *vt* saquear.

looting ['lu:tɪŋ] *n* saqueo *m*.

lop [lɒp] *vt* podar. ◆ **lop off** *vt sep* cortar.

lop-sided [-'saɪdɪd] *adj* **-1.** [uneven] ladeado(da), torcido(da). **-2.** *fig* [biased] desequilibrado(da).

lord [lɔːd] *n Br* [man of noble rank] lord *m*. ◆ **Lord** *n* **-1.** RELIG: **the Lord** [God] el Señor; **good Lord!** *Br* ¡Dios mío! **-2.** [in titles] lord *m*; [as form of address]: **my Lord** [bishop] su Ilustrísima; [judge] su Señoría. ◆ **Lords** *npl Br* POL: **the Lords** la Cámara de los Lores.

Lordship ['lɔːdʃɪp] *n*: **your/his** ~ su Señoría *f*.

lore [lɔːʳ] *n* (*U*) saber *m* OR tradición *f* popular.

lorry ['lɒrɪ] *n Br* camión *m*.

lorry driver *n Br* camionero *m*, -ra *f*.

lose [lu:z] (*pt & pp* **lost**) ◇ *vt* [gen] perder; [subj: clock, watch] atrasarse; **to** ~ **sight of sthg/sb** *lit* & *fig* perder de vista algo/a alguien; **to** ~ **one's way** perderse. ◇ *vi* [fail to win] perder.

loser ['lu:zəʳ] *n* **-1.** [of competition] perdedor *m*, -ra *f*. **-2.** *inf pej* [unsuccessful person] desgraciado *m*, -da *f*.

loss [lɒs] *n* **-1.** [gen] pérdida *f*; **to make a** ~ sufrir pérdidas. **-2.** [failure to win] derrota *f*. **-3.** *phr*: **to be at a** ~ **to explain sthg** no saber cómo explicar algo.

lost [lɒst] ◇ *pt & pp* → **lose**. ◇ *adj* **-1.** [unable to find way] perdido(da); **to get** ~ perderse; **get** ~! *inf* ¡vete a la porra!

-2. [that cannot be found] extraviado(da), perdido(da).

lost-and-found office *n Am* oficina *f* de objetos perdidos.

lost property office *n Br* oficina *f* de objetos perdidos.

lot [lɒt] *n* **-1.** [large amount]: **a** ~ **of, ~s of** mucho(cha); **a** ~ **of people** mucha gente, muchas personas; **a** ~ **of problems** muchos problemas; **the** ~ todo. **-2.** [group, set] grupo *m*. **-3.** [destiny] destino *m*, suerte *f*. **-4.** *Am* [of land] terreno *m*; [car park] aparcamiento *m*. **-5.** [at auction] partida *f*, lote *m*. **-6.** *phr*: to draw ~s echar a suerte. ◆ **a lot** *adv* mucho.

lotion ['ləʊʃn] *n* loción *f*.

lottery ['lɒtərɪ] *n* lotería *f*.

loud [laʊd] ◇ *adj* **-1.** [voice, music] alto(ta); [bang] fuerte; [person] ruidoso(sa). **-2.** [emphatic]: **to be** ~ **in one's criticism of** ser enérgico(ca) en la crítica de. **-3.** [too bright] chillón(ona). ◇ *adv* fuerte; **out** ~ en voz alta.

loudhailer [,laʊd'heɪləʳ] *n Br* megáfono *m*.

loudly ['laʊdlɪ] *adv* **-1.** [shout] a voz en grito; [talk] en voz alta. **-2.** [gaudily] con colores chillones OR llamativos.

loudspeaker [,laʊd'spi:kəʳ] *n* altavoz *m*.

lounge [laʊndʒ] ◇ *n* **-1.** [in house] salón *m*. **-2.** [in airport] sala *f* de espera. ◇ *vi* repantigarse.

lounge bar *n Br* salón-bar *m*.

louse [laʊs] (*pl* **lice**) *n* [insect] piojo *m*.

lousy ['laʊzɪ] *adj inf* [poor quality] fatal, pésimo(ma).

lout [laʊt] *n* gamberro *m*.

louvre *Br*, **louver** *Am* ['lu:vəʳ] *n* persiana *f*.

lovable ['lʌvəbl] *adj* adorable.

love [lʌv] ◇ *n* **-1.** [gen] amor *m*; **give her my** ~ dale un abrazo de mi parte; ~ **from** [at end of letter] un abrazo de; **to be in** ~ **(with)** estar enamorado(da) (de); **to fall in** ~ enamorarse; **to make** ~ hacer el amor. **-2.** [liking, interest] pasión *f*; **a** ~ **of** OR **for** una pasión por. **-3.** *inf* [form of address] cariño *m y f*. **-4.** TENNIS: **30** ~ 30 a nada. ◇ *vt* **-1.** [feel affection for] amar, querer. **-2.** [like]: **I** ~ **football** me encanta el fútbol; **I** ~ **going to** OR **to go to the theatre** me encanta ir al teatro.

love affair *n* aventura *f* amorosa.

love life *n* vida *f* amorosa.

lovely ['lʌvlɪ] *adj* **-1.** [beautiful - person]

encantador(ra); [- dress, place] precioso(sa). **-2.** [pleasant] estupendo(da).

lover ['lʌvə'] n **-1.** [sexual partner] amante m y f. **-2.** [enthusiast] amante m y f, apasionado m, -da f.

loving ['lʌvɪŋ] adj cariñoso(sa).

low [ləu] ◇ adj **-1.** [gen] bajo(ja); **in the ~ twenties** 20 y algo; **a ~ trick** una mala jugada. **-2.** [little remaining] escaso(sa). **-3.** [unfavourable - opinion] malo(la); [- esteem] poco(ca). **-4.** [dim] tenue. **-5.** [dress, neckline] escotado(da). **-6.** [depressed] deprimido(da). ◇ adv **-1.** [gen] bajo; **morale is very ~** la moral está por los suelos; **~ paid** mal pagado. **-2.** [speak] en voz baja. ◇ n **-1.** [low point] punto m más bajo. **-2.** METEOR área f de bajas presiones.

low-calorie adj light (inv), bajo(ja) en calorías.

low-cut adj escotado(da).

lower ['ləuə'] ◇ adj inferior. ◇ vt **-1.** [gen] bajar; [flag] arriar. **-2.** [reduce] reducir.

low-fat adj bajo(ja) en grasas.

low-key adj discreto(ta).

lowly ['ləulɪ] adj humilde.

low-lying adj bajo(ja).

loyal ['lɔɪəl] adj leal, fiel.

loyalty ['lɔɪəltɪ] n lealtad f.

lozenge ['lɒzɪndʒ] n **-1.** [tablet] tableta f, pastilla f. **-2.** [shape] rombo m.

LP (abbr of **long-playing record**) n LP m.

L-plate n Br placa f L (de prácticas).

Ltd, ltd (abbr of **limited**) S.L.

lubricant ['lu:brɪkənt] n lubricante m.

lubricate ['lu:brɪkeɪt] vt lubricar, engrasar.

lucid ['lu:sɪd] adj **-1.** [clear] claro(ra). **-2.** [not confused] lúcido(da).

luck [lʌk] n suerte f; **good/bad ~** [good, bad fortune] buena/mala suerte; **good ~!** [said to express best wishes] ¡buena suerte!; **bad** OR **hard ~!** ¡mala suerte!; **to be in ~** estar de suerte; **with (any) ~** con un poco de suerte.

luckily ['lʌkɪlɪ] adv afortunadamente.

lucky ['lʌkɪ] adj **-1.** [fortunate - person] afortunado(da); [- event] oportuno(na). **-2.** [bringing good luck] que trae buena suerte.

lucrative ['lu:krətɪv] adj lucrativo(va).

ludicrous ['lu:dɪkrəs] adj absurdo(da).

lug [lʌg] vt inf arrastrar, tirar con dificultad.

luggage ['lʌgɪdʒ] n Br equipaje m.

luggage rack n Br [of car] baca f, portaequipajes m inv; [in train] redecilla f.

lukewarm ['lu:kwɔ:m] adj **-1.** [tepid] tibio(bia), templado(da). **-2.** [unenthusiastic] indiferente, desapasionado(da).

lull [lʌl] ◇ n: ~ (in) [activity] respiro m OR pausa f (en); [fighting] tregua f (en). ◇ vt: **to ~ sb into a false sense of security** infundir una sensación de falsa seguridad a alguien; **to ~ sb to sleep** adormecer OR hacer dormir a alguien.

lullaby ['lʌləbaɪ] n nana f, canción f de cuna.

lumber ['lʌmbə'] n (U) **-1.** Am [timber] maderos mpl. **-2.** Br [bric-a-brac] trastos mpl. ◆ **lumber with** vt sep Br inf: **to ~ sb with sthg** cargar a alguien con algo.

lumberjack ['lʌmbədʒæk] n leñador m, -ra f.

luminous ['lu:mɪnəs] adj luminoso(sa).

lump [lʌmp] ◇ n **-1.** [of coal, earth] trozo m; [of sugar] terrón m; [in sauce] grumo m. **-2.** [on body] bulto m. **-3.** fig [in throat] nudo m. ◇ vt: **to ~ sthg together** [things] amontonar algo; [people, beliefs] agrupar OR juntar algo.

lump sum n suma f OR cantidad f global.

lumpy ['lʌmpɪ] (compar **-ier**, superl **-iest**) adj [sauce] grumoso(sa); [mattress] lleno(na) de bultos.

lunacy ['lu:nəsɪ] n locura f.

lunar ['lu:nə'] adj lunar.

lunatic ['lu:nətɪk] n **-1.** pej [fool] idiota m y f. **-2.** [insane person] loco m, -ca f.

lunch [lʌntʃ] ◇ n comida f, almuerzo m. ◇ vi almorzar, comer.

luncheon ['lʌntʃən] n fml comida f, almuerzo m.

luncheon meat n carne de cerdo en lata troceada.

luncheon voucher n Br vale m del almuerzo.

lunch hour n hora f del almuerzo.

lunchtime ['lʌntʃtaɪm] n hora f del almuerzo.

lung [lʌŋ] n pulmón m.

lunge [lʌndʒ] vi lanzarse, abalanzarse; **to ~ at sb** arremeter contra alguien.

lurch [lɜ:tʃ] ◇ n [of boat] bandazo m; [of person] tumbo m; **to leave sb in the ~** dejar a alguien en la estacada. ◇ vi [boat] dar bandazos; [person] tambalearse.

lure [ljuə'] ◇ n atracción f. ◇ vt atraer OR convencer con engaños.

lurid ['ljuərɪd] adj **-1.** [brightly coloured]

chillón(ona). -2. [shockingly unpleasant] espeluznante.

lurk [lɜːk] *vi* **-1.** [person] estar al acecho. **-2.** [memory, danger, fear] ocultarse.

luscious ['lʌʃəs] *adj* lit & fig apetitoso(sa).

lush [lʌʃ] *adj* [luxuriant] exuberante.

lust [lʌst] *n* **-1.** [sexual desire] lujuria f. **-2.** [strong desire]: ~ **for sthg** ansia f de algo. **◆ lust after, lust for** *vt fus* **-1.** [desire - wealth, success] codiciar. **-2.** [desire sexually] desear.

lusty ['lʌstɪ] *adj* vigoroso(sa), fuerte.

Luxembourg ['lʌksəm,bɜːg] *n* Luxemburgo.

luxuriant [lʌg'ʒʊərɪənt] *adj* exuberante.

luxurious [lʌg'ʒʊərɪəs] *adj* **-1.** [expensive] lujoso(sa). **-2.** [pleasurable] voluptuoso(sa).

luxury ['lʌkʃərɪ] ◇ *n* lujo *m.* ◇ *comp* de lujo.

LW (*abbr of* **long wave**) *n* OL f.

Lycra® ['laɪkrə] *n* lycra® f.

lying ['laɪɪŋ] ◇ *adj* mentiroso(sa), falso(sa). ◇ *n* (U) mentira f.

lynch [lɪntʃ] *vt* linchar.

lyric ['lɪrɪk] *adj* lírico(ca).

lyrical ['lɪrɪkl] *adj* [poetic] lírico(ca).

lyrics ['lɪrɪks] *npl* letra f.

M

m¹ (*pl* **m's** OR **ms**), **M** (*pl* **M's** OR **Ms**) [em] *n* [letter] m f, M f. **◆ M** *abbr of* **motorway**.

m² **-1.** (*abbr of* **metre**) m. **-2.** (*abbr of* **million**) m. **-3.** *abbr of* **mile**.

MA *n abbr of* **Master of Arts**.

mac [mæk] (*abbr of* **mackintosh**) *n* Br inf [coat] impermeable *m.*

macaroni [,mækə'rəʊnɪ] *n* (U) macarrones *mpl.*

mace [meɪs] *n* **-1.** [ornamental rod] maza f. **-2.** [spice] macis f inv.

machine [mə'ʃiːn] ◇ *n* **-1.** [power-driven device] máquina f. **-2.** [organization] aparato *m.* ◇ *vt* **-1.** SEWING coser a máquina. **-2.** TECH hacer con una máquina.

machinegun [mə'ʃiːngʌn] *n* ametralladora f.

machine language *n* COMPUT lenguaje *m* máquina.

machinery [mə'ʃiːnərɪ] *n* lit & fig maquinaria f.

macho ['mætʃəʊ] *adj* inf macho.

mackerel ['mækrəl] (*pl inv* OR **-s**) *n* caballa f.

mackintosh ['mækɪntɒʃ] *n* Br impermeable *m.*

mad [mæd] *adj* **-1.** [gen] loco(ca); [attempt, idea] disparatado(da); **to be ~ about sb/sthg** estar loco(ca) por alguien/algo; **to go ~** volverse loco. **-2.** [furious] furioso(sa). **-3.** [hectic] desenfrenado(da).

Madagascar [,mædə'gæskə'] *n* Madagascar.

madam ['mædəm] *n* señora f.

madcap ['mædkæp] *adj* descabellado(da).

madden ['mædn] *vt* volver loco(ca).

made [meɪd] *pt & pp →* **make**.

Madeira [mə'dɪərə] *n* **-1.** [wine] madeira *m,* madera *m.* **-2.** GEOGR Madeira.

made-to-measure *adj* hecho(cha) a la medida.

made-up *adj* **-1.** [with make-up - face, person] maquillado(da); [- lips, eyes] pintado(da). **-2.** [invented] inventado(da).

madly ['mædlɪ] *adv* [frantically] enloquecidamente; **~ in love** locamente enamorado.

madman ['mædmən] (*pl* **-men** [-mən]) *n* loco *m.*

madness ['mædnɪs] *n* locura f.

Madrid [mə'drɪd] *n* Madrid.

Mafia ['mæfɪə] *n*: **the ~** la mafia.

magazine [,mægə'ziːn] *n* **-1.** [periodical] revista f. **-2.** [news programme] magazín *m.* **-3.** [on a gun] recámara f.

maggot ['mægət] *n* gusano *m,* cresa f.

magic ['mædʒɪk] ◇ *adj* [gen] mágico(ca). ◇ *n* magia f.

magical ['mædʒɪkl] *adj* lit & fig mágico(ca).

magician [mə'dʒɪʃn] *n* **-1.** [conjuror] prestidigitador *m,* -ra f. **-2.** [wizard] mago *m.*

magistrate ['mædʒɪstreɪt] *n* magistrado *m,* -da f.

magistrates' court *n* Br juzgado *m* de primera instancia.

magnanimous [mæg'nænɪməs] *adj* magnánimo(ma).

magnate ['mægneɪt] *n* magnate *m.*

magnesium [mæg'niːzɪəm] *n* magnesio *m.*

magnet ['mægnɪt] *n* imán *m.*

magnetic [mæg'netɪk] *adj* **-1.** [attracting iron] **magnético(ca). -2.** *fig* [appealingly forceful] **atrayente, carismático(ca).**

magnetic tape *n* **cinta** *f* **magnetofónica.**

magnificent [mæg'nɪfɪsənt] *adj* [building, splendour] **grandioso(sa);** [idea, book, game] **magnífico(ca).**

magnify ['mægnɪfaɪ] *vt* **-1.** [in vision] **aumentar. -2.** [in the mind] **exagerar.**

magnifying glass ['mægnɪfaɪɪŋ-] *n* **lupa** *f.*

magnitude ['mægnɪtjuːd] *n* **magnitud** *f.*

magpie ['mægpaɪ] *n* **urraca** *f.*

mahogany [mə'hɒgənɪ] *n* **-1.** [wood] **caoba** *f.* **-2.** [colour] **caoba** *m.*

maid [meɪd] *n* [in hotel] **camarera** *f*; [domestic] **criada** *f.*

maiden ['meɪdn] ◇ *adj* **inaugural.** ◇ *n literary* **doncella** *f.*

maiden aunt *n* **tía** *f* **soltera.**

maiden name *n* **nombre** *m* **de soltera.**

mail [meɪl] ◇ *n* **-1.** [letters, parcels received] **correspondencia** *f.* **-2.** [system] **correo** *m*; **by ~ por correo.** ◇ *vt* [send] **mandar por correo;** [put in mail box] **echar al buzón.**

mailbox ['meɪlbɒks] *n Am* **buzón** *m.*

mailing list ['meɪlɪŋ-] *n* **lista** *f* **de distribución de publicidad** OR **información.**

mailman ['meɪlmən] (*pl* **-men** [-mən]) *n Am* **cartero** *m.*

mail order *n* **pedido** *m* **por correo.**

mailshot ['meɪlʃɒt] *n* **folleto** *m* **de publicidad (por correo).**

maim [meɪm] *vt* **mutilar.**

main [meɪn] ◇ *adj* **principal.** ◇ *n* [pipe] **tubería** *f* **principal;** [wire] **cable** *m* **principal.** ◆ **mains** *npl*: **the ~s** [gas, water] **la tubería principal;** [electricity] **la red eléctrica. -2.** ◆ **in the main** *adv* **por lo general.**

main course *n* **plato** *m* **fuerte.**

mainframe (computer) ['meɪnfreɪm-] *n* **unidad** *f* **central.**

mainland ['meɪnlənd] ◇ *adj* **continental; ~ Spain la Península.** ◇ *n*: **the ~ el continente.**

mainly ['meɪnlɪ] *adv* **principalmente.**

main road *n* **carretera** *f* **principal.**

mainstay ['meɪnsteɪ] *n* **fundamento** *m.*

mainstream ['meɪnstriːm] ◇ *adj* [gen] **predominante;** [taste] **corriente;** [political party] **convencional.** ◇ *n*: **the ~ la tendencia general.**

maintain [meɪn'teɪn] *vt* **-1.** [gen] **mantener. -2.** [support, provide for] **sostener. -3.** [assert]: **to ~ (that) sostener que.**

maintenance ['meɪntənəns] *n* **-1.** [gen] **mantenimiento** *m.* **-2.** [money] **pensión** *f* **alimenticia.**

maize [meɪz] *n* **maíz** *m.*

majestic [mə'dʒestɪk] *adj* **majestuoso(sa).**

majesty ['mædʒəstɪ] *n* [grandeur] **majestad** *f.* ◆ **Majesty** *n*: **His/Her/Your Majesty Su Majestad.**

major ['meɪdʒər] ◇ *adj* **-1.** [important] **principal. -2.** MUS **mayor.** ◇ *n* MIL **comandante** *m.*

Majorca [mə'jɔːkə, mə'dʒɔːkə] *n* **Mallorca.**

majority [mə'dʒɒrətɪ] *n* **mayoría** *f.*

make [meɪk] (*pt & pp* **made**) ◇ *vt* **-1.** [produce] **hacer; she ~s her own clothes se hace su propia ropa. -2.** [perform - action] **hacer; to ~ a speech pronunciar** OR **dar un discurso; to ~ a decision tomar una decisión; to ~ a mistake cometer un error. -3.** [cause to be, cause to do] **hacer; it ~s me sick me pone enfermo; it made him angry hizo que se enfadara; you made me jump! ¡vaya susto que me has dado!; to ~ sb happy hacer a alguien feliz; to ~ sb sad entristecer a alguien. -4.** [force]: **to ~ sb do sthg hacer que alguien haga algo, obligar a alguien a hacer algo. -5.** [construct]: **to be made of sthg estar hecho(cha) de algo; made in Spain fabricado en España. -6.** [add up to] **hacer, ser; 2 and 2 ~ 4 2 y 2 hacen** OR **son 4. -7.** [calculate] **calcular; I ~ it 50/ six o'clock calculo que serán 50/las seis; what time do you ~ it? ¿qué hora es? -8.** [earn] **ganar; to ~ a profit obtener beneficios; to ~ a loss sufrir pérdidas. -9.** [have the right qualities for] **ser; she'd ~ a good doctor seguro que sería una buena doctora. -10.** [reach] **llegar a. -11.** [gain - friend, enemy] **hacer; to ~ friends with sb hacerse amigo de alguien. -12.** *phr*: **to ~ it** [arrive in time] **conseguir llegar a tiempo;** [be a success] **alcanzar el éxito;** [be able to attend] **venir/ir; to ~ do with sthg apañarse** OR **arreglarse con algo.** ◇ *n* [brand] **marca.** ◆ **make for** *vt fus* **-1.** [move towards] **dirigirse a** OR **hacia. -2.** [contribute to] **contribuir a.** ◆ **make of** *vt sep* **-1.** [understand] **entender; what do you ~ of this word? ¿qué entiendes tú por esta palabra? -2.** [have opinion of] **opinar de.** ◆ **make off** *vi* **darse a la fuga.** ◆ **make out** ◇ *vt sep* **-1.** *inf* [see] **distinguir;** [hear] **entender, oír. -2.** *inf*

manhandle

[understand - word, number] **descifrar;** [- person, attitude] **comprender. -3.** [fill out - form] **rellenar;** [- cheque, receipt] **extender;** [- list] **hacer.** ◆ **make up** ◇ *vt sep* **-1.** [compose, constitute] **componer, constituir. -2.** [invent] **inventar. -3.** [apply cosmetics to] **maquillar. -4.** [prepare - parcel, prescription, bed] **preparar. -5.** [make complete - amount] **completar;** [- difference] **cubrir.** ◇ *vi* [become friends again]: **to ~ up (with sb)** hacer las paces (con alguien). ◆ **make up for** *vt fus* **compensar.** ◆ **make up to** *vt sep*: **to ~ it up to sb (for sthg)** recompensar a alguien (por algo).

make-believe *n* invención *f*.

maker ['meɪkəʳ] *n* [of film, programme] creador *m*, -ra *f*; [of product] fabricante *m y f*.

makeshift ['meɪkʃɪft] *adj* [temporary] provisional; [improvized] improvisado(da).

make-up *n* **-1.** [cosmetics] maquillaje *m*; ~ **remover** loción *f* OR leche *f* desmaquilladora. **-2.** [person's character] carácter *m*. **-3.** [structure] estructura *f*; [of team] composición *f*.

making ['meɪkɪŋ] *n* [of product] fabricación *f*; [of film] rodaje *m*; [of decision] toma *f*; **this is history in the ~** esto pasará a la historia; **your problems are of your own ~** tus problemas te los has buscado tú mismo; **to have the ~s of** tener madera de.

malaise [mə'leɪz] *n fml* malestar *m*.

malaria [mə'leərɪə] *n* malaria *f*.

Malaya [mə'leɪə] *n* Malaya.

Malaysia [mə'leɪzɪə] *n* Malaisia.

male [meɪl] ◇ *adj* **-1.** [animal] macho. **-2.** [human] masculino(na), varón. **-3.** [concerning men] masculino(na). ◇ *n* **-1.** [animal] macho *m*. **-2.** [human] varón *m*.

male nurse *n* enfermero *m*.

malevolent [mə'levələnt] *adj* malévolo(la).

malfunction [mæl'fʌŋkʃn] ◇ *n* funcionamiento *m* defectuoso. ◇ *vi* funcionar mal.

malice ['mælɪs] *n* malicia *f*.

malicious [mə'lɪʃəs] *adj* malicioso(sa).

malign [mə'laɪn] ◇ *adj* maligno(na), perjudicial. ◇ *vt fml* difamar.

malignant [mə'lɪgnənt] *adj* **-1.** *fml* [full of hate] malvado(da). **-2.** MED maligno(na).

mall [mɔːl] *n*: **(shopping)** ~ centro *m* comercial peatonal.

mallet ['mælɪt] *n* mazo *m*.

malnutrition [,mælnjuː'trɪʃn] *n* malnutrición *f*.

malpractice [,mæl'præktɪs] *n* (U) JUR negligencia *f*.

malt [mɔːlt] *n* **-1.** [grain] malta *f*. **-2.** [whisky] whisky *m* de malta.

Malta ['mɔːltə] *n* Malta.

mammal ['mæml] *n* mamífero *m*.

mammoth ['mæməθ] ◇ *adj* descomunal. ◇ *n* mamut *m*.

man [mæn] (*pl* **men**) ◇ *n* hombre *m*; **the ~ in the street** el hombre de la calle, el ciudadano de a pie. ◇ *vt* [gen] manejar; [ship, plane] tripular; **manned 24 hours a day** [telephone] en servicio las 24 horas del día.

manage ['mænɪdʒ] ◇ *vi* **-1.** [cope] poder; **can you ~ that box?** ¿puedes con la caja? **-2.** [survive] apañárselas. ◇ *vt* **-1.** [succeed]: **to ~ to do sthg** conseguir hacer algo. **-2.** [company] dirigir, llevar; [money] administrar, manejar; [pop star] representar; [time] organizar.

manageable ['mænɪdʒəbl] *adj* [task] factible, posible; [children] dominable; [inflation, rate] controlable.

management ['mænɪdʒmənt] *n* **-1.** [control, running] gestión *f*. **-2.** [people in control] dirección *f*.

manager ['mænɪdʒəʳ] *n* **-1.** [of company] director *m*, -ra *f*; [of shop] jefe *m*, -fa *f*; [of pop star] manager *m y f*. **-2.** SPORT entrenador *m*, -ra *f*.

manageress [,mænɪdʒə'res] *n Br* [of company] directora *f*; [of shop] jefa *f*.

managerial [,mænɪ'dʒɪərɪəl] *adj* directivo(va).

managing director ['mænɪdʒɪŋ-] *n* director *m*, -ra *f* gerente.

mandarin ['mændərɪn] *n* [fruit] mandarina *f*.

mandate ['mændeɪt] *n* **-1.** [elected right or authority] mandato *m*. **-2.** [task] misión *f*.

mandatory ['mændətrɪ] *adj* obligatorio(ria).

mane [meɪn] *n* [of horse] crin *f*; [of lion] melena *f*.

maneuver *Am* = **manoeuvre**.

manfully ['mænfʊlɪ] *adv* valientemente.

mangle ['mæŋgl] *vt* [crush] aplastar; [tear to pieces] despedazar.

mango ['mæŋgəʊ] (*pl* **-es** OR **-s**) *n* mango *m*.

mangy ['meɪndʒɪ] *adj* sarnoso(sa).

manhandle ['mæn,hændl] *vt* [person] maltratar.

manhole ['mænhəʊl] *n* boca *f* (del alcantarillado).

manhood ['mænhʊd] *n* **-1.** [state] virilidad *f.* **-2.** [time] edad *f* viril OR adulta.

manhour ['mæn,aʊər] *n* hora *f* de trabajo (realizada por una persona).

mania ['meɪnjə] *n* **-1.** [excessive liking]: ~ (**for**) manía *f* (por). **-2.** PSYCH manía *f.*

maniac ['meɪnɪæk] *n* **-1.** [madman] maníaco *m*, -ca *f.* **-2.** [fanatic] fanático *m*, -ca *f.*

manic ['mænɪk] *adj* maníaco(ca).

manicure ['mænɪ,kjʊər] *n* manicura *f.*

manifest ['mænɪfest] *fml* ◇ *adj* manifiesto(ta). ◇ *vt* manifestar.

manifesto [,mænɪ'festəʊ] (*pl* **-s** OR **-es**) *n* manifiesto *m.*

manipulate [mə'nɪpjʊleɪt] *vt* **-1.** [control for personal benefit] manipular. **-2.** [machine] manejar; [controls, lever] accionar.

mankind [mæn'kaɪnd] *n* la humanidad, el género humano.

manly ['mænlɪ] *adj* varonil, viril.

man-made *adj* [environment, problem, disaster] producido(da) por el hombre; [fibre] artificial.

manner ['mænər] *n* **-1.** [method] manera *f*, forma *f.* **-2.** [bearing, attitude] comportamiento *m.* **-3.** *esp literary* [type, sort] tipo *m*, clase *f.* ◆ **manners** *npl* modales *mpl*; **it's good/bad ~s** to do sthg es de buena/mala educación hacer algo.

mannerism ['mænərɪzm] *n* costumbre *f* (típica de uno).

mannish ['mænɪʃ] *adj* [woman] hombruno(na).

manoeuvre *Br*, **maneuver** *Am* [mə'nu:vər] ◇ *n lit* & *fig* maniobra *f.* ◇ *vt* maniobrar. ◇ *vi* maniobrar.

manor ['mænər] *n* [house] casa *f* solariega.

manpower ['mæn,paʊər] *n* [manual workers] mano *f* de obra; [white-collar workers] personal *m.*

mansion ['mænʃn] *n* [manor] casa *f* solariega; [big house] casa grande.

manslaughter ['mæn,slɔːtər] *n* homicidio *m* involuntario.

mantelpiece ['mæntlpiːs] *n* repisa *f* (de la chimenea).

manual ['mænjʊəl] ◇ *adj* manual. ◇ *n* manual *m.*

manual worker *n* obrero *m*, -ra *f.*

manufacture [,mænjʊ'fæktʃər] ◇ *n* fabricación *f.* ◇ *vt* [make] fabricar.

manufacturer [,mænjʊ'fæktʃərər] *n* fabricante *m y f.*

manure [mə'njʊər] *n* estiércol *m.*

manuscript ['mænjʊskrɪpt] *n* **-1.** [gen] manuscrito *m.* **-2.** [in exam] hoja *f* de examen.

many ['menɪ] (*compar* **more**, *superl* **most**) ◇ *adj* muchos(chas); ~ **people** muchas personas, mucha gente; **how ~?** ¿cuántos(tas)?; **I wonder how ~ people went** me pregunto cuánta gente fue; **too ~** demasiados(das); **there weren't too ~ students** no había muchos estudiantes; **as ~ ... as** tantos(tas) ... como; **so ~** tantos(tas); **I've never seen so ~ people** nunca había visto tanta gente; **a good OR great ~** muchísimos(mas). ◇ *pron* muchos(chas).

map [mæp] *n* mapa *m.* ◆ **map out** *vt sep* planear, planificar.

maple ['meɪpl] *n* arce *m.*

mar [mɑːr] *vt* deslucir.

marathon ['mærəθn] *n* maratón *m.*

marauder [mə'rɔːdər] *n* merodeador *m*, -ra *f.*

marble ['mɑːbl] *n* **-1.** [stone] mármol *m.* **-2.** [for game] canica *f*, bolita *f* Amer.

march [mɑːtʃ] ◇ *n* **-1.** MIL marcha *f.* **-2.** [of demonstrators] manifestación *f.* **-3.** [steady progress] avance *m*, progreso *m.* ◇ *vi* **-1.** [in formation] marchar. **-2.** [in protest] manifestarse. **-3.** [speedily]: **to ~ up to sb** abordar a alguien decididamente. ◇ *vt* llevar por la fuerza.

March [mɑːtʃ] *n* marzo *m*; *see also* **September**.

marcher ['mɑːtʃər] *n* [protester] manifestante *m y f.*

mare [meər] *n* yegua *f.*

margarine [,mɑːdʒə'riːn, ,mɑːgə'riːn] *n* margarina *f.*

marge [mɑːdʒ] *n inf* margarina *f.*

margin ['mɑːdʒɪn] *n* [gen] margen *m.*

marginal ['mɑːdʒɪnl] *adj* **-1.** [unimportant] marginal. **-2.** *Br* POL: ~ **seat** OR **constituency** *escaño vulnerable a ser perdido en las elecciones por tener una mayoría escasa.*

marginally ['mɑːdʒɪnəlɪ] *adv* ligeramente.

marigold ['mærɪgəʊld] *n* caléndula *f.*

marihuana, marijuana [,mærɪ'wɑːnə] *n* marihuana *f.*

marine [mə'riːn] ◇ *adj* marino(na). ◇ *n* soldado *m* de infantería de marina.

marital ['mærɪtl] *adj* matrimonial.

marital status *n* estado *m* civil.

maritime ['mærɪtaɪm] *adj* marítimo(ma).

mark [mɑːk] ◇ *n* **-1.** [stain] mancha *f.* **-2.** [written symbol - on paper] marca *f;* [- in the sand] señal *f.* **-3.** [in exam] nota *f;* **to get good ~s** sacar buenas notas. **-4.** [stage, level]: **once past the halfway ~** una vez llegado a medio camino. **-5.** [sign - of respect] señal *f;* [- of illness, old age] huella *f.* **-6.** [currency] marco *m.* ◇ *vt* **-1.** [stain] manchar. **-2.** [label - with initials etc] señalar. **-3.** [exam, essay] puntuar, calificar. **-4.** [identify - place] señalar; [- beginning, end] marcar. **-5.** [commemorate] conmemorar. **-6.** [characterize] caracterizar. ◆ **mark off** *vt sep* [cross off] tachar.

marked [mɑːkt] *adj* [improvement] notable; [difference] acusado(da).

marker ['mɑːkər] *n* [sign] señal *f.*

marker pen *n* rotulador *m.*

market ['mɑːkɪt] ◇ *n* mercado *m.* ◇ *vt* comercializar.

market garden *n* [small] huerto *m;* [large] huerta *f.*

marketing ['mɑːkɪtɪŋ] *n* marketing *m.*

marketplace ['mɑːkɪtpleɪs] *n lit & fig* mercado *m.*

market research *n* estudio *m* de mercados.

market value *n* valor *m* actual OR en venta.

marking ['mɑːkɪŋ] *n* [of exams etc] corrección *f.* ◆ **markings** *npl* [of flower, animal] pintas *fpl;* [on road] señales *fpl.*

marksman ['mɑːksmən] (*pl* **-men** [-mən]) *n* tirador *m.*

marmalade ['mɑːməleɪd] *n* mermelada *f* (*de cítricos*).

maroon [mə'ruːn] *adj* granate.

marooned [mə'ruːnd] *adj* incomunicado(da), aislado(da).

marquee [mɑː'kiː] *n* carpa *f,* toldo *m* grande.

marriage ['mærɪdʒ] *n* **-1.** [act] boda *f.* **-2.** [state, institution] matrimonio *m.*

marriage bureau *n Br* agencia *f* matrimonial.

marriage certificate *n* certificado *m* de matrimonio.

marriage guidance *n* asesoría *f* matrimonial.

married ['mærɪd] *adj* **-1.** [wedded] casado(da). **-2.** [of marriage] matrimonial.

marrow ['mærəʊ] *n* **-1.** *Br* [vegetable] calabacín *m* grande. **-2.** [in bones] médula *f.*

marry ['mærɪ] ◇ *vt* casar; **to get married** casarse. ◇ *vi* casarse.

Mars [mɑːz] *n* Marte *m.*

marsh [mɑːʃ] *n* **-1.** [area of land] zona *f* pantanosa. **-2.** [type of land] pantano *m.*

marshal ['mɑːʃl] ◇ *n* **-1.** MIL mariscal *m.* **-2.** [steward] oficial *m y f,* miembro *m y f* del servicio de orden. **-3.** *Am* [officer] jefe *m,* -fa *f* de policía. ◇ *vt* [people] dirigir, conducir; [thoughts] ordenar.

martial arts [,mɑːʃl-] *npl* artes *fpl* marciales.

martial law [,mɑːʃl-] *n* ley *f* marcial.

martyr ['mɑːtər] *n* mártir *m y f.*

martyrdom ['mɑːtədəm] *n* martirio *m.*

marvel ['mɑːvl] ◇ *n* maravilla *f.* ◇ *vi:* **to ~ (at)** maravillarse OR asombrarse (ante).

marvellous *Br,* **marvelous** *Am* ['mɑːvələs] *adj* maravilloso(sa).

Marxism ['mɑːksɪzm] *n* marxismo *m.*

Marxist ['mɑːksɪst] ◇ *adj* marxista. ◇ *n* marxista *m y f.*

marzipan ['mɑːzɪpæn] *n* mazapán *m.*

mascara [mæs'kɑːrə] *n* rímel *m.*

masculine ['mæskjʊlɪn] *adj* [gen] masculino(na); [woman, appearance] hombruno(na).

mash [mæʃ] *vt* triturar.

mashed potatoes [mæʃt-] *npl* puré *m* de patatas.

mask [mɑːsk] ◇ *n lit & fig* máscara *f.* ◇ *vt* **-1.** [to hide] enmascarar. **-2.** [cover up] ocultar, disfrazar.

masochist ['mæsəkɪst] *n* masoquista *m y f.*

mason ['meɪsn] *n* **-1.** [stonemason] cantero *m.* **-2.** [freemason] masón *m.*

masonry ['meɪsnrɪ] *n* [stones] albañilería *f.*

masquerade [,mæskə'reɪd] *vi:* **to ~ as** hacerse pasar por.

mass [mæs] ◇ *n* **-1.** [gen] masa *f.* **-2.** [large amount] cantidad *f,* montón *m.* ◇ *adj* [unemployment] masivo(va); [communication] de masas. ◇ *vi* agruparse, concentrarse. ◆ **Mass** *n* [religious ceremony] misa *f.* ◆ **masses** *npl* **-1.** *inf* [lots] montones *mpl.* **-2.** [workers]: **the ~es** las masas.

massacre ['mæsəkər] ◇ *n* matanza *f,* masacre *f.* ◇ *vt* masacrar.

massage [*Br* 'mæsɑːʒ, *Am* mə'sɑːʒ] ◇ *n* masaje *m.* ◇ *vt* dar masajes a.

massive ['mæsɪv] *adj* [gen] enorme; [majority] aplastante.

mass media *n or npl:* **the ~** los medios de comunicación de masas.

mass production *n* producción *f* OR fabricación *f* en serie.

mast [mɑːst] *n* **-1.** [on boat] mástil *m*. **-2.** RADIO & TV poste *m*, torre *f*.

master ['mɑːstəʳ] ◇ *n* **-1.** [of people, animals] amo *m*, dueño *m*; [of house] señor *m*. **-2.** *fig* [of situation] dueño *m*, -ña *f*. **-3.** *Br* [teacher - primary school] maestro *m*; [- secondary school] profesor *m*. ◇ *adj* maestro(tra). ◇ *vt* **-1.** [situation] dominar, controlar; [difficulty] superar. **-2.** [technique etc] dominar.

master key *n* llave *f* maestra.

masterly ['mɑːstəlɪ] *adj* magistral.

mastermind ['mɑːstəmaɪnd] ◇ *n* cerebro *m*. ◇ *vt* ser el cerebro de, dirigir.

Master of Arts (*pl* **Masters of Arts**) *n* **-1.** [degree] maestría *f* OR máster *m* en Letras. **-2.** [person] licenciado *m*, -da *f* con maestría en Letras.

Master of Science (*pl* **Masters of Science**) *n* **-1.** [degree] maestría *f* OR máster *m* en Ciencias. **-2.** [person] licenciado *m*, -da *f* con maestría en Ciencias.

masterpiece ['mɑːstəpiːs] *n* *lit* & *fig* obra *f* maestra.

master's degree *n* máster *m*.

mastery ['mɑːstərɪ] *n* dominio *m*.

mat [mæt] *n* **-1.** [beer mat] posavasos *m inv*; [tablemat] salvamanteles *m inv*. **-2.** [doormat] felpudo *m*; [rug] alfombrilla *f*.

match [mætʃ] ◇ *n* **-1.** [game] partido *m*. **-2.** [for lighting] cerilla *f*. **-3.** [equal]: **to be no ~ for** no poder competir con. ◇ *vt* **-1.** [be the same as] coincidir con. **-2.** [pair off]: **to ~ sthg (to)** emparejar algo (con). **-3.** [be equal with] competir con. **-4.** [go well with] hacer juego con. ◇ *vi* **-1.** [be the same] coincidir. **-2.** [go together well] hacer juego.

matchbox ['mætʃbɒks] *n* caja *f* de cerillas.

matching ['mætʃɪŋ] *adj* a juego, que combina bien.

mate [meɪt] ◇ *n* **-1.** *inf* [friend] amigo *m*, -ga *f*, compañero *m*, -ra *f*. **-2.** *Br inf* [term of address] colega *m* y *f*. **-3.** [of animal] macho *m*, hembra *f*. **-4.** NAUT: **(first) ~** (primer) oficial *m*. ◇ *vi* [animals]: **to ~ (with)** aparearse (con).

material [mə'tɪərɪəl] ◇ *adj* **-1.** [physical] material. **-2.** [important] sustancial. ◇ *n* **-1.** [substance] material *m*. **-2.** [type of substance] materia *f*. **-3.** [fabric] tela *f*, tejido *m*. **-4.** [type of fabric] tejido *m*. **-5.** (*U*) [ideas, information] información *f*, documentación *f*. ◆ **materials** *npl*: **building ~s** materiales *mpl* de construcción; **writing ~s** objetos *mpl* de es-

critorio; **cleaning ~s** productos *mpl* de limpieza.

materialistic [mə,tɪərɪə'lɪstɪk] *adj* materialista.

maternal [mə'tɜːnl] *adj* [gen] maternal; [grandparent] materno(na).

maternity [mə'tɜːnətɪ] *n* maternidad *f*.

maternity dress *n* vestido *m* premamá.

maternity hospital *n* hospital *m* de maternidad.

math *Am* = **maths**.

mathematical [,mæθə'mætɪkl] *adj* matemático(ca).

mathematics [,mæθə'mætɪks] *n* (*U*) matemáticas *fpl*.

maths *Br* [mæθs], **math** *Am* [mæθ] (*abbr of* **mathematics**) *inf n* (*U*) mates *fpl*.

matinée ['mætɪneɪ] *n* [at cinema] primera sesión *f*; [at theatre] función *f* de tarde.

mating season ['meɪtɪŋ-] *n* época *f* de celo.

matrices ['meɪtrɪsiːz] *pl* → **matrix**.

matriculation [mə,trɪkjʊ'leɪʃn] *n* matrícula *f*.

matrimonial [,mætrɪ'məʊnjəl] *adj* matrimonial.

matrimony ['mætrɪmənɪ] *n* (*U*) matrimonio *m*.

matrix ['meɪtrɪks] (*pl* **matrices** OR **-es**) *n* matriz *f*.

matron ['meɪtrən] *n* **-1.** *Br* [in hospital] enfermera *f* jefa. **-2.** [in school] ama *f* de llaves.

matronly ['meɪtrənlɪ] *adj* *euphemism* corpulenta y de edad madura.

matt *Br*, **matte** *Am* [mæt] *adj* mate.

matted ['mætɪd] *adj* enmarañado(da).

matter ['mætəʳ] ◇ *n* **-1.** [question, situation] asunto *m*; **that's another** OR **a different ~** es otra cuestión OR cosa; **as a ~ of course** automáticamente; **to make ~s worse** para colmo de desgracias; **a ~ of opinion** una cuestión de opiniones. **-2.** [trouble, cause of pain]: **what's the ~ (with it/her)?** ¿qué (le) pasa?; **something's the ~ with my car** algo le pasa a mi coche. **-3.** PHYSICS materia *f*. **-4.** (*U*) [material] material *m*. ◇ *vi* [be important] importar; **it doesn't ~** no importa. ◆ **as a matter of fact** *adv* en realidad. ◆ **for that matter** *adv* de hecho. ◆ **no matter** *adv*: **no ~ how hard I try** por mucho que lo intente; **no ~ what he does** haga lo que haga; **we must win, no ~ what** tenemos que ganar como sea.

Matterhorn ['mætə,hɔːn] *n*: **the ~** el monte Cervino.

matter-of-fact *adj* pragmático(ca).

mattress ['mætrɪs] *n* colchón *m*.

mature [mə'tjʊəʳ] ◇ *adj* [person, wine] maduro(ra); [cheese] **curado(da).** ◇ *vi* madurar.

mature student *n* Br UNIV estudiante *m* y *f* en edad adulta.

maul [mɔːl] *vt* [savage] herir gravemente.

mauve [məʊv] *adj* malva.

max. [mæks] (*abbr of* **maximum**) máx.

maxim ['mæksɪm] (*pl* **-s**) *n* máxima *f*.

maximum ['mæksɪməm] (*pl* **maxima** OR **-s**) ◇ *adj* máximo(ma). ◇ *n* máximo *m*.

may [meɪ] *modal vb* poder; **the coast ~ be seen** se puede ver la costa; **you ~ like it** puede OR es posible que te guste; **I ~ come, I ~ not** puede que venga, puede que no; **it ~ be done in two different ways** puede hacerse de dos maneras (distintas); **~ I come in?** ¿se puede (pasar)?; **~ I?** ¿me permite?; **it ~ be cheap, but it's good** puede que sea barato, pero es bueno; **~ all your dreams come true!** ¡que todos tus sueños se hagan realidad!; **be that as it ~** aunque así sea; **come what ~** pase lo que pase; *see also* **might**.

May [meɪ] *n* mayo *m*; *see also* **September**.

maybe ['meɪbɪ] *adv* **-1.** [perhaps] quizás, tal vez; **~ she'll come tal vez venga. -2.** [approximately] más o menos.

May Day *n* Primero *m* de Mayo.

mayhem ['meɪhem] *n* alboroto *m*.

mayonnaise [,meɪə'neɪz] *n* mayonesa *f*.

mayor [meəʳ] *n* alcalde *m*, -esa *f*.

mayoress ['meərɪs] *n* alcaldesa *f*.

maze [meɪz] *n* lit & fig laberinto *m*.

MB (*abbr of* **megabyte**) MB *m*.

MD *n abbr of* **managing director**.

me [miː] *pers pron* **-1.** (*direct, indirect*) me; **can you see/hear ~?** ¿me ves/ oyes?; **it's ~** soy yo; **they spoke to ~** hablaron conmigo; **she gave it to ~** me lo dio; **give it to ~!** ¡dámelo! **-2.** (*stressed*): **you can't expect** ME **to do it** no esperarás que YO lo haga. **-3.** (*after prep*): mí; **they went with/without ~** fueron conmigo/sin mí. **-4.** (*in comparisons*) yo; **she's shorter than ~** (ella) es más baja que yo.

meadow ['medəʊ] *n* prado *m*, pradera *f*.

meagre Br, **meager** Am ['miːgəʳ] *adj* miserable, escaso(sa).

meal [miːl] *n* comida *f*.

mealtime ['miːltaɪm] *n* hora *f* de la comida.

mean [miːn] (*pt & pp* **meant**) ◇ *vt* **-1.** [signify] significar, querer decir; **it ~s nothing to me** no significa nada para mí. **-2.** [have in mind] querer decir, referirse a; **what do you ~?** ¿qué quieres decir?; **to ~ to do sthg** tener la intención de OR querer hacer algo; **to be meant for** estar destinado(da) a; **to be meant to do sthg** deber hacer algo; **that's not meant to be there** esto no debería estar allí; **it was meant to be a joke** era solamente una broma; **to ~ well** tener buenas intenciones. **-3.** [be serious about]: **I ~ it** hablo OR lo digo en serio. **-4.** [be important, matter] significar. **-5.** [entail] suponer, implicar. **-6.** *phr*: **I ~** quiero decir, o sea. ◇ *adj* **-1.** [miserly] tacaño(ña). **-2.** [unkind] mezquino(na), malo(la); **to be ~ to sb** ser malo con alguien. **-3.** [average] medio(dia). ◇ *n* [average] promedio *m*, media *f*; *see also* **means**.

meander [mɪ'ændəʳ] *vi* **-1.** [river, road] serpentear. **-2.** [walk aimlessly] vagar; [write, speak aimlessly] divagar.

meaning ['miːnɪŋ] *n* **-1.** [sense - of a word etc] significado *m*. **-2.** [significance] intención *f*, sentido *m*. **-3.** [purpose, point] propósito *m*, razón *f* de ser.

meaningful ['miːnɪŋfʊl] *adj* **-1.** [expressive] significativo(va). **-2.** [profound] profundo(da).

meaningless ['miːnɪŋlɪs] *adj* **-1.** [without meaning, purpose] sin sentido. **-2.** [irrelevant, unimportant] irrelevante.

means [miːnz] ◇ *n* [method, way] medio *m*; **we have no ~ of doing it** no tenemos manera de hacerlo; **by ~ of** por medio de. ◇ *npl* [money] recursos *mpl*. ◆ **by all means** *adv* por supuesto. ◆ **by no means** *adv fml* en absoluto.

meant [ment] *pt & pp* → **mean**.

meantime ['miːn,taɪm] *n*: **in the ~** mientras tanto.

meanwhile ['miːn,waɪl] *adv* mientras tanto, entre tanto.

measles ['miːzlz] *n*: **(the) ~** sarampión *m*.

measly ['miːzlɪ] *adj inf* raquítico(ca).

measure ['meʒəʳ] ◇ *n* **-1.** [step, action] medida *f*. **-2.** [of alcohol] medida *f*. **-3.** [indication, sign]: **a ~ of** una muestra de. ◇ *vt* [object] medir; [damage, impact etc] determinar, juzgar. ◇ *vi* medir.

measurement ['meʒəmənt] *n* medida *f*.

meat [miːt] *n* carne *f*; **cold ~** fiambre *m*.

meatball ['miːtbɔːl] *n* albóndiga *f*.

meat pie *n Br* pastel *m* de carne.

meaty ['miːtɪ] *adj fig* sustancioso(sa).

Mecca ['mekə] *n* GEOGR La Meca; *fig* meca *f*.

mechanic [mɪ'kænɪk] *n* mecánico *m*, -ca *f*. ◆ **mechanics** ◇ *n* (U) [study] mecánica *f*. ◇ *npl fig* mecanismos *mpl*.

mechanical [mɪ'kænɪkl] *adj* [worked by machinery, routine] mecánico(ca).

mechanism ['mekənɪzm] *n lit & fig* mecanismo *m*.

medal ['medl] *n* medalla *f*.

medallion [mɪ'dæljən] *n* medallón *m*.

meddle ['medl] *vi*: **to ~ (in)** entrometerse OR interferir (en); **to ~ with sthg** manosear algo.

media ['miːdjə] ◇ *pl* → **medium**. ◇ *n or npl*: **the ~** los medios de comunicación.

mediaeval [ˌmedɪ'iːvl] = **medieval**.

median ['miːdjən] ◇ *adj* mediano(na). ◇ *n Am* [of road] mediana *f*.

mediate ['miːdɪeɪt] *vi*: **to ~ (for/between)** mediar (por/entre).

mediator ['miːdɪeɪtə'] *n* mediador *m*, -ra *f*.

Medicaid ['medɪkeɪd] *n Am* sistema estatal de ayuda médica.

medical ['medɪkl] ◇ *adj* médico(ca). ◇ *n* reconocimiento *m* médico.

Medicare ['medɪkeə'] *n Am* ayuda médica estatal para ancianos.

medicated ['medɪkeɪtɪd] *adj* medicinal.

medicine ['medsɪn] *n* -1. [treatment of illness] medicina *f*; **Doctor of Medicine** UNIV doctor *m*, -ra *f* en medicina. -2. [substance] medicina *f*, medicamento *m*.

medieval [ˌmedɪ'iːvl] *adj* medieval.

mediocre [ˌmiːdɪ'əukə'] *adj* mediocre.

meditate ['medɪteɪt] *vi*: **to ~ (on** OR **upon)** meditar OR reflexionar (sobre).

Mediterranean [ˌmedɪtə'reɪnjən] ◇ *n* [sea]: **the ~ (Sea)** el (mar) Mediterráneo. ◇ *adj* mediterráneo(a).

medium ['miːdjəm] (*pl sense 1* **media**, *pl sense 2* **mediums**) ◇ *adj* mediano(na). ◇ *n* -1. [way of communicating] medio *m*. -2. [spiritualist] médium *m y f*.

medium-sized [-saɪzd] *adj* de tamaño mediano.

medium wave *n* onda *f* media.

medley ['medlɪ] (*pl* **medleys**) *n* -1. [mixture] mezcla *f*. -2. [selection of music] popurrí *m*.

meek [miːk] *adj* sumiso(sa), dócil.

meet [miːt] (*pt & pp* **met**) ◇ *vt* -1. [by chance] encontrarse con; [for first time, come across] conocer; [by arrangement, for a purpose] reunirse con. -2. [go to meet - person] ir/venir a buscar. -3. [need, demand] satisfacer. -4. [deal with - problem, challenge] hacer frente a. -5. [costs, debts] pagar. -6. [experience - problem, situation] encontrarse con. -7. [hit, touch] darse OR chocar contra. -8. [join] juntarse OR unirse con. ◇ *vi* -1. [by chance] encontrarse; [by arrangement] verse; [for a purpose] reunirse. -2. [get to know sb] conocerse. -3. [hit in collision] chocar; [touch] tocar. -4. [eyes] cruzarse. -5. [join - roads etc] juntarse. ◇ *n Am* [meeting] encuentro *m*. ◆ **meet up** *vi*: **to ~ up (with sb)** quedarse en verse (con alguien). ◆ **meet with** *vt fus* -1. [refusal, disappointment] recibir; **to ~ with success** tener éxito; **to ~ with failure** fracasar. -2. *Am* [by arrangement] reunirse con.

meeting ['miːtɪŋ] *n* -1. [for discussions, business] reunión *f*. -2. [by chance, in sport] encuentro *m*; [by arrangement] cita *f*; [formal] entrevista *f*.

megabyte ['megəbaɪt] *n* COMPUT megaocteto *m*.

megaphone ['megəfəun] *n* megáfono *m*.

melancholy ['melənkəlɪ] ◇ *adj* melancólico(ca). ◇ *n* melancolía *f*.

mellow ['meləu] ◇ *adj* [sound, colour, light] suave; [wine] añejo(ja). ◇ *vi* suavizarse; [person] ablandarse.

melody ['melədɪ] *n* melodía *f*.

melon ['melən] *n* melón *m*.

melt [melt] ◇ *vt* -1. [make liquid] derretir. -2. *fig* [soften] ablandar. ◇ *vi* -1. [become liquid] derretirse. -2. *fig* [soften] ablandarse. -3. [disappear]: **to ~ away** [savings] esfumarse; [anger] desvanecerse. ◆ **melt down** *vt sep* fundir.

meltdown ['meltdaun] *n* -1. [act of melting] fusión *f*. -2. [incident] fuga *f* radiactiva.

melting pot ['meltɪŋ-] *n fig* crisol *m*.

member ['membə'] *n* -1. [of social group] miembro *m y f*. -2. [of party, union] afiliado *m*, -da *f*, miembro *m y f*; [of organization, club] socio *m*, -cia *f*.

Member of Congress (*pl* **Members of Congress**) *n* miembro *m y f* del Congreso (*de los Estados Unidos*).

Member of Parliament (*pl* **Members of Parliament**) *n Br* diputado *m*, -da *f* (*del parlamento británico*).

membership ['membəʃɪp] n **-1.** [of party, union] afiliación f; [of club] calidad f de miembro OR socio. **-2.** [number of members] número m de socios. **-3.** [people themselves]: **the ~** [of organization] los miembros; [of club] los socios.

membership card n carnet m de socio, -cia f.

memento [mɪ'mentəu] (pl -s) n recuerdo m.

memo ['meməu] (pl -s) n memorándum m.

memoirs ['memwɑːz] npl memorias fpl.

memorandum [,memə'rændəm] (pl -da [-də] OR -dums) n fml memorándum m.

memorial [mɪ'mɔːrɪəl] ◇ adj conmemorativo(va). ◇ n monumento m conmemorativo.

memorize, -ise ['meməraɪz] vt memorizar, aprender de memoria.

memory ['memərɪ] n **-1.** [faculty, of computer] memoria f. **-2.** [thing or things remembered] recuerdo m; **from ~** de memoria.

men [men] pl → **man.**

menace ['menəs] ◇ n **-1.** [threat] amenaza f; [danger] peligro m. **-2.** inf [nuisance, pest] pesadez f. ◇ vt amenazar.

menacing ['menəsɪŋ] adj amenazador(ra).

mend [mend] ◇ n inf: **to be on the ~** ir recuperándose. ◇ vt [shoes, toy] arreglar; [socks] zurcir; [clothes] remendar.

menial ['miːnjəl] adj servil, bajo(ja).

meningitis [,menɪn'dʒaɪtɪs] n (U) meningitis f.

menopause ['menəpɔːz] n: **the ~** la menopausia.

men's room n Am: **the ~** los servicios de caballeros.

menstruation [,menstru'eɪʃn] n menstruación f.

menswear ['menzweər] n ropa f de caballeros.

mental ['mentl] adj mental.

mental hospital n hospital m psiquiátrico.

mentality [men'tælətɪ] n mentalidad f.

mentally handicapped ['mentəlɪ-] npl: **the ~** los disminuidos psíquicos.

mention ['menʃn] ◇ vt: **to ~ sthg (to)** mencionar algo (a); **not to ~** sin mencionar; **don't ~ it!** ¡de nada!, ¡no hay de qué! ◇ n mención f.

menu ['menjuː] n **-1.** [in restaurant] carta f. **-2.** COMPUT menú m.

meow Am = miaow.

MEP (abbr of **Member of the European Parliament**) n eurodiputado m, -da f.

mercenary ['mɜːsɪnrɪ] ◇ adj mercenario(ria). ◇ n mercenario m, -ria f.

merchandise ['mɜːtʃəndaɪz] n (U) mercancías fpl, géneros mpl.

merchant ['mɜːtʃənt] ◇ adj [seaman, ship] mercante. ◇ n comerciante m y f.

merchant bank n Br banco m comercial.

merchant navy Br, **merchant marine** Am n marina f mercante.

merciful ['mɜːsɪful] adj **-1.** [showing mercy] compasivo(va). **-2.** [fortunate] afortunado(da).

merciless ['mɜːsɪlɪs] adj despiadado(da).

mercury ['mɜːkjurɪ] n mercurio m.

Mercury ['mɜːkjurɪ] n Mercurio m.

mercy ['mɜːsɪ] n **-1.** [kindness, pity] compasión f, misericordia f; **at the ~ of** fig a merced de. **-2.** [blessing] suerte f.

mere [mɪər] adj simple, mero(ra); **she's a ~ child** no es más que una niña.

merely ['mɪəlɪ] adv simplemente, sólo.

merge [mɜːdʒ] ◇ vt **-1.** [gen] mezclar. **-2.** COMM & COMPUT fusionar. ◇ vi **-1.** [join, combine]: **to ~ (with)** [company] fusionarse (con); [roads, branches] unirse OR convergir (con). **-2.** [blend - colours] fundirse; **to ~ into** confundirse con.

merger ['mɜːdʒər] n fusión f.

meringue [mə'ræŋ] n merengue m.

merit ['merɪt] ◇ n mérito m. ◇ vt merecer, ser digno(na) de. ◆ **merits** npl ventajas fpl.

mermaid ['mɜːmeɪd] n sirena f.

merry ['merɪ] adj **-1.** literary [gen] alegre. **-2.** [party] animado(da); **Merry Christmas!** ¡feliz Navidad! **-3.** inf [tipsy] achispado(da).

merry-go-round n tiovivo m.

mesh [meʃ] ◇ n malla f. ◇ vi encajar.

mesmerize, -ise ['mezməraɪz] vt: **to be ~d (by)** estar fascinado(da) (por).

mess [mes] n **-1.** [untidy state] desorden m. **-2.** [muddle, problematic situation] lío m. **-3.** MIL [room] comedor m; [food] rancho m. ◆ **mess about, mess around** inf ◇ vt sep fastidiar. ◇ vi **-1.** [waste time] pasar el rato; [fool around] hacer el tonto. **-2.** [interfere]: **to ~ about with sthg** manosear algo. ◆ **mess up** vt sep inf **-1.** [clothes] ensuciar; [room] desordenar. **-2.** [plan, evening] echar a perder.

message ['mesɪdʒ] n -1. [piece of information] recado m, mensaje m. -2. [of book etc] mensaje m.

messenger ['mesɪndʒər] n mensajero m, -ra f.

Messrs, Messrs. ['mesəz] (abbr of messieurs) Sres.

messy ['mesɪ] adj [dirty] sucio(cia), desordenado(da).

met [met] pt & pp → meet.

metal ['metl] ◇ n metal m. ◇ comp de metal, metálico(ca).

metallic [mɪ'tælɪk] adj -1. [gen] metálico(ca). -2. [paint, finish] metalizado(da).

metalwork ['metəlwɜːk] n [craft] metalistería f.

metaphor ['metəfər] n metáfora f.

mete [miːt] ◆ **mete out** vt sep: to ~ sthg out to sb imponer algo a alguien.

meteor ['miːtɪər] n bólido m.

meteorology [,miːtjə'rɒlədʒɪ] n meteorología f.

meter ['miːtər] n -1. [device] contador m. -2. Am = metre.

method ['meθəd] n método m.

methodical [mɪ'θɒdɪkl] adj metódico(ca).

Methodist ['meθədɪst] ◇ adj metodista. ◇ n metodista m y f.

meths [meθs] n Br inf alcohol m metilado OR desnaturalizado.

methylated spirits ['meθɪleɪtɪd-] n alcohol m metilado OR desnaturalizado.

meticulous [mɪ'tɪkjʊləs] adj meticuloso(sa), minucioso(sa).

metre Br, **meter** Am ['miːtər] n metro m.

metric ['metrɪk] adj métrico(ca).

metronome ['metrənəʊm] n metrónomo m.

metropolitan [,metrə'pɒlɪtn] adj [of a metropolis] metropolitano(na).

Metropolitan Police npl policía de Londres.

mettle ['metl] n: to be on one's ~ estar dispuesto(ta) a hacer lo mejor posible; to show OR prove one's ~ mostrar el valor de uno.

mew [mjuː] = miaow.

mews [mjuːz] (pl inv) n Br callejuela de antiguas caballerizas convertidas en viviendas de lujo.

Mexican ['meksɪkn] ◇ adj mejicano(na). ◇ n mejicano m, -na f.

Mexico ['meksɪkəʊ] n Méjico m.

MI5 (abbr of Military Intelligence 5) n organismo británico de contraespionaje.

MI6 (abbr of Military Intelligence 6) n organismo británico de espionaje.

miaow Br [miːˈaʊ], **meow** Am [mɪ'aʊ] ◇ n maullido m. ◇ vi maullar.

mice [maɪs] pl → mouse.

mickey ['mɪkɪ] n: to take the ~ out of sb Br inf tomar el pelo a alguien.

microchip ['maɪkrəʊtʃɪp] n COMPUT microchip m.

microcomputer [,maɪkrəʊkəm'pjuːtər] n microordenador m.

microfilm ['maɪkrəʊfɪlm] n microfilm m.

microphone ['maɪkrəfəʊn] n micrófono m.

microscope ['maɪkrəskəʊp] n microscopio m.

microscopic [,maɪkrə'skɒpɪk] adj lit & fig microscópico(ca).

microwave (oven) ['maɪkrəweɪv-] n (horno m) microondas m inv.

mid- [mɪd] prefix medio(dia); (in) ~morning a media mañana; (in) ~August a mediados de agosto; (in) ~winter en pleno invierno; she's in her ~twenties tiene unos 25 años.

midair [mɪd'eər] n: in ~ en el aire.

midday ['mɪddeɪ] n mediodía m.

middle ['mɪdl] ◇ adj [gen] del medio. ◇ n -1. [of room, town etc] medio m, centro m; in the ~ of the month/the 19th century a mediados del mes/del siglo XIX; to be in the ~ of doing sthg estar haciendo algo; in the ~ of the night en plena noche. -2. [waist] cintura f.

middle-aged adj de mediana edad.

Middle Ages npl: the ~ la Edad Media.

middle-class adj de clase media.

middle classes npl: the ~ la clase media.

Middle East n: the ~ el Oriente Medio.

middleman ['mɪdlmæn] (pl -men [-men]) n intermediario m.

middle name n segundo nombre m (en un nombre compuesto).

middleweight ['mɪdlweɪt] n peso m medio.

middling ['mɪdlɪŋ] adj regular, mediano(na).

Mideast [,mɪd'iːst] n Am: the ~ el Oriente Medio.

midfield [,mɪd'fiːld] n FTBL medio campo m.

midge [mɪdʒ] n (tipo m de) mosquito m.

midget ['mɪdʒɪt] n enano m, -na f.

midi system ['mɪdɪ-] n minicadena f.

Midlands ['mɪdləndz] *npl*: **the** ~ *la región central de Inglaterra*.

midnight ['mɪdnaɪt] *n* medianoche *f*.

midriff ['mɪdrɪf] *n* diafragma *m*.

midst [mɪdst] *n* -1. [in space]: **in the** ~ **of** *literary* en medio de. -2. [in time]: **in the** ~ **of** en medio de.

midsummer ['mɪd,sʌmə'] *n* pleno verano *m*.

Midsummer Day *n* Día *m* de San Juan (*24 de junio*).

midway [,mɪd'weɪ] *adv* -1. [in space]: ~ **(between)** a medio camino (entre). -2. [in time]: ~ **(through)** a la mitad (de).

midweek [*adj* mɪd'wi:k, *adv* 'mɪdwi:k] ◇ *adj* de entre semana. ◇ *adv* entre semana.

midwife ['mɪdwaɪf] (*pl* -**wives** [-waɪvz]) *n* comadrona *f*.

midwifery ['mɪd,wɪfərɪ] *n* obstetricia *f*.

might [maɪt] ◇ *modal vb* -1. [expressing possibility]: **he** ~ **be armed** podría estar armado; **I** ~ **do it** puede que OR quizás lo haga; **we** ~ **have been killed, had we not been careful** si no hubiéramos tenido cuidado, podríamos haber muerto. -2. [expressing suggestion]: **you** ~ **have told me!** ¡podrías habérmelo dicho!; **it** ~ **be better to wait** quizás sea mejor esperar. -3. *fml* [asking permission]: **he asked if he** ~ **leave the room** pidió permiso para salir. -4. [expressing concession]: **you** ~ **well be right, but ...** puede que tengas razón, pero .... -5. *phr*: **I** ~ **have known** OR **guessed** podría haberlo sospechado. ◇ *n* (U) fuerza *f*, poder *m*.

mighty ['maɪtɪ] ◇ *adj* [strong] fuerte; [powerful] poderoso(sa). ◇ *adv* muy.

migraine ['miːgreɪn, 'maɪgreɪn] *n* jaqueca *f*.

migrant ['maɪgrənt] ◇ *adj* -1. [bird, animal] migratorio(ria). -2. [workers] emigrante. ◇ *n* [person] emigrante *m y f*.

migrate [*Br* maɪ'greɪt, *Am* 'maɪgreɪt] *vi* emigrar.

mike [maɪk] (*abbr of* **microphone**) *n inf* micro *m*.

mild [maɪld] *adj* -1. [taste, disinfectant, wind] suave; [effect, surprise, illness] leve. -2. [person, nature] apacible; [tone of voice] sereno(na). -3. [climate] templado(da).

mildew ['mɪldjuː] *n* [gen] moho *m*; [on plants] añublo *m*.

mildly ['maɪldlɪ] *adv* -1. [gen] ligeramente, levemente; **to put it** ~ por no decir más. -2. [talk] suavemente.

mile [maɪl] *n* milla *f*; **to be** ~**s away** *fig* estar en la luna.

mileage ['maɪlɪdʒ] *n* distancia *f* en millas.

mileometer [maɪ'lɒmɪtə'] *n* cuentamillas *m inv*, ≃ cuentakilómetros *m inv*.

milestone ['maɪlstəʊn] *n* -1. [marker stone] mojón *m*. -2. *fig* [event] hito *m*.

militant ['mɪlɪtənt] ◇ *adj* militante. ◇ *n* militante *m y f*.

military ['mɪlɪtrɪ] ◇ *adj* militar. ◇ *n*: **the** ~ los militares.

militia [mɪ'lɪʃə] *n* milicia *f*.

milk [mɪlk] ◇ *n* leche *f*. ◇ *vt* -1. [cow etc] ordeñar. -2. [use to own ends] sacar todo el jugo a; **they** ~**ed him for every penny he had** le chuparon hasta el último centavo.

milk chocolate *n* chocolate *m* con leche.

milkman ['mɪlkmən] (*pl* -**men** [-mən]) *n* lechero *m*.

milk shake *n* batido *m*.

milky ['mɪlkɪ] *adj* -1. *Br* [with milk] con mucha leche. -2. [pale white] lechoso(sa).

Milky Way *n*: **the** ~ la Vía Láctea.

mill [mɪl] ◇ *n* -1. [flour-mill] molino *m*. -2. [factory] fábrica *f*. -3. [grinder] molinillo *m*. ◇ *vt* moler. ◆ **mill about, mill around** *vi* arremolinarse.

millennium [mɪ'lenɪəm] (*pl* -**nnia** [-nɪə]) *n* milenio *m*.

miller ['mɪlə'] *n* molinero *m*, -ra *f*.

millet ['mɪlɪt] *n* mijo *m*.

milligram(me) ['mɪlɪgræm] *n* miligramo *m*.

millimetre *Br*, **millimeter** *Am* ['mɪlɪ,miːtə'] *n* milímetro *m*.

millinery ['mɪlɪnrɪ] *n* sombrerería *f* (de señoras).

million ['mɪljən] *n* millón *m*; **a** ~, ~**s of** *fig* millones de.

millionaire [,mɪljə'neə'] *n* millonario *m*.

millstone ['mɪlstəʊn] *n* piedra *f* de molino, muela *f*.

milometer [maɪ'lɒmɪtə'] = **mileometer**.

mime [maɪm] ◇ *n* [acting] mímica *f*. ◇ *vt* describir con gestos. ◇ *vi* hacer mímica.

mimic ['mɪmɪk] (*pt & pp* -**ked**, *cont* -**king**) ◇ *n* imitador *m*, -ra *f*. ◇ *vt* imitar.

mimicry ['mɪmɪkrɪ] *n* imitación *f*.

min. [mɪn] -1. (*abbr of* **minute**) min. -2. (*abbr of* **minimum**) mín.

mince [mɪns] ◇ *n Br* carne *f* picada. ◇ *vt* picar. ◇ *vi* andar dando pasitos.

mincemeat ['mɪnsmiːt] n **-1.** [fruit] mezcla de fruta confitada y especias. **-2.** Am [minced meat] carne f picada.

mince pie n pastelillo m de fruta confitada.

mincer ['mɪnsər] n máquina f de picar carne.

mind [maɪnd] ◇ n **-1.** [gen] mente f; state of ~ estado m de ánimo; to come into OR to cross sb's ~ pasársele a alguien por la cabeza; to have sthg on one's ~ estar preocupado por algo; to keep an open ~ tener una actitud abierta; to take sb's ~ off sthg hacer olvidar algo a alguien; to make one's ~ up decidirse. **-2.** [attention] atención f; to put one's ~ to sthg poner empeño en algo. **-3.** [opinion]: to change one's ~ cambiar de opinión; to my ~ en mi opinión; to be in two ~s about sthg no estar seguro(ra) de algo; to speak one's ~ hablar sin rodeos. **-4.** [memory] memoria f; to bear sthg in ~ tener presente algo. **-5.** [intention]: to have sthg in ~ tener algo en mente; to have a ~ to do sthg estar pensando en hacer algo. ◇ vi [be bothered]: do you ~? ¿te importa?; I don't ~ ... no me importa ...; never ~ [don't worry] no te preocupes; [it's not important] no importa. ◇ vt **-1.** [be bothered about, dislike]: do you ~ if I leave? ¿te molesta si me voy?; I don't ~ waiting no me importa esperar; I wouldn't ~ a ... no me vendría mal un .... **-2.** [pay attention to] tener cuidado con. **-3.** [take care of] cuidar. ◆ **mind you** adv: he's a bit deaf; ~ you, he is old está un poco sordo; te advierto que es ya mayor.

minder ['maɪndər] n Br inf [bodyguard] guardaespaldas m y f.

mindful ['maɪndful] adj: ~ of consciente de.

mindless ['maɪndlɪs] adj **-1.** [stupid] absurdo(da), sin sentido. **-2.** [not requiring thought] aburrido(da).

mine[1] [maɪn] poss pron mío (mía); that money is ~ ese dinero es mío; his car hit ~ su coche chocó contra el mío; it wasn't your fault, it was MINE la culpa no fue tuya sino MÍA; a friend of ~ un amigo mío.

mine[2] [maɪn] ◇ n mina f. ◇ vt **-1.** [excavate - coal] extraer. **-2.** [lay mines in] minar.

minefield ['maɪnfiːld] n lit & fig campo m de minas.

miner ['maɪnər] n minero m, -ra f.

mineral ['mɪnərəl] ◇ adj mineral. ◇ n mineral m.

mineral water n agua f mineral.

minesweeper ['maɪn,swiːpər] n dragaminas m inv.

mingle ['mɪŋgl] vi **-1.** [combine]: to ~ (with) mezclarse (con). **-2.** [socially]: to ~ (with) alternar (con).

miniature ['mɪnətʃər] ◇ adj en miniatura. ◇ n **-1.** [painting] miniatura f. **-2.** [of alcohol] botellín de licor en miniatura.

minibus ['mɪnɪbʌs] (pl -es) n microbús m.

minicab ['mɪnɪkæb] n Br taxi que se puede pedir por teléfono, pero no se puede parar en la calle.

minima ['mɪnɪmə] pl → minimum.

minimal ['mɪnɪml] adj mínimo(ma).

minimum ['mɪnɪməm] (pl -mums OR -ma) ◇ adj mínimo(ma). ◇ n mínimo m.

mining ['maɪnɪŋ] ◇ n minería f. ◇ adj minero(ra).

miniskirt ['mɪnɪskɜːt] n minifalda f.

minister ['mɪnɪstər] n **-1.** POL: ~ (for) ministro m, -tra f (de). **-2.** RELIG pastor m, -ra f. ◆ **minister to** vt fus atender a.

ministerial [,mɪnɪ'stɪərɪəl] adj ministerial.

minister of state n: ~ (for) ministro m, -tra f de estado (para).

ministry ['mɪnɪstrɪ] n **-1.** POL ministerio m. **-2.** RELIG: the ~ el clero.

mink [mɪŋk] (pl inv) n visón m.

minnow ['mɪnəu] n pececillo m (de agua dulce).

minor ['maɪnər] ◇ adj menor. ◇ n menor m y f (de edad).

Minorca [mɪ'nɔːkə] n Menorca f.

minority [maɪ'nɒrətɪ] n minoría f.

mint [mɪnt] ◇ n **-1.** [herb] menta f, hierbabuena f. **-2.** [peppermint] pastilla f de menta. **-3.** [for coins]: the ~ la Casa de la Moneda; in ~ condition en perfecto estado, como nuevo(va). ◇ vt acuñar.

minus ['maɪnəs] (pl -es) ◇ prep **-1.** MATH [less]: 4 ~ 2 is 2 4 menos 2 es 2. **-2.** [in temperatures]: it's ~ 5°C estamos a 5° bajo cero. ◇ n **-1.** MATH signo m (de) menos. **-2.** [disadvantage] pega f, desventaja f.

minus sign n signo m (de) menos.

minute[1] ['mɪnɪt] n minuto m; at any ~ en cualquier momento; this ~ ahora mismo. ◆ **minutes** npl acta f; to take ~s levantar OR tomar acta.

minute[2] [maɪ'njuːt] adj diminuto(ta).

miracle ['mɪrəkl] *n lit & fig* milagro *m*.

miraculous [mɪ'rækjʊləs] *adj* milagroso(sa).

mirage [mɪ'rɑːʒ] *n lit & fig* espejismo *m*.

mire [maɪəʳ] *n* fango *m*, lodo *m*.

mirror ['mɪrəʳ] ◇ *n* espejo *m*. ◇ *vt* reflejar.

mirth [mɜːθ] *n* risa *f*.

misadventure [,mɪsəd'ventʃəʳ] *n* desgracia *f*; **death by ~** JUR muerte *f* accidental.

misapprehension ['mɪs,æprɪ'henʃn] *n* **-1.** [misunderstanding] malentendido *m*. **-2.** [mistaken belief] creencia *f* errónea.

misappropriation ['mɪsə,prəʊprɪ'eɪʃn] *n*: **~ (of)** malversación *f* (de).

misbehave [,mɪsbɪ'heɪv] *vi* portarse mal.

miscalculate [,mɪs'kælkjʊleɪt] *vt & vi* calcular mal.

miscarriage [,mɪs'kærɪdʒ] *n* [at birth] aborto *m* (natural).

miscarriage of justice *n* error *m* judicial.

miscellaneous [,mɪsə'leɪnjəs] *adj* diverso(sa).

mischief ['mɪstʃɪf] *n* (*U*) **-1.** [playfulness] picardía *f*. **-2.** [naughty behaviour] travesuras *fpl*. **-3.** [harm] daño *m*.

mischievous ['mɪstʃɪvəs] *adj* **-1.** [playful] lleno(na) de picardía. **-2.** [naughty] travieso(sa).

misconception [,mɪskən'sepʃn] *n* concepto *m* erróneo.

misconduct [,mɪs'kɒndʌkt] *n* mala conducta *f*.

misconstrue [,mɪskən'struː] *vt fml* malinterpretar.

miscount [,mɪs'kaʊnt] *vt & vi* contar mal.

misdeed [,mɪs'diːd] *n literary* fechoría *f*.

misdemeanour *Br*, **misdemeanor** *Am* [,mɪsdɪ'miːnəʳ] *n fml* delito *m* menor.

miser ['maɪzəʳ] *n* avaro *m*, -ra *f*.

miserable ['mɪzrəbl] *adj* **-1.** [unhappy] infeliz, triste. **-2.** [wretched, poor] miserable. **-3.** [weather] horrible. **-4.** [pathetic] lamentable.

miserly ['maɪzəlɪ] *adj* miserable, mezquino(na).

misery ['mɪzərɪ] *n* **-1.** [unhappiness] desdicha *f*. **-2.** [wretchedness] miseria *f*.

misfire [,mɪs'faɪəʳ] *vi* **-1.** [car engine] no arrancar. **-2.** [plan] fracasar.

misfit ['mɪsfɪt] *n* inadaptado *m*, -da *f*.

misfortune [mɪs'fɔːtʃuːn] *n* **-1.** [bad luck]

mala suerte *f*. **-2.** [piece of bad luck] desgracia *f*, infortunio *m*.

misgivings [mɪs'gɪvɪŋz] *npl* recelos *mpl*.

misguided [,mɪs'gaɪdɪd] *adj* [person] descaminado(da); [attempt] equivocado(da).

mishandle [,mɪs'hændl] *vt* **-1.** [person, animal] maltratar. **-2.** [affair] llevar mal.

mishap ['mɪshæp] *n* contratiempo *m*.

misinterpret [,mɪsɪn'tɜːprɪt] *vt* malinterpretar.

misjudge [,mɪs'dʒʌdʒ] *vt* **-1.** [guess wrongly] calcular mal. **-2.** [appraise wrongly] juzgar mal.

mislay [,mɪs'leɪ] (*pt & pp* **-laid**) *vt* extraviar, perder.

mislead [,mɪs'liːd] (*pt & pp* **-led**) *vt* engañar.

misleading [,mɪs'liːdɪŋ] *adj* engañoso(sa).

misled [,mɪs'led] *pt & pp* → **mislead**.

misnomer [,mɪs'nəʊməʳ] *n* término *m* equivocado.

misplace [,mɪs'pleɪs] *vt* extraviar.

misprint ['mɪsprɪnt] *n* errata *f*, error *m* de imprenta.

miss [mɪs] ◇ *vt* **-1.** [fail to see - TV programme, film] perderse; [- error, person in crowd] no ver. **-2.** [shot] fallar; [ball] no dar a. **-3.** [feel absence of] echar de menos OR en falta. **-4.** [opportunity] perder, dejar pasar; [turning] pasarse. **-5.** [train, bus] perder. **-6.** [appointment] faltar a. **-7.** [avoid] evitar. ◇ *vi* fallar. ◇ *n*: **to give sthg a ~** *inf* pasar de algo. ◆ **miss out** ◇ *vt sep* pasar por alto. ◇ *vi*: **to ~ out (on sthg)** perderse (algo).

Miss [mɪs] *n* señorita *f*.

misshapen [,mɪs'ʃeɪpn] *adj* deforme.

missile [*Br* 'mɪsaɪl, *Am* 'mɪsəl] *n* **-1.** [weapon] misil *m*. **-2.** [thrown object] proyectil *m*.

missing ['mɪsɪŋ] *adj* **-1.** [lost] perdido(da), extraviado(da). **-2.** [not present] que falta; **to be ~** faltar.

mission ['mɪʃn] *n* misión *f*.

missionary ['mɪʃənrɪ] *n* misionero *m*, -ra *f*.

misspend [,mɪs'spend] (*pt & pp* **-spent**) *vt* malgastar.

mist [mɪst] *n* [gen] neblina *f*; [at sea] bruma *f*. ◆ **mist over**, **mist up** *vi* [windows, spectacles] empañarse; [eyes] llenarse de lágrimas.

mistake [mɪ'steɪk] (*pt* **-took**, *pp* **-taken**) ◇ *n* error *m*; **to make a ~** equivocarse, cometer un error; **by ~** por error. ◇ *vt* **-1.** [misunderstand] entender mal. **-2.**

[fail to recognize]: **to ~ sthg/sb for** confundir algo/a alguien con.
mistaken [mɪ'steɪkn] ◇ *pp* → **mistake**. ◇ *adj* equivocado(da); **to be ~ about** sb/sthg estar equivocado respecto a alguien/algo.
mister ['mɪstər] *n inf* amigo *m*. ◆ **Mister** *n* señor *m*.
mistletoe ['mɪsltəu] *n* muérdago *m*.
mistook [mɪ'stuk] *pt* → **mistake**.
mistreat [ˌmɪs'triːt] *vt* maltratar.
mistress ['mɪstrɪs] *n* **-1.** [woman in control] señora *f*. **-2.** [female lover] amante *f*. **-3.** *Br* [school teacher - primary] maestra *f*; [- secondary] profesora *f*.
mistrust [ˌmɪs'trʌst] ◇ *n* desconfianza *f*, recelo *m*. ◇ *vt* desconfiar de.
misty ['mɪstɪ] *adj* [gen] neblinoso(sa); [at sea] brumoso(sa).
misunderstand [ˌmɪsʌndə'stænd] (*pt & pp* **-stood**) *vt & vi* entender OR comprender mal.
misunderstanding [ˌmɪsʌndə'stændɪŋ] *n* malentendido *m*.
misunderstood [ˌmɪsʌndə'stud] *pt & pp* → **misunderstand**.
misuse [*n* ˌmɪs'juːs, *vb* ˌmɪs'juːz] ◇ *n* uso *m* indebido. ◇ *vt* hacer uso indebido de.
miter *Am* = **mitre**.
mitigate ['mɪtɪgeɪt] *vt fml* mitigar.
mitre *Br*, **miter** *Am* ['maɪtər] *n* [hat] mitra *f*.
mitt [mɪt] *n* manopla *f*.
mitten ['mɪtn] *n* manopla *f*.
mix [mɪks] ◇ *vt*: **to ~ sthg (with)** mezclar algo (con). ◇ *vi* **-1.** [substances] mezclarse; [activities] ir bien juntos(tas). **-2.** [socially]: **to ~ with** alternar OR salir con. ◇ *n* mezcla *f*. ◆ **mix up** *vt sep* **-1.** [confuse] confundir. **-2.** [disorder] mezclar.
mixed [mɪkst] *adj* **-1.** [of different kinds] surtido(da), variado(da). **-2.** [of different sexes] mixto(ta).
mixed-ability *adj Br* de varios niveles.
mixed grill *n* parrillada *f* mixta.
mixed up *adj* **-1.** [confused] confuso(sa). **-2.** [involved]: **~ in** [fight, crime] involucrado(da) en.
mixer ['mɪksər] *n* **-1.** [for food] batidora *f*; [for cement] hormigonera *f*. **-2.** [non-alcoholic drink] *bebida no alcohólica para mezclar con bebidas alcohólicas*.
mixture ['mɪkstʃər] *n* [gen] mezcla *f*; [of sweets] surtido *m*.
mix-up *n inf* lío *m*, confusión *f*.
mm (*abbr of* millimetre) mm.

moan [məun] ◇ *n* [of pain, sadness] gemido *m*. ◇ *vi* **-1.** [in pain, sadness] gemir. **-2.** *inf* [complain]: **to ~ (about)** quejarse (de).
moat [məut] *n* foso *m*.
mob [mɒb] ◇ *n* muchedumbre *f*. ◇ *vt* asediar.
mobile ['məubaɪl] ◇ *adj* [able to move] móvil. ◇ *n* móvil *m*.
mobile home *n* caravana *f*.
mobile phone *n* teléfono *m* portátil.
mobilize, -ise ['məubɪlaɪz] *vt* movilizar.
mock [mɒk] ◇ *adj* fingido(da); **~ (exam)** simulacro *m* de examen. ◇ *vt* burlarse de. ◇ *vi* burlarse.
mockery ['mɒkərɪ] *n* burla *f*.
mod cons [ˌmɒd-] (*abbr of* **modern conveniences**) *npl Br inf*: **all ~** con todas las comodidades.
mode [məud] *n* modo *m*.
model ['mɒdl] ◇ *n* **-1.** [gen] modelo *m*. **-2.** [small copy] maqueta *f*. **-3.** [for painter, in fashion] modelo *m y f*. ◇ *adj* **-1.** [exemplary] modelo (*inv*). **-2.** [reduced-scale] en miniatura. **-3.** [shape] modelar. **-2.** [wear] lucir (*en pase de modelos*). **-3.** [copy]: **to ~ o.s. on sb** tener a alguien como modelo. ◇ *vi* trabajar de modelo.
modem ['məudem] *n* COMPUT módem *m*.
moderate [*adj & n* 'mɒdərət, *vb* 'mɒdəreɪt] ◇ *adj* moderado(da). ◇ *n* POL moderado *m*, -da *f*. ◇ *vt* moderar. ◇ *vi* moderarse.
moderation [ˌmɒdə'reɪʃn] *n* moderación *f*; **in ~** con moderación.
modern ['mɒdən] *adj* moderno(na).
modernize, -ise ['mɒdənaɪz] ◇ *vt* modernizar. ◇ *vi* modernizarse.
modern languages *npl* lenguas *fpl* modernas.
modest ['mɒdɪst] *adj* **-1.** [gen] modesto(ta). **-2.** [improvement] ligero(ra); [price] módico(ca).
modesty ['mɒdɪstɪ] *n* modestia *f*.
modicum ['mɒdɪkəm] *n fml*: **a ~ of** un mínimo de.
modify ['mɒdɪfaɪ] *vt* modificar.
module ['mɒdjuːl] *n* módulo *m*.
mogul ['məugl] *n* magnate *m y f*.
mohair ['məuheər] *n* mohair *m*.
moist [mɔɪst] *adj* húmedo(da).
moisten ['mɔɪsn] *vt* humedecer.
moisture ['mɔɪstʃər] *n* humedad *f*.
moisturizer ['mɔɪstʃəraɪzər] *n* (crema *f*) hidratante *m*.
molar ['məulər] *n* muela *f*.
molasses [mə'læsɪz] *n* (*U*) melaza *f*.

mold *etc Am* = mould.

mole [məʊl] *n* -1. [animal, spy] topo *m*. -2. [spot] lunar *m*.

molecule ['mɒlɪkjuːl] *n* molécula *f*.

molest [mə'lest] *vt* -1. [attack sexually] acosar sexualmente. -2. [attack] atacar.

mollusc, mollusk *Am* ['mɒləsk] *n* molusco *m*.

mollycoddle ['mɒlɪ,kɒdl] *vt inf* mimar.

molt *Am* = moult.

molten ['məʊltn] *adj* fundido(da).

mom [mɒm] *n Am inf* mamá *f*.

moment ['məʊmənt] *n* momento *m*; **at any** ~ de un momento a otro; **at the** ~ en este momento; **for the** ~ de momento.

momentarily ['məʊməntərɪlɪ] *adv* -1. [for a short time] momentáneamente. -2. *Am* [soon] pronto.

momentary ['məʊməntrɪ] *adj* momentáneo(a).

momentous [mə'mentəs] *adj* trascendental.

momentum [mə'mentəm] *n* (*U*) -1. PHYSICS momento *m*. -2. *fig* [speed, force] ímpetu *m*, impulso *m*; **to gather** ~ cobrar intensidad.

momma ['mɒmə], **mommy** ['mɒmɪ] *n Am* mamá *f*.

Monaco ['mɒnəkəʊ] *n* Mónaco.

monarch ['mɒnək] *n* monarca *m y f*.

monarchy ['mɒnəkɪ] *n* -1. [gen] monarquía *f*. -2. [royal family]: **the** ~ la familia real.

monastery ['mɒnəstrɪ] *n* monasterio *m*.

Monday ['mʌndɪ] *n* lunes *m inv*; *see also* **Saturday**.

monetary ['mʌnɪtrɪ] *adj* monetario(ria).

money ['mʌnɪ] *n* dinero *m*; **to make** ~ hacer dinero; **to get one's** ~**'s worth** sacarle provecho al dinero de uno.

moneybox ['mʌnɪbɒks] *n* hucha *f*.

moneylender ['mʌnɪ,lendər] *n* prestamista *m y f*.

money order *n* giro *m* postal.

money-spinner [-,spɪnər] *n inf* mina *f* (de dinero).

mongol ['mɒŋgəl] *dated & offensive n* mongólico *m*, -ca *f*.

Mongolia [mɒŋ'gəʊlɪə] *n* Mongolia.

mongrel ['mʌŋgrəl] *n* perro *m* cruzado OR sin pedigrí.

monitor ['mɒnɪtər] ◇ *n* [gen & COMPUT] monitor *m*. ◇ *vt* -1. [check] controlar. -2. [listen in to] escuchar.

monk [mʌŋk] *n* monje *m*.

monkey ['mʌŋkɪ] (*pl* **monkeys**) *n* mono *m*.

monkey nut *n* cacahuete *m*.

monkey wrench *n* llave *f* inglesa.

mono ['mɒnəʊ] *adj* mono (*inv*).

monochrome ['mɒnəkrəʊm] *adj* monocromo(ma).

monocle ['mɒnəkl] *n* monóculo *m*.

monologue, monolog *Am* ['mɒnəlɒg] *n* monólogo *m*.

monopolize, -ise [mə'nɒpəlaɪz] *vt* monopolizar.

monopoly [mə'nɒpəlɪ] *n*: ~ **(on** OR **of)** monopolio *m* (de).

monotone ['mɒnətəʊn] *n*: **in a** ~ con voz monótona.

monotonous [mə'nɒtənəs] *adj* monótono(na).

monotony [mə'nɒtənɪ] *n* monotonía *f*.

monsoon [mɒn'suːn] *n* monzón *m*.

monster ['mɒnstər] *n* [imaginary creature, cruel person] monstruo *m*.

monstrosity [mɒn'strɒsətɪ] *n* monstruosidad *f*.

monstrous ['mɒnstrəs] *adj* -1. [very unfair, frightening, ugly] monstruoso(sa). -2. [very large] gigantesco(ca).

Mont Blanc [mɔ̃blɑ̃] *n* Mont Blanc.

month [mʌnθ] *n* mes *m*.

monthly ['mʌnθlɪ] (*pl* **-ies**) ◇ *adj* mensual. ◇ *adv* mensualmente.

monument ['mɒnjumənt] *n* monumento *m*.

monumental [,mɒnjʊ'mentl] *adj* -1. [gen] monumental. -2. [error] descomunal.

moo [muː] (*pl* **-s**) *vi* mugir.

mood [muːd] *n* [of individual] humor *m*; [of public, voters] disposición *f*; **in a (bad)** ~ de mal humor; **in a good** ~ de buen humor.

moody ['muːdɪ] *adj pej* -1. [changeable] de humor variable. -2. [bad-tempered] malhumorado(da).

moon [muːn] *n* luna *f*.

moonlight ['muːnlaɪt] *n* luz *f* de la luna.

moonlighting ['muːnlaɪtɪŋ] *n* pluriempleo *m*.

moonlit ['muːnlɪt] *adj* [night] de luna; [landscape] iluminado(da) por la luna.

moor [mɔːr] ◇ *n* páramo *m*. ◇ *vt* amarrar. ◇ *vi* echar las amarras.

Moor [mɔːr] *n* moro *m*, -ra *f*.

Moorish ['mɔːrɪʃ] *adj* moro(ra), morisco(ca).

moorland ['mɔːlənd] *n* páramo *m*, brezal *m*.

moose [muːs] (*pl inv*) *n* [North American] alce *m*.

mop [mɒp] ◇ *n* **-1.** [for cleaning] fregona *f*. **-2.** *inf* [of hair] pelambrera *f*. ◇ *vt* **-1.** [clean with mop] pasar la fregona por. **-2.** [dry with cloth - sweat] enjugar. ◆ **mop up** *vt sep* [clean up] limpiar.

mope [məup] *vi pej* estar deprimido(da).

moped ['məuped] *n* ciclomotor *m*, motoneta *f Amer*.

moral ['mɒrəl] ◇ *adj* moral. ◇ *n* [lesson] moraleja *f*. ◆ **morals** *npl* [principles] moral *f*.

morale [mə'rɑːl] *n* (*U*) moral *f*.

morality [mə'rælətɪ] *n* **-1.** [gen] moralidad *f*. **-2.** [system of principles] moral *f*.

morass [mə'ræs] *n* cenagal *m*.

morbid ['mɔːbɪd] *adj* morboso(sa).

more [mɔːʳ] ◇ *adv* **-1.** (*with adjectives and adverbs*) más; ~ **important (than)** más importante (que); ~ **quickly/often (than)** más rápido/a menudo (que). **-2.** [to a greater degree] más; **we were ~ hurt than angry** más que enfadados estábamos heridos. **-3.** [another time]: **once/twice ~** una vez/dos veces más. ◇ *adj* más; ~ **food than drink** más comida que bebida; ~ **than 70 people died** más de 70 personas murieron; **have some ~ tea** toma un poco más de té; **I finished two ~ chapters today** acabé otros dos capítulos hoy. ◇ *pron* más; ~ **than five** más de cinco; **he's got ~ than I have** él tiene más que yo; **there's no ~ (left)** no queda nada (más); **(and) what's ~** (y lo que) es más. ◆ **any more** *adv*: **not ... any ~** ya no .... ◆ **more and more** *adv, adj & pron* cada vez más. ◆ **more or less** *adv* más o menos.

moreover [mɔː'rəuvəʳ] *adv fml* además.

morgue [mɔːg] *n* depósito *m* de cadáveres.

Mormon ['mɔːmən] *n* mormón *m*, -ona *f*.

morning ['mɔːnɪŋ] *n* **-1.** [first part of day] mañana *f*; **in the ~** por la mañana; **six o'clock in the ~** las seis de la mañana. **-2.** [between midnight and dawn] madrugada *f*. **-3.** [tomorrow morning]: **in the ~** mañana por la mañana. ◆ **mornings** *adv Am* por la mañana.

Moroccan [mə'rɒkən] ◇ *adj* marroquí. ◇ *n* marroquí *m y f*.

Morocco [mə'rɒkəu] *n* Marruecos.

moron ['mɔːrɒn] *n inf* imbécil *m y f*.

morose [mə'rəus] *adj* malhumorado(da).

morphine ['mɔːfiːn] *n* morfina *f*.

Morse (code) [mɔːs-] *n* (alfabeto *m*) Morse *m*.

morsel ['mɔːsl] *n* bocado *m*.

mortal ['mɔːtl] ◇ *adj* [gen] mortal. ◇ *n* mortal *m y f*.

mortality [mɔː'tælətɪ] *n* mortalidad *f*.

mortar ['mɔːtəʳ] *n* **-1.** [cement mixture] argamasa *f*. **-2.** [gun, bowl] mortero *m*.

mortgage ['mɔːgɪdʒ] ◇ *n* hipoteca *f*. ◇ *vt* hipotecar.

mortified ['mɔːtɪfaɪd] *adj* muerto(ta) de vergüenza.

mortuary ['mɔːtʃuərɪ] *n* depósito *m* de cadáveres.

mosaic [mə'zeɪɪk] *n* mosaico *m*.

Moscow ['mɒskəu] *n* Moscú.

Moslem ['mɒzləm] = Muslim.

mosque [mɒsk] *n* mezquita *f*.

mosquito [mə'skiːtəu] (*pl* -es OR -s) *n* mosquito *m*, zancudo *m Amer*.

moss [mɒs] *n* musgo *m*.

most [məust] (*superl of* many) ◇ *adj* **-1.** [the majority of] la mayoría de; ~ **people** la mayoría de la gente. **-2.** [largest amount of]: **(the) ~** más; **who has got (the) ~ money?** ¿quién es el que tiene más dinero? ◇ *pron* **-1.** [the majority]: ~ **(of)** la mayoría (de); ~ **of the time** la mayor parte del tiempo. **-2.** [largest amount]: **(the) ~** lo más, lo máximo; **at ~** como mucho, todo lo más. **-3.** *phr*: **to make the ~ of sthg** sacarle el mayor partido a algo. ◇ *adv* **-1.** [to the greatest extent] ◇ **the ~** el/la/lo más; **what I like ~** lo que más me gusta. **-2.** *fml* [very] muy; ~ **certainly** con toda seguridad. **-3.** *Am* [almost] casi.

mostly ['məustlɪ] *adv* [in the main part] principalmente; [usually] normalmente.

MOT (*abbr of* **Ministry of Transport test**) *n* ≈ ITV *f*.

motel [məu'tel] *n* motel *m*.

moth [mɒθ] *n* polilla *f*.

mothball ['mɒθbɔːl] *n* bola *f* de naftalina.

mother ['mʌðəʳ] ◇ *n* madre *f*. ◇ *vt usu pej* [spoil] mimar.

motherhood ['mʌðəhud] *n* maternidad *f*.

mother-in-law (*pl* **mothers-in-law** OR **mother-in-laws**) *n* suegra *f*.

motherly ['mʌðəlɪ] *adj* maternal.

mother-of-pearl *n* nácar *m*.

mother-to-be (*pl* **mothers-to-be**) *n* futura madre *f*.

mother tongue *n* lengua *f* materna.

motif [məʊˈtiːf] *n* ART & MUS motivo *m*.

motion [ˈməʊʃn] ◇ *n* **-1.** [gen] movimiento *m*; **to set sthg in ~** poner algo en marcha. **-2.** [proposal] moción *f*. ◇ *vt*: **to ~ sb to do sthg** indicar a alguien con un gesto que haga algo. ◇ *vi*: **to ~ to sb** hacer una señal (con la mano) a alguien.

motionless [ˈməʊʃənlɪs] *adj* inmóvil.

motion picture *n Am* película *f*.

motivated [ˈməʊtɪveɪtɪd] *adj* motivado(da).

motivation [ˌməʊtɪˈveɪʃn] *n* motivación *f*.

motive [ˈməʊtɪv] *n* [gen] motivo *m*; [for crime] móvil *m*.

motley [ˈmɒtlɪ] *adj pej* variopinto(ta).

motor [ˈməʊtəʳ] ◇ *adj Br* [industry, accident] automovilístico(ca); [mechanic] de automóviles. ◇ *n* motor *m*.

motorbike [ˈməʊtəbaɪk] *n inf* moto *f*.

motorboat [ˈməʊtəbəʊt] *n* lancha *f* motora.

motorcar [ˈməʊtəkɑːʳ] *n* automóvil *m*.

motorcycle [ˈməʊtəˌsaɪkl] *n* motocicleta *f*.

motorcyclist [ˈməʊtəˌsaɪklɪst] *n* motociclista *m y f*.

motoring [ˈməʊtərɪŋ] *n dated* automovilismo *m*.

motorist [ˈməʊtərɪst] *n* automovilista *m y f*, conductor *m*, -ra *f*.

motor racing *n* automovilismo *m* deportivo.

motor scooter *n* Vespa® *f*, escúter *m*.

motor vehicle *n* vehículo *m* de motor.

motorway [ˈməʊtəweɪ] *Br n* autopista *f*.

mottled [ˈmɒtld] *adj* moteado(da).

motto [ˈmɒtəʊ] (*pl* **-s** OR **-es**) *n* lema *m*.

mould, mold *Am* [məʊld] ◇ *n* **-1.** [growth] moho *m*. **-2.** [shape] molde *m*. ◇ *vt lit* & *fig* moldear.

moulding, molding *Am* [ˈməʊldɪŋ] *n* [decoration] moldura *f*.

mouldy, moldy *Am* [ˈməʊldɪ] *adj* mohoso(sa).

moult, molt *Am* [məʊlt] *vi* [bird] mudar la pluma; [dog] mudar el pelo.

mound [maʊnd] *n* **-1.** [small hill] montículo *m*. **-2.** [untidy pile] montón *m*.

mount [maʊnt] ◇ *n* **-1.** [gen] montura *f*; [for photograph] marco *m*; [for jewel] engaste *m*. **-2.** [mountain] monte *m*. ◇ *vt* **-1.** [horse, bike] subirse a, montar en. **-2.** [attack] lanzar. **-3.** [exhibition] montar. **-4.** [jewel] engastar; [photograph] enmarcar. ◇ *vi* [increase] aumentar.

mountain [ˈmaʊntɪn] *n lit* & *fig* montaña *f*.

mountain bike *n* bicicleta *f* de montaña.

mountaineer [ˌmaʊntɪˈnɪəʳ] *n* montañero *m*, -ra *f*, andinista *m y f* Amer.

mountaineering [ˌmaʊntɪˈnɪərɪŋ] *n* montañismo *m*, andinismo *m* Amer.

mountainous [ˈmaʊntɪnəs] *adj* montañoso(sa).

mourn [mɔːn] ◇ *vt* [person] llorar por; [thing] lamentarse de. ◇ *vi* afligirse; **to ~ for sb** llorar la muerte de alguien.

mourner [ˈmɔːnəʳ] *n* doliente *m y f*.

mournful [ˈmɔːnfʊl] *adj* [face, voice] afligido(da), lúgubre; [sound] lastimero(ra).

mourning [ˈmɔːnɪŋ] *n* luto *m*; **in ~** de luto.

mouse [maʊs] (*pl* **mice**) *n* ZOOL & COMPUT ratón *m*.

mousetrap [ˈmaʊstræp] *n* ratonera *f*.

mousse [muːs] *n* **-1.** [food] mousse *m*. **-2.** [for hair] espuma *f*.

moustache *Br* [məˈstɑːʃ], **mustache** *Am* [ˈmʌstæʃ] *n* bigote *m*.

mouth [maʊθ] *n* [gen] boca *f*; [of river] desembocadura *f*.

mouthful [ˈmaʊθfʊl] *n* [of food] bocado *m*; [of drink] trago *m*.

mouthorgan [ˈmaʊθˌɔːgən] *n* armónica *f*.

mouthpiece [ˈmaʊθpiːs] *n* **-1.** [of telephone] micrófono *m*. **-2.** [of musical instrument] boquilla *f*. **-3.** [spokesperson] portavoz *m y f*.

mouthwash [ˈmaʊθwɒʃ] *n* elixir *m* bucal.

mouth-watering [-ˌwɔːtərɪŋ] *adj* muy apetitoso(sa).

movable [ˈmuːvəbl] *adj* movible.

move [muːv] ◇ *n* **-1.** [movement] movimiento *m*; **to get a ~ on** *inf* espabilarse, darse prisa. **-2.** [change - of house] mudanza *f*; [- of job] cambio *m*. **-3.** [in board game] jugada *f*. **-4.** [course of action] medida *f*. ◇ *vt* **-1.** [shift] mover. **-2.** [change - house] mudarse de; [- job] cambiar de. **-3.** [affect] conmover. **-4.** [in debate - motion] proponer. **-5.** [cause]: **to ~ sb to do sthg** mover OR llevar a alguien a hacer algo. ◇ *vi* **-1.** [gen] moverse; [events] cambiar. **-2.** [change house] mudarse; [change job] cambiar de trabajo. ◆ **move about** *vi* **-1.** [fidget] ir de aquí para allá. **-2.** [travel] viajar. ◆ **move along** ◇ *vt sep*

hacer circular. ◇ *vi* **-1.** [move towards front or back] hacerse a un lado. **-2.** [move away - crowd, car] circular.
◆ **move around** = **move about**.
◆ **move away** *vi* [leave] marcharse.
◆ **move in** ◇ *vi* **-1.** [to new house] instalarse. **-2.** [take control, attack] prepararse para el ataque. ◆ **move on** ◇ *vi* **-1.** [go away] reanudar la marcha. **-2.** [progress] avanzar. ◆ **move out** ◇ *vi* mudarse. ◆ **move over** *vi* hacer sitio.
◆ **move up** *vi* [on bench etc] hacer sitio.

moveable = **movable**.

movement ['mu:vmənt] *n* **-1.** [gen] movimiento *m*. **-2.** [transportation] transporte *m*.

movie ['mu:vi] *n* película *f*.

movie camera *n* cámara *f* cinematográfica.

moving ['mu:vɪŋ] *adj* **-1.** [touching] conmovedor(ra). **-2.** [not fixed] móvil.
◆ **mow down** *vt sep* acribillar.

mow [məʊ] (*pt* **-ed**, *pp* **-ed** OR **mown**) *vt* [grass, lawn] cortar; [corn] segar.
◆ **mow down** *vt sep* acribillar.

mower ['məʊəʳ] *n* cortacésped *m o f*.

mown [məʊn] *pp* → **mow**.

MP *n* **-1.** (*abbr of* **Military Police**) PM *f*. **-2.** *Br abbr of* **Member of Parliament**.

mpg (*abbr of* **miles per gallon**) millas/galón.

mph (*abbr of* **miles per hour**) mph.

Mr ['mɪstəʳ] *n* Sr.; ~ **Jones** el Sr. Jones.

Mrs ['mɪsɪz] *n* Sra.; ~ **Jones** la Sra. Jones.

Ms [mɪz] *n* abreviatura utilizada delante de un apellido de mujer cuando no se quiere especificar si está casada o no.

MS, ms *n abbr of* **multiple sclerosis**.

MSc (*abbr of* **Master of Science**) *n* (titular de un) título postuniversitario de unos dos años de duración en el campo de las ciencias.

much [mʌtʃ] (*compar* **more**, *superl* **most**) ◇ *adj* mucho(cha); **there isn't** ~ **rice left** no queda mucho arroz; **as** ~ **time as** ... tanto tiempo como ...; **how** ~ **money?** ¿cuánto dinero?; **so** ~ tanto(ta); **too** ~ demasiado(da); **how** ...? ¿cuánto(ta) ...? ◇ *pron*: **have you got** ~? ¿tienes mucho?; **I don't see** ~ **of him** no lo veo mucho; **I don't think** ~ **of it** no me parece gran cosa; **as** ~ **as** tanto como; **too** ~ demasiado; **how** ~? ¿cuánto?; **this isn't** ~ **of a party** esta fiesta no es nada del otro mundo; **so** ~ **for** tanto con; **I thought as** ~ ya me lo imaginaba. ◇ *adv* mucho; **I don't go out** ~ no salgo mucho; ~ **too**

cold demasiado frío; **so** ~ tanto; **thank you very** ~ muchas gracias; **as** ~ **as** tanto como; **he is not so** ~ **stupid as** **lazy** más que tonto es vago; **too** ~ demasiado; **without so** ~ **as** ... sin siquiera .... ◆ **much as** *conj*: ~ **as (I like him)** por mucho OR más que (me guste).

muck [mʌk] *n inf* (U) **-1.** [dirt] mugre *f*, porquería *f*. **-2.** [manure] estiércol *m*.
◆ **muck about, muck around** *Br inf vi* hacer el indio OR tonto. ◆ **muck up** *vt sep inf Br* fastidiar.

mucky ['mʌkɪ] *adj* guarro(rra).

mucus ['mju:kəs] *n* mucosidad *f*.

mud [mʌd] *n* barro *m*, lodo *m*.

muddle ['mʌdl] ◇ *n* **-1.** [disorder] desorden *m*. **-2.** [confusion] lío *m*, confusión *f*; **to be in a** ~ estar hecho un lío. ◇ *vt* **-1.** [put into disorder] desordenar. **-2.** [confuse] liar, confundir. ◆ **muddle along** *vi* apañárselas más o menos.
◆ **muddle through** *vi* arreglárselas.
◆ **muddle up** *vt sep* [put into disorder] desordenar; [confuse] liar, confundir.

muddy ['mʌdɪ] *adj* [gen] lleno(na) de barro; [river] cenagoso(sa).

mudguard ['mʌdgɑ:d] *n* guardabarros *m inv*, tapabarro *m Amer*.

mudslinging ['mʌd,slɪŋɪŋ] *n* (U) *fig* insultos *mpl*, improperios *mpl*.

muesli ['mju:zlɪ] *n Br* muesli *m*.

muff [mʌf] ◇ *n* manguito *m*. ◇ *vt inf* [catch] fallar; [chance] dejar escapar.

muffin ['mʌfɪn] *n* **-1.** *Br* [bread roll] panecillo *m*. **-2.** *Am* [cake] especie de magdalena que se come caliente.

muffle ['mʌfl] *vt* [sound] amortiguar.

muffler ['mʌfləʳ] *n Am* [for car] silenciador *m*.

mug [mʌg] ◇ *n* **-1.** [cup] taza *f* (alta). **-2.** *inf* [fool] primo *m*, -ma *f*. ◇ *vt* asaltar, atracar.

mugging ['mʌgɪŋ] *n* [single attack] atraco *m*; [series of attacks] atracos *mpl*.

muggy ['mʌgɪ] *adj* bochornoso(sa).

mule [mju:l] *n* mula *f*.

mull [mʌl] ◆ **mull over** *vt sep* reflexionar sobre.

mulled [mʌld] *adj*: ~ **wine** vino caliente con azúcar y especias.

multicoloured *Br*, **multicolored** *Am* [,mʌltɪ'kʌləd] *adj* multicolor.

multilateral [,mʌltɪ'lætərəl] *adj* multilateral.

multinational [,mʌltɪ'næʃənl] *n* multinacional *f*.

multiple ['mʌltɪpl] ◇ *adj* múltiple. ◇ *n* múltiplo *m*.

multiple sclerosis [-sklɪ'rəusɪs] n esclerosis f inv múltiple.

multiplex cinema ['mʌltɪpleks-] (cine m) multisalas m inv.

multiplication [ˌmʌltɪplɪ'keɪʃn] n multiplicación f.

multiply ['mʌltɪplaɪ] ◇ vt multiplicar. ◇ vi [increase, breed] multiplicarse.

multistorey Br, **multistory** Am [ˌmʌltɪ'stɔːrɪ] adj de varias plantas.

multitude ['mʌltɪtjuːd] n multitud f.

mum [mʌm] Br inf ◇ n mamá f. ◇ adj: to keep ~ no decir ni pío.

mumble ['mʌmbl] ◇ vt mascullar. ◇ vi musitar, hablar entre dientes.

mummy ['mʌmɪ] n -1. Br inf [mother] mamá f. -2. [preserved body] momia f.

mumps [mʌmps] n (U) paperas fpl.

munch [mʌntʃ] vt & vi masticar.

mundane [mʌn'deɪn] adj trivial.

municipal [mjuː'nɪsɪpl] adj municipal.

municipality [mjuːˌnɪsɪ'pælətɪ] n municipio m.

mural ['mjuːərəl] n mural m.

murder ['mɜːdər] ◇ n asesinato m. ◇ vt asesinar.

murderer ['mɜːdərər] n asesino m.

murderous ['mɜːdərəs] adj asesino(na).

murky ['mɜːkɪ] adj -1. [water, past] turbio(bia). -2. [night, street] sombrío(a), lúgubre.

murmur ['mɜːmər] ◇ n [low sound] murmullo m. ◇ vt & vi murmurar.

muscle ['mʌsl] n -1. MED músculo m. -2. fig [power] poder m. ♦ **muscle in** vi entrometerse.

muscular ['mʌskjʊlər] adj -1. [of muscles] muscular. -2. [strong] musculoso(sa).

muse [mjuːz] ◇ n musa f. ◇ vi meditar.

museum [mjuː'ziːəm] n museo m.

mushroom ['mʌʃrʊm] ◇ n BOT seta f, hongo m; CULIN champiñón m. ◇ vi extenderse rápidamente.

music ['mjuːzɪk] n música f.

musical ['mjuːzɪkl] ◇ adj -1. [gen] musical. -2. [talented in music] con talento para la música. ◇ n musical m.

musical instrument n instrumento m musical.

music centre n cadena f (musical).

music hall n Br teatro m de variedades OR de revista.

musician [mjuː'zɪʃn] n músico m, -ca f.

Muslim ['mʊzlɪm] ◇ adj musulmán(ana). ◇ n musulmán m, -ana f.

muslin ['mʌzlɪn] n muselina f.

mussel ['mʌsl] n mejillón m.

must [mʌst] ◇ aux vb -1. [have to, intend to] deber, tener que; I ~ go tengo que OR debo irme. -2. [as suggestion] tener que; you ~ come and see us tienes que venir a vernos. -3. [to express likelihood] deber (de); it ~ be true debe (de) ser verdad; they ~ have known deben de haberlo sabido. ◇ n inf: a ~ algo imprescindible.

mustache Am = moustache.

mustard ['mʌstəd] n mostaza f.

muster ['mʌstər] vt reunir.

mustn't ['mʌsnt] = must not.

must've ['mʌstəv] = must have.

musty ['mʌstɪ] adj [room] que huele a cerrado; [book] que huele a viejo.

mute [mjuːt] ◇ adj mudo(da). ◇ n mudo m, -da f.

muted ['mjuːtɪd] adj -1. [not bright] apagado(da). -2. [subdued] contenido(da).

mutilate ['mjuːtɪleɪt] vt mutilar.

mutiny ['mjuːtɪnɪ] ◇ n motín m. ◇ vi amotinarse.

mutter ['mʌtər] ◇ vt musitar, mascullar. ◇ vi murmurar.

mutton ['mʌtn] n (carne f de) cordero m.

mutual ['mjuːtʃʊəl] adj -1. [reciprocal] mutuo(tua). -2. [common] común.

mutually ['mjuːtʃʊəlɪ] adv mutuamente.

muzzle ['mʌzl] ◇ n -1. [animal's nose and jaws] hocico m, morro m. -2. [wire guard] bozal m. -3. [of gun] boca f. ◇ vt [put muzzle on] poner bozal a.

MW (abbr of medium wave) OM f.

my [maɪ] poss adj -1. [gen] mi, mis (pl); ~ house/sister mi casa/hermana; ~ children mis hijos; ~ name is Sarah me llamo Sarah; it wasn't MY fault no fue culpa mía OR mi culpa; I washed ~ hair me lavé el pelo. -2. [in titles]: ~ Lord milord; ~ Lady milady.

myriad ['mɪrɪəd] literary adj innumerables.

myself [maɪ'self] pron -1. (reflexive) me; (after prep) mí mismo(ma); with ~ conmigo mismo. -2. (for emphasis) yo mismo(ma); I did it ~ lo hice yo solo(la).

mysterious [mɪ'stɪərɪəs] adj misterioso(sa).

mystery ['mɪstərɪ] n misterio m.

mystical ['mɪstɪkl] adj místico(ca).

mystified ['mɪstɪfaɪd] adj desconcertado(da), perplejo(ja).

mystifying ['mɪstɪfaɪɪŋ] *adj* desconcertante.

mystique [mɪ'stiːk] *n* misterio *m*.

myth [mɪθ] *n* mito *m*.

mythical ['mɪθɪkl] *adj* **-1.** [imaginary] mítico(ca). **-2.** [untrue] falso(sa).

mythology [mɪ'θɒlədʒɪ] *n* [collection of myths] mitología *f*.

N

n (*pl* **n's** OR **ns**), **N** (*pl* **N's** OR **Ns**) [en] *n* [letter] n *f*, N *f*. ◆ **N** (*abbr of* **north**) N.

n/a, N/A (*abbr of* **not applicable**) no interesa.

nab [næb] *vt inf* **-1.** [arrest] pillar, echar el guante a. **-2.** [get quickly] coger.

nag [næg] *vt* dar la lata a.

nagging ['nægɪŋ] *adj* **-1.** [thought, doubt] persistente. **-2.** [person] gruñón(ona).

nail [neɪl] ◇ *n* **-1.** [for fastening] clavo *m*. **-2.** [of finger, toe] uña *f*. ◇ *vt*: **to ~ sthg to sthg** clavar algo en OR a algo. ◆ **nail down** *vt sep* **-1.** [fasten] clavar. **-2.** [person]: **I couldn't ~ him down** no pude hacerle concretar.

nailbrush ['neɪlbrʌʃ] *n* cepillo *m* de uñas.

nail file *n* lima *f* de uñas.

nail polish *n* esmalte *m* para las uñas.

nail scissors *npl* tijeras *fpl* para las uñas.

nail varnish *n* esmalte *m* para las uñas.

nail varnish remover [-rɪ'muːvər] *n* quitaesmaltes *m inv*.

naive, naïve [naɪ'iːv] *adj* ingenuo(nua).

naked ['neɪkɪd] *adj* **-1.** [gen] desnudo(da); **~ flame** llama *f* sin protección. **-2.** [blatant - hostility, greed] abierto(ta); [- facts] sin tapujos. **-3.** [unaided]: **with the ~ eye** a simple vista.

name [neɪm] ◇ *n* [gen] nombre *m*; [surname] apellido *m*; **what's your ~?** ¿cómo te llamas?; **my ~ is John** me llamo John; **by ~** por el nombre; **in sb's ~** a nombre de alguien; **in the ~ of** en nombre de; **to call sb ~s** llamar de todo a alguien. ◇ *vt* **-1.** [christen] poner nombre a; **to ~ sb after sb** *Br*, **to ~ sb for sb** *Am* poner a alguien el

nombre de alguien. **-2.** [identify] nombrar. **-3.** [date, price] poner, decir. **-4.** [appoint] nombrar.

nameless ['neɪmlɪs] *adj* [unknown - person, author] anónimo(ma); [- disease] desconocido(da).

namely ['neɪmlɪ] *adv* a saber.

namesake ['neɪmseɪk] *n* tocayo *m*, -ya *f*.

nanny ['nænɪ] *n* niñera *f*.

nap [næp] ◇ *n* siesta *f*. ◇ *vi*: **we were caught napping** *inf* nos pilló desprevenidos.

nape [neɪp] *n*: **~ of the neck** nuca *f*.

napkin ['næpkɪn] *n* servilleta *f*.

nappy ['næpɪ] *n Br* pañal *m*.

nappy liner *n parte desechable de un pañal de gasa.*

narcissi [nɑː'sɪsaɪ] *pl* → **narcissus**.

narcissus [nɑː'sɪsəs] (*pl* **-cissuses** OR **-cissi**) *n* narciso *m*.

narcotic [nɑː'kɒtɪk] *n* narcótico *m*.

narrative ['nærətɪv] ◇ *adj* narrativo(va). ◇ *n* **-1.** [account] narración *f*. **-2.** [art of narrating] narrativa *f*.

narrator [*Br* nə'reɪtər, *Am* 'næreɪtər] *n* narrador *m*, -ra *f*.

narrow ['nærəʊ] ◇ *adj* **-1.** [not wide] estrecho(cha). **-2.** [limited] estrecho(cha) de miras. **-3.** [victory, defeat] por un estrecho margen; [escape, miss] por muy poco. ◇ *vi* **-1.** [become less wide] estrecharse. **-2.** [eyes] entornarse. **-3.** [gap] reducirse. ◆ **narrow down** *vt sep* reducir.

narrowly ['nærəʊlɪ] *adv* [barely] por muy poco.

narrow-minded [-'maɪndɪd] *adj* estrecho(cha) de miras.

nasal ['neɪzl] *adj* nasal.

nasty ['nɑːstɪ] *adj* **-1.** [unkind] malintencionado(da). **-2.** [smell, taste, feeling] desagradable; [weather] horrible. **-3.** [problem, decision] peliagudo(da). **-4.** [injury, disease] doloroso(sa); [fall] malo(la).

nation ['neɪʃn] *n* nación *f*.

national ['næʃənl] ◇ *adj* nacional. ◇ *n* súbdito *m*, -ta *f*.

national anthem *n* himno *m* nacional.

national dress *n* traje *m* típico (de un país).

National Front *n*: **the ~** *partido político minoritario de extrema derecha en Gran Bretaña.*

National Health Service *n Br*: **the ~** *organismo gestor de la salud pública*, ≃ el Insalud.

National Insurance *n Br* ≃ Seguridad *f* Social.

nationalism ['næʃnəlɪzm] *n* nacionalismo *m*.

nationalist ['næʃnəlɪst] ◇ *adj* nacionalista. ◇ *n* nacionalista *m* y *f*.

nationality [,næʃə'næləti] *n* nacionalidad *f*.

nationalize, -ise ['næʃnəlaɪz] *vt* nacionalizar.

national park *n* parque *m* nacional.

national service *n Br* MIL servicio *m* militar.

National Trust *n Br*: **the** ~ *organización británica encargada de la preservación de edificios históricos y lugares de interés*, ≃ el Patrimonio Nacional.

nationwide ['neɪʃənwaɪd] ◇ *adj* a escala nacional. ◇ *adv* [travel] por todo el país; [be broadcast] a todo el país.

native ['neɪtɪv] ◇ *adj* **-1.** [country, area] natal. **-2.** [speaker] nativo(va); ~ **language** lengua *f* materna. **-3.** [plant, animal]: ~ **(to)** originario(ria) (de). ◇ *n* natural *m* y *f*, nativo *m*, -va *f*.

Native American *n* indio americano *m*, india americana *f*.

Nativity [nə'tɪvəti] *n*: **the** ~ la Natividad.

NATO ['neɪtəʊ] (*abbr of* **North Atlantic Treaty Organization**) *n* OTAN *f*.

natural ['nætʃrəl] *adj* **-1.** [gen] natural. **-2.** [comedian, musician] nato(ta).

natural gas *n* gas *m* natural.

naturalize, -ise ['nætʃrəlaɪz] *vt* naturalizar; **to be** ~**d** naturalizarse.

naturally ['nætʃrəli] *adv* **-1.** [as expected, understandably] naturalmente. **-2.** [unaffectedly] con naturalidad. **-3.** [instinctively] por naturaleza.

natural wastage *n* (*U*) *reducción de plantilla por jubilación escalonada.*

nature ['neɪtʃə'] *n* **-1.** [gen] naturaleza *f*. **-2.** [disposition] modo *m* de ser, carácter *m*; **by** ~ por naturaleza.

nature reserve *n* reserva *f* natural.

naughty ['nɔːti] *adj* **-1.** [badly behaved] travieso(sa), malo(la). **-2.** [rude] verde.

nausea ['nɔːsjə] *n* náusea *f*.

nauseam ['nɔːzɪæm] → **ad nauseam**.

nauseating ['nɔːsɪeɪtɪŋ] *adj lit* & *fig* nauseabundo(da).

nautical ['nɔːtɪkl] *adj* náutico(ca), marítimo(ma).

naval ['neɪvl] *adj* naval.

nave [neɪv] *n* nave *f*.

navel ['neɪvl] *n* ombligo *m*.

navigate ['nævɪgeɪt] ◇ *vt* **-1.** [steer] pilotar, gobernar. **-2.** [travel safely across]

surcar, navegar por. ◇ *vi* [in plane, ship] dirigir, gobernar; [in car] guiar, dirigir.

navigation [,nævɪ'geɪʃn] *n* gobierno *m*.

navigator ['nævɪgeɪtə'] *n* oficial *m* y *f* de navegación, navegante *m* y *f*.

navvy ['nævɪ] *n Br inf* peón *m* caminero.

navy ['neɪvɪ] ◇ *n* armada *f*. ◇ *adj* [in colour] azul marino (*inv*).

navy blue *adj* azul marino (*inv*).

Nazi ['nɑːtsɪ] (*pl* **-s**) ◇ *adj* nazi. ◇ *n* nazi *m* y *f*.

NB (*abbr of* **nota bene**) N.B.

near [nɪə'] ◇ *adj* **-1.** [close in distance, time] cerca; **in the** ~ **future** en un futuro próximo. **-2.** [related] cercano(na), próximo(ma). **-3.** [almost happened]: **it was a** ~ **thing** poco le faltó. ◇ *adv* **-1.** [close in distance, time] cerca; **nowhere** ~ ni de lejos, ni mucho menos; **to draw** OR **come** ~ acercarse. **-2.** [almost] casi. ◇ *prep* **-1.** [close in position]: ~ **(to)** cerca de. **-2.** [close in time]: ~ **(to)** casi; ~ **the end** casi al final; ~**er the time** cuando se acerque la fecha. **-3.** [on the point of]: ~ **(to)** al borde de. **-4.** [similar to]: ~ **(to)** cerca de. ◇ *vt* acercarse OR aproximarse a. ◇ *vi* acercarse, aproximarse.

nearby [nɪə'baɪ] ◇ *adj* cercano(na). ◇ *adv* cerca.

nearly ['nɪəlɪ] *adv* casi; **I** ~ **fell** por poco me caigo.

near miss *n* **-1.** [nearly a hit]: **to be a** ~ fallar por poco. **-2.** [nearly a collision] incidente *m* aéreo (sin colisión).

nearside ['nɪəsaɪd] ◇ *adj* [right-hand drive] del lado izquierdo; [left-hand drive] del lado derecho. ◇ *n* [right-hand drive] lado *m* izquierdo; [left-hand drive] lado derecho.

nearsighted [,nɪə'saɪtɪd] *adj Am* miope, corto(ta) de vista.

neat [niːt] *adj* **-1.** [tidy, precise - gen] pulcro(cra); [- room, house] arreglado(da); [- handwriting] esmerado(da). **-2.** [smart] arreglado(da), pulcro(cra). **-3.** [skilful] hábil. **-4.** [undiluted] solo(la). **-5.** *Am inf* [very good] guay, de buten (*inv*).

neatly ['niːtlɪ] *adv* **-1.** [tidily, smartly] con pulcritud. **-2.** [skilfully] hábilmente.

nebulous ['nebjʊləs] *adj fml* nebuloso(sa).

necessarily [*Br* 'nesəsrəlɪ, ,nesə'serəlɪ] *adv* necesariamente.

necessary ['nesəsrɪ] *adj* **-1.** [required] necesario(ria). **-2.** [inevitable] inevitable.

necessity [nɪ'sesətɪ] *n* necesidad *f*; **of ~ por fuerza**, por necesidad. ◆ **necessities** *npl* artículos *mpl* de primera necesidad.

neck [nek] ◇ *n* [of person] cuello *m*; [of animal] pescuezo *m*, cuello. ◇ *vi inf* pegarse el lote.

necklace ['neklɪs] *n* collar *m*.

neckline ['neklaɪn] *n* escote *m*.

necktie ['nektaɪ] *n Am* corbata *f*.

nectarine ['nektərɪn] *n* nectarina *f*.

née [neɪ] *adj* de soltera.

need [niːd] ◇ *n*: ~ **(for sthg/to do sthg)** necesidad *f* (de algo/de hacer algo); **to be in** OR **to have ~ of sthg** necesitar algo; **there's no ~ for you to cry** no hace falta que llores; **if ~ be** si hace falta; **in ~** necesitado(da). ◇ *vt* **-1.** [require] necesitar; **I ~ a haircut** me falta un corte de pelo. **-2.** [be obliged]: **to ~ to do sthg** tener que hacer algo. ◇ *modal vb*: **to ~ to do sthg** necesitar hacer algo; **~ we go?** ¿tenemos que irnos?; **it ~ not happen** no tiene por qué ser así.

needle ['niːdl] ◇ *n* aguja *f*. ◇ *vt inf* pinchar.

needless ['niːdlɪs] *adj* innecesario(ria); **~ to say ...** está de más decir que ....

needlework ['niːdlwɜːk] *n* **-1.** [embroidery] bordado *m*. **-2.** (U) [activity] costura *f*.

needn't ['niːdnt] = **need not**.

needy ['niːdɪ] *adj* necesitado(da).

negative ['negətɪv] ◇ *adj* negativo(va). ◇ *n* **-1.** PHOT negativo *m*. **-2.** LING negación *f*; **to answer in the ~** decir que no.

neglect [nɪ'glekt] ◇ *n* [of garden, work] descuido *m*; [of duty] incumplimiento *m*; **a state of ~** un estado de abandono. ◇ *vt* **-1.** [ignore] desatender. **-2.** [duty, work] no cumplir con; **to ~ to do sthg** dejar de hacer algo.

neglectful [nɪ'glektful] *adj* descuidado(da), negligente.

negligee ['neglɪʒeɪ] *n* salto *m* de cama.

negligence ['neglɪdʒəns] *n* negligencia *f*.

negligible ['neglɪdʒəbl] *adj* insignificante.

negotiate [nɪ'gəʊʃɪeɪt] ◇ *vt* **-1.** [obtain through negotiation] negociar. **-2.** [obstacle] salvar, franquear; [hill] superar; [bend] tomar. ◇ *vi*: **to ~ (with sb for sthg)** negociar (con alguien algo).

negotiation [nɪ,gəʊʃɪ'eɪʃn] *n* negociación *f*. ◆ **negotiations** *npl* negociaciones *fpl*.

Negress ['niːgrɪs] *n* negra *f*.

Negro ['niːgrəʊ] (*pl* **-es**) ◇ *adj* negro(gra). ◇ *n* negro *m*, -gra *f*.

neigh [neɪ] *vi* relinchar.

neighbour *Br*, **neighbor** *Am* ['neɪbəʳ] *n* vecino *m*, -na *f*.

neighbourhood *Br*, **neighborhood** *Am* ['neɪbəhʊd] *n* **-1.** [of town] barrio *m*, vecindad *f*. **-2.** [approximate figure]: **in the ~ of** alrededor de.

neighbouring *Br*, **neighboring** *Am* ['neɪbərɪŋ] *adj* vecino(na).

neighbourly *Br*, **neighborly** *Am* ['neɪbəlɪ] *adj* de buen vecino.

neither ['naɪðəʳ, 'niːðəʳ] ◇ *adv*: **I don't drink – me** no bebo – yo tampoco; **the food was ~ good nor bad** la comida no era ni buena ni mala; **to be ~ here nor there** no tener nada que ver. ◇ *pron* ninguno(na); **~ of us/them** ninguno de nosotros/ellos. ◇ *adj*: **~ cup is blue** ninguna de las dos tazas es azul. ◇ *conj*: **~ ... nor ...** ni ... ni ...; **she could ~ eat nor sleep** no podía ni comer ni dormir.

neon ['niːɒn] *n* neón *m*.

neon light *n* lámpara *f* OR luz *f* de neón.

nephew ['nefjuː] *n* sobrino *m*.

Neptune ['neptjuːn] *n* Neptuno *m*.

nerve [nɜːv] *n* **-1.** ANAT nervio *m*. **-2.** [courage] valor *m*; **to keep one's ~** mantener la calma, no perder los nervios; **to lose one's ~** echarse atrás, perder el valor. **-3.** [cheek] cara *f*. ◆ **nerves** *npl* nervios *mpl*; **to get, on sb's ~s** sacar de quicio OR poner los nervios de punta a alguien.

nerve-racking [-,rækɪŋ] *adj* crispante.

nervous ['nɜːvəs] *adj* **-1.** ANAT & PSYCH nervioso(sa). **-2.** [apprehensive] inquieto(ta), aprensivo(va).

nervous breakdown *n* crisis *f inv* nerviosa.

nest [nest] ◇ *n* nido *m*; **wasps' ~** avispero *m*; **~ of tables** mesas *fpl* nido. ◇ *vi* anidar.

nest egg *n* ahorros *mpl*.

nestle ['nesl] *vi* [settle snuggly - in chair] arrellanarse; [- in bed] acurrucarse.

net [net] ◇ *adj* [weight, price, loss] neto(ta). ◇ *n* red *f*. ◇ *vt* **-1.** [catch] coger con red. **-2.** [acquire] embolsarse.

netball ['netbɔːl] *n deporte parecido al baloncesto femenino*.

net curtains *npl* visillos *mpl*.

Netherlands ['neðələndz] *npl*: **the ~** los Países Bajos.

net revenue n Am facturación f.
nett [net] adj = **net**.
netting ['netɪŋ] n red f, malla f.
nettle ['netl] n ortiga f.
network ['netwɜːk] ◇ n **-1.** [gen & COMPUT] red f. **-2.** RADIO & TV [station] cadena f. ◇ vt COMPUT conectar a la red.
neurosis [,njʊə'rəʊsɪs] (pl **-ses** [-siːz]) n neurosis f inv.
neurotic [,njʊə'rɒtɪk] ◇ adj neurótico(ca). ◇ n neurótico m, -ca f.
neuter ['njuːtəʳ] ◇ adj neutro(tra). ◇ vt castrar.
neutral ['njuːtrəl] ◇ adj **-1.** [gen] neutro(tra); [shoe cream] incoloro(ra). **-2.** [non-allied] neutral. ◇ n AUT punto m muerto.
neutrality [njuː'trælətɪ] n neutralidad f.
neutralize, -ise ['njuːtrəlaɪz] vt neutralizar.
never ['nevəʳ] adv **-1.** [at no time] nunca, jamás; ~ **ever** nunca jamás; **well I** ~! ¡vaya!, ¡caramba! **-2.** inf [as negative] no; **you** ~ **did!** ¡no (me digas)!
never-ending adj inacabable.
nevertheless [,nevəðə'les] adv sin embargo, no obstante.
new [adj njuː, n njuːz] adj nuevo(va); [baby] recién nacido (recién nacida); **as good as** ~ como nuevo. ◆ **news** n (U) noticias fpl; **a piece of** ~s una noticia; **the** ~s las noticias; **that's** ~s **to me** me coge de nuevas.
newborn ['njuːbɔːn] adj recién nacido (recién nacida).
newcomer ['njuː,kʌməʳ] n: ~ **(to)** recién llegado m, recién llegada f (a).
newfangled [,njuː'fæŋgld] adj inf pej novedoso(sa).
new-found adj [gen] recién descubierto (recién descubierta); [friend] reciente.
newly ['njuːlɪ] adv recién.
newlyweds ['njuːlɪwedz] npl recién casados mpl.
new moon n luna f nueva.
news agency n agencia f de noticias.
newsagent Br ['njuːzeɪdʒənt], **newsdealer** Am ['njuːzdiːlər] n [person] vendedor m, -ra f de periódicos; ~**'s (shop)** ≃ quiosco m de periódicos.
newscaster ['njuːzkɑːstəʳ] n presentador m, -ra f, locutor m, -ra f.
newsdealer Am = **newsagent**.
newsflash ['njuːzflæʃ] n flash m informativo, noticia f de última hora.
newsletter ['njuːz,letəʳ] n boletín m, hoja f informativa.

newspaper ['njuːz,peɪpəʳ] n **-1.** [publication, company] periódico m, diario m. **-2.** [paper] papel m de periódico.
newsprint ['njuːzprɪnt] n papel m de periódico.
newsreader ['njuːz,riːdəʳ] n presentador m, -ra f, locutor m, -ra f.
newsreel ['njuːzriːl] n noticiario m cinematográfico.
newsstand ['njuːzstænd] n puesto m de periódicos.
newt [njuːt] n tritón m.
new technology n nueva tecnología f.
new town n Br ciudad nueva construida por el gobierno.
New Year n Año m Nuevo; **Happy** ~! ¡Feliz Año Nuevo!
New Year's Day n día m de Año Nuevo.
New Year's Eve n Nochevieja f.
New York [-'jɔːk] n **-1.** [city]: ~ **(City)** Nueva York. **-2.** [state]: ~ **(State)** (el estado de) Nueva York.
New Zealand [-'ziːlənd] n Nueva Zelanda.
New Zealander [-'ziːləndəʳ] n neozelandés m, -esa f.
next [nekst] ◇ adj **-1.** [in time] próximo(ma); **the** ~ **day** el día siguiente; ~ **Tuesday/year** el martes/el año que viene; ~ **week** la semana próxima OR que viene; **the** ~ **week** los próximos siete días. **-2.** [in space - page etc] siguiente; [- room] de al lado. ◇ pron el siguiente (la siguiente); **the day after** ~ pasado mañana; **the week after** ~ la semana que viene no, la otra. ◇ adv **-1.** [afterwards] después. **-2.** [again] de nuevo. **-3.** [with superlatives]: ~ **best/biggest** etc el segundo mejor/más grande etc. ◇ prep Am al lado de, junto a. ◆ **next to** prep al lado de, junto a; ~ **to nothing** casi nada.
next door adv (en la casa de) al lado. ◆ **next-door** adj: **next-door neighbour** vecino m, -na f de al lado.
next of kin n pariente más cercano m, pariente más cercana f.
NHS n abbr of **National Health Service**.
NI n abbr of **National Insurance**. ◇ n abbr of **Northern Ireland**.
nib [nɪb] n plumilla f.
nibble ['nɪbl] vt mordisquear.
Nicaragua [,nɪkə'rægjʊə] n Nicaragua.
Nicaraguan [,nɪkə'rægjʊən] ◇ adj nicaragüense. ◇ n nicaragüense m y f.
nice [naɪs] adj **-1.** [attractive] bonito(ta); [good] bueno(na). **-2.** [kind] amable;

[pleasant, friendly] agradable, simpático(ca), dije *Amer*; **to be ~ to sb** ser agradable con alguien.

nice-looking [-'lʊkɪŋ] *adj* [person] guapo(pa); [car, room] bonito(ta).

nicely ['naɪslɪ] *adv* **-1.** [well, attractively] bien. **-2.** [politely] educadamente, con educación. **-3.** [satisfactorily] bien; **that will do ~** esto irá de perlas.

niche [niːʃ] *n* **-1.** [in wall] nicho *m*, hornacina *f*. **-2.** [in life] buena posición *f*.

nick [nɪk] ◇ *n* **-1.** [cut] cortecito *m*; [notch] muesca *f*. **-2.** *phr:* **in the ~ of time** justo a tiempo. ◇ *vt* **-1.** [cut] cortar; [make notch in] mellar. **-2.** *Br inf* [steal] birlar.

nickel ['nɪkl] *n* **-1.** [metal] níquel *m*. **-2.** *Am* [coin] moneda *f* de cinco centavos.

nickname ['nɪkneɪm] ◇ *n* apodo *m*. ◇ *vt* apodar.

nicotine ['nɪkətiːn] *n* nicotina *f*.

niece [niːs] *n* sobrina *f*.

Nigeria [naɪ'dʒɪərɪə] *n* Nigeria *f*.

Nigerian [naɪ'dʒɪərɪən] ◇ *adj* nigeriano(na). ◇ *n* nigeriano *m*, -na *f*.

niggle ['nɪgl] *vt Br* **-1.** [worry] inquietar. **-2.** [criticize] meterse con, criticar.

night [naɪt] *n* noche *f*; [evening] tarde *f*; **last ~** anoche, ayer por la noche; **at ~** por la noche, de noche; **to have an early/a late ~** irse a dormir pronto/tarde. ◆ **nights** *adv* **-1.** *Am* [at night] por las noches. **-2.** *Br* [nightshift]: **to work ~s** hacer el turno de noche.

nightcap ['naɪtkæp] *n* [drink] *bebida que se toma antes de ir a dormir.*

nightclub ['naɪtklʌb] *n* club *m* nocturno.

nightdress ['naɪtdres] *n* camisón *m*.

nightfall ['naɪtfɔːl] *n* anochecer *m*.

nightgown ['naɪtgaʊn] *n* camisón *m*.

nightie ['naɪtɪ] *n inf* camisón *m*.

nightingale ['naɪtɪŋgeɪl] *n* ruiseñor *m*.

nightlife ['naɪtlaɪf] *n* vida *f* nocturna.

nightly ['naɪtlɪ] ◇ *adj* nocturno(na), de cada noche. ◇ *adv* cada noche.

nightmare ['naɪtmeəʳ] *n lit & fig* pesadilla *f*.

night porter *n* recepcionista *m y f* del turno de noche.

night school *n* (U) escuela *f* nocturna.

night shift *n* turno *m* de noche.

nightshirt ['naɪtʃɜːt] *n* camisa *f* de dormir (masculina).

nighttime ['naɪttaɪm] *n* noche *f*.

nil [nɪl] *n* **-1.** [nothing] nada *f*. **-2.** *Br* SPORT cero *m*.

Nile [naɪl] *n*: **the ~** el Nilo.

nimble ['nɪmbl] *adj* **-1.** [person, fingers] ágil. **-2.** [mind] rápido(da).

nine [naɪn] *num* nueve; *see also* **six**.

nineteen [,naɪn'tiːn] *num* diecinueve; *see also* **six**.

ninety ['naɪntɪ] *num* noventa; *see also* **sixty**.

ninth [naɪnθ] ◇ *num adj* noveno(na). ◇ *num n* **-1.** [fraction] noveno *m*. **-2.** [in order] noveno *m*, -na *f*; *see also* **sixth**.

nip [nɪp] ◇ *n* [of drink] trago *m*. ◇ *vt* [pinch] pellizcar; [bite] mordisquear.

nipple ['nɪpl] *n* **-1.** [of woman] pezón *m*. **-2.** [of baby's bottle, man] tetilla *f*.

nit [nɪt] *n* [in hair] liendre *f*.

nitpicking ['nɪtpɪkɪŋ] *inf n* (U) nimiedades *fpl*.

nitrogen ['naɪtrədʒən] *n* nitrógeno *m*.

nitty-gritty [,nɪtɪ'grɪtɪ] *n inf*: **to get down to the ~** ir al grano.

no [nəʊ] (*pl* **-es**) ◇ *adv* [gen] no; **you're ~ better than me** tú no eres mejor que yo. ◇ *adj* no; **I have ~ time** no tengo tiempo; **that's ~ excuse** esa no es excusa que valga; **there are ~ taxis** no hay taxis; **he's ~ fool** no es ningún tonto; **she's ~ friend of mine** no es amiga mía; **"~ smoking/parking/ cameras"** "prohibido fumar/aparcar/ hacer fotos". ◇ *n* no *m*; **he/she won't take ~ for an answer** no acepta una respuesta negativa.

No., no. (*abbr of* **number**) n.º.

nobility [nə'bɪlətɪ] *n* nobleza *f*.

noble ['nəʊbl] ◇ *adj* noble. ◇ *n* noble *m y f*.

nobody ['nəʊbədɪ] ◇ *pron* nadie. ◇ *n pej* don nadie *m*.

nocturnal [nɒk'tɜːnl] *adj* nocturno(na).

nod [nɒd] ◇ *vt*: **to ~ one's head** [in agreement] asentir con la cabeza; [as greeting] saludar con la cabeza. ◇ *vi* **-1.** [in agreement] asentir con la cabeza. **-2.** [to indicate sthg] indicar con la cabeza. **-3.** [as greeting] saludar con la cabeza. ◆ **nod off** *vi* dar cabezadas.

noise [nɔɪz] *n* ruido *m*; **to make a ~** armar OR hacer ruido.

noisy ['nɔɪzɪ] *adj* ruidoso(sa).

no-man's-land *n* tierra *f* de nadie.

nominal ['nɒmɪnl] *adj* nominal.

nominate ['nɒmɪneɪt] *vt* **-1.** [propose]: **to ~ sb (for** OR **as)** proponer a alguien (por OR como). **-2.** [appoint]: **to ~ sb (to sthg)** nombrar a alguien (algo).

nomination [,nɒmɪ'neɪʃn] *n* **-1.** [proposal] nominación *f*. **-2.** [appointment]: **~ (to sthg)** nombramiento *m* (a algo).

nominee [ˌnɒmɪ'niː] n nominado m, -da f.

non- [nɒn] prefix no.

nonalcoholic [ˌnɒnælkə'hɒlɪk] adj sin alcohol.

nonaligned [ˌnɒnə'laɪnd] adj no alineado(da).

nonchalant [Br 'nɒnʃələnt, Am ˌnɒnʃə'lɑːnt] adj despreocupado(da).

noncommittal [ˌnɒnkə'mɪtl] adj que no compromete a nada, evasivo(va).

nonconformist [ˌnɒnkən'fɔːmɪst] ◇ adj inconformista. ◇ n inconformista m y f.

nondescript [Br 'nɒndɪskrɪpt, Am ˌnɒndɪ'skrɪpt] adj anodino(na), soso(sa).

none [nʌn] ◇ pron -1. [not any] nada; **there is ~ left** no queda nada; **it's ~ of your business** no es asunto tuyo. -2. [not one - object, person] ninguno(na); **~ of us/the books** ninguno de nosotros/ de los libros; **I had ~** no tenía ninguno. ◇ adv: **I'm ~ the worse/better** no me ha perjudicado/ayudado en nada; **I'm ~ the wiser** no lo he entendido nada. ♦ **none too** adv no demasiado.

nonentity [nɒ'nentətɪ] n cero m a la izquierda.

nonetheless [ˌnʌnðə'les] adv sin embargo, no obstante.

non-event n fracaso m.

nonexistent [ˌnɒnɪg'zɪstənt] adj inexistente.

nonfiction [ˌnɒn'fɪkʃn] n no ficción f.

no-nonsense adj práctico(ca).

nonpayment [ˌnɒn'peɪmənt] n impago m.

nonplussed, nonplused Am [ˌnɒn'plʌst] adj perplejo(ja).

nonreturnable [ˌnɒnrɪ'tɜːnəbl] adj no retornable, sin retorno.

nonsense ['nɒnsəns] ◇ n (U) -1. [gen] tonterías fpl, bobadas fpl; **it is ~ to suggest that ...** es absurdo sugerir que ...; **to make (a) ~ of sthg** dar al traste con algo. -2. [incomprehensible words] galimatías m inv. ◇ excl ¡tonterías!

nonsensical [nɒn'sensɪkl] adj disparatado(da), absurdo(da).

nonsmoker [ˌnɒn'sməukər] n no fumador m, no fumadora f.

nonstick [ˌnɒn'stɪk] adj antiadherente.

nonstop [ˌnɒn'stɒp] ◇ adj [activity, rain] continuo(nua), incesante; [flight] sin escalas. ◇ adv sin parar.

noodles ['nuːdlz] npl fideos mpl.

nook [nʊk] n [of room]: **every ~ and cranny** todos los recovecos.

noon [nuːn] n mediodía m.

no one pron = **nobody**.

noose [nuːs] n [loop] nudo m corredizo; [for hanging] soga f.

no-place Am = **nowhere**.

nor [nɔːr] conj -1. → **neither**. -2. [and not] ni; **I don't smoke - ~ do I** no fumo - yo tampoco; **I don't know, ~ do I care** ni lo sé, ni me importa, ~

norm [nɔːm] n norma f; **the ~** lo normal.

normal ['nɔːml] adj normal.

normality [nɔː'mælɪtɪ], **normalcy** Am ['nɔːmlsɪ] n normalidad f.

normally ['nɔːməlɪ] adv normalmente.

north [nɔːθ] ◇ n -1. [direction] norte m. -2. [region]: **the North** el norte. ◇ adj del norte; **North London** el norte de Londres. ◇ adv: **~ (of)** al norte (de).

North Africa n África del Norte.

North America n Norteamérica.

North American ◇ adj norteamericano(na). ◇ n norteamericano m, -na f.

northeast [ˌnɔːθ'iːst] ◇ n -1. [direction] nordeste m. -2. [region]: **the Northeast** el nordeste. ◇ adj del nordeste. ◇ adv: **~ (of)** al nordeste (de).

northerly ['nɔːðəlɪ] adj del norte.

northern ['nɔːðən] adj del norte, norteño(ña).

Northern Ireland n Irlanda del Norte.

northernmost ['nɔːðənməust] adj más septentrional OR al norte.

North Korea n Corea del Norte.

North Pole n: **the ~** el Polo Norte.

North Sea n: **the ~** el Mar del Norte.

northward ['nɔːθwəd] ◇ adj hacia el norte. ◇ adv = **northwards**.

northwards ['nɔːθwədz] adv hacia el norte.

northwest [ˌnɔːθ'west] ◇ n -1. [direction] noroeste m. -2. [region]: **the Northwest** el noroeste. ◇ adj del noroeste. ◇ adv: **~ (of)** al noroeste (de).

Norway ['nɔːweɪ] n Noruega.

Norwegian [nɔː'wiːdʒən] ◇ adj noruego(ga). ◇ n -1. [person] noruego m, -ga f. -2. [language] noruego m.

nose [nəuz] n [of person] nariz f; [of animal] hocico m; [of plane, car] morro m; **to keep one's ~ out of sthg** no meter las narices en algo; **to look down one's ~ at sb/sthg** mirar por encima del hombro a alguien/algo; **to poke OR stick one's ~ in** inf meter las narices; **to turn up one's ~ at sthg** hacerle ascos a algo. ♦ **nose about**, **nose around** vi curiosear.

nosebleed ['nəʊzbliːd] *n* hemorragia *f* nasal.

nosedive ['nəʊzdaɪv] ◇ *n* [of plane] picado *m*. ◇ *vi lit* & *fig* bajar en picado.

nosey ['nəʊzɪ] = **nosy**.

nostalgia [nɒ'stældʒə] *n*: ~ **(for)** nostalgia *f* (de).

nostril ['nɒstrəl] *n* ventana *f* de la nariz.

nosy ['nəʊzɪ] *adj* fisgón(ona), curioso(sa).

not [nɒt] *adv* no; **this is** ~ **the first time** no es la primera vez; **it's green, isn't it?** es verde, ¿no?; **I hope/think** ~ espero/creo que no; ~ **a chance de ninguna manera;** ~ **even a ...** ni siquiera un (una) ...; ~ **all** OR **every** no todos(das); ~ **always** no siempre; ~ **that ...** no es que ...; ~ **at all** [no] en absoluto; [to acknowledge thanks] de nada.

notable ['nəʊtəbl] *adj* notable; **to be** ~ **for sthg** destacar por algo.

notably ['nəʊtəblɪ] *adv* **-1.** [in particular] especialmente. **-2.** [noticeably] marcadamente.

notary ['nəʊtərɪ] *n*: ~ **(public)** notario *m*, -ria *f*.

notch [nɒtʃ] *n* [cut] muesca *f*.

note [nəʊt] ◇ *n* **-1.** [gen] nota *f*; **to take** ~ **of sthg** tener algo presente. **-2.** [paper money] billete *m*. **-3.** [tone] tono *m*. ◇ *vt* **-1.** [observe] notar. **-2.** [mention] mencionar. ◆ **notes** *npl* [written record] apuntes *mpl*; **to take** ~**s** tomar apuntes; [in book] notas *fpl*. ◆ **note down** *vt sep* anotar, apuntar.

notebook ['nəʊtbʊk] *n* **-1.** [for taking notes] libreta *f*, cuaderno *m*. **-2.** COMPUT: ~ **(computer)** ordenador *m* portátil.

noted ['nəʊtɪd] *adj* destacado(da); **to be** ~ **for** distinguirse por.

notepad ['nəʊtpæd] *n* bloc *m* de notas.

notepaper ['nəʊtpeɪpə*] *n* papel *m* de escribir OR de cartas.

noteworthy ['nəʊt,wɜːðɪ] *adj* digno(na) de mención.

nothing ['nʌθɪŋ] ◇ *pron* nada; **I've got** ~ **to do** no tengo nada que hacer; **for** ~ [free] gratis; [for no purpose] en vano, en balde; **he's** ~ **if not generous** otra cosa no será pero desde luego generoso sí que es; ~ **but** tan sólo; **there's** ~ **for it (but to do sthg)** *Br* no hay más remedio (que hacer algo). ◇ *adv*: **to be** ~ **like sb/sthg** no parecerse en nada a alguien/algo; **I'm** ~ **like finished** no he terminado ni mucho menos.

notice ['nəʊtɪs] ◇ *n* **-1.** [on wall, door] letrero *m*, cartel *m*; [in newspaper] anuncio *m*. **-2.** [attention] atención *f*; **to take** ~ **(of)** hacer caso (de), prestar atención (a). **-3.** [warning] aviso *m*; **at short** ~ casi sin previo aviso; **until further** ~ hasta nuevo aviso. **-4.** [at work]: **to be given one's** ~ ser despedido(da); **to hand in one's** ~ presentar la dimisión. ◇ *vt* [sense, smell] notar; [see] fijarse en, ver; **to** ~ **sb doing sthg** fijarse en alguien que está haciendo algo.

noticeable ['nəʊtɪsəbl] *adj* notable.

notice board *n* tablón *m* de anuncios.

notify ['nəʊtɪfaɪ] *vt*: **to** ~ **sb (of sthg)** notificar OR comunicar (algo) a alguien.

notion ['nəʊʃn] *n* noción *f*. ◆ **notions** *npl Am* artículos *mpl* de mercería.

notorious [nəʊ'tɔːrɪəs] *adj* notorio(ria), célebre.

notwithstanding [,nɒtwɪθ'stændɪŋ] *fml* ◇ *prep* a pesar de. ◇ *adv* sin embargo.

nougat ['nuːgɑː] *n* dulce hecho a base de nueces y frutas.

nought [nɔːt] *num* cero.

noun [naʊn] *n* nombre *m*, sustantivo *m*.

nourish ['nʌrɪʃ] *vt* **-1.** [feed] nutrir. **-2.** [entertain] alimentar, albergar.

nourishing ['nʌrɪʃɪŋ] *adj* nutritivo(va).

nourishment ['nʌrɪʃmənt] *n* alimento *m*, sustento *m*.

novel ['nɒvl] ◇ *adj* original. ◇ *n* novela *f*.

novelist ['nɒvəlɪst] *n* novelista *m* y *f*.

novelty ['nɒvltɪ] *n* **-1.** [gen] novedad *f*. **-2.** [cheap object] baratija *f* (poco útil).

November [nə'vembə*] *n* noviembre *m*; *see also* **September**.

novice ['nɒvɪs] *n* **-1.** [inexperienced person] principiante *m* y *f*. **-2.** RELIG novicio *m*, -cia *f*.

now [naʊ] ◇ *adv* **-1.** [at this time, at once] ahora; **do it** ~ hazlo ahora; **he's been away for two weeks** ~ lleva dos semanas fuera; **any day** ~ cualquier día de éstos; **any time** ~ en cualquier momento; **for** ~ por ahora, por el momento; ~ **and then** OR **again** de vez en cuando. **-2.** [at a particular time in the past] entonces. **-3.** [to introduce statement] vamos a ver ... ◇ *conj*: ~ **(that)** ahora que, ya que. ◇ *n* ahora; **from now on** a partir de ahora; **they should be here by** ~ ya deberían estar aquí; **up until** ~ hasta ahora.

nowadays ['nauədeɪz] *adv* hoy en día, actualmente.

nowhere *Br* ['nəuweə'], **no-place** *Am adv* en ninguna parte; ~ **else** en ninguna otra parte; **to be getting** ~ no estar avanzando nada, no ir a ninguna parte; **(to be)** ~ **near (as ... as ...)** (no ser) ni mucho menos (tan ... como ...).

nozzle ['nɒzl] *n* boquilla *f*.

nuance [nju:'ɑːns] *n* matiz *m*.

nuclear ['nju:klɪə'] *adj* nuclear.

nuclear bomb *n* bomba *f* atómica.

nuclear disarmament *n* desarme *m* nuclear.

nuclear energy *n* energía *f* nuclear.

nuclear power *n* energía *f* nuclear.

nuclear reactor *n* reactor *m* nuclear.

nucleus ['nju:klɪəs] (*pl* **-lei** [-lɪaɪ]) *n lit & fig* núcleo *m*.

nude [nju:d] ◇ *adj* desnudo(da). ◇ *n* ART desnudo *m*; **in the** ~ desnudo(da), en cueros.

nudge [nʌdʒ] *vt* [with elbow] dar un codazo a.

nudist ['nju:dɪst] *n* nudista *m y f*.

nudity ['nju:dətɪ] *n* desnudez *f*.

nugget ['nʌgɪt] *n* [of gold] pepita *f*.

nuisance ['nju:sns] *n* [thing] fastidio *m*, molestia *f*; [person] pesado *m*; **to make a** ~ **of o.s.** dar la lata.

nuke [nju:k] *inf* ◇ *n* bomba *f* atómica. ◇ *vt* atacar con arma nuclear.

null [nʌl] *adj*: ~ **and void** nulo(la) y sin efecto.

numb [nʌm] ◇ *adj* [gen] entumecido(da); [leg, hand] dormido(da); **to be** ~ **with cold** estar helado(da) de frío; **to be** ~ **with fear** estar paralizado(da) de miedo. ◇ *vt* entumecer.

number ['nʌmbə'] ◇ *n* -**1.** [gen] número *m*; **a** ~ **of** varios(rias); **any** ~ **of** la mar de. -**2.** [of car] matrícula *f*. ◇ *vt* -**1.** [amount to] ascender a. -**2.** [give a number to] numerar. -**3.** [include]: **to be** ~ed **among** figurar entre.

number one ◇ *adj* principal, número uno. ◇ *n inf* [oneself] uno mismo (una misma).

numberplate ['nʌmbəpleɪt] *n* matrícula *f* (de vehículo).

Number Ten *n* el número 10 de Downing Street, residencia oficial del primer ministro británico.

numeral ['nju:mərəl] *n* número *m*, cifra *f*.

numerate ['nju:mərət] *adj Br* competente en aritmética.

numerical [nju:'merɪkl] *adj* numérico(ca).

numerous ['nju:mərəs] *adj* numeroso(sa).

nun [nʌn] *n* monja *f*.

nurse [nɜːs] ◇ *n* MED enfermero *m*, -ra *f*; [nanny] niñera *f*. ◇ *vt* -**1.** [care for] cuidar, atender. -**2.** [try to cure - a cold] curarse. -**3.** [nourish] abrigar. -**4.** [subj: mother] amamantar.

nursery ['nɜːsərɪ] *n* -**1.** [at home] cuarto *m* de los niños; [away from home] guardería *f*. -**2.** [for plants] semillero *m*, vivero *m*.

nursery rhyme *n* poema *m* OR canción *f* infantil.

nursery school *n* parvulario *m*.

nursery slopes *npl* pista *f* para principiantes.

nursing ['nɜːsɪŋ] *n* [profession] profesión *f* de enfermero; [of patient] asistencia *f*, cuidado *m*.

nursing home *n* [for old people] clínica *f* de reposo (privada); [for childbirth] clínica *f* (privada) de maternidad.

nurture ['nɜːtʃə'] *vt* -**1.** [child, plant] criar. -**2.** [plan, feelings] alimentar.

nut [nʌt] *n* -**1.** [to eat] nuez *f*. -**2.** [of metal] tuerca *f*. -**3.** *inf* [mad person] chiflado *m*, -da *f*. ◆ **nuts** *inf* ◇ *adj*: **to be** ~s estar chalado(da). ◇ *excl Am* ¡maldita sea!

nutcrackers ['nʌt,krækəz] *npl* cascanueces *m inv*.

nutmeg ['nʌtmeg] *n* nuez *f* moscada.

nutritious [nju:'trɪʃəs] *adj* nutritivo(va).

nutshell ['nʌtʃel] *n*: **in a** ~ en una palabra.

nuzzle ['nʌzl] ◇ *vt* rozar con el hocico. ◇ *vi*: **to** ~ **(up) against** arrimarse a.

nylon ['naɪlɒn] ◇ *n* nylon *m*. ◇ *comp* de nylon.

o (*pl* **o's** OR **os**), **O** (*pl* **O's** OR **Os**) [əu] *n* -**1.** [letter] o *f*, O *f*. -**2.** [zero] cero *m*.

oak [əuk] ◇ *n* roble *m*. ◇ *comp* de roble.

OAP *n abbr of* **old age pensioner**.

oar [ɔː'] *n* remo *m*.

oasis [əʊ'eɪsɪs] (*pl* **oases** [əʊ'eɪsiːz]) *n lit & fig* oasis *m inv*.

oatcake ['əʊtkeɪk] *n* galleta *f* de avena.

oath [əʊθ] *n* **-1.** [promise] juramento *m*; **on** OR **under** ~ bajo juramento. **-2.** [swearword] palabrota *f*.

oatmeal ['əʊtmiːl] *n* harina *f* de avena.

oats [əʊts] *npl* [grain] avena *f*.

obedience [ə'biːdjəns] *n*: ~ **(to sb)** obediencia *f* (a alguien).

obedient [ə'biːdjənt] *adj* obediente.

obese [əʊ'biːs] *adj fml* obeso(sa).

obey [ə'beɪ] *vt & vi* obedecer.

obituary [ə'bɪtʃʊərɪ] *n* nota *f* necrológica, necrología *f*.

object [*n* 'ɒbdʒɪkt, *vb* ɒb'dʒekt] ◇ *n* **-1.** [gen] objeto *m*. **-2.** [aim] objeto *m*, propósito *m*. **-3.** GRAMM complemento *m*. ◇ *vt* objetar. ◇ *vi*: **to** ~ **(to sthg/to doing sthg)** oponerse (a algo/a hacer algo).

objection [əb'dʒekʃn] *n* objeción *f*, reparo *m*; **to have no** ~ **(to sthg/to doing sthg)** no tener inconveniente (en algo/en hacer algo).

objectionable [əb'dʒekʃənəbl] *adj* [person] desagradable; [behaviour] censurable.

objective [əb'dʒektɪv] ◇ *adj* objetivo(va). ◇ *n* objetivo *m*.

obligation [,ɒblɪ'geɪʃn] *n* **-1.** [compulsion] obligación *f*; **to be under an** ~ **to do sthg** tener la obligación de hacer algo. **-2.** [duty] deber *m*.

obligatory [ə'blɪgətrɪ] *adj* obligatorio(ria).

oblige [ə'blaɪdʒ] *vt* **-1.** [force]: **to** ~ **sb to do sthg** obligar a alguien a hacer algo. **-2.** *fml* [do a favour to] hacer un favor a.

obliging [ə'blaɪdʒɪŋ] *adj* servicial, atento(ta).

oblique [ə'bliːk] ◇ *adj* **-1.** [indirect - reference] indirecto(ta). **-2.** [slanting] oblicuo(cua). ◇ *n* TYPO barra *f*.

obliterate [ə'blɪtəreɪt] *vt* arrasar.

oblivion [ə'blɪvɪən] *n* olvido *m*.

oblivious [ə'blɪvɪəs] *adj* inconsciente; **to be** ~ **to** OR **of sthg** no ser consciente de algo.

oblong ['ɒblɒŋ] ◇ *adj* rectangular, oblongo(ga). ◇ *n* rectángulo *m*.

obnoxious [əb'nɒkʃəs] *adj* detestable.

oboe ['əʊbəʊ] *n* oboe *m*.

obscene [əb'siːn] *adj* obsceno(na).

obscure [əb'skjʊər] ◇ *adj lit & fig* oscuro(ra). ◇ *vt* **-1.** [make difficult to understand] oscurecer. **-2.** [hide] esconder.

obsequious [əb'siːkwɪəs] *adj fml & pej* servil.

observance [əb'zɜːvəns] *n* observancia *f*, cumplimiento *m*.

observant [əb'zɜːvnt] *adj* observador(ra).

observation [,ɒbzə'veɪʃn] *n* **-1.** [by police] vigilancia *f*; [by doctor] observación *f*. **-2.** [comment] comentario *m*.

observatory [əb'zɜːvətrɪ] *n* observatorio *m*.

observe [əb'zɜːv] *vt* **-1.** [gen] observar. **-2.** [obey] cumplir con, observar.

observer [əb'zɜːvər] *n* observador *m*, -ra *f*.

obsess [əb'ses] *vt* obsesionar; **to be** ~**ed by** OR **with** estar obsesionado con.

obsessive [əb'sesɪv] *adj* obsesivo(va).

obsolescent [,ɒbsə'lesnt] *adj* obsolescente.

obsolete ['ɒbsəliːt] *adj* obsoleto(ta).

obstacle ['ɒbstəkl] *n* **-1.** [object] obstáculo *m*. **-2.** [difficulty] estorbo *m*.

obstetrics [ɒb'stetrɪks] *n* obstetricia *f*.

obstinate ['ɒbstənət] *adj* **-1.** [stubborn] obstinado(da), terco(ca). **-2.** [persistent] tenaz.

obstruct [əb'strʌkt] *vt* **-1.** [block] obstruir, bloquear. **-2.** [hinder] estorbar.

obstruction [əb'strʌkʃn] *n* [gen] obstrucción *f*; [in road] obstáculo *m*.

obtain [əb'teɪn] *vt* obtener, conseguir.

obtainable [əb'teɪnəbl] *adj* que se puede conseguir, asequible.

obtrusive [əb'truːsɪv] *adj* [smell] penetrante; [colour] chillón(ona); [person] entrometido(da).

obtuse [əb'tjuːs] *adj lit & fig* obtuso(sa).

obvious ['ɒbvɪəs] *adj* obvio(via), evidente.

obviously ['ɒbvɪəslɪ] *adv* **-1.** [of course] evidentemente, obviamente; ~ **not** claro que no. **-2.** [clearly] claramente.

occasion [ə'keɪʒn] *n* **-1.** [time] vez *f*, ocasión *f*; **on one** ~ una vez, en una ocasión; **on several** ~**s** varias veces, en varias ocasiones. **-2.** [important event] acontecimiento *m*; **to rise to the** ~ ponerse a la altura de las circunstancias. **-3.** *fml* [opportunity] ocasión *f*.

occasional [ə'keɪʒənl] *adj* [trip, drink] poco frecuente, esporádico(ca); [showers] ocasional.

occasionally [ə'keɪʒnəlɪ] *adv* de vez en cuando.

occult [ɒ'kʌlt] *adj* oculto(ta).

occupant ['ɒkjʊpənt] n **-1.** [of building, room] inquilino m, -na f. **-2.** [of chair, vehicle] ocupante m y f.

occupation [ˌɒkjʊ'peɪʃn] n **-1.** [job] empleo m, ocupación f. **-2.** [pastime] pasatiempo m. **-3.** MIL [of country, building] ocupación f.

occupational hazard [ɒkjʊˌpeɪʃənl-] n: ~s gajes mpl del oficio.

occupational therapy [ɒkjʊˌpeɪʃənl-] n terapia f ocupacional.

occupier ['ɒkjʊpaɪəʳ] n inquilino m, -na f.

occupy ['ɒkjʊpaɪ] vt **-1.** [gen] ocupar. **-2.** [live in] habitar. **-3.** [entertain]: **to ~ o.s.** entretenerse.

occur [ə'kɜːʳ] vi **-1.** [happen] ocurrir, suceder. **-2.** [be present] encontrarse. **-3.** [thought, idea]: **to ~ to sb** ocurrírsele a alguien.

occurrence [ə'kʌrəns] n [event] acontecimiento m.

ocean ['əʊʃn] n océano m; Am [sea] mar m o f.

oceangoing ['əʊʃnˌgəʊɪŋ] adj de alta mar.

ochre Br, **ocher** Am ['əʊkəʳ] adj ocre.

o'clock [ə'klɒk] adv: **it's one ~** es la una; **it's two/three ~** son las dos/las tres; **at one/two ~** a la una/las dos.

octave ['ɒktɪv] n octava f.

October [ɒk'təʊbəʳ] n octubre m; see also **September**.

octopus ['ɒktəpəs] (pl **-puses** OR **-pi** [-paɪ]) n pulpo m.

OD -1. abbr of **overdose**. **-2.** abbr of **overdrawn**.

odd [ɒd] adj **-1.** [strange] raro(ra), extraño(ña). **-2.** [not part of pair] sin pareja. **-3.** [number] impar. **-4.** inf [leftover] sobrante. **-5.** inf [occasional]: **I play the ~ game** juego alguna que otra vez. **-6.** inf [approximately]: **30 ~ years** 30 y tantos OR y pico años. ◆ **odds** npl **-1.** the ~s [probability] las probabilidades; [in betting] las apuestas; **the ~s are that ...** lo más probable es que ...; **against all ~s** contra viento y marea. **-2.** [bits]: ~s **and ends** chismes mpl, cosillas fpl. **-3.** phr: **to be at ~s with sb** estar reñido con alguien.

oddity ['ɒdɪtɪ] (pl **-ies**) n rareza f.

odd jobs npl chapuzas fpl.

oddly ['ɒdlɪ] adv extrañamente; ~ **enough** aunque parezca mentira.

oddments ['ɒdmənts] npl retales mpl.

odds-on ['ɒdz-] adj inf: **the ~ favourite** el favorito indiscutible.

odometer [əʊ'dɒmɪtəʳ] n cuentakilómetros m inv.

odour Br, **odor** Am ['əʊdəʳ] n [gen] olor m; [of perfume] fragancia f.

of [unstressed əv, stressed ɒv] prep **-1.** [gen] de; **the cover ~ a book** la portada de un libro; **both ~ us** nosotros dos; **to die ~ sthg** morir de algo. **-2.** [expressing quantity, referring to container] de; **thousands ~ people** miles de personas; **a cup ~ coffee** un café, una taza de café. **-3.** [indicating amount, age, time] de; **a child ~ five** un niño de cinco (años); **an increase ~ 6%** un incremento del 6%; **the 12th ~ February** el 12 de febrero. **-4.** [made from] de; **a dress ~ silk** un vestido de seda. **-5.** [with emotions, opinions]: **fear ~ ghosts** miedo a los fantasmas; **love ~ good food** amor por la buena mesa; **it was very kind ~ you** fue muy amable de OR por tu parte.

off [ɒf] ◇ adv **-1.** [away]: **to drive ~** alejarse conduciendo; **to turn ~ (the road)** salir de la carretera; **I'm ~!** ¡me voy! **-2.** [at a distance - in time]: **it's two days ~** quedan dos días; **that's a long time ~** aún queda mucho para eso; [- in space]: **it's ten miles ~** está a diez millas; **far ~** lejos. **-3.** [so as to remove]: **to take ~** [gen] quitar; [one's clothes] quitarse; **to cut ~** cortar; **could you help me ~ with my coat?** ¿me ayudas a quitarme el abrigo? **-4.** [so as to complete]: **to finish ~** terminar, acabar; **to kill ~** rematar. **-5.** [not at work] libre, de vacaciones; **a day ~** un día libre; **time ~** tiempo m libre. **-6.** [so as to separate]: **to fence ~** vallar; **to wall ~** tapiar. **-7.** [discounted]: **£10 ~** 10 libras de descuento. **-8.** [having money]: **to be well/badly ~** andar bien/mal de dinero. ◇ prep **-1.** [away from]: **to get ~ sthg** bajarse de algo; **to keep ~ sthg** mantenerse alejado de algo; **"keep ~ the grass"** "prohibido pisar el césped". **-2.** [close to]: **just ~ the coast** muy cerca de la costa; **it's ~ Oxford Street** está al lado de Oxford Street. **-3.** [removed from]: **to cut a slice ~ sthg** cortar un pedazo de algo; **take your hands ~ me!** ¡quítame las manos de encima! **-4.** [not attending]: **to be ~ work/duty** no estar trabajando/de servicio. **-5.** inf [no longer liking]: **she's ~ coffee/her food** no le apetece café/comer. **-6.** [deducted from]: **there's 10% ~ the price** hay un 10% de rebaja so-

bre el precio. **-7.** *inf* [from]: **I bought it
~ him** se lo compré a él. ◇ *adj* **-1.**
[gone bad - meat, cheese] **pasado(da)**, es-
tropeado(da); [- milk] **cortado(da)**. **-2.**
[not operating] **apagado(da)**. **-3.** [can-
celled] **suspendido(da)**.

offal ['ɒfl] *n* (*U*) **asaduras** *fpl*.

off-chance *n*: **on the ~** **por si acaso**.

off colour *adj* **indispuesto(ta)**.

off duty *adj* **fuera de servicio**.

offence *Br*, **offense** *Am* [ə'fens] *n* **-1.**
[crime] **delito** *m*. **-2.** [cause of upset]
ofensa *f*; **to take ~** **ofenderse**.

offend [ə'fend] *vt* **ofender**.

offender [ə'fendər] *n* **-1.** [criminal] **delincuente** *m y f*. **-2.** [culprit] **culpable** *m y f*.

offense *Am* [sense 2 'ɒfens] *n* **-1.** = of-
fence. **-2.** SPORT **ataque** *m*.

offensive [ə'fensɪv] ◇ *adj* **-1.** [remark,
behaviour] **ofensivo(va)**; [smell] **repugnante**. **-2.** [aggressive] **atacante**. ◇ *n* MIL
ofensiva *f*.

offer ['ɒfər] ◇ *n* **oferta** *f*; **on ~** [available]
disponible; [at a special price] **en oferta**.
◇ *vt* **ofrecer**; **to ~ sthg to sb, to ~ sb
sthg** ofrecer algo a alguien; [be willing]:
to ~ to do sthg ofrecerse a hacer algo.
◇ *vi* **ofrecerse**.

offering ['ɒfərɪŋ] *n* **-1.** [thing offered]
ofrecimiento *m*; [gift] **regalo** *m*. **-2.**
[sacrifice] **ofrenda** *f*.

off-guard *adj* **desprevenido(da)**.

offhand [,ɒf'hænd] ◇ *adj* **brusco(ca)**,
descortés. ◇ *adv* **de improviso**.

office ['ɒfɪs] *n* **-1.** [gen] **oficina** *f*. **-2.**
[room] **despacho** *m*, **oficina** *f*. **-3.** [posi-
tion of authority] **cargo** *m*; **in ~** [political
party] **en el poder**; [person] **en el cargo**;
to take ~ [political party] **subir al poder**;
[person] **asumir el cargo**.

office automation *n* **ofimática** *f*.

office block *n* **bloque** *m* **de oficinas**.

office hours *npl* **horas** *fpl* **de oficina**.

officer ['ɒfɪsər] *n* **-1.** MIL **oficial** *m y f*.
-2. [in organization] **director** *m*, **-ra** *f*. **-3.**
[in police force] **agente** *m y f* **de policía**.

office worker *n* **oficinista** *m y f*.

official [ə'fɪʃl] ◇ *adj* **oficial**. ◇ *n* [of un-
ion] **delegado** *m*, **-da** *f*; [of government]
funcionario *m*, **-ria** *f*.

officialdom [ə'fɪʃəldəm] *n* **burocracia** *f*.

offing ['ɒfɪŋ] *n*: **to be in the ~** **estar al
caer** OR **a la vista**.

off-licence *n* *Br* **tienda donde se venden
bebidas alcohólicas para llevar**.

off-line *adj* COMPUT **desconectado(da)**.

off-peak *adj* [electricity, phone call, travel]

de tarifa reducida; [period] **económi-
co(ca)**.

off-putting [-,pʊtɪŋ] *adj* **repelente**.

off season *n*: **the ~** **la temporada baja**.

offset ['ɒfset] (*pt & pp* **offset**) *vt* **compensar**, **contrarrestar**.

offshoot ['ɒfʃuːt] *n* **retoño** *m*.

offshore ['ɒfʃɔːr] ◇ *adj* [wind] **coste-
ro(ra)**; [fishing] **de bajura**; [oil rig] **maríti-
mo(ma)**; [banking] **en bancos extranje-
ros**. ◇ *adv* **mar adentro**; **two miles ~** **a
dos millas de la costa**.

offside [,ɒf'saɪd] ◇ *adj* **-1.** [part of vehicle -
right-hand drive] **izquierdo(da)**; [- left-hand
drive] **derecho(cha)**. **-2.** SPORT **fuera de
juego**. ◇ *adv* SPORT **fuera de juego**.

offspring ['ɒfsprɪŋ] (*pl inv*) *n* **-1.** [of
people - child] *fml or hum* **descendiente**
m y f; [- children] **descendencia** *f*. **-2.** [of
animals] **crías** *fpl*.

offstage [,ɒf'steɪdʒ] *adj & adv* **entre
bastidores**.

off-the-cuff ◇ *adj* **improvisado(da)**. ◇
adv **improvisadamente**.

off-the-peg *adj* *Br* **confeccionado(da)**.

off-the-record ◇ *adj* **extraoficial**. ◇
adv **extraoficialmente**.

off-white *adj* **blancuzco(ca)**.

often ['ɒfn, 'ɒftn] *adv* [many times] **a menudo**, **con frecuencia**; **how ~ do you
go?** **¿cada cuánto** OR **con qué frecuencia vas?**; **I don't ~ see him** **no lo veo
mucho**. ◆ **as often as not** *adv* **muchas
veces**. ◆ **every so often** *adv* **cada cierto tiempo**. ◆ **more often than not** *adv*
la mayoría de las veces.

ogle ['əʊgl] *vt pej* **comerse con los ojos**.

oh [əʊ] *excl* **-1.** [to introduce comment]
¡ah!; **~ really?** **¿de verdad?** **-2.** [express-
ing joy, surprise, fear] **¡oh!**; **~ no!** **¡no!**

oil [ɔɪl] ◇ *n* **-1.** [gen] **aceite** *m*. **-2.** [pe-
troleum] **petróleo** *m*. ◇ *vt* **engrasar**.

oilcan ['ɔɪlkæn] *n* **aceitera** *f*.

oilfield ['ɔɪlfiːld] *n* **yacimiento** *m* **petrolífero**.

oil filter *n* **filtro** *m* **del aceite**.

oil-fired [-,faɪəd] *adj* **de fuel-oil**.

oil painting *n* **pintura** *f* **al óleo** *m*.

oilrig ['ɔɪlrɪg] *n* **plataforma** *f* **petrolífera**.

oilskins ['ɔɪlskɪnz] *npl* [gen] **prenda** *f* **de
hule**; [coat] **impermeable** *m*, **chubasquero** *m*.

oil slick *n* **marea** *f* **negra**.

oil tanker *n* **-1.** [ship] **petrolero** *m*. **-2.**
[lorry] **camión** *m* **cisterna**.

oil well *n* **pozo** *m* **petrolífero** OR **de petróleo**.

oily ['ɔɪlɪ] *adj* [food] aceitoso(sa); [rag, cloth] grasiento(ta).

ointment ['ɔɪntmənt] *n* pomada *f*, ungüento *m*.

OK (*pt* & *pp* **OKed**, *cont* **OKing**), **okay** [,əʊ'keɪ] *inf* ◇ *adj*: **is it ~ with you?** ¿te parece bien? ◇ *excl* **-1.** [gen] vale, de acuerdo. **-2.** [to introduce new topic] bien, vale. ◇ *vt* dar el visto bueno a.

old [əʊld] ◇ *adj* **-1.** [gen] viejo(ja); **how ~ are you?** ¿cuántos años tienes?, ¿qué edad tienes?; **I'm 20 years ~** tengo 20 años. **-2.** [former] antiguo(gua). ◇ *npl*: **the ~** los ancianos.

old age *n* vejez *f*.

old age pensioner *n Br* pensionista *m y f*, jubilado *m*, -da *f*.

Old Bailey [-'beɪlɪ] *n*: **the ~** el juzgado criminal central de Inglaterra.

old-fashioned [-'fæʃnd] *adj* **-1.** [outmoded] pasado(da) de moda, anticuado(da). **-2.** [traditional] tradicional.

old people's home *n* residencia *f* OR hogar *m* de ancianos.

O level *n Br* ≈ Bachillerato *m*, ≈ BUP *m*.

olive ['ɒlɪv] ◇ *adj* verde oliva. ◇ *n* [fruit] aceituna *f*, oliva *f*.

olive green *adj* verde oliva.

olive oil *n* aceite *m* de oliva.

Olympic [ə'lɪmpɪk] *adj* olímpico(ca). ◆ **Olympics** *npl*: **the ~s** los Juegos Olímpicos.

Olympic Games *npl*: **the ~** los Juegos Olímpicos.

ombudsman ['ɒmbʊdzmən] (*pl* **-men** [-mən]) *n* ≈ Defensor *m* del Pueblo.

omelet(te) ['ɒmlɪt] *n* tortilla *f*.

omen ['əʊmen] *n* presagio *m*, agüero *m*.

ominous ['ɒmɪnəs] *adj* siniestro(tra), de mal agüero.

omission [ə'mɪʃn] *n* **-1.** [thing left out] olvido *m*, descuido *m*. **-2.** [act of omitting] omisión *f*.

omit [ə'mɪt] *vt* omitir; [name - from list] pasar por alto; **to ~ to do sthg** olvidar hacer algo.

omnibus ['ɒmnɪbəs] *n* **-1.** [book] antología *f*. **-2.** *Br* RADIO & TV *programa que emite varios capítulos seguidos.*

on [ɒn] ◇ *prep* **-1.** [indicating position - gen] en; [- on top of] sobre, en; **~ a chair** en OR sobre una silla; **~ the wall/ground** en la pared/el suelo; **he was lying ~ his side/back** estaba tumbado de costado/de espaldas; **~ the left/right** a la izquierda/derecha; **I haven't got any money ~ me** no llevo nada de dinero encima. **-2.** [indicating means]: **it runs ~ diesel** funciona con diesel; **~ TV/the radio** en la tele/la radio; **she's ~ the telephone** está al teléfono; **he lives ~ fruit** vive (a base) de fruta; **to hurt o.s. ~ sthg** hacerse daño con algo. **-3.** [indicating mode of transport]: **to travel ~ a bus/train/ship** viajar en autobús/tren/barco; **I was ~ the bus** iba en el autobús; **to get ~ a bus/train/ship** subirse a un autobús/tren/barco; **~ foot** a pie. **-4.** [indicating time, activity]: **~ Thursday** el jueves; **~ my birthday** el día de mi cumpleaños; **~ the 10th of February** el 10 de febrero; **~ my return**, **~ returning** al volver; **~ business/holiday** de negocios/vacaciones. **-5.** [concerning] sobre, acerca de; **a book ~ astronomy** un libro acerca de OR sobre astronomía. **-6.** [indicating influence] en, sobre; **the impact ~ the environment** el impacto en OR sobre el medio ambiente. **-7.** [using, supported by]: **to be ~ social security** cobrar dinero de la seguridad social; **he's ~ tranquillizers** está tomando tranquilizantes; **to get ~ a bus/** drugs [addicted] drogarse. **-8.** [earning]: **she's ~ £25,000 a year** gana 25.000 libras al año. **-9.** [referring to musical instrument] con; **~ the violin** con el violín; **~ the piano** al piano. **-10.** *inf* [paid by]: **the drinks are ~ me** yo pago las copas, a las copas invito yo. ◇ *adv* **-1.** [indicating covering, clothing]: **put the lid ~** pon la tapa; **what did she have ~?** ¿qué llevaba encima OR puesto?; **put your coat ~** ponte el abrigo. **-2.** [being shown]: **what's ~ at the cinema?** ¿qué echan OR ponen en el cine? **-3.** [working - machine] funcionando; [- radio, TV, light] encendido(da); [- tap] abierto(ta); [- brakes] puesto(ta); **turn ~ the power** pulse el botón de encendido. **-4.** [indicating continuing action]: **he kept ~ walking** siguió caminando. **-5.** [forward]: **send my mail ~ (to me)** reenvíame el correo; **later ~** más tarde, después; **earlier ~** con anterioridad, antes. **-6.** *inf* [referring to behaviour]: **it's just not ~!** ¡es una pasada! ◆ **from ... on** *adv*: **from now ~** de ahora en adelante; **from that moment/time ~** desde aquel momento/aquella vez. ◆ **on and off** *adv* de vez en cuando. ◆ **on to, onto** *prep* (*only written as* **onto** *for senses 4 and 5*) **-1.** [to a position on top of] encima de, sobre; **she jumped ~ to the chair** salto encima de OR sobre la silla. **-2.**

[to a position on a vehicle]: **to get ~ to a bus/train/plane** subirse a un autobús/tren/avión. **-3.** [to a position attached to] a; **stick the photo ~ to the page** pega la foto a la hoja. **-4.** [aware of wrongdoing]: **to be onto sb** andar detrás de alguien. **-5.** [into contact with]: **get onto the factory** ponte en contacto con la fábrica.

once [wʌns] ◇ *adv* **-1.** [on one occasion] una vez; **~ a week** una vez a la semana; **~ again** OR **more** otra vez; **for ~** por una vez; **~ and for all** de una vez por todas; **~ or twice** alguna que otra vez; **~ in a while** de vez en cuando. **-2.** [previously] en otro tiempo, antiguamente; **~ upon a time** érase una vez. ◇ *conj* una vez que; **~ you have done it** una vez que lo hayas hecho. ◆ **at once** *adv* **-1.** [immediately] en seguida, inmediatamente. **-2.** [at the same time] a la vez, al mismo tiempo; **all at ~** de repente, de golpe.

oncoming ['ɒn,kʌmɪŋ] *adj* [traffic] que viene en dirección contraria; [danger, event] venidero(ra).

one [wʌn] ◇ *num* [the number 1] un (una); **I only want ~** sólo quiero uno; **~ fifth** un quinto, una quinta parte; **~ of my friends** uno de mis amigos; **on page a hundred and ~** en la página ciento uno; **(number)** ~ el uno. ◇ *adj* **-1.** [only] único(ca); **it's her ~ ambition** es su única ambición. **-2.** [indefinite]: **~ of these days** un día de éstos. ◇ *pron* **-1.** [referring to a particular thing or person] uno (una); **I want the red ~** yo quiero el rojo; **the ~ with the blond hair** la del pelo rubio; **which ~ do you want?** ¿cuál quieres?; **this ~** éste (ésta); **that ~** ése (ésa); **she's the ~ I told you about** es (ésa) de la que te hablé. **-2.** *fml* [you, anyone] uno (una); **to do ~'s duty** cumplir uno con su deber. ◆ **for one** *adv*: **I for ~ remain unconvinced** yo, por lo menos OR por mi parte, sigo poco convencido.

one-armed bandit *n* (máquina *f*) tragaperras *f inv*.

one-man *adj* individual, en solitario.

one-man band *n* [musician] hombre *m* orquesta.

one-off *inf* ◇ *adj* único(ca). ◇ *n* caso *m* excepcional.

one-on-one *Am* = **one-to-one**.

one-parent family *n* familia *f* monoparental.

oneself [wʌn'self] *pron* **-1.** (*reflexive, after prep*) uno mismo (una misma); **to buy presents for ~** hacerse regalos a sí mismo. **-2.** (*for emphasis*): **by ~** [without help] solo(la).

one-sided [-'saɪdɪd] *adj* **-1.** [unequal] desigual. **-2.** [biased] parcial.

one-to-one *Br*, **one-on-one** *Am adj* [relationship, discussion] entre dos; [tuition] individual.

one-upmanship [,wʌn'ʌpmənʃɪp] *n* habilidad para ganar ventaja sin hacer trampas.

one-way *adj* **-1.** [street] de dirección única. **-2.** [ticket] de ida.

ongoing ['ɒn,gəʊɪŋ] *adj* actual, en curso.

onion ['ʌnjən] *n* cebolla *f*.

online ['ɒnlaɪn] *adj & adv* COMPUT en línea.

onlooker ['ɒn,lʊkəʳ] *n* espectador *m*, -ra *f*.

only ['əʊnlɪ] ◇ *adj* único(ca); **an ~ child** hijo único. ◇ *adv* [exclusively] sólo, solamente; **I was ~ too willing to help** estaba encantado de poder ayudar; **I ~ wish I could!** ¡ojalá pudiera!; **it's ~ natural** es completamente normal; **not ~ ... but no sólo ... sino;** **~ just** apenas. ◇ *conj* sólo OR solamente que; **I would go, ~ I'm too tired** iría, lo que pasa es que estoy muy cansado.

onset ['ɒnset] *n* comienzo *m*.

onshore ['ɒnʃɔːʳ] *adj* [wind] procedente del mar; [oil production] en tierra firme.

onslaught ['ɒnslɔːt] *n lit & fig* acometida *f*.

onto [*unstressed before consonant* 'ɒntə, *unstressed before vowel* 'ɒntʊ, *stressed* 'ɒntuː] = **on to**.

onus ['əʊnəs] *n* responsabilidad *f*.

onward ['ɒnwəd] ◇ *adj* [in time] progresivo(va); [in space] hacia delante. ◇ *adv* = **onwards**.

onwards ['ɒnwədz] *adv* [in space] adelante, hacia delante; [in time]: **from now/then ~** de ahora/allí en adelante.

ooze [uːz] ◇ *vt fig* rebosar. ◇ *vi*: **to ~ (from** OR **out of)** rezumar (de); **to ~ with sthg** *fig* rebosar OR irradiar algo.

opaque [əʊ'peɪk] *adj* **-1.** [not transparent] opaco(ca). **-2.** *fig* [obscure] oscuro(ra).

OPEC ['əʊpek] (*abbr of* **Organization of Petroleum Exporting Countries**) *n* OPEP *f*.

open ['əʊpn] ◇ *adj* **-1.** [gen] abierto(ta); [curtains] descorrido(da); [view, road] despejado(da). **-2.** [receptive]: **to be ~ to** [ideas, suggestions] **estar abierto a**; [blame, criticism, question] **prestarse a**. **-3.** [frank] **sincero(ra), franco(ca)**. **-4.** [uncovered - car] **descubierto(ta)**. **-5.** [available - subj: choice, chance]: **to be ~ to sb estar disponible para alguien**. ◇ *n*: **in the ~** [fresh air] **al aire libre**; **to bring sthg out into the ~ sacar a luz algo**. ◇ *vt* **-1.** [gen] **abrir**; **to ~ fire abrir fuego**. **-2.** [inaugurate - public area, event] **inaugurar**. ◇ *vi* **-1.** [door, flower] **abrirse**. **-2.** [shop, office] **abrir**. **-3.** [event, play] **dar comienzo**. ◆ **open on to** *vt fus* **dar a**. ◆ **open up** ◇ *vt sep* **abrir**. ◇ *vi* **-1.** [become available] **surgir**. **-2.** [unlock door] **abrir**.

opener ['əupnə']ʳ *n* [gen] **abridor** *m*; [for tins] **abrelatas** *m inv*; [for bottles] **abrebotellas** *m inv*.

opening ['əupnɪŋ] ◇ *adj* **inicial**. ◇ *n* **-1.** [beginning] **comienzo** *m*, **principio** *m*. **-2.** [gap - in fence] **abertura** *f*. **-3.** [opportunity] **oportunidad** *f*. **-4.** [job vacancy] **puesto** *m* **vacante**.

opening hours *npl* **horario** *m* (de apertura).

openly ['əupənlɪ] *adv* **abiertamente**.

open-minded [-'maɪndɪd] *adj* **sin prejuicios**.

open-plan *adj* **de plan abierto, sin tabiques**.

Open University *n Br*: **the ~ ≃ la Universidad Nacional de Educación a Distancia**.

opera ['ɒpərə] *n* **ópera** *f*.

opera house *n* **teatro** *m* **de la ópera**.

operate ['ɒpəreɪt] ◇ *vt* **-1.** [machine] **hacer funcionar**. **-2.** [business, system] **dirigir**. ◇ *vi* **-1.** [carry out trade, business] **operar, actuar**. **-2.** [function] **funcionar**. **-3.** MED: **to ~ (on sb/sthg) operar (a alguien/de algo)**.

operating theatre *Br*, **operating room** *Am* ['ɒpəreɪtɪŋ-] *n* **quirófano** *m*.

operation [ˌɒpə'reɪʃn] *n* **-1.** [planned activity - police, rescue, business] **operación** *f*; [- military] **maniobra** *f*. **-2.** [running - of business] **administración** *f*. **-3.** [functioning - of machine] **funcionamiento** *m*; **to be in ~** [machine] **funcionar**; [law, system] **estar en vigor**. **-4.** MED **operación** *f*, **intervención** *f* **quirúrgica**; **to have an ~ (for/on) operarse (de)**.

operational [ˌɒpə'reɪʃənl] *adj* [ready for use] **operacional, en estado de funcionamiento**.

operative ['ɒprətɪv] ◇ *adj* **en vigor, vigente**. ◇ *n* **operario** *m*, **-ria** *f*.

operator ['ɒpəreɪtə'] *n* **-1.** TELEC **operador** *m*, **-ra** *f*, **telefonista** *m y f*. **-2.** [employee] **operario** *m*, **-ria** *f*. **-3.** [person in charge - of business] **encargado** *m*, **-da** *f*.

opinion [ə'pɪnjən] *n* **opinión** *f*; **to be of the ~ that opinar** OR **creer que**; **in my ~ a mi juicio, en mi opinión**.

opinionated [ə'pɪnjəneɪtɪd] *adj pej* **terco(ca)**.

opinion poll *n* **sondeo** *m*, **encuesta** *f*.

opponent [ə'pəunənt] *n* **-1.** POL **adversario** *m*, **-ria** *f*. **-2.** SPORT **contrincante** *m y f*.

opportune ['ɒpətjuːn] *adj* **oportuno(na)**.

opportunist [ˌɒpə'tjuːnɪst] *n* **oportunista** *m y f*.

opportunity [ˌɒpə'tjuːnətɪ] *n* **oportunidad** *f*, **ocasión** *f*; **to take the ~ to do** OR **of doing sthg aprovechar la ocasión de** OR **para hacer algo**.

oppose [ə'pəuz] *vt* **oponerse a**.

opposed [ə'pəuzd] *adj* **opuesto(ta)**; **to be ~ to oponerse a**; **as ~ to en vez de, en lugar de**; **I like beer as ~ to wine me gusta la cerveza y no el vino**.

opposing [ə'pəuzɪŋ] *adj* **opuesto(ta), contrario(ria)**.

opposite ['ɒpəzɪt] ◇ *adj* **-1.** [facing - side, house] **de enfrente**. **-2.** [very different]: **~ (to) opuesto(ta)** OR **contrario(ria) (a)**. ◇ *adv* **enfrente**. ◇ *prep* **enfrente de**. ◇ *n* **contrario** *m*.

opposite number *n* **homólogo** *m*, **-ga** *f*.

opposition [ˌɒpə'zɪʃn] *n* **-1.** [gen] **oposición** *f*. **-2.** [opposing team] **oponentes** *mpl y fpl*. ◆ **Opposition** *n Br* POL: **the Opposition la oposición**.

oppress [ə'pres] *vt* **-1.** [persecute] **oprimir**. **-2.** [depress] **agobiar, deprimir**.

oppressive [ə'presɪv] *adj* **-1.** [unjust] **tiránico(ca), opresivo(va)**. **-2.** [stifling] **agobiante, sofocante**. **-3.** [causing unease] **opresivo(va), agobiante**.

opt [ɒpt] ◇ *vt*: **to ~ to do sthg optar por** OR **elegir hacer algo**. ◇ *vi*: **to ~ for sthg optar por** OR **elegir algo**. ◆ **opt in** *vi*: **to ~ in (to sthg) optar por participar (en algo)**. ◆ **opt out** *vi*: **to ~ out (of sthg) decidir no tomar parte (en algo)**.

optical ['ɒptɪkl] *adj* **óptico(ca)**.

optician [ɒp'tɪʃn] *n* **óptico** *m*, **-ca** *f*; **~'s (shop) la óptica**.

optimist ['ɒptɪmɪst] *n* **optimista** *m y f*.

optimistic [ˌɒptɪ'mɪstɪk] *adj* **optimista**.

optimum ['ɒptɪməm] *adj* **óptimo(ma)**.

option ['ɒpʃn] *n* opción *f*; **to have the ~ to do** OR **of doing sthg** tener la opción OR la posibilidad de hacer algo.

optional ['ɒpʃənl] *adj* facultativo(va), optativo(va); **~ extra** extra *m* opcional.

or [ɔːʳ] *conj* **-1.** [gen] o; (*before "o" or "ho"*) u; **~ (else)** o de lo contrario, si no. **-2.** (*after negative*): **he cannot read ~ write** no sabe ni leer ni escribir.

oral ['ɔːrəl] ◇ *adj* **-1.** [spoken] oral. **-2.** [relating to the mouth] bucal. ◇ *n* examen *m* oral.

orally ['ɔːrəlɪ] *adv* **-1.** [in spoken form] oralmente. **-2.** [via the mouth] por vía oral.

orange ['ɒrɪndʒ] ◇ *adj* naranja. ◇ *n* [fruit] naranja *f*.

orator ['ɒrətəʳ] *n* orador *m*, -ra *f*.

orbit ['ɔːbɪt] ◇ *n* órbita *f*. ◇ *vt* girar alrededor de.

orchard ['ɔːtʃəd] *n* huerto *m*.

orchestra ['ɔːkɪstrə] *n* orquesta *f*.

orchestral [ɔːˈkestrəl] *adj* orquestal.

orchid ['ɔːkɪd] *n* orquídea *f*.

ordain [ɔːˈdeɪn] *vt* **-1.** *fml* [decree] decretar, ordenar. **-2.** RELIG: **to be ~ed** ordenarse (sacerdote).

ordeal [ɔːˈdiːl] *n* calvario *m*, experiencia *f* terrible.

order ['ɔːdəʳ] ◇ *n* **-1.** [instruction] orden *f*; **to be under ~s to do sthg** tener órdenes de hacer algo. **-2.** COMM [request] pedido *m*; **to ~** por encargo. **-3.** [sequence, discipline, system] orden *m*; **in ~** en orden; **in ~ of importance** por orden de importancia. **-4.** [fitness for use]: **in working ~** en funcionamiento; **"out of ~"** "no funciona"; **to be out of ~** [not working] estar estropeado(da); [incorrect behaviour] ser improcedente; **in ~** [correct] en regla. **-5.** RELIG orden *f*. **-6.** *Am* [portion] ración *f*. ◇ *vt* **-1.** [command]: **to ~ sb (to do sthg)** ordenar a alguien (que haga algo); **to ~ that** ordenar que. **-2.** [request - drink, taxi] pedir. **-3.** COM encargar. ◆ **in the order of** *Br*, **on the order of** *Am prep* del orden de. ◆ **in order that** *conj* para que. ◆ **in order to** *conj* para. ◆ **order about, order around** *vt sep* mangonear.

order form *n* hoja *f* de pedido.

orderly ['ɔːdəlɪ] ◇ *adj* [person, crowd] obediente; [room] ordenado(da), en orden. ◇ *n* [in hospital] auxiliar *m y f* sanitario.

ordinarily ['ɔːdənrəlɪ] *adv* de ordinario.

ordinary ['ɔːdənrɪ] ◇ *adj* **-1.** [normal] corriente, normal. **-2.** *pej* [unexcep-

tional] mediocre, ordinario(ria). ◇ *n*: **out of the ~** fuera de lo común.

ordnance ['ɔːdnəns] *n* (*U*) **-1.** [military supplies] pertrechos *mpl* de guerra. **-2.** [artillery] artillería *f*.

ore [ɔːʳ] *n* mineral *m*.

oregano [ˌɒrɪˈgɑːnəʊ] *n* orégano *m*.

organ ['ɔːgən] *n* órgano *m*.

organic [ɔːˈgænɪk] *adj* orgánico(ca).

organization [ˌɔːgənaɪˈzeɪʃn] *n* organización *f*.

organize, -ise ['ɔːgənaɪz] *vt* organizar.

organizer ['ɔːgənaɪzəʳ] *n* organizador *m*, -ra *f*.

orgasm ['ɔːgæzm] *n* orgasmo *m*.

orgy ['ɔːdʒɪ] *n* *lit* & *fig* orgía *f*.

Orient ['ɔːrɪənt] *n*: **the ~** el Oriente.

oriental [ˌɔːrɪˈentl] ◇ *adj* oriental. ◇ *n* oriental *m y f* (*atención: el término "oriental" se considera racista*).

orienteering [ˌɔːrɪənˈtɪərɪŋ] *n* deporte *m* de orientación, orienteering *m*.

origami [ˌɒrɪˈgɑːmɪ] *n* papiroflexia *f*.

origin ['ɒrɪdʒɪn] *n* origen *m*; **country of ~** país *m* de origen. ◆ **origins** *npl* origen *m*.

original [əˈrɪdʒənl] ◇ *adj* original; **the ~ owner** el primer propietario. ◇ *n* original *m*.

originally [əˈrɪdʒənəlɪ] *adv* [at first] originariamente; [with originality] originalmente.

originate [əˈrɪdʒəneɪt] ◇ *vt* originar, producir. ◇ *vi*: **to ~ (in)** nacer OR surgir (de); **to ~ from** nacer OR surgir de.

Orkney Islands ['ɔːknɪ-], **Orkneys** ['ɔːknɪz] *npl*: **the ~** las Orcadas.

ornament ['ɔːnəmənt] *n* adorno *m*.

ornamental [ˌɔːnəˈmentl] *adj* ornamental, decorativo(va).

ornate [ɔːˈneɪt] *adj* [style] recargado(da); [decoration, vase] muy vistoso(sa).

ornithology [ˌɔːnɪˈθɒlədʒɪ] *n* ornitología *f*.

orphan ['ɔːfn] ◇ *n* huérfano *m*, -na *f*. ◇ *vt*: **to be ~ed** quedarse huérfano.

orphanage ['ɔːfənɪdʒ] *n* orfelinato *m*.

orthodox ['ɔːθədɒks] *adj* ortodoxo(xa).

orthopaedic [ˌɔːθəˈpiːdɪk] *adj* ortopédico(ca).

orthopedic [ˌɔːθəˈpiːdɪk] *etc* = **orthopaedic** *etc*.

oscillate ['ɒsɪleɪt] *vi* *lit* & *fig*: **to ~ (between)** oscilar (entre).

Oslo ['ɒzləʊ] *n* Oslo.

ostensible [ɒˈstensəbl] *adj* aparente.

ostentatious [ˌɒstən'teɪʃəs] *adj* **-1.** [life-style, wealth] ostentoso(sa). **-2.** [person] ostentativo(va). **-3.** [behaviour] ostensible.

osteopath ['ɒstɪəpæθ] *n* osteópata *m* y *f*.

ostracize, -ise ['ɒstrəsaɪz] *vt* [colleague etc] marginar, hacer el vacío a; POL condenar al ostracismo.

ostrich ['ɒstrɪtʃ] *n* avestruz *m*.

other ['ʌðər] ◇ *adj* otro (otra); **the ~ one** el otro (la otra); **the ~ day** el otro día. ◇ *pron* **-1.** [different one]: ~s otros (otras). **-2.** [remaining, alternative one]: **the ~** el otro (la otra); **the ~s** los otros (las otras), los demás (las demás); **one after the ~** uno tras otro; **one or ~** uno u otro; **to be none ~ than** no ser otro(tra) sino. ◆ **something or other** *pron* una cosa u otra. ◆ **somehow or other** *adv* de una u otra forma. ◆ **other than** *conj* excepto, salvo.

otherwise ['ʌðəwaɪz] ◇ *adv* **-1.** [or else] si no. **-2.** [apart from that] por lo demás. **-3.** [differently] de otra manera; **deliberately or ~** adrede o no. ◇ *conj* sino, de lo contrario.

otter ['ɒtər] *n* nutria *f*.

ouch [aʊtʃ] *excl* ¡ay!

ought [ɔːt] *aux vb* deber; **you ~ to go/ to be nicer** deberías irte/ser más amable; **she ~ to pass the exam** tiene probabilidades de aprobar el examen.

ounce [aʊns] *n* [unit of measurement] = 28,35g, ≃ onza *f*.

our ['aʊər] *poss adj* nuestro(tra), nuestros(tras) (*pl*); ~ **money** nuestro dinero; ~ **house** nuestra casa; ~ **children** nuestros hijos; **it wasn't OUR fault** no fue culpa nuestra OR nuestra culpa; **we washed ~ hair** nos lavamos el pelo.

ours ['aʊəz] *poss pron* nuestro(tra); **that money is ~** ese dinero es nuestro; **those keys are ~** esas llaves son nuestras; **it wasn't their fault, it was OURS** no fue culpa de ellos sino de nosotros; **a friend of ~** un amigo nuestro; **their car hit ~** suyo coche chocó contra el nuestro.

ourselves [aʊə'selvz] *pron pl* **-1.** (*reflexive*) nos *mpl* y *fpl*; (*after prep*) nosotros *mpl*, nosotras *fpl*. **-2.** (*for emphasis*) nosotros mismos *mpl*, nosotras mismas *fpl*; **we did it by ~** lo hicimos nosotros solos.

oust [aʊst] *vt fml*: **to ~ sb (from)** [job] desbancar a alguien (de); [land] desalojar a alguien (de).

out [aʊt] *adv* **-1.** [not inside, out of doors] fuera; **we all went ~** todos salimos fuera; **I'm going ~ for a walk** voy a salir a dar un paseo; **they ran ~** salieron corriendo; **he poured the water ~** sirvió el agua; ~ **here/there** aquí/allí fuera. **-2.** [away from home, office] fuera; **John's ~ at the moment** John está fuera ahora mismo. **-3.** [extinguished] apagado(da); **the fire went ~** el fuego se apagó. **-4.** [of tides]: **the tide had gone ~** la marea estaba baja. **-5.** [out of fashion] pasado(da) de moda. **-6.** [published, released - book] publicado(da); **they've got a new record ~** han sacado un nuevo disco. **-7.** [in flower] en flor. **-8.** *inf* [on strike] en huelga. **-9.** [determined]: **to be ~ to do sthg** estar decidido(da) a hacer algo. ◆ **out of** *prep* **-1.** [away from, outside] fuera de; **to go ~ of the room** salir de la habitación. **-2.** [indicating cause] por; ~ **of spite/love** por rencor/amor. **-3.** [indicating origin, source] de; **a page ~ of a book** una página de un libro. **-4.** [without] sin; **we're ~ of sugar** estamos sin azúcar, se nos ha acabado el azúcar. **-5.** [made from] de; **it's made ~ of plastic** está hecho de plástico. **-6.** [sheltered from] a resguardo de. **-7.** [to indicate proportion]: **one ~ of ten people** una de cada diez personas; **ten ~ of ten** [mark] diez de OR sobre diez.

out-and-out *adj* [disgrace, lie] infame; [liar, crook] redomado(da).

outback ['aʊtbæk] *n*: **the ~** los llanos del interior de Australia.

outboard (motor) ['aʊtbɔːd-] *n* (motor *m*) fueraborda *m*.

outbreak ['aʊtbreɪk] *n* [of war] comienzo *m*; [of crime] ola *f*; [of illness] epidemia *f*; [of spots] erupción *f*.

outburst ['aʊtbɜːst] *n* **-1.** [sudden expression of emotion] explosión *f*, arranque *m*. **-2.** [sudden occurrence] estallido *m*.

outcast ['aʊtkɑːst] *n* marginado *m*, -da *f*, paria *m* y *f*.

outcome ['aʊtkʌm] *n* resultado *m*.

outcrop ['aʊtkrɒp] *n* afloramiento *m*.

outcry ['aʊtkraɪ] *n* protestas *fpl*.

outdated [ˌaʊt'deɪtɪd] *adj* anticuado(da), pasado(da) de moda.

outdid [ˌaʊt'dɪd] *pt* → **outdo**.

outdo [ˌaʊt'duː] (*pt* **-did**, *pp* **-done** [-dʌn]) *vt* aventajar, superar.

outdoor ['aʊtdɔːr] *adj* [life, swimming pool] al aire libre; [clothes] de calle.

outdoors [aʊt'dɔːz] *adv* al aire libre.

outer ['aʊtər] *adj* exterior, externo(na).

outer space *n* espacio *m* exterior.

outfit ['aʊtfɪt] *n* **-1.** [clothes] conjunto *m*, traje *m*. **-2.** *inf* [organization] equipo *m*.

outfitters ['aʊt,fɪtəz] *n dated* tienda *f* de confección.

outgoing ['aʊt,gəʊɪŋ] *adj* **-1.** [chairman] saliente. **-2.** [sociable] extrovertido(da).

◆ **outgoings** *npl* gastos *mpl*.

outgrow [,aʊt'grəʊ] (*pt* **-grew**, *pp* **-grown**) *vt* **-1.** [grow too big for]: **he has ~n his shirts** las camisas se le han quedado pequeñas. **-2.** [grow too old for] ser demasiado mayor para.

outhouse ['aʊthaʊs, *pl* -haʊzɪz] *n* dependencia *f*.

outing ['aʊtɪŋ] *n* [trip] excursión *f*.

outlandish [aʊt'lændɪʃ] *adj* estrafalario(ria).

outlaw ['aʊtlɔː] ◇ *n* proscrito *m*, -ta *f*. ◇ *vt* [make illegal] ilegalizar.

outlay ['aʊtleɪ] *n* desembolso *m*.

outlet ['aʊtlet] *n* **-1.** [for emotions] salida *f*. **-2.** [for water] desagüe *m*; [for gas] salida *f*. **-3.** [shop] punto *m* de venta. **-4.** *Am* ELEC toma *f* de corriente.

outline ['aʊtlaɪn] ◇ *n* **-1.** [brief description] esbozo *m*, resumen *m*; **in ~** en líneas generales. **-2.** [silhouette] contorno *m*. ◇ *vt* [describe briefly] esbozar, resumir.

outlive [,aʊt'lɪv] *vt* [subj: person] sobrevivir a.

outlook ['aʊtlʊk] *n* **-1.** [attitude, disposition] enfoque *m*, actitud *f*. **-2.** [prospect] perspectiva *f* (de futuro).

outlying ['aʊt,laɪɪŋ] *adj* [remote] lejano(na), remoto(ta); [on edge of town] periférico(ca).

outmoded [,aʊt'məʊdɪd] *adj* anticuado(da), pasado(da) de moda.

outnumber [,aʊt'nʌmbə'] *vt* exceder en número.

out-of-date *adj* **-1.** [clothes, belief] anticuado(da), pasado(da) de moda. **-2.** [passport, season ticket] caducado(da).

out of doors *adv* al aire libre.

out-of-the-way *adj* [far away] remoto(ta); [unusual] poco común.

outpatient [aʊt,peɪʃnt] *n* paciente externo *m*, paciente externa *f*.

outpost ['aʊtpəʊst] *n* puesto *m* avanzado.

output ['aʊtpʊt] *n* **-1.** [production] producción *f*, rendimiento *m*. **-2.** [COMPUT - printing out] salida *f*; [- printout] impresión *f*.

outrage ['aʊtreɪdʒ] ◇ *n* **-1.** [anger] indig-

nación *f*. **-2.** [atrocity] atrocidad *f*, escándalo *m*. ◇ *vt* ultrajar, atropellar.

outrageous [aʊt'reɪdʒəs] *adj* **-1.** [offensive, shocking] indignante, escandaloso(sa). **-2.** [very unusual] extravagante.

outright [*adj* 'aʊtraɪt, *adv* ,aʊt'raɪt] ◇ *adj* **-1.** [categoric] categórico(ca). **-2.** [total - disaster] completo(ta); [- victory, winner] indiscutible. ◇ *adv* **-1.** [ask] abiertamente; [deny] categóricamente. **-2.** [win, ban] totalmente; [be killed] en el acto.

outset ['aʊtset] *n*: **at the ~** al principio; **from the ~** desde el principio.

outside [*adv* aʊt'saɪd, *adj*, *prep & n* 'aʊtsaɪd] ◇ *adj* **-1.** [gen] exterior. **-2.** [opinion, criticism] independiente. **-3.** [chance] remoto(ta). ◇ *adv* fuera; **to go/run/look ~** ir/correr/mirar fuera. ◇ *prep* fuera de; **we live half an hour ~ London** vivimos a media hora de Londres. ◇ *n* [exterior] exterior *m*.

◆ **outside of** *prep Am* [apart from] aparte de.

outside lane *n* carril *m* de adelantamiento.

outside line *n* línea *f* exterior.

outsider [,aʊt'saɪdə'] *n* **-1.** [stranger] forastero *m*, -ra *f*. **-2.** [in horse race] *caballo que no es uno de los favoritos.*

outsize ['aʊtsaɪz] *adj* **-1.** [bigger than usual] enorme. **-2.** [clothes] de talla muy grande.

outskirts ['aʊtskɜːts] *npl*: **the ~** las afueras.

outspoken [,aʊt'spəʊkn] *adj* franco(ca).

outstanding [,aʊt'stændɪŋ] *adj* **-1.** [excellent] destacado(da). **-2.** [not paid, unfinished] pendiente.

outstay [,aʊt'steɪ] *vt*: **to ~ one's welcome** quedarse más tiempo de lo debido.

outstretched [,aʊt'stretʃt] *adj* extendido(da).

outstrip [,aʊt'strɪp] *vt lit & fig* aventajar, dejar atrás.

out-tray *n* cubeta o bandeja de asuntos ya resueltos.

outward ['aʊtwəd] ◇ *adj* **-1.** [journey] de ida. **-2.** [composure, sympathy] aparente. **-3.** [sign, proof] visible, exterior. ◇ *adv Am* = **outwards**.

outwardly ['aʊtwədlɪ] *adv* [apparently] aparentemente, de cara al exterior.

outwards *Br* ['aʊtwədz], **outward** *Am adv* hacia fuera.

outweigh [,aʊt'weɪ] *vt* pesar más que.

outwit [ˌaʊt'wɪt] *vt* ser más listo(ta) que.

oval ['əʊvl] ◇ *adj* oval, ovalado(da). ◇ *n* óvalo *m*.

Oval Office *n*: **the ~** el Despacho Oval, *oficina que tiene el presidente de Estados Unidos en la Casa Blanca.*

ovary ['əʊvərɪ] *n* ovario *m*.

ovation [əʊ'veɪʃn] *n* ovación *f*; **a standing ~** una ovación de gala (con el público en pie).

oven ['ʌvn] *n* horno *m*.

ovenproof ['ʌvnpruːf] *adj* refractario(ria).

over ['əʊvər] ◇ *prep* **-1.** [directly above, on top of] encima de; **a fog hung ~ the river** una espesa niebla flotaba sobre el río; **put your coat ~ the chair** pon el abrigo encima de la silla. **-2.** [to cover] sobre; **she wore a veil ~ her face** un velo le cubría el rostro. **-3.** [on other side of] al otro lado de; **he lives ~ the road** vive enfrente. **-4.** [across surface of] por encima de; **they sailed ~ the ocean** cruzaron el océano en barco. **-5.** [more than] más de; **~ and above** además de. **-6.** [senior to] por encima de. **-7.** [with regard to] por; **a fight ~ a woman** una pelea por una mujer. **-8.** [during] durante; **~ the weekend** (en) el fin de semana. ◇ *adv* **-1.** [short distance away]: **~ here** aquí; **~ there** allí. **-2.** [across]: **to cross ~** cruzar; **to go ~** ir. **-3.** [down]: **to fall ~** caerse; **to push ~** empujar, tirar. **-4.** [round]: **to turn sthg ~** dar la vuelta a algo; **to roll ~** darse la vuelta. **-5.** [more] más. **-6.** [remaining]: **to be (left) ~** quedar, sobrar. **-7.** [at sb's house]: **invite them ~** invítalos a casa. **-8.** RADIO: **~ (and out)!** ¡cambio (y cierro)! **-9.** [involving repetitions]: **(all) ~ again** otra vez desde el principio; **~ and ~ (again)** una y otra vez. ◇ *adj* [finished] terminado(da). ◆ **all over** ◇ *prep* por todo(da). ◇ *adv* [everywhere] por todas partes. ◇ *adj* [finished] terminado(da).

overall [*adj & n* 'əʊvərɔːl, *adv* ˌəʊvər'ɔːl] ◇ *adj* [general] global, total. ◇ *adv* en conjunto. ◇ *n* **-1.** [gen] guardapolvo *m*. **-2.** *Am* [for work] mono *m*. ◆ **overalls** *npl* **-1.** [for work] mono *m*. **-2.** *Am* [dungarees] pantalones *mpl* de peto.

overawe [ˌəʊvər'ɔː] *vt* intimidar.

overbalance [ˌəʊvə'bæləns] *vi* perder el equilibrio.

overbearing [ˌəʊvə'beərɪŋ] *adj pej* despótico(ca).

overboard ['əʊvəbɔːd] *adv*: **to fall ~** caer al agua OR por la borda.

overbook [ˌəʊvə'bʊk] *vi* hacer overbooking.

overcame [ˌəʊvə'keɪm] *pt* → **overcome.**

overcast ['əʊvəkɑːst] *adj* cubierto(ta), nublado(da).

overcharge [ˌəʊvə'tʃɑːdʒ] *vt*: **to ~ sb (for sthg)** cobrar a alguien en exceso (por algo).

overcoat ['əʊvəkəʊt] *n* abrigo *m*.

overcome [ˌəʊvə'kʌm] (*pt* **-came,** *pp* **-come**) *vt* **-1.** [deal with] vencer, superar. **-2.** [overwhelm]: **to be ~ (by** OR **with)** [fear, grief, emotion] estar abrumado(da) (por); [smoke, fumes] estar asfixiado(da) (por).

overcrowded [ˌəʊvə'kraʊdɪd] *adj* [room] atestado(da) de gente; [country] superpoblado(da).

overcrowding [ˌəʊvə'kraʊdɪŋ] *n* [of country] superpoblación *f*; [of prison] hacinamiento *m*.

overdo [ˌəʊvə'duː] (*pt* **-did** [-dɪd], *pp* **-done**) *vt* **-1.** *pej* [exaggerate] exagerar. **-2.** [do too much]: **to ~ one's work/the walking** trabajar/andar demasiado. **-3.** [overcook] hacer demasiado.

overdone [ˌəʊvə'dʌn] ◇ *pp* → **overdo.** ◇ *adj* muy hecho(cha).

overdose ['əʊvədəʊs] *n* sobredosis *f inv*.

overdraft ['əʊvədrɑːft] *n* [sum owed] saldo *m* deudor; [loan arranged] (giro *m* OR crédito *m* en) descubierto *m*.

overdrawn [ˌəʊvə'drɔːn] *adj*: **to be ~** tener un saldo deudor.

overdue [ˌəʊvə'djuː] *adj* **-1.** [late]: **to be ~** [train] ir con retraso; [library book] estar con el plazo de préstamo caducado; **I'm ~ (for) a bit of luck** va siendo hora de tener un poco de suerte. **-2.** [awaited]: **(long) ~** (largamente) esperado(da), ansiado(da). **-3.** [unpaid] vencido(da) y sin pagar.

overestimate [ˌəʊvər'estɪmeɪt] *vt* sobreestimar.

overflow [*vb* ˌəʊvə'fləʊ, *n* 'əʊvəfləʊ] ◇ *vi* **-1.** [spill over] rebosar; [river] desbordarse. **-2.** [go beyond limits]: **to ~ (into)** rebosar (hacia). **-3.** [be very full]: **to be ~ing (with)** rebosar (de). ◇ *n* [pipe] cañería *f* de desagüe.

overgrown [ˌəʊvə'grəʊn] *adj* cubierto(ta) de matojos.

overhaul [*n* 'əʊvəhɔːl, *vb* ˌəʊvə'hɔːl] ◇ *n* **-1.** [of car, machine] revisión *f*. **-2.** [of method, system] repaso *m* general. ◇ *vt* revisar.

overhead [*adv* ˌəʊvəˈhed, *adj & n* ˈəʊvəhed] ◇ *adj* aéreo(a). ◇ *adv* por lo alto, por encima. ◇ *n Am* (*U*) gastos *mpl* generales. ◆ **overheads** *npl* gastos *mpl* generales.

overhead projector *n* retroproyector *m*.

overhear [ˌəʊvəˈhɪəʳ] (*pt & pp* **-heard** [-ˈhɜːd]) *vt* oír por casualidad.

overheat [ˌəʊvəˈhiːt] *vi* recalentarse.

overjoyed [ˌəʊvəˈdʒɔɪd] *adj*: **to be ~ (at sthg)** estar encantado(da) (con algo).

overkill [ˈəʊvəkɪl] *n* exageración *f*, exceso *m*.

overladen [ˌəʊvəˈleɪdn] *pp* → **overload**.

overland [ˈəʊvəlænd] ◇ *adj* terrestre. ◇ *adv* por tierra.

overlap [ˌəʊvəˈlæp] *vi* **-1.** [cover each other] superponerse. **-2.** [be similar]: **to ~ (with sthg)** coincidir en parte (en algo).

overleaf [ˌəʊvəˈliːf] *adv* al dorso.

overload [ˌəʊvəˈləʊd] (*pp* **-loaded** OR **-laden**) *vt* sobrecargar.

overlook [ˌəʊvəˈlʊk] *vt* **-1.** [look over] mirar o dar a. **-2.** [disregard, miss] pasar por alto. **-3.** [forgive] perdonar.

overnight [*adj* ˈəʊvənaɪt, *adv* ˌəʊvəˈnaɪt] ◇ *adj* **-1.** [for all of night] de noche, nocturno(na). **-2.** [for a night's stay - clothes] para una noche. **-3.** [very sudden] súbito(ta). ◇ *adv* **-1.** [for all of night] durante la noche. **-2.** [very suddenly] de la noche a la mañana.

overpass [ˈəʊvəpɑːs] *n Am* paso *m* elevado.

overpower [ˌəʊvəˈpaʊəʳ] *vt* **-1.** [in fight] vencer, subyugar. **-2.** *fig* [overwhelm] sobreponerse a, vencer.

overpowering [ˌəʊvəˈpaʊərɪŋ] *adj* arrollador(ra), abrumador(ra).

overran [ˌəʊvəˈræn] *pt* → **overrun**.

overrated [ˌəʊvəˈreɪtɪd] *adj* sobreestimado(da).

override [ˌəʊvəˈraɪd] (*pt* **-rode**, *pp* **-ridden**) *vt* **-1.** [be more important than] predominar sobre. **-2.** [overrule] desautorizar.

overriding [ˌəʊvəˈraɪdɪŋ] *adj* predominante.

overrode [ˌəʊvəˈrəʊd] *pt* → **override**.

overrule [ˌəʊvəˈruːl] *vt* [person] desautorizar; [decision] anular; [request] denegar.

overrun [ˌəʊvəˈrʌn] (*pt* **-ran**, *pp* **-run**) ◇ *vt* **-1.** MIL [enemy, army] apabullar, arrasar; [country] ocupar, invadir. **-2.** *fig*

[cover]: **to be ~ with** estar invadido(da) de. ◇ *vi* rebasar el tiempo previsto.

oversaw [ˌəʊvəˈsɔː] *pt* → **oversee**.

overseas [*adj* ˈəʊvəsiːz, *adv* ˌəʊvəˈsiːz] ◇ *adj* **-1.** [in or to foreign countries - market] exterior; [- sales, aid] al extranjero; [- network, branches] en el extranjero. **-2.** [from abroad] extranjero(ra). ◇ *adv* [go, travel] al extranjero; [study, live] en el extranjero.

oversee [ˌəʊvəˈsiː] (*pt* **-saw**, *pp* **-seen** [-ˈsiːn]) *vt* supervisar.

overseer [ˈəʊvəˌsiːəʳ] *n* supervisor *m*, -ra *f*.

overshadow [ˌəʊvəˈʃædəʊ] *vt* **-1.** [be more important than]: **to be ~ed by** ser eclipsado(da) por. **-2.** [mar]: **to be ~ed by sthg** ser ensombrecido(da) por algo.

overshoot [ˌəʊvəˈʃuːt] (*pt & pp* **-shot**) *vt* [go past] pasarse.

oversight [ˈəʊvəsaɪt] *n* descuido *m*.

oversleep [ˌəʊvəˈsliːp] (*pt & pp* **-slept** [-ˈslept]) *vi* no despertarse a tiempo, quedarse dormido(da).

overspill [ˈəʊvəspɪl] *n* exceso *m* de población.

overstep [ˌəʊvəˈstep] *vt* pasar de; **to ~ the mark** pasarse de la raya.

overt [ˈəʊvɜːt] *adj* abierto(ta), evidente.

overtake [ˌəʊvəˈteɪk] (*pt* **-took**, *pp* **-taken** [-ˈteɪkn]) *vt* **-1.** AUT adelantar. **-2.** [subj: event] coger de improviso.

overthrow [ˌəʊvəˈθrəʊ] (*pt* **-threw**, *pp* **-thrown**) *vt* [oust] derrocar.

overtime [ˈəʊvətaɪm] ◇ *n* (*U*) **-1.** [extra work] horas *fpl* extra. **-2.** *Am* SPORT (tiempo *m* de) descuento *m*. ◇ *adv*: **to work ~** trabajar horas extra.

overtones [ˈəʊvətəʊnz] *npl* matiz *m*.

overtook [ˌəʊvəˈtʊk] *pt* → **overtake**.

overture [ˈəʊvəˌtjʊəʳ] *n* MUS obertura *f*.

overturn [ˌəʊvəˈtɜːn] ◇ *vt* **-1.** [turn over] volcar. **-2.** [overrule] rechazar. **-3.** [overthrow] derrocar, derrumbar. ◇ *vi* [vehicle] volcar; [boat] zozobrar.

overweight [ˌəʊvəˈweɪt] *adj* grueso(sa), gordo(da).

overwhelm [ˌəʊvəˈwelm] *vt* **-1.** [make helpless] abrumar. **-2.** [defeat] aplastar.

overwhelming [ˌəʊvəˈwelmɪŋ] *adj* **-1.** [despair, kindness] abrumador(ra). **-2.** [defeat, majority] aplastante.

overwork [ˌəʊvəˈwɜːk] ◇ *n* trabajo *m* excesivo. ◇ *vt* [give too much work to] hacer trabajar demasiado.

overwrought [ˌəʊvəˈrɔːt] *adj fml* nerviosísimo(ma), sobreexcitado(da).

owe [əʊ] *vt*: **to ~ sthg to sb, to ~ sb
sthg** deber algo a alguien.
owing ['əʊɪŋ] *adj* que se debe.
◆ **owing to** *prep* debido a.
owl [aʊl] *n* búho *m*, lechuza *f*.
own [əʊn] ◇ *adj*: **my/your/his** *etc* ~ **car**
mi/tu/su *etc* propio coche. ◇ *pron*: **my**
~ el mío (la mía); **his/her** ~ el suyo (la
suya); **a house of my/his** ~ mi/su propia casa; **on one's** ~ solo(la); **to get
one's** ~ **back** *inf* tomarse la revancha,
desquitarse. ◇ *vt* poseer, tener. ◆ **own
up** *vi*: **to** ~ **up (to sthg)** confesar (algo).
owner ['əʊnəʳ] *n* propietario *m*, -ria *f*.
ownership ['əʊnəʃɪp] *n* propiedad *f*.
ox [ɒks] (*pl* **oxen**) *n* buey *m*.
Oxbridge ['ɒksbrɪdʒ] *n* (*U*) *las universidades de Oxford y Cambridge*.
oxen ['ɒksn] *pl* → **ox**.
oxtail soup ['ɒksteɪl-] *n* sopa *f* de rabo
de buey.
oxygen ['ɒksɪdʒən] *n* oxígeno *m*.
oxygen mask *n* máscara *f* de oxígeno.
oxygen tent *n* tienda *f* de oxígeno.
oyster ['ɔɪstəʳ] *n* ostra *f*.
oz. *abbr of* **ounce**.
ozone ['əʊzəʊn] *n* ozono *m*.
ozone-friendly *adj* que no daña a la
capa de ozono.
ozone layer *n* capa *f* de ozono.

P

p¹ (*pl* **p's** OR **ps**), **P** (*pl* **P's** OR **Ps**) [piː]
n [letter] p *f*, P *f*.
p² (*abbr of* **page**) p. **-2.** *abbr of* **penny, pence**.
pa [pɑː] *n inf* papá *m*.
p.a. (*abbr of* **per annum**) p.a.
PA *n* **-1.** *Br abbr of* **personal assistant**.
-2. *abbr of* **public-address system**.
pace [peɪs] ◇ *n* paso *m*, ritmo *m*; **to
keep** ~ **(with sthg)** [change, events]
mantenerse al corriente (de algo); **to
keep** ~ **(with sb)** llevar el mismo paso
(que alguien). ◇ *vi*: **to** ~ **(up and
down)** pasearse de un lado a otro.
pacemaker ['peɪs,meɪkəʳ] *n* **-1.** MED
marcapasos *m inv*. **-2.** [in race] liebre *f*.
Pacific [pə'sɪfɪk] ◇ *adj* del Pacífico. ◇
n: **the** ~ **(Ocean)** el (océano) Pacífico.

pacifier ['pæsɪfaɪəʳ] *n Am* [for child] chupete *m*.
pacifist ['pæsɪfɪst] *n* pacifista *m y f*.
pacify ['pæsɪfaɪ] *vt* [person, mob] calmar,
apaciguar.
pack [pæk] ◇ *n* **-1.** [bundle] lío *m*, fardo
m; [rucksack] mochila *f*. **-2.** [packet] paquete *m*. **-3.** [of cards] baraja *f*. **-4.** [of
dogs] jauría *f*; [of wolves] manada *f*; *pej*
[of people] banda *f*. ◇ *vt* **-1.** [for journey
- bags, suitcase] hacer; [- clothes, etc] meter (en la maleta). **-2.** [put in parcel] empaquetar; [put in container] envasar. **-3.**
[fill] llenar, abarrotar; **to be ~ed into**
estar apretujados dentro de. ◇ *vi* hacer las maletas. ◆ **pack in** *inf* ◇ *vt sep
Br* [stop] dejar; ~ **it in!** ¡déjalo!, ¡ya
basta! ◇ *vi* parar. ◆ **pack off** *vt sep inf*
enviar, mandar.
package ['pækɪdʒ] ◇ *n* [gen & COMPUT]
paquete *m*. ◇ *vt* [wrap up] envasar.
package deal *n* convenio *m* OR acuerdo *m* global.
package tour *n* vacaciones *fpl* con
todo incluido.
packaging ['pækɪdʒɪŋ] *n* [wrapping] envasado *m*.
packed [pækt] *adj*: ~ **(with)** repleto(ta)
(de).
packed lunch *n Br* almuerzo preparado
de antemano que se lleva uno al colegio, la
oficina *etc*.
packed-out *adj Br inf* a tope.
packet ['pækɪt] *n* [gen] paquete *m*; [of
crisps, sweets] bolsa *f*.
packing ['pækɪŋ] *n* **-1.** [protective ma-
terial] embalaje *m*. **-2.** [for journey]: **to
do the** ~ hacer el equipaje.
packing case *n* cajón *m* de embalaje.
pact [pækt] *n* pacto *m*.
pad [pæd] ◇ *n* **-1.** [of material] almoha-
dillado *m*. **-2.** [of paper] bloc *m*. **-3.**
SPACE: (launch) ~ plataforma *f* de lanzamiento). **-4.** *inf dated* [home] casa *f*.
◇ *vt* acolchar, rellenar. ◇ *vi* [walk soft-
ly] andar con suavidad.
padding ['pædɪŋ] *n* (*U*) **-1.** [in jacket,
chair] relleno *m*. **-2.** [in speech] paja *f*.
paddle ['pædl] ◇ *n* **-1.** [for canoe,
dinghy] pala *f*, canalete *m*. **-2.** [walk in
sea] paseo *m* por la orilla. ◇ *vt* remar.
◇ *vi* **-1.** [in canoe] remar. **-2.** [person - in
sea] pasear por la orilla.
paddle boat, **paddle steamer** *n* vapor
m de paletas OR ruedas.
paddling pool ['pædlɪŋ-] *n Br* **-1.** [in
park] estanque *m* para chapotear. **-2.**
[inflatable] piscina *f* inflable.

paddock ['pædək] n -1. [small field] potrero m, corral m. -2. [at racecourse] paddock m.

paddy field ['pædɪ-] n arrozal m.

padlock ['pædlɒk] ◇ n candado m. ◇ vt cerrar con candado.

paediatrics [ˌpiːdɪ'ætrɪks] = pediatrics.

pagan ['peɪgən] ◇ adj pagano(na). ◇ n pagano m, -na f.

page [peɪdʒ] ◇ n página f. ◇ vt [in hotel, airport] llamar por megafonía.

pageant ['pædʒənt] n desfile m.

pageantry ['pædʒəntrɪ] n boato m.

paid [peɪd] ◇ pt & pp → pay. ◇ adj [holiday, leave] pagado(da); [work, staff] remunerado(da).

pail [peɪl] n cubo m.

pain [peɪn] n -1. [ache] dolor m; to be in ~ dolerse, sufrir dolor. -2. [mental suffering] pena f, sufrimiento m. -3. inf [annoyance - person] pesado m, -da f; [- thing] pesadez f. ◆ pains npl [effort, care] esfuerzos mpl; to be at ~s to do sthg afanarse por hacer algo; to take ~s to do sthg esforzarse en hacer algo.

pained [peɪnd] adj apenado(da).

painful ['peɪnfʊl] adj [back, eyes] dolorido(da); [injury, exercise, memory] doloroso(sa).

painfully ['peɪnfʊlɪ] adv -1. [causing pain] dolorosamente. -2. [extremely] terriblemente.

painkiller ['peɪnˌkɪlər] n calmante m.

painless ['peɪnlɪs] adj -1. [physically] indoloro(ra). -2. [emotionally] sin complicaciones.

painstaking ['peɪnzˌteɪkɪŋ] adj meticuloso(sa), minucioso(sa).

paint [peɪnt] ◇ n pintura f. ◇ vt pintar; to ~ the ceiling white pintar el techo de blanco.

paintbrush ['peɪntbrʌʃ] n -1. ART pincel m. -2. [of decorator] brocha f.

painter ['peɪntər] n pintor m, -ra f.

painting ['peɪntɪŋ] n -1. [picture] cuadro m, pintura f. -2. (U) [art form, trade] pintura f.

paint stripper n quitapinturas f inv.

paintwork ['peɪntwɜːk] n (U) pintura f.

pair [peər] n -1. [of shoes, socks, wings] par m; [of aces] pareja f. -2. [two-part object]: a ~ of scissors unas tijeras; a ~ of trousers unos pantalones. -3. [couple - of people] pareja f.

pajamas [pə'dʒɑːməz] = pyjamas.

Pakistan [Br ˌpɑːkɪ'stɑːn, Am ˌpækɪ'stæn] n (el) Paquistán.

Pakistani [Br ˌpɑːkɪ'stɑːnɪ, Am ˌpækɪ'stænɪ] ◇ adj paquistaní. ◇ n paquistaní m y f.

pal [pæl] n inf [friend] amiguete m, -ta f, colega m y f.

palace ['pælɪs] n palacio m.

palatable ['pælətəbl] adj -1. [pleasant to taste] sabroso(sa). -2. [acceptable] aceptable.

palate ['pælət] n paladar m.

palaver [pə'lɑːvər] n inf [fuss] follón m.

pale [peɪl] ◇ adj -1. [colour, clothes, paint] claro(ra); [light] tenue. -2. [person] pálido(da). ◇ vi palidecer.

Palestine ['pælɪˌstaɪn] n Palestina.

Palestinian [ˌpælə'stɪnɪən] ◇ adj palestino(na). ◇ n [person] palestino m, -na f.

palette ['pælət] n paleta f.

palings ['peɪlɪŋz] npl empalizada f.

pall [pɔːl] ◇ n -1. [of smoke] nube f, cortina f. -2. Am [coffin] féretro m. ◇ vi hacerse pesado(da).

pallet ['pælɪt] n plataforma f de carga.

pallor ['pælər] n literary palidez f.

palm [pɑːm] n -1. [tree] palmera f. -2. [of hand] palma f. ◆ palm off vt sep inf: to ~ sthg off on sb endosar OR encasquetar algo a alguien; to ~ sb off with despachar a alguien con.

Palm Sunday n Domingo m de Ramos.

palm tree n palmera f.

palpable ['pælpəbl] adj palpable.

paltry ['pɔːltrɪ] adj mísero(ra).

pamper ['pæmpər] vt mimar.

pamphlet ['pæmflɪt] n [political] panfleto m; [publicity, information] folleto m.

pan [pæn] ◇ n -1. [saucepan] cazuela f, cacerola f; [frying pan] sartén f. -2. Am [for bread, cakes etc] molde m. ◇ vt inf [criticize] poner por los suelos. ◇ vi CINEMA tomar vistas panorámicas.

panacea [ˌpænə'sɪə] n: a ~ (for) la panacea (de).

Panama [ˌpænə'mɑː] n Panamá.

Panama Canal n: the ~ el canal de Panamá.

panama (hat) n panamá m.

pancake ['pæŋkeɪk] n torta f, crepe f.

Pancake Day n Br ≃ Martes m inv de Carnaval.

panda ['pændə] (pl inv OR -s) n panda m.

Panda car n Br coche m patrulla.

pandemonium [ˌpændɪ'məʊnjəm] n pandemónium m, jaleo m.

pander ['pændər] vi: to ~ to complacer a.

pane [peɪn] n (hoja f de) cristal m.

panel ['pænl] n **-1.** [group of people] equipo m; [in debates] mesa f. **-2.** [of a material] panel m. **-3.** [of a machine] tablero m, panel m.

panelling Br, **paneling** Am ['pænəlɪŋ] n (U) [on a ceiling] artesonado m; [on a wall] paneles mpl.

pang [pæŋ] n punzada f.

panic ['pænɪk] (pt & pp **-ked**, cont **-king**) ◇ n pánico m. ◇ vi aterrarse.

panicky ['pænɪkɪ] adj [person] aterrado(da), nervioso(sa); [feeling] de pánico.

panic-stricken adj preso(sa) OR víctima del pánico.

panorama [,pænə'rɑːmə] n panorama m, vista f.

pansy ['pænzɪ] n **-1.** [flower] pensamiento m. **-2.** pej inf [man] marica m.

pant [pænt] vi jadear.

panther ['pænθəʳ] (pl inv OR **-s**) n pantera f.

panties ['pæntɪz] npl inf bragas fpl.

pantihose ['pæntɪhəʊz] = **panty hose**.

pantomime ['pæntəmaɪm] n Br obra musical humorística para niños celebrada en Navidad.

pantry ['pæntrɪ] n despensa f.

pants [pænts] npl **-1.** Br [underpants] calzoncillos mpl. **-2.** Am [trousers] pantalones mpl.

panty hose ['pæntɪ-] npl Am medias fpl.

papa [Br pə'pɑː, Am 'pæpə] n papá m.

paper ['peɪpəʳ] ◇ n **-1.** (U) [material] papel m; **piece of ~** [sheet] hoja f de papel; [scrap] trozo m de papel; **on ~** [written down] por escrito; [in theory] sobre el papel. **-2.** [newspaper] periódico m. **-3.** [in exam] examen m. **-4.** [essay-gen] estudio m, ensayo m; [- for conference] ponencia f. ◇ adj [made of paper] de papel. ◇ vt empapelar. ◆ **papers** npl [official documents] documentación f.

paperback ['peɪpəbæk] n libro m en rústica.

paper clip n clip m.

paper handkerchief n pañuelo m de papel, klínex® m inv.

paper knife n abrecartas m inv.

paper shop n Br quiosco m de periódicos.

paperweight ['peɪpəweɪt] n pisapapeles m inv.

paperwork ['peɪpəwɜːk] n papeleo m.

papier-mâché [,pæpjeɪ'mæʃeɪ] n cartón m piedra.

paprika ['pæprɪkə] n pimentón m.

par [pɑːʳ] n **-1.** [parity]: **on a ~ with** al mismo nivel que. **-2.** GOLF par m. **-3.** [good health]: **below** OR **under ~** pachucho(cha).

parable ['pærəbl] n parábola f.

parachute ['pærəʃuːt] n paracaídas m inv.

parade [pə'reɪd] ◇ n [procession] desfile m. ◇ vt **-1.** [soldiers] hacer desfilar; [criminals, captives] pasear. **-2.** fig [flaunt] hacer alarde de. ◇ vi desfilar.

paradise ['pærədaɪs] n fig paraíso m.

paradox ['pærədɒks] n paradoja f.

paradoxically [,pærə'dɒksɪklɪ] adv paradójicamente.

paraffin ['pærəfɪn] n parafina f.

paragon ['pærəgən] n dechado m.

paragraph ['pærəgrɑːf] n párrafo m.

Paraguay ['pærəgwaɪ] n (el) Paraguay.

Paraguayan [,pærə'gwaɪən] ◇ adj paraguayo(ya). ◇ n paraguayo m, -ya f.

parallel ['pærəlel] ◇ adj: **~ (to** OR **with)** paralelo(la) (a). ◇ n **-1.** [parallel line, surface] paralela f. **-2.** [something, someone similar]: **to have no ~** no tener precedente. **-3.** [similarity] semejanza f. **-4.** GEOGR paralelo m.

paralyse Br, **-yze** Am ['pærəlaɪz] vt lit & fig paralizar.

paralysis [pə'rælɪsɪs] (pl **-lyses** [-lɪsiːz]) n parálisis f inv.

paramedic [,pærə'medɪk] n auxiliar sanitario m, auxiliar sanitaria f.

parameter [pə'ræmɪtəʳ] n parámetro m.

paramount ['pærəmaʊnt] adj vital, fundamental; **of ~ importance** de suma importancia.

paranoid ['pærənɔɪd] adj paranoico(ca).

paraphernalia [,pærəfə'neɪljə] n parafernalia f.

parasite ['pærəsaɪt] n parásito m, -ta f.

parasol ['pærəsɒl] n sombrilla f.

paratrooper ['pærətruːpəʳ] n paracaidista m y f (del ejército).

parcel ['pɑːsl] n paquete m. ◆ **parcel up** vt sep empaquetar.

parcel post n (servicio m de) paquete m postal.

parched [pɑːtʃt] adj **-1.** [throat, mouth] seco(ca); [lips] quemado(da). **-2.** inf [very thirsty] seco(ca).

parchment ['pɑːtʃmənt] n [paper] pergamino m.

pardon ['pɑːdn] ◇ n **-1.** JUR perdón m, indulto m. **-2.** [forgiveness] perdón m; **I beg your ~?** [showing surprise, asking for repetition] ¿perdón?, ¿cómo (dice)?; **I beg your ~** [to apologize] le ruego me

disculpe, perdón. ◇ *vt* **-1.** [forgive]: **to
~ sb (for sthg)** perdonar a alguien (por
algo); **~?** ¿perdón?, ¿cómo (dice)?; **~
me** [touching sb accidentally, belching]
discúlpeme, perdón; [excuse me] con
permiso. **-2.** JUR indultar.

parent ['peǝrǝnt] *n* [father] padre *m*;
[mother] madre *f*. ◆ **parents** *npl* padres
mpl.

parental [pǝ'rentl] *adj* [paternal] paterno(na); [maternal] materno(na).

parenthesis [pǝ'renθısıs] (*pl* **-theses**
[-θısi:z]) *n* paréntesis *m inv*.

Paris ['pærıs] *n* París.

parish ['pærıʃ] *n* **-1.** [of church] parroquia *f*. **-2.** Br [area of local government]
municipio *m*.

parity ['pærǝtı] *n*: **~ (with/between)**
igualdad *f* (con/entre).

park [pɑ:k] ◇ *n* parque *m*. ◇ *vt & vi*
aparcar, parquear *Amer*.

parking ['pɑ:kıŋ] *n* aparcamiento *m*;
"no ~" "prohibido aparcar".

parking lot *n* Am aparcamiento *m* (al
aire libre).

parking meter *n* parquímetro *m*.

parking ticket *n* multa *f* por aparcamiento indebido.

parlance ['pɑ:lǝns] *n*: **in common/legal
etc ~** en el habla común/legal *etc*, en el
lenguaje común/legal *etc*.

parliament ['pɑ:lǝmǝnt] *n* **-1.** [assembly,
institution] parlamento *m*. **-2.** [session]
legislatura *f*.

parliamentary [,pɑ:lǝ'mentǝrı] *adj* parlamentario(ria).

parlour Br, **parlor** Am ['pɑ:lǝ'] *n* dated
salón *m*.

parochial [pǝ'rǝukjǝl] *adj pej* de miras
estrechas.

parody ['pærǝdı] ◇ *n* parodia *f*. ◇ *vt*
parodiar.

parole [pǝ'rǝul] *n* libertad *f* condicional
(bajo palabra); **on ~** en libertad condicional.

parquet ['pɑ:keı] *n* parqué *m*.

parrot ['pærǝt] *n* loro *m*, papagayo *m*.

parry ['pærı] *vt* [blow] parar; [attack]
desviar.

parsimonious [,pɑ:sı'mǝunjǝs] *adj fml &
pej* mezquino(na), tacaño(ña).

parsley ['pɑ:slı] *n* perejil *m*.

parsnip ['pɑ:snıp] *n* chirivía *f*.

parson ['pɑ:sn] *n* párroco *m*.

part [pɑ:t] ◇ *n* **-1.** [gen] parte *f*; **for the
most ~** en su mayoría. **-2.** [component]
pieza *f*. **-3.** THEATRE papel *m*. **-4.** [involvement]: **~ (in)** participación *f* (en);

to play an important ~ (in) desempeñar OR jugar un papel importante (en);
to take ~ (in) tomar parte (en); **for
my/his ~** por mi/su parte. **-5.** Am [hair
parting] raya *f*. ◇ *adv* en parte. ◇ *vt* **-1.**
[lips, curtains] abrir. **-2.** [hair] peinar con
raya. ◇ *vi* **-1.** [leave one another] separarse. **-2.** [separate - lips, curtains] abrirse. ◆ **parts** *npl* [place] pagos *mpl*.
◆ **part with** *vt fus* separarse de.

part exchange *n sistema de pagar parte
de algo con un artículo usado*; **in ~** como
parte del pago.

partial ['pɑ:ʃl] *adj* **-1.** [incomplete,
biased] parcial. **-2.** [fond]: **~ to** amigo(ga) de, aficionado(da) a.

participant [pɑ:'tısıpǝnt] *n* participante
m y f.

participate [pɑ:'tısıpeıt] *vi*: **to ~ (in)**
participar (en).

participation [pɑ:,tısı'peıʃn] *n* participación *f*.

participle ['pɑ:tısıpl] *n* participio *m*.

particle ['pɑ:tıkl] *n* partícula *f*.

particular [pǝ'tıkjulǝ'] *adj* **-1.** [specific,
unique] especial, en concreto OR particular. **-2.** [extra, greater] especial. **-3.**
[difficult] exigente. ◆ **particulars** *npl* [of
person] datos *mpl*; [of thing] detalles
mpl. ◆ **in particular** *adv* en particular.

particularly [pǝ'tıkjulǝlı] *adv* especialmente.

parting ['pɑ:tıŋ] *n* **-1.** [separation] despedida *f*. **-2.** Br [in hair] raya *f*.

partisan [,pɑ:tı'zæn] ◇ *adj* partidista. ◇
n [freedom fighter] partisano *m*, -na *f*.

partition [pɑ:'tıʃn] ◇ *n* **-1.** [wall] tabique *m*; [screen] separación *f*. **-2.** [of a
country] división *f*. ◇ *vt* **-1.** [room] dividir con tabiques. **-2.** [country] dividir.

partly ['pɑ:tlı] *adv* en parte.

partner ['pɑ:tnǝ'] *n* **-1.** [spouse, lover]
pareja *f*. **-2.** [in an activity] compañero
m, -ra *f*. **-3.** [in a business] socio *m*, -cia
f. **-4.** [ally] colega *m y f*.

partnership ['pɑ:tnǝʃıp] *n* **-1.** [relationship] asociación *f*. **-2.** [business] sociedad *f*.

partridge ['pɑ:trıdʒ] *n* perdiz *f*.

part-time ◇ *adj* a tiempo parcial. ◇
adv a tiempo parcial.

party ['pɑ:tı] *n* **-1.** POL partido *m*. **-2.**
[social gathering] fiesta *f*. **-3.** [group] grupo *m*. **-4.** JUR parte *f*.

party line *n* **-1.** POL línea *f* (política) del
partido. **-2.** TELEC línea *f* (telefónica)
compartida.

patent

pass [pɑːs] ◇ *n* **-1.** SPORT pase *m*. **-2.** [document, permit] pase *m*; **travel** ~ tarjeta *f* OR abono *m* de transportes. **-3.** *Br* [successful result] aprobado *m*. **-4.** [route between mountains] vía *f*, desfiladero *m*. **-5.** *phr*: **to make a** ~ **at sb** intentar ligar con alguien. ◇ *vt* **-1.** [gen] pasar; **to** ~ **sthg (to sb), to** ~ **(sb) sthg** pasar OR pasarle algo (a alguien). **-2.** [move past - thing] pasar por (delante de); [- person] pasar delante de; **to** ~ **sb in the street** cruzarse con alguien. **-3.** AUT adelantar. **-4.** [exceed] sobrepasar. **-5.** [exam, candidate, law] aprobar; **to** ~ **sthg fit (for)** dar algo por bueno (para). **-6.** [opinion, judgement] formular; [sentence] dictar. ◇ *vi* **-1.** [gen] pasar. **-2.** AUT adelantar. **-3.** [in exam] pasar, aprobar. **-4.** [occur] transcurrir. ◆ **pass as** *vt fus* pasar por. ◆ **pass away** *vi* fallecer. ◆ **pass by** ◇ *vt sep* [people] hacer caso omiso a; [subj: events, life] pasar desapercibido(da) a. ◇ *vi* pasar cerca. ◆ **pass for = pass as. ◆ pass on** ◇ *vt sep*: **to** ~ **sthg on (to)** pasar algo (a). ◇ *vi* **-1.** [move on] continuar. **-2.** = **pass away**. ◆ **pass out** *vi* **-1.** [faint] desmayarse. **-2.** *Br* MIL graduarse. ◆ **pass over** *vt fus* pasar por alto. ◆ **pass up** *vt sep* dejar pasar OR escapar.

passable ['pɑːsəbl] *adj* **-1.** [satisfactory] pasable. **-2.** [not blocked] transitable.

passage ['pæsɪdʒ] *n* **-1.** [corridor - between houses] pasadizo *m*, pasaje *m*; [- between rooms] pasillo *m*. **-2.** [clear path] paso *m*, hueco *m*. **-3.** MED conducto *m*, tubo *m*. **-4.** [of music, speech] pasaje *m*. **-5.** *fml* [of vehicle, person, time] paso *m*. **-6.** [sea journey] travesía *f*.

passageway ['pæsɪdʒweɪ] *n* [between houses] pasadizo *m*, pasaje *m*; [between rooms] pasillo *m*.

passbook ['pɑːsbʊk] *n* ≃ cartilla *f* OR libreta *f* de banco.

passenger ['pæsɪndʒər] *n* pasajero *m*, -ra *f*.

passerby [ˌpɑːsə'baɪ] (*pl* **passersby** [ˌpɑːsəz'baɪ]) *n* transeúnte *m y f*.

passing ['pɑːsɪŋ] ◇ *adj* [fad] pasajero(ra); [remark] de pasada. ◇ *n* transcurso *m*. ◆ **in passing** *adv* de pasada.

passion ['pæʃn] *n*: ~ **(for)** pasión *f* (por).

passionate ['pæʃənət] *adj* apasionado(da).

passive ['pæsɪv] *adj* pasivo(va).

Passover ['pɑːsˌəʊvər] *n*: **(the)** ~ **(la)** Pascua judía.

passport ['pɑːspɔːt] *n* pasaporte *m*.

passport control *n* control *m* de pasaportes.

password ['pɑːswɜːd] *n* [gen & COMPUT] contraseña *f*.

past [pɑːst] ◇ *adj* **-1.** [former] anterior. **-2.** [most recent] pasado(da); **over the** ~ **week** durante la última semana. **-3.** [finished] terminado(da). ◇ *adv* **-1.** [telling the time]: **it's ten** ~ son y diez. **-2.** [beyond, in front] por delante; **to walk/run** ~ pasar andando/corriendo. ◇ *n* **-1.** [time]: **the** ~ el pasado. **-2.** [personal history] pasado *m*. ◇ *prep* **-1.** [telling the time]: **it's five/half/a quarter** ~ **ten** son las diez y cinco/media/cuarto. **-2.** [alongside, in front of] por delante de. **-3.** [beyond] más allá de; **it's** ~ **the bank** está pasado el banco.

pasta ['pæstə] *n* (*U*) pasta *f*.

paste [peɪst] ◇ *n* **-1.** [smooth mixture] pasta *f*. **-2.** [food] paté *m*, pasta *f*. **-3.** [glue] engrudo *m*. ◇ *vt* [labels, stamps] pegar; [surface] engomar, engrudar.

pastel ['pæstl] ◇ *adj* pastel (*inv*). ◇ *n* ART [crayon] pastel *m*.

pasteurize, -ise ['pɑːstʃəraɪz] *vt* pasteurizar.

pastille ['pæstɪl] *n* pastilla *f*.

pastime ['pɑːstaɪm] *n* pasatiempo *m*.

pastor ['pɑːstər] *n* pastor *m* RELIG.

past participle *n* participio *m* pasado.

pastry ['peɪstrɪ] *n* **-1.** [mixture] pasta *f*. **-2.** [cake] pastel *m*.

past tense *n*: **the** ~ el pasado.

pasture ['pɑːstʃər] *n* pasto *m*.

pasty¹ ['peɪstɪ] *adj* pálido(da).

pasty² ['pæstɪ] *n Br* empanada *f*.

pat [pæt] ◇ *n* [of butter etc] porción *f*. ◇ *vt* [gen] golpear ligeramente; [dog] acariciar; [back, hand] dar palmaditas a.

patch [pætʃ] ◇ *n* **-1.** [for mending] remiendo *m*; [to cover eye] parche *m*. **-2.** [part of surface] área *f*. **-3.** [area of land] bancal *m*, parcela *f*. **-4.** [period of time] periodo *m*. ◇ *vt* remendar. ◆ **patch up** *vt sep* **-1.** [mend] reparar. **-2.** [resolve - quarrel] resolver.

patchwork ['pætʃwɜːk] *adj* de trozos de distintos colores y formas.

patchy ['pætʃɪ] *adj* **-1.** [uneven - fog, sunshine] irregular; [- colour] desigual. **-2.** [incomplete] deficiente, incompleto(ta). **-3.** [good in parts] irregular.

pâté ['pæteɪ] *n* paté *m*.

patent [*Br* 'peɪtənt, *Am* 'pætənt] ◇ *adj* [obvious] patente, evidente. ◇ *n* patente *f*. ◇ *vt* patentar.

patent leather *n* charol *m*.

paternal [pə'tɜːnl] *adj* [love, attitude] paternal; [grandmother, grandfather] paterno(na).

paternity [pə'tɜːnətɪ] *n* paternidad *f*.

path [pɑːθ, *pl* pɑːðz] *n* **-1.** [track, way ahead] camino *m*. **-2.** [trajectory - of bullet] trayectoria *f*; [- of flight] rumbo *m*. **-3.** [course of action] curso *m*.

pathetic [pə'θetɪk] *adj* **-1.** [causing pity] patético(ca), lastimoso(sa). **-2.** [attempt, person] inútil; [actor, film] malísimo(ma).

pathological [ˌpæθə'lɒdʒɪkl] *adj* patológico(ca).

pathology [pə'θɒlədʒɪ] *n* patología *f*.

pathos ['peɪθɒs] *n* patetismo *m*.

pathway ['pɑːθweɪ] *n* camino *m*, sendero *m*.

patience ['peɪʃns] *n* **-1.** [quality] paciencia *f*. **-2.** [card game] solitario *m*.

patient ['peɪʃnt] ◇ *adj* paciente. ◇ *n* paciente *m y f*.

patio ['pætɪəʊ] (*pl* -s) *n* patio *m*.

patriotic [*Br* ,pætrɪ'ɒtɪk, *Am* ,peɪtrɪ'ɒtɪk] *adj* patriótico(ca).

patrol [pə'trəʊl] ◇ *n* patrulla *f*. ◇ *vt* patrullar.

patrol car *n* coche *m* patrulla.

patrolman [pə'trəʊlmən] (*pl* -men [-mən]) *n Am* policía *m*, guardia *m*.

patron ['peɪtrən] *n* **-1.** [of arts] mecenas *m y f inv*. **-2.** *Br* [of charity, campaign] patrocinador *m*, -ra *f*. **-3.** *fml* [customer] cliente *m y f*.

patronize, -ise ['pætrənaɪz] *vt* **-1.** *pej* [talk down to] tratar con aire paternalista OR condescendiente. **-2.** *fml* [back financially] patrocinar.

patronizing ['pætrənaɪzɪŋ] *adj pej* paternalista, condescendiente.

patter ['pætər] ◇ *n* **-1.** [of raindrops] repiqueteo *m*; [of feet] pasitos *mpl*. **-2.** [sales talk] charlatanería *f*. ◇ *vi* [dog, feet] corretear; [rain] repiquetear.

pattern ['pætən] *n* **-1.** [design] dibujo *m*, diseño *m*. **-2.** [of life, work] estructura *f*; [of illness, events] desarrollo *m*, evolución *f*. **-3.** [for sewing, knitting] patrón *m*. **-4.** [model] modelo *m*.

paunch [pɔːntʃ] *n* barriga *f*, panza *f*.

pauper ['pɔːpər] *n* indigente *m y f*.

pause [pɔːz] ◇ *n* pausa *f*. ◇ *vi* **-1.** [stop speaking] hacer una pausa. **-2.** [stop moving, doing sthg] detenerse.

pave [peɪv] *vt* pavimentar; **to ~ the way for** preparar el terreno para.

pavement ['peɪvmənt] *n* **-1.** *Br* [at side of road] acera *f*, andén *m Amer*. **-2.** *Am* [roadway] calzada *f*.

pavilion [pə'vɪljən] *n* **-1.** *Br* [at sports field] vestuarios *mpl*. **-2.** [at exhibition] pabellón *m*.

paving ['peɪvɪŋ] *n* (*U*) pavimento *m*.

paving stone *n* losa *f*.

paw [pɔː] *n* [foot] pata *f*; [claw] zarpa *f*.

pawn [pɔːn] ◇ *n* **-1.** [chesspiece] peón *m*. **-2.** [unimportant person] marioneta *f*. ◇ *vt* empeñar.

pawnbroker ['pɔːn,brəʊkər] *n* prestamista *m y f*.

pawnshop ['pɔːnʃɒp] *n* monte *m* de piedad.

pay [peɪ] (*pt & pp* **paid**) ◇ *vt* **-1.** [gen] pagar; **to ~ sb for sthg** pagar a alguien por algo; **he paid £20 for it** pagó 20 libras por ello. **-2.** *Br* [put into bank account]: **to ~ sthg into** ingresar algo en. **-3.** [be profitable to] ser rentable a. **-4.** [compliment, visit] hacer; [respects] ofrecer; [attention] prestar; [homage] rendir. ◇ *vi* **-1.** [gen] pagar; **to ~ dearly for sthg** pagar caro (por) algo. **-2.** [be profitable] ser rentable. ◇ *n* paga *f*. ◆ **pay back** *vt sep* **-1.** [money] devolver, reembolsar. **-2.** [revenge oneself]: **to ~ sb back (for sthg)** hacer pagar a alguien (por algo). ◆ **pay off** ◇ *vt sep* **-1.** [repay - debt] liquidar, saldar. **-2.** [dismiss] despedir con indemnización. **-3.** [bribe] comprar, sobornar. ◇ *vi* salir bien, tener éxito. ◆ **pay up** *vi* pagar.

payable ['peɪəbl] *adj* **-1.** [to be paid] pagadero(ra). **-2.** [on cheque]: **~ to** a favor de.

paycheck ['peɪtʃek] *n Am* paga *f*.

payday ['peɪdeɪ] *n* día *m* de paga.

payee [peɪ'iː] *n* beneficiario *m*, -ria *f*.

pay envelope *n Am* sobre *m* de paga.

payment ['peɪmənt] *n* pago *m*.

pay packet *n Br* **-1.** [envelope] sobre *m* de paga. **-2.** [wages] paga *f*.

pay phone, pay station *Am n* teléfono *m* público.

payroll ['peɪrəʊl] *n* nómina *f*.

payslip ['peɪslɪp] *n Br* hoja *f* de paga.

pay station *Am* = **pay phone**.

pc (*abbr of* **per cent**) p.c.

PC *n* **-1.** (*abbr of* **personal computer**) PC *m*. **-2.** *abbr of* **police constable**.

PE (*abbr of* **physical education**) *n* EF *f*.

pea [piː] *n* guisante *m*, arveja *f Amer*.

peace [piːs] *n* **-1.** [gen] paz *f*. **-2.** [quiet] calma *f*, tranquilidad *f*. **-3.** [freedom from disagreement] orden *m*; **to make (one's) ~ (with)** hacer las paces (con).

peaceable ['piːsəbl] *adj* [not aggressive] pacífico(ca).

peaceful ['piːsfʊl] *adj* **-1.** [quiet, calm] tranquilo(la). **-2.** [not aggressive] pacífico(ca).

peacetime ['piːstaɪm] *n* (*U*) tiempos *mpl* de paz.

peach [piːtʃ] ◇ *adj* [in colour] de color melocotón. ◇ *n* **-1.** [fruit] melocotón *m*. **-2.** [colour] color *m* melocotón.

peacock ['piːkɒk] *n* pavo *m* real.

peak [piːk] ◇ *n* **-1.** [mountain top] pico *m*, cima *f*. **-2.** [highest point] apogeo *m*. **-3.** [of cap] visera *f*. ◇ *adj* [season] alto(ta); [condition] perfecto(ta). ◇ *vi* alcanzar el máximo.

peaked [piːkt] *adj* con visera.

peak hour *n* hora *f* punta.

peak period *n* [of electricity etc] periodo *m* de tarifa máxima; [of traffic] horas *fpl* punta.

peak rate *n* tarifa *f* máxima.

peal [piːl] ◇ *n* [of bells] repique *m*; ~ (of laughter) carcajada *f*. ◇ *vi* repicar.

peanut ['piːnʌt] *n* cacahuete *m*, maní *m* *Amer*.

peanut butter *n* manteca *f* de cacahuete.

pear [peəʳ] *n* pera *f*.

pearl [pɜːl] *n* perla *f*.

peasant ['peznt] *n* [in countryside] campesino *m*, -na *f*.

peat [piːt] *n* turba *f*.

pebble ['pebl] *n* guijarro *m*.

peck [pek] ◇ *n* **-1.** [with beak] picotazo *m*. **-2.** [kiss] besito *m*. ◇ *vt* [with beak] picotear. ◇ *vi* picotear.

pecking order ['pekɪŋ-] *n* jerarquía *f*.

peckish ['pekɪʃ] *adj* *Br inf*: **to feel** ~ estar algo hambriento(ta).

peculiar [pɪ'kjuːljəʳ] *adj* **-1.** [odd] singular, extraño(ña). **-2.** [slightly ill] raro(ra), indispuesto(ta). **-3.** [characteristic]: **to be** ~ **to** ser propio(pia) de.

peculiarity [pɪ,kjuːlɪ'ærətɪ] *n* **-1.** [eccentricity] extravagancia *f*. **-2.** [characteristic] peculiaridad *f*.

pedal ['pedl] ◇ *n* pedal *m*. ◇ *vi* pedalear.

pedal bin *n* cubo *m* de basura con pedal.

pedantic [pɪ'dæntɪk] *adj* *pej* puntilloso(sa).

peddle ['pedl] *vt* [drugs] traficar con; [wares] vender de puerta en puerta.

pedestal ['pedɪstl] *n* pedestal *m*.

pedestrian [pɪ'destrɪən] ◇ *adj* *pej* mediocre. ◇ *n* peatón *m*.

pedestrian crossing *n* *Br* paso *m* de peatones.

pedestrian precinct *Br*, **pedestrian zone** *Am* *n* zona *f* peatonal.

pediatrics [,piːdɪ'ætrɪks] *n* pediatría *f*.

pedigree ['pedɪgriː] ◇ *adj* de raza. ◇ *n* **-1.** [of animal] pedigrí *m*. **-2.** [of person] linaje *m*.

pedlar *Br*, **peddler** *Am* ['pedləʳ] *n* vendedor *m*, -ra *f* ambulante.

pee [piː] *inf* ◇ *n* pis *m*. ◇ *vi* mear.

peek [piːk] *inf* ◇ *n* mirada *f*, ojeada *f*. ◇ *vi* mirar a hurtadillas.

peel [piːl] ◇ *n* [gen] piel *f*; [of orange, lemon] corteza *f*; [once removed] mondaduras *fpl*. ◇ *vt* pelar, mondar. ◇ *vi* [walls, paint] desconcharse; [wallpaper] despegarse; [skin, nose] pelarse.

peelings ['piːlɪŋz] *npl* peladuras *fpl*.

peep [piːp] ◇ *n* **-1.** [look] mirada *f* furtiva, ojeada *f*. **-2.** *inf* [sound] pío *m*. ◇ *vi* [look] mirar furtivamente. ◆ **peep out** *vi* asomar.

peephole ['piːphəʊl] *n* mirilla *f*.

peer [pɪəʳ] ◇ *n* **-1.** [noble] par *m*. **-2.** [equal] igual *m*. ◇ *vi* mirar con atención.

peerage ['pɪərɪdʒ] *n* **-1.** [rank] rango *m* de par. **-2.** [group]: **the** ~ la nobleza.

peer group *n* grupo generacional o social.

peeved [piːvd] *adj* *inf* disgustado(da).

peevish ['piːvɪʃ] *adj* malhumorado(da).

peg [peg] *n* **-1.** [hook] gancho *m*. **-2.** [for washing line] pinza *f*. **-3.** [on tent] estaca *f*.

pejorative [pɪ'dʒɒrətɪv] *adj* peyorativo(va), despectivo(va).

pekinese [,piːkə'niːz], **pekingese** [,piːkɪŋ'iːz] (*pl inv* OR **-s**) *n* [dog] pequinés *m*.

Peking [piː'kɪŋ] *n* Pekín *m*.

pelican ['pelɪkən] (*pl inv* OR **-s**) *n* pelícano *m*.

pelican crossing *n* *Br* paso de peatones con semáforo accionado por el usuario.

pellet ['pelɪt] *n* **-1.** [small ball] bolita *f*. **-2.** [for gun] perdigón *m*.

pelmet ['pelmɪt] *n* *Br* galería *f*.

pelt [pelt] ◇ *n* [animal skin] piel *f*. ◇ *vt*: **to** ~ **sb with sthg** acribillar a alguien con algo, arrojar algo a alguien. ◇ *vi* **-1.** [rain] llover a cántaros. **-2.** [run very fast] correr a toda pastilla.

pelvis ['pelvɪs] (*pl* **-vises** OR **-ves** [-viːz]) *n* pelvis *f*.

pen [pen] ◇ *n* **-1.** [ballpoint] bolígrafo *m*, lapicera *f* *Amer*; [fountain pen] pluma *f*; [felt-tip] rotulador *m*. **-2.** [enclosure] redil *m*, corral *m*. ◇ *vt* [enclose] encerrar.

penal ['pi:nl] *adj* penal.

penalize, -ise ['pi:nəlaɪz] *vt* [gen] penalizar; SPORT penalizar, castigar.

penalty ['penltɪ] *n* **-1.** [punishment] pena *f*; **to pay the ~ (for sthg)** *fig* pagar las consecuencias (de algo). **-2.** [fine] multa *f*. **-3.** SPORT penalty *m*; **~ (kick)** FTBL penalty *m*; RUGBY golpe *m* de castigo.

penance ['penəns] *n* penitencia *f*.

pence [pens] *Br pl* → **penny**.

penchant [*Br* pɑ̃ʃɑ̃, *Am* 'pentʃənt] *n*: **to have a ~ for** tener debilidad por.

pencil ['pensl] *n* lápiz *m*, lapicero *m*; **in ~** a lápiz.

pencil case *n* estuche *m*, plumero *m*.

pencil sharpener *n* sacapuntas *m inv*.

pendant ['pendənt] *n* [jewel on chain] colgante *m*.

pending ['pendɪŋ] *fml* ◇ *adj* **-1.** [about to happen] inminente. **-2.** [waiting to be dealt with] pendiente. ◇ *prep* a la espera de.

pendulum ['pendjʊləm] (*pl* **-s**) *n* [of clock] péndulo *m*.

penetrate ['penɪtreɪt] *vt* **-1.** [barrier] atravesar; [jungle, crowd] penetrar en. **-2.** [infiltrate - organization] infiltrarse en.

pen friend *n* amigo *m*, -ga *f* por correspondencia.

penguin ['peŋgwɪn] *n* pingüino *m*.

penicillin [,penɪ'sɪlɪn] *n* penicilina *f*.

peninsula [pə'nɪnsjʊlə] (*pl* **-s**) *n* península *f*.

penis ['pi:nɪs] (*pl* **penises** ['pi:nɪsɪz]) *n* pene *m*.

penitentiary [,penɪ'tenʃərɪ] *n Am* penitenciaría *f*.

penknife ['pennaɪf] (*pl* **-knives** [-naɪvz]) *n* navaja *f*.

pen name *n* seudónimo *m*.

pennant ['penənt] *n* banderín *m*.

penniless ['penɪlɪs] *adj* sin dinero.

penny ['penɪ] (*pl sense 1* **-ies**, *pl sense 2* **pence**) *n* **-1.** [coin] *Br* penique *m*; *Am* centavo *m*. **-2.** *Br* [value] penique *m*.

pen pal *n inf* amigo *m*, -ga *f* por correspondencia.

pension ['penʃn] *n* **-1.** *Br* [gen] pensión *f*. **-2.** [disability pension] subsidio *m*.

pensioner ['penʃənər] *n Br*: **(old-age) ~** pensionista *m y f*.

pensive ['pensɪv] *adj* pensativo(va).

pentagon ['pentəgən] *n* pentágono *m*. ◆**Pentagon** *n Am*: **the Pentagon** el Pentágono, *sede del ministerio de Defensa estadounidense*.

Pentecost ['pentɪkɒst] *n* Pentecostés *m*.

penthouse ['penthaus, *pl* -hauzɪz] *n* ático *m*.

pent up ['pent-] *adj* reprimido(da).

penultimate [pe'nʌltɪmət] *adj* penúltimo(ma).

people ['pi:pl] ◇ *n* [nation, race] pueblo *m*. ◇ *npl* **-1.** [gen] gente *f*; [individuals] personas *fpl*; **a table for eight ~** una mesa para ocho personas; **~ say that ...** dice la gente que .... **-2.** [inhabitants] habitantes *mpl*. **-3.** POL: **the ~** el pueblo. ◇ *vt*: **to be ~d by** OR **with** estar poblado(da) de.

pep [pep] *n inf* vitalidad *f*. ◆**pep up** *vt sep* animar.

pepper ['pepər] *n* **-1.** [spice] pimienta *f*. **-2.** [vegetable] pimiento *m*.

pepperbox *Am* = **pepper pot**.

peppermint ['pepəmɪnt] *n* **-1.** [sweet] pastilla *f* de menta. **-2.** [herb] menta *f*.

pepper pot *Br*, **pepperbox** *Am* ['pepəbɒks] *n* pimentero *m*.

pep talk *n inf* palabras *fpl* de ánimo.

per [pɜːr] *prep* [expressing rate, ratio] por; **~ hour/kilo/person** por hora/kilo/persona; **~ day** al día; **as ~ instructions** de acuerdo con OR según las instrucciones.

per annum *adv* al OR por año.

per capita [pə'kæpɪtə] ◇ *adj* per cápita. ◇ *adv* por cabeza.

perceive [pə'si:v] *vt* **-1.** [notice] percibir, apreciar. **-2.** [understand, realize] advertir, apreciar. **-3.** [see]: **to ~ sthg/sb as** ver algo/a alguien como.

per cent *adv* por ciento.

percentage [pə'sentɪdʒ] *n* porcentaje *m*.

perception [pə'sepʃn] *n* **-1.** [act of seeing] percepción *f*. **-2.** [insight] perspicacia *f*. **-3.** [opinion] idea *f*.

perceptive [pə'septɪv] *adj* perspicaz.

perch [pɜːtʃ] ◇ *n* **-1.** [for bird] percha *f*, vara *f*. **-2.** [fish] perca *f*. ◇ *vi*: **to ~ (on)** [bird] posarse (en); [person] sentarse (en).

percolator ['pɜːkəleɪtər] *n* percolador *m*.

percussion [pə'kʌʃn] *n* MUS percusión *f*.

perennial [pə'renjəl] ◇ *adj* [gen & BOT] perenne. ◇ *n* BOT planta *f* perenne.

perfect [*adj & n* 'pɜːfɪkt, *vb* pə'fekt] ◇ *adj* perfecto(ta); **he's a ~ stranger to me** me es completamente desconocido. ◇ *n* GRAMM: **the ~ (tense)** el perfecto. ◇ *vt* perfeccionar.

perfection [pə'fekʃn] *n* perfección *f*; **to ~** a la perfección.

perfectionist [pə'fekʃənɪst] *n* perfeccionista *m y f*.

perfectly ['pɜːfɪktlɪ] *adv* **-1.** [for emphasis] absolutamente; ~ **well** perfectamente bien. **-2.** [to perfection] perfectamente.

perforate ['pɜːfəreɪt] *vt* perforar.

perforation [,pɜːfə'reɪʃn] *n* [in paper] perforación *f*.

perform [pə'fɔːm] ◇ *vt* **-1.** [carry out] llevar a cabo, realizar. **-2.** [music, dance] interpretar; [play] representar. ◇ *vi* **-1.** [function - car, machine] funcionar; [- person, team] desenvolverse. **-2.** [in front of audience] actuar.

performance [pə'fɔːməns] *n* **-1.** [carrying out] realización *f*. **-2.** [show] representación *f*. **-3.** [of actor, singer etc] interpretación *f*, actuación *f*. **-4.** [of car, engine] rendimiento *m*.

performer [pə'fɔːməʳ] *n* [actor, singer etc] intérprete *m y f*.

perfume ['pɜːfjuːm] *n* perfume *m*.

perfunctory [pə'fʌŋktərɪ] *adj* superficial.

perhaps [pə'hæps] *adv* **-1.** [maybe] quizás, quizá; ~ **she'll do it** quizás ella lo haga; ~ **so/not** tal vez sí/no. **-2.** [in polite requests, suggestions, remarks]: ~ **you could help?** ¿te importaría ayudar?; ~ **you should start again** ¿por qué no empiezas de nuevo?

peril ['perɪl] *n literary* peligro *m*.

perimeter [pə'rɪmɪtəʳ] *n* perímetro *m*.

period ['pɪərɪəd] ◇ *n* **-1.** [of time] período *m*, periodo *m*. **-2.** HISTORY época *f*. **-3.** SCH clase *f*, hora *f*. **-4.** [menstruation] período *m*. **-5.** *Am* [full stop] punto *m*. ◇ *comp* de época.

periodic [,pɪərɪ'ɒdɪk] *adj* periódico(ca).

periodical [,pɪərɪ'ɒdɪkl] ◇ *adj* = **periodic**. ◇ *n* [magazine] revista *f*.

peripheral [pə'rɪfərəl] ◇ *adj* **-1.** [of little importance] marginal. **-2.** [at edge] periférico(ca). ◇ *n* COMPUT periférico *m*.

perish ['perɪʃ] *vi* **-1.** [die] perecer. **-2.** [decay] deteriorar.

perishable ['perɪʃəbl] *adj* perecedero(ra). ◆ **perishables** *npl* productos *mpl* perecederos.

perjury ['pɜːdʒərɪ] *n* JUR perjurio *m*.

perk [pɜːk] *n inf* extra *m*, beneficio *m* adicional. ◆ **perk up** *vi* animarse.

perky ['pɜːkɪ] *adj inf* alegre, animado(da).

perm [pɜːm] *n* permanente *f*.

permanent ['pɜːmənənt] ◇ *adj* **-1.** [gen] permanente; [job, address] fijo(ja). **-2.** [continuous, constant] constante. ◇ *n Am* [perm] permanente *f*.

permeate ['pɜːmɪeɪt] *vt* impregnar.

permissible [pə'mɪsəbl] *adj* permisible.

permission [pə'mɪʃn] *n*: ~ **(to do sthg)** permiso *m* (para hacer algo).

permissive [pə'mɪsɪv] *adj* permisivo(va).

permit [*vb* pə'mɪt, *n* 'pɜːmɪt] ◇ *vt* permitir; **to** ~ **sb sthg/to do sthg** permitir a alguien algo/hacer algo. ◇ *n* permiso *m*.

pernicious [pə'nɪʃəs] *adj fml* pernicioso(sa).

pernickety [pə'nɪkətɪ] *adj inf* quisquilloso(sa).

perpendicular [,pɜːpən'dɪkjʊləʳ] ◇ *adj* **-1.** MATH: ~ **(to)** perpendicular (a). **-2.** [upright] vertical. ◇ *n* MATH perpendicular *f*.

perpetrate ['pɜːpɪtreɪt] *vt fml* perpetrar.

perpetual [pə'petʃʊəl] *adj* **-1.** *pej* [constant] constante. **-2.** [everlasting] perpetuo(tua).

perplex [pə'pleks] *vt* dejar perplejo(ja).

perplexing [pə'pleksɪŋ] *adj* desconcertante.

persecute ['pɜːsɪkjuːt] *vt* perseguir.

perseverance [,pɜːsɪ'vɪərəns] *n* perseverancia *f*.

persevere [,pɜːsɪ'vɪəʳ] *vi*: **to** ~ **(with sthg/in doing sthg)** perseverar (en algo/en hacer algo).

Persian ['pɜːʃn] *adj* persa.

persist [pə'sɪst] *vi* **-1.** [problem, rain] persistir. **-2.** [person]: **to** ~ **in doing sthg** empeñarse en hacer algo.

persistence [pə'sɪstəns] *n* **-1.** [continuation] persistencia *f*. **-2.** [determination] perseverancia *f*.

persistent [pə'sɪstənt] *adj* **-1.** [constant] continuo(nua). **-2.** [determined] persistente.

person ['pɜːsn] (*pl* **people** OR **persons** *fml*) *n* **-1.** [man, woman] persona *f*; **in** ~ en persona. **-2.** [body]: **about one's** ~ en su cuerpo.

personable ['pɜːsnəbl] *adj* agradable.

personal ['pɜːsənl] *adj* **-1.** [gen] personal. **-2.** [private - life, problem] privado(da). **-3.** *pej* [rude] ofensivo(va); **to be** ~ hacer alusiones personales.

personal assistant *n* asistente *m*, -ta *f* personal.

personal column *n* sección *f* de asuntos personales.

personal computer *n* ordenador *m* personal.

personality [ˌpɜːsəˈnælətɪ] *n* personalidad *f*.

personally [ˈpɜːsnəlɪ] *adv* personalmente; **to take sthg** ~ tomarse algo como algo personal.

personal organizer *n* agenda *f* (personal).

personal property *n* (U) bienes *mpl* muebles.

personal stereo *n* walkman® *m inv*.

personify [pəˈsɒnɪfaɪ] *vt* personificar.

personnel [ˌpɜːsəˈnel] ◇ *n* (U) [department] personal *m*. ◇ *npl* [staff] personal *m*.

perspective [pəˈspektɪv] *n* perspectiva *f*.

Perspex® [ˈpɜːspeks] *n Br* ≃ plexiglás® *m*.

perspiration [ˌpɜːspəˈreɪʃn] *n* transpiración *f*.

persuade [pəˈsweɪd] *vt*: **to** ~ **sb (of sthg/to do sthg)** persuadir a alguien (de algo/a hacer algo); **to** ~ **sb that** convencer a alguien (de) que.

persuasion [pəˈsweɪʒn] *n* **-1.** [act of persuading] persuasión *f*. **-2.** [belief] creencia *f*.

persuasive [pəˈsweɪsɪv] *adj* persuasivo(va).

pert [pɜːt] *adj* vivaracho(cha).

pertain [pəˈteɪn] *vi fml*: ~**ing to** relacionado(da) con.

pertinent [ˈpɜːtɪnənt] *adj* pertinente.

perturb [pəˈtɜːb] *vt fml* perturbar.

Peru [pəˈruː] *n* (el) Perú.

peruse [pəˈruːz] *vt* [read carefully] leer detenidamente; [browse through] leer por encima.

Peruvian [pəˈruːvjən] ◇ *adj* peruano(na). ◇ *n* [person] peruano *m*, -na *f*.

pervade [pəˈveɪd] *vt* impregnar.

perverse [pəˈvɜːs] *adj* [delight, enjoyment] perverso(sa); [contrary] puñetero(ra).

perversion [*Br* pəˈvɜːʃn, *Am* pəˈvɜːrʒn] *n* **-1.** [sexual deviation] perversión *f*. **-2.** [of justice, truth] tergiversación *f*.

pervert [*n* ˈpɜːvɜːt, *vb* pəˈvɜːt] ◇ *n* pervertido *m*, -da *f*. ◇ *vt* **-1.** [course of justice] tergiversar. **-2.** [corrupt sexually] pervertir.

pessimist [ˈpesɪmɪst] *n* pesimista *m y f*.

pessimistic [ˌpesɪˈmɪstɪk] *adj* pesimista.

pest [pest] *n* **-1.** [insect] insecto *m* nocivo; [animal] animal *m* nocivo. **-2.** *inf* [annoying person] pesado *m*, -da *f*; [annoying thing] lata *f*.

pester [ˈpestəʳ] *vt* dar la lata a.

pet [pet] ◇ *adj* [subject, theory] preferido(da); ~ **hate** gran fobia *f*. ◇ *n* **-1.** [domestic animal] animal *m* doméstico. **-2.** [favourite person] preferido *m*, -da *f*. ◇ *vt* acariciar. ◇ *vi* besuquearse.

petal [ˈpetl] *n* pétalo *m*.

peter [ˈpiːtəʳ] ◆ **peter out** *vi* [supplies, interest] agotarse; [path] desaparecer.

petite [pəˈtiːt] *adj* [woman] chiquita.

petition [pɪˈtɪʃn] ◇ *n* petición *f*. ◇ *vi* JUR: **to** ~ **for divorce** pedir el divorcio.

petrified [ˈpetrɪfaɪd] *adj* [terrified] petrificado(da).

petrol [ˈpetrəl] *n Br* gasolina *f*, nafta *f* Amer.

petrol bomb *n Br* bomba *f* de gasolina.

petrol can *n Br* lata *f* de gasolina.

petroleum [pɪˈtrəʊljəm] *n* petróleo *m*.

petrol pump *n Br* surtidor *m* de gasolina, bomba *f* Amer.

petrol station *n Br* gasolinera *f*, grifo *m* Amer.

petrol tank *n Br* depósito *m* de gasolina.

petticoat [ˈpetɪkəʊt] *n* [underskirt] enaguas *fpl*; [full-length] combinación *f*.

petty [ˈpetɪ] *adj* **-1.** [small-minded] mezquino(na). **-2.** [trivial] insignificante.

petty cash *n* dinero *m* para gastos menores.

petty officer *n* sargento *m* de la marina.

petulant [ˈpetjʊlənt] *adj* cascarrabias (*inv*).

pew [pjuː] *n* banco *m*.

pewter [ˈpjuːtəʳ] *n* peltre *m*.

phantom [ˈfæntəm] ◇ *adj* ilusorio(ria). ◇ *n* [ghost] fantasma *m*.

pharmaceutical [ˌfɑːməˈsjuːtɪkl] *adj* farmacéutico(ca).

pharmacist [ˈfɑːməsɪst] *n* farmacéutico *m*, -ca *f*.

pharmacy [ˈfɑːməsɪ] *n* [shop] farmacia *f*.

phase [feɪz] ◇ *n* fase *f*. ◇ *vt* escalonar. ◆ **phase in** *vt sep* introducir progresivamente. ◆ **phase out** *vt sep* retirar progresivamente.

PhD (*abbr of* **Doctor of Philosophy**) *n* (titular de un) doctorado en el campo de las humanidades.

pheasant [ˈfeznt] (*pl inv* OR **-s**) *n* faisán *m*.

phenomena [fɪˈnɒmɪnə] *pl* → **phenomenon**.

phenomenal [fɪˈnɒmɪnl] *adj* fenomenal.

phenomenon [fɪˈnɒmɪnən] (*pl* **-mena**) *n* lit & fig fenómeno *m*.

phial [ˈfaɪəl] *n* frasco *m* (pequeño).

philanthropist [fɪ'lænθrəpɪst] *n* filantrópico *m*, -ca *f*.

philately [fɪ'lætəlɪ] *n* filatelia *f*.

Philippine ['fɪlɪpiːn] *adj* filipino(na).
◆ **Philippines** *npl*: **the ~s** las Filipinas.

philosopher [fɪ'lɒsəfəʳ] *n* filósofo *m*, -fa *f*.

philosophical [,fɪlə'sɒfɪkl] *adj* filosófico(ca).

philosophy [fɪ'lɒsəfɪ] *n* filosofía *f*.

phlegm [flem] *n* [mucus] flema *f*.

phlegmatic [fleg'mætɪk] *adj* flemático(ca).

phobia ['fəʊbjə] *n* fobia *f*.

phone [fəʊn] ◇ *n* teléfono *m*; **to be on the ~** [speaking] estar al teléfono; *Br* [connected to network] tener teléfono. ◇ *vt & vi* telefonear, llamar. ◆ **phone up** *vt sep & vi* llamar.

phone book *n* guía *f* telefónica.

phone booth *n* teléfono *m* público.

phone box *n Br* cabina *f* telefónica.

phone call *n* llamada *f* telefónica; **to make a ~** hacer una llamada.

phonecard ['fəʊnkɑːd] *n* tarjeta *f* telefónica.

phone-in *n* RADIO & TV programa *m* a micrófono abierto.

phone number *n* número *m* de teléfono.

phonetics [fə'netɪks] *n* (U) fonética *f*.

phoney *Br*, **phony** *Am* ['fəʊnɪ] (*compar* -**ier**, *superl* -**iest**) ◇ *adj inf* falso(sa). ◇ *n* farsante *m y f*.

phosphorus ['fɒsfərəs] *n* fósforo *m*.

photo ['fəʊtəʊ] *n* foto *f*; **to take a ~ (of)** sacar una foto (de).

photocopier [,fəʊtəʊ'kɒpɪəʳ] *n* fotocopiadora *f*.

photocopy ['fəʊtəʊ,kɒpɪ] ◇ *n* fotocopia *f*. ◇ *vt* fotocopiar.

photograph ['fəʊtəgrɑːf] ◇ *n* fotografía *f*; **to take a ~ (of)** sacar una fotografía (de). ◇ *vt* fotografiar.

photographer [fə'tɒgrəfəʳ] *n* fotógrafo *m*, -fa *f*.

photography [fə'tɒgrəfɪ] *n* (U) fotografía *f*.

phrasal verb ['freɪzl-] *n* verbo *m* con preposición.

phrase [freɪz] ◇ *n* -**1.** [group of words] locución *f*, frase *f*. -**2.** [expression] expresión *f*. ◇ *vt* [apology, refusal] expresar; [letter] redactar.

phrasebook ['freɪzbʊk] *n* libro *m* de frases.

physical ['fɪzɪkl] ◇ *adj* físico(ca). ◇ *n* [examination] examen *m* médico.

physical education *n* educación *f* física.

physically ['fɪzɪklɪ] *adv* físicamente.

physically handicapped *npl*: **the ~** los minusválidos.

physician [fɪ'zɪʃn] *n* médico *m y f*.

physicist ['fɪzɪsɪst] *n* físico *m*, -ca *f*.

physics ['fɪzɪks] *n* (U) física *f*.

physiotherapy [,fɪzɪəʊ'θerəpɪ] *n* fisioterapia *f*.

physique [fɪ'ziːk] *n* físico *m*.

pianist ['pɪənɪst] *n* pianista *m y f*.

piano [pɪ'ænəʊ] (*pl* -**s**) *n* [instrument] piano *m*.

piccolo ['pɪkələʊ] (*pl* -**s**) *n* flautín *m*.

pick [pɪk] ◇ *n* -**1.** [tool] piqueta *f*. -**2.** [selection]: **take your ~** escoge el que quieras. -**3.** [best]: **the ~ of** lo mejor de. ◇ *vt* -**1.** [team, winner] seleccionar; [time, book, dress] elegir. -**2.** [fruit, flowers] coger. -**3.** [remove - hairs etc]: **to ~ sthg off sthg** quitar algo de algo. -**4.** [nose] hurgarse; [teeth] mondarse. -**5.** [provoke]: **to ~ a fight/quarrel (with)** buscar pelea/bronca (con). -**6.** [open - lock] forzar (con ganzúa). ◆ **pick on** *vt fus* meterse con. ◆ **pick out** *vt sep* -**1.** [recognize] reconocer, identificar. -**2.** [select] escoger. ◆ **pick up** ◇ *vt sep* -**1.** [gen] recoger. -**2.** [buy, acquire] adquirir; **to ~ up speed** [car] acelerar. -**3.** [learn - tips, language] aprender. -**4.** *inf* [approach] ligar con. -**5.** RADIO & TELEC captar. -**6.** [start again] reanudar. ◇ *vi* -**1.** [improve] mejorar. -**2.** [start again] proseguir.

pickaxe *Br*, **pickax** *Am* ['pɪkæks] *n* piqueta *f*.

picket ['pɪkɪt] ◇ *n* piquete *m*. ◇ *vt* formar piquetes en.

picket line *n* piquete *m* (de huelga).

pickle ['pɪkl] ◇ *n* -**1.** [vinegar preserve] encurtido *m*; [sweet vegetable sauce] *salsa espesa agridulce con trozos de cebolla etc*. -**2.** *inf* [difficult situation]: **to be in a ~** estar en un lío. ◇ *vt* encurtir.

pickpocket ['pɪk,pɒkɪt] *n* carterista *m y f*.

pick-up *n* -**1.** [of record player] fonocaptor *m*. -**2.** [truck] furgoneta *f*.

picnic ['pɪknɪk] (*pt & pp* -**ked**, *cont* -**king**) ◇ *n* comida *f* campestre, picnic *m*. ◇ *vi* ir de merienda al campo.

pictorial [pɪk'tɔːrɪəl] *adj* ilustrado(da).

picture ['pɪktʃəʳ] ◇ *n* -**1.** [painting] cuadro *m*; [drawing] dibujo *m*. -**2.** [photograph] foto *f*. -**3.** [on TV] imagen *f*. -**4.** [cinema film] película *f*. -**5.** [in mind]

idea f, imagen f. **-6.** [situation] situación f. **-7.** phr: **to get the ~** inf entenderlo; **to put sb in the ~** poner a alguien al corriente. ◇ vt **-1.** [in mind] imaginarse. **-2.** [in media]: **to be ~d** aparecer en la foto. ◆ **pictures** npl Br: **the ~s** el cine.

picture book n libro m ilustrado.

picturesque [ˌpɪktʃə'resk] adj pintoresco(ca).

pie [paɪ] n [sweet] tarta f (cubierta de hojaldre); [savoury] empanada f, pastel m.

piece [piːs] n **-1.** [individual part or portion] trozo m, pedazo m; **to come to ~s** deshacerse; **to take sthg to ~s** desmontar algo; **in ~s** en pedazos; **in one ~** [intact] intacto(ta); [unharmed] sano y salvo (sana y salva). **-2.** (with uncountable noun) [individual object]: **~ of furniture** mueble m; **~ of clothing** prenda f de vestir; **~ of advice** consejo m; **~ of news** noticia f; **~ of luck** golpe m de suerte. **-3.** [in board game] pieza f. **-4.** [of journalism] artículo m. **-5.** [coin] moneda f. ◆ **piece together** vt sep [discover] componer.

piecemeal ['piːsmiːl] ◇ adj poco sistemático(ca). ◇ adv por etapas.

piecework ['piːswɜːk] n (U) trabajo m a destajo.

pie chart n gráfico m circular OR de sectores.

pier [pɪə] n [at seaside] paseo marítimo en un malecón.

pierce [pɪəs] vt **-1.** [subj: bullet, needle] perforar; **to have one's ears ~d** hacerse agujeros en las orejas. **-2.** [subj: voice, scream] romper.

piercing ['pɪəsɪŋ] adj **-1.** [scream] desgarrador(ra); [sound, voice] agudo(da). **-2.** [wind] cortante. **-3.** [look, eyes] penetrante.

piety ['paɪətɪ] n piedad f.

pig [pɪg] n **-1.** [animal] cerdo m, puerco m, chancho m Amer. **-2.** inf pej [greedy eater] tragón m, -ona f. **-3.** inf pej [unkind person] cerdo m, -da f.

pigeon ['pɪdʒɪn] (pl inv OR -s) n paloma f.

pigeonhole ['pɪdʒɪnhəʊl] ◇ n [compartment] casilla f. ◇ vt [classify] encasillar.

piggybank ['pɪgɪbæŋk] n hucha f con forma de cerdito.

pigheaded [ˌpɪg'hedɪd] adj cabezota.

pigment ['pɪgmənt] n pigmento m.

pigpen Am = pigsty.

pigskin ['pɪgskɪn] n piel f de cerdo.

pigsty ['pɪgstaɪ], **pigpen** Am ['pɪgpen] n lit & fig pocilga f.

pigtail ['pɪgteɪl] n [girl's] trenza f; [Chinese, bullfighter's] coleta f.

pike [paɪk] (pl sense 1 only inv OR -s) n **-1.** [fish] lucio m. **-2.** [weapon] pica f.

pilchard ['pɪltʃəd] n sardina f.

pile [paɪl] ◇ n **-1.** [heap] montón m; **a ~ OR ~s of** un montón de. **-2.** [neat stack] pila f. **-3.** [of carpet, fabric] pelo m. ◇ vt amontonar. ◆ **piles** npl MED almorranas fpl. ◆ **pile into** vt fus inf amontonarse OR meterse en. ◆ **pile up** vt sep amontonar. ◇ vi **-1.** [form a heap] amontonarse. **-2.** [mount up] acumularse.

pileup ['paɪlʌp] n accidente m en cadena.

pilfer ['pɪlfə] ◇ vt sisar. ◇ vi: **to ~ (from)** sisar (de).

pilgrim ['pɪlgrɪm] n peregrino m, -na f.

pilgrimage ['pɪlgrɪmɪdʒ] n peregrinación f.

pill [pɪl] n **-1.** MED píldora f, pastilla f. **-2.** [contraceptive]: **the ~** la píldora (anticonceptiva); **to be on the ~** tomar la píldora.

pillage ['pɪlɪdʒ] vt saquear, pillar.

pillar ['pɪlə] n lit & fig pilar m.

pillar box n Br buzón m.

pillion ['pɪljən] n: **to ride ~** ir en el asiento trasero (de una moto).

pillow ['pɪləʊ] n **-1.** [for bed] almohada f. **-2.** Am [on sofa, chair] cojín m.

pillowcase ['pɪləʊkeɪs], **pillowslip** ['pɪləʊslɪp] n funda f de almohada.

pilot ['paɪlət] ◇ n **-1.** AERON & NAUT piloto m. **-2.** TV programa m piloto. ◇ comp piloto (inv), de prueba. ◇ vt AERON & NAUT pilotar.

pilot burner, pilot light n piloto m, luz f indicadora.

pilot study n estudio m piloto.

pimp [pɪmp] n inf chulo m, padrote m Amer.

pimple ['pɪmpl] n grano m.

pin [pɪn] ◇ n **-1.** [for sewing] alfiler m; **~s and hormigueo** m. **-2.** [of plug] polo m. **-3.** TECH clavija f. ◇ vt **-1.** [fasten]: **to ~ sthg to OR on** [notice] clavar con alfileres algo en; [medal, piece of cloth] prender algo en. **-2.** [trap]: **to ~ sb against OR to** inmovilizar a alguien contra. **-3.** [apportion]: **to ~ sthg on OR upon sb** endosar algo a alguien. ◆ **pin down** vt sep **-1.** [identify] determinar, identificar. **-2.** [force to make a decision]: **to ~ sb down (to)** obligar a alguien a comprometerse (a).

pinafore ['pɪnəfɔːr] n -1. [apron] delantal m. -2. Br [dress] pichi m.

pinball ['pɪnbɔːl] n millón m, flípper m.

pincers ['pɪnsəz] npl -1. [tool] tenazas fpl. -2. [front claws] pinzas fpl.

pinch [pɪntʃ] ◇ n -1. [nip] pellizco m. -2. [small quantity] pizca f. ◇ vt -1. [nip] pellizcar; [subj: shoes] apretar. -2. inf [steal] mangar. ◆at a pinch Br, in a pinch Am adv si no hay más remedio.

pincushion ['pɪn,kuʃn] n acerico m.

pine [paɪn] ◇ n pino m. ◇ vi: to ~ for suspirar por. ◆pine away vi morirse de pena.

pineapple ['paɪnæpl] n piña f, ananá m Amer.

pinetree ['paɪntriː] n pino m.

ping [pɪŋ] n [of bell] tilín m; [of metal] sonido m metálico.

Ping-Pong® [-pɒŋ] n ping-pong® m.

pink [pɪŋk] ◇ adj rosa. ◇ n -1. [colour] rosa m. -2. [flower] clavel m.

pinnacle ['pɪnəkl] n -1. [high point] cumbre f. -2. [mountain peak, spire] pináculo m, cima f.

pinpoint ['pɪnpɔɪnt] vt determinar, identificar.

pin-striped [-,straɪpt] adj a rayas.

pint [paɪnt] n -1. [unit of measurement] Br = 0,568 litros; Am = 0,473 litros, ≃ pinta f. -2. Br [beer]: they went out for a ~ salieron a tomar una caña.

pioneer [,paɪə'nɪər] n pionero m, -ra f.

pious ['paɪəs] adj -1. [religious] piadoso(sa). -2. pej [sanctimonious] mojigato(ta).

pip [pɪp] n -1. [seed] pepita f. -2. Br [bleep] señal f.

pipe [paɪp] ◇ n -1. [for gas, water] tubería f. -2. [for smoking] pipa f. ◇ vt [transport via pipes] conducir por tuberías. ◆pipes npl MUS gaita f. ◆pipe down vi inf cerrar la boca. ◆pipe up vi inf: to ~ up with a suggestion saltar con una sugerencia.

pipe cleaner n limpiapipas m inv.

pipe dream n sueño m imposible.

pipeline ['paɪplaɪn] n [for gas] gasoducto m; [for oil] oleoducto m; [for water] tuberías fpl.

piper ['paɪpər] n gaitero m, -ra f.

piping hot ['paɪpɪŋ-] adj humeante, calentito(ta).

piquant ['piːkənt] adj -1. [food] picante. -2. [story] intrigante; [situation] que suscita un placer mordaz.

pique [piːk] n resentimiento m.

pirate ['paɪrət] ◇ adj [gen & COMPUT] pirata. ◇ n [sailor] pirata m y f. ◇ vt piratear.

pirate radio n Br radio f pirata.

pirouette [,pɪru'et] n pirueta f.

Pisces ['paɪsiːz] n Piscis m inv.

piss [pɪs] vulg ◇ n [urine] meada f. ◇ vi mear.

pissed [pɪst] adj vulg -1. Br [drunk] pedo (inv). -2. Am [annoyed] irritado(da).

pissed off adj vulg: to be OR to feel ~ estar cabreado(da).

pistol ['pɪstl] n pistola f.

piston ['pɪstən] n pistón m, émbolo m.

pit [pɪt] ◇ n -1. [large hole] hoyo m. -2. [small hole - in metal, glass] señal f, marca f; [- on face] picadura f. -3. [for orchestra] foso m de la orquesta. -4. [mine] mina f. -5. Am [of fruit] hueso m. ◇ vt: to be pitted against ser enfrentado(da) con. ◆pits npl [in motor racing]: the ~s el box.

pitch [pɪtʃ] ◇ n -1. SPORT campo m. -2. MUS tono m. -3. [level, degree] grado m, punto m. -4. [selling place] puesto m. -5. inf [sales talk] labia f de comerciante. ◇ vt -1. [throw] lanzar, arrojar. -2. [speech] dar un tono a; [price] establecer un precio para. -3. [tent] montar, poner. ◇ vi -1. [ball] tocar el suelo; to ~ forwards [person] precipitarse hacia delante. -2. [ship, plane] dar un bandazo.

pitch-black adj negro(gra) como boca de lobo.

pitched battle [,pɪtʃt-] n HISTORY batalla f campal; fig [bitter struggle] lucha f encarnizada.

pitcher ['pɪtʃər] n Am [jug] cántaro m.

pitchfork ['pɪtʃfɔːk] n horca f.

piteous ['pɪtɪəs] adj lastimero(ra).

pitfall ['pɪtfɔːl] n peligro m, escollo m.

pith [pɪθ] n parte blanca de la piel de una fruta.

pithy ['pɪθɪ] adj conciso(sa) y contundente.

pitiful ['pɪtɪful] adj [condition, excuse, effort] lamentable; [person, appearance] lastimoso(sa).

pitiless ['pɪtɪlɪs] adj [person] despiadado(da), cruel; [weather] deplorable.

pit stop n [in motor racing] parada f en boxes.

pittance ['pɪtəns] n miseria f.

pity ['pɪtɪ] ◇ n [compassion] compasión f; [shame] pena f, lástima f; what a ~! ¡qué pena!; to take OR have ~ on compadecerse de. ◇ *vt* compadecerse de, sentir pena por.

pivot ['pɪvət] *n* pivote *m*, eje *m*; *fig* eje *m*.

pizza ['piːtsə] *n* pizza *f*.

placard ['plækɑːd] *n* pancarta *f*.

placate [plə'keɪt] *vt* aplacar, apaciguar.

place [pleɪs] ◇ *n* -1. [gen] lugar *m*, sitio *m*; ~ **of birth** lugar de nacimiento. -2. [proper position] sitio *m*. -3. [suitable occasion, time] momento *m*. -4. [home] casa *f*. -5. [specific seat] asiento *m*; THEATRE localidad *f*. -6. [setting at table] cubierto *m*. -7. [on course, at university] plaza *f*. -8. [on committee, team] puesto *m*. -9. [role, function] papel *m*; **to have an important ~ in** desempeñar un papel importante en. -10. [rank] lugar *m*, posición *f*. -11. [in book] página *f*; [in speech] momento *m*; **to lose one's ~** no saber (uno) dónde estaba. -12. MATH: **decimal ~** punto *m* decimal. -13. [instance]: **in the first ~** [from the start] desde el principio; **in the first ~ ... and in the second ~ ...** [firstly, secondly] en primer lugar ... y en segundo lugar .... -14. *phr*: **to take ~** tener lugar; **to take the ~ of** sustituir a. ◇ *vt* -1. [position, put] colocar, poner; **to be well ~d to** do sthg estar en buena posición para hacer algo. -2. [lay, apportion]: **to ~ pressure on** ejercer presión sobre. -3. [identify]: **I recognize the face, but I can't ~ her** me suena su cara, pero no sé de qué. -4. [bet, order etc] hacer. -5. [in horse racing]: **to be ~d** llegar entre los tres primeros. ◆ **all over the place** *adv* por todas partes. ◆ **in place** *adv* -1. [in proper position] en su sitio. -2. [established, set up] en marcha OR funcionamiento. ◆ **in place of** *prep* en lugar de. ◆ **out of place** *adv* -1. [in wrong position]: **to be out of ~** no estar en su sitio. -2. [inappropriate, unsuitable] fuera de lugar.

place mat *n* mantel *m* individual.

placement ['pleɪsmənt] *n* colocación *f*.

placid ['plæsɪd] *adj* -1. [even-tempered] apacible. -2. [peaceful] tranquilo(la).

plagiarize, -ise ['pleɪdʒəraɪz] *vt* plagiar.

plague [pleɪg] ◇ *n* -1. [attack of disease] peste *f*. -2. [disease]: **(the) ~** la peste. -3. [of rats, insects] plaga *f*. ◇ *vt*: **to ~ sb with** [complaints, requests] acosar a alguien con; [questions] coser a alguien a; **to be ~d by** [ill health] estar acosado de; [doubts] estar atormentado de.

plaice [pleɪs] (*pl inv*) *n* platija *f*.

plaid [plæd] *n* tejido *m* escocés.

Plaid Cymru [,plaɪd'kʌmri] *n Br* POL *partido nacionalista galés.*

plain [pleɪn] ◇ *adj* -1. [not patterned] liso(sa). -2. [simple - gen] sencillo(lla); [- yoghurt] natural. -3. [clear] evidente, claro(ra). -4. [speaking, statement] franco(ca). -5. [absolute - madness etc] total, auténtico(ca). -6. [not pretty] sin atractivo. ◇ *adv inf* completamente. ◇ *n* GEOGR llanura *f*, planicie *f*.

plain chocolate *n Br* chocolate *m* amargo.

plain-clothes *adj* vestido(da) de paisano.

plain flour *n Br* harina *f* (sin levadura).

plainly ['pleɪnlɪ] *adv* -1. [upset, angry] evidentemente. -2. [visible, audible] claramente. -3. [frankly] francamente. -4. [simply] sencillamente.

plaintiff ['pleɪntɪf] *n* demandante *m y f*.

plait [plæt] ◇ *n* trenza *f*. ◇ *vt* trenzar.

plan [plæn] ◇ *n* -1. [strategy] plan *m*, proyecto *m*; **to go according to ~** salir según lo previsto. -2. [of story, essay] esquema *m*. -3. [of building etc] plano *m*. ◇ *vt* -1. [organize] planear, organizar. -2. [career, future] planificar; **to ~ to do sthg** tener la intención de hacer algo. -3. [design, devise] trazar un esquema OR boceto de. ◇ *vi* hacer planes OR proyectos. ◆ **plans** *npl* planes *mpl*; **to have ~s for** tener planes para. ◆ **plan on** *vt fus*: **to ~ on doing sthg** pensar hacer algo.

plane [pleɪn] ◇ *adj* plano(na). ◇ *n* -1. [aircraft] avión *m*. -2. GEOM [flat surface] plano *m*. -3. *fig* [level - intellectual] plano *m*. -4. [tool] cepillo *m*. -5. [tree] plátano *m*.

planet ['plænɪt] *n* planeta *m*.

plank [plæŋk] *n* [piece of wood] tablón *m*, tabla *f*.

planning ['plænɪŋ] *n* [gen] planificación *f*.

planning permission *n* permiso *m* de construcción OR de obras.

plant [plɑːnt] ◇ *n* -1. BOT planta *f*. -2. [factory] planta *f*, fábrica *f*. -3. [heavy machinery] maquinaria *f*. ◇ *vt* -1. [seed, tree, vegetable]: **to ~ sthg (in)** plantar algo (en). -2. [field, garden]: **to ~ sthg with** sembrar algo de. -3. [bomb, bug] colocar secretamente.

plantation [plæn'teɪʃn] *n* plantación *f*.

plaque [plɑːk] *n* placa *f*.

plaster ['plɑːstər] ◇ *n* -1. [for wall, ceiling] yeso *m*. -2. [for broken bones] escayola f. **-3.** Br [bandage] **tirita**® f, **espara-drapo** m. ◇ vt **-1.** [put plaster on] **enye-sar. -2.** [cover]: **to ~ sthg (with)** cubrir algo (de).

plaster cast n **-1.** [for broken bones] escayola f. **-2.** [model, statue] vaciado m en yeso.

plastered ['plɑːstəd] adj inf [drunk] cocido(da).

plasterer ['plɑːstərər] n yesero m, -ra f.

plastic ['plæstɪk] ◇ adj [made from plastic] de plástico. ◇ n plástico m.

Plasticine® ['plæstɪsiːn] n Br plastilina® f.

plastic surgery n cirugía f plástica.

plate [pleɪt] ◇ n **-1.** [dish, plateful] plato m. **-2.** [on machinery, wall, door] placa f. **-3.** (U) [metal covering]: **gold/silver ~** chapa f de oro/plata. **-4.** [photograph] lámina f. **-5.** [in dentistry] dentadura f postiza. ◇ vt: **to be ~d (with)** estar chapado(da) (en OR de).

plateau ['plætəʊ] (pl -s OR -x [-z]) n [high, flat land] meseta f.

plate glass n vidrio m cilindrado.

platform ['plætfɔːm] n **-1.** [gen] plataforma f; [stage] estrado m; [at meeting] tribuna f. **-2.** RAIL andén m. **-3.** POL programa m electoral.

platform ticket n Br billete m de andén.

platinum ['plætɪnəm] n platino m.

platitude ['plætɪtjuːd] n tópico m.

platoon [plə'tuːn] n pelotón m.

platter ['plætər] n [dish] fuente f.

plausible ['plɔːzəbl] adj plausible, admisible.

play [pleɪ] ◇ n **-1.** (U) [amusement] juego m. **-2.** [piece of drama] obra f. **-3.** [game]: **~ on words** juego m de palabras. **-4.** TECH juego m. ◇ vt **-1.** [game, sport] jugar a. **-2.** [play game against]: **to ~ sb (at sthg)** jugar contra alguien (a algo). **-3.** [perform for amusement]: **to ~ a joke on** gastar una broma a; **to ~ a dirty trick on** jugar una mala pasada a. **-4.** [act - part, character] representar; **to ~ a part** OR **role in** fig desempeñar un papel en; **to ~ the fool** hacer OR hacerse el tonto. **-5.** [instrument, tune] tocar; [record, cassette] poner. **-6.** phr: **to ~ it safe** actuar sobre seguro. ◇ vi **-1.** [gen]: **to ~ (with/against)** jugar (con/contra); **to ~ for sb/a team** jugar para alguien/ con un equipo. **-2.** [MUS - person] tocar; [- music] sonar. ◆ **play along** vi: **to ~ along (with)** seguir la corriente (a). ◆ **play down** vt sep quitar importancia

a. ◆ **play up** ◇ vt sep [emphasize] hacer resaltar. ◇ vi [machine, part of body, child] dar guerra.

play-act vi fingir, hacer comedia.

playboy ['pleɪbɔɪ] n playboy m.

player ['pleɪər] n **-1.** [of sport, game] jugador m, -ra f. **-2.** MUS intérprete m y f. **-3.** THEATRE actor m, actriz f.

playful ['pleɪfʊl] adj juguetón(ona).

playground ['pleɪgraʊnd] n patio m de recreo.

playgroup ['pleɪgruːp] n jardín m de infancia, guardería f.

playing card ['pleɪɪŋ-] n naipe m, carta f.

playing field ['pleɪɪŋ-] n campo m de juego.

playmate ['pleɪmeɪt] n compañero m, -ra f de juego.

play-off n partido m de desempate.

playpen ['pleɪpen] n parque m (de niños) (tipo cuna).

playschool ['pleɪskuːl] n jardín m de infancia, guardería f.

plaything ['pleɪθɪŋ] n lit & fig juguete m.

playtime ['pleɪtaɪm] n recreo m.

playwright ['pleɪraɪt] n dramaturgo m, -ga f.

plc abbr of **public limited company**.

plea [pliː] n **-1.** [appeal] súplica f, petición f. **-2.** JUR declaración por parte del acusado de culpabilidad o inocencia.

plead [pliːd] (pt & pp **-ed** OR **pled**) ◇ vt **-1.** JUR [one's cause] defender; **to ~ guilty/not guilty** declararse culpable/ inocente. **-2.** [give as excuse] pretender. ◇ vi **-1.** [beg]: **to ~ (with sb to do sthg)** rogar OR implorar (a alguien que haga algo); **to ~ for sthg** pedir algo. **-2.** JUR declarar.

pleasant ['pleznt] adj **-1.** [smell, taste, view] agradable; [surprise, news] grato(ta). **-2.** [person, smile, face] simpático(ca).

pleasantry ['plezntrɪ] n: **to exchange pleasantries** intercambiar cumplidos.

please [pliːz] ◇ vt complacer, agradar; **he always ~s himself** él siempre hace lo que le da la gana; **~ yourself!** ¡como quieras! ◇ vi **-1.** [give satisfaction] satisfacer, agradar. **-2.** [think appropriate]: **to do as one ~s** hacer como a uno le parezca. ◇ adv por favor.

pleased [pliːzd] adj: **to be ~ (about/ with)** estar contento(ta) (por/con); **~ to meet you!** ¡encantado(da) de conocerle!, ¡mucho gusto!

pleasing ['pliːzɪŋ] *adj* agradable, grato(ta).

pleasure ['pleʒər] *n* **-1.** [feeling of happiness] gusto *m*; **to take ~ in sthg** disfrutar haciendo algo. **-2.** [enjoyment] diversión *f*. **-3.** [delight] placer *m*; **it's a ~, my ~** no hay de qué.

pleat [pliːt] ◇ *n* pliegue *m*. ◇ *vt* plisar.

pled [pled] *pt & pp* → **plead**.

pledge [pledʒ] ◇ *n* **-1.** [promise] promesa *f*. **-2.** [token] señal *f*, prenda *f*. ◇ *vt* **-1.** [promise] prometer. **-2.** [make promise]: **to ~ sb to sthg** hacer jurar a alguien algo; **to ~ o.s.** comprometerse a. **-3.** [pawn] empeñar.

plentiful ['plentɪful] *adj* abundante.

plenty ['plentɪ] ◇ *n* (U) abundancia *f*. ◇ *pron*: **we've got ~** tenemos de sobra; **~ of** mucho(cha).

pliable ['plaɪəbl], **pliant** ['plaɪənt] *adj* flexible.

pliers ['plaɪəz] *npl* alicates *mpl*.

plight [plaɪt] *n* grave situación *f*.

plimsoll ['plɪmsəl] *n Br* playera *f*, zapato *m* de tenis.

plinth [plɪnθ] *n* [for statue] peana *f*; [for pillar] plinto *m*.

PLO (*abbr of* **Palestine Liberation Organization**) *n* OLP *f*.

plod [plɒd] *vi* **-1.** [walk slowly] caminar con paso cansino. **-2.** [work slowly] llevar a cabo un trabajo pesado.

plodder ['plɒdər] *n pej* persona *f* mediocre pero voluntariosa (en el trabajo).

plonk [plɒŋk] *n* (U) *Br inf* [wine] vino *m* peleón. ◆ **plonk down** *vt sep inf* dejar caer.

plot [plɒt] ◇ *n* **-1.** [plan] complot *m*, conspiración *f*. **-2.** [story] argumento *m*, trama *f*. **-3.** [of land] parcela *f*. ◇ *vt* **-1.** [plan] tramar, urdir. **-2.** [on map, graph] trazar. ◇ *vi*: **to ~ (to do sthg)** tramar (hacer algo); **to ~ against** conspirar contra.

plotter ['plɒtər] *n* [schemer] conspirador *m*, -ra *f*.

plough *Br*, **plow** *Am* [plaʊ] ◇ *n* arado *m*. ◇ *vt* arar. ◆ **plough into** ◇ *vt sep* [invest] invertir. ◇ *vt fus* [hit] chocar contra.

ploughman's ['plaʊmənz] (*pl inv*) *n Br*: **~ (lunch)** queso, cebolletas y ensalada con pan.

plow *etc Am* = **plough** *etc*.

ploy [plɔɪ] *n* táctica *f*, estratagema *f*.

pluck [plʌk] ◇ *vt* **-1.** [fruit, flower] coger. **-2.** [pull sharply] arrancar. **-3.** [bird] desplumar. **-4.** [eyebrows] depilar. **-5.** [instrument] puntear. ◇ *n dated* valor *m*. ◆ **pluck up** *vt fus*: **to ~ up the courage to do sthg** armarse de valor para hacer algo.

plucky ['plʌkɪ] *adj dated* valiente.

plug [plʌg] ◇ *n* **-1.** ELEC enchufe *m*, clavija *f*. **-2.** [for bath or sink] tapón *m*. ◇ *vt* **-1.** [hole, leak] tapar. **-2.** *inf* [mention favourably] dar publicidad a. ◆ **plug in** *vt sep* enchufar.

plughole ['plʌghəʊl] *n* desagüe *m*.

plum [plʌm] ◇ *adj* **-1.** [colour] de color ciruela. **-2.** [choice]: **~ job** chollo *m*. ◇ *n* [fruit] ciruela *f*.

plumb [plʌm] ◇ *adv* **-1.** *Br* [exactly]: **~ in the middle** justo en medio. **-2.** *Am* [completely] completamente. ◇ *vt*: **to ~ the depths of** alcanzar las cotas más bajas de.

plumber ['plʌmər] *n* fontanero *m*, -ra *f*, gásfiter *m Amer*.

plumbing ['plʌmɪŋ] *n* (U) **-1.** [fittings] tubería *f*. **-2.** [work] fontanería *f*.

plume [pluːm] *n* **-1.** [feather] pluma *f*. **-2.** [decoration, of smoke] penacho *m*.

plummet ['plʌmɪt] *vi* caer en picado.

plump [plʌmp] *adj* regordete(ta). ◆ **plump for** *vt fus* optar OR decidirse por. ◆ **plump up** *vt sep* ahuecar.

plum pudding *n* budín navideño con pasas.

plunder ['plʌndər] ◇ *n* **-1.** [stealing, raiding] saqueo *m*, pillaje *m*. **-2.** [stolen goods] botín *m*. ◇ *vt* saquear.

plunge [plʌndʒ] ◇ *n* [fall, dive] chapuzón *m*, zambullida *f*; **to take the ~** dar el paso decisivo. ◇ *vt* **-1.** [knife etc]: **to ~ sthg into** hundir algo en. **-2.** [into darkness, water]: **to ~ sthg into** sumergir algo en. ◇ *vi* **-1.** [fall, dive] hundirse, zambullirse. **-2.** [decrease] bajar vertiginosamente.

plunger ['plʌndʒər] *n* [for blocked pipes] desatascador *m*.

pluperfect [ˌpluːˈpɜːfɪkt] *n*: **~ (tense)** (pretérito *m*) pluscuamperfecto *m*.

plural ['plʊərəl] ◇ *adj* [gen] plural. ◇ *n* plural *m*.

plus [plʌs] (*pl* **-es** OR **-ses**) ◇ *adj* [or more]: **35-~** 35 o más. ◇ *n* **-1.** MATH [sign] signo *m* más. **-2.** *inf* [bonus] ventaja *f*. ◇ *prep* más. ◇ *conj* además.

plush [plʌʃ] *adj* lujoso(sa).

plus sign *n* signo *m* más.

Pluto ['pluːtəʊ] *n* [planet] Plutón *m*.

plutonium [pluːˈtəʊnɪəm] *n* plutonio *m*.

ply [plaɪ] ◇ vt **-1.** [trade] ejercer. **-2.** [supply, provide]: **to ~ sb with sthg** [questions] acosar a alguien con algo; [food, drink] no parar de ofrecer a alguien algo. ◇ vi navegar.

plywood ['plaɪwʊd] n contrachapado m.

p.m., pm (abbr of post meridiem): **at 3 ~** a las tres de la tarde.

PM n abbr of **prime minister**.

PMT, PMS (abbr of **premenstrual tension, premenstrual syndrome**) n SPM m.

pneumatic [njuːˈmætɪk] adj [tyre, chair] neumático(ca).

pneumatic drill n martillo m neumático.

pneumonia [njuːˈməʊnjə] n (U) pulmonía f.

poach [pəʊtʃ] ◇ vt **-1.** [game] cazar en vedado; [fish] pescar en vedado. **-2.** [copy] plagiar. **-3.** CULIN [salmon] hervir; [egg] escalfar. ◇ vi [for game] cazar en vedado; [for fish] pescar en vedado.

poacher ['pəʊtʃər] n [hunter] cazador furtivo m, cazadora furtiva f; [fisherman] pescador furtivo m, pescadora furtiva f.

poaching ['pəʊtʃɪŋ] n [for game] caza f furtiva; [for fish] pesca f furtiva.

PO Box (abbr of **Post Office Box**) n apdo. m.

pocket ['pɒkɪt] ◇ n **-1.** [in clothes] bolsillo m; **to be £10 out of ~** salir perdiendo 10 libras; **to pick sb's ~** vaciar a alguien el bolsillo. **-2.** [in car door etc] bolsa f, bolsillo m. **-3.** [of resistance] foco m; [of air] bolsa f. ◇ vt **-1.** [place in pocket] meterse en el bolsillo. **-2.** [steal] birlar. ◇ adj de bolsillo.

pocketbook ['pɒkɪtbʊk] n **-1.** [notebook] libreta f. **-2.** Am [handbag] bolso m.

pocketknife ['pɒkɪtnaɪf] (pl **-knives** [-naɪvz]) n navaja f (de bolsillo).

pocket money n propina f, dinero m para gastar.

pockmark ['pɒkmɑːk] n marca f OR señal f (en la cara).

pod [pɒd] n [of plants] vaina f.

podgy ['pɒdʒɪ] adj inf gordinflón(ona).

podiatrist [pəˈdaɪətrɪst] n Am podólogo m, -ga f.

podium ['pəʊdɪəm] (pl **-diums** OR **-dia** [-dɪə]) n podio m.

poem ['pəʊɪm] n poema m, poesía f.

poet ['pəʊɪt] n poeta m y f.

poetic [pəʊˈetɪk] adj poético(ca).

poet laureate n poeta m laureado.

poetry ['pəʊɪtrɪ] n poesía f.

poignant ['pɔɪnjənt] adj patético(ca), conmovedor(ra).

point [pɔɪnt] ◇ n **-1.** [gen] punto m; **at that ~** en aquel momento. **-2.** [tip] punta f. **-3.** [detail, argument]: **to make a ~** hacer una observación; **to have a ~** tener razón. **-4.** [main idea]: **the ~ is ...** lo fundamental OR más importante es ...; **to miss the ~ of** no coger la idea de; **to get** OR **come to the ~** ir al grano; **it's beside the ~** no viene al caso. **-5.** [feature] cualidad f; **weak/strong ~** punto m débil/fuerte. **-6.** [purpose] sentido m; **what's the ~?** ¿para qué?; **there's no ~ in it** no tiene sentido. **-7.** [decimal point] coma f; **two ~ six** dos coma seis. **-8.** Br ELEC toma f de corriente. **-9.** phr: **to make a ~ of doing sthg** poner empeño en hacer algo. ◇ vt: **to ~ a gun at sthg/sb** apuntar a algo/alguien con una pistola; **to ~ one's finger at sthg/sb** señalar algo/a alguien con el dedo. ◇ vi **-1.** [indicate with finger]: **to ~ at sthg/sb, to ~ to sthg/sb** señalar algo/a alguien con el dedo. **-2.** fig [suggest]: **everything ~s to her guilt** todo indica que ella es la culpable. ◆ **points** npl Br RAIL agujas fpl. ◆ **up to a point** adv hasta cierto punto. ◆ **on the point of** prep: **to be on the ~ of doing sthg** estar a punto de hacer algo. ◆ **point out** vt sep [person, object, fact] señalar, indicar; [mistake] hacer notar.

point-blank adv **-1.** [refuse, deny] categóricamente. **-2.** [at close range] a quemarropa.

pointed ['pɔɪntɪd] adj **-1.** [sharp, angular] en punta, puntiagudo(da). **-2.** [cutting, incisive] intencionado(da).

pointer ['pɔɪntər] n **-1.** [piece of advice] consejo m. **-2.** [needle] aguja f. **-3.** COMPUT puntero m.

pointless ['pɔɪntlɪs] adj sin sentido.

point of view (pl **points of view**) n **-1.** [opinion] punto m de vista. **-2.** [aspect, perspective] perspectiva f.

poise [pɔɪz] n [self-assurance] aplomo m, serenidad f; [elegance] elegancia f.

poised [pɔɪzd] adj **-1.** [ready]: **to be ~ to do sthg** estar listo(ta) para hacer algo. **-2.** [calm and dignified] sereno(na).

poison ['pɔɪzn] ◇ n veneno m. ◇ vt [gen - intentionally] envenenar; [- unintentionally] intoxicar.

poisoning ['pɔɪznɪŋ] n [intentional] envenenamiento *m*; [unintentional] intoxicación *f*.

poisonous ['pɔɪznəs] *adj* **-1.** [substance, gas] tóxico(ca). **-2.** [snake] venenoso(sa).

poke [pəʊk] ◇ *vt* **-1.** [with finger, stick] empujar; [with elbow] dar un codazo a; [fire] atizar; **to ~ sb in the eye** meter el dedo en el ojo de alguien. **-2.** [push, stuff]: **to ~ sthg into** meter algo en. ◇ *vi* [protrude]: **to ~ out of sthg** sobresalir por algo. ◆ **poke about, poke around** *vi inf* fisgonear, hurgar.

poker ['pəʊkə'] *n* **-1.** [game] póker *m*. **-2.** [for fire] atizador *m*.

poker-faced [-,feɪst] *adj* con cara inexpresiva.

poky ['pəʊkɪ] *adj pej*: **a ~ little room** un cuartucho.

Poland ['pəʊlənd] *n* Polonia.

polar ['pəʊlə'] *adj* polar.

Polaroid® ['pəʊlərɔɪd] *n* **-1.** [camera] polaroid® *f*. **-2.** [photograph] fotografía *f* polaroid.

pole [pəʊl] *n* **-1.** [rod, post] palo *m*; **telegraph ~** poste *m* telegráfico. **-2.** ELEC & GEOGR polo *m*.

Pole [pəʊl] *n* polaco *m*, -ca *f*.

pole vault *n*: **the ~** el salto con pértiga.

police [pə'liːs] ◇ *npl* [police force]: **the ~** la policía. ◇ *vt* mantener el orden en, vigilar.

police car *n* coche *m* patrulla.

police constable *n Br* policía *m y f*.

police force *n* cuerpo *m* de policía.

policeman [pə'liːsmən] (*pl* **-men** [-mən]) *n* policía *m*.

police officer *n* agente *m y f* de la policía.

police record *n*: **(to have a) ~** (tener) antecedentes *mpl* policiales.

police station *n* comisaría *f* (de policía).

policewoman [pə'liːs,wʊmən] (*pl* **-women** [-,wɪmɪn]) *n* (mujer *f*) policía *f*.

policy ['pɒləsɪ] *n* **-1.** [plan, practice] política *f*. **-2.** [document, agreement] póliza *f*.

polio ['pəʊlɪəʊ] *n* polio *f*.

polish ['pɒlɪʃ] ◇ *n* **-1.** [for floor] cera *f*; [for shoes] betún *m*; [for window] limpiacristales *m inv*; [for nails] esmalte *m*. **-2.** [shine] brillo *m*, lustre *m*. **-3.** *fig* [refinement] refinamiento *m*. ◇ *vt* [floor] encerar; [shoes, window, car] limpiar; [cutlery, silver, glasses] sacar brillo a. ◆ **polish**

off *vt sep inf* [food] zamparse; [job] despachar.

Polish ['pəʊlɪʃ] ◇ *adj* polaco(ca). ◇ *n* [language] polaco *m*. ◇ *npl*: **the ~** los polacos *mpl*.

polished ['pɒlɪʃt] *adj* **-1.** [person, manner] refinado(da). **-2.** [performance, speech] esmerado(da).

polite [pə'laɪt] *adj* educado(da), cortés.

politic ['pɒlətɪk] *adj fml* oportuno(na), conveniente.

political [pə'lɪtɪkl] *adj* [concerning politics] político(ca).

politically correct [pə,lɪtɪklɪ-] *adj* políticamente correcto(ta), *conforme a la ética según la cual se sustituyen términos considerados sexistas, racistas etc por otros considerados aceptables*.

politician [,pɒlɪ'tɪʃn] *n* político *m*, -ca *f*.

politics ['pɒlətɪks] ◇ *n* (*U*) **-1.** [gen] política *f*. **-2.** [field of study] ciencias *fpl* políticas. ◇ *npl* **-1.** [personal beliefs] ideas *fpl* políticas. **-2.** [of a group, area] política *f*.

polka ['pɒlkə] *n* polca *f*.

polka dot *n* lunar *m* (*en un vestido*).

poll [pəʊl] ◇ *n* [vote] votación *f*; [of opinion] encuesta *f*. ◇ *vt* **-1.** [people] sondear. **-2.** [votes] obtener. ◆ **polls** *npl*: **the ~s** los comicios.

pollen ['pɒlən] *n* polen *m*.

polling booth ['pəʊlɪŋ-] *n* cabina *f* electoral.

polling day ['pəʊlɪŋ-] *n Br* día *m* de elecciones.

polling station ['pəʊlɪŋ-] *n* mesa *f* OR centro *m* electoral.

pollute [pə'luːt] *vt* contaminar.

pollution [pə'luːʃn] *n* (*U*) **-1.** [process of polluting] contaminación *f*. **-2.** [impurities] substancias *fpl* contaminantes.

polo ['pəʊləʊ] *n* polo *m*.

polo neck *Br n* **-1.** [neck] cuello *m* alto. **-2.** [jumper] jersey *m* de cuello alto.

polyethylene *n Am* = **polythene**.

Polynesia [,pɒlɪ'niːzə] *n* Polinesia.

polystyrene [,pɒlɪ'staɪriːn] *n* poliestireno *m*.

polytechnic [,pɒlɪ'teknɪk] *n Br* politécnico *m*, escuela *f* politécnica.

polythene *Br* ['pɒlɪθiːn], **polyethylene** *Am* ['pɒlɪ'eθɪliːn] *n* polietileno *m*.

polythene bag *n Br* bolsa *f* de plástico.

pomegranate ['pɒmɪ,grænɪt] *n* granada *f*.

pomp [pɒmp] *n* pompa *f*.

pompom ['pɒmpɒm] *n* borla *f*, pompón *m*.

pompous ['pɒmpəs] *adj* **-1.** [self-important] presumido(da). **-2.** [style] pomposo(sa); [building] ostentoso(sa).

pond [pɒnd] *n* estanque m.

ponder ['pɒndər] *vt* considerar.

ponderous ['pɒndərəs] *adj* **-1.** [speech, book] pesado(da). **-2.** [action, walk] lento(ta) y torpe.

pong [pɒŋ] *Br inf n* (olor m a) peste f.

pontoon [pɒn'tuːn] *n* **-1.** [bridge] pontón m. **-2.** *Br* [game] veintiuna f.

pony ['pəʊnɪ] *n* poni m.

ponytail ['pəʊnɪteɪl] *n* coleta f (de caballo).

pony-trekking [-,trekɪŋ] *n* (U) excursión f en poni.

poodle ['puːdl] *n* caniche m.

pool [puːl] ◇ *n* **-1.** [of water, blood, ink] charco m; [pond] estanque m. **-2.** [swimming pool] piscina f. **-3.** [of light] foco m. **-4.** COMM [fund] fondos mpl comunes. **-5.** [of people, things]: **typing** ~ servicio m de mecanografía; **car** ~ parque m de automóviles. **-6.** [game] billar m americano. ◇ *vt* [resources, funds] juntar; [knowledge] poner en común.
◆ **pools** *npl Br*: **the** ~**s** las quinielas.

poor [pɔːr] ◇ *adj* **-1.** [gen] pobre; ~ **old John!** ¡el pobre de John! **-2.** [quality, result] malo(la). ◇ *npl*: **the** ~ los pobres.

poorly ['pɔːlɪ] ◇ *adj Br* pachucho(cha). ◇ *adv* mal.

pop [pɒp] ◇ *n* **-1.** [music] (música f) pop m. **-2.** (U) *inf* [fizzy drink] gaseosa f. **-3.** *inf* [father] papá m. **-4.** [sound] pequeña explosión f. ◇ *vt* **-1.** [balloon, bubble] pinchar. **-2.** [put quickly]: **to** ~ **sthg into** meter algo en. ◇ *vi* **-1.** [balloon] reventar; [cork, button] saltar. **-2.** [eyes] salirse de las órbitas. **-3.** [go quickly]: **I'm just popping round to the shop** voy un momento a la tienda.
◆ **pop in** *vi* entrar un momento.
◆ **pop up** *vi* aparecer de repente.

pop concert *n* concierto m de música pop.

popcorn ['pɒpkɔːn] *n* palomitas fpl (de maíz).

pope [pəʊp] *n* papa m.

pop group *n* grupo m (de música) pop.

poplar ['pɒplər] *n* álamo m.

poppy ['pɒpɪ] *n* amapola f.

Popsicle® ['pɒpsɪkl] *n Am* polo m.

populace ['pɒpjʊləs] *n*: **the** ~ [masses] el populacho; [people] el pueblo.

popular ['pɒpjʊlər] *adj* **-1.** [gen] popular; [person] estimado(da). **-2.** [belief, atti-

tude, discontent] generalizado(da). **-3.** [newspaper, politics] para las masas.

popularize, -ise ['pɒpjʊləraɪz] *vt* **-1.** [make popular] popularizar. **-2.** [simplify] vulgarizar.

population [,pɒpjʊ'leɪʃn] *n* población f.

porcelain ['pɔːsəlɪn] *n* porcelana f.

porch [pɔːtʃ] *n* **-1.** [entrance] porche m, pórtico m. **-2.** *Am* [verandah] terraza f.

porcupine ['pɔːkjʊpaɪn] *n* puerco m espín.

pore [pɔːr] *n* poro m. ◆ **pore over** *vt fus* estudiar esmeradamente.

pork [pɔːk] *n* carne f de cerdo.

pork pie *n* empanada f de carne de cerdo.

pornography [pɔː'nɒgrəfɪ] *n* pornografía f.

porous ['pɔːrəs] *adj* poroso(sa).

porridge ['pɒrɪdʒ] *n* papilla f OR gachas fpl de avena.

port [pɔːt] *n* **-1.** [coastal town, harbour] puerto m. **-2.** NAUT [left-hand side] babor m. **-3.** [drink] oporto m. **-4.** COMPUT conexión f.

portable ['pɔːtəbl] *adj* portátil.

portent ['pɔːtənt] *n literary* presagio m.

porter ['pɔːtər] *n* **-1.** *Br* [in block of flats] portero m, -ra f; [in public building, hotel] conserje m y f. **-2.** [for luggage] mozo m.

portfolio [,pɔːt'fəʊljəʊ] (*pl* **-s**) *n* **-1.** ART, FIN & POL cartera f. **-2.** [sample of work] carpeta f.

porthole ['pɔːthəʊl] *n* portilla f.

portion ['pɔːʃn] *n* **-1.** [part, section] porción f. **-2.** [of chips, vegetables etc] ración f.

portly ['pɔːtlɪ] *adj* corpulento(ta).

port of call *n* **-1.** NAUT puerto m de escala. **-2.** *fig* [on journey] escala f.

portrait ['pɔːtreɪt] *n* retrato m.

portray [pɔː'treɪ] *vt* **-1.** [represent - in a play, film] representar. **-2.** [describe] describir. **-3.** [paint] retratar.

Portugal ['pɔːtʃʊgl] *n* Portugal.

Portuguese [,pɔːtʃʊ'giːz] ◇ *adj* portugués(esa). ◇ *n* [language] portugués m. ◇ *npl*: **the** ~ los portugueses.

pose [pəʊz] ◇ *n* **-1.** [position, stance] postura f. **-2.** *pej* [pretence, affectation] pose f. ◇ *vt* **-1.** [problem, threat] presentar. **-2.** [question] formular. ◇ *vi* **-1.** [model] posar. **-2.** *pej* [behave affectedly] adoptar una pose. **-3.** [pretend to be]: **to** ~ **as sb/sthg** fingir ser alguien/algo.

posh [pɒʃ] *adj inf* **-1.** [hotel, area etc] de lujo, elegante. **-2.** *Br* [person, accent] afectado(da).

position [pə'zɪʃn] ◇ *n* **-1.** [gen] posición *f*. **-2.** [right place] sitio *m*, lugar *m*. **-3.** [status] rango *m*. **-4.** [job] puesto *m*. **-5.** [in a race, competition] lugar *m*. **-6.** [state, situation] situación *f*. **-7.** [stance, opinion]: ~ **on** opinión *f* respecto a. ◇ *vt* colocar.

positive ['pɒzətɪv] *adj* **-1.** [gen] positivo(va). **-2.** [sure]: **to be ~ (about)** estar seguro(ra) (de). **-3.** [optimistic, confident]: **to be ~ (about)** ser optimista (respecto a). **-4.** [definite - action] decisivo(va); [- decision] categórico(ca). **-5.** [irrefutable - evidence, fact] irrefutable; [- proof] concluyente.

posse ['pɒsɪ] *n Am* **-1.** [to pursue criminal] grupo *m* de hombres a caballo. **-2.** [group] grupo *m*.

possess [pə'zes] *vt* **-1.** [gen] poseer. **-2.** [subj: emotion] adueñarse de.

possession [pə'zeʃn] *n* posesión *f*. ◆ **possessions** *npl* bienes *mpl*.

possessive [pə'zesɪv] *adj* **-1.** [gen] posesivo(va). **-2.** *pej* [selfish] egoísta.

possibility [,pɒsə'bɪlətɪ] *n* posibilidad *f*.

possible ['pɒsəbl] *adj* **-1.** [gen] posible; **as soon as** ~ cuanto antes; **as much as** ~ todo lo posible; **it's ~ that she'll come** es posible que venga. **-2.** [viable - plan etc] viable, factible.

possibly ['pɒsəblɪ] *adv* **-1.** [perhaps] posiblemente, quizás. **-2.** [within one's power]: **could you ~ help me?** ¿te importaría ayudarme? **-3.** [to show surprise]: **how could he ~ do that?** ¿cómo demonios pudo hacer eso? **-4.** [for emphasis]: **I can't ~ do it** no puedo hacerlo de ninguna manera.

post [pəʊst] ◇ *n* **-1.** [service]: **the ~** el correo; **by ~** por correo. **-2.** (*U*) [letters etc] cartas *fpl*. **-3.** [delivery] reparto *m*. **-4.** *Br* [collection] colecta *f*. **-5.** [pole] poste *m*. **-6.** [position, job] puesto *m*. **-7.** MIL puesto *m*. ◇ *vt* **-1.** [by mail] echar al correo. **-2.** [transfer] enviar, destinar.

postage ['pəʊstɪdʒ] *n* franqueo *m*, porte *m*; ~ **and packing** gastos *mpl* de envío.

postal ['pəʊstl] *adj* postal.

postal order *n* giro *m* postal.

postbox ['pəʊstbɒks] *n Br* buzón *m*.

postcard ['pəʊstkɑːd] *n* postal *f*.

postcode ['pəʊstkəʊd] *n Br* código *m* postal.

postdate [,pəʊst'deɪt] *vt* poner posfecha a.

poster ['pəʊstər] *n* cartel *m*, póster *m*.

poste restante [,pəʊst'restɑːnt] *n* lista *f* de correos.

posterior [pɒ'stɪərɪər] *n hum* trasero *m*.

postgraduate [,pəʊst'grædʒuət] *n* posgraduado *m*, -da *f*.

posthumous ['pɒstjuməs] *adj* póstumo(ma).

postman ['pəʊstmən] (*pl* **-men** [-mən]) *n* cartero *m*.

postmark ['pəʊstmɑːk] *n* matasellos *m inv*.

postmaster ['pəʊst,mɑːstər] *n* administrador *m* de correos.

postmortem [,pəʊst'mɔːtəm] ◇ *adj* post-mórtem (*inv*). ◇ *n* [autopsy] autopsia *f*.

post office *n* **-1.** [organization]: **the Post Office** ≃ Correos *m inv*. **-2.** [building] oficina *f* de correos.

post office box *n* apartado *m* de correos, casilla *f* de correos *Amer*.

postpone [,pəʊst'pəʊn] *vt* posponer.

postscript ['pəʊstskrɪpt] *n* [additional message] posdata *f*; *fig* [additional information] nota *f* final.

posture ['pɒstʃər] *n lit & fig* postura *f*; ~ **on sthg** postura hacia algo.

postwar [,pəʊst'wɔːr] *adj* de (la) posguerra.

posy ['pəʊzɪ] *n* ramillete *m*.

pot [pɒt] ◇ *n* **-1.** [for cooking] olla *f*. **-2.** [for tea] tetera *f*; [for coffee] cafetera *f*. **-3.** [for paint] bote *m*; [for jam] tarro *m*. **-4.** [flowerpot] tiesto *m*, maceta *f*. **-5.** (*U*) *inf* [cannabis] maría *f*, hierba *f*. **-6.** *phr*: **to go to ~** ir al traste. ◇ *vt* plantar (en un tiesto).

potassium [pə'tæsɪəm] *n* potasio *m*.

potato [pə'teɪtəʊ] (*pl* **-es**) *n* patata *f*.

potato peeler [-,piːlər] *n* pelapatatas *m inv*.

potent ['pəʊtənt] *adj* **-1.** [powerful, influential] poderoso(sa). **-2.** [drink, drug] fuerte. **-3.** [sexually capable] potente.

potential [pə'tenʃl] ◇ *adj* potencial, posible. ◇ *n* (*U*) potencial *m*; **to have ~** tener posibilidades, prometer.

potentially [pə'tenʃəlɪ] *adv* en potencia.

pothole ['pɒthəʊl] *n* **-1.** [in road] bache *m*. **-2.** [underground] cueva *f*.

potholing ['pɒt,həʊlɪŋ] *n Br* espeleología *f*.

potion ['pəʊʃn] *n* poción *f*.

potluck [,pɒt'lʌk] *n*: **to take ~** [gen] elegir a ojo; [at meal] conformarse con lo que haya.

potshot ['pɒt,ʃɒt] *n*: **to take a ~ (at sthg/sb)** disparar (a algo/alguien) sin apuntar.

potted ['pɒtɪd] *adj* **-1.** [plant] en tiesto. **-2.** [meat, fish] en conserva.

potter ['pɒtəʳ] *n* alfarero *m*, -ra *f*. ◆ **potter about, potter around** *vi Br* entretenerse.

pottery ['pɒtərɪ] *n* **-1.** [gen] cerámica *f*, alfarería *f*. **-2.** [factory] fábrica *f* de cerámica.

potty ['pɒtɪ] *Br inf* ◇ *adj* [person] chalado(da). ◇ *n* orinal *m*.

pouch [pautʃ] *n* **-1.** [small bag] bolsa *f* pequeña; [for tobacco] petaca *f*. **-2.** [on animal's body] bolsa *f* (abdominal).

poultry ['pəultrɪ] ◇ *n* [meat] carne *f* de pollería. ◇ *npl* [birds] aves *fpl* de corral.

pounce [pauns] *vi* [leap]: **to ~ (on** OR **upon)** abalanzarse (sobre).

pound [paund] ◇ *n* **-1.** [unit of money, weight] libra *f*. **-2.** [for cars] depósito *m* (de coches); [for dogs] perrera *f*. ◇ *vt* **-1.** [hammer on] golpear, aporrear. **-2.** [pulverize] machacar. ◇ *vi* **-1.** [hammer]: **to ~ on sthg** golpear OR aporrear algo. **-2.** [beat, throb] palpitar.

pound sterling *n* libra *f* esterlina.

pour [pɔːʳ] ◇ *vt* [cause to flow]: **to ~ sthg (into)** echar OR verter algo (en); **to ~ sb a drink, to ~ a drink for sb** servirle una copa a alguien. ◇ *vi* **-1.** [liquid] chorrear; [smoke] salir a borbotones. **-2.** *fig* [rush]: **to ~ in/out** entrar/salir en manada. ◇ *v impers* [rain hard] llover a cántaros. ◆ **pour in** *vi* llegar a raudales. ◆ **pour out** *vt sep* **-1.** [empty] echar, vaciar. **-2.** [serve] servir.

pouring ['pɔːrɪŋ] *adj* [rain] torrencial.

pout [paut] *vi* [showing displeasure] hacer pucheros; [being provocative] hacer un gesto provocador con los labios.

poverty ['pɒvətɪ] *n lit* & *fig* pobreza *f*.

poverty-stricken *adj* necesitado(da).

powder ['paudəʳ] ◇ *n* polvo *m*; [makeup] polvos *mpl*. ◇ *vt* poner polvos en; **to ~ o.s.** darse polvos, empolvarse.

powder compact *n* polvera *f*.

powdered ['paudəd] *adj* [in powder form] en polvo.

powder puff *n* borla *f*.

powder room *n* servicios *mpl* de señoras.

power ['pauəʳ] ◇ *n* **-1.** (*U*) [authority, control] poder *m*; **to come to/take ~** llegar al/hacerse con el poder; **to be in ~** estar en el poder. **-2.** [ability] facultad *f*; **it isn't within my ~ to do it** no está dentro de mis posibilidades hacerlo. **-3.** [legal authority] autoridad *f*, competencia *f*. **-4.** [physical strength] fuerza *f*.

-5. [energy - solar, steam etc] energía *f*. **-6.** [electricity] corriente *f*; **to turn the ~ on/off** dar/cortar la corriente. **-7.** [powerful nation, person, group] potencia *f*. ◇ *vt* impulsar.

powerboat ['pauəbəut] *n* motora *f*.

power cut *n* apagón *m*.

power failure *n* corte *m* de corriente.

powerful ['pauəful] *adj* **-1.** [gen] poderoso(sa). **-2.** [blow, voice, drug] potente. **-3.** [speech, film] conmovedor(ra).

powerless ['pauəlɪs] *adj* **-1.** [helpless] impotente. **-2.** [unable]: **to be ~ to do sthg** no poder hacer algo.

power point *n Br* toma *f* (de corriente).

power station *n* central *f* eléctrica.

power steering *n* dirección *f* asistida.

pp (*abbr of* **per procurationem**) p.p.

p & p *abbr of* **postage and packing**.

PR *n* **-1.** *abbr of* **proportional representation**. **-2.** *abbr of* **public relations**.

practicable ['præktɪkəbl] *adj* factible.

practical ['præktɪkl] ◇ *adj* **-1.** [gen] práctico(ca). **-2.** [skilled with hands] hábil, mañoso(sa). ◇ *n* práctica *f*.

practicality [‚præktɪ'kælətɪ] *n* viabilidad *f*.

practical joke *n* broma *f* pesada.

practically ['præktɪklɪ] *adv* **-1.** [in a practical way] de manera práctica. **-2.** [almost] prácticamente, casi.

practice, practise *Am* ['præktɪs] *n* **-1.** [training, training session] práctica *f*; SPORT entrenamiento *m*; MUS ensayo *m*; **I'm out of ~** me falta práctica. **-2.** [reality]: **to put sthg into ~** llevar algo a la práctica; **in ~** [in fact] en la práctica. **-3.** [habit, regular activity] costumbre *f*. **-4.** [of profession] ejercicio *m*. **-5.** [business - of doctor] consulta *f*; [- of lawyer] bufete *m*, despacho *m*.

practicing *Am* = **practising**.

practise, practice *Am* ['præktɪs] ◇ *vt* **-1.** SPORT entrenar; MUS & THEATRE ensayar. **-2.** [religion, economy, safe sex] practicar. **-3.** [medicine, law] ejercer. ◇ *vi* **-1.** [train - gen] practicar; [- SPORT] entrenarse. **-2.** [as doctor] practicar; [as lawyer] ejercer.

practising, practicing *Am* ['præktɪsɪŋ] *adj* **-1.** [Catholic, Jew etc] practicante. **-2.** [doctor, lawyer] en ejercicio. **-3.** [homosexual] activo(va).

practitioner [præk'tɪʃnəʳ] *n*: **medical ~** médico *m*, -ca *f*.

Prague [prɑːg] *n* Praga.

prairie ['preərɪ] *n* pradera *f*, prado *m*.

praise [preɪz] ◇ *n* (U) elogio *m*, alabanza *f*. ◇ *vt* elogiar, alabar.

praiseworthy ['preɪz,wɜːðɪ] *adj* encomiable.

pram [præm] *n* cochecito *m* de niño.

prance [prɑːns] *vi* **-1.** [person] ir dando brincos. **-2.** [horse] hacer cabriolas.

prank [præŋk] *n* travesura *f*.

prawn [prɔːn] *n* gamba *f*.

pray [preɪ] *vi* rezar, orar; **to ~ to sb** rogar a alguien; **to ~ for sthg/for sthg to happen** *lit* & *fig* rogar algo/que pase algo.

prayer [preəʳ] *n* **-1.** RELIG oración *f*. **-2.** *fig* [strong hope] ruego *m*, súplica *f*.

prayer book *n* misal *m*.

preach [priːtʃ] ◇ *vt* [gen] predicar; [sermon] dar. ◇ *vi* **-1.** RELIG: **to ~ (to)** predicar (a). **-2.** *pej* [pontificate]: **to ~ (at)** sermonear (a).

preacher ['priːtʃəʳ] *n* predicador *m*, -ra *f*.

precarious [prɪ'keərɪəs] *adj* precario(ria).

precaution [prɪ'kɔːʃn] *n* precaución *f*.

precede [prɪ'siːd] *vt* preceder.

precedence ['presɪdəns] *n*: **to take ~ over** tener prioridad sobre.

precedent ['presɪdənt] *n* precedente *m*.

precinct ['priːsɪŋkt] *n* **-1.** *Br* [shopping area] zona *f* comercial. **-2.** *Am* [district] distrito *m*. ◆ **precincts** *npl* recinto *m*.

precious ['preʃəs] *adj* **-1.** [gen] precioso(sa). **-2.** [memories, possessions] preciado(da). **-3.** [affected] afectado(da).

precipice ['presɪpɪs] *n* *lit* & *fig* precipicio *m*.

precipitate [prɪ'sɪpɪteɪt] *fml* *vt* precipitar.

precise [prɪ'saɪs] *adj* preciso(sa), exacto(ta).

precisely [prɪ'saɪslɪ] *adv* **-1.** [with accuracy] exactamente. **-2.** [exactly, literally] precisamente. **-3.** [as confirmation]: ~! ¡eso es!

precision [prɪ'sɪʒn] *n* precisión *f*.

preclude [prɪ'kluːd] *vt* *fml* evitar, impedir; [possibility] excluir; **to ~ sthg/sb from doing sthg** impedir que algo/alguien haga algo.

precocious [prɪ'kəʊʃəs] *adj* precoz.

preconceived [,priːkən'siːvd] *adj* preconcebido(da).

precondition [,priːkən'dɪʃn] *n* *fml*: ~ **(for)** requisito *m* previo (para).

predator ['predətəʳ] *n* depredador *m*, -ra *f*; *fig* buitre *m* y *f*.

predecessor ['priːdɪsesəʳ] *n* antecesor *m*, -ra *f*.

predicament [prɪ'dɪkəmənt] *n* apuro *m*.

predict [prɪ'dɪkt] *vt* predecir, pronosticar.

predictable [prɪ'dɪktəbl] *adj* **-1.** [result etc] previsible. **-2.** [film, book, person] poco original.

prediction [prɪ'dɪkʃn] *n* pronóstico *m*.

predispose [,priːdɪs'pəʊz] *vt*: **to be ~d to sthg/to do sthg** [by nature] estar predispuesto(ta) a algo/a hacer algo.

predominant [prɪ'dɒmɪnənt] *adj* predominante.

predominantly [prɪ'dɒmɪnəntlɪ] *adv* fundamentalmente.

preempt [,priː'empt] *vt* [make ineffective] adelantarse a.

preemptive [,priː'emptɪv] *adj* preventivo(va).

preen [priːn] *vt* **-1.** [subj: bird] arreglar (con el pico). **-2.** *fig* [subj: person]: **to ~ o.s.** acicalarse.

prefab ['priːfæb] *n* *inf* casa *f* prefabricada.

preface ['prefɪs] *n*: ~ **(to)** prólogo *m* OR prefacio *m* (a).

prefect ['priːfekt] *n* *Br* [pupil] delegado *m*, -da *f* de curso.

prefer [prɪ'fɜːʳ] *vt*: **to ~ sthg (to)** preferir algo (a); **to ~ to do sthg** preferir hacer algo.

preferable ['prefrəbl] *adj*: **to be ~ (to)** ser preferible (a).

preferably ['prefrəblɪ] *adv* preferentemente.

preference ['prefərəns] *n*: ~ **(for)** preferencia *f* (por).

preferential [,prefə'renʃl] *adj* preferente.

prefix ['priːfɪks] *n* prefijo *m*.

pregnancy ['pregnənsɪ] *n* embarazo *m*.

pregnant ['pregnənt] *adj* [carrying unborn baby] embarazada.

prehistoric [,priːhɪ'stɒrɪk] *adj* prehistórico(ca).

prejudice ['predʒʊdɪs] ◇ *n*: ~ **(against)** prejuicio *m* (contra), **in favour of** predisposición *f* a favor de. ◇ *vt* **-1.** [bias]: **to ~ sb (in favour of/against)** predisponer a alguien (a favor de/en contra de). **-2.** [harm] perjudicar.

prejudiced ['predʒʊdɪst] *adj* parcial; **to be ~ in favour of/against** estar predispuesto a favor de/en contra de.

prejudicial [,predʒʊ'dɪʃl] *adj*: ~ **(to)** perjudicial (para).

preliminary [prɪ'lɪmɪnərɪ] *adj* preliminar.

prelude ['prelju:d] *n* [event]: ~ (to) preludio *m* (a).

premarital [,pri:'mærɪtl] *adj* prematrimonial.

premature ['premə,tjʊəʳ] *adj* prematuro(ra).

premeditated [,pri:'medɪteɪtɪd] *adj* premeditado(da).

premenstrual syndrome, premenstrual tension [pri:'menstruəl-] *n* síndrome *m* premenstrual.

premier ['premjəʳ] ◇ *adj* primero(ra). ◇ *n* primer ministro *m*, primera ministra *f*.

premiere ['premɪeəʳ] *n* estreno *m*.

premise ['premɪs] *n* premisa *f*. ◆ **premises** *npl* local *m*; **on the** ~**s** en el local.

premium ['pri:mjəm] *n* prima *f*; **at a** ~ [above usual value] por encima de su valor; [in great demand] muy solicitado(da).

premium bond *n* Br *boleto numerado emitido por el Estado que autoriza a participar en sorteos mensuales de dinero hasta su amortización.*

premonition [,premə'nɪʃn] *n* premonición *f*.

preoccupied [pri:'ɒkjʊpaɪd] *adj*: ~ (**with**) preocupado(da) (por).

prep [prep] (*abbr of* **preparation**) *n* (*U*) Br *inf* tarea *f*, deberes *mpl*.

prepaid ['pri:peɪd] *adj* [post paid] porte pagado.

preparation [,prepə'reɪʃn] *n* [act of preparing] preparación *f*. ◆ **preparations** *npl* preparativos *mpl*; **to make** ~**s for** hacer los preparativos para.

preparatory [prɪ'pærətrɪ] *adj* preparatorio(ria), preliminar.

preparatory school *n* [in UK] *colegio de pago para niños de 7 a 12 años;* [in US] *colegio privado que prepara a sus alumnos para estudios superiores.*

prepare [prɪ'peəʳ] ◇ *vt* preparar. ◇ *vi*: **to** ~ **for sthg/to do sthg** prepararse para algo/para hacer algo.

prepared [prɪ'peəd] *adj* -**1.** [gen] preparado(da). -**2.** [willing]: **to be** ~ **to do sthg** estar dispuesto(ta) a hacer algo.

preposition [,prepə'zɪʃn] *n* preposición *f*.

preposterous [prɪ'pɒstərəs] *adj* absurdo(da).

prep school *n* inf *abbr of* **preparatory school**.

prerequisite [,pri:'rekwɪzɪt] *n*: ~ (**for**) requisito *m* (para).

prerogative [prɪ'rɒgətɪv] *n* prerrogativa *f*.

Presbyterian [,prezbɪ'tɪərɪən] ◇ *adj* presbiteriano(na). ◇ *n* presbiteriano *m*, -na *f*.

preschool [,pri:'sku:l] ◇ *adj* preescolar. ◇ *n* Am parvulario *m*.

prescribe [prɪ'skraɪb] *vt* -**1.** MED recetar. -**2.** [order] ordenar, mandar.

prescription [prɪ'skrɪpʃn] *n* receta *f*; **on** ~ con receta médica.

presence ['prezns] *n* presencia *f*; **to be in sb's** ~ OR **in the** ~ **of sb** estar en presencia de alguien.

presence of mind *n* aplomo *m*.

present [*adj & n* 'preznt, *vb* prɪ'zent] ◇ *adj* -**1.** [current] actual. -**2.** [in attendance] presente; **to be** ~ **at sthg** asistir a algo, estar presente en algo. ◇ *n* -**1.** [current time]: **the** ~ el presente; **at** ~ actualmente. -**2.** LING: ~ (**tense**) (tiempo *m*) presente *m*. -**3.** [gift] regalo *m*. ◇ *vt* -**1.** [gen] presentar; **to** ~ **sb with sthg, to** ~ **sthg to sb** [challenge, opportunity] representar para alguien; **to** ~ **sb to sb** presentar a alguien a alguien; **to** ~ **o.s.** [arrive] presentarse. -**2.** [give]: **to** ~ **sb with sthg, to** ~ **sthg to sb** [as present] obsequiar algo a alguien; [at ceremony] entregar algo a alguien. -**3.** [play etc] representar.

presentable [prɪ'zentəbl] *adj* presentable; **to make o.s.** ~ arreglarse.

presentation [,prezn'teɪʃn] *n* -**1.** [gen] presentación *f*. -**2.** [ceremony] entrega *f*. -**3.** [performance] representación *f*.

present day *n*: **the** ~ el presente. ◆ **present-day** *adj* de hoy en día.

presenter [prɪ'zentəʳ] *n* Br presentador *m*, -ra *f*.

presently ['prezntlɪ] *adv* -**1.** [soon] dentro de poco. -**2.** [now] actualmente.

preservation [,prezə'veɪʃn] *n* preservación *f*, conservación *f*.

preservative [prɪ'zɜ:vətɪv] *n* conservante *m*.

preserve [prɪ'zɜ:v] ◇ *vt* conservar. ◇ *n* [jam] mermelada *f*. ◆ **preserves** *npl* [jam] mermelada *f*; [vegetables] conserva *f*.

preset [,pri:'set] (*pt & pp* **preset**) *vt* programar.

president ['prezɪdənt] *n* presidente *m*, -ta *f*.

presidential [,prezɪ'denʃl] *adj* presidencial.

press [pres] ◇ *n* -**1.** [push]: **to give sthg a** ~ apretar algo. -**2.** [newspapers, reporters]: **the ~** la prensa. **-3.** [machine] prensa *f.* ◇ *vt* **-1.** [gen] apretar; **to ~ sthg against sthg** apretar algo contra algo. **-2.** [grapes, flowers] prensar. **-3.** [iron] planchar. **-4.** [urge]: **to ~ sb (to do sthg** OR **into doing sthg)** presionar a alguien (para que haga algo). **-5.** [pursue - claim] insistir en. ◇ *vi* **-1.** [gen]: **to ~ (on sthg)** apretar (algo). **-2.** [crowd]: **to ~ forward** empujar hacia adelante. **◆ press for** *vt fus* exigir, reclamar. **◆ press on** *vi* [continue]: **to ~ on (with)** proseguir (con).

press agency *n* agencia *f* de prensa.

press conference *n* rueda *f* de prensa.

pressed [prest] *adj*: **to be ~ (for time/ money)** andar escaso(sa) (de tiempo/ de dinero).

pressing ['presɪŋ] *adj* apremiante.

press officer *n* jefe *m*, -fa *f* de prensa.

press release *n* comunicado *m* de prensa.

press-stud *n Br* automático *m*.

press-up *n Br* flexión *f*.

pressure ['preʃər] *n* presión *f*; **to put ~ on sb (to do sthg)** presionar a alguien (para que haga algo).

pressure cooker *n* olla *f* a presión.

pressure gauge *n* manómetro *m*.

pressure group *n* grupo *m* de presión.

pressurize, -ise ['preʃəraɪz] *vt* **-1.** TECH presurizar. **-2.** *Br* [force]: **to ~ sb to do** OR **into doing sthg** presionar a alguien para que haga algo.

prestige [pre'stiːʒ] *n* prestigio *m*.

presumably [prɪ'zjuːməblɪ] *adv*: **~ you've read it** supongo que los has leído.

presume [prɪ'zjuːm] *vt* suponer; **he is ~d dead** se supone que está muerto.

presumption [prɪ'zʌmpʃn] *n* **-1.** [assumption] suposición *f.* [of innocence] presunción *f.* **-2.** (U) [audacity] presunción *f*, osadía *f.*

presumptuous [prɪ'zʌmptʃuəs] *adj* presuntuoso(sa).

pretence, pretense *Am* [prɪ'tens] *n* fingimiento *m*, simulación *f*; **to make a ~ of doing sthg** fingir hacer algo; **under false ~s** con engaños, con falsos pretextos.

pretend [prɪ'tend] ◇ *vt*: **to ~ to do sthg** fingir hacer algo. ◇ *vi* fingir, simular.

pretense *Am* = **pretence**.

pretension [prɪ'tenʃn] *n* pretensión *f.*

pretentious [prɪ'tenʃəs] *adj* pretencioso(sa).

pretext ['priːtekst] *n* pretexto *m*; **on** OR **under the ~ that ...**/**of doing sthg** con el pretexto de que ...**/**de estar haciendo algo.

pretty ['prɪtɪ] ◇ *adj* bonito(ta). ◇ *adv* bastante; **~ much** más o menos; **~ well** [almost] casi.

prevail [prɪ'veɪl] *vi* **-1.** [be widespread] predominar, imperar. **-2.** [triumph]: **to ~ (over)** prevalecer (sobre). **-3.** [persuade]: **to ~ on** OR **upon sb to do sthg** persuadir a alguien para que haga algo.

prevailing [prɪ'veɪlɪŋ] *adj* predominante.

prevalent ['prevələnt] *adj* predominante.

prevent [prɪ'vent] *vt* impedir; [event, illness, accident] evitar; **to ~ sthg (from) happening** impedir OR evitar que algo pase; **to ~ sb (from) doing sthg** impedir a alguien que haga algo.

preventive [prɪ'ventɪv] *adj* preventivo(va).

preview ['priːvjuː] *n* [of film, exhibition] preestreno *m.*

previous ['priːvjəs] *adj* previo(via), anterior; **the ~ week/president** la semana/el presidente anterior.

previously ['priːvjəslɪ] *adv* **-1.** [formerly] anteriormente. **-2.** [before]: **two years ~** dos años antes.

prewar [ˌpriːˈwɔːr] *adj* de preguerra.

prey [preɪ] *n* presa *f*, víctima *f.* **◆ prey on** *vt fus* **-1.** [live off] cazar, alimentarse de. **-2.** [trouble]: **to ~ on sb's mind** atormentar a alguien.

price [praɪs] ◇ *n lit & fig* precio *m*; **to go up/down in ~** subir/bajar de precio; **at any ~** a toda costa, a cualquier precio; **at a ~** a un alto precio. ◇ *vt* poner precio a.

priceless ['praɪslɪs] *adj lit & fig* que no tiene precio, inestimable.

price list *n* lista *f* OR tarifa *f* de precios.

price tag *n* [label] etiqueta *f* (del precio).

pricey ['praɪsɪ] (*compar* **-ier**, *superl* **-est**) *adj* caro(ra).

prick [prɪk] ◇ *n* **-1.** [wound] pinchazo *m.* **-2.** *vulg* [penis] polla *f.* **-3.** *vulg* [stupid person] gilipollas *m y f inv.* ◇ *vt* **-1.** [gen] pinchar. **-2.** [sting] picar. **◆ prick up** *vt fus*: **to ~ up one's ears** [subj: animal] levantar las orejas; [subj: person] aguzar el oído.

prickle ['prɪkl] ◇ *n* **-1.** [thorn] espina *f.* **-2.** [sensation] comezón *f.* ◇ *vi* picar.

prickly ['prɪklɪ] *adj* **-1.** [thorny] espinoso(sa). **-2.** *fig* [touchy] susceptible, enojadizo(za).

prickly heat *n* (U) *sarpullido por causa del calor.*

pride [praɪd] ◇ *n* orgullo *m*; **to take ~ in sthg/in doing sthg** enorgullecerse de algo/de hacer algo. ◇ *vt*: **to ~ o.s. on sthg** enorgullecerse de algo.

priest [priːst] *n* sacerdote *m*.

priestess ['priːstɪs] *n* sacerdotisa *f*.

priesthood ['priːsthʊd] *n* **-1.** [position, office]: **the ~** el sacerdocio. **-2.** [priests collectively]: **the ~** el clero.

prig [prɪg] *n* mojigato *m*, -ta *f*.

prim [prɪm] *adj* remilgado(da).

primarily ['praɪmərɪlɪ] *adv* principalmente.

primary ['praɪmərɪ] ◇ *adj* **-1.** [main] principal. **-2.** SCH primario(ria). ◇ *n Am* POL primaria *f*.

primary school *n* escuela *f* primaria.

primate ['praɪmeɪt] *n* **-1.** ZOOL primate *m*. **-2.** RELIG primado *m*.

prime [praɪm] ◇ *adj* **-1.** [main] primero(ra), principal. **-2.** [excellent] excelente; [quality] primero(ra). ◇ *n*: **in one's ~** en la flor de la vida. ◇ *vt* **-1.** [inform]: **to ~ sb about sthg** preparar a alguien a fondo para algo. **-2.** [surface] preparar. **-3.** [gun, pump] cebar.

prime minister *n* primer ministro *m*, primera ministra *f*.

primer ['praɪmər] *n* **-1.** [paint] imprimación *f*. **-2.** [textbook] cartilla *f*.

primeval [praɪ'miːvl] *adj* [ancient] primitivo(va).

primitive ['prɪmɪtɪv] *adj* [tribe, species etc] primitivo(va); [accommodation, sense of humour] rudimentario(ria).

primrose ['prɪmrəʊz] *n* primavera *f*, prímula *f*.

Primus stove® ['praɪməs-] *n* hornillo *m* de camping.

prince [prɪns] *n* príncipe *m*.

princess [prɪn'ses] *n* princesa *f*.

principal ['prɪnsəpl] ◇ *adj* principal. ◇ *n* SCH director *m*, -ra *f*.

principle ['prɪnsəpl] *n* **-1.** [gen] principio *m*. **-2.** (U) [integrity] principios *mpl*; **on ~, as a matter of ~** por principio. ◆ **principle** *adv* en principio.

print [prɪnt] ◇ *n* **-1.** (U) [type] caracteres *mpl* (de imprenta); **in ~** [available] disponible; [in printed characters] en letra impresa; **to be out of ~** estar agotado. **-2.** [piece of artwork] grabado *m*. **-3.** [reproduction] reproducción *f*. **-4.** [photograph] fotografía *f*. **-5.** [fabric] estampado *m*. **-6.** [mark - of foot etc] huella *f*. ◇ *vt* TYPO imprimir. **-2.** [produce by printing - book, newspaper] tirar. **-3.** [publish] publicar. **-4.** [decorate - cloth etc] estampar. **-5.** [write in block letters] escribir con letra de imprenta. ◇ *vi* imprimir. ◆ **print out** *vt sep* COMPUT imprimir.

printer ['prɪntər] *n* **-1.** [person] impresor *m*, -ra *f*; [firm] imprenta *f*. **-2.** [machine] impresora *f*.

printing ['prɪntɪŋ] *n* **-1.** (U) [act of printing] impresión *f*. **-2.** [trade] imprenta *f*.

printout ['prɪntaʊt] *n* COMPUT salida *f* de impresora.

prior ['praɪər] ◇ *adj* **-1.** [previous] anterior, previo(via). **-2.** [more important] preferente. ◇ *n* [monk] prior *m*. ◆ **prior to** *prep* antes de.

priority [praɪ'ɒrətɪ] *n* prioridad *f*; **to have** OR **take ~ (over)** tener prioridad (sobre).

prise [praɪz] *vt*: **to ~ sthg open/away** abrir/separar algo haciendo palanca.

prison ['prɪzn] *n* cárcel *f*, prisión *f*.

prisoner ['prɪznər] *n* **-1.** [convict] preso *m*, -sa *f*. **-2.** [captive] prisionero *m*, -ra *f*.

prisoner of war (*pl* **prisoners of war**) *n* prisionero *m*, -ra *f* de guerra.

privacy [*Br* 'prɪvəsɪ, *Am* 'praɪvəsɪ] *n* intimidad *f*.

private ['praɪvɪt] ◇ *adj* **-1.** [gen] privado(da); [class] particular; [telephone call, belongings] personal. **-2.** [thoughts, plans] secreto(ta). **-3.** [secluded] retirado(da). **-4.** [unsociable - person] reservado(da). ◇ *n* **-1.** [soldier] soldado *m* raso. **-2.** (**to do sthg) in ~** [in secret] (hacer algo) en privado.

private enterprise *n* (U) empresa *f* privada.

private eye *n* detective privado *m*, -da *f*.

privately ['praɪvɪtlɪ] *adv* **-1.** [not by the state] de forma privada; **~ owned** de propiedad privada. **-2.** [confidentially] en privado.

private property *n* propiedad *f* privada.

private school *n* colegio *m* privado.

privatize, -ise ['praɪvɪtaɪz] *vt* privatizar.

privet ['prɪvɪt] *n* alheña *f*.

privilege ['prɪvɪlɪdʒ] *n* privilegio *m*.

privy ['prɪvɪ] *adj*: **to be ~ to sthg** estar enterado(da) de algo.

Privy Council *n Br*: **the ~** en Gran Bre-

taña, consejo privado que asesora al monarca.

prize [praɪz] ◇ *adj* de primera. ◇ *n* premio *m*. ◇ *vt*: **to be ~d** ser apreciado(da).

prize-giving [-ˌgɪvɪŋ] *n* Br entrega *f* de premios.

prizewinner ['praɪzˌwɪnəʳ] *n* premiado *m*, -da *f*.

pro [prəʊ] (*pl* **-s**) *n* **-1.** *inf* [professional] profesional *m* y *f*. **-2.** [advantage]: **the ~s and cons** los pros y los contras.

probability [ˌprɒbə'bɪlətɪ] *n* probabilidad *f*.

probable ['prɒbəbl] *adj* probable.

probably ['prɒbəblɪ] *adv* probablemente.

probation [prə'beɪʃn] *n* **-1.** [of prisoner] libertad *f* condicional; **to put sb on ~** poner a alguien en libertad condicional. **-2.** [trial period] periodo *m* de prueba; **to be on ~** estar en periodo de prueba.

probe [prəʊb] ◇ *n* **-1.** [investigation]: **~ (into)** investigación *f* (sobre). **-2.** MED & SPACE sonda *f*. ◇ *vt* **-1.** [investigate] investigar. **-2.** [with tool] sondar; [with finger, stick] hurgar en.

problem ['prɒbləm] *n* problema *m*; **no ~!** *inf* ¡por supuesto!, ¡desde luego!

procedure [prə'siːdʒəʳ] *n* procedimiento *m*.

proceed [*vb* prə'siːd, *npl* 'prəʊsiːdz] *vi* **-1.** [do subsequently]: **to ~ to do sthg** proceder a hacer algo. **-2.** [continue]: **to ~ (with sthg)** proseguir (con algo). **-3.** *fml* [advance] avanzar. ◆ **proceeds** *npl* ganancias *fpl*, beneficios *mpl*.

proceedings [prə'siːdɪŋz] *npl* **-1.** [series of events] acto *m*. **-2.** [legal action] proceso *m*.

process ['prəʊses] ◇ *n* proceso *m*; **in the ~** en el intento; **to be in the ~ of doing sthg** estar en vías de hacer algo. ◇ *vt* **-1.** [gen & COMPUT] procesar. **-2.** [application] tramitar.

processing ['prəʊsesɪŋ] *n* **-1.** [gen & COMPUT] procesamiento *m*. **-2.** [of applications etc] tramitación *f*.

procession [prə'seʃn] *n* desfile *m*; [religious] procesión *f*.

proclaim [prə'kleɪm] *vt* [gen] proclamar; [law] promulgar.

procrastinate [prə'kræstɪneɪt] *vi* andarse con dilaciones.

procure [prə'kjʊəʳ] *vt* [obtain] obtener.

prod [prɒd] *vt* [push, poke] dar golpecitos a.

prodigal ['prɒdɪgl] *adj* [son, daughter] pródigo(ga).

prodigy ['prɒdɪdʒɪ] *n* [person] prodigio *m*.

produce [*n* 'prɒdjuːs, *vb* prə'djuːs] ◇ *n* (U) productos *mpl* agrícolas. ◇ *vt* **-1.** [gen] producir; [offspring, flowers] engendrar. **-2.** [bring out] mostrar, enseñar. **-3.** THEATRE poner en escena.

producer [prə'djuːsəʳ] *n* **-1.** [gen] productor *m*, -ra *f*. **-2.** THEATRE director *m*, -ra *f* de escena.

product ['prɒdʌkt] *n* producto *m*.

production [prə'dʌkʃn] *n* **-1.** [gen] producción *f*. **-2.** (U) THEATRE puesta *f* en escena.

production line *n* cadena *f* de producción.

productive [prə'dʌktɪv] *adj* **-1.** [efficient] productivo(va). **-2.** [rewarding] provechoso(sa).

productivity [ˌprɒdʌk'tɪvətɪ] *n* productividad *f*.

profane [prə'feɪn] *adj* [disrespectful] obsceno(na).

profession [prə'feʃn] *n* profesión *f*; **by ~** de profesión.

professional [prə'feʃənl] ◇ *adj* profesional. ◇ *n* profesional *m* y *f*.

professor [prə'fesəʳ] *n* **-1.** Br [head of department] catedrático *m*, -ca *f*. **-2.** Am & Can [lecturer] profesor *m*, -ra *f* (de universidad).

proficiency [prə'fɪʃənsɪ] *n*: **~ (in)** competencia *f* (en).

profile ['prəʊfaɪl] *n* perfil *m*; **high ~** notoriedad *f*.

profit ['prɒfɪt] ◇ *n* **-1.** [financial gain] beneficio *m*, ganancia *f*; **to make a ~** sacar un beneficio. **-2.** [advantage] provecho *m*. ◇ *vi*: **to ~ (from** OR **by)** sacar provecho (de).

profitability [ˌprɒfɪtə'bɪlətɪ] *n* rentabilidad *f*.

profitable ['prɒfɪtəbl] *adj* **-1.** [making a profit] rentable. **-2.** [beneficial] provechoso(sa).

profiteering [ˌprɒfɪ'tɪərɪŋ] *n* especulación *f*.

profound [prə'faʊnd] *adj* profundo(da).

profusely [prə'fjuːslɪ] *adv* profusamente.

profusion [prə'fjuːʒn] *n* profusión *f*.

progeny ['prɒdʒənɪ] *n* progenie *f*.

prognosis [prɒg'nəʊsɪs] (*pl* **-noses** [-'nəʊsiːz]) *n* pronóstico *m*.

program ['prəʊgræm] (*pt* & *pp* **-med** OR **-ed**, *cont* **-ming** OR **-ing**) ◇ *n* **-1.** COMPUT

programa *m.* **-2.** *Am* = **programme.** ◇ *vt* **-1.** COMPUT programar. **-2.** *Am* = **programme.** ◇ *vi* COMPUT programar.

programer *Am* = **programmer.**

programme *Br*, **program** *Am* ['prəʊɡræm] ◇ *n* programa *m.* ◇ *vt:* to ~ **sthg (to do sthg)** programar algo (para que haga algo).

programmer *Br*, **programer** *Am* ['prəʊɡræmər] *n* COMPUT programador *m*, -ra *f.*

programming ['prəʊɡræmɪŋ] *n* programación *f.*

progress [*n* 'prəʊɡres, *vb* prə'ɡres] ◇ *n* **-1.** [gen] progreso *m*; **in** ~ en curso; **to make** ~ hacer progresos. **-2.** [forward movement] avance *m.* ◇ *vi* **-1.** [gen] progresar; [pupil etc] hacer progresos. **-2.** [move forward] avanzar.

progressive [prə'ɡresɪv] *adj* **-1.** [enlightened] progresista. **-2.** [gradual] progresivo(va).

prohibit [prə'hɪbɪt] *vt* prohibir; **to** ~ **sb from doing sthg** prohibirle a alguien hacer algo.

project [*n* 'prɒdʒekt, *vb* prə'dʒekt] ◇ *n* **-1.** [plan, idea] proyecto *m.* **-2.** SCH: ~ **(on)** estudio *m* OR trabajo *m* (sobre). ◇ *vt* **-1.** [gen] proyectar. **-2.** [estimate - statistic, costs] estimar. **-3.** [company, person] dar una imagen de; [image] proyectar. ◇ *vi* proyectarse.

projectile [prə'dʒektaɪl] *n* proyectil *m.*

projection [prə'dʒekʃn] *n* **-1.** [gen] proyección *f.* **-2.** [protrusion] saliente *m.*

projector [prə'dʒektər] *n* proyector *m.*

proletariat [ˌprəʊlɪ'teərɪət] *n* proletariado *m.*

prolific [prə'lɪfɪk] *adj* prolífico(ca).

prologue, **prolog** *Am* ['prəʊlɒɡ] *n* prólogo *m.*

prolong [prə'lɒŋ] *vt* prolongar.

prom [prɒm] *n* **-1.** *abbr of* **promenade concert.** **-2.** (*abbr of* **promenade**) *Br inf* [road by sea] paseo *m* marítimo. **-3.** *Am* [ball] baile *m* de gala (en la escuela).

promenade [ˌprɒmə'nɑːd] *n Br* [by sea] paseo *m* marítimo.

promenade concert *n Br* concierto sinfónico en donde parte del público está de pie.

prominent ['prɒmɪnənt] *adj* **-1.** [important] destacado(da), importante. **-2.** [noticeable] prominente.

promiscuous [prɒ'mɪskjʊəs] *adj* promiscuo(cua).

promise ['prɒmɪs] ◇ *n* promesa *f.* ◇ *vt:* to ~ **(to do sthg)** prometer (hacer

algo); **to** ~ **sb sthg** prometer a alguien algo. ◇ *vi:* **I** ~ te lo prometo.

promising ['prɒmɪsɪŋ] *adj* prometedor(ra).

promontory ['prɒməntrɪ] *n* promontorio *m.*

promote [prə'məʊt] *vt* **-1.** [foster] fomentar, promover. **-2.** [push, advertise] promocionar. **-3.** [in job]: **to** ~ **sb (to sthg)** ascender a alguien (a algo). **-4.** SPORT: **to be** ~**d** subir.

promoter [prə'məʊtər] *n* **-1.** [organizer] organizador *m*, -ra *f.* **-2.** [supporter] promotor *m*, -ra *f.*

promotion [prə'məʊʃn] *n* **-1.** [in job] ascenso *m.* **-2.** [advertising] promoción *f.* **-3.** [campaign] campaña *f* de promoción.

prompt [prɒmpt] ◇ *adj* rápido(da). ◇ *adv* en punto. ◇ *vt* **-1.** [motivate]: **to** ~ **sb (to do sthg)** inducir OR impulsar a alguien (a hacer algo). **-2.** THEATRE apuntar. ◇ *n* THEATRE [line] apunte *m.*

promptly ['prɒmptlɪ] *adv* **-1.** [reply, react, pay] inmediatamente, rápidamente. **-2.** [arrive, leave] puntualmente.

prone [prəʊn] *adj* **-1.** [susceptible]: **to be** ~ **to sthg/to do sthg** ser propenso(sa) a algo/a hacer algo. **-2.** [lying flat] boca abajo.

prong [prɒŋ] *n* diente *m*, punta *f.*

pronoun ['prəʊnaʊn] *n* pronombre *m.*

pronounce [prə'naʊns] ◇ *vt* **-1.** [gen] pronunciar. **-2.** [declare] declarar. ◇ *vi:* to ~ **on sthg** pronunciarse sobre algo.

pronounced [prə'naʊnst] *adj* pronunciado(da), marcado(da).

pronouncement [prə'naʊnsmənt] *n* declaración *f.*

pronunciation [prəˌnʌnsɪ'eɪʃn] *n* pronunciación *f.*

proof [pruːf] ◇ *n* **-1.** [gen & TYPO] prueba *f.* **-2.** [of alcohol]: **to be 10%** ~ tener 10 grados. ◇ *adj* [secure]: ~ **against** a prueba de.

prop [prɒp] ◇ *n* **-1.** [physical support] puntal *m*, apoyo *m.* **-2.** *fig* [supporting thing, person] sostén *m.* ◇ *vt:* to ~ **sthg on** OR **against sthg** apoyar algo contra algo. ♦ **props** *npl* accesorios *mpl.* ♦ **prop up** *vt sep* **-1.** [physically support] apuntalar. **-2.** *fig* [sustain] apoyar.

propaganda [ˌprɒpə'ɡændə] *n* propaganda *f.*

propel [prə'pel] *vt* propulsar, impulsar.

propeller [prə'pelər] *n* hélice *f.*

propelling pencil [prə'pelɪŋ-] *n Br* portaminas *m inv.*

propensity [prə'pensətɪ] *n fml*: ~ **(for** OR **to sthg)** propensión *f* (a algo).

proper ['prɒpər] *adj* **-1.** [real] de verdad. **-2.** [correct - gen] correcto(ta); [- time, place, equipment] adecuado(da).

properly ['prɒpəlɪ] *adv* **-1.** [satisfactorily, correctly] bien. **-2.** [decently] correctamente.

proper noun *n* nombre *m* propio.

property ['prɒpətɪ] *n* **-1.** [gen] propiedad *f*. **-2.** [estate] finca *f*. **-3.** *fml* [house] inmueble *m*.

property owner *n* propietario *m*, -ria *f* de un inmueble.

prophecy ['prɒfɪsɪ] *n* profecía *f*.

prophesy ['prɒfɪsaɪ] *vt* profetizar.

prophet ['prɒfɪt] *n* profeta *m y f*.

proportion [prə'pɔːʃn] *n* **-1.** [part] parte *f*. **-2.** [ratio, comparison] proporción *f*. **-3.** [correct relationship]: **out of** ~ desproporcionado(da); **sense of** ~ *fig* sentido *m* de la medida.

proportional [prə'pɔːʃənl] *adj*: ~ **(to)** proporcional (a).

proportional representation *n* representación *f* proporcional.

proportionate [prə'pɔːʃnət] *adj*: ~ **(to)** proporcional (a).

proposal [prə'pəuzl] *n* **-1.** [plan, suggestion] propuesta *f*. **-2.** [offer of marriage] proposición *f*.

propose [prə'pəuz] ◇ *vt* **-1.** [suggest] proponer; [motion] presentar. **-2.** [intend]: **to** ~ **doing** OR **to do sthg** tener la intención de hacer algo. ◇ *vi* [make offer of marriage] declararse; **to** ~ **to sb** pedir la mano de alguien.

proposition [ˌprɒpə'zɪʃn] *n* [suggestion] propuesta *f*.

proprietor [prə'praɪətər] *n* propietario *m*, -ria *f*.

propriety [prə'praɪətɪ] *n* (*U*) *fml* **-1.** [moral correctness] propiedad *f*. **-2.** [rightness] conveniencia *f*, oportunidad *f*.

pro rata [-'rɑːtə] *adj & adv* a prorrata.

prose [prəuz] *n* **-1.** (*U*) LITERATURE prosa *f*. **-2.** SCH traducción *f* inversa.

prosecute ['prɒsɪkjuːt] ◇ *vt* procesar, enjuiciar. ◇ *vi* **-1.** [bring a charge] entablar una acción judicial. **-2.** [represent in court] representar al demandante.

prosecution [ˌprɒsɪ'kjuːʃn] *n* **-1.** [gen] procesamiento *m*. **-2.** [lawyers]: **the** ~ la acusación.

prosecutor ['prɒsɪkjuːtər] *n* fiscal *m y f*.

prospect [*n* 'prɒspekt, *vb* prə'spekt] ◇ *n* **-1.** [gen] perspectiva *f*. **-2.** [possibility] posibilidad *f*. ◇ *vi*: **to** ~ **(for)** hacer

prospecciones (de). ◆ **prospects** *npl*: ~**s (for)** perspectivas *fpl* (de).

prospecting [prə'spektɪŋ] *n* (*U*) prospecciones *fpl*.

prospective [prə'spektɪv] *adj* posible.

prospector [prə'spektər] *n* prospector *m*, -ra *f*.

prospectus [prə'spektəs] (*pl* -es) *n* prospecto *m*, folleto *m* informativo.

prosper ['prɒspər] *vi* prosperar.

prosperity [prɒ'sperətɪ] *n* prosperidad *f*.

prosperous ['prɒspərəs] *adj* próspero(ra).

prostitute ['prɒstɪtjuːt] *n* prostituta *f*.

prostrate ['prɒstreɪt] *adj* postrado(da).

protagonist [prə'tægənɪst] *n* **-1.** *fml* [supporter] partidario *m*, -ria *f*. **-2.** [main character] protagonista *m y f*.

protect [prə'tekt] *vt*: **to** ~ **sthg/sb (against/from)** proteger algo/a alguien (contra/de).

protection [prə'tekʃn] *n*: ~ **(against/ from)** protección *f* (contra/de).

protective [prə'tektɪv] *adj* protector(ra).

protégé ['prɒteʒeɪ] *n* protegido *m*.

protein ['prəutiːn] *n* proteína *f*.

protest [*n* 'prəutest, *vb* prə'test] ◇ *n* protesta *f*. ◇ *vt* **-1.** [state] manifestar, aseverar. **-2.** *Am* [oppose] protestar en contra de. ◇ *vi*: **to** ~ **(about/against/at)** protestar (por/en contra de/por).

Protestant ['prɒtɪstənt] ◇ *adj* protestante. ◇ *n* protestante *m y f*.

protester [prə'testər] *n* manifestante *m y f*.

protest march *n* manifestación *f*.

protocol ['prəutəkɒl] *n* protocolo *m*.

prototype ['prəutətaɪp] *n* prototipo *m*.

protracted [prə'træktɪd] *adj* prolongado(da).

protrude [prə'truːd] *vi*: **to** ~ **(from)** sobresalir (de).

protuberance [prə'tjuːbərəns] *n* protuberancia *f*.

proud [praud] *adj* **-1.** [gen]: ~ **(of)** orgulloso(sa) (de). **-2.** *pej* [arrogant] soberbio(bia), arrogante.

prove [pruːv] (*pp* -d OR **proven**) *vt* **-1.** [show to be true] probar, demostrar. **-2.** [show oneself to be]: **to** ~ **(to be) sthg** demostrar ser algo; **to** ~ **o.s.** demostrar (uno) sus cualidades.

proven ['pruːvn, 'prəuvn] ◇ *pp* → **prove**. ◇ *adj* probado(da).

proverb ['prɒvɜːb] *n* refrán *m*.

provide [prə'vaɪd] *vt* proporcionar, proveer; **to** ~ **sb with sthg** proporcionar a alguien algo; **to** ~ **sthg for sb** ofrecer algo a alguien. ◆ **provide for** vt fus **-1.** [support] **mantener. -2.** fml [make arrangements for] **prevenir, tomar medidas para.**

provided [prə'vaɪdɪd] ◆ **provided (that)** conj con tal (de) que.

providing [prə'vaɪdɪŋ] ◆ **providing (that)** conj = **provided.**

province ['prɒvɪns] n **-1.** [part of country] **provincia** f. **-2.** [speciality] **campo** m, **competencia** f.

provincial [prə'vɪnʃl] adj **-1.** [of a province] **provincial. -2.** pej [narrowminded] **provinciano(na).**

provision [prə'vɪʒn] n **-1.** [gen] **suministro** m. **-2.** (U) [arrangement]: **to make ~ for** [eventuality, future] **tomar medidas para. -3.** [in agreement, law] **disposición** f. ◆ **provisions** npl [supplies] **víveres** mpl.

provisional [prə'vɪʒənl] adj **provisional.**

proviso [prə'vaɪzəu] (pl **-s**) n **condición** f; **with the ~ that ...** con la condición de que ....

provocative [prə'vɒkətɪv] adj **-1.** [controversial] **provocador(ra). -2.** [sexy] **provocativo(va).**

provoke [prə'vəuk] vt **provocar; to ~ sb to do sthg** **provocar a alguien a que haga algo.**

prow [prau] n **proa** f.

prowess ['prauɪs] n fml **proezas** fpl.

prowl [praul] ◇ n: **on the ~** **merodeando.** ◇ vt **merodear por.** ◇ vi **merodear.**

prowler ['praulər] n **merodeador** m, **-ra** f.

proxy ['prɒksɪ] n: **by ~** **por poderes.**

prudent ['pru:dnt] adj **prudente.**

prudish ['pru:dɪʃ] adj **mojigato(ta).**

prune [pru:n] ◇ n [fruit] **ciruela** f **pasa.** ◇ vt **podar.**

pry [praɪ] vi **fisgonear; to ~ into sthg** **entrometerse en algo.**

PS (abbr of **postscript**) n P.D.

psalm [sɑ:m] n **salmo** m.

pseudonym ['sju:dənɪm] n **seudónimo** m.

psyche ['saɪkɪ] n **psique** f.

psychiatric [,saɪkɪ'ætrɪk] adj **psiquiátrico(ca).**

psychiatrist [saɪ'kaɪətrɪst] n **psiquiatra** m y f.

psychiatry [saɪ'kaɪətrɪ] n **psiquiatría** f.

psychic ['saɪkɪk] adj **-1.** [clairvoyant] **clarividente. -2.** [mental] **psíquico(ca).**

psychoanalysis [,saɪkəuə'næləsɪs] n **psicoanálisis** m inv.

psychoanalyst [,saɪkəu'ænəlɪst] n **psicoanalista** m y f.

psychological [,saɪkə'lɒdʒɪkl] adj **psicológico(ca).**

psychologist [saɪ'kɒlədʒɪst] n **psicólogo** m, **-ga** f.

psychology [saɪ'kɒlədʒɪ] n **psicología** f.

psychopath ['saɪkəpæθ] n **psicópata** m y f.

psychotic [saɪ'kɒtɪk] ◇ adj **psicótico(ca).** ◇ n **psicótico** m, **-ca** f.

pt -1. abbr of **pint. -2.** abbr of **point.**

PTO (abbr of **please turn over**) sigue.

pub [pʌb] (abbr of **public house**) n **pub** m (británico).

puberty ['pju:bətɪ] n **pubertad** f.

pubic ['pju:bɪk] adj **púbico(ca).**

public ['pʌblɪk] ◇ adj **público(ca).** ◇ n **público** m; **in ~** **en público; the ~** **el gran público.**

public-address system n **sistema** m de **megafonía.**

publican ['pʌblɪkən] n Br **patrón** m, **-ona** f de un "pub".

publication [,pʌblɪ'keɪʃn] n **publicación** f.

public bar n Br en ciertos pubs y hoteles, bar de sencilla decoración con precios más bajos que los del "saloon bar".

public company n **sociedad** f **anónima** (con cotización en Bolsa).

public convenience n Br **aseos** mpl **públicos.**

public holiday n **fiesta** f **nacional.**

public house n Br fml **pub** m (británico).

publicity [pʌb'lɪsɪtɪ] n **publicidad** f.

publicize, -ise ['pʌblɪsaɪz] vt **divulgar.**

public limited company n **sociedad** f **anónima** (con cotización en Bolsa).

public opinion n (U) **opinión** f **pública.**

public prosecutor n **fiscal** m y f del Estado.

public relations ◇ n (U) **relaciones** fpl **públicas.** ◇ npl **relaciones** fpl **públicas.**

public school n **-1.** Br [private school] **colegio** m **privado. -2.** Am [state school] **escuela** f **pública.**

public-spirited adj **con sentido cívico.**

public transport n **transporte** m **público.**

publish ['pʌblɪʃ] vt **-1.** [gen] **publicar. -2.** [make known] **hacer público(ca).**

publisher ['pʌblɪʃər] n [person] **editor** m, **-ra** f; [firm] **editorial** f.

publishing ['pʌblɪʃɪŋ] n (U) industria f editorial.

pub lunch n almuerzo servido en un "pub".

pucker ['pʌkəʳ] vt fruncir.

pudding ['pudɪŋ] n -1. [sweet] pudín m; [savoury] pastel m. -2. (U) Br [course] postre m.

puddle ['pʌdl] n charco m.

Puerto Rico [,pwɜːtəʊ'riːkəʊ] n Puerto Rico.

puff [pʌf] ◇ n -1. [of cigarette, pipe] calada f. -2. [gasp] jadeo m. -3. [of air] soplo m; [of smoke] bocanada f. ◇ vt dar caladas a. ◇ vi -1. [smoke]: to ~ at OR on dar caladas a. -2. [pant] jadear. ◆ **puff out** vt sep [cheeks, chest] hinchar; [feathers] ahuecar.

puffed [pʌft] adj [swollen]: ~ (up) hinchado(da).

puffin ['pʌfɪn] n frailecillo m.

puff pastry, puff paste Am n hojaldre m.

puffy ['pʌfɪ] adj hinchado(da).

pugnacious [pʌg'neɪʃəs] adj fml pugnaz.

pull [pul] ◇ vt -1. [gen] tirar de; [trigger] apretar. -2. [tooth, cork] sacar, extraer. -3. [muscle] sufrir un tirón en. -4. [attract] atraer. -5. [gun] sacar y apuntar ◇ vi tirar. ◇ n -1. [tug with hand] tirón m. -2. (U) [influence] influencia f. ◆ **pull apart** vt sep [machine etc] desmontar. ◆ **pull at** vt fus dar tirones de. ◆ **pull away** vi [from roadside] alejarse (de la acera). ◆ **pull down** vt sep [building] derribar. ◆ **pull in** vi [train] pararse (en el andén). ◆ **pull off** vt sep [succeed in] conseguir llevar a cabo. ◆ **pull out** ◇ vt sep retirar. ◇ vi -1. [vehicle] alejarse (de la acera). -2. [withdraw] retirarse. ◆ **pull over** vi AUT hacerse a un lado. ◆ **pull through** vi recobrarse. ◆ **pull together** vt sep: to ~ o.s. together calmarse, serenarse. ◆ **pull up** ◇ vt sep [move closer] acercar. ◇ vi parar, detenerse.

pulley ['pulɪ] (pl pulleys) n polea f.

pullover ['pul,əʊvəʳ] n jersey m.

pulp [pʌlp] n -1. [soft mass] papilla f. -2. [of fruit] pulpa f. -3. [of wood] pasta f de papel.

pulpit ['pulpɪt] n púlpito m.

pulsate [pʌl'seɪt] vi palpitar.

pulse [pʌls] ◇ n -1. [in body] pulso m. -2. TECH impulso m. ◇ vi latir. ◆ **pulses** npl [food] legumbres fpl.

puma ['pjuːmə] (pl inv OR -s) n puma m.

pumice (stone) ['pʌmɪs-] n piedra f pómez.

pummel ['pʌml] vt aporrear.

pump [pʌmp] ◇ n -1. [machine] bomba f. -2. [for petrol] surtidor m. ◇ vt [convey by pumping] bombear. ◆ **pumps** npl [shoes] zapatillas fpl de tenis.

pumpkin ['pʌmpkɪn] n calabaza f.

pun [pʌn] n juego m de palabras.

punch [pʌntʃ] ◇ n -1. [blow] puñetazo m. -2. [tool - for leather etc] punzón m; [- for tickets] máquina f para picar billetes. -3. [drink] ponche m. ◇ vt -1. [hit] dar un puñetazo a. -2. [ticket] picar. -3. [hole] perforar.

Punch-and-Judy show [-'dʒuːdɪ-] n teatro de guiñol para niños con personajes arquetípicos y representado normalmente en la playa.

punch(ed) card [pʌntʃ(t)-] n tarjeta f perforada.

punch line n remate m (de un chiste).

punch-up n Br inf pelea f.

punchy ['pʌntʃɪ] adj inf efectista, resultón(ona).

punctual ['pʌŋktʃʊəl] adj puntual.

punctuation [,pʌŋktʃʊ'eɪʃn] n puntuación f.

punctuation mark n signo m de puntuación.

puncture ['pʌŋktʃəʳ] ◇ n pinchazo m; [in skin] punción f. ◇ vt pinchar.

pundit ['pʌndɪt] n experto m, -ta f.

pungent ['pʌndʒənt] adj [strong-smelling] penetrante, fuerte.

punish ['pʌnɪʃ] vt: to ~ sb (for sthg/for doing sthg) castigar a alguien (por algo/por haber hecho algo).

punishing ['pʌnɪʃɪŋ] adj penoso(sa).

punishment ['pʌnɪʃmənt] n [for crime] castigo m.

punk [pʌŋk] ◇ adj punk. ◇ n -1. [music]: ~ (rock) punk m. -2. [person]: ~ (rocker) punki m y f. -3. Am inf [lout] gamberro m.

punt [pʌnt] n batea f.

punter ['pʌntəʳ] n Br -1. [gambler] apostante m y f. -2. inf [customer] cliente m, -ta f, parroquiano m, -na f.

puny ['pjuːnɪ] adj [person, limbs] enclenque, raquítico(ca); [effort] penoso(sa), lamentable.

pup [pʌp] n -1. [young dog] cachorro m. -2. [young seal, otter] cría f.

pupil ['pjuːpl] n -1. [student] alumno m, -na f. -2. [follower] pupilo m, -la f. -3. [of eye] pupila f.

puppet ['pʌpɪt] n lit & fig títere m.

puppy ['pʌpɪ] n cachorro m, perrito m.
purchase ['pɜːtʃəs] fml ◇ n compra f, adquisición f. ◇ vt comprar, adquirir.
purchaser ['pɜːtʃəsəʳ] n comprador m, -ra f.
purchasing power ['pɜːtʃəsɪŋ-] n poder m adquisitivo.
pure [pjʊəʳ] adj puro(ra).
puree ['pjʊəreɪ] n puré m.
purely ['pjʊəlɪ] adv puramente.
purge [pɜːdʒ] ◇ n POL purga f. ◇ vt: to ~ sthg (of) purgar algo (de).
purify ['pjʊərɪfaɪ] vt purificar.
purist ['pjʊərɪst] n purista m y f.
puritan ['pjʊərɪtən] ◇ adj puritano(na). ◇ n puritano m, -na f.
purity ['pjʊərətɪ] n pureza f.
purl [pɜːl] n (U) punto m del revés.
purple ['pɜːpl] adj morado(da).
purport [pə'pɔːt] vi fml: to ~ to do/be sthg pretender hacer/ser algo.
purpose ['pɜːpəs] n [gen] propósito m; it serves no ~ carece de sentido; to no ~ en vano. ◆ **on purpose** adv a propósito, adrede.
purposeful ['pɜːpəsfʊl] adj resuelto(ta).
purr [pɜːʳ] vi -1. [cat, person] ronronear. -2. [engine, machine] zumbar.
purse [pɜːs] ◇ n -1. [for money] monedero m. -2. Am [handbag] bolso m. ◇ vt fruncir (con desagrado).
purser ['pɜːsəʳ] n contador m, -ra f.
pursue [pə'sjuː] vt -1. [follow] perseguir. -2. fml [policy] llevar a cabo; [aim, pleasure etc] ir en pos de, buscar; [topic, question] profundizar en; [hobby, studies] dedicarse a.
pursuer [pə'sjuːəʳ] n perseguidor m, -ra f.
pursuit [pə'sjuːt] n -1. (U) fml [attempt to achieve] búsqueda f. -2. [chase, in cycling] persecución f. -3. [occupation, activity] ocupación f; leisure ~ pasatiempo m.
pus [pʌs] n pus m.
push [pʊʃ] ◇ vt -1. [shove] empujar; to ~ sthg into sthg meter algo en algo; to ~ sthg open/shut abrir/cerrar algo empujándolo. -2. [press - button] apretar, pulsar. -3. [encourage]: to ~ sb (to do sthg) empujar a alguien (a hacer algo). -4. [force]: to ~ sb (into doing sthg) obligar a alguien (a hacer algo). -5. inf [promote] promocionar. ◇ vi [press forward] empujar; [on button] apretar, pulsar. ◇ n lit & fig empujón m. ◆ **push around** vt sep inf mandonear. ◆ **push for** vt fus [demand] reclamar. ◆ **push in**

vi [in queue] colarse. ◆ **push off** vi inf largarse. ◆ **push on** vi seguir adelante sin parar. ◆ **push through** vt sep [law etc] conseguir que se apruebe.
pushchair ['pʊʃtʃeəʳ] n Br silla f (de paseo).
pushed [pʊʃt] adj inf: to be ~ for sthg andar corto(ta) de algo; to be hard ~ to do sthg tenerlo difícil para hacer algo.
pusher ['pʊʃəʳ] n inf camello m.
pushover ['pʊʃ,əʊvəʳ] n inf: it's a ~ está chupado.
push-up n flexión f.
pushy ['pʊʃɪ] adj pej agresivo(va), insistente.
puss [pʊs], **pussy (cat)** ['pʊsɪ-] n inf gatito m, minino m.
put [pʊt] (pt & pp put) vt -1. [gen] poner; to ~ sthg into sthg meter algo en algo. -2. [place exactly] colocar. -3. [send - to prison etc] meter; to ~ **the children to bed** acostar a los niños. -4. [express] expresar, formular. -5. [ask - question] hacer. -6. [estimate]: to ~ sthg at calcular algo en. -7. [invest]: to ~ sthg into sthg poner algo en algo, dedicar algo a algo. -8. [apply]: to ~ **pressure on** presionar a. ◆ **put across** vt sep transmitir. ◆ **put away** vt sep [tidy away] poner en su sitio, guardar. ◆ **put back** vt sep -1. [replace] volver a poner en su sitio. -2. [postpone] aplazar. -3. [clock, watch] atrasar. ◆ **put by** vt sep ahorrar. ◆ **put down** vt sep -1. [lay down] dejar (encima de algún sitio). -2. [quell] sofocar, reprimir. -3. Br [animal] matar (a un animal que es viejo o está enfermo). -4. [write down] apuntar. ◆ **put down to** vt sep achacar a. ◆ **put forward** vt sep -1. [plan, theory, name] proponer; [proposal] someter. -2. [clock, meeting, event] adelantar. ◆ **put in** vt sep -1. [spend - time] dedicar. -2. [submit] presentar. ◆ **put off** vt sep -1. [postpone] posponer, aplazar. -2. [cause to wait] hacer esperar. -3. [discourage] disuadir. -4. [cause to dislike]: to ~ sb off sthg hacerle pasar a alguien las ganas de algo. ◆ **put on** vt sep -1. [wear] ponerse. -2. [show, play] representar; [exhibition] hacer. -3. [gain]: to ~ **on weight** engordar. -4. [radio, light] encender; to ~ **on the brakes** poner el freno, frenar. -5. [record, tape] poner. -6. [start cooking] empezar a hacer OR cocinar. -7. [bet] apostar por. -8. [add] añadir. -9. [feign - air, accent] fingir. ◆ **put out** vt sep -1.

[place outside] **sacar. -2.** [issue - statement] **hacer público. -3.** [extinguish] **apagar. -4.** [switch off] **quitar, apagar. -5.** [prepare for use - clothes] **sacar. -6.** [extend - hand, leg] **extender;** [- tongue] **sacar. -7.** [upset]: **to be ~ out** estar enfadado(da). **-8.** [inconvenience] **causar molestias a. ◆ put through** *vt sep* TELEC [call] **poner; to ~ sb through to sb** poner a alguien con alguien. **◆ put up** ◇ *vt sep* **-1.** [build] **construir. -2.** [umbrella] **abrir;** [flag] **izar. -3.** [poster] **fijar;** [painting] **colgar. -4.** [provide - money] **poner. -5.** [propose - candidate] **proponer. -6.** [increase] **subir, aumentar. -7.** [provide accommodation for] **alojar, hospedar.** ◇ *vt fus* [resistance] **ofrecer; to ~ up a fight** resistir. **◆ put up with** *vt fus* **aguantar.**

putrid ['pjuːtrɪd] *adj fml* **putrefacto(ta).**

putt [pʌt] *n* **putt** *m*, **tiro** *m* **al hoyo.**

putting green ['pʌtɪŋ-] *n* **minigolf** *m* (*sin obstáculos*).

putty ['pʌtɪ] *n* **masilla** *f*.

puzzle ['pʌzl] ◇ *n* **-1.** [toy, game] **rompecabezas** *m inv*. **-2.** [mystery] **misterio** *m*, **enigma** *m*. ◇ *vt* **dejar perplejo, desconcertar.** ◇ *vi*: **to ~ over sthg** romperse la cabeza con algo. **◆ puzzle out** *vt sep* **descifrar.**

puzzling ['pʌzlɪŋ] *adj* **desconcertante.**

pyjamas [pə'dʒɑːməz] *npl* **pijama** *m*.

pylon ['paɪlən] *n* **torre** *f* (*de conducción eléctrica*).

pyramid ['pɪrəmɪd] *n* **-1.** [structure] **pirámide** *f*. **-2.** [pile] **montón** *m*, **pila** *f*.

Pyrenees [,pɪrə'niːz] *npl*: **the ~** **los Pirineos.**

Pyrex® ['paɪreks] *n* **pírex®** *m*.

python ['paɪθn] (*pl inv* OR **-s**) *n* **pitón** *m*.

Q

q (*pl* **q's** OR **qs**), **Q** (*pl* **Q's** OR **Qs**) [kjuː] *n* [letter] **q** *f*, **Q** *f*.

quack [kwæk] *n* **-1.** [noise] **graznido** *m* (*de pato*). **-2.** *inf* [doctor] **matasanos** *m inv*.

quad [kwɒd] *n abbr of* **quadrangle.**

quadrangle ['kwɒdræŋgl] *n* **-1.** [figure] **cuadrángulo** *m*. **-2.** [courtyard] **patio** *m*.

quadruple [kwɒ'druːpl] ◇ *vt* **cuadruplicar.** ◇ *vi* **cuadruplicarse.**

quadruplets ['kwɒdruplɪts] *npl* **cuatrillizos** *mpl*, **-zas** *fpl*.

quads [kwɒdz] *npl inf* **cuatrillizos** *mpl*, **-zas** *fpl*.

quagmire ['kwægmaɪəʳ] *n* **lodazal** *m*.

quail [kweɪl] (*pl inv* OR **-s**) ◇ *n* **codorniz** *f*. ◇ *vi literary* **amedrentarse.**

quaint [kweɪnt] *adj* **pintoresco(ca).**

quake [kweɪk] ◇ *n inf* **terremoto** *m*. ◇ *vi* **temblar, estremecerse.**

Quaker ['kweɪkəʳ] *n* **cuáquero** *m*, **-ra** *f*.

qualification [,kwɒlɪfɪ'keɪʃn] *n* **-1.** [examination, certificate] **título** *m*. **-2.** [ability, skill] **aptitud** *f*. **-3.** [qualifying statement] **modificación** *f*.

qualified ['kwɒlɪfaɪd] *adj* **-1.** [trained] **cualificado(da). -2.** [limited] **limitado(da).**

qualify ['kwɒlɪfaɪ] ◇ *vt* **-1.** [modify] **modificar. -2.** [entitle]: **to ~ sb to do sthg** **capacitar a alguien para hacer algo.** ◇ *vi* **-1.** [pass exams] **sacar el título. -2.** [be entitled]: **to ~ (for)** **tener derecho (a). -3.** SPORT **clasificarse.**

quality ['kwɒlətɪ] ◇ *n* **-1.** [standard] **calidad** *f*. **-2.** [characteristic] **cualidad** *f*. ◇ *comp* **de calidad.**

qualms [kwɑːmz] *npl* **escrúpulos** *mpl*.

quandary ['kwɒndərɪ] *n*: **to be in a ~ about** OR **over sthg** **estar en un dilema sobre algo.**

quantify ['kwɒntɪfaɪ] *vt* **cuantificar.**

quantity ['kwɒntətɪ] *n* **cantidad** *f*.

quantity surveyor *n* **aparejador** *m*, **-ra** *f*.

quarantine ['kwɒrəntiːn] *n* **cuarentena** *f*.

quark [kwɑːk] *n* CULIN *tipo de queso blando bajo en grasas.*

quarrel ['kwɒrəl] ◇ *n* **pelea** *f*, **disputa** *f*. ◇ *vi* **pelearse, reñir; to ~ with sb** **pelearse con alguien; to ~ with sthg** **no estar de acuerdo con algo.**

quarrelsome ['kwɒrəlsəm] *adj* **pendenciero(ra).**

quarry ['kwɒrɪ] *n* **-1.** [place] **cantera** *f*. **-2.** [prey] **presa** *f*.

quart [kwɔːt] *n* **cuarto** *m* **de galón.**

quarter ['kwɔːtəʳ] *n* **-1.** [fraction] **cuarto** *m*. **-2.** [in telling time]: **~ past two** *Br*, **~ after two** *Am* **las dos y cuarto; ~ to two** *Br*, **~ of two** *Am* **las dos menos cuarto. -3.** [of year] **trimestre** *m*. **-4.** *Am* [coin] **moneda** *f* **de 25 centavos. -5.** [four ounces] **cuatro onzas** *fpl*. **-6.** [area in town] **barrio** *m*. **-7.** [group of people]

lugar *m*, **parte** *f*. ◆ **quarters** *npl* [rooms] residencia *f*, alojamiento *m*. ◆ **at close quarters** *adv* muy de cerca.

quarterfinal [ˌkwɔːtəˈfaɪnl] *n* cuarto *m* de final.

quarterly [ˈkwɔːtəlɪ] ◇ *adj* trimestral. ◇ *adv* trimestralmente. ◇ *n* trimestral *f*.

quartermaster [ˈkwɔːtəˌmɑːstər] *n* oficial *m* de intendencia.

quartet [kwɔːˈtet] *n* cuarteto *m*.

quartz [kwɔːts] *n* cuarzo *m*.

quartz watch *n* reloj *m* de cuarzo.

quash [kwɒʃ] *vt* **-1.** [reject] anular, invalidar. **-2.** [quell] reprimir, sofocar.

quasi- [ˈkweɪzaɪ] *prefix* cuasi-.

quaver [ˈkweɪvər] ◇ *n* MUS corchea *f*. ◇ *vi* temblar.

quay [kiː] *n* muelle *m*.

quayside [ˈkiːsaɪd] *n* muelle *m*.

queasy [ˈkwiːzɪ] *adj* mareado(da).

queen [kwiːn] *n* **-1.** [gen] reina *f*. **-2.** [playing card] dama *f*.

Queen Mother *n*: **the ~** la reina madre.

queer [kwɪər] ◇ *adj* [odd] raro(ra), extraño(ña). ◇ *n* *inf pej* marica *m*.

quell [kwel] *vt* **-1.** [rebellion] sofocar, reprimir. **-2.** [feelings] dominar, contener.

quench [kwentʃ] *vt* apagar.

querulous [ˈkwerʊləs] *adj* *fml* quejumbroso(sa).

query [ˈkwɪərɪ] ◇ *n* pregunta *f*, duda *f*. ◇ *vt* poner en duda.

quest [kwest] *n* *literary*: ~ **(for)** búsqueda *f* (de).

question [ˈkwestʃn] ◇ *n* **-1.** [query, problem in exam] pregunta *f*; **to ask (sb) a ~** hacer una pregunta (a alguien). **-2.** [doubt] duda *f*; **to call sthg into ~** poner algo en duda; **without ~** sin duda; **beyond ~** fuera de toda duda. **-3.** [issue, matter] cuestión *f*, asunto *m*. **-4.** *phr*: **there's no ~ of ...** es imposible que .... ◇ *vt* **-1.** [interrogate] interrogar. **-2.** [express doubt about] cuestionar. ◆ **in question** *adv*: **the matter in ~** el asunto en cuestión. ◆ **out of the question** *adv* imposible.

questionable [ˈkwestʃənəbl] *adj* [gen] cuestionable; [taste] dudoso(sa).

question mark *n* (signo *m* de) interrogación *f*.

questionnaire [ˌkwestʃəˈneər] *n* cuestionario *m*.

queue [kjuː] *Br* ◇ *n* cola *f*. ◇ *vi*: **to ~ (up for sthg)** hacer cola (para algo).

quibble [ˈkwɪbl] *pej* *vi* quejarse por tonterías.

quiche [kiːʃ] *n* quiche *f*.

quick [kwɪk] ◇ *adj* **-1.** [gen] rápido(da); **be ~!** ¡date prisa! **-2.** [clever - person] espabilado(da); [- wit] agudo(da). **-3.** [irritable]: **a ~ temper** un genio vivo. ◇ *adv* rápidamente.

quicken [ˈkwɪkn] ◇ *vt* apretar, acelerar. ◇ *vi* acelerarse, apresurarse.

quickly [ˈkwɪklɪ] *adv* **-1.** [rapidly] rápidamente, de prisa. **-2.** [without delay] rápidamente, en seguida.

quicksand [ˈkwɪksænd] *n* arenas *fpl* movedizas.

quick-witted [-ˈwɪtɪd] *adj* agudo(da).

quid [kwɪd] (*pl inv*) *n* *Br* *inf* libra *f* (esterlina).

quiet [ˈkwaɪət] ◇ *adj* **-1.** [silent - gen] silencioso(sa); [- room, place] tranquilo(la); **be ~!** ¡cállate!; **in a ~ voice** en voz baja; **to keep ~ about sthg** guardar silencio sobre algo. **-2.** [not talkative] callado(da). **-3.** [tranquil, uneventful] tranquilo(la). **-4.** [unpublicized - wedding etc] privado(da), íntimo(ma). ◇ *n* tranquilidad *f*, silencio *m*; **on the ~** a escondidas. ◇ *vt* *Am* tranquilizar. ◆ **quiet down** ◇ *vt* *sep* tranquilizar. ◇ *vi* tranquilizarse.

quieten [ˈkwaɪətn] *vt* tranquilizar. ◆ **quieten down** ◇ *vt* *sep* tranquilizar. ◇ *vi* tranquilizarse.

quietly [ˈkwaɪətlɪ] *adv* **-1.** [without noise] silenciosamente, sin hacer ruido; **to speak ~** hablar en voz baja. **-2.** [without moving] sin moverse. **-3.** [without excitement] tranquilamente. **-4.** [without fuss] discretamente.

quilt [kwɪlt] *n* edredón *m*.

quinine [kwɪˈniːn] *n* quinina *f*.

quins *Br* [kwɪnz], **quints** *Am* [kwɪnts] *npl* *inf* quintillizos *mpl*, -zas *fpl*.

quintet [kwɪnˈtet] *n* quinteto *m*.

quints *Am* = **quins**.

quintuplets [kwɪnˈtjuːplɪts] *npl* quintillizos *mpl*, -zas *fpl*.

quip [kwɪp] *n* ocurrencia *f*, salida *f*.

quirk [kwɜːk] *n* **-1.** [habit] manía *f*, rareza *f*. **-2.** [strange event] extraña coincidencia *f*.

quit [kwɪt] (*Br pt & pp* quit OR -ted, *Am pt & pp* quit) ◇ *vt* **-1.** [resign from] dejar, abandonar. **-2.** [stop]: **to ~ doing sthg** dejar de hacer algo. ◇ *vi* [resign] dimitir.

quite [kwaɪt] *adv* **-1.** [completely] totalmente, completamente. **-2.** [fairly] bastante; ~ **a lot of people** bastante gente. **-3.** [after negative]: **it's not ~ big enough** no es todo lo grande que tendría que ser; **I don't ~ understand/ know** no entiendo/sé muy bien. **-4.** [to emphasize]: **~ a ...** todo un (toda una) .... **-5.** [to express agreement]: **~ (so)!** ¡efectivamente!, ¡desde luego!

quits [kwɪts] *adj inf*: **to be ~ (with sb)** estar en paz (con alguien); **to call it ~** quedar en paz.

quiver ['kwɪvə^r] ◇ *n* [for arrows] carcaj *m*. ◇ *vi* temblar, estremecerse.

quiz [kwɪz] (*pl* **-zes**) ◇ *n* **-1.** [gen] concurso *m*. **-2.** *Am* SCH control *m*. ◇ *vt*: **to ~ sb (about)** interrogar a alguien (sobre).

quizzical ['kwɪzɪkl] *adj* [smile] burlón(ona); [look, glance] interrogativo(va).

quota ['kwəʊtə] *n* cuota *f*.

quotation [kwəʊ'teɪʃn] *n* **-1.** [citation] cita *f*. **-2.** COMM presupuesto *m*.

quotation marks *npl* comillas *fpl*.

quote [kwəʊt] ◇ *n* **-1.** [citation] cita *f*. **-2.** COMM presupuesto *m*. ◇ *vt* **-1.** [cite] citar. **-2.** [figures, example, price] dar; **he ~d £100** fijó un precio de 100 libras. ◇ *vi* **-1.** [cite]: **to ~ (from)** citar (de). **-2.** COMM: **to ~ for** dar un presupuesto por.

quotient ['kwəʊʃnt] *n* cociente *m*.

R

r (*pl* **r's** OR **rs**), **R** (*pl* **R's** OR **Rs**) [ɑː^r] *n* [letter] r *f*, R *f*.

rabbi ['ræbaɪ] *n* rabino *m*.

rabbit ['ræbɪt] *n* conejo *m*.

rabbit hutch *n* conejera *f*.

rabble ['ræbl] *n* chusma *f*, populacho *m*.

rabies ['reɪbiːz] *n* rabia *f*.

RAC (*abbr of* **Royal Automobile Club**) *n* asociación británica del automóvil, ≃ RACE *m*.

race [reɪs] ◇ *n* **-1.** *lit* & *fig* [competition] carrera *f*. **-2.** [people, descent] raza *f*. ◇ *vt* **-1.** [compete against] competir con (*corriendo*); **they ~d each other to the door** echaron una carrera hasta la puerta. **-2.** [cars, pigeons] hacer carreras de; [horses] hacer correr. ◇ *vi* **-1.** [rush] ir corriendo. **-2.** [beat fast] acelerarse.

race car *Am* = **racing car**.

racecourse ['reɪskɔːs] *n* hipódromo *m*.

race driver *Am* = **racing driver**.

racehorse ['reɪshɔːs] *n* caballo *m* de carreras.

racetrack ['reɪstræk] *n* [for horses] hipódromo *m*; [for cars] autódromo *m*; [for runners] pista *f* (de carreras).

racial discrimination ['reɪʃl-] *n* discriminación *f* racial.

racing ['reɪsɪŋ] *n* carreras *fpl*; **motor ~** carreras de coches.

racing car *Br*, **race car** *Am n* coche *m* de carreras.

racing driver *Br*, **race driver** *Am n* piloto *m* y *f* de carreras.

racism ['reɪsɪzm] *n* racismo *m*.

racist ['reɪsɪst] ◇ *adj* racista. ◇ *n* racista *m* y *f*.

rack [ræk] ◇ *n* **-1.** [for plates] escurreplatos *m inv*; [for clothes] percha *f*; [for magazines] revistero *m*; [for bottles] botellero *m*. **-2.** [for luggage] portaequipajes *m inv*. ◇ *vt*: **to ~ one's brains** *Br* devanarse los sesos.

racket ['rækɪt] *n* **-1.** [noise] jaleo *m*, alboroto *m*. **-2.** [swindle] timo *m*. **-3.** [illegal activity] negocio *m* sucio. **-4.** SPORT raqueta *f*.

racquet ['rækɪt] *n* SPORT = **racket**.

racy ['reɪsɪ] *adj* entretenido(da) y picante.

radar ['reɪdɑː^r] *n* radar *m*.

radial (tyre) ['reɪdjəl-] *n* neumático *m* radial.

radiant ['reɪdjənt] *adj* **-1.** [happy] radiante. **-2.** *literary* [brilliant] resplandeciente.

radiate ['reɪdɪeɪt] ◇ *vt lit* & *fig* irradiar. ◇ *vi* **-1.** [be emitted] ser irradiado(da). **-2.** [spread from centre] salir, extenderse.

radiation [,reɪdɪ'eɪʃn] *n* radiación *f*.

radiator ['reɪdɪeɪtə^r] *n* radiador *m*.

radical ['rædɪkl] ◇ *adj* radical. ◇ *n* POL radical *m* y *f*.

radically ['rædɪklɪ] *adv* radicalmente.

radii ['reɪdɪaɪ] *pl* → **radius**.

radio ['reɪdɪəʊ] (*pl* **-s**) ◇ *n* radio *f*. ◇ *comp* de radio, radiofónico(ca).

radioactive [,reɪdɪəʊ'æktɪv] *adj* radiactivo(va).

radio alarm *n* radiodespertador *m*.

radio-controlled [-kən'trəʊld] *adj* teledirigido(da).

radiography [,reɪdɪ'ɒgrəfɪ] *n* radiografía *f*.

radiology [ˌreɪdɪˈɒlədʒɪ] n radiología f.
radiotherapy [ˌreɪdɪəʊˈθerəpɪ] n radioterapia f.
radish [ˈrædɪʃ] n rábano m.
radius [ˈreɪdɪəs] (pl **radii**) n [gen & ANAT] radio m.
RAF [ɑːreɪˈef, ræf] n abbr of **Royal Air Force**.
raffle [ˈræfl] ◇ n rifa f, sorteo m. ◇ comp: ~ **ticket** boleto m. ◇ vt rifar.
raft [rɑːft] n [craft] balsa f.
rafter [ˈrɑːftər] n par m (de armadura de tejido).
rag [ræg] n **-1.** [piece of cloth] trapo m, harapo m. **-2.** pej [newspaper] periodicucho m. ◆ **rags** npl [clothes] trapos mpl.
rag-and-bone man n trapero m.
rag doll n muñeca f de trapo.
rage [reɪdʒ] ◇ n **-1.** [fury] rabia f, ira f. **-2.** inf [fashion]: **it's all the** ~ es la última moda. ◇ vi **-1.** [behave angrily] estar furioso(sa). **-2.** [subj: storm, sea] enfurecerse; [subj: disease] hacer estragos; [subj: argument, controversy] continuar con violencia.
ragged [ˈrægɪd] adj **-1.** [wearing torn clothes] andrajoso(sa), harapiento(ta). **-2.** [torn] hecho(cha) jirones.
rag week n Br semana en que los universitarios organizan actividades divertidas con fines benéficos.
raid [reɪd] ◇ n **-1.** [attack] incursión f. **-2.** [forced entry - by robbers] asalto m; [- by police] redada f. ◇ vt **-1.** [attack] atacar por sorpresa. **-2.** [subj: robbers] asaltar; [subj: police] hacer una redada en.
raider [ˈreɪdər] n **-1.** [attacker] invasor m, -ra f. **-2.** [thief] ladrón m, -ona f.
rail [reɪl] n **-1.** [on staircase] barandilla f. **-2.** [bar] barra f; **towel** ~ toallero m. **-3.** [of railway line] carril m, riel m. **-4.** (U) [form of transport] ferrocarril m; **by** ~ por ferrocarril.
railcard [ˈreɪlkɑːd] n Br tarjeta que permite algunos descuentos al viajar en tren.
railing [ˈreɪlɪŋ] n reja f.
railway Br [ˈreɪlweɪ], **railroad** Am [ˈreɪlrəʊd] n **-1.** [company] ferrocarril m. **-2.** [route] línea f de ferrocarril.
railway line n línea f de ferrocarril.
railwayman [ˈreɪlweɪmən] (pl **-men** [-mən]) n Br ferroviario m.
railway station n estación f de ferrocarril.
railway track n vía f férrea.

rain [reɪn] ◇ n lluvia f. ◇ v impers METEOR llover. ◇ vi caer.
rainbow [ˈreɪnbəʊ] n arco m iris.
rain check n Am: **I'll take a** ~ **(on that)** no lo quiero ahora, pero igual me apunto la próxima vez.
raincoat [ˈreɪnkəʊt] n impermeable m.
raindrop [ˈreɪndrɒp] n gota f de lluvia.
rainfall [ˈreɪnfɔːl] n pluviosidad f.
rain forest n bosque m tropical.
rainy [ˈreɪnɪ] adj lluvioso(sa).
raise [reɪz] ◇ vt **-1.** [lift up] levantar; **to** ~ **o.s.** levantarse. **-2.** [increase - level] aumentar; **to** ~ **one's voice** levantar la voz. **-3.** [improve] elevar. **-4.** [obtain - from donations] recaudar; [- by selling, borrowing] conseguir. **-5.** [memory, thoughts] traer; [doubts] levantar. **-6.** [bring up, breed] criar. **-7.** [crops] cultivar. **-8.** [mention] plantear. **-9.** [build] construir. ◇ n Am aumento m.
raisin [ˈreɪzn] n pasa f.
rake [reɪk] ◇ n **-1.** [implement] rastrillo m. **-2.** dated & literary [immoral man] libertino m. ◇ vt [smooth] rastrillar.
rally [ˈrælɪ] ◇ n **-1.** [meeting] mitin m, reunión f. **-2.** [car race] rally m. **-3.** [in tennis etc] peloteo m. ◇ vt reunir. ◇ vi **-1.** [come together] reunirse. **-2.** [recover] recuperarse. ◆ **rally round** ◇ vt fus formar una piña con. ◇ vi inf formar una piña.
ram [ræm] ◇ n carnero m. ◇ vt **-1.** [crash into] chocar con OR contra. **-2.** [force] embutir.
RAM [ræm] (abbr of **random access memory**) n COMPUT RAM f.
ramble [ˈræmbl] ◇ n paseo m por el campo. ◇ vi **-1.** [walk] pasear. **-2.** [talk] divagar. ◆ **ramble on** vi divagar sin parar.
rambler [ˈræmblər] n [walker] excursionista m y f.
rambling [ˈræmblɪŋ] adj **-1.** [building, house] laberíntico(ca); [town] desparramado(da). **-2.** [speech, writing] confuso(sa), incoherente.
ramp [ræmp] n **-1.** [slope] rampa f. **-2.** AUT [in road] rompecoches m inv.
rampage [ræmˈpeɪdʒ] n: **to go on the** ~ desbandarse.
rampant [ˈræmpənt] adj desenfrenado(da).
ramparts [ˈræmpɑːts] npl murallas fpl.
ramshackle [ˈræmˌʃækl] adj destartalado(da).
ran [ræn] pt → **run**.
ranch [rɑːntʃ] n rancho m.

rancher ['rɑːntʃəʳ] n ranchero m, -ra f.

rancid ['rænsɪd] adj rancio(cia).

rancour Br, **rancor** Am ['ræŋkəʳ] n rencor m.

random ['rændəm] ◇ adj fortuito(ta), hecho(cha) al azar. ◇ n: **at** ~ al azar.

random access memory n COMPUT memoria f de acceso aleatorio.

R and R (abbr of **rest and recreation**) n Am permiso militar.

randy ['rændɪ] adj inf cachondo(da), caliente.

rang [ræŋ] pt → **ring**.

range [reɪndʒ] ◇ n -1. [of missile, telescope] alcance m; [of ship, plane] autonomía f; **at close** ~ de cerca. -2. [variety] variedad f, gama f. -3. [of prices, salaries] escala f. -4. [of mountains] sierra f, cordillera f. -5. [shooting area] campo m de tiro. -6. [of voice] registro m. ◇ vt alinear. ◇ vi -1. [vary]: **to** ~ **from ... to ...**, **to** ~ **between ... and ...** oscilar OR fluctuar entre ... y .... -2. [deal with, include]: **to** ~ **over sthg** comprender algo.

ranger ['reɪndʒəʳ] n guardabosques m y f inv.

rank [ræŋk] ◇ adj -1. [utter, absolute - bad luck, outsider] absoluto(ta); [- disgrace, injustice] flagrante. -2. [foul] pestilente. ◇ n -1. [position, grade] grado m, graduación f. -2. [social class] clase f, categoría f; **the** ~ **and file** las bases (del partido). -3. [row] fila f. ◇ vt [class]: **to be** ~**ed** estar clasificado(da). ◇ vi: **to** ~ **as** estar considerado(da) (como); **to** ~ **among** encontrarse entre. ◆ **ranks** npl -1. MIL: **the** ~**s** los soldados rasos. -2. fig [members] filas fpl.

rankle ['ræŋkl] vi amargar, doler.

ransack ['rænsæk] vt [search] registrar a fondo; [plunder] saquear.

ransom ['rænsəm] n rescate m; **to hold sb to** ~ fig hacer chantaje a alguien.

rant [rænt] vi despotricar.

rap [ræp] ◇ n -1. [knock] golpecito m. -2. [type of music] rap m. ◇ vt dar golpecitos en.

rape [reɪp] ◇ n -1. [crime] violación f. -2. BOT colza f ◇ vt violar.

rapeseed ['reɪpsiːd] n semilla f de colza.

rapid ['ræpɪd] adj rápido(da). ◆ **rapids** npl rápidos mpl.

rapidly ['ræpɪdlɪ] adv rápidamente.

rapist ['reɪpɪst] n violador m, -ra f.

rapport [ræ'pɔːʳ] n compenetración f.

rapture ['ræptʃəʳ] n arrobamiento m.

rapturous ['ræptʃərəs] adj muy entusiasta.

rare [reəʳ] adj -1. [scarce] poco común, raro(ra). -2. [infrequent] poco frecuente, raro(ra). -3. [exceptional] raro(ra), excepcional. -4. CULIN poco hecho(cha).

rarely ['reəlɪ] adv raras veces.

raring ['reərɪŋ] adj: **to be** ~ **to go** estar ansioso(sa) por empezar.

rarity ['reərətɪ] n rareza f.

rascal ['rɑːskl] n pícaro m, -ra f.

rash [ræʃ] ◇ adj precipitado(da). ◇ n -1. MED erupción f (cutánea), sarpullido m. -2. [spate] aluvión m.

rasher ['ræʃəʳ] n loncha f.

rasp [rɑːsp] n [harsh sound] chirrido m.

raspberry ['rɑːzbərɪ] n [fruit] frambuesa f.

rat [ræt] n [animal] rata f.

rate [reɪt] ◇ n -1. [speed] velocidad f; **at this** ~ a este paso. -2. [of birth, death] índice m; [of unemployment, inflation] tasa f. -3. [price] precio m, tarifa f; [of interest] tipo m. ◇ vt -1. [consider]: **to** ~ **sthg/sb (as/among)** considerar algo/a alguien (como/entre). -2. [deserve] merecer. ◆ **rates** npl Br ≈ contribución f urbana. ◆ **at any rate** adv -1. [at least] al menos. -2. [anyway] de todos modos.

ratepayer ['reɪt,peɪəʳ] n Br contribuyente m y f.

rather ['rɑːðəʳ] adv -1. [to quite a large extent] bastante. -2. [to a limited extent] algo; **he's** ~ **like you** se parece (en) algo a ti. -3. [as preference]: **I would** ~ **wait** preferiría esperar; **I'd** ~ **not** mejor que no. -4. [more exactly]: **or** ~ ... o más bien ..., o mejor dicho .... -5. [on the contrary]: **(but)** ~ ... (sino) más bien OR por el contrario .... ◆ **rather than** conj antes que.

ratify ['rætɪfaɪ] vt ratificar.

rating ['reɪtɪŋ] n [standing] clasificación f, posición f.

ratio ['reɪʃɪəʊ] (pl -s) n proporción f, relación f.

ration ['ræʃn] ◇ n ración f. ◇ vt racionar. ◆ **rations** npl víveres mpl.

rational ['ræʃənl] adj racional.

rationale [,ræʃə'nɑːl] n lógica f, razones fpl.

rationalize, **-ise** ['ræʃənəlaɪz] vt racionalizar.

rat race n mundo despiadadamente competitivo de los negocios.

rattle ['rætl] ◇ n -1. [of engine, metal] ruido m, traqueteo m; [of glass] tintineo *m*; [of typewriter] **repiqueteo** *m*. **-2.** [toy] **sonajero** *m*. ◇ *vt* **-1.** [make rattle] **hacer sonar. -2.** [unsettle] **desconcertar.** ◇ *vi* **golpetear;** [gunfire] **tabletear.**

rattlesnake ['rætlsneɪk], **rattler** *Am* ['rætlər] *n* serpiente *f* de cascabel.

raucous ['rɔːkəs] *adj* ronco(ca) y estridente.

ravage ['rævɪdʒ] *vt* estragar, asolar. ◆ **ravages** *npl* estragos *mpl*.

rave [reɪv] ◇ *n Br inf* [party] juerga *f*. ◇ *vi* **-1.** [talk angrily]: **to ~ against sb/sthg** despotricar contra alguien/algo. **-2.** [talk enthusiastically]: **to ~ about sthg** deshacerse en alabanzas sobre algo.

raven ['reɪvn] *n* cuervo *m*.

ravenous ['rævənəs] *adj* [person, animal] **famélico(ca);** [appetite] **voraz.**

ravine [rə'viːn] *n* barranco *m*.

raving ['reɪvɪŋ] *adj* [lunatic] de atar; [fantasy] **delirante.**

ravioli [,rævɪ'əʊlɪ] *n* (*U*) raviolis *mpl*.

ravishing ['rævɪʃɪŋ] *adj* [sight, beauty] de ensueño; [person] **bellísimo(ma).**

raw [rɔː] *adj* **-1.** [uncooked] **crudo(da). -2.** [untreated] **en bruto. -3.** [painful - wound] **en carne viva. -4.** [inexperienced] **novato(ta). -5.** [cold] **crudo(da).**

raw deal *n*: **to get a ~** recibir un trato injusto.

raw material *n* materia *f* prima.

ray [reɪ] *n* rayo *m*; **~ of hope** resquicio *m* de esperanza.

rayon ['reɪɒn] *n* rayón *m*.

raze [reɪz] *vt* arrasar.

razor ['reɪzər] *n* [wet shaver] navaja *f*; [electric machine] **maquinilla** *f* de afeitar.

razor blade *n* hoja *f* de afeitar.

RC *abbr of* **Roman Catholic.**

Rd *abbr of* **road.**

R & D (*abbr of* **research and development**) *n* I & D *f*.

re [riː] *prep* Ref.

RE *n* (*abbr of* **religious education**) religión *f*.

reach [riːtʃ] ◇ *n* alcance *m*; **he has a long ~** tiene los brazos largos; **within (sb's) ~** [easily touched] al alcance (de alguien); [easily travelled to] a poco distancia (de alguien); **out of OR beyond sb's ~** fuera del alcance de alguien. ◇ *vt* **-1.** [gen] alcanzar, llegar a; **to ~ an agreement/a decision** llegar a un acuerdo/una decisión. **-2.** [arrive at - place etc] llegar a. **-3.** [get by stretching - object, shelf] alcanzar. **-4.** [contact] localizar. ◇ *vi*: **to ~ out/across** alargar la mano; **to ~ down** agacharse.

react [rɪ'ækt] *vi* **-1.** [respond]: **to ~ (to)** reaccionar (a OR ante). **-2.** [rebel]: **to ~ against** reaccionar en contra de. **-3.** CHEM: **to ~ with** reaccionar con.

reaction [rɪ'ækʃn] *n*: **~ (to/against)** reacción *f* (a/contra).

reactionary [rɪ'ækʃənrɪ] ◇ *adj* reaccionario(ria). ◇ *n* reaccionario *m*, -ria *f*.

reactor [rɪ'æktər] *n* reactor *m*.

read [riːd] (*pt & pp* **read** [red]) ◇ *vt* **-1.** [gen] leer. **-2.** [subj: sign, words] poner, decir. **-3.** [interpret] interpretar. **-4.** [subj: thermometer, meter etc] marcar. **-5.** *Br* UNIV estudiar. ◇ *vi* **-1.** [person] leer. **-2.** [read aloud]: **to ~ (to sb)** leerle (a alguien). **-3.** [piece of writing] leerse. ◆ **read out** *vt sep* leer en voz alta. ◆ **read up on** *vt fus* leer OR documentarse sobre.

readable ['riːdəbl] *adj* ameno(na), que se lee con agrado.

reader ['riːdər] *n* [person who reads] lector *m*, -ra *f*.

readership ['riːdəʃɪp] *n* [total number of readers] lectores *mpl*.

readily ['redɪlɪ] *adv* **-1.** [willingly] de buena gana. **-2.** [easily] en seguida.

reading ['riːdɪŋ] *n* **-1.** [gen] lectura *f*. **-2.** [recital] recital *m*.

readjust [,riːə'dʒʌst] ◇ *vt* reajustar. ◇ *vi*: **to ~ (to)** volverse a adaptar (a).

readout ['riːdaʊt] *n* COMPUT texto *m* en pantalla.

ready ['redɪ] ◇ *adj* **-1.** [prepared] listo(ta), preparado(da); **to be ~ for sthg/to do sthg** estar listo para algo/para hacer algo. **-2.** [willing]: **to be ~ to do sthg** estar dispuesto(ta) a hacer algo. **-3.** [in need of]: **to be ~ for sthg** necesitar algo. **-4.** [likely]: **to be ~ to do sthg** estar a punto de hacer algo. **-5.** [cash] contante; [smile] pronto(ta). ◇ *vt* preparar.

ready cash *n* dinero *m* contante.

ready-made *adj* [products] hecho(cha); [clothes] confeccionado(da).

ready money *n* dinero *m* contante.

ready-to-wear *adj* confeccionado(da).

reafforestation ['riːə,fɒrɪ'steɪʃn] *n* repoblación *f* forestal.

real ['rɪəl] ◇ *adj* **-1.** [not imagined, actual] real; **the ~ thing** lo auténtico; **for ~ de verdad;** **in ~ terms** en términos reales. **-2.** [genuine, proper] auténtico(ca). ◇ *adv Am* muy.

real estate *n* propiedad *f* inmobiliaria.

realign [,riːə'laɪn] *vt* volver a alinear.

realism ['rɪəlɪzm] *n* realismo *m*.

realistic [ˌrɪə'lɪstɪk] *adj* realista.
reality [rɪ'ælətɪ] *n* realidad *f*.
realization [ˌrɪəlaɪ'zeɪʃn] *n* **-1.** [recognition] comprensión *f*. **-2.** [achievement] consecución *f*.
realize, -ise ['rɪəlaɪz] *vt* **-1.** [become aware of] darse cuenta de. **-2.** [produce, achieve, make profit of] realizar.
really ['rɪəlɪ] ◇ *adv* **-1.** [for emphasis] de verdad; ~ **good** buenísimo. **-2.** [actually, honestly] realmente. **-3.** [to sound less negative] en realidad. ◇ *excl* **-1.** [expressing doubt]: ~? [in affirmatives] ¿ah sí?; [in negatives] ¿ah no? **-2.** [expressing surprise, disbelief]: ~? ¿de verdad?
realm [relm] *n* **-1.** [field] campo *m*, esfera *f*. **-2.** [kingdom] reino *m*.
realtor ['rɪəltər] *n Am* agente inmobiliario *m*, agente inmobiliaria *f*.
reap [riːp] *vt lit & fig* cosechar.
reappear [ˌriːə'pɪər] *vi* reaparecer.
rear [rɪər] ◇ *adj* trasero(ra), de atrás. ◇ *n* [back] parte *f* de atrás; **to bring up the** ~ cerrar la marcha. ◇ *vt* criar. ◇ *vi*: **to** ~ **(up)** encabritarse.
rearm [ˌriː'ɑːm] *vi* rearmarse.
rearmost ['rɪəməʊst] *adj* último(ma).
rearrange [ˌriːə'reɪndʒ] *vt* **-1.** [room, furniture] colocar de otro modo; [system, plans] reorganizar. **-2.** [meeting] volver a concertar.
rearview mirror ['rɪəvjuː-] *n* (espejo *m*) retrovisor *m*.
reason ['riːzn] ◇ *n* **-1.** [cause]: ~ **(for)** razón *f* (para); **for some** ~ por alguna razón. **-2.** [justification]: **to have** ~ **to do sthg** tener motivo para hacer algo. **-3.** [rationality] razón *f*, sensatez *f*; **it stands to** ~ es razonable; **to listen to** ~ avenirse a razones. ◇ *vt & vi* razonar. ◆ **reason with** *vt fus* razonar con.
reasonable ['riːznəbl] *adj* razonable.
reasonably ['riːznəblɪ] *adv* razonablemente.
reasoned ['riːznd] *adj* razonado(da).
reasoning ['riːznɪŋ] *n* razonamiento *m*.
reassess [ˌriːə'ses] *vt* reconsiderar.
reassurance [ˌriːə'ʃɔːrəns] *n* **-1.** (*U*) [comfort] palabras *fpl* tranquilizadoras. **-2.** [promise] promesa *f*, compromiso *m*.
reassure [ˌriːə'ʃɔːr] *vt* tranquilizar.
reassuring [ˌriːə'ʃɔːrɪŋ] *adj* tranquilizador(ra).
rebate ['riːbeɪt] *n* devolución *f*, bonificación *f*.
rebel [*n* 'rebl, *vb* rɪ'bel] ◇ *n* rebelde *m y*

f. ◇ *vi*: **to** ~ **(against)** rebelarse (contra).
rebellion [rɪ'beljən] *n* rebelión *f*.
rebellious [rɪ'beljəs] *adj* rebelde.
rebound [*n* 'riːbaʊnd, *vb* ˌrɪ'baʊnd] ◇ *n*: **on the** ~ [ball] de rebote *m*. ◇ *vi* [bounce back] rebotar.
rebuff [rɪ'bʌf] *n* desaire *m*, negativa *f*.
rebuild [ˌriː'bɪld] *vt* reconstruir.
rebuke [rɪ'bjuːk] ◇ *n* reprimenda *f*, reprobación *f*. ◇ *vt*: **to** ~ **sb (for)** reprender a alguien (por).
rebuttal [riː'bʌtl] *n* refutación *f*.
recalcitrant [rɪ'kælsɪtrənt] *adj* recalcitrante.
recall [rɪ'kɔːl] ◇ *n* [memory] memoria *f*. ◇ *vt* **-1.** [remember] recordar, acordarse de. **-2.** [ambassador] retirar.
recant [rɪ'kænt] *vi* [deny statement] retractarse; [deny religion] renegar de la fe.
recap ['riːkæp] *inf* ◇ *n* resumen *m*, recapitulación *f*. ◇ *vt* [summarize] recapitular, resumir. ◇ *vi* recapitular, resumir.
recapitulate [ˌriːkə'pɪtjʊleɪt] *vt & vi* recapitular, resumir.
recd, rec'd *abbr of* received.
recede [riː'siːd] *vi* **-1.** [person, car] alejarse; [coastline] retroceder. **-2.** *fig* [disappear] esfumarse.
receding [rɪ'siːdɪŋ] *adj* [chin] medida hacia dentro; [forehead] hundida; ~ **hairline** entradas *fpl*.
receipt [rɪ'siːt] *n* recibo *m*; **to acknowledge** ~ acusar recibo. ◆ **receipts** *npl* recaudación *f*.
receive [rɪ'siːv] *vt* **-1.** [gen] recibir. **-2.** [reaction] tener; [injury, setback] sufrir. **-3.** [greet]: **to be well/badly** ~**d** tener una buena/mala acogida.
receiver [rɪ'siːvər] *n* **-1.** [of telephone] auricular *m*. **-2.** [radio, TV set] receptor *m*. **-3.** [criminal] perista *m y f*. **-4.** FIN síndico *m*, -ca *f*.
recent ['riːsnt] *adj* reciente.
recently ['riːsntlɪ] *adv* recientemente.
receptacle [rɪ'septəkl] *n* receptáculo *m*.
reception [rɪ'sepʃn] *n* recepción *f*.
reception desk *n* recepción *f*.
receptionist [rɪ'sepʃənɪst] *n* recepcionista *m y f*.
recess ['riːses, *Br* rɪ'ses] *n* **-1.** [vacation] periodo *m* vacacional; **to be in** ~ estar clausurado(da). **-2.** [alcove] nicho *m*, hueco *m*. **-3.** *Am* SCH recreo *m*. ◆ **recesses** *npl* [of mind, heart] recovecos *mpl*; [of building] escondrijos *mpl*.

recession [rɪ'seʃn] n recesión f.
recharge [,ri:'tʃɑ:dʒ] vt recargar.
recipe ['resɪpɪ] n CULIN & fig receta f.
recipient [rɪ'sɪpɪənt] n [of letter, cheque] destinatario m, -ria f.
reciprocal [rɪ'sɪprəkl] adj recíproco(ca).
recital [rɪ'saɪtl] n recital m.
recite [rɪ'saɪt] vt **-1.** [poem] recitar. **-2.** [list] enumerar.
reckless ['reklɪs] adj imprudente, temerario(ria).
reckon ['rekn] vt **-1.** inf [think]: to ~ (that) pensar que, suponer que. **-2.** [consider, judge]: to be ~ed to be sthg ser considerado(da) algo. **-3.** [calculate] calcular. ◆**reckon on** vt fus contar con. ◆**reckon with** vt fus **-1.** [expect] contar con.
reckoning ['rekənɪŋ] n [calculation] cálculo m.
reclaim [rɪ'kleɪm] vt **-1.** [claim back] reclamar. **-2.** [recover]: to ~ land from the sea ganarle tierra al mar.
recline [rɪ'klaɪn] vi reclinarse.
reclining [rɪ'klaɪnɪŋ] adj reclinable.
recluse [rɪ'klu:s] n solitario m, -ria f.
recognition [,rekəg'nɪʃn] n reconocimiento m; **beyond** OR **out of all** ~ de modo irreconocible; **in** ~ **of** en reconocimiento a.
recognizable ['rekəgnaɪzəbl] adj reconocible.
recognize, -ise ['rekəgnaɪz] vt reconocer.
recoil [vb rɪ'kɔɪl, n 'ri:kɔɪl] ◇ vi **-1.** [draw back] retroceder, echarse atrás. **-2.** fig [shrink from]: to ~ from OR at sthg [truth, bad news] esquivar OR rehuir algo; [idea, suggestion] estremecerse ante algo. ◇ n [of gun] retroceso m.
recollect [,rekə'lekt] vt recordar.
recollection [,rekə'lekʃn] n recuerdo m.
recommend [,rekə'mend] vt recomendar.
recompense ['rekəmpens] ◇ n: ~ **(for)** compensación f OR indemnización f (por). ◇ vt: to ~ **sb (for)** recompensar a alguien (por).
reconcile ['rekənsaɪl] vt **-1.** [find agreement between] conciliar; to ~ **sthg with** hacer compatible algo con. **-2.** [make friendly again] reconciliar. **-3.** [accept]: to ~ **o.s. to sthg** resignarse a.
reconditioned [,ri:kən'dɪʃnd] adj revisado(da), reparado(da).
reconnaissance [rɪ'kɒnɪsəns] n reconocimiento m.

reconnoitre Br, **reconnoiter** Am [,rekə'nɔɪtər] ◇ vt reconocer. ◇ vi hacer un reconocimiento.
reconsider [,ri:kən'sɪdər] vt & vi reconsiderar.
reconstruct [,ri:kən'strʌkt] vt [building, crime] reconstruir.
record [n & adj 'rekɔ:d, vb rɪ'kɔ:d] ◇ n **-1.** [of event, piece of information] registro m, anotación f; [of meeting] actas fpl; **on** ~ [on file] archivado; [ever recorded] de que se tiene constancia; **off the** ~ confidencial. **-2.** [vinyl disc] disco m. **-3.** [best achievement] récord m. **-4.** [history] historial m; **criminal** ~ antecedentes mpl penales. ◇ vt **-1.** [write down] anotar, tomar nota de. **-2.** [put on tape] grabar. ◇ adj récord (inv).
recorded delivery [rɪ'kɔ:dɪd-] n correo m certificado.
recorder [rɪ'kɔ:dər] n [musical instrument] flauta f.
record holder n plusmarquista m y f.
recording [rɪ'kɔ:dɪŋ] n grabación f.
record player n tocadiscos m inv.
recount [n 'ri:kaunt, vt sense 1 rɪ'kaunt, sense 2 ,ri:'kaunt] ◇ n recuento m. ◇ vt **-1.** [narrate] narrar. **-2.** [count again] volver a contar.
recoup [rɪ'ku:p] vt recuperar.
recourse [rɪ'kɔ:s] n fml: to have ~ to recurrir a.
recover [rɪ'kʌvər] ◇ vt **-1.** [retrieve, recoup] recuperar. **-2.** [regain - calm etc] recobrar. ◇ vi: to ~ **(from)** recuperarse (de).
recovery [rɪ'kʌvərɪ] n recuperación f.
recreation [,rekrɪ'eɪʃn] n [leisure] esparcimiento m, recreo m.
recrimination [rɪ,krɪmɪ'neɪʃn] n recriminación f.
recruit [rɪ'kru:t] ◇ n recluta m y f. ◇ vt **-1.** [gen] reclutar; to ~ **sb (for sthg/to do sthg)** reclutar a alguien (para algo/para hacer algo). **-2.** [find, employ] contratar. ◇ vi buscar empleados nuevos.
recruitment [rɪ'kru:tmənt] n [gen] reclutamiento m; [of staff] contratación f.
rectangle ['rek,tæŋgl] n rectángulo m.
rectangular [rek'tæŋgjulər] adj rectangular.
rectify ['rektɪfaɪ] vt fml rectificar.
rector ['rektər] n **-1.** [priest] párroco m. **-2.** Scot [head - of school] director m, -ra f; [- of college, university] rector m, -ra f.
rectory ['rektərɪ] n rectoría f.
recuperate [rɪ'ku:pəreɪt] vi fml: to ~ **(from)** recuperarse (de).

recur [rɪ'kɜːr] vi repetirse.

recurrence [rɪ'kʌrəns] n fml repetición f.

recurrent [rɪ'kʌrənt] adj que se repite.

recycle [ˌriː'saɪkl] vt reciclar.

red [red] ◇ adj rojo(ja); [hair] pelirrojo(ja). ◇ n [colour] rojo m; **to be in the ~** inf estar en números rojos.

red card n FTBL: **to show sb the ~** mostrarle a alguien (la) tarjeta roja.

red carpet n: **to roll out the ~ for sb** recibir a alguien con todos los honores. ◆ **red-carpet** adj: **to give sb the red-carpet treatment** dispensar a alguien un gran recibimiento.

Red Cross n: **the ~** la Cruz Roja.

redcurrant ['redkʌrənt] n **-1.** [fruit] grosella f. **-2.** [bush] grosellero m.

redden ['redn] ◇ vt [make red] teñir de rojo. ◇ vi [flush] enrojecer.

redecorate [ˌriː'dekəreɪt] vt & vi volver a pintar (o empapelar).

redeem [rɪ'diːm] vt **-1.** [save, rescue] salvar, rescatar. **-2.** fml [at pawnbroker's] desempeñar.

redeeming [rɪ'diːmɪŋ] adj: **his only ~** feature lo único que le salva.

redeploy [ˌriːdɪ'plɔɪ] vt reorganizar.

red-faced [-'feɪst] adj **-1.** [flushed] rojo(ja), colorado(da). **-2.** [with embarrassment] rojo(ja) de vergüenza.

red-haired [-'heəd] adj pelirrojo(ja).

red-handed [-'hændɪd] adj: **to catch sb ~** coger a alguien con las manos en la masa.

redhead ['redhed] n pelirrojo m, -ja f.

red herring n fig [unhelpful clue] pista f falsa; [means of distracting attention] ardid m para distraer la atención.

red-hot adj [metal, person, passion] al rojo (vivo); [zeal] fervoroso(sa).

redid [ˌriː'dɪd] pt → **redo**.

redirect [ˌriːdɪ'rekt] vt **-1.** [retarget] redirigir. **-2.** [send elsewhere] enviar a otro lugar. **-3.** [forward] reexpedir.

rediscover [ˌriːdɪ'skʌvər] vt **-1.** [re-experience] volver a descubrir. **-2.** [make popular, famous again]: **to be ~ed** ser descubierto(ta) de nuevo.

red light n [traffic signal] semáforo m rojo.

red-light district n barrio m chino.

redo [ˌriː'duː] (pt **-did**, pp **-done**) vt [do again] volver a hacer.

redolent ['redələnt] adj literary **-1.** [reminiscent]: **~ of** evocador(ra) de. **-2.** [smelling]: **~ of** con olor a.

redouble [ˌriː'dʌbl] vt: **to ~ one's efforts (to do sthg)** redoblar esfuerzos (para hacer algo).

redraft [ˌriː'drɑːft] vt volver a redactar.

redress [rɪ'dres] fml ◇ n (U) reparación f, desagravio m. ◇ vt: **to ~ the balance (between)** equilibrar la balanza (entre).

red tape n fig papeleo m.

reduce [rɪ'djuːs] ◇ vt reducir; **to be ~d to doing sthg** verse rebajado OR forzado a hacer algo; **to be ~d to** verse sumido OR hundido en. ◇ vi Am [diet] (intentar) adelgazar.

reduction [rɪ'dʌkʃn] n **-1.** [gen]: **~ (in)** reducción f (de). **-2.** COMM: **~ (of)** descuento m (de).

redundancy [rɪ'dʌndənsɪ] n **-1.** Br [job loss] despido m. **-2.** [unemployment] desempleo m.

redundant [rɪ'dʌndənt] adj **-1.** Br [jobless]: **to be made ~** perder el empleo. **-2.** [not required - equipment, factory] innecesario(ria); [- comment] redundante.

reed [riːd] n **-1.** [plant] carrizo m, cañavera f. **-2.** [of musical instrument] lengüeta f.

reef [riːf] n arrecife m.

reek [riːk] vi: **to ~ (of)** apestar (a).

reel [riːl] ◇ n [of cotton, film, on fishing rod] carrete m. ◇ vi **-1.** [stagger] tambalearse. **-2.** [be stunned]: **to ~ from sthg** quedarse atónito(ta) por algo. ◆ **reel in** vt sep sacar enrollando el carrete (en pesca). ◆ **reel off** vt sep recitar al corrido.

reenact [ˌriːɪ'nækt] vt representar de nuevo.

ref [ref] n **-1.** (abbr of **referee**) inf SPORT árbitro m. **-2.** (abbr of **reference**) ADMIN ref.

refectory [rɪ'fektərɪ] n refectorio m.

refer [rɪ'fɜːr] vt **-1.** [send, direct]: **to ~ sb to** [to place, person] enviar a alguien a; [to source of information] remitir a alguien a. **-2.** [report, submit]: **to ~ sthg to** remitir algo a. ◆ **refer to** vt fus **-1.** [mention, speak about] referirse a. **-2.** [consult] consultar.

referee [ˌrefə'riː] ◇ n **-1.** SPORT árbitro m. **-2.** Br [for job application] persona que recomienda a alguien para un trabajo. ◇ vt & vi SPORT arbitrar.

reference ['refrəns] n **-1.** [mention, reference number]: **to make ~ to** hacer referencia a; **with ~ to** fml con referencia a. **-2.** (U) [for advice, information]: **~ (to)** consulta f (a). **-3.** [for job - letter] referencias *fpl*; [- person] *persona que recomienda a alguien para un trabajo.*

reference book *n* libro *m* de consulta.

reference number *n* número *m* de referencia.

referendum [,refə'rendəm] (*pl* -s OR -da [-də]) *n* referéndum *m*.

refill [*n* 'ri:fɪl, *vb* ,ri:'fɪl] ◇ *n inf*: would you like a ~? ¿te apetece otra copa? ◇ *vt* volver a llenar.

refine [rɪ'faɪn] *vt* -1. [oil, food] refinar. -2. [plan, speech] pulir.

refined [rɪ'faɪnd] *adj* -1. [oil, food, person] refinado(da). -2. [equipment, theory] perfeccionado(da).

refinement [rɪ'faɪnmənt] *n* -1. [improvement]: ~ (on) mejora *f* (de). -2. (*U*) [gentility] refinamiento *m*.

reflect [rɪ'flekt] ◇ *vt* -1. [gen] reflejar. -2. [think, consider]: to ~ that ... considerar que .... ◇ *vi*: to ~ (on OR upon) reflexionar (sobre).

reflection [rɪ'flekʃn] *n* -1. [gen] reflejo *m*. -2. [criticism]: ~ on crítica *f* de. -3. [thinking] reflexión *f*; on ~ pensándolo bien.

reflector [rɪ'flektər] *n* reflector *m*.

reflex ['ri:fleks] *n*: ~ (action) (acto *m*) reflejo *m*.

reflexive [rɪ'fleksɪv] *adj* GRAMM reflexivo(va).

reforestation [riː,fɒrɪ'steɪʃn] = **reafforestation**.

reform [rɪ'fɔːm] ◇ *n* reforma *f*. ◇ *vt* reformar. ◇ *vi* reformarse.

Reformation [,refə'meɪʃn] *n*: the ~ la Reforma.

reformatory [rɪ'fɔːmətrɪ] *n Am* reformatorio *m*, centro *m* de menores.

reformer [rɪ'fɔːmər] *n* reformador *m*, -ra *f*.

refrain [rɪ'freɪn] ◇ *n* [chorus] estribillo *m*. ◇ *vi fml*: to ~ from doing sthg abstenerse de hacer algo.

refresh [rɪ'freʃ] *vt* refrescar.

refreshed [rɪ'freʃt] *adj* descansado(da).

refresher course [rɪ'freʃər-] *n* cursillo *m* de reciclaje.

refreshing [rɪ'freʃɪŋ] *adj* [change, honesty, drink] refrescante; [sleep] vigorizante.

refreshments [rɪ'freʃmənts] *npl* refrigerio *m*.

refrigerator [rɪ'frɪdʒəreɪtər] *n* refrigerador *m*.

refuel [,riː'fjʊəl] ◇ *vt* llenar de carburante. ◇ *vi* repostar.

refuge ['refjuːdʒ] *n* refugio *m*; to seek OR take ~ (in) *fig* buscar refugio (en).

refugee [,refjʊ'dʒiː] *n* refugiado *m*, -da *f*.

refund [*n* 'riːfʌnd, *vb* rɪ'fʌnd] ◇ *n* reembolso *m*. ◇ *vt*: to ~ sthg to sb, to ~ sb sthg reembolsar algo a alguien.

refurbish [,riː'fɜːbɪʃ] *vt* [building] restaurar; [office, shop] renovar.

refusal [rɪ'fjuːzl] *n* -1. [disagreement, saying no]: ~ (to do sthg) negativa *f* (a hacer algo). -2. [withholding, denial] denegación *f*. -3. [non-acceptance]: to meet with ~ ser rechazado(da).

refuse[1] [rɪ'fjuːz] ◇ *vt* -1. [withhold, deny]: to ~ sb sthg, to ~ sthg to sb denegar a alguien algo. -2. [decline, reject] rechazar. -3. [not agree, be completely unwilling]: to ~ to do sthg negarse a hacer algo. ◇ *vi* negarse.

refuse[2] ['refjuːs] *n* [rubbish] basura *f*.

refuse collection ['refjuːs-] *n* recogida *f* de basuras.

refute [rɪ'fjuːt] *vt fml* refutar.

regain [rɪ'geɪn] *vt* [leadership, first place] recuperar; [health, composure] recobrar.

regal ['riːgl] *adj* regio(gia).

regalia [rɪ'geɪljə] *n* (*U*) *fml* ropaje *m*.

regard [rɪ'gɑːd] ◇ *n* -1. *fml* [respect, esteem]: ~ (for) estima *f* OR respeto *m* (por). -2. [aspect]: in this/that ~ a este/ese respecto. ◇ *vt* -1. [consider]: to ~ o.s. as sthg considerarse algo; to ~ sthg/sb as considerar algo/a alguien como. -2. [look at, view]: to be highly ~ed estar muy bien considerado. ◆ **regards** *npl* [in greetings] recuerdos *mpl*. ◆ **as regards** *prep* en cuanto a, por lo que se refiere a. ◆ **in regard to, with regard to** *prep* respecto a, en cuanto a.

regarding [rɪ'gɑːdɪŋ] *prep* respecto a, en cuanto a.

regardless [rɪ'gɑːdlɪs] *adv* a pesar de todo. ◆ **regardless of** *prep* sin tener en cuenta; ~ of the cost cueste lo que cueste.

regime [reɪ'ʒiːm] *n* régimen *m*.

regiment ['redʒɪmənt] *n* MIL regimiento *m*.

region ['riːdʒən] *n* región *f*; in the ~ of alrededor de.

regional ['riːdʒənl] *adj* regional.

register ['redʒɪstər] ◇ *n* [of electors etc] registro *m*; [at school] lista *f*. ◇ *vt* -1. [record - gen] registrar; [- car] matricular. -2. [express] mostrar, reflejar. ◇ *vi* -1. [be put on official list]: to ~ (as/for) inscribirse (como/para). -2. [book in - at hotel] **registrarse**; [- at conference] **inscribirse**. **-3.** *inf* [be noticed]: **I told him but it didn't seem to ~** se lo dije, pero no pareció que lo captara.

registered ['redʒɪstəd] *adj* **-1.** [officially listed] **inscrito(ta) oficialmente**. **-2.** [letter, parcel] **certificado(da)**.

registered trademark *n* **marca** *f* **registrada**.

registrar [,redʒɪ'strɑːʳ] *n* **-1.** [keeper of records] **registrador** *m*, **- ra** *f* **oficial**. **-2.** UNIV **secretario** *m*, **-ria** *f* **general**. **-3.** [doctor] **médico** *m*, **-ca** *f* **de hospital**.

registration [,redʒɪ'streɪʃn] *n* **-1.** [gen] **registro** *m*. **-2.** AUT = **registration number**.

registration number *n* **número** *m* **de matrícula**.

registry ['redʒɪstrɪ] *n* **registro** *m*.

registry office *n* **registro** *m* **civil**.

regret [rɪ'gret] ◇ *n* **-1.** *fml* [sorrow] **pesar** *m*. **-2.** [sad feeling]: **I've no ~s about it** no lo lamento en absoluto. ◇ *vt* [be sorry about]: **to ~ sthg/doing sthg** lamentar algo/haber hecho algo.

regretfully [rɪ'gretfʊlɪ] *adv* **con pesar**; **~, we have to announce ...** lamentamos tener que anunciar ....

regrettable [rɪ'gretəbl] *adj fml* **lamentable**.

regroup [,riː'gruːp] *vi* **reagruparse**.

regular ['regjʊləʳ] ◇ *adj* **-1.** [gen] **regular**. **-2.** [customer] **habitual, asiduo(dua)**. **-3.** [time, place] **acostumbrado(da)**; [problem] **usual, normal**. **-4.** *Am* [pleasant] **legal**. ◇ *n* **cliente** *m* **habitual**.

regularly ['regjʊləlɪ] *adv* **-1.** [gen] **con regularidad**. **-2.** [equally spaced] **de manera uniforme**.

regulate ['regjʊleɪt] *vt* **regular**.

regulation [,regjʊ'leɪʃn] *n* **-1.** [rule] **regla** *f*, **norma** *f*. **-2.** (*U*) [control] **regulación** *f*.

rehabilitate [,riːə'bɪlɪteɪt] *vt* **rehabilitar**.

rehearsal [rɪ'hɜːsl] *n* **ensayo** *m*.

rehearse [rɪ'hɜːs] *vt* **ensayar**.

reign [reɪn] *lit & fig* ◇ *n* **reinado** *m*. ◇ *vi*: **to ~ (over)** **reinar (sobre)**.

reimburse [,riːɪm'bɜːs] *vt*: **to ~ sb (for sthg)** **reembolsar a alguien (algo)**.

rein [reɪn] *n fig*: **to give (a) free ~ to sb, to give sb free ~** **dar rienda suelta a alguien**. ◆ **reins** *npl* [for horse] **riendas** *fpl*.

reindeer ['reɪn,dɪəʳ] (*pl inv*) *n* **reno** *m*.

reinforce [,riːɪn'fɔːs] *vt* **reforzar**.

reinforced concrete [,riːɪn'fɔːst-] *n* **cemento** *m* OR **hormigón** *m* **armado**.

reinforcement [,riːɪn'fɔːsmənt] *n* **refuerzo** *m*. ◆ **reinforcements** *npl* **refuerzos** *mpl*.

reinstate [,riːɪn'steɪt] *vt* **-1.** [give job back to] **restituir** OR **reintegrar en su puesto a**. **-2.** [bring back] **restablecer**.

reissue [riː'ɪʃuː] *vt* [gen] **reeditar, reimprimir**; [film] **reestrenar**.

reiterate [riː'ɪtəreɪt] *vt fml* **reiterar**.

reject [*n* 'riːdʒekt, *vb* rɪ'dʒekt] ◇ *n* **desecho** *m*; **~s** **artículos** *mpl* **defectuosos**. ◇ *vt* **rechazar**.

rejection [rɪ'dʒekʃn] *n* **rechazo** *m*.

rejoice [rɪ'dʒɔɪs] *vi*: **to ~ (at** OR **in)** **alegrarse** OR **regocijarse (con)**.

rejuvenate [rɪ'dʒuːvəneɪt] *vt* **rejuvenecer**.

rekindle [,riː'kɪndl] *vt fig* **reavivar**.

relapse [rɪ'læps] ◇ *n* **recaída** *f*. ◇ *vi*: **to ~ into** **volver a caer en**.

relate [rɪ'leɪt] ◇ *vt* **-1.** [connect]: **to ~ sthg (to)** **relacionar algo (con)**. **-2.** [tell] **contar, relatar**. ◇ *vi* **-1.** [be connected]: **to ~ to** **estar relacionado(da) con**. **-2.** [concern]: **to ~ to** **referirse a**. **-3.** [empathize]: **to ~ (to sb)** **tener mucho en común (con alguien)**. ◆ **relating to** *prep* **concerniente** OR **referente a**.

related [rɪ'leɪtɪd] *adj* **-1.** [in same family] **emparentado(da)**; **to be ~ to sb** **ser pariente de alguien**. **-2.** [connected] **relacionado(da)**.

relation [rɪ'leɪʃn] *n* **-1.** [connection]: **~ (to/between)** **relación** *f* **(con/entre)**; **to bear no ~ to** **no tener nada que ver con**. **-2.** [family member] **pariente** *m y f*, **familiar** *m y f*. ◆ **relations** *npl* [family, race, industrial] **relaciones** *fpl*.

relationship [rɪ'leɪʃnʃɪp] *n* **relación** *f*; **a good ~** **buenas relaciones**.

relative ['relətɪv] ◇ *adj* **relativo(va)**. ◇ *n* **pariente** *m y f*, **familiar** *m y f*. ◆ **relative to** *prep fml* **con relación a**.

relatively ['relətɪvlɪ] *adv* **relativamente**.

relax [rɪ'læks] ◇ *vt* **-1.** [gen] **relajar**. **-2.** [loosen - grip] **aflojar**. ◇ *vi* **-1.** [gen] **relajarse**. **-2.** [loosen] **aflojarse**.

relaxation [,riːlæk'seɪʃn] *n* **-1.** [recreation] **relajación** *f*, **esparcimiento** *m*. **-2.** [slackening - of discipline] **relajación** *f*.

relaxed [rɪ'lækst] *adj* [gen] **relajado(da)**; [person] **tranquilo(la)**; [atmosphere] **desenfadado(da)**.

relaxing [rɪ'læksɪŋ] *adj* **relajante**.

relay ['riːleɪ] ◇ *n* **-1.** SPORT: **~ (race)** **carrera** *f* **de relevos**. **-2.** RADIO & TV **retransmisión** *f*. ◇ *vt* **-1.** [broadcast] **re-**

transmitir. **-2.** [repeat]: **to ~ sthg (to)** transmitir algo (a).

release [rɪ'liːs] ◇ n **-1.** [setting free] puesta f en libertad, liberación f. **-2.** [relief] liberación f. **-3.** [statement] comunicado m. **-4.** [emitting - of gas] escape m; [- of heat, pressure] emisión f. **-5.** [thing issued, issuing - of film] estreno m; [- of record] emisión f. ◇ vt **-1.** [set free]: **to ~ sb (from)** liberar a alguien (de). **-2.** [lift restriction on]: **to ~ sb from** descargar OR liberar a alguien de. **-3.** [make available - funds, resources] entregar. **-4.** [let go - rope, reins, person] soltar; [- grip] aflojar; [- brake, lever] soltar; [- mechanism, trigger] disparar. **-5.** [emit - gas, heat] despedir. **-6.** [issue - film] estrenar; [- record] sacar.

relegate ['relɪgeɪt] vt **-1.** [demote]: **to ~ sthg/sb (to)** relegar algo/a alguien (a). **-2.** Br FTBL: **to be ~d** descender (a una división inferior).

relent [rɪ'lent] vi [person] ablandarse; [wind, storm] remitir, aminorar.

relentless [rɪ'lentlɪs] adj implacable.

relevant ['reləvənt] adj **-1.** [connected]: **~ (to)** relacionado(da) (con), pertinente (a). **-2.** [important]: **~ (to)** importante OR relevante (para). **-3.** [appropriate] pertinente, oportuno(na).

reliable [rɪ'laɪəbl] adj **-1.** [dependable] fiable. **-2.** [information] fidedigno(na).

reliably [rɪ'laɪəblɪ] adv **-1.** [dependably] sin fallar. **-2.** [correctly]: **to be ~ informed about sthg** saber algo de fuentes fidedignas.

reliant [rɪ'laɪənt] adj: **to be ~ on sb/sthg** depender de alguien/de algo.

relic ['relɪk] n **-1.** [gen] reliquia f. **-2.** [custom still in use] vestigio m.

relief [rɪ'liːf] n **-1.** [comfort] alivio m. **-2.** [for poor, refugees] ayuda f (benéfica). **-3.** (U) Am [social security] subsidio m.

relieve [rɪ'liːv] vt **-1.** [ease, lessen] aliviar. **-2.** [take away from]: **to ~ sb of sthg** liberar a alguien de algo.

religion [rɪ'lɪdʒn] n religión f.

religious [rɪ'lɪdʒəs] adj religioso(sa).

relinquish [rɪ'lɪŋkwɪʃ] vt [power, claim] renunciar a; [hold] soltar.

relish ['relɪʃ] ◇ n **-1.** [enjoyment]: **with (great) ~** con (gran) deleite. **-2.** [pickle] salsa rojiza agridulce con pepinillo etc. ◇ vt disfrutar con; **to ~ the thought** OR **idea** OR **prospect of doing sthg** disfrutar con antemano la idea de hacer algo.

relocate [,riːləʊ'keɪt] ◇ vt trasladar. ◇ vi trasladarse.

reluctance [rɪ'lʌktəns] n desgana f.

reluctant [rɪ'lʌktənt] adj reacio(cia); **to be ~ to do sthg** estar poco dispuesto a hacer algo.

reluctantly [rɪ'lʌktəntlɪ] adv con desgana.

rely [rɪ'laɪ] ◆ **rely on** vt fus **-1.** [count on] contar con; **to ~ on sb/sthg to do sthg** estar seguro de que alguien/algo hará algo. **-2.** [be dependent on]: **to ~ on sb/sthg for sthg** depender de alguien/algo para algo.

remain [rɪ'meɪn] ◇ vt continuar como; **to ~ the same** continuar siendo igual. ◇ vi **-1.** [stay] quedarse, permanecer. **-2.** [survive - custom, problem] quedar, continuar. **-3.** [be left]: **to ~ to be done/proved** quedar por hacer/probar. ◆ **remains** npl restos mpl.

remainder [rɪ'meɪndər] n **-1.** [rest]: **the ~** el resto. **-2.** MATH resto m.

remaining [rɪ'meɪnɪŋ] adj restante.

remand [rɪ'mɑːnd] JUR ◇ n: **on ~** detenido(da) en espera de juicio. ◇ vt: **to be ~ed in custody** estar bajo custodia.

remark [rɪ'mɑːk] ◇ n [comment] comentario m. ◇ vt: **to ~ (that)** comentar que.

remarkable [rɪ'mɑːkəbl] adj excepcional, extraordinario(ria).

remarry [,riː'mærɪ] vi volverse a casar.

remedial [rɪ'miːdjəl] adj **-1.** SCH [class, teacher] de refuerzo; [pupil] atrasado(da). **-2.** [corrective] correctivo(va).

remedy ['remədɪ] ◇ n lit & fig: **~ (for)** remedio m (para). ◇ vt remediar.

remember [rɪ'membər] ◇ vt [gen] recordar, acordarse de; **to ~ to do sthg** acordarse de hacer algo; **to ~ doing sthg** recordar OR acordarse de haber hecho algo. ◇ vi [gen] recordar, acordarse.

remembrance [rɪ'membrəns] n fml: **in ~ of** en conmemoración de.

Remembrance Day n en Gran Bretaña, día en conmemoración por los caídos en las dos guerras mundiales.

remind [rɪ'maɪnd] vt: **to ~ sb (about sthg/to do sthg)** recordar a alguien (algo/que haga algo); **she ~s me of my sister** me recuerda a mi hermana.

reminder [rɪ'maɪndər] n **-1.** [to jog memory] recordatorio m, recuerdo m. **-2.** [letter, note] notificación f, aviso m.

reminisce [,remɪ'nɪs] vi: **to ~ (about sthg)** rememorar (algo).

reminiscent [,remɪ'nɪsnt] adj [similar to]: **~ of** evocador(ra) de.

remiss [rɪ'mɪs] *adj* negligente, remiso(sa); **it was ~ of me** fue una negligencia por mi parte.

remit¹ [rɪ'mɪt] *vt* [money] remitir.

remit² ['riːmɪt] *n* [responsibility] misión *f*.

remittance [rɪ'mɪtns] *n* giro *m*.

remnant ['remnənt] *n* **-1.** [remaining part] resto *m*. **-2.** [of cloth] retal *m*.

remold *n & vt Am* = **remould**.

remorse [rɪ'mɔːs] *n* (*U*) remordimiento *m*.

remorseful [rɪ'mɔːsful] *adj* lleno(na) de remordimiento.

remorseless [rɪ'mɔːslɪs] *adj* **-1.** [pitiless] despiadado(da). **-2.** [unstoppable] implacable.

remote [rɪ'məut] *adj* **-1.** [place, time possibility] remoto(ta). **-2.** [from reality etc]: **~ (from)** apartado(da) OR alejado(da) (de).

remote control *n* mando *m* a distancia.

remotely [rɪ'məutlɪ] *adv* **-1.** [in the slightest]: **not ~** ni remotamente, en lo más mínimo. **-2.** [far off] muy lejos.

remould *Br*, **remold** *Am* ['riːməuld] *n* neumático *m* recauchutado.

removable [rɪ'muːvəbl] *adj* [detachable] separable.

removal [rɪ'muːvl] *n* **-1.** (*U*) [act of removing] separación *f*, extracción *f*; [of threat, clause] supresión *f*. **-2.** *Br* [change of house] mudanza *f*.

removal van *n Br* camión *m* de mudanzas.

remove [rɪ'muːv] *vt* **-1.** [take away, clean away]: **to ~ sthg (from)** quitar algo (de). **-2.** [take off] quitarse, sacarse. **-3.** [from a job, post]: **to ~ sb (from)** destituir a alguien (de). **-4.** [problem] eliminar, resolver; [suspicion] disipar.

remuneration [rɪ,mjuːnə'reɪʃn] *n fml* remuneración *f*.

Renaissance [rə'neɪsəns] *n*: **the ~** el Renacimiento.

render ['rendər] *vt* **-1.** [make]: **to ~ sthg useless** hacer OR volver algo inútil. **-2.** [give - help] prestar, dar.

rendering ['rendərɪŋ] *n* interpretación *f*.

rendezvous ['rɒndɪvuː] (*pl inv*) *n* [meeting] cita *f*.

renegade ['renɪgeɪd] ◇ *adj* renegado(da). ◇ *n* renegado *m*, -da *f*.

renew [rɪ'njuː] *vt* **-1.** [attempt, attack] reemprender. **-2.** [relationship] reanudar, renovar. **-3.** [licence, contract] renovar. **-4.** [strength, interest] reavivar.

renewable [rɪ'njuːəbl] *adj* renovable.

renewal [rɪ'njuːəl] *n* **-1.** [of an activity] reanudación *f*. **-2.** [of a contract, licence etc] renovación *f*.

renounce [rɪ'nauns] *vt* renunciar a.

renovate ['renəveɪt] *vt* reformar, renovar.

renown [rɪ'naun] *n* renombre *m*.

renowned [rɪ'naund] *adj*: **~ (for)** célebre (por).

rent [rent] ◇ *n* alquiler *m*. ◇ *vt* alquilar, rentar *Amer*.

rental ['rentl] ◇ *adj* de alquiler. ◇ *n* alquiler *m*.

renunciation [rɪ,nʌnsɪ'eɪʃn] *n* renuncia *f*.

reorganize, -ise [,riː'ɔːgənaɪz] *vt* reorganizar.

rep [rep] *n* **-1.** *abbr of* **representative**. **-2.** *abbr of* **repertory**.

repaid [riː'peɪd] *pt & pp* → **repay**.

repair [rɪ'peər] ◇ *n* reparación *f*, refacción *f Amer*; **in good/bad ~** en buen/mal estado. ◇ *vt* reparar, refaccionar *Amer*.

repair kit *n* caja de herramientas de una bicicleta.

repartee [,repɑː'tiː] *n* intercambio *m* de réplicas ingeniosas.

repatriate [,riː'pætrɪeɪt] *vt* repatriar.

repay [riː'peɪ] (*pt & pp* **repaid**) *vt* devolver; **to ~ sb sthg, to ~ sthg to sb** devolver a alguien algo.

repayment [riː'peɪmənt] *n* **-1.** [act of paying back] devolución *f*, reembolso *m*. **-2.** [sum] pago *m*.

repeal [rɪ'piːl] ◇ *n* revocación *f*, abrogación *f*. ◇ *vt* revocar, abrogar.

repeat [rɪ'piːt] ◇ *vt* **-1.** [gen] repetir. **-2.** [TV, radio programme] volver a emitir. ◇ *n* reposición *f*.

repeatedly [rɪ'piːtɪdlɪ] *adv* repetidamente.

repel [rɪ'pel] *vt* [disgust] repeler.

repellent [rɪ'pelənt] ◇ *adj* repelente. ◇ *n* espray *m* anti-insectos.

repent [rɪ'pent] ◇ *vt* arrepentirse de. ◇ *vi*: **to ~ of** arrepentirse de.

repentance [rɪ'pentəns] *n* arrepentimiento *m*.

repercussions [,riːpə'kʌʃnz] *npl* repercusiones *fpl*.

repertoire ['repətwɑːr] *n* repertorio *m*.

repertory ['repətrɪ] *n* repertorio *m*.

repetition [,repɪ'tɪʃn] *n* repetición *f*.

repetitious [,repɪ'tɪʃəs], **repetitive** [rɪ'petɪtɪv] *adj* repetitivo(va).

replace [rɪ'pleɪs] *vt* **-1.** [take the place of] sustituir. **-2.** [change for something else]: **to ~ sthg (with)** cambiar algo (por). **-3.** [change for somebody else]: **to ~ sb (with)** sustituir a alguien (por). **-4.** [supply another]: **to ~ sthg** dar otro(tra). **-5.** [put back] poner en su sitio.

replacement [rɪ'pleɪsmənt] *n* **-1.** [act of replacing] sustitución *f*. **-2.** [something new]: **~ (for)** sustituto *m*, -ta *f* (para). **-3.** [somebody new]: **~ (for)** sustituto *m*, -ta *f* OR suplente *m y f* (de).

replay [*n* 'ri:pleɪ, *vb* ,ri:'pleɪ] ◇ *n* repetición *f* (*de un partido*). ◇ *vt* [film, tape] volver a poner.

replenish [rɪ'plenɪʃ] *vt fml*: **to ~ sthg (with)** reaprovisionar OR reponer algo (de).

replica ['replɪkə] *n* réplica *f*.

reply [rɪ'plaɪ] ◇ *n*: **~ (to)** respuesta *f* (a). ◇ *vt* responder, contestar. ◇ *vi*: **to ~ (to sb/sthg)** responder (a alguien/algo).

reply coupon *n* cupón *m* de respuesta.

report [rɪ'pɔːt] ◇ *n* **-1.** [gen] informe *m*; PRESS & TV reportaje *m*. **-2.** *Br* SCH boletín *m* de evaluación. ◇ *vt* **-1.** [say, make known]: **to ~ that** informar que, reportar que *Amer*; **to ~ sthg (to)** informar de algo (a). **-2.** [complain about]: **to ~ sb (to sb for sthg)** denunciar a alguien (a alguien por algo), reportar a alguien (a alguien por algo) *Amer*. ◇ *vi* **-1.** [give account]: **to ~ on** informar sobre. **-2.** [present oneself]: **to ~ to sb/for sthg** presentarse a alguien/para algo.

report card *n* boletín *m* de evaluación.

reportedly [rɪ'pɔːtɪdlɪ] *adv* según se afirma.

reporter [rɪ'pɔːtəʳ] *n* reportero *m*, -ra *f*.

repose [rɪ'pəʊz] *n literary* reposo *m*.

repossess [,ri:pə'zes] *vt* requisar la posesión de.

reprehensible [,reprɪ'hensəbl] *adj fml* reprensible.

represent [,reprɪ'zent] *vt* [gen] representar; [person, country] representar a.

representation [,reprɪzen'teɪʃn] *n* [gen] representación *f*. ◆ **representations** *npl fml*: **to make ~s to** presentar una queja a.

representative [,reprɪ'zentətɪv] ◇ *adj*: **~ (of)** representativo(va) (de). ◇ *n* representante *m y f*.

repress [rɪ'pres] *vt* reprimir.

repression [rɪ'preʃn] *n* represión *f*.

reprieve [rɪ'priːv] *n* **-1.** [delay] tregua *f*. **-2.** [of death sentence] indulto *m*.

reprimand ['reprɪmɑːnd] ◇ *n* reprensión *f*. ◇ *vt* reprender.

reprisal [rɪ'praɪzl] *n* represalia *f*.

reproach [rɪ'prəʊtʃ] ◇ *n* reproche *m*. ◇ *vt*: **to ~ sb (for OR with sthg)** reprochar a alguien (algo).

reproachful [rɪ'prəʊtʃfʊl] *adj* de reproche.

reproduce [,ri:prə'djuːs] ◇ *vt* reproducir. ◇ *vi* BIOL reproducirse.

reproduction [,ri:prə'dʌkʃn] *n* reproducción *f*.

reproof [rɪ'pruːf] *n* **-1.** [words of blame] reprobación *f*. **-2.** [disapproval] reproche *m*.

reprove [rɪ'pruːv] *vt*: **to ~ sb (for)** reprobar a alguien (por).

reptile ['reptaɪl] *n* reptil *m*.

republic [rɪ'pʌblɪk] *n* república *f*.

republican [rɪ'pʌblɪkən] ◇ *adj* republicano(na). ◇ *n* republicano *m*, -na *f*. ◆ **Republican** ◇ *adj* **-1.** [in US] republicano(na); **the Republican Party** el partido republicano. **-2.** [in Northern Ireland] independentista. ◇ *n* **-1.** [in US] republicano *m*, -na *f*. **-2.** [in Northern Ireland] independentista *m y f*.

repudiate [rɪ'pjuːdɪeɪt] *vt fml* repudiar.

repulse [rɪ'pʌls] *vt* rechazar.

repulsive [rɪ'pʌlsɪv] *adj* repulsivo(va).

reputable ['repjʊtəbl] *adj* de buena fama OR reputación.

reputation [,repjʊ'teɪʃn] *n* reputación *f*.

repute [rɪ'pjuːt] *n fml*: **of good/ill ~** de buena/mala fama.

reputed [rɪ'pjuːtɪd] *adj* reputado(da); **to be ~ to be/do sthg** tener fama de ser/hacer algo.

reputedly [rɪ'pjuːtɪdlɪ] *adv* según se dice.

request [rɪ'kwest] ◇ *n*: **~ (for)** petición *f* (de); **on ~** a petición del interesado. ◇ *vt* solicitar, pedir; **to ~ sb to do sthg** rogar a alguien que haga algo.

request stop *n Br* parada *f* discrecional.

require [rɪ'kwaɪəʳ] *vt* necesitar, requerir; **to ~ sb to do sthg** exigir a alguien que haga algo.

requirement [rɪ'kwaɪəmənt] *n* requisito *m*.

requisition [,rekwɪ'zɪʃn] *vt* requisar.

rerun ['riː,rʌn] *n* **-1.** [film, programme] reposición *f*. **-2.** [repeated situation] repetición *f*.

resat [,riː'sæt] *pt & pp* → **resit**.

rescind [rɪ'sɪnd] *vt* JUR [contract] rescindir; [law] revocar.

rescue ['reskjuː] ◇ n rescate m. ◇ vt: **to ~ sb/sthg (from)** rescatar a alguien/algo (de).

rescuer ['reskjuəʳ] n rescatador m, -ra f.

research [,rɪ'sɜːtʃ] ◇ n (U): **~ (on** OR **into)** investigación f (de OR sobre); **~ and development** investigación y desarrollo. ◇ vt investigar.

researcher [rɪ'sɜːtʃəʳ] n investigador m, -ra f.

resemblance [rɪ'zembləns] n parecido m, semejanza f.

resemble [rɪ'zembl] vt parecerse a.

resent [rɪ'zent] vt tomarse a mal.

resentful [rɪ'zentful] adj resentido(da).

resentment [rɪ'zentmənt] n resentimiento m.

reservation [,rezə'veɪʃn] n **-1.** [booking] reserva f. **-2.** [uncertainty]: **without ~** sin reserva. **-3.** Am [for Native Americans] reserva f. ◆ **reservations** npl [doubts] reservas fpl.

reserve [rɪ'zɜːv] ◇ n **-1.** [gen] reserva f; **in ~** en reserva. **-2.** SPORT suplente m y f. ◇ vt **-1.** [save, book] reservar. **-2.** [retain]: **to ~ the right to do sthg** reservarse el derecho a hacer algo.

reserved [rɪ'zɜːvd] adj reservado(da).

reservoir ['rezəvwɑːʳ] n [lake] pantano m, embalse m.

reset [,riː'set] (pt & pp reset) vt [clock] poner en hora; [meter, controls, computer] reinicializar.

reshape [,riː'ʃeɪp] vt [policy, thinking] reformar, rehacer.

reshuffle [,riː'ʃʌfl] n remodelación f; **cabinet ~** remodelación del gabinete.

reside [rɪ'zaɪd] vi fml [live] residir.

residence ['rezɪdəns] n **-1.** [house] residencia f. **-2.** [state of residing]: **to be in ~ (at)** residir (en).

residence permit n permiso m de residencia.

resident ['rezɪdənt] ◇ adj **-1.** [settled, living] residente. **-2.** [on-site, live-in] que vive en su lugar de trabajo. ◇ n residente m y f.

residential [,rezɪ'denʃl] adj [live-in] en régimen de internado.

residential area n zona f residencial.

residue ['rezɪdjuː] n residuo m.

resign [rɪ'zaɪn] ◇ vt **-1.** [give up] dimitir de, renunciar a. **-2.** [accept calmly]: **to ~ o.s. to sthg** resignarse a algo. ◇ vi [quit]: **to ~ (from)** dimitir (de).

resignation [,rezɪg'neɪʃn] n **-1.** [from job] dimisión f. **-2.** [calm acceptance] resignación f.

resigned [rɪ'zaɪnd] adj: **~ (to)** resignado(da) (a).

resilient [rɪ'zɪlɪənt] adj [person] resistente, fuerte; [rubber] elástico(ca).

resin ['rezɪn] n resina f.

resist [rɪ'zɪst] vt **-1.** [refuse to accept] resistir, oponerse a. **-2.** [fight against] resistir a. **-3.** [refuse to give in to - temptation] resistir.

resistance [rɪ'zɪstəns] n: **~ (to)** resistencia f (a).

resit [n 'riːsɪt, vb ,riː'sɪt] (pt & pp **-sat**) Br ◇ n (examen m de) repesca f. ◇ vt volver a presentarse a.

resolute ['rezəluːt] adj resuelto(ta), determinado(da).

resolution [,rezə'luːʃn] n **-1.** [gen] resolución f. **-2.** [vow, promise] propósito m.

resolve [rɪ'zɒlv] ◇ n (U) resolución f. ◇ vt **-1.** [vow, promise]: **to ~ that** resolver que; **to ~ to do sthg** resolver hacer algo. **-2.** [solve] resolver.

resort [rɪ'zɔːt] n **-1.** [for holidays] lugar m de vacaciones. **-2.** [solution]: **as a ~ in the last ~** como último recurso. ◆ **resort to** vt fus recurrir a.

resound [rɪ'zaʊnd] vi **-1.** [noise] resonar. **-2.** [place]: **the room ~ed with laughter** la risa resonaba por la habitación.

resounding [rɪ'zaʊndɪŋ] adj **-1.** [loud - noise, knock] retumbante; [- crash] estruendoso(sa). **-2.** [very great] clamoroso(sa).

resource [rɪ'sɔːs] n recurso m.

resourceful [rɪ'sɔːsful] adj de recursos.

respect [rɪ'spekt] ◇ n **-1.** [gen]: **~ (for)** respeto m (por); **with ~** con respeto. **-2.** [aspect] aspecto m; **in this ~** a este respecto; **in that ~** en cuanto a esto. ◇ vt [admire] respetar; **to ~ sb for sthg** respetar a alguien por algo. ◆ **respects** npl: **to pay one's ~s (to)** presentar uno sus respetos (a). ◆ **with respect to** prep con respecto a.

respectable [rɪ'spektəbl] adj respetable.

respectful [rɪ'spektful] adj respetuoso(sa).

respective [rɪ'spektɪv] adj respectivo(va).

respectively [rɪ'spektɪvlɪ] adv respectivamente.

respite ['respaɪt] n **-1.** [lull] respiro m. **-2.** [delay] aplazamiento m.

resplendent [rɪ'splendənt] adj literary resplandeciente.

respond [rɪ'spɒnd] vi: **to ~ (to)** responder (a); **to ~ by doing sthg** responder haciendo algo.

response [rɪ'spɒns] n respuesta f.
responsibility [rɪ,spɒnsə'bɪlətɪ] n: ~ **(for)** responsabilidad f (de).
responsible [rɪ'spɒnsəbl] adj **-1.** [gen] responsable; ~ **(for)** responsable (de). **-2.** [answerable]: ~ **to sb** responsable ante alguien. **-3.** [job, position] de responsabilidad.
responsibly [rɪ'spɒnsəblɪ] adv de manera responsable.
responsive [rɪ'spɒnsɪv] adj **-1.** [quick to react] que responde muy bien. **-2.** [aware]: ~ **(to)** sensible OR perceptivo(va) (a).
rest [rest] ◇ n **-1.** [remainder]: **the ~ (of)** el resto (de). **-2.** [relaxation, break] descanso m; **to have a ~** descansar. **-3.** [support - for feet] descanso m; [- for head] respaldo m. ◇ vt **-1.** [relax - eyes, feet] descansar. **-2.** [support] apoyar, descansar. ◇ vi **-1.** [relax, be still] descansar. **-2.** [depend]: **to ~ on** OR **upon** depender de. **-3.** [be supported] apoyarse, descansar. **-4.** phr: ~ **assured that** ... tenga la seguridad de que ....
restaurant ['restərɒnt] n restaurante m.
restaurant car n Br coche m OR vagón m restaurante.
restful ['restful] adj tranquilo(la), apacible.
rest home n [for the elderly] asilo m de ancianos; [for the sick] casa f de reposo.
restive ['restɪv] adj inquieto(ta).
restless ['restlɪs] adj **-1.** [bored, dissatisfied] impaciente, desasosegado(da). **-2.** [fidgety] inquieto(ta), agitado(da). **-3.** [sleepless] en blanco, agitado(da).
restoration [,restə'reɪʃn] n restauración f.
restore [rɪ'stɔːr] vt **-1.** [reestablish] restablecer. **-2.** [to a previous position or condition]: **to ~ sb to sthg** restaurar a alguien en algo; **to ~ sthg to sthg** volver a poner algo en algo. **-3.** [renovate] restaurar. **-4.** [give back] devolver.
restrain [rɪ'streɪn] vt controlar; **to ~ o.s. from doing sthg** contenerse para no hacer algo.
restrained [rɪ'streɪnd] adj comedido(da).
restraint [rɪ'streɪnt] n **-1.** [rule, check] restricción f. **-2.** [control] (U) control m.
restrict [rɪ'strɪkt] vt [limit] restringir, limitar; **to ~ sthg/sb to** restringir algo/a alguien a.
restriction [rɪ'strɪkʃn] n restricción f.
restrictive [rɪ'strɪktɪv] adj restrictivo(va).

rest room n Am aseos mpl.
result [rɪ'zʌlt] ◇ n resultado m; **as a ~** como resultado. ◇ vi **-1.** [cause]: **to ~ (in sthg)** tener como resultado (algo). **-2.** [be caused]: **to ~ (from)** resultar (de).
resume [rɪ'zjuːm] ◇ vt [start again] reanudar. ◇ vi volver a empezar.
résumé ['rezjuːmeɪ] n **-1.** [summary] resumen m. **-2.** Am [of career, qualifications] currículum m (vitae).
resumption [rɪ'zʌmpʃn] n reanudación f.
resurgence [rɪ'sɜːdʒəns] n resurgimiento m.
resurrection [,rezə'rekʃn] n resurrección f.
resuscitate [rɪ'sʌsɪteɪt] vt resucitar.
retail ['riːteɪl] ◇ n venta f al por menor OR al detalle. ◇ adv al por menor.
retailer ['riːteɪlər] n minorista m y f, detallista m y f.
retail price n precio m de venta al público.
retain [rɪ'teɪn] vt retener.
retainer [rɪ'teɪnər] n [fee] anticipo m.
retaliate [rɪ'tælɪeɪt] vi desquitarse, tomar represalias.
retaliation [rɪ,tælɪ'eɪʃn] n (U) represalias fpl.
retarded [rɪ'tɑːdɪd] adj retrasado(da).
retch [retʃ] vi tener náuseas.
retentive [rɪ'tentɪv] adj retentivo(va).
reticent ['retɪsənt] adj reticente, reservado(da).
retina ['retɪnə] (pl **-nas** OR **-nae** [-niː]) n retina f.
retinue ['retɪnjuː] n séquito m.
retire [rɪ'taɪər] vi **-1.** [from work] jubilarse. **-2.** fml [to another place, to bed] retirarse.
retired [rɪ'taɪəd] adj jubilado(da).
retirement [rɪ'taɪəmənt] n jubilación f, retiro m.
retiring [rɪ'taɪərɪŋ] adj [shy] retraído(da).
retort [rɪ'tɔːt] ◇ n [sharp reply] réplica f. ◇ vt: **to ~ (that)** replicar (que).
retrace [rɪ'treɪs] vt: **to ~ one's steps** desandar lo andado.
retract [rɪ'trækt] ◇ vt **-1.** [withdraw, take back] retractarse de. **-2.** [pull in - claws] retraer. ◇ vi [subj: claws] meterse, retraerse; [subj: wheels] replegarse.
retrain [,riː'treɪn] vt reciclar.
retraining [,riː'treɪnɪŋ] n reciclaje m.
retread ['riːtred] n neumático m recauchutado.

retreat [rɪ'triːt] ◇ n -1. MIL: ~ (from) retirada f (de). -2. [peaceful place] refugio m. ◇ vi [move away]: to ~ (from) [gen] retirarse (de); [from a person] apartarse (de).

retribution [,retrɪ'bjuːʃn] n castigo m merecido.

retrieval [rɪ'triːvl] n COMPUT recuperación f.

retrieve [rɪ'triːv] vt -1. [get back] recobrar. -2. COMPUT recuperar. -3. [rescue - situation] salvar.

retriever [rɪ'triːvər] n perro m cobrador.

retrograde ['retrəgreɪd] adj fml [gen] retrógrado(da); [step] hacia atrás.

retrospect ['retrəspekt] n: in ~ retrospectivamente, mirando hacia atrás.

retrospective [,retrə'spektɪv] adj -1. fml [gen] retrospectivo(va). -2. [law, pay rise] con efecto retroactivo.

return [rɪ'tɜːn] ◇ n -1. (U) [arrival back] vuelta f, regreso m. -2. Br [ticket] billete m de ida y vuelta. -3. [profit] ganancia f, rédito m. ◇ vt -1. [book, visit, compliment] devolver. -2. [reciprocate] corresponder a. -3. [replace] volver a poner en su sitio. -4. JUR [verdict] pronunciar. -5. POL [candidate] elegir. ◇ vi: to ~ (from/to) volver (de/a), regresar (de/a). ◆ returns npl -1. COMM réditos mpl. -2. phr: many happy ~s (of the day)! ¡y que cumplas muchos más! ◆ in return adv en recompensa. ◆ in return for prep en recompensa por.

return (key) n COMPUT tecla f de retorno de carro.

return ticket n Br billete m de ida y vuelta.

reunification [,riːjuːnɪfɪ'keɪʃn] n reunificación f.

reunion [,riː'juːnjən] n reunión f.

reunite [,riːjuː'naɪt] vt [people]: to be ~d with volver a encontrarse OR verse con; [factions, parts] reunir.

rev [rev] inf ◇ n (abbr of revolution) revolución f (motriz). ◇ vt: to ~ sthg (up) acelerar algo. ◇ vi: to ~ (up) acelerar el motor.

revamp [,riː'væmp] vt inf renovar.

reveal [rɪ'viːl] vt revelar.

revealing [rɪ'viːlɪŋ] adj revelador(ra).

reveille [Br rɪ'vælɪ, Am 'revəlɪ] n toque m de diana.

revel ['revl] vi: to ~ in deleitarse en.

revelation [,revə'leɪʃn] n revelación f.

revenge [rɪ'vendʒ] n venganza f; to take ~ (on sb) vengarse (en alguien).

revenue ['revənjuː] n ingresos mpl.

reverberate [rɪ'vɜːbəreɪt] vi -1. [reecho] resonar, retumbar. -2. [have repercussions] repercutir.

reverberations [rɪ,vɜːbə'reɪʃnz] npl -1. [echoes] reverberación f. -2. [repercussions] repercusiones fpl.

revere [rɪ'vɪər] vt fml venerar.

reverence ['revərəns] n fml reverencia f.

Reverend ['revərənd] n reverendo m.

reverie ['revərɪ] n fml ensueño m.

reversal [rɪ'vɜːsl] n -1. [turning around] cambio m total. -2. [ill fortune] contratiempo m.

reverse [rɪ'vɜːs] ◇ adj inverso(sa). ◇ n -1. AUT: ~ (gear) marcha f atrás. -2. [opposite]: the ~ lo contrario. -3. [opposite side, back]: the ~ [gen] el revés; [of coin] el reverso; [of piece of paper] el dorso. ◇ vt -1. AUT dar marcha atrás a. -2. [change usual order] invertir. -3. [change to opposite] cambiar completamente. -4. Br TELEC: to ~ the charges llamar a cobro revertido. ◇ vi AUT dar marcha atrás.

reverse-charge call n Br llamada f a cobro revertido.

reversing light [rɪ'vɜːsɪŋ-] n Br luz f de marcha atrás.

revert [rɪ'vɜːt] vi: to ~ to volver a.

review [rɪ'vjuː] ◇ n -1. [examination] revisión f, repaso m. -2. [critique] reseña f. ◇ vt -1. [reexamine] revisar. -2. [consider] reconsiderar. -3. [write an article on] reseñar. -4. Am [study again] repasar.

reviewer [rɪ'vjuːər] n crítico m, -ca f.

revile [rɪ'vaɪl] vt literary injuriar.

revise [rɪ'vaɪz] ◇ vt -1. [reconsider] revisar. -2. [rewrite] modificar, corregir. -3. Br [study] repasar. ◇ vi Br: to ~ (for sthg) repasar (para algo).

revision [rɪ'vɪʒn] n -1. [alteration] corrección f, modificación f. -2. Br [study] repaso m.

revitalize, -ise [,riː'vaɪtəlaɪz] vt revivificar.

revival [rɪ'vaɪvl] n reactivación f.

revive [rɪ'vaɪv] ◇ vt -1. [person, plant] resucitar; [economy] reactivar. -2. [tradition, play, memories] restablecer. ◇ vi reponerse.

revolt [rɪ'vəʊlt] ◇ n rebelión f. ◇ vt repugnar. ◇ vi: to ~ (against) rebelarse OR sublevarse (contra).

revolting [rɪ'vəʊltɪŋ] adj repugnante, asqueroso(sa).

revolution [,revə'luːʃn] n revolución f.

revolutionary [revə'luːʃnərɪ] ◇ *adj* revolucionario(ria). ◇ *n* revolucionario *m*, -ria *f*.

revolve [rɪ'vɒlv] *vi* [go round] dar vueltas, girar.

revolver [rɪ'vɒlvəʳ] *n* revólver *m*.

revolving [rɪ'vɒlvɪŋ] *adj* giratorio(ria).

revolving door *n* puerta *f* giratoria.

revue [rɪ'vjuː] *n* revista *f* (teatral).

revulsion [rɪ'vʌlʃn] *n* asco *m*, repugnancia *f*.

reward [rɪ'wɔːd] ◇ *n* recompensa *f*, premio *m*. ◇ *vt*: **to ~ sb (for/with)** recompensar a alguien (por/con).

rewarding [rɪ'wɔːdɪŋ] *adj* gratificador(ra).

rewind [,riː'waɪnd] (*pt* & *pp* **rewound**) *vt* rebobinar.

rewire [,riː'waɪəʳ] *vt* cambiar la instalación eléctrica de.

reword [,riː'wɜːd] *vt* expresar de otra forma.

rewound [,riː'waʊnd] *pt* & *pp* → **rewind**.

rewrite [,riː'raɪt] (*pt* **rewrote** [,riː'rəʊt], *pp* **rewritten** [,riː'rɪtn]) *vt* volver a escribir.

Reykjavik ['rekjəvɪk] *n* Reykjavik.

rhapsody ['ræpsədɪ] *n* MUS rapsodia *f*.

rhetoric ['retərɪk] *n* retórica *f*.

rhetorical question [rɪ'tɒrɪkl-] *n* pregunta *f* retórica (*a la que no se espera contestación*).

rheumatism ['ruːmətɪzm] *n* reumatismo *m*.

Rhine [raɪn] *n*: **the ~** el Rin.

rhino ['raɪnəʊ] (*pl inv* OR **-s**), **rhinoceros** [raɪ'nɒsərəs] (*pl inv* OR **-es**) *n* rinoceronte *m*.

rhododendron [,rəʊdə'dendrən] *n* rododendro *m*.

Rhône [rəʊn] *n*: **the (River) ~** el (río) Ródano.

rhubarb ['ruːbɑːb] *n* ruibarbo *m*.

rhyme [raɪm] ◇ *n* **-1.** [gen] rima *f*. **-2.** [poem] poesía *f*, versos *mpl*. ◇ *vi*: **to ~ (with)** rimar (con).

rhythm ['rɪðm] *n* ritmo *m*.

rib [rɪb] *n* **-1.** ANAT costilla *f*. **-2.** [of umbrella] varilla *f*.

ribbed [rɪbd] *adj* de canalé.

ribbon ['rɪbən] *n* cinta *f*.

rice [raɪs] *n* arroz *m*.

rice pudding *n* arroz *m* con leche.

rich [rɪtʃ] ◇ *adj* **-1.** [gen] rico(ca). **-2.** [full]: **to be ~ in** abundar en. **-3.** [fertile] fértil. **-4.** [indigestible] pesado(da). ◇

npl: **the ~** los ricos. ◆ **riches** *npl* **-1.** [natural resources] riquezas *fpl*. **-2.** [wealth] riqueza *f*.

richly ['rɪtʃlɪ] *adv* **-1.** [well - rewarded] ricamente. **-2.** [plentifully] copiosamente.

richness ['rɪtʃnɪs] *n* **-1.** [gen] riqueza *f*. **-2.** [fertility] fertilidad *f*. **-3.** [indigestibility] pesadez *f*.

rickety ['rɪkətɪ] *adj* desvencijado(da).

rickshaw ['rɪkʃɔː] *n* jinrikisha *f*.

ricochet ['rɪkəʃeɪ] (*pt* & *pp* **-ed** OR **-ted**, *cont* **-ing** OR **-ting**) ◇ *n* rebote *m*. ◇ *vi*: **to ~ (off)** rebotar (de).

rid [rɪd] (*pt* **rid** OR **-ded**, *pp* **rid**) *vt*: **to ~ sthg/sb** of librar algo/a alguien de; **to get ~ of** deshacerse de.

ridden ['rɪdn] *pp* → **ride**.

riddle ['rɪdl] *n* **-1.** [verbal puzzle] acertijo *m*. **-2.** [mystery] enigma *m*.

riddled ['rɪdld] *adj*: **to be ~ with** estar plagado(da) de.

ride [raɪd] (*pt* **rode**, *pp* **ridden**) ◇ *n* paseo *m*; **to go for a ~** [on horseback] darse un paseo a caballo; [on bike] darse un paseo en bicicleta; [in car] darse una vuelta en coche; **to take sb for a ~ inf** *fig* embaucar a alguien. ◇ *vt* **-1.** [horse] montar a. **-2.** [bicycle, motorbike] montar en; **he rode his bike to the station** fue a la estación en bici. **-3.** *Am* [bus, train] ir en; [elevator] subir/bajar en. **-4.** [distance] recorrer. ◇ *vi* **-1.** [on horseback] montar a caballo; **she rode over to see me** vino a verme a caballo. **-2.** [on bicycle] ir en bici; [on motorbike] ir en moto. **-3.** [in car]: **we rode to London in a jeep** fuimos a Londres en jeep.

rider ['raɪdəʳ] *n* **-1.** [on horseback] jinete *m*, amazona *f*. **-2.** [on bicycle] ciclista *m* y *f*; [on motorbike] motorista *m* y *f*.

ridge [rɪdʒ] *n* **-1.** [on mountain] cresta *f*. **-2.** [on flat surface] rugosidad *f*.

ridicule ['rɪdɪkjuːl] ◇ *n* (*U*) burlas *fpl*. ◇ *vt* ridiculizar.

ridiculous [rɪ'dɪkjʊləs] *adj* ridículo(la).

riding ['raɪdɪŋ] *n* equitación *f*.

riding school *n* escuela *f* de equitación.

rife [raɪf] *adj* extendido(da); **to be ~ with** estar lleno de.

riffraff ['rɪfræf] *n* gentuza *f*.

rifle ['raɪfl] ◇ *n* rifle *m*, fusil *m*. ◇ *vt* desvalijar.

rifle range *n* campo *m* de tiro.

rift [rɪft] *n* **-1.** GEOL hendedura *f*, grieta *f*. **-2.** [quarrel] desavenencia *f*. **-3.** POL: **~ between/in** escisión *f* entre/en.

rig [rɪg] ◇ n: **(oil)** ~ [onshore] torre f de perforación; [offshore] **plataforma** f petrolífera. ◆ vt [falsify] **amañar, falsificar.** ◆**rig up** vt sep construir, armar.

rigging ['rɪgɪŋ] n cordaje m.

right [raɪt] ◇ adj **-1.** [correct] **correcto(ta), bueno(na); to be ~ (about)** tener razón (respecto a); **get it ~!** ¡hazlo bien! **-2.** [satisfactory] **bien. -3.** [morally correct, socially acceptable] **apropiado(da); to be ~ to do sthg** hacer bien en hacer algo. **-4.** [uppermost]: ~ **side** cara f anterior OR de arriba. **-5.** [on right-hand side] **derecho(cha). ◇ n -1.** (U) [moral correctness] **bien** m; **to be in the ~** tener razón. **-2.** [entitlement, claim] **derecho** m; **by ~s** en justicia. **-3.** [right-hand side] **derecha** f. ◇ adv **-1.** [correctly] **bien, correctamente. -2.** [to right-hand side] **a la derecha. -3.** [emphatic use]: ~ **here** aquí mismo; ~ **at the top** arriba del todo; ~ **in the middle** justo en el medio. **-4.** [immediately]: **I'll be ~ back** ahora mismo vuelvo; ~ **before/after (sthg)** justo antes/después (de algo); ~ **now** ahora mismo, ahorita Amer; ~ **away** en seguida. ◇ vt **-1.** [correct] **corregir, rectificar. -2.** [make upright] **enderezar.** ◇ excl **¡bien!** ◆**Right** n POL: **the Right** la derecha.

right angle n ángulo m recto; **at ~s (to)** en ángulo recto (con).

righteous ['raɪtʃəs] adj [anger] **justo(ta);** [person] **honrado(da).**

rightful ['raɪtfʊl] adj **legítimo(ma).**

right-hand adj **derecho(cha); the ~ side** el lado derecho, la derecha.

right-hand drive adj que se conduce por la derecha.

right-handed [-'hændɪd] adj **diestro(tra).**

right-hand man n **brazo** m derecho.

rightly ['raɪtlɪ] adv **-1.** [correctly] **correctamente. -2.** [appropriately] **debidamente, bien. -3.** [morally] **con razón.**

right of way n **-1.** AUT **prioridad** f. **-2.** [access] **derecho** m de paso.

right-on adj inf **esnob.**

right wing n: **the ~** la derecha. ◆**right-wing** adj **derechista.**

rigid ['rɪdʒɪd] adj **-1.** [stiff] **rígido(da). -2.** [harsh, unbending] **inflexible.**

rigmarole ['rɪgmərəʊl] n inf pej **-1.** [process] **ritual** m. **-2.** [story] **galimatías** m inv.

rigor Am = **rigour.**

rigorous ['rɪgərəs] adj **riguroso(sa).**

rigour Br, **rigor** Am ['rɪgər] n [firmness] **rigor** m, **severidad** f.

rile [raɪl] vt **irritar, sacar de quicio.**

rim [rɪm] n **-1.** [of container] **borde** m. **-2.** [of spectacles] **montura** f.

rind [raɪnd] n **corteza** f.

ring [rɪŋ] (pt **rang**, pp **rung** vt senses 1 & 2 & vi, pt & pp **ringed** vt senses 3 & 4 only) ◇ n **-1.** [telephone call]: **to give sb a ~** llamar a alguien (por teléfono). **-2.** [sound of doorbell] **timbrazo** m. **-3.** [metal hoop] **aro** m; [for curtains] **anilla** f. **-4.** [on finger] **anillo** m. **-5.** [circle - of trees] **círculo** m; [- of people] **corro** m. **-6.** [for boxing] **cuadrilátero** m. **-7.** [illegal group] **cartel** m. ◇ vt **-1.** Br [phone] **llamar por teléfono, telefonear. -2.** [bell] **tocar. -3.** [draw a circle round] **señalar con un círculo. -4.** [surround] **rodear.** ◇ vi **-1.** Br [phone] **llamar por teléfono, telefonear. -2.** [bell] **sonar. -3.** [to attract attention]: **to ~ (for)** llamar (para). **-4.** [resound]: **to ~ with** resonar con. ◆**ring back** vt sep & vi Br volver a llamar. ◆**ring off** vi Br colgar. ◆**ring up** vt sep Br llamar (por teléfono).

ring binder n carpeta f de anillas.

ringing ['rɪŋɪŋ] n [of bell] **repique** m, **tañido** m; [in ears] **zumbido** m.

ringing tone n tono m de llamada.

ringleader ['rɪŋ,liːdər] n cabecilla m y f.

ringlet ['rɪŋlət] n rizo m, tirabuzón m.

ring road n Br carretera f de circunvalación.

rink [rɪŋk] n pista f.

rinse [rɪns] vt **-1.** [dishes, vegetables] **enjuagar;** [clothes] **aclarar. -2.** [wash out]: **to ~ one's mouth out** enjuagarse la boca.

riot ['raɪət] ◇ n disturbio m; **to run ~** desbocarse. ◇ vi **amotinarse.**

rioter ['raɪətər] n amotinado m, -da f.

riotous ['raɪətəs] adj **ruidoso(sa).**

riot police npl brigada f antidisturbios.

rip [rɪp] ◇ n rasgón m. ◇ vt **-1.** [tear] **rasgar, desgarrar. -2.** [remove violently] **quitar de un tirón.** ◇ vi **rasgarse, romperse.**

RIP (abbr of **rest in peace**) RIP.

ripe [raɪp] adj **maduro(ra); to be ~ (for sthg)** estar listo (para algo).

ripen ['raɪpn] vt & vi **madurar.**

rip-off n inf **estafa** f.

ripple ['rɪpl] ◇ n **-1.** [in water] **onda** f, **rizo** m. **-2.** [of laughter, applause] **murmullo** m. ◇ vt **rizar.**

rise [raɪz] (pt **rose**, pp **risen** ['rɪzn]) ◇ n **-1.** [increase] **ascenso** m. **-2.** Br [increase in salary] **aumento** m. **-3.** [to fame etc] **subida** f. **-4.** phr: **to give ~ to sthg** dar origen a algo. ◇ vi **-1.** [gen] **elevarse. -2.** [sun, moon] **salir. -3.** [price, wage, temperature] **subir. -4.** [stand up, get out of bed] **levantarse. -5.** [street, ground] **subir. -6.** [respond]: **to ~ to reaccionar ante. -7.** [rebel] **sublevarse. -8.** [move up in status] **ascender; to ~ to power/ fame** ascender al poder/a la gloria.

rising ['raɪzɪŋ] ◇ adj **-1.** [sloping upwards] **ascendente. -2.** [increasing] **creciente. -3.** [increasingly successful] **prometedor(ra).** ◇ n **rebelión** f.

risk [rɪsk] ◇ n [gen] **riesgo** m; [danger] **peligro** m; **to run the ~ of sthg/of doing sthg** correr el riesgo de algo/de hacer algo; **to take a ~** **arriesgarse; at your own ~** bajo tu cuenta y riesgo; **at ~ en peligro.** ◇ vt **-1.** [put in danger] **arriesgar. -2.** [take the chance of]: **to ~ doing sthg** exponerse a hacer algo.

risky ['rɪskɪ] adj **peligroso(sa), arriesgado(da).**

risqué ['riːskeɪ] adj **subido(da)** de tono.

rissole ['rɪsəʊl] n Br especie de albóndiga de carne o verduras.

rite [raɪt] n **rito** m.

ritual ['rɪtʃʊəl] ◇ adj **ritual.** ◇ n **ritual** m.

rival ['raɪvl] ◇ adj **rival, opuesto(ta).** ◇ n **rival** m y f, **competidor** m, **-ra** f. ◇ vt **rivalizar** OR **competir con.**

rivalry ['raɪvlrɪ] n **rivalidad** f, **competencia** f.

river ['rɪvər] n **río** m.

river bank n **orilla** f OR **margen** f del río.

riverbed ['rɪvəbed] n **cauce** m OR **lecho** m del río.

riverside ['rɪvəsaɪd] n: **the ~** la ribera OR orilla del río.

rivet ['rɪvɪt] ◇ n **remache** m. ◇ vt **-1.** [fasten] **remachar. -2.** fig [fascinate]: **to be ~ed by sthg** estar fascinado(da) con algo.

Riviera [ˌrɪvɪ'eərə] n: **the French ~** la Riviera francesa.

road [rəʊd] n [minor] **camino** m; [major] **carretera** f; [street] **calle** f; **to be on the ~ to** fig estar en camino de.

roadblock ['rəʊdblɒk] n **control** m.

road hog n inf pej conductor rápido y negligente.

road map n **mapa** m de carreteras.

road safety n **seguridad** f en carretera.

roadside ['rəʊdsaɪd] n: **the ~** el borde de la carretera.

road sign n **señal** f de carretera.

road tax n **impuesto** m de circulación.

roadway ['rəʊdweɪ] n **calzada** f.

road works npl **obras** fpl de carretera.

roadworthy ['rəʊdˌwɜːðɪ] adj **apto(ta)** para circular.

roam [rəʊm] ◇ vt **vagar.** ◇ vi **vagar por.**

roar [rɔːr] ◇ vi [make a loud noise] **rugir, bramar; to ~ with laughter** reírse a carcajadas. ◇ vt **rugir, decir a voces.** ◇ n **-1.** [of traffic] **fragor** m. **-2.** [of lion, person] **rugido** m.

roaring ['rɔːrɪŋ] adj **-1.** [loud] **clamoroso(sa). -2.** [fire] **espectacular. -3.** [as emphasis]: **to do a ~ trade** hacer un gran negocio.

roast [rəʊst] ◇ adj **asado(da).** ◇ n **asado** m. ◇ vt **-1.** [potatoes, meat] **asar. -2.** [nuts, coffee beans] **tostar.**

roast beef n **rosbif** m.

rob [rɒb] vt **robar; to ~ sb of sthg** lit & fig robar a alguien algo.

robber ['rɒbər] n **ladrón** m, **-ona** f.

robbery ['rɒbərɪ] n **robo** m.

robe [rəʊb] n **-1.** [towelling] **albornoz** m. **-2.** [of student] **toga** f. **-3.** [of priest] **sotana** f. **-4.** Am [dressing gown] **bata** f.

robin ['rɒbɪn] n **petirrojo** m.

robot ['rəʊbɒt] n **robot** m.

robust [rəʊ'bʌst] adj **robusto(ta), fuerte.**

rock [rɒk] ◇ n **-1.** (U) [substance] **roca** f. **-2.** [boulder] **peñasco** m. **-3.** Am [pebble] **guijarro** m. **-4.** [music] **rock** m. **-5.** Br [sweet] **palo** m de caramelo. ◇ comp de rock. ◇ vt [cause to move] **mecer, balancear.** ◇ vi **mecerse.** ◆ **Rock** n inf [Gibraltar]: **the Rock** el Peñón. ◆ **on the rocks** adv **-1.** [drink] **con hielo. -2.** [marriage, relationship] **que va mal.**

rock and roll n **rock and roll** m.

rock bottom n **el fondo; to hit ~ tocar fondo.** ◆ **rock-bottom** adj: **rock-bottom prices** precios muy bajos.

rockery ['rɒkərɪ] n **jardín** m de rocas.

rocket ['rɒkɪt] n **cohete** m.

rocket launcher [-ˌlɔːntʃər] n **lanzacohetes** m inv.

rocking chair ['rɒkɪŋ-] n **mecedora** f.

rocking horse ['rɒkɪŋ-] n **caballo** m de balancín.

rock'n'roll [ˌrɒkən'rəʊl] = **rock and roll.**

rocky ['rɒkɪ] adj [full of rocks] **rocoso(sa).**

Rocky Mountains npl: **the ~** las montañas Rocosas.

rod [rɒd] n [wooden] vara f; [metal] barra f; [for fishing] caña f.
rode [rəʊd] pt → ride.
rodent ['rəʊdənt] n roedor m.
roe [rəʊ] n hueva f.
roe deer n corzo m.
rogue [rəʊg] n [likeable rascal] picaruelo m, -la f.
role [rəʊl] n THEATRE & fig papel m.
roll [rəʊl] ◇ n -1. [gen] rollo m; [of paper, banknotes] fajo m; [of cloth] pieza f. -2. [of bread] panecillo m. -3. [list] lista f; [payroll] nómina f. -4. [of drums] redoble m; [of thunder] retumbo m. ◇ vt -1. [turn over] hacer rodar. -2. [roll up] enrollar. -3. [cigarette] liar. ◇ vi -1. [ball, barrel] rodar. -2. [vehicle] ir, avanzar. -3. [ship] balancearse. -4. [thunder] retumbar; [drum] redoblar. ◆ **roll about**, **roll around** vi: to ~ about OR around (on) rodar (por). ◆ **roll in** vi inf llegar a raudales. ◆ **roll over** vi darse la vuelta. ◆ **roll up** ◇ vt sep -1. [make into roll] enrollar. -2. [sleeves] remangarse. ◇ vi -1. [vehicle] llegar. -2. inf [person] presentarse, aparecer.
roll call n: to take a ~ pasar lista.
roller ['rəʊlər] n -1. [cylinder] rodillo m. -2. [curler] rulo m.
roller coaster n montaña f rusa.
roller skate n patín m de ruedas.
rolling ['rəʊlɪŋ] adj -1. [undulating] ondulante. -2. phr: to be ~ in it inf nadar en la abundancia.
rolling pin n rodillo m (de cocina).
rolling stock n material m rodante.
roll-on adj [deodorant etc] de bola.
ROM [rɒm] (abbr of read only memory) n ROM f.
Roman ['rəʊmən] ◇ adj romano(na). ◇ n romano m, -na f.
Roman Catholic ◇ adj católico (romano) (católica (romana)). ◇ n católico (romano) m, católica (romana) f.
romance [rəʊˈmæns] n -1. [romantic quality] lo romántico. -2. [love affair] amorío m. -3. [in fiction - modern] novela f romántica.
Romania [ruːˈmeɪnjə] n Rumanía.
Romanian [ruːˈmeɪnjən] ◇ adj rumano(na). ◇ n -1. [person] rumano m, -na f. -2. [language] rumano m.
Roman numerals npl números mpl romanos.
romantic [rəʊˈmæntɪk] adj romántico(ca).
Rome [rəʊm] n Roma.

romp [rɒmp] ◇ n retozo m, jugueteo m. ◇ vi retozar, juguetear.
rompers ['rɒmpəz] npl, **romper suit** ['rɒmpər-] n pelele m.
roof [ruːf] n -1. [of building] tejado m; [of vehicle] techo m; **to go through** OR **hit the ~** [person] subirse por las paredes. -2. [of mouth] paladar m.
roofing ['ruːfɪŋ] n techumbre f.
roof rack n baca f, portaequipajes m inv.
rooftop ['ruːftɒp] n tejado m.
rook [rʊk] n -1. [bird] grajo m. -2. [chess piece] torre f.
rookie ['rʊkɪ] n Am inf novato m, -ta f.
room [ruːm, rʊm] n -1. [in house, building] habitación f. -2. [for conferences etc] sala f. -3. [bedroom] habitación f, cuarto m. -4. (U) [space] sitio m, espacio m.
rooming house ['ruːmɪŋ-] n Am casa f de huéspedes, pensión f.
roommate ['ruːmmeɪt] n compañero m, -ra f de habitación.
room service n servicio m de habitación.
roomy ['ruːmɪ] adj espacioso(sa), amplio(plia).
roost [ruːst] n percha f, palo m.
rooster ['ruːstər] n gallo m.
root [ruːt] ◇ n lit & fig raíz f; **to take ~** lit & fig arraigar. ◇ vi [pig etc] hozar; [person] hurgar, escarbar. ◆ **roots** npl [origins] raíces fpl. ◆ **root for** vt fus Am inf apoyar a. ◆ **root out** vt sep [eradicate] desarraigar.
rope [rəʊp] ◇ n [thin] cuerda f; [thick] soga f; NAUT maroma f, cable m; **to know the ~s** saber de qué va el asunto. ◇ vt atar con cuerda. ◆ **rope in** vt sep inf arrastrar OR enganchar a.
rosary ['rəʊzərɪ] n rosario m.
rose [rəʊz] ◇ pt → rise. ◇ adj [pink] rosa, color de rosa. ◇ n [flower] rosa f.
rosé ['rəʊzeɪ] n rosado m.
rosebud ['rəʊzbʌd] n capullo m de rosa.
rose bush n rosal m.
rosemary ['rəʊzmərɪ] n romero m.
rosette [rəʊˈzet] n [badge] escarapela f.
roster ['rɒstər] n lista f.
rostrum ['rɒstrəm] (pl **-trums** OR **-tra** [-trə]) n tribuna f.
rosy ['rəʊzɪ] adj -1. [pink] sonrosado(da). -2. [hopeful] prometedor(ra).
rot [rɒt] ◇ n (U) -1. [of wood, food] podredumbre f; [in society, organization] decadencia f. -2. Br dated [nonsense] tonterías fpl. ◇ vt pudrir. ◇ vi pudrirse.

rota ['rəʊtə] *n* lista *f* (de turnos).

rotary ['rəʊtərɪ] ◇ *adj* giratorio(ria), rotativo(va). ◇ *n Am* [roundabout] glorieta *f*, cruce *m* de circulación giratoria.

rotate [rəʊ'teɪt] ◇ *vt* [turn] hacer girar, dar vueltas a. ◇ *vi* [turn] girar, dar vueltas.

rotation [rəʊ'teɪʃn] *n* [gen] rotación *f*.

rote [rəʊt] *n*: by ~ de memoria.

rotten ['rɒtn] *adj* -1. [decayed] podrido(da). -2. *inf* [poor-quality] malísimo(ma), fatal. -3. *inf* [unpleasant] despreciable. -4. *inf* [unwell]: to feel ~ sentirse fatal OR muy mal.

rouge [ruːʒ] *n* colorete *m*.

rough [rʌf] ◇ *adj* -1. [not smooth - surface, skin] áspero(ra); [- ground, road] desigual. -2. [not gentle, brutal] bruto(ta). -3. [crude, not refined - person, manner] grosero(ra), tosco(ca); [- shelter] precario(ria); [- food, living conditions] simple. -4. [approximate - plan, sketch] a grandes rasgos; [- estimate, translation] aproximado(da). -5. [unpleasant] duro(ra), difícil. -6. [wind] violento(ta); [sea] picado(da); [weather, day] tormentoso(sa). -7. [harsh - wine, voice] áspero(ra). -8. [violent - area] peligroso(sa); [- person] violento(ta). ◇ *adv*: to sleep ~ dormir a raso. ◇ *n* -1. GOLF: the ~ el rough. -2. [undetailed form]: in ~ en borrador. ◇ *vt phr*: to ~ it vivir sin comodidades.

roughage ['rʌfɪdʒ] *n* (U) fibra *f*.

rough and ready *adj* tosco(ca).

roughcast ['rʌfkɑːst] *n* mortero *m* grueso.

roughen ['rʌfn] *vt* poner áspero(ra).

roughly ['rʌflɪ] *adv* -1. [approximately] más o menos. -2. [not gently] brutalmente. -3. [crudely] toscamente.

roulette [ruː'let] *n* ruleta *f*.

round [raʊnd] ◇ *adj* redondo(da). ◇ *prep* -1. [surrounding] alrededor de. -2. [near] cerca de; ~ here por aquí. -3. [all over - the world etc] por todo(da). -4. [in circular movement]: ~ (and ~) alrededor de. -5. [in measurements]: she's 30 inches ~ the waist mide 30 pulgadas de cintura. -6. [at or to the other side of]: they were waiting ~ the corner esperaban a la vuelta de la esquina; to drive ~ the corner doblar la esquina; to go ~ sthg rodear algo. -7. [so as to avoid]: he drove ~ the pothole condujo esquivando el bache. ◇ *adv* -1. [on all sides]: all ~ por todos lados. -2. [near]: ~ about alrededor, en las proximida-

des. -3. [all over]: to travel ~ viajar por ahí. -4. [in circular movement]: ~ (and ~) en redondo; to go OR spin ~ girar. -5. [in measurements] en redondo. -6. [to the other side] al otro lado; to go ~ dar un rodeo. -7. [at or to nearby place]: he came ~ to see us vino a vernos. ◇ *n* -1. [of talks, drinks] ronda *f*; a ~ of applause una salva de aplausos. -2. [in championship] vuelta *f*. -3. [of doctor] visita *f*; [of milkman, postman] recorrido *m*. -4. [of ammunition] cartucho *m*. -5. [in boxing] asalto *m*. -6. [in golf] vuelta *f*. ◇ *vt* doblar. ◆ **rounds** *npl* [of doctor] visitas *fpl*; [of postman] recorrido *m*; to do OR go the ~s [joke, rumour] divulgarse; [illness] estar rodando. ◆ **round off** *vt sep* terminar. ◆ **round up** *vt sep* -1. [gather together] reunir. -2. MATH redondear.

roundabout ['raʊndəbaʊt] *n Br* -1. [on road] glorieta *f*, cruce *m* de circulación giratoria. -2. [at fairground] tiovivo *m*.

rounders ['raʊndəz] *n Br juego parecido al béisbol.*

roundly ['raʊndlɪ] *adv* rotundamente.

round-shouldered [-'ʃəʊldəd] *adj* cargado(da) de espaldas.

round trip *n* viaje *m* de ida y vuelta.

roundup ['raʊndʌp] *n* [summary] resumen *m*.

rouse [raʊz] *vt* -1. *fml* [wake up] despertar. -2. [impel]: to ~ sb/o.s. to do sthg animar a alguien/animarse a hacer algo. -3. [excite] excitar.

rousing ['raʊzɪŋ] *adj* [speech] conmovedor(ra); [cheer] entusiasta.

rout [raʊt] ◇ *n* derrota *f* aplastante. ◇ *vt* derrotar, aplastar.

route [ruːt] ◇ *n* [gen] ruta *f*; [of bus] línea *f*, recorrido *m*; [of ship] rumbo *m*.

route map *n* plano *m* (del camino).

routine [ruː'tiːn] ◇ *adj* rutinario(ria). ◇ *n* rutina *f*.

roving ['rəʊvɪŋ] *adj* volante, itinerante.

row[1] [rəʊ] ◇ *n* -1. [line] fila *f*, hilera *f*. -2. [succession] serie *f*; three in a ~ tres seguidos. ◇ *vt* [boat] remar. ◇ *vi* remar.

row[2] [raʊ] ◇ *n* -1. [quarrel] pelea *f*, bronca *f*. -2. *inf* [noise] estruendo *m*, ruido *m*. ◇ *vi* [quarrel] reñir, pelearse.

rowboat ['rəʊbəʊt] *n Am* bote *m* de remos.

rowdy ['raʊdɪ] *adj* [noisy] ruidoso(sa); [quarrelsome] pendenciero(ra).

row house [rəʊ-] *n Am* casa *f* adosada.

rowing ['rəʊɪŋ] *n* remo *m*.

rowing boat n bote m de remo.

royal ['rɔɪəl] ◇ adj real. ◇ n inf miembro m de la familia real.

Royal Air Force n: the ~ las Fuerzas Aéreas de Gran Bretaña.

royal family n familia f real.

Royal Mail n Br: the ~ ≃ Correos m.

Royal Navy n: the ~ la Armada de Gran Bretaña.

royalty ['rɔɪəltɪ] n realeza f. ◆ **royalties** npl derechos mpl de autor.

rpm (abbr of **revolutions per minute**) r.p.m. fpl.

RSPCA (abbr of **Royal Society for the Prevention of Cruelty to Animals**) n sociedad británica protectora de animales, ≃ SPA f.

RSVP (abbr of **répondez s'il vous plaît**) s.r.c.

Rt Hon (abbr of **Right Honourable**) su Sría.

rub [rʌb] ◇ vt: to ~ sthg (against OR on) frotar algo (en OR contra); to ~ sthg on OR onto frotar algo en; to ~ sthg in OR into frotar algo en; to ~ sb up the wrong way Br, to ~ sb the wrong way Am sacar a alguien de quicio. ◇ vi: to ~ (against sthg) rozar (algo); to ~ (together) rozarse. ◆ **rub off on** vt fus [subj: quality] influir en. ◆ **rub out** vt sep [erase] borrar.

rubber ['rʌbə'] n -1. [substance] goma f, caucho m. -2. Br [eraser] goma f de borrar. -3. Am inf [condom] goma f. -4. [in bridge] partida f.

rubber band n gomita f, goma f.

rubber plant n ficus m inv.

rubber stamp n estampilla f. ◆ **rubber-stamp** vt aprobar oficialmente.

rubbish ['rʌbɪʃ] n (U) -1. [refuse] basura f. -2. inf fig [worthless matter] porquería f. -3. inf [nonsense] tonterías fpl.

rubbish bin n Br cubo m de la basura.

rubbish dump n Br vertedero m, basurero m.

rubble ['rʌbl] n (U) escombros mpl.

ruby ['ru:bɪ] n rubí m.

rucksack ['rʌksæk] n mochila f.

ructions ['rʌkʃnz] npl inf bronca f.

rudder ['rʌdə'] n timón m.

ruddy ['rʌdɪ] adj -1. [reddish] rojizo(za). -2. Br dated [for emphasis] maldito(ta).

rude [ru:d] adj -1. [impolite - person, manners, word] grosero(ra), liso(sa) Amer; [- joke] verde. -2. [shocking] violento(ta), brusco(ca).

rudimentary [,ru:dɪ'mentərɪ] adj rudimentario(ria).

rueful ['ru:ful] adj arrepentido(da).

ruffian ['rʌfjən] n rufián m.

ruffle ['rʌfl] vt -1. [hair] despeinar; [water] agitar; [feathers] encrespar. -2. [composure, nerves] encrespar.

rug [rʌg] n -1. [carpet] alfombra f. -2. [blanket] manta f de viaje.

rugby ['rʌgbɪ] n rugby m.

rugged ['rʌgɪd] adj -1. [wild, inhospitable] escabroso(sa). -2. [sturdy] fuerte. -3. [roughly handsome] duro y atractivo (dura y atractiva).

rugger ['rʌgə'] n Br inf rugby m.

ruin ['ru:ɪn] ◇ n ruina f. ◇ vt -1. [destroy] arruinar, estropear. -2. [bankrupt] arruinar. ◆ **in ruin(s)** adv en ruinas.

rule [ru:l] ◇ n -1. [regulation, guideline] regla f, norma f. -2. [norm]: the ~ la norma; as a ~ por regla general. -3. [government] dominio m. -4. [ruler] regla f. ◇ vt -1. fml [control] regir. -2. [govern] gobernar. -3. [decide]: to ~ that decidir OR ordenar que. ◇ vi -1. [give decision] decidir, fallar. -2. fml [be paramount] ser primordial. -3. [govern] gobernar. ◆ **rule out** vt sep descartar.

ruled [ru:ld] adj rayado(da).

ruler ['ru:lə'] n -1. [for measurement] regla f. -2. [monarch] soberano m, -na f.

ruling ['ru:lɪŋ] ◇ adj en el poder. ◇ n fallo m, decisión f.

rum [rʌm] n ron m.

Rumania [ru:'meɪnjə] = **Romania**.

Rumanian [ru:'meɪnjən] = **Romanian**.

rumble ['rʌmbl] ◇ n [gen] estruendo m; [of stomach] ruido m. ◇ vi [gen] retumbar; [stomach] hacer ruido.

rummage ['rʌmɪdʒ] vi hurgar, rebuscar.

rumour Br, **rumor** Am ['ru:mə'] n rumor m.

rumoured Br, **rumored** Am ['ru:məd] adj: to be ~ rumorearse; she is ~ to be very rich se rumorea que es muy rica.

rump [rʌmp] n -1. [of animal] grupa f, ancas fpl. -2. inf [of person] trasero m.

rump steak n filete m de lomo.

rumpus ['rʌmpəs] n inf lío m, jaleo m.

run [rʌn] (pt **ran**, pp **run**) ◇ n -1. [on foot] carrera f; to go for a ~ ir a correr; on the ~ en fuga. -2. [journey - in car] paseo m OR vuelta f (en coche); [- in plane, ship] viaje m. -3. [series - of wins, disasters] serie f; [- of luck] racha f. -4. THEATRE: the play had a 6-week ~ la obra estuvo en cartelera 6 semanas. -5. [great demand]: ~ on sthg gran demanda de algo. **-6.** [in tights] **carrera** *f.* **-7.** [in cricket, baseball] **carrera** *f.* **-8.** [for skiing etc] **pista** *f.* **-9.** [term]: **in the short/long** ~ **a corto/largo plazo.** ◇ *vt* **-1.** [on foot] **correr. -2.** [manage - business] **dirigir, administrar;** [- life, event] **organizar. -3.** [operate - computer program, machine, film] **poner. -4.** [have and use - car etc] **hacer funcionar. -5.** [open - tap] **abrir; to** ~ **a bath llenar la bañera. -6.** [publish] **publicar. -7.** [move]: **to** ~ **sthg along** OR **over pasar algo por.** ◇ *vi* **-1.** [on foot] **correr. -2.** [follow a direction] **seguir. -3.** [in election]: **to** ~ **(for) presentarse como candidato(ta) (a). -4.** [factory, machine] **funcionar;** [engine] **estar encendido(da); to** ~ **on** OR **off sthg funcionar con algo; to** ~ **smoothly ir bien. -5.** [bus, train] **ir. -6.** [flow] **correr. -7.** [tap] **gotear;** [nose] **moquear;** [eyes] **llorar. -8.** [colour] **desteñir. -9.** [pass - gen] **pasar. -10.** [continue to be] **seguir. -11.** [remain valid] **ser válido(da).** ◆ **run across** *vt fus* [meet] **encontrarse con.** ◆ **run away** *vi* **-1.** [flee]: **to** ~ **away (from) huir** OR **fugarse (de).** ◆ **run down** ◇ *vt sep* **-1.** [run over] **atropellar. -2.** [criticize] **hablar mal de. -3.** [allow to decline] **debilitar.** ◇ *vi* [battery] **acabarse;** [clock] **pararse;** [project, business] **debilitarse.** ◆ **run into** *vt fus* **-1.** [problem] **encontrar;** [person] **tropezarse con. -2.** [in vehicle] **chocar con.** ◆ **run off** ◇ *vt sep* **imprimir.** ◇ *vi*: **to** ~ **off (with) fugarse (con).** ◆ **run out** *vi* **-1.** [become used up] **acabarse. -2.** [expire] **caducar.** ◆ **run out of** *vt fus* **quedarse sin.** ◆ **run over** *vt sep* **atropellar.** ◆ **run through** *vt fus* **-1.** [be present in] **recorrer, atravesar. -2.** [practise] **ensayar. -3.** [read through] **echar un vistazo a.** ◆ **run to** *vt fus* **-1.** [amount to] **ascender a.** ◆ **run up** *vt fus* [amass] **incurrir en.** ◆ **run up against** *vt fus* **tropezar con.**

runaway ['rʌnəweɪ] ◇ *adj* **-1.** [gen] **fugitivo(va);** [horse] **desbocado(da);** [train] **fuera de control;** [inflation] **desenfrenado(da). -2.** [victory] **fácil.** ◇ *n* **fugitivo** *m,* **-va** *f.*

rundown ['rʌndaʊn] *n* [report] **informe** *m,* **resumen** *m.* ◆ **run-down** *adj* **-1.** [dilapidated] **en ruinas. -2.** [tired] **agotado(da).**

rung [rʌŋ] ◇ *pp* → **ring.** ◇ *n lit* & *fig* **peldaño** *m.*

runner ['rʌnə'] *n* **-1.** [athlete] **corredor** *m,* **-ra** *f.* **-2.** [smuggler] **contrabandista** *m*

y *f.* **-3.** [on skate] **cuchilla** *f;* [on sledge] **carril** *m;* [of drawer, sliding seat] **carro** *m.*

runner bean *n Br* **judía** *f* **escarlata.**

runner-up (*pl* **runners-up**) *n* **subcampeón** *m,* **-ona** *f.*

running ['rʌnɪŋ] ◇ *adj* **-1.** [continuous] **continuo(nua). -2.** [consecutive] **seguidos(das). -3.** [water] **corriente.** ◇ *n* **-1.** [act of running] **el correr; to go** ~ **hacer footing. -2.** SPORT **carreras** *fpl.* **-3.** [management] **dirección** *f,* **organización** *f.* **-4.** [operation] **funcionamiento** *m.* **-5.** *phr:* **to be in/out of the** ~ **(for sthg) tener/ no tener posibilidades (de algo).**

runny ['rʌnɪ] *adj* **-1.** [food] **derretido(da). -2.** [nose] **que moquea;** [eyes] **llorosos(as).**

run-of-the-mill *adj* **normal y corriente.**

runt [rʌnt] *n* **-1.** [animal] **cría** *f* **más pequeña y débil. -2.** *pej* [person] **renacuajo** *m.*

run-up *n* **-1.** [preceding time] **periodo** *m* **previo. -2.** SPORT **carrera** *f.*

runway ['rʌnweɪ] *n* **pista** *f.*

rupture ['rʌptʃə'] *n* MED **hernia** *f.*

rural ['rʊərəl] *adj* **rural.**

ruse [ruːz] *n* **ardid** *m.*

rush [rʌʃ] ◇ *n* **-1.** [hurry] **prisa** *f;* **to be in a** ~ **tener prisa. -2.** [burst of activity]: ~ **(for** OR **on sthg) avalancha** *f* **(en busca de algo). -3.** [busy period] **hora** *f* **punta. -4.** [surge - of air] **ráfaga** *f;* [- of water] **torrente** *m;* [- mental] **arrebato** *m;* **to make a** ~ **for sthg ir en desbandada hacia algo.** ◇ *vt* **-1.** [hurry] **apresurar. -2.** [send quickly] **llevar rápidamente.** ◇ *vi* **-1.** [hurry] **ir de prisa, correr; to** ~ **into sthg meterse de cabeza en algo. -2.** [surge] **precipitarse.** ◆ **rushes** *npl* **-1.** BOT **juncos** *mpl.*

rush hour *n* **hora** *f* **punta.**

rusk [rʌsk] *n* **galleta** *que se da a los niños pequeños para que acostumbran a masticar.*

Russia ['rʌʃə] *n* **Rusia.**

Russian ['rʌʃn] ◇ *adj* **ruso(sa).** ◇ *n* **-1.** [person] **ruso** *m,* **-sa** *f.* **-2.** [language] **ruso** *m.*

rust [rʌst] ◇ *n* **moho** *m,* **óxido** *m.* ◇ *vi* **oxidarse.**

rustic ['rʌstɪk] *adj* **rústico(ca).**

rustle ['rʌsl] ◇ *vt* **-1.** [paper] **hacer crujir. -2.** *Am* [cattle] **robar.** ◇ *vi* [wind, leaves] **susurrar;** [paper] **crujir.**

rusty ['rʌstɪ] *adj lit* & *fig* **oxidado(da).**

rut [rʌt] *n* [track] **rodada** *f;* **to get into/ be in a** ~ *fig* **caer/estar metido en una rutina.**

ruthless ['ruːθlɪs] *adj* despiadado(da).
RV *n Am* (*abbr of* **recreational vehicle**) casa-remolque *f*.
rye [raɪ] *n* [grain] centeno *m*.
rye bread *n* pan *m* de centeno.

S

s (*pl* **ss** OR **s's**), **S** (*pl* **Ss** OR **S's**) [es] *n* [letter] s *f*, S *f*. ◆ **S** (*abbr of* **south**) S.
Sabbath ['sæbəθ] *n*: **the** ~ [for Christians] el domingo; [for Jews] el sábado.
sabbatical [sə'bætɪkl] *n* sabático *m*; **on** ~ de sabático.
sabotage ['sæbətɑːʒ] ◇ *n* sabotaje *m*. ◇ *vt* sabotear.
saccharin(e) ['sækərɪn] *n* sacarina *f*.
sachet ['sæʃeɪ] *n* bolsita *f*.
sack [sæk] ◇ *n* **-1.** [bag] saco *m*. **-2.** *Br inf* [dismissal]: **to get** OR **be given the** ~ ser despedido(da). ◇ *vt Br inf* despedir.
sacking ['sækɪŋ] *n* [fabric] harpillera *f*.
sacred ['seɪkrɪd] *adj lit & fig* sagrado(da).
sacrifice ['sækrɪfaɪs] RELIG & *fig* ◇ *n* sacrificio *m*. ◇ *vt* sacrificar.
sacrilege ['sækrɪlɪdʒ] *n* RELIG & *fig* sacrilegio *m*.
sacrosanct ['sækrəusæŋkt] *adj* sacrosanto(ta).
sad [sæd] *adj* triste.
sadden ['sædn] *vt* entristecer.
saddle ['sædl] ◇ *n* **-1.** [for horse] silla *f* (de montar). **-2.** [of bicycle, motorcycle] sillín *m*, asiento *m*. ◇ *vt* **-1.** [horse] ensillar. **-2.** *fig* [burden]: **to** ~ **sb with sthg** cargar a alguien con algo.
saddlebag ['sædlbæg] *n* alforja *f*.
sadistic [sə'dɪstɪk] *adj* sádico(ca).
sadly ['sædlɪ] *adv* tristemente.
sadness ['sædnɪs] *n* tristeza *f*.
s.a.e., sae *n abbr of* **stamped addressed envelope**.
safari [sə'fɑːrɪ] *n* safari *m*.
safe [seɪf] ◇ *adj* **-1.** [gen] seguro(ra); ~ **and sound** sano y salvo (sana y salva). **-2.** [without harm] sin contratiempos. **-3.** [not causing disagreement]: **it's** ~ **to say that ...** se puede afirmar con seguridad que ...; **to be on the** ~ **side** por mayor seguridad. **-4.** [reliable] dig-

no(na) de confianza. ◇ *n* caja *f* (de caudales).
safe-conduct *n* salvoconducto *m*.
safe-deposit box *n* caja *f* de seguridad.
safeguard ['seɪfgɑːd] ◇ *n* salvaguardia *f*, protección *f*; ~ **against sthg** protección contra algo. ◇ *vt*: **to** ~ **sthg/sb (against sthg)** salvaguardar OR proteger algo/a alguien (contra algo).
safekeeping [,seɪf'kiːpɪŋ] *n* protección *f*.
safely ['seɪflɪ] *adv* **-1.** [with no danger] con seguridad. **-2.** [not in danger] seguramente. **-3.** [unharmed] sin novedad. **-4.** [for certain]: **I can** ~ **say that** puedo decir con toda confianza que.
safe sex *n* sexo *m* sin riesgo.
safety ['seɪftɪ] *n* seguridad *f*.
safety belt *n* cinturón *m* de seguridad.
safety pin *n* imperdible *m*, seguro *m Amer*.
saffron ['sæfrən] *n* [spice] azafrán *m*.
sag [sæg] *vi* [sink downwards] hundirse, combarse.
sage [seɪdʒ] ◇ *adj* sabio(bia). ◇ *n* **-1.** [herb] salvia *f*. **-2.** [wise man] sabio *m*.
Sagittarius [,sædʒɪ'teərɪəs] *n* Sagitario *m*.
Sahara [sə'hɑːrə] *n*: **the** ~ **(Desert)** el (desierto del) Sáhara.
said [sed] *pt & pp* → **say**.
sail [seɪl] ◇ *n* **-1.** [of boat] vela *f*; **to set** ~ zarpar. **-2.** [journey by boat] paseo *m* en barco de vela. ◇ *vt* **-1.** [boat, ship] gobernar. **-2.** [sea] cruzar. ◇ *vi* **-1.** [travel by boat] navegar. **-2.** [move - boat]: **the ship** ~**ed across the ocean** el barco cruzó el océano. **-3.** [leave by boat] zarpar. ◆ **sail through** *vt fus* hacer con facilidad.
sailboat *Am* = **sailing boat**.
sailing ['seɪlɪŋ] *n* **-1.** (*U*) SPORT vela *f*. **-2.** [trip by ship] travesía *f*.
sailing boat *Br*, **sailboat** *Am* ['seɪlbəut] *n* barco *m* de vela.
sailing ship *n* (buque *m*) velero *m*.
sailor ['seɪlər] *n* marinero *m*, -ra *f*.
saint [seɪnt] *n* RELIG & *fig* santo *m*, -ta *f*.
saintly ['seɪntlɪ] *adj* santo(ta), piadoso(sa).
sake [seɪk] *n*: **for the** ~ **of** por (el bien de); **for God's** OR **heaven's** ~ ¡por el amor de Dios!
salad ['sæləd] *n* ensalada *f*.
salad bowl *n* ensaladera *f*.
salad cream *n Br* salsa *parecida a la mahonesa para aderezar la ensalada*.
salad dressing *n* aliño *m* (para la ensalada).

salami [səˈlɑːmɪ] n salami m.

salary [ˈsælərɪ] n sueldo m.

sale [seɪl] n **-1.** [gen] venta f; **on ~** en venta; **(up) for ~** en venta; **"for ~"** "se vende". **-2.** [at reduced prices] liquidación f, saldo m. ◆ **sales** npl **-1.** ECON ventas fpl. **-2.** [at reduced prices]: **the ~s** las rebajas.

saleroom Br [ˈseɪlrʊm], **salesroom** Am [ˈseɪlzrʊm] n sala f de subastas.

sales assistant [ˈseɪlz-], **salesclerk** Am [ˈseɪlzklɜːrk] n dependiente m, -ta f.

salesman [ˈseɪlzmən] (pl **-men** [-mən]) n [in shop] dependiente m, vendedor m; [travelling] viajante m.

sales rep n inf representante m y f.

salesroom Am = **saleroom**.

saleswoman [ˈseɪlz,wʊmən] (pl **-women** [-,wɪmɪn]) n [in shop] dependienta f, vendedora f; [travelling] viajante f.

salient [ˈseɪljənt] adj fml sobresaliente.

saliva [səˈlaɪvə] n saliva f.

sallow [ˈsæləʊ] adj cetrino(na).

salmon [ˈsæmən] (pl inv OR **-s**) n salmón m.

salmonella [,sælməˈnelə] n salmonelosis f inv.

salon [ˈsælɒn] n salón m.

saloon [səˈluːn] n **-1.** Br [car] turismo m. **-2.** Am [bar] bar m. **-3.** Br [in pub]: ~ **(bar)** en ciertos pubs y hoteles, bar elegante con precios más altos que los del 'public bar'. **-4.** [in ship] salón m.

salt [sɔːlt, sɒlt] ◇ n sal f. ◇ vt [food] salar; [roads] echar sal en (las carreteras etc para evitar que se hielen). ◆ **salt away** vt sep inf ahorrar.

salt cellar Br, **salt shaker** Am [-,ʃeɪkər] n salero m.

saltwater [ˈsɔːlt,wɔːtər] adj de agua salada.

salty [ˈsɔːltɪ] adj salado(da), salobre.

salutary [ˈsæljʊtrɪ] adj saludable.

salute [səˈluːt] ◇ n **-1.** [with hand] saludo m. MIL [firing of guns] salva f, saludo m. ◇ vt **-1.** MIL [with hand] saludar. **-2.** [acknowledge formally] reconocer.

Salvadoran, **Salvadorian** [,sælvə-ˈdɔːrɪən] ◇ adj salvadoreño(ña). ◇ n salvadoreño m, -ña f.

salvage [ˈsælvɪdʒ] ◇ n (U) **-1.** [rescue of ship] salvamento m. **-2.** [property rescued] objetos mpl recuperados OR rescatados. ◇ vt lit & fig: **to ~ sthg (from)** salvar algo (de).

salvation [sælˈveɪʃn] n salvación f.

Salvation Army n: **the ~** el Ejército de Salvación.

same [seɪm] ◇ adj mismo(ma); **the ~ colour as his** el mismo color que el suyo; **at the ~ time** [simultaneously] al mismo tiempo; [yet] aún así; **one and the ~** el mismo (la misma). ◇ pron: **the ~** el mismo (la misma); **she did the ~** hizo lo mismo; **the ingredients are the ~** los ingredientes son los mismos OR iguales; **I'll have the ~ (again)** tomaré lo mismo (que antes); **all** OR **just the ~** [nevertheless, anyway] de todos modos; **it's all the ~ to me** me da igual; **it's not the ~** no es lo mismo. ◇ adv: **the ~** lo mismo.

sample [ˈsɑːmpl] ◇ n muestra f. ◇ vt [food, wine, attractions] probar.

sanatorium (pl **-riums** OR **-ria** [-rɪə]), **sanitorium** Am (pl **-riums** OR **-ria** [-rɪə]) [,sænəˈtɔːrɪəm] n sanatorio m.

sanctimonious [,sæŋktɪˈməʊnjəs] adj pej santurrón(ona).

sanction [ˈsæŋkʃn] ◇ n sanción f. ◇ vt sancionar.

sanctity [ˈsæŋktətɪ] n santidad f.

sanctuary [ˈsæŋktʃʊərɪ] n **-1.** [for birds, wildlife] reserva f. **-2.** [refuge] refugio m. **-3.** [holy place] santuario m.

sand [sænd] ◇ n arena f. ◇ vt lijar.

sandal [ˈsændl] n sandalia f.

sandalwood [ˈsændlwʊd] n sándalo m.

sandbox Am = **sandpit**.

sandcastle [ˈsænd,kɑːsl] n castillo m de arena.

sand dune n duna f.

sandpaper [ˈsænd,peɪpər] ◇ n (U) papel m de lija. ◇ vt lijar.

sandpit Br [ˈsændpɪt], **sandbox** Am [ˈsændbɒks] n cuadro m de arena.

sandstone [ˈsændstəʊn] n piedra f arenisca.

sandwich [ˈsænwɪdʒ] ◇ n [made with roll etc] bocadillo m; [made with sliced bread] sandwich m frío. ◇ vt fig apretujar.

sandwich board n cartelón m (de hombre-anuncio).

sandwich course n Br curso universitario que incluye un cierto tiempo de experiencia profesional.

sandy [ˈsændɪ] adj **-1.** [covered in sand] arenoso(sa). **-2.** [sand-coloured] rojizo(za).

sane [seɪn] adj **-1.** [not mad] cuerdo(da). **-2.** [sensible] prudente, sensato(ta).

sang [sæŋ] pt → **sing**.

sanitary ['sænɪtrɪ] *adj* **-1.** [connected with health] **sanitario(ria).** **-2.** [clean, hygienic] **higiénico(ca).**

sanitary towel, sanitary napkin *Am n* [disposable] **compresa** *f* (higiénica); [made of cloth] **paño** *m* (higiénico).

sanitation [,sænɪ'teɪʃn] *n* sanidad *f*.

sanitorium *Am* = **sanatorium.**

sanity ['sænətɪ] *n* **-1.** [saneness] cordura *f*. **-2.** [good sense] sensatez *f*.

sank [sæŋk] *pt* → **sink.**

Santa (Claus) ['sæntə(,klaʊz)] *n* Papá *m* Noel.

sap [sæp] ◇ *n* [of plant] savia *f*. ◇ *vt* [weaken] minar.

sapling ['sæplɪŋ] *n* árbol *m* nuevo, arbolito *m*.

sapphire ['sæfaɪəʳ] *n* zafiro *m*.

Saragossa [,særə'gɒsə] *n* Zaragoza.

sarcastic [sɑː'kæstɪk] *adj* sarcástico(ca).

sardine [sɑː'diːn] *n* sardina *f*.

sardonic [sɑː'dɒnɪk] *adj* sardónico(ca).

SAS (*abbr of* **Special Air Service**) *n* unidad especial del ejército británico encargada de operaciones de sabotaje.

SASE *n abbr of* **self-addressed stamped envelope.**

sash [sæʃ] *n* faja *f*.

sat [sæt] *pt & pp* → **sit.**

SAT [sæt] *n* **-1.** (*abbr of* **Standard Assessment Test**) examen de aptitud que se realiza a los siete, once y catorce años en Inglaterra y Gales. **-2.** (*abbr of* **Scholastic Aptitude Test**) examen de ingreso a la universidad en Estados Unidos.

Satan ['seɪtn] *n* Satanás *m*.

satchel ['sætʃəl] *n* cartera *f*.

satellite ['sætəlaɪt] *n lit & fig* satélite *m*.

satellite TV *n* televisión *f* por satélite.

satin ['sætɪn] ◇ *n* satén *m*, raso *m*. ◇ *comp* de satén, de raso.

satire ['sætaɪəʳ] *n* sátira *f*.

satisfaction [,sætɪs'fækʃn] *n* satisfacción *f*.

satisfactory [,sætɪs'fæktərɪ] *adj* satisfactorio(ria).

satisfied ['sætɪsfaɪd] *adj* satisfecho(cha).

satisfy ['sætɪsfaɪ] *vt* **-1.** [gen] satisfacer. **-2.** [convince] convencer; **to ~ sb that** convencer a alguien (de) que.

satisfying ['sætɪsfaɪɪŋ] *adj* agradable, satisfactorio(ria).

satsuma [,sæt'suːmə] *n* satsuma *f, tipo de mandarina.*

saturate ['sætʃəreɪt] *vt* **-1.** [drench]: **to ~ sthg (with)** empapar algo (de). **-2.** [fill completely]: **to ~ sthg (with)** saturar algo (de).

Saturday ['sætədɪ] ◇ *n* sábado *m*; **what day is it? - it's ~** ¿a qué estamos hoy? - estamos a sábado; **on ~** el sábado; **on ~s** los sábados; **last ~** el sábado pasado; **this ~** este sábado, el sábado que viene; **next ~** el sábado de la semana que viene; **every ~** todos los sábados; **every other ~** cada dos sábados; **the ~ before** el sábado anterior; **the ~ after next** no este sábado sino el siguiente; **the ~ before last** hace dos sábados; **~ week, a week on ~** del sábado en ocho días. ◇ *comp* del sábado.

Saturn ['sætən] *n* Saturno *m*.

sauce [sɔːs] *n* CULIN salsa *f*.

saucepan ['sɔːspən] *n* [with two handles] cacerola *f*; [with one long handle] cazo *m*.

saucer ['sɔːsəʳ] *n* platillo *m*.

saucy ['sɔːsɪ] *adj inf* descarado(da), fresco(ca).

Saudi Arabia [,saʊdɪə'reɪbjə] *n* Arabia Saudí.

Saudi (Arabian) ['saʊdɪ-] ◇ *adj* saudí, saudita. ◇ *n* [person] saudí *m y f*, saudita *m y f*.

sauna ['sɔːnə] *n* sauna *f*.

saunter ['sɔːntəʳ] *vi* pasearse (tranquilamente).

sausage ['sɒsɪdʒ] *n* salchicha *f*.

sausage roll *n Br* salchicha envuelta en masa como de empanadilla.

sauté [*Br* 'səʊteɪ, *Am* səʊ'teɪ] (*pt & pp* **sautéed** OR **sautéd**) *vt* saltear.

savage ['sævɪdʒ] ◇ *adj* [cruel, fierce] feroz, salvaje *m y f*. ◇ *n pej* salvaje *m y f*. ◇ *vt* **-1.** [subj: animal] embestir, atacar. **-2.** [subj: person] atacar con ferocidad.

save [seɪv] ◇ *vt* **-1.** [rescue] salvar, rescatar; **to ~ sb from sthg** salvar a alguien de algo. **-2.** [prevent waste of - time, money, energy] ahorrar; [- food, strength] guardar, reservar. **-3.** [set aside - money] ahorrar; [- food, strength] guardar, reservar. **-4.** [avoid] evitar; **to ~ sb from doing sthg** evitar a alguien (el) hacer algo. **-5.** SPORT parar. **-6.** COMPUT guardar. ◇ *vi* ahorrar. ◇ *n* SPORT parada *f*. ◇ *prep fml*: **~ (for)** excepto.
◆ **save up** *vi* ahorrar.

saving grace ['seɪvɪŋ-] *n* lo único positivo.

savings ['seɪvɪŋz] *npl* ahorros *mpl*.

savings account *n Am* cuenta *f* de ahorros.

savings and loan association *n Am* sociedad *f* de préstamos inmobiliarios.

savings bank *n* ≃ caja *f* de ahorros.

saviour *Br*, **savior** *Am* ['seɪvjər] *n* salvador *m*, -ra *f*.

savour *Br*, **savor** *Am* ['seɪvər] *vt lit* & *fig* saborear.

savoury *Br*, **savory** *Am* ['seɪvərɪ] ◇ *adj* **-1.** [not sweet] salado(da). **-2.** [respectable, pleasant] agradable. ◇ *n* comida *f* de aperitivo.

saw [sɔː] (*Br pt* **-ed**, *pp* **sawn**, *Am pt* & *pp* **-ed**) ◇ *pt* → **see**. ◇ *n* sierra *f*. ◇ *vt* serrar.

sawdust ['sɔːdʌst] *n* serrín *m*.

sawed-off shotgun *Am* = **sawn-off shotgun**.

sawmill ['sɔːmɪl] *n* aserradero *m*.

sawn [sɔːn] *pp Br* → **saw**.

sawn-off shotgun *Br*, **sawed-off shotgun** *Am* [sɔːd-] *n* arma *f* de cañones recortados.

saxophone ['sæksəfəʊn] *n* saxofón *m*.

say [seɪ] (*pt* & *pp* **said**) ◇ *vt* **-1.** [gen] decir; **to ~ yes** decir que sí; **he's said to be good** se dice que es bueno; **let's ~ you were to win** pongamos que ganaras; **that goes without ~ing** ni que decir tiene; **it has a lot to be said for it** tiene muy buenos puntos en su favor. **-2.** [indicate - clock, meter] marcar. ◇ *n*: **to have a/no ~ in sthg** tener/no tener voz y voto en algo; **let me have my ~** déjame decir lo que pienso. ◆ **that is to say** *adv* es decir.

saying ['seɪɪŋ] *n* dicho *m*.

scab [skæb] *n* **-1.** MED costra *f*. **-2.** *pej* [non-striker] esquirol *m*.

scaffold ['skæfəʊld] *n* **-1.** [around building] andamio *m*. **-2.** [for execution] cadalso *m*.

scaffolding ['skæfəldɪŋ] *n* (*U*) andamios *mpl*, andamiaje *m*.

scald [skɔːld] *vt* escaldar.

scale [skeɪl] ◇ *n* **-1.** [gen] escala *f*. **-2.** [size, extent] tamaño *m*, escala *f*; **to ~ a** escala. **-3.** [of fish, snake] escama *f*. **-4.** *Am* = **scales**. ◇ *vt* **-1.** [climb] escalar. **-2.** [remove scales from] escamar. ◆ **scales** *npl* **-1.** [for weighing food] balanza *f*. **-2.** [for weighing person] báscula *f*. ◆ **scale down** *vt fus* reducir.

scale model *n* maqueta *f*.

scallop ['skɒləp] ◇ *n* ZOOL vieira *f*. ◇ *vt* [decorate edge of] festonear.

scalp [skælp] ◇ *n* cuero *m* cabelludo. ◇ *vt* escalpar.

scalpel ['skælpəl] *n* bisturí *m*.

scamper ['skæmpər] *vi* correr.

scampi ['skæmpɪ] *n* (*U*): **(breaded) ~** gambas *fpl* a la gabardina.

scan [skæn] ◇ *n* exploración *f* ultrasónica. ◇ *vt* **-1.** [examine carefully] examinar. **-2.** [glance at] dar un vistazo a. **-3.** ELECTRON & TV registrar.

scandal ['skændl] *n* **-1.** [scandalous event, outrage] escándalo *m*. **-2.** [scandalous talk] habladurías *fpl*.

scandalize, **-ise** ['skændəlaɪz] *vt* escandalizar.

Scandinavia [ˌskændɪ'neɪvjə] *n* Escandinavia.

Scandinavian [ˌskændɪ'neɪvjən] ◇ *adj* escandinavo(va). ◇ *n* [person] escandinavo *m*, -va *f*.

scant [skænt] *adj* escaso(sa).

scanty ['skæntɪ] *adj* [amount, resources] escaso(sa); [dress] ligero(ra); [meal] insuficiente.

scapegoat ['skeɪpgəʊt] *n* cabeza *f* de turco.

scar [skɑːr] *n* **-1.** [physical] cicatriz *f*. **-2.** *fig* [mental] señal *f*.

scarce ['skeəs] *adj* escaso(sa).

scarcely ['skeəslɪ] *adv* apenas; **~ anyone/ever** casi nadie/nunca.

scare [skeər] ◇ *n* **-1.** [sudden fear] susto *m*, sobresalto *m*. **-2.** [public fear] temor *m*. ◇ *vt* asustar, sobresaltar. ◆ **scare away**, **scare off** *vt sep* ahuyentar.

scarecrow ['skeəkrəʊ] *n* espantapájaros *m inv*.

scared ['skeəd] *adj* **-1.** [frightened] asustado(da); **to be ~ stiff** OR **to death** estar muerto de miedo. **-2.** [worried]: **to be ~ that** tener miedo que.

scarf [skɑːf] (*pl* **-s** OR **scarves**) *n* [for neck] bufanda *f*; [for head] pañuelo *m* de cabeza.

scarlet ['skɑːlət] *adj* color escarlata.

scarlet fever *n* escarlatina *f*.

scarves [skɑːvz] *pl* → **scarf**.

scathing ['skeɪðɪŋ] *adj* mordaz.

scatter ['skætər] ◇ *vt* esparcir, desparramar. ◇ *vi* dispersarse.

scatterbrained ['skætəbreɪnd] *adj inf* atolondrado(da).

scavenger ['skævɪndʒər] *n* **-1.** [animal] carroñero *m*, -ra *f*. **-2.** [person] persona *f* que rebusca en las basuras.

scenario [sɪ'nɑːrɪəʊ] (*pl* **-s**) *n* **-1.** [possible situation] situación *f* hipotética. **-2.** [of film, play] resumen *m* del argumento.

scene [siːn] *n* **-1.** [gen] escena *f*; **behind the ~s** entre bastidores. **-2.** [painting of place] panorama *m*, paisaje *m*. **-3.** [location] sitio *m*. **-4.** [show of emotion] jaleo *m*, escándalo *m*. **-5.** *phr*: **to set the ~** [for person] describir la escena; [for event] crear el ambiente propicio.

scenery ['si:nərɪ] *n* (*U*) **-1.** [of countryside] paisaje *m*. **-2.** THEATRE decorado *m*.

scenic ['si:nɪk] *adj* [view] pintoresco(ca); [tour] turístico(ca).

scent [sent] *n* **-1.** [smell - of flowers] fragancia *f*; [- of animal] rastro *m*. **-2.** *fig* [track] pista *f*. **-3.** [perfume] perfume *m*.

scepter *Am* = **sceptre**.

sceptic *Br*, **skeptic** *Am* ['skeptɪk] *n* escéptico *m*, -ca *f*.

sceptical *Br*, **skeptical** *Am* ['skeptɪkl] *adj* escéptico(ca); **to be ~ about** tener muchas dudas acerca de.

sceptre *Br*, **scepter** *Am* ['septər] *n* cetro *m*.

schedule [*Br* 'ʃedju:l, *Am* 'skedʒʊl] ◇ *n* **-1.** [plan] programa *m*, plan *m*; **on ~** sin retraso; **ahead of ~** con adelanto; **behind ~** con retraso. **-2.** [of prices, contents] lista *f*; [of times] horario *m*. ◇ *vt*: **to ~ sthg (for)** fijar algo (para).

scheduled flight [*Br* 'ʃedju:ld-, *Am* 'skedʒʊld-] *n* vuelo *m* regular.

scheme [ski:m] ◇ *n* **-1.** [plan] plano *m*, proyecto *m*. **-2.** *pej* [dishonest plan] intriga *f*. **-3.** [arrangement, decoration - of room] disposición *f*; [- of colours] combinación *f*. ◇ *vi pej*: **to ~ (to do sthg)** intrigar (para hacer algo).

scheming ['ski:mɪŋ] *adj* intrigante.

schism ['sɪzm, 'skɪzm] *n* cisma *f*.

schizophrenic [,skɪtsə'frenɪk] *adj* esquizofrénico(ca).

scholar ['skɒlər] *n* **-1.** [expert] erudito *m*, -ta *f*. **-2.** *dated* [student] alumno *m*, -na *f*.

scholarship ['skɒləʃɪp] *n* **-1.** [grant] beca *f*. **-2.** [learning] erudición *f*.

school [sku:l] *n* **-1.** [gen] colegio *m*, escuela *f*; [for driving, art] escuela *f*; [for medicine, law] facultad *f*. **-2.** *Am* [university] universidad *f*.

school age *n* edad *f* escolar.

schoolbook ['sku:lbʊk] *n* libro *m* de texto.

schoolboy ['sku:lbɔɪ] *n* colegial *m*.

schoolchild ['sku:ltʃaɪld] (*pl* **-children** [-tʃɪldrən]) *n* colegial *m*, -la *f*.

schooldays ['sku:ldeɪz] *npl* años *mpl* de colegio.

schoolgirl ['sku:lgɜ:l] *n* colegiala *f*.

schooling ['sku:lɪŋ] *n* educación *f* escolar.

school-leaver [-,li:vər] *n Br* joven *que ha terminado la enseñanza obligatoria*.

schoolmaster ['sku:l,mɑ:stər] *n dated* [at primary school] maestro *m*; [at secondary school] profesor *m*.

schoolmistress ['sku:l,mɪstrɪs] *n dated* [at primary school] maestra *f*; [at secondary school] profesora *f*.

school of thought *n* corriente *f* de opinión.

schoolteacher ['sku:l,ti:tʃər] *n* [primary] maestro *m*, -tra *f*; [secondary] profesor *m*, -ra *f*.

school year *n* año *m* escolar.

schooner ['sku:nər] *n* **-1.** [ship] goleta *f*. **-2.** *Br* [sherry glass] copa *f* larga (para jerez).

sciatica [saɪ'ætɪkə] *n* ciática *f*.

science ['saɪəns] *n* ciencia *f*.

science fiction *n* ciencia *f* ficción.

scientific [,saɪən'tɪfɪk] *adj* científico(ca).

scientist ['saɪəntɪst] *n* científico *m*, -ca *f*.

scintillating ['sɪntɪleɪtɪŋ] *adj* brillante, chispeante.

scissors ['sɪzəz] *npl* tijeras *fpl*; **a pair of ~** unas tijeras.

sclerosis → **multiple sclerosis**.

scoff [skɒf] ◇ *vt Br inf* zamparse, tragarse. ◇ *vi*: **to ~ (at sb/sthg)** mofarse OR burlarse (de alguien/de algo).

scold [skəʊld] *vt* regañar, reñir.

scone [skɒn] *n bollo tomado con té a la hora de la merienda*.

scoop [sku:p] ◇ *n* **-1.** [utensil - for sugar] cucharita *f* plana; [- for ice cream] pinzas *fpl* (*de helado*); [- for flour] paleta *f*. **-2.** PRESS exclusiva *f*. ◇ *vt* **-1.** [with hands] recoger. **-2.** [with utensil] recoger con cucharilla. ◆ **scoop out** *vt sep* sacar con cuchara.

scooter ['sku:tər] *n* **-1.** [toy] patinete *m*. **-2.** [motorcycle] Vespa® *f*, motoneta *f Amer*.

scope [skəʊp] *n* (*U*) **-1.** [opportunity] posibilidades *fpl*. **-2.** [range] alcance *m*.

scorch [skɔ:tʃ] *vt* **-1.** [dress, meat] chamuscar; [face, skin] quemar. **-2.** [dry out] secar.

scorching ['skɔ:tʃɪŋ] *adj inf* abrasador(ra).

score [skɔ:r] ◇ *n* **-1.** [in test] calificación *f*, nota *f*; [in competition] puntuación *f*. **-2.** SPORT resultado *m*; **what's the ~?** ¿cómo van? **-3.** *dated* [twenty] veintena *f*. **-4.** MUS partitura *f*. **-5.** [subject]: **on that ~** a ese respecto. ◇ *vt* **-1.** SPORT marcar. **-2.** [achieve - success, victory] obtener. **-3.** [cut] grabar. ◇ *vi* **-1.** SPORT marcar. **-2.** [in test etc] obtener una puntuación. ◆ **score out** vt sep Br tachar.

scoreboard ['skɔːbɔːd] n marcador m.

scorer ['skɔːrəʳ] n **-1.** [official] tanteador m, -ra f. **-2.** [player - in football] goleador m, -ra f; [- in other sports] marcador m, -ra f.

scorn [skɔːn] ◇ n menosprecio m, desdén m. ◇ vt menospreciar, desdeñar.

scornful ['skɔːnful] adj despectivo(va); **to be ~ of** sthg desdeñar algo.

Scorpio ['skɔːpɪəu] (pl **-s**) n Escorpión m.

scorpion ['skɔːpjən] n alacrán m.

Scot [skɒt] n escocés m, -esa f.

scotch [skɒtʃ] vt [rumour] desmentir; [idea] desechar.

Scotch [skɒtʃ] ◇ adj escocés(esa). ◇ n whisky m escocés.

Scotch (tape)® n Am cinta f adhesiva.

scot-free adj inf: **to get off ~** salir impune.

Scotland ['skɒtlənd] n Escocia.

Scots [skɒts] ◇ adj escocés(esa). ◇ n [dialect] escocés m.

Scotsman ['skɒtsmən] (pl **-men** [-mən]) n escocés m.

Scotswoman ['skɒtswumən] (pl **-women** [-ˌwɪmɪn]) n escocesa f.

Scottish ['skɒtɪʃ] adj escocés(esa).

Scottish National Party n: **the ~** el Partido Nacionalista Escocés.

scoundrel ['skaundrəl] n dated sinvergüenza m, canalla m.

scour [skauəʳ] vt **-1.** [clean] fregar, restregar. **-2.** [search] registrar, batir.

scourge [skɜːdʒ] n **-1.** [cause of suffering] azote m. **-2.** [critic] castigador m, -ra f.

scout [skaut] n MIL explorador m. ◆ **Scout** n [boy scout] explorador m. ◆ **scout around** vi: **to ~ around (for)** explorar el terreno (en busca de).

scowl [skaul] vi fruncir el ceño; **to ~ at sb** mirar con ceño a alguien.

scrabble ['skræbl] vi **-1.** [scramble, scrape] escarbar. **-2.** [feel around]: **to ~ around for** sthg hurgar en busca de algo.

Scrabble® ['skræbl] n Scrabble® m.

scraggy ['skrægɪ] adj inf flaco(ca).

scramble ['skræmbl] ◇ n [rush] pelea f. ◇ vi **-1.** [climb] trepar. **-2.** [move clumsily]: **to ~ to one's feet** levantarse rápidamente y tambaleándose.

scrambled eggs ['skræmbld-] npl huevos mpl revueltos.

scrap [skræp] ◇ n **-1.** [small piece] trozo m, pedazo m. **-2.** [metal] chatarra f. **-3.** inf [fight, quarrel] pelotera f. ◇ vt desechar, descartar. ◆ **scraps** npl [food] sobras fpl.

scrapbook ['skræpbuk] n álbum m de recortes.

scrap dealer n chatarrero m, -ra f.

scrape [skreɪp] ◇ n **-1.** [noise] chirrido m. **-2.** dated [difficult situation] apuro m. ◇ vt **-1.** [remove]: **to ~ sthg off sthg** raspar algo de algo. **-2.** [vegetables] raspar. **-3.** [car, bumper, glass] rayar; [knee, elbow, skin] rasguñar. ◇ vi **-1.** [rub]: **to ~ against/on sthg** rozar contra/en algo. **-2.** [save money] economizar. ◆ **scrape through** vt fus aprobar por los pelos.

scraper ['skreɪpəʳ] n raspador m.

scrap merchant n Br chatarrero m, -ra f.

scrap paper Br, **scratch paper** Am n (U) papel m usado.

scrapyard ['skræpjɑːd] n [gen] depósito m de chatarra; [for cars] cementerio m de coches.

scratch [skrætʃ] ◇ n **-1.** [wound] arañazo m, rasguño m. **-2.** [mark] raya f, surco m. **-3.** phr: **to do sthg from ~** hacer algo partiendo desde el principio; **to be up to ~** estar a la altura requerida. ◇ vt **-1.** [wound] arañar, rasguñar. **-2.** [mark] rayar. **-3.** [rub - head, leg] rascar. ◇ vi [rub] rascarse.

scratch paper Am = scrap paper.

scrawl [skrɔːl] ◇ n garabatos mpl. ◇ vt garabatear.

scrawny ['skrɔːnɪ] adj flaco(ca).

scream [skriːm] ◇ n **-1.** [cry, shout] grito m, chillido m. **-2.** [noise] chirrido m. ◇ vt vociferar. ◇ vi [person] chillar.

scree [skriː] n montón de piedras desprendidas de la ladera de una montaña.

screech [skriːtʃ] ◇ n **-1.** [of person] chillido m; [of bird] chirrido m. **-2.** [of car, tyres] chirrido m, rechinar m. ◇ vt gritar. ◇ vi **-1.** [person, bird] chillar. **-2.** [car, tyres] chirriar, rechinar.

screen [skriːn] ◇ n **-1.** TV, CINEMA & COMPUT pantalla f. **-2.** [panel] biombo m. ◇ vt **-1.** [show in cinema] proyectar. **-2.** [broadcast on TV] emitir. **-3.** [shield]: **to ~ sthg/sb (from)** proteger algo/a alguien (de). **-4.** [candidate, patient] examinar.

screening ['skriːnɪŋ] n **-1.** [of film] proyección f. **-2.** [of TV programme] emisión *f.* **-3.** [for security] examen *m.* **-4.** MED [examination] chequeo *m.*

screenplay ['skri:npleɪ] *n* guión *m.*

screw [skru:] ◇ *n* [for fastening] tornillo *m.* ◇ *vt* **-1.** [fix]: **to ~ sthg to** atornillar algo a. **-2.** [twist] enroscar. **-3.** *vulg* [woman] follar, coger *Amer.* ◆ **screw up** *vt sep* **-1.** [sheet of paper etc] arrugar. **-2.** [eyes] entornar; [face] arrugar. **-3.** *v inf* [ruin] jorobar.

screwdriver ['skru:,draɪvəʳ] *n* destornillador *m.*

scribble ['skrɪbl] ◇ *n* garabato *m.* ◇ *vt & vi* garabatear.

script [skrɪpt] *n* **-1.** [of play, film etc] guión *m.* **-2.** [system of writing] escritura *f.* **-3.** [handwriting] letra *f.*

Scriptures ['skrɪptʃəz] *npl*: **the ~** las Sagradas Escrituras.

scriptwriter ['skrɪpt,raɪtəʳ] *n* guionista *m y f.*

scroll [skrəʊl] ◇ *n* rollo *m* de pergamino/papel. ◇ *vt* COMPUT desplazar.

scrounge [skraʊndʒ] *inf vt* gorronear.

scrounger ['skraʊndʒəʳ] *n inf* gorrón *m*, -ona *f.*

scrub [skrʌb] ◇ *n* **-1.** [rub] restregón *m.* **-2.** [undergrowth] maleza *f.* ◇ *vt* restregar.

scruff [skrʌf] *n*: **by the ~ of the neck** por el pescuezo.

scruffy ['skrʌfɪ] *adj* [person] dejado(da); [clothes] andrajoso(sa); [room] desordenado(da).

scrum(mage) ['skrʌm(ɪdʒ)] *n* RUGBY melé *f.*

scruples ['skru:plz] *npl* escrúpulos *mpl.*

scrutinize, -ise ['skru:tɪnaɪz] *vt* escudriñar.

scrutiny ['skru:tɪnɪ] *n* (U) escrutinio *m*, examen *m.*

scuff [skʌf] *vt* [damage - shoes] pelar; [- furniture, floor] rayar.

scuffle ['skʌfl] *n* refriega *f*, reyerta *f.*

scullery ['skʌlərɪ] *n* trascocina *f.*

sculptor ['skʌlptəʳ] *n* escultor *m*, -ra *f.*

sculpture ['skʌlptʃəʳ] *n* escultura *f.*

scum [skʌm] *n* **-1.** [froth] espuma *f.* **-2.** *v inf pej* [worthless person] escoria *f.*

scupper ['skʌpəʳ] *vt* NAUT & *fig* hundir.

scurrilous ['skʌrələs] *adj fml* injurioso(sa), difamatorio(ria).

scurry ['skʌrɪ] *vi*: **to ~ off** OR **away** escabullirse.

scuttle ['skʌtl] ◇ *n* cubo *m* del carbón. ◇ *vi* [rush]: **to ~ off** OR **away** escabullirse.

scythe [saɪð] *n* guadaña *f.*

SDLP (*abbr of* **Social Democratic and Labour Party**) *n* partido político norirlandés que defiende la integración pacífica en la república de Irlanda.

sea [si:] ◇ *n* **-1.** [not land] mar *m o f*; **at ~** en el mar; **by ~** en barco; **by the ~** a orillas del mar; **out to ~** [away from shore] mar adentro; [across the water] hacia el mar. **-2.** [not ocean] mar *m.* **-3.** *phr*: **to be all at ~** estar totalmente perdido(da). ◇ *comp* de mar.

seabed ['si:bed] *n*: **the ~** el lecho marino.

seaboard ['si:bɔ:d] *n fml* litoral *m.*

sea breeze *n* brisa *f* marina.

seafood ['si:fu:d] *n* (U) mariscos *mpl.*

seafront ['si:frʌnt] *n* paseo *m* marítimo.

seagull ['si:gʌl] *n* gaviota *f.*

seal [si:l] (*pl inv* OR **-s**) ◇ *n* **-1.** [animal] foca *f.* **-2.** [official mark] sello *m.* **-3.** [on bottle, meter] precinto *m*; [on letter] sello *m.* ◇ *vt* **-1.** [envelope] sellar, cerrar. **-2.** [opening, tube, crack] tapar, cerrar. ◆ **seal off** *vt sep* [entrance, exit] cerrar; [area] acordonar.

sea level *n* nivel *m* del mar.

sea lion (*pl inv* OR **-s**) *n* león *m* marítimo.

seam [si:m] *n* **-1.** SEWING costura *f.* **-2.** [of coal] veta *f.*

seaman ['si:mən] (*pl* **-men** [-mən]) *n* marinero *m.*

seamy ['si:mɪ] *adj* sórdido(da).

séance ['seɪɒns] *n* sesión *f* de espiritismo.

seaplane ['si:pleɪn] *n* hidroavión *m.*

seaport ['si:pɔ:t] *n* puerto *m* de mar.

search [sɜ:tʃ] ◇ *n* [gen] búsqueda *f*; [of room, drawer] registro *m*; [of person] cacheo *m*; **~ for sthg** búsqueda de algo; **in ~ of** en busca de. ◇ *vt* [gen] registrar; [one's mind] escudriñar; **to ~ sthg for sthg** buscar algo en algo. ◇ *vi*: **to ~ (for sthg/sb)** buscar (algo/a alguien).

searching ['sɜ:tʃɪŋ] *adj* [question] agudo(da); [look] penetrante.

searchlight ['sɜ:tʃlaɪt] *n* reflector *m.*

search party *n* equipo *m* de búsqueda.

search warrant *n* mandamiento *m* de registro.

seashell ['si:ʃel] *n* concha *f* (marina).

seashore ['si:ʃɔ:ʳ] *n*: **the ~** la orilla del mar.

seasick ['si:sɪk] *adj* mareado(da).

seaside ['si:saɪd] *n*: **the ~** la playa.

seaside resort *n* lugar *m* de veraneo (en la playa).

season ['siːzn] ◇ n -1. [of year] estación f. -2. [particular period] época f. -3. [of holiday] temporada f. -4. [of food]: **out of/in ~** fuera de/en sazón. -5. [of talks, films] temporada f. ◇ vt sazonar.

seasonal ['siːzənl] adj [work] temporal; [change] estacional.

seasoned ['siːznd] adj [experienced] veterano(na).

seasoning ['siːznɪŋ] n condimento m.

season ticket n abono m.

seat [siːt] ◇ n -1. [gen] asiento m. -2. [of trousers, skirt] trasero m. -3. POL [in parliament] escaño m. ◇ vt -1. [sit down] sentar; **be ~ed!** ¡siéntese! -2. [subj: building, vehicle] tener cabida para.

seat belt n cinturón m de seguridad.

seating ['siːtɪŋ] n (U) [capacity] asientos mpl.

seawater ['siː,wɔːtər] n agua f de mar.

seaweed ['siːwiːd] n (U) alga f marina.

seaworthy ['siː,wɜːðɪ] adj en condiciones de navegar.

sec. (abbr of second) seg.

secede [sɪ'siːd] vi fml: **to ~ (from sthg)** separarse (de algo).

secluded [sɪ'kluːdɪd] adj apartado(da).

seclusion [sɪ'kluːʒn] n aislamiento m.

second ['sekənd] ◇ n -1. [gen] segundo m. -2. Br UNIV ≃ licenciatura f con notable. ◇ num segundo(da); see also **sixth**. ◇ vt secundar. ◆ **seconds** npl -1. COMM artículos mpl defectuosos. -2. [of food]: **to have ~s** repetir (en una comida).

secondary ['sekəndrɪ] adj -1. [SCH - school] secundario(ria); [- education] medio(dia). -2. [less important]: **to be ~ to** ser secundario(ria) a.

secondary school n escuela f de enseñanza media.

second-class ['sekənd-] adj -1. [gen] de segunda clase. -2. Br UNIV nota global de licenciatura equivalente a un notable o un aprobado alto.

second hand ['sekənd-] n [of clock] segundero m.

second-hand ['sekənd-] ◇ adj [goods, information] de segunda mano. ◇ adv [not new] de segunda mano.

secondly ['sekəndlɪ] adv en segundo lugar.

secondment [sɪ'kɒndmənt] n Br traslado m temporal.

second-rate ['sekənd-] adj pej de segunda categoría, mediocre.

second thought ['sekənd-] n: **to have ~s about sthg** tener dudas acerca de

algo; **on ~s** Br, **on ~** Am pensándolo bien.

secrecy ['siːkrəsɪ] n (U) secreto m.

secret ['siːkrɪt] ◇ adj secreto(ta). ◇ n secreto m; **in ~** en secreto.

secretarial [,sekrə'teərɪəl] adj [course, training] de secretariado; [staff] administrativo(va).

secretary [Br 'sekrətrɪ, Am 'sekrə,terɪ] n -1. [gen] secretario m, -ria f. -2. POL [minister] ministro m.

Secretary of State n -1. Br: **~ (for)** ministro m (de). -2. Am ministro m estadounidense de Asuntos Exteriores.

secretive ['siːkrətɪv] adj [person] reservado(da); [organization] secreto(ta).

secretly ['siːkrɪtlɪ] adv [hope, think] secretamente; [tell] en secreto.

sect [sekt] n secta f.

sectarian [sek'teərɪən] adj sectario(ria).

section ['sekʃn] n sección f.

sector ['sektər] n sector m.

secular ['sekjʊlər] adj [education, life] laico(ca), secular; [music] profano(na).

secure [sɪ'kjʊər] ◇ adj [gen] seguro(ra). ◇ vt -1. [obtain] conseguir, obtener. -2. [make safe] proteger. -3. [fasten] cerrar bien.

security [sɪ'kjʊərətɪ] n -1. seguridad f. -2. [for loan] garantía f. ◆ **securities** npl FIN valores mpl.

security guard n guardia m jurado OR de seguridad.

sedan [sɪ'dæn] n Am (coche m) utilitario m.

sedate [sɪ'deɪt] ◇ adj sosegado(da). ◇ vt sedar.

sedation [sɪ'deɪʃn] n (U) sedación f.

sedative ['sedətɪv] n sedante m.

sediment ['sedɪmənt] n sedimento m.

seduce [sɪ'djuːs] vt: **to ~ sb (into doing sthg)** seducir a alguien (a hacer algo).

seductive [sɪ'dʌktɪv] adj seductor(ra).

see [siː] (pt saw, pp seen) ◇ vt -1. [gen] ver. -2. [visit - friend, doctor] ir a ver, visitar; **~ you soon/later/tomorrow** etc! ¡hasta pronto/luego/mañana etc!; **~ you!** ¡hasta luego!; **~ below/p 10** véase más abajo/pág. 10. -3. [accompany - to door etc] acompañar. -4. [make sure]: **to ~ (to it) that ...** encargarse de que .... ◇ vi [gen] ver; [understand] entender; **let's ~, let me ~** vamos a ver, veamos; **you ~ ...** verás, es que ...; **I ~** ya veo. ◆ **seeing as, seeing that** prep inf como. ◆ **see about** vt fus [arrange] encargarse de. ◆ **see off** vt sep -1. [say goodbye to] despedir. -2. Br [chase away] ahuyentar.

◆ **see through** *vt fus* [person] ver claramente las intenciones de. ◆ **see to** *vt fus* ocuparse de.

seed [siːd] *n* [of plant] semilla *f*. ◆ **seeds** *npl fig* [of doubt] semilla *f*; [of idea] germen *m*.

seedling ['siːdlɪŋ] *n* plantón *m*.

seedy ['siːdɪ] *adj* [room, area] sórdido(da); [person] desaliñado(da).

seek [siːk] (*pt & pp* **sought**) *fml vt* **-1.** [look for, try to obtain] buscar. **-2.** [ask for] solicitar. **-3.** [try]: **to ~ to do sthg** procurar hacer algo.

seem [siːm] ◇ *vi* parecer; **it ~s (to be) good** parece (que es) bueno; **I can't ~ to do it** no puedo hacerlo (por mucho que lo intente). ◇ *v impers*: **it ~s (that)** parece que.

seemingly ['siːmɪŋlɪ] *adv* aparentemente.

seen [siːn] *pp* → **see**.

seep [siːp] *vi* rezumarse, filtrarse.

seesaw ['siːsɔː] *n* balancín *m*.

seethe [siːð] *vi* **-1.** [person] rabiar. **-2.** [place]: **to be seething with** estar a rebosar de.

see-through *adj* transparente.

segment ['segmənt] *n* **-1.** [proportion, section] segmento *m*. **-2.** [of fruit] gajo *m*.

segregate ['segrɪgeɪt] *vt* segregar.

Seine [seɪn] *n*: **the (River) ~** el (río) Sena.

seize [siːz] *vt* **-1.** [grab] agarrar, coger. **-2.** [capture - control, power, town] tomar, hacerse con. **-3.** [arrest] detener. **-4.** [take advantage of] aprovechar. ◆ **seize (up)on** *vt fus* valerse de. ◆ **seize up** *vi* agarrotarse.

seizure ['siːʒər] *n* **-1.** MED ataque *m*. **-2.** [taking, capturing] toma *f*.

seldom ['seldəm] *adv* raramente.

select [sɪ'lekt] ◇ *adj* selecto(ta). ◇ *vt* [gen] elegir, escoger; [team] seleccionar.

selection [sɪ'lekʃn] *n* **-1.** [gen] selección *f*. **-2.** [fact of being selected] elección *f*. **-3.** [in shop] surtido *m*.

selective [sɪ'lektɪv] *adj* selectivo(va).

self [self] (*pl* **selves**) *n* uno mismo *m*, una misma *f*; **the ~** el yo.

self-addressed stamped envelope [-ə,drest'stæmpt-] *n Am* sobre con sus señas y franqueo.

self-assured *adj* seguro de sí mismo (segura de sí misma).

self-catering *adj* sin pensión.

self-centred [-'sentəd] *adj* egocéntrico(ca).

self-confessed [-kən'fest] *adj* confeso(sa).

self-confident *adj* [person] seguro de sí mismo (segura de sí misma); [attitude, remark] lleno(na) de seguridad.

self-conscious *adj* cohibido(da).

self-contained [-kən'teɪnd] *adj* autosuficiente.

self-control *n* control *m* de sí mismo/misma.

self-defence *n* defensa *f* propia; **in ~** en defensa propia.

self-discipline *n* autodisciplina *f*.

self-employed [-ɪm'plɔɪd] *adj* autónomo(ma), que trabaja por cuenta propia.

self-esteem *n* amor *m* propio.

self-evident *adj* evidente, patente.

self-explanatory *adj* evidente.

self-government *n* autogobierno *m*.

self-important *adj pej* engreído(da).

self-indulgent *adj pej* que se permite excesos.

self-interest *n pej* (U) interés *m* propio.

selfish ['selfɪʃ] *adj* egoísta.

selfishness ['selfɪʃnɪs] *n* egoísmo *m*.

selfless ['selflɪs] *adj* desinteresado(da).

self-made *adj* que ha triunfado por su propio esfuerzo.

self-opinionated *adj pej* que siempre tiene que decir la suya.

self-pity *n pej* lástima *f* de uno mismo/una mismo.

self-portrait *n* autorretrato *m*.

self-possessed [-pə'zest] *adj* dueño de sí mismo (dueña de sí misma).

self-raising flour *Br* [-,reɪzɪŋ-], **self-rising flour** *Am n* harina *f* con levadura.

self-reliant *adj* independiente.

self-respect *n* amor *m* propio.

self-respecting [-rɪs'pektɪŋ] *adj* que se precie, digno(na).

self-restraint *n* dominio *m* de sí mismo/misma.

self-righteous *adj pej* santurrón(ona).

self-rising flour *Am* = **self-raising flour**.

self-sacrifice *n* abnegación *f*.

self-satisfied *adj pej* [person] satisfecho de sí mismo (satisfecha de sí misma); [smile] lleno(na) de suficiencia.

self-service *comp* de autoservicio.

self-sufficient *adj*: **~ (in)** autosuficiente (en).

self-taught *adj* autodidacta.

sell [sel] (*pt* & *pp* **sold**) ◇ *vt* **-1.** [gen] vender; **to ~ sthg to sb, to ~ sb sthg** vender algo a alguien; **to ~ sthg for** vender algo por. ◇ *vi* **-1.** [exchange for money] vender. **-2.** [be bought]: **to ~ (for** OR **at)** venderse (a). ◆ **sell off** *vt sep* liquidar. ◆ **sell out** ◇ *vt sep* [performance]: **to have sold out** estar agotado(da). ◇ *vi* **-1.** [shop]: **to ~ out (of sthg)** agotar las existencias (de algo). **-2.** [be disloyal, unprincipled] venderse.

sell-by date *n Br* fecha *f* de caducidad.

seller ['selə'] *n* vendedor *m*, -ra *f*.

selling price ['selɪŋ-] *n* precio *m* de venta.

Sellotape® ['seləteɪp] *n Br* celo® *m*, cinta *f* adhesiva.

sell-out *n* [performance, match] lleno *m*.

selves [selvz] *pl* → **self**.

semaphore ['seməfɔː'] *n* (*U*) semáforo *m*.

semblance ['sembləns] *n fml* apariencia *f*.

semen ['siːmen] *n* semen *m*.

semester [sɪ'mestə'] *n* semestre *m*.

semicircle ['semɪ,sɜːkl] *n* semicírculo *m*.

semicolon [,semɪ'kəʊlən] *n* punto *m* y coma.

semidetached [,semɪdɪ'tætʃt] ◇ *adj* adosado(da). ◇ *n Br* casa *f* adosada (a otra).

semifinal [,semɪ'faɪnl] *n* semifinal *f*.

seminar ['semɪnɑː'] *n* seminario *m*.

seminary ['semɪnərɪ] *n* RELIG seminario *m*.

semiskilled [,semɪ'skɪld] *adj* semicualificado(da).

semolina [,semə'liːnə] *n* sémola *f*.

Senate ['senɪt] *n* POL: **the (United States) ~** el Senado (de los Estados Unidos).

senator ['senətə'] *n* senador *m*, -ra *f*.

send [send] (*pt* & *pp* **sent**) *vt* **-1.** [gen] mandar; **to ~ sb sthg, to ~ sthg to sb** mandar a alguien algo. **-2.** [tell to go, arrange for attendance]: **to ~ sb (to)** enviar OR mandar a alguien (a). ◆ **send for** *vt fus* [person] mandar llamar a. ◆ **send in** *vt sep* mandar, enviar. ◆ **send off** *vt sep* **-1.** [by post] mandar (por correo). **-2.** SPORT expulsar. ◆ **send off for** *vt fus* [goods, information] pedir, encargar. ◆ **send up** *vt sep Br inf* [imitate] parodiar.

sender ['sendə'] *n* remitente *m* y *f*.

send-off *n* despedida *f*.

senile ['siːnaɪl] *adj* senil.

senior ['siːnjə'] ◇ *adj* **-1.** [highest-ranking] superior, de rango superior. **-2.** [higher-ranking]: **~ to sb** superior a alguien. **-3.** SCH [pupil] mayor; [class, common room] de los mayores. ◇ *n* **-1.** [older person]: **I'm five years his ~** le llevo cinco años. **-2.** SCH mayor *m* y *f*.

senior citizen *n* ciudadano *m*, -na *f* de la tercera edad.

sensation [sen'seɪʃn] *n* sensación *f*.

sensational [sen'seɪʃənl] *adj* [gen] sensacional.

sensationalist [sen'seɪʃnəlɪst] *adj pej* sensacionalista.

sense [sens] ◇ *n* **-1.** [faculty, meaning] sentido *m*; **to make ~** [have meaning] tener sentido. **-2.** [feeling - of guilt, terror] sentimiento *m*; [- of urgency] sensación *f*; [- of honour, duty] sentido *m*. **-3.** [natural ability]: **business ~** talento *m* para los negocios; **~ of humour/style** sentido *m* del humor/estilo. **-4.** [wisdom, reason] juicio *m*, sentido *m* común; **to make ~** [be sensible] ser sensato. ◇ *vt* sentir, percibir; **to ~ (that)** percibir OR sentir que. ◆ **in a sense** *adv* en cierto sentido.

senseless ['senslɪs] *adj* **-1.** [stupid] sin sentido. **-2.** [unconscious] inconsciente.

sensibilities [,sensɪ'bɪlətɪz] *npl* [delicate feelings] sensibilidad *f*.

sensible ['sensəbl] *adj* [person, decision] sensato(ta); [clothes] práctico(ca).

sensitive ['sensɪtɪv] *adj* **-1.** [understanding]: **~ (to)** comprensivo(va) (hacia). **-2.** [easily hurt, touchy]: **~ (to/about)** susceptible (a/acerca de). **-3.** [controversial] delicado(da). **-4.** [easily damaged, tender]: **~ (to)** sensible (a). **-5.** [responsive - instrument] sensible.

sensual ['sensjʊəl] *adj* sensual.

sensuous ['sensjʊəs] *adj* sensual.

sent [sent] *pt* & *pp* → **send**.

sentence ['sentəns] ◇ *n* **-1.** [group of words] frase *f*, oración *f*. **-2.** JUR sentencia *f*. ◇ *vt*: **to ~ sb (to)** condenar a alguien (a).

sentiment ['sentɪmənt] *n* **-1.** [feeling] sentimiento *m*. **-2.** [opinion] opinión *f*.

sentimental [,sentɪ'mentl] *adj* sentimental.

sentry ['sentrɪ] *n* centinela *m*.

separate [*adj* & *n* 'seprət, *vb* 'sepəreɪt] ◇ *adj* **-1.** [not joined, apart]: **~ (from)** separado(da) (de). **-2.** [individual, distinct] distinto(ta). ◇ *vt* **-1.** [keep or move apart]: **to ~ sthg/sb (from)** separar algo/a alguien (de). **-2.** [distinguish]: **to**

~ sthg/sb from diferenciar algo/a alguien de. -3. [divide]: to ~ sthg/sb into dividir algo/a alguien en. ◇ vi -1. [gen]: to ~ (from) separarse (de). -2. [divide]: to ~ (into) dividirse (en). ◆ separates npl Br piezas fpl (de vestir que combinan).

separately ['seprǝtli] adv -1. [on one's own] independientemente. -2. [one by one] por separado.

separation [ˌsepǝ'reiʃn] n separación f.

September [sep'tembǝʳ] n septiembre m, setiembre m; 1 ~ 1992 [in letters etc] 1 de septiembre de 1992; by/in ~ para/en septiembre; last/this/next ~ en septiembre del año pasado/de este año/del año que viene; every ~ todos los años en septiembre; during ~ en septiembre; at the beginning/end of ~ a principios/finales de septiembre; in the middle of ~ a mediados de septiembre.

septic ['septik] adj séptico(ca).

septic tank n fosa f séptica.

sequel ['si:kwǝl] n -1. [book, film]: ~ (to) continuación f (de). -2. [consequence]: ~ (to) secuela f (de).

sequence ['si:kwǝns] n -1. [series] sucesión f. -2. [order, of film] secuencia f.

Serb = Serbian.

Serbia ['sɜ:bjǝ] n Serbia.

Serbian ['sɜ:bjǝn], **Serb** [sɜ:b] ◇ adj serbio(bia). ◇ n -1. [person] serbio m, -bia f. -2. [dialect] serbio m.

serene [si'ri:n] adj sereno(na).

sergeant ['sɑ:dʒǝnt] n -1. MIL sargento m. -2. [in police] ≃ subinspector m de policía.

sergeant major n sargento m mayor.

serial ['siǝriǝl] n serial m.

serial number n número m de serie.

series ['siǝri:z] (pl inv) n serie f.

serious ['siǝriǝs] adj -1. [gen] serio(ria); are you ~? ¿hablas en serio? -2. [very bad] grave.

seriously ['siǝriǝsli] adv -1. [honestly] en serio. -2. [very badly] gravemente. -3. [in a considered, earnest, solemn manner] seriamente. -4. phr: to take sthg/sb ~ tomar algo/a alguien en serio.

seriousness ['siǝriǝsnis] n -1. [gravity] gravedad f. -2. [solemnity] seriedad f.

sermon ['sɜ:mǝn] n RELIG & pej sermón m.

serrated [si'reitid] adj dentado(da).

servant ['sɜ:vǝnt] n sirviente m, -ta f.

serve [sɜ:v] ◇ vt -1. [work for] servir. -2. [have effect]: to ~ to do sthg servir para hacer algo. -3. [fulfil]: to ~ a purpose cumplir un propósito. -4. [provide for] abastecer. -5. [food, drink]: to ~ sthg to sb, to ~ sb sthg servir algo a alguien. -6. [in shop, bar etc] despachar, servir. -7. JUR: to ~ sb with sthg, to ~ sthg on sb entregar a alguien algo. -8. [prison sentence] cumplir; [apprenticeship] hacer; [term of office] ejercer. -9. SPORT servir, sacar. -10. phr: that ~s you right! ¡bien merecido lo tienes! ◇ vi -1. [work, give food or drink] servir. -2. [function]: to ~ as servir de. -3. [in shop, bar etc] despachar. -4. SPORT sacar. ◇ n saque m. ◆ serve out, serve up vt sep servir.

service ['sɜ:vis] ◇ n -1. [gen] servicio m; in ~ en funcionamiento; out of ~ fuera de servicio. -2. [mechanical check] revisión f. -3. RELIG oficio m, servicio m. -4. [set of plates etc] servicio m, juego m. -5. SPORT saque m. -6. [use]: to be of ~ (to sb) servir (a alguien). ◇ vt [car, machine] revisar. ◆ services ◇ npl -1. [on motorway] área f de servicios. -2. [armed forces]: the ~s las fuerzas armadas. -3. [efforts, work] servicios mpl.

serviceable ['sɜ:visǝbl] adj útil, práctico(ca).

service area n área f de servicios.

service charge n servicio m.

serviceman ['sɜ:vismǝn] (pl -men [-mǝn]) n militar m.

service station n estación f de servicio.

serviette [ˌsɜ:vi'et] n servilleta f.

sesame ['sesǝmi] n sésamo m.

session ['seʃn] n -1. [gen] sesión f; in ~ en sesión. -2. Am [school term] trimestre m.

set [set] (pt & pp set) ◇ adj -1. [fixed - expression, amount] fijo(ja); [- pattern, method] establecido(da). -2. Br SCH [text etc] asignado(da). -3. [ready, prepared]: ~ (for sthg/to do sthg) listo(ta) (para algo/para hacer algo). -4. [determined]: to be ~ on sthg/doing sthg estar empeñado(da) en algo/hacer algo. ◇ n -1. [collection - gen] juego m; [- of stamps] serie f. -2. [TV, radio] aparato m. -3. THEATRE decorado m; CINEMA plató m. -4. TENNIS set m. ◇ vt -1. [position, place] poner, colocar. -2. [fix, insert]: to ~ sthg in OR into montar algo en. -3. [cause to be or start]: to ~ free poner en libertad; to ~ fire to prender fuego a; to ~ sthg in motion poner algo en marcha. -4. [trap, table, essay] poner. -5.

[alarm, meter] **poner. -6.** [time, wage] **fijar. -7.** [example] **dar;** [precedent] **sentar;** [trend] **imponer, dictar. -8.** [target] **fijar. -9.** MED [bones, leg] **componer. -10.** [book, play, film] **situar, ambientar.** ◇ *vi* **-1.** [sun] **ponerse. -2.** [jelly] **cuajarse;** [glue, cement] **secarse.** ◆ **set about** *vt fus* [start - task] **comenzar;** [- problem] **atacar; to ~ about doing sthg** ponerse a hacer algo. ◆ **set aside** *vt sep* **-1.** [keep, save] **reservar. -2.** [dismiss - enmity, differences] **dejar de lado.** ◆ **set back** *vt sep* **-1.** [delay] **retrasar.** ◆ **set off** ◇ *vt sep* **-1.** [initiate, cause] **provocar. -2.** [ignite - bomb] **hacer estallar.** ◇ *vi* **ponerse en camino.** ◆ **set out** ◇ *vt sep* **-1.** [arrange] **disponer. -2.** [explain] **exponer.** ◇ *vi* **-1.** [on journey] **ponerse en camino. -2.** [intend]: **to ~ out to do sthg** proponerse a hacer algo. ◆ **set up** ◇ *vt sep* **-1.** [business] **poner, montar;** [committee, organization] **crear;** [procedure] **establecer;** [interview, meeting] **organizar. -2.** [statue, roadblock] **levantar. -3.** [prepare for use] **preparar. -4.** *inf* [frame] **tender una trampa a.**

setback ['setbæk] *n* revés *m*, contratiempo *m*.

set menu *n* menú *m* del día.

settee [se'ti:] *n* sofá *m*.

setting ['setɪŋ] *n* **-1.** [surroundings] escenario *m*. **-2.** [of dial, control] posición *f*.

settle ['setl] ◇ *vt* **-1.** [conclude, decide] **resolver. -2.** [pay] **ajustar, saldar. -3.** [calm - nerves] **tranquilizar.** ◇ *vi* **-1.** [stop travelling] **instalarse. -2.** [make o.s. comfortable] **acomodarse. -3.** [dust, sediment] **depositarse. -4.** [calm down - person] **calmarse.** ◆ **settle down** *vi* **-1.** [concentrate on]: **to ~ down to doing sthg** ponerse a hacer algo. **-2.** [become respectable] **sentar la cabeza. -3.** [calm oneself] **calmarse.** ◆ **settle for** *vt fus* **conformarse con.** ◆ **settle in** *vi* [in new home] **instalarse;** [in new job] **adaptarse.** ◆ **settle on** *vt fus* [choose] **decidirse por.** ◆ **settle up** *vi*: **to ~ up (with sb)** ajustar las cuentas (con alguien).

settlement ['setlmənt] *n* **-1.** [agreement] **acuerdo** *m*. **-2.** [village] **poblado** *m*.

settler ['setlə'] *n* colono *m*.

set-up *n inf* **-1.** [system, organization] **sistema** *m*. **-2.** [frame, trap] **trampa** *f*.

seven ['sevn] *num* siete *m*; *see also* **six**.

seventeen [,sevn'ti:n] *num* diecisiete *m*; *see also* **six**.

seventh ['sevnθ] *num* séptimo(ma); *see also* **sixth**.

seventy ['sevntɪ] *num* setenta *m*; *see also* **sixty**.

sever ['sevə'] *vt* **-1.** [cut through] **cortar. -2.** [finish completely] **romper.**

several ['sevrəl] ◇ *adj* varios(rias). ◇ *pron* varios *mpl*, -rias *fpl*.

severance ['sevrəns] *n fml* ruptura *f*.

severance pay *n* despido *m*.

severe [sɪ'vɪə'] *adj* [gen] severo(ra); [pain] fuerte, agudo(da).

severity [sɪ'verətɪ] *n* [gen] gravedad *f*; [of shortage, problem] severidad *f*.

Seville [sə'vɪl] *n* Sevilla.

sew [səʊ] (*Br pp* **sewn**, *Am pp* **sewed** OR **sewn**) *vt & vi* coser. ◆ **sew up** *vt sep* [cloth] **coser.**

sewage ['su:ɪdʒ] *n* (U) aguas *fpl* residuales.

sewer ['suə'] *n* alcantarilla *f*, cloaca *f*.

sewing ['səʊɪŋ] *n* (U) **-1.** [activity] labor *f* de costura. **-2.** [items] costura *f*.

sewing machine *n* máquina *f* de coser.

sewn [səʊn] *pp* → **sew**.

sex [seks] *n* sexo *m*; **to have ~** tener relaciones sexuales.

sexist ['seksɪst] ◇ *adj* sexista. ◇ *n* sexista *m y f*.

sexual ['sekʃʊəl] *adj* sexual.

sexual harassment *n* acoso *m* sexual.

sexual intercourse *n* (U) relaciones *fpl* sexuales.

sexy ['seksɪ] *adj inf* sexi (*inv*).

shabby ['ʃæbɪ] *adj* **-1.** [clothes, briefcase] **desastrado(da);** [street] de aspecto **abandonado. -2.** [person] **andrajoso(sa).**

shack [ʃæk] *n* chabola *f*.

shackle ['ʃækl] *vt* [enchain] **poner grilletes a.** ◆ **shackles** *npl* [metal rings] **grilletes** *mpl*.

shade [ʃeɪd] ◇ *n* **-1.** (U) [shadow] sombra *f*. **-2.** [lampshade] **pantalla** *f*. **-3.** [of colour, meaning] **matiz** *m*. ◇ *vt* [from light] **dar sombra a.** ◆ **shades** *npl inf* [sunglasses] **gafas** *fpl* de sol.

shadow ['ʃædəʊ] *n* **-1.** [dark shape, form] **sombra** *f*. **-2.** [darkness] **oscuridad** *f*. **-3.** *phr*: **there's not a** OR **the ~ of a doubt** no hay la menor duda.

shadow cabinet *n* gobierno *m* en la **sombra,** *directiva del principal partido de la oposición en Gran Bretaña.*

shadowy ['ʃædəʊɪ] *adj* **-1.** [dark] **sombrío(a). -2.** [hard to see] **vago(ga).**

shady ['ʃeɪdɪ] *adj* **-1.** [sheltered from sun] **sombreado(da). -2.** *inf* [dishonest - businessman] **sospechoso(sa);** [- deal] **turbio(bia).**

shaft [ʃɑːft] n **-1.** [vertical passage] pozo m. **-2.** [rod - of propeller etc] eje m. **-3.** [of light] rayo m.

shaggy ['ʃægɪ] adj [dog] peludo(da).

shake [ʃeɪk] (pt **shook**, pp **shaken** ['ʃeɪkən]) ◇ vt **-1.** [move vigorously] sacudir; **to ~ sb's hand** dar OR estrechar la mano a alguien; **to ~ hands** darse OR estrecharse la mano; **to ~ one's head** [in refusal] negar con la cabeza; [in disbelief] mover la cabeza mostrando incredulidad. **-2.** [shock] trastornar, conmocionar. ◇ vi temblar. ◆ **shake off** vt sep [pursuer] deshacerse de; [cold] quitarse de encima; [illness] superar.

shaken ['ʃeɪkn] pp → **shake**.

shaky ['ʃeɪkɪ] adj **-1.** [weak, nervous] tembloroso(sa). **-2.** [unconfident, insecure - start] incierto(ta); [- argument] poco sólido(da).

shall [weak form ʃəl, strong form ʃæl] aux vb **-1.** (1st person sg & 1st person pl) [to express future tense]: **we ~ be there tomorrow** mañana estaremos ahí; **I shan't be home till ten** no estaré en casa hasta las diez. **-2.** (esp 1st person sg & 1st person pl) [in questions]: **~ we go for a walk?** ¿vamos a dar una vuelta?; **~ I give her a ring?** ¿la llamo?; **I'll do that,** ~ **I?** hago esto, ¿vale? **-3.** [in orders]: **you ~ do as I tell you!** ¡harás lo que yo te diga!; **no one ~ leave until I say so** que nadie salga hasta que yo lo diga.

shallow ['ʃæləʊ] adj **-1.** [in size] poco profundo(da). **-2.** pej [superficial] superficial.

sham [ʃæm] ◇ n farsa f. ◇ vi fingir.

shambles ['ʃæmblz] n desbarajuste m, follón m.

shame [ʃeɪm] ◇ n **-1.** (U) [remorse] vergüenza f, pena f Amer. **-2.** [dishonour]: **to bring ~ on** OR **upon sb** deshonrar a alguien. **-3.** [pity]: **what a ~!** ¡qué pena OR lástima!; **it's a ~** es una pena OR lástima. ◇ vt **-1.** [fill with shame] avergonzar. **-2.** [force by making ashamed]: **to ~ sb into doing sthg** conseguir que alguien haga algo avergonzándole.

shamefaced [ˌʃeɪm'feɪst] adj avergonzado(da).

shameful ['ʃeɪmfʊl] adj vergonzoso(sa).

shameless ['ʃeɪmlɪs] adj desvergonzado(da).

shampoo [ʃæm'puː] (pl **-s**) ◇ n [liquid] champú m. ◇ vt lavar (con champú).

shamrock ['ʃæmrɒk] n trébol m.

shandy ['ʃændɪ] n cerveza f con gaseosa, clara f.

shan't [ʃɑːnt] = **shall not**.

shantytown ['ʃæntɪtaʊn] n barrio m de chabolas, cantegril m Amer.

shape [ʃeɪp] ◇ n **-1.** [outer form] forma f. **-2.** [definite form, silhouette] figura f. **-3.** [structure] configuración f; **to take ~** tomar forma. **-4.** [form, health]: **to be in good/bad ~** [person] estar/no estar en forma; [business etc] estar en buen/mal estado. ◇ vt **-1.** [mould]: **to ~ sthg (into)** dar a algo forma (de). **-2.** [cause to develop] desarrollar. ◆ **shape up** vi [develop] desarrollarse.

-shaped ['ʃeɪpt] suffix: **egg/star~** en forma de huevo/estrella.

shapeless ['ʃeɪplɪs] adj sin forma.

shapely ['ʃeɪplɪ] adj bien hecho(cha).

share [ʃeəʳ] ◇ n **-1.** [portion]: **~ (of** OR **in)** parte f (de). **-2.** [contribution, quota]: **to have/do one's ~ of sthg** tener/hacer la parte que a uno le toca de algo. ◇ vt [gen]: **to ~ sthg (with)** compartir algo (con). ◇ vi compartir. ◆ **shares** npl acciones fpl. ◆ **share out** vt sep repartir, distribuir.

shareholder ['ʃeəˌhəʊldəʳ] n accionista m y f.

shark [ʃɑːk] (pl inv OR **-s**) n tiburón m; fig estafador m, -ra f.

sharp [ʃɑːp] ◇ adj **-1.** [not blunt] afilado(da). **-2.** [well-defined - outline] definido(da); [- photograph] nítido(da); [- contrast] marcado(da). **-3.** [intelligent, keen - person] listo(ta); [- eyesight] penetrante; [- hearing] fino(na); [- intelligence] vivo(va). **-4.** [abrupt, sudden] brusco(ca). **-5.** [quick, firm - blow] seco(ca). **-6.** [angry, severe] cortante. **-7.** [piercing, acute - sound, cry, pain] agudo(da); [- cold, wind] penetrante. **-8.** [bitter] ácido(da). **-9.** MUS desafinado(da). ◇ adv **-1.** [punctually] en punto. **-2.** [quickly, suddenly] bruscamente. ◇ n MUS sostenido m.

sharpen ['ʃɑːpn] vt **-1.** [make sharp] afilar; [pencil] sacar punto a. **-2.** [make keener, quicker, greater] agudizar.

sharpener ['ʃɑːpnəʳ] n [for pencils] sacapuntas m inv; [for knives] afilador m.

sharp-eyed [-'aɪd] adj perspicaz.

sharply ['ʃɑːplɪ] adv **-1.** [distinctly] claramente. **-2.** [suddenly] repentinamente. **-3.** [harshly] duramente.

shat [ʃæt] pt & pp → **shit**.

shatter ['ʃætəʳ] ◇ vt **-1.** [smash] hacer

añicos. **-2.** [hopes etc] echar por tierra. ◇ *vi* hacerse añicos.

shattered ['ʃætəd] *adj* **-1.** [shocked, upset] destrozado(da). **-2.** *Br inf* [very tired] hecho(cha) polvo.

shave [ʃeɪv] ◇ *n* afeitado *m*; **to have a ~** afeitarse. ◇ *vt* **-1.** [face, body] afeitar. **-2.** [cut pieces off] raspar. ◇ *vi* afeitar.

shaver ['ʃeɪvə^r] *n* maquinilla *f* (de afeitar) eléctrica.

shaving brush ['ʃeɪvɪŋ-] *n* brocha *f* de afeitar.

shaving cream ['ʃeɪvɪŋ-] *n* crema *f* de afeitar.

shaving foam ['ʃeɪvɪŋ-] *n* espuma *f* de afeitar.

shavings ['ʃeɪvɪŋz] *npl* virutas *fpl*.

shawl [ʃɔ:l] *n* chal *m*.

she [ʃi:] ◇ *pers pron* **-1.** [referring to woman, girl, animal] ella; **~'s tall** es alta; SHE **can't do it** ella no puede hacerlo; **there ~ is** allí está; **if I were** OR **was ~** *fml* si (yo) fuera ella. **-2.** [referring to boat, car, country]: **~'s a fine ship** es un buen barco. ◇ *comp*: **~-elephant** elefanta *f*; **~ bear** osa *f*.

sheaf [ʃi:f] (*pl* **sheaves**) *n* **-1.** [of papers, letters] fajo *m*. **-2.** [of corn, grain] gavilla *f*.

shear [ʃɪə^r] (*pp* **-ed** OR **shorn**) *vt* [sheep] esquilar. ◆ **shears** *npl* [for garden] tijeras *fpl* de podar. ◆ **shear off** *vi* romperse.

sheath [ʃi:θ] (*pl* **-s**) *n* **-1.** [covering for knife] vaina *f*. **-2.** *Br* [condom] preservativo *m*.

sheaves [ʃi:vz] *pl* → **sheaf**.

shed [ʃed] (*pt* & *pp* **shed**) ◇ *n* cobertizo *m*. ◇ *vt* **-1.** [skin] mudar de; [leaves] despejarse de. **-2.** [discard] deshacerse de. **-3.** [tears, blood] derramar.

she'd [weak form ʃɪd, strong form ʃi:d] = **she had, she would.**

sheen [ʃi:n] *n* brillo *m*, lustre *m*.

sheep [ʃi:p] (*pl inv*) *n* [animal] oveja *f*; *fig* [person] borrego *m*, cordero *m*.

sheepdog ['ʃi:pdɒg] *n* perro *m* pastor.

sheepish ['ʃi:pɪʃ] *adj* avergonzado(da).

sheepskin ['ʃi:pskɪn] *n* piel *f* de carnero.

sheer [ʃɪə^r] *adj* **-1.** [absolute] puro(ra). **-2.** [very steep - cliff] escarpado(da); [- drop] vertical. **-3.** [delicate] diáfano(na).

sheet [ʃi:t] *n* **-1.** [for bed] sábana *f*. **-2.** [of paper] hoja *f*. **-3.** [of glass, metal, wood] lámina *f*.

sheik(h) [ʃeɪk] *n* jeque *m*.

shelf [ʃelf] (*pl* **shelves**) *n* estante *m*.

shell [ʃel] ◇ *n* **-1.** [of egg, nut] cáscara *f*. **-2.** [of tortoise, crab] caparazón *m*; [of snail, mussels] concha *f*. **-3.** [on beach] concha *f*. **-4.** [of building] esqueleto *m*; [of boat] casco *m*; [of car] armazón *m*, chasis *m inv*. **-5.** MIL [missile] proyectil *m*. ◇ *vt* **-1.** [peas] desvainar; [nuts, eggs] quitar la cáscara a. **-2.** MIL [fire shells at] bombardear.

she'll [ʃi:l] = **she will, she shall.**

shellfish ['ʃelfɪʃ] (*pl inv*) *n* **-1.** [creature] crustáceo *m*. **-2.** (*U*) [food] mariscos *mpl*.

shell suit *n Br* chandal *m* (de nailon).

shelter ['ʃeltə^r] ◇ *n* [building, protection] refugio *m*. ◇ *vt* **-1.** [protect]: **to be ~ed by/from** estar protegido(da) por/de. **-2.** [provide place to live for] dar asilo OR cobijo a. **-3.** [hide] proteger, esconder. ◇ *vi*: **to ~ from/in** resguardarse de/en, protegerse de/en.

sheltered ['ʃeltəd] *adj* [place, existence] protegido(da).

shelve [ʃelv] *vt* dar carpetazo a.

shelves [ʃelvz] *pl* → **shelf**.

shepherd ['ʃepəd] ◇ *n* pastor *m*. ◇ *vt fig* acompañar.

shepherd's pie ['ʃepədz-] *n* carne picada cubierta de puré de patatas.

sheriff ['ʃerɪf] *n Am* sheriff *m*.

sherry ['ʃerɪ] *n* jerez *m*.

she's [ʃi:z] = **she is, she has.**

Shetland ['ʃetlənd] *n*: **(the) ~ (Islands)** las islas Shetland.

shield [ʃi:ld] ◇ *n* [armour, sports trophy] escudo *m*. ◇ *vt*: **to ~ sb (from)** proteger a alguien (de).

shift [ʃɪft] ◇ *n* **-1.** [slight change] cambio *m*. **-2.** [period of work, workers] turno *m*. ◇ *vt* **-1.** [furniture etc] cambiar de sitio, mover. **-2.** [attitude, belief] cambiar de. ◇ *vi* **-1.** [person] moverse; [wind, opinion] cambiar. **-2.** *Am* AUT cambiar de marcha.

shiftless ['ʃɪftlɪs] *adj* vago(ga).

shifty ['ʃɪftɪ] *adj inf* [person] con pinta deshonesta; [behaviour] sospechoso(sa); [look] huidizo(za).

shilling ['ʃɪlɪŋ] *n* chelín *m*.

shilly-shally ['ʃɪlɪˌʃælɪ] (*pt* & *pp* **-ied**) *vi* titubear, vacilar.

shimmer ['ʃɪmə^r] *vi* rielar, brillar con luz trémula.

shin [ʃɪn] *n* espinilla *f*.

shinbone ['ʃɪnbəʊn] *n* espinilla *f*.

shine [ʃaɪn] (*pt* & *pp* **shone**) ◇ *n* brillo

m. ◇ *vt* [torch, lamp] dirigir. ◇ *vi* [gen] brillar.

shingle ['ʃɪŋgl] *n* (U) [on beach] guijarros *mpl*. ◆ **shingles** *n* (U) herpes *m inv.*

ship [ʃɪp] ◇ *n* barco *m*, buque *m*. ◇ *vt* enviar por barco.

shipbuilding ['ʃɪp,bɪldɪŋ] *n* construcción *f* naval.

shipment ['ʃɪpmənt] *n* envío *m*.

shipper ['ʃɪpər] *n* compañía *f* naviera.

shipping ['ʃɪpɪŋ] *n* (U) **-1.** [transport] envío *m*, transporte *m*. **-2.** [ships] barcos *mpl*, buques *mpl*.

shipshape ['ʃɪpʃeɪp] *adj* en orden.

shipwreck ['ʃɪprek] ◇ *n* **-1.** [destruction of ship] naufragio *m*. **-2.** [wrecked ship] barco *m* náufrago. ◇ *vt*: **to be ~ed** naufragar.

shipyard ['ʃɪpjɑːd] *n* astillero *m*.

shire [ʃaɪər] *n* [county] condado *m*.

shirk [ʃɜːk] *vt* eludir.

shirt [ʃɜːt] *n* camisa *f*.

shirtsleeves ['ʃɜːtsliːvz] *npl*: **to be in (one's) ~** ir en mangas de camisa.

shit [ʃɪt] (*pt & pp* **shit** OR **-ted** OR **shat**) *vulg* ◇ *n* **-1.** [excrement] mierda *f*. **-2.** (U) [nonsense] gilipolleces *fpl*. ◇ *vi* cagar. ◇ *excl* ¡mierda!

shiver ['ʃɪvər] ◇ *n* escalofrío *m*. ◇ *vi*: **to ~ (with)** [fear] temblar OR estremecerse (de); [cold] tiritar (de).

shoal [ʃəʊl] *n* banco *m*.

shock [ʃɒk] ◇ *n* **-1.** [unpleasant surprise, reaction, emotional state] susto *m*; **it came as a ~** fue un duro golpe. **-2.** (U) MED: **to be suffering from ~** estar en un estado de choque. **-3.** [impact] choque *m*. **-4.** [electric shock] descarga *f* OR sacudida *f* (eléctrica). ◇ *vt* **-1.** [upset] conmocionar. **-2.** [offend] escandalizar.

shock absorber [-əb,zɔːbər] *n* amortiguador *m*.

shocking ['ʃɒkɪŋ] *adj* **-1.** [very bad] pésimo(ma). **-2.** [behaviour, film] escandaloso(sa); [price] de escándalo.

shod [ʃɒd] ◇ *pt & pp* → **shoe.** ◇ *adj* calzado(da).

shoddy ['ʃɒdɪ] *adj* [work] chapucero(ra); [goods] de pacotilla; *fig* [treatment] vil, despreciable.

shoe [ʃuː] (*pt & pp* **shod** OR **shoed**) ◇ *n* zapato *m*. ◇ *vt* herrar.

shoebrush ['ʃuːbrʌʃ] *n* cepillo *m* para los zapatos.

shoehorn ['ʃuːhɔːn] *n* calzador *m*.

shoelace ['ʃuːleɪs] *n* cordón *m* del zapato.

shoe polish *n* betún *m*.

shoe shop *n* zapatería *f*.

shoestring ['ʃuːstrɪŋ] *n* *fig*: **on a ~** con cuatro cuartos, con muy poco dinero.

shone [ʃɒn] *pt & pp* → **shine.**

shoo [ʃuː] ◇ *vt* [animal] espantar, ahuyentar; [person] mandar a otra parte. ◇ *excl* ¡fuera!

shook [ʃʊk] *pt* → **shake.**

shoot [ʃuːt] (*pt & pp* **shot**) ◇ *n* **-1.** *Br* [hunting expedition] cacería *f*. **-2.** [new growth] brote *m*, retoño *m*. ◇ *vt* **-1.** [fire gun at] disparar contra, abalear *Amer*; [injure] herir a tiros; [kill] matar a tiros; **to ~ o.s.** pegarse un tiro. **-2.** *Br* [hunt] cazar. **-3.** [arrow] disparar. **-4.** CINEMA rodar, filmar. ◇ *vi* **-1.** [fire gun]: **to ~ (at)** disparar (contra). **-2.** *Br* [hunt] cazar. **-3.** [move quickly]: **to ~ in/out/past** entrar/salir/pasar disparado(da). **-4.** CINEMA rodar, filmar. **-5.** SPORT chutar. ◆ **shoot down** *vt sep* **-1.** [plane] derribar. **-2.** [person] matar a tiros. ◆ **shoot up** *vi* **-1.** [child, plant] crecer rápidamente. **-2.** [prices] dispararse.

shooting ['ʃuːtɪŋ] *n* **-1.** [killing] asesinato *m* (*a tiros*). **-2.** (U) [hunting] caza *f*, cacería *f*.

shooting star *n* estrella *f* fugaz.

shop [ʃɒp] ◇ *n* **-1.** [store] tienda *f*. **-2.** [workshop] taller *m*. ◇ *vi* comprar; **to go shopping** ir de compras.

shop assistant *n* *Br* dependiente *m*, -ta *f*.

shop floor *n*: **the ~** el personal, los obreros.

shopkeeper ['ʃɒp,kiːpər] *n* tendero *m*, -ra *f*.

shoplifting ['ʃɒp,lɪftɪŋ] *n* (U) robo *m* en una tienda.

shopper ['ʃɒpər] *n* comprador *m*, -ra *f*.

shopping ['ʃɒpɪŋ] *n* (U) **-1.** [purchases] compras *fpl*. **-2.** [act of shopping] compra *f*.

shopping bag *n* bolsa *f* de la compra.

shopping centre *Br*, **shopping mall** *Am*, **shopping plaza** *Am* [-,plɑːzə] *n* centro *m* comercial.

shopsoiled *Br* ['ʃɒpsɔɪld], **shopworn** *Am* ['ʃɒpwɔːn] *adj* deteriorado(da).

shop steward *n* enlace *m* y *f* sindical.

shopwindow [,ʃɒp'wɪndəʊ] *n* escaparate *m*.

shopworn *Am* = **shopsoiled.**

shore [ʃɔːr] *n* **-1.** [of sea, lake, river] orilla *f*. **-2.** [land]: **on ~** en tierra. ◆ **shore up** *vt sep* apuntalar.

shorn [ʃɔːn] ◇ *pp* → **shear**. ◇ *adj* [grass, hair] corto(ta); [head] rapado(da).

short [ʃɔːt] ◇ *adj* **-1.** [gen] corto(ta). **-2.** [not tall] bajo(ja). **-3.** [curt]: **to be ~ (with sb)** ser seco(ca) (con alguien). **-4.** [lacking] escaso(sa); **to be ~ on sthg** no andar sobrado de algo; **to be ~ of** estar OR andar mal de. **-5.** [be shorter form]: **to be ~ for** ser el diminutivo de. ◇ *adv* **-1.** [out of]: **we are running ~ of water** se nos está acabando el agua. **-2.** [suddenly, abruptly]: **to cut sthg ~** interrumpir algo antes de acabar; **to stop ~** parar en seco OR de repente; **to bring** OR **pull sb up ~** hacer a alguien parar en seco. ◇ *n* **-1.** *Br* [alcoholic drink] licor *m*. **-2.** [film] cortometraje *m*. ◆ **shorts** *npl* **-1.** [gen] pantalones *mpl* cortos. **-2.** *Am* [underwear] calzoncillos *mpl*. ◆ **for short** *adv* para abreviar. ◆ **in short** *adv* en resumen. ◆ **nothing short of** *prep*: **it was nothing ~ of madness/a disgrace** fue una auténtica locura/vergüenza. ◆ **short of** *prep* **-1.** [just before] cerca de. **-2.** [without]: **~ of asking, I can't see how you'll find out** salvo que preguntes, no sé cómo lo vas a averiguar.

shortage [ʃɔːtɪdʒ] *n* falta *f*, escasez *f*.

shortbread [ʃɔːtbred] *n* especie de torta hecha de azúcar, harina y mantequilla.

short-change *vt* [in shop] dar mal el cambio a; *fig* [reward unfairly] estafar.

short circuit *n* cortocircuito *m*.

shortcomings [ʃɔːtˌkʌmɪŋz] *npl* defectos *mpl*.

shortcrust pastry [ʃɔːtkrʌst-] *n* pasta *f* quebrada.

short cut *n* **-1.** [quick way] atajo *m*. **-2.** [quick method] método *m* rápido.

shorten [ʃɔːtn] ◇ *vt* acertar. ◇ *vi* acortarse.

shortfall [ʃɔːtfɔːl] *n*: **~ (in** OR **of)** déficit *m* (de).

shorthand [ʃɔːthænd] *n* [writing system] taquigrafía *f*.

shorthand typist *n Br* taquimecanógrafo *m*, -fa *f*.

short list *n Br* [for job] lista *f* de candidatos seleccionados; [for prize] relación *f* de finalistas.

shortly [ʃɔːtlɪ] *adv* [soon] dentro de poco; **~ before/after** poco antes/después de.

shortsighted [ˌʃɔːtˈsaɪtɪd] *adj* [myopic] miope, corto(ta) de vista; *fig* [lacking foresight] corto de miras.

short-staffed [-ˈstɑːft] *adj*: **to be ~** estar falto(ta) de personal.

short story *n* cuento *m*.

short-tempered [-ˈtempəd] *adj* de mal genio.

short-term *adj* a corto plazo.

short wave *n* (*U*) onda *f* corta.

shot [ʃɒt] ◇ *pt & pp* → **shoot**. ◇ *n* **-1.** [gunshot] tiro *m*, disparo *m*; **like a ~** [quickly] en el acto. **-2.** [marksman] tirador *m*, -ra *f*. **-3.** [in football] chut *m*, tiro *m*; [in golf, tennis] golpe *m*. **-4.** [photograph] foto *f*. **-5.** CINEMA plano *m*, toma *f*. **-6.** *inf* [try, go] intento *m*. **-7.** [injection] inyección *f*.

shotgun [ʃɒtɡʌn] *n* escopeta *f*.

should [ʃʊd] *aux vb* **-1.** [be desirable]: **we ~ leave now** deberíamos irnos ya OR ahora. **-2.** [seeking advice, permission]: **~ I go too?** ¿voy yo también? **-3.** [as suggestion]: **I ~ deny everything** yo lo negaría todo. **-4.** [indicating probability]: **she ~ be home soon** tiene que llegar a casa pronto. **-5.** [have been expected]: **they ~ have won the match** tendrían que OR deberían haber ganado el partido. **-6.** [indicating intention, wish]: **I ~ like to come with you** me gustaría ir contigo. **-7.** (*as conditional*): **you ~ go if you were invited** tendrías que OR deberías ir si te han invitado. **-8.** (*in 'that' clauses*): **we decided that you ~ do it** decidimos que lo hicieras tú. **-9.** [expressing uncertain opinion]: **I ~ think he's about 50 (years old)** yo diría que tiene unos 50 (años).

shoulder [ʃəʊldər] ◇ *n* **-1.** [part of body, clothing] hombro *m*. **-2.** CULIN espaldilla *f*. ◇ *vt* [accept - responsibility] cargar con.

shoulder blade *n* omóplato *m*.

shoulder strap *n* **-1.** [on dress] tirante *m*. **-2.** [on bag] correa *f*, bandolera *f*.

shouldn't [ʃʊdnt] = **should not**.

should've [ʃʊdəv] = **should have**.

shout [ʃaʊt] ◇ *n* grito *m*. ◇ *vt* gritar. ◇ *vi*: **to ~ (at)** gritar (a). ◆ **shout down** *vt sep* acallar a gritos.

shouting [ʃaʊtɪŋ] *n* (*U*) gritos *mpl*.

shove [ʃʌv] ◇ *n*: **(to give sthg/sb) a ~** (dar a algo/a alguien) un empujón. ◇ *vt* empujar; **to ~ sthg/sb in** meter algo/a alguien a empujones; **to ~ sthg/sb out** sacar algo/a alguien a empujones. ◆ **shove off** *vi* [go away] *inf* largarse.

shovel [ʃʌvl] ◇ *n* pala *f*. ◇ *vt* remover con la pala OR a paletadas.

show [ʃəʊ] (*pp* **shown** OR **-ed**) ◇ *n* **-1.** [display, demonstration] demostración *f.* **-2.** [piece of entertainment - at theatre] espectáculo *m*; [- on radio, TV] programa *m.* **-3.** [performance] función *f.* **-4.** [of dogs, flowers, art] exposición *f.* ◇ *vt* **-1.** [gen] mostrar; **to ~ sb sthg, to ~ sthg to sb** enseñar OR mostrar a alguien algo. **-2.** [escort]: **to ~ sb to sthg** llevar OR acompañar a alguien hasta algo. **-3.** [make visible, reveal] dejar ver. **-4.** [indicate - increase, profit, loss] arrojar, registrar. **-5.** [broadcast - film] proyectar; [- TV programme] emitir. ◇ *vi* **-1.** [indicate, make clear] indicar, mostrar. **-2.** [be visible] verse. **-3.** [film] proyectarse. ◆ **show off** ◇ *vt sep* lucir, presumir de. ◇ *vi* presumir. ◆ **show up** ◇ *vt sep* poner en evidencia. ◇ *vi* **-1.** [stand out] resaltar. **-2.** [turn up] aparecer.

show business *n* (*U*) mundo *m* del espectáculo.

showdown ['ʃəʊdaʊn] *n*: **to have a ~ with** enfrentarse abiertamente a OR con.

shower ['ʃaʊəʳ] ◇ *n* **-1.** [device] ducha *f.* **-2.** [wash]: **to have** OR **take a ~** ducharse. **-3.** [of rain] chubasco *m*, chaparrón *m.* **-4.** [stream] lluvia *f.* ◇ *vt* **-1.** [sprinkle] rociar. **-2.** [bestow]: **to ~ sb with sthg, to ~ sthg on** OR **upon sb** [present, compliments] colmar a alguien de algo; [insults] acribillar a alguien a algo. ◇ *vi* ducharse.

shower cap *n* gorro *m* de baño.

showing ['ʃəʊɪŋ] *n* [of film] pase *m*, proyección *f*; [of paintings] exposición *f.*

show jumping [-,dʒʌmpɪŋ] *n* concurso *m* hípico de salto.

shown [ʃəʊn] *pp* → **show.**

show-off *n inf* presumido *m*, -da *f.*

showpiece ['ʃəʊpiːs] *n* pieza *f* de mayor interés.

showroom ['ʃəʊrʊm] *n* salón *m* OR sala *f* de exposición.

shrank [ʃræŋk] *pt* → **shrink.**

shrapnel ['ʃræpnl] *n* metralla *f.*

shred [ʃred] ◇ *n* [small piece - of material] jirón *m*; [- of paper] pedacito *m*; *fig* [scrap] pizca *f.* ◇ *vt* [paper] hacer trizas; [food] rallar.

shredder ['ʃredəʳ] *n* [for paper] destructora *f*; [for food] rallador *m.*

shrewd [ʃruːd] *adj* astuto(ta).

shriek [ʃriːk] ◇ *n* chillido *m*, grito *m.* ◇ *vi*: **to ~ (with** OR **in)** chillar (de).

shrill [ʃrɪl] *adj* [high-pitched] estridente, agudo(da).

shrimp [ʃrɪmp] *n* camarón *m.*

shrine [ʃraɪn] *n* santuario *m.*

shrink [ʃrɪŋk] (*pt* **shrank,** *pp* **shrunk**) ◇ *vt* encoger. ◇ *vi* **-1.** [become smaller] encoger. **-2.** *fig* [contract, diminish] disminuir. **-3.** [recoil]: **to ~ away from** retroceder OR arredrarse ante. **-4.** [be reluctant]: **to ~ from sthg** eludir algo.

shrinkage ['ʃrɪŋkɪdʒ] *n* [loss in size] encogimiento *m*; *fig* [contraction] reducción *f.*

shrink-wrap *vt precintar o envasar con plástico termoretráctil.*

shrivel ['ʃrɪvl] ◇ *vt*: **to ~ (up)** secar, marchitar. ◇ *vi*: **to ~ (up)** secarse, marchitarse.

shroud [ʃraʊd] ◇ *n* [cloth] mortaja *f*, sudario *m.* ◇ *vt*: **to be ~ed in sthg** estar envuelto(ta) en.

Shrove Tuesday ['ʃrəʊv-] *n* martes *m inv* de carnaval.

shrub [ʃrʌb] *n* arbusto *m.*

shrubbery ['ʃrʌbərɪ] *n* (zona *f* de) arbustos *mpl.*

shrug [ʃrʌg] ◇ *vt*: **to ~ one's shoulders** encogerse de hombros. ◇ *vi* encogerse de hombros. ◆ **shrug off** *vt sep* quitar importancia a.

shrunk [ʃrʌŋk] *pp* → **shrink.**

shudder ['ʃʌdəʳ] *vi* [tremble]: **to ~ (with)** estremecerse (de).

shuffle ['ʃʌfl] ◇ *vt* **-1.** [feet] arrastrar. **-2.** [cards] barajar. ◇ *vi* [walk by dragging feet]: **to ~ in/out/along** entrar/salir/andar arrastrando los pies.

shun [ʃʌn] *vt* rehuir, esquivar.

shunt [ʃʌnt] *vt* RAIL cambiar de vía; *fig* [move] llevar (de un sitio a otro).

shut [ʃʌt] (*pt* & *pp* **shut**) ◇ *adj* cerrado(da). ◇ *vt* cerrar. ◇ *vi* **-1.** [close] cerrarse. **-2.** [close for business] cerrar. ◆ **shut away** *vt sep* guardar bajo llave. ◆ **shut down** *vt sep* & *vi* cerrar. ◆ **shut out** *vt sep* **-1.** [person, cat] dejar fuera a; [light, noise] no dejar entrar. ◆ **shut up** *inf* ◇ *vt sep* [silence] hacer callar. ◇ *vi* callarse.

shutter ['ʃʌtəʳ] *n* **-1.** [on window] postigo *m.* **-2.** [in camera] obturador *m.*

shuttle ['ʃʌtl] ◇ *adj*: **~ service** [of planes] puente *m* aéreo; [of buses, trains] servicio *m* regular. ◇ *n* [plane] avión *m* (de puente aéreo).

shuttlecock ['ʃʌtlkɒk] *n* volante *m.*

shy [ʃaɪ] ◇ *adj* [timid] tímido(da). ◇ *vi* espantarse.

Siberia [saɪ'bɪərɪə] *n* Siberia.

sibling ['sɪblɪŋ] *n* hermano *m*, -na *f.*

Sicily ['sɪsɪlɪ] n Sicilia.

sick [sɪk] adj **-1.** [ill] enfermo(ma). **-2.** [nauseous]: **to feel ~** marearse. **-3.** [vomiting]: **to be ~** Br devolver, vomitar. **-4.** [fed up]: **to be ~ of** sthg/of doing sthg estar harto(ta) de algo/de hacer algo. **-5.** [offensive] de mal gusto.

sickbay ['sɪkbeɪ] n enfermería f.

sicken ['sɪkn] ◇ vt poner enfermo(ma), asquear. ◇ vi Br: **to be ~ing for** sthg estar cogiendo algo.

sickening ['sɪknɪŋ] adj **-1.** [disgusting] asqueroso(sa). **-2.** [infuriating] exasperante.

sickle ['sɪkl] n hoz f.

sick leave n (U) baja f por enfermedad.

sickly ['sɪklɪ] adj **-1.** [unhealthy] enfermizo(za). **-2.** [unpleasant] nauseabundo(da).

sickness ['sɪknɪs] n **-1.** [illness] enfermedad f. **-2.** Br (U) [nausea, vomiting] mareo m.

sick pay n (U) paga f por enfermedad.

side [saɪd] ◇ n **-1.** [gen] lado m; **at** OR **by one's ~** al lado de uno; **on every ~, on all ~s** por todos los lados; **from ~ to ~** de un lado a otro; **~ by ~** juntos, uno al lado de otro. **-2.** [of person] costado m; [of animal] ijada f. **-3.** [edge] lado m, borde m. **-4.** [of hill, valley] falda f, ladera f. **-5.** [bank] orilla f. **-6.** [page] cara f. **-7.** [participant - in war, game] lado m, bando m; [- in sports match] equipo m. **-8.** [viewpoint] punto m de vista; **to take sb's ~** ponerse del lado OR de parte de alguien. **-9.** [aspect] aspecto m; **to be on the safe ~** para estar seguro. ◇ adj lateral. ◆ **side with** vt fus ponerse de parte de.

sideboard ['saɪdbɔːd] n aparador m.

sideboards Br ['saɪdbɔːdz], **sideburns** Am ['saɪdbɜːnz] npl patillas fpl.

side effect n MED & fig efecto m secundario.

sidelight ['saɪdlaɪt] n luz f lateral.

sideline ['saɪdlaɪn] n **-1.** [extra business] negocio m suplementario. **-2.** [on tennis court] línea f lateral; [on football pitch] línea de banda.

sidelong ['saɪdlɒŋ] adj & adv de reojo OR soslayo.

sidesaddle ['saɪd,sædl] adv: **to ride ~** montar a sentadillas OR mujeriegas.

sideshow ['saɪdʃəʊ] n barraca f OR caseta f de feria.

sidestep ['saɪdstep] vt **-1.** [in football,

rugby] regatear. **-2.** fig [problem, question] esquivar.

side street n calle f lateral.

sidetrack ['saɪdtræk] vt: **to be ~ed** desviarse OR salirse del tema.

sidewalk ['saɪdwɔːk] n Am acera f.

sideways ['saɪdweɪz] ◇ adj [movement] hacia un lado; [glance] de soslayo. ◇ adv [move] de lado; [look] de reojo.

siding ['saɪdɪŋ] n vía f muerta.

sidle ['saɪdl] ◆ **sidle up** vi: **to ~ up to** acercarse furtivamente a.

siege [siːdʒ] n **-1.** [by army] sitio m, cerco m. **-2.** [by police] cerco m policial.

sieve [sɪv] ◇ n [utensil] colador m. ◇ vt [soup] colar; [flour, sugar] tamizar.

sift [sɪft] ◇ vt **-1.** [sieve] tamizar. **-2.** fig [examine carefully] examinar cuidadosamente. ◇ vi: **to ~ through** sthg examinar cuidadosamente algo.

sigh [saɪ] ◇ n suspiro m. ◇ vi suspirar.

sight [saɪt] ◇ n **-1.** [vision] vista f. **-2.** [act of seeing]: **her first ~ of the sea** la primera vez que vio el mar; **in ~** a la vista; **to disappear out of ~** perderse de vista; **at first ~** a primera vista. **-3.** [something seen] imagen f. **-4.** [on gun] mira f. ◇ vt divisar, avistar. ◆ **sights** npl atracciones fpl turísticas.

sightseeing ['saɪt,siːɪŋ] n (U) recorrido m turístico.

sightseer ['saɪt,siːə'] n turista m y f.

sign [saɪn] ◇ n **-1.** [written symbol] signo m. **-2.** [gesture] señal f. **-3.** [of pub, shop] letrero m; [on road] señal f; [notice] cartel m. **-4.** [indication] señal f, indicio m. ◇ vt firmar. ◆ **sign on** vi **-1.** [enrol, register]: **to ~ on (for)** [army] alistarse (en); [job] firmar el contrato (de); [course] matricularse (en). **-2.** [register as unemployed] firmar para cobrar el paro. ◆ **sign up** ◇ vt sep [employee] contratar; [recruit] alistar. ◇ vi: **to ~ up (for)** [army] alistarse (en); [job] firmar el contrato (de); [course] matricularse (en).

signal ['sɪgnl] ◇ n señal f. ◇ vt **-1.** [indicate] indicar. **-2.** [tell]: **to ~ sb (to do** sthg) hacer señas a alguien (para que haga algo). ◇ vi **-1.** AUT señalizar. **-2.** [indicate]: **to ~ to sb (to do sthg)** hacer señas a alguien (para que haga algo).

signalman ['sɪgnlmən] (pl **-men** [-mən]) n RAIL guardavía m.

signature ['sɪgnətʃə'] n firma f.

signature tune n sintonía f.

signet ring ['sɪgnɪt-] n (anillo m de) sello m.

significance [sɪg'nɪfɪkəns] n trascendencia f, importancia f.

significant [sɪg'nɪfɪkənt] adj -1. [considerable, meaningful] significativo(va). -2. [important] trascendente.

signify ['sɪgnɪfaɪ] vt significar.

signpost ['saɪnpəʊst] n letrero m indicador.

Sikh [siːk] ◇ adj sij. ◇ n [person] sij m y f.

silence ['saɪləns] ◇ n silencio m. ◇ vt [person, critic] acallar; [gun] silenciar.

silencer ['saɪlənsə'] n silenciador m.

silent ['saɪlənt] adj -1. [gen] silencioso(sa). -2. [not revealing anything]: **to be ~ about** quedar en silencio respecto a. -3. CINEMA & LING mudo(da).

silhouette [,sɪluː'et] n silueta f.

silicon chip [,sɪlɪkən-] n chip m de silicio.

silk [sɪlk] ◇ n seda f. ◇ comp de seda.

silky ['sɪlkɪ] adj [hair, dress, skin] sedoso(sa); [voice] aterciopelado(da).

sill [sɪl] n [of window] alféizar m.

silly ['sɪlɪ] adj estúpido(da).

silo ['saɪləʊ] (pl -s) n silo m.

silt [sɪlt] n cieno m, légamo m.

silver ['sɪlvə'] ◇ adj [of colour] plateado(da). ◇ n (U) -1. [metal, silverware] plata f. -2. [coins] monedas fpl plateadas. ◇ comp de plata.

silver foil, silver paper n (U) papel m de plata.

silver-plated [-'pleɪtɪd] adj plateado(da).

silversmith ['sɪlvəsmɪθ] n platero m, -ra f.

silverware ['sɪlvəweə'] n (U) -1. [dishes etc] plata f. -2. Am [cutlery] cubertería f de plata.

similar ['sɪmɪlə'] adj: ~ **(to)** parecido(da) OR similar (a).

similarly ['sɪmɪlɪə] adv [likewise] asimismo; [equally] igualmente.

simmer ['sɪmə'] vt & vi hervir a fuego lento.

simpering ['sɪmpərɪŋ] adj [person] que sonríe con cara de tonto(ta); [smile] bobo(ba).

simple ['sɪmpl] adj -1. [gen] sencillo(lla). -2. dated [mentally retarded] simple. -3. [plain - fact] mero(ra); [- truth] puro(ra).

simple-minded [-'maɪndɪd] adj simple.

simplicity [sɪm'plɪsətɪ] n sencillez f.

simplify ['sɪmplɪfaɪ] vt simplificar.

simply ['sɪmplɪ] adv -1. [merely] sencillamente, simplemente. -2. [for emphasis]: ~ **dreadful/wonderful** francamente terrible/maravilloso. -3. [in a simple way] de manera sencilla.

simulate ['sɪmjʊleɪt] vt simular.

simultaneous [Br ,sɪmʊl'teɪnjəs, Am ,saɪməl'teɪnjəs] adj simultáneo(a).

sin [sɪn] ◇ n pecado m. ◇ vi: **to ~ (against)** pecar (contra).

since [sɪns] ◇ adv desde entonces. ◇ prep desde; **he has worked here ~ 1975** trabaja aquí desde 1975. ◇ conj -1. [in time] desde que; **it's ages ~ I saw you** hace siglos que no te veo. -2. [because] ya que, puesto que.

sincere [sɪn'sɪə'] adj sincero(ra).

sincerely [sɪn'sɪəlɪ] adv sinceramente; **Yours ~** [at end of letter] atentamente.

sincerity [sɪn'serətɪ] n sinceridad f.

sinew ['sɪnjuː] n tendón m.

sinful ['sɪnful] adj -1. [person] pecador(ra). -2. [thought, act] pecaminoso(sa).

sing [sɪŋ] (pt **sang**, pp **sung**) vt & vi cantar.

Singapore [,sɪŋə'pɔː'] n Singapur.

singe [sɪndʒ] vt chamuscar.

singer ['sɪŋə'] n cantante m y f.

singing ['sɪŋɪŋ] n (U) canto m.

single ['sɪŋgl] ◇ adj -1. [only one] único(ca). -2. [individual]: **every ~ penny** todos y cada uno de los peniques. -3. [unmarried] soltero(ra). -4. Br [one-way] de ida. ◇ n -1. Br [one-way ticket] billete m de ida. -2. MUS [record] sencillo m, single m. ◆ **singles** npl TENNIS (partido m) individual m. ◆ **single out** vt sep: **to ~ sb out (for)** escoger a alguien (para).

single bed n cama f individual.

single-breasted [-'brestɪd] adj recto(ta).

single cream n Br nata f líquida.

single file n: **in ~** en fila india.

single-handed [-'hændɪd] adv sin ayuda.

single-minded [-'maɪndɪd] adj resuelto(ta).

single-parent family n familia f en la que falta uno de los padres.

single room n habitación f individual.

singlet ['sɪŋglɪt] n Br camiseta f sin mangas.

singular ['sɪŋgjʊlə'] ◇ adj singular. ◇ n singular m.

sinister ['sɪnɪstə'] adj siniestro(tra).

sink [sɪŋk] (pt **sank**, pp **sunk**) ◇ n -1. [in kitchen] fregadero m. -2. [in bathroom] lavabo m. ◇ vt -1. [cause to go under water] hundir. -2. [cause to penetrate]: **to ~ sthg into** [knife, claws] clavar algo en; [teeth] hincar algo en. ◇ vi -1.

[go down - ship, sun] hundirse. **-2.**
[slump - person] hundirse. **-3.** [decrease]
bajar. ◆ **sink in** *vi* hacer mella.

sink unit *n* fregadero *m* (con mueble
debajo).

sinner ['sɪnəʳ] *n* pecador *m*, -ra *f*.

sinus ['saɪnəs] (*pl* **-es**) *n* seno *m*.

sip [sɪp] ◇ *n* sorbo *m*. ◇ *vt* beber a sor-
bos.

siphon ['saɪfn] *n* sifón *m*. ◆ **siphon off**
vt sep **-1.** [liquid] sacar con sifón. **-2.** *fig*
[funds] desviar.

sir [sɜːʳ] *n* **-1.** [form of address] señor *m*.
-2. [in titles]: **Sir Philip Holden** Sir Philip Holden.

siren ['saɪərən] *n* [alarm] sirena *f*.

sirloin (steak) ['sɜːlɔɪn] *n* solomillo *m*.

sissy ['sɪsɪ] *inf n* mariquita *m*.

sister ['sɪstəʳ] *n* **-1.** [gen] hermana *f*. **-2.**
Br [senior nurse] enfermera *f* jefe.

sister-in-law (*pl* **sisters-in-law** OR
sister-in-laws) *n* cuñada *f*.

sit [sɪt] (*pt* & *pp* **sat**) ◇ *vi* **-1.** [be seated,
sit down] sentarse. **-2.** [be member]: **to
~ on** ser miembro de. **-3.** [be in session]
reunirse. ◇ *vt Br* [exam] presentarse a.
◆ **sit about, sit around** *vi* estar senta-
do(da) sin hacer nada. ◆ **sit down** *vi*
sentarse. ◆ **sit in on** *vt fus* estar presente en (*sin tomar parte*). ◆ **sit
through** *vt fus* aguantar (hasta el final).
◆ **sit up** *vi* **-1.** [sit upright] incorporarse.
-2. [stay up] quedarse levantado(da).

sitcom ['sɪtkɒm] *n inf* comedia *f* de situación.

site [saɪt] ◇ *n* [place] sitio *m*, lugar *m*;
[of construction work] obra *f*. ◇ *vt* situar.

sit-in *n* sentada *f*.

sitting ['sɪtɪŋ] *n* **-1.** [serving of meal] turno *m* (para comer). **-2.** [session] sesión
f.

sitting room *n* sala *f* de estar.

situated ['sɪtjʊeɪtɪd] *adj* [located]: **to be
~** estar situado(da).

situation [ˌsɪtjʊ'eɪʃn] *n* **-1.** [gen] situación *f*. **-2.** [job] colocación *f*; **"Situations Vacant"** *Br* "Ofertas de trabajo".

six [sɪks] ◇ *num adj* seis (*inv*); **she's ~
(years old)** tiene seis años. ◇ *num n*
-1. [the number six] seis *m inv*; **two hundred and ~** doscientos seis; **~ comes
before seven** el seis va antes que el
siete. **-2.** [in times]: **it's ~ (thirty)** son
las seis (y media); **we arrived at ~** llegamos a las seis. **-3.** [in addresses]: **~
Peyton Place** Peyton Place número
seis. **-4.** [in scores]: **~-nil** seis a cero. ◇

num pron seis *m y f*; **there are ~ of us**
somos seis.

sixteen [sɪks'tiːn] *num* dieciséis; *see also*
six.

sixth [sɪksθ] ◇ *num adj* sexto(ta). ◇
num adv sexto(ta). ◇ *num pron* sexto *m*,
-ta *f*. ◇ *n* **-1.** [fraction]: **a ~** OR **one ~ of**
un sexto de, la sexta parte de. **-2.** [in
dates]: **the ~** el (día) seis; **the ~ of September** el seis de septiembre.

sixth form *n Br* SCH *curso optativo de dos
años de enseñanza secundaria con vistas al
examen de ingreso a la universidad,* ≃
COU *m*.

sixth form college *n Br centro público
para alumnos de 16 a 18 años donde se
preparan para los 'A levels' o para exámenes de formación profesional.*

sixty ['sɪkstɪ] *num* sesenta; *see also* **six**.
◆ **sixties** *npl* **-1.** [decade]: **the sixties** los
años sesenta. **-2.** [in ages]: **to be in
one's sixties** tener más de sesenta
años.

size [saɪz] *n* **-1.** [gen] tamaño *m*. **-2.** [of
clothes] talla *f*; [of shoes] número *m*.
◆ **size up** *vt sep* [situation] evaluar; [per-
son] juzgar.

sizeable ['saɪzəbl] *adj* considerable.

sizzle ['sɪzl] *vi* chisporrotear.

skate [skeɪt] (*pl sense 2 only inv* OR **-s**)
◇ *n* **-1.** [ice skate, roller skate] patín *m*.
-2. [fish] raya *f*. ◇ *vi* [on skates] patinar.

skateboard ['skeɪtbɔːd] *n* monopatín *m*.

skater ['skeɪtəʳ] *n* patinador *m*, -ra *f*.

skating ['skeɪtɪŋ] *n* patinaje *m*.

skating rink *n* pista *f* de patinaje.

skeleton ['skelɪtn] *n* ANAT esqueleto *m*.

skeleton key *n* llave *f* maestra.

skeleton staff *n* personal *m* mínimo.

skeptic *etc Am* = **sceptic** *etc*.

sketch [sketʃ] ◇ *n* **-1.** [drawing, brief
outline] esbozo *m*, bosquejo *m*. **-2.** [hu-
morous scene] sketch *m*. ◇ *vt* esbozar.

sketchbook ['sketʃbʊk] *n* cuaderno *m*
de dibujo.

sketchpad ['sketʃpæd] *n* bloc *m* de dibujo.

sketchy ['sketʃɪ] *adj* incompleto(ta).

skewer ['skjʊəʳ] *n* brocheta *f*.

ski [skiː] (*pt* & *pp* **skied**, *cont* **skiing**) ◇
n esquí *m*. ◇ *vi* esquiar.

ski boots *npl* botas *fpl* de esquí.

skid [skɪd] ◇ *n* patinazo *m*. ◇ *vi* patinar.

skier ['skiːəʳ] *n* esquiador *m*, -ra *f*.

skies [skaɪz] *pl* → **sky**.

skiing ['skiːɪŋ] *n* (*U*) esquí *m*.

ski jump n -1. [slope] pista f para saltos de esquí. -2. [event] saltos mpl de esquí.

skilful, skillful Am ['skɪlfʊl] adj hábil.

ski lift n telesilla m.

skill [skɪl] n -1. (U) [expertise] habilidad f, destreza f. -2. [craft, technique] técnica f.

skilled [skɪld] adj -1. [skilful] habilidoso(sa). -2. [trained] cualificado(da).

skillful etc Am = **skilful** etc.

skim [skɪm] ⋄ vt -1. [remove - cream] desnatar. -2. [fly above] volar rozando. ⋄ vi: **to ~ through sthg** hojear algo, leer algo por encima.

skim(med) milk [skɪm(d)-] n leche f desnatada.

skimp [skɪmp] ⋄ vt [gen] escatimar; [work] hacer de prisa y corriendo. ⋄ vi: **to ~ on sthg** [gen] escatimar algo; [work] hacer algo de prisa y corriendo.

skimpy ['skɪmpɪ] adj [clothes] muy corto y estrecho (muy corta y estrecha); [meal, facts] escaso(sa).

skin [skɪn] ⋄ n -1. [gen] piel f; [on face] cutis m. -2. [on milk, pudding] nata f; [on paint] capa f, película f. ⋄ vt -1. [animal] despellejar. -2. [knee, elbow etc] rasguñarse.

skin-deep adj superficial.

skin diving n buceo m, submarinismo m (sin traje ni escafandra).

skinny ['skɪnɪ] adj inf flaco(ca).

skin-tight adj muy ajustado(da).

skip [skɪp] ⋄ n -1. [little jump] brinco m, saltito m. -2. Br [large container] contenedor m, container m. ⋄ vt saltarse. ⋄ vi -1. [move in little jumps] ir dando brincos. -2. Br [jump over rope] saltar a la comba.

ski pants npl pantalones mpl de esquí.

ski pole n bastón m para esquiar.

skipper ['skɪpǝʳ] n NAUT & SPORT capitán m, -ana f.

skipping rope ['skɪpɪŋ-] n Br comba f, cuerda f de saltar.

skirmish ['skɜːmɪʃ] n lit & fig escaramuza f.

skirt [skɜːt] ⋄ n falda f. ⋄ vt -1. [border] rodear, bordear. -2. [go round - obstacle] sortear; [- person, group] esquivar. -3. [avoid dealing with] eludir. ◆ **skirt round** vt fus -1. [obstacle] sortear. -2. [issue, problem] evitar, eludir.

skit [skɪt] n: **~ (on)** parodia f (de).

skittle ['skɪtl] n Br bolo m. ◆ **skittles** n (U) bolos mpl.

skive [skaɪv] vi Br inf: **to ~ (off)** escaquearse.

skulk [skʌlk] vi esconderse.

skull [skʌl] n [gen] calavera f; ANAT cráneo m.

skunk [skʌŋk] n mofeta f.

sky [skaɪ] n cielo m.

skylight ['skaɪlaɪt] n claraboya f, tragaluz m.

skyscraper ['skaɪˌskreɪpǝʳ] n rascacielos m inv.

slab [slæb] n [of stone] losa f; [of cheese] pedazo m; [of chocolate] tableta f.

slack [slæk] ⋄ adj -1. [rope, cable] flojo(ja). -2. [business] inactivo(va). -3. [person - careless] descuidado(da). ⋄ n [in rope] parte f floja.

slacken ['slækn] ⋄ vt [speed, pace] reducir; [rope] aflojar. ⋄ vi [speed, pace] reducirse.

slag [slæg] n [waste material] escoria f.

slagheap ['slæghiːp] n escorial m.

slain [sleɪn] pp → **slay.**

slam [slæm] ⋄ vt -1. [shut] cerrar de golpe. -2. [place with force]: **to ~ sthg on** OR **onto sthg** dar un golpe con algo contra algo violentamente. ⋄ vi [shut] cerrarse de golpe.

slander ['slɑːndǝʳ] ⋄ n calumnia f, difamación f. ⋄ vt calumniar, difamar.

slang [slæŋ] n argot m, jerga f.

slant [slɑːnt] ⋄ n -1. [diagonal angle] inclinación f. -2. [perspective] enfoque m. ⋄ vi inclinarse.

slanting ['slɑːntɪŋ] adj inclinado(da).

slap [slæp] ⋄ n [in face] bofetada f; [on back] palmada f. ⋄ vt -1. [person, face] abofetear; [back] dar una palmada a. -2. [place with force]: **to ~ sthg on** OR **onto sthg** dar un golpe con algo contra. ⋄ adv inf [directly] de narices.

slapdash ['slæpdæʃ], **slaphappy** ['slæpˌhæpɪ] adj inf chapucero(ra).

slapstick ['slæpstɪk] n (U) payasadas fpl.

slap-up adj Br inf: **~ meal** comilona f.

slash [slæʃ] ⋄ n -1. [long cut] raja f, tajo m. -2. [oblique stroke] barra f oblicua. ⋄ vt -1. [material] rasgar; [wrists] cortar. -2. inf [prices etc] recortar drásticamente.

slat [slæt] n tablilla f.

slate [sleɪt] ⋄ n pizarra f. ⋄ vt [criticize] poner por los suelos.

slaughter ['slɔːtǝʳ] ⋄ n lit & fig matanza f. ⋄ vt matar.

slaughterhouse ['slɔːtǝhaʊs, pl -haʊzɪz] n matadero m.

slave [sleɪv] ◇ *n* esclavo *m*, -va *f*. ◇ *vi* [work hard]: **to ~ (over)** trabajar como un negro (en).

slavery ['sleɪvərɪ] *n lit* & *fig* esclavitud *f*.

slay [sleɪ] (*pt* **slew**, *pp* **slain**) *vt literary* asesinar, matar.

sleazy ['sliːzɪ] *adj* [disreputable] de mala muerte.

sledge [sledʒ], **sled** *Am* [sled] *n* trineo *m*.

sledgehammer ['sledʒ,hæmər] *n* almádena *f*.

sleek [sliːk] *adj* **-1.** [hair] suave y brillante; [fur] lustroso(sa). **-2.** [shape] de línea depurada.

sleep [sliːp] (*pt* & *pp* **slept**) ◇ *n* sueño *m*; **to go to ~** [doze off] dormirse. ◇ *vi* dormir. ◆ **sleep in** *vi* levantarse tarde. ◆ **sleep with** *vt fus euphemism* acostarse con.

sleeper ['sliːpər] *n* **-1.** [person]: **to be a heavy/light ~** tener el sueño profundo/ligero. **-2.** [sleeping compartment] coche-cama *m*. **-3.** [train] tren *m* nocturno (con literas). **-4.** *Br* [on railway track] traviesa *f*.

sleeping bag ['sliːpɪŋ-] *n* saco *m* de dormir.

sleeping car ['sliːpɪŋ-] *n* coche-cama *m*.

sleeping pill ['sliːpɪŋ-] *n* pastilla *f* para dormir.

sleepless ['sliːplɪs] *adj* en blanco.

sleepwalk ['sliːpwɔːk] *vi* [be a sleepwalker] ser somnámbulo(la); [walk in one's sleep] andar mientras uno duerme.

sleepy ['sliːpɪ] *adj* [person] soñoliento(ta).

sleet [sliːt] ◇ *n* aguanieve *f*. ◇ *v impers*: **it's ~ing** cae aguanieve.

sleeve [sliːv] *n* **-1.** [of garment] manga *f*. **-2.** [for record] cubierta *f*.

sleigh [sleɪ] *n* trineo *m*.

sleight of hand [,slaɪt-] *n* (*U*) *lit* & *fig* juego *m* de manos.

slender ['slendər] *adj* **-1.** [thin] esbelto(ta). **-2.** [scarce] escaso(sa).

slept [slept] *pt* & *pp* → **sleep**.

slew [sluː] ◇ *pt* → **slay**. ◇ *vi* girar bruscamente.

slice [slaɪs] ◇ *n* **-1.** [of bread] rebanada *f*; [of cheese] loncha *f*; [of sausage] raja *f*; [of lemon] rodaja *f*; [of meat] tajada *f*. **-2.** [of market, glory] parte *f*. ◇ *vt* [gen] cortar; [bread] rebanar.

slick [slɪk] *adj* **-1.** [smooth, skilful] logrado(da). **-2.** *pej* [superficial - talk] aparentemente brillante; [- person] de labia fácil.

slide [slaɪd] (*pt* & *pp* **slid** [slɪd]) ◇ *n* **-1.** [decline] descenso *m*. **-2.** PHOT diapositiva *f*. **-3.** [in playground] tobogán *m*. **-4.** *Br* [for hair] pasador *m*. ◇ *vt* deslizar. ◇ *vi* **-1.** [slip] resbalar. **-2.** [glide] deslizarse. **-3.** [decline gradually] caer.

sliding door [,slaɪdɪŋ-] *n* puerta *f* corredera.

sliding scale [,slaɪdɪŋ-] *n* escala *f* móvil.

slight [slaɪt] ◇ *adj* **-1.** [improvement, hesitation etc] ligero(ra); [wound] superficial; **not in the ~est** *fml* en absoluto. **-2.** [slender] menudo(da). ◇ *n* desaire *m*. ◇ *vt* menospreciar, desairar.

slightly ['slaɪtlɪ] *adv* [to small extent] ligeramente.

slim [slɪm] ◇ *adj* **-1.** [person, object] delgado(da). **-2.** [chance, possibility] remoto(ta). ◇ *vi* (intentar) adelgazar.

slime [slaɪm] *n* [in pond etc] lodo *m*, cieno *m*; [of snail, slug] baba *f*.

slimming ['slɪmɪŋ] *n* adelgazamiento *m*.

sling [slɪŋ] (*pt* & *pp* **slung**) ◇ *n* **-1.** [for injured arm] cabestrillo *m*. **-2.** [for carrying things] braga *f*, honda *f*. ◇ *vt* **-1.** [hang roughly] colgar descuidadamente. **-2.** *inf* [throw] tirar.

slip [slɪp] ◇ *n* **-1.** [mistake] descuido *m*, desliz *m*; **a ~ of the pen/tongue** un lapsus. **-2.** [of paper - gen] papelito *m*; [- form] hoja *f*. **-3.** [underskirt] enaguas *fpl*. **-4.** *phr*: **to give sb the ~** *inf* dar esquinazo a alguien. ◇ *vt*: **to ~ sthg into** meter algo rápidamente en; **to ~ into sthg, to ~ sthg on** [clothes] ponerse rápidamente algo. ◇ *vi* **-1.** [lose one's balance] resbalar, patinar. **-2.** [slide] escurrirse, resbalar. **-3.** [decline] empeorar. ◆ **slip up** *vi* cometer un error (poco importante).

slipped disc [,slɪpt-] *n* hernia *f* discal.

slipper ['slɪpər] *n* zapatilla *f*.

slippery ['slɪpərɪ] *adj* resbaladizo(za).

slip road *n Br* [for joining motorway] acceso *m*; [for leaving motorway] salida *f*.

slipshod ['slɪpʃɒd] *adj* chapucero(ra).

slip-up *n inf* fallo *m* poco importante.

slipway ['slɪpweɪ] *n* grada *f*.

slit [slɪt] (*pt* & *pp* **slit**) ◇ *n* ranura *f*, hendidura *f*. ◇ *vt* abrir, cortar (a lo largo).

slither ['slɪðər] *vi* deslizarse.

sliver ['slɪvər] *n* [of glass] esquirla *f*; [of wood] astilla *f*; [of cheese, ham] tajada *f* muy fina.

slob [slɒb] *n inf* guarro *m*, -rra *f*.

slog [slɒg] *inf* ◇ *n* [work] curro *m*, trabajo *m* pesado. ◇ *vi* [work]: **to ~ (away) at** trabajar sin descanso en.

slogan ['sləʊgən] *n* eslogan *m*.

slop [slɒp] ◇ *vt* derramar. ◇ *vi* derramarse.

slope [sləʊp] ◇ *n* cuesta *f*, pendiente *f*. ◇ *vi* inclinarse.

sloping ['sləʊpɪŋ] *adj* [gen] inclinado(da); [ground] en pendiente.

sloppy ['slɒpɪ] *adj* [person] descuidado(da); [work] chapucero(ra); [appearance] dejado(da).

slot [slɒt] *n* **-1.** [opening - gen & COMPUT] ranura *f*. **-2.** [groove] muesca *f*. **-3.** [place in schedule] espacio *m*.

slot machine *n* **-1.** [vending machine] máquina *f* automática *(de bebidas, cigarrillos etc)*. **-2.** [arcade machine] máquina *f* tragaperras.

slouch [slaʊtʃ] *vi* ir con los hombros caídos.

Slovakia [slə'vækɪə] *n* Eslovaquia.

slovenly ['slʌvnlɪ] *adj* [unkempt] desaliñado(da); [careless] descuidado(da).

slow [sləʊ] ◇ *adj* **-1.** [not fast] lento(ta). **-2.** [not prompt]: **to be ~ to do sthg** tardar en hacer algo. **-3.** [clock etc] atrasado(da). **-4.** [not intelligent] corto(ta) (de alcances). ◇ *vt* aminorar, ralentizar. ◇ *vi* ir más despacio. ◆ **slow down**, **slow up** ◇ *vt sep* [growth] retrasar; [car] reducir la velocidad de. ◇ *vi* [walker] ir más despacio; [car] reducir la velocidad.

slowdown ['sləʊdaʊn] *n* ralentización *f*.

slowly ['sləʊlɪ] *adv* despacio, lentamente.

slow motion *n*: **in ~** a cámara lenta.

sludge [slʌdʒ] *n* (*U*) [mud] fango *m*, lodo *m*; [sewage] aguas *fpl* residuales.

slug [slʌg] *n* **-1.** [animal] babosa *f*. **-2.** *Am inf* [bullet] bala *f*.

sluggish ['slʌgɪʃ] *adj* [movement, activity] lento(ta); [feeling] aturdido(da).

sluice [sluːs] *n* [passage] canal *m* de desagüe; [gate] compuerta *f*.

slum [slʌm] *n* [area] barrio *m* bajo.

slumber ['slʌmbə] *literary vi* dormir.

slump [slʌmp] ◇ *n* **-1.** [decline]: **~ (in)** bajón *m* (en). **-2.** ECON crisis *f* económica. ◇ *vi* **-1.** [fall in value] dar un bajón. **-2.** [fall heavily - person] desplomarse, dejarse caer.

slung [slʌŋ] *pt & pp* → **sling**.

slur [slɜːr] ◇ *n* [insult] agravio *m*. ◇ *vt* mascullar.

slush [slʌʃ] *n* nieve *f* medio derretida.

slush fund, **slush money** *Am n* fondos utilizados para actividades corruptas.

slut [slʌt] *n* **-1.** *inf* [dirty or untidy woman] marrana *f*. **-2.** *v inf* [sexually immoral woman] ramera *f*.

sly [slaɪ] (*compar* **slyer** OR **slier**, *superl* **slyest** OR **sliest**) *adj* **-1.** [look, smile] furtivo(va). **-2.** [person] astuto(ta).

smack [smæk] ◇ *n* **-1.** [slap] cachete *m*. **-2.** [impact] golpe *m*. ◇ *vt* **-1.** [slap] pegar, dar un cachete a. **-2.** [place violently] tirar de golpe.

small [smɔːl] *adj* [gen] pequeño(ña); [person] bajo(ja); [matter, attention] de poca importancia; [importance] poco(ca).

small ads [-ædz] *npl Br* anuncios *mpl* clasificados.

small change *n* cambio *m*, suelto *m*.

smallholder ['smɔːl,həʊldər] *n Br* minifundista *m y f*.

small hours *npl* primeras horas *fpl* de la madrugada.

smallpox ['smɔːlpɒks] *n* viruela *f*.

small print *n*: **the ~** la letra pequeña.

small talk *n* (*U*) conversación *f* trivial.

smarmy ['smɑːmɪ] *adj* cobista.

smart [smɑːt] ◇ *adj* **-1.** [neat, stylish] elegante. **-2.** [clever] inteligente. **-3.** [fashionable, exclusive] elegante. **-4.** [quick, sharp] rápido(da). ◇ *vi* **-1.** [eyes, wound] escocer. **-2.** [person] sentir resquemor.

smarten ['smɑːtn] ◆ **smarten up** *vt sep* arreglar.

smash [smæʃ] ◇ *n* **-1.** [sound] estrépito *m*. **-2.** *inf* [car crash] accidente *m*. **-3.** TENNIS mate *m*, smash *m*. ◇ *vt* **-1.** [break into pieces] romper, hacer pedazos. **-2.** [hit, crash]: **to ~ one's fist into sthg** dar un puñetazo en algo. **-3.** *fig* [defeat] aplastar. ◇ *vi* **-1.** [break into pieces] romperse, hacerse pedazos. **-2.** [crash, collide]: **to ~ into sthg** chocar violentamente con algo.

smashing ['smæʃɪŋ] *adj inf* fenomenal.

smattering ['smætərɪŋ] *n* nociones *fpl*; **he has a ~ of Spanish** habla cuatro palabras de español.

smear [smɪər] ◇ *n* **-1.** [dirty mark] mancha *f*. **-2.** MED frotis *m*. **-3.** [slander] calumnia *f*, difamación *f*. ◇ *vt* **-1.** [smudge] manchar. **-2.** [spread]: **to ~ sthg onto sthg** untar algo con algo. **-3.** [slander] calumniar, difamar.

smell [smel] (*pt & pp* **-ed** OR **smelt**) ◇ *n* **-1.** [odour] olor *m*. **-2.** [sense of smell] olfato *m*. ◇ *vt lit & fig* oler. ◇ *vi* **-1.**

[gen] oler; **to ~ of/like** oler a/como; **to ~ good/bad** oler bien/mal. **-2.** [smell unpleasantly] apestar.

smelly ['smelɪ] *adj* maloliente.

smelt [smelt] ◇ *pt & pp* → **smell**. ◇ *vt* fundir.

smile [smaɪl] ◇ *n* sonrisa *f*. ◇ *vi* sonreír.

smirk [smɜːk] *n* sonrisa *f* desdeñosa.

smock [smɒk] *n* blusón *m*.

smog [smɒg] *n* niebla *f* baja, smog *m*.

smoke [sməʊk] ◇ *n* [gen] humo *m*. ◇ *vt* **-1.** [cigarette, cigar] fumar. **-2.** [fish, meat, cheese] ahumar. ◇ *vi* **-1.** [smoke tobacco] fumar. **-2.** [give off smoke] echar humo.

smoked [sməʊkt] *adj* ahumado(da).

smoker ['sməʊkər] *n* **-1.** [person] fumador *m*, -ra *f*. **-2.** RAIL [compartment] compartimiento *m* de fumadores.

smokescreen ['sməʊkskriːn] *n fig* cortina *f* de humo.

smoke shop *n Am* estanco *m*.

smoking ['sməʊkɪŋ] *n*: ~ **is bad for you** fumar es malo; **"no ~"** "prohibido fumar".

smoky ['sməʊkɪ] *adj* **-1.** [full of smoke] lleno(na) de humo. **-2.** [taste, colour] ahumado(da).

smolder *Am* = **smoulder**.

smooth [smuːð] ◇ *adj* **-1.** [surface] liso(sa); [skin] terso(sa). **-2.** [mixture] sin grumos. **-3.** [movement, taste] suave. **-4.** [flight, ride] tranquilo(la). **-5.** *pej* [person, manner] meloso(sa). **-6.** [trouble-free] sin problemas. ◇ *vt* alisar. ◆ **smooth out** *vt sep* alisar.

smother ['smʌðər] *vt* **-1.** [cover thickly]: **to ~ sthg in** OR **with** cubrir algo de. **-2.** [kill] asfixiar. **-3.** [extinguish] sofocar, apagar. **-4.** *fig* [control] contener.

smoulder *Br*, **smolder** *Am* ['sməʊldər] *vi* **-1.** [fire] arder sin llama. **-2.** *fig* [person, feelings] arder.

smudge [smʌdʒ] ◇ *n* [dirty mark] mancha *f*; [ink blot] borrón *m*. ◇ *vt* [by blurring] emborronar; [by dirtying] manchar.

smug [smʌg] *adj pej* pagado(da) OR satisfecho(cha) de sí mismo(ma).

smuggle ['smʌgl] *vt* [across frontiers] pasar de contrabando.

smuggler ['smʌglər] *n* contrabandista *m y f*.

smuggling ['smʌglɪŋ] *n (U)* contrabando *m*.

smutty ['smʌtɪ] *adj inf pej* guarro(rra).

snack [snæk] *n* bocado *m*, piscolabis *m inv*.

snack bar *n* bar *m*, cafetería *f*.

snag [snæg] ◇ *n* [problem] **pega** *f*. ◇ *vi*: **to ~ (on)** engancharse (en).

snail [sneɪl] *n* caracol *m*.

snake [sneɪk] *n* [large] serpiente *f*; [small] culebra *f*.

snap [snæp] ◇ *adj* repentino(na). ◇ *n* **-1.** [act or sound] crujido *m*, chasquido *m*. **-2.** *inf* [photograph] foto *f*. ◇ *vt* **-1.** [break] partir (en dos). **-2.** [move with a snap]: **to ~ sthg open** abrir algo de golpe. ◇ *vi* **-1.** [break] partirse (en dos). **-2.** [attempt to bite]: **to ~ at sthg/sb** intentar morder algo/a alguien. **-3.** [speak sharply]: **to ~ (at sb)** contestar bruscamente OR de mala manera a alguien. ◆ **snap up** *vt sep* no dejar escapar.

snap fastener *n* cierre *m* (*en la ropa etc*).

snappy ['snæpɪ] *adj inf* **-1.** [stylish] con estilo. **-2.** [quick] rápido(da); **make it ~!** ¡date prisa!

snapshot ['snæpʃɒt] *n* foto *f*.

snare [sneər] *n* trampa *f*.

snarl [snɑːl] *vi* gruñir.

snatch [snætʃ] ◇ *n* [of conversation, song] fragmento *m*. ◇ *vt* [grab] agarrar; **to ~ sthg from sb** arrancarle OR arrebatarle algo a alguien.

sneak [sniːk] (*Am pt* **snuck**) ◇ *n Br inf* acusica *m y f*, chivato *m*, -ta *f*. ◇ *vt* colar, pasar a escondidas. ◇ *vi*: **to ~ in/out** entrar/salir a escondidas.

sneakers ['sniːkəz] *npl Am* zapatos *mpl* de lona.

sneaky ['sniːkɪ] *adj inf* solapado(da).

sneer [snɪər] *vi* [smile unpleasantly] sonreír con desprecio.

sneeze [sniːz] *vi* estornudar.

snide [snaɪd] *adj* sarcástico(ca).

sniff [snɪf] ◇ *vt* **-1.** [smell] oler. **-2.** [drug] esnifar. ◇ *vi* [to clear nose] sorber por la nariz.

snigger ['snɪgər] ◇ *n* risa *f* disimulada. ◇ *vi* reírse por lo bajo.

snip [snɪp] ◇ *n inf* [bargain] ganga *f*. ◇ *vt* cortar con tijeras.

sniper ['snaɪpər] *n* francotirador *m*, -ra *f*.

snippet ['snɪpɪt] *n* retazo *m*.

snivel ['snɪvl] *vi* lloriquear.

snob [snɒb] *n* esnob *m y f*.

snobbish ['snɒbɪʃ], **snobby** ['snɒbɪ] *adj* esnob.

snooker ['snuːkər] *n* snooker *m*, *juego parecido al billar*.

snoop [snuːp] *vi inf* fisgonear.

snooty ['snuːtɪ] *adj* engreído(da).

snooze [snuːz] ◇ n cabezada f. ◇ vi dormitar.

snore [snɔːʳ] ◇ n ronquido m. ◇ vi roncar.

snoring ['snɔːrɪŋ] n (U) ronquidos mpl.

snorkel ['snɔːkl] n tubo m respiratorio.

snort [snɔːt] ◇ n resoplido m. ◇ vi resoplar.

snout [snaʊt] n hocico m.

snow [snəʊ] ◇ n nieve f. ◇ v impers nevar.

snowball ['snəʊbɔːl] ◇ n bola f de nieve. ◇ vi fig aumentar rápidamente.

snowbound ['snəʊbaʊnd] adj bloqueado(da) por la nieve.

snowdrift ['snəʊdrɪft] n montón m de nieve.

snowdrop ['snəʊdrɒp] n campanilla f blanca.

snowfall ['snəʊfɔːl] n nevada f.

snowflake ['snəʊfleɪk] n copo m de nieve.

snowman ['snəʊmæn] (pl -men [-men]) n muñeco m de nieve.

snowplough Br, **snowplow** Am ['snəʊplaʊ] n quitanieves m inv.

snowshoe ['snəʊʃuː] n raqueta f de nieve.

snowstorm ['snəʊstɔːm] n tormenta f de nieve.

SNP n abbr of **Scottish National Party**.

Snr, **snr** (abbr of **senior**) sén.

snub [snʌb] ◇ n desaire m. ◇ vt desairar.

snuck [snʌk] Am pt → **sneak**.

snuff [snʌf] n [tobacco] rapé m.

snug [snʌg] adj **-1.** [person] cómodo y calentito (cómoda y calentita); [feeling] de bienestar. **-2.** [place] acogedor(ra). **-3.** [close-fitting] ajustado(da).

snuggle ['snʌgl] vi: to ~ up to sb arrimarse a alguien acurrucándose.

so [səʊ] ◇ adv **-1.** [to such a degree] tan; ~ **difficult (that)** tan difícil (que); **don't be** ~ **stupid!** ¡no seas bobo!; **I've never seen** ~ **much money/many cars** en mi vida he visto tanto dinero/tantos coches. **-2.** [in referring back to previous statement, event etc]: ~ **what's the point then?** entonces ¿qué sentido tiene?; ~ **you knew already?** ¿así que ya lo sabías?; **I don't think** ~ no creo, me parece que no; **I'm afraid** ~ me temo que sí; **if** ~ de ser así; **is that** ~? ¿es así? **-3.** [also] también; ~ **can I** y yo (también puedo); ~ **do I** y yo (también); **she speaks French and** ~ **does her husband** ella habla francés y su

marido también. **-4.** [in such a way]: **(like)** ~ así, de esta forma. **-5.** [in expressing agreement]: ~ **there is!** ¡pues (sí que) es verdad!; ¡sí que lo hay, sí!; ~ **I see** ya lo veo. **-6.** [unspecified amount, limit]: **they pay us** ~ **much a week** nos pagan tanto a la semana; **it's not** ~ **much the money as the time involved** no es tanto el dinero como el tiempo que conlleva; **or** ~ o así. ◇ conj **-1.** [with the result that, therefore] así que, por lo tanto. **-2.** [to introduce a statement] (bueno) pues; ~ **what have you been up to?** bueno, ¿y qué has estado haciendo?; ~ **that's who she is!** ¡anda! ¡o sea que ella!; ~ **what?** inf ¿y qué?; ~ **there** inf ¡(y si no te gusta,) te chinchas! ◆ **and so on, and so forth** adv y cosas por el estilo. ◆ **so as** conj para; **we didn't knock** ~ **as not to disturb them** no llamamos para no molestarlos. ◆ **so that** conj para que; **he lied** ~ **that she would go free** mintió para que ella saliera en libertad.

soak [səʊk] ◇ vt **-1.** [leave immersed] poner en remojo. **-2.** [wet thoroughly] empapar. ◇ vi **-1.** [become thoroughly wet]: **to leave sthg to** ~, **to let sthg** ~ dejar algo en remojo. **-2.** [spread]: **to** ~ **into** OR **through sthg** calar algo. ◆ **soak up** vt sep [liquid] absorber.

soaking ['səʊkɪŋ] adj empapado(da).

so-and-so n inf **-1.** [to replace a name] fulano m, -na f de tal. **-2.** [annoying person] hijo m, -ja f de tal.

soap [səʊp] n **-1.** (U) [for washing] jabón m. **-2.** TV culebrón m.

soap flakes npl escamas fpl de jabón.

soap opera n culebrón m.

soap powder n jabón m en polvo.

soapy ['səʊpɪ] adj [full of soap] jabonoso(sa).

soar [sɔːʳ] vi **-1.** [bird] remontar el vuelo. **-2.** [rise into the sky] elevarse. **-3.** [increase rapidly] alcanzar cotas muy altas.

sob [sɒb] ◇ n sollozo m. ◇ vi sollozar.

sober ['səʊbəʳ] adj **-1.** [gen] sobrio(bria). **-2.** [serious] serio(ria). ◆ **sober up** vi pasársele a uno la borrachera.

sobering ['səʊbərɪŋ] adj que hace reflexionar.

so-called [-kɔːld] adj **-1.** [misleadingly named] mal llamado(da), supuesto(ta). **-2.** [widely known as] así llamado(da).

soccer ['sɒkəʳ] n (U) fútbol m.

sociable ['səʊʃəbl] adj sociable.

social ['səʊʃl] adj social.

social club n local m social de una empresa.

socialism ['səʊʃəlɪzm] n socialismo m.

socialist ['səʊʃəlɪst] ◇ adj socialista. ◇ n socialista m y f.

socialize, -ise ['səʊʃəlaɪz] vi: **to ~ (with)** alternar (con).

social security n seguridad f social.

social services npl servicios mpl sociales.

social worker n asistente m, -ta f social.

society [sə'saɪətɪ] n -1. [gen] sociedad f. -2. [club, organization] sociedad f, asociación f.

sociology [,səʊsɪ'ɒlədʒɪ] n sociología f.

sock [sɒk] n calcetín m.

socket ['sɒkɪt] n -1. ELEC enchufe m. -2. [of eye] cuenca f; [of joint] glena f.

sod [sɒd] n -1. [of turf] tepe m. -2. v inf [person] cabroncete m.

soda ['səʊdə] n -1. [gen] soda f. -2. Am [fizzy drink] gaseosa f.

soda water n soda f.

sodden ['sɒdn] adj empapado(da).

sodium ['səʊdɪəm] n sodio m.

sofa ['səʊfə] n sofá m.

Sofia ['səʊfjə] n Sofía f.

soft [sɒft] adj -1. [pliable, not stiff, not strict] blando(da). -2. [smooth, gentle, not bright] suave.

soft drink n refresco m.

soften ['sɒfn] ◇ vt suavizar. ◇ vi -1. [substance] ablandarse. -2. [expression] suavizarse.

softhearted [,sɒft'hɑːtɪd] adj de buen corazón.

softly ['sɒftlɪ] adv -1. [gently] con delicadeza. -2. [quietly, not brightly] suavemente. -3. [leniently] con indulgencia.

soft-spoken adj de voz suave.

software ['sɒftweəʳ] n COMPUT software m.

soggy ['sɒgɪ] adj inf empapado(da).

soil [sɔɪl] ◇ n [earth] tierra f, suelo m. ◇ vt ensuciar.

soiled [sɔɪld] adj sucio(cia).

solace ['sɒləs] n literary consuelo m.

solar ['səʊləʳ] adj solar.

sold [səʊld] pt & pp → **sell**.

solder ['səʊldəʳ] ◇ n (U) soldadura f. ◇ vt soldar.

soldier ['səʊldʒəʳ] n soldado m.

sold-out adj agotado(da); **the theatre was ~** se agotaron las localidades.

sole [səʊl] (pl sense 2 only inv OR **-s**) ◇ adj -1. [only] único(ca). -2. [exclusive] exclusivo(va). ◇ n -1. [of foot] planta f; [of shoe] suela f. -2. [fish] lenguado m.

solemn ['sɒləm] adj solemne.

solicit [sə'lɪsɪt] ◇ vt fml [request] solicitar. ◇ vi [prostitute] ofrecer sus servicios.

solicitor [sə'lɪsɪtəʳ] n Br JUR abogado que lleva casos administrativos y legales, pero que no acude a los tribunales superiores.

solid ['sɒlɪd] ◇ adj -1. [gen] sólido(da). -2. [rock, wood, gold] macizo(za). -3. [reliable, respectable] serio(ria), formal. -4. [without interruption] sin interrupción. ◇ n sólido m.

solidarity [,sɒlɪ'dærətɪ] n solidaridad f.

solitaire [,sɒlɪ'teəʳ] n -1. [jewel, board game] solitario m. -2. Am [card game] solitario m.

solitary ['sɒlɪtrɪ] adj solitario(ria).

solitary confinement n: **to be in ~** estar incomunicado(da) (en la cárcel).

solitude ['sɒlɪtjuːd] n soledad f.

solo ['səʊləʊ] (pl **-s**) ◇ adj & adv a solas. ◇ n solo m.

soloist ['səʊləʊɪst] n soloista m y f.

soluble ['sɒljʊbl] adj soluble.

solution [sə'luːʃn] n: **~ (to)** solución f (a).

solve [sɒlv] vt resolver.

solvent ['sɒlvənt] ◇ adj FIN solvente. ◇ n disolvente m.

Somalia [sə'mɑːlɪə] n Somalia.

sombre Br, **somber** Am ['sɒmbəʳ] adj sombrío(a).

some [sʌm] ◇ adj -1. [a certain amount, number of]: **would you like ~ coffee?** ¿quieres café?; **give me ~ money** dame algo de dinero; **there are ~ good articles in it** tiene algunos artículos buenos; **I bought ~ socks** [one pair] me compré unos calcetines; [more than one pair] me compré calcetines. -2. [fairly large number or quantity of]: **I've known him for ~ years** no lo conozco desde hace bastantes años; **I had ~ difficulty getting here** me costó lo mío llegar aquí. -3. (contrastive use) [certain] algunos(as), ciertos(as); **~ jobs are better paid than others** algunos trabajos están mejor pagados que otros; **~ people say that ...** los hay que dicen que .... -4. [in imprecise statements] algún(una); **there must be ~ mistake** debe haber un OR algún error; **she married ~ writer or other** se casó con no sé qué escritor. -5. inf [very good] menudo(da); **that's ~ car he's got** ¡menudo coche tiene! ◇ pron -1. [a certain amount]: **can I have** ~? [money, milk, coffee etc] ¿puedo coger un poco?; ~ **of** parte de. **-2.** [a certain number] algunos(as); **can I have** ~? [books, potatoes etc] ¿puedo coger algunos?; ~ **(of them) left early** algunos se fueron temprano; ~ **say he lied** hay quien dice que mintió. ◇ *adv* unos(as); **there were** ~ **7,000 people there** habría unas 7.000 personas.

somebody ['sʌmbədɪ] *pron* alguien.

someday ['sʌmdeɪ] *adv* algún día.

somehow ['sʌmhaʊ], **someway** *Am* ['sʌmweɪ] *adv* **-1.** [by some action] de alguna manera. **-2.** [for some reason] por alguna razón.

someone ['sʌmwʌn] *pron* alguien; ~ **or other** alguien, no sé quien.

someplace *Am* = **somewhere**.

somersault ['sʌməsɔːlt] *n* [in air] salto *m* mortal; [on ground] voltereta *f*.

something ['sʌmθɪŋ] ◇ *pron* algo; **or** ~ *inf* o algo así. ◇ *adv*: ~ **like**, ~ **in the region of** algo así como.

sometime ['sʌmtaɪm] *adv* en algún momento; ~ **next week** durante la semana que viene.

sometimes ['sʌmtaɪmz] *adv* a veces.

someway *Am* = **somehow**.

somewhat ['sʌmwɒt] *adv fml* algo.

somewhere *Br* ['sʌmweəʳ], **someplace** *Am* ['sʌmpleɪs] *adv* **-1.** [unknown place - with verbs of position] en alguna parte; [- with verbs of movement] a alguna parte; **it's** ~ **else** está en otra parte; **shall we go** ~ **else**? ¿nos vamos a otra parte? **-2.** [in approximations]: ~ **between five and ten** entre cinco y diez; ~ **around 20** alrededor de 20.

son [sʌn] *n* hijo *m*.

song [sɒŋ] *n* **-1.** [gen] canción *f*. **-2.** [of bird] canto *m*.

sonic ['sɒnɪk] *adj* sónico(ca).

son-in-law (*pl* **sons-in-law** OR **son-in-laws**) *n* yerno *m*.

sonnet ['sɒnɪt] *n* soneto *m*.

sonny ['sʌnɪ] *n inf* hijo *m*, chico *m*.

soon [suːn] *adv* pronto; **how** ~ **will it be ready**? ¿para cuándo estará listo?; ~ **after** poco después; **as** ~ **as** tan pronto como; **as** ~ **as possible** cuanto antes.

sooner ['suːnəʳ] *adv* **-1.** [in time] antes; **no** ~ **did he arrive than ...** apenas había llegado cuando ...; ~ **or later** (más) tarde o (más) temprano; **the** ~ **the better** cuanto antes mejor. **-2.** [expressing preference]: **I'd** ~ **...** preferiría ....

soot [sʊt] *n* hollín *m*.

soothe [suːð] *vt* **-1.** [pain] aliviar. **-2.** [nerves etc] calmar.

sophisticated [sə'fɪstɪkeɪtɪd] *adj* [gen] sofisticado(da).

sophomore ['sɒfəmɔːʳ] *n Am* estudiante *m* y *f* del segundo curso.

soporific [,sɒpə'rɪfɪk] *adj* soporífico(ca).

sopping ['sɒpɪŋ] *adj*: ~ **(wet)** chorreando.

soppy ['sɒpɪ] *adj inf pej* sentimentaloide.

soprano [sə'prɑːnəʊ] (*pl* **-s**) *n* soprano *f*.

sorbet ['sɔːbeɪ] *n* sorbete *m*.

sorcerer ['sɔːsərəʳ] *n* brujo *m*, -ja *f*.

sordid ['sɔːdɪd] **-1.** [immoral] obsceno(na). **-2.** [dirty, unpleasant] sórdido(da).

sore [sɔːʳ] ◇ *adj* **-1.** [painful] dolorido(da); **to have a** ~ **throat** tener dolor de garganta. **-2.** *Am* [upset] enfadado(da). ◇ *n* llaga *f*, úlcera *f*.

sorely ['sɔːlɪ] *adv literary* enormemente.

sorrow ['sɒrəʊ] *n* pesar *m*, pena *f*.

sorry ['sɒrɪ] ◇ *adj* **-1.** [expressing apology]: **to be** ~ **about sthg** sentir OR lamentar algo; **I'm** ~ **for what I did** siento lo que hice; **I'm** ~ **lo siento. -2.** [expressing shame, disappointment]: **to be** ~ **that** sentir que; **we were** ~ **about his resignation** sentimos que dimitiera; **to be** ~ **for arrepentirse de. -3.** [expressing regret]: **I'm** ~ **to have to say that ...** siento tener que decir que .... **-4.** [expressing pity]: **to be** OR **feel** ~ **for sb** sentir lástima por alguien. **-5.** [expressing polite disagreement]: **I'm** ~, **but ...** perdón, pero .... **-6.** [poor, pitiable] lamentable, penoso(sa). ◇ *excl* **-1.** [pardon]: ~? ¿perdón? **-2.** [to correct oneself]: **a girl,** ~, **a woman** una chica, perdón, una mujer.

sort [sɔːt] ◇ *n* tipo *m*, clase *f*; **all** ~**s of** todo tipo de; ~ **of** más o menos, así así; **a** ~ **of** una especie de. ◇ *vt* clasificar. ◆ **sort out** *vt sep* **-1.** [classify] clasificar. **-2.** [solve] solucionar, resolver.

sorting office ['sɔːtɪŋ-] *n* oficina *f* de clasificación del correo.

SOS (*abbr of* **save our souls**) *n* SOS *m*.

so-so *adj & adv inf* así así.

soufflé ['suːfleɪ] *n* suflé *m*.

sought [sɔːt] *pt & pp* ⊢ **seek**.

soul [səʊl] *n* **-1.** [gen] alma *f*. **-2.** [music] música *f* soul.

soul-destroying [-dɪ,strɔɪɪŋ] *adj* desmoralizador(ra).

soulful ['səʊlfʊl] *adj* lleno(na) de sentimiento.

sound [saʊnd] ◇ *adj* **-1.** [healthy] sano(na). **-2.** [sturdy] sólido(da). **-3.** [reliable] fiable, seguro(ra). ◇ *adv*: to be ~ **asleep** estar profundamente dormido(da). ◇ *n* **-1.** [gen] sonido *m*. **-2.** [particular noise] ruido *m*. **-3.** [impression]: **by the** ~ **of it** por lo que parece. ◇ *vt* [bell etc] hacer sonar, tocar. ◇ *vi* **-1.** [gen] sonar. **-2.** [give impression]: **it ~s like fun** suena divertido. ◆ **sound out** *vt sep*: **to** ~ **sb out** (**on** OR **about**) sondear a alguien (sobre).

sound barrier *n* barrera *f* del sonido.

sound effects *npl* efectos *mpl* sonoros.

sounding ['saʊndɪŋ] *n* NAUT sondeo *m* marino.

soundly ['saʊndlɪ] *adv* **-1.** [severely beat] totalmente. **-2.** [deeply] profundamente.

soundproof ['saʊndpruːf] *adj* insonorizado(da).

soundtrack ['saʊndtræk] *n* banda *f* sonora.

soup [suːp] *n* [thick] sopa *f*; [clear] caldo *m*.

soup plate *n* plato *m* hondo OR sopero.

soup spoon *n* cuchara *f* sopera.

sour [saʊəʳ] ◇ *adj* **-1.** [acidic] ácido(da). **-2.** [milk, person, reply] agrio(gria). ◇ *vt* agriar.

source [sɔːs] *n* **-1.** [gen] fuente *f*. **-2.** [cause] origen *m*.

sour grapes *n* (*U*) *inf*: **it's ~!** ¡están verdes!

south [saʊθ] ◇ *n* **-1.** [direction] sur *m*. **-2.** [region]: **the South** el sur. ◇ *adj* del sur. ◇ *adv*: ~ (**of**) al sur (de).

South Africa *n*: (**the Republic of**) ~ (la república de) Suráfrica.

South African ◇ *adj* surafricano(na). ◇ *n* [person] surafricano *m*, -na *f*.

South America *n* Sudamérica.

South American ◇ *adj* sudamericano(na). ◇ *n* [person] sudamericano *m*, -na *f*.

southeast [,saʊθ'iːst] ◇ *n* **-1.** [direction] sudeste *m*. **-2.** [region]: **the Southeast** el sudeste. ◇ *adj* del sudeste. ◇ *adv*: ~ (**of**) hacia el sudeste (de).

southerly ['sʌðəlɪ] *adj* del sur.

southern ['sʌðən] *adj* del sur, sureño(ña).

South Korea *n* Corea del Sur.

South Pole *n*: **the** ~ el polo Sur.

southward ['saʊθwəd] ◇ *adj* sur. ◇ *adv* = **southwards**.

southwards ['saʊθwədz] *adv* hacia el sur.

southwest [,saʊθ'west] ◇ *n* **-1.** [direction] suroeste *m*. **-2.** [region]: **the Southwest** el suroeste. ◇ *adj* del suroeste. ◇ *adv*: ~ (**of**) hacia el suroeste (de).

souvenir [,suːvə'nɪəʳ] *n* recuerdo *m*.

sovereign ['sɒvrɪn] ◇ *adj* soberano(na). ◇ *n* **-1.** [ruler] soberano *m*, -na *f*. **-2.** [coin] soberano *m*.

soviet ['saʊvɪət] *n* soviet *m*. ◆ **Soviet** ◇ *adj* soviético(ca). ◇ *n* [person] soviético *m*, -ca *f*.

Soviet Union *n*: **the (former)** ~ la (antigua) Unión Soviética.

sow[1] [saʊ] (*pt* **-ed**, *pp* **sown** OR **-ed**) *vt lit* & *fig* sembrar.

sow[2] [saʊ] *n* cerda *f*, puerca *f*.

sown [səʊn] *pp* → **sow**[1].

soya ['sɔɪə] *n* soja *f*.

soy(a) bean ['sɔɪ(ə)-] *n* semilla *f* de soja.

spa [spɑː] *n* balneario *m*.

space [speɪs] ◇ *n* espacio *m*. ◇ *comp* espacial. ◇ *vt* espaciar. ◆ **space out** *vt sep* [arrange with spaces between] espaciar.

spacecraft ['speɪskrɑːft] (*pl inv*) *n* nave *f* espacial.

spaceman ['speɪsmæn] (*pl* **-men** [-men]) *n inf* astronauta *m*.

spaceship ['speɪsʃɪp] *n* nave *f* espacial.

space shuttle *n* transbordador *m* espacial.

spacesuit ['speɪssuːt] *n* traje *m* espacial.

spacing ['speɪsɪŋ] *n* TYPO espacio *m*.

spacious ['speɪʃəs] *adj* espacioso(sa).

spade [speɪd] *n* [tool] pala *f*. ◆ **spades** *npl* picas *fpl*.

spaghetti [spə'getɪ] *n* (*U*) espaguetis *mpl*.

Spain [speɪn] *n* España.

span [spæn] ◇ *pt* → **spin**. ◇ *n* **-1.** [in time] lapso *m*, periodo *m*. **-2.** [range] gama *f*. **-3.** [of wings] envergadura *f*. **-4.** [of bridge, arch] ojo *m*. ◇ *vt* **-1.** [in time] abarcar. **-2.** [subj: bridge etc] cruzar, atravesar.

Spaniard ['spænjəd] *n* español *m*, -la *f*.

spaniel ['spænjəl] *n* perro *m* de aguas.

Spanish ['spænɪʃ] ◇ *adj* español(la). ◇ *n* [language] español *m*, castellano *m*. ◇ *npl* [people]: **the** ~ los españoles.

spank [spæŋk] *vt* zurrar.

spanner ['spænəʳ] *n* llave *f* inglesa.

spar [spɑːʳ] ◇ n palo m, verga f. ◇ vi BOXING: **to ~ (with)** entrenarse (con).

spare [speəʳ] ◇ adj **-1.** [surplus] de sobra. **-2.** [free - chair, time] libre. ◇ n **-1.** [spare object] **(pieza f de) recambio m**, **repuesto m. -2.** inf [part] pieza f de recambio OR repuesto. ◇ vt **-1.** [time] conceder; [money] dejar; **we can't ~ any time/money** no tenemos tiempo/ dinero; **to ~ de** sobra. **-2.** [not harm - person, life] perdonar; [- company, city] salvar. **-3.** [not use, not take]: **to ~ no expense/effort** no escatimar gastos/ esfuerzos. **-4.** [save from]: **to ~ sb sthg** ahorrarle a alguien algo.

spare part n AUT pieza f de recambio OR repuesto.

spare time n tiempo m libre.

spare wheel n rueda f de recambio.

sparing ['speərɪŋ] adj: **~ with** OR **of** parco(ca) en.

sparingly ['speərɪŋlɪ] adv con moderación.

spark [spɑːk] n lit & fig chispa f.

sparking plug ['spɑːkɪŋ-] Br = **spark plug**.

sparkle ['spɑːkl] ◇ n (U) [of diamond] destello m; [of eyes] brillo m. ◇ vi [star, jewels] centellear; [eyes] brillar.

sparkling wine ['spɑːklɪŋ-] n vino m espumoso.

spark plug n bujía f.

sparrow ['spærəʊ] n gorrión m.

sparse ['spɑːs] adj escaso(sa).

spasm ['spæzm] n **-1.** MED [state] espasmo m. **-2.** MED [attack] acceso m.

spastic ['spæstɪk] MED n espástico m, -ca f.

spat [spæt] pt & pp → **spit**.

spate [speɪt] n cadena f, serie f.

spatter ['spætəʳ] vt salpicar.

spawn [spɔːn] ◇ n (U) huevas fpl. ◇ vt fig engendrar. ◇ vi desovar, frezar.

speak [spiːk] (pt **spoke**, pp **spoken**) ◇ vt **-1.** [say] decir. **-2.** [language] hablar. ◇ vi hablar; **to ~ to** OR **with** hablar con; **to ~ to sb (about)** hablar con alguien (de); **to ~ about** hablar de; **to ~ to sb (on sthg)** [give speech] hablar ante alguien (sobre algo). ◆ **so to speak** adv por así decirlo. ◆ **speak for** vt fus [represent] hablar en nombre de. ◆ **speak up** vi **-1.** [speak out]: **to ~ up for** salir en defensa de. **-2.** [speak louder] hablar más alto.

speaker ['spiːkəʳ] n **-1.** [person talking] persona f que habla. **-2.** [person making a speech - at meal etc] orador m, -ra f;

[- at conference] conferenciante m y f. **-3.** [of a language] hablante m y f. **-4.** [of radio] altavoz m.

speaking ['spiːkɪŋ] adv: **generally ~** en general; **legally ~** desde una perspectiva legal.

spear [spɪəʳ] ◇ n [gen] lanza f; [for hunting] jabalina f. ◇ vt [animal] atravesar; [piece of food] pinchar.

spearhead ['spɪəhed] vt encabezar.

spec [spek] n Br inf: **to buy on ~** comprar sin garantías.

special ['speʃl] adj **-1.** [gen] especial. **-2.** [particular, individual] particular.

special delivery n correo m urgente.

specialist ['speʃəlɪst] ◇ adj [doctor] especialista; [literature] especializado(da). ◇ n especialista m y f.

speciality [ˌspeʃɪ'ælətɪ], **specialty** Am ['speʃltɪ] n especialidad f.

specialize, -ise ['speʃəlaɪz] vi: **to ~ (in)** especializarse (en).

specially ['speʃəlɪ] adv especialmente.

specialty Am = **speciality**.

species ['spiːʃiːz] (pl inv) n especie f.

specific [spə'sɪfɪk] adj **-1.** [particular] determinado(da). **-2.** [precise] específico(ca). **-3.** [unique]: **~ to** específico(ca) de.

specifically [spə'sɪfɪklɪ] adv **-1.** [particularly] expresamente. **-2.** [precisely] específicamente.

specify ['spesɪfaɪ] vt: **to ~ (that)** especificar (que).

specimen ['spesɪmən] n **-1.** [example] espécimen m, ejemplar m. **-2.** [sample] muestra f.

speck [spek] n **-1.** [small stain] manchita f. **-2.** [small particle] mota f.

speckled ['spekld] adj: **~ (with)** moteado(da) (de).

specs [speks] npl Br inf [glasses] gafas fpl.

spectacle ['spektəkl] n [gen] espectáculo m. ◆ **spectacles** npl Br gafas fpl.

spectacular [spek'tækjʊləʳ] adj espectacular.

spectator [spek'teɪtəʳ] n espectador m, -ra f.

spectre Br, **specter** Am ['spektəʳ] n lit & fig fantasma m.

spectrum ['spektrəm] (pl **-tra** [-trə]) n **-1.** [gen] espectro m. **-2.** fig [variety] gama f.

speculation [ˌspekjʊ'leɪʃn] n especulación f.

sped [sped] pt & pp → **speed**.

speech [spiːtʃ] n **-1.** [gen] habla f. **-2.** [formal talk] discurso m. **-3.** THEATRE parlamento m. **-4.** [manner of speaking] manera f de hablar. **-5.** [dialect] dialecto m, habla f.

speechless ['spiːtʃlɪs] adj: **to be ~ (with)** enmudecer (de).

speed [spiːd] (pt & pp **-ed** OR **sped**) ◇ n **-1.** [rate of movement] velocidad f; **at top ~** a toda velocidad. **-2.** [rapidity] rapidez f. ◇ vi **-1.** [move fast]: **to ~ (along/away/by)** ir/alejarse/pasar a toda velocidad. **-2.** AUT [go too fast] conducir con exceso de velocidad. ◆ **speed up** ◇ vt sep [gen] acelerar; [person] meter prisa a. ◇ vi [gen] acelerarse; [person] darse prisa.

speedboat ['spiːdbəʊt] n lancha f motora.

speeding ['spiːdɪŋ] n (U) exceso m de velocidad.

speed limit n límite m de velocidad.

speedometer [spɪ'dɒmɪtər] n velocímetro m.

speedway ['spiːdweɪ] n **-1.** (U) SPORT carreras fpl de moto. **-2.** Am [road] autopista f.

speedy ['spiːdɪ] adj rápido(da).

spell [spel] (Br pt & pp **spelt** OR **-ed**, Am pt & pp **-ed**) ◇ n **-1.** [of time] temporada f; [of weather] racha f. **-2.** [enchantment] hechizo m; **to cast** OR **put a ~ on sb** hechizar a alguien. **-3.** [magic words] conjuro m. ◇ vt **-1.** [form by writing] deletrear. **-2.** fig [signify] significar. ◇ vi escribir correctamente. ◆ **spell out** vt sep **-1.** [read aloud] deletrear. **-2.** [explain]: **to ~ sthg out (for** OR **to sb)** decir algo por las claras (a alguien).

spellbound ['spelbaʊnd] adj hechizado(da), embelesado(da).

spelling ['spelɪŋ] n ortografía f; **~ mistake** falta f de ortografía.

spelt [spelt] Br pt & pp → **spell**.

spend [spend] (pt & pp **spent**) vt **-1.** [gen] gastar; **to ~ sthg on** gastar algo en. **-2.** [time, life] pasar.

spendthrift ['spendθrɪft] n derrochador m, -ra f.

spent [spent] ◇ pt & pp → **spend**. ◇ adj [matches, ammunition] usado(da); [patience] agotado(da).

sperm [spɜːm] (pl inv OR **-s**) n esperma f.

spew [spjuː] vt arrojar, escupir.

sphere [sfɪər] n **-1.** [gen] esfera f. **-2.** [of people] círculo m.

spice [spaɪs] n CULIN especia f.

spick-and-span [ˌspɪkən'spæn] adj inmaculado(da).

spicy ['spaɪsɪ] adj CULIN & fig picante.

spider ['spaɪdər] n araña f.

spike [spaɪk] n **-1.** [on railing etc] punta f; [- on wall] clavo m. **-2.** [on plant] pincho m; [of hair] pelo m de punta.

spill [spɪl] (Br pt & pp **spilt** OR **-ed**, Am pt & pp **-ed**) ◇ vt derramar, verter. ◇ vi [flow] derramarse, verterse.

spilt [spɪlt] Br pt & pp → **spill**.

spin [spɪn] (pt **span** OR **spun**, pp **spun**) ◇ n **-1.** [turn] vuelta f. **-2.** AERON barrena f. **-3.** inf [in car] vuelta f. ◇ vt **-1.** [cause to rotate] girar, dar vueltas a. **-2.** [clothes, washing] centrifugar. **-3.** [wool, yarn] hilar. ◇ vi [rotate] girar, dar vueltas. ◆ **spin out** vt sep [food, story] alargar, prolongar; [money] estirar.

spinach ['spɪnɪdʒ] n (U) espinacas fpl.

spinal column ['spaɪnl-] n columna f vertebral.

spinal cord ['spaɪnl-] n médula f espinal.

spindly ['spɪndlɪ] adj larguirucho(cha).

spin-dryer n Br centrifugadora f.

spine [spaɪn] n **-1.** ANAT espina f dorsal. **-2.** [of book] lomo m. **-3.** [spike, prickle] espina f, púa f.

spinning ['spɪnɪŋ] n hilado m.

spinning top n peonza f.

spin-off n [by-product] resultado m OR efecto m indirecto.

spinster ['spɪnstər] n soltera f.

spiral ['spaɪərəl] ◇ adj en espiral. ◇ n [curve] espiral f. ◇ vi [move in spiral curve] moverse en espiral.

spiral staircase n escalera f de caracol.

spire [spaɪər] n aguja f.

spirit ['spɪrɪt] n **-1.** [gen] espíritu m. **-2.** [vigour] vigor m, valor m. ◆ **spirits** npl **-1.** [mood] humor m; **to be in high/low ~s** estar exultante/alicaído. **-2.** [alcohol] licores mpl.

spirited ['spɪrɪtɪd] adj enérgico(ca).

spirit level n nivel m de burbuja de aire.

spiritual ['spɪrɪtʃʊəl] adj espiritual.

spit [spɪt] (Br pt & pp **spat**, Am pt & pp **spit**) ◇ n **-1.** [saliva] saliva f. **-2.** [skewer] asador m. ◇ vi escupir. ◇ v impers Br [rain lightly]: **it's spitting** está chispeando.

spite [spaɪt] ◇ n rencor m. ◇ vt fastidiar, molestar. ◆ **in spite of** prep a pesar de.

spiteful ['spaɪtful] adj [person, behaviour] rencoroso(sa); [action, remark] malintencionado(da).

spittle ['spɪtl] n saliva f.

splash [splæʃ] ◇ n -1. [sound] chapoteo m. -2. [of colour, light] mancha f. ◇ vt salpicar. ◇ vi -1. [person]: to ~ about OR around chapotear. -2. [water, liquid]: to ~ on OR against sthg salpicar algo. ◆ **splash out** ◇ vi inf: to ~ out (on sthg) gastar un dineral (en algo).

spleen [spliːn] n ANAT bazo m; fig [anger] cólera f.

splendid ['splendɪd] adj -1. [marvellous] espléndido(da). -2. [magnificent, beautiful] magnífico(ca).

splint [splɪnt] n tablilla f.

splinter ['splɪntər] ◇ n [of wood] astilla f; [of glass, metal] fragmento m. ◇ vi astillarse.

split [splɪt] (pt & pp **split**) ◇ n -1. [crack - in wood] grieta f; [- in garment] desgarrón m. -2. [division]: ~ (**in**) escisión f (en). -3. [difference]: ~ (**between**) diferencia f (entre). ◇ vt -1. [tear] desgarrar, rasgar; [crack] agrietar. -2. [break in two] partir. -3. [party, organization] escindir. -4. [share] repartir. ◇ vi -1. [break up - road] bifurcarse; [- object] partirse. -2. [party, organization] escindirse. -3. [wood] agrietarse; [fabric] desgarrarse. ◆ **split up** vi separarse.

split second n fracción f de segundo.

splutter ['splʌtər] vi -1. [person] balbucear. -2. [fire, oil] chisporrotear.

spoil [spɔɪl] (pt & pp **-ed** OR **spoilt**) vt -1. [ruin] estropear, echar a perder. -2. [child etc] mimar. ◆ **spoils** npl botín m.

spoiled [spɔɪld] = **spoilt**.

spoilsport ['spɔɪlspɔːt] n aguafiestas m y f inv.

spoilt [spɔɪlt] ◇ pt & pp → **spoil**. ◇ adj mimado(da), consentido(da).

spoke [spəʊk] ◇ pt → **speak**. ◇ n radio m.

spoken ['spəʊkn] pp → **speak**.

spokesman ['spəʊksmən] (pl **-men** [-mən]) n portavoz m.

spokeswoman ['spəʊks,wʊmən] (pl **-women** [-,wɪmɪn]) n portavoz f.

sponge [spʌndʒ] ◇ n -1. [for cleaning, washing] esponja f. -2. [cake] bizcocho m. ◇ vt limpiar con una esponja. ◇ vi inf: to ~ off vivir a costa de.

sponge bag n Br neceser m.

sponge cake n bizcocho m.

sponsor ['spɒnsər] ◇ n patrocinador m,

-ra f. ◇ vt -1. [gen] patrocinar. -2. [support] respaldar.

sponsored walk [,spɒnsəd-] n marcha f benéfica.

sponsorship ['spɒnsəʃɪp] n patrocinio m.

spontaneous [spɒn'teɪnjəs] adj espontáneo(a).

spooky ['spuːkɪ] adj inf escalofriante.

spool [spuːl] n [gen & COMPUT] bobina f.

spoon [spuːn] n -1. [piece of cutlery] cuchara f. -2. [spoonful] cucharada f.

spoon-feed vt [feed with spoon] dar de comer con cuchara a.

spoonful ['spuːnful] (pl **-s** OR **spoonsful** ['spuːnzful]) n cucharada f.

sporadic [spə'rædɪk] adj esporádico(ca).

sport [spɔːt] n -1. [game] deporte m. -2. dated [cheerful person] persona f amable.

sporting ['spɔːtɪŋ] adj lit & fig deportivo(va); **to give sb a** ~ **chance** dar a alguien la oportunidad de ganar.

sports car ['spɔːts-] n coche m deportivo.

sports jacket ['spɔːts-] n chaqueta f de esport.

sportsman ['spɔːtsmən] (pl **-men** [-mən]) n deportista m.

sportsmanship ['spɔːtsmənʃɪp] n deportividad f.

sportswear ['spɔːtsweər] n ropa f deportiva.

sportswoman ['spɔːts,wʊmən] (pl **-women** [-,wɪmɪn]) n deportista f.

sporty ['spɔːtɪ] adj inf [fond of sports] aficionado(da) a los deportes.

spot [spɒt] ◇ n -1. [stain] mancha f, mota f; [dot] punto m. -2. [pimple] grano m. -3. [drop] gota f. -4. inf [bit, small amount] pizca f. -5. [place] lugar m; **on the** ~ en el lugar; **to do sthg on the** ~ hacer algo en el acto. -6. RADIO & TV espacio m. ◇ vt [notice] notar, ver.

spot check n control m aleatorio.

spotless ['spɒtlɪs] adj [thing] inmaculado(da); [reputation] intachable.

spotlight ['spɒtlaɪt] n [of car] faro m auxiliar; [in theatre, home] foco m, reflector m de luz; **to be in the** ~ fig ser el centro de atención.

spotted ['spɒtɪd] adj de lunares.

spotty ['spɒtɪ] adj Br [skin] con granos.

spouse [spaʊs] n cónyuge m y f.

spout [spaʊt] ◇ n [of kettle, teapot] pitorro m; [of jug] pico m; [of pipe] caño m. ◇ vi: to ~ from OR out of [liquid] salir a chorros de; [smoke, flames] salir incesantemente de.

sprain [spreɪn] ◇ *n* torcedura *f*. ◇ *vt* torcerse.

sprang [spræŋ] *pt* → **spring**.

sprawl [sprɔːl] *vi* [sit] repantigarse, arrellanarse; [lie] echarse, tumbarse.

spray [spreɪ] ◇ *n* **-1.** [small drops - of liquid] rociada *f*; [- of sea] espuma *f*; [- of aerosol] pulverización *f*. **-2.** [pressurized liquid] líquido *m* pulverizado, espray *m*. **-3.** [can, container - gen] atomizador *m*; [- for garden] pulverizador *m*. **-4.** [of flowers] ramo *m*. ◇ *vt* rociar, vaporizar.

spread [spred] (*pt* & *pp* **spread**) ◇ *n* **-1.** [soft food]: **cheese** ~ queso *m* para untar. **-2.** [of fire, disease] propagación *f*. ◇ *vt* **-1.** [rug, tablecloth] extender; [map] desplegar. **-2.** [legs, fingers etc] estirar. **-3.** [butter, jam] untar; [glue] repartir; **to** ~ **sthg over sthg** extender algo por algo. **-4.** [disease] propagar; [news] difundir, diseminar. **-5.** [wealth, work] repartir equitativamente. ◇ *vi* **-1.** [disease, fire, news] extenderse, propagarse. **-2.** [gas, cloud] esparcirse. ◆ **spread out** *vi* diseminarse, dispersarse.

spread-eagled [-,iːgld] *adj* despatarrado(da).

spreadsheet ['spredʃiːt] *n* COMPUT hoja *f* de cálculo electrónica.

spree [spriː] *n* jarana *f*.

sprightly ['spraɪtlɪ] *adj* animado(da).

spring [sprɪŋ] (*pt* **sprang**, *pp* **sprung**) ◇ *n* **-1.** [season] primavera *f*. **-2.** [coil] muelle *m*. **-3.** [jump] salto *m*. **-4.** [water source] manantial *m*, vertiente *f* *Amer*. ◇ *vi* **-1.** [jump] saltar. **-2.** [move suddenly] moverse de repente. ◆ **spring up** *vi* surgir de repente.

springboard ['sprɪŋbɔːd] *n* *lit* & *fig* trampolín *m*.

spring-clean *vt* limpiar a fondo.

spring onion *n* *Br* cebolleta *f*.

springtime ['sprɪŋtaɪm] *n*: **in (the)** ~ en primavera.

springy ['sprɪŋɪ] *adj* [carpet, mattress, grass] mullido(da); [rubber] elástico(ca).

sprinkle ['sprɪŋkl] *vt* rociar, salpicar; **to** ~ **sthg over** OR **on sthg, to** ~ **sthg with sthg** rociar algo sobre algo.

sprinkler ['sprɪŋklər] *n* aspersor *m*.

sprint [sprɪnt] ◇ *n* **-1.** SPORT esprint *m*. **-2.** [fast run] carrera *f*. ◇ *vi* SPORT esprintar; [run fast] correr a toda velocidad.

sprout [spraʊt] ◇ *n* **-1. (Brussels)** ~s coles *fpl* de Bruselas. **-2.** [shoot] brote *m*, retoño *m*. ◇ *vt* [subj: plant] echar. ◇

vi **-1.** [plants, vegetables] crecer. **-2.** [leaves, shoots] brotar.

spruce [spruːs] ◇ *adj* pulcro(cra). ◇ *n* picea *f*. ◆ **spruce up** *vt sep* arreglar.

sprung [sprʌŋ] *pp* → **spring**.

spry [spraɪ] *adj* ágil, activo(va).

spun [spʌn] *pt* & *pp* → **spin**.

spur [spɜːr] ◇ *n* **-1.** [incentive]: ~ **(to sthg)** estímulo *m* (para conseguir algo). **-2.** [on rider's boot] espuela *f*. ◇ *vt* [encourage]: **to** ~ **sb to do sthg** animar a alguien a hacer algo. ◆ **on the spur of the moment** *adv* sin pensarlo dos veces. ◆ **spur on** *vt sep*: **to** ~ **sb on** animar a alguien.

spurious ['spʊərɪəs] *adj* falso(sa).

spurn [spɜːn] *vt* rechazar.

spurt [spɜːt] ◇ *n* **-1.** [of water] chorro *m*; [of flame] llamarada *f*. **-2.** [of activity, effort] arranque *m*. **-3.** [of speed] acelerón *m*. ◇ *vi* [gush]: **to** ~ **(out of** OR **from)** [liquid] salir a chorros de; [flame] salir incesantemente de.

spy [spaɪ] ◇ *n* espía *m y f*. ◇ *vt inf* divisar. ◇ *vi*: **to** ~ **(on)** espiar (a), aguaitar (a) *Amer*.

spying ['spaɪɪŋ] *n* espionaje *m*.

Sq., sq. *abbr of* **square**.

squabble ['skwɒbl] ◇ *n* riña *f*. ◇ *vi*: **to** ~ **(about** OR **over)** reñir (por).

squad [skwɒd] *n* **-1.** [of police] brigada *f*. **-2.** MIL pelotón *m*. **-3.** [SPORT - of club] plantilla *f*, equipo *m* completo; [- of national team] seleccionado *m*.

squadron ['skwɒdrən] *n* [of planes] escuadrilla *f*; [of warships] escuadra *f*; [of soldiers] escuadrón *m*.

squalid ['skwɒlɪd] *adj* [filthy] miserable, sórdido(da).

squall [skwɔːl] *n* [storm] turbión *m*.

squalor ['skwɒlər] *n* (U) miseria *f*.

squander ['skwɒndər] *vt* [opportunity] desaprovechar; [money] despilfarrar; [resources] malgastar.

square [skweər] ◇ *adj* **-1.** [gen] cuadrado(da). **-2.** [not owing money]: **we're** ~ **now** ya estamos en paz. ◇ *n* **-1.** [shape] cuadrado *m*. **-2.** [in town, city] plaza *f*. **-3.** *inf* [unfashionable person] carroza *m y f*. ◇ *vt* **-1.** MATH elevar al cuadrado. **-2.** [balance, reconcile]: **how can you** ~ **that with your principles?** ¿cómo encajas esto con tus principios? ◆ **square up** *vi* [settle up]: **to** ~ **up with** saldar cuentas con.

squarely ['skweəlɪ] *adv* [directly] justo, exactamente.

square meal *n* comida *f* satisfactoria.

squash [skwɒʃ] ◇ *n* **-1.** [game] squash *m*. **-2.** *Br* [drink] zumo *m*. **-3.** *Am* [vegetable] cucurbitácea *f*. ◇ *vt* [squeeze, flatten] aplastar.

squat [skwɒt] ◇ *adj* achaparrado(da). ◇ *vi* [crouch]: **to ~ (down)** agacharse, ponerse en cuclillas.

squatter ['skwɒtər] *n Br* ocupante *m* y *f* ilegal, squatter *m* y *f*.

squawk [skwɔːk] *n* [of bird] graznido *m*.

squeak [skwiːk] *n* **-1.** [of animal] chillido *m*. **-2.** [of hinge] chirrido *m*.

squeal [skwiːl] *vi* **-1.** [person, animal] chillar, gritar. **-2.** [brakes] chirriar.

squeamish ['skwiːmɪʃ] *adj* aprensivo(va).

squeeze [skwiːz] ◇ *n* [pressure] apretón *m*. ◇ *vt* **-1.** [press firmly] apretar. **-2.** [force out - toothpaste] sacar (estrujando); [- juice] exprimir. **-3.** [cram]: **to ~ sthg into sthg** [into place] conseguir meter algo en algo; [into time] arreglárselas para hacer algo en algo.

squelch [skweltʃ] *vi*: **to ~ through mud** cruzar el barro chapoteando.

squid [skwɪd] (*pl inv* OR **-s**) *n* **-1.** ZOOL calamar *m*. **-2.** (*U*) [food] calamares *mpl*.

squiggle ['skwɪgl] *n* garabato *m*.

squint [skwɪnt] ◇ *n* estrabismo *m*, bizquera *f*. ◇ *vi*: **to ~ at** mirar con los ojos entrecerrados.

squire ['skwaɪər] *n* [landowner] terrateniente *m* y *f*.

squirm [skwɜːm] *vi* [wriggle] retorcerse.

squirrel [*Br* 'skwɪrəl, *Am* 'skwɜːrəl] *n* ardilla *f*.

squirt [skwɜːt] ◇ *vt* [force out] sacar a chorro de. ◇ *vi*: **to ~ out of** salir a chorro.

Sr *abbr of* **senior**.

Sri Lanka [ˌsriːˈlæŋkə] *n* Sri Lanka.

St -1. (*abbr of* **saint**) Sto. (Sta.). **-2.** (*abbr of* **Street**) c/.

stab [stæb] ◇ *n* **-1.** [with knife] puñalada *f*. **-2.** *inf* [attempt]: **to have a ~ (at sthg)** probar (a hacer algo). **-3.** [twinge] punzada *f*. ◇ *vt* **-1.** [with knife] apuñalar. **-2.** [jab] pinchar.

stable ['steɪbl] ◇ *adj* **-1.** [unchanging] estable. **-2.** [not moving] fijo(ja). **-3.** MED [condition] estacionario(ria); [mental health] equilibrado(da). ◇ *n* [building] cuadra *f*.

stack [stæk] ◇ *n* [pile] pila *m*. ◇ *vt* [pile up] apilar.

stadium ['steɪdjəm] (*pl* **-diums** OR **-dia** [-djə]) *n* estadio *m*.

staff [stɑːf] ◇ *n* [employees] empleados *mpl*, personal *m*. ◇ *vt*: **the shop is ~ed by women** la tienda está llevada por una plantilla de mujeres.

stag [stæg] (*pl inv* OR **-s**) *n* ciervo *m*, venado *m*.

stage [steɪdʒ] ◇ *n* **-1.** [part of process, phase] etapa *f*. **-2.** [in theatre, hall] escenario *m*, escena *f*. **-3.** [acting profession]: **the ~** el teatro. ◇ *vt* **-1.** THEATRE representar. **-2.** [event, strike] organizar.

stagecoach ['steɪdʒkəʊtʃ] *n* diligencia *f*.

stage fright *n* miedo *m* al público.

stage-manage *vt* **-1.** THEATRE dirigir. **-2.** *fig* [orchestrate] urdir, maquinar.

stagger ['stægər] ◇ *vt* **-1.** [astound] dejar atónito(ta). **-2.** [arrange at different times] escalonar. ◇ *vi* tambalearse.

stagnant ['stægnənt] *adj lit* & *fig* estancado(da).

stagnate [stæg'neɪt] *vi* estancarse.

stag party *n* despedida *f* de soltero.

staid [steɪd] *adj* recatado y conservador (recatada y conservadora).

stain [steɪn] ◇ *n* mancha *f*. ◇ *vt* manchar.

stained glass [ˌsteɪnd-] *n* (*U*) vidrio *m* de color.

stainless steel [ˌsteɪnlɪs-] *n* acero *m* inoxidable.

stain remover [-rɪˌmuːvər] *n* quitamanchas *m inv*.

stair [steər] *n* peldaño *m*, escalón *m*. ◆ **stairs** *npl* escaleras *fpl*, escalera *f*.

staircase ['steəkeɪs] *n* escalera *f*.

stairway ['steəweɪ] *n* escalera *f*.

stairwell ['steəwel] *n* hueco *m* OR caja *f* de la escalera.

stake [steɪk] ◇ *n* **-1.** [share]: **to have a ~ in** tener intereses en. **-2.** [wooden post] estaca *f*. **-3.** [in gambling] apuesta *f*. ◇ *vt* **-1.** [risk]: **to ~ sthg (on** OR **upon)** arriesgar OR jugarse algo (en). **-2.** [in gambling] apostar. ◆ **at stake** *adv*: **to be at ~** estar en juego.

stale [steɪl] *adj* [bread] duro(ra); [food] pasado(da); [air] viciado(da).

stalemate ['steɪlmeɪt] *n* **-1.** [deadlock] punto *m* muerto. **-2.** CHESS tablas *fpl*.

stalk [stɔːk] ◇ *n* **-1.** [of flower, plant] tallo *m*. **-2.** [of leaf, fruit] pecíolo *m*, rabillo *m*. ◇ *vt* [hunt] acechar, seguir sigilosamente. ◇ *vi*: **to ~ in/out** entrar/salir con paso airado.

stall [stɔːl] ◇ *n* [in market, at exhibition] puesto *m*, caseta *f*. ◇ *vt* AUT calar. ◇ *vi* **-1.** AUT calarse. **-2.** [delay] andar con evasivas. ◆ **stalls** *npl Br* platea *f*.

stallion ['stæljən] *n* semental *m*.

stalwart ['stɔːlwət] *n* partidario *m*, -ria *f* incondicional.

stamina ['stæmɪnə] *n* resistencia *f*.

stammer ['stæmə'] ◇ *n* tartamudeo *m*. ◇ *vi* tartamudear.

stamp [stæmp] ◇ *n* -1. [gen] sello *m*, estampilla *f Amer*. -2. [tool] tampón *m*. ◇ *vt* -1. [mark by stamping] timbrar. -2. [stomp]: **to ~ one's feet** patear. ◇ *vi* -1. [stomp] patalear. -2. [tread heavily]: **to ~ on sthg** pisotear OR pisar algo.

stamp album *n* álbum *m* de sellos.

stamp-collecting [-kə,lektɪŋ] *n* filatelia *f*.

stamped addressed envelope ['stæmptə,drest-] *n Br* sobre con sus señas y franqueo.

stampede [stæm'piːd] ◇ *n lit* & *fig* estampida *f*. ◇ *vi* salir de estampida.

stance [stæns] *n* -1. [way of standing] postura *f*. -2. [attitude]: **~ (on)** postura *f* (ante).

stand [stænd] (*pt* & *pp* **stood**) ◇ *n* -1. [stall] **puesto** *m*; [selling newspapers] quiosco *m*. -2. [supporting object] soporte *m*; **coat ~** perchero *m*. -3. SPORT tribuna *f*. -4. [act of defence]: **to make a ~** resistir al enemigo. -5. [publicly stated view] postura *f*. -6. *Am* JUR estrado *m*. ◇ *vt* -1. [place upright] colocar (verticalmente). -2. [withstand, tolerate] soportar. ◇ *vi* -1. [be upright - person] estar de pie; [- object] estar (*en posición vertical*). -2. [get to one's feet] ponerse de pie, levantarse. -3. [liquid] reposar. -4. [still be valid] seguir vigente OR en pie. -5. [be in particular state]: **as things ~** tal como están las cosas. -6. *Br* POL [be a candidate] presentarse; **to ~ for Parliament** presentarse para las elecciones al Parlamento. -7. *Am* AUT: **"no ~ing"** "prohibido aparcar". ◆ **stand back** *vi* echarse para atrás. ◆ **stand by** ◇ *vt fus* -1. [person] seguir al lado de. -2. [promise, decision] mantener. ◇ *vi* -1. [in readiness]: **to ~ by (for sthg/to do sthg)** estar preparado(da) (para algo/para hacer algo). -2. [remain inactive] quedarse sin hacer nada. ◆ **stand down** *vi* [resign] retirarse. ◆ **stand for** *vt fus* -1. [signify] significar. -2. [tolerate] aguantar, tolerar. ◆ **stand in** *vi*: **to ~ in for sb** sustituir a alguien. ◆ **stand out** *vi* sobresalir, destacarse. ◆ **stand up** ◇ *vt sep inf* [boyfriend etc] dejar plantado(da). ◇ *vi* [rise from seat] levantarse. ◆ **stand up for** *vt fus* salir en defensa

de. ◆ **stand up to** *vt fus* -1. [weather, heat etc] resistir. -2. [person] hacer frente a.

standard ['stændəd] ◇ *adj* -1. [normal] corriente, estándar. -2. [accepted] establecido(da). ◇ *n* -1. [acceptable level] nivel *m*. -2. [point of reference - moral] criterio *m*; [- technical] norma *f*. -3. [flag] estandarte *m*. ◆ **standards** *npl* [principles] valores *mpl* morales.

standard lamp *n Br* lámpara *f* de pie.

standard of living (*pl* **standards of living**) *n* nivel *m* de vida.

standby ['stændbaɪ] (*pl* **standbys**) ◇ *n* recurso *m*; **on ~** preparado(da). ◇ *comp*: **~ ticket** billete *m* en lista de espera.

stand-in *n* [stuntman] doble *m* y *f*; [temporary replacement] sustituto *m*, -ta *f*.

standing ['stændɪŋ] ◇ *adj* [permanent] permanente. ◇ *n* -1. [reputation] reputación *f*. -2. [duration] duración *f*; **friends of 20 years' ~** amigos desde hace 20 años.

standing order *n* domiciliación *f* de pago.

standing room *n* (*U*) [on bus] sitio *m* para estar de pie; [at theatre, sports ground] localidades *fpl* de pie.

standoffish [,stænd'ɒfɪʃ] *adj* distante.

standpoint ['stændpɔɪnt] *n* punto *m* de vista.

standstill ['stændstɪl] *n*: **at a ~** [not moving] parado(da); *fig* [not active] en un punto muerto; **to come to a ~** [stop moving] pararse; *fig* [cease] llegar a un punto muerto.

stank [stæŋk] *pt* → **stink**.

staple ['steɪpl] ◇ *adj* [principal] básico(ca), de primera necesidad. ◇ *n* -1. [item of stationery] grapa *f*. -2. [principal commodity] producto *m* básico OR de primera necesidad. ◇ *vt* grapar.

stapler ['steɪplə'] *n* grapadora *f*.

star [stɑː'] ◇ *n* [gen] estrella *f*. ◇ *comp* estelar. ◇ *vi*: **to ~ (in)** hacer de protagonista en. ◆ **stars** *npl* horóscopo *m*.

starboard ['stɑːbəd] ◇ *adj* de estribor. ◇ *n*: **to ~** a estribor.

starch [stɑːtʃ] *n* -1. [gen] almidón *m*. -2. [in potatoes etc] fécula *f*.

stardom ['stɑːdəm] *n* estrellato *m*.

stare [steə'] ◇ *n* mirada *f* fija. ◇ *vi*: **to ~ (at sthg/sb)** mirar fijamente (algo/a alguien).

stark [stɑːk] ◇ *adj* -1. [landscape, decoration, room] austero(ra). -2. [harsh -

reality] crudo(da). ◇ *adv*: ~ **naked** en cueros.

starling ['stɑːlɪŋ] *n* estornino *m*.

starry ['stɑːrɪ] *adj* estrellado(da).

starry-eyed [-'aɪd] *adj* [optimism etc] iluso(sa); [lovers] encandilado(da).

Stars and Stripes *n*: **the** ~ la bandera de las barras y estrellas.

start [stɑːt] ◇ *n* **-1.** [beginning] principio *m*, comienzo *m*; **at the** ~ **of the year** a principios de año. **-2.** [jerk, jump] sobresalto *m*. **-3.** [starting place] salida *f*. **-4.** [time advantage] ventaja *f*. ◇ *vt* **-1.** [begin] empezar, comenzar; **to** ~ **doing** OR **to do sthg** empezar a hacer algo; **to** ~ **with** empezar por. **-2.** [turn on - machine, engine] poner en marcha; [- vehicle] arrancar. **-3.** [set up] formar, crear; [business] montar. ◇ *vi* **-1.** [begin] empezar, comenzar. **-2.** [machine, tape] ponerse en marcha; [vehicle] arrancar. **-3.** [begin journey] ponerse en camino. **-4.** [jerk, jump] sobresaltarse. ◆ **start off** ◇ *vt sep* [discussion, rumour] desencadenar; [meeting] empezar; [person]: **this should be enough to** ~ **you off** con esto tienes suficiente trabajo para empezar. ◇ *vi* **-1.** [begin] empezar, comenzar. **-2.** [leave on journey] salir, ponerse en camino. ◆ **start out** *vi* **-1.** [originally be] empezar, comenzar. **-2.** [leave on journey] salir, ponerse en camino. ◆ **start up** ◇ *vt sep* **-1.** [business] montar; [shop] poner; [association] crear. **-2.** [car, engine] arrancar. ◇ *vi* **-1.** [begin] empezar. **-2.** [car, engine] arrancar.

starter ['stɑːtər] *n* **-1.** *Br* [of meal] primer plato *m*, entrada *f*. **-2.** AUT (motor *m* de) arranque *m*. **-3.** [person participating in race] participante *m y f*.

starting point ['stɑːtɪŋ-] *n lit & fig* punto *m* de partida.

startle ['stɑːtl] *vt* asustar.

startling ['stɑːtlɪŋ] *adj* asombroso(sa).

starvation [stɑː'veɪʃn] *n* hambre *m*, inanición *f*.

starve [stɑːv] ◇ *vt* [deprive of food] privar de comida. ◇ *vi* **-1.** [have no food] pasar hambre. **-2.** *inf* [be hungry]: **I'm starving!** ¡me muero de hambre!

state [steɪt] ◇ *n* estado *m*; **not to be in a fit** ~ **to do sthg** no estar en condiciones de hacer algo; **to be in a** ~ tener los nervios de punta. ◇ *comp* [ceremony] oficial, de Estado; [control, ownership] estatal. ◇ *vt* **-1.** [gen] indicar; [reason, policy] plantear; [case] exponer.

-2. [time, date, amount] fijar. ◆ **State** *n*: **the State** el Estado. ◆ **States** *npl*: **the States** los Estados Unidos.

State Department *n Am* ≃ Ministerio *m* de Asuntos Exteriores.

stately ['steɪtlɪ] *adj* majestuoso(sa).

statement ['steɪtmənt] *n* **-1.** [gen] declaración *f*. **-2.** [from bank] extracto *m* OR estado *m* de cuenta.

state of mind (*pl* **states of mind**) *n* estado *m* de ánimo.

statesman ['steɪtsmən] (*pl* **-men** [-mən]) *n* estadista *m*.

static ['stætɪk] ◇ *adj* estático(ca). ◇ *n* (*U*) interferencias *fpl*, parásitos *mpl*.

static electricity *n* electricidad *f* estática.

station ['steɪʃn] ◇ *n* **-1.** [gen] estación *f*. **-2.** RADIO emisora *f*. **-3.** [centre of activity] centro *m*, puesto *m*. **-4.** *fml* [rank] rango *m*. ◇ *vt* **-1.** [position] situar, colocar. **-2.** MIL estacionar, apostar.

stationary ['steɪʃnərɪ] *adj* inmóvil.

stationer ['steɪʃnər] *n* papelero *m*, -ra *f*; ~**'s (shop)** papelería *f*.

stationery ['steɪʃnərɪ] *n* (*U*) objetos *mpl* de escritorio.

stationmaster ['steɪʃn,mɑːstər] *n* jefe *m* de estación.

station wagon *n Am* furgoneta *f* familiar.

statistic [stə'tɪstɪk] *n* estadística *f*. ◆ **statistics** *n* (*U*) estadística *f*.

statistical [stə'tɪstɪkl] *adj* estadístico(ca).

statue ['stætʃuː] *n* estatua *f*.

stature ['stætʃər] *n* **-1.** [height] estatura *f*, talla *f*. **-2.** [importance] categoría *f*.

status ['steɪtəs] *n* (*U*) **-1.** [position, condition] condición *f*, estado *m*. **-2.** [prestige] prestigio *m*, estatus *m inv*.

status symbol *n* símbolo *m* de posición social.

statute ['stætjuːt] *n* estatuto *m*.

statutory ['stætjutrɪ] *adj* reglamentario(ria).

staunch [stɔːntʃ] ◇ *adj* fiel, leal. ◇ *vt* restañar.

stave [steɪv] (*pt & pp* **-d** OR **stove**) *n* MUS pentagrama *m*. ◆ **stave off** *vt sep* [disaster, defeat] retrasar; [hunger, illness] aplacar temporalmente.

stay [steɪ] ◇ *vi* **-1.** [not move away]: **to** ~ **put** permanecer en el mismo sitio. **-2.** [as visitor] alojarse. **-3.** [continue, remain] permanecer. ◇ *n* estancia *f*. ◆ **stay in** *vi* quedarse en casa. ◆ **stay on** *vi* permanecer, quedarse. ◆ **stay**

out vi [from home] **quedarse fuera.**
◆ **stay up** vi **quedarse levantado(da).**

staying power ['steɪɪŋ-] n **resistencia** f.

stead [sted] n: **to stand sb in good ~**
servir de mucho a alguien.

steadfast ['stedfɑːst] adj [supporter] **fiel;**
[gaze] **fijo(ja);** [resolve] **inquebrantable.**

steadily ['stedɪlɪ] adv -1. [gradually]
constantemente. -2. [regularly - breathe,
move] **normalmente.** -3. [calmly - look]
fijamente; [- speak] **con tranquilidad.**

steady ['stedɪ] ◇ adj -1. [gradual]
gradual. -2. [regular, constant] **constan-**
te, continuo(nua). -3. [not shaking]
firme. -4. [voice] **sereno(na);** [stare]
fijo(ja). -5. [relationship] **estable, se-**
rio(ria); [boyfriend, girlfriend] **formal; a ~**
job un trabajo fijo. -6. [reliable, sensible]
sensato(ta). ◇ vt -1. [stop from shaking]
mantener firme; to ~ o.s. dejar de
temblar. -2. [nerves, voice] **dominar,**
controlar.

steak [steɪk] n -1. (U) [meat] **bistec** m,
filete m, **bife** m Amer. -2. [piece of meat,
fish] **filete** m.

steal [stiːl] (pt **stole,** pp **stolen**) ◇ vt
[gen] **robar;** [idea] **apropiarse de; to ~**
sthg from sb robar algo a alguien. ◇ vi
[move secretly] **moverse sigilosamente.**

stealthy ['stelθɪ] adj **cauteloso(sa), sigi-**
loso(sa).

steam [stiːm] ◇ n (U) **vapor** m, **vaho**
m. ◇ vt CULIN **cocer al vapor.** ◇ vi [wa-
ter, food] **echar vapor.** ◆ **steam up** ◇ vt
sep [mist up] **empañar.** ◇ vi **empañarse.**

steamboat ['stiːmbəʊt] n **buque** m **de**
vapor.

steam engine n **máquina** f **de vapor.**

steamer ['stiːmər] n [ship] **buque** m **de**
vapor.

steamroller ['stiːm,rəʊlər] n **apisonado-**
ra f.

steamy ['stiːmɪ] adj -1. [full of steam]
lleno(na) de vaho. -2. inf [erotic] **calien-**
te, erótico(ca).

steel [stiːl] ◇ n **acero** m. ◇ comp **de**
acero.

steelworks ['stiːlwɜːks] (pl inv) n **fun-**
dición f **de acero.**

steep [stiːp] ◇ adj -1. [hill, road] **empi-**
nado(da). -2. [considerable - increase, fall]
considerable. -3. inf [expensive] **muy**
caro(ra), abusivo(va). ◇ vt **remojar.**

steeple ['stiːpl] n **aguja** f (de un campanario).

steeplechase ['stiːpltʃeɪs] n **carrera** f **de**
obstáculos.

steer ['stɪər] ◇ n **buey** m. ◇ vt -1. [vehi-
cle] **conducir.** -2. [person, discussion etc]
dirigir. ◇ vi: **the car ~s well el coche**
se conduce bien; to ~ clear of sthg/sb
evitar algo/a alguien.

steering ['stɪərɪŋ] n (U) **dirección** f.

steering wheel n **volante** m, **timón** m
Amer.

stem [stem] ◇ n -1. [of plant] **tallo** m.
-2. [of glass] **pie** m. -3. [of pipe] **tubo** m.
-4. GRAMM **raíz** f. ◇ vt [flow] **contener;**
[blood] **restañar.** ◆ **stem from** vt fus **de-**
rivarse de.

stench [stentʃ] n **hedor** m.

stencil ['stensl] ◇ n **plantilla** f. ◇ vt **es-**
tarcir.

stenographer [stə'nɒgrəfər] n Am **taquí-**
grafo m, **-fa** f.

step [step] ◇ n -1. [gen] **paso** m; **~ by**
~ paso a paso; to be in/out of ~
llevar/no llevar el paso; fig **estar/no es-**
tar al tanto. -2. [action] **medida** f. -3.
[stair, rung] **peldaño** m. ◇ vi -1. [move
foot] **dar un paso; he stepped off the**
bus se bajó del autobús. -2. [tread]: **to**
~ on sthg pisar algo; to ~ in sthg me-
ter el pie en algo. ◆ **steps** npl -1. [stairs
- indoors] **escaleras** fpl; [- outside] **escali-**
nata f. -2. Br [stepladder] **escalera** f **de**
tijera. ◆ **step down** vi [leave job] **renun-**
ciar. ◆ **step in** vi **intervenir.** ◆ **step up**
vt sep **aumentar.**

stepbrother ['step,brʌðər] n **hermanas-**
tro m.

stepdaughter ['step,dɔːtər] n **hijastra** f.

stepfather ['step,fɑːðər] n **padrastro** m.

stepladder ['step,lædər] n **escalera** f **de**
tijera.

stepmother ['step,mʌðər] n **madrastra** f.

stepping-stone ['stepɪŋ-] n [in river] **pa-**
sadera f.

stepsister ['step,sɪstər] n **hermanastra** f.

stepson ['stepsʌn] n **hijastro** m.

stereo ['sterɪəʊ] (pl -s) ◇ adj **estéreo**
(inv). ◇ n -1. [record player] **equipo** m
estereofónico. -2. [stereo sound] **estéreo**
m.

stereotype ['sterɪətaɪp] n **estereotipo** m.

sterile ['steraɪl] adj -1. [germ-free] **esteri-**
lizado(da). -2. [unable to produce off-
spring] **estéril.**

sterilize, -ise ['sterəlaɪz] vt **esterilizar.**

sterling ['stɜːlɪŋ] ◇ adj -1. [of British
money] **esterlina.** -2. [excellent] **excelen-**
te. ◇ n (U) **libra** f **esterlina.**

sterling silver n **plata** f **de ley.**

stern [stɜːn] ◇ adj **severo(ra).** ◇ n **popa**
f.

steroid ['stɪərɔɪd] n esteroide m.

stethoscope ['steθəskəup] n estetoscopio m.

stew [stjuː] ◇ n estofado m, guisado m. ◇ vt [meat, vegetables] estofar, guisar; [fruit] hacer una compota de.

steward ['stjuəd] n **-1.** [on plane] auxiliar m de vuelo; [on ship, train] camarero m. **-2.** Br [organizer] ayudante m y f de organización.

stewardess ['stjuədɪs] n auxiliar f de vuelo, azafata f.

stick [stɪk] (pt & pp **stuck**) ◇ n **-1.** [of wood, for playing sport] palo m. **-2.** [of dynamite] cartucho m; [of liquorice, rock] barra f. **-3.** [walking stick] bastón m. ◇ vt **-1.** [push]: **to ~ sthg in** OR **into sthg** [knife, pin] clavar algo en algo; [finger] meter algo en algo. **-2.** [make adhere]: **to ~ sthg (on** OR **to sthg)** pegar algo (en algo). **-3.** inf [put] meter. **-4.** Br inf [tolerate] soportar, aguantar. ◇ vi **-1.** [adhere]: **to ~ (to)** pegarse (a). **-2.** [jam] atrancarse. ◆ **stick out** ◇ vt sep **-1.** [make protrude] sacar. **-2.** [endure] aguantar. ◇ vi [protrude] sobresalir. ◆ **stick to** vt fus **-1.** [follow closely] seguir. **-2.** [principles] ser fiel a; [promise, agreement] cumplir con; [decision] atenerse a. ◆ **stick up** vi salir, sobresalir. ◆ **stick up for** vt fus defender.

sticker ['stɪkər] n [piece of paper] pegatina f.

sticking plaster ['stɪkɪŋ-] n esparadrapo m.

stickler ['stɪklər] n: ~ **for sthg** maniático m, -ca f de algo.

stick shift n Am palanca f de cambios.

stick-up n inf atraco m a mano armada.

sticky ['stɪkɪ] adj **-1.** [tacky] pegajoso(sa). **-2.** [adhesive] adhesivo(va). **-3.** inf [awkward] engorroso(sa).

stiff [stɪf] ◇ adj **-1.** [inflexible] rígido(da). **-2.** [door, drawer] atascado(da). **-3.** [aching] agarrotado(da); **to be ~ tener agujetas. -4.** [formal - person, manner] estirado(da); [- smile] rígido(da). **-5.** [severe, intense] severo(ra). **-6.** [difficult - task] duro(ra). ◇ adv inf: **bored/frozen ~** muerto(ta) de aburrimiento/frío.

stiffen ['stɪfn] vi **-1.** [become inflexible] endurecerse. **-2.** [bones] entumecerse; [muscles] agarrotarse. **-3.** [become more severe, intense] intensificarse.

stifle ['staɪfl] vt **-1.** [prevent from breathing] ahogar, sofocar. **-2.** [prevent from happening] reprimir.

stifling ['staɪflɪŋ] adj sofocante.

stigma ['stɪgmə] n estigma m.

stile [staɪl] n escalones mpl para pasar una valla.

stiletto heel [stɪ'letəu-] n Br tacón m fino OR de aguja.

still [stɪl] ◇ adv **-1.** [up to now, up to then, even now] todavía. **-2.** [to emphasize remaining amount] aún; **I've ~ got two left** aún me quedan dos. **-3.** [nevertheless, however] sin embargo, no obstante. **-4.** [with comparatives] aún. **-5.** [motionless] sin moverse. ◇ adj **-1.** [not moving] inmóvil. **-2.** [calm, quiet] tranquilo(la), sosegado(da). **-3.** [not windy] apacible. **-4.** [not fizzy] sin gas. ◇ n **-1.** PHOT vista f fija. **-2.** [for making alcohol] alambique m.

stillborn ['stɪlbɔːn] adj nacido muerto (nacida muerta).

still life (pl **-s**) n bodegón m, naturaleza f muerta.

stilted ['stɪltɪd] adj forzado(da).

stilts [stɪlts] npl **-1.** [for person] zancos mpl. **-2.** [for building] pilotes mpl.

stimulate ['stɪmjuleɪt] vt [gen] estimular; [interest] excitar.

stimulating ['stɪmjuleɪtɪŋ] adj [physically] estimulante; [mentally] interesante.

stimulus ['stɪmjuləs] (pl **-li** [-laɪ]) n estímulo m.

sting [stɪŋ] (pt & pp **stung**) ◇ n **-1.** [by bee] picadura f. **-2.** [of bee] aguijón m. **-3.** [sharp pain] escozor m. ◇ vt **-1.** [subj: bee, nettle] picar. **-2.** [cause sharp pain to] escocer. ◇ vi picar.

stingy ['stɪndʒɪ] adj inf tacaño(ña), roñoso(sa).

stink [stɪŋk] (pt **stank** OR **stunk**, pp **stunk**) ◇ n peste f, hedor m. ◇ vi [have unpleasant smell] apestar, heder.

stinking ['stɪŋkɪŋ] inf fig ◇ adj asqueroso(sa). ◇ adv increíblemente.

stint [stɪnt] ◇ n periodo m. ◇ vi: **to ~ on sthg** escatimar algo.

stipulate ['stɪpjuleɪt] vt estipular.

stir [stɜːr] ◇ n [public excitement] revuelo m. ◇ vt **-1.** [mix] remover. **-2.** [move gently] agitar, mover. **-3.** [move emotionally] conmover. ◇ vi **-1.** [move gently] moverse, agitarse. ◆ **stir up** vt sep **-1.** [cause to rise] levantar. **-2.** [cause] provocar.

stirrup ['stɪrəp] n estribo m.

stitch [stɪtʃ] ◇ n **-1.** SEWING puntada f. **-2.** [in knitting] punto m. **-3.** MED punto m (de sutura). **-4.** [stomach pain]: **to have a ~** sentir pinchazos (en el estómago). ◇ vt **-1.** SEWING coser. **-2.** MED suturar.

stoat [stəʊt] n armiño m.

stock [stɒk] ◇ n **-1.** [supply] reserva f. **-2.** (U) COMM [reserves] existencias fpl; [selection] surtido m; **in ~** en existencia; **out of ~** agotado(da). **-3.** FIN [of company] capital m; **~s and shares** acciones fpl, valores mpl. **-4.** [ancestry] linaje m, estirpe f. **-5.** CULIN caldo m. **-6.** [livestock] ganado m, ganadería f. **-7.** phr: **to take ~ (of sthg)** evaluar (algo). ◇ adj estereotipado(da). ◇ vt **-1.** COMM abastecer de, tener en el almacén. **-2.** [shelves] llenar; [lake] repoblar. ◆ **stock up** vi: **to ~ up (with)** abastecerse (de).

stockbroker ['stɒk,brəʊkəʳ] n corredor m, -ra f de bolsa.

stock cube n Br pastilla f de caldo.

stock exchange n bolsa f.

stockholder ['stɒk,həʊldəʳ] n Am accionista m y f.

Stockholm ['stɒkhəʊm] n Estocolmo.

stocking ['stɒkɪŋ] n [for woman] media f.

stockist ['stɒkɪst] n Br distribuidor m, -ra f.

stock market n bolsa f, mercado m de valores.

stock phrase n frase f estereotipada.

stockpile ['stɒkpaɪl] ◇ n reservas fpl. ◇ vt almacenar, acumular.

stocktaking ['stɒk,teɪkɪŋ] n (U) inventario m, balance m.

stocky ['stɒkɪ] adj corpulento(ta), robusto(ta).

stodgy ['stɒdʒɪ] adj [indigestible] indigesto(ta).

stoical ['stəʊɪkl] adj estoico(ca).

stoke [stəʊk] vt [fire] avivar, alimentar.

stole [stəʊl] ◇ pt → **steal**. ◇ n estola f.

stolen ['stəʊln] pp → **steal**.

stolid ['stɒlɪd] adj impasible.

stomach ['stʌmək] ◇ n **-1.** [organ] estómago m. **-2.** [abdomen] vientre m. ◇ vt tragar, aguantar.

stomachache ['stʌməkeɪk] n dolor m de estómago.

stomach upset [-'ʌpset] n trastorno m gástrico.

stone [stəʊn] (pl sense 4 only inv OR **-s**) ◇ n **-1.** [mineral] piedra f. **-2.** [jewel] piedra f preciosa. **-3.** [seed] hueso m. **-4.** Br [unit of measurement] = 6,35 kilos. ◇ comp de piedra. ◇ vt apedrear.

stone-cold adj helado(da).

stonewashed ['stəʊnwɒʃt] adj lavado(da) a la piedra.

stonework ['stəʊnwɜːk] n mampostería f.

stood [stʊd] pt & pp → **stand**.

stool [stuːl] n [seat] taburete m.

stoop [stuːp] ◇ n [bent back]: **to walk with a ~** caminar encorvado(da). ◇ vi **-1.** [bend] inclinarse, agacharse. **-2.** [hunch shoulders] encorvarse.

stop [stɒp] ◇ n **-1.** [gen] parada f; **to put a ~ to sthg** poner fin a algo. **-2.** [full stop] punto m. ◇ vt **-1.** [gen] parar; **to ~ doing sthg** dejar de hacer algo. **-2.** [prevent] impedir; **to ~ sb/sthg from doing sthg** impedir que alguien/algo haga algo. **-3.** [cause to stop moving] detener. ◇ vi [gen] pararse; [rain, music] cesar. ◆ **stop off** vi hacer una parada. ◆ **stop up** vt sep [block] taponar, tapar.

stopgap ['stɒpgæp] n [thing] recurso m provisional; [person] sustituto m, -ta f.

stopover ['stɒp,əʊvəʳ] n [gen] parada f; [of plane] escala f.

stoppage ['stɒpɪdʒ] n **-1.** [strike] paro m, huelga f. **-2.** Br [deduction] retención f.

stopper ['stɒpəʳ] n tapón m.

stop press n noticias fpl de última hora.

stopwatch ['stɒpwɒtʃ] n cronómetro m.

storage ['stɔːrɪdʒ] n almacenamiento m.

storage heater n Br calentador por almacenamiento térmico.

store [stɔːʳ] ◇ n **-1.** [shop] tienda f. **-2.** [supply] provisión f, reserva f. **-3.** [place of storage] almacén m. ◇ vt **-1.** [gen & COMPUT] almacenar. **-2.** [keep] guardar. ◆ **store up** vt sep [provisions, goods] almacenar; [information] acumular.

storekeeper ['stɔː,kiːpəʳ] n Am tendero m, -ra f.

storeroom ['stɔːrʊm] n [gen] almacén m; [for food] despensa f.

storey Br (pl **storeys**), **story** Am ['stɔːrɪ] n planta f.

stork [stɔːk] n cigüeña f.

storm [stɔːm] ◇ n **-1.** [bad weather] tormenta f. **-2.** [violent reaction] torrente m. ◇ vi **-1.** MIL asaltar. ◇ vi **-1.** [go angrily]: **to ~ out** salir echando pestes. **-2.** [say angrily] vociferar.

stormy ['stɔːmɪ] adj **-1.** [weather] tormentoso(sa). **-2.** [meeting] acalorado(da); [relationship] tempestuoso(sa).

story ['stɔːrɪ] n **-1.** [tale] cuento m. **-2.** [history] historia f. **-3.** [news article] artículo m. **-4.** Am = **storey**.

storybook ['stɔːrɪbʊk] adj de cuento.

storyteller ['stɔːrɪ,teləʳ] n [teller of story] narrador m, -ra f, cuentista m y f.

stout [staut] ◇ adj -1. [rather fat] corpulento(ta). -2. [strong, solid] fuerte, sólido(da). -3. [resolute] firme. ◇ n (U) cerveza f negra.

stove [stəʊv] ◇ pt & pp → stave. ◇ n [for heating] estufa f; [for cooking] cocina f.

stow [stəʊ] vt: to ~ sthg (away) guardar algo.

stowaway ['stəʊəweɪ] n polizón m.

straddle ['strædl] vt [subj: person] sentarse a horcajadas sobre.

straggle ['strægl] vi -1. [sprawl] desparramarse. -2. [dawdle] rezagarse.

straggler ['stræglər] n rezagado m, -da f.

straight [streɪt] ◇ adj -1. [not bent] recto(ta). -2. [hair] liso(sa). -3. [honest, frank] sincero(ra). -4. [tidy] arreglado(da). -5. [choice, swap] simple, fácil. -6. [alcoholic drink] solo(la). ◇ adv -1. [in a straight line - horizontally] directamente; [- vertically] recto(ta); ~ ahead todo recto. -2. [directly] directamente; [immediately] inmediatamente. -3. [frankly] francamente. -4. [tidy] en orden. -5. [undiluted] solo(la). -6. phr: let's get things ~ vamos a aclarar las cosas. ◆ straight off adv en el acto. ◆ straight out adv sin tapujos.

straightaway [,streɪtə'weɪ] adv en seguida.

straighten ['streɪtn] vt -1. [tidy - room] ordenar; [- hair, dress] poner bien. -2. [make straight - horizontally] poner recto(ta); [- vertically] enderezar. ◆ straighten out vt sep [mess] arreglar; [problem] resolver.

straight face n: to keep a ~ aguantar la risa.

straightforward [,streɪt'fɔ:wəd] adj -1. [easy] sencillo(lla). -2. [frank - answer] directo(ta); [- person] sincero(ra).

strain [streɪn] ◇ n -1. [weight] peso m; [pressure] presión f. -2. [mental stress] tensión f nerviosa. -3. [physical injury] torcedura f. -4. [worry, difficulty] esfuerzo m. ◇ vt -1. [overtax - budget] estirar; [- enthusiasm] agotar. -2. [use hard]: to ~ one's eyes/ears aguzar la vista/el oído. -3. [injure - eyes] cansar; [- muscle, back] torcerse. -4. [drain] colar. ◇ vi: to ~ to do sthg esforzarse por hacer algo. ◆ strains npl literary [of music] acordes mpl.

strained [streɪnd] adj -1. [worried] preocupado(da). -2. [unfriendly] tirante, tenso(sa). -3. [insincere] forzado(da).

strainer ['streɪnər] n colador m.

strait [streɪt] n estrecho m. ◆ straits npl: in dire OR desperate ~s en un serio aprieto.

straitjacket ['streɪt,dʒækɪt] n [garment] camisa f de fuerza.

straitlaced [,streɪt'leɪst] adj pej mojigato(ta).

strand [strænd] n [thin piece] hebra f; a ~ of hair un pelo del cabello.

stranded ['strændɪd] adj [ship] varado(da); [person] colgado(da).

strange [streɪndʒ] adj -1. [unusual] raro(ra), extraño(ña). -2. [unfamiliar] extraño(ña), desconocido(da).

stranger ['streɪndʒər] n -1. [unfamiliar person] extraño m, -ña f, desconocido m, -da f. -2. [outsider] forastero m, -ra f.

strangle ['stræŋgl] vt [kill] estrangular.

stranglehold ['stræŋglhəʊld] n fig [strong influence] dominio m absoluto.

strap [stræp] ◇ n -1. [of handbag, rifle] bandolera f. -2. [of watch, case] correa f; [of dress, bra] tirante m. ◇ vt [fasten] atar con correa.

strapping ['stræpɪŋ] adj robusto(ta).

Strasbourg ['stræzbɜːg] n Estrasburgo.

strategic [strə'ti:dʒɪk] adj estratégico(ca).

strategy ['strætɪdʒɪ] n estrategia f.

straw [strɔ:] n -1. AGR paja f. -2. [for drinking] pajita f, paja f. -3. phr: the last ~ el colmo.

strawberry ['strɔ:bəri] ◇ n fresa f, frutilla f Amer. ◇ comp de fresa.

stray [streɪ] ◇ adj -1. [animal - without owner] callejero(ra); [- lost] extraviado(da). -2. [bullet] perdido(da); [example] aislado(da). ◇ vi -1. [from path] desviarse; [from group] extraviarse. -2. [thoughts, mind] perderse.

streak [stri:k] ◇ n -1. [of hair] mechón m; [of lightning] rayo m; [of grease] raya f. -2. [in character] vena f. ◇ vi [move quickly] ir como una rayo.

stream [stri:m] ◇ n -1. [small river] riachuelo m. -2. [of liquid, smoke] chorro m; [of light] raudal m. -3. [current] corriente f. -4. [of people, cars] torrente m. -5. [continuous series] sarta f, serie f. -6. Br SCH grupo m. ◇ vi -1. [liquid, smoke, light]: to ~ into entrar a raudales en; to ~ out of brotar de. -2. [people, cars]: to ~ into entrar atropelladamente en; to ~ out of salir atropelladamente de. ◇ vt Br SCH agrupar de acuerdo con el rendimiento escolar.

streamer ['stri:mər] n [for party] serpentina f.

streamlined ['striːmlaɪnd] *adj* **-1.** [aerodynamic] aerodinámico(ca). **-2.** [efficient] racional.

street [striːt] *n* calle *f*.

streetcar ['striːtkɑːʳ] *n Am* tranvía *m*.

street lamp, **street light** *n* farola *f*.

street plan *n* plano *m* (de la ciudad).

streetwise ['striːtwaɪz] *adj inf* espabilado(da).

strength [streŋθ] *n* **-1.** [physical or mental power] fuerza *f*. **-2.** [power, influence] poder *m*. **-3.** [quality] punto *m* fuerte. **-4.** [solidity - of material structure] solidez *f*. **-5.** [intensity - of feeling, smell, wind] intensidad *f*; [- of accent, wine] fuerza *f*; [- of drug] potencia *f*. **-6.** [credibility, weight] peso *m*, fuerza *f*.

strengthen ['streŋθn] *vt* **-1.** [gen] fortalecer. **-2.** [reinforce - argument, bridge] reforzar. **-3.** [intensify] acentuar, intensificar. **-4.** [make closer] estrechar.

strenuous ['strenjʊəs] *adj* agotador(ra).

stress [stres] ◇ *n* **-1.** [emphasis]: ~ (on) hincapié *m* OR énfasis *m inv* (en). **-2.** [tension, anxiety] estrés *m*. **-3.** [physical pressure]: ~ (on) presión *f* (en). **-4.** LING [on word, syllable] acento *m*. ◇ *vt* **-1.** [emphasize] recalcar, subrayar. **-2.** LING [word, syllable] acentuar.

stressful ['stresfʊl] *adj* estresante.

stretch [stretʃ] ◇ *n* **-1.** [of land, water] extensión *f*; [of road, river] tramo *m*, trecho *m*. **-2.** [of time] periodo *m*. ◇ *vt* **-1.** [gen] estirar. **-2.** [overtax - person] extender. **-3.** [challenge] hacer rendir al máximo. ◇ *vi* [area]: **to ~ over/from ...** **to** extenderse   por/desde   ...   hasta. ◆ **stretch out** ◇ *vt sep* [foot, leg] estirar; [hand, arm] alargar. ◇ *vi* **-1.** [lie down] tumbarse. **-2.** [reach out] estirarse.

stretcher ['stretʃəʳ] *n* camilla *f*.

strew [struː] (*pp* **strewn** [struːn] OR **-ed**) *vt*: **to be strewn with** estar cubierto(ta) de.

stricken ['strɪkn] *adj*: **to be ~ by** OR **with** [illness] estar aquejado(da) de(de); [grief] estar afligido(da) por; [doubts, horror] estar atenazado(da) por.

strict [strɪkt] *adj* **-1.** [gen] estricto(ta). **-2.** [precise] exacto(ta), estricto(ta).

strictly ['strɪktlɪ] *adv* **-1.** [severely] severamente. **-2.** [absolutely - prohibited] terminantemente; [- confidential] absolutamente. **-3.** [exactly] exactamente; ~ **speaking** en el sentido estricto de la palabra. **-4.** [exclusively] exclusivamente.

stride [straɪd] (*pt* **strode**, *pp* **stridden** ['strɪdn]) ◇ *n* zancada *f*. ◇ *vi* andar a zancadas.

strident ['straɪdnt] *adj* **-1.** [harsh] estridente. **-2.** [vociferous] exaltado(da).

strife [straɪf] *n* (*U*) *fml* conflictos *mpl*.

strike [straɪk] (*pt* & *pp* **struck**) ◇ *n* **-1.** [refusal to work etc] huelga *f*; **to be (out) on** ~ estar en huelga; **to go on** ~ declararse en huelga. **-2.** MIL ataque *m*. **-3.** [find] descubrimiento *m*. ◇ *vt* **-1.** *fml* [hit - deliberately] golpear, pegar; [- accidentally] chocar contra. **-2.** [subj: disaster, earthquake] asolar; [subj: lightning] fulminar. **-3.** [subj: thought, idea] ocurrírsele a. **-4.** [deal, bargain] cerrar. **-5.** [match] encender. ◇ *vi* **-1.** [stop working] estar en huelga. **-2.** *fml* [hit accidentally]: **to ~ against** chocar contra. **-3.** [hurricane, disaster] sobrevenir; [lightning] caer. **-4.** *fml* [attack] atacar. **-5.** [chime] dar la hora; **the clock struck six** el reloj dio las seis. ◆ **strike down** *vt sep* fulminar. ◆ **strike out** *vt sep* tachar. ◆ **strike up** *vt fus* **-1.** [friendship] trabar; [conversation] entablar. **-2.** [tune] empezar a tocar.

striker ['straɪkəʳ] *n* **-1.** [person on strike] huelguista *m y f*. **-2.** FTBL delantero *m*, -ra *f*.

striking ['straɪkɪŋ] *adj* **-1.** [noticeable, unusual] chocante, sorprendente. **-2.** [attractive] llamativo(va), atractivo(va).

string [strɪŋ] (*pt* & *pp* **strung**) *n* **-1.** [thin rope] cuerda *f*; **a (piece of)** ~ un cordón; **to pull** ~s utilizar uno sus influencias. **-2.** [of beads, pearls] sarta *f*. **-3.** [series] serie *f*, sucesión *f*. **-4.** [of musical instrument] cuerda *f*. ◆ **strings** *npl* MUS: **the** ~s los instrumentos de cuerda. ◆ **string out** *vt fus*: **to be strung out** alinearse. ◆ **string together** *vt sep* enlazar.

string bean *n* judía *f* verde.

stringed instrument ['strɪŋd-] *n* instrumento *m* de cuerda.

stringent ['strɪndʒənt] *adj* estricto(ta), severo(ra).

strip [strɪp] ◇ *n* **-1.** [narrow piece] tira *f*. **-2.** [narrow area] franja *f*. **-3.** *Br* SPORT camiseta *f*, colores *mpl*. ◇ *vt* **-1.** [undress] desnudar. **-2.** [paint, wallpaper] quitar. ◇ *vi* [undress] desnudarse. ◆ **strip off** *vi* desnudarse.

strip cartoon *n Br* historieta *f*, tira *f* cómica.

stripe [straɪp] *n* **-1.** [band of colour] raya *f*, franja *f*. **-2.** [sign of rank] galón *m*.

striped [straipt] *adj* a rayas.

strip lighting *n* alumbrado *m* fluorescente.

stripper ['strɪpəʳ] *n* **-1.** [performer of striptease] artista *m* y *f* de striptease. **-2.** [for paint] disolvente *m*.

striptease ['striptiːz] *n* striptease *m*.

strive [straɪv] (*pt* strove, *pp* striven ['strɪvn]) *vi fml*: **to ~ for sthg** luchar por algo; **to ~ to do sthg** esforzarse por hacer algo.

strode [strəʊd] *pt* → stride.

stroke [strəʊk] ◇ *n* **-1.** MED apoplejía *f*, derrame *m* cerebral. **-2.** [of pen] trazo *m*; [of brush] pincelada *f*. **-3.** [style of swimming] estilo *m*. **-4.** [in tennis, golf etc] golpe *m*. **-5.** [of clock] campanada *f*. **-6.** *Br* [oblique] barra *f*. **-7.** [piece]: **a ~ of genius** una genialidad; **a ~ of luck** un golpe de suerte; **at a ~** de una vez, de golpe. ◇ *vt* acariciar.

stroll [strəʊl] ◇ *n* paseo *m*. ◇ *vi* pasear.

stroller ['strəʊləʳ] *n Am* [for baby] sillita *f* (de niño).

strong [strɒŋ] *adj* **-1.** [gen] fuerte. **-2.** [material, structure] sólido(da), resistente. **-3.** [feeling, belief] profundo(da); [opposition, denial] firme; [support] acérrimo(ma); [accent] marcado(da). **-4.** [discipline, policy] estricto(ta). **-5.** [argument] convincente. **-6.** [in numbers]: **the crowd was 2,000 ~** la multitud constaba de 2.000 personas. **-7.** [good, gifted]: **one's ~ point** el punto fuerte de uno. **-8.** [concentrated] concentrado(da).

strongbox ['strɒŋbɒks] *n* caja *f* fuerte.

stronghold ['strɒŋhəʊld] *n fig* [bastion] bastión *m*, baluarte *m*.

strongly ['strɒŋlɪ] *adv* **-1.** [sturdily] fuertemente. **-2.** [in degree] intensamente. **-3.** [fervently]: **to support/oppose sthg ~** apoyar/oponerse a algo totalmente.

strong room *n* cámara *f* acorazada.

strove [strəʊv] *pt* → strive.

struck [strʌk] *pt & pp* → strike.

structure ['strʌktʃəʳ] *n* **-1.** [arrangement] estructura *f*. **-2.** [building] construcción *f*.

struggle ['strʌgl] ◇ *n* **-1.** [great effort]: **~ (for sthg/to do sthg)** lucha *f* (por algo/por hacer algo). **-2.** [fight, tussle] forcejeo *m*. ◇ *vi* **-1.** [make great effort]: **to ~ (for sthg/to do sthg)** luchar (por algo/por hacer algo). **-2.** [to free o.s.]: **to ~ free** forcejear para soltarse. **-3.** [move with difficulty]: **to ~ with sthg** llevar algo con dificultad.

strum [strʌm] *vt & vi* rasguear.

strung [strʌŋ] *pt & pp* → string.

strut [strʌt] ◇ *n* CONSTR puntal *m*. ◇ *vi* andar pavoneándose.

stub [stʌb] ◇ *n* **-1.** [of cigarette] colilla *f*; [of pencil] cabo *m*. **-2.** [of ticket] resguardo *m*; [of cheque] matriz *f*. ◇ *vt*: **to ~ one's toe on** darse con el pie en.

◆ stub out *vt sep* apagar.

stubble ['stʌbl] *n* (U) **-1.** [in field] rastrojo *m*. **-2.** [on chin] barba *f* incipiente OR de tres días.

stubborn ['stʌbən] *adj* [person] terco(ca), testarudo(da).

stuck [stʌk] ◇ *pt & pp* → stick. ◇ *adj* **-1.** [jammed - lid, window] atascado(da). **-2.** [unable to progress] atascado(da). **-3.** [stranded] colgado(da). **-4.** [in a meeting, at home] encerrado(da).

stuck-up *adj inf pej* engreído(da).

stud [stʌd] *n* **-1.** [metal decoration] tachón *m*. **-2.** [earring] pendiente *m*. **-3.** *Br* [on boot, shoe] taco *m*. **-4.** [horse] semental *m*.

studded ['stʌdɪd] *adj*: **~ (with)** tachonado(da) (con).

student ['stjuːdnt] ◇ *n* **-1.** [at college, university] estudiante *m* y *f*. **-2.** [scholar] estudioso *m*, -sa *f*. ◇ *comp* estudiantil.

studio ['stjuːdɪəʊ] (*pl* -s) *n* estudio *m*.

studio flat *Br*, **studio apartment** *Am n* estudio *m*.

studious ['stjuːdjəs] *adj* estudioso(sa).

studiously ['stjuːdjəslɪ] *adv* cuidadosamente.

study ['stʌdɪ] ◇ *n* estudio *m*. ◇ *vt* **-1.** [learn] estudiar. **-2.** [examine - report, sb's face] examinar, estudiar. ◇ *vi* estudiar.

stuff [stʌf] ◇ *n* (U) *inf* **-1.** [things, belongings] cosas *fpl*. **-2.** [substance]: **what's that ~ in your pocket?** ¿qué es eso que llevas en el bolsillo? ◇ *vt* **-1.** [push, put] meter. **-2.** [fill, cram]: **to ~ sthg (with)** [box, room] llenar algo (de); [pillow, doll] rellenar algo (de). **-3.** CULIN rellenar.

stuffed [stʌft] *adj* **-1.** [filled, crammed]: **~ with** atestado(da) de. **-2.** *inf* [subj: person - with food] lleno(na), inflado(da). **-3.** CULIN relleno(na). **-4.** [preserved - animal] disecado(da).

stuffing ['stʌfɪŋ] *n* (U) relleno *m*.

stuffy ['stʌfɪ] *adj* **-1.** [atmosphere] cargado(da); [room] mal ventilado(da). **-2.** [old-fashioned] retrógrado(da), carca.

stumble ['stʌmbl] *vi* [trip] tropezar.

◆ stumble across, **stumble on** *vt fus*

[thing] dar con; [person] encontrarse con.

stumbling block ['stʌmblɪŋ-] *n* obstáculo *m*, escollo *m*.

stump [stʌmp] ◇ *n* [of tree] tocón *m*; [of limb] **muñón** *m*. ◇ *vt* [subj: question, problem] dejar perplejo(ja).

stun [stʌn] *vt lit & fig* aturdir.

stung [stʌŋ] *pt & pp* → **sting**.

stunk [stʌŋk] *pt & pp* → **stink**.

stunning ['stʌnɪŋ] *adj* **-1.** [very beautiful] imponente. **-2.** [shocking] pasmoso(sa).

stunt [stʌnt] ◇ *n* **-1.** [for publicity] truco *m* publicitario. **-2.** CINEMA escena *f* arriesgada OR peligrosa. ◇ *vt* atrofiar.

stunted ['stʌntɪd] *adj* esmirriado(da).

stunt man *n* especialista *m*, doble *m*.

stupefy ['stjuːpɪfaɪ] *vt* **-1.** [tire, bore] aturdir, atontar. **-2.** [surprise] dejar estupefacto(ta).

stupendous [stjuːˈpendəs] *adj inf* [wonderful] estupendo(da); [very large] enorme.

stupid ['stjuːpɪd] *adj* **-1.** [foolish] estúpido(da). **-2.** *inf* [annoying] puñetero(ra).

stupidity [stjuːˈpɪdətɪ] *n* (U) estupidez *f*.

sturdy ['stɜːdɪ] *adj* [person, shoulders] fuerte; [furniture, bridge] firme, sólido(da).

stutter ['stʌtəʳ] *vi* tartamudear.

sty [staɪ] *n* [pigsty] pocilga *f*.

stye [staɪ] *n* orzuelo *m*.

style [staɪl] ◇ *n* **-1.** [characteristic manner] estilo *m*. **-2.** (U) [smartness, elegance] clase *f*. **-3.** [design] modelo *m*. ◇ *vt* [hair] peinar.

stylish ['staɪlɪʃ] *adj* elegante, con estilo.

stylist ['staɪlɪst] *n* [hairdresser] peluquero *m*, -ra *f*.

stylus ['staɪləs] (*pl* **-es**) *n* [on record player] aguja *f*.

suave [swɑːv] *adj* [well-mannered] afable, amable; [obsequious] zalamero(ra).

sub [sʌb] *n inf* SPORT (*abbr of* **substitute**) reserva *m y f*.

subconscious [ˌsʌbˈkɒnʃəs] *adj* subconsciente.

subcontract [ˌsʌbkənˈtrækt] *vt* subcontratar.

subdivide [ˌsʌbdɪˈvaɪd] *vt* subdividir.

subdue [səbˈdjuː] *vt* **-1.** [enemy, nation] sojuzgar. **-2.** [feelings] contener.

subdued [səbˈdjuːd] *adj* **-1.** [person] apagado(da). **-2.** [colour, light] tenue.

subject [*adj, n & prep* 'sʌbdʒekt, *vt* səbˈdʒekt] ◇ *adj* [affected]: ~ **to sthg** [taxes, changes, law] sujeto(ta) a; [illness]

proclive a. ◇ *n* **-1.** [topic] tema *m*. **-2.** GRAMM sujeto *m*. **-3.** SCH & UNIV asignatura *f*. **-4.** [citizen] súbdito *m*, -ta *f*. ◇ *vt* **-1.** [bring under control] someter, dominar. **-2.** [force to experience]: **to ~ sb to sthg** someter a alguien a algo. ◆ **subject to** *prep* dependiendo de.

subjective [səbˈdʒektɪv] *adj* subjetivo(va).

subject matter ['sʌbdʒekt-] *n* (U) tema *m*, contenido *m*.

subjunctive [səbˈdʒʌŋktɪv] *n* GRAMM: ~ **(mood)** (modo *m*) subjuntivo *m*.

sublet [ˌsʌbˈlet] (*pt & pp* **sublet**) *vt & vi* subarrendar.

sublime [səˈblaɪm] *adj* [wonderful] sublime.

submachine gun [ˌsʌbməˈʃiːn-] *n* metralleta *f*.

submarine [ˌsʌbməˈriːn] *n* submarino *m*.

submerge [səbˈmɜːdʒ] ◇ *vt* **-1.** [in water] sumergir. **-2.** *fig* [in activity]: **to ~ o.s. in sthg** dedicarse de lleno a algo. ◇ *vi* sumergirse.

submission [səbˈmɪʃn] *n* **-1.** [capitulation] sumisión *f*. **-2.** [presentation] presentación *f*.

submissive [səbˈmɪsɪv] *adj* sumiso(sa).

submit [səbˈmɪt] ◇ *vt* presentar. ◇ *vi*: **to ~ (to sb)** rendirse (a alguien); **to ~ (to sthg)** someterse (a algo).

subnormal [ˌsʌbˈnɔːml] *adj* subnormal.

subordinate [səˈbɔːdɪnət] ◇ *adj fml* [less important]: ~ **(to)** subordinado(da) (a). ◇ *n* subordinado *m*, -da *f*.

subpoena [səˈpiːnə] JUR ◇ *n* citación *f*. ◇ *vt* citar.

subscribe [səbˈskraɪb] *vi* **-1.** [to magazine, newspaper]: **to ~ (to)** suscribirse (a). **-2.** [to belief]: **to ~ to** estar de acuerdo con.

subscriber [səbˈskraɪbəʳ] *n* **-1.** [to magazine, newspaper] suscriptor *m*, -ra *f*. **-2.** [to service] abonado *m*, -da *f*.

subscription [səbˈskrɪpʃn] *n* [to magazine] suscripción *f*; [to service] abono *m*; [to society, club] cuota *f*.

subsequent ['sʌbsɪkwənt] *adj* subsiguiente, posterior.

subsequently ['sʌbsɪkwəntlɪ] *adv* posteriormente.

subservient [səbˈsɜːvjənt] *adj* [servile]: ~ **(to sb)** servil (ante alguien).

subside [səbˈsaɪd] *vi* **-1.** [anger] apaciguarse; [pain] calmarse; [grief] pasarse; [storm, wind] amainar. **-2.** [noise] apagarse. **-3.** [river] **bajar, descender;** [building, ground] **hundirse.**

subsidence [səb'saɪdn̩s, 'sʌbsɪdn̩s] *n* CONSTR **hundimiento** *m*.

subsidiary [səb'sɪdjərɪ] ◇ *adj* **secundario(ria).** ◇ *n*: ~ **(company) filial** *f*.

subsidize, -ise ['sʌbsɪdaɪz] *vt* **subvencionar.**

subsidy ['sʌbsɪdɪ] *n* **subvención** *f*.

substance ['sʌbstəns] *n* **-1.** [gen] **sustancia** *f*. **-2.** [essence] **esencia** *f*.

substantial [səb'stænʃl] *adj* **-1.** [large, considerable] **sustancial, considerable;** [meal] **abundante. -2.** [solid] **sólido(da).**

substantially [səb'stænʃəlɪ] *adv* **-1.** [quite a lot] **sustancialmente, considerablemente. -2.** [fundamentally] **esencialmente;** [for the most part] **en gran parte.**

substantiate [səb'stænʃɪeɪt] *vt fml* **justificar.**

substitute ['sʌbstɪtjuːt] ◇ *n* **-1.** [replacement]: ~ **(for) sustituto** *m*, **-ta** *f* **(de). -2.** SPORT **suplente** *m y f*, **reserva** *m y f*. ◇ *vt*: **to** ~ **sthg/sb for sustituir algo/a alguien por.**

subtitle ['sʌb,taɪtl] *n* **subtítulo** *m*.

subtle ['sʌtl] *adj* **-1.** [gen] **sutil;** [taste, smell] **delicado(da). -2.** [plan, behaviour] **ingenioso(sa).**

subtlety ['sʌtltɪ] *n* **-1.** [gen] **sutileza** *f*; [of taste, smell] **delicadeza** *f*. **-2.** [of plan, behaviour] **ingenio** *m*.

subtract [səb'trækt] *vt*: **to** ~ **sthg (from)** **restar algo (de).**

subtraction [səb'trækʃn] *n* **resta** *f*.

suburb ['sʌbɜːb] *n* **barrio** *m* **residencial.** ◆ **suburbs** *npl*: **the** ~**s las afueras.**

suburban [sə'bɜːbn] *adj* **-1.** [of suburbs] **de los barrios residenciales. -2.** *pej* [boring] **convencional, burgués(esa).**

suburbia [sə'bɜːbɪə] *n* (U) **barrios** *mpl* **residenciales.**

subversive [səb'vɜːsɪv] ◇ *adj* **subversivo(va).** ◇ *n* **subversivo** *m*, **-va** *f*.

subway ['sʌbweɪ] *n* **-1.** *Br* [underground walkway] **paso** *m* **subterráneo. -2.** *Am* [underground railway] **metro** *m*.

succeed [sək'siːd] ◇ *vt* **suceder a.** ◇ *vi* **-1.** [gen] **tener éxito. -2.** [achieve desired result]: **to** ~ **in sthg/in doing sthg conseguir algo/hacer algo. -3.** [plan, tactic] **salir bien. -4.** [go far in life] **triunfar.**

succeeding [sək'siːdɪŋ] *adj fml* **sucesivo(va).**

success [sək'ses] *n* **-1.** [gen] **éxito** *m*; **to be a** ~ **tener éxito. -2.** [in career, life] **triunfo** *m*.

successful [sək'sesful] *adj* [gen] **de éxito;** [attempt] **logrado(da);** [politician] **popular.**

succession [sək'seʃn] *n* **sucesión** *f*.

successive [sək'sesɪv] *adj* **sucesivo(va).**

succinct [sək'sɪŋkt] *adj* **sucinto(ta).**

succumb [sə'kʌm] *vi*: **to** ~ **(to) sucumbir (a).**

such [sʌtʃ] ◇ *adj* **-1.** [like that] **semejante, tal;** ~ **stupidity tal** OR **semejante estupidez. -2.** [like this]: **have you got** ~ **a thing as a tin opener? ¿tendrías acaso un abrelatas?;** ~ **words as "duty" and "honour" palabras (tales) como "deber" y "honor". -3.** [whatever]: **I've spent** ~ **money as I had he gastado el poco dinero que tenía. -4.** [so great, so serious]: **there are** ~ **differences that ... las diferencias son tales que ...;** ~ **... that tal ... que.** ◇ *adv* **tan;** ~ **a lot of books tantos libros;** ~ **nice people una gente tan amable;** ~ **a good car un coche tan bueno;** ~ **a long time tanto tiempo.** ◇ *pron*: **and** ~ **(like) y otros similares** OR **por el estilo.** ◆ **as such** *pron* **propiamente dicho(cha).** ◆ **such and such** *adj*: **at** ~ **and** ~ **a time a tal hora.**

suck [sʌk] *vt* **-1.** [by mouth] **chupar. -2.** [subj: machine] **aspirar.**

sucker ['sʌkər] *n* **-1.** [of animal] **ventosa** *f*. **-2.** *inf* [gullible person] **primo** *m*, **-ma** *f*, **ingenuo** *m*, **-nua** *f*.

suction ['sʌkʃn] *n* [gen] **succión** *f*; [by machine] **aspiración** *f*.

Sudan [suː'dɑːn] *n* **(el) Sudán.**

sudden ['sʌdn] *adj* [quick] **repentino(na);** [unforeseen] **inesperado(da); all of a** ~ **de repente.**

suddenly ['sʌdnlɪ] *adv* **de repente.**

suds [sʌdz] *npl* **espuma** *f* **del jabón.**

sue [suː] *vt*: **to** ~ **sb (for) demandar a alguien (por).**

suede [sweɪd] *n* [for jacket, shoes] **ante** *m*; [for gloves] **cabritilla** *f*.

suet ['suɪt] *n* **sebo** *m*.

suffer ['sʌfər] ◇ *vt* **sufrir.** ◇ *vi* **-1.** [gen] **sufrir. -2.** [experience negative effects] **salir perjudicado(da). -3.** MED: **to** ~ **from** [illness] **sufrir** OR **padecer de.**

sufferer ['sʌfrər] *n* **enfermo** *m*, **-ma** *f*.

suffering ['sʌfrɪŋ] *n* [gen] **sufrimiento** *m*; [pain] **dolor** *m*.

suffice [sə'faɪs] *vi fml* **ser suficiente, bastar.**

sufficient [sə'fɪʃnt] *adj fml* **suficiente, bastante.**

sufficiently [sə'fɪʃntlɪ] *adv fml* **suficientemente, bastante.**

suffocate ['sʌfəkeɪt] ◇ *vt* asfixiar, ahogar. ◇ *vi* asfixiarse, ahogarse.

suffrage ['sʌfrɪdʒ] *n* sufragio *m*.

suffuse [sə'fjuːz] *vt*: ~**d with** bañado de.

sugar ['ʃʊgəʳ] ◇ *n* azúcar *m o f*. ◇ *vt* echar azúcar a.

sugar beet *n* remolacha *f* (azucarera).

sugarcane ['ʃʊgəkeɪn] *n* (U) caña *f* de azúcar.

sugary ['ʃʊgərɪ] *adj* [high in sugar] azucarado(da), dulce.

suggest [sə'dʒest] *vt* -1. [propose] sugerir; **to ~ that sb do sthg** sugerir que alguien haga algo. -2. [imply] insinuar.

suggestion [sə'dʒestʃn] *n* -1. [proposal] sugerencia *f*. -2. [implication] insinuación *f*.

suggestive [sə'dʒestɪv] *adj* [implying sexual connotation] provocativo(va), insinuante.

suicide ['suːɪsaɪd] *n lit & fig* suicidio *m*; **to commit ~** suicidarse.

suit [suːt] ◇ *n* -1. [clothes - for men] traje *m*; [- for women] traje de chaqueta. -2. [in cards] palo *m*. -3. JUR pleito *m*. ◇ *vt* -1. [look attractive on] favorecer, sentar bien a. -2. [be convenient or agreeable to] convenir. -3. [be appropriate to] ser adecuado(da) para; **that job ~s you perfectly** ese trabajo te va de perlas.

suitable ['suːtəbl] *adj* adecuado(da); **the most ~ person** la persona más indicada.

suitably ['suːtəblɪ] *adv* adecuadamente.

suitcase ['suːtkeɪs] *n* maleta *f*, petaca *f Amer*.

suite [swiːt] *n* -1. [of rooms] suite *f*. -2. [of furniture] juego *m*; **dining-room ~** comedor *m*.

suited ['suːtɪd] *adj*: ~ **to/for** adecuado(da) para; **the couple are ideally ~** forman una pareja perfecta.

suitor ['suːtəʳ] *n dated* pretendiente *m*.

sulfur *Am* = **sulphur**.

sulk [sʌlk] *vi* estar de mal humor.

sulky ['sʌlkɪ] *adj* malhumorado(da).

sullen ['sʌlən] *adj* hosco(ca), antipático(ca).

sulphur *Br*, **sulfur** *Am* ['sʌlfəʳ] *n* azufre *m*.

sultana [səl'tɑːnə] *n Br* [dried grape] pasa *f* de Esmirna.

sultry ['sʌltrɪ] *adj* [hot] bochornoso(sa), sofocante.

sum [sʌm] *n* suma *f*. ◆ **sum up** *vt sep & vi* [summarize] resumir.

summarize, -ise ['sʌməraɪz] *vt & vi* resumir.

summary ['sʌmərɪ] *n* resumen *m*.

summer ['sʌməʳ] ◇ *n* verano *m*. ◇ *comp* de verano.

summerhouse ['sʌməhaʊs, *pl* -haʊzɪz] *n* cenador *m*.

summer school *n* escuela *f* de verano.

summertime ['sʌmətaɪm] *n*: **(the) ~** (el) verano.

summit ['sʌmɪt] *n* -1. [mountain-top] cima *f*, cumbre *f*. -2. [meeting] cumbre *f*.

summon ['sʌmən] *vt* [person] llamar; [meeting] convocar. ◆ **summon up** *vt sep* [courage] armarse de.

summons ['sʌmənz] (*pl* **summonses**) JUR ◇ *n* citación *f*. ◇ *vt* citar.

sump [sʌmp] *n* cárter *m*.

sumptuous ['sʌmptʃʊəs] *adj* suntuoso(sa).

sun [sʌn] *n* sol *m*; **in the ~** al sol.

sunbathe ['sʌnbeɪð] *vi* tomar el sol.

sunbed ['sʌnbed] *n* camilla *f* de rayos ultravioletas.

sunburn ['sʌnbɜːn] *n* (U) quemadura *f* de sol.

sunburned ['sʌnbɜːnd], **sunburnt** ['sʌnbɜːnt] *adj* quemado(da) por el sol.

Sunday ['sʌndɪ] *n* domingo *m*; ~ **lunch** *comida del domingo que generalmente consiste en rosbif, patatas asadas etc*; *see also* **Saturday**.

Sunday school *n* catequesis *f inv*.

sundial ['sʌndaɪəl] *n* reloj *m* de sol.

sundown ['sʌndaʊn] *n* anochecer *m*.

sundries ['sʌndrɪz] *npl fml* [gen] artículos *mpl* diversos; FIN gastos *mpl* diversos.

sundry ['sʌndrɪ] *adj fml* diversos(sas); **all and ~** todos sin excepción.

sunflower ['sʌn,flaʊəʳ] *n* girasol *m*.

sung [sʌŋ] *pp* → **sing**.

sunglasses ['sʌn,glɑːsɪz] *npl* gafas *fpl* de sol.

sunk [sʌŋk] *pp* → **sink**.

sunlight ['sʌnlaɪt] *n* luz *f* del sol.

sunlit ['sʌnlɪt] *adj* iluminado(da) por el sol.

sunny ['sʌnɪ] *adj* -1. [day] de sol; [room] soleado(da). -2. [cheerful] alegre.

sunrise ['sʌnraɪz] *n* -1. (U) [time of day] amanecer *m*. -2. [event] salida *f* del sol.

sunroof ['sʌnruːf] *n* [on car] techo *m* corredizo; [on building] azotea *f*.

sunset ['sʌnset] *n* -1. (U) [time of day]

anochecer *m*. **-2.** [event] puesta *f* del sol.

sunshade ['sʌnʃeɪd] *n* sombrilla *f*.

sunshine ['sʌnʃaɪn] *n* (luz *f* del) sol *m*.

sunstroke ['sʌnstrəʊk] *n* (U) insolación *f*.

suntan ['sʌntæn] ◇ *n* bronceado *m*. ◇ *comp* bronceador(ra).

suntrap ['sʌntræp] *n* lugar *m* muy soleado.

super ['suːpər] *adj* **-1.** *inf* [wonderful] estupendo(da), fenomenal. **-2.** [better than normal - size etc] superior.

superannuation ['suːpə,rænjʊ'eɪʃn] *n* (U) jubilación *f*, pensión *f*.

superb [suː'pɜːb] *adj* excelente, magnífico(ca).

supercilious [,suːpə'sɪliəs] *adj* altanero(ra).

superficial [,suːpə'fɪʃl] *adj* superficial.

superfluous [suː'pɜːflʊəs] *adj* superfluo(flua).

superhuman [,suːpə'hjuːmən] *adj* sobrehumano(na).

superimpose [,suːpərɪm'pəʊz] *vt*: **to ~ sthg on** superponer OR sobreponer algo a.

superintendent [,suːpərɪn'tendənt] *n* **-1.** *Br* [of police] ≃ subjefe *m*, -fa *f* (de policía). **-2.** *fml* [of department] supervisor *m*, -ra *f*.

superior [suː'pɪərɪər] ◇ *adj* **-1.** [gen]: **~ (to)** superior (a). **-2.** *pej* [arrogant] altanero(ra), arrogante. ◇ *n* superior *m* y *f*.

superlative [suː'pɜːlətɪv] ◇ *adj* [of the highest quality] supremo(ma). ◇ *n* GRAMM superlativo *m*.

supermarket ['suːpə,mɑːkɪt] *n* supermercado *m*.

supernatural [,suːpə'nætʃrəl] *adj* sobrenatural.

superpower ['suːpə,paʊər] *n* superpotencia *f*.

supersede [,suːpə'siːd] *vt* suplantar.

supersonic [,suːpə'sɒnɪk] *adj* supersónico(ca).

superstitious [,suːpə'stɪʃəs] *adj* supersticioso(sa).

superstore ['suːpəstɔːr] *n* hipermercado *m*.

supertanker ['suːpə,tæŋkər] *n* superpetrolero *m*.

supervise ['suːpəvaɪz] *vt* [person] vigilar; [activity] supervisar.

supervisor ['suːpəvaɪzər] *n* [gen] supervisor *m*, -ra *f*; [of thesis] director *m*, -ra *f*.

supper ['sʌpər] *n* [evening meal] cena *f*.

supple ['sʌpl] *adj* flexible.

supplement [*n* 'sʌplɪmənt, *vb* 'sʌplɪment] ◇ *n* suplemento *m*. ◇ *vt* complementar.

supplementary [,sʌplɪ'mentərɪ] *adj* suplementario(ria).

supplementary benefit *n Br* subsidio *m* social.

supplier [sə'plaɪər] *n* proveedor *m*, -ra *f*.

supply [sə'plaɪ] ◇ *n* **-1.** [gen] suministro *m*; [of jokes etc] surtido *m*. **-2.** (U) ECON oferta *f*. ◇ *vt*: **to ~ sthg (to)** suministrar OR proveer algo (a); **to ~ sb (with)** proveer a alguien (de).
◆ **supplies** *npl* MIL pertrechos *mpl*; [food] provisiones *fpl*; [for office etc] material *m*.

support [sə'pɔːt] ◇ *n* **-1.** (U) [physical, moral, emotional] apoyo *m*. **-2.** (U) [financial] ayuda *f*. **-3.** (U) [intellectual] respaldo *m*. **-4.** TECH soporte *m*. ◇ *vt* **-1.** [physically] sostener. **-2.** [emotionally, morally, intellectually] apoyar. **-3.** [financially - oneself, one's family] mantener; [- company, organization] financiar. **-4.** SPORT seguir.

supporter [sə'pɔːtər] *n* **-1.** [gen] partidario *m*, -ria *f*. **-2.** SPORT hincha *m* y *f*.

suppose [sə'pəʊz] ◇ *vt* suponer. ◇ *vi* suponer; **I ~ (so)** supongo (que sí); **I ~ not** supongo que no.

supposed [sə'pəʊzd] *adj* **-1.** [doubtful] supuesto(ta). **-2.** [intended]: **he was ~ to be here at eight** debería haber estado aquí a las ocho. **-3.** [reputed]: **it's ~ to be very good** se supone OR se dice que es muy bueno.

supposedly [sə'pəʊzɪdlɪ] *adv* según cabe suponer.

supposing [sə'pəʊzɪŋ] *conj*: **~ your father found out?** ¿y si se entera tu padre?

suppress [sə'pres] *vt* **-1.** [uprising] reprimir. **-2.** [emotions] contener.

supreme [sʊ'priːm] *adj* supremo(ma).

Supreme Court *n*: **the ~** [in US] el Tribunal Supremo (de los Estados Unidos).

surcharge ['sɜːtʃɑːdʒ] *n*: **~ (on)** recargo *m* (en).

sure [ʃʊər] ◇ *adj* **-1.** [gen] seguro(ra). **-2.** [certain - of outcome]: **to be ~ of** poder estar seguro(ra) de; **make ~ (that) you do it** asegúrate de que lo haces. **-3.** [confident]: **to be ~ of o.s.** estar seguro(ra) de uno mismo. ◇ *adv* **-1.** *inf* [yes] por supuesto, pues claro. **-2.** *Am* [really] realmente. ◆ **for sure** *adv* a ciencia cierta. ◆ **sure enough** *adv* efectivamente.

surely ['ʃʊəlɪ] *adv* sin duda; ~ **you remember him?** ¡no me digas que no te acuerdas de él!

surety ['ʃʊərətɪ] *n* (U) fianza *f*.

surf [sɜːf] *n* espuma *f* (*de las olas*).

surface ['sɜːfɪs] ◇ *n* **-1.** [gen] superficie *f*. **-2.** *fig* [immediately visible part]: **on the ~** a primera vista. ◇ *vi* [gen] salir a la superficie.

surface mail *n* correo *m* por vía terrestre/marítima.

surfboard ['sɜːfbɔːd] *n* plancha *f* OR tabla *f* de surf.

surfeit ['sɜːfɪt] *n fml* exceso *m*.

surfing ['sɜːfɪŋ] *n* surf *m*.

surge [sɜːdʒ] ◇ *n* **-1.** [of waves, people] oleada *f*; [of electricity] sobrecarga *f* momentánea. **-2.** [of emotion] arrebato *m*. **-3.** [of interest, support, sales] aumento *m* súbito. ◇ *vi* [people, vehicles] avanzar en masa; [sea] encresparse.

surgeon ['sɜːdʒən] *n* cirujano *m*, -na *f*.

surgery ['sɜːdʒərɪ] *n* **-1.** (U) MED [performing operations] cirugía *f*. **-2.** *Br* MED [place] consultorio *m*; [consulting period] consulta *f*.

surgical ['sɜːdʒɪkl] *adj* [gen] quirúrgico(ca).

surgical spirit *n Br* alcohol *m* de 90°.

surly ['sɜːlɪ] *adj* hosco(ca), malhumorado(da).

surmount [sɜːˈmaʊnt] *vt* [overcome] superar, vencer.

surname ['sɜːneɪm] *n* apellido *m*.

surpass [səˈpɑːs] *vt fml* [exceed] superar, sobrepasar.

surplus ['sɜːpləs] ◇ *adj* excedente, sobrante. ◇ *n* [gen] excedente *m*, sobrante *m*; [in budget] superávit *m*.

surprise [səˈpraɪz] ◇ *n* sorpresa *f*. ◇ *vt* sorprender.

surprised [səˈpraɪzd] *adj* [person, expression] asombrado(da).

surprising [səˈpraɪzɪŋ] *adj* sorprendente.

surrender [səˈrendər] ◇ *n* rendición *f*. ◇ *vi lit & fig*: **to ~ (to)** rendirse OR entregarse (a).

surreptitious [ˌsʌrəpˈtɪʃəs] *adj* subrepticio(cia).

surrogate ['sʌrəgeɪt] ◇ *adj* sustitutorio(ria). ◇ *n* sustituto *m*, -ta *f*.

surrogate mother *n* madre *f* de alquiler.

surround [səˈraʊnd] *vt lit & fig* rodear.

surrounding [səˈraʊndɪŋ] *adj* **-1.** [area, countryside] circundante. **-2.** [controversy, debate] relacionado(da).

surroundings [səˈraʊndɪŋz] *npl* [physical] alrededores *mpl*; [social] entorno *m*.

surveillance [sɜːˈveɪləns] *n* vigilancia *f*.

survey [*n* 'sɜːveɪ, *vb* səˈveɪ] ◇ *n* **-1.** [of public opinion, population] encuesta *f*. **-2.** [of land] medición *f*; [of building] inspección *f*. ◇ *vt* **-1.** [contemplate] contemplar. **-2.** [investigate statistically] hacer un estudio de. **-3.** [examine - land] medir; [- building] inspeccionar.

surveyor [səˈveɪər] *n* [of property] perito *m* tasador de la propiedad; [of land] agrimensor *m*, -ra *f*.

survival [səˈvaɪvl] *n* [gen] supervivencia *f*.

survive [səˈvaɪv] ◇ *vt* sobrevivir a. ◇ *vi* [person] sobrevivir; [custom, project] perdurar.

survivor [səˈvaɪvər] *n* [person who escapes death] superviviente *m y f*.

susceptible [səˈseptəbl] *adj* **-1.** [to pressure, flattery]: ~ **(to)** sensible (a). **-2.** MED: ~ **(to)** propenso(sa) (a).

suspect [*adj & n* 'sʌspekt, *vb* səˈspekt] ◇ *adj* sospechoso(sa). ◇ *n* sospechoso *m*, -sa *f*. ◇ *vt* **-1.** [distrust] sospechar. **-2.** [think likely] imaginar. **-3.** [consider guilty]: **to ~ sb (of)** considerar a alguien sospechoso(sa) (de).

suspend [səˈspend] *vt* [gen] suspender; [payments, work] interrumpir; [schoolchild] expulsar temporalmente.

suspended sentence [səˈspendɪd-] *n* condena *f* condicional.

suspender belt [səˈspendər-] *n Br* liguero *m*.

suspenders [səˈspendəz] *npl* **-1.** *Br* [for stockings] ligas *fpl*. **-2.** *Am* [for trousers] tirantes *mpl*.

suspense [səˈspens] *n* [gen] incertidumbre *f*; CINEMA suspense *m*.

suspension [səˈspenʃn] *n* **-1.** [gen & AUT] suspensión *f*. **-2.** [from job, school] expulsión *f* temporal.

suspension bridge *n* puente *m* colgante.

suspicion [səˈspɪʃn] *n* **-1.** [gen] sospecha *f*; [distrust] recelo *m*. **-2.** [small amount] pizca *f*.

suspicious [səˈspɪʃəs] *adj* **-1.** [having suspicions] receloso(sa). **-2.** [causing suspicion] sospechoso(sa).

sustain [səˈsteɪn] *vt* **-1.** [gen] sostener. **-2.** *fml* [injury, damage] sufrir.

sustenance ['sʌstɪnəns] n (U) fml sustento m.

SW (abbr of **short wave**) OC.

swab [swɒb] n (trozo m de) algodón m.

swagger ['swægəʳ] vi pavonearse.

Swahili [swɑː'hiːlɪ] n [language] suahili m.

swallow ['swɒləʊ] ◇ n [bird] golondrina f. ◇ vt [food, drink] tragar.

swam [swæm] pt → **swim**.

swamp [swɒmp] ◇ n pantano m, ciénaga f. ◇ vt -1. [flood - boat] hundir; [- land] inundar. -2. [overwhelm]: to ~ sthg (with) [office] inundar algo (de); to ~ sb (with) agobiar a alguien (con).

swan [swɒn] n cisne m.

swap [swɒp] vt -1. [of one thing]: to ~ sthg (for/with) cambiar algo (por/con). -2. [of two things]: to ~ sthg (over OR round) [hats, chairs] cambiarse algo. -3. fig [stories, experiences] intercambiar.

swarm [swɔːm] ◇ n [of bees] enjambre m; fig [of people] multitud f. ◇ vi -1. fig [people] ir en tropel. -2. fig [place]: to be ~ing (with) estar abarrotado(da) (de).

swarthy ['swɔːðɪ] adj moreno(na).

swastika ['swɒstɪkə] n esvástica f, cruz f gamada.

swat [swɒt] vt aplastar.

sway [sweɪ] ◇ vt [influence] convencer. ◇ vi balancearse.

swear [sweəʳ] (pt swore, pp sworn) ◇ vt: to ~ (to do sthg) jurar (hacer algo). ◇ vi -1. [state emphatically] jurar. -2. [use swearwords] decir tacos, jurar.

swearword ['sweəwɜːd] n palabrota f.

sweat [swet] ◇ n [perspiration] sudor m. ◇ vi [perspire] sudar.

sweater ['swetəʳ] n suéter m, jersey m.

sweatshirt ['swetʃɜːt] n sudadera f.

sweaty ['swetɪ] adj [skin] sudoroso(sa); [clothes] sudado(da).

swede [swiːd] n Br nabo m sueco.

Swede [swiːd] n sueco m, -ca f.

Sweden ['swiːdn] n Suecia f.

Swedish ['swiːdɪʃ] ◇ adj sueco(ca). ◇ n [language] sueco m. ◇ npl: **the** ~ los suecos.

sweep [swiːp] (pt & pp swept) ◇ n -1. [movement - of broom] barrido m; [- of arm, hand] movimiento m OR gesto m amplio. -2. [chimney sweep] deshollinador m, -ra f. ◇ vt -1. [with brush] barrer. -2. [with light-beam] rastrear; [with eyes] recorrer. ◇ vi -1. [wind, rain]: to ~ over OR across sthg azotar algo. -2. [person]: to ~ past pasar como un rayo.

◆ **sweep away** vt sep [destroy] destruir completamente. ◆ **sweep up** vt sep & vi barrer.

sweeping ['swiːpɪŋ] adj -1. [effect, change] radical. -2. [statement] demasiado general. -3. [curve] amplio(plia).

sweet [swiːt] ◇ adj -1. [gen] dulce; [sugary] azucarado(da). -2. [feelings] placentero(ra). -3. [smell - of flowers, air] fragante, perfumado(da). -4. [sound] melodioso(sa). -5. [character, person] amable. ◇ n Br -1. [candy] caramelo m, golosina f. -2. [dessert] postre m.

sweet corn n maíz m.

sweeten ['swiːtn] vt endulzar.

sweetheart ['swiːthɑːt] n -1. [term of endearment] cariño m. -2. [boyfriend or girlfriend] amor m, novio m, -via f.

sweetness ['swiːtnɪs] n -1. [gen] dulzura f. -2. [of taste] dulzor m.

sweet pea n guisante m de olor.

swell [swel] (pp swollen OR -ed) ◇ vi -1. [become larger] hincharse. -2. [population, sound] aumentar. ◇ vt [numbers etc] aumentar. ◇ n [of sea] oleaje m. ◇ adj Am inf estupendo(da).

swelling ['swelɪŋ] n hinchazón f.

sweltering ['sweltərɪŋ] adj -1. [weather] abrasador(ra), sofocante. -2. [person] achicharrado(da).

swept [swept] pt & pp → **sweep**.

swerve [swɜːv] vi virar bruscamente.

swift [swɪft] ◇ adj -1. [fast] rápido(da). -2. [prompt] pronto(ta). ◇ n [bird] vencejo m.

swig [swɪg] inf n trago m.

swill [swɪl] ◇ n [pig food] bazofia f. ◇ vt Br [wash] enjuagar.

swim [swɪm] (pt swam, pp swum) ◇ n baño m; **to go for a** ~ ir a nadar OR a darse un baño. ◇ vi -1. [in water] nadar. -2. [head, room] dar vueltas.

swimmer ['swɪməʳ] n nadador m, -ra f.

swimming ['swɪmɪŋ] n natación f.

swimming cap n gorro m de baño.

swimming costume n Br bañador m, traje m de baño.

swimming pool n piscina f, alberca f Amer.

swimming trunks npl bañador m.

swimsuit ['swɪmsuːt] n bañador m, traje m de baño.

swindle ['swɪndl] ◇ n estafa f, timo m. ◇ vt estafar, timar; to ~ sb out of sthg estafar a alguien algo.

swine [swaɪn] n inf pej [person] cerdo m, -da f, canalla m y f.

swing [swɪŋ] ⟨ *pt & pp* **swung**⟩ ◇ *n* **-1.** [child's toy] columpio *m*. **-2.** [change] viraje *m*. **-3.** [sway] meneo *m*, balanceo *m*. **-4.** *phr*: **to be in full ~** estar en plena marcha. ◇ *vt* **-1.** [move back and forth] balancear. **-2.** [move in a curve - car etc] hacer virar bruscamente. ◇ *vi* **-1.** [move back and forth] balancearse, oscilar. **-2.** [move in a curve] girar. **-3.** [turn]: **to ~ (round)** volverse, girarse. **-4.** [change] virar, cambiar.

swing bridge *n* puente *m* giratorio.

swing door *n* puerta *f* oscilante.

swingeing ['swɪndʒɪŋ] *adj* severo(ra).

swipe [swaɪp] ◇ *vt inf* [steal] birlar. ◇ *vi*: **to ~ at sthg** intentar golpear algo.

swirl [swɜːl] *vi* arremolinarse.

swish [swɪʃ] *vt* [tail] agitar, menear.

Swiss [swɪs] ◇ *adj* suizo(za). ◇ *n* [person] suizo *m*, -za *f*. ◇ *npl*: **the ~** los suizos.

switch [swɪtʃ] ◇ *n* **-1.** [control device] interruptor *m*. **-2.** [change] cambio *m* completo, viraje *m*. ◇ *vt* **-1.** [change] cambiar de. **-2.** [swap] intercambiar. ◆ **switch off** *vt sep* [light, radio etc] apagar; [engine] parar. ◆ **switch on** *vt sep* [light, radio etc] encender; [engine] poner en marcha.

switchboard ['swɪtʃbɔːd] *n* centralita *f*, conmutador *m Amer*.

Switzerland ['swɪtsələnd] *n* Suiza.

swivel ['swɪvl] ◇ *vt* hacer girar. ◇ *vi* girar.

swivel chair *n* silla *f* giratoria.

swollen ['swəʊln] ◇ *pp* → **swell**. ◇ *adj* [ankle, leg etc] hinchado(da); [river] crecido(da).

swoop [swuːp] ◇ *n* [raid] redada *f*. ◇ *vi* **-1.** [move downwards] caer en picado. **-2.** [move quickly] atacar por sorpresa.

swop [swɒp] = **swap**.

sword [sɔːd] *n* espada *f*.

swordfish ['sɔːdfɪʃ] (*pl inv* OR **-es**) *n* pez *m* espada.

swore [swɔːr] *pt* → **swear**.

sworn [swɔːn] ◇ *pp* → **swear**. ◇ *adj* JUR jurado(da).

swot [swɒt] *Br inf* ◇ *n pej* empollón *m*, -ona *f*. ◇ *vi*: **to ~ (for)** empollar (para).

swum [swʌm] *pp* → **swim**.

swung [swʌŋ] *pt & pp* → **swing**.

sycamore ['sɪkəmɔːr] *n* sicomoro *m*.

syllable ['sɪləbl] *n* sílaba *f*.

syllabus ['sɪləbəs] (*pl* **-buses** OR **-bi** [-baɪ]) *n* programa *m* (de estudios).

symbol ['sɪmbl] *n* símbolo *m*.

symbolize, -ise ['sɪmbəlaɪz] *vt* simbolizar.

symmetry ['sɪmətrɪ] *n* simetría *f*.

sympathetic [ˌsɪmpə'θetɪk] *adj* **-1.** [understanding] comprensivo(va). **-2.** [willing to support] favorable; **~ to** bien dispuesto(ta) hacia.

sympathize, -ise ['sɪmpəθaɪz] *vi* **-1.** [feel sorry]: **to ~ (with)** compadecerse (de). **-2.** [understand]: **to ~ (with sthg)** comprender (algo). **-3.** [support]: **to ~ with sthg** apoyar algo.

sympathizer, -iser ['sɪmpəθaɪzər] *n* simpatizante *m y f*.

sympathy ['sɪmpəθɪ] *n* **-1.** [understanding]: **~ (for)** comprensión *f* (hacia); [compassion] compasión *f* (por). **-2.** [agreement] solidaridad *f*. ◆ **sympathies** *npl* [to bereaved person] pésame *m*.

symphony ['sɪmfənɪ] *n* sinfonía *f*.

symposium [sɪm'pəʊzjəm] (*pl* **-siums** OR **-sia** [-zjə]) *n fml* simposio *m*.

symptom ['sɪmptəm] *n lit & fig* síntoma *m*.

synagogue ['sɪnəgɒg] *n* sinagoga *f*.

syndicate ['sɪndɪkət] *n* sindicato *m*.

syndrome ['sɪndrəʊm] *n* síndrome *m*.

synonym ['sɪnənɪm] *n*: **~ (for** OR **of)** sinónimo *m* (de).

synopsis [sɪ'nɒpsɪs] (*pl* **-ses** [-siːz]) *n* sinopsis *f inv*.

syntax ['sɪntæks] *n* sintaxis *f inv*.

synthesis ['sɪnθəsɪs] (*pl* **-ses** [-siːz]) *n* síntesis *f inv*.

synthetic [sɪn'θetɪk] *adj* **-1.** [man-made] sintético(ca). **-2.** *pej* [insincere] artificial.

syphilis ['sɪfɪlɪs] *n* sífilis *f inv*.

syphon ['saɪfn] = **siphon**.

Syria ['sɪrɪə] *n* Siria.

syringe [sɪ'rɪndʒ] *n* jeringa *f*, jeringuilla *f*.

syrup ['sɪrəp] *n* (U) **-1.** CULIN almíbar *m*. **-2.** MED jarabe *m*.

system ['sɪstəm] *n* [gen] sistema *m*; [of central heating etc] instalación *f*.

systematic [ˌsɪstə'mætɪk] *adj* sistemático(ca).

system disk *n* COMPUT disco *m* del sistema.

systems analyst ['sɪstəmz-] *n* COMPUT analista *m y f* de sistemas.

t (*pl* **t's** OR **ts**), **T** (*pl* **T's** OR **Ts**) [tiː] *n* [letter] t *f*, T *f*.

ta [tɑː] *excl Br inf* ¡gracias!

tab [tæb] *n* **-1.** [of cloth] etiqueta *f*. **-2.** [of metal, card etc] lengüeta *f*. **-3.** *Am* [bill] cuenta *f*. **-4.** *phr:* **to keep ~s on sb** vigilar de cerca a alguien.

tabby ['tæbɪ] *n:* **~ (cat)** gato *m* atigrado.

table ['teɪbl] *n* **-1.** [piece of furniture] mesa *f*; [small] mesilla *f*. **-2.** [diagram] tabla *f*. ◇ *vt Br* [propose] presentar.

tablecloth ['teɪblklɒθ] *n* mantel *m*.

table lamp *n* lámpara *f* de mesa.

tablemat ['teɪblmæt] *n* salvamanteles *m inv*.

tablespoon ['teɪblspuːn] *n* **-1.** [spoon] cuchara *f* grande (*para servir*). **-2.** [spoonful] cucharada *f* (grande).

tablet ['tæblɪt] *n* **-1.** [pill, piece of soap] pastilla *f*. **-2.** [piece of stone] lápida *f*.

table tennis *n* tenis *m* de mesa.

table wine *n* vino *m* de mesa.

tabloid ['tæblɔɪd] *n:* **the ~s** los periódicos sensacionalistas; **~ (newspaper)** tabloide *m*.

tabulate ['tæbjʊleɪt] *vt* tabular.

tacit ['tæsɪt] *adj fml* tácito(ta).

taciturn ['tæsɪtɜːn] *adj fml* taciturno(na).

tack [tæk] ◇ *n* **-1.** [nail] tachuela *f*. **-2.** *fig* [course of action] táctica *f*. ◇ *vt* **-1.** [fasten with nail] fijar con tachuelas. **-2.** [in sewing] hilvanar. ◇ *vi* NAUT virar.

tackle ['tækl] ◇ *n* **-1.** FTBL entrada *f*. **-2.** RUGBY placaje *m*. **-3.** (*U*) [equipment] equipo *m*, aparejos *mpl*. **-4.** [for lifting] aparejo *m*. ◇ *vt* **-1.** [deal with - job] emprender; [- problem] abordar. **-2.** FTBL entrar. **-3.** RUGBY placar. **-4.** [attack] atacar, arremeter.

tacky ['tækɪ] *adj* **-1.** *inf* [cheap and nasty] cutre; [ostentatious and vulgar] hortera. **-2.** [sticky] pegajoso(sa).

tact [tækt] *n* (*U*) tacto *m*, discreción *f*.

tactful ['tæktfʊl] *adj* discreto(ta).

tactic ['tæktɪk] *n* táctica *f*. ◆ **tactics** *n* (*U*) MIL táctica *f*.

tactical ['tæktɪkl] *adj* estratégico(ca); [weapons] táctico(ca).

tactless ['tæktlɪs] *adj* indiscreto(ta).

tadpole ['tædpəʊl] *n* renacuajo *m*.

tag [tæg] *n* [of cloth, paper] etiqueta *f*. ◆ **tag along** *vi inf* pegarse, engancharse.

tail [teɪl] ◇ *n* [gen] cola *f*; [of coat, shirt] faldón *m*. ◇ *vt inf* [follow] seguir de cerca. ◆ **tails** *npl* **-1.** [formal dress] frac *m*. **-2.** [side of coin] cruz *f*. ◆ **tail off** *vi* [voice] ir debilitándose; [sound] ir disminuyendo.

tailback ['teɪlbæk] *n Br* cola *f*.

tailcoat [ˌteɪl'kəʊt] *n* frac *m*.

tail end *n* parte *f* final.

tailgate ['teɪlgeɪt] *n* [of hatchback car] portón *m*.

tailor ['teɪlə'] ◇ *n* sastre *m*. ◇ *vt* adaptar.

tailor-made *adj* (hecho(cha)) a la medida.

tailwind ['teɪlwɪnd] *n* viento *m* de cola.

tainted ['teɪntɪd] *adj* **-1.** [reputation] manchado(da). **-2.** *Am* [food] estropeado(da).

Taiwan [ˌtaɪ'wɑːn] *n* Taiwán.

take [teɪk] (*pt* **took**, *pp* **taken**) ◇ *vt* **-1.** [gen] tomar; **to ~ a photo** hacer OR tomar una foto; **to ~ a walk** dar un paseo; **to ~ a bath** bañarse; **to ~ a test** hacer un examen; **to ~ offence** ofenderse. **-2.** [bring, carry, accompany] llevar. **-3.** [steal] quitar, robar. **-4.** [buy] coger, quedarse con; [rent] alquilar. **-5.** [receive] recibir. **-6.** [take hold of] coger; **to ~ sb prisoner** capturar a alguien. **-7.** [accept - offer, cheque, criticism] aceptar; [- advice] seguir; [- responsibility, blame] asumir; **the machine only ~s 50p pieces** la máquina sólo admite monedas de 50 peniques. **-8.** [have room for - passengers, goods] tener cabida para. **-9.** [bear - pain etc] soportar, aguantar. **-10.** [require - time, courage] requerir; [- money] costar; **it will ~ a week/three hours** llevará una semana/tres horas. **-11.** [travel by - means of transport, route] tomar, coger. **-12.** [wear - shoes] calzar; [- clothes] usar. **-13.** [consider] considerar. **-14.** [assume]: **I ~ it (that)** ... supongo que .... ◇ *n* CINEMA toma *f*. ◆ **take after** *vt fus* parecerse a. ◆ **take apart** *vt sep* [dismantle] desmontar. ◆ **take away** *vt sep* **-1.** [remove] quitar. **-2.** [deduct] restar, sustraer. ◆ **take back** *vt sep* **-1.** [return] devolver. **-2.** [accept - faulty goods] aceptar la devolución de. **-3.** [admit as wrong] retirar. ◆ **take down** vt sep **-1.** [dismantle] desmontar. **-2.** [write down] tomar nota de. ◆ **take in** vt sep **-1.** [deceive] engañar. **-2.** [understand] comprender, asimilar. **-3.** [include] incluir, abarcar. **-4.** [provide accommodation for] acoger. ◆ **take off** ◇ vt sep **-1.** [clothes, glasses] quitarse. **-2.** [have as holiday] tomarse. **-3.** Br inf [imitate] imitar. ◇ vi **-1.** [plane] despegar. **-2.** [go away suddenly] irse, marcharse. ◆ **take on** ◇ vt sep **-1.** [accept - work, job] aceptar; [- responsibility] asumir. **-2.** [employ] emplear, coger. **-3.** [confront] desafiar. ◆ **take out** vt sep **-1.** [from container, pocket] sacar. **-2.** [go out with]: **to ~ sb out** invitar a salir a alguien. ◆ **take over** ◇ vt sep **-1.** [company, business] absorber, adquirir; [country, government] apoderarse de. **-2.** [job] asumir. ◇ vi **-1.** [take control] tomar el poder. **-2.** [in job] entrar en funciones. ◆ **take to** vt fus **-1.** [feel a liking for - person] coger cariño a; [- activity] aficionarse a. **-2.** [begin]: **to ~ to doing sthg** empezar a hacer algo. ◆ **take up** vt sep **-1.** [begin]: **to ~ up singing** dedicarse a cantar; [job] aceptar, tomar. **-2.** [use up - time, space] ocupar; [- effort] requerir. ◆ **take up on** vt sep [accept]: **to ~ sb up on an offer** aceptar una oferta de alguien.

takeaway Br ['teɪkə,weɪ], **takeout** Am ['teɪkaʊt] n [food] comida f para llevar.

taken ['teɪkn] pp → take.

takeoff ['teɪkɒf] n [of plane] despegue m.

takeout Am = takeaway.

takeover ['teɪk,əʊvər] n [of company] adquisición f.

takings npl [of shop] venta f; [of show] recaudación f.

talc [tælk], **talcum (powder)** ['tælkəm-] n talco m.

tale [teɪl] n **-1.** [fictional story] cuento m. **-2.** [anecdote] anécdota f.

talent ['tælənt] n: ~ **(for sthg)** talento m (para algo).

talented ['tæləntɪd] adj con talento.

talk [tɔːk] ◇ n **-1.** [conversation] conversación f. **-2.** (U) [gossip] habladurías fpl. **-3.** [lecture] charla f, conferencia f. ◇ vi **-1.** [gen] hablar; **to ~ to/of** hablar con/de; **to ~ on** OR **about** hablar acerca de OR sobre. **-2.** [gossip] chismorrear. ◇ vt hablar de. ◆ **talks** npl conversaciones fpl. ◆ **talk into** vt sep: **to ~ sb into doing sthg** convencer a alguien para que haga algo. ◆ **talk out of** vt

sep: **to ~ sb out of doing sthg** disuadir a alguien de que haga algo. ◆ **talk over** vt sep discutir, hablar de.

talkative ['tɔːkətɪv] adj hablador(ra).

talk show Am n programa m de entrevistas.

tall [tɔːl] adj alto(ta); **she's 2 metres ~** mide 2 metros.

tall story n cuento m (increíble).

tally ['tælɪ] ◇ n cuenta f; **to keep a ~** llevar la cuenta. ◇ vi concordar.

talon ['tælən] n garra f.

tambourine [,tæmbə'riːn] n pandereta f.

tame [teɪm] ◇ adj **-1.** [domesticated] doméstico(ca). **-2.** pej [unexciting] soso(sa). ◇ vt **-1.** [domesticate] domesticar. **-2.** [bring under control] dominar.

tamper ['tæmpər] ◆ **tamper with** vt fus [lock] intentar forzar; [records, file] falsear; [machine] manipular.

tampon ['tæmpɒn] n tampón m.

tan [tæn] ◇ adj de color marrón claro. ◇ n bronceado m. ◇ vi broncearse.

tang [tæŋ] n [smell] olor m fuerte; [taste] sabor m fuerte.

tangent ['tændʒənt] n GEOM tangente f; **to go off at a ~** salirse por la tangente.

tangerine [,tændʒə'riːn] n mandarina f.

tangible ['tændʒəbl] adj tangible.

tangle ['tæŋgl] n [mass] maraña f; fig [mess] enredo m, embrollo m.

tank [tæŋk] n **-1.** [container] depósito m, tanque m. **-2.** MIL tanque m, carro m de combate.

tanker ['tæŋkər] n **-1.** [ship - gen] barco m cisterna, tanque m; [- for oil] petrolero m. **-2.** [truck] camión m cisterna.

tanned [tænd] adj bronceado(da).

Tannoy® ['tænɔɪ] n (sistema m de) altavoces mpl.

tantalizing ['tæntəlaɪzɪŋ] adj tentador(ra).

tantamount ['tæntəmaʊnt] adj: ~ **to** equivalente a.

tantrum ['tæntrəm] (pl -s) n rabieta f.

Tanzania [,tænzə'nɪə] n Tanzania.

tap [tæp] ◇ n **-1.** [device] grifo m. **-2.** [light blow] golpecito m. ◇ vt **-1.** [hit] golpear ligeramente. **-2.** [strength, resources] utilizar. **-3.** [phone] intervenir.

tap dance n claqué m.

tape [teɪp] ◇ n **-1.** [cassette, magnetic tape, strip of cloth] cinta f. **-2.** [adhesive plastic] cinta f adhesiva. ◇ vt **-1.** [on tape recorder, video recorder] grabar. **-2.** [with adhesive tape] pegar con cinta adhesiva.

tape measure n cinta f métrica.

taper ['teɪpər] ◇ *n* [candle] vela *f.* ◇ *vi* afilarse.

tape recorder *n* magnetófono *m.*

tapestry ['tæpɪstrɪ] *n* **-1.** [piece of work] tapiz *m.* **-2.** [craft] tapicería *f.*

tar [tɑːʳ] *n* alquitrán *m.*

target ['tɑːgɪt] *n* **-1.** [of missile, goal, aim] objetivo *m.* **-2.** [in archery, shooting, of criticism] blanco *m.*

tariff ['tærɪf] *n* tarifa *f.*

Tarmac® ['tɑːmæk] *n* [material] alquitrán *m.* ◆ **tarmac** *n* AERON: **the tarmac** la pista.

tarnish ['tɑːnɪʃ] *vt* [make dull] deslustrar; *fig* [damage] empañar, manchar.

tarpaulin [tɑːˈpɔːlɪn] *n* lona *f* alquitranada.

tart [tɑːt] ◇ *adj* [bitter] agrio (agria). ◇ *n* **-1.** [sweet pastry] tarta *f.* **-2.** *v inf* [prostitute] furcia *f,* fulana *f.* ◆ **tart up** *vt sep Br inf pej* emperejilar.

tartan ['tɑːtn] ◇ *n* tartán *m.* ◇ *comp* de tartán.

tartar(e) sauce ['tɑːtəʳ-] *n* salsa *f* tártara.

task [tɑːsk] *n* tarea *f.*

task force *n* MIL destacamento *m* de fuerzas.

tassel ['tæsl] *n* borla *f.*

taste [teɪst] ◇ *n* **-1.** [physical sense, discernment] gusto *m*; **in bad/good** ~ de mal/buen gusto. **-2.** [flavour] sabor *m.* **-3.** [try]: **have a** ~ pruébalo. **-4.** *fig* [for success, fast cars etc]: ~ **(for)** afición *f* (a), gusto *m* (por). **-5.** *fig* [experience] experiencia *f.* ◇ *vt* **-1.** [food] notar un sabor a. **-2.** [test, try] probar. **-3.** *fig* [experience] conocer. ◇ *vi* saber; **to** ~ **of** OR **like** saber a.

tasteful ['teɪstful] *adj* de buen gusto.

tasteless ['teɪstlɪs] *adj* **-1.** [offensive, cheap and unattractive] de mal gusto. **-2.** [without flavour] insípido(da), soso(sa).

tasty ['teɪstɪ] *adj* sabroso(sa).

tatters ['tætəz] *npl*: **in** ~ [clothes] andrajoso(sa), *fig* [confidence, reputation] por los suelos.

tattoo [tə'tuː] (*pl* **-s**) ◇ *n* **-1.** [design] tatuaje *m.* **-2.** *Br* [military display] desfile *m* militar. ◇ *vt* tatuar.

tatty ['tætɪ] *adj Br inf pej* desastrado(da).

taught [tɔːt] *pt & pp* → **teach**.

taunt [tɔːnt] ◇ *vt* zaherir a. ◇ *n* pulla *f.*

Taurus ['tɔːrəs] *n* Tauro *m.*

taut [tɔːt] *adj* tenso(sa).

tawdry ['tɔːdrɪ] *adj pej* de oropel.

tax [tæks] ◇ *n* impuesto *m.* ◇ *vt* **-1.** [goods, profits] gravar. **-2.** [business, person] imponer contribuciones a. **-3.** [strain, test] poner a prueba.

taxable ['tæksəbl] *adj* imponible.

tax allowance *n* desgravación *f* fiscal.

taxation [tæk'seɪʃn] *n* (*U*) **-1.** [system] sistema *m* tributario. **-2.** [amount] impuestos *mpl.*

tax avoidance [-ə'vɔɪdəns] *n* evasión *f* fiscal.

tax collector *n* recaudador *m,* -ra *f* de impuestos.

tax disc *n Br* pegatina del impuesto de circulación.

tax evasion *n* fraude *m* fiscal, evasión *f* de impuestos.

tax-exempt *Am* = **tax-free**.

tax-free *Br,* **tax-exempt** *Am adj* exento(ta) de impuestos.

taxi ['tæksɪ] ◇ *n* taxi *m.* ◇ *vi* [plane] rodar por la pista.

taxi driver *n* taxista *m y f.*

tax inspector *n* ≃ inspector *m,* -ra *f* de Hacienda.

taxi rank *Br,* **taxi stand** *n* parada *f* de taxis.

taxpayer ['tæks,peɪəʳ] *n* contribuyente *m y f.*

tax relief *n* (*U*) desgravación *f* fiscal.

tax return *n* declaración *f* de renta.

TB *n abbr of* **tuberculosis**.

tea [tiː] *n* **-1.** [drink, leaves] té *m.* **-2.** *Br* [afternoon snack] té *m,* merienda *f.* **-3.** *Br* [evening meal] merienda cena *f.*

teabag ['tiːbæg] *n* bolsita *f* de té.

tea break *n Br* descanso *m* (*durante la jornada laboral*).

teach [tiːtʃ] (*pt & pp* **taught**) ◇ *vt* **-1.** [give lessons to] dar clases a; **to** ~ **sb sthg** enseñar algo a alguien; **to** ~ **sb to do sthg** enseñar a alguien a hacer algo. **-2.** [give lessons in] dar clases de. ◇ *vi* ser profesor(ra).

teacher ['tiːtʃəʳ] *n* [at primary school] maestro *m,* -tra *f*; [at secondary school] profesor *m,* -ra *f.*

teachers college *Am* = **teacher training college**.

teacher training college *Br,* **teachers college** *Am n* escuela *f* normal.

teaching ['tiːtʃɪŋ] *n* enseñanza *f.*

tea cloth *n Br* **-1.** [tablecloth] mantel *m.* **-2.** [tea towel] paño *m* de cocina.

tea cosy *Br,* **tea cozy** *Am n* cubretetera *f.*

teacup ['tiːkʌp] *n* taza *f* de té.

teak [tiːk] *n* teca *f.*

team [ti:m] *n* equipo *m*.

teammate ['ti:mmeɪt] *n* compañero *m*, -ra *f* de equipo.

teamwork ['ti:mwɜ:k] *n* (*U*) trabajo *m* en equipo.

teapot ['ti:pɒt] *n* tetera *f*.

tear¹ [tɪər] *n* lágrima *f*; **in ~s** llorando.

tear² [teər] (*pt* **tore**, *pp* **torn**) ◇ *vt* **-1.** [rip] rasgar, romper. **-2.** [remove roughly] arrancar. ◇ *vi* **-1.** [rip] romperse, rasgarse. **-2.** *inf* [move quickly] ir a toda pastilla. ◇ *n* rasgón *m*, desgarrón *m*. ♦ **tear apart** *vt sep* **-1.** [rip up] despedazar. **-2.** [upset greatly] desgarrar. ♦ **tear down** *vt sep* echar abajo. ♦ **tear up** *vt sep* hacer pedazos.

teardrop ['tɪədrɒp] *n* lágrima *f*.

tearful ['tɪəful] *adj* [person] lloroso(sa).

tear gas [tɪə-] *n* (*U*) gas *m* lacrimógeno.

tearoom ['ti:rum] *n* salón *m* de té.

tease [ti:z] *vt* [mock]: **to ~ sb (about)** tomar el pelo a alguien (acerca de).

tea service, tea set *n* servicio *m* OR juego *m* de té.

teaspoon ['ti:spu:n] *n* **-1.** [utensil] cucharilla *f*. **-2.** [amount] cucharadita *f*.

teat [ti:t] *n* **-1.** [of animal] tetilla *f*. **-2.** [of bottle] tetina *f*.

teatime ['ti:taɪm] *n* *Br* hora *f* del té.

tea towel *n* paño *m* de cocina.

technical ['teknɪkl] *adj* técnico(ca).

technical college *n* *Br* ≃ centro *m* de formación profesional.

technicality [,teknɪ'kælətɪ] *n* detalle *m* técnico.

technically ['teknɪklɪ] *adv* **-1.** [gen] técnicamente. **-2.** [theoretically] teóricamente, en teoría.

technician [tek'nɪʃn] *n* técnico *m*, -ca *f*.

technique [tek'ni:k] *n* técnica *f*.

technological [,teknə'lɒdʒɪkl] *adj* tecnológico(ca).

technology [tek'nɒlədʒɪ] *n* tecnología *f*.

teddy ['tedɪ] *n*: **~ (bear)** oso *m* de peluche.

tedious ['ti:djəs] *adj* tedioso(sa).

tee [ti:] *n* tee *m*.

teem [ti:m] *vi* **-1.** [rain] llover a cántaros. **-2.** [be busy]: **to be ~ing with** estar inundado(da) de.

teenage ['ti:neɪdʒ] *adj* adolescente.

teenager ['ti:n,eɪdʒər] *n* adolescente *m y f*, quinceañero *m*, -ra *f*.

teens [ti:nz] *npl* adolescencia *f*.

tee shirt *n* camiseta *f*.

teeter ['ti:tər] *vi* *lit & fig* tambalearse.

teeth [ti:θ] *npl* → **tooth**.

teethe [ti:ð] *vi* echar los dientes.

teething troubles ['ti:ðɪŋ-] *npl* *fig* problemas *mpl* iniciales.

teetotaller *Br*, **teetotaler** *Am* [ti:'təʊtlər] *n* abstemio *m*, -mia *f*.

TEFL ['tefl] (*abbr of* **teaching of English as a foreign language**) *n* enseñanza de inglés para extranjeros.

tel. (*abbr of* **telephone**) tfno.

telecommunications ['telɪkə,mju:nɪ'keɪʃnz] *npl* telecomunicaciones *fpl*.

telegram ['telɪgræm] *n* telegrama *m*.

telegraph ['telɪgrɑ:f] *n* telégrafo *m*.

telegraph pole, telegraph post *Br n* poste *m* de telégrafos.

telepathy [tɪ'lepəθɪ] *n* telepatía *f*.

telephone ['telɪfəʊn] ◇ *n* teléfono *m*; **to be on the ~** *Br* [connected to network] tener teléfono; [speaking] estar al teléfono. ◇ *vt & vi* telefonear.

telephone book *n* guía *f* telefónica.

telephone booth *n* teléfono *m* público.

telephone box *n* *Br* cabina *f* (telefónica).

telephone call *n* llamada *f* telefónica.

telephone directory *n* guía *f* telefónica.

telephone number *n* número *m* de teléfono.

telephonist [tɪ'lefənɪst] *n* *Br* telefonista *m y f*.

telephoto lens [,telɪ'fəʊtəʊ-] *n* teleobjetivo *m*.

telescope ['telɪskəʊp] *n* telescopio *m*.

teletext ['telɪtekst] *n* teletexto *m*.

televise ['telɪvaɪz] *vt* televisar.

television ['telɪ,vɪʒn] *n* televisión *f*.

television set *n* televisor *m*, (aparato *m* de) televisión *f*.

telex ['teleks] ◇ *n* télex *m*. ◇ *vt* [message] transmitir por télex; [person] mandar un télex a.

tell [tel] (*pt & pp* **told**) ◇ *vt* **-1.** [gen] decir; **to ~ sb (that)** decir a alguien que; **to ~ sb sthg, to ~ sthg to sb** decir a alguien algo; **to ~ sb to do sthg** decir a alguien que haga algo. **-2.** [joke, story] contar. **-3.** [judge, recognize]: **to ~ what sb is thinking** saber en qué está pensando alguien; **to ~ the time** decir la hora. ◇ *vi* [have effect] surtir efecto. ♦ **tell apart** *vt sep* distinguir. ♦ **tell off** *vt sep* reñir, reprender.

telling ['telɪŋ] *adj* **-1.** [speech, argument] efectivo(va). **-2.** [remark, incident] revelador(ra).

telltale ['telteɪl] ◇ adj revelador(ra). ◇ n chivato m, -ta f, acusica m y f.

telly ['telɪ] (abbr of **television**) n Br inf tele f.

temp [temp] ◇ n inf Br (abbr of **temporary (employee)**) secretario m eventual, secretaria f eventual (por horas). ◇ vi: **she's ~ing** está de secretaria eventual.

temper ['tempər] ◇ n -1. [state of mind, mood] humor m; **to lose one's ~** enfadarse, perder la paciencia. -2. [angry state]: **to be in a ~** estar de mal humor. -3. [temperament] temperamento m. ◇ vt fml templar, suavizar.

temperament ['temprəmənt] n temperamento m.

temperamental [,temprə'mentl] adj [volatile] temperamental.

temperate ['temprət] adj templado(da).

temperature ['temprətʃər] n temperatura f; **to have a ~** tener fiebre.

tempestuous [tem'pestjuəs] adj lit & fig tempestuoso(sa).

template ['templɪt] n plantilla f.

temple ['templ] n -1. RELIG templo m. -2. ANAT sien f.

temporarily [,tempə'rerəlɪ] adv temporalmente, provisionalmente.

temporary ['tempərərɪ] adj [gen] temporal, provisional; [improvement, problem] pasajero(ra).

tempt [tempt] vt [entice]: **to ~ sb (to do sthg)** tentar a alguien (a hacer algo).

temptation [temp'teɪʃn] n tentación f.

tempting ['temptɪŋ] adj tentador(ra).

ten [ten] num diez; see also **six**.

tenable ['tenəbl] adj [reasonable, credible] sostenible.

tenacious [tɪ'neɪʃəs] adj tenaz.

tenancy ['tenənsɪ] n [period - of house] alquiler m; [- of land] arrendamiento m.

tenant ['tenənt] n [of house] inquilino m, -na f; [of pub] arrendatario m, -ria f.

tend [tend] vt -1. [have tendency]: **to ~ to do sthg** soler hacer algo, tender a hacer algo. -2. [look after] cuidar.

tendency ['tendənsɪ] n -1. [trend]: **~ (for sb/sthg to do sthg)** tendencia f (de alguien/algo a hacer algo). -2. [leaning, inclination] inclinación f.

tender ['tendər] ◇ adj [gen] tierno(na); [sore] dolorido(da). ◇ n COMM propuesta f, oferta f. ◇ vt fml [resignation] presentar; [apology, suggestion] ofrecer.

tendon ['tendən] n tendón m.

tenement ['tenəmənt] n bloque de viviendas modestas.

Tenerife [,tenə'riːf] n Tenerife.

tenet ['tenɪt] n fml principio m.

tennis ['tenɪs] ◇ n tenis m. ◇ comp de tenis; **~ player** tenista m y f.

tennis ball n pelota f de tenis.

tennis court n pista f de tenis.

tennis racket n raqueta f de tenis.

tenor ['tenər] n [singer] tenor.

tense [tens] ◇ adj tenso(sa). ◇ n tiempo m. ◇ vt tensar.

tension ['tenʃn] n tensión f.

tent [tent] n tienda f (de campaña).

tentacle ['tentəkl] n tentáculo m.

tentative ['tentətɪv] adj -1. [person] indeciso(sa); [step, handshake] vacilante. -2. [suggestion, conclusion etc] provisional.

tenterhooks ['tentəhʊks] npl: **to be on ~** estar sobre ascuas.

tenth [tenθ] num décimo(ma); see also **sixth**.

tent peg n estaca f.

tent pole n mástil m de tienda.

tenuous ['tenjuəs] adj [argument] flojo(ja); [evidence, connection] débil, insignificante; [hold] ligero(ra).

tenure ['tenjər] n (U) fml -1. [of property] arrendamiento m. -2. [of job] ocupación f, ejercicio m.

tepid ['tepɪd] adj [liquid] tibio(bia).

term [tɜːm] ◇ n -1. [word, expression] término m. -2. SCH & UNIV trimestre m. -3. POL mandato m. -4. [period of time] periodo m; **in the long/short ~** a largo/corto plazo. ◇ vt: **to ~ sthg sthg** calificar algo de algo. ◆ **terms** npl -1. [of contract, agreement] condiciones fpl. -2. [basis]: **in international/real ~s** en términos internacionales/reales; **to be on good ~s (with sb)** mantener buenas relaciones (con alguien); **to come to ~s with sthg** aceptar algo. ◆ **in terms of** prep por lo que se refiere a.

terminal ['tɜːmɪnl] ◇ adj MED incurable, terminal. ◇ n -1. [transport] terminal f. -2. COMPUT terminal m.

terminate ['tɜːmɪneɪt] ◇ vt fml [gen] poner fin a; [pregnancy] interrumpir. ◇ vi -1. [bus, train] finalizar el trayecto. -2. [contract] terminarse.

termini ['tɜːmɪnaɪ] pl → **terminus**.

terminus ['tɜːmɪnəs] (pl **-ni** OR **-nuses**) n (estación f) terminal f.

terrace ['terəs] n -1. [gen] terraza f. -2. Br [of houses] hilera f de casas adosadas. ◆ **terraces** npl FTBL: **the ~s** las gradas.

terraced ['terəst] *adj* **-1.** [hillside] a terrazas. **-2.** [house, housing] adosado(da).

terraced house *n* Br casa *f* adosada.

terrain [te'reɪn] *n* terreno *m*.

terrible ['terəbl] *adj* **-1.** [crash, mess, shame] terrible, espantoso(sa). **-2.** [unwell, unhappy, very bad] fatal.

terribly ['terəblɪ] *adv* [sing, play, write] malísimamente; [injured, sorry, expensive] terriblemente.

terrier ['terɪəʳ] *n* terrier *m*.

terrific [tə'rɪfɪk] *adj* **-1.** [wonderful] estupendo(da). **-2.** [enormous] enorme.

terrified ['terɪfaɪd] *adj* aterrorizado(da); **to be ~ (of)** tener terror a.

terrifying ['terɪfaɪɪŋ] *adj* aterrador(ra).

territory ['terətrɪ] *n* **-1.** [political area] territorio *m*. **-2.** [terrain] terreno *m*. **-3.** [area of knowledge] esfera *f*.

terror ['terəʳ] *n* [fear] terror *m*.

terrorism ['terərɪzm] *n* terrorismo *m*.

terrorist ['terərɪst] *n* terrorista *m y f*.

terrorize, -ise ['terəraɪz] *vt* aterrorizar.

terse [tɜːs] *adj* seco(ca).

Terylene® ['terəliːn] *n* terylene® *m*.

test [test] ◇ *n* **-1.** [trial] prueba *f*. **-2.** [examination] examen *m*, prueba *f*. **-3.** MED [of blood, urine] análisis *m inv*; [of eyes] revisión *f*. ◇ *vt* **-1.** [try out] probar, poner a prueba. **-2.** [examine] examinar; **to ~ sb on** examinar a alguien de.

testament ['testəmənt] *n* [will] testamento *m*.

test-drive *vt* someter a prueba de carretera.

testicles ['testɪklz] *npl* testículos *mpl*.

testify ['testɪfaɪ] *vi* **-1.** JUR prestar declaración; **to ~ that** declarar que. **-2.** [be proof]: **to ~ to sthg** dar fe de OR atestiguar algo.

testimony [Br 'testɪmənɪ, Am 'testəməʊnɪ] *n* JUR testimonio *m*, declaración *f*.

testing ['testɪŋ] *adj* duro(ra).

test match *n* Br partido *m* internacional.

test pilot *n* piloto *m y f* de pruebas.

test tube *n* probeta *f*.

test-tube baby *n* bebé *m y f* probeta.

tetanus ['tetənəs] *n* tétanos *m inv*.

tether ['teðəʳ] ◇ *vt* atar. ◇ *n*: **to be at the end of one's ~** estar uno que ya no puede más.

text [tekst] *n* **-1.** [gen] texto *m*. **-2.** [textbook] libro *m* de texto.

textbook ['tekstbʊk] *n* libro *m* de texto.

textile ['tekstaɪl] *n* textil *m*, tejido *m*.

texture ['tekstʃəʳ] *n* textura *f*.

Thai [taɪ] ◇ *adj* tailandés(esa). ◇ *n* **-1.** [person] tailandés *m*, -esa *f*. **-2.** [language] tailandés *m*.

Thailand ['taɪlænd] *n* Tailandia.

Thames [temz] *n*: **the ~** el Támesis.

than [weak form ðən, strong form ðæn] ◇ *prep* que; **you're older ~ me** eres mayor que yo; **you're older ~ I thought** eres mayor de lo que pensaba. ◇ *conj* que; **I'd sooner read ~ sleep** prefiero leer que dormir; **no sooner did he arrive ~ she left** tan pronto llegó él, ella se fue; **more ~ three/once** más de tres/de una vez; **rather ~ stay, he chose to go** en vez de quedarse, prefirió irse.

thank [θæŋk] ◇ *vt*: **to ~ sb (for sthg)** dar las gracias a alguien (por algo), agradecer a alguien (algo); **~ God** OR **goodness** OR **heavens!** ¡gracias a Dios!, ¡menos mal! ◆ **thanks** ◇ *npl* agradecimiento *m*. ◇ *excl* ¡gracias! ◆ **thanks to** *prep* gracias a.

thankful ['θæŋkfʊl] *adj* **-1.** [relieved] aliviado(da). **-2.** [grateful]: **~ (for)** agradecido(da) (por).

thankless ['θæŋklɪs] *adj* ingrato(ta).

thanksgiving ['θæŋks,gɪvɪŋ] *n* acción *f* de gracias. ◆ **Thanksgiving (Day)** *n* Día *m* de Acción de Gracias.

thank you *excl* ¡gracias!; **~ for** gracias por.

that [ðæt, weak form of pron and conj ðət] (*pl* **those**) ◇ *pron* **-1.** (*demonstrative use: pl 'those'*) ése *m*, ésa *f*, ésos *mpl*, ésas *fpl*; (*indefinite*) eso; **~ sounds familiar** eso me resulta familiar; **who's ~?** [who is it?] ¿quién es?; **what's ~?** ¿qué es eso?; **~'s a shame** es una pena; **is ~ Maureen?** [asking someone else] ¿es ésa Maureen?; [asking person in question] ¿eres Maureen?; **do you like these or those?** ¿te gustan éstos o ésos? **-2.** [further away in distance, time] aquél *m*, aquélla *f*, aquéllos *mpl*, aquéllas *fpl*; (*indefinite*) aquello; **~ was the life!** ¡aquello sí que era vida!; **all those who helped me** todos aquellos que me ayudaron. **-3.** (*to introduce relative clauses*) que; **a path ~ led into the woods** un sendero que conducía al bosque; **everything ~ I have done** todo lo que he hecho; **the room ~ I sleep in** el cuarto donde OR en (el) que duermo; **the day ~ he arrived** el día en que llegó; **the firm ~ he's applying to** la empresa a la que solicita trabajo. ◇ *adj* (*demonstrative: pl 'those'*) ese (esa), esos (esas) (*pl*); [further away in distance, time] aquel (aquella), aquellos (aquellas) (*pl*); **those chocolates are delicious** esos bombones están exquisitos; **I'll have ~ book at the back** yo cogeré aquel libro del fondo; **later ~ day** más tarde ese/aquel mismo día. ◇ *adv* tan; **it wasn't ~ bad** no estuvo tan mal; **it doesn't cost ~ much** no cuesta tanto; **it was ~ big** fue así de grande. ◇ *conj* que; **he recommended ~ I phone you** aconsejó que te telefoneara; **it's time ~ we were leaving** deberíamos irnos ya, ya va siendo hora de irse. ◆ **that is** *adv* es decir.

thatched [θætʃt] *adj* con techo de paja.

that's [ðæts] = **that is**.

thaw [θɔː] ◇ *vt* [snow, ice] derretir; [frozen food] descongelar. ◇ *vi* [snow, ice] derretirse; [frozen food] descongelarse; *fig* [people, relations] distenderse. ◇ *n* deshielo *m*.

the [*weak form* ðə, *before vowel* ði, *strong form* ðiː] *def art* **-1.** [gen] el (la), (*pl*) los (las); (*before feminine nouns beginning with stressed "a" or "ha" = **el**; "a" + "el" = **al**; "de" + "el" = **del**): **~ boat** el barco; **~ Queen** la reina; **~ men** los hombres; **~ women** las mujeres; **~ (cold) water** el agua (fría); **to ~ end of ~ world** al fin del mundo; **to play ~ piano** tocar el piano; **the Joneses are coming to supper** los Jones vienen a cenar. **-2.** (*with an adjective to form a noun*): **~ old/young** los viejos/jóvenes; **~ impossible** lo imposible. **-3.** [in dates]: **~ twelfth of May** el doce de mayo; **~ forties** los cuarenta. **-4.** (*in comparisons*): **~ more I see her, ~ less I like her** cuanto más la veo, menos me gusta; **~ sooner ~ better** cuanto antes mejor. **-5.** [in titles]: **Catherine ~ Great** Catalina la Grande; **George ~ First** Jorge Primero.

theatre, theater *Am* ['θɪətər] *n* **-1.** [for plays etc] teatro *m*. **-2.** *Br* [in hospital] quirófano *m*. **-3.** *Am* [cinema] cine *m*.

theatregoer, theatergoer *Am* ['θɪətə‚ɡəʊər] *n* aficionado *m*, -da *f* al teatro.

theatrical [θɪ'ætrɪkl] *adj lit* & *fig* teatral.

theft [θeft] *n* [more serious] robo *m*; [less serious] hurto *m*.

their [ðeər] *poss adj* su, sus (*pl*); **~ house** su casa; **~ children** sus hijos; **it wasn't THEIR fault** no fue culpa suya

OR su culpa; **they washed ~ hair** se lavaron el pelo.

theirs [ðeəz] *poss pron* suyo (suya); **that money is ~** ese dinero es suyo; **our car hit ~** nuestro coche chocó contra el suyo; **it wasn't our fault, it was THEIRS** no fue culpa nuestra sino suya OR de ellos; **a friend of ~** un amigo suyo OR de ellos.

them [*weak form* ðəm, *strong form* ðem] *pers pron pl* **-1.** (*direct*) los *mpl*, las *fpl*; **I know ~** los conozco; **I like ~** me gustan; **if I were** OR **was ~** si (yo) fuera ellos. **-2.** (*indirect - gen*) les *mpl y fpl*; (*- with other third person prons*) se *mpl y fpl*; **she sent ~ a letter** les mandó una carta; **we spoke to ~** hablamos con ellos; **I gave it to ~** se lo di (a ellos). **-3.** (*stressed, after prep, in comparisons etc*) ellos *mpl*, ellas *fpl*; **you can't expect THEM to do it** no esperarás que ELLOS lo hagan; **with/without ~** con/sin ellos; **we're not as wealthy as ~** no somos tan ricos como ellos.

theme [θiːm] *n* **-1.** [gen] tema *m*. **-2.** [signature tune] sintonía *f*.

theme tune *n* tema *m* musical.

themselves [ðəm'selvz] *pron* **-1.** (*reflexive*) se; (*after preposition*) sí; **they enjoyed ~** se divirtieron. **-2.** (*for emphasis*) ellos mismos *mpl*, ellas mismas *fpl*; **they did it ~** lo hicieron ellos mismos. **-3.** [alone] solos(las); **they organized it (by) ~** lo organizaron ellas solas.

then [ðen] *adv* **-1.** [not now] entonces. **-2.** [next, afterwards] luego, después. **-3.** [in that case] entonces; **all right ~** de acuerdo, pues. **-4.** [therefore] entonces, por lo tanto. **-5.** [furthermore, also] además.

theology [θɪ'ɒlədʒɪ] *n* teología *f*.

theoretical [θɪə'retɪkl] *adj* teórico(ca).

theorize, -ise ['θɪəraɪz] *vi*: **to ~ (about sthg)** teorizar (sobre algo).

theory ['θɪərɪ] *n* teoría *f*; **in ~** en teoría.

therapist ['θerəpɪst] *n* terapeuta *m y f*.

therapy ['θerəpɪ] *n* terapia *f*.

there [ðeər] ◇ *pron* [indicating existence]: **~ is/are** hay; **~'s someone at the door** hay alguien en la puerta; **~ must be some mistake** debe (de) haber un error; **~ are five of us** somos cinco. ◇ *adv* **-1.** [in existence, available] ahí; **is anybody ~?** ¿hay alguien ahí?; **is John ~, please?** [when telephoning] ¿está John? **-2.** [referring to place - near speaker] ahí; [- further away] allí, allá; **I'm going ~ next week** voy para allá OR allí la semana que viene; ~ **it is** ahí está; **over** ~ por allí; **it's six miles** ~ **and back** hay seis millas entre ir y volver. ◇ *excl*: ~, **I knew he'd turn up** ¡mira!, sabía que aparecería; ~, ~ **(don't cry)** ¡venga, venga (no llores)! ◆ **there and then, then and there** *adv* en el acto.

thereabouts [,ðeərə'bauts], **thereabout** *Am* [,ðeər'baut] *adv*: **or** ~ por ahí.

thereafter [,ðeər'ɑ:ftər] *adv fml* después, a partir de entonces.

thereby [,ðeər'baɪ] *adv fml* de ese modo.

therefore ['ðeəfɔ:r] *adv* por lo tanto.

there's [ðeəz] = **there is**.

thermal ['θɜ:ml] *adj* térmico(ca).

thermometer [θə'mɒmɪtər] *n* termómetro *m*.

Thermos (flask)® ['θɜ:məs-] *n* termo *m*.

thermostat ['θɜ:məstæt] *n* termostato *m*.

thesaurus [θɪ'sɔ:rəs] (*pl* **-es**) *n* diccionario *m* de sinónimos y voces afines.

these [ði:z] *pl* → **this**.

thesis ['θi:sɪs] (*pl* **theses** ['θi:si:z]) *n* tesis *f inv*.

they [ðeɪ] *pers pron pl* **-1.** [gen] ellos *mpl*, ellas *fpl*; ~'**re pleased** (ellos) están satisfechos; ~'**re pretty earrings** son unos pendientes bonitos; THEY **can't do it** ELLOS no pueden hacerlo; **there** ~ **are** allí están. **-2.** [unspecified people]: ~ **say it's going to snow** dicen que va a nevar.

they'd [ðeɪd] = **they had, they would**.

they'll [ðeɪl] = **they shall, they will**.

they're [ðeər] = **they are**.

they've [ðeɪv] = **they have**.

thick [θɪk] ◇ *adj* **-1.** [not thin] grueso(sa); **it's 3 cm** ~ tiene 3 cm de grueso; **how** ~ **is it?** ¿qué espesor tiene? **-2.** [dense - hair, liquid, fog] espeso(sa). **-3.** *inf* [stupid] necio(cia). ◇ *n*: **to be in the** ~ **of** estar en el centro OR meollo de.

thicken ['θɪkn] ◇ *vt* espesar. ◇ *vi* [gen] espesarse.

thicket ['θɪkɪt] *n* matorral *m*.

thickness ['θɪknɪs] *n* espesor *m*.

thickset [,θɪk'set] *adj* fornido(da).

thick-skinned [-'skɪnd] *adj* insensible.

thief [θi:f] (*pl* **thieves**) *n* ladrón *m*, -ona *f*.

thieve [θi:v] *vt & vi* robar, hurtar.

thieves [θi:vz] *pl* → **thief**.

thigh [θaɪ] *n* muslo *m*.

thimble ['θɪmbl] *n* dedal *m*.

thin [θɪn] *adj* **-1.** [not thick] delgado(da), fino(na). **-2.** [skinny] delgado(da), flaco(ca). **-3.** [watery] claro(ra), aguado(da). **-4.** [sparse - crowd, vegetation, mist] poco denso (poco densa); [- hair] ralo(la). ◆ **thin down** *vt sep* aclarar.

thing [θɪŋ] *n* **-1.** [gen] cosa *f*; **the next** ~ **on the list** lo siguiente de la lista; **the (best)** ~ **to do would be ...** lo mejor sería ...; **the** ~ **is ...** el caso es que .... **-2.** [anything]: **not a** ~ nada. **-3.** [person]: **poor** ~! ¡pobrecito *m*, -ta *f* ! ◆ **things** *npl* **-1.** [clothes, possessions] **cosas** *fpl*. **-2.** *inf* [life]: **how are** ~**s?** ¿qué tal (van las cosas)?

think [θɪŋk] (*pt & pp* **thought**) ◇ *vt* **-1.** [believe]: **to** ~ **(that)** creer OR pensar que; **I** ~ **so/not creo** que sí/no. **-2.** [have in mind] pensar; **what are you** ~**ing?** ¿en qué piensas? **-3.** [imagine] entender, hacerse una idea de; **I thought so** ya me lo imaginaba. **-4.** [in polite requests] creer; **do you** ~ **you could help me?** ¿cree que podría ayudarme? ◇ *vi* **-1.** [use mind] pensar. **-2.** [have stated opinion]: **what do you** ~ OR **about his new film?** ¿qué piensas de su nueva película?; **to** ~ **a lot of sthg/sb** tener en mucha estima algo/a alguien. **-3.** *phr*: **to** ~ **twice** pensárselo dos veces. ◆ **think about** *vt fus* pensar en; **I'll have to** ~ **about it** tendré que pensarlo; **to** ~ **about doing sthg** pensar en hacer algo. ◆ **think of** *vt fus* **-1.** [consider]: **to** ~ **of doing sthg** pensar en hacer algo. **-2.** [remember] acordarse de. **-3.** [conceive] pensar en; **how did you** ~ **of (doing) that?** ¿cómo se te ocurrió (hacer) esto? ◆ **think out**, **think through** *vt sep* [plan] elaborar; [problem] examinar. ◆ **think over** *vt sep* pensarse. ◆ **think up** *vt sep* idear.

think tank *n* grupo de expertos convocados por una organización para aconsejar sobre un tema determinado.

third [θɜ:d] ◇ *num adj* tercer(ra). ◇ *num n* **-1.** [fraction] tercio *m*. **-2.** [in order] tercero *m*, -ra *f*. **-3.** UNIV ≃ aprobado *m* (*en un título universitario*); *see also* **sixth**.

thirdly ['θɜ:dlɪ] *adv* en tercer lugar.

third party insurance *n* seguro *m* a terceros.

third-rate *adj pej* de poca categoría.

Third World *n*: **the** ~ el Tercer Mundo.

thirst [θɜ:st] *n lit & fig*: ~ **(for)** sed *f* (de).

thirsty ['θɜːstɪ] *adj* [parched]: **to be** OR **feel** ~ tener sed.

thirteen [,θɜː'tiːn] *num* trece; *see also* **six**.

thirty ['θɜːtɪ] *num* treinta; *see also* **sixty**.

this [ðɪs] (*pl* **these**) ◇ *pron* [gen] éste *m*, ésta *f*, éstos *mpl*, éstas *fpl*; (*indefinite*) esto; ~ **is/these are for you** esto es/ éstos son para tí; ~ **can't be true** esto no puede ser cierto; **do you prefer these or those?** ¿prefieres éstos o aquéllos?; ~ **is Daphne Logan** [introducing another person] ésta es OR te presento a Daphne Logan; [introducing oneself on phone] soy Daphne Logan; **what's** ~? ¿qué es eso? ◇ *adj* **-1.** [gen] este (esta), estos (estas) (*pl*); ~ **country** este país; **these thoughts** estos pensamientos; **I prefer** ~ **one** prefiero éste; ~ **morning/week** esta mañana/ semana; ~ **Sunday/summer** este domingo/verano. **-2.** *inf* [a certain] un (una); **there's a** ~ **woman I know** hay una tía que conozco. ◇ *adv*: **it was** ~ **big** era así de grande; **you'll need about** ~ **much** te hará falta un tanto así.

thistle ['θɪsl] *n* cardo *m*.

thong [θɒŋ] *n* [of leather] correa *f*.

thorn [θɔːn] *n* [prickle] espina *f*.

thorough ['θʌrə] *adj* **-1.** [investigation etc] exhaustivo(va). **-2.** [person, work] minucioso(sa).

thoroughbred ['θʌrəbred] *n* pura sangre *m y f*.

thoroughfare ['θʌrəfeə] *n fml* calle *f* mayor.

thoroughly ['θʌrəlɪ] *adv* **-1.** [fully, in detail] a fondo. **-2.** [completely, utterly] completamente.

those [ðəʊz] *pl* → **that**.

though [ðəʊ] ◇ *conj* aunque; **even** ~ aunque; **as** ~ como si. ◇ *adv* sin embargo.

thought [θɔːt] ◇ *pt & pp* → **think**. ◇ *n* **-1.** [notion, idea] idea *f*. **-2.** [act of thinking]: **after much** ~ después de pensarlo mucho. **-3.** [philosophy, thinking] pensamiento *m*. ◆ **thoughts** *npl* **-1.** [reflections] reflexiones *fpl*. **-2.** [views] opiniones *fpl*.

thoughtful ['θɔːtful] *adj* **-1.** [pensive] pensativo(va). **-2.** [considerate] considerado(da).

thoughtless ['θɔːtlɪs] *adj* desconsiderado(da).

thousand ['θaʊznd] *num* mil; **a** OR **one** ~ **mil**; **two** ~ dos mil; ~**s of miles** de; *see also* **six**.

thousandth ['θaʊzntθ] ◇ *num adj* milésimo(ma). ◇ *num n* [fraction] milésima *f*; *see also* **sixth**.

thrash [θræʃ] *vt lit & fig* dar una paliza a. ◆ **thrash about, thrash around** *vi* agitarse violentamente. ◆ **thrash out** *vt sep* darle vueltas a, discutir.

thread [θred] ◇ *n* **-1.** [of cotton, argument] hilo *m*. **-2.** [of screw] rosca *f*, filete *m*. ◇ *vt* [needle] enhebrar.

threadbare ['θredbeə] *adj* raído(da).

threat [θret] *n*: ~ **(to/of)** amenaza *f* (para/de).

threaten ['θretn] ◇ *vt* amenazar; **to** ~ **sb (with)** amenazar a alguien (con); **to** ~ **to do sthg** amenazar con hacer algo. ◇ *vi* amenazar.

three [θriː] *num* tres; *see also* **six**.

three-dimensional [-dɪ'menʃənl] *adj* tridimensional.

threefold ['θriːfəʊld] ◇ *adj* triple. ◇ *adv* tres veces.

three-piece *adj* de tres piezas; ~ **suite** tresillo *m*.

three-ply *adj* [wood] de tres capas; [rope, wool] de tres hebras.

thresh [θreʃ] *vt* trillar.

threshold ['θreʃhəʊld] *n* **-1.** [doorway] umbral *m*. **-2.** [level] límite *m*.

threw [θruː] *pt* → **throw**.

thrifty ['θrɪftɪ] *adj* [person] ahorrativo(va); [meal] frugal.

thrill [θrɪl] ◇ *n* **-1.** [sudden feeling] estremecimiento *m*. **-2.** [exciting experience]: **it was a** ~ **to see it** fue emocionante verlo. ◇ *vt* entusiasmar.

thrilled [θrɪld] *adj*: ~ **(with sthg/to do sthg)** encantado(da) (de algo/de hacer algo).

thriller ['θrɪlə] *n* novela *f*/película *f*/ obra *f* de suspense.

thrilling ['θrɪlɪŋ] *adj* emocionante.

thrive [θraɪv] (*pt* **-d** OR **throve**) *vi* [plant] crecer mucho; [person] rebosar de salud; [business] prosperar.

thriving ['θraɪvɪŋ] *adj* [plant] que crece bien.

throat [θrəʊt] *n* garganta *f*.

throb [θrɒb] *vi* **-1.** [heart, pulse] latir; [head] palpitar. **-2.** [engine, music] vibrar, resonar.

throes [θrəʊz] *npl*: **to be in the** ~ **of** estar en medio de.

throne [θrəʊn] *n* trono *m*.

throng [θrɒŋ] ◇ *n* multitud *f*. ◇ *vt* llegar en tropel a.

throttle ['θrɒtl] ◇ n válvula f reguladora. ◇ vt [strangle] estrangular.

through [θruː] ◇ adj [finished]: **to be ~ with** sthg haber terminado algo. ◇ adv **-1.** [in place] de parte a parte, de un lado a otro; **they let us ~** nos dejaron pasar; **I read it ~** lo leí hasta el final. **-2.** [in time] hasta el final. ◇ prep **-1.** [relating to place, position] a través de; **to cut/travel ~** sthg cortar/viajar por algo. **-2.** [during] durante; **to go ~ an experience** pasar por una experiencia. **-3.** [because of] a causa de, por. **-4.** [by means of] gracias a, por medio de; **I got it ~ a friend** lo conseguí a través de un amigo. **-5.** Am [up to and including]: **Monday ~ Friday** de lunes a viernes. ◆ **through and through** adv de pies a cabeza.

throughout [θruː'aʊt] ◇ prep **-1.** [during] a lo largo de, durante todo (durante toda). ◇ adv **-1.** [all the time] todo el tiempo. **-2.** [everywhere] por todas partes.

throve [θrəʊv] pt → **thrive.**

throw [θrəʊ] (pt **threw,** pp **thrown**) ◇ vt **-1.** [gen] tirar; [ball, hammer, javelin] lanzar. **-2.** [subj: horse] derribar, desmontar. **-3.** fig [confuse] desconcertar. ◇ n lanzamiento m, tiro m. ◆ **throw away** vt sep [discard] tirar; fig [waste] desperdiciar. ◆ **throw out** vt sep **-1.** [discard] tirar. **-2.** [force to leave] echar. ◆ **throw up** vi inf [vomit] vomitar.

throwaway ['θrəʊə,weɪ] adj **-1.** [bottle, product] desechable. **-2.** [remark, gesture] hecho(cha) como quien no quiere la cosa.

throw-in n Br FTBL saque m de banda.

thrown [θrəʊn] pp → **throw.**

thru [θruː] Am inf = **through.**

thrush [θrʌʃ] n **-1.** [bird] tordo m. **-2.** MED [vaginal] hongos mpl (vaginales).

thrust [θrʌst] n **-1.** [of sword] estocada f; [of knife] cuchillada f; [of troops] arremetida f. **-2.** TECH (fuerza f de) propulsión f. **-3.** [main meaning] esencia f. ◇ vt [shove]: **he ~ the knife into his enemy** hundió el cuchillo en el cuerpo de su enemigo.

thud [θʌd] vi dar un golpe seco.

thug [θʌg] n matón m.

thumb [θʌm] ◇ n [of hand] pulgar m. ◇ vt inf [hitch]: **to ~ a lift** hacer dedo. ◆ **thumb through** vt fus hojear.

thumbs down [,θʌmz-] n: **to get OR be**

given the ~ [plan] ser rechazado(da); [play] ser recibido(da) con descontento.

thumbs up [,θʌmz-] n: **we got OR were given the ~** nos dieron luz verde OR el visto bueno.

thumbtack ['θʌmtæk] n Am chincheta f.

thump [θʌmp] ◇ n **-1.** [blow] puñetazo m. **-2.** [thud] golpe m seco. ◇ vt [punch] dar un puñetazo a. ◇ vi [heart, head] latir con fuerza.

thunder ['θʌndər] ◇ n (U) **-1.** METEOR truenos mpl. **-2.** fig [loud sound] estruendo m. ◇ v impers METEOR tronar. ◇ vi [make loud sound] retumbar.

thunderbolt ['θʌndəbəʊlt] n rayo m.

thunderclap ['θʌndəklæp] n trueno m.

thunderstorm ['θʌndəstɔːm] n tormenta f.

thundery ['θʌndərɪ] adj tormentoso(sa).

Thursday ['θɜːzdɪ] n jueves m inv; see also **Saturday.**

thus [ðʌs] adv fml **-1.** [therefore] por consiguiente, así que. **-2.** [in this way] así, de esta manera.

thwart [θwɔːt] vt frustrar.

thyme [taɪm] n tomillo m.

thyroid ['θaɪrɔɪd] n tiroides m inv.

tiara [tɪ'ɑːrə] n tiara f.

Tibet [tɪ'bet] n (el) Tibet.

tic [tɪk] n tic m.

tick [tɪk] ◇ n **-1.** [written mark] marca f OR señal f de visto bueno. **-2.** [sound] tictac m. ◇ vt marcar (con una señal). ◇ vi [make ticking sound] hacer tictac. ◆ **tick off** vt sep **-1.** [mark off] marcar (con una señal de visto bueno). **-2.** [tell off]: **to ~ sb off (for sthg)** echar una bronca a alguien (por algo). ◆ **tick over** vi funcionar al ralentí.

ticket ['tɪkɪt] n **-1.** [for bus, train etc] billete m, boleto m Amer; [for cinema, football match] entrada f. **-2.** [for traffic offence] multa f.

ticket collector n Br revisor m, -ra f.

ticket inspector n Br revisor m, -ra f.

ticket machine n máquina f automática para la venta de billetes.

ticket office n taquilla f, boletería f Amer.

tickle ['tɪkl] vt **-1.** [touch lightly] hacer cosquillas a. **-2.** fig [amuse] divertir.

ticklish ['tɪklɪʃ] adj [sensitive to touch]: **to be ~** tener cosquillas.

tidal ['taɪdl] adj de la marea.

tidal wave n maremoto m.

tidbit Am = **titbit.**

tiddlywinks ['tɪdlɪwɪŋks], **tiddledy-**

winks *Am* ['tɪdldɪwɪŋks] *n* juego *m* de la pulga.

tide [taɪd] *n* **-1.** [of sea] marea *f*. **-2.** *fig* [of protest, feeling] oleada *f*.

tidy ['taɪdɪ] ◇ *adj* **-1.** [room, desk etc] ordenado(da). **-2.** [person, dress, hair] arreglado(da). ◇ *vt* ordenar, arreglar.
◆ **tidy up** *vt sep* ordenar, arreglar.

tie [taɪ] (*pt* & *pp* **tied**, *cont* **tying**) ◇ *n* **-1.** [necktie] corbata *f*. **-2.** [string, cord] atadura *f*. **-3.** [bond, link] vínculo *m*, lazo *m*. **-4.** SPORT [draw] empate *m*. ◇ *vt* **-1.** [attach, fasten]: **to ~ sthg (to** OR **onto sthg)** atar algo (a algo); **to ~ sthg round/with sthg** atar algo a/con algo. **-2.** [do up - shoelaces] atar; [- knot] hacer. **-3.** *fig* [link]: **to be ~d to** estar ligado(da) a. ◇ *vi* [draw]: **to ~ (with)** empatar (con). ◆ **tie down** *vt sep fig* atar. ◆ **tie in with** *vt fus* concordar con. ◆ **tie up** *vt sep* **-1.** [gen] atar. **-2.** *fig* [money, resources] inmovilizar. **-3.** *fig* [link]: **to be ~d up with** estar ligado(da) a.

tiebreak(er) ['taɪbreɪk(ə')] *n* **-1.** TENNIS muerte *f* súbita, tiebreak *m*. **-2.** [in game, competition] *pregunta adicional para romper un empate*.

tiepin ['taɪpɪn] *n* alfiler *m* de corbata.

tier [tɪə'] *n* [of seats] hilera *f*; [of cake] piso *m*.

tiff [tɪf] *n* pelea *f* (*de poca importancia*).

tiger ['taɪgə'] *n* tigre *m*.

tight [taɪt] ◇ *adj* **-1.** [gen] apretado(da); [shoes] estrecho(cha). **-2.** [string, skin] tirante. **-3.** [budget] ajustado(da). **-4.** [rules, restrictions] riguroso(sa). **-5.** [corner, bend] cerrado(da). **-6.** [match, finish] reñido(da). **-7.** *inf* [drunk] cocido(da). **-8.** *inf* [miserly] agarrado(da). ◇ *adv* **-1.** [hold, squeeze] con fuerza; **to hold ~** agarrarse (fuerte); **to shut** OR **close sthg ~** cerrar algo bien. **-2.** [pull, stretch] de modo tirante. ◆ **tights** *npl* medias *fpl*.

tighten ['taɪtn] ◇ *vt* **-1.** [hold, grip]: **to ~ one's hold** OR **grip on sthg** coger con más fuerza algo. **-2.** [rope, chain] tensar. **-3.** [knot] apretar; [belt] apretarse. **-4.** [rules, system] intensificar. ◇ *vi* [rope, chain] tensarse.

tightfisted [,taɪt'fɪstɪd] *adj inf pej* agarrado(da).

tightly ['taɪtlɪ] *adv* **-1.** [hold, squeeze] con fuerza; [fasten] bien. **-2.** [pack] apretadamente.

tightrope ['taɪtrəʊp] *n* cuerda *f* floja.

tile [taɪl] *n* **-1.** [on roof] teja *f*. **-2.** [on floor] baldosa *f*; [on wall] azulejo *m*.

tiled [taɪld] *adj* [roof] tejado(da); [floor] embaldosado(da); [wall] alicatado(da).

till [tɪl] ◇ *prep* hasta; **~ now/then** hasta ahora/entonces. ◇ *conj* hasta que; **wait ~ he arrives** espera hasta que llegue. ◇ *n* caja *f* (registradora).

tiller ['tɪlə'] *n* NAUT caña *f* del timón.

tilt [tɪlt] ◇ *vt* inclinar. ◇ *vi* inclinarse.

timber ['tɪmbə'] *n* **-1.** (*U*) [wood] madera *f* (*para la construcción*). **-2.** [beam - of ship] cuaderna *f*; [- of house] viga *f*.

time [taɪm] ◇ *n* **-1.** [gen] tiempo *m*; **ahead of ~** temprano; **in good ~** con tiempo; **on ~** puntualmente; **to take ~** llevar tiempo; **it's (about) ~ to ...** ya es hora de ...; **to have no ~ for** no poder con, no aguantar; **to pass the ~** pasar el rato; **to play for ~** intentar ganar tiempo; **to take one's ~ (doing sthg)** tomarse uno mucho tiempo (para hacer algo). **-2.** [as measured by clock] hora *f*; **what ~ is it?, what's the ~?** ¿qué hora es?; **the ~ is three o'clock** son las tres; **in a week's/year's ~** dentro de una semana/un año. **-3.** [length of time] rato *m*; **it was a long ~ before he came** pasó mucho tiempo antes de que viniera; **for a ~** durante un tiempo. **-4.** [point in time in past, era] época *f*; **at that ~** en aquella época; **before my ~** antes de que yo naciera. **-5.** [occasion] vez *f*; **three ~s a week** tres veces a la semana; **from ~ to ~** de vez en cuando; **~ after ~, ~ and again** una y otra vez. **-6.** [experience]: **we had a good/bad ~** lo pasamos bien/mal. **-7.** MUS compás *m*. ◇ *vt* **-1.** [schedule] programar. **-2.** [race, runner] cronometrar. **-3.** [arrival, remark] elegir el momento oportuno para. ◆ **times** ◇ *n*: **four ~s as much as me** cuatro veces más que yo. ◇ *prep* MATH: **4 ~s 4** 4 por 5. ◆ **about time** *adv*: **it's about ~** ya va siendo hora. ◆ **at a time** *adv*: **for months at a ~** durante meses seguidos; **one at a ~** de uno en uno. ◆ **at times** *adv* a veces. ◆ **at the same time** *adv* al mismo tiempo. ◆ **for the time being** *adv* de momento. ◆ **in time** *adv* **-1.** [not late]: **in ~ (for)** a tiempo (para). **-2.** [eventually] con el tiempo.

time bomb *n* [bomb] bomba *f* de relojería; *fig* [dangerous situation] bomba *f*.

time lag *n* intervalo *m*.

timeless ['taɪmlɪs] *adj* eterno(na).

time limit *n* plazo *m*.

timely ['taɪmlɪ] *adj* oportuno(na).

time off *n* tiempo *m* libre.

time out n Am SPORT tiempo m muerto.

timer ['taɪmə'] n temporizador m.

time scale n tiempo m de ejecución.

time-share n Br copropiedad f.

time switch n interruptor m de reloj.

timetable ['taɪm,teɪbl] n -1. [of buses, trains, school] horario m. -2. [schedule of events] programa m.

time zone n huso m horario.

timid ['tɪmɪd] adj tímido(da).

timing ['taɪmɪŋ] n (U) -1. [judgment]: **she made her comment with perfect ~** su comentario fue hecho en el momento más oportuno. -2. [scheduling]: **the ~ of the election is crucial** es crucial que las elecciones se celebren en el momento oportuno. -3. [measuring] cronometraje m.

timpani ['tɪmpənɪ] npl timbales mpl.

tin [tɪn] n -1. [metal] estaño m; **~ plate** hojalata f. -2. Br [can, container] lata f.

tin can n lata f.

tinfoil ['tɪnfɔɪl] n (U) papel m de aluminio.

tinge [tɪndʒ] n -1. [of colour] matiz m. -2. [of feeling] ligera sensación f.

tinged [tɪndʒd] adj: **~ with** con un toque de.

tingle ['tɪŋgl] vi: **my feet are tingling** siento hormigueo en los pies.

tinker ['tɪŋkə'] ◇ n Br pej [gypsy] gitano m, -na f. ◇ vi hacer chapuzas; **to ~ with** enredar con.

tinkle ['tɪŋkl] vi [ring] tintinear.

tinned [tɪnd] adj Br enlatado(da), en conserva.

tin opener n Br abrelatas m inv.

tinsel ['tɪnsl] n (U) oropel m.

tint [tɪnt] n tinte m, matiz m.

tinted ['tɪntɪd] adj [glasses, windows] tintado(da), ahumado(da).

tiny ['taɪnɪ] adj diminuto(ta), pequeñito(ta).

tip [tɪp] ◇ n -1. [end] punta f. -2. Br [dump] vertedero m. -3. [gratuity] propina f. -4. [piece of advice] consejo m. ◇ vt -1. [tilt] inclinar, ladear. -2. [spill, pour] vaciar, verter. -3. [give a gratuity to] dar una propina a. ◇ vi -1. [tilt] inclinarse, ladearse. -2. [spill] derramarse. ◆ **tip over** ◇ vt sep volcar. ◇ vi volcarse.

tip-off n información f (confidencial).

tipped [tɪpt] adj [cigarette] con filtro.

tipsy ['tɪpsɪ] adj inf dated piripi.

tiptoe ['tɪptəʊ] n: **on ~** de puntillas.

tip-top adj inf dated de primera.

tire ['taɪə'] ◇ n Am = tyre. ◇ vt cansar. ◇ vi: **to ~ (of)** cansarse (de).

tired ['taɪəd] adj: **~ of sthg/of doing sthg** cansado(da) (de algo/de hacer algo).

tireless ['taɪəlɪs] adj incansable.

tiresome ['taɪəsəm] adj pesado(da).

tiring ['taɪərɪŋ] adj cansado(da).

tissue ['tɪʃuː] n -1. [paper handkerchief] pañuelo m de papel. -2. (U) BIOL tejido m. -3. [paper] papel m de seda.

tissue paper n (U) papel m de seda.

tit [tɪt] n -1. [bird] herrerillo m. -2. vulg [breast] teta f.

titbit Br ['tɪtbɪt], **tidbit** Am ['tɪdbɪt] n -1. [of food] golosina f. -2. fig [of news] noticia f breve e interesante.

tit for tat [-'tæt] n: **it's ~** donde las dan las toman.

titillate ['tɪtɪleɪt] vt & vi excitar.

title ['taɪtl] n título m.

title deed n título m de propiedad.

title role n papel m principal.

titter ['tɪtə'] vi reírse por lo bajo.

TM abbr of **trademark**.

to [unstressed before consonant tə, unstressed before vowel tʊ, stressed tuː] ◇ prep -1. [indicating place, direction] a; **to go ~ Liverpool/Spain/school** ir a Liverpool/España/la escuela; **to go ~ the doctor's/John's** ir al médico/a casa de John; **the road ~ Glasgow** la carretera de Glasgow; **the left/right** a la izquierda/derecha; **~ the east/west** hacia el este/oeste. -2. (to express indirect object) a; **to give sthg ~ sb** darle algo a alguien; **to talk ~ sb** hablar con alguien; **a threat ~ sb** una amenaza para alguien; **we were listening ~ the radio** escuchábamos la radio. -3. [as far as] hasta, a; **to count ~ ten** contar hasta diez; **we work from nine ~ five** trabajamos de nueve a cinco. -4. [in expressions of time]: **it's ten/a quarter ~ three** son las tres menos diez/cuarto. -5. [per] por; **40 miles ~ the gallon** un galón (por) cada 40 millas. -6. [of] de; [for] para; **the key ~ the car** la llave del coche; **a letter ~ my daughter** una carta OR a mi hija. -7. [indicating reaction, effect]: **~ my surprise** para sorpresa mía. -8. [in stating opinion]: **it seemed quite unnecessary ~ me/him** etc para mí/él etc aquello parecía del todo innecesario. -9. [indicating state, process]: **to drive sb ~ drink** llevar a alguien a la bebida; **to lead ~ trouble** traer problemas. ◇ adv [shut]: **push the**

door ~ cierra la puerta. ◇ *with infinitive* **-1.** (*forming simple infinitive*): ~ **walk** andar. **-2.** (*following another verb*): **to begin** ~ do sthg empezar a hacer algo; **to try/want** ~ **do sthg** intentar/querer hacer algo; **to hate** ~ do sthg odiar tener que hacer algo. **-3.** (*following an adjective*): **difficult** ~ do difícil de hacer; **ready** ~ go listos para marchar. **-4.** (*indicating purpose*) para; **I'm doing it** ~ **help you** lo hago para ayudarte; **he came** ~ **see me** vino a verme. **-5.** (*substituting for a relative clause*): **I have a lot** ~ do tengo mucho que hacer; **he told me** ~ **leave me** dijo que me fuera. **-6.** (*to avoid repetition of infinitive*): **I meant to call him but I forgot** ~ tenía intención de llamarle pero se me olvidó. **-7.** [in comments]: ~ **be honest** ... para ser honesto ...; ~ **sum up** ... para resumir ..., resumiendo .... ◆ **to and fro** *adv* de un lado para otro.

toad [təʊd] *n* sapo *m*.

toadstool ['təʊdstuːl] *n* seta *f* venenosa.

toast [təʊst] ◇ *n* **-1.** (U) [bread] pan *m* tostado; **a slice of** ~ una tostada. **-2.** [drink] brindis *m*. ◇ *vt* **-1.** [bread] tostar. **-2.** [person] brindar por.

toasted sandwich [,təʊstɪd-] *n* sándwich *m* tostado.

toaster ['təʊstər] *n* tostador *m*, -ra *f*.

tobacco [tə'bækəʊ] *n* tabaco *m*.

tobacconist [tə'bækənɪst] *n* estanquero *m*, -ra *f*; ~'s (shop) estanco *m*.

toboggan [tə'bɒgən] *n* tobogán *m*, trineo *m*.

today [tə'deɪ] ◇ *n* **-1.** [this day] hoy *m*. **-2.** [nowadays] hoy (en día). ◇ *adv* **-1.** [this day] hoy. **-2.** [nowadays] hoy (en día).

toddler ['tɒdlər] *n* niño pequeño *m*, niña pequeña *f* (que empieza a andar).

toddy ['tɒdɪ] *n* ponche *m*.

to-do (*pl* -s) *n inf dated* jaleo *m*.

toe [təʊ] ◇ *n* **-1.** [of foot] dedo *m* (del pie). **-2.** [of sock] punta *f*; [of shoe] puntera *f*. ◇ *vt*: **to** ~ **the line** acatar las normas.

toenail ['təʊneɪl] *n* uña *f* del dedo del pie.

toffee ['tɒfɪ] *n* caramelo *m*.

toga ['təʊgə] *n* toga *f*.

together [tə'geðər] *adv* **-1.** [gen] juntos(tas); **all** ~ todos juntos; **to stick** ~ pegar; **to go (well)** ~ combinar bien. **-2.** [at the same time] a la vez, juntos(tas). ◆ **together with** *prep* junto con.

toil [tɔɪl] *fml* ◇ *n* trabajo *m* duro. ◇ *vi* trabajar sin descanso.

toilet ['tɔɪlɪt] *n* [at home] wáter *m*, lavabo *m*; [in public place] servicios *mpl*, lavabo *m*; **to go to the** ~ ir al wáter.

toilet bag *n* neceser *m*.

toilet paper *n* (U) papel *m* higiénico.

toiletries ['tɔɪlɪtrɪz] *npl* artículos *mpl* de tocador.

toilet roll *n* [roll] rollo *m* de papel higiénico.

toilet water *n* (agua *f* de) colonia *f*.

token ['təʊkn] ◇ *adj* simbólico(ca). ◇ *n* **-1.** [voucher] vale *m*; [disk] ficha *f*. **-2.** [symbol] muestra *f*, símbolo *m*. ◆ **by the same token** *adv* del mismo modo.

told [təʊld] *pt* & *pp* → **tell**.

tolerable ['tɒlərəbl] *adj* tolerable, pasable.

tolerance ['tɒlərəns] *n* tolerancia *f*.

tolerant ['tɒlərənt] *adj* tolerante.

tolerate ['tɒləreɪt] *vt* **-1.** [put up with] soportar, tolerar. **-2.** [permit] tolerar.

toll [təʊl] ◇ *n* **-1.** [number] **death** ~ número *m* de víctimas. **-2.** [fee] peaje *m*. **-3.** *phr*: **to take its** ~ hacer mella. ◇ *vi* tocar, doblar.

toll-free *Am adv*: **to call a number** ~ llamar a un número gratis.

tomato [*Br* tə'mɑːtəʊ, *Am* tə'meɪtəʊ] (*pl* -es) *n* tomate *m*.

tomb [tuːm] *n* tumba *f*, sepulcro *m*.

tomboy ['tɒmbɔɪ] *n* niña *f* poco feminina.

tombstone ['tuːmstəʊn] *n* lápida *f*.

tomcat ['tɒmkæt] *n* gato *m* (macho).

tomorrow [tə'mɒrəʊ] ◇ *n lit* & *fig* mañana; **the day after** ~ pasado mañana; ~ **night** mañana por la noche. ◇ *adv* mañana.

ton [tʌn] (*pl inv* OR -s) *n* **-1.** [imperial] *Br* = 1016 kg, *Am* = 907,2 kg, ≃ tonelada *f*. **-2.** [metric] = 100 kg, tonelada *f*. ◆ **tons** *npl inf*: ~s (of) un montón (de).

tone [təʊn] *n* **-1.** [gen] tono *m*. **-2.** [on phone] señal *f*. ◆ **tone down** *vt sep* suavizar, moderar. ◆ **tone up** *vt sep* poner en forma.

tone-deaf *adj* que no tiene (buen) oído.

tongs [tɒŋz] *npl* [for coal] tenazas *fpl*; [for sugar] pinzas *fpl*, tenacillas *fpl*.

tongue [tʌŋ] *n* **-1.** [gen] lengua *f*; **to hold one's** ~ *fig* quedarse callado(da). **-2.** [of shoe] lengüeta *f*.

tongue-in-cheek *adj*: **it was only** ~ no iba en serio.

total

tongue-tied [-,taɪd] *adj* incapaz de hablar (*por timidez o nervios*).

tongue twister [-,twɪstər] *n* trabalenguas *m inv*.

tonic ['tɒnɪk] *n* **-1.** [gen] tónico *m*. **-2.** [tonic water] tónica *f*.

tonic water *n* agua *f* tónica.

tonight [tə'naɪt] ◇ *n* esta noche *f*. ◇ *adv* esta noche.

tonnage ['tʌnɪdʒ] *n* tonelaje *m*.

tonne [tʌn] (*pl inv* OR **-s**) *n* tonelada *f* métrica.

tonsil ['tɒnsl] *n* amígdala *f*.

tonsil(l)itis [,tɒnsɪ'laɪtɪs] *n* (U) amigdalitis *f inv*.

too [tuː] *adv* **-1.** [also] también. **-2.** [excessively] demasiado; ~ **much** demasiado; ~ **many things** demasiadas cosas; **it finished all** OR **only ~ soon** terminó demasiado pronto; **I'd be only ~ happy to help** me encantaría ayudarte; **not ~ ...** no muy ....

took [tʊk] *pt* → **take**.

tool [tuːl] *n* [implement] herramienta *f*; **garden ~s** útiles *mpl* del jardín.

tool box *n* caja *f* de herramientas.

tool kit *n* juego *m* de herramientas.

toot [tuːt] ◇ *n* bocinazo *m*. ◇ *vi* tocar la bocina.

tooth [tuːθ] (*pl* **teeth**) *n* [in mouth, of saw, gear wheel] diente *m*.

toothache ['tuːθeɪk] *n* dolor *m* de muelas.

toothbrush ['tuːθbrʌʃ] *n* cepillo *m* de dientes.

toothpaste ['tuːθpeɪst] *n* pasta *f* de dientes.

toothpick ['tuːθpɪk] *n* palillo *m*.

top [tɒp] ◇ *adj* **-1.** [highest - step, floor] de arriba; [- object on pile] de encima. **-2.** [most important, successful] importante; **she got the ~ mark** sacó la mejor nota. **-3.** [maximum] máximo(ma). ◇ *n* **-1.** [highest point] parte *f* superior OR de arriba; [of list] cabeza *f*, principio *m*; [of tree] copa *f*; [of hill, mountain] cumbre *f*, cima *f*; on ~ encima; **at the ~ of one's voice** a voz en grito. **-2.** [lid, cap - of jar, box] tapa *f*; [- of bottle, tube] tapón *m*; [- of pen] capuchón *m*. **-3.** [upper side] superficie *f*. **-4.** [blouse] blusa *f*; [T-shirt] camiseta *f*; [of pyjamas] parte *f* de arriba. **-5.** [toy] peonza *f*. **-6.** [most important level] cúpula *f*. **-7.** [of league, table, scale] cabeza *f*. ◇ *vt* **-1.** [be first in] estar a la cabeza de. **-2.** [better] superar. **-3.** [exceed] exceder. ◆ **on top of** *prep* **-1.** [in space] encima de. **-2.** [in

addition to] además de. ◆ **top up** *Br*, **top off** *Am vt sep* volver a llenar.

top floor *n* último piso *m*.

top hat *n* sombrero *m* de copa.

top-heavy *adj* demasiado pesado(da) en la parte de arriba.

topic ['tɒpɪk] *n* tema *m*, asunto *m*.

topical ['tɒpɪkl] *adj* actual.

topless ['tɒplɪs] *adj* topless (*inv*).

top-level *adj* de alto nivel.

topmost ['tɒpməʊst] *adj* más alto(ta).

topping ['tɒpɪŋ] *n* capa *f*; **with a ~ of cream** cubierto de nata.

topple ['tɒpl] ◇ *vt* [government, pile] derribar; [president] derrocar. ◇ *vi* venirse abajo.

top-secret *adj* sumamente secreto (sumamente secreta).

topspin ['tɒpspɪn] *n* TENNIS liftado *m*.

topsy-turvy [,tɒpsɪ'tɜːvɪ] ◇ *adj* [messy] patas arriba (*inv*). ◇ *adv* [messily] en desorden, de cualquier manera.

torch [tɔːtʃ] *n* **-1.** *Br* [electric] linterna *f*. **-2.** [burning] antorcha *f*.

tore [tɔːr] *pt* → **tear²**.

torment [*n* 'tɔːment, *vb* tɔː'ment] ◇ *n* tormento *m*. ◇ *vt* **-1.** [worry greatly] atormentar. **-2.** [annoy] fastidiar.

torn [tɔːn] *pp* → **tear²**.

tornado [tɔː'neɪdəʊ] (*pl* **-es** OR **-s**) *n* tornado *m*.

torpedo [tɔː'piːdəʊ] (*pl* **-es**) *n* torpedo *m*.

torrent ['tɒrənt] *n* torrente *m*.

torrid ['tɒrɪd] *adj* [hot] tórrido(da); *fig* [passionate] apasionado(da).

tortoise ['tɔːtəs] *n* tortuga *f* (de tierra).

tortoiseshell ['tɔːtəʃel] ◇ *adj*: ~ **cat** gato *m* pardo atigrado. ◇ *n* (U) [material] carey *m*, concha *f*.

torture ['tɔːtʃər] ◇ *n* tortura *f*. ◇ *vt* torturar.

Tory ['tɔːrɪ] ◇ *adj* tory, del partido conservador (británico). ◇ *n* tory *m y f*, miembro *m* del partido conservador (británico).

toss [tɒs] ◇ *vt* **-1.** [throw carelessly] tirar. **-2.** [move from side to side - head, boat] sacudir. **-3.** [salad] remover; [pancake] dar la vuelta en el aire. **-4.** [coin]: **to ~ a coin** echar a cara o cruz. ◇ *vi* [move rapidly]: **to ~ and turn** dar vueltas (en la cama). ◆ **toss up** *vi* jugar a cara o cruz.

tot [tɒt] *n* **-1.** *inf* [small child] nene *m*, nena *f*. **-2.** [of drink] trago *m*.

total ['təʊtl] ◇ *adj* total. ◇ *n* total *m*. ◇

vt [add up] **sumar.** ◇ *vi* [amount to] **ascender a.**

totalitarian [,təʊtælɪ'teərɪən] *adj* totalitario(ria).

totally ['təʊtəlɪ] *adv* [entirely] **totalmente.**

totter ['tɒtər] *vi lit* & *fig* **tambalearse.**

touch [tʌtʃ] ◇ *n* **-1.** [sense, act of feeling] **tacto** *m*. **-2.** [detail, skill, knack] **toque** *m*. **-3.** [contact]: **to get/keep in ~ (with)** ponerse/mantenerse en contacto (con); **to lose ~ (with)** perder el contacto (con); **to be out of ~ with** no estar al tanto de. **-4.** SPORT: **in ~** fuera de banda. **-5.** [small amount]: **a ~** un poquito. ◇ *vt* **-1.** [gen] **tocar. -2.** [emotionally] **conmover.** ◇ *vi* [be in contact] **tocarse.** ◆ **touch down** *vi* [plane] **aterrizar.** ◆ **touch on** *vt fus* **tratar por encima.**

touch-and-go *adj* **dudoso(sa), poco seguro (poco segura).**

touchdown ['tʌtʃdaʊn] *n* **-1.** [of plane] **aterrizaje** *m*. **-2.** [in American football] **ensayo** *m*.

touched [tʌtʃt] *adj* [grateful] **emocionado(da).**

touching ['tʌtʃɪŋ] *adj* **conmovedor(ra).**

touchline ['tʌtʃlaɪn] *n* **línea** *f* **de banda.**

touchy ['tʌtʃɪ] *adj* **-1.** [person]: **~ (about)** **susceptible (con). -2.** [subject, question] **delicado(da).**

tough [tʌf] *adj* **-1.** [resilient] **fuerte. -2.** [hard-wearing] **resistente. -3.** [meat, regulations, policies] **duro(ra). -4.** [difficult to deal with] **difícil. -5.** [rough - area] **peligroso(sa).**

toughen ['tʌfn] *vt* **endurecer.**

toupee ['tu:peɪ] *n* **peluquín** *m*.

tour [tʊər] ◇ *n* **-1.** [long journey] **viaje** *m* **largo. -2.** [of pop group etc] **gira** *f*. **-3.** [for sightseeing] **recorrido** *m*, **visita** *f*. ◇ *vt* [museum] **visitar**; [country] **recorrer, viajar por.** ◇ *vi* **estar de gira.**

touring ['tʊərɪŋ] *n* **viajes** *mpl* **turísticos.**

tourism ['tʊərɪzm] *n* **turismo** *m*.

tourist ['tʊərɪst] *n* **turista** *m y f*.

tourist (information) office *n* **oficina** *f* **de turismo.**

tournament ['tɔ:nəmənt] *n* **torneo** *m*.

tour operator *n* **touroperador** *m*.

tousle ['taʊzl] *vt* **despeinar, alborotar.**

tout [taʊt] ◇ *n* **revendedor** *m*, **-ra** *f*. ◇ *vt* **revender.** ◇ *vi*: **to ~ for sthg** **solicitar algo.**

tow [təʊ] ◇ *n*: **on ~** *Br* [car] **a remolque.** ◇ *vt* **remolcar.**

towards *Br* [tə'wɔ:dz], **toward** *Am* [tə'wɔ:d] *prep* **-1.** [gen] **hacia. -2.** [for the purpose or benefit of] **para.**

towel ['taʊəl] *n* **toalla** *f*.

towelling *Br*, **toweling** *Am* ['taʊəlɪŋ] *n* (U) (tejido *m* de) **toalla** *f*.

towel rail *n* **toallero** *m*.

tower ['taʊər] ◇ *n* **torre** *f*. ◇ *vi*: **to ~ (over sthg)** **elevarse (por encima de algo).**

tower block *n Br* **bloque** *m* (*de pisos u oficinas*).

towering ['taʊərɪŋ] *adj* **altísimo(ma).**

town [taʊn] *n* **-1.** [gen] **ciudad** *f*; [smaller] **pueblo** *m*. **-2.** [centre of town, city] **centro** *m* **de la ciudad; to go out on the ~** **irse de juerga; to go to ~** *fig* [to put in a lot of effort] **emplearse a fondo**; [spend a lot of money] **tirar la casa por la ventana.**

town centre *n* **centro** *m* **(de la ciudad).**

town council *n* **ayuntamiento** *m*.

town hall *n* **ayuntamiento** *m*.

town plan *n* **plano** *m* **de la ciudad.**

town planning *n* [study] **urbanismo** *m*.

township ['taʊnʃɪp] *n* **-1.** [in South Africa] **zona urbana asignada por el gobierno para la población negra. -2.** [in US] ≈ **municipio** *m*.

towpath ['təʊpɑ:θ, *pl* -pɑ:ðz] *n* **camino** *m* **de sirga.**

towrope ['təʊrəʊp] *n* **cable** *m* **de remolque.**

tow truck *n Am* **(coche** *m*) **grúa** *f*.

toxic ['tɒksɪk] *adj* **tóxico(ca).**

toy [tɔɪ] *n* **juguete** *m*. ◆ **toy with** *vt fus* [idea] **acariciar**; [food, coin etc] **jugetear con.**

toy shop *n* **juguetería** *f*.

trace [treɪs] ◇ *n* **-1.** [evidence, remains] **rastro** *m*, **huella** *f*. **-2.** [small amount] **pizca** *f*. ◇ *vt* **-1.** [find] **localizar, encontrar. -2.** [follow progress of] **describir. -3.** [on paper] **calcar.**

tracing paper ['treɪsɪŋ-] *n* (U) **papel** *m* **de calcar.**

track [træk] ◇ *n* **-1.** [path] **sendero** *m*. **-2.** SPORT **pista** *f*. **-3.** RAIL **vía** *f*. **-4.** [mark, trace] **rastro** *m*, **huella** *f*. **-5.** [on record, tape] **canción** *f*. **-6.** *phr*: **to keep/lose ~ of sb** **no perder/perder la pista a alguien; to be on the right/wrong ~** **ir por el buen/mal camino.** ◇ *vt* [follow tracks of] **seguir la pista de.** ◆ **track down** *vt sep* **localizar.**

track record *n* **historial** *m*.

tracksuit ['træksu:t] *n* **chandal** *m*.

tract [trækt] *n* **-1.** [pamphlet] artículo *m* breve. **-2.** [of land, forest] extensión *f*.

traction ['trækʃn] *n* tracción *f*; **to have one's leg in ~** tener la pierna escayolada en alto.

tractor ['træktər] *n* tractor *m*.

trade [treɪd] ◇ *n* **-1.** (*U*) [commerce] comercio *m*. **-2.** [job] oficio *m*; **by ~ de** oficio. ◇ *vt* [exchange]: **to ~ sthg (for)** cambiar algo (por). ◇ *vi* COMM: **to ~ (with)** comerciar (con). ◆ **trade in** *vt sep* [exchange] dar como entrada.

trade fair *n* feria *f* de muestras.

trade-in *n* artículo usado que se entrega como entrada al comprar un artículo nuevo.

trademark ['treɪdmɑːk] *n* COMM marca *f* comercial.

trade name *n* COMM nombre *m* comercial.

trader ['treɪdər] *n* comerciante *m y f*.

tradesman ['treɪdzmən] (*pl* **-men** [-mən]) *n* [trader] comerciante *m*; [shopkeeper] tendero *m*.

trade(s) union *n Br* sindicato *m*.

Trades Union Congress *n Br*: **the ~** *la asociación británica de sindicatos*.

trade(s) unionist *n Br* sindicalista *m y f*.

trading ['treɪdɪŋ] *n* (*U*) comercio *m*.

trading estate *n Br* polígono *m* industrial.

tradition [trə'dɪʃn] *n* tradición *f*.

traditional [trə'dɪʃənl] *adj* tradicional.

traffic ['træfɪk] (*pt & pp* **-ked**, *cont* **-king**) ◇ *n* **-1.** [vehicles] tráfico *m*. **-2.** [illegal trade]: **~ (in)** tráfico *m* (de). ◇ *vi*: **to ~ in** traficar con.

traffic circle *n Am* glorieta *f*.

traffic jam *n* embotellamiento *m*.

trafficker ['træfɪkər] *n*: **~ (in)** traficante *m y f* (de).

traffic lights *npl* semáforos *mpl*.

traffic warden *n Br* ≃ guardia *m y f* de tráfico.

tragedy ['trædʒədɪ] *n* tragedia *f*.

tragic ['trædʒɪk] *adj* trágico(ca).

trail [treɪl] ◇ *n* **-1.** [path] sendero *m*, camino *m*. **-2.** [trace, track] rastro *m*, huellas *fpl*. ◇ *vt* **-1.** [drag] arrastrar. **-2.** [lose to] ir por detrás de. ◇ *vi* **-1.** [drag] arrastrarse. **-2.** [move slowly] andar con desgana. **-3.** [lose] ir perdiendo. ◆ **trail away**, **trail off** *vi* apagarse.

trailer ['treɪlər] *n* **-1.** [vehicle for luggage] remolque *m*. **-2.** [for living in] roulotte *m*, caravana *f*. **-3.** CINEMA trailer *m*.

train [treɪn] ◇ *n* **-1.** RAIL tren *m*. **-2.** [of dress] cola *f*. ◇ *vt* **-1.** [teach]: **to ~ sb (to**

do sthg) enseñar a alguien (a hacer algo); **to ~ sb in sthg** preparar a alguien para algo. **-2.** [for job]: **to ~ sb (as sthg)** formar a alguien (como algo). **-3.** SPORT: **to ~ sb (for)** entrenar a alguien (para). **-4.** [aim - gun] apuntar. ◇ *vi* **-1.** [for job] estudiar; **to ~ as** formarse OR prepararse como. **-2.** SPORT: **to ~ (for)** entrenarse (para).

trained [treɪnd] *adj* cualificado(da).

trainee [treɪ'niː] *n* aprendiz *m*, -za *f*.

trainer ['treɪnər] *n* **-1.** [of animals] amaestrador *m*, -ra *f*. **-2.** SPORT entrenador *m*, -ra *f*. ◆ **trainers** *npl Br* zapatillas *fpl* de deporte.

training ['treɪnɪŋ] *n* (*U*) **-1.** [for job]: **~ (in)** formación *f* OR preparación *f* (para). **-2.** SPORT entrenamiento *m*.

training college *n Br* [gen] centro *m* de formación especializada; [for teachers] escuela *f* normal.

training shoes *npl Br* zapatillas *fpl* de deporte.

train of thought *n* hilo *m* del razonamiento.

traipse [treɪps] *vi* andar con desgana.

trait [treɪt] *n* rasgo *m*, característica *f*.

traitor ['treɪtər] *n*: **~ (to)** traidor *m*, -ra *f* (a).

trajectory [trə'dʒektərɪ] *n* trayectoria *f*.

tram [træm], **tramcar** ['træmkɑːr] *n Br* tranvía *m*.

tramp [træmp] ◇ *n* **-1.** [homeless person] vagabundo *m*, -da *f*. **-2.** *Am inf* [woman] fulana *f*. ◇ *vi* andar pesadamente.

trample ['træmpl] *vt* pisar, pisotear.

trampoline ['træmpəliːn] *n* cama *f* elástica.

trance [trɑːns] *n* trance *m*.

tranquil ['træŋkwɪl] *adj literary* tranquilo(la), apacible.

tranquillizer *Br*, **tranquilizer** *Am* ['træŋkwɪlaɪzər] *n* tranquilizante *m*.

transaction [træn'zækʃn] *n* transacción *f*.

transcend [træn'send] *vt fml* ir más allá de.

transcript ['trænskrɪpt] *n* transcripción *f*.

transfer [*n* 'trænsfɜːr, *vb* træns'fɜːr] ◇ *n* **-1.** [gen] transferencia *f*. **-2.** [for job] traslado *m*. **-3.** SPORT traspaso *m*. **-4.** [design] calcomanía *f*. ◇ *vt* **-1.** [from one place to another] trasladar. **-2.** [from one person to another] **transferir.** ◇ *vi* [to different job etc]: **he transferred to a different department** lo trasladaron a otro departamento.

transfix [træns'fɪks] vt [immobilize] paralizar.

transform [træns'fɔ:m] vt: **to ~ sthg/sb (into)** transformar algo/a alguien (en).

transfusion [træns'fju:ʒn] n transfusión f.

transient ['trænzɪənt] adj fml [fleeting] transitorio(ria), pasajero(ra).

transistor [træn'zɪstər] n transistor m.

transistor radio n dated transistor m.

transit ['trænsɪt] n: **in ~** de tránsito.

transition [træn'zɪʃn] n: **~ (from sthg to sthg)** transición f (de algo a algo).

transitive ['trænzɪtɪv] adj GRAMM transitivo(va).

transitory ['trænzɪtrɪ] adj transitorio(ria).

translate [træns'leɪt] vt [languages] traducir.

translation [træns'leɪʃn] n traducción f.

translator [træns'leɪtər] n traductor m, -ra f.

transmission [trænz'mɪʃn] n transmisión f.

transmit [trænz'mɪt] vt transmitir.

transmitter [trænz'mɪtər] n ELECTRON transmisor m.

transparency [trans'pærənsɪ] n transparencia f.

transparent [træns'pærənt] adj **-1.** [see-through] transparente. **-2.** [obvious] claro(ra).

transpire [træn'spaɪər] fml ◇ vt: **it ~s that ...** resulta que .... ◇ vi [happen] ocurrir.

transplant ['trænsplɑ:nt] n trasplante m.

transport [n 'trænspɔ:t, vb træn'spɔ:t] ◇ n transporte m. ◇ vt transportar.

transportation [,trænspɔ:'teɪʃn] n transporte m.

transport cafe ['trænspɔ:t-] n Br bar m de camioneros.

transpose [træns'pəʊz] vt [change round] invertir.

trap [træp] ◇ n trampa f. ◇ vt **-1.** [catch - animals, birds] coger con trampa. **-2.** [trick] atrapar, engañar.

trapdoor [,træp'dɔ:r] n [gen] trampilla f, trampa; THEATRE escotillón m.

trapeze [trə'pi:z] n trapecio m.

trappings ['træpɪŋz] npl atributos mpl.

trash [træʃ] n Am lit & fig basura f.

trashcan ['træʃkæn] n Am cubo m de la basura.

traumatic [trɔ:'mætɪk] adj traumático(ca).

travel ['trævl] ◇ n (U) viajes mpl. ◇ vt [place] viajar por; [distance] recorrer. ◇ vi viajar.

travel agency n agencia f de viajes.

travel agent n empleado m, -da f de una agencia de viajes; **~'s** agencia f de viajes.

traveller Br, **traveler** Am ['trævlər] n [person on journey] viajero m, -ra f.

traveller's cheque n cheque m de viajero.

travelling Br, **traveling** Am ['trævlɪŋ] adj [theatre, showman] ambulante.

travelsick ['trævəlsɪk] adj que se marea al viajar.

travesty ['trævəstɪ] n burda parodia f.

trawler ['trɔ:lər] n trainera f.

tray [treɪ] n bandeja f.

treacherous ['tretʃərəs] adj **-1.** [plan, action] traicionero(ra); [person] traidor(ra). **-2.** [dangerous] peligroso(sa).

treachery ['tretʃərɪ] n traición f.

treacle ['tri:kl] n Br melaza f.

tread [tred] (pt trod, pp trodden) ◇ n **-1.** [on tyre, shoe] banda f. **-2.** [sound of walking] pasos mpl; [way of walking] modo m de andar. ◇ vi **-1.** [step]: **to ~ on sthg** pisar algo. **-2.** [walk] andar.

treason ['tri:zn] n traición f.

treasure ['treʒər] ◇ n lit & fig tesoro m. ◇ vt guardar como oro en paño.

treasurer ['treʒərər] n tesorero m, -ra f.

treasury ['treʒərɪ] n [room] habitación donde se guarda el tesoro de un castillo, de una catedral etc. ◆ **Treasury** n: **the Treasury** ≃ el Ministerio de Hacienda.

treat [tri:t] ◇ vt **-1.** [gen] tratar; **to ~ sb as/like** tratar a alguien como. **-2.** [give sthg special]: **to ~ sb (to)** invitar a alguien (a). ◇ n [something special] regalo m; **he took me out to dinner as a ~** me invitó a cenar.

treatise ['tri:tɪs] n fml: **~ (on)** tratado m (sobre).

treatment ['tri:tmənt] n **-1.** MED tratamiento m. **-2.** [manner of dealing] trato m.

treaty ['tri:tɪ] n tratado m.

treble ['trebl] ◇ adj **-1.** MUS de tiple. **-2.** [with numbers] triple. ◇ n MUS [range, singer] tiple m. ◇ vt triplicar. ◇ vi triplicarse.

treble clef n clave f de sol.

tree [tri:] n BOT & COMPUT árbol m.

treetop ['tri:top] n copa f (de árbol).

tree-trunk n tronco m (de árbol).

trek [trek] n viaje m largo y difícil.

trellis ['trelɪs] n enrejado m, espaldera f.

tremble ['trembl] *vi* temblar.

tremendous [trɪ'mendəs] *adj* **-1.** [impressive, large] enorme, tremendo(da). **-2.** *inf* [really good] estupendo(da).

tremor ['tremər] *n* **-1.** [of person, body, voice] estremecimiento *m*. **-2.** [small earthquake] temblor *m*.

trench [trentʃ] *n* **-1.** [narrow channel] zanja *f*. **-2.** MIL trinchera *f*.

trench coat *n* trinchera *f*.

trend [trend] *n* [tendency] tendencia *f*; [fashion] moda *f*.

trendy ['trendɪ] *inf adj* [person] moderno(na); [clothes] de moda.

trepidation [,trepɪ'deɪʃn] *n fml*: **in** OR **with ~** con ansiedad OR agitación.

trespass ['trespəs] *vi* entrar ilegalmente; "no ~ing" "prohibido el paso".

trespasser ['trespəsər] *n* intruso *m*, -sa *f*.

trestle ['tresl] *n* caballete *m*.

trestle table *n* mesa *f* de caballete.

trial ['traɪəl] *n* **-1.** JUR juicio *m*, proceso *m*; **to be on ~ (for)** ser procesado(da) (por). **-2.** [test, experiment] prueba *f*; **on ~ de prueba; by ~ and error** a base de probar. **-3.** [unpleasant experience] suplicio *m*, fastidio *m*.

triangle ['traɪæŋgl] *n* GEOM & MUS triángulo *m*.

tribe [traɪb] *n* tribu *f*.

tribunal [traɪ'bjuːnl] *n* tribunal *m*.

tributary ['trɪbjutrɪ] *n* afluente *m*.

tribute ['trɪbjuːt] *n* **-1.** [credit] tributo *m*; **to be a ~ to** hacer honor a. **-2.** (U) [respect, admiration]: **to pay ~ (to)** rendir homenaje (a).

trice [traɪs] *n*: **in a ~** en un dos por tres.

trick [trɪk] ◇ *n* **-1.** [to deceive] truco *m*; [to trap] trampa *f*; [joke] broma *f*; **to play a ~ on sb** gastarle una broma a alguien. **-2.** [in magic] juego *m* (de manos). **-3.** [knack] truco *m*; **that should do the ~** eso es lo que necesitamos. ◇ *vt* engañar; **to ~ sb into doing sthg** engañar a alguien para que haga algo.

trickery ['trɪkərɪ] *n* (U) engaño *m*.

trickle ['trɪkl] ◇ *n* [of liquid] hilo *m*. ◇ *vi* **-1.** [liquid] resbalar (*formando un hilo*). **-2.** [people, things]: **to ~ in/out** llegar/salir poco a poco.

tricky ['trɪkɪ] *adj* [difficult] difícil.

tricycle ['traɪsɪkl] *n* triciclo *m*.

tried [traɪd] *adj*: **~ and tested** probado(da).

trifle ['traɪfl] *n* **-1.** *Br* CULIN postre *m* de bizcocho con gelatina, crema, frutas y nata. **-2.** [unimportant thing] nadería *f*. ◆ **a trifle** *adv fml* un poco, ligeramente.

trifling ['traɪflɪŋ] *adj pej* trivial.

trigger ['trɪgər] *n* [on gun] gatillo *m*. ◆ **trigger off** *vt sep* desencadenar.

trill [trɪl] *n* trino *m*.

trim [trɪm] ◇ *adj* **-1.** [neat and tidy] limpio y arreglado (limpia y arreglada). **-2.** [slim] esbelto(ta). ◇ *n* [of hair] recorte *m*. ◇ *vt* **-1.** [nails, moustache] recortar. **-2.** [decorate]: **to ~ sthg (with)** adornar algo (con).

trimmings ['trɪmɪŋz] *npl* **-1.** [on clothing] adornos *mpl*. **-2.** [with food] guarnición *f*.

trinket ['trɪŋkɪt] *n* baratija *f*.

trio ['triːəʊ] (*pl* **-s**) *n* trío *m*.

trip [trɪp] ◇ *n* [gen & *drugs sl*] viaje *m*. ◇ *vt* [make stumble] hacer la zancadilla a. ◇ *vi* [stumble] tropezar; **to ~ over sthg** tropezar con algo. ◆ **trip up** *vt sep* [make stumble] hacer tropezar, hacer la zancadilla a.

tripe [traɪp] *n* (U) **-1.** CULIN callos *mpl*. **-2.** *inf* [nonsense] tonterías *fpl*.

triple ['trɪpl] ◇ *adj* triple. ◇ *vt* triplicar. ◇ *vi* triplicarse.

triple jump *n*: **the ~** el triple salto.

triplets ['trɪplɪts] *npl* trillizos *mpl*, -zas *fpl*.

triplicate ['trɪplɪkət] *n*: **in ~** por triplicado.

tripod ['traɪpɒd] *n* trípode *m*.

trite [traɪt] *adj pej* trillado(da).

triumph ['traɪəmf] ◇ *n* triunfo *m*. ◇ *vi*: **to ~ (over)** triunfar (sobre).

trivia ['trɪvɪə] *n* (U) trivialidades *fpl*.

trivial ['trɪvɪəl] *adj pej* trivial.

trod [trɒd] *pt* → **tread**.

trodden ['trɒdn] *pp* → **tread**.

trolley ['trɒlɪ] (*pl* **trolleys**) *n* **-1.** *Br* [for shopping, food, drinks] carrito *m*. **-2.** *Am* [train] tranvía *m*.

trombone [trɒm'bəʊn] *n* trombón *m*.

troop [truːp] ◇ *n* [of people] grupo *m*, bandada *f*; [of animals] manada *f*. ◇ *vi* ir en grupo. ◆ **troops** *npl* tropas *fpl*.

trooper ['truːpər] *n* **-1.** MIL soldado *m* de caballería. **-2.** *Am* [policeman] miembro *m* de la policía estatal.

trophy ['trəʊfɪ] *n* SPORT trofeo *m*.

tropical ['trɒpɪkl] *adj* tropical.

tropics ['trɒpɪks] *npl*: **the ~** el trópico.

trot [trɒt] ◇ *n* **-1.** [of horse] trote *m*. **-2.** [of person] paso *m* rápido. ◇ *vi* **-1.** [horse] trotar. **-2.** [person] andar con pasos rápidos. ◆ **on the trot** *adv inf*:

three times on the ~ tres veces seguidas.

trouble ['trʌbl] ◇ n (U) **-1.** [bother] molestia f; [difficulty, main problem] problema m; **would it be too much ~ to ask you to ...?** ¿tendría inconveniente en ...?; **to be in ~** tener problemas; **to take the ~ to do sthg** tomarse la molestia de hacer algo. **-2.** (U) [pain] dolor m; [illness] enfermedad f. **-3.** (U) [violence, unpleasantness] problemas mpl. ◇ vt **-1.** [worry, upset] preocupar. **-2.** [disturb, give pain to] molestar. ◆ **troubles** npl **-1.** [problems, worries] problemas mpl. **-2.** POL conflicto m.

troubled ['trʌbld] adj **-1.** [worried, upset] preocupado(da). **-2.** [disturbed, problematic] agitado(da), turbulento(ta).

troublemaker ['trʌbl,meɪkə'] n alborotador m, -ra f.

troubleshooter ['trʌbl,ʃuːtə'] n [for machines] especialista en la localización y reparación de averías; [in organizations] persona contratada para resolver problemas.

troublesome ['trʌblsəm] adj molesto(ta).

trough [trɒf] n **-1.** [for drinking] abrevadero m; [for eating] comedero m. **-2.** [low point] punto m más bajo.

troupe [truːp] n compañía f.

trousers ['traʊzəz] npl pantalones mpl.

trousseau ['truːsəʊ] (pl **-x** [-z] OR **-s**) n ajuar m.

trout [traʊt] (pl inv OR **-s**) n trucha f.

trowel ['traʊəl] n **-1.** [for the garden] desplantador m. **-2.** [for cement, plaster] paleta f, palustre m.

truant ['truːənt] n [child] alumno m, -na f que hace novillos; **to play ~** hacer novillos.

truce [truːs] n: ~ **(between)** tregua f (entre).

truck [trʌk] n **-1.** [lorry] camión m. **-2.** RAIL vagón m de mercancías.

truck driver n camionero m, -ra f.

trucker ['trʌkə'] n Am camionero m, -ra f.

truck farm n Am puesto de verduras y frutas para la venta.

truculent ['trʌkjʊlənt] adj agresivo(va), pendenciero(ra).

trudge [trʌdʒ] vi caminar con dificultad.

true [truː] adj **-1.** [gen] verdadero(ra); **it's ~** es verdad; **to come ~** hacerse realidad. **-2.** [genuine] auténtico(ca); [friend] de verdad. **-3.** [exact] exacto(ta).

truffle ['trʌfl] n trufa f.

truly ['truːlɪ] adv verdaderamente; **yours ~** le saluda atentamente.

trump [trʌmp] n triunfo m (en cartas).

trumped-up ['trʌmpt-] adj pej inventado(da).

trumpet ['trʌmpɪt] n trompeta f.

truncheon ['trʌntʃən] n porra f.

trundle ['trʌndl] vi rodar lentamente.

trunk [trʌŋk] n **-1.** [of tree, person] tronco m. **-2.** [of elephant] trompa f. **-3.** [box] baúl m. **-4.** Am [of car] maletero m, cajuela f Amer. ◆ **trunks** npl bañador m (de hombre).

trunk call n Br conferencia f, llamada f interurbana.

trunk road n ≃ carretera f nacional.

truss [trʌs] n MED braguero m.

trust [trʌst] ◇ vt **-1.** [believe in] confiar en. **-2.** [have confidence in]: **to ~ sb to do sthg** confiar en alguien para que haga algo. **-3.** [entrust]: **to ~ sb with sthg** confiar algo a alguien. **-4.** [accept as safe, reliable] fiarse de. ◇ n **-1.** (U) [faith, responsibility]: ~ **(in)** confianza f (en). **-2.** FIN trust m; **in ~** en fideicomiso.

trusted ['trʌstɪd] adj de confianza.

trustee [trʌs'tiː] n FIN & JUR fideicomisario m, -ria f.

trust fund n fondo m de fideicomiso.

trusting ['trʌstɪŋ] adj confiado(da).

trustworthy ['trʌst,wɜːðɪ] adj digno(na) de confianza.

truth [truːθ] n verdad f; **in (all) ~** en verdad, verdaderamente.

truthful ['truːθfʊl] adj **-1.** [person] sincero(ra). **-2.** [story] verídico(ca).

try [traɪ] ◇ vt **-1.** [attempt] intentar; **to ~ to do sthg** tratar de OR intentar hacer algo. **-2.** [sample, test] probar. **-3.** JUR [case] ver; [criminal] juzgar, procesar. **-4.** [put to the test - person] acabar con la paciencia de; [- patience] acabar con. ◇ vi intentar; **to ~ for sthg** tratar de conseguir algo. ◇ n **-1.** [attempt] intento m, tentativa f. **-2.** [sample, test]: **to give sthg a ~** probar algo. **-3.** RUGBY ensayo m. ◆ **try on** vt sep probarse. ◆ **try out** vt sep [car, machine] probar; [plan] poner a prueba.

trying ['traɪɪŋ] adj difícil, pesado(da).

T-shirt n camiseta f.

T-square n escuadra f en forma de T.

tub [tʌb] n **-1.** [container - small] bote m; [- large] tina f. **-2.** inf [bath] bañera f.

tubby ['tʌbɪ] adj inf regordete(ta).

tube [tjuːb] n **-1.** [cylinder, container]

tubo *m.* **-2.** ANAT conducto *m.* **-3.** *Br* RAIL metro *m*; **by ~** en metro.

tuberculosis [tju:,bɜ:kjʊ'ləʊsɪs] *n* tuberculosis *f.*

tubing ['tju:bɪŋ] *n* (U) tubos *mpl.*

tubular ['tju:bjʊləʳ] *adj* tubular.

TUC *n abbr of* **Trades Union Congress.**

tuck [tʌk] *vt* [place neatly] meter. ◆ **tuck away** *vt sep* [money etc] guardar. ◆ **tuck in** ◇ *vt sep* **-1.** [person - in bed] arropar. **-2.** [clothes] meterse. ◇ *vi inf* comer con apetito. ◆ **tuck up** *vt sep* arropar.

tuck shop *n Br* confitería *f* (*emplazada cerca de un colegio*).

Tuesday ['tju:zdɪ] *n* martes *m inv*; *see also* **Saturday.**

tuft [tʌft] *n* [of hair] mechón *m*; [of grass] manojo *m.*

tug [tʌg] ◇ *n* **-1.** [pull] tirón *m.* **-2.** [boat] remolcador *m.* ◇ *vt* tirar de. ◇ *vi*: **to ~ (at)** tirar de.

tug-of-war *n* juego *m* de la cuerda (*en el que dos equipos compiten tirando de ella*).

tuition [tju:'ɪʃn] *n* enseñanza *f*; **private ~** clases *fpl* particulares.

tulip ['tju:lɪp] *n* tulipán *m.*

tumble ['tʌmbl] ◇ *vi* [person] caerse (rodando). ◇ *n* caída *f.* ◆ **tumble to** *vt fus Br inf* caerse en la cuenta de.

tumbledown ['tʌmbldaʊn] *adj* ruinoso(sa).

tumble-dryer [-,draɪəʳ] *n* secadora *f.*

tumbler ['tʌmbləʳ] *n* [glass] vaso *m.*

tummy ['tʌmɪ] *n inf* barriga *f.*

tumour *Br*, **tumor** *Am* ['tju:məʳ] *n* tumor *m.*

tuna [*Br* 'tju:nə, *Am* 'tu:nə] (*pl inv* OR **-s**) *n* atún *m.*

tune [tju:n] ◇ *n* **-1.** [song, melody] melodía *f.* **-2.** [harmony]: **in ~** MUS afinado(da); **out of ~** MUS desafinado(da); **to be out of/in ~ (with sb/sthg)** *fig* no avenirse/avenirse (con alguien/algo). ◇ *vt* **-1.** MUS afinar. **-2.** RADIO & TV sintonizar. **-3.** [engine] poner a punto. ◆ **tune in** *vi* RADIO & TV: **to ~ in (to sthg)** sintonizar (algo). ◆ **tune up** *vi* MUS concertar OR afinar los instrumentos.

tuneful ['tju:nfʊl] *adj* melodioso(sa).

tuner ['tju:nəʳ] *n* **-1.** RADIO & TV sintonizador *m.* **-2.** MUS afinador *m*, -ra *f.*

tunic ['tju:nɪk] *n* túnica *f.*

tuning fork ['tju:nɪŋ-] *n* diapasón *m.*

Tunisia [tju:'nɪzɪə] *n* Túnez *m.*

tunnel ['tʌnl] ◇ *n* túnel *m.* ◇ *vi* hacer un túnel.

turban ['tɜ:bən] *n* turbante *m.*

turbine ['tɜ:baɪn] *n* turbina *f.*

turbocharged ['tɜ:bəʊtʃɑ:dʒd] *adj* provisto(ta) de turbina; [car] turbo (*inv*).

turbulence ['tɜ:bjʊləns] *n* (U) *lit* & *fig* turbulencia *f.*

turbulent ['tɜ:bjʊlənt] *adj lit* & *fig* turbulento(ta).

tureen [tə'ri:n] *n* sopera *f.*

turf [tɜ:f] (*pl* **-s** OR **turves**) ◇ *n* **-1.** [grass surface] césped *m.* **-2.** [clod] tepe *m.* ◇ *vt* encespedar. ◆ **turf out** *vt sep Br inf* [person] dar la patada a, echar; [old clothes] tirar.

turgid ['tɜ:dʒɪd] *adj fml* [over-solemn] ampuloso(sa).

Turk [tɜ:k] *n* turco *m*, -ca *f.*

turkey ['tɜ:kɪ] (*pl* **turkeys**) *n* pavo *m.*

Turkey ['tɜ:kɪ] *n* Turquía.

Turkish ['tɜ:kɪʃ] ◇ *adj* turco(ca). ◇ *n* [language] turco *m.* ◇ *npl* [people]: **the ~** los turcos.

Turkish delight *n* rahat lokum *m*, *dulce de una sustancia gelatinosa, cubierto de azúcar glas.*

turmoil ['tɜ:mɔɪl] *n* confusión *f*, alboroto *m.*

turn [tɜ:n] ◇ *n* **-1.** [in road, river] curva *f.* **-2.** [of knob, wheel] vuelta *f.* **-3.** [change] cambio *m.* **-4.** [in game] turno *m*; **it's my ~** me toca a mí; **in ~** sucesivamente, uno tras otro. **-5.** [performance] número *m.* **-6.** MED ataque *m.* **-7.** *phr*: **to do sb a good ~** hacerle un favor a alguien. ◇ *vt* **-1.** [chair, page, omelette] dar la vuelta a. **-2.** [knob, wheel] girar. **-3.** [corner] doblar. **-4.** [thoughts, attention]: **to ~ sthg to** dirigir algo hacia. **-5.** [change]: **to ~ sthg into** convertir OR transformar algo en. **-6.** [cause to become]: **the cold ~ed his fingers blue** se le pusieron los dedos azules por el frío. **-7.** [become]: **it ~ed black** se volvió negro. ◇ *vi* **-1.** [car] girar; [road] torcer; [person] volverse, darse la vuelta. **-2.** [wheel] dar vueltas. **-3.** [turn page over]: **~ to page two** pasen a la página dos. **-4.** [thoughts, attention]: **to ~ to** dirigirse hacia. **-5.** [seek consolation]: **to ~ to sb/sthg** buscar consuelo en alguien/algo. **-6.** [change]: **to ~ into** convertirse OR transformarse en. **-7.** [go sour] cortarse. ◆ **turn around** = **turn round.** ◆ **turn away** *vt sep* [refuse entry to] no dejar entrar. ◆ **turn back** ◇ *vt sep* [person, vehicle] hacer volver. ◇ *vi* volver, volverse. ◆ **turn down** *vt sep* **-1.** [offer, person] rechazar. **-2.**

[volume etc] bajar. ◆ **turn in** *vi inf* [go to bed] irse a dormir. ◆ **turn off** ◇ *vt fus* [road, path] desviarse de. ◇ *vt sep* [radio, heater] apagar; [engine] parar; [gas, tap] cerrar. ◇ *vi* [leave road] desviarse. ◆ **turn on** ◇ *vt sep* **-1.** [radio, TV, engine] encender; [gas, tap] abrir. **-2.** *inf* [excite sexually] poner cachondo(da). ◇ *vt fus* [attack] atacar. ◆ **turn out** ◇ *vt sep* **-1.** [extinguish] apagar. **-2.** [empty - pockets, bag] vaciar. ◇ *vt fus*: **to ~ out to be** resultar ser. ◇ *vi* **-1.** [end up] salir. **-2.** [arrive]: **to ~ out (for)** venir OR presentarse (a). ◆ **turn over** ◇ *vt sep* **-1.** [turn upside down] dar la vuelta a; [page] volver. **-2.** [consider] darle vueltas a. **-3.** *Br* RADIO & TV cambiar. **-4.** [hand over]: **to ~ sthg/sb over (to)** entregar algo/a alguien (a). ◇ *vi* **-1.** [roll over] darse la vuelta. **-2.** *Br* RADIO & TV cambiar de canal. ◆ **turn round** ◇ *vt sep* **-1.** [gen] dar la vuelta a. **-2.** [knob, key] hacer girar. ◇ *vi* [person] darse la vuelta, volverse. ◆ **turn up** ◇ *vt sep* [volume, heating] subir. ◇ *vi inf* aparecer.

turning ['tɜːnɪŋ] *n* [road] bocacalle *f*.

turning point *n* momento *m* decisivo.

turnip ['tɜːnɪp] *n* nabo *m*.

turnout ['tɜːnaʊt] *n* número *m* de asistentes, asistencia *f*.

turnover ['tɜːn,əʊvə*r*] *n* (*U*) **-1.** [of personnel] movimiento *m* de personal. **-2.** *Br* FIN volumen *m* de ventas, facturación *f*.

turnpike ['tɜːnpaɪk] *n Am* autopista *f* de peaje.

turnstile ['tɜːnstaɪl] *n* torniquete *m*.

turntable ['tɜːn,teɪbl] *n* plato *m* giratorio.

turn-up *n Br* [on trousers] vuelta *f*; **a ~ for the books** *inf* una auténtica sorpresa.

turpentine ['tɜːpəntaɪn] *n* trementina *f*.

turquoise ['tɜːkwɔɪz] ◇ *adj* turquesa. ◇ *n* [mineral, gem] turquesa *f*.

turret ['tʌrɪt] *n* torreta *f*, torrecilla *f*.

turtle ['tɜːtl] (*pl inv* OR **-s**) *n* tortuga *f* (marina).

turtleneck ['tɜːtlnek] *n* cuello *m* (de) cisne.

turves [tɜːvz] *Br pl* → **turf**.

tusk [tʌsk] *n* colmillo *m*.

tussle ['tʌsl] ◇ *n* lucha *f*, pelea *f*. ◇ *vi*: **to ~ (over)** pelearse (por).

tutor ['tjuːtə*r*] *n* **-1.** [private] profesor particular *m*, profesora particular *f*, tutor *m*, -ra *f*. **-2.** UNIV profesor universi-

tario *m*, profesora universitaria *f* (*de un grupo pequeño*).

tutorial [tjuːˈtɔːrɪəl] *n* tutoría *f*, clase *f* con grupo reducido.

tuxedo [tʌkˈsiːdəʊ] (*pl* **-s**) *n* esmoquin *m*.

TV (*abbr of* **television**) ◇ *n* televisión *f*; **on ~** en la televisión. ◇ *comp* de televisión.

twang [twæŋ] *n* **-1.** [of guitar] tañido *m*; [of string, elastic] sonido *m* vibrante. **-2.** [accent] gangueo *m*, acento *m* nasal.

tweed [twiːd] *n* tweed *m*.

tweezers ['twiːzəz] *npl* pinzas *fpl*.

twelfth [twelfθ] *num* duodécimo(ma); *see also* **sixth**.

twelve [twelv] *num* doce; *see also* **six**.

twentieth ['twentɪəθ] *num* vigésimo(ma); *see also* **sixth**.

twenty ['twentɪ] *num* veinte; *see also* **sixty**.

twice [twaɪs] ◇ *num adv* dos veces; **~ a week** dos veces por semana; **it costs ~ as much** cuesta el doble. ◇ *num adj* dos veces; **~ as big** el doble de grande.

twiddle ['twɪdl] ◇ *vt* dar vueltas a. ◇ *vi*: **to ~ with** juguetear con.

twig [twɪg] *n* ramita *f*.

twilight ['twaɪlaɪt] *n* crepúsculo *m*.

twin [twɪn] ◇ *adj* gemelo(la). ◇ *n* gemelo *m*, -la *f*.

twin-bedded [-ˈbedɪd] *adj* de dos camas.

twine [twaɪn] ◇ *n* (*U*) bramante *m*. ◇ *vt*: **to ~ sthg round sthg** enrollar algo en algo.

twinge [twɪndʒ] *n* [of pain] punzada *f*; [of guilt] remordimiento *m*.

twinkle ['twɪŋkl] *vi* **-1.** [star] centellear, parpadear. **-2.** [eyes] brillar.

twin room *n* habitación *f* con dos camas.

twin town *n* ciudad *f* hermanada.

twirl [twɜːl] ◇ *vt* dar vueltas a. ◇ *vi* dar vueltas rápidamente.

twist [twɪst] ◇ *n* **-1.** [in road] vuelta *f*, recodo *m*; [in river] meandro *m*. **-2.** [of head, lid, knob] giro *m*. **-3.** [shape] espiral *f*. **-4.** *fig* [in plot] giro *m* imprevisto. ◇ *vt* **-1.** [cloth, rope] retorcer; [hair] enroscar. **-2.** [face etc] torcer. **-3.** [dial, lid] dar vueltas a; [head] volver. **-4.** [ankle, knee etc] torcerse. **-5.** [misquote] tergiversar. ◇ *vi* **-1.** [person] retorcerse; [road, river] serpentear. **-2.** [face] contorsionarse; [frame, rail] torcerse. **-3.** [turn - head, hand] volverse.

twit [twɪt] *n Br inf* imbécil *m y f.*

twitch [twɪtʃ] ◇ *n* contorsión *f;* **nervous ~ tic** *m* (nervioso). ◇ *vi* contorsionarse.

two [tuː] *num* dos; **in ~** en dos; *see also* **six**.

two-door *adj* [car] de dos puertas.

twofaced [ˌtuːˈfeɪst] *adj pej* hipócrita.

twofold [ˈtuːfəʊld] ◇ *adj* doble; **a ~ increase** un incremento del doble. ◇ *adv:* **to increase ~** duplicarse.

two-piece *adj* [suit] de dos piezas.

twosome [ˈtuːsəm] *n inf* pareja *f.*

two-way *adj* [traffic] en ambas direcciones; [agreement, cooperation] mutuo(tua).

tycoon [taɪˈkuːn] *n* magnate *m.*

type [taɪp] ◇ *n* **-1.** [gen] tipo *m.* **-2.** (*U*) TYPO tipo *m,* letra *f.* ◇ *vt* **-1.** [on typewriter] escribir a máquina, mecanografiar. **-2.** [on computer] escribir en el ordenador; **to ~ sthg into sthg** entrar algo en algo. ◇ *vi* escribir a máquina.

typecast [ˈtaɪpkɑːst] (*pt & pp* **typecast**) *vt:* **to ~ sb (as)** encasillar a alguien (como).

typeface [ˈtaɪpfeɪs] *n* tipo *m,* letra *f.*

typescript [ˈtaɪpskrɪpt] *n* copia *f* mecanografiada.

typeset [ˈtaɪpset] (*pt & pp* **typeset**) *vt* componer.

typewriter [ˈtaɪpˌraɪtər] *n* máquina *f* de escribir.

typhoid (fever) [ˈtaɪfɔɪd-] *n* fiebre *f* tifoidea.

typhoon [taɪˈfuːn] *n* tifón *m.*

typical [ˈtɪpɪkl] *adj:* **~ (of)** típico(ca) (de).

typing [ˈtaɪpɪŋ] *n* mecanografía *f.*

typist [ˈtaɪpɪst] *n* mecanógrafo *m,* -fa *f.*

typography [taɪˈpɒgrəfɪ] *n* [process, job] tipografía *f.*

tyranny [ˈtɪrənɪ] *n* tiranía *f.*

tyrant [ˈtaɪrənt] *n* tirano *m,* -na *f.*

tyre *Br,* **tire** *Am* [ˈtaɪər] *n* neumático *m.*

tyre pressure *n* presión *f* de los neumáticos.

U

u (*pl* **u's** OR **us**), **U** (*pl* **U's** OR **Us**) [juː] *n* [letter] u *f,* U *f.*

U-bend *n* sifón *m.*

udder [ˈʌdər] *n* ubre *f.*

UFO (*abbr of* **unidentified flying object**) *n* OVNI *m.*

Uganda [juːˈgændə] *n* Uganda.

ugh [ʌg] *excl* ¡puaf!

ugly [ˈʌglɪ] *adj* **-1.** [unattractive] feo(a). **-2.** *fig* [unpleasant] desagradable.

UHF (*abbr of* **ultra-high frequency**) UHF.

UK (*abbr of* **United Kingdom**) *n* RU *m;* **the ~** el Reino Unido.

Ukraine [juːˈkreɪn] *n:* **the ~** Ucrania.

ulcer [ˈʌlsər] *n* úlcera *f.*

ulcerated [ˈʌlsəreɪtɪd] *adj* ulceroso(sa).

Ulster [ˈʌlstər] *n* (el) Úlster.

ulterior [ʌlˈtɪərɪər] *adj:* **~ motive** motivo *m* oculto.

ultimata [ˌʌltɪˈmeɪtə] *pl* → **ultimatum.**

ultimate [ˈʌltɪmət] ◇ *adj* **-1.** [final, longterm] final, definitivo(va). **-2.** [most powerful] máximo(ma). ◇ *n:* **the ~ in** el colmo de.

ultimately [ˈʌltɪmətlɪ] *adv* finalmente, a la larga.

ultimatum [ˌʌltɪˈmeɪtəm] (*pl* **-s** OR **-ta**) *n* ultimátum *m.*

ultrasound [ˈʌltrəsaʊnd] *n* ultrasonido *m.*

ultraviolet [ˌʌltrəˈvaɪələt] *adj* ultravioleta.

umbilical cord [ʌmˈbɪlɪkl-] *n* cordón *m* umbilical.

umbrella [ʌmˈbrelə] ◇ *n* **-1.** [for rain] paraguas *m inv.* **-2.** [on beach] parasol *m.* ◇ *adj* que engloba a otros (otras).

umpire [ˈʌmpaɪər] *n* árbitro *m.*

umpteen [ˌʌmpˈtiːn] *num adj inf:* **~ times** la tira de veces.

umpteenth [ˌʌmpˈtiːnθ] *num adj inf* enésimo(ma); **for the ~ time** por enésima vez.

UN (*abbr of* **United Nations**) *n:* **the ~** la ONU.

unabated [ˌʌnəˈbeɪtɪd] *adj* incesante.

unable [ʌn'eɪbl] *adj*: to be ~ to do sthg no poder hacer algo.

unacceptable [ˌʌnək'septəbl] *adj* inaceptable.

unaccompanied [ˌʌnə'kʌmpənɪd] *adj* -1. [child] que no va acompañado(da); [luggage] desatendido(da). -2. [song] sin acompañamiento.

unaccountably [ˌʌnə'kaʊntəblɪ] *adv* inexplicablemente.

unaccounted [ˌʌnə'kaʊntɪd] *adj*: 12 people are ~ for hay 12 personas aún sin localizar.

unaccustomed [ˌʌnə'kʌstəmd] *adj* [unused]: to be ~ to no estar acostumbrado(da) a.

unadulterated [ˌʌnə'dʌltəreɪtɪd] *adj* -1. [unspoilt] sin adulterar. -2. [absolute] completo(ta), absoluto(ta).

unanimous [juː'nænɪməs] *adj* unánime.

unanimously [juː'nænɪməslɪ] *adv* unánimemente.

unanswered [ˌʌn'ɑːnsəd] *adj* sin contestar.

unappetizing, -ising [ˌʌn'æpɪtaɪzɪŋ] *adj* poco apetitoso(sa).

unarmed [ˌʌn'ɑːmd] *adj* desarmado(da).

unarmed combat *n* lucha *f* OR combate *m* a brazo partido.

unashamed [ˌʌnə'ʃeɪmd] *adj* descarado(da).

unassuming [ˌʌnə'sjuːmɪŋ] *adj* sin pretensiones.

unattached [ˌʌnə'tætʃt] *adj* -1. [not fastened, linked] independiente; ~ to que no está ligado a. -2. [without partner] libre, sin compromiso.

unattended [ˌʌnə'tendɪd] *adj* desatendido(da).

unattractive [ˌʌnə'træktɪv] *adj* poco atractivo(va).

unauthorized, -ised [ˌʌn'ɔːθəraɪzd] *adj* no autorizado(da).

unavailable [ˌʌnə'veɪləbl] *adj* que no está disponible.

unavoidable [ˌʌnə'vɔɪdəbl] *adj* inevitable, ineludible.

unaware [ˌʌnə'weər] *adj* inconsciente; to be ~ of no ser consciente de.

unawares [ˌʌnə'weəz] *adv*: to catch OR take sb ~ coger a alguien desprevenido(da).

unbalanced [ˌʌn'bælənst] *adj* desequilibrado(da).

unbearable [ʌn'beərəbl] *adj* insoportable, inaguantable.

unbeatable [ˌʌn'biːtəbl] *adj* [gen] insuperable; [prices, value] inmejorable.

unbeknown(st) [ˌʌnbɪ'nəʊn(st)] *adv*: ~ to sin conocimiento de.

unbelievable [ˌʌnbɪ'liːvəbl] *adj* increíble.

unbending [ʌn'bendɪŋ] *adj* resoluto(ta).

unbia(s)sed [ˌʌn'baɪəst] *adj* imparcial.

unborn [ˌʌn'bɔːn] *adj* [child] no nacido(da) aún.

unbreakable [ˌʌn'breɪkəbl] *adj* irrompible.

unbridled [ˌʌn'braɪdld] *adj* desmesurado(da), desenfrenado(da).

unbutton [ˌʌn'bʌtn] *vt* desabrochar.

uncalled-for [ˌʌn'kɔːld-] *adj* injusto(ta), inmerecido(da).

uncanny [ʌn'kænɪ] *adj* extraño(ña).

unceasing [ˌʌn'siːsɪŋ] *adj fml* incesante.

unceremonious ['ʌnˌserɪ'məʊnjəs] *adj* [curt] brusco(ca).

uncertain [ʌn'sɜːtn] *adj* [gen] incierto(ta); [undecided, hesitant] indeciso(sa); in no ~ terms de forma vehemente.

unchanged [ˌʌn'tʃeɪndʒd] *adj* sin alterar.

unchecked [ˌʌn'tʃekt] ◇ *adj* [unrestrained] desenfrenado(da). ◇ *adv* [unrestrained] libremente, sin restricciones.

uncivilized, -ised [ˌʌn'sɪvɪlaɪzd] *adj* [society] incivilizado(da); [person] inculto(ta).

uncle ['ʌŋkl] *n* tío *m*.

unclear [ˌʌn'klɪər] *adj* poco claro(ra); to be ~ about sthg no tener claro algo.

uncomfortable [ˌʌn'kʌmftəbl] *adj* -1. [gen] incómodo(da). -2. *fig* [fact, truth] inquietante, desagradable.

uncommon [ʌn'kɒmən] *adj* [rare] poco común, raro(ra).

uncompromising [ˌʌn'kɒmprəmaɪzɪŋ] *adj* inflexible, intransigente.

unconcerned [ˌʌnkən'sɜːnd] *adj* [not anxious] indiferente.

unconditional [ˌʌnkən'dɪʃənl] *adj* incondicional.

unconscious [ʌn'kɒnʃəs] ◇ *adj* inconsciente; to be ~ of sthg ser inconsciente de OR ignorar algo. ◇ *n* inconsciente *m*.

unconsciously [ʌn'kɒnʃəslɪ] *adv* inconscientemente.

uncontrollable [ˌʌnkən'trəʊləbl] *adj* [gen] incontrolable; [desire, hatred] irrefrenable; [laughter] incontenible.

unconventional [ˌʌnkən'venʃənl] *adj* poco convencional.

unconvinced [ˌʌnkən'vɪnst] *adj*: to remain ~ seguir sin convencerse.

uncouth [ʌn'kuːθ] *adj* grosero(ra).

uncover [ʌn'kʌvəʳ] *vt* [gen] descubrir; [jar, tin etc] **destapar**.

undecided [ˌʌndɪ'saɪdɪd] *adj* **-1.** [person] indeciso(sa). **-2.** [issue] pendiente.

undeniable [ˌʌndɪ'naɪəbl] *adj* innegable.

under ['ʌndəʳ] ◇ *prep* **-1.** [beneath] debajo de. **-2.** [with movement] bajo; **they walked ~ the bridge** pasaron por debajo del puente. **-3.** [subject to, undergoing, controlled by] bajo; ~ **the circumstances** dadas las circunstancias; ~ **discussion** en proceso de discusión; **he has 20 men ~ him** tiene 20 hombres a su cargo. **-4.** [less than] menos de. **-5.** [according to] según. **-6.** [in headings, classifications]: **he filed it ~ "D"** lo archivó en la "D". **-7.** [name, title]: ~ **an alias** bajo nombre supuesto. ◇ *adv* **-1.** [gen] debajo; **to go ~** [business] irse a pique. **-2.** [less]: **children of 12 years and ~** niños menores de 13 años.

underage [ʌndər'eɪdʒ] *adj* [person] menor de edad; [sex, drinking] en menores de edad.

undercarriage ['ʌndəˌkærɪdʒ] *n* tren *m* de aterrizaje.

undercharge [ˌʌndə'tʃɑːdʒ] *vt* cobrar menos del precio estipulado.

underclothes ['ʌndəkləʊðz] *npl* ropa *f* interior.

undercoat ['ʌndəkəʊt] *n* [of paint] primera mano *f* OR capa *f*.

undercover ['ʌndəˌkʌvəʳ] *adj* secreto(ta).

undercurrent ['ʌndəˌkʌrənt] *n* fig sentimiento *m* oculto.

undercut [ˌʌndə'kʌt] (*pt & pp* **undercut**) *vt* [in price] vender más barato que.

underdeveloped [ˌʌndədɪ'veləpt] *adj* subdesarrollado(da).

underdog ['ʌndədɒg] *n*: **the ~** el que lleva las de perder.

underdone [ˌʌndə'dʌn] *adj* poco hecho(cha).

underestimate [ʌndər'estɪmeɪt] *vt* subestimar.

underexposed [ˌʌndərɪk'spəʊzd] *adj* PHOT subexpuesto(ta).

underfoot [ˌʌndə'fʊt] *adj*: **it's wet ~** el suelo está mojado.

undergo [ˌʌndə'gəʊ] (*pt* **-went**, *pp* **-gone**) *vt* [pain, change, difficulties] **sufrir**, experimentar; [operation, examination] someterse a.

undergraduate [ˌʌndə'grædʒʊət] *n* estudiante universitario no licenciado *m*, estudiante universitaria no licenciada *f*.

underground [*adj & n* 'ʌndəgraʊnd, *adv* ˌʌndə'graʊnd] ◇ *adj* **-1.** [below the ground] subterráneo(a). **-2.** fig [secret, illegal] clandestino(na). ◇ *adv*: **to go ~** pasar a la clandestinidad. ◇ *n* **-1.** *Br* [railway system] metro *m*. **-2.** [activist movement] movimiento *m* clandestino.

undergrowth ['ʌndəgrəʊθ] *n* (*U*) maleza *f*.

underhand [ˌʌndə'hænd] *adj* turbio(bia), poco limpio(pia).

underline [ˌʌndə'laɪn] *vt* subrayar.

underlying [ˌʌndə'laɪɪŋ] *adj* subyacente.

undermine [ˌʌndə'maɪn] *vt* fig minar, socavar.

underneath [ˌʌndə'niːθ] ◇ *prep* **-1.** [beneath] debajo de. **-2.** [with movement] bajo. ◇ *adv* [under, below] debajo. ◇ *adj inf* inferior, de abajo. ◇ *n* [underside]: **the ~** la superficie inferior.

underpaid ['ʌndəpeɪd] *adj* mal pagado(da).

underpants ['ʌndəpænts] *npl* calzoncillos *mpl*.

underpass ['ʌndəpɑːs] *n* paso *m* subterráneo.

underprivileged [ˌʌndə'prɪvɪlɪdʒd] *adj* desvalido(da), desamparado(da).

underrated [ˌʌndə'reɪtɪd] *adj* subestimado(da), infravalorado(da).

undershirt ['ʌndəʃɜːt] *n* *Am* camiseta *f*.

underside ['ʌndəsaɪd] *n*: **the ~** la superficie inferior.

underskirt ['ʌndəskɜːt] *n* enaguas *fpl*.

understand [ˌʌndə'stænd] (*pt & pp* **-stood**) ◇ *vt* **-1.** [gen] comprender, entender. **-2.** [know all about] entender de. **-3.** *fml* [to be informed]: **to ~ that** tener entendido(da) que. ◇ *vi* comprender, entender.

understandable [ˌʌndə'stændəbl] *adj* comprensible.

understanding [ˌʌndə'stændɪŋ] ◇ *n* **-1.** [knowledge] entendimiento *m*, comprensión *f*. **-2.** [sympathy] comprensión *f* mutua. **-3.** [informal agreement] acuerdo *m*. ◇ *adj* comprensivo(va).

understatement [ˌʌndə'steɪtmənt] *n* **-1.** [inadequate statement] atenuación *f*; **it's an ~ to say he's fat** decir que es gordo es quedarse corto. **-2.** (*U*) [quality of understating]: **he's a master of ~** puede quitarle importancia a cualquier cosa.

understood [ˌʌndə'stʊd] *pt & pp* → **understand**.

understudy ['ʌndə,stʌdɪ] n suplente m y f.

undertake [,ʌndə'teɪk] (pt -took, pp -taken) vt -1. [task] emprender; [responsibility, control] asumir, tomar. -2. [promise]: to ~ to do sthg comprometerse a hacer algo.

undertaker ['ʌndə,teɪkəʳ] n director m, -ra f de pompas fúnebres.

undertaking [,ʌndə'teɪkɪŋ] n -1. [task] tarea f, empresa f. -2. [promise] promesa f.

undertone ['ʌndətəʊn] n -1. [quiet voice] voz f baja. -2. [vague feeling] matiz m.

undertook [,ʌndə'tʊk] pt → undertake.

underwater [,ʌndə'wɔːtəʳ] ◇ adj submarino(na). ◇ adv bajo el agua.

underwear ['ʌndəweəʳ] n ropa f interior.

underwent [,ʌndə'went] pt → undergo.

underworld ['ʌndə,wɜːld] n [criminal society]: the ~ el hampa, los bajos fondos.

underwriter ['ʌndə,raɪtəʳ] n asegurador m, -ra f.

undid [,ʌn'dɪd] pt → undo.

undies ['ʌndɪz] npl inf paños mpl menores.

undisputed [,ʌndɪ'spjuːtɪd] adj indiscutible.

undistinguished [,ʌndɪ'stɪŋgwɪʃt] adj mediocre.

undo [,ʌn'duː] (pt -did, pp -done) vt -1. [unfasten - knot] desatar, desanudar; [- button, clasp] desabrochar; [- parcel] abrir. -2. [nullify] anular, deshacer.

undoing [,ʌn'duːɪŋ] n (U) fml ruina f, perdición f.

undone [,ʌn'dʌn] ◇ pp → undo. ◇ adj -1. [coat] desabrochado(da); [shoes] desatado(da). -2. fml [not done] por hacer.

undoubted [ʌn'daʊtɪd] adj indudable.

undoubtedly [ʌn'daʊtɪdlɪ] adv fml indudablemente, sin duda (alguna).

undress [,ʌn'dres] ◇ vt desnudar. ◇ vi desnudarse.

undue [,ʌn'djuː] adj fml indebido(da).

undulate ['ʌndjʊleɪt] vi fml ondular.

unduly [,ʌn'djuːlɪ] adv fml indebidamente.

unearth [,ʌn'ɜːθ] vt [dig up] desenterrar; fig [discover] descubrir.

unearthly [ʌn'ɜːθlɪ] adj inf [hour] intempestivo(va).

unease [ʌn'iːz] n malestar m.

uneasy [ʌn'iːzɪ] adj -1. [person, feeling] intranquilo(la). -2. [peace] inseguro(ra).

uneconomic ['ʌn,iːkə'nɒmɪk] adj poco rentable.

uneducated [,ʌn'edjʊkeɪtɪd] adj ignorante, inculto(ta).

unemployed [,ʌnɪm'plɔɪd] ◇ adj parado(da), desempleado(da). ◇ npl: the ~ los parados.

unemployment [,ʌnɪm'plɔɪmənt] n desempleo m, paro m.

unemployment benefit Br, **unemployment compensation** Am n subsidio m de desempleo OR paro.

unerring [,ʌn'ɜːrɪŋ] adj infalible.

uneven [,ʌn'iːvn] adj -1. [not flat - road] lleno(na) de baches; [- land] escabroso(sa). -2. [inconsistent, unfair] desigual.

unexpected [,ʌnɪk'spektɪd] adj inesperado(da).

unexpectedly [,ʌnɪk'spektɪdlɪ] adv inesperadamente.

unfailing [ʌn'feɪlɪŋ] adj indefectible.

unfair [,ʌn'feəʳ] adj injusto(ta).

unfaithful [,ʌn'feɪθfʊl] adj [sexually] infiel.

unfamiliar [,ʌnfə'mɪljəʳ] adj -1. [not well-known] desconocido(da). -2. [not acquainted]: to be ~ with sthg/sb desconocer algo/a alguien.

unfashionable [,ʌn'fæʃnəbl] adj [clothes, ideas] pasado(da) de moda; [area of town] poco popular.

unfasten [,ʌn'fɑːsn] vt [garment, buttons] desabrochar; [rope, tie] desatar, soltar; [door] abrir.

unfavourable Br, **unfavorable** Am [,ʌn'feɪvrəbl] adj desfavorable.

unfeeling [ʌn'fiːlɪŋ] adj insensible.

unfinished [,ʌn'fɪnɪʃt] adj sin terminar.

unfit [,ʌn'fɪt] adj -1. [injured] lesionado(da); [in poor shape] que no está en forma. -2. [not suitable - thing] impropio(pia); [- person]: ~ to incapaz de; ~ for no apto para.

unfold [ʌn'fəʊld] ◇ vt -1. [open out] desplegar, desdoblar. -2. [explain] revelar. ◇ vi [become clear] revelarse.

unforeseen [,ʌnfɔː'siːn] adj imprevisto(ta).

unforgettable [,ʌnfə'getəbl] adj inolvidable.

unforgivable [,ʌnfə'gɪvəbl] adj imperdonable.

unfortunate [ʌn'fɔːtʃnət] adj -1. [unlucky] desgraciado(da), desdichado(da). -2. [regrettable] inoportuno(na).

unfortunately [ʌn'fɔːtʃnətlɪ] adv desgraciadamente, desafortunadamente.

unfounded [ˌʌnˈfaʊndɪd] *adj* infundado(da).

unfriendly [ˌʌnˈfrendlɪ] *adj* poco amistoso(sa).

unfurnished [ˌʌnˈfɜːnɪʃt] *adj* desamueblado(da).

ungainly [ʌnˈɡeɪnlɪ] *adj* desgarbado(da).

ungodly [ˌʌnˈɡɒdlɪ] *adj inf* [hour] intempestivo(va).

ungrateful [ʌnˈɡreɪtful] *adj* desagradecido(da), ingrato(ta).

unhappy [ʌnˈhæpɪ] *adj* -1. [sad] triste; [wretched] desdichado(da), infeliz. -2. [uneasy]: **to be ~ (with** OR **about)** estar inquieto(ta) (por). -3. *fml* [unfortunate] desafortunado(da).

unharmed [ˌʌnˈhɑːmd] *adj* [person] ileso(sa); [thing] indemne.

unhealthy [ʌnˈhelθɪ] *adj* -1. [in bad health] enfermizo(za). -2. [causing bad health] insalubre. -3. *fig* [interest etc] morboso(sa).

unheard-of [ʌnˈhɜːd-] *adj* -1. [unknown, completely absent] inaudito(ta). -2. [unprecedented] sin precedente.

unhook [ˌʌnˈhʊk] *vt* -1. [unfasten hooks of] desabrochar. -2. [remove from hook] descolgar, desenganchar.

unhurt [ˌʌnˈhɜːt] *adj* ileso(sa).

unhygienic [ˌʌnhaɪˈdʒiːnɪk] *adj* antihigiénico(ca).

unidentified flying object *n* objeto *m* volador no identificado.

unification [ˌjuːnɪfɪˈkeɪʃn] *n* unificación *f*.

uniform [ˈjuːnɪfɔːm] ◇ *adj* uniforme, constante. ◇ *n* uniforme *m*.

unify [ˈjuːnɪfaɪ] *vt* unificar, unir.

unilateral [ˌjuːnɪˈlætərəl] *adj* unilateral.

unimportant [ˌʌnɪmˈpɔːtənt] *adj* sin importancia, insignificante.

uninhabited [ˌʌnɪnˈhæbɪtɪd] *adj* deshabitado(da).

uninjured [ˌʌnˈɪndʒəd] *adj* ileso(sa).

unintelligent [ˌʌnɪnˈtelɪdʒent] *adj* poco inteligente.

unintentional [ˌʌnɪnˈtenʃənl] *adj* involuntario(ria).

union [ˈjuːnjən] ◇ *n* -1. [trade union] sindicato *m*. -2. [alliance] unión *f*, alianza *f*. ◇ *comp* sindical.

Union Jack *n*: **the ~** la bandera del Reino Unido.

unique [juːˈniːk] *adj* -1. [gen] único(ca). -2. *fml* [peculiar, exclusive]: **~ to** peculiar de.

unison [ˈjuːnɪzn] *n* unísono *m*; **in ~** [simultaneously] al unísono.

unit [ˈjuːnɪt] *n* -1. [gen] unidad *f*. -2. [piece of furniture] módulo *m*, elemento *m*.

unite [juːˈnaɪt] ◇ *vt* [gen] unir; [country] unificar. ◇ *vi* unirse, juntarse.

united [juːˈnaɪtɪd] *adj* unido(da).

United Kingdom *n*: **the ~** el Reino Unido.

United Nations *n*: **the ~** las Naciones Unidas.

United States *n*: **the ~ (of America)** los Estados Unidos (de América).

unit trust *n Br* fondo *m* de inversión mobiliaria.

unity [ˈjuːnətɪ] *n* (*U*) unidad *f*, unión *f*.

universal [ˌjuːnɪˈvɜːsl] *adj* universal.

universe [ˈjuːnɪvɜːs] *n*: **the ~** el universo.

university [ˌjuːnɪˈvɜːsətɪ] ◇ *n* universidad *f*. ◇ *comp* universitario(ria); **~ student** (estudiante) universitario *m*, (estudiante) universitaria *f*.

unjust [ˌʌnˈdʒʌst] *adj* injusto(ta).

unkempt [ˌʌnˈkempt] *adj* [person] desaseado(da); [hair] despeinado(da); [clothes] descuidado(da).

unkind [ʌnˈkaɪnd] *adj* [uncharitable] poco amable, cruel.

unknown [ˌʌnˈnəʊn] *adj* desconocido(da).

unlawful [ˌʌnˈlɔːful] *adj* ilegal, ilícito(ta).

unleaded [ˌʌnˈledɪd] *adj* sin plomo.

unleash [ˌʌnˈliːʃ] *vt literary* desatar.

unless [ənˈles] *conj* a menos que; **~ I say so** a menos que yo lo diga; **~ I'm mistaken** si no me equivoco.

unlike [ˌʌnˈlaɪk] *prep* -1. [different from] distinto(ta) a, diferente a. -2. [differently from] a diferencia de. -3. [not typical of] poco característico(ca) de.

unlikely [ʌnˈlaɪklɪ] *adj* -1. [not probable] poco probable. -2. [bizarre] inverosímil.

unlisted [ʌnˈlɪstɪd] *adj Am* [phone number] que no figura en la guía telefónica.

unload [ˌʌnˈləʊd] *vt* [goods, car] descargar.

unlock [ˌʌnˈlɒk] *vt* abrir (con llave).

unlucky [ʌnˈlʌkɪ] *adj* -1. [unfortunate] desgraciado(da). -2. [number, colour etc] de la mala suerte.

unmarried [ˌʌnˈmærɪd] *adj* que no se ha casado.

unmistakable [ˌʌnmɪˈsteɪkəbl] *adj* inconfundible.

unmitigated [ʌnˈmɪtɪɡeɪtɪd] *adj* absoluto(ta).

unnatural [ʌn'nætʃrəl] *adj* **-1.** [unusual, strange] anormal. **-2.** [affected] afectado(da).

unnecessary [ʌn'nesəsərɪ] *adj* innecesario(ria).

unnerving [ˌʌn'nɜːvɪŋ] *adj* desconcertante.

unnoticed [ˌʌn'nəʊtɪst] *adj* inadvertido(da), desapercibido(da).

unobtainable [ˌʌnəb'teɪnəbl] *adj* inasequible.

unobtrusive [ˌʌnəb'truːsɪv] *adj* discreto(ta).

unofficial [ˌʌnə'fɪʃl] *adj* extraoficial.

unorthodox [ʌn'ɔːθədɒks] *adj* poco ortodoxo(xa).

unpack [ˌʌn'pæk] ◇ *vt* **-1.** [box] desempaquetar, desembalar; [suitcases] deshacer. **-2.** [clothes] sacar (de la maleta). ◇ *vi* deshacer las maletas.

unpalatable [ʌn'pælətəbl] *adj* [food] incomible; [drink] imbebible; *fig* [difficult to accept] desagradable.

unparalleled [ʌn'pærəleld] *adj* incomparable, sin precedente.

unpleasant [ʌn'pleznt] *adj* **-1.** [disagreeable] desagradable. **-2.** [unfriendly, rude - person] antipático(ca); [- remark] mezquino(na).

unplug [ʌn'plʌg] *vt* desenchufar, desconectar.

unpopular [ˌʌn'pɒpjʊləʳ] *adj* poco popular.

unprecedented [ʌn'presɪdəntɪd] *adj* sin precedentes, inaudito(ta).

unpredictable [ˌʌnprɪ'dɪktəbl] *adj* imprevisible.

unprofessional [ˌʌnprə'feʃənl] *adj* poco profesional.

unqualified [ˌʌn'kwɒlɪfaɪd] *adj* **-1.** [not qualified] sin título, no cualificado(da). **-2.** [total, complete] incondicional.

unquestionable [ʌn'kwestʃənəbl] *adj* incuestionable, indiscutible.

unquestioning [ʌn'kwestʃənɪŋ] *adj* incondicional.

unravel [ʌn'rævl] *vt lit & fig* desenmarañar.

unreal [ˌʌn'rɪəl] *adj* irreal.

unrealistic [ˌʌnrɪə'lɪstɪk] *adj* [person] poco realista; [idea, plan] impracticable.

unreasonable [ʌn'riːznəbl] *adj* **-1.** [person, behaviour, decision] poco razonable. **-2.** [demand, price] excesivo(va).

unrelated [ˌʌnrɪ'leɪtɪd] *adj:* **to be ~ (to)** no tener conexión (con).

unrelenting [ˌʌnrɪ'lentɪŋ] *adj* implacable, inexorable.

unreliable [ˌʌnrɪ'laɪəbl] *adj* que no es de fiar.

unremitting [ˌʌnrɪ'mɪtɪŋ] *adj* incesante.

unrequited [ˌʌnrɪ'kwaɪtɪd] *adj* no correspondido(da).

unreserved [ˌʌnrɪ'zɜːvd] *adj* [wholehearted] incondicional, absoluto(ta).

unresolved [ˌʌnrɪ'zɒlvd] *adj* sin resolver, pendiente.

unrest [ˌʌn'rest] *n* (U) malestar *m*, inquietud *f*.

unrivalled *Br*, **unrivaled** *Am* [ʌn'raɪvld] *adj* incomparable, sin par.

unroll [ˌʌn'rəʊl] *vt* desenrollar.

unruly [ʌn'ruːlɪ] *adj* **-1.** [person, behaviour] revoltoso(sa). **-2.** [hair] rebelde.

unsafe [ˌʌn'seɪf] *adj* [gen] inseguro(ra); [risky] arriesgado(da).

unsaid [ˌʌn'sed] *adj:* **to leave sthg ~** dejar algo sin decir.

unsatisfactory ['ʌnˌsætɪs'fæktərɪ] *adj* insatisfactorio(ria).

unsavoury, **unsavory** *Am* [ˌʌn'seɪvərɪ] *adj* desagradable.

unscathed [ˌʌn'skeɪðd] *adj* ileso(sa).

unscrew [ˌʌn'skruː] *vt* **-1.** [lid, top] abrir. **-2.** [sign, hinge] desatornillar.

unscrupulous [ʌn'skruːpjʊləs] *adj* desaprensivo(va), poco escrupuloso(sa).

unseemly [ʌn'siːmlɪ] *adj* indecoroso(sa).

unselfish [ˌʌn'selfɪʃ] *adj* altruista.

unsettle [ˌʌn'setl] *vt* perturbar.

unsettled [ˌʌn'setld] *adj* **-1.** [person] nervioso(sa), intranquilo(la). **-2.** [weather] variable. **-3.** [argument, matter, debt] pendiente. **-4.** [situation] inestable.

unshak(e)able [ʌn'ʃeɪkəbl] *adj* inquebrantable.

unshaven [ˌʌn'ʃeɪvn] *adj* sin afeitar.

unsightly [ʌn'saɪtlɪ] *adj* [building] feo (fea); [scar, bruise] desagradable.

unskilled [ˌʌn'skɪld] *adj* [person] no cualificado(da); [work] no especializado(da).

unsociable [ˌʌn'səʊʃəbl] *adj* poco sociable.

unsocial [ˌʌn'səʊʃl] *adj:* **to work ~ hours** trabajar a horas intempestivas.

unsound [ˌʌn'saʊnd] *adj* **-1.** [conclusion, method] erróneo(a). **-2.** [building, structure] defectuoso(sa).

unspeakable [ʌn'spiːkəbl] *adj* [crime] incalificable; [pain] indecible.

unstable [ˌʌn'steɪbl] *adj* inestable.

unsteady [ˌʌn'stedɪ] *adj* [gen] inestable; [hands, voice] tembloroso(sa); [footsteps] vacilante.

unstoppable [ˌʌn'stɒpəbl] *adj* irrefrenable.

unstuck [ˌʌn'stʌk] *adj*: **to come ~** [notice, stamp, label] despegarse, desprenderse; *fig* [plan, system, person] fracasar.

unsuccessful [ˌʌnsək'sesfʊl] *adj* [person] fracasado(da); [attempt, meeting] infructuoso(sa).

unsuccessfully [ˌʌnsək'sesfʊlɪ] *adv* sin éxito, en vano.

unsuitable [ˌʌn'suːtəbl] *adj* inadecuado(da), inapropiado(da); **he is ~ for the job** no es la persona indicada para el trabajo; **I'm afraid 3 o'clock would be ~** lo siento, pero no me va bien a las 3.

unsure [ˌʌn'ʃɔːr] *adj* **-1.** [not confident]: **to be ~ of o.s.** sentirse inseguro(ra). **-2.** [not certain]: **to be ~ (about OR of)** no estar muy seguro (de).

unsuspecting [ˌʌnsə'spektɪŋ] *adj* desprevenido(da), confiado(da).

unsympathetic ['ʌnˌsɪmpə'θetɪk] *adj*: **~ to** indiferente a.

untangle [ˌʌn'tæŋgl] *vt* desenmarañar.

untapped [ˌʌn'tæpt] *adj* sin explotar.

untenable [ˌʌn'tenəbl] *adj* insostenible.

unthinkable [ʌn'θɪŋkəbl] *adj* impensable, inconcebible.

untidy [ʌn'taɪdɪ] *adj* [room, desk] desordenado(da); [person, appearance] desaliñado(da).

untie [ˌʌn'taɪ] (*cont* **untying**) *vt* desatar.

until [ən'tɪl] ◇ *prep* hasta; **~ now/then** hasta ahora/entonces. ◇ *conj* **-1.** [gen] hasta que. **-2.** (*after negative*): **don't leave ~ you've finished** no te vayas hasta que no hayas terminado.

untimely [ʌn'taɪmlɪ] *adj* **-1.** [premature] prematuro(ra). **-2.** [inappropriate] inoportuno(na).

untold [ˌʌn'təʊld] *adj* [incalculable, vast] incalculable; [suffering, joy] indecible.

untoward [ˌʌntə'wɔːd] *adj* [event] adverso(sa); [behaviour] fuera de lugar.

untrue [ˌʌn'truː] *adj* [not true] falso(sa).

unused [*sense 1* ˌʌn'juːzd, *sense 2* ʌn'juːst] *adj* **-1.** [not previously used] nuevo(va), sin usar. **-2.** [unaccustomed]: **to be ~ to sthg/to doing sthg** no estar acostumbrado(da) a algo/a hacer algo.

unusual [ʌn'juːʒl] *adj* [rare] insólito(ta), poco común.

unusually [ʌn'juːʒəlɪ] *adv* **-1.** [exceptionally] extraordinariamente. **-2.** [surprisingly] sorprendentemente.

unveil [ˌʌn'veɪl] *vt* **-1.** [statue, plaque] descubrir. **-2.** *fig* [plans, policy] revelar.

unwanted [ˌʌn'wɒntɪd] *adj* [clothes, furniture] **superfluo(flua)**; [child, pregnancy] no deseado(da).

unwavering [ʌn'weɪvərɪŋ] *adj* [determination, feeling] firme, inquebrantable; [concentration] constante; [gaze] fijo(ja).

unwelcome [ʌn'welkəm] *adj* inoportuno(na).

unwell [ˌʌn'wel] *adj*: **to be/feel ~** estar/sentirse mal.

unwieldy [ʌn'wiːldɪ] *adj* **-1.** [object] abultado(da); [tool] poco manejable. **-2.** *fig* [system, organization] poco eficiente.

unwilling [ˌʌn'wɪlɪŋ] *adj*: **to be ~ to do sthg** no estar dispuesto a hacer algo.

unwind [ˌʌn'waɪnd] (*pt & pp* **unwound**) ◇ *vt* desenrollar. ◇ *vi fig* [person] relajarse.

unwise [ˌʌn'waɪz] *adj* imprudente.

unwitting [ʌn'wɪtɪŋ] *adj fml* inconsciente.

unworkable [ˌʌn'wɜːkəbl] *adj* impracticable.

unworthy [ʌn'wɜːðɪ] *adj* [undeserving]: **to be ~ of** no ser digno(na) de.

unwound [ˌʌn'waʊnd] *pt & pp* → **unwind**.

unwrap [ˌʌn'ræp] *vt* [present] desenvolver; [parcel] desempaquetar.

unwritten law [ˌʌn'rɪtn-] *n* ley *f* no escrita.

up [ʌp] ◇ *adv* **-1.** [towards a higher position] hacia arriba; [in a higher position] arriba; **to throw sthg ~** lanzar algo hacia arriba; **she's ~ in her room** está arriba en su cuarto; **pick it ~!** ¡cógelo!, ¡agárralo! *Amer*; **we walked ~ to the top** subimos hasta arriba del todo; **prices are going ~** los precios están subiendo. **-2.** [into an upright position]: **to stand ~** levantarse. **-3.** [northwards]: **I'm going ~ to York next week** voy a subir a York la semana próxima; **~ north** en el norte. **-4.** [along a road or river] **their house is 100 metres further ~** su casa está 100 metros más adelante. ◇ *prep* **-1.** [towards a higher position]: **we went ~ the mountain** subimos por la montaña; **I went ~ the stairs** subí las escaleras. **-2.** [in a higher position] en lo alto de; **~ a tree** en un árbol. **-3.** [at far end of] al final de; **they live ~ the road from us** viven al final de nuestra calle. **-4.** [against current of river]: **~ the Amazon** Amazonas arriba. ◇ *adj* **-1.** [out of bed] levantado(da); **I was ~ at six today** hoy me levanté a las seis. **-2.** [at an end] terminado(da). **-3.** *inf* [wrong]: **is something ~?** ¿pasa algo?, ¿algo va mal?; **what's ~?** ¿qué pasa? ◇ *n*: **~s and downs** altibajos *mpl*. ◆ **up and down** ◇ *adv*: **to jump ~ and down** saltar para arriba y para abajo; **to walk ~ and down** andar para un lado y para otro. ◇ *prep*: **we walked ~ and down the avenue** estuvimos caminando arriba y abajo de la avenida. ◆ **up to** *prep* **-1.** [indicating level] hasta; **it could take ~ to six weeks** podría tardar hasta seis semanas; **it's not ~ to standard** no tiene el nivel necesario. **-2.** [well or able enough for]: **to be ~ to doing sthg** sentirse con fuerzas (como) para hacer algo; **my French isn't ~ to much** mi francés no es gran cosa. **-3.** *inf* [secretly doing something]: **what are you ~ to?** ¿qué andas tramando? **-4.** [indicating responsibility]: **it's not ~ to me to decide** no depende de mí el decidir. ◆ **up to, up until** *prep* hasta.

up-and-coming *adj* prometedor(ra).

upbringing ['ʌp,brɪŋɪŋ] *n* educación *f*.

update [,ʌp'deɪt] *vt* actualizar.

upheaval [ʌp'hiːvl] *n* trastorno *m*, agitación *f*.

upheld [ʌp'held] *pt & pp* → **uphold**.

uphill [,ʌp'hɪl] ◇ *adj* [rising] empinado(da), cuesta arriba; *fig* [difficult] arduo(dua), difícil. ◇ *adv* cuesta arriba.

uphold [ʌp'həʊld] (*pt & pp* **-held**) *vt* sostener, apoyar.

upholstery [ʌp'həʊlstərɪ] *n* tapicería *f*.

upkeep ['ʌpkiːp] *n* mantenimiento *m*.

uplifting [ʌp'lɪftɪŋ] *adj* inspirador(ra).

up-market *adj* de clase superior.

upon [ə'pɒn] *prep fml* en, sobre; **~ entering the room** al entrar en el cuarto; **question ~ question** pregunta tras pregunta; **summer is ~ us** ya tenemos el verano encima.

upper ['ʌpə'] ◇ *adj* superior. ◇ *n* [of shoe] pala *f*.

upper class *n*: **the ~** la clase alta. ◆ **upper-class** *adj* de clase alta.

upper hand *n*: **to have/gain the ~ (in)** llevar/empezar a llevar la ventaja (en).

uppermost ['ʌpəməʊst] *adj* **-1.** [highest] más alto(ta). **-2.** [most important]: **to be ~ in one's mind** ser lo más importante para uno.

upright [*adj senses 1 & 2 & adv* ,ʌp'raɪt, *adj sense 3 & n* 'ʌpraɪt] ◇ *adj* **-1.** [erect - person, chair] derecho(cha). **-2.** [standing vertically - object] vertical. **-3.** *fig* [honest]

recto(ta), honrado(da). ◇ *adv* erguidamente. ◇ *n* poste *m*.

uprising ['ʌp,raɪzɪŋ] *n* sublevación *f*.

uproar ['ʌprɔːʳ] *n* **-1.** (U) [commotion] alboroto *m*. **-2.** [protest] escándalo *m*.

uproot [ʌp'ruːt] *vt* **-1.** [person] desplazar, mudar. **-2.** BOT [plant] desarraigar.

upset [ʌp'set] (*pt & pp* **upset**) ◇ *adj* **-1.** [distressed] disgustado(da). **-2.** MED: **to have an ~ stomach** sentirse mal del estómago. ◇ *n*: **to have a stomach ~** sentirse mal del estómago. ◇ *vt* **-1.** [distress] disgustar, perturbar. **-2.** [mess up] dar al traste con. **-3.** [overturn, knock over] volcar.

upshot ['ʌpʃɒt] *n* resultado *m*.

upside down [,ʌpsaɪd-] ◇ *adj* al revés. ◇ *adv* al revés; **to turn sthg ~** revolver algo, desordenar algo.

upstairs [,ʌp'steəz] ◇ *adj* de arriba. ◇ *adv* arriba. ◇ *n* el piso de arriba.

upstart ['ʌpstɑːt] *n* advenedizo *m*, -za *f*.

upstream [,ʌp'striːm] *adv* río arriba.

upsurge ['ʌpsɜːdʒ] *n*: **~ of** OR **in** aumento *m* considerable de.

uptake ['ʌpteɪk] *n*: **to be quick on the ~** cogerlas al vuelo; **to be slow on the ~** ser un poco torpe.

uptight [ʌp'taɪt] *adj inf* tenso(sa), nervioso(sa).

up-to-date *adj* **-1.** [modern] moderno(na). **-2.** [most recent] actual, al día. **-3.** [informed]: **to keep ~ with** mantenerse al día de.

upturn ['ʌptɜːn] *n*: **~ (in)** mejora *f* (de).

upward ['ʌpwəd] ◇ *adj* hacia arriba. ◇ *adv Am* = **upwards**.

upwards ['ʌpwədz] *adv* hacia arriba. ◆ **upwards of** *prep* más de.

uranium [jʊ'reɪnjəm] *n* uranio *m*.

Uranus ['jʊərənəs] *n* Urano *m*.

urban ['ɜːbən] *adj* urbano(na).

urbane [ɜː'beɪn] *adj* cortés, urbano(na).

urchin ['ɜːtʃɪn] *n dated* pilluelo *m*, -la *f*.

Urdu ['ʊəduː] *n* urdu *m*.

urge [ɜːdʒ] ◇ *n* impulso *m*, deseo *m*; **to have an ~ to do sthg** desear ardientemente hacer algo. ◇ *vt* **-1.** [try to persuade]: **to ~ sb to do sthg** instar a alguien a hacer algo. **-2.** [advocate] recomendar encarecidamente.

urgency ['ɜːdʒənsɪ] *n* (U) urgencia *f*.

urgent ['ɜːdʒənt] *adj* **-1.** [pressing] urgente. **-2.** [desperate] apremiante.

urinal [,jʊə'raɪnl] *n* [place] urinario *m*; [vessel] orinal *m*.

urinate ['jʊərɪneɪt] *vi* orinar.

urine ['jʊərɪn] *n* orina *f*.

urn [ɜːn] *n* **-1.** [for ashes] urna *f*. **-2.** [for tea, coffee] *cilindro o barril con grifo para servir té o café en grandes cantidades*.

Uruguay ['juərəgwaɪ] *n* Uruguay.

Uruguayan [,juərə'gwaɪən] ◇ *adj* uruguayo(ya). ◇ *n* uruguayo *m*, -ya *f*.

us [ʌs] *pers pron* **-1.** (*direct, indirect*) nos; **can you see/hear** ~? ¿puedes vernos/oírnos?; **it's** ~ somos nosotros; **he sent** ~ **a letter** nos mandó una carta; **she gave it to** ~ nos lo dio. **-2.** (*stressed, after prep, in comparisons etc*) nosotros(tras); **you can't expect US to do it** no esperarás que lo hagamos NOSOTROS; **with/without** ~ con/sin nosotros; **they are more wealthy than** ~ son más ricos que nosotros; **all of** ~ todos (nosotros); **some of** ~ algunos de nosotros.

US (*abbr of* United States) *n* EEUU *mpl*.

USA *n* (*abbr of* United States of America) EEUU *mpl*.

usage ['juːzɪdʒ] *n* uso *m*.

use [*n & aux vb* juːs, *vt* juːz] ◇ *n* uso *m*; **to be in** ~ usarse; **to be out of** ~ no usarse; **"out of** ~**"** "no funciona"; **to make** ~ **of sthg** utilizar OR aprovechar algo; **to be of/no** ~ ser útil/inútil; **what's the** ~ (**of doing sthg**)? ¿de qué sirve (hacer algo)? ◇ *aux vb* soler, acostumbrar; **he** ~**d to be fat** antes estaba gordo; **I** ~**d to go swimming** solía OR acostumbraba ir a nadar. ◇ *vt* **-1.** [utilize, employ] usar, emplear. **-2.** [exploit] usar, manejar. ◆ **use up** *vt sep* agotar.

used [*sense 1* juːzd, *sense 2* juːst] *adj* **-1.** [dirty, second-hand] usado(da). **-2.** [accustomed]: **to be** ~ **to** estar acostumbrado(da) a; **to get** ~ **to** acostumbrarse a.

useful ['juːsful] *adj* **-1.** [handy] útil. **-2.** [helpful - person] valioso(sa).

useless ['juːslɪs] *adj* **-1.** [gen] inútil. **-2.** *inf* [hopeless] incompetente.

user ['juːzər] *n* usuario *m*, -ria *f*.

user-friendly *adj* [gen & COMPUT] fácil de utilizar.

usher ['ʌʃər] ◇ *n* [at wedding] ujier *m*; [at theatre, concert] acomodador *m*, -ra *f*. ◇ *vt*: **to** ~ **sb in** hacer pasar a alguien; **to** ~ **sb out** acompañar a alguien hasta la puerta.

usherette [,ʌʃə'ret] *n* acomodadora *f*.

USSR (*abbr of* Union of Soviet Socialist Republics) *n*: **the (former)** ~ la (antigua) URSS.

usual ['juːʒəl] *adj* habitual; **as** ~ [as normal] como de costumbre; [as often happens] como siempre.

usually ['juːʒəlɪ] *adv* por regla general.

usurp [juː'zɜːp] *vt fml* usurpar.

utensil [juː'tensl] *n* utensilio *m*.

uterus ['juːtərəs] (*pl* **-ri** [-raɪ] OR **-ruses**) *n* útero *m*.

utility [juː'tɪlətɪ] *n* **-1.** [gen & COMPUT] utilidad *f*. **-2.** [public service] servicio *m* público.

utility room *n* trascocina *f*.

utilize, -ise ['juːtəlaɪz] *vt* utilizar.

utmost ['ʌtməʊst] ◇ *adj* mayor, supremo(ma). ◇ *n*: **to do one's** ~ hacer lo imposible; **to the** ~ al máximo, a más no poder.

utter ['ʌtər] ◇ *adj* puro(ra), completo(ta). ◇ *vt* [word] pronunciar; [sound, cry] emitir.

utterly ['ʌtəlɪ] *adv* completamente.

U-turn *n lit & fig* giro *m* de 180°.

v¹ (*pl* **v's** OR **vs**), **V** (*pl* **V's** OR **Vs**) [viː] *n* [letter] v *f*, V *f*.

v² **-1.** (*abbr of* verse) v. **-2.** (*abbr of* volt) v. **-3.** (*abbr of* vide) [cross-reference] v. **-4.** *abbr of* versus.

vacancy ['veɪkənsɪ] *n* **-1.** [job, position] vacante *f*. **-2.** [room available] habitación *f* libre; **"no vacancies"** "completo".

vacant ['veɪkənt] *adj* **-1.** [room, chair, toilet] libre. **-2.** [job, post] vacante. **-3.** [look, expression] distraído(da).

vacant lot *n* terreno *m* disponible.

vacate [və'keɪt] *vt* **-1.** [job, post] dejar vacante. **-2.** [room, seat, premises] desocupar.

vacation [və'keɪʃn] *n* vacaciones *fpl*.

vacationer [və'keɪʃənər] *n Am*: **summer** ~ veraneante *m y f*.

vaccinate ['væksɪneɪt] *vt*: **to** ~ **sb (against sthg)** vacunar a alguien (de OR contra algo).

vaccine [*Br* 'væksiːn, *Am* væk'siːn] *n* vacuna *f*.

vacuum ['vækjuəm] ◇ *n* **-1.** TECH & *fig*

vacío *m*. **-2.** [cleaner] aspiradora *f*. ◇ *vt* pasar la aspiradora por.

vacuum cleaner *n* aspiradora *f*.

vacuum-packed *adj* envasado(da) al vacío.

vagina [və'dʒaɪnə] *n* vagina *f*.

vagrant ['veɪgrənt] *n* vagabundo *m*, -da *f*.

vague [veɪg] *adj* **-1.** [imprecise] vago(ga), impreciso(sa). **-2.** [person] poco claro(ra). **-3.** [feeling] leve. **-4.** [evasive] evasivo(va). **-5.** [absent-minded] distraído(da). **-6.** [outline] borroso(sa).

vaguely ['veɪglɪ] *adv* **-1.** [imprecisely] vagamente. **-2.** [slightly, not very] levemente.

vain [veɪn] *adj* **-1.** *pej* [conceited] vanidoso(sa). **-2.** [futile] vano(na). ◆ **in vain** *adv* en vano.

valentine card ['væləntaɪn-] *n* tarjeta *f* que se manda el Día de los Enamorados.

Valentine's Day ['væləntaɪnz-] *n*: **(St)** ~ San Valentín *m*, Día *m* de los Enamorados.

valet ['væleɪ, 'vælɪt] *n* ayuda *m* de cámara.

valiant ['væljənt] *adj* valeroso(sa).

valid ['vælɪd] *adj* **-1.** [argument, explanation] válido(da). **-2.** [ticket, driving licence] valedero(ra).

valley ['vælɪ] (*pl* **valleys**) *n* valle *m*.

valour *Br*, **valor** *Am* ['vælə] *n* (U) *fml & literary* valor *m*.

valuable ['væljuəbl] *adj* valioso(sa). ◆ **valuables** *npl* objetos *mpl* de valor.

valuation [,vælju'eɪʃn] *n* **-1.** [pricing, estimated price] valuación *f*. **-2.** [opinion, judging of worth] valoración *f*.

value ['vælju:] ◇ *n* valor *m*; **to be good** ~ estar muy bien de precio; **to be** ~ **for money** estar muy bien de precio. ◇ *vt* **-1.** [estimate price of] valorar, tasar. **-2.** [cherish] apreciar. ◆ **values** *npl* [morals] valores *mpl* morales.

value-added tax [-ædɪd-] *n* impuesto *m* sobre el valor añadido.

valued ['vælju:d] *adj* apreciado(da).

valve [vælv] *n* [in pipe, tube] válvula *f*.

van [væn] *n* **-1.** AUT furgoneta *f*, camioneta *f*. **-2.** *Br* RAIL furgón *m*.

vandal ['vændl] *n* vándalo *m*, gamberro *m*, -rra *f*.

vandalism ['vændəlɪzm] *n* vandalismo *m*, gamberrismo *m*.

vandalize, -ise ['vændəlaɪz] *vt* destruir, destrozar.

vanguard ['vængɑːd] *n* vanguardia *f*; **in the** ~ **of** a la vanguardia de.

vanilla [və'nɪlə] *n* vainilla *f*.

vanish ['vænɪʃ] *vi* desaparecer.

vanity ['vænətɪ] *n pej* vanidad *f*.

vantagepoint ['vɑːntɪdʒ,pɔɪnt] *n* posición *f* ventajosa.

vapour *Br*, **vapor** *Am* ['veɪpə] *n* (U) vapor *m*.

variable ['veərɪəbl] *adj* variable.

variance ['veərɪəns] *n fml*: **at** ~ **(with)** en desacuerdo (con).

variation [,veərɪ'eɪʃn] *n*: ~ **(in/on)** variación *f* (en/sobre).

varicose veins ['værɪkəʊs-] *npl* varices *fpl*.

varied ['veərɪd] *adj* variado(da).

variety [və'raɪətɪ] *n* **-1.** [gen] variedad *f*; **for a** ~ **of reasons** por razones varias. **-2.** (U) THEATRE variedades *fpl*.

variety show *n* espectáculo *m* de variedades.

various ['veərɪəs] *adj* **-1.** [several] varios(rias). **-2.** [different] diversos(sas).

varnish ['vɑːnɪʃ] ◇ *n* barniz *m*. ◇ *vt* [with varnish] barnizar; [with nail varnish] pintar.

vary ['veərɪ] ◇ *vt* variar. ◇ *vi*: **to** ~ **(in/with)** variar (de/con).

vase [*Br* vɑːz, *Am* veɪz] *n* florero *m*.

Vaseline® ['væsəliːn] *n* vaselina® *f*.

vast [vɑːst] *adj* enorme, inmenso(sa).

vat [væt] *n* cuba *f*, tina *f*.

VAT [væt, viːeɪ'tiː] (*abbr of* **value added tax**) *n* IVA *m*.

Vatican ['vætɪkən] *n*: **the** ~ el Vaticano.

vault [vɔːlt] ◇ *n* **-1.** [in bank] cámara *f* acorazada. **-2.** [in church] cripta *f*. **-3.** [roof] bóveda *f*. ◇ *vt* saltar. ◇ *vi*: **to** ~ **over sthg** saltar por encima de algo.

VCR (*abbr of* **video cassette recorder**) *n* vídeo *m*.

VD (*abbr of* **venereal disease**) *n* ETS *f*.

VDU (*abbr of* **visual display unit**) *n* monitor *m*.

veal [viːl] *n* (U) ternera *f*.

veer [vɪə] *vi* virar.

vegan ['viːgən] *n* vegetariano que no consume ningún producto que provenga de un animal, como huevos, leche etc.

vegetable ['vedʒtəbl] ◇ *n* **-1.** BOT vegetal *m*. **-2.** [food] hortaliza *f*, legumbre *f*; ~**s** verduras *fpl*. ◇ *adj* vegetal.

vegetarian [,vedʒɪ'teərɪən] ◇ *adj* vegetariano(na). ◇ *n* vegetariano *m*, -na *f*.

vegetation [,vedʒɪ'teɪʃn] *n* vegetación *f*.

vehement ['viːəmənt] *adj* [person, denial] vehemente; [attack, gesture] violento(ta).

vehicle ['viːəkl] *n* [for transport] vehículo *m*.

veil [veɪl] *n lit* & *fig* velo *m*.

vein [veɪn] *n* **-1.** ANAT & BOT vena *f*. **-2.** [of mineral] filón *m*, veta *f*.

velocity [vɪ'lɒsətɪ] *n* velocidad *f*.

velvet ['velvɪt] *n* terciopelo *m*.

vendetta [ven'detə] *n* enemistad *f* mortal.

vending machine ['vendɪŋ-] *n* máquina *f* de venta.

vendor ['vendɔːʳ] *n* vendedor *m*, -ra *f*.

veneer [və'nɪəʳ] *n* [of wood] chapa *f*; *fig* [appearance] apariencia *f*.

venereal disease [vɪ'nɪərɪəl-] *n* enfermedad *f* venérea.

venetian blind *n* persiana *f* veneciana.

Venezuela [ˌvenɪz'weɪlə] *n* Venezuela.

Venezuelan [ˌvenɪz'weɪlən] ◇ *adj* venezolano(na). ◇ *n* venezolano *m*, -na *f*.

vengeance ['vendʒəns] *n* venganza *f*; **with a ~** con creces.

venison ['venɪzn] *n* carne *f* de venado.

venom ['venəm] *n* [poison] veneno *m*; *fig* [spite] malevolencia *f*.

vent [vent] ◇ *n* [opening] abertura *f* de escape; [grille] rejilla *f* de ventilación; **to give ~ to sthg** dar rienda suelta a algo. ◇ *vt*: **to ~ sthg (on)** desahogar algo (contra).

ventilate ['ventɪleɪt] *vt* ventilar.

ventilator ['ventɪleɪtəʳ] *n* ventilador *m*.

ventriloquist [ven'trɪləkwɪst] *n* ventrílocuo *m*, -cua *f*.

venture ['ventʃəʳ] ◇ *n* empresa *f*. ◇ *vt* aventurar; **to ~ to do sthg** aventurarse a hacer algo. ◇ *vi* **-1.** [go somewhere dangerous]: **she ~d outside** se atrevió a salir. **-2.** [take a risk]: **to ~ into** lanzarse a.

venue ['venjuː] *n* lugar *m* (*en que se celebra algo*).

Venus ['viːnəs] *n* [planet] Venus *m*.

veranda(h) [və'rændə] *n* veranda *f*.

verb [vɜːb] *n* verbo *m*.

verbal ['vɜːbl] *adj* verbal.

verbatim [vɜː'beɪtɪm] ◇ *adj* literal. ◇ *adv* literalmente, palabra por palabra.

verbose [vɜː'bəʊs] *adj fml* [person] verboso(sa); [report] prolijo(ja).

verdict ['vɜːdɪkt] *n* **-1.** JUR veredicto *m*, fallo *m*. **-2.** [opinion]: **~ (on)** juicio *m* OR opinión *f* (sobre).

verge [vɜːdʒ] *n* **-1.** [edge, side] borde *m*. **-2.** [brink]: **on the ~ of sthg** al borde de algo; **on the ~ of doing sthg** a punto de hacer algo. ◆ **verge (up)on** *vt fus* rayar en.

verify ['verɪfaɪ] *vt* **-1.** [check] verificar, comprobar. **-2.** [confirm] confirmar.

veritable ['verɪtəbl] *adj hum* or *fml* verdadero(ra).

vermin ['vɜːmɪn] *npl* bichos *mpl*.

vermouth ['vɜːməθ] *n* vermut *m*.

versa → **vice versa**.

versatile ['vɜːsətaɪl] *adj* **-1.** [person] polifacético(ca). **-2.** [machine, tool] que tiene muchos usos.

verse [vɜːs] *n* **-1.** (*U*) [poetry] versos *mpl*, poesía *f*. **-2.** [stanza] estrofa *f*. **-3.** [in Bible] versículo *m*.

versed [vɜːst] *adj*: **well ~ in** versado(da) en.

version ['vɜːʃn] *n* versión *f*.

versus ['vɜːsəs] *prep* SPORT contra.

vertebra ['vɜːtɪbrə] (*pl* **-brae** [-briː]) *n* vértebra *f*.

vertical ['vɜːtɪkl] *adj* vertical.

vertigo ['vɜːtɪgəʊ] *n* vértigo *m*.

verve [vɜːv] *n* brío *m*, entusiasmo *m*.

very ['verɪ] ◇ *adv* **-1.** [as intensifier] muy; **~ much** mucho. **-2.** [as euphemism]: **not ~ often** OR **much** no mucho; **he's not ~ intelligent** no es muy inteligente; **is it good? - not ~** ¿es bueno? - no mucho. ◇ *adj* mismísimo(ma); **the ~ thing I was looking for** justo lo que estaba buscando; **the ~ thought makes me ill** sólo con pensarlo me pongo enfermo; **fighting for his ~ life** luchando por su propia vida; **the ~ best** el mejor (de todos); **at the ~ least** como muy poco; **a house of my ~ own** mi propia casa. ◆ **very well** *adv* muy bien; **you can't ~ well stop him now** es un poco tarde para impedírselo.

vessel ['vesl] *n fml* **-1.** [boat] nave *f*. **-2.** [container] vasija *f*, recipiente *m*.

vest [vest] *n* **-1.** *Br* [undershirt] camiseta *f*. **-2.** *Am* [waistcoat] chaleco *m*.

vested interest ['vestɪd-] *n*: **~ (in)** intereses *mpl* creados (en).

vestibule ['vestɪbjuːl] *n fml* [entrance hall] vestíbulo *m*.

vestige ['vestɪdʒ] *n fml* vestigio *m*.

vestry ['vestrɪ] *n* sacristía *f*.

vet [vet] ◇ *n Br* (*abbr of* **veterinary surgeon**) veterinario *m*, -ria *f*. ◇ *vt* someter a una investigación.

veteran ['vetrən] *n* veterano *m*, -na *f*.

veterinarian [ˌvetərɪ'neərɪən] *n Am* veterinario *m*, -ria *f*.

veterinary surgeon ['vetərɪnrɪ-] *n Br fml* veterinario *m*, -ria *f.*

veto ['viːtəʊ] (*pl* **-es**) ◇ *n* veto *m.* ◇ *vt* vetar.

vex [veks] *vt fml* molestar.

vexed question [,vekst-] *n* manzana *f* de la discordia.

vg (*abbr of* **very good**) MB.

VHF (*abbr of* **very high frequency**) VHF.

VHS (*abbr of* **video home system**) *n* VHS *m.*

via ['vaɪə] *prep* **-1.** [travelling through] vía. **-2.** [by means of] a través de, por.

viable ['vaɪəbl] *adj* viable.

vibrate [vaɪ'breɪt] *vi* vibrar.

vicar ['vɪkəʳ] *n* [in Church of England] párroco *m*; [in Roman Catholic Church] vicario *m.*

vicarage ['vɪkərɪdʒ] *n* casa *f* del párroco.

vicarious [vɪ'keərɪəs] *adj* indirecto(ta).

vice [vaɪs] *n* **-1.** [immorality, moral fault] vicio *m.* **-2.** [tool] torno *m* de banco.

vice-chairman *n* vicepresidente *m.*

vice-chancellor *n* UNIV rector *m*, -ra *f.*

vice-president *n* vicepresidente *m*, -ta *f.*

vice versa [,vaɪsɪ'vɜːsə] *adv* viceversa.

vicinity [vɪ'sɪnətɪ] *n*: **in the ~ (of)** cerca (de).

vicious ['vɪʃəs] *adj* [dog] furioso(sa); [person, ruler] **cruel**; [criticism, attack] despiadado(da).

vicious circle *n* círculo *m* vicioso.

victim ['vɪktɪm] *n* víctima *f.*

victimize, -ise ['vɪktɪmaɪz] *vt* [retaliate against] tomar represalias contra; [pick on] mortificar.

victor ['vɪktəʳ] *n literary* vencedor *m*, -ra *f.*

victorious [vɪk'tɔːrɪəs] *adj* victorioso(sa).

victory ['vɪktərɪ] *n*: **~ (over)** victoria *f* (sobre).

video ['vɪdɪəʊ] (*pl* **-s**) ◇ *n* **-1.** [recording, medium, machine] **vídeo** *m.* **-2.** [cassette] videocasete *m.* ◇ *comp* vídeo. ◇ *vt* **-1.** [using video recorder] grabar en vídeo. **-2.** [using camera] hacer un vídeo de.

video camera *n* videocámara *f.*

video cassette *n* videocasete *m.*

video game *n* videojuego *m.*

videorecorder ['vɪdɪəʊrɪ,kɔːdəʳ] *n* vídeo *m.*

video shop *n* tienda *f* de vídeos.

videotape ['vɪdɪəʊteɪp] *n* videocinta *f.*

vie [vaɪ] (*pt* & *pp* **vied**, *cont* **vying**) *vi*: **to ~ (with sb for sthg/to do sthg)** competir (con alguien por algo/para hacer algo).

Vienna [vɪ'enə] *n* Viena.

Vietnam [*Br* ,vjet'næm, *Am* ,vjet'nɑːm] *n* (el) Vietnam.

Vietnamese [,vjetnə'miːz] ◇ *adj* vietnamita. ◇ *n* **-1.** [person] vietnamita *m y f.* **-2.** [language] vietnamita *m.*

view [vjuː] ◇ *n* **-1.** [opinion] parecer *m*, opinión *f*; **in my ~** en mi opinión. **-2.** [attitude]: **~ (of)** actitud *f* (frente a). **-3.** [scene] vista *f*, panorama *m.* **-4.** [field of vision] vista *f*; **to come into ~** aparecer. ◇ *vt* **-1.** [consider] ver, considerar. **-2.** *fml* [examine, look at - stars etc] observar; [- house, flat] visitar, ver. ◆ **in view of** *prep* en vista de. ◆ **with a view to** *conj* con miras OR vistas a.

viewer ['vjuːəʳ] *n* **-1.** [person] espectador *m*, -ra *f.* **-2.** [apparatus] visionador *m.*

viewfinder ['vjuː,faɪndəʳ] *n* visor *m.*

viewpoint ['vjuːpɔɪnt] *n* **-1.** [opinion] punto *m* de vista. **-2.** [place] mirador *m.*

vigil ['vɪdʒɪl] *n* **-1.** [watch] vigilia *f.* **-2.** RELIG Vigilia *f.*

vigilante [,vɪdʒɪ'læntɪ] *n persona que extraoficialmente patrulla un área para protegerla, tomándose la justicia en sus manos.*

vigorous ['vɪgərəs] *adj* enérgico(ca).

vile [vaɪl] *adj* [person, act] vil, infame; [food, smell] repugnante; [mood] de perros.

villa ['vɪlə] *n* [in country] villa *f*; [in town] chalet *m.*

village ['vɪlɪdʒ] *n* aldea *f*, pueblecito *m.*

villager ['vɪlɪdʒəʳ] *n* aldeano *m*, -na *f.*

villain ['vɪlən] *n* **-1.** [of film, book] malo *m*, -la *f.* **-2.** *dated* [criminal] criminal *m y f.*

vinaigrette [,vɪnɪ'gret] *n* vinagreta *f.*

vindicate ['vɪndɪkeɪt] *vt* justificar.

vindictive [vɪn'dɪktɪv] *adj* vindicativo(va).

vine [vaɪn] *n* [on ground] vid *f*; [climbing plant] parra *f.*

vinegar ['vɪnɪgəʳ] *n* vinagre *m.*

vineyard ['vɪnjəd] *n* viña *f*, viñedo *m.*

vintage ['vɪntɪdʒ] ◇ *adj* **-1.** [wine] añejo(ja). **-2.** [classic] clásico(ca). ◇ *n* cosecha *f* (*de vino*).

vintage wine *n* vino *m* añejo.

vinyl ['vaɪnɪl] *n* vinilo *m.*

viola [vɪ'əʊlə] *n* viola *f.*

violate ['vaɪəleɪt] vt **-1.** [law, treaty, rights] violar, infringir. **-2.** [peace, privacy] invadir.

violence ['vaɪələns] n violencia f.

violent ['vaɪələnt] adj **-1.** [gen] violento(ta). **-2.** [emotion, anger] intenso(sa).

violet ['vaɪələt] ◇ adj violeta, violado(da). ◇ n [flower] violeta f.

violin [,vaɪə'lɪn] n violín m.

violinist [,vaɪə'lɪnɪst] n violinista m y f.

VIP (abbr of **very important person**) n celebridad f.

viper ['vaɪpər] n víbora f.

virgin ['vɜːdʒɪn] ◇ adj literary [spotless] virgen. ◇ n virgen m y f.

Virgo ['vɜːgəʊ] (pl **-s**) n Virgo m.

virile ['vɪraɪl] adj viril.

virtually ['vɜːtʃʊəlɪ] adv prácticamente.

virtual reality n realidad f virtual.

virtue ['vɜːtjuː] n **-1.** [morality, good quality] virtud f. **-2.** [benefit] ventaja f. ◆ **by virtue of** prep fml en virtud de.

virtuous ['vɜːtʃʊəs] adj virtuoso(sa).

virus ['vaɪrəs] n COMPUT & MED virus m.

visa ['viːzə] n visado m.

vis-à-vis [,viːzɑː'viː] prep fml con relación a.

viscose ['vɪskəʊs] n viscosa f.

visibility [,vɪzɪ'bɪlətɪ] n visibilidad f.

visible ['vɪzəbl] adj visible.

vision ['vɪʒn] n **-1.** (U) [ability to see] visión f, vista f. **-2.** [foresight] clarividencia f. **-3.** [impression, dream] visión f.

visit ['vɪzɪt] ◇ n visita f; **on a ~** de visita. ◇ vt visitar.

visiting hours ['vɪzɪtɪŋ-] npl horas fpl de visita.

visitor ['vɪzɪtər] n **-1.** [to one's home, hospital] visita f. **-2.** [to museum, town etc] visitante m y f.

visitors' book n libro m de visitas.

visitor's passport n Br pasaporte m provisional.

visor ['vaɪzər] n visera f.

vista ['vɪstə] n [view] vista f, perspectiva f; fig [wide range] perspectiva f.

visual ['vɪʒʊəl] adj [gen] visual; [of the eyes] ocular.

visual aids npl medios mpl visuales.

visual display unit n monitor m.

visualize, -ise ['vɪʒʊəlaɪz] vt visualizar; **to ~ (sb) doing sthg** imaginar (a alguien) haciendo algo.

vital ['vaɪtl] adj **-1.** [essential] vital, esencial. **-2.** [full of life] enérgico(ca).

vitally ['vaɪtəlɪ] adv sumamente.

vital statistics npl inf medidas fpl (del cuerpo de la mujer).

vitamin [Br 'vɪtəmɪn, Am 'vaɪtəmɪn] n vitamina f.

vivacious [vɪ'veɪʃəs] adj vivaz.

vivid ['vɪvɪd] adj **-1.** [colour] vivo(va). **-2.** [description, memory] vívido(da).

vividly ['vɪvɪdlɪ] adv **-1.** [brightly] con colores muy vivos. **-2.** [clearly] vívidamente.

vixen ['vɪksn] n zorra f.

VLF (abbr of **very low frequency**) VLF.

V-neck n [sweater, dress] jersey m con cuello de pico.

vocabulary [və'kæbjʊlərɪ] n vocabulario m.

vocal ['vəʊkl] adj **-1.** [outspoken] vociferante. **-2.** [of the voice] vocal.

vocal cords npl cuerdas fpl vocales.

vocalist ['vəʊkəlɪst] n [in orchestra] vocalista m y f; [in pop group] cantante m y f.

vocation [vəʊ'keɪʃn] n vocación f.

vocational [vəʊ'keɪʃənl] adj profesional.

vociferous [və'sɪfərəs] adj fml ruidoso(sa).

vodka ['vɒdkə] n [drink] vodka m.

vogue [vəʊg] n moda f; **in ~** en boga.

voice [vɔɪs] ◇ n voz f. ◇ vt [opinion, emotion] expresar.

void [vɔɪd] ◇ adj **-1.** [invalid] inválido(da); → **null**. **-2.** fml [empty]: **~ of** falto(ta) de. ◇ n literary vacío m.

volatile [Br 'vɒlətaɪl, Am 'vɒlətl] adj [situation] volátil; [person] voluble.

vol-au-vent ['vɒləʊvɒŋ] n volován m.

volcano [vɒl'keɪnəʊ] (pl **-es** OR **-s**) n volcán m.

volition [və'lɪʃn] n fml: **of one's own ~** por voluntad propia.

volley ['vɒlɪ] (pl **volleys**) ◇ n **-1.** [of gunfire] ráfaga f. **-2.** fig [rapid succession] torrente m. **-3.** SPORT volea f. ◇ vt volear.

volleyball ['vɒlɪbɔːl] n voleibol m.

volt [vəʊlt] n voltio m.

voltage ['vəʊltɪdʒ] n voltaje m.

voluble ['vɒljʊbl] adj fml locuaz.

volume ['vɒljuːm] n [gen & COMPUT] volumen m.

voluntarily [Br 'vɒləntrɪlɪ, Am ,vɒlən'terəlɪ] adv voluntariamente.

voluntary ['vɒləntrɪ] adj voluntario(ria); **~ organization** organización f benéfica.

volunteer [,vɒlən'tɪər] ◇ n [person who volunteers] voluntario m, -ria f. ◇ vt **-1.**

[offer of one's free will]: **to ~ to do sthg** ofrecerse para hacer algo. **-2.** [information, advice] **dar**, ofrecer. ◇ vi **-1.** [freely offer one's services]: **to ~ (for)** ofrecerse (para). **-2.** MIL alistarse.

vomit ['vɒmɪt] ◇ n vómito m. ◇ vi vomitar.

vote [vəʊt] ◇ n **-1.** [gen] voto m; **~ for/against** voto a favor de/en contra de. **-2.** [session, ballot, result] votación f. **-3.** [votes cast]: **the ~ los votos.** ◇ vt **-1.** [person, leader] **elegir. -2.** [choose]: **to ~ to do sthg** votar hacer algo. ◇ vi: **to ~ (for/against)** votar (a favor de/en contra de).

vote of thanks (pl **votes of thanks**) n palabras fpl de agradecimiento.

voter ['vəʊtə'] n votante m y f.

voting ['vəʊtɪŋ] n votación f.

vouch [vaʊtʃ] ◆ **vouch for** vt fus **-1.** [person] responder por. **-2.** [character, accuracy] dar fe de.

voucher ['vaʊtʃə'] n vale m.

vow [vaʊ] ◇ n RELIG voto m; [solemn promise] promesa f solemne. ◇ vt: **to ~ to do sthg** jurar hacer algo; **to ~ that** jurar que.

vowel ['vaʊəl] n vocal f.

voyage ['vɔɪɪdʒ] n viaje m.

vs abbr of **versus**.

VSO (abbr of **Voluntary Service Overseas**) n organización británica de voluntarios que ayuda a países en vías de desarrollo.

vulgar ['vʌlgə'] adj **-1.** [in bad taste] ordinario(ria). **-2.** [offensive] grosero(ra).

vulnerable ['vʌlnərəbl] adj: **~ (to)** vulnerable (a).

vulture ['vʌltʃə'] n lit & fig buitre m.

w (pl **w's** OR **ws**), **W** (pl **W's** OR **Ws**) ['dʌbljuː] n [letter] w f, W f. ◆ **W -1.** (abbr of **west**) O. **-2.** (abbr of **watt**) w.

wad [wɒd] n **-1.** [of paper] taco m. **-2.** [of banknotes, documents] fajo m. **-3.** [of cotton, cotton wool, tobacco] bola f.

waddle ['wɒdl] vi anadear.

wade [weɪd] vi caminar por el agua. ◆ **wade through** vt fus fig: he was

wading through the documents le costaba mucho leer los documentos.

wading pool ['weɪdɪŋ-] n Am piscina f para niños.

wafer ['weɪfə'] n [thin biscuit] barquillo m.

waffle ['wɒfl] ◇ n **-1.** CULIN gofre m. **-2.** Br inf [vague talk] paja f. ◇ vi enrollarse.

waft [wɑːft, wɒft] vi flotar.

wag [wæg] ◇ vt menear. ◇ vi menearse.

wage [weɪdʒ] ◇ n [gen] salario m; [daily] jornal m. ◇ vt: **to ~ war** hacer la guerra. ◆ **wages** npl [gen] salario m; [daily] jornal m.

wage earner [-,ɜːnə'] n asalariado m, -da f.

wage packet n Br **-1.** [envelope] sobre m de pago. **-2.** fig [pay] paga f.

wager ['weɪdʒə'] n apuesta f.

waggle ['wægl] inf vt menear.

waggon ['wægən] Br = **wagon**.

wagon ['wægən] n **-1.** [horse-drawn vehicle] carro m. **-2.** Br RAIL vagón m.

wail [weɪl] ◇ n lamento m, gemido m. ◇ vi lamentarse, gemir.

waist [weɪst] n cintura f.

waistcoat ['weɪskəʊt] n chaleco m.

waistline ['weɪstlaɪn] n cintura f, talle m.

wait [weɪt] ◇ n espera f. ◇ vi: **to ~ (for sthg/sb)** esperar (algo/a alguien); **to be unable to ~ to do sthg** estar impaciente por hacer algo; **to ~ and see** esperar y ver lo que pasa. ◆ **wait for** vt fus esperar. ◆ **wait on** vt fus [serve food to] servir. ◆ **wait up** vi quedarse despierto(ta) esperando.

waiter ['weɪtə'] n camarero m.

waiting list ['weɪtɪŋ-] n lista f de espera.

waiting room ['weɪtɪŋ-] n sala f de espera.

waitress ['weɪtrɪs] n camarera f.

waive [weɪv] vt fml [rule] no aplicar.

wake [weɪk] (pt **woke** OR **-d**, pp **woken** OR **-d**) ◇ n [of ship, boat] estela f. ◇ vt despertar. ◇ vi despertarse. ◆ **wake up** ◇ vt sep despertar. ◇ vi [wake] despertarse.

waken ['weɪkən] fml ◇ vt despertar. ◇ vi despertarse.

Wales [weɪlz] n (el país de) Gales.

walk [wɔːk] ◇ n **-1.** [way of walking] andar m, paso m. **-2.** [journey on foot] paseo m; **to go for a ~** dar un paseo; **it's ten minutes' ~ away** está a diez minutos andando. ◇ vt **-1.** [dog] pasear. **-2.** [streets] **andar por**; [distance] recorrer, andar. ◇ *vi* **-1.** [move on foot] andar, caminar. **-2.** [for pleasure] pasear. ◆ **walk out** *vi* **-1.** [leave suddenly] salirse. **-2.** [go on strike] **declararse en huelga.** ◆ **walk out on** *vt fus* abandonar.

walker ['wɔːkə'] *n* caminante *m y f*, paseante *m y f*.

walkie-talkie [ˌwɔːkɪ'tɔːkɪ] *n* walki-talki *m*.

walking ['wɔːkɪŋ] *n* (*U*) [for sport] marcha *f*; [for pleasure] andar *m*.

walking shoes *npl* zapatos *mpl* para caminar.

walking stick *n* bastón *m*.

Walkman® ['wɔːkmən] *n* walkman® *m*.

walk of life (*pl* **walks of life**) *n*: people from all walks of life gente de toda condición.

walkout ['wɔːkaʊt] *n* huelga *f*.

walkover ['wɔːkˌəʊvə'] *n* victoria *f* fácil.

walkway ['wɔːkweɪ] *n* [on ship, oilrig, machine] pasarela *f*; [between buildings] paso *m*.

wall [wɔːl] *n* **-1.** [inside building, of cell, stomach] pared *f*. **-2.** [outside] muro *m*.

wallchart ['wɔːltʃɑːt] *n* (gráfico *m*) mural *m*.

walled [wɔːld] *adj* amurallado(da).

wallet ['wɒlɪt] *n* cartera *f*, billetera *f*.

wallflower ['wɔːlˌflaʊə'] *n* **-1.** [plant] alhelí *m*. **-2.** *inf fig* [person] *persona tímida que queda al margen de una fiesta.*

wallop ['wɒləp] *inf vt* [child] pegar una torta a; [ball] golpear fuerte.

wallow ['wɒləʊ] *vi* [in liquid] revolcarse.

wallpaper ['wɔːlˌpeɪpə'] ◇ *n* papel *m* de pared OR de empapelar. ◇ *vt* empapelar.

Wall Street *n* Wall Street *f*, *zona financiera neoyorquina.*

wally ['wɒlɪ] *n Br inf* imbécil *m y f*.

walnut ['wɔːlnʌt] *n* **-1.** [nut] nuez *f*. **-2.** [wood, tree] nogal *m*.

walrus ['wɔːlrəs] (*pl inv* OR **-es**) *n* morsa *f*.

waltz [wɔːls] ◇ *n* vals *m*. ◇ *vi* [dance] bailar el vals.

wan [wɒn] *adj* pálido(da).

wand [wɒnd] *n* varilla *f* mágica.

wander ['wɒndə'] *vi* vagar; my mind kept ~ing se me iba la mente en otras cosas.

wane [weɪn] *vi* [influence, interest] disminuir, decrecer.

wangle ['wæŋgl] *vt inf* agenciarse.

want [wɒnt] *fml* ◇ *n* **-1.** [need] necesidad *f*. **-2.** [lack] falta *f*; **for ~ of** por OR a falta de. **-3.** [deprivation] indigencia *f*, miseria *f*. ◇ *vt* [desire] querer; **to ~ to do sthg** querer hacer algo; **to ~ sb to do sthg** querer que alguien haga algo.

wanted ['wɒntɪd] *adj*: **to be ~ (by the police)** ser buscado(da) (por la policía).

wanton ['wɒntən] *adj fml* gratuito(ta), sin motivo.

war [wɔː'] ◇ *n lit* & *fig* guerra *f*. ◇ *vi* estar en guerra.

ward [wɔːd] *n* **-1.** [in hospital] sala *f*. **-2.** *Br* POL distrito *m* electoral. **-3.** JUR pupilo *m*, -la *f*. ◆ **ward off** *vt fus* protegerse de.

warden ['wɔːdn] *n* **-1.** [of park] guarda *m y f*. **-2.** *Br* [of youth hostel, hall of residence] encargado *m*, -da *f*. **-3.** [of monument] guardián *m*, -ana *f*. **-4.** *Am* [prison governor] director *m*, -ra *f*.

warder ['wɔːdə'] *n* [in prison] carcelero *m*, -ra *f*.

wardrobe ['wɔːdrəʊb] *n* **-1.** [piece of furniture] armario *m*, guardarropa *m*. **-2.** [collection of clothes] guardarropa *m*, vestuario *m*.

warehouse ['weəhaʊs, *pl* -haʊzɪz] *n* almacén *m*.

wares [weəz] *npl literary* mercancías *fpl*.

warfare ['wɔːfeə'] *n* (*U*) guerra *f*.

warhead ['wɔːhed] *n* ojiva *f*, cabeza *f*.

warily ['weərəlɪ] *adv* con cautela.

arm [wɔːm] ◇ *adj* **-1.** [pleasantly hot gen] caliente; [- weather, day] caluroso(sa); **it's/I'm ~** hace/tengo calor; [lukewarm] tibio(bia), templado(da). **-2.** [clothes etc] que abriga. **-3.** [colour, sound] cálido(da). **-4.** [friendly - person, atmosphere, smile] afectuoso(sa); [- congratulations] efusivo(va). ◇ *vt* calentar. ◆ **warm up** ◇ *vt sep* calentar. ◇ *vi* [gen] entrar en calor; [weather, room, engine] calentarse.

warm-hearted [-'hɑːtɪd] *adj* afectuoso(sa).

warmly ['wɔːmlɪ] *adv* **-1.** [in warm clothes]: **to dress ~** vestirse con ropa de abrigo. **-2.** [in a friendly way] calurosamente.

warmth [wɔːmθ] *n* **-1.** [heat] calor *m*. **-2.** [of clothes] abrigo *m*. **-3.** [friendliness] cordialidad *f*.

warn [wɔːn] *vt* prevenir, advertir; **to ~ sb of sthg** prevenir a alguien algo; **to ~ sb not to do sthg** advertir a alguien que no haga algo.

warning ['wɔːnɪŋ] *n* aviso *m*, advertencia *f*.

warning light *n* piloto *m*.

warning triangle *n* Br triángulo *m* de avería.

warp [wɔːp] ◇ *vt* **-1.** [wood] alabear. **-2.** [personality] torcer, deformar. ◇ *vi* alabearse.

warrant ['wɒrənt] ◇ *n* orden *f* OR mandamiento *m* judicial. ◇ *vt fml* merecer.

warranty ['wɒrəntɪ] *n* garantía *f*.

warren ['wɒrən] *n* zona *f* de conejos.

warrior ['wɒrɪəʳ] *n* guerrero *m*, -ra *f*.

Warsaw ['wɔːsɔː] *n* Varsovia; **the ~ Pact** el Pacto de Varsovia.

warship ['wɔːʃɪp] *n* buque *m* de guerra.

wart [wɔːt] *n* verruga *f*.

wartime ['wɔːtaɪm] *n* tiempos *mpl* de guerra.

wary ['weərɪ] *adj*: ~ **(of)** receloso(sa) (de).

was [*weak form* wəz, *strong form* wɒz] *pt* → **be**.

wash [wɒʃ] ◇ *n* **-1.** [act of washing] lavado *m*. **-2.** [things to wash] ropa sucia. **-3.** [from boat] estela *f*. ◇ *vt* **-1.** [gen] lavar; [hands, face] lavarse. **-2.** [carry - subj: waves etc] arrastrar, llevarse. ◇ *vi* **-1.** [clean oneself] lavarse. **-2.** [waves, oil]: **to ~ over sthg** bañar algo. ◆ **wash away** *vt sep* [subj: water, waves] llevarse, barrer. ◆ **wash up** ◇ *vt sep* Br [dishes] lavar, fregar. ◇ *vi* **-1.** Br [wash the dishes] fregar OR lavar los platos. **-2.** Am [wash o.s.] lavarse.

washable ['wɒʃəbl] *adj* lavable.

washbasin Br ['wɒʃ,beɪsn], **washbowl** Am ['wɒʃbəʊl] *n* lavabo *m*.

washcloth ['wɒʃ,klɒθ] *n* Am toallita *f* para lavarse la cara.

washer ['wɒʃəʳ] *n* TECH arandela *f*.

washing ['wɒʃɪŋ] *n* (U) **-1.** [operation] colada *f*. **-2.** [clothes - dirty] ropa *f* sucia OR para lavar; [- clean] colada *f*.

washing line *n* tendedero *m*.

washing machine *n* lavadora *f*.

washing powder *n* Br detergente *m*, jabón *m* en polvo.

Washington ['wɒʃɪŋtən] *n* [town]: ~ **D.C.** ciudad *f* de Washington.

washing-up *n* **-1.** Br [crockery, pans etc] platos *mpl* para fregar. **-2.** [operation] fregado *m*; **to do the ~** fregar los platos.

washing-up liquid *n* Br detergente *m* para vajillas.

washout ['wɒʃaʊt] *n inf* desastre *m*.

washroom ['wɒʃrum] *n* Am aseos *mpl*.

wasn't [wɒznt] = **was not**.

wasp [wɒsp] *n* [insect] avispa *f*.

wastage ['weɪstɪdʒ] *n* desperdicio *m*.

waste [weɪst] ◇ *adj* [land] yermo(ma); [material, fuel] de desecho. ◇ *n* **-1.** [misuse, incomplete use] desperdicio *m*, derroche *m*; **a ~ of time** una pérdida de tiempo. **-2.** (U) [refuse] desperdicios *mpl*; [chemical, toxic etc] residuos *mpl*. ◇ *vt* [time] perder; [money] malgastar, derrochar; [food, energy, opportunity] desperdiciar. ◆ **wastes** *npl literary* yermos *mpl*.

wastebasket Am = **wastepaper basket**.

waste disposal unit *n* triturador *m* de basuras.

wasteful ['weɪstful] *adj* derrochador(ra).

waste ground *n* (U) descampados *mpl*.

wastepaper basket [,weɪst'peɪpəʳ-], **wastepaper bin** [,weɪst'peɪpəʳ-], **wastebasket** Am ['weɪst,bɑːskɪt] *n* papelera *f*.

watch [wɒtʃ] ◇ *n* **-1.** [timepiece] reloj *m*. **-2.** [act of watching]: **to keep ~** estar de guardia; **to keep ~ on sthg/sb** vigilar algo/a alguien. **-3.** MIL [group of people] guardia *f*. ◇ *vt* **-1.** [look at - gen] ver; [- sunset] contemplar; [- football match, TV] mirar. **-2.** [spy on] vigilar. **-3.** [be careful about] tener cuidado con, vigilar. ◇ *vi* mirar, observar. ◆ **watch out** *vi* tener cuidado.

watchdog ['wɒtʃdɒg] *n* **-1.** [dog] perro *m* guardián. **-2.** *fig* [organization] comisión *f* de vigilancia.

watchful ['wɒtʃful] *adj* atento(ta).

watchmaker ['wɒtʃ,meɪkəʳ] *n* relojero *m*, -ra *f*.

watchman ['wɒtʃmən] (*pl* **-men** [-mən]) *n* vigilante *m*.

water ['wɔːtəʳ] ◇ *n* [gen] agua *f*. ◇ *vt* regar. ◇ *vi* **-1.** [eyes]: **my eyes are ~ing** me lloran los ojos. **-2.** [mouth]: **my mouth is ~ing** se me hace la boca agua. ◆ **waters** *npl* aguas *fpl*. ◆ **water down** *vt sep* **-1.** [dilute] diluir, aguar. **-2.** *usu pej* [moderate] moderar.

water bottle *n* cantimplora *f*.

water closet *n dated* wáter *m*.

watercolour ['wɔːtə,kʌləʳ] *n* acuarela *f*.

watercress ['wɔːtəkres] *n* berro *m*.

waterfall ['wɔːtəfɔːl] *n* cascada *f*, salto *m* de agua.

water heater *n* calentador *m* de agua.

waterhole ['wɔːtəhəʊl] *n* balsa *f* (donde acuden a beber los animales).

watering can ['wɔːtərɪŋ-] *n* regadera *f*.

water level *n* nivel *m* del agua.

water lily *n* nenúfar *m*.

waterline ['wɔːtəlaɪn] *n* NAUT línea *f* de flotación.

waterlogged ['wɔːtəlɒgd] *adj* inundado(da).

water main *n* cañería *f* principal.

watermark ['wɔːtəmɑːk] *n* **-1.** [in paper] filigrana *f*. **-2.** [showing water level] marca *f* del nivel del agua.

watermelon ['wɔːtə,melən] *n* sandía *f*.

water polo *n* water-polo *m*.

waterproof ['wɔːtəpruːf] ◇ *adj* impermeable. ◇ *n* impermeable *m*.

watershed ['wɔːtəʃed] *n fig* momento *m* decisivo.

water skiing *n* esquí *m* acuático.

water tank *n* reserva *f* de agua.

watertight ['wɔːtətaɪt] *adj* [waterproof] hermético(ca).

waterway ['wɔːtəweɪ] *n* vía *f* navegable.

waterworks ['wɔːtəwɜːks] (*pl inv*) *n* [building] central *f* de agua.

watery ['wɔːtərɪ] *adj* **-1.** [food] soso(sa); [drink] aguado(da). **-2.** [pale] desvaído(da).

watt [wɒt] *n* vatio *m*.

wave [weɪv] ◇ *n* **-1.** [of hand] ademán *m* OR señal *f* (con la mano). **-2.** [of water] ola *f*. **-3.** [of emotion, nausea, panic] arranque *m*; [of immigrants, crime etc] oleada *f*. **-4.** [of light, sound, heat] onda *f*. **-5.** [in hair] ondulación *f*. ◇ *vt* **-1.** [move about as signal] agitar. **-2.** [signal to] hacer señales OR señas a. ◇ *vi* **-1.** [with hand - in greeting] saludar con la mano; [- to say goodbye] decir adiós con la mano; **to** ~ **at** OR **to sb** saludar a alguien con la mano. **-2.** [flag] ondear; [trees] agitarse.

wavelength ['weɪvleŋθ] *n* longitud *f* de onda; **to be on the same** ~ *fig* estar en la misma onda.

waver ['weɪvər] *vi* **-1.** [falter - resolution, confidence] flaquear. **-2.** [hesitate] dudar, vacilar. **-3.** [fluctuate] oscilar.

wavy ['weɪvɪ] *adj* ondulado(da).

wax [wæks] ◇ *n* cera *f*. ◇ *vt* encerar.

wax paper *n Am* papel *m* de cera.

waxworks ['wæksw3ːks] (*pl inv*) *n* museo *m* de cera.

way [weɪ] ◇ *n* **-1.** [manner, method] manera *f*, modo *m*; **in the same** ~ del mismo modo, igualmente; **this/that** ~ así; **in a** ~ en cierto modo; **to get** OR **have one's** ~ salirse uno con la suya. **-2.** [route, path] camino *m*; **to lose one's** ~ perderse; ~ **in** entrada *f*; ~ **out** salida *f*; **it's out of my** ~ no me pilla de

camino; **it's out of the** ~ [place] está algo aislado; **on the** OR **on one's** ~ de camino; **I'm on my** ~ voy de camino; **to be under** ~ [ship] estar navegando; *fig* [meeting] estar en marcha; **to get under** ~ [ship] zarpar; [meeting] ponerse en marcha; **to be in the** ~ estar en medio; **to go out of one's** ~ **to do sthg** tomarse muchas molestias para hacer algo; **to keep out of the** ~ mantenerse alejado; **to make** ~ **for** dar paso a. **-3.** [direction] dirección *f*; **come this** ~ ven por aquí; **go that** ~ ve por ahí; **which** ~ **do we go?** ¿hacia dónde vamos?; **the wrong** ~ **up** OR **round** al revés; **the right** ~ **up** OR **round** del derecho. **-4.** [distance]: **all the** ~ todo el camino OR trayecto; **it's a long** ~ **away** está muy lejos; **we have a long** ~ **to go** queda mucho camino por recorrer. **-5.** *phr*: **to give** ~ [under weight, pressure] ceder; "**give** ~" *Br* AUT "ceda el paso"; **no** ~! ¡ni hablar! ◇ *adv inf* [far] mucho; **it's** ~ **too big** es toda de grande. ◆ **ways** *npl* [customs, habits] costumbres *fpl*, hábitos *mpl*. ◆ **by the way** *adv* por cierto.

waylay [,weɪ'leɪ] (*pt & pp* **-laid**) *vt* abordar.

wayward ['weɪwəd] *adj* [person, behaviour] incorregible.

WC (*abbr of* **water closet**) WC.

we [wiː] *pers pron* nosotros *mpl*, -tras *fpl*; **WE can't do it** NOSOTROS no podemos hacerlo; **as** ~ **say in France** como decimos en Francia; ~ **British** nosotros los británicos.

weak [wiːk] *adj* **-1.** [gen] débil. **-2.** [material, structure] frágil. **-3.** [argument, tea etc] flojo(ja). **-4.** [lacking knowledge, skill]: **to be** ~ **on sthg** estar flojo(ja) en algo.

weaken ['wiːkn] ◇ *vt* debilitar. ◇ *vi* **-1.** [become less determined] ceder, flaquear. **-2.** [physically] debilitarse.

weakling ['wiːklɪŋ] *n pej* enclenque *m* y *f*.

weakness ['wiːknɪs] *n* **-1.** [gen] debilidad *f*. **-2.** [imperfect point] defecto *m*.

wealth [welθ] *n* **-1.** [riches] riqueza *f*. **-2.** [abundance] profusión *f*.

wealthy ['welθɪ] *adj* rico(ca).

wean [wiːn] *vt* [from mother's milk] destetar.

weapon ['wepən] *n* arma *f*.

weaponry ['wepənrɪ] *n* (*U*) armamento *m*.

wear [weər] (*pt* **wore**, *pp* **worn**) ◇ *n* (*U*) **-1.** [use] uso *m*. **-2.** [damage] desgaste *m*; ~ **and tear** desgaste. **-3.** [type of clothes] **ropa** *f.* ◇ *vt* **-1.** [clothes, hair] llevar; [shoes] **calzar**; **to** ~ **red** vestirse de rojo. **-2.** [damage] desgastar. ◇ *vi* **-1.** [deteriorate] **desgastarse. -2.** [last]: **to** ~ **well/badly** durar mucho/poco. ◆**wear away** ◇ *vt sep* desgastar. ◇ *vi* desgastarse. ◆**wear down** *vt sep* **-1.** [reduce size of] desgastar. **-2.** [weaken] agotar. ◆**wear off** *vi* desaparecer, disiparse. ◆**wear out** ◇ *vt sep* **-1.** [shoes, clothes] gastar. **-2.** [person] agotar. ◇ *vi* gastarse.

weary ['wɪərɪ] *adj* fatigado(da), cansado(da); **to be** ~ **of sthg/of doing sthg** estar cansado de algo/de hacer algo.

weasel ['wiːzl] *n* comadreja *f.*

weather ['weðər] ◇ *n* tiempo *m*; **to be under the** ~ no encontrarse muy bien. ◇ *vt* [crisis etc] superar.

weather-beaten [-,biːtn] *adj* [face, skin] curtido(da).

weathercock ['weðəkɒk] *n* veleta *f.*

weather forecast *n* parte *m* meteorológico.

weatherman ['weðəmæn] (*pl* **-men** [-men]) *n* hombre *m* del tiempo.

weather vane [-veɪn] *n* veleta *f.*

weave [wiːv] (*pt* **wove**, *pp* **woven**) ◇ *vt* [using loom] tejer. ◇ *vi* [move]: **to** ~ **through** colarse por entre.

weaver ['wiːvər] *n* tejedor *m*, -ra *f.*

web [web] *n* **-1.** [cobweb] telaraña *f.* **-2.** *fig* [of lies etc] urdimbre *f.*

wed [wed] (*pt* & *pp* **-ded** OR **wed**) *literary* ◇ *vt* desposar. ◇ *vi* desposarse.

we'd [wiːd] = **we had, we would.**

wedding ['wedɪŋ] *n* boda *f*, casamiento *m.*

wedding anniversary *n* aniversario *m* de boda.

wedding cake *n* tarta *f* nupcial.

wedding dress *n* traje *m* de novia.

wedding ring *n* anillo *m* de boda, argolla *f* *Amer.*

wedge [wedʒ] ◇ *n* **-1.** [for steadying or splitting] cuña *f.* **-2.** [triangular slice] porción *f*, trozo *m.* ◇ *vt*: **to** ~ **sthg open/ shut** dejar algo abierto/cerrado con una cuña.

Wednesday ['wenzdɪ] *n* miércoles *m inv; see also* **Saturday.**

wee [wiː] ◇ *adj Scot* pequeño(ña). ◇ *n v inf* pipí *m.* ◇ *vi v inf* hacer pipí.

weed [wiːd] ◇ *n* **-1.** [wild plant] mala hierba *f.* **-2.** *Br inf* [feeble person] canijo *m*, -ja *f.* ◇ *vt* desherbar, escardar.

weedkiller ['wiːd,kɪlər] *n* herbicida *m.*

weedy ['wiːdɪ] *adj Br inf* [feeble] enclenque.

week [wiːk] *n* [gen] semana *f.*

weekday ['wiːkdeɪ] *n* día *m* laborable.

weekend [,wiːk'end] *n* fin *m* de semana.

weekly ['wiːklɪ] ◇ *adj* semanal. ◇ *adv* semanalmente. ◇ *n* semanario *m.*

weep [wiːp] (*pt* & *pp* **wept**) ◇ *vt* derramar. ◇ *vi* llorar.

weeping willow [,wiːpɪŋ-] *n* sauce *m* llorón.

weigh [weɪ] *vt* **-1.** [gen] pesar. **-2.** [consider carefully] sopesar. ◆**weigh down** *vt sep* **-1.** [physically] sobrecargar. **-2.** [mentally]: **to be** ~**ed down by** OR **with** estar abrumado(da) de OR por. ◆**weigh up** *vt sep* **-1.** [consider carefully] sopesar. **-2.** [size up] hacerse una idea de.

weight [weɪt] *n* **-1.** [gen] peso *m*; **to put on** OR **gain** ~ engordar; **to lose** ~ adelgazar; **to pull one's** ~ poner (uno) de su parte. **-2.** [metal object] pesa *f.*

weighted ['weɪtɪd] *adj*: **to be** ~ **in favour of/against** inclinarse a favor/en contra de.

weighting ['weɪtɪŋ] *n* prima por vivir en una ciudad con alto coste de vida.

weightlifting ['weɪt,lɪftɪŋ] *n* levantamiento *m* de pesos, halterofilia *f.*

weighty ['weɪtɪ] *adj* [serious] de peso.

weir [wɪər] *n* presa *f*, dique *m.*

weird [wɪəd] *adj* raro(ra), extraño(ña).

welcome ['welkəm] ◇ *adj* **-1.** [guest] bienvenido(da). **-2.** [free]: **you're** ~ **to come si quieres, puedes venir. -3.** [appreciated]: **to be** ~ ser de agradecer. **-4.** [in reply to thanks]: **you're** ~ de nada. ◇ *n* bienvenida *f.* ◇ *vt* **-1.** [receive] dar la bienvenida a. **-2.** [approve, support] recibir bien. ◇ *excl* ¡bienvenido(da)!

weld [weld] ◇ *n* soldadura *f.* ◇ *vt* soldar.

welfare ['welfeər] ◇ *adj* de asistencia social. ◇ *n* **-1.** [state of well-being] bienestar *m.* **-2.** *Am* [income support] subsidio *m* de la seguridad social.

welfare state *n*: **the** ~ el Estado de bienestar.

well [wel] (*compar* **better**, *superl* **best**) ◇ *adj* bien; **to be** ~ [healthy] estar bien (de salud); **all is** ~ todo va bien; **(it's) just as** ~ menos mal. ◇ *adv* **-1.** [satisfactorily, thoroughly] bien; **they were** ~ **beaten** fueron ampliamente derrotados; **to go** ~ ir bien; ~ **done!** ¡muy bien!; ~ **and truly** completamente. **-2.**

[definitely, certainly] **claramente, definitivamente**; **it was ~ worth it** sí que valió la pena. **-3.** [as emphasis]: **you know perfectly ~ (that)** sabes de sobra (que). **-4.** [very possibly]: **it could ~ rain** es muy posible que llueva. ◇ *n* **pozo** *m*. ◇ *excl* **-1.** [gen] **bueno; oh ~!** ¡en fin! **-2.** [in surprise] ¡vaya! ◆ **as well** *adv* **-1.** [in addition] **también. -2.** [with same result]: **you may** OR **might as ~ (do it)** ¿y por qué no (lo haces)? ◆ **as well as** *conj* **además de.** ◆ **well up** *vi* **brotar.**

we'll [wiːl] = **we shall, we will.**

well-advised [-əd'vaɪzd] *adj* **sensato(ta); you would be ~ to do it** sería aconsejable que lo hicieras.

well-behaved [-bɪ'heɪvd] *adj* **formal, bien educado(da).**

wellbeing [ˌwel'biːɪŋ] *n* **bienestar** *m*.

well-built *adj* **fornido(da).**

well-done *adj* [thoroughly cooked] **muy hecho(cha).**

well-dressed [-'drest] *adj* **bien vestido(da).**

well-earned [-'ɜːnd] *adj* **bien merecido(da).**

well-heeled [-hiːld] *adj* *inf* **ricachón(ona).**

wellington boots ['welɪŋtən-], **wellingtons** ['welɪŋtənz] *npl* **botas** *fpl* **de agua.**

well-kept *adj* **-1.** [neat, tidy] **bien cuidado(da). -2.** [not revealed] **bien guardado(da).**

well-known *adj* **conocido(da).**

well-mannered [-'mænəd] *adj* **de buenos modales.**

well-meaning *adj* **bienintencionado(da).**

well-nigh [-naɪ] *adv* **casi.**

well-off *adj* **-1.** [rich] **acomodado(da), rico(ca). -2.** [well-provided]: **to be ~ for sthg** **tener bastante de algo.**

well-read [-'red] *adj* **instruido(da), culto(ta).**

well-rounded [-'raʊndɪd] *adj* [varied] **completo(ta).**

well-timed *adj* **oportuno(na).**

well-to-do *adj* **adinerado(da).**

wellwisher ['wel,wɪʃəʳ] *n* **simpatizante** *m y f* (que da muestras de apoyo).

Welsh [welʃ] ◇ *adj* **galés(esa).** ◇ *n* [language] **galés** *m*. ◇ *npl*: **the ~** los galeses.

Welshman ['welʃmən] (*pl* **-men** [-mən]) *n* **galés** *m*.

Welshwoman ['welʃ,wʊmən] (*pl* **-women** [-,wɪmɪn]) *n* **galesa** *f*.

went [went] *pt* → **go.**

wept [wept] *pt & pp* → **weep.**

were [wɜːʳ] *pt* → **be.**

we're [wɪəʳ] = **we are.**

weren't [wɜːnt] = **were not.**

west [west] ◇ *n* **-1.** [direction] **oeste** *m*. **-2.** [region]: **the West** el Oeste. ◇ *adj* **del oeste.** ◇ *adv*: ~ **(of)** al oeste (de). ◆ **West** *n* POL: **the ~** el Oeste Occidente.

West Bank *n*: **the ~** Cisjordania.

West Country *n Br*: **the ~** el sudoeste de Inglaterra.

West End *n Br*: **the ~** zona central de Londres, famosa por sus teatros, tiendas etc.

westerly ['westəlɪ] *adj* **del oeste.**

western ['westən] ◇ *adj* **occidental.** ◇ *n* [book] **novela** *f* **del oeste;** [film] **película** *f* **del oeste, western** *m*.

West German ◇ *adj* **de la Alemania Occidental.** ◇ *n* [person] **alemán** *m*, **-ana** *f* **occidental.**

West Germany *n*: **(the former) ~** (la antigua) Alemania Occidental.

West Indian ◇ *adj* **antillano(na).** ◇ *n* [person] **antillano** *m*, **-na** *f*.

West Indies [-'ɪndiːz] *npl*: **the ~** las Antillas.

Westminster ['westmɪnstəʳ] *n* **barrio londinense en que se encuentra el parlamento británico; por extensión éste.**

westward ['westwəd] ◇ *adj* **hacia el oeste.** ◇ *adv* = **westwards.**

westwards ['westwədz] *adv* **hacia el oeste.**

wet [wet] (*pt & pp* **wet** OR **-ted**) ◇ *adj* **-1.** [soaked] **mojado(da);** [damp] **húmedo(da). -2.** [rainy] **lluvioso(sa). -3.** [paint, cement] **fresco(ca). -4.** *Br inf pej* [weak, feeble] **ñoño(ña).** ◇ *n inf* POL *político conservador moderado.* ◇ *vt* [soak] **mojar;** [dampen] **humedecer.**

wet blanket *n inf pej* **aguafiestas** *m y f*.

wet suit *n* **traje** *m* **de submarinista.**

we've [wiːv] = **we have.**

whack [wæk] *inf n* [hit] **castañazo** *m*.

whale [weɪl] *n* [animal] **ballena** *f*.

wharf [wɔːf] (*pl* **-s** OR **wharves** [wɔːvz]) *n* **muelle** *m*, **embarcadero** *m*.

what [wɒt] ◇ *adj* **-1.** (*in direct, indirect questions*) **qué;** ~ **shape is it?** ¿qué forma tiene?; **he asked me ~ shape it was** me preguntó qué forma tenía; ~ **colour is it?** ¿de qué color es? **-2.** (*in exclamations*) **qué;** ~ **a surprise!** ¡qué sorpresa!; ~ **a stupid idea!** ¡qué idea más tonta! ◇ *pron* **-1.** (*interrogative*) **qué;** ~ **are they doing?** ¿qué hacen?; ~ **are they talking about?** ¿de qué están hablando?; ~ **is it called?** ¿cómo se llama?; ~ **does it cost?** ¿cuánto cuesta?; ~ **is it like?** ¿cómo es?; ~'s **the Spanish for "book"?** ¿cómo se dice "book" en español?; ~ **about another drink/ going out for a meal?** ¿qué tal otra copa/si salimos a comer?; ~ **about me?** ¿y yo qué?; ~ **if nobody comes?** ¿y si no viene nadie, qué? **-2.** (*relative*) lo que; **I saw** ~ **happened/he did** yo vi lo que ocurrió/hizo; **I don't know** ~ **to do** no sé qué hacer. ◇ *excl* [expressing disbelief] ¿qué?; ~, **no milk!** ¿cómo? ¿que no hay leche?

whatever [wɒt'evəʳ] ◇ *adj* cualquier; **eat** ~ **food you find** come lo que encuentres; **no chance** ~ ni la más remota posibilidad; **nothing** ~ nada en absoluto. ◇ *pron* **-1.** [no matter what]: ~ **they may offer** ofrezcan lo que ofrezcan; ~ **you like** lo que (tú) quieras; ~ **happens** pase lo que pase. **-2.** [indicating surprise]: ~ **do you mean?** ¿qué diablos quieres decir? **-3.** [indicating ignorance]: ~ **that is** OR **may be sea lo** que sea eso; **or** ~ o lo que sea.

whatsoever [,wɒtsəʊ'evəʳ] *adj*: **nothing** ~ nada en absoluto; **none** ~ ni uno.

wheat [wiːt] *n* trigo *m*.

wheedle ['wiːdl] *vt* decir con zalamería; **to** ~ **sb into doing sthg** camelar OR engatusar a alguien para que haga algo; **to** ~ **sthg out of sb** sonsacarle algo a alguien.

wheel [wiːl] ◇ *n* **-1.** [gen] rueda *f*. **-2.** [steering wheel] volante *m*. ◇ *vt* empujar (*algo sobre ruedas*). ◇ *vi* **-1.** [move in circle] dar vueltas. **-2.** [turn round]: **to** ~ **round** darse la vuelta.

wheelbarrow ['wiːl,bærəʊ] *n* carretilla *f*.

wheelchair ['wiːl,tʃeəʳ] *n* silla *f* de ruedas.

wheelclamp ['wiːl,klæmp] *n* cepo *m*.

wheeze [wiːz] *vi* resollar.

whelk [welk] *n* buccino *m*.

when [wen] ◇ *adv* (*in direct, indirect question*) cuándo; ~ **does the plane arrive?** ¿cuándo llega el avión?; **he asked me** ~ **I would be in London** me preguntó cuándo estaría en Londres. ◇ *conj* cuando; **tell me** ~ **you've read it** avísame cuando lo hayas leído; **on the day** ~ **it happened** el día (en) que pasó; **you said it was black** ~ **it was actually white** dijiste que era negro cuando en realidad era blanco.

whenever [wen'evəʳ] ◇ *conj* [no matter when] cuando; [every time] cada vez

que; ~ **you like** cuando quieras. ◇ *adv* cuando sea.

where [weəʳ] ◇ *adv* (*in direct, indirect questions*) dónde; ~ **do you live?** ¿dónde vives?; **do you know** ~ **he lives?** ¿sabes dónde vive?; ~ **are we going?** ¿adónde vamos?; **I don't know** ~ **to start** no sé por dónde empezar. ◇ *conj* [referring to place, situation] donde; **this is** ~ **... es** aquí donde ...; **go** ~ **you like** vete (a) donde quieras.

whereabouts [*adv* ,weərə'bauts, *n* 'weərəbauts] ◇ *adv* (por) dónde. ◇ *npl* paradero *m*.

whereas [weər'æz] *conj* mientras que.

whereby [weə'bai] *conj fml* por el/la cual.

whereupon [,weərə'pɒn] *conj fml* tras OR con lo cual.

wherever [weər'evəʳ] ◇ *conj* [no matter where] dondequiera que; ~ **you go** dondequiera que vayas; **sit** ~ **you like** siéntate donde quieras. ◇ *adv* **-1.** [no matter where] en cualquier parte. **-2.** [indicating surprise]: ~ **did you hear that?** ¿dónde diablos habrás oído eso?

wherewithal ['weəwɪðɔːl] *n fml*: **to have the** ~ **to do sthg** disponer de los medios para hacer algo.

whet [wet] *vt*: **to** ~ **sb's appetite (for sthg)** despertar el interés de alguien (por algo).

whether ['weðəʳ] *conj* **-1.** [indicating choice, doubt] si; **I doubt** ~ **she'll do it** dudo que lo haga. **-2.** [no matter if]: ~ **I want to or not** tanto si quiero como si no.

which [wɪtʃ] ◇ *adj* **-1.** (*in direct, indirect questions*) qué; ~ **house is yours?** ¿cuál es tu casa?; ~ **one?** ¿cuál?; ~ **ones?** ¿cuáles? **-2.** [to refer back to]: **in** ~ **case** en cuyo caso. ◇ *pron* **-1.** (*in direct, indirect questions*) cuál, cuáles (*pl*); ~ **do you prefer?** ¿cuál prefieres? **I can't decide** ~ **to have** no sé cuál coger. **-2.** (*in relative clause replacing noun*) que; **the table,** ~ **was made of wood, ...** la mesa, que OR la cual era de madera, ...; **the world in** ~ **we live** el mundo en que OR en el cual vivimos. **-3.** (*to refer back to a clause*) lo cual; **she denied it,** ~ **surprised me** lo negó, lo cual me sorprendió.

whichever [wɪtʃ'evəʳ] ◇ *adj* **-1.** [no matter which]: ~ **route you take** vayas por donde vayas. **-2.** [the one which]: ~ **colour you prefer** el color que prefieras. ◇ *pron* el que (la que), los que (las que) (*pl*); **take ~ you like** coge el que quieras.

whiff [wɪf] *n* [smell] olorcillo *m*.

while [waɪl] ◇ *n* rato *m*; **it's a long ~ since I did that** hace mucho que no hago eso; **for a ~** un rato; **after a ~** después de un rato; **in a ~** dentro de poco; **once in a ~** de vez en cuando. ◇ *conj* **-1.** [during the time that] mientras. **-2.** [whereas] mientras que. **-3.** [although] aunque. ◆ **while away** *vt sep* pasar.

whilst [waɪlst] *conj* = **while**.

whim [wɪm] *n* capricho *m*.

whimper ['wɪmpər] *vt & vi* gimotear.

whimsical ['wɪmzɪkl] *adj* [idea, story] fantasioso(sa); [remark] juguetón(ona).

whine [waɪn] *vi* [child, dog] gemir; [siren] ulular.

whinge [wɪndʒ] *vi Br*: **to ~ (about)** quejarse (de).

whip [wɪp] ◇ *n* **-1.** [for hitting] látigo *m*; [for horse] fusta *f*. **-2.** *Br POL* miembro de un partido encargado de asegurar que otros miembros voten en el parlamento. ◇ *vt* **-1.** [gen] azotar. **-2.** [take quickly]: **to ~ sthg out/off** sacar/quitar algo rápidamente. **-3.** [whisk] batir.

whipped cream [wɪpt-] *n* nata *f* montada.

whip-round *n Br inf*: **to have a ~** hacer una colecta.

whirl [wɜːl] ◇ *n* fig [of activity, events] torbellino *m*. ◇ *vt*: **to ~ sb/sthg round** hacer dar vueltas a alguien/algo. ◇ *vi* [move around] arremolinarse; [dancers] girar vertiginosamente.

whirlpool ['wɜːlpuːl] *n* remolino *m*.

whirlwind ['wɜːlwɪnd] *n* torbellino *m*.

whirr [wɜːr] *vi* zumbar.

whisk [wɪsk] ◇ *n* CULIN varilla *f*. ◇ *vt* **-1.** [move quickly]: **to ~ sthg away/out** llevarse/sacar algo rápidamente. **-2.** CULIN batir.

whisker ['wɪskər] *n* [pelo *m* del] bigote *m*. ◆ **whiskers** *npl* [of person] patillas *fpl*; [of cat] bigotes *mpl*.

whisky *Br*, **whiskey** *Am & Irish* (*pl* **whiskeys**) ['wɪskɪ] *n* whisky *m*.

whisper ['wɪspər] ◇ *vt* susurrar. ◇ *vi* cuchichear.

whistle ['wɪsl] ◇ *n* **-1.** [sound] silbido *m*, pitido *m*. **-2.** [device] silbato *m*, pito *m*. ◇ *vt* silbar. ◇ *vi* [person] silbar, chiflar *Amer*; [referee] pitar; [bird] piar.

white [waɪt] ◇ *adj* **-1.** [gen] blanco(ca). **-2.** [coffee, tea] con leche. ◇ *n* **-1.** [colour] blanco *m*. **-2.** [person] blanco *m*,

-ca *f*. **-3.** [of egg] clara *f*. **-4.** [of eye] blanco *m*.

white-collar *adj* de oficina; **~ worker** oficinista *m y f*.

white elephant *n* fig mamotreto *m* (*caro e inútil*).

Whitehall ['waɪthɔːl] *n* calle londinense en que se encuentra la Administración británica; por extensión ésta.

white-hot *adj* incandescente.

White House *n*: **the ~** la Casa Blanca.

white lie *n* mentira *f* piadosa.

whiteness ['waɪtnɪs] *n* blancura *f*.

white paper *n POL* libro *m* blanco.

white sauce *n* (salsa *f*) bechamel *f*.

white spirit *n Br* especie de aguarrás.

whitewash ['waɪtwɒʃ] ◇ *n* **-1.** (*U*) [paint] blanqueo *m*, lechada *f* (de cal). **-2.** *pej* [cover-up] encubrimiento *m*. ◇ *vt* [paint] blanquear.

whiting ['waɪtɪŋ] (*pl inv* OR **-s**) *n* pescadilla *f*.

Whitsun ['wɪtsn] *n* [day] Pentecostés *m*.

whittle ['wɪtl] *vt* [reduce]: **to ~ down** OR **away** reducir gradualmente.

whiz, whizz [wɪz] *vi*: **to ~ past** OR **by** pasar muy rápido OR zumbando.

whiz(z) kid *n inf* genio *m*, prodigio *m*.

who [huː] *pron* **-1.** (*in direct, indirect questions*) quién, quiénes (*pl*); **~ are you?** ¿quién eres tú?; **~ did you see?** ¿a quién viste?; **I didn't know ~ she was** no sabía quién era. **-2.** (*in relative clauses*) que; **he's the doctor ~ treated me** es el médico que me atendió; **those ~ are in favour** los que están a favor.

who'd [huːd] = **who had**, **who would**.

whodu(n)nit [ˌhuːˈdʌnɪt] *n inf* historia *f* policíaca de misterio.

whoever [huːˈevər] *pron* **-1.** [unknown person] quienquiera, (*pl*) quienesquiera; **~ finds it** quienquiera que lo encuentre; **tell ~ you like** díselo a quien quieras. **-2.** [indicating surprise, astonishment]: **~ can that be?** ¿quién podrá ser? **-3.** [no matter who]: **come in, ~ you are** pasa, seas quién seas.

whole [həʊl] ◇ *adj* **-1.** [entire, complete] entero(ra). **-2.** [for emphasis]: **a ~ lot taller** muchísimo más alto; **a ~ new idea** una idea totalmente nueva. ◇ *n* **-1.** [all]: **the ~ of the school/summer** el colegio/verano entero. **-2.** [unit, complete thing] todo *m*. ◆ **as a whole** *adv* en conjunto. ◆ **on the whole** *adv* en general.

wholefood ['həʊlfuːd] *n* Br comida *f* integral.

whole-hearted [-'hɑːtɪd] *adj* profundo(da).

wholemeal ['həʊlmiːl] *adj* Br integral.

wholesale ['həʊlseɪl] ◇ *adj* -1. COMM al por mayor. -2. *pej* [indiscriminate] indiscriminado(da). ◇ *adv* -1. COMM al por mayor. -2. *pej* [indiscriminately] indiscriminadamente.

wholesaler ['həʊl,seɪlər] *n* mayorista *m* y *f*.

wholesome ['həʊlsəm] *adj* sano(na).

whole wheat *Am* = wholemeal.

who'll [huːl] = who will.

wholly ['həʊlɪ] *adv* completamente.

whom [huːm] *pron* -1. (*in direct, indirect questions*) *fml* quién, quiénes (*pl*); **from ~ did you receive it?** ¿de quién lo recibiste?; **for/of/to ~** por/de/a quién. -2. (*in relative clauses*) que; **the man ~ I saw** el hombre que vi; **the man to ~ I gave it** el hombre al que se lo di; **several people came, none of ~ I knew** vinieron varias personas, de las que no conocía a ninguna.

whooping cough ['huːpɪŋ-] *n* tos *f* ferina.

whopping ['wɒpɪŋ] *inf* ◇ *adj* enorme. ◇ *adv*: **a ~ great lorry/lie, a ~ big lorry/lie** un camión/una mentira enorme.

whore [hɔːr] *n pej* zorra *f*, puta *f*.

who're ['huːər] = who are.

whose [huːz] ◇ *pron* -1. (*in direct, indirect questions*) de quién, (*pl*) de quiénes; **~ is this?** ¿de quién es esto?; **I wonder ~ they are** me pregunto de quién serán. -2. (*in relative clauses*) cuyo(ya), cuyos(yas) (*pl*); **that's the boy ~ father's an MP** ese es el chico cuyo padre es diputado; **the woman ~ daughters are twins** la mujer cuyas hijas son gemelas. ◇ *adj* de quién; **~ car is that?** ¿de quién es ese coche?

who's who [huːz-] *n* [book] Quién es Quién *m*.

who've [huːv] = who have.

why [waɪ] ◇ *adv* por qué; **~ did you lie to me?** ¿por qué me mentiste?; **~ don't you all come?** ¿por qué no venís todos?; **~ not?** ¿por qué no? ◇ *conj* por qué; **I don't know ~ he said that** no sé por qué dijo eso. ◇ *pron*: **there are several reasons ~ he left** hay varias razones por las que se marchó; **that's ~ she did it** por eso es por lo que lo hizo; **I don't know the reason**

~ no se por qué razón. ◇ *excl* ¡hombre!, ¡vaya! ◆ **why ever** *adv*: **~ did you do that?** ¿por qué diablos has hecho eso?

wick [wɪk] *n* mecha *f*.

wicked ['wɪkɪd] *adj* -1. [evil] malvado(da). -2. [mischievous, devilish] travieso(sa).

wicker ['wɪkər] *adj* de mimbre.

wickerwork ['wɪkəwɜːk] *n* (U) artículos *mpl* de mimbre.

wicket ['wɪkɪt] *n* CRICKET [stumps] palos *mpl*.

wide [waɪd] ◇ *adj* -1. [broad] ancho(cha); **it's 50 cm ~** tiene 50 cm de ancho. -2. [range, choice etc] amplio(plia). -3. [gap, difference, implications] grande, considerable. -4. [off-target] desviado(da). ◇ *adv* -1. [broadly]: **to open/spread sthg ~** abrir/desplegar algo completamente. -2. [off target]: **to go** OR **be ~** salir desviado.

wide-angle lens *n* gran angular *m*.

wide-awake *adj* completamente despierto(ta).

widely ['waɪdlɪ] *adv* -1. [travel, read] extensamente. -2. [believed, known, loved] generalmente. -3. [differ, vary] mucho.

widen ['waɪdn] *vt* [gen] ampliar; [road, bridge] ensanchar.

wide open *adj* -1. [window, door] abierto(ta) de par en par. -2. [eyes] completamente abierto(ta).

wide-ranging [-'reɪndʒɪŋ] *adj* [changes, survey, consequences] de gran alcance; [discussion, interests] de gran variedad; [selection] amplio(plia).

widespread ['waɪdspred] *adj* extendido(da), general.

widow ['wɪdəʊ] *n* [woman] viuda *f*.

widowed ['wɪdəʊd] *adj* viudo(da).

widower ['wɪdəʊər] *n* viudo *m*.

width [wɪdθ] *n* -1. [breadth] anchura *f*; **it's 50 cm in ~** tiene 50 cm de ancho. -2. [in swimming pool] ancho *m*.

wield [wiːld] *vt* -1. [weapon] esgrimir; [implement] manejar. -2. [power] ejercer.

wife [waɪf] (*pl* **wives**) *n* mujer *f*, esposa *f*.

wig [wɪg] *n* peluca *f*.

wiggle ['wɪgl] *inf vt* menear; [hips etc] contonear.

wild [waɪld] *adj* -1. [gen] salvaje; [plant, flower] silvestre; [bull] bravo(va). -2. [landscape, scenery] agreste. -3. [weather, sea] borrascoso(sa). -4. [crowd, laughter, applause] frenético(ca). -5. [hair] alborotado(da). -6. [hope, idea, plan] descabellado(da). **-7.** [guess, exaggeration] extravagante. ◆ **wilds** *npl*: the ~s las tierras remotas.

wilderness ['wɪldənɪs] *n* **-1.** [barren land] yermo *m*, desierto *m*. **-2.** [overgrown land] jungla *f*.

wild-goose chase *n inf* búsqueda *f* infructuosa.

wildlife ['waɪldlaɪf] *n* (U) fauna *f*.

wildly ['waɪldlɪ] *adv* **-1.** [enthusiastically] frenéticamente. **-2.** [without discipline, inaccurately] a lo loco. **-3.** [very] extremadamente.

wilful *Br*, **willful** *Am* ['wɪlfʊl] *adj* **-1.** [stubborn] que siempre se tiene que salir con la suya. **-2.** [deliberate] deliberado(da).

will¹ [wɪl] ◇ *n* **-1.** [gen] voluntad *f*. **-2.** [document] testamento *m*. ◇ *vt*: **to ~ sthg to happen** desear mucho que ocurra algo; **to ~ sb to do sthg** desear mucho que alguien haga algo.

will² [wɪl] *modal vb* **-1.** [to express future tense]: **they say it ~ rain tomorrow** dicen que lloverá OR va a llover mañana; **when ~ we get paid?** ¿cuándo nos pagarán?; **~ they come? - yes, they ~** ¿vendrán? - sí. **-2.** [indicating willingness]: **~ you have some more tea?** ¿te apetece más té?; **I won't do it** no lo haré. **-3.** [in commands, requests]: **you ~ leave this house at once** vas a salir de esta casa ahora mismo; **close that window, ~ you?** cierra la ventana, ¿quieres?; **~ you be quiet!** ¿queréis hacer el favor de callaros? **-4.** [indicating possibility, what usually happens]: **the hall ~ hold up to 1,000 people** la sala tiene cabida para 1.000 personas. **-5.** [expressing an assumption]: **that'll be your father** ese va a ser OR será tu padre. **-6.** [indicating irritation]: **she ~ keep phoning me** ¡y venga a llamarme!

willful *Am* = **wilful**.

willing ['wɪlɪŋ] *adj* **-1.** [prepared]: **to be ~ (to do sthg)** estar dispuesto(ta) (a hacer algo). **-2.** [eager] servicial.

willingly ['wɪlɪŋlɪ] *adv* de buena gana.

willow (tree) ['wɪləʊ-] *n* sauce *m*.

willpower ['wɪl,paʊəʳ] *n* fuerza *f* de voluntad.

willy-nilly [,wɪlɪ'nɪlɪ] *adv* pase lo que pase.

wilt [wɪlt] *vi* [plant] marchitarse; [person] desfallecer, extenuarse.

wily ['waɪlɪ] *adj* astuto(ta).

wimp [wɪmp] *n pej inf* blandengue *m y f*.

win [wɪn] (*pt & pp* **won**) ◇ *n* victoria *f*, triunfo *m*. ◇ *vt* ganar. ◇ *vi* ganar. ◆ **win over**, **win round** *vt sep* convencer.

wince [wɪns] *vi* hacer una mueca de dolor; **to ~ at/with sthg** estremecerse ante/de algo.

winch [wɪntʃ] *n* torno *m*.

wind¹ [wɪnd] ◇ *n* **-1.** METEOR viento *m*. **-2.** [breath] aliento *m*, resuello *m*. **-3.** (U) [in stomach] gases *mpl*. ◇ *vt* [knock breath out of] dejar sin aliento.

wind² [waɪnd] (*pt & pp* **wound**) ◇ *vt* **-1.** [string, thread] enrollar; **to ~ sthg around sthg** enrollar algo alrededor de algo. **-2.** [clock, watch] dar cuerda a. ◇ *vi* serpentear. ◆ **wind down** ◇ *vt sep* **-1.** [car window] bajar. **-2.** [business] cerrar poco a poco. ◇ *vi* [person] relajarse, descansar. ◆ **wind up** ◇ *vt sep* **-1.** [finish - activity] finalizar, concluir; [business] liquidar. **-2.** [clock, watch] dar cuerda a. **-3.** [car window] subir. **-4.** *Br inf* [annoy] vacilar, tomar el pelo a. ◇ *vi inf* [end up] terminar, acabar.

windfall ['wɪndfɔːl] *n* [unexpected gift] dinero *m* llovido del cielo.

winding ['waɪndɪŋ] *adj* tortuoso(sa).

wind instrument [wɪnd-] *n* instrumento *m* de viento.

windmill ['wɪndmɪl] *n* [building] molino *m* de viento.

window ['wɪndəʊ] *n* **-1.** [gen & COMPUT] ventana *f*. **-2.** AUT ventanilla *f*. **-3.** [of shop] escaparate *m*.

window box *n* jardinera *f* (de ventana).

window cleaner *n* limpiacristales *m y f inv*.

window ledge *n* alféizar *m*.

window pane *n* cristal *m* (de la ventana).

windowsill ['wɪndəʊsɪl] *n* alféizar *m*.

windpipe ['wɪndpaɪp] *n* tráquea *f*.

windscreen *Br* ['wɪndskriːn], **windshield** *Am* ['wɪndʃiːld] *n* parabrisas *m inv*.

windscreen washer *n* lavaparabrisas *m inv*.

windscreen wiper *n* limpiaparabrisas *m inv*.

windshield *Am* = **windscreen**.

windsurfing ['wɪnd,sɜːfɪŋ] *n* windsurf *m*.

windswept ['wɪndswept] *adj* [scenery] azotado(da) por el viento.

windy ['wɪndɪ] *adj* [day, weather] vento-

so(sa), de mucho viento; [place] expuesto(ta) al viento; **it's ~** hace viento.
wine [waɪn] *n* vino *m*; **red/white ~** vino tinto/blanco.
wine bar *n Br* bar de cierta elegancia especializado en vinos que suele servir comidas.
wine cellar *n* bodega *f*.
wineglass ['waɪnglɑːs] *n* copa *f* OR vaso *m* (de vino).
wine list *n* lista *f* de vinos.
wine merchant *n Br* vinatero *m*, -ra *f*.
wine tasting [-ˌteɪstɪŋ] *n* cata *f* de vinos.
wine waiter *n* sommelier *m*.
wing [wɪŋ] *n* **-1.** [gen] ala *f*. **-2.** AUT guardabarros *m inv*. **-3.** SPORT [side of pitch] banda *f*; [winger] extremo *m*. ◆ **wings** *npl* THEATRE: **the ~s** los bastidores.
winger ['wɪŋər] *n* SPORT extremo *m*.
wing mirror *n* retrovisor *m*.
wink [wɪŋk] ◇ *n* guiño *m*. ◇ *vi* [eye]: **to ~ (at sb)** guiñar (a alguien).
winkle ['wɪŋkl] *n* bígaro *m*.
winner ['wɪnər] *n* ganador *m*, -ra *f*.
winning ['wɪnɪŋ] *adj* **-1.** [team, competitor] vencedor(ra); [goal, point] de la victoria; [ticket, number] premiado(da). **-2.** [smile, ways] atractivo(va). ◆ **winnings** *npl* ganancias *fpl*.
winning post *n* meta *f*.
winter ['wɪntər] ◇ *n* (*U*) invierno *m*. ◇ *comp* de invierno, invernal.
winter sports *npl* deportes *mpl* de invierno.
wintertime ['wɪntətaɪm] *n* (*U*) invierno *m*.
wint(e)ry ['wɪntrɪ] *adj* [gen] de invierno, invernal; [showers] con nieve.
wipe [waɪp] ◇ *n*: **give the table a ~** pásale un trapo a la mesa. ◇ *vt* [rub to clean] limpiar, pasar un trapo a; [rub to dry] secar. ◆ **wipe out** *vt sep* **-1.** [erase] borrar. **-2.** [eradicate] aniquilar. ◆ **wipe up** *vt sep* empapar, limpiar.
wire ['waɪər] ◇ *n* **-1.** [gen] alambre *m*; ELEC cable *m*. **-2.** [telegram] telegrama *m*. ◇ *vt* **-1.** [connect]: **to ~ sthg to sthg** conectar algo a algo. **-2.** [ELEC - house] poner la instalación eléctrica de; [- plug] conectar el cable a. **-3.** [send telegram to] enviar un telegrama a.
wireless ['waɪəlɪs] *n dated* radio *f*.
wiring ['waɪərɪŋ] *n* (*U*) instalación *f* eléctrica.
wiry ['waɪərɪ] *adj* **-1.** [hair] estropajoso(sa). **-2.** [body, man] nervudo(da).

wisdom ['wɪzdəm] *n* **-1.** [learning] sabiduría *f*. **-2.** [good sense] sensatez *f*.
wisdom tooth *n* muela *f* del juicio.
wise [waɪz] *adj* **-1.** [learned] sabio(bia). **-2.** [sensible] prudente.
wisecrack ['waɪzkræk] *n pej* broma *f*, chiste *m*.
wish [wɪʃ] ◇ *n*: **~ (for sthg/to do sthg)** deseo *m* (de algo/de hacer algo). ◇ *vt*: **to ~ to do sthg** *fml* desear hacer algo; **to ~ sb sthg** desear a alguien algo; **I ~ (that) you had told me before!** ¡ojalá me lo hubieras dicho antes!; **I ~ (that) I were** OR **was rich** ojalá fuera rico. ◇ *vi* [by magic]: **to ~ for sthg** pedir (como deseo) algo. ◆ **wishes** *npl*: **(with) best ~es** [in letter] muchos recuerdos.
wishful thinking [ˌwɪʃfʊl-] *n* (*U*): **it's just ~** no son más que (vanas) ilusiones.
wishy-washy ['wɪʃɪˌwɒʃɪ] *adj inf pej* soso(sa), insípido(da).
wisp [wɪsp] *n* **-1.** [of hair] mechón *m*; [of grass] brizna *f*. **-2.** [cloud] nubecilla *f*; [of smoke] voluta *f*.
wistful ['wɪstfʊl] *adj* melancólico(ca).
wit [wɪt] *n* **-1.** [humour] ingenio *m*, agudeza *f*. **-2.** [intelligence]: **to have the ~ to do sthg** tener el buen juicio de hacer algo. ◆ **wits** *npl*: **to have** OR **keep one's ~s about one** mantenerse alerta.
witch [wɪtʃ] *n* bruja *f*.
with [wɪð] *prep* **-1.** [in company of] con; **we stayed ~ them for a week** estuvimos con ellos una semana; **~ me** conmigo; **~ you** contigo; **~ himself/herself** consigo. **-2.** [indicating opposition] con; **to argue ~ sb** discutir con alguien. **-3.** [indicating means, manner, feelings] con; **I washed it ~ detergent** lo lavé con detergente; **he filled it ~ wine** lo llenó de vino; **covered ~ mud** cubierto de barro; **she was trembling ~ fear** temblaba de miedo. **-4.** [having - gen] con; **a man ~ a beard** un hombre con barba; **the woman ~ the black hair/big dog** la señora del pelo negro/perro grande. **-5.** [regarding] con; **he's very mean ~ money** es muy tacaño con el dinero; **the trouble ~ her is that ...** su problema es que .... **-6.** [because of] con; **~ my luck, I'll probably lose** con la suerte que tengo seguro que pierdo. **-7.** [indicating understanding]: **are you ~ me?** ¿me sigues? **-8.** [indicating support] con; **I'm ~ Dad on this** en eso estoy con papá.

withdraw [wɪð'drɔː] (*pt* **-drew**, *pp* **-drawn**) ◇ *vt* **-1.** [gen]: **to ~ sthg (from)** retirar algo (de). **-2.** [money] sacar. ◇ *vi*: **to ~ (from/to)** retirarse (de/a).

withdrawal [wɪð'drɔːəl] *n* **-1.** [gen & MIL] retirada *f*. **-2.** [retraction] retractación *f*. FIN reintegro *m*.

withdrawal symptoms *npl* síndrome *m* de abstinencia.

withdrawn [wɪð'drɔːn] ◇ *pp* → **withdraw**. ◇ *adj* [shy, quiet] reservado(da).

withdrew [wɪð'druː] *pt* → **withdraw**.

wither ['wɪðər] *vi* **-1.** [dry up] marchitarse. **-2.** [become weak] debilitarse.

withhold [wɪð'həʊld] (*pt* & *pp* **-held** [-'held]) *vt* [gen] **retener**; [consent, permission] **negar**.

within [wɪ'ðɪn] ◇ *prep* **-1.** [gen] dentro de; **~ reach** al alcance de la mano. **-2.** [less than - distance] a menos de; [- time] en menos de; **it's ~ walking distance** se puede ir andando; **~ the next six months** en los próximos seis meses; **it arrived ~ a week** llegó en una semana. ◇ *adv* dentro.

without [wɪð'aʊt] ◇ *prep* sin; **~ sthg/doing sthg** sin algo/hacer algo; **it happened ~ my realizing** pasó sin que me diera cuenta. ◇ *adv*: **to go** OR **do ~ sthg** pasar sin algo.

withstand [wɪð'stænd] (*pt* & *pp* **-stood** [-'stʊd]) *vt* resistir, aguantar.

witness ['wɪtnɪs] ◇ *n* **-1.** [person] testigo *m* y *f*. **-2.** [testimony]: **to bear ~ to** sthg atestiguar algo, dar fe de algo. ◇ *vt* **-1.** [see] presenciar. **-2.** [countersign] firmar (como testigo).

witness box *Br*, **witness stand** *Am n* tribuna *f* (de los testigos).

witticism ['wɪtɪsɪzm] *n* ocurrencia *f*.

witty ['wɪtɪ] *adj* ingenioso(sa), ocurrente.

wives [waɪvz] *pl* → **wife**.

wizard ['wɪzəd] *n* **-1.** [magician] mago *m* (*en cuentos*). **-2.** [skilled person] genio *m*.

wobble ['wɒbl] *vi* [gen] tambalearse; [furniture] cojear; [legs] temblar.

woe [wəʊ] *n literary* aflicción *f*.

woke [wəʊk] *pt* → **wake**.

woken ['wəʊkn] *pp* → **wake**.

wolf [wʊlf] (*pl* **wolves**) *n* ZOOL lobo *m*.

wolves [wʊlvz] *pl* → **wolf**.

woman ['wʊmən] (*pl* **women**) ◇ *n* **-1.** [female] mujer *f*. **-2.** [womanhood] la mujer. ◇ *comp*: **~ doctor** médica *f*.

womanly ['wʊmənlɪ] *adj* femenino(na).

womb [wuːm] *n* matriz *f*, útero *m*.

women ['wɪmɪn] *pl* → **woman**.

women's lib [-'lɪb] *n* liberación *f* de la mujer.

women's liberation *n* liberación *f* de la mujer.

won [wʌn] *pt* & *pp* → **win**.

wonder ['wʌndər] ◇ *n* **-1.** [amazement] asombro *m*, admiración *f*. **-2.** [cause for surprise]: **it's a ~ (that)** ... es un milagro que ...; **no** OR **little** OR **small ~** ... no es de extrañar que .... **-3.** [amazing thing, person] maravilla *f*. ◇ *vt* **-1.** [speculate]: **to ~ (if** OR **whether)** preguntarse (si). **-2.** [in polite requests]: **I ~ if** OR **whether I could ask you a question?** ¿le importaría que le hiciera una pregunta? ◇ *vi* [speculate]: **I was only ~ing** (preguntaba) sólo por curiosidad; **to ~ about** sthg preguntarse por algo.

wonderful ['wʌndəfʊl] *adj* maravilloso(sa), estupendo(da).

wonderfully ['wʌndəfʊlɪ] *adv* **-1.** [very well] estupendamente. **-2.** [very] extremadamente.

won't [wəʊnt] = **will not**.

woo [wuː] *vt* **-1.** *literary* [court] cortejar. **-2.** [try to win over] granjearse el apoyo de.

wood [wʊd] *n* **-1.** [timber] madera *f*; [for fire] leña *f*. **-2.** [group of trees] bosque *m*. ◆ **woods** *npl* bosque *m*.

wooded ['wʊdɪd] *adj* arbolado(da).

wooden ['wʊdn] *adj* **-1.** [of wood] de madera. **-2.** *pej* [actor] envarado(da).

woodpecker ['wʊd,pekər] *n* pájaro *m* carpintero.

woodwind ['wʊdwɪnd] *n*: **the ~** los instrumentos de viento de madera.

woodwork ['wʊdwɜːk] *n* carpintería *f*.

woodworm ['wʊdwɜːm] *n* carcoma *f*.

wool [wʊl] *n* lana *f*; **to pull the ~ over sb's eyes** *inf fig* dar a alguien gato por liebre.

woollen *Br*, **woolen** *Am* ['wʊlən] *adj* de lana. ◆ **woollens** *npl* géneros *mpl* de lana.

woolly ['wʊlɪ] *adj* **-1.** [woollen] de lana. **-2.** *inf* [fuzzy, unclear] confuso(sa).

word [wɜːd] ◇ *n* **-1.** LING palabra *f*; **~ for ~** palabra por palabra, en otras palabras; **in a ~** en una palabra; **too ... for ~s** de lo más ...; **she doesn't mince her ~s** no tiene pelos en la lengua; **to have a ~ with sb** hablar con alguien; **I couldn't get a ~ in edgeways** no pude meter baza. **-2.** (U) [news] noticia *f*. **-3.** [promise] palabra *f*;

to give sb one's ~ dar (uno) su palabra a alguien. ◇ *vt* redactar, expresar.

wording ['wɜːdɪŋ] *n* (U) términos *mpl*, forma *f* (de expresión).

word processing *n* (U) proceso *m* de textos.

word processor [-'prəʊsesəʳ] *n* procesador *m* de textos.

wore [wɔːʳ] *pt* → **wear**.

work [wɜːk] ◇ *n* **-1.** (U) [employment] trabajo *m*, empleo *m*; **to be out of ~** estar desempleado; **at ~** en el trabajo. **-2.** [activity, tasks] trabajo *m*; **at ~** trabajando. **-3.** [of art, literature etc] obra *f*. ◇ *vt* **-1.** [employees, subordinates] hacer trabajar. **-2.** [machine] manejar, operar. **-3.** [wood, metal, land] trabajar. ◇ *vi* **-1.** [person]: **to ~ (on sthg)** trabajar (en algo). **-2.** [machine, system, idea] funcionar. **-3.** [drug] surtir efecto. **-4.** [become by movement]: **to ~ loose** soltarse; **to ~ free** desprenderse. ◆ **works** ◇ *n* [factory] fábrica *f*. ◇ *npl* [mechanism] mecanismo *m*. ◆ **work on** *vt fus* **-1.** [pay attention to] trabajar en. **-2.** [take as basis] partir de. ◆ **work out** ◇ *vt sep* **-1.** [plan, schedule] elaborar. **-2.** [total, amount] calcular; [answer] dar con. ◇ *vi* **-1.** [figure etc]: **to ~ out at** salir a. **-2.** [turn out] resolverse. **-3.** [be successful] salir bien. **-4.** [train, exercise] hacer ejercicio. ◆ **work up** ◇ *vt sep* **-1.** [excite]: **to ~ o.s. up into a frenzy** ponerse frenético(ca). **-2.** [generate] despertar.

workable ['wɜːkəbl] *adj* factible, viable.

workaholic [ˌwɜːkə'hɒlɪk] *n* adicto *m*, -ta *f* al trabajo.

workday ['wɜːkdeɪ] *n* [not weekend] día *m* laborable.

worked up [ˌwɜːkt-] *adj* nervioso(sa).

worker ['wɜːkəʳ] *n* [person who works] trabajador *m*, -ra *f*; [manual worker] obrero *m*, -ra *f*.

workforce ['wɜːkfɔːs] *n* mano *f* de obra.

working ['wɜːkɪŋ] *adj* **-1.** [in operation] funcionando. **-2.** [having employment] empleado(da). **-3.** [relating to work - gen] laboral; [- day] laborable. ◆ **workings** *npl* mecanismo *m*.

working class *n*: **the ~** la clase obrera. ◆ **working-class** *adj* obrero(ra).

working order *n*: **to be in (good) ~** funcionar (bien).

workload ['wɜːkləʊd] *n* cantidad *f* de trabajo.

workman ['wɜːkmən] (*pl* **-men** [-mən]) *n* obrero *m*.

workmanship ['wɜːkmənʃɪp] *n* artesanía *f*.

workmate ['wɜːkmeɪt] *n* compañero *m*, -ra *f* de trabajo, colega *m* y *f*.

work permit [-ˌpɜːmɪt] *n* permiso *m* de trabajo.

workplace ['wɜːkpleɪs] *n* lugar *m* de trabajo.

workshop ['wɜːkʃɒp] *n* taller *m*.

workstation ['wɜːkˌsteɪʃn] *n* COMPUT estación *f* de trabajo.

worktop ['wɜːktɒp] *n* Br mármol *m*, encimera *f*.

work-to-rule *n* Br huelga *f* de celo.

world [wɜːld] ◇ *n* mundo *m*; **the best in the ~** el mejor del mundo; **to think the ~ of sb** querer a alguien con locura; **a ~ of difference** una diferencia enorme. ◇ *comp* mundial.

world-class *adj* de primera categoría.

world-famous *adj* famoso(sa) en el mundo entero.

worldly ['wɜːldlɪ] *adj* literary mundano(na).

World War I *n* la Primera Guerra Mundial.

World War II *n* la Segunda Guerra Mundial.

worldwide ['wɜːldwaɪd] ◇ *adj* mundial. ◇ *adv* en todo el mundo.

worm [wɜːm] *n* [animal] gusano *m*; [earthworm] lombriz *f* (de tierra).

worn [wɔːn] ◇ *pp* → **wear**. ◇ *adj* **-1.** [threadbare] gastado(da). **-2.** [tired] ajado(da).

worn-out *adj* **-1.** [old, threadbare]: **to be ~** estar ya para tirar. **-2.** [tired] agotado(da).

worried ['wʌrɪd] *adj* preocupado(da).

worry ['wʌrɪ] ◇ *n* preocupación *f*. ◇ *vt* [trouble] preocupar. ◇ *vi*: **to ~ (about)** preocuparse (por); **not to ~!** ¡no importa!

worrying ['wʌrɪɪŋ] *adj* preocupante.

worse [wɜːs] ◇ *adj* peor; **to get ~** empeorar. ◇ *adv* peor; **~ off** [gen] en peor situación; [financially] peor económicamente. ◇ *n*: **~ was to come** lo peor estaba aún por venir; **for the ~** para peor.

worsen ['wɜːsn] *vt & vi* empeorar.

worship ['wɜːʃɪp] ◇ *vt lit & fig* adorar. ◇ *n lit & fig*: **~ (of)** culto *m* (a), adoración *f* (por). ◆ **Worship** *n*: **Your/Her/ His Worship** su señoría; **his Worship the Mayor** el Excelentísimo Señor alcalde.

worst [wɜːst] ◇ *adj* peor; **the ~ thing is ...** lo peor es que .... ◇ *adv* peor; **the ~ affected area** la región más afectada. ◇ *n:* **the ~** [thing] lo peor; [person] el peor *m*, la peor *f*; **if the ~ comes to the ~** en último extremo. ◆ **at (the) worst** *adv* en el peor de los casos.

worth [wɜːθ] ◇ *prep* **-1.** [having the value of]: **it's ~ £50** vale 50 libras; **how much is it ~?** ¿cuánto vale? **-2.** [deserving of] digno(na) de; **the museum is ~ visiting** OR **a visit, it's ~ visiting the museum** el museo merece una visita. ◇ *n* **-1.** [amount]: **£50,000 ~ of antiques** antigüedades por valor de 50.000 libras; **a month's ~ of groceries** provisiones para un mes. **-2.** *fml* [value] valor *m*.

worthless [ˈwɜːθlɪs] *adj* **-1.** [object] sin valor. **-2.** [person] despreciable.

worthwhile [ˌwɜːθˈwaɪl] *adj* que vale la pena; [cause] noble, digno(na).

worthy [ˈwɜːðɪ] *adj* **-1.** [gen] digno(na). **-2.** [good but unexciting] encomiable.

would [wʊd] *modal vb* **-1.** (*in reported speech*): **she said she ~ come** dijo que vendría. **-2.** [indicating likelihood]: **what ~ you do?** ¿qué harías?; **he ~ have resigned** habría dimitido. **-3.** [indicating willingness]: **she ~n't go** no quiso/quería ir; **he ~ do anything for her** haría cualquier cosa por ella. **-4.** (*in polite questions*): **~ you like a drink?** ¿quieres beber algo?; **~ you mind closing the window?** ¿le importaría cerrar la ventana?; **help me shut this suitcase, ~ you?** ayúdame a cerrar esta maleta, ¿quieres? **-5.** [indicating inevitability]: **he WOULD** say that, **~n't he?** hombre, era de esperar que dijera eso, ¿no? **-6.** [expressing opinions]: **I ~ have thought (that) it ~ be easy** hubiera pensado que sería fácil; **I ~ prefer ...** preferiría ...; **I ~ like ...** quisiera ..., quiero .... **-7.** [giving advice]: **I ~ report it if I were you** yo en tu lugar lo denunciaría. **-8.** [indicating habit]: **he ~ smoke a cigar after dinner** solía fumar un puro después de la cena; **she ~ often complain about the neighbours** se quejaba a menudo de los vecinos.

would-be *adj:* **a ~ author** un aspirante a literato.

wouldn't [ˈwʊdnt] = **would not**.

would've [ˈwʊdəv] = **would have**.

wound¹ [wuːnd] ◇ *n* herida *f*. ◇ *vt lit & fig* herir.

wound² [waʊnd] *pt & pp* → **wind²**.

wove [wəʊv] *pt* → **weave**.

woven [ˈwəʊvn] *pp* → **weave**.

WP -1. *abbr of* **word processing. -2.** *abbr of* **word processor.**

wrangle [ˈræŋgl] ◇ *n* disputa *f*. ◇ *vi:* **to ~ (with sb over sthg)** discutir OR pelearse (con alguien por algo).

wrap [ræp] ◇ *vt* **-1.** [cover] envolver; **to ~ sthg in sthg** envolver algo en algo; **to ~ sthg around** OR **round sthg** liar algo alrededor de algo. **-2.** [encircle]: **he wrapped his hands around it** lo rodeó con sus manos. ◇ *n* [garment] echarpe *m*. ◆ **wrap up** ◇ *vt sep* [cover] envolver. ◇ *vi* [put warm clothes on]: **~ up well** OR **warmly** abrígate bien.

wrapper [ˈræpər] *n* envoltorio *m*.

wrapping [ˈræpɪŋ] *n* envoltorio *m*.

wrapping paper *n* (U) papel *m* de envolver.

wrath [rɒθ] *n literary* ira *f*, cólera *f*.

wreak [riːk] *vt* causar; **to ~ havoc** hacer estragos; **to ~ revenge** OR **vengeance** tomar la revancha.

wreath [riːθ] *n* corona *f* (de flores).

wreck [rek] ◇ *n* **-1.** [of car, plane] restos *mpl* del siniestro; [of ship] restos del naufragio. **-2.** *inf* [person] guiñapo *m*. ◇ *vt* **-1.** [destroy] destrozar. **-2.** NAUT hacer naufragar; **to be ~ed** naufragar. **-3.** [spoil] dar al traste con; [health] acabar con.

wreckage [ˈrekɪdʒ] *n* (U) [of plane, car] restos *mpl*; [of building] escombros *mpl*.

wren [ren] *n* chochín *m*.

wrench [rentʃ] ◇ *n* **-1.** [tool] llave *f* inglesa. **-2.** [injury] torcedura *f*. ◇ *vt* **-1.** [pull violently]: **to ~ sthg (off)** arrancar algo; **to ~ sthg open** abrir algo de un tirón. **-2.** [twist and injure] torcer.

wrestle [ˈresl] *vi lit & fig:* **to ~ (with)** luchar (con).

wrestler [ˈreslər] *n* luchador *m*, -ra *f*.

wrestling [ˈreslɪŋ] *n* lucha *f* libre.

wretch [retʃ] *n* desgraciado *m*, -da *f*.

wretched [ˈretʃɪd] *adj* **-1.** [miserable] miserable. **-2.** *inf* [damned] maldito(ta).

wriggle [ˈrɪgl] *vi* **-1.** [move about] menearse. **-2.** [twist] escurrirse, deslizarse.

wring [rɪŋ] (*pt & pp* **wrung**) *vt* **-1.** [wet clothes etc] estrujar, escurrir. **-2.** [neck] retorcer.

wringing [ˈrɪŋɪŋ] *adj:* **~ (wet)** empapado(da).

wrinkle [ˈrɪŋkl] ◇ *n* arruga *f*. ◇ *vt* arrugar. ◇ *vi* arrugarse.

wrist [rɪst] *n* muñeca *f*.

wristwatch ['rɪstwɒtʃ] *n* reloj *m* de pulsera.

writ [rɪt] *n* mandato *m* judicial.

write [raɪt] (*pt* **wrote**, *pp* **written**) ◇ *vt* **-1.** [gen & COMPUT] escribir. **-2.** *Am* [person] escribir a. ◇ *vi* [gen & COMPUT] escribir. ◆ **write back** *vt sep* & *vi* contestar. ◆ **write down** *vt sep* apuntar. ◆ **write into** *vt sep* incluir en. ◆ **write off** *vt sep* **-1.** [plan, hopes] abandonar. **-2.** [debt] cancelar, anular. **-3.** [person - as failure] considerar un fracaso. **-4.** *Br inf* [wreck] cargarse. ◆ **write up** *vt sep* redactar.

write-off *n*: the car was a ~ el coche quedó totalmente destrozado.

writer ['raɪtə'] *n* **-1.** [as profession] escritor *m*, -ra *f*. **-2.** [of letter, article, story] autor *m*, -ra *f*.

writhe [raɪð] *vi* retorcerse.

writing ['raɪtɪŋ] *n* **-1.** (*U*) [handwriting] letra *f*, caligrafía *f*. **-2.** [something written] escrito *m*; **in ~** por escrito. **-3.** [activity] escritura *f*.

writing paper *n* (*U*) papel *m* de carta.

written ['rɪtn] ◇ *pp* → **write**. ◇ *adj* **-1.** [not oral] escrito(ta). **-2.** [official] por escrito.

wrong [rɒŋ] ◇ *adj* **-1.** [not normal, not satisfactory] malo(la); **the clock's ~** el reloj anda mal; **what's ~?** ¿qué pasa?; **there's nothing ~ with me** no me pasa nada. **-2.** [not suitable, not correct] equivocado(da); [moment, time] inoportuno(na); **to be ~** equivocarse; **to do sthg** cometer un error al hacer algo. **-3.** [morally bad] malo(la); **it's ~ to steal/lie** robar/mentir está mal; **what's ~ with being a communist?** ¿qué tiene de malo ser comunista? ◇ *adv* [incorrectly] mal; **to get sthg ~** entender mal algo; **to go ~** [make a mistake] cometer un error; [stop functioning] estropearse. ◇ *n* **-1.** [evil] mal *m*; **to be in the ~** haber hecho mal. **-2.** [injustice] injusticia *f*. ◇ *vt* ser injusto(ta) con, agraviar.

wrongful ['rɒŋful] *adj* [dismissal] improcedente; [arrest, imprisonment] ilegal.

wrongly ['rɒŋlɪ] *adv* equivocadamente.

wrong number *n*: sorry, ~ lo siento, se ha equivocado de número.

wrote [rəut] *pt* → **write**.

wrought iron [rɔːt-] *n* hierro *m* forjado.

wrung [rʌŋ] *pt* & *pp* → **wring**.

wry [raɪ] *adj* **-1.** [amused] irónico(ca). **-2.** [displeased] de asco.

x (*pl* **x's** OR **xs**), **X** (*pl* **X's** OR **Xs**) [eks] *n* [letter] x *f inv*, X *f inv*.

xenophobia [ˌzenə'fəubjə] *n* xenofobia *f*.

Xmas ['eksməs] ◇ *n* Navidad *f*. ◇ *comp* de Navidad.

X-ray ◇ *n* **-1.** [ray] rayo *m* X. **-2.** [picture] radiografía *f*. ◇ *vt* examinar con rayos X, radiografiar.

xylophone ['zaɪləfəun] *n* xilófono *m*.

y (*pl* **y's** OR **ys**), **Y** (*pl* **Y's** OR **Ys**) [waɪ] *n* [letter] y *f*, Y *f*.

yacht [jɒt] *n* yate *m*; [for racing] balandro *m*.

yachting ['jɒtɪŋ] *n* balandrismo *m*.

yachtsman ['jɒtsmən] (*pl* **-men** [-mən]) *n* balandrista *m*.

Yank [jæŋk] *n inf* término peyorativo que designa a un estadounidense, yanqui *m* y *f*.

Yankee ['jæŋkɪ] *n Br inf* término peyorativo que designa a un estadounidense, yanqui *m* y *f*.

yap [jæp] *vi* [dog] ladrar.

yard [jɑːd] *n* **-1.** [unit of measurement] = 91,44 cm, yarda *f*. **-2.** [walled area] patio *m*. **-3.** [shipyard] astillero *m*; **builder's/goods ~** depósito *m* de materiales/de mercancías. **-4.** *Am* [attached to house] jardín *m*.

yardstick ['jɑːdstɪk] *n* criterio *m*, pauta *f*.

yarn [jɑːn] *n* [thread] hilo *m*, hilaza *f*.

yawn [jɔːn] ◇ *n* [when tired] bostezo *m*. ◇ *vi* **-1.** [when tired] bostezar. **-2.** [gap, chasm] abrirse.

yd *abbr of* **yard**.

yeah [jeə] *adv inf* sí.

year [jɪəʳ] *n* **-1.** [gen] año *m*; **he's 25 ~s old** tiene 25 años; **all (the) ~ round** todo el año. **-2.** SCH curso *m*; **he's in (his) first ~** está en primero. ◆**years** *npl* [ages] años *mpl*; **it's ~s since I last saw you** hace siglos que no te veo.

yearly ['jɪəlɪ] ◇ *adj* anual. ◇ *adv* **-1.** [once a year] una vez al año. **-2.** [every year] cada año.

yearn [jɜ:n] *vi*: **to ~ for sthg/to do sthg** ansiar algo/hacer algo.

yearning ['jɜ:nɪŋ] *n*: **~ (for sb/sthg)** anhelo *m* (de alguien/algo).

yeast [ji:st] *n* levadura *f*.

yell [jel] ◇ *n* grito *m*, alarido *m*. ◇ *vt & vi* vociferar.

yellow ['jeləʊ] ◇ *adj* [in colour] amarillo(lla). ◇ *n* amarillo *m*.

yellow card *n* FTBL tarjeta *f* amarilla.

yelp [jelp] ◇ *n* aullido *m*. ◇ *vi* aullar.

yeoman of the guard ['jəʊmən-] (*pl* **yeomen of the guard** ['jəʊmən-]) *n* alabardero de la Casa Real británica.

yes [jes] ◇ *adv* sí; **to say ~** decir que sí; **to say ~ to sthg** consentir algo. ◇ *n* sí *m*.

yesterday ['jestədɪ] ◇ *n* ayer *m*. ◇ *adv* ayer; **~ afternoon** ayer por la tarde; **the day before ~** anteayer.

yet [jet] ◇ *adv* **-1.** [gen] todavía, aún; **have you had lunch ~?** ¿has comido ya?; **their worst defeat ~** la mayor derrota que han sufrido hasta la fecha; **as ~** de momento, hasta ahora; **not ~** todavía OR aún no. **-2.** [even]: **~ another car** otro coche más; **~ again** otra vez más; **~ more** aún más. ◇ *conj* pero, sin embargo.

yew [ju:] *n* tejo *m*.

Yiddish ['jɪdɪʃ] ◇ *adj* yídish (*inv*). ◇ *n* yídish *m*.

yield [ji:ld] ◇ *n* **-1.** AGR cosecha *f*. **-2.** FIN rédito *m*. ◇ *vt* **-1.** [gen] producir, dar. **-2.** [give up] ceder. ◇ *vi* **-1.** [shelf, lock etc] ceder. **-2.** *fml* [person, enemy] rendirse; **to ~ to sb/sthg** claudicar ante alguien/algo. **-3.** *Am* AUT [give way]: "~" "ceda el paso".

YMCA (*abbr of* **Young Men's Christian Association**) *n* asociación internacional de jóvenes cristianos.

yoga ['jəʊgə] *n* yoga *m*.

yoghourt, yoghurt, yogurt [*Br* 'jɒgət, *Am* 'jəʊgərt] *n* yogur *m*.

yoke [jəʊk] *n lit & fig* yugo *m*.

yolk [jəʊk] *n* yema *f*.

you [ju:] *pers pron* **-1.** (*subject - sg*) tú, vos (*+ pl vb*) *Amer*; (*- formal use*) us-

ted; (*- pl*) vosotros *mpl*, - tras *fpl*; (*- formal use*) ustedes (*pl*); **~'re a good cook** eres/usted es un buen cocinero; **are ~ French?** ¿eres/es usted francés?; **~ idiot!** ¡imbécil!; **if I were** OR **was ~** si (yo) fuera tú/usted, yo en tu/su lugar; **excuse me, Madam, have ~ got the time?** perdone, señora, ¿tiene usted hora?; **there ~ are** [you've appeared] ¡ya estás/está usted aquí!; [have this] ahí tienes/tiene; **that jacket isn't really ~** esa chaqueta no te/le pega. **-2.** (*direct object - unstressed - sg*) te; (*- pl*) os; (*- formal use*) le *m*, la *f*; (*- pl*) les *mpl*, las *fpl*; **I can see ~** te/os veo; **yes, Madam, I understand ~** sí, señora, la comprendo. **-3.** (*direct object - stressed*): **I don't expect YOU to do it** no te voy a pedir que TÚ lo hagas. **-4.** (*indirect object - sg*) te; (*- pl*) os; (*- formal use*) le; (*- pl*) les; **she gave it to ~** te/os lo dio; **can I get ~ a chair, sir?** ¿le traigo una silla, señor? **-5.** (*after prep, in comparisons etc - sg*) ti; (*- pl*) vosotros *mpl*, -tras *fpl*; (*- formal use*) usted; (*- pl*) ustedes; **we shall go with/without ~** iremos contigo/sin ti, iremos con/sin vosotros (*pl*); **I'm shorter than ~** soy más bajo que tú/vosotros. **-6.** [anyone, one] uno; **wouldn't have thought so** uno no lo habría pensado; **exercise is good for ~** el ejercicio es bueno.

you'd [ju:d] = **you had, you would.**

you'll [ju:l] = **you will.**

young [jʌŋ] ◇ *adj* [not old] joven. ◇ *npl* **-1.** [young people]: **the ~** los jóvenes. **-2.** [baby animals] crías *fpl*.

younger ['jʌŋgəʳ] *adj*: **Pitt the ~** Pitt el joven, Pitt hijo.

youngster ['jʌŋstəʳ] *n* joven *m y f*.

your [jɔ:ʳ] *poss adj* **-1.** (*everyday use - referring to one person*) tu; (*- referring to more than one person*) vuestro(tra); **~ dog** tu/vuestro perro; **~ children** tus niños; **what's ~ name?** ¿cómo te llamas?; **it wasn't YOUR fault** no fue culpa tuya/vuestra; **you didn't wash ~ hair** no te lavaste/os lavasteis el pelo. **-2.** (*formal use*) su; **~ dog** su perro; **what are ~ names?** ¿cuáles son sus nombres? **-3.** (*impersonal use*): **~ attitude changes as you get older** la actitud de uno cambia con la vejez; **it's good for ~ teeth/hair** es bueno para los dientes/el pelo; **~ average English-man** el inglés medio.

you're [jɔ:ʳ] = **you are.**

yours [jɔːz] *poss pron* **-1.** (*everyday use - referring to one person*) tuyo (tuya); (*- referring to more than one person*) vuestro (vuestra); **that money is** ~ ese dinero es tuyo/vuestro; **those keys are** ~ esas llaves son tuyas/vuestras; **my car hit** ~ mi coche chocó contra el tuyo/el vuestro; **it wasn't her fault, it was** YOURS no fue culpa de ella sino TUYA/ VUESTRA; **a friend of** ~ un amigo tuyo/ vuestro. **-2.** (*formal use*) suyo (suya). ◆ **Yours** *adv* [in letter] un saludo; *see also* **faithfully, sincerely** *etc.*

yourself [jɔːˈself] (*pl* **-selves** [-ˈselvz]) *pron* **-1.** (*as reflexive sg*) te; (*-pl*) os; (*- formal use*) se; **did you hurt** ~? ¿te hiciste/se hizo daño? **-2.** (*after prep - sg*) ti mismo (ti misma); (*- pl*) vosotros mismos (vosotras mismas); (*- formal use*) usted mismo (usted misma); **with** ~ contigo mismo/misma. **-3.** (*for emphasis*): **you** ~ tú mismo (tú misma); (*formal use*) usted mismo(ma); **you yourselves** vosotros mismos (vosotras mismas); (*formal use*) ustedes mismos(mas). **-4.** [without help] solo(la); **did you do it (by)** ~? ¿lo hiciste solo?

youth [juːθ] *n* **-1.** [gen] juventud *f.* **-2.** [boy, young man] joven *m.*

youth club *n* club *m* juvenil.

youthful [ˈjuːθfʊl] *adj* juvenil.

youth hostel *n* albergue *m* juvenil.

you've [juːv] = **you have.**

YTS (*abbr of* **Youth Training Scheme**) *n* programa gubernamental de promoción del empleo juvenil en Gran Bretaña.

Yugoslav = **Yugoslavian.**

Yugoslavia [ˌjuːgəˈslɑːvɪə] *n* Yugoslavia.

Yugoslavian [ˌjuːgəˈslɑːvɪən], **Yugoslav** [ˌjuːgəˈslɑːv] ◇ *adj* yugoslavo(va). ◇ *n* yugoslavo *m*, -va *f.*

yuppie, yuppy [ˈjʌpɪ] (*abbr of* **young urban professional**) *n* yuppy *m* y *f.*

YWCA (*abbr of* **Young Women's Christian Association**) *n* asociación internacional de jóvenes cristianas.

Z

z (*pl* **z's** OR **zs**), **Z** (*pl* **Z's** OR **Zs**) [*Br* zed, *Am* ziː] *n* [letter] z *f*, Z *f.*

Zambia [ˈzæmbɪə] *n* Zambia.

zany [ˈzeɪnɪ] *adj inf* [humour, trick] disparatado(da); [person] loco(ca).

zap [zæp] *inf vi*: **to** ~ **off (somewhere)** hacer una escapada (a algún sitio).

zeal [ziːl] *n fml* celo *m.*

zealous [ˈzeləs] *adj fml* entusiasta.

zebra [*Br* ˈzebrə, *Am* ˈziːbrə] (*pl inv* OR **-s**) *n* cebra *f.*

zebra crossing *n Br* paso *m* cebra.

zenith [*Br* ˈzenɪθ, *Am* ˈziːnəθ] *n* ASTRON & *fig* cenit *m.*

zero [*Br* ˈzɪərəʊ, *Am* ˈziːrəʊ] (*pl inv* OR **-es**) ◇ *adj* cero (*inv*),. nulo(la). ◇ *n* cero *m*; **below** ~ bajo cero.

zest [zest] *n* (*U*) **-1.** [excitement, eagerness] entusiasmo *m.* **-2.** [of orange, lemon] cáscara *f.*

zigzag [ˈzɪgzæg] ◇ *n* zigzag *m.* ◇ *vi* zigzaguear.

Zimbabwe [zɪmˈbɑːbwɪ] *n* Zimbabue.

zinc [zɪŋk] *n* cinc *m*, zinc *m.*

zip [zɪp] *n Br* [fastener] cremallera *f*, cierre *m* relámpago *Amer.* ◆ **zip up** *vt sep* cerrar la cremallera de.

zip code *n Am* código *m* postal.

zip fastener *Br* = **zip.**

zipper [ˈzɪpər] *n Am* = **zip.**

zodiac [ˈzəʊdɪæk] *n*: **the** ~ el zodiaco.

zone [zəʊn] *n* zona *f.*

zoo [zuː] *n* zoo *m.*

zoology [zəʊˈɒlədʒɪ] *n* zoología *f.*

zoom [zuːm] *vi inf* [move quickly]: **to** ~ **past** pasar zumbando.

zoom lens *n* zoom *m.*

zucchini [zuːˈkiːnɪ] (*pl inv*) *n Am* calabacín *m.*

Achevé d'imprimer par l'Imprimerie
Maury-Eurolivres S.A. à Manchecourt
Décembre 1994 – N° d'éditeur : 18394
Dépôt légal : Janvier 1994 – N° d'imprimeur : 94/12/M5618
Imprimé en France - (Printed in France)